The University of LAW

14 Store Street
London
WC1E 7DE

ROOK & WARD
ON
SEXUAL OFFENCES
LAW AND PRACTICE

Fifth Edition

ROOK & WARD
ON
SEXUAL OFFENCES
LAW AND PRACTICE

Fifth Edition

HH Judge Peter Rook QC, M.A. (Cantab.),
a Judge at the Old Bailey
and Robert Ward, CBE, M.A., LL.B. (Cantab.),
LL.M. (U.B.C.), of the Middle Temple, Barrister,
Formerly Fellow of Gonville and Caius College,
Cambridge

SWEET & MAXWELL  THOMSON REUTERS

First edition	*1990 by Peter Rook and Robert Ward*
Second edition	*1997 by Peter Rook and Robert Ward*
Third edition	*2004 by Peter Rook and Robert Ward*
Fourth edition	*2010 by Peter Rook and Robert Ward*

This edition published in 2016 by
Thomson Reuters (Professional) UK Limited trading as
Sweet & Maxwell, Friars House, 160 Blackfriars Road, London SE1 8EZ
(Registered in England & Wales. Company No. 1679046
Registered Office and address for service:
2nd floor, 1 Mark Square, Leonard Street, London EC2A 4EG)

For further information on our products and services, visit
http://www.sweetandmaxwell.co.uk

Typeset by Wright and Round Ltd., Gloucestershire
Printed and bound by CPI Group (UK) Ltd, Croydon, CR0 4YY

ISBN: 978 0 414 05074 7

No natural forests were destroyed to make this product;
only farmed timber was used and replanted.

A CIP catalogue record of this book is available from the British Library.

Dedicated to
Susanna, Annabel, Clifton, Sophie, Luke, Joshua and Freya
and
Mai, Ruby and Honor
for their ever continuing forbearance and support.

Foreword

By Lord Justice Fulford
Senior Presiding Judge of England and Wales
Royal Courts of Justice
May 23, 2016

The rise in prosecutions for sexual offences presents one of the most profound challenges for the courts in England and Wales in the early 21st century. These cases are almost invariably of the upmost importance because of the direct impact of offending of this kind on victims and the indirect impact it has on the well-being of our society. They are often difficult to prosecute, for a myriad of reasons, and they frequently result in contested trials, not least because of the consequences for those who are guilty if they admit their offending (for instance, the likely custodial sentence and the inevitable public opprobrium). The numbers of reported incidents rise year after year, and the best predictions are that this increase is set to continue. Many judges spend 50% or more of their time trying cases involving serious sexual allegations. This represents a considerable professional burden.

The apparent increased ability of members of our society to report these offences is, at least in part, a reflection of the many improvements that have been made in the treatment of alleged victims, in the standards of investigation, in a far more coherent and enlightened approach to prosecutions than in yesteryear and in improved court processes and procedures. The experience of being a complainant, albeit still far from perfect, is much improved on the historical position. For instance, witnesses in these cases increasingly give evidence from remote locations and the section 28 pilot (pre-recorded questioning) has been an unqualified success; indeed, I have – cautious – high hopes that the government will implement this provision across England and Wales on a permanent basis in the near future. However, no firm decision has been made at the time of penning this Foreword.

Not only is this work increasing in quantity, but arguably it has become more complex because of notable shifts in the jurisprudential sands. Over the last 12 months, there have been a number of important decisions from the Court of Appeal which are superbly analysed by the authors, and the Chapter List reveals the wide range of subjects about which the practitioner must be wholly familiar. The latter is daunting. This book is a true "one-stop-shop" for those who conduct cases in this complex area. It is critical, for instance, that judges and lawyers are fully familiar with the impact of *R. v FNC* as regards DNA evidence, a case that has received detailed and incisive analysis. Similarly, there have been significant developments as regards the courts approach to trafficking (e.g. *Ali (Yasir)*). The extensive assistance provided in the text on the multiple complexities of sentencing is particularly notable.

There is much that still needs to be done to refine and improve the ways in which these cases are handled, from the first report to the authorities right up to the last decision of the Court of Appeal, but this edition of this important book yet again shines a bright light on a truly complicated landscape and it will help us once again reflect on the areas in which further improvements can be made. I find it difficult to contemplate anyone operating in this field without this text being within arm's length or a mouse-click away.

Foreword to the Fourth Edition

By the Rt Hon. Lord Justice Pitchford,
Lord Justice of Appeal

I have read in draft much of the 2010 edition of Rook and Ward on Sexual Offences, always with respect and admiration, particularly for the scope and depth of the treatment of its subject. Since the authors published their first edition in 1990, Rook and Ward has become a standard work for those who practise in this area of criminal law and for those who have a serious academic or other interest in the subject. The authors have been in the vanguard of analysis and comment upon many new and sometimes controversial developments both in the law and in the conduct of trials of sexual offences. Their expertise in the field has enabled them to make an invaluable contribution to the learning and comprehension of the professions and the judiciary.

The investigation of offences, the admissibility of evidence and the conduct of criminal trials involving those who have or are alleged to have been victims of sexual offences have all been the subject of much authoritative research and Parliamentary activity since HH Judge Peter Rook QC and Robert Ward first embarked on their project. The detailed attention they have, in successive editions, given to these developments by tracing the history of changes and by offering searching analysis of them, has been of great benefit. The landscape for the administration of criminal justice in this field has changed dramatically since the enactment of the Sexual Offences Act 2003 and this book continues to keep us engaged and informed.

For advocates who conduct criminal trials for the prosecution or the defence, Rook and Ward has become an essential reference. Its treatment in depth of the requirements of investigation, the preparation and delivery of evidence and the responsibilities of the advocates leaves the reader in no doubt of the dedication with which advocates are required to approach their task of assisting the court and the participants in the trial of and sentencing for a sexual offence.

Judges who preside in the Crown Court over trials of sexual offences are required to undertake specialised training to which both the authors have made distinguished contributions. Expertise in the trial of sexual offences is, however, only part of the story. Judges require constant access to authoritative works of reference. This is one of them.

I have no doubt that this fourth edition of Rook and Ward will be received with relief and enthusiasm.

Foreword to the Third Edition

By the Rt Hon. Lord Justice Rose.
Vice-President of the Court of Appeal, Criminal Division

The Sexual Offences Act 2003 is only part of the current legislative torrent. Such torrents require careful navigation if judges, magistrates and practitioners are to stay afloat. As the two previous editions of this book have shown, Peter Rook and Robert Ward are reliable pilots with particular expertise in this area. This third edition provides a most welcome chart to the law on sexual offences in the light of the recent Act.

New offences and sentences, issues in relation to previous sexual history, disclosure, medical and DNA evidence, and the regime for vulnerable witnesses are among the many subjects helpfully discussed by reference to statutes, English and Commonwealth authorities and academic writings.

I warmly commend the new edition of this admirable book.

Foreword to the Second Edition

By the Rt Hon. Mr Justice Blofeld

It is a privilege to pay tribute to such a useful book as this. It is essential for practitioners to have available books on specific areas of law accurately set out and clearly expounded. Since the publication of the first edition of this book there have been a number of subjects in the law relating to sexual offences which have needed updating. Until the arrival of this book it has been difficult to find all the relevant information gathered together in one place. It is, therefore, a necessary tool for all criminal practitioners.

It is invidious to select one part of this book above another, but I find that the chapters concerning Public Interest Immunity disclosure, the procedures relating to evidence about children and DNA evidence particularly helpful. They set out the matters clearly, explain the problems and bring together the differing strands of statutory law, case law and academic criticism that fall for consideration. Some of these subjects will certainly develop further in the future. I would single out the chapters concerning DNA evidence, specifically the passages dealing with its scientific evaluation and its statistical relevance, as being of particular importance.

I have already found the first edition of this work to be a useful and valuable tool and I am confident that this second edition will prove even more valuable than its predecessor. I would like to commend the co-authors for all their hard work.

Preface

In previous editions, we have covered the substantive law governing sexual offences and also focused on evidence, procedure and medical issues. We have now widened the scope of this work in the face of the demands of the current climate in respect of the trials of sexual offences. For instance, the police investigative process, CPS policy, historic cases and advocacy all warrant dedicated chapters.

Fifty years ago, prosecutions of sexual offences only accounted for a limited proportion of the daily work of the criminal courts. Today, in 2016, the opposite is true. It is the most common type of contested case at many Crown Court centres.

The increase in prosecutions can be explained, in part, by a more sympathetic environment in which complainants can report. There has been a surge in the number of sexual offending allegations that are being reported to police. Figures released by the Office for National Statistics on April 21, 2016 reveal that police recorded more than 100,000 sex offences in a single year for the first time in 2015, with recorded rapes up by 30% to 34,700.

High profile cases and documentaries about them may have a tendency to encourage further reporting.

Some types of offending represent new phenomena, such as the particularly concerning development of the misuse of the internet and the use of social networking sites (SNS) to facilitate the grooming and sexual exploitation of children. A further undesirable consequence of the digital revolution is the surge in the viewing of online imagery of child sex abuse. However, these developments cannot explain such a steep rise in prosecutions.

Further important reasons include the abolition of the rule requiring corroboration in sexual cases and a greater concentration upon sexual offending where the parties are or have been in a relationship. The change in CPS prosecution policy in 2013 so that the primary focus is the nature of the offending, rather than the credibility of the complainant, is also significant.

However, even in combination, these factors cannot provide a full answer as to why there has been such an exponential rise in cases coming before the courts and, in particular, why, given that sexual offending is not new, there were not more prosecutions in the past.

In our view, the answer must lie, to some extent, in a change in society's attitudes which manifests itself now in the investigation and trial of sexual offending that occurred often many years ago. Public concern over issues raised by sexual offending has never been higher. However, this change has not been consistent, and many people still adhere to more outmoded values. As Dame Elish Angiolini pointed out, in her independent review of how the Metropolitan Police Service and the Crown Prosecution Service investigate and prosecute rape in London:

"While experts in this field have made considerable progress in understanding rape, including the deliberate targeting by perpetrators of vulnerable complainants and its serious psychological impact, this understanding has not filtered down into public awareness."

Of particular concern is that children's and young people's understanding of consent continues to be influenced by societal stereotypes which diminish the perpetrator's responsibility and blame the complainant.

The Court of Appeal has continued to support the development of judicial directions to prevent the false assumptions which many people still make, although despite such directions some remain in a state of denial. We are grateful to Sir David Maddison, Professor David Ormerod QC, HH Judge John Wait and Simon Tonkin for their permission to reproduce appropriate parts of the Crown Court Compendium 2016, which is intended to replace all the guidance previously provided by the Judicial College. We commend Chapter 20(1) of the Compendium (to be found Appendix G of this work), which sets out areas where judicial guidance may be necessary to prevent unwarranted assumptions and provides non-prescriptive examples.

There may be a case for some of these directions to be given at the outset of the case when their impact is likely to be greater, rather than during the summing up. Such an approach has now been encouraged by Sir Brian Leveson P in his recent *Review of Efficiency in Criminal Proceedings*. Sir Brian encourages (i) identification for the jury of the issues in the case, by both prosecution and defence, before the evidence is called; and (ii) the giving of directions at a point or points in the trial when they are of most use to the jury. This approach has been formally adopted in the Criminal Procedure Rules, in a new rule 25.14.

The tsunami of prosecutions has been accompanied by changes in almost every aspect of how cases involving allegations of sexual offending are pursued, tried in court, and sentenced.

There has been a marked increase in the levels of sentences imposed upon sexual offenders during the last two decades reflecting a much greater understanding of the harm such offending can cause. Nevertheless, sentences in this area still lead to public concern. Recently there have been more References by the Attorney-General on the basis that more unduly lenient sentences have been passed in respect of sexual offending as compared with any other type of case. In many of these cases, sentences have been increased. No doubt, in part, this is due to the greater volume of cases, but it also reveals a significant number of unjustified departures from the Sentencing Council guideline.

The Court of Appeal has had an opportunity over the last decade or so to address all the key definitions in the Sexual Offences Act 2003, which has led to greater clarity in most areas of the law governing sexual offences.

Non-consensual offences

There has been important case law during the last five years, including some clarification of the law governing absence of consent where it is alleged that there has been psychological coercion rather than violence or the threat of violence.

After the implementation of the 2003 Act in May 2004, there were concerns that the new statutory definition of consent in s.74 might not be apt to cover circumstances where a teenager had been groomed for sex. However, those concerns have proved not to be well-founded. The last few years have seen successful prosecutions of gangs who sexually exploited young girls in various cities such as Oxford, Rotherham and Rochdale. As always with consent, context is all-important. In the context of grooming, an apparent consent may well not be a genuine consent. In *Ali (Yasir)*,[1] the Court of Appeal acknowledged that one of the consequences of grooming is that it has a tendency to limit or subvert a complainant's capacity to make free decisions, and it creates the risk that he or she simply submitted because of the environment of dependency created by those responsible for treating him or her in this way. An individual may have been manipulated to the extent that he or she is unaware of, or confused about, the distinction between acquiescence and genuine agreement at the time the incident occurred. Importantly, Fulford L.J. explained that in a case in which a vulnerable or immature individual has allegedly been groomed, the question of whether real or proper consent was given will usually be for the jury unless the evidence clearly indicates that proper consent was given.

In *Assange v Swedish Prosecution Authority*,[2] the Divisional Court, when ruling upon an extradition request, clarified that deceptions falling short of deceptions within the scope of s.76 of the 2003 Act may entitle a jury to conclude there was no genuine consent. However, the elusive principle that would enable easy identification of a deception capable of vitiating consent has yet to be found. An active and intended deception as to gender can do so,[3] as can a deception as to whether a condom was to be worn[4] or whether the defendant would ejaculate,[5] whereas deception as to wealth cannot.

The advocates of an interpretation of the s.74 definition of consent, which seeks to protect a complainant's autonomy by treating as relevant all active and intended deceptions as to any material fact, appear to have the ascendancy.

Trafficking

This is a hugely important and topical area. The Modern Slavery Act received Royal Assent in March 2015 and came into force on July 31, 2015.

---

[1] [2015] EWCA Crim 1279.
[2] [2011] EWHC 2489 (Admin).
[3] *Justine McNally v The Queen* [2013] EWCA Crim 1051.
[4] *Assange v Swedish Prosecution Authority* [2011] EWHC 2489 (Admin).
[5] *R (F) v DPP* [2013] EWHC 945 (Admin).

The effects of the new Act are: (i) to consolidate the hitherto disparate law around slavery and trafficking offences, replacing the offences in s.59A (formerly ss.57–59) of the Sexual Offence Act 2003 (trafficking into, out of and within the UK for the purposes of sexual exploitation); (ii) to bring the UK into line with international instruments on human trafficking and slavery, servitude, and forced compulsory labour; (iii) to enhance the prospects of eradicating slavery, servitude, trafficking and exploitation (both work and sexual); (iv) to rescue and protect victims of modern slavery (both trafficking and exploitation); and (v) to provide measures to encourage victims of these offences to come forward. In addressing these developments (in Chapter 11), we welcome to our team Riel Karmy-Jones QC of 18 Red Lion Chambers, a much respected expert in this area.

Section 45 of the Modern Slavery Act 2015 provides a new statutory defence for victims of slavery and trafficking, whereas in the past the only remedy available to a victim was to apply for a stay. The defence builds upon the CPS guidance, with the purpose of encouraging victims to come forward and give evidence without fear of being convicted of offences connected to their own slavery or trafficking situation. The defence does not, however, supersede the CPS guidance, nor remove the requirement for the proper exercise of prosecutorial discretion before proceedings are brought against a possible victim of trafficking.

Given the scale of trafficking, evidence may emerge that a convicted defendant is and was a credible victim of trafficking. This may lead to applications for leave to appeal out of time on the basis that, had this been known, the CPS would not have prosecuted and the court would have found that to bring proceedings was an abuse of process. These cases may require careful guidance from the Court of Appeal in the future.

A measure of the rapid changes made to the law to combat slavery and trafficking can be found in the imposition of the first "international" Slavery and Trafficking Prevention Orders (STPOs) at the Central Criminal Court in early 2016, in order to protect persons from physical or psychological harm which would be likely to occur if the offenders committed a slavery or human trafficking offence. The potential for the wide ambit of STPOs is well illustrated by these orders, which prevented nationals of the Republic of Slovakia from returning to their own home towns where they had recruited their victims.

Child sexual abuse imagery

Vast numbers of web pages have been taken down as a result of reports to watchdogs such as the Internet Watch Foundation, but cases of exploitative imagery continue to proliferate before the courts. As well as addressing developments in the law in this area, we explain the new approach to sentencing indecent image cases set out in the Sentencing Council guideline. But the problem remains deeply concerning, the more so given the increasing use of levels of encryption that law enforcement cannot access and the trading of imagery on the unpoliced dark web.

Evidence

Since our 4th edition, as more cases have reached the Court of Appeal, there have been many decisions illustrating the operation of the provisions on bad character, hearsay and previous sexual history (s.41 of the Youth Justice and Criminal Evidence Act 1999). Two judgments of Hughes L.J. (as he then was) are of particular importance. First, *R. v D, P and U*[6] provides valuable guidance as to the approach to be adopted in determining the admissibility of bad character evidence in respect of the possession of indecent photographs where a defendant is charged with a contact offence. Second, *Riat*[7] is in our view required reading, not only because of its clear exposition of the statutory framework governing hearsay evidence, but also because it provides three instructive examples of the application of law in sex cases.

The operation of s.41 of the 1999 Act (evidence of the complainant's previous sexual history) has for the most part become smoother. It is rare for evidence of a complainant's sexual experience with a third party to be admissible under s.41.

Inevitably, issues concerning the posting of entries on social networking sites have been considered by the Court of Appeal, which has held that a sexual entry may constitute sexual behaviour which engages s.41 of the YJCEA 1999.[8]

There have also been important developments since our 4th edition in relation to the admissibility of expert evidence in criminal proceedings. In 2011, the Law Commission recommended the introduction by statute of a new reliability-based test of admissibility for such evidence. Although the Government declined to legislate, the matter has not rested there, as the Rule Committee has filled the gap by adopting many of the Law Commission's recommendations in the Criminal Procedure Rules. We have revised our chapter on the subject (Chapter 24) in order to explain the genesis and impact of the new provisions in the Rules and accompanying Criminal Practice Directions.

Historic cases

Whilst many complainants may take matters to their grave without revealing abuse they endured when they were young, in the wake of high profile investigations such as Operation Yewtree, there is evidence of greater disclosure.

---

[6] [2011] EWCA Crim 1474.
[7] [2012] EWCA 1509.
[8] *Ben-Rejab* [2011] EWCA Crim 1136; *R v D* [2011] EWCA Crim 2305.

However, the law governing the trial of historic cases has developed in a haphazard way, with different constitutions of the Court of Appeal adopting different approaches both to applications to stay for abuse of process on grounds of delay and to sentencing.

The five-judge Court of Appeal in *R. v F(S)*[9] gave clear guidance as to the approach to be taken to an application for a stay due to delay. This guidance has provided enormous assistance to the courts during the last five years, at a time when there are more and more historic cases involving sexual offending. Points which simply go to whether there is sufficient evidence and whether the *Galbraith* test is satisfied are now reserved for submissions at the close of the prosecution case.

The Court of Appeal revisited the sentencing of historic sexual offending in *R. H(J)*,[10] where the then Lord Chief Justice, Lord Judge, set out the principles underpinning the correct approach. Notwithstanding this important guidance, judges frequently face difficult sentencing exercises in sex cases. The use by Lord Judge of the expression "measured reference" does not mean that the court should create a notional guideline, scaling down the starting point to a figure in the middle of the sentencing range that would have been available at the time of committing the offences.[11] The judge must follow the clear and structured decision-making process set out in the current guideline whenever the offence was committed and reflect modern attitudes to historic offences.[12] This can pose difficulties, particularly where the defendant was under 18 at the time of the offences. This area is likely to receive more attention from the Court of Appeal in the near future.

Medical chapters

We are deeply grateful to our two medical contributors. Dr Catherine White OBE, the Clinical Director of the Sexual Assault Referral Centre, St Mary's Hospital, Manchester, has expanded her brief so as to cover the medical evidence in respect of both adults (Chapter 21) and children (Chapter 22.) She has done so with her usual authority and clarity.

The fundamental messages to be drawn from the pioneering work of Professor Fiona Mason on the psychological impact of the trauma of sexual assault upon victims remains as powerful as ever (Chapter 23). We are grateful to her and Dr Paula Murphy for updating the chapter so as to include new research and developments in the area.

[9] [2011] EWCA Crim 1844.
[10] [2012] EWCA Crim 2753.
[11] *Attorney General's Reference (No.27 of 2015)* [2015] EWCA Crim 1538.
[12] *Clifford* [2014] EWCA Crim 2245.

Sentencing

The approach taken by the courts when dealing with sex offenders has been transformed over the last 15 years. Sex offenders have received special attention from successive Parliaments, and a number of measures have been introduced with the aim of protecting the public from them.

We published a supplement to our 4th edition in January 2014 to cover significant changes in the substantive law and in evidential, procedural and medical developments. The supplement included the Sentencing Council's new Definitive Sentencing Guideline, which has applied to all adult[13] sex offenders, whenever the offence was committed, from April 1, 2014.

The new guideline represents a new approach with major differences from its predecessor, the *Sexual Offences Act: Definitive Guideline,* which had been in place since April 2007. The Council adopted the decision-making process for sentencing that it developed for the *Assault: Definitive Guideline.* It is a step-by-step process with nine steps to be followed for each offence. An emphasis is placed on harm and culpability, and the structure for determining these varies according to the offence concerned so that the guideline is tailored to the particular offending behaviour. It focuses on the extent of the harm to the victim rather than on the nature of the particular physical activity. It uses a number of models for addressing harm and culpability, each different from the model used in the previous guideline. The model used for the majority of offences, including rape and sexual assault, has a lowest level (a baseline) where inherent harm and culpability are assumed.

Two years on, we have had the opportunity to consider Court of Appeal decisions in respect of sentences passed under the new guideline. Whilst most cases will turn on their own facts, some provide useful illustrations of the proper application of the guideline, whilst others, such as *Attorney General's Reference (No. 51 of 2015) (Whitmore),*[14] assist in interpreting factors which may be critical when evaluating harm or culpability. With this in mind, we have included some recent decisions in respect of the new guideline in the chapters dealing with specific offences. We have also decided that the different approach adopted in the new guideline justifies giving the subject a separate chapter in the sentencing section of this edition (Section C, Chapter 33).

Tim Moloney QC has provided two excellent chapters. One deals with the complex subject of sentencing sex offending in the wake of the final demise of imprisonment for public protection (IPP) and the advent of the new type of extended sentence, which is deployed frequently in cases of sexual offenders who represent a continuing danger to the public, whenever the

---

[13] The previous guideline (i.e. the Sentencing Guidelines Council's *Sexual Offences Act 2003 Definitive Guideline* relating to offenders sentenced after May 14, 2007) has been superseded by the 2014 guidelines only as far as adults are concerned, and is still in force in respect young offenders. See *R. v GB* [2015] EWCA Crim 1501.

[14] [2015] EWCA Crim 1699.

offence was committed (Chapter 34). The other contains a thorough exposition on the complex law relating to notification requirements (Chapter 35).

HH Judge Picton joined our team at the time of the last supplement. As Course Director of the Judicial College's seminar on serious sexual offences, he is well-placed to cover the various preventative orders available to the courts in these cases, and we are very grateful for his lucid treatment of the subject. Of particular note, Sexual Offences Prevention Orders (SOPOs) have been the subject of a re-branding exercise so as to become Sexual Harm Prevention Orders (SHPOs). As HH Judge Picton explains, the hurdle that has to be surmounted for orders to be made has been lowered. Furthermore, the scope of the provisions has been widened so that orders can be made that prohibit qualifying offenders from foreign travel. These orders continue to give rise to drafting challenges. The current approach of the Court of Appeal appears to favour the inclusion of a non-contact clause even in a case solely concerning indecent images, where there has been no current or previous instance of physical sexual contact.

Crown Prosecution Service (CPS)

In the light of the exponential rise in the number of cases, we felt that we should cover both investigation and policy in respect of the decision to prosecute. This has led to the recruitment of more specialist contributors and the inclusion of two further chapters: (i) one on the police investigation of rape and serious sexual offences by Assistant Commissioner Martin Hewitt QPM, which covers the structure of police investigations, the investigative process and police decision–making (Chapter 16); and (ii) one on CPS policy and decision-making on the prosecution of rape and serious sexual offences by Alison Levitt QC[15] and Tim Thompson[16] Alison and Tim cover the Victims' Right to Review scheme introduced by the CPS in response to the Court of Appeal's invitation in *Killick*.[17]

Advocacy and the vulnerable

We are writing at a critical time for the adversarial system. It must adapt so as to ensure that the vulnerable (whether complainant, witness or defendant) are treated with appropriate sensitivity in court. The need for many more advocates to undertake these cases has exposed continuing flaws in the treatment of the vulnerable in court.

Over the last decade or so, special measures to assist vulnerable witnesses to give their best evidence have been a conspicuous success. Witnesses have

[15] Principal Legal Advisor to the Director of Public Prosecutions 2009–2014.
[16] Deputy Chief Crown Prosecutor CPS until 2015. (Chapter 17).
[17] [2011] EWCA 1608.

been able to give evidence where even half a generation ago it would have been inconceivable.

The dark days of traditional adversarial cross-examination of the vulnerable are over. Some advocates have already acquired the necessary specialist skills. First class material has been developed, such as the Advocate's Gateway toolkits. We are deeply grateful to the Advocacy Training Council for giving us their enthusiastic support by permitting us to include some of the most important of the toolkits in Appendix F.

However, there are strong and justified concerns that advocacy has not evolved so as to ensure best practice is universally adopted in respect of the handling and questioning of vulnerable witnesses and defendants. Questioning that contravenes principles for obtaining accurate information from a witness by exploiting his or her developmental limitations is not only wholly inconsistent with a fair trial, but also contravenes the respective Codes of Conduct of both the Bar and the Law Society.

In late 2013, the Advocacy Training Council (ATC) set up a working party to devise a pan-profession training course for all advocates who undertake cases involving the vulnerable. As we write this Preface, following the preparation and piloting of materials, trainers and facilitators are being trained by the ATC so as to enable the course to be undertaken by all advocates during the next two years or so.

The importance of these developments has led us to devote more space to advocacy and the vulnerable, so as to assist practitioners to develop the appropriate and necessary skills when cross-examining. With the collaboration of Alexandra Ward and Angela Rafferty QC, we have written a chapter on advocacy and the vulnerable explaining how the Court of Appeal, through a number of ground-breaking decisions,[18] has explained the correct approach that advocates should adopt in cases involving the vulnerable (Chapter 28).

With the help of Alexandra Ward, we have also kept pace with the rapid changes in respect of the vulnerable in court. Her chapter on vulnerable witnesses, dealing with special measures and related matters, covers all the significant developments in the area, including Ground Rules Hearings, which have become an essential part of the pre-trial process in cases involving the vulnerable (Chapter 27). The successful piloting of pre-trial cross-examination under s.28 of the Youth Justice and Criminal Evidence Act 1999 has demonstrated the effectiveness of all parties complying with ground rules laid down by the judge, including through early judicial scrutiny of proposed questions.

---

[18] *Barker* [2010] EWCA Crim 4; *W and M* [2010] EWCA Crim 1926; *Wills* [2011] EWCA Crim 1938; *R. v E* [2012] EWCA Crim 563; *Lumemba* [2015] 1 Cr. App. R. 12 ; *Jonas* [2015] EWCA Crim 562.

Anonymity and reporting restrictions

The period since our 4th edition has seen the enactment of important new provisions relating to reporting restrictions, as a result of which we have completely revised our chapter on the topic (Chapter 29). The new provisions include an important new power to impose lifetime reporting restrictions in relation to witnesses and victims under the age of 18. In the revised chapter, we also explain current policy and good practice on the naming of suspects pre-charge, which remains an intensely controversial subject.

Other important developments

HH Judge Johannah Cutts QC, now the Resident Judge at Reading Crown Court, has found time to cover all significant developments in respect of disclosure, including the *Protocol and Good Practice Model: Disclosure of information in cases of alleged child abuse and linked criminal and care directions*, which has helped to achieve consistency of approach in this critical area (Chapter 18).

We are delighted that Jonathan Rees QC, with his recent experience of high profile DNA cases, has built on the work of Victoria Oakes and updated Graham Cooke's much admired chapter on *DNA, Law and Statistics* (Chapter 24).

Gillian Jones and Naomi Parsons, both of Red Lion Chambers, have updated the chapter on sexual offences cases in the Youth Court, where many trials of sexual offences take place (Chapter 31).

Similarly, HH Judge David McFarland, the Recorder of Belfast, has provided his expertise in respect of developments in Northern Ireland (Chapter 32).

We would like to give special thanks to the Law Commissioner Professor David Ormerod QC, who has always been ready to discuss, assist and shed light should a particular legal problem arise. We have also been greatly assisted by Laura Hoyano, Fellow and Tutor in Law at Wadham College, Oxford, for sharing her expertise on such subjects as the relevance of behavioural evidence of victims of abuse where the defence attacks the complainant's credibility on the basis of aberrant behaviour following alleged incidents.

We would also like to express our gratitude to the many other colleagues who have been prepared to act as sounding boards on difficult issues as they have emerged during the preparation of this work. We mention in particular in this connection the valuable contributions of HH Judge Martin Picton, HH Judge Mark Lucraft QC and HH Judge Patricia Lees.

Given the scope of this work, we needed the assistance of two able researchers. We found them at Red Lion Chambers, where Samantha Wright and Elizabeth Campbell were in the middle of their pupillages. Quite apart from their general assistance, Elizabeth carried out important research on certain areas on which developments elsewhere in the Commonwealth shed light, whilst Samantha Wright took responsibility for the appendices, including her own work on Revenge Pornography (Appendix I).

HH Judge Peter Rook QC,   Robert Ward CBE QC,
The Old Bailey   *Cambridge*

April 25, 2016

Preface to the Third Edition

A major part of the legal landscape in respect of the law governing sexual offences has been re-designed during the seven years since the publication of the second edition of this work. The landscaping culminated in the Sexual Offences Act 2003 (the new Act), which represents the most important overhaul of the law at least since Victorian times.

Even before the first reading of the then Sexual Offences Bill 2003 in the House of Lords in January 2003, we were planning a third edition which would deal not only with the new substantive law, but also with relevant procedural, sentencing, evidential and medical issues. We felt that readers would wish us to include as many of these matters as possible. For instance, the vulnerable witnesses legislation (contained in the Youth Justice and Criminal Evidence Act 1999) is of immense importance in sex cases and so we have devoted a chapter to it. The complicated restrictions on evidence of the complainant's previous sexual history (to be found in ss.41–43 of the same Act) warrant a chapter in their own right. Similarly, subjects such as disclosure, DNA and medical evidence deserve significant coverage.

The new Act came into force on May 1, 2004.[1] Its provisions derive largely from the recommendations of a Home Office review which put in an immense amount of work, meeting on 35 occasions between February 1999 and April 2000. The eventual report of the Sexual Offences Review was handed to Ministers as long ago as April 2000, and was published as *Setting the Boundaries: Reforming the Law on Sex Offences.*[2] It contained a total of 62 recommendations, and invited further views in 11 areas. The consultation period resulted in over 700 responses. The Review was followed by a White Paper, *Protecting the Public: Strengthening Protection against Sex Offenders and Reforming the Law on Sexual Offences,*[3] the proposals in which formed the basis of the first draft of the Bill.

In *Protecting the Public* the Government stated:

> "The law on sex offences, as it stands, is archaic, incoherent and discriminatory. Much of it is contained in the Sexual Offences Act 1956, and most of that was simply a consolidation of nineteenth-century law. It does not reflect the changes in society and social attitudes that have taken place since the Act became law and it is widely considered to be inadequate and out of date."

It would be difficult to disagree with these sentiments. In fact academics and practitioners have been calling for this overhaul for a long time. In the

---

[1] It is understood that an inquiry into these investigations is not being pursued: *The Times*, September 15, 2010, *Rape case reform is shelved to cut costs.*

[2] Home Office, The Stern Review: *A Report by Baroness Stern CBE of an independent review into how rape complaints are handled by public authorities in England and Wales*, March 2010.

[3] For instance, the London Metropolitan University has reported that 6.5 per cent is the lowest rate amongst 33 European countries.

preface to the second edition, in 1997, we stated that there was a strong case for general reform and a fresh codification of the law governing sexual offences. Previous reform proposals, including the Fifteenth Report of the Criminal Law Revision Committee,[4] had been largely ignored. Despite some important incremental development, both at common law[5] and by legislation,[6] a comprehensive reform of the law governing sexual offences was long overdue. The 1956 Act failed to reflect the morality and prevalent sexual practices of the present day. The issue climbed the political agenda in the 1990s. There is now a much greater public awareness of the nature and effect of sexual assaults, combined with an increase in reporting sexual crimes. Falling conviction rates were said to be at least in part a consequence of the inadequacies of the old law (quite apart from shortcomings in respect of the law of evidence[7] and procedure and investigations).[8] The new Act redefines many of the offences found in the old legislation, but introduces a great number of new offences. It is not a complete codification of all sexual offences. Some regulation remains elsewhere, for example in relation to prostitution[9] and indecent photographs,[10] albeit the new Act does make some changes in these areas.

The Bill was introduced into the Lords, where it received vigorous scrutiny. The debates were informed by a high level of legal and social expertise on all sides of the House. In addition to the Parliamentary debates, the Bill was scrutinised by the House of Commons Home Affairs Committee.[11] It ended its passage through Parliament substantially intact, but with some important changes made at various stages, particularly in relation to the new mental element required for non-consensual offences and the list of circumstances, now set out in s.75 of the Act, in which there is an evidential presumption of absence of consent.

The key objective of the Bill was to modernise the law of sexual offences, by refocusing it on critical issues such as consent and the protection of sexual autonomy. The main principles underpinning the Bill were (i) non-discrimination between men and women and non-discrimination between those of different sexual orientation (some existing offences were discriminatory on this basis, *e.g.* the separate offence of "buggery" for non-consensual homosexual acts); (ii) protection of the public, especially the vulnerable (particularly children and the mentally disordered, *e.g.* the law designed to protect "defectives" was both inadequate and offensive, and (iii) compliance with the

---

[4] *H (Karl Anthony)* [2005] EWCA Crim 732, "sexual assault", "touching"; *Heard* [2007] EWCA Crim 125, "intentional touching".
[5] [2009] 1 A.C. 92.
[6] [2004] Crim. L.R. 342 at p.353.
[7] [2009] UKHL 42.
[8] *Gavin White* [2010] EWCA Crim 1929; *Shanji Zhang* [2010] EWCA Crim 2018.
[9] *Convicting Rapists and Protecting Victims – Justice for Victims of Rape* (Spring 2006).
[10] [2007] EWCA Crim 804.
[11] *Hysa* [2007] EWCA Crim 2056; Appendix G of this work.

European Convention on Human Rights, *e.g.* the offence of gross indecency was in breach of Article 8.[12]

The Act largely achieves its aims, but is far from problem-free. The areas of particular difficulty are undue complexity and density of drafting, excessive overlap between offences, and excessive breadth of offences, resulting in over-dependence on prosecutorial discretion to ensure offences are charged only where the intervention of the criminal law is justified. Furthermore, there is an undue emphasis on the means by which harm is caused rather than the harm itself.

The Act creates over 50 offences, some carrying different maximum sentences depending upon the facts proved. Under the principle in *Courtie*[13] this means yet more offences, and prosecutors will therefore need to be careful in drafting charges and indictments. Throughout the Act the maximum sentences are generally higher than for comparable offences under the previous law.[14] As we write, consideration is being given to the newly-formed Sentencing Advisory Panel's *Consultation Paper on the Sexual Offences Act 2003* (available at *www.sentencing-guidelines.gov.uk*).

The Act does away with many ancient offences that have been part of the legal landscape for centuries, including incest, indecent assault, buggery, bestiality and gross indecency between men. It is with a twinge of regret that we see the passing of "abduction of an heiress for the sake of her fortune." Many are replaced by new offences that are essentially modernised versions of the old ones. Rape is retained, label and all, but is redefined. Some areas of the law are left largely unaffected, in particular the law of child pornography contained in the Protection of Children Act 1978 and Criminal Justice Act 1988—though the protection of these statutes is extended from children under 16 to children under 18. The law of prostitution is also largely unaffected, although important new trafficking offences are created and the Government is conducting a separate review of the law in this area.

The abuse of trust offences build on the offence introduced in the Sexual Offences (Amendment) Act 2000 but extend its protection to children under 18. There is a series of new offences to protect children under 13 and under 16, and in addition the Act creates a series of familial child sex offences with an extended definition of family no longer dependent on the existence of a blood relationship. Offences of sex with an adult relative replace incest. The Act brings about major changes to offences designed to protect those with mental disorders. The demise of the term "defective" is to be welcomed, not just because it was offensive and pejorative, but also because it led to terminological confusion and set too high a threshold by requiring severe impairment of social functioning as minimum conditions. No fewer than 12 offences are created to protect the mentally disordered, with three categories

---

[12] [2008] EWCA Crim 2394.
[13] *R. v ER* [2010] EWCA Crim 2522; *see also Miller* [2010] EWCA Crim 1578.
[14] Chapter 23.

of exploitative contexts each comprising four offences. Finally, the prosecutor's armoury is further strengthened with three widely drafted preparatory offences.

A preface is not the place to discuss the detail of the new law. However, we do wish to comment on the significant changes embodied in the non-consensual offences. First, we welcome the demise of the principle in *Morgan v DPP*.[15] The diehard subjectivists have lost the battle, and we believe rightly so. In 1997, in the preface to our second edition, we indicated that we felt this reform was overdue. In the complicated area of sexual relations where individuals should be expected to respect each other's autonomy, it was offensive that in the early 21st century a defendant's wholly unreasonable belief that a complainant was consenting could provide them with a defence, if the belief may have been genuine. We also feel that it is absolutely correct that the harshness of a purely objective test has been avoided and that juries will be able to take into account a defendant's relevant characteristics in determining the reasonableness of their belief.

The Government deserves fewer plaudits for the way the Act deals with the concept of consent. Despite the avowed objective to bring crystal clarity to this difficult area, the new legislation falls well short of this. Section 74, which defines consent, is not a model of tight drafting, leaving juries to grapple with concepts such as freedom, choice and capacity. It remains for the jury to resolve as issues of fact such questions as whether the degree of coercion and/or abuse of power or authority exercised upon the complainant's mind was such that he or she did not agree by choice with the freedom to make that choice. That said, this aspect of the new law represents a significant improvement on the approach advocated in *Olugboja*,[16] which left juries with very little guidance apart from being told that submission is not necessarily consent.

The Sexual Offences Review in *Setting the Boundaries* felt that the arguments for both defining and explaining consent in statute were overwhelming. In particular, they thought that the approach adopted in a number of Australian states (and the Penal Code) of setting a list of examples of circumstances where consent was not present would be helpful to practitioners and juries. The Review's list was designed to complement and buttress a definition of consent based on free agreement. The grand design of the Review was to set out those areas that are well-established in case law as to when consent is not present, and those where it should be clear that consent would be present. The Review recognised the challenge of considering whether other types of behaviour ought to be included, in order to produce a robust and appropriate list of circumstances over and above the major components of the common law. It did include in its recommended, non-exhaustive list several examples which went significantly further than the

[15] London: Royal College of Paediatrics and Child Health, 2008.
[16] Chapter 24.

common law, including (i) submission of the complainant because of threats or fear of serious detriment of any type to themselves or another person, (ii) complainant too affected by alcohol or drugs to give free agreement, and (iii) complainant has agreement given for them by a third party.

The Review clearly envisaged that where one or more of the circumstances in the list was established, consent would be taken as being absent and would no longer be an issue. *Protecting the Public* reproduced a similar list of circumstances, but framed as presumptions. The Sexual Offences Bill as introduced included provisions which, if they had become law, would have had the effect of reversing the burden of proof if the prosecution established the relevant sexual activity, one of the list of circumstances and the defendant's knowledge of that circumstance. Responding to pressure in the House of Lords, Baroness Scotland moved a Government amendment on Third Reading so that the presumptions, if established, placed an evidential rather than persuasive burden upon the defendant. By this time the original list of circumstances as recommended by the Review had been significantly eroded.

We have serious misgivings as to the extent to which the s.75 list will assist juries on the issue of consent. A direction in accordance with the definition in s.74, tailor-made for the particular case, will often be clearer than the additional s.75 direction which will be necessary if the judge decides at the close of the evidence that the presumption of absence of consent and/or reasonable belief in consent has not been rebutted. We are, in short, concerned as to whether the s.75 list will in practice prove effective or simply cosmetic.

In many cases, the evidential burden will no doubt be discharged and the s.75 route to proving absence of consent and/or reasonable belief in consent will be barred. For instance, a defendant can do this by means of his own evidence. Even if the presumption is not discharged, the jury will need to be directed as to the three elements that have to be proved before the s.75 route is available. One of these is the defendant's knowledge of the circumstance. We fail to follow the relevance of this to the issue of whether a complainant may have been consenting or not. Furthermore, some of the circumstances, such as when the complainant was asleep, hardly need a s.75 direction. All sexual activity requires a fresh consent.

In some respects, the new Act is an undeniable improvement on the previous law: the offences are better targeted, there is more coherence[17] and far fewer idiosyncrasies. There is also an absence of discrimination based on gender or sexual orientation. However, the complexity of the new offence structure,[18] the excessive overlap between offences and the substantial reliance on prosecutorial discretion are likely to lead to problems.

---

[17] Chapter 18.
[18] [2010] EWCA Crim 1824.

The Crown Prosecution Service will need to ensure that there is a countrywide even-handed approach to decisions as to whether it is in the public interest to prosecute, and as to which charges are appropriate when there is significant overlapping. This discretion will be important in respect of sexual conduct not only between the young, but also between the mentally disordered, and (in the case of consensual sexual penetration) between adult relatives. The Director of Public Prosecutions, Ken Macdonald Q.C., has already indicated the principles that will govern the exercise of the discretion to prosecute in these difficult areas,[19] and the legal guidance will soon be published on the Internet. In respect of child sex offences, where a person's conduct towards the complainant is exploitative, or coercive, or he or she is much older than the complainant, the balance may be in favour of prosecution, whereas if the sexual activity is truly of the complainant's own free will it may not be in public interest to prosecute. It will not be in the public interest to prosecute children who are of the same or similar age and understanding who engage in sexual activity, where the activity is truly consensual for both parties and there are no aggravating features, such as coercion or corruption. In such cases, protection will normally be best achieved by providing education for the children and young people and providing them and their families with access to advisory and counselling services.

Multiple charging options could lead to confusion and inhibit development of case law, with the Crown Prosecution Service and the courts treating different types of sexual conduct in an inconsistent manner. Much will turn on the effectiveness of the Crown Prosecution Service's guidance to prosecutors on the approach to particular cases, extracts from which (in its current form) we produce in Appendix E. For instance, where a child is under 13, an under–13 offence should be charged, if appropriate, notwithstanding the fact that the new familial offences under ss. 25 and 26 cover children under 13. If there may be difficulty in proving the child was under 13, then the appropriate familial offence should be charged, so long as the other elements of the offence can be proved. Where the child is 13 or over, if possible the familial offence should be charged, and where the child is 16 or 17 this will be the only charge available, unless the case comes within the abuse of position of trust provisions (ss. 16 to 24). Where there is difficulty in proving a "family" relationship, the equivalent offence requiring no proof of such a relationship should be charged (s.9 or 10).

While the provisions that impose evidential burdens, such as ss. 75 and 38(2), are not incompatible with the presumption of innocence under Article 6(2), it is quite possible that the criminalisation of sexual conduct between those aged 13–16 may lead to a successful ECHR challenge.[20] Article 8 is engaged when the law seeks to regulate a person's sexual behaviour, and it is

---

[19] [2010] EWCA Crim 4; see also *Malicki* [2009] EWCA Crim 365 which is likely now to be regarded as a case on its own facts.

[20] Christopher Kinch QC, *Nuffield Foundation Seminar*, June 10, 2010.

doubtful whether the full range of offences against children is "necessary" and "proportionate" to a legitimate aim such as the protection of health or morals.[21] For instance, the Parliamentary Joint Committee on Human Rights suggested that s.7 was overbroad in criminalising all sexual touching of children under 13.[22]

In some parts of the Act there is an obsession with exhaustive definition, whilst in others, such as in the s.74 definition of "consent", the drafting is far from tight. The courts may resolve through interpretation at least some of the problems to which the Act might otherwise give rise. But over time other difficulties are likely to emerge that are not yet apparent. The Government has announced that it proposes to scrutinise closely the operation of the new Act, and it is safe to predict that it will not be another century before the next Parliamentary foray into this territory. It is with regret that we note that Parliament has missed the opportunity in the Criminal Justice Act 2003 to make the evidence of a complainant's first complaint admissible even if not made as soon as can reasonably be expected. Complainants may be slow to report, for a number of good and compelling reasons, and a jury will often be assisted by hearing the circumstances of the first reporting. We have come a long way since the days of hue and cry, and it is somewhat surprising that a Government adopting an inclusionary approach to evidence should allow this anachronistic rule to remain.[23]

It is perhaps wise to remember that reforms to the substantive law will not on their own improve conviction rates. High quality investigation and clear presentation in court are of fundamental importance. Similarly, it is vital that victims feel that they will receive appropriate support from the criminal justice system.[24] Already much has been achieved in some areas, but proper resources are needed, and it is to be hoped that funding will allow sexual assault referral centres to be available throughout the country. From July 12, 2004, Havens will be providing over the whole of London such services as acute, round-the-clock forensic on-call cover and medical aftercare to victims of sexual assault.[25]

Myths cut both ways. The bad old days when complainants were unfairly cross-examined about their previous sexual history have gone. The "twin myths", as described in Canadian Jurisprudence,[26] "that unchaste women were more likely to consent to intercourse and, in any event, were less worthy of belief" are outlawed lines of reasoning. Notwithstanding this, we still hear

---

[21] It is understood that ACPO are currently introducing a new system of shorter interviews. In many cases the prosecution will rely solely upon the complainant's account given in answer to the initial open-ended questions rather than the later line by line dissection of that account.

[22] Home Office, Report on the advisory group on video-recorded evidence (1989), Chairman His Honour Thomas Pigot QC.

[23] J. Spencer, "Children's Evidence: the Barker case and the case for Pigot" 3 *Archbold News* 5-8 (2010).

[24] See *The Framework Decision on the Rights of Victims* (2001).

[25] Chapter 26.

[26] [2010] EWCA Crim 1926.

speeches from politicians suggesting that complainants are not sufficiently protected by the regime that regulates previous sexual history evidence. Such suggestions misrepresent the true position and do a disservice to victims. All who operate in the courts know that, whatever the situation was in the past, the current regime is very tight, and it is irresponsible to mislead the public into thinking otherwise. If Parliament re-visits this difficult area in the wake of *R. v A (No.2)*,[27] the words of Lord Steyn should be borne in mind: "while the statute pursued desirable goals, the methods adopted amounted to legislative overkill."[28] In Canada, the Hon. Mrs. Justice McLachlin reached a similar conclusion in *Seaboyer*,[29] when the Canadian Supreme Court declared a blanket exclusion to be unconstitutional. Her words give us great insight:

> "In achieving its purpose—the abolition of the outmoded, sexist based use of sexual conduct evidence—it overshoots the mark and renders inadmissible evidence that may be essential to the presentation of legitimate defences and hence to a fair trial. In exchange for the elimination of the possibility that the judge and jury may draw illegitimate inferences from the evidence, it exacts as a price the real risk that an innocent person may be convicted. The price is too great in relation to the benefit secured, and cannot be tolerated in a society that does not countenance in any form the conviction of the innocent."

We wish to acknowledge the significant assistance that we have received from colleagues and friends. Disclosure issues are constantly arising in child sex cases, particularly in relation to local authority and health records, school reports and records held by counsellors. Johannah Cutts has updated our disclosure chapter so as to provide a lucid exposition of the current law. Graham Cooke has again come up trumps with a practical chapter on how best to approach DNA evidence. Alexandra Ward undertook much of the work on "Vulnerable Witnesses, Special Measures and related matters." She also did the groundwork on "Sexual offences against those with a Mental Disorder." Ruby Hamid provided valuable assistance in respect of "Familial offences." Tim Maloney has lent us his expertise on criminology and sentencing by writing no less than three chapters, Chapter 22—*Sentencing of sex offenders*, Chapter 23—*Notification and notification orders*, and Chapter 24—*Sexual Offences Prevention Orders, Foreign Travel Orders and risk of Sexual Harm Orders*. For the first time we have included a chapter on the medical aspects of sexual assault, and we are grateful to Dr Beata Cybulksa, Associate Specialist in Forensic Gynaecology/ Genitourinary Medicine based at the Haven Whitechapel, for finding time to write this for us whilst busy with the launch of the Paddington Haven.

We have had requests from a number of colleagues who feel that advocates would gain from a checklist of important points likely to arise in sex cases. In response to this, with the encouragement of our publishers, we have for the

[27] In fact the Old Bailey.
[28] [2008] EWCA Crim 2310.
[29] Chapter 30.

first time included a practical guide for advocates (whether prosecution or defence) who undertake sex cases. The guide is both the brainchild of and compiled by Patricia Lees. She has drawn upon her experience as both prosecution and defence counsel in such cases, and we are very grateful to her for providing this helpful new addition, which is to be found in Appendix C.

Others deserve special thanks: Katie Dennison for her research into Commonwealth cases which are highly relevant in some areas of the new Act; Sandra Villani for her vital role as a research assistant and proof reader; Professor David Ormerod for both reading and providing constructive comments on some of our draft chapters; Neil Kibble of the University of Wales for reading and giving insightful comments upon our draft chapter on previous sexual history; Sheelagh Morton, formerly of the Crown Prosecution Service Policy Directorate, for reading and providing valuable assistance with our chapter on Vulnerable Witnesses; Jeremy Carter Manning Q.C., leading counsel for the appellant in *Mohammed Dica*,[30] for keeping us abreast of developments in the law governing consent to run the risk of contracting HIV, and offences under Offences against the Person Act 1861; Anthony Jennings, Q.C., for his ideas on how to approach historic cases; Nigel Gibbs of the Crown Prosecution Service Policy Directorate for his assistance in respect of Appendix E; Emmanuel Vincent for his research into historic cases; and Mohammed Fakrul Islam, the librarian at 18 Red Lion Court, whose constant willingness to track down obscure publications at short notice, made an enormous difference to our task.

Finally, we have once again tested our publishers' forbearance to the full. They have responded with full support, understanding and efficiency. We would like to record our deep gratitude to Nicky Meech and Johanna Whelehan of Sweet and Maxwell who demonstrated all these qualities.

P.R.   R.W.
18, Red Lion Court,   *Godmanchester*
London EC4A 3EB   July 9, 2004

---

[30] With the Central and North West London NHS Foundation Trust.

Preface to the Second Edition

It is now over six years since the publication of the first edition of this work. We welcome this opportunity to up-date the law, which is stated as at February 1, 1997. We have also added various chapters in order to assist the busy practitioner with the practical problems that frequently occur during trials for sexual offences.

Since 1990 there have been a number of significant changes in this area of the law. However, the Government has refrained from considering the existing law in the round. Whilst there have been reforms in certain areas, other somewhat antique legislation remains on the statute book. Many proposals for reform, particularly those adopted in the draft Criminal Code Bill, have not become law. The Law Commission Consultation Paper *Consent in the Criminal Law* No. 139 (1995) has made significant progress by putting forward provisional proposals to reform a difficult area of the law. We hope that one of these proposals will bring about the overdue demise of the principle that a wholly unreasonable but genuine belief that a complainant was consenting affords a defence to rape. There remains a strong case for general reform and a fresh codification of the law of sexual offences.

In *R. v. R.* the anachronism that a woman could not in law refuse sexual intercourse with her husband was brought to a timely end. The Criminal Justice and Public Order Act 1994 subsequently altered the basis of the offence of rape by enacting that rape includes the penetration of the anus, with the result that a man as well as a woman may be the victim of the offence. The widening of the definition of rape has the effect of confining the offences of buggery to cases of anal intercourse with consent; in other cases the appropriate charge is now rape. The scope of buggery is further limited by the reduction of the age of homosexual consent from 21 to 18, a change also brought about by the 1994 Act. The effect of this reduction is to prevent homosexual acts in private between consenting parties, both of whom have reached the age of 18, from constituting an offence.

In the first edition we took the view that as evidential considerations are of such importance to trials for sexual offences, we should devote an entire chapter to a concise explanation of the relevant rules of evidence. In this edition, we have gone one stage further and have included two chapters on the subject, one dealing concisely with the general rules of evidence and one with the particular issues associated with the evidence of children.

In the supplement to the first edition, published in late 1993, we included a chapter on DNA profiling evidence, in recognition of its frequent use in sexual cases. In this we were greatly assisted by Dr Patrick Lincoln, a highly esteemed expert in this area who is well-known to practitioners. For this edition, we have invited Dr Lincoln to contribute a chapter on DNA profiling, in which he explains the basis of DNA evidence and covers recent scientific advances. In view of the practical difficulties that many practitioners encounter when wrestling with issues of DNA evidence, we have also included a chapter on DNA, Law and Statistics. We are delighted that this chapter has been contributed by Graham Cooke, a barrister with great experience of statistics and many DNA cases. He has been able to include the recent guideline case on presenting DNA evidence to a jury (*Doheny and Adams*).

In the supplement, we also included a chapter on disclosure in sexual cases, so often a problem to the practitioner, particularly when vital material is in the hands of third parties. The positive response to this chapter has encouraged us to cover the subject in this edition. The chapter takes into account the imminent changes to the law of disclosure to be brought about by the Criminal Procedure and Investigations Act 1996. We are particularly grateful to Dominic Bowen for the substantial contribution he made to this chapter.

Whilst we have dealt with sentencing in relation to particular sexual offences in the chapters relating to those offences, we have covered in a separate chapter the provisions of the Criminal Justice Act 1991 on protective sentences for sex offenders and on extended periods of supervision upon release. This chapter also covers the Government's proposed reforms to sentencing in this area, whereby certain second offenders will receive automatic life sentences. At the time of writing, these proposals are before Parliament in the shape of the Crime (Sentences) Bill.

Also at the time of writing, the Government has just published the Sex Offenders Bill, which provides in Part I for the keeping of registers of sex offenders and in Part II for the extension of jurisdiction over certain sexual acts committed against children abroad. Part II of the Bill is intended to complete the work begun by the Sexual Offences (Conspiracy and Incitement) Act 1996, which made it an offence to conspire with or incite others to commit certain sexual acts against children abroad. The 1996 Act and the Bill are set out in full in Appendices C and D.

We should like to express our gratitude to all those who helped in the production of this book, and in particular to the following, who assisted us by commenting on draft chapters, reading proofs or raising unresolved points of law: Alisdair Williamson, Gillian Jones, Adrian Turner and Stephen Leslie Q.C.

Finally, we are particularly indebted to our ever-understanding publishers, who have provided us with support, encouragement and tolerance.

P.R.
Temple

R.W.
Godmanchester
February 16, 1997.

Preface to the First Edition

It was originally intended that this series should cover all offences against the person, including sexual offences, in a single volume. However, it gradually became clear that the law of sexual offences, although generally given a low priority by textbooks on criminal law, in fact deserves extensive treatment in its own right. The sheer size and scope of the subject, and its importance at a time of great public concern over sexual violence and the sexual abuse of children, led eventually to the decision to devote to it an entire volume. As a result we have been able to deal in suitable detail with virtually every facet of the relevant law, from rape through to "streaking" and "mooning" (which may amount to an offence under the Public Order Act 1986 or at common law). We hope that by so doing we have filled a significant gap in the literature.

We have not confined ourselves simply to describing the substantive law. First, evidential considerations are of such particular importance in trials for sexual offences that no book on this subject is really complete unless it contains an explanation of the relevant rules of evidence. We have therefore taken the opportunity to explain those rules in concise terms and to illustrate the problems to which they may give rise. We have not, however, set out to give the law of evidence exhaustive consideration, but simply to steer busy practitioners towards a solution to the problems they are likely to face; anything more we leave to monographs on the law of evidence. Secondly, in writing the book we have been acutely aware of the increased and sometimes intense public interest that has been focussed in recent years on the law of sexual offences, especially as it relates to the abuse and exploitation of children. In anticipation of continuing public debate we have taken the opportunity to describe and comment on proposals for reform, in particular those adopted in the draft Criminal Code Bill.

We have endeavoured to state the law as at May 1, 1990. In a few cases our ever-understanding publishers have allowed us to amend the proofs to incorporate the effects of decisions handed down between that date and October 1990. For the most part we have confined ourselves to adding references to the footnotes, in order simply to put the reader on notice of recent applications or refinements of the law. But where there has been a significant development, such as a departure from earlier authorities, we have dealt with this in the text; as for example, with *R. v. R.* (unreported, July 30, 1990) and *R. v. C. and another* (*The Independent*, October 19, 1990), where judges at first instance have taken a robust line on the vexed question of the scope of the marital exemption in rape. At well past the eleventh hour we were permitted to make short reference to the Law Commission working paper on Rape within Marriage published in November 1990.

We should like to express our gratitude to all those who helped in the production of this book, and in particular to the following, who assisted us by commenting on draft chapters, typing endless drafts or reading proofs: Professor John Andrews; Anthony Arlidge Q.C.; Tracy Ayling; Jenny Driscoll; Nicholas Browne; Peter Carter; Justin Gau; Michael Grieve; Ruth Harrison; Kate Hitchcock; Elizabeth Hudson; Dr Hubert Lacey; Mark Lucraft; Naomi Perry; Howard Shaw; Linda Stern; and Sarah Ward.

Finally, our thanks go to Waterlows, whose constant support and encouragement eased us through what was, at times, an anxious gestation.

P.R.
Temple

R.W.
Godmanchester
October 9, 1990.

CONTENTS

	Page
Foreword	vii
Foreword to the Fourth Edition	ix
Foreword to the Third Edition	xi
Foreword to the Second Edition	xiii
Preface	xv
Preface to the Third Edition	xxvii
Preface to the Second Edition	xxxvii
Preface to the First Edition	xxxix
Table of Cases	li
Table of Statutes	cxlvii
Table of Statutory Instruments	clxxxix

	Para.

1. RAPE

The Evolution of the Definition of Rape	1.14
Sentencing	1.35
Absence of Consent	1.169
Mental Element	1.371

2. SEXUAL ASSAULTS AND SEXUAL ACTIVITY WITHOUT CONSENT

Assault by Penetration	2.07
Sexual Assault	2.38
Causing a Person to Engage in Sexual Activity without Consent	2.84
Consent and Public Policy	2.109

3. OFFENCES AGAINST CHILDREN UNDER 13

Rape of a Child under 13	3.29
Assault of a Child under 13 by Penetration	3.79
Sexual Assault of a Child under 13	3.104
Causing or Inciting a Child under 13 to Engage in Sexual Activity	3.131

4. CHILD SEX OFFENCES

Sexual Activity with a Child	4.20
Causing or Inciting a Child to Engage in Sexual Activity	4.67

Engaging in Sexual Activity in the Presence of a Child   4.94
Causing a Child to Watch a Sexual Act   4.121
Child Sex Offences Committed by Children or Young Persons   4.144
Arranging or Facilitating Commission of a Child Sex Offence   4.160
Meeting a Child Following Sexual Grooming Etc   4.186
Sexual Communication with a Child   4.225
Possession of a Paedophile Manual   4.248

5. ABUSE OF POSITION OF TRUST

Abuse of Position of Trust: Sexual Activity with a Child   5.07
Abuse of Position of Trust: Causing or Inciting a Child to Engage in
    Sexual Activity   5.51
Abuse of Position of Trust: Engaging in Sexual Activity in the
    Presence of a Child   5.75
Abuse of Position of Trust: Causing a Child to Watch a Sexual Act   5.103
Abuse of Position of Trust: Acts Done in Scotland or Northern
    Ireland   5.126

6. FAMILIAL SEX OFFENCES

Sexual Activity with a Child Family Member   6.12
Inciting a Child Family Member to Engage in Sexual Activity   6.54
Jurisdiction   6.63
Sex with an Adult Relative: Penetration   6.72
Sex with an Adult Relative: Consenting to Penetration   6.94

7. SEXUAL OFFENCES AGAINST THOSE WITH A MENTAL DISORDER

Overview of the Mental Disorder Offences   7.12
Sexual Activity with a Person with a Mental Disorder Impeding
    Choice   7.47
Causing or Inciting a Person, with a Mental Disorder Impeding
    Choice, to Engage in Sexual Activity   7.91
Engaging in Sexual Activity in the Presence of a Person with a Mental
    Disorder Impeding Choice   7.106
Causing a Person, with a Mental Disorder Impeding Choice, to Watch
    a Sexual Act   7.126
Inducement, Threat or Deception to Procure Sexual Activity with a
    Person with a Mental Disorder   7.142
Causing a Person with a Mental Disorder to Engage in or Agree to
    Engage in Sexual Activity by Inducement, Threat or Deception   7.160
Engaging in Sexual Activity in the Presence, Procured by Inducement,
    Threat or Deception, of a Person with a Mental Disorder   7.173
Causing a Person with a Mental Disorder to Watch a Sexual Act by
    Inducement, Threat or Deception   7.193

CONTENTS

Offences Relating to Care Workers: Sexual Activity with a Person with
    a Mental Disorder   7.209
Care Workers: Causing or Inciting Sexual Activity   7.237
Care Workers: Sexual Activity in the Presence of a Person with a
    Mental Disorder   7.252
Care Workers: Causing a Person with a Mental Disorder to Watch a
    Sexual Act   7.272

8. INDECENT PHOTOGRAPHS OF CHILDREN

Taking (etc.) an Indecent Photograph or Pseudo-Photograph of a
    Child   8.03
Possession of an Indecent Photograph or Pseudo-Photograph of a
    Child   8.119

9. OFFENCES OF CHILD ABDUCTION

Child Abduction   9.07
Abduction of Child in Care   9.52

10. SEXUAL EXPLOITATION OF CHILDREN AND ADULTS

Child Sexual Exploitation   10.03
Paying for Sexual Services of a Child   10.10
Causing or Inciting Sexual Exploitationof a Child   10.35
Controlling a Child in relation to Sexual Exploitation   10.69
Arranging or Facilitating Sexual Exploitationof a Child   10.88
Sexual Exploitation Of Adults   10.105
Causing or Inciting Prostitution for Gain   10.111
Controlling Prostitution for Gain   10.143
Paying for Sexual Services of a Prostitute Subjected to Force etc.   10.163

11. MODERN SLAVERY AND TRAFFICKING

Prosecution of the Victims of Trafficking   11.22
Modern Slavery Act 2015   11.44
Slavery, Servitude and Forced Compulsory Labour   11.59
Human Trafficking   11.72
Committing an Offence with Intent to Commit a Human Trafficking
    Offence   11.114
Powers Available Under the Modern Slavery Act 2015   11.117

12. STREET-BASED PROSTITUTION

Keeping a Brothel   12.21
Keeping a Brothel used for Prostitution   12.42

Landlord Letting Premises for Use as a Brothel   12.57
Tenant Permitting Premises to Be Used as a Brothel   12.65
Tenant Permitting Premises to Be Used for Prostitution   12.76
Keeping a Disorderly House   12.85
Allowing a Person under 16 to be in a Brothel   12.97
Knowingly Permitting Prostitutes to Meet and Remain in House of
    Refreshment   12.104

13. STREET PROSTITUTION

Loitering or Soliciting for the Purpose of Prostitution   13.25
Advertising by or on Behalf of Prostitutes   13.54
Soliciting for the Purpose of Obtaining the Sexual Services of a
    Prostitute   13.60
Anti-Social Behaviour Orders   13.73
Binding Over   13.83

14. PREPARATORY OFFENCES

Administering a Substance with Intent to Stupefy or Overpower   14.08
Committing an Offence with Intent to Commit a Sexual Offence   14.37
Trespass with Intent to Commit a Sexual Offence   14.51

15. OFFENCES AGAINST PUBLIC DECENCY

Outraging Public Decency   15.26
Exposure   15.69
Voyeurism   15.90
Intercourse with an Animal   15.126
Sexual Penetration of a Corpse   15.145
Sexual Activity in a Public Lavatory   15.156
Insulting Behaviour under Section 4 of the Public Order Act 1986   15.163
Insulting Behaviour with Intent to Harass, Alarm or Distress under
    Section 4A of the Public Order Act 1986   15.171
Abusive or Disorderly Behaviour under Section 5 of the Public Order
    Act 1986   15.179
Other Relevant Offences   15.199

16. POLICE INVESTIGATION OF RAPE AND SERIOUS SEXUAL OFFENCES

The Structure of Police Rape Investigations   16.07
Primary Guidance Documents   16.11
The Investigative Process   16.12
Conclusion   16.35

CONTENTS

17. PROSECUTING RAPE AND SERIOUS SEXUAL OFFENCES—CPS POLICY AND DECISION-MAKING

The Full Code Test   17.03
The Evidential Stage: Common Myths and Stereotypes and The
    "Merit-Based" Approach   17.06
Withdrawal of Allegations   17.17
Cases Involving Children   17.21
Abuse of Process, Reconsideration of Decisions Not to Prosecute and
    the Victims' Right of Review Scheme   17.28
The Public Interest Stage of the Full Code Test   17.35
False Rape Allegations   17.48
Breaches of the Non-Reporting Provisions   17.66

18. DISCLOSURE

Prosecution Duty to Disclose   18.10
Material in the Hands of Third Parties   18.32
Documents Held by the Family Court   18.39
Documents Not Held by the Family Court   18.67
Article 8 ECHR and Issues of Confidentiality   18.92
Conclusion   18.99

19. EVIDENCE: GENERAL

Joinder and Severance   19.04
Hearsay Evidence   19.28
Collateral Questions and the Rule of Finality   19.91
Corroboration and Warnings about Reliance on a Complainant's
    Evidence   19.106
Evidence of Defendant's Spouse or Civil Partner   19.123

20. EVIDENCE OF BAD CHARACTER

The Criminal Justice Act 2003   20.01
Notice Requirements   20.03
Proving the Details of a Previous Sexual Offence   20.07
The Definition of "Bad Character"   20.13
The Gateways   20.24
Exclusionary Discretion under Section 101(3)   20.92
Jury Direction   20.109
Cross-Admissibility and Bad Character   20.111
Non-Defendant's Bad Character   20.139
Overlap Between Section 100 of the Criminal Justice Act 2003 and
    Section 41 of the Youth Justice and Criminal Evidence Act 1999   20.151

21. MEDICAL EVIDENCE: ADULTS

Prevalence   21.04
Presentation   21.12
SARCs   21.16
Forensic Medical Examination   21.18
Forensic Samples   21.37
Drug-Facilitated Sexual Assault   21.40
Aftercare   21.41
Psychological Sequelae of Sexual Violence   21.55

22. MEDICAL EVIDENCE: CHILDREN

The Medical Response to an Allegation or Suspicion of Child Sexual
    Abuse   22.04
The Medical Examination   22.25
Interpretation of Ano-Genital Findings   22.42
Sexually Transmitted Infections   22.67
Female Genital Mutilation   22.68
Child Sexual Exploitation   22.75
Learning Disability and Sexual Exploitation   22.78
Conclusion   22.79

23. PSYCHOLOGICAL EFFECTS OF RAPE AND SERIOUS SEXUAL ASSAULT

Myths and Stereotypes   23.18
Psychological Reactions During Rape and Serious Sexual Assault   23.32
Psychological Reactions Following Sexual Assault   23.36
Legal Implications   23.59
Late Reporting   23.73
Re-Traumatisation   23.76
Inconsistencies and Lies   23.78
The Trial   23.80
What Do Victims Need?   23.83

24. EXPERT EVIDENCE

Expert Evidence   24.02

25. DNA EVIDENCE

The Nature of DNA Evidence   25.02
Admissibility of DNA Evidence   25.24
Criminal Prodedure Rules 2015   25.29
Assessing the Weight of DNA Evidence   25.39
Low Template DNA   25.46
Evaluation of Mixed Samples   25.56

CONTENTS

The Forensic Science Regulator   25.60
The National DNA Database   25.63
Preparing for a Case involving DNA Evidence   25.67

26. RESTRICTIONS ON EVIDENCE OR QUESTIONS ABOUT THE COMPLAINANT'S SEXUAL HISTORY

Sections 41 to 43 of the Youth Justice and Criminal Evidence Act
    1999   26.21
The Four Gateways and Two Restrictions   26.50
The Canadian Experience   26.168
The Future of Section 41   26.177

27. VULNERABLE WITNESSES, "SPECIAL MEASURES" AND RELATED MATTERS

Vulnerable Witnesses and "Special Measures"   27.12
Types of Special Measures   27.55
Procedural Matters   27.116
Vulnerable Witnesses: Practicalities   27.125
Competence to Give Evidence   27.143
Prohibition on Cross-Examination by the Defendant in Person 27.157

28. ADVOCACY AND THE VULNERABLE

The Correct Approach—Adaptation   28.10
Confrontation—Putting the Case   28.22
Case Management—Ground Rules Hearing   28.31
Questioning—Practical Suggestions   28.41

29. ANONYMITY IN SEX CASES AND REPORTING RESTRICTIONS RELATING TO CHILDREN AND YOUNG PERSONS

Anonymity of Complainants in Sex Cases   29.12
Anonymity and the Defendant   29.33
Reporting Restrictions Relating to Children and Young Persons 29.58
Lifetime Reporting Restrictions Relating to Witnesses and Victims
    under 18   29.108
Reporting Restrictions Relating to Adult Witnesses   29.123

30. HISTORIC CASES

The Indictment   30.15
Disclosure   30.24
Abuse of Process   30.26
Directions   30.83
Sentencing   30.109

31. SEXUAL OFFENCES IN THE YOUTH COURT

Preliminary Matters	31.03
Trial in the Youth Court	31.31
Mode of Trial	31.64
Sentencing Youths for Sexual Offences	31.100
Annex 1: Sentencing Options Available to the Youth Court	31.139
Annex 2: Classification of Sexual Offences Involving Youths	31.140

32. SEXUAL OFFENCES IN NORTHERN IRELAND

Sexual Offences (Northern Ireland) Order 2008	32.07
Application of Sexual Offences Act 2003 to Northern Ireland	32.22
Commencement	32.26
Sentencing Provisions	32.29
Sentencing Generally	32.47
Evidence	32.57
Delay	32.69
Receiving Verdicts	32.74
Annex: Equivalent Sections in Sexual Offences Act 2003 to Articles in Sexual Offences (NI) Order 2008	32.75

33. THE SENTENCING OF SEX OFFENDERS: THE DEFINITIVE GUIDELINE

Sentencing under the Sexual Offences Act 2003 and Historic Cases: General	33.06
Approach to Harm and Culpability	33.12
Ostensible or Apparent Consent	33.15
Offences Committed Online	33.18
Increase in Sentencing Levels for Some Offences of Rape	33.19
Approach to Good Character and/or Exemplary Conduct	33.20
Other Relevant Guidelines	33.21
The Principle in *Canavan*: Offender may be Sentenced Only for Offences of which he has been Convicted or which he has Admitted	33.24

34. SENTENCING OF SEX OFFENDERS

Offences Committed on or after April 4, 2005	34.06
Offences Committed on Dates Straddling either May 1, 2004 or April 4, 2005	34.52
Miscellaneous	34.56

35. NOTIFICATION AND NOTIFICATION ORDERS

Notification	35.07

CONTENTS

36. SEXUAL HARM PREVENTION ORDERS AND SEXUAL RISK ORDERS

Introduction   36.01
Sexual Harm Prevention Orders   36.13
Sexual Risk Orders   36.66

Appendix A

Criminal Justice Act 2003: Schs 15 and 15B   A.01

Appendix B

Approach to Sentencing Historic Sexual Offences   B.01

Appendix C

Offences and Penalties: Comparative Table of Offences under the Old
    Law and Current Law   C.01

Appendix D

The Crown Prosecution Service: Index to the CPS Rape and Sexual
    Offences Guidance   D.01

Appendix E

CPS Legal Guidance: Rape and Sexual Offences — Chapter 11:
    Youths   E.01

Appendix F

The Advocate's Gateway: Toolkits 1, 1a, 1b, 2, 6 and 10   F.01

Appendix G

The Crown Court Compendium Part 1   G.01

Appendix H

Draft Directions in Multiple Defendant Grooming Cases   H.01

Appendix I

"Revenge Pornography"   I.01

TABLE OF CASES

All references are to paragraph numbers.

A (A Child) (Application for Reporting Restrictions), Re; sub nom. A
Local Authority v A Mother; A (A Child) (Reporting Restriction
Order), Re [2011] EWHC 1764 (Fam); [2012] 1 F.L.R. 239; [2011]
3 F.C.R. 176; [2011] Fam. Law 1076 ....29.100
A (Criminal Proceedings: Disclosure), Re [1996] 1 F.L.R. 221; [1996]
Fam. Law 142 CA (Civ Div) 18.49
A (Prosecutor's Appeal), Re. *See* R. v C; sub nom. R. v A (Prose-
cutor's Appeal)
A Council v M (Children) (Reporting Restriction Order: Adoption:
Artificial Insemination) [2012] EWHC 2038 (Fam); [2013] 2
F.L.R. 1270; [2013] Fam. Law 970 ....29.102
A District Council v M (West Yorkshire Police as interveners) [2007]
EWHC 3471 (Fam) 18.53
A Local Authority v A Mother. *See* X (Children) (Disclosure of
Judgment to Police), Re
A Local Authority v H [2012] EWHC 49 (COP); [2012] 1 F.C.R. 590;
(2012) 124 B.M.L.R. 98 .... 7.10
A Local Authority v W. *See* W (Children) (Identification: Restrictions
on Publication), Re
A Local Authority v X [2013] EWHC 3274 (Fam); [2014] 2 F.L.R. 123;
[2014] Fam. Law 293 .... 4.17
A v British Broadcasting Corp. *See* BBC, Re
A v DPP [2002] EWHC 403 (Admin); [2002] 2 Cr. App. R. (S.) 88;
[2002] Crim. L.R. 434 ....31.114
A v R. [2015] EWCA Crim 1177 .... 1.30, 1.31, 19.25, 30.23
AB (A Minor) (Medical Issues: Expert Evidence), Re [1995] 1 F.L.R.
181; [1995] 1 F.C.R. 280; [1995] Fam. Law 62 Fam Div 24.17
Abbas v Crown Prosecution Service 2015] EWHC 579 (Admin); [2015]
2 Cr. App. R. 11; (2015) 179 J.P. 295 .... 20.148, 27.161
Abbott v Smith [1965] 2 Q.B. 662 (Note); [1965] 3 W.L.R. 362; [1964]
3 All E.R. 762; (1965) 129 J.P. 3 QBD 12.31, 12.36
Abdul v DPP [2011] EWHC 247 (Admin); (2011) 175 J.P. 190; [2011]
H.R.L.R. 16; [2011] Crim. L.R. 553; [2011] A.C.D. 45 ....15.183
Abrahams v Cavey [1968] 1 Q.B. 479; [1967] 3 W.L.R. 1229; [1967] 3
All E.R. 179; (1967) 111 S.J. 654 DC 15.202

ADT v United Kingdom (Application No.35765/97) [2000] 2 F.L.R. 697; (2001) 31 E.H.R.R. 33; 9 B.H.R.C. 112; [2000] Crim. L.R. 1009; [2000] Fam. Law 797 ECtHR 2.118

Ahdel Ali and Mubarek Ali. *See* R. v A(A)

Aitken v DPP [2015] EWHC 1079 (Admin); [2016] 1 W.L.R. 297; [2015] 2 Cr. App. R. 18; (2015) 179 J.P. 223; [2015] E.M.L.R. 23; [2015] Crim. L.R. 719; [2015] A.C.D. 77 .... 29.09

AJA v Commissioner of Police of the Metropolis; AKJ v Commissioner of Police of the Metropolis [2013] EWCA Civ 1342; [2014] 1 W.L.R. 285; [2014] 1 All E.R. 882 .... 1.215

Al-Khawaja v United Kingdom (26766/05) (2009) 49 E.H.R.R. 1; 26 B.H.R.C. 249; [2009] Crim. L.R. 352 ECtHR 19.36, 19.37

Aldis v DPP. *See* A v DPP

Alhaji Mohamed v Knott; sub nom M v Knott; Mohamed v Knott [1969] 1 Q.B. 1; [1968] 2 W.L.R. 1446; [1968] 2 All E.R. 563; (1968) 132 J.P. 349; (1968) 112 S.J. 332 DC 1.167, 4.17

Ali v Crown Prosecution Service [2007] EWCA Crim 691 .... 30.79

Allen v Whitehead [1930] 1 K.B. 211 KBD 12.107

Alphacell Ltd v Woodward [1972] A.C. 824; [1972] 2 W.L.R. 1320; [1972] 2 All E.R. 475; 70 L.G.R. 455; [1972] Crim. L.R. 41; (1972) 116 S.J. 431 HL 2.98

Amrani. *See* R. v A (Ashraf)

Anderton v Cooper (1981) 72 Cr. App. R. 232; [1981] Crim. L.R. 177 DC 12.24

Andrew M (No.99/6651/Y3) unreported 27 January 2000 CA 15.181

Armhouse Lee Ltd v Chappell, *Times*, 7 August 1996; *Independent*, 26 July 1996 CA (Civ Div) 13.48, 13.49

Arnott v McFadyen, 2002 S.C.C.R. 96 HCJ Appeal 8.98

Assange v Sweden; sub nom. Assange v Swedish Prosecution Authority [2012] UKSC 22; [2012] 2 A.C. 471; [2012] 2 W.L.R. 1275; [2012] 4 All E.R. 1249; [2013] 1 C.M.L.R. 4; (2012) 109(24) L.S.G. 22 .... 1.07, 1.209, 1.211, 1.212, 1.213, 1.343

Associated Provincial Picture Houses Ltd v Wednesbury Corp [1948] 1 K.B. 223; [1947] 2 All E.R. 680; (1947) 63 T.L.R. 623; (1948) 112 J.P. 55; 45 L.G.R. 635; [1948] L.J.R. 190; (1947) 177 L.T. 641; (1948) 92 S.J. 26 HL 17.30, 19.108, 20.110

Atkin v DPP (1989) 89 Cr. App. R. 199; (1989) 153 J.P. 383; [1989] Crim. L.R. 581; (1989) 153 J.P.N. 451 DC 15.165

Atkins v DPP; Goodland v DPP; sub nom. DPP v Atkins [2000] 1 W.L.R. 1427; [2000] 2 All E.R. 425; [2000] 2 Cr. App. R. 248; (2000) 97(13) L.S.G. 42; (2000) 144 S.J.L.B. 148 Div 8.56, 8.61, 8.88, 8.91, 8.96, 8.97, 8.99

Attorney General for Akrotiri and Dhekelia v Steinhoff [2005] UKPC 31 .... 27.58

Attorney General for Jersey v Holley [2005] UKPC 23; [2005] 2 A.C. 580; [2005] 3 W.L.R. 29; [2005] 3 All E.R. 371; [2005] 2 Cr. App. R. 36; [2005] Crim. L.R. 966; (2005) 155 N.L.J. 1009; (2005) 149 S.J.L.B. 774 .... 1.387

Attorney General of Northern Ireland's Reference (No.1 of 1998), Re [1998] N.I. 232 CA (Crim Div) (NI) 32.33

Attorney General v Greater Manchester Newspapers Ltd. *See* Venables v News Group International (Breach of Injunction)

Attorney General v Hitchcock, 154 E.R. 38; (1847) 1 Ex. 91 Ex Ct 19.91

Attorney General's Reference (No.6 of 1980), Re [1981] Q.B. 715; [1981] 3 W.L.R. 125; [1981] 2 All E.R. 1057; (1981) 73 Cr. App. R. 63; [1981] Crim. L.R. 553; (1981) 125 S.J. 426 CA (Crim Div) 2.110, 2.115

Attorney General's Reference (No.1 of 1990), Re [1992] Q.B. 630; [1992] 3 W.L.R. 9; [1992] 3 All E.R. 169; (1992) 95 Cr. App. R. 296; (1992) 156 J.P. 593; [1993] Crim. L.R. 37; (1992) 156 J.P.N. 476; (1992) 89(21) L.S.G. 28; (1992) 142 N.L.J. 563 CA (Crim Div) 30.38

Attorney General's Reference (No.1 of 1992), Re [1993] 1 W.L.R. 274; [1993] 2 All E.R. 190; (1993) 96 Cr. App. R. 298; [1993] Crim. L.R. 274; (1992) 136 S.J.L.B. 304 CA (Crim Div) 1.137

Attorney General's Reference (No.1 of 1994), Re [1995] 1 W.L.R. 599; [1995] 2 All E.R. 1007; (1995) 159 J.P. 584; [1995] Env. L.R. 356; 93 L.G.R. 349; (1995) 159 J.P.N. 387; (1995) 92(10) L.S.G. 37; (1995) 139 S.J.L.B. 56 CA (Crim Div) 2.98

Attorney General's Reference (No.32 of 1996); sub nom. R. v Whittaker (Steven Alan) [1997] 1 Cr. App. R. (S.) 261; [1996] Crim. L.R. 917; (1996) 93(38) L.S.G. 42 CA (Crim Div) 1.131, 1.135, 30.162

Attorney General's Reference (No.50 of 1997); sub nom. R. v V (David Victor) [1998] 2 Cr. App. R. (S.) 155 CA (Crim Div) 35.07

Attorney General's Reference (No.3 of 1998) [2000] Q.B. 401; [1999] 3 W.L.R. 1194; [1999] 3 All E.R. 40; [1999] 2 Cr. App. R. 214; (1999) 49 B.M.L.R. 124; [1999] Crim. L.R. 986; (1999) 96(19) L.S.G. 27; (1999) 149 N.L.J. 522; (1999) 143 S.J.L.B. 130 CA (Crim Div) 15.97

Attorney General's Reference (No.3 of 2000), Re; R. v Looseley (Grant Spencer) (No.2); sub nom. R. v Loosely (Grant Spencer); R. v G (Entrapment); R. v Loosley (Grant Spencer) (No.2) [2001] UKHL 53; [2001] 1 W.L.R. 2060; [2001] 4 All E.R. 897; [2002] 1 Cr. App. R. 29; [2002] H.R.L.R. 8; [2002] U.K.H.R.R. 333; [2002] Crim. L.R. 301; (2001) 98(45) L.S.G. 25; (2001) 145 S.J.L.B. 245 ... 3.16, 11.30

Attorney General's Reference (No.4 of 2002), Re. *See* Sheldrake v DPP

Attorney General's Reference (No.3 of 2003) [2004] EWCA Crim 868;
    [2005] Q.B. 73; [2004] 3 W.L.R. 451; [2005] 4 All E.R. 303; [2004]
    2 Cr. App. R. 23 .... 12.64, 15.154
Attorney General's Reference (Nos 37, 38, 44, 54, 51, 53, 35, 40, 43, 45,
    41 and 42 of 2003); sub nom. R. v HN; R. v TG; R. v Coles; R.
    v RD; R. v Hodgkins; R. v EE; R. v EM; R. v AC; R. v TC; R.
    v JC; R. v GS; R. v DS [2003] EWCA Crim 2973; [2004] 1 Cr.
    App. R. (S.) 84 .... 1.129
Attorney General's Reference (No.2 of 2004) [2004] NICA 15 .... 32.49
Attorney General's Reference (No.104 of 2004); sub nom. R. v Garvey
    (Wayne) [2004] EWCA Crim 2672; [2005] 1 Cr. App. R. (S.) 117;
    [2005] Crim. L.R. 150; (2004) 148 S.J.L.B. 1283 .... 1.82
Attorney General's Reference (No.3 of 2006), Re [2006] NICA 36 .... 32.49
Attorney General's Reference (Nos 14 and 15 of 2006); sub nom. R. v
    Webster (Alan); R. v French (Tanya) [2006] EWCA Crim 1335;
    [2007] 1 All E.R. 718; [2007] 1 Cr. App. R. (S.) 40; [2006] Crim.
    L.R. 943 .... 1.127
Attorney General's Reference (No.31 of 2006); sub nom. R. v Spall
    (Rohail) [2007] EWCA Crim 1623; [2008] 1 Cr. App. R. (S.) 46 ..... 14.23
Attorney General's Reference (No.79 of 2006) (Application for Leave
    to Make Reference), Re; sub nom. R. v Whitta (Adam George)
    [2006] EWCA Crim 2626; [2007] 1 Cr. App. R. (S.) 122 ...... 2.34, 2.35
Attorney General's Reference (No.145 of 2006); sub nom. R. v C
    (Stephen) [2007] EWCA Crim 692 ....234.37
Attorney General's Reference (Nos 74 and 83 of 2007), Re; sub nom.
    R. v Fenn (Keith); R. v Foster (Simon James) [2007] EWCA Crim
    2550; [2008] 1 Cr. App. R. (S.) 110 .... 3.50, 3.55, 3.56, 3.58
Attorney General's Reference (No.107 of 2007); sub nom. R. v
    Bouguenoune (Mohandzine) [2008] EWCA Crim 198; [2008] 2 Cr.
    App. R. (S.) 373 .... 1.87
Attorney General's Reference (No.20 of 2008), Re; sub nom. R. v W
    [2008] EWCA Crim 1383; [2009] 1 Cr. App. R. (S.) 58 .... 4.46
Attorney General's Reference (No.55 of 2008); R. v PC; R. v P; R. v
    D; R. v W; R. v R; R. v A; R. v F; R. v CD; sub nom. R. v C
    [2008] EWCA Crim 2790; [2009] 1 W.L.R. 2158; [2009] 2 All E.R.
    867; [2009] 2 Cr. App. R. (S.) 22; [2009] Prison L.R. 353; [2009]
    Crim. L.R. 221 .... 1.78, 32.44, 34.32
Attorney General's Reference (No.67 of 2008), Re; sub nom. R. v E
    [2009] EWCA Crim 132; [2009] 2 Cr. App. R. (S.) 60 .... 4.50
Attorney General's Reference (Nos 7, 8 and 9 of 2009), Re; R. v
    Raymond (Yusuf); R. v Brew (Jason); R. v Muaimba (Hector); R.
    v Denton (O'Neil); sub nom. R. v McMorris (Rogel) [2009]
    EWCA Crim 1490; [2010] 1 Cr. App. R. (S.) 67 .... 1.90
Attorney General's Reference (No.43 of 2009), Re; R. v Ali; R. v
    Olawaiye; R. v Bennett; sub nom. R. v Wilkinson [2009] EWCA

Crim 1925; [2010] 1 Cr. App. R. (S.) 100; [2010] Crim. L.R. 69;
(2009) 153(38) S.J.L.B. 28 .... 1.93, 34.07
Attorney General's Reference (No.67 of 2009); sub nom. R. v P [2009]
EWCA Crim 2221; [2010] 1 Cr. App. R. (S.) 106 .... 6.24
Attorney General's Reference (Nos 3, 73 and 75 of 2010); sub nom. R.
v Anigbugu (Michael); R. v Pyo (Hyung-Woo); R. v McGee
(Mark Stuart) [2011] EWCA Crim 633; [2011] 2 Cr. App. R. (S.)
100; [2011] Crim. L.R. 580 .... 1.42, 1.50, 1.81, 1.136
Attorney General's Reference (No.28 of 2010); sub nom. R. v Charn-
ley (Michael Anthony) [2010] EWCA Crim 1996; [2011] 1 Cr.
App. R. (S.) 58 .... 3.154
Attorney General's Reference (Nos 37, 38 and 65 of 2010); sub nom.
R. v Khan (Shahnawaz Ali); R. v Khan (Raza Ali); R. v Khan
(Perveen) [2010] EWCA Crim 2880; [2011] 2 Cr. App. R. (S.) 31;
[2011] M.H.L.R. 14; [2011] Crim. L.R. 336; (2010) 108(2) L.S.G.
18 .... 11.65
Attorney General's Reference (No.124 of 2010); sub nom. R. v JW
[2011] EWCA Crim 337 .... 6.25, 6.27
Attorney General's Reference (No.1 of 2011); sub nom. R. v A [2011]
EWCA Crim 930; [2011] 2 Cr. App. R. (S.) 112 .... 33.26
Attorney General's Reference (No.18 of 2011) [2011] EWCA Crim
1300; [2012] 1 Cr. App. R. (S.) 27; [2011] Crim. L.R. 721 .... 3.63
Attorney General's Reference (No.24 of 2011) [2011] EWCA Crim
1960 .... 3.150, 4.34, 4.77, 4.79
Attorney General's Reference (No.64 of 2011) [2011] EWCA Crim
2277 ....30.120
Attorney General's Reference (No.66 of 2011) [2011] EWCA Crim
2697 .... 1.73
Attorney General's Reference (Nos 11 and 12 of 2012); sub nom. R. v
Channer (Roshane); R. v Monteiro (Ruben) [2012] EWCA Crim
1119; [2013] 1 Cr. App. R. (S.) 43; [2012] Crim. L.R. 719 .... 3.54, 3.55,
3.57, 3.58, 4.31, 33.15
Attorney General's Reference (No.77 of 2012); sub nom. R. v H [2013]
EWCA Crim 202 .... 1.85
Attorney General's Reference (Nos 2, 3, 4 and 5 of 2013); R. v
Connors (William); R. v Connors (Miles); R. v Connors (John);
R. v Connors (James) [2013] EWCA Crim 324; [2013] 2 Cr. App.
R. (S.) 71; [2013] Crim. L.R. 611 .... 11.65
Attorney General's Reference (No.27 of 2013); R. v P (Anthony); R. v
Ahmad (Goran Kamal); R. v Hanson (John); R. v Donegan
(David); R. v Smith (Paul Simon); R. v Mathews (Michael
Richard); R. v C; sub nom. R. v Burinskas (Gintas) [2014] EWCA
Crim 334; [2014] 1 W.L.R. 4209; [2015] 1 All E.R. 93; [2014] 2 Cr.
App. R. (S.) 45 ...... 1.78, 1.94, 1.103, 1.104, 1.105, 1.107, 1.112, 1.121,
1.123, 1.124, 34.09, 34.21

Attorney General's Reference (No.35 of 2013); sub nom. R. v Knight
(Francis) [2013] EWCA Crim 1757 .... 3.150, 4.77
Attorney General's Reference (No.38 of 2013); sub nom. R. v Hall
(James Stuart) [2013] EWCA Crim 1450; [2014] 1 Cr. App. R. (S.)
61 .... 1.75, 15.77, 30.07, 30.127, 33.20
Attorney General's Reference (No.53 of 2013); sub nom. R. v Wilson
(Neil) [2013] EWCA Crim 2544; [2014] 2 Cr. App. R. (S.) 1 .... 4.58, 5.27,
6.42, 9.26, 33.16
Attorney General's Reference (No.48 of 2014); sub nom. R. v Storey
(Timothy) [2014] EWCA Crim 1591 .... 4.43, 4.55
Attorney General's Reference (No.54 of 2014); sub nom. R. v Hill
(Aiden Gareth) [2014] EWCA Crim 2999 .... 7.59
Attorney General's Reference (No.61 of 2014); sub nom. R. v H [2014]
EWCA Crim 1933; [2015] 1 Cr. App. R. (S.) 25 .... 30.118, 30.118E,
30.135, 30.138
Attorney General's Reference (No.64 of 2014) [2015] EWCA Crim
128 .... 1.75
Attorney General's Reference (No.85 of 2014); sub nom. R. v Ackland
(Karen) [2014] EWCA Crim 2088; [2015] 1 Cr. App. R. (S.) 14 .... 1.83,
1.88, 4.51
Attorney General's Reference (No.94 of 2014) [2014] EWCA Crim
2752 .... 3.153, 4.80, 4.81, 4.83
Attorney General's Reference (No.95 of 2014) unreported 12 Novem-
ber 2014 .... 6.26
Attorney General's Reference (No.105 of 2014); sub nom. R. v Harrak
(Musa) [2014] EWCA Crim 2751; [2015] 1 Cr. App. R. (S.) 45 .... 3.57
Attorney General's Reference (No.115 of 2014); sub nom. R. v Long
(Linton Lee) [2015] EWCA Crim 200 .... 1.69, 33.20
Attorney General's Reference (No.118 of 2014) [2014] EWCA Crim
2898 .... 2.59
Attorney General's Reference (No.126 of 2014); sub nom. R. v Jumale
(Omar); R. v Zakaria (Said); Attorney General's Reference (Nos
126 and 127 of 2014) [2015] EWCA Crim 128; [2015] 1 Cr. App.
R. (S.) 65; [2015] Crim. L.R. 465 .... 1.44, 1.45, 11.91
Attorney General's Reference (No.7 of 2015); sub nom. R. v F [2015]
EWCA Crim 963; [2015] Crim. L.R. 827 .... 3.124
Attorney General's Reference (Nos 12 and 13 of 2015); R. v McClaren
(Kristofer Ryan); sub nom. R. v Whitelaw (Craig Matthew) [2015]
EWCA Crim 1223 .... 2.23
Attorney General's Reference (No.14 of 2015) [2015] EWCA Crim
949; [2015] All E.R. (D.) 04 (May) 30.134
Attorney General's Reference (No.21 of 2015) [2015] EWCA Crim
953; [2015] 2 Cr. App. R. (S.) 41 .... 30.133, 30.141
Attorney General's Reference (No.27 of 2015); sub nom. R. v U [2015]
EWCA Crim 1538 .... 30.06, 30.114, 30.145, 33.06

Attorney General's Reference (No.32 of 2015); sub nom. R. v Salisbury (Caroline Jane) [2015] EWCA Crim 1110 .... 4.36
Attorney General's Reference (No.41 of 2015); sub nom. R. v Hepworth (Adam Daniel) [2015] EWCA Crim 1510 .... 2.60
Attorney General's Reference (No.51 of 2015) (Whitmore) [2015] EWCA Crim 1699 .... 1.43, 33.11
Attorney General's Reference (No.80 of 2015); sub nom. R. v Fernandes (Lawrence) [2015] EWCA Crim 2026; [2015] All E.R. (D.) 300 (Nov) 33.10
Attorney General's Reference (No.104 of 2015); R. v Jade Hatt unreported 8 December 2015 .... 4.50, 4.51
Attorney General's Reference (No.121 of 2015) (Jonathan R) [2016] EWCA Crim 173 .... 1.47, 30.115, 30.117
Attorney General's Reference (No.122 of 2015) [2016] EWCA Crim 392 .... 1.68
Attorney General's Reference (No.142 of 2015); sub nom. R. v Brown (Jack Joseph) [2016] EWCA Crim 80 .... 3.53, 3.60
Attorney General's Reference (No.1 of 2016) (GG) [2016] EWCA Crim 62 .... 30.114, 30.133
Attorney General's Reference (No.16 of 2016); R. v W [2016] EWCA Crim 58, [2016] All ER (D) 184 (Mar) 4.37
Attorney General's Reference (No.32 of 2016) unreported 7 April 2016 .... 30.118E, 30.135, 30.138
Atwal v Massey [1971] 3 All E.R. 881; (1972) 56 Cr. App. R. 6 DC 9.61, 12.63

B v The Queen. See R. v M [2013]
B (A Child: Disclosure of Evidence in Care Proceedings), Re [2012] 1 F.L.R. 142; [2011] Fam. Law 1200 Fam Div 18.46
B (A Child) v DPP [2000] 2 A.C. 428; [2000] 2 W.L.R. 452; [2000] 1 All E.R. 833; [2000] 2 Cr. App. R. 65; [2000] Crim. L.R. 403; (2000) 97(11) L.S.G. 36; (2000) 144 S.J.L.B. 108 HL 8.98, 10.142, 32.04, 34.34
B v Chief Constable of Avon and Somerset [2001] 1 W.L.R. 340; [2001] 1 All E.R. 562; [2000] Po. L.R. 98 DC 36.19
Balazsy (1981) 54 Can.C.C. (2d) 346 Prov Ct (Ont) 15.44, 15.48
Barker v R. (1986) 153 C.L.R. 338 H Ct (Aus) 14.70
Barking and Dagenham LBC v Bass Taverns [1993] C.O.D. 453 DC 8.63
Barking and Dagenham LBC v SS; sub nom. SS (Secure Accommodation Order), Re [2014] EWHC 4436 (Fam); [2015] 2 F.L.R. 1358; [2015] Fam. Law 279 .... 4.18
Barnaby v DPP [2015] EWHC 232 (Admin); [2015] 2 Cr. App. R. 4; (2015) 179 J.P. 143; [2015] Crim. L.R. 729; [2015] A.C.D. 50 ..... 19.63
Barnett v Covell (1903) 68 J.P. 93 .... 13.37
BBC, Re; sub nom. A v Secretary of State for the Home Department; A v BBC [2014] UKSC 25; [2015] A.C. 588; [2014] 2 W.L.R. 1243;

[2014] 2 All E.R. 1037; 2014 S.C. (U.K.S.C.) 151; 2014 S.L.T. 613; 2014 S.C.L.R. 593; [2014] E.M.L.R. 25; 37 B.H.R.C. 664; 2014 G.W.D. 15–266 .... 29.31

Beal v Kelley [1951] 2 All E.R. 763; [1951] 2 T.L.R. 865; (1951) 35 Cr. App. R. 128; (1951) 115 J.P. 566; 49 L.G.R. 833; [1951] W.N. 505; (1951) 95 S.J. 685 DC 2.63

Beckford v Queen, The [1988] A.C. 130; [1987] 3 W.L.R. 611; [1987] 3 All E.R. 425; (1987) 85 Cr. App. R. 378; [1988] Crim. L.R. 116; (1987) 84 L.S.G. 2192; (1987) 137 N.L.J. 591; (1987) 131 S.J. 1122 PC (Jam) 9.48

Behrendt v Burridge [1977] 1 W.L.R. 29; [1976] 3 All E.R. 285; (1976) 63 Cr. App. R. 202; [1976] Crim. L.R. 522; (1976) 120 S.J. 538 DC 13.36, 13.39

Bell v Alfred Franks & Bartlett Co Ltd [1980] 1 W.L.R. 340; [1980] 1 All E.R. 356; (1980) 39 P. & C.R. 591; (1979) 253 E.G. 903; (1979) 123 S.J. 804 CA (Civ Div) 12.64

Bellerby v Carle [1983] 2 A.C. 101; [1983] 2 W.L.R. 687; [1983] 1 All E.R. 1031; 81 L.G.R. 425 HL 8.71

Bennett (1976) 29 Can.C.C. (2d) 403 .... 15.44

Birmingham City Council v Riaz [2014] EWHC 4247 (Fam); [2015] 2 F.L.R. 763; [2015] Fam. Law 271 .... 4.18, 29.100, 36.08, 36.77

Black (1921) 21 S.R. (N.S.W.) 748 .... 15.59

Blake v DPP; Austin v DPP (1993) 97 Cr. App. R. 169; [1993] Crim. L.R. 283 QBD 15.202

Bond v Evans (1888) L.R. 21 Q.B.D. 249 QBD 12.108

Bowman. See R. v B [2006]

Bracey v Read [1963] Ch. 88; [1962] 3 W.L.R. 1194; [1962] 3 All E.R. 472; (1962) 106 S.J. 878 Ch D 14.71

Briffett v DPP; sub nom. Briffett v Crown Prosecution Service; Briffet v DPP [2001] EWHC Admin 841; (2002) 166 J.P. 66; [2002] E.M.L.R. 12; (2002) 166 J.P.N. 92 .... 29.84

Bright v Secretary of State for Justice. See R. (on the application of Bright) v Secretary of State for Justice

Brushett. See R. v B (Derek Anthony)

Brutus v Cozens [1973] A.C. 854; [1972] 3 W.L.R. 521; [1972] 2 All E.R. 1297; (1972) 56 Cr. App. R. 799; [1973] Crim. L.R. 56; (1972) 116 S.J. 647 HL 9.38, 15.166, 15.185

Bryan Marshall unreported 2 November 2009 Crown Ct (Woolwich) 1.33

Bryan v Robinson [1960] 1 W.L.R. 506; [1960] 2 All E.R. 173; (1960) 124 J.P. 310; (1960) 104 S.J. 389 DC 15.166

Buckinghamshire CC v Trigg [1963] 1 W.L.R. 155; [1963] 1 All E.R. 403; (1963) 127 J.P. 171; 61 L.G.R. 189; (1963) 107 S.J. 36 DC 13.37

Bull v The Queen [2002] H.C.A. 24; (2000) 201 C.L.R. 443; 110 A. Crim. R. 562; 74 A.L.J.R. 836; 171 A.L.R. 613 High Ct (Aus) 26.111

Burge v DPP [1962] 1 W.L.R. 265; [1962] 1 All E.R. 666 (Note); (1962)
    106 S.J. 198 DC 13.35
Burnby, Ex p. [1901] 2 K.B. 458 KBD 12.24
Burns v Nowell (1880) 5 Q.B.D. 444 CA 8.71
Burrell v Harmer [1967] Crim. L.R. 169; (1966) 116 N.L.J. 1658 DC 15.63
C (A Minor) (Care Proceedings: Disclosure), Re; sub nom. EC (A
    Minor) (Care Proceedings: Disclosure), Re; EC (Disclosure of
    Material), Re [1997] Fam. 76; [1997] 2 W.L.R. 322; [1996] 2 F.L.R.
    725; [1996] 3 F.C.R. 521; [1997] Fam. Law 160 CA (Civ Div) 18.46,
                                                                    18.51, 18.52
C (A Minor) v DPP; sub nom. Curry v DPP [1996] A.C. 1; [1995] 2
    W.L.R. 383; [1995] 2 All E.R. 43; [1995] 2 Cr. App. R. 166; (1995)
    159 J.P. 269; [1995] R.T.R. 261; [1995] 1 F.L.R. 933; [1995] Crim.
    L.R. 801; [1995] Fam. Law 400; (1995) 159 J.P.N. 248; (1995) 145
    N.L.J. 416 HL 1.151
C (Adult: Refusal of Medical Treatment), Re [1994] 1 W.L.R. 290;
    [1994] 1 All E.R. 819; [1994] 1 F.L.R. 31; [1994] 2 F.C.R. 151 Fam
    Div 1.232, 7.19, 7.75
C v C [1942] N.Z.L.R. 356 .... 1.331
C v R. See R. v C; sub nom. R. v AC [2012]
Caird v Sime (1887) L.R. 12 App. Cas. 326 HL 8.74
Caldwell v Leach (1913) 77 J.P. 254; 23 Cox C.C. 510; [1911–13] All
    E.R. Rep. 703; 109 L.T. 188; 29 T.L.R. 457 DC 12.31
Cambridgeshire and Isle of Ely CC v Rust [1972] 2 Q.B. 426; [1972] 3
    W.L.R. 226; [1972] 3 All E.R. 232; 70 L.G.R. 444; [1972] Crim.
    L.R. 433; (1972) 116 S.J. 564 DC 9.29
Cambridgeshire CC v Associated Lead Mills Ltd [2005] EWHC 1627
    (Admin); (2005) 169 J.P. 489; [2006] R.T.R. 8; [2006] A.C.D. 7;
    (2005) 169 J.P.N. 778 .... 8.104
Campbell v Mirror Group Newspapers Ltd; sub nom. Campbell v
    MGN Ltd [2004] UKHL 22; [2004] 2 A.C. 457; [2004] 2 W.L.R.
    1232; [2004] 2 All E.R. 995; [2004] E.M.L.R. 15; [2004] H.R.L.R.
    24; [2004] U.K.H.R.R. 648; 16 B.H.R.C. 500; (2004) 101(21)
    L.S.G. 36; (2004) 154 N.L.J. 733; (2004) 148 S.J.L.B. 572 .... 29.98
Canada (Attorney General) v Bedford [2013] SCC 72 ..... 12.15, 12.19, 13.20,
                                                                           13.23
Carltona Ltd v Commissioners of Works [1943] 2 All E.R. 560 CA 35.27
Carter v Boehm (1766) 3 Burr. 1905; 97 E.R. 1162 KB 24.02
Case of P (T129/92) (1993) 10 CRNZ 250 .... 1.385
CC (A Minor) v DPP [1996] 1 Cr. App. R. 375 QBD 1.151
Central Estates (Belgravia) Ltd v Woolgar (No.2) [1972] 1 W.L.R.
    1048; [1972] 3 All E.R. 610; (1972) 24 P. & C.R. 103; (1972) 116
    S.J. 566 CA (Civ Div) 12.64
Chambers v DPP [1995] Crim. L.R. 896; [1995] C.O.D. 321 DC ... 15.166,
                                                                          15.185

Chambers v DPP; Edwards v DPP [1995] Crim. L.R. 896; [1995]
    C.O.D. 321 DC 15.196
Cheesman v DPP [1992] Q.B. 83; [1991] 2 W.L.R. 1105; [1991] 3 All
    E.R. 54; (1991) 93 Cr. App. R. 145; (1991) 155 J.P. 469; [1991]
    Crim. L.R. 296; (1991) 155 J.P.N. 91 QBD 15.51, 15.56, 15.166,
                                                                                    15.193
Chief Constable of Cleveland v H. See Chief Constable of Cleveland
    v Haggas
Chief Constable of Cleveland v Haggas; sub nom. R. (on the
    application of Cleveland Police) v Haggas [2009] EWHC 3231
    (Admin); [2010] 3 All E.R. 506; (2010) 174 J.P. 132 .... 36.19
Chief Constable of Hampshire v Mace (1987) 84 Cr. App. R. 40;
    (1986) 150 J.P. 470; (1986) 150 J.P.N. 574 QBD 4.174
Chief Constable of Lancashire v Potter [2003] EWHC 2272 (Admin);
    [2003] Po. L.R. 379; (2003) 100(42) L.S.G. 31 ..... 13.74, 13.82, 15.169,
                                                                                    15.193
Chorherr v Austria (A/266-B) (1994) 17 E.H.R.R. 358 ECtHR 13.86
Christison (George) v Hogg, 1974 J.C. 55; 1974 S.L.T. (Notes) 33
    HJC 12.68
City and County of Swansea v XZ [2014] EWHC 212 (Fam); [2014] 2
    F.L.R. 1091; [2015] 2 F.C.R. 369; [2014] Fam. Law 972 ....29.100
Cole v Coulton (1860) 24 J.P. 596; 2 E. & E. 695; 29 L.J.M.C. 125; 6
    Jur. N.S. 698; 8 W.R. 412; 2 L.T. 216 ....12.106
Collins v Wilcock [1984] 1 W.L.R. 1172; [1984] 3 All E.R. 374; (1984)
    79 Cr. App. R. 229; (1984) 148 J.P. 692; [1984] Crim. L.R. 481;
    (1984) 81 L.S.G. 2140; (1984) 128 S.J. 660 DC 13.53
Commissioner of Police of the Metropolis v Ebanks [2012] EWHC
    2368 (Admin); (2012) 176 J.P. 751; [2012] A.C.D. 111 ...... 36.19, 36.69
Cooper and Schaub. See R. v Schaub (Mark Tony)
CPS v LR. See R. v LR
Craig Pedley. See R. v P (Craig)
Crawford v Crown Prosecution Service [2008] EWHC 854 (Admin);
    (2008) 172 J.P. 273 .... 29.95, 29.98, 29.99
Crook v Edmondson; sub nom. Crook v Edmonson [1966] 2 Q.B. 81;
    [1966] 2 W.L.R. 672; [1966] 1 All E.R. 833; (1978) 66 Cr. App. R.
    90; (1966) 130 J.P. 191; (1966) 110 S.J. 147 QBD 13.06, 13.84
Crown Prosecution Service v CE [2006] EWCA Crim 1410 .... 19.66, 27.80,
                                                                                    27.103
D County Council v LS [2010] EWHC 1544 (Fam); [2010] Med. L.R.
    499 .... 7.10
Darroch v DPP (1990) 91 Cr. App. R. 378; (1990) 154 J.P. 844; [1990]
    Crim. L.R. 814; [1990] C.O.D. 406; (1990) 154 J.P.N. 578 QBD 13.69
David Oakes v R. See R. v Oakes (David)
Dial v Trinidad and Tobago; Dottin v Trinidad and Tobago [2005]
    UKPC 4; [2005] 1 W.L.R. 1660; (2005) 102(15) L.S.G. 32 .... 22.46

Dias v O'Sullivan [1949] A.L.R. 586 .... 12.84
Doheny and Adams. *See* R. v Doheny (Alan James)
Donovan v Gavin [1965] 2 Q.B. 648; [1965] 3 W.L.R. 352; [1965] 2 All
    E.R. 611; (1965) 129 J.P. 404; (1965) 109 S.J. 373 QBD 12.29, 12.30,
                                                                12.57, 12.64
Doorson v Netherlands (1996) 22 E.H.R.R. 330 ECtHR 27.76, 27.88
DPP for Northern Ireland v Lynch [1975] A.C. 653; [1975] 2 W.L.R.
    641; [1975] 1 All E.R. 913; (1975) 61 Cr. App. R. 6; [1975] Crim.
    L.R. 707; (1975) 119 S.J. 233 HL 15.142
DPP v Anderson (Keith Anthony); sub nom. R. v Anderson (Keith
    Anthony); Anderson (Keith Anthony) v DPP [1978] A.C. 964;
    [1978] 2 All E.R. 512; (1978) 67 Cr. App. R. 185; [1978] Crim.
    L.R. 568; (1978) 122 S.J. 400 HL 34.34
DPP v Armstrong (Andrew) [2000] Crim. L.R. 379; (1999) 96(45)
    L.S.G. 32; (1999) 143 S.J.L.B. 279 QBD 8.68
DPP v Boardman; sub nom. R. v Boardman (Derrick Rowland);
    Boardman v DPP [1975] A.C. 421; [1974] 3 W.L.R. 673; [1974] 3
    All E.R. 887; (1974) 60 Cr. App. R. 165; [1975] Crim. L.R. 36;
    (1974) 118 S.J. 809 HL 19.11, 19.14, 26.86, 26.87
DPP v Bull [1995] Q.B. 88; [1994] 3 W.L.R. 1196; [1994] 4 All E.R. 411;
    [1995] 1 Cr. App. R. 413; (1994) 158 J.P. 1005; [1994] Crim. L.R.
    762; (1994) 158 J.P.N. 453 DC 13.05, 13.29
DPP v Bulmer [2015] EWHC 2323 (Admin); [2015] 1 W.L.R. 5159;
    [2016] 1 Cr. App. R. (S.) 12; (2015) 179 J.P. 519; [2015] Crim. L.R.
    986 .... 13.75, 13.78, 13.80
DPP v Chand [2007] EWHC 90 (Admin); (2007) 171 J.P. 285; (2007)
    171 J.P.N. 565 ....20.110
DPP v Clarke; DPP v Lewis; DPP v O'Connell; DPP v O'Keefe (1992)
    94 Cr. App. R. 359; (1992) 156 J.P. 267; [1992] Crim. L.R. 60;
    [1992] C.O.D. 103; (1991) 135 S.J. 135 QBD ... 15.166, 15.169, 15.170,
                                                        15.177, 15.197, 15.198
DPP v Curley and Farrelly [1991] C.O.D. 186 DC 12.39
DPP v Fearon [2010] EWHC 340 (Admin); [2010] 2 Cr. App. R. 22;
    (2010) 174 J.P. 145; [2010] Crim. L.R. 646; [2010] A.C.D. 39 ..... 13.16
DPP v Gawecki and Bazar [1993] Crim. L.R. 202; [1993] C.O.D. 27
    DC 15.201
DPP v K [1997] 1 Cr. App. R. 36; [1997] Crim. L.R. 121 DC 1.145, 1.150,
                                                                15.142
DPP v Majewski; sub nom. R. v Majewski (Robert Stefan) [1977] A.C.
    443; [1976] 2 W.L.R. 623; [1976] 2 All E.R. 142; (1976) 62 Cr. App.
    R. 262; [1976] Crim. L.R. 374; (1976) 120 S.J. 299 HL 1.398, 2.81,
                                                            2.82, 14.49, 14.73
DPP v Merriman; sub nom. R. v Merriman (John) [1973] A.C. 584;
    [1972] 3 W.L.R. 545; [1972] 3 All E.R. 42; (1972) 56 Cr. App. R.
    766; [1972] Crim. L.R. 784; (1972) 116 S.J. 745 HL 1.144

DPP v Morgan; DPP v McDonald; DPP v McLarty; DPP v Parker;
    sub nom. R. v Morgan (William Anthony) [1976] A.C. 182; [1975]
    2 W.L.R. 913; [1975] 2 All E.R. 347; (1975) 61 Cr. App. R. 136;
    [1975] Crim. L.R. 717; (1975) 119 S.J. 319 HL 1.10, 1.17, 1.145,
                                    1.374, 1.388, 1.391, 1.392, 1.398, 26.10
DPP v Morgan; DPP v McDonald; DPP v McLarty; DPP v Parker;
    sub nom. R. v Morgan (William Anthony) [1975] 1 All E.R. 8 CA
    (Crim Div) 1.145
DPP v Ollerenshaw, *Independent*, 6 January 1992 DC 13.68
DPP v Orum [1989] 1 W.L.R. 88; [1988] 3 All E.R. 449; (1989) 88 Cr.
    App. R. 261; (1989) 153 J.P. 85; [1988] Crim. L.R. 848; (1989) 153
    J.P.N. 107; (1988) 132 S.J. 1637 QBD 15.166, 15.169, 15.193
DPP v P; sub nom. R. v P (A Father) [1991] 2 A.C. 447; [1991] 3
    W.L.R. 161; [1991] 3 All E.R. 337; (1991) 93 Cr. App. R. 267;
    (1992) 156 J.P. 125; [1992] Crim. L.R. 41; (1991) 155 J.P.N. 572;
    (1991) 141 N.L.J. 928; (1991) 135 S.J.L.B. 69 HL 19.14, 20.31, 26.86,
                                                                      26.87
DPP v R [2007] EWHC 1842 (Admin) 7.37, 19.51, 27.146
DPP v Ramos [2000] Crim. L.R. 768; [2000] C.O.D. 287 DC 15.168
DPP v Rogers [1953] 1 W.L.R. 1017; [1953] 2 All E.R. 644; (1953) 37
    Cr. App. R. 137; (1953) 117 J.P. 424; (1953) 97 S.J. 541 QBD 2.04,
                                                                2.63, 2.64
DPP v Speede; R. v Liverpool Magistrates Court Ex p. Collins; R. v
    Liverpool Magistrates Court Ex p. Santos; sub nom. Crown
    Prosecution Service v Speede [1998] 2 Cr. App. R. 108 DC 13.83
DPP v Taylor (Keith Richard); DPP v Little [1992] Q.B. 645; [1992] 2
    W.L.R. 460; [1992] 1 All E.R. 299; (1992) 95 Cr. App. R. 28;
    (1991) 155 J.P. 713; [1991] Crim. L.R. 900; [1991] Crim. L.R. 904;
    [1992] C.O.D. 26; [1992] Fam. Law 377; (1991) 155 J.P.N. 523;
    (1991) 141 N.L.J. 964 QBD 2.44
DPP v Vivier [1991] 4 All E.R. 18; (1991) 155 J.P. 970; [1991] R.T.R.
    205; [1991] Crim. L.R. 637; (1991) 155 L.G. Rev. 588 DC 13.41,
                                                                      13.42
DPP v Whitehouse. *See* R. v Whitehouse (Arthur)
DPP's Reference (No.18 of 2013), Re; sub nom. R. v Finnegan (Colin)
    [2014] NICA 20 .... 32.47, 32.51, 32.52
DPP's Reference (No.4 of 2012), Re; sub nom. R. v D [2013] NICA
    10 .... 32.53
Drew unreported December 2006 CC (Southwark) 10.157, 10.161
DS v HM Advocate; sub nom. HM Advocate v DS [2007] UKPC D1;
    2007 S.C. (P.C.) 1; 2007 S.L.T. 1026; 2007 S.C.C.R. 222; [2007]
    H.R.L.R. 28; 24 B.H.R.C. 412 .... 20.49
Dudgeon v United Kingdom (A/45) (1982) 4 E.H.R.R. 149 ECtHR 7.42,
                                                                      18.92

Durose v Wilson (1907) 71 J.P. 263; 21 Cox C.C. 421; 96 L.T. 645
  DC 12.28, 12.30, 12.60
Dyer v Watson; K (A Juvenile) v HM Advocate; sub nom. HM
  Advocate v JK; Procurator Fiscal, Linlithgow v Watson; HM
  Advocate v K (A Juvenile); K v Lord Advocate [2002] UKPC D
  1; [2004] 1 A.C. 379; [2002] 3 W.L.R. 1488; [2002] 4 All E.R. 1;
  2002 S.C. (P.C.) 89; 2002 S.L.T. 229; 2002 S.C.C.R. 220; [2002]
  H.R.L.R. 21; [2002] U.K.H.R.R. 542; 2002 G.W.D. 5–153 .... 32.71
E v DPP [2005] EWHC 147 (Admin); (2005) 102(14) L.S.G. 26 .... 4.15
E, S and R, R. (on the application of) v DPP. See R. (on the
  application of E) v DPP
Ebrahim v Feltham Magistrates' Court. See R. (on the application of
  Ebrahim) v Feltham Magistrates Court
Ecclesiastical Commissioners for England's Conveyance, Re; sub nom.
  Law of Property Act 1925, Re [1936] Ch. 430; (1957) 7 P. & C.R.
  298 Ch D 13.37
Elkins v Cartlidge [1947] 1 All E.R. 829; 177 L.T. 519; (1947) 91 S.J.
  573 KBD 13.41
Elliott v DPP, Times, 19 January 1989 QBD 12.39
Empress Car Co (Abertillery) Ltd v National Rivers Authority. See
  Environment Agency (formerly National Rivers Authority) v
  Empress Car Co (Abertillery) Ltd
Environment Agency (formerly National Rivers Authority) v Empress
  Car Co (Abertillery) Ltd; sub nom. Empress Car Co (Abertillery)
  Ltd v National Rivers Authority [1999] 2 A.C. 22; [1998] 2 W.L.R.
  350; [1998] 1 All E.R. 481; [1998] Env. L.R. 396; [1988] E.H.L.R.
  3; [1998] E.G. 16 (C.S.); (1998) 95(8) L.S.G. 32; (1998) 148 N.L.J.
  206; (1998) 142 S.J.L.B. 69; [1998] N.P.C. 16 HL 8.74
Exchange Telegraph Co Ltd v Central News Ltd [1897] 2 Ch. 48 Ch
  D 8.74
F v Newsquest Ltd; sub nom. X and Y (Children), Re [2004] EWHC
  762 (Fam); [2004] E.M.L.R. 29 ....29.101
F v The Queen. See R. v F [2008]
Fagan v Commissioner of Police of the Metropolis [1969] 1 Q.B. 439;
  [1968] 3 W.L.R. 1120; [1968] 3 All E.R. 442; (1968) 52 Cr. App. R.
  700; (1969) 133 J.P. 16; (1968) 112 S.J. 800 DC 2.127
Fairclough v Whipp [1951] 2 All E.R. 834; [1951] 2 T.L.R. 909; (1951)
  35 Cr. App. R. 138; (1951) 115 J.P. 612; 49 L.G.R. 836; [1951]
  W.N. 528; (1951) 95 S.J. 699 CCA 2.63, 30.155
Fairweather v Commissioner of Police of the Metropolis [2008]
  EWHC 3073 (Admin) 36.27
Farrington v Thomson and Bridgland [1959] V.R. 286 .... 14.70
Faulkner v Talbot [1981] 1 W.L.R. 1528; [1981] 3 All E.R. 468; (1982)
  74 Cr. App. R. 1; [1981] Crim. L.R. 705; (1981) 125 S.J. 859
  DC 2.63

Felix v DPP [1998] Crim. L.R. 657; [1998] E.H.L.R. Dig. 278 DC 13.57
Fenwick (1953) 54 S.R. (N.S.W.) 147 .... 1.144
Ferricks v Guzikowski (1990) 51 A. Crim. R. 78 Sup Ct Full Ct
    (Qld). 12.84
Field v Chapman [1953] C.L.Y. 787 DC 13.34
Fisher v Bell [1961] 1 Q.B. 394; [1960] 3 W.L.R. 919; [1960] 3 All E.R.
    731; (1961) 125 J.P. 101; (1960) 104 S.J. 981 DC 8.64
Flynn (Patrick Anthony) v HM Advocate (No.1); McMurray (Peter) v
    HM Advocate (No.1); Nicol (John Gary) v HM Advocate (No.1);
    Meek (Peter Mitchell) v HM Advocate (No.1) [2004] UKPC D 1;
    2004 S.C. (P.C.) 1; 2004 S.L.T. 863; 2004 S.C.C.R. 281; [2004]
    H.R.L.R. 17; [2005] 1 Prison L.R. 154; 2004 G.W.D. 16–360 ....30.113
Forbes v Secretary of State for the Home Department [2006] EWCA
    Civ 962; [2006] 1 W.L.R. 3075; [2006] 4 All E.R. 799; [2007] 1 Cr.
    App. R. (S.) 72; [2006] U.K.H.R.R. 1053; [2006] Crim. L.R. 1085;
    (2006) 103(30) L.S.G. 30 .... 35.12
Foster v DPP; Rutherford v DPP [2004] EWHC 2955 (Admin); [2005]
    1 W.L.R. 1400; [2005] 1 F.C.R. 153; [2005] Crim. L.R. 639; [2005]
    A.C.D. 63 .... 9.07, 9.31, 9.38, 9.43, 9.44, 9.45, 9.46, 9.50, 9.52
G (A Minor) (Social Worker: Disclosure), Re; sub nom. G (A Minor)
    (Care Proceedings: Disclosure), Re; G (A Minor) (Child Protec-
    tion: Investigations), Re [1996] 1 W.L.R. 1407; [1996] 2 All E.R.
    65; [1996] 1 F.L.R. 276; [1996] 3 F.C.R. 77; (1996) 31 B.M.L.R.
    175; [1996] Fam. Law 143; (1996) 146 N.L.J. 85 CA (Civ Div) 18.42
G v DPP [1998] Q.B. 919; [1998] 2 W.L.R. 609; [1997] 2 All E.R. 755;
    [1997] 2 Cr. App. R. 78; (1997) 161 J.P. 498; [1997] 2 F.L.R. 810;
    [1998] Fam. Law 12 DC 27.83
G v F (Non Molestation Order: Jurisdiction); sub nom. G v G (Non
    Molestation Order: Jurisdiction) [2000] Fam. 186; [2000] 3 W.L.R.
    1202; [2000] 2 F.L.R. 533; [2000] 2 F.C.R. 638; [2000] Fam. Law
    519; [2000] Fam. Law 703; (2000) 97(25) L.S.G. 40 .... 6.35
G v United Kingdom (Application No 37334/08) [2011] E.H.H.R.
    1308 ECtHR 3.20
Gaviria. See R. v G [2010]
Giambalvo (1983) 70 Can.C.C. (2d) 324 CA (Ont) 15.42, 15.44
Gillick v West Norfolk and Wisbech AHA [1986] A.C. 112; [1985] 3
    W.L.R. 830; [1985] 3 All E.R. 402; [1986] Crim. L.R. 113; (1985)
    82 L.S.G. 3531; (1985) 135 N.L.J. 1055; (1985) 129 S.J. 738 HL 4.181,
                                                           4.182, 22.21, 22.22
Girgawy (Fillobbos Fahmy) v Strathern, 1925 J.C. 31; 1925 S.L.T. 84,
    HJC 12.83
GMS Syndicate Ltd v Gary Elliott Ltd [1982] Ch. 1; [1981] 2 W.L.R.
    478; [1981] 1 All E.R. 619; (1981) 41 P. & C.R. 124; (1980) 258
    E.G. 25; (1980) 124 S.J. 776 Ch D 12.64
Goodbarne v Buck [1940] 1 K.B. 771; (1940) 66 Ll. L. Rep. 129 CA 8.63

Goodland v DPP. *See* Atkins v DPP

Gorman v Standen; Palace Clark v Standen; sub nom. Gordon v
    Standen [1964] 1 Q.B. 294; [1963] 3 W.L.R. 917; [1963] 3 All E.R.
    627; (1964) 48 Cr. App. R. 30; (1964) 128 J.P. 28; (1963) 107 S.J.
    811 QBD 12.27, 12.31, 12.33, 12.37

Gough v DPP [2013] EWHC 3267 (Admin); (2013) 177 J.P. 669; [2014]
    Crim. L.R. 371; [2014] A.C.D. 49 .... 15.45, 15.186

Gough v United Kingdom (49327/11), 2015 S.C.C.R. 1; (2015) 61
    E.H.R.R. 8; 38 B.H.R.C. 281 ECtHR 15.190, 15.191

Gowan, March 3, 1998; Doc. Ottawa 97–20544 (Ontario Court of
    Justice, Provincial Division) 15.47

Gray (1982) 65 Can.C.C. (2d) 353 H Ct (Ont) 15.42, 15.45

Gray's Haulage Co Ltd v Arnold [1966] 1 W.L.R. 534; [1966] 1 All
    E.R. 896; (1966) 130 J.P. 196; (1966) 110 S.J. 112 QBD 8.94

Greater Manchester Police v Andrews [2011] EWHC 1966 (Admin);
    [2012] A.C.D. 18 .... 8.117

Green 4.134

Gully v Dix; sub nom. Dix (Deceased), Re [2004] EWCA Civ 139;
    [2004] 1 W.L.R. 1399; [2004] 1 F.L.R. 918; [2004] 1 F.C.R. 453;
    [2004] W.T.L.R. 331; [2004] Fam. Law 334; (2004) 101(6) L.S.G.
    32; (2004) 148 S.J.L.B. 116 .... 6.35

H (Children) (Care Proceedings: Disclosure), Re [2009] EWCA Civ
    704; [2009] 2 F.L.R. 1531; [2009] Fam. Law 925 .... 18.43, 18.50

H (L), Re [1997] 1 Cr. App. R. 176 CC (Reading) 18.82

H and R v R. *See* R. v H; R. v R

Hamilton v R. *See* R. v H [2014]

Hammond v DPP; sub nom. DPP v Hammond [2004] EWHC 69
    (Admin); (2004) 168 J.P. 601; (2004) 168 J.P.N. 877 ...... 15.166, 15.187

Harris v Tippett, 170 E.R. 1277; (1811) 2 Camp. 637 KB 19.91

Harvey v DPP [2011] EWHC 3992 (Admin); (2012) 176 J.P. 265; [2012]
    Crim. L.R. 553 .... 15.185, 15.193

Hashman and Harrup v United Kingdom (25594/94) (2000) 30
    E.H.R.R. 241; 8 B.H.R.C. 104; [2000] Crim. L.R. 185 ECtHR 13.85,
                                                                                    13.86, 13.87

Hawtrey v Beaufront Ltd [1946] K.B. 280 KBD 12.107

Hellstrom v Commonwealth, 825 SW 2d 612 (1992) Sup Ct
    (Kentucky) 19.121

Herring v Walround, 22 E.R. 870; (1682) 2 Ch. Cas. 110 Ct of
    Chancery 15.26

Hillen v ICI (Alkali) Ltd; Pettigrew v ICI (Alkali) Ltd [1936] A.C. 65;
    (1935) 52 Ll. L. Rep. 179 HL 14.70

HKSAR v Chan Yau Hei [2014] HKCFA 18 .... 15.60, 15.61

HM Queen v JA and Attorney General of Canada and Women's Legal
    Education and Action Fund [2011] 2 S.C.R. 440 .... 1.182

Hodgetts v Chiltern DC; sub nom. Chiltern DC v Hodgetts [1983] 2
A.C. 120; [1983] 2 W.L.R. 577; [1983] 1 All E.R. 1057; (1983) 147
J.P. 372; (1983) 45 P. & C.R. 402; [1983] J.P.L. 377 HL 9.40
Holloway v DPP [2004] EWHC 2621 (Admin); (2005) 169 J.P. 14;
(2004) 168 J.P.N. 956 ....15.194
Hols v Netherlands (App. No.25206/94) 19 October 1995 .... 27.58
Honeysett v The Queen [2014] H.C.A. 29; (2014) 253 C.L.R. 122; 237
A. Crim. R. 589; 88 A.L.J.R. 786; 311 A.L.R. 320; [2014]
A.L.M.D. 5281; [2014] A.L.M.D. 5291; [2014] A.L.M.D. 5460
High Ct (Aus) 24.08
Horton v Mead [1913] 1 K.B. 154 KBD 13.35
Howker v Robinson [1973] Q.B. 178; [1972] 3 W.L.R. 234; [1972] 2 All
E.R. 786; [1972] Crim. L.R. 377; (1972) 116 S.J. 354 DC 12.107
Huckerby v Elliott [1970] 1 All E.R. 189; (1969) 113 S.J. 1001 QBD 8.42
Hughes v Holley (1988) 86 Cr. App. R. 130; (1987) 151 J.P. 233; [1987]
Crim. L.R. 253; (1987) 151 J.P.N. 124 DC 13.84, 13.85
Hulme v DPP [2006] EWHC 1347 (Admin); (2006) 170 J.P. 598; (2006)
170 J.P.N. 997 .... 7.78
Hunt v DPP (1990) 154 J.P. 762; [1990] Crim. L.R. 812; (1990) 154
J.P.N. 548 DC 15.83
Ibbotson v United Kingdom (40146/98) [1999] Crim. L.R. 153; (1999)
27 E.H.R.R. CD332 Eur HR Comm 35.14
Ikarian Reefer, The. See National Justice Compania Naviera SA v
Prudential Assurance Co Ltd
IM v (1) LM (by her Litigation Friend, the Official Solicitor (2) AB (3)
Liverpool City Council. See M (An Adult) (Capacity: Consent to
Sexual Relations), Re
IM v LM, AB, Liverpool City Council. See M (An Adult) (Capacity:
Consent to Sexual Relations), Re
Inco Europe Ltd v First Choice Distribution [2000] 1 W.L.R. 586;
[2000] 2 All E.R. 109; [2000] 1 All E.R. (Comm) 674; [2000] 1
Lloyd's Rep. 467; [2000] C.L.C. 1015; [2000] B.L.R. 259; (2000) 2
T.C.L.R. 487; 74 Con. L.R. 55; (2000) 97(12) L.S.G. 39; (2000)
144 S.J.L.B. 134; [2000] N.P.C. 22 HL 26.24
Invicta Plastics Ltd v Clare [1976] R.T.R. 251; [1976] Crim. L.R. 131;
(1975) 120 S.J. 62 DC 3.158
ITN News Ltd, Re. See R. v ITN News
Jacob, 142 D.L.R. (4th) 411; 112 C.C.C. (3d) 1 .... 15.47
James & Son v Smee; Green v Burnett [1955] 1 Q.B. 78; [1954] 3
W.L.R. 631; [1954] 3 All E.R. 273; (1954) 118 J.P. 536; 52 L.G.R.
545; (1954) 98 S.J. 771 QBD 8.94
James v R. (1971) 55 Cr. App. R. 299 PC 19.118
JC v Central Criminal Court. See R. (on the application of JC) v
Central Criminal Court
Jenks v Turpin (1884) 13 Q.B.D. 505 QBD 12.92

Jones v DPP; sub nom. R. v Jones (Arthur Albert) [1962] A.C. 635;
  [1962] 2 W.L.R. 575; [1962] 1 All E.R. 569; (1962) 46 Cr. App. R.
  129; (1962) 126 J.P. 216; 96 I.L.T. 207; (1962) 106 S.J. 192 HL 34.40
Jones v DPP; Wood v DPP (1993) 96 Cr. App. R. 130 QBD 12.38
JP v Crown Prosecution Service; sub nom. R. v P [2010] EWCA Crim
  2438; [2011] Crim. L.R. 502 .... 18.84
K v News Group Newspapers Ltd [2011] EWCA Civ 439; [2011] 1
  W.L.R. 1827; [2011] E.M.L.R. 22; (2011) 108(18) L.S.G. 18 ...... 29.99
Kaitamaki v R. [1985] A.C. 147; [1984] 3 W.L.R. 137; [1984] 2 All E.R.
  435; (1984) 79 Cr. App. R. 251; [1984] Crim. L.R. 564; (1984) 81
  L.S.G. 1915; (1984) 128 S.J. 331 PC (NZ) 1.158
Kelly v Purvis [1983] Q.B. 663; [1983] 2 W.L.R. 299; [1983] 1 All E.R.
  525; (1983) 76 Cr. App. R. 165; (1983) 147 J.P. 135; [1983] Crim.
  L.R. 185; (1983) 127 S.J. 52 DC 12.34, 12.35
Kennedy [1981] V.R. 565 Sup Ct FC (Vict). 9.46
Kevin Gallagher, Re [2003] NIQB 26 .... 35.12
Kirk and Kirk. See R. v PK
KL (A Juvenile) v DPP; LAK (A Juvenile) v DPP [2001] EWHC
  Admin 1112; (2002) 166 J.P. 369; (2002) 166 J.P.N. 470; (2002) 166
  J.P.N. 351 .... 27.60
Knight v Fryer [1976] Crim. L.R. 322 DC 13.50
Knuller (Publishing, Printing and Promotions) Ltd v DPP; Hall
  (David) v DPP; Stansill (Peter) v DPP; Keen (Graham) v DPP;
  sub nom. R. v Knuller (Publishing, Printing and Promotions) Ltd
  [1973] A.C. 435; [1972] 3 W.L.R. 143; [1972] 2 All E.R. 898; (1972)
  56 Cr. App. R. 633; [1975] Crim. L.R. 704; (1972) 116 S.J. 545
  HL 13.53, 15.26, 15.42, 15.43, 15.45
Konig v Germany (No.1) (A/27) (1979–80) 2 E.H.R.R. 170 ECtHR 32.71
Konrad Cole and Rocky Keet. See R. v Cole (Konrad)
Kyselka (1962) 133 C.C.C. 103 CA (Ont). 19.103
L (A Minor) (Police Investigation: Privilege), Re; sub nom. L (Minors)
  (Disclosure of Medical Reports), Re; L (Minors) (Police Inves-
  tigation: Privilege), Re [1997] A.C. 16; [1996] 2 W.L.R. 395; [1996]
  2 All E.R. 78; [1996] 1 F.L.R. 731; [1996] 2 F.C.R. 145; (1996) 32
  B.M.L.R. 160; [1996] Fam. Law 400; (1996) 160 L.G. Rev. 417;
  (1996) 93(15) L.S.G. 30; (1996) 146 N.L.J. 441; (1996) 140 S.J.L.B.
  116 HL 18.56
L (Care: Confidentiality), Re [1999] 1 F.L.R. 165; [1999] Fam. Law 81
  Fam Div 18.53
Laskey v United Kingdom; Jaggard v United Kingdom; Brown v
  United Kingdom (1997) 24 E.H.R.R. 39 ECtHR 2.118
Lawrence v Lawrence. See Lawrence v Ridsdale
Lawrence v Ridsdale [1968] 2 Q.B. 93; [1968] 2 W.L.R. 1062; [1968] 1
  All E.R. 1191; (1968) 132 J.P. 277; (1968) 112 S.J. 212 Div 3.112, 9.18,
                                                                   14.43

Lightbound v Higher Bebington Local Board (1885) 16 Q.B.D. 577
   CA 13.37
Liverpool Society for the Prevention of Cruelty to Children v Jones
   [1914] 3 K.B. 813 KBD 12.100
Local Authority X v M; sub nom. MM (An Adult), Re; A Local
   Authority v MM [2007] EWHC 2003 (Fam); [2009] 1 F.L.R. 443;
   [2008] 3 F.C.R. 788; (2008) 11 C.C.L. Rep. 119; [2008] Fam. Law
   213 .... 1.229, 1.230, 7.74
Lodge v DPP, Times, 26 October 1988 DC 15.196
Lord Baltimore's Case (1768) 1 Black.W. 648 .... 1.149
Love (Alexander) v HM Advocate, 2000 J.C. 1; 1999 S.C.C.R. 783;
   1999 G.W.D. 30–1409 HCJ 26.78
Lovelace v DPP [1954] 1 W.L.R. 1468; [1954] 3 All E.R. 481; (1955)
   119 J.P. 21; (1954) 98 S.J. 852 DC 8.104
Ludlow v Commissioner of Police of the Metropolis; sub nom.
   Ludlow v Metropolitan Police Commissioner; R. v Ludlow
   (Edward Alexander) [1971] A.C. 29; [1970] 2 W.L.R. 521; [1970] 1
   All E.R. 567; (1970) 54 Cr. App. R. 233; (1970) 114 S.J. 148
   HL 19.05, 19.06, 20.111
M (A Minor) (Disclosure of Material), Re [1990] 2 F.L.R. 36; [1990]
   F.C.R. 485; 88 L.G.R. 841; [1990] Fam. Law 259; (1990) 154 J.P.N.
   410; (1990) 154 L.G. Rev. 496 CA (Civ Div) 18.89
M (An Adult) (Capacity: Consent to Sexual Relations), Re; sub nom.
   IM v LM (Capacity to Consent to Sexual Relations) [2014]
   EWCA Civ 37; [2015] Fam. 61; [2014] 3 W.L.R. 409; [2014] 3 All
   E.R. 491; [2014] 2 F.C.R. 13; [2014] C.O.P.L.R. 246; (2014) 17
   C.C.L. Rep. 39; [2014] Med. L.R. 345; (2014) 158(5) S.J.L.B.
   37 .... 1.234, 1.235, 1.237, 7.09, 7.11, 7.44
M v Chief Constable of Hampshire; sub nom. R. (on the application
   of M) v Chief Constable of Hampshire [2014] EWCA Civ 1651;
   [2015] 1 W.L.R. 1176; [2015] 1 Cr. App. R. 20 .... 35.44, 36.37
M, Re [2007]. See Local Authority X v M
MacLennan v HM Advocate [2012] HCJAC 94 .... 8.141
Madercine (1899) 20 N.S.W. Law Rep. 36 .... 15.59
Maidstone Building Provisions, Re [1971] 1 W.L.R. 1085; [1971] 3 All
   E.R. 363; (1971) 115 S.J. 464 Ch D 12.64
Main v Scottish Ministers [2015] CSIH 41; 2015 S.C. 639; 2015 S.L.T.
   349; 2015 S.C.L.R. 732; 2015 G.W.D. 18–307 .... 35.27
Makin v Attorney General of New South Wales [1894] A.C. 57 NSW
   PC (Aus) 20.02
Mallows v Harris [1979] R.T.R. 404; [1979] Crim. L.R. 320 DC 35.48,
                                                                                                    36.60
Marsh v Arscott (1982) 75 Cr. App. R. 211; [1982] Crim. L.R. 827
   QBD 15.169

Masterman v Commissioner of Police of the Metropolis [2010] EWHC
806 (Admin) 35.60
Masterson v Holden [1986] 1 W.L.R. 1017; [1986] 3 All E.R. 39; (1986)
83 Cr. App. R. 302; [1986] Crim. L.R. 688; (1986) 83 L.S.G. 2326;
(1986) 130 S.J. 592 QBD 15.167
Mattison v Johnson (1916) 85 L.J.K.B. 741 .... 12.83
May v DPP [2005] EWHC 1280 (Admin) 13.42
MB (Caesarean Section), Re; sub nom. MB (Medical Treatment), Re
[1997] 2 F.L.R. 426; [1997] 2 F.C.R. 541; [1997] 8 Med. L.R. 217;
(1997) 38 B.M.L.R. 175; [1997] Fam. Law 542; (1997) 147 N.L.J.
600 CA (Crim Div) 1.232
McGowan v Longmuir, 1931 S.C.(J.) 10 .... 15.38, 15.44
McKenzie v Whyte (1864) 4 Irv. 570 .... 15.45
McKerry v Teesdale and Wear Valley Justices; sub nom. McKerry v
DPP (2000) 164 J.P. 355; [2001] E.M.L.R. 5; [2000] Crim. L.R.
594; [2000] C.O.D. 199; (2000) 97(11) L.S.G. 36; (2000) 144
S.J.L.B. 126 DC 31.41
McR's Application for Judicial Review, Re [2002] NIQB 58; [2003] N.I.
1 .... 32.02
MH v R. See R. v MH
MM (An Adult), Re. See Local Authority X v M
MM v R. See R. v M(M)
Moloney v Mercer [1971] 2 N.S.W.L.R. 207 .... 15.42, 15.44, 15.62
Moores v DPP [1992] Q.B. 125; [1991] 1 W.L.R. 549; [1991] 4 All E.R.
521; (1992) 94 Cr. App. R. 173; (1992) 156 J.P. 113; [1992] Crim.
L.R. 49; [1992] C.O.D. 364; (1991) 155 J.P.N. 474 QBD 12.89, 12.95
Moyna v Secretary of State for Work and Pensions; sub nom. Moyna
v Secretary of State for Social Security [2003] UKHL 44; [2003] 1
W.L.R. 1929; [2003] 4 All E.R. 162; (2003) 73 B.M.L.R. 201 .... 9.38
N(H) v R. See R. v N [2011]
National Justice Compania Naviera SA v Prudential Assurance Co
Ltd (The Ikarian Reefer) (No.1) [1993] 2 Lloyd's Rep. 68; [1993]
F.S.R. 563; [1993] 37 E.G. 158 QBD 24.16
New Jersey v JQ, 617 A 2d 1196 (1993) Sup Ct (New Jersey) 19.121
New Plymouth BC v Taranaki Electric-Power Board [1933] A.C. 680
PC (NZ) 13.37
NHS Trust v P [2013] EWHC 50 (COP) 1.235, 7.11
Nicholson v Gage (1985) 80 Cr. App. R. 40 DC 15.169
Niman (1975) 31 C.R. (N.S.) 51 Prov Ct (Ont) 15.45
Niwar Doski v R. See R. v Doski (Niwar)
North Somerset Council v LW [2014] EWHC 1670 (Fam) 29.100
Norwood v DPP [2003] EWHC 1564 (Admin); [2003] Crim. L.R.
888 ....15.194
Norwood v United Kingdom (Admissibility) (23131/03) (2005) 40
E.H.R.R. SE11 ECtHR 15.194

O v Governor of Holloway Prison; sub nom. O v Governor of Brixton
    Prison [2000] 1 Cr. App. R. 195; [2000] 1 F.L.R. 147; [2000] Fam.
    Law 10 QBD 9.27, 9.31, 9.42, 9.45
O'Riordan v DPP [2005] EWHC 1240 (Admin); *Times*, 31 May
    2005 .... 29.19, 29.28
Owen v DPP [1994] Crim. L.R. 192 ....15.200
Owners, Re. *See* O v Governor of Holloway Prison
Pacurar (2016) 160(19) S.J. 37 ....14.52A
Parker v Jeffrey Ex p. Parker [1963] Q.W.N Qd. S.C.F.C 12.84
Parkin v Norman; Valentine v Lilley [1983] Q.B. 92; [1982] 3 W.L.R.
    523; [1982] 2 All E.R. 583; [1982] Crim. L.R. 528; (1982) 126 S.J.
    359 DC 15.166, 15.169, 15.193
Patel v K&J Restaurants Ltd [2010] EWCA Civ 1211; [2011] L. & T.R.
    6; [2011] 1 P. & C.R. DG7 .... 12.64
Patnaik [2000] 3 Archbold News 2 CA 1.137
Peebles (Glen John) v HM Advocate [2007] HCJAC 6; 2007 J.C. 93;
    2007 S.L.T. 197; 2007 G.W.D. 3–43 .... 8.102
Peebles v HM Advocate [2007] HCJAC 6 .... 8.67
People v Brophy [1992] ILRM 709 .... 32.02
People v Hackett, 365 NW 2d 120 (1984) 26.148, 26.183
Pepper (Inspector of Taxes) v Hart; sub nom. Pepper v Hart [1993]
    A.C. 593; [1992] 3 W.L.R. 1032; [1993] 1 All E.R. 42; [1992] S.T.C.
    898; [1993] I.C.R. 291; [1993] I.R.L.R. 33; [1993] R.V.R. 127;
    (1993) 143 N.L.J. 17; [1992] N.P.C. 154 HL 8.87
Percy v DPP [1995] 1 W.L.R. 1382; [1995] 3 All E.R. 124; (1995) 159
    J.P. 337; [1995] Crim. L.R. 714; (1995) 159 J.P.N. 228; (1995) 92(9)
    L.S.G. 38; (1995) 139 S.J.L.B. 34 DC 13.83, 13.84
PI [1998] C.Law 27.85
Planton v DPP. *See* R. (on the application of Planton) v DPP
PNM v Times Newspapers Ltd; sub nom. M v Times Newspapers Ltd
    [2014] EWCA Civ 1132; [2014] C.P. Rep. 48; [2015] 1 Cr. App. R.
    1; [2014] E.M.L.R. 30 .... 29.57, 29.99, 29.100
Police Service for Northern Ireland v MacRitchie [2010] NICA 26 ......15.118
Polychronakis v Richards & Jerrom Ltd [1998] Env. L.R. 346; [2001]
    L.L.R. 538; [1998] J.P.L. 588 DC 35.48, 36.60
Pora v R. [2015] UKPC 9; [2016] 1 Cr. App. R. 3; [2015] Crim. L.R.
    884 .... 24.03, 24.33
Practice Direction (CA (Crim Div): Criminal Proceedings: Amend-
    ment No.3); sub nom. Practice Direction (CA (Crim Div):
    Criminal Proceedings: Various Amendments) [2015] EWCA Crim
    1567 .... 27.22
Practice Direction (CA (Crim Div): Criminal Proceedings: General
    Matters) (Amendment No.1) [2016] EWCA Crim 97; [2016] All
    E.R. (D.) 199 (Mar) 27.08, 27.32, 27.35, 27.63, 27.78, 27.81

Practice Direction (Fam Div: Applications for Reporting Restriction
    Orders) [2005] 2 F.L.R. 120 Fam Div 29.105
Price v Cromack [1975] 1 W.L.R. 988; [1975] 2 All E.R. 113; (1975) 119
    S.J. 458 QBD 2.98, 8.74
Prince Albert v Strange, 47 E.R. 1302; (1849) 1 H. & Tw. 1 Ct of
    Chancery 8.74
Pugh v Pugh [1951] P. 482; [1951] 2 All E.R. 680; [1951] 2 T.L.R. 806;
    (1951) 95 S.J. 468 PDAD 4.17
R. (A) v St Albans Crown Court Ex p. T. See R. (on the application
    of T) v St Albans Crown Court
R. (on the application of A) v Lowestoft Magistrates' Court [2013]
    EWHC 659 (Admin); [2014] 1 W.L.R. 1489; (2013) 177 J.P. 377;
    [2013] E.M.L.R. 20; [2013] L.L.R. 407; [2013] Crim. L.R. 763;
    [2013] A.C.D. 72 .... 29.96
R. (on the application of AS) v Great Yarmouth Youth Court [2011]
    EWHC 2059 (Admin); [2012] Crim. L.R. 478 .... 27.21, 27.32
R. (on the application of Axon) v Secretary of State for Health [2006]
    EWHC 37 (Admin); [2006] Q.B. 539; [2006] 2 W.L.R. 1130; [2006]
    2 F.L.R. 206; [2006] 1 F.C.R. 175; [2006] H.R.L.R. 12; (2006) 88
    B.M.L.R. 96; [2006] A.C.D. 58; [2006] Fam. Law 272; (2006)
    103(8) L.S.G. 25 .... 4.181
R. (on the application of B) v Ashworth Hospital Authority [2005]
    UKHL 20; [2005] 2 A.C. 278; [2005] 2 W.L.R. 695; [2005] 2 All
    E.R. 289; (2005) 8 C.C.L. Rep. 287; (2005) 83 B.M.L.R. 160;
    [2005] M.H.L.R. 47; (2005) 155 N.L.J. 546; (2005) 149 S.J.L.B.
    359 .... 7.25
R. (on the application of B) v DPP [2009] EWHC 106 (Admin); [2009]
    1 W.L.R. 2072; [2009] 1 Cr. App. R. 38; [2009] U.K.H.R.R. 669;
    (2009) 106 B.M.L.R. 152; [2009] M.H.L.R. 61; [2009] Crim. L.R.
    652; [2009] A.C.D. 19; (2009) 153(5) S.J.L.B. 29 .... 17.11, 17.16, 17.23
R. (on the application of B) v Richmond on Thames Youth Court. See
    R. (on the application of W) v Brent Youth Court
R. (on the application of B) v Stafford Combined Court; sub nom. R.
    (on the application of TB) v Stafford Crown Court [2006] EWHC
    1645 (Admin); [2007] 1 W.L.R. 1524; [2007] 1 All E.R. 102; [2006]
    2 Cr. App. R. 34 .... 18.95
R. (on the application of BH (A Child)) v Llandudno Youth Court
    [2014] EWHC 1833 (Admin); (2014) 178 J.P. 305 .... 31.89
R. (on the application of Bright) v Secretary of State for Justice; R. (on
    the application of Keeley) v Secretary of State for Justice; sub
    nom. Bright v Governor of Whitemoor Prison [2014] EWCA Civ
    1628; [2015] 1 W.L.R. 723 ....15.166
R. (on the application of C) v Sevenoaks Youth Court [2009] EWHC
    3088 (Admin); [2010] 1 All E.R. 735; (2010) 174 J.P. 224 .... 27.25, 27.32,
                                                                                      27.33, 27.36, 31.49

R. (on the application of C) v Sheffield Youth Court. *See* R. (on the application of D) v Sheffield Youth Court
R. (on the application of CM) v Crown Prosecution Service [2014] EWHC 4457 (Admin); [2015] A.C.D. 55 .... 3.13
R. (on the application of Cooke) v DPP; sub nom. Cooke v DPP [2008] EWHC 2703 (Admin); (2008) 172 J.P. 596; [2008] M.H.L.R. 348 .... 36.27
R. (on the application of Crown Prosecution Service) v South East Surrey Youth Court; sub nom. R. (on the application of DPP) v South East Surrey Youth Court; Crown Prosecution Service v MLG [2005] EWHC 2929 (Admin); [2006] 1 W.L.R. 2543; [2006] 2 All E.R. 444; [2006] 2 Cr. App. R. (S.) 26; (2006) 170 J.P. 65; [2006] Crim. L.R. 367; (2006) 179 J.P.N. 95 .... 31.96, 31.98, 31.99
R. (on the application of Cunliffe) v West London Magistrates Court; R. (on the application of Cunliffe) v Ealing Magistrates Court; R. (on the application of Cunliffe) v Hastings Magistrates Court [2006] EWHC 2081 (Admin) 18.78
R. (on the application of D) v Camberwell Green Youth Court; R. (on the application of R) v Balham Youth Court; R. (on the application of N) v Camberwell Green Youth Court; R. (on the application of DPP) v Camberwell Green Youth Court; R. (on the application of G) v Camberwell Green Youth Court [2005] UKHL 4; [2005] 1 W.L.R. 393; [2005] 1 All E.R. 999; [2005] 2 Cr. App. R. 1; (2005) 169 J.P. 105; [2005] 1 F.C.R. 365; [2005] H.R.L.R. 9; [2005] U.K.H.R.R. 302; 17 B.H.R.C. 625; [2005] Crim. L.R. 497; (2005) 169 J.P.N. 257; (2005) 102(13) L.S.G. 27; (2005) 149 S.J.L.B. 146 .... 27.20, 27.26, 27.30, 27.40, 27.51, 27.76
R. (on the application of D) v Manchester City Youth Court [2003] 1 Cr. App. R. (S.) 323 .... 31.89
R. (on the application of D) v Sheffield Youth Court; R. (on the application of N) v Sheffield Youth Court; sub nom. R. (on the application of C) v Sheffield Youth Court [2003] EWHC 35 (Admin); (2003) 167 J.P. 159; [2003] A.C.D. 22; (2003) 167 J.P.N. 251; (2003) 100(12) L.S.G. 298 31.81
R. (on the application of Denny) [2004] EWHC 948 (Admin); [2004] 1 W.L.R. 3051; [2004] 2 All E.R. 961; [2005] 1 Cr. App. R. (S.) 6; (2004) 168 J.P. 388; (2004) 168 J.P.N. 556; (2004) 101(21) L.S.G. 35 ....31.114
R. (on the application of DPP) v Redbridge Youth Court; R. (on the application of L (A Child)) v Bicester Youth Court [2001] EWHC Admin 209; [2001] 1 W.L.R. 2403; [2001] 4 All E.R. 411; [2001] 2 Cr. App. R. 25; [2001] 3 F.C.R. 615; [2001] Crim. L.R. 473; [2001] A.C.D. 81 .... 27.52, 27.75
R. (on the application of DPP) v South Tyneside Youth Court [2015] EWHC 1455 (Admin); [2015] 2 Cr. App. R. (S.) 59; [2015] Crim.

L.R. 746 .... 31.81

R. (on the application of E) v Birmingham Magistrates' Court; R. (on the application of M) v Birmingham Magistrates' Court; sub nom. R. (on the application of NE) v Birmingham Magistrates' Court; R. (on the application of NM) v Birmingham Magistrates' Court [2015] EWHC 688 (Admin); [2015] 1 W.L.R. 4771; [2015] 2 Cr. App. R. (S.) 25; (2015) 179 J.P. 187; [2015] A.C.D. 56 .... 35.29

R. (on the application of E) v DPP [2011] EWHC 1465 (Admin); [2012] 1 Cr. App. R. 6; [2012] Crim. L.R. 39; (2011) 155(24) S.J.L.B. 43 .... 3.10, 3.13, 3.21

R. (on the application of Ebrahim) v Feltham Magistrates Court; R. v Feltham Magistrates Court Ex p. DPP; Mouat v DPP; sub nom. R. v Feltham Magistrates Court Ex p. Ebrahim [2001] EWHC Admin 130; [2001] 1 W.L.R. 1293; [2001] 1 All E.R. 831; [2001] 2 Cr. App. R. 23; [2002] R.T.R. 7; [2001] Crim. L.R. 741; (2001) 151 N.L.J. 304 .... 30.24

R. (on the application of F) v Crown Prosecution Service [2003] EWHC 3266 (Admin); (2004) 168 J.P. 93; (2004) 168 J.P.N. 174 .... 31.21

R. (on the application of F) v DPP [2013] EWHC 945 (Admin); [2014] Q.B. 581; [2014] 2 W.L.R. 190; [2013] 2 Cr. App. R. 21; [2013] A.C.D. 86 .... 1.07, 1.209, 1.213, 1.214

R. (on the application of F) v Secretary of State for the Home Department; R. (on the application of Thompson) v Secretary of State for the Home Department; sub nom. R. (on the application of F) v Secretary of State for Justice [2010] UKSC 17; [2010] 2 W.L.R. 992; [2010] 2 All E.R. 707; [2010] H.R.L.R. 23; [2010] U.K.H.R.R. 809; (2010) 113 B.M.L.R. 209; (2010) 154(16) S.J.L.B. 27 .... 32.24, 35.26, 35.29, 36.52

R. (on the application of FB) v DPP. See R. (on the application of B) v DPP

R. (on the application of Gazette Media Co Ltd) v Teesside Crown Court; sub nom. Gazette Media Co Ltd, Re [2005] EWCA Crim 1983; [2005] E.M.L.R. 34; [2006] Crim. L.R. 157 ..... 29.19, 29.21, 29.90, 29.92

R. (on the application of Gosport BC) v Fareham Magistrates Court [2006] EWHC 3047 (Admin); [2007] 1 W.L.R. 634; (2007) 171 J.P. 102; (2007) 171 J.P.N. 3638 13.77

R. (on the application of Grant) v Kingston Crown Court [2015] EWHC 767 (Admin); [2015] 2 Cr. App. R. (S.) 11; [2015] A.C.D. 87 .... 36.12

R. (on the application of Green) v City of Westminster Magistrates' Court [2007] EWHC 2785 (Admin); [2008] E.M.L.R. 15; [2008] H.R.L.R. 12; (2007) 157 N.L.J. 1767 .... 15.50

R. (on the application of Guest) v DPP [2009] EWHC 594 (Admin); [2009] 2 Cr. App. R. 26; (2009) 173 J.P. 511; [2009] Crim. L.R.

730 .... 17.28

R. (on the application of H) v South and South East Hants Youth
Court Justices & the Crown Prosecution Service [2006] EWHC
1147 (Admin) 31.89

R. (on the application of H) v Southampton Youth Court [2004]
EWHC 2912 (Admin); [2005] 2 Cr. App. R. (S.) 30; (2005) 169 J.P.
37; [2005] Crim. L.R. 395; [2005] A.C.D. 45; (2005) 169 J.P.N.
159 .... 31.80, 31.89

R. (on the application of Hamberger) v Crown Prosecution Service
[2014] EWHC 2814 (Admin); [2015] M.H.L.R. 439 .... 27.32

R. (on the application of Hamill) v Chelmsford Magistrates' Court;
sub nom. Hamill v Chelmsford Magistrates' Court; R. (on the
application of Hamill) v Chelmsford Justices [2014] EWHC 2799
(Admin); [2015] 1 W.L.R. 1798; (2014) 178 J.P. 401; (2014) 158(33)
S.J.L.B. 41 .... 35.27, 35.29

R. (on the application of JC) v Central Criminal Court; sub nom. JC
v Central Criminal Court [2014] EWCA Civ 1777; [2015] 1
W.L.R. 2865; (2015) 179 J.P. 205 .... 29.09, 29.87, 31.28

R. (on the application of M) v Secretary of State for Work and
Pensions [2008] UKHL 63; [2009] 1 A.C. 311; [2008] 3 W.L.R.
1023; [2009] 2 All E.R. 556; [2009] P.T.S.R. 336; [2009] H.R.L.R.
5; [2009] U.K.H.R.R. 117; 26 B.H.R.C. 587 .... 19.36

R. (on the application of McCann) v Manchester Crown Court;
Clingham v Kensington and Chelsea RLBC; sub nom. R. (on the
application of M (A Child)) v Manchester Crown Court; R. v
Manchester Crown Court Ex p. M (A Child) [2002] UKHL 39;
[2003] 1 A.C. 787; [2002] 3 W.L.R. 1313; [2002] 4 All E.R. 593;
[2003] 1 Cr. App. R. 27; (2002) 166 J.P. 657; [2002] U.K.H.R.R.
1286; 13 B.H.R.C. 482; [2003] H.L.R. 17; [2003] B.L.G.R. 57;
[2003] Crim. L.R. 269; (2002) 166 J.P.N. 850; (2002) 146 S.J.L.B.
239 .... 11.131, 13.74

R. (on the application of Minter) v Chief Constable of Hampshire
[2013] EWCA Civ 697; [2014] 1 W.L.R. 179 .... 35.21

R. (on the application of Morgan Grenfell & Co Ltd) v Special
Commissioners of Income Tax; sub nom. R. v Inland Revenue
Commissioners Ex p. Morgan Grenfell & Co Ltd; R. v Special
Commissioners of Income Tax Ex p. Morgan Grenfell & Co Ltd
[2002] UKHL 21; [2003] 1 A.C. 563; [2002] 2 W.L.R. 1299; [2002]
3 All E.R. 1; [2002] S.T.C. 786; [2002] H.R.L.R. 42; 74 T.C. 511;
[2002] B.T.C. 223; 4 I.T.L. Rep. 809; [2002] S.T.I. 806; (2002)
99(25) L.S.G. 35; (2002) 146 S.J.L.B. 126; [2002] N.P.C. 70 .... 34.34

R. (on the application of NE) v Birmingham Magistrates' Court. See
R. (on the application of E) v Birmingham Magistrates' Court

R. (on the application of Nicolaou) v Redbridge Magistrates' Court
[2012] EWHC 1647 (Admin); [2012] 2 Cr. App. R. 23; (2012) 176

J.P. 441; [2012] 3 F.C.R. 378; [2013] Crim. L.R. 54; [2012] A.C.D.
96 .... 9.36
R. (on the application of O) v Central Criminal Court [2006] EWHC
3542 (Admin) 20.04
R. (on the application of O) v Coventry Magistrates' Court [2004]
Crim. L.R. 948 DC 8.106
R. (on the application of O) v Harrow Crown Court; sub nom. O (Writ
of Habeas Corpus), Re; R. (on the application of O) v Crown
Court at Harrow [2006] UKHL 42; [2007] 1 A.C. 249; [2006] 3
W.L.R. 195; [2006] 3 All E.R. 1157; [2007] 1 Cr. App. R. 9; [2006]
H.R.L.R. 35; [2006] U.K.H.R.R. 1062; [2007] Crim. L.R. 63;
(2006) 103(32) L.S.G. 22; (2006) 150 S.J.L.B. 1021 .... 1.25
R. (on the application of OP) v Secretary of State for Justice [2014]
EWHC 1944 (Admin); [2015] 1 Cr. App. R. 7; (2014) 178 J.P. 377;
[2015] M.H.L.R. 421; [2015] Crim. L.R. 79 .... 27.35, 27.111
R. (on the application of P) v Derby Youth Court; sub nom. R. (on the
application of TP) v Derby Youth Court [2015] EWHC 573
(Admin); (2015) 179 J.P. 139 .... 31.79
R. (on the application of P) v West London Youth Court; sub nom. R.
(on the application of TP) v West London Youth Court [2005]
EWHC 2583 (Admin); [2006] 1 W.L.R. 1219; [2006] 1 All E.R.
477; [2006] 1 Cr. App. R. 25; (2006) 170 J.P. 82; [2006] M.H.L.R.
40; (2006) 170 J.P.N. 333; (2006) 170 J.P.N. 355 ..... 27.33, 31.48, 31.49
R. (on the application of Paul Richards) v Teesside Magistrates' Court
[2015] EWCA Civ 7; [2015] 1 W.L.R. 1695; [2015] 1 Cr. App. R.
(S.) 60; (2015) 179 J.P. 119; [2015] Crim. L.R. 461 .... 36.43
R. (on the application of Planton) v DPP; sub nom. Planton v DPP
[2001] EWHC Admin 450; (2002) 166 J.P. 324; [2002] R.T.R. 9;
(2002) 166 J.P.N. 370; (2001) 98(27) L.S.G. 40 .... 13.42
R. (on the application of Press Association) v Cambridge Crown
Court; sub nom. Press Association, Re [2012] EWCA Crim 2434;
[2013] 1 W.L.R. 1979; [2013] 1 All E.R. 1361; [2013] 1 Cr. App. R.
16; [2013] E.M.L.R. 9; [2013] Crim. L.R. 323 ...... 29.18, 29.23, 29.24,
29.26, 29.30, 29.32, 29.33
R. (on the application of Prothero) v Secretary of State for the Home
Department [2013] EWHC 2830 (Admin); [2014] 1 W.L.R. 1195;
[2014] A.C.D. 40; (2013) 157(37) S.J.L.B. 37 .... 35.36
R. (on the application of R) v A Chief Constable [2013] EWHC 2864
(Admin); [2014] 1 Cr. App. R. 16; (2013) 134 B.M.L.R. 98; [2014]
Crim. L.R. 524; [2014] A.C.D. 28 .... 25.66
R. (on the application of R) v DPP [2006] EWHC 1375 (Admin);
(2006) 170 J.P. 661; (2007) 171 J.P.N. 140 ....15.196
R. (on the application of Robinson) v Sutton Coldfield Magistrates
Court [2006] EWHC 307 (Admin); [2006] 4 All E.R. 1029; [2006]
2 Cr. App. R. 13; (2006) 170 J.P. 336; [2006] Crim. L.R. 742; [2006]

A.C.D. 53; (2006) 170 J.P.N. 634 .... 20.03

R. (on the application of S) v Crown Prosecution Service; S v Oxford Magistrates' Court; sub nom. S v Crown Prosecution Service [2015] EWHC 2868 (Admin); [2016] 1 W.L.R. 804; [2016] 1 Cr. App. R. 14; [2016] Crim. L.R. 215; [2016] A.C.D. 3 .... 17.34

R. (on the application of S) v DPP; sub nom. S v DPP [2006] EWHC 2231 (Admin) 3.22, 3.78, 31.09, 31.21

R. (on the application of S) v Waltham Forest Youth Court [2004] EWHC 715 (Admin); [2004] 2 Cr. App. R. 21; (2004) 168 J.P. 293; (2004) 168 J.P.N. 438 .... 27.30

R. (on the application of T) v Secretary of State for Justice [2013] EWHC 1119 (Admin); [2013] A.C.D. 88 ....27.136

R. (on the application of T) v St Albans Crown Court; Chief Constable of Surrey v JHG [2002] EWHC 1129 (Admin); [2002] All E.R. (D.) 308 (May) 29.76, 29.87

R. (on the application of TB) v Stafford Crown Court. See R. (on the application of B) v Stafford Combined Court

R. (on the application of the Crown Prosecution Service) v Brentford Youth Court [2003] EWHC 2409 (Admin); (2003) 167 J.P. 614; [2004] Crim. L.R. 159; (2003) 167 J.P.N. 934 .... 27.78

R. (on the application of the Crown Prosecution Service) v Redbridge Youth Court [2005] EWHC 1390 (Admin); (2005) 169 J.P. 393; (2005) 169 J.P.N. 557 .... 31.89

R. (on the application of TP) v West London Youth Court. See R. (on the application of P) v West London Youth Court

R. (on the application of Trinity Mirror Plc) v Croydon Crown Court; sub nom. Trinity Mirror Plc, Re [2008] EWCA Crim 50; [2008] Q.B. 770; [2008] 3 W.L.R. 51; [2008] 2 All E.R. 1159; [2008] 2 Cr. App. R. 1; [2009] E.M.L.R. 3; [2008] Crim. L.R. 554 ..... 29.32, 29.75, 29.98, 29.99, 29.107

R. (on the application of Uttley) v Secretary of State for the Home Department [2004] UKHL 38; [2004] 1 W.L.R. 2278; [2004] 4 All E.R. 1; [2005] 1 Cr. App. R. 15; [2005] 1 Cr. App. R. (S.) 91; [2004] H.R.L.R. 42; [2004] U.K.H.R.R. 1031; 17 B.H.R.C. 379; [2005] 1 Prison L.R. 234; (2004) 101(35) L.S.G. 33; (2004) 154 N.L.J. 1255; (2004) 148 S.J.L.B. 977 ....30.113

R. (on the application of W) v Brent Youth Court; R. (on the application of S) v Enfield Youth Court; R. (on the application of B) v Richmond on Thames Youth Court [2006] EWHC 95 (Admin); (2006) 170 J.P. 198; [2006] A.C.D. 40; (2006) 170 J.P.N. 297 .... 31.82, 31.83, 31.85, 31.86, 31.89

R. (on the application of W) v Caernarfon Youth Court [2013] EWHC 1466 (Admin); (2013) 177 J.P. 534; [2013] A.C.D. 111 ....31.104

R. (on the application of W) v DPP. See W v DPP

R. (on the application of W) v Leeds Crown Court [2011] EWHC 2326
(Admin); [2012] 1 W.L.R. 2786; [2012] 1 Cr. App. R. 13; (2011)
175 J.P. 467; [2012] Crim. L.R. 160; [2012] A.C.D. 8 .... 31.99
R. (on the application of W) v Oldham Youth Court [2010] EWHC
661 (Admin) 31.83, 31.89
R. (on the application of W) v Thetford Youth Court; R. (on the
application of M) v Waltham Forest Youth Court [2002] EWHC
1252 (Admin); [2003] 1 Cr. App. R. (S.) 67; (2002) 166 J.P. 453;
[2002] Crim. L.R. 681; (2002) 166 J.P.N. 573 .... 31.89
R. (on the application of Y) v Aylesbury Crown Court [2012] EWHC
1140 (Admin); [2012] E.M.L.R. 26; [2012] Crim. L.R. 893; [2012]
A.C.D. 70 .... 29.74, 29.75, 29.76, 29.77, 29.78, 29.79, 29.87
R. (on the application of Yam) v Central Criminal Court [2015] UKSC
76 .... 29.87
R. (on the prosecution of Lambeth BC) v South Eastern Rly Co (1910)
74 J.P. 137 CA 13.37
R. v A (Alec Edward) [2009] EWCA Crim 513 ..... 20.37, 20.50, 20.55, 20.140
R. v A (Ashraf) [2011] EWCA Crim 1517; (2011) 175 J.P. 437 .... 19.78
R. v A (Child Abduction) [2000] 1 W.L.R. 1879; [2000] 2 All E.R. 177;
[2000] 1 Cr. App. R. 418; [2000] Crim. L.R. 169; (1999) 96(40)
L.S.G. 42 CA (Crim Div) 9.34
R. v A (Complainant's Sexual History); sub nom. R. v A (No.2); R. v
Y (Sexual Offence: Complainant's Sexual History) [2001] UKHL
25; [2002] 1 A.C. 45; [2001] 2 W.L.R. 1546; [2001] 3 All E.R. 1;
[2001] 2 Cr. App. R. 21; (2001) 165 J.P. 609; [2001] H.R.L.R. 48;
[2001] U.K.H.R.R. 825; 11 B.H.R.C. 225; [2001] Crim. L.R. 908;
(2001) 165 J.P.N. 750 .... 1.287, 26.02, 26.04, 26.05, 26.06, 26.07, 26.09,
26.17, 26.43, 26.55, 26.62, 26.68, 26.70, 26.72, 26.75, 26.82,
26.86, 26.87, 26.92, 26.99, 26.100, 26.101, 26.102, 26.103,
26.104, 26.107, 26.108, 26.109, 26.112, 26.114, 26.116,
26.124, 26.127, 26.141, 26.143, 26.147, 26.176, 26.179,
26.180, 26.181, 26.183
R. v A (No.2). See R. v A (Complainant's Sexual History)
R. v A (Patrick) [2000] 2 All E.R. 185 CA (Crim Div) 32.03
R. v A (Prosecutor's Appeal). See R. v C; sub nom. R. v A
(Prosecutor's Appeal)
R. v A [2008] EWCA Crim 2908; [2009] 1 W.L.R. 1947; [2009] 2 All
E.R. 898; [2009] 1 Cr. App. R. 26; [2009] Crim. L.R. 739 .... 1.143
R. v A [2010] EWCA Crim 2913 .... 17.53
R. v A [2011] EWCA Crim 1943 .... 19.78
R. v A [2012] EWCA Crim 434; [2012] 2 Cr. App. R. 8; [2013] Crim.
L.R. 240 .... 17.50, 17.63
R. v A [2014] EWCA Crim 299; [2014] 1 W.L.R. 2469; [2014] 2 Cr.
App. R. 5 .... 1.226, 1.236, 7.09, 7.18, 7.23, 7.44, 7.46, 7.84, 7.86
R. v A [2014] NICA 2 .... 32.66, 32.74

R. v A [2015] EWCA Crim 177; [2015] 2 Cr. App. R. (S.) 12; [2015] Crim. L.R. 555 .... 33.24, 33.25

R. v A [2015]. *See* A v R. [2015]

R. v A; sub nom. R. v BA [2012] EWCA Crim 1529; [2012] 1 W.L.R. 3378; [2013] 1 All E.R. 280; [2012] 2 Cr. App. R. 34; (2012) 176 J.P. 615; [2013] Crim. L.R. 168 ....19.124

R. v A(A) [2014] EWCA Crim 140 .... 19.34, 26.153

R. v AA [2007] EWCA Crim 1779 .... 19.77, 19.78, 19.80, 19.81, 30.103

R. v AB [2011] EWCA Crim 3331 .... 19.09

R. v AB [2015] EWCA Crim 1042 .... 30.08, 30.125

R. v Abadom (Steven) [1983] 1 W.L.R. 126; [1983] 1 All E.R. 364; (1983) 76 Cr. App. R. 48; [1983] Crim. L.R. 254; (1982) 79 L.S.G. 1412; (1983) 133 N.L.J. 132; (1982) 126 S.J. 562 CA (Crim Div) 25.36

R. v Abbott (Charles Clement) [1955] 2 Q.B. 497; [1955] 3 W.L.R. 369; [1955] 2 All E.R. 899; (1955) 39 Cr. App. R. 141; (1955) 119 J.P. 526; (1955) 99 S.J. 544 CCA 17.54

R. v Abdelrahman (Samir) [2005] EWCA Crim 1367; *Times*, 15 June 2005 ....26.155

R. v Abdullahi (Osmund Mohammed) [2006] EWCA Crim 2060; [2007] 1 W.L.R. 225; [2007] 1 Cr. App. R. 14; [2007] Crim. L.R. 184 .... 4.139, 4.239

R. v Abdulle (Ayanle); sub nom. R. v Adbulle (Ayanle) [2013] EWCA Crim 1069 .... 19.49

R. v Aboulkadir [2009] EWCA Crim 956 .... 27.83

R. v Abu Hamza [2006] EWCA Crim 2918; [2007] Q.B. 659; [2007] 2 W.L.R. 226; [2007] 3 All E.R. 451; [2007] 1 Cr. App. R. 27; [2007] Crim. L.R. 320 .... 17.31, 17.32, 30.67

R. v AD (A Juvenile) [2001] 1 Cr. App. R. (S.) 59; [2000] Crim. L.R. 867 CA (Crim Div) 31.77

R. v AD [2002] EWCA Crim 1789 .... 19.99

R. v AD [2016] EWCA Crim 454 .... 1.34

R. v Adams (Christopher) [2003] EWCA Crim 3231; [2004] 2 Cr. App. R. (S.) 15 .... 35.50

R. v Adams (Denis John) (No.1) [1996] 2 Cr. App. R. 467; [1996] Crim. L.R. 898 CA (Crim Div) 25.43, 25.45

R. v Adams (Denis John) (No.2) [1998] 1 Cr. App. R. 377 CA (Crim Div) 25.43

R. v Adams (John) [2014] EWCA Crim 1898 ....15.110

R. v Adenusi (Oladele) [2006] EWCA Crim 1059; (2007) 171 J.P. 169; [2006] Crim. L.R. 929; (2007) 171 J.P.N. 428; (2007) 171 J.P.N. 514 .... 20.54

R. v Adeojo (Sodiq) [2013] EWCA Crim 41 .... 19.49

R. v Adey (No.97/5306/Y3) unreported 3 March 1998 ....19.115

R. v Adkins. *See* R. v A (Patrick)

R. v AG [2010] NICA 20 .... 32.60, 32.72

R. v Ahmed and Khan [1994] Crim. L.R. 669 CA (Crim Div) 19.99

R. v Ainscough (Zane Roy) [2006] EWCA Crim 694; (2006) 170 J.P. 517; [2006] Crim. L.R. 635; (2006) 170 J.P.N. 894 .... 20.09

R. v AJC [2006] EWCA Crim 284 .... 20.19

R. v Akin (No.96/1196/W3) unreported 23 September 1996 .... 19.74

R. v Alary (Bruno) [2012] EWCA Crim 1534 .... 35.24

R. v Alderson (No.97/4008/22) unreported 6 May 1988 .... 19.16

R. v Alderton (Michael Thomas) [2014] EWCA Crim 2204 .... 4.109

R. v Aldridge (Trevor); R. v Eaton (Thomas) [2012] EWCA Crim 1456 .... 36.56

R. v Alexander (Leon) (1912) 107 L.T. 240 .... 9.35

R. v Ali (Yasir Ifran); R. v Ashraf (Daaim Ali) [2015] EWCA Crim 1279; [2015] 2 Cr. App. R. 33 ...... 1.07, 1.185, 1.194, 4.117, 11.92, 11.97, 11.100, 11.111, 19.50, 33.16

R. v Ali Sed. See R. v Sed (Ali Dahir)

R. v Alibhai (Akbal); R. v Bakir (Nabil); R. v Collier (Adam); R. v Dias (Chaim Nathan) [2004] EWCA Crim 681 .... 18.72

R. v All-Hilly (Salaam David) [2014] EWCA Crim 1614; [2014] 2 Cr. App. R. 33 .... 26.158, 26.161

R. v Allen (Henry) (1839) 9 C. & P. 31 .... 1.156

R. v AM and MG [2014] EWCA Crim 1970 ...... 1.73, 30.120, 30.124, 30.126

R. v AM. See R. v M [2009]

R. v Amado-Taylor. See R. v IWAT

R. v Ambrose (Peter Thomas) (1973) 57 Cr. App. R. 538 CA (Crim Div) 15.166

R. v Anderson (Anthony) [2008] EWCA Crim 12; [2008] 2 Cr. App. R. (S.) 57 .... 15.26

R. v Anderson (Keith Anthony). See DPP v Anderson (Keith Anthony)

R. v Anderson (Stephen) [2012] EWCA Crim 1785 .... 24.41

R. v Andrade [2015] EWCA Crim 1722; [2015] All E.R. (D.) 122 (Nov) 19.30, 26.47

R. v Andreous (Andreas Nicholas) [2014] EWCA Crim 2886 .... 1.369

R. v Andrews (Donald Joseph); sub nom. R. v Andrews [1987] A.C. 281; [1987] 2 W.L.R. 413; [1987] 1 All E.R. 513; (1987) 84 Cr. App. R. 382; [1987] Crim. L.R. 487; (1987) 151 J.P.N. 254 HL 19.63

R. v Angel (Robert Charles) [1968] 1 W.L.R. 669; [1968] 2 All E.R. 607 (Note); (1968) 52 Cr. App. R. 280; (1968) 112 S.J. 310 CA (Crim Div) 8.10, 30.160

R. v Ansell (Richard James) [1975] Q.B. 215; [1974] 3 W.L.R. 430; [1974] 3 All E.R. 568; (1974) 60 Cr. App. R. 45; [1974] Crim. L.R. 616; (1974) 118 S.J. 715 CA (Crim Div) 10.153, 10.161

R. v Antoine (Pierre Harrison) [2001] 1 A.C. 340; [2000] 2 W.L.R. 703; [2000] 2 All E.R. 208; [2000] 2 Cr. App. R. 94; (2000) 54 B.M.L.R. 147; [2000] M.H.L.R. 28; [2000] Crim. L.R. 621; (2000) 97(18) L.S.G. 36; (2000) 144 S.J.L.B. 212 HL 15.97, 15.100

R. v Arcuri, 2001 SCC 54, [2001] 2 S.C.R. 828 .... 1.291

R. v Arundel Justices Ex p. Westminster Press [1986] 1 W.L.R. 676; [1985] 1 W.L.R. 708; [1985] 2 All E.R. 390; (1985) 149 J.P. 299; (1985) 82 L.S.G. 1781; (1985) 129 S.J. 274 DC 29.32

R. v Ashes (Stephen Kenny) [2007] EWCA Crim 1848; [2008] 1 All E.R. 113; [2008] 1 Cr. App. R. (S.) 86; [2008] Crim. L.R. 68 ..... 34.43

R. v Ashford (Derek) [2013] EWCA Crim 720 .... 15.77

R. v Ashton (John); R. v O'Reilly (Darren); R. v Draz (Omar) [2006] EWCA Crim 794; [2007] 1 W.L.R. 181; [2006] 2 Cr. App. R. 15; [2006] Crim. L.R. 1004 .... 8.10

R. v Ashton (Robert Vincent) [2015] EWCA Crim 1799; [2016] 1 Cr. App. R. (S.) 32 .... 2.22

R. v Asi-Akram (Paiwand) [2005] EWCA Crim 1543; [2006] 1 Cr. App. R. (S.) 47 .... 1.90

R. v AT [2013] EWCA Crim 1850 .... 20.111, 20.127, 20.128, 20.133

R. v Athwal (Bachan Kaur); R. v Athwal (Sukhdave Singh) [2009] EWCA Crim 789; [2009] 1 W.L.R. 2430; [2009] 2 Cr. App. R. 14; [2009] Crim. L.R. 726 .... 19.81, 19.89, 19.90

R. v Aubrey-Fletcher Ex p. Thompson [1969] 1 W.L.R. 872; [1969] 2 All E.R. 846; (1969) 53 Cr. App. R. 380; (1969) 133 J.P. 450; (1969) 113 S.J. 364 DC 13.83

R. v Avery (Richard Sean) [2007] EWCA Crim 1830 .... 19.80

R. v Ayeva (Sharif) [2009] EWCA Crim 2640; [2010] 2 Cr. App. R. (S.) 22 .... 2.98

R. v Aziz (Kazim); R. v Tosun (Ali Yener); R. v Yorganci (Metin) [1996] A.C. 41; [1995] 3 W.L.R. 53; [1995] 3 All E.R. 149; [1995] 2 Cr. App. R. 478; (1995) 159 J.P. 669; [1995] Crim. L.R. 897; (1995) 159 J.P.N. 756; (1995) 92(28) L.S.G. 41; (1995) 145 N.L.J. 921; [1995] 139 S.J.L.B. 158 HL 19.103

R. v B (Brian S) [2003] EWCA Crim 319; [2003] 2 Cr. App. R. 13; (2003) 147 S.J.L.B. 237 .... 30.69

R. v B (David) [2005] EWCA Crim 158; [2005] 2 Cr. App. R. (S.) 65 .... 35.52, 35.55

R. v B (Derek Anthony) [2001] Crim. L.R. 471 .... 18.89, 18.91

R. v B (Dwayne Clinton) [2006] EWCA Crim 330; [2006] 2 Cr. App. R. (S.) 60 .... 1.90

R. v B (Kuldip) [2002] EWCA Crim 2140 .... 27.77, 27.93

R. v B (Lee) [2005] EWCA Crim 3146 ....26.167

R. v B (MT). See R. v MB (Appeal Against Conviction)

R. v B (P) [2012] EWCA Crim 2451 .... 20.78

R. v B (Peter Alexander) [2012] EWCA Crim 1659 ...... 20.60, 20.76, 20.78

R. v B (Richard William) [2008] EWCA Crim 1850 .... 20.46, 20.85
R. v B [2005] EWCA Crim 29 .... 30.32, 30.53, 30.55
R. v B [2006] EWCA Crim 2945; [2007] 1 W.L.R. 1567; [2007] 1 Cr.
    App. R. 29; (2006) 150 S.J.L.B. 1392 ... 1.209, 1.210, 1.211, 1.318, 1.338,
                                1.339, 1.343, 1.344, 1.345, 1.348, 1.349
R. v B [2006] EWCA Crim 417; [2006] 2 Cr. App. R. 3; [2006] Inquest
    L.R. 45; [2006] Crim. L.R. 745; (2006) 150 S.J.L.B. 361 ...... 24.38, 32.73
R. v B [2008] EWCA Crim 1144; *Times,* 22 May 2008 .... 30.59
R. v B [2009] EWCA Crim 1690 ....20.108
R. v B [2009] EWCA Crim 2291; [2010] Crim. L.R. 489 .... 30.24
R. v B [2012] EWCA Crim 1874; [2013] 1 Cr. App. R. (S.) 96 .... 4.107
R. v B [2012] EWCA Crim 328 .... 6.82
R. v B [2013] EWCA Crim 2301 .... 4.24
R. v B [2013] EWCA Crim 823; [2013] 2 Cr. App. R. 29 .... 1.08, 1.278, 1.323,
                                                                  1.324
R. v B [2015] EWCA Crim 319 .... 3.123
R. v B unreported 2 February 2015 .... 3.132
R. v B, 1955 (3) S.A. 494 .... 15.59
R. v B; R. v S [2008] EWCA Crim 365 .... 19.69
R. v B; sub nom. R. v AB [2003] EWCA Crim 951; [2003] 1 W.L.R.
    2809; (2003) 100(18) L.S.G. 34 .... 19.95
R. v B; sub nom. R. v MB [2012] EWCA Crim 770; [2013] 1 W.L.R.
    499; [2012] 3 All E.R. 1093; [2012] 2 Cr. App. R. 15; (2012) 176
    J.P. 312; [2015] M.H.L.R. 105; [2013] Crim. L.R. 90; (2012)
    109(19) L.S.G. 20 ...... 2.43, 15.96, 15.111, 15.114, 15.122, 15.123, 15.124
R. v B(K). *See* R. v B (Kuldip)
R. v BA. *See* R. v A
R. v Bahador (Hussein) [2005] EWCA Crim 396 .... 26.57, 26.65
R. v Baird (Paul) (1993) 97 Cr. App. R. 308; [1993] Crim. L.R. 778 CA
    (Crim Div) 19.06, 19.07
R. v Balazs [2014] EWCA Crim 937 .... 20.47, 20.51
R. v Ball [2005]. *See* R. v Renda (Raymond)
R. v Bannister (1993) 10 W.A.R. 484 ....26.111
R. v Bao (Chunxia) [2007] EWCA Crim 2781; [2008] 2 Cr. App. R. (S.)
    10; [2008] Crim. L.R. 234 ....30.113
R. v Barclay (David) [2012] EWCA Crim 2375 .... 14.65
R. v Barker (1829) 3 C. & P. 589 .... 19.91
R. v Barker (No.9705014 Z5) unreported 27 March 1998 CA (Crim
    Div) 8.67
R. v Barker [2010] EWCA Crim 4; [2011] Crim. L.R. 233 ..... 19.51, 27.47,
                27.143, 27.146, 27.147, 27.149, 27.150, 27.151, 27.152, 28.06,
                                        28.10, 28.14, 28.17, 28.23, 28.26
R. v Barker. *See* R. v B [2010]
R. v Barlow [2013] EWCA Crim 920 ....20.147

R. v Barnes (Mark) [2004] EWCA Crim 3246; [2005] 1 W.L.R. 910; [2005] 2 All E.R. 113; [2005] 1 Cr. App. R. 30; [2005] Crim. L.R. 381; (2005) 102(4) L.S.G. 30 .... 1.337, 2.113, 2.132

R. v Barnett (Graham) [2007] EWCA Crim 1625; [2008] 1 Cr. App. R. (S.) 61 .... 4.206

R. v Barrett (1862) 26 J.P. 805; Le. & Ca. 263; 32 L.J.M.C. 36; 9 Cox C.C. 255; 1 New Rep. 335; 11 W.R. 124; 169 E.R. 1389; 7 L.T. 435 .... 12.88, 12.96

R. v Barrett (1873) L.R. 2 C.C.R. 81; 43 L.J.M.C. 7; 12 Cox C.C. 498; 22 W.R. 136; [1861–73] All E.R. Rep. 792; 29 L.T. 409 .... 1.226

R. v Barrie [1978] 2 N.Z.L.R. 78 CA (NZ) 12.26

R. v Barrow (1868) L.R. 1 C.C.R. 156; 38 L.J.M.C. 20; 11 Cox C.C. 191; 17 W.R. 102; 19 L.T. 293 .... 1.329

R. v Barton (Kevin John) (1987) 85 Cr. App. R. 5; [1987] Crim. L.R. 399; (1987) 84 L.S.G. 574 CA (Crim Div) 26.60, 26.68

R. v Bashir (Mohammed) (1983) 77 Cr. App. R. 59; [1982] Crim. L.R. 687 CA (Crim Div) 1.287

R. v Bashir (Mohammed); R. v Manzur (Mohammed) [1969] 1 W.L.R. 1303; [1969] 3 All E.R. 692; (1970) 54 Cr. App. R. 1; (1969) 133 J.P. 687; (1969) 113 S.J. 703 Assizes (Leeds) 19.91, 26.08

R. v Bassett (Kevin) [2008] EWCA Crim 1174; [2009] 1 W.L.R. 1032; [2009] 1 Cr. App. R. 7; (2008) 172 J.P. 491; [2008] Crim. L.R. 998; (2008) 172 J.P.N. 708 .... 15.114, 15.117

R. v Bates (Richard) (Application for Leave to Appeal) [2006] EWCA Crim 1395 .... 25.37

R. v Bayliss (Simon Philip) [2012] EWCA Crim 269; [2012] 2 Cr. App. R. (S.) 61 .... 4.169

R. v BD [2007]. See R. v D; sub nom. R. v BD

R. v BD [2015] EWCA Crim 1415 .... 1.115

R. v BDG [2012] EWCA Crim 1283; [2013] 1 Cr. App. R. (S.) 26; [2012] Crim. L.R. 814 .... 33.27, 34.58

R. v Beaney (Andrew David) [2004] EWCA Crim 449; [2004] 2 Cr. App. R. (S.) 82; [2004] Crim. L.R. 480 .... 8.16

R. v Beaney (Ben) [2010] EWCA Crim 2551 .... 1.138, 1.139, 1.140

R. v Beedall (Lee James) [2007] EWCA Crim 23; [2007] Crim. L.R. 910 .... 26.126, 26.147, 26.148

R. v Beeden (Jeffrey Richard) [2013] EWCA Crim 63 .... 36.56, 36.63

R. v Beggs (William Frederick) (1990) 90 Cr. App. R. 430; [1989] Crim. L.R. 898 CA (Crim Div) 19.14

R. v Bellis (Frederick Arthur) (1911) 6 Cr. App. R. 283 CA 3.74

R. v Ben-Rejab (Anouar); R. v Baccar (Nizar) [2011] EWCA Crim 1136; [2012] 1 W.L.R. 2364; [2012] 1 Cr. App. R. 4 .... 26.34, 26.40

R. v Benabbou (Fouad) [2012] EWCA Crim 1256 .... 20.94, 20.98

R. v Bennett (Simon Adam); R. v Turner (Christopher Andrew) [2008] EWCA Crim 248 .... 19.65, 19.69

R. v Bennett, 176 E.R. 925; (1866) 4 F. & F. 1105 Assizes 1.334

R. v Benney (John Rundle) [2010] EWCA Crim 1288 .... 1.84

R. v Benson unreported 14 February 2003 .... 32.33

R. v Berberi (Leart); R. v Mirsini (Shiro); R. v McLeod (Keef Matti) [2014] EWCA Crim 2961; [2015] 2 Cr. App. R. 2 .... 24.14

R. v Berg (Alexander); R. v Lummies (Bert); R. v Carre (Constance); R. v Britt (Robert) (1928) 20 Cr. App. R. 38 CCA 12.92, 12.94

R. v Bernard [1997] 1 Cr. App. R. (S.) 135 ....30.139

R. v Berry (Arthur John) (1988) 10 Cr. App. R. (S.) 13; [1988] Crim. L.R. 325 CA (Crim Div) 1.83

R. v Berry (Thomas Clive) (Abduction) [1996] 2 Cr. App. R. 226; [1996] Crim. L.R. 574 CA (Crim Div) 9.24, 9.27, 9.31

R. v Berry (William George) (1925) 18 Cr. App. R. 65 CCA 19.106

R. v Best (No.98/6932/X5) unreported 7 December 1999 .... 27.59, 27.85

R. v Bevan (John) [2011] EWCA Crim 654 .... 1.152, 30.13

R. v Beverley (Elijah) [2006] EWCA Crim 1287; [2006] Crim. L.R. 1064 .... 20.27

R. v Billam (Keith) [1986] 1 W.L.R. 349; [1986] 1 All E.R. 985; (1986) 82 Cr. App. R. 347; (1986) 8 Cr. App. R. (S.) 48; [1986] Crim. L.R. 347 CA (Crim Div) 1.46, 31.85, 31.86

R. v Birch (Stephen) [2007] EWCA Crim 1008; [2008] 1 Cr. App. R. (S.) 13 .... 15.36

R. v Black (Joseph Christopher); R. v Gowan (Lloyd) [2006] EWCA Crim 2306; (2006) 103(37) L.S.G. 30; (2006) 150 S.J.L.B. 1255 ...... 34.39

R. v Blackstock (Stuart) (1980) 70 Cr. App. R. 34 CA (Crim Div) 19.06

R. v Blake [2006] EWCA Crim 871; [2006] All E.R. (D.) 361 (Feb) 20.48

R. v Blasiak (Slawomir) [2010] EWCA Crim 2620 ....19.116

R. v Blore. See R. v B [2013]

R. v Boakye (Christiana); R. v Alleyne (Rebekah); R. v Nwude (Ifeoma Kalistar); R. v Nasri (Sbida); R. v Latchman (Dona Narisa); R. v Jagne (Shireen) [2012] EWCA Crim 838; [2013] 1 Cr. App. R. (S.) 2; [2012] Crim. L.R. 626 .... 33.09

R. v Boal (Francis Steven) [1992] Q.B. 591; [1992] 2 W.L.R. 890; [1992] 3 All E.R. 177; [1992] B.C.L.C. 872; (1992) 95 Cr. App. R. 272; (1992) 156 J.P. 617; [1992] I.C.R. 495; [1992] I.R.L.R. 420; (1992) 156 L.G. Rev. 763; (1992) 136 S.J.L.B. 100 .... 8.42

R. v Boardman (David) [2015] EWCA Crim 175; [2015] 1 Cr. App. R. 33; [2015] Crim. L.R. 451 ....18.100

R. v Bogie [1992] Crim. L.R. 301 CA (Crim Div) 26.145

R. v Bolduc and Bird (1967) 63 D.L.R. (2d) 82 .... 1.327, 2.75

R. v Boness (Dean); R. v Bebbington (Shaun Anthony) [2005] EWCA Crim 2395; [2006] 1 Cr. App. R. (S.) 120; (2005) 169 J.P. 621; [2006] Crim. L.R. 160; [2006] A.C.D. 5; (2005) 169 J.P.N. 937 .... 13.79

R. v Bonnick (Derek Denton) (1978) 66 Cr. App. R. 266; [1978] Crim.
L.R. 246; (1977) 121 S.J. 79 CA (Crim Div) 1.284
R. v Bonython (1984) 38 SASR 45 .... 24.05
R. v Booth (1872) 12 Cox C.C. 231 .... 9.29
R. v Bounekhla (Samir) [2006] EWCA Crim 1217 .... 2.63, 2.65
R. v Bourne (Sydney Joseph) (1952) 36 Cr. App. R. 125 CA 15.138,
15.140, 15.142
R. v Bowden (Jonathan) [2001] Q.B. 88; [2000] 2 W.L.R. 1083; [2000]
2 All E.R. 418; [2000] 1 Cr. App. R. 438; [2000] 2 Cr. App. R. (S.)
26; [2000] Crim. L.R. 381; (1999) 96(47) L.S.G. 29; (2000) 144
S.J.L.B. 5 CA (Crim Div) 8.61, 8.140
R. v Bowen (Cecil) [1997] 1 W.L.R. 372; [1996] 4 All E.R. 837; [1996]
2 Cr. App. R. 157; [1996] Crim. L.R. 577; (1996) 93(15) L.S.G. 31;
(1996) 146 N.L.J. 442; (1996) 140 S.J.L.B. 1007 CA (Crim Div) 1.384
R. v Bowers (Stephen) [1999] 2 Cr. App. R. (S.) 97; [1999] Crim. L.R.
234 CA (Crim Div) 1.133
R. v Bowman (Maximus John) [2005] EWCA Crim 3612; [2006] 2 Cr.
App. R. (S.) 40 .... 35.52
R. v Boxer (Michael) [2015] EWCA Crim 1684 .... 27.84
R. v Boyea (1992) 156 J.P. 505; [1992] Crim. L.R. 574; (1992) 156 J.P.N.
442 CA (Crim Div) 2.121, 2.122, 2.124, 2.126, 2.127, 2.128, 2.131,
2.132
R. v Boyesen (Peregrine) [1982] A.C. 768; [1982] 2 W.L.R. 882; [1982]
2 All E.R. 161; (1982) 75 Cr. App. R. 51; [1982] Crim. L.R. 596;
(1982) 126 S.J. 308 HL 8.96
R. v Bradbury (Myles James) [2015] EWCA Crim 1176; [2015] 2 Cr.
App. R. (S.) 72; [2015] Crim. L.R. 1005 .... 4.36, 4.54
R. v Bradley (David Benjamin) [2005] EWCA Crim 20; [2005] 1 Cr.
App. R. 24; (2005) 169 J.P. 73; [2005] Crim. L.R. 411; (2005) 169
J.P.N. 200; (2005) 102(8) L.S.G. 29 .... 20.02
R. v Brady (James Richard); R. v Ram (Gurdas) [1964] 3 All E.R. 616;
(1963) 47 Cr. App. R. 196; (1965) 129 J.P. 1 CA 12.90
R. v Braithwaite (Stephen) [2010] EWCA Crim 1082; [2010] 2 Cr. App.
R. 18; (2010) 174 J.P. 387; [2010] Crim. L.R. 855 .... 20.143, 20.148
R. v Brand (Paul James) [2009] EWCA Crim 2878 .... 20.16
R. v Bree (Benjamin) [2007] EWCA Crim 804; [2008] Q.B. 131; [2007]
3 W.L.R. 600; [2007] 2 All E.R. 676; [2007] 2 Cr. App. R. 13;
[2007] Crim. L.R. 900; (2007) 104(15) L.S.G. 23; (2007) 151
S.J.L.B. 432 .... 1.187, 1.188, 1.244, 1.245, 1.246, 1.250, 1.260
R. v Breeze (Steven) [2009] EWCA Crim 255; [2009] All E.R. (D) 206
(Jan) 1.363
R. v Brewster (Neil) [2010] EWCA Crim 1194; [2011] 1 W.L.R. 601;
[2010] 2 Cr. App. R. 20; (2010) 174 J.P. 353; [2011] Crim. L.R.
58 ....20.146
R. v Bridge (Damien Ross) [2012] EWCA Crim 2270 .... 1.42

R. v Bright (Michael John) : [2008] EWCA Crim 462; [2008] 2 Cr. App.
R. (S.) 102; [2008] Lloyd's Rep. F.C. 323; [2008] Crim. L.R. 482 ....30.142
R. v Brima (Jimmy) [2006] EWCA Crim 408; [2007] 1 Cr. App. R.
24 .... 20.92
R. v Broadfoot (Joseph James) [1976] 3 All E.R. 753; (1977) 64 Cr.
App. R. 71; [1977] Crim. L.R. 690 CA (Crim Div) 10.63, 10.135,
10.136
R. v Brock (John Terrence); R. v Wyner (Ruth Avril) [2001] 1 W.L.R.
1159; [2001] 2 Cr. App. R. 3; [2001] 2 Cr. App. R. (S.) 48; (2001)
165 J.P. 331; [2001] Crim. L.R. 320; (2001) 165 J.P.N. 225; (2001)
98(8) L.S.G. 43; (2001) 145 S.J.L.B. 44 CA (Crim Div) 12.82
R. v Brocklebank (Andrew) [2013] EWCA Crim 1813 .... 4.34, 4.77
R. v Broughton (Mel) [2010] EWCA Crim 549 .... 25.53
R. v Broughton (Thomas Michael) [2007] EWCA Crim 566; [2007] 2
Cr. App. R. (S.) 72 .... 2.99, 3.132, 3.165
R. v Brown (1889) 24 Q.B.D. 357 CCR 15.137
R. v Brown (Anthony Joseph) [1994] 1 A.C. 212; [1993] 2 W.L.R. 556;
[1993] 2 All E.R. 75; (1993) 97 Cr. App. R. 44; (1993) 157 J.P. 337;
(1993) 157 J.P.N. 233; (1993) 143 N.L.J. 399 HL 2.63, 2.114, 2.115,
2.118, 2.119, 2.120, 2.121, 2.122, 2.123, 2.124, 2.131, 2.132,
20.19
R. v Brown (Christian Thomas); R. v Grant (Jason) [2004] EWCA
Crim 1620 .... 27.19, 27.60, 27.61
R. v Brown (Craig William) [2006] EWCA Crim 1996; [2007] 1 Cr.
App. R. (S.) 77; [2006] Crim. L.R. 1082 ... 30.165, 34.41, 34.44, 34.50
R. v Brown (Graham) [2001] EWCA Crim 724; [2002] 1 Cr. App. R.
(S.) 1 .... 36.62
R. v Brown (Kevin) (1984) 1 B.C.C. 98970; (1984) 79 Cr. App. R. 115;
[1984] Crim. L.R. 167 CA (Crim Div) 1.26, 1.27, 1.157, 14.52A
R. v Brown (Raymond Andrew) [1984] 1 W.L.R. 1211; [1984] 3 All
E.R. 1013; (1985) 80 Cr. App. R. 36; [1984] Crim. L.R. 627; (1984)
81 L.S.G. 2617; (1984) 128 S.J. 736 CA (Crim Div) 10,63, 10.142
R. v Brown (Richard) [2013] UKSC 43; [2013] 4 All E.R. 860; [2013]
N.I. 265 .... 32.04
R. v Brown (Uriah Samuel) (1989) 89 Cr. App. R. 97; [1988] Crim.
L.R. 828 CA (Crim Div) 26.20
R. v Brownless unreported 9 May 2000 .... 2.43, 9.18
R. v Brusch (Martin); R. v Horvat (Dusan) [2011] EWCA Crim 1554;
[2012] 1 Cr. App. R. (S.) 47 .... 11.93
R. v Brustenga-Vilaseca (Maria Rosario) [2011] EWCA Crim 1099;
[2012] 1 Cr. App. R. (S.) 3 .... 34.57
R. v Bryan (Delroy) [2015] EWCA Crim 548 .... 1.140
R. v Bryon (Michael David) [2015] EWCA Crim 997; [2015] 2 Cr. App.
R. 21 .... 25.45
R. v BT and MH. See R. v T (Complainant's Sexual History)

R. v Buchanan (Richard Kenneth) [2015] EWCA Crim 172; [2015] 2
    Cr. App. R. (S.) 13; [2015] Crim. L.R. 551 .... 4.41, 4.80, 4.82
R. v Buckingham. *See* R. v B [2012]
R. v Bullas. *See* R. v B (Peter Alexander)
R. v Bullen (Lee David) [2008] EWCA Crim 4; [2008] 2 Cr. App. R. 25;
    [2008] Crim. L.R. 472; (2008) 158 N.L.J. 147 .... 20.53
R. v Bunyan and Morgan (1844) 1 Cox C.C. 74; 3 L.T.O.S. 453 ...... 15.53,
                                                                                    15.67
R. v Burdess 2014] EWCA Crim 270 .... 20.46
R. v Burgess (Bertram Fraser) (1956) 40 Cr. App. R. 144; [1956] Crim.
    L.R. 699 CCA 19.106
R. v Burk (CO/2286/96) unreported 12 December 1996 .... 30.74
R. v Burke (John) [2008] EWCA Crim 1077 .... 1.110
R. v Burke. *See* R. v B [2005]
R. v Burns (1994) Can LII 127 (SCC); (1994) 1 S.C.R. 656 ....19.122
R. v Burrows (Basil Pipe Turner) [1952] 1 All E.R. 58 (Note); [1952] 1
    T.L.R. 51; (1951) 35 Cr. App. R. 180; (1952) 116 J.P. 47; [1952]
    W.N. 21; (1952) 96 S.J. 122 CCA 2.63
R. v Burrows (Craig Martin) [2015] EWCA Crim 2046 .... 36.47
R. v Burt (Sean David) (1997) 161 J.P. 77; [1996] Crim. L.R. 660;
    (1996) 160 J.P.N. 1156 CA (Crim Div) 2.43, 9.18
R. v Buswell [1972] 1 W.L.R. 64; [1972] 1 All E.R. 75; (1972) 116 S.J.
    36 CA (Crim Div) 8.99
R. v Butcher (Keith James) [2009] EWCA Crim 1458 ... 2.99, 3.132, 3.150,
                                                                                    4.34, 4.77
R. v Butler (Carl) [2015] EWCA Crim 854 .... 18.33, 18.78
R. v Butterwasser (Abraham) [1948] 1 K.B. 4; [1947] 2 All E.R. 415; 63
    T.L.R. 463; (1948) 32 Cr. App. R. 81; (1947) 111 J.P. 527; (1947)
    91 S.J. 586 CCA 20.87
R. v Byczko [1997] 16 S.A.S.R. 506 ....26.125
R. v Byrne (Frankie) [2009] EWCA Crim 1555; [2010] 1 Cr. App. R.
    (S.) 65 .... 36.61
R. v C (1992) 14 Cr. App. R. (S.) 562 .... 30.122, 30.124
R. v C (Barry) [2004] EWCA Crim 292; [2004] 1 W.L.R. 2098; [2004]
    3 All E.R. 1; [2004] 2 Cr. App. R. 15; [2004] 1 F.C.R. 759; [2005]
    Crim. L.R. 238; (2004) 101(15) L.S.G. 27 .... 1.168
R. v C (Brian William) [2005] EWCA Crim 3121 .... 27.93
R. v C (David Alexander) [2005] EWCA Crim 2827; [2006] 1 Cr. App.
    R. 20; [2006] Crim. L.R. 345 .... 8.68, 30.14
R. v C (John Francis) (1993) 14 Cr. App. R. (S.) 562 CA (Crim Div) 1.73
R. v C (Joining Counts), *Times*, 4 February 1993 .... 19.07
R. v C [1992] Crim. L.R. 642 CA (Crim Div) 2.81
R. v C [2006] EWCA Crim 2132; [2007] Crim. L.R. 235 .... 8.69

R. v C [2007] EWCA Crim 2581; [2008] 1 W.L.R. 966; [2008] 1 Cr.
    App. R. 22; (2007) 104(45) L.S.G. 31 .... 26.23, 26.24, 27.159
R. v C [2007] EWCA Crim 3463 .... 19.65
R. v C [2010] EWCA Crim 2578; [2011] 3 All E.R. 509; [2011] Crim.
    L.R. 396 .... 25.34, 25.52, 25.53
R. v C [2012] EWCA Crim 1478 .... 24.27
R. v C [2014]. See Attorney General's Reference (No.27 of 2013)
R. v C [2015] EWCA Crim 1856 .... 3.42
R. v C unreported 10 September 2014 .... 3.43, 4.37, 4.156
R. v C; R. v Bartley (Anthony Michael); R. v Baldrey (Danny); R. v
    Price (Robert William); R. v Broad (Wayne Malcolm) [2007]
    EWCA Crim 680; [2007] 3 All E.R. 735; [2007] 2 Cr. App. R. (S.)
    98; [2008] Prison L.R. 35; [2007] Crim. L.R. 581 .... 34.42, 34.45
R. v C; R. v T [2010] EWCA Crim 2402; [2010] Crim. L.R. 858 ...... 19.61
R. v C; sub nom. R. v A (Prosecutor's Appeal) [2005] EWCA Crim
    3533; [2006] 1 Cr. App. R. 28 .... 19.18, 26.24, 34.52
R. v C; sub nom. R. v AC [2012] EWCA Crim 2034; [2013] Crim. L.R.
    358 .... 1.07, 1.32, 1.191, 19.18
R. v C(G) (1997) 8 CR (5th) 21 (Ontario Gen Div) 44 .... 19.121
R. v Cairns (James Philip); R. v Firfire (Asif); R. v Rafiq (Shahid); R.
    v Morris (Nigel Leonard) [2013] EWCA Crim 467; [2013] 2 Cr.
    App. R. (S.) 73; [2013] Crim. L.R. 616 .... 36.39
R. v Caldwell (James); sub nom. Commissioner of Police of the
    Metropolis v Caldwell [1982] A.C. 341; [1981] 2 W.L.R. 509;
    [1981] 1 All E.R. 961; (1981) 73 Cr. App. R. 13; [1981] Crim. L.R.
    392; (1981) 125 S.J. 239 HL 1.398
R. v Calver (Philip) unreported 5 December 2012 .... 7.220
R. v Camelleri [1922] 2 K.B. 122 CA 19.74
R. v Campbell (Kenneth George) [2007] EWCA Crim 1472; [2007] 1
    W.L.R. 2798; [2007] 2 Cr. App. R. 28; (2007) 171 J.P. 525; [2008]
    Crim. L.R. 303; (2008) 172 J.P.N. 33; (2007) 104(28) L.S.G. 28 .... 20.79,
                                                                  20.110
R. v Campbell and Campbell [1982] Crim. L.R. 595 CC 12.69
R. v Campbell unreported 26.103
R. v Camplin, 169 E.R. 163; (1845) 1 Den. 89 CCR 1.169, 1.301
R. v Camplin, 174 E.R. 1016; (1845) 1 Car. & K. 746; (1846) 1 Cox
    C.C. 220 QBD 1.16
R. v Canavan (Darren Anthony); R. v Shaw (Dennis); R. v Kidd
    (Philip Richard) [1998] 1 W.L.R. 604; [1998] 1 All E.R. 42; [1998]
    1 Cr. App. R. 79; [1998] 1 Cr. App. R. (S.) 243; (1997) 161 J.P. 709;
    [1997] Crim. L.R. 766; (1997) 161 J.P.N. 838; (1997) 94(35) L.S.G.
    33; (1997) 147 N.L.J. 1457; (1997) 141 S.J.L.B. 169 CA (Crim Div)
    .... 1.31, 3.26, 3.28, 4.43, 4.44, 19.27, 30.22, 30.23, 33.24, 33.26, 33.27,
                        33.29, 33.30, 33.31, 34.34, 34.36, 34.58, 34.62

R. v Cannan (John David) (1991) 92 Cr. App. R. 16; [1990] Crim. L.R.
    869 CA (Crim Div) 19.14, 19.15
R. v Cannings (Angela) [2004] EWCA Crim 1; [2004] 1 W.L.R. 2607;
    [2004] 1 All E.R. 725; [2004] 2 Cr. App. R. 7; [2004] 1 F.C.R. 193;
    [2005] Crim. L.R. 126; (2004) 101(5) L.S.G. 27; (2004) 148 S.J.L.B.
    114 .... 24.06, 25.27
R. v Canns (Jason) [2005] EWCA Crim 2264 .... 1.384
R. v Carman (Philip) [2004] EWCA Crim 540 .... 19.07
R. v Carnell (Simon) [2012] EWCA Crim 248 .... 35.53, 35.55
R. v Carr (Anthony Jacob) [2008] EWCA Crim 1283 ....20.143
R. v Carr (Roger John) [2009] EWCA Crim 224; [2009] 2 Cr. App. R.
    (S.) 72 .... 36.61
R. v Carroll (Peter) [2014] EWCA Crim 2818; [2015] 1 Cr. App. R. (S.)
    54 .... 1.39, 1.58

R. v Carton (Keith John) [2012] EWCA Crim 3199 .... 15.35
R. v Cartwright. *See* R. v C [2007]
R. v Case, 169 E.R. 381; (1850) 1 Den. 580 .... 1.318
R. v Cash (Stephen) [2014] EWCA Crim 1981 .... 9.23
R. v CE [2012] EWCA Crim 1324 .... 1.357, 1.361
R. v Central Criminal Court Ex p. Crook; sub nom. Crook, Ex p.; R.
    v Central Criminal Court Ex p. Godwin [1995] 1 W.L.R. 139;
    [1995] 1 All E.R. 537; [1995] 2 Cr. App. R. 212; (1995) 159 J.P.
    295; [1995] 1 F.L.R. 132; [1995] 2 F.C.R. 153; [1995] Crim. L.R.
    509; [1995] Fam. Law 73; (1995) 159 J.P.N. 249; (1994) 91(39)
    L.S.G. 39; (1994) 138 S.J.L.B. 199 .... 29.66, 29.84
R. v Central Criminal Court Ex p. S; R. v Central Criminal Court Ex
    p. P (1999) 163 J.P. 776; [1999] 1 F.L.R. 480; [1999] Crim. L.R.
    159; [1999] Fam. Law 93 .... 29.76
R. v Central Criminal Court Ex p. W [2001] 1 Cr. App. R. 2; [2000]
    C.O.D. 442 DC 29.76, 29.87
R. v Chakwane (Tonderai) [2013] NICA 24 .... 32.60
R. v Chance (Terence Easton) [1988] Q.B. 932; [1988] 3 W.L.R. 661;
    [1988] 3 All E.R. 225; (1988) 87 Cr. App. R. 398; [1988] Crim.
    L.R. 745; (1988) 138 N.L.J. Rep. 249 CA (Crim Div) 19.106
R. v Chaney (David John) [2009] EWCA Crim 52 .... 1.33
R. v Channing [1994] Crim. L.R. 924 .... 19.14
R. v Chapman (Frank) [1959] 1 Q.B. 100; [1958] 3 W.L.R. 401; [1958]
    3 All E.R. 143; (1958) 42 Cr. App. R. 257; (1958) 122 J.P. 462;
    (1958) 102 S.J. 621 CA 1.161, 1.166, 1.167
R. v Chapman (Jamie Lee) [2000] 1 Cr. App. R. 77; [2000] 1 Cr. App.
    R. (S.) 377; [1999] Crim. L.R. 852 CA (Crim Div) 1.135
R. v Chargot Ltd (t/a Contract Services) [2008] UKHL 73; [2009] 1
    W.L.R. 1; [2009] 2 All E.R. 645; [2009] I.C.R. 263; (2009) 153(1)
    S.J.L.B. 32 .... 8.43, 29.28, 29.71, 29.117, 29.131

R. v Charles (Chuks Emmanuel) [2009] EWCA Crim 1570; [2010] 1
    W.L.R. 644; [2010] 1 Cr. App. R. 2; (2009) 173 J.P. 481; [2010]
    Crim. L.R. 303 .... 13.81, 35.48, 36.60
R. v Chauhan (Ramesh) (1981) 73 Cr. App. R. 232 CA (Crim Div) 19.119
R. v Chedwyn Evans [2012] EWCA Crim 2559 .... 1.253
R. v Cheema (Julie Mary) [1994] 1 W.L.R. 147; [1994] 1 All E.R. 639;
    (1994) 98 Cr. App. R. 195; [1994] Crim. L.R. 206; (1993) 143
    N.L.J. 1439; (1993) 137 S.J.L.B. 231 CA (Crim Div) 19.107
R. v Cheshire (John) [2014] EWCA Crim 627; [2014] 2 Cr. App. R. (S.)
    53 .... 8.33
R. v Chief Constable of Kent Ex p. L; R. v DPP Ex p. B [1993] 1 All
    E.R. 756; (1991) 93 Cr. App. R. 416; [1991] Crim. L.R. 841; [1991]
    C.O.D. 446; (1991) 155 J.P.N. 636; (1992) 136 S.J.L.B. 136 DC 31.08,
                                                                            31.14
R. v Chief Constable of the West Midlands Ex p. Wiley; R. v Chief
    Constable of Nottinghamshire Ex p. Sunderland [1995] 1 A.C.
    274; [1994] 3 W.L.R. 433; [1994] 3 All E.R. 420; [1995] 1 Cr. App.
    R. 342; [1994] C.O.D. 520; (1994) 91(40) L.S.G. 35; (1994) 144
    N.L.J. 1008; (1994) 138 S.J.L.B. 156 HL 18.85
R. v Chinn (Michael) [2012] EWCA Crim 501; [2012] 1 W.L.R. 3401;
    [2012] 3 All E.R. 502; [2012] 2 Cr. App. R. 4; (2012) 176 J.P. 209;
    [2012] Crim. L.R. 707 .... 19.69
R. v Chohan. See R. v Edwards (Karl Adrian)
R. v Choi [1999] EWCA Crim 1279 .... 15.16, 15.26, 15.39, 15.151
R. v Chopra (Manoj Kumar) [2006] EWCA Crim 2133; [2007] 1 Cr.
    App. R. 16; [2007] Crim. L.R. 380 ...... 20.113, 20.118, 20.119, 20.120,
                                                                            20.121
R. v Christian (1913) 78 J.P. 112; (1913) 23 Cox C.C. 541 CCC 10.135
R. v Christou (George) [1997] A.C. 117; [1996] 2 W.L.R. 620; [1996] 2
    All E.R. 927; [1996] 2 Cr. App. R. 360; [1996] Crim. L.R. 911;
    (1996) 93(20) L.S.G. 30; (1996) 146 N.L.J. 750; (1996) 140 S.J.L.B.
    129 HL 1.146, 19.15, 22.46
R. v Ciccarelli (Yuri) [2011] EWCA Crim 2665; [2012] 1 Cr. App. R.
    15 .... 1.09, 1.285
R. v Cilla [2013] EWCA Crim 1810 .... 36.34
R. v Cinous [2002] S.C.C. 29; [2002] 2 S.C.R. 3 .... 1.290, 1.291
R. v CK (A Minor) [2009] NICA 17; [2010] N.I. 15 CA (NI) 32.47, 32.54,
                                                                            36.25
R. v Clarence (Charles James) (1888) 22 Q.B.D. 23 CCR 1.168, 1.318,
                                                                      1.334, 1.335
R. v Clark (1883) 15 Cox C.C. 171 .... 15.37
R. v Clark (James) [2002] EWCA Crim 1009; [2003] 1 Cr. App. R. (S.)
    2 .... 35.52
R. v Clark (Nigel Paul) [2006] EWCA Crim 231 .... 24.49

R. v Clark (Raymond Dennis) [1996] 2 Cr. App. R. 282; [1996] 2 Cr.
App. R. (S.) 351; [1996] Crim. L.R. 448 CA (Crim Div) 3.26, 4.43,
33.24

R. v Clark (Sally) (Appeal against Conviction) (No.2) [2003] EWCA
Crim 1020; [2003] 2 F.C.R. 447; (2003) 147 S.J.L.B. 473 .... 24.06

R. v Clark (Trevor Anthony) [2014] EWCA Crim 1891 .... 14.38

R v Clarke [1992] 1 N.Z.L.R. 147 CA (NZ) 1.380

R. v Clarke (Michael) [2006] EWCA Crim 491 .... 35.51

R. v Clarke (Richard Anthony) [2012] EWCA Crim 2354 .... 19.49

R. v Clarke (Robert) [2012] EWCA Crim 9 ....30.113

R. v Clarke (Ronald Augustus); R. v McDaid (James Andrew) [2008]
UKHL 8; [2008] 1 W.L.R. 338; [2008] 2 All E.R. 665; [2008] 2 Cr.
App. R. 2; [2008] Crim. L.R. 551; (2008) 105(7) L.S.G. 31; (2008)
152(6) S.J.L.B. 28 .... 8.12, 8.13, 30.160

R. v Clay (1851) 5 Cox C.C. 146 .... 19.91, 26.08

R. v Claydon. See R. v C (David Alexander)

R. v Clements [2009] EWCA Crim 2726; Times, 4 December 2009 ...... 20.39,
20.40

R. v Cleobury (Dean Charles) [2012] EWCA Crim 17; [2012] Crim.
L.R. 615 .... 25.33

R. v Clifford (Frank Maxwell) [2014] EWCA Crim 2245; [2015] 1 Cr.
App. R. (S.) 32; [2015] Crim. L.R. 167 ..... 30.06, 30.114, 30.130, 30.145,
30.153, 33.06, 33.26, 34.61

R. v Clifford [1988] 8 C.L. 86 .... 15.31, 15.44

R. v Clifford, Times, 5 December 2003 .... 2.43

R. v Clowes (Peter) (No.1) [1992] 3 All E.R. 440; [1992] B.C.L.C. 1158;
(1992) 95 Cr. App. R. 440 CCC 18.80

R. v CM; R. v N [2011] EWCA Crim 1458; 175 C.L. & J. 405 .... 19.64

R. v Coates (Phillip) [2007] EWCA Crim 1471; [2008] 1 Cr. App. R. 3;
[2007] Crim. L.R. 887 .... 1.250, 19.68, 19.70, 19.79, 24.29

R. v Cogan (John Rodney); R. v Leak (Michael Edward) [1976] Q.B.
217; [1975] 3 W.L.R. 316; [1975] 2 All E.R. 1059; (1975) 61 Cr.
App. R. 217; [1975] Crim. L.R. 584; (1975) 119 S.J. 473 CA (Crim
Div) 1.145, 1.149, 1.413

R. v Coid [1998] Crim. L.R. 199 .... 12.68

R. v Cole (Konrad); R. v Keet (Rocky) [2007] EWCA Crim 1924;
[2007] 1 W.L.R. 2716; [2008] 1 Cr. App. R. 5 .... 19.52

R. v Coles (Martyn) [2010] EWCA Crim 320 .... 1.121, 1.124

R. v Collard (Jonathan Richard) [2004] EWCA Crim 1664; [2005] 1 Cr.
App. R. (S.) 34; [2004] Crim. L.R. 757; (2004) 148 S.J.L.B. 663 .... 36.21,
36.22

R. v Collier (David William) [2013] EWCA Crim 1038 .... 1.128

R. v Collier (Edward John) [2004] EWCA Crim 1411; [2005] 1 W.L.R.
843; [2005] 1 Cr. App. R. 9; (2004) 101(27) L.S.G. 29 .... 8.86, 8.89, 8.90,
8.98

R. v Collins (David) [2015] EWCA Crim 915; [2015] 2 Cr. App. R. (S.)
50 .... 4.169, 4.178
R. v Collins (Stephen William George) [1973] Q.B. 100; [1972] 3
W.L.R. 243; [1972] 2 All E.R. 1105; (1972) 56 Cr. App. R. 554;
[1972] Crim. L.R. 498; (1972) 116 S.J. 432 CA (Crim Div) 14.68
R. v Collinson (Alfred Charles) (1932) 23 Cr. App. R. 49 CCA 13.41
R. v Colwill (Jamie Lee) [2002] EWCA Crim 1320 .... 19.99
R. v Congdon, unreported, 1990 CC (Portsmouth) 10.152
R. v Considine (Lawrence Philip); R. v Davis (Jay) [2007] EWCA Crim
1166; [2008] 1 W.L.R. 414; [2007] 3 All E.R. 621; [2008] 1 Cr. App.
R. (S.) 41; [2007] Crim. L.R. 824 .... 34.36, 34.37
R. v Constanza (Gaetano) [1997] 2 Cr. App. R. 492; [1997] Crim. L.R.
576 CA (Crim Div) 1.294, 2.64
R. v Cooke (Stephen) [1995] 1 Cr. App. R. 318; [1995] Crim. L.R. 497;
(1994) 91(36) L.S.G. 37; (1994) 138 S.J.L.B. 168 CA 25.67
R. v Cooper [2009] UKHL 42; [2009] 1 W.L.R. 1786; [2009] 4 All E.R.
1033; [2010] 1 Cr. App. R. 7; [2010] Crim. L.R. 75; (2009) 153(31)
S.J.L.B. 30 ... 1.230, 1.231, 1.241, 1.181, 1.183, 1.231, 1.238, 1.304, 7.06,
7.09, 7.16, 7.19, 7.22, 7.25, 7.29, 7.30, 7.31, 7.32, 7.33, 7.34,
7.70, 7.75, 7.77, 7.156
R. v Cooper. See R. v C
R. v Cornick (William) [2014] EWHC 3623 (QB); [2015] E.M.L.R.
9 .... 29.78
R. v Cornwall (Joseph Matthew) [2012] EWCA Crim 1227; [2013] 1
Cr. App. R. (S.) 30 .... 5.15, 5.20, 5.21
R. v Corran (Ben); R. v C; R. v Heard (Kevin Phillip); R. v Williams
(Anthony Michael) [2005] EWCA Crim 192; [2005] 2 Cr. App. R.
(S.) 73; [2005] Crim. L.R. 404 .... 3.50, 3.52
R. v Correia de Oliveira (Joao Luis) [2009] EWCA Crim 378 .... 20.10
R. v Corrigan (Patrick) [2014] NICA 85 .... 12.63
R. v Cosco (Michael Nicola) [2005] EWCA Crim 207; [2005] 2 Cr.
App. R. (S.) 66 .... 15.04, 15.36
R. v Coshall, Times, 17 February 1995 .... 27.97
R. v Cottrell (Steven); R. v Fletcher (Joseph) [2007] EWCA Crim 2016;
[2007] 1 W.L.R. 3262; [2008] 1 Cr. App. R. 7; [2008] Crim. L.R.
50 .... 4.03, 30.157
R. v Coull (Ian) [2012] EWCA Crim 2893 ....20.127
R. v Coulthread (1934) 24 Cr. App. R. 44 CCA 19.74
R. v Court (Bernard); R. v Gu (Xiufen) [2012] EWCA Crim 133;
[2012] 1 W.L.R. 2260; [2012] 1 Cr. App. R. 36; [2012] L.L.R.
454 .... 12.87, 12.94
R. v Court (Robert Christopher) [1987] Q.B. 156; [1986] 3 W.L.R.
1029; [1987] 1 All E.R. 120; (1987) 84 Cr. App. R. 210; [1987]
Crim. L.R. 134 CA (Crim Div) 8.49

R. v Court (Robert Christopher) [1989] A.C. 28; [1988] 2 W.L.R. 1071; [1988] 2 All E.R. 221; (1988) 87 Cr. App. R. 144; (1988) 152 J.P. 422; [1988] Crim. L.R. 537; (1988) 152 J.P.N. 414; (1988) 138 N.L.J. Rep. 128 HL 2.04, 2.64, 2.68, 2.72, 2.74, 15.42

R. v Courtie (Thomas) [1984] A.C. 463; [1984] 2 W.L.R. 330; [1984] 1 All E.R. 740; (1984) 78 Cr. App. R. 292; (1984) 148 J.P. 502; [1984] Crim. L.R. 366 HL 2.85, 3.132, 4.68, 6.56, 10.13

R. v Cox (1968–1969) 5 C.R. (N.S.) 395 CA (Ont) 9.28

R. v Cox (Anthony Russell) [2012] EWCA Crim 549; [2012] 2 Cr. App. R. 6; (2012) 176 J.P. 549; [2015] M.H.L.R. 402; [2012] Crim. L.R. 621 .... 27.33, 27.34

R. v Cox (David) (1987) 84 Cr. App. R. 132; (1986) 150 J.P. 336 CA (Crim Div) 26.153

R. v Cox (John Anthony) [2007] EWCA Crim 3365 .... 20.51

R. v Cox [1898] 1 Q.B. 179 CCR 3.75

R. v Coyles [2010] NICA 48 .... 32.47

R. v Cracknell (1866) 10 Cox C.C. 408 .... 19.91

R. v Critchley [1982] Crim. L.R. 524 DC 1.284

R. v Cronshaw (Michael George) [2004] EWCA Crim 2057; [2005] 1 Cr. App. R. (S.) 89 .... 4.03

R. v Crosby [1995] 2 S.C.R. 912 Sup Ct (Can) 26.109

R. v Croydon Justices Ex p. Dean [1993] Q.B. 769; [1993] 3 W.L.R. 198; [1993] 3 All E.R. 129; (1994) 98 Cr. App. R. 76; (1993) 157 J.P. 975; [1993] Crim. L.R. 759; [1993] C.O.D. 290; (1993) 157 J.P.N. 457; (1993) 143 N.L.J. 508 DC 30.75

R. v Crunden, 170 E.R. 1091; (1809) 2 Camp. 89 Assizes 15.45, 15.66

R. v Cruttenden (Roger Christian) [1991] 2 Q.B. 66; [1991] 2 W.L.R. 921; [1991] 3 All E.R. 242; (1991) 93 Cr. App. R. 119; (1991) 155 J.P. 798; [1991] Crim. L.R. 537; (1991) 155 J.P.N. 236 CA (Crim Div) 19.127

R. v Cuerrier [1998] S.C.R. 371; [1991] 2 L.R.C. 29 Sup Ct (Canada) 1.346

R. v Curran [1998] EWCA Crim. 3048 .... 15.26, 15.31, 15.43

R. v Curtis (James Daniel) [2010] EWCA Crim 123; [2010] 3 All E.R. 849; [2010] 1 Cr. App. R. 31; [2010] Crim. L.R. 638 ....15.196

R. v Cushing [2006] EWCA Crim 1221; [2006] All E.R. (D.) 22 (May) 20.110

R. v CW and MM. See R. v Welsh (Christopher)

R. v D (Clifford Robin) (Joined Charges: Evidence) [2003] EWCA Crim 2424; [2004] 1 Cr. App. R. 19; [2005] Crim. L.R. 163; (2003) 147 S.J.L.B. 1088 .... 19.17, 20.134

R. v D (George Ernest) (1993) 14 Cr. App. R. (S.) 776 CA (Crim Div) 10.13

R. v D (Keith) [2005] EWCA Crim 3043 .... 19.66

R. v D (Michael); R. v S (Anthony) [2002] EWCA Crim 1460; (2002) 166 J.P. 792 .... 27.85

R. v D (Sexual Offences Prevention Order) [2005] EWCA Crim 3660; [2006] 1 W.L.R. 1088; [2006] 2 All E.R. 726; [2006] 2 Cr. App. R. (S.) 32; [2006] 1 F.L.R. 1085; [2006] Crim. L.R. 364; [2006] Fam. Law 273 .... 36.25, 36.44

R. v D (Video Testimony) [2002] EWCA Crim 990; [2003] Q.B. 90; [2002] 3 W.L.R. 997; [2002] 2 Cr. App. R. 36; (2002) 166 J.P. 489; [2003] Crim. L.R. 274; (2002) 166 J.P.N. 630; (2002) 99(23) L.S.G. 27; (2002) 146 S.J.L.B. 123 .... 1.236, 7.38, 7.40, 19.51, 19.66, 19.68, 27.10, 27.103, 27.146

R. v D [2005] EWCA Crim 2282 .... 34.26

R. v D [2006] EWCA Crim 111; [2006] 2 Cr. App. R. (S.) 52 ....31.124

R. v D [2007] Crim. L.R. 240 .... 8.11

R. v D [2008] EWCA Crim 1156; [2009] 2 Cr. App. R. 17; (2008) 172 J.P. 358; (2008) 172 J.P.N. 509 .... 20.26

R. v D [2011] EWCA Crim 2305 .... 26.39, 26.41

R. v D [2012] EWCA Crim 2370; [2013] 1 Cr. App. R. (S.) 127; [2013] Crim. L.R. 159 .... 1.133, 1.134, 30.162

R. v D [2013] EWCA Crim 465; [2014] 1 W.L.R. 525; [2013] 3 All E.R. 242; (2013) 177 J.P. 361; [2014] M.H.L.R. 148; [2014] Crim. L.R. 141 .... 28.14

R. v D unreported 3 November 1995 CA 24.33

R. v D; R. v P; R. v U [2011] EWCA Crim 1474; [2013] 1 W.L.R. 676; [2011] 4 All E.R. 568; [2012] 1 Cr. App. R. 8; (2012) 176 J.P. 11 .... 20.01, 20.27, 20.28, 20.33, 20.34, 20.35, 20.37, 20.38, 20.82, 20.88

R. v D; sub nom. R. v BD [2007] EWCA Crim 4 ....26.157

R. v D. See R. v Bridge (Damien Ross)

R. v D(E). See R. v ED

R. v Dalby (Louis) [2012] EWCA Crim 701 .... 20.03, 20.17

R. v Dale (John Luke) [2014] EWCA Crim 2286 .... 2.57

R.. v Danga (Harbeer Singh) [1992] Q.B. 476; [1992] 2 W.L.R. 277; [1992] 1 All E.R. 624; (1992) 94 Cr. App. R. 252; (1992) 13 Cr. App. R. (S.) 408; (1992) 156 J.P. 382; [1992] Crim. L.R. 219; (1992) 156 J.P.N. 382 CA (Crim Div) 31.115

R. v Danielle Smith unreported 2 February 2016 CC (Shrewsbury) 15.55

R. v Darnell [2002] EWCA Crim 176; [2003] All E.R. (D.) 24 (Feb) 26.73, 26.75, 26.142

R. v Darrach (1998) 38 O.R. (3d) 1 CA (Ont) 26.109

R. v Darrach [2000] 2 S.C.R. 443; 2000 S.C.C. 46 Sup Ct (Can) ... 26.174, 26.176

R. v Davies (Dewi John) [2014] EWCA Crim 2243 .... 3.60

R. v Davies (John Cedric) [2011] EWCA Crim 1177; [2011] Crim. L.R. 732 .... 27.75

R. v Davis [2008]. See R. v D [2008]

R. v Davison (Anthony) [2008] EWCA Crim 2795; [2009] 2 Cr. App.
R. (S.) 13; [2009] Crim. L.R. 208 .... 35.13
R. v Day (1841) 9 C. & P. 722; 173 All E.R. Rep. 1026 .... 1.170
R. v Day (Adrian Harold) [2013] EWCA Crim 1648; [2013] All E.R.
(D) 98 (Sep); [2014] 1 Cr. App. R. (S.) 72 .... 1.48, 35.55
R. v Day (Jennifer Sylvia) [2009] EWCA Crim 2445; [2010] 2 Cr. App.
R. (S.) 12 .... 34.57
R. v DB [2012] EWCA Crim 1235 ....26.128
R. v De Munck (Augusta) [1918] 1 K.B. 635; (1919) 13 Cr. App. R. 113
CCA 13.47
R. v Dean [[2000] 2 Cr. App. R. 253 .... 9.20
R. v Dee (1884) 15 Cox C.C. 579 .... 1.329
R. v Delahaye-Bryan [2015] EWCA Crim 1987 .... 3.23, 3.30
R. v Delaval, 97 E.R. 913; (1763) 3 Burr. 1434 KB 15.26
R. v Delay (Timothy) [2006] EWCA Crim 1110; (2006) 170 J.P. 581;
(2006) 170 J.P.N. 997 .... 20.03, 20.124
R. v Delroy Grant unreported March 2011 Crown Ct (Woolwich) 1.110
R. v Dent (Jim) [1943] 2 All E.R. 596; (1944) 29 Cr. App. R. 120
CCA 19.106
R. v Derby Magistrates Court Ex p. B [1996] A.C. 487; [1995] 3 W.L.R.
681; [1995] 4 All E.R. 526; [1996] 1 Cr. App. R. 385; (1995) 159
J.P. 785; [1996] 1 F.L.R. 513; [1996] Fam. Law 210; (1995) 159
J.P.N. 778; (1995) 145 N.L.J. 1575; [1995] 139 S.J.L.B. 219 .... 18.54,
18.55, 18.78
R. v Devenney [2001] 10 BNIL 90 .... 32.33
R. v Devonald (Stephen) [2008] EWCA Crim 527; [2008] All E.R. (D)
241 (Feb) 1.322, 1.324
R. v DGF. See R. v F [2008]
R. v Dhooper (Avtar Singh) [2008] EWCA Crim 2892 .... 20.49
R. v Dica (Mohammed) [2004] EWCA Crim 1103; [2004] Q.B. 1257;
[2004] 3 W.L.R. 213; [2004] 3 All E.R. 593; [2004] 2 Cr. App. R.
28; (2004) 77 B.M.L.R. 243; (2004) 101(21) L.S.G. 35; (2004) 148
S.J.L.B. 570 .... 1.334, 1.335, 1.336, 1.337, 1.340, 1.347, 2.112, 2.124,
2.127, 2.131, 2.132
R. v Dickson [1994] 1 S.C.R. 153 Sup Ct (Can) 26.106
R. v Dimes (Clifford) (1912) 7 Cr. App. R. 43 CCA 1.16
R. v Dixon. See R. v D [2013]
R. v Dizaei (Jamshid Ali) [2013] EWCA Crim 88; [2013] 1 W.L.R.
2257; [2013] 1 Cr. App. R. 31 ....20.150
R. v DJ [2010] EWCA Crim 385; [2010] 2 Cr. App. R. 2; [2010] Crim.
L.R. 769 .... 20.24, 30.25
R. v DJ [2015] EWCA Crim 563; [2015] 2 Cr. App. R. (S.) 16; [2015]
Crim. L.R. 650 .... 1.118, 1.121, 1.122, 1.123, 1.124, 3.70

R. v Dlugosz (Kuba); sub nom. R. v Pickering (Mark Lee) [2013]
EWCA Crim 2; [2013] 1 Cr. App. R. 32; [2013] Crim. L.R. 684 .... 24.05,
25.02, 25.58, 25.61

R. v DM; sub nom. DPP's Reference (No.1 of 2012), Re [2012] NICA
36 .... 32.50, 32.53

R. v DM. *See* R. v M [2011]

R. v DO; sub nom. R. v O [2014] EWCA Crim 2202; [2015] 1 Cr. App.
R. (S.) 41; [2015] Crim. L.R. 379 .... 1.47

R. v Dodd (Jonathan James) [2013] EWCA Crim 660 .... 8.46

R. v Doheny (Alan James); R. v Adams (Gary Andrew) [1997] 1 Cr.
App. R. 369; [1997] Crim. L.R. 669 CA (Crim Div) ... 19.108, 19.117,
25.11, 25.42, 25.45

R. v Donaldson [2008] EWCA Crim 1269 .... 30.37, 30.52

R. v Dones [1987] Crim. L.R. 682 CCC 14.28

R. v Donovan (John George) [1934] 2 K.B. 498; (1936) 25 Cr. App. R.
1 CA 2.110, 2.112, 2.113, 2.115, 2.121, 2.123, 2.124, 2.125, 2.126,
2.127, 2.129, 2.130, 2.131, 2.132

R. v Doody [2008] EWCA Crim 2394 .... 1.356, 1.357, 30.10, 30.105

R. v Doody [2008] EWCA Crim 2557; [2009] Crim. L.R. 591 .... 1.187, 1.366,
1.367, 1.368, 24.25, 24.28

R. v Dooley (Michael) (Appeal against Conviction) [2005] EWCA
Crim 3093; [2006] 1 W.L.R. 775; [2006] 1 Cr. App. R. 21; [2006]
Crim. L.R. 544 .... 8.100

R. v Doski (Niwar) [2011] EWCA Crim 987; [2011] Crim. L.R. 712 .... 18.89,
18.91

R. v Dougal unreported November 2005 Crown Ct (Swansea) 1.243,
1.245

R. v Dowley [1983] Crim. L.R. 168 ....19.119

R. v Doyle (Danny) [2010] EWCA Crim 119 .... 1.220, 1.221

R. v DP. *See* R. v P; sub nom. R. v DP

R. v DPMC and DJW [2010] NICA 22 .... 32.73

R. v DPP Ex p. Kebeline; R. v DPP Ex p. Boukemiche (Farid); R. v
DPP Ex p. Souidi (Sofiane); R. v DPP Ex p. Rechachi (Fatah);
sub nom. R. v DPP Ex p. Kebelene; R. v DPP Ex p. Kebilene
[2000] 2 A.C. 326; [1999] 3 W.L.R. 972; [1999] 4 All E.R. 801;
[2000] 1 Cr. App. R. 275; [2000] H.R.L.R. 93; [2000] U.K.H.R.R.
176; (2000) 2 L.G.L.R. 697; (1999) 11 Admin. L.R. 1026; [2000]
Crim. L.R. 486; (1999) 96(43) L.S.G. 32 HL ... 15.177, 15.193, 15.197

R. v Drew (Martin Ralph) [2000] 1 Cr. App. R. 91; [1999] Crim. L.R.
581 CA (Crim Div) 8.67

R. v Drew unreported December 2006 Crown Ct (Southwark) 10.156,
10.161

R. v Drury (Alfred) (1974) 60 Cr. App. R. 195; [1975] Crim. L.R. 655
CA (Crim Div) 2.98

R. v DS [2008] NICA 19 .... 32.64

R. v DS [2010] NICA 18 .... 32.69
R. v DS, TS. *See* R. v Salt (Daryl)
R. v DT unreported 17 February 2000 .... 1.216
R. v Duffy (Paula) (No.1) [1999] Q.B. 919; [1998] 3 W.L.R. 1060;
    [1999] 1 Cr. App. R. 307; [1998] Crim. L.R. 650; (1998) 95(20)
    L.S.G. 33; (1998) 142 S.J.L.B. 149 CA (Crim Div) 27.103
R. v Dunkova (Alzberta) [2010] EWCA Crim 1318; [2011] 1 Cr. App.
    R. (S.) 40 .... 11.94
R. v Dunn (Christopher) [2015] EWCA Crim 724; [2015] 2 Cr. App. R.
    13 ....30.155
R. v Dutton [1994] Crim. L.R. 910 .... 30.95
R. v E (Dennis Andrew) [2004] EWCA Crim 1313; [2005] Crim. L.R.
    227 .... 26.29, 26.154
R. v E (John) (Sexual Abuse: Delay) [1996] 1 Cr. App. R. 88; (1995)
    92(28) L.S.G. 40; (1995) 139 S.J.L.B. 158 CA (Crim Div) 30.95
R. v E (Stephen) [2009] EWCA Crim 2668 ....26.157
R. v E [2009] EWCA Crim 1370 .... 24.02, 24.39, 24.40, 24.41
R. v E [2011] EWCA Crim 3028; [2012] Crim. L.R. 563 .... 28.06, 28.27,
    28.30
R. v E [2012] EWCA Crim 563 .... 28.14
R. v E; sub nom. R. v TE [2004] EWCA Crim 1441; [2004] 2 Cr. App.
    R. 36; [2005] Crim. L.R. 74 .... 30.48
R. v E(T). *See* R. v E; sub nom. R. v TE
R. v Eastlake (Nicky) [2007] EWCA Crim 603; (2007) 151 S.J.L.B.
    258 .... 20.48
R. v EB [2010] NICA 40 .... 32.44, 32.55
R. v ED [2010] EWCA Crim 1213; (2010) 174 J.P. 289; [2010] Crim.
    L.R. 862 .... 19.38, 19.61
R. v ED [2015] EWCA Crim 1092 .... 26.41
R. v Edwards (Karl Adrian) R. v Edwards (Karl Adrian); R. v Fysh
    (Stephen John); R. v Duggan (James Edward); R. v Chohan
    (Naveed Nasir) [2005] EWCA Crim 1813; [2006] 1 Cr. App. R.
    3 .... 20.27
R. v Edwards (Stewart Dean); R. v Gray (Rosalind); R. v Enright
    (Kevin James); R. v Smith (David Reginald); R. v McLean
    (Michael); R. v Rowlands (Tony) [2005] EWCA Crim 3244; [2006]
    1 W.L.R. 1524; [2006] 3 All E.R. 882; [2006] 2 Cr. App. R. 4;
    [2006] Crim. L.R. 531; (2006) 103(5) L.S.G. 28 .... 20.14, 20.23, 20.25,
    20.27, 20.80
R. v Edwards. *See* R. v E [2011]
R. v EF [2002] EWCA Crim 1773 .... 19.99
R. v Elbekkay [1995] Crim. L.R. 163 .... 1.329, 1.330, 1.331
R. v Eldridge and Salmon [1999] Crim. L.R. 166 .... 27.95
R. v Elliot and White (1861) Le. & Ca. 103 .... 15.37, 15.52, 15.53
R. v Ellis (Thomas) [2010] EWCA Crim 163 .... 20.79

R. v Emmett (Stephen Roy) [1999] EWCA Crim 1710 ..... 2.123, 2.124, 2.131, 2.132

R. v England (Rosanne) [2010] EWCA Crim 1408; [2011] 1 Cr. App. R. (S.) 51 .... 34.57

R. v Enright [2005]. *See* R. v Edwards (Stewart Dean)

R. v ER [2010] EWCA Crim 2522 ..... 1.354, 1.370, 24.26, 24.27, 24.28, 24.30

R. v Esau [1997] 2 S.C.R. 443 .... 26.62

R. v ET. *See* R. v T (Child Pornography)

R. v Etches. *See* R. v E (Dennis Andrew)

R. v Evans (1924) 18 Cr. App. R. 123 CCA 19.74

R. v Evans (Dorothy Gertrude) [2004] EWCA Crim 3102; [2005] 1 W.L.R. 1435; [2005] 1 Cr. App. R. 32; (2005) 169 J.P. 129; [2005] Crim. L.R. 654; (2005) 169 J.P.N. 222; (2005) 102(7) L.S.G. 26 ..... 9.38

R. v Evans (Stephen). *See* R. v E (Stephen)

R. v Evans [1995] Crim. L.R. 245 .... 3.25

R. v Evans [2012] EWCA Crim 2183; 176 C.L. & J. 595; [2012] All E.R. (D) 143 (Sep) 4.82

R. v Ewanchuck [1999] 1 S.C.R. 330 Cup Ct (Can) 1.183, 1.283, 1.293, 26.68

R. v F (David Charles) [2005] EWCA Crim 3217 .... 19.17, 20.134

R. v F [2005] EWCA Crim 493; [2005] 1 W.L.R. 2848; [2005] 2 Cr. App. R. 13; [2005] Crim. L.R. 564; (2005) 102(18) L.S.G. 22 .... 26.28, 26.53, 26.75, 26.143

R. v F [2008] EWCA Crim 2859 .... 26.77, 26.118

R. v F [2008] EWCA Crim 994; [2008] All E.R. (D) 380 (Apr) 1.33

R. v F [2010] EWCA Crim 2243; (2010) 174 J.P. 582 .... 15.52, 15.55

R. v F [2014] EWCA Crim 878 .... 1.372

R. v F; sub nom. Crown Prosecution Service v F [2011] EWCA Crim 1844; [2012] Q.B. 703; [2012] 2 W.L.R. 1038; [2012] 1 All E.R. 565; [2011] 2 Cr. App. R. 28; [2012] Crim. L.R. 282 .... 30.03, 30.30, 30.31, 30.32, 30.37, 30.38, 30.39, 30.47, 30.48, 30.49, 30.52

R. v F; sub nom. R. v JRF [2013] EWCA Crim 424; [2013] 1 W.L.R. 2143; [2013] 2 Cr. App. R. 13; (2013) 177 J.P. 406; [2014] Crim. L.R. 136 .... 27.147

R. v F(DS), 1999 Can L II 3704 (Ont CA); 43 O.R. (3d) 609 .... 19.121

R. v F(S). *See* R. v F; sub nom. Crown Prosecution Service v F

R. v F(TB) [2011] EWCA Crim 726; [2011] 2 Cr. App. R. 13 .... 30.34

R. v Fagan (Keith Michael) [2014] EWCA Crim 2728 .... 4.79

R. v Fagan (Taariq); R. Fergus (Michael) [2012] EWCA Crim 2248 ..... 19.49

R. v Farooqi (Munir Ahmed); R. v Malik (Israr Hussain); R. v Newton (Matthew) [2013] EWCA Crim 1649; [2014] 1 Cr. App. R. 8; [2014] Crim. L.R. 239 .... 28.38, 28.42

R. v Farrant [1973] Crim. L.R. 240 CA (Crim Div) 15.202

R. v Farrar (Stuart) [2006] EWCA Crim 3261; [2007] 2 Cr. App. R. (S.)
35; [2007] Crim. L.R. 308 .... 34.33, 34.36

R. v Farrell (1862) 9 Cox C.C. 446 CCA 15.52

R. v Fellows (Alban); R. v Arnold (Stephen) [1997] 2 All E.R. 548;
[1997] 1 Cr. App. R. 244; [1998] Masons C.L.R. Rep. 121; [1997]
Crim. L.R. 524 CA 8.52, 8.64, 8.67

R. v Fenton (David George) [1996] Crim. L.R. 257 CA (Crim Div) 19.15,
19.16

R. v Fenton (Steven) [2006] EWCA Crim 2156; [2007] 1 Cr. App. R.
(S.) 97 .... 36.60, 36.61

R. v Ferguson (Mark Brandon) [2008] EWCA Crim 2940; [2009] 2 Cr.
App. R. (S.) 8 .... 15.48

R. v Ferriter (Maurice) [2012] EWCA Crim 2211 .... 1.139, 1.140

R. v Fethney [2010] EWCA Crim 3096; [2010] All ER (D) 240
(Nov) 1.150, 1.152, 30.12, 30.14

R. v Field (Brian John); R. v Young (Alfred) [2002] EWCA Crim 2913;
[2003] 1 W.L.R. 882; [2003] 3 All E.R. 769; [2003] 2 Cr. App. R.
3; [2003] 2 Cr. App. R. (S.) 35; [2003] U.K.H.R.R. 271; [2003]
Crim. L.R. 201; (2003) 100(7) L.S.G. 35; (2003) 147 S.J.L.B. 25 ...27.111

R. v Field (Mark Anthony) [2016] EWCA Crim 385 ....20.118

R. v Figg (Joseph Albert) [2003] EWCA Crim 2751; [2004] 1 Cr. App.
R. (S.) 68; [2004] Crim. L.R. 386 .... 4.03

R. v Filice (1999) Carswell Ont. 1262 .... 1.289

R. v Filor (David John) [2012] EWCA Crim 850 .... 36.30

R. v Finnegan (Colin). See DPP's Reference (No.18 of 2013), Re

R. v Fitzmaurice (Robert) [1983] Q.B. 1083; [1983] 2 W.L.R. 227;
[1983] 1 All E.R. 189; (1983) 76 Cr. App. R. 17 CA (Crim Div) 3.158

R. v Flattery (John) (1877) 2 Q.B.D. 410; (1887) 13 Cox C.C. 388
CCR 1.318

R. v Fletcher (1859) Bell 63 .... 1.169, 1.301

R. v Fletcher (1884) 15 Cox C.C. 579 .... 7.67

R. v Fletcher (Richard), 169 E.R. 1168; (1859) Bell C.C. 63 CCR 1.226

R. v Flook (Robert Daniel) [2009] EWCA Crim 682; [2010] 1 Cr. App.
R. 30; [2010] Crim. L.R. 148 .... 18.21

R. v FN [2012] NICA 38 .... 32.68

R. v FNC [2015] EWCA Crim 1732; [2016] 1 W.L.R. 980; [2016] 1 Cr.
App. R. 12; [2016] Crim. L.R. 275 .... 25.44, 25.45

R. v Fontaine [2004] S.C.C. 27; [2004] 1 S.C.R. 702 .... 1.291

R. v Foster [1995] Crim. L.R. 333 .... 27.59

R. v Fotheringham (William Bruce) (1989) 88 Cr. App. R. 206; [1988]
Crim. L.R. 846 CA (Crim Div) 1.399

R. v Fowler (Alan) [2002] EWCA Crim 620; [2002] 2 Cr. App. R. (S.)
99; [2002] Crim. L.R. 521 .... 1.133

R. v Fowler unreported 20–27 September 1994 CC (Luton) 8.92

R. v Fox (Charles Frederick) [2009] EWCA Crim 653; [2009] Crim.
L.R. 881 .... 2.74, 8.125, 20.21, 20.22

R. v Francis (Malachi Augustus); R. v Lawrence (Calvin Angelo)
[2014] EWCA Crim 631 .... 34.51

R. v Freebody (John Edward) (1936) 25 Cr. App. R. 69 CCA 19.106

R. v Freeman (Daniel Robert); R. v Crawford (Jerome) [2008] EWCA
Crim 1863; [2009] 1 W.L.R. 2723; [2009] 2 All E.R. 18; [2009] 1 Cr.
App. R. 11; (2008) 172 J.P. 529; [2009] Crim. L.R. 103; (2008) 172
J.P.N. 757 .... 1.146, 20.32, 20.118, 20.119, 20.121

R. v Frew (Wayne Gary) [2008] EWCA Crim 1029; [2009] 1 Cr. App.
R. (S.) 17 .... 4.46, 36.25

R. v Funderburk (Roy) [1990] 1 W.L.R. 587; [1990] 2 All E.R. 482;
(1990) 90 Cr. App. R. 466; [1990] Crim. L.R. 405; (1990) 87(17)
L.S.G. 31; (1990) 134 S.J. 578 CA 19.91, 19.92, 19.96, 19.97, 19.102,
19.103, 19.104, 19.105, 20.141, 26.140

R. v Fung (Chee Hin) [2012] EWCA Crim 761 .... 36.40

R. v G (Paul) [2012] EWCA Crim 1296 .... 9.12

R. v G (Raymond) [2008] EWCA Crim 3123 ....30.142

R. v G [2004] EWCA Crim 1240; [2004] 2 Cr. App. R. 38 .... 24.07

R. v G [2007] EWCA Crim 2468 ....20.150

R. v G [2008] UKHL 37; [2009] 1 A.C. 92; [2008] 1 W.L.R. 1379; [2008]
3 All E.R. 1071; [2009] 1 Cr. App. R. 8; [2008] H.R.L.R. 36; [2009]
U.K.H.R.R. 72; [2008] Crim. L.R. 818; (2008) 152(25) S.J.L.B.
31 .... 3.09, 3.14, 3.15, 3.19, 3.20, 3.21, 3.22, 3.23, 3.78, 4.16, 31.17

R. v G [2009] EWCA Crim 265; [2009] 2 Cr. App. R. (S.) 77 .... 3.66

R. v G [2012] EWCA Crim 1756; [2013] Crim. L.R. 678 .... 1.410, 3.37

R. v G And F. *See* R. v G [2012]

R. v G; R. v R [2003] UKHL 50; [2004] 1 A.C. 1034; [2003] 3 W.L.R.
1060; [2003] 4 All E.R. 765; [2004] 1 Cr. App. R. 21; (2003) 167
J.P. 621; [2004] Crim. L.R. 369; (2003) 167 J.P.N. 955; (2003)
100(43) L.S.G. 31 ....15.143

R. v G(H) [2010] EWCA Crim 1693; [2011] Crim LR 339; [2010] All
E.R. (D) 199 (Jul) 1.192, 3.43, 4.37, 4.52, 4.211, 4.221, 11.112

R. v GA. *See* R. v A [2014]

R. v Galbraith (George Charles) [1981] 1 W.L.R. 1039; [1981] 2 All
E.R. 1060; (1981) 73 Cr. App. R. 124; [1981] Crim. L.R. 648;
(1981) 125 S.J. 442 CA (Crim Div) 19.38, 30.30, 30.38

R. v Gammon (Dennis) (1959) 43 Cr. App. R. 155; (1959) 123 J.P. 410
CCA 19.106

R. v Garaxo (Shino) [2005] EWCA Crim 1170; [2005] Crim. L.R.
883 ....26.160

R. v Garnham (Jamie Richard) [2008] EWCA Crim 266 ....20.144

R. v Gauthier, 2013 SCC 32, [2013] 2 S.C.R. 403 .... 1.291, 2.73

R. v Gaviria. *See* R. v G(H)

R. v GB [2015] EWCA Crim 1501; [2016] 1 Cr. App. R. (S.) 17 .... 30.118,
33.23

R. v George [1956] Crim. L.R. 52 Assizes (Lincoln) 2.72

R. v Gersh (Daniel) [2008] EWCA Crim 1150 .... 36.25

R. v Ghafoor (Imran Hussain) [2002] EWCA Crim 1857; [2003] 1 Cr.
App. R. (S.) 84; (2002) 166 J.P. 601; [2002] Crim. L.R. 739; (2002)
166 J.P.N. 744 .... 31.115, 31.133

R. v Ghani (No.99/04599/Z4) unreported 25 October 1999 CA 27.60

R. v Gibson (Richard Norman); R. v Sylveire (Peter Sebastian) [1990]
2 Q.B. 619; [1990] 3 W.L.R. 595; [1991] 1 All E.R. 439; (1990) 91
Cr. App. R. 341; (1991) 155 J.P. 126; [1990] Crim. L.R. 738; (1990)
154 J.P.N. 596; (1990) 134 S.J. 1123 CA (Crim Div) 15.26, 15.66,
15.67

R. v Giga (Zulfikar) [2008] EWCA Crim 703; [2008] 2 Cr. App. R. (S.)
112; [2008] Crim. L.R. 579 ....30.142

R. v Gilfoyle (Norman Edward) (Appeal against Conviction) [2001] 2
Cr. App. R. 5; [2001] Crim. L.R. 312 CA (Crim Div) 19.102, 26.152

R. v Gilfoyle (Norman Edward) (Appeal against Conviction) [2001] 2
Cr. App. R. 5; [2001] Crim. L.R. 312 .... 24.05

R. v Gillard (Simon Paul) (1988) 87 Cr. App. R. 189; [1988] Crim. L.R.
531 CA (Crim Div) 14.28

R. v Gillooley (Joseph) [2009] EWCA Crim 671 .... 19.81

R. v Gisson (George), 175 E.R. 327; (1847) 2 Car. & K. 781 Assizes 14.05

R. v GJB [2011] EWCA Crim 867 .... 1.357, 30.101

R. v Gjoni (Kujtim) [2014] EWCA Crim 691; [2014] Crim. L.R. 765 ... 26.65,
26.66, 26.67, 26.68

R. v GM [2004] EWCA Crim 1393 .... 26.47, 26.80, 26.125

R. v Gnango (Armel) [2011] UKSC 59; [2012] 1 A.C. 827; [2012] 2
W.L.R. 17; [2012] 2 All E.R. 129; [2012] 1 Cr. App. R. 18; (2012)
109(2) L.S.G. 16; (2011) 155(48) S.J.L.B. 31 ...... 2.119, 4.57, 5.26, 6.41

R. v Goddard (Leigh) [2007] EWCA Crim 3134 ....20.140

R. v Goddard (Nigel) (1991) 92 Cr. App. R. 185; [1991] Crim. L.R. 299
CA (Crim Div) 13.06

R. v Gold and Cohen (1907) 71 J.P. 360 .... 10.63, 10.136

R. v Goldman (Terence) [2001] EWCA Crim 1684; [2001] Crim. L.R.
822 .... 3.158, 3.159, 8.69, 8.70

R. v Goodyear (Karl) [2005] EWCA Crim 888; [2005] 1 W.L.R. 2532;
[2005] 3 All E.R. 117; [2005] 2 Cr. App. R. 20; [2006] 1 Cr. App.
R. (S.) 6; [2005] Crim. L.R. 659 .... 34.38, 34.39

R. v Gowans (Paul); R. v Hillman (Barry Kenneth) [2015] EWCA
Crim 952; [2016] Crim. L.R. 206 ....30.160

R. v GP [2015] EWCA Crim 594 .... 3.42

R. v Graham [1997] 1 Cr. App. R. (S.) 302 .... 30.16

R. v Graham-Kerr (John) [1988] 1 W.L.R. 1098; (1989) 88 Cr. App. R.
    302; (1989) 153 J.P. 171; (1989) 153 J.P.N. 170; (1988) 132 S.J.
    1299 .... 8.44, 8.49, 8.50, 8.91, 8.92, 9.100, 11.110
R. v Grainge (Albert Robert Burns) [1974] 1 W.L.R. 619; [1974] 1 All
    E.R. 928; (1974) 59 Cr. App. R. 3; [1974] Crim. L.R. 180; (1974)
    118 S.J. 116 CA (Crim Div) 9.61, 12.63
R. v Grant (Alan Ian) [2008] EWCA Crim 1890 .... 25.45
R. v Greatbanks [1959] Crim. L.R. 450 CCC 26.08
R. v Greaves (Patrick Kennedy) [2007] EWCA Crim 1348 .... 20.12
R. v Green (John Francis) [2007] EWCA Crim 2172; [2008] 1 Cr. App.
    R. (S.) 97; [2008] Crim. L.R. 66 .... 34.24
R. v Green (Peter Donovan) [2002] EWCA Crim 1501; [2002] All E.R.
    (D) 94 (Aug) 1.322, 1.322
R. v Greene [2010] NICA 47 .... 32.60, 32.69
R. v Grewal (Amanpreet Singh) [2010] EWCA Crim 2448 ...... 1.11, 1.401,
                                                                      26.58
R. v Grey (1864) 4 F. & F. 73; 176 E.R. 472 Assizes 15.26
R. v Gribben (Daniel Peter) [2015] EWCA Crim 736 .... 10.53, 10.61
R. v Griffiths (Leslie George) (1974) 60 Cr. App. R. 14 CA (Crim
    Div) 9.61, 12.63
R. v Grizzle [1991] Crim. L.R. 553 CA (Crim Div) 10.152, 10.159
R. v Grosvenor (Steven Victor) [2010] EWCA Crim 560; [2010] 2 Cr.
    App. R. (S.) 100 .... 35.52, 35.53, 35.54, 35.55
R. v Grout (Phillip) [2011] EWCA Crim 299; [2011] 1 Cr. App. R. 38;
    (2011) 175 J.P. 209; [2011] Crim. L.R. 584 ... 2.99, 2.105, 3.133, 3.158,
                                              3.164, 3.165, 3.169, 26.27, 26.34
R. v Guled Yusuf [2010] EWCA Crim 359 .... 26.153, 26.165
R. v Gyima (Edward); R. v Adjei (Francis) [2007] EWCA Crim 429;
    [2007] Crim. L.R. 890 .... 20.92
R. v H (Arthur Henry); sub nom. R. v H (Sexual Assault); R. v H
    (Henry) [1998] 2 Cr. App. R. 161; [1998] Crim. L.R. 409 .... 30.94
R. v H (Childhood Amnesia); sub nom. R. v JRH; R. v TG
    (Deceased), R. v X (Childhood Amnesia) [2005] EWCA Crim
    1828; [2006] 1 Cr. App. R. 10 .... 24.35, 24.37, 24.39, 24.41, 24.42
R. v H (Christopher) [2006] EWCA Crim 2898 .... 20.46
R. v H (David Thomas) [2007] EWCA Crim 1863 .... 5.22
R. v H (Karl Anthony); sub nom. R. v H (Sexual Assault: Touching)
    [2005] EWCA Crim 732; [2005] 1 W.L.R. 2005; [2005] 2 All E.R.
    859; [2005] 2 Cr. App. R. 149; [2005] Crim. L.R. 735; (2005)
    102(14) L.S.G. 26; (2005) 149 S.J.L.B. 179 .... 2.63, 2.69
R. v H (Peter) [2002] EWCA Crim 730; [2002] Crim. L.R. 578 .... 22.46
R. v H (Special Measures), Times 15 April 2003 .... 27.31
R. v H [2003] EWCA Crim 1209 .... 27.25, 27.31
R. v H [2006] EWCA Crim 853; [2006] All E.R. (D) 220 (Apr); (2006)
    150 S.J.L.B. 571 .... 1.353

R. v H [2007] EWCA Crim 2056 .... 1.187, 1.255, 1.261, 1.262
R. v H [2011] EWCA Crim 2344; [2012] 1 Cr. App. R. 30; [2013] Crim.
      L.R. 681 .... 19.17, 19.78, 19.79, 20.132, 20.134, 24.40, 24.41, 30.134
R. v H [2014] EWCA Crim 1555; [2014] All E.R. (D.) 249 (Jul); [2014]
      Crim. L.R. 905; 140 B.M.L.R. 59 .... 24.13, 24.46
R. v H [2015] EWCA Crim 1579; [2016] 1 Cr. App. R. (S.) 13; [2016]
      Crim. L.R. 138 .... 3.66, 3.68, 29.59, 29.74, 29.76, 33.23
R. v H [2015] EWCA Crim 54; [2015] 1 Cr. App. R. (S.) 59 .... 1.56
R. v H; R. v C [2004] UKHL 3; [2004] 2 A.C. 134; [2004] 2 W.L.R. 335;
      [2004] 1 All E.R. 1269; [2004] 2 Cr. App. R. 10; [2004] H.R.L.R.
      20; 16 B.H.R.C. 332; (2004) 101(8) L.S.G. 29; (2004) 148 S.J.L.B.
      183 .... 18.22, 18.68
R. v H; R. v P; R. v Robertson; R. v S; R. v Dan; R. v Walker (P); R.
      v W; R. v F [2011] EWCA Crim 2753; [2012] 1 W.L.R. 1416;
      [2012] 2 All E.R. 340; [2012] 2 Cr. App. R. (S.) 21; [2012] Crim.
      L.R. 149 ..... 1.35, 1.70, 1.130, 30.04, 30.05, 30.06, 30.07, 30.111, 30.113,
                             30.115, 30.118D, 30.141, 30.142, 30.144, 30.149, 33.01,
                             33.06, 34.02
R. v H; R. v R [2008] EWCA Crim 1202 .... 2.100
R. v H(J). See R. v H; R. v P
R. v H(L). See H(L), Re
R. v Hadley [2012] EWCA Crim 1997; [2012] All E.R. (D.) 46
      (Aug) 36.65
R. v Haigh (Tara Elizabeth) [2010] EWCA Crim 90 .... 20.15, 20.26
R. v Hakala. See R. v H (Peter)
R. v Halahan (Maxwell Crosby) [2014] EWCA Crim 2079 .... 30.43
R. v Hall (Edward Leonard) (1985) 81 Cr. App. R. 260; [1985] Crim.
      L.R. 377; (1985) 82 L.S.G. 1485; (1985) 136 N.L.J. 604; (1985) 128
      S.J. 283 CA (Crim Div) 9.61, 12.63
R. v Hall (James Stuart). See Attorney General's Reference (No.38 of
      2013)
R. v Hall (John Hamilton) (1988) 86 Cr. App. R. 159 CA (Crim Div) ... 7.84,
                                                                                                        7.85
R. v Hall-Chung (Teon) [2007] EWCA Crim 3429; (2007) 151 S.J.L.B.
      1020 .... 20.19
R. v Hamadi (Zeeyad) [2007] EWCA Crim 3048 ..... 26.89, 26.120, 26.121,
                                                                                                  26.123
R. v Hamilton (Simon Austin) [2007] EWCA Crim 2062; [2008] Q.B.
      224; [2008] 2 W.L.R. 107; [2008] 1 All E.R. 1103; [2008] 1 Cr. App.
      R. 13; [2008] Crim. L.R. 225; (2007) 104(34) L.S.G. 28; (2007) 157
      N.L.J. 1234 .... 15.26, 15.52, 15.53, 15.55, 15.57, 15.58
R. v Hamilton [2011] NICA 46 .... 32.04
R. v Hamilton, Times, 25 July 1998 ....19.103
R. v Hammond (Paul Churchill) [2008] EWCA Crim 1358 .... 36.51

R. v Hanson (Nicky); R. v P (Robert Alan); R. v Gilmore (Vincent
Martin) [2005] EWCA Crim 824; [2005] 1 W.L.R. 3169; [2005] 2
Cr. App. R. 21; (2005) 169 J.P. 250; [2005] Crim. L.R. 787; (2005)
169 J.P.N. 380; (2005) 149 S.J.L.B. 392 .... 20.10, 20.42, 20.43, 20.44,
20.47, 20.50, 20.51, 20.79, 20.91, 20.92, 20.98, 20.110,
20.118, 20.120, 20.144
R. v Hanton (Donald Adrian) [2005] EWCA Crim 2009 .... 27.83
R. v Harbinson [2012] NICA 20 .... 32.74
R. v Hardy (James) [2013] EWCA Crim 2125; [2014] 1 Cr. App. R. (S.)
70 .... 15.04, 15.181
R. v Harley (1830) 4 C. & P. 369 .... 14.29
R. v Harling (Ronald) [1938] 1 All E.R. 307; (1938) 26 Cr. App. R. 127
CCA 1.16, 1.217
R. v Harms [1944] 2 D.L.R. 61 .... 1.326
R. v Harold (Christopher John) (1984) 6 Cr. App. R. (S.) 30 CA (Crim
Div) 1.208
R. v Harries (Michael John); R. v S (Robert Michael); R. v B; R. v S;
R. v Kai Ho Fan [2007] EWCA Crim 1622; [2008] 1 Cr. App. R.
(S.) 47; [2007] Crim. L.R. 820 .... 30.21, 30.167, 34.53, 34.55
R. v Harris (1871) 11 Cox C.C. 659 .... 15.59
R. v Harris (Joshua Bryan John) [2014] EWCA Crim 2873 ...... 1.192, 4.52
R. v Harris (Lorraine); R. v Faulder (Michael Ian); R. v Cherry (Alan
Barry); R. v Rock (Raymond Charles) [2005] EWCA Crim 1980;
[2006] 1 Cr. App. R. 5; [2008] 2 F.L.R. 412; (2005) 85 B.M.L.R.
75; [2008] Fam. Law 842 .... 24.17
R. v Harris (Wayne Lee) [2009] EWCA Crim 434; [2010] Crim. L.R.
54 .... 26.90, 26.96
R. v Harrison (Carl Richardson) [2006] EWCA Crim 1543 .... 26.63
R. v Harrison (Neil John) [2007] EWCA Crim 2976; [2008] 1 Cr. App.
R. 29 .... 8.62
R. v Harrow Crown Court Ex p. Perkins; R. v Cardiff Crown Court Ex
p. M (A Minor) (1998) 162 J.P. 527; (1998) 162 J.P.N. 483 CA
(Crim Div) 29.87
R. v Hartley (John) [2011] EWCA Crim 1299; [2012] 1 Cr. App. R. 7;
[2012] 1 Cr. App. R. (S.) 28; [2011] Crim. L.R. 726 ...... 1.29, 1.30, 33.26,
33.27, 33.28, 33.29
R. v Hashi (Adam); R. v Idle (Abdirhan Abdull); R. v Khalif
(Mahaddayib); R. v Pirabakaran (Piratheepan) [2014] EWCA
Crim 2119; [2015] 1 Cr. App. R. (S.) 17 .... 13.77
R. v Haslam (Lee Anthony) [2014] EWCA Crim 2179 .... 2.58
R. v Hassett (Kevin); R. v Hassett (Richard John) [2008] EWCA Crim
1634 .... 20.03
R. v Haughian (Anthony Edward); R. v Pearson (Arthur Reginald)
(1984) 80 Cr. App. R. 334 CA (Crim Div) 1.287
R. v Hawkins (Stephen Arthur) [1995] C.L.Y. 946 CA (Crim Div) 27.86

R. v Hayford (John Robert) [2015] EWCA Crim 782 .... 30.46
R. v Haywood (Craig Callan) [2000] 2 Cr. App. R. (S.) 418; [2000]
    Crim. L.R. 490 CA (Crim Div) 34.40
R. v Healey (Robert); R. v Bolton (Mark); R. v McGregor (Alex-
    ander); R. v Brearley (Gary); R. v Taylor (Matthew) [2012]
    EWCA Crim 1005; [2013] 1 Cr. App. R. (S.) 33; [2012] Crim. L.R.
    640 .... 33.10
R. v Heard (Lee) [2007] EWCA Crim 125; [2008] Q.B. 43; [2007] 3
    W.L.R. 475; [2007] 3 All E.R. 306; [2007] 1 Cr. App. R. 37; [2007]
    Crim. L.R. 654; (2007) 104(9) L.S.G. 32; (2007) 151 S.J.L.B.
    259 ... 1.372, 2.32, 2.37, 2.78, 2.81, 2.82, 2.105, 2.107, 3.77, 3.103, 3.130,
              3.168, 3.170, 4.65, 4.92, 4.120, 4.141, 4.224, 4.247, 5.50, 5.74,
                  5.102, 6.47, 6.69, 6.106, 7.87, 7.104, 7.125, 7.141, 7.192,
              7.208, 7.234, 7.250, 7.270, 7.286, 8.103, 14.34, 14.49, 14.73,
                            15.67, 15.89, 15.112, 15.144, 15.155, 15.162
R. v Heard [2004] Crim. L.R. 342 .... 3.77
R. v Hearn [1970] Crim. L.R. 175 CA (Crim Div) 1.141
R. v Hecker (1981) 58 Can.C.C. (2d) 66 Yukon T. Ct 15.42, 15.44, 15.48
R. v Hedgcock (Alan Peter); R. v Dyer (David Charles); R. v Mayers
    (Robert) [2007] EWCA Crim 3486; [2007] All E.R. (D) 400
    (Nov) 1.409, 1.140, 3.37
R. v Hemsley (Daniel Mark) [2010] EWCA Crim 225; [2010] 3 All
    E.R. 965 .... 36.25, 36.51
R. v Henderson (Keran Louise); R. v Butler (Ben); R. v Oyediran
    (Oladapo) [2010] EWCA Crim 1269; [2010] 2 Cr. App. R. 24;
    [2010] 1 F.L.R. 547; (2010) 115 B.M.L.R. 139; [2010] Crim. L.R.
    945; [2010] Fam. Law 917; (2010) 107(26) L.S.G. 16 .... 24.21
R. v Henry (Neville Benson); R. v Manning (Jeffrey Patrick) (1969) 53
    Cr. App. R. 150; [1969] Crim. L.R. 142; (1969) 113 S.J. 12 CA
    (Crim Div) 19.106
R. v Heys (Carl John); R. v Murtagh (Kevin John) [2011] EWCA Crim
    2112 .... 9.48
R. v HG. See R. v G(H)
R. v Hibbert (Christopher Keith) [2015] EWCA Crim 507; [2015] 2 Cr.
    App. R. (S.) 15 .... 34.50, 34.51
R. v Hickmet (Mustapha) [1996] Crim. L.R. 588 CA (Crim Div) 19.108
R. v Hicks (Robert Lwellyn) [2009] EWCA Crim 733; (2009) 106(18)
    L.S.G. 18 .... 36.35
R. v Higgins [1996] 1 F.L.R. 137; [1996] 2 F.C.R. 612; [1996] Fam. Law
    144; (1996) 146 N.L.J. 918 CA (Crim Div) 18.89
R. v Higginson (1762) 2 Burr. 1272 .... 12.85
R. v Highton (Edward Paul); R. v Carp (Anthony Mark); R. v Van
    Nguyen (Dong) [2005] EWCA Crim 1985; [2005] 1 W.L.R. 3472;
    [2006] 1 Cr. App. R. 7; [2006] Crim. L.R. 52 .... 20.108, 20.109
R. v Higson, *Times*, 21 January 1984 .... 15.133, 15.134

R. v Hill (William); R. v Churchman (Frank) [1914] 2 K.B. 386; (1914)
10 Cr. App. R. 56 CCA 10.77

R. v Hills (Christopher Carl); R. v Pomfret (Marvin Emeka); R. v
Davies (Stephen David) [2008] EWCA Crim 1871; [2012] 1
W.L.R. 2121; [2009] 1 Cr. App. R. (S.) 75; [2010] 1 Prison L.R.
122; [2009] Crim. L.R. 116 .... 34.49

R. v Hinton (Roy) (1995) 16 Cr. App. R. (S.) 523 CA (Crim Div) 4.03

R. v Hoath (Terence); R. v Standage (Terence Edward) [2011] EWCA
Crim 274; [2011] 1 W.L.R. 1656; [2011] 4 All E.R. 306 .... 36.55, 36.56,
                                                                          36.57

R. v Hobson (Andrew Craig) [2013] EWCA Crim 819; [2013] 1 W.L.R.
3733; [2013] 2 Cr. App. R. 27; [2014] Crim. L.R. 83 .... 1.29, 33.30, 33.31

R. v Hodgson (Roger Harry Watson); R. v Marshall (Roger Johnson);
R. v Hadden (David Douglas); R. v Moon (Kevin Alan) [1973]
Q.B. 565; [1973] 2 W.L.R. 570; [1973] 2 All E.R. 552; (1973) 57 Cr.
App. R. 502; [1973] Crim. L.R. 364; (1973) 117 S.J. 283 CA (Crim
Div) 3.74

R. v Hodgson (Rowland Jack) (1968) 52 Cr. App. R. 113; [1968] Crim.
L.R. 46 CA (Crim Div) 1.131, 1.133, 1.135, 30.162

R. v Hogg (Brian Maurice) [2007] EWCA Crim 1357; [2008] 1 Cr. App.
R. (S.) 22; [2007] Crim. L.R. 990 .... 1.110

R. v Holley (Michael William); R. v Smith (Leslie); R. v Paul
(Frederick Charles) (1969) 53 Cr. App. R. 519; [1969] Crim. L.R.
437; (1969) 119 N.L.J. 602; (1969) 113 S.J. 524 CA (Crim Div) 1.144

R. v Holmes (Henry); R. v Furness (Joseph Frederick) (1871) L.R. 1
C.C.R. 334 CCR 19.91, 26.08

R. v Holmes, 175 E.R. 589; (1850) 3 Car. & K. 360 Assizes 15.59

R. v Hookway (Steven James); R. v Noakes (Gavin) [2011] EWCA
Crim 1989; [2012] Crim. L.R. 130 .... 25.27

R. v Hooper (Derek) [2003] EWCA Crim 2427 .... 30.48, 30.52

R. v Hopkins (No.97/5836/Y3) unreported 16 February 1998 ....19.114

R. v Hopkins, 174 E.R. 495; (1842) Car. & M. 254 .... 9.28

R. v Horley [1999] Crim. L.R. 488 .... 27.91, 27.93

R. v Horncastle (Michael Christopher); R. v Graham (Joseph David);
R. v Marquis (Abijah); R. v Carter (David Michael); R. v
Blackmore (David Lee) [2009] UKSC 14; [2010] 2 A.C. 373;
[2010] 2 W.L.R. 47; [2010] 2 All E.R. 359; [2010] 1 Cr. App. R. 17;
[2010] H.R.L.R. 12; [2010] U.K.H.R.R. 1; [2010] Crim. L.R. 496;
(2009) 153(48) S.J.L.B. 32 .... 19.35, 19.37, 19.40, 19.49

R. v Horseferry Road Magistrates Court Ex p. Siadatan; sub nom. R.
v Metropolitan Magistrate Ex p. Siadatan [1991] 1 Q.B. 260;
[1990] 3 W.L.R. 1006; [1991] 1 All E.R. 324; (1991) 92 Cr. App. R.
257; [1990] Crim. L.R. 598; (1990) 87(17) L.S.G. 40; (1990) 140
N.L.J. 704 QBD 1.274, 15.168

R. v Howard (Robert Lesarian) [1966] 1 W.L.R. 13; [1965] 3 All E.R.
684; (1966) 50 Cr. App. R. 56; (1966) 130 J.P. 61; (1965) 109 S.J.
920 CA 1.17, 1.217, 1.225, 1.235, 1.246, 1.298, 1.302
R. v Howells. *See* R. v H (David Thomas)
R. v Howes (Joseph Michael) [1996] 2 Cr. App. R. 490 CA (Crim
Div) 26.145
R. v HSD [2006] EWCA Crim 1703 .... 20.92
R. v Hudd (Stevan) [2012] EWCA Crim 846 .... 3.64
R. v Hughes (1841) 9 C. & P. 752; 2 Mood. C.C. 190 CCR 1.156
R. v Hughes [2008] NICA 17 .... 32.72
R. v Humphris (Andrew James) [2005] EWCA Crim 2030; (2005) 169
J.P. 441; (2005) 169 J.P.N. 718 .... 20.07
R. v Hunt (Richard Selwyn) [1987] A.C. 352; [1986] 3 W.L.R. 1115;
[1987] 1 All E.R. 1; (1987) 84 Cr. App. R. 163; [1987] Crim. L.R.
263 HL 15.177, 15.197
R. v Hunter (Sam Jordan) [2015] EWCA Crim 372 .... 9.51
R. v Hussain (Mohammed Blayat) [1969] 2 Q.B. 567; [1969] 3 W.L.R.
134; [1969] 2 All E.R. 1117; (1969) 53 Cr. App. R. 448; (1969) 113
S.J. 424 CA (Crim Div) 8.71
R. v Hussain (Mohammed) [2015] EWCA Crim 383 ....20.145
R. v Hutchinson (1988) 10 Cr. App. R.(S) 50 ....30.121
R. v Hutchinson (Arthur) (1986) 82 Cr. App. R. 51; [1985] Crim. L.R.
730; (1985) 82 L.S.G. 2332; (1985) 129 S.J. 700 CA (Crim Div) 20.90
R. v Hutchinson [2014] NICA 75 .... 32.67
R. v Hutchison [2015] EWCA Crim 947 .... 36.31, 36.36, 36.49
R. v Hysa. *See* R. v H
R. v I [2012] EWCA Crim 1288; [2012] Crim. L.R. 886 .... 24.06
R. v IA [2013] EWCA Crim 1308 .... 28.06
R. v Ibrahim (Dahir) [2012] EWCA Crim 837; [2012] 4 All E.R. 225;
[2012] 2 Cr. App. R. 32; (2012) 176 J.P. 470; [2012] Crim. L.R.
793 .... 19.36, 19.37, 19.39, 19.49
R. v IJ [2011] EWCA Crim 2734 .... 20.59, 20.60, 20.67, 20.77, 20.78
R. v Imiela [2013] EWCA Crim 2171 .... 20.98
R. v Ingram (Matthew) [2015] EWCA Crim 1375 .... 1.192
R. v Inner London Crown Court Ex p. B. *See* R. v Inner London
Crown Court Ex p. Barnes (Anthony)
R. v Inner London Crown Court Ex p. Barnes (Anthony); sub nom. R.
v Inner London Crown Court Ex p. B [1996] C.O.D. 17 DC 29.76
R. v Instone [2012] EWCA Crim 1792; [2012] All E.R. (D.) 161
(Jul) 36.58
R. v Ireland (Robert Matthew); R. v Burstow (Anthony Christopher)
[1998] A.C. 147; [1997] 3 W.L.R. 534; [1997] 4 All E.R. 225; [1998]
1 Cr. App. R. 177; (1997) 161 J.P. 569; [1998] 1 F.L.R. 105; [1997]
Crim. L.R. 810; [1998] Fam. Law 137; (1997) 161 J.P.N. 816;
(1997) 147 N.L.J. 1273; (1997) 141 S.J.L.B. 205 HL 1.274, 2.64

R. v Isa (Mustapha Abdi) [2005] EWCA Crim 3330; [2006] 2 Cr. App.
R. (S.) 29; [2006] Crim. L.R. 356 .... 34.30

R. v Isichei (Marvin) [2006] EWCA Crim 1815; (2006) 170 J.P. 753;
(2007) 171 J.P.N. 235 .... 19.32

R. v Islam (Abdul Khair) [1999] 1 Cr. App. R. 22; (1998) 162 J.P. 391;
[1998] Crim. L.R. 575; (1998) 162 J.P.N. 445; (1998) 95(17) L.S.G.
29; (1998) 142 S.J.L.B. 123 CA (Crim Div) 19.74

R. v Islington North Juvenile Court Ex p. Daley; sub nom. Daley, Re
[1983] 1 A.C. 347; [1982] 3 W.L.R. 344; [1982] 2 All E.R. 974;
(1982) 75 Cr. App. R. 280; [1982] Crim. L.R. 760; (1982) 79 L.S.G.
1412; (1982) 126 S.J. 524 HL 31.71

R. v Ismail (Abokar Ahmed); sub nom. R. v Ismail (Abokor Ahmed)
[2005] EWCA Crim 397; [2005] 2 Cr. App. R. (S.) 542; [2005]
Crim. L.R. 491 .... 1.89

R. v ITN News; sub nom. ITN News Ltd, Re [2013] EWCA Crim 773;
[2014] 1 W.L.R. 199; [2013] 2 Cr. App. R. 22; [2013] E.M.L.R. 22;
[2014] Crim. L.R. 375 .... 29.123, 29.124, 29.127, 29.136

R. v IWAT (No.1) [2000] 2 Cr. App. R. 189; [2000] Crim. L.R. 618 CA
(Crim Div) 26.126

R. v IWAT (No.2) [2001] EWCA Crim 1898 ....26.125

R. v J (BJ) (1996) 193 A.R. 151 Sup Ct (Alta) 2.73

R. v J [2004] UKHL 42; [2005] 1 A.C. 562; [2004] 3 W.L.R. 1019;
[2005] 1 All E.R. 1; [2005] 1 Cr. App. R. 19; (2004) 101(40) L.S.G.
28; (2004) 148 S.J.L.B. 1216 .... 4.03, 30.157

R. v J [2005] EWCA Crim 362 ....31.135

R. v J [2012] EWCA Crim 3025; [2013] 2 Cr. App. R. (S.) 42 .... 4.47

R. v J(I) [2012] EWCA Crim 2268 .... 1.48

R. v J(S) [2009] EWCA Crim 1869 .... 19.53

R. v Jabbar (Abdul) [2013] EWCA Crim 801 .... 19.49

R. v Jackson (Joseph), 168 E.R. 911; (1822) Russ. & Ry. 487 CCR 1.329

R. v Jackson (Paul Maitland) [1997] Crim. L.R. 293 CA (Crim Div) 8.09

R. v Jackson (Phillip Michael); sub nom. R. v Jackson (Philip
Michael) [2012] EWCA Crim 2602; (2013) 177 J.P. 147 .... 36.26

R. v Jackson (Terry Paul) [1996] 2 Cr. App. R. 420; [1996] Crim. L.R.
732 CA (Crim Div) 24.02

R. v Jackson [1891] 1 Q.B. 671 CA 1.168

R. v James (Christopher Michael) [2012] EWCA Crim 81 .... 36.40

R. v James (Steven Vincent) [2013] EWCA Crim 847 .... 36.59

R. v Jasionis (Vytautas) [2010] EWCA Crim 2981 .... 20.51

R. v Javaherifard (Mohammed); R. v Miller (Joanne) [2005] EWCA
Crim 3231; [2006] Imm. A.R. 185; [2006] I.N.L.R. 302 ...... 11.17, 11.98,
11.99

R. v JD [2002] 6 BNIL 98 .... 32.48

R. v Jeeves [2014] EWCA Crim 2059 .... 36.34

R. v JF [2002] EWCA Crim 2936; [2002] All E.R. (D) 234 (Dec) 1.156

R. v JH and TG. *See* R. v H (Childhood Amnesia)

R. v JH. *See* R. v H

R. v Jheeta (Harvinder Singh) [2007] EWCA Crim 1699; [2008] 1
W.L.R. 2582; [2007] 2 Cr. App. R. 34; [2008] Crim. L.R. 144 ..... 1.08,
1.12, 1.207, 1.208, 1.210, 1.211, 1.263, 1.314, 1.317, 1.320,
1.322, 1.323, 1.324, 1.327, 1.332

R. v JM [2016] 1 Cr. App. (S.) 145 .... 3.42

R. v JM [2015] EWCA Crim 1928 .... 19.13, 30.96

R. v JM unreported 1997 .... 32.49

R. v Jobe (Ismael Alhagie) [2004] EWCA Crim 3155 ....30.106

R. v JOC [2012] EWCA Crim 2458; [2012] All E.R. (D) 39 (Nov) 1.152

R. v John Tinkler, 175 E.R. 832; (1859) 1 F. & F. 513 .... 9.29

R. v Johnson (Gerald Ivan) [1964] 2 Q.B. 404; [1963] 3 W.L.R. 1031;
[1963] 3 All E.R. 577; (1964) 48 Cr. App. R. 25; (1963) 127 J.P.
556; (1963) 107 S.J. 1042 CA 10.63, 10.136

R. v Johnson (Paul Anthony) [2006] EWCA Crim 2486; [2007] 1
W.L.R. 585; [2007] 1 All E.R. 1237; [2007] 1 Cr. App. R. (S.) 112;
(2007) 171 J.P. 172; [2007] Crim. L.R. 177; (2007) 171 J.P.N.
410 .... 31.94, 32.44, 34.29, 34.31, 34.32, 34.36

R. v Johnstone (Robert Alexander); R. v Harrison (Richard James);
R. v Mayron Multimedia Ltd; R. v Eley (Charles Thomas); R. v
Ho (Toon Chin); R. v Croxson (Matthew Louis) [2003] UKHL
28; [2003] 1 W.L.R. 1736; [2003] 3 All E.R. 884; [2003] 2 Cr. App.
R. 33; (2003) 167 J.P. 281; [2004] E.T.M.R. 2; [2003] H.R.L.R. 25;
[2003] U.K.H.R.R. 1239; [2003] F.S.R. 42; [2004] Crim. L.R. 244;
(2003) 167 J.P.N. 453; (2003) 100(26) L.S.G. 36; (2003) 147
S.J.L.B. 625 .... 15.177, 15.197

R. v Jolleys (Robert) Ex p. Press Association [2013] EWCA Crim 1135;
[2014] 1 Cr. App. R. 15; [2014] E.M.L.R. 16 .... 29.81

R. v Jonas (Sandor) [2015] EWCA Crim 562; [2015] Crim. L.R. 742 ... 28.04,
28.16, 28.36, 28.37

R. v Jones (1903) 6 O.L.R. 35 CA (Ont) 10.32

R. v Jones (Christopher John) [2015] EWCA Crim 31 .... 4.53

R. v Jones (David William) [2014] EWCA Crim 1859; [2015] 1 Cr. App.
R. (S.) 9 .... 8.36

R. v Jones (Ian Anthony) [2007] EWCA Crim 1118; [2008] Q.B. 460;
[2007] 3 W.L.R. 907; [2007] 4 All E.R. 112; [2007] 2 Cr. App. R.
21; [2007] Crim. L.R. 979; (2007) 104(22) L.S.G. 24 .... 3.156, 3.160,
4.190, 14.05, 14.47

R. v Jones (James William) [1973] Crim. L.R. 621 CC (Stafford) 9.04

R. v Jones (John); R. v Smith (Christopher) [1976] 1 W.L.R. 672;
[1976] 3 All E.R. 54; (1976) 63 Cr. App. R. 47; (1976) 120 S.J. 299
CA (Crim Div) 14.68

R. v Jones (Thomas James) (1927) 19 Cr. App. R. 40 CCA 19.106

R. v Jones (William) (1924) 17 Cr. App. R. 117 CCA 20.91

R. v Jones [2011] NICA 62 .... 32.55

R. v Joof (Adam) [2012] EWCA Crim 1475 .... 18.20

R. v Jordan (Nicholas James) [2006] EWCA Crim 3311; [2007] 2 Cr.
App. R. (S.) 33 .... 4.169, 4.173

R. v Joshi (Udaykamaur) [2012] NICA 56 .... 19.111, 32.66, 32.69

R. v Joy (David) [2007] EWCA Crim 3281 .... 8.32

R. v Joyce (Richard James); R. v Joyce (James Paul) [2005] EWCA
Crim 1785 .... 19.64, 19.65

R. v Joynson (Frank) [2008] EWCA Crim 3049 ...... 30.29, 30.48, 30.57, 30.97

R. v JR [2008] EWCA Crim 2912 .... 4.174

R. v JSK [2011] NICA 44 .... 32.60, 32.69

R. v JTB. See R. v T; sub nom. R. v JTB

R. v Juneidi [2014] EWCA Crim 966 .... 36.41, 36.51

R. v K (Age of Consent: Reasonable Belief); sub nom. Crown
Prosecution Service v K (Age of Consent: Reasonable Belief)
[2001] UKHL 41; [2002] 1 A.C. 462; [2001] 3 W.L.R. 471; [2001]
3 All E.R. 897; [2002] 1 Cr. App. R. 13; [2001] 3 F.C.R. 115; [2001]
Crim. L.R. 993; (2001) 98(34) L.S.G. 39; (2001) 145 S.J.L.B.
202 .... 32.04

R. v K (Howard) (Evidence: Child Video Interview) [2006] EWCA
Crim 472; [2006] 2 Cr. App. R. 10; (2006) 170 J.P. 558; (2006) 170
J.P.N. 975 .... 27.83, 27.84

R. v K [2007] EWCA Crim 911; [2007] All E.R. (D.) 205 (Jan) 20.06

R. v K [2009] 1 Cr. App. R. 331 .... 1.26, 1.157

R. v K [2009] EWCA Crim 1931; [2009] All E.R. (D) 158 (Aug) 4.131,
4.132

R. v K. See R. v King (Alan Robert)

R. v K(P) and K(T). See R. v PK

R. v Kamki (Gael Tameu) [2013] EWCA Crim 2335 .... 1.252, 1.253

R. v Kane (Desmond Anthony) [1965] 1 All E.R. 705; (1965) 129 J.P.
170 Assizes (Stafford) 13.41

R. v Kapezi (Tamanda) [2013] EWCA Crim 560 .... 1.09, 1.265

R. v Karam (Mawawe Ibrahim) [2013] EWCA Crim 138; [2013] 2 Cr.
App. R. (S.) 65; [2013] Crim. L.R. 998 .... 1.43

R. v Karrar (Bassam Abdu); R. v Dogar (Akhtar Javid); R. v Dogar
(Anjum Javaid); R. v Jamil (Kamar) [2015] EWCA Crim 850 ...... 1.124,
11.92, 33.17

R. v Karshe (J) [2014] EWCA Crim 1733 .... 2.22

R. v Kauffman (1904) 68 J.P. 189 .... 9.35

R. v Kavanagh (Paul Thomas) [2008] EWCA Crim 855; [2008] 2 Cr.
App. R. (S.) 86 .... 33.08

R. v Keast [1998] Crim. L.R. 748 ....19.121

R. v Keeton (Geoffrey Wayne) [1995] 2 Cr. App. R. 241 CA (Crim
Div) 1.28

R. v Kehoe (Bridie Joanna) [2008] EWCA Crim 819; [2009] 1 Cr. App.
R. (S.) 9; [2008] Crim. L.R. 728 .... 1.93
R. v Kelly (Paul Mark) [2015] EWCA Crim 817 ....20.148
R. v Kennedy (Simon) [2007] UKHL 38; [2008] 1 A.C. 269; [2007] 3
W.L.R. 612; [2007] 4 All E.R. 1083; [2008] 1 Cr. App. R. 19; [2007]
Inquest L.R. 234; [2008] Crim. L.R. 222; (2007) 104(42) L.S.G.
33; (2007) 151 S.J.L.B. 1365 .... 14.28
R. v Ketteridge (Nicholas) [2014] EWCA Crim 1962; [2015] 1 Cr. App.
R. (S.) 11; [2015] R.T.R. 5 .... 15.82
R. v Khan (Arslan) [2015] EWCA Crim 831 .... 10.54, 11.91
R. v Khan (Mohammed Iqbal); R. v Dhokia (Mahesh); R. v Banga
(Jaswinder Singh); R. v Faiz (Navaid) [1990] 1 W.L.R. 813; [1990]
2 All E.R. 783; (1990) 91 Cr. App. R. 29; (1990) 154 J.P. 805;
[1990] Crim. L.R. 519; (1990) 154 J.P.N. 548; (1990) 87(9) L.S.G.
42; (1990) 134 S.J. 401 CA 1.399, 1.404, 1.406
R. v Khan (Mohammed) [2009] EWCA Crim 86 .... 19.61
R. v Killick (Christopher) [2011] EWCA Crim 1608; [2012] 1 Cr. App.
R. 10 .... 17.32, 27.113, 30.69, 30.70, 30.74
R. v Killick (William John) (1925) 18 Cr. App. R. 120 CCA 19.106
R. v Kimber (David Michael) [1983] 1 W.L.R. 1118; [1983] 3 All E.R.
316; (1983) 77 Cr. App. R. 225; [1983] Crim. L.R. 630; (1984) 148
J.P.N. 11 CA (Crim Div) 2.127
R. v King (Alan Robert) [2008] EWCA Crim 3301; [2009] Crim. L.R.
517 ....20.126
R. v Kingsbury (1870) 9 S.C.R. (N.S.W.) 278 Sup Ct FC (NSW) 9.28
R. v Kingston (Barry) [1995] 2 A.C. 355; [1994] 3 W.L.R. 519; [1994]
3 All E.R. 353; (1994) 99 Cr. App. R. 286; (1994) 158 J.P. 717;
[1994] Crim. L.R. 846; (1994) 158 J.P.N. 552; (1994) 144 N.L.J.
1044 HL 2.81, 14.34, 14.49, 14.73
R. v Kirk (Andrew Patrick) [2006] EWCA Crim 725; [2006] Crim. L.R.
850 .... 15.38
R. v KJC [2012] EWCA Crim 1669 ....26.163
R. v Kloss (Richard James) [2008] EWCA Crim 2873 .... 4.49
R. v Knight [2013] EWCA Crim 2486; [2013] All E.R. (D.) 333
(Oct) 26.162
R. v Knights (Richard Michael); R. v Sekhon (Daljit Singh); R. v
McFaul (Kevin); R. v Maguire (Kevin); R. v Dhnoay (Gurdev
Singh); R. v Singh (Satnam); R. v Singh (Shangara) [2002] EWCA
Crim 2954; [2003] 1 W.L.R. 1655; [2003] 3 All E.R. 508; [2003] 1
Cr. App. R. 34; [2003] 2 Cr. App. R. (S.) 38; [2003] Crim. L.R.
642; (2003) 100(8) L.S.G. 29; (2003) 147 S.J.L.B. 148 .... 8.10
R. v Koli (Raj); sub nom. R. v Koli (Rak) [2012] EWCA Crim 1869;
[2013] 1 Cr. App. R. (S.) 6; [2012] Crim. L.R. 903 .... 35.55
R. v Konzani (Feston) [2005] EWCA Crim 706; [2005] 2 Cr. App. R.
14; (2005) 149 S.J.L.B. 389 .... 1.337, 1.349

R. v Kordasinski (Leszek); sub nom. R. v Kordansinki (Leszek) [2006]
EWCA Crim 2984; [2007] 1 Cr. App. R. 17; (2007) 171 J.P. 206;
[2007] Crim. L.R. 794; (2007) 171 J.P.N. 479; (2006) 103(46)
L.S.G. 34 .... 20.09
R. v Korie [1966] 1 All E.R. 50 CC 12.41
R. v Krausky (1989) 45 A.Crim.R. 41 CCA (Qd) 12.31
R. v Krausz (Francis Leonard) (1973) 57 Cr. App. R. 466; [1973] Crim.
L.R. 581 CA (Crim Div) 19.91
R. v Krezolek (Mariusz); R. v Luczak (Magdalena) [2014] EWCA
Crim 2782; [2015] 2 Cr. App. R. (S.) 2; [2015] Crim. L.R. 628 .... 27.84
R. v Kulah (Mustafa Nour) [2007] EWCA Crim 1701; [2008] 1 W.L.R.
2517; [2008] 1 All E.R. 16; [2008] 1 Cr. App. R. (S.) 85; [2007]
Crim. L.R. 907 .... 34.38
R. v Kumar (Sachidanand) [2006] EWCA Crim 1946; (2006) 150
S.J.L.B. 1053 .... 2.75
R. v L (Graham) [2003] EWCA Crim 1512 .... 1.168
R. v L (Mark) [2014] EWCA Crim 1669 .... 33.09
R. v L (William Frederick); R. v C (Carole Anne) [2009] EWCA Crim
2688 .... 20.15
R. v L [2006] EWCA Crim 2988 .... 20.53
R. v L [2007] EWCA Crim 764 ....30.108
R. v L [2007]. See R. v Levey (Stephen)
R. v L [2008] EWCA Crim 973; [2009] 1 W.L.R. 626; [2008] 2 Cr. App.
R. 18; [2008] Crim. L.R. 823 ....19.129
R. v L [2012] EWCA Crim 316; (2012) 176 J.P. 231 .... 20.28
R. v L [2015] EWCA Crim 741 .... 26.77, 26.161
R. v L; R. v T; R. v THN; R. v HVN [2013] EWCA Crim 991; [2014]
1 All E.R. 113; [2013] 2 Cr. App. R. 23; [2014] Crim. L.R. 150 ..... 11.12,
11.29, 11.35, 11.36
R. v L(GB) (No.00/1697/21) unreported 28 November 2000 .... 19.74
R. v L(P) [2014] EWCA Crim 207 .... 20.38
R. v Lafayette (Anthony Lascelles) [2008] EWCA Crim 3238; [2009]
Crim. L.R. 809 .... 20.89, 20.109
R. v Lamaletie (Mervyn); R. v Royce (Karen) [2008] EWCA Crim 314;
(2008) 172 J.P. 249; (2008) 172 J.P.N. 491; (2008) 152(10) S.J.L.B.
28 .... 20.07
R. v Lamb (Mark) [2007] EWCA Crim 1766 .... 20.130, 30.108
R. v Lambert (Steven); R. v Jordan (Shirley); R. v Ali (Mudassir
Mohammed) [2001] UKHL 37; [2002] 2 A.C. 545; [2001] 3 W.L.R.
206; [2001] 3 All E.R. 577; [2002] 1 All E.R. 2; [2001] 2 Cr. App.
R. 28; [2001] H.R.L.R. 55; [2001] U.K.H.R.R. 1074; [2001] Crim.
L.R. 806; (2001) 98(33) L.S.G. 29; (2001) 145 S.J.L.B. 174 ... 1.09, 1.278,
15.177, 15.197
R. v Lamont (James Bruce) [2010] EWCA Crim 2144 .... 30.24

R. v Land (Michael) [1999] Q.B. 65; [1998] 3 W.L.R. 322; [1998] 1 All
    E.R. 403; [1998] 1 Cr. App. R. 301; (1998) 162 J.P. 29; [1998] 1
    F.L.R. 438; [1998] Crim. L.R. 70; [1998] Fam. Law 133; (1997)
    161 J.P.N. 1173; (1997) 94(42) L.S.G. 32 CA 8.58, 8.89, 8.98
R. v Lane [1961] N.Z.L.R. 989 .... 9.28
R. v Lang (Christopher Michael) (1975) 62 Cr. App. R. 50 CA (Crim
    Div) 1.246, 1.302, 14.32
R. v Lang (Stephen Howard); R. v D; R. v Edwards (Kyle Frederick);
    R. v Guidera (Michael); R. v Sheppard (James); R. v Collier
    (Edward); R. v Glave (Heathcliffe); R. v Armitage (Lewis); R. v
    Smith (Gary); R. v Wright (Robert); R. v Feihn (Steven); R. v
    Carasco (Charles); R. v Winters (Keith); R. v Abdi (Hassan)
    [2005] EWCA Crim 2864; [2006] 1 W.L.R. 2509; [2006] 2 All E.R.
    410; [2006] 2 Cr. App. R. (S.) 3; [2006] Crim. L.R. 174 .... 31.95, 31.96,
                              32.44, 34.25, 34.26, 34.29, 34.30, 34.31, 34.54
R. v Larmour unreported 22 June 2001 .... 32.35
R. v Larter and Castleton [1995] Crim. L.R. 75 CA (Crim Div) 1.298,
                                                                             1.302
R. v Lashley unreported 8 February 2000 .... 25.45
R. v Latham [2014]. See R. v L(P) [2014]
R. v Lawrence (Karl) [2011] EWCA Crim 3185 .... 36.16
R. v Lawrence [1977] Crim. L.R. 492 CC (Nottingham) 26.15
R. v Laws-Chapman (William George) [2013] EWCA Crim 1851 .... 20.59,
                                                                     20.61, 20.67
R. v Lawson (Jonathan Eric) [2006] EWCA Crim 2572; [2007] 1
    W.L.R. 1191; [2007] 1 Cr. App. R. 11; (2007) 171 J.P. 43; [2007]
    Crim. L.R. 232; (2007) 171 J.P.N. 323; (2006) 150 S.J.L.B. 1152 .... 20.81
R. v Lea (Nicholas) [2011] EWCA Crim 487 .... 36.40
R. v Leach [2005] EWCA Crim 58 .... 19.66
R. v Leather (John Holdsworth) (1994) 98 Cr. App. R. 179; [1993] 2
    F.L.R. 770; [1994] 1 F.C.R. 877; [1993] Crim. L.R. 516; [1994]
    Fam. Law 70; (1993) 137 S.J.L.B. 54 CA (Crim Div) 9.41, 9.43, 9.45
R. v Leaver [2006]. See R. v L [2006]
R. v Leboe (1965) 46 C.R. 375 Co Ct (BC) 9.35
R. v Lee (2006) 22 C.R.N.Z. 568 CA (NZ) 2.118
R. v Lee (Anthony William) (A Minor) [1993] 1 W.L.R. 103; [1993] 2
    All E.R. 170; (1993) 96 Cr. App. R. 188; (1993) 157 J.P. 533; [1993]
    Crim. L.R. 65; (1992) 156 J.P.N. 746 CA (Crim Div) 29.74, 29.87,
                                                                             29.88
R. v Lee (John) (1912) 7 Cr. App. R. 31 CA 19.85
R. v Lee (Terence Michael) [2008] EWCA Crim 1350 .... 3.55, 3.56, 3.58, 3.61
R. v Lee. See R. v L [2007]
R. v Leeks (David Edward) [2009] EWCA Crim 1612; [2010] 1 Cr.
    App. R. 5; [2010] R.T.R. 16; [2010] Crim. L.R. 641 .... 8.12
R. v Lefeuvre (Christopher) [2011] EWCA Crim 1253 ....26.162

R. v Leicester Crown Court Ex p. S (A Minor) [1993] 1 W.L.R. 111;
    [1992] 2 All E.R. 659; (1992) 94 Cr. App. R. 153; [1991] Crim.
    L.R. 365; [1991] C.O.D. 231; (1991) 155 J.P.N. 139 QBD 29.87
R. v Leonard (John) [2012] EWCA Crim 277; [2012] 2 Cr. App. R.
    12 .... 8.142
R. v Levey (Stephen) [2006] EWCA Crim 1902; [2006] 1 W.L.R. 3092;
    [2007] 1 Cr. App. R. 1; [2007] 1 F.L.R. 462; [2006] 2 F.C.R. 724;
    [2007] Crim. L.R. 472; [2006] Fam. Law 1021 .... 30.50, 30.51
R. v Lewis (John Michael) [2012] EWCA Crim 1071; [2013] 1 Cr. App.
    R. (S.) 23 .... 33.08
R. v Lewis (Leroy) [2013] EWCA Crim 2596; [2014] 1 W.L.R. 2027;
    [2014] 1 Cr. App. R. 25 .... 2.44
R. v LF; R. v DS [2016] EWCA Crim 561 .... 30.164, 34.55
R. v Lillyman [1896] 2 Q.B. 167 CCR 19.74
R. v Linekar (Gareth) [1995] Q.B. 250; [1995] 2 W.L.R. 237; [1995] 3
    All E.R. 69; [1995] 2 Cr. App. R. 49; [1995] Crim. L.R. 320; (1995)
    92(2) L.S.G. 35; (1994) 138 S.J.L.B. 227 CA 1.207, 1.320
R. v Lines, 174 E.R. 861; (1844) 1 Car. & K. 393Assizes 1.156
R. v Lipman (Robert) [1970] 1 Q.B. 152; [1969] 3 W.L.R. 819; [1969] 3
    All E.R. 410; (1969) 53 Cr. App. R. 600; (1969) 133 J.P. 712;
    (1969) 113 S.J. 670 CA (Crim Div) 2.79
R. v Llorenz (2000) 145 CCC (3d) 535 CA (Ont) 19.121
R. v Lloyd (James Peter) [2005] EWCA Crim 1111 .... 26.32
R. v Lloyd (No.99/7714/Z1) unreported 18 February 2000 .... 19.94
R. v LM; R. v YT; R. v BT; R. v DG; R. v MB [2010] EWCA Crim
    2327; [2011] 1 Cr. App. R. 12; [2011] Crim. L.R. 425 ..... 11.12, 11.24,
                                                                        11.25, 11.26, 11.36
R. v Loftus. R. v L (William Frederick)
R. v Longworth (Gary Dean) [2006] UKHL 1; [2006] 1 W.L.R. 313;
    [2006] 1 All E.R. 887; [2006] 2 Cr. App. R. (S.) 62; [2006] Crim.
    L.R. 553; (2006) 103(6) L.S.G. 35; (2006) 150 S.J.L.B. 132 .... 35.07,
                                                                        35.09, 35.22
R. v Looseley. See Attorney General's Reference (No.3 of 2000), Re
R. v Lovell (George) (1923) 17 Cr. App. R. 163 CA 19.74
R. v LR; sub nom. Crown Prosecution Service v LR [2010] EWCA
    Crim 924; [2011] 1 W.L.R. 359; [2010] 3 All E.R. 969; [2010] 2 Cr.
    App. R. 9; (2010) 174 J.P. 271; [2011] Crim. L.R. 319 .... 18.31
R. v Lubemba (Cokesix); R. v JP [2014] EWCA Crim 2064; [2015] 1
    W.L.R. 1579; [2015] 1 Cr. App. R. 12; [2015] Crim. L.R. 237 ... 27.07,
              27.130, 27.151, 27.161, 28.02, 28.06, 28.14, 28.16, 28.25,
                                                                        28.32
R. v Lunderbech [1991] Crim. L.R. 784 CA (Crim Div) 15.51, 15.56,
                                                                        15.62
    v Lunney (Daniel) [1999] NI 158 .... 32.33

R. v Lynn (1788) 2 Durn. & E. 733 .... 15.26

R. v Lynsey (Jonathan Simon) [1995] 3 All E.R. 654; [1995] 2 Cr. App.
R. 667; (1995) 159 J.P. 437; (1995) 159 J.P.N. 317 CA (Crim
Div) 2.44

R. v M (Alexander) [2006] EWCA Crim 1509 .... 20.05, 20.19, 20.153

R. v M (Brian) [2000] 1 Cr. App. R. 49; [1999] Crim. L.R. 922; (1999)
96(28) L.S.G. 25 CA (Crim Div) 30.94

R. v M (Donald Gordon) [2006] EWCA Crim 3388 .... 20.32, 20.54

R. v M (John) [1996] 2 Cr. App. R. 56; (1996) 140 S.J.L.B. 37 CA (Crim
Div) 27.89, 27.93

R. v M (John) [2013] EWCA Crim 2238 ....20.148

R. v M (Michael) [2006] EWCA Crim 3408; [2007] Crim. L.R. 637 ..... 20.50,
20.52

R. v M (Patrick) [2004] EWCA Crim 1679; [2005] 1 Cr. App. R. (S.)
218 .... 1.90

R. v M [2009] EWCA Crim 618; [2010] Crim. L.R. 792; (2009) 173
C.L. & J. 237 .... 20.152, 26.156, 26.157, 26.160

R. v M [2010] EWCA Crim 1578; [2011] Crim. L.R. 79 .... 1.187, 1.361,
1.362, 20.46, 30.105

R. v M [2011] EWCA Crim 2752; [2012] Crim. L.R. 789 ...... 8.09, 8.11, 8.79,
8.81

R. v M [2011]. See R. v CM

R. v M [2012] EWCA Crim 852 .... 36.59

R. v M [2013] EWCA Crim 3; [2013] All E.R. (D) 24 (Feb); [2013] 1 Cr.
App. R. 36; [2014] M.H.L.R. 12; [2014] Crim. L.R. 312 .... 1.11, 1.74,
1.388, 1.389, 26.58

R. v M [2014] EWCA Crim 1457; [2014] Crim. L.R. 823 .... 20.140, 20.147

R. v M [2015] EWCA Crim 353; [2015] 2 Cr. App. R. 22 .... 8.44, 8.46, 20.35,
20.36

R. v M unreported 11 November 2014 .... 4.86

R. v M; R. v B; R. v H [2010] EWCA Crim 42 .... 35.22

R. v M'Rue (1838) 8 C. & P. 641 .... 1.156

R. v M(A) [2012] EWCA Crim 899; [2013] 1 Cr. App. R. 17 .... 27.78

R. v M(H) [2013] EWCA Crim 1642 .... 1.46

R. v M(H). See R. v Day (Adrian Harold)

R. v M(M) [2011] EWCA Crim 1291 .... 1.358, 1.361, 1.386, 26.88

R. v M(M) Superior Ct of Justice (Ontario) 26.109

R. v MA [2012] EWCA Crim 1646 .... 1.84

R. v MA, PA and RS unreported 22 January 2015 Crown Ct
(Lincoln) 1.262

R. v MacKreth (Kenneth Tom) [2009] EWCA Crim 1849; [2010] Crim.
L.R. 226 ..... 30.28, 30.29, 30.37, 30.52, 30.57, 30.61, 30.77, 30.78, 30.81
30.

R. v MacPherson (Ian) [2005] EWCA Crim 3605; [2006] 1 Cr. App. R.
30; [2007] Crim. L.R. 504 .... 27.143, 27.146, 27.148, 31.52

R. v Mailer (Stephen Paul) [2006] EWCA Crim 665; [2006] 2 Cr. App.
R. (S.) 84 .... 15.77

R. v Makanjuola (Oluwanfunso); R. v Easton (Christopher John)
[1995] 1 W.L.R. 1348; [1995] 3 All E.R. 730; [1995] 2 Cr. App. R.
469; (1995) 159 J.P. 701; (1995) 92(22) L.S.G. 40; (1995) 139
S.J.L.B. 179 CA (Crim Div) 19.108, 19.110, 19.111, 19.112, 19.115,
19.117, 30.106

R. v Malicki (Janusz Marian) [2009] EWCA Crim 365 .... 27.146, 27.152

R. v Malone (Thomas Patrick) [1998] 2 Cr. App. R. 447; [1998] Crim.
L.R. 834 CA (Crim Div) 1.17, 1.185, 1.203, 1.261

R. v Manchester Crown Court Ex p. H (A Juvenile); sub nom. H (A
Minor) (Reporting Restrictions), Re; D (A Minor) (Reporting
Restrictions), Re [2000] 1 W.L.R. 760; [2000] 2 All E.R. 166;
[2000] 1 Cr. App. R. 262 QBD 29.87

R. v Manister. See R. v Weir (Antony Albert)

R. v Manktelow (1853) 6 Cox C.C. 143 .... 9.35

R. v Mapstone [1964] 1 W.L.R. 439 (Note); [1963] 3 All E.R. 930
(Note); (1964) 128 J.P. 94 Assizes (Monmouthshire) 13.43

R. v Marlow (Michael David) [1998] 1 Cr. App. R. (S.) 273; [1997]
Crim. L.R. 897 CA (Crim Div) 3.158

R. v Marriott (Charles Percival) [1971] 1 W.L.R. 187; [1971] 1 All E.R.
595; (1971) 55 Cr. App. R. 82; (1970) 115 S.J. 11 CA (Crim
Div) 8.96

R. v Marsh (Stephen) [2009] EWCA Crim 2696 .... 20.19, 20.23

R. v Marshall (Francis Denham) (1925) 18 Cr. App. R. 164 CCA 19.106

R. v Martin (Durwayne Nathan) [2004] EWCA Crim 916; [2004] 2 Cr.
App. R. 22 .... 26.75, 26.143, 26.183

R. v Martindale (Clive) [1986] 1 W.L.R. 1042; [1986] 3 All E.R. 25;
(1987) 84 Cr. App. R. 31; (1986) 150 J.P. 548; [1986] Crim. L.R.
736; (1986) 150 J.P.N. 573; (1986) 130 S.J. 613 CA (Crim Div) 8.99

R. v Mason (Dulcie Irene) (1969) 53 Cr. App. R. 12 Assizes
(Shropshire) 2.63

R. v Masood (Asif) [1997] 2 Cr. App. R. (S.) 137 CA (Crim Div) 1.87

R. v Massey (Steven John) [2007] EWCA Crim 2664; [2008] 1 W.L.R.
937; [2008] 2 All E.R. 969; [2008] 1 Cr. App. R. 28; (2008) 172 J.P.
25; [2008] Crim. L.R. 719; (2008) 172 J.P.N. 237 .... 10.155, 10.156

R. v Matrix (Billy) [1997] EWCA Crim 2058; [1997] Crim. L.R. 901
CA (Crim Div) 8.89, 8.96, 8.97

R. v Matt (Christopher) [2015] EWCA Crim 162 .... 1.325

R. v Matthews (Alex Joseph) [2011] EWCA Crim 3110; [2012] 2 Cr.
App. R. (S.) 33 ....30.142

R. v Matthews unreported October 1996 CC (Reading) 1.155

R. v Matthews. See R. v M (John)

R. v May (John) (1990) 91 Cr. App. R. 157; [1990] Crim. L.R. 415 CA
(Crim Div) 10.30, 15.26, 15.27, 15.31, 15.33, 15.37, 15.40, 15.51,
15.52, 15.59, 15.62, 15.63, 15.65

R. v Maybery (John) [2003] EWCA Crim 782 .... 30.10, 30.82

R. v Mayers (1872) 12 Cox C.C.C. 311 .... 1.298

R. v Mayling (Cyril) [1963] 2 Q.B. 717; [1963] 2 W.L.R. 709; [1963] 1
All E.R. 687; (1963) 47 Cr. App. R. 102; (1963) 127 J.P. 269;
(1963) 107 S.J. 177 CA 15.26, 15.29, 15.31, 15.37, 15.51, 15.52, 15.59

R. v Mayuran, 2012 SCC 31, [2012] 2 S.C.R. 162 .... 1.291

R. v MB 1.237

R. v MB (Appeal Against Conviction) [2000] Crim. L.R. 181 CA
(Crim Div) 19.118

R. v Mba (Lewis) [2012] EWCA Crim 2773 .... 1.09, 1.265

R. v MC [2012] EWCA Crim 213 .... 26.164, 30.16, 30.17

R. v MC [2015] EWCA Crim 717 .... 30.93

R. v McAllister (David) [2008] EWCA Crim 1544; [2009] 1 Cr. App. R.
10 .... 20.32, 20.118, 20.120

R. v McAllister [1997] Crim. L.R. 233 CA (Crim Div) 1.173, 1.218

R. v McC [2014] EWCA Crim 909 .... 35.55, 35.56

R. v McCaffrey [2015] EWCA Crim 792 .... 34.62

R. v McCalmont [2010] NICA 27 .... 24.39, 32.72

R. v McCandles [2004] NICA 1 .... 32.43

R. v McCaughey (Thomas) [2014] NICA 61 .... 32.50

R. v McColgan [2006] NICA 41 .... 32.31

R. v McConnell [2014] NICA 14 .... 32.55

R. v McCormack (Patrick Eugene) [1969] 2 Q.B. 442; [1969] 3 W.L.R.
175; [1969] 3 All E.R. 371; (1969) 53 Cr. App. R. 514; (1969) 133
J.P. 630; (1969) 113 S.J. 507 CA (Crim Div) 2.63

R. v McCormick (Gerard) [2015] NICA 14 .... 32.50

R. v McDonald [1989] NI 37 .... 32.48

R. v McDonnell [2001] NI 168 .... 32.33

R. v McFarlane (Eric) [1994] Q.B. 419; [1994] 2 W.L.R. 494; [1994] 2
All E.R. 283; (1994) 99 Cr. App. R. 8; (1994) 158 J.P. 310; [1994]
Crim. L.R. 532; (1994) 144 N.L.J. 270; (1994) 138 S.J.L.B. 19 CA
(Crim Div) 13.49

R. v McGowan [2000] NIJB 305 .... 32.35

R. v McGrade [2014] NICA 8 .... 32.50

R. v McK [2013] NICA 11 .... 32.69, 32.70

R. v McKendrick. *See* R. v GM

R. v McKenning (Zara Louise) [2008] EWCA Crim 2301; [2009] 1 Cr.
App. R. (S.) 106 .... 34.56, 34.57

R. v McKenzie (Mark Anthony) [2008] EWCA Crim 758; (2008) 172
J.P. 377; [2008] R.T.R. 22; (2008) 172 J.P.N. 559 ....20.103

R. v McKeown (Gary); R. v HL; sub nom. DPP's Reference (No.2 of
2013), Re [2013] NICA 28 .... 32.38, 32.50

R. v McKinnell (John) [2013] NICA 52 .... 32.51
R. v McKintosh (Demoy) [2006] EWCA Crim 193 .... 20.15, 20.26
R. v McNally (Justine) [2013] EWCA Crim 1051; [2014] Q.B. 593;
    [2014] 2 W.L.R. 200; [2013] 2 Cr. App. R. 28 .... 1.07, 1.209, 1.214
R. v McNamara (James) (1988) 87 Cr. App. R. 246; (1988) 152 J.P. 390;
    [1988] Crim. L.R. 440; (1988) 152 J.P.N. 350; (1988) 132 S.J. 300
    CA (Crim Div) 8.96
R. v McNeill (Tracy) [2007] EWCA Crim 2927; (2008) 172 J.P. 50;
    (2008) 172 J.P.N. 257 .... 20.15
R. v McQuiston (James Wallace) [1998] 1 Cr. App. R. 139; [1998]
    Crim. L.R. 69; (1997) 161 J.P.N. 1173 .... 27.93
R. v MD [2015] EWCA Crim 818 .... 20.46
R. v Meachen (David Nigel) [2006] EWCA Crim 2414 .... 2.129
R. v Meachen (David Nigel) [2009] EWCA Crim 1701 ..... 2.125, 2.127, 2.130
R. v Mearns (John Ronald) [1991] 1 Q.B. 82; [1990] 3 W.L.R. 569;
    [1990] 3 All E.R. 989; (1990) 91 Cr. App. R. 312; (1990) 154 J.P.
    447; [1990] Crim. L.R. 708; (1990) 154 J.P.N. 378 CA (Crim
    Div) 2.43, 2.44, 9.18
R. v Merritt (Kelvin James) [2014] EWCA Crim 2384 .... 8.36
R. v MF [2005] EWCA Crim 3376 .... 26.80
R. v MH [2003] EWCA Crim 1066 .... 26.71
R. v MH [2012] EWCA Crim 2725; [2013] Crim. L.R. 849 .... 19.56, 19.81,
    19.90, 27.74, 27.153
R. v Miah (Abdal); R. v Mohammed (Liban) [2014] EWCA Crim 938;
    (2014) 178 J.P. 297 ....19.121
R. v Miah (Masuk) [2006] EWCA Crim 132; [2006] 2 Cr. App. R. (S.)
    46 .... 15.37
R. v Miah (Mukith) [2015] EWCA Crim 1628; [2016] 1 Cr. App. R. (S.)
    27 .... 14.66
R. v Miah (Zunur); R. v Uddin (Syed Ebad) [2006] EWCA Crim 1168;
    (2006) 150 S.J.L.B. 702 .... 26.61
R. v Mickle [1978] 1 N.Z.L.R. 720 Sup Ct (NZ) 12.26
R. v Miles [2015]. See R. v M [2015]
R. v Miles. See R. v M [2015]
R. v Millard and Vernon [1987] Crim. L.R. 393 CA (Crim Div) 1.404,
    1.406
R. v Millberry (William Christopher); R. v Lackenby (Ian Stuart); R.
    v Morgan (Paul Robert) [2002] EWCA Crim 2891; [2003] 1
    W.L.R. 546; [2003] 2 All E.R. 939; [2003] 1 Cr. App. R. 25; [2003]
    2 Cr. App. R. (S.) 31; [2003] Crim. L.R. 207; (2003) 100(7) L.S.G.
    34; (2003) 147 S.J.L.B. 28 .... 1.54, 1.69, 1.73, 1.82, 1.83, 1.86, 1.129,
    30.04, 30.06, 30.113
R. v Miller (David) [2010] EWCA Crim 2883 .... 8.138, 8.139
R. v Miller (Gary) [2010] EWCA Crim 809; [2011] 1 Cr. App. R. (S.)
    2; [2010] Crim. L.R. 648 ....20.148

R. v Miller. *See* R. v M [2010]
R. v Mills (Leroy) (1979) 68 Cr. App. R. 327 CA (Crim Div) 26.15
R. v Millward (Sidney Booth) (1994) 158 J.P. 1091; [1994] Crim. L.R. 527 CA (Crim Div) 15.142
R. v Milton Brown (No.97/8393/Z4) unreported 6 May 1998 .... 19.16
R. v Mitchell (John Irvine) (1952) 36 Cr. App. R. 79 CCA 19.106
R. v ML [2013] NICA 23 .... 32.06
R. v ML [2013] NICA 27 .... 32.47
R. v MM [2007] EWCA Crim 1558 .... 1.355, 1.388, 1.391, 1.394, 30.105
R. v Mogford [1970] 1 W.L.R. 988; (1970) 114 S.J. 318 Assizes (Glamorgan) 12.69
R. v Mohammed Zafar (No.92/2762/W2) unreported 18 June 1993 CA (Crim Div) 1.218, 1.219
R. v Mohan (John Patrick) [1976] Q.B. 1; [1975] 2 W.L.R. 859; [1975] 2 All E.R. 193; (1974) 60 Cr. App. R. 272; [1975] R.T.R. 337; [1975] Crim. L.R. 283; (1975) 119 S.J. 219 CA (Crim Div) 1.406
R. v Mokrecovas (Andrius) [2001] EWCA Crim 1644; [2002] 1 Cr. App. R. 20; [2001] Crim. L.R. 911 .... 26.70, 26.71, 26.74, 26.142
R. v Molloy [1997] NIJB 241 .... 32.49
R. v Montila (Steven William); sub nom. R. v Montilla (Steven William) [2004] UKHL 50; [2004] 1 W.L.R. 3141; [2005] 1 All E.R. 113; [2005] 1 Cr. App. R. 26; [2005] Crim. L.R. 479; (2005) 102(3) L.S.G. 30; (2004) 148 S.J.L.B. 1403 .... 10.64, 14.05
R. v Moore (Andrew Neish) [2004] EWCA Crim 2574; [2005] 1 Cr. App. R. (S.) 101 .... 36.62
R. v Moore and Grazier (1971) 1 Can.C.C. (2d) 521 CA (BC) 9.38
R. v Moran (Noel) [2007] EWCA Crim 2947 .... 20.03
R. v Morgan (Graham) [2009] EWCA Crim 2705 .... 20.57
R. v Morgan [1970] V.R. 337 Sup Ct (Vic) 1.227, 1.228, 1.237, 7.68, 7.69
R. v Morris (1963) 47 Cr. App. R. 202 Assizes 13.44
R. v Morris (Charles) [1951] 1 K.B. 394; [1950] 2 All E.R. 965; 66 T.L.R. (Pt. 2) 1050; (1950) 34 Cr. App. R. 210; (1951) 115 J.P. 5; 49 L.G.R. 95; (1950) 94 S.J. 708 CCA 12.86, 15.28
R. v Morris (Richard John) [2013] EWCA Crim 350 .... 36.62
R. v Morris (Richard) [2011] EWCA Crim 2639 .... 36.34
R. v Morris [1998] Crim. L.R. 416 .... 27.97
R. v Morris [2013]. *See* R. v Cairns (James Philip)
R. v Morris-Lowe (Brian John) [1985] 1 W.L.R. 29; [1985] 1 All E.R. 400; (1985) 80 Cr. App. R. 114; [1985] Crim. L.R. 50; (1984) 81 L.S.G. 3336; (1984) 128 S.J. 872 CA (Crim Div) 13.46
R. v Mortimer (Jason Christopher) [2010] EWCA Crim 1303 .... 36.29
R. v Mortimore (Aaron George) [2013] EWCA Crim 1639 .... 9.39
R. v Mousir [1987] Crim. L.R. 561; (1987) 84 L.S.G. 1328 CA (Crim Div) 9.42, 9.45

R. v Moys (Robert) (1984) 79 Cr. App. R. 72; [1984] Crim. L.R. 494; (1984) 128 S.J. 548 CA (Crim Div) 9.61, 12.63

R. v MR (No.98/6035/W5) unreported 21 February 2000 .... 27.91

R. v Muir (William) [1938] 2 All E.R. 516; (1938) 26 Cr. App. R. 164 CCA 1.146

R. v Mukadi (Patrick) [2003] EWCA Crim 3765; [2004] Crim. L.R. 373 .... 26.30, 26.31, 26.80, 26.140

R. v Mullen (James Arthur) [2004] EWCA Crim 602; [2004] 2 Cr. App. R. 18; [2005] Crim. L.R. 76; (2004) 148 S.J.L.B. 386 .... 27.89, 27.94

R. v Murphy (1996) 919 P.2d 26.126

R. v Murphy and Bieneck (1981) 21 C.R.(3d) 39 CA (Alta) 10.152

R. v Murray (Arthur Alan) [2004] EWCA Crim 2211; [2005] Crim. L.R. 387 .... 8.51

R. v Musone (Ibrahim) [2007] EWCA Crim 1237; [2007] 1 W.L.R. 2467; [2007] 2 Cr. App. R. 29; (2007) 171 J.P. 425; [2007] Crim. L.R. 972; (2007) 171 J.P.N. 689; (2007) 151 S.J.L.B. 709 .... 20.81

R. v N (Andrew) [2004] EWCA Crim 1236 .... 1.151

R. v N (Child Witnesses: Unsworn Evidence) [1998] N.I. 261 CA (Crim Div) (NI) 32.65

R. v N (Kenneth) [2006] EWCA Crim 3309; (2007) 171 J.P. 158; (2007) 171 J.P.N. 382 .... 19.33

R. v N (No.97/6290/Z3) unreported 8 April 1998 .... 19.91, 19.96, 19.99

R. v N [2011] EWCA Crim 730; [2012] Crim. L.R. 158 ...... 20.124, 20.125

R. v N; R. v L; R. v D [2010] EWCA Crim 941; [2010] 2 Cr. App. R. 14; [2011] 1 Cr. App. R. (S.) 22 .... 1.90, 1.147

R. v N; R. v Le (Vinh Cong); sub nom. R. v AN [2012] EWCA Crim 189; [2013] Q.B. 379; [2012] 3 W.L.R. 1159; [2012] 1 Cr. App. R. 35; [2012] Crim. L.R. 958 .... 11.12, 11.26, 11.27, 11.28

R. v Nagrecha (Chandu) [1997] 2 Cr. App. R. 401; [1998] Crim. L.R. 65 .... 19.100, 19.101, 19.102, 26.152

R. v Naillie (Yabu Hurerali); R. v Kanesarajah (Rajaratnam) [1993] A.C. 674; [1993] 2 W.L.R. 927; [1993] 2 All E.R. 782; (1993) 97 Cr. App. R. 388; (1993) 143 N.L.J. 848 HL 11.17

R. v Nangle (Brendan Francis) (Appeal against Sentence) [2001] EWCA Crim 1587 .... 24.20

R. v Narif [1987] 2 N.Z.L.R. 122 CA (NZ) 1.380

R. v Nathaniel (Lonsdale) [1995] 2 Cr. App. R. 565 CA 25.67

R. v Neal (Stephen) [2011] EWCA Crim 461 .... 8.44, 8.93

R. v Neish (Nathan) [2012] EWCA Crim 62 .... 36.59

R. v Nelson (Ashley George) [2006] EWCA Crim 3412; [2007] Crim. L.R. 709 .... 20.87

R. v Nestoros (Costos) [2015] EWCA Crim 1424; [2016] 1 Cr. App. R. (S.) 5 .... 8.37

R. v Neville (Christina); R. v Bailey (Venita) (1995) 16 Cr. App. R. (S.) 647 CA (Crim Civ) 10.157

R. v Newbon [2005] Crim. L.R. 738 .... 1.32, 19.18

R. v Newsome (Peter Alan) [1997] 2 Cr. App. R. (S.) 69; [1997] Crim.
L.R. 237 CA (Crim Div) 9.11

R. v Newton (Robert John) (1983) 77 Cr. App. R. 13; (1982) 4 Cr. App.
R. (S.) 388; [1983] Crim. L.R. 198 CA (Crim Div) 3.30

R. v Ngwata (Esther Faraja) [2012] EWCA Crim 2015; [2013] 1 Cr.
App. R. (S.) 111 .... 34.57

R. v NH [2006] EWCA Crim 3294; [2007] 2 Cr. App. R. (S.) 27 ....31.115

R. v Nicholas unreported 13 December 1994 CA 27.59

R. v Nicholls (1867) 10 Cox C.C. 476 .... 3.75

R. v Nicholson (Gavin) [2012] EWCA Crim 1568; [2012] 2 Cr. App. R.
31 ....20.135

R. v Nicholson (George Desmond) [2014] EWCA Crim 834 .... 33.09

R. v Nicklass (Karl Christopher) [2006] EWCA Crim 2613 .... 8.44

R. v Nightingale (Alan) [2010] EWCA Crim 111; [2010] 2 Cr. App. R.
(S.) 59 .... 1.48

R. v Norcott (Richard) [1917] 1 K.B. 347; (1917) 12 Cr. App. R. 166;
(1916) 86 L.J. K.B. 7 CA 19.86

R. v Norris (Colin) [2009] EWCA Crim 2697 ....20.137

R. v North (Mark Edward) [2011] EWCA Crim 88 ..... 18.33, 18.77, 18.78,
18.81

R. v Norton (Joseph) [2014] EWCA Crim 1275; [2014] 2 Cr. App. R.
(S.) 79 .... 35.56

R. v Novac (Andrew); R. v Raywood (Malcolm Jack); R. v Andrew-
Cohen (Basil John); R. v Archer (David) (1976) 65 Cr. App. R.
107 CA (Crim Div) 19.14

R. v Noye (Kenneth) [2011] EWCA Crim 650; (2011) 119 B.M.L.R.
151 .... 22.46

R. v O (Ian) [2006] EWCA Crim 556; [2006] 2 Cr. App. R. 27; [2006]
Crim. L.R. 918 .... 19.85, 30.103

R. v O [2008] EWCA Crim 2835; Times, 2 October 2008 .... 11.11, 11.22,
11.31

R. v O unreported 4 December 2012 CA 30.113

R. v O'Boyle [1973] R.T.R. 445 CA (Crim Div) 35.48, 36.60

R. v O'Brien (Edward Vincent) [1974] 3 All E.R. 663 CC (Bristol) 1.166

R. v O'Brien (Karl) [2006] EWCA Crim 1741; [2007] 1 W.L.R. 833;
[2006] 4 All E.R. 1012; [2007] 1 Cr. App. R. (S.) 75; [2006] Crim.
L.R. 1074 .... 34.40, 34.41, 34.42, 34.44

R. v O'Brien (Robert Francis) [2000] Crim. L.R. 863 CA (Crim
Div) 19.08

R. v O'Conner (Daniel) [2015] EWCA Crim 515 .... 14.45

R. v O'Dell (Leslie Philip) unreported 10 November 2000 CA (Crim
Div) 30.60

R. v O'Dowd (Kevin) [2009] EWCA Crim 905; [2009] 2 Cr. App. R. 16;
(2009) 173 J.P. 640; [2009] Crim. L.R. 827 .... 19.71, 20.104, 20.106,
20.107
R. v O'Grady (Patrick Gerald) [1987] Q.B. 995; [1987] 3 W.L.R. 321;
[1987] 3 All E.R. 420; (1987) 85 Cr. App. R. 315; [1987] Crim.
L.R. 706; (1987) 131 S.J. 887 CA (Crim Div) 1.399
R. v O'Hare (Martin Timothy) [2006] EWCA Crim 2512 .... 19.61
R. v O'Keefe unreported 3 March 2000 .... 32.33
R. v O'Leary (Patrick) [2013] EWCA Crim 1371 .... 7.38, 20.119, 27.146
R. v O'Reilly (John Joseph) [1967] 2 Q.B. 722; [1967] 3 W.L.R. 191;
[1967] 2 All E.R. 766; (1967) 51 Cr. App. R. 345; (1967) 131 J.P.
370; (1967) 111 S.J. 314 CA (Crim Div) 19.106
R. v O'Shea (1898) 19 Cox C.C. 76 .... 1.318
R. v O(D). See R. v DO
R. v Oakes (David); R. v Restivo (Daniel); R. v Roberts (Michael
John); R. v Simmons (David); R. v Stapleton (Kiaran Mark)
[2012] EWCA Crim 2435; [2013] Q.B. 979; [2013] 3 W.L.R. 137;
[2013] 2 All E.R. 30; [2013] 2 Cr. App. R. (S.) 22; [2013] H.R.L.R.
9; [2013] Crim. L.R. 252 .... 1.111, 34.59
R. v Oakes (Paul) [2011] EWCA Crim 818; [2011] 2 Cr. App. R. (S.)
588 .... 9.21
R. v Odam (Soloman Alexander) [2008] EWCA Crim 1087; [2009] 1
Cr. App. R. (S.) 22 .... 35.13
R. v Offen (Matthew Barry) (No.2); R. v McGilliard (Peter Wilson);
R. v McKeown (Darren); R. v Okwuegbunam (Kristova); R. v S
(Stephen Peter) [2001] 1 W.L.R. 253; [2001] 2 All E.R. 154; [2001]
1 Cr. App. R. 24; [2001] 2 Cr. App. R. (S.) 10; [2000] Prison L.R.
283; [2001] Crim. L.R. 63; (2001) 98(1) L.S.G. 23; (2000) 144
S.J.L.B. 288 CA (Crim Div) 34.26
R. v Ogbodo (Uwal Silus) [2011] EWCA Crim 564 .... 26.47, 26.112
R. v Ogden (Robert) [2013] EWCA Crim 1294 .... 25.45
R. v Olifier (1886) 10 Cox C.C. 402 .... 9.35
R. v Oliver (Mark David); R. v Hartrey (Michael Patrick); R. v
Baldwin (Leslie) [2002] EWCA Crim 2766; [2003] 1 Cr. App. R.
28; [2003] 2 Cr. App. R. (S.) 15; [2003] Crim. L.R. 127 ...... 8.19, 8.20,
8.31, 8.46, 8.124, 33.12
R. v Olu (Nicholas Andreas); R. v Wilson (Leon Tony); R. v Brooks
(David) [2010] EWCA Crim 2975; [2011] 1 Cr. App. R. 33; (2011)
175 J.P. 1 .... 20.08
R. v Olugboja (Stephen) [1982] Q.B. 320; [1981] 3 W.L.R. 585; [1981]
1 All E.R. 443; (1981) 73 Cr. App. R. 344 CA (Crim) 1.05, 1.170,
1.171, 1.172, 1.174, 1.175, 1.177
R. v Openshaw. See R. v O (Ian)
R. v Orchard and Thurtle (1848) 3 Cox C.C. 248 .... 15.59
R. v Osborne (Mark Williams) [2010] EWCA Crim 1981 .... 19.65

R. v Osborne (William Henry) [1905] 1 K.B. 551 CCR 19.74, 19.86
R. v Osbourne (Gary Ozzy) [2007] EWCA Crim 481; [2007] Crim.
   L.R. 712 .... 20.18
R. v Osolin [1993] 4 S.C.R. 595 Sup Ct (Can) 1.288
R. v Owen (Alan Carl) (1986) 83 Cr. App. R. 100 CA (Crim Div) 20.91
R. v Owen (Anthony Robert) [2007] EWCA Crim 694 .... 36.25
R. v Owen (Charles William) [1988] 1 W.L.R. 134; (1988) 86 Cr. App.
   R. 291; [1988] Crim. L.R. 120; (1987) 131 S.J. 1696 .... 8.47, 8.48, 8.49,
                                                   8.50, 8.52
R. v P (Craig) [2014] EWCA Crim 848 .... 20.91
R. v P (G) [2006] EWCA Crim 1980 .... 27.90
R. v P (John James) [2008] EWCA Crim 1806; [2009] 1 Cr. App. R. (S.)
   45 .... 2.19, 3.100
R. v P (Mark Geoffrey) [2006] EWCA Crim 2517 .... 20.26
R. v P (Pamela Jean) (1992) 13 Cr. App. R. (S.) 369 CA (Crim Div) 15.133
R v P(R). See R. v P
R. v P (Stephen) [2013] EWCA Crim 913 .... 20.40
R. v P [1990] Crim. L.R. 323 .... 14.06
R. v P [2009] EWCA Crim 1327; [2009] All E.R. (D.) 79 (Jul) 20.127
R. v P [2013] EWCA Crim 2331; [2014] 1 W.L.R. 3058; [2014] 1 Cr.
   App. R. 28; [2014] Crim. L.R. 547 .... 26.28
R. v P [2013]. See R. v P (Stephen)
R. v P [2015] EWCA Crim 753; [2015] 2 Cr. App. R. (S.) 28 ... 7.60, 7.147
R. v P; sub nom. R. v DP [2013] EWCA Crim 1143; [2013] 2 Cr. App.
   R. (S.) 63; [2013] Crim. L.R. 860 .... 1.131, 30.163, 30.164
R. v P(J). See R. v Lubemba (Cokesix)
R. v P(P) [2009] EWCA Crim 1048 .... 1.118, 1.120, 1.123
R. v Pace (Martin Edward); R. v Rogers (Simon Peter) [2014] EWCA
   Crim 186; [2014] 1 W.L.R. 2867; [2014] 1 Cr. App. R. 34; (2014)
   178 J.P. 133; [2014] Lloyd's Rep. F.C. 319 .... 1.406
R. v Packer (1886) 16 Cox C.C. 57 .... 9.36
R. v Page (1846) 2 Cox C.C. 133 .... 1.300
R. v Panayiotou (No.97/5500/W2) unreported 19 June 1998 .... 19.16
R. v Papadimitropoulos (1957) 98 C.L.R. 249 .... 1.326
R. v Pappajohn [1980] 2 S.C.R. 120 Sup Ct (Can) 1.287, 1.290, 26.68
R. v Pappas [2013] S.C.C. 56 .... 1.291
R. v Park [1995] 2 S.C.R. 836 Sup Ct (Can) 1.288, 26.68
R. v Park [2008] See R. v P (John James)
R. v Park. See R. v P (John James)
R. v Parker (Francis) [1996] Crim. L.R. 511 CA (Crim Div) 27.87
R. v Parnell (Brian Michael) [2004] EWCA Crim 2523; [2005] 1
   W.L.R. 853 .... 35.11
R. v Pashley (Adam) [2015] EWCA Crim 1540 .... 36.28, 36.36

R. v Payne (Cynthia) (1980) 2 Cr. App. R. (S.) 161; [1980] Crim. L.R.
595 CA (Crim Div) 12.87
R. v Payne (Trevor Bernard) unreported 29 January 2015 CA (Crim
Div) 3.66
R. v Pearce (Stephen John) (1981) 72 Cr. App. R. 295; [1981] Crim.
L.R. 639 CA (Crim Div) 8.10
R. v Pedley (Dean); R. v Hamadi (Zeeyad); R. v Martin (Lee) [2009]
EWCA Crim 840; [2009] 1 W.L.R. 2517; [2010] 1 Cr. App. R. (S.)
24; [2010] 1 Prison L.R. 258; [2009] Crim. L.R. 669 .... 34.32
R. v Pelletier (Paul) [2012] EWCA Crim 1060 .... 36.52
R. v Pendleton (Donald) [2001] UKHL 66; [2002] 1 W.L.R. 72; [2002]
1 All E.R. 524; [2002] 1 Cr. App. R. 34; [2002] Crim. L.R. 398;
(2002) 99(7) L.S.G. 34; (2002) 146 S.J.L.B. 20 .... 22.46
R. v Percival (Brian) (1998) 95(27) L.S.G. 25; (1998) 142 S.J.L.B. 190
CA (Crim Div) 30.94
R. v Perry and Pledger [1920] N.Z.L.R. 21 CA (NZ) 4.66

R. v Petherick (Rosie Lee) [2012] EWCA Crim 2214; [2013] 1 W.L.R.
1102; [2013] 1 Cr. App. R. (S.) 116; (2013) 177 J.P. 94; [2013] Crim.
L.R. 80 .... 1.76
R. v Petraitis (Mindaugas) [2013] EWCA Crim 997 .... 35.54
R. v Pettman unreported 2 May 1985 CA 20.30, 26.103
R. v PF [2009] EWCA Crim 1086 .... 22.46
R. v PG [2016] EWCA Crim 250 .... 36.12, 36.32
R. v Phillips (Graham Alistair) [2007] EWCA Crim 485 .... 4.03, 30.157
R. v Phillips (Paul Edward) [2011] EWCA Crim 2935; [2012] 1 Cr.
App. R. 25; [2012] Lloyd's Rep. F.C. 179; [2012] Crim. L.R.
460 .... 20.143
R. v Pikos [1967] V.R. 89 Sup Ct (Vict) 10.135
R. v Pinnell (Paul Leslie); R. v Joyce (Martin Peter Francis) [2010]
EWCA Crim 2848; [2012] 1 W.L.R. 17; [2011] 2 Cr. App. R. (S.)
30; [2011] Crim. L.R. 253 .... 30.165, 34.50, 34.51
R. v Pipe (Steven Allan) [2014] EWCA Crim 2570; [2015] 1 Cr. App.
R. (S.) 42; [2015] Crim. L.R. 304 .... 4.43, 4.44, 33.26
R. v Piskadlo (Robert) [2014] EWCA Crim 76 .... 35.55
R. v Pitt (Ian Barry) 1983] Q.B. 25; [1982] 3 W.L.R. 359; [1982] 3 All
E.R. 63; (1982) 75 Cr. App. R. 254; [1982] Crim. L.R. 513; (1982)
12 Fam. Law 152; (1982) 79 L.S.G. 953; (1982) 126 S.J. 447 CA
(Crim Div) 19.128
R. v PK [2015] EWCA Crim 648 .... 30.118C, 30.141
R. v PK; R. v TK [2008] EWCA Crim 434; [2008] All E.R. (D.) 29
(Mar) 1.190, 1.216, 19.89, 26.28
R. v Pollins (Paul Duncan) [2014] NICA 62 .... 32.45
R. v Popescu (Nicolae Lucian) [2010] EWCA Crim 1230; [2011] Crim.
L.R. 227 .... 27.98, 27.100, 27.102

R. v Porter (Ross Warwick) [2006] EWCA Crim 560; [2006] 1 W.L.R. 2633; [2007] 2 All E.R. 625; [2006] 2 Cr. App. R. 25; [2006] Crim. L.R. 748; (2006) 103(14) L.S.G. 28 ..... 8.71, 8.72, 8.135, 8.136, 8.137, 8.138, 8.139, 8.140, 8.141, 8.142

R. v Powell (Carl Michael) [2014] EWCA Crim 642; [2014] 1 W.L.R. 2757; [2014] 2 Cr. App. R. 31 .... 19.04, 20.111

R. v Powell (Michael John) [2006] EWCA Crim 3; [2006] 1 Cr. App. R. 31; [2006] Crim. L.R. 781 .... 27.146, 27.152, 31.53

R. v PR [2010] EWCA Crim 2741 ....20.129

R. v Pratt [1984] Crim. L.R. 41 CC 2.36, 2.80

R. v Price (David Arthur) [2003] EWCA Crim 2405; [2004] 1 Cr. App. R. 12; (2003) 100(36) L.S.G. 38 .... 2.73

R. v Price (David Ryan) [2006] EWCA Crim 3363 .... 8.95, 8.96

R. v Prince (Henry) (1875) L.R. 2 C.C.R. 154 CCR 9.29, 9.31, 9.46, 9.48

R. v Prince (Ricky Ernest) unreported 6 May 2015 CA (Crim Div) 8.35

R. v Prince (Shayne) [2013] EWCA Crim 1768 .... 4.77, 33.18

R. v Pritchett [2007] EWCA Crim 586; [2008] Crim. L.R. 214 .... 12.24, 12.45

R. v Proctor (Adrian) [2014] EWCA Crim 162 .... 36.65

R. v PS [2013] EWCA Crim 992 .... 30.01, 30.52, 30.85, 30.99

R. v Qazi (Saraj); R. v Hussain (Majid) [2010] EWCA Crim 2579; [2011] 2 Cr. App. R. (S.) 8; [2011] H.R.L.R. 4; [2011] Crim. L.R. 159 ....30.139

R. v Quayle (Simon Kevin) (1993) 14 Cr. App. R. (S.) 726 CA (Crim Div) 4.03

R. v Quinn (Geoffrey Anthony); R. v Bloom (Samuel) [1962] 2 Q.B. 245; [1961] 3 W.L.R. 611; [1961] 3 All E.R. 88; (1961) 45 Cr. App. R. 279; (1961) 125 J.P. 565; (1961) 105 S.J. 590 CCA 12.92, 12.94

R. v R (Amer); R. v V (Abolghasem); R. v L (Abraham); R. v S (Imran); R. v C (James); R. v O (Claire); R. v M (Faisal Jamil) [2006] EWCA Crim 1974; [2007] 1 Cr. App. R. 10; [2007] Crim. L.R. 79 ....30.160

R. v R (Blood Sample: Privilege) [1994] 1 W.L.R. 758; [1994] 4 All E.R. 260; [1995] 1 Cr. App. R. 183; (1994) 138 S.J.L.B. 54 CA (Crim Div) 25.38

R. v R (Paul Brian) (1993) 14 Cr. App. R. (S.) 772; [1993] Crim. L.R. 541 CA (Crim Div) 30.21

R. v R (Peter) (Abuse of Process) [2001] EWCA Crim 2844 ....26.138

R. v R (Rape: Marital Exemption); sub nom. R. v R (A Husband) [1992] 1 A.C. 599; [1991] 3 W.L.R. 767; [1991] 4 All E.R. 481; (1992) 94 Cr. App. R. 216; (1991) 155 J.P. 989; [1992] 1 F.L.R. 217; [1992] Crim. L.R. 207; [1992] Fam. Law 108; (1991) 155 J.P.N. 752; (1991) 141 N.L.J. 1481; (1991) 135 S.J.L.B. 181 HL 1.03, 1.162, 1.164, 1.165, 1.166, 1.329, 30.01

R. v R [1996] Crim. L.R. 815 ....19.108

R. v R [2003] EWCA Crim 2754 .... 26.100, 26.110

R. v R [2008] EWCA Crim 619; [2009] 1 W.L.R. 713; [2008] 2 Cr. App.
R. 38; (2008) 172 J.P. 441 .... 4.132, 4.173
R. v R unreported 30 July 1990 CA 1.166, 1.168
R. v R; sub nom. R. v R (SA) [2008] EWCA Crim 678; [2008] 1 W.L.R.
2044; [2008] 2 Cr. App. R. 10 .... 27.41
R. v Rackham (Terrance John) [1997] 2 Cr. App. R. 222; [1997] Crim.
L.R. 592 CA (Crim Div) 3.25, 19.99, 30.15
R. v Rae [2013] EWCA Crim 2056; [2013] All E.R. (D) 346 (Oct) 4.22
R. v Raheem Ul Nasir Jamal Muhammed unreported, 10 September
2015 CA (Crim Div) 1.40
R. v Rakib (Mohammed) [2011] EWCA Crim 870; [2012] 1 Cr. App.
R. (S.) 1; [2011] Crim. L.R. 570 .... 15.84, 15.85
R. v Ralphs (James) (1914) 9 Cr. App. R. 86 CCA 2.98
R. v Ram (1893) 17 Cox C.C. 609 .... 1.149
R. v Rampley (Kim) [2006] EWCA Crim 2203; [2007] 1 Cr. App. R.
(S.) 87; [2007] Crim. L.R. 84 .... 32.36
R. v Ramzan. See R. v R (Amer)
R. v Randall (Heath) [2006] EWCA Crim 1413 .... 20.48
R. v Ransford (1874) 31 L.T. 488 .... 3.159
R. v Rawlings (Royston George); R. v Broadbent (Timothy Charles)
[1995] 1 W.L.R. 178; [1995] 1 All E.R. 580; [1995] 2 Cr. App. R.
222; (1995) 92(2) L.S.G. 36; (1994) 144 N.L.J. 1626; (1994) 138
S.J.L.B. 223 CA (Crim Div) 27.90, 27.91, 27.92, 27.93, 27.95, 27.97
R. v RD [2013] EWCA Crim 1592 .... 30.01, 30.08, 30.39, 30.48
R. v Reading Justices Ex p. Berkshire CC [1996] 1 Cr. App. R. 239;
[1996] 1 F.L.R. 149; [1996] 2 F.C.R. 535; [1996] Crim. L.R. 347;
[1995] C.O.D. 385; [1996] Fam. Law 84 DC 18.77, 18.80, 18.81, 18.91
R. v Redbridge Youth Court. See R. (on the application of DPP) v
Redbridge Youth Court
R. v Redguard [1991] Crim. L.R. 213 CA (Crim Div) 26.125
R. v Redpath (Alan) (1962) 46 Cr. App. R. 319; (1962) 106 S.J. 412
CA 19.74, 19.119
R. v Reed (1871) 12 Cox C.C. 1 .... 15.45
R. v Reed (David); R. v Reed (Terence); R. v Garmson (Neil) [2009]
EWCA Crim 2698; [2010] 1 Cr. App. R. 23; [2010] Crim. L.R.
716 .... 25.02, 25.07, 25.23, 25.25, 25.32, 25.34, 25.51, 25.52, 25.53
R. v Rees (Gareth) [2014] EWCA Crim 2363 .... 4.203
R. v Rehman (Zakir); R. v Wood (Gary Dominic) [2005] EWCA Crim
2056; [2006] 1 Cr. App. R. (S.) 77; [2005] Crim. L.R. 878 .... 32.19
R. v Renda (Raymond); R. v Ball (Nathan); R. v Akram (Adil); R. v
Osbourne (Lee); R. v Razaq (Ajaz); R. v Razaq (Abdul) [2005]
EWCA Crim 2826; [2006] 1 W.L.R. 2948; [2006] 2 All E.R. 553;
[2006] 1 Cr. App. R. 24; [2006] Crim. L.R. 534 .... 20.18, 20.87, 20.87,
20.91
R. v Rhule (James) [2010] EWCA Crim 2177 ....30.142

R. v Riat (Jaspal); R. v Doran (James); R. v Wilson (Martin Paul); R.
v Clare (William Henry); R. v Bennett (John) [2012] EWCA Crim
1509; [2013] 1 W.L.R. 2592; [2013] 1 All E.R. 349; [2013] 1 Cr.
App. R. 2; [2013] Crim. L.R. 60 .... 7.221, 19.28, 19.37, 19.38, 19.40.
19.41, 19.42, 19.47, 19.49, 19.61
R. v Riby (No.94/4933/Y5), unreported 6 February 1995 CA 27.87
R. v Richard W [2003] EWCA Crim 3490 .... 24.44, 24.45, 24.46
R. v Richards (Christopher Andrew) [2006] EWCA Crim 2519; [2007]
1 W.L.R. 847; [2007] 1 Cr. App. R. (S.) 120; [2007] Crim. L.R.
173 .... 32.36
R. v Richards (Randall) (1999) 163 J.P. 246; [1999] Crim. L.R. 764 CA
(Crim Div) 27.66
R. v Richardson (Diane) [1999] Q.B. 444; [1998] 3 W.L.R. 1292; [1998]
2 Cr. App. R. 200; (1998) 43 B.M.L.R. 21; [1999] Crim. L.R. 62;
(1998) 95(17) L.S.G. 30; (1998) 142 S.J.L.B. 131 CA (Crim
Div) 1.321, 1.332
R. v Riley (1887) 18 Q.B.D. 481 CCR 19.91, 26.08
R. v Riley (Dennis) [2006] EWCA Crim 2030 ....20.144
R. v Rimmington; R. v Goldstein (Harry Chaim) [2005] UKHL 63;
[2006] 1 A.C. 459; [2005] 3 W.L.R. 982; [2006] 2 All E.R. 257;
[2006] 1 Cr. App. R. 17; [2006] H.R.L.R. 3; [2006] U.K.H.R.R. 1;
[2006] Crim. L.R. 153; (2005) 102(43) L.S.G. 28; (2005) 155 N.L.J.
1685 .... 15.03, 15.04, 15.27
R. v Robb, 176 E.R. 466; (1864) 4 F. & F. 59 Assizes 9.35
R. v Robbins [1988] Crim. L.R. 744 CA (Crim Div) 7.85
R. v Roberts (William) (1987) 84 Cr. App. R. 117; [1986] Crim. L.R.
188 CA (Crim Div) 1.166
R. v Robertshaw [2013] EWCA Crim 635 .... 1.131
R. v Robinson (Dennis) [2005] EWCA Crim 3233; [2006] 1 Cr. App. R.
32; [2006] Crim. L.R. 431 .... 20.81
R. v Robinson (Raymond) [1994] 3 All E.R. 346; (1994) 98 Cr. App. R.
370; [1994] Crim. L.R. 356; (1993) 143 N.L.J. 1643 CA (Crim
Div) 19.103
R. v Robinson (Sean) [2011] EWCA Crim 916 .... 11.07,.193, 1.194, 1.200,
33.17
R. v Robson (Kevin) [2006] EWCA Crim 1414; [2007] 1 All E.R. 506;
[2007] 1 Cr. App. R. (S.) 54; (2006) 170 J.P. 637; [2006] Crim. L.R.
935; (2007) 171 J.P.N. 123 ....31.115
R. v Robson (Thomas Anthony); R. v Robson (George); R. v Wilson
(Robert) [2006] EWCA Crim 2754; [2007] Crim. L.R. 478; (2007)
151 S.J.L.B. 60 .... 30.27, 30.49, 30.83
R. v Robson [2012] EWCA Crim 2753 .... 30.27
R. v Rogers (Isaac) (1914) 10 Cr. App. R. 276 CA 3.74
R. v Rogier (1823) 2 Dow. & Ry 431 .... 12.92
R. v Rolfe (Kenneth) (1952) 36 Cr. App. R. 4 CA 2.04, 2.64

R. v Romeo (Cornelius Donovan) [2003] EWCA Crim 2844; [2004] 1
  Cr. App. R. 30; [2004] Crim. L.R. 302 ....19.119
R. v Rooney. *See* R. v R (Peter) (Abuse of Process)
R. v Rosato (Carlo) [2008] EWCA Crim 1243 .... 20.81
R. v Rossi (Alexander) [2009] EWCA Crim 2406 .... 20.18
R. v Round (Terence); R. v Dunn (Vincent David) [2009] EWCA Crim
  2667; [2010] 2 Cr. App. R. (S.) 45; [2010] Crim. L.R. 329 ....30.142
R. v Rouverard (1830) 15.52
R. v Rowe [2008] EWCA Crim 2712 .... 8.72, 8.137
R. v Rowed, 114 E.R. 476; (1842) 3 Q.B. 180 QB 15.26
R. v Rowell (Michael Charles) [1978] 1 W.L.R. 132; [1978] 1 All E.R.
  665; (1977) 65 Cr. App. R. 174; [1977] Crim. L.R. 681; (1977) 121
  S.J. 790 CA (Crim Div) 17.58
R. v Rowley (Michael) [1991] 1 W.L.R. 1020; [1991] 4 All E.R. 649;
  (1992) 94 Cr. App. R. 95; (1992) 156 J.P. 319; [1991] Crim. L.R.
  785; (1991) 155 J.P.N. 672; (1991) 135 S.J.L.B. 84 CA (Crim
  Div) 3.159, 15.41
R. v RT; R. v MH. *See* R. v T (Complainant's Sexual History)
R. v Rudge (John) (1924) 17 Cr. App. R. 113 CCA 19.106
R. v Ryan (1846) 2 Cox C.C. 115; 8 L.T.O.S. 5 .... 1.226
R. v Ryder (David Robert) [1994] 2 All E.R. 859; (1994) 98 Cr. App.
  R. 242; (1993) 157 J.P. 1095; [1993] Crim. L.R. 601; (1993) 157
  J.P.N. 557 CA (Crim Div) 30.108
R. v S (Andrew Benjamin) (A Juvenile) [2001] 1 Cr. App. R. (S.) 18;
  (2000) 164 J.P. 681; [2000] Crim. L.R. 613 CA (Crim Div) 31.77
R. v S (Andrew) [2006] EWCA Crim 1303; [2007] 1 W.L.R. 63; [2006]
  2 Cr. App. R. 31 ....20.145
R. v S (Jonathan Charles); R. v W (Malcolm) [2006] EWCA Crim
  1404; [2007] 2 All E.R. 974 .... 24.32, 24.37, 24.39, 24.40, 24.41
R. v S (Paul Martin) [2012] EWCA Crim 2668 ....30.113
R. v S (Stephen Paul) [2006] EWCA Crim 756; [2006] 2 Cr. App. R. 23;
  (2006) 170 J.P. 434; [2007] Crim. L.R. 296; (2006) 170 J.P.N.
  760 .... 20.30, 30.28, 30.37, 30.38
R. v S [1992] Crim. L.R. 307 CA (Crim Div) 19.98, 26.152
R. v S [1992] Crim. L.R. 309 .... 19.94, 19.101
R. v S [2003]. *See* R. v Singh (Gulab)
R. v S [2007] EWCA Crim 2105; (2007) 151 S.J.L.B. 1260 .... 20.12
R. v S [2007] EWCA Crim 335; [2008] 2 Cr. App. R. 26 .... 20.09
R. v S [2008] EWCA Crim 2177; [2009] 1 W.L.R. 1489; [2009] 1 All
  E.R. 716; [2009] 1 Cr. App. R. 18; [2009] Crim. L.R. 191; (2008)
  158 N.L.J. 1459 .... 8.117
R. v S [2008] EWCA Crim 544 ....20.118
R. v S [2008] EWCA Crim 600; [2008] 2 Cr. App. R. (S.) 91 .... 4.205
R. v S [2009] EWCA Crim 2457 .... 20.141, 20.143, 20.151
R. v S [2010] EWCA Crim 1462 ....30.166

R. v S [2010] EWCA Crim 1579; [2011] Crim. L.R. 671 ..... 26.114, 26.116
R. v S [2011] EWCA Crim 1238; [2012] 1 Cr. App. R. (S.) 14 .... 3.62
R. v S [2012] EWCA Crim 1433; (2012) 127 B.M.L.R. 164 .... 22.46
R. v S; R. v Burt (Scott-Rab John); R. v Parsons (John David); R. v
    Carr (Craig Edward); R. v Hargreaves (Stephen Lee); R. v
    Denton (Vincent); R. v Taylor (Timothy Nicholas); R. v Coyne
    (Timothy Malcolm); R. v H [2005] EWCA Crim 3616; [2006] 2 Cr.
    App. R. (S.) 35; (2006) 170 J.P. 145; [2006] Crim. L.R. 459; (2006)
    170 J.P.N. 234 .... 34.40
R. v S; R. v C [2015] NICA 51 .... 32.74
R. v S; sub nom. R. v CS [2012] EWCA Crim 389; [2012] 1 W.L.R.
    3081; [2012] 1 Cr. App. R. 31; [2012] Crim. L.R. 623 .... 9.30
R. v S(C). See R. v S; sub nom. R. v CS
R. v Sadiq (Sajid Ali); R. v Hussain (Noweed) [2009] EWCA Crim
    712; (2009) 173 J.P. 471 .... 19.71
R. v Sadique (Omar) [2013] EWCA Crim 1150; [2014] 1 W.L.R. 986;
    [2013] 4 All E.R. 924; [2013] 2 Cr. App. R. 31; [2014] Crim. L.R.
    61 .... 1.416
R. v Sadique (Omar); R. v Hussain (Zakir) [2011] EWCA Crim 2872;
    [2012] 1 W.L.R. 1700; [2012] 2 All E.R. 793; [2012] 1 Cr. App. R.
    19; [2012] Crim. L.R. 449 .... 1.416
R. v Saint (Robert) [2010] EWCA Crim 1924 .... 20.26
R. v Salkeld (Michael) [2015] EWCA Crim 163 .... 3.122
R. v Salt (Daryl); R. v Salt (Thomas) [2015] EWCA Crim 662; [2015]
    1 W.L.R. 4905; [2015] 2 Cr. App. R. 27; [2015] Crim. L.R. 814 ..... 17.40,
                                                            18.100, 18.103
R. v Sampson (Albert); R. v Kelly (Mason) [2014] EWCA Crim
    1968 .... 25.45
R. v Sand H. See R. v Sadique (Omar)
R. v Sardar (Aamir) [2012] EWCA Crim 134; [2012] Crim. L.R.
    618 ....27.102
R. v Sarouji (Mohamad Modar) [2014] EWCA Crim 2670 .... 2.56
R. v Saunders (Red); R. v Edwards (Ian Peter); R. v G [2013] EWCA
    Crim 1027; [2014] 1 Cr. App. R. (S.) 45; [2013] Crim. L.R. 930 .... 1.50,
                        1.92, 1.96, 1.97, 1.106, 3.69, 30.162, 34.07, 34.08, 34.09
R. v Saunders [2013] Crim. L.R. 935 ....30.161
R. v Savage (Susan); R. v Parmenter (Philip Mark) (No.1); sub nom.
    DPP v Parmenter (Philip Mark) [1992] 1 A.C. 699; [1991] 3
    W.L.R. 914; [1991] 4 All E.R. 698; (1992) 94 Cr. App. R. 193;
    (1991) 155 J.P. 935; [1992] Crim. L.R. 288; (1991) 155 J.P.N. 770;
    (1991) 141 N.L.J. 1553 HL 2.126, 2.127
R. v Scarrott (Ernest Theodore) [1978] Q.B. 1016; [1977] 3 W.L.R. 629;
    [1978] 1 All E.R. 672; (1977) 65 Cr. App. R. 125; [1977] Crim.
    L.R. 745; (1977) 121 S.J. 558 CA (Crim Div) 19.14, 19.15

R. v Schaub (Mark Tony); sub nom. R. v Cooper (Joey) [1994] Crim.
L.R. 531; (1994) 91(5) L.S.G. 35; (1994) 138 S.J.L.B. 11 CA (Crim
Div) 1.159, 27.59

R. v Scott. *See* R. v S

R. v Seaboyer (1991) 83 D.L.R. (4th) 193; [1991] 2 S.C.R. 577 Sup Ct
(Can) 26.04, 26.56, 26.170, 26.172, 26.173, 26.174, 26.184, 26.140,
26.183

R. v Sed (Ali Dahir) [2004] EWCA Crim 1294; [2004] 1 W.L.R. 3218;
[2005] 1 Cr. App. R. 4; (2004) 148 S.J.L.B. 756 .... 1.236, 7.38, 19.51,
19.66, 19.68, 24.49, 27.146

R. v Sedley, 17 St. Tr. 155n 15.26

R. v Selvey (Wilfred George) (No.1); sub nom. Selvey v DPP (No.1)
[1970] A.C. 304; [1968] 2 W.L.R. 1494; [1968] 2 All E.R. 497;
(1968) 52 Cr. App. R. 443; (1968) 132 J.P. 430; (1968) 112 S.J. 461
HL 20.90

R. v SG [2010] NICA 32 .... 32.50

R. v Shabir (Mohammed Haness) [2012] EWCA Crim 2564; (2013)
177 J.P. 271 .... 19.48, 19.49

R. v Shaffi (Zulfiqar) [2006] EWCA Crim 418; [2006] 2 Cr. App. R. (S.)
92; [2006] Crim. L.R. 6658 34.30

R. v Shannon [2008] NICA 38 .... 36.25

R. v Sharman (Peter Edward) [1998] 1 Cr. App. R. 406; (1998) 162 J.P.
110; [1998] 1 F.L.R. 785; [1998] Fam. Law 315; (1998) 162 J.P.N.
187 CA (Crim Div) 32.65

R. v Sheehan (Michael); R. v Moore (George Alan) [1975] 1 W.L.R.
739; [1975] 2 All E.R. 960; (1974) 60 Cr. App. R. 308; [1975] Crim.
L.R. 339; (1975) 119 S.J. 271 CA (Crim Div) ... 2.78, 14.34, 14.49, 14.73

R. v Shehu [2011] All E.R. (D) 79 (Aug) CA (Crim Div) 1.251

R. v Sheikh (Anver Daud) [2006] EWCA Crim 2625 .... 30.29, 30.53

R. v Sheppard (James Martin); R. v Sheppard (Jennifer Christine)
[1981] A.C. 394; [1980] 3 W.L.R. 960; [1980] 3 All E.R. 899; (1981)
72 Cr. App. R. 82; [1981] Crim. L.R. 171; (1980) 124 S.J. 864
HL 12.64

R. v Sheppard (Simon Guy); R. v Whittle (Stephen) [2010] EWCA
Crim 65; [2010] 1 W.L.R. 2779; [2010] 2 All E.R. 850; [2010] 1 Cr.
App. R. 26; [2010] 2 Cr. App. R. (S.) 68; [2010] Crim. L.R. 720 ..... 8.65

R. v Sherif (Abdul); R. v Fardosa (Abdullahi); R. v Abdurahman
(Ismail); R. v Mohamed (Wahbi); R. v Ali (Muhedin); R. v Ali
(Siraj) [2008] EWCA Crim 2653; [2009] 2 Cr. App. R. (S.) 33 ..... 9.61,
12.63

R. v Shiekh (Sabir) [2013] EWCA Crim 907 .... 20.29

R. v Shillingford (Holly); R. v Vanderwall (Rayonne Niel) [1968] 1
W.L.R. 566; [1968] 2 All E.R. 200; (1968) 52 Cr. App. R. 188;
(1968) 132 J.P. 264; (1968) 112 S.J. 170 CA (Crim Div) 14.36

R. v Shivpuri (Pyare) [1987] A.C. 1; [1986] 2 W.L.R. 988; [1986] 2 All
  E.R. 334; (1986) 83 Cr. App. R. 178; (1986) 150 J.P. 353; [1986]
  Crim. L.R. 536; (1986) 150 J.P.N. 510; (1986) 83 L.S.G. 1896;
  (1986) 136 N.L.J. 488; (1986) 130 S.J. 39 HL 3.162, 4.190, 10.142
R. v Sidley (1663) 1 Sid. 168; 82 E.R. 1036 KB 15.26
R. v Simmonds (Phillip Anthony) [2015] EWCA Crim 1068; [2015] 2
  Cr. App. R. (S.) 60 .... 36.63
R. v Simpson (Jodie) [2013] EWCA Crim 1250 .... 34.57
R. v Simpson (Michael) [2014] NICA 83 .... 32.55
R. v Sinclair (1867) 13 Cox C.C. 28 .... 1.334
R. v Singh (Amar Jit); R. v Meeuwsen (Johannes Hendrikus) [1972] 1
  W.L.R. 1600; [1973] 1 All E.R. 122; (1973) 57 Cr. App. R. 180;
  [1973] Crim. L.R. 49; (1972) 116 S.J. 863 CA (Crim Div) 11.99
R. v Singh (Bukhtor) [2012] EWCA Crim 1274; [2013] 1 Cr. App. R.
  (S.) 44 .... 2.19, 2.22
R. v Singh (Gulab) [2003] EWCA Crim 485 ..... 26.42, 26.125, 26.142, 26.167
R. v Skinner (Philip) [2005] EWCA Crim 1439; [2006] Crim. L.R.
  56 .... 8.107
R. v Slingsby [1995] Crim L.R. 570 Crown Ct (Nottingham) 2.128, 2.129
R. v Sloan [2008] NICA 46 .... 32.50
R. v Slocombe (Nicholas) [2005] EWCA Crim 2997; [2006] 1 W.L.R.
  328; [2006] 1 All E.R. 670; [2006] 1 Cr. App. R. 33 .... 31.129, 35.22
R. v Smethurst (John Russell) [2001] EWCA Crim 772; [2002] 1 Cr.
  App. R. 6; (2001) 165 J.P. 377; [2001] Crim. L.R. 657; (2001) 165
  J.P.N. 408 .... 8.44, 8.80, 8.91
R. v Smith (2000). See R. v S (Andrew Benjamin) (A Juvenile)
R. v Smith (Andrew) [2014] EWCA Crim 2383 .... 8.34
R. v Smith (Christopher Robert) [2009] EWCA Crim 785; [2009] 2 Cr.
  App. R. (S.) 110; [2009] Crim. L.R. 600 .... 36.35
R. v Smith (Gavin) [2015] EWCA Crim 398 .... 8.74
R. v Smith (Graham Westgarth); R. v Jayson (Mike) [2002] EWCA
  Crim 683; [2003] 1 Cr. App. R. 13; [2002] Crim. L.R. 659 ...... 8.61, 8.90,
                                                                                8.91, 8.92, 8.140
R. v Smith (Mark Anthony) [2015] EWCA Crim 722 .... 3.42
R. v Smith (Paul) [2015] EWCA Crim 1627 ....30.165
R. v Smith (Steven); R. v Clarke (Wayne); R. v Hall (Bryan); R. v
  Dodd (Jonathan) [2011] EWCA Crim 1772; [2012] 1 W.L.R. 1316;
  [2012] 1 All E.R. 451; [2012] 1 Cr. App. R. (S.) 82; [2011] Crim.
  L.R. 967 ..... 36.17, 36.23, 36.29, 36.30, 36.32, 36.33, 36.34, 36.36, 36.38,
                    36.39, 36.40, 36.48, 36.49, 36.51, 36.55, 36.56, 36.58, 36.59,
                                                                                                36.63
R. v Smith (Wallace Duncan) (No.4) [2004] EWCA Crim 631; [2004]
  Q.B. 1418; [2004] 3 W.L.R. 229; [2004] 2 Cr. App. R. 17 ..... 4.238, 5.128,
                                                                                8.65, 10.80, 10.98
R. v Smith [1994] Crim. L.R. 458 .... 27.59

R. v Smith [2005]. *See* R. v Edwards (Stewart Dean)

R. v Smith [2006] All E.R. (D.) 280 (Feb) 20.48

R. v Smith [2012] EWCA Crim 1772 .... 32.55

R. v Smolinski (Mark Paul); sub nom. R. v Smolenski (Mark Paul)
[2004] EWCA Crim 1270; [2004] 2 Cr. App. R. 40 .... 30.32, 30.38

R. v SMS [1992] Crim. L.R. 310 .... 26.20, 26.125

R. v Somanathan. *See* R. v Weir (Antony Albert)

R. v Somers (Patrick) [1963] 1 W.L.R. 1306; [1963] 3 All E.R. 808;
(1964) 48 Cr. App. R. 11; (1964) 128 J.P. 20; 61 L.G.R. 598; (1963)
107 S.J. 813 CA 24.02, 25.36

R. v Soneji (Kamlesh Kumar); R. v Bullen (David Frederick); sub
nom. R. v Soneiji (Kamalesh Kumar) [2005] UKHL 49; [2006] 1
A.C. 340; [2005] 3 W.L.R. 303; [2005] 4 All E.R. 321; [2006] 2 Cr.
App. R. 20; [2006] 1 Cr. App. R. (S.) 79; [2006] Crim. L.R. 167;
(2005) 102(31) L.S.G. 26; (2005) 155 N.L.J. 1315; (2005) 149
S.J.L.B. 924 .... 8.10

R. v Soroya (Naveed) [2006] EWCA Crim 1884; [2007] Crim. L.R. 181;
(2006) 150 S.J.L.B. 1054 .... 26.49

R. v Souter (Raymond John) [1971] 1 W.L.R. 1187; [1971] 2 All E.R.
1151; (1971) 55 Cr. App. R. 403; (1971) 115 S.J. 548 CA (Crim
Div) 8.94

R. v South Shields Licensing Justices [1911] 2 K.B. 1 KBD 13.26

R. v Southwark Crown Court Ex p. Godwin; R. v Southwark Crown
Court Ex p. Daily Telegraph; R. v Southwark Crown Court Ex p.
MGN Ltd; R. v Southwark Crown Court Ex p. Associated
Newspapers; R. v Southwark Crown Court Ex p. Newspaper
Publishing; sub nom. Godwin, Re [1992] Q.B. 190; [1991] 3
W.L.R. 689; [1991] 3 All E.R. 818; (1992) 94 Cr. App. R. 34;
(1992) 156 J.P. 86; [1991] Crim. L.R. 302; (1991) 155 J.P.N. 834;
(1991) 141 N.L.J. 963; (1991) 135 S.J.L.B. 28 CA (Crim Div) 29.89

R. v Speck (Harry) [1977] 2 All E.R. 859; (1977) 65 Cr. App. R. 161;
[1977] Crim. L.R. 689; (1977) 121 S.J. 221 CA (Civ Div) 4.60

R. v Spencer (Alan Widdison); R. v Smails (George Glenville); R. v
Ball (Kenneth); R. v Mason (Michael Dennis); R. v White (Paul)
[1987] A.C. 128; [1986] 3 W.L.R. 348; [1986] 2 All E.R. 928; (1986)
83 Cr. App. R. 277; (1986) 130 S.J. 572 HL 19.106

R. v Spratt (Robert Michael) [1990] 1 W.L.R. 1073; [1991] 2 All E.R.
210; (1990) 91 Cr. App. R. 362; (1990) 154 J.P. 884; [1990] Crim.
L.R. 797; (1990) 154 J.P.N. 561; (1990) 134 S.J. 869 CA (Div
Crim) 2.127

R. v Springer [1996] Crim. L.R. 903 .... 27.96

R. v Squirrel (No.97/3618/Z4) unreported 22 January 1998 .... 19.86

R. v SR [2011] NICA 49 .... 32.71

R. v Stafford Crown Court Ex p. BBC Litigation Dept [2002] EWCA
Crim 962 .... 29.84

R. v Stanley (Alan Basil) [1965] 2 Q.B. 327; [1965] 2 W.L.R. 917; [1965]
    1 All E.R. 1035; (1965) 49 Cr. App. R. 175; (1965) 129 J.P. 279;
    (1965) 109 S.J. 193 CA 15.38, 15.42, 15.44
R. v Stannard (1863) 9 Cox C.C. 405 .... 12.88
R. v Stannard (Raymond) [2008] EWCA Crim 2789; [2009] 2 Cr. App.
    R. (S.) 21; [2009] Crim. L.R. 217 .... 34.29, 34.54
R. v Steed (Gareth) (1990–91) 12 Cr. App. R. (S.) 230; [1990] Crim.
    L.R. 816 CA (Crim Div) 11.30
R. v Steele (Peter Edward) (1977) 65 Cr. App. R. 22; [1977] Crim. L.R.
    290 CA (Crim Div) 1.166
R. v Steen (George) [2014] EWCA Crim 1390 .... 8.45, 8.91
R. v Steidl and Baxendale-Walker unreported 27 June 2002 CC
    (Southwark) 30.51
R. v Stephenson (David); sub nom. R. v Stevenson (David) [2006]
    EWCA Crim 2325; (2006) 103(36) L.S.G. 34; (2006) 150 S.J.L.B.
    1151 .... 20.144, 26.159
R. v Stephenson (Joseph) [1912] 3 K.B. 341; (1913) 8 Cr. App. R. 36
    CA 3.74
R. v Stewart (John) (1986) 83 Cr. App. R. 327; [1986] Crim. L.R. 805
    CA (Crim Div) 10.152, 10.153, 10.161
R. v Stewart, Times, 21 May 2012 CA (Crim Div) 30.17
R. v Stocker (Keith Anthony) [2013] EWCA Crim 1993; [2014] 1 Cr.
    App. R. 18; [2014] Crim. L.R. 319 .... 1.34
R. v Stocker unreported 23 November 2004 CCC 30.51
R. v Stratton (Geoffrey Lawrence) [2007] EWCA Crim 2984 .... 20.06
R. v Strotten (Rupert Brian) [2015] EWCA Crim 1101 .... 19.57
R. v Suchy (Tibor); R. v Sana (Rene) [2014] EWCA Crim 1245 .... 11.54
R. v Suchy; R. v, Sana; R. v Sanova; R. v Ziga; R. v Ziga; R. v Boros,
    June 2015 CCC 11.110, 11.124
R. v Suleman (Omar Mohammed) [2012] EWCA Crim 1569; [2012] 2
    Cr. App. R. 30; [2014] Crim. L.R. 66 ....20.132
R. v Sullivan [2015] EWCA Crim 1565; 179 J.P. 552 .... 20.15
R. v Sully (George Raymond) [2007] EWCA Crim 3512; (2007) 151
    S.J.L.B. 1564 .... 20.53
R. v Sutton (Richard Keith) [2005] EWCA Crim 190 .... 30.80
R. v SW [2004] EWCA Crim 2979 .... 24.96
R. v SW [2011]. See R. v W [2011]
R. v Sweet-Escott (Robin Patrick) (1971) 55 Cr. App. R. 316 Assizes
    (Derby) 19.93, 20.141
R. v Swyer [2007] EWCA Crim 204 ....15.117
R. v Symmons (Derek) [2009] EWCA Crim 1304; [2010] 1 Cr. App. R.
    (S.) 68; (2009) 153(27) S.J.L.B. 28 .... 1.73, 30.123, 30.124
R. v Szczerba (Ian Michael) [2002] EWCA Crim 440; [2002] 2 Cr. App.
    R. (S.) 86; [2002] Crim. L.R. 429 .... 34.40
R. v T (Abdul) [2004] EWCA Crim 1220; [2004] 2 Cr. App. R. 32 .... 26.85

R. v T (Child Pornography); sub nom. R. v ET (Child Pornography)
(1999) 163 J.P. 349; [1999] Crim. L.R. 749; (1999) 163 J.P.N. 619
CA 8.67, 8.73
R. v T (Complainant's Sexual History); R. v H (Complainant's Sexual
History); sub nom. R. v MH R. v RT [2001] EWCA Crim 1877;
[2002] 1 W.L.R. 632; [2002] 1 All E.R. 683; [2002] 1 Cr. App. R.
22; [2002] Crim. L.R. 73 .... 20.152, 26.72, 26.74, 26.135, 26.142, 26.153,
26.154, 26.157
R. v T [2008] EWCA Crim 484; [2008] All E.R. (D.) 122 (May) 19.84,
19.89, 19.90
R. v T [2011] EWCA Crim 729 .... 8.118, 8.140
R. v T; sub nom. R. v JTB; R. v B [2009] UKHL 20; [2009] 1 A.C.
1310; [2009] 2 W.L.R. 1088; [2009] 3 All E.R. 1; [2009] 2 Cr. App.
R. 13; (2009) 173 J.P. 289; [2009] Crim. L.R. 581; (2009) 159
N.L.J. 672; (2009) 153(18) S.J.L.B. 27 .... 1.151
R. v Tabassum (Naveed); sub nom. R. v Tabassum (Navid) [2000] 2 Cr.
App. R. 328; [2000] Lloyd's Rep. Med. 404; [2000] Crim. L.R. 686;
(2000) 97(22) L.S.G. 43 CA (Crim Div) 1.321
R. v Tambedou (Seedy) [2014] EWCA Crim 954 .... 1.262
R. v Tan (Moira); R. v Greaves (Brian Edwin); R. v Greaves (Gloria
Gina) [1983] Q.B. 1053; [1983] 3 W.L.R. 361; [1983] 2 All E.R. 12;
(1983) 76 Cr. App. R. 300; (1983) 147 J.P. 257; [1983] Crim. L.R.
404; (1983) 127 S.J. 390 CA (Crim Div) 12.85, 12.93, 12.94
R. v Tao (Ben Nien) [1977] Q.B. 141; [1976] 3 W.L.R. 25; [1976] 3 All
E.R. 65; (1976) 63 Cr. App. R. 163; [1976] Crim. L.R. 516; (1976)
120 S.J. 420 CA (crim Div) 12.68, 12.69
R. v Taran (Farid) [2006] EWCA Crim 1498 .... 1.403
R. v Taylor (Alan Edward) [2015] EWCA Crim 322 .... 7.219
R. v Taylor (Alan) [1995] 1 Cr. App. R. 131; (1994) 158 J.P. 317; [1994]
Crim. L.R. 527; (1994) 158 J.P.N. 354; (1994) 138 S.J.L.B. 54 CA
(Crim Div) 8.64
R. v Taylor (Gary David) [2012] EWCA Crim 1326; [2013] 1 Cr. App.
R. (S.) 55 .... 14.65
R. v Taylor (Gary) [1995] Crim. L.R. 253 CA (Crim Div) 27.58
R. v Taylor (Paul Barry) [2013] EWCA Crim 2398 .... 30.01, 30.76
R. v Taylor (Robert Peter) (1985) 80 Cr. App. R. 327 CA (Crim
Div) 1.287
R. v TB (No.99/1447/Y2), unreported 11 November 1999 .... 19.08
R. v Tegerdine (Colin) (1982) 75 Cr. App. R. 298; [1983] Crim. L.R.
163 CA (Crim Div) 9.29, 9.31
R. v Terrell (Alexander James) [2007] EWCA Crim 3079; [2008] 2 All
E.R. 1065; [2008] 2 Cr. App. R. (S.) 49; [2008] Crim. L.R. 320 .... 8.32,
8.33, 36.25
R. v TH [2015] NICA 48 .... 32.50

R. v Thallman (1863) 9 Cox C.C. 388 .... 15.59
R. v Thick [1907] Q.S.R. 198 Qd. S.C.F.C 12.84
R. v Thomas (Andrew Babatunde) [1957] 1 W.L.R. 747; [1957] 2 All
    E.R. 342 (Note); (1957) 41 Cr. App. R. 121; (1957) 121 J.P. 338;
    (1957) 101 S.J. 430 CCA 10.153
R. v Thomas (John) (1949) 33 Cr. App. R. 74; (1949) 93 S.J. 89 CA 1.146
R. v Thompson (Andrew) [2014] EWCA Crim 836 .... 24.50
R. v Thompson (Edward) [2009] EWCA Crim 3258 .... 36.35, 36.36
R. v Thompson (Richard) [2004] EWCA Crim 669; [2004] 2 Cr. App.
    R. 16; [2005] 1 Cr. App. R. (S.) 1; (2004) 148 S.J.L.B. 417 ...... 8.14, 8.124
R. v Tierney (Kevin) (1990–91) 12 Cr. App. R. (S.) 216 CA (Crim
    Div) 15.134
R. v Timmins (Mark) [2005] EWCA Crim 2909; [2006] 1 W.L.R. 756;
    [2006] 1 Cr. App. R. 18 .... 4.03, 30.157
R. v Tirnaveanu (Cornel) [2007] EWCA Crim 1239; [2007] 1 W.L.R.
    3049; [2007] 4 All E.R. 301; [2007] 2 Cr. App. R. 23; (2007) 171
    J.P. 621; [2007] Crim. L.R. 969; (2008) 172 J.P.N. 134 .... 20.15
R. v TM; R. v PAM; R. v B; sub nom. R. v M (Admissibility:
    Background Evidence) [2000] 1 W.L.R. 421; [2000] 1 All E.R. 148;
    [2000] 2 Cr. App. R. 266; [1999] Crim. L.R. 982 .... 20.30
R. v Tobierre (Joseph Wayne) [1986]1 W.L.R. 125; [1986] 1 All E.R.
    346; (1986) 82 Cr. App. R. 212; [1986] Crim. L.R. 243; (1986) 83
    L.S.G. 116; (1986) 130 S.J. 35 CA (Crim Div) 14.33
R. v Tobin (Steven David) [2003] EWCA Crim 190; [2003] Crim. L.R.
    408 .... 19.103, 19.105, 26.125
R. v Tovey (David); R. v Smith (Peter John) [2005] EWCA Crim 530;
    [2005] 2 Cr. App. R. (S.) 100; [2005] Crim. L.R. 575 ..... 3.26, 4.43, 33.24
R. v TS [2008] EWCA Crim 6; [2008] All E.R. (D) 139 (Jan) 1.391, 24.50
R. v Tully (Stephen); R. v Wood (Kevin) [2006] EWCA Crim 2270;
    (2007) 171 J.P. 25; (2007) 171 J.P.N. 306 .... 20.45
R. v Turbill (Maxine); R. v Broadway (Gail Julie) [2013] EWCA Crim
    1422; [2014] 1 Cr. App. R. 7; (2013) 134 B.M.L.R. 13; [2014]
    M.H.L.R. 177; [2014] Crim. L.R. 388 .... 12.64
R. v Turnbull (Julian) [2010] EWCA Crim 3149 .... 36.34, 36.40
R. v Turner (James) [1944] K.B. 463; [1944] 1 All E.R. 599; (1945) 30
    Cr. App. R. 9 CA 19.91, 20.90, 20.91
R. v Turner (Martin Lance) [2013] EWCA Crim 1869 .... 36.40
R. v Turner (Michael John) [2000] Crim. L.R. 832 CA (Crim Div) 30.61,
    30.62, 30.78
R. v Turner (Terence Stuart) [1975] Q.B. 834; [1975] 2 W.L.R. 56;
    [1975] 1 All E.R. 70; (1974) 60 Cr. App. R. 80; [1975] Crim. L.R.
    98; (1974) 118 S.J. 848 CA (Crim Div) 1.370, 24.04, 24.07, 24.20,
    24.24
R. v Tutt (Tony) [2015] EWCA Crim 391 .... 4.40, 4.48

R. v Twist (Andrew Terence); R. v Boothman (Richard); R. v Tomlinson (Rhys); R. v Kelly (Lewis Bradley); R. v L [2011] EWCA Crim 1143; [2011] 3 All E.R. 1055; [2011] 2 Cr. App. R. 17; (2011) 175 J.P. 257; [2011] Crim. L.R. 793 .... 19.29, 19.30, 19.31

R. v Tyndale [1999] Crim. L.R. 320 .... 19.88

R. v Tyne Tees Television Ltd [1997] EWCA Crim 2395; *Times*, 20 October 1997 .... 29.71

R. v Tyrrell [1894] 1 Q.B. 710 CCR 1.418, 2.119, 4.57, 4.58, 5.26, 5.27, 6.41, 6.42, 9.26, 10.152

R. v Ubolcharoen (Phanida) [2009] EWCA Crim 3263 .... 10.63, 10.136

R. v Ukpabio (Roland Thompson) [2007] EWCA Crim 2108; [2008] 1 W.L.R. 728; [2008] 1 Cr. App. R. 6; (2007) 171 J.P. 692; (2008) 172 J.P.N. 188 .... 27.30

R. v Ul-Haq (Miftah Fazal) [2010] EWCA Crim 1683 ....20.145

R. v Utting (John Benjamin) [1987] 1 W.L.R. 1375; (1988) 86 Cr. App. R. 164; [1987] Crim. L.R. 636; (1987) 84 L.S.G. 2529; (1987) 131 S.J. 1154 CA (Crim Div) 14.33

R. v Uxbridge Youth Court Ex p. H (1998) 162 J.P. 327 DC 31.71

R. v V (Bernard) [2003] EWCA Crim 3917 .... 24.03, 24.45, 24.46

R. v V [2006] EWCA Crim 1901 ...... 20.152, 26.33, 26.146, 26.160, 26.166

R. v Vaiculevicius (Andrius) [2013] EWCA Crim 185; [2013] 2 Cr. App. R. (S.) 55 .... 15.34

R. v Valentine (Anthony) [1996] 2 Cr. App. R. 213 CA (Crim Div) 19.74

R. v Valujevs (Juris); R. v Mezals (Ivars) [2014] EWCA Crim 2888; [2015] Q.B. 745; [2015] 3 W.L.R. 109 .... 11.53

R. v van Dao (Vinh); R. v Muoi Thi Nguyen; R. v Hoang Mai [2012] EWCA Crim 1717; [2013] Crim. L.R. 234 .... 11.26

R. v Velasquez (Campo Elkin) [1996] 1 Cr. App. R. 155 CA (Crim Div) 1.141

R. v Venna (Henson George) [1976] Q.B. 421; [1975] 3 W.L.R. 737; [1975] 3 All E.R. 788; (1975) 61 Cr. App. R. 310; [1975] Crim. L.R. 701; (1975) 119 S.J. 679 CA (Crim Div) 2.127

R. v Verdol [2015] EWCA Crim 502 .... 20.82

R. v Vine (Michelle Kelly) [2011] EWCA Crim 1860; [2012] 1 Cr. App. R. (S.) 78 .... 34.57

R. v Viola (Michael) [1982] 1 W.L.R. 1138; [1982] 3 All E.R. 73; (1982) 75 Cr. App. R. 125; [1982] Crim. L.R. 515; (1982) 126 S.J. 536 CA (Crim Div) 26.16, 26.20, 26.74

R. v W (Daniel) [2009] EWCA Crim 153 .... 1.90

R. v W (No.97/0806/Y3) unreported 25 March 1997 .... 19.99

R. v W (No.98/7675/W3) unreported 13 December 1999 ....19.102

R. v W (Robert) [2015] EWCA Crim 629 .... 1.128, 4.49

R. v W [2006]. *See* R. v Watson (Demaine Colin)

R. v W [2010] EWCA Crim 1926 .... 28.14, 28.18, 28.20, 31.90
R. v W [2011] EWCA Crim 1142 .... 27.92
R. v W [2011] EWCA Crim 2463; [2011] All E.R. (D.) 02 (Nov) 19.12,
                                                            19.14, 20.111, 20.131
R. v W [2013] NICA 6 .... 32.69, 32.70
R. v W [2015] All E.R. (D.) 46 (Feb) 20.23
R. v W and M. See R. v W [2010]
R. v W; R. v T [2005] EWCA Crim 2448 .... 4.117
R. v W(G) and W(E). See R. v Whittle (George Alfred)
R. v Waddon, unreported 8.69
R. v Wakeman (Timothy) [2011] EWCA Crim 1649; (2011) 175 J.P.
    353 .... 9.22, 9.32, 9.42, 9.45
R. v Walker (Haughton Alfonso) [1996] Crim. L.R. 742 CA (Crim
    Div) 19.113
R. v Walker (Simon John) [2006] EWCA Crim 1907 ..... 3.132, 3.169, 4.68,
                                4.162, 5.53, 10.37, 10.89, 10.112, 12.21, 13.25
R. v Walker (Steven) [1996] 1 Cr. App. R. 111; [1995] Crim. L.R. 826;
    (1995) 159 J.P.N. 406; (1995) 92(17) L.S.G. 47; (1995) 139 S.J.L.B.
    118 CA (Crim Div) 15.58, 15.59
R. v Wall (Barry) [2005] EWCA Crim 3251 .... 19.17
R. v Wallace (James Andrew) [2007] EWCA Crim 1760; [2008] 1
    W.L.R. 572; [2007] 2 Cr. App. R. 30; (2007) 171 J.P. 543; [2007]
    Crim. L.R. 976 .... 20.32, 20.117
R. v Wallwork (William Evans) (1958) 42 Cr. App. R. 153; (1958) 122
    J.P. 299 CA 19.74
R. v Wang (Cheong) [2005] UKHL 9; [2005] 1 W.L.R. 661; [2005] 1 All
    E.R. 782; [2005] 2 Cr. App. R. 8; (2005) 169 J.P. 224; [2005] Crim.
    L.R. 645; (2005) 169 J.P.N. 339; (2005) 102(10) L.S.G. 29 .... 1.280, 1.282
R. v Wannell (Robert Charles) (1923) 17 Cr. App. R. 53 CA 19.74
R. v Warbutton [2012] EWCA Crim 3146 .... 36.32, 36.57
R. v Warner unreported 5 June 2007 CC (Birmingham) 26.23, 26.24
R. v Warnick (Mark Andrew) [2013] EWCA Crim 2320 .... 19.61
R. v Warnock (Cyril) [2013] NICA 34 .... 32.60
R. v Warren (Adam Michael) [2015] EWCA Crim 434 .... 36.59
R. v Warren (Leslie Gordon) [2005] EWCA Crim 659 ....26.153
R. v Warren (Peter) [2007] EWCA Crim 2733 .... 4.205
R. v Waters (John James) (1963) 47 Cr. App. R. 149; [1963] Crim. L.R.
    437; (1963) 107 S.J. 275 CA 13.42
R. v Watford Magistrates Court Ex p. Lenman [1993] Crim. L.R. 388;
    [1992] C.O.D. 474 DC 27.58
R. v Watkins (Ian) [2014] EWCA Crim 1677; [2015] 1 Cr. App. R. (S.)
    6 .... 1.118, 1.119, 1.123, 3.69, 3.70, 34.50, 34.51
R. v Watson (1847) 2 Cox C.C. 376 .... 15.52, 15.58, 15.59

R. v Watson (Demaine Colin) [2006] EWCA Crim 2308 .... 20.16, 20.32

R. v Watson (NM) [2015] EWCA Crim 559; [2015] All E.R. (D) 87 (Apr) 1.221

R. v Watson unreported 17 October 2013 CA (Crim Div) 14.17, 14.24, 14.61

R. v Watts (James Michael) [2010] EWCA Crim 1824; [2011] Crim. L.R. 68 .... 7.38, 17.15, 27.10, 27.101

R. v Waya (Terry); sub nom. R. v Waya Solicitors [2012] UKSC 51; [2013] 1 A.C. 294; [2012] 3 W.L.R. 1188; [2013] 1 All E.R. 889; [2013] 2 Cr. App. R. (S.) 20; [2013] H.R.L.R. 5; [2013] Lloyd's Rep. F.C. 187; 35 B.H.R.C. 293; [2013] Crim. L.R. 256 .... 11.30

R. v WCA unreported November 2003 .... 1.150

R. v Weaver (1876) L.R. 2 C.C.R. 85 CCR 3.74

R. v Webb (1848) 2 Car. & K. 933; (1848) 3 Cox C.C. 183; 175 E.R. 391 QB 15.52

R. v Webb (Walter Henry); sub nom. Webb v Commissioner of Police of the Metropolis [1964] 1 Q.B. 357; [1963] 3 W.L.R. 638; [1963] 3 All E.R. 177; (1963) 47 Cr. App. R. 265; (1963) 127 J.P. 516; (1963) 107 S.J. 597 CCA 12.34, 13.47

R. v Webb, 169 E.R. 271; (1848) 1 Den. 338 CCR 15.52

R. v Weinstein (1916) 28 D.L.R. 327 Qc. Ct. of Sessions 9.35

R. v Weir (Antony Albert); R. v Somanathan (Ramanathan); R. v Yaxley-Lennon (Stephen); R. v Manister (Simon Charles); R. v Hong Qiang He [2005] EWCA Crim 2866; [2006] 1 W.L.R. 1885; [2006] 2 All E.R. 570; [2006] 1 Cr. App. R. 19; [2006] Crim. L.R. 433 .... 20.19, 20.20, 20.22, 20.31, 20.45, 20.84, 20.73, 20.142

R. v Wellard (1884) 14 Q.B.D. 63; 49 J.P. 296; 54 L.J.M.C. 14; 15 Cox C.C. 559; 33 W.R. 156; [1881–5] All E.R. Rep. 1018; 51 L.T. 604 CCR 13.41, 15.59

R. v Weller (Peter) [2010] EWCA Crim 1085 .... 25.36

R. v Wells (Marc Martin); R. v Kail (Tony Nicholas); R. v Hone (Susan); R. v Masud (Sarfraz) [2015] EWCA Crim 2; [2015] 1 W.L.R. 2797; [2015] 1 Cr. App. R. 27; [2015] Crim. L.R. 359 .... 2.43

R. v Welsh (Christopher Mark) [2015] EWCA Crim 1516; [2016] 4 W.L.R. 13; [2016] 1 Cr. App. R. 9; [2016] Crim. L.R. 43 ....30.160

R. v Welsh (Christopher); R. v MM [2015] EWCA Crim 906; [2016] 1 Cr. App. R. 8; [2015] Crim. L.R. 806 .... 8.13

R. v Welstead (Stephen Paul) [1996] 1 Cr. App. R. 59 CA (Crim Div) 27.96

R. v Wendell Wilberforce Baker [2014] EWCA Crim 242 .... 1.42, 1.133, 30.162

R. v White (Andre Barrington) [2004] EWCA Crim 946; (2004) 148 S.J.L.B. 300 .... 26.98, 26.145, 26.149, 26.181, 26.183

R. v White (Andrew Mark) [2015] EWCA Crim 98 .... 8.38

R. v White (Gavin) [2010] EWCA Crim 1929 ..... 1.09, 1.263, 1.264, 1.280,
            1.282, 1.299, 5.48, 5.49, 5.72, 5.73, 5.100, 5.101, 5.123, 5.124,
                                                                    6.48
R. v Whitehead (Job) [1929] 1 K.B. 99; (1930) 21 Cr. App. R. 23 CA 19.118
R. v Whitehouse (Arthur) [1977] Q.B. 868; [1977] 2 W.L.R. 925; [1977]
    3 All E.R. 737; (1977) 65 Cr. App. R. 33; [1977] Crim. L.R. 689;
    (1977) 121 S.J. 171 CA (Crim Div) 4.57, 5.26, 6.01, 6.41
R. v Whittaker (Steven Alan). See Attorney General's Reference
    (No.32 of 1996)
R. v Whittle (George Alfred); R. v Whittle (Elaine Ann); sub nom. R.
    v W (G); R. v W (E) [1997] 1 Cr. App. R. 166; [1996] Crim. L.R.
    904; (1996) 93(28) L.S.G. 29; (1996) 140 S.J.L.B. 168 CA (Crim
    Div) 18.83
R. v Whittle (Martin) [2007] EWCA Crim 539; [2007] 2 Cr. App. R.
    (S.) 88; [2007] Crim. L.R. 499; (2007) 151 S.J.L.B. 398 ....30.142
R. v Wilbourne (Ernest Wardman) (1917) 12 Cr. App. R. 280 CA 19.85
R. v Wilcox (Terry John) [2002] EWCA Crim 1430; [2003] 1 Cr. App.
    R. (S.) 43 .... 35.50
R. v Wilkinson (Thomas McBride) [2006] EWCA Crim 1332 .... 20.48
R. v Wilkinson [2011] NICA 29 .... 32.03
R. v Williams (Bruce Martin) [2009] EWCA Crim 1034 .... 36.25
R. v Williams (Edmond Selwyn) [2012] EWCA Crim 2516; [2012] All
    E.R. (D) 346 (Nov) 1.26, 1.29
R. v Williams (Gladstone) [1987] 3 All E.R. 411; (1984) 78 Cr. App. R.
    276; [1984] Crim. L.R. 163; (1984) 81 L.S.G. 278 CA (Crim
    Div) 2.127, 9.48
R. v Williams (No.99/4704/R1) unreported 22 October 1999 .... 2.27
R. v Williams (Owen Richard) [1923] 1 K.B. 340; (1924) 17 Cr. App.
    R. 56 CCA 1.318
R. v Williams [1974] Crim. L.R. 558 CA (Crim Div) 15.133
R. v Williams [2007] EWCA Crim 3030 .... 20.89
R. v Williamson (John Michael) [2005] EWCA Crim 2151 .... 36.25
R. v Wills (Alan Paul) [2011] EWCA Crim 1938; [2012] 1 Cr. App. R.
    2; [2012] Crim. L.R. 565 .... 28.06, 28.14, 28.26, 28.30, 28.39
R. v Wilson (Alan Thomas) [1997] Q.B. 47; [1996] 3 W.L.R. 125; [1996]
    2 Cr. App. R. 241; [1996] Crim. L.R. 573; (1996) 140 S.J.L.B. 93
    CA (Crim Div) 2.122, 2.123
R. v Wilson (Clarence George); R. v Jenkins (Ronald Patrick); R. v
    Jenkins (Edward John) [1984] A.C. 242; [1983] 3 W.L.R. 686;
    [1983] 3 All E.R. 448; (1983) 77 Cr. App. R. 319; [1984] Crim.
    L.R. 36; (1983) 133 N.L.J. 1016; (1983) 127 S.J. 712 HL 7.16
R. v Wilson (Daniel Rushton) [2007] EWCA Crim 2762; [2008] 1 Cr.
    App. R. (S.) 90 .... 5.23
R. v Wilson (Donald Theodore) (1984) 78 Cr. App. R. 247 CA (Crim
    Div) 10.159, 10.162

R. v Wilson (Michael) [2013] EWCA Crim 1780; [2014] Q.B. 704;
[2014] 2 W.L.R. 1180; [2014] 1 Cr. App. R. 10; [2014] Crim. L.R.
368 .... 8.42
R. v Wilson (No.98/1938/Y4) unreported 6 October 1998 .... 27.93
R. v Wilson (Simon Tyler) [2009] EWCA Crim 999; [2010] 1 Cr. App.
R. (S.) 11; [2009] Crim. L.R. 665 .... 1.113
R. v Winchester Crown Court Ex p. B (A Minor) [1999] 1 W.L.R. 788;
[1999] 4 All E.R. 53; [2000] 1 Cr. App. R. 11; (1999) 96(5) L.S.G.
35; (1999) 143 S.J.L.B. 31 .... 29.76, 29.78, 29.86, 29.87
R. v Winfield (Albert George) [1939] 4 All E.R. 164; (1940) 27 Cr. App.
R. 139 CCA 19.106
R. v Winter (Robert Michael) [2008] EWCA Crim 3; [2008] Crim. L.R.
971; (2008) 152(4) S.J.L.B. 29 .... 26.59
R. v Witty [2014] EWCA Crim 2333 .... 20.93, 20.94
R. v WM [2012] NICA 33 .... 32.60
R. v Wollaston (1872) 12 Cox C.C. 180 .... 15.62
R. v Wood (Clive) [2009] EWCA Crim 651; [2010] 1 Cr. App. R. (S.)
2; [2009] Crim. L.R. 543 .... 1.93
R. v Woodhouse (Rupert Giles) [2009] EWCA Crim 498; (2009) 173
J.P. 337 .... 20.09, 20.10, 20.51, 20.52
R. v Woodland. See R. v W (Robert)
R. v Woods (Walter) (1982) 74 Cr. App. R. 312; [1982] Crim. L.R. 42
CA (Crim Div) 1.398, 1.400
R. v Woollin (Stephen Leslie) [1999] 1 A.C. 82; [1998] 3 W.L.R. 382;
[1998] 4 All E.R. 103; [1999] 1 Cr. App. R. 8; [1998] Crim. L.R.
890; (1998) 95(34) L.S.G. 32; (1998) 148 N.L.J. 1178; (1998) 142
S.J.L.B. 248; (1998) 142 S.J.L.B. 230 HL 2.125, 15.192
R. v Worrall (Robert) [2012] EWCA Crim 1150 .... 12.22
R. v WR [2005] EWCA Crim 1907 .... 4.03, 30.157
R. v Wrench (Peter) [1996] 1 Cr. App. R. 340; [1996] 1 Cr. App. R. (S.)
145; [1995] Crim. L.R. 265 CA (Crim Div) 9.11
R. v Wright (Albert Edward); R. v Ormerod (Sidney George) (1990) 90
Cr. App. R. 91 CA (Crim Div) 19.74
R. v Wright (Michael Anthony) [2006] EWCA Crim 2672; [2007] 1 Cr.
App. R. (S.) 109 .... 14.22
R. v Wright (Nathan) [2007] EWCA Crim 3473 .... 1.250
R. v Wright (Paul John) (1990) 90 Cr. App. R. 325 CA (Crim Div) 20.55
R. v Wynes (Andrew Charles) [2014] EWCA Crim 2585; (2015) 179 J.P.
42 .... 20.23, 20.35
R. v X [2007] EWCA Crim 3226 .... 24.28
R. v X [2010] EWCA Crim 2367 .... 9.45
R. v X; R. v Z; R. v Y (1990) 91 Cr. App. R. 36; [1990] Crim. L.R. 515
CA (Crim Div) 27.59

R. v Xhabri (Agrol) [2005] EWCA Crim 3135; [2006] 1 All E.R. 776; [2006] 1 Cr. App. R. 26; 20 B.H.R.C. 233 .... 19.83

R. v Yaxley-Lennon. *See* R. v Weir (Antony Albert)

R. v Younas (Mohammed Zahir) [2007] EWCA Crim 1676 .... 34.48

R. v Z (Prior Acquittal); sub nom. R. v X (Prior Acquittal) [2000] 2 A.C. 483; [2000] 3 W.L.R. 117; [2000] 3 All E.R. 385; [2000] 2 Cr. App. R. 281; (2000) 164 J.P. 533; [2001] Crim. L.R. 222; (2000) 164 J.P.N. 824; (2000) 97(28) L.S.G. 31; (2000) 150 N.L.J. 984 HL 20.23

R. v Z [2009] EWCA Crim 20; [2009] 3 All E.R. 1015; [2009] 1 Cr. App. R. 34; (2009) 173 J.P. 145; [2009] Crim. L.R. 519 .... 19.61, 19.71

R. v Zala (Navin Naran) [2014] EWCA Crim 2181 ....19.120

R. v ZBT [2012] EWCA Crim 1727; [2013] 1 Cr. App. R. (S.) 85 ..... 1.48

R. v Zhang (Shanjil) [2007] EWCA Crim 2018 .... 1.265, 1.282

Rantsev v Cyprus (25965/04) (2010) 51 E.H.R.R. 1; 28 B.H.R.C. 313 ECtHR 11.02

Rawlings v Smith [1938] 1 K.B. 675 KBD 13.33

Read v DPP [1997] C.L.Y. 1202 .... 12.68

Read v Jones (1983) 77 Cr. App. R. 246; [1983] Crim. L.R. 809 DC 15.169

Reading BC v D (Angela) [2006] EWHC 1465 (Fam); [2007] 1 W.L.R. 1932; [2007] 1 All E.R. 293; [2006] 2 F.L.R. 1053; [2007] 1 F.C.R. 105; (2006) 92 B.M.L.R. 1; [2006] Fam. Law 738 ..... 18.43, 18.44, 18.45, 18.46

Red Saunders v R. *See* R. v Saunders (Red)

Reed and Reed. *See* R. v Reed (David)

Reid (Lindsey) v HM Advocate, 1999 J.C. 54; 1999 S.L.T. 1275; 1999 S.C.C.R. 19; 1999 G.W.D. 2–84, HJC 10.152

Reinsch [1978] 1 N.S.W.L.R. 483 .... 15.59

Reynolds (1881) 1 L.R. (N.S.W.) 129 Sup Ct (NSW) 15.137

Roberts v DPP [1994] R.T.R. 31; [1994] Crim. L.R. 926 DC 12.40

Rochford Rural DC v Port of London Authority [1914] 2 K.B. 916 KBD 12.108

Ropemaker Properties Ltd v Noonhaven Ltd [1989] 2 E.G.L.R. 50; [1989] 34 E.G. 39 Ch D 12.64

Rose v DPP; sub nom. R. (on the application of Rose) v DPP [2006] EWHC 852 (Admin); [2006] 1 W.L.R. 2626; [2006] 2 Cr. App. R. 29; (2007) 171 J.P. 57; [2006] Crim. L.R. 993; (2007) 171 J.P.N. 323 .... 15.54, 15.55

Ross Hillman Ltd v Bond [1974] Q.B. 435; [1974] 2 W.L.R. 436; [1974] 2 All E.R. 287; (1974) 59 Cr. App. R. 42; [1974] R.T.R. 279; (1974) 118 S.J. 243 DC 8.104

Rukwira, Rukwira, Mosoke and Johnson v DPP (1994) 158 J.P. 65; [1993] Crim. L.R. 882; (1993) 157 J.P.N. 709 DC 15.164, 15.172, 15.194

S (A Child) (Identification: Restrictions on Publication), Re; sub nom.
S (A Child) (Identification: Restriction on Publication), Re [2004]
UKHL 47; [2005] 1 A.C. 593; [2004] 3 W.L.R. 1129; [2004] 4 All
E.R. 683; [2005] E.M.L.R. 2; [2005] 1 F.L.R. 591; [2004] 3 F.C.R.
407; [2005] H.R.L.R. 5; [2005] U.K.H.R.R. 129; 17 B.H.R.C. 646;
[2005] Crim. L.R. 310; (2004) 154 N.L.J. 1654; (2004) 148 S.J.L.B.
1285 .... 29.57, 29.95, 29.98, 29.99, 29.101, 29.103
S and G v United Kingdom (App No.17634/91) unreported 15.26
S CC v B [2000] Fam. 76; [2000] 3 W.L.R. 53; [2000] 2 F.L.R. 161;
[2000] 1 F.C.R. 536; [2000] Fam. Law 462 .... 18.56
S v CPS. *See* R. (on the application of S) v Crown Prosecution
Service
S v DPP. *See* R. (on the application of S) v DPP
S v HM Advocate, 1989 S.L.T. 469; 1989 S.C.C.R. 248 HCJ 1.164
S v K, 1983 (1) S.A. 65 .... 15.45
S, B, C and R v R. *See* R. v S [2012]
Sadler v Worcestershire Magistrates' Court [2014] EWHC 1715
(Admin) 36.59
Salabiaku v France (A/141-A) (1991) 13 E.H.R.R. 379 ECtHR 3.78
Samuels v Bosch (1972) 127 C.L.R. 517 H Ct (Aus) 11.84
Santos v Santos [1972] Fam. 247; [1972] 2 W.L.R. 889; [1972] 2 All
E.R. 246; (1972) 116 S.J. 196 CA (Civ Div) 6.35
Saunders v United Kingdom (19187/91); sub nom. Saunders v United
Kingdom (43/1994/490/572) [1997] B.C.C. 872; [1998] 1 B.C.L.C.
362; (1997) 23 E.H.R.R. 313; 2 B.H.R.C. 358 ECtHR 8.117
SC v United Kingdom (60958/00) [2005] 1 F.C.R. 347; (2005) 40
E.H.R.R. 10; 17 B.H.R.C. 607; [2005] Crim. L.R. 130 ECtHR 27.32,
31.48
Secretary of State for Defence v Warn; sub nom. R. v Warn (Peter
John) [1970] A.C. 394; [1968] 3 W.L.R. 609; [1968] 2 All E.R. 300;
(1968) 52 Cr. App. R. 366; (1968) 112 S.J. 461 HL 8.10
Shaw v DPP; sub nom. R. v Shaw (Frederick Charles) [1962] A.C. 220;
[1961] 2 W.L.R. 897; [1961] 2 All E.R. 446; (1961) 45 Cr. App. R.
113; (1961) 125 J.P. 437; (1961) 105 S.J. 421 HL 10.153, 13.53
Sheldrake v DPP; Attorney General's Reference (No.4 of 2002), Re
[2004] UKHL 43; [2005] 1 A.C. 264; [2004] 3 W.L.R. 976; [2005]
1 All E.R. 237; [2005] 1 Cr. App. R. 28; (2004) 168 J.P. 669; [2005]
R.T.R. 2; [2004] H.R.L.R. 44; [2005] U.K.H.R.R. 1; 17 B.H.R.C.
339; [2005] L.L.R. 198; [2005] Crim. L.R. 215; (2005) 169 J.P.N.
19; (2004) 101(43) L.S.G. 33; (2004) 148 S.J.L.B. 1216 ..... 15.177, 15.197
Singleton v Ellison [1895] 1 Q.B. 607 QBD 12.27, 12.31, 12.96
Siviour v Napolitano [1931] 1 K.B. 636 KBD 12.68, 12.79
Smart v HM Advocate, 2007 J.C. 119 .... 8.61, 8.91
Smith v Hughes; Smith v Caiels; Tolan v Hughes; Tolan v Caiels;
Tolan v Thomas; Tolan v Mackinnon [1960] 1 W.L.R. 830; [1960]

2 All E.R. 859; (1960) 124 J.P. 430; (1960) 104 S.J. 606 QBD ... 13.38, 13.40

Snell and Wilson. *See* R. v S (Jonathan Charles)

Somerset v Wade [1894] 1 Q.B. 574 QBD 12.107, 12.108

Sopp v Long; sub nom. Long v Sopp [1970] 1 Q.B. 518; [1969] 2 W.L.R. 587; [1969] 1 All E.R. 855; 67 L.G.R. 389; (1969) 113 S.J. 123 QBD 8.104

Southard v DPP [2006] EWHC 3449 (Admin); [2007] A.C.D. 53 ... 15.185, 15.193

Springer (1975) 31 C.R. (N.S.) 48 Dist Ct (Sask) 15.45

Stanford v United Kingdom (App. No.16757/90) 23 February 1994 ..... 27.58

State of Missouri v Kevin Murray, 842 S.W. Reporter (2d) 122 .... 26.81

State v Obeta, 796 N.W.2d 282 (Minn. 2011) 23.70

Stevens v Christy (1987) 85 Cr. App. R. 249; (1987) 151 J.P. 366; [1987] Crim. L.R. 503; (1987) 151 J.P.N. 271 DC 12.28, 12.27, 12.31

Storey v Wick [1977] W.A.R. 47 .... 12.84

Strath v Foxon [1956] 1 Q.B. 67; [1955] 3 W.L.R. 659; [1955] 3 All E.R. 398; (1955) 39 Cr. App. R. 162; (1955) 119 J.P. 581 DC 12.30, 12.61

Street v Mountford [1985] A.C. 809; [1985] 2 W.L.R. 877; [1985] 2 All E.R. 289; (1985) 17 H.L.R. 402; (1985) 50 P. & C.R. 258; [1985] 1 E.G.L.R. 128; (1985) 274 E.G. 821; [2008] B.T.C. 7094; (1985) 82 L.S.G. 2087; (1985) 135 N.L.J. 460; (1985) 129 S.J. 348 L 12.68

Strong v Russell (1904) 24 N.Z.L.R. 916 .... 14.70

Stubing v Germany (43547/08) [2013] 1 F.C.R. 107; (2012) 55 E.H.R.R. 24; 33 B.H.R.C. 440 ECtHR 6.10, 6.11

Sunday Times v United Kingdom (A/30) (1979–80) 2 E.H.R.R. 245; (1979) 76 L.S.G. 328 ECtHR 18.92

Surrey CC v ME [2014] EWHC 489 (Fam); [2014] 2 F.L.R. 1267; [2014] Fam. Law 815 ....29.100

SW v United Kingdom (A/355-B); CR v United Kingdom; sub nom. SW v United Kingdom (20166/92) [1996] 1 F.L.R. 434; (1996) 21 E.H.R.R. 363; [1996] Fam. Law 275 ECtHR 1.168

Swanston v DPP (1997) 161 J.P. 203; [1997] C.O.D. 180; (1997) 161 J.P.N. 212 DC 15.165

T v DPP [2003] EWHC 2408 (Admin); (2004) 168 J.P. 194; [2005] Crim. L.R. 739; (2004) 168 J.P.N. 186 .... 29.09

T v R. *See* R. v T [2011]

Tabernacle v Secretary of State for Defence [2008] EWHC 416 (Admin); *Times*, 9 April 2008 .... 13.86

Taylor v DPP [2006] EWHC 1202 (Admin); (2006) 170 J.P. 485; (2006) 170 J.P.N. 856 .... 15.193, 15.194

Taylor v Jackson (1898) 78 L.T. 555 .... 14.70

TB (Minors) (Care Proceedings: Criminal Trial), Re [1995] 2 F.L.R. 801; [1996] 1 F.C.R. 101; (1995) 159 J.P.N. 796 CA (Crim Div) 30.51

Tesco Supermarkets Ltd v Nattrass [1972] A.C. 153; [1971] 2 W.L.R. 1166; [1971] 2 All E.R. 127; 69 L.G.R. 403; (1971) 115 S.J. 285 HL 8.42
The People v Williams, 841 P.2d 961 (1992) 26.62
The Queen on the Application of JRP v The Crown Prosecution Service. *See* JP v Crown Prosecution Service
Thompson v Lodwick [1983] R.T.R. 76 DC 8.63
Three Rivers DC v Bank of England (Disclosure) (No.3) [2003] EWCA Civ 474; [2003] Q.B. 1556; [2003] 3 W.L.R. 667; [2003] C.P.L.R. 349; (2003) 100(23) L.S.G. 37 .... 18.54
Three Rivers DC v Bank of England (Disclosure) (No.4) [2004] UKHL 48; [2005] 1 A.C. 610; [2004] 3 W.L.R. 1274; [2005] 4 All E.R. 948; (2004) 101(46) L.S.G. 34; (2004) 154 N.L.J. 1727; (2004) 148 S.J.L.B. 1369 .... 18.54
Tipu Sultan. *See* R. v TS [2008]
Toohey v Commissioner of Police of the Metropolis; sub nom. R. v Toohey [1965] A.C. 595; [1965] 2 W.L.R. 439; [1965] 1 All E.R. 506; (1965) 49 Cr. App. R. 148; (1965) 129 J.P. 181; (1965) 109 S.J. 130 .... 24.33, 24.50
Trewin. *See* R. v T [2008]
Trochym v The Queen (2007) 216 C.C.C.(3d) 225 Sup Ct (Can) 25.26
Tsang Ping-Nam v Queen, The [1981] 1 W.L.R. 1462; (1982) 74 Cr. App. R. 139; [1982] Crim. L.R. 46 PC 17.54
US v Diodoro (Anthony) (November 2, 2006) (Pennsylvania) 8.97
US v Kuchinski (John Charles) (November 27, 2006) (9th Cir. (US)) 8.97
Usai (Enrico) v Russell, 2000 J.C. 144; 2000 S.C.C.R. 57; 1999 G.W.D. 32–1519 HCJ 15.67
V, W, X, Y and Z v UK (Application No.22170/93) unreported 18 January 1995 EComHR 2.118
Van Mechelen v Netherlands (Art.6) (1998) 25 E.H.R.R. 647; 2 B.H.R.C. 486 ECtHR 27.58
Vehicle Inspectorate v Nuttall; sub nom. Secretary of State for Transport v Nuttall (t/a Redline Coaches); Wing v Nuttall; Nuttall v Vehicle Inspectorate [1999] 1 W.L.R. 629; [1999] 3 All E.R. 833; [1999] R.T.R. 264; [1999] I.R.L.R. 656; [1999] Crim. L.R. 674; (1999) 96(16) L.S.G. 36; (1999) 149 N.L.J. 521; (1999) 143 S.J.L.B. 111 HL 8.63
Venables v News Group International (Breach of Injunction); Thompson v News Group International; sub nom. Attorney General v Greater Manchester Newspapers Ltd (2002) 99(6) L.S.G. 30; (2001) 145 S.J.L.B. 279 QBD 29.19
Vernon v Bosley (No.2) [1999] Q.B. 18; [1997] 3 W.L.R. 683; [1997] 1 All E.R. 614; [1997] R.T.R. 275; [1998] 1 F.L.R. 304; [1997] P.I.Q.R. P326; (1997) 35 B.M.L.R. 174; [1997] Fam. Law 476;

(1997) 94(4) L.S.G. 26; (1997) 147 N.L.J. 89; (1997) 141 S.J.L.B. 27
CA (Civ Div) 18.56
Vigon v DPP (1998) 162 J.P. 115; [1998] Crim. L.R. 289; (1998) 162
J.P.N. 88 DC 15.16, 15.181, 15.187
W (Children) (Identification: Restrictions on Publication), Re; sub
nom. A Local Authority v W [2005] EWHC 1564 (Fam); [2006] 1
F.L.R. 1; [2007] 3 F.C.R. 69; [2005] Fam. Law 868 ...... 29.101, 29.102
W v DPP; sub nom. R. (on the application of W) v DPP [2005] EWHC
1333 (Admin); (2005) 169 J.P. 435; (2005) 169 J.P.N. 635 .... 36.65
W v Warrington Magistrates' Court [2009] EWHC 1538 (Admin);
(2009) 173 J.P. 561 .... 31.84, 31.87, 31.89, 31.98
Wakefield Local Board of Health v Lee (1876) 1 Ex. D. 336 .... 13.37
Waltham Forest LBC v AD [2014] EWHC 1985 (Fam); [2014] Fam.
Law 1253 .... 29.104, 29.106
Warner v Commissioner of Police of the Metropolis; sub nom. R. v
Warner (Reginald Charles) [1969] 2 A.C. 256; [1968] 2 W.L.R.
1303; [1968] 2 All E.R. 356; (1968) 52 Cr. App. R. 373; (1968) 132
J.P. 378; (1968) 112 S.J. 378 HL 8.96, 9.61, 12.63
Weisz v Monahan [1962] 1 W.L.R. 262; [1962] 1 All E.R. 664; (1962)
126 J.P. 184; (1962) 106 S.J. 114 DC 13.35, 13.36
Westminster City Council v Croyalgrange Ltd [1986] 1 W.L.R. 674;
[1986] 2 All E.R. 353; (1986) 83 Cr. App. R. 155; (1986) 150 J.P.
449; 84 L.G.R. 801; [1986] Crim. L.R. 693; (1986) 83 L.S.G. 2089;
(1986) 136 N.L.J. 491; (1986) 130 S.J. 409 HL 9.61, 12.63
Whaley, 1993 WL 167342 ....26.148
Whitley v Stumbles; sub nom. Stumbles v Whitley [1930] A.C. 544
HL 14.71
Williams v R. See R. v Williams (Edmond Selwyn)
Williamson (James) v Wright, 1924 J.C. 57; 1924 S.L.T. 363 HJC 13.33
Winn v DPP (1992) 156 J.P. 881; (1992) 156 J.P.N. 554; (1992) 142
N.L.J. 527 DC 15.163
Winter v Woolfe [1931] 1 K.B. 549 KBD 12.33, 12.34, 12.35, 12.55
Woodhouse v Hall (1981) 72 Cr. App. R. 39; [1980] Crim. L.R. 645
DC 12.40
Wychavon DC v National Rivers Authority [1993] 1 W.L.R. 125;
[1993] 2 All E.R. 440; (1994) 158 J.P. 190; [1993] Env. L.R. 330; 91
L.G.R. 517; [1993] Crim. L.R. 766; [1993] C.O.D. 37; (1994) 158
L.G. Rev. 181; (1992) 136 S.J.L.B. 260; [1992] N.P.C. 121 QBD 8.74
X (Children) (Disclosure for Purposes of Criminal Proceedings), Re
[2008] EWHC 242 (Fam); [2008] 3 All E.R. 958; [2008] 2 F.L.R.
944; [2008] 3 F.C.R. 23; [2008] Fam. Law 725 .... 18.53
X (Children) (Disclosure of Judgment to Police), Re; sub nom. A
Local Authority v A Mother [2014] EWHC 278 (Fam); [2015] 1
F.L.R. 1218; [2014] Fam. Law 96 .... 18.46, 18.51, 18.52,. 18.53

X (Children), Re [2007] EHWC 1719 (Fam); [2008] 1 F.L.R. 589;
    [2008] Fam. Law 23 .... 18.51
X City Council v MB [2006] EWHC 168 (Fam); [2006] 2 F.L.R. 968;
    [2007] 3 F.C.R. 371; [2006] Fam. Law 637 .... 1.226, 1.229, 7.74
X NHS Trust v T (Adult Patient: Refusal of Medical Treatment) [2004]
    EWHC 1279 (Fam); [2005] 1 All E.R. 387; [2004] 3 F.C.R. 297;
    (2005) 8 C.C.L. Rep. 38; [2004] Lloyd's Rep. Med. 433; (2004) 80
    B.M.L.R. 184 .... 1.232
X v Netherlands (A/91); Y v Netherlands (A/91); sub nom. X v
    Netherlands (8978/80) (1986) 8 E.H.R.R. 235 ECtHR 7.05, 7.43
Z v News Group Newspapers Ltd [2013] EWHC 1150 (Fam); [2013]
    Fam. Law 1130 .... 29.95, 29.96, 29.103
Z v News Group Newspapers Ltd [2013] EWHC 1371 (Fam); [2013]
    Fam. Law 1132 .... 29.95, 29.96, 29.103
Zubair Anwar. See R. v X [2007]

TABLE OF STATUTES

All references are to paragraph numbers.
References in bold indicate where legislation is reproduced in full.

1275 Statute of Westminster
(3 Edw. 1 c.13) 1.14

1285 Statute of Westminster
(13 Edw. 1 c.33) ... 1.14

1361 Justices of the Peace
Act (34 Edw 3
c.1) 13.83, 13.84

1751 Disorderly Houses Act
(c.36)–
s.81 ....31.140

1824 Vagrancy Act (5 Geo. 4
c.83) 15.12
s.3 .... 13.02, 13.04
s.4 .... 13.33, 15.83

1828 Offences Against the
Person Act (9
Geo.4 c.31) 9.02

1839 Metropolitan Police
Act (2 & 3 Vict.
c.47)–
s.44 ... 12.04, **12.104**, 12.015,
12.108, 31.140
s.58 ....15.202

1839 City of London Police
Act (2 & 3 Vict.
c.94)–
s.28 .... 12.04, 12.104, 31.140

1847 Town Police Clauses
Act (10 & 11 Vict.
c.89) 15.12
s.28 ...... 12.04, 15.02, 15.200
s.29 ....15.202
s.35 .... 12.05, 12.106

1851 Evidence Act (14 & 15
Vict. c.99)–
s.7 .... 20.09

1860 Ecclesiastical Courts
Jurisdiction (23 &
24 Vict. c.32)–
s.2 ....15.202

1861 Offences Against the
Person Act (24 &
25 Vict. c.100) 1.274,
1.334, 1.337, 2.112,
2.114, 2.117, 4.58,
5.27, 6.42, 11.105,
14.28
s.18 .... 1.337, 2.30, 2.76,
3.100, 3.127, 20.144
s.20 .... 1.334, 1.335, 1.336,
1.337, 1.340, 1.349, 2.30,
2.76, 2.114, 2.115, 2.124,
2.129, 2.131, 3.100, 3.127,
29.101
s.21 .... 14.38
s.22 .... 14.03
s.23 .... 14.28, 14.29, 14.33
s.24 .... 14.28, 14.29
s.47 .... 1.334, 2.30, 2.114,
2.115, 2.117, 2.126, 3.100,
3.127
s.48 .... 1.15
s.52 .... 32.02
s.58 .... 14.28, 14.29
s.61 .... 32.02
s.62 .... 32.02

1865 Criminal Procedure Act (28 & 29 Vict. c.18)–
s.4 .... 18.78, 19.96, 26.33, 26.166, 26.167

1885 Criminal Law Amendment Act (48 & 49 Vict. c.69)–
s.4 .... 1.329, 32.02
s.5 .... 32.02

1898 Criminal Evidence Act (61 & 62 Vict. c.36)–
s.1(f)(ii) 20.87

1902 Licensing Act (2 Edw. 7 c.28)–
s.2(1) 29.96

1908 Punishment of Incest Act (8 Edw. 7 c.45) 6.01, 6.07

1911 Perjury Act (1 & 2 Geo. 5 c.6)–
s.1 .... 27.37

1915 Indictments Act (5 & 6 Geo. 5 c.90) 19.15
s.5(3) 1.146, **19.10**, 19.14

1922 Criminal Law Amendment Act (12 & 13 Geo. 5 c.56) –
s.2 .... 32.04

1923 Criminal Law (Amendment) Act (Northern Ireland) (c.8)–
s.2 .... 32.02

1933 Evidence (Foreign, Dominion and Colonial Documents) Act (23 & 24 Geo. 5 c.4) 3.74

1933 Children and Young Persons Act (23 & 24 Geo. 5 c.12) 11.105, 31.04
s.3 ...... 12.04, 12.100, 31.140

(1) **12.97**, 12.98, 12.101
s.17 ....**12.100**
s.31 ....27.136
s.34A(1) 31.36
(2) 31.26
s.39 .... 29.07, 29.09, 29.59, 29.62, 26.63, 29.66, 29.71, 29.74, 29.75, 29.76, 29.77, 29.78, 29.81, 29.82, 29.84, 29.87, 29.88, 29.90, 29.92, 29.95, 29.96, 29.103, 29.104
s.41(1) 30.118B, 33.23
s.44 .... 4.154, 29.75, 31.06, 36.77
(1) 3.65, 31.116
s.45 .... 31.02, 31.32
s.47(2) 31.35
s.49 .... 29.07, 29.09, 29.64, **31.38**, 31.40
(3) **31.38**
(4) 31.40
(4A) 31.40, 31.41
(5) 31.40
(a) 31.40
(5)–(7) 31.40
s.99(1) 11.36, 31.71
(2) 3.74, 8.57, 8.131, 9.41, 12.101
Sch.1 .... 3.74, 8.57, 9.41, 12.101

1933 Administration of Justice (Miscellaneous Provisions) Act (23 & 24 Geo. 5 c.36)–
s.2(1) 8.12

1936 Public Health Act (26 Geo. 5 & 1 Edw. 8 c.49)–
s.5 .... 15.166, 15.167, 15.169
(1) 15.169
s.231(1)(d) 15.199

1948 Attempted Rape Act
(11 & 12 Geo. 6
c.19) 30.151
1949 Marriage Act (12, 13 &
14 Geo. 6 c.76) ... 6.28
s.2 .... 4.17
1953 Births and Deaths Registration Act (1 &
2 Eliz.2 c.20)–
s.34 .... 3.74
1953 Post Office Act (1 & 2
Eliz.2 c.36)–
s.11 .... 15.38
1955 Army Act (3 & 4 Eliz. 2
c.18) 29.49
1955 Air Force Act (3 & 4
Eliz. 2 c.19) 29.49
1956 Sexual Offences Act (4
& 5 Eliz.2 c.69) ... 1.109,
1.132, 1.161, 1.166,
1.175, 1.190, 4.02,
6.01, 7.07, 7.25,
7.29, 9.03, 9.04,
9.48, 10.108,
10.152, 11.05,
12.02, 12.04,
12.23, 12.27,
12.35, 12.44,
14.36, 19.106,
26.22, 27.14,
30.16, 30.109,
30.114, 30.143,
30.146, 30.155,
31.64, 31.74,
34.19, 34.55
s.1 .... 1.24, 1.142, 34.55
(1) 1.15, 1.34, 30.147
(2) 1.15, 1.17, 1.18,
1.329, 1.330
(3) **1.330**
s.2 .... 1.12, 1.208
(1) 1.352
ss.2–7 .... 29.20
s.3 .... 1.12, 1.208, 1.326,
1.350, 1.352

(1) 1.314, 1.317, 1.320,
1.350
s.4 .... 14.01
s.5 ... 1.142, 1.167, 3.02, 3.29,
30.156, 34.55
s.6 .... 4.17, 4.181, **12.32**,
30.156, 30.157
(1) 4.15
s.7 .... 1.238, 7.81
s.9–12 .... 29.20
s.10 .... 1.142, 6.01
s.11 .... 6.01
s.12 .... 15.06, 15.19, 15.20,
20.61, 34.55, 35.05
s.13 ..... 2.114, 15.06, 15.200,
15.201, 35.05
s.14 .... 2.02, 27.75, 30.152
(1) 1.34, 30.16, 30.114
ss.14–17 .... 29.20
s.15 ... 2.02, 30.152, 30.118E,
34.55
s.17 .... 9.03, 9.38
s.18 .... 9.03
s.19 .... 1.161, 1.166, 9.03
s.20 .... 9.03, 9.04, 9.28, 9.29,
9.31, 9.35, 9.46
s.21 .... 9.03
s.22 ... 10.63, 10.135, 10.142,
11.05
s.24 .... 11.05
s.28 .... 2.98, 10.06, 11.05
s.30 ... 10.77, 10.105, 10.149,
10.152, 10.153, 10.159,
10.161, 11.05
s.31 .... 10.105, 11.05
s.32 .... 13.05, 13.06, 13.09,
13.34, 13.84, 15.06
ss.33–36 .... 12.96, 31.61
s.33 .... 12.02, 12.03, **12.21**,
12.22, 12.23, 12.24, 12.25,
12.35, 12.39, 12.42, 12.58,
12.66, 12.75, 12.77, 12.85,
12.87, 12.93, 31.140

s.33A .. 10.108, 12.02, 12.03,
12.23, 12.35, 12.42, 12.43,
12.44, 12.45, 12.46, 12.47,
12.48, 12.49, 12.50, 12.52,
12.55, 12.56, 12.75, 12.85,
12.87, 12.93, 12.94, 31.98,
31.125, 31.140
(1) **12.42**
(2) 12.55
s.34 .... 12.02, 12.22, **12.57**,
12.58, 12.59, 12.64, 12.66,
12.77, 12.79, 12.84,
31.140
s.35 .... 12.02, 12.22, 12.58,
12.77, 31.140
(1) **12.65**, 12.66, 12.67,
12.70, 12.80, 12.82
(2) **12.74**, 12.75
(3) **12.74**
s.36 .... 12.02, 12.22, 12.58,
12.66, 12.75, **12.76**, 12.77,
12.78, 12.79, 12.80, 12.83,
12.84, 12.84, 12.94,
31.140
s.37 .... 1.20, 12.22, 12.43,
12.58, 12.66, 12.77,
30.152, 30.157
(2) 30.151
s.45 .... 7.25, 7.81
Sch.1 .... 12.74
Sch.2 ... 1.20, 30.152, 30.157
para.(1)(b) 30.151
para.33 .... 12.22
para.33A 12.43
para.34 .... 12.58
para.35 .... 12.66
para.36 .... 12.77
1957 Naval Discipline Act (5
& 6 Eliz. 2 c.53) ... 29.49
1959 Street Offences Act (7
& 8 Eliz.2 c.57) ... 13.04,
13.05, 13.06, 13.09,
13.13, 13.16,
13.27, 13.33,
13.35, 13.41,
13.46, 13.51, 13.53
s.1 .... 13.11, 13.16, 13.49
(1) **13.25**, 13.26, 13.27,
13.29, 13.30, 13.33, 13.38,
13.46, 13.51, 13.53, 13.54,
13.55, 13.66, 13.67, 13.72,
32.07, 32.75
(2A)–(2D) 13.27
(2) 13.26
(3) 13.53
(4) 13.37, 13.38
(a) **13.31**
(b) **13.45**
(c) **13.37**
s.1A 13.27
s.2 .... 13.16
s.3 .... 12.05
1959 Obscene Publications
Act (7 & 8 Eliz.2
c.66) 8.74, 13.54
s.2(1) 8.64
1959 Mental Health Act (7
& 8 Eliz.2 c.72) ... 7.06
1960 Road Traffic Act (8 & 9
Eliz.2 c.16) 13.42
1960 Indecency with Children Act (8 & 9
Eliz.2 c.33) 4.02,
15.27, 27.14,
30.155
s.1 ....30.158
(1) 4.60, 15.27, 20.61,
20.133, 30.155
s.2 ....30.152
1960 Administration of Jus-
tice Act (8 & 9
Eliz.2 c.65)–
s.12 .... 18.39
1961 Criminal Justice Act (9
& 10 Eliz.2 c.39)–
s.160 ....31.125
1963 Betting, Gaming and
Lotteries   Act
(c.2)–

s.8(1) 13.33

1963 Children and Young
    Persons Act
    (c.37) 31.04
s.2 .... 4.17
s.29 ....31.114

1963 Local Government (Fi-
    nancial Provi-
    sions) Act (c.46)–
s.76(1) 12.104

1964 Licensing Act (c.26)–
s.175 .... 12.05
s.176 .... 12.05

1964 Criminal Procedure
    (Insanity) Act
    (c.84)–
s.4 .... 36.28
  (5) 15.96
  (5) 15.96
s.4A 7.23, 7.46, 15.99
  (2) 2.43, 15.96, **15.97**,
       15.98, 15.100
s.5 .... 15.99

1965 Criminal Procedure
    (Attendance of
    Witnesses) Act
    (c.69)–
s.2 .... 18.68, 18.70, 18.78,
      18.80, 18.82
  (1) **18.76**
  (b) 18.79
  (3) 18.76
  (5) **18.76**

1965 Dangerous Drugs Act
    (c.15)–
s.5 .... 12.69

1967 Criminal Law Act
    (c.58) 2.44
s.3(1) 15.168
s.5(2) 17.58
s.6(3) 1.141, 2.44, 7.16,
      9.18, 30.157
  (3A) 2.44, 9.18

  (3B) 2.44, 9.18
  (4) 1.141

1967 Sexual Offences Act
    (c.60) 27.14
s.6 .... 12.32
s.8 .... 8.10, **30.159**

1967 Criminal Justice Act
    (c.80)–
s.9 .... 19.39

1968 Criminal Appeal Act
    (c.19)–
s.2 .... 25.38
s.3 .... 30.16
s.11(3) 34.55, 36.57
s.23 .... 26.39

1968 Firearms Act (c.27)–
s.16 ....11.112
s.51A 31.65

1968 Children and Young
    Persons Act
    (c.38)–
s.22 .... 32.02

1968 Theatres Act (c.54) 15.49,
      15.63
s.2(4) 15.49, 15.50
s.18 .... 15.50
  (1) 15.49

1968 Theft Act (c.60)–
s.9 .... 14.07, 14.68, 31.75,
      31.140
  (1)(a) 14.07

1968 Justices of the Peace
    Act (c.69)–
s.1(7) 13.83

1969 Family Law Reform
    Act (c.46)–
s.9(1) 3.73, 4.56, 4.84,
    4.110, 4.129, 4.157, 4.207,
    4.237, 5.24, 5.59, 5.86,
    5.110, 8.57, 8.131, 9.41,
    9.55, 12.101
s.11(c) 9.03

1969 Late Night Refresh-
     ment Houses Act
     (c.53)–
     s.9(1) 12.05
1971 Misuse of Drugs Act
     (c.38)–
     s.8 .... 12.68, 12.69, 12.70,
                                    12.82
1971 Immigration   Act
     (c.77)–
     s.25 .... 11.17, 11.47, 11.54,
          11.98, 11.99, 11.132
1972 Local Government Act
     (c.70)–
     s.235 ....15.199
     (3) 15.200
1973 Matrimonial   Causes
     Act (c.18)–
     s.11 .... 4.17
1973 Employment   and
     Training   Act
     (c.50)–
     ss.8–10 .... 5.34
1974 Health and Safety at
     Work   etc.   Act
     (c.37) 8.43
     s.37 .... 8.43
1974 Rehabilitation of Of-
     fenders   Act
     (c.53)–
     s.5(2)–(8) 13.28
1976 Adoption Act (c.36)–
     s.39 .... 6.30, 6.88
     s.47(1) 6.88
     s.50(2) 3.74
1976 Bail Act (c.63) 31.29
     s.4 .... 31.29
     Sch.1 .... 1.25
     para.3 .... 31.29
1976 Sexual   Offences
     (Amendment) Act
     (c.82) 1.166, 26.17,
          26.22, 29.02, 29.04,
               29.13, 30.147
     s.1 .... 1.163, 1.398

     (1) 1.17, 1.161, 1.163,
          1.164, 1.165, 1.166
     (2) 1.398
     s.2 .... 26.05, 26.07, 26.09,
     26.14, 26.15, 26.17, 26.18,
     26.19, 26.20, 26.22, 26.26,
          26.60, 26.74, 26.168,
                              26.181
     (4) 26.14
     s.4(1) 29.02, 29.13
     s.6(1) 29.34
1977 Criminal   Law   Act
     (c.45)–
     s.1 .... 1.406, 8.67
     (1) 10.152
     (2) **1.407**, 1.408
     (a) 10.152
     s.4 .... 8.13
     s.54 .... 27.14
     (1) 6.01, 6.02
1978 Oaths Act (c.19)
     s.1 .... 32.58
1978 Interpretation   Act
     (c.30)–
     s.5 .... 2.44
     Sch.1 .... 2.44
1978 Protection of Children
     Act (c.37) .. 4.136, 6.34,
          8.01, 8.02, 8.09,
          8.11, 8.14, 8.53,
          8.54, 8.57, 8.58,
          8.66, 8.74, 8.75,
          8.83, 8.105, 8.123,
               8.124, 8.130,
          8.131, 19.123,
               27.14, 29.21,
          29.92, 31.61, 31.64
     s.1 ... 4.54, 4.55, 4.249, 4.261,
          20.45, 27.15, 29.92,
          31.125, 31.129, 31.140
     (1) 4.263, **8.03**, 8.04,
     8.06, 8.07, 8.16, 8.23, 8.27,
     8.32, 8.39, 8.40, 8.41,
                         8.44, 8.53

(a) 8.11, 8.18, 8.47,
8.57, 8.61, 8.63, 8.75, 8.76,
8.79, 8.80, 8.82, 8.83,
8.84, 8.90, 8.92, 8.94,
8.97, 8.104, 8.117, 8.125,
8.140, 10.57, 20.21
(b) 8.57, 8.65, 8.67,
8.69, 8.75, 8.86, 8.90, 8.95,
8.98
(b)–(d) 8.79
(c) 8.18, 8.57, 8.64,
8.71, 8.73, 8.75, 8.86, 8.90,
8.96, 8.98, 8.100, 8.101,
8.102, 8.103, 11.110
(d) 8.57, 8.60, 8.74,
8.76, 8.104
(2) **8.64**, 8.69
(3) 4.245, 8.09, 8.10,
8.11, 8.13, 8.123
(4) 4.263, **8.86**
(a) 8.87, 8.88
(b) 8.89, 8.98
(5) 8.57
s.1A ... 8.75, 8.77, 8.79, 8.80,
8.81
s.1B 8.82, 8.85
s.2(3) 8.58, 8.132
s.3 ..... 8.39, **8.42**, 8.43, 8.129
s.4 .... 4.252, 8.08, 8.122
s.5 .... 4.252, 8.08, 8.122
s.6(1) 8.04
(2) 8.04
(3) 8.04
s.7 .... 8.130
(2) 8.52
(3) **8.52**
(4) 8.52
(4A) **8.53**
(a) 8.56
(6) 8.57, 8.131
(7) 8.55, 8.56
(8) 8.53, 8.55, 8.58
(9) 8.55
s.9 .... 8.66
Sch. 4.252, 8.08

1979 Customs and Excise
Management Act
(c.2)–
s.170(2)(b) 35.12
1980 Magistrates' Court Act
(c.43) 12.86
s.24 .... 1.20, 31.71, 31.86
(1) **31.64**, 31.72, 31.87
(a) 31.86
ss.24A–24D 31.68
s.32 .... 8.04
(1) 15.28
s.97 .... 18.78
s.115 .... 13.83
s.150 .... 11.36
Sch.1 .... 8.04
1981 Indecent Displays
(Control) Act
(c.42) 13.54, 13.55
s.1(1) 13.55, 13.56
(2) 13.55
(3) 13.55
(4) 13.55
(5) 13.55
(6) 13.55
1981 Criminal Attempts Act
(c.47) 30.151
s.1 .... 1.405, 1.406
(1) **1.404**, 1.406
(2) 10.142
(3) 10.142
1981 Contempt of Court
Act (c.49)–
s.4(2) 29.29, **29.30**, 29.32,
29.57, 29.82
s.11 .... **29.31**, 29.32
1981 Senior Courts Act
(c.54)–
s.29(3) 29.87
s.45(4) 29.107
1981 British Nationality Act
(c.61) 1.154, 2.25,
3.72, 4.59, 5.28,
6.43, 7.62, 8.41,
10.26, 14.26

1982 Civic Government (Scotland) Act (c.45)–
s.52(1)(c) 8.102, 8.141
1982 Criminal Justice Act (c.48) 13.12, 13.26
s.1(6) 11.36
s.35(3) ... 12.22, 12.58, 12.66, 12.77
s.38 ....12.105
s.46 .... 12.22, 12.58, 12.66, 12.77, 12.105
s.71 .... 13.04, 13.26
1983 Mental Health Act (c.20) .. 7.25, 7.28, 7.70, 34.28
s.1 .... 1.238, 7.25, 27.17
(2) 7.80, **27.17**
(3) 7.25
(4) 7.25
1984 Child Abduction Act (c.37) ... 9.28, 9.38, 9.39
s.1 .... 9.30
(1) 9.36
(2)(c)–(e) 9.24
s.2 ...... 9.04, 9.08, 9.09, 9.16, 9.22, 19.123
(1) ... **9.07**, 9.09, 9.10, 9.12, 9.15, 9.24, 9.29, 9.30, 9.31, 9.36, 9.38, 9.39, 9.41, 9.42, 9.45, 9.46, 9.50, 9.51, 9.53, 9.58
(a) 9.07, 9.08, 9.09, 9.22, 9.42, 9.43, 9.45, 9.50
(b) 9.07, 9.08, 9.21, 9.39, 9.42, 9.45
(2) **9.24**
(3)(a) 9.24, 9.31
(b) 9.36, 9.40, **9.47**, 9.48, 9.49, 9.50
s.3(a) ... **9.33**, 9.34, 9.35, 9.36
(c) 9.09, **9.37**, 9.39
s.4(1) 9.10, 9.11
(a) 9.10

(b) 9.10
1984 Police and Criminal Evidence Act (c.60) 8.113, 25.67
s.10 .... 25.38
(1) 25.38
s.24 .... 13.53
(4) 13.53
(5)(c) 13.53
(6) 13.53
s.26 .... 13.53
s.62 .... 25.66
s.63 .... 25.66
s.63A 25.66
s.63D 25.64
(3)–(4) 25.64
ss.63D–63U 25.64
ss.63E–63O 25.64
s.63R 25.64
(4) 25.64
s.63T 25.64
s.64 .... 25.67
s.74 .... 20.12
(3) 20.105
s.78 .... 1.339, 7.38, 19.30, 19.32, 19.38, 19.39, 19.45, 19.49, 19.70, 19.79, 20.81, 20.108, 25.34, 25.52, 26.49, 27.149, 27.150, 27.152
s.80 .... 19.123, 19.129
(2) 19.123
(2A) 19.123
(3) 19.123
(a) 19.124
(4) 19.125
(4A) 19.125
(5) 19.127
(5A) 19.127
(6) 19.123
(7) 19.123
s.80A 19.126
s.81 .... 25.29
Sch.2 .... 13.53
Sch.2A 25.66

1985 Prosecution of Of-
        fences Act (c.23)–
    s.1(7) 8.09, 30.159
    s.10 .... 17.01
    s.15(2) 29.61
1985 Sexual Offences Act
        (c.44) 13.08, 13.15,
                13.16, 13.61, 13.62,
                    13.67, 13.72,
                13.84, 30.148
    s.1(1) 13.31, 13.61, 13.68,
                            32.75
    s.2(1) 13.61, 13.69, 32.07,
                            32.75
    s.3 ....30.151
    (2) 1.20
    s.5(5) 30.151
1986 Public Order Act
        (c.64) 8.65
    s.4 .... 1.274, 1.279, 15.05,
            15.166, 15.167, 15.193
    (1) 15.163, 15.164,
        15.166, 15.167, 15.168,
        15.169, 15.170, 15.179
    (2) 15.164
    (4) 15.164
    s.4A 15.05, 15.176
    (1) 15.196
        (a) 15.171, 15.173,
                        15.182
    (2) 15.172
    (3) 15.177
    (5) 15.173
    s.5 .... 15.05, 15.06, 15.07,
            15.09, 15.10, 15.45,
        15.180, 15.183, 5.186,
        15.190, 15.193, 15.196,
            15.198, 15.200
    (1) ... 15.16, 15.53, 15.179,
        15.181, 15.183, 15.184,
        15.186, 15.189, 15.192,
            15.193, 15.195
    (2) 15.195
    (3) 15.197
        (c) 15.187, 15.190

    (6) 15.184
    s.6(3) 15.170
    (4) 15.183, 15.198
    (5) 15.170, 15.198
    s.8 ....15.168
    s.19 .... 8.65
    s.42 .... 8.65, 8.66
1988 Malicious Communi-
        cations   Act
        (c.27)–
    s.1 .... 4.228
1988 Criminal Justice Act
        (c.33) .. 2.44, 7.38, 8.01,
            8.02, 8.73, 11.18,
                14.66, 29.34
    s.23 .... 7.38, 19.51, 19.66,
                        27.10
    s.26 .... 7.38
    s.27 .... 8.107, 8.108, 8.109,
                        8.110
    s.32A 27.52, 27.83, 27.86
    (3)(c) 27.52
    s.39 .... 2.44, 9.18
    s.40 .... 2.44, 9.18
    s.139(1) 14.66
    s.159 .... 29.86, 29.88
    (1)(c) 29.136
    s.160 .... 4.249, 8.01, 8.132,
            19.123, 27.15, 31.140
    (1) ... 8.11, 8.14, 8.16, 8.18,
        8.23, 8.27, 8.103, 8.107,
    8.119, 8.120, 8.121, 8.123,
    8.124, 8.126, 8.128, 8.129,
    8.130, 8.131, 8.136, 8.140,
                8.143, 29.21
    (2) 4.263, 8.135, 8.144
        (b) 8.89
        (c) 8.140
    (2A) 8.120
    (3) 8.120
    (4) 8.123, 8.130, 8.131,
                        8.132
    s.160A 8.143
    s.170(1) 9.41
    s.177(5) 35.13

Sch.15 para.9 .... 9.41

1988 Road Traffic Act
(c.52) 13.42
s.185(1) 13.65

1989 Children Act (c.41) 5.36,
18.39, 30.50, 30.51,
36.44
s.7 .... 5.35
s.20 .... 5.35
s.21 .... 5.35
s.22C 6.32
(6) 5.33
(a) 6.32
(b) 6.32
s.23(2) 5.33
s.23B(2) 5.35
Pt IV 9.05, 9.55, 18.56
s.31(2) 18.59
s.36 .... 5.36
s.41(1) 5.36
s.43 .... 9.55
s.46 .... 9.05, 9.55, 9.60
s.49 .... 9.05, 9.12, 9.16
(1) **9.52**, 9.55
(b) 9.58, 9.59
(c) 9.59
(2) 9.55, **9.60**
(3) 9.53
s.51 .... 9.24
s.53 .... 5.33
s.59(1) 5.33
(a) 6.32
s.60(3) 5.33
s.66(1)(b) 6.32
s.82(5) 5.33
s.98 .... 18.40
(2) 18.40, 18.53, 18.57
s.105(1) 9.55
s.108(2) 9.52
(3) 9.52
(5) 12.97, 12.98, 12.100
Sch.2 para.19C 5.35
Sch.13 para.3 .... 12.97
para.5 .... 12.98, 12.100

1989 Statute Law (Repeals)
Act (c.43)–
s.1 .... 13.04
Sch.1 .... 13.04

1990 Broadcasting Act
(c.42) 15.49, 15.50,
15.63, 29.51,
29.117, 29.131
Sch.15 para.6 .... 15.49

1990 Environmental Protection Act (c.43)–
s.87 .... 13.57

1991 Criminal Justice Act
(c.53) 30.142, 30.163,
32.29

1992 Sexual Offences
(Amendment) Act
(c.34) 29.02, 29.03,
29.13, 29.14, 29.17,
29.21, 29.92
s.1 .... 29.15, **29.16**, 29.22,
29.23, 29.25, 29.26, 29.27,
29.92, 31.42
(1) 29.33
(2) 29.19, 29.23, 29.30
(3A) 29.14
s.2(1) 29.14, **29.20**, 31.42
(a) **29.20**
(2) **29.20**
s.3 .... 29.25, 31.42
(1) 29.25
(2) 29.25
(4) 29.25
(7) 29.25
s.5 .... 29.27, 28.28
(2) 29.28
(3) 29.28
(4) 29.28
(5) 29.28
(6) 29.28
(7) 29.28

1993 Sexual Offences Act
(c.30) 17.66, 17.67,
17.68, 17.69
s.1 .... 1.150, 30.14

(4) 17.69
1994 Criminal Justice and
    Public Order Act
    (c.33) 1.03, 1.18,
        1.155, 1.330, 8.01,
            8.52, 30.106
s.25 .... 1.24, 1.25, 2.13, 2.90,
        3.36, 3.86, 3.141, 7.52,
            7.96, 31.29
    (2) 1.24
    (d) 1.24
    (e) 1.24
    (3) 31.29
s.32 .... 10.152, 19.107
    (1) **19.107**, 19.108
    (b) 30.01, 30.106
    (3) 19.107
s.33 .... 19.107, 30.01
s.57 .... 25.67
s.84(1) 8.03, 8.52, 8.55,
        8.86, 8.119, 8.144
    (2) 8.03, 8.86
    (3) 8.52, 8.55
    (4) 8.119, 8.144
s.86(1) 8.120
s.142 .... 1.03, 1.18, 1.153,
                1.162
    (3) 1.330
s.154 .... 15.171, 15.179
s.168(1) 29.20
Sch.9 para.52(2) 29.20
1995 Merchant Shipping
    Act (c.21)–
s.108 .... 3.74
1995 Criminal Appeal Act
    (c.35)–
s.23(1) 18.91
1995 Criminal Procedure
    (Scotland) Act
    (c.46)–
s.210F(1) 31.132
1996 Law Reform (Year and
    a Day Rule) Act
    (c.19)–
s.2 ....30.160

1996 Criminal Procedure
    and Investigations
    Act (c.25) 18.01,
        18.13, 18.16, 18.21,
            18.22, 18.43,
                18.68, 18.91,
            27.127, 30.24,
                31.44
s.1(1) 18.27
s.3 .... 18.13, 18.26
    (2) 18.13
    (6) 18.22
s.4(2)(b) 18.28
s.5 .... 30.24
s.6 .... 31.45
    (2) 31.45
s.6A 31.45
s.7 .... 18.13
s.7A(2) 18.16
    (3) 18.16
    (8) 18.22
s.8 .... 18.17, 30.24, 31.45
    (5) 18.22
s.21(2) 18.26
Pt II 18.13
s.35 .... 19.13
1997 Protection from Har-
    assment Act
    (c.40)–
s.4(1) 15.196
1997 Crime (Sentences) Act
    (c.43)–
s.34 .... 34.18
1997 Sex Offenders Act
    (.51) 18.26, 35.01,
        35.02, 35.04, 35.09,
            35.11, 35.12,
                35.14, 35.55,
                36.01, 36.03
Pt I 36.02
s.5A 36.02
    (2) 36.02
    (3) 36.02
    (4)–(7) 36.02
    (8) 36.02

(9) 36.02
Sch.1 .... 36.02
1998 Data Protection Act
(c.29) 18.05, 18.68
s.29(1)(b) 18.05
1998 Crime and Disorder
Act (c.37) 13.73,
35.01, 36.02, 36.03
s.1(10) 13.81
s.1C 36.27
s.2(1) 36.03
(3) 36.03
(4) 36.03
(5) 36.03
(7) 36.03
(8) 36.03
s.8 ....31.138
s.34 .... 1.150, 1.151
s.37 ...... 4.154, **31.05**, 31.121
(1) 3.65, 31.116, 33.23
s.39 .... 31.07
s.41 .... 31.07
s.51(7)(b) 31.66, 31.99
s.51A 31.96, 31.98
(2) **31.91**, 31.96
(3) **31.65**, 31.72, 31.76,
31.79
(d) 31.91, 31.96
(12) 31.65
s.51B 31.65
s.51C 31.65
s.53A 31.98
s.65 .... 31.08, 31.21
s.66 .... 31.08, 31.21
(4) 31.139
s.66A 31.21
ss.66A–66E 31.24
s.66B(3) 31.24
s.66BA 31.24
s.66E(2) 31.24
s.66ZA 31.21
(1)(a)–(c) 31.22
s.67(8) 31.08
s.71 .... 31.98
s.80(1)(d) 31.23

s.113(1) 31.23
1998 Human Rights Act
(c.42) 6.10, 15.167,
15.177, 15.197,
17.015, 18.51,
29.75, 29.97, 36.52
s.3 ... 8.04, 8.80, 8.120, 26.04,
26.72, 26.99, 26.181
s.12(1) 29.106
(4) 29.102, 29.103
1999 Youth Justice and
Criminal Evidence
Act (c.23) 11.19,
11.68, 26.20, 26.28,
26.66, 26.72,
26.147, 27.10,
27.10, 27.11,
27.16, 27.20,
27.32, 27.51,
27.53, 27.59,
27.157, 29.02,
29.06, 29.11,
29.13, 29.14,
29.58, 29.124,
29.129
Pt II 27.01, 27.02, 27.03,
27.04, 27.12, 27.32
s.16 ...... 27.13, 27.115, 31.56
(1) 27.15
(a) .. 27.15, 31.56, 31.58,
31.61
(b) 27.17, 27.18,
27.139, 31.56, 31.58
(2) 27.17, 31.58
(3) 31.61
(4) 27.18
(5) 27.18
ss.16–30 .... 27.12
ss.16–32 .... 31.56
s.17 .... 27.13, 27.19, 31.56
(1) 31.56, 31.58
(2) 27.19, 31.58
(3) 27.19
(4) 27.19, 31.56, 31.58
(5) 27.19

s.18(1) 27.106
  (a) 27.116
  (2) 27.41
s.19 .... 19.49, 27.116, 27.143
  (2) 27.50, 27.55, 27.75
  (a) 27.49
  (b) 27.49
  (3)(a) 27.49
  (b) 27.49
s.20(1) 27.123
  (2) 27.123
  (a) 27.123
  (b) 27.123
s.21 .... 27.14, 27.55, 31.61
  (2) 27.50
  (3) 27.14, 27.82, 31.61
  (4)(b) 27.82
  (4A) 27.50
  (4B)(a) 27.50
  (b) 27.50
  (4C) 27.50
  (8) 27.123
  (9) 27.123
s.22 .... 27.55, 31.61
  (1)(a) 27.16
  (2) 27.50
  (a) 27.16
s.22A 27.55
s.23 .... 27.57, 31.59
ss.23–27 .... 27.41
ss.23–30 .... 31.59
s.24 .... 27.62, 31.59
  (1A) 27.62
  (1B) 27.62
  (3) 27.51
s.25 .... 27.66
  (2) 27.66
  (4) 27.66
  (a) 27.49
s.26 .... 27.67
s.27 .... 27.41, 27.42, 27.55,
  27.68, 31.59, 31.60
  (2) 27.51, 27.53, 27.82
  (3) 27.82
  (4) 27.79

  (ii) 27.103
  (5) 27.54, 27.151
  (b) 27.54
s.28 .... 18.08, 18.72, 27.09,
  27.41, 27.43, 27.103,
  28.22A, 31.60
  (1) 27.104
  (2) 27.104
  (5) 27.104
  (6)(a) 27.105
  (b) 27.105
s.29 ..... 27.41, 27.105, 31.59,
  31.63
  (2) 27.106
s.30 ...... 27.41, 27.115, 31.59
s.33(5) 27.15
  (6) 27.15
ss.33A–33C 27.25
s.33A 27.12, 27.26, 27.30,
  31.50
  (2)(b) 27.26
  (3)(c) 27.52
  (4)(a) 27.26
  (b) 27.26
  (5)(a) 27.28
  (b) 27.28
  (c) 18.28
  (6) 18.29
  (7) 18.29
ss.33BA–33BC 27.25
s.33BA ... 27.09, 27.12, 27.35,
  27.36, 27.37, 31.51
  (5) 27.37
  (6) 27.37
  (7) 27.37
  (9) 27.37
  (10) 27.37
s.33BB 27.37
  (2) 27.37
s.34 .. 27.158, 27.159, 27.160,
  27.161, 27.162, 27.163
s.35 .. 27.159, 27.160, 27.161,
  27.162, 27.163
  (1) 27.159
  (2) 27.158

(3) 27.159
(a) 27.14, 27.159,
31.61
(b)–(d) 27.159
(4) 27.159
s.36 .. 27.160, 27.161, 27.162
27.163
(1) 27.160
s.38 ....27.161
(1) 27.161
(2) 27.161
(3) 27.161
(4) 27.161
(5) 27.161
s.39 .... 29.59
s.41 .... 1.384, 19.02, 19.91,
20.151, 20.152, 20.153,
26.02, 26.03, 26.04, 26.06,
26.07, 26.18, 26.23, 26.24,
26.25, 26.27, 26.28, 26.29,
26.31, 26.33, 26.34, 26.37,
26.40, 26.41, 26.43, 26.44,
26.45, 26.47, 26.49, 26.53,
26.59, 26.63, 26.69, 26.72,
26.74, 26.80, 26.105,
26.125, 26.132, 26.146,
26.149, 26.150, 26.151,
26.152, 26.154, 26.155,
26.163, 26.164, 26.166,
26.173, 26.176, 26.177,
26.179, 26.180, 26.181,
26.182, 26.184
(1) 26.06, 26.21, 26.22,
26.25, 26.26, 26.154
(c) 26.146
(2)–(6) **26.50**
(2) 26.45
(a) 26.127
(b) 26.03, 26.34,
26.51, 26.53, 26.57, 26.76,
26.118, 26.122, **26.127**,
26.180
(3) 26.37, 26.73, 26.83,
26.98, 26.127

(a) .. 26.51, 26.52, 26.54,
26.58, 26.105, 26.143
(b) 26.31, 26.51,
26.52, **26.80**, 26.85, 26.98,
26.105
(c) ... 26.51, 26.52, **26.83**,
26.85, 26.90, 26.91, 26.94,
26.98, 26.99, 26.109,
26.110, 26.114, 26.146,
26.150, 26.181
(4) 26.03, 26.34. 26.40,
26.52, 26.53, 26.67, 26.70,
26.71, 26.72, 26.73, 26.75,
26.76, 26.118, 26.125,
26.132, 26.133, 26.136,
26.139, 26.141, 26.142,
26.152, 26.178, 26.183
(5) 26.34, 26.41, 26.42,
26.43, 26.51, **26.117**,
26.118, 26.119, 26.120,
26.122, 26.124, 26.125,
26.127, 26.140
(a) 26.125
(b) 26.118
(6) 26.52, 26.64, 26.73,
26.97, 26.118, 26.142,
26.144, 26.145, 26.146,
26.147, 26.149, 26.178
(7) **26.25**
ss.41–43 .... 26.01, 26.20,
26.21, 32.64
s.42(1)(a) 26.54, 26.73,
26.127, 26.135, 26.142
(b) 26.136
(c) **26.26**, 26.34
(3) **26.44**
s.43 .... 26.45
(1)(a) 26.70
(b) 26.82
(3) **26.46**
s.44 .... 29.03, 29.05, 29.47,
29.48, 29.50, 29.52, 29.60
(1) 29.47
(b) 29.49
(2) 29.47

(3) 29.47
(4) 29.47
(5) 29.47
(6) 29.47
(7) 29.47, 29.52
(8) 29.47
(9) 29.47, 29.49
(11) 29.47
(12) 29.47
s.45 .... 29.03, 29.07, 29.10,
    29.14, 29.21, 29.33, 29.47,
    29.59, 29.62, 29.64, 29.65,
    29.66, 29.67, **29.68**, 29.69,
    29.72, 29.73, 29.74, 29.75,
    29.76, 29.82, 29.84, 29.85,
    29.86, 29.87, 29.88, 29.89,
    29.90, 29.95, 29.97, 29.99,
    29.108, 29.129, 31.39
(1) 29.64
(3) 29.64
(4) 29.67
(5) 29.67
(6) 29.66, 29.67
(7) 29.64
(8) 29.66
(9) 29.67
(10) 29.67
(11) 29.67
s.45A 29.08, 29.09, 29.47,
    29.59, 29.62, 29.64,
    29.108, 29.110, 29.112,
    29.113, 29.114, 29.115,
    29.116, 29.118, 29.119,
    29.120, 29.121, 29.122,
    31.38
(2) 29.109
(3) 29.109
(4) 29.109
(5) 29.110
(6) 29.110
(7) 29.110
(10) 29.111
(11) 29.111
(13) 29.111
(14) 29.111

s.46 .... 26.45, 29.08, 29.11,
    29.123, 29.124, 29.125,
    29.126, 29.127, 29.130,
    29.132, 29.133, 29.134,
    29.135, 29.136
(4) 29.124
(5) 29.124
(6) 29.125
(7) 29.127
(8) 29.128
(9) 29.127, **29.128**
(12) 29.136
s.47(1) 27.124
(3) 27.124
(4) 27.124
(5) 27.124
(6) 27.124
s.48 .... 29.14, 31.28
(d) 29.16, 29.20
s.49 ..... 27.124, 29.50, 29.51,
    29.52, 29.70, 29.73,
    29.116, 29.117, 29.118,
    29.119, 29.130, 29.131,
    29.133
(1A) 29.117
(2) ... 29.51, 29.71, 29.117,
    29.131
(6) 27.124
s.50(1) 29.52, 29.73,
    29.119, 29.133
(2) 29.52
(3) 29.52
(6) 29.52
(6A) 29.119
(6B) 29.119
(7)–(14) 29.133
(8) .. 29.52, 29.119, 29.133
(8)–(14) 29.52
s.51 ..... 29.51, 29.71, 29.117,
    29.131
s.52 .... 29.67, 29.112, 29.126
s.53 .. 27.144, 27.149, 27.156,
    31.52
(1) 7.36, 27.143
(3) 7.36, 27.143, 31.52

(4) 27.143
(5) 27.143
s.54 ....27.143
(3) 7.36, 31.52
(4) 27.143
(5) 7.36, 27.143
(6) 27.143, 27.151
s.55 .... 27.155, 27.156
(2) 27.155, 31.55
(3) 27.151, 27.155
(4) 27.155
(5) 27.151
(5)–(7) 27.155
(8) 27.155
s.56(1) 27.156
(2) 27.156, 31.55
(3) 27.156
(4) 27.156
(5) 27.156
s.62 .... 26.22, 27.15
(1) 26.22, **26.23**, 26.24
(1A)(a)–(e) **26.22**
(2) **26.22**
s.63(1) 29.65, 29.114
s.64(3) 29.47
s.65(3) 27.155
s.67 .... 29.02, 29.62
(1) 19.123
(3) 29.16, 29.20
(4) 29.16, 29.20
s.68(6) ... 29.51, 29.71, 29.131
Sch.1A 27.19
Sch.2 .... 29.14, 31.28
para.6 .... 29.16, 29.20
paras 6–14 .... 29.16, 29.20
Sch.2A 29.118
Sch.4 para.13 ....19.123
Sch.6 .... 29.02
Sch.7 para.6(3) 29.62
2000 Powers of Criminal
Courts (Sentenc-
ing) Act (c.6) .. 30.118E,
30.163, 31.04,
31.69, 34.24

s.3B(1) .. 31.69, 31.81, 31.97,
31.101
s.3C 31.88, 31.97, 31.101
s.8(2) 31.101
(6) 31.101
(7) 31.101
(8) 31.101
s.9 .... 1.107, 31.114
ss.16–17 .... 31.88, 31.110
s.16(1)(a) 31.111
(b)–(c) 31.111
s.17(1) 31.111
(b) 31.111
(2)(b) 31.112
s.20(1) 31.139
(2) 31.139
(3) 31.139
s.80(2)(b) 9.11, 30.161,
30.166
s.82A 34.40
(3)(a) 34.40
s.85 .... 30.164, 31.135
s.90 ....31.102
s.91 ... 30.118B, 31.27, 31.29,
31.67, 31.69, 31.72, 31.79,
31.82, 31.90, 31.92, 31.97,
31.101, 31.102, 31.135
(1) 31.65, 31.72
(a) 31.73, 31.74
(b)–(e) 31.75
(b) 31.73, 31.140
(c) 31.140
(d) 31.140
(e) 31.140
(3) 31.65, 31.76, 31.78
s.100 .... 4.154, 31.77
(2)(b) 31.139
ss.100–107 .... 31.104, 31.139
s.101(1) 31.77, 31.104
(4) 31.77, 31.104
s.102(2) 31.104, 35.22
(b) 31.104
s.109(2) 34.20
s.116 .... 34.40
s.118 ....30.138

ss.130–134	11.117
s.135(1)	31.113
s.143	4.252
s.147	15.82
s.154	34.49
s.165(1)	1.20
Sch.9 para.64	1.20

2000 Care Standards Act (c.14) 5.33
    s.1 .... 5.33
    s.2 .... 5.33
    (3) 5.33

2000 Regulation of Investigatory Powers Act (c.23)– 36.34
    s.49 .... 8.112, 8.113, 8.116, 8.117
    (2)(c) 8.117
    s.50 .... 8.114
    s.51 .... 8.114, 8.115
    s.53 .... 8.116
    Sch.2 .... 8.113

2000 Postal Services Act (c.26)–
    s.85(4) 15.38

2000 Criminal Justice and Court Services Act (c.43) .. 8.04, 8.120, 34.63, 36.49
    s.26 .... 36.48
    s.28 .... 5.20
    s.41 .... 32.02
    (1) 8.04
    (3) 8.120
    s.66 .... 36.02
    Sch.5 para.6(1) 36.02

2000 Sexual Offences (Amendment) Act (c.44) .. 5.03, 5.04, 5.05, 5.06, 5.37, 5.127

2001 Criminal Justice and Police Act (c.16)–
    s.46 .... 13.58
    (1) 13.57, 13.59
    (2) 13.57
    (3) 13.57
    (4) 13.57
    (5) 13.57
    s.47(1) 13.58
    (2) 13.58

2002 Proceeds of Crime Act (c.29) 10.42, 10.76, 10.95, 10.117, 10.148, 11.64, 11.78, 12.22, 12.43, 12.86
    s.6 ....11.117
    s.327 .... 1.406
    s.340(3) 1.406
    Sch.2 .... 10.42, 10.76, 10.95, 10.117, 10.148, 11.64, 11.78

2002 Education Act (c.32) ... 29.05
    s.141F 29.45, 29.46
    s.141G 29.46

2002 Adoption and Children Act (c.38) 6.88
    s.67 .... 6.30
    s.77(5) 3.74

2002 Nationality, Asylum and Immigration Act (c.41)–
    s.145 .... 11.08

2003 Licensing Act (c.17) ... 12.05
    s.140 .... 12.05
    s.199 .... 12.05
    Sch.7 .... 12.05

2003 Female Genital Mutilation Act (c.31) 22.68, 22.69, 22.70
    s.1 .... 22.70
    (2) 22.69
    (3) 22.69
    ss.1–3 .... 22.71
    s.2 .... 22.70
    s.3 .... 22.70, 22.72
    s.4 .... 22.71, 22.72

2003 Courts Act (c.39)–
    s.66 .... 31.34

s.109(1) 29.48
Sch.8 para.386 .... 29.48
2003 Communications Act
(c.21)–
s.127 .... 4.228
2003 Sexual Offences Act
(c.42) .. 1.03, 1.05, 1.06,
1.07, 1.10, 1.12,
1.13, 1.23, 1.24,
1.33, 1.34, 1.90,
1.108, 1.153,
1.156, 1.170,
1.185, 1.187,
1.190, 1.208,
1.210, 1.217,
1.220, 1.222,
1.223, 1.225,
1.229, 1.243,
1.248, 1.280,
1.281, 1.299,
1.303, 1.306,
1.317, 1.318,
1.320, 1.321,
1.326, 1.331,
1.334, 1.339,
1.340, 1.352,
1.385, 1.388,
1.391, 2.01, 2.02,
2.12, 2.35, 2.36,
2.42, 2.80, 2.81,
2.89, 2.112, 3.19,
3.30, 3.35, 3.50,
3.56, 3.85, 3.111,
3.140, 4.01, 4.02,
4.03, 4.07, 4.08,
4.15, 4.17, 4.29,
4.74, 4.98, 4.126,
4.150, 4.166,
4.194, 4.228,
4.235, 5.01, 5.06,
5.12, 5.37, 5.49,
5.57, 5.80, 5.108,
5.127, 5.128, 6.01,
6.02, 6.03, 6.05,
6.07, 6.17, 6.42,

6.60, 6.76, 6.88, 6.98, 7.05,
7.09, 7.12, 7.22, 7.25, 7.27,
7.28, 7.30, 7.45, 7.51,
7.58, 7.69, 7.75, 7.80,
7.95, 7.130, 7.146, 7.164,
7.177, 7.197, 7.213, 7.241,
7.256, 7.276, 8.01, 8.06,
8.57, 8.82, 8.121, 8.143,
9.03, 9.04, 9.11, 10.01,
10.05, 10.07, 10.12, 10.15,
10.16, 10.36, 10.40, 10.41,
10.44, 10.71, 10.90,
10.106, 10.108, 10.109,
10.119, 10.155, 10.164,
11.07, 11.08, 11.16, 11.60,
11.61, 11.75, 11.90, 11.98,
11.112, 12.03, 12.06,
12.09, 13.05, 13.15, 13.29,
14.01, 14.12, 14.42, 14.56,
15.02, 15.04, 15.27, 15.72,
15.94, 15.119, 15.133,
15.148, 15.159, 19.18,
19.19, 19.36, 24.50, 24.51,
26.23, 26.33, 26.24, 26.57,
26.58, 26.62, 26.63, 26.65,
26.161, 26.180, 27.159,
29.04, 29.13, 29.36, 29.40,
30.04, 30.16, 30.17, 30.21,
30.109, 30.115, 30.118A,
30.118E, 30.143, 30.144,
30.155, 31.04, 31.12,
31.20, 31.42, 31.64, 31.74,
31.75, 31.106, 31.131,
31.140, 32.07, 32.22,
32.27, 32.50, 33.01, 33.03,
33.23, 34.05, 34.40, 34.49,
34.52, 35.01, 35.04, 35.06,
35.14, 35.22, 35.26, 35.27,
35.30, 35.55, 36.04, 36.05,
36.44, 36.52
Pt 1 ... 1.06, 1.32, 1.179, 2.63,
4.117, 4.178, 4.186, 4.243,
4.261, 5.39, 5.67, 5.95,
5.118, 6.104, 11.103,
14.04, 14.05, 14.37, 14.52,

14.52A, 15.111, 15.161,
19.123, 27.14, 27.15,
31.42, 31.61, 34.63
s.1 .... 1.04, 1.19, 1.24, 1.142,
1.145, 1.224, 1.242, 1.378,
1.380, 3.30, 3.39, 3.77,
7.32, 7.34, 31.74, 31.139,
31.140, 32.75
(1) 1.10, 1.34, 1.314
(c) 1.10, 1.239, 1.283,
1.374, 1.400, 1.401, 7.88
(2) 1.09, 1.10, 1.11,
1.264, 1.283, 1.299, 1.313,
1.319, **1.382**, 1.387, 1.388,
1.396, 1.400, 26.58
(4) 1.20
ss.1–3 .... 4.64, 5.25, 7.30,
7.53, 14.52A
ss.1–4 ...... 1.06, 1.179, 1.239,
1.241, 1.263, 3.03, 4.13,
4.24, 5.13, 7.21, 7.29,
17.39
ss.1–79 ... 4.219, 14.37, 14.52
s.2 .... 1.24, 1.138, 1.142,
1.214, 2.01, 2.03, 2.07,
2.25, 2.27, 2.28, 2.32,
2.33, 2.34, 2.36, 2.91,
3.80, 3.88, 15.135, 31.74,
31.139, 31.140, 32.75,
33.19
(1) **2.07**
(2) 2.34
(3) 2.31
(4) 2.09
s.3 .... 1.137, 2.01, 2.04, 2.63,
2.78, 2.80, 3.105, 3.113,
4.54, 7.78, 15.112, 31.75,
31.86, 31.125, 31.129,
31.140, 32.75, 33.13
(1) **2.38**
(c) 2.77
(2) **2.33**, **2.83**
(3) 2.77
(4) 2.39, 2.99

s.4 ... 1.24, 1.142, 1.322, 2.01,
2.05, 2.85, 2.86, 2.88, 2.89,
2.91, 2.92, 2.93, 2.94,
2.96, 2.97, 2.98, 2.100,
2.102, 2.104, 2.107, 2.108,
3.134, 3.142, 3.168,
31.140, 32.75
(1) 1.48, 1.323, **2.84**,
31.74
(2) **2.108**
(3) 2.104
(4) 2.85, 31.74, 31.139,
31.140
(a)–(d) 1.24
(5) 2.85
s.5 ... 1.24, 1.98, 1.100, 1.102,
1.142, 1.153, 1.217, 1.224,
1.361, 3.01, 3.05, 3.14,
3.15, 3.16, 3.17, 3.19,
3.20, 3.22, 3.23, 3.30,
3.31, 3.32, 3.33, 3.34,
3.35, 3.39, 3.40, 3.41,
3.47, 3.50, 3.51, 3.52,
3.53, 3.56, 3.57, 3.58,
3.59, 3.60, 3.61, 3.62,
3.64, 3.66, 3.69, 3.77,
3.78, 3.135, 4.16, 4.30,
5.08, 5.13, 30.118E,
30.135, 31.17, 31.74,
31.139, 31.140, 32.75,
33.17, 34.55
(1) **3.29**, **3.79**, 31.129
(a) 3.30, 3.80
(b) 3.80
(2) 3.32
ss.5–7 ...... 4.21, 5.25, 14.52A
ss.5–8 .... 3.01, 3.03, 3.04,
3.23, 3.78, 4.07, 4.22, 4.23,
4.24, 4.30, 4.178, 5.41,
6.03, 10.12, 10.17, 10.36,
10.71, 10.90, 17.39, 31.04,
31.15, 31.18, 31.19
s.6 .... 1.24, 1.142, 2.08, 3.01,
3.58, 3.80, 3.84, 3.85, 3.88,
3.90, 3.92, 3.97, 3.98,

3.103, 4.30, 5.08, 5.13,
15.135, 30.163, 31.74,
31.139, 31.140, 32.75,
34.55
(1) 30.163
(2) 3.82
s.7 ...... 1.40, 1.99, 2.61, 3.01,
3.57, 3.58, 3.105, 3.106,
3.107, 3.108, 3.109, 3.110,
3.111, 3.113, 3.115, 3.119,
3.122, 3.124, 3.125, 3.130,
4.25, 4.54, 5.08, 5.13,
31.74, 31.125, 31.129,
31.140, 32.75
(1) **3.104**
(a) 3.105
(b) 3.105
(2) 3.107
s.8 .... 1.142, 2.74, 2.96, 2.99,
2.101, 2.105, 3.01, 3.57,
3.81, 3.106, 3.124, 3.132,
3.134, 3.136, 3.137, 3.138,
3.138, 3.140, 3.142, 3.144,
3.146, 3.147, 3.150, 3.151,
3.152, 3.153, 3.155, 3.156,
3.157, 3.159, 3.162, 3.163,
3.165, 3.168, 3.170, 4.22,
4.30, 4.55, 4.60, 4.68,
4.69, 4.75, 4.84, 4.162,
5.52, 5.53, 5.60, 5.73,
6.55, 10.36, 10.37, 10.62,
10.89, 10.112, 11.73,
26.34, 31.74, 31.140,
32.75, 33.18
(1) **3.131**
(a) 3.134
(b) 3.134
(2) 3.136
(3) 3.137
(4) 31.139
ss.8–12 ....31.129
s.9 ...... 1.40, 2.08, 2.61, 2.96,
3.05, 3.16, 3.22, 3.30, 3.53,
3.59, 3.61, 3.78, 3.151,
4.01, 4.21, 4.22, 4.23,

4.24, 4.26, 4.27, 4.28, 4.29,
4.30, 4.32, 4.34, 4.35, 4.39,
4.40, 4.41, 4.45, 4.46,
4.48, 4.49, 4.50, 4.52,
4.53, 4.54, 4.56, 4.57,
4.58, 4.59, 4.60, 4.64,
4.65, 4.70, 4.76, 4.77,
4.78, 4.139, 4.146, 4.155,
4.156, 4.169, 4.203, 5.08,
5.13, 5.15, 5.16, 5.25,
5.27, 5.41, 5.42, 5.69,
5.96, 5.120, 6.03, 6.42,
7.147, 7.216, 9.26, 10.17,
10.19, 10.20, 10.57,
11.112, 30.16, 31.21,
31.124, 31.140, 32.75,
33.16, 33.18
(1) 1.372, **4.20**
(c) 3.15
(2) 4.26, 4.34
(3) 4.26
ss.9–10 .... 4.151
ss.9–12 .... 1.35, 4.144, 4.145,
4.151, 4.155, 4.159, 4.168,
4.230, 5.02, 5.06, 7.12,
17.39, 31.04, 31.18,
31.140
ss.9–13 .... 4.17, 4.160, 4.161,
4.170, 4.178, 4.179, 4.185
ss.9–15 .... 3.04, 4.02
s.10 .... 2.96, 2.101, 3.78,
3.151, 3.153, 3.160, 3.163,
4.01, 4.32, 4.34, 4.35,
4.39, 4.40, 4.41, 4.45,
4.50, 4.53, 4.54, 4.55,
4.60, 4.68, 4.69, 4.70,
4.71, 4.72, 4.73, 4.75,
4.76, 4.77, 4.78, 4.81,
4.83, 4.84, 4.85, 4.86,
4.91, 4.92, 4.110, 4.146,
4.155, 4.156, 5.52, 5.60,
5.73, 6.03, 6.55, 7.147,
10.36, 10.54, 10.62,
11.112, 31.124, 31.140,
32.75, 33.18

(1) **4.67**
(2) 4.71
(3) 4.71
s.11 .... 2.36, 2.80, 4.01, 4.41,
4.95, 4.96, 4.97, 4.98, 4.99,
4.100, 4.102, 4.103, 4.105,
4.106, 4.107, 4.109, 4.110,
4.111, 4.115, 4.116, 4.120,
4.128, 4.129, 4.134, 4.155,
4.229, 4.239, 5.76, 5.81,
5.82, 5.83, 5.87, 5.95,
7.112, 20.118, 31.124,
31.140, 32.75
(1) **4.94**
(2) 4.95
ss.11–12 .... 4.151
s.12 ... 2.36, 2.80, 2.101, 3.65,
4.01, 4.41, 4.100, 4.102,
4.103, 4.105, 4.106, 4.107,
4.122, 4.123, 4.124, 4.125,
4.126, 4.127, 4.128, 4.129,
4.130, 4.131, 4.133, 4.134,
4.135, 4.138, 4.139, 4.141,
4.155, 4.229, 4.230, 4.239,
5.81, 5.82, 5.83, 5.104,
5.111, 7.112, 31.124,
31.140, 32.75
(1) **4.121**
(2) 4.123
s.13 .... 1.35, 2.08, 2.61, 2.96,
3.15, 3.16, 3.17, 3.19, 3.22,
3.23, 3.30, 4.01, 4.12,
4.21, 4.23, 4.56, 4.69,
4.75, 4.84, 4.110, 4.146,
4.147, 4.148, 4.149, 4.150,
4.151, 4.152, 4.153, 4.156,
4.157, 4.158, 4.230, 5.25,
5.60, 5.87, 5.111,
30.118A, 30.118C,
30.118D, 31.17, 31.18,
31.19, 31.21, 31.75,
31.129, 31.140, 32.75,
35.22
(1) **4.144**
s.14 .... 4.01, 4.132, 4.139,

4.162, 4.163, 4.164, 4.165,
4.166, 4.167, 4.168, 4.169,
4.169, 4.170, 4.171, 4.172,
4.173, 4.174, 4.175, 4.176,
4.177, 4.178, 4.179, 4.180,
4.181, 4.182, 10.28, 31.74,
31.129, 31.140, 32.75,
34.34
(1) **4.160**
(2) 4.145, **4.180**
(2)–(3) 4.182
(3) **4.180**
(d) 4.183
(4) 4.163
s.15 ... 4.01, 4.41, 4.49, 4.178,
4.187, 4.188, 4.190, 4.191,
4.192, 4.193, 4.194, 4.195,
4.196, 4.197, 4.198, 4.199,
4.200, 4.201, 4.203, 4.204,
4.207, 4.208, 4.211, 4.213,
4.220, 4.221, 4.223, 4.224,
4.230, 11.112, 31.140,
33.12
(1) ... **4.186**, 31.140, 32.75,
34.34
(2)(a) **4.209**
(b) 4.219
(4) 4.191
ss.15–24 .... 32.22
s.15A .. 2.29, 2.66, 4.01, 4.08,
4.135, 4.189, 4.211, 4.227,
4.229, 4.230, 4.231, 4.232,
4.234, 4.235, 4.236, 4.237,
4.238, 4.239, 4.242, 4.244,
4.245, 4.246, 4.247,
15.161, 31.140, 32.75
(1) **4.225**, 31.140
(2) **4.243**, 4.244
(3)(a) 4.232
(b) 4.232
s.16 .... 2.08, 2.61, 5.01, 5.02,
5.08, 5.09, 5.10, 5.14, 5.15,
5.16, 5.17, 5.19, 5.24,
5.25, 5.26, 5.28, 5.42,
5.50, 5.58, 5.83, 5.84,

6.03, 31.140, 32.75
(1) **5.07**, 31.140
(d) 5.39
(2) **5.39**, 5.48
(3) 5.49
(4) **5.39**, 5.48
(5) 5.09
ss.16–19 ..... 5.40, 5.43, 5.68,
5.95, 5.119, 5.127, 7.12,
36.39
ss.16–20 .... 5.02
s.17 .... 2.96, 5.01, 5.02, 5.14,
5.15, 5.16, 5.17, 5.19, 5.20,
5.22, 5.23, 5.52, 5.53,
5.54, 5.55, 5.56, 5.57,
5.58, 5.59, 5.60, 5.61,
5.62, 5.69, 5.74, 5.84,
6.03, 6.55, 31.140, 32.75
(1) **5.51**, 31.140
(d) 5.67
(2) **5.67**, 5.72
(3) 5.73
(4) 4.191, **5.67**, 5.72
(5) 5.54
s.18 .... 1.24, 2.36, 2.80, 5.01,
5.76, 5.77, 5.78, 5.79, 5.80,
5.81, 5.82, 5.83, 5.84,
5.86, 5.87, 5.88, 5.89,
5.98, 5.102, 5.109, 31.140,
32.75
(1) **5.75**, 31.140
(c) 5.98
(e) 5.94
(2) **5.94**, 5.100
(3) 5.101
(a)–(d) 1.24
(4) **5.94**, 5.100
(5) 5.77
s.19 .... 2.36, 2.80, 5.01, 5.81,
5.82, 5.83, 5.84, 5.104,
5.104, 5.106, 5.107, 5.108,
5.109, 5.110, 5.112, 5.113,
5.120, 5.125, 31.140,
32.75
(1) **5.103**, 31.140

(d) 5.118
(2) **5.118**, 5.123
(3) 5.124
(4) **5.118**, 5.123
(5) 5.105
s.20 .... 5.01, **5.126**, 5.127,
5.128, 32.75
s.21 .... 5.32, 5.38, 32.75
(1) **5.31**, 5.38
(b) 5.32
(2)–(5) 5.39, 5.67, 5.94,
5.118
(2)–(13) 5.32
(2) 5.32
(3) 5.33
(4) 5.33
(5) 5.34
(7) 5.34
(9) 5.35
(10) 5.35
(11) 5.36, 5.37
(12) 5.36, 5.37
(13) 5.36
s.22 .... 32.75
(2) 5.38
(3) 5.34
(4) 5.34
(5) 5.33, 5.36
(6) 5.33
s.23 ... 5.40, 5.68, 5.95, 5.119,
32.75
(1) .. 5.40, 5.68, 5.95, 5.119
(2) .. 5.40, 5.68, 5.95, 5.119
s.24 ... 5.42, 5.69, 5.96, 5.120,
32.75
(1) .. 5.42, 5.69, 5.96, 5.120
(2) .. 5.42, 5.69, 5.96, 5.120
(3) .. 5.42, 5.69, 5.96, 5.120
s.25 .... 6.02, 6.03, 6.05, 6.06,
6.13, 6.14, 6.15, 6.16, 6.17,
6.18, 6.19, 6.20, 6.21,
6.23, 6.25, 6.26, 6.27,
6.29, 6.32, 6.38, 6.39,
6.40, 6.41, 6.43, 6.46,

6.50, 6.51, 6.52, 6.55, 6.56,
6.61, 6.68, 6.83, 6.84,
30.118A, 30.118B,
30.118D, 31.19, 31.75,
31.124, 31.140, 32.75,
36.39
(1) **6.12**
  (d) 6.48
  (e) 6.49
(2) 6.49
(3) 6.48
(4)–(6) 6.13
ss.25–26 .... 31.04, 31.19,
31.129
ss.25–29 .... 5.38
s.26 .... 6.02, 6.03, 6.05, 6.06,
6.18, 6.19, 6.20, 6.21, 6.25,
6.29, 6.32, 6.38, 6.40,
6.41, 6.43, 6.51, 6.52,
6.52, 6.56, 6.57, 6.58,
6.59, 6.60, 6.61, 6.62,
6.63, 6.84, 31.19, 31.75,
30.118A, 30.118D,
31.124, 31.140, 32.75,
36.39
(1) **6.54**
(4)–(6) 6.56
s.27 .... 6.04, 6.28, 6.29, 6.34,
6.36, 6.48, 32.75
(1) **6.29**
  (b) 6.30
(2)–(4) 6.29, 6.30
(2) **6.31**, 6.32, 6.53
(3) ... **6.33**, 6.34, 6.35, 6.36
(4) 6.32, **6.37**, 6.39
(5)(a) 6.32
  (c) 6.32
  (d) 6.34
  (e) 6.32
s.28 .... 6.28, 6.51, 32.75
(2) 6.51
s.29 .... 6.52, 32.75
(1)(a) 6.53
  (b) 6.53
(3) 6.52

s.30 .... 1.24, 1.142, 1.231,
1.232, 1.239, 1.241, 7.16,
7.29, 7.30, 7.31, 7.32,
7.48, 7.49, 7.50, 7.51,
7.54, 7.55, 7.56, 7.59,
7.60, 7.61, 7.62, 7.65,
7.78, 7.87, 7.97, 7.105,
7.124, 7.140, 7.156, 7.159,
7.172, 7.191, 7.207,
31.140, 32.75
(1) **7.47**
  (d) 1.239
(2) 1.240, 1.241, 1.304,
7.18, **7.65**, 7.69, 7.78
  (a) 1.225, 7.19, 7.66,
7.75
  (b) 7.20
(3) 7.48
  (a)–(d) 1.24
(4) 1.238, 7.48
ss.30–31 .... 31.74
ss.30–33 .... 1.241, 7.12, 7.15,
7.16, 7.18, 7.27, 7.29, 7.30,
7.31, 7.45, 7.58, 7.65,
7.70, 7.90, 7.236
ss.30–41 .... 1.238, 7.01, 7.12,
7.41
s.31 ... 1.24, 1.142, 7.54, 7.55,
7.56, 7.59, 7.92, 7.93, 7.94,
7.95, 7.96, 7.97, 7.99,
7.100, 7.104, 31.140,
32.75
(1) **7.91**
(2) 7.69, **7.102**
(3) 7.92
  (a)–(d) 1.24
(4) 7.92
ss.31–34 .... 7.18
s.32 .... 2.36, 2.80, 7.107,
7.108, 7.109, 7.110, 7.112,
7.114, 7.117, 7.125, 7.131,
31.140, 32.75
(1) **7.106**
(2) 7.69, **7.121**
(4) 7.107

s.33 .... 2.36, 2.80, 7.112,
7.114, 7.127, 7.128, 7.129,
7.130, 7.131, 7.133, 7.141,
24.49, 31.140, 32.75
(1) **7.126**
(2) 7.69, **7.137**
(3) 7.127
s.34 .... 1.240, 7.16, 7.29,
7.143, 7.144, 7.145, 7.146,
7.147, 7.149, 7.150, 7.153,
7.156, 7.165, 7.170,
31.140, 32.75
(1) **7.142**
(2) 7.143
(3) 7.143
ss.34–35 .... 31.74
ss.34–37 ..... 7.13, 7.16, 7.29,
7.45, 7.58
ss.34–41 .... 7.15
s.35 .... 7.147, 7.149, 7.150,
7.161, 7.163, 7.164, 7.165,
7.167, 7.170, 31.140,
32.75
(1) **7.160**
(2) 7.161
(3) 7.161
s.36 .... 2.36, 2.80, 7.174,
7.175, 7.176, 7.177, 7.178,
7.180, 7.181, 7.184, 7.192,
7.198, 31.140, 32.75
(1) **7.173**
(2) 7.174
s.37 .... 2.36, 2.80, 7.178,
7.180, 7.181, 7.193, 7.194,
7.195, 7.196, 7.197, 7.198,
7.200, 7.208, 31.140,
32.75
(1) **7.193**
(2) 7.194
s.38 .... 7.210, 7.211, 7.212,
7.213, 7.214, 7.216, 7.217,
7.219, 7.220, 7.221, 7.223,
7.242, 31.140, 32.75
(1) **7.209**
(2) **7.232**

(3) 7.210, 31.140
(4) 7210
ss.38–39 .... 31.74
ss.38–41 ..... 7.14, 7.17, 7.58,
7.224, 31.129
s.39 .... 7.214, 7.216, 7.217,
7.238, 7.239, 7.240, 7.241,
7.242, 7.244, 7.245, 7.250,
7.251, 31.140, 32.75
(1) **7.237**
(2) 7.232, 7.249
(3) 7.238, 31.140
(4) 7.238
s.40 .... 2.36, 2.80, 7.253,
7.254, 7.255, 7.256, 7.257,
7.259, 7.260, 7.270, 7.271,
7.277, 31.140, 32.75
(1) **7.252**
(2) 7.232, 7.269
(3) 7.253
s.41 .... 2.36, 2.80, 7.257,
7.259, 7.260, 7.273, 7.274,
7.275, 7.246, 7.277, 7.279,
7.286, 7.287, 31.140,
32.75
(1) **7.272**
(2) 7.226, 7.232, 7.285
(3) 7.226, 7.273
(4) 7.227
s.42 .... **7.224**, 7.225, 29.20,
32.75
(2)–(4) 7.225
s.43 .... 7.17, **7.235**, **7.251**,
7.271, 7.287, 32.75
s.44 .... 7.17, **7.326**, 7.271,
7.287, 32.75
s.45 .... 8.133, 32.75
(2) 8.57, 8.58, 8.131
s.46 .... 8.82
s.47 .... 10.05, 10.11, 10.14,
10.15, 10.16, 10.17, 10.19,
10.20, 10.21, 10.22, 10.23,
10.25, 10.26, 10.27, 10.28,
10.29, 10.31, 10.32, 10.53,

10.57, 10.61, 31.129,
31.140, 32.75
(1) **10.10**
(2) **10.32**, 10.60
(3) 31.140
(3)–(6) 10.11
(4) 31.140
ss.47–50 .... 10.01, 10.36,
10.44, 10.71, 10.90,
10.119, 31.20, 31.74
ss.47–54 .... 32.22
s.48 .... 10.05, 10.27, 10.28,
10.36, 10.37, 10.38, 10.39,
10.40, 10.41, 10.42, 10.53,
10.54, 10.56, 10.57, 10.61,
10.62, 10.63, 10.64, 10.65,
10.68, 10.133, 31.140,
32.75
(1) **10.35**
(2) 10.38
ss.48–50 .... 10.43, 10.45,
10.46, 10.50, 10.51, 10.68,
10.78, 10.96, 10.138,
31.125
ss.48–51 .... 10.01
s.49 .... 10.05, 10.72, 10.73,
10.74, 10.75, 10.76, 10.77,
10.79, 10.80, 10.81, 10.84,
10.87, 10.151, 31.140,
32.75
(1) **10.69**
(2) 10.72, 10.91
s.50 .... 4.169, 10.05, 10.28,
10.36, 10.68, 10.89, 10.91,
10.93, 10.94, 10.95, 10.97,
10.98, 10.99, 10.101,
10.104, 10.153, 31.140,
32.75
(1) **10.88**
s.51 .... 32.75
(2) **10.59**, 10.60, 10.61,
10.63, 10.64, 10.136,
10.138, 12.55
(a) 10.61
(b) 10.62

(3) **10.60**
s.51A 13.16, **13.60**, 13.62,
13.63, 13.64, 13.65, 13.72,
14.05, 31.140, 32.08
(2) **13.65**, 13.66
(3) 13.63
(4) 13.65
s.52 .... 10.47, 10.51, 10.63,
10.68, 10.106, 10.107,
10.112, 10.113, 10.114,
10.115, 10.116, 10.117,
10.118, 10.120, 10.121,
10.127, 10.128, 10.135,
10.136, 10.138, 10.139,
10.141, 10.150, 10.153,
10.164, 10.168, 12.03,
12.47, 12.48, 12.50,
31.125, 31.140, 32.75
(1) **10.111**
(2) 10.113
ss.52–53 .... 10.46
ss.52–53A 10.01
s.53 .... 10.47, 10.51, 10.86,
10.106, 10.118, 10.120,
10.121, 10.122, 10.125,
10.127, 10.128, 10.130,
10.142, 10.144, 10.145,
10.146, 10.147, 10.148,
10.149, 10.150, 10.152,
10.153, 10.154, 10.155,
10.156, 10.157, 10.159,
10.160, 10.161, 12.03,
12.47, 12.48, 12.50,
31.125, 31.140, 32.75
(1) **10.143**
(2) 10.144
s.53A 10.109, **10.163**,
10.164, 12.09, 31.140,
32.08, 32.75
(2) 10.169
(b) 10.171
(3) **10.169**
(4) 10.164
s.54(1) **10.140**, **10.170**
(a) 10.141

(b) 10.141
(2) **10.137**, 10.138,
10.159, 10.168
(3) **10.137**, 10.138,
10.159, 10.167
s.55 .... 12.03, 12.42, 32.75
s.56 .... 11.76, 13.05, 13.25,
13.29
s.57 .... 11.07, 11.17, 11.98,
32.13
(1) 11.21
ss.57–59 .... 11.08, 11.16,
11.47, 11.79, 11.90, 32.13
s.58 .... 10.54, 11.07, 11.92,
11.100, 32.13
s.58A 32.13
s.59 .... 11.07, 32.13
s.59A 11.16, 11.17, 11.19,
11.21, 11.47, 11.72, 11.79,
11.80, 11.85, 11.86, 11.90,
11.110, 11.111, 11.112,
32.13
s.61 .... 14.01, 14.03, 14.09,
14.10, 14.11, 14.13, 14.15,
14.17, 14.18, 14.19, 14.21,
14.22, 14.23, 14.24, 14.25,
14.26, 14.28, 14.31, 14.34,
14.57, 31.140, 32.75,
33.12
(1) **14.08**
s.62 .... 3.156, 3.160, 14.01,
14.03, 14.04, 14.05, 14.06,
14.07, 14.37, 14.38, 14.39,
14.40, 14.41, 14.42, 14.43,
14.44, 14.45, 14.46, 14.47,
14.48, 14.49, 14.50, 14.52,
14.66, 31.74
(1) **14.37**, 31.140, 32.75
(2) 14.09, 14.37
(3) 31.140
ss.62–63 ....31.129
s.63 .... 14.01, 14.07, 14.25,
14.52A, 14.53, 14.54,
14.55, 14.56, 14.57, 14.58,
14.59, 14.60, 14.61, 14.62,

14.63, 14.65, 14.66, 14.67,
14.68, 14.69, 14.70, 14.71,
14.73, 14.74, 31.140,
32.75, 33.12
(1) **14.51**
(c) 14.68
(2) 14.52, 14.71
(3) 14.39
(4) 14.39
s.64 .... 6.05, 6.06, 6.11, 6.73,
6.74, 6.75, 6.76, 6.77, 6.78,
6.79, 6.80, 6.83, 6.84,
6.85, 6.86, 6.88, 6.91,
6.99, 6.100, 31.42, 31.129,
31.140, 32.75, 33.12
(1) **6.72**
(2) 6.85
(3) **6.86**, 14.53
(3A) **6.86**
(4) **6.92**, 6.105
(5) 6.73
ss.64–65 .... 31.19
s.65 .... 6.05, 6.06, 6.11, 6.77,
6.78, 6.79, 6.80, 6.83, 6.84,
6.88, 6.95, 6.97, 6.98,
6.99, 6.100, 6.101, 6.106,
31.42, 31.140, 32.75,
33.12
(1) **6.94**
(2) 6.100, 6.105
(3) **6.101**
(3A) **6.101**
(4) 6.105
(5) 6.95
s.66 .... 4.109, 14.13, 15.02,
15.04, 15.34, 15.36, 15.45,
15.71, 15.72, 15.73, 15.76,
15.80, 15.83, 15.84, 15.89,
15.103, 15.107, 15.151,
15.192, 31.125, 31.129,
31.140, 33.12
(1) **15.69**, 15.70, 32.75,
34.62
(2) 15.70
ss.66–71 .... 32.22

s.67 ... 2.36, 2.80, 4.54, 14.13,
15.02, 15.18, 15.75, **15.90**,
15.91, 15.92, 15.93, 15.94,
15.95, 15.104, 15.107,
15.108, 15.111, 15.113,
15.121, 15.122, 15.125,
15.181, 31.125, 31.129,
31.140, 32.75, 33.12
(1) 15.91, 15.96, 15.68,
15.100, 15.101, 15.112,
15.122
(a) 15.122, 15.123
(b) 15.122, 15.124
(2) .. 15.91, 15.122, 15.125
(3) 15.91, 15.125
(4) 15.91
(5) 15.92
(7) 15.91
s.68 .. 15.117, 15.118, 31.129,
32.75
(1) 15.113, 15.114,
15.117
(2) 15.121
s.69 .... 15.02, 15.19, 15.22,
15.126, 15.128, 15.129,
15.130, 15.132, 15.133,
15.137, 15.141, 15.142,
15.144, 31.42, 31.129,
31.140, 32.75
(1) 15.131, 15.136,
15.143
(2) ... 2.27, 15.131, 15.135,
15.139, 15.140, 15.143
(3) 15.128
ss.69–71 .... 15.132, 15.151,
15.159
s.70 ..... 15.24, 15.25, 15.143,
15.147, 15.149, 15.151,
15.154, 15.155, 31.140,
32.75
(1) **15.145**
(2) 15.147
s.71 .... 2.29, 2.66, 4.243,
15.02, 15.10, 15.34,
15.159, 15.162, 31.42,

31.125, 31.140, 32.75
(1) **15.156**, 15.157
(2) **15.161**
(3) 15.157
s.72 ... 1.154, 2.25, 2.62, 2.97,
3.72, 3.98, 3.126, 3.157,
4.59, 4.85, 4.111, 4.130,
4.158, 4.171, 4.177, 4.208,
4.238, 4.257, 5.28, 5.62,
5.89, 5.113, 6.43, 6.63,
7.62, 7.99, 7.117, 7.133,
7.153, 7.167, 7.184, 7.200,
7.223, 7.244, 7.263, 7.279,
8.41, 8.128, 10.26, 10.56,
10.80, 10.98, 14.26, 14.46,
14.67, 32.22, 32.75
(6)–(8) ... 1.154, 2.26, 3.72,
4.59, 5.28, 6.43, 7.62, 8.41,
10.26, 14.30
(9) 1.154, 2.26, 3.72,
4.59, 5.28, 6.43, 7.62, 8.41,
10.26, 14.26, 15.136
(10) 15.136
s.73 .... 4.182, 32.75
s.74 .... 1.06, 1.07, 1.08, 1.09,
1.12, 1.13, 1.179, 1.183,
1.185, 1.186, 1.187, 1.206,
1.207, 1.208, 1.209, 1.210,
1.211, 1.213, 1.214, 1.215,
1.219, 1.220, 1.222, 1.225,
1.238, 1.241, 1.242, 1.244,
1.248, 1.263, 1.264, 1.265,
1.274, 1.281, 1.299, 1.313,
1.316, 1.317, 1.319, 1.339,
1.343, 1.344, 1.345, 1.348,
1.349, 1.355, 2.31, 2.77,
2.104, 7.29, 7.32, 7.33,
14.31, 16.26, 32.75
s.75 .... 1.08, 1.09, 1.179,
1.210, 1.263, 1.264, 1.265,
1.266, 1.277, 1.278, 1.281,
1.282, 1.283, 1.285, 1.299,
1.310, 1.313, 1.319, 2.31,
2.64, 2.77, 2.98, 2.104,
14.31, 16.28, 32.75

(1) 1.285, 7.21
  (a) 1.282
  (b) 1.282
  (c) 1.278, 1.282
(2) 1.269, 1.278, 1.282,
           1.292, 1.295
  (a)–(f) 1.278
  (a) .. 1.284, 1.293, 1.296
  (b) .. 1.293, 1.294, 1.296
  (c) 1.297
  (d) 1.263, 1.298,
           1.299, 1.303
  (e) 1.304, 7.21, 7.34
  (f) 1.306
(3) 1.296
s.76 .... 1.07, 1.08, 1.179,
1.205, 1.206, 1.207, 1.208,
1.209, 1.210, 1.211, 1.212,
1.214, 1.215, 1.277, 1.310,
1.311, 1.313, 1.315, 1.316,
1.318, 1.320, 1.322, 1.323,
1.324, 1.332, 1.343, 1.348,
     2.31, 2.77, 2.104, 7.33,
           14.31, 32.75
  (1) **1.310**
  (2) 1.205, 1.214, 1.311
  (a) .. 1.207, 1.313, 1.314,
1.318, 1.320, 1.321, 1.322,
.325, 1.326, 1.327, 1.328,
           1.334
s.77 .... 1.277, 1.279, 1.282,
           1.292, 32.75
s.78 .... **2.29**, 2.36, **2.66**, 2.67,
     2.68, 2.72, 2.80, 2.99,
4.243, 7.123, 7.139, 7.190,
     7.268, 10.29, 10.30,
     15.161, 26.31, 32.75
  (a) 2.67, 2.68
  (b) ... 2.68, 2.69, 2.70, 2.72,
     2.73, 2.74, 2.75, 15.41,
           15.42
s.79 .... 32.75
  (2) 1.158, 1.169, 1.213,
           15.154
  (3) 1.155, 2.63

(4) 4.115, 4.136, 15.111
(5) 4.136
(6) 1.238, 7.25, 7.80
(7) 4.115, 15.111
(8) 2.63
(9) 1.155, 21.30, 22.35
Pt 2 .... 3.14, 8.59, 8.133,
     11.120, 16.33, 32.23
s.80 .... 1.23, 2.12, 2.42, 2.89,
     3.35, 3.85, 3.110, 3.140,
     4.29, 4.74, 4.97, 4.126,
4.150, 4.166, 4.194, 4.235,
     4.253, 5.12, 5.57, 5.80,
     5.108, 6.17, 6.60, 6.76,
     6.98, 7.51, 7.95, 7.110,
     7.130, 7.146, 7.164, 7.177,
     7.197, 7.213, 7.241, 7.256,
     7.276, 8.06, 8.121, 10.17,
     10.41, 10.75, 10.94, 14.12,
     14.42, 14.56, 15.72, 15.94,
     15.129, 15.148, 35.07,
           35.08
  (1)(c) 15.99
  (d) 31.132
s.81 .... 35.14. **35.15**, 35.58
  (7) 35.14
  (8) 35.14
s.82 .... **35.16**, 35.23, 35.26,
           35.58
  (1) 31.132, 35.26
  (2) 35.18
  (3) 35.19
  (4) 35.19
  (5) 35.25
  (6) 31.133, 35.17
  (7) 32.24
s.83 .... 35.31, **35.33**
  (1) 35.31
  (2) 35.32
  (4) 35.32
  (5) 35.31, 35.33, 35.41
  (6) 35.31
ss.83–85 .... 35.43
s.84 .... 35.04, 35.37, **35.39**,
           35.41

(1) 35.38
(2) 35.38
(3) 35.38
(4) 35.38
s.85 .... 35.04, 35.41, **35.42**
(5)(a) 35.41
s.86 .... 35.04, 35.45
(14) 4.232
s.87 .... 35.34
(4) 35.34
s.88(3) 35.34
s.89 ...... 31.131, 35.04, 35.46
s.90 ... 31.139, 31.140, 35.04,
35.47
s.91 .. 31.125, 31.139, 31.140,
35.49, 35.50, 35.51
(3) 35.48
s.91A 35.27, **35.28**
ss.91A–91C 35.27
s.91A–91F 35.21, 35.27
s.91B 35.27, **35.28**
s.91C 35.27, **35.28**, 35.29
s.91D 35.27, **35.28**
(1)(b) 35.29
s.91E 35.27, **35.28**
s.91F 35.27, **35.28**
(1) 32.24
s.94 .... 35.43
s.95 .... 35.43
s.96 .... 35.43
s.96B 35.44, 36.37
s.97 .... 35.57, **35.59**, 35.61,
35.66
(1) 35.58
(2)–(4) 35.58
(3)(c) 35.60
ss.97–103 .... 35.04
s.98 .... 35.63, **35.64**
(3) 35.63
s.99 .... 35.61, **35.62**
(3) 35.61
s.100 .... 18.33, 35.65
s.101 .... 19.04, 35.66
s.103 .... 19.04
s.103A **36.13**, 36.27

(2) 36.15, 36.17, 36.23
(3) 36.23
ss.103A–103K 36.06
s.103B(1) 36.15, 36.18
(3) 36.18
s.103C 36.53
(1) 36.53
(2) 36.49
(3)(b) 36.50
(4) 36.53
(6) 36.53
s.103D(1) 36.45
(3) 36.45
(4) 36.45
(5) 36.45
s.103E 36.57
(5) 36.54
(7) 36.54
s.103F 36.20
s.103G 36.51
(5) 36.52
s.103H 36.55
(3)(a) 36.57
s.103I 36.60
ss.104–129 .... 36.06
s.107(1)(b) 32.54
s.108 .... 36.55, 36.57
s.109(1) 11.16
(2) 11.16
s.110(3)(a) 36.57
s.113 ....31.140
(1) 20.29
s.122 ....31.140
s.122A **36.66**
(7) 36.70
(8) 36.70
ss.122A–122K 36.06
s.122C 36.70
(4) 36.70
s.122D 36.71
(5) 36.71
s.122F 36.70
s.122G 36.72
s.122H 36.73
(1) 36.73

(3) 36.73
(4) 36.73
s.122I(1) 36.73
(1)–(3) 36.73
(2) 36.73
(4) 36.73
s.122J 36.74
s.122K(1)(a) 36.75
(b) 36.75, 36.76
s.123(3) 36.08
s.128 .... 36.73
s.131 ....31.106
(a) 31.129, 35.22
s.132A 36.19
s.133(1) 31.130
s.134 .... 35.09
s.139 .... 1.24, 6.88, 8.119,
10.42, 10.76, 10.95,
10.117, 10.148, 19.123,
26.23, 29.13, 31.29, 31.42
s.141 .... 1.32, 19.18
s.142(2)(c) 32.23
Sch.1 .... 13.05, 13.25, 13.29
Pt 1 .... 11.60
Sch.2 . .. 2.25, 2.62, 2.97,
3.72, 3.98, 3.126, 3.157,
4.59, 4.85, 4.111, 4.130,
4.158, 4.171, 4.208, 4.238,
5.28, 5.62, 5.89, 5.113,
6.43, 6.63, 7.62, 7.99,
7.117, 7.133, 7.153, 7.167,
7.184, 7.200, 7.223, 7.244,
7.263, 7.279, 8.41, 8.128,
10.26, 10.56, 10.80, 10.98,
14.26, 14.46, 14.67
Sch.3 .. 1.23, 2.12, 2.42, 2.89,
3.35, 3.80, 3.110, 3.140,
4.29, 4.74, 4.97, 4.126,
4.150, 4.166, 4.194, 4.235,
4.253, 5.12, 5.57, 5.80,
5.108, 6.17, 6.60, 6.76,
6.98, 7.51, 7.95, 7110,
7.130, 7.146, 7.164, 7.177,
7.197, 7.213, 7.241, 7.256,
7.276, 8.06, 8.121, 10.17,

10.41, 10.75, 10.94, 14.12,
14.42, 14.56, 15.72, 15.94,
15.129, 15.146, 31.128,
31.135, 31.140, 35.07,
35.10, 35.27, 35.34, 35.61,
35.65, 36.15, 36.18
para.18(b)(ii)(c) 35.13
para.22 .... 35.22
Sch.3A 32.24
Sch.5 .... 31.135, 31.140,
36.15, 36.18
para.5(2) 11.21
Sch.6 .... 29.13, 31.29
para.31 .... 29.20, 31.42
para.24 .... 8.03
para.28 ....19.123
para.29 .... 8.119
para.32(2) 1.24
para.41 .... 26.23
para.46 .... 10.42, 10.76,
10.95, 10.117, 10.148
para.47 .... 6.88
para.52 .... 32.02
Sch.15 .... 11.75, 31.140
2003 Criminal Justice Act
(c.44) 1.22, 1.92,
1.106, 1.108, 1.146,
2.11, 2.74, 3.34,
3.84, 3.109, 3.139,
4.28, 4.73, 4.97,
4.165, 4.193,
4.235, 6.16, 6.59,
8.32, 8.33, 9.11,
10.74, 10.93,
12.23, 12.44,
12.86, 15.01,
15.09, 15.29,
18.01, 19.02,
19.16, 19.38,
19.39, 19.51,
19.118, 20.02,
20.06, 20.57,
20.90, 20.91,
27.10, 27.103,
27.146, 30.25,

30.103, 30.121, 30.142,
30.144, 30.161, 30.167,
31.27, 31.68, 31.91, 31.98,
31.116, 32.29, 32.40,
32.57, 34.04, 34.06, 34.13,
34.16, 34.30, 34.34, 34.36,
34.52, 34.53, 34.54
s.8(1) 20.21
Pt 5 .... 18.10
s.41 .... 31.64, 31.65, 31.66,
31.99
s.58 ...... 1.255, 27.147, 30.32
s.76 .... 1.134, 1.142
s.78 .... 1.143
Pt 11 .... 19.28
s.98 ..... **20.13**, 20.15, 20.117,
20.140, 26.165
(a) 20.15, 20.16, 20.33
s.99 .... **20.13**
s.100 .. 19.91, 20.140, 20.142,
20.143, 20.144, 20.145,
20.148, 20.150, 20.151,
20.152, 20.153, 26.165
(1)(b) 20.143, 20.145,
20.147, 26.165
(3) 20.143
(a)–(d) 20.143
s.101 .. 20.14, 20.111, 20.117,
20.145, 20.150
(1) 20.34, 20.112
(a)–(g) 20.02
(b) 20.25, 20.143
(c) ... 1.150, 20.15, 20.26,
20.29
(d) 1.143, 1.146,
19.71, 20.10, 20.11, 20.16,
20.18, 20.31, 20.80, 20.89,
20.100, 20.104, 20.117
(e) 20.80
(f) 20.84
(g) 20.07, 20.87
(3) 20.40, 20.49, 20.81,
20.92, 20.93, 20.94, 20.99,
20.103, 20.105, 20.108
(4) 20.49, 20.99

s.102 .... 20.26, 20.28
s.103 ..... 20.09, 20.41, 20.43,
20.45, 20.111
(1) **20.41**
(2) **20.41**, 20.43
(3) 20.40, 20.49
s.105 .... 20.82
(1)(a) 20.83
(2)(b) 20.83
(3) 20.83
s.106 .... 20.87, 20.91
(1)(c) 20.51, 20.87
s.109 ....20.148
s.110 .... 20.20
s.112 .... 20.22
(1) .. 20.13, 20.18, 20.31
(2) 20.112, 20.113
s.114 .... 19.53
(1) 19.53
(d) 19.32, 19.38,
19.44, 19.49, 19.53, 19.54,
19.56, 19.59, 19.61, 19.62,
19.69, 19.71, 19.83,
19.129, 20.09, 20.107
(2) 19.38, 19.44, 19.49,
19.52, 19.53, 19.81, 20.09
(a)–(i) 19.49
s.115 .... 19.33
ss.116–118 .... 19.38
s.116 ... 7.37, 7.38, 7.40, 7.90,
19.38, 19.39, 19.51, 19.54,
19.61, 19.66, 19.71, 20.09,
24.49, 27.10
(1) 19.39
(b) 19.49
(2) 20.09
(a) .. 19.39, 19.41, 19.61
(b) 7.31, 7.37, 19.47
(e) 19.49, 19.50
(3) 19.49
(4) 19.49
(a)–(c) 19.49
(c) 19.49
s.117 .... 18.78, 20.07
(2)(b) 18.78

s.118(1) 19.62
   (d) 19.63
   (4) 19.62
   (8) 24.02
s.119 ..... 19.64, 19.65, 19.69,
            19.70, 27.80
   (1) 19.64, 19.70
s.120 .... 7.40, 19.72, 19.75,
   19.76, 19.77, 19.87, 19.88,
               19.102
   (2) 19.72, **19.89**, 19.90
   (4) 19.80, 19.82, 19.88,
           19.90, 30.102
     (a) 7.40
     (b) 7.40
   (4)–(7) 19.72
   (5) 7.40, 19.82
   (6) 19.82
   (7) 7.40, **19.82**, 19.83,
       19.84, 19.88, 19.90,
            30.102
    (d) 19.76, 19.83,
            30.103
    (e) 19.85
    (f) 19.87
   (8) 19.85
s.123 ..... 7.38, 19.51, 27.146,
             27.146
   (1) **19.51**
s.124 ...... 19.38, 19.49, 19.50
s.125 ...... 19.38, 19.40, 19.50
   (4) 33.08
   (7) 33.07
s.126 .... 19.38
s.127 .... 25.31, 25.35
s.129 .... **8.111**
s.133 ...... 8.107, 8.110, **8.111**
s.139 .... 27.81
s.142 .... 30.138, 31.116
s.142A 31.116
s.143(1) 1.94
   (2) 1.94
s.144 .... 1.77
s.146 .... 7.41
s.147(2) 4.155

s.148(1) 31.108
   (5) 31.108
s.152(2) 31.105
s.153 .... 1.106
   (2) 34.12
s.154(1) 11.60, 11.74
s.156(3) 31.104
   (5) 31.103
s.163 .... 11.60, 11.74
s.172 ....30.113
   (1) 33.07
s.174 ... 1.80, 2.21, 2.55, 2.95,
    3.49, 3.95, 3.121, 3.149,
    4.42, 4.108, 4.202, 5.18,
    5.85, 6.22, 6.81, 7.57,
   7.115, 7.151, 7.182, 7.218,
   7.261, 8.30, 10.15, 10.24,
   10.52, 10.132, 11.89,
  12.51, 14.20, 14.64, 15.81,
            15.109
   (1)(a) 33.10, 34.26
   (2)(a) 33.10
    (aa) 33.10
   (4B) 31.105
   (6) 33.10
s.179 .... 31.91
s.189(6) 35.23
s.202 .... 2.18, 2.51, 2.93,
    3.117, 4.39, 4.106, 5.16,
    5.83, 6.20, 6.79, 7.113,
   7.149, 7.180, 7.216, 7.259,
   8.24, 10.22, 10.49, 10.126,
   11.84, 12.49, 15.73,
            15.107
s.224 ... 1.22, 2.11, 2.88, 3.34,
    3.84, 3.108, 3.139, 4.28,
    4.73, 4.97, 4.125, 4.149,
   4.165, 4.193, 4.234, 6.16,
    6.59, 7.50, 7.94, 7.145,
   7.163, 9.11, 10.14, 10.40,
  10.74, 10.93, 12.23, 12.44,
  12.86, 14.41, 15.29, 31.65,
            31.91
ss.224–229 .... 34.25, 34.30,
       34.31, 34.40, 34.41

s.224A 1.22, 1.78, 1.96,
    1.107, 1.109, 2.11, 2.21,
    2.88, 2.95, 3.34, 3.49,
    3.84, 3.95, 3.109, 3.121,
    3.139, 3.149, 4.28, 4.42,
    4.73, 4.97, 4.108, 4.125,
    4.149, 4.165, 4.193, 4.202,
    6.16, 6.22, 6.59, 7.50,
    7.57, 7.94, 7.145, 7.151,
    7.163, 8.07, 10.15, 10.40,
    10.52, 10.74, 10.93, 11.61,
    11.75, 14.41, 34.08, 34.11,
    34.17, 34.20, 34.21, **34.22**
  (2) 34.21
  (a) 34.20
  (b) 34.20
  (10) 34.18
s.225 .... 1.92, 1.94, 1.114,
    1.131, 34.06, 34.07, 34.09,
                         34.23
  (1) 1.92, 1.95, 1.96,
    1.106, 34.07, 34.08, 34.32
  (2) ... 1.22, 1.78, 1.92, 1.95,
    1.96, 1.106, 2.11, 2.21,
    2.88, 2.95, 3.34, 3.49,
    3.84, 3.95, 3.139, 3.149,
    7.50, 7.57, 7.94, 7.145,
    7.151, 7.163, 14.41, 34.07,
                  34.08, 34.11
  (b) 1.94, 1.105
s.226 .... 31.105, 31.139
  (1) 34.45
s.226A 1.22, 1.78, 1.94,
    1.95, 2.11, 2.21, 2.41, 2.55,
    2.88, 2.95, 3.34, 3.49,
    3.84, 3.95, 3.109, 3.121,
    3.139, 3.149, 4.28, 4.42,
    4.73, 4.97, 4.108, 4.125,
    4.165, 4.193, 4.202, 5.11,
    5.18, 5.56, 5.79, 5.85,
    5.107, 6.16, 6.22, 6.59,
    6.75, 6.81, 6.97, 7.50,
    7.57, 7.94, 7.115, 7.129,
    7.145, 7.151, 7.163, 7.176,
    7.182, 7.196, 7.212, 7.218,

    7.240, 7.255, 7.261, 7.275,
    8.07, 8.30, 10.15, 10.24,
    10.40, 10.52, 10.74, 10.93,
    10.115, 10.132, 10.146,
    11.61, 11.75, 11.89, 14.11,
    14.20, 14.41, 14.45, 14.55,
    14.64, 15.71, 15.81, 15.93,
    15.109, 30.161, 34.10,
    34.13, 34.14, **34.16**, 34.23
  (1) 34.11
  (3) 34.11
  (4) 34.11
  (5) 34.12
  (6) 34.12
  (7) 34.12
  (7A) 34.12
  (8) 34.12
  (9) 34.12
  (11) 1.78
s.226B 1.78, 31.66, 31.91,
    31.92, 31.102, 34.14,
                         34.16
  (1) **31.92**
  (b) 31.93
s.227 .... 1.78, 1.95, 34.10,
                         34.26
  (3)(b) 34.38
s.228 .. 31.105, 31.139, 34.26
  (3)(b) 34.38
s.229 ..... **31.93**, **34.24**, 34.26,
    34.30, 34.33, 34.36
  (2) 34.26, 34.33, 34.36
  (a) 31.94
  (aa) 31.94
  (b) 34.33, 34.34
  (c) 31.94, 34.33
  (3) 34.26, 34.26, 34.30
s.233 .... 34.24
s.235 .... 34.14
s.236A 30.164, 34.55
s.240 .... 34.47
s.240A 1.80, 2.21, 2.55,
    2.95, 3.49, 3.95, 3.121,
    3.149, 4.42, 4.108, 4.202,
    5.18, 5.85, 6.22, 6.81,

7.57, 7.115, 7.151, 7.182,
7.218, 7.261, 8.30, 10.24,
10.52, 10.132, 11.89,
12.51, 14.20, 14.64, 15.81,
15.109
s.244 .... 34.40
s.244A 34.55
s.246A 1.79, **34.16**
(2) 34.13
(6)(b) 34.13
s.247 .... 34.41
s.282(2) 2.39, 2.86, 3.107,
3.137, 4.26, 4.71, 4.95,
4.123, 4.147, 4.163, 4.191,
4.232, 4.250, 5.09, 5.54,
5.77, 5.105, 6.14, 6.57,
6.73, 6.95, 7.48, 7.92,
7.107, 7.127, 7.143, 7.161,
7.174, 7.194, 7.210, 7.238,
7.253, 7.273, 8.04, 8.120,
9.10, 9.53, 10.11, 10.38,
10.72, 10.91, 10.113,
10.144, 12.43, 13.57,
14.09, 14.39, 14.53, 15.28,
15.70, 15.92, 15.128,
15.147, 35.48
(3) 2.39, 2.86, 3.107,
3.137, 4.26, 4.71, 4.95,
4.123, 4.147, 4.163, 4.191,
4.232, 4.250, 5.09, 5.54,
5.77, 5.105, 6.14, 6.57,
6.73, 6.95, 7.48, 7.92,
7.107, 7.127, 7.143, 7.161,
7.174, 7.194, 7.210, 7.238,
7.253, 7.273, 8.04, 8.120,
9.10, 9.53, 10.11, 10.38,
10.72, 10.91, 10.113,
10.144, 12.43, 13.57,
14.09, 14.39, 14.53, 15.28,
15.70, 15.92, 15.128,
15.147, 35.48
(4) 2.39, 2.86, 3.107,
3.137, 4.26, 4.71, 4.95,
4.123, 4.147, 4.163, 4.191,
4.232, 4.250, 5.09, 5.54,

5.77, 5.105, 6.14, 6.57,
6.73, 6.95, 7.48, 7.92,
7.107, 7.127, 7.143, 7.161,
7.174, 7.194, 7.210, 7.238,
7.253, 7.273, 8.04, 8.120,
9.10, 9.53, 10.11, 10.38,
10.72, 10.91, 10.113,
10.144, 12.43, 13.57,
14.09, 14.39, 14.53, 15.28,
15.70, 15.92, 15.128,
15.147, 35.48
s.305(2) 11.36
s.320(1) 15.01
(2) 15.01
Sch.3 para.9 ....
para.18 .... 31.65, 31.66,
31.99
Sch.4 .... 1.142
Sch.5 .... 1.142
Sch.8 para.15 .... 31.91
Sch.15 ... 9.11, 12.23, 34.11,
34.38
Pt 1 ....31.140
Pt 2 .... 1.22, 2.11, 2.88,
3.34, 3.84, 3.109, 3.139,
4.28, 4.73, 4.97, 4.125,
4.149, 4.165, 4.193, 4.234,
6.16, 6.59, 7.50, 7.94,
7.145, 7.163, 10.15, 10.40,
10.74, 10.93, 12.23, 12.44,
12.86, 14.41, 15.29, 31.40,
31.91, 31.140
Sch.15A 1.78, 34.10
Sch.15B 1.78, 1.96, 1.109,
11.75, 34.08, 34.10, 34.14,
34.17
Pt 1 ..... 1.22, 1.108, 1.109,
2.11, 2.88, 3.34, 3.84,
3.109, 3.139, 4.28, 4.73,
4.97, 4.125, 4.149, 4.165,
4.193, 6.16, 6.59, 7.50,
7.94, 7.145, 7.163, 8.07,
10.40, 10.74, 10.93, 11.61,
11.75, 14.41, 34.17, 34.19
Pt 2 .... 1.109

Sch.18A 34.55

2004 Asylum and Immigra-
tion (Treatment of
Claimants, etc.)
Act (c.19) 11.13
s.4 .... 11.47, 11.72

2004 Domestic Violence,
Crime and Victims
Act (c.28)–
s.11 .... 2.44, 9.18
s.17 .... 34.34

2004 Children Act (c.31)–
s.11 .... 36.77

2004 Civil Partnerships Act
(c.33)–
s.3 .... 5.40
s.215 .... 5.40
s.217 .... 5.40
s.246(1) 6.34
s.247(1) 6.34
s.261(1) 5.39, 5.68, 5.95,
5.119, 6.51, 7.235, 8.75,
19.123
s.263 ....19.123
Sch.21 para.61 .... 6.34
Sch.27 para.60 .... 8.75
para.97 ....19.123
para.173 .... 5.39, 5.68,
5.95, 5.119
para.174(2) 6.51
(3) 6.51
para.175(2) 7.235
(3) 7.235

2005 Mental Capacity Act
(c.9) 1.229, 1.223,
7.08, 7.10, 7.11,
21.20
s.1(2) **7.24**
(4) 1.235
s.2 .... 7.10
(1) 1.223
(4) **7.24**
s.3 .... 7.10
(1) 1.223
(c) 1.235

2005 Serious Organised
Crime and Police
Act (c.15) 13.53
s.70(1) 22.72
s.73 .... 1.77
s.74 .... 1.77
s.110 .... 13.53
s.111 .... 13.53
Sch.7 para.14 .... 13.53

2005 Prohibition of Female
Genital Mutila-
tion (Scotland)
Act (asp 8) 22.68

2005 Protection of Children
and Prevention of
Sexual Offences
(Scotland) Act
(asp 9)–
s.2 .... 36.73
s.5 .... 36.73
s.7 .... 36.73

2006 Fraud Act (c.35)–
s.4 .... 11.53

2006 Violent Crime Reduc-
tion Act (c.38)
s.29(3) 31.65
s.55 .... 1.33, 19.18, 32.27,
32.28, **34.52**
(1)(c) 32.27
s.57(1) 35.16
s.58(1) 35.44

2006 National Health Service Act (c.41)–
s.275 .... 5.33

2006 National Health Service (Wales) Act
(c.42)–
s.206 .... 5.33

2006 Safeguarding Vulner-
able Groups Act
(c.47) 5.38, 34.63,
36.49
s.2 .... 36.49
s.7 .... 34.64
(3) 34.64

(4) 34.64
s.9 .... 34.64
Sch.3 .... 34.63, 36.49
Sch.4 Pt 1 .... 34.63
Pt 2 .... 34.63
2006 Police and Justice Act
(c.48)–
s.47 .... 27.25, 27.26
2006 Armed Forces Act
(c.52)–
s.378 .... 29.48, 35.08
s.383(2) 35.08
Sch.16 para.158 .... 29.48
Sch.17 .... 35.08
2006 Police, Public Order
and Criminal Jus-
tice (Scotland) Act
(asp 10)–
s.78 .... 35.34, 35.39, 35.49
(2) 35.33
s.104 ..... 35.33, 35.34, 35.39,
35.49
2007 Mental Health Act
(c.12) .. 7.25, 7.80, 27.17
s.2(3) 7.25
s.3 .... 7.25
2007 Serious Crime Act
(c.27) 1.418, 2.100
Pt 2 .... 11.39, 29.20
ss.44–46 .... 1.145, 1.149,
1.418, 4.161, 14.03, 15.91,
15.141
s.44 .... 1.411, 1.412, 1.413,
3.31, 3.81, 3.106, 4.70,
8.68, 8.69, 8.70
s.45 .... 1.411, 1.414
s.46 .... 1.411, 1.415, 1.416
s.47 .... 1.412
(4) 1.415
(5) 1.415
(b) 1.413
s.48(2) 1.415
s.49(7) 1.415
s.50 .... 1.417

(3) 1.417
s.51 .... 1.418
s.59 .... 1.411
s.63(1) 29.20
(2) 35.10
s.65(2)(b) 1.411
s.94 .... 35.10
Sch.6 para.20(a) 29.20
para.63(2) 35.10
Sch.13 para.5 .... 35.10
2007 Local Government and
Public Involve-
ment in Health
Act (c.28) 15.199
s.135 ....15.199
s.241 ....15.199
Sch.6 para.2(c) 15.199
Sch.18 Pt 7 ....15.199
2007 UK Borders Act
(c.30) 11.17
s.31(3) 11.17
2008 Criminal Justice and
Immigration Act
(c.4) 4.187, 6.88,
27.159, 31.107,
34.50
s.1 ....31.107
(1)(a) 31.139
(b) 31.139
(c) 31.139
(d) 31.139
(e) 31.139
(f) 31.139
(g) 31.139
(h) 31.139
(i) 31.139
(j) 31.139
(k) 31.139
(m) 31.139
(n) 31.139
(o) 31.139
(2) 31.139

(3) 31.139
  (a) 31.107
  (b) 31.107
(4) 31.108, 31.139
s.9 ....31.116
s.17 .... 34.24, 34.26
s.35 .... 31.88, 31.110
s.63 .... 4.103, 15.127, 15.146
  (3) .. 4.103, 15.127, 15.146
  (5A) 4.103, 15.127,
                  15.146
  (7) .. 4.103, 15.127, 15.146
  (7A) 4.103
s.65 .... 4.263
s.67 .... 15.127, 15.146
s.69 .... 8.53
  (1) 8.55
  (2) 8.82
  (4) 8.55
s.72 ... 1.154, 2.25, 2.62, 2.97,
    3.72, 3.98, 3.126, 3.157,
    4.59, 4.85, 4.111, 4.130,
    4.158, 4.171, 4.208, 4.238,
    5.28, 7.62, 7.99, 7.117,
    7.133, 7.153, 7.167, 7.184,
    7.200, 7.223, 7.244, 7.263,
    7.279, 8.41, 8.128, 10.26,
    10.56, 10.80, 10.98, 14.26,
             14.46, 14.67
s.73 .... 4.186, 5.67, 5.89,
    5.113, 6.29, 6.43, 6.51,
    6.63, 6.72, 6.86, 6.94,
    6.100, 35.33, 35.39, 35.42
s.142(1) 35.33
  (3)–(5) 35.39
  (7)–(9) 35.42
s.148(1) ... 35.10, 35.33, 35.42
s.149 .... 31.93
s.153(7) ... 35.10, 35.39, 35.42
Sch.1 para.2 ....31.139
  (2) 31.139
  para.3 ....31.139
  (2) 31.139

para.4 ....31.139
paras 6–8 ....31.139
  (3) 31.139
para.9 ....31.139
para.10 ....31.139
para.12 ....31.139
para.13 ....31.139
  (1) 31.139
  (2) 31.139
para.14 ....31.139
  (4) 31.139
para.15 ....31.139
para.16 ....31.139
para.17 ....31.139
  (6)(b) 31.139
para.20 ....31.139
para.22 ....31.139
para.23 ....31.139
para.24 ....31.139
para.25 ....31.139
  (5) 31.139
para.26 ....31.139
  (1) 31.139
  (7) 31.139
Sch.2 ....31.109
  paras 6–8 ....31.105
Sch.4 para.80(3) 31.105
Sch.15 para.1 .... 4.186
  para.3 .... 6.30
  para.4 .... 6.51
  para.5(2) 6.72
  (3) 6.86, 6.100
  para.6(2) 6.94
Sch.26 para.36 ....27.159
  para.55 .... 35.42
  para.58(2) 35.10
Sch.28 para.1 .... 31.93

2008   Children and Young
        Persons   Act
        (c.23)–
    s.8(2) 5.33, 6.32
    Sch.1 para.15 .... 5.33

	para.16	6.32
2008	Education and Skills Act (c.25)–	
	s.68	5.34
	s.70(1)(b)	5.34
	s.74	5.34
2009	Coroners and Justice Act (c.25)	27.59
	s.62	8.01, 8.37
	s.69(1)	8.75
	(2)	8.143
	s.71	11.21, 11.47, 11.59
	s.98	31.58
	s.99(1)	27.19
	(2)	27.19
	s.100(1)	27.50
	(4)(ba)	27.50
	(5)	27.50
	(6)	27.14, 27.50
	(8)	27.50
	s.101	27.55
	s.102	27.62
	s.104	27.37
	(1)	27.12, 27.25
	s.105	27.159
	s.112	19.76, 30.103
	s.125	30.04, 31.119, 31.120, 33.07, 33.10
	(1)	30.113, 33.07
	(3)	33.08
	s.144	20.09
	s.177	33.07
	(1)	35.10
	s.182(5)	35.10
	Sch.17	20.09
	Sch.21 para.62(2)	35.10
	Sch.22 para.27	33.07
2009	Policing and Crime Act (c.26)	10.109, 10.163, 12.09, 13.15, 13.27, 32.75
	s.14	10.109, 32.08
	s.15	32.08
	s.16	13.25
	(1)	13.31, 13.45
	(3)	13.31, 13.45
	s.17	13.27
	s.19	13.60, 32.08
	s.20	32.08
	s.81	34.63
	s.112(1)	10.170
	s.116(1)	10.170
	Sch.7 para.24(d)	10.170
2009	Sexual Offences (Scotland) Act (asp 9)	4.229, 5.128
	s.3(1)(d)	2.63
	s.9	15.125
	s.17	7.30
2010	Department of Justice Act (Northern Ireland) (c.3)	32.01
2010	Criminal Justice and Licensing (Scotland) Act (asp 13)–	
	s.41(3)(b)	35.10
	s.206(1)	35.10
2011	Education Act (c.21)–	
	s.13(1)	29.45
2011	Justice Act (Northern Ireland) (c.24)–	
	Pt 1 Ch.1	32.39
	s.7	32.61
	s.9	32.62
	s.12	32.62
2012	Health and Social Care Act (c.7)–	
	s.55(2)	7.224
	Sch.5 para.117	7.224
2012	Protection of Freedoms Act (c.9)	11.16, 25.63, 25.64
	ss.1–17	25.64

s.87(1) 34.63
s.109 .... 11.16, 32.13

2012   Legal Aid, Sentencing
     and   Punishment
     of Offenders Act
     (c.10) .. 1.78, 1.79, 1.94,
           1.95, 1.102, 1.106,
           30.161, 30.164,
           34.06, 34.07,
           34.09, 34.13, 34.16
s.85 .... 2.39, 2.86, 3.107,
       3.137, 4.26, 4.71, 4.95,
     4.123, 4.147, 4.163, 4.191,
       5.09, 5.54, 5.77, 5.105,
         6.14, 6.57, 6.73, 6.95,
       7.48, 7.92, 7.107, 7.127,
     7.143, 7.161, 7.174, 7.194,
     7.210, 7.238, 7.253, 7.273,
       8.04, 8.120, 9.10, 9.53,
     10.11, 10.38, 10.72, 10.91,
       10.113, 10.144, 12.43,
     13.56, 13.57, 14.09, 14.39,
     14.53, 15.28, 15.70, 15.92,
     15.128, 15.147, 15.157,
     15.164, 15.173, 27.124,
       29.27, 29.46, 29.50,
       29.116, 29.130
s.90 .... 2.13, 2.90, 3.35, 3.86,
         3.141, 7.52, 7.96
ss.91–102 .... 31.30
ss.92–97 .... 31.30
s.93(2) 31.30
s.94 .... 31.30
s.98 .... 31.30
s.102 .... 31.30
s.122 .... 1.96, 1.107, 1.108,
       2.11, 2.88, 3.34, 3.84,
       3.109, 4.28, 4.73, 4.97,
     4.125, 4.149, 4.165, 4.193,
       6.16, 6.59, 7.50, 7.94,
     7.145, 7.163, 8.07, 10.15,
     10.40, 10.74, 10.93, 11.60,
     11.75, 14.41, 34.08, 34.17
     (1) 34.22

s.124 ... 1.22, 2.11, 2.41, 2.88,
     3.34, 3.84, 3.109, 3.139,
     4.28, 4.73, 4.97, 4.125,
     4.165, 4.193, 5.11, 5.56,
     5.79, 5.107, 6.16, 6.59,
       6.74, 6.97, 7.50, 7.94,
   7.109, 7.129, 7.196, 7.212,
     7.240, 7.255, 7.275, 8.07,
   10.15, 10.40, 10.74, 10.93,
     10.115, 10.146, 11.60,
   11.75, 14.11, 14.41, 14.55,
   15.71, 15.92, 31.92, 34.10,
                 34.16
s.125(3) 34.16
s.135 .... 31.21
s.139 .... 13.28
s.141 .... 13.28
Sch.11 para.33 .... 2.13, 2.90,
     3.36, 3.86, 3.141, 7.52,
     7.96, 7.145, 7.163, 7.176
Sch.18 .... 1.108
Sch.19 para.24(2) 34.22
Sch.21 para.36(2) 34.16
Sch.25 Pt 2 .... 13.28

2012   Local   Government
     Byelaws   (Wales)
     Act (anaw. 2)–
s.2 ....15.199
s.20 ....15.199
Sch.2 para.9(1) 15.199
     (2) 15.199

2013   Criminal   Justice   Act
     (Northern   Ire-
     land) (c.7)–
s.1 .... 32.24
s.2 .... 32.25
s.5 .... 32.56
s.6 .... 32.13

2013   Crime and Courts Act
     (c.22)–
s.57 .. 15.179, 15.180, 15.198

2013   Marriage (Same   Sex
     Couples)   Act
     (c.30)–
s.11 .... 8.75, 8.143

Sch.3 Pt 1 para.1 .... 8.75,
8.143
2014 Offender Rehabilita-
tion Act (c.11)–
s.8(2) 34.16
(3) 34.16
2014 Anti-social Behaviour,
Crime and Polic-
ing Act (c.12) 25.64,
26.05
Pt 1 .... 13.73
s.1 .... 13.74
ss.1–21 .... 13.74
s.3 .... 13.76
s.8 .... 13.76
s.22 .... 13.77
s.23(2) 13.79
s.25 .... 13.79
s.27 .... 13.79
s.30 .... 13.79
s.114 .... 36.06
(5) 36.06
2015 Human Trafficking
and Exploitation
(Criminal Justice
and Support for
Victims) Act
(Northern Ire-
land) (c.2) 32.09,
32.18, 32.75
s.2 .... 32.13, 32.15, 32.18
s.3 .... 32.18
s.4 .... 32.15
s.15(4) 32.09
(5) 32.09
Sch.3 .... 32.21
para.1(2) 32.21
para.4(1) 32.21
2015 Criminal Justice and
Courts Act
(c.2) 4.187, 4.213,
12.23, 12.44, 13.52,
29.08, 29.09,
32.12, 34.08,
34.13, 34.50

s.2(1) 12.23, 12.44
(5) 12.23, 12.44
(6) 12.23, 12.44
s.4 .... 30.165, 34.13
(2) 34.16
(3) 34.16
s.6 .... 34.55
s.17(2) 2.09
(3) 2.39, 2.86, 3.107,
3.137, 4.26, 4.71, 4.95,
4.123, 4.163, 4.191, 5.09,
5.54, 5.77, 5.105, 6.14,
6.57, 8.04, 8.120, 10.11,
10.38, 10.72, 10.91
(4) 13.52
(5) 13.52
(6) 13.52
s.33 .... 8.81, 15.91, 15.125
s.36 .... 4.186
(2) 4.187
s.37 .... 4.103
s.53 .... 31.69, 31.81, 31.97
s.67 .... 4.225
s.78 ....29.108
s.79 .... 29.07, 29.62
(12) 29.62
s.80 ....29.118
Sch.1 .... 34.55
Sch.15 ....29.118
2015 Justice Act (Northern
Ireland) (c.9)–
s.55 .... 32.21
s.89 .... 32.12
s.90 .... 32.11
2015 Serious Crime Act
(c.9) ... 4.08, 9.25, 10.01,
10.05, 10.62, 10.63,
10.64, 10.138,
13.13, 13.30, 32.11
s.45 .... 11.53
s.58 .... 31.20
s.68 .... 10.01
(1) 10.35, 10.59, 10.69,
10.88, 13.25
(3) 10.35

(4) 10.69
(5) 10.88
(6) 10.59
(7) 13.25, 13.30
(11) 13.30
s.69 .... 4.01, 4.09, 4.249,
    4.250, 4.253, 4.255, 4.256,
    4.257, 4.258, 4.261, 4.264,
    9.15
(1) **4.248**
(2) **4.262**
    (a) 4.263
    (b) 4.263
(3) 4.250
    (b) 4.250
    (c) 4.250
(4)(a) 4.254
(5) 4.252
(8) 4.259, **4.261**
s.85 .... 2.29, 2.66, 4.234,
    4.253, 10.42, 10.76, 10.95,
    10.117, 10.138, 10.148,
    35.10
s.86(14) 4.250
Sch.3 .... 4.256
Sch.4 para.58 ... 10.42, 10.76,
    10.95, 10.117, 10.148
para.62 ....10.138
para.66(1) 4.234, 4.253,
    35.10
    (2) 4.234
    (3) 4.253, 35.10
para.63 .... 2.29, 2.66
para.68(1) 4.234
    (2) 4.234
2015 Modern Slavery Act
    (c.30) 11.21, 11.36,
        11.44, 11.46, 11.48,
        11.53, 11.59,
        11.64, 11.78,
        11.79, 11.117,
        11.119, 11.127
Pt 1 .... 11.50

s.1 .... 11.21, 11.51, 11.52,
    11.59, 11.60, 11.61, 11.64,
    11.65, 11.66, 11.68,
    11.104, 11.105, 11.108,
    11.115, 11.117, 11.120,
    27.15, 27.19, 31.140
(1)(a) 11.71
    (b) 11.71
(3) 11.66
(4) 11.104
    (a) 11.66
    (b) 11.66
(5) 11.67, 11.100
ss.1–4 .... 11.56
s.2 .... 10.46, 10.54, 11.19,
    11.21, 11.52, 11.66, 11.68,
    11.72, 11.73, 11.74, 11.75,
    11.79, 11.85, 11.90, 11.95,
    11.98, 11.99, 11.100,
    11.102, 11.103, 11.104,
    11.105, 11.111, 11.113,
    11.114, 11.115, 11.116,
    11.117, 11.118, 11.120,
    27.15, 27.19, 31.140
(1) 11.96
(2) 11.108
(3) 11.97
(4) 11.96, 11.107
(5) 11.96
(6) 11.95
(7) 11.95
s.3 ...... 11.52, **11.101**, 11.104
(3) 11.103, 31.140
    (b) 11.103
(3)–(6) 11.66, 11.104
s.4 .... **11.114**, 11.115, 11.117
s.5 ....11.114
(1) 11.60, 11.74
    (a) 11.60, 11.74
    (b) 11.60, 11.74
(2) 11.115
(3) 11.115
(4) 11.60, 11.74, 11.115
s.6(1) 11.60
(1)–(3) 11.75

(2) 11.60
s.7 .... 11.64, 11.78
s.8(3) 11.117
(7)(a) 11.117
(b) 11.117
(5) 11.117
(6) 11.117
(8)(b) 11.117
(c) 11.117
ss.8–10 ....11.117
s.9 ....11.117
(5) 11.117
s.10 .... 11.64, 11.78
(2) 11.117
s.11 ....11.118
Pt 2 .... 11.50
s.14 .. 11.120, 11.121, 11.127
ss.14–22 ....11.120
s.15 ....11.121
(4) 11.121
(7) 11.121
(8) 11.121
s.17(1) 11.122
(2) 11.122
(3) 11.122
(4) 11.122
(5) 11.122
s.18 ....11.123
(4)–(6) 11.123
s.19 .... 11.120, 11.124
(6) 11.123
(7) 11.123
s.20 ....11.123
s.21 ....11.124
s.22 ....11.123
s.23(1) 11.128

(2) 11.128
ss.23–29 ....11.128
s.24(1) 11.128
(4) 11.128
s.25(1) 11.128
s.27 ....11.128
s.29 ....11.128
s.30 .. 11.125, 11.127, 11.129
Pt 3 .... 11.50
Pt 4 .... 11.50
s.43 .... 11.49
Pt 5 .... 11.50
s.45 .... 11.22, 11.24, 11.37
(1) 11.38
(2) 11.38
(3) 11.38
(4) 11.39
(5) 11.38
(7) 11.40, 11.39
s.46 .... 11.68
(2) 27.19
(4) 27.15
s.48 .... 11.69
ss.49–54 .... 11.70
Pt 6 .... 11.50
Pt 7 .... 11.50
s.57 .... 11.72
(1) 29.20
Sch.1 .... 11.120, 11.121
Sch.2 .... 11.64
Sch.3 .... 11.49
Sch.4 .... 11.39
paras 1–37 .... 11.40
Sch.5 .... 11.75
para.4 .... 29.20

TABLE OF STATUTORY INSTRUMENTS

All references are to paragraph numbers.
References in bold indicate where legislation is reproduced in full.

1971 Indictment Rules (SI
     1971/1253) 19.22
     r.9 .... 1.146, 19.04, 19.05,
          19.06, 19.08
1978 Protection of Children
     (Northern Ire-
     land) Order (SI
     1978/1047)–
     art.3(1) 32.02
1979 Merchant Shipping
     (Returns of Births
     and Deaths) Reg-
     ulations (SI
     1979/1577) 3.74
1982 Homosexual Offences
     (Northern Ire-
     land) Order (SI
     1982/1536 (NI
     19))–
     art.3 .... 32.02
1984 Adoption Rules (SI
     1984/265)–
     r.6 .... 5.36
     r.18 .... 5.36
1987 Prosecution of Of-
     fences (Custody
     Time-limits) Reg-
     ulations (SI
     1987/299)–
     reg.6(6) 1.25
1989 Police and Criminal
     Evidence (North-
     ern Ireland) Order
     (SI 1989/1314 (NI

     12))–
     art.81A 32.65
     art.81B 32.64
1989 Treatment of Offenders
     (Northern Ire-
     land) Order (SI
     1989/1344 (NI
     15))–
     art.12 .... 32.02
1991 Children Act 1989
     (Commencement
     and Transitional
     Provisions) Order
     (SI 1991/828)–
     art.3(2) 9.52
1991 Family Proceedings
     Rules (SI
     1991/1247) 18.41,
          18.43
     r.4.23 .... 18.42
     r.9.5 .... 5.36
1995 Criminal Justice and
     Public Order Act
     1994 (Commence-
     ment No.5 and
     Transitional Pro-
     visions) Order (SI
     1995/127) 19.107
1995 Children's Evidence
     (Northern Ire-
     land) Order (SI
     1995/757 (NI 3))–
     art.4 .... 32.59
     art.5 .... 32.65

1996 Criminal Justice
(Northern Ire-
land) Order (SI
1996/3160 (NI
24)) 32.29, 32.30,
32.35, 32.36, 32.37,
32.46
art.2(2) 32.21
arts 4–7 .... 32.30
arts 8–17 .... 32.30
art.20 .... **32.31**
(2)(b) 32.36
art.23 .... 32.53
art.24 .... **32.32**
art.26 .... **32.34**, 32.35, 32.37,
32.46
(1)(b) 32.36
(3) 32.35
(4) 32.35
art.27 .... 32.35
1997 Crown Court Rules
(Northern Ire-
land) (SR
1979/90) 32.64
r.44H 32.64
1998 Criminal Justice (Children) (Northern
Ireland) Order (SI
1998/1504 (NI
9))–
art.1(2) 32.06
art.3 .... 32.06
art.19(1) 32.58
art.20 .... 32.58
art.21(1) 32.58
art.23 .... 32.59
Sch.1 .... 32.31
1999 Criminal Evidence
(Northern Ire-
land) Order (SI
1999/2789 (NI
8))–
arts.4–21 .... 32.61
art.10A 32.62
art.17 .... 32.63

art.21BA 32.63
arts.22–27 .... 32.64
arts.28–30 .... 32.64
2000 Criminal Justice and
Court Services
Act 2000 (Com-
mencement No.1)
Order (SI
2000/3302) ... 8.04, 8.120
2000 National Police Re-
cords (Recordable
Offences) Regula-
tions (SI
2000/1139) 13.51
2001 Life Sentence (Northern Ireland) Order
(SI 2001/2564) 32.30,
32.43
2002 Youth Justice and
Criminal Evidence
Act 1999 (Com-
mencement No.7)
Order (SI
2002/1739) 27.02
2002 Electronic Commerce
(EC Directive)
Regulations (SI
2002/2013) 29.132
reg.17 .... 29.72, 29.132
2003 Criminal Justice (2003
Order) (Com-
mencement No.2)
Order (Northern
Ireland) (SI
2003/352) 32.05
2003 Criminal Justice
(Northern Ire-
land) Order (SI
2003/1247 (NI
13))–
art.4(a) 32.02
(b) 32.02
art.18(4) 32.02
art.19 .... 32.02
art.21 .... 32.02

art.22 .... 32.02
(1) 32.02
art.23 .... 32.05
Sch.1 para.19 .... 32.31
para.23 .... 29.48
2004 Criminal Justice Act
2003 (Commence-
ment No.2 and
Saving Provisions)
Order (SI
2004/81) 15.01
2004 Crown Court (Special
Measures Direc-
tions and Direc-
tions Prohibiting
Cross-examina-
tion) (Amend-
ment) Rules (SI
2004/185) 18.01
2004 Youth Justice and
Criminal Evidence
Act 1999 (Com-
mencement No.9)
Order (SI
2004/299) 27.02,
27.105
2004 Sexual Offences Act
2003 (Commence-
ment) Order (SI
2004/874) 1.32
2004 Magistrates' Courts
(Sexual Offences
Prevention Or-
ders) Rules (SI
2004/1054) 36.19
2004 Sexual Offences Act
2003 (Travel Noti-
fication Require-
ments) Regula-
tions (SI
2004/1220) 35.45
reg.5(1) 35.45
(3) 35.45

2004 Criminal Justice (Evidence) (Northern
Ireland) Order (SI
2004/1501 (NI
10)) 32.57
2004 Youth Justice and
Criminal Evidence
Act 1999 (Com-
mencement
No.10) (England
and Wales) Order
(SI 2004/2428) 29.02
2004 Criminal Justice Act
2003 (Categories
of Offences) Order
(SI 2004/3346) 20.45,
20.51
2005 Family Proceedings
(Amendment
No.4) Rules (SI
2005/1976) 18.43,
18.46
2005 Remand in Custody
(Effect of Concur-
rent and Consec-
utive Sentences of
Imprisonment)
Rules (SI
2005/2054) 34.47
2005 Family Procedure
(Adoption) Rules
(SI 2005/2795)
r.59 .... 5.36
2005 Civil Partnership Act
2004 (Relation-
ships Arising
Through Civil
Partnership)
Order (SI
2005/3137) 6.34
2007 Criminal Procedure
(Amendment)
Rules (SI
2007/699) .. 3.27, 19.05,
19.22, 30.18, 33.25

2007 References to Health
Authorities Order
(SI 2007/961)–
art.3 .... 7.224
Sch. 7.224

2007 Sexual Offences Act
2003 (Amendment
of Schedules 3 and
5) Order (SI
2007/296)–
art.1(1) 35.10
art.2(2) 35.10

2007 Youth Courts (Constitution of Commit-
tees and Rights to
Preside) Rules (SI
2007/1611) 31.33
r.10(1) 31.33
r.11(1) 31.33

2008 Criminal Justice
(Northern Ire-
land) Order 2008
(Commencement
No.1 and Savings
and Transitory
Provisions) Order
(S I2008/217)
(c.8) 32.36

2008 Sexual Offences
(Northern Ire-
land) Order 2008
(Commencement)
Order (SI
2008/510
(c.30)) 32.01, 32.26

2008 Police and Justice Act
2006 (Commence-
ment No.1, Tran-
sitional and Sav-
ings Provisions)
Order (SI
2008/617) .. 27.25, 27.26

2008 Criminal Justice
(Northern Ire-
land) Order (SI
2008/1216) 32.20,
32.29, 32.40, 32.41,
32.46
art.3(3) 32.36
art.7(2) 32.37
art.8 .... 32.37, 32.38
(2) 32.37
(3) 32.37
(5) 32.37
art.13(1)(a) 32.41
(b) 32.44
(3) 32.43, 32.45
(a) 32.45
(b) 32.43
art.14(1)(a) 32.41
(b) 32.44, 32.45
(2) 32.45
(3)(b) 32.42
(4)(b) 32.42
(8)(b) 32.42
(9) 32.42
art.15(1)(b) 32.36, 32.44
art.18(2)(a) 32.43
(b) 32.42
(3) 32.42, 32.43
(4)(b) 32.43
art.22(4) 32.43
art.24(3)(b) 32.42, 32.43
(5) 32.42, 32.43
art.34 .... 32.35
Sch.1 .... 32.41
Pt 2 .... 32.41
para.35 .... 32.41
Sch.2 .... 32.41
Pt 2 .... 32.41

2008 Criminal Justice and
Immigration Act
2008 (Commence-
ment No.2 and
Transitional and
Saving Provisions)
Order (SI

2008/1586) 31.93

2008 Sexual Offences
(Northern Ire-
land) Order (SI
2008/1769) 32.01,
32.07, 32.22, 32.26,
32.28
art.1 .... 32.75
art.2 .... 32.75
art.3 .... 32.75
art.4 .... 32.75
art.5 .... 32.75
(6) 32.28
art.6 .... 32.75
art.7 .... 32.75
art.8 .... 32.75
art.9 .... 32.75
art.10 .... 32.75
art.11 .... 32.75
art.12 .... 32.75
art.13 .... 32.75
art.14 .... 32.75
art.15 .... 32.75
art.16 .... 32.75
art.17 .... 32.75
art.18 .... 32.75
art.19 .... 32.75
art.20 .... 32.75
art.21 .... 32.75
art.22 .... 32.12, 32.75
art.22A 32.11, 32.75
art.23 .... 32.75
arts 23–26 .... 32.75
art.24 .... 32.75
art.25 .... 32.75
art.26 .... 32.75
art.27 .... 32.75
art.28 .... 32.75
art.29 .... 32.75
art.30 .... 32.75
art.31 .... 32.75
art.32 .... 32.75
art.33 .... 32.75
art.34 .... 32.75

art.35 .... 32.75
art.36 .... 32.75
art.37 .... 32.75
art.38 .... 32.75
arts 38–40 .... 32.75
art.39 .... 32.75
art.40 .... 32.75
art.41 .... 32.75
art.42 .... 32.75
art.43 .... 32.75
art.44 .... 32.75
art.45 .... 32.75
art.46 .... 32.75
art.47 .... 32.75
art.48 .... 32.75
art.49 .... 32.75
art.50 .... 32.75
art.51 .... 32.75
arts 51–54 .... 32.75
art.52 .... 32.75
art.53 .... 32.75
art.54 .... 32.75
art.55 .... 32.75
art.56 .... 32.75
art.57 .... 32.75
art.58 .... 32.75
(3) 32.10
art.59 ..... 32.07, 32.09, 32.75
art.60 ..... 32.07, 32.08, 32.75
art.61 ..... 32.07, 32.08, 32.75
art.62 .... 32.10, 32.75
art.63 .... 32.10, 32.75
art.64 .... 32.75
art.64A ... 32.08, 32.09, 32.75
art.65 .... 32.75
art.66 .... 32.75
art.67 .... 32.75
art.68 .... 32.75
art.69 .... 32.75
art.70 .... 32.75
art.71 .... 32.75
art.72 .... 32.75

art.73 .... 32.75
art.74 .... 32.75
art.75 .... 32.75
art.76 .... 32.75
art.77 .... 32.75
art.82 .... 32.28
art.83 .... 32.22
Sch.1 para.35 .... 32.41
Sch.2 .... 32.28
   para.1(2) 32.01
Sch.3 .... 32.22

2008 Sexual Offences (Northern Ireland Consequential Amendments) Order (SI 2008/1779) 32.04
art.4 .... 4.219
art.5 .... 5.124
art.11 .... 32.13

2009 Safeguarding Vulnerable Groups Act (Prescribed Criteria and Miscellaneous Provisions) Regulations (SI 2009/37) 34.63, 36.49

2009 Criminal Justice (Northern Ireland) Order 2008 (Commencement No.5 and Saving Provisions) Order (SI 2009/120) (c.6)–
art.2 .... 32.37
Sch.2 para.2 .... 32.37

2009 Armed Forces Act 2006 (Transitional Provisions etc.) Order (SI 2009/1059)–

art.205 .... 29.49
Sch.1 para.44(1) 29.49

2009 Youth Justice and Criminal Evidence Act 1999 (Application to Service Courts) Order (SI 2009/2083) 29.69, 29.115, 29.129
art.7 .... 26.25

2009 Court Martial and Service Civilian Court (Youth Justice and Criminal Evidence Act 1999) Rules (SI 2009/2100) 29.69, 29.115, 29.129

2009 Sexual Offences (Northern Ireland) Order 2008 (Transitional Provisions) Order (SR 2009/265) 32.28

2010 Local Government and Public Involvement in Health Act 2007 (Commencement No.9) Order (SI 2010/112) 15.199

2010 Offences Act 2003 (Prescribed Police Stations) Regulations (SI 2010/207) 28.23

2010 Policing and Crime Act 2009 (Commencement No.4) Order 2010 (SI 2010/507) 13.25, 13.27, 13.45, 32.08

2010 Health and Social Care Act 2008 (Consequential Amendments No.2) Order (SI 2010/813)–
    art.13(4) 7.224

2010 Northern Ireland Act 1998 (Devolution of Policing and Justice Functions) Order (SI 2010/976) 32.01
    Sch.14 para.43 .... 29.48

2010 Family Procedure Rules (SI 2010/2955) 18.37
    Pt 12 Ch.7 .... 18.41
    r.12.73 .... 18.37
    (1) **18.41**
    (a) .. 18.46, 18.48, 18.57
    (b) 18.48
    (c) 18.47, 18.48
    PD12G 18.41, 18.47
    para.2.1 .... 18.47
    para.6(1) 18.47
    r.16.3(1)(ii) 5.36
    r.16.4 .... 5.36
    r.27.10 .... 18.39

2010 Children and Young Persons Act 2008 (Commencement No.3, Saving and Transitional Provisions) Order (SI 2010/2981) 5.33

2011 Family Procedure (Modification of Enactments) Order (SI 2011/1045)–
    art.15 .... 5.36

2011 Coroners and Justice Act 2009 (Commencement No.7) Order (SI 2011/1452) 27.55, 27.62, 27.159

2012 Justice (2011 Act) (Commencement No.4 and Transitory Provision) Order (Northern Ireland) (SI 2012/214 (c.18)) ... 32.39

2012 Sexual Offences Act 2003 (Prescribed Police Stations) Regulations (Northern Ireland) (SI 2012/325) 35.34

2012 Criminal Justice Act 2003 (Commencement No.28 and Saving Provisions) Order (SI 2012/1320) 31.64, 31.65

2012 Criminal Justice Act 1988 (Reviews of Sentencing) (Amendment) Order (SI 2012/1833) 11.18

2012 Sexual Offences Act 2003 (Notification Requirements) (England and Wales) Regulations (SI 2012/1876) 35.01, 35.06, 35.45
    reg.5(a) 35.45
    (b) 35.45
    reg.9 .... 35.41
    reg.10 .... 35.40

reg.11 .... 35.40
reg.12 .... 35.35, 35.36
  (1) 35.35
  (2)–(7) 35.35
reg.13 .... 35.35
2012 Sexual Offences Act
    2003 (Remedial)
    Order 2012 (SI
    2012/1883) 32.24,
      35.27, 36.52
2012 Magistrates' Courts
    (Sexual Offences
    Act 2003) (Miscel-
    laneous Amend-
    ments) Rules (SI
    2012/2018) 36.18
2012 Criminal Justice Act
    2003 (Commence-
    ment No.29 and
    Saving Provisions)
    Order (SI
    2012/2574) 31.64,
      31.65
2012 Legal Aid, Sentencing
    and Punishment
    of Offenders Act
    2012 (Commence-
    ment No.4 and
    Saving Provisions)
    Order (SI
    2012/2906) ... 1.22, 2.11,
      2.41, 2.88, 3.34,
      3.84, 3.109, 3.139,
      3.141, 4.28, 4.73,
      4.97, 4.125, 4.149,
      4.165, 4.193, 5.11,
      5.56, 5.79, 5.107,
      6.16, 6.59, 6.75,
      6.97, 7.50, 7.94,
      7.109, 7.129,
      7.145, 7.163,
      7.176, 7.196,
      7.212, 7.240,
      7.255, 7.275, 8.07,
      10.15, 10.40,

      10.74, 10.93, 10.115,
      10.146, 11.60, 11.75,
    14.11, 14.41, 14.55, 15.71,
      15.92, 31.92
2013 Criminal Evidence
    (Northern Ire-
    land) Order 1999
    (Commencement
    No.8) Order (SI
    2013/126 (c.8)) 32.63
2013 Protection of Free-
    doms Act 2012
    (Commencement
    No.5 and Saving
    and Transitional
    Provision) Order
    (SI 2013/470) 11.16
2013 Trafficking People for
    Exploitation Reg-
    ulations (SI
    2013/554) 11.19
reg.3 .... **11.20**
reg.4 .... **11.20**
2013 Criminal Justice Act
    2003 (Commence-
    ment No.31 and
    Saving Provisions)
    Order (SI
    2013/1103) 31.64,
      31.65
2013 Criminal Procedure
    Rules (SI
    2013/1554) 18.37
2013 Special Measures for
    Child Witnesses
    (Sexual Offences)
    Regulations (SI
    2013/2971) 10.09
reg.2(b) 27.15
2013 Working with Children
    (Exchange of
    Criminal Convic-
    tion Information)
    (England and
    Wales and North-

ern Ireland) Regulations (SI 2013/2945) 10.09

2013 Youth Justice and Criminal Evidence Act 1999 (Commencement No.13) Order (SI 2013/3236) 27.43

2014 Criminal Justice (2013 Act) (Commencement No.3) Order (Northern Ireland) (SI 2014/53 (c.2)) 32.24

2014 Marriage (Same Sex Couples) Act 2013 (Commencement No.2 and Transitional Provision) Order (SI 2014/93) 8.75

2014 Criminal Justice (2013 Act) (Commencement No.4) Order (Northern Ireland) (SI 2014/179 (c.11)) 32.25, 32.56

2014 Legal Aid, Sentencing and Punishment of Offenders Act 2012 (Commencement No.9, Saving Provision and Specification of Commencement Date) Order (SI 2014/423) 13.28

2014 Sexual Offences Act 2003 (Prescribed Police Stations) (Scotland) Regulations (SSI 2014/147) 35.34

2015 Sexual Offences Act 2003 (Prescribed Police Stations) Regulations (SI 2015/82) 35.34

2015 Anti-social Behaviour, Crime and Policing Act 2014 (Commencement No.8, Saving and Transitional Provisions) Order (SI 2015/373) .. 13.73, 36.06

2015 Criminal Justice and Courts Act 2015 (Commencement No.1, Saving and Transitional Provisions) Order (SI 2015/778) 4.103, 4.186, 29.07

2015 Criminal Justice and Courts Act 2015 (Simple Cautions) (Specification of Either-Way Offences) Order (SI 2015/790) 2.39, 2.86, 3.107, 3.137, 4.26, 4.71, 4.95, 4.123, 4.163, 4.191, 5.09, 5.54, 5.77, 5.105, 6.14, 6.57, 8.04, 8.120, 10.11, 10.38, 10.72, 10.91, 11.60, 11.77

2015 Youth Justice and Criminal Evidence Act 1999 (Commencement No.14) (England and Wales) Order (SI 2015/818) 29.07

2015 Serious Crime Act 2015 (Commencement No.1) Regulations (SI 2015/820) 4.249, 4.253, 10.35, 10.59, 10.69, 10.88, 10.138, 13.25, 13.30

2015 Criminal Justice and Courts Act 2015 (Simple Cautions) (Specification of Police Ranks) Order (SI 2015/830) 13.52

2015 Local Government Byelaws (Wales) Act 2012 (Commencement No.2, Transitional Provisions and Savings) Order (SI 2015/1025) 15.199

2015 Modern Slavery Act 2015 (Consequential Amendments) Regulations (SI 2015/1472) 11.19
reg.20 .... 11.63, 11.77
reg.21 .... 11.63, 11.77

2015 Modern Slavery Act 2015 (Commencement No.1, Saving and Transitional Provisions) Regulations (SI 2015/1476) 11.22, 11.59, 27.15

2015 Criminal Procedure Rules (SI 2015/1490) 18.24, 18.37, 20.03, 24.09, 27.07, 27.117, 27.121, 28.06,

31.49
r.1.1 .... 27.76
(2)(b) 27.76, 31.49
(d) 27.76
r.3.2(2)(b) 27.07
r.3.10(3)(b) 31.49
r.3.11(c)(iv) 27.07
(v) 27.07
r.3.9(3)(b) 27.21, 28.24
(6) 27.21
(7) 28.32, 28.44
Pt 6 .... 29.26, 29.80
r.6.1 .... 29.26
r.6.2 .... **29.80**
(3) **29.80**
(b) 29.81
r.6.4(3)(e) 29.124
Pt 10 .... 19.27
r.10.2(1)(a)(ii) 1.34
(2) 1.30, 3.27, 19.05, 19.22, 19.27, 30.18, 30.125, 33.25, 33.28
(3) 1.146, 19.04, 19.05
Pt 15 ..... 18.12, 18.22, 19.22, 31.43
r.15.2 .... 18.15
r.15.3 .... 18.23
(2)(b)(ii) 18.88
Pt 17 ..... 18.37, 18.66, 18.68, 18.73, 18.74, 18.96
r.17.3 .... **18.74**
(2)(b) 18.79
r.17.4 .... **18.74**
r.17.5 .... **18.74**
(3) 18.68
(b)(i) 18.94
(4)(b) 18.94
r.17.6 .... 18.75
(3)(b) 18.94
Pt 18 ... 27.32, 27.55, 27.116, 27.126
r.18.1(1)(a) 27.116
r.18.3 .... 31.62
(a) 27.116
(b) 27.116

r.18.4(1) 27.119
  (2) 27.119
r.18.5 ....27.116
r.18.7 ....27.111
r.18.9 .... 27.117, 31.62
r.18.10 ....27.117
r.18.11 ....27.121
r.18.12 ....27.120
r.18.13 ....27.118
  (4) 27.118
  (5) 27.121
Pt 19 .... 25.34, 25.35
r.19.2 .... **24.16**
  (1) 25.30
  (3) 25.30
rr.19.3–19.5 .... 24.19
r.19.4 .... 24.14, 25.30, **25.31**,
                                    25.36
r.19.6 .... 24.12, 25.32
r.19.6 ....27.122
Pt 22 .... 26.47
r.22.1 .... **26.48**
r.22.2 .... **26.48**

r.22.3 .... **26.48**
r.22.4 .... **26.48**
r.22.5 .... **26.48**
r.22.6 .... **26.48**
Pt 23 ....27.162
r.23.2(4)(b) 27.162
Pt 24 .... 31.47
r.24.2 .... 31.47
r.24.11(2)(b) 31.101
  (7) 31.103
r.24.12(3)(b) 31.47
r.25.2(c) 31.35
r.28.3 .... 35.07
Pt 31 .... 36.16, 36.23
r.31.3 .... 36.23
Pt 35 .... 20.03

2004 Sexual Offences Act
        2003 (Travel Noti-
        fication Require-
        ments) (Scotland)
        Regulations (SSI
        2004/205) 35.45

CHAPTER 1

RAPE

Introduction...................................... 1.01
The Evolution of the Definition of
  Rape.. 1.14
The Definition of Rape in the
  Sexual Offences Act 2003............ 1.19
Form and Content of the
  Indictment.................................... 1.26
Sentencing....................................... 1.35
Alternative Verdicts 1.137
Double Jeopardy.............................. 1.142
Allegation of Joint Offence.............. 1.144
Parties to the Offence 1.148
Jurisdiction 1.154

"Penetrates the Vagina, Anus or
  Mouth" 1.155
History of the Demise of the
  Marital Exemption...................... 1.160
Absence of Consent......................... 1.169
Consent and "Capacity" under The
  Sexual Offences Act 2003............. 1.222
Evidential Presumptions as to
  Consent 1.263
Conclusive Presumptions as to
  Consent 1.310
Permissible Judicial Comment in
  Rape Cases.................................. 1.354
Mental Element.............................. 1.371

INTRODUCTION

In recent years, sexual offending has been revealed of a nature and scale not   1.01
previously contemplated and there has been a significant increase in such
cases being brought to trial.[1] The Crime Survey for England and Wales
showed that in the year to June 2015, sexual offences recorded by the police
continued to rise with the latest figures up 41 per cent on the previous year,
equivalent to an additional 27,602 offences (up from 67,880 to 95,482).[2] The
numbers of rapes (31,621) and other sexual offences (63,861) were at the
highest level since the introduction of the National Crime Recording
Standard in 2002/03.[2a] As well as improvements in recording, this is also

---

[1] See *An Overview of Sexual Offending in England and Wales* (MoJ, Home Office and ONS,
January 10, 2013), p.34. In 2011, 7,061 defendants were tried at the Crown Court for sexual
offences, of whom 2,713 (38.4 per cent) pleaded guilty; 1,639 (23.2 per cent) pleaded not guilty
and were found guilty; and 2,592 (36.7 per cent) pleaded not guilty and were acquitted. These
figures represent an overall 61.6 per cent conviction rate, which is a 7.1 per cent increase since
2005.
[2] The CSEW is available at *http://www.ons.gov.uk/ons/rel/crime-stats/crime-statistics/year-ending-june-2015/stb-crime–ye-june-2015.html* [Accessed March 19, 2016].
[2a] *http://webarchive.nationalarchives.gov.uk/20110218135832/http:/rds.homeoffice.gov.uk/rds/pdfs2/rdsolr3103.pdf* [Accessed March 19, 2016].

thought to reflect a greater willingness of victims to come forward to report such crimes. Since 2005 there has been an exponential increase in the numbers of rape and penetrative offences recorded by the Metropolitan Police Service. In the following eight years the recorded figure for "total allegations" of rape and penetration offences increased by 173 per cent.[3] These cases include rapes where there has been an established relationship between the parties, allegations in respect of events that took place a generation or more ago, often involving those in a position of trust, and cases where men have targeted vulnerable girls on a substantial scale. For instance, in August 2014 an independent review[4] reported that in Rotherham over 1,400 under-age girls had been groomed and subjected to grotesque levels of violence and abuse over 16 years. On a different level, Operation Yewtree has disclosed abuse of young girls by those enjoying celebrity status against a background of collusion.[5]

1.02   Rape continues to be regarded as the most serious sexual offence, although there may be severe degradation of the victim during assault by penetration or sexual assault where there is no penetration of the vagina, anus or mouth and thus no rape. The Stern Review described rape as "unique in the way it strikes at the bodily integrity and self-respect of the victim, in the demands it makes on public authorities and in the controversy it generates."[6] To this could be added, that it is also unique in the way it attracts popular misconceptions as to the nature of the offence itself and the behaviour of perpetrators and victims.

1.03   The law of rape underwent significant changes during the 1990s, even before the implementation of the Sexual Offences Act 2003. Those changes went some way towards addressing criticisms of the way sexual offences were defined in England and Wales. Their effect was, first to widen the category of persons who could be raped and secondly, to widen the definition of what constituted rape. In *R. v R*,[7] the exception to the law of rape whereby a man could not be found guilty of raping his wife was finally and completely abrogated. In the Criminal Justice and Public Order Act 1994, Parliament altered the basis of the offence by enacting that rape included the penetration of the anus, with the result that a man as well as a woman could be the victim of rape.[8] Notwithstanding these changes, rape was the subject of a significant proportion of the submissions to the review of sex offences announced by the

---

[3] *Report of the Independent Review into The Investigation and Prosecution of Rape in London*, Rt Hon Dame Elish Angiolini DBE QC, April 30, 2015, para.242 (p.62).
[4] Professor Alexis Jay OBE, *Independent Inquiry into Child Sexual Exploitation in Rotherham (1997–2013)*, available at *http://www.rotherham.gov.uk/downloads/file/1407/independent_inquiry_cse_in_rotherham* [Accessed March 19, 2016].
[5] For background, see *https://en.wikipedia.org/wiki/Operation_Yewtree*.
[6] Home Office, The Stern Review: *A report by Baroness Stern CBE of an independent review of into how rape complaints are handled by public authorities in England and Wales*, March 2010.
[7] [1992] 1 A.C. 599, HL.
[8] s.142.

Home Secretary on January 25, 1999. The Sexual Offences Review discovered that the increase in the reporting of rape and the reduction of
conviction rates had generated substantial public disquiet about the way that
rape offences were dealt with by the criminal justice system.[9] A variety of
problems were identified, including some which derived from the substantive
law. In addition the Review found that the nature and effect of sexual assaults
of all kinds on the victims, both men and women, were still not sufficiently
understood by the law, despite the significant advances in understanding
made in recent years. This impacted throughout the criminal justice system,
including sentencing. The increase in the reporting of rape and the reduction
in the rate of convictions had reduced confidence in the ability of the law to
deliver justice to victims. Although the numbers of reported rapes had
increased significantly, the number of successful prosecutions had risen only
slightly.[10]

In addition, it was accepted by the Sexual Offences Review that forced oral   **1.04**
sex can be as horrible, as demeaning and as traumatising as other forms of
penile penetration,[11] and yet the law did not offer appropriate protection
against such very serious sexual assaults because the definition of rape was
confined to penile penetration of the vagina and anus. Section 1 of the Sexual
Offences Act 2003 ("the 2003 Act") provided a new, extended definition of
rape. In particular, it extended the definition to cover non-consensual penile
penetration of the mouth of a woman or a man, which in the past would have
been indecent assault.

Until the 2003 Act there was no statutory definition of "consent" in   **1.05**
respect of the law governing sexual offences. The leading authority of
Olugboja[12] had left juries to grapple with the concept of consent by giving it
its "ordinary meaning", even though it covers a wide spectrum of states of
mind ranging from enthusiastic desire on the one hand to reluctant
acquiescence on the other.[13] Whilst the courts had recognised that the
concept of consent is not entirely straightforward, and that the difference
between consent and submission should be explained to juries, in many cases
judges gave little further guidance. The Sexual Offences Review, responding
to severe criticism of the absence of a definition of consent, stressed that "in
the most private and difficult area of sexual relationships the law should be

---

[9] *Setting the Boundaries: Reforming the law on sexual offences* (Home Office, July 2000).
[10] *Setting the Boundaries*, paras 2.3 and 2.8.5. See also *Report on the Joint Inspection into the
Investigation and Prosecution of Rape Offences in England and Wales* (April 2002), where it is
stated that the rate of convictions of rape, after trial, had decreased from one in three cases
reported in 1977 to one in 13 in 1999.
[11] It also carries similar risks in respect of disease transmission.
[12] [1981] 3 All. E. R 443.
[13] In Richard Card, Alisdair A. Gillespie and Michael Hirst, *Sexual Offences* (Bristol:
Jordans, 2008), para.3.10, the authors point out that *Olugboja* took a modern and enlightened
approach to the concept of consent, rejecting any suggestion that physical resistance or
insensibility was required to negate it. However the distinction between "reluctant acquiescence"
and "mere submission" inevitably gave rise to uncertainty.

as clear as possible so the boundaries of what is acceptable, and of criminally culpable behaviour, are all well understood".[14]

1.06   The 2003 Act seeks to define "consent" to the extent that it provides in s.74 that "a person consents if he agrees by choice, and has the freedom and capacity to make that choice". A definition in terms of free agreement was favoured by the Review since any free agreement would necessarily be voluntary and genuine. It also felt that use of the concept of free agreement would assist in making it clear that absence of protest, resistance or injury does not necessarily mean the complainant consented. This definition applies for the purposes of Pt 1 of the Act, including the non-consensual offences in ss.1-4 of rape, assault by penetration, sexual assault and causing a person to engage in sexual activity without consent.

1.07   The last few years have seen important case law giving a wide interpretation to the definition of consent in s.74 of the Act. The decisions have underlined that context is all-important, illuminated how evidence of "grooming" may be relevant to the issue of consent[15] and clarified that deceptions falling short of s.76 deceptions may entitle a jury to conclude that there was no genuine consent.[16] This wide interpretation has led to academic criticism on the grounds that juries are again finding themselves having to interpret concepts that are not defined with precision, as they had to do in the days before the enactment of the 2003 Act. The counter-argument, however, is that the definition in s.74 as now interpreted is the natural consequence of a focus on the autonomy of the complainant, and a further definition is inapt when dealing with this area of human behaviour.

1.08   This general definition of consent is supplemented by ss.75 and 76 of the Act, which represented a new departure in the law governing sexual offences in that they set out respectively evidential and conclusive presumptions about consent which arise in certain specified circumstances. Section 76 is the less radical in that the conclusive presumptions about absence of consent in the main simply reflect the common law and the pre-existing statute law. The Court of Appeal, recognising that the provisions on deception in s.76 effectively extended the definition of rape, has taken a restrictive view when interpreting that section.[17] An indirect result of this restrictive view of s.76 appears to be a wider interpretation of s.74.[18]

1.09   In contrast, s.75 was a new phenomenon. It lists six sets of circumstances which, if established to have existed with the defendant's knowledge, will

---

[14] *Setting the Boundaries,* 2000, from para.2.7.3.
[15] *Ali (Yazir)* [2015] EWCA Crim 1279; [2015] 2 Cr. App. R. 33; *C v R.* [2012] EWCA Crim 2034; *Robinson* [2011] EWCA Crim 916.
[16] *Assange v Swedish Prosecution Authority* [2011] EWHC 2489 (admin); *R. v (F) v DPP* [2013] EWHC 945 (Admin): *Justine McNally v The Queen* [2013] EWCA Crim 1051.
[17] *Jheeta* [2007] EWCA Crim 1699; *R v B* [2013] EWCA Crim 823.
[18] Karl Laird, *Rapist or Rogue? Deception, consent and the Sexual Offences Act 2003* [2014] Crim. L.R. 492. The author refers to how the applicability of s.76 has been reduced to vanishing point.

create an evidential presumption that the complainant did not consent and that the defendant did not reasonably believe the complainant consented. This means that the prosecution can rely upon the presumption unless the defendant discharges an evidential burden to the contrary.[19] The potential operation of s.75 is confined to these six specific sets of circumstances. In reality, the years since implementation have shown that the s.75 presumptions very rarely arise in practice,[20] although a case has come before the Court of Appeal in which the trial judge was held to have been right to hold that s.75 applied.[21] Normally, there will be sufficient evidence from the defendant or some other source to raise the issue of consent and/or reasonable belief as to consent, and the issue of consent will be determined in accordance with s.74. In those circumstances, the s.75 route is barred and the judge will direct the jury in accordance with the provisions of s.74 and s.1(2), which is explained below.

The 2003 Act also made a major change to the mental element required for rape. Many submissions to the Sexual Offences Review were highly critical of the defence of honest but mistaken belief in consent as established in *DPP v Morgan*.[22] The Review felt that this defence was in direct conflict with the perception of many in the community who consider that, in the particular circumstances of rape and serious sexual assault, the defence of belief in consent should be fettered. The Act accordingly brought about the overdue demise of the principle that a wholly unreasonable but genuinely held belief that a complainant was consenting affords a defence to rape, thereby overruling *Morgan*. Under s.1(1) of the Act the prosecution has to prove intentional penetration of the vagina, anus or mouth of the complainant, and the absence of a *reasonable* belief that the complainant was consenting. However, the change has not swept away entirely any notion of subjectivity or any consideration of the defendant's personal characteristics. Section 1(1)(c) focuses on whether the defendant had a reasonable belief in consent and, by virtue of s.1(2), whether a defendant's belief is reasonable is to be determined having regard to all the circumstances, including any steps the defendant has taken to ascertain whether the complainant consents. Ministerial statements in Parliament suggested that the reference to "all the

1.10

---

[19] In earlier versions of the Sexual Offences Bill, the defendant was to have to discharge legal burden of proof to displace the presumption. This provoked serious opposition and was abandoned by the Government. There were concerns about the compatibility of such reverse onus provisions with the presumption of innocence in art.6 of the European Convention of Human Rights as interpreted by the House of Lords in *Lambert* [2002] 2 A.C. 545.

[20] The leading case on the operation of s.75 is *Gavin White* [2010] EWCA Crim 1929. See also *Kapezi* [2013] EWCA Crim 560 and *Lewis Mba* [2012] EWCA Crim 2773 for examples where it should not have arisen and *Ciccarelli* [2011] EWCA Crim 2665 where, on the exceptional facts of that case, the Court of Appeal held that the trial judge had been correct to rule that s.75 did arise.

[21] *Ciccarelli* [2011] EWCA Crim 2665.

[22] [1976] A.C.182.

circumstances" will allow juries to take account, where necessary and subject to any directions of the judge, of any relevant characteristics of the defendant so as to determine whether it was reasonable for him to have held the beliefs he claims to have held.[23]

1.11   It was always clear that s.1(2) had not turned the clock back so as to allow the jury to consider a defendant's voluntary intoxication through drink or drugs as a relevant characteristic.[24] However, the issue as to what personal characteristics are relevant when considering the reasonableness of a defendant's belief that the complainant was consenting was left unresolved until the Court of Appeal's judgment in *B v The Queen*[25] in January 2013. In that case, it was held that the reasonableness of an asserted belief should be determined independently of any psychosis or delusional thinking. The Court did, however, acknowledge that there may be cases in which the personality and abilities of the defendant may be relevant to the question of whether a positive belief was reasonable, and the dividing-line is difficult to identify. Cases could arise in which the reasonableness of such a belief depends upon the reading by a defendant of subtle social signals, and in which his impaired ability to do so is relevant to the reasonableness of his belief. The Court did not attempt exhaustively to foresee what circumstances might arise in which a belief might be held which is not in any sense irrational, even though most people would not have held it.

1.12   The Review also recommended that ss.2 and 3 of the Sexual Offences Act 1956 (procuring a woman by threat or intimidation (s.2) or by false pretences or false representations (s.3) to have sexual intercourse in any part of the world) should be replaced by an offence of obtaining sexual penetration by threats or deception in any part of the world.[26] Despite this, the Act repealed both sections without creating any replacement offence. Although the two offences, which owe their origins to concerns about the "white slave trade", had been rarely used, offences of this sort in which absence of consent is not an essential ingredient had a continuing role to play in the law governing serious sexual offences. Whilst it has now been clarified that deceptions falling short of s.76 deceptions may vitiate consent, it does not automatically follow that they will do so. Threats or deceptions used to procure sexual intercourse, but falling short of what is sufficient to vitiate consent and allow rape to be charged, may well have been within ss.2 or 3 and of the Review's replacement offence. Arguably, the definition of consent in s.74, whilst bolstered by the presumptions, has still left significant examples of procuring sex by threats or by deceptions outside the scope of the Sexual Offences Act

---

[23] *Hansard,* HL Vol.648, col.1073, Lord Falconer of Thoroton (June 2, 2003); Vol.649, col. 677, Baroness Scotland of Asthal (June 17, 2003).

[24] *Grewal* [2010] EWCA Crim 2448, at [30] per Elias LJ.

[25] [2013] EWCA Crim 3.

[26] *Setting the Boundaries,* 2000, para.2.18.7.

2003.[27] The omission is all the more surprising in the light of the fact that the 2003 Act created specific offences of causing a mentally disordered person to engage in sexual activity by threats, inducement or deception.

The Court of Appeal has had an opportunity over the last decade to   **1.13** address all the key definitions in the 2003 Act, which has led to greater clarity in most areas of the law governing sexual offences. Current issues relate to the application of the law to areas such as absence of consent where it is alleged that there has been psychological coercion rather than violence or the threat of violence. Courts still struggle to find any principle to enable the identification of deceptions that negate consent. The advocates of an interpretation of the s.74 definition of consent which seeks to protect a complainant's autonomy by including all active and intended deceptions as to any material fact appear to have the ascendancy.

THE EVOLUTION OF THE DEFINITION OF RAPE

The punishment for rape has varied over the centuries reflecting different   **1.14** attitudes to the nature and seriousness of the offence. In Norman and Plantagenet times the seriousness of the offence derived from the fact that virginity and chastity had been defiled.[28] Whilst it had been punishable with death before the Norman Conquest, in the days of William the Conqueror the offence attracted a punishment of mutilation involving castration and loss of the eyes.[29] During the reign of Edward I, the ravishment of a woman became a trespass with a punishment of two years' imprisonment and a fine at the king's will.[30] This leniency appears to have lasted only 10 years, as in 1285 rape became a capital felony[31] and it remained so until 1841 when the punishment was reduced to transportation overseas. The maximum punishment is now life imprisonment.

Until 1976 there was no statutory definition of rape. Section 1(1) of the   **1.15** Sexual Offences Act 1956[32] simply provided: "It is a felony for a man to rape a woman". Section 1(2) provided: "A man who induces a married woman to have sexual intercourse with him by impersonating her husband commits rape."

---

[27] For discussion of the nature of deceit sufficient to vitiate consent, see *Jheeta* [2007] EWCA Crim 1699. On one interpretation of recent authorities, this omission has led to a position where virtually all forms of active and intentional deception are capable of negating consent. In *Rapist or rogue? Deception, consent and Sexual Offences Act 2003* [2014] Crim. L.R. 492, Karl Laird takes the entirely understandable view that the failure to enact a moderated version of s.3 made the current situation inevitable.

[28] Jennifer Temkin, *Rape and the Legal Process*, 2nd edn (Oxford: Oxford University Press, 2002), p.57.

[29] *Ancient Laws and Institutions of England 1840: The Laws of King William the Conqueror*, XII, XVIII.

[30] 3 Edw. 1 c.13 (1275).

[31] 13 Edw. 1 c. 34.

[32] Which replaced s.48 of the Offences Against the Person Act 1861.

1.16   Rape was defined at common law as unlawful sexual intercourse with a woman without her consent, by force, fear or fraud.[33] Once rape ceased to be a capital felony, the judges became prepared to widen its scope. In *Camplin*[34] in 1845 it was established that the use or threat of force was not an essential ingredient of the offence.[35] The essence of the offence was and remains the absence of consent, whether or not the complainant resists and struggles, is in fear or deceived.

1.17   In 1975, widespread concern expressed by the public, the media and in Parliament about the decision of the House of Lords in *DPP v Morgan*[36] led the Home Secretary to appoint a committee under the chairmanship of Mrs Justice Heilbron to give urgent consideration to the law of rape. The Heilbron Report was published in December 1975,[37] with the Committee recommending that the time had come for a definition of rape to be declared in statutory form:

> " . . . this would provide the opportunity to clarify the existing law and in particular to bring out the importance of recklessness as a mental element in the crime. Such a definition would also emphasise that a lack of consent (and not violence) is the crux of the matter."[38]

Section 1(1) of the Sexual Offences (Amendment) Act 1976 incorporated the Committee's recommendations into the Sexual Offences Act 1956, s.1(2) of which provided:

> "A man commits rape if—
>   (a) he has unlawful sexual intercourse with a woman who at the time of the intercourse does not consent to it; and
>   (b) at the time he knows that she does not consent to the intercourse or he is reckless as to whether she consents to it."

1.18   Then, in response to rising public concern over incidents of male "rape", s.142 of the Criminal Justice and Public Order Act 1994 re-defined the offence by bringing anal intercourse within its scope. As substituted by the 1994 Act, s.1(2) of the Sexual Offences Act 1956 provided:

> "A man commits rape if—
>   (a) he has sexual intercourse with a person (whether vaginal or anal) who at the time of the intercourse does not consent to it; and

---

[33] 1 Hale 626; East P.C. 434.

[34] (1845) 1 Cox CC 220. Tindal CJ and Parke B were of the view that rape was ravishing a woman "where she did not consent" and not ravishing her "against her will".

[35] Notwithstanding *Camplin*, some courts appear to have continued to direct juries that the use of force by the defendant and resistance by the complainant were essential ingredients of the offence of rape: see *Dimes*, 7 Cr. App. R. 43; *Harling* [1938] 1 All E.R. 307; *Howard* [1965] 3 All E.R. 684. However, any enduring misconceptions were put right in *Malone* [1998] 2 Cr. App. R. 447.

[36] [1976] A.C. 182.

[37] *Report of the Advisory Group on the Law of Rape* (1975), Cmnd. 6352.

[38] *Report of the Advisory Group on the Law of Rape* (1975), VIII Summary of Recommendations, para.1 (p.36). The proposed definition was also designed to pre-empt the argument that the question of recklessness did not directly arise for decision in *Morgan* in view of the question certified.

(b) at the time he knows that the person does not consent to the intercourse or is reckless as to whether that person consents to it."

A further effect of the amendment was to remove the word "unlawful" from the statutory definition of rape, thereby confirming that rape within marriage is an offence.

THE DEFINITION OF RAPE IN THE SEXUAL OFFENCES ACT 2003

Section 1 of the Sexual Offences Act 2003 re-defined rape as follows: **1.19**

"(1) A person (A) commits an offence if—
　(a) he intentionally penetrates the vagina, anus or mouth of another person (B) with his penis,
　(b) B does not consent to the penetration, and
　(c) A does not reasonably believe B consents.
(2) Whether a belief is reasonable is to be determined having regard to all the circumstances, including any steps A has taken to ascertain whether B consents."

MODE OF TRIAL AND PUNISHMENT

Both rape and attempted rape are triable only on indictment, except for certain cases where there is provision for trial in the Youth Court.[39] The maximum penalty for rape and attempted rape is life imprisonment.[40]   **1.20**

For the purposes of listing, cases of rape[41] fall within Class 2B, save for complex cases involving many complainants (often under age, in care or otherwise particularly vulnerable) and/or many defendants who are alleged to have systematically groomed and abused them, often over a long period of time, which fall within Class 1C.[42] Cases in Class 1C must be referred to the Resident Judge, and by the Resident Judge to a Presiding Judge. Cases in Class 2B must be similarly referred in certain specified circumstances, including where the case is unusually grave or complex or a novel and important point of law is to be raised; where the defendant is a police officer, a member of the legal profession or a high profile figure; or where for any reason the case is likely to attract exceptional media attention.   **1.21**

Rape is a serious specified offence for the purposes of the dangerousness provisions of the Criminal Justice Act 2003.[43] Accordingly, the offence falls   **1.22**

[39] Sexual Offences Act 2003 s.1(4); Magistrates' Court Act 1980 s.24, as amended by the Powers of Criminal Courts (Sentencing) Act 2000 s.165(1) and Sch.9, para.64. For detailed discussion see Ch.31.
[40] Sexual Offences Act 2003, s.1(4). Attempted rape formerly carried a maximum of seven years' imprisonment: Sexual Offences Act 1956, s.37 and Sch.2. The maximum was increased to life by the Sexual Offences Act 1985 s.3(2).
[41] And of soliciting, inciting, encouraging or assisting, attempting or conspiring to commit the offence or assisting an offender having committed the offence.
[42] *Consolidated Criminal Practice Directions*, Part XIII Listing B: CLASSIFICATION, available at *https://www.judiciary.gov.uk/publications/criminal-practice-directions-2015* [Accessed March 19, 2016].
[43] Criminal Justice Act 2003 s.224 and Sch.15, Pt 2.

within the scope of s.225(2) of that Act (life sentences for serious offences). Further, an offence of rape, whenever committed, may be made the subject of an extended sentence under s.226A of that Act.[44] The offence is also listed in Pt 1 of Sch.15B to the Criminal Justice Act 2003 for the purposes of s.224A of the Act (life sentence for a second listed offence).[45]

1.23   A person convicted of rape, cautioned, found not guilty by reason of insanity or found to be under a disability and to have done the act charged, is automatically subject to the notification requirements in the Sexual Offences Act 2003.[46]

BAIL

1.24   Section 25 of the Criminal Justice and Public Order Act 1994 provides that a person charged with or convicted of certain offences who has a previous conviction for any such offence shall be granted bail only if the court, or as the case may be, the constable considering the grant of bail, is of the opinion that there are exceptional circumstances which justify it. Section 25(2) as enacted covered, in s.25(2)(d) and (e), rape and attempted rape. The 2003 Act[47] substituted the following for s.25(2)(d) and (e):

> "(d) rape under the law of Scotland or Northern Ireland;
> (e) an offence under section 1 of the Sexual Offences Act 1956 (rape);
> (f) an offence under section 1 of the Sexual Offences Act 2003 (rape);
> (g) an offence under section 2 of that Act (assault by penetration);
> (h) an offence under section 4 of that Act (causing a person to engage in sexual activity without consent), where the activity caused involved penetration within subsection (4)(a) to (d) of that section;
> (i) an offence under section 5 of that Act (rape of a child under 13);
> (j) an offence under section 6 of that Act (assault of a child under 13 by penetration);
> (k) an offence under section 18 of that Act (causing or inciting a child under 13 to engage in sexual activity), where an activity involving penetration within subsection (3)(a) to (d) of that section was caused;
> (l) an offence under section 30 of that Act (sexual activity with a person with a mental disorder impeding choice), where the touching involved penetration within subsection (3)(a) to (d) of that section;
> (m) an offence under section 31 of that Act (causing or inciting a person, with a mental disorder impeding choice, to engage in sexual activity), where an activity involving penetration within subsection (3)(a) to (d) of that section was caused;
> (n) an attempt to commit an offence within any of paragraphs (d) to (m)."

1.25   Section 25 was considered in *R. (O) v Harrow Crown Court*[48] where the House of Lords noted that it appears to create a statutory presumption

---

[44] Inserted by the Legal Aid, Sentencing and Punishment of Offenders Act 2012 s.124, brought into force on December 3, 2012, by SI 2012/2906.
[45] Inserted by the Legal Aid, Sentencing and Punishment of Offenders Act 2012 s.122, brought into force on December 3, 2012, by SI 2012/2906.
[46] s.80 and Sch.3, discussed in Ch.35, below.
[47] s.139 and Sch.6, para.32(2).
[48] [2007] 1 A.C. 249.

against the grant of bail in those cases to which it applies and so to be incompatible with art.5(3) ECHR. The House held that the section should be construed and applied essentially as a guide to the proper operation of the Bail Act 1976 in those cases. The section places a burden on the defendant to rebut a presumption and if he fails to do so he is to be denied bail. In the vast majority of cases arising before the expiry of the custody time limit, the court will reach a clear view one way or the other whether the conditions for withholding bail specified by Sch.1 to the Bail Act are satisfied. But should the court be left unsure as to whether the defendant should be released on bail—the only situation in which the burden of proof assumes any relevance- —bail would then have to be granted as the "default position". Section 25 should be read down to make that plain.[49] As for cases where the custody time-limit has expired, the House held that s.25 operates to disapply the ordinary requirement under reg.6(6) of the Prosecution of Offences (Custody Time-limits) Regulations 1987[50] that bail should be granted automatically in such circumstances. The House did not expect there to be many cases where bail is refused notwithstanding the court's refusal to extend the custody time limit; but there is no necessary inconsistency here and art.5(3) is not necessarily breached in such cases.

FORM AND CONTENT OF THE INDICTMENT

Specimen counts

Specimen counts are frequently used in trials of sexual offences. They are   **1.26** appropriate where a complainant cannot particularise any specific incident and merely alleges a pattern of similar conduct, and there is no room for the jury to focus on one incident rather than another because no single occasion is sufficiently distinct. However, care must be taken to identify cases in which separate particularised incidents are wrapped up in one count within a pattern of conduct, where it may be necessary for the judge to give a *Brown*[51] direction along the lines that the jury have to be unanimous about the same incident. In most cases where a specimen count is relied on, it is enough for the judge to tell the jury that they may convict if they are sure that the offence has been committed at least once.[52] *Williams v R.*[53] is a classic example of the

---

[49] At [35] per Lord Brown of Eaton-under-Heywood. Lord Carswell stated at [12] that, where an application for bail is made during the currency of the custody time-limit, s.25 should be read as placing an evidential burden upon the defendant to "point to or produce material which supports the existence of exceptional circumstances".

[50] SI 1987/299.

[51] [1984] 79 Cr. App. R. 115.

[52] See *R. v K* [2009] 1 Cr. App. R. 331, where the Court of Appeal held that a trial judge's direction to the jury in respect of a count alleging a single episode involving the penetration of the six-year-old complainant's vagina or anus could not be criticised. The judge had directed the jury that they could convict the defendant if they were sure he had penetrated either the vagina or the anus. It did not matter if they disagreed as to which was penetrated as long as they were sure that one of them was penetrated. See para.1.157, below.

[53] [2012] EWCA Crim 2516.

use of specimen counts in a sex case, and the submissions that arise at the close of evidence when the defence ask for a direction in accordance with *Brown*. The appellant was convicted on one count of oral rape and one count of vaginal rape. These were specimen counts because the victim alleged that she had been orally and vaginally raped several times during the night she spent in the appellant's home. The allegations covered a single night, the same parties, the same place, and the same defence was put forward in relation to the activity in each count. In relation to the allegation of oral rape, it was agreed the activity took place and the issue was consent. In relation to the allegation of vaginal rape, the issue was whether there had been any vaginal sexual intercourse. The trial judge explained to the jury that the prosecution had selected one example of each allegation instead of loading up the indictment with counts that charged numerous offences of the same kind. He directed them that they could only convict the defendant if they were sure that he committed the particular offence charged in that particular count, whether or not they were sure that he also committed other offences.

1.27   On appeal, it was submitted on behalf of the appellant that this was a misdirection and that the judge should specifically have directed the jury that they could not convict upon any specimen count unless they were all agreed as to which offending incident they were sure the appellant committed. His failure so to direct them meant the jury might have been divided as to which course of conduct they were sure the appellant committed. For example, they might have been divided as to whether the complainant's account in relation to matters later in the evening after admittedly taking crack cocaine and alcohol was accurate. Some jury members might have been sure that she had been raped vaginally or orally at some point, but not agreed as to precisely when. It was argued, citing *Brown*,[54] that the judge's direction left it open to the jury to convict of rape, with some members being sure of an account of one incident and others only being sure in relation to a different incident later on that night.

1.28   The Court of Appeal pointed out that *Brown* was concerned with the situation that arises where a count contains a number of different ingredients, representing alternative ways in which an offence may be committed. In those circumstances, the judge must direct the jury that where a number of matters are specified in the count as together constituting an ingredient in the offence, and any one of them was capable of doing so, any individual matter must be proved to the satisfaction of the whole jury. It would not, where an indictment alleges different types of activity, be sufficient for six members of the jury to find one activity proved and another six members to find a different activity proved. As was observed in *Keeton*[55]:

> "... it is only in cases where truly alternative bases for a finding of guilt are being put forward by the Crown and where there is a risk that the jury might feel

---

[54] [1984] 79 Cr. App. R. 115.
[55] [1995] 2 Cr. App. R. 241, at p.259G.

it is permissible for some of them to be satisfied by one basis and others by another, that the *Brown* direction need be given. It is not appropriate to complicate what are essentially straightforward cases with a *Brown* direction."

As this was not a case where the counts specified a number of different ingredients, the Court of Appeal concluded that a *Brown* direction was not necessary, and the judge's direction was sufficient. There was no disparity as to time, place, particulars or nature of the act required to prove a count. The separate allegations of oral and vaginal rape stood or fell together within each count. At no stage was the case conducted on the basis that some jurors might be satisfied in relation to one episode, with some being satisfied in relation to another.

The situation in *Williams* should be contrasted with that in *Hobson*,[56]   **1.29** where the complainants gave evidence identifying specific occasions alleged to be part of a pattern of conduct, and there was evidence which could have caused a reasonable jury to acquit on the specimen count but convict on the particularised occasion, or vice versa. In those circumstances it was possible that the jury was not at one in relation to any specific occasion. Where this occurs, an obvious solution is for the prosecution to apply to amend the indictment in order to add the particular incident or incidents as separate counts. However, if the specific occasions are not particularised on the indictment, it will be incumbent on the judge to tell the jury that they can only convict if they are sure the offence has been committed on the same occasion, either an occasion in the course of the unspecified pattern of offending or one of the particular occasions identified in the evidence. The nature of the incidents alleged in *Hobson* was such that the jury could, on the evidence, have been satisfied about the course of conduct but not about the specific occasions, or vice versa. In such circumstances, it could not be said that the verdicts were safe.

Course of conduct/multiple incident counts

By virtue of the Criminal Procedure Rules 2015, r.10.2(2),[57] more than one   **1.30** incident of the commission of an offence may be included in a count if those incidents taken together amount to a course of conduct having regard to the time, place or purpose of commission. This provision allows the prosecution to reflect the offending in a single count rather than a specimen count which, in turn, should assist the prosecution in striking the right balance between including sufficient counts to give the court adequate sentencing powers and unduly burdening the indictment. It is a departure from the common law and to that extent a modification of what used to be called the rule against duplicity.[58] In *A v R*.[59] the Court of Appeal explained that the purpose

---

[56] [2013] EWCA Crim 819. See commentary at [2014] Crim. L.R. 83, and the guidance given by Hughes LJ (as he then was) in *Hartley* [2011] EWCA Crim 1299.
[57] Supplemented by the Criminal Practice Directions 2015, para.10A.13.
[58] *Hartley* [2011] EWCA Crim 1299.
[59] [2015] EWCA Crim 1177.

underpinning multiple counts is to enable the prosecution to reflect the defendant's alleged criminality when the offences are so similar and numerous that it is inappropriate to indict each occasion, or a large number of different occasions, in separate charges. Fulford LJ observed that when the prosecution fails to specify a sufficient minimum number of occasions within the multiple incident count or counts, they are not making proper use of the procedure. In cases of sustained abuse it will often be unhelpful to draft the count as representing, potentially, no more than two incidents. The prosecution needs to ensure that there are one or more sufficiently broad course of conduct counts, or a mix of individual counts and course of conduct counts, such that the judge will be able to sentence the defendant appropriately on the basis of his criminality as revealed by the counts on which he is convicted.

1.31   *A v R.* is an example of a case where the prosecution did not make proper use of multiple incident counts by drafting them to cover a sufficient minimum number of occasions, so that the extent and timespan of the offending was unclear from the jury's verdicts. The appellant was alleged to have raped and sexually assaulted his wife on many occasions. He was convicted on one multiple incident count of rape and one multiple incident count of assault by penetration. In evidence, the victim had given some particulars of the occasions when the offending occurred. The incidents were broadly similar in nature and represented a pattern of behaviour rather than clearly identifiable incidents. The judge had directed the jury that in respect of the multiple incident counts, the jury needed to be sure the defendant carried out the activity on more than one occasion. Upon sentence, the judge found that the appellant had committed multiple rapes against the complainant, as well as further acts of degradation by penetrating her vagina with his finger on several occasions. It was held that the verdicts on the two multiple incident counts did not entitle the judge to sentence on that factual basis. The appellant should have been sentenced for two offences of rape and two of assault by penetration. A defendant can only be sentenced in respect of matters of which he has been convicted or which have been taken into consideration.[60] For further discussion see paras 30.18 and following, below.

IMPLEMENTATION DATE: WHERE UNCLEAR WHETHER OFFENCE UNDER THE OLD OR NEW LAW

1.32   The Sexual Offences Act 2003 (Commencement Order) 2004[61] brought the Act fully into force on May 1, 2004. On that day, the majority of existing sexual offences were abolished, others such as rape were re-defined, and over 50 new offences in Pt 1 of the 2003 Act came into force. Section 141 of the Act empowered the Secretary of State to make transitional provisions, but no

---

[60] *Canavan* [1998] 1 Cr. App. R. 79.
[61] SI 2004/874.

such provisions were enacted. It followed that, where there was a doubt as to whether the events occurred before or after the coming into force of the Act, the prosecution would fail, because it could not be proved whether an offence was committed under the old law or the new law.[62]

This lacuna was filled by s.55 of the Violent Crime Reduction Act 2006,   **1.33** which came into effect on February 12, 2007. This deeming provision covers the situation where an accused is charged in respect of the same conduct both with an offence under the 2003 Act and an offence under the old law, and the only thing preventing him being found guilty of the 2003 Act offence is the fact that it has not been proved beyond a reasonable doubt that the time when the conduct took place was after the coming into force of that Act, and the only thing preventing him being found guilty of the offence under the old law is the fact that it has not been proved beyond a reasonable doubt that the time when the conduct took place was before the repeal of that law. In such circumstances, for the purpose of determining guilt, it will be conclusively presumed that the time when the conduct took place was when the old law applied, if the offence attracted a lesser maximum penalty; otherwise, it will be presumed that the conduct took place after the implementation of the new law. Where the evidence is such that it is unclear whether the offence should be charged under the new or the old law, then in order to rely upon s.55 each offence should be charged in the alternative under the new and old regimes. It is plain from the authorities that when the appropriate procedures are not followed and the evidence is inconclusive as to when the offences were committed, any conviction must be held to be unsafe.[63] Adopting a procedural device with particulars of an offence under both the old law and the new law in the same count is not an appropriate solution. It would be duplicitous, would impede the proper working of s.55 and directions to the jury would be difficult, if not impossible.[64]

WHERE ACCUSED CONVICTED UNDER WRONG STATUTE

In *Stocker*,[65] the appellant was convicted of rape, contrary to s.1(1) of the   **1.34** Sexual Offences Act 1956. The offence was committed in 2008 and so the relevant statutory provision had been wrongly identified: it should have been s.1(1) of the 2003 Act. The question for the Court of Appeal was whether this was a purely technical defect or whether the count was fundamentally flawed

---

[62] *A (Prosecutor's Appeal)* [2006] 1 Cr. App. R. 433; *Newbon* [2005] Crim. L.R. 738.
[63] *F v The Queen* [2008] EWCA 994; *Chaney* [2009] EWCA Crim 52.
[64] *Bryan Marshall*, Woolwich Crown Court, November 2, 2009 (HH Judge Peter Murphy).
[65] [2013] EWCA Crim 1993. For a useful discussion of defective indictments, see also *R. v AD* [2016] EWCA Crim 454, where the statement of offence had wrongly referred to s.14(1) of the Sexual Offences Act 1956, rather than s.15(1), in respect of two offences committed by the appellant against his son. The Court of Appeal confirmed the growing trend towards prioritisation of substance over form. The slip in drafting had not caused the appellant any prejudice, breached his ECHR rights or otherwise rendered the trial process unfair. The defect in the indictment, whilst reflecting a degree of culpable oversight, did not render the convictions unsafe.

because it breached the provision now contained in r.10.2(1)(a)(ii) of the Criminal Procedure Rules 2015 by failing to identify accurately the legislation contravened. From the beginning to the end of the process, the charge was, in substance, one of rape under the 2003 Act. The error could have been cured easily by an amendment at any time. The Court of Appeal did not accept that an error in the date of the statute on these facts was so fundamental as to render the proceedings a nullity, or that the drafter of the Rules would have intended such an outcome for a breach of this kind. Nothing had occurred during the trial to render the indictment a nullity or the conviction unsafe. Clearly, the situation will be different if the jury is inappropriately directed to apply the present law in respect of the mental element of rape to a case predating the 2003 Act, when the test of belief in consent was purely subjective.

SENTENCING

Definitive Guideline

1.35 Two years after it was established in 2010, the Sentencing Council conducted a timely review of the *Sexual Offences Act 2003: Definitive Guideline*, which had been issued by the Sentencing Guidelines Council ("SGC") on April 30, 2007. Following a thorough consultation process, the Council issued a new Definitive Guideline on February 12, 2014: for general discussion, see Ch.33, below. The guideline applies in respect of the sentencing of offenders aged 18 and older convicted of sexual offences, whenever committed,[66] who are sentenced on or after April 1, 2014. It follows that the earlier SGC guideline will only now be relevant in appeals out of time against sentences passed before that date.[67]

Step One—Harm and culpability

1.36 The guideline requires the sentencing court to go through a series of steps in order to determine the appropriate sentence. Step one involves determining the offence category by reference to the degree of harm caused to the victim and then the culpability level for the offence. This approach differs from the SGC's Definitive Guideline in that gravity is not to be evaluated by considering only the physical activity concerned, as the Sentencing Council considered that this does not fully reflect the seriousness or complexity of the offence. The court should determine harm and culpability by reference only to the tables set out in the guideline. In relation to the offence of rape, these are as follows:

---

[66] See *R. v H(J)* [2011] EWCA Crim 2753, where Lord Judge CJ summarised the principles underpinning the correct approach to sentencing in historic cases. These are set out in Annex B of the *Sexual Offences: Definitive Guideline*. See also Ch.30, below (Historic cases).

[67] The SGC guideline has not been replaced insofar as it deals with child sex offences committed by children or young persons (s13 read with ss.9-12 of the Sexual offences Act 2003).

Harm		Culpability	
Category 1	The extreme nature of one or more category 2 factors or the extreme impact caused by a combination of category 2 factors **may** elevate to category 1	A	
		Significant degree of planning	
		Offender acts together with others to commit the offence	
		Use of alcohol/drugs on victim to facilitate the offence	
Category 2	• Severe psychological or physical harm • Pregnancy or STI as a consequence of offence • Additional degradation/ humiliation • Abduction • Prolonged detention/sustained incident • Violence or threats of violence (beyond that which is inherent in the offence) • Forced/uninvited entry into victim's home • Victim is particularly vulnerable due to personal circumstances* *for children under 13 please refer to the guideline on page 27	Abuse of trust	
		Previous violence against victim	
		Offence committed in course of burglary	
		Recording of the offence	
		Commercial exploitation and/or motivation	
		Offence racially or religiously aggravated	
		Offence motivated by, or demonstrating, hostility to the victim based on his or her sexual orientation (or presumed sexual orientation) or transgender identity (or presumed transgender identity)	
		Offence motivated by, or demonstrating, hostility to the victim based on his or her disability (or presumed disability)	
		B	
Category 3	Factor(s) in categories 1 and 2 not present	Factor(s) in category A not present	

1.37   The Guideline recognises that all rape is extremely harmful to the victim by assuming there is *always* a baseline of harm. This is reflected in category 3 harm, which covers offences in which the harm factors identified in categories 1 and 2 are not present. The existence of category 3 is designed to indicate to the sentencer that, once an offender has been found guilty of rape, they do not need to identify additional factors for the offence to be deemed harmful or serious. The Council felt that the violation of the victim through the act of rape is harm in itself and it would be unhelpful to articulate this as "lesser harm", as these offences are inherently harmful. However, the Council also recognised that the level of harm caused by rape can vary, and categories 1 and 2 therefore build upon the baseline of harm assumed in category 3.

Category 1 harm—extreme nature or extreme impact of category 2 factors

1.38   The guideline adopts a different approach from the previous SGC guideline, which placed repeated rape of the same victim *or* rape involving multiple victims in the category with the highest starting point. The Sentencing Council took the view that the guideline is concerned with sentencing levels for a single offence. If there are multiple rapes or victims, these should be charged as separate instances of rape with the overall sentence subject to the principle of totality. In particularly serious cases, this may have the effect of taking the sentence above the top bracket.

1.39   In contrast with other guidelines issued by the Council, category 1 does not rely on new factors to increase the severity of the sentence, but instead permits a combination of category 2 factors to elevate a case. The Council believes that many of the factors set out in category 2, when combined, will increase the psychological and/or physical harm to the victim. This approach relies on the sentencer, in full possession of all the facts of the case, being best placed to determine when either the extreme nature of a factor in category 2, or the extreme impact of a combination of such factors, justifies the elevation of the case to category 1. In *Carroll*,[68] it was argued that the violence was not of an extreme nature. The victim of the rape was a 20-year-old prostitute who was 17 weeks pregnant at the time. The appellant, aged 56, was a customer. They were having vaginal sex in a lay-by. The appellant put his hands around his victim's neck, pressed his thumb to the front of her throat and began to strangle her. She struggled and tried to kick him between the legs. She scratched his face to try to stop him. At this stage his penis was still inside her vagina. She then lost consciousness. When she regained consciousness, she was on the ground half-naked and he had disappeared. The appellant left her severely traumatised. Although her physical injuries were not serious, the psychological damage which the appellant had done to her was extreme. The appellant sought to rely upon the expert's evidence that only a short period

---

[68] [2014] EWCA Crim 2818.

of strangulation would lead to a loss of consciousness, and if strangulation continued death would be likely within a short period of time. Therefore, the appellant must have released his hold on the victim's neck shortly after she lost consciousness. It was also argued that there was no evidence of an extreme impact beyond the inevitable consequence of being raped by a stranger. The Court of Appeal was quite satisfied that rape offence was a category 1 offence, and the nature of the violence was correctly categorised as extreme. Albeit the strangling may not have lasted a long time, the violence and fear induced by throttling a victim cannot be underestimated.

Category 2 harm

● **Severe psychological or physical harm**   1.40
The Council was sensitive to the fact that individuals will have different psychological responses and that assumptions should not be made about the severity of rape based solely upon the resilience or lack of resilience of a victim.[69] It therefore included severe psychological harm in the consultation draft guideline as an aggravating factor at step two. Some respondents to the consultation argued that severe psychological or physical harm should be reflected at step one. The Council did not wish to propagate the myth that a lack of physical harm makes rape less serious and so in the published guideline it moved severe psychological harm to step one, to allow sentencers to reflect the severe nature of the harm in selecting the offence category. The judge should focus upon the harm caused to the particular individual in deciding whether it amounts to severe psychological harm so as to place the case in category 2 at step one, or whether it amounts to an aggravating feature under step two. It is clear from *Ul Nasir*[70] that the harm can be aggravated by the impact upon the victim and their family within their particular community. That does not mean that offences are aggravated by reason of the victim's ethnic and religious origins. As Walker J explained in that case, the point taken by the applicant's counsel that there had been an uplift in sentence because of the complainant's ethnic and religious background was a misconception. In her sentencing remarks the judge had observed that the victim was finding it difficult at school because her friends knew what had happened leading to problems and shame for her. For the family as a whole there had been enormous implications. The father had said that he and her mother were struggling and felt socially isolated because, within their particular community, it brought shame on the whole family. He was also concerned about the marriage prospects for his daughters. The

---

[69] In this respect the Council cite Dr. Fiona Mason in *Psychological effects of rape and serious sexual assault,* which was Ch.23 in our 4th edition. See now Ch.23, below.

[70] Unreported, September 10, 2015 (renewed application for leave to appeal against sentence). The applicant had been convicted of two offences of sexual assault on a child under 13, contrary to s.7 of the SOA 2003, and four offences of sexual activity with a child contrary to s.9 of that Act.

applicant, coming from their family, knew only too well the effect upon the children and the family, and this was an aggravating feature.

- **Pregnancy or STI as a consequence of offence**

The Council treated pregnancy or STI as principal factual elements which, where present, may exacerbate still further the long-term harm experienced by the victim. It did not keep the specific reference in the SGC's guideline to "ejaculation", on the basis that harm to the victim occurs at the point penetration takes place, whether or not the offender subsequently ejaculates. However, "ejaculation" is included as an aggravating factor at step two, enabling the starting point to be increased where this has occurred. This does not mean that mitigation is available in the absence of ejaculation. In order to deal with any concerns about double counting where "pregnancy or STI as a consequence" is present at step one, the step two factor is worded as: "ejaculation (where not taken into account at step one)".

- **Additional degradation/humiliation**

This factor relates to cases where the offender has subjected the victim to further acts of degradation and humiliation not inherent in all rape cases. Examples given by the Council are: urinating or ejaculating over the victim, leaving the victim naked in a public place, or forcing the victim to dress up or strip for the offender.

- **Abduction**

This factor reflects the increased psychological harm that being detained or abducted would have on the victim. It includes preventing the victim from leaving their home during an attack.

- **Prolonged detention/sustained incident**

The Council separated prolonged detention from abduction in recognition that it is a different and distinct factor. This factor reflects the fact that a prolonged or sustained incident may increase the psychological harm to the victim where there is a fear of escalation and the psychological trauma of not knowing when and if they may escape from the offender. The feature in the SGC guideline of repeated rape in the course of one attack is not included. It follows that where there is vaginal and anal rape in the course of one attack, this should in the Council's view be treated as two offences of rape.

- **Violence or threats of violence (beyond that which is inherent in the offence)**

This reflects the fact that not all rapes are accompanied by violence and that fear of violence following a threat can be as harmful as the violence itself.

1.41
- **Forced/uninvited entry into victim's home**

This factor covers not only an offender who breaks into the victim's home but also an ex-partner who enters the victim's home uninvited. Where the ex-partner has been invited, this factor would not apply. However, at step two the Council have retained the location of the offence as an aggravating factor, so that if the sentencer feels that the harm to the victim is increased by virtue of the fact it occurred in their home, this can be taken into account at that stage.

"Forced/uninvited entry into the victim's home" was not dealt with **1.42** directly in the SGC guideline, which may have led to under-sentencing in such cases until the decision in *Attorney General's Reference (Nos 73, 75 and 03 of 2010) (Anigbugu)*,[71] in which the Court of Appeal took the opportunity to amplify the guideline. The Court stated that rape of a person by an intruder in the safe haven of their own home is a serious aggravating feature. Even if there were no additional features beyond the rape and the burglary, the starting point would rarely be less than 12 years' imprisonment and, where there were additional aggravating features, the starting point for consideration would increase to 15 years and beyond. Lord Judge CJ stated[72]:

> "As these cases show, in many such cases where rape or serious sexual assault is perpetrated in the course of a burglary, several additional aggravating features are usually present. We have referred to the taking of photographs in two of these cases. We shall identify a number of differing aggravating features in the course of the judgment dealing with the individual cases. In such cases, where there are aggravating features, the starting point for consideration will increase to fifteen years' imprisonment and beyond. In all such cases the question of dangerousness must be carefully examined."

The Sentencing Council's guideline is consistent with Lord Judge's approach in *Anigbugu*. In *Wendell Baker*[73] the trial judge had had to consider how far beyond 15 years to go in respect of an extremely serious example of a rape by an intruder. The case was heard after *Anigbugu* but before the new guideline. The Court of Appeal, whilst acknowledging that culpability and harm were very high indeed, held that a starting point of 20 years rather than 24 years was appropriate for a rape where the intruder had broken into a house in the early hours of the morning where a 68-year-old lady lived on her own. The victim had then been subjected to gratuitous violence both before and after an anal rape, as well as threats to her life. She was also locked in a small cupboard which could only be opened from the outside. She remained there for many hours in acute discomfort expecting to die. She was not found until early evening the next day when, fortuitously, a friend called and rescued her. The Court of Appeal showed gruesome imagination by suggesting that it might be possible to imagine a worse case in which the victim had been burgled and then subjected to the dreadful indignity of a pitiless and life-scarring violent sexual assault. The Court did, however, uphold the life sentence, recognising that the applicant was dangerous and might be so for many years.

- **Victim is particularly vulnerable due to personal circumstances**

---

[71] [2011] EWCA Crim 633. See also *R. v D* [2012] EWCA Crim 2270, where the appellant as a youth had broken into his grandmother's home and raped her. The Court of Appeal took the view that the trial judge might well have passed a longer minimum sentence had *Anigbugu* been brought to his notice.

[72] At [8].

[73] [2014] EWCA Crim 242.

1.43 This factor elevates to category 2 a rape committed against someone who has been subjected to habitual sexual abuse. It is broad enough to include those particularly vulnerable because of a background of emotional or physical abuse or vulnerability through age and/or disability. It has been made clear that the factor is not qualified by a requirement of something such as "permanent disability" or circumstances that are more than "temporary". It can, for instance, include a young female who is alone at night and very intoxicated. In *Attorney General's Reference (No.51 of 2015) (Whitmore)*,[74] prosecution counsel had appeared to concede that the fact that the victim was alone, drunk and vulnerable was not a factor that could place the case in category 2 as it was "part of the offence anyway". The Court of Appeal agreed with submissions made on behalf of the Solicitor General that the judge had been led into error by the submissions of the parties to the effect that this rape was not a category 2 offence. Defence counsel, who had conducted research into the production of the Definitive Guideline, used consultation documents to argue that for someone to be particularly vulnerable due to personal circumstances, there has to be some kind of condition which is "immutable", for example a permanent physical disability or vulnerability through age. The Vice President, Hallett LJ, rejected this argument, holding that the court should look at the terms of the guideline as finally produced as opposed to discussions that took place during the consultation period. The words "victim is particularly vulnerable due to personal circumstances" are not so qualified and can cover temporary circumstances such as those of the complainant in this case.

Culpability

1.44 The Sentencing Council took the view that the use of the term "lower culpability" would not be appropriate in a rape case, as an offender who carries out a rape necessarily demonstrates a high degree of culpability. It therefore set out an exhaustive list of factors which may take rape beyond the culpability inherent in the act of rape itself. Accordingly, culpability B has no factors listed. This is to reflect the fact that the act of rape inherently involves a high level of culpability. It is not a lower culpability category but reflects the absence of any of the additional factors found in culpability B and indicates a baseline of culpability that exists whenever rape is committed. The culpability A factors are considered below.
   - **Significant degree of planning**
Research showed that the public saw this factor as increasing the culpability of the offender. The SGC guideline had stated that the planning of an offence indicated a higher level of culpability than an opportunistic or impulsive

---

[74] [2015] EWCA Crim 1699. The sentence was increased from four to six years on the basis that the case fell within category 2B rather than category 3B. See also *Karam* [2013] 2. Cr. App. R.(S.) 65, where the complainant was in a similar state to this complainant and the court had proceeded on the same basis.

offence. Clearly the issue of planning needs to be considered in the overall context. In *Attorney General's Reference (No. 126 of 2014) (Omar Jumale and Said Zakaria)*,[75] the trial judge had declined to find that two rapes which took place in a hotel had been planned. The context was the sustained sexual abuse of a 13-year-old who had become a sexual plaything of a group of associated men. What had been planned was a sex party in which this 13-year-old girl was to be a compliant participant. The Court of Appeal stated[76]:

> "The very fact that further sexual abuse of an already abused and vulnerable 13-year-old girl was plainly planned is itself a feature of the case which renders it as a serious one. In any event, as the situation developed it turned to rape. The rapes left the victim injured and this physically small girl was humiliated in what the judge described as a cynical, callous and very nasty manner. The judge assessed the rapes as falling within category 2B. It appears to us that in the circumstances there would have been a justification for finding that the case came within category 2A: not least by the presence of others in the vicinity, and taking account of, (if not a culpability A factor), the significant aggravating factor of the planned sexual abuse of a 13 year old."

- **Offender acts together with others to commit the offence**

This area is the subject of recent and continuing research, especially in **1.45** relation to the exploitation of young children, particularly young teenagers, by groups. There have been a number of high profile cases of this type during the last few years. The Sentencing Council cites the emerging findings of the Children's Commissioner for England:[77]

> " . . . that children are being victimised through gang and group sexual exploitation from the age of 10 upwards, and are both female and male (although predominantly female). They come from a full range of ethnic backgrounds represented in England, and some are disabled. The abuse is taking place in urban, rural and metropolitan areas. Children are being sexually exploited by groups and gangs made up of people who are both the same, and different, ages, ethnicities and social backgrounds from those that characterise them as victims."

This factor identifies situations where two or more offenders act together, irrespective of the nature or formal structure of the grouping. It reflects the enhanced fear and intimidation created by the presence of more than one offender. Again, the overall context is important. This factor is different from "the presence of others in the vicinity" which features at step two of the guideline which is concerned with the movement from the starting point arising from an assessment of the aggravating and mitigating features. The guideline requires a determination of culpability and harm at step one by reference *only* to the particular factors listed. Nevertheless, in *Attorney*

---

[75] [2015] EWCA Crim 128.
[76] At [25] per Treacy LJ.
[77] *Emerging findings from the inquiry into gangs and groups* (Children's Commissioner, July 2012).

General's Reference (No. 126 of 2014)[78] the Court of Appeal identified "the presence of others in the vicinity" as part of the circumstances that would have justified a finding that the case came within category 2A. Lyndon Harris had described this as a misapplication of the guideline.[79] However, there clearly will be cases where there is an overlap between these factors, particularly where there has been systematic abuse of a victim by a group of associated men. In *Attorney General's Reference (No. 126 of 2014)*, even though others were not present in the hotel room where the offender raped the victim, a sex party with a compliant 13 year-old victim had been planned. Numerous men had been present at the flat from where the offender collected the 13-year-old victim to take her to the hotel where he had organised a room for the purpose of sexual abuse. No one else was present but CCTV footage showed that a group of men were in close proximity within the hotel and it is clear the victim was aware of their presence.

- **Use of alcohol/drugs on victim to facilitate the offence**

1.46 This factor reflects the increased culpability of someone who, in a common scenario, gets the victim drunk, stupefied or intoxicated, or administers some form of drug in order to render the victim incapable of consenting to sexual activity. It reflects an element of deliberation and planning which is always an aggravating factor. *R. v M (H)*[80] provides a good example of this factor being given weight under the previous guideline. The offender contacted his two female victims via a social networking site, took each of them to a hotel room, gave them alcohol to the extent they were rendered unconscious and then took sexual advantage of them. He filmed his offending against one victim and photographed the other while she was naked and unconscious. It followed that, not only were there two separate victims, but there were aggravating features in the use of alcohol and the photographing. On an Attorney General's reference, the Court of Appeal increased the total sentence from six to nine years' imprisonment.

- **Abuse of trust**

1.47 An offender's culpability is increased if they are in a position of responsibility towards the victim.[81] The term "abuse of trust" is wider than the term "abuse of position of trust" which was a factor indicating higher culpability in the consultation draft of the guideline. In *R. v O(D)*,[82] the Court of Appeal considered whether use of the broader term in the published guideline required that a rape within a relationship would automatically constitute an abuse of trust such as to bring the case within culpability A. It was held that

---

[78] [2015] EWCA Crim 128 at [10] and [25].
[79] [2015] Crim L.R. 465.
[80] [2013] EWCA Crim 1642.
[81] A number of examples are given in *Billam* [1986] 1 W.L.R. 349.
[82] [2014] EWCA Crim 2202; [2014] 1 Cr. App. R.(S.) 41. See also *Attorney General's Reference (No.121 of 2015)(Jonathan R)* [2016] EWCA Crim 173 at [19], where the Court of Appeal agreed with the trial judge's rejection of the prosecution submission that the abuse committed by the offender when he was 14 upon his much younger twin sisters amounted to an inherent "abuse of trust".

was not the intention of the Sentencing Council. The change to the term "abuse of trust" was intended to include circumstances where the offender may not hold a formal position of trust in relation to the victim but they have abused the trust engendered by their status and/or standing. In *R. v O(D)* the fact that the rape took place within a relationship was not sufficient for the offence to represent an abuse of trust, but it did constitute a gross betrayal which was itself an aggravating factor. As an aggravating factor it would come into play at step two rather than being one of the listed factors which elevate the case into culpability A. The Court was, however, satisfied that the case fell into category 2 harm on the basis of the severe psychological harm caused. The rape was committed against the mother of one of the children whom the appellant was abusing at the time. In her statement the victim described the psychological injury that the appellant had caused her and her family as "immeasurable".

The Court of Appeal considered the scope of the term "abuse of trust" on **1.48** a number of occasions in respect of the SGC guideline. In *R. v ZBT*[83] the Court indicated that in their experience abuse of trust contemplated, for example, abuse of teacher/student or parent/child relationships. It did not cover a case where the complainant and the appellant were step-siblings in a familial context. In *R. v J(I)*[84] the Court considered that abuse of trust required a relationship involving inequality between the parties to some substantive degree. Despite the fact that the appellant was in a position equivalent to the victim's father-in-law and was a workmate as shop fitter, it was a relationship between equal adults. The abuse of their relationship as friends and work mates was to an extent an aggravating feature, particularly as it resulted in more serious consequences to the victim, but it was not an abuse of trust of a nature or significance to warrant the starting point being raised from three to eight years for an offence under s.4(1) of the 2003 Act (causing a person to engage in sexual activity without consent). We do not consider that either of these examples would amount to an abuse of trust under the Sentencing Council guideline.

- **Previous violence against victim**

The culpability factors are not just weighted towards rape by someone **1.49** unknown to the victim but also recognise the reality that rape is more often committed by someone known to them. This explains the inclusion of "previous violence against victim", although this factor could also apply to "stranger" rape. The SGC guideline relating to domestic violence remains in force and should be considered in respect of offences committed in the domestic context.

- **Recording of the offence**

The Sentencing Council believed that creating a permanent record of the **1.50** attack, thereby subjecting the victim to re-victimisation, should be reflected

[83] [2012] EWCA Crim 1727.
[84] [2012] EWCA Crim 2268. See also *Nightingale* [2010] EWCA Crim 111.

at step one. It noted that this activity has become more prevalent since the SGC guideline was published. In *Attorney General's Reference (Nos 73, 75 and 03 of 2010) (Anigbuju)*, Lord Judge CJ said[85]:

> "A pernicious new habit has developed by which criminals take photographs of their victims—often just to show off to their friends: often just to add something to the humiliation which the victim is already suffering; and sometimes . . . either as a form of pressure to discourage any complaint . . . but also possibly for the purposes of blackmail. Anyone can understand what a powerful lever may be given to the criminal by his possession of photographs taken of the victim when, as in these cases, she has been subject to degrading treatment . . . We make it clear that from now onwards the taking of photographs should always be treated as an aggravating feature of any case and in particular of any sexual cases. Photography in these circumstances usually constitutes a very serious aggravating feature of the case."

To this should be added the filming by the offender of his sexual abuse of the victim and later editing it for the purposes of his own further sexual gratification.[86]

- **Commercial exploitation and/or motivation**

1.51   This is frequently a feature in cases involving grooming.

- **Offence racially or religiously aggravated**
- **Offence motivated by, or demonstrating, hostility to the victim based on his or her sexual orientation (or presumed sexual orientation) or transgender identity (or presumed transgender identity)**
- **Offence motivated by, or demonstrating, hostility to the victim based on his or her disability (or presumed disability)**

1.52   These are factors found in the *Assault: Definitive Guideline*. The Sentencing Council considered that if an offender demonstrates motivation on one of these grounds, that increases his culpability and should therefore be reflected at step one.

Step Two—Starting point and category range

1.53   Once the court has determined the offence category and culpability level, at step two it should use the corresponding starting point specified in the guideline in order to reach a sentence within the category range. The starting point applies to all offenders irrespective of plea or previous convictions. Once the starting point has been determined, step two allows further adjustment for aggravating or mitigating features as set out below. A case of particular gravity, reflected by multiple features of culpability or harm, could merit upward adjustment from the starting point before further adjustment for aggravating or mitigating features.

---

[85] [2011] EWCA Crim 633, at [7]. See also *R. v M(H)* [2013] EWCA Crim 1648, where both victims were photographed.

[86] cf. *Red Saunders v R.* [2013] EWCA Crim 1027.

In relation to rape, having considered the application of the SGC guideline 1.54 based on *Millberry*,[87] the Sentencing Council decided to keep the starting points of five and eight years' imprisonment with a clearer articulation of the culpability of the offender. This means that where any of the culpability A factors are present, the starting point is likely to be seven and ten years, not five and eight, before any further adjustment for aggravating or mitigating features.

The highest category, with a starting point of 15 years' imprisonment, can 1.55 now be used for single rapes of particular severity, so providing the opportunity for a full reflection of harm in these cases. In the SGC guideline, a starting point of 15 years was reserved for multiple rapes. The Council took the view that multiple rapes should be charged and sentenced separately. This would entitle the sentencer, subject to the principle of totality, to pass overall sentences above the sentencing range where there are a series of extremely serious counts reflecting a truly grave course of conduct.

At the beginning of the guideline for rape is to be found the following 1.56 rubric: "Offences may be of such severity, for example involving a campaign of rape, that sentences of 20 years and above may be appropriate." This statement is not confined to "campaign" cases. For instance, it may apply to repeat very serious offending against a very young victim. In *R. v JH*[88] the applicant had been convicted of five offences of rape and three of indecent assault committed against his daughter when she was aged between 11 and 15. The Court of Appeal held that an overall sentence of 22 years was not at all too long for this series of offences. It was unnecessary to consider whether the case should be elevated into category 1, reserved for cases with category 2 factors of an extreme nature or causing an extreme impact upon the victim, as in cases involving multiple counts of rape, it is important to focus on the rubric. This case fell within the category justifying 20 years and above. The judge was right to treat the case as one of indescribable depravity.

The starting points and category ranges for rape are as follows: 1.57

	A	B
Category 1	Starting point 15 years' custody	Starting point 12 years' custody
	Category range 13–19 years' custody	Category range 10–15 years' custody

[87] [2002] EWCA Crim 2891.
[88] [2015] EWCA Crim 54; [2015] 1 Cr. App. R.(S.) 59.

	A	*B*
Category 2	*Starting point* 10 years' custody	*Starting point* 8 years' custody
	Category range 9–13 years' custody	*Category range* 7–9 years' custody
Category 3	*Starting point* 7 years' custody	*Starting point* 5 years' custody
	Category range 6–9 years' custody	*Category range* 4–7 years' custody

Aggravating and mitigating factors

1.58 After identifying the starting point and category range, the court should consider whether the presence of aggravating or mitigating factors should result in an upward or downward adjustment from the starting point or the imposition of a sentence outside the category range. In particular, relevant recent convictions are likely to result in an upward adjustment. Unlike the exercise at step one, the list of aggravating and mitigating factors for rape is not exhaustive and any factors not considered at step one, but which the sentencer considers relevant to either the harm to the victim or the culpability of the offender, can be taken into account. It is a matter for the sentencer whether such a factor should be taken into account and, if so, how much weight should be given to it. It is envisaged that in exceptional cases the impact of these factors may lead to a sentence outside the category range identified for category 1. The sentencer should be careful to make sure that aggravating factors are not double-counted. For example, in *Carroll*[89] the Court of Appeal took the view that after correctly taking into account the severe psychological harm, violence and vulnerability which placed the case in category 1 (harm), there was nothing at this stage of the sentencing exercise which suggested departing from the 12-year custody starting point for category 1B. The Court disagreed with the judge that the case fell at the top end of culpability B. As for mitigating factors, the mere presence of such a factor does not lead to an automatic reduction in the sentence, because the precise weight to be attached, if any, will depend upon the individual circumstances of the case.

1.59   The non-exhaustive list of aggravating and mitigating factors for assault by penetration is as follows:

[89] [2014] EWCA Crim 2818.

Aggravating factors
Statutory aggravating factors
Previous convictions, having regard to a) the nature of the offence to which the conviction relates and its relevance to the current offence; and b) the time that has elapsed since the conviction
Offence committed whilst on bail
Other aggravating factors
Specific targeting of a particularly vulnerable victim
Ejaculation (where not taken into account at a step one)
Blackmail or other threats made (where not taken into account at step one)
Location of offence
Timing of offence
Use of weapon or other item to frighten or injure
Victim compelled to leave their home (including victims of domestic violence)
Failure to comply with current court orders
Offence committed whilst on licence
Exploiting contact arrangements with a child to commit an offence
Presence of others, especially other children
Any steps taken to prevent the victim reporting an incident, obtaining assistance and/or from assisting or supporting the prosecution
Attempts to dispose of or conceal evidence
Commission of offence whilst under the influence of alcohol or drugs

Mitigating factors
No previous convictions *or* no relevant/recent convictions
Remorse
Previous good character and/or exemplary conduct*

Age and/or lack of maturity where it affects the responsibility of the offender
Mental disorder or learning disability, particularly where linked to the commission of the offence

* Previous good character/exemplary conduct is different from having no previous convictions. The more serious the offence, the less the weight which should normally be attributed to this factor. Where previous good character/exemplary conduct has been used to facilitate the offence, this mitigation should not normally be allowed and such conduct may constitute an aggravating factor.

In the context of this offence, previous good character/exemplary conduct should not normally be given any significant weight and will not normally justify a reduction in what would otherwise be the appropriate sentence.

Aggravating factors

- **Previous convictions**
- **Offence committed whilst on bail**

1.60   There is a statutory requirement for sentencers to take these factors into account when assessing the seriousness of an offence. As with other guidelines, the Council recommends that these factors are considered at step two, only after the starting point has been established. Previous convictions for sexual offences will be regarded as particularly aggravating, as will an offence committed on bail for an offence against the same victim.

- **Ejaculation (where not taken into account at step one)**

1.61   This does not mean mitigation is available if there is an absence of ejaculation. In order to deal with any concerns about double counting where "Pregnancy or STI as a consequence" is present at step one, the step two factor is worded as: "Ejaculation (where not taken into account at step one)".

- **Blackmail or other threats made (where not taken into account at step one)**

1.62   This reflects the fact that not all rapes are accompanied by actual violence and that threats which induce a fear of violence or cause inner torment can be as harmful as violence itself.

- **Location of offence**
- **Timing of offence**

1.63   The Council deliberately framed these factors in a non-prescriptive way to allow the sentencer to decide whether in the circumstances of the individual case before them the offence is aggravated by its location or timing. This adopts the approach set out in the *Assault: Definitive Guideline*.

- **Use of weapon or other item to frighten or injure**

1.64   The Council believed that this means of controlling a victim should be reflected as an aggravating factor.

- **Victim compelled to leave their home (including victims of domestic violence)**

The Council concluded that a particularly aggravating feature is the physical   **1.65**
removal of the victim from a place that should be their place of safety.
Compulsion to leave home might apply not only to an offence within a
domestic relationship but also where, following a stranger attack in the home,
the victim feels unable to return there. It should be noted that the factors at
step two are non-exhaustive, enabling a court to take into account the wider
circumstances of the particular case, such as where the victim wants to leave
their home as a result of the offence but feels compelled to stay for financial
reasons.

- **Failure to comply with current court orders**
- **Offence committed whilst on licence**
- **Exploiting contact arrangements with a child to commit an offence**
- **Presence of others, especially children**

These are all factors found in other guidelines and have their roots in the   **1.66**
SGC guideline on domestic violence. The Council believed it was important
to include aggravating features that pertain to a rape that has occurred within
a relationship, particularly because such rapes are far more prevalent than
"stranger rape".

- **Any steps taken to prevent the victim reporting an incident, obtaining assistance and/or from assisting or supporting the prosecution**
- **Attempts to dispose of or conceal evidence**

These factors are intended to reflect the serious aggravation created where an   **1.67**
offender attempts to intimidate their victim into remaining silent. This is a
very frequent occurrence. Steps taken to prevent reporting cover a wide range
of scenarios and could, in the case of rape, include threats of physical harm,
or threats to circulate photographs taken during the offence, if a report is
made.

- **Commission of offence whilst under the influence of alcohol or drugs**

This factor has been included as intoxication generally aggravates offences,   **1.68**
and in the context of rape may mean the offender has lost self-control,
thereby demonstrating a degree of recklessness. In any event, the fact that an
offender may have drunk himself into such a state that he could not recognise
that the person he was with was incapable of giving consent does not provide
any mitigation.[89a]

Mitigating factors

- **No previous convictions or no relevant/recent convictions**

The following caveat is applied to all offences: **1.69**

> "Previous good character/exemplary conduct is different from having no pre-
> vious convictions. The more serious the offence, the less the weight which should

[89a] *Attorney General's Reference (No.122 of 2015)* [2016] EWCA Crim 392.

normally be attributed to this factor. Where previous good character/exemplary conduct has been used to facilitate the offence, this mitigation should not normally be allowed and such conduct may constitute an aggravating factor."

In addition, further wording is added to all offences carrying a maximum of life or 14 years, including rape

"In the context of this offence, good character/exemplary conduct should not normally be given any significant weight and will not normally justify a substantial reduction in what would otherwise be the appropriate sentence."[90]

The principle that only limited weight should be attached to previous good character cannot be avoided by enhancing its value as a mitigating factor by combining it with the courage shown by entering a plea of guilty. In *Attorney General's Reference (No. 115 of 2014)*,[91] the offender had pleaded guilty on the date set down for trial to one offence of vaginal rape, two offences of oral rape, one offence of assault by penetration, and robbery. The victim had been walking home alone in the early hours of the morning, when the offender followed her. He punched her twice and then took her down a deserted alleyway where over a period of about 15 minutes he raped her vaginally and orally and also digitally penetrated her vagina. Having ejaculated onto the ground, he blindfolded her with her scarf and then made off with her handbag. He was sentenced to a total sentence of seven years and two months' imprisonment. The offender was a man of previous good character aged 40. The judge stated that he was taking into account that for anyone faced with the shame and gravity of his position, it had taken a level of courage to plead guilty, albeit on the day of trial. He indicated that a series of positive testimonials coupled with the courage the offender had shown in pleading guilty would have an impact upon sentence. The judge placed the case in category 2A of the guideline and took 11 years as the starting point. He then took into account the previous good character and courage shown so as to reduce the sentence to eight years, before applying a 10 per cent discount for the late plea. The Court of Appeal took the view that the three year discount for good character and/or courage was wrong in principle, and substituted a sentence of 10 years' imprisonment.

1.70   The difficulties raised by previous and/or subsequent good character in historic cases were highlighted by Lord Judge CJ in *R. v H*[92]:

"The passing of the years may demonstrate aggravating features if, for example, the defendant has continued to commit sexual crime or he represents a continuing risk to the public. On the other hand, mitigation may be found in an unblemished life over the years since the offences were committed, particularly if accompanied by evidence of positive good character."

● **Remorse**

[90] cf *Millberry* [2002] EWCA Crim 2891, at [29]: "[T]he defendant's good character, although it should not be ignored, does not justify a substantial reduction of what would otherwise be the appropriate sentence."
[91] [2015] EWCA Crim 200.
[92] [2011] EWCA Crim 2753, at [47(e)].

A number of respondents to the Sentencing Council's consultation queried   **1.71**
the inclusion of "remorse" on the basis it could be easily faked and "switched
on" by manipulative offenders. These comments confirmed the Council's
experience that the consideration of remorse is nuanced, and all the
circumstances of the case will be considered by the sentencer in deciding
whether any expressed remorse is in fact genuine.

- **Age and/or lack of maturity where it affects the responsibility of the offender**

This is a standard factor in Sentencing Council guidelines. It is intended to   **1.72**
deal with those offenders who are just over the age of 18 or those over 18 who
are not as mature as others in their peer group.

The age factor can also be applied to offenders who are very elderly at the   **1.73**
time of sentence, when they are sentenced decades after their offences have
taken place. The cases establish that in some circumstances there will be
scope for a degree of mercy. However, the court is not to engage in an
actuarial calculation and has to have regard to the particular circumstances
of each case.[93] In *Attorney General's Reference (No. 65 of 2011)*, Hughes LJ
(as he then was) observed that prison bites differently and harder and deeper
on someone of advanced age or significant infirmity. In *Millberry*,[94] the
Court of Appeal said:

> "In addition, the court is always entitled to show a limited degree of mercy to an
> offender who is of advanced years, because of the impact that a sentence of
> imprisonment can have on an offender of that age."

There is, however, no principle that the term of imprisonment must seek to
avoid the likelihood that the defendant will die in prison. It is inevitable that
if there is a substantial delay in investigating and prosecuting historic sexual
offences, the mere passage of time is going to increase the risk that, when
prosecuted to conviction, elderly offenders will spend their declining years in
prison and may die there.[95]

- **Mental disorder or learning disability, where linked to the commission of the offence**

The research commissioned by the Sentencing Council indicated this was the   **1.74**
only mitigating factor on which there was broad agreement. It was felt that
it should influence the nature but not the duration of the custodial sentence
suggested, with an emphasis on treatment or care under supervision.[96] The
Court of Appeal in *R. v B*[97]—whilst concluding that a defendant's belief in
consent arising from a condition such as a delusional psychotic illness or

---

[93] *R. v AM and MG* [2014] EWCA Crim 1970.
[94] [2002] EWCA Crim 2891.
[95] *R. v AM and MG* [2014] EWCA Crim 1970, at [39] per Hallett LJ. See also *R. v C* [1993]
14 Cr. App. R.(S.) 562; *Symmons* [2009] EWCA Crim 1304.
[96] Natcen research, cited in the Sentencing Council's consultation document, December 2012,
p.24.
[97] [2013] EWCA Crim 3, at [40] per Hughes LJ (as he then was).

personality disorder must be judged by objective standards of reason-ableness—observed that a defendant's mental condition, and its impact on his behaviour, is of course extremely relevant to sentence. If punishment is appropriate, a non-custodial sentence may result when otherwise there would be a substantial sentence of imprisonment, whether or not a hospital order is needed by time of trial. In other cases the defendant's mental condition may significantly mitigate the punishment required. In yet others, it may result in a substantial custodial sentence in recognition of the danger the defendant poses.

- **Request for leniency by victim**

1.75 This is not listed in the guideline as a mitigating factor. However, the guideline issued by the Sentencing Guidelines Council in relation to domestic violence remains in force (see para.33.22, below) and in relation to the wishes of the victim provides in terms:

> "4.1 As a matter of general principle, a sentence imposed for an offence of violence should be determined by the seriousness of the offence, not by the expressed wishes of the victim.
>
> 4.2 There are a number of reasons why it may be particularly important that this principle is observed in a case of domestic violence:
>
> - it is undesirable that a victim should feel a responsibility for the sentence imposed;
> - there is a risk that a plea for mercy made by a victim will be induced by threats made by, or by fear of, the offender;
> - the risk of such threats will be increased if it is generally believed that the severity of the sentence may be affected by the wishes of the victim.
>
> 4.3 Nonetheless, there may be circumstances in which the court can properly mitigate a sentence to give effect to the expressed wish of the victim that the relationship be permitted to continue.
>
> 4.4 Either the offender or the victim (or both) may ask the court to take into consideration the interests of any children and to impose a less severe sentence. The court will wish to have regard not only to the effect on the children if the relationship is disrupted but also to the likely effect on the children of any further incidents of domestic violence."

The extent of the relevance of the victim's wishes was stated with some force by Lord Judge CJ in *Hall*[98]:

> "We must, of course, consider the harm done to victims, but victims do not and cannot decide sentences. We cannot have sentences which depend upon whether a victim feels particularly vengeful, moderately vengeful, not vengeful at all, filled with mercy, or even, as some do, believes that there should not be a prison sentence."

This statement of principle was followed in *Attorney General's Reference (No. 64 of 2014)*,[99] where the victim had, prior to trial, made a withdrawal statement saying that in hindsight she believed that what the offender had done to her had been accidental because they both had been drinking. She said that although the relationship was over she wanted the offender to have

---

[98] [2013] EWCA Crim 1450, at [86].
[99] [2014] EWCA Crim 2050.

regular contact with his children because he was a good father; she did not want him to go to prison. The Court of Appeal took the view that the judge had ignored the overarching principles on domestic violence in reducing the sentence significantly by taking into account the plea made by the victim herself. The case involved a horrific sexual assault by penetration against a background of a relationship blighted by episodes of domestic violence.

- **Impact upon the offender's dependents**

This is also not listed as a mitigating factor. However, the court will have   1.76
regard to the offender's family circumstances and the impact upon them of
a sentence of immediate imprisonment, particularly the likely effect upon the
younger members of the offender's family. But as Hughes VP (as he then was)
said in *Petherick*,[100] if the offence committed is grave, the more likely it is that
a lengthy sentence of imprisonment is proportionate, notwithstanding the
contrary interests of the children.

Steps Three to Nine

The remaining steps cover the following points. At step three the court   1.77
should consider any factors which would indicate a reduction in sentence, e.g.
assistance to the prosecution (ss.73 and 74 of the Serious Organised Crime
and Police Act 2005). At step four it should consider any reduction for a
guilty plea (s.144 of the Criminal Justice Act 2003 and the Guilty Plea
guideline).

At step five the court should consider dangerousness, i.e. whether it would   1.78
be appropriate to award a life sentence (s.224A or s.225(2) of the Criminal
Justice Act 2003) or an extended sentence (s.226A). Following the approach
in *Attorney General's Reference (No.55 of 2008)*,[101] where the dangerousness
criteria are satisfied, if an extended sentence, with, if required, the additional
support of other orders such as a sexual harm prevention order (SHPO), can
achieve appropriate public protection against the risk posed by an individual
offender, then an extended sentence rather than a life sentence should be
imposed. Extended sentences were formerly provided for by s.227 of the
Criminal Justice Act 2003. Section 227 was replaced by a new s.226A (adults)
and s.226B (persons under 18) inserted by the Legal Aid, Sentencing and
Punishment of Offenders Act 2012 in relation to anyone convicted on or after
December 3, 2012, whenever the offence was committed.[102] The conditions
for the imposition of an extended sentence remain exactly the same as before,
except that they require a conviction under new Sch.15B to the Act (and not
Sch.15A as previously) at the time the offence was committed. Schedule 15B

---

[100] [2013] 1 Cr. App. R.(S.) 116.
[101] [2008] EWCA Crim 3123. See also paras 34.23 and following, below.
[102] See s.226A(11) The new extended sentence is available even for offences committed before April 4, 2005. This was confirmed at in *R. v C* [2014] EWCA Crim 334, at [176] (one of the conjoined appeals heard together with *Attorney General's Reference (No. 27 of 2013) (Gintas Burinskas)* [2014] EWCA Crim 334).

is set out at Appendix A, below. The alternative pre-condition is that if the court imposed an extended sentence, it would specify a custodial term of at least four years.

1.79   However, s.246A of the 2003 Act, also inserted by the Legal Aid, Sentencing and Punishment of Offenders Act 2012, makes a radical change in the operation of the new extended sentence in respect of the provisions for release upon licence. The earliest possible release is after two-thirds of the custodial term. Even then, if the custodial term is 10 years or more, or the sentence imposed is for any of the offences listed in Sch.15B, release is when the Parole Board considers the offender is no longer dangerous, or the end of the custodial term, whichever is the earlier. The extension period must not exceed eight years in the case of a specified sexual offence.

1.80   Step six requires the court to consider whether the total sentence is just and proportionate to the offending behaviour. At step seven it should consider whether to make an ancillary order (e.g. a compensation order, a SHPO or a restraining order). At this step the court should inform the offender of any notification requirements that apply. Step eight requires the court to fulfil its duty under s.174 of the Criminal Justice Act 2003 to give reasons for, and explain the effect of, the sentence. Finally, at step nine the court should consider whether to give credit for time spent on bail in accordance with s.240A of that Act.

Sentences passed under the SGC Definitive Guideline

1.81   Sentences passed under the previous guideline need to be treated with some caution in light of the changes made in the Sentencing Council guideline. In any event, cases are fact-specific. However, some decisions in sentencing appeals remain significant in that the principles have not changed. Additionally some decisions and/or the reasoning underpinning them were expressly adopted by the Sentencing Council in framing its guideline.[103]

No distinction between male and female rape

1.82   In *Millberry*[104] the Court of Appeal agreed with the Sentencing Advisory Panel's recommendation that the same guidelines should apply to all victims of rape, whether male or female, with gender-specific factors, such as pregnancy as a result of rape, left to be considered on a case-by-case basis. This approach was followed by the Court in *Attorney General's Reference (No.104 of 2004) (Garvey)*[105] and underpins the approach taken in the SGC and Sentencing Council guidelines. At least since 2008 the Court of Appeal

---

[103] Notably *Attorney General's References (Nos 73, 75 and 03 of 2010) (Anigbugu)* [2011] EWCA Crim 633.
[104] [2002] EWCA Crim 2891.
[105] [2005] 1 Cr. App. R.(S.) 666.

has proceeded on the basis that the sexual offence guidelines are gender-neutral.[106]

Relevance of relationship between the defendant and the victim

It is a fundamental principle that the starting point for "relationship rape" or   **1.83**
"acquaintance rape" is the same as for "stranger rape". In the past, courts
had been reluctant to place the culpability of these forms of rape on precisely
the same footing.[107] This debate was finally laid to rest in *Millberry*.[108] The
SGC guideline stated:

> "Any rape is a traumatic and humiliating experience and, although the particular
> circumstances in which the rape takes place may affect the sentence imposed, the
> starting-point for the sentence should be the same."

Victim the defendant's partner/wife

In *R. v MA*,[109] the Court of Appeal, Lord Judge CJ presiding, emphatically   **1.84**
rejected counsel's submission that a man who raped his wife should be
treated less severely if he came from a culture which instilled in him a belief
that he had a right to do so. The Court stated[110]:

> "No man, whatever his background, whatever his race, whatever his creed, has
> the right to rape his wife."

In *Benney*,[111] the Court observed that marital rape is a serious as other forms
of rape. It can be a violent, predatory and shocking event and, if the facts
support it, a serious sentence for marital rape as it is for is as appropriate a
rape outside any such relationship. However, in *Benney* pleas had been
entered in a rather unusual case on a very specific basis accepted by the
prosecution. On five occasions during the marriage, the defendant admitted
that he had carried on having sexual intercourse with his wife, after she told
him to stop, having withdrawn her consent. Sexual intercourse had commenced on a consensual basis. The Court concluded that the starting point
should have been three rather than six years.[112]

In *Attorney General's Reference (No.77 of 2012)*,[113] leave was refused to   **1.85**
refer as unduly lenient the defendant's sentence of two years' imprisonment

---

[106] *Attorney General's Reference (No.85 of 2014) (R. v A)* [2014] EWCA Crim 2088; [2015] 1
Cr. App. R.(S.) 14 at p.119.
[107] See *Berry* (1988) 10 Cr. App. R.(S.) 13, at 15 per Mustill LJ. The approach in *Berry* has
been criticised for its lack of proper foundation: Philip N.S. Rumney, *When Rape isn't Rape:
Court of Appeal sentencing practice in cases of marital and relationship rape*, O.J.L.S., Vol.19,
Summer 1999, p.243.
[108] [2002] EWCA Crim 2891.
[109] [2012] EWCA Crim 1646.
[110] At [21] per Griffith Williams J.
[111] [2010] EWCA Crim 1288.
[112] The Court referred to the SGC guideline, p.24, in respect of pre-existing consensual sexual
activity.
[113] [2013] EWCA Crim 202.

for the rape of his wife. The Court of Appeal described the offence as one occasion of unwanted sexual intercourse during a period of consensual relations. After the offence, and when the offence was known, consensual relations continued over a not inconsiderable period. The Court noted remarkable distinctive facts that the judge had been correct in identifying, and in particular, there was no evidence of psychological harm, nor, as far as the Court could see, of anger. This case should be treated with care as the circumstances were exceptional and in other cases the seriousness of the non-consensual act may overwhelm any other consideration, particularly if the rape involved violence.

Previous consensual activity between offender and victim

1.86 It is the particular circumstances in which the rape was committed that may affect the sentence imposed. In the SGC guideline it was noted that in *Millberry*[114] the Court of Appeal established that the offender's culpability in a case of rape would be "somewhat less" in cases where the victim had consented to sexual familiarity with the offender on the occasion in question than in cases where the offender set out with the intention of committing rape. Save in cases of breach of trust or grooming, an offender's culpability may be reduced if the offender and victim engaged in consensual activity on the same occasion and immediately before the offence took place. Factors relevant to culpability in such circumstances include the type of consensual activity that occurred, similarity to what then occurs and timing. However, previous consensual sex on another occasion is unlikely to provide any mitigation.

Victim a prostitute

1.87 In *Attorney General's Reference (No. 107 of 2007)*,[115] the Court of Appeal took the view that the status of the victim as a prostitute on the streets in the early hours neither mitigated nor aggravated the offence. This confirmed the approach adopted in *Masood (Asif)*.[116]

Victim a child/victim not sexually experienced

1.88 The guideline is designed to protect children, sometimes from themselves, and is to be applied whatever the history of the child. In *Attorney General's Reference (No. 85 of 2014) (R v A)*,[117] the judge was made aware that the victim was not sexually naïve. There had been sexual activity with children of approximately his own age. The issue was raised in argument as to whether

[114] [2002] EWCA Crim 2891.
[115] [2008] 2 Cr. App. R.(S.) 373.
[116] [1997] 2 Cr. App. R.(S.) 137.
[117] [2014] EWCA Crim 2088.

that experience might constitute a mitigating factor because it might result in less harm to the victim, or whether it might be taken into account only as the absence of the aggravating factor of taking a child's virginity. In the Court of Appeal's judgment, the proper approach is to treat that factor as an absence of aggravation which otherwise might have existed. The risk of harm is always present. The existence of present harm will vary from case to case.

Form of penetration

The SGC guideline stated that it is impossible to say that any one form of   **1.89**
non-consensual penetration is inherently a more serious violation of the victim's sexual autonomy than another. Whilst this is not expressly repeated in the Sentencing Council guideline, the position is now well settled and no distinction is made as between types of penetration. This is in line with the approach adopted by the Court of Appeal in *Ismail*,[118] a case of forcible oral rape where the Court observed that, although there was no pregnancy risk from oral rape, there remains the danger of sexually transmitted diseases and that amounts itself to an aggravating feature. In that case a sentence of six years' detention in a young offenders' institution was upheld in respect of an 18-year-old with no previous convictions who pleaded guilty at a Plea and Directions Hearing to raping a 16-year-old in a public place at night.

Young offenders

For the general approach when sentencing youths, see the *Sentencing*   **1.90**
Guidelines Council Definitive Guideline: Overarching Principles—Sentencing Youths, which applies to the sentencing of offenders on or after November 30, 2009. The Sentencing Council guideline does *not* supersede the SGC's Sexual Offences Act 2003 Definitive Guideline in respect of offences under the 2003 Act which have a lower maximum penalty when committed by a person under 18.[119] The youth and immaturity of the offender must be taken into account.[120] When sentencing an offender under 18, the court has to have regard to the principal aim of the youth justice system to avoid future offending. In some cases the maturity of the offender will be at least as important as his chronological age.[121] In *Lang* the Court of Appeal said that when sentencing young offenders it is important to bear in mind that they may change and develop in a shorter time than an adult. It is well established

---

[118] [2005] 2 Cr. App. R.(S.) 542.
[119] See the Sentencing Guidelines Council definitive guideline (April 2007), Part 7: Sentencing Young Offenders—Offences with a Lower Statutory Maximum (available on the Sentencing Council website).
[120] See *Daniel W* [2009] EWCA Crim 153 where the Court of Appeal held that in light of the evidence of the 20-year-old appellant's learning difficulties and serious immaturity, it was inappropriate to take into account an abuse of trust as an aggravating feature when sentencing him for three counts of rape of a child under 13.
[121] *R. v N, D, L* [2010] EWCA Crim 941, at [28] per Lord Judge CJ.

that the youth of an offender should normally result in a more lenient sentence. However, whilst normally a sentence for rape will be significantly shorter than that for an adult, this will not always be the case. Where the facts of the case are particularly serious, the youth of the offender will not necessarily amount to significant mitigation.[122] In *R. v B*[123] the Court of Appeal upheld an indeterminate sentence in respect of a 15-year-old offender who, as a pupil, had forced a teacher to perform oral sex twice, having dragged her from the classroom and told her he would kill her. The sentencing judge fixed a notional sentence of nine years with a specified term of three years and eight months. The Court of Appeal held that the case was unique, that exceptional violence had been used and that the offender's young age had to be balanced against the seriousness of the crime. While the age of the offender was something a court had to take strongly into account, it could not be a matter that prevented an appropriate sentence on particular facts. In *Raymond and Denton*[124] the Court of Appeal stated that the trial judge had been correctly concerned at the gang mentality which had infused offenders aged 14 and 15. This was echoed in *R. v N, D, L*,[125] where the victim had been aged 14 at the time and the assailants, who were convicted of rape, had been between 14 and 16. The Court of Appeal stated that the judge had been entirely justified in disregarding the youth of the leader of this ugly group action, where there had been an element of gratuitous cruelty.

Life imprisonment

1.91 Life imprisonment remains the ultimate sentence to be reserved for the most serious and grave cases.

"Discretionary" life sentence under s.225(1) and (2) of the Criminal Justice Act 2003

1.92 A sentence of life imprisonment must be imposed under s.225(1) and (2) of the Criminal Justice Act 2003 ("CJA 2003") if the court is of the opinion that there is "a significant risk to members of the public occasioned by the commission by [the offender] of further specified offences" and concludes that "the seriousness of the offence, or of the offence and one or more offences associated with it, is such as to justify the imposition of a sentence of imprisonment for life". In *Red Saunders v R.*[126] Lord Judge CJ, giving the judgment of the Court, explained that the sentence of life imprisonment under s.225 continues in force after the changes made to the CJA 2003 by the Legal Aid, Sentencing and Punishment of Offenders Act 2012, and has been

---

[122] *Asi-Akram* [2005] EWCA Crim 1543; *Patrick M* [2005] 1 Cr. App. R.(S.) 218.
[123] [2006] EWCA Crim 330.
[124] [2009] EWCA Crim 1490.
[125] [2010] EWCA Crim 941.
[126] [2013] EWCA Crim 1027.

frequently described as the discretionary life sentence, although once the statutory conditions in s.225(1) and (2) are established it "must" be imposed. His Lordship said[127]:

> "In that broad sense, therefore, this sentence is also statutory, but it may only be imposed if justified by reference to the seriousness of the offence and the protection of the public in accordance with s.225(1) and (2)".

The impact of the abolition of imprisonment for public protection ("IPP")

Life imprisonment remains the sentence of last resort. In *Wilkinson*,[128] at a   **1.93**
time when the sentence of IPP was an available alternative, the Court of Appeal said:

> "In our judgment it is clear that as a matter of principle the discretionary life sentence under section 225 should continue to be reserved for offences of the utmost gravity. Without being prescriptive, we suggest that the sentence should come into contemplation when the judgment of the court is that the seriousness is such that the life sentence would have . . . a 'denunciatory' value, reflective of public abhorrence of the offence, and where, because of its seriousness, the notional determinate sentence would be very long, measured in very many years."

Considerations of public protection were irrelevant to a decision whether to impose a sentence of life imprisonment rather than a sentence of IPP. In *Kehoe (Bridie Joanna)*,[129] which was later to be followed by a five-judge Court in *Wood*,[130] Openshaw J stated:

> "When, as here, an offender meets the criteria of dangerousness, there is no longer any need to protect the public by passing a sentence of life imprisonment for the public are now properly protected by the imposition of a sentence of imprisonment for public protection. In such cases, therefore, the cases decided before the Criminal Justice Act 2003 came into effect no longer offer guidance on when a life sentence should be imposed. We think that now, when the court finds that the defendant satisfies the criteria for dangerousness, a life sentence should be reserved for those cases where the culpability of the offender is particularly high or the offence itself particularly grave."

The abolition of IPP by the Legal Aid, Sentencing and Punishment of   **1.94**
Offenders Act 2012 with effect from December 3, 2012,[131] is leading to more sentences of life imprisonment being passed under s.225 where the sentencer concludes that an extended sentence under the new s.226A of the CJA 2003 would not afford sufficient public protection. In *Attorney General's Reference (No.27 of 2013) (Gintas Burinskas)*,[132] Lord Thomas CJ, giving the judgment of the Court, observed that it was inevitable that the application of

---

[127] At [9].
[128] [2009] EWCA Crim 1925, at [19] per Lord Judge CJ.
[129] [2008] EWCA Crim 819, at [17].
[130] [2009] EWCA Crim 651.
[131] There is an exception which will become increasingly rare where a defendant was convicted before December 3, 2012, but was not sentenced before that date.
[132] [2014] EWCA Crim 334.

s.225 in its current form would lead to the imposition of life sentences in circumstances where previously the sentence would have been one of IPP. Although the provisions of s.225 in respect of life sentences remain the same, the statutory context in which they are to be interpreted has changed fundamentally. The new extended sentence is not a direct replacement of the old IPP. He explained that the question in s.225(2)(b) as to whether the seriousness of the offence (or of the offence and one or more offences associated with it) is such as to justify a life sentence requires consideration of:

(i) The seriousness of the offence itself, on its own or with other offences associated with it in accordance with the provisions of s.143(1). This is always a matter for the judgment of the court. The express requirement that the seriousness of the offence should be considered with other offences associated with it should not be overlooked.[133]

(ii) The defendant's previous convictions (in accordance with s.143(2)).

(iii) The level of danger posed to the public by the defendant and whether there is a reliable estimate of the length of time he will remain a danger. This point is well-illustrated by *Burinskas*, the facts of which are set out at paras 1.103 and following, below.

(iv) The available alternative sentences.

1.95   In the past, in the overwhelming majority of cases, the relatively minor distinctions between life imprisonment and IPP were irrelevant, and so IPP was normally sufficient to address the protection of the public from a dangerous offender who would, if made subject to the order, continue to be detained until the Parole Board was satisfied he no longer represented a risk to the public. Now, where a dangerous offender is convicted of rape, the sentencing options will be a sentence of life imprisonment imposed under s.225(1) and (2) of the CJA 2003, an extended sentence imposed under s.226A of the CJA 2003 (inserted in place of s.227 by the Legal Aid, Sentencing and Punishment of Offenders Act 2012 ("LASPO")),[134] or a determinate sentence.

1.96   In *Red Saunders v R.*,[135] Lord Judge CJ explained the impact of the removal of IPP as a sentencing option as follows:

"The new statutory life sentence[136] has not replaced the IPP. Many offenders who represent a danger to the public may not 'qualify' for the statutory life sentence. Yet, for some offenders, the imperative of public protection continues undiminished, and is not wholly met by the 'new' extended sentence. Very long term public protection must therefore be provided by the imposition of a discretionary life sentence. That is consequent on s.225(1) and (2) which, in the

[133] See the conjoined appeal of *Goran Kamal Ahmad* at [84].
[134] The new LASPO extended sentence is explained in paras 34.17 and following, below.
[135] [2013] EWCA Crim 1027, at [15].
[136] Under s.224A of the CJA 2003, inserted by s.122 of the Legal Aid, Sentencing and Punishment of Offenders Act 2012: see paras 1.107 and following, below.

context of the discretionary life sentence for serious offences continue, as we have explained, in full force."

His Lordship noted that under the new LASPO extended sentence the offender will not be released during the custodial term until at least the two-thirds point of it has been reached. Where the custodial term is 10 years or more, or the offences for which the sentence was imposed included one in Sch.15B to the CJA 2003, he will not be released until the Parole Board has directed his release on the ground that his continued incarceration is no longer necessary for public protection. Under the old form of extended sentence, release was automatic half way through the custodial term. In relation to public protection as it arises under the new extended sentence, having assessed the appropriate custodial term, the extension period during which the offender would be subject to licence is limited, in the context of a specified sexual offence, to eight years. Further, in relation to some of the specified sexual offences, the maximum available term is 10 years', or 14 years' imprisonment, and that term may not be exceeded. His Lordship said that it is therefore clear that in relation to the offender who will continue to represent a significant risk to the safety of the public for an indefinite period, the new extended sentence cannot be treated as a direct replacement for the old IPP. He continued[137]:

> "Accordingly, in cases in which, prior to the enactment of LASPO, the court would have been driven to the conclusion that an IPP was required for public protection (on the basis on a judgment made on the particular facts rather than one to which the court was driven by some of the more troublesome assumptions required by the legislation in its original form) the discretionary life sentence will arise for consideration, and where appropriate, if the necessary level of public protection cannot be achieved by the new extended sentence, ordered. The 'denunciatory' ingredient identified to distinguish between the circumstances in which the discretionary life sentence rather than the IPP should be imposed is no longer apposite. By that we mean that although the 'denunciatory' element of the sentencing decision may continue to justify the discretionary life sentence, its absence does not preclude such an order. As every judge appreciates, however, the life sentence remains the sentence of last resort."

In *Red Saunders*, the Court of Appeal took the view that a life sentence was **1.97** correctly imposed even though the option of an IPP or an extended sentence had been available to the judge. The Lord Chief Justice noted the appalling nature of the offences. He observed that the evidence underlined that, for an indefinite period, the appellant would represent a very high risk to children. There was no getting away from the stark, profoundly disturbing facts.

The appellant had been sentenced to life imprisonment with a minimum **1.98** term of eight years for the rape of a child under 13, contrary to s.5 of the 2003 Act. He was given concurrent sentences for various other sexual offences. There were two child victims. The appellant, a photography student, was aged 23. In 2005, when he was only 16, he was convicted of a sexual assault

---

[137] At [18].

upon a five-year-old girl. He had admitted downloading sexual images of children since he was 12. The probation officer described him as having an entrenched pattern of sexual offending against children.

1.99   In the autumn of 2011, the appellant answered an advertisement on the internet for a baby sitter for G, a little girl then aged six. He provided the parents with a bogus employment history and bogus references. He said, again untruthfully, that he would provide the relevant criminal records check when it was available. To the parents and prospective employers, he appeared plausible, even charming; he seemed to interact with the child in a natural way. This was all a front, for he had always intended to abuse G whilst the parents were out, and indeed, he wrote a script in advance describing what he planned to do. Following his script, he introduced G to a so-called game. As he lay on the bed, fully clothed, but with an obviously erect penis, he made her sit astride him and tried to persuade her to open her legs, but the girl was reluctant. This was charged as sexual assault upon a child under 13 contrary to s.7 of the 2003 Act. There was a further sexual assault when they were both on the floor and he tried to lift the child's skirt. All this he filmed using his photographic skills. He later edited the footage giving it various crude titles. He increased the speed of the film so as to give the impression that he was having intercourse with her.

1.100   The appellant then obtained similar employment with another family who had a daughter, D, aged seven. Again he wrote himself a script. The offences occurred on two consecutive days in April 2012. He invited D to perform various games and he filmed her. He made her wear a blindfold. He put various phallic objects in her mouth asking her to guess the taste. He then covered his erect penis in chocolate and twice put it in the child's mouth. This was charged as oral rape of a child under 13 contrary to s.5 of the 2003 Act. At one stage he got the child to sit astride him, bouncing her up and down on his exposed erect penis. Later he professionally edited the film footage of the abuse, giving it such titles as "Pedo Productions". When police searched his house, they found the films and 4,000 indecent images of children, some at level 4 or 5 on the Copine scale. When the appellant was asked in interview about the indecent images, he said that he considered the children to be willing participants. He told the writer of the pre-sentence report that, after a time, viewing was not enough and he wanted to be part of it.

1.101   Police also found a diary in which the appellant set out in disturbing detail how to abduct, sexually abuse, kill and dispose of a child. He wrote of selecting a girl at a particular primary school and that whoever discovered the material had discovered his heart's intent. When asked about this, he said that these writings were just fantasy and that he would never have carried them out. The author of the pre-sentence report did not accept that his expressions of remorse were genuine. He was plainly dangerous.

1.102   In his sentencing remarks the judge observed that these were truly grave sexual offences and concluded that the public would consider the s.5 offence warranted a sentence of denunciatory value and accordingly imposed a sentence of life imprisonment on the s.5 count. If sentence had been passed one month later, after the coming into force of the relevant provisions of LASPO and the abolition of IPP, it would no longer have been apposite to identify a "denunciatory" ingredient to distinguish between the circumstances in which discretionary life should be imposed rather than IPP. However, as the Court of Appeal agreed with the judge's decision, even if the judge had not found the "denunciatory" element, its absence would not have precluded the imposition of a life sentence.

Gintas Burinskas[138] is an instructive example of a case where the Court of   **1.103**
Appeal held that an extended sentence for a violent rape would not provide adequate protection for the public and so was unduly lenient, and substituted a life sentence. The offender, a Lithuanian national aged 37, had pleaded guilty to rape and causing grievous bodily harm with intent. He had been released from prison in Lithuania in August 2012 having served a 10 year prison sentence for participating in the gang rape of a prostitute. The instant case involved a sustained and brutal attack on a very vulnerable young woman in the early hours of the morning as she walked along the street. He put his hands around her neck, squeezed her throat, and took her to an area surrounded by trees and bushes where he proceeded to rape her. Afterwards she tried to run away, but the offender caught her, kicked her to the head some four or five times, stamped on her body and punched her to the stomach. He then dragged her across the road and tipped alcohol over her. The victim was devastated by the incident. She thought that she was going to die. She sustained three fractures of the jaw, one of them displaced. A consultant forensic scientist concluded that the offender was suffering from a personality disorder and that he posed a significant risk of future harm to members of the public. It was accepted that he met the dangerousness criteria, but it was submitted that no attempt at rehabilitation had been made whilst the offender had been a serving prisoner in Lithuania, and an extended sentence was right in principle. In rejecting that submission and substituting a life sentence, the Court observed that an extended sentence that required his release at the end of the custodial term did not adequately protect the public. Even assuming that there would be long term work done in prison with which the offender might well engage it was not possible to say with any degree of confidence when he would no longer be dangerous.

The conjoined appeal of *Anthony Phillips*[139] is an illustration of a case   **1.104**
where the Court of Appeal took the view that the judge had been correct to pass a life sentence upon an appellant who had carried out a planned, sustained campaign of violence, including sexual violence, designed to take revenge on his partner. He had previously raped his brother's girlfriend on two occasions. This rape was a gratuitous attack. The fact that the appellant

[138] *Attorney General's Reference (No.27 of 2013) (Gintas Burinskas)* [2014] EWCA Crim 334, at [45].
[139] *Attorney General's Reference (No.27 of 2013) (Gintas Burinskas)* [2014] EWCA Crim 334, at [68].

had not used exceptional violence to overcome his victim on this occasion did not matter. By the time he committed the rape, the appellant had already inflicted over 50 injuries. She had been in bed on medication. This was the final humiliation. The appellant was dangerous. Given his previous history, this offence and the offences associated with it plainly justified a life sentence. An extended sentence would not adequately protect the public.

1.105   In the conjoined appeal of *Goran Kamal Ahmad*,[140] the Court of Appeal rejected the submission that rape was not sufficiently serious to justify a sentence of life imprisonment. The appellant was convicted of two grave offences, a rape and a sexual assault approximately four months later. There was deliberate targeting of vulnerable victims who had been dragged to a relatively secluded spot. The pre-sentence report indicated a developing pattern and an escalation in seriousness. It could not be said when the appellant could be safely released. The approach of the appellant's advocate had overlooked the express requirement in s.225(2)(b) that the seriousness of the offence should be considered together with other offences associated with it.

The second form of discretionary life sentence

1.106   In *Red Saunders v R.*,[141] Lord Judge CJ concluded that the jurisdiction to impose a life sentence in an appropriate case (where the maximum sentence for the particular offence is life) has survived the enactment of the CJA 2003 and the changes to the sentencing regime affected by the Legal Aid, Sentencing and Punishment of Offenders Act 2012 (LASPO). He pointed out that if it had been intended to abolish that jurisdiction, the appropriate legislative change could readily have been made by the provisions restricting the life sentence (other than the mandatory sentence) to the statutory sentence or the discretionary life sentence under s.225(1) and (2) of the CJA 2003. Neither that Act nor LASPO imposed any limit on the power of the court to impose a sentence of life imprisonment in such cases. In *Attorney General's Reference (No.2 of 2013) (Gintas Burinskas)*,[142] Lord Thomas CJ made reference to Lord Judge's conclusions as to the continued existence of this jurisdiction. He observed that, whilst some commentators have questioned this view in light of the provisions of s.153 of the CJA 2003 (custodial sentence must be for the shortest term commensurate with the seriousness of the offence), this questioning runs contrary to the then guideline of the Sentencing Guidelines Council. However, the occasions when this second form of discretionary life sentence is likely to be imposed will be rare. In the

---

[140] *Attorney General's Reference (No.27 of 2013) (Gintas Burinskas)* [2014] EWCA Crim 334, at [84].

[141] [2013] EWCA Crim 1027.

[142] [2014] EWCA Crim 334, at [6]. The SGC's guideline stated (p.24, para.1(b)): "Life imprisonment is the maximum for the offence [of rape]. Such a sentence may be imposed either as a result of the offence itself where a number of aggravating factors are present, or because the offender meets the dangerousness criterion."

vast majority of cases, offenders who represent a danger to the public requiring long term public protection will be sentenced in accordance with s.225(1) and (2) of the CJA 2003.

The "new automatic life sentence"—statutory life under s.224A of the Criminal Justice Act 2003 following conviction for a second listed offence

Under s.224A of the CJA 2003, inserted by s.122 of LASPO, a sentence of   **1.107** imprisonment for life "must" be imposed following conviction for a second listed offence, unless particular circumstances would make it unjust. It follows that there is a discretionary power in the court to disapply what would otherwise be a provision requiring an obligatory sentence. In contrast to the original automatic life sentence under s.9 of the Powers of Criminal Courts (Sentencing) Act 2000, the sentencer does not have to find "exceptional circumstances".

To qualify for an automatic life sentence, the offender must be aged 18 or   **1.108** over and must be convicted of an offence listed in Pt 1 of new Sch.15B to the CJA 2003.[143] The offence must have been committed on or after December 3, 2012. The Schedule lists a large number of offences, some of which are not punishable with life imprisonment in normal circumstances. It includes numerous offences contrary to the Sexual Offences Act 2003.

The "sentence condition" and the "previous offence condition" which   **1.109** must be met before s.224A is engaged will ensure that this new "automatic" life sentence is of limited application, although those who commit a second rape and/or second child sex offence could, in certain circumstances, qualify. For the "sentence condition" to be satisfied, the sentencer must conclude that a sentence of 10 years' imprisonment or more is appropriate after taking into account all relevant considerations, including the offender's plea, and disregarding any extension period which might be imposed as part of an extended sentence. For the "previous offence condition" to be satisfied, the offender at the time the latest offence was committed must have been convicted of an offence in Sch.15B[144] (not just in Pt 1 of that Schedule) *and* a "relevant life sentence" or a "relevant sentence of imprisonment or detention for a determinate period" must have been imposed on the offender for the previous offence. A determinate sentence of imprisonment or detention is "relevant" for this purpose if it was for a period of 10 years or more. An extended sentence is relevant if the custodial sentence was five years or more. A life sentence or other indeterminate sentence will be relevant if the minimum sentence, disregarding any time spent in custody on remand, was at least five years.

---

[143] Added to the Criminal Justice Act 2003 by the Legal Aid, Sentencing and Punishment of Offenders Act 2012, s.122 and Sch.18, and set out at para.34.17, below.
[144] Pt 2 of Sch.15B includes various offences under the Sexual Offences Act 1956, including rape. See Appendix A, below.

Whole life order

1.110   Whole life sentences (with no minimum term specified) are reserved for rare
and exceptional cases, and the sentence must be justified by the extreme
seriousness of the offence as opposed to the dangerousness of the offender.[145]
Normally a minimum term should be specified.[146] It follows that a whole life
order is most unlikely to be appropriate in a sexual case, however grave,
unless the sexual offences are accompanied by a homicide. For example, in
the "night stalker" case of *Delroy Grant*,[147] tried at Woolwich Crown Court
in March 2011, in which 17 elderly victims, mostly living alone, had been
subjected to serious sexual assaults over a period of over 10 years, concurrent
life sentences with minimum terms of 27 years were passed on a man in his
fifties.

1.111   In *David Oakes v R.*,[148] the Court of Appeal considered whether a whole
life order was appropriate in cases involving very grave crimes. It noted that
among the cases in which such orders had been imposed, none could be
found in the context of sexual crime where one or more of the victims had
not been murdered. Lord Judge CJ observed:

> "It is regrettably possible to envisage, and there have been cases, where dreadful
> sexual assaults have been followed by murderous violence. The whole life order
> is reserved for the most exceptional cases. Without suggesting that the court is
> prohibited from making a whole life order unless the defendant is convicted of
> at least one murder, such an order will, inevitably be a very rare event
> indeed."

1.112   In one of the conjoined appeals (*Michael Roberts*), the Court agreed with
the submission that a whole life order should be reserved for cases where the
criminal had gone even further than the appellant. Roberts, then aged 45,
had been convicted at Southwark Crown Court of a series of rapes which had
multiple aggravating features. There were three rape victims. A fourth victim
was 84 when she was severely assaulted, although there was no evidence of
sexual assault. All four victims were women, no longer young, and living
alone, who were attacked in their homes during the course of burglaries. The
rapes involved a high level of violence, including terrible facial injuries to the
first victim. Each was subjected to an ordeal which would have been likely to
have blighted the remainder of their lives. The offences, together with some
of the appellant's earlier convictions, confirmed that he was cruel and
ruthless and a real and continuing danger to vulnerable people. The Court of
Appeal quashed the whole life order and substituted a minimum term of 25
years. Lord Judge CJ observed that the Court was not be taken as implying
anything less than that the appellant was highly dangerous, and on the

---

[145] *Hogg* [2007] EWCA Crim 1357.
[146] *Burke* [2008] EWCA Crim 1077.
[147] There was no appeal against conviction or sentence.
[148] [2012] EWCA Crim 2435.

evidence before him at that time, it seemed highly improbable that he would, after the expiry of 25–30 or more years, or indeed ever, be safe for release.

Assistance can be derived from *Wilson*[149] as to the weight to be given to **1.113** previous convictions of the utmost gravity when deciding whether a whole life sentence is appropriate. The appellant had pleaded guilty to attempted rape, wounding with intent and causing a person to engage in sexual activity without her consent. He was born in the UK in 1957 but emigrated to Australia when he was a boy. In Australia he accumulated 17 convictions for a variety of offences. These included raping and causing grievous bodily harm to an elderly lady in 1985, for which he was sentenced to 10 years' imprisonment. Following his release on licence from that sentence, he murdered another elderly lady and left her body naked in a park. He was sentenced in 1992 to life imprisonment for that murder. He was released on licence in 2008 and deported to the UK. A few months after his return, he committed the offences which were the subject of the appeal. He followed and attacked a 71-year-old lady as she entered her home. He threatened her with a knife, punched her in the face, cut off her clothes and forced her to handle his penis. She attempted to resist and suffered serious lacerations to her hand as a result of grabbing the knife. The attack stopped when two boys disturbed the appellant. The victim sustained serious injuries including two significant cuts and a fractured cheekbone.

On appeal, it was conceded that the appellant satisfied the dangerousness **1.114** criteria for the purposes of s.225 of the CJA 2003. It was not argued that a life sentence was inappropriate, but the whole life order was challenged on the basis that (i) the offences, taken on their own, did not justify a whole life order, and (ii) the appellant's previous convictions were not of immediate relevance. The Lord Chief Justice agreed with the sentencing judge that the appellant was "exceptionally dangerous". However, the Court accepted that a whole life order remained a sentence of last resort for cases of the most extreme gravity. The offences were very serious indeed but, taken on their own, would not justify a whole life term. However, they were committed by a man with a lengthy criminal record which included the rape and murder of elderly females. Each of the earlier offences was properly to be treated as a serious aggravating feature of the instant, very serious crimes. The seriousness of the latest offences was significantly greater because they were committed by the same man who had committed the earlier offences. However, without wishing to minimise the instant horrific offences, the earlier offences needed to be treated with caution proportionate to the fact that the appellant was not being sentenced for them. The Court concluded that the punitive element of the offence should be fixed by the court and it substituted a minimum period of 10 years.

---

[149] *Wilson* [2009] EWCA Crim 999.

Extended sentences

1.115   There will be many serious sexual offences where an extended sentence may be appropriate if the dangerousness criteria are satisfied. For further discussion of extended sentences, see paras 34.10 and following, below. When deciding whether an extended sentence is necessary to provide the appropriate level of public protection, it is important that consideration be given as to whether a carefully drafted SHPO might sufficiently control the defendant's future behaviour so as to eliminate or substantially reduce any risk of serious harm to the public by the commission further specified offences. In *R. v BD*,[150] the appellant had been convicted of serious sexual offences (including two rapes) against two young girls. On the rape counts he was sentenced to an extended sentence of 22 years comprising a custodial term of 17 years and an extension period of five years. An indefinite Sexual Offences Prevention Order was made. The Court of Appeal observed that neither counsel had addressed the judge specifically on the interrelation of the SOPO and the difficult task of deciding whether an extended sentence was required. Taking into account the stringent terms of the SOPO, which would suitably constrain opportunities for future sexual offending, the Court concluded there was no necessity to impose an extended sentence in that case. The terms of the SOPO had a direct bearing upon the likelihood of the appellant re-offending in a sexual way. The Court did, however, approve the 17-year custodial sentence.

Cases of exceptional gravity

1.116   In the vast majority of cases, sentences will be within the ranges suggested by the guideline. However, the ranges are not rigid, and the Court of Appeal has acknowledged the need for flexibility in applying them. If there is to be a significant departure from the guideline, the sentencer must explain this and give full reasons for such departure.

1.117   Cases of exceptional gravity arise where the scale of the offending and the multiplicity of aggravating features mean that they fall in a category where the guideline was not intended to apply and previous decisions can only provide limited assistance. It follows that exceptional aggravating features can lead to a starting point above the range suggested in the guideline.

1.118   In *R. v DJ*,[151] the Court of Appeal reviewed the appropriate level of sentence for campaigns of rape and offending of extreme severity. All the cases considered were decided whilst the Sentencing Guidelines Council's guideline was in force. In that guideline, for repeated rape of the same victim over a course of time, or rape involving multiple victims, the starting point was 15 years with a range of 13–19 years. In *R. v DJ*, the earlier decisions in

---

[150] [2015] EWCA Crim 1415.
[151] [2015] EWCA Crim 563.

Watkins[152] and *R. v P(P)*[153] were described as representing cases at the extreme end of the spectrum of offending.

Watkins was described as a case which "plumbed the depths of depravity". **1.119** The first applicant, Ian Watkins, was the lead singer of a band called "Lost Prophets". The band toured extensively and the applicant used his fame to secure sexual encounters with fans and, later, with their children. He recorded his sexual encounters and retained and stored the recordings. The pleasure he derived from the commission of the most serious sexual offences against babies was clear. The second applicant, P, and B were sexual partners of Watkins. Acting independently of one another, both allowed Watkins to commit sexual assaults upon their infant children. With Watkins' encouragement and for his gratification they sexually assaulted their own children. Watkins dominated his sexual partners and exercised a corrupting influence over them. The judge concluded that the multiplicity of aggravating factors justified a departure from the guideline range. He ordered that the sentences on the offences committed with P and those with B should be consecutive, making a total sentence of 29 years with an extended licence period of six years. The offences included two attempted rapes of a baby for which Watkins received concurrent 15-year custodial sentences and offences of digital penetration and conspiracy to rape in relation to a female child aged just over 12 months, for which he received concurrent 14-year sentences to be served consecutively to the sentences for the rapes. The judge also imposed an extended sentence of six years, making a sentence of 35 years in all. He ordered all other sentences to run concurrently. The issue arose as to whether the judge imposed a total sentence that, in a just and proportionate manner, reflected the whole of the applicant's offending. The Court of Appeal was satisfied the judge did apply the principle of totality, and the application for leave to appeal sentence was refused.

In *R. v P(P)*, a case involving serial rape and other sexual abuse of two **1.120** daughters from the age of about eight through to their early 30's, the Court of Appeal indicated that a 33-year notional term would have been appropriate after a trial. The case was aggravated by significant violence, causing serious physical injury, regular pregnancies, the isolation of the victims and the blighting of their lives.

Also referred to in *R. v DJ* were the decisions in *Coles*[154] and *Coleman*.[155] **1.121** In *Coles*, five girls aged between 11 and 15 had been subjected to rape and sexual abuse over an eight-year period and had been corrupted. The Court of Appeal described the case as "dreadful" but said the offences "could not properly be regarded as sexual offences of the utmost gravity". It nonetheless

---

[152] [2014] EWCA Crim 1677.
[153] [2009] EWCA Crim 1048. A life sentence was imposed.
[154] [2010] EWCA Crim 320. A sentence of imprisonment for public protection (IPP) was imposed.
[155] Part of the Court of Appeal's decision in *Attorney General's Reference (No.27 of 2013) (Gintas Burinskas)* [2014] EWCA Crim 334.

held that a 20-year notional determinate term after trial was appropriate. *Coleman* involved countless rapes of a single victim, a step-daughter, over a 10-year-period when she was between the ages of five and 16. The custodial term of an extended sentence was reduced to 27 years prior to credit for a guilty plea. About two years of the 27 years was attributable to indecent images offences. The case involved the use of significant violence including the hospitalisation of the victim. Lord Thomas CJ observed that, given the very prolonged period of time over which the offences continued, the custodial period must be "well above the sentencing range in the first bracket of the rape guideline".

1.122   In *R. v DJ*, Treacy LJ, after reviewing these cases, stated that care needs to be taken in relying on phrases such as "the depths of depravity" as if that established a particular category of offence. He explained that there will in any given case be a number of factors to be taken into account. A case may reach the level of utmost seriousness by a variety of routes and the attaching of labels is not a particularly good guide.

1.123   In *R. v DJ*, an extended sentence of 39 years (comprising a custodial term of 33 years and an extension period of six years) was imposed for serious sexual offending committed against children aged between five and 15 over a period of approximately 10 years. There were no less than nine separate victims. The multiple aggravating features involved breach of trust, recording of the offending, threats to victims, deceit, grooming and controlling, the suborning of a victim's sisters to give false evidence at trial, the isolation of a victim within the family and the exploitation of the vulnerable. The Court of Appeal took the view that the judge had been entitled to pass a series of consecutive sentences reflecting offending against different individuals. None of the sentences imposed in relation to any of those individuals was open to criticism. In the light of *Coleman*, a longer sentence might have been justified in one case (SJ) had it stood alone. It was clear from the judge's sentencing remarks that she had been acutely conscious of the need to recognise the principles of totality and proportionality. That was why she passed a series of concurrent sentences in relation to five of the victims as well as in relation to the serious indecent image offences. The duration and scale of the offending was particularly substantial. Whilst the features which made the case very serious might not have been as eye catching as those in *Watkins,* or as extreme as in *R. v P(P)*, the offences approached a comparable level of gravity for different reasons. However, the violence used in the case of SJ was not of the order found in those cases. Also, there were no aggravating features such as sadism, pregnancy or sexually transmitted disease. The Court concluded that the overall sentence was too long and reduced the custodial term to 30 years.

1.124   A high profile example of a case where sentencing outside the guideline was appropriate is the Oxford grooming case, *Bassam Karrar*,[156] which

---

[156] [2015] EWCA Crim 850. See Appendix H, below.

involved the sustained exploitation and corruption of girls by a group of men
in the Oxford area. The four appellants were convicted of rape and
conspiracy to rape. The Court of Appeal was referred to the judgment of
Treacy LJ in *R. v DJ.* The appellants placed reliance upon *Coles* and
Coleman. However, grave sexual crimes tend to have a variety of aggravating
features, and this case included men operating in gangs deliberately targeting
and grooming vulnerable children both for their own self-gratification and
for brutal and humiliating sexual exploitation by others. The men targeted
vulnerable girls as young as 11 with troubled upbringings. They used a
number of methods to groom the girls: giving them time, showing them
apparent affection, and supplying them with drugs such as cannabis, cocaine
and heroin so that some became addicted. The men would exercise extreme
physical and sexual violence upon them and threaten them should they ever
seek to escape.

The men raped the girls both alone and with others. The girls were taken   1.125
to other men for sex often in groups and often in return for money. The
sexual activity included vaginal, anal and oral rape. It involved the use of a
variety of objections such as knives, meat cleavers, baseball bats and various
sex toys that caused physical injury. It was often accompanied by humiliating
and degrading contact such as girls being bitten, scratched, urinated upon,
suffocated, tied, burnt or branded. Some had to endure men licking the
blood from their injured vaginas and smelling their dirty or stained
underwear.

The appellants were each sentenced to imprisonment for life and in   1.126
relation to each minimum terms were specified of between eight and 20 years.
It was submitted on appeal that, grave though the offences were, sentences of
such a length were disproportionate to the level of offending. Hallett LJ, in
dismissing the appeals, described the case as one of the worst cases of child
exploitation to come before the courts in recent years. These were crimes of
the utmost gravity whatever the role played by the applicants. She saw
considerable force in the Crown's submission that this was one of those cases
for which the guidelines were not intended and previous decisions would only
be of limited assistance. She continued[157]:

> "If they were of any relevance, the circumstances of the offences committed by
> the applicants themselves upon each victim, considered in isolation, would place
> them at the highest end of the range in the most culpable category. Similarly, the
> offences which involved making arrangements for other men to commit sexual
> offences upon the victims would have merited sentences at or beyond the highest
> range in the most culpable category. However, the offending went much further:
> there was more than one victim of each of the offenders and a multiplicity of
> aggravating features to be factored in."

It follows that exceptional aggravating features can lead to a starting point   1.127
above the range suggested in the guideline. In *Attorney General's Reference*

[157] At [67].

(Nos 14 and 15 of 2006) (Tanya French and Alan Webster),[158] the Court of Appeal agreed with the trial judge's remarks and the Attorney General's submission that the case went beyond that envisaged by the then guideline. The case combined the aggravating features of repeated rape of a victim over a period of time, breach of trust, and the most vulnerable victim possible, a tiny baby. The Court held that this last feature should be treated as an additional aggravating feature, and that the extraordinary and abhorrent treatment of this victim called for a starting point of 24 years.

Attempted rape

1.128   In certain circumstances, the fact that there was no actual penetration will provide little or no mitigation. The commission of the full offence may only have been prevented by the resistance of the complainant or the actions of a third party. A recent example, decided under the SGC guideline, is *Collier*,[159] which involved convictions of attempted rape, assault occasioning actual bodily harm and theft. The victim suffered from learning difficulties and the appellant had entered her home without permission and attacked her, attempting to rape her both orally and anally, before leaving with her phone and laptop computer. The Court of Appeal held that a total sentence with a starting point of 13 years' imprisonment that was reduced to eight-and-a-half years' imprisonment on account of early pleas of guilty, was not manifestly excessive. However, where an offender has a positive change of mind and consciously draws back from committing the full offence, a reduction is appropriate.[160] In *Woodland*,[161] the Court of Appeal reduced the starting point where the full offence of attempted rape was not thwarted by the intervention of a third party, but rather by physical steps the young victim took to make penetration more difficult. The appellant took his nephew, who was just short of 16, to the carnival where he plied him with alcohol. On return he lured the victim into his bedroom, pulled down the victim's trousers, pushed him onto his front, and tried to force his penis into the victim's anus. The victim resisted by clenching his buttocks. The appellant then thrust his penis between the victim's thighs and ejaculated rather than force his penis into the victim's anus. The Court of Appeal reduced the sentence from 10 years' to eight years' imprisonment.

Historic cases

1.129   In *Millberry*,[162] the Court of Appeal accepted that historic cases of abuse where the offence is reported many years after it was committed should not

[158] [2006] EWCA Crim 1335.
[159] [2013] EWCA Crim 1038.
[160] *R. v C(RA)* [2015] Crim 1856.
[161] [2015] EWCA Crim 629.
[162] *Millberry* [2002] EWCA Crim 2891.

necessarily attract a lesser sentence. They should be considered on a case-by-case basis, with the court being entitled to show a "limited degree of mercy" where the offender is advanced in years.[163] In a later case, the Court added: "it is important to emphasise the word 'limited' and sentencers should be careful not to make too great an allowance in that regard".[164] The Court of Appeal has also stated that this ought to apply to other serious forms of sexual offending.[165]

In *R. v H(J)*,[166] the Court of Appeal considered sentencing issues in the   **1.130**
context of crimes brought to justice many years after they were committed, sometimes described as "historic" or "cold" cases. Although Lord Judge CJ, delivering the judgment of the Court, gave sentencing guidance of general application, he specifically considered a number of "historic" sex cases of which three involved sentencing decisions following convictions for rape. His Lordship stated that sentence will be imposed at the date of the sentencing hearing on the basis of the legislative provisions then current, and by measured reference to any definitive sentencing guideline relevant to the situation revealed by established facts. Although sentence must be limited to the maximum sentence at the date when the offence was committed, it is wholly unrealistic to attempt an assessment of sentence by seeking to identify at the time of sentencing what the sentence for the individual offence was likely to have been if the offence had come to light at or shortly after the date when it was committed. For fuller discussion of the approach to sentencing in historic cases, see paras 30.110 and following, below.

Life sentences in cases before the implementation of the "dangerousness provisions" under the Criminal Justice Act 2003

There will, though, be some very grave sexual offences committed before the   **1.131**
implementation of s.225 of the Criminal Justice Act 2003 where a discretionary life sentence will be appropriate, provided the case was sufficiently grave and the offender might remain a serious danger to the public for a period which cannot be reliably estimated at sentence time.[167]

The limitation to the then maximum sentence does not affect the full   **1.132**
offence of rape as the maximum sentence was discretionary life under the

[163] At 17.
[164] *Attorney General's References (Nos 37, 38, 44, 54, 51, 53, 35, 40, 43, 45, 41 and 42 of 2003)* [2003] EWCA Crim 2973; [2004] 1 Cr. App. R.(S.) 84.
[165] *Attorney General's References (Nos 37, 38, 44, 54, 51, 53, 35, 40, 43, 45, 41 and 42 of 2003)* [2003] EWCA Crim 2973; [2004] 1 Cr. App. R.(S.) 84.
[166] [2011] EWCA Crim 2753, discussed more fully in paras 30.111 and following, below. *Cp. Fowler* [2002] EWCA Crim 620; *Bowers* [1999] 2 Cr. App. R.(S.) 97 (in a historic case, where the defendant would have been a young offender had the matter been discovered and dealt with timeously, the likely sentence at the time of the offence is a useful starting point and will be a "powerful factor" in deciding the proper sentence.
[167] See the criteria in *Hodgson* (1968) 52 Cr. App. R. 113 (referred to below); *Whittaker* [1997] 1 Cr. App. R.(S.) 261. For recent examples, see *R. v DP* [2013] EWCA Crim 1143 and *Robertshaw* [2013] EWCA Crim 635.

Sexual Offences Act 1956. However, the maximum sentence for attempted rape was seven years' imprisonment until 1985, when it was increased to life. As the Sentencing Council guideline frequently recommends sentences significantly higher than those that would have been passed 20 or even 10 years ago, the appropriate sentence for "historic" cases of rape may be very much higher than if the matter had been dealt with at the time.

1.133   In respect of offences committed before April 4, 2005, a life sentence is justified where (i) the offence itself was grave enough to require a very long sentence, (ii) it appeared from the nature of the offence or from the offender's record that he was a person of unstable character who was likely to commit such offences in the future and (iii) if such offences were committed, the consequences to others would be especially injurious, as in the case of sexual or violent crimes.[168] In *Wendell Baker*,[169] the applicant had been convicted of a particularly violent rape committed nearly 17 years before in early 1997. The victim, who lived on her own and was aged 68, was subjected to the dreadful indignity of a pitiless and life-scarring violent sexual assault. At night the applicant had broken into her home and raped her anally before locking her into a small cupboard which could be opened only from the outside. The victim remained there for many hours in acute discomfort, fearing she was about to die. She was rescued alive only because a friend visited the premises. Her face was so badly beaten she was unrecognisable to her son. It was submitted on the applicant's behalf that, since the applicant (now aged 56) had not committed any offences since 2005, there was evidence that he was a changed man. The Court of Appeal took the view that the judge was entitled to reject this submission and form the view that a life sentence was appropriate as the applicant was an unstable character who might commit serious offences in the future involving serious physical or psychological harm.

1.134   In *R. v D*,[170] the Court of Appeal upheld a sentence of discretionary life imprisonment passed in August 2011 in respect of a rape committed approximately 30 years earlier. The appellant had pleaded guilty to the rape of his grandmother in 1982 when she was 64 and the appellant was 16. The appellant was tried for her rape in 1983 but was found not guilty. His grandmother died in 1992. In 2002 the appellant was arrested on suspicion of rape of his step-daughter. The appellant absconded and left the country. Subsequent investigation of the rape of his grandmother resulted in the production of a DNA profile which was found to match that of the appellant. He was surrendered to the UK and in 2008 pleaded guilty to the rape of his step-daughter. His acquittal of the rape of his grandmother was quashed

---

[168] See *Hodgson* (1968) 52 Cr. App. R. 113, applied in *R. v D* [2013] 1 Cr. App. R.(S.) 127.
[169] [2014] EWCA Crim 242. The Court did, nevertheless, reduce the minimum term on the basis that the judge's starting point of 24 years if the sentence had been a determinative sentence was too long, and the correct starting point was 20 years. This translated into a minimum term of eight and a half years, taking into account other factors. See para.1.42, above.
[170] [2012] EWCA Crim 2370.

under s.76 of the CJA 2003. The appellant subsequently pleaded guilty to that rape and was sentenced to life imprisonment with a minimum term of three-and-a-half years. The sentencing judge considered that if the appellant had been adult at the time of the offence in 1982 and there was no mitigation, the appropriate determinate sentence would have been 11 years. However, taking account of the aggravating and mitigating circumstances, in particular the fact that the appellant was 16 when the offence was committed, the judge said that the determinate sentence would have been seven years.

Leave to appeal was granted so that the Court of Appeal could consider   **1.135**
whether the conditions laid down in *Hodgson*,[171] which must be satisfied before a discretionary sentence may be imposed, were satisfied in this case. The Court of Appeal in *Hodgson* said that a life sentence would be justified where the offence or offences were in themselves grave enough to require a very long sentence, where it appeared from the nature of the offences and from the defendant's history that he was a person of unstable character likely to commit such offences in the future, and where if such offences were committed the consequences to others might be especially injurious.

On appeal it was submitted that the first condition was not satisfied, as the   **1.136**
offence was committed when the appellant was 16 and it could not be said to be grave enough to require a very long sentence of imprisonment. The Court rejected this argument, taking into account the statements of Lord Judge CJ in *Attorney General's References (Nos 3, 73, and 75 of 2010) (Anigbugu)*[172] on how seriously the courts regard offences of rape committed against a lone woman in her home at night after forced entry into the house, and the guidance given by his Lordship on the length of the determinate sentence that such offences will attract. The Court concluded that it was impossible to argue that the offence committed in 1982 was not "grave enough to require a very long sentence".[173]

ALTERNATIVE VERDICTS

If the jury are not sure that there was penile penetration, they may   **1.137**
nevertheless bring in a verdict of guilty of attempted rape if the defendant's conduct amounted to more than mere preparation and the defendant had the requisite intent. It is not necessary that the defendant should have done an

---

[171] (1968) 52 Cr. App. R. 113. These conditions had been considered and confirmed in subsequent cases, in particular *(No.32 of 1996) (Whitaker)* [1997] 1 Cr. App. R.(S.) 261 and *Chapman* [2000] 1 Cr. App. R.(S.) 377.
[172] [2011] EWCA Crim 633.
[173] It appears that the sentencing judge was not referred to *Anigbugu*, where it was said that in a case where rape was committed after or in the course of burglary in the home, the starting point would rarely be less than 12 years' imprisonment and the presence of aggravating features would increase the starting point to 15 years' imprisonment and beyond. The Court of Appeal took the view that if this authority had been drawn to the attention of the judge, it was possible that the determinate sentence might have been higher.

act of an unequivocally sexual nature.[174] In order to raise a prima facie case of attempted rape, it is not necessary to prove that the defendant with the requisite intent had necessarily gone as far as to attempt physical preparation of the vagina, mouth or anus with his penis. It is sufficient if there is evidence from which an intent can be inferred and there are proven acts which a jury could properly regard as more than merely preparatory to the commission of the offence. In *Attorney General's Reference (No.1 of 1992)*,[175] there was no evidence of any penile penetration in that it was the doctor's opinion that a recent bruise just outside the hymen but inside the labia could have been caused by finger pressure. The Court of Appeal stated that the evidence of the young woman's distress, the state of her clothing (her knickers were around her ankles) and the position in which she was seen, together with the respondent's acts of dragging her up the steps, lowering his trousers and interfering with her private parts, and his answers to the police, left it open to the jury to conclude that the respondent had the necessary intent and had done acts which were more than merely preparatory. Similarly, in a trial for an offence of rape, a jury may bring in an alternative verdict of sexual assault under s.3 of the 2003 Act if they are sure that there was intentional sexual touching but are unsure whether there was attempted penetration or an intention to penetrate. In cases where the complainant's evidence leaves the issue open as to whether there was penetration by the defendant's penis or by another part of his body (or anything else), it would be advisable to include an alternative count of assault by penetration contrary to s.2 of the 2003 Act.

1.138   In *Beaney*,[176] the appellant was convicted of attempted rape in relation to an incident in which he had already pleaded guilty to robbery. He had accosted the complainant in a station car park at 1.15am. She described herself as "merrily drunk but not paralytic". He held a weapon against her throat and told her to get into some bushes. He robbed her of her shoulder bag and an Ipod. He used his body to manoeuvre her towards the bushes. The complainant remembered seeing his hand coming up her right leg. She broke free. There was some evidence he then followed her but desisted when he saw a man on the road. She had marks on her arms consistent with a grip by fingers. Her shoes were found in the grassy area. It was submitted on his behalf that the appellant had admitted snatching the bag and the evidence of an intention to rape was entirely speculative. The Court of Appeal held that there was sufficient evidence of an intention to carry out a sexual attack over and above the robbery, but the evidence did not go beyond sufficient evidence to support an intention to commit a sexual assault. In the circumstances, the Court felt it was appropriate to substitute a conviction for attempted sexual assault.

---

[174] *Patnaik* [2000] 3 *Archbold News* 2, CA. See also *Beaney* [2010] EWCA Crim 2551.
[175] 96 Cr. App. R. 298.
[176] [2010] EWCA Crim 2551.

The approach adopted by the Court of Appeal in *Beaney* was followed in **1.139**
Ferriter,[177] which also involved an appeal against conviction for attempted
rape. The appellant spent a night drinking in a bar where the complainant
was the barmaid. When he was the last customer, he walked behind the bar
and struggled with the complainant. Both ended up on the floor. The
complainant escaped and the appellant stole spirits and cash from the till. He
was charged with theft and with attempted rape or sexual assault in the
alternative, based on the complainant's evidence that he had tried during the
struggle to pull her trousers down more than once. The appellant, who
pleaded guilty to the thefts, denied this and claimed he just wanted to take
money from the tills. The trial judge refused to accede to a submission of no
case on the charge of attempted rape. It was submitted on appeal on behalf
of the appellant that (a) there had been insufficient evidence to leave to the
jury that he had gone beyond mere preparation, and (b) even assuming that
he had gone beyond mere preparation, there had been insufficient evidence to
leave to the jury to justify the inference that his intent had not been to assault
the complainant sexually, but to commit the specific offence of rape. The
Court of Appeal allowed the appeal. It took the view that there was not the
slightest doubt that the appellant's acts went well beyond mere preparation
and into trying to commit a sexual offence. However, although there was
ample evidence on which a jury could conclude that the appellant's intent
was sexual molestation, there was no evidence which pointed to an intent to
commit rape rather than some other sexual offence. The Court observed that
although the defendant's activities were more explicit than in *Beaney* in that
the defendant had molested the complainant and was in the act of removing
her trousers, the evidence was equally consistent with an intention to commit
sexual assault as with an intention to commit rape. The Court accordingly
quashed the conviction for attempted rape and substituted a conviction for
sexual assault.

However, in *Delroy Bryan*[178] the Court of Appeal implicitly disapproved **1.140**
the approach adopted in *Ferriter* (and, by implication, in *Beaney*) in relation
to cases where the evidence is equivocal as to the form of sexual offence
intended. In *Delroy Bryan* the appellant had been convicted of attempted
rape. The complainant had fallen asleep on a London bus in the early hours
of the morning. The appellant was alleged to have placed a mobile device
between her legs up her skirt whilst she was asleep. She awoke and realised
that she had missed her stop. The appellant befriended her and reassured her
that he would look after her and help her to get home. He guided her to a
secluded area of a public park. They were walking with their arms interlinked
through the park when the appellant hit her in the face and she fell to the
ground. The appellant lay on her with one hand covering her mouth and

---

[177] [2012] EWCA Crim 2211.
[178] [2015] EWCA Crim 548.

nose. She struggled to breathe and felt faint. The complainant was certain that he was about to rape her as he was preventing her from screaming and had his hand on her thigh. She eventually managed to force his hand from her mouth and shouted "police" and the appellant ran away. The complainant discovered that her tights had been torn, but she stated that she had not felt his hand inside her knickers nor had she seen his penis at any time. She was satisfied that there had been no vaginal penetration. The appellant denied he was the attacker. He gave "no comment" interviews, he did not give any evidence before the jury, nor did he call any witnesses. The ground of appeal related to a submission at the close of the prosecution case that there was insufficient evidence to leave the count of attempted rape to the jury. It was contended, relying on *Ferriter*, that it would not be legitimate for the jury to infer, on the basis of the evidence adduced by the prosecution, that the appellant had the relevant intent. The only interference with the complainant, at its highest, was the hand on the thigh and possibly an attempt to rip her tights on the crotch. There was no evidence that he was seeking to remove his clothes or to release his penis. The Court of Appeal rejected this submission, confining itself to considering whether there was sufficient evidence for the attempted rape properly to be left to the jury. The Court, agreeing with the trial judge, noted that *Ferriter* was factually a very different case. In *Delroy Bryan*, whilst there was no single feature of the evidence which taken in isolation signified or signalled the relevant intent, taking the evidence in the round and looking at the totality of the facts, there was evidence from which a jury could be sure there was an intention to rape. As for *Ferriter*, the Court said that it was a very different case in that the facts were much more equivocal as to the appellant's intention. In *Delroy Bryan*, by contrast, there was the lead up to the incident which was potentially important, as well as the ripping of tights, the grabbing of the thigh, the lying on top of the complainant and attempting to stop her from shouting. However, the Court went on respectfully to query how helpful the approach suggested in *Ferriter* is. Evidence of an intent to rape will necessarily constitute evidence of some lesser sexual offence. The relevant question is not whether there is any particularly piece of evidence which is consistent with the more serious offence of rape but not with a lesser sexual offence. The evidence will often be consistent with both offences. The only question for the judge in a submission of no case to answer is whether the evidence taken at its highest is capable of sustaining a conviction for the offence charged. In answering that essentially straightforward question, the Court thought it an unnecessary, unhelpful and potentially confusing distraction to focus on distinctions which may be drawn between the evidence necessary to sustain an intent to rape and the evidence necessary to sustain some lesser sexual offence.

1.141   If a defendant is tried on a charge of rape and the jury return a general verdict of not guilty, he may not thereafter be tried for attempted rape, since it was open to the jury to convict of the attempt on the charge of the full offence[179] and by their general verdict the jury acquitted the defendant not only of the crime expressly charged, but also of any other crime which they could have convicted on that indictment. Where, however, the jury acquit a defendant of rape but are unable to agree on an alternative of attempted rape which has been specifically left to them, the prosecution may seek a re-trial and the acquittal is no bar to a subsequent indictment on the same facts for attempted rape.[180] Where a defendant is acquitted (or convicted) of attempted rape, he cannot thereafter be charged with the full offence on a second indictment.[181]

DOUBLE JEOPARDY

Schedule 5 to the Criminal Justice Act 2003[182] lists 12 sexual offences as "qualifying offences" in respect of which the prosecution may apply to the Court of Appeal, under s.76 of the Act, for an order quashing an acquittal where there is new and compelling evidence against the acquitted person. The listed offences include rape under s.1 of the Sexual Offences Act 1956 and s.1 of the Sexual Offences Act 2003, attempted rape and conspiracy to rape.[183]   1.142

In *R. v A*,[184] the Court of Appeal granted an application under these provisions for an order quashing an acquittal of rape and an order for a re-trial. At a trial in 2004, the respondent had been acquitted of two counts of indecent assault and one count of rape. The offences were alleged to have taken place when the complainant was 15 at a residential camp for her church youth group. After the trial, on seeing an article about it in a local newspaper, the respondent's first wife contacted the police. She told them that long before the trial the respondent had been arrested for indecent assaults on three children when working at a school. An extensive police investigation followed which led to a 17-count indictment being preferred against the respondent. The trial on these counts was due to begin shortly after the application. Seven different complainants, both girls and boys, were identified in the particulars. The allegations encompassed offences of inde-cent assault on young males and females, buggery and indecency with a child. The evidence in support of the new indictment demonstrated that in reality the original complaint formed part of a series, and occurred approx-imately half-way through the lengthy history of the respondent's alleged misconduct with children, as he moved around the country. The evidence of   1.143

---

[179] Criminal Law Act 1967 s.6(3), (4).
[180] *Hearn* [1970] Crim. L.R. 175.
[181] *Velasquez* [1996] 1 Cr. App. R. 155.
[182] See Sch.4.
[183] Sch.5 also includes the offences in ss.5 and 10 (where alleged to have been committed on a girl under 13) of the SOA 1956 and ss.2, 5, 6 of the SOA 2003 and ss.4, 8, 30 and 31 of that Act where the activity or touching involved penetration.
[184] [2008] EWCA Crim 2908. At the re-trial the defendant was acquitted.

the new complainants, and the supporting evidence available to the prosecution at the forthcoming trial, was admissible to support the original complainant. Some of the details bore significant similarities to her allegations, and the evidence would undermine the respondent's contention that he had spent his adult life blamelessly working with children. During the investigation the respondent had made a number of apparent admissions, but continued to deny he had raped the original complainant. It was accepted that the new evidence, taken cumulatively, was compelling both as similar fact evidence and as evidence of the respondent's propensities under s.101(1)(d) of the Criminal Justice Act 2003. However, it was argued that such material could not be described as being evidence "in relation to a qualifying offence" within the meaning of s.78 of the Act, unlike e.g. a new DNA analysis which provides direct evidence. The Lord Chief Justice rejected this submission, stating that the stark question under the Act was whether the evidence was "highly probative" of the respondent's guilt of the qualifying offence. In this case there was not the slightest possibility of collusion or contamination between the different groups of complainants. For the purposes of s.78, the evidence was "new" and also "compelling" in that it was reliable, substantial and highly probative of the case against the respondent in the 2004 trial, demonstrating that the complaint was far from isolated. The acquittals of indecent assault (not qualifying offences) would not make a re-trial of the rape allegation unfair. Although there were aspects of the complainant's evidence that might remain open to criticism, her credibility was far from destroyed. It is not unusual for victims of sexual abuse to exhibit fragility, especially where the trial takes place long after the abuse ceased.

ALLEGATION OF JOINT OFFENCE

1.144   Where a person has been raped by more than one man on the same occasion, it is permissible and often advisable to charge one offence of rape as against all defendants without reference to aiding and abetting, rather than to charge rape in respect of each act of penetration.[185] Then, on appropriate facts, the prosecution will be entitled to present its case on the basis that either (a) the defendants acted in concert in pursuance of a common design, or (b) each defendant was individually guilty of rape independently of whether they were acting in pursuance of a common design. In *Fenwick*,[186] a decision of the Court of Criminal Appeal in New South Wales which was approved by the House of Lords in *DPP v Merriman*,[187] the two appellants were jointly charged with one count of rape, and the indictment did not contain separate counts alleging independent crimes of rape by each of them. The two

[185] *DPP v Merriman* [1973] A.C. 584, overruling, inter alia, *Holley* (1969) 53 Cr. App. R. 519.
[186] (1953) 54 S.R. (N.S.W.) 147.
[187] [1973] A.C. 584.

appellants were driving a girl home after a dance. Both of them had intercourse with her. The trial judge told the jury that the Crown's case was presented in two ways: (1) the appellants acted in concert, in pursuance of a common design (in which case it did not matter whether both achieved penetration, provided there was penetration by one and the other assisted or encouraged the one who actually committed the act of rape), or (2) each was individually guilty of rape independently of whether or not they were acting with a common purpose (in which case the Crown would have to prove that each committed the full act of rape). One ground of appeal by each appellant was that it was not open to the jury if they found no common design to consider the appellant's individual cases as separate charges. Street CJ held that the point taken was technical and could be dealt with by way of a technical answer. Indictments are to be read jointly and severally. It followed that a finding of fact that there was no common design would not preclude a guilty verdict against each appellant in respect of his own conduct if he committed the physical act of rape. If separate counts are charged in respect of each penetration, with the defendant responsible for that penetration charged as principal and the other or others as aiders and abettors,[188] then in the absence of evidence as to which defendant committed the physical act of penetration, all the defendants would have to be acquitted notwithstanding the fact of the jury being satisfied that all were active participants in the offence. If there is just one joint charge, the jury need not be directed that each defendant must have had a common purpose or design or that one is to be regarded as a principal and the other or others as aiding and abetting. All that matters is that they should be satisfied (a) that there was penetration and (b) that in respect of any particular defendant he was actively participating in some way in the offence, if not by himself penetrating then at least by encouraging or assisting his co-defendant, and that, in doing the act or in helping his co-defendant, he himself had the necessary criminal intent.

A defendant who aids, abets, counsels or procures a man to penetrate a   1.145
person knowing that he or she does not consent cannot escape conviction for rape on the basis that the man who penetrated the person reasonably believed he or she was consenting. The leading authority is *Cogan and Leek*,[189] where L procured C to have intercourse with his (L's) wife. At their trial on a charge of rape, C maintained that he had thought the wife was consenting. The trial judge, when dealing with the mental element in relation to C, directed the jury on the basis of the Court of Appeal's decision in *Morgan*,[190] namely that a mistaken belief in consent could provide a defence only if based on reasonable grounds. However, appreciating that the Court of Appeal had given leave to appeal in *Morgan*, the judge asked the jury to make a finding whether any belief in consent C may have had was based on such grounds.

---

[188] This practice was recommended by Lord Parker CJ in *Holley* (1969) 53 Cr. App. R. 519 (now overruled).
[189] [1975] 2 All E.R. 1059.
[190] [1975] 1 All E.R. 8.

The jury returned a verdict of guilty with respect to C, finding that he had believed the wife was consenting, but that he had no reasonable grounds for such a belief. In the light of the House of Lords' decision in *DPP v Morgan*,[191] the Court of Appeal allowed C's appeal against conviction. However, despite C's state of mind, L, who had known that his wife was not consenting, was guilty of rape as an aider and abettor and L's appeal against conviction was dismissed.[192] As the offence of rape is now defined in s.1 of the 2003 Act, C would not have a defence as he did not have a reasonable belief in consent. L's position would be unaffected, though as an alternative to rape as an accessory he could under the new law be charged with causing a person to engage in sexual activity without consent (s.4), or encouraging or assisting rape under ss.44–46 of the Serious Crime Act 2007.

JOINDER OF OTHER OFFENCES IN AN INDICTMENT CHARGING RAPE

1.146 The position is governed by the Criminal Procedure Rules 2015, r.10.2(3). This is the successor to Rule 9 of the Indictment Rules 1971 and is drafted in similar terms:

> "An indictment may contain more than one count if all the offences charged—
> (a) are founded on the same facts; or
> (b) form or are a part of a series of offences of the same or a similar character."

By s.5(3) of the Indictments Act 1915 the court has the duty to order the separate trial of offences that are properly joined in one indictment where the court is of the opinion that the defendant might otherwise be prejudiced or embarrassed. Where there is a strong danger of unfair prejudice, charges of a different nature should not be tried together on the same indictment.[193] There may be such a danger where unconnected sexual offences are tried together with a count of rape, and there is no cross-admissibility as between counts under s.101(1)(d) of the Criminal Justice Act 2003. The critical issue is frequently whether the nature of the evidence on one count is such that it is capable of being probative in relation to another, in the sense that it makes it more likely that the offence was committed or that the defendant committed it.[194] However, there is no hard and fast rule that a judge should

---

[191] [1976] A.C. 182.

[192] Lawton LJ stated, obiter, that, "had L been indicted as a principal offender, the case against him would have been clear beyond argument". This reasoning appears not to have been accepted by the Divisional Court in *DPP v K and C* [1997] 1 Cr. App. R. 36, at 42.

[193] *Muir* (1936) 26 Cr. App. R. 164, where a charge of indecent assault was so unconnected with a charge of rape that it could not have been given in evidence to support it. However, the position has been changed by the bad character regime in the Criminal Justice Act 2003. In many cases now unconnected allegations may be cross-admissible under s.101(1)(d) of that Act.

[194] See *Freeman* and *Crawford* [2008] EWCA Crim 1863.

order severance where there is no cross-admissibility.[195] For further discussion, see paras 10.04 and following (joinder and severence).

Substantially less serious offences involving different considerations   1.147
should not clutter up an indictment containing a count of rape.[196] Nor
should a count be included which adds nothing to the rape in that it is
necessarily part of the allegation. *R. v N(P)*[197] is a good example, involving
as it did a count of false imprisonment as well as rape. In reality, anyone
involved directly or indirectly in the rape of the victim was party to false
imprisonment, and the inclusion of a count to reflect that was an unnecessary
makeweight.

PARTIES TO THE OFFENCE

Only a male can commit the offence of rape as a principal. The Sexual   1.148
Offences Review did consider whether there was evidence that a woman
could force a man to penetrate her against his will. Whilst they found a little
anecdotal evidence, they did not discover sufficient to be convinced that this
was the equivalent of rape.[198] The Review was uneasy about extending the
definition of the offence to all forms of penetration. It felt that rape was
clearly understood by the public as an offence that was committed by men on
women and on men. Furthermore, it took the view that the offence of penile
penetration was of a particularly personal kind, carrying risks of pregnancy
and disease transmission, and should properly be treated separately from
other penetrative assaults. This led the Review to set aside in this context its
presumption of gender-neutrality as regards the perpetrator of offences and
to propose that the offence of rape be limited to penile penetration.

A woman who encourages or assists a man to penetrate another woman   1.149
knowing that the other woman does not consent may be convicted of aiding
and abetting rape[199] or of encouraging or assisting it contrary to ss.44–46 of
the Serious Crime Act 2007.[200] This is so notwithstanding that the man is
acquitted of rape on the ground that he may have reasonably believed that
the woman was consenting.[201]

[195] *Christou* [1996] 2 Cr. App. R. 360.
[196] *Thomas* (1949) 33 Cr. App. R. 74.
[197] [2010] EWCA Crim 941.
[198] *Setting the Boundaries* (2000), para.2.8.4. In her feature *A Tiger by the Tail: Sexual Offences in the CJPOA 1994*, *Archbold News*, Issue 2, March 1, 1995 p.5, Nicola Padfield described the fact that a woman cannot be convicted as a principal as an anomaly. She asks the rhetorical question: "Even if it is unlikely that a woman successfully rapes a man, why should this mean that the law itself is not gender neutral?"
[199] *Ram* (1893) 17 Cox C.C. 609; *Lord Baltimore's Case* (1768) 1 Black.W. 648. In *Lord Baltimore's Case* two women who were alleged to have forcibly lifted a woman into Lord Baltimore's bed were admitted to trial; all parties were acquitted at the next Assizes.
[200] Under these complex provisions, which were implemented on October 1, 2008, the defendant is liable as soon as he or she has performed an act capable of assisting or encouraging a potential offender. The offence is committed even if the potential offender does not go on and commit the anticipated offence. It is irrelevant that a woman cannot commit the offence as a principal. See further paras 1.411 and following, below.
[201] cf. *Cogan and Leak* [1975] 2 All E.R. 1059, discussed in para.1.145, above.

Boys under the age of 14

1.150   Section 1 of the Sexual Offences Act 1993 provides:

> "The presumption of the criminal law that a boy under the age of fourteen is incapable of sexual intercourse (whether natural or unnatural) is hereby abolished."

This provision did away with the common law presumption that boys under the age of 14 were incapable of sexual intercourse, whether vaginal or anal. It follows that boys under that age (but not those under the age of 10) can be convicted of a sexual offence involving penile penetration of the vagina, anus or mouth.[202] However, a conviction is not possible if the act of penetration occurred before the presumption was abolished on September 20, 1993.[203] But in such cases, evidence of penetration can be adduced and so the case may be dealt with as an indecent assault or, in appropriate cases, the evidence may be adduced as background evidence or, in appropriate cases, under s.101(1)(c) of the Criminal Justice Act 2003 as important explanatory evidence. A boy under 10 cannot commit an offence and so cannot commit or be procured to commit rape.[204]

1.151   At common law there was a rebuttable presumption that a child aged not less than 10 but under 14 was doli incapax, i.e. incapable of committing a crime. The presumption was rebutted only if the prosecution proved beyond reasonable doubt not only that the child committed the actus reus with appropriate mens rea, but also that he knew that the particular act was "seriously wrong" and not merely naughty or mischievous. This presumption was abolished by s.34 of the Crime and Disorder Act 1998 with effect from September 30, 1998. The intention was to put children aged 10 and above on the same footing as adults from the time of implementation of s.34. The doctrine of doli incapax has not survived s.34, although the section only expressly abolishes the presumption.[205] However, the presumption will still apply to pre-abolition historic abuse cases.[206]

---

[202] s.34 of the Crime and Disorder Act 1998 abolished the rebuttable presumption that a child aged between 10 and 14 was incapable of committing a criminal offence (the presumption of doli incapax): see para.1.151, below.

[203] cf. *R. v WCA*, Unreported, November 2003, following the argument advanced by Professor David Ormerod in *A Presumption of Intercourse*, *Archbold News*, Issue 1, February 3, 2003, p.8; *Fethney* [2010] EWCA Crim 3906.

[204] *DPP v K and C* [1997] 1 Cr. App. R. 36 at 42, but see commentary at [1997] Crim. L.R. 121, where it is argued it should make no difference whether there is a rebuttable or irrebuttable presumption that the child is doli incapax.

[205] *R. v JTB* [2009] UKHL 20, where the House of Lords rejected the argument that s.34 merely reversed the burden of proof rather than abolishing the concept of doli incapax.

[206] *R. v N (Andrew)* [2004] EWCA Crim 1236. For guidance as to the correct approach to doli incapax in respect of offences committed before September 30, 1998, see *CC (a Minor) v DPP* [1996] 1 Cr. App. R. 375; *C (a Minor) v DPP* [1996] 1 A.C. 1; Croft, T., *Rebutting the presumption of doli incapax* (1998) 62 *Journal of Criminal Law* at p.185. See also paras 30.12 and following, below.

The Court of Appeal has recently considered the two presumptions based   **1.152**
on age (that a boy under 14 was incapable of sexual intercourse and that a
child aged 10–14 was doli incapax) in three historic cases of rape. In
Fethney,[207] the Court observed that neither presumption had been abolished
retrospectively. If the act of penetration alleged had been committed before
September 20, 1993, but could not be shown to have been committed after
the appellant's fourteenth birthday, he could not be convicted of the offence.
With respect to doli incapax, a failure to direct as to the doctrine in this case
rendered convictions unsafe relating to conduct committed before September
30, 1998, when the appellant was aged between 10 and 14. In *R. v. J.OC*[208] a
lawyer in the Criminal Appeals Office noticed that one of 14 counts was a
rape upon the appellant's five-year-old sister, alleged to have taken place
when the appellant was aged 10 or 11. In light of the irrebuttable presumption, the conviction on that count had to be quashed. A similar situation
arose in *Bevan*,[209] where the Court of Appeal had no choice but to quash a
conviction for rape alleged to have been committed by the appellant when he
may have been aged under 14, thereby engaging the irrebuttable presumption
of penetrative incapacity. However, the Court held that other convictions
which did not involve penile penetration were safe. Although the jury should
have been directed that the rebuttable presumption of doli incapax applied,
a number of features of the evidence led the court to conclude that there was
no prospect that the jury would not have been convinced that the appellant
had known his actions were seriously wrong. The decision therefore shows
that, when there is a failure to direct as to the rebuttable presumption, the
Court of Appeal will look at the circumstances to see if it was inevitable that
the presumption would have been rebutted.

Victims of rape

Changes made to the definition of rape in 1994 enabled the offence to be   **1.153**
committed against another male as well as against a female.[210] This remains
the case under the 2003 Act. Section 5 of that Act creates a separate offence
of rape of a child under 13.[211] Absence of consent is not an element, so the
offence is committed by intentional penile penetration of the vagina, anus or
mouth of a child under the age of 13.

JURISDICTION

By virtue of s.72 of the 2003 Act, as amended,[212] it is an offence of rape for   **1.154**
a UK national to do an act in a country outside the UK which would

---

[207] [2010] EWCA Crim 3906.
[208] [2012] EWCA 2458.
[209] [2011] EWCA Crim 654.
[210] See s.142 of the Criminal Justice and Public Order Act 1994.
[211] See paras 3.29 and following, below.
[212] By the Criminal Justice and Immigration Act 2008 s.72, with effect from July 14, 2008.

constitute an offence of rape of a person under 18 if done in England and Wales or in Northern Ireland. One effect of the amendments, made in 2008, is that s.72 is no longer restricted to offences against children below the age of 16. In respect of non-consensual offences, such as rape, the new age limit is 18. Furthermore the amended provision deprives UK nationals of any defence based on lack of double criminality. This means that the fact that the overseas jurisdiction does not criminalise acts of non-consensual sex with a child aged 17 or under will not prevent a UK national being criminally liable in England and Wales for such acts. However, the double criminality requirement is retained in respect of the prosecution of UK residents and those who become UK residents or nationals after the doing of the relevant act. For the purposes of s.72 a "country" includes a territory and a "United Kingdom national" means a British citizen, a British overseas territories citizen, a British National (Overseas), a British Overseas citizen, a person who under the British Nationality Act 1981 is a British subject, or a British protected person within the meaning of that Act.[213] An act is taken to be an offence in the country in which it was done unless the defendant serves a notice putting the prosecution to proof on the point.[214]

"PENETRATES THE VAGINA, ANUS OR MOUTH"

1.155   The prosecution must establish penetration of the vagina, anus or mouth of another person by the defendant's penis. By virtue of s.79(9) of the Act, the "vagina" is not restricted to its strict medical anatomical meaning[215] and is to be interpreted as including the vulva (the outer end of the vagina or the external female genitals which include the labia majora, labia minora and vestibule of the vagina.) It also includes sexual organs, whether male or female, provided by modern surgical techniques.[216] It follows that penile penetration of a vagina surgically constructed through gender reassignment surgery is within the scope of the offence. This gives statutory confirmation to the ruling of Hooper J (as he then was) in *Matthews*,[217] that an artificially constructed vagina was included within the definition of rape in s.142 of the Criminal Justice and Public Order Act 1994. The gender of the victim is irrelevant.

1.156   The Sexual Offences Act 2003 does not address issues such as the extent of penetration required or whether there needs to be ejaculation. However, there can be no doubt that the common law in this area should be followed. The slightest penetration is sufficient. In respect of penetration of the vagina it is

---

[213] s.72(9).
[214] s.72(6)–(8).
[215] The medical definition of the vagina is the lowest part of the female genital tract, the muscular tube which has the cervix (neck of the womb) at its upper end and the hymen (or hymenal remnants) at its outer end. See para.21.30, below.
[216] s.79(3).
[217] Unreported, October 1996, Reading Crown Court. See also M. Hicks and G. Branston, *Transexual Rape—A Loophole Closed?* [1997] Crim. L.R. 565.

not necessary to show the hymen was ruptured.[218] Whether the defendant ejaculated or not is irrelevant.

A count relating to a single act that alleges that the defendant committed   1.157
rape by penetrating the complainant vaginally or anally is not duplicitous. The jury needs to be sure that one of the proscribed orifices has been penetrated. They do not need to be satisfied as to which. In *R. v K*[219] the trial judge allowed an amendment to the indictment so it alleged that the defendant had committed rape by penetrating the complainant (his six-year-old daughter) vaginally or anally. He then directed the jury that they could convict the defendant if they were sure he had penetrated either the vagina or the anus. It did not matter if they disagreed as to which was penetrated as long as they were all sure that one had been penetrated. The Court of Appeal dismissed the appeal on the basis there was no question of duplicity in the count that was left to the jury. The count related to one occasion and one act of penetration. The only doubt was whether the penetration was of the anus or the vagina, which was of no materiality. The defendant denied that the act had taken place at all, and so the possibility of doubt as to which orifice had been penetrated caused him no prejudice. The judge's direction could not be criticised.

Section 79(2) of the Act provides that penetration is a continuing act from   1.158
entry to withdrawal. This puts on a statutory footing the Privy Council's decision in *Kaitamaki v R.*[220] That decision was criticised by the late Professor Sir John Smith on the ground that, although rape is not an instantaneous act, penetration without consent is an essential part of the actus reus and this must be accompanied by the mens rea.[221] Section 79(2) puts the point beyond argument. It follows that a defendant can commit the offence of rape by "omission", in the sense that he becomes liable to conviction if upon acquiring the appropriate state of mind he does not withdraw immediately.

In *Cooper and Schaub*,[222] the Court of Appeal again emphasised that   1.159
penetration is a continuing act and that although the initial penetration may have been with consent, if the woman withdraws that consent and the man continues to penetrate her then he commits rape (the other elements being present). The appeal was allowed, however, on the ground that the question

---

[218] This follows from the wide legal definition of vagina as including the vulva. See also *R. v JF* [2002] EWCA Crim 2936 and *Hughes* (1841) 9 C. & P. 752; *Lines* (1844) 1 C. & K. 393. In *Lines* the victim's hymen had not been ruptured, but a venereal sore had developed upon it. Parke B ruled that if any part of the virile member of the defendant was within the *labia* of the *pudendum* of the victim, no matter how little, this would be sufficient to constitute penetration. See also *Allen (Henry)* (1839) 9 C. & P. 31; *M'Rue* (1838) 8 C. & P. 641.

[219] [2009] 1 Cr. App. R. 331. The Court of Appeal held that this was not a case for a *Brown* direction requiring the jury to be unanimous on the basis upon which they find the defendant guilty: see *Brown* (1984) 79 Cr. App. R. 115.

[220] [1985] A.C. 147.

[221] [1984] Crim. L.R. 565.

[222] [1994] Crim. L.R. 531. The trial judge unwisely answered the jury's question without consulting counsel.

whether consent had been withdrawn had not been canvassed before the jury, and so when the jury asked a question as to the law on the withdrawal of consent, the judge should have directed them to dismiss that matter from their minds.

HISTORY OF THE DEMISE OF THE MARITAL EXEMPTION

1.160 The traditional rule was that a man could not rape his wife, subject to certain exceptions where the law had placed (or recognised) some barrier between the parties. The rule derived from Hale, who wrote as follows in the 1650s, at a time when the only way a marriage could be dissolved was by death, and the only way a marriage could be avoided was by a private Act of Parliament:

> "But the husband cannot be guilty of a rape committed by himself upon his lawful wife, for by their mutual matrimonial consent and contract the wife hath given up herself in this kind unto her husband, which she cannot retract."[223]

1.161 The preservation of this rule up to the 1990s derived from the inclusion of the word "unlawful" before "sexual intercourse" in the definition of rape. In codifying that definition, s.1(1) of the Sexual Offences (Amendment) Act 1976 used the term "unlawful sexual intercourse" without providing any explanation as to when sexual intercourse was "unlawful". Accordingly this continued to be governed by the common law. In relation to other offences under the 1956 Act, "unlawful" was construed as meaning outside marriage.[224] This construction was accepted as applying also to rape.

The decision in *R. v R*

1.162 During the second half of the last century, the marital immunity from rape was gradually eroded by judicial decisions until, finally, the anachronism that a woman could not in law refuse sexual intercourse with her husband unless the law had placed some barrier between them was swept away. A unanimous House of Lords confirmed Owen J's decision in *R. v R*[225] that, if a woman refused her husband sexual intercourse, he could be guilty of rape if he nonetheless decided to proceed.[226] Shortly afterwards, s.142 of the Criminal Justice and Public Order Act 1994 removed the word "unlawful" from the then statutory definition of rape, thereby confirming that rape may occur within marriage.

---

[223] 1 Hale 629. For a detailed history of the abolition of the exemption in England and Wales, see Temkin, *Rape and Legal Process*, 2002, p.82.
[224] *Chapman* [1959] 1 Q.B. 100 (decided under s.19 of the 1956 Act).
[225] [1992] 1 A.C. 599.
[226] In its report in January 1992, the Law Commission recommended that legislation be introduced to confirm the removal of the marital exemption as a defence to the charge of rape: *Rape Within Marriage*, Law Com. No.205 (1992).

The justice of the decision in *R. v R* and its simplification of the law were   1.163
very welcome. If the House had sought to preserve the marital immunity, its
decision would have been greeted with a chorus of contempt. That said,
strictly speaking, the manner by which the House circumvented the wording
of s.1(1) of the Sexual Offences (Amendment) Act 1976 was dubious.[227]

The vital matter to be decided by the House was the meaning to be   1.164
attached to the word "unlawful" in s.1(1) of the 1976 Act. Lord Keith (who
gave the leading speech) began by looking at the supposed marital exemption
in the light of changing social, economic and cultural values:

> "Hale's proposition involves that by marriage a wife gives her irrevocable consent
> to sexual intercourse with her husband under all circumstances and irrespective
> of her state of health or how she happens to be feeling at the time. In modern
> times any reasonable person must regard that conception as quite unaccept-
> able."[228]

He then referred with approval to the reasoning of the High Court of
Justiciary in Scotland in *S v HM Advocate*[229] to justify his approach in
changing the common law. In that case, the Lord Justice-General, Lord
Emslie, delivering the judgment of the court, held that the fiction of implied
consent no longer had any useful purpose to serve in the law of rape in
Scotland, and there was no longer any justification for the husband's
immunity.

Having reviewed the English case law, Lord Keith went on to state: 1.165

> "The position then is that that part of Hale's proposition which asserts that a
> wife cannot retract the consent to sexual intercourse which she gives on marriage
> has been departed from in a series of decided cases. On grounds of principle there
> is no good reason why the whole proposition should not be held inapplicable in
> modern times. The only question is whether section 1(1) of the Act of 1976
> presents an insuperable obstacle to that sensible course. The argument is that
> 'unlawful' in the subsection means outside the bond of marriage. That is not the
> most natural meaning of the word which normally describes something which is
> contrary to some law or enactment or is done without some lawful justification
> or excuse. Certainly in modern times sexual intercourse outside marriage would
> not ordinarily be described as unlawful. If the subsection proceeds on the basis
> that a woman on marriage gives general consent to sexual intercourse, there can
> never be any question of intercourse with her by her husband being without her
> consent. There would thus be no point in enacting that only intercourse without
> consent outside marriage is to constitute rape."[230]

Lord Keith noted the decision of the Court of Criminal Appeal in *Chap-*   1.166
man,[231] where in the context of s.19 of the Sexual Offences Act 1956
(abduction of an unmarried girl under 18), the Court had reached the
conclusion that "unlawful" sexual intercourse meant intercourse which takes

---

[227] See M. Giles, *Judicial Law-Making in the Criminal Courts: the Case of Marital Rape* [1992]
Crim. L.R. 407.
[228] [1992] 1 A.C. 599, at 616.
[229] 1989 S.L.T. 469.
[230] [1992] 1 A.C. 599, at 621.
[231] [1959] 1 Q.B. 100.

place outside the bond of marriage. But Lord Keith took the view that there was a further important context to s.1(1) of the Act of 1976 as compared to the 1956 Act. This was the line of cases on the existence of exceptions to the marital exemption which were decided between the passing of the two Acts.[232] He held that an interpretation of "unlawful" in the 1976 Act as meaning "outside the bond of marriage" would indicate that the draftsman had intended, by implication, either to abolish the exceptions to the marital exemption or to put a significant gloss on the meaning of the word "unlawful".[233] He continued:

> "If the intention of Parliament was to abolish the exceptions it would have been expected to do so expressly, and it is in fact inconceivable that Parliament should have had such an intention. In order that the exceptions might be preserved, it would be necessary to construe 'unlawful' as meaning 'outside marriage or within marriage in a situation covered by one of the exceptions to the marital exemption'".[234]

Further:

> " . . . the gloss which the suggested construction would place on the word unlawfully would give it a meaning unique to the particular subsection, and if the mind of the draftsman had been directed to the existence of the exceptions he would surely have dealt with them specifically and not in such an oblique fashion."[235]

1.167 Lord Keith found further support for his contextual interpretation in Donovan J's acceptance in *Chapman*[236] that the word "unlawful" in s.5 of the Sexual Offences Act 1956 (unlawful sexual intercourse with a girl under 13) was surplusage because nobody under that age would be lawfully married.[237] He concluded:

> "The fact is that it is clearly unlawful to have sexual intercourse with any woman without her consent, and that the use of the word in the subsection adds nothing. In my opinion there are no rational grounds for putting the suggested gloss on the word, and it should be treated as being mere surplusage in this enactment, as it clearly fell to be in those referred to by Donovan J."

---

[232] *O'Brien* [1974] 3 All E.R. 663; *Steele* (1976) 65 Cr. App. R. 22; *Roberts* [1986] Crim. L.R. 188.

[233] cf. *Giles*, op. cit. n.228: "He sidesteps the analogous point that had the draftsman intended to abolish marital rape immunity it is likely that he would have made specific provision for that."

[234] [1992] 1 A.C. 599, at 622.

[235] ibid. The attractiveness of this argument was acknowledged by the late Professor J.C. Smith in his commentary at [1992] Crim. L.R. 209, although he points out that "unlawful" had probably acquired a limited meaning prior to *R. v R* which squared with the existing authorities.

[236] [1959] 1 Q.B. 100 at 102–103.

[237] Under Muslim law it is in fact possible for a child aged nine to be legally married and thus, strictly speaking, the word was not surplusage. See Keith Hodkinson, *Muslim Family Law* (London: Croom Helm 1987), p.92; also *Alhaji Mohamed v Knott* [1969] 1 Q.B. 1, referred to in para.4.17, above.

Retrospective effect of removal of marital immunity from rape

A husband can be guilty of raping his wife even if the sexual intercourse took   1.168
place before Owen J's ruling in *R. v R* on July 30, 1990, or the Court of
Appeal's decision in that case on March 14, 1991. Such a conviction would
not amount to a violation of art.7(1) ECHR, which provides that: "No one
shall be guilty of any criminal offence on account of any act or omission
which did not constitute a criminal offence under national or international
law at the time when it was committed." In the European Court of Human
Rights in *SW v UK, CR v UK*,[238] the applicants both maintained that the
general common law principle that a husband could not be found guilty of
rape of his wife, albeit subject to certain exceptions, was still effective on
September 18, 1990 and November 12, 1989 respectively, when they committed the acts which gave rise to the rape charges in *SW v UK* and the
charge of attempted rape in *CR v UK*. It was argued that *R. v R* had altered
the law retrospectively, and the applicants should be entitled under art.7(1) to
invoke immunity to escape conviction. The Strasbourg Court held that
art.7(1) could not be read as outlawing the gradual clarification of the rules
of criminal liability through judicial interpretation from case to case,
provided that the resultant development was consistent with the essence of
the offence and could reasonably be foreseen. The decisions of the Court of
Appeal and then the House of Lords did no more than continue a perceptible
line of case law dismantling the immunity of a husband from prosecution for
the rape of his wife. Furthermore, the evolution had reached a stage where
judicial recognition of the absence of immunity had become a reasonably
foreseeable development of the law. The Court of Appeal has since held that
a man may properly be convicted of raping his wife even though the offence
was committed over 20 years before the final demise of the marital exemption
in *R. v R*.[239]

ABSENCE OF CONSENT

MEANING OF "CONSENT"

The prosecution must prove that at the time of the penetration the person did   1.169
not consent to it.[240] Penile penetration of the vagina, anus or mouth and
absence of consent are the vital ingredients of the actus reus of the offence.
Use of force, although often present in rape, is not an essential ingredient.

---

[238] [1996] 21 E.H.R.R. 363. See also *Graham L.* [2003] EWCA Crim 1512.

[239] *Barry C.* [2004] EWCA Crim 292. The rape had occurred between 1967 and 1971. In his
historical analysis, Judge LJ (as he then was) noted that Hale's statement of principle was not
accepted by all the judges in *Clarence* (1888) 22 QBD 23, and that it would have been hard
pressed to withstand the approach of the Court of Appeal in *Jackson* [1891] 1 Q.B. 671, dealing
with the concept of a husband's supposed "dominion" over his wife.

[240] This must be read where appropriate together with s.79(2) of the Act which provides that
penetration is a continuing act from entry to withdrawal: see para.1.158, above.

Before the middle of the nineteenth century, judges would direct juries that rape was sexual intercourse against a woman's will by force, fear or fraud. After rape ceased to be a capital offence in 1841,[241] the definition of rape was widened to include cases where intercourse had taken place without the woman's consent even though there had been no force, fear or fraud. Non-consensual sexual intercourse with a woman when she had been rendered insensible by drink[242] and when she was asleep[243] were held to be rape.

Consent before the Sexual Offences Act 2003: Olugboja

1.170　Until the Sexual Offences Act 2003 there was no statutory definition of "consent" for the purposes of rape. The decision in *Olugboga*[244] represented the approach to absence of consent in rape. It left the parameters of absence of consent undefined, and placed the burden on the jury to decide whether consent was absent in any particular case by giving the word "consent" its ordinary meaning. The Court of Appeal in *Olugboja* did recognise that consent is not an entirely straightforward concept for a jury, covering as it does a wide spectrum of states of mind ranging from actual desire on the one hand to reluctant acquiescence on the other. Dunn LJ, delivering the judgment of the Court, stated that the issue of consent should not be left to the jury without some further direction:

> "What this should be will depend on the circumstances of each case ... [The jury] should be directed that consent, or the absence of it, is to be given its ordinary meaning and if need be, by way of example there is a difference between consent and submission; every consent involves a submission, but it by no means follows that a mere submission involves a consent.[245] In the majority of cases, where the allegation is that intercourse was by force or the fear of force, such a direction coupled with specific references to and comments on the evidence relevant to the absence of real consent will clearly suffice."

1.171　Dunn LJ recognised that the issue of consent may be much more intractable where the defendant confines himself to threatening something other than violence, but he failed to resolve the problem:[246]

> "In the less common type of case where intercourse takes place after threats not involving violence or the fear of it ... we think that an appropriate direction to a jury will have to be fuller. They should be directed to concentrate on the state of mind of the victim immediately before the act of sexual intercourse, having

---

[241] In 1841 the punishment was reduced to transportation overseas: see K.L. Koh, *Consent and Responsibility in Sexual Offences* [1968] Crim. L.R. 81.

[242] *Camplin* (1845) 1 Den. 89. This was the first instance of the wider interpretation of rape. Tindal CJ and Parke B were of the view that rape was ravishing a woman "where she did not consent" and not ravishing her "against her will".

[243] *Fletcher* (1859) Bell 63.

[244] [1981] 3 All E.R. 443.

[245] Citing *Day* (1841) 9 C. & P. 722 at 724; 173 All E.R. Rep. 1026 at 1027, per Coleridge J.

[246] [1981] 3 All E.R. 443 at 448–9.

regard to all the relevant circumstances, and in particular the events leading up to the act, and her reaction to them showing the impact upon her mind."

This approach meant that the jury had to decide whether a particular threat had such an impact on the victim that she did not truly consent. No attempt was made by the Court to categorise the forms of threat or pressure that could be capable of having this effect. Moral or economic pressure was unlikely to have been enough. However, the employer who threatened a female employee with dismissal unless she had intercourse with him could be convicted of rape if the jury were satisfied that there was an absence of consent.

Dunn LJ continued[247]:   1.172

> "In addition to the general direction about consent which we have outlined, the jury will probably be helped in such cases by being reminded that in this context consent does comprehend the wide spectrum of states of mind to which we earlier referred and that the dividing line in such circumstances between real consent on the one hand and mere submission on the other may not be easy to draw. Where it is to be drawn in a given case is for the jury to decide, applying their combined good sense, experience and knowledge of human nature and modern behaviour to all the relevant facts of that case."

In *McAllister*,[248] a case of indecent assault, the jury sent the trial judge a note   1.173
asking about the difference between submission and consent. Counsel for the appellant persuaded the judge not to give the following dictionary definitions to the jury: "to submit . . . to give way, resign oneself, yield, cease or abstain from resistance" contrasted with "to consent . . . to express willingness, give permission, agree." On appeal, the Court of Appeal held that the judge could not have been faulted if he had given the jury the proposed definitions. It also said that the jury would not necessarily have been helped by a reference to reluctant acquiescence and that the focus of inquiry in all such cases is the sexual autonomy of the complainant.

Criticisms of Olugboja

The approach in *Olugboja* provoked fierce academic criticism. For instance,   1.174
Professor Glanville Williams wrote[249]:

> "The court assumes that fear can vitiate consent in rape even though it is not fear of violence (or presumably, of force short of violence); and yet the court makes no effort to specify the sort of fear or threat that has this effect . . . Questions of policy are involved in deciding what pressures are sufficient to nullify consent, and guidance must be given by rules of law . . . This is one more manifestation of the deplorable tendency of the criminal courts to leave important questions of legal policy to the jury."

---

[247] [1981] 3 All E.R. 443 at 449.
[248] [1997] Crim. L.R. 233.
[249] Glanville Williams, *Textbook of Criminal Law*, 2nd edn (London: Stevens & Sons Ltd, 1983), p.551, para.25.3.

1.175 The difficult relationship between "consent" and "submission" has been highlighted in Smith and Hogan[250]:

> "Under the 1956 Act, in *Olugboja* the court placed considerable emphasis on the difference between consent and submission, but never fully identified what the distinction was."

1.176 The Sexual Offences Review identified as a problem that the full legal meaning of consent was not clearly understood. The absence of a definition of such a key concept generated uncertainty.[251] In particular, the Review concluded that rape and sexual assault are primarily crimes against the sexual autonomy of others, and that consent is the essential issue in that the offences are essentially those of violating another person's freedom to withhold sexual contact. It stressed that[252]:

> "[I]n this most private and difficult area of sexual relationships the law should be as clear as possible so that the boundaries of what is acceptable, and of criminally culpable behaviour are all well understood."

1.177 The Review forcefully rejected the *Olugboja* approach[253]:

> "The law sets the ground rules of what is and is not criminal behaviour, and all citizens need to know and understand what these are. This is particularly important because consent to sexual activity is so much part of a private relationship where verbal and non-verbal messages can be mistaken and where assumptions about what is and is not appropriate can lead to significant misunderstanding and, in extreme cases, to forced and unwelcome sex."

It went on to expose the inadequacy of simply relying on the continuing development of the common law to meet society's needs:[254]

> "... that process can lead to uncertainty, as in the case of *Olugboja*. In an area of human behaviour where there are debates within society about what is and is not appropriate, it is more than ever important that the law is clear and well understood, particularly about what behaviour is criminal."

1.178 The Review recommended that the meaning of "consent" be clarified in statute, which would enable judges to explain what the law said and juries to understand just what is meant by consent. This would also enable Parliament to consider and recommend what should and should not form acceptable standards of behaviour in a modern society. The Review stressed[255]:

> "In today's world it is important to recognise that sexual partners are each responsible for their own actions and that there should be parity of status. In defining consent we are not seeking to *change* its meaning, rather to clarify the law so it is clearly understood."

---

[250] David Ormerod QC and Karl Laird, *Smith and Hogan's Criminal Law*, 14th edn (Oxford: OUP, 2015), pp.822. The discussion of the case echoes criticisms to be found in earlier editions.
[251] *Setting the Boundaries*, 2000, para.2.3.
[252] *Setting the Boundaries*, 2000, from para.2.7.2.
[253] *Setting the Boundaries*, 2000, para.2.10.
[254] *Setting the Boundaries*, 2000, para.2.10.1.
[255] *Setting the Boundaries*, 2000, para.2.10.3.

The 2003 Act definition of consent

Section 74 of the 2003 Act defines consent for the purposes of rape and the   **1.179**
other offences in Pt 1 of the Act, to the extent that it provides:

> "For the purposes of this Part, a person consents if he agrees by choice, and has
> the freedom and capacity to make that choice."

This follows the recommendation of the Sexual Offences Review, which
emphasised that "any free agreement would necessarily be voluntary and
genuine".[256] The Review felt that the use of "free agreement" to define
consent would assist in making it clear that absence of protest, resistance or
injury does not necessarily mean that the complainant consented. It also
serves to underline the fact that a complainant who simply freezes but utters
no protest and offers no physical resistance may nevertheless not be
consenting. The definition in s.74 applies for the purposes of the whole of Pt
1 of the Act, including the non-consensual offences in ss.1–4 of rape, assault
by penetration, sexual assault and causing a person to engage in sexual
activity without consent. This general definition of consent is supplemented
by ss.75 and 76 of the Act which set out respectively evidential and conclusive
presumptions: see paras 1.263 and following, and 1.310 and following,
below.

The Review noted that the Oxford dictionary defines the verb "to consent"   **1.180**
as "to acquiesce, or agree" and the noun "consent" as "voluntary agreement,
compliance or permission". It recognised that these definitions cover a range
of behaviour from whole-hearted enthusiastic agreement to reluctant acquiescence, but that in this context the core element is that there is an agreement
between two people to engage in sex:

> "People have devised a complex set of messages to convey agreement and lack of
> it—agreement is not necessarily verbal, but it must be understood by both
> parties. Each must respect the right of the other to say 'no'—and mean it."

The Law Commission had suggested "subsisting free and genuine agreement". This was rejected by the Review as being too complex and as
introducing an unnecessary semi-contractual complication. It recommended
a definition based on "free agreement" because of its simplicity and clarity
and the fact that it included all the necessary ingredients.

The relevant time for the purposes of determining consent

The relevant time is the time of penetration, and any consent at that time   **1.181**
must relate to penetration. To borrow the pellucid words of Baroness Hale in
Cooper[257] delivered in the context of the potentially fluctuating capacity of
mentally disordered complainants:

---

[256] *Setting the Boundaries,* 2000, para.2.10.5.
[257] [2010] 1 Cr. App. R. 7 at [27].

"My Lords, it is difficult to think of an activity which is more person and situation specific than sexual relations. One does not consent to sex in general. One consents to this act of sex with this person at this time and in this place."

Whilst these observations may appear self-evident, they apply to all sexual activity and are worthy of emphasis, as in some cases there is a risk of undue focus being placed upon earlier conduct rather than the complainant's state of mind at the critical time. For instance, an assumption that earlier disinhibited and flirtatious behaviour by a complainant means that the complainant would be prepared to engage in later penetrative sexual activity is ill-founded.

1.182 The Court of Appeal has yet to tackle the problem of a pre-arranged sober agreement to have sex followed by the complainant losing consciousness. Would this be an exception to the normal rule that the relevant time for the purposes of determining consent is the time of the sexual activity? The Supreme Court of Canada in *HM Queen v JA and Attorney General of Canada and Women's Legal Education and Action Fund*[258] had to resolve the issue of whether a person can lawfully perform sexual acts on an unconscious person if the person consented to those acts in advance of being rendered unconscious. In that case, the complainant had consciously agreed to engage in a sexual practice involving transitory unconsciousness (erotic asphyxiation), and lost consciousness before JA inserted a dildo into her anus. The Supreme Court decided that Parliament had defined consent in a way that required the complainant be conscious throughout the sexual activity in question; the definition did not extend to advance consent to sexual acts committed while the complainant was unconscious. The legislation required ongoing, conscious consent to ensure that women and men are not the victims of sexual exploitation, and that individuals engaging in sexual activity are capable of asking their partners to stop at any point.

1.183 There are significant differences between the definitions of consent in the Canadian Criminal Code, where it is limited by stipulated circumstances, and in s.74 of the 2003 Act. However, under both, consent for this purpose is actual subjective consent in the mind of the complainant at the time of the sexual activity in question.[259] We therefore consider it likely that the courts in this jurisdiction would interpret the meaning of consent in the same way as the Canadian Supreme Court. This would be in line with the approach taken by Baroness Hale in *R. v C*,[260] admittedly in the different context of the potentially fluctuating capacity of mentally disordered complainants. The necessity for the prosecution to prove that the defendant did not reasonably believe that the complainant was consenting will ensure that no injustice arises.

---

[258] [2011] 2 S.C.R. 440.
[259] *Criminal Code*, s.273; *Ewanchuk* [1999] 1 S.C.R. 330.
[260] [2009] UKHL 42 at [27].

Consent to a particular sexual activity

Similarly, the existence of consent to some form of sexual activity does not   1.184
necessarily mean that there is a later consent to penetration. Nor does it
necessarily follow that consent to vaginal penetration is consent to anal or
oral penetration. A person may withdraw consent at any time and is entitled
to exercise a free choice as to how far he or she will go, and will not go, at
the time of the particular sexual activity in question.[261]

Complainant's evidence as to absence of consent

Whilst, in most cases, evidence to establish absence of consent will, at least in   1.185
part, come from the complainant, it is not necessarily essential for the
prosecution to call overt evidence from the complainant to the effect that she
or he did not consent. In *Malone*[262] Roche LJ, when considering a non-
exhaustive list of different and diverse circumstances which might establish
lack of consent under the law predating the Sexual Offences Act 2003,
observed that there would be cases where there may be evidence that by
reason of age and lack of understanding due to mental disorder the
complainant did not give consent. The logical extension of this would be
cases where there is evidence to suggest that the victim has been successfully
groomed for sexual exploitation and may have had a limited or distorted
appreciation of his or her role in the sexual relations and the true nature of
what occurred.[263] Furthermore, many complainants, particularly the young
and vulnerable, may have had an understanding of the meaning of consent
wholly inconsistent with the legal definition in s.74. For instance, there are
complainants who believe that a failure to say "no" or to protest will mean
they were consenting at the time. As Roche LJ stated in *Malone*:

> "[These illustrations] suffice to demonstrate that it is not the law that the
> prosecution in order to obtain a conviction for rape have to show that the
> complainant was either incapable of saying no or putting up some physical
> resistance or did say no or put up some physical resistance."

What are the boundaries of "free agreement"?

In *Protecting the Public*, the Government stated its intention that there   1.186
should be a clear and unambiguous statutory definition of consent.[264]
Despite this, s.74 is not a model of tight drafting. Whilst the use of the phrase
"freedom . . . to make that choice" signifies that "consent" cannot be

---

[261] See illustration of an appropriate direction in the *Crown Court Compendium*, Pt 1, Ch.20,
Direction 10 (see Appendix G, below).
[262] (1998) 2 Cr App R 447 at 457G.
[263] *Ali (Yasir)* [2015] EWCA Crim 1279; [2015] 2 Cr. App. R. 33 at [56]. See also discussion
in paras 1.192 and following, below, of how grooming for sexual exploitation may affect a
complainant's perception of their own actions.
[264] Home Office, *Protecting the Public* (HMSO, 2002), Cm 5668, para.30.

obtained by duress,[265] the parameters of "freedom" are not clear.[266] It must follow that to have freedom to make a choice a person must be free from physical pressure, but the definition does not address the issue of whether absence of economic, cultural or even religious freedom will be sufficient to vitiate consent.

1.187   Since consent involves free agreement by choice, simply to comply or to submit is not necessarily to consent. Consent must be freely given. The definition therefore serves to emphasise the focus upon the complainant's autonomy. Section 74 certainly gives juries more guidance than they gained from the *Olugboja* approach. Further, developments since the implementation of the 2003 Act[267] mean that juries now receive significantly greater assistance from judges as to how they should approach the issue of consent, with particular stress on alerting the jury to the danger of assumptions. In particular[268]:

> "Judges have, as a result of their own experience, in recent years adopted the course of cautioning juries against applying stereotypical images of how an alleged victim or an alleged perpetrator of a sexual offence ought to have behaved at the time, or ought to appear while giving evidence, and to judge the evidence on its intrinsic merits. This is not to invite juries to suspend their own judgement but to approach the evidence without prejudice."

1.188   However, the concept of "free agreement" remains capable of a wide interpretation and ultimately it will be for juries to decide its boundaries. For instance, whilst an evidential presumption arises in respect of a complainant intoxicated to a level of unconsciousness, or where drugs or alcohol have been administered surreptitiously without the complainant's knowledge,[269] the Act provides no specific guidance in respect of those who may have been heavily but voluntarily intoxicated. However, arguably this is a justifiable omission as capacity is an integral part of the definition of consent. If through drink (or for any other reason), a complainant has temporarily lost her capacity to choose whether to have intercourse on the relevant occasion,

---

[265] Law Commission, *Consent in Sex Offences* (HMSO, 2000), para.2.10.

[266] In their article *The Sexual Offences Act 2003 (1): Rape, Sexual Assaults and the Problems of Consent* [2004] Crim. L.R. 328 at p.336, Professors Jennifer Temkin and Andrew Ashworth make the point that "freedom" and "choice" are ideas which raise philosophical issues of such complexity as to be ill-suited to the needs of criminal justice. For strong criticism by David Ormerod QC and Karl Laird of the use of the word "freedom" in defining the crucial element of such serious offences, see *Smith and Hogan's Criminal Law*, 14th edn (Oxford: OUP, 2015), p.822. They submit that "freedom" is too loose a word. It is a term which is heavily context-dependent and always implies "freedom from something."

[267] See *Bree* [2007] EWCA Crim 804, where the trial judge was criticised for simply giving the jury a mere recital of the definition of consent; *Doody* [2008] EWCA Crim 2557, where the Court of Appeal approved balanced judicial comment in areas which are well-established.

[268] This passage from the *Crown Court Bench Book* (2010), Ch.17, p.353, was endorsed by the Court of Appeal in *Miller* [2010] EWCA Crim 1578. The 2010 Bench Book has now been replaced by the *Crown Court Compendium* 2016, but the passage is repeated in Pt 1, Ch.20.1, Sexual offences. See Appendix G, below, and also Appendix H (draft direction in multiple defendant cases). *Hysa* [2007] EWCA Crim 2056 is an excellent example of these principles in operation.

[269] See paras 1.243 and following, below.

she is not consenting. As Sir Igor Judge P (as he then was) said in *Bree*,[270] some areas of human behaviour remain inapt for legislative structures.

What degree of coercion and/or abuse of position, power or authority has   1.189 to be exercised upon a person's mind before he or she is not agreeing by choice with the freedom to make that choice? This is a matter of fact for the jury to resolve. Is a penniless employee, who is threatened with the sack by her employer unless she grants him sexual favours, giving her free agreement if she grants those favours? The availability to a complainant of alternative courses of action may be highly relevant. In situations where the complainant complies out of fear of the consequences of refusal, with no alternative course available, there is likely to be no free agreement. In contrast, an employee who fears discrimination if she does not comply with her employer's wishes has alternative courses of action available.

Context is all-important when considering whether an apparent consent   1.190 was in fact a genuine consent. Key factors can be the condition of the complainant as a result of the way he or she was treated at the time and/or in the past. For instance, there will be cases where there was no free agreement by a vulnerable complainant because of psychological coercion. In *Kirk and Kirk*,[271] a vulnerable and destitute 14-year-old girl submitted to sexual intercourse with the appellant for money in order that she could buy food. The appellant (and his brother) had abused her in the past. A rape conviction (under the 1956 Act) was upheld by the Court of Appeal even though there was no evidence of pressure, threats or deception by the appellant. Clearly, the result would have been the same had the charge been under the 2003 Act. In distilling the issues for the jury, the trial judge explained that the prosecution case was that the appellant had taken advantage of a hungry and vulnerable child whom he knew had been abused by his brother and to a lesser extent himself, which meant that she was submitting because her will was overcome by hunger and desperation, and that did not represent a true consent. The judge summarised the defence case, making it clear that "his defence is that sexual intercourse with this grubby and smelly girl was all lies". Jo Miles has noted[272] that *Kirk and Kirk* is of particular interest in that it provides an unusual example of a problem often discussed by textbook writers, namely a rape conviction where there was no evidence of threat, pressure or deception. She argues that it is perhaps debatable whether the case could properly have been left to the jury if there had been no prior history of abuse between the parties, which must have left the complainant in a psychologically vulnerable state. The decision has been strongly criticised elsewhere.[273] However, where the prior history of abuse left

---

[270] [2007] EWCA Crim 804.

[271] [2008] EWCA Crim 434.

[272] Jo Miles, *Sexual offences: consent, capacity and children*, *Archbold News*, Issue 10, December 5, 2008.

[273] James Richardson in *Criminal Law Week*, Issue 46, December 15, 2008.

the complainant in a psychologically vulnerable state, surely "free agreement" was an issue for the jury.

1.191   *C v R.*[274] provides a further strong example of the importance of context when considering evidence of apparent consent. The appellant was charged with 18 offences relating to the sexual abuse of his step-daughter over a period of about 20 years, from when she was five until she was 25. His defence was there had been no sexual activity of any kind between them before she was 16, and that thereafter there was a sexual relationship between them in which all the sexual activity was entirely consensual. There was a substantial body of evidence available in respect of the later counts (relating to the period after the complainant reached 16) which tended to show apparent consent. This included photographs of the complainant posing naked and, by her smile and demeanour, appearing to indicate that she was willing for the appellant to take these photographs of her. A video film was available which showed her apparently performing oral sex on the appellant. There were intimate text messages using pet names and uninhibited sexually explicit language. The appellant's counsel submitted that there was evidence that during the later period the appellant did not oblige her to participate in sexual activity if she was reluctant. The trial judge directed the jury that they could only proceed to consider their verdicts on the later counts if they were sure of earlier sexual abuse. The convictions were upheld on appeal. The Court of Appeal, in a judgment delivered by Lord Judge CJ, held that the reality of the case could not be understood without reference to the long years of the complainant's childhood during which she was the victim of repeated sexual abuse by the appellant. The appellant was domineering, aggressive and controlling. The evidence of prolonged grooming and potential corruption of the complainant when she was a child provided the context in which the evidence of her apparent consent after she had grown up should be examined and assessed. Properly analysed, the evidence of apparent consent did not undermine the credibility of the complainant's evidence that she had never consented. Once the jury were satisfied that sexual activity of the type alleged had occurred when the complainant was a child, and that it impacted on and reflected the appellant's dominance and control over the complainant, it was open to them to conclude that the evidence of apparent consent when the complainant was no longer a child was indeed apparent, not real, and that the appellant was well aware that in reality she was not consenting.

Grooming and consent

1.192   Evidence of grooming may be an important part of the overall context and will be highly relevant to the issue as to whether there was a genuine consent. Grooming may take a variety of different forms. The classic cases of

[274] [2012] EWCA Crim 2034.

grooming tend to involve the manipulation of an individual, often a teenage girl, so as to achieve and/or obtain opportunities for sexual exploitation of that individual. It can manifest itself in incremental steps such as providing (i) time, attention and apparent friendship, sometimes over the internet; (ii) gifts; (iii) alcohol; and (iv) drugs. It may evolve into violence and threats of violence to ensure the sexual objective. If sex is obtained by violence or the threat of violence, clearly there is no genuine consent. However, there will be cases where some or all of these steps have been taken with a view to obtaining sex, but there has been no resort to violence or the threat of violence. Grooming behaviour does not have to be, and frequently is not, coercive. It is often rather more insidious and subtle[275] involving using an opportunity for contact in a way which opens the door to sexual offending. It involves trying to obtain the confidence of the intended victim and to break down their inhibitions.[276] The essence of this sort of conduct has been described as involving, to a greater or lesser degree, elements of manipulation and control, with the offender treating the victim as an object for his own self-gratification.[277]

Whilst evidence of grooming will not necessarily establish absence of **1.193** consent, in cases where it is practised upon a complainant who is immature and vulnerable, it may well do so. This was recognised by Elias LJ in *Robinson*,[278] a case involving the grooming of a teenager by her then stepfather. In the course of his judgment, Elias LJ made some significant observations about grooming, which are likely to be helpful in respect of other young complainants, including those older than the complainant in *Robinson*, where grooming involves providing alcohol and drugs to a targeted victim[279]:

> "Grooming is not a term of art, but it suggests cynical and manipulative behaviour designed to achieve a particular sexual objective. Not all relationships with underage children can fairly be characterised as involving grooming, although many will. But even where they can, the fact of grooming plainly does not vitiate consent. Many a seducer achieves his objectives with the liberal and cynical employment of gifts, insincere compliments and false promises. But such manipulative and deceitful methods could not be relied upon to establish a lack of consent whenever the seduction was successful. The situation will often be no different where the complainant is under age. But where the exploitation is of a girl who is of an age where she does not, or may not, have the capacity to understand the full significance of what she is doing, and, in particular, where, as here, there was evidence of acquiescence or acceptance rather than positive consent, we think that, as the judge found, it would be open to the jury to conclude that the complainant, perhaps out of embarrassment or some other reason, had in reality unwillingly gone along with the acts which she did not in fact wish to engage in."

[275] [2015] EWCA Crim 1375 at paras [12]ff per Treacy LJ.
[276] *R. v HG* [2010] EWCA Crim 1693, at [16].
[277] *Harris* [2014] EWCA Crim 2873 at [20] per Cox J.
[278] [2011] EWCA Crim 916 at [21]. For a fuller discussion of the facts, see paras 1.200 and following, below.
[279] At [22].

1.194   In *Ali (Yasir)*,[280] the Court of Appeal went on to consider the position when vulnerable people are groomed for sexual exploitation, in a case where the jury had been given directions on how to approach consent based to a significant extent on the observations of Elias LJ in *Robinson*. The case involved the targeting of young girls whom the defendants had befriended and groomed for sexual purposes. The prosecution alleged that the girls were selected because of their circumstances, including such factors as their ages, troubled backgrounds, and humdrum lives which made them susceptible to the advances of older males, who plied them with alcohol, flattered them, drove them to various out-of-the-way locations and took them to "parties" at hotels. At the core of the prosecution's case was the allegation that the victims became sexually compliant, and that any apparent consent on their part was not genuine or real. The defence contended that there was clear evidence of consent, and that no reasonable jury could conclude that the complainant had not consented, still less that the defendant did not reasonably believe she consented. The thrust of the defence submission was that the prosecution impermissibly invited the jury to ignore the evidence of the alleged victims, and to substitute their own moral judgment about the sexual relations that had occurred. For example, a complainant such as SS (see below) did not at any stage assert she had not consented. Fulford LJ observed that, in these circumstances, compliance can mask the lack of true consent on the part of the victim. He continued:

> " . . . Although, as Elias LJ observed [in *Robinson*], grooming does not necessarily vitiate consent, it starkly raises the possibility that a vulnerable or immature individual may have been placed in a position in which he or she is led merely to acquiesce rather than to give proper and real consent. One of the consequences of grooming is that it has a tendency to limit or subvert the alleged victim's capacity to make free decisions, and it creates the risk that he or she simply submitted because of the environment of dependency created by those responsible for treating the alleged victim in this way. Indeed, the individual may have been manipulated to the extent that he or she is unaware of, or confused about, the distinction between acquiescence and genuine agreement at the time the incident occurred."

1.195   Fulford LJ summarised the position by explaining that in a case in which a vulnerable or immature individual has allegedly been groomed by the defendant, the question of whether real or proper consent was given will usually be for the jury unless the evidence clearly indicates that proper consent was given. He explained that it is particularly important in cases in which vulnerable people are involved that the admissible evidence is considered in the round. Cases should not be withdrawn from the jury because the judge is led artificially to focus on limited areas of evidence.

1.196   This approach is well illustrated by the trial judge's analysis of the evidence in respect of the allegation of the rape of SS. She gave evidence which, at face value, appeared to indicate she consented.

---

[280] [2015] EWCA Crim 1279.

"The first time there was sex, she said, was in about March. She remembered losing her virginity to him. She was in town, and had been at a friend's birthday party. She had been drinking, and he picked her up. They parked near to the Ramada. He came to her on the seat. They had planned to have sex. He was like 'When are we going to have sex?' And she had said 'Well, tonight.' And that was when they had planned to meet up after the party. She was fine with it, but nervous as it was her first time. It was a mutual thing. She did not feel under any pressure, and she said a condom was used. She was on the passenger seat and he was on top of her, and he had put his penis in her vagina.

As to how she felt afterwards, she said she honestly could not remember. She was quite drunk. She had been drinking vodka. She used to drink quite a bit. And she put herself at six or seven in terms of a scale out of ten. She could remember what was going on. It hurt as it was the first time. He dropped her off home about ten minutes later. He knew it was her first time. He had the condom."

Although SS described having "fallen" for the appellant and said that she did **1.197** not feel under pressure to have sex (the appellant sulked rather than forcing himself on her), she gave the following description of their contact, as summarised by the judge:

"She did not want to say no to him. When she was asked why not, she said she did not know. 'I just wanted to please him. And I thought if I weren't going to give it he'd probably go and find it elsewhere.'

Sex then took place every time she saw him. He would make the first move, but she was fine about that. There was a time when she did not want it, he got into a mood about it, and just dropped her off. That made her feel angry, as it felt like he just wanted sex.

They were together for about nine months. They split in October 2010 just after her 16th birthday. He said that he did not want to be with her any more, and a couple of weeks later he was with someone else.

She said her relationship with Yas was not a nice relationship. Things started to change, and he would call her a retard and everything and it felt like he only wanted sex. But she did not want to say anything as she did not want to lose him. She told him she loved him, and he said he didn't love her. He said he really liked her, but love was a strong word. She was upset, but she didn't want to be with him, and he had not ever forced sex on her.

She now regretted what had happened and she knew it was wrong. At the time, it did not feel wrong. Looking back, she thinks it is wrong, as he knew how old she was and he knew it was against the law."

It was contended on behalf of the appellant that, on the basis of her age, **1.198** there was no evidence that SS was "immature", since she was 15 at the relevant time. The decision to embark on a sexual relationship was mutual, having been agreed in advance, and there was a lack of evidence of grooming, as demonstrated by their habit of driving around Peterborough drinking alcohol.

However, the Court of Appeal said that her evidence needed to be viewed **1.199** in the context of her account of meeting the appellant, the way he treated her, how often they met, her consumption of alcohol, and the particular events that led to sex on the first occasion. In the Court's view it was for the jury to assess SS's suggested immaturity, the extent to which she was groomed by the appellant and the other defendants and the effect of the consumption by her of a considerable quantity of alcohol at the time of these events, and whether these and other factors materially had an impact on her ability truly to agree to what occurred. The Court acknowledged that the appellant had a potentially powerful argument that SS had participated in the planning of this event, but held that single factor was not determinative of the issue. It was one of the competing considerations that the jury needed to weigh when deciding whether there had been a proper consent. This was a complex factual situation leading to credible competing submissions as to whether there had been a true consent.

1.200 The facts of *Robinson*[281] provide a further illustration of the appropriate way to approach consent where there is evidence of grooming. The appellant was charged with rape and other sexual offences allegedly committed against the daughter of his former partner in the 1990s. The appellant had formed a relationship with the complainant's mother following the breakdown of her marriage. He formed a particularly close relationship with the complainant, ZK. She would visit him at his flat and play computer games when she was 11 or 12. She referred to a particular occasion when she got into bed with the appellant and her mother and he touched her legs under the cover. He would kiss and stroke her leg when they were in the car together. He showed her pornographic films on television when she was at his flat. Gradually this developed into a fuller sexual relationship and they had sexual intercourse, first when she was 12, and thereafter the relationship continued for some three years. The appellant denied that anything untoward had occurred or that there was anything inappropriate in the relationship.

1.201 The trial judge rejected an application that there was insufficient evidence for the rape charges to be left to the jury because the evidence suggested that the complainant had been a willing participant. In his ruling, the judge referred to passages in the complainant's ABE interview. The complainant had said that she did not initiate sexual intercourse. During the act she felt detached from it. When asked whether she had said "no" to having sex with the appellant, she said:

> "I remember sort of half-heartedly saying no, and then—especially to things I didn't want to do, or at first just being very like 'no, I don't think so'. And it was, I remember, it was being him definitely persuading me a lot, but not, maybe not really forcibly, just like 'oh, come on, what are you worried about?' and almost talking me through it, like 'why are you so nervous? Why don't you want me to do this?'"

There were passages in the ABE interview that clearly demonstrated that the child was infatuated with the appellant, that she thought he had fallen in love with her, and that she wanted to be with him, at least at various stages during the period of their relationship. The trial judge observed that the interviewing

---

[281] [2011] EWCA Crim 916.

officers had not in terms asked the complainant whether she had consented. Whilst she was being cross-examined, he asked her about the first occasion of sexual intercourse when she was 12. She answered:

> "I did not ask the defendant not to, I did not move to stop him. He reassured me it was okay. I did not make it plain to him I did not want to. There was no occasion when I said that I didn't want him to do it, at least not before I met T [a boyfriend with whom she started a relationship when aged 15]."

The judge said that it would be open to the jury on these facts to infer that the complainant did not genuinely consent, or, put the other way, that what happened was mere submission on her part, having been comprehensively groomed by the appellant: **1.202**

> "The defendant spent a great deal of time with her, he played with her, watched films with her, and enjoyed her company, and indeed continually praised her, said how pretty she was and clever she was, and indeed how much he loved her. They held hands, he sat her on his lap, stroked her hair and so on. Clear evidence of grooming."

On appeal, counsel for the appellant submitted that there was no evidence of submission of the kind falling within the situations described by Roche LJ in *Malone*,[282] referred to in para.1.185, above. He accepted that the fact that the complainant was a 12-year-old at the time of the first act of sexual intercourse was potentially relevant when considering whether there was true consent. However, here the judge had found on the evidence that she was a mature 12-year-old, who plainly understood the nature of the sexual act and was capable of making up her own mind, and so the only proper inference was that she had full capacity. She never expressed any lack of enthusiasm for sex and did not at any stage say she was an unwilling participant. Counsel for the appellant criticised the judge for putting some weight in his ruling on his finding that the girl may have been groomed by the appellant. He submitted that this was not necessarily pertinent to the question of consent at all. He asked rhetorically whether, if she positively asserted that she had consented, the issue of consent could have been left to the jury because she was being groomed.   **1.203**

Elias LJ, giving the judgment of the Court of Appeal, said that some 12-year-olds plainly do not have the capacity to consent, and whilst the complainant did not fall into that category, there was evidence on which a jury was entitled to find that her immaturity, coupled with the evidence of acquiescence rather than enthusiastic consent, particularly in the context of what could be perceived as grooming, meant there was no proper consent. Dismissing the appeal, he stated that the trial judge had taken the only sensible view that could be taken.   **1.204**

---

[282] [1998] 2 Cr. App. R. 447.

Deceptions falling short of deceptions as to the nature or purpose of the act: does s.76 limit the definition of consent in s.74?

1.205   Section 76 of the 2003 Act, discussed in paras 1.310 and following, below, identifies two cases where it will be conclusively presumed that the complainant was not consenting and the defendant did not reasonably believe he or she was consenting. By s.76(2) the circumstances are that: (a) the defendant intentionally deceived the complainant as to the nature or purpose of the relevant act; or (b) the defendant intentionally induced the complainant to consent as to the relevant act by impersonating a person known personally to the complainant.

1.206   Jo Miles had argued[283] that the basic definition of consent in s.74 must be read subject to s.76, which identifies two cases in which it will be conclusively presumed that the complainant was not consenting and the defendant did not reasonably believe she was consenting. However, it is now clear that s.76 goes no further than establishing that lesser deceptions, i.e. those falling outside the ambit of the section, do not automatically vitiate consent.

1.207   The Miles interpretation, in limiting the ambit of the general definition of consent in s.74, exaggerates the scope of s.76. Section 76, which in many ways replicates the common law, simply identifies the relatively rare situations in which the conclusive presumptions arise. It cannot found a principle that a "but for" mistake without more can never vitiate consent. The whole purpose of the definition in s.74 is to focus upon the autonomy of the complainant. The presumptions were designed to buttress s.74, not to limit it. In *Jheeta*,[284] Sir Igor Judge P, as he then was, acknowledged that in most cases, the absence of consent and the appropriate state of the defendant's mind will be proved without reference to evidential or conclusive presumptions. When they do apply, the presumptions are directed to the process of proving the absence of consent to whichever sexual act is alleged. They are concerned with proof of consent rather than its definition. It follows that whether there was free agreement in a particular case is fact specific. In *Jheeta*, the Court considered the facts of *Linekar*,[285] a rape case under the old law, in order to demonstrate the rarity of the occasions on which the conclusive presumption in s.76(2)(a) will apply. The appellant had tricked a prostitute to have intercourse with him by promising to pay her £25. He never intended to keep that promise. However, notwithstanding his lies, she was undeceived about the nature or purpose of the act, i.e. intercourse. The conclusive presumption in s.76 would have no application. Clearly, the Court was applying a strict approach to the scope of s.76 in indicating that the facts of *Linekar* would not generate a conclusive presumption. But it did not go so far as to say that deceptions outside s.76 can never vitiate consent (although,

---

[283] *Sexual offences: consent, capacity and children*, *Archbold News*, Issue 10, Dec 5, 2008.
[284] [2007] 2 Cr. App. R. 34, at 486. The case is discussed in the next paragraph.
[285] [1995] 2 Cr. App. R. 49, considered in *Jheeta* at [27].

in practical terms, it would be difficult to establish absence of consent on the facts of *Linekar,* whatever view the original jury may have taken[286]).

As David Ormerod QC and Karl Laird observe, the most intractable point   **1.208** that remains unresolved is whether deception as to any condition at all has the potential to fall within s.74 and vitiate consent.[287] The facts of *Jheeta* itself support the view that deceptions outside the scope of s.76 may lead to an absence of consent within the definition of s.74. In that case, the appellant's persuasion took the form of pressures imposed upon the complainant by a complicated scheme he had fabricated. The complainant was not deceived as to the nature or purpose of the intercourse, but she was deceived as to the situation in which she found herself. The Court held that the appellant's pleas of guilty had been properly entered. His actions had deprived the complainant of the freedom to choose whether or not to have intercourse with him. His course of deceptive conduct had led her to have intercourse with him more frequently than otherwise would have been the case. It follows that evidence of a deception falling outside s.76 may be relevant to whether there was a free agreement under s.74, as it will be part of the relevant circumstances. Under the old law, sexual intercourse procured by threats insufficient to vitiate consent could have been prosecuted under s.2 of the 1956 Act (procurement of a woman by threats).[288] Alternatively, sexual intercourse procured by deceptions which did go to the nature of the act and so vitiate consent, could have been prosecuted under s.3. However, ss.2 and 3 were repealed and not replaced by the 2003 Act.

The position has now been clarified in *Assange v Swedish Prosecution*   **1.209** *Authority.*[289] The Divisional Court, in considering an appeal against extradition, had to consider whether the conduct alleged to amount to the Swedish offence of sexual molestation was an offence under the law of England and Wales. The essence of the offence as described in the European arrest warrant was that the appellant knew that the complainant would consent to sexual

---

[286] See Temkin and Ashworth in *The Sexual Offences Act 2003 (1) Rape, Sexual Assaults and the Problems of Consent* [2004] Crim. L.R. 328, at p.329, where the authors take the view that other cases of deception outside s.76 fall to be dealt with under the broad definition of consent as agreement by choice (s.74). They stress the fact that a pivotal element in the new law, the definition of consent in s.74, is vague in its terms leaving much to the interpretation of juries. They consider that a jury, if left with the words of s.74, might conclude that the prostitute in *Linekar* did not agree by choice. The article was written just before the implementation of the new law, and before *R. v B.*

[287] *Smith and Hogan's Criminal Law,* 14th edn (Oxford: OUP, 2015), p.831.

[288] See *Harold* (1984) 6 Cr. App. R.(S.) 30, where H was prosecuted under s.2 for threatening to tell the complainant's employer that she had been a prostitute.

[289] [2011] EWHC 2849 (Admin). Jonathan Rogers in *The effect of "deception" in the Sexual Offences Act 2003, Archbold Review,* Issue 4, May 14, 2013, argues that *Assange* was wrongly decided and an alternative interpretation of the legislation should be preferred. Rogers argues that it is a mistake to conflate concerns about sexual health and/or pregnancy with sexual autonomy. He expresses the hope that *Assange* will not be followed and that liability for nonconsensual offences will arise only where the sexual autonomy of the victim has been compromised. In fact *Assange* has been followed: see *McNally* [2013] EWCA Crim 1051 and *R(F) v DPP* [2013] EWHC 945 (Admin), discussed below. It is quite clear that s.74 is being given a wide interpretation unrestricted by s.76.

intercourse only if he used a condom throughout but, nevertheless, went on to have unprotected sexual intercourse with her. The appellant submitted that the conduct described in the warrant was not an offence under the law of England and Wales, in that a consent to sexual intercourse on condition that the appellant wore a condom remained a consent to sexual intercourse, even if he had not used a condom or had removed or damaged the condom he had used. The appellant relied heavily upon *R. v B*,[290] in which the Court of Appeal held that deception as to HIV status was not a deception as to the nature or purpose of the act of sexual intercourse, and accordingly the conclusive presumption in s.76 did not apply: the act remained a consensual act. Furthermore, the Court in *R. v B* had gone on to hold that the fact that B had not disclosed he was HIV positive was not in any way relevant to the issue of consent to sexual intercourse under s.74. It was submitted that the present case was analogous, as the complainant had consented to sexual intercourse and it did not matter that she had consented only on the basis that the appellant would use a condom, as that did not change the nature of the act. It was accepted on the appellant's behalf that this contention might not be one that contemporary society would readily understand or consider justifiable, but Parliament had enacted the law in those terms and the duty of the courts was to apply the law.

1.210   The Divisional Court, in deciding that the extradition requirement of dual criminality was satisfied, rejected the appellant's submissions based on *R. v B*. It noted that in *Jheeta*[291] the Court of Appeal had made it clear that in most cases, the absence of consent and of a reasonable belief in consent would be proved without reference to the presumptions set out in ss.75 and 76. In the Divisional Court's view, s.76 had no application to this case. The section should be given a stringent construction because it provides for a conclusive presumption. The question of consent, and the issue of the materiality of the use of a condom, fell to be determined by reference to s.74. It would be open to a jury to hold that, if the complainant had made clear that she would consent to sexual intercourse only if the appellant used a condom, then there would be no consent if, without her consent, he did not use a condom, or removed or tore it. Thus his conduct would amount to an offence under the 2003 Act, whatever the position may have been prior to the Act.

1.211   In short, if a deception is not within s.76 (i.e. it is not a deception as to the nature or purpose of the act or a case of impersonation), that does not preclude reliance upon s.74. Section 76 simply establishes a conclusive presumption in the very limited circumstances to which it applies. In *Assange*, the Divisional Court rejected the argument that if the deception was not a

---

[290] [2007] 1 Cr. App. R. 29, discussed in paras 1.339 and following, below.
[291] [2007] 2 Cr. App. R. 34, discussed in para.1.208, above.

deception within s.76, then it could not be taken into account for the purposes of s.74. Sir John Thomas P, as he then was, stated[292]:

> "It appears to have been contended by Mr Assange, that if, in accordance with the conclusion we have reached, the deception was not a deception within s.76 (a deception as to the nature or quality of the act or a case of impersonation), then the deception could not be taken into account for the purposes of s.74. It would, in our view, have been extraordinary if Parliament had legislated in terms that, if conduct that was not deceptive could be taken into account for the purposes of s.74, conduct that was deceptive could not be. There is nothing in *R v B* that suggests that. All the court said at paragraph 21 was: 'All we need to say is that, as a matter of law, the fact that the defendant may not have disclosed his HIV status is not a matter which could in any way be relevant to the issue of consent under section 74 in relation to the sexual activity in this case.'
>
> The editors of Smith & Hogan in the passage to which we have referred regard it as self evident that deception in relation to the use of a condom would 'be likely to be held to remove any purported free agreement by the complainant under s.74'. A very similar view is expressed in Rook and Ward on Sexual Offences (4th edition) at paragraph 1.216. Moreover *Jheeta* makes clear the limited scope of s.76. The complainant was deceived in a manner which did not go to the nature or purpose of the act; s.76 was therefore of no application (see paragraph 28). The evidence in relation to the fabricated scheme was sufficient, in the court's view, to negative consent for the purposes of s.74 (see paragraph 29).
>
> In our view s.76 deals simply with a conclusive presumption in the very limited circumstances to which it applies. If the conduct of the defendant is not within s.76, that does not preclude reliance on s.74. *R v B* goes no further than deciding that failure to disclose HIV infection is not of itself relevant to consent under s.74. *R v B* does not permit Mr Assange to contend that, if he deceived ΛΛ as to whether he was using a condom or one that he had not damaged, that was irrelevant to the issue of AA's consent to sexual intercourse as a matter of the law of England and Wales or his belief in her consent. On each of those issues, it is clear that it is the prosecution case she did not consent and he had no or no reasonable belief in that consent. Those are issues to which s.74 and not s.76 is relevant; there is nothing in *R v B* which compels any other conclusion. Furthermore it does not matter whether the sexual contact is described as molestation, assault or, since it involved penile penetration, rape. The dual criminality issue is the absence of consent and the absence of a reasonable belief in consent. Those issues are the same regardless of the description of the conduct."

Assange clarifies the relevance of deceptions, falling short of s.76 deceptions, to the question of consent. This has led to academic criticism suggesting that the line between frauds that can vitiate consent and those that cannot is "murky and uncertain".[293]. As the law stands, it is a matter for the jury to determine whether a particular deception operating upon the mind of a

1.212

---

[292] At [88].
[293] See Professor J.R. Spencer, *Sex by deception*, *Archbold Review*, Issue 9, Nov 14, 2013, pp.6–9, where it is pointed out that the 2003 Act, in repealing the offence of procuring a woman by false representations to have unlawful sexual intercourse in any part of the world, has left a gap in the criminal law governing sexual misconduct.

complainant means that the complainant was not agreeing by choice. Two subsequent cases illustrate this process in action.

1.213   In *R.(F) v DPP*,[294] the claimant challenged a decision not to prosecute her former partner for rape and/or sexual assault where the allegation was that consent was forthcoming on the basis that ejaculation would take place outside the body. There was evidence that the former partner, the intervener in the proceedings, knew and understood that the claimant was consenting only on the basis that he withdrew before ejaculation, and that he deliberately ignored the basis of her consent as a manifestation of his control over her. Lord Judge CJ, giving the judgment of the Divisional Court, observed[295]:

> "What *Assange* underlines is that 'choice' is crucial to the issue of 'consent' . . . The evidence relating to 'choice' and the 'freedom' to make any particular choice must be approached in a broad common sense way. If before penetration began the intervener had made up his mind that he would penetrate and ejaculate within the claimant's vagina, or even, because 'penetration is a continuing act from entry to withdrawal' (see s.79(2) of the 2003 Act) he decided that he would not withdraw at all, just because he deemed the claimant subservient to his control, she was deprived of choice relating to the crucial feature on which her original consent to sexual intercourse was based. Accordingly her consent was negated. Contrary to her wishes, and knowing that she would not have consented, and did not consent to penetration or the continuation of penetration if she had any inkling of his intention, he deliberately ejaculated within her vagina. In law, this combination of circumstances falls within the statutory definition of rape."

1.214   In *Justine McNally v R.*,[296] the appellant had pleaded guilty to six counts of assault by penetration under s.2 of the Sexual Offences Act 2003. The appellant and the complainant were both young teenage girls. They met on

---

[294] [2013] EWHC 945 (Admin). Jonathan Rogers, in *Further developments under the Sexual Offences Act*, Archbold Review, Issue 7, August 7, 2013, pp.7–9, whilst acknowledging that the alleged facts in *R.(F) v DPP* make the case hard to distinguish from *Assange*, argues that liability for non-consensual sexual offences should only arise where the victim has not been willing to be used for the sexual gratification of another in a way that shows regard to his or her sexual preferences. He contends that in both *Assange* and *R.(F) v DPP*, the sexual intercourse itself was in accordance with the complainants' own sexual preference. This criticism ignores the width of s.74 as described above.

[295] At [26].

[296] [2013] EWCA Crim 1051. This decision is criticised by Jonathan Rogers in his article in *Archbold Review*, Issue 7, August 7, 2013, pp.7–9, on the basis that *McNally* was a s.76 case and s.74 did not arise. The thrust of the argument is that if the core "agreement" to the acts is present, then s.74 says nothing about any deception making any difference. Where a competent person has freely agreed to the sexual activity which takes place, then, if any type of misunderstanding is to make any difference at all, it should be the result of intentional deception by the defendant. This type of misunderstanding, on the face of the statute, is the exclusive province of s.76. A difference in gender, as in *McNally*, should only make a difference to the "nature of the act" under s.76(2) of the Act. If s.76 applied, the prosecution would have had to prove that the appellant intentionally induced the complainant's mistake, which was not a pre-condition under s.74. This argument again ignores the wide ambit of s.74, which focuses on a jury's decision whether the particular complainant agreed to the particular sexual activity alleged. Sections 74 and 76 are not mutually exclusive.

the internet through a social networking game. The appellant led the complainant to believe she was a boy called "Scott Hill" from Glasgow. Arrangements were made for them to meet in London once the complainant was 16. Over four visits it was alleged that various forms of penetration took place. On the fourth visit, the appellant was confronted by the complainant's mother, and the complainant learnt the appellant's true gender. It was the prosecution case that the complainant had only consented because she believed she was engaging in sex with a boy called Scott. The Court of Appeal, in a judgment delivered by Leveson LJ, rejected the appellant's argument that deception as to gender cannot vitiate consent. The Court did accept that some deceptions (such as, for example, in relation to wealth) would obviously not be sufficient to vitiate consent, but did not explain why such a deception would necessarily fall outside s.74. However, the Court accepted the respondent's contention that a deception did not have to be relevant to the definition of the offence, nor relate to features of the particular act. The Court adopted the approach set out by Lord Judge CJ in *R. (F) v DPP* that the evidence as to "choice" and the "freedom" to make any particular choice must be approached in a broad common sense way. While, in a physical sense, the acts of assault by penetration of the vagina are the same whether perpetrated by a male or a female, the sexual nature of the acts is, on any common sense view, different where the complainant is deliberately deceived by a defendant into believing that the latter is a male. Leveson LJ concluded[297]:

> "Assuming the facts to be proved as alleged, [the complainant] chose to have sexual encounters with a boy and her preference (her freedom to choose whether or not to have a sexual encounter with a girl) was removed by the appellant's deception."

David Ormerod QC and Karl Laird have identified the importance of **1.215** *McNally* as its confirmation by implication that only an active deception (as opposed to a failure to disclose) falls within the scope of s.74, which, in one sense, brings s.74 and s.76 closer together in that the latter requires intentional deception.[298] However, apart from this, as with *R(F) v DPP*, *McNally* does not shed light on any principle underpinning the scope of s.74, and, in particular, whether there is any limit on what is capable of constituting a crucial feature for the purposes of choice under s.74. It follows that the law remains, that whilst some deceptions such as lies about wealth and a promise to pay are acknowledged as insufficient to vitiate consent, it is a matter for a jury whether an intended deception did in fact do so. It follows

---

[297] At [26].
[298] *Smith and Hogan's Criminal Law*, 14th edn (Oxford: OUP, 2015), p.830. The authors acknowledge that the distinction between active deception and failure to disclose may be difficult to draw.

that areas which are unlikely to be within a juror's perception of rape are capable of being rape as a matter of law.[299]

The use of the words "want" and "willing"

1.216 When explaining the meaning of consent, judges should avoid using the words "want" and "willing", as they may mislead the jury. In *Kirk and Kirk*[300] the trial judge directed the jury:

"Just where the line is to be drawn between real consent and submission, albeit willing submission, may not be easy to draw, but the law leaves it to juries who have heard all the evidence of the witnesses to say where the line is to be drawn and whether in any case lack of consent is proved."

That was followed by the further direction:

"Therefore, I will leave it to you to draw that line. Was it consent or was it submission and therefore not consent."

The judge had appropriately stressed that consent must be freely given and that it covers a wide spectrum of states of mind from actual desire on the one hand to reluctant acquiescence on the other. However, giving the judgment of the Court of Appeal, Pill LJ had reservations about the use of the phrase "willing submission"[301]:

"The expression 'willing submission' is not an easy one in this context. Willingness is usually associated with consent. However, we are satisfied the jury would not, in the context of this very full direction, have been misled by the use of the word 'willing'. This was not a case where it was alleged that submission had been achieved by physical force. It was willing in the sense that there was no attempt at resistance by the complainant and the judge used it in that sense. That leaves open the possibility that the circumstances were such that the complainant submitted to sexual intercourse rather than consented to it. That was the overall effect of the direction. We are satisfied that, having regard to the full direction given, the jury would not have been misled or distracted, by the use of the expression 'willing submission', from the question they were told they had to

---

[299] See the facts of the civil case *AJA v Commissioner of Police for the Metropolis* [2013] EWCA Civ 1342, where it was alleged that an undercover police officer established and maintained intimate sexual relationships with the appellants for the covert purpose of obtaining intelligence. The officer used a false identity to deceive committed environmental activists into embarking on sexual relationships with him while he was performing his duties as an undercover officer. He used his sexual relationships with the claimants to enable him to gather intelligence and/or for personal gratification. He pretended to be a confidant, empathiser and source of close support. He exploited vulnerabilities and sought to encourage the claimants to become emotionally dependent upon him. None of the claimants would have entered into a relationship and consented to sex if they had known his true identity or purpose. It was not argued that there was a deception within the meaning of s.76. However, since a deception does not have to relate to the nature of the act, we find ourselves searching for the principle that would exclude such active and intended deception from being capable of vitiating consent under s.74. See David Ormerod QC and Karl Laird, *Smith and Hogan's Criminal Law*, 14th edn (2015), p.831 (n.103).
[300] [2008] EWCA Crim 434.
[301] At 92.

answer. It is not, however, an expression we would commend for use on other occasions."

This was not the first time that the Court of Appeal has recommended that the words "want" or "willing" should not be used in summing up on the definition of consent in a rape case. It is possible not to want something and yet to freely agree to it by choice.[302]

Consent of children

Where the complainant is aged 13 or over the prosecution must prove that   1.217
she did not consent. Until the 2003 Act, there was no fixed age limit below which a child was incapable of consenting as a matter of law, although in many cases the prosecution did not have to prove much more than the age of the child.[303] Now, s.5 of the Act creates an offence of rape of a child under 13, where consent is not an issue. The question whether a child would have been capable of consenting is less likely to arise in relation to a child of 13 or over. However, extreme youth may be relevant to a particular child's capacity to make the choice to agree, in which case it may be necessary to focus on the child's understanding and knowledge. Complainants cannot consent to what they do not understand.[304]

Consent and rape where the parties are married or have a long-standing relationship

Many rape cases are brought nowadays where the parties are in or have   1.218
recently been in a relationship. In *Mohammed Zafar*,[305] the Court of Appeal considered the extent to which it could give assistance to judges in dealing with the issue of consent in marital rape cases. The Court's comments apply equally to any established relationship between a couple, whatever their sexual orientation. The Court described the trial judge's summing-up as an admirable exposition of the law and of the approach a jury should adopt in a case where marital rape is alleged. In the very first sentence of the summing-up the trial judge, Pill J, as he then was, had said:

> "Members of the jury, the defendant and [the complainant] had a long standing relationship, they lived together in Cardiff, they had two children and they had many acts of sexual intercourse."

Later he said:

---

[302] See *R. v DT*, Unreported, February 17, 2000.
[303] See e.g. *Harling* (1938) 26 Cr. App. R. 127, where Humphreys J held that the age of the girl (13 and a half) coupled with the fact that she was a weakling was enough to prove that there was no consent on her part.
[304] cf. *Howard* (1965) 50 Cr. App. R. 56.
[305] Unreported, June 18, 1993, CA (No.92/2762/W2). Pill J's direction was commended in *McAllister* [1997] Crim. L.R. 233, CA.

"It is a relevant fact (you may think) that they had lived together (the defendant and the complainant) in a long standing relationship, relevant that is to the charge. When sexual intercourse occurs between a man and a woman your approach to the questions of consent which arise may well be different in a situation where the parties live together and have lived together for a long time from a situation where, for example, they have just met. The questions on the law of rape are the same in each case; but the answers will be given in the light of all the circumstances and all the evidence, including the fact that they have had a long standing relationship. They were living (you may think on the evidence) as if they were man and wife. And that being so the question whether they are actually married in English law is not a question which you need or should decide or one which is relevant to the issues in the case."

He continued:

"In law a husband or a long-term partner . . . short-term partner for that matter . . . can be convicted of rape of his partner if the constituents of the offence are proved notwithstanding his relationship with the victim."

He concluded:

"In considering whether it is proved that the complainant did not consent, bear in mind when considering the evidence, the relationship between them. When people enter into long-term relationships either within or outside marriage they usually contemplate regular sexual relations. In most partnerships, even not entirely happy ones, there is often a give and take between the partners on sexual as on other matters. A female partner may not particularly want sexual intercourse on a particular occasion but because it is her husband or her partner who is asking for it she will consent to sexual intercourse. The fact that such consent is given reluctantly or out of a sense of duty to her partner, is still a consent.

However, a woman is entitled to say 'no' and to refuse to consent even to her husband or long-term partner. There is a dividing line between a real consent on the one hand and a lack of consent or mere submission on the other. It is for you to decide whether the absence of consent is proved in this case by applying your combined good sense, experience and knowledge of human nature and modern behaviour to all the relevant facts of the case."

1.219   Where the parties are in a long-standing relationship, Pill J's approach in *Mohammed Zafar*[306] remains useful provided it is appropriately updated in the light of the statutory definition of consent in s.74 of the 2003 Act. An example of such a direction, addressing the issue of reluctant consent within or immediately after a long-term relationship, is included in the *Crown Court Compendium*[307]

"It is common ground that D and V have had a long-term sexual relationship. This is plainly relevant to the question of whether or not, on this occasion, V consented to D \specify act\, because the situation between two people who have/ had such a relationship is quite different from a situation in which two people are strangers or have met one another only a few times.

When two people have/have had such a relationship, there is likely to be some give and take between them in relation to any number of things, including their

---

[306] Unreported, June 18, 1993, CA (No.92/2762, W2).
[307] 2016, Ch.20.4, para.4, Direction 6: see Appendix G, below.

sexual relationship, and sometimes a partner who is not feeling enthusiastic may nevertheless reluctantly give consent.

This is not to say however that when two people are/ have been in such a relationship it must follow that both of them will consent to any sexual activity which takes place. One party is fully entitled to say "no" to the other notwithstanding their relationship. What you must decide in this case is (a) whether V consented freely and by choice, albeit reluctantly, to what took place or whether she did not consent but submitted to it and (b) whether, in the light of all the evidence including the nature of the [previous] relationship between V and D, D may have reasonably believed that she was consenting."

This full direction will not be required in every case where there has been a **1.220** prior relationship, particularly where the prosecution and defence cases are diametrically opposed and the complainant alleges violence. In *Doyle*[308] the Court of Appeal upheld a conviction for the violent rape of an ex-girlfriend where it had emerged during the course of the evidence that the relationship was volatile with moments of violence and unpleasantness followed by making up. In summing up, the judge had distinguished between consent as defined in s.74 and "mere submission to something she did not want". It was submitted that the judge should have assisted the jury on how to approach the issue of consent in the context of a consensual sexual relationship, but that he failed to give any further explanation as to the distinction between submission and consent freely given by choice. In particular, it was argued that submission was a concept which pre-dated the Sexual Offences Act 2003 and that the use of the expression without further explanation, in the context of a continuing sexual relationship, was unhelpful and, as a result, unfair and adverse to the appellant. The Court of Appeal concluded that the judge had directed the jury appropriately in the context of the case. There would be circumstances where a jury would require assistance with the distinction between reluctant but free exercise of choice, especially in a long-term loving relationship, and unwilling submission due to fear of worse circumstances. However, here the judge had drawn clear distinctions between the complainant's and the accused's accounts and there was no possibility that he might have given the jury the wrong impression or that they had convicted the accused on the basis of a misunderstanding about the difference between consent and submission.

In *Watson*,[309] however, the overall effect of the judge's directions was to **1.221** leave a real possibility that the jury may have misunderstood the distinction

---

[308] [2010] EWCA Crim 119.
[309] [2015] EWCA Crim 559. Even without the misdirection discussed here, the Court of Appeal considered that the convictions were not safe in the face of deficiencies in the summing up. In particular, the Court felt that at some stage the judge should have drawn together the relevance and importance to the issues of a series of text messages that passed between the appellant and the complainant which appeared inconsistent with the complainant's evidence that there was non-consensual activity on the dates of two of the alleged rapes. The Court also concluded that the judge ought to have reminded the jury of the reasons advanced by the appellant as to why the complainant may have lied.

between consent and submission. The appellant had a consensual relation-ship with his biological daughter almost immediately after he first met her when she was 34 and he was approaching his 52nd birthday. The admitted consensual sexual activity included bondage. It was alleged that he had raped her on a number of occasions during the course of the relationship. He pleaded guilty to three counts of having sex with an adult relative. However, his case was that all sexual activity with his daughter was with her freely given consent. When directing the jury, the trial judge had explained that consent "can taking many forms from willing enthusiasm to reluctant acquiescence". He correctly summarised the statutory definition of consent. However, later in his summing up, he set up this dichotomy for the jury:

> "Was the complainant freely consenting to sexual intercourse or was she submitting to a demand she felt unable to resist?"

The Court of Appeal considered that this sentence was apt to confuse. This dichotomy did not accurately summarise what had gone before and did not reflect the law. The Court observed that it is possible for a person to submit to a demand which he or she feels unable to resist, but without lacking the capacity or freedom to make a choice. That would be an example of reluctant consent. The Court acknowledged that the words should be considered in their context, and the temptation to isolate particular phrases and subject them to over-refined analysis should be resisted.[310] However, here the potential vice of the formulation was that it set up a clear choice for the jury that did not accurately reflect the law. As the dichotomy stood, the jury could have convicted the appellant upon the basis that the complainant was reluctant to engage in the sexual activity. If the jury found that she was submitting to a demand she felt unable to resist, that was not enough. They should have gone on to consider why she felt unable to resist, and whether in the circumstances as they found them to have been, she was freely con-senting.

CONSENT AND "CAPACITY" UNDER THE SEXUAL OFFENCES ACT 2003

1.222 Since "capacity" is now an integral part of the definition of consent in s.74 of the 2003 Act, it is clear that a valid consent may be given only by a person who has the capacity to give it. The Sexual Offences Review recommended that there should be a statutory definition of capacity to consent,[311] specifically adopting the Law Commission definition[312] which would reflect both the complainant's knowledge and understanding of sex and its broad

---

[310] [2015] EWCA Crim 559, at [35]. Burnett LJ referred to *Doyle* [2010] EWCA 119, where a sentence in the consent direction, if taken in isolation rather than in context, would have been problematic.
[311] *Setting the Boundaries*, 2000, from para.4.5.
[312] *Consent in Sex Offences*, 2000, paras 4.71–4.81.

implications. The Review recognised that this is an area fraught with difficulty. It noted that "there is a very real tension between the right to a private life and the need to protect people who are susceptible and easily taken advantage of". Notwithstanding its recommendation, "capacity" is not defined in the 2003 Act. Nevertheless, it would appear that capacity is intended to mean mental capacity. The Explanatory Notes to the Act state that a person might not have sufficient capacity because of his age or because of a mental disorder.[313]

However, two of the main areas where lack of capacity to consent may **1.223** arise, i.e. youth and mental disorder, are catered for in the 2003 Act by specially tailored offences. Indeed, the wide nature of these distinct offences and the substantial maximum sentences they carry may be a reason for there being no definition of capacity.

Incapacity by reason of youth

By virtue of s.5 of the Act, a person who intentionally penetrates with his **1.224** penis the vagina, anus or mouth of a person under the age of 13 commits rape. The issue of consent is irrelevant in a prosecution under s.5. A child under 13 is irrebuttably presumed not to have the capacity to consent: see paras 3.02 and following, below. However, if a prosecution is brought under s.1 rather than s.5, the issue is technically still live.

Incapacity by reason of mental disorder

The 2003 Act addresses the issue of capacity in relation to the mentally **1.225** disordered by creating specific offences turning on the term "unable to refuse". For instance, s.30(2)(a) states that B is unable to refuse if he lacks the capacity to choose whether to agree to the touching (whether because he lacks sufficient understanding of the nature or reasonably foreseeable consequences of what is being done, or for any other reason). The Act does not define capacity in the context of the definition of consent, apart from making it clear in s.74 that capacity is an integral part of consent. It follows that if a mentally disordered person does not have the capacity to agree by choice to sexual activity they will not be consenting to it. The test of capacity in this context is likely to be similar to the approach taken to lack of capacity as a result of the consumption of alcohol and/or drugs. If a complainant has no real understanding of what is involved, or has such a limited knowledge, awareness or understanding as to be in no position to be able to agree, they will not have the capacity to consent.[314]

---

[313] para.139.
[314] *Howard* (1966) 50 Cr. App. R. 56.

Capacity under the common law

1.226 What will be the correct approach if in a prosecution for rape there is a live issue as to whether the complainant lacked capacity by reason of mental disorder? The burden of proving lack of capacity will fall upon the prosecution.[315] As there is no definition of capacity in the Act, the courts may look for assistance to the common law. However, the common law developed no clear principles governing whether a person had capacity to consent to sexual acts: it was a question of fact for the jury to determine in accordance with their interpretation of the ordinary meaning of the word "consent". Clearly, a person's capacity to consent depends upon their understanding and the degree to which it is impaired.[316] Nineteenth century English cases addressed the issue in terms of a woman's capability to express consent, and stated that a man who had sexual intercourse with a woman who was incapable of expressing consent or dissent by reason of her condition and who did not consent, committed rape; but a consent produced by a mere animal instinct on the part of a mentally ill or subnormal woman would be sufficient to prevent the act constituting rape.[317] According to Platt B, in his summing up in *Ryan*,[318] probability of consent might be inferred from loose and indecent habits. In *Fletcher*,[319] however, a conviction for rape was upheld in respect of sexual intercourse with a girl of weak intellect. The jury found that she was incapable of giving consent due to her defect in reasoning.

1.227 Other jurisdictions refined the approach to capacity. A useful test was formulated in the Australian case of *Morgan*,[320] where Winneke CJ, delivering the judgment of the Supreme Court of Victoria, stated that in order to establish that a woman lacks capacity to consent to sexual intercourse:

> "It must be proved that she has not sufficient knowledge or understanding to comprehend:
>   (a) that what is proposed to be done is the physical fact of penetration of her body by the male organ, or, if that is not proved,
>   (b) that the act of penetration proposed is one of sexual connection as distinct from an act of a totally different character."

[315] *R. v A* [2014] EWCA Crim 299 (*held*, the burden of proving incapacity falls upon the party asserting it). It follows that in criminal proceedings the prosecution must make the jury sure the complainant lacked capacity to consent or it will be assumed that he or she had such capacity.

[316] *Barratt* (1873) L.R. 2 C.C.R. 81.

[317] *Fletcher* (1859) Bell C.C. 63. The "animal instincts" test was condemned by Munby J in *X City Council v MB, NB and MAB* [2006] EWHC 168 (Fam).

[318] (1846) 2 Cox C.C. 115.

[319] (1859) Bell C.C. 63.

[320] [1970] V.R. 337 at 341, approved by Munby J in *X City Council v MB, NB and MAB* [2006] EWHC 168 (Fam), a case which concerned whether a 25-year-old man with marked autistic spectrum disorder had the capacity to consent to marriage. Capacity to consent to sexual activity was a live issue. For a very clear analysis of *Morgan*, see Tracey Elliott, *Capacity, sex and the mentally disordered*, Archbold News, Issue 8, 2008, p.3.

The Court went on to consider the extent of the knowledge and understanding required:[321]

> "That knowledge or understanding need not, of course, be a complete or sophisticated one. It is enough that she has sufficient 'rudimentary knowledge' of what the act comprises and of its character to enable her to decide whether to give or withhold consent."

This test removes the difficulty of deciding whether a woman who is incapable of expressing consent does in fact consent to sexual intercourse. If, on application of the test proposed in *Morgan*, a woman is found to be incapable of consenting, then a man having sexual intercourse with her commits rape if he does not reasonably believe she is capable of consenting. Professor Glanville Williams argued[322] that although the test in *Morgan* was greatly superior to the English pronouncements of the nineteenth century, the rule would be more clearly expressed in positive terms: the woman must both know the physical facts and know that the connection is sexual; failing knowledge of either fact, she would not consent in law.[323]   **1.228**

Some assistance in identifying the common law approach to capacity may be derived from two decisions of Munby J sitting in the Family Division, namely *X City Council v MB, NA and MAB*[324] in 2006 and *Re MM (an adult)*[325] in 2007. Both cases were decided before the implementation of the Mental Capacity Act 2005. Tracey Elliott has suggested[326] that the test in *Morgan* requires only a relatively low level of understanding and she illustrates this proposition by reference to *Re MM (an adult)*. In that case, Munby J decided that, although MM lacked the capacity to make decisions in relation to most significant aspects of her life, she did have the capacity to consent to sexual relations on the basis that she understood the nature of the act of sexual intercourse and its risks, including pregnancy and sexually transmitted disease, and therefore satisfied the test for capacity to consent to sexual relations, which depended upon a person "having sufficient knowledge and understanding . . . of the sexual nature and character . . . of the act of sexual intercourse, and of the reasonably foreseeable consequences of sexual intercourse, to have the capacity whether or not to engage in it." As Munby J acknowledged in *X City Council v MB, NA and MAB*,[327] although, in a criminal context, there might be some difference between the common law test and the test of "unable to refuse" in the 2003 Act, they come to very much the same thing: the first involving "the capacity to choose, to decide   **1.229**

---

[321] At 342.
[322] Williams, *The Vitiation of Consent by Fear*, p.571.
[323] See Law Com. Consultation Paper No.139 (1995), paras 5.01–5.22, where it is provisionally proposed that there should be legislation stating that a valid consent may not be given by a person without capacity.
[324] [2006] EWHC 168 (Fam).
[325] [2007] EWHC 2003 (Fam).
[326] In *Capacity, sex and the mentally disordered*, Archbold News, Issue 8, 2008, p.3.
[327] [2006] EWHC 168 (Fam), described by Tracey Elliott as producing a sensible and workable test for capacity to consent to sexual relations.

whether to give or withhold consent, dependent upon the capacity to understand the nature and character of the act, crucially the capacity to understand the sexual nature of the act", and the second involving "the capacity to choose, dependent upon the capacity to understand the nature and reasonably foreseeable consequences of the act."

Capacity is specific to the issue, person (partner) and situation

1.230   Munby J had taken the view in *MM (an adult)* that capacity to consent to sexual relations is issue specific. Someone may have capacity for one purpose but lack capacity for another purpose. That proposition is well-established. He went on to say that, in contrast, it is not person (partner) specific. The Court of Appeal in *Cooper*[328] agreed and added that capacity cannot be situation specific. In so doing, the Court took a narrow view by holding that the complainant's irrational fear preventing her from exercising choice did not amount to a lack of capacity to choose.

1.231   The decision in *Cooper* was reversed by the House of Lords.[329] The decision relates to capacity in the context of an offence under s.30 of the 2003 Act (sexual activity with a person with a mental disorder impeding choice). For a full discussion of the case and how it has widened the scope of s.30, see Ch.7, below. However, *Cooper* is also of significance in explaining the meaning of mental capacity in respect of consent in relation to the non-consensual offences. Baroness Hale felt that the Court of Appeal had been led astray by the view that capacity could not be situation-specific. She stated[330]:

> "The object of the 2003 act was to get away from the previous 'status'-based approach which assumed that all 'defectives' lacked capacity while failing to protect those whose mental disorder deprived them of autonomy in other ways."

It follows that a jury must consider whether the complainant had capacity to choose to perform the particular sexual act with the particular person at the particular time.

1.232   Baroness Hale observed that the case law on capacity has for some time recognised that to be able to make a decision the person concerned must be able not only (a) to understand the information relevant to making it but also (b) to weigh that information in the balance to arrive at a choice. She referred to a line of authorities in respect of refusal of medical treatment.[331] In particular, she provided the graphic example based upon an analogous situation in *NHS Trust v T (Adult Patient: Refusal of Medical Treatment)*[332]

---

[328] [2009] 1 Cr. App. R. 15.
[329] [2009] UKHL 42 at [24].
[330] At [27].
[331] *Re C (Adult: Refusal of Medical Treatment)* [1994] 1 W.L.R. 290 at 295; *Re MB (Medical Treatment)* [1997] 2 F.L.R. 426 at 433.
[332] [2005] 1 All E.R. 387.

where a patient was refusing a blood transfusion even though she knew she might die without it; but she believed that her blood was evil and that the healthy blood given her in a transfusion would become contaminated and increase the volume of evil blood in her and, as a consequence, the danger of her committing acts of evil. Charles J concluded that the patient was unable to use and weigh the relevant information, and thus the competing factors, in the process of arriving at her decision whether to undergo a transfusion. Baroness Hale argued that, in the same way, a person's delusion that she was commanded by God to have sexual intercourse, an act which she was perfectly capable of understanding, might make her incapable of exercising an autonomous choice in the matter. Baroness Hale expressly refrained from deciding the appropriate test at common law, but for the purposes of s.30, which was the subject of the appeal, the 2003 Act had put the matter beyond doubt.

Relevance of the Mental Capacity Act 2005

The words used by Baroness Hale when considering the case law on capacity are close to the statutory test for capacity found in the Mental Capacity Act 2005.[333] The Act is not specifically applied to the Sexual Offences Act 2003. Indeed, the Code of Practice under the 2005 Act[334] makes it clear that, although the Act applies in relation to financial, healthcare or welfare decisions, it does not replace existing common law tests relating to such matters as marriage and the ability to enter into a contract, and judges considering cases upon these issues may retain existing common law tests or adopt the new statutory definition. Section 2(1) of the Act provides: **1.233**

> "For the purposes of this Act, a person lacks capacity in relation to a matter if at the material time he is unable to make a decision for himself in relation to the matter because of an impairment of, or disturbance in the functioning of, the mind or brain."

Section 3(1) defines "unable to make a decision" as follows:

> "For the purposes of section 2, a person is unable to make a decision for himself if he is unable—
> (a) to understand the information relevant to the decision,
> (b) to retain that information,
> (c) to use or weigh that information as part of the process of making the decision, or
> (d) to communicate his decision (whether by talking, using sign language or any other means)."

The Act illustrates that the modern approach to capacity is to focus upon not only the degree of understanding of information relevant to a decision, but also the ability to use or weigh that information as part of the process of decision-making, whatever the quality of the actual decision.

[333] Which came into force on October 1, 2007.
[334] para.4.33.

1.234   When considering authorities in this context, it is important to acknowledge the difference of approach between the Court of Protection and the
criminal courts. In *IM v (1) LM (by her Litigation Friend, the Official
Solicitor (2) AB (3) Liverpool City Council*,[335] the Court of Appeal (Civil
Division), whilst considering an appeal from the Court of Protection,
addressed the apparent conflict of judicial opinion at first instance on the
issue of capacity to sexual relations. Sir Brian Leveson P, giving the judgment
of the Court, acknowledged the critical importance of the distinction
between the criminal law, which is act, person and situation-sensitive and
operates only retrospectively, and the civil law which requires prospective
assessment in the light of the particular circumstances of the affected
individual. In the Court's view, the reason why the words used are diametrically opposed to each other has arisen from the two distinct and different
contexts in which the respective judgments were given. The necessary
forward-looking focus of the Court of Protection is upon the general
capacity to give or withhold consent to sexual relations whilst the focus of the
criminal law is upon a person, time and place-specific occasion when that
capacity is actually deployed and consent is either given or withheld.

The ability to use or weigh information

1.235   The Court in *IM* made some very important observations in respect of the
approach to s.3(1)(c) of the Mental Capacity Act 2005, which refers to the
ability to use or weigh information as part of the process of making the
decision. Section 1(4) of the Act provides that a person is not to be treated
as unable to make a decision merely because he makes an unwise decision.
The Court adopted the observation of Hedley J in *A NHS Trust v P*[336] that
s.1(4) is a very powerful qualification of the powers of the court in the field
of personal relationships. In his words:

> "The intention of the Act is not to dress an incapacitous person in forensic
> cotton wool but to allow them as far as possible to make the same mistakes that
> all other human beings are at liberty to make and not infrequently do."

This led the Court to take the view that the ability to use and weigh
information is unlikely to loom large in the evaluation of capacity to consent
to sexual relations. Sir Brian Leveson continued:

> "It is not an irrelevant consideration; indeed (as we have emphasised) the statute
> mandates that it be taken into account, but the notional process of using and
> weighing information attributed to the protected person should not involve a refined
> analysis of the sort which does not typically inform the decision to consent to sexual
> relations made by a person of full capacity."

In most cases in which a defendant is charged with raping a severely mentally
disordered complainant, and the prosecution allege lack of capacity, the test

---

[335] [2014] EWCA Civ 37.
[336] [2013] EWHC 50 (COP).

of capacity set out in *Howard*[337] will be sufficient, i.e. if the complainant had no real understanding of what was involved or had such limited awareness or understanding as to be in no position to agree, they will have lacked capacity. An example of where this approach would be appropriate is a case in which the complainant was suffering from an advanced form of a severe degenerative condition such as Alzheimer's.[338]

Where the mental disorder is less severe, it may be appropriate that the jury is given more assistance. In *R. v A*[339] Macur LJ, when considering the issue of lack of capacity through mental disorder in criminal proceedings, explained that the requirement that a complainant should understand the nature of the act of sexual engagement will be a relatively simple issue to address. She then adopted the approach of the court in *IM*:

> "The question relating to the understanding of reasonable foreseeable consequences obviously should not become divorced from the actual decision-making process carried out in that regard on a daily basis by persons of full capacity. In the opinion of this court, adopting the opinion of the Court of Appeal Civil Division in *IM,* this process is 'largely visceral rather than cerebral, and owes more to instinct and emotion rather than to analysis.'"

One option would be to adopt the test set out by the Supreme Court of   **1.237**
Victoria in *Morgan* as approved by Munby J in *X City Council v MB, NB and MAB*[339a] as to the level of understanding required in order to have capacity, whilst approaching the issue of the ability to weigh up information that has to be understood as part of the decision-making process in the manner suggested in *IM*. Such a test would read: a person has capacity to make a choice to agree to a sexual act where (i) they understand the nature and character of the act (particularly its sexual character) and (ii) they understand the information relevant to the choice and are able to use that information and weigh it in the balance to arrive at a choice, though not necessarily the right choice. When considering (ii) it is important to bear in mind that people with capacity may well understand information and weigh it in the balance, but still make mistakes and arrive at unwise decisions. Furthermore, when persons of full capacity make decisions about whether to engage in sexual relations, the decisions are often instinctive and emotional, and so it would be wrong to decide this issue on the basis of whether the person is capable of refined analysis.

Comparison with prosecutions under ss.30–41 of the 2003 Act

Sections 30 to 41 of the 2003 Act create a series of offences concerned with   **1.238**
the protection of those with mental disorders.[340] "Mental disorder" is defined

---

[337] (1966) 50 Cr. App. R. 56, discussed in paras 1.246 and 1.302, above.
[338] See *R. v D* [2002] EWCA Crim 990; and *R. v Sed* [2004] EWCA Crim 1294.
[339] [2014] EWCA Crim 299.
[339a] [2006] EWHC 168 (Fam).
[340] For detailed discussion of these offences see Ch.7.

by reference to s.1 of the Mental Health Act 1983.[341] The definition includes people suffering from a wide variety of mental disorders, including learning disability, and is substantially wider than the definition of "defective" which formed the basis of the previous offence under s.7 of the Sexual Offences Act 1956. Section 30 of the Act creates an offence of intentional sexual touching of a person who is unable to refuse because of, or for a reason related to, mental disorder. By virtue of s.30(4), if the touching involves penile penetration of the vagina, anus or mouth the defendant is liable on conviction on indictment to life imprisonment.[342] In stark contrast, the maximum punishment for an offence under s.7 of the 1956 Act (unlawful sexual intercourse with a defective) was two years' imprisonment. This means that where a defendant has had penetrative sex with a person who is unable to refuse because of, or for a reason related to, mental disorder, an appropriately serious alternative offence may be charged which obviates the need to charge rape. This ensures that the jury do not have to grapple with the issue of whether the complainant had the capacity to consent. In *Cooper*,[343] Baroness Hale noted that the appellant had originally been charged with rape, but that charges under s.30 were substituted at a later stage. She considered that the view may have been taken that s.30 is somewhat easier to prove. The prosecution has to prove only the inability to refuse rather than that the complainant actually did not consent. She also noted that this might not make much difference in practice given that both offences relate to a specific sexual act, and the definition of consent in s.74.

1.239   In particular, Baroness Hale observed that proof of the appropriate mental element is less onerous for the prosecution under s.30 than in respect of the non-consensual offences (ss.1–4.) Both have a hybrid objective/subjective test, requiring the jury to focus on the defendant and consider either whether he reasonably believed in consent (s.1(1)(c) of the Act) or whether he could reasonably have been expected to know that the complainant had a mental disorder and was likely to be unable to refuse (s.30(1)(d) of the Act). However, as Baroness Hale states, the test under s.30(1)(d) puts a greater burden of restraint upon people who know or ought to know a person's mental disorder is likely to affect their ability to choose.

1.240   It should be noted that where there is evidence of the sexual activity being procured by inducement, threat or deception upon a person with a mental disorder, a charge under s.34 may be preferable because it obviates the need to prove that the complainant was "unable to refuse" within the meaning of s.30(2) because of or for a reason related to a mental disorder.

---

[341] s.79(6) of the 2003 Act.
[342] Other forms of penetration also carry a maximum penalty of life imprisonment: see para.7.48, below.
[343] [2009] UKHL 42 at [32].

Will there ever be a need to charge rape if there is evidence that the complainant was suffering from mental disorder?

If there is no likely issue as to mental disorder, a charge under s.30 may well 1.241 be appropriate. However, there remains significant scope for a rape charge. The narrow interpretation of the meaning of "unable to refuse" in s.30(2) adopted by the Court of Appeal in *R. v C*[344] had left prosecutors in a position where they might have preferred the option of proceeding under ss.1–4 in cases where the complainant's mental condition would fluctuate or where an inability to communicate was not a physical inability to communicate. The broader interpretation by the House of Lords of "unable to refuse" will increase the number of cases in which a charge under s.30 will be appropriate. Presumably, where a complainant is "unable to refuse" or "lacks the capacity to choose", they will not have agreed by choice to the sexual activity and will not have had the capacity to make that choice. However, there will be cases where a jury might decide that a person with a mental disorder may have had the ability to refuse, in that they may have had the capacity to choose, but, nevertheless, did not freely agree within the meaning of s.74. In such a case, the prosecution may prefer the option of bringing alternative charges under both ss.30–33 and ss.1–4.

Because lack of capacity provides an alternative route to establishing 1.242 absence of consent in a non-consensual sexual offence, a rape charge has the advantage of enabling the prosecution to run their case in the alternative whilst simply having one charge. Where the prosecution charge a defendant with rape and there is evidence that the complainant has a mental disorder, the prosecution may seek to rely on evidence of that mental disorder as (i) showing that she did not have the capacity to agree by choice to sex within the meaning of s.74, or (ii) as part of the circumstances, to show that she was not freely agreeing to sex. It follows that they may present a rape case under s.1 on the alternative bases that the complainant did not freely agree to sex and, in any event, she did not have the mental capacity to agree by choice.

Lack of capacity through voluntary consumption of alcohol and/or drugs

Whilst a drunken consent is still a consent, if a complainant becomes so 1.243 intoxicated that they no longer have the capacity to choose, there can be no consent. The issue was put under the spotlight not long after the 2003 Act came into force in the case of *Dougal* tried at Swansea Crown Court in November 2005. The defendant had been charged with the rape of a university student, who had consumed a significant amount of alcohol. Following cross-examination of the complainant, prosecution counsel, after taking instructions from the CPS, informed the judge that he did not propose to offer any further evidence, as the prosecution were unable to prove the

---

[344] [2009] 1 Cr. App. R. 211 at [53]–[55].

complainant had not given consent because of her level of alcohol consumption. The trial judge directed the jury to enter a "not guilty" verdict. The Home Office subsequently consulted on a proposal that there should be a statutory definition of "incapacity through intoxication".[345] In the event, whilst no statutory definition of incapacity has been introduced, the Court of Appeal did provide an important steer in *Bree*[346] as to how such cases should be approached. The Judicial Studies Board followed this with some guidance as to appropriate judicial directions in such cases.

1.244   In *Bree,* the complainant, a student, shared a flat with the appellant's brother. One weekend, the appellant visited and went out with a group of his brother's friends, which included the complainant. She drank to excess and on returning to the flat, was violently ill. She recalled being in bed and said that, when she was lying there, she became aware that the appellant's face was between her legs and he was placing his tongue in her vagina. She then remembered him coming towards her and inserting his penis into her vagina. She said that she did not consent, but did not know how to stop the activity. She did not resist and said nothing. She felt uncoordinated. She could remember being asked whether she had a condom and saying "ow" when the appellant penetrated her, but her recollection was "very patchy" because of her intoxication. The appellant was charged with rape and the issue at trial was consent. At the start of the trial the prosecution had alleged that the complainant's alcohol consumption was so great that she was effectively unconscious and lacked the capacity to consent. By the end of the evidence, the case had changed. The prosecution no longer claimed that the complainant lacked the capacity to consent, but put the case to the jury on the basis that she had not consented. She knew what was happening. She knew that she did not want to have sexual intercourse and, so far as she could, she had

[345] Consultation Paper, *Convicting Rapists and Protecting Victims—Justice for Victims of Rape,* Office for Criminal Justice Reform (Spring 2006). See Clare Gunby, Anna Carline, and Caryl Beynon, *Alcohol-related Rape Cases: Barristers' Perspectives on the Sexual Offences Act 2003 and its Impact on Practice,* J. Crim. L. 2010, 74(6), 579–600, a study in which 14 barristers were interviewed about the "law-in-action reality" of rape cases involving alcohol intoxication. The conclusion reports that advocates were reluctant to see additional legislative changes being brought into the area of voluntary intoxication and rape, as legal reform was not a cure-all solution. Education and awareness at societal level were deemed paramount in order to allow the legislation to have its best impact. Barristers felt the best way to tackle the issue of rape following voluntary intoxication was to promote societal messages that dispel rape myths, which highlight the importance of acting ethically when drinking, of acceptable behaviour and social responsibility on the part of men as well as women. Barristers felt that such messages should be built into the educational programme and this was the critical factor in developing a society that could negotiate sexual consent and openly discuss sexual issues, expectations and intentions. In practice, attitudinal change may be difficult to foster, particularly because attitudes around consumption of alcohol are embedded within complex social beliefs that link alcohol use with sex. The authors call for greater public education and awareness of the provisions of the 2003 Act to help enlighten the lay public in their understanding of sexual offences and to make clear what is acceptable and unacceptable sexual behaviour.

[346] [2007] EWCA Crim 804; [2007] 2 Cr. App. R. 13.

made that clear, but severe intoxication had hampered her ability to resist. The appellant's case was that, although the complainant had been intoxicated, she was not so drunk as to be incapable of consenting, she had been conscious throughout and she had in fact consented. The judge directed the jury simply in terms of the definition of consent in s.74 of the 2003 Act. "Capacity" is not defined by the Act and the judge did not direct the jury on its meaning or effect in the context of the case. The appellant was convicted and appealed on the basis that the judge had directed the jury inadequately.

The Court of Appeal quashed the conviction, and in doing so made a number of observations on the operation of the law on the issue of "capacity". In particular, the Court stated that some of the hugely critical discussion arising after *Dougal* missed the essential point.[347] In that case, neither counsel for the Crown nor, for that matter, the judge was saying that a complainant who through drink is incapable of consenting to intercourse must nevertheless be deemed to have consented to it. Nor were they saying that a man is at liberty to have sexual intercourse with a woman who happens to be drunk, on the basis that her drunkenness deprives her of her right to choose whether to have intercourse or not. Such ideas were wrong in law and offensive.   1.245

However, the decision in *Bree* does not represent a fresh interpretation of the law governing the issue. Sir Igor Judge P, as he then was, giving the judgment of the Court, pointed out that the relevant principle was summarised in *Lang*,[348] where the Court had held that the critical question was whether an intoxicated complainant understood her situation and was capable of making up her own mind. The Court approved the passage from *Howard*[349], where Lord Parker CJ said in respect of young complainants that the prosecution must prove that the complainant's "understanding and knowledge were such that she was not in a position to decide whether to consent or resist". Scarman LJ (as he then was) widened the application of Lord Parker CJ's words to cover complainants who had taken drink or drugs as well as those who were very young. He stressed that the critical question is not how a drunk complainant came to take the drink but whether she understood her situation and was capable of making up her mind.   1.246

Sir Igor stated that: 1.247

" . . . it would be unrealistic to endeavour to create some kind of grid system which would enable the answer to these questions to be related to some

---

[347] The Court of Appeal stated (at [32]): "Without knowing all the details of the case, and focusing exclusively upon the observations of Counsel for the Crown in *Dougal*, it would be open to question whether the inability of the complainant to remember whether she gave consent or not might on further reflection be approached rather differently."
[348] (1975) 62 Cr. App. R. 50.
[349] (1966) 50 Cr. App. R. 56.

prescribed level of alcohol consumption. Experience shows that different individuals have a greater or lesser capacity to cope with alcohol than others, and indeed the ability of a single individual to do so may vary from day to day. The practical reality is that there are some areas of human behaviour which are inapt for legislative structures. In this context, provisions intended to protect women from sexual assaults might very well be conflated into a system which would provide patronising interference with the right of autonomous adults to make personal decisions for themselves."

1.248 It was the Court's view that the 2003 Act provided a clear definition of "consent" for the purposes of the law of rape, and by defining it with reference to "capacity to make that choice", it sufficiently addresses the issue of consent in the context of voluntary consumption by the complainant. The Court went on to observe:

"In our judgement, the proper construction of section 74 of the 2003 Act . . . leads to clear conclusions. If, through drink (or for any other reason) the complainant has temporarily lost her capacity to choose whether to have intercourse on the relevant occasion, she is not consenting, and subject to questions about the defendant's state of mind, if intercourse takes place, this would be rape. However, where the complainant has voluntarily consumed even substantial quantities of alcohol, but nevertheless remains capable of choosing whether or not to have intercourse, and in drink agrees to do so, this would not be rape. We should perhaps underline that, as a matter of practical reality, capacity to consent may well evaporate well before a complainant becomes unconscious. Whether this is so or not, however, is fact specific, or more accurately, depends on the actual state of mind of the individuals involved on the particular occasion."

1.249 The Court nonetheless took the view that the jury should have been given some assistance with the meaning of "capacity" in circumstances where the complainant was affected by her own voluntarily induced intoxication, and also with the question whether, and to what extent they could take that into account in deciding whether she had consented. The only specific feature of the complainant's alcohol consumption identified by the judge was its possible relevance to her reliability as a witness. The judge had referred to evidence that the complainant had been unconscious at times without giving any direction as to its significance. It was therefore possible that the jury had proceeded on the basis that the complainant was indeed unconscious, contrary to the prosecution case in its developed form. The critical aspect of the defence case was that the complainant had drunk far more than she was accustomed to which may have led her to behave in a way, which if sober, she would not. This was not sufficiently addressed in the summing up and the conviction was accordingly quashed.

1.250 It follows that in all cases where there is evidence upon which the jury could find that the complainant was voluntarily intoxicated by drink or drugs, a mere recital of the elements of the offence will not suffice. The jury should be given directions as to the possibility that intoxication may have swept away inhibitions and led the complainant to behave in an uncharacteristic way. As the Court of Appeal stated in *Bree*, a drunken consent is still a consent.[350] Further, in cases in which the jury might properly decide that the complainant did not have the capacity to agree by choice, the judge should direct them on the issue of "capacity". But it remains unnecessary to give a direction on "capacity" where the complainant's and the accused's respective accounts are completely at odds and the issue does not arise on the evidence. In *Wright*[351] the trial judge in a rape case was held to have correctly summed up the case on the basis that the jury had a stark choice, namely, that either (i) the complainant had been unconscious at the time of the sexual intercourse, in which case she had not consented and, if the accused had known of her unconscious state, he would be guilty, or (ii) the complainant had been affected by her own voluntarily induced intoxication, but nevertheless remained capable of choosing whether or not to have intercourse, and, in drink, had agreed to do so, in which case the accused would be not guilty.

On appropriate evidence the prosecution is entitled to put its case in respect of absence of consent on an alternative basis alleging (i) lack of capacity and, in any event, (ii) absence of consent, i.e. no agreement by choice. However, it is important for the trial judge not to leave lack of capacity as a route to a guilty verdict where the prosecution has not put its case on that basis and where the defence have not had an opportunity to cross-examine the complainant on the issue of capacity or to make submissions to the jury on the issue. In *Shehu*,[352] the Court of Appeal dismissed an appeal against conviction of rape and assault by penetration in circumstances where the judge had made reference to the issue of capacity in his summing up, notwithstanding that the prosecution case was simply that the complainant had not consented, and it had not advanced its case on the basis of lack of capacity to consent. The judge provided a route to verdict referring to the issue of capacity when it was not a live issue in the case. Whilst the Court of Appeal felt that, looking at the summing up as a whole, the direction had not left the issue of capacity to the jury, clearly it would have been wiser not to risk leaving an alternative route to conviction on a basis which had not been a live issue during the trial. **1.251**

Cases in which one or both parties are heavily intoxicated are so fact specific, there are dangers in slavishly following a prescriptive specimen direction.[353] However, these points (lack of capacity and absence of consent) often arise in such cases and when they do, they need to be addressed in the **1.252**

---

[350] At [32], where Sir Igor Judge P stated that, in the context of consent to intercourse, the phrase lacks delicacy, but, properly understood, it provides a useful shorthand accurately encapsulating the legal position. The same point arose in *Coates* [2008] 1 Cr. App. R. 31, where the President suggested that directions to the Board of the Court Martial should have been directed inter alia to the possibility that the complainant's consumption of alcohol may have led her to behave differently from the way she would have done if entirely sober.

[351] [2007] EWCA Crim 3473.

[352] [2011] All E.R.(D.) 79.

[353] For a helpful direction, see the *Crown Court Compendium* 2016, Ch.20.5 (sexual offences – capacity and voluntary intoxication).

judge's summing up. In *Kamki*,[354] the Court of Appeal considered the various elements included in the trial judge's summing up when directing a jury on the issue of consent and capacity to consent in a rape case, and concluded that the relevant propositions had been put to the jury in a correct way. We have refined the direction suggested in our last edition by reference to the propositions set out in *Kamki*. Directions must be tailor-made to cover the facts of the case so it may not be necessary to include every proposition:

(i) If a person is asleep, or has lost consciousness through drink or drugs, they cannot consent (as there is no freedom and capacity to choose), and that is so even though their body responds to the defendant's advances.

(ii) A person can still have the capacity to make a choice and have sex even where they have had a considerable amount to drink.

(iii) Consumption of alcohol or drugs may cause someone to become disinhibited and behave differently from the way they would normally behave. If they are aware of what is happening, but the consumption of alcohol or drugs has caused them to consent to activity which they would ordinarily refuse, then they have consented no matter how much they may later regret it. The fact that a person makes an unwise choice does not mean that they lacked the capacity to make it. A drunken consent is still a consent, if a person has the capacity to make the decision whether to agree by choice.

(iv) However, a person may lose the capacity to consent through the consumption of drink or drugs before a complete loss of consciousness arises.[355]

(v) Consideration then has to be given to the degree of consciousness or otherwise to determine the issue of capacity. Clearly a complainant will not have had the capacity to agree by choice where, due to intoxication through drink or drugs, their understanding and knowledge are so limited that they are not in a position to decide whether or not to agree.

(vi) Thus, if a complainant becomes so intoxicated that they no longer have the capacity to agree, there will be no consent. For instance, a person may be in a state where they know they do not want to take part in any sexual activity with someone, but they are incapable of saying so. Alternatively, they may have been affected to such a degree that, whilst having some limited awareness of what is happening, they are incapable of making any decision at all.

---

[354] [2013] EWCA Crim 2335.
[355] See Professor J.R. Spencer, *Three new cases on consent*, Cambridge Law Journal [2007] 490. The traveller on the road to alcoholic oblivion may reach the point where freedom and capacity is lost.

(vii) If it is determined that the complainant may have had the capacity to make a choice, consideration will then have to be given as to whether she did or may have consented to sexual intercourse.

In *Chedwyn Evans*,[356] Lord Judge CJ observed that on occasions when the words "drunken consent" are used or the issue is put in that way, it causes umbrage and indeed distress. Similarly, the Court of Appeal in *Kamki*[357] observed that it is not necessary when the elements of capacity have been addressed appropriately for the judge to direct the jury that a drunken consent remains a consent. For example, in *Chedwyn Evans*, the Court of Appeal took the view that the trial judge had amply encapsulated the concept of the drunken consent amounting to consent without using the express words "a drunken consent is still a consent". He had referred to two ways in which drink and/or drugs can affect an individual who is intoxicated: **1.253**

> "First it can remove inhibitions and a person may do things which she would not do or be less likely to do if sober. Secondly, she may consume so much alcohol and/or drugs that it affects her state of awareness. So you need to reach a conclusion upon what was the complainant's state of intoxication as you find it to be. Was she just disinhibited, or had what she had taken removed her capacity to exercise a choice?"

The judge went on to explain: **1.254**

> "A woman clearly does not have the capacity to make a choice if she is completely unconscious through the effects of drink and drugs, but there are various stages of consciousness, from being wide awake to dim awareness of reality. In a state of dim and drunken awareness you may, or may not, be in a condition to make choices. So you will need to consider the evidence of the complainant's state and decide these two questions: was she in a condition in which she was capable of making any choice one way or another? If you are sure that she was not, then she did not consent. If, on the other hand, you conclude she chose to agree to sexual intercourse, or may have done, then you must find the defendant not guilty."

Consent and capacity to consent—withdrawal of case from the jury

The issues of consent and capacity to consent in rape cases should normally be left to the jury to determine. *Hysa*[358] is a highly instructive case in which, on an interlocutory appeal by the CPS under s.58 of the Criminal Justice Act 2003, the Court of Appeal decided that it was not reasonable for the trial judge to have withdrawn the case from the jury. Whilst the case does not establish any new principle, it is a graphic illustration of how issues in relation to consent and capacity to consent should be approached where the complainant was heavily intoxicated. **1.255**

---

[356] [2012] EWCA Crim 2559.
[357] [2013] EWCA 2335.
[358] [2007] EWCA Crim 2056 (sub nom *R. v H*). The Court allowed the appeal against the trial judge's ruling and remitted the case for trial at the Crown Court. When the trial resumed, the defendant chose not to give evidence, and was convicted by the jury after a short retirement.

1.256   The complainant was a 16-year-old girl who had come to London to celebrate the New Year. She was drunk, became separated from her friends and ended up on her own at White City. On the opposite side of the road was a car containing three men, one of whom called her over. For some reason, possibly problems with a former boyfriend, she got into the car with complete strangers. The car drove off. During the journey, a man in the front passenger seat penetrated her vagina with his fingers. She said that she did not know when this started or how it happened. She told the jury that this unknown man must have undone her jeans without her knowledge. All she could say was that when she saw his hand between her legs, she pulled it out and told him to get off. She said that she did not consent to what the man did. The prosecution case was that 10 minutes later the defendant asked her for sex. She described what happened in her video recorded interview as follows:

> "... I just remember the man in the back saying, 'Can I have sex?' but I can't remember what I said to him and all of a sudden my trousers were like yanked down and then he was like, he'd like pulled them down to my knee and then he just like pushed my legs forward and my like jeans were like covering my face and my nose, and he was just like having sex with me and I remember I couldn't breathe or anything."

Later she said:

> "I think I tried, I think I might have tried to say get off me but I don't think he could hear me because like the jeans was over my face and there was some music playing."

1.257   She confirmed in her evidence that she did not want to have sex with the man, she did not think that she did so willingly and she did not think that she would have consented. She said that she could not remember what she had said to the man because she was drunk. When pressed by defence counsel in cross-examination, she said she could not recall what she was thinking or saying. The prosecution argued that when she said that she did not think she would have "consented", it was clear that the complainant meant she could not say whether she actually said "yes" or "no". The defence objected to this interpretation of the evidence. They argued that the complainant was clearly unable to exclude the possibility that she had said "yes" to sex.

1.258   At the close of the prosecution case, the defence submitted to the trial judge that there was no case to answer because the prosecution had not established that intercourse had taken place without consent. The complainant clearly had the capacity to consent because she rejected the advances of the first and third man. At its highest, the prosecution case was that she could not remember whether she had not consented. The prosecution simply could not exclude the possibility that the complainant had said "yes". The prosecution submitted that there was sufficient evidence from which the jury could conclude that consent had never been given. There was no requirement that the prosecution must establish that the complainant said "no". Furthermore, in the alternative, there was ample evidence from which the jury could have concluded that she did not have capacity. She was a small girl, just 5'3" in height, weighing 8 stone 3 pounds, aged 16, who had consumed half-a-litre of vodka and smoked cannabis prior to the incident.

The trial judge, in his ruling, observed that, at its highest, the complain- **1.259** ant's evidence was that she did not think she would have consented. He stated that the prosecution accepted the complainant could not say that she did not say "yes". In respect of the issue as to whether she lacked the capacity to agree by choice as a result of taking drink or drugs, he found that although there was evidence of drunkenness, it was insufficient to allow a jury safely to conclude that the complainant had lacked the capacity to consent.

The Court of Appeal allowed the prosecution's appeal against the termi- **1.260** nating ruling. It held, citing *Bree*, that there was sufficient evidence of rape to be left to the jury. The complainant's evidence was that she did not want to have sex when she got into the car, she did not want to have sex when she found her jeans on her face and she told or may have told the man to get off during the course of intercourse. The fact that she did not say "no" at the moment of initial penetration was not fatal to the prosecution case, nor was the fact that she could not remember whether she had consented or not. The judge had trespassed too far into the jury's territory by withdrawing the case from them. They should have been left to decide whether the complainant had capacity to consent and whether she had in fact consented. The points made by the defence were all good jury points and would no doubt be deployed to good effect in defence counsel's closing speech. The Court said:

> "Issues of consent and capacity to consent to intercourse in cases of alleged rape should normally be left to the jury to determine. It would be a rare case indeed where it would be appropriate for a judge to stop a case in which, on one view, a 16-year-old girl, alone at night and vulnerable through drink, is picked up by a stranger who has sex with her within minutes of meeting her and she says repeatedly she would not have consented to sex in these circumstances."

Hysa serves as an important reminder of some fundamental principles which **1.261** should underpin a jury's approach to the issue of consent. These principles were set out by Roche LJ in *Malone*.[359] To establish absence of consent, the prosecution does not have to show that the complainant did something to demonstrate that she is not consenting. Nor does the prosecution have to show that absence of consent was communicated to the defendant. It follows that it does not matter that the prosecution cannot prove that the complainant did not say "no" or was incapable of saying "no". There is no requirement for a complainant to resist or be incapable of resisting. If a complainant does not have capacity, the fact that she cannot remember if she "consented" or not is not necessarily fatal to the prosecution. The Court also made it clear that a provable lie, such as the defendant's denial in interview

---

[359] *Malone* [1998] 2 Cr. App. R. 447 at 457.

that he had had sex with the complainant, could be evidence of absence of consent.

1.262   A further example of these principles in operation in a case where the complainant was strongly affected by alcohol can be found in the interlocutory appeal of *R. v MA, PA and RS*.[360] The case is of particular significance because it demonstrates that a complainant's lack of memory and her acceptance in evidence that sexual activity "could have happened consensually" is not necessarily fatal to a prosecution.[361] The case involved an allegation of rape of the same complainant by the three respondents. The trial judge indicated at the close of the prosecution case that he proposed to withdraw the case from the jury as there was insufficient evidence upon which a jury could say the complainant lacked capacity as opposed to simply having no recollection of events to which she may have consented. The complainant was aged 23. The defendants, aged between 40 and 48, were strangers to her. The complainant had gone out and during the course of an evening at a club she had consumed up to about 12 shots of vodka. After leaving the nightclub at about 2.10 am, she met the three respondents and took a taxi to their flat where she drank more vodka. In interview, each respondent admitted having sexual intercourse with her at the flat and all stated that any sexual activity was consensual. The complainant remained at the flat until 11.00 pm the same day. Once taken to the police station, she made complaints of rape. The toxicology evidence suggested that her blood alcohol concentration was likely to have been well over twice the drink driving limit at that time (most likely concentration 208 milligrams per 100 mls of blood). The toxicologist gave evidence that memory loss from which she said she was suffering did not of itself mean a person would have been incapable or unable to make decisions. Alcohol at a blood concentration of around 200 milligrams and above may interfere with the way in which long-term memories are stored. The complainant gave evidence that owing to the amount of drink consumed she had little memory of what happened at the flat. She only remembered having sexual intercourse with one of the respondents. She had told him to stop and he ignored her. During cross-examination she accepted that sexual activity could have happened consensually and she may just have had a blank in her memory. Two mobile phones were seized by the police showing sexual activity including sexual intercourse with one of the respondents. The Court of Appeal took the view that in the video clips the complainant was depicted throughout as being sufficiently inert and unresponsive as to leave it open to a properly directed jury to be sure that at the relevant times she was not consenting and that she did not have the freedom and capacity to do so. In the context of what the respondents had said about the timings of their respective acts of sexual

---

[360] Unreported, January 22, 2015. Appeal from Lincoln Crown Court.
[361] The same point arose in *Seedy Tambedou* [2014] EWCA Crim 954 (lack of memory does not establish whether sexual activity was consensual or not).

intercourse with the complainant, the clips provided evidence of the complainant's condition for the jury to assess in relation to all three complainants. Such an approach would be consonant with the observations in *Hysa* in that issues of consent and capacity should normally be left to a jury to determine. The Court of Appeal reversed the ruling in relation to all three respondents. It found, after a close analysis of the evidence in the case, that there was a case to answer in each case and that the rulings were not reasonable in that the judge's failure to refer to the video clips was a serious and significant omission. It was a matter for the jury to assess the video footage and the overall evidence of the alcohol taken by the complainant and its effects upon her. An important and appropriate concession was made in the course of argument before the Court of Appeal that the complainant's answer in cross-examination as to the possibility of having consented to intercourse but failing to recall it could not be determinative.

EVIDENTIAL PRESUMPTIONS AS TO CONSENT

Section 75 of the Sexual Offences Act 2003

Section 75 of the Sexual Offences Act 2003 creates evidential presumptions   1.263
regarding the issues of consent and reasonable belief in consent. The section applies to the offences under ss.1–4 of the Act, i.e. rape, assault by penetration, sexual assault and causing a person to engage in sexual activity without consent. It does not appear to apply to inchoate offences.[362] The presumptions in s.75 arise very rarely in practice.[363] They continue to require the prosecution to disprove consent if, in the circumstances defined in the section, there is sufficient evidence to raise the issue.[364] The defendant will usually be in a position to point to sufficient evidence, from whatever source, to raise an issue as to whether the complainant consented and/or whether the defendant reasonably believed that the complainant consented, in which case the direction to the jury should be on the basis of s.74.[365] For instance, in a case where the complainant states she was asleep, thereby establishing the circumstance set out in s.75(2)(d), an issue as to consent would nevertheless be raised if the defendant then gives evidence that he had a mutual understanding with the complainant that they would wake each other up

---

[362] This problem is highlighted in HH Judge Rodwell QC, *Problems with the Sexual Offences Act 2003* [2005] Crim. L.R. 290.

[363] It is the authors' experience that many barristers feel that s.75 arises in circumstances where it clearly does not. For the proper application of s.75, see *Gavin White* [2010] EWCA Crim 1929.

[364] *Jheeta* [2007] EWCA Crim 1699 at [23] per Sir Igor Judge P.

[365] David Ormerod QC and Karl Laird point out in *Smith and Hogan's Criminal Law*, 14th edn (2015), p.832, that the nature of the presumptions means that a defendant can raise sufficient evidence to rebut a presumption without necessarily challenging the actual circumstances. A is obliged not to rebut the *fact* giving rise to the presumption, but the *legal consequences* of the presumption.

with sex. But in practical terms, the existence of s.75 may mean that the defendant is obliged to enter the witness box to provide an explanation where one or more of the circumstances has been established without contradiction, and sufficient evidence to raise an issue has not emerged during cross-examination.

1.264   In *Gavin White*[366] the Court of Appeal approved a passage from *Blackstone's*[367] dealing with the operation of s.75, stating that it is vital to appreciate that where the judge concludes at the close of evidence that there is sufficient evidence to raise an issue as to consent, the s.75 route to verdict is closed, and the judge must direct the jury in accordance with s.74 and s.1(2). In *Gavin White*, at trial, both counsel and the trial judge appear not to have understood how this difficult section operates. The case is instructive as to the extent to which s.75 is still frequently misunderstood. The appellant had been convicted of sexual assault by penetration after the trial judge directed the jury in accordance with s.75. In fact, as the respondents conceded at the appeal (although not at trial), a s.75 direction was inappropriate as there was no doubt that there was sufficient evidence to raise an issue as to consent. The appellant had given evidence that the complainant was not asleep and the digital penetration was consensual. Furthermore, had a s.75 direction been appropriate, the direction given by the judge was inadequate.

1.265   A s.75 presumption must *not*, however, be elevated into an irrebuttable presumption: see *Kapezi*,[368] where the trial judge corrected his earlier direction to the jury in appropriate terms. In *Shanji Zhang*,[369] the Court of Appeal upheld a rape conviction even though the trial judge had mistakenly referred to the evidential presumptions in his summing up, on the basis that the jury could have been in no doubt as to what they had to decide. To similar effect is *Lewis Mba*[370] where a conviction was upheld following a hybrid s.74/s.75 direction. This should not be interpreted as an endorsement of such directions; rather, it was an acceptable direction on the special facts of that case

1.266   Section 75 states:

> "(1) If in proceedings for an offence to which this section applies it is proved—
>> (a) that the defendant did the relevant act,
>> (b) that any of the circumstances specified in subsection (2) existed, and
>> (c) that the defendant knew that those circumstances existed,
>
> the complainant is to be taken not to have consented to the relevant act unless sufficient evidence is adduced to raise an issue as to whether he consented, and the defendant is to be taken not to have reasonably believed that the complainant

---

[366] [2010] EWCA Crim 1929.
[367] 2010 edn, para.B3.19, now 2016 edn, para.B3.31.
[368] [2013] EWCA Crim 560.
[369] [2007] EWCA Crim 2018.
[370] [2012] EWCA Crim 2773.

consented unless sufficient evidence is adduced to raise an issue as to whether he reasonably believed it.

(2) The circumstances are that—

    (a) any person was, at the time of the relevant act or immediately before it began, using violence against the complainant or causing the complainant to fear that immediate violence would be used against him;

    (b) any person was, at the time of the relevant act or immediately before it began, causing the complainant to fear that violence was being used, or that immediate violence would be used, against another person;

    (c) the complainant was, and the defendant was not, unlawfully detained at the time of the relevant act;

    (d) the complainant was asleep or otherwise unconscious at the time of the relevant act;

    (e) because of the complainant's physical disability, the complainant would not have been able at the time of the relevant act to communicate to the defendant whether the complainant consented;

    (f) any person had administered to or caused to be taken by the complainant, without the complainant's consent, a substance which, having regard to when it was administered or taken, was capable of causing or enabling the complainant to be stupefied or overpowered at the time of the relevant act.

(3) In subsection (2)(a) and (b), the reference to the time immediately before the relevant act began is, in the case of an act which is one of a continuous series of sexual activities, a reference to the time immediately before the first sexual activity began."

The Sexual Offences Review

The Sexual Offences Review felt that the arguments for both defining and explaining consent in statute were overwhelming. In particular, it thought that the approach adopted in a number of Australian states (and the US Model Penal Code) of setting out a list of examples of circumstances where consent was not present was helpful to all concerned. The Review stressed that any such list would be a set of examples only: it would not be complete and would not cover each and every circumstance where consent is not present. The Review felt that such a list should help both practitioners and juries in coming to decisions in particular cases, and give broad guidelines for considering the issue.[371]   **1.267**

The Review's list was designed to complement and buttress a definition of consent based upon free agreement. The grand design was to set out those areas that are well-established in case law as to when consent is not present, and those where it should be clear that consent would not be present. The courts would have the benefit of a more detailed statute, in which Parliament would have given a clear indication to the courts and society about the bounds of acceptable behaviour.   **1.268**

The Review recognised the challenge of considering whether other types of behaviour and situations ought to be included, over and above the major   **1.269**

[371] *Setting the Boundaries*, 2000, para.2.10.6.

components of the common law, in order to produce a robust and appropriate list. It thought that any list should be as comprehensive as possible, but the question would be exactly which examples to include and where to stop.[372] The Review's suggested list was, in fact, significantly wider than the circumstances enacted in s.75(2) of the 2003 Act. The recommended examples which were not included in the legislation were where a person submits because of threats or fear of serious harm or serious detriment of any type to themselves or another person; is too affected by alcohol or drugs to give free agreement; or has agreement given for them by a third party.[373]

Protecting the Public

1.270   In the White Paper *Protecting the Public*,[374] the Government indicated that it would be including in the proposed statute a list of circumstances in which it should be presumed that consent was most unlikely to have been present. These broadly reflected the examples given by the Review, although intoxication was removed from the list. The Home Secretary stated:

> "I have rejected the suggestion that someone who is inebriated could claim they were unable to give consent—as opposed to someone who was unconscious for whatever reason, including because of alcohol—on the ground that we do not want mischievous accusations."

1.271   However, whilst the Government's list was similar to the Review's, it had a different approach to how the list would operate. Under the Government's scheme it would be for the prosecution to prove, beyond reasonable doubt, that sexual activity took place in one of the circumstances on the list. If that was proved, it would then be for the defendant to show, on the balance of probabilities, that in the particular circumstances in question the complainant did indeed give their consent.

1.272   The Sexual Offences Review had not dealt with the burden of proof, and appears to have intended its list to operate so that, if one or more of the listed circumstances was established by the prosecution, consent would be taken as being absent and no longer be an issue. *Protecting the Public*, whilst reproducing a similar list of circumstances, framed them as presumptions.

The Sexual Offences Bill

1.273   The Sexual Offences Bill as introduced included provisions which, if they had become law, would have had the effect of reversing the burden of proof if both relevant sexual activity and at least one of the listed circumstances were established. However, it was vehemently argued during the Bill's passage

[372] *Setting the Boundaries*, 2000, para.2.10.8.
[373] *Setting the Boundaries*, 2000, para.2.10.9.
[374] *Protecting the Public*, 2002, para.32.

through the House of Lords that the rebuttable and conclusive presumptions set out in the Bill were an attack on the presumption of innocence.[375] Another major criticism was that the provision creating rebuttable presumptions was muddled and would be difficult for juries to understand, because of the way in which the burden of proof shifted between the prosecution and the defence. In order to alleviate these concerns, on Third Reading the Government tabled amendments altering the rebuttable presumptions so that they placed an evidential rather than a persuasive burden on the defendant.[376]

Another feature of the Bill was its erosion of the list of circumstances recommended by the Sexual Offences Review.[377] First, the Review's list had included the case where the complainant was put in fear of violence. The Bill confined this circumstance to cases where the fear was of violence that was "immediate". This will clearly have a limiting effect, though the word "immediate" is capable of being interpreted broadly, as in the context of the Offences Against the Person Act 1861 where it has come to mean "imminent".[378] Further, the jury will also have the assistance of s.74, which may lead them to conclude that the violence, though not immediate, nonetheless affected the complainant's freedom to choose to consent.   1.274

Secondly, the Review's list included the case where a person submits or is unable to resist "because of threats or fear of serious harm or serious detriment of any type to themselves or another person". This wording had the potential to encompass a wide range of threats, including the threat of serious economic harm such as the loss of a job.[379] However, the Government took the view that in this respect the Review's list was too wide and that there were difficulties in covering such a wide range of threats. Lord Falconer, in resisting the suggestion that the list should be more comprehensive, said[380]:   1.275

"The rebuttable presumptions should be limited sensibly. Something that might frighten someone in a particular condition might not frighten someone else."

Finally, the Review's list included the situation "where agreement is expressed by a third party not a victim". This found its way into the Bill as introduced,   1.276

---

[375] *Hansard*, HL Vol.648, cols 1062–1063, Lord Thomas of Gresford (June 2, 2003).

[376] *Hansard*, HL Vol.649, col.670 (June 17, 2003).

[377] For argument that the list should have been more extensive and non-exhaustive (as in Canada and Australia), leaving scope for further situations to be added through the common law, see Professors Jennifer Temkin and Andrew Ashworth, *The Sexual Offences Act 2003 (1): Rape, Sexual Assaults and the Problems of Consent* [2004] Crim. L.R. 328 at p.338.

[378] cf. *Ireland* [1998] A.C. 147 HL. See also *R. v Horseferry Road Magistrates Court Ex p. Siadatan* [1991] 1 Q.B. 260, where Watkins LJ, while dealing with the construction of s.4 of the Public Order Act 1986, stated that "immediate" does not mean "instantaneous".

[379] *Setting the Boundaries*, 2000, para.2.10.9. The Review said it would be for the court to consider in each case what the nature of the threat was and whether the victim would think that she or he would suffer serious harm. These could vary from case to case: the threat of loss of employment might be far more serious in a small community with few other opportunities, for example. The Review drew a distinction between threats and inducements, saying that promising rewards for sex did not preclude free agreement and was unlikely to be a coercive situation.

[380] *Hansard*, HL Vol.648, col.1082 (June 2, 2003).

but was subsequently removed by Government amendment. This was because the argument was accepted that it would be unfair to impose a presumption in relation to absence of reasonable belief in consent where the defendant was a person with a mental disorder or learning disability and was told by another person that the complainant consented to sexual activity. Such a person could not necessarily be expected to understand that the third party was deceiving him.[381]

Section 77 of the Sexual Offences Act 2003: "relevant acts"

1.277   Section 77 of the 2003 Act provides:

"Sections 75 and 76: relevant acts
In relation to an offence to which sections 75 and 76 apply, references in those sections to the relevant act and to the complainant are to be read as follows—

Offence	Relevant Act
An offence under section 1 (rape).	The defendant intentionally penetrating, with his penis, the vagina, anus or mouth of another person ('the complainant').
An offence under section 2 (assault by penetration).	The defendant intentionally penetrating, with a part of his body or anything else, the vagina or anus of another person ('the complainant'), where the penetration is sexual.
An offence under section 3 (sexual assault).	The defendant intentionally touching another person ('the complainant'), where the touching is sexual.
An offence under section 4 (causing a person to engage in sexual activity without consent).	The defendant intentionally causing another person ('the complainant') to engage in an activity, where the activity is sexual."

1.278   Section 75 is designed to make absolutely clear the circumstances in which consent is unlikely to have been present. Evidential presumptions are created that in certain circumstances there was no consent. The list is exhaustive in the sense that circumstances outside those that fall within s.75(2)(a)–(f), however compelling, will not raise the presumption. Once any of these presumptions is triggered, an evidential burden will lie upon the defendant to

---

[381] cf. *Hansard*, HL Vol.649, col.671 (June 17, 2003), where Baroness Scotland of Asthal accepted Lord Carlisle's argument.

rebut the presumption.[382] Three matters have to be proved before the presumption arises. Section 77 sets out the relevant act that must be proved. Section 75(2) sets out the circumstances that will give rise to the presumptions, if it is proved that any of them existed. It is sufficient for any of the circumstances to be proved. Section 75(1)(c) stipulates that for the presumption to arise, it must be proved that the defendant knew that the relevant circumstances existed.

Professor David Ormerod[383] has criticised the drafting of s.77 which   **1.279**
defines the "relevant act" for the purposes of the s.4 offence as the defendant intentionally causing the complainant to engage in sexual activity. Professor Ormerod describes the question that the Act forces us to ask as rather odd: "Has the defendant deceived the complainant as to the nature or purpose of him intentionally causing her to engage in sexual activity?"

How will a defendant satisfy a judge that the presumption does not apply?

The defendant must be in a position to point to sufficient evidence to raise   **1.280**
an issue as to whether the complainant consented. In practical terms this may well mean that the defendant is obliged to enter the witness box to provide an explanation, if sufficient evidence has not been established during the cross-examination of prosecution witnesses.[384] Whilst it is not clear how demanding the evidential burden upon the defendant will be, in Parliament Baroness Scotland of Asthal stated:[385]

> "In order for these presumptions not to apply, the defendant will need to satisfy the judge from the evidence that there is a real issue about consent that is worth putting to the jury. The evidence relied on may be, for example, evidence that the defendant himself gives in the witness box, or evidence given on his behalf by a defence witness, or evidence given by the complainant during cross-examination. If the judge is satisfied that there is sufficient evidence to justify putting the issue of consent to the jury, then the issues will have to be proved by the prosecution is the normal way. If the judge does not think the evidence relied on by the defendant meets the threshold, he will direct the jury to find the defendant guilty."[386]

Whilst Baroness Scotland of Asthal referred to the need to raise a real issue about consent, that wording is not included in the legislation, which simply refers to "sufficient evidence".

---

[382] Since these are evidential presumptions there is no conflict with European jurisprudence and no incompatibility with ECHR, art.6(2) (the presumption of innocence): see *Lambert* [2002] A.C. 545.

[383] In a commentary on *R. v B* [2013] EWCA Crim 823.

[384] The Explanatory Notes to the 2003 Act, paras 140–141, make clear the Government's view that evidence given by the defendant himself may constitute "sufficient evidence". This was confirmed in *Gavin White* [2010] EWCA Crim 1929 where the Court of Appeal agreed with the respondent's concession that the appellant had raised sufficient evidence at trial by his own evidence.

[385] *Hansard*, HL Vol.649, col.670 (June 17, 2003).

[386] It is now settled that the final sentence of this extract is incorrect: see para.1.282, below (citing *Wang* [2005] UKHL 9).

1.281   Section 75 creates presumptions relating to both the issue of consent and the issue of reasonable belief in consent. If the trial judge decides (presumably at the close of the evidence) that there is sufficient evidence to raise an issue as to whether the complainant consented, the judge will put the issue of consent before the jury, and the s.75 route is barred. Similarly, if the judge decides that there is sufficient evidence to raise an issue as to whether the defendant reasonably believed that the complainant consented, the judge will put this issue before the jury. Again, the s.75 route is barred, and the evidential presumptions have no further role to play. The case returns to the key sections, ss.74 and 1(2). Conversely, if the judge decides there is insufficient evidence to raise an issue as to either consent or reasonable belief in consent, he will give the jury a s.75 direction on that issue.

1.282   The judge must be careful not to raise a s.75 evidential presumption into a conclusive presumption.[387] The jury must be directed that if they are sure of three matters, they will find, as appropriate, absence of consent and/or absence of reasonable belief in consent. Those three matters are: (i) the defendant did the relevant act (the relevant acts are set out in s.77) (s.75(1)(a)); (ii) any of the s.75(2) circumstances existed (s.75(1)(b)); and (iii) the defendant knew those circumstances existed (s.75(1)(c)). It is important to remember that, even in those rare cases where there is insufficient evidence to raise an issue as to consent, these three matters must be left to the jury, and the judge must never direct the jury to convict.[388] In *Gavin White*,[389] in the light of the appellant's evidence, a s.75 direction should not have been given at all. However, the Court of Appeal pointed out that the direction given must, in any event, have been baffling for the jury. The judge gave the direction twice, once in the summing up and once in answer to a question. He told the jury that if they were satisfied the complainant was asleep, it placed an evidential burden upon the defendant to satisfy the jury on the balance of probabilities that he reasonably believed she was consenting. First, even if s.75 applies, it does not reverse the burden of proof. Secondly, it appears to have been treated by the judge as a conclusive presumption in relation to the issue of absence of consent. Thirdly, even in those rare cases when it does arise, the jury must be sure of the three matters before they can convict, and a s.75 direction should be tailored to the facts.

1.283   It may often be easier for the defendant to establish sufficiency of evidence as to the reasonableness of belief in consent as opposed to consent itself, as it is easier to give evidence of one's own state of mind than of the state of mind of another. For the presumption to arise in respect of absence of consent, the prosecution must prove not only the particular circumstances

---

[387] In *Shanji Zhang* [2007] EWCA Crim 2018, the trial judge inappropriately directed the jury on the evidential presumption. The conviction was upheld on the basis that the jury could have been in no doubt whatsoever as to what they had to decide, namely whether the complainant did not consent and whether the defendant did not reasonably believe that she had consented.

[388] *Wang* [2005] UKHL 9.

[389] [2010] EWCA Crim 1929.

giving rise to the presumption but also that the defendant knew of those circumstances. However, whilst the defendant's knowledge that those circumstances existed will be highly relevant to whether he had a reasonable belief in consent, it is less than clear why it should have a bearing on the issue of consent itself. How could the defendant's knowledge shed light on the complainant's state of mind? This point was made in the Canadian case of *Ewanchuck*[390]:

> "Absence of consent is purely subjective and determined by reference to the complainant's subjective internal state of mind . . . The accused's perception of the complainant's state of mind is not relevant and only becomes so when a defence . . . is raised in the *mens rea* stage of the inquiry."

There may accordingly be cases where the judge will conclude there is insufficient evidence to raise the issue of actual consent, and will therefore give a s.75 direction to the jury, but give a direction relating to reasonable belief in consent in accordance with ss.1(1)(c) and 1(2).

What constitutes "sufficient evidence"?

No indication is given in the Act as to where the "sufficient evidence" threshold might lie. Even if a defendant does not give evidence putting forward a particular defence, whether as to consent or belief in it, the threshold may still be satisfied if sufficient evidence to raise such a defence can reasonably be inferred from the other evidence. Although the evidence may be adduced in rebuttal of the s.75 circumstances upon which the prosecution seek to rely, it need not necessarily be so specific provided it raises an issue as to consent and/or reasonable belief in consent. For example, a defendant might claim that although he knew the complainant was asleep, he reasonably believed that she was consenting based on past consensual sex with her in such circumstances. This does not mean that there is an obligation for judges to leave to the jury defences that are "fanciful or speculative". An example of where there might be sufficient evidence to rebut a presumption under s.75(2)(a) would be where a defendant raises some evidence of consensual sado-masochistic sex. There must be some foundation in the evidence. The point is illustrated by *Critchley*,[391] where the appellant, a drug-taker, was charged with murder. He stated that he had no recollection of what had happened but denied the killing. Counsel for the defence suggested that self-defence was a possibility if the jury rejected the defendant's denial. The Court of Appeal held that, although there are circumstances where a judge should leave a defence not raised by the defendant to the jury, in this case there was insufficient evidence to justify the judge leaving the issue of self-defence to them. A defence which has not been raised by the

1.284

---

[390] [1999] 1 S.C.R. 330, Can. S.Ct.
[391] [1982] Crim. L.R. 524. See in particular the commentary by Di Birch at p.525. See also *Bonnick* (1978) 66 Cr. App. R. 266.

defendant should only be left to the jury where there is evidence from which the jury could reasonably infer that the defendant acted in a way which provided a defence in law; a judge is under no duty to leave to a jury a defence which is fanciful or speculative.

1.285   *Ciccarelli*[392] is an example of a s.75 presumption arising as there was insufficient evidence that the appellant's belief that the complainant was consenting was reasonable. It was alleged that he had sexually assaulted a young woman who was fast asleep or unconscious through drink and/or drugs. There had been no previous relationship between the parties, not even a short sexual relationship of any kind. It was accepted that the complainant had not consented. There was only one issue in the case, which was whether the appellant might have reasonably believed that she was consenting. At the end of the evidence, including the appellant's, the trial judge concluded that no sufficient evidence had been adduced in accordance with s.75(1) on which the appellant could argue that he had reasonably believed the complainant was consenting. The judge indicated that she would give appropriate directions to the jury. Following her ruling, the appellant pleaded guilty. On appeal, the Court of Appeal held that the trial judge's approach had been entirely correct. Lord Judge CJ stated[393] that the basis of the appellant's submission was that it was enough for him to give the evidence he gave that he believed the complainant was consenting. Thereafter, whether or not the belief was reasonable was a matter for the jury. In other words, his asserted belief was sufficient to raise an issue. However, the trial judge had carried out a careful evaluation of the evidence and, on the facts of the case, her conclusion was entirely justified. These were two strangers and, before he touched the complainant sexually, the appellant made no attempt to awaken her. The reasonableness of his asserted belief was based on the single advance she had made to him (according to his account) at an earlier stage in the evening when she was awake, in a different place, before she was taken to the flat he shared with his girlfriend and put to bed in the spare room to sleep off her drunken stupor. There must be some evidence that the belief was reasonable. The evidence here did not raise an issue for the consideration of the jury.

Canadian "air of reality" test

1.286   Canadian cases may be instructive as to what the courts in England and Wales may consider to constitute "sufficient evidence" to raise a defence of reasonable belief in consent. In Canada it is not sufficient that a defendant merely asserts that he believed the defendant was consenting, he must satisfy the evidential burden by giving the defence an "air of reality".[394] However,

---

[392] [2011] EWCA Crim 2665.
[393] At [19]–[20].
[394] For further discussion, see Jennifer Temkin, *Rape and the Legal Process*, 2nd edn (Oxford: Oxford University Press, 2002), p.132.

there is no evidence to suggest that English courts have so far adopted such an approach.

Where the versions of events offered by the complainant and the defendant **1.287** differ greatly, and the only issue is that of consent or lack of consent, the Canadian courts have held that the judge need not put the issue of belief in consent before the jury. For example, the Supreme Court of Canada in *Pappajohn*[395] held that a trial judge must put before the jury any defences which may be open to the defendant upon the evidence, but that the judge is not bound to put before the jury every defence that is raised by counsel. The judge should only put the defence before the jury if there is some basis in evidence upon which the defence can rest.[396] For this purpose, the judge must consider whether there is some evidence which would convey a sense of reality to the submission. In *Pappajohn*, the appellant appealed against his conviction for rape on the ground that the trial judge failed to put the defence of mistake of fact to the jury. The complainant was a real estate saleswoman who was responsible for the sale of the appellant's home. The complainant alleged that she was raped whilst inside the appellant's property, despite her protests and struggles. In contrast, the appellant stated that the complainant consented to sexual intercourse a number of times. The complainant ran out of the house naked wearing a man's bow tie with her hands tied behind her back. The Court held that because the two versions were so different, and because the only issue was that of consent or no consent, the trial judge was right not to put the defence of mistake of fact to the jury.[397] If that approach is also taken in this jurisdiction, it follows that in cases where the prosecution and defence cases on the issue of consent are dramatically opposed, there may be insufficient evidence to raise an issue as to reasonable belief in consent.[398]

In the case of *Osolin*,[399] Cory J held that there need not be independent **1.288** evidence to corroborate the defendant's version of events, but that a mere assertion of mistaken belief will not suffice.[400] Similarly, in the case of *Park*[401] the Supreme Court reiterated the need for a "real factual basis" to support the mistaken belief defence.

An interesting example where the court held that the "air of reality" test **1.289** had been met, and that the honest belief in consent defence should be left to the jury, is *Filice*.[402] The complainant stated that the defendant raped her, whereas the defendant claimed that the complainant had consented. Prior to

---

[395] [1980] 2 S.C.R. 120.
[396] [1980] 2 S.C.R. 120 at 126, per McIntyre J.
[397] cf. *R. v A (No. 2)* [2002] 1 A.C. 45 at [67], per Lord Steyn.
[398] cf. *Haughian and Pearson* (1984) 80 Cr. App. R. 334; *Taylor* (1985) 80 Cr. App. R. 327; cf. *Bashir (Mohamed)* (1983) Cr. App. R. 59.
[399] [1993] 4 S.C.R. 595, Can. S.Ct.
[400] See Don Stuart, *Canadian Criminal Law: A Treatise*, 4th edn (Toronto: Carswell, 2001), p.283.
[401] [1995] 2 S.C.R. 836.
[402] (1999) Carswell Ont. 1262.

the sexual intercourse the complainant had removed her false teeth. The defendant claimed that she had done this on previous occasions immediately prior to having sexual intercourse, and he took it to be an indication that she was consenting. The court held that the removal of the false teeth and the absence of resistance provided reasonable grounds for an honest belief in consent.

1.290 The Supreme Court again considered the "air of reality" test in *Cinous*[403]:

> "The basic requirement of an evidential foundation for defences gives rise to two well-established principles. First, a trial judge must put to the jury all defences that arise on the facts, whether or not they have been specifically raised by an accused. Where there is an air of reality to a defence, it should go to the jury. Second, a trial judge has a positive duty to keep from the jury defences lacking an evidential foundation. A defence that lacks an air of reality should be kept from the jury ... This is so even when the defence lacking an air of reality represents the accused's only chance for an acquittal, as illustrated by *R. v. Latimer*, [2001] 1 S.C.R. 3, 2001 SCC 1."

The Court went on to hold that:

> "the authorities after *Pappajohn* continue to support a two-pronged question for determining whether there is an evidential foundation warranting that a defence be put to a jury. The question remains whether there is (1) evidence (2) upon which a properly instructed jury acting reasonably could acquit if it believed the evidence to be true. The second part of this question can be rendered by asking whether the evidence put forth is reasonably capable of supporting the inferences required to acquit the accused. This is the current state of the law, uniformly applicable to all defences."

1.291 While the case law had affirmed that a trial judge applying the "air of reality" test should not consider issues of credibility and reliability, weigh evidence substantively, make findings of fact or draw determinate factual inferences,[404] this has now been qualified. In 2013 the Supreme Court in *Pappas*[405] established that, where the evidence requires the drawing of inferences in order to establish the objective or subjective elements of a defence, the trial judge may engage in a limited weighing to determine whether the elements of the defence can reasonably be inferred from the evidence[406]:

> "The air of reality test requires courts to tread a fine line: it requires more than 'some' or 'any' evidence of the elements of a defence, yet it does not go so far as to allow a weighing of the substantive merits of a defence: *R. v. Mayuran*, 2012 SCC 31, [2012] 2 S.C.R. 162, at para. 21. A trial judge applying the air of reality test cannot consider issues of credibility and reliability, weigh evidence substantively, make findings of fact, or draw determinate factual inferences: *R. v. Cinous*, 2002 SCC 29, [2002] 2 S.C.R. 3, at para. 87; *R. v. Fontaine*, 2004 SCC 27, [2004] 1 S.C.R. 702, at para. 12. However, where appropriate, the trial judge can

---

[403] [2002] 2 S.C.R. 3.
[404] *Cinous* [2002] S.C.C. 29; *Fontaine* [2004] S.C.C. 27, [2004] 1 S.C.R. 702 at [12].
[405] [2013] S.C.C. 56.
[406] At [22]–[26].

engage in a 'limited weighing' of the evidence, similar to that conducted by a preliminary inquiry judge when deciding whether to commit an accused to trial: see *R. v. Arcuri*, 2001 SCC 54, [2001] 2 S.C.R. 828, cited by McLachlin C.J. and Bastarache J. in *Cinous*, at para. 91.

The ability of the trial judge to engage in 'limited weighing' depends on the type of evidence on the record. 'If there is direct evidence as to every element of the defence, whether or not it is adduced by the accused, the trial judge must put the defence to the jury': *Cinous*, at para. 88. The trial judge may not engage in any weighing of direct evidence, since this would require a consideration of the inherent reliability of the evidence.

'Direct evidence is evidence which, if believed, resolves a matter in issue': *Cinous*, at para. 88, citing D. Watt, *Watt's Manual of Criminal Evidence* (2001), at § 8.0. However, 'the mere assertion by the accused of the elements of a defence does not constitute direct evidence, and will not be sufficient to put the defence before a jury': *Cinous*, at para. 88. An air of reality 'cannot spring from what amounts to little more than a bare, unsupported assertion by the accused', which is otherwise inconsistent with the totality of the accused's own evidence: *R. v. Park*, [1995] 2 S.C.R. 836, at para. 35, *per* L'Heureux-Dubé J. For example, in *R. v. Gauthier*, 2013 SCC 32, [2013] 2 S.C.R. 403, this Court, *per* Wagner J., suggested that a single statement made by an accused that is otherwise inconsistent with the accused's 'principal narrative' is insufficient to give an air of reality to a defence: paras. 60-61.

Where the evidence instead requires the drawing of inferences in order to establish the elements of a defence, the trial judge may engage in a limited weighing to determine whether the elements of the defence can reasonably be inferred from the evidence. 'The judge does not draw determinate factual inferences, but rather comes to a conclusion about the field of factual inferences that could reasonably be drawn from the evidence': *Cinous*, at para. 91. In conducting this limited weighing, the trial judge must examine the totality of the evidence: *Cinous*, at para. 53; *Park*, at para. 13, *per* L'Heureux-Dubé J.

. . . The fact remains that the trial judge exercises a gatekeeper role in keeping from the jury defences that have no evidential foundation. Defences supported only by bald assertions that cannot reasonably be borne out by the evidence, viewed in its totality, should be kept from the jury."

The list of circumstances in s.75(2)

The prosecution may establish an evidential presumption as to absence of consent and reasonable belief in consent simply by proving the relevant act under s.77, one of the list of circumstances in s.75(2) and the defendant's knowledge of those circumstances. There is no additional requirement to prove that the existence of the relevant circumstances caused the complainant not to consent. What are the circumstances?   **1.292**

Violence

Section 75(2)(a) and (b) deal with situations where violence is used or threatened against the complainant or another person. Section 75(2)(a) applies where any person was, at the time of the relevant act or immediately before it began, using violence against the complainant or causing the complainant to fear that immediate violence would be used against him. The   **1.293** use of the term "any person" means that the violence need not have been used or threatened by the defendant. Nor need it have caused the complainant to submit. Where the complainant is caused to fear violence, the fear must be of "immediate" violence. There is no stipulation that the complainant's fear must be based upon reasonable grounds, and so it would seem that an honest but unreasonable fear of immediate violence will suffice. As the Canadian Supreme Court said in *Ewanchuk*[407]:

> "As irrational as a complainant's motive might be, if she subjectively felt fear, it must lead to a legal finding of absence of consent."

1.294 Section 75(2)(b) focuses on the situation where violence is used or threatened against a person other than the complainant. It applies where any person was, at the time of the relevant act or immediately before it began, causing the complainant to fear that violence was being used, or that immediate violence would be used, against another person. Again, the violence need not have been threatened or used by the defendant, nor need it have caused the complainant to submit. But in the case of future violence, the fear must be of "immediate" violence. Again, there is no stipulation that the complainant's fear must have been based upon reasonable grounds, and so it would seem that an honest but unreasonable fear will suffice. "Immediately" needs to be interpreted in the context of the circumstances of the particular case.[408]

1.295 Neither paragraph deals with the situation where a complainant fears future violence, although in such circumstances the fear may well mean that the complainant does not consent. The justification for this omission is less than clear. But the circumstances set out in s.75(2) are not exhaustive of the cases where consent will be absent. In circumstances outside the list, the prosecution may establish absence of consent in the normal way. Although threats of future violence do not appear in the list, they may well be capable of preventing free agreement such that the prosecution are able to prove absence of consent without reliance on the presumptions.

1.296 Section 75(3) extends the meaning of "immediately before it began" in s.75(2)(a) and (b) to cover the time immediately before the first sexual activity began, if there is a continuous series of sexual activities. This ensures that the presumption of absence of consent may be established where violence is used or threatened immediately before a series of sexual acts done by the defendant to the complainant which only culminate in penetration.

Unlawful detention

1.297 Section 75(2)(c) applies where the complainant was, and the defendant was not, unlawfully detained at the time of the relevant act. Clearly, in such a coercive situation the complainant would be unlikely to be in a position to

---

[407] [1999] 1 S.C.R. 330, Can. S.Ct.
[408] *Constanza* (1997) 2 Cr. App. R. 492.

give free agreement. Cases do arise where a previous partner of a complainant finds it impossible to accept that a relationship is over and to release control. In such circumstances there may be allegations of both false imprisonment and rape. However, for the presumption to arise, the detention does not have to have been brought about by the defendant.

Sleep or unconsciousness

Section 75(2)(d) applies where the complainant was asleep or otherwise **1.298** unconscious at the time of the relevant act. It is arguable that in this area the law has taken a step backwards.[409] At common law, if a complainant was asleep or unconscious for any reason at the time of penetration, she was incapable of consenting.[410]

Although under the 2003 Act the issue of consent will still be live if **1.299** sufficient evidence is adduced, in most cases the reality will be that the complainant will not have had the capacity to make any choice if the jury find that he or she was asleep. Classically the defendant will deny that the complainant was asleep, leaving a stark choice for the jury between the prosecution case that the complainant was unconscious and the defence case that he or she was conscious and willing. Resort to a presumption in these circumstances would only complicate issues unnecessarily. The position is less straightforward where the defence accepts that the complainant was asleep but the defendant gives evidence that there was a subsisting agreement that the parties would have sex which would include the defendant waking the complainant with sex. The presumption will then be displaced, as there will be sufficient evidence to raise an issue as to both consent and reasonable belief as to consent, and it will be for the jury to resolve these issues under s.74 and s.1(2) in the usual way. In *Gavin White*,[411] the appellant had been charged with assault by penetration. He had taken an intimate photo showing the complainant's vagina being penetrated by two of his fingers at a time when the prosecution contended his sexual relationship with the complainant was over, and the complainant must have been asleep. The appellant gave evidence that the complainant was awake and posing for the photograph, and the digital penetration was consensual. Notwithstanding this evidence, the trial judge erroneously gave the jury a s.75 direction in his summing up on the basis of s.75(2)(d). He repeated the direction in response to a jury question: "If she gave consent beforehand, and she fell asleep during the photo preparation, is the consent still current?" The Court of Appeal, whilst making it clear that a s.75 direction was not appropriate, and, in any

[409] See Ashworth and Temkin, *The Sexual Offences Act 2003: (1) Rape, Sexual Assaults and the Problems of Consent* [2004] Crim. L.R. 328, where it is argued, with some force, that the circumstance of "unconsciousness" should give rise to a conclusive presumption.
[410] *Mayers* (1872) 12 Cox C.C.C. 311; *Larter and Castleton* [1995] Crim. L.R. 75; *Howard* (1965) 50 Cr. App. R. 56, see para.1.252, above, for a suggested direction where a complainant was unconscious through drink.
[411] [2010] EWCA Crim 1929.

event, the direction given was inadequate, acknowledged that in the situation suggested by the jury question the defendant would have a defence on the issue of consent. The Court observed that the jury may have been given the impression that they should convict if they were sure the complainant was asleep.

1.300　　In any event, where the parties have regularly slept together and had consensual intercourse in the past, although there may not be a particular consent, the required mental element for rape may not be present.[412] However, in the light of the continuing nature of the act of penetration, it would be rape to continue sexual intercourse with a partner who was asleep at the outset but who awakes during intercourse and does not consent to it, if there is no reasonable belief in consent.

1.301　　If the complainant is in a severe state of alcoholic inebriation and so affected by the alcohol as not to be in a position to give free agreement, but is nonetheless conscious, whilst the presumption does not arise, the complainant will not have had the capacity to agree by choice, and so will not have consented. Since capacity is an integral element of consent, here the common law has in fact been replicated without resort to a presumption.[413]

1.302　　The common law is illustrated by *Lang*,[414] where the case for the prosecution was that the complainant had submitted willingly, but only after a struggle and in the belief that further resistance was useless. The defence introduced the question of her drinking in an attempt to show that she might well have consented, being in a less inhibited state of mind than she would have been had she taken no drink. The trial judge in his summing-up invited the jury to think it might be necessary to determine how she came to take the drink, whether she took it willingly knowing what she was doing, whether she had been deceived by her seducer, not appreciating that she was being given alcohol to drink, and whether she took it knowingly but was actively encouraged by the defendant in the hope that her resistance might collapse. The conviction was quashed on appeal, as the trial judge had given the jury no assistance as to the state of mind that the complainant must have been in before it could be said that her apparent consent was not a real consent. He had encouraged the jury to think it was necessary to determine how she came to take the drink, when the critical question was whether she understood her situation and was capable of making up her own mind. The Court approved the passage from *Howard*[415] in which Lord Parker CJ said there is no rape unless the complainant's "understanding and knowledge were such that she

---

[412] *Page* (1846) 2 Cox C.C. 133.
[413] *Camplin* (1845) 1 Den. 89. See also *Fletcher* (1859) Bell 63 at 71, per Lord Campbell CJ.
[414] (1975) 62 Cr. App. R. 50.
[415] (1965) 50 Cr. App. R. 56.

was not in a position to decide whether to consent or resist".[416] In *Lang*,[417] Scarman LJ (as he then was) widened the application of Lord Parker CJ's words to cover complainants who have taken drink or drugs as well as those who are very young.

It follows that under the common law, if a complainant by reason of **1.303** alcohol or drugs was not capable of exercising a judgment on consent, absence of consent was established. In reality the law has not changed in practical terms since such a complainant would not have had capacity. Indeed, lack of capacity is not confined to those who are unconscious. As the Court of Appeal in *Bree* observed, capacity to consent can evaporate well before unconsciousness occurs. Whilst it may be argued that, since a state of unconsciousness is a circumstance within s.75(2)(d), it is not necessarily conclusive as to the issue of consent under the 2003 Act, the 2003 Act correctly focuses upon "capacity" by including it in the s.74 definition as a pre-requisite for consent.[418]

Physical disability

Section 75(2)(e) applies where, because of the complainant's physical disabil-   **1.304** ity, the complainant would not have been able at the time of the relevant act to communicate to the defendant whether he or she consented.[419] The provision is confined to those with physical disability and does not refer to complainants with a mental disorder who are not capable of communicating whether or not they consent. Presumably it was felt that such persons are sufficiently protected by the offences protecting those with mental disorder[420] and/or they will not have had the mental capacity to consent. In *Cooper*,[421] Lord Rodger of Earlsferry observed that where there is an inability to communicate choice because of physical disability as opposed to mental disorder, the ordinary non-consensual offences in ss.1–4 apply as opposed to the special offences in ss.30–33. Baroness Hale[422] accepted this but pointed out that some physical disorders of the brain lead to disorders of the mind. These observations do not, however, acknowledge the rarity of the evidential presumptions and how, in reality, they are easily rebutted. For instance, this presumption could be displaced by evidence of some form of communication indicating consent.

---

[416] The words "or resist" should be replaced with the words "or not": *Larter and Castleton* [1995] Crim. L.R. 75.

[417] *Lang* (1975) 62 Cr. App. R. 50.

[418] See *Setting The Boundaries*, 2000, para.2.10.7 where it was envisaged that the complainant's unconsciousness would give rise to a conclusive presumption.

[419] Examples might be those suffering from cerebral palsy or the effects of a stroke.

[420] See e.g. s.30(2) of the Sexual Offences Act 2003, where a person is unable to refuse because of, or for a reason related to, a mental disorder if he is unable to communicate a choice to agree to sexual touching. See Ch.7.

[421] [2009] UKHL 42 at [4].

[422] At [30].

Drug-assisted rape

1.305   The problem of drug-assisted rape has been recognised for some time.[423] Certain drugs have the capacity to lead complainants to consent to acts which they would normally find repugnant.[424] They may also cause sexual arousal and a sense of enjoyment. They can be mixed with other drugs or alcohol to avoid detection.

1.306   Section 75(2)(f) applies where *any* person has administered to or caused to be taken by the complainant, without the complainant's consent, a substance which, having regard to when it was administered or taken, was capable of causing or enabling the complainant to be stupefied or overpowered at the time of the relevant act. This represents the one circumstance where the 2003 Act goes further than recommended by the Sexual Offences Review, albeit the Review did include in its original list of circumstances the situation where a complainant is too affected by alcohol or drugs to give free agreement.[425]

1.307   The substance must, having regard to when it was administered or taken, have been capable of causing or enabling the complainant to be stupefied or overpowered at the time of the relevant act. The substance need not be an illegal substance. This wide definition includes laced drinks.

1.308   The substance must have been administered etc. without the complainant's consent. Voluntary consumption of the substance will not suffice. However, for the complainant to have consented to the administration etc., they would have to have freely agreed to its administration etc., knowing its nature and effect. Deception of the complainant as to the nature or effect of the substance would vitiate consent.

1.309   If the substance was administered etc. but no sexual activity actually took place and none was attempted, the defendant may still be charged with the preparatory offence of administering a substance with intent.[426]

CONCLUSIVE PRESUMPTIONS AS TO CONSENT

1.310   In contrast to the rebuttable presumptions of s.75 of the 2003 Act, which the defendant may challenge if there is sufficient evidence, s.76 of the Act creates conclusive presumptions. It provides:

---

[423] P. Sturman, *Drug Assisted Sexual Assault: A study for the Home Office* (Chardon: Metropolitan Police, 2000). For further discussion see Temkin, *Rape and the Legal Process*, 2nd edn, (2002) p.103. See also E. Finch and V.E. Munro, *Intoxicated Consent and the Boundaries of Drug Assisted Rape* [2003] Crim. L.R. 773 and *Intoxicated Consent and the Boundaries of Drug Assisted Rape Revisited* [2004] Crim. L.R. 789.
[424] Rohypnol or GHB (Gamma hydroxyl butyrate acid).
[425] In their article *The Sexual Offences Act 2003: (1) Rape, Sexual Assaults, and Problems of Consent* [2004] Crim. L.R. 328 at p.337, Professors Jennifer Temkin and Andrew Ashworth make a powerful case that this circumstance should raise an irrebuttable presumption.
[426] See Ch.14, below.

"(1) If in proceedings for an offence to which this section applies it is proved that the defendant did the relevant act and that any of the circumstances specified in subsection (2) existed, it is to be conclusively presumed—
   (a) that the complainant did not consent to the relevant act, and
   (b) that the defendant did not believe that the complainant consented to the relevant act.
(2) The circumstances are that—
   (a) the defendant intentionally deceived the complainant as to the nature or purpose of the relevant act;
   (b) the defendant intentionally induced the complainant to consent to the relevant act by impersonating a person known personally to the complainant."

Section 76 essentially replicates the common law, although both limbs of **1.311** s.76(2) in some respects go further. Where the prosecution are able to prove that the defendant did a relevant act (in the case of rape, intentional penile penetration of the complainant's vagina, anus or mouth), and that either of the circumstances set out in s.76(2) existed, it is conclusively presumed that the complainant did not consent to the relevant act and that the defendant did not believe that the complainant consented to the relevant act. The jury should be directed to convict the defendant if they find either of these matters proved. The judge should give the jury clear directions as to the meaning of the word "purpose" and identify the relevant evidence going to that issue. Since this section creates conclusive presumptions, it is arguable that its contents should not have been treated as matters of evidence but should have been included in the definition of the offence. The circumstances that give rise to the conclusive presumptions are not necessarily the worst type of rape.

The deception or impersonation must be shown to have operated upon the **1.312** mind of the complainant so as to induce consent. Lies as to the nature or purpose of the act or as to identity are not sufficient in themselves to trigger the presumptions. The presumption relating to impersonation does not arise if the complainant was not in fact induced to consent by the impersonation, and consented irrespective of it.

Deception as to the nature or purpose of the relevant act

As the conclusive presumptions in s.76 of the 2003 Act provide an alternative **1.313** route for a jury to convict a defendant, they require careful scrutiny. The presumption in s.76(2)(a) is relevant only in the comparatively rare case where the defendant has deliberately deceived the complainant about the nature or purpose of the relevant sexual act. The ambit of the provision is limited to the "act" to which the deception relates, and to deceptions as to the "nature or purpose" of the act as opposed to its quality. Beyond this very limited type of case, and assuming that none of the evidential presumptions in s.75 applies, the issue of consent in rape must be addressed by reference to the definition of consent in s.74 and the provision as to reasonable belief in consent in s.1(2).

1.314   Section 76(2)(a) applies where the defendant intentionally deceived the
complainant as to the nature or purpose of the relevant act. In *Jheeta*[427] the
presumption was held not to have arisen where the defendant deceived the
complainant by creating a bizarre fantasy which led her into having sexual
intercourse with him more often than she would otherwise have done. The
appellant pleaded guilty to two counts of procuring the complainant to have
sexual intercourse with him by false pretences, contrary to s.3(1) of the
Sexual Offences Act 1956, four counts of rape, contrary to s.1(1) of the
Sexual Offences Act 2003, and one count of blackmail. The complainant and
appellant had met while students and started a sexual relationship. To
prevent the complainant from breaking off the relationship the appellant sent
her threatening text messages. The complainant had no idea who was sending
the messages, and shared her worries about them with the appellant. He tried
to reassure her that he and his friends would protect her. When the
complainant wanted to involve the police, he said he would lodge a
complaint on her behalf. Over a period of four years, the appellant sent her
numerous text messages appearing to be sent by different police officers. The
police officers were fictitious. The messages were designed to encourage her
to maintain the relationship with the appellant and to sleep with him.

1.315   The appellant was arrested and, when interviewed, eventually admitted
that he had been responsible for the creation of the entire fictitious scheme.
There had been occasions when sexual intercourse had taken place while the
complainant was not truly consenting. Following advice from his counsel as
to the effect of s.76, the appellant pleaded guilty to four counts of rape. In his
basis of plea, he acknowledged that he had persuaded the complainant to
have sexual intercourse with him more frequently than she would otherwise
have done and that the persuasion had taken the form of pressures imposed
on her by the complicated scheme he had fabricated.

1.316   On appeal against conviction, the appellant argued that the deception did
not amount to a deception as to the nature or purpose of the act, and
accordingly the appellant had been wrongly advised as to the law by his then
counsel, the ambit of his behaviour was not caught by s.76 and the conclusive
presumption did not arise. The Court of Appeal agreed, holding that the
complainant had been deceived not as to the nature or purpose of the sexual
intercourse, but as to the situation in which she had found herself. No
conclusive presumption arises merely because a complainant is deceived in
some way or other by disingenuous blandishments or common-or-garden lies
told by the defendant. Lies of that type may well be deceptive and persuasive,
but they will rarely go to the nature or purpose of intercourse. However, the
Court dismissed the appeal on the basis that, in the light of the appellant's
admissions, the complainant had not exercised a free choice or consent for
the purposes of s.74 of the 2003 Act. There was no doubt that, on some

---

[427] [2007] EWCA Crim 1699.

occasions at least, the complainant had not consented and that the appellant was perfectly aware of that. This appears to be an acknowledgement by the Court of Appeal that some deceptions, when considered in the context of all the circumstances prevailing at the time, may lead to a complainant not exercising a free choice under s.74, even though those deceptions fall short of those engaging the s.76 presumptions. For further discussion see paras 1.205ff above.

It is of interest that the appellant's earlier deceptions in *Jheeta* were 1.317 charged under the old law as procuring sexual intercourse by false pretences, contrary to s.3(1) of the Sexual Offences Act 1956. The 2003 Act does not contain this offence, which was accordingly abolished as from May 1, 2004. The decision in *Jheeta* reveals a gap in the law[428] in that it is not at present properly equipped to deal with the procuring of sexual intercourse by fraud, which falls short of the limited categories of fraud that vitiate consent. However, the wider definition of consent in s.74, with its emphasis on freedom of choice, may be sufficient to catch cases where there is evidence that a complainant's choice was very far from informed.

Deception as to the nature of the act within the meaning of s.76

Section 76(2)(a) of the 2003 Act is relevant only in those comparatively rare 1.318 cases where the defendant deliberately deceived the complainant about the nature or purpose of one or other form of sexual intercourse. The ambit of s.76 is limited to the "act" to which the deception relates and to deceptions as to the "nature or purpose" of the act, as opposed to the act's quality. With regard to the nature of the act, the 2003 Act follows the common law, which established that if the victim was induced to consent on the basis of a fraudulent misrepresentation as to the nature of the act, there was no consent. In *Flattery*,[429] the defendant ran an open stall at Halifax market from which he professed to give medical and surgical advice for money. The victim, a girl of 19, consulted him with respect to an illness from which she was suffering. He advised that a surgical operation should be performed and, under the pretence of performing it, had sexual intercourse with her. She submitted to what was done in the belief that the defendant was merely treating her medically. It was adjudged that in the circumstances the girl had only consented to a surgical operation, and the conviction for rape was

---

[428] See the observations of Professor John Spencer in *Three new cases on consent*, *Cambridge Law Journal* [2007] 490.
[429] (1877) 1 QBD 410. See also *Case* (1850) 1 Den. 580, where a 14-year-old girl believed that she was submitting to medical treatment and made no resistance when her medical practitioner had sexual intercourse with her. Wilde CJ said (at 582): "She consented to one thing, he did another materially different, on which she had been prevented by his fraud from exercising her judgement and will".

upheld. *Flattery* was followed in *Williams*[430] where the appellant, who was a choirmaster in a Presbyterian church, was engaged by the parents of a 16-year-old girl to give her lessons in singing and voice production. The appellant had sexual intercourse with her under the pretence that her breathing was not quite right, and that he had to perform an operation to make an air passage to enable her to produce her voice properly. The girl submitted to what was done under the belief fraudulently induced by the appellant that she was being medically and surgically treated, and not with the intention that he should have sexual intercourse with her. In contrast, a fraudulent misrepresentation that a person has been found to be free from HIV and/or other sexually transmitted diseases does not nullify consent, because there is no deception as to the nature of the act.[431]

1.319   Beyond this limited type of case, and assuming that none of the evidential presumptions in s.75 apply, the issue of consent must be addressed by reference to the definition of consent in s.74 and the provision as to reasonable belief in consent in s.1(2).

Sexual intercourse induced by a fraudulent promise

1.320   It follows from the preceding paragraph that at common law, where a complainant consented to sexual intercourse knowing full well what the nature of the act was, but deceived by a promise never intended to be fulfilled, the complainant's consent was not vitiated by the deception. This is illustrated by *Linekar*,[432] where the defendant had approached a prostitute outside a cinema and they had agreed a price; they eventually had sexual intercourse with him promising to pay afterwards. He failed to pay. He was convicted of rape and appealed. It was held, allowing the appeal, that an essential ingredient of rape was proof that the woman did not consent to the act of sexual intercourse with the man who penetrated her; that the only types of fraud which could vitiate consent in a case of rape were frauds as to the nature of the act itself or as to the identity of the agent; that it was the absence of consent to sexual intercourse, rather than fraud, which constituted the offence of rape; and that accordingly, the reality of the complainant's consent in the present case was not destroyed by the defendant's pretence that he would pay her. In *Jheeta*,[433] the Court of Appeal confirmed that the facts of *Linekar* would not fall within the ambit of s.76(2)(a) and that the

---

[430] [1923] 1 K.B. 340, overruling *O'Shea* (1898) 19 Cox C.C. 76, in which Ridley J appeared to say that *Flattery* was no longer law. The decision in *Williams* was criticised by Professor Glanville Williams on the ground that the girl was deceived only as to the effects of the defendant's act rather than as to its essential nature: *Textbook of Criminal Law*, 2nd edn, (1983) pp.561–562. See also *Clarence* (1888) 22 QBD 13 at 44, per Stephen J: "Consent in such cases does not exist at all, because the act consented to is not the act done".

[431] For this reason, the Law Commission invited views as to whether this should be a further exception to the general rule: Law. Com. Consultation Paper No.139, paras 6.19 and 6.80. See also *R. v B* [2006] EWCA Crim 2945.

[432] [1995] 2 Cr. App. R. 49.

[433] [2007] EWCA Crim 1699 at [27] per Sir Igor Judge P.

position reached by the common law has not been changed by the 2003 Act. Similarly, consent induced by a promise to marry the complainant, or to give the complainant a lift home afterwards, an expensive holiday or a part in a film, is still consent to the relevant act albeit the person making the promise never intended to keep it. Accordingly, s.76 would not apply. Such conduct could have amounted to an offence under s.3(1) of the Sexual Offences Act 1956 if it involved sexual intercourse procured by false pretences or false representation. However, as noted above, that offence was repealed and not replaced by the 2003 Act.

Deception as to the purpose of the act not the quality of the act

By including in s.76(2)(a) deception as to the "purpose" of the act, **1.321** Parliament arguably extended the pre-existing common law. The extension was proposed by the Sexual Offences Review, citing as an example a false representation that the purpose of the act is a medical examination.[434] A deception of this sort is unlikely to feature in a rape case, but it could arise in cases of assault by penetration or sexual assault, where a complainant is induced by deception as to the purpose of the act to undergo an intimate medical examination. The inclusion in s.76(2)(a) of deception as to purpose has the virtue that it will eliminate the need to determine whether the complainant was deceived as to the nature of the act or its purpose. In particular, it renders academic any question as to whether the difficult case of *Tabassum*[435] was correctly decided as, on any view, the Court of Appeal in *Tabassum* applied a test different from the present law. The appellant in that case deceived women by pretending in one case that he was a fully qualified breast cancer specialist, and in other cases that he was doing a survey on breast cancer. The representations led the women to allow him to examine their breasts. In fact, although he had no medical qualifications, it was held by the Court of Appeal that the victims had consented to the nature of the defendant's acts, but not to their quality, since they believed he was medically qualified or had trained at the cancer hospital and that the touching was for a medical purpose; and that accordingly, there was no true consent. The late Professor Sir John Smith was highly critical of the decision, stating that the distinction drawn between "nature" and "quality" was new and highly suspect.[436] Arguably, this concern is dispelled by the Sexual Offences Act 2003, which, by adding the words "or purpose" to "nature", enables a jury to decide whether there was no consent due to deception as to the purpose of the relevant act. However, the Court of Appeal in *Jheeta*, when reviewing the pre-2003 Act authorities, pointed out that s.76(2)(a) does not address the

---

[434] *Setting the Boundaries*, 2000, para.2.10.9.
[435] [2000] Crim. L.R. 686.
[436] [2000] Crim. L.R. 686 at p.687. Arguably *Tabassum* is inconsistent with *Richardson* [1998] 2 Cr. App. R. 200 where a struck-off dentist who carried out work on patients without disclosing her status was held not to have committed an assault.

"quality" of the act but confines itself to its "purpose". The Court preferred *Green*[437] to *Tabassum* as an example where s.76(2)(a) would operate. In that case, a qualified doctor carried out bogus medical examinations of young men in the course of which they were wired up to monitors while they were masturbated. As the purported object was to assess their potential for impotence, there was a clear deception as to the "purpose" of the physical act.

1.322   The decision in *Jheeta* suggested that the Court of Appeal was adopting a restrictive interpretation of "the purpose of the act". The Court stated that since the s.76 presumptions are conclusive of guilt, they require the most stringent scrutiny. However, a considerably broader approach was taken by the Court of Appeal in *Devonald*,[438] in a reserved judgement, where it upheld the trial judge's decision that s.76(2)(a) applied where the appellant had persuaded the complainant, a 16-year-old boy, to masturbate in front of a webcam. The appellant believed that the boy had treated his daughter badly so he decided to teach him a lesson. He corresponded with the boy over the internet pretending to be a young woman and persuaded him to masturbate in front of a webcam. The appellant was convicted under s.4 of the 2003 Act of causing a person to engage in sexual activity without consent, having changed his plea following a ruling by the judge. The Court of Appeal, here, gave s.76(2)(a) a very wide interpretation as the complainant undoubtedly masturbated for a sexual purpose, albeit he was doing it for a young woman. It held that it would have been open to the jury to conclude that the complainant had been deceived as to the purpose of the masturbation. The Court regarded the case as analogous to *Green*, although in *Green* the complainants were induced to masturbate for non-sexual purposes. It said that the concept of "purpose" encompasses rather more than the specific purpose of sexual gratification by the defendant in the act of masturbation. *Devonald* has been the subject of significant academic criticism. Professor Ormerod argued that it is out of step with *Jheeta*.[439] If correctly decided, it would mean that lies about a defendant's state of mind could trigger the conclusive presumption, whereas they should simply be part of the evidence to be considered when the jury evaluate absence of consent. Jo Miles has echoed this criticism in observing that the implication of *Devonald* is that where a defendant intentionally induces the complainant's participation in sexual activity on the basis of some ostensible purpose other than his genuine purpose, the s.76 presumption would be triggered.[440]

---

[437] [2002] EWCA Crim 1501, identified by David Ormerod QC and Karl Laird in *Smith and Hogan's Criminal Law*, 14th edn (Oxford: OUP, 2015), p.840, as a relatively easy case in that the true purpose was not medical but sexual gratification.

[438] [2008] EWCA Crim 527.

[439] *Smith and Hogan's Criminal Law*, 14th edn (Oxford: OUP, 2015), p.842, where David Ormerod QC and Karl Laird argue that there are dangers in taking a wider reading of "purpose", as many bigamists and adulterers would thereby become rapists on the basis of a conclusive presumption.

[440] Jo Miles, *Sexual offences: consent, capacity and children*, Archbold News, Issue 10, December 5, 2008.

Subsequently, in *R. v B*[441] the Court of Appeal confirmed the restrictive   1.323
interpretation of the "purpose" of the act adopted in *Jheeta*.[442] The facts are
instructive. The appellant was convicted on seven counts of causing the
complainant, his girlfriend, to engage in sexual activity without consent,
contrary to s.4(1) of the 2003 Act. He established a fake Facebook account
and under a pseudonym ("G") established an online relationship with the
complainant. She had no idea that G was in reality the appellant. Using the
pseudonym he persuaded her to share sexual photos with him, and then
blackmailed her into performing more sexual acts. She confided in the
appellant as to what had happened. He told her he had dealt with the matter
by killing G. The appellant then established another fake online account
purporting to be a friend of G. Through that account he contacted the
complainant online and blackmailed her into providing yet more sexually
explicit photographs of herself. At trial, the appellant admitted setting up the
accounts and persuading the complainant to engage in the sexual activity,
but claimed that he believed she was consenting. The Crown sought to rely
upon the conclusive presumption in s.76 on the basis that the appellant had
intentionally deceived the complainant as to the purpose of the relevant acts
(it was not contended that she was deceived as to the *nature* of the acts). The
trial judge agreed that a s.76 issue arose for the jury to consider. He decided
he would leave to the jury the issue of whether the complainant had been
deceived as to the purpose of the acts and that he would direct them that, if
they found deceit proved, the conclusive presumption applied. The complainant was not asked at trial what she understood the purpose or the motive of
the person at the end of the webcam to be. The Court of Appeal quashed the
convictions and ordered a re-trial. Hallett LJ stated:[443]

> "Reliance upon section 76 in this case, on these facts and this evidence, was
> misplaced. The prosecution needed to look no further than the provisions of
> section 74. It provides that 'a person consents if he agrees by choice and has the
> freedom and capacity to make that choice'. If the complainant only complied
> because she was being blackmailed, the prosecution might argue forcefully she
> did not agree by choice."

In *R. v B*, there was no deception as to the "nature" of the acts: the   1.324
complainant knew that they were sexual acts of vaginal and anal penetration.
There was, undoubtedly, a deception as to the identity of the person who was
intentionally causing her to engage in sexual activity. Could there have been
a deception as to identity within the meaning of s.76? The obstacle to that
argument is that the conclusive presumption in s.76 has to be restrictively
interpreted as it effectively widens the definition of rape. Parliament has
provided that a fraud as to identity will trigger the application of s.76 only
where a defendant impersonates someone "known personally to the complainant". The identities used in this case were not the true identities of

---

[441] [2013] EWCA Crim 823.
[442] [2007] EWCA Crim 1699.
[443] At [24].

anyone known personally to the complainant. Arguably, there was in *R. v B* a deception as to motivation, in that it is likely that the girlfriend thought she was being intentionally caused to engage in the sexual acts for someone's sexual gratification, whereas the true motivation was to test her fidelity or to humiliate her. Clearly, the deception as to identity was inextricably linked to the appellant's motivation or purpose. However, on these facts, the Court of Appeal suggested that if the complainant had assumed that the motive of the other person was sexual gratification, she would not have been misled as to the purpose. The Court of Appeal distinguished *Devonald*,[444] and preferred *Jheeta* to the extent that there is a conflict between the two decisions.

1.325   The recent case of *Matt*[445] provides a clear cut example of a deception as to purpose. The complainant answered an advertisement placed by the applicant on a respectable website to appear in a pilot programme for a television series. The applicant was not a film maker but a plumber. He deceived the complainant into believing she was undergoing a casting process and induced her to carry out sexual acts with him, short of sexual intercourse, in a London hotel room. The Court of Appeal, in refusing an application for leave to appeal, had no difficulty in finding that there was a deception as to purpose falling within s.76(2)(a) in that the applicant's ostensible purpose was not sexual pleasure but simulated sexual pleasure for commercial purposes.

1.326   Two Commonwealth cases are instructive in this context. In the Canadian case of *Harms*[446] the appellant had posed as a doctor and obtained consent to sexual intercourse by falsely representing it as a necessary medical treatment for a condition for which he had given a false diagnosis. The Court upheld the conviction. Such conduct would clearly be rape under the 2003 Act as there was deception as to the purpose of the Act. In contrast, in the Australian case of *Papadimitropoulos*[447] the defendant went through a bogus ceremony of marriage with the complainant, inducing her thereby to have sexual intercourse with him. The High Court refused to find that the deception invalidated the woman's consent. This would be a clear example of the old offence under s.3 of the 1956 Act. Equally s.76(2)(a) of the 2003 Act might apply on these facts as arguably there was a deception as to the purpose of the act, the consummation of the marriage.

1.327   Section 76(2)(a) seems to assume that an act can have only one purpose. For instance, a doctor with a gynaecological sexual obsession might tell the complainant truthfully that an intimate medical examination is necessary. That doctor would not have deceived the complainant as to one of his purposes, but he would have failed to reveal that his secondary purpose was to obtain sexual gratification from the examination. If the evidence were to

---

[444] [2008] EWCA Crim 527. For further criticism of *Devonald*, see para.1.322, above.
[445] [2015] EWCA Crim 162.
[446] [1944] 2 D.L.R. 61.
[447] (1957) 98 C.L.R. 249. "Once the consent is comprehending and actual the inducing causes cannot destroy its reality and leave the man guilty of rape."

establish that sexual gratification was an additional purpose, and the complainant was deceived as to this and would not have consented had it been known, it is at least arguable that the presumption would operate, albeit the need for the medical examination was genuine. In the Canadian case of *Bolduc and Bird*,[448] a doctor deliberately allowed a voyeuristic friend, falsely representing himself to be a medical student, to be present at a vaginal examination. The woman's consent to the examination was held to be valid. Arguably, if the same set of facts arose in this jurisdiction, under the 2003 Act there would have been a deception as to the ulterior sexual purpose of the act even if the examination was necessary, so that the conclusive presumption would be engaged. The position would be different if the defendant had multiple purposes, but the complainant actually understood one of the purposes to be sexual gratification.[449]

Impersonation

Section 76(2)(b) appears to extend the common law by widening the **1.328** categories of impersonation sufficient to vitiate consent beyond the complainant's husband or regular sexual partner to "a person known to the complainant".

Before the Act, the law had developed to a stage where, in cases of **1.329** impersonation, the offence of rape would be committed whether the person impersonated was the complainant's husband or any other welcome sexual partner. Section 1(2) of the Sexual Offences Act 1956 provided that it was rape for a man to have sexual intercourse with a woman by a fraud which induced her to suppose he was her husband.[450] On the face of it, this provision was limited to impersonation of the complainant's husband. The position at common law with respect to people with whom the complainant had had a relationship falling short of marriage was for a long time unclear. However, in *Elbekkay*[451] it was decided that s.1(2) of the 1956 Act was not limited to husbands, as the section was derived from s.4 of the Criminal Law Amendment Act 1885, which was declaratory of the common law and was in itself designed to resolve the conflict between two conflicting judicial

---

[448] (1967) 63 D.L.R. (2nd) 82.

[449] See Jo Miles, *Sexual offences: consent, capacity and children*, Archbold News, Issue 10, December 5, 2008, where it is argued, on the basis of the outcome in *Jheeta*, that a complainant's ignorance of one of the defendant's multiple purposes, will not vitiate consent, at least where one purpose actually was, and was actually understood by the complainant to be, sexual gratification.

[450] A line of cases starting with *Jackson* (1822) Russ. & Ry. 487 and culminating in *Barrow* (1868) 11 Cox C.C. 191 (where the Court for Crown Cases Reserved held that the woman's consent to sexual intercourse was a defence even though she was deceived into thinking that the defendant was her husband) resulted in the passing of s.4 of the Criminal Law Amendment Act 1885 (later re-enacted as s.1(2) of the Sexual Offences Act 1956) which extended rape to cover this situation and so put an end to the vexed question of consent in this area.

[451] [1995] Crim. L.R. 163.

decisions.[452] It was limited to husbands solely because there was no need to include the unmarried, as the problem had just not arisen. The declaration was repeated in s.1(2) of the Sexual Offences Act 1956. The Court of Appeal held that it was very unlikely that in 1956 Parliament was deliberately and consciously deciding that it was rape to impersonate a husband but not, for example, a man who had been living with a woman for many years. The vital question was whether there was an absence of consent. The Court wholly agreed with the trial judge that to find that it is rape to impersonate a husband, but not if the person impersonated was the partner of the woman, would be extraordinary. In respect of the nineteenth century authorities, the Court adopted the words of Lord Keith in *R. v R*[453] that "the common law is . . . capable of changing in the light of changing social, economic and cultural developments". The decision in *Elbekkay* was welcome; any other interpretation would have been an anachronism.

1.330 What was s.1(2) of the 1956 Act was reproduced in s.1(3) of that Act when the definition of rape was amended by s.142(3) of the Criminal Justice and Public Order Act 1994. Section 1(3) provides that:

> "A man also commits rape if he induces a married woman to have sexual intercourse with him by impersonating her husband."

The Criminal Law Revision Committee had recommended in 1984 that consent obtained by impersonating *another man* (not just a husband) should be included amongst the cases where consent obtained by fraud amounts to rape.[454] This recommendation was adopted in Clause 89(2)(b)(ii) of the draft Criminal Code Bill.[455] Nevertheless, Parliament did not take the opportunity when amending the definition of rape in 1994 to extend the impersonation rule to all cases. That was unfortunate because, although it was likely that the courts would follow *Elbekkay*, it was at the very least arguable that the 1994 Act had implicitly overruled that decision by excluding from the new s.1(3) of the 1956 Act any reference to other welcome partners.[456]

"A person known to the complainant"

1.331 The 2003 Act uses the term "a person known to the complainant". This puts beyond doubt the position of sexual partners, both heterosexual and homosexual. Indeed, the term appears significantly to extend the pre-existing law. It could embrace a wide spectrum of people, from those the complainant has never met but has heard of to those with whom the complainant has had

---

[452] *Barrow* (1868) 11 Cox C.C. 191 and *Dee* (1884) 15 Cox C.C. 579.

[453] [1992] 1 A.C. 599 at 616C.

[454] Criminal Law Revision Committee, Fifteenth Report on *Sexual Offences* (1984), Cmnd.9213, para.2.102.

[455] Law Com.No.177 (1989).

[456] See Professor Sir John Smith's commentary on *Elbekkay* [1995] Crim. L.R. 163, at p.164. See also Nicola Padfield, *A Tiger by the Tail: Sexual Offences in the CJPOA 1994*, Archbold *News*, Issue 2, March 1, 1995 ("Such is the price for hasty Parliamentary reform.")

some degree of intimacy. It is unclear what degree of prior knowledge and/or intimacy is required. It is certainly not necessary for the person impersonated to be someone who has previously engaged in sexual activity with the complainant.[457] Nor would it appear necessary from the wording of the statute for the person impersonated to be someone the complainant has met,[458] although this would mean that an undisclosed last-minute stand-in on a date set up over the internet would be at risk of a conclusive presumption that the complainant did not consent to any subsequent sexual activity. It remains to be seen whether the courts will be tempted to apply *Elbekkay* so as to restrict persons known to the complainant to regular partners. However, a natural reading of the new provision suggests they will not so restrict it.

Section 76 does not address the problem of where there is a deception as to the defendant's professional qualifications or authority to do the act. The Law Commission recommended that this situation should be included within deception as to identity.[459] However, there is no specific provision in the Act to cover it. Whilst deception as to the "nature or purpose" of the act may cover bogus medical examinations, it does not necessarily follow that a deception solely as to qualifications or other attributes is a deception as to "nature or purpose". Nor is it necessarily a deception as to identity. This appears from the decision in *Richardson*,[460] where the defendant had continued to practise as a dentist despite being suspended. Patients claimed that they would not have allowed her to treat them if they had known of her suspension. She pleaded guilty to assault after the trial judge ruled that her deception had vitiated the patients' consent. The judge rejected the defence submission that the patients had consented to treatment despite their ignorance of the circumstances. The Court of Appeal quashed the conviction. The Court felt that the prosecution submission that the concept of identity encompassed a person's qualifications and other attributes would be straining and distorting the definition of identity even though it was clear that patients would not have consented had they known the dentist was suspended.

1.332

---

[457] cf. H.O. Circular 21/2004, *Guidance as to Part 1 of the Sexual Offences Act 2003*, para.337 (giving as an example a man impersonating his twin brother in order to engage in sexual activity with a woman whom he knows would be willing to engage in sexual activity with his brother).

[458] In this context, it is worth noting that family courts have been prepared to find no consent to marriage where the parties had only corresponded by letter before the wedding day: see the New Zealand case *C v C* [1942] NZLR 356, 358–9. The authors are grateful to Jo Miles for bringing the point to their attention.

[459] *Consent in Sex Offences* (2000), para.5.25. The Commission concluded "that it should be open to a jury to decide that, for the purposes of a particular act, the 'identity' of the actor included the possession of a professional qualification or other authority to do the act in question, and that if the defendant had no such authority then he or she did it without consent."

[460] [1998] 2 Cr. App. R. 200.

1.333   There are risks in taking the analogy of consent to bogus medical examinations too far. In the context of rape, deceptions as to attributes should never trigger presumptions.

Deception as to HIV status

Sexual Offences Act 2003 and Offences Against the Person Act 1861

1.334   A person who lies about or knowingly conceals their HIV positive status before embarking upon penetrative sex is putting the other party's life at risk. Nevertheless, the deception would appear not to be a deception as to the "nature or purpose" of the relevant act under s.76(2)(a) and so the conclusive presumption about consent would not be triggered.[461] Furthermore, any implied deception arising from a failure to reveal HIV positive status is irrelevant to the issue of consent in the context of sexual offences.[462] The position is very different under the Offences Against the Person Act 1861. It is true that in *Clarence*[463] it was held that the only type of deceptions which would vitiate consent were those relating to the nature of the act or the identity of the perpetrator. In that case, the defendant infected his wife with gonorrhoea. She stated, not unreasonably, that she would not have consented to sexual intercourse with her husband if she had been aware of his condition. The defendant was charged under ss.20 and 47 of the Offences Against the Person Act 1861.[464] The prosecution case was that by concealing his gonorrhoea the defendant had obtained consent by fraud, which was no consent at all. He was convicted, but on appeal the convictions were quashed.[465] Wills J held[466]:

> "Consent obtained by fraud is no consent at all is not true as a general proposition either in fact or in law".

1.335   However, the law has since moved on and in *Mohammed Dica* the Court of Appeal said that *Clarence* is of "no continuing relevance" in the context of offences against the person.[467] The defendant was convicted of two offences under s.20 of the Offences Against the Person Act 1861 on the basis that he concealed his HIV positive status from his two victims before he had unprotected sexual intercourse with them. Both complainants were subsequently diagnosed as HIV positive. Both had been willing to have sexual

---

[461] See *Jheeta* [2007] EWCA Crim 1699.

[462] *R. v B* [2007] 1 Cr. App. R. 29.

[463] (1888) 22 QBD 23, overruling *Sinclair* (1867) 13 Cox C.C. 28 and *Bennett* (1866) 4 F. & F. 1105.

[464] Rape was not an option as the marital exemption would have applied.

[465] By a majority of 9:4.

[466] In *Mohammed Dica* [2004] EWCA Crim 1103, Judge LJ (as he then was) noted that the observations of the Court in *Clarence* have to be put into the context of the perceived requirement that the husband could be convicted under s.20 only if he had committed an assault, and the deemed consent of the wife to have sexual intercourse with her husband.

[467] [2004] EWCA Crim 1103.

intercourse with the defendant. The prosecution case was that the complainants would not have consented had they known he was HIV positive. The appellant's case was that he told both women of his condition and they were nonetheless willing to have sexual intercourse with him. The trial judge, notwithstanding defence submissions based on *Clarence*, had allowed the case to continue on the basis that the passing of the HIV virus by consensual sexual intercourse is capable of being a matter that comes within s.20.[468] He also withdrew the defence of consent from the jury. On appeal against conviction, the Court of Appeal held that whilst the trial judge had been correct to rule that the spreading of HIV could come within s.20, he had been wrong to rule that the possible consent of the victims to run the risk of infection was irrelevant to a charge under s.20. The convictions were quashed and a retrial was ordered.

It is to be stressed that the Court of Appeal in *Mohammed Dica* was considering consent in the context of charges of causing grievous bodily harm under s.20 of the Offences against the Person Act 1861 and not in respect of non-consensual sexual offences. The Court identified the question for decision as whether the victim's consent to sexual intercourse, which as a result of the appellant's concealment was given in ignorance of the facts of his condition, necessarily amounted to consent to the risk of being infected by him. Judge LJ (as he then was) stated[469]:   **1.336**

> "In our view, on the assumed facts now being considered, the answer is entirely straightforward. These victims consented to sexual intercourse. Accordingly, the appellant was not guilty of rape. Given the long-term nature of the relationships, if the appellant concealed the truth about his condition from them, and therefore kept them in ignorance of it, there was no reason for them to think that they were running any risk of infection, and they were not consenting to it. On this basis, there would be no consent sufficient in law to provide the appellant with a defence to a charge under section 20."

It is important to distinguish between s.18 and s.20 of the 1861 Act in this context. Following *Mohammed Dica*, it is clear that when a defendant infects a sexual partner with HIV or another sexually transmissible disease by penetrative sex, it may be possible to bring charges under the Offences against the Person Act 1861. Deliberate and intentional spreading of HIV with intent to cause grievous bodily harm will amount to an offence under s.18 of the 1861 Act. An agreement on the part of the other participant to run the risk of infection will not amount to a defence. If a defendant knows that   **1.337**

---

[468] It was argued that criminalisation would have a serious and negative effect for reporting and detecting the virus. It would put any person infected with HIV who has unprotected consensual sexual intercourse at risk of prosecution for at least an attempt to commit an offence under s.20 of the 1861 Act, whether or not the partner is him/herself infected with a strain of the virus. The effect of an interpretation which criminalises such conduct could be that a woman who is known to be HIV positive would be criminally liable for breast-feeding her child. It was also argued that criminalisation would discourage testing, or only those who had been tested would have "actual knowledge".

[469] [2004] EWCA Crim 1103 at [39].

he is suffering from HIV or some other serious sexual disease, recklessly decides to take the risk of its transmission through consensual sexual intercourse, and inflicts grievous bodily harm on a person from whom the risk is concealed and who does not consent to run it, he commits an offence under s.20 of the 1861 Act. Consent to sexual intercourse is not of itself to be regarded as consent to the risk of consequent disease. Whilst it is unlikely that someone would consent to a risk of a major illness, if the victim consents to the risk of disease, this continues to be a defence under s.20.[470] In *Barnes*[471] Lord Woolf CJ summarised the effect of the decision in *Mohammed Dica*. An HIV positive defendant who infected a sexual partner with the HIV virus would be guilty of an offence "contrary to s.20 of the 1861 Act if, being aware of his condition, he had sexual intercourse . . . without disclosing his condition." On the other hand, he would have a defence if he had made his partner aware of his condition, or if she had learnt of his condition from another source, and she "with that knowledge consented to sexual intercourse with him because she was still prepared to accept the risks involved". In *Konzani*[472] the Court of Appeal made it clear that for a complainant's consent to the risk of contracting HIV to be a defence, their consent must be an informed consent. Where a defendant deliberately conceals his HIV positive status, he cannot then assert he had an honest belief in his partner's informed consent to the risk of the transmission of the disease, unless there is some evidence that might form the basis of such a belief. Normally, silence in these circumstances is incongruous with an informed consent.

1.338 In its second consultation paper,[473] the Law Commission acknowledged that there is a case for treating a deception as to a person's HIV status or freedom from other sexually transmissible disease as of such fundamental importance to his or her partner that it should nullify consent altogether. However, in its report to the Sex Offences Review[474] the Commission felt that this was a delicate issue requiring expertise in public health and social policy rather than law. In particular, there was a concern that such an extension of the law might discourage people from discovering their HIV status.[475] The Commission did not feel qualified to express a view and made no recommendation on the issue.

---

[470] At [59].

[471] [2004] EWCA Crim 3246.

[472] [2005] 2 Cr. App. R. 14. For discussion see Mathew Wait, *Knowledge, autonomy and consent: R v Konzani* [2005] Crim. L.R. 763; Samantha Ryan, *Reckless transmission of HIV: Knowledge and culpability* [2006] Crim. L.R. 981.

[473] Law Commission (1995), paras 6.19 and 6.80.

[474] (2000), para.5.27. The Court of Appeal agreed with this approach in *R. v B* [2007] 1 Cr. App. R. 29.

[475] The Law Commission was also concerned that there should be no anomalies as between rape and offences against the person: see para.5.29. The Terence Higgins Trust is against the involvement of the criminal law in these circumstances as it could act as a deterrent to regular testing.

R. v B

The issue has arisen in a case under the Sexual Offences Act 2003. In *R. v*   1.339
B[476] the appellant was convicted of rape. The prosecution case was that the
complainant was subjected to a prolonged assault which culminated in
vaginal intercourse. At no stage did she consent to that sexual activity. The
appellant's account was that they had had consensual intercourse. It was
established in 2001 that the appellant was HIV positive. He knew about his
HIV status and he did not inform the complainant about it. At trial the
prosecution had applied to put the appellant's HIV status in evidence. The
defence objected on the basis that it was irrelevant, and even if it had any
relevance, it was so prejudicial it should be excluded under s.78 of the Police
and Criminal Evidence Act 1984. The trial judge, in ruling the evidence
admissible, referred to the statutory definition of consent in s.74 and said:
"the definition involves the person . . . being in a position to make a reasoned
choice in the matter, and for such a person to be in that position that person
has to be in possession of all relevant facts, and a relevant fact is the prospect
that he or she might, by dint of sexual intimacy, become infected with HIV
thereafter". He held that the fact that the appellant had not informed the
complainant of his HIV status was a matter the jury was entitled to take into
account when determining whether or not she had in truth consented on the
one hand, or whether he had a reasonable belief in her consent on the
other.

It was submitted by the appellant that since the Sexual Offences Act makes   1.340
no reference to implied deceptions, nor to behaviour relating to or in the
context of transmissible diseases, the Act does not purport to change the law
in that respect. Implied deceptions have little relevance to the issue of
consent. The appellant relied upon *Mohammed Dica*[477] where, in the
judgement of the Court, Judge LJ (as he then was) had observed that the
appellant's concealment of his HIV status from his partners meant that he
would have no defence to a charge under s.20 of the Offences against the
Person Act, but as the victims had consented to sexual intercourse, he was
not guilty of rape.

The Court of Appeal accepted this submission and held that where one   1.341
party to sexual activity has a sexually transmissible disease which is not
disclosed to the other party, any consent that may have been given to that
activity by the other party is not thereby vitiated. However, the party
suffering from the sexually transmissible disease will not have any defence to
any charge which may result from harm created by the sexual activity, merely
by virtue of that consent, because such consent did not include consent to
infection by that disease.

---

[476] [2007] 1 Cr. App. R. 29. The conviction was quashed and a re-trial was ordered. The
defendant was re-convicted.
[477] [2004] Q.B. 1257.

1.342   The Court took the view that the consequences of a law that a failure to disclose HIV status vitiated consent was a matter which required debate, not in a court of law but as a matter of public and social policy, bearing in mind all the factors that are concerned, including questions of personal autonomy, in delicate personal relationships. It agreed with the view of the Law Commission that there would appear to be good reasons for considering the extent to which it would be right to criminalise sexual activity by those with sexually transmissible diseases who do not disclose it to their partners. But the extent to which such activity should result in charges such as rape, as opposed to tailor-made charges of deception in relation to the particular sexual activity, seemed to the Court to be a matter which was properly for public debate.

1.343   *R. v B*[478] needs to be considered in the context of the decision of the Divisional Court in *Assange v Swedish Prosecution Authority*.[479] The Court in that case rejected the argument that, if a deception does not fall within s.76, it cannot be taken into account for the purposes of s.74 of the Act. Sir John Thomas P, as he then was, observed that all the court had said in *R. v B* was that[480]:

> " . . . as a matter of law, the fact that the defendant may not have disclosed his HIV status is not a matter which could in any way be relevant to the issue of consent under section 74 in relation to sexual activity in this case."

Sir John continued[481]:

> "*R v B* goes no further than deciding that failure to disclose HIV infection is not of itself relevant to consent under s.74. *R v B* does not permit Mr Assange to contend that, if he deceived AA as to whether he was using a condom or one that he had not damaged, that was irrelevant to the issue of AA's consent to sexual intercourse as a matter of the law of England and Wales or his belief in her consent. On each of those issues, it is clear that it is the prosecution case she did not consent and he had no or no reasonable belief in that consent. Those are issues to which s.74 and not s.76 is relevant; there is nothing in *R v B* which compels any other conclusion. Furthermore it does not matter whether the sexual contact is described as molestation, assault or, since it involved penile penetration, rape. The dual criminality issue is the absence of consent and the absence of a reasonable belief in consent. Those issues are the same regardless of the description of the conduct."

It remains to be seen whether the decision in *Assange* will have any impact upon the situation where there is an established sexual relationship between the parties, and the defendant does not reveal to his partner that he has just been diagnosed as HIV positive. Whilst the effect of the decision would be that the failure to reveal his HIV status would not be relevant in itself to the issue of consent, there may be circumstances in which the failure to disclose would, when considered with other evidence, be relevant to that issue.

---

[478] [2006] EWCA Crim 2945.
[479] [2011] EWHC 2849 (Admin), at [88]ff.
[480] At [21].
[481] At [90].

The implications of R. v B for non-consensual offences under the Sexual Offences Act 2003

Whereas *R. v B* appears to have settled the law for the time being in the   **1.344**
context of sexual offences where there has been no deception as to the
defendant's HIV status, it is clear that s.74 of the 2003 Act was intended to
and has provided a new definition of consent, which is now a concept
significantly wider than simply awareness of the physical nature of the act
and agreement to it. It follows that there may be circumstances where
concealment of HIV status will be relevant to the issue of consent.

Professor Leigh has mounted a powerful argument that the Court of   **1.345**
Appeal in *R. v B* accepted too readily that s.74 was not intended to mark a
change in the previous law according to which consent in rape means no
more than consent to the act of intercourse.[482] He suggests that the Court
was influenced, not only by a reluctance to venture into issues of social
policy, but also by the outmoded view that it is only appreciation of the
barest physical nature of the act and the willingness to perform it that counts.
He states:

> "One can conceive of few situations in which active misrepresentation as to HIV
> status or indeed STI infection would not be relevant to consent. Consent need
> not be seen simply in terms of awareness of the physical nature of the sexual act
> but also in terms of the victim's awareness and agreement to some of its collateral
> aspects."

To provide graphic support for his argument, Professor Leigh goes to   **1.346**
Canadian jurisprudence. He cites the following passage from the minority
judgement of McLachlin J in *Cuerrier*[483]:

> "With the greatest of deference to the learned judges in these cases, an
> explanation may be suggested as to why deceit as to venereal disease may vitiate
> consent while deceit as to other inducements, like promises of marriage or fur
> coats, does not. Consent to unprotected sexual intercourse is consent to sexual
> intercourse with a certain person and to the transmission of bodily fluids from
> that person. Where the person represents that he or she is disease-free, and
> consent is given on that basis, deception on that matter goes to the very act of
> assault. The complainant does not consent to the transmission of diseased fluid
> into his or her body. This deception in a very real sense goes to the nature of the
> sexual act, changing it from an act that has certain natural consequences
> (whether pleasure, pain, or pregnancy), to a potential sentence of death. It differs
> fundamentally from deception as to the consideration that will be given for
> consent, like marriage, money or a fur coat, in that it relates to the physical act
> itself. It differs, moreover, in a profoundly serious way that merits the criminal
> sanction."

Professor Leigh argues that it would be possible for an English court to   **1.347**
adopt similar reasoning and to conclude that a person cannot be said to have

---

[482] Professor Leigh, *Two cases on consent in rape*, Archbold News, Issue 5, June 8, 2007.
[483] [1998] S.C.R. 371; [1991] 2 L.R.C. 29 (Canada SC), Gonthier J concurring. McLachlin J
was later to become Chief Justice.

agreed by choice to intercourse where she has been actively misled or is unaware of the fact that her partner suffers from HIV or other STI, on the basis that the deception goes to the very nature of the sexual act, albeit slightly more broadly conceived than was the case in *Dica*. That form of deception qualifies the essential character of the act.

1.348   Professor Leigh's trenchant criticism of *R. v B* is, in part, based upon an interpretation of *R. v B* that it established that a positive misrepresentation about HIV status would not vitiate consent. In fact, in *R. v B* there was no deception. The ratio was confined to the fact that failure to reveal HIV status was not relevant to consent under s.74 of the 2003 Act in that case. However, Professor Leigh suggests that the Court also meant to preclude any argument that positive misrepresentation is relevant to consent. This suggestion is based upon the Court's invocation of the Law Commission's submission, where no distinction was made between concealment and active mis-representation. But the position is likely to be different where a defendant does not conceal his HIV positive status but tells lies about it. In those circumstances, there is a compelling argument that the lie is relevant to whether the complainant is consenting, i.e. agreeing by choice with the freedom and capacity to make that choice in accordance with s.74 of the 2003 Act. The evidence will not be conclusive as to the vitiation of consent, but, at the very least, it is arguable that a lie about HIV status would be relevant to the complainant's state of mind, unless he or she was willing to run the risk of contracting the disease. The counter-argument is that s.76 confines the scope of s.74 so that deceptions falling short of being deceptions as to the nature or purpose of the relevant act can never, on their own, vitiate consent. We do not favour this interpretation as it runs counter to the purpose of definition in s.74 which is designed to focus upon the autonomy of the complaint. For further discussion see paras 1.205 and following, above.

1.349   The situation is more difficult where there is an established relationship between the parties, the defendant becomes HIV positive and he fails to reveal it to his sexual partner. It could be argued that this amounts to an implied deception in that the continuing consensual sexual relationship depends upon openness about such a fundamental matter. In the context of offences against the person, in *Konzani*[484] the Court of Appeal considered the position of a defendant charged under s.20 of the Offences against the Person Act 1861 with having recklessly transmitted the HIV virus to his partner through consensual intercourse. The Court acknowledged that, on any view, the concealment of this fact from a partner almost inevitably means that she is deceived as to his HIV positive status and so is not in a position to give an informed consent to take the risk of contracting the disease. This begs the question whether depriving a sexual partner of the opportunity to decide whether to take such a risk is relevant for a jury in a rape case, when deciding whether the partner consented to penetration. Following *R. v B*, such implied

---

[484] [2005] 2 Cr. App. R. 14 (p.198).

deception as result of a stark moral omission would not be relevant to the issue of consent in rape. It remains to be seen whether the issue of the potential width of s.74 will be re-visited in the context of an omission to tell an established partner after discovery of infection.

Section 3 of the Sexual Offences Act 1956

Under s.3(1) of the Sexual Offences Act 1956 it was an offence for a person   **1.350** to procure a woman, by false pretences or false representations, to have sexual intercourse in any part of the world. The Law Commission recommended that s.3 should be extended to procuring any form of penetration by deception, leaving open whether this should include deception as to HIV status.[485]

The Sexual Offences Review recommended that there should be an offence   **1.351** of obtaining sexual penetration by threats or deception in any part of the world.[486] It stated:

> "We envisage that this kind of deception is of a lower level or a different kind than in our list of situations where consent is absent (which includes deception as to the identity of the person, or the nature or purpose of the act), and could relate to going through a sham ceremony of marriage."

The Review pointed out that the offence could be used in situations such as advertising in the UK for waitresses or entertainers overseas, when the real requirement is to provide sex.

Section 3 of the Sexual Offences Act 1956 was repealed but not replaced by   **1.352** the Sexual Offences Act 2003.[487] The lack of a replacement offence is to be regretted. Although the origin of the offence may have been concern about the white slave trade, and the offence was rarely used, its absence leaves a gap in the law governing serious sexual offences. In particular, such an offence would have addressed the situation where there is deception which is not of a nature necessarily to vitiate consent for the purposes of rape.

IS IT NECESSARY FOR THE JUDGE TO DIRECT THE JURY UPON THE ISSUE OF CONSENT WHERE THE PROSECUTION AND DEFENCE CASES ARE DIAMETRICALLY OPPOSED?

Even where the defence is a simple denial that the incidents ever occurred, the   **1.353** issue of consent should not be withdrawn from the jury. In *R. v H*[488] the appellant had been charged with rape and his defence was that the alleged conduct (oral penetration) had simply not happened at all. The judge

---

[485] Law Commission (1995), para.5.45.
[486] *Setting the Boundaries*, 2000, para.2.18.7.
[487] The same is true of s.2(1) of the 1956 Act (procuring a woman, by threats or intimidation, to have sexual intercourse).
[488] [2006] EWCA Crim 853.

directed the jury properly as to the ingredients of the offence (including consent) and then suggested:

> "You may think that the issue of consent does not arise in this case, it being the defendant's case that it never happened at all. So you may think that your task can be simplified by asking yourself [whether the defendant did the act alleged]. If the answer is yes, the defendant would be guilty. If the answer is no, he would be not guilty."

While the Court had some sympathy with the judge's natural wish to identify for the jury the central issue between the parties, it would have been better had he been less emphatic. However, it could not be said that the issue of consent had been withdrawn from the jury: the judge had left them to decide whether they could simplify their task, and they would only have done so if they were sure that consent was not an issue.

PERMISSIBLE JUDICIAL COMMENT IN RAPE CASES

1.354 In *Convicting Rapists and Protecting Victims—Justice for Victims of Rape*,[489] the Office for Criminal Justice Reform invited responses on the merits of making generic expert evidence admissible to counter myths and stereotypes regarding victims of rape. The support for such a change in the law derived from the growing belief that complainants were being evaluated without juries appreciating the potential effects of the trauma of serious assault and how it might affect a victim's evidence, these being matters outside a juror's normal experience. Whilst the position remains that parties are not permitted to introduce generic expert evidence of the range of known reactions to non-consensual offences,[490] there has been significant development in the use of balanced judicial comment to address areas where rape myths are sufficiently well-established.

1.355 During the years following the introduction of the s.74 definition of consent, it has become increasingly recognised that it is appropriate for judges to provide juries with assistance in non-consensual cases as to the way evidence should be approached. This stems from a much greater awareness of the dangers of stereotyping and illegitimate lines of reasoning, which could lead a jury to view a complainant's evidence with unwarranted scepticism.[491] Lawyers have become used to addressing these issues in the evidence they adduce and in their speeches. Balanced judicial comment enables juries to be warned about unjustified assumptions without the danger of generic expert evidence deflecting from the critical issues in the case. However, Neil Kibble

---

[489] Consultation paper published in 2006.
[490] *R. v ER* [2010] EWCA Crim 2522.
[491] *Crown Court Bench Book* 2010, Ch.17, p.356; *Crown Court Compendium* 2016, Pt.1, Ch.20.

has noted that there is a view that a brief judicial statement to juries rejecting myths may not be sufficient to overcome entrenched attitudes or beliefs.[492]

In *Doody*[493] the Court of Appeal addressed the limits of permissible comment when a judge is summing up in a rape case. It said that balanced directions aimed at correcting misconceptions can be given where there is a danger of the jury coming to an unjustified conclusion without an appropriate warning. The situation is analogous to those in which the trial judge warns the jury against apparently persuasive, but possibly mistaken, evidence of identification (the *Turnbull* direction) or against jumping to a conclusion from a defendant's lie (the *Lucas* direction). The only difference is that in non-consensual sex cases, the comment is made to ensure fairness to the complainant rather than to the defendant. **1.356**

There have been significant developments in the seven years since *Doody*[494] Judicial comment to prevent false assumptions has become a regular feature in sex cases and is positively encouraged by the Judicial College and the *Crown Court Bench Book* 2010, now replaced by the *Crown Court Compendium* 2016.[495] Any comment must be balanced, as its purpose is to warn the jury against the unfairness of approaching the evidence with *any* preformed assumptions. For instance, in *R. v GJB*[496] the trial judge gave a direction examining possible reasons why the complainant did not make disclosure for several years, but failed to strike a balance by putting the defence case before the jury in the same context. Similarly, in *R. v CE*[497] the judge directed the jury that it was a common misconception that victims of sexual abuse are eager to complain to the police about what has been done to them. That made it sound as if there are no victims of sexual abuse who are eager to complain to the police, which would, as the Court of Appeal **1.357**

---

[492] [2009] Crim. L.R. 591. Some commentators still maintain a preference for the Government's original proposal of expert evidence, on the ground that such evidence would enable a more detailed explanation of why certain ideas are mythical and misconceived to be put before the jury. See also Louise Ellison and Vanessa Munro, *Turning Mirrors into Windows? Assessing the Impact of (Mock) Juror Education in Rape Trials*, Br. J Criminology 49, which examined the impact of expert guidance upon jurors in the form of both general expert evidence and judicial comment. They concluded that their findings give cause for optimism in terms of the ability of either general expert testimony and/or extended judicial instruction to inform jurors about the disparate reactions of victims of rape, and to generate less prejudicial assessments of the relevance of counter-intuitive behaviours, such as delayed reporting or a calm courtroom demeanour. Expectations of physical resistance and/or injury may be less amenable to judicial direction.

[493] [2008] EWCA Crim 2557. See also *R. v MM* [2007] EWCA Crim 1558 for an example of a case where the Court of Appeal said that the trial judge had not gone beyond the bounds of permissible comment when the defence had been fabrication in respect allegations of rape and indecent assault upon the defendant's step-children. The defence had criticised the complainants for the delay in making complaints.

[494] [2008] EWCA Crim 2557.

[495] See *Crown Court Bench Book* 2010, Appendix E—Directing the jury, Ch.17 at E.06; *Crown Court Compendium* 2016, Pt.1, Ch.20 Sexual offences—The dangers of assumptions. For an article written by counsel experienced in these cases supporting these directions, see Felicity Gerry and Catarina Sjolin, *Rape Trauma Direction*, *Counsel Magazine*, April 2011, p.27.

[496] [2011] EWCA Crim 867.

[497] [2012] EWCA Crim 1324.

pointed out, be to significantly overstate the position. It is essential that the direction does not implant in the jury's mind any contrary assumption.[498] However, the Court of Appeal held that, although the wording was not ideal, it did not so far depart from what is acceptable as to render the conviction unsafe.

1.358   It is important that directions are tailored to the facts of the particular case, that they are confined to matters which are well-established and that the judge does not exceed legitimate comment. *MM v R*.[499] is an illustration of a rape case where the trial judge went further than was legitimate. The judge gave appropriate directions cautioning the jury against stereotyping, pointing out that the image of rape as an attack by a stranger is a myth. However, he continued[500]:

> "Rapes occur in a whole variety of situations. Evidence shows us that in over 90% of allegations that come before the court, the two principal people involved know each other and have often on occasions known each [other] for a long time and very well. It is sadly not unheard of that those that love each other can rape each other. Those in relationships can attack each other. It is nothing, it is human nature."

The Court of Appeal accepted that the judge exceeded legitimate comment in respect of his reference to the proportion of cases. However, apart from this reference, about which there was no evidence before the jury and no source known to the Court of Appeal, the judge's remarks were unexceptional. The effect of the judge's words read as a whole was simply to caution the jury against stereotyping, and the Court did not consider the mention of the proportion deprived his direction of balance.

1.359   It has become common practice for judges to provide juries with written directions on matters of law. We suggest that there is no reason why directions designed to prevent false assumptions should not also be provided in written form,[501] and it should become routine in more complex cases. The use of expressive and emotive language should, of course, be avoided.[502]

1.360   The authors of the *Crown Court Compendium* state that such directions must be crafted with care and should always be discussed with the advocates. Thought should be given as to when may be the most appropriate time to give such directions: at the outset of the trial or in the course of the summing up.[503] We are of the view that there is a strong case for general directions to

---

[498] This is stressed in the *Crown Court Compendium* 2016, Part 1, Ch.20 Sexual Offences—The dangers of assumptions, para 7.

[499] [2011] EWCA Crim 1291.

[500] At [39].

[501] Research by Professor Cheryl Thomas has revealed juries' strong preference for written directions: see *http://www.ucl.ac.uk/news/news-articles/1002/10011701* [Accessed March 19, 2016].

[502] See *Joseph* [2010] EWCA Crim 2445, where the Court of Appeal upheld the conviction but noted that through some of his comments the judge had expressed some judicial hostility in strong terms. This was a strong case where the points of criticism of the summing up did not undermine the safety of the conviction.

[503] Ch.20.1 Sexual offences—The dangers of assumptions, para 9.

prevent false assumptions being given early in the trial—for instance, before the prosecution opening. Delivered at that stage they are likely to have greater impact, whereas if delivered later the illegitimate lines of reasoning will have had some time to become embedded. Dr Emily Henderson and Judge Duncan Harvey have observed[504] that research in other jurisdictions[505] suggests both that jurors' preconceptions have a strong impact upon their decision-making, and that the timing of the delivery of the judicial directions may be vital. Some of these directions, however, where there is a particular need to tailor them to the evidence in the case, may be better deployed during the summing up.

The Court of Appeal indicated in *Miller*[506] that, although such directions **1.361** have been given for some years, it would have been better if the judge had discussed them as part of the routine analysis of the directions to be contained in the summing up, which should take place before counsel's speeches in almost every case and certainly in every case of this type. In *Miller* the appellant was convicted on five counts of rape of a child under 13, contrary to s.5 of the 2003 Act. The trial judge had given directions on late reporting and the reaction of children to abuse in the context of the family. On appeal, it was submitted that judicial comment designed to question stereotypical assumptions about the behaviour of rape case complainants offended the common law principle that judicial notice can only be taken of facts of particular notoriety or common knowledge. This submission was given short shrift. The countering of generalisations was the intent of such judicial observations.

As Pitchford LJ pointed out in the *Crown Court Bench Book*,[507] such **1.362** directions are given in the interests of securing the overriding objective of dealing with cases "justly". He writes:

> "The experience of judges who try sexual offences is that an image of stereotypical behaviour and demeanour by a victim or the perpetrator of a non-consensual offence such as rape held by some members of the public can be misleading and capable of leading to injustice. That experience has been gained by judges, expert in the field, presiding over many such trials during which guilt has been established but in which the behaviour and demeanour of complainants and defendants, both during the incident giving rise to the charge and in evidence, has been widely variable. Judges have, as a result of their experience, in recent years adopted the course of cautioning juries against applying stereotypical images [of] how an alleged victim or an alleged perpetrator of a sexual

---

[504] *Myth-busting in Sex Trials: Judicial Directions or Expert Evidence?*, Archbold Review, Issue 5, June 5, 2015. The authors stress this by literary analogy: "Jurors' first impressions, like those of Mr Darcy, rarely alter and their good opinion, once lost, is lost forever."

[505] E. McDonald and Y. Tinsley (eds), *From Real Rape to Real Justice: Prosecuting Rape in New Zealand* (Wellington, VUP, 2011).

[506] [2010] EWCA Crim 1578, at [26] per Leveson LJ. See also *R. v CE* [2012] EWCA Crim 1324, at [27]; *MM v R.* [2011] EWCA Crim 1291, at [39], where the Court of Appeal noted that perhaps if the matter had been raised in discussions with counsel before speeches, the error would have been avoided.

[507] This passage was endorsed by the Court of Appeal in *Miller* [2010] EWCA Crim 1578. It is repeated in the *Crown Court Compendium* 2016, Ch.20, para.3.

offence ought to have behaved at the time, or ought to appear while giving evidence, and to judge the evidence on its intrinsic merits. This is not to invite juries to suspend their own judgement but to approach the evidence without prejudice."

1.363 The judge should not support any particular conclusion, but should focus upon warning the jury against the unfairness of approaching the evidence with any pre-formed and unjustified assumptions. The comment should be balanced[508] and not controversial. It should deal with areas where the position is sufficiently well-known to justify comment. The *Crown Court Compendium,* as was the case with its predecessor, the *Crown Court Bench Book*, drawing upon research by experts in this area,[509] identifies the following "supposed indicators" as to where, depending upon the evidence and arguments advanced in the case, guidance may be necessary relating to the evidence of the complainant so as to prevent unwarranted assumptions:

"(1) Of untruthfulness:
    (a) Delay in making a complaint.
    (b) Complaint made for the first time in giving evidence.
    (c) Inconsistent accounts given by the complainant.
    (d) Lack of emotion/ distress when giving evidence.
(2) Of truthfulness
    (a) A consistent account given by the complainant.
    (b) Emotion/ distress when giving evidence.
(3) Of consent and/ or belief in consent:
    (a) Clothing worn by the complainant said to be revealing or provocative.
    (b) Intoxication (drink and/or drugs) on the part of the complainant whilst in the company of others.
    (c) Previous knowledge of, or friendship/ sexual relationship between the complainant and the defendant. In this regard it may be necessary to alert the jury to the distinction between submission and consent.
    (d) Some consensual sexual activity on the occasion of the alleged offence.
(4) Of consent and/ or belief in consent and/or lack of involvement.
    (a) Lack of any use or threat of force, physical struggle and/or injury. In this regard it will be necessary to alert the jury to the distinction between submission and consent.
    (b) A defendant who is in an established sexual relationship."

These "supposed indicators" overlap with the non-exhaustive list of subjects which may lead to unjustified stereotyping previously set out in the *Crown Court Bench Book*:

---

[508] See *Breeze* [2009] EWCA Crim 255, where the trial judge was held to have gone too far in his drum-like repetition that there was no obvious motivation for the complainant to tell lies. The Court of Appeal could not exclude the possibility that the jury may have been influenced by the "refrain".

[509] See Ch.23, citing Temkin and Krahe, *Sexual assault and the Justice Gap: A question of Attitude* (Oxford: Hart Publishing, 2008). This illuminating research showed that some jurors may have difficulty accepting lack of violence by the defendant and lack of resistance by the complainant as being consistent with absence of consent.

- The complainant got drunk in male company; therefore he/she must have been prepared for sex.
- An attractive male does not need to have sex without consent.
- A complainant in a relationship with the alleged attacker is likely to have consented.
- Rape takes place between strangers.
- Rape does not take place without physical resistance from a victim.
- If it is rape there must be injuries.
- A person who has been sexually assaulted remembers events consistently.
- A person who has been sexually assaulted reports it as soon as possible.

It is of fundamental importance to appreciate that there is no classic 1.364
reaction to rape or other serious sexual assaults. The following provide good
examples.

Presentation in court

Experience shows that people react differently when speaking about such an 1.365
assault in court. Some will display obvious signs of distress, others will not.
The reason for this is that people develop different ways of coping.
Conversely, it does not follow that signs of distress displayed by a witness
confirm the truth and accuracy of the evidence given. In other words,
demeanour is not necessarily a clue to the truth of the witness's account. It
depends on the character and the personality of the individual concerned.

Late reporting

In *Doody*, where the defendant raised the issue of late reporting as 1.366
undermining the credibility of the complainant, Latham LJ approved the
suggested direction below as providing, in very general terms, an appropriate
form of direction which should be tailored to the facts of the particular
case:

> "Experience shows that people react differently to the trauma of a serious sexual
> assault. There is no classic response. The defence say that the reason the
> complainant did not report this until her boyfriend returned from Dubai ten
> days after the incident is because she has made up a false story. That is a matter
> for you. You may think that some people may complain immediately to the first
> person they see, whilst others may feel shame and shock and not complain for
> some time. A late complaint does not necessarily mean it is a false complaint.
> That is a matter for you."

The Court did, however, conclude that the judge's extensive comments on
possible reasons for the delay in reporting should have been balanced by
reference to the appellant's case on the significance of the delay.

Feelings of shame and guilt

1.367   The Court in *Doody* acknowledged that it is sufficiently well-known that the trauma of rape can cause feelings of shame and guilt which might inhibit a woman from making a complaint, and that a comment to that effect is justified. In that case the trial judge had been entitled to add to that general comment, a reference to the particular feelings of shame and embarrassment which may arise when the allegation is of sexual assault by a partner.

Forced sex within a relationship

1.368   The Court in *Doody* also stated that there was no need to emphasise the effects of "relationship rape" in as much detail as the trial judge had done and, in any event, it should have been done in a more measured way. In his commentary on the case, Neil Kibble has suggested that the Court of Appeal's criticism of the judge's comments on forced sex within a relationship may have been unduly harsh[510]:

> "In relation to the appropriate level of detail on the effect of forced sex in a relationship, it is arguable that the judge's comments were directed at correcting another common rape 'myth', namely that relationship rape is not as traumatic and serious as 'stranger' rape, which is why he referred to breach of trust and 'the invasion'."

No stereotypical sex offender or victim of sexual offences

1.369   A jury should not approach a case with pre-formed assumptions about the likely social or cultural background of a person who commits a sex offence or a person who is likely to be a victim of such an offence. A judge is entitled to direct a jury that there is no fixed type of those who have these offences committed against them or commit them. In *Andreous*[511] the appellant had been convicted of sexual assault, but acquitted of rape. He was a dentist. The complainant had an appointment with him for a "deep clean". It was alleged that whilst pretending to carry out treatment upon her, he placed his erect penis against the inside of her mouth. When summing up, the judge directed the jury that those who have these offences committed against them or commit them come from every possible culture, age, class or profession. He observed that there was no way of saying a particular person is or is not more likely to commit such an offence because of these sort of factors and added that it was the clear experience of the courts that nothing could be further from the truth, and both those who commit them and those against whom they are committed come from as wide a range of society as it is possible to imagine. The Court of Appeal rejected the appellant's argument that the direction in some way diminished the judge's earlier direction on the

---

[510] [2009] Crim. L.R. 590, at p.595.
[511] [2014] EWCA Crim 2886.

standard of proof. The direction conformed with the approved approach of directing the jury so as to prevent pre-conceived assumptions.

Expert evidence inadmissible if matter can properly be covered by balanced judicial direction even if outwith a jury's experience—a gloss on the rule in Turner[512]

It follows that the last few years have seen the Court of Appeal allow balanced judicial directions to develop for the purpose of correcting erroneous beliefs or assumptions that a jury may hold and which, if uncorrected, may lead to illegitimate reasoning. In *R. v ER*[513] the Court of Appeal endorsed balanced judicial direction at the expense of allowing expert evidence to prevent false assumptions.[514] *R. v ER* was a historical sex abuse case. The appellant was convicted of serious sexual assaults committed against his sister-in-law in the 1970s when she was aged between 11 and 13. The trial judge in *R. v ER* had allowed a psychotherapist (a specialist in counselling in child abuse cases) to give evidence in respect of complainant behaviour and reasons for delay in such cases. Hughes LJ, as he then was, giving the judgment of the Court, stated that the psychotherapist's evidence should not have been called. The remedy was a neutral judicial warning. Expert evidence carries the danger that it invests the warning with special weight. It may lack any consideration of the appellant's contrary assertion. Expert evidence may divert attention away from critical witnesses. Hughes LJ put a new gloss on the general rule in *Turner*: unless this kind of expert evidence is directed to something which is quite outside both the experience of the jury and the ability of the judge to explain common understanding and common patterns of behaviour, it should not be adduced.

1.370

MENTAL ELEMENT

INTENTIONAL PENETRATION

The prosecution must establish that the defendant intentionally penetrated the complainant's vagina, anus or mouth with his penis. In the vast majority of cases, if penetration is proved there will be no issue as to whether it was intentional. Some of the more difficult aspects of intention are dealt with below. In the rare case where there is an issue, the prosecution need prove no

1.371

---

[512] [1975] Q.B. 834, referred to in para.24.04, below.
[513] [2010] EWCA Crim 2522. For further analysis of *R. v ER*, see paras 24.26 and following, below.
[514] In New Zealand, "counter-intuitive" expert evidence as to complainant behaviour can be admitted if it is "substantially helpful": see s.25 of the Evidence Act 2006. For a clear and powerful article on the merits of allowing such evidence, see Dr Emily Henderson and Judge Duncan Harvey, *Myth-busting in Sex Trials: Judicial Directions or Expert Evidence?*, Archbold Review, Issue 5, June 15, 2015.

more than deliberate penetration, meaning simply voluntarily willed movement.[515] Self-induced intoxication does not provide a defence.

1.372   A jury is likely to have difficulty in accepting that a defendant, who admits sexual intercourse, was a passive and unconscious participant. In *R. v F*[516] the issue arose as to whether penile penetration of the complainant's vagina was voluntary as the appellant had maintained at trial that he must have been an unconscious and passive participant. The appellant was charged with an offence of engaging in sexual activity with a child aged (14 or 15) contrary to s.9(1) of the Sexual Offences Act 2003. DNA analysis established that the appellant was the father of the complainant's child. The appellant accepted that he was the father of the child, but claimed that he had done nothing wrong because the complainant had "raped" him. The appellant had arranged a big family party at a travellers' caravan site where he lived with his partner. The appellant embarked upon a prolonged bout of drinking and drug taking after which he announced he was going to bed. He woke up the next morning to find both his partner and the complainant on his bed. The prosecution case was that the appellant had invented the party as a circumstantial invention and had been in a sexual relationship with the complainant for a period of time leading to the conception of their daughter. The trial judge explained to the jury that the prosecution must prove an intentional and voluntary act by the appellant. There could be circumstances in which an act may not be intentional and voluntary, such as where a person is sleep-walking. The judge said that the only way the appellant could have an arguable defence in these circumstances was if the jury took the view that intercourse occurred or may have occurred when he was unconscious through sleep. The judge did comment that it was a little difficult to envisage how a man could gain an erection and persist in an act of intercourse to the point of ejaculation without waking up, and there had been no expert evidence upon the point. He acknowledged that a man could obtain an erection when asleep and ejaculate, but pointed out that that was a rather different circumstance from an act of intercourse which, upon the basis of what the appellant recounted the complainant had said to him, involved her climbing on top of him, having first aroused him in some way so as to obtain an erection.

1.373   On behalf of the appellant, it was submitted that the judge was adopting the prosecution case and preferring it to the defence case. Furthermore, it was contended that the judge's reference to "expert evidence" appeared to amount to a criticism of the defence for not calling an expert to demonstrate the scientific possibility that the appellant's defence was true. The Court of Appeal rejected the submissions. It took the view that the judge was doing no more than he was required to do as the trial judge, namely to identify the issues for the jury's decision on an application of his legal direction to the

---

[515] *Heard* [2007] EWCA Crim 125, a sexual assault case but the same reasoning applies: see further paras 2.78 and following, below.
[516] [2014] EWCA Crim 878.

facts of the case as it emerged in evidence. The judge was correct to invite the jury to confront the problem of how the complainant's child was conceived if the appellant was, as he maintained, a passive and unconscious participant. There had not been a hint of criticism of the defence when the judge pointed out there had been no expert evidence. The judge identified for the jury the difficulty for the appellant's defence of unconsciousness if that was the way intercourse took place, and he pointed out that that was the only explanation given as to how the intercourse took place. Common sense seemed to dictate that if the jury could not accept the appellant's account of unconsciousness, a guilty verdict must follow.

ABSENCE OF REASONABLE BELIEF IN CONSENT

By virtue of s.1(1)(c) of the Act, the prosecution must establish that the defendant did not reasonably believe that the complainant was consenting at the time of the penetration. Section 1(1)(c) is designed to reverse the decision in *DPP v Morgan*,[517] which established that a person could avoid conviction for rape if he had an honest but mistaken belief in consent. The continuing existence of this defence provoked strong criticism amongst many of those who responded to the Sexual Offences Review, and also amongst members of the Review. Many felt that a requirement of reasonableness should be re-introduced into the law, so as to confine the defence to cases of honest and reasonable belief. Any suggestion that there is analogy with the defence of self-defence is fallacious as the sexual context is totally different. In particular, it was argued that the subjective test undermined the fundamental concept of sexual autonomy by implicitly authorising the assumption of consent, regardless of the views of the victim or what they say or do. The arguments against the subjective test included the following[518]:

> "The mistaken belief arises in a situation where it is easy to seek consent and the cost to the victim of the forced penetration is very high. It is not unfair to any person to make them take care that their partner is consenting and be at risk of a prosecution if they do not do so."

Avoidance of the reasonable man test

Notwithstanding that the defendant's belief in consent must now be reasonable, it is clear that the wording of the section leaves scope for consideration by the jury of the defendant's relevant personal characteristics. The Act does not adopt a test based on what a reasonable man would have believed, and in so doing acknowledges that the objective test at its harshest is not appropriate in this context.

1.374

1.375

---

[517] [1976] A.C. 182 HL.
[518] *Setting the Boundaries*, 2000, para.2.13.7.

1.376   However, for some time this seemed an unlikely legislative outcome, and the objective test looked set to prevail. In *Protecting the Public*[519] the Government indicated that the reasonableness of a defendant's belief in consent would be judged by reference to what an objective third party would think in the circumstances. The Sexual Offences Bill as introduced sought to present an objective test which would be determined by reference to a reasonable person. Clause 1(3) read:

> "This subsection applies if—
> (a) a reasonable person would in all the circumstances doubt whether B consents, and
> (b) A does not act in a way that a reasonable person would consider sufficient in all the circumstances to resolve such doubt."

1.377   Even before this clause was amended and replaced by the present section, Lord Falconer of Thoroton stated[520]:

> "The jury's consideration will also take account, where necessary, and subject to any directions of the judge, of any relevant characteristics of the defendant . . . I have indicated that the judge and the jury together can be relied on to identify those characteristics which would be taken into account, and I stand by that . . . It is for the jury to decide whether any of the defendant's attributes are relevant to their deliberations, subject to the judge's directions where necessary."

Lord Falconer stated that it would be unwise for him to seek to restrict the precise characteristics upon which a judge could direct a jury. It would depend upon the circumstances of a particular case. Whilst accepting the relevance of such enduring characteristics as age and mental impairment, he did not rule out others, stating "one will have to leave it to the good sense of judges and juries".[521]

1.378   When moving the amendment to Clause 1 which substituted the text of what became s.1 of the 2003 Act, Baroness Scotland of Asthal acknowledged that the Government had taken on board concerns about basing the test on what a "reasonable person would have thought" or how a "reasonable person would have acted" in the circumstances. In particular, she acknowledged that there had been criticism that it was not clear what characteristics should be assumed by the jury in seeking to determine the role of the "reasonable person". She explained that, in order to satisfy those concerns, the Government was tabling an amendment to revise the reasonableness test so as to it move away from the concept of the reasonable person.[522]

---

[519] 2002 (Cm. 5668).
[520] *Hansard*, HL Vol.648, col.1073 (June 2, 2003). The debate concerned an amendment moved by Lord Thomas of Gresford introducing the mental element "A does not reasonably believe B consents". Lord Falconer stated that his comments applied equally to Lord Thomas's amendment.
[521] *Hansard*, HL Vol.648, col.1076 (June 2, 2003).
[522] *Hansard*, HL Vol.649, col.669 (June 17, 2003).

Comparison with the New Zealand test

Many common law jurisdictions do not have a wholly subjective test of   1.379
reasonableness of belief.[523] In New Zealand, the test in relation to sexual
violation by rape is that the accused does not believe on reasonable grounds
that the victim is consenting. This test was introduced in 1985, when the
Crimes Act 1961 was amended so as to abolish the specific offence of rape
and replace it with the offence of sexual violation.[524] The legislature declined
to adopt the subjective test as set out in *DPP v Morgan*, and s.128(2) of the
Crimes Act 1961[525] accordingly states:

> "Person A rapes person B if person A has sexual connection with person B,
> effected by the penetration of person B's genitalia by person A's penis—
>   (a) without person B's consent to the connection; and
>   (b) without believing on reasonable grounds that person B consents to the
>   connection."

In *Clarke*,[526] it was held that there must be objectively valid grounds for a   1.380
belief in consent. The Court held that the requirement that the belief be
reasonably held does not leave room for a belief based on drunken
indifference or mistake nor, perhaps, on an intellectual impairment. In
contrast to s.1 of the Sexual Offences Act 2003, where the question is whether
the accused held a reasonable belief in consent, in New Zealand the
reasonableness of the accused's belief is not relevant except to the extent that
it impacts on the assessment of whether the accused did believe that there
was consent.[527]

Concerns were expressed in Parliament during the passage of the Sexual   1.381
Offences Bill that the New Zealand approach might be followed by our own
courts.[528] Baroness Scotland of Asthal provided reassurance[529]:

> "[W]e fully expect that characteristics such as mental incapacity and extreme
> youth will be taken into account in line with existing case law on such issues. We
> would not expect our courts to follow the New Zealand approach. We believe we
> can rely principally on case law as regards reasonableness."

The defendant's characteristics

Section 1(2) of the 2003 Act provides: 1.382

> "Whether a belief is reasonable is to be determined having regard to all the
> circumstances, including any steps A has taken to ascertain whether B con-
> sents."

[523] For example the common law States in Australia (ACT, Victoria, NSW and South Australia).
[524] Crimes Amendment Act (No.3) 1983, s.2, which introduced a new s.128(2), (3) into the
Crimes Act 1961.
[525] As replaced on May 20, 2005, by s.7 of the Crimes Amendment Act 2005 (2005 No 41).
[526] *Clarke* [1992] 1 N.Z.L.R. 147, NZCA.
[527] *Narif* [1987] 2 N.Z.L.R. 122, NZCA.
[528] *Hansard*, HL Vol.649, col.673, Lady Noakes and Lord Campbell of Alloway (June 17,
2003).
[529] *Hansard*, HL Vol.649, col.678, Baroness Scotland of Asthal.

1.383   The Act does not state that the belief must be one that would have been held by a reasonable man. Since the provision focuses on the particular defendant, and regard is to be had to "all the circumstances", it is clear that in deciding whether a belief was reasonable the jury may take into account relevant characteristics of the defendant. This was confirmed by Ministerial statements in Parliament.[530] However, Ministers stated that the jury should not be asked to take into account characteristics that should not absolve a defendant from guilt.[531]

1.384   How far can the jury go in taking the defendant's characteristics into account? Which characteristics are properly relevant to the defendant's ability to appreciate the risk that the complainant was not consenting? It is instructive to consider the reasoning in decisions, such as *Bowen*,[532] dealing with the application of the reasonable man test in the law of duress. If a similar approach were to be adopted in the present context, it would mean that characteristics of a defendant that would be so contradictory to the notion of a person forming a reasonable belief about consent as to render it absurd, should not be taken into account. In many cases, it is probably only the age of the defendant that is capable of being relevant. Furthermore, it is highly unlikely that any characteristic which leads to beliefs which conflict with the reasoning that underpins s.41 of the Youth Justice and Criminal Evidence Act 1999, which outlawed the "twin myths", will be relevant. See further Ch.26.

Is a psychological condition that affects the defendant's ability to determine whether the complainant was consenting relevant to the reasonableness of his belief in consent?

1.385   What characteristics might exceptionally be relevant? At this level of analysis the analogy with duress is less helpful, as duress is concerned with conditions that make a person more susceptible to pressure and threats, whilst here the concern is with the ability to recognise that someone might not be consenting. To what extent would a mental disorder which might have affected the defendant's ability to understand the true situation be a relevant characteristic when considering whether a belief in consent was reasonable? Clearly, the reasonableness of an asserted belief should be determined independently

[530] *Hansard*, HL Vol.648, col.1073, Lord Falconer of Thoroton (June 2, 2003); Vol.649, col.674, Baroness Scotland of Asthal Hansard (June 17, 2003).

[531] *Hansard*, HL Vol.648, cols 1073–4 (June 2, 2003), where Lord Falconer of Thoroton stated: "Introducing a requirement that all of the personal characteristics of the defendant should be taken into account would mean that the jury would be asked to take into account characteristics that should not absolve him from his guilt: for example, the fact that he has a quick temper or that the sight of a girl in a miniskirt will always turn him on and make him unable to resist her. That cannot be the intention."

[532] [1996] 2 Cr. App. R. 157. See also the approach to the relevance of psychiatric evidence to the reasonableness of a defendant's use of excessive force in self-defence. A defendant's psychiatric condition should not be taken into account when considering whether his reaction was reasonable: *Canns* [2005] EWCA Crim 2264.

of any psychosis or delusional thinking.[533] A good example of an irrelevant
characteristic is erotomania,[534] the delusional belief that another person,
usually of some social prominence, has fallen in love with the sufferer. But
what of other forms of mental disorder?

The issue was identified by the Court of Appeal in *R. v MM*,[535] in which 1.386
the appellant was convicted of raping his ex-girlfriend three days after she
had broken off the relationship. At his first trial, defence psychiatric medical
experts concluded that he had possibly been suffering from bi-polar affective
disorder at the relevant time. The trial judge indicated that it was his
intention to direct the jury that the appellant's psychiatric condition was not
relevant to whether his belief in the complainant's consent to sexual
intercourse was reasonable. The judge then discharged the jury to enable the
defence to consider the appellant's best interests. At the appellant's re-trial,
one expert concluded that the appellant's mental condition meant that he did
not understand the complainant's signals that she did not consent to sex. The
same expert's opinion was that the appellant was not guilty by virtue of
insanity. However, the appellant's counsel informed the judge that he was not
instructed to adduce any psychiatric evidence as the appellant wished to rely
on the defence of consent. The appellant was convicted.

The Court of Appeal decided the appeal without having to interpret s.1(2). 1.387
It held that the appellant had not been prevented from adducing evidence at
trial and had chosen not to do so. A close analysis of the psychiatric evidence
revealed that it would inevitably have resulted in a finding that he knew the
complainant was not consenting. As to whether the appellant's mental
disorder was relevant to the issue of whether he had a reasonable belief in
consent, Pitchford LJ (giving the judgment of the Court) stated[536]:

> "There is, we recognise, an interesting argument to be addressed as to whether
> there is a material difference between (1) an honest belief held by a defendant
> which may have been reasonable in the circumstances and (2) a belief which a
> reasonable man, placed in the defendant's circumstances, may have held. A
> statutory reasonable man test was held by the Privy Council in *Attorney General
> for Jersey v Holley*[537] to be stricter than the 'looser' concept of an honest belief
> which was reasonable in the circumstances . . . In the latter case it is arguable that
> the circumstances may include a mental illness which materially affected the
> defendant's ability to interpret the complainant's lack of consent. This, however,

---

[533] In Richard Card, Alisdair A. Gillespie and Michael Hirst, *Sexual Offences* (2008), the
powerful point is made that the psychotic delusions of a mentally ill defendant, however
understandable in medical terms, cannot be described as "reasonable" without doing extreme
violence to the English language. They cite the New Zealand case of *P (T129/92) (1993)* 10
CRNZ 250, where it was held that mental illness must be disregarded. However, as they point
out, the New Zealand statute does not refer (as does the Sexual Offences Act 2003) to "all the
circumstances" being taken into consideration.

[534] Anderson, Camp and Filey, *Erotomania and Aneurysmal Subarachnoid Hemorrhage; Case
Report and Literature Review*, Journal of Neuropsychiatry and Clinical Neurosciences, 1998,
Vol.10, no.3.

[535] [2011] EWCA Crim 1291.

[536] At [54].

[537] [2005] A.C. 580. See [17]–[25] per Lord Nicholls.

is not the time to engage in that argument since, on the facts of this case, a permissive construction of the section would not have availed the defendant."

1.388   *R. v MM* left the stage open for the issue to be considered by the Court of Appeal in *B v The Queen*[538] which has, to some extent, settled whether a mental disorder that might affect a defendant's ability to understand the true nature of a situation may be a relevant characteristic. The Court held that delusional thinking, psychotic or otherwise, can never be considered to be reasonable. Such a permissive construction would fly in the face of the legislative intention to reverse the decision of *DPP v Morgan*.[539] The 2003 Act represented a deliberate departure from the model of criminal offences where a defendant was judged only by his subjective state of mind. It deliberately does not make a genuine belief in consent a complete defence to rape. There was a conscious departure from the former law which may well have been because it is not unreasonable to require a person to take care to establish that a sexual event was consensual; the cost to him was very slight whilst the cost to a victim of forced sexual activity was very high indeed.[540] The Court of Appeal concluded that, unless and until the state of mind of a defendant amounts to insanity in law, then under the rule enacted in s.1(2) of the 2003 Act, beliefs in consent arising from conditions such as delusional psychotic illness or personality disorders must be judged by objective standards of reasonableness and not by taking into account a mental disorder which induced a belief which could not reasonably arise without it. Once a belief could be judged reasonable only by a process which labelled a plainly irrational belief as reasonable, it cannot be open to a jury to conclude that it was reasonable without straying outside the Act.

Point left open: autism, Asperger's syndrome

1.389   The Court in *B v The Queen* did, however, acknowledge that there may be cases in which the personality and abilities of the defendant may be relevant to whether his positive belief in consent was reasonable. Cases could arise in which the reasonableness of such a belief depends on the reading by the defendant of subtle social signals, and in which his impaired ability to do so is relevant to the reasonableness of his belief. The Court did not attempt exhaustively to foresee what circumstances might arise in which a belief

---

[538] [2013] EWCA Crim 3.

[539] [1976] A.C. 182.

[540] The then Government's view expressed by Lord Falconer during the debate as the Bill was passing through Parliament. See *B v The Queen* [2013] EWCA Crim 3 at [28], [37]. See also the analysis of the distinction between self-defence and sexual cases by David Ormerod QC and Karl Laird in *Smith and Hogan's Criminal Law* 14th edn (2015), p.853, cited (in a previous edition) in *B v The Queen* (at [37]): "The generosity of the law, extends to accepting a defendant's genuine but unreasonable mistakes in, for example matters of self defence, need not be replicated in sexual cases because the conduct in question calls for a qualitatively different degree of vigilance on his part."

might be held which is not in any sense irrational, even though most people would not have held it.

The Court illustrated the difficulty in identifying the dividing line in such   1.390
cases. It gave as a possible example the case of a defendant of less than ordinary intelligence or with a demonstrated inability to recognise behavioural cues. However, the Court indicated that whether such a defendant's belief ought properly to be characterised as unreasonable must await a decision on the facts of a particular case. The Court felt that it is possible that beliefs generated by such factors may not properly be described as irrational and might be judged by a jury not to be unreasonable on the particular facts. This has left open the possible relevance of conditions such as autism spectrum disorder and Asperger's syndrome, which might lead to an impaired or distorted perception of a complainant's behaviour.

Tipu Sultan[541] is an example of a rape case under the old law in which, had   1.391
it been tried under the 2003 Act, there would have been a strong argument, following the steer in *B v The Queen*, that the appellant's psychological condition at the relevant time was a relevant factor for the jury to consider when deciding if his belief may have been reasonable. Evidence that the appellant was suffering from Asperger's syndrome, which might have affected his ability to determine another's intentions, beliefs or desires in ambiguous situations, would have been a relevant factor for a jury to consider. In that case, the appellant was convicted in 2005 of the rape of his estranged wife. His conviction was quashed in the light of a fresh diagnosis in 2007 that he had had Asperger's syndrome at the time. The original diagnosis had been delusional jealousy, which would be irrelevant following *R. v MM*. On appeal, it was successfully argued that the appellant, as a sufferer from Asperger's syndrome, would have been liable to misunderstand in real time the signs and even straightforward indications of those with whom he came into contact. Clearly, this was relevant and admissible at a time when the test was the purely subjective one of honest belief in consent. There is a mounting body of evidence that a person with Asperger's may misinterpret a victim's response to sexual overtures.[542] It remains to be seen whether the courts will consider such a characteristic as relevant where there is evidence that because of Asperger's disorder, a defendant has failed to appreciate cues and communications which would have alerted others that their behaviour was distressing or not resulting in consent. We suggest that, in contrast to an irrational belief arising from a psychotic belief which could never be reasonable, a misinterpretation of behaviour due to a development disorder such as Asperger's falls into a different category. Such a condition is constant, causes significant impairment in social functioning, and can properly be taken into account by a jury.

[541] [2008] EWCA Crim 6.
[542] Dr Ian Freckleton SC and David List, *Asperger's Disorder, Criminal Responsibility and Criminal Culpability*, Psychiatry, Psychology and Law (2009).

1.392   It is instructive to consider the facts of *B v The Queen* as it provides an
example where evidence of a psychiatric condition was not relevant to
whether a defendant's belief was reasonable. The appellant was convicted of
two rapes upon his partner following the deterioration in his behaviour
which, with hindsight, would suggest his illness was developing. They had
been in a relationship since 2004 and had a child. The prosecution case was
that the complainant had objected and she had simply submitted in the face
of his insistence. The defence was consent. The appellant did not give
evidence and so there was no direct evidence that he believed that his partner
was consenting. However, the appellant had told the police in interview that
he never had intercourse with her without her consent. A consultant
psychiatrist gave evidence that the appellant was a paranoid schizophrenic
harbouring a number of delusional beliefs. The psychiatrist stated that when
ill, the appellant lacked insight into his condition. The acts of intercourse
might have been motivated by delusional beliefs that he had sexual healing
powers. They might also have been motivated by delusional beliefs that the
complainant was having improper contact with men at work. The appellant
might have believed that although she was saying no to sexual intercourse, it
would still be good for her, and so he might have continued notwithstanding
her response. Any such delusional beliefs did not, however, extend to a belief
that she was consenting; his illness was not relevant to his understanding
whether she was consenting to sexual intercourse or saying no. However, the
consultant psychiatrist did give evidence that at the time the appellant had an
impaired ability to interpret events normally. His ability to read signals and
see things as others did had been impaired by illness.

1.393   The trial judge ruled that the psychiatric evidence was only relevant to the
genuineness of the appellant's belief. It should be left out of the equation
when considering reasonableness. A delusional belief in consent or a belief in
consent as a result of his mental illness could not be a reasonable belief. He
directed the jury that, as a matter of public policy, the law does not permit
defendants suffering from mental illness to avoid the consequences of their
crimes by relying upon the explanation: "I only did it because I was mentally
ill."

1.394   The Court of Appeal, in dismissing the appeal, decided that the issue had
not arisen on the facts as the psychiatrist's opinion was that the appellant's
illness did not affect his ability to understand whether or not his partner was
saying "no". The fact that defence counsel had skilfully elicited the evidence
that the appellant had an impaired ability to interpret events normally did
not alter the position. The Court added that, if they were wrong about that,
and the appellant's delusional beliefs could have led him to believe that his
partner consented when she did not, they took the clear view that such
delusional beliefs cannot in law render reasonable a belief that his partner
was consenting when in fact she was not. A delusional belief in consent, if
entertained, would be by definition irrational and thus *un*reasonable and not
reasonable. If such delusional beliefs were capable of being described as

reasonable, then the more irrational the belief of a defendant, the better would be its prospects of being held reasonable. The Court said that the possible condition of the defendant in *R. v MM* might afford an example. It seemed that he may have been suffering from a bi-polar affective disorder which disinhibited him and made him grossly impulsive. He apparently believed he was entitled to have intercourse with his former girlfriend despite her objections because those objections were, to him, invalid.

In the light of the above, the dividing-line has become clearer. Character-   1.395
istics such as a condition in which defendant has psychotic episodes and/or periods of delusional thinking will not be relevant. Nor will character defects such as alcoholism or excessive vanity. We suggest extreme youth at the time, and constant conditions such as blindness and learning disability, may be relevant to the extent that they have a bearing on a particular defendant's ability to appreciate the risk that a person is not consenting to sex. It will then be a matter for the jury to decide whether any such characteristic has a bearing on the issue of reasonable belief.

Section 1(2) states that whether a belief is reasonable is to be determined   1.396
having regard to all the circumstances, "including any steps A has taken to ascertain whether B consents". These words were inserted by amendment at the time the Government abandoned the reasonable man test in favour of the test of whether the defendant's belief in consent was reasonable. Section 1(2) does not positively require a defendant to have taken steps to ascertain whether the complainant consents. However, this is something the jury will consider when considering the reasonableness of his belief. More steps are likely to be expected where there is no established relationship. It is likely that police interviews with those suspected of rape will now focus more than in the past on what steps, if any, the suspect took to ascertain whether the complainant was consenting. Baroness Scotland of Asthal, in moving the amendment, stated[543]:

> "The test is supported by an explanation of the type of criteria to be used to determine whether the defendant's belief in consent was reasonable in relation to the alleged offence. The jury is directed to have regard to all the circumstances at the time, including any steps that the defendant may have taken to establish that the complainant consented to the sexual activity.
>
> Although we recognise that not every sexual act has to be preceded by specific actions on the part of the defendant, especially where the defendant and complainant are in a well-established, consensual sexual relationship, it is still imperative that the defendant must be certain that his partner consents to the sexual activity at the time in question. Doubt is most likely to arise in those cases where the defendant and the complainant are not in a well-established relationship and where it would be reasonable to expect the defendant to take steps to ensure consent. Our reasonableness test does not require the defendant to have taken any specific steps but makes it clear that where such steps have been taken they must be taken into account by the jury in deciding whether the defendant's claimed belief in consent was reasonable. Some might argue that that goes

[543] *Hansard*, HL Vol.649, col.669 (June 3, 2003).

> without saying, but we believe that it is important to send a clear message to everyone that sexual acts with another person must be mutually agreed and that we all have an individual responsibility to ensure that that is the case."

1.397 When discussing the introduction of a test of reasonableness, *Protecting the Public* stated[544]:

> "The jury would however have to take into account the actions of both parties, the circumstances in which they have placed themselves and the level of responsibility exercised by both. The jury would also expect, where relevant, to take account of the circumstances in which the accusation or revelation is delivered (including any media involvement) and the time that has elapsed."

Media involvement and delayed disclosure would, however, seem to be more relevant to the complainant's credibility than to whether the defendant's belief was reasonable.

CAN SELF-INDUCED INTOXICATION EVER BE A DEFENCE TO RAPE?

1.398 Under the old law rape was held to be a crime of basic intent.[545] Accordingly, the principles laid down in *DPP v Majewski*[546] applied, and self-induced intoxication could not be used as the basis of a denial of mens rea. In *Woods (W)*[547] the Court of Appeal confirmed that the position had not been changed by the passing of s.1 of the Sexual Offences (Amendment) Act 1976. It was argued in *Woods (W)* that s.1(2) of the 1976 Act[548] permitted the jury to take into account the defendant's drunken state as a possible reasonable ground for his belief that a woman was consenting to intercourse. The Court of Appeal rejected this argument, and held that a defendant's self-induced intoxication is not a relevant matter which a jury are entitled to take into account in deciding whether there are grounds for his alleged belief. "Reasonable grounds" are grounds that would have been reasonable if the defendant had been sober.

1.399 It was held in *Fotheringham*[549] that no mistake, whether as to consent or any other matter, arising from self-induced intoxication can provide a defence to rape. The appellant was charged with raping a 14-year-old girl, who had been baby-sitting for him and his wife. His defence was, inter alia, that he had been so drunk at the time of the offence that he thought he was having sexual intercourse with his wife. The jury was directed that in

---

[544] 2002 (Cm 5668), para.34. At that point it was proposed that reasonableness would be judged by reference to what an objective third party would think in the circumstances.

[545] *Morgan* [1976] A.C. 182 at 218, per Lord Simon of Glaisdale.

[546] [1977] A.C. 443; in *Caldwell* [1982] A.C. 341 at 355, Lord Diplock stated that self-induced intoxication is no defence to a crime in which recklessness is enough to constitute the necessary mens rea.

[547] (1982) 74 Cr. App. R. 312.

[548] Section 1(2) provided: "It is hereby declared that if at a trial for a rape offence the jury has to consider whether a man believed a woman was consenting to sexual intercourse, the presence or absence of reasonable grounds for such a belief is a matter to which the jury is to have regard, in conjunction with any other relevant matters, in considering whether he so believed".

[549] (1989) 88 Cr. App. R. 206.

considering whether the appellant may have believed that he was sleeping with his wife, they had to ask themselves whether there were reasonable grounds for that belief, i.e. grounds which would be reasonable to a sober man, and that in deciding that issue they should disregard the appellant's self-induced intoxication. It was argued before the Court of Appeal that the judge had effectively withdrawn the appellant's defence from the jury, and that self-induced intoxication may ground a defence when the vital issue in a case of rape is whether the defendant held an honest, although mistaken, belief that he was having conjugal relations. It was conceded in argument that (a) a defendant's self-induced intoxication was not a relevant matter which the jury were entitled to take into account in deciding whether there were reasonable grounds for the defendant's belief that the complainant consented, and (b) rape is a crime of basic intent to which self-induced intoxication is no defence. Nevertheless, it was submitted that mistake as a defence falls into a different category from the issues of intention and consent, and stands alone unmentioned and untouched by legislation. The Court rejected this argument as running counter to authority,[550] upheld the trial judge's direction to the jury to ignore the effects of the drink, and held that a mistake arising from self-induced intoxication is no defence in rape.[551]

It would appear that self-induced intoxication can never be a factor which **1.400** can properly be taken into account when considering whether A does not reasonably believe that B consents under s.1(1)(c) of the 2003 Act. Whilst s.1(2) does stipulate that whether a belief is reasonable is to be determined having regard to all the circumstances, the Court of Appeal's line of reasoning in *Woods (W)* applies and the test is whether the belief would have been reasonable had the defendant been sober.

In *Grewal*[552] the Court of Appeal confirmed that there is a two-stage test **1.401** under s.1(1)(c), as was proposed in our 4th edition. Essentially there are two questions[553]:

(i) May the defendant have genuinely believed that the complainant was consenting? Here, the jury are entitled to take into account any evidence of intoxication. If the jury are sure that the defendant did not have such a belief, the prosecution have proved the mental element. If the defendant may have had such a belief, the jury need to consider question (ii).

(ii) Was the defendant's belief reasonable in all the circumstances? Here intoxication is irrelevant. The reasonableness of the defendant's belief must be evaluated as if he had been sober. Of course, this does not preclude a jury finding that a drunken man may have had a reasonable belief provided that the belief was reasonable.

---

[550] *O'Grady* (1987) 85 Cr. App. R. 315.
[551] [1990] 1 W.L.R. 813.
[552] [2010] EWCA Crim 2448, at [30] per Elias LJ.
[553] For an example direction, see Crown Court Bench Book 2010, Ch.17, p.374.

Reasonable belief where complainant lacks the capacity to consent through drink or drugs

1.402   Where there is a live issue for the jury as to whether the complainant was so affected by drink or drugs that she did not have the capacity to agree to sex, the jury will need to be directed on what the prosecution must establish in order to disprove reasonable belief in consent. Frequently, the defendant will also have been affected by alcohol. The jury will need to focus upon whether the defendant should have realised that the complainant was in no condition to make a choice[554] (or that the complainant was not agreeing by choice). The jury needs to consider all the circumstances as they would have appeared to the defendant had he been sober. Would or should the defendant have realised the condition of the complainant? If so, would it have been reasonable or unreasonable for the defendant to believe she was consenting?

In a case where consent is contested, is it necessary to direct the jury upon absence of reasonable belief?

1.403   The judge is not bound to give a direction on absence of reasonable belief in every case. In *Taran*[555] the Court of Appeal stressed that the judge's task is not to read the jury an abstract lecture upon the law but to explain to them in simple terms those parts of the law that apply in the case they are trying. A direction on absence of reasonable belief falls to be given when, but only when, there is material on which a jury might come to the conclusion that (a) the complainant did not in fact consent, but (b) the defendant thought that she was consenting. In *Taran* there was no such material: the complainant's evidence was that she was struggling to get away and making it abundantly clear that she did not consent, and the appellant's case was that, far from giving the impression of hesitant consent, the complainant was throwing herself at him. There was simply no room, on the case of either party, for any misunderstanding by the appellant as to the presence of consent.

MENTAL ELEMENT OF ATTEMPTED RAPE

1.404   Despite an undercurrent of academic controversy during the 1980s,[556] the proposition that a man could attempt to rape recklessly appears not to have been seriously challenged in the Court of Appeal until *Khan*[557] at the end of the decade. In that case the trial judge had directed the jury that the

---

[554] *Crown Court Compendium* 2016, Ch.20.5.
[555] [2006] EWCA Crim 1498.
[556] G. Williams, *The Problem of Reckless Attempts* [1983] Crim. L.R. 365; R. Buxton, *Circumstances, Consequences and Attempted Rape* [1984] Crim. L.R. 25.
[557] [1990] 1 W.L.R. 813. The question had been raised but left unanswered by Mustill LJ in *Millard and Vernon* [1987] Crim. L.R. 393.

principles relevant to recklessness and consent applied in exactly the same way to attempted rape as to the full offence. In the Court of Appeal it was argued that this amounted to a material misdirection, for recklessness, as a state of mind on the part of the offender, has no place in the offence of attempted rape. This is because s.1(1) of the Criminal Attempts Act 1981 provides:

> "If, with intent to commit an offence to which this section applies, a person does an act which is more than merely preparatory to the commission of the offence, he is guilty of attempting to commit the offence."

The argument developed on behalf of the appellants was that the phrase "with intent to commit an offence" requires an intent as to every element constituting the crime and thus recklessness as to lack of consent was insufficient. The Court held, however, that the mens rea for attempted rape was precisely the same as for rape, namely an intention to have sexual intercourse plus knowledge of or recklessness as to the absence of consent.

It followed from this that in attempted rape, as in rape, it was sufficient that **1.405** the man was reckless as to the circumstance of the women's consent, though he must have intended to perform the act of sexual intercourse. Russell LJ said:

> "In our judgment, however, the words 'with intent to commit the offence' to be found in section 1 of the 1981 Act mean, when applied to rape, 'with intent to have sexual intercourse with a woman in circumstances where she does not consent and the defendant knows or could not care less about her absence of consent'. The only 'intent', giving that word its natural and ordinary meaning, of the rapist is to have sexual intercourse. He commits the offence because of the circumstances in which he manifests that intent—*i.e.* when the woman is not consenting and he either knows it or could not care less about the absence of the consent."

The decision in *Khan* appeared to clarify the position. However, the **1.406** argument deployed unsuccessfully by the appellants in *Khan* was recently adopted by the Court of Appeal in *Pace and Rogers*.[558] The Court was considering an appeal against conviction for attempting to commit money laundering offences under s.327 of the Proceeds of Crime Act 2002 by concealing, disguising or converting "criminal property". The appellants were alleged to have attempted to deal in scrap metal they suspected was stolen. Since the metal belonged to the police, it was not stolen and the full offence could not be committed. The trial judge directed the jury that they should convict if they were sure the appellants suspected the goods were stolen. The Court of Appeal allowed the appeal on the basis that in order to establish an attempt to commit an offence under s.327, the prosecution must prove an intention to commit all the elements of the actus reus. If this line of reasoning were to be applied to attempted rape, it would reverse *Khan*. It would mean that in respect of the mental element, where the jury is sure that

[558] [2014] EWCA Crim 186.

the defendant did not reasonably believe the complainant was consenting but cannot conclude that he intended to have non-consensual sex with her, he would escape criminal liability.[559] However, whilst the Court of Appeal rejected the reasoning in *Khan* (where the mental element of the substantive offence included recklessness) as incapable of providing assistance in respect of a case under s.327 (where the mental element included suspicion), it did not venture so far as to re-consider the mental element required in attempted rape. The Court focused on the mental element required under s.340(3) of the Proceeds of Crime Act 2002 (an interpretation provision), observing that it specified no mental element other than knowledge or suspicion, and that "suspicion is a lesser state of awareness than belief". It acknowledged that in *Khan* the Court had recognised that its reasoning would not apply to all attempts. It distinguished *Khan*[560] on the basis that the appellants intended to penetrate the victim, and, if they had been successful, the full offence would have been committed. In our view, *Pace and Rogers* goes no further than establishing that for the purposes of attempted money laundering, the proof of a mental element of suspicion (only) does not suffice. The precise requirement of the mental element will continue to turn upon the distinction between acts (or omissions) and their circumstances[561] and we believe the courts will continue to follow the approach in *Khan* in applying the new law of rape, since although recklessness is no longer an element of the offence it has effectively been embraced in the requirement of absence of reasonable belief. Since an absence of reasonable belief relates to the circumstances of the offence, as opposed to the act of penetration itself, on the basis of *Khan* a defendant can be guilty of attempted rape if he intends to penetrate the complainant and does not reasonably believe the complainant is consenting at the time. It follows that the mental element of attempted rape is identical to that of rape.

MENTAL ELEMENT OF CONSPIRACY TO RAPE

1.407   It would appear that a defendant can only conspire to rape if he agrees to the penetration of the complainant and he knows that the complainant is not consenting. Section 1(2) of the Criminal Law Act 1977 provides:

[559] See Matthew Dyson, *Scrapping Khan?* [2014] Crim. L R. 445, where it is argued that whilst *Pace and Rogers* represents a plausible interpretation of s.1(1) of the Criminal Attempt Act 1981, as a matter of policy it should not be followed. It cannot be right that a defendant who, doing more than preparatory acts to rape a complainant, should only be liable to conviction of attempted rape if he intends that she does not consent, rather than if he has no reasonable belief that she does. Dyson also notes that s.1 of the Criminal Law Act 1977 is not drafted in the same way as s.1 of the Criminal Attempts Act 1981.

[560] [2014] EWCA Crim 186 at [52].

[561] See also *Millard and Vernon* [1987] Crim. L.R. 393. An example of an offence that could not be recklessly attempted is *Mohan* [1976] Q.B. 1 (attempt to cause bodily harm by wanton driving).

"Where liability for any offence may be incurred without knowledge on the part of the person committing it of any particular fact or circumstance necessary for the commission of the offence, a person shall nonetheless not be guilty of conspiracy to commit that offence by virtue of subsection (1) above unless he and at least one other party to the agreement intend or know that the fact or circumstances shall or will exist at the time when the conduct constituting the offence is to take place."

The effect of s.1(2) of the 1977 Act is to ensure that lack of reasonable belief **1.408** that the complainant is consenting is not sufficient mens rea for conspiracy to rape. Knowledge is required of all the circumstances of the actus reus, including the circumstance of absence of consent. Accordingly, for conspiracy to rape to be established there must be an agreement with at least one other, to penetrate the complainant's vagina, anus or mouth, knowing that there is a lack of consent. If the agreement is to have sexual intercourse with a complainant not knowing whether there is consent, there is no conspiracy to rape, but as soon as acts are done in pursuance of the agreement which are more than merely preparatory, an attempted rape is committed.

To prove conspiracy to rape, the prosecution must establish that the **1.409** defendants actually intended to carry out the agreement to rape. In *Hedgcock, Dyer and Mayers*[562] the Court of Appeal quashed convictions for conspiracy to rape obtained on the basis of web conversations between the three appellants over the internet and pornographic images exchanged between them and downloaded from their computers. Although the web chats appeared to demonstrate an agreement to commit rape, there was no evidence fit to go to the jury that the agreement was intended to be carried out, as opposed to fantasy. The probability from the terms of the chats was that it was fantasy, and there was no extraneous evidence upon which a jury could reasonably conclude that the appellants actually intended to carry out the agreement to rape. The computer discs on their own could only carry the case so far. The judge ought to have accepted the submission of no case to answer.

To similar effect is *R. v G and F*.[563] The Court of Appeal quashed **1.410** convictions for conspiracy to rape as the actions of the appellants in exchanging text messages were as consistent with nothing more than fantasy in the appellants' minds about raping a young boy from which each gained sexual pleasure as they were with an intent to carry out the plan. The prosecution sought to distinguish *Hedgcock, Dyer and Mayers*, where the Court stated that the jury could only conclude that the participants in the "chat room" conversations actually intended to carry out the agreement to rape if there was some extraneous evidence favouring that interpretation, and the other "objective circumstances" if anything pointed the other way. In *R. v G and F* the prosecution case was that the text messages were evidence of an agreement to rape a six-year-old boy. The messages referred to one of the

[562] [2007] EWCA Crim 3486.
[563] [2012] EWCA Crim 1756.

appellants being "best friends with his Mum" and the possibility of drugging the boy. The prosecution contended that, unlike in *Hedgcock,* a particular boy was the target of the rape plan, and F had access to the boy through his relationship with the boy's mother. Furthermore, again unlike in *Hedgcock,* no visual pornographic material was exchanged between the two defendants. However, the Court of Appeal came to the same conclusion as in *Hedgcock.* No reasonable jury, taking the prosecution case at its highest, could infer that the appellants intended to carry out the agreement. The evidence was equivocal. It was particularly striking that these men never met at any stage, either before or after the text exchange, nor did they even suggest meeting to discuss the plan further. Nor was there any evidence that they took any steps to advance the plan beyond suggesting "Friday night". No place or time or practical details were identified. Nothing at all happened after the exchange of text messages.

ENCOURAGING OR ASSISTING RAPE

1.411 The common law of incitement was abolished by s.59 of the Serious Crime Act 2007 with effect from October 1, 2008. For most offences (including rape) it has been replaced by the inchoate offences created by ss.44, 45 and 46 of the 2007 Act.[564] Under the new law it becomes an offence to provide assistance to a potential offender, even if he does not go on to commit the anticipated offence. This has significant repercussions for the law of sexual offences, in that it criminalises facilitation of an offence by assisting its commission without encouraging it and without the substantive offence actually being committed. Sections 44, 45 and 46 are all wide enough to include doing an act which is capable of assisting or encouraging the anticipated offence, where the full offence is not committed. The person assisted or encouraged need not have been aware of this. There are no definitions of either "encouraging" or "assisting",[565] but taken together they will cover a very wide range of acts. It would appear that any act capable of encouraging or assisting another person to any extent will be sufficient. For instance, in the context of rape, this could cover the provision of condoms and/or providing accommodation for under age sex, or facilitating sex with those who have been the victims of trafficking and have been institutionally coerced into sex. Accordingly, although a woman cannot be guilty of rape as a principal, she can be guilty of encouraging or assisting rape.

---

[564] See R. Fortson, *Blackstone's Guide to the Serious Crime Act 2007* (Oxford: OUP, 2008), Ch.6. For criticism of the provisions by Professor David Ormerod QC and Karl Laird , see *Smith and Hogan's Criminal Law*, 14th edn (2015), pp.526ff; and David Ormerod and Rudi Fortson, *Serious Crime Act 2007: The Part 2 Offences* [2009] Crim. L.R. 389, where the authors describe ss.44–46 as "tortuously difficult offences" and question whether they are really necessary.

[565] There is an extended definition of "assisting" in s.65(2)(b) so that it includes taking steps to reduce the prospect of criminal proceedings being brought or deliberately failing to take steps to discharge a duty.

These new offences are complex, particularly in respect of the provisions   **1.412**
relating to mental element.[566] This can be demonstrated by looking at what
the prosecution will need to prove in respect of the offence of encouraging or
assisting rape (s.44), ironically the least complex of the three offences.

Under s.44, to have assisted or encouraged rape, the defendant must have   **1.413**
done an act capable of encouraging or assisting rape. The mental element has
three components: (i) He must have intended to encourage or assist its
commission. (ii) He must also have believed or been reckless as to whether
the other person would penetrate the vagina, anus or mouth of the
complainant without the complainant's consent[567] *or*, if the penetration was
non-consensual but was done by a person who reasonably believed the
complainant was consenting, he must have intended the penetration not
reasonably believing the complainant was consenting. (iii) Finally, since rape
is an offence which requires proof of particular circumstances (penetration
without consent), by virtue of s.47(5)(b) the prosecution must prove either
that the defendant believed that, were the act to be done, it would be done in
those circumstances *or* that he was reckless as to whether or not it would be
done in those circumstances. The particular circumstances must be penetration without consent.

Section 45 covers doing an act capable of encouraging or assisting such an   **1.414**
offence, believing it will be committed and that the act will encourage or
assist its commission. This could include providing advice, information or
practical support, e.g. contraceptives. This offence focuses upon belief. The
prosecution do not need to establish that the defendant intended the
commission of the substantive offence. Again, there are three components in
the mental element. The prosecution must prove (i) that the defendant
believed that non-consensual penetration would be committed, (ii) that his
act would encourage or assist non-consensual penetration and (iii) that he
believed or was reckless as to whether the non-consensual penetration would
be performed deliberately without a reasonable belief that the complainant
was consenting *or* if the non-consensual penetration was carried out by a
person who reasonably believed the complainant was consenting, he himself
believed that there would be deliberate penetration with no reasonable belief
in consent.

Section 46 is the broadest offence as it covers doing such an act capable of   **1.415**
encouraging or assisting the commission of one or more of a number of
offences, believing one or more will be committed and that the act will
encourage or assist the commission of one or more of them. This has an
obvious attraction to prosecutors where the nature of the anticipated

---

[566] See s.47 of the 2007 Act.
[567] This means that the offence covers the *Cogan and Leak* style scenario where a female
defendant encourages a man to penetrate another woman without her consent not reasonably
believing that the other woman is consenting. The female defendant would be guilty of this
offence even if the man does not reasonably believe the complainant was consenting. See
para.1.149, above.

proscribed sexual activity is not clear. The prosecution need not prove that any of the anticipated offences occurred. Again the mental element is complex in that the defendant must have believed that his act would encourage or assist one of the offences, and that one or more of the offences would be committed.[568] Furthermore the defendant must *either* have believed or been reckless as to whether another person would act with the appropriate mental element *or* have had the appropriate mental element, if he had done it himself.[569] Finally, the defendant must have believed or been reckless as to the circumstances (i.e. non-consensual penetration).

1.416   In *R. v S and H*,[570] the Court of Appeal attempted to resolve a number of problems of construction and application of the offence under s.46 of the Serious Crime Act 2007 in the context of supplying Class A or Class B drugs. Section 46 should only be used if it might be that it was the defendant's belief at the time of doing the act that one or more offences would be committed, but he had no belief as to which. The prosecution has to identify which offences the defendant's act was capable of encouraging and assisting and upon which it wishes to rely. Assuming the acts are X, Y and Z (it could be two or more of them), there should be a separate s.46 count for each of X, Y and Z. It is clear that s.46 should be used sparingly, and, in many cases in the context of sexual offences, there may be clear evidence as to which offence the defendant believed would be committed. However, there may be circumstances where a number of different sexual offences could have been anticipated.

Defence of "acting reasonably"

1.417 Section 50 of the 2007 Act provides a defence to these offences where the defendant proves either (a) that he knew certain circumstances existed and it was reasonable for him to act as he did in those circumstances or (b) that he believed certain circumstances to exist, his belief was reasonable, and it was reasonable for him to act as he did in the circumstances as he believed them to be. Section 50(3) sets out a non-exhaustive list of factors to be considered in determining whether it was reasonable for a person to act as he did. These include the seriousness of the anticipated offence and the purpose for which and any authority by which he claims to have been acting. This could be an important defence in cases where contraceptives or contraceptive advice have been given in circumstances where under-age sex is likely or inevitable, and it is questionable whether such a fundamental issue should reverse the burden of proof. Arguably it is not compliant with art.6 of the ECHR as interpreted by the European Court in Strasbourg. The counter-argument is that often

---

[568] See s.49(7), s.47(4).
[569] s.48(2), s.47(5).
[570] [2011] EWCA Crim 2872; [2011] Crim. L.R. 449 (for valuable commentary). See also *Sadique (Omar)* [2013] EWCA Crim 1150; [2014] Crim. L.R. 61.

the details which might found such a special defence are only within the knowledge of the defendant.

Potential victims of "protective offences"

The principle in *Tyrrell*[571] is expressly preserved by s.51 of the 2007 Act so   **1.418** that a "victim" of rape, such as a child under the age of 13, who actively encouraged the sex will have a complete defence to a charge under ss.44–46. This principle should apply equally to a person who is mentally disordered and does not have the capacity to consent, as clearly the victim of an offence under s.30 of the 2003 Act who is "unable to refuse by reason of mental disorder" will have a complete defence to a charge under the 2007 Act even though they instigated the sex.

[571] [1894] 1 Q.B. 710.

CHAPTER 2

SEXUAL ASSAULTS AND SEXUAL ACTIVITY WITHOUT CONSENT

Introduction	2.01	Causing a Person to Engage in	
Assault by Penetration	2.07	Sexual Activity without Consent..	2.84
Sexual Assault	2.38	Consent and Public Policy	2.109

INTRODUCTION

This chapter considers the following offences contained in the Sexual **2.01** Offences Act 2003:

- assault by penetration (s.2),
- sexual assault (s.3), and
- causing a person to engage in sexual activity without consent (s.4).

These offences resulted from the work of the Sexual Offences Review, which **2.02** was established by the Home Secretary in 1999 to make recommendations on reform of the law of sexual offences and reported the following year.[1] The two assault offences replaced the offences of indecent assault on a man and indecent assault on a woman formerly contained in ss.14 and 15 of the Sexual Offences Act 1956. The overlap between the two sets of offences is not, however, complete. The most serious form of indecent assault, i.e. penile penetration of a person's mouth without their consent (or non-consensual fellatio) now falls within the expanded definition of rape. There are also a small number of circumstances, discussed below in the context of sexual assault, in which conduct that would have been capable of prosecution as indecent assault falls outside the scope of the 2003 Act offences (though in appropriate circumstances it may be prosecutable as an attempt to commit one of those offences).

---

[1] *Setting the Boundaries: Reforming the law on sexual offences* (Home Office, July 2000), paras 3.1.5, 3.1.6. The report is available at *http://webarchive.nationalarchives.gov.uk/+/http:/www. homeoffice.gov.uk/documents/vol1main.pdf?view=Binary* [Accessed April 30, 2016].

Assault by penetration

2.03   The Sexual Offences Review recognised that non-consensual penetration by objects or by parts of the body other than the penis can be as serious in its impact on the victim as rape. The offences of indecent assault were inadequate, it thought, to tackle this problem: they covered a wide spread of behaviour, from touching to truly appalling violations, and carried a maximum sentence of only 10 years' imprisonment, which was insufficient for the worst cases. The Review accordingly recommended the creation of a new offence of assault by penetration, defined to cover penetration of the anus or genitalia, including surgically constructed genitalia.[2] It also recommended that the offence should be defined in a way that would enable it to be used where there is doubt as to the nature of the penetration, e.g. where a child or mentally impaired adult is unable to say exactly what penetrated them, whether the defendant's penis or something else. These recommendations were accepted by the Government[3] and enacted in s.2 of the 2003 Act as the offence of assault by penetration. The importance attached to the offence by the Government is reflected in the comment of Lord Falconer of Thoroton, then Minister of State at the Home Office, that s.2 covers:

> "extremely serious offending behaviour that can inflict as much, if not more, pain and physical damage on a victim as penile penetration [and] is likely to result in similar psychological trauma."[4]

Sexual assault

2.04   The Sexual Offences Review also considered a range of other sexual behaviour that it considered unacceptable, from "frottage", fondling and groping, to quite serious assaults. All of these, it said, are distressing to the victim because of the sexual motivation and the fact that they are often directed at the more sensitive and private parts of the body or carried out by the use of the private parts of the perpetrator. The Review wished to penalise this sort of activity by means of an offence that retained the concept of an assault, so as to cover not only touching but also behaviour which puts the victim in fear of being touched. It recommended the creation of a new offence of sexual assault to cover sexual touching, defined as behaviour that a reasonable bystander would consider to be sexual, which is done without the consent of the victim.[5] This recommendation was accepted by the Government[6] and enacted in s.3 of the 2003 Act. However, the offence falls short of the Review's stated objective in that it is confined to physical

---

[2] *Setting the Boundaries,* para.2.9.
[3] In the White Paper, *Protecting the Public: strengthening protection against sex offenders and reforming the law on sexual offences* (Cm 5668) (Nov 2002), para.44.
[4] *Hansard,* HL Vol.646, col.1186 (April 1, 2003).
[5] *Setting the Boundaries,* para.2.14.
[6] *Protecting the Public,* para.45.

touching and so, unlike the offence of indecent assault, does not extend to cases where the victim is put in fear of being touched.[7]

Causing a person to engage in sexual activity without consent

Another potentially very serious form of sexual behaviour which the Review 2.05 thought should be criminalised was compelling another person to perform a sexual act against their will, whether the act is performed by the victim on himself, on the person exercising the compulsion, on a third party, or even on an animal.[8] There was evidence before the Review of conduct which it considered should be caught by the new offence, including forced masturbation and cases of women compelling men to penetrate them, which the Review regarded not as rape but as a serious assault on the man's sexual autonomy. The Review thought it necessary to structure any new offence to reflect the seriousness of the compelled acts: a compelled touching may be comparatively minor, but compelled sexual penetration would be very serious. It therefore recommended that there should be two offences with different penalties: a more serious offence of compelling sexual penetration of a person or an animal by a person, an object or an animal, and a lesser offence of compelling other sexual acts (including sexual touching). The recommendation was broadly adopted by the Government, which agreed that it should be possible to prosecute someone who "forces" another to perform sexual or indecent acts. It proposed to cover such conduct in a single offence of "causing another person to perform an indecent act without consent".[9] The word "causing" would, of course, extend the offence beyond cases involving the use of force to those where some other means is used to make a person perform a sexual act, e.g. a threat of something other than force or the abuse of a position of authority. The Government's proposed offence was in due course enacted in s.4 of the 2003 Act, which creates an offence of causing another person to engage in sexual activity without consent. Although on the face of the Act there is only one offence, rather than two as recommended by the Review, the Review's aim is essentially met by a provision for the offence to carry a higher maximum penalty where penetration is involved, which, as explained below, has the effect of creating two separate offences.

Consent and public policy

Finally, at the end of the chapter we consider the circumstances in which 2.06 consent to sexual activity that is freely given by a person of full capacity will

---

[7] See the old cases of *Rolfe* (1952) 36 Cr. App. R. 4; *DPP v Rogers* [1953] 1 W.L.R. 1017 at 1019; *Court* [1989] A.C. 28 at 41G-42A, per Lord Ackner; at 47E-H per Lord Goff. Such conduct may of course be prosecuted as an attempted sexual assault in appropriate circumstances.

[8] *Setting the Boundaries*, para.2.20.

[9] *Protecting the Public*, para.46.

nonetheless be regarded by the law as ineffective on grounds of public policy.

Aꜱꜱᴀᴜʟᴛ ʙʏ Pᴇɴᴇᴛʀᴀᴛɪᴏɴ

Dᴇꜰɪɴɪᴛɪᴏɴ

2.07   Section 2(1) of the Sexual Offences Act 2003 provides as follows:

"A person (A) commits an offence if—
(a) he intentionally penetrates the vagina or anus of another person (B) with a part of his body or anything else,
(b) the penetration is sexual,
(c) B does not consent to the penetration, and
(d) A does not reasonably believe that B consents."

2.08   If B was under 13 at the relevant time, A should be charged not under s.2 but under s.6 of the Act (assault of a child under 13 by penetration), which carries no requirement to prove absence of consent. This is so regardless of A's age at the time. If B was 13, 14 or 15, and consent is in issue, it may be appropriate to charge A in the alternative under s.2 and s.9 of the Act (or s.9 read with s.13, if A was under 18), so that if the jury find that B consented, A may nonetheless be convicted of sexual activity with a child: see para.4.24, below. Similarly, if A was 18 or over and in a position of trust in relation to B, who was 16 or 17, it may be more appropriate to charge A under s.16 (abuse of position of trust: sexual activity with a child).

Mᴏᴅᴇ ᴏꜰ Tʀɪᴀʟ ᴀɴᴅ Pᴜɴɪꜱʜᴍᴇɴᴛ

2.09   Assault by penetration is an indictable-only offence with a maximum sentence of life imprisonment.[10] The offence cannot be dealt with by way of a caution save in exceptional circumstances relating to the person or the offence and with the consent of the Director of Public Prosecutions.[11]

2.10   For the purposes of listing, cases of assault by penetration[12] fall within Class 2B, save for complex cases involving many complainants (often under age, in care or otherwise particularly vulnerable) and/or many defendants who are alleged to have systematically groomed and abused them, often over a long period of time, which fall within Class 1C.[13] Cases in Class 1C must be referred to the Resident Judge, and by the Resident Judge to a Presiding Judge. Cases in Class 2B must be similarly referred in certain specified

---

[10] s.2(4).
[11] Criminal Justice and Courts Act 2015 s.17(2).
[12] And of soliciting, inciting, encouraging or assisting, attempting or conspiring to commit the offence or assisting an offender having committed the offence.
[13] *Consolidated Criminal Practice Directions*, Part XIII Listing B: CLASSIFICATION, available at *https://www.judiciary.gov.uk/publications/criminal-practice-directions-2015/* [Accessed April 30, 2016].

circumstances, including where the case is unusually grave or complex or a novel and important point of law is to be raised; where the defendant is a police officer, a member of the legal profession or a high profile figure; or where for any reason the case is likely to attract exceptional media attention.

An offence of assault by penetration is a serious specified offence for the purposes of ss.224 and 225(2) (life sentence for serious offences) of the Criminal Justice Act 2003.[14] An offence of assault by penetration, whenever committed, may be made the subject of an extended sentence under s.226A of that Act.[15] The offence is also listed in Pt 1 of Sch.15B to the Criminal Justice Act 2003 for the purposes of s.224A of the Act (life sentence for a second listed offence).[16]   **2.11**

A person convicted of assault by penetration, cautioned, found not guilty by reason of insanity or found to be under a disability and to have done the act charged, is automatically subject to the notification requirements in the Sexual Offences Act 2003.[17]   **2.12**

BAIL

Section 25 of the Criminal Justice and Public Order Act 1994[18] provides that a person charged with or convicted of certain offences who has a previous conviction for any such offence shall be granted bail only if the court, or as the case may be, the constable considering the grant of bail, is of the opinion that there are exceptional circumstances which justify it. The offences in question include assault by penetration and an attempt to commit that offence. For the full list of offences covered by s.25 of the 1994 Act, see paras 1.24 and following, above.   **2.13**

ALTERNATIVE VERDICT

A defendant indicted for assault by penetration may, on appropriate facts, be acquitted of the offence charged and convicted in the alternative of the lesser offence of sexual assault.[19] As to when a conviction in the alternative of common assault may be brought in, see para.2.44, below.   **2.14**

---

[14] Criminal Justice Act 2003 s.224 and Sch.15, Pt 2.

[15] Inserted by the Legal Aid, Sentencing and Punishment of Offenders Act 2012 s.124, brought into force on December 3, 2012, by SI 2012/2906.

[16] Inserted by the Legal Aid, Sentencing and Punishment of Offenders Act 2012 s.122, brought into force on December 3, 2012, by SI 2012/2906.

[17] s.80 and Sch.3, discussed in Ch.35, below.

[18] As amended with effect from December 3, 2012, by the Legal Aid, Sentencing and Punishment of Offenders Act 2012 s.90 and Sch.11 para.33.

[19] For which see paras 2.38 and following, below.

Sentencing

2.15 For the Sentencing Council guideline relating to the sentencing of sexual offences committed by offenders aged 18 and over, see Ch.33. In consulting on its draft guideline,[20] the Council noted that the types of penetration and offending behaviours that may be involved in assault by penetration are wider than in relation to rape, and range from acts as severe as the highest category rape (for example, a violent sexual attack involving penetration of the victim with an object intended or likely to cause significant injury), to an activity that, whilst involving severe sexual violation of the victim, is more akin to a serious sexual assault (e.g. momentary penetration with fingers). The Council noted that research had found a general view among the public and victims that assault by penetration is akin to rape and should be sentenced accordingly. Participants described penetration by objects such as bottles or knives as a particularly aggravated form of rape, potentially more serious and more physically damaging than penetration with a penis. The Council agreed that there is a high degree of crossover between the two offences. However, because the range of potential types of offending is wider for assault by penetration, the Council favoured treating the two offences separately in the guideline.

2.16 Under the previous guideline, issued in 2007 by the Sentencing Guidelines Council ("SGC"), a lower sentence would be given for penetration with a body part, such as a finger or tongue, where no other physical harm was sustained. A higher sentence would be given for penetration with an object (the larger or more dangerous the object, the higher the sentence would be) or penetration combined with abduction, detention, abuse of trust or more than one offender acting together. However, the Sentencing Council agreed with the conclusions of public research that stated:

> "Generally where penetration of genitals had occurred, the public and victims/survivors felt this was akin to rape regardless of what had been used to penetrate due to the level of violation inherent."[21]

The Council therefore proposed that such assaults should generally be treated in very similar terms to rape in terms of the harm caused. Indeed, there are only two differences in the harm factors specified in relation to the two offences. First, the factor relating to pregnancy or an STI occurring as a consequence of the offence is included in the guideline for rape, but not for assault by penetration, because that offence does not involve penile penetration and so these risks do not arise. Secondly, "penetration using large or dangerous object(s)" is included as a harm factor in relation to assault by penetration because, whilst psychological harm results whatever the means of penetration, the Council was of the view that where a large or dangerous

---

[20] *Sexual Offences Guideline: Consultation* (December 6, 2012). The consultation document is available on the Sentencing Council's website.

[21] *Attitudes to sentencing sexual offences*: Sentencing Council Research series 01/12, available at *https://www.sentencingcouncil.org.uk/publications/item/sexual-offences-attitudes-to-sentencing-sexual-offences/* [Accessed April 30, 2016].

object is used, this increases the physical consequences of the attack and also the psychological harm, and so should increase the starting point for sentence.

Sentencing guideline

Step One—Harm and culpability

The guideline requires the sentencing court to go through a series of steps in order to determine the appropriate sentence. Step one involves determining the offence category by reference to the degree of harm caused and then the culpability level for the offence. In relation to the offence of assault by penetration, the harm and culpability factors are as follows:

2.17

Harm		Culpability	
Category 1	The extreme nature of one or more category 2 factors or the extreme impact caused by a combination of category 2 factors *may* elevate to category 1	A	
		Significant degree of planning	
		Offender acts together with others to commit the offence	
		Use of alcohol/drugs on victim to facilitate the offence	
Category 2	• Severe psychological or physical harm • Penetration using large or dangerous object(s) • Additional degradation/ humiliation • Abduction • Prolonged detention/sustained incident • Violence or threats of violence (beyond that which is inherent in the offence) • Forced/uninvited entry into victim's home	Abuse of trust	
		Previous violence against victim	
		Offence committed in course of burglary	
		Recording of the offence	
		Commercial exploitation and/or motivation	
		Offence racially or religiously aggravated	
		Offence motivated by, or demonstrating, hostility to the victim based on his or her sexual orientation (or presumed sexual orientation) or transgender identity (or presumed transgender identity)	

	• Victim is particularly vulnerable due to personal circumstances* *for children under 13 please refer to the guideline on page 33	Offence motivated by, or demonstrating, hostility to the victim based on his or her disability (or presumed disability)
		B Factor(s) in category A not present
Category 3	Factor(s) in categories 1 and 2 not present	

Step Two—Starting point and category range

2.18 Once the court has determined the offence category and culpability level, at step two it should use the corresponding starting point specified in the guideline in order to reach a sentence within the category range. The starting point applies to all offenders irrespective of plea or previous convictions. Once the starting point has been determined, step two allows further adjustment for aggravating or mitigating features as set out below. A case of particular gravity, reflected by multiple features of culpability or harm, could merit upward adjustment from the starting point before further adjustment for aggravating or mitigating features. Where there is a sufficient prospect of rehabilitation, a community order with a sex offender treatment programme requirement under s.202 of the Criminal Justice Act 2003 can be a proper alternative to a short or moderate length custodial sentence. The starting points and category ranges for assault by penetration are as follows:

	A	*B*
Category 1	*Starting point* 15 years' custody *Category range* 13–19 years' custody	*Starting point* 12 years' custody *Category range* 10–15 years' custody
Category 2	*Starting point* 8 years' custody *Category range* 5–13 years' custody	*Starting point* 6 years' custody *Category range* 4–9 years' custody

	A	*B*
Category 3	*Starting point* 4 years' custody	*Starting point* 2 years' custody
	Category range 2–9 years' custody	*Category range* High level community order – 4 years' custody

As noted above, the Sentencing Council considered that the violation **2.19** incurred by reason of penetration is equally severe whether the means used is the penis, another body part or an object. Accordingly, the Council saw no justification for any difference in sentencing between rape and assault by penetration for the most serious offences, i.e. those in category 1, and the same starting points therefore apply. In categories 2 and 3, the ranges are broader than those for rape in order to accommodate the broader range of offending that can be encompassed by this offence. For example, category 2 assault by penetration could include an assault where the victim has been detained in their home by a partner for a prolonged period and there has been very brief penetration with a finger. But it could also include a scenario where an ex-partner has broken into the victim's home and carried out a violent assault and penetrated the victim with his fist. As for category 3, the starting points are higher than in the SGC guideline for offences where any of the culpability A factors are present (4 years' imprisonment as opposed to 2 years'). In the SGC guideline this category was focused solely on the type of penetration, e.g. by fingers, toes or tongue. The Sentencing Council's aim was to move away from a focus on the physical acts involved and instead to reflect the harm caused to the victim by the penetration, irrespective of the way in which it is carried out. Category 3 therefore reflects a baseline of harm without the need for the presence of any other factors. It is evident from the Council's comments on categories 2 and 3 that brief penetration with a finger, toe or tongue, where no harm is caused to the victim (not simply no *physical* harm, as under the SGC guideline), will continue to attract a sentence towards the lower end of the range.[22]

Aggravating and mitigating factors

After identifying the starting point and category range, the court should **2.20** consider whether the presence of aggravating or mitigating factors should

---

[22] For the approach to such cases under the SGC guideline, see, e.g. *Bukhtor Singh* [2012] EWCA Crim 1274, mentioned in para.2.22, below; *Park* [2008] EWCA Crim 1806.

result in an upward or downward adjustment from the starting point or the imposition of a sentence outside the category range. In particular, relevant recent convictions are likely to result in an upward adjustment. When sentencing appropriate category 3 offences, the court should also consider whether the custody threshold has been passed; if so, whether a custodial sentence is unavoidable; and if it is, whether that sentence can be suspended. The non-exhaustive list of aggravating and mitigating factors for assault by penetration is as follows:

Aggravating factors
Statutory aggravating factors
Previous convictions, having regard to a) the nature of the offence to which the conviction relates and its relevance to the current offence; and b) the time that has elapsed since the conviction
Offence committed whilst on bail
Other aggravating factors
Specific targeting of a particularly vulnerable victim
Blackmail or other threats made (where not taken into account at step one)
Location of offence
Timing of offence
Use of weapon or other item to frighten or injure
Victim compelled to leave their home (including victims of domestic violence)
Failure to comply with current court orders
Offence committed whilst on licence
Exploiting contact arrangements with a child to commit an offence
Presence of others, especially other children
Any steps taken to prevent the victim reporting an incident, obtaining assistance and/or from assisting or supporting the prosecution
Attempts to dispose of or conceal evidence
Commission of offence whilst under the influence of alcohol or drugs

Mitigating factors
No previous convictions *or* no relevant/recent convictions
Remorse
Previous good character and/or exemplary conduct*
Age and/or lack of maturity where it affects the responsibility of the offender
Mental disorder or learning disability, particularly where linked to the commission of the offence

* Previous good character/exemplary conduct is different from having no previous convictions. The more serious the offence, the less the weight which should normally be attributed to this factor. Where previous good character/exemplary conduct has been used to facilitate the offence, this mitigation should not normally be allowed and such conduct may constitute an aggravating factor.
In the context of this offence, previous good character/exemplary conduct should not normally be given any significant weight and will not normally justify a reduction in what would otherwise be the appropriate sentence.

Steps Three to Nine

The remaining steps cover the following points. At step three the court should consider any factors which would indicate a reduction in sentence, e.g. assistance to the prosecution. At step four it should consider any reduction for a guilty plea. At step five the court should consider dangerousness, i.e. whether it would be appropriate to award a life sentence (s.224A or s.225(2) of the Criminal Justice Act 2003) or an extended sentence (s.226A). Step six requires the court to consider whether the total sentence is just and proportionate to the offending behaviour. At step seven it should consider whether to make an ancillary order (e.g. a compensation order, a sexual harm prevention order ("SHPO") or a restraining order). Step eight requires the court to fulfil its duty under s.174 of the Criminal Justice Act 2003 to give reasons for, and explain the effect of, the sentence. Finally, at step nine the court should consider whether to give credit for time spent on bail in accordance with s.240A of that Act. **2.21**

Sentencing examples

The decision in *Karshe*[23] illustrates the operation of the culpability factor abuse of trust. The appellant, aged 37, a taxi driver, was convicted of two offences of assault by penetration and sentenced to terms of seven years' **2.22**

[23] [2014] EWCA Crim 1733. See also *Ashton* [2015] EWCA Crim 1799, in which it was held that the existence of an employment relationship between the parties did not give rise to an abuse of trust.

imprisonment to run concurrently. The 16-year-old victim had been out drinking one evening in Cardiff. Two women put her into the appellant's taxi and told him to make sure that she got home. She asked to be taken to Caerphilly and sat in the rear of the taxi. At some stage during the journey the appellant stopped the taxi, got in the back and digitally penetrated the victim's anus and vagina while she was asleep. When the victim awoke the appellant immediately desisted, returned to the driver's seat and drove her home. The victim did not remember the rest of the journey. She went to bed and the next morning told friends that she thought she had been raped. The police were contacted and traces of semen matching the appellant's DNA were found in her anal canal. In interview, the appellant denied digitally penetrating the victim but could not explain the presence of his semen. In the course of his sentencing remarks, the judge said that the appellant had been trying to masturbate himself, although no "ejaculatory event" occurred. The appellant was of previous good character. A pre-sentence report noted that he strongly denied the offences and so did not admit any sexual motivation. He had arrived in this country from Somalia in 1992, aged 13 or 14. He currently lived with his wife and six children, who were between 14 years and 16 months old, and his wife was pregnant with their seventh child. The report expressed the view that the appellant was a sexual predator who presented a high risk of harm to women who were alone. The appellant was reported to be fearful of the impact of a custodial sentence on his family. In passing sentence the judge noted that for an offence of this gravity personal circumstances were of limited weight. He observed that no physical harm had been caused to the victim and that the appellant had desisted when he realised she was awake. However the assaults plainly involved a serious abuse of trust and fell into category 1A of the guideline. The public, particularly women who rely on taxis to get home at night, would be horrified to hear that a taxi driver had taken advantage of the particular vulnerability of a young woman who was intoxicated. The experience of waking up in an isolated place with him assaulting her would have been an absolutely terrifying experience for the victim. She had been significantly affected as a result of knowing that he knew her address: the family had moved home and her behaviour had altered as a result of the attack. She was now worried about being left alone and no longer took taxis. Her attendance at school had suffered. The offences had affected her confidence badly. The conviction, however, had vindicated her and had assisted in her recovery from the effects of the offences. An immediate custodial sentence was inevitable. The judge took the starting point of eight years, which he reduced to seven years to reflect the appellant's previous good character and the other mitigation. On appeal, it was submitted that the judge failed to pay sufficient regard to three factors: first, the penetration was by the use of fingers and lasted a relatively short time; second, there was no force or threat of force, indeed the victim was unaware of what was happening, and he desisted; third, there was no premeditation and he was of previous good character. The Court noted that, as counsel for the appellant accepted, the case involved an abuse of the trust which members of society repose in taxi and other professional drivers: they are trusted to take people to their destination safely, and the more vulnerable the people are, the greater the degree of trust. The victim was suffering from the effects of drink, she was effectively unconscious and thus particularly vulnerable to the assaults. This was a significantly aggravating circumstance, which struck at the heart of the relationship between all taxi drivers and their customers. As the Court had recognised in *Bukhtor Singh*[24]:

> " . . . it is important that those who drive in taxis feel safe. Moreover offences of this kind damage the interests of taxi drivers as a community."

Bukhtor Singh also involved the digital penetration of a young woman by a taxi driver in his taxi. The Court in that case considered that the sentencing judge had been justified in placing the case in the most serious level in the SGC guideline in view of the breach of trust. However, it also drew a distinction between penile and non-penile penetration, with the latter being sentenced less severely in view of the lesser harm caused by such offences: there is no risk of impregnation or infection and no substantial physical harm. The Court in *Bukhtor Singh* reduced the sentence from seven years to five years. In *Karshe*, the Court was also persuaded that the sentence of seven years was too high by a factor which entitled it to intervene. Although in *Bukhtor Singh* there was the additional aggravating factor that the victim was awake during the assault, the present case was aggravated by the presence of semen on the victim's body, the double penetration and the fact that the victim was taken to a lonely and secluded spot. Taking those matters into account, the Court concluded that the correct sentence following a trial was a term of six years' imprisonment and accordingly, it quashed the sentence of seven years and substitute a sentence of six years.

The operation of the totality principle where digital penetration takes place in the course of an incident of rape is illustrated by *Attorney General's Reference (Nos 12 and 13 of 2015) (McClaren and Whitelaw)*.[25] M and W (both 21) had met the victim at a club when she was intoxicated. She went with them into an alleyway where both offenders digitally penetrated her vagina, and both put their penises in her mouth and in her vagina. W also put his finger in her anus. Both offenders contended that the sexual activity had been consensual. The jury found M guilty of rape and W guilty of rape and assault by penetration. The judge placed the offending in category 2A of the guideline for several reasons: it occurred over an extended period; degradation and humiliation were inflicted on the victim by the anal penetration and because she was menstruating; and the offenders' culpability was high as they had committed the rapes together. Each was sentenced to nine years' imprisonment for rape, and W received a concurrent term of four years for the digital anal penetration. The Attorney General submitted that

2.23

---

[24] [2012] EWCA Crim 1274, at [13].
[25] [2015] EWCA Crim 1223.

the sentences were unduly lenient as the judge had failed to have sufficient regard to a number of aggravating factors, and a consecutive sentence should have been imposed on W for the assault by penetration to mark the distinction between the offenders. The Court of Appeal declined to interfere with the sentences. As for the concurrent sentence imposed on W for the assault by penetration, this could not be categorised as wrong in principle, and the judge was entitled to regard the sentence he imposed as appropriate for the total of both the penile and digital sexual offending.

Parties to the Offence

2.24   The offence of assault by penetration may be committed by and against persons of either sex. There is no requirement that the defendant (A) must be above a certain age or the victim (B) below a certain age.

Jurisdiction

2.25   By virtue of s.72 of and Sch.2 to the Sexual Offences Act 2003, as amended,[26] it is an offence under s.2 for a UK national to do an act in a country outside the UK which would constitute a s.2 offence committed against a child under 18 if done in England and Wales. The amendments, made in 2008, expanded the scope of s.72 in two respects. First, they removed the limitation on s.72 as enacted that it applied only to offences committed against victims aged under 16 (the relevant age is now 18). Secondly, they abolished, in respect of UK nationals, the "double criminality" requirement that the act must have been an offence in the country in which it was done. However, this requirement is retained in respect of the prosecution of UK residents and those who become UK residents or nationals after the doing of the relevant act. For the purposes of s.72 a "country" includes a territory and a "United Kingdom national" means a British citizen, a British overseas territories citizen, a British National (Overseas), a British Overseas citizen, a person who under the British Nationality Act 1981 is a British subject, or a British protected person within the meaning of that Act.[27] An act is taken to be an offence in the country in which it was done unless the defendant serves a notice putting the prosecution to proof on the point.[28]

"Penetrates the Vagina or Anus of another Person"

2.26   For discussion of this phrase in the context of rape, see paras 1.55 and following, above.

---

[26] By the Criminal Justice and Immigration Act 2008, s.72, with effect from July 14, 2008.
[27] s.72(9).
[28] s.72(6)–(8).

"WITH A PART OF HIS BODY OR ANYTHING ELSE"

If a person (A) penetrates the vagina or anus of another person (B) with his **2.27**
penis without consent, the correct charge is rape. If he uses any other part of
his body, e.g. his finger, fist or tongue, a charge of assault by penetration will
lie. So, too, if A penetrates B with an object or instrument, such as a bottle,
knife or vibrator. The term "anything else" is apt to include an animal or
other living organism.[29] Thus if A penetrates B's vagina or anus with the
penis (or any other part) of an animal, the appropriate charge is under s.2.
The offence of intercourse with an animal in s.69(2) of the Sexual Offences
Act 2003 applies only where A causes or allows A's own vagina or anus to be
penetrated by an animal's penis.

It is not necessary for the prosecution to establish what penetrated B, only **2.28**
that he was penetrated by something. This means that the offence under s.2
can be prosecuted where, for example, B is a child or a person with a learning
disability who is sure that he was penetrated but not whether it was by A's
penis or something else, so that there is insufficient evidence for a charge of
rape.

"THE PENETRATION IS SEXUAL"

Section 78 of the 2003 Act provides: **2.29**

> "For the purposes of this Part (except section 71[30]), penetration, touching or any
> other activity is sexual if a reasonable person would consider that—
> (a) whatever its circumstances or any person's purpose in relation to it, it is
>   because of its nature sexual, or
> (b) because of its nature it may be sexual and because of its circumstances or
>   the purpose of any person in relation to it (or both) it is sexual."

For the meaning and effect of this provision, see paras 2.66 and following, **2.30**
below. If A penetrates B's vagina or anus in circumstances where there is no
or insufficient evidence that the penetration is sexual, it may be appropriate
to charge one of the offences against the person, i.e. (depending on the level
of harm caused by the penetration) common assault, assault occasioning
actual bodily harm contrary to s.47 of the Offences Against the Person Act
1861, maliciously causing grievous bodily harm contrary to s.20 of the 1861
Act or inflicting grievous bodily harm with intent contrary to s.18 of that
Act.[31]

---

[29] cf. *Williams*, unreported, October 22, 1999 (No.99/4704/R1), which deserves to be buried in
a footnote, where the appellant committed indecent assault by inserting live maggots into the
victim's vagina. See also the reference to "felching" in para.15.135, below.
[30] On a date to be appointed s.78 will be amended by the Serious Crime Act 2015 s.85 and
Sch.4, para.63, to replace the words "except section 71" with "except sections 15A and 71". For
s.15A of the 2003 Act, see paras 4.225 and following, below.
[31] cf. *Hansard*, HC, Standing Committee B, col.49, Beverley Hughes MP and col.103, Paul
Goggins MP (September 9, 2003).

Consent

2.31   It is an element of the offence that B does not consent to the penetration. For this purpose, a person consents if he agrees by choice and has the freedom and capacity to make that choice.[32] The presumptions relating to absence of consent in ss.75 and 76 of the 2003 Act apply to this offence.[33] On consent, see further paras 1.169 and following, above.

Mental Element

2.32   An offence is committed under s.2 only if the penetration is intentional. It will suffice if the defendant's acts were deliberate.[34] If the penetration is accidental, careless or even reckless, no offence will be committed.

2.33   It is a requirement of the s.2 offence that A does not reasonably believe that B consents. Section 3(2) provides:

> "Whether a belief is reasonable is to be determined having regard to all the circumstances, including any steps A has taken to ascertain whether B consents."

For the effect of this provision, see paras 1.382 and following, above.

2.34   The effect of a mistake of identity on the requirement of absence of reasonable belief in consent was considered, briefly, in the strange case of *Attorney General's Reference (No.79 of 2006) (Whitta)*.[35] On the appellant's version of events,[36] he met a girl at a party and an understanding developed that they would have sex later. The girl went to bed. After some time the appellant followed her. He entered the bedroom in which he thought the girl was sleeping, took off his glasses, got into bed and digitally penetrated the vagina of the occupant, who turned out to be the mother of the party host. She protested and the appellant left the room. He pleaded guilty to assault by penetration, following a ruling by the trial judge that the jury was not entitled, on the facts asserted by the appellant, to consider the mistake of identity as a relevant circumstance in assessing whether the appellant had had a reasonable belief in consent. The basis of the learned judge's reasoning was that the only relevant consent, for the purposes of s.2, is that of the complainant, and in this case the appellant could not reasonably have believed that he had the complainant's consent. The position was unaffected by s.2(2), which states that whether a belief is reasonable is to be determined having regard to "all the circumstances", including any steps A has taken to ascertain whether B consents. The judge held that this provision cannot

---

[32] s.74 of the Act, discussed in paras 1.179 and following, above.
[33] s.2(3).
[34] *Heard* [2007] EWCA Crim 125, discussed in paras 2.78 and following, below.
[35] [2006] EWCA Crim 2626.
[36] The prosecution version was never presented to the court, as the appellant pleaded guilty following a preliminary ruling made by the judge on the assumption that the appellant's version was correct.

widen the scope of the jury's consideration so as to allow for the defendant's state of mind in relation to a third party.

The matter came before the Court of Appeal on an appeal against **2.35** sentence, and the Court was therefore not concerned with the correctness of the judge's ruling. But it noted in passing that an alternative way of dealing with this "very rare set of circumstances" would be to hold that the offence is committed if a reasonable (and therefore sober) person would have realised that the person being penetrated was not the person whom the defendant thought he was penetrating. This amounts to a rejection of the judge's analysis, under which there is no scope for reasonable belief in consent to operate unless the defendant believed that the person he actually penetrated was consenting. But the Court of Appeal was surely right implicitly to reject that analysis and to allow scope for mistake as to identity to operate in this way. The judge appears to have been misled by the unusual drafting style of the 2003 Act, which throughout refers to the offender as "A" and the victim as "B", into concluding that any belief in consent must relate to "B", i.e. the complainant, and cannot relate to a third person. This reads too much into what is ultimately a matter of drafting technique. If Parliament had intended to produce the result achieved in *Whitta*, which may fairly be regarded as harsh, it would surely have said so expressly.

Must A intend the penetration to be sexual? As a matter of principle, it **2.36** seems not. On a natural reading of s.2, the requirement of intention is linked only to the act of penetration and not to the requirement that the penetration is sexual. Further, the effect of s.78[37] is that penetration may be sexual by virtue of its nature, or its nature combined with its circumstances, regardless of A's intention in carrying it out. Finally, certain offences in the 2003 Act expressly require the defendant to act for the purpose of sexual gratification,[38] and the implication is that where this is *not* an element of the offence, such a purpose need not be proved. It is, however, difficult to conceive of circumstances in which a jury is likely to find A's penetration of B to be sexual without being satisfied that it had a sexual purpose. Evidence that A had a non-sexual purpose is therefore likely to be of real practical significance.[39]

In *Heard*,[40] dealing with the offence of sexual assault, for which an **2.37** intentional touching is required, the Court of Appeal upheld the trial judge's direction to the jury that it was not open to the defendant to contend that voluntary intoxication through drink or drugs prevented him from intending to touch the victim. We suggest that the same will apply to the offence of assault by penetration.

[37] Discussed in paras 2.66 and following, below.

[38] See ss.11, 12, 18, 19, 32, 33, 36, 37, 40, 41, and 67.

[39] cf. *Pratt* [1984] Crim. L.R. 41 (man charged with indecent assault for compelling two young boys to undress and shine a torch on each other's private parts; *held*, evidence from the man that his motive had been to search the boys for cannabis that he suspected them of taking from him was admissible to challenge the prosecution case that he acted with an indecent intention).

[40] [2007] EWCA Crim 125, discussed in paras 2.78 and following, below.

Sexual Assault

Definition

2.38 Section 3(1) of the Sexual Offences Act 2003 provides as follows:

"A person (A) commits an offence if—
(a) he intentionally touches another person (B),
(b) the touching is sexual,
(c) B does not consent to the touching, and
(d) A does not reasonably believe that B consents."

Mode of Trial and Punishment

2.39 Sexual assault is triable either way. The maximum sentence on conviction on indictment is 10 years' imprisonment and on summary conviction is six months' imprisonment or a fine, or both.[41] As from a day to be appointed the maximum sentence of imprisonment on summary conviction will increase to 12 months' imprisonment.[42] The increase will have no application to offences committed before it takes effect.[43] Until recently, the maximum fine on summary conviction was a fine not exceeding the statutory maximum (i.e. £5,000). The effect of s.85 of the Legal Aid, Sentencing and Punishment of Offenders Act 2012 is that, from March 12, 2015, a fine of any amount may be imposed. An offence of sexual assault committed against a victim under the age of 16 cannot be dealt with by way of a simple caution.[44]

2.40 For the purposes of listing, cases of sexual assault[45] fall within Class 2B, save for complex cases involving many complainants (often under age, in care or otherwise particularly vulnerable) and/or many defendants who are alleged to have systematically groomed and abused them, often over a long period of time, which fall within Class 1C.[46] Cases in Class 1C must be referred to the Resident Judge, and by the Resident Judge to a Presiding Judge. Cases in Class 2B must be similarly referred in certain specified circumstances, including where the case is unusually grave or complex or a novel and important point of law is to be raised; where the defendant is a police officer, a member of the legal profession or a high profile figure; or where for any reason the case is likely to attract exceptional media attention.

---

[41] s.3(4).

[42] Criminal Justice Act 2003 s.282(2), (3).

[43] Criminal Justice Act 2003 s.282(4)

[44] Criminal Justice and Courts Act 2015 s.17(3), and the Criminal Justice and Courts Act 2015 (Simple Cautions) (Specification of Either-Way Offences) Order 2015 (SI 2015/790).

[45] And of soliciting, inciting, encouraging or assisting, attempting or conspiring to commit the offence or assisting an offender having committed the offence.

[46] *Consolidated Criminal Practice Directions*, Part XIII Listing B: CLASSIFICATION, available at *https://www.judiciary.gov.uk/publications/criminal-practice-directions-2015/* [Accessed April 30, 2016].

An offence of sexual assault, whenever committed, is a specified offence   2.41
for the purposes of s.226A of the Criminal Justice Act 2003 (extended
sentence for certain violent or sexual offences).[47]

A person convicted of sexual assault, cautioned, found not guilty by   2.42
reason of insanity or found to be under a disability and to have done the act
charged, is automatically subject to the notification requirements in the
Sexual Offences Act 2003, if:

- they were under 18 at the time of the offence and are sentenced to at
  least 12 months' imprisonment, or
- in any other case, the victim was under 18 or the offender is sentenced
  to a term of imprisonment, detained in a hospital or given a
  community sentence of at least 12 months.[48]

Fitness to plead

Where, in the context of an alleged sexual assault, a jury is determining for   2.43
the purposes of s.4A(2) of the Criminal Procedure (Insanity) Act 1964
whether a person committed "the act ... charged against him as the
offence", the requirement of an absence of reasonable belief in the victim's
consent is not part of the "act charged" and so does not require a finding.[49]

ALTERNATIVE VERDICT

A defendant indicted for sexual assault may be convicted in the alternative of   2.44
battery if the "sexual" element of the offence is not established. On the face
of it this is surprising, since under s.6(3) of the Criminal Law Act 1967 a jury
may bring in an alternative verdict only in relation to "another offence falling
within the jurisdiction of the court of trial", and battery, which used to be
triable either way, was turned into a summary offence by s.39 of the Criminal
Justice Act 1988.[50] However, s.40 of the 1988 Act, as construed in *Lynsey*,[51]
makes provision for a count charging battery to be included on an indictment

---

[47] Inserted by the Legal Aid, Sentencing and Punishment of Offenders Act 2012 s.124,
brought into force on December 3, 2012, by SI 2012/2906.

[48] s.80 and Sch.3, discussed in Ch.35, below.

[49] *Wells* [2015] EWCA Crim 2, citing *R. v B* [2012] EWCA Crim 770 (relating to the offence
of voyeurism).

[50] Thus in *Mearns* [1991] 1 Q.B. 82 it was held that an alternative verdict of guilty of common
assault was not available on an indictment charging assault occasioning actual bodily harm.
Mearns was followed in *Burt* (1996) 161 J.P. 77; *Brownless*, unreported, May 9, 2000; *Clifford*,
The Times, December 5, 2003.

[51] [1995] 2 Cr. App. R. 667. See also *Lewis* [2014] 1 Cr. App. R. 345 (25), holding that s.40 does
not require the defendant to be put in charge of the jury on the count relating to the indictable
offence, the section being directed rather to the stage when the indictment is drawn up;
accordingly, where an indictment contained one count of attempted theft and two of battery, and
after the defendant had been arraigned the prosecution offered no evidence on the attempted
theft count, this did not deprive the indictment of validity and the Crown Court had jurisdiction
to try the two summary counts.

if it is founded on the same facts or evidence as a count charging an indictable offence. The term "indictable offence" is defined to include offences triable either way.[52] As a result, a count of battery[53] may be included as an alternative count on any indictment charging sexual assault. Moreover, by virtue of subsequent changes to the Criminal Law Act 1967, an alternative verdict of guilty of battery may now be brought in if the prosecutor *could* have included a count charging that offence on the indictment in accordance with s.40 of the 1988 Act, even if that was not in fact done.[54] The net result is that, whenever sexual assault is indicted, the jury may convict of battery. However, the Crown Court may only deal with the offender for the assault in a manner in which a magistrates' court could have dealt with him. On a summary charge, the magistrates have no jurisdiction to find the defendant guilty of a lesser offence.

SENTENCING

2.45 For the Sentencing Council guideline relating to the sentencing of sexual offences committed by offenders aged 18 and over, see Ch.33. The previous guideline, issued in 2007 by the Sentencing Guidelines Council ("SGC"), categorised the offence of sexual assault purely by reference to the type of touching involved, e.g. "contact between either the clothed genitalia of offender and naked genitalia of victim or naked genitalia of offender and clothed genitalia of victim". In consulting on its draft guideline,[55] the Sentencing Council said that this focus on the activity in question was too narrow and could make it difficult for sentences to reflect fully the harm caused to the victim, in particular the fear and intimidation they may have suffered. The published guideline is accordingly intended to reflect the emotional and physical harm that can be caused by this offence.

Sentencing guideline

Step One—Harm and culpability

2.46 The guideline requires the sentencing court to go through a series of steps in order to determine the appropriate sentence. Step one involves determining the offence category by reference to the degree of harm caused and then the culpability level for the offence. In relation to the offence of sexual assault the harm and culpability factors are as follows:

---

[52] Interpretation Act 1978 s.5 and Sch.1.

[53] Preferably expressed as "assault by beating" in order to distinguish it from common assault: *DPP v Taylor* [1992] Q.B. 645, at 651 per Mann LJ.

[54] Criminal Law Act 1967 s.6(3A), (3B), inserted by the Domestic Violence, Crime and Victims Act 2004 s.11, which was introduced to overturn *Mearns*, above.

[55] *Sexual Offences Guideline: Consultation* (December 6, 2012). The consultation document is available on the Sentencing Council's website.

Harm		Culpability
Category 1	• Severe psychological or physical harm • Abduction • Violence or threats of violence • Forced/uninvited entry into victim's home	**A**
		Significant degree of planning
		Offender acts together with others to commit the offence
		Use of alcohol/drugs on victim to facilitate the offence
		Abuse of trust
Category 2	• Touching of naked genitalia or naked breasts • Prolonged detention/sustained incident • Additional degradation/ humiliation • Victim is particularly vulnerable due to personal circumstances* *for children under 13 please refer to the guideline on page 37	Previous violence against victim
		Offence committed in course of burglary
		Recording of the offence
		Commercial exploitation and/or motivation
		Offence racially or religiously aggravated
		Offence motivated by, or demonstrating, hostility to the victim based on his or her sexual orientation (or presumed sexual orientation) or transgender identity (or presumed transgender identity)
Category 3	Factor(s) in categories 1 and 2 not present	
		Offence motivated by, or demonstrating, hostility to the victim based on his or her disability (or presumed disability)
		B
		Factor(s) in category A not present

2.47 The factors identified in category 1 in this guideline are placed in category 2 in the guidelines for rape and assault by penetration. The reason for the difference of approach is that the Sentencing Council considered that category 1 sexual assaults will never be as severe as category 1 rapes or assaults by penetration, as reflected by the lower statutory maximum (10 years' imprisonment rather than life). For example, a rape during the course of a forced entry into a home would warrant a starting point of 10 years and is placed in category 2. For sexual assault, forced entry into the home has to be placed in category 1 in order to enable a sentence to be passed that reflects the severity of this aggravation.

2.48 The factor "violence or threats of violence" is included in category 1 because the Council thought that fear of escalation of an attack is likely to increase the psychological harm to the victim, to the extent that it should affect the starting point. For example, an offender may seek to control the victim using threatening language, and especially violent sexual language, to force compliance.

2.49 The factor "touching of naked genitalia or naked breasts" in category 2 was expressed in the consultation draft of the guideline simply as "touching of genitalia". The Sentencing Council said that, whilst the type of physical touching should not be the only determinant of harm, the degree of violation inherent in the touching of genitalia is such that an offence with that feature should always fall within category 2 (i.e. should never fall within category 3). The previous SGC guideline drew a distinction between clothed and unclothed genitalia, but the Council did not believe that a clear distinction can always be drawn between the two in terms of harm caused. For example, where the victim is followed home at night by a stranger who, on a quiet street, grabs the victim between the legs, touches their clothed genitalia and pulls them to the ground, the degree of psychological harm caused by the isolation and the fear of escalation should bring the offence within category 2, irrespective of the fact the victim's genitalia are touched over their clothing. Accordingly, the draft guideline did not distinguish between clothed and naked genitalia. This produced mixed responses from respondents to the consultation. Some felt that assaults over clothing are less harmful, a lesser violation and show a lower level of intent to harm, and that category 2 should cover only offences involving naked genitalia. Others supported the Council's approach of drawing no distinction. Given the differences of view and the need for clarity, the Council decided to amend the factor to "touching of naked genitalia or naked breasts". As a result, touching of clothed genitalia or breasts, without more, will fall within category 3. The Council did, however, express the hope that when the context of the offence makes touching of clothed genitalia or breasts more threatening, this will be captured by the other factors in the harm categories, as in the example given above of the victim followed home at night.

2.50 Finally, as with rape and assault by penetration, category 3 does not list any factors in order to reflect the fact that any sexual assault will cause some degree of harm to the victim.

Step Two—Starting point and category range

Once the court has determined the offence category and culpability level, at step two it should use the corresponding starting point specified in the guideline in order to reach a sentence within the category range. The starting point applies to all offenders irrespective of plea or previous convictions. Once the starting point has been determined, step two allows further adjustment for aggravating or mitigating features, set out below. A case of particular gravity, reflected by multiple features of culpability or harm, could merit upward adjustment from the starting point before further adjustment for aggravating or mitigating features. Where there is a sufficient prospect of rehabilitation, a community order with a sex offender treatment programme requirement under s.202 of the Criminal Justice Act 2003 can be a proper alternative to a short or moderate length custodial sentence. The starting points and category ranges for sexual assault are as follows: **2.51**

	A	B
Category 1	*Starting point* 4 years' custody	*Starting point* 2 years' 6 months' custody
	Category range 3–7 years' custody	*Category range* 2–4 years' custody
Category 2	*Starting point* 2 years' custody	*Starting point* 1 years' custody
	Category range 1–4 years' custody	*Category range* High level community order – 2 years' custody
Category 3	*Starting point* 26 weeks' custody	*Starting point* High level community order
	Category range High level community order – 1 year's custody	*Category range* Medium level community order – 26 weeks' custody

2.52   The starting points and ranges for culpability A offences are slightly higher than under the SGC guideline. This reflects the inclusion in the new guideline of a broader range of harm and culpability factors, as a result of the Sentencing Council's view that sentencing should reflect more than just the physical activity that has taken place.

2.53   In its consultation document, the Council said that it had included community orders at the bottom of the range of available sentences for sexual assaults in categories 2B and 3 in order to reflect the very wide range of offending behaviour that can come before the courts. Whilst all cases are serious, the aims of preventing reoffending and rehabilitating the offender may be better achieved by imposing a community sentence rather than a short custodial sentence which is likely to leave the offender's behaviour unaddressed. The Council gave as an example an offender with no previous convictions who approaches a woman at a crowded bus stop and grabs her breast over her clothing. This would be a very distressing experience for the victim, and the sentencer would want to impose a sentence that prevents the offender from assaulting other women in a similar way. For this type of case, the Council thought the judge may wish to impose a community order for a period of up to two years with a requirement to attend a sex offender treatment programme where the offender's behaviour can be challenged and addressed.

Aggravating and mitigating factors

2.54   After identifying the starting point and category range, the court should consider whether the presence of aggravating or mitigating factors should result in an upward or downward adjustment from the starting point or the imposition of a sentence outside the category range. In particular, relevant recent convictions are likely to result in an upward adjustment. When sentencing appropriate category 2 or 3 offences, the court should also consider whether the custody threshold has been passed; if so, whether a custodial sentence is unavoidable; and if it is, whether that sentence can be suspended. The non-exhaustive list of aggravating and mitigating factors for sexual assault is as follows:

Aggravating factors
Statutory aggravating factors
Previous convictions, having regard to a) the nature of the offence to which the conviction relates and its relevance to the current offence; and b) the time that has elapsed since the conviction
Offence committed whilst on bail

Other aggravating factors
Specific targeting of a particularly vulnerable victim
Blackmail or other threats made (where not taken into account at step one)
Location of offence
Timing of offence
Use of weapon or other item to frighten or injure
Victim compelled to leave their home (including victims of domestic violence)
Failure to comply with current court orders
Offence committed whilst on licence
Exploiting contact arrangements with a child to commit an offence
Presence of others, especially other children
Any steps taken to prevent the victim reporting an incident, obtaining assistance and/or from assisting or supporting the prosecution
Attempts to dispose of or conceal evidence
Commission of offence whilst under the influence of alcohol or drugs

Mitigating factors
No previous convictions or no relevant/recent convictions
Remorse
Previous good character and/or exemplary conduct*
Age and/or lack of maturity where it affects the responsibility of the offender
Mental disorder or learning disability, particularly where linked to the commission of the offence
Demonstration of step taken to address offending behaviour

* Previous good character/exemplary conduct is different from having no previous convictions. The more serious the offence, the less the weight which should normally be attributed to this factor. Where previous good character/exemplary conduct has been used to facilitate the offence, this mitigation should not normally be allowed and such conduct may constitute an aggravating factor.

Steps Three to Nine

2.55   The remaining steps cover the following points. At step three the court should consider any factors which would indicate a reduction in sentence, e.g. assistance to the prosecution. At step four it should consider any reduction for a guilty plea. At step five the court should consider dangerousness, i.e. whether it would be appropriate to award an extended sentence (s.226A of the Criminal Justice Act 2003). Step six requires the court to consider whether the total sentence is just and proportionate to the offending behaviour. At step seven it should consider whether to make an ancillary order (e.g. a compensation order, a SHPO or a restraining order). Step eight requires the court to fulfil its duty under s.174 of the Criminal Justice Act 2003 to give reasons for, and explain the effect of, the sentence. Finally, at step nine the court should consider whether to give credit for time spent on bail in accordance with s.240A of that Act.

Sentencing examples

2.56   In *Mohamad Modar Sarouji*,[56] the appellant, aged 20, pleaded guilty to sexual assault and was sentenced to two-and-a-half years' detention in a young offender institution. He saw the victim in the centre of Watford in the early hours of the morning and followed her through the town for some five to seven minutes. When the victim was alone in an alleyway she felt the appellant touch her bottom; he then grabbed her arms and stood facing her. The fly of his jeans was undone and his penis was exposed and erect. He quietly repeated to her "come here, come here". She tried to get away but the appellant was stronger than she was. She lived nearby and knew her landlord was at home so she screamed his name. The appellant let go and she was able to run home, extremely upset and shaking. The appellant was traced and made full admissions. He said that he became sexually aroused when following the victim and wanted her to give him oral sex. He had not been drunk or under the influence of drugs. In a victim personal statement, the victim explained that as a result of the offence she was scared of walking home at night and so had to take a taxi. The pre-sentence report identified a high risk of re-conviction for a sexual offence. The appellant's capacity for change was low and his attitude in interview was both arrogant and blasé. The appellant had no previous convictions. The sentencing judge took into account the appellant's age and that he had a liver condition for which he continued to be treated. However, the judge said that young women were entitled to walk the streets of our towns and cities in safety. The appellant had targeted the victim as someone to satisfy his sexual needs. The judge took account of the appellant's remorse, the fact that he made immediate admissions and his plea of guilty at the first reasonable opportunity. The

---

[56] [2014] EWCA Crim 2670.

judge also commented that the victim could be said to have suffered severe psychological harm, as she thought that she was going to be raped. She was particularly vulnerable because she was walking home in the early hours of the morning. The location of the offence was also an aggravating feature. On appeal, the appellant contended that the offence fell into category 3B. He conceded there were serious aggravating factors which took the offending outside the sentence for a category 3B offence, but contended that the sentence imposed had been manifestly excessive. The Court of Appeal held that this was a very serious offence, but it was impressed by two features advanced on behalf of the appellant, namely his age and his serious illness, which was possibly fatal and required constant medical attention. In all the circumstances, the appropriate sentence would have been two (rather than two-and-a-half) years' detention in a young offender institution, and the Court allowed the appeal and substituted that sentence for the one imposed by the judge.

In *Dale (John Luke)*,[57] the appellant pleaded guilty to a single count of sexual assault and was sentenced to nine months' imprisonment. At the material time he was a student. He spent the evening in question with a friend from his home town, H, and other fellow students. He drank heavily and was intoxicated at the time of the events giving rise to the indictment. The group of friends and the victim, who was the girlfriend of one of them, ended up at a student flat where the appellant was then living. The victim went to sleep in a bedroom. She was naked, lying under a duvet. Her boyfriend left the flat for a short time, telling the appellant and H not to go into the bedroom. In disobedience to that instruction, they went into the room, drew the duvet from the victim's body and filmed her as she lay on her side using H's mobile phone. The appellant took off all of his clothes apart from his boxer shorts and climbed onto the bed, where he took out his penis and brought it into contact with the victim's forehead as if striking her with it. It was this conduct which gave rise to the count of sexual assault. H, for his part, touched her vagina. The offence came to light when H showed the film to work colleagues, who informed the police. The appellant was arrested and made untruthful denials in interview. On appeal, it was argued that the sentence was manifestly excessive as the mitigation available to the appellant was so powerful as to make it inappropriate for him to be sentenced to imprisonment, at least with immediate effect. The appellant pointed to an the impressive bundle of testimonials; the fact that his behaviour had caused him loss of career opportunity; his remorse, as evidenced by an apologetic and contrite letter to the victim and his decision to absent himself from the university for the then current academic year in order to spare her the anxiety of running into him, though the Court noted that the remorse was not immediate; and he took up employment and built up savings in order to offer a sum by way of financial compensation. However, there was also before the

2.57

---

[57] [2014] EWCA Crim 2286.

Court a victim personal statement in which the victim said that it had made her feel sick and violated that two men she did not know would come into the room she was sleeping in and sexually assault her and record themselves doing so; and the possibility that the video could still exist petrified her. The Court held that the offence fell within the category 2A of the guideline. There were two culpability factors: the offence was committed jointly by two offenders and, of particular importance, it was recorded. Accordingly, the appropriate sentencing range was from one to four years with a starting point of two years. Whilst there was considerable mitigation available to the appellant, there were also other aggravating features: the assault was on a sleeping woman who was therefore vulnerable; it was in a private room, from which the appellant had been specifically instructed to stay out, and so the location factor was present; and the appellant was the worse for drink. The task with which the judge had to grapple was to answer the questions posed in the guideline in relation to offences in categories 2 and 3. First, was the custody threshold passed? The Court held that it manifestly had been passed in this case. Secondly, was it unavoidable that a custodial sentence be imposed, and if so, could that sentence be suspended? The sentencing judge determined that an immediate custodial sentence was unavoidable. She assessed that the correct sentence after trial, in the absence of the appellant's personal mitigation, would have been 18 months' imprisonment. The Court of Appeal held that, given the presence of two culpability factors and three aggravating factors, an uplift of six months from the lowest end of the range was probably generous to the appellant. This was, after all, a reduction from the starting point, not an increase from it as those factors would have merited. The judge then assessed the weight to be given to the mitigating factors in combination with the guilty plea. Her determination, with which the Court agreed, was that a reduction of 50 per cent from the notional sentence of 18 months represented a just and proportionate sentencing outcome. The sentence which she imposed could not possibly be categorised as wrong in principle or manifestly excessive.

2.58   The decision in *Haslam (Lee Anthony)*[58] demonstrates the difficulty that can face sentencers when two offences of a different nature are committed at the same time, each of which is subject to a guideline, and each of which aggravates the effect of the other. The appellant, aged 29, pleaded guilty to one count of sexual assault and one of robbery and was sentenced to six years' imprisonment and three years' imprisonment respectively, the sentences to run concurrently. The judge gave a 25 per cent discount for the guilty plea. The 19-year-old victim was walking home in an alley leading to a bridge in the early hours of the morning when the appellant grabbed her from behind, placed a hand over her mouth and tripped her so she fell and landed hard on the ground, hitting her head as she did so. She was screaming and was scared. The appellant leaned over her with one hand firmly on her

---

[58] [2014] EWCA Crim 2179.

mouth and pulled down her leggings and knickers. She struggled, kicking and screaming. He kept holding her down with his hand over her face and she thought that she was going to be raped. She felt the appellant's skin against her thighs and legs. He grabbed her by the ankles and dragged her from the wall where she was propped up in the middle of the bridge. Her thighs were apart and her vagina exposed. At that point, the appellant appeared to abandon his sexual assault and instead took money from her bag and the mobile phone she had in her hand and ran off. She managed to get up and make her way to a friend's house. The appellant was arrested and interviewed but initially denied the offences and gave an alibi and, when that was disproved, he made no comment. The appellant pleaded guilty, though he did so between the PCMH and the trial date and so the 25 per cent discount was generous. He had a long criminal record and was subject to a suspended sentence at the relevant time. On the night in question, he had smoked heroin, taken crack cocaine and drunk 10 cans of cider. He ran out of cocaine and decided to commit a burglary at a shop when he came across the complainant and decided to rob her. He pleaded guilty to the sexual assault only because of the DNA evidence. In her victim impact statement, the victim said that four months after the incident she was still unable to go out on her own and could not cross the road or go 100 yards to the shops. She felt that the appellant had taken away her freedom, social life and relationships. In passing sentence, the judge commented that it was an unusual case in which two serious offences were committed at the same time. Counsel had argued that this was a sexual offence committed in the course of a robbery but the judge saw it the other way round, as a robbery in the course of a sexual offence: the appellant had first thrown his victim to the ground and attempted a sexual assault, and it was abundantly clear she feared she might be raped. The judge observed that there were two sets of guidelines, but noted the observation in the sexual assault guideline that "Cases of particular gravity reflected by multiple features of culpability or harm could merit an upward adjustment from the starting point". That upward adjustment was appropriate in this case. Before the Court of Appeal, it was argued, in relation to the six year sentence imposed for the sexual assault, that the judge must have started with a minimum of eight years' imprisonment, given the 25 per cent discount for the guilty plea. That exceeded the guideline by a considerable distance and failed adequately to reflect the facts that an initial allegation of attempted rape had been abandoned and there had been no actual contact with the victim's genitalia. The Court held that the judge had been perfectly entitled to move outside the category range for this combination of offences, given that he intended to pass a concurrent term. The appellant admitted that the offences were aggravated by the vulnerability of the victim in an isolated area, late at night, by the significant emotional trauma to her, the physical injury, and the fact that the offence was committed whilst the appellant was subject to a suspended sentence. The Court held that in all the circumstances, the judge's formulation of the sentence as a concurrent term was entirely justified and was neither wrong in principle nor manifestly excessive.

2.59   In *Attorney General's Reference (No.118 of 2014)*,[59] the offender, S, aged 75 at the time of sentence, sexually assaulted four victims, aged between 16 and 30, who were all employed by him, between 2004 and 2012. The offending included touching, holding and squeezing breasts and bottoms under and over clothing; putting his hands down their tops or trousers and underneath underwear and nipple-sucking. On one occasion S pushed one of the victims onto her back, climbed on top of her, kissed her and pulled down her leggings and underwear to try to touch her vagina. Following a *Goodyear* indication, S pleaded guilty to 11 offences, with the agreement of the prosecution, on the understanding that he would receive a 24-month suspended prison sentence. The judge said that the offences had been aggravated by the fact that S had abused his position as employer, there were four victims, the offending was protracted and predatory, the victims were assaulted at their place of work, S had manipulated opportunities to assault them, the victims were vulnerable and the offending had a considerable impact on them. In mitigation, the judge took into account S's guilty pleas, age and lack of previous convictions. S received sentences of between six and eight months, some concurrent and others consecutive, totalling 24 months, and the whole term was suspended for 24 months. The Solicitor General referred the sentence to the Court of Appeal as unduly lenient, submitting that the sentence remained open to challenge despite the fact that it had been imposed after a *Goodyear* indication. He argued that the sentencing judge had given too much weight to the mitigating factors and that the sentence failed to reflect the aggravating features. He said the offences came within category 2A, which had a starting point of two years' imprisonment with a range of one to four years; that consecutive sentences should have been given to reflect the multiple victims; and that suspending the sentences was wrong. In reply, S argued that the Solicitor General could not argue that the sentence was unduly lenient as the prosecution had agreed to S's pleas and to the sentencing indication given by the judge. He said the offending fell into category 2A of the guideline only by virtue of one element, namely the touching of naked breasts. He argued that it was a matter for the judge whether to impose concurrent sentences and that it was unlikely he would offend again. The Court allowed the Reference. The offending encompassed a broad range of actions, but by virtue of the fact that there had been touching of naked breasts it fell within category 2A, for which the starting point was two years' imprisonment. The judge should have considered the cumulative effect of the offending and then looked at any mitigation. The suspended sentences were quashed and replaced with immediate 15-month custodial sentences on each count to run concurrently.

[59] [2014] EWCA Crim 2898.

The decision in *Attorney General's Reference (No.41 of 2015) (Hepworth)*[60] throws light on the application of the culpability factor "abuse of trust". The offender had met the complainant on a night out. She and her friend stayed at the offender's house and went to bed with their clothes on. Whilst the complainant was asleep, her friend saw the offender twice go under the covers and start moving up and down. She did not see any penetration, or the offender's penis, but noted that he was moaning. The offender was later seen masturbating himself until he ejaculated. The complainant had no recollection of the events but on waking, noticed that her tights had been pulled down, her top that fastened between the legs had been undone and pulled up, and that her underwear was twisted. Delays in obtaining forensic evidence meant that expert reports were not served for five years. In that time the offender was sentenced to two years' imprisonment for sexual activity with a girl under the age of 16. He undertook a sex offenders' course. When charged with the instant offence he pleaded guilty in the face of DNA evidence. The pre-sentence report recommended a community order in light of his positive response to his sex offenders' course, and that any custodial penalty should be suspended; it also noted that the offender had admitted to entering the bed uninvited and touching the complainant's genitals. The sentencing judge concluded that he had insufficient information about the offence to categorise it within the guideline, and adopted the lowest possible categorisation, category 3B, before imposing the community order. The Solicitor-General submitted that the offence had involved the touching of naked genitalia and fell within the range of higher culpability on the basis that there had been an abuse of trust. The Court of Appeal allowed the Reference. There was ample and compelling evidence that the offence was a sexual assault involving naked genitalia of a comatose victim. The offending fell within category 2. It was not an abuse of trust; there was nothing which elevated the situation between the offender and the complainant into a relationship of trust. It was an opportunistic offence, albeit carried out in aggravating circumstances. Applying the sentencing guideline, the offending fell within category 2B, with a starting point of one year's custody and a range from a high-level community order to two years' custody. An argument that the community order was not so far outside the range as to be unduly lenient was only tenable in the absence of the aggravating factors which had been present. The complainant had been asleep in a stranger's house. The offence was sordid and committed in her friend's presence. The offender had been under the influence of alcohol, but he had been aware that the complainant was incapable of resistance or consent. The mitigating factors were the steps taken to address the offending behaviour, the guilty plea, albeit late, and the fact that the sentence had been long delayed. The sentence was unduly lenient and the offending warranted an immediate custodial sentence. The considerable aggravation elevated the starting point to at least 18

---

[60] [2015] EWCA Crim 1510.

months. The steps the offender had taken to address his offending behaviour was not sufficient to justify a reduction in the starting point.

Parties to the Offence

2.61 The offence of sexual assault may be committed by and against persons of either sex. There is no requirement that the defendant (A) must be above a certain age or the victim (B) below a certain age. However, if B is under 13, the appropriate charge is under s.7 of the 2003 Act (sexual assault of a child under 13). This is so regardless of the age of A. If B is 13, 14 or 15, and consent is in issue, it may be appropriate to charge A in the alternative under s.3 and under s.9 (sexual activity with a child),[61] so that if the jury find that B consented, A may be nonetheless convicted of sexual activity with a child. Similarly, if A is 18 or over and in a position of trust in relation to B, who is 16 or 17, it may sometimes be appropriate to charge A under s.16 (abuse of position of trust: sexual activity with a child). See further the discussion of these offences in Chs 3 to 5.

Jurisdiction

2.62 By virtue of s.72 of and Sch.2 to the Sexual Offences Act 2003, as amended,[62] it is an offence under s.3 for a UK national to do an act in a country outside the UK which would constitute an offence of sexual assault committed against a child under 18 if done in England and Wales. See further para.2.25, above.

"Touches another Person"

2.63 Section 79(8) of the 2003 Act provides that for the purposes of Pt 1 of the Act, touching includes touching with any part of the body, with anything else or through anything. By virtue of s.79(3), the reference to part of the body includes a reference to a part surgically constructed (in particular, through gender reassignment surgery). For the purposes of sexual assault, touching will therefore include touching with an object or an instrument or with part of another person's body (whether or not surgically constructed): e.g. where A places C's hand on B's breast. Touching through anything, e.g. rubbing or stroking a person's body through their clothes or a bed sheet, will suffice. Indeed, in *R. v H*[63] the Court of Appeal held that touching the clothing that another person is wearing (in that case, pulling their tracksuit bottoms) may be a "touching" for this purpose. The better view is that the effect of the

---

[61] Or, if A is below the age of 18, under s.13 read with s.9 (child sex offences committed by children or young persons).
[62] By the Criminal Justice and Immigration Act 2008 s.72, with effect from July 14, 2008.
[63] [2005] 2 Cr. App. R. 149.

words "touching . . . with anything" in s.79(8), read with *R. v H*, is that ejaculating onto the clothing worn by another person is a sexual assault.[64] Section 3 contains no requirement of force or violence: the lightest touching will suffice. Nor is there a need for any element of "hostility", as was required by one line of cases on indecent assault.[65] Section 79(8) also provides that touching includes touching amounting to penetration. However, touching which involves penile penetration of the vagina, anus or mouth is properly charged as rape and other forms of penetration of the vagina or anus as assault by penetration.

It is not enough to constitute sexual assault for A to cause B to think that he is about to touch her, if the touching does not in fact occur. So, for example, if B sees A's hand moving towards her breast and about to touch it, and manages to move out of the way just in time, there is no completed offence, although this might constitute an attempt. This is one area where the offence of sexual assault is narrower than the repealed offence of indecent assault, which could be committed if A, by action and/or word, caused B to apprehend that he was about to touch her indecently.[66]   **2.64**

There is no requirement that B must be aware of the touching, and so the offence of sexual assault may be committed against someone who is asleep or otherwise unconscious[67] or who simply does not notice that the touching has occurred. An example is *Bounekhla*,[68] which involved a plea under s.3 where the allegation was that the defendant had surreptitiously taken his penis out of his trousers and ejaculated onto a woman's clothing when pressed up against her on the dance floor of a nightclub.   **2.65**

"THE TOUCHING IS SEXUAL"

Section 78 of the 2003 Act provides: **2.66**

> "For the purposes of this Part (except section 71[69]), penetration, touching or any other activity is sexual if a reasonable person would consider that—

---

[64] See *Bounekhla* [2006] EWCA Crim 1217, referred to in para.2.65, below. The Sexual Offences (Scotland) Act 2009 s.3(2)(d) provides that it is a sexual assault for A intentionally or recklessly to ejaculate semen onto B. The context makes it clear that ejaculation onto B's clothing will not suffice.

[65] cf. *Beal v Kelley* (1951–52) 35 Cr. App. R. 128; *Fairclough v Whipp* (1951–52) 35 Cr. App. R. 138; *Burrows* (1951–52) 35 Cr. App. R. 180; *DPP v Rogers* [1953] 1 W.L.R. 1017; *Mason* (1968) 53 Cr. App. R. 12; *cp. McCormack* [1969] 2 Q.B. 442; *Faulkner v Talbot* [1981] 1 W.L.R. 1528; *Brown* [1993] 2 W.L.R. 556. The authorities are fully discussed in the second edition of this work, from para.1.37.

[66] cf. *Rolfe* (1952) 36 Cr. App. R. 4 (A exposed himself to B and walked towards her, making indecent suggestions); *DPP v Rogers* [1953] 1 W.L.R. 1017 at 1019; *Court* [1989] A.C. 28 at 41G–42A, per Lord Ackner; 47E–H per Lord Goff; *Constanza* [1997] 2 Cr. App. R. 576; *Ireland*; *Burstow* [1997] Crim. L.R. 810.

[67] In which case the evidential presumption of absence of consent in s.75 will apply: see paras 1.263 and following, above.

[68] [2006] EWCA Crim 1217.

[69] On a date to be appointed s.78 will be amended by the Serious Crime Act 2015 s.85 and Sch.4, para.63, to replace the words "except section 71" with "except sections 15A and 71". For s.15A of the 2003 Act, see paras 4.225 and following, below.

    (a) whatever its circumstances or any person's purpose in relation to it, it is because of its nature sexual, or

    (b) because of its nature it may be sexual and because of its circumstances or the purpose of any person in relation to it (or both) it is sexual."

This definition derives from the law of indecent assault, under which an assault might be indecent either (i) because it was "inherently indecent", (ii) because it was rendered indecent by the circumstances in which it was carried out, or (iii) because it was capable of being indecent and was in fact indecent because of the defendant's purpose in carrying it out.[70]

Section 78(a)

2.67   In a trial for sexual assault it is a question of fact for the jury (or magistrates) whether the touching meets the requirements of s.78. If the judge considers that no reasonable jury properly directed could find that it does, he or she should stop the case. If the defence submit that this is the proper course, in a case where the prosecution rely on s.78(a), the judge will need to decide whether a reasonable person could find the alleged touching was because of its nature sexual. If the judge concludes that a reasonable person could possibly answer that question adversely to the defendant, then the matter must be left to the jury.

2.68   It is noteworthy that s.78(a) requires the jury to focus only on the nature of the touching, while s.78(b) requires them to consider its nature in combination with its circumstances and/or the purpose of A (and anyone else) in relation to it. The implication is that in applying s.78(a), the circumstances of the touching and A's purpose in carrying it out are not relevant. It follows that the jury will need careful direction in cases where both limbs of s.78 are in issue and evidence of A's purpose is adduced in relation to the second, e.g an admission by A that he obtains sexual pleasure from the conduct alleged against him. In such a case, the judge must direct the jury to ignore that admission in considering s.78(a) but to take it into account in considering s.78(b). This may not be an easy direction to follow, with a consequent risk to A where there is a dispute as to whether the first limb is satisfied.

Section 78(b)

2.69   The correct approach to the application of s.78(b) was considered in *R. v H.*[71] The complainant in that case was walking along a path when the appellant approached and asked her the time. She answered him and he then said: "Do

---

[70] *Court* [1989] A.C. 28 HL.
[71] [2005] 2 Cr. App. R. 149.

you fancy a shag?''. The complainant kept walking but the appellant followed her, came up beside her and asked if she was shy. He then grabbed her tracksuit bottoms by the fabric in the area of the right pocket and attempted to pull her towards him. At trial, the appellant submitted there was no case to answer as nothing had occurred that a reasonable person could regard as "sexual" within the meaning of the Act. The judge took the view that there were clearly circumstances in what had occurred, including the words alleged to have been spoken beforehand, which could result in what had occurred properly being regarded as sexual within the meaning of s.78(b). The appellant was duly convicted.

On appeal, the Court of Appeal said that the judge's approach to s.78(b)   **2.70** had been inappropriate. The provision contains two requirements: first, that the touching (or other activity) because of its nature *may* be sexual, and secondly, that the touching because of its circumstances or the purpose of any person in relation to it (or both) *is* sexual. If there is a submission of "no case", the judge must decide whether there is a case to be left to the jury by determining, first, whether it would be possible for a reasonable person to consider that the touching because of its nature may be sexual, and secondly, whether it would be possible for a reasonable person to conclude, because of the circumstances of the touching or the purpose of any person in relation to it (or both), that it is sexual. If the judge concludes that a reasonable person could possibly answer those questions adversely to the defendant, then the matter must be left to the jury. In approaching the matter as he had, the judge had not adopted the required two-stage approach to s.78(b) but had rather looked at the matter as a whole. The problem with this was that, in a borderline case, a person's intention or other circumstances may appear to show that what had happened was sexual, although the nature of the touching might *not* have been sexual. The Court did, however, recognise that in the great majority of cases the answer will be the same whether the two-stage approach is adopted or the position is looked at as a whole. On that basis it went on to hold that, despite the judge's misdirection, the appellant's conviction was safe.

In the course of its decision the Court suggested that, when directing the   **2.71** jury on s.78(b), the judge should identify two distinct questions for them, as follows. First, would they, as reasonable people, consider that because of its nature the touching could be sexual? If the answer to that question was "No", then they would find the defendant not guilty. If "Yes", they would have to go on and ask themselves (again as reasonable people) whether in view of the circumstances and/or the purpose of any person in relation to the touching, the touching was in fact sexual. If they were satisfied that it was, they would find the defendant guilty. If they were not so satisfied, they would find him not guilty. The Court added that in this suggested approach, the reference in the first question to the nature of the touching is a reference to the actual touching that took place. The jury should be directed that in answering that question, they are not concerned with the circumstances that pertained before or after the touching took place, nor with any evidence as to the purpose of any person in relation to the touching.[72]

2.72   In the course of its decision the Court referred to the old case of *George*,[73] in which it was held that the act of a shoe fetishist in removing a woman's shoe from her foot was not capable of being indecent. Lord Ackner had cited *George* with apparent approval in *Court*,[74] the indecent assault case from which the definition of "sexual" in s.78 derives. However, the Court in *R. v H* expressed the view that under the new law, it would be for the jury to decide whether the act that took place in that case could be sexual.[75] This highlights the potentially wide scope of the application of s.78(b), as a result of which the offence of sexual assault is capable of catching a broader range of conduct than the repealed offence of indecent assault. As Professor Ormerod has commented:

> "Fetishism knows no bounds [and] it will only be the most unusual fetishes where A derives sexual gratification from the most innocuous conduct that will definitely fall outside the scope of the [offence]."[76]

2.73   Whether touching (or other activity) that is capable of being considered sexual is indeed sexual under s.78(b), as interpreted in *R. v H*, will depend upon the jury's assessment of the circumstances in which the touching took place and the purpose of those involved. In short, the context will be determinative. Some examples may illustrate the point. Most juries are, we suggest, likely to consider that slapping another person on the buttock is capable of being a sexual act. Yet a slap given by a team coach as the athletes are leaving the field after a hard-fought game, accompanied by words of congratulation or encouragement, is most unlikely to be found to be a sexual assault.[77] A slap in the dressing room as the athlete emerges from the shower, however, perhaps accompanied by a lascivious laugh, might well be viewed differently. Again, most juries are likely to find that stroking a person's leg is capable of being a sexual act. But they are likely to see a clear difference between a father's affectionate stroking of his child and a fetishist's compulsive stroking of a stranger.[78]

2.74   By virtue of s.78(b), a touching may be established to be sexual by evidence of the defendant's purpose in carrying it out. In some cases there will be direct evidence of purpose, notably where the defendant has made an admission as to what it was. A useful example is the indecent assault case of

---

[72] There is an obvious potential difficulty with this suggestion, in that before one can say that a touching may be sexual in nature it may be necessary to know something of the circumstances in which it was carried out. In such cases the judge will need to be careful in directing the jury as to the circumstances that they should and should not take into account.

[73] [1956] Crim. L.R. 52.

[74] [1989] A.C. 28.

[75] Presumably on the basis that a reasonable person could find that it might be.

[76] [2005] Crim. L.R. 737.

[77] cf. *Gauthier* Can.Cr.L.Digest 42887; and see *J (BJ)* (1996) 193 A.R. 151 (Alta SC).

[78] As in *Price (David)* [2004] 1 Cr. App. R. 145. The fetishist's purpose would be taken into account under s.78(b).

Court,[79] where the appellant, a shop-assistant, had smacked a young girl who visited the shop 12 times on her buttocks over her shorts. When asked by the police to explain his conduct, he said "I don't know—buttock fetish". The House of Lords held that evidence of this admission could be adduced to establish that the spanking, an "equivocal action" that might have either an innocent or an indecent explanation, was in fact indecent. In a case where there is no direct evidence of the defendant's purpose, the prosecution might seek to establish what it was by inference from other evidence admissible either at common law or under the "bad character" provisions of the Criminal Justice Act 2003. An instructive case is *Fox*,[80] which concerned charges under s.8 of the Sexual Offences Act 2003 of causing a child under 13 to engage in sexual activity. The appellant had caused young girls to adopt provocative poses and had then taken photographs of them. The prosecution case was that the appellant had caused the girls to engage in activity that could be sexual, and it was in fact sexual because he had the intention of obtaining sexual gratification; but the appellant denied obtaining such gratification and claimed that he had been undertaking an artistic project. In order to prove that his purpose was in fact sexual, the prosecution adduced in evidence the following items found in his van, in which he lived: (1) photographs that he had taken of older girls and which the prosecution said were indecent, (2) a notebook with entries showing an interest in pubescent and pre-pubescent girls and (3) certain other contents of the van, in particular items of girls' underwear and photographs of women in sexual poses, some of them designed to make the women look younger than their true age. The judge admitted this material in evidence under the "bad character" provisions and the appellant was convicted. His conviction was, however, quashed by the Court of Appeal on the basis that the judge had not assessed the items of evidence separately in order to determine in relation to each whether it was properly admissible under the 2003 Act or at common law, and had failed carefully to explain to the jury how they should approach each item and what it might prove.

It is important to note that a defendant's purpose is capable of making an **2.75** activity sexual only if the activity because of its nature *could* be sexual. So if a doctor carries out an intimate medical examination of a female patient, which is in fact unnecessary, and there is evidence that he has a sexual purpose, the case will fall readily within the scope of s.78(b) and the doctor will be liable to conviction of sexual assault.[81] But if the examination is a necessary one, the fact that the doctor secretly obtains sexual gratification from it will not make it a sexual assault. This point was raised in *Kumar*,[82] in

---

[79] [1989] A.C. 28 HL.
[80] [2009] EWCA Crim 653, discussed in more detail at paras 20.21 and following, below.
[81] cf. *Court* [1989] A.C. 28, at 43G–44C per Lord Ackner; at 35D, E per Lord Griffiths.
[82] [2006] EWCA Crim 1946. See also *Bolduc and Bird* (1967) 63 D.L.R. (2d) 82, where a doctor was held to have committed an indecent assault by carrying out a proper vaginal examination whilst allowing a friend, masquerading as a medical student, to be present for the purpose of obtaining sexual gratification.

which the appellant, a general practitioner, was convicted of indecent assault in relation to a breast examination he had conducted on a female patient. He appealed on the ground that it had wrongly been left open to the jury to convict if they thought that the examination might have been legitimate, but that the appellant used it as "cover" for a secret intention to obtain sexual gratification. Such a secret intention, he argued, could not turn a legitimate examination into an indecent assault. The appeal was rejected on the basis that the Crown's case throughout had been that, whilst a breast examination was required, it was improperly conducted. It had never been suggested that this was a "secret intent" case and in those circumstances the judge's direction did not render the conviction unsafe. The Court of Appeal did, however, say that a necessary medical examination properly conducted, but with the secret intention of gaining sexual gratification, would not constitute an indecent assault, since if the examination was necessary the defendant's act in carrying it out could not bear an indecent interpretation. The same logic would apply where the allegation is of sexual assault, since under s.78(b) the admissibility of evidence of a defendant's purpose will turn on whether his conduct because of its nature may be sexual, and that question could not be answered adversely to the defendant in relation to a necessary and properly conducted medical examination.

2.76   If A touches B without B's consent, and the circumstances are such that it is doubtful whether it can be proved that the touching was sexual, the appropriate charge is likely to be common assault. Even if sufficient proof is available to charge sexual assault, if the assault causes serious harm to B it may be more appropriate to charge A instead with maliciously causing grievous bodily harm (s.20 of the Offences against the Person Act 1861) or inflicting grievous bodily harm with intent (s.18 of the 1861 Act).[83]

Consent

2.77   It is an element of the offence of sexual assault that B does not consent to the touching.[84] For this purpose, a person consents if he agrees by choice and has the freedom and capacity to make that choice.[85] The presumptions relating to absence of consent in ss.75 and 76 of the Act apply to this offence.[86] On consent, see further paras 1.69 and following, above. For the circumstances in which a consent will not be effective for public policy reasons, see paras 2.109 and following, below.

---

[83] cf. *Hansard*, HC, Standing Committee B, col.49, Beverley Hughes MP, and col.103, Paul Goggins MP (September 9, 2003).
[84] s.3(1)(c).
[85] s.74 of the Act, discussed in paras 1.179 and following, above.
[86] s.3(3).

MENTAL ELEMENT

Requirement of intention

For an offence of sexual assault to be committed, the touching by A must be   2.78
intentional; an accidental, careless or reckless touching will not suffice. This
requirement was considered in *Heard*,[87] where the appellant, who had been
drinking heavily, undid his trousers, took his penis in his hand and rubbed it
up and down the thigh of a police officer. He was convicted of sexual assault
on a direction by the trial judge that s.3 requires a deliberate touching and
creates an offence of basic rather than specific intent, so that drunkenness
can provide no defence. The Court of Appeal held that the judge had been
right to rule that the touching must be deliberate. Reckless touching will not
do. On the evidence, the appellant plainly intended to touch the police officer
with his penis. That he was drunk may have meant that he was disinhibited
and did something he would not have done if sober, and/or that he did not
remember it afterwards. Neither of those matters would destroy the intentional character of the touching, on the basis that "[i]n the homely language
employed daily in directions to juries in cases of violence and sexual
misbehaviour, 'a drunken intent is still an intent'".[88] The judge's direction
amounted to telling the jury that they must be sure the appellant's mind
(drunken or otherwise) had gone with his physical act of touching. It seemed
to the Court that in the great majority of alleged sexual assaults, or
comparable sexual crimes, the defendant's mind, albeit in some cases a
drunken mind, will have gone with the touching, penetration or other
prohibited act.

The Court did, however, say that it was possible to envisage exceptional   2.79
cases in which the defendant's intoxication was such that his mind did not go
with his act, so that his touching was not truly intentional. It referred to
Lipman,[89] in which the appellant contended that when he killed his victim by
stuffing bedclothes down her throat he was under the illusion, induced by
hallucinatory drugs voluntarily taken, that he was fighting for his life against
snakes. If the equivalent state of mind were to exist in someone who
committed an act of sexual touching or penetration, the question whether
their act was intentional would be directly in point. Another potential
example would be an intoxicated person whose control of his limbs is
uncoordinated or impaired, so that in consequence he stumbles or flails
about against another person, touching them in a sexual way—e.g. he

---

[87] [2007] EWCA Crim 125.
[88] cf. *Sheehan and Moore* (1975) 60 Cr. App. R. 308, at 312: "A drunken intent is nevertheless
an intent".
[89] (1969) 53 Cr. App. R. 600.

touches a woman on her private parts. The Court said that in a case of that sort there is no offence whether the person is intoxicated or sober[90]:

> "To flail about, stumble or barge around in an unco-ordinated manner which results in an unintended touching, objectively sexual, is not this offence. If to do so when sober is not this offence, then nor is it this offence to do so when intoxicated. It is also possible that such an action would not be judged by the jury to be objectively sexual, on the basis that it was clearly accidental, but whether that is so or not, we are satisfied that in such a case this offence is not committed. The intoxication, in such a situation, has not impacted on intention. Intention is simply not in question. What is in question is impairment of control of the limbs . . . We would expect that in some cases where this was in issue the Judge might well find it useful to add to the previously-mentioned direction that 'a drunken intent is still an intent', the corollary that 'a drunken accident is still an accident'. To the limited, and largely theoretical, extent that a reckless sexual touching is possible the same would apply to that case also. Whether, when a defendant claims accident, he is doing so truthfully, or as a means of disguising the reality that he intended to touch, will be what the jury has to decide on the facts of each such case."

2.80 Must A intend the touching to be sexual? As a matter of principle, it seems not. On a natural reading of s.3, the requirement of intention is linked only to the touching and not to the requirement that the touching is sexual. Further, the effect of s.78[91] is that the touching may be sexual by virtue of its nature, or its nature combined with its circumstances, regardless of A's intention in carrying it out. Finally, certain offences in the 2003 Act expressly require the defendant to act for the purpose of sexual gratification,[92] and the implication is that where this is *not* an element of the offence, such a purpose need not be proved. It is, however, difficult to conceive of circumstances in which a jury is likely to find that A's touching of B was sexual without being satisfied that A had a sexual purpose. Evidence that A had a non-sexual purpose is therefore likely to be of real practical significance.[93]

Intoxication

2.81 If at the time he touched B, A lacked the necessary mental element for the offence due to involuntary intoxication, e.g. his drink had been spiked, then he is not liable to conviction of the offence.[94] If A's intoxication was self-induced, i.e. he simply over-indulged, he cannot rely on his intoxication to support a claim that he reasonably believed that B was consenting to being touched, as a drunken mistake can never found a defence to the charge.[95] The

---

[90] At 23.
[91] Discussed in paras 2.66 and following.
[92] See ss.11, 12, 18, 19, 32, 33, 36, 37, 40, 41, and 67.
[93] cf. *Pratt* [1984] Crim. L.R. 41, n.39, above.
[94] cf. *Kingston* [1995] 2 A.C. 355 HL.
[95] cf. para.1.399, above.

position is the same if the issue is whether the touching was intentional. As noted above, it was established in *Heard*[96] that if A touches B whilst in a state of voluntary intoxication due to drink or drugs, he is nonetheless liable to conviction if, despite his condition, his act was deliberate in the sense that his mind went with it. It will not assist A that he acted as he did only because of a loss of self-control or disinhibition caused by the intoxication. The Court of Appeal in *Heard* held that the trial judge had been right to direct the jury that sexual assault is an offence of basic intent, to which drunkenness is not a defence, rather than an offence of specific intent, which, citing *DPP v Majewski*,[97] the Court defined as an offence requiring proof of a state of mind addressing something beyond the prohibited act itself, namely its consequences. The Court recognised that there is a large element of policy in the decision whether voluntary intoxication can or cannot be relied upon in relation to an offence. It noted the decision in *R. v C*[98] that indecent assault was a crime of basic intent, and expressed itself satisfied that Parliament had not intended the 2003 Act to change the law by allowing voluntary intoxication to provide a defence where previously it did not. It concluded that voluntary intoxication, whether through the taking of drink, drugs or other mind-altering substances, cannot be relied upon as negating intention on a charge of sexual assault.

Though it is difficult to quarrel with the conclusion reached in *Heard*, the decision is open to criticism for the way in which the Court defined the concept of specific intent. The generally accepted understanding, worked out through the case law following *Majewski*, is that offences of specific intent are those requiring proof of intention, whilst offences of basic intent, to which voluntary intoxication can provide no defence, are those requiring some lesser form of mens rea, including recklessness. On this analysis, one might plausibly argue that sexual assault is a crime of specific intent in relation to the element of intentional touching. However, it was always likely that the courts would look for a way to categorise the offence as one of basic intent, in order to discourage unmeritorious defences based upon intoxication. The Court of Appeal in *Heard* did just that. But its definition of specific intent as requiring a state of mind addressing not merely the prohibited act, but also its consequences, threatens to unsettle the law relating to mens rea and voluntary intoxication generally. It ought, for example, to mean that murder is an offence of basic intent and not, as it has long been considered, one of specific intent.[99] The implications for other sexual offences of the Court's

2.82

---

[96] [2007] EWCA Crim 125.
[97] [1977] A.C. 443.
[98] [1992] Crim. L.R. 642.
[99] See Smith and Hogan, *Criminal Law*, 14th edn, (2015), pp.360–1. This point goes beyond the scope of this book, but those who wish to pursue it should start with the trenchant and persuasive commentary on *Heard* by David Ormerod at [2007] Crim. L.R. 654.

approach to the distinction between offences of specific and basic intent are nonetheless noted as appropriate below.

Consent

2.83 It is a requirement of the offence that A does not reasonably believe that B consents. Section 3(2) provides:

> "Whether a belief is reasonable is to be determined having regard to all the circumstances, including any steps A has taken to ascertain whether B consents."

For the effect of this provision, see paras 1.382 and following and 2.34 and following, above.

CAUSING A PERSON TO ENGAGE IN SEXUAL ACTIVITY WITHOUT CONSENT

DEFINITION

2.84 Section 4(1) of the Sexual Offences Act 2003 provides as follows:

> "A person (A) commits an offence if—
> (a) he intentionally causes another person (B) to engage in an activity,
> (b) the activity is sexual,
> (c) B does not consent to engaging in the activity, and
> (d) A does not reasonably believe that B consents."

MODE OF TRIAL AND PUNISHMENT

2.85 If the activity in which A causes B to engage involves any of the following, a s.4 offence is triable only on indictment and the maximum penalty is life imprisonment:
   (a) penetration of B's anus or vagina,
   (b) penetration of B's mouth with a person's penis,
   (c) penetration of a person's anus or vagina with a part of B's body or by B with anything else, or
   (d) penetration of a person's mouth with B's penis.[100]
In other cases, offences under s.4 are triable either way with a maximum sentence on indictment of 10 years' imprisonment and on summary conviction of six months' imprisonment or a fine, or both.[101] The effect of the decision in *Courtie*[102] is that the provision of a higher maximum punishment where certain forms of penetration occur is to create two separate offences,

---

[100] s.4(4).
[101] s.4(5).
[102] [1984] A.C. 463.

one involving those forms of penetration and the other not. It is important in cases tried on indictment that the relevant count specifies which of the two offences is being charged.

As from a day to be appointed the maximum sentence of imprisonment on summary conviction will increase to 12 months' imprisonment.[103] The increase will have no application to offences committed before it takes effect.[104] Until recently, the maximum fine on summary conviction was a fine not exceeding the statutory maximum (i.e. £5,000). The effect of s.85 of the Legal Aid, Sentencing and Punishment of Offenders Act 2012 is that, from March 12, 2015, a fine of any amount may be imposed. An offence under s.4 committed against a victim under the age of 16 cannot be dealt with by way of a simple caution.[105]   **2.86**

For the purposes of listing, cases under s.4[106] fall within Class 2B, save for complex cases involving many complainants (often under age, in care or otherwise particularly vulnerable) and/or many defendants who are alleged to have systematically groomed and abused them, often over a long period of time, which fall within Class 1C.[107] Cases in Class 1C must be referred to the Resident Judge, and by the Resident Judge to a Presiding Judge. Cases in Class 2B must be similarly referred in certain specified circumstances, including where the case is unusually grave or complex or a novel and important point of law is to be raised; where the defendant is a police officer, a member of the legal profession or a high profile figure; or where for any reason the case is likely to attract exceptional media attention.   **2.87**

An offence under s.4 is a serious specified offence for the purposes of s.224 and, where the offence involved penetration, s.225(2) (life sentence for serious offences) of the Criminal Justice Act 2003.[108] A s.4 offence, whenever committed, may be made the subject of an extended sentence under s.226A of that Act.[109] The offence is also listed in Pt 1 of Sch.15B to the Criminal Justice Act 2003 for the purposes of s.224A of that Act (life sentence for a second listed offence).[110]   **2.88**

A person convicted under s.4, cautioned, found not guilty by reason of insanity or found to be under a disability and to have done the act charged,   **2.89**

---

[103] Criminal Justice Act 2003 s.282(2), (3).

[104] Criminal Justice Act 2003 s.282(4)

[105] Criminal Justice and Courts Act 2015 s.17(3), and the Criminal Justice and Courts Act 2015 (Simple Cautions) (Specification of Either-Way Offences) Order 2015 (SI 2015/790).

[106] And of soliciting, inciting, encouraging or assisting, attempting or conspiring to commit the offence or assisting an offender having committed the offence.

[107] *Consolidated Criminal Practice Directions*, Part XIII Listing B: CLASSIFICATION, available at *https://www.judiciary.gov.uk/publications/criminal-practice-directions-2015/* [Accessed April 30, 2016].

[108] Criminal Justice Act 2003 s.224 and Sch.15, Pt 2.

[109] Inserted by the Legal Aid, Sentencing and Punishment of Offenders Act 2012 s.124, brought into force on December 3, 2012, by SI 2012/2906.

[110] Inserted by the Legal Aid, Sentencing and Punishment of Offenders Act 2012 s.122, brought into force on December 3, 2012, by SI 2012/2906.

is automatically subject to the notification requirements in the Sexual Offences Act 2003.[111]

BAIL

2.90 Section 25 of the Criminal Justice and Public Order Act 1994[112] provides that a person charged with or convicted of certain offences who has a previous conviction for any such offence shall be granted bail only if the court, or as the case may be, the constable considering the grant of bail is of the opinion that there are exceptional circumstances which justify it. The offences in question include offences under s.4, where the activity caused by A involved penetration as set out in para.2.85 above, and an attempt to commit such an offence. For the full list of offences covered by s.25 of the 1994 Act, see para.1.24, above.

SENTENCING

2.91 For the Sentencing Council guideline relating to the sentencing of sexual offences committed by offenders aged 18 and over, see Ch.33. In consulting on its draft guideline,[113] the Council proposed that s.4 offences should be sentenced according to the approach and sentence levels specified for the offence of assault by penetration (s.2 of the 2003 Act), given the closeness of the range of behaviours covered by the two offences. This is the approach followed in the published guideline, and reference should accordingly be made to the discussion, above, of the guideline for assault by penetration.

Sentencing guideline

Step One—Harm and culpability

2.92 The guideline requires the sentencing court to go through a series of steps in order to determine the appropriate sentence. Step one involves determining the offence category by reference to the degree of harm caused and then the culpability level for the offence. In relation to offences under s.4, the harm and culpability factors are as follows:

---

[111] s.80 and Sch.3, discussed in Ch.35, below.
[112] As amended with effect from December 3, 2012, by the Legal Aid, Sentencing and Punishment of Offenders Act 2012 s.90 and Sch.11 para.33.
[113] *Sexual Offences Guideline: Consultation* (December 6, 2012). The consultation document is available on the Sentencing Council's website.

Harm	
Category 1	The extreme nature of one or more category 2 factors or the extreme impact caused by a combination of category 2 factors **may** elevate to category 1
Category 2	• Severe psychological or physical harm • Penetration using large or dangerous object(s) • Pregnancy or STI as consequence of the offence • Additional degradation/ humiliation • Abduction • Prolonged detention/sustained incident • Violence or threats of violence • Forced/uninvited entry into victim's home • Victim is particularly vulnerable due to personal circumstances* *for children under 13 please refer to the guideline on page 41
Category 3	Factor(s) in categories 1 and 2 not present

Culpability
A
Significant degree of planning
Offender acts together with others to commit the offence
Use of alcohol/drugs on victim to facilitate the offence
Abuse of trust
Previous violence against victim
Offence committed in course of burglary
Recording of the offence
Commercial exploitation and/or motivation
Offence racially or religiously aggravated
Offence motivated by, or demonstrating, hostility to the victim based on his or her sexual orientation (or presumed sexual orientation) or transgender identity (or presumed transgender identity)
Offence motivated by, or demonstrating, hostility to the victim based on his or her disability (or presumed disability)
B
Factor(s) in category A not present

Step Two—Starting point and category range

2.93   Once the court has determined the offence category and culpability level, at step two it should use the corresponding starting point specified in the guideline in order to reach a sentence within the category range. The starting point applies to all offenders irrespective of plea or previous convictions. Once the starting point has been determined, step two allows further adjustment for aggravating or mitigating features, set out below. A case of particular gravity, reflected by multiple features of culpability or harm, could merit upward adjustment from the starting point before further adjustment for aggravating or mitigating features. Where there is a sufficient prospect of rehabilitation, a community order with a sex offender treatment programme requirement under s.202 of the Criminal Justice Act 2003 can be a proper alternative to a short or moderate length custodial sentence. The starting points and category ranges for offences under s.4 are as follows:

Where offence involved penetration		
	A	*B*
Category 1	*Starting point* 15 years' custody *Category range* 13–19 years' custody	*Starting point* 12 years' custody *Category range* 10–15 years' custody
Category 2	*Starting point* 8 years' custody *Category range* 5–13 years' custody	*Starting point* 6 years' custody *Category range* 4–9 years' custody
Category 3	*Starting point* 4 years' custody *Category range* 2–6 years' custody	*Starting point* 2 years' custody *Category range* High level community order – 4 years' custody

Where offence did not involve penetration		
	A	*B*
Category 1	*Starting point* 4 years' custody *Category range* 3–7 years' custody	*Starting point* 2 years' 6 month's custody *Category range* 2–4 years' custody
Category 2	*Starting point* 2 years' custody *Category range* 1–4 years' custody	*Starting point* 1 years' custody *Category range* High level community order – 2 years' custody
Category 3	*Starting point* 26 weeks' custody *Category range* High level community order – 1 year's custody	*Starting point* High level community order *Category range* Medium level community order – 26 weeks' custody

Aggravating and mitigating factors

After identifying the starting point and category range, the court should   **2.94**
consider whether the presence of aggravating or mitigating factors should
result in an upward or downward adjustment from the starting point or the
imposition of a sentence outside the category range. In particular, relevant
recent convictions are likely to result in an upward adjustment. When
sentencing appropriate category 2 or 3 offences, the court should also
consider whether the custody threshold has been passed; if so, whether a
custodial sentence is unavoidable; and if it is, whether that sentence can be
suspended. The non-exhaustive list of aggravating and mitigating factors for
offences under s.4 is as follows:

Aggravating factors
Statutory aggravating factors
Previous convictions, having regard to a) the nature of the offence to which the conviction relates and its relevance to the current offence; and b) the time that has elapsed since the conviction
Offence committed whilst on bail
Other aggravating factors
Specific targeting of a particularly vulnerable victim
Ejaculation (where not taken into account at step one)
Blackmail or other threats made (where not taken into account at step one)
Location of offence
Timing of offence
Use of weapon or other item to frighten or injure
Victim compelled to leave their home (including victims of domestic violence)
Failure to comply with current court orders
Offence committed whilst on licence
Exploiting contact arrangements with a child to commit an offence
Presence of others, especially other children
Any steps taken to prevent the victim reporting an incident, obtaining assistance and/or from assisting or supporting the prosecution
Attempts to dispose of or conceal evidence
Commission of offence whilst under the influence of alcohol or drugs

Mitigating factors
No previous convictions *or* no relevant/recent convictions
Remorse
Previous good character and/or exemplary conduct*

Age and/or lack of maturity where it affects the responsibility of the offender
Mental disorder or learning disability, particularly where linked to the commission of the offence

* Previous good character/exemplary conduct is different from having no previous convictions. The more serious the offence, the less the weight which should normally be attributed to this factor. Where previous good character/exemplary conduct has been used to facilitate the offence, this mitigation should not normally be allowed and such conduct may constitute an aggravating factor.
In the context of this offence, previous good character/exemplary conduct should not normally be given any significant weight and will not normally justify a reduction in what would otherwise be the appropriate sentence.

Steps Three to Nine

The remaining steps cover the following points. At step three the court   **2.95**
should consider any factors which would indicate a reduction in sentence, e.g.
assistance to the prosecution. At step four it should consider any reduction
for a guilty plea. At step five the court should consider dangerousness, i.e.
whether it would be appropriate to award a life sentence (s.224A or s.225(2)
of the Criminal Justice Act 2003) or an extended sentence (s.226A). Step six
requires the court to consider whether the total sentence is just and
proportionate to the offending behaviour. At step seven it should consider
whether to make an ancillary order (e.g. a compensation order, a SHPO or
a restraining order). Step eight requires the court to fulfil its duty under s.174
of the Criminal Justice Act 2003 to give reasons for, and explain the effect of,
the sentence. Finally, at step nine the court should consider whether to give
credit for time spent on bail in accordance with s.240A of that Act.

PARTIES TO THE OFFENCE

An offence under s.4 may be committed by and against persons of either sex.   **2.96**
There is no requirement that the defendant (A) must be above a certain age
or the victim (B) below a certain age. However, if B is under 13, the
appropriate charge is under s.8 of the 2003 Act (causing or inciting a child
under 13 to engage in sexual activity). This is so regardless of the age of A.
If B is 13, 14 or 15, it may be appropriate to charge A in the alternative under
s.4 and s.10 (causing or inciting a child to engage in sexual activity),[114] so that
if the jury find that B consented A may nonetheless be convicted of an
offence. Similarly, if A is 18 or over and in a position of trust in relation to
B, who is 16 or 17, it may sometimes be more appropriate to charge A under

---

[114] Or, if A is below the age of 18, under s.13 read with s.9 (child sex offences committed by children or young persons).

s.17 (abuse of position of trust: causing or inciting a child to engage in sexual activity). See further the discussion of these offences in Chs 3 to 5.

Jurisdiction

2.97 By virtue of s.72 of and Sch.2 to the Sexual Offences Act 2003, as amended,[115] it is an offence under s.4 for a UK national to do an act in a country outside the UK which would constitute a s.4 offence committed against a child under 18 if done in England and Wales. See further para.2.25, above.

"Causes another Person . . . "

2.98 The offence covers the situation where A causes B to engage in a sexual activity without B's consent, whether or not A also engages in it. The word "causes" is not defined and so any causative conduct by A may suffice, including the use of physical force[116] or of words alone, as where A threatens B with violence or some economic or other harm, or uses inducements or persuasion.[117] The question whether A caused B to engage in the activity in one of fact, the determination of which is dependent on the application of common sense.[118] In principle, A's conduct need not be the only operative cause. However, "causing" requires proof of an act and "mere tacit standing by and looking on" is therefore insufficient.[119] Thus A is not guilty of the "causing" offence under s.4 if he fails to prevent a third party (C) from engaging in sexual activity with B without B's consent. This is so even if A owes a legal duty of care to B or has a right to exercise control over C. However, for A to stand passively by in those circumstances is likely to make him an accessory to any offence committed by C against B. See further para.4.86, below.

---

[115] By the Criminal Justice and Immigration Act 2008 s.72, with effect from July 14, 2008.

[116] As in *Ayeva* [2009] EWCA Crim 2640, where the appellant forced the complainant's hand onto his penis and moved it up and down.

[117] Proof of the causal element of the offence cannot, however, be supplied simply by proving one of the circumstances sufficient to bring into play the evidential presumptions about consent in s.75 of the Act, e.g. that immediately before B engaged in the relevant activity, A had threatened him with immediate violence. This is because s.75 does not require the proof of a causal link between the circumstances specified in it and B's conduct: it is sufficient merely to prove one of the circumstances to bring the presumption into play. Accordingly, whilst the prosecution may deal with the consent requirements of the s.4 offence by proving, e.g. a threat of immediate violence by A, in order to prove the causal element of the offence they must go further and satisfy the jury that the threat caused B to engage in the activity.

[118] *Alphacell Ltd v Woodward* [1972] A.C. 824.

[119] *Price v Cromack* [1975] 1 W.L.R. 988; *(No. 1 of 1994)* [1995] 1 W.L.R. 599. *Cp. Ralphs* (1913) 9 Cr. App. R. 86 and *Drury* (1974) 60 Cr. App. R. 195, in which it was held that a person could commit the repealed offence of causing or encouraging sexual intercourse with, or an indecent assault on, a girl under 16 for whom he was responsible (s.28 of the Sexual Offences Act 1956) by failing to prevent the intercourse or assault. However, both decisions turned on the "encouragement" limb of the offence.

" . . . TO ENGAGE IN AN ACTIVITY"

The term "activity" is not defined in the Act. It will include penetration and   **2.99**
touching.[120] But there is no reason to limit it to activities of this sort, and in
principle any conduct in which B is caused to engage will qualify provided
only that it is "sexual". So the term is apt to cover the case where A causes
B to take intimate images of herself and send them by phone to A,[121] to
display her private parts and/or to masturbate for A to watch by webcam,[122]
or to engage in conversation with A of a sexual nature. In *Grout*,[123] decided
under s.8 of the 2003 Act, the Court of Appeal said:

> "We are prepared to accept, for the purposes of this appeal, that 'activity' on the
> part of the child could embrace 'the activity' of conversation or sending text or
> MSN messages, depending on the circumstances."

It is also clear that the activity in which B is caused to engage may involve B   **2.100**
alone, as in the examples just given, or may be activity by B with A, with a
third person or even with an animal.[124] In principle, the s.4 offence may be
used to prosecute cases of "female rape", in which A causes a non-consenting
B to penetrate her vagina with his penis. The offence may also be prosecuted
where B can himself be convicted of a sexual offence in relation to the sexual
activity in question, on the basis that, although he did not consent to the
activity, he nonetheless committed the actus reus of the relevant sexual
offence with the necessary mens rea in circumstances where he cannot avail
himself of the defence of duress. However, in those circumstances it would be
more natural to prosecute B for the sexual offence in question and A under
the Serious Crime Act 2007 for encouraging him to commit it.

The effect of the term "engage in an activity" is that the offence will not be   **2.101**
committed where A causes B simply to watch sexual activity by others. This
reading is supported by the existence in s.12 of the 2003 Act of an offence of
causing a child to watch a sexual act. If watching a sexual act was intended
to constitute "engaging in sexual activity", s.12 would be unnecessary as the
conduct in question would be adequately covered by s.10 (causing or inciting
a child to engage in sexual activity) and, in relation to children under 13, s.8
(causing or inciting a child under 13 to engage in sexual activity).

It seems clear that B will "engage in" an activity for the purposes of the   **2.102**
offence by passively allowing a third person to perform a sexual act upon
him, e.g. by allowing himself to be masturbated. What if B's conduct is
involuntary or unconscious? If in those circumstances B did not "engage in"

---

[120] cf. s.78, discussed in paras 2.66 and following, above: "penetration, touching *or any other
activity*" (our emphasis); and see the various types of penetration identified in s.4(4), as set out
in para.2.85, above.
[121] cf. *Broughton* [2007] EWCA Crim 566.
[122] cf. *Butcher* [2009] EWCA Crim 1458.
[123] [2011] EWCA Crim 299 at [29].
[124] For an example of a s.4 offence committed by causing another person to engage in sexual
activity with an animal, see *H and R v R*. [2008] EWCA Crim 1202.

an activity, then A would commit no s.4 offence where he causes B to do a sexual act whilst B is in a drugged or hypnotised state, such that B does not realise what he is doing. We anticipate that the courts would strive to avoid this result by interpreting the concept of "engaging in an activity" in a purely physical sense, i.e. so that there is no requirement for B's mind to "go with" the activity.

"The Activity is Sexual"

2.103   For the meaning of "sexual", see paras 2.66 and following, above. It is the activity in which A causes B to engage that must be sexual, and it is not sufficient for A to engage in sexual activity directed towards B: see further para.3.165, below.

Consent

2.104   It is an element of the s.4 offence that B does not consent to engaging in the activity. For this purpose, a person consents if he agrees by choice and has the freedom and capacity to make that choice.[125] The presumptions relating to absence of consent in ss.75 and 76 of the Act apply to this offence:[126] see further paras 1.263 and following, above. Professor John Spencer has called for the enactment of offences of obtaining sexual activity by threats and obtaining sexual activity by false pretences, on the basis that s.4 is an "imperfect instrument" for penalising such conduct as it applies only where the threat or pretence is such as to nullify consent.[127]

Mental Element

2.105   A must "intentionally" cause B to engage in the activity; if he does so accidentally or carelessly or recklessly, the offence is not committed. Thus in *Grout*,[128] decided under s.8 of the 2003 Act, the Court of Appeal said:

> "The causing or inciting must be intentional, i.e. deliberate; recklessness or less will not do."

2.106   Must A intend or know that the activity he causes B to engage in is sexual? As a matter of principle, it seems not: see the discussion in para.2.80, above.

2.107   As to whether A is liable to conviction if he causes B to engage in sexual activity whilst he (A) is in a state of intoxication due to drink or drugs, see

---

[125] s.74 of the Act, discussed in paras 1.179 and following, above.
[126] s.4(3).
[127] *Sex by Deception, Archbold Review*, Issue 9, November 14, 2013, pp.6–9.
[128] [2011] EWCA Crim 299, at [26], citing *Heard*; [2007] EWCA Crim 125, at [22] per Hughes LJ.

the discussion of *Heard*[129] in paras 2.78 and following, above. In the light of that discussion, voluntary intoxication through drink or drugs will provide no defence to a charge under s.4.

It is a requirement of the s.4 offence that A does not reasonably believe 2.108 that B consents. Section 4(2) provides:

> "Whether a belief is reasonable is to be determined having regard to all the circumstances, including any steps A has taken to ascertain whether B consents."

For the effect of this provision, see paras 1.382 and following and 2. 34 and following, above.

Consent and Public Policy

No Consent to the Infliction of Actual Bodily Harm

The offences considered in this chapter are non-consensual, in that they are 2.109 committed only if the person who is penetrated, touched etc. does not consent to the penetration or touching. There are, however, circumstances in which consent, although full, informed and freely given, will not be recognised by the law as valid for this purpose. In short, the law will in certain circumstances protect individuals from themselves on grounds of public policy, by declining to recognise their consent as effective to prevent an offence being committed against them.

This limitation on personal autonomy was first clearly identified, though 2.110 not in fact applied, in *Donovan*,[130] a case of indecent assault in which it was held that a person cannot give an effective consent to the infliction on himself of actual bodily harm. The appellant in that case had persuaded a girl of 17 to submit to a caning. Evidence was given that he was addicted to such behaviour, from which he derived sexual pleasure. His conviction was quashed on the ground that the trial judge had misdirected the jury on the burden of proof with respect to absence of consent, but the Court also dealt with the prosecution argument that the case was one in which proof of absence of consent was not necessary. It said:

> "As a general rule, although it is a rule to which there are well established exceptions, it is an unlawful act to beat another person with such a degree of violence that the infliction of bodily harm is a probable consequence, and when such an act is proved, consent is immaterial."[131]

The Court later summarised this general rule by saying "an act likely or intended to cause bodily harm is an unlawful act". For this purpose, bodily harm was defined as:

---

[129] [2007] EWCA Crim 125.
[130] [1934] 2 K.B. 498, DC. See also *(No.6 of 1980)* [1981] Q.B. 715, a case of common assault.
[131] [1934] 2 K.B. 498, DC at 507.

"any hurt or injury calculated to interfere with the health or comfort of the [victim]. Such hurt or injury need not be permanent, but must . . . be more than merely transient or trifling."[132]

2.111   It followed that the jury should have been directed to consider first of all whether they were satisfied that the blows struck by the appellant were likely or intended to do bodily harm, and if so to convict him. Only if they were not so satisfied should they have gone on to consider whether the prosecution had proved absence of consent. In fact, the jury had not been directed to consider the first question, and the Court found it impossible to say that they would inevitably have decided it against the appellant: there are, said Swift J, many gradations between a light tap and a severe blow. The Court therefore declined to uphold the appellant's conviction on the basis that this was a case where consent could not operate, and accordingly the judge's misdirection as to the burden of proof made the conviction unsafe.

2.112   Although the decision concerned the repealed offence of indecent assault, there is nothing in the Sexual Offences 2003 to suggest that Parliament intended the rule in *Donovan* not to apply to the offences of assault by penetration or sexual assault. HH Judge Peter Murphy has argued that, as the Act makes absence of consent an element of those offences, a defendant charged with one of them must be allowed to run a consent "defence"[133] even in circumstances where the rule identified in *Donovan* would otherwise apply.[134] This argument is, with respect, flawed. The fact is that absence of consent had to be proved in order to secure a conviction of indecent assault, and the same is true of the subsisting offences under the Offences against the Person Act 1861 of which assault is a constituent element, yet this has not prevented the rule in *Donovan* applying to those offences. In truth, regardless of the context, where the elements of an offence, whatever its origins, include absence of consent, it is clearly established that the defendant may rely only upon a consent which the courts recognise as capable of being legally effective.

2.113   It is nonetheless true that the Court in *Donovan* accepted that there were "well established exceptions" to the rule it identified, including "manly diversions" such as friendly contests at wrestling or with foils, and "rough and undisciplined horseplay", provided in both cases that there is no intent to cause bodily harm.[135] Perhaps unsurprisingly, it held that the appellant's "corrupt motive" was not within any of the recognised exceptions. But times move on, and modern sexual mores are very different from those that

---

[132] [1934] 2 K.B. 498, DC at 507.

[133] Though as absence of consent is an element of the offence, its presence could not supply a "defence", properly so-called.

[134] *Flogging Live Complainants and Dead Horses: We May No Longer Need to Be in Bondage To Brown* [2011] Crim. L.R. 758.

[135] The categories of exception are not closed: see *Mohammed Dica* [2004] EWCA Crim 1103, at 41. The exceptions also include physical injury inflicted during contact sports, where the conduct that causes the injury does not go beyond what a player might reasonably be considered to have accepted: *Barnes* [2004] EWCA Crim 3246; [2005] Crim. L.R. 381.

prevailed in the inter-war period when *Donovan* was decided. Sexual autonomy is now a keystone of the law of sexual offences, and is also protected by art.8 ECHR. One might perhaps expect these developments to be reflected in a more liberal judicial approach to the operation of consent in the context of sexual encounters. In fact, this is not the case. We go on below to look at this topic under two broad headings: sado-masochism and rough sex.

Sado-masochism: the decision in Brown

The leading authority on the operation of consent in relation to injuries **2.114** caused during sado-masochistic encounters is the decision of the House of Lords in *Brown*.[136] The appellants, who were homosexual, were in the habit of meeting together secretly and practising on each other a variety of sado-masochistic acts, which included bondage, genital torture (including the use of hot wax, fish hooks and needles), beating, branding, blood-letting and the smearing of blood. The "victims" all volunteered for this treatment because they enjoyed the pain, humiliation and degradation involved. Each was given a codeword that he could use if excessive harm or pain was caused, and the instruments employed by the sadists were clean and sterilised before use. The police became aware of the group because they came across videos made by group members recording some of their activities. Although the videos clearly showed acts of gross indecency, charges under s.13 of the Sexual Offences Act 1956 were time-barred and the appellants were accordingly charged instead with offences of assault occasioning actual bodily harm and/ or wounding under the Offences Against the Person Act 1861. They were convicted and their convictions were upheld by the Court of Appeal, which certified the following point of law of general public importance:

> "Where A wounds or assaults B occasioning him actual bodily harm in the course of a sado-masochistic encounter, does the prosecution have to prove lack of consent on the part of B before they can establish A's guilt under section 20 or section 47 of the Offences Against the Person Act 1861?"

The House answered this question in the negative and dismissed the appeals **2.115** by a bare majority.[137] Their Lordships all treated the matter as turning upon considerations of policy and public interest. The majority based their opinions on the proposition, for which they found support in *Donovan*[138] and

[136] [1993] 2 W.L.R. 556.

[137] Lords Templeman, Jauncey of Tullichettle and Lowry; Lords Mustill and Slynn dissenting.

[138] [1934] 2 K.B. 498. In *Brown*, Lords Lowry (at 575) and Mustill (at 584) questioned the correctness of the decision in *Donovan*, though not the principle enunciated in the case, on the basis that the appellant had been charged not with assault occasioning actual bodily harm but with common and indecent assault, to both of which consent is a defence. This criticism seems misconceived. The appellant had set out to inflict bodily harm, so his conduct must have been unlawful, in accordance with the reasoning in *Brown*, regardless of the form of assault with which he was ultimately charged. See further Sir John Smith in [1993] Crim. L.R. 586; but cp. Clarkson, C.M.V., *Violence and the Law Commission* [1994] Crim. L.R. 324 at 332 (fn.74).

Attorney-General's Reference (No.6 of 1980),[139] that as a general rule a person cannot validly consent to the infliction on himself of actual bodily harm. The question was therefore whether sado-masochism should be added to the list of established exceptions. The majority were clear that it should not. Lord Templeman said[140] that to add it:

".. would be acceptable if sado-masochism were only concerned with sex, as the appellants contend. In my opinion sado-masochism is not only concerned with sex. Sado-masochism is also concerned with violence . . . In principle there is a difference between violence which is incidental and violence which is inflicted for the indulgence of cruelty. The violence of sado-masochistic encounters involves the indulgence of cruelty by sadists and the degradation of victims. Such violence is injurious to the participants and unpredictably dangerous. I am not prepared to invent a defence of consent for sado-masochistic encounters which breed and glorify cruelty and result in offences under sections 47 and 20 of the Act of 1861."

Lord Jauncey said[141]:

". . . in considering the public interest it would be wrong to look only at the activities of the appellants alone . . . This House must . . . consider the possibility that these activities are practised by others and by others who are not so controlled or responsible as the appellants are claimed to be. Without going into details of all the rather curious activities in which the appellants engaged it would appear to be good luck rather than good judgment which has prevented serious injury from occurring. Wounds can easily become septic if not properly treated, the free flow of blood from a person who is H.I.V. positive or who has Aids can infect another and an inflictor who is carried away by sexual excitement or by drink or drugs could very easily inflict pain and injury beyond the level to which the receiver has consented . . . Furthermore, the possibility of proselytisation and corruption of young men is a real danger even in the case of these appellants . . . I have no doubt that it would not be in the public interest that deliberate infliction of actual bodily harm during the course of consensual sado-masochistic activities should be held to be lawful."

Lord Lowry agreed with Lords Templeman and Jauncey, but added[142]:

"What the appellants are obliged to propose is that the deliberate and painful infliction of physical injury should be exempted from the operation of statutory provisions the object of which is to prevent or punish that very thing, the reason for the proposed exemption being that both those who will inflict and those who will suffer the injury wish to satisfy a perverted and depraved sexual desire. Sado-masochistic homosexual activity cannot be regarded as conducive to the enhancement or enjoyment of family life or conducive to the welfare of society. A relaxation of the prohibitions in sections 20 and 47 can only encourage the practice of homosexual sado-masochism and the physical cruelty that it must involve . . . by withdrawing the legal penalty and giving the activity a judicial imprimatur. As well as all this, one cannot overlook the physical danger to those who may indulge in sado-masochism. In this connection, and also generally, it is idle for the appellants to claim that they are educated exponents of 'civilised

[139] [1981] Q.B. 715.
[140] [1993] 2 W.L.R. 556, at 564.
[141] At 574.
[142] At 583.

cruelty'. A proposed *general* exemption is to be tested by considering the likely *general* effect. This must include the probability that some sado-masochistic activity, under the powerful influence of the sexual instinct, will get out of hand and result in serious physical damage to the participants and that some activity will involve a danger of infection such as these particular exponents do not contemplate for themselves."

The fact that the case involved some quite extreme activities seems clearly to have coloured the approach of the majority, whose principal concern was the pain, cruelty, humiliation and degradation involved. It is also apparent from the comments cited above that Lord Jauncey and Lord Lowry were influenced at least in part by the fact that the sado-masochistic activity with which they were dealing was homosexual in nature. The answer given by the majority to the certified question was not, however, confined to homosexual acts, and it follows that any act undertaken in the course of a sado-masochistic encounter, whether heterosexual or homosexual, that is intended or likely to cause more than "transient or trifling" harm will in principle constitute a sexual offence and/or an offence of violence. **2.116**

The tone of the dissenting opinions is very different. Lord Mustill, after an exhaustive examination of the case law, concluded that there is no general principle that the infliction of bodily harm is invariably criminal in the absence of some specific factor that decrees otherwise. Instead, each individual category of consensual violence must be addressed in the light of the situation as a whole. His Lordship accordingly felt free to consider afresh whether the public interest demanded that s.47 of the 1861 Act be interpreted in such a way as to render criminal the appellants' activities. He considered that it did not. Those activities involved the infliction of actual, not grievous bodily harm; they were carried out in private; they took place not only with the consent of the recipient but with his willing and glad co-operation; the harm was inflicted for the gratification of sexual desire, not in a spirit of animosity or rage; and the activities were not engaged in for profit. Leaving aside repugnance and moral objection, neither of which were grounds upon which the courts could properly create new crimes, his Lordship could visualise only the following reasons for making the appellant's activities criminal: **2.117**

1. Some of the practices obviously created a risk of genito-urinary infection, and others of septicaemia. These might indeed have been grave in former times, but the risk of serious harm must surely have been greatly reduced by modern medical science.
2. The possibility that matters might get out of hand, with grave results. It has been acknowledged throughout the present proceedings that the appellants' activities were performed as a pre-arranged ritual, which at the same time enhanced their excitement and minimised the risk that the infliction of injury would go too far. Of course things might go wrong and serious injury or death might ensue. If this happened, those responsible would be punished according to the ordinary law, in the same way as those who kill or injure in the course of more ordinary sexual activities are regularly punished. But to penalise the appellants' conduct even if the extreme consequences do not ensue, just because they might have done so would

require an assessment of the degree of risk, and the balancing of this risk against the interests of individual freedom. Such a balancing is in my opinion for Parliament, not the courts . . .

3. I would give the same answer to the suggestion that these activities involved a risk of accelerating the spread of [Aids] and that they should be brought within the Act of 1861 in the interests of public health. The consequence would be strange, since what is currently the principal cause of the transmission of this scourge, namely consenting buggery between males, is now legal. Nevertheless, I would have been compelled to give this proposition the most anxious consideration if there had been any evidence to support it. But there is none, since the case for the respondent was advanced on an entirely different ground.

4. There remains an argument to which I have given much greater weight. As the evidence in the present case has shown, there is a risk that strangers (and especially young strangers) may be drawn into these activities at an early age and will then become established in them for life. This is indeed a disturbing prospect, but I have come to the conclusion that it is not a sufficient ground for declaring these activities to be criminal under the Act of 1861. The element of the corruption of youth is already catered for by the existing legislation; and if there is a gap in it which needs to be filled the remedy surely lies in the hands of Parliament, not in the application of a statute which is aimed at other forms of wrong-doing."[143]

Lord Slynn also thought that the earlier authorities did not conclusively resolve the certified question. Considering the matter as one of principle, his Lordship could see no significant reason for denying a consent defence in any case falling short of grievous bodily harm or death. That being so, the appellants should have been permitted to run a defence of consent. As to whether activities of the sort carried out by the appellants should be criminalised, that was a matter of policy for the legislature:

"It is not for the courts in the interests of 'paternalism' . . . or in order to protect people from themselves, to introduce, into existing statutory crimes relating to offences *against* the person, concepts which do not properly fit there."[144]

2.118 Ultimately, however, these more liberal voices did not prevail. As a result, the decision in *Brown* proved controversial and has been regarded by many as a missed opportunity for a reappraisal of this sensitive area of the law.[145] The decision nonetheless survived a challenge before the European Court of

[143] At 600–1.
[144] At 608.
[145] For proposed alternatives, see e.g. Simon Cooper and Mark James, *Entertainment—The Painful Process of Rethinking Consent* [2012] Crim. L.R. 188, arguing that activities that involve the intentional infliction of harm or carry a significant risk of unintended injury should be lawful if undertaken in circumstances which are tolerated by society, but not otherwise; Julia Tolmie, *Consent to Harmful Assaults: The Case for Moving Away from Category Based Decision Making* [2012] Crim. L.R. 656, advocating the approach adopted by the New Zealand Court of Appeal in *Lee* (2006) 22 C.R.N.Z. 568, under which consent presumptively renders lawful the intentional or reckless infliction of grievous bodily harm, but the presumption can be displaced in respect of dangerous categories of activity with limited social utility or which society will not tolerate. For comment on these articles, see the First Supplement to our Fourth Edition (2014), pp.72–3.

Human Rights. In *Laskey, Jaggard and Brown v UK*,[146] three of the appellants lodged applications in Strasbourg claiming that their prosecution and conviction amounted to a violation of their right to respect for private life guaranteed by art.8 ECHR. The Court rejected the applications, holding that, although the criminal proceedings constituted an interference with the applicants' right to respect for private life, the UK authorities had been entitled to consider the interference "necessary in a democratic society" for the protection of health, within the meaning of art.8(2). It added that Member States are entitled to regulate, through the operation of the criminal law, activities which involve the infliction of physical harm, whether the activities occur in the course of sexual conduct or otherwise. The determination of the level of harm which should be tolerated by the law in situations where the victim consents is in the first instance a matter for the State concerned, since at stake are public health considerations, the general deterrent effect of the criminal law and, on the other side, individual autonomy. The Court rejected the applicants' argument that their behaviour formed part of private morality which it is not the State's business to regulate. It commented that the activities involved a significant degree of injury, which distinguished the case from those involving consensual homosexual conduct in private where no such feature was present.[147] It said that, in any event, the State authorities are entitled to have regard not only to the actual seriousness of the injuries, but also to the potential for harm inherent in the incident in question.

It would also be wrong to assume that in *Brown*, in relation to sado-   **2.119**
masochistic encounters, only those who inflict harm are liable to prosecution. On the contrary it seems that the masochist may also be convicted as an accessory to the offence or of encouraging or assisting it. This follows from the reasoning of the majority of the Supreme Court in the case of *Gnango*.[148] In that case, which involved very different facts, the majority (Lord Kerr dissenting) held that where D1 and D2 voluntarily enter into a fight against each other, each intending to kill or cause grievous bodily harm to the other and each foreseeing that the other has a reciprocal intention, and where D1 mistakenly kills a third party (V) in the course of the fight, then not only D1 but also D2 is guilty of murdering V. The significance of the decision for present purposes is that in the course of its reasoning the majority held that

---

[146] [1997] E.H.R.L.R. 411 (Applications Nos 21627/93, 21826/93 and 21974/93). See also *V, W, X, Y and Z v UK*, January 18, 1995 (Application No.22170/93), where the European Commission on Human Rights held inadmissible similar applications brought under art.8 by a variety of unidentified sado-masochists, both homosexual and heterosexual. The Commission held that the applications were manifestly ill-founded, as *Brown* did not have a direct or continuous impact on the applicants' private lives, so that they could not claim to be victims of a violation of the Convention.

[147] cf. *ADT v UK* [2000] 2 F.L.R. 697 (Application No.35765/97), holding that art.8 was infringed by the applicant's conviction for gross indecency for engaging in non-violent group homosexual activity in private in circumstances which gave rise to no public health considerations.

[148] [2011] UKSC 59.

there is no general statutory or common law bar to a defendant being convicted as an accessory to a crime of which he was the actual or intended victim. The only exception is the rule,[149] illustrated by the decision in *Tyrrell*,[150] that where legislation creates an offence that is intended to protect a class of persons, a member of that class cannot be convicted as an accessory to the offence committed in respect of him. How should the Supreme Court's reasoning be applied where the victim is a willing participant in a sado-masochistic encounter? *Brown* establishes that his consent to the infliction on himself of actual bodily harm cannot provide a defence to a criminal charge brought against the person who inflicted the injury. As the rule in *Tyrrell* has no application in this context, the effect of *Gnango* is that, not only does the sadist have no defence, but the masochist is party to the sadist's offence, which was committed in respect of him. In this connection it is worth noting that the view of the majority in *Gnango* was that D2, by voluntarily entering into the gun fight, encouraged or assisted D1 to kill or seriously injure him. This proposition is, with respect, wholly artificial, given that D2's whole purpose was to avoid being killed and instead to kill D1, and the decision may be criticised for that reason. However, the circumstances in that case are clearly distinguishable in this respect from a sado-masochistic encounter, in which the masochist may well be encouraging and perhaps also assisting the infliction of injury upon himself. Will the CPS regard *Gnango* as shifting the boundaries in this area so as to justify the prosecution of all those involved in sado-masochistic encounters, including those on whom pain is inflicted? One hopes not, given the lack of any compelling public interest in such prosecutions. There is currently no guidance on the CPS website that bears upon the issue.

2.120   *Brown* is an unsatisfactory decision, and we hope that in due course the Supreme Court will have an opportunity to re-consider the boundaries of consent in relation to sado-masochistic sexual activity. Whether and when this happens is likely to depend ultimately on the wisdom of the exercise of prosecutorial discretion in this sensitive area. If the Supreme Court does become seized of the matter, it will no doubt be told that, shortly after the decision in *Brown*, the Law Commission considered the extent to which intentionally inflicted injuries should be within the scope of the criminal law. The Commission proposed that it should be possible to give a valid consent to any injury less than one which is "seriously disabling", and that this should apply inter alia to injuries resulting from sado-masochism indulged in for sexual pleasure, except where the injured person was under 18.[151]

---

[149] Identified by Professor Glanville Williams in his article *Victims and other exempt parties in crime* (1990) 10 Legal Studies at p.245.
[150] [1894] 1 Q.B. 710.
[151] *Consent in the Criminal Law*, Law Com Consultation Paper No.139 (1995), paras 3.1–3.11, 10.16–10.54.

Rough sex

Brown establishes that the operation of consent is limited in relation to sado-   **2.121**
masochistic encounters, i.e. those in which the participants derive pleasure
from the infliction and receipt of pain. Is there any reason why the same
limits should not apply where pain is inflicted as an incident of what might
otherwise be regarded as a conventional sexual encounter? The authorities
suggest not, though in this context the courts have at least stated a
willingness in principle to accommodate changes in sexual mores. Thus
Donovan was followed in *Boyea*,[152] where, in the course of sexual activity, the
appellant injured the victim by inserting his hand into her vagina and
twisting it. He was convicted of indecent assault, on a direction by the judge
that the question whether the victim had consented was not relevant if the
jury were satisfied that the appellant's actions were intended or likely to cause
bodily harm. On appeal, it was argued that this had been a misdirection and
that the issue of consent should have been left to the jury. The Court of
Appeal considered *Donovan* and said that, in determining whether any
intended or likely harm was "transient or trifling" within the meaning of that
case, account must be taken of the fact that social attitudes had changed
since that case was decided, particularly in the field of sexual relations
between adults. It accepted that the "level of vigour in sexual congress"
which was generally acceptable, and therefore the voluntarily accepted risk of
incurring some injury, was probably higher in 1992 than it was in 1934, and
accordingly the phrase "transient or trifling" had to be understood in the
light of present day conditions rather than those of nearly 60 years earlier.
However, even with that qualification, the Court considered that the extent of
the violence inflicted in *Boyea* went far beyond the risk of minor injury to
which, if the victim had consented, her consent would have been a defence.
Moreover, it was inconceivable that she would have consented to the injuries
that were in fact inflicted on her. This is a useful indication of modern
judicial attitudes, although in a trial, the question whether a particular
degree of harm is to be regarded as "transient or trifling" is of course one for
the jury.

Boyea preceded the decision in *Brown*, but the courts have declined to   **2.122**
extrapolate from the later decision an absolute rule that there can be no
consent to injury inflicted during sexual or other intimate activity carried out
in private. The most significant decision in this respect is *Wilson*,[153] where the
appellant, at his wife's instigation, had used a knife to brand his initials onto
each of her buttocks. He was charged with assault occasioning actual bodily
harm. At the close of the prosecution case, the judge rejected a submission of
no case to answer based on the wife's consent, citing *Brown*. The appellant
was convicted, but his conviction was quashed on appeal on the ground that

---

[152] [1992] Crim. L.R. 574.
[153] [1996] 3 W.L.R. 125. For criticism of the reasoning employed in this nonetheless "happy
decision", see Professor Griew, *Archbold News*, May 3, 1996, p.1.

in the circumstances the defence of consent had been available to him. The Court of Appeal said that *Brown* is not authority for the proposition that consent is no defence to a charge of assault occasioning actual bodily harm whenever the harm is deliberately inflicted. It also observed that the certified question in *Brown* related only to a sado-masochistic encounter, that their Lordships had recognised that there must be exceptions to what was no more than a general proposition, and in that context some of them had specifically mentioned tattooing. The Court added that in its view, consensual activity between husband and wife in the privacy of the matrimonial home is not a proper matter for criminal investigation or prosecution. The material facts underpinning its decision appear to have been that the wife had suffered no significant harm; that she had not just consented to what the appellant did, but had instigated it; and that there was no aggressive intent on the part of the appellant, on the contrary his desire was to assist his wife in acquiring what she regarded as a "desirable personal adornment".

2.123   Another indicator of judicial attitudes is *Emmett*,[154] where again the Court seemed unwilling to regard *Brown* as establishing the limits of consent in the area of private sexual activity. The appellant was convicted on two counts of assault occasioning actual bodily harm in relation to injuries inflicted during sexual activity with his partner. The first count related to an occasion when he had placed a plastic bag over his partner's head and tied it around her neck with a ligature. During the ensuing sexual activity the partner became distressed due to loss of oxygen and may have lost consciousness. The following day her eyes became increasingly bloodshot and she visited her doctor, who found haemorrhaging in both eyes and bruising around her neck. The second count related to an occasion when, again during sexual activity, the appellant had poured lighter fuel on his partner's breasts and set light to it. She suffered a burn, which became infected, and as a result she again visited the doctor. The doctor thought she had a third degree burn that would require a skin graft, but fortunately the wound had healed without scarring by the time of the trial. The judge directed the jury to convict on the first count on the basis that the appellant could not rely on consent, and the appellant had accordingly pleaded guilty to the second count. On appeal against conviction, the appellant, citing *Wilson*, argued that he should have been able to rely on his partner's consent. The Court of Appeal rejected this argument, holding that the actual or potential harm to which the partner was exposed went far beyond that in *Wilson* and was well over the line beyond which consent becomes immaterial. But as to where that line falls to be drawn, the Court was less than clear, declining to decide whether it is at the point where common assault becomes assault occasioning actual bodily harm, as suggested by the majority in *Brown*, or at some "higher level", where the evidence looked at objectively reveals a realistic risk of a more than transient or trivial injury. This is, with respect, difficult to follow. In

[154] [1999] EWCA Crim 1710.

particular, it is not obvious why "a realistic risk of a more than transient or trivial injury" is at a "higher level" than the point at which an assault becomes an assault occasioning actual bodily harm, given that "bodily harm" means harm which is "more than transient or trivial".[155] In truth the two levels of harm identified by the Court appear remarkably similar, if not identical.

Sexual activity carrying a risk to health

It is important in this context to note the decision in *Mohamed Dica*,[156] in which the Court of Appeal helpfully clarified that the limits on the operation of consent identified in *Donovan* and *Brown* apply only to physical injuries and not to other health-related consequences of sexual activity, such as the contraction of an infectious disease. The appellant, who was HIV positive, had engaged in penetrative sex with two different women, both of whom had themselves become infected with HIV. He was convicted of two offences of causing grievous bodily harm contrary to s.20 of the Offences Against the Person Act 1861. The appellant intended to run a defence of consent, but the judge accepted the prosecution's argument, based on *Brown*, that the complainants could not consent to the harm they had suffered. This decision was overturned on appeal, the Court holding that the judge should not have withdrawn the issue of consent from the jury. On the assumption, made for the purposes of argument, that the complainants consented to have sex with the appellant knowing that he was HIV positive and of the risk to themselves, Judge LJ (as he then was), giving the judgment of the Court, said[157]:

2.124

> "In our judgment the impact of the authorities dealing with sexual gratification[158] can too readily be misunderstood. It does not follow from them, and they do not suggest, that consensual acts of sexual intercourse are unlawful merely because there may be a known risk to the health of one or other participant. These participants are not intent on spreading or becoming infected with disease through sexual intercourse. They are not indulging in serious violence for the purposes of sexual gratification. They are simply prepared, knowingly, to run the risk—not the certainty—of infection, as well as all the other risks inherent in and possible consequences of sexual intercourse, such as, and despite the most careful precautions, an unintended pregnancy . . . These, and similar risks, have always been taken by adults consenting to sexual intercourse . . . Modern society has not thought to criminalise those who have willingly accepted the risks . . . In our judgment, interference of this kind with personal autonomy, and its level and extent, may only be made by Parliament."

---

[155] See *Donovan*, discussed in para.2.110, above.
[156] [2004] EWCA Crim 1103; [2004] Crim. L.R. 944. For further discussion see paras 2.131 and following, below.
[157] At 47ff.
[158] The Court cited *Brown* [1993] 2 W.L.R. 556, *Boyea* [1992] Crim. L.R. 574 and *Emmett* [1999] EWCA Crim 1710.

An issue of mens rea

2.125   As explained above, the rule of public policy identified in *Donovan* is that a person cannot give an effective consent to an act that is likely or intended to cause him harm that is more than "transient or trifling". For this purpose, the infliction of harm by A on B will be intentional if it is deliberate.[159] If A does not intend to inflict such harm, is it sufficient to engage the rule of public policy that his acts are deliberate and likely to cause B more than transient or trifling harm ? Or must A foresee that his actions may cause B such harm, i.e. must he be reckless as to its infliction?

2.126   This issue arose in the unsatisfactory decision in *Boyea*,[160] a case of indecent assault, where the trial judge directed the jury in accordance with *Donovan* that if they were satisfied that the appellant's actions were likely or intended to cause bodily harm, then he was guilty, whether or not the victim consented. It was argued on appeal that the judge should also have directed the jury not to convict unless they were satisfied that the appellant was reckless as to whether such harm would be caused, i.e. unless he realised that his act might cause bodily harm but went ahead anyway. The Court of Appeal dismissed this argument. It relied on the decision in *Savage*,[161] where the House of Lords held that on a charge of assault occasioning actual bodily harm (s.47 of the Offences Against the Person Act 1861), it is sufficient to prove that actual bodily harm was occasioned by the assault, and that there is no requirement to prove that the defendant intended to cause such harm or was reckless as to causing it. Drawing on this decision, the Court held that, for the purposes of the rule in *Donovan*, the question whether an act is likely to cause bodily harm is to be answered by giving "likely" an objective meaning and not by introducing the concept of recklessness.

2.127   There is a serious flaw in this reasoning. In *Savage*, it was not disputed that the appellant had committed an assault or that the assault had caused actual bodily harm. The question was whether it was necessary for the prosecution to prove mens rea with respect to the harm. The House of Lords held that it was not. In *Boyea*, the whole question was whether or not an assault had been committed, given the issue of consent. On that point, the argument advanced by the appellant seems unanswerable. It is settled that assault requires proof of mens rea (intention or recklessness) and for this purpose recklessness involves an element of foresight or appreciation of risk.[162] The requirement of mens rea applies to the absence of a valid consent as it does to the other elements of assault. It should follow, in the light of *Donovan*, that

---

[159] The jury may infer that harm was inflicted intentionally if they feel sure that A's actions were virtually certain to result in harm and A appreciated that to be the case: *Woolin* [1999] 1 A.C. 82. For an example, see *Meachen* [2009] EWCA Crim 1701.

[160] [1992] Crim. L.R. 574.

[161] [1992] 1 A.C. 699.

[162] *Fagan v Metropolitan Police Commissioner* [1969] 1 Q.B. 439 at 444, per James LJ; *Venna* [1976] Q.B. 421 at 429; *Kimber* [1983] 1 W.L.R. 1118 at 1121; *Williams (Gladstone)* [1987] 3 All E.R. 411 at 413; *Spratt* (1990) 91 Cr. App. R. 362; *Savage and Parmenter* [1992] 1 A.C. 699.

if a person does an act which is likely to cause more than "transient or trifling" harm to another, with the other's consent, he commits an offence only if he foresees that such harm may be caused. If he foresees no harm, or only harm that is "transient or trifling", he does not have the requisite mens rea for the offence.[163]

More satisfactory than *Boyea*, in this respect, is the ruling of Judge J (as   **2.128** he then was) in *Slingsby*.[164] The defendant and the victim had engaged in vigorous sexual activity during which the defendant had penetrated the victim's vagina and rectum with his hand. The victim was cut by a signet ring on the defendant's finger, and as a result she ultimately died of septicaemia. At trial, the prosecution invited the judge to rule that the defendant was liable to conviction of "unlawful act" manslaughter, since the sexual activity had been likely to cause significant injury and the victim's consent to that activity could not prevent the defendant's acts amounting to an assault. The learned judge rejected this argument. The sexual activity had not involved the deliberate infliction of injury, and neither party had anticipated or considered that injury might be caused. The victim's injuries were an accidental, if tragic, consequence of the sexual activity. It would be contrary to principle to treat an activity as an assault merely because an injury occurred in the course of it, without being intended or foreseen, and accordingly a manslaughter charge could not be sustained.

The distinction between intentional, reckless and accidental injuries   **2.129** surfaced again in *Meachen*,[165] but with a more equivocal outcome. The complainant and the appellant met at a club and returned to the complainant's house. She had been drinking and had no recollection of events at the house, save that the appellant was with her at one point on her living room sofa. When she awoke alone the next morning she was in immense pain and had suffered considerable blood loss from her perianal area. The medical evidence was that she had suffered serious anal injuries most likely caused by "fisting" or penetration by a blunt object. The appellant's case was that they had both willingly taken the drug GHB before becoming sexually intimate. The complainant had, he said, enjoyed penetration of her vagina and anus with his fingers. She had ended up astride him with three of his fingers in her anus and his thumb in her vagina, and she had thrust up and down on his fingers for some four or five minutes before giving every sign of reaching a climax. He noticed some blood on his fingers and assumed the complainant was having her period. When he left the house, he did not know that she was injured. The appellant was charged inter alia with indecent assault and maliciously inflicting grievous bodily harm (s.20 of the 1860 Act). At the end of the prosecution case the judge ruled that, given the position established by

---

[163] *Boyea* was said in *Dica* [2004] EWCA Crim 1103 and *Meachen* [2009] EWCA Crim 1701 to be "on close analysis" a case in which the complainant did not in fact consent. This is not, with respect, a convincing explanation for the decision.

[164] [1995] Crim. L.R. 570 (Nottingham Crown Court).

[165] [2006] EWCA Crim 2414. See also *Slingsby*, last footnote.

Donovan and subsequent cases, there was no defence in law to these counts. In the light of that ruling, the appellant pleaded guilty. The convictions were, however, quashed by the Court of Appeal which held, after an extensive citation of authority, that while consent cannot provide a defence where the incident in question involved the intentional or reckless infliction of harm, it can provide a defence if the harm was unintentionally and accidentally caused. In this case, at the time the judge made his ruling there was, on the appellant's account, an issue as to whether he had been reckless as to the risk of causing harm, or whether the serious injury that occurred was the unintentional and accidental result of consensual sexual activity. In those circumstances, the appellant should have been permitted to run a consent defence and the judge's ruling to the contrary was incorrect.

2.130   *Meachen* is therefore fully consistent with the view that the rule in *Donovan* applies to the intentional or reckless infliction of harm. However, at the very end of its judgment the Court said that it was unnecessary for it to consider the further question of whether consent is ruled out only where harm is deliberately inflicted, so that it may operate where the defendant was reckless as to causing actual bodily harm and the complainant consented to the risk of that level of harm. This comment is somewhat surprising, as there is nothing earlier in the judgment to indicate that this further question has been argued. This comment was obiter and, we suggest, should not be taken to indicate any uncertainty on the point.

2.131   The point did however arise again in *Mohammed Dica*,[166] which concerned an appeal against conviction on two counts of maliciously inflicting grievous bodily harm (s.20 of the Offences Against the Person Act 1861). The appellant was an HIV-positive man who had infected two women with the virus by having unprotected sex with them. His evidence would have been that both complainants were aware of his condition at the time the sex took place. However, at the close of the prosecution case the judge ruled, following *Brown*, that the women's consent could provide no defence. The appellant therefore gave no evidence and was convicted on both counts. His appeal was allowed on the ground that the judge should not have withdrawn the issue of consent from the jury. The Court of Appeal, having cited *Brown*, *Donovan*, *Boyea* and *Emmett*, drew a distinction between the intentional and the reckless infliction of harm. It said:[167]

> "These authorities demonstrate that violent conduct involving the deliberate and intentional infliction of bodily harm is . . . unlawful notwithstanding that its purpose is the sexual gratification of one or both participants . . . It does not follow from them, and they do not suggest, that consensual acts of sexual intercourse are unlawful merely because there may be a known risk to the health of one or other participant . . . At one extreme there is casual sex between complete strangers, sometimes protected, sometimes not, when the attendant risks are known to be higher, and at the other, there is sexual intercourse between

[166] [2004] EWCA Crim 1103; [2004] Crim. L.R. 944.
[167] At [46]–[52].

couples in a long-term and loving, and trusting relationship, which may from time to time also carry risks.

The first of these categories is self-explanatory and needs no amplification. By way of illustration we shall provide two examples of cases which would fall within the second.

In the first, one of a couple suffers from HIV. It may be the man: it may be the woman. The circumstances in which HIV was contracted are irrelevant. They could result from a contaminated blood transfusion, or an earlier relationship with a previous sexual partner, who unknown to the sufferer with whom we are concerned, was himself or herself infected with HIV. The parties are Roman Catholics. They are conscientiously unable to use artificial contraception. They both know of the risk that the healthy partner may become infected with HIV. Our second example is that of a young couple, desperate for a family, who are advised that if the wife were to become pregnant and give birth, her long-term health, indeed her life itself, would be at risk. Together the couple decide to run that risk, and she becomes pregnant. She may be advised that the foetus should be aborted, on the grounds of her health, yet, nevertheless, decide to bring her baby to term. If she does, and suffers ill health, is the male partner to be criminally liable for having sexual intercourse with her, notwithstanding that he knew of the risk to her health? If he is liable to be prosecuted, was she not a party to whatever crime was committed? And should the law interfere with the Roman Catholic couple, and require them, at the peril of criminal sanctions, to choose between bringing their sexual relationship to an end or violating their consciences by using contraception?

These, and similar risks, have always been taken by adults consenting to sexual intercourse . . . Modern society has not thought to criminalise those who have willingly accepted the risks, and we know of no cases where one or other of the consenting adults has been prosecuted, let alone convicted, for the consequences of doing so.

The problems of *criminalising* the consensual taking of risks like these include the sheer impracticability of enforcement and the haphazard nature of its impact. The process would undermine the general understanding of the community that sexual relationships are pre-eminently private and essentially personal to the individuals involved in them. And if adults were to be liable to prosecution for the consequences of taking known risks with their health, it would seem odd that this should be confined to risks taken in the context of sexual intercourse, while they are nevertheless permitted to take the risks inherent in so many other aspects of everyday life, including, again for example, the mother or father of a child suffering a serious contagious illness, who holds the child's hand, and comforts or kisses him or her goodnight.

In our judgement, interference of this kind with personal autonomy, and its level and extent, may only be made by Parliament."

Dica has been cited as authority that "the law treats . . . consent as invalid   **2.132** only in respect of intentionally inflicted harms".[168] This is, with respect, too wide a reading. The language and examples used by the Court indicate that it was addressing the operation of consent in relation to the reckless infliction of harm in the context of heterosexual intercourse. Its apparent focus was the risk to health, through disease or pregnancy, involved in this form of sexual activity. It does not deal with the reckless infliction of harm in other sexual

---

[168] See Professor David Ormerod's commentaries on *Barnes* [2005] Crim. L.R. 381, at p.383.

contexts, e.g. a sado-masochistic encounter or rough sex. Indeed, the Court's citation of *Brown*, *Donovan*, *Boyea* and *Emmett* strongly suggests that it was not intending to break new ground and that it would incline against allowing consent to operate in such circumstances. If that is right, the decision is consistent with the long-established disposition of the courts to regulate the operation of consent as a defence to the infliction of harm in the context of sexual activity in accordance with their assessment of the relevant public policy considerations, including the nature and extent of the risks involved. Despite the ringing terms of the last sentence of the extract from the judgment set out above, the decision is unlikely to mark a change of direction in favour of absolute personal autonomy in relation to all forms of sexual activity.

CHAPTER 3

OFFENCES AGAINST CHILDREN UNDER 13

Introduction.................................... 3.01
Multiple Offending and Form of
   Indictment.................................. 3.24
Rape of a Child Under 13.............. 3.29

Assault of a Child Under 13 by
   Penetration 3.79
Sexual Assault of a Child Under 13 3.104
Causing or Inciting a Child Under
   13 to Engage in Sexual Activity... 3.131

INTRODUCTION

This chapter deals with the offences in ss.5–8 of the Sexual Offences Act   3.01
2003, which are designed to protect children under 13. The offences are:

- rape of a child under 13 (s.5),
- assault of a child under 13 by penetration (s.6),
- sexual assault of a child under 13 (s.7), and
- causing or inciting a child under 13 to engage in sexual activity (s.8).

Background

These offences had their genesis in the Sexual Offences Review, which   3.02
reported in 2000.[1] The Review identified overwhelmingly strong arguments
for a set of gender-neutral sex offences relating to children, to mark their
particular need for protection and society's disapproval of adult sexual
activity with them.[2] The offences relating to children in force at that time,
together with the well-founded criticisms made of them by the Review, are set
out in paras 4.02 and following, below. The Review reached a number of
conclusions about how the law relating to sexual offences against children
should be shaped. One was that it should state that a child under the age of
13 cannot effectively consent to sexual activity. Although the Review
considered that the legal age of consent should remain at 16, it recognised

---

[1] *Setting the Boundaries. Reforming the Law on Sexual Offences* (Home Office, July 2000).
[2] *Setting the Boundaries*, 2000, paras 3.1.5, 3.1.6.

251

that, whatever the law might say, children under 16 may well engage in consensual sexual activity. It nonetheless saw a strong case for setting a lower age beneath which the law would recognise no consent whatsoever, in order to provide absolute protection for younger children. This age had to be one below which it could safely be said that there was no mutual agreement (because one or both parties were too young to possess the necessary knowledge, understanding and maturity to know what they were agreeing to). The Review decided that the thirteenth birthday provided a benchmark that was already established in law[3] and recognised by society as the entry to teenage years, and accordingly adopted 13 as the age below which no consent should be recognised.

3.03   This recommendation was adopted in the White Paper *Protecting the Public* and enacted in ss.5–8 of the 2003 Act, which create a set of offences mirroring the non-consensual offences in ss.1–4 of the Act but applicable specifically where the victim is under 13. Any apparent consent by the child is legally insignificant and there is no defence of mistaken belief in age.[4]

Overlap between the under-13 offences and the child sex offences

3.04   The under-13 offences overlap to a very significant extent with the child sex offences (ss.9–15 of the 2003 Act), which are designed to protect children under 16. However, the Government's wish and expectation as expressed during the debates on the Bill was that someone who engages in sexual activity with a child under 13 should be prosecuted for one of the offences specifically designed to protect such children, i.e. under ss.5–8, and not with a child sex offence.[5] This is to ensure the availability of the higher maximum penalties applicable to the under-13 offences.

3.05   In fact, the Bill as introduced contained no overlap between the two sets of offences, as the child sex offences were limited to children aged 13 or over and under 16. The Government realised after some time that this created an inflexible scheme which could in certain cases achieve the opposite of what was intended. Suppose, for example, a man had apparently consensual sexual intercourse with a girl whom the prosecutor believed was 13 at the time of the alleged offence. He would be charged under what became s.9. If it should emerge at trial that the girl was, in fact, only 12 at the relevant time, the prosecution would have to apply to amend the indictment to include a charge of rape of a child under 13, contrary to what became s.5. A judge might be reluctant to amend the indictment during the course of the trial, especially where the effect would be to add a more serious offence; and the later the application, the less likely it would be to succeed. If leave to amend were

---

[3] cf. the offence under s.5 of the Sexual Offences Act 1956 of unlawful sexual intercourse with a girl under the age of 13.

[4] See the discussion in paras 3.06 and following, below.

[5] *Hansard*, HL Vol.648, col.1097, Lord Falconer of Thoroton (June 2, 2003). For judicial endorsement of this approach, see *Collins* [2015] EWCA Crim 915 at [16].

refused, then under the offence scheme as originally created the man would have to be acquitted, despite having had sex with a 12-year-old. Once this potential problem was identified, the Government introduced amendments to extend the child sex offences to cover children under 13, with no mistake of age defence.[6] This ensured that where, in a prosecution for a child sex offence, it emerges that the child was under 13 at the relevant time, the defendant may still be convicted of the offence charged. The logical next step might have been to combine the two sets of offences, which would have had the beneficial effect of removing the duplication between them and simplifying the legislative scheme. But the Government did not take this step and came under no Parliamentary pressure to do so.

Under-13 offences committed by children

The Sexual Offences Review thought it could safely be said that children **3.06** under 13 are too young to consent to sexual activity. It is, however, undeniable that children under that age may engage with other young children in sexual activity that is at least apparently consensual, and during the passage of the Sexual Offences Bill, considerable concern was expressed about the potentially dramatic impact of the under-13 offences on such children. Humphrey Malins MP put the point trenchantly during the Committee debates:

> "If a boy and girl aged 12 indulge in French kissing to which each consents, they will be committing an offence under [section 7]. If a boy fondles a girl sexually over her clothes, or vice versa, both will be committing a sexual offence under [section 7], and that offence will be punishable—yes, punishable—by 14 years' imprisonment. I am not being flippant, but if two 12-and-a-half-year-old boys relieve the boredom of their first year at boarding school by indulging in mutual masturbation—which has happened—a serious offence will have taken place. If, at the suggestion of a girl aged 12, a boy of the same age puts his finger into her vagina, the boy will be committing an offence punishable under [section 6] by imprisonment for life. We think that that is a preposterous proposition".[7]

To address this issue, Baroness Walmsley tabled amendments in the Lords **3.07** designed to limit the scope of the under-13 offences to cases where the offender was 16 or over.[8] Her purpose was to prevent the prosecution of children under that age who engage in sexual activity with children under 13, on the basis that such cases call for alternative forms of disposal. The noble Baroness thought the application of the offences in those circumstances could produce "appalling injustices", e.g. where a boy of 12 has intercourse initiated by a girl of the same age. She also argued that the offences could pose risks to children's health and welfare, since girls under the age of 13 might avoid approaching a doctor for contraceptive and other health advice,

---

[6] *Hansard*, HL Vol.646, col.1197, Lord Falconer of Thoroton (April 1, 2003).
[7] *Hansard*, HL, Standing Committee B, col.94 (September 11, 2003).
[8] *Hansard*, HL, Standing Committee B, col.1174, Baroness Walmsley (September 11, 2003).

knowing that all sexual activity with them will be defined as serious child abuse and that accordingly their "boyfriend" might get into serious trouble.

3.08   The Government resisted the amendments, Lord Falconer of Thoroton responding as follows:

> "I recognize . . . that children under 13 engage in mutually agreed sex. I have listened to those who argue with real conviction that it is completely unfair for the law to make it possible for a boy aged 14, for example, to be charged with raping a 12 year-old girl following mutually agreed sexual intercourse. It is worth pointing out that prosecution is certainly not the inevitable outcome where two minors of the ages I have described engage in sexual activity. In those cases where sexual activity between minors is truly mutually agreed and there is nothing to suggest that the activity is in any way exploitative, we would not expect and we would not want the full weight of the criminal law to be used against them. Our overriding concern is to protect children, not to punish them unnecessarily. Where sexual relationships between minors are not abusive, prosecuting either or both children is highly unlikely to be in the public interest. Nor would it be in the best interests of the children involved . . . Even where the sexual activity is abusive, the Crown Prosecution Service may consider that it was not in the public interest to prosecute someone under 16 if other courses of action were likely to be more effective. The CPS has a discretion about whether or not to prosecute in such cases. We would expect it to continue to use that discretion wisely . . . Having said all that, if the law is to be effective, there will be cases in which under 16 year-olds commit such crimes where prosecution is appropriate. We must remember that not only children aged 12 and 14 but also children very much younger will be protected by this provision against teenagers of 16 and under. That is where we need the clarity and protection of the criminal law. That is why we believe it would be wrong to accede to the amendment[s]".[9]

3.09   This argument is very similar to the one deployed to justify the exceptionally wide reach of the child sex offences, considered in the next chapter. It has utilitarian merit, since the wide drafting of the under-13 offences will ensure that no case involving sexual activity with a child under that age which is deserving of prosecution will fall outside their scope. But one must ask whether it is consonant with the rule of law to create offences in such broad terms and then rely on the discretion of prosecutors to decide when to invoke them.[10]

CPS charging guidance

3.10   The Government's position rested on the expectation that the Crown Prosecution Service would exercise its prosecutorial discretion wisely. The CPS did indeed issue guidance to prosecutors following the commencement

---

[9] Hansard, HL, Standing Committee B, cols 1176–1177 (September 11, 2003).
[10] An objection to the under-13 offences based on art.8 ECHR cannot be sustained in light of the decision of the House of Lords in *R. v G* [2008] UKHL 37, discussed in paras 3.14 and following, below.

of the Act. The current guidance[11] was revised in 2013. It notes (in Chapter 2) that the overriding public concern is to protect children, and that it was not Parliament's intention to punish children unnecessarily or for the criminal law to intervene where it is wholly inappropriate. The guidance states that CPS Youth Offender Specialists should review all files involving youth offenders and take all major decisions in relation to those cases, in particular, whether or not a prosecution should take place. In addition, Chief Crown Prosecutors must be notified of any case where at least one of the complainants and at least one of the suspects are under the age of 13. This includes cases which are diverted from prosecution, whether on evidential or public interest grounds. All such cases must be reviewed by a prosecutor who is both a rape specialist and a youth specialist. The principles of the decision-making process are the same as in all cases under the Code for Crown Prosecutors, i.e. if there is sufficient evidence of a sexual offence committed by a child to justify instituting proceedings, the public interest must be considered with care before a prosecution is commenced.

The guidance states that, when a sexual offence committed by a child **3.11** passes the evidential stage of the Full Code test, it is essential that when considering the public interest, prosecutors have as much information as possible from sources including the police, Youth Offending Teams and any professionals assisting those agencies, about the defendant's background and the circumstances surrounding the alleged offence, as well as any information known about the victim. Views expressed by the victim, and where appropriate the victim's family, should be taken into account in accordance with the Code, as should the interests of the alleged offender. Furthermore, in deciding whether or not to prosecute, prosecutors should have careful regard to the following factors, the weight to be attached to which will vary depending on the circumstances of the case:

- The age and understanding of the offender. This may include whether the offender has been subjected to any exploitation, coercion, threat, deception, grooming or manipulation by another which has led him or her to commit the offence;
- The relevant ages and levels of maturity of the parties, i.e. the same or no significant disparity in age;
- Whether the complainant entered into sexual activity willingly, i.e. did the complainant understand the nature of his or her actions and that she/he was able to communicate his or her willingness freely;
- Parity between the parties in regard to sexual, physical, emotional and educational development;

[11] Available at *http://www.cps.gov.uk/legal/p_to_r/rape_and_sexual_offences/soa_2003_and_ soa_1956/£a20* [Accessed April 30, 2016]. An earlier iteration of the guidance was held to be consistent with the UK's international obligations including under the UN Convention on the Rights of the Child: *E, S and R, R. (on the application of) v DPP* [2011] EWHC 1465 (Admin). See also the CPS guidance on Youth Offenders, available at *http://www.cps.gov.uk/legal/v_to_ z/youth_offenders/* [Accessed April 30, 2016].

- The relationship between the parties, its nature and duration and whether this represents a genuine transitory phase of adolescent development;
- Whether there is any element of exploitation, coercion, threat, deception, grooming, seduction, manipulation or breach of trust in the relationship;
- Whether the child under 13 freely consented (even though in law this is not a defence) or a genuine mistake as to her/ his age was in fact made;
- The nature of the activity e.g. penetrative or non-penetrative activity;
- The sexual and emotional maturity of the parties and any emotional or physical effects resulting from the conduct; and
- The likely impact of any prosecution on the parties.

3.12　Finally, the guidance states (in Chapter 11):

> "If the sexual act or activity was in fact genuinely consensual and the youth and the child under 13 concerned are fairly close in age and development, a prosecution is unlikely to be appropriate. Action falling short of prosecution may be appropriate. In such cases, the parents and/or welfare agencies may be able to deal with the situation informally. There is a fine line between sexual experimentation and offending and in general, children under the age of 13 should not be criminalised for sexual behaviour in the absence of coercion, exploitation or abuse of trust.
>
> However, if a very young child has been seduced by a youth, or a baby-sitter in a position of responsibility has taken advantage of a child under 13 in his/her care, prosecution is likely to be in the public interest. Where a child under 13 has not given ostensible consent to the activity, then a prosecution contrary to sections 5 to 8 is likely to be the appropriate course of action."

3.13　This guidance is, with respect, entirely sensible and focused on the right points. However, it cannot in itself guarantee that prosecutorial decisions relating to child suspects will be beyond reproach. So in *E, S and R, R. (on the application of) v DPP*,[12] the Court quashed a decision by the CPS, made contrary to the advice of a multi-agency strategy group, to prosecute a 12-year-old victim of sexual exploitation who was persuaded by a paedophile to abuse her own younger sisters. Laura Hoyano has described the CPS decision as "perturbing and perplexing".[13] Yet it was purportedly made in accordance with the CPS's own guidance. In any event, however wisely CPS prosecutors may exercise their prosecutorial discretion, the possibility cannot

---

[12] [2011] EWHC 1465 (Admin). cp. *R. (on the application of CM) v Crown Prosecution Service* [2014] EWHC 4457 (Admin), in which it was held that a decision to prosecute a 10-year-old boy for sexual offences committed against a boy of eight was not irrational. The CPS had been entitled to bear in mind that the charge was of some seriousness, that CM was denying it and that he had a history of sexually inappropriate behaviour. Some reports identified him as "an intelligent and highly controlling person who manipulated those more vulnerable" and as a sexual predator. Given those matters, together with the highly exceptional nature of the court's jurisdiction to intervene, there were no grounds for quashing the decision to prosecute.
[13] [2012] Crim. L.R. 42.

be ruled out that an inappropriate private prosecution will be brought, for example, by an outraged parent. Lastly, and perhaps most importantly, a police investigation, or even the mere possibility of one, may itself damage the children involved in the ways suggested by Baroness Walmsley, long before the stage at which the CPS may be called upon to make a decision on the public interest. For these reasons, we remain concerned at the potential for the under-13 offences to have an adverse impact on the interests of young people.

Article 8 ECHR

In terms of legal analysis those interests are most likely to be identified with   3.14
the right to private life protected by art.8 ECHR. Sure enough, not long after the 2003 Act was commenced, in the case of *R. v G*,[14] the courts were called upon to consider the compatibility with art.8 of the prosecution and conviction of a youth under s.5 of the Act. The appellant was 15 at the time of the incident and the complainant 12. The offence took place in the appellant's bedroom relatively shortly after the two had met. The complainant maintained that she had not consented. In due course the appellant pleaded guilty on the following basis:

"(i) The complainant willingly agreed to have sexual intercourse with the defendant.
(ii) At the time the defendant believed the complainant was 15 years old. She told him so on an earlier occasion.
(iii) The defendant nonetheless pleads guilty to the SOA 2003 offence having been advised that, by reason of the fact that the complainant was under 13 at the relevant time, the offence is committed irrespective of:
(a) consent,
(b) reasonable belief in consent,
(c) a reasonable belief as to age."

The prosecution initially declined to accept this basis of plea, but did so after the complainant acknowledged that she had indeed told the appellant that she was 15 and in the light of her reluctance to attend court to give evidence. The judge imposed a 12-month detention and training order, the effect of which was to make the appellant subject to the notification requirements under Pt 2 of the 2003 Act.

Before the Court of Appeal,[15] the appellant argued inter alia that his   3.15
prosecution and conviction for rape under s.5 were incompatible with his right to respect for private life under art.8. He was, he said, morally blameless but would carry with him the stigma of a rape conviction for the rest of his life. Although the initial charge under s.5 had not breached art.8, as the information before the prosecutor at that stage was that the complainant had

---

[14] [2008] UKHL 37. The decision is considered in Dr Bharat Malkani, *Article 8 of the European Convention on Human Rights, and the Decision to Prosecute* [2011] Crim. L.R. 943.
[15] [2006] EWCA Crim 821.

not consented to intercourse, once it became clear that she had changed her account of the incident, the prosecutor should have proceeded instead under s.13 read with s.9(1)(c)(ii) of the Act (sexual activity with a child by a person under 18), which would not have carried the same stigma. The failure to do so was incompatible with art.8, despite the guilty plea and the fact that the appellant, once his plea was accepted, did not seek either to stay the proceedings or to argue abuse of process. The Court (Lord Phillips LCJ presiding) accepted the possibility that the prosecution of a child under s.5 rather than under s.13, or indeed their prosecution at all, in relation to consensual sexual intercourse might, on the particular facts, produce consequences that amounted to an interference with the child's art.8 rights that were not justified under art.8(2). However, where, as in this case, no criticism could be made of the initial charge under s.5, the judge was not necessarily required to substitute an alternative charge under s.13 if it transpired that the sexual activity was, or had to be treated as, consensual. In those circumstances, the judge should normally be able, by an appropriate sentence, to ensure that there was no interference with the defendant's art.8 rights that could not be justified under art.8(2). The Court accordingly rejected the argument on this ground.[16]

3.16   The appellant then took the argument to the House of Lords, which, by a bare majority, upheld the Court of Appeal's decision that the failure of the prosecutor, once the basis of plea was accepted, to substitute a charge under ss.13 and 9 had not infringed the appellant's right to private life. Unfortunately, their Lordships' reasoning shows a surprising variety of approaches to this issue. The minority (Lord Hope, with whom Lord Carswell agreed) accepted the appellant's argument and would have quashed his conviction. They held that the appellant's prosecution under s.5, whilst interfering with his art.8 rights (in ways their Lordships do not explain), was justified for so long as the complainant maintained that she did not consent. However, once the appellant's basis of plea was accepted, the continuation of the prosecution was an unjustified interference with those rights, as the offence then fell properly within the ambit of s.13 rather than s.5.

3.17   Of the majority, Lord Hoffman held that art.8 is simply inapplicable to prosecutorial policy and sentencing. Baroness Hale held that the appellant's conviction under s.5 did not engage his art.8 rights, but if it did, the interference was entirely justified. She said:

> "The concept of private life 'covers the physical and moral integrity of the person, including his or her sexual life' (*X and Y v The Netherlands*, para.22). This does not mean that every sexual relationship, however brief or unsymmetrical, is worthy of respect, nor is every sexual act which a person wishes to perform. It does mean that the physical and moral integrity of the complainant, vulnerable by reason of her age if nothing else, was worthy of respect. The state would have been open to criticism if it did not provide her with adequate

---

[16] It did however quash the DTO and substituted an immediate conditional discharge for a period of 12 months.

protection. This it attempts to do by a clear rule that children under 13 are incapable of giving any sort of consent to sexual activity and treating penile penetration as a most serious form of such activity. This does not in my view amount to a lack of respect for the private life of the penetrating male.

Even supposing that it did, it cannot be an unjustified interference with that right to label the offence which he has committed 'rape'. The word 'rape' does indeed connote a lack of consent. But the law has disabled children under 13 from giving their consent. So there was no consent. In view of all the dangers resulting from under age sexual activity, it cannot be wrong for the law to apply that label even if it cannot be proved that the child was in fact unwilling. The fact that the appellant was under 16 is obviously relevant to his relative blameworthiness and has been reflected in the second most lenient disposal available to a criminal court. But it does not alter the fact of what he did or the fact that he should not have done it. In my view the prosecution, conviction and sentence were both rational and proportionate in the pursuit of the legitimate aims of the protection of health and morals and of the rights and freedoms of others."

The third member of the majority, Lord Mance, held that art.8 was engaged **3.18** because the appellant's conviction under s.5 carried a stigma, the consequences of which would affect his ability to establish and develop his personality and relations with others. But he went on to hold that, having regard to the "strong protective needs" of children under 13, and the conditional discharge substituted by the Court of Appeal, the appellant's conviction under s.5 was neither unjustified nor disproportionately prejudicial to him in a way that could involve a breach of art.8.

The divergent approaches taken by their Lordships to the application of **3.19** art.8 are unfortunate, given the provision's importance to the law of sexual offences generally. Leaving aside Lord Hoffman, with whose narrow construction of art.8 none of the other speeches agreed, the House was evenly split on the main point at issue, i.e. whether, in the light of the complainant's consent and the appellant's mistaken belief that she was 15, the requirements of art.8 were met by a prosecution under s.13 or s.5. The reasoning of the minority on this point is not highly developed. By contrast, Baroness Hale and Lord Mance gave art.8 much fuller treatment, and in drawing their conclusions both emphasised the positive obligation it places on the State to give children under 13 adequate protection from premature sexual activity. This is, of course, a highly relevant consideration. However, their Lordships did not explain why the obligation would not have been discharged, on the facts of this case as set out in the basis of plea, by means of a charge under s.13. This is the more disappointing given the comments of Lord Falconer in the House of Lords during the passage of the 2003 Act about the importance of the wise exercise of the prosecutorial discretion. In any event, as it is difficult to conceive of a factual scenario that would be more propitious for an art.8 argument, the effect of *R. v G* is that there cannot now be any valid art.8 objection to the prosecution and conviction of a young person for an offence under s.5, or for any of the other under-13 offences.[17]

---

[17] Young offenders convicted in such cases can of course expect substantial mitigation of sentence.

3.20   By way of coda, the European Court of Human Rights subsequently declared inadmissible an application by the convicted defendant in *R. v G* in which he rehearsed the argument based upon art.8 that had been rejected by the House of Lords.[18] The Court held, also by a majority, that the applicant's prosecution for the conduct at issue in this case constituted an interference with his "private life" within the meaning of art.8(1). However, in determining whether such an interference was "necessary in a democratic society" within the meaning of art.8(2), it took into account that Member States enjoy a wide margin of appreciation as regards the means of ensuring adequate protection against rape, especially where, as in this case, the public interest at stake was the need to protect the complainant and other children in her position against premature sexual activity, exploitation and abuse. The authorities could not be said to have exceeded that margin of appreciation by creating the s.5 offence, nor by deciding to prosecute the applicant for it, particularly as the possible sentences covered a broad range from absolute discharge to detention for life, and the Court of Appeal had taken fully into account the applicant's mitigating circumstances.

3.21   Several months before the Strasbourg decision, *R. v G* was cited in *E, S and R, R. (on the application of) v DPP*, referred to in para.3.13, above. One argument advanced by the mother of the three girls for quashing the decision to prosecute the 12-year-old was that it failed to have proper regard to the girls' rights under arts 3 and 8 of the ECHR. The Court declined to decide the point on the basis that it had already determined to quash the decision on another ground. It did, however, note that the decision and reasoning in *R. v G* presented "formidable obstacles" to the success of any art.8 challenge to a decision to prosecute.

3.22   Contrast with *R. v G* the earlier decision in *S v DPP*.[19] The claimant was charged under s.5 following an incident in which, aged 15, he had sexual intercourse with a girl of 12. Following representations from his solicitors, the CPS amended the charge to one under s.13 read with s.9. The reasons for this decision are not given in the judgment, but it appears to have been influenced by a psychologist's report to the effect that the only inappropriate element in the claimant's behaviour was that he had engaged in sexual behaviour with a partner who was not a peer. The claimant then sought to quash the decision to prosecute at all. The Administrative Court refused his application on the ground that, if the prosecution were able to prove the allegation that he had known the complainant's age, the circumstances could be described as exploitative such that a reasonable prosecutor could consider a prosecution (under s.13) to be in the public interest.

3.23   Given the apparent element of exploitation, the claimant in *S v DPP* was perhaps fortunate to have persuaded the CPS to amend the charge in his favour. Following the decision of the House of Lords in *R. v G*, others who

---

[18] [2011] E.H.H.R. 1308 (Application No.37334/08).
[19] [2006] EWHC 2231 (Admin).

try the same tactic are unlikely to be so lucky. In this connection, current CPS guidance[20] states:

> "Where the Full Code Test is satisfied in a case in which a youth is suspected of committing a sexual offence involving a child under the age of 13, the appropriate charge will be an offence contrary to sections 5 to 8 Sexual Offences Act 2003, depending on the act, and not the lesser offence contrary to section 13 Sexual Offences Act 2003."

For an unsuccessful challenge to a conviction under s.5 obtained in such circumstances, see *Delahaye-Bryan*,[21] discussed in para.3.30, below.

MULTIPLE OFFENDING AND FORM OF INDICTMENT

It can be especially difficult to frame an indictment in cases involving multiple offences committed against a child over a period of perhaps years, where the complainant is unable to recall other than in vague terms when the various offences took place. How should the prosecution proceed in such cases?   **3.24**

The aim should be to draft an indictment that identifies the alleged offences as specifically as possible but is not so lengthy and complicated as to make the trial, and the jury's task, unmanageable. In *Rackham*,[22] convictions for sexual offences committed by the appellant against his two step-daughters over a period of nearly 10 years were quashed on the ground that the trial judge should have acceded to an application for identification of the incidents to which the various counts related. The Court of Appeal said that in such cases the indictment should be drawn so that the defendant will know with as much particularity as the circumstances permit what case he must meet on each count, and so that the judge, in the event of a conviction, will know precisely what the jury has found proved. The Court said that it should not be too difficult in most cases to settle an indictment that steers a safe course between prejudicial uncertainty and over-loading. It added that it is common to lay a count alleging, say, a rape on a day between the complainant's one birthday and the next. This is permissible on the basis that a difficulty in being precise in every respect is not a reason not to be precise when one can.   **3.25**

One way to achieve a degree of precision without over-loading an indictment is to rely upon specimen charges. However, in *Canavan*[23] the Court of Appeal held that it is a fundamental principle that a person should be sentenced only for the offences of which he has been convicted, or which he has admitted, and not for other offences of which those were specimens.   **3.26**

---

[20] Available at *http://www.cps.gov.uk/legal/p_to_r/rape_and_sexual_offences/soa_2003_and_soa_1956/£a20* [Accessed April 30, 2016].

[21] [2015] EWCA Crim 1987.

[22] [1997] 2 Cr. App. R. 222; and see *Evans* [1995] Crim. L.R. 245.

[23] [1998] 1 Cr. App. R. 79, discussed in paras 34.24 and following, below. See also *Clark* [1996] 2 Cr. App. R.(S.) 351; *Tovey and Smith* [2005] EWCA Crim 530.

The Court clearly appreciated that its decision would encourage prosecutors to include more counts in their indictments, so that there would be sufficient proof of the offender's criminality to enable the court to pass an appropriate sentence. However, it did not think this "need be unduly burdensome or render the trial unmanageable". But the decision created a dilemma for prosecutors and the courts in cases involving multiple offences in which an accurate picture of the defendant's criminality could be given only by framing the indictment in a way that would require the defendant to plead to too many offences, or the jury to bring in verdicts in respect of too many counts. It is inevitable in the light of *Canavan* that, in at least some cases, the need to ensure a fair trial and the practicalities of trial management will compel the prosecutor to draw up an indictment that gives something less than the full picture.[24]

3.27   This problem has been mitigated, if not wholly resolved, by the amendment of the Criminal Procedure Rules in 2007 to permit more than one incident of the same offence to be charged in a single count if the incidents taken together amount to a course of conduct having regard to the time, place or purpose of their commission: see r.10.2(2) of the Criminal Procedure Rules 2015, discussed in paras 19.22 and following, below. The Criminal Procedure Rules Committee stated that this facility may be used "when, for example, a defendant is alleged to have repeatedly assaulted the same victim in the same way over a period of time".[25] The Committee's intention in creating this new rule was to take account, amongst other things, of the potential of the old rules to create a perceived unfairness to a victim of multiple offending where, out of many alleged offences, only a few were prosecuted as examples, giving the impression that the victim's distress had been underestimated or that he or she had not been believed.[26]

3.28   The fundamental principle set out in *Canavan* is, however, still frequently overlooked by the courts. For full discussion, see paras 33.24 and following, below.

Rape of a Child Under 13

Definition

3.29   Section 5(1) of the Sexual Offences Act 2003 provides as follows:

"A person commits an offence if—
(a) he intentionally penetrates the vagina, anus or mouth of another person with his penis, and
(b) the other person is under 13."

---

[24] cf. *Tovey and Smith*, last note, at [36].
[25] See guidance to the Rules, dated March 27, 2007.
[26] Taken from a note prepared by the Secretariat to the Committee dated March 27, 2007 and published with the guidance, above.

This offence has its roots in the repealed offence of unlawful sexual intercourse with a girl under 13 (s.5 of the Sexual Offences Act 1956). The old offence is in effect expanded to cover boys and penetration of the anus and mouth, and redefined as rape.

The elements of s.5(1)(a) are also elements of the offence of rape (s.1) and reference should accordingly be made to the discussion of that offence in Ch.1. Problems have arisen in certain cases where the child was close to their thirteenth birthday at the relevant time and the accused maintains that the sexual activity was consensual, i.e. he was not guilty of rape contrary to s.1 of the 2003 Act. Some judges have been reluctant to deprive the jury of the opportunity to decide the issue of consent, which, in relation to a child of that age, may be relevant for sentencing purposes, and so they have encouraged the prosecution to charge the defendant under s.1 with the s.5 offence as an alternative. This is the wrong way to proceed. In so far as consent may be relevant to sentence,[27] the issue is properly one for the judge to determine in a *Newton* hearing. The CPS's legal guidance on charging under the 2003 Act[28] says: **3.30**

> "In cases where a defendant admits sexual activity with a child under 13 but states that the victim consented, the proper course is to invite the court to hold a *Newton* hearing. On no account should a section 1 rape count be added as an alternative."

An earlier version of the guidance elaborated the point as follows:

> "Juries should not be asked to deliberate upon issues that are critical to sentence and which are not necessary to substantiate a charge in law. Rather these are questions that a judge should consider by hearing evidence on the relevant point, and according to the procedure as set out in *R v Newton* 77 Cr. App. R. 13."[29]

We respectfully agree with the CPS guidance and the elaboration that used to accompany it, which reflects the intention of Parliament in creating the under-13 offences specifically to protect young children without any require- ment on the prosecution to prove absence of consent. This approach is supported by the recent decision of the Court of Appeal in *Delahaye-Bryan*,[30] in which the 16-year-old applicant was convicted under s.5 in relation to sexual activity with a girl of 12 which he claimed had been consensual. At trial he had offered a plea under s.13 read with s.9 of the Act (child sex offences committed by children or young persons) but this was rejected. On conviction under s.5, he sought leave to appeal on the ground that he had been denied a fair trial as the possibility of convicting him under s.13 read

---

[27] As to which see paras 3.50 and following, below.
[28] Ch.2. The guidance is available at *http://www.cps.gov.uk/legal/p_to_r/rape_and_sexual_ offences/soa_2003_and_soa_1956/£a20* [Accessed April 30, 2016].
[29] *http://webarchive.nationalarchives.gov.uk/20120229131134/http://www.cps.gov.uk/legal/s_to_ u/sexual_offences_act/#OFFENCES_AGAINST_CHILDREN* [Accessed April 30, 2016].
[30] [2015] EWCA Crim 1987.

with s.9 should have been left to the jury as an alternative. Rejecting this argument, the Court said that the applicant had no defence to the s.5 charge and his counsel's only option[31]:

" . . . was to advise [him] to plead guilty and offer a basis of plea. Any significant issues such as consent could then be determined at a *Newton* hearing (as they were)."

3.31   Illustrations of the potential application of the s.5 offence are:

- A, aged 16, has sexual intercourse with B, a 12-year-old girl he meets at a party. A commits the offence. This is so even if B told A that she was 16, and she looks it, so that A reasonably believed she had reached the age of consent.
- A, aged 12, has sexual intercourse with B, his 12-year-old girlfriend. C, also aged 12, knows what A and B are doing and keeps watch to make sure no adults are around. A commits the offence and C aids and abets it.
- A, aged 16, asks B, aged 12, to fellate him. She does so. A commits the offence whether or not B acted willingly.
- A and C are friends and B is A's girlfriend. They are all aged 12. C urges A to ask B to fellate him. C encourages the s.5 offence for the purposes of s.44 of the Serious Crime Act 2007.

Mode of Trial and Punishment

3.32   The s.5 offence of rape of a child under 13 is triable only on indictment and the maximum sentence is life imprisonment.[32]

3.33   For the purposes of listing, cases under s.5[33] fall within Class 2B, save for complex cases involving many complainants (often under age, in care or otherwise particularly vulnerable) and/or many defendants who are alleged to have systematically groomed and abused them, often over a long period of time, which fall within Class 1C.[34] Cases in Class 1C must be referred to the Resident Judge, and by the Resident Judge to a Presiding Judge. Cases in Class 2B must be similarly referred in certain specified circumstances, including where the case is unusually grave or complex or a novel and important point of law is to be raised; where the defendant is a police officer, a member of the legal profession or a high profile figure; or where for any reason the case is likely to attract exceptional media attention.

---

[31] at [19] per Hallett LJ.
[32] s.5(2).
[33] And of soliciting, inciting, encouraging or assisting, attempting or conspiring to commit the offence or assisting an offender having committed the offence.
[34] *Consolidated Criminal Practice Directions*, Part XIII Listing B: CLASSIFICATION, available at *https://www.judiciary.gov.uk/publications/criminal-practice-directions-2015/* [Accessed April 30, 2016].

The offence under s.5 is a serious specified offence for the purposes of the   3.34
dangerousness provisions of the Criminal Justice Act 2003.[35] Accordingly,
the offence falls within the scope of s.225(2) of that Act, relating to the
imposition of life sentences for serious offences. Further, a s.5 offence,
whenever committed, may be made the subject of an extended sentence
under s.226A of that Act.[36] The offence is also listed in Pt 1 of Sch.15B to the
Criminal Justice Act 2003 for the purposes of s.224A of that Act (life
sentence for a second listed offence).[37]

A person convicted under s.5, cautioned, found not guilty by reason of   3.35
insanity or found to be under a disability and to have done the act charged,
is automatically subject to the notification requirements in the Sexual
Offences Act 2003.[38]

BAIL

Section 25 of the Criminal Justice and Public Order Act 1994[39] provides that   3.36
a person charged with or convicted of certain offences who has a previous
conviction for any such offence shall be granted bail only if the court, or as
the case may be, the constable considering the grant of bail is of the opinion
that there are exceptional circumstances which justify it. The offences in
question include the s.5 offence and an attempt to commit it. For the full list
of offences covered by s.25 of the 1994 Act, see para.1.24, above.

CONSPIRACY

In *R. v G and F*,[40] the appellants were convicted of conspiracy to rape a male   3.37
child under 13 in circumstances where they had communicated only by text
message. They did not meet at any stage, either before or after the text
exchange, nor did they suggest meeting to discuss the plan. There was no
evidence that they had taken any steps to advance the plan. No place or time
or other details were identified. They were arrested some three years after the
text exchange. They were silent in interview. At trial, the judge rejected a half-
time submission of no case to answer. The convictions were quashed on

---

[35] Criminal Justice Act 2003 s.224 and Sch.15, Pt 2.
[36] Inserted by the Legal Aid, Sentencing and Punishment of Offenders Act 2012 s.124,
brought into force on December 3, 2012, by SI 2012/2906.
[37] Inserted by the Legal Aid, Sentencing and Punishment of Offenders Act 2012 s.122,
brought into force on December 3, 2012, by SI 2012/2906.
[38] s.80 and Sch.3, discussed in Ch.35, below.
[39] As amended with effect from December 3, 2012, by the Legal Aid, Sentencing and
Punishment of Offenders Act 2012 s.90 and Sch.11 para.33.
[40] [2012] EWCA Crim 1756; see also *Hedgcock, Dyer and Mayers* [2007] EWCA Crim 3486.
The cases are discussed in paras 1.409 and following, above.

appeal. The Court of Appeal said that as regards the submission of no case to answer, the vital question in this case was whether a jury could be sure that both the appellants intended to carry out the agreement to rape a male child under 13. The Court's view was that no reasonable jury, taking the prosecution evidence at its highest, could infer that the appellants did so intend. The evidence was all equivocal and was as consistent with fantasy as with an intent to carry out the plan. The appellants' silence in interview and their failure to mention it was all a fantasy could be taken into account, but it was of little weight given the other facts, or rather lack of them.

Alternative Verdict

3.38   See the discussion in para.1.137 and following, above.

Sentencing

Sentencing guideline

3.39   For the Sentencing Council guideline relating to the sentencing of sexual offences committed by offenders aged 18 and over, see Ch.33, below. In consulting on its draft guideline,[41] the Council noted that the previous guideline, issued in 2007 by the Sentencing Guidelines Council ("SGC"), covered the under-13 offences and the equivalent offences for victims aged over 13 together; for example, there was a single guideline covering both rape (s.1) and rape of a child under 13 (s.5). The Council proposed instead to issue separate guidelines for the two sets of offences, in recognition that "there are issues and sensitivities unique to offences against children under 13 that require a separate guideline to ensure clarity for sentencers as to the factors to be taken into account and to provide a transparent process for others concerned with these cases".[42] This is the approach taken in the published guideline.

3.40   The consultation document noted that s.5 offences may involve a range of factual circumstances that will influence the type and length of sentence awarded, and the draft guideline sought to deal with the most common of these factual circumstances which can range from:

> "forced non-consensual activity seen in the equivalent offences for victims aged 13 and over . . . to instances where an adult offender has exploited or groomed

---

[41] *Sexual Offences Guideline: Consultation* (December 6, 2012). The consultation document is available on the Sentencing Council's website.
[42] *Sexual Offences Guideline: Consultation* (December 6, 2012), p.36.

a child to the extent that the child maintains they have consented to the activity and may even regard themselves as being in a 'genuine' relationship with the offender, or where, over time, the child has become habituated to the activity."

The Council felt it important that cases in which a child under the age of 13 has been groomed into acquiescence are treated equally for sentencing purposes with cases of forced non-consensual activity, given evidence that younger children are increasingly at risk of sexual exploitation. As for the exceptional case of a truly non-exploitative relationship, the Council considered that such cases should be sentenced outside the guideline. In order to give sentencers the confidence to do so, it included in the guideline the following highly important narrative, the impact of which we consider below:

When dealing with the statutory offence of rape of a child under 13, the court may be faced with a wide range of offending behaviour.

Sentencers should have particular regard to the fact that these offences are not only committed through force or fear of force but may include exploitative behaviour towards a child which should be considered to indicate high culpability.

This guideline is designed to deal with the majority of offending behaviour which deserves a significant custodial sentence; the starting points and ranges reflect the fact that such offending merits such an approach. There may also be *exceptional* cases, where a lengthy community order with a requirement to participate in a sex offender treatment programme may be the best way of changing the offender's behaviour and of protecting the public by preventing any repetition of the offence. This guideline may not be appropriate where the sentencer is satisfied that on the available evidence, and in the absence of exploitation, a young or particularly immature defendant genuinely believed, on reasonable grounds, that the victim was aged 16 or over and that they were engaging in lawful sexual activity.

Sentencers are reminded that if sentencing outside the guideline they must be satisfied that it would be contrary to the interests of justice to follow the guideline.

It is important to note that in referring to a "young" defendant the narrative must be taken to mean a young adult, rather than a child or young person, since the guideline is applicable only to offenders aged 18 and over. For the sentencing of young offenders, see paras 3.51 and following, below.

Step One—Harm and culpability

The guideline requires the sentencing court to go through a series of steps in order to determine the appropriate sentence. Step one involves determining the offence category by reference to the degree of harm caused and then the culpability level for the offence. In relation to the s.5 offence, the harm and culpability factors are as follows:

3.41

Harm		Culpability
Category 1	The extreme nature of one or more category 2 factors or the extreme impact caused by a combination of category 2 factors **may** elevate to category 1	A
		Significant degree of planning
		Offender acts together with others to commit the offence
		Use of alcohol/drugs on victim to facilitate the offence
Category 2	• Severe psychological or physical harm • Pregnancy or STI as a consequence of offence • Additional degradation/ humiliation • Abduction • Prolonged detention/sustained incident • Violence or threats of violence • Forced/uninvited entry into victim's home • Child is particularly vulnerable due to extreme youth and/ or personal circumstances	Grooming behaviour used against victim
		Abuse of trust
		Previous violence against victim
		Offence committed in course of burglary
		Sexual images of victim recorded, retained, solicited or shared
		Deliberate isolation of victim
		Commercial exploitation and/or motivation
		Offence racially or religiously aggravated
		Offence motivated by, or demonstrating, hostility to the victim based on his or her sexual orientation (or presumed sexual orientation) or transgender identity (or presumed transgender identity)
Category 3	Factor(s) in categories 1 and 2 not present	
		Offence motivated by, or demonstrating, hostility to the victim based on his or her disability (or presumed disability)

B
Factor(s) in category A not present

Categories 1 and 2 contain a list of factors indicating additional harm; these **3.42** are the same factors as those in the rape guideline. Category 3 has no factors listed, in order to reflect the fact that any rape of a child under the age of 13 will cause some degree of harm to the victim. It has been held that in the factor "severe psychological or physical harm", "severe" means "more than significant", in the sense of more than the psychological harm that will inevitably be caused when a young child is raped.[43] A suicide attempt as a result of the offending will demonstrate "severe psychological harm".[44] As for "extreme youth", this has been said to be a flexible expression which prima facie applies to someone under the age of 12, though the younger the child, the greater the vulnerability.[45]

With respect to culpability, the offence of rape of a child under 13 can, as **3.43** noted above, cover a very wide range of offending behaviours, including exploitative behaviour used to obtain the victim's acquiescence. For this reason, the culpability factors in this guideline are wider than those in the guideline for rape. In its consultation document, the Sentencing Council indicated the possible scope of some of these factors:

- In relation to "use of alcohol/drugs on victim to facilitate the offence" it noted that in addition to the use of alcohol to incapacitate the victim, offenders may use access to alcohol and/or drugs as part of the grooming process in order to gain the trust or friendship of a child by allowing them to behave in a way that would not be permitted by their parents or other responsible adults.
- "Grooming behaviour used against victim" is included as a factor to cover a wide variety of sexual exploitation, of which the use of alcohol and gifts are examples. There is no legal definition of the term "grooming" and the courts have said that it would be unwise to create one.[46] The term is used in relation to sexual offences to mean preparing a victim for a particular sexual activity. The acts of preparation that constitute grooming do not in themselves need to be sexual.[47]
- As for "abuse of trust", in relation to children under 13 trust may arise not only from a position of formal responsibility but also from a relationship with the child, e.g. as babysitter or family friend who has been trusted to look after the child on a day out.

---

[43] *R. v GP* [2015] EWCA Crim 594, at [23].
[44] *R. v. JM* [2016] 1 Cr.App.(S.) 145(21).
[45] *R. v C* [2015] EWCA Crim 1856; *Smith* [2015] EWCA Crim 722.
[46] *R. v C*, unreported, September 10, 2014.
[47] *R. v C*, unreported, September 10, 2014, following *R. v G* [2010] EWCA Crim 1693.

Step Two—Starting point and category range

3.44 Once the court has determined the offence category and culpability level, at step two it should use the corresponding starting point specified in the guideline in order to reach a sentence within the category range. The starting point applies to all offenders irrespective of plea or previous convictions. Once the starting point has been determined, step two allows further adjustment for aggravating or mitigating features, set out below. A case of particular gravity, reflected by multiple features of culpability or harm, could merit upward adjustment from the starting point before further adjustment for aggravating or mitigating features.

3.45   The starting points and category ranges for rape of a child under 13 are set out in the table below. The Sentencing Council set them higher than the starting points and ranges in the rape guideline, in order to reflect the increased harm and culpability that exist when an adult offender decides to engage in penetrative sexual activity with a child under the age of 13. The Council did, however, recognise that the wide range of offending behaviour with which a sentencer may be faced means there is a need for flexibility in the sentencing regime.

	A	*B*
Category 1	*Starting point* 16 years' custody *Category range* 13–19 years' custody	*Starting point* 13 years' custody *Category range* 11–17 years' custody
Category 2	*Starting point* 13 years' custody *Category range* 11–17 years' custody	*Starting point* 10 years' custody *Category range* 8–13 years' custody
Category 3	*Starting point* 10 years' custody *Category range* 8–13 years' custody	*Starting point* 8 years' custody *Category range* 6–11 years' custody

3.46 The SGC guideline suggested higher starting points and ranges for victims of rape under the age of 13, except in the highest category, where the starting point was 15 years' custody whatever the age of the victim. The reason given for this was that when a rape has factors placing it in the highest category, the age of the victim becomes secondary to the extreme nature of those other factors. The Sentencing Council, in its consultation document, said that it appreciated the logic of this approach but felt that there should be a differential in the level of sentence to reflect the inherent vulnerability of a young victim and the harm done to them by the commission of this offence. It therefore raised the starting point in the highest category to 16 years' custody for victims under the age of 13, as compared to 15 years' custody for victims over the age of 13. The highest sentence level in the SGC guideline was reserved for multiple rapes, but the current guideline moves away from that by making the 16-year starting point available for single rapes.

Aggravating and mitigating factors

After identifying the starting point and category range, the court should   **3.47** consider whether the presence of aggravating or mitigating factors should result in an upward or downward adjustment from the starting point or the imposition of a sentence outside the category range. In particular, relevant recent convictions are likely to result in an upward adjustment. The non-exhaustive list of aggravating and mitigating factors for the s.5 offence is as follows:

Aggravating factors
Statutory aggravating factors
Previous convictions, having regard to a) the nature of the offence to which the conviction relates and its relevance to the current offence; and b) the time that has elapsed since the conviction
Offence committed whilst on bail
Other aggravating factors
Specific targeting of a particularly vulnerable victim
Ejaculation (where not taken into account at step one)
Blackmail or other threats made (where not taken into account at step one)
Location of offence
Timing of offence
Use of weapon or other item to frighten or injure
Victim compelled to leave their home, school etc
Failure to comply with current court orders

Offence committed whilst on licence
Exploiting contact arrangements with a child to commit an offence
Presence of others, especially other children
Any steps taken to prevent the victim reporting an incident, obtaining assistance and/or from assisting or supporting the prosecution
Attempts to dispose of or conceal evidence
Commission of offence whilst under the influence of alcohol or drugs
Victim encouraged to recruit others

Mitigating factors
No previous convictions *or* no relevant/recent convictions
Remorse
Previous good character and/or exemplary conduct*
Age and/or lack of maturity where it affects the responsibility of the offender
Mental disorder or learning disability, particularly where linked to the commission of the offence

* Previous good character/exemplary conduct is different from having no previous convictions. The more serious the offence, the less the weight which should normally be attributed to this factor. Where previous good character/exemplary conduct has been used to facilitate the offence, this mitigation should not normally be allowed and such conduct may constitute an aggravating factor.

In the context of this offence, previous good character/exemplary conduct should not normally be given any significant weight and will not normally justify a reduction in what would otherwise be the appropriate sentence.

3.48   The Sentencing Council noted that the caveat, stating that it may be more appropriate to treat previous good character/exemplary conduct as an aggravating factor rather than as mitigation where it has been used to facilitate the offence, is especially pertinent to some historic child sex offences that have come before the courts in recent years, in which status and "good character" have been one of the main reasons the offender has been able to evade justice for such a significant amount of time (cf. the notorious cases of the broadcasters Jimmy Savile and Stuart Hall).

Steps Three to Nine

3.49 The remaining steps cover the following points. At step three the court should consider any factors which would indicate a reduction in sentence, e.g. assistance to the prosecution. At step four it should consider any reduction for a guilty plea. At step five the court should consider dangerousness, i.e. whether it would be appropriate to award a life sentence (s.224A or s.225(2) of the Criminal Justice Act 2003) or an extended sentence (s.226A). Step six requires the court to consider whether the total sentence is just and proportionate to the offending behaviour. At step seven it should consider whether to make an ancillary order (e.g. a compensation order, a SHPO or a restraining order). Step eight requires the court to fulfil its duty under s.174 of the Criminal Justice Act 2003 to give reasons for, and explain the effect of, the sentence. Finally, at step nine the court should consider whether to give credit for time spent on bail in accordance with s.240A of that Act.

Sentencing where penetration was consensual and/or offender reasonably believed child to be 16

Almost from the enactment of the 2003 Act, and before any sentencing   **3.50** guideline was in place, the Court of Appeal indicated that, especially (but not only) in the case of young offenders, the sentence for an under-13 offence would be mitigated by the presence of consent and/or a reasonable belief that the victim was 16 or over. Thus in *Corran*[48] the Court said in relation to the s.5 offence:[49]

> "Although absence of consent is not an ingredient of the offence, presence of consent is, in our judgment, material in relation to sentence, particularly in relation to young defendants ... A very short period of custody is likely to suffice for a teenager where the other party consents ... A reasonable belief that the victim was 16 will also be a mitigating factor, particularly where the defendant is young."

The Sentencing Council guideline does not explicitly identify as a mitigating   **3.51** factor either the victim's apparent consent or the offender's reasonable belief that she was 16. However, as noted in para.3.40, above, recognition of the broad scope of the s.5 offence led the Council to include in the guideline a narrative acknowledging that there may be:

> " ... exceptional cases, where a lengthy community order with a requirement to participate in a sex offender treatment programme may be the best way of changing the offender's behaviour and of protecting the public by preventing any repetition of the offence, for example where the sentencer is satisfied that on the available evidence, and in the absence of exploitation, a young or particularly immature defendant genuinely believed, on reasonable grounds, that the victim was aged 16 or over and that they were engaging in lawful sexual activity."

This narrative was well received by those who responded to the Sentencing Council's consultation, though a number of judges requested the inclusion of

---

[48] [2005] EWCA Crim 192; and see *Attorney General's References (Nos 74 and 83 of 2007)* [2007] EWCA Crim 2550.

[49] [2005] EWCA Crim 192, at [8]–[9].

the SGC guideline's mitigating factor "reasonable belief (by a young offender) that the victim was aged 16 or over". The Council declined this request, saying that it had considered the point with great care but did not believe that specifying this as a mitigating factor would be as effective as the narrative approach in identifying the very limited factual circumstances in which a sentencer might be warranted in imposing a sentence below the category range.[50] The Council added that mitigation is normally used to move down the sentencing range, not to move significantly outside it; and the mitigating factors were intended to capture the factors most often relevant to the offence, whereas cases of the sort that concerned the judges are unusual and fact-specific.

3.52   The pre-guideline case of *Corran*, referred to above, provides a good example of the sort of case to which the Sentencing Council's narrative is intended to apply. One of the appellants in that case, aged 20, pleaded guilty to one offence under s.5. He met the 12-year-old victim in the company of other girls all of whom were aged 15 or 16. They spoke and exchanged telephone numbers. For the next few weeks they saw each other every day and, during that period, the victim told the appellant that she was 16, was in year 11 and was shortly leaving school. One day when they were alone together the victim removed her clothing and said it would be O.K. for the appellant to have sex with her. They had consensual sex, the appellant using a condom. The victim was not a virgin and later described the sex as pleasurable. She told her mother what had happened and her mother went to the police. The appellant was arrested and immediately admitted having had sex with the victim, saying he would not have done so had he known her age. He felt disgusted, ashamed and misled. The pre-sentence report recommended a community rehabilitation order. In passing sentence, the judge referred to the early guilty plea, the appellant's good work record and his respectable family background. He passed a sentence of two years' detention in a young offender institution. On appeal against sentence, the Court of Appeal observed that, apart from the difference in age, the case contained every feature of mitigation which could be imagined and that the learned judge might very well have thought it appropriate to take the wholly exceptional course of imposing a non-custodial penalty, whether by way of a community punishment order or otherwise. As it was, the appellant had spent five-and-a-half months in custody, and in those circumstances the Court quashed the sentence of detention and substituted a six-month conditional discharge, which, as it ran from the date of sentencing, had all but expired.

3.53   The Sentencing Council's narrative was misapplied by the judge in *Attorney General's Reference (No.142 of 2015) (Jack Joseph Brown)*.[51] The

---

[50] *Sexual Offences: Response to Consultation* (December 2013), p.25. The document is available at *https://www.sentencingcouncil.org.uk/wp-content/uploads/Final_Sexual_Offences_Response_to_Consultation_web1.pdf* [Accessed April 30, 2016].
[51] [2016] EWCA Crim 80.

12-year-old victim willingly engaged in sexual intercourse with the offender, who was 19. His condom split and the victim became pregnant as a result. She underwent an abortion. At the preliminary hearing, the offender pleaded guilty to one s.5 offence. The recorder found that the offence fell within category 2B but that the sex had been in a "genuine boyfriend and girlfriend relationship", that the victim had not been subjected to fear, manipulation or coercion and that she had been a few months away from her thirteenth birthday. Having considered the guideline for the offence of sexual activity with a child (s.9 of the 2003 Act), in order to compare the sentence which the offender would have received had the victim been 13 at the time of the offending, the recorder was satisfied that the facts were "exceptional". He sentenced the offender to a three-year community order, with a supervision requirement for two years and a rehabilitation activity requirement for 30 days. The Attorney General referred the sentence to the Court of Appeal as unduly lenient. The Court considered the aggravating features, including that the offender had told the victim not to tell anyone of their relationship and had known that she was under 13. Consideration was also given to the mitigating features, including that the offender had shown clear and genuine remorse; was relatively young at the time of the offending; had significant learning difficulties and immaturity; had no previous convictions; and was due credit for his early guilty plea. The Court nonetheless held that the sentence was unduly lenient. The recorder had been wrong to refer to the guideline for s.9 of the 2003 Act by way of comparison. He had also been wrong to assess the case as "exceptional" on the basis that there had been no force, manipulation or coercion on the offender's part. The whole purpose of the s.5 offence was to protect young victims from themselves. The victim had had a termination and so had undergone harm. The recorder had also been wrong to place emphasis upon apparent consent. Although the offender was immature, he was 19 at the time and had known that the victim was under age and had, therefore, taken advantage of her willingness. The facts had not amounted to exceptional circumstances. However, as no force, manipulation or coercion had taken place, the recorder would have been entitled to go below the sentencing range of a category 2B offence. Accordingly, before credit, a starting point of six years' custody would have been appropriate. Giving credit for the guilty plea gave a sentence of four years' custody. That was further reduced to 42 months' custody to reflect, amongst other things, the offender's successful engagement with probation officers in relation to the previously imposed community order requirements.

Where the offender claims that the victim consented and/or that he **3.54** believed she was older than her true age, it is important that the claim is properly tested. As Pitchford LJ said in *Attorney General's References (Nos 11 and 12 of 2012) (Channer and Monteiro)*[52]:

---

[52] [2012] EWCA Crim 1119 at [34].

"Careful analysis of the circumstances of a section 5 offence is always required and a *Newton* hearing may be necessary when the claim is made that the victim was consenting in fact and/or that the offender believed the victim to be significantly older than her chronological age. The prosecutor bears a burden of responsibility to ensure that factual concessions to a basis of plea or mitigation of the offence are made only when justified and that, if made, the precise import of the concession is understood by the offender and the court . . . ".

The rise and decline of "ostensible consent"

3.55 The language of "ostensible consent" was used in the SGC guideline and also by the Court of Appeal in *Attorney General's References (Nos 74 and 83 of 2007) (Fenn and Foster)*,[53] where the Court held that such consent would mitigate an under-13 offence to the extent that it was a true consent, as opposed to one obtained opportunistically or by means of coercion or exploitation.[54] But the Court in *Channer and Monteiro* struck a cautionary note[55]:

"Exploitative sexual behaviour towards a child under 13 without consideration for the vulnerability of that child may be just as serious as submission obtained by the use of force or the threat of force. 'Ostensible consent' and 'willingness' are terms which, in the context of offences against the young in particular, are susceptible to misunderstanding and, even if accurately used, are liable to obscure the true nature of the encounter between the offender and the victim . . . ".

The Sentencing Council agreed with this comment and decided to adopt language that focuses not on the behaviour of the victim but on the behaviour and culpability of the offender. Its narrative therefore deliberately departs from the SGC guideline by omitting any reference to the victim's "ostensible consent" and focuses instead on the absence of exploitation[56] and the offender's belief that the sexual activity was lawful, i.e. consensual. This approach is to be welcomed, and was well received by respondents to the Council's consultation draft.

Adult offenders and belief that victim 16 or over

3.56 The Sentencing Council's narrative acknowledges that an offence may attract a sentence below the category range where a young or particularly immature offender reasonably believed that the victim was 16 or over and was consenting, there being no element of exploitation. It leaves unaddressed the question whether an offence may be mitigated to any degree in circumstances of this sort where the offender is a mature adult. We suggest that in a case of this sort the sentencer may properly look for guidance to *Fenn and Foster*,[57]

[53] [2007] EWCA Crim 2550, applied in *Lee* [2008] EWCA Crim 1350.
[54] [2007] EWCA Crim 2550, at [11].
[55] At [34], per Pitchford LJ.
[56] Which will include grooming: see the discussion in paras 1.192 and following, above.
[57] [2007] EWCA Crim 2550, applied in *Lee* [2008] EWCA Crim 1350.

a carefully reasoned decision which repays attention. In that case, the Court noted that the SGC guideline only referred to a reasonable belief that the victim was 16 or over as being capable of being a mitigating factor in the case of a young offender, i.e. one under the age of 18.[58] It said this reflected two aspects of the scheme of the Sexual Offences Act 2003[59]:

"The first is that there is a special sentencing regime for young offenders ... which does not apply to offences under s.5. Secondly, in relation to offences against those aged between 13 and 16, it is a defence to establish a reasonable belief that the other person is 16 or over. It seems to us that inherent in this approach is the view that any adult who embarks on sexual activity with a young person does so at their own risk. Just as anyone in relation to consent has to give due consideration as to whether the victim was able to or did in fact give consent, failure to give due consideration to age will in itself be a substantial element in the culpability of the offence."

The Court added, however, that this did not mean that a reasonable belief that the victim is 16 or over can never be a mitigating factor for an adult offender, though the older the offender, the less relevant a mistaken belief as to age, even if reasonably held, will be. We suggest this continues to be the case. For an example of circumstances in which a young adult might expect to rely on such a belief in mitigation, see para.3.52 above.

Belief that victim aged 13–15

The Sentencing Council's narrative also leaves unaddressed the question   3.57 whether an offence may be mitigated to any degree where the offender believed the victim to be older than her true age but still under 16. In *Channer and Monteiro*,[60] the Court said[61]:

"The [SGC] guideline does not ... recognise as a mitigating factor a belief by the offender that the victim was aged 13-15 years. There is a good reason for this. Such an offender knew that the victim was not in law consenting."

The Court went on to hold that no significant mitigation was available to the offenders in that case on the basis of mistaken belief in the victim's age, as they could not have thought that she was older than 14, and so they knew that she was incapable of consenting in law to the activity in which they required her to engage. We suggest that these comments remain valid and that, save perhaps in a truly exceptional case, a belief that the victim was aged between 13 and 15 will be incapable of providing significant mitigation, even to a young offender. This proposition derives support from *Attorney General's Reference (No.105 of 2014) (Harrak Musa)*,[62] in which the offender (18) was charged with committing offences under ss.5, 7 and 8

---

[58] SGC Definitive Guideline (2007), para.2.18. This is in contrast to the current guideline: see para.3.40, above.
[59] [2007] EWCA Crim 2550, at [13].
[60] [2012] EWCA Crim 1119.
[61] At 34, per Pitchford LJ.
[62] [2014] EWCA Crim 2751.

against a victim aged 12. On the first occasion they kissed and the victim masturbated the offender; on the other, they kissed, he touched her breast under her clothing, and she masturbated him and performed oral sex on him. The offender pleaded guilty on the morning of trial on the basis that he had thought the victim was older than 12, although he had known she was still at school and suspected she was under 16. He was of previous good character, had expressed remorse and had a supportive family. The pre-sentence report referred to him as having been disgusted with himself on learning the victim's age and as very immature. The judge said that those factors enabled him to take an exceptional course and impose a two-year community order with supervision and specified activity requirements. The Attorney General referred the sentence to the Court of Appeal as unduly lenient. The Court agreed. The sentencing guideline indicated that a custodial sentence of some length was the starting point for such offences. Although there had been no "grooming", the offender had known that the victim was under age and his eagerness to have sexual intercourse with her was indicative of his culpability. Taking into account the offender's mitigation and the effect of an order placing him in custody for the first time after initially being given a non-custodial sentence, a sentence of two-and-a-half years in a young offender institution for the offence under s.8 committed on the first occasion, with concurrent two-year terms on the remaining three counts, was just and proportionate.

Examples

3.58   Any sentencer called upon to deal with issues of consent and mistaken belief in age is likely to benefit from considering the Court of Appeal decisions in *Fenn and Foster*[63] and *Channer and Monteiro,*[64] which, although decided by reference to the SGC guideline, and so not a reliable guide to current sentencing levels, nonetheless contain practical guidance of continuing relevance:

- In *Fenn*, the offender, aged 24, pleaded guilty to two offences under s.5, one involving oral penetration and the other vaginal penetration. The victim was a girl of 10 years and nine months who could pass for someone much older: she was tall for her age and physically mature, and dressed and made herself up in a way which further disguised her real age. The victim absconded from the children's home where she lived and went into the centre of town, where she approached the offender and his co-defendant. She told them she was 16 and had been thrown out of her home. The offender took her to a recreation ground where they kissed and cuddled and eventually the offences were committed. The victim had been a virgin before the offences.

[63] [2007] EWCA Crim 2550, applied in *Lee* [2008] EWCA Crim 1350.
[64] [2012] EWCA Crim 1119.

When asked whether she consented to the sexual activity, she said "I don't actually know". Asked whether the offender would have thought that she did consent, she replied "probably did". In interview, the offender said he thought the victim was over 16. In sentencing, the judge observed that the victim made the running socially when she met the offender and his co-defendant. The judge found that they had not given a thought to her age and it would not have been unreasonable for them to think that she was 16. He concluded that the wholly exceptional circumstances of the case merited a sentence of two years' imprisonment. The Court of Appeal held this sentence to be unduly lenient. In terms of the victim's apparent age, the Court was prepared to accept that the offender may have been lulled into a "sense of false security" by her looks, and by her account of how she had come to be in town that evening. She was nonetheless young and the offender was 24. As to consent, the offender's conduct was an opportunistic piece of sexual gratification, and properly recognised as such by the judge. This was just the sort of case in which young girls required the protection of the courts in the form of significant sentences. The offences were aggravated by the fact that the victim was a virgin, and the offender ejaculated and did not use a condom. The case required a sentence of six years' imprisonment which, with the discount for plea, resulted in a sentence of four years.

- In *Foster*, the offender, 26, pleaded guilty to two offences under s.5, one under s.6 of assaulting a child under 13 by digital penetration and one under s.7 of sexual assault on a child under 13 by sexual touching. The offender made contact with the victim, a girl aged 12 and a half years, through an internet chat room. He said he was 19 and the victim said that she was 15. Their messages increased in intimacy and the offender told the victim that he would like to have sex with her. They met once, the victim accompanied by a friend, and nothing of a sexual nature took place. A few days later they met again, when they kissed and the offender put his hand inside her trousers. At a third meeting they went to a secluded area where the offender placed two fingers inside the victim's vagina and persuaded her to perform oral sex on him. He ejaculated into her mouth. She later told the police: "He wouldn't take no for an answer. I let him do it because I just wanted to go." The offender then attempted to penetrate the victim vaginally but did not manage to do so fully. In interview the offender claimed to have believed that the victim was 16, but he told the author of the pre-sentence report that he had suspected she was under that age. In sentencing, the judge observed that a report indicated that the girl looked older than her years and behaved in a way which was consistent with that. However, he concluded that the offender did not really think she was 16 but rather suspected that she was lying about her age. He imposed a sentence of two years' imprisonment. The

Court of Appeal held this to be unduly lenient. The case involved a man of 26, pretending to be 19, grooming a girl about whose age he clearly had doubts, for the purposes of sex. A minimum of six years' imprisonment, before any discount for plea, would have been appropriate—indeed, a sentence of between six and eight years would not have been surprising in view of the offender's deliberate grooming of the victim. The Court was, however, prepared to accept that the offender was not someone who deliberately preyed on young people without any concern for their age and, taking into account his plea, it considered the appropriate sentence was one of four years' imprisonment.

- The offenders in *Channer and Monteiro*, 20, both pleaded guilty to one s.5 offence committed on the same occasion. They victim was 11 at the time, but the offenders claimed they thought she was much older and that she had been a "willing participant". The judge found that they could reasonably have believed the victim to be 14, but no older. He found the offences aggravated by the fact that there was more than one offender each committing an offence in the presence of the other; they gave implicit approval to the filming of the incident by other young males, and they used the victim for casual sex not caring what her age was. In mitigation, the judge cited the "willingness" of the victim, the early guilty pleas, some remorse and the absence of previous convictions for sexual offences. He said that the case was not an exceptional one which required him to depart from the SGC guideline, which specified a starting point of 13 years' custody and a range of 11–17 years. However, as the offence "was consensual in the sense that [the victim] was a willing participant" and the offenders reasonably believed her to be 14, he took a starting point of five years' detention which, after a discount of one-third for the guilty pleas, produced sentences of 40 months. The Court of Appeal held these to be unduly lenient. The judge had identified the factual basis for sentence in an exemplary manner, but he had reached the wrong conclusion as to the seriousness of the offences given the following facts[65]:

> "(1)   These offenders could not have thought that the complainant was older than 14 years of age. It follows that no significant mitigation was available to them on the basis of a mistaken belief in the girl's age. They knew that the girl was incapable of consenting in law to the activity in which they required her to engage.
> (2)   They did not care how old she was. They did not make any enquiry of the girl. The circumstances were such that they must have realised that she was a child and, therefore, vulnerable.
> (3)   There was a substantial disparity between their ages and the complainant's actual age; there was a significant disparity between

---

[65] [2012] EWCA Crim 1119 at [38]–[39].

their ages and the complainant's age as they might reasonably have believed it to be. We use these descriptions in order to emphasise the gulf in maturity between an 11 or 14 year old victim and the 20 year old offenders. Nonetheless these offenders were still young men.

(4) The only mitigating feature available to the offenders was the complainant's willingness to engage in sexual activity. As explained in *Fenn and Foster,* however, such 'willingness' is of little value in mitigation where the offence amounts to the exploitation of a young child. The circumstances here were that two adults jointly took advantage of a child in degrading circumstances.

(5) The group nature of the activity (which should not be double-counted) and the recording of the event constituted serious aggravating features of an already exploitative offence.

(6) The harm done by the offenders will be long-lasting, perhaps permanent."

In those circumstances, the starting point for sentencing purposes should not have been below 11 years' custody and may have been somewhat higher. The Court therefore quashed the sentences imposed by the judge and substituted sentences of seven years' detention.

Victim nearly 13—does this mitigate the offence?

May the fact that the victim was just short of her thirteenth birthday at the **3.59** relevant time ever mitigate an under-13 offence? If the victim was 13 or just over, the offence would not be statutory rape but sexual activity with a child (s.9 of the Sexual Offences Act 2003), for which the maximum sentence is considerably lower (14 years' rather than life imprisonment), as reflected in the starting points and sentencing ranges in the sentencing guideline for s.9. On the other hand, it might be argued that the offender must take his victim as he finds her, and that if she is under 13, however marginally, he is to be sentenced in accordance with the s.5 guideline just as if she was considerably younger, with no account taken of what the position would have been if she had been slightly older.

The s.5 guideline explicitly acknowledges that the courts may be faced with **3.60** a wide range of offending behaviour, but it contains nothing to suggest that the offence will be mitigated if the victim was just under 13 at the relevant time. It is certainly clear that ordinarily this fact will have no effect upon sentence, given that the offence necessarily involves exploitation of the child. A good illustration of the point is *Davies (Dewi John)*,[66] in which the appellant, 18, pleaded guilty to three s.5 offences and received concurrent sentences of six years' detention in a young offender institution. The offences occurred over a period of about 19 days, the victim being a girl of 12 who would have been 13 the following month. The appellant was effectively of good character. He was aware of the victim's age before the offences were committed. They initially communicated on Facebook, their conversations

[66] [2014] EWCA Crim 2243. See also *Attorney General's Reference (No.142 of 2015) (Jack Joseph Brown)* [2016] EWCA Crim 80, discussed in para.3.53, above.

gradually becoming sexual in nature. The first offence was committed in a country area where they both drank alcohol and smoked cannabis provided by the appellant. He penetrated the victim's vagina with his fingers and then inserted his penis into her mouth before withdrawing and ejaculating over her clothed shoulder. A week later they arranged to go camping together. Vaginal intercourse occurred, the appellant using a condom and ejaculating inside it. Ten days later, at the appellant's home, they again consumed alcohol and smoked cannabis before engaging in unprotected sexual intercourse, the appellant ejaculating onto the bed clothes. In her victim impact statement, the victim said that the offences had had a marked effect on her life: she felt ashamed of what had happened, it had affected her temper, she had had suicidal thoughts, felt physically and emotionally drained and no longer trusted people. The sentencing judge considered that the offences fell within category 3A of the guideline. While accepting that what occurred was in fact consensual, he said that the element of grooming and the provision of alcohol and cannabis to the victim both placed the offences in category A so far as culpability was concerned. The judge took a starting point of 10 years which he increased to 12 years as a result of aggravating factors, namely the fact that sexual intercourse had taken place on three occasions, the appellant had taken the victim's virginity, the risk of pregnancy and the fact of ejaculation. He then took into account the appellant's age, which reduced the starting point back to 10 years. Giving full credit for the pleas reduced the starting point to six-and-a-half years, which the judge reduced further to six years on account of what he described as totality. On appeal, it was submitted that the sentence was excessive given that all the sexual activity was in fact consensual. The Court of Appeal acknowledged the appellant's youth and immaturity, but said that he had engaged in exploitative behaviour towards the victim: the fact that he knew her to be 12 showed that he was essentially interested in satisfying his own sexual urges and paid no attention to the requirements of the law or the victim's interests. The judge was right to impose an immediate custodial sentence and to conclude that there were features which placed the offending in category 3A. That said, the sentence of six years' detention was manifestly excessive given the mitigating factors of the appellant's lack of maturity and his mental health issues highlighted in the pre-sentence report. The Court took a starting point of eight years, which it reduced to six years on account of these factors. Giving full credit for the pleas, the appropriate sentence was one of four years' detention, which sufficiently underlined the degree of exploitation present in the offences and the fact that the appellant knew that the complainant was 12 years of age. The Court regarded the latter as of particular importance: "It would have to be a truly exceptional case for other than an immediate custodial sentence to be imposed where the offender knows the victim is under 13 years of age."

3.61   However, as demonstrated by the following cases,[67] when the SGC guideline was in place the Court of Appeal was sometimes willing to

[67] See also *Lee* [2008] EWCA Crim 1350.

contemplate a reduced sentence where the offender and the victim were in a relationship in which consensual sexual intercourse took place immediately before and after the victim became 13, essentially so as to "taper" the sentences applicable to the offences (under s.5 and s.9 respectively) committed by the offender either side of the victim's thirteenth birthday. As the SGC guideline was, like the current guideline, silent on the point addressed in this section, we do not anticipate that the introduction of the current guideline will lead to a material change in approach, at least in cases where none of the aggravating features listed in the guideline apply. The following cases illustrate the point.

In *R. v S*,[68] the appellant (S, aged 16) pleaded guilty to one offence under   **3.62**
s.5. S and the victim had developed a relationship and first had sexual intercourse one week before the victim's thirteenth birthday. Their relationship continued for six weeks. The victim became pregnant and had a termination. The evidence suggested conception was likely to have occurred during one of the earliest acts of intercourse. During the interview the victim admitted initiating the sexual activity. S admitted that although he had initially believed the victim to be around his own age, he had been aware of her true age before the first act of sexual intercourse. A pre-sentence report said that S's actions were not predatory, the couple had been in a stable, caring relationship at the relevant time, and S had demonstrated remorse. The report suggested that the matter could properly be dealt with by a non-custodial sentence. The sentencing judge took a starting point for a convicted adult of over 15 years' imprisonment and determined that, taking into account S's mitigation and in particular his age, a minimum sentence of nine years' detention could have been imposed on conviction after trial. Allowing a full discount for the guilty plea entered at the earliest opportunity, the judge arrived at a sentence of six years. S successfully appealed. The Court of Appeal held that the judge had been right to reject the suggestion that the matter could properly be dealt with by a non-custodial sentence; for all the mitigation, it was statutory rape and the victim had become pregnant. However, the judge had erred in his approach. First, he had treated the case as a course of rape of the same victim on a significant number of occasions, resulting in the sentencing starting point of 15 years. Although statutory rape occurred on one or two occasions before the victim's thirteenth birthday, what occurred thereafter was not rape but sexual activity with a child. It was unrealistic to approach S's sentencing solely on the basis of events that occurred before the victim's thirteenth birthday, having regard to the basis on which a guilty plea was entered. It was also wrong in principle to regard the totality of S's behaviour as rape; the vast majority was not. Secondly, in taking 15 years as the starting point, in accordance with the SGC guideline, the judge had treated the sexual intercourse as non-consensual behaviour, which it was not. Further, some 85 per cent of the sexual activity occurred

[68] [2011] EWCA Crim 1238.

after the victim's thirteenth birthday, for which conduct the guideline suggested a maximum sentence after conviction, allowing for the aggravating feature of pregnancy, of two years' detention. The maximum sentence in view of S's early guilty plea and full expression of remorse would not have exceeded one year and four months. It was also of some relevance that the victim had appeared to S to be physically and emotionally older than her chronological age, which was how the relationship had developed. However, the fact remained that there had been a rape of a 12-year-old girl that was likely to have resulted in her becoming pregnant. 12-year-old girls are vulnerable and need to be protected, which was why they were deemed incapable of consenting to sexual intercourse. Taking those matters into account, the Court quashed the sentence of six years' detention and substituted one of two years and three months' detention.

3.63   To similar effect is *Attorney General's Reference (No.18 of 2011)*,[69] where the Attorney General referred to the Court as unduly lenient the six-year custodial element of a 10-year extended sentence imposed on the offender (X) following her conviction for sexual offences against a boy of 12. X had begun a sexual relationship with the victim shortly before his thirteenth birthday. She was 31, in an adult relationship and had children of a similar age to the victim, who was the son of family friends. The relationship had lasted four months and involved full, consensual intercourse. X was charged with one offence of intercourse before, and a number after, the victim's thirteenth birthday. The Attorney General identified as aggravating features the 18-year age disparity; the breach of the trust between the victim's parents and X; the marked effect the relationship had had on the victim's mother; the fact that X had encouraged the victim to miss school to spend time with her; and the fact that the relationship was unbalanced and exploitative. In mitigation, X was of previous good character and was immature and child-like; there had been no element of coercion; and the relationship had ended before it was discovered. The Attorney General submitted that, as one of the offences had been committed before the victim's thirteenth birthday, the six-year custodial element was unduly lenient and one of nine years would have been appropriate. The Court of Appeal disagreed. While Parliament had set a watershed age of 13 for the purpose of defining sexual offences against children, it did not follow that there had to be a fundamental difference in sentencing where identical offences occurred a few days before, then a few days after, a child's thirteenth birthday. Indeed, any such difference would be unjust and irrational. The judge had examined the guidelines and had applied them intelligently to the facts of the case, attempting to synthesise the differing guidance for the offences committed before, and those committed after, the victim's thirteenth birthday. That was undoubtedly the right approach and the six-year sentence was absolutely correct.

---

[69] [2011] EWCA Crim 1300.

A more dubious decision is *Hudd*,[70] in which, given his predatory **3.64** behaviour, the appellant (H) was perhaps fortunate to achieve a discount simply on the basis that his victim was just under 13. The Court of Appeal appears to have been influenced by the sentence passed on H's friend, R, who had sexual intercourse with the victim after she reached 13. But it is difficult to see why R's sentence had any relevance to the sentence passed on H, given that the two were convicted of different offences that had no direct connection. H was convicted of four offences under s.5 and received concurrent sentences of 10 years' imprisonment. He was aged 23 or 24 when the offences took place and had no previous convictions for sexual offences. The victim was approaching her thirteenth birthday. H befriended her and had sexual intercourse with her five times over the course of one week. He did not use contraception. He later introduced her to R, who also had sexual intercourse with her on two occasions several months later. R received concurrent sentences of five years' imprisonment because by the date of his offences the victim was over the age of 13. On appeal against sentence, H submitted that the judge had taken insufficient account of the victim's proximity to her thirteenth birthday, and there was a large disparity between the sentences imposed upon him and R for similar offences. The appeal was allowed. The Court of Appeal said that the judge could legitimately have attached more weight to the peculiar circumstance that the victim was within a few weeks or days of her thirteenth birthday at the time of the statutory rapes. The significance of the age 13 was demonstrated by the fact that R received sentences of five years for each of his two offences, committed when the victim was aged 13-and-a-half. There were striking similarities between the circumstances of H's and R's offences. They were both men with no previous convictions for sexual offences. They both had positive reports and references. Their offending had occurred over a short period of time. The critical distinguishing factor was that in H's case the offences occurred before the victim's thirteenth birthday, and in R's case, some months after that. In addition, R had committed two offences whereas H had committed five, which would have merited a different sentence. However, having regard to the similarities between the two sets of offences, and the two offenders, the disparity was such that it was exceptionally possible for the Court to intervene and to substitute sentences of eight years for the sentences of 10 years.

Young offenders

The Sentencing Council guideline applies only to offenders aged 18 and older **3.65** but, in relation to the sentencing of youths, it directs the reader to the general

---

[70] [2012] EWCA Crim 846.

principles in the SGC's definitive guideline, *Overarching Principles—Sentencing Youths*.[71] That guideline notes that when sentencing an offender aged under 18, a court must have regard to the principal aim of the youth justice system (to prevent offending by children and young persons)[72] and the welfare of the offender.[73] It states[74]:

> "there is an expectation that, generally, a young person will be dealt with less severely than an adult offender, although this distinction diminishes as the offender approaches age 18 (subject to an assessment of maturity and criminal sophistication). In part, this is because young people are unlikely to have the same experience and capacity as an adult to realise the effect of their actions on other people or to appreciate the pain and distress caused and because a young person is likely to be less able to resist temptation, especially where peer pressure is exerted."

The guideline provides[75]:

> "In determining the sentence, the key elements are:
> - the age of the offender (chronological and emotional),
> - the seriousness of the offence,
> - the likelihood of further offences being committed, and
> - the extent of harm likely to result from those further offences.
>
> The approach to sentence will be individualistic.
>
> Proper regard should be had to the mental health and capability of the young person, and to any learning disability, learning difficulty, speech and language difficulty or other disorder, any of which is likely to affect the likelihood of those purposes being achieved."

3.66 For an example of youth being explicitly taken into account as a mitigating factor, see *Payne (Trevor Bernard)*,[76] where the appellant appealed against a sentence of 13 years' imprisonment following conviction for two s.5 offences. The offences had been committed in the 1960s over a five-year period, when the appellant was aged between 13 and 17 and the victim was aged between eight and 13. They were specimen offences. The rapes stopped shortly before the victim's twelfth birthday, when she began to menstruate. The appellant threatened the victim with violence if she told anyone. She eventually told her husband. She suffered severe psychiatric harm as a result of the offences and

---

[71] November 2009, available at *https://www.sentencingcouncil.org.uk/wp-content/uploads/web_overarching_principles_sentencing_youths.pdf* [Accessed April 30, 2016].

[72] Crime and Disorder Act 1998 s.37(1).

[73] Children and Young Persons Act 1933 s.44(1).

[74] para. 3.1.

[75] para. 4.1.

[76] Unreported, January 29, 2015. See also *R. v H* [2015] EWCA Crim 1579, discussed below; *R. v G* [2009] EWCA Crim 265, in which the appellant, 14, was convicted of three offences of rape of a child under 13 and two of sexual assault on a child under 13, committed in the course of one month against a girl of 10 who lived near him. The offending was serious, in that it involved the use of coercion and force and the appellant ejaculated during four of the incidents. In consequence the judge imposed concurrent sentences of four years' detention in respect of the rape offences and two years' in respect of the sexual assaults. The Court of Appeal reduced the sentences for the rape offences to three years' detention. In doing so it said that although the victim was only 10, the appellant was naïve, fragile, unsophisticated and immature; and he had no previous convictions, warnings or reprimands.

had been unable to have a normal sex life. The sentencing judge classified the offence as falling within category 2A of the guideline. Aggravating factors included the targeting of a vulnerable victim, ejaculation and a lack of remorse. In mitigation the appellant, then 67, had no previous convictions and had committed no further offences in the intervening years. He submitted that the judge had failed to take sufficient account of his age at the time of the offending, had failed to make sufficient adjustments to account for the length of time since the offending, and failed to give sufficient credit for his exemplary life for the last 50 years. The appeal was allowed. The offences had been committed over a sustained period of time and had a lifelong effect on the victim, but the appellant was young at the time, with the rapes ending before he reached 17. The starting point for an adult would have been 15 years' imprisonment. The appropriate discount given the appellant's age should have been one-third. The sentence of 13 years was quashed and replaced with one of 10 years.

The sexual offences guideline published by the SGC in 2007, which **3.67** preceded the current Sentencing Council guideline, provided that the significance of the offender's age for sentencing purposes would be particularly acute:

> "in relation to the strict liability offences such as 'rape of a child under 13', where the maximum penalty is life imprisonment, especially if an offender is very young and the disparity in age between the offender and the victim is very small."

Disparity of age is not, however, specifically mentioned in *Overarching Principles—Sentencing Youths*, which places the focus on the chronological and emotional age of the offender alone. Similarly, the Sentencing Council guideline, in relation to offenders aged 18 or over, states simply that the age and/or lack of maturity of the offender will mitigate the offence only where it affects his responsibility. So on a strict reading of the current guidelines, it might seem that the age gap between a young offender and their child victim is no longer relevant to sentencing. We nonetheless confidently expect the courts to continue to regard this gap, both in terms of chronological age and of maturity, as relevant to the offender's culpability and so to sentence.

Support for this proposition can be found in *R. v H*,[77] where the appellant, **3.68** 16, pleaded guilty to four specimen counts of rape of a child under 13, in circumstances where he had, over a period of six months, regularly engaged in sexual intercourse and oral sex with his 12-year-old girlfriend, in full knowledge of her age. When sentencing, the judge referred to the number of occasions on which the offences had been committed, the gap in age between the appellant and the victim, the fact that the appellant had misled his parents as to the victim's age and the fact that the purpose of the legislation was to protect children under 13 from themselves. Concluding that the appellant knew exactly what he was doing, and that it was wrong, he imposed an 18-month detention and training order. The Court of Appeal allowed the

[77] [2015] EWCA Crim 1579.

appeal in part. As to whether the judge's decision to impose a custodial sentence was wrong in principle or manifestly excessive, there were many mitigating features, including the appellant's good character, his positive attitude in custody, the absence of force, his remorse and candour, his low-risk of re-offending and his educational ambitions. Furthermore, he was aged 16 at the time of the offence and was described as having been "emotionally immature". Those considerations were balanced by the disparity in age between the appellant and the victim, the fact that he misled his parents as to the victim's age, so demonstrating that he knew what he was doing was wrong, and the fact that the behaviour was not merely experimentation but was, on the contrary, a settled and relatively frequent course of conduct that had taken place over several months. What had taken place did not involve coercion or obvious exploitation, but the victim's participation nevertheless had to be seen in the context of someone of her chronological age who needed to be protected from her own immature urges and inclinations. On the facts, the judge's conclusion that an immediate custodial sentence was required was neither wrong in principle nor manifestly excessive. However, the judge did not make sufficient allowance for the available mitigation and the need to keep custody to a minimum. Accordingly, the Court reduced the detention and training order to a period of 12 months.[78]

Very young victims and other cases "of the utmost seriousness"

3.69   In the sentencing guideline for the s.5 offence, it is a category 2 harm factor that the victim "is particularly vulnerable due to extreme youth". An extreme case may even be elevated to category 1 harm. On this basis, offences against very young victims, i.e. babies and toddlers, are likely to attract very substantial sentences. A notorious example of such a case is *Watkins (Ian)*,[79] in which the applicants (W and P) sought leave to appeal against sentences imposed following their guilty pleas to various sexual offences against children and babies. W had been the lead singer in a rock band and had used his fame to secure sexual encounters with fans and, later, with their children. P was one of W's sexual partners who allowed him to commit sexual assaults on her 12-month-old baby daughter. They discussed over the internet plans for P to allow W to rape the baby. Devices seized from W's home contained indecent images and films involving W and various children and also photographs of P sexually abusing her daughter, which she had sent to W. W

---

[78] In his commentary on the case at [2016] Crim. L.R. 139, Professor Andrew Ashworth points out that the judgment makes no reference to two important paragraphs in the guideline. Paragraph 11.11 reminds sentencers of the statutory requirement that custody should not be imposed unless a youth rehabilitation order with intensive supervision and surveillance cannot be justified. Paragraph 11.2 summarises the law by stating that the statutory tests for custody are likely to be satisfied only where a custodial sentence will be more effective in preventing offending by children and young persons.

[79] [2014] EWCA Crim 1677. See also *Red Saunders v R.* [2013] EWCA Crim 1027, discussed in paras 1.196 and following, above.

and P pleaded guilty on the first day of trial. Having given W a discount of 10 per cent for his guilty pleas, the judge imposed on him consecutive sentences of 15 years' imprisonment for the attempted oral and anal rape of another 12-month-old baby, and 14 years' imprisonment for his assault by penetration of and conspiracy to rape P's child, making a total sentence of 29 years' imprisonment. Concurrent sentences were imposed for various other offences committed by W, including concurrent sentences of 12 months' imprisonment for two offences of taking indecent photographs of a child. The judge also imposed a six-year extended licence period. P was sentenced on counts of assault by penetration and conspiracy to rape to concurrent terms of 14 years and four months' imprisonment. She was also sentenced to a consecutive term of two years and eight months' imprisonment for sexual assault, making a total of 17 years' imprisonment. Concurrent terms were also imposed on her in respect of other offences. W submitted the total sentence imposed was disproportionate to his overall offending. P argued that the internet conversations between herself and W were clearly fantasy and that she had not intended to expose her daughter to W's sexual assaults. She further submitted that she was vulnerable, inadequate and under W's malign influence. The Court of Appeal refused the applications. W's offences "plumbed the depths of depravity" such that a very lengthy sentence of imprisonment was demanded. The judge plainly applied the principle of totality by concentrating on the appropriate total sentence for the combined seriousness of the attempted rapes, the conspiracy to rape and the sexual assault. Were it not for the principle of totality, the judge would have been justified in imposing consecutive sentences for the indecent photograph offences that were significantly in excess of 12 months' imprisonment, instead of ordering those sentences to run concurrently. It was not arguable that the total sentence of 29 years' custody with an extended licence period of six years was manifestly excessive. As for P, she was in no sense a victim. She knew of W's reputation and offered her child as the sacrifice for W's continued interest in her. The sexual assault of her daughter was a price that she was willing to pay to get from W the gratification that she wanted. There was no sign of coercion, only of willing corruption and complicity. The judge had not erred in assessing the seriousness of P's offending; she had acknowledged her agreement with W that her daughter should be raped by him, and that was not an expression of fantasy but a criminal agreement of the utmost seriousness, made against the background that P had already abused her own daughter for W's sexual gratification. The judge had not erred in principle and it was not arguable that the total sentence imposed was manifestly excessive.

However in *R. v DJ*,[80] referring to the decision in *Watkins*, the Court of 　**3.70** Appeal said that care must be taken in relying on phrases such as "the depths of depravity" as if they establish a particular category of offence. In any given

---

[80] [2015] EWCA Crim 563.

case there will be a number of factors to take into account and a case may reach the level of the utmost seriousness by a variety of routes. The attaching of labels is not a particularly good guide; what is required is a careful assessment of the facts. The applicant in *R. v DJ* (49 and with no previous convictions) appealed against an extended sentence of 39 years imposed after he pleaded guilty to numerous serious sexual offences committed against children aged five to 15, including rape, rape of a child under 13, sexual assault of a child under 13, sexual activity with a child, causing or inciting a child to engage in sexual activity, and indecent image offences. The applicant was also convicted of further offences over the course of two trials, including rape, causing or inciting a child under 13 to engage in sexual activity, abducting a child and sexual assault. The offending included the repeated rape of his daughter on a regular basis over a period of approximately 10 years, beginning when she was five. The applicant had told her that the rapes were punishment for her "being bad". The activity also included the applicant holding her nose, thereby forcing her to open her mouth so that he could insert his penis and force her to perform oral sex on him. Another girl, aged 15, who had run away from home, entered into a sexual relationship with the applicant. She had "mental deficits" which meant that she had a "functioning level of a six to eight-year-old". Intercourse occurred on a regular basis, with the applicant recording still and moving images of their activities on his mobile phone. Other victims included the applicant's niece, a friend of his daughter and four other girls whom he had contacted via the internet. In addition, the applicant's mobile phone was found to contain 500 indecent still and moving images of children, 200 of which he had recorded himself. The judge found that the applicant satisfied the test for dangerousness and imposed an extended sentence of 39 years, comprising a custodial term of 33 years and an extension period of six years. He also imposed an indefinite SOPO. On appeal against sentence, the applicant submitted that: (a) notwithstanding the very grave nature of the offences and the numerous aggravating features, the judge had made insufficient allowance for the principle of totality resulting in a manifestly excessive custodial term; (b) notwithstanding an upward adjustment for the aggravating features, the sentence was too long having regard to the sentencing guideline for rape, which provides that "[o]ffences may be of such severity, for example involving a campaign of rape, that sentences of 20 years and above may be appropriate"; and (c) sentences of the duration imposed on the applicant should be reserved for the very worse type of cases, exemplified by *Watkins*, and the instant case fell short of such cases. The appeal was allowed in part. Considering the SGC's rape guideline,[81] the Court of Appeal said that the instant case not only involved the repeated rape of the same victim, which would lead to a starting point of 15 years, but also the repeated rapes of more

---

[81] The applicant was sentenced shortly before April 1, 2014, when the Sentencing Council guideline came into effect.

than one victim, together with the rape of a further victim, and a large number of other serious sexual offences committed against young girls. For this reason the custodial period had to be well above the sentencing range in the guideline of 13-19 years. Nine victims could be identified and there were multiple aggravating features, including breaches of trust, recording of the offending, threats to victims, deceit, grooming and controlling vulnerable individuals. The duration and scale of the offending was particularly substantial. Whilst the features which made the case so very serious were not as eye catching as those in *Watkins*, the case approached a comparable level of gravity for different reasons. None of the sentences imposed on the applicant was open to criticism. However, in the particular circumstances of the case the Court considered that the judge had not made sufficient allowance for totality. Accordingly, it reduced the sentence to an extended sentence of 36 years, comprising a custodial term of 30 years with an extended licence of six years.

Parties to the Offence

The offence of rape of a child under 13 requires penile penetration and so   **3.71** only males can commit it. As the penetration may be of the vagina, anus or mouth of the victim, the offence may be committed against persons of either sex. As to whether a child victim is liable to prosecution as an accessory if they encourage the offence, see the discussion in paras 4.57 and following, below.

Jurisdiction

By virtue of s.72 of and Sch.2 to the Sexual Offences Act 2003, as amended,[82]   **3.72** it is an offence under s.5 for a UK national to do an act in a country outside the UK which would constitute a s.5 offence if done in England and Wales. The amendments, made in 2008, expanded the scope of s.72 in two respects. First, they removed the limitation on s.72 as enacted that it applied only to offences committed against victims aged under 16 (the relevant age is now 18). Secondly, they abolished, in respect of UK nationals, the "double criminality" requirement that the act must have been an offence in the country in which it was done. This requirement is, however, retained in respect of the prosecution of UK residents and those who become UK residents or nationals after the doing of the relevant act. For the purposes of s.72 a "country" includes a territory and a "United Kingdom national" means a British citizen, a British overseas territories citizen, a British National (Overseas), a British Overseas citizen, a person who under the British Nationality Act 1981 is a British subject, or a British protected person

---

[82] By the Criminal Justice and Immigration Act 2008 s.72, with effect from July 14, 2008.

within the meaning of that Act.[83] An act is taken to be an offence in the country in which it was done unless the defendant serves a notice putting the prosecution to proof on the point.[84]

"Child under 13"

3.73   A child attains the age of 13 at the commencement of the thirteenth anniversary of his or her birth.[85]

3.74   The indictment must contain an averment that the victim was under 13 on the relevant date.[86] In seeking to prove this averment the prosecution may rely on s.99(2) of the Children and Young Persons Act 1933, which enables the court to draw from the victim's appearance a rebuttable presumption that he was under 13 at the date of the alleged offence.[87] Alternatively, age may be proved by the production of a certified copy of an entry in the Register of Births, sealed or stamped with the seal of the General Register Office.[88] The age of an adopted child may be proved by production of a certified copy of an entry in the Adopted Children Register, similarly sealed or stamped.[89] In either case, evidence must be given identifying the victim with the person to whom the copy relates.[90]

3.75   Age may also be proved by direct evidence from someone who was present at the birth. In *Nicholls*,[91] it was held that the evidence of a girl's mother was some evidence of her age, although it was subsequently shown on cross-examination that the mother's knowledge was far from certain. In *Cox*,[92] the age of a child was held to have been sufficiently proved by evidence of belief given by two witnesses who had seen the child and a third who was the mistress of the elementary school which the child attended.

Consent

3.76   The offence is committed regardless of whether the child consents. For the effect of consent on sentence, see paras 3.50 and following, above.

---

[83] s.72(9).

[84] s.72(6)–(8).

[85] Family Law Reform Act 1969 s.9(1).

[86] cf. *Hodgson* [1973] 1 Q.B. 565; *Stephenson* [1912] 3 K.B. 341.

[87] 1933 Act s.99(2) and Sch.1, as amended.

[88] Births and Deaths Registration Act 1953 s.34; and see the Evidence (Foreign, Dominion and Colonial Documents) Act 1933 and, for births at sea, the Merchant Shipping Act 1995 s.108, and the Merchant Shipping (Returns of Births and Deaths) Regulations 1979 (SI 1979/1577).

[89] Adoption Act 1976 s.50(2); Adoption and Children Act 2002 s.77(5).

[90] *Bellis* [1911] 6 Cr. App. R. 283 (held, sufficient to identify girl with the person to whom the certificate related that the girl had always been treated as being that person); *Rogers* (1914) 10 Cr. App. R. 276; *Weaver* (1876) L.R. 2 C.C.R. 85.

[91] (1867) 10 Cox C.C. 476.

[92] [1898] 1 Q.B. 179.

MENTAL ELEMENT

See the discussion in paras 1.371 and following, above (mental element of 3.77
rape). In prosecutions for an offence contrary to s.5, as in rape prosecutions,
it must be proved that the penetration was intentional. It will suffice if the
defendant's acts were deliberate.[93] If the penetration is accidental, careless or
even reckless no offence will be committed. In *Heard*,[94] dealing with the
offence of sexual assault, for which an intentional act is also required, the
Court of Appeal upheld the trial judge's direction to the jury that it was not
open to the defendant to contend that voluntary intoxication through drink
or drugs prevented him from intending to touch the victim. We suggest that
this must apply equally to the s.5 offence. As consent provides no defence to
a charge under s.5, there is no requirement (as there is with rape contrary to
s.1) for the prosecution to prove that the defendant did not reasonably believe
that the victim consented.

Must it be proved that A knew or was reckless as to B's age? As explained 3.78
above, this was not the intention of the Sexual Offences Review nor of the
Government expressed during the passage of the Bill. Shortly after the Bill
became an Act, Professor John Spencer identified a "plausible argument"
based on a comparison of ss.5–8 with ss.9 and 10 that the former created
offences of mens rea, so that a defendant would not be liable to conviction if
he was labouring under a mistaken belief that the child was 13 or over.[95]
Whatever the merits of this argument, it did not prevail: it was settled by the
House of Lords in *R. v G*[96] that the s.5 offence does not require mens rea as
to age and a defendant will therefore be liable to conviction even if he
mistakenly believed at the relevant time that the child was 13 or over. The
facts of the case are set out in para.3.14, above. The appellant accepted
before the House that s.5 contains no express requirement of mens rea as to
age but argued that, if the provision could not be "read down" through the
introduction of such a requirement, it was incompatible with art.6(2) of the
ECHR (right to a fair trial). Their Lordships agreed that s.5 creates an
offence of strict liability with respect to the age of the victim, which they
clearly thought desirable. Baroness Hale made this telling comment:

> "Every male has a choice about where he puts his penis. It may be difficult for
> him to restrain himself when aroused but he has a choice. There is nothing unjust
> or irrational about a law which says that if he chooses to put his penis inside a
> child who turns out to be under 13 he has committed an offence . . . The object
> is to make him take responsibility for what he chooses to do with what is capable

[93] *Heard* [2007] EWCA Crim 125, discussed in paras 2.78 and following, above.
[94] [2007] EWCA Crim 125, discussed in paras 2.81 and following, above.
[95] [2004] Crim. L.R. 342 at p.353. This argument was based the fact that ss.9 and 10 of the Act
confine the mistake of age defence to children of 13 or over, and so make clear that where the
child is under 13 there is strict liability with respect to age, whereas ss.5–8 are silent on the
question of mistake of age, with the result, says Professor Spencer, that on ordinary principles
the courts should interpret them as offences of mens rea.
[96] [2008] UKHL 37.

of being, not only an instrument of great pleasure, but also a weapon of great danger."

The Court went on to consider the appellant's argument that s.5 should be "read down" so as to require the prosecution to establish that the defendant did not believe the victim to be 13 or over. The appellant, citing *Salabiaku v France*,[97] submitted that an absolute offence is capable of infringing art.6(2) unless it is "within reasonable limits". Section 5 did not fall within reasonable limits because it can have consequences which are wholly unreasonable, i.e. by making a 15-year-old who has had sexual intercourse with a consenting 12-year-old, whom he reasonably believed to be 15, liable to conviction for rape of a child, carrying with it the stigma to which such a conviction gives rise, the requirement to comply with the notification provisions and a potential sentence of life imprisonment. The House rejected this argument in fairly short terms on the ground that art.6(2) is concerned with the procedural fairness of a trial, not with the substantive law that falls to be applied in the course of it. It follows that a trial will not be rendered unfair for the purposes of art.6(2) merely because the offence in question is an absolute one.[98]

ASSAULT OF A CHILD UNDER 13 BY PENETRATION

DEFINITION

3.79 Section 6(1) of the Sexual Offences Act 2003 provides as follows:

"A person commits an offence if—
(a) he intentionally penetrates the vagina or anus of another person with a part of his body or anything else,
(b) the penetration is sexual, and
(c) the other person is under 13."

3.80 The elements of s.6(1)(a) and (b) are the same as those of the offence of assault by penetration (s.2) and reference should accordingly be made to the discussion of that offence in paras 2.07 and following, above. For the question whether, where the child was close to her thirteenth birthday and the accused asserts that the sexual activity was consensual, it may be appropriate to charge under s.2 with an alternative charge under s.6, see para.3.30, above.

3.81 The following are illustrations of the possible application of the s.6 offence[99]:

- A, aged 19, penetrates with his finger the vagina of B, a 12-year-old girl he meets at a party. A commits the offence, whether or not B consents.

---

[97] (1988) 13 E.H.R.R. 379.
[98] *R. v G* was followed on this point in *S v DPP* [2006] EWHC 2231 (Admin).
[99] They assume that the penetration in each case is "sexual".

- A, aged 10, penetrates with his finger the vagina of B, his 12-year-old girlfriend. A commits the offence, whether or not B consents.
- A and C are friends and B is A's girlfriend. They are all aged 12. C urges A to penetrate B's vagina with his finger. C encourages the offence for the purposes of s.44 of the Serious Crime Act 2007 (and also commits the s.8 offence of inciting a child under 13 to engage in sexual activity).
- A, aged 12, performs oral sex on B, his 12-year-old girlfriend. C, also aged 12, knows that A intends to engage in such activity with B and keeps watch to make sure they are not interrupted. A commits the offence and C aids and abets it.
- A and B are boyfriend and girlfriend aged 12. B asks A to use a vibrator on her, and he does so. A commits the offence. In principle, B commits the s.8 offence of inciting a child under 13 to engage in sexual activity.

Mode of Trial and Punishment

The s.6 offence is triable only on indictment and the maximum sentence is life imprisonment.[100]   **3.82**

For the purposes of listing, cases under s.6[101] fall within Class 2B, save for complex cases involving many complainants (often under age, in care or otherwise particularly vulnerable) and/or many defendants who are alleged to have systematically groomed and abused them, often over a long period of time, which fall within Class 1C.[102] Cases in Class 1C must be referred to the Resident Judge, and by the Resident Judge to a Presiding Judge. Cases in Class 2B must be similarly referred in certain specified circumstances, including where the case is unusually grave or complex or a novel and important point of law is to be raised; where the defendant is a police officer, a member of the legal profession or a high profile figure; or where for any reason the case is likely to attract exceptional media attention.   **3.83**

An offence under s.6 is a serious specified offence for the purposes of the dangerousness provisions of the Criminal Justice Act 2003.[103] Accordingly, the offence falls within the scope of s.225(2) of that Act, relating to the imposition of life sentences for serious offences. Further, a s.6 offence, whenever committed, may be made the subject of an extended sentence under s.226A of that Act.[104] The offence is also listed in Pt 1 of Sch.15B to   **3.84**

---

[100] s.6(2).

[101] And of soliciting, inciting, encouraging or assisting, attempting or conspiring to commit the offence or assisting an offender having committed the offence.

[102] *Consolidated Criminal Practice Directions*, Part XIII Listing B: CLASSIFICATION, available at *https://www.judiciary.gov.uk/publications/criminal-practice-directions-2015/* [Accessed April 30, 2016].

[103] Criminal Justice Act 2003 s.224 and Sch.15, Pt 2.

[104] Inserted by the Legal Aid, Sentencing and Punishment of Offenders Act 2012 s.124, brought into force on December 3, 2012, by SI 2012/2906.

the Criminal Justice Act 2003 for the purposes of s.224A of that Act (life sentence for a second listed offence).[105]

3.85 A person convicted under s.6, cautioned, found not guilty by reason of insanity or found to be under a disability and to have done the act charged, is automatically subject to the notification requirements in the Sexual Offences Act 2003.[106]

Bail

3.86 Section 25 of the Criminal Justice and Public Order Act 1994[107] provides that a person charged with or convicted of certain offences who has a previous conviction for any such offence shall be granted bail only if the court, or as the case may be, the constable considering the grant of bail is of the opinion that there are exceptional circumstances which justify it. The offences in question include the s.6 offence and an attempt to commit it. For the full list of offences covered by s.25 of the 1994 Act, see para.1.24, above.

Alternative Verdict

3.87 A defendant indicted for assault of a child under 13 by penetration may, on appropriate facts, be acquitted of the offence charged and convicted in the alternative of the lesser offence of sexual assault. As to when a conviction in the alternative of common assault may be brought in, see para.2.44, above.

Sentencing

3.88 For the Sentencing Council guideline relating to the sentencing of sexual offences committed by offenders aged 18 and over, see Ch.33, below. In consulting on its draft guideline,[108] the Council noted that the previous guideline, issued in 2007 by the Sentencing Guidelines Council ("SGC"), covered the under-13 offences and the equivalent offences for victims aged 13 and over together; for example, there was a single guideline covering assault by penetration (s.2) and assault of a child under 13 by penetration (s.6). The Sentencing Council proposed instead to issue separate guidelines for the two sets of offences, in recognition that "there are issues and sensitivities unique to offences against children under 13 that require a separate guideline to ensure clarity for sentencers as to the factors to be taken into account and to

---

[105] Inserted by the Legal Aid, Sentencing and Punishment of Offenders Act 2012 s.122, brought into force on December 3, 2012, by SI 2012/2906.

[106] s.80 and Sch.3, discussed in Ch.35, below.

[107] As amended with effect from December 3, 2012, by the Legal Aid, Sentencing and Punishment of Offenders Act 2012 s.90 and Sch.11 para.33.

[108] *Sexual Offences Guideline: Consultation* (December 6, 2012). The consultation document is available on the Sentencing Council's website.

provide a transparent process for others concerned with these cases".[109] This is the approach taken in the published guideline.

The guideline for assault by penetration of a child under 13 nonetheless   3.89 follows the format of the guideline for the offence against victims aged 13 and over, but with the addition of factors to reflect that the under-13 offence may involve a child being coerced and groomed into sexual activity. The starting points and category ranges for the under-13 offence are higher than those for the offence against victims aged 13 and over; but the guideline also acknowledges that the potential range of offending behaviours is such that there may be exceptional cases where a greater degree of flexibility is required. On this aspect see the discussion, above, of the guideline for rape of a child under 13.

Sentencing guideline

Step One—Harm and culpability

The guideline requires the sentencing court to go through a series of steps in   3.90 order to determine the appropriate sentence. Step one involves determining the offence category by reference to the degree of harm caused and then the culpability level for the offence. In relation to the s.6 offence of assault by penetration of a child under 13, the harm and culpability factors are as follows:

Harm		*Culpability*
Category 1	The extreme nature of one or more category 2 factors or the extreme impact caused by a combination of category 2 factors **may** elevate to category 1	*A*
		Significant degree of planning
		Offender acts together with others to commit the offence
		Use of alcohol/drugs on victim to facilitate the offence
Category 2	• Severe psychological or physical harm	Grooming behaviour used against the victim
	• Penetration using large or dangerous object(s)	Abuse of trust

---

[109] *Sexual Offences Guideline: Consultation* (December 6, 2012), p.36.

		Previous violence against victim
	• Additional degradation/ humiliation • Abduction • Prolonged detention/sustained incident • Violence or threats of violence • Forced/uninvited entry into victim's home • Child is particularly vulnerable due to extreme youth and/ or personal circumstances	Offence committed in course of burglary
		Sexual images of victim recorded, retained, solicited or shared
		Deliberate isolation of victim
		Commercial exploitation and/or motivation
		Offence racially or religiously aggravated
Category 3	Factor(s) in categories 1 and 2 not present	Offence motivated by, or demonstrating, hostility to the victim based on his or her sexual orientation (or presumed sexual orientation) or transgender identity (or presumed transgender identity)
		Offence motivated by, or demonstrating, hostility to the victim based on his or her disability (or presumed disability)
		B
		Factor(s) in category A not present

3.91   Categories 1 and 2 contain a list of factors indicating additional harm, but category 3 does not list any factors, in order to reflect the fact that any assault by penetration of a child under the age of 13 will cause some degree of harm to the victim. For the meaning of "severe" in the factor "severe psychological or physical harm" and of "extreme youth", see para.3.42, above. For discussion of the factors "use of alcohol/drugs on victim to facilitate the offence", "grooming behaviour used against victim" and "abuse of trust", see para.3.43, above.

Step Two—Starting point and category range

3. 92   Once the court has determined the offence category and culpability level, at step two it should use the corresponding starting point specified in the

guideline in order to reach a sentence within the category range. The starting point applies to all offenders irrespective of plea or previous convictions. Once the starting point has been determined, step two allows further adjustment for aggravating or mitigating features, set out below. A case of particular gravity, reflected by multiple features of culpability or harm, could merit upward adjustment from the starting point before further adjustment for aggravating or mitigating features. The starting points and category ranges for offences under s.6 are as follows:

	A	*B*
Category 1	*Starting point* 16 years' custody *Category range* 13–19 years' custody	*Starting point* 13 years' custody *Category range* 11–17 years' custody
Category 2	*Starting point* 11 years' custody *Category range* 7–15 years' custody	*Starting point* 8 years' custody *Category range* 5–13 years' custody
Category 3	*Starting point* 6 years' custody *Category range* 4–9 years' custody	*Starting point* 4 years' custody *Category range* 2–6 years' custody

Aggravating and mitigating factors

After identifying the starting point and category range, the court should **3.93** consider whether the presence of aggravating or mitigating factors should result in an upward or downward adjustment from the starting point or the imposition of a sentence outside the category range. In particular, relevant recent convictions are likely to result in an upward adjustment. The non-exhaustive list of factors relevant to offences under s.6 is as follows:

Aggravating factors
Statutory aggravating factors
Previous convictions, having regard to a) the nature of the offence to which the conviction relates and its relevance to the current offence; and b) the time that has elapsed since the conviction
Offence committed whilst on bail
Other aggravating factors
Specific targeting of a particularly vulnerable victim
Blackmail or other threats made (where not taken into account at step one)
Location of offence
Timing of offence
Use of weapon or other item to frighten or injure
Victim compelled to leave their home, school etc
Failure to comply with current court orders
Offence committed whilst on licence
Exploiting contact arrangements with a child to commit an offence
Presence of others, especially other children
Any steps taken to prevent the victim reporting an incident, obtaining assistance and/or from assisting or supporting the prosecution
Attempts to dispose of or conceal evidence
Commission of offence whilst under the influence of alcohol or drugs
Victim encouraged to recruit others

Mitigating factors
No previous convictions *or* no relevant/recent convictions
Remorse
Previous good character and/or exemplary conduct*

Age and/or lack of maturity where it affects the responsibility of the offender
Mental disorder or learning disability, particularly where linked to the commission of the offence

* Previous good character/exemplary conduct is different from having no previous convictions. The more serious the offence, the less the weight which should normally be attributed to this factor. Where previous good character/exemplary conduct has been used to facilitate the offence, this mitigation should not normally be allowed and such conduct may constitute an aggravating factor.

In the context of this offence, previous good character/exemplary conduct should not normally be given any significant weight and will not normally justify a reduction in what would otherwise be the appropriate sentence.

The Sentencing Council included the factor "victim compelled to leave   3.94
their home, school, etc" in order to reflect the fact that where a child has to
move from their home, place of care or school as a result of the offence it can
create even longer term harm, as they will have had their education disrupted
or been uprooted from friendship and support networks.

Steps Three to Nine

The remaining steps cover the following points. At step three the court   3.95
should consider any factors which would indicate a reduction in sentence, e.g.
assistance to the prosecution. At step four it should consider any reduction
for a guilty plea. At step five the court should consider dangerousness, i.e.
whether it would be appropriate to award a life sentence (s.224A or s.225(2)
of the Criminal Justice Act 2003) or an extended sentence (s.226A). Step six
requires the court to consider whether the total sentence is just and
proportionate to the offending behaviour. At step seven it should consider
whether to make an ancillary order (e.g. a compensation order, a SHPO or
a restraining order). Step eight requires the court to fulfil its duty under s.174
of the Criminal Justice Act 2003 to give reasons for, and explain the effect of,
the sentence. Finally, at step nine the court should consider whether to give
credit for time spent on bail in accordance with s.240A of that Act.

As regards the possible relevance to sentence of the offender's belief that   3.96
the victim consented and/or that she was older than her true age, see paras
3.50 and following, above.

Parties to the Offence

The s.6 offence may be committed by and (given that the penetration may be   3.97
of the vagina or the anus) against persons of either sex. As to whether the
child victim is liable to prosecution as an accessory if she encourages the
offence, see para.4.57 and following, below.

Jurisdiction

3.98   By virtue of s.72 of and Sch.2 to the Sexual Offences Act 2003, as amended,[110] it is an offence under s.6 for a UK national to do an act in a country outside the UK which would constitute a s.6 offence if done in England and Wales. See further para.3.72, above.

"Penetrates the Vagina or Anus of another Person"

3.99   For discussion of this phrase in the context of rape, see paras 1.155 and following, above.

"The Penetration is Sexual"

3.100 For the meaning of "penetration", see paras 1.156 and following, above. The slightest penetration is sufficient.[111] For the meaning of "sexual", see paras 2.66 and following, above. If a person penetrates the vagina or anus of a child under 13 in circumstances where there is no or insufficient evidence that the penetration is sexual, it may be appropriate to charge one of the offences against the person, i.e. (depending on the level of harm caused by the penetration) common assault, assault occasioning actual bodily harm contrary to s.47 of the Offences Against the Person Act 1861, maliciously causing grievous bodily harm contrary to s.20 of the 1861 Act or inflicting grievous bodily harm with intent contrary to s.18 of that Act.[112]

"Child under 13"

3.101 For the meaning of this term and proof of age, see paras 3.73 and following, above.

Consent

3.102 The offence is committed regardless of whether the child consents. For the effect of consent on sentence, see paras 3.50 and following, above.

Mental Element

3.103 See the discussion in paras 2.32 and following (mental element of the offence of assault by penetration) and 3.77 and following (mental element of rape of

---

[110] By the Criminal Justice and Immigration Act 2008 s.72, with effect from July 14, 2008.
[111] *Park* [2008] EWCA Crim 1806 at [6]; and see para.1.156, above.
[112] cf. *Hansard*, HC, Standing Committee B, col.49, Beverley Hughes MP, and col.103, Paul Goggins MP (September 9, 2003).

a child under 13), above. In *Heard*,[113] dealing with the offence of sexual assault, for which an intentional act is also required, the Court of Appeal upheld the trial judge's direction to the jury that it was not open to the defendant to contend that voluntary intoxication through drink or drugs prevented him from intending to touch the victim. We suggest that this must apply equally to the s.6 offence.

SEXUAL ASSAULT OF A CHILD UNDER 13

DEFINITION

Section 7(1) of the Sexual Offences Act 2003 provides as follows: **3.104**

> "A person commits an offence if—
> (a) he intentionally touches another person,
> (b) the touching is sexual,
> (c) the other person is under 13."

The elements of s.7(1)(a) and (b) are the same as those of the offence of **3.105** sexual assault (s.3) and reference should accordingly be made to the discussion of that offence in paras 2.38 and following, above. For the question whether, where the child was close to her thirteenth birthday and the accused asserts that the sexual activity was consensual, it may be appropriate to charge under s.3 with an alternative charge under s.7, see para.3.30, above.

The following are illustrations of the possible application of the s.7 **3.106** offence[114]:

- A, aged 18, passionately kisses a 12-year-old girl he meets at a party. A commits the offence. This is so even if B told A that she was 16, and she looks it, so that A reasonably believes she has reached the age of consent.
- A, aged 12, gropes the breasts of B, his 12-year-old girlfriend. A commits the offence, whether or not B consents to his actions.
- A and C are friends and B is A's girlfriend. They are all aged 12. C urges A to grope B's breasts. C encourages the offence for the purposes of s.44 of the Serious Crime Act 2007 (and also commits the s.8 offence of inciting a child under 13 to engage in sexual activity).
- A and B, both aged 12, share a passionate kiss. They both commit the offence.
- A, aged 12, engages in heavy petting with B, his 12-year-old girlfriend. C, also aged 12, knows what A and B intend to do and keeps watch to make sure no adults are around. A and B both commit the offence and C aids and abets it.

---

[113] [2007] EWCA Crim 125, discussed in paras 2.81 and following, above.
[114] They assume that the touching in each case is "sexual".

Mode of Trial and Punishment

3.107   The s.7 offence is triable either way. The maximum sentence on conviction on indictment is 14 years' imprisonment and on summary conviction is six months' imprisonment or a fine, or both.[115] As from a day to be appointed the maximum sentence of imprisonment on summary conviction will increase to 12 months.[116] The increase will have no application to offences committed before it takes effect.[117] Until recently, the maximum fine on summary conviction was a fine not exceeding the statutory maximum (i.e. £5,000). The effect of s.85 of the Legal Aid, Sentencing and Punishment of Offenders Act 2012 is that, from March 12, 2015, a fine of any amount may be imposed. A s.7 offence cannot be dealt with by way of a simple caution.[118]

3.108   For the purposes of listing, cases under s.7[119] fall within Class 2B, save for complex cases involving many complainants (often under age, in care or otherwise particularly vulnerable) and/or many defendants who are alleged to have systematically groomed and abused them, often over a long period of time, which fall within Class 1C.[120] Cases in Class 1C must be referred to the Resident Judge, and by the Resident Judge to a Presiding Judge. Cases in Class 2B must be similarly referred in certain specified circumstances, including where the case is unusually grave or complex or a novel and important point of law is to be raised; where the defendant is a police officer, a member of the legal profession or a high profile figure; or where for any reason the case is likely to attract exceptional media attention.

3.109   An offence under s.7 is a specified offence for the purposes of the dangerousness provisions of the Criminal Justice Act 2003.[121] Accordingly, a s.7 offence, whenever committed, may be made the subject of an extended sentence under s.226A of that Act.[122] The offence is also listed in Pt 1 of Sch.15B to the Criminal Justice Act 2003 for the purposes of s.224A of that Act (life sentence for a second listed offence) if he was 18 or over at the time of the offence or is sentenced to at least 12 months' imprisonment.[123]

---

[115] s.7(2).

[116] Criminal Justice Act 2003 s.282(2), (3).

[117] Criminal Justice Act 2003 s.282(4)

[118] Criminal Justice and Courts Act 2015 s.17(3), and the Criminal Justice and Courts Act 2015 (Simple Cautions) (Specification of Either-Way Offences) Order 2015 (SI 2015/790).

[119] And of soliciting, inciting, encouraging or assisting, attempting or conspiring to commit the offence or assisting an offender having committed the offence.

[120] *Consolidated Criminal Practice Directions*, Part XIII Listing B: CLASSIFICATION, available at *https://www.judiciary.gov.uk/publications/criminal-practice-directions-2015/* [Accessed April 30, 2016].

[121] Criminal Justice Act 2003 s.224 and Sch.15, Pt 2.

[122] Inserted by the Legal Aid, Sentencing and Punishment of Offenders Act 2012 s.124, brought into force on December 3, 2012, by SI 2012/2906.

[123] Inserted by the Legal Aid, Sentencing and Punishment of Offenders Act 2012 s.122, brought into force on December 3, 2012, by SI 2012/2906.

A person convicted under s.7, cautioned, found not guilty by reason of insanity or found to be under a disability and to have done the act charged, is automatically subject to the notification requirements in the Sexual Offences Act 2003.[124]   3.110

During the passage of the Sexual Offences Bill, Baroness Noakes tabled a probing amendment designed to discover when the Government thought a summary prosecution under s.7 might be appropriate.[125] In response, Lord Falconer said that where, for example, an 18-year-old kisses a 12-year-old with the latter's consent, he could envisage circumstances where it might be appropriate for the case to be dealt with in a magistrates' court.[126] The point is not covered in the CPS guidance to prosecutors on charging under the 2003 Act, but in the present climate of public concern about child sexual exploitation, it will be rare for any case involving an adult defendant that reaches the threshold for prosecution to be thought suitable for trial in the magistrates' court. The *Code for Crown Prosecutors* requires prosecutors to bear in mind that youths should be tried in the youth court wherever possible and states that a trial of a youth in the Crown Court should be reserved for the most serious cases or where the interests of justice require a youth to be jointly tried with an adult.[127]   3.111

Alternative Verdict

As to when a conviction in the alternative of common assault may be brought in, see para.2.44, above. On a summary charge, the magistrates have no jurisdiction to find the defendant guilty of a lesser offence.[128]   3.112

Sentencing

For the Sentencing Council guideline relating to the sentencing of sexual offences committed by offenders aged 18 and over, see Ch.33, below. In consulting on its draft guideline,[129] the Council noted that the previous guideline, issued by the Sentencing Guidelines Council ("SGC") in 2007, covered the under-13 offences and the equivalent offences for victims aged 13 and over together; for example, there was a single guideline covering sexual assault (s.3) and sexual assault of a child under 13 (s.7). The Sentencing Council proposed instead to issue separate guidelines for the two sets of offences, in recognition that "there are issues and sensitivities unique to offences against children under 13 that require a separate guideline to ensure   3.113

---

[124] s.80 and Sch.3, discussed in Ch.35, below.
[125] *Hansard*, HL Vol.646, col.1193 (April 1, 2003).
[126] *Hansard*, HL Vol.646, col.1194 (April 1, 2003).
[127] *Code for Crown Prosecutors* (Jan 2013), para.8.3.
[128] *Lawrence v Lawrence* [1968] 2 Q.B. 93.
[129] *Sexual Offences Guideline: Consultation* (December 6, 2012). The consultation document is available on the Sentencing Council's website.

clarity for sentencers as to the factors to be taken into account and to provide a transparent process for others concerned with these cases".[130] This is the approach taken in the published guideline.

3.114   The guideline for sexual assault of a child under 13 nonetheless follows the format of the guideline for the offence against victims aged 13 and over, but with the addition of factors to reflect that the under-13 offence may involve a child being coerced and groomed into sexual activity. The starting points and category ranges for the under-13 offence are higher than for the offence against victims aged 13 and over; but the guideline also acknowledges that the potential range of offending behaviours is such that there may be exceptional cases where a greater degree of flexibility is required. On this aspect see the discussion, above, of the guideline for rape of a child under 13.

Sentencing guideline

Step One—Harm and culpability

3.115   The guideline requires the sentencing court to go through a series of steps in order to determine the appropriate sentence. Step one involves determining the offence category by reference to the degree of harm caused and then the culpability level for the offence. In relation to the s.7 offence of sexual assault of a child under 13, the harm and culpability factors are as follows:

Harm		*Culpability*
Category 1	• Severe psychological or physical harm • Abduction • Violence or threats of violence • Forced/uninvited entry into victim's home	*A*
		Significant degree of planning
		Offender acts together with others to commit the offence
		Use of alcohol/drugs on victim to facilitate the offence
Category 2	• Touching of naked genitalia or naked breast area	Grooming behaviour used against the victim
		Abuse of trust

---

[130] *Sexual Offences Guideline: Consultation* (December 6, 2012), p.36.

	• Prolonged detention/sustained incident • Additional degradation/humiliation • Child is particularly vulnerable due to extreme youth and/or personal circumstances	Previous violence against victim
		Offence committed in course of burglary
		Sexual images of victim recorded, retained, solicited or shared
		Deliberate isolation of victim
		Commercial exploitation and/or motivation
Category 3	Factor(s) in categories 1 and 2 not present	Offence racially or religiously aggravated
		Offence motivated by, or demonstrating, hostility to the victim based on his or her sexual orientation (or presumed sexual orientation) or transgender identity (or presumed transgender identity)
		Offence motivated by, or demonstrating, hostility to the victim based on his or her disability (or presumed disability)
		B
		Factor(s) in category A not present

Categories 1 and 2 contain a list of factors indicating additional harm but   **3.116**
category 3 does not list any factors, in order to reflect the fact that any sexual
assault of a child under the age of 13 will cause some degree of harm to the
victim. For the meaning of "severe" in the factor "severe psychological or
physical harm" and of "extreme youth", see para.3.42, above. For discussion
of the factors "use of alcohol/drugs on victim to facilitate the offence",
"grooming behaviour used against victim" and "abuse of trust", see
para.3.43, above.

Step Two—Starting point and category range

Once the court has determined the offence category and culpability level, at   **3.117**
step two it should use the corresponding starting point specified in the

guideline in order to reach a sentence within the category range. The starting point applies to all offenders irrespective of plea or previous convictions. Once the starting point has been determined, step two allows further adjustment for aggravating or mitigating features, set out below. A case of particular gravity, reflected by multiple features of culpability or harm, could merit upward adjustment from the starting point before further adjustment for aggravating or mitigating features. Where there is a sufficient prospect of rehabilitation, a community order with a sex offender treatment programme requirement under s.202 of the Criminal Justice Act 2003 can be a proper alternative to a short or moderate length custodial sentence.

3.118   The starting points and category ranges for offences under s.7 are as follows:

	A	*B*
Category 1	*Starting point* 6 years' custody	*Starting point* 4 years' custody
	Category range 4–9 years' custody	*Category range* 3–7 years' custody
Category 2	*Starting point* 4 years' custody	*Starting point* 2 years' custody
	Category range 3–7 years' custody	*Category range* 1–4 years' custody
Category 3	*Starting point* 1 years' custody	*Starting point* 26 weeks' custody
	Category range 26 weeks'–2 years' custody	*Category range* High level community order – 1 years' custody

Aggravating and mitigating factors

3.119 After identifying the starting point and category range, the court should consider whether the presence of aggravating or mitigating factors should result in an upward or downward adjustment from the starting point or the imposition of a sentence outside the category range. In particular, relevant recent convictions are likely to result in an upward adjustment. The non-exhaustive list of factors relevant to offences under s.7 is as follows:

Aggravating factors
Statutory aggravating factors
Previous convictions, having regard to a) the nature of the offence to which the conviction relates and its relevance to the current offence; and b) the time that has elapsed since the conviction
Offence committed whilst on bail
Other aggravating factors
Specific targeting of a particularly vulnerable victim
Blackmail or other threats made (where not taken into account at step one)
Location of offence
Timing of offence
Use of weapon or other item to frighten or injure
Victim compelled to leave their home, school etc
Failure to comply with current court orders
Offence committed whilst on licence
Exploiting contact arrangements with a child to commit an offence
Presence of others, especially other children
Any steps taken to prevent the victim reporting an incident, obtaining assistance and/or from assisting or supporting the prosecution
Attempts to dispose of or conceal evidence
Commission of offence whilst under the influence of alcohol or drugs
Victim encouraged to recruit others

Mitigating factors
No previous convictions *or* no relevant/recent convictions
Remorse
Previous good character and/or exemplary conduct*

Age and/or lack of maturity where it affects the responsibility of the offender
Mental disorder or learning disability, particularly where linked to the commission of the offence

* Previous good character/exemplary conduct is different from having no previous convictions. The more serious the offence, the less the weight which should normally be attributed to this factor. Where previous good character/exemplary conduct has been used to facilitate the offence, this mitigation should not normally be allowed and such conduct may constitute an aggravating factor.

In the context of this offence, previous good character/exemplary conduct should not normally be given any significant weight and will not normally justify a reduction in what would otherwise be the appropriate sentence.

3.120　　The Sentencing Council included "victim compelled to leave their home, school, etc" in order to reflect the fact that where a child has to move from their home, place of care or school as a result of the offence it can create even longer term harm, as they will have had their education disrupted or been uprooted from friendship and support networks.

Steps Three to Nine

3.121　　The remaining steps cover the following points. At step three the court should consider any factors which would indicate a reduction in sentence, e.g. assistance to the prosecution. At step four it should consider any reduction for a guilty plea. At step five the court should consider dangerousness, i.e. whether it would be appropriate to award a life sentence (s.224A of the Criminal Justice Act 2003) or an extended sentence (s.226A). Step six requires the court to consider whether the total sentence is just and proportionate to the offending behaviour. At step seven it should consider whether to make an ancillary order (e.g. a compensation order, a SHPO or a restraining order). Step eight requires the court to fulfil its duty under s.174 of the Criminal Justice Act 2003 to give reasons for, and explain the effect of, the sentence. Finally, at step nine the court should consider whether to give credit for time spent on bail in accordance with s.240A of that Act.

Sentencing examples

3.122　　In *Salkeld*,[131] the appellant (47) was convicted of one offence under s.7 and one of false imprisonment. In 1995 he had been convicted of attempted rape of a boy under 16 and gross indecency with a child, for which he received a total of five years' imprisonment. In 2002 he was convicted of false imprisonment for which he received eight years' imprisonment. That offence was serious: he had physically picked up a seven-year-old boy in a GP's

---

[131] [2015] EWCA Crim 163.

surgery and placed him in a cubicle in the male lavatory. He was disturbed by another man coming in. It was only because of that interruption that the appellant left the boy, telling him to stay there. It was clear that he was hoping to come back and sexually assault the child. Fortunately that child escaped unharmed. The appellant was made the subject of a SOPO as a consequence. He breached the order and in 2010 he went to prison again, this time for eight months for failing to inform the authorities of his whereabouts. As regards the present offence, on the day in question the appellant was working in a junk shop. The victim and his father went into the shop. The victim was interested in a horn that was for sale in the shop but the father did not have the money to pay for it. The following day, the appellant spotted the victim near the shop, approached him and asked if he was still interested in the horn. The victim said he was and the appellant told him to come into the shop, which the victim did. The appellant then pulled the shutter at the front entrance half-way down and locked the door. He put his hand down inside the front of the victim's trousers and underpants and touched his penis. The victim broke away and managed to unlock the door and get out beneath the shutter. In interview the appellant alleged that the victim had stolen the horn and then made up the allegations to cover up the theft. He was convicted at trial. A pre-sentence report found there was a very high risk of re-offending and of serious harm being caused. The appellant displayed no empathy or understanding of the effect of his offending on his victims. In passing sentence the judge observed that it was clear the appellant was a dangerous offender and that the case called for extended sentences. He imposed, in relation to the sexual assault, a 10-year extended sentence made up of a seven year custodial element and three year extended licence. For the false imprisonment offence, he imposed a 14-year extended sentence made up of a 10-year custodial element with a four year extended licence. The sentences were ordered to be served concurrently. On appeal, the appellant conceded that it had been proper for the judge to pass extended sentences, but contended that the custodial sentences were too long. In relation to the sexual assault, he argued that the offence involved touching of the naked genitalia and so fell within category 2 of the guidelines, which indicates a starting point of four years' custody. If the factors involved in the culpability table arose, it was only with limited effect: there was some degree of planning, but it was not significant, and if abuse of trust arose here it would arise in any case where the child is in the company of an adult. The Court of Appeal agreed that this was a category 2 offence. As regards aggravating factors, the truly striking factors here related to the appellant's previous offending, his denials and his attitude to the offence. Whilst these bore directly on risk, they had also to be taken into account when considering culpability. The Court concluded that the appellant's culpability was very high, based on his offending history, the attitudes expressed by him and his knowledge of the consequences of such offending. These factors in combination rendered proper the sentence passed on the assault. The Court also concluded, particularly in the light of the offending history, that it was entirely proper for there to be an additional period of imprisonment to reflect the false imprisonment, reflecting the very high culpability of that offence over and above the sexual assault. Whilst the sentences were clearly severe and intended to be so, they were not manifestly excessive.

3.123   In *R. v B*,[132] the appellant appealed against a total sentence of six years' imprisonment imposed for causing or inciting a child under 13 to engage in sexual activity, taking indecent photographs of a child and sexual assault of a child under 13. The appellant was in a relationship with a woman who had two daughters. The relationship broke down but the appellant maintained contact with the girls. On the occasion in question they came to stay with him overnight, when the younger was aged seven. While she was asleep the appellant took photos of her naked genitalia and of his naked, erect penis touching skin close to her vagina. In the morning the appellant asked her to pose for indecent photographs. The girl told her mother what had happened and police officers attended the appellant's home, where they discovered 393 indecent images of the girl on his mobile. The appellant pleaded guilty to causing or inciting the girl to engage in sexual activity and to taking indecent photographs. He subsequently pleaded guilty to a fourth count, of sexual assault of a child under 13, after initially denying such conduct. The judge imposed concurrent one-year sentences for causing or inciting a child to engage in sexual activity and for taking indecent photographs. As for the sexual assault, he decided that the offence fell within category 2A of the guideline and took a starting point of six years' imprisonment, which he reduced by one-sixth to five years' imprisonment to take account of the guilty plea. The concurrent one-year sentences were ordered to run consecutively to the five-year sentence, giving a total sentence of six years' imprisonment. The appellant submitted that the judge had erred in treating the sexual assault as falling within category 2A rather than category 3 and that he should have applied a discount of one-quarter, rather than one-sixth, in respect of the guilty plea to that count. The appeal was allowed. The Court of Appeal held that there was a combination of factors in the case which made it every bit as serious as the cases contemplated by category 2; for example, the appellant had touched, not just with his hands but with his erect penis, skin which was very close to the victim's vagina. Further, although it was impossible to tell precisely how sustained the contact had been, it had clearly lasted long enough for him take the photographs. As for vulnerability, the victim was aged only seven and was in the appellant's care in circumstances where he could do what he wished. The case clearly fell within category 2. However, the judge should have given credit of one-quarter rather than one-sixth for the plea. The Court accordingly reduced the sentence from five years to four-and-a-half years' imprisonment, so reducing the total term from six to five-and-a-half years' imprisonment. We would note that the particular

---

[132] [2015] EWCA Crim 319.

vulnerability of the child in this case was beyond doubt, as she was only seven and was away from her mother in the appellant's home and in his sole care. These factors were, we suggest, sufficient by themselves to place the sexual assault in category 2. The Court of Appeal nonetheless sought to reinforce its decision by finding other category 2 factors present. But in touching with his erect penis the child's skin near her vagina, the appellant was some way from touching her naked genitalia as specified in category 2. Further, to treat his conduct as "sustained" because it lasted long enough for him to take a photograph robs the word "sustained" of almost all sensible meaning. We suggest that the Court should have rested its decision on the basis of the child's particular vulnerability and not strained to bolster it by unconvincing elaboration of the language of the guideline.

In *Attorney General's Reference (No.7 of 2015) (R. v F)*,[133] F was **3.124** convicted of three offences under s.7 and five more under s.8 of causing a child under 13 to engage in sexual activity. F was married with two small children and of good character. The victim, aged 12, was one of F's neighbours. F would knock on the door of the victim's house to see if he wanted to play out in the street. They would regularly play badminton together and the neighbourhood was one in which children would play in the street and would interact with adults. Over the course of some five or six months, F committed a number of offences against the victim. These included instructing the victim to touch his penis, instructing the victim to masturbate him, and instructing the victim to suck his penis. The victim complied with the earlier requests, but refused to perform oral sex upon F. Additionally, F required the victim to remove his trousers and underwear and bend over, upon which F placed his penis between the victim's buttocks in order to masturbate himself. F then turned away and masturbated himself manually to ejaculation. Finally, F touched the victim's bottom and reached for his penis; however, the victim resisted. As a result of the offending the victim began to dread physical expressions of affection from his family. The judge found that F had groomed the victim under the guise of friendship, and tht the victim was vulnerable. With the agreement of both counsel, he placed the sexual assault offences into category 2A of the guideline, with a starting point of four years' custody, and the offences of causing sexual activity into category 3A, with a starting point of five years' custody. The judge imposed a sentence of three years and six months' imprisonment. The Court of Appeal held the sentence unduly lenient. The most serious of the offences, the sexual assault in which F placed his penis between the victim's buttocks, was to be placed within category 2A of the guideline by virtue of the grooming behaviour, breach of trust and isolation of the victim. That provided a starting point of four years. However, the guideline stated that multiple features of culpability could merit upward adjustment from the starting point. On the particular facts, the multiple features listed in the

---

[133] [2015] EWCA Crim 963.

assessment of culpability in the guideline required an adjusted starting point of five years' imprisonment. A further aggravating feature was that F committed multiple offences against the victim over a period of months. The mitigation comprised only F's hitherto good character, the effect of which was limited given the seriousness of the offences that he committed against a child member of his local community. The appropriate sentence, reflecting the totality of the offending, was one of five years and six months' imprisonment.

Parties to the Offence

3.125   The s.7 offence may be committed by and against persons of either sex. As to whether the child victim is liable to prosecution as an accessory if she encourages the offence, see paras 4.57 and following, below.

Jurisdiction

3.126   By virtue of s.72 of and Sch.2 to the Sexual Offences Act 2003, as amended,[134] it is an offence under s.7 for a UK national to do an act in a country outside the UK which would constitute a s.7 offence if done in England and Wales. See further para.3.72, above.

"The Touching is Sexual"

3.127   For the meaning of "sexual", see paras 2.66 and following, above. If a person were to touch a child under 13 without the child's consent in circumstances where there is no or insufficient evidence that the touching was sexual, it may be appropriate to charge one of the offences against the person, i.e. common assault or, where bodily harm is caused, assault occasioning actual bodily harm contrary to s.47 of the Offences Against the Person Act 1861, maliciously causing grievous bodily harm contrary to s.20 of the 1861 Act or inflicting grievous bodily harm with intent contrary to s.18 of that Act.[135]

"Child under 13"

3.128   For the meaning of this term and proof of age, see paras 3.73 and following, above.

Consent

3.129   The offence is committed regardless of whether the child consents. For the effect of consent on sentence, see paras 3.50 and following, above.

[134] By the Criminal Justice and Immigration Act 2008 s.72, with effect from July 14, 2008.
[135] cf. *Hansard*, HC, Standing Committee B, col.49, Beverley Hughes MP and col.103, Paul Goggins MP (September 9, 2003).

Mental Element

See the discussion in paras 2.78 and following (mental element of the offence   3.130
of sexual assault) and 3.77 and following (mental element of rape of a child
under 13), above. In *Heard*,[136] dealing with the offence of sexual assault, for
which an intentional touching is also required, the Court of Appeal upheld
the trial judge's direction to the jury that it was not open to the defendant to
contend that voluntary intoxication through drink or drugs prevented him
from intending to touch the victim. We suggest that this must apply equally
to the s.7 offence.

Causing or Inciting a Child Under 13 to Engage in Sexual Activity

Definition

Section 8(1) of the Sexual Offences Act 2003 provides as follows: 3.131

> "A person commits an offence if—
> (a) he intentionally causes or incites another person (B) to engage in an
>   activity,
> (b) the activity is sexual, and
> (c) B is under 13."

It was held in *Walker*[137] that s.8 creates two offences, one of intentionally   3.132
causing and one of intentionally inciting a person under 13 to engage in
sexual activity. It follows that a count alleging that the defendant "caused or
incited" the relevant activity is in principle duplicitous and should be
amended or struck out; though in practice counts in this form are,
unfortunately, common and rarely challenged.[138] Further, the effect of the
decision in *Courtie*[139] is that the provision by s.8 of a higher maximum
punishment where certain forms of penetration occur (see para.3.136, below)
creates separate offences, one involving the specified forms of penetration
and the other not. The combined effect of the two authorities is that s.8 in
principle creates four offences: causing penetrative sexual activity, inciting
penetrative sexual activity, causing non-penetrative sexual activity and
inciting non-penetrative sexual activity. It is important that the charge or
indictment specifies which of these offences is being charged.

The preceding two sentences[140] were cited with approval by Aikens LJ,   3.133
giving the judgment of the Court of Appeal in *Grout*.[141] In that case the
appellant was convicted on a count (count 1) charging that between specified

---

[136] [2007] EWCA Crim 125, discussed in paras 2.81 and following, above.
[137] [2006] EWCA Crim 1907.
[138] See e.g. *Broughton* [2007] EWCA Crim 566; *Butcher* [2009] EWCA Crim 1458; *R. v B*, unreported, 2 February 2015.
[139] [1984] A.C. 463.
[140] As they appeared in para.3.92 of our 4th edition.
[141] [2011] EWCA Crim 299, at [27].

dates he had "intentionally caused or incited [H] a child under the aged of 13, namely 12 years, to engage in sexual activity, namely taking part in a webcam conversation when you asked [H] to show you her bra and asked her if she would take off clothing". The Court of Appeal quashed the conviction on this count, saying[142]:

> "On any view count 1 alleges at least four different offences. These are: (1) intentionally *causing* H to engage in sexual activity in taking part in a webcam conversation when the defendant asked H to show her bra; (2) intentionally *inciting* H to engage in sexual activity in taking part in a webcam conversation when the defendant asked H to show her bra; (3) intentionally *causing* H to engage in sexual activity in taking part in a webcam conversation and asking her to take off clothing; and (4) intentionally *inciting* H to engage in sexual activity in taking part in a webcam conversation and asking her to take off clothing. It might be thought that the count also contains allegations of (a) intentionally causing and (b) intentionally inciting H to engage in 'sexual activity' in the form of a webcam conversation in the circumstances alleged. Technically speaking, the count was bad because it contained within it allegations regarding a multiplicity of offences, which depended on proof of different facts and different actions, and a different state of mind by the defendant (an intention to cause and an intention to incite) for each allegation. More importantly and practically, this jumble of offences in one count created difficulties for both judge and jury.
>
> The count should have been broken down. In essence there were two prosecution allegations that mattered in this case. The first allegation was that the appellant had intentionally *caused* H to engage in 'sexual activity' by asking her to show her bra on the webcam, which, all were agreed, she had actually done by showing her bra strap. The two key questions in relation to that allegation were whether, in the circumstances, the action of showing the bra strap amounted to 'sexual activity' and whether the appellant had 'intentionally caused' H to engage in such 'sexual activity'.
>
> The second relevant allegation was that the appellant had intentionally *incited* H to engage in 'sexual activity' by asking her if she would take off clothing. Whether that activity was meant to be on the webcam or otherwise is not clear. H did not, of course, take off clothing. The key questions in relation to that allegation would be whether, in the circumstances, 'taking off clothing' amounted to 'sexual activity' by H and whether the appellant had 'intentionally incited' H to engage in that 'sexual activity'.
>
> In our view the judge erred in not making this analysis of count 1 at the beginning of the trial. He should have directed the prosecution to decide what specific offences it wished to allege. Then, for the benefit of the jury, if not to ensure that there was no 'duplicity' or even 'quadruplicity' or 'sextuplicity' in the count, he should have directed that there be separate counts for each specific alleged offence. If this analysis had been undertaken, it would have become immediately clear that there was no evidence at all to support an allegation that the appellant had intentionally caused H to engage in 'sexual activity' in the form of taking off clothing. H had not done so at any stage, so the appellant could not have 'intentionally caused' her to do so. In addition, in our view, the evidence in support of an allegation that the appellant had 'intentionally incited' H actually to take off clothing, i.e. deliberately encouraged her to do so by a text or MSN message which asked her if she would do that, was either non-existent or so vague that no jury could have safely convicted of that offence. We note that

---

[142] At [32]–[37] per Aitkens LJ.

nowhere in the summing up did the judge refer to any MSN or text exchange in which the appellant even asked H the question 'would you take off clothing'.

Therefore, if a careful analysis of count 1 had been undertaken at the outset of the trial, the judge would have had to conclude that two out of the four parts of it should not go before the jury, viz. those alleging that the appellant had intentionally caused or had intentionally incited H to engage in 'sexual activity' by taking off clothing. Those allegations, should have been withdrawn on the simple ground that there was insufficient evidence on which a jury, properly directed, could convict of those offences. Moreover, it is clear that the offence of 'intentionally inciting' H to show her bra was itself duplication, because the evidence was that she had actually shown her bra strap, so that the offence of 'intentionally causing' H to do so was sufficient to cover those facts.

We have concluded that this failure in itself makes the conviction unsafe because the jury were asked to consider, within the one count, two possible offences which they should not have been asked to consider. We do not know on what basis the jury did, in fact, convict the appellant."

A key difference between s.8 and s.4, the equivalent provision relating to   **3.134**
victims aged 13 and over, is that whilst both provisions make it an offence to cause the victim to engage in sexual activity, s.8 also makes it an offence to incite the victim to engage in such activity. Apart from that difference, the elements of s.8(1)(a) and (b) and of s.4 are the same, and reference should accordingly be made to the discussion of s.4 in paras 2.84 and following, above. For the question whether, where the offence is one of "causing", the child was close to her thirteenth birthday and the accused asserts that the activity was consensual, it may be appropriate to charge under s.4 with an alternative charge under s.8, see para.3.30, above.

The following are illustrations of the possible application of s.8[143]:   **3.135**

- A and B are 12-year-old boys. A encourages B to grope the breasts of B's girlfriend C, also aged 12. A commits the offence by inciting non-penetrative sexual activity.
- B, aged 12, asks her older sister, A, whether she should have sexual intercourse with C, her 16-year-old boyfriend, as he wishes. A suggests that as she is only 12 she should confine herself to heavy petting. A commits the offence by inciting non-penetrative sexual activity.
- A and B are boyfriend and girlfriend, both aged 12. A persuades B to perform oral sex on him. He commits the offence by causing penetrative activity, though he also commits the s.5 offence of rape of a child under 13. It does not matter whether B acts willingly or unwillingly.
- A, aged 16, persuades B, aged 12, to masturbate herself. A commits the offence by causing sexual activity (which may or may not be penetrative, depending on the facts). This is so whether or not he is physically present when the masturbation takes place.

[143] They assume that the activity in each case is "sexual".

Mode of Trial and Punishment

3.136 If the activity caused or incited involves any of the following, an offence under s.8 is triable only on indictment and the maximum sentence is life imprisonment:

(a) penetration of B's anus or vagina,

(b) penetration of B's mouth with a person's penis,

(c) penetration of a person's anus or vagina with a part of B's body or by B with anything else, or

(d) penetration of a person's mouth with B's penis.[144]

3.137 In other cases, the offence is triable either way. The maximum sentence on conviction on indictment is 14 years' imprisonment and on summary conviction is six months' imprisonment or a fine, or both.[145] As from a day to be appointed the maximum sentence of imprisonment on summary conviction will increase to 12 months.[146] The increase will have no application to offences committed before it takes effect.[147] Until recently, the maximum fine on summary conviction was a fine not exceeding the statutory maximum (i.e. £5,000). The effect of s.85 of the Legal Aid, Sentencing and Punishment of Offenders Act 2012 is that, from March 12, 2015, a fine of any amount may be imposed. A s.8 offence cannot be dealt with by way of a simple caution.[148]

3.138 For the purposes of listing, cases under s.8[149] fall within Class 2B, save for complex cases involving many complainants (often under age, in care or otherwise particularly vulnerable) and/or many defendants who are alleged to have systematically groomed and abused them, often over a long period of time, which fall within Class 1C.[150] Cases in Class 1C must be referred to the Resident Judge, and by the Resident Judge to a Presiding Judge. Cases in Class 2B must be similarly referred in certain specified circumstances, including where the case is unusually grave or complex or a novel and important point of law is to be raised; where the defendant is a police officer, a member of the legal profession or a high profile figure; or where for any reason the case is likely to attract exceptional media attention.

3.139 An offence under s.8 is a serious specified offence for the purposes of the dangerousness provisions of the Criminal Justice Act 2003.[151] An offence under s.8 that involves penetration falls within the scope of s.225(2) of that

---

[144] s.8(2).

[145] s.8(3).

[146] Criminal Justice Act 2003 s.282(2), (3).

[147] Criminal Justice Act 2003 s.282(4)

[148] Criminal Justice and Courts Act 2015 s.17(3), and the Criminal Justice and Courts Act 2015 (Simple Cautions) (Specification of Either-Way Offences) Order 2015 (SI 2015/790).

[149] And of soliciting, inciting, encouraging or assisting, attempting or conspiring to commit the offence or assisting an offender having committed the offence.

[150] *Consolidated Criminal Practice Directions*, Part XIII Listing B: CLASSIFICATION, available at *https://www.judiciary.gov.uk/publications/criminal-practice-directions-2015/* [Accessed April 30, 2016].

[151] Criminal Justice Act 2003 s.224 and Sch.15, Pt 2.

Act, relating to the imposition of life sentences for serious offences. Further, a s.8 offence, whenever committed, may be made the subject of an extended sentence under s.226A of that Act.[152] The offence is also listed in Pt 1 of Sch.15B to the Criminal Justice Act 2003 for the purposes of s.224A of that Act (life sentence for a second listed offence) if he was 18 or over at the time of the offence or is sentenced to at least 12 months' imprisonment.[153]

A person convicted under s.8, cautioned, found not guilty by reason of   **3.140** insanity or found to be under a disability and to have done the act charged, is automatically subject to the notification requirements in the Sexual Offences Act 2003.[154]

BAIL

Section 25 of the Criminal Justice and Public Order Act 1994[155] provides that   **3.141** a person charged with or convicted of certain offences who has a previous conviction for any such offence shall be granted bail only if the court, or as the case may be, the constable considering the grant of bail is of the opinion that there are exceptional circumstances which justify it. The offences in question include s.8 offences in which the sexual activity caused or incited involved penetration as set out in para.3.136 above, and an attempt to commit that offence. For the full list of offences covered by s.25 of the 1994 Act, see para.1.24, above.

SENTENCING

For the Sentencing Council guideline relating to the sentencing of sexual   **3.142** offences committed by offenders aged 18 and over, see Ch.33, below. In consulting on its draft guideline,[156] the Council noted that the previous guideline, issued by the Sentencing Guidelines Council ("SGC") in 2007, covered the under-13 offences and the equivalent offences for victims aged 13 and over together; for example, there was a single guideline covering causing a person to engage in sexual activity without consent (s.4) and causing or inciting a child under 13 to engage in sexual activity (s.8). The Sentencing Council proposed instead to issue separate guidelines for the two sets of offences, in recognition that "there are issues and sensitivities unique to offences against children under 13 that require a separate guideline to ensure

---

[152] Inserted by the Legal Aid, Sentencing and Punishment of Offenders Act 2012 s.124, brought into force on December 3, 2012, by SI 2012/2906.
[153] Inserted by the Legal Aid, Sentencing and Punishment of Offenders Act 2012 s.122, brought into force on December 3, 2012, by SI 2012/2906.
[154] s.80 and Sch.3, discussed in Ch.35, below.
[155] As amended by the Legal Aid, Sentencing and Punishment of Offenders Act 2012 s.90 and Sch.11 para.33, which was brought into force by the Legal Aid, Sentencing and Punishment of Offenders Act 2012 (Commencement No.4 and Saving Provisions) Order 2012, last note.
[156] *Sexual Offences Guideline: Consultation* (December 6, 2012). The consultation document is available on the Sentencing Council's website.

clarity for sentencers as to the factors to be taken into account and to provide a transparent process for others concerned with these cases".[157] This is the approach taken in the published guideline.

3.143   The guideline for causing or inciting a child under 13 to engage in sexual activity nonetheless follows the format of the guideline for the offence against victims aged 13 and over, but with the addition of factors to reflect that the under-13 offence may involve a child being coerced and groomed into sexual activity. The starting points and category ranges for the under-13 offence are higher than for the offence against victims aged 13 and over; but the guideline also acknowledges that the potential range of offending behaviours is such that there may be exceptional cases where a greater degree of flexibility is required. On this aspect see further the discussion, above, of the guideline for rape of a child under 13.

Sentencing guideline

Step One—Harm and culpability

3.144   The guideline requires the sentencing court to go through a series of steps in order to determine the appropriate sentence. Step one involves determining the offence category by reference to the degree of harm caused and then the culpability level for the offence. In relation to offences under s.8, the offence categories are as follows:

Harm		*Culpability*
Category 1	The extreme nature of one or more category 2 factors or the extreme impact caused by a combination of category 2 factors **may** elevate to category 1	*A*
		Significant degree of planning
		Offender acts together with others to commit the offence
		Use of alcohol/drugs on victim to facilitate the offence
Category 2	• Severe psychological or physical harm • Penetration of vagina or anus (using body or object) by, or of, victim	Grooming behaviour used against the victim
		Abuse of trust
		Previous violence against victim

[157] *Sexual Offences Guideline: Consultation* (December 6, 2012), p.36.

	• Penile penetration of mouth by, or of, victim • Additional degradation/ humiliation • Abduction • Prolonged detention/sustained incident • Violence or threats of violence • Forced/uninvited entry into victim's home • Child is particularly vulnerable due to extreme youth and/ or personal circumstances	Offence committed in course of burglary
		Sexual images of victim recorded, retained, solicited or shared
		Deliberate isolation of victim
		Commercial exploitation and/or motivation
		Offence racially or religiously aggravated
		Offence motivated by, or demonstrating, hostility to the victim based on his or her sexual orientation (or presumed sexual orientation) or transgender identity (or presumed transgender identity)
Category 3	Factor(s) in categories 1 and 2 not present	Offence motivated by, or demonstrating, hostility to the victim based on his or her disability (or presumed disability)
		B
		Factor(s) in category A not present

Category 3 has no factors listed, to reflect the fact that any offence of **3.145** causing or inciting a child under 13 to engage in sexual activity involves inherent serious harm. For the meaning of "severe" in the factor "severe psychological or physical harm" and of "extreme youth", see para.3.42, above. For discussion of the factors "use of alcohol/drugs on victim to facilitate the offence", "grooming behaviour used against victim" and "abuse of trust", see para.3.43, above.

Step Two—Starting point and category range

Once the court has determined the offence category and culpability level, at **3.146** step two it should use the corresponding starting point specified in the guideline in order to reach a sentence within the category range. The starting point applies to all offenders irrespective of plea or previous convictions. Once the starting point has been determined, step two allows further adjustment for aggravating or mitigating features, set out below. A case of particular gravity, reflected by multiple features of culpability or harm, could merit upward adjustment from the starting point before further adjustment for aggravating or mitigating features. The starting points and category ranges for offences under s.8 are:

	A	*B*
Category 1	*Starting point* 13 years' custody *Category range* 11–17 years' custody	*Starting point* 11 years' custody *Category range* 10–15 years' custody
Category 2	*Starting point* 8 years' custody *Category range* 5–10 years' custody	*Starting point* 6 years' custody *Category range* 3–9 years' custody
Category 3	*Starting point* 5 years' custody *Category range* 3–8 years' custody	*Starting point* 2 years' custody *Category range* 1–4 years' custody

Aggravating and mitigating factors

3.147 After identifying the starting point and category range, the court should consider whether the presence of aggravating or mitigating factors should result in an upward or downward adjustment from the starting point or the imposition of a sentence outside the category range. In particular, relevant recent convictions are likely to result in an upward adjustment. The non-exhaustive list of factors relevant to offences under s.8 is as follows:

Aggravating factors
Statutory aggravating factors
Previous convictions, having regard to a) the nature of the offence to which the conviction relates and its relevance to the current offence; and b) the time that has elapsed since the conviction
Offence committed whilst on bail

Other aggravating factors
Specific targeting of a particularly vulnerable victim
Ejaculation (where not taken into account at step one)
Blackmail or other threats made (where not taken into account at step one)
Location of offence
Timing of offence
Use of weapon or other item to frighten or injure
Victim compelled to leave their home, school etc
Failure to comply with current court orders
Offence committed whilst on licence
Exploiting contact arrangements with a child to commit an offence
Presence of others, especially other children
Any steps taken to prevent the victim reporting an incident, obtaining assistance and/or from assisting or supporting the prosecution
Attempts to dispose of or conceal evidence
Commission of offence whilst under the influence of alcohol or drugs
Victim encouraged to recruit others

Mitigating factors
No previous convictions *or* no relevant/recent convictions
Remorse
Previous good character and/or exemplary conduct*
Age and/or lack of maturity where it affects the responsibility of the offender
Mental disorder or learning disability, particularly where linked to the commission of the offence
Sexual activity was incited but no activity took place because the offender voluntarily desisted or intervened to prevent it

* Previous good character/exemplary conduct is different from having no previous convictions. The more serious the offence, the less the weight which should normally be attributed to this factor. Where previous good character/exemplary conduct has been used to facilitate the offence, this mitigation should not normally be allowed and such conduct may constitute an aggravating factor.

In the context of this offence, previous good character/exemplary conduct should not normally be given any significant weight and will not normally justify a reduction in what would otherwise be the appropriate sentence.

3.148   The Sentencing Council included "victim compelled to leave their home, school, etc" in order to reflect the fact that where a child has to move from their home, place of care or school as a result of the offence it can create even longer term harm, as they will have had their education disrupted or been uprooted from friendship and support networks.

Steps Three to Nine

3.149   The remaining steps cover the following points. At step three the court should consider any factors which would indicate a reduction in sentence, e.g. assistance to the prosecution. At step four it should consider any reduction for a guilty plea. At step five the court should consider dangerousness, i.e. whether it would be appropriate to award a life sentence (s.224A or s.225(2) of the Criminal Justice Act 2003) or an extended sentence (s.226A). Step six requires the court to consider whether the total sentence is just and proportionate to the offending behaviour. At step seven it should consider whether to make an ancillary order (e.g. a compensation order, a SHPO or a restraining order). Step eight requires the court to fulfil its duty under s.174 of the Criminal Justice Act 2003 to give reasons for, and explain the effect of, the sentence. Finally, at step nine the court should consider whether to give credit for time spent on bail in accordance with s.240A of that Act.

Online or "cyber" offending

3.150   The sentencing ranges suggested in the SGC guideline for s.8 all presupposed physical contact between the offender and the victim and so gave no guidance to a court required to sentence for offences committed remotely using the internet. As a result, different courts reached different conclusions as to how the sentencing of those cases should be approached. In *Attorney General's Reference (No.24 of 2011)*,[158] the Vice-President, Hughes LJ, said that:

---

[158] [2011] EWCA Crim 1960, at 8. See also *Butcher* [2009] EWCA Crim 1458, in which the Court said that where, as in that case, the offender had no physical contact with the victim and the offending amounted to "no more than incitement" over the internet, there had to be a significant reduction in the starting point and sentencing range.

" . . . offences of 'cyber sex', serious as they are, are, in ordinary terms at least, likely to be less serious than physical contact offences. There are a number of reasons for that. The obvious ones include the greater freedom of activity for any child when connected only electronically; correspondingly the reduced opportunities for coercion or influence and of course the absence of health risks or pregnancy."

However, in *Attorney General's Reference (No.35 of 2013)*[159] the Court said it did not construe the earlier decision "as intending in any way to dilute the seriousness on their own facts of offences such as these". It added that whilst offences of cyber sex are in one sense less serious than physical contact offences, they are arguably more difficult to prevent; and contact offences could be readily envisaged which are less serious than some cyber sex offences, particularly where those offences are in number. Further, the long-term effect on a child confronting personal exposure to a stranger is likely to be severe.

The Sentencing Council, by contrast, designed its guideline explicitly to cater for cyber offending. As the Council stated in the Preface to its consultation document[160]:   **3.151**

" . . . the Council has been mindful of the significant rise in sexual offences committed via the internet involving new and developing technologies, and has sought to tailor its approach to accommodate the factors and circumstances of a wide variety of offending behaviour."

Accordingly, the new s.8 guideline deliberately contemplates a wider range of possible harm than the SGC guideline, and as such is fully apt to cover cyber as well as contact offending. We therefore suggest that in sentencing cyber offences the courts should focus on the terms of the guideline itself and be cautious in citing earlier judicial comment on the subject. In short, the sentence for any particular cyber offence should turn, like that for a contact offence, on the application of the harm and culpability factors specified in the guideline; and the offence ought not to be regarded as mitigated (or aggravated) by reason of the fact that it was committed online. The fly in the ointment, as regards cyber offences contrary to s.8, is the statement in the new guideline for ss.9 and 10 (sexual activity with a child and causing or inciting a child to engage in sexual activity) that: "This guideline also applies to offences committed remotely/online". It is unfortunate that a similar statement was not included in the s.8 guideline.[161] But given the clear statement in the Preface to the consultation document cited above, we trust that its absence will not mislead sentencing courts into thinking that the s.8 guideline does not cater for cyber offending.

---

[159] [2013] EWCA Crim 1757.
[160] Sexual Offences Guideline Consultation, Dec 2012, p.5.
[161] Though its inclusion in the guideline for ss.9 and 10 has not resolved all problems arising in relation to the sentencing of cyber offences committed under s.10: see the discussion in paras 4.77 and following, below.

Should offences of "incitement" attract lower sentences than offences of "causing"?

3.152   There is nothing in the new guideline to suggest that a s.8 offence should attract a lesser sentence merely because it involved inciting rather than causing sexual activity. If the Sentencing Council had intended offences of incitement routinely to attract a lesser sentence than offences of causing, it would surely have said so. In fact, all it said was that an offence will be mitigated where "sexual activity was incited but no activity took place because the offender voluntarily desisted or intervened to prevent it". Although the mitigating factors specified in the guideline are not exhaustive, the implication of this wording is that if sexual activity was incited but did not take place for some *other* reason, e.g. the victim refused or the police intervened, the offender cannot expect a reduction in sentence.

3.153   It is, however, clear from the decision in *Attorney General's Reference (No.94 of 2014)*,[162] relating to the s.10 offence of inciting sexual activity with a child, that an offence of incitement under s.8 in which no sexual activity occurred should not be placed in category 2 merely because the activity incited involved penetration. Instead, in accordance with the reasoning in that decision, such an offence will fall within category 3, regardless of the nature of the sexual activity incited, unless one or more of the *other* harm factors specified in the guideline applies, i.e. severe psychological or physical harm, additional degradation/humiliation, abduction, prolonged detention/ sustained incident, violence or threats of violence, forced/uninvited entry into the victim's home, or the child is particularly vulnerable due to extreme youth and/or personal circumstances. See further the discussion in paras 4.81 and following, below.

3.154   In this context it is worth mentioning *Attorney General's Reference (No.28 of 2010)* (also known as *Charnley*),[163] which predates the Sentencing Council guideline but nonetheless is instructive as to the sentencing of s.8 offences committed by an offender who commissions the horrific sexual exploitation of vulnerable children overseas in order to view it by webcam for his own sexual gratification. In that case the Attorney General referred as unduly lenient a total sentence of five years' imprisonment imposed after C pleaded guilty to 23 counts relating to the horrific sexual abuse of vulnerable children aged 2–17 in many different countries. Counts 1–19 charged him with making indecent photographs of a child, counts 20–22 with causing or inciting a child under 13 to engage in sexual activity not involving penetration, and count 23 with causing or inciting a child under 13 to engage in sexual activity involving penetration.[164] Over a period of 18 months C had made, downloaded and retained 110,000 still images and 356 films depicting

---

[162] [2014] EWCA Crim 2752.
[163] [2010] EWCA Crim 1996.
[164] The charges are so described in the official transcript. However, if C was indeed charged with "causing or inciting" then the indictment was duplicitous: see para.3.132, above.

indecent acts with children. The children lived in dire circumstances and C had exploited their vulnerability. He had paid adults to sexually abuse them and, using his computer, he had directed, watched and filmed the activities in real time, issuing instructions about the abuse that he wanted to see. That abuse involved children being tied up and penetrated, vaginally, anally and orally. The judge sentenced C, who was of previous good character, to a total of four years' imprisonment on counts 1–19, three years on counts 20–22 and five years on count 23, the terms to run concurrently. The Court of Appeal allowed the Reference on the ground that the judge had made two major errors. First, he had made no reference to the aggravating features. The offences were planned, they involved acts of penetration, there were multiple victims and there were sustained and repeated assaults on vulnerable children. The overall sentence was wholly inadequate and did not begin to meet the gravity of the offences or reflect the fact that the victims were young, vulnerable children. The fact that the victims were on the other side of the world and that the offences were enabled by modern communications was no mitigation, indeed, it was an aggravating factor. Secondly, the judge had erred in ordering the sentences to run concurrently. They were separate offences committed against separate children, and each merited severe punishment. Offenders such as C needed to be deterred and their victims needed protection. Nothing in the previous authorities or in the SGC guideline grappled with offending like C's. In respect of counts 1–19, the starting point after a trial would have been around seven years' imprisonment. Given the guilty plea, the four-year sentence would not be altered. On counts 20–22 the starting point after a trial would again have been around seven years' imprisonment. The three-year sentence was too low and would be replaced with a consecutive four-year term. The starting point on count 23, after a trial, would have been around 13 years' imprisonment, with a range of 11–17 years. Allowing for the guilty plea, the appropriate sentence was one of eight years' imprisonment, to be served consecutively to the four-year sentence on counts 1–19 and concurrently with the four-year sentence on counts 20–22. Those were the very minimum sentences that could be imposed. There was no room for any deduction for double jeopardy or personal mitigation. The total sentence imposed was therefore one of 12 years' imprisonment.

PARTIES TO THE OFFENCE

Offences under s.8 may be committed by and against persons of either sex. **3.155**

In *Jones*,[165] the Court of Appeal rejected the argument that an offence of **3.156** incitement under s.8 requires proof that the defendant incited an identified or identifiable child. Thus, the offence can be committed by a person who, with the requisite intention, makes a statement which in specific terms directly

---

[165] [2007] EWCA Crim 1118.

incites a child under the age of 13 to engage in sexual activity, whether or not the statement is addressed to any specific or identifiable person. The appellant in *Jones* had left graffiti messages on toilet doors in trains and at stations seeking girls aged 8 to 13 for sex and giving a mobile telephone number. He was charged under s.62 of the 2003 Act in relation to these messages, but the Court indicated that he could properly have been charged with incitement contrary to s.8. It follows by analogy that the incitement offence will be committed by a person who posts a message of this sort on an internet website or in a blog.

JURISDICTION

3.157   By virtue of s.72 of and Sch.2 to the Sexual Offences Act 2003, as amended,[166] it is an offence under s.8 for a UK national to do an act in a country outside the UK which would constitute a s.8 offence if done in England and Wales. See further para.3.72, above.

"CAUSES OR INCITES ANOTHER PERSON . . ."

3.158   For the meaning of "causes another person", see para.2.98, above. As for "incite", its usual meaning is to suggest, propose, persuade or induce.[167] Incitement involves some form of encouragement and includes the use of threats or other forms of pressure.[168] In *Grout*,[169] the Court of Appeal said that the essence of the s.8 offence of "incitement" is "the intentional seeking to bring about something by encouragement or persuasion". The Home Office guidance on the Act states:

> "Examples of an adult causing or inciting a child to engage in sexual activity could be promising a reward, persuading a child that it is perfectly acceptable behaviour that other children engage in all the time and he/she would be abnormal not to agree, or saying that it was necessary to check the child's body for bruises/lice etc., or to try on clothes."[170]

3.159   A person (A) may convicted of the incitement offence even where the sexual activity does not for any reason take place, e.g. because B refuses to engage in it, or a third party intervenes, or A changes his mind and countermands the pressure he previously placed on B. As a matter of principle, the offence is complete only if the incitement comes to the attention of B. Thus if A sends B, aged 12, an email or text message encouraging him to engage in sexual activity, but the message for some reason does not reach B (e.g. it is sent to the wrong email address or phone, or is intercepted and deleted by B's

---

[166] By the Criminal Justice and Immigration Act 2008 s.72, with effect from July 14, 2008.
[167] *Goldman* [2001] Crim. L.R. 822.
[168] *Fitzmaurice* [1983] Q.B. 1083; *Invicta Plastics Ltd v Clare* [1976] Crim. L.R. 131; *Marlow* [1997] Crim. L.R. 897.
[169] [2011] EWCA Crim 299, at [26].
[170] H.O. Circular 21/2004: *Guidance on Part 1 of the Sexual Offences Act 2003*, para.40.

parents), A cannot be convicted under s.8 of inciting B, though he may be guilty of an attempt.[171] If the message does not itself incite sexual activity but merely seeks to engineer a preliminary meeting at which A intends that incitement will take place, then the sending of the message will be at most an act preparatory to incitement and will not qualify as an attempt.[172] It is clear that A may be convicted under s.8 even if it was B who took the initiative. Suppose B, aged 12, places a message on the internet inviting interested people to contact him for sex. If A sends B an email taking him up on his invitation, he will be guilty of attempting to commit the s.8 incitement offence when he sends the email, and of committing that offence once it is received.[173]

An instructive case is *Jones*,[174] in which the appellant left graffiti messages   **3.160** on toilet doors in trains and at stations seeking girls aged 8 to 13 for sex and giving a mobile telephone number. A journalist who saw one of the messages texted him and the appellant replied in terms indicating that he was looking for an opportunity to incite a child to have penetrative sex. The journalist reported the matter to the police, who commenced an undercover operation in which a police officer posing as a 12-year-old girl called "Amy" exchanged text messages with the appellant. By this means a meeting was arranged at which the appellant was arrested. He was charged in relation to the graffiti messages under s.62 of the 2003 Act (committing an offence with intent to commit a sexual offence) and, in relation to Amy, with attempting to cause or incite a child under the age of 13 to engage in penetrative sexual activity.[175] The prosecution case in relation to the attempt charge was that, based upon the text messages exchanged, the appellant had intended to meet "Amy" and engage in penetrative sex with her. The appellant applied for this count to be stayed as an abuse of process on a number of grounds, including, first, that this was a case of entrapment by the police, and secondly, that he lacked the intention necessary for an attempt because he did not intend to incite an actual child to sexual activity, but an adult pretending to be a child. The stay was refused and the appellant was duly convicted. He appealed, renewing the two arguments that had failed at trial and adding a third, that he should have been charged instead with an attempt to commit the less serious offence under s.10 of the 2003 Act (causing or inciting a child under 16 to engage in sexual activity).

The Court of Appeal dismissed all these arguments. On entrapment,   **3.161** following an extensive citation of authority[176] it held that by sending the text messages the police had neither incited nor instigated the crime nor lured the

---

[171] cf. *Ransford* (1874) 31 L.T. 488.
[172] cf. *Rowley* (1992) 94 Cr. App. R. 95.
[173] *Goldman* [2001] Crim. L.R. 822.
[174] [2007] EWCA Crim 1118.
[175] This was inappropriate, as "causing" and "inciting" are two separate offences: see para.3.132, above. It is clear from the facts that the appropriate charge was attempting to incite a child, etc, since no sexual activity took place, i.e. none was caused.
[176] Including in particular *Looseley* [2001] UKHL 53.

appellant into committing it. They had simply provided him with an opportunity to commit an offence which he had already attempted to commit in his text exchanges with the journalist, but in circumstances in which no harm could come to the victim.

3.162   Secondly, in relation to the appellant's argument that he had not intended to incite an actual child under 13, the Court followed the decision of the House of Lords in *Shivpuri*[177] to the effect that a person may be convicted of an attempt if they do an act that is more than merely preparatory to the full offence, intending to commit that offence, although the commission of the full offence is, on the true facts, impossible. It was clear on the evidence that the appellant had intended to incite a child under 13 to engage in penetrative sexual activity and he had done an act more than merely preparatory to the commission of a s.8 offence. It was impossible for him to complete the offence only because the person whom he intended to incite, Amy, was not in fact aged under 13. This impossibility did not preclude his conviction for attempted incitement.

3.163   The appellant's third argument was that he had been charged with a more serious offence than was warranted. It was, he said, only because the police had chosen Amy's age as 12 that he was charged with attempting the offence under s.8. If they had instead chosen to tell him that Amy was 13, he would have been charged with attempting the less serious offence under s.10. There was no evidence that it mattered to him that Amy was 12 rather than 13, nor that he would have behaved any differently had Amy claimed to be 13. In rejecting this argument the Court said that the police had not acted improperly by choosing 12 rather than 13 as Amy's age. The appellant's graffiti messages were directed to girls aged 8 to 13. It was the appellant who asked Amy her age and, when she gave it as 12, from that point on the appellant believed that he was inciting a child under 13. In those circumstances he was properly charged with attempting the more serious offence under s.8.

" . . . To Engage in an Activity"

3.164 For the meaning of this term, see paras 2.99 and following, above. In *Grout*,[178] the Court of Appeal accepted for the purposes of that case that:

> "'activity' on the part of the child could embrace 'the activity' of conversation or sending text or MSN messages, depending on the circumstances."

"The Activity is Sexual"

3.165 A must cause or incite B to engage in sexual activity; it is not sufficient for A to engage in sexual activity directed towards B. This is so even if A's

---

[177] [1987] A.C. 1.
[178] [2011] EWCA Crim 299, at [29].

activity is designed to groom B or "soften him up" in preparation for engaging in sexual activity, if it falls short of actually inciting such activity. Thus in *Grout*[179] the Court of Appeal said:

> "The . . . offences created by section 8 are directed towards a defendant who intentionally causes or incites *the child*, that is (B) himself or herself, to engage in 'sexual activity'. The offence is not concerned with whether the defendant engages in sexual activity."

For the meaning of "sexual" in this context, see paras 2.66 and following, above. To take a simple example, if A asks B to show him her underwear, this is likely (depending on the context) to amount to inciting sexual activity; but if he asks her what colour underwear she is wearing, he is most unlikely, without more, to be inciting activity of a sexual nature and no offence will be committed.[180] The point is well illustrated by *Broughton*,[181] where the appellant pleaded guilty to a number of counts under s.8 relating to text messages that he had exchanged with a young girl. Specifically, the appellant had (a) sent the girl "rude" messages, which she acknowledged in neutral terms, in which he spoke of "feeling her up", having her in bed with him and wanting her to have an orgasm, (b) pestered her to take a photograph of her vagina and send it to him, which she eventually did, and (c) sent her in response two images of his erect penis. On his appeal against sentence, the Court of Appeal considered what sexual activity the appellant had caused or incited the girl to engage in[182]:

> "The text messages were not coupled with any direct suggestion of meeting for sexual activity, although there were clearly messages which were expressions of the appellant's fantasies to that effect. It does not seem to us that sending the child such photographs of himself for her simply to look at necessarily involved the causing or inciting *her* to engage in sexual activity; whereas the taking of the photograph of herself, which he also incited, in our judgment was sexual activity in the light of the definitions contained in s.8 of the 2003 Act. Count 2 . . . alleged that the appellant committed this offence by sending her the sexually explicit text messages over the full period. Those were expressions of his sexual fantasies, unhealthy and unpleasant as they were, including fantasies about sexual activity with this child, rather than acts that positively incited, let alone caused *her* to engage in sexual activity."

These comments are, with respect, well-founded. On the evidence, a guilty plea was appropriate only in respect of the appellant's conduct in persuading the girl to take and send to him a photograph of her vagina, which was properly to be regarded as causing her to engage in sexual activity. The other counts related to conduct that, whilst reprehensible, fell short of a s.8 offence. If the girl had responded to the appellant's messages with texts of a sexual

---

[179] [2011] EWCA Crim 299, at [28].
[180] cf. *Grout* [2011] EWCA Crim 299, in which a count under s.8 alleging that the defendant asked the complainant the colour of her underwear was not left to the jury for this reason. The authors are indebted to HH Judge Leonard QC for drawing their attention to this point.
[181] [2007] EWCA Crim 566.
[182] At [12].

nature, this could have qualified as "sexual activity" caused by him. But in fact her texts were "neutral" in tone. As to whether the appellant's conduct in sending the girl images of his erect penis could have been the subject of a charge under s.12 of the 2003 Act, see para.4.135, below.

"Child under 13"

3.166 For the meaning of this term and proof of age, see paras 3.73 and following, above.

Consent

3.167 The offence is committed regardless of whether B consents. For the effect of consent on sentence, see paras 3.50 and following, above.

Mental Element

3.168 In *Grout*,[183] the Court of Appeal said that for the purposes of s.8:

> "The causing or inciting must be intentional, i.e. deliberate; recklessness or less will not do."

See further the discussion in paras 2.105 and following (mental element of the s.4 offence of causing a person to engage in sexual activity without consent) and 3.77 and following (mental element of rape of a child under 13), above.

3.169 In *Walker*,[184] the appellant rang a telephone box near to which children were playing and, when the complainant answered, asked her to show him her "fanny". He was convicted of the incitement offence under s.8 but appealed on the basis that he had not intended the girl to act on his words. The Court of Appeal upheld the conviction, on the basis that the offence may be committed although the defendant did not intend that the incited activity should take place. This is a surprising decision, given that incitement is usually defined as seeking to bring something about through encouragement or persuasion: see para.3.158, above.

3.170 In the light of the decision in *Heard*,[185] the authors suggest that it is not open to a defendant charged under s.8 to contend that voluntary intoxication through drink or drugs prevented him from intending to incite the victim to engage in sexual activity.

---

[183] [2011] EWCA Crim 299, at [26], citing *Heard*; [2007] EWCA Crim 125, at [22] per Hughes LJ.
[184] [2006] EWCA Crim 1907.
[185] [2007] EWCA Crim 125, discussed in paras 2.81 and following, above.

CHAPTER 4

CHILD SEX OFFENCES

Introduction.................................... 4.01
Development of the Child Sex
    Offences...................................... 4.02
Child Sex Offences Committed by
    Children...................................... 4.10
Demise of the Marriage Exception:
    Where Does This Leave the Law? 4.17
Use of Civil Orders to Protect
    Children from Sexual
    Exploitation................................ 4.18
Multiple Offending and Form of
    Indictment................................... 4.19
Sexual Activity with a Child............ 4.20
Causing or Inciting a Child to
    Engage in Sexual Activity........... 4.67
Engaging in Sexual Activity in the
    Presence of a Child.................... 4.94
Causing a Child to Watch a Sexual
    Act... 4.121
Child Sex Offences Committed by
    Children or Young Persons......... 4.144
Arranging or Facilitating the
    Commission of a Child Sex
    Offence...................................... 4.160
Meeting a Child Following Sexual
    Grooming etc. 4.186
Sexual Communication with a
    Child.. 4.225
Possession of a Paedophile Manual. 4.248

INTRODUCTION

This chapter deals with the sex offences which protect children under the age **4.01**
of 16. The offences, most of which are found in the Sexual Offences Act 2003,
are as follows:

- Sexual activity with a child (s.9 of the 2003 Act)
- Causing or inciting a child to engage in sexual activity (s.10)
- Engaging in sexual activity in the presence of a child (s.11)
- Causing a child to watch a sexual act (s.12)
- Child sex offences committed by children or young persons (s.13)
- Arranging or facilitating the commission of a child sex offence (s.14)
- Meeting a child following sexual grooming etc. (s.15)
- Sexual communication with a child (s.15A)
- Possession of a paedophile manual (s.69 of the Serious Crime Act 2015).

DEVELOPMENT OF THE CHILD SEX OFFENCES

Sexual Offences Review

4.02   The offences in ss.9–15 of the Sexual Offences Act 2003 arose out of the Sexual Offences Review, established by the Home Secretary in 1999. The Review identified overwhelmingly strong arguments for a establishing a set of gender-neutral sex offences relating to children, to mark their particular need for protection and society's disapproval of adult sexual activity with them.[1] The major offences relating specifically to children at the time of the review, all of which were abolished by the 2003 Act, were as follows:

Sexual Offences Act 1956

- Unlawful sexual intercourse with a girl under 13 (maximum penalty life imprisonment)
- Unlawful sexual intercourse with a girl under 16 (maximum penalty two years' imprisonment)
- Anal intercourse (buggery) with a child under 18 (maximum penalty life imprisonment where the child was under 16)
- Indecent assault (a child under 16 could not in law consent so as to prevent an act being such an assault) (maximum penalty 10 years' imprisonment)

Indecency with Children Act 1960

- Gross indecency with or towards a child under 14 (maximum penalty 10 years' imprisonment)

4.03   Although these offences provided fairly comprehensive protection for children, they were open to criticism on a number of grounds identified by the Review:

Lack of coherence: the offences had been created piecemeal over time and dealt differently with different kinds of abuse depending on the nature of the act, so providing varying and incoherent levels of protection for boys and girls. The Review's starting point was that the law should provide protection for all children under the age of 16.

Differing defences: defences were available to some of the offences but not others. Particularly controversial was the so-called "young man's defence" to the offence of unlawful sexual intercourse with a girl under 16, which was available to a man aged between 16 and 24 who had not previously been charged with a like offence who reasonably believed the girl to be 16 or over.

---

[1] *Setting the Boundaries* (Home Office, July 2000), paras 3.1.5, 3.1.6. The report is available at *http://webarchive.nationalarchives.gov.uk/-/http:/www.homeoffice.gov.uk/documents/vol1main.pdf-?view=Binary* [Accessed April 30, 2016].

This defence hindered the protection the law gave to girls and was not mirrored in respect of offences against boys.

Anomalous maximum penalties: there was no coherent relationship between the maxima for the offences: for example, a man who had unlawful sexual intercourse with a girl under 16 faced a maximum of two years' imprisonment, but if he indecently assaulted her (i.e. committed what would generally be a lesser offence) the maximum was 10 years, and if he buggered her it was life imprisonment.

Differing age thresholds: the age thresholds for the different offences varied, with no overall scheme being apparent.

Variable time-limits: there were 12-month time limits for two of the offences, unlawful sexual intercourse with a girl under 16 and gross indecency with a child. These time limits were a hindrance to effective child protection, particularly given the recognition that children may delay complaining about abuse until they feel in a safe position to do so, which may be many years after the offence. In relation to out-of-time offences of unlawful sexual intercourse, it was long-standing prosecutorial practice to charge indecent assault instead. This had the incidental effect of enhancing the maximum penalty for the conduct in question from two years' to 10 years' imprisonment, and in recognition of this, the Court of Appeal had ruled that sentencing in such cases should be carried out on the basis of the tariff for the "lesser" offence.[2] However, in *R. v J*,[3] the House of Lords held that the practice of charging indecent assault where the offence of unlawful sexual intercourse was time-barred was impermissible, because it deprived the statutory bar of meaningful effect. The current state of the law in the light of that decision and subsequent authorities is that, where intercourse with a girl under the age of 16 took place before the commencement of the Sexual Offences Act 2003 (May 1, 2004) and a charge of unlawful sexual intercourse is now time-barred, indecent assault cannot be charged instead, either on its own (as in *R. v J*) or as an alternative to a charge of rape.[4] But if in such a case the defendant is charged with rape, the judge may properly leave indecent assault to the jury as an alternative verdict.[5] The Court of Appeal in *Cottrell and Fletcher* noted the fortuitous impact of the case law where indecent assault is charged as an alternative to rape (unacceptable) and where it is left to the jury as an alternative verdict (acceptable). In *Timmins* it certified the point as one of general public importance, but the House of Lords refused leave to appeal. One may speculate that this was because the number of cases in which the distinction could be significant was small even

---

[2] cf. *Quayle* (1993) 14 Cr. App. R.(S.) 726; *Hinton* (1995) 16 Cr. App. R.(S.) 523; *Figg* [2003] EWCA Crim 2751; *Cronshaw* [2004] EWCA Crim 2057.

[3] [2004] UKHL 42; [2005] 1 A.C. 562.

[4] *R. v WR* [2005] EWCA Crim 1907; *Cottrell and Fletcher* [2007] EWCA Crim 2016.

[5] *Timmins* [2005] EWCA Crim 2909; [2006] 1 Cr. App. R. 18; *Phillips* [2007] EWCA Crim 485.

at that time and was destined to get smaller, being confined to cases predating the 2003 Act. The law is nonetheless in an unsatisfactory state.[6]

4.04   The Sexual Offences Review concluded that the law, with its distinctions based on the sex and age of the child and the nature of the act involved, was unnecessarily complex and confusing. It reached a number of conclusions about how the law should be re-shaped:

Age of consent: as a matter of public policy the age of legal consent should remain at 16. The Review recognised that children now mature physically much earlier than they used to and are exposed to sexual images and pressure to engage in sexual activity by the media and by their peers when they are very young. However, it considered that the overriding need is to protect children from inappropriate sexual activity at too early an age when it has the potential to cause physical, emotional and psychological harm. The existing age of consent, at 16, was well established, well understood and well supported, and should be retained.

Under 13s unable to give effective consent: the law relating to sexual offences against children should state that below the age of 13, a child cannot effectively consent to sexual activity. This aspect is considered further in para.3.02, above.

Offence of adult sexual abuse of a child: the Review said that one of the key issues to emerge from its consultation was the need for the law to establish beyond any doubt that adults should not engage in sexual activity with children, and that this warranted the creation of a serious offence. It concluded that the non-consensual offences of rape, assault by penetration and sexual assault should be available for use as needed, but that there should be a separate offence covering behaviour that would not be an offence if committed between consenting adults but that was wrong and inappropriate where children were involved. The offence should apply where a person of 18 or over (a) was involved in penetration of a child under 16, (b) undertook any sexual act towards or with such a child, (c) incited, induced or compelled a child to carry out a sexual act, whether on the adult, another person or the child himself, or (d) made a child witness a sexual act (whether live or recorded). Only the adult should be liable to conviction; the child should not be criminally liable, however much they might appear to have consented, aided or abetted the offence.

4.05   *Defence of mistaken belief as to age*: the Review recognised that the question whether there should be a defence of mistaken belief as to age involved addressing a tension between the interests of justice and of fairness to defendants and the interests of child protection. On the one hand, an adult may meet a child in a situation where they expect them to be over 16, e.g. in a pub or club, and the child may appear and claim to be older than they are. If the meeting leads to a sexual relationship, the adult may have sex with an

---

[6] For trenchant but well-aimed criticism of *R. v J* and its consequences, see Jonathan Rogers, *Fundamentally objectionable* [2007] N.L.J. 1252–3.

under-age child with no intention to do so. On the other hand, it is all too easy falsely to claim an honest mistake. The Review concluded that there should be a defence of mistake as to the age of the child, restricted to cases where the belief was honest and reasonable and the defendant had taken all reasonable steps to ascertain the child's age.

Defence of marriage: the Review noted that it was a defence to unlawful sexual intercourse with a girl under 16 that the defendant reasonably believed the girl to be his wife, even where the marriage was invalid under UK law. The Review's aim of increasing the protection of children from sexual abuse made it reluctant to agree to the continuation of this defence. However, it recognised that some countries have a low legal age of marriage, and that a man who has married a young girl in one of those countries would believe that he was acting quite properly in having sex with his wife. Moreover, the UK has obligations under international law to recognise valid overseas marriages, and it would be difficult to claim to be doing this if sexual contact between the spouses was criminalised. The Review therefore "very reluctantly" concluded that it should be a defence to the child sex offences that the defendant was or believed he was validly married to the child. But it noted that the proposal for an absolute age of "no consent" at 13 meant that the defence would not be available where the child-spouse was below that age.

Offence of sexual activity between minors: the Review considered how the law should deal with sexual activity by those under 18 with children under 16. It recognised that children can and do coerce and abuse each other, and that sexual relations between children are capable of being exploitative. But it also acknowledged that much sexual activity between teenagers is sexual experimentation carried out with mutual agreement, where there is no public interest in prosecuting and criminalisation might deter the individuals concerned from seeking help and advice relating to their sexual health. There was a very difficult balance to be struck between ensuring that the law is appropriate, fair and effective in enabling a range of coercive activity to be dealt with, and avoiding the criminalisation of young people for mutually agreed sexual behaviour. It concluded that, in addition to the non-consensual offences of rape, assault by penetration and sexual assault, there should be a separate offence mirroring the offence of adult sexual abuse of a child and covering behaviour by those aged under 18 with those under 16. The offence should be used where behaviour was not mutually agreed, but was exploitative and coercive. This would make the law clearer and more accessible to children and, the Review hoped, provide better protection by acting as a more effective deterrent to underage sexual activity.

The Government broadly accepted these recommendations in the White **4.06** Paper *Protecting the Public*.[7] However, the White Paper's proposals went beyond *Setting the Boundaries* in one key respect, by proposing a new offence

---

[7] *Protecting the Public: strengthening protection against sex offenders and reforming the law on sexual offences* (Cm 5668) (Nov 2002).

of sexual grooming designed to catch adults who undertake a course of conduct with a child under 16 leading to a meeting where the adult intends to engage in sexual activity with the child. This would, the Government said, enable the law to tackle those who take advantage of the innocence of children by grooming them for sexual abuse, including by misuse of the internet.

Overlap between child sex offences and under-13 offences

4.07 When the Bill that became the Sexual Offences Act 2003 was introduced, it contained a set of child sex offences designed to implement the White Paper proposals in order to protect children aged 13 and over but under 16. A separate set of offences (which became ss.5 to 8 of the Act) was introduced to protect children under 13. However, as explained in para.3.05, above, the Government realised after some time that making these two sets of offences mutually exclusive could frustrate the objective of child protection, since it would be possible for a person charged with one of the child sex offences to defend himself on the basis that the child was, in fact, under 13 at the relevant time. Once this potential problem was identified, the Government introduced amendments to extend the child sex offences to cover children under 13, but with no mistake of age defence in relation to such children.[8] The result is that where, in a prosecution for a child sex offence, it emerges that the child was under 13 at the relevant time, the defendant may still be convicted of the offence charged.[9] The logical next step might have been to combine the two sets of offences, which would have had the beneficial effect of removing the duplication between them and simplifying the legislative scheme. But the Government did not take this step and came under no Parliamentary pressure to do so.

Developments subsequent to the 2003 Act

4.08 Since the enactment of the Sexual Offences Act 2003, there have been two important additions to the list of child sex offences. Both offences were created by the Serious Crime Act 2015. The first, which is not yet in force at the time of writing (April 29, 2016), is the offence of sexual communication with a child, contained in a new s.15A inserted in the 2003 Act. The offence had its origins in a campaign run in 2014 by the National Society for the Prevention of Cruelty to Children, with the aim of enhancing the protection

---

[8] cf. *Hansard*, HL, vol.646, col.1197ff, Lord Falconer of Thoroton (April 1, 2003).

[9] If the child is known to have been under 13 at the relevant time, the Government's wish and expectation as expressed during the debates on the Sexual Offences Bill was that the defendant should be prosecuted under ss.5–8, which are specifically designed to protect such children, and not with a child sex offence: cf. *Hansard*, HL, vol.648, col.1097, Lord Falconer of Thoroton (June 2, 2003). This position is reflected in the CPS's guidance to prosecutors: see *http://www.cps.gov.uk/legal/p_to_r/rape_and_sexual_offences/soa_2003_and_soa_1956/£a20* [Accessed April 30, 2016], under "Selecting charges".

of children from paedophiles who send them sexual messages, particularly online in the form of "sexualised chat", but without asking them to respond or act in any sexual way. After initial resistance, the Government conceded that there was a gap in the law relating to activity of this sort, and it amended the Serious Crime Bill to create the new offence.[10]

The second new offence, contained in s.69 of the Serious Crime Act 2015, **4.09** prohibits the possession of what is commonly referred to as a "paedophile manual", defined in the Act as "any item that contains advice or guidance about abusing children sexually." The offence owes its origins to a growing awareness of the existence, particularly online, of deeply disturbing material giving practical advice to paedophiles about how to commit a sexual offence against a child, e.g. how to entrap or "groom" them, where to find a child to abuse, and how to offend and escape capture. There was previously no offence that prohibited the possession of this sort of material. The Prime Minister announced in April 2014 that he intended to fill this gap,[11] and what became s.69 of the 2015 Act was duly included in the Serious Crime Bill on introduction.

CHILD SEX OFFENCES COMMITTED BY CHILDREN

The child sex offences were among the most closely scrutinised provisions of **4.10** the Sexual Offences Bill as it went through Parliament. The greatest controversy arose over what became s.13, which penalises child sex offences committed by children or young persons. This provision was keenly debated in both Houses, due to its effect in criminalising all consensual sexual activity between teenagers. Views were polarised on the wisdom and desirability of such a sweeping provision. Many members of both Houses took the view that teenage sexual activity is a fact of modern life and that the Act should acknowledge this.[12] Various examples were given to illustrate the width of the offence: it would, for example, criminalise children playing postman's knock, a young boyfriend and girlfriend engaged in experimental sexual fumbling and a schoolboy who shows his friend a pornographic magazine. As Dominic Grieve MP commented during the Second Reading debate:

> "things appear in a pretty stark light when we end up with five-year penalties for those who go behind the bicycle sheds to engage in some French kissing".[13]

---

[10] The origins of the new offence is explained more fully in paras 4.227 and following, below.

[11] *http://www.telegraph.co.uk/news/politics/10791387/Cameron-to-close-legal-loophole-that-lets-paedophiles-download-child-grooming-manuals.html* [Accessed April 30, 2016].

[12] See e.g. *Hansard*, HL, vol.646, col.1214, Baroness Walmsley, col.1216, the Earl of Listowel and col.1221, Baroness Howarth of Breckland (April 1, 2003); HL, vol.648, col.1103, Baroness Walmsley and col.1105, Baroness Howarth of Breckland (June 2, 2003). See also Nicola Lacey, *Beset by Boundaries: The Home Office Review of Sexual Offences* [2001] Crim. L.R. 3, at p.9.

[13] *Hansard*, HC, vol.409, col.194 (July 15, 2003).

In fact, the French element is not essential: any kissing involving a child under 16 will fall within the scope of the offence provided the jury consider it to be "sexual".

4.11 The then Home Secretary, David Blunkett MP, responded to the barrage of criticism with a "champagne challenge", offering a magnum of champagne to anyone who solved the conundrum of how to protect children aged 13 to 16 from inappropriate sexual behaviour by their peers whilst not criminalising activity that is widely regarded as a normal part of adolescent development.[14] A number of amendments were tabled during the passage of the Bill that would have addressed the issue in different ways, including by removing the offence altogether; adding a requirement of absence of consent; imposing an obligation on the Attorney General to issue guidance to prosecutors on when the offence should be prosecuted; and requiring the consent of the Director of Public Prosecutions for particular prosecutions. But the Government was not persuaded by any of these proposals and the Home Secretary's magnum remained in the fridge.

4.12 In defending s.13, the Government noted that approximately one third of sexual assaults against children were committed by other young people,[15] and said that there had to be adequate sanctions to protect children from such abuse.[16] To be effective in achieving this, the law had to be clear that sexual activity below the age of consent is not lawful. Legalising sexual activity between minors would tend to undermine the age of consent, by sending the message that sexual activity below that age is normal and acceptable That would encourage more children to engage in such activity before they are emotionally and physically ready to cope with the consequences.

4.13 The Government conceded that under-age sexual activity covers a wide variety of circumstances and asserted that, where it is genuinely consensual, it is "extraordinarily unlikely"[17] that the Crown Prosecution Service will decide that prosecution is in the public interest. It noted that there had been no problem about this issue under the existing law, in the sense that there was no body of complaint that cases were being wrongly prosecuted. There may, though, be cases involving children in which there is insufficient evidence to support a charge of a non-consensual offence (i.e. an offence under ss.1 to 4 of the 2003 Act), but there *is* evidence to suggest the activity is exploitative or coercive, such that prosecution is appropriate. Those cases, said the Government, cannot be defined by Parliament, as legislation cannot capture the complexity of every situation that may arise; decisions on prosecution

[14] *Hansard*, HC, vol.409, col.195, the Home Secretary (July 15, 2003).
[15] cf. NSPCC Report (2000), finding that between 25 per cent and 40 per cent of all sexual assaults on youths are committed by juveniles.
[16] *Hansard*, HL, vol.646, col.1223ff, Lord Falconer of Thoroton (April 1, 2003); vol.648, col.1107, Lord Falconer of Thoroton (June 2, 2003); vol.649, col.689, Baroness Scotland of Asthal (June 17, 2003). See also *Hansard*, HL, vol.646, col.1213, Baroness Blatch and col.1220, the Bishop of Guildford (April 1, 2003); HL, vol.648, col.1106, Baroness Blatch and col.1106, the Bishop of Chester (June 2, 2003).
[17] *Hansard*, HL vol.646, col.1224, Lord Falconer of Thoroton (April 1, 2003).

need to be taken by the CPS after a thorough assessment of the circumstances of each case. The Government's wish and expectation, however, was that children engaging in under-age sexual activity should not be prosecuted, nor issued with a reprimand or final warning, unless there is clear evidence of exploitation, and it undertook that published guidance to that effect would be issued to the CPS.[18] In the light of this assurance, none of the amendments was put to a vote.

The Government's argument has utilitarian merit, since the wide drafting **4.14** of the under-16 offences will ensure that no case involving a child under that age which is deserving of prosecution falls outside their scope. But one must ask whether it is consonant with the rule of law to create offences in such broad terms and then rely on the wisdom of prosecutors to decide when to invoke them.[19] The Government's position rested on the expectation that the Crown Prosecution Service would exercise its prosecutorial discretion wisely. The CPS did indeed issue guidance to prosecutors following the commencement of the Act.[20] For comment on that guidance, as it applies to decisions as to the prosecution of child suspects, see para.3.13, above.

The key question here, in legal terms, is when the prosecution of a child for **4.15** committing a child sex offence will and will not be compatible with the child's rights under art.8 of the ECHR. There has been no reported decision on this point since the 2003 Act was passed. In the pre-Act decision in *E v DPP*,[21] a prosecution was held compatible with art.8 in a case involving consensual sexual activity between teenagers. Two 15-year-olds had consensual sex and the boy was convicted by the magistrates of unlawful sexual intercourse with a girl under 16 (contrary to s.6(1) of the Sexual Offences Act 1956). On appeal, the Divisional Court rejected the argument that the prosecution breached the boy's art.8 rights. It held that, having regard to the "tender age" of those involved, proscription of consensual sexual intercourse between 15-year-olds does not constitute an interference with private life within the meaning of art.8(1). Moreover, even if it did, the proscription would be justified under art.8(2) because of the need to protect girls from the risk of pregnancy. The decision is very short and not fully satisfactory. It is hard to see how the fact that those affected are of "tender age" prevented the offence from interfering with their art.8 rights. The age of the individuals concerned, and the legislative aim of protecting the young, are surely relevant to whether the offence could be justified under art.8(2) rather than to whether it interfered with private life, which it would seem clearly to do. As for

[18] See *Hansard*, HL, vol.649, col.689, Baroness Scotland of Asthal (June 17, 2003); HC, Standing Committee B, September 11, 2003, col.123, Paul Goggins M.P. See also H.O. Circular 21/2004: *Guidance on Part 1 of the Sexual Offences Act 2003*, para.72.
[19] An objection to the under-13 offences based on art.8 ECHR cannot be sustained in light of the decision of the House of Lords in *R. v. G* [2008] UKHL 37, discussed in paras 3.14 and following, above.
[20] See *http://www.cps.gov.uk/legal/p_to_r/rape_and_sexual_offences/* [Accessed April 30, 2016].
[21] [2005] EWHC 147 (Admin).

justification, the Court simply assumed that pregnancy risk was sufficient for this purpose without the benefit of evidence, e.g. as to the availability and use of contraception among children under 16 who engage in sexual activity. Further, the Court focused on the justification of the offence itself and did not consider whether its prosecution in this case was proportionate. For all these reasons, we suggest that the decision should not be regarded as of instructive value as and when the point arises again.

4.16   Finally, the decision of the House of Lords in *R. v G*,[22] relating to the compatibility with art.8 of the ECHR of a prosecution under s.5 of the 2003 Act, does not determine the position as regards the child sex offences. In that case, a 15-year-old boy was prosecuted under s.5 after he had sexual intercourse with a girl of 12 who (on the basis of plea eventually accepted by the CPS) consented to the act and whom he reasonably believed also to be 15. The House of Lords held that there had been no breach of art.8. The majority opinions emphasise the need to protect children under 13, with the result that young people who engage in sexual activity with each other must take the risk that the other party is in fact under that age, in which case a prosecution for an under-13 offence will be justified under art.8. It is by no means self-evident that the same reasoning should apply where both parties are over 13 but under 16. Indeed, we submit that it should not, and that in such circumstances the compatibility of a prosecution with art.8 should turn on the merits of the particular case. Further, we suggest that art.8 should operate to prevent a prosecution in the case of truly consensual, non-exploitative sexual activity between such children, at least where they are close in age and maturity or understanding.

DEMISE OF THE MARRIAGE EXCEPTION: WHERE DOES THIS LEAVE THE LAW?

4.17   The Sexual Offences Bill, when introduced, contained an exception for conduct between married couples which would otherwise involve an offence under what became ss.9 to 13 of the 2003 Act. This exception was removed by Government amendment at a late stage, on the basis that "someone should not be able to engage in sexual activity with a child under the age of consent just because the two are married".[23] This runs counter to the line taken, albeit "very reluctantly", by the Sexual Offences Review and staunchly defended by the Government in the face of strong criticism at earlier stages of the Bill's passage.[24] In dropping the exception, the Government made no mention of the UK's obligations under international law to recognise valid marriages. In the absence of specific provision on the point in the 2003 Act, the better view is that the existence of a valid and subsisting

---

[22] [2008] UKHL 37, discussed in paras 3.14 and following, above.
[23] *Hansard*, HL, vo. 654, col.1627, Baroness Scotland of Asthal (November 13, 2003).
[24] See e.g. Standing Committee B, September 16, 2003, col.275ff.

marriage between the parties cannot provide a defence to a prosecution for a child sex offence. However, the right to private and family life guaranteed by art.8 ECHR must, in the case of lawfully married spouses, include a right to engage in sexual congress together. Accordingly, if the CPS were to prosecute for a child sex offence a person who had engaged in sexual conduct with their child spouse, its decision could be challenged by way of judicial review as an unnecessary or disproportionate interference with the parties' art.8 rights.[25] In the event of such a challenge, the court would be required to rule on whether, in effect, the international law obligation to recognise the marriage ought to prevail over international law obligations to protect children from sexual exploitation, as reflected in the 2003 Act. To be clear, this issue relates only to marriages validly contracted overseas between persons domiciled in the relevant jurisdiction. An individual domiciled in England and Wales cannot contract a valid marriage here or in any other jurisdiction if they or the other person are under the age of 16.[26]

USE OF CIVIL ORDERS TO PROTECT CHILDREN FROM SEXUAL EXPLOITATION

A notable recent development has been the use of the civil law to protect **4.18** abused children from continued sexual exploitation. The subject falls outside the scope of this work, but it is important to mention the decision in *Birmingham City Council v Riaz*,[27] which involved a "bold and innovative" application by the Council, made with the support of West Midlands police, for the Family Court to use its inherent jurisdiction to make injunctive orders to prevent men who had abused a girl of 17 ("AB") from contacting her or other young females. The application was made because there was insufficient evidence to prosecute any of the men. Keehan J found to the civil standard that all 10 respondents had been engaged in the sexual exploitation of AB, and that there was a real risk that, unless prohibited from doing so, each of them would seek to exploit sexually other vulnerable young females under 18. Accordingly, the judge was satisfied that it was fair, necessary and proportionate to make orders which, in essence, prohibited each of the men

[25] cf. *Alhaji Mohamed v Knott* [1969] 1 Q.B. 1, DC, in which the appellant, a Nigerian citizen, cohabited in England with a girl of 13 to whom he was married under Nigerian law. The question before the court was whether the girl was in need of care, protection or control in that she was exposed to "moral danger" within the meaning of s.2 of the Children and Young Persons Act 1963. The court recognised the marriage as valid and held that the girl could not be in moral danger merely because she carried out her "wifely duties". It was suggested in argument by the respondent that each time the couple had intercourse, the appellant committed an offence of unlawful sexual intercourse with a girl under 16 (s.6 of the Sexual Offences Act 1956). Lord Parker, CJ reached no concluded view on this point, but said he did not "think the police could ever properly prosecute in a case such as that if the marriage is a marriage recognised by this country" (at 16B–17A).
[26] Marriage Act 1949 s.2; Matrimonial Causes Act 1973 s.11; *Pugh v Pugh* [1951] P 482; and see *A local authority v X* [2013] EWHC 3274 (Fam).
[27] [2014] EWHC 4247 (Fam).

from contacting or approaching AB or from approaching in a public place any other female under the age of 18 not previously associated with him. The decision demonstrates the potential value of the civil injunction as a means of curtailing the activities of those who exploit children sexually. However, as pointed out in para.36.77, below, in many cases it is likely to be more efficient and economical for the police to seek a Sexual Risk Order against the exploiter. In any event the decision in *Riaz* should be contrasted with that in *Barking and Dagenham LBC v SS*,[28] in which Hayden J held that it was inappropriate to make a secure accommodation order in respect of a 15-year-old girl who had been the victim of sex trafficking and had twice absconded from her foster home in order to return to those who had exploited her. Although there was a real possibility of further absconding, with a risk of emotional and physical harm, a secure accommodation order would be an unjustified restriction of her liberty and she required therapeutic support which could be provided in her foster home. It would be possible to read too much into these decisions, but taken together they may indicate a welcome recognition by the Family Court that in so far as the civil law has a role in this area, it lies in constraining the unlawful activities of the exploiters of children rather than in restricting the liberties of their child victims in order, as it were, to protect the children from themselves.

MULTIPLE OFFENDING AND FORM OF INDICTMENT

4.19 It can be especially difficult to frame an indictment in cases involving multiple offences committed against a child over a period of perhaps years, where the complainant is unable to recall other than in vague terms when the various offences took place. For a discussion of how the prosecution should proceed in such cases, see paras 33.24 and following, below.

SEXUAL ACTIVITY WITH A CHILD

DEFINITION

4.20 Section 9(1) of the Sexual Offences Act 2003 provides:

"A person aged 18 or over (A) commits an offence if—
  (a) he intentionally touches another person (B),
  (b) the touching is sexual, and
  (c) either—
    (i) B is under 16 and A does not reasonably believe that B is 16 or over, or
    (ii) B is under 13."

---

[28] [2014] EWHC 4436 (Fam).

The s.9 offence should be contrasted with the offences in ss.5–7 of the Act,   4.21
which all deal with sexual conduct relating to children under 13. There is an
ostensible difference between these offences in that those in ss.5–7 may be
committed by anyone over the age of criminal responsibility, while the
offence in s.9 may only be committed by those aged 18 or over. However, a
person under 18 who engages in the sexual touching of a child under 13 may
in principle be convicted under s.13 of the 2003 Act read with s.9.[29] This has
the effect that the offences in ss.5–7 and s.9 overlap in relation to the sexual
touching of children under the age of 13. However, in such cases the
appropriate charge will be under ss.5–7, which are specifically designed to
protect children under 13 and carry a higher maximum penalty to reflect the
fact that the child is particularly young and cannot legally consent to sexual
activity.[30]

In *Rae*,[31] Pitchford LJ, giving the judgment of the Court of Appeal, said   4.22
that in a case involving a child under the age of 13, there may be a dilemma
as to whether to charge the defendant under ss.5–8 (in that case, an offence
under s.8 of causing a child under 13 to engage in sexual activity) or under
s.9, and that s.9 is often charged where the child was or may have been
ostensibly consenting and an under-13 offence where there was manifestly no
consent. If this is indeed prosecutorial practice, we suggest it is wrong, and
that where a child victim was under the age of 13 it will always be appropriate
to charge under ss.5–8: see the discussion in para.3.30, above. *Rae* is an
unfortunate example of a charge being brought under s.9, rather than s.8,
where the victim was 12 at the relevant time. The judge then highlighted the
error by determining sentence by reference to the guideline for s.8, rather
than s.9. The Court of Appeal held that he had been wrong to do so, but that
he had been entitled to regard the absence of "ostensible consent" as an
aggravating factor, even though it was not specified as such in the sentencing
guideline for the s.9 offence then current. The net result was that the Court
reduced the sentence from 10 to seven years' imprisonment, i.e. a sentence at
the top end of the range specified in the s.9 guideline. By that means, justice
was as nearly served as it could be in these confused circumstances.

What if there is an issue as to whether the child was under 13 at the   4.23
relevant time? It follows from the previous paragraph that the appropriate
course in such circumstances is to charge the defendant in the alternative
under s.9 and ss.5–8 (rather than simply under s.9, even though that offence
protects all children under the age of 16). However, the case will need to be
left to the jury on the basis that, if they are satisfied that the child had
reached the age of 13, they can convict under s.9 only if they are also satisfied
that the defendant did not reasonably believe that the child consented. What
if there is an issue as to the age of the defendant, i.e. as to whether he was

[29] For s.13, see paras 4.144 and following, below.
[30] See fn.9, above.
[31] [2013] EWCA Crim 2056, at [11]–[13].

under or over 18? Suppose, for example, a child of 15 complains that when she was about 10 she was digitally penetrated by her male cousin, who is eight years older than her. In a case of this sort the defendant should be charged in the alternative under s.9 and s.13 read with s.9. This will prevent an acquittal should the jury be sure about the penetration but not about whether the defendant was 18 or over at the time it occurs.

4.24   The s.9 offence is designed for use in cases involving apparently consensual sexual activity with a child aged 13, 14 or 15. Where consent is in issue, it may be appropriate to charge the defendant both with a non-consensual offence, i.e. under ss.1–4 of the 2003 Act, and in the alternative under s.9, so that the jury can determine the issue of consent. An example of this being done is *Blore*,[32] where an alternative charge under s.9 was added in response to evidence suggestive of consent that emerged during the course of a trial for rape. However, where the child was under 13 at the relevant time, if the defendant states that the child consented, it will *not* be appropriate to charge him under s.9 in the alternative to a charge under ss.5–8. This is because absence of consent is not an element of s.9, any more than it is of ss.5–8, and so adding to the indictment an alternative charge under s.9 would achieve nothing. Rather, in any case involving a complainant under the age of 13, one of the under-13 offences should be charged and any issue as to consent, in so far as relevant to sentence (as to which see paras 3.50 and following, above), should be resolved in a *Newton* hearing.[33]

4.25   Illustrations of the possible application of the s.9 offence are:

- A, aged 18, penetrates with his finger the vagina of B, his 15-year-old girlfriend. B consents. A commits the offence.
- A, aged 18, kisses and caresses B, his 15-year-old girlfriend, with her consent. A commits the offence if the jury consider the touching "sexual".
- A, aged 18, kisses and caresses a girl, aged 13, with her consent. A commits the offence if the jury consider the touching "sexual". However, if she told him she was 16 and he reasonably believed her, A does not commit the offence.
- A, aged 18, kisses and caresses a girl, aged 12, with her consent. She told him she was 16 and he reasonably believed her. A commits the offence. But he should be charged under s.7 with sexual assault on a child under 13.

---

[32] [2013] EWCA Crim 2301.

[33] In *Rae* [2013] EWCA Crim 2056, Pitchford LJ noted (at [13]) what he said was the suggestion in para.4.18 of our 4th edition that, where a defendant admits conduct in relation to a child under 13 but there is an issue as to consent, it may be appropriate to include in the indictment an alternative charge under s.9, i.e. alternative to one under ss.5–8. His Lordship merely observed that there was no admission in that case as to the nature of the alleged conduct. We regret that a lack of clarity in our 4th edition may have misled his Lordship and have sought to correct it here.

MODE OF TRIAL AND PUNISHMENT

Where the touching involved any of the following, the s.9 offence is triable **4.26** only on indictment and the maximum sentence is 14 years' imprisonment:

- penetration of B's anus or vagina with a part of A's body or anything else,
- penetration of B's mouth with A's penis,
- penetration of A's anus or vagina with a part of B's body, or
- penetration of A's mouth with B's penis.[34]

Otherwise, the offence is triable either way. The maximum sentence on conviction on indictment is 14 years' imprisonment and on summary conviction is six months' imprisonment or a fine, or both.[35] As from a day to be appointed the maximum sentence of imprisonment on summary conviction will increase to 12 months.[36] The increase will have no application to offences committed before it takes effect.[37] Until recently, the maximum fine on summary conviction was a fine not exceeding the statutory maximum (i.e. £5,000). The effect of s.85 of the Legal Aid, Sentencing and Punishment of Offenders Act 2012 is that, from March 12, 2015, a fine of any amount may be imposed. The s.9 offence cannot be dealt with by way of a simple caution.[38]

For the purposes of listing, cases under s.9[39] fall within Class 2B, save for **4.27** complex cases involving many complainants (often under age, in care or otherwise particularly vulnerable) and/or many defendants who are alleged to have systematically groomed and abused them, often over a long period of time, which fall within Class 1C.[40] Cases in Class 1C must be referred to the Resident Judge, and by the Resident Judge to a Presiding Judge. Cases in Class 2B must be similarly referred in certain specified circumstances, including where the case is unusually grave or complex or a novel and important point of law is to be raised; where the defendant is a police officer, a member of the legal profession or a high profile figure; or where for any reason the case is likely to attract exceptional media attention.

The offence under s.9 is a serious specified offence for the purposes of the **4.28** dangerousness provisions of the Criminal Justice Act 2003.[41] A s.9 offence, whenever committed, may be made the subject of an extended sentence

---

[34] s.9(2).

[35] s.9(3).

[36] Criminal Justice Act 2003 s.282(2), (3).

[37] Criminal Justice Act 2003 s.282(4).

[38] Criminal Justice and Courts Act 2015 s.17(3), and the Criminal Justice and Courts Act 2015 (Simple Cautions) (Specification of Either-Way Offences) Order 2015 (SI 2015/790).

[39] And of soliciting, inciting, encouraging or assisting, attempting or conspiring to commit the offence or assisting an offender having committed the offence.

[40] *Consolidated Criminal Practice Directions*, Part XIII Listing B: CLASSIFICATION, available at *https://www.judiciary.gov.uk/wp-content/uploads/2015/09/crim-pd-2015.pdf* [Accessed April 30, 2016].

[41] Criminal Justice Act 2003 s.224 and Sch.15, Pt 2.

under s.226A of that Act.[42] The offence is also listed in Pt 1 of Sch.15B to the Criminal Justice Act 2003 for the purposes of s.224A of that Act (life sentence for a second listed offence).[43]

4.29   A person convicted under s.9, cautioned, found not guilty by reason of insanity or found to be under a disability and to have done the act charged, is automatically subject to the notification requirements in the Sexual Offences Act 2003.[44]

4.30   An amendment tabled in the House of Lords when the Sexual Offences Bill was before Parliament would have raised the maximum penalty under s.9 to life imprisonment in cases involving penetration of or by a child under 13, to bring it into line with the maximum penalties for the offences under ss.5, 6 and 8.[45] The Government resisted the amendment on the basis that those offences, which are specifically designed to protect children under 13, will normally be charged in cases of this sort and so the desired maximum will in any event be available.[46] A conviction under s.9 will occur only in exceptional cases, where a mistake has been made about the age of the child and it becomes apparent only during the proceedings, and too late to amend the indictment, that the child was under 13 at the relevant time. Also, raising the maximum to life imprisonment to ensure consistency with ss.5, 6 and 8 would raise questions about consistency with other sections of the Act which could be charged in cases involving penetration of or by a child under 13, e.g. the familial child sex and abuse of trust offences—though it was "very unlikely" that such charges would be brought in preference to a charge under ss.5–8. These arguments are not very compelling. The fact that convictions under s.9 involving penetration of or by a child under the age of 13 are likely to be rare does not make it any the less desirable that, when they occur, the maximum penalty should be that which Parliament sought fit to apply to such cases under ss.5, 6 and 8. It also seems of little importance that making the penalties consistent between those sections and s.9 would give rise to possible inconsistencies with other offences which are "very unlikely" to be charged, and are expected not to be charged.[47]

Sentencing

4.31 For the Sentencing Council guideline relating to the sentencing of sexual offences committed by offenders aged 18 and over, see Ch.33, below. In its

[42] Inserted by the Legal Aid, Sentencing and Punishment of Offenders Act 2012 s.124, brought into force on December 3, 2012, by SI 2012/2906.

[43] Inserted by the Legal Aid, Sentencing and Punishment of Offenders Act 2012 s.122, brought into force on December 3, 2012, by SI 2012/2906.

[44] s.80 and Sch.3, discussed in Ch.35, below.

[45] *Hansard*, HL, vol.649, col.679ff, Baroness Noakes (June 17, 2003).

[46] *Hansard*, HL, vol.648, col.1101, Lord Falconer of Thoroton (June 2, 2003); vol.649, col.680, Baroness Scotland of Asthal (June 17, 2003).

[47] See fn.9, above.

consultation on the draft guideline,[48] the Council noted that the offence of sexual activity with a child (and the other child sex offences) will normally be charged where the victim is aged 13 to 15 and maintains that they agreed to the sexual activity. Where a victim is over 13, lack of consent must be proved to obtain a conviction of rape (or assault by penetration or sexual assault), and where the victim maintains that they consented to the sexual activity, a rape prosecution is unlikely to be successful. However, the offence of sexual activity with a child can be charged instead, as it requires proof only that the offender engaged in the sexual activity, irrespective of whether the child maintains that they agreed to it. Indeed, the previous guideline, issued in 2007 by the Sentencing Guidelines Council ("SGC"), referred to this offence and the others discussed in this chapter as "ostensible consent offences".[49] In *Attorney General's Reference (Nos. 11 and 12 of 2012) (R. v Channer and Monteiro)*,[50] Pitchford LJ said:

> "'Ostensible consent' and 'willingness' are terms which, in the context of offences against the young in particular, are susceptible to misunderstanding and, even if accurately used, are liable to obscure the true nature of the encounter between the offender and the victim."

As noted in para.3.53, above, the Sentencing Council decided to move away from the language used by the SGC so that the focus of the current guideline is not the behaviour of the victim but the behaviour and culpability of the offender. This approach is to be welcomed, and was well received by respondents to the Council's consultation draft.

Sentencing guideline

A single guideline covers the offences of sexual activity with a child (s.9 of the   **4.32** 2003 Act) and causing or inciting a child to engage in sexual activity (s.10). For the avoidance of doubt, the guideline for these offences contains a prominent note that it "also applies to offences committed remotely/online". For online or "cyber" offending, see paras 4.77 and following, below.

Step One—Harm and culpability

The guideline requires the sentencing court to go through a series of steps in   **4.33** order to determine the appropriate sentence. Step one involves determining the offence category by reference to the degree of harm caused and then the culpability level for the offence.

---

[48] *Sexual Offences Guideline: Consultation* (December 6, 2012). The consultation document is available on the Sentencing Council's website.
[49] Sentencing Guidelines Council, *Sexual Offences Act 2003: Definitive Guideline*, pp.48–58. The Definitive Guideline is available on the Sentencing Council's website.
[50] [2012] EWCA Crim 1119, at [34].

Harm

4.34   Throughout the guideline, the Sentencing Council has generally sought to avoid identifying harm by reference to the nature of the sexual activity in question, on the basis that this would not fully reflect the seriousness or complexity of the offending. For offences under ss.9 and 10, however, the Council decided that harm should be determined by reference to the relevant sexual activity, on the ground that, in relation to these offences, the child may not see him/herself as a victim. They may see the offender as their "boyfriend" and may be unable or reluctant to articulate or recognise that they have suffered any psychological or emotional harm. The guideline therefore correlates harm to the nature of the sexual activity, on the basis that penetrative sexual activity will generally harm and corrupt the child more than non-penetrative activity will. The offence categories for these offences are accordingly as follows:

Harm	
Category 1	• Penetration of vagina or anus (using body or object) • Penile penetration of mouth In either case by, or of, the victim
Category 2	• Touching, or exposure, of naked genitalia or naked breasts by, or of, the victim
Category 3	Other sexual activity

Category 1 is confined to cases involving penetration on the ground that the consequences of this type of sexual activity are the most harmful to victims. The law already recognises the increased severity if penetration occurs, as the offence is then triable only in the Crown Court.[51] As for category 2, the Council proposed in its consultation that this should refer only to masturbation, as its analysis of case law showed that masturbation and penetrative activity are involved in the majority of cases that come before the courts for sentence. It was also keen to move away from the complex formulation of physical contact found in the SGC guideline, for example, "contact between naked genitalia of offender and naked genitalia or another part of victim's body, particularly face or mouth". Although the Council did not mention this, the concentration in the SGC guideline on physical contact had also made it difficult for the courts to identify the appropriate sentence for s.10 offences committed over the internet, where the offender incited the child to perform some sexual act such as masturbating or exposing themselves, and

---

[51] s.9(2) of the 2003 Act.

no physical contact between the parties was even possible.[52] The growing incidence of "cyber offending" of this sort was highlighted in responses to the consultation, as was the fact that the draft guideline placed touching of naked genitalia in category 3, which would have had the effect of lowering the sentences awarded for such activity. As a result, the Council revised category 2 by replacing "masturbation by or of the victim" with "touching, or exposure, of naked genitalia or naked breasts by, or of, the victim". It said that the new wording captures a range of offending, both contact and remote, that is serious but was not catered for in the original proposal, including the situation where a victim has been blackmailed via webcam into stripping. The Council said it was "confident the guideline can cope with both online and face to face offending".

Culpability

The culpability factors specified in the guideline for offences under ss.9 and   **4.35**
10 are as follows:

CULPABILITY
A
• Significant degree of planning • Offender acts together with others to commit the offence • Use of alcohol/drugs on victim to facilitate the offence • Grooming behaviour used against victim • Abuse of trust • Use of threats (including blackmail) • Sexual images of victim recorded, retained, solicited or shared • Specific targeting of a particularly vulnerable child • Offender lied about age • Significant disparity in age • Commercial exploitation and/or motivation • Offence racially or religiously aggravated • Offence motivated by, or demonstrating, hostility to the victim based on his or her sexual orientation (or presumed sexual orientation) or transgender identity (or presumed transgender identity)

---

[52] cf. *Butcher* [2009] EWCA Crim 1458; *Attorney General's Reference (No.24 of 2011)* [2011] EWCA Crim 1960; *Brocklebank* [2013] EWCA Crim 1813.

• Offence motivated by, or demonstrating, hostility to the victim based on his or her disability (or presumed disability)
B
Factor(s) in category A not present

4.36 In its consultation, the Sentencing Council elaborated its reasons for adopting some of the culpability A factors:

- "Use of alcohol/drugs on victim to facilitate the offence" is included because, in addition to the use of alcohol to incapacitate the victim, offenders may use access to alcohol and/or drugs as part of the grooming process, in order to gain the child's trust or friendship by allowing them to behave in a way that would not be permitted by their parents or other responsible adults.
- "Abuse of trust" is used rather than "abuse of position of trust" because trust may arise in relation to children not only from a position of formal responsibility but also from the offender's relationship with the child, e.g. as a family friend who has been trusted to look after the child on a day out. Examples of abuse of trust for the purposes of the guideline are where a paediatrician used his position to commit offences against child patients[53] and where a school bus monitor developed a sexual relationship with a child who used the bus.[54]
- "Use of threats (including blackmail)" will cover the case where the offender threatens to tell others about the activity as a way of controlling the victim.
- "Sexual images of victim recorded, retained, solicited or shared" is wider than "recording of the offence", found in the rape and assault guidelines. The reason is that, in committing an offence of sexual activity with a child, the offender may persuade the victim to take naked pictures of him/herself, in which case the images will be recorded by the victim rather than the offender. The words "sexual images solicited" were included on the basis that an offender is culpable if he solicits such images from his victim, regardless of whether the victim is robust enough to turn down the request.
- "Specific targeting of a particularly vulnerable child" may be relevant where, for example, an offender targets a child who is in care or whose home life is chaotic or dysfunctional, knowing the child is likely to be more susceptible to the attention of an adult who befriends them and professes to care for them.

---

[53] *Bradbury (Myles James)* [2015] EWCA Crim 1176.
[54] *Attorney General's Reference (No.32 of 2015)* [2015] EWCA Crim 1110.

- "Offender lied about age" is included to cover those cases where an offender misleads the victim about his age so that the victim believes they are in contact with a peer. This factor may be particularly relevant where contact is made online.
- Finally, the Council felt it important to acknowledge "significant disparity in age" as a culpability factor, although, as the offence may be committed only by offenders over the age of 18, it thought there will be very few instances where the disparity in age is not significant. The implication of this comment is, of course, that the Council believed that very few cases will *not* fall within culpability A.

As for "grooming behaviour used against victim", there is no legal **4.37** definition of the term "grooming" and the courts have said that it would be unwise to create one.[55] The term is used in relation to sexual offences to mean preparing a victim for a particular sexual activity. The acts of preparation that constitute grooming do not in themselves need to be sexual.[56]

Finally, as with other guidelines, no factors are listed under culpability B. **4.38** The Sentencing Council envisaged the type of offender who would fall within this category as one who is in an unlawful and inappropriate relationship with their victim, but where there is no significant disparity in age and no sign of exploitation.

Step Two—Starting point and category range

Once the court has determined the offence category and culpability level, at **4.39** step two it should use the corresponding starting point specified in the guideline in order to reach a sentence within the category range. The starting point applies to all offenders irrespective of plea or previous convictions. Once the starting point has been determined, step two allows further adjustment for aggravating or mitigating features as set out below. A case of particular gravity, reflected by multiple features of culpability or harm, could merit upward adjustment from the starting point before further adjustment for aggravating or mitigating features. Where there is a sufficient prospect of rehabilitation, a community order with a sex offender treatment programme requirement under s.202 of the Criminal Justice Act 2003 may be a proper alternative to a short or moderate length custodial sentence. The starting points and category ranges for offences under ss.9 and 10 of the Act are as follows:

---

[55] *R. v C*, unreported, September 10, 2014; *Attorney General's Reference (No.16 of 2016) (R. v W)* [2016] All E.R.(D.) 184 (Mar).
[56] *R. v C*, unreported, September 10, 2014, following *R. v G* [2010] EWCA Crim 1693; and see *Attorney General's Reference (No.16 of 2016) (R. v W)* [2016] All E.R.(D.) 184 (Mar), where it was held that there was no grooming, the Court noting that W had not sought out the child or her trust, nor had he brought her gifts or treats of any sort.

	A	*B*
Category 1	*Starting point* 5 years' custody *Category range* 4–10 years' custody	*Starting point* 1 year's custody *Category range* High level community order – 2 years' custody
Category 2	*Starting point* 3 years' custody *Category range* 2–6 years' custody	*Starting point* 26 weeks' custody *Category range* High level community order – 1 year's custody
Category 3	*Starting point* 26 weeks' custody *Category range* High level community order – 3 years' custody	*Starting point* Medium level community order *Category range* Low level community order – High level community order

In its consultation, the Sentencing Council said these starting points and category ranges are influenced more by culpability than harm, and that sentence levels are substantially lower where the offence does not involve the exploitation or grooming of the victim than when it does. For culpability B, a non-custodial option will be open to the sentencer as part of the available range. The sentencer must assess the facts in the case before them and be able to pass a sentence that will not only punish the offender but also protect the public and any future victims by addressing the offender's behaviour and thinking, to best ensure they do not reoffend. In some cases the sentencer may decide that the best way to do this is through a lengthy community order with punitive elements and a requirement to engage in a sexual offender treatment programme. Where, however, there has been penetrative sexual activity, there is always a custodial starting point, as there is where there is evidence of exploitation or grooming. Additionally, for the top category, the SGC guideline's 4 year starting point and 3–7 year range is increased to a 5 year starting point with a range of 4–10 years. The Council believed this increase was representative of sentences already being passed by the courts and was needed in order to address what can be very serious offending.

Aggravating and mitigating factors

After identifying the starting point and category range, the court should **4.40** consider whether the presence of aggravating or mitigating factors should result in an upward or downward adjustment from the starting point or the imposition of a sentence outside the category range. In particular, relevant recent convictions are likely to result in an upward adjustment. When sentencing appropriate category 2 or 3 offences, the court should also consider whether the custody threshold has been passed; if so, whether a custodial sentence is unavoidable; and if it is, whether that sentence can be suspended. The non-exhaustive list of aggravating and mitigating factors for offences under ss.9 and 10 is as follows:

Aggravating factors
Statutory aggravating factors
• Previous convictions, having regard to a) the nature of the offence to which the conviction relates and its relevance to the current offence; and b) the time that has elapsed since the conviction • Offence committed whilst on bail
Other aggravating factors
• Severe psychological or physical harm • Ejaculation • Pregnancy or STI as a consequence of offence • Location of offence • Timing of offence • Victim compelled to leave their home, school, etc. • Failure to comply with current court orders • Offence committed whilst on licence • Exploiting contact arrangements with a child to commit an offence • Presence of others, especially other children • Any steps taken to prevent the victim reporting an incident, obtaining assistance and/or from assisting or supporting the prosecution • Attempts to dispose of or conceal evidence • Failure of offender to respond to previous warnings

- Commission of offence whilst under the influence of alcohol or drugs
- Victim encouraged to recruit others
- Period over which offence committed

Mitigating factors

- No previous convictions **or** no relevant/recent convictions
- Remorse
- Previous good character and/or exemplary conduct*
- Age and/or lack of maturity where it affects the responsibility of the offender
- Mental disorder or learning disability, particularly where linked to the commission of the offence
- Sexual activity was incited but no activity took place because the offender voluntarily desisted or intervened to prevent it

* Previous good character/exemplary conduct is different from having no previous convictions. The more serious the offence, the less the weight which should normally be attributed to this factor. Where previous good character/exemplary conduct has been used to facilitate the offence, this mitigation should not normally be allowed and such conduct may constitute an aggravating factor.
In the context of this offence, previous good character/exemplary conduct should not normally be given any significant weight and will not normally justify a reduction in what would otherwise be the appropriate sentence.

It is notable that "pregnancy or STI as a consequence of offence" is included as an aggravating factor at step two, whereas for other offences it is at step one. This is because, for offences under ss.9 and 10, penetrative sexual activity places the offender in the highest category of harm. If pregnancy or STI resulted from the penetrative activity, and was placed at step one, there would be no opportunity for the sentencer to aggravate the sentence to take it into account as an additional factor. Placing it at step two allows the sentencer to move upwards from the starting point from the highest category by treating pregnancy or STI as an aggravating factor.[57]

4.41   As for the mitigating factors, the consultation draft included "determination and/or demonstration of steps taken to address sexual behaviour", as the Council thought it appropriate to give an offender some credit for recognising and trying to address their behaviour and to prevent future offending. This factor does not appear in the published guideline, though it does appear in the guidelines for certain other offences, including the child sex offences in ss.11, 12 and 15 of the 2003 Act and the abuse of trust offences in ss.16–19. We suggest, however, that this comparison should not preclude a court from treating an offender's attempts to address his offending behaviour as a mitigating factor in relation to ss.9 and 10, given that the

[57] cf. *Tutt (Tony)* [2015] EWCA Crim 391 (pregnancy and consequent abortion treated as aggravating factors).

mitigating factors specified in the guideline are said not to be exhaustive. The Court of Appeal has certainly been prepared to treat such attempts as providing mitigation in appropriate circumstances.[58]

Steps Three to Nine

The remaining steps cover the following points. At step three the court 4.42 should consider any factors which would indicate a reduction in sentence, e.g. assistance to the prosecution. At step four it should consider any reduction for a guilty plea. At step five the court should consider dangerousness, i.e. whether it would be appropriate to award a life sentence (s.224A of the Criminal Justice Act 2003) or an extended sentence (s.226A). Step six requires the court to consider whether the total sentence is just and proportionate to the offending behaviour. At step seven it should consider whether to make an ancillary order (e.g. a compensation order, a SHPO or a restraining order). Step eight requires the court to fulfil its duty under s.174 of the Criminal Justice Act 2003 to give reasons for, and explain the effect of, the sentence. Finally, at step nine the court should consider whether to give credit for time spent on bail in accordance with s.240A of that Act.

Offender should be sentenced only for offences of which he has been convicted or which he has admitted

Caution is required in relation to the decision in *Pipe*,[59] in which the Court 4.43 of Appeal completely overlooked the principle in *Canavan*[60] that a person should be sentenced only for the offences of which he has been convicted, or which he has admitted, and not for other offences of which those were specimens. In *Pipe*, the appellant (31) was convicted of three specimen offences under s.9 committed in relation to a girl of 15. He was sentenced to a total of 9 years' imprisonment. The defence was fabrication. The complainant was the sister of one of the appellant's work colleagues. She moved in with the appellant and his wife for some months and thereafter continued to see the appellant up to and beyond her sixteenth birthday. When the complainant lived with the appellant there were numerous instances of digital penetration (count 1) and sexual intercourse (count 2). Count 3 related to further incidents of sexual intercourse after the complainant had moved away but before her sixteenth birthday. In sentencing, the judge noted that, before the complainant moved in with him, the appellant began grooming her by text, eyeing her as a potential source of sexual gratification. She was a vulnerable young girl, unhappy, naïve, immature, quiet and lonely.

---

[58] cf. *Buchanan* [2015] EWCA Crim 172; *Attorney General's Reference (No.48 of 2014) (Timothy Storey)* [2014] EWCA Crim 1591.

[59] [2014] EWCA Crim 2570.

[60] [1998] 1 Cr. App. R. 70, discussed in paras 33.24 and following, below; and see *Clark* [1996] 2 Cr. App. R.(S.) 351; *Tovey and Smith* [2005] EWCA Crim 530.

The appellant had taken advantage of her vulnerability, and, despite the fact that she was living at his house, where she should have been under his protection, he forced his attentions upon her. He plied her with alcohol and filled her head with "spiritual mumbo-jumbo". There were many offences of digital penetration and full sexual intercourse in which the complainant was not a truly willing participant. She was confused and did not know what to do, how to react, or how to extricate herself. The appellant knew that she was 15. Her distress when giving evidence had been tangible. On appeal the appellant submitted that, as he had no previous convictions and there had been no violence, the term of 9 years was manifestly excessive. The Court of Appeal held that the offending fell within category 1A. The harm was in category 1 because it involved the penetration of the complainant's vagina by the appellant's fingers and subsequently his penis. Culpability was in category A because the offending involved planning, the use of alcohol, grooming behaviour and a gross abuse of trust. There were also additional aggravating factors which took the offending toward the top, if not to the very top, of category 1A, including the fact that the appellant ejaculated, that fact that the offending occurred in his own home, the threats he made to the complainant if she told anyone about what they had done, and the period of time over which the offending occurred. The principal mitigating factor was the absence of previous convictions. But the Court held that the critical factor for sentencing purposes was that these were far from being one-off offences. The appellant's offending resulted from an extensive campaign of sexual abuse against a vulnerable 15-year-old. The three counts on which he was convicted were specimen charges. Both his digital penetration of the complainant, and the subsequent full sexual intercourse, occurred repeatedly throughout the months that she was living at the appellant's house, and afterwards. The Court said that the guideline starts from the position of a single offence and if, as here, an offender is convicted of numerous, repeat offences, then he or she can expect a sentence which is towards, or at the very top of, the recommended range. The range for category 1A went up to 10 years, and even allowing for the appellant's good character, the Court considered the total term of 9 years' imprisonment identified by the judge as the appropriate sentence in this case.

4.44   The problem with *Pipe* is that, in accordance with the principle in *Canavan*, the Court should have had regard for sentencing purposes only to the three offences of which the appellant had been convicted, and should have disregarded the fact that these were specimen offences. The guideline assumes a single offence, and the Court should therefore have applied it to each of the three offences, making the sentences consecutive or concurrent as it considered just and proportionate,[61] and not inflating them to reflect other offences of which the appellant had *not* been convicted.

---

[61] For guidance see the Sentencing Council's *Offences Taken Into Consideration and Totality: Definitive Guideline* (2012).

Victim nearly 16—does this mitigate the offence?

May the fact that the victim was just short of her sixteenth birthday at the **4.45** relevant time ever mitigate an offence under s.9 or s.10? This is not one of the mitigating factors specified in the guideline, though those factors are expressed to be non-exhaustive. The same was true of the SGC guideline. However, in cases decided under that guideline the Court of Appeal was sometimes prepared to treat the fact that the victim was just under age at the relevant time as a factor which mitigated the offence.

An example is *Frew*,[62] where the offender (28) pleaded guilty to one s.9 **4.46** offence relating to an act of sexual intercourse with girl of 15 years and 7 months. The appellant and the victim were members of a martial arts club. He knew she had a crush on him. The incident took place after a party when the appellant was drunk. The victim became pregnant and suffered a traumatic and painful late abortion. The appellant had no recent convictions and none for sexual offences. He was sentenced to two years' imprisonment. The Court of Appeal held that the offence was aggravated by the pregnancy and its consequences, the appellant's knowledge of the victim's age and the age disparity between them. But in terms of mitigation, there had been only one act of intercourse, which was consensual. Further, the victim's age was such that if the incident had happened five months later, there would have been no offence. On those facts the sentence of two years' imprisonment was held manifestly excessive and was reduced to 18 months.

To similar effect is *R. v J*,[63] where the appellant (38) pleaded guilty to one **4.47** offence under s.9 committed when he had consensual sexual intercourse with the victim, his next-door-neighbour, who was aged 15 years and 10 months. They had known each other for eight years. A year or so earlier, the victim had developed feelings for the appellant. At first he did not agree to have sex with her because of her age; however, they met secretly in his van, where talking progressed to hugging and kissing and eventually to intercourse. The appellant was sentenced to three years' imprisonment. The Court of Appeal held that this sentence was too high. In assessing seriousness, an important consideration was that the victim had been almost 16 and was a mature 15-year-old. Additional mitigating factors were that she had pursued the appellant and he had, for a long time, resisted her advances; it was a single act; and he was of previous good character. On the other hand, there was a considerable disparity in age between them, and the appellant had met the victim surreptitiously when he knew she wanted a sexual relationship and when he had been warned about his behaviour by the police, who had been alerted by her parents. In all the circumstances, the Court substituted a sentence of six months' imprisonment.

---

[62] [2008] EWCA Crim 1029. See also *Attorney General's Reference (No.20 of 2008)* [2008] EWCA Crim 1383.
[63] [2012] EWCA Crim 3025.

4.48   It is likely that a similar approach will be taken in cases decided under the Sentencing Council guideline. An example where this was done is *Tutt (Tony)*,[64] in which the appellant (19) pleaded guilty to five s.9 offences committed against a girl of 15. They had full sexual intercourse on many occasions. The appellant knew the victim's age and asked her to tell a neighbour that she was 16. She became pregnant and had an abortion. In passing sentence the judge stated that the offences fell within category 1B. They were aggravated by the victim's pregnancy and the consequent abortion. There was mitigation in the appellant's guilty pleas, immaturity, good character and remorse. The judged passed sentences of 30 months' imprisonment concurrent on each count. On appeal against sentence, the Court of Appeal said that the case was serious and merited a custodial sentence, but that the judge had failed to give sufficient allowance for the mitigating factors. In particular, the Court mentioned the appellant's good character and the fact that "while [the victim] was still below the age at which she could lawfully give consent, she was not much below it". The Court accordingly quashed the sentences imposed by the judge and substituted sentences of 20 months concurrent on each count.

4.49   It is notable that these decisions all involved acts of intercourse by a man of good character with a victim who appeared freely to consent. The Court of Appeal has been much less inclined to treat as mitigation the fact that the victim was nearly 16 where the offence involved grooming, deception or other abuse.[65] An example is *Kloss*,[66] where the appellant (32) pleaded guilty to three offences under s.9, two under s.15 (grooming), four of making indecent photographs of a child and four of possession of such photographs, committed in relation to a girl aged 15 years and eight months. They had met in an internet chatroom and the appellant subsequently contacted the victim by mobile phone, MSN and Skype. He knew she was 15. After about a week she exposed her breasts to him over the webcam. Shortly afterwards they met and had unprotected vaginal intercourse at his home. A couple of weeks later, again at his home, they engaged in a variety of sexual acts including masturbation and oral sex, which he recorded on his webcam. There were a number of aggravating features: the evidence of grooming, the indecent photograph offences and the offences taken into consideration showed a progression towards the offences of which he was convicted; the sexual activity was unprotected; there was a 17-year disparity in age; the appellant knew the victim was 15 at the time of the offences, and she was vulnerable. As for mitigation, the sexual activity took place on two occasions in one month and then stopped; and the filming was consensual and intended for the appellant's use only. The appellant pleaded at the first opportunity, was

[64] [2015] EWCA Crim 391.
[65] In the case of a non-consensual offence, the fact that the victim was nearly 16 can never avail the offender: see *Woodland* [2015] EWCA Crim 629 (a case of attempted rape).
[66] [2008] EWCA Crim 2873.

effectively of previous good character and had substantial personal mitigation. The pre-sentence report described him as acting in a predatory and manipulative manner by grooming children of 14 and 15 to fulfil his sexual interest in them. He was sentenced to five-and-a-half years' imprisonment concurrent for the s.9 offences, four years concurrent for the grooming offences, 12 months' consecutive for one offence of making indecent photographs and shorter concurrent sentences for the other photograph offences. The judge took into consideration five further offences involving other girls. On appeal against sentence, the appellant noted that under the SGC guideline the starting point for a single s.9 offence of the sort he had committed was four years' imprisonment. He submitted, however, that this starting point was too high where the offence involved a girl who was almost 16 and was a willing participant. The Court of Appeal accepted that in certain circumstances the starting point will be substantially reduced, for example where the offender is 18 and the sexual activity is part of an ongoing relationship. This appellant, however, had behaved in a predatory manner and his offences were serious. The Court nonetheless held that the total sentence was manifestly excessive and it substituted sentences of four-and-a-half years' imprisonment for the s.9 offences and three years concurrent for the grooming offences.

Guideline is gender neutral

The guideline for ss.9 and 10 applies irrespective of the gender of the offender   **4.50**
or the victim.[67] In particular, it contains nothing that would justify a different
approach to sentencing male and female offenders simply on the basis of
their gender.

An illustration of the application of the guideline to a female offender is   **4.51**
Attorney General's Reference (No.85 of 2014).[68] The Attorney General
referred as unduly lenient a suspended total sentence of nine months'
imprisonment imposed on an offender (44) following her plea of guilty to
three offences of sexual activity with a boy of 14. The offender was good
friends with the victim's mother. She had instigated the offences, which took
place at the victim's home when the offender was drunk after spending the
evening with the family. The victim had also been drinking and the offender
had flirted with him throughout the evening. She performed oral sex upon
him twice and they had sexual intercourse. When the victim's brother found
them in bed together, the offender apologised and left, though she later
denied that any sexual activity had occurred. She initially pleaded not guilty
but changed her plea after the judge informed her that if she pleaded guilty

---

[67] *Attorney General's Reference (No.104 of 2015) (R. v Jade Hatt)*, unreported, December 8, 2015; *Attorney General's Reference (No.67 of 2008)* [2009] EWCA Crim 132 (decided under the SGC guideline).
[68] [2014] EWCA Crim 2088; and see *Attorney General's Reference (No.104 of 2015) (R. v Jade Hatt)*, unreported, December 8, 2015.

he could place the offences in category 1B of the guideline rather than category 1A, and would not be compelled to impose an immediate custodial sentence. He decided that the offences were a drunken isolated incident and that the offender was remorseful. He took into account that the victim had also been drinking, was sexually active with his peers and had expressed a wish that the offender should not be punished. He imposed a sentence of nine months' imprisonment on each count concurrent, suspended for 12 months. The Attorney General submitted that there were no grounds on which the offences could be placed in category 1B, and the circumstances were so serious that only an immediate custodial sentence was appropriate. The Court of Appeal allowed the reference. The offender's sentence was plainly unduly lenient. Although the offences had been out of character, there were several aggravating features, including the disparity in age, the offender's persistent seduction of the victim throughout the evening, several acts of penetration, ejaculation, taking advantage of the victim's inebriation, and the breach of trust that had happened in his own home. The fact that the victim had already been sexually active should be treated as an absence of aggravation that otherwise might have existed, not a mitigating feature. His anxiety that the offender should not be punished was unsurprising because she was his mother's friend and it was common for children in such situations to feel guilty. Further, the judge's reference to the offender's remorse was misplaced: remorse had been her first reaction but had been supplanted by an attitude of denial. The lowest possible sentence in the circumstances was two years' imprisonment to be served immediately.

"Grooming behaviour" and "significant disparity in age"

4.52 In *Harris (Joshua)*[69] the Court of Appeal gave helpful guidance on the meaning of "grooming behaviour" and "significant disparity in age", which are factors in the guideline that will raise an offence to culpability level A. The appellant (nearly 29) had pleaded guilty to three s.9 offences committed against a girl of 14, with whom he had come into contact on social media through a mutual friend when he was 18. She told him she was 14. The appellant suggested that they engage in sexual activity. The victim agreed and they arranged to meet. She took him back to her home and, while her family were away, they had consensual vaginal sexual intercourse in the living room and bedroom. This incident was the subject of the first count on the indictment. The victim told her parents that she was seeing the appellant and had some concerns. They advised her to stop seeing him. However, about three months later, the appellant got in touch with her via text message and suggested they meet up. She agreed on condition that there was no sexual activity between them. They met in an alley. The appellant suggested that

[69] [2014] EWCA Crim 2873.

they go into some woods. They arrived at a clearing and sat down on a bench. The appellant then pulled down his jogging bottoms, exposing his penis, and stood in front of the victim, holding the back of her head with one hand and his penis with the other. She turned her head away but then he did it again, and, although reluctant, she put his penis into her mouth. He pushed her head down and about 3 minutes later ejaculated into her mouth, causing her to gag. This incident formed the subject of the second count on the indictment. The appellant then asked the victim if he could have sexual intercourse. She said "no" because he did not have a condom. The appellant took her wrists and lifted her from the bench, unbuttoned her shorts and took her underwear down to her knees. He then had vaginal sex from behind, touching her breasts over her clothing at the same time. Again he ejaculated inside her. This was the third count on the indictment. Afterwards they went their separate ways. The victim was afraid she might be pregnant and told her parents what had happened, and the matter was reported to the police. The victim's personal statement described the serious psychological effects upon her of the appellant's actions, including considerable anxiety and distress at the possibility that she could be pregnant. Her relationship with her parents had suffered. She had started to self-harm and her academic progress and psychological stability generally had been impaired. The appellant had no previous convictions. The pre-sentence report noted that he took full responsibility for his actions and their impact on the victim, but assessed him as posing a high risk of harm to children and to the general public, with a significant risk of sexual assaults against women. In passing sentence the judge observed that the appellant was almost 19 at the time of the first offence. In terms of the guideline, the judge said the offences fell within category 1A as they involved a significant degree of planning, grooming behaviour and a significant disparity in age, given that the appellant was almost a third older than the victim. The victim was inexperienced and the appellant had taken advantage of her naivety, acting solely for his own gratification. There were favourable character references before the court and the judge accepted that the appellant was in most respects honest and decent, but he had let himself down and had to pay the price, partly as punishment and partly to make other young men realise that they must leave children to develop into adults in an innocent way, without having sex thrust upon them in such an unwelcome and damaging manner. With credit for his early guilty plea, the appellant was sentenced to 40 months' detention in a young offender institution on each count, to run concurrently. On appeal, it was submitted that the judge erred in placing the offences in category 1A and that they properly fell within category 1B. As such, and allowing credit for the early plea of guilty, the sentence of 40 months was manifestly excessive. It was also submitted that the judge erred in concluding that there was a significant disparity of age between the victim and the appellant, as they were both teenagers, engaged in an immature sexual relationship, and were sufficiently close in age to have mutual friends and acquaintances. Similarly, although the meeting had been planned, the offences had not required a significant degree of planning of the kind envisaged by the guideline. Nor could the appellant be said to have engaged in "grooming behaviour" of the kind contemplated in the guideline. They met through a mutual friend and communicated through a social network. After the first offence, the appellant had contacted the victim in the hope she would agree to meet again. She did agree and when they met, the other two offences were committed. In addressing these submissions the Court of Appeal declined to attempt any definition of "grooming behaviour" or of "planning", terms which are not themselves defined in the guideline. It noted that in previous cases the Court had observed that "grooming" involves trying to obtain the confidence of the intended victim and to break down their inhibitions.[70] The Court agreed, and added that in its judgment, the essence of this sort of conduct involves elements of manipulation and control, the offender treating the victim as an object for his own self-gratification. As for the offences before the Court, these were serious offences committed by a young adult against a child of 14 and the judge had been right to place them in category 1A. Age disparity involves consideration of maturity and responsibility, as well as the chronological ages of the parties. While the pre-sentence report noted that the appellant had a tendency to socialise with persons younger than himself, his character references indicated that he was a hard-working, reliable and responsible young adult. In the Court's view, he was sufficiently mature to be well aware that what he was doing was wrong. The judge was therefore right to regard the disparity in age as significant. In addition there were elements of grooming and planning. The appellant undoubtedly had his own self-gratification in mind when suggesting sexual activity to the victim, initially and when persuading her to meet him again three months later. He used his influence to overcome her initial reluctance to meet him again and agreed to her request that there should be no sexual activity between them, while no doubt intending that such activity would take place. The victim was obviously reluctant throughout both the sexual acts which occurred; the appellant would have been well aware of this, and yet he persisted. After the act of oral sex, following which she gagged, he had vaginal intercourse with her from behind, even after she had initially said "no" because he did not have a condom. This was manipulative and controlling behaviour by a young adult male taking advantage of the 14-year-old victim's naivety. His conduct indicated a high degree of culpability. The personal statement revealed the serious effects of the appellant's actions upon the victim. The judge had been right to stress that the law is there to protect young girls from themselves and from being exploited and used for sex in this way. For all these reasons, the Court held that the judge had been entirely right to sentence as he did.

---

[70] Citing *R. v HG* [2010] EWCA Crim 1693, at [16].

Sentencing examples

In *Jones (Christopher John)*,[71] the appellant (28) pleaded guilty to a number	4.53
of sexual offences committed against 13-year-old twin sisters, A and O. They
lived with their mother, who started seeing the appellant's flatmate. In
consequence, the victims came into regular contact with the appellant. They
got on well with him. They told him they were 13. He told A that he wished
she was older and he kissed and touched her a number of times. He also
started flirting with O and kissed and touched her. When interviewed, A said
she had thought she was "going out" with the appellant. Count 2 on the
indictment, relating to A, was a specimen count under s.9 reflecting repeated
incidents of kissing her. Count 3 was a specimen count under s.9 reflecting
incidents of kissing and hugging. Count 5, again under s.9, related to a
specific occasion when the appellant and A were alone watching television
and he rubbed her thigh in a sexual manner over her clothing. Count 6, again
under s.9, related to a specific occasion when they were watching television
on a sofa whilst others were also in the room and he began rubbing her
vaginal area over her clothing and also touched her breast over her clothing.
He then he placed A's hand on his erect penis over his clothing, which was
count 7. She felt embarrassed and quickly removed her hand. Count 8 was a
specimen count under s.9 reflecting incidents of kissing O. Count 9, again
under s.9, reflected a specific occasion when the appellant and O were on the
sofa watching television whilst A and others were upstairs. They were kissing.
He massaged her vagina over her clothing, which was a "onesie". There was
a hole in the crotch and he inserted his finger through it and touched O's
vagina over her knickers. She pushed his hand away. He tried to do it again
a couple of times, but she again pushed his hand away. Count 10, an attempt
to commit a s.9 offence, related to an occasion when the appellant and O
were in a bedroom and he tried to touch her vagina over her clothing whilst
on the bed. He then put her hand on his erect penis over his clothing, which
was count 11, under s.10. The appellant eventually fell out with his flatmate
and went to stay at the home of the victims and their mother, sleeping in the
lounge. Count 12, also under s.10, reflected an incident when the appellant
was lying in bed and he pulled back the covers and showed O his erect penis
inside his underpants. When the offences came to light, the appellant initially
denied any wrongdoing. He subsequently entered guilty pleas at the plea and
case management hearing. The judge gave a 25 per cent discount for the
pleas. In reviewing the facts the judge noted that the case plainly involved an
element of breach of trust. He decided that the offending fell within category
3A of the guideline. The judge took a particularly severe view of count 9, the
"onesie" incident, which he described as being "prolonged, in the sense it was
persistent in that [he] attempted to continue and to touch her for a little
time". In fact, the incident lasted for around one minute. The judge noted

[71] [2015] EWCA Crim 31.

that the appellant used no force or violence at any time, nor did he make any threats. He also referred to the pre-sentence report indicating the appellant's lack of insight into his offending. As regards A, the appellant was sentenced to four months' imprisonment concurrent on counts 2, 3 and 5 and 18 months' concurrent on counts 6 and 7, making a total sentence in relation to A of 18 months' imprisonment. As for O, the appellant was sentenced to four months' imprisonment on count 8; 24 months' concurrent on count 9; 12 months' concurrent on count 10; 18 months' concurrent on count 11; and, finally, 6 months' consecutive on count 12, making a total sentence in relation to O of 30 months' imprisonment. The sentences in relation to O were ordered to run consecutively to those relating to A, so that the total sentence was four years' imprisonment. On appeal, counsel for the appellant accepted that an immediate custodial sentence was justified, as were consecutive sentences, given there were two victims. She acknowledged that there were a number of aggravating factors: the difference in age between the appellant and the victims, an element of grooming, the element of abuse of trust and the fact that the offending continued for some four weeks. However, the total sentence of four years' imprisonment connoted a starting point in the order of five-and-a-half years, which was too long given that at no stage had the appellant touched the girls on their naked skin nor exposed himself other than under his own clothing. In particular, the sentences of 18 months' imprisonment on counts 6 and 7, and two years' imprisonment on count 9, were unjustified. Also, the sentence of six months on count 12 should have been concurrent rather than consecutive given that this offence was part and parcel of the overall conduct, although it was committed after the appellant had moved into the family home. The Court agreed that, having regard to the circumstances both of the offences and of the appellant, the starting point of five and a half years' imprisonment was significantly too long and should have been around three and a half years. It therefore reduced the sentences on counts 6, 7, 9 and 11 to 16 months' imprisonment, and made the sentence of six months' imprisonment on count 12 concurrent rather than consecutive, giving a total sentence of two years and eight months' imprisonment.

4.54   In *Bradbury (Myles James)*,[72] the appellant (B, aged 41) appealed against a total sentence of 22 years' imprisonment imposed for numerous sexual offences against children. B was a doctor specialising in paediatric haematology. He cared for children who were seriously ill or recovering from illness. B exploited his position to indulge in sexual contact with his patients under the pretext of monitoring their genital and sexual development. On occasions he misled victims into believing that they needed more appointments than were necessary. The offences spanned a period of four-and-a-half years and involved 18 boys aged between 10 and 16. B had required some of the victims to masturbate themselves in order to have an erection, and had asked others to remove their clothing before fondling their genitalia. B had also attempted

---

[72] [2015] EWCA Crim 1176.

to use a camera pen to obtain images of the boys when partially clothed. He was suspended when one boy told his family what had happened. B pleaded guilty at an early stage to two counts of making an indecent image (Protection of Children Act 1978 s.1), one count of voyeurism (s.67 of the 2003 Act), three counts of causing or inciting a child to engage in sexual activity (s.10), 12 counts of sexual activity with a child (s.9), seven counts of sexual assault of a child under 13 (s.7) and one count of sexual assault (s.3). A pre-sentence report assessed B as posing a high risk of serious harm to children. The sentencing judge found that he was dangerous but was satisfied that the overall length of the sentence offered sufficient protection for the public, and so did not impose an extended sentence. A one-third discount was given for B's early guilty pleas. On appeal, B disputed the finding of dangerousness, contending that he had insight into his paedophilic tendencies and was prepared to engage with the help on offer to him in order to lower the risk he posed. He also argued that he had limited his offending to non-penetrative sexual activity, which he claimed was not sufficiently serious to merit categorisation as dangerous and did not merit a term of imprisonment of the length imposed. The Court of Appeal allowed his appeal in part. Although the sexual activity, taken in isolation, was not of the most serious kind, the surrounding circumstances made the offending grave. B had been entrusted with the care of children, many of whom were very seriously ill. An intelligent and educated man, he had exploited and manipulated his position for his own sexual gratification. He must have known he had paedophilic tendencies when he accepted his position. He appeared to have targeted the particularly vulnerable, for whom the consequences of his offending would be most severe. The Court had yet to encounter a more egregious breach of trust. The harm caused by B's conduct went far beyond his immediate victims and had far reaching consequences for their families, the hospital, the practice of paediatrics and the health service in its management of child patients. Precious resources that should have been used for treating the sick had been diverted into enquiries and attempts to restore public confidence. In light of the scale and consequences of B's offending, the judge had not been wrong to conclude that he was dangerous. An offence did not have to involve penetration to cause serious psychological harm and for the offender to qualify as dangerous. Moreover, B had admitted that he was addicted to his behaviour and that it was escalating. There was no doubt that he posed a significant risk of serious harm to other boys. The relevant category of the guideline for the most serious offences was category 2A, with a starting point (depending on the offence) of three or four years and a range of two to six or three to seven years. However, the Court was obliged to bear in mind the question of totality and was not entitled simply to multiply the figures provided in the guideline by the number of victims. There were many aggravating features, including planning, targeting vulnerable children, exploitation of position, taking photographs with a hidden camera and attempts to have the assaults kept a secret. One grossly aggravating feature was that B led a child and his parents to believe that he was more seriously ill than he was in order to gain greater access to the child. The only mitigating feature was B's early guilty pleas, which had spared his victims the ordeal of giving evidence. Although a total figure of 22 years was appropriate, the Court restructured that sentence so that the custodial element was 16 years. It reduced seven-year terms imposed for causing or inciting sexual activity with a child, sexual activity with child and sexual assault of a child under 13 to five years, to run consecutively to each other and to a 12-month term for making an indecent photograph. Finally, it attached an extended licence period of six years to the total term.

4.55   In *Attorney General's Reference (No 48 of 2014) (Timothy Storey)*,[73] the Attorney General referred as unduly lenient a three-year community order imposed on an offender who pleaded guilty to one count under s.8 of the 2003 Act of inciting a child under 13 to engage in sexual activity, six counts under s.10 of inciting a child under 16 to engage in sexual activity and two counts under s.1 of the Protection of Children Act 1978 of making indecent images of children. Nine further offences of inciting a child to engage in sexual activity were taken into consideration, eight committed in relation to children under 16 and one in relation to a child under 13. The offender (32) pretended to be a teenage boy and used social media to seek out and befriend a very large number of young girls under the age of 16 and incite them to engage in sexual activity. The offender had showed his penis to some of the victims. On one occasion he masturbated himself to ejaculation. On another, the victim sent him an image of her vagina with a finger inserted into it. In total he had made about 775 young girls his Facebook friends, with about 20 of whom he had sexual conversations. The offender made admissions when interviewed. He said that he was addicted to the sexual aspects of the conversations and was seeking professional help. The victims' impact statements showed a loss of social confidence and anxiety as a result of the offender's behaviour. Two of the victims had self-harmed and school work, sleep and personal relationships had been generally affected. The pre-sentence report recorded that the offender had expressed remorse and shame. Importantly, he had become concerned about his behaviour prior to his arrest. He had disclosed to his GP the extent to which had been accessing adult pornography although he had not disclosed the activities which were the subject of the proceedings. His GP had referred him to a clinic and a hospital and following his arrest he had been in contact with a counsellor, had a number of sessions with a psychiatrist and had contacted a charitable organisation which provides treatment programmes for sex offenders. In the light of this, the sentencing judge was satisfied that the offender had taken steps to address his offending behaviour. There were a number of aggravating features: the number of offences involved and the duration of the offending

---

[73] [2014] EWCA Crim 1591.

over a period of about a year; the multiple, persistent contacts with victims; grooming behaviour; and a significant degree of planning and premeditation. The victims were by definition at a vulnerable stage of their sexual development and two were under the age of 13. The girls had been deceived by the offender into thinking he was a teenager. As for mitigation, the offender could claim the benefit of early guilty pleas; he was of previous good character; his expressions of shame and remorse were accepted as genuine; he had acknowledged his misconduct in interview and thus before the matter first came to court; and he had voluntarily sought assistance in dealing with what had led him to offend in this way. The judge sentenced the offender to a three-year community order in relation to each count to run concurrently. He attached requirements to the order, namely that the offender attend a sex offender group work programme for 100 days or sessions and that he be supervised by the probation service for three years. In addition the offender was made the subject of an indefinite SOPO. Before the Court of Appeal, the Attorney General submitted that the community order failed to reflect the gravity of the offending, particularly when the aggravating features were taken into account. The Court recognised that in cases of this type it may be legitimate to pass a non-custodial sentence where the custodial threshold has been crossed. This will particularly be so in the case of an offender of previous good character who has exhibited remorse and where there is a good prospect of rehabilitation. In those circumstances, as the guideline demonstrates, a community order with a sex offender treatment programme requirement may be a proper alternative to a short or moderate length custodial sentence. The Court also recognised that the purposes of sentencing to which a court must have regard include the reduction of crime and the reform and rehabilitation of offenders, as well as punishment and the protection of the public. However, the difficulty for the offender in this case was the length of time over which he offended and the significant number of victims who were subjected to his persistent and manipulative conduct. He had put his own sexual needs above the predictable harm and damage likely to be caused to his victims. The Court was clear that offending of this nature, frequency and persistence must be met with an immediate custodial sentence, particularly where the case involved girls who were under the age of 13. It therefore held that the community order was unduly lenient. A sentence of at least five years after a trial would have been appropriate, taking account of the mitigation. Giving full credit for the early guilty pleas, the Court quashed the community order made below and substituted in relation to the offences under ss.8 and 10 a term of three years on each count to run concurrently, saying that it had decided to sentence by reference to the totality rather than to distinguish between individual counts. As for the counts relating to indecent images, the Court substituted terms of imprisonment of three months on each count to run concurrently with one another and with the sentences for the other counts. The effect was to impose a custodial sentence of three years' imprisonment.

Parties to the Offence

4.56 The s.9 offence may be committed by and against persons of either sex. The defendant (A) must be 18 or over and the child (B) must be under 16. A person attains the age of 16 at the commencement of the sixteenth anniversary of her birth and the age of 18 at the commencement of its eighteenth anniversary.[74] For proof of age, see paras 3.73 and following, above. If A is under 18, the appropriate charge is under s.13 (child sex offences committed by children or young persons) read with s.9.

Is the child victim liable to prosecution if they encourage the offence?

4.57 If the child who is the victim of the activity encourages or assists the offence, are they liable to conviction as an accessory? This turns on the application of the principle in *Tyrrell*,[75] in which it was held that a young girl could not be convicted as accessory to an offence of having unlawful carnal knowledge with a girl under 16 committed against herself, as the offence was created to protect girls against men and there was no indication in the statute of an intention to criminalise the girls themselves. The s.9 offence was clearly created to protect children under 18 from sexual exploitation by adults, and there is nothing in the Act that indicates an intention to criminalise the children concerned. This strongly suggests that the principle in *Tyrrell* should apply in relation to s.9.

4.58 The point has been settled for all practical purposes by the decision in *Attorney General's Reference (No.53 of 2013) (Neil Wilson)*,[76] in which the offender pleaded guilty to one s.9 offence committed against a girl aged 13 and was sentenced to eight months' imprisonment. The girl was sexually experienced and prosecuting counsel described her in the course of the sentencing hearing as "predatory", a term picked up by the judge in his sentencing remarks. On a reference by the Attorney General, the Court of Appeal held that the sentence was plainly unduly lenient. In doing so, it accepted the Attorney General's submission that the fact that the victim had initiated what had happened was an aggravating rather than a mitigating factor. Lord Thomas CJ said[77]:

> "It has been clear since at least the Offences Against the Person Act 1861, and subsequent nineteenth century legislation, that the purpose of Parliament in passing legislation to make it a crime punishable with imprisonment to have

---

[74] Family Law Reform Act 1969 s.9(1).

[75] [1894] 1 Q.B. 710; and see *DPP v Whitehouse* [1977] Q.B. 868. In *Gnango* [2011] UKSC 59, a majority of the Supreme Court said that *Tyrrell* is an illustration of a general rule, identified by Professor Glanville Williams in his article *Victims and other exempt parties in crime* (1990) 10 Legal Studies at p.245, that where legislation creates an offence that is intended to protect a class of persons, a member of that class cannot be convicted as an accessory to such an offence committed in respect of him.

[76] [2013] EWCA Crim 2544.

[77] At [19]–[20].

sexual relations with those under 16 was to protect those under 16. Indeed the Criminal Law Amendments [*sic*] Act 1885 makes it expressly clear that that was the purpose of the legislation. That can be seen from the preamble to the Act and was made clear by this court in *R. v Tyrrell* [1894] 1 QB 710.

That long-standing principle is well-known. The reduction of punishment on the basis that the person who needed protection encouraged the commission of an offence is therefore simply wrong. We agree with the submission of the Attorney General that an underage person who encourages sexual relations with her needs more protection, not less. Accepting that as the basis for sentencing for the reasons we have explained, the fact that the offender took advantage of what he asserted the victim did aggravated the offence."

Although his Lordship did not engage in elaborate legal analysis, his reference to *Tyrrell* clearly indicates that he considered the s.9 offence, and by inference all the other child sex offences, to fall within the scope of the principle in that case, such that there can be no question of the child victim of such an offence being prosecuted for any part she may have played in encouraging it.

Jurisdiction

By virtue of s.72 of and Sch.2 to the Sexual Offences Act 2003, as amended,[78]   **4.59** it is an offence under s.9 for a UK national to do an act in a country outside the UK which would constitute a s.9 offence if done in England and Wales. The amendments, made in 2008, expanded the scope of s.72 in two respects. First, they removed the limitation on s.72 as enacted that it applied only to offences committed against victims aged under 16 (the relevant age is now 18). Secondly, they abolished, in respect of UK nationals, the "double criminality" requirement that the act must have been an offence in the country in which it was done. This requirement is, however, retained in respect of the prosecution of UK residents and those who become UK residents or nationals after the doing of the relevant act. For the purposes of s.72 a "country" includes a territory and a "United Kingdom national" means a British citizen, a British overseas territories citizen, a British National (Overseas), a British Overseas citizen, a person who under the British Nationality Act 1981 is a British subject, or a British protected person within the meaning of that Act.[79] An act is taken to be an offence in the country in which it was done unless the defendant serves a notice putting the prosecution to proof on the point.[80]

"Touches another Person"

For the meaning of "touches", see paras 2.63 and following, above. Suppose   **4.60** an adult allows a child to touch him in a sexual way, e.g. to masturbate him.

[78] By the Criminal Justice and Immigration Act 2008 s.72, with effect from July 14, 2008.
[79] s.72(9).
[80] s.72(6)–(8).

Does the adult commit an offence under s.9? In the old case of *Speck*,[81] the Court of Appeal upheld the appellant's conviction of committing an act of gross indecency with or towards a child, contrary to s.1(1) of the Indecency with Children Act 1960, after she had placed her hand on his penis outside his trousers and kept it there for some five minutes. The Court held that the appellant's inactivity once the child had placed her hand on his lap was capable of constituting an invitation to her to go on acting in that way, and the invitation was capable of being an "act" for the purposes of the offence. This was a startling linguistic contortion. But the decision is of little direct assistance in the present context, since on similar facts the question is not whether the adult has committed an indecent "act" towards the child, but whether he has "touched" her. If the adult is passive throughout, the better view must be that he does not commit the s.9 offence, as the only touching is by the child. Any other result would place unreasonable strain on the statutory language. However, the adult might well commit an offence of causing or inciting the child to engage in sexual activity contrary to s.10 (or s.8, in the case of a child under 13). This will certainly be so if he causes the child to undertake her actions, or to continue them once she has started, for example by cajoling, pressurising or threatening her. Further, even if he does nothing of the sort, he will commit the incitement offence if, on the facts, his passive acceptance of her conduct after she commences it amounts to encouraging her to go on with it.

"THE TOUCHING IS SEXUAL"

4.61   For the meaning of "sexual", see paras 2.66 and following, above.

"PENETRATION"

4.62   For the meaning of this term, see paras 1.156 and following, above.

"VAGINA"

4.63   For the meaning of this term, see para.1.155, above.

CONSENT

4.64   Absence of consent is not an element of the s.9 offence. Accordingly, the offence is committed regardless of whether the child agrees to the touching. But if she does not consent, the appropriate charge will be under ss.1–3 of the Act (the non-consensual offences).

---

[81] [1977] 2 All E.R. 859.

MENTAL ELEMENT

The touching must be intentional. For the meaning of "intention" and the   **4.65**
question whether A must intend the activity he causes or incites to be sexual,
see paras 2.78 and following, above. Recklessness will not suffice.[82] In
Heard,[83] dealing with the offence of sexual assault, for which an intentional
touching is also required, the Court of Appeal upheld the trial judge's
direction to the jury that the touching had to be deliberate, and that it was
not open to the defendant to contend that voluntary intoxication through
drink or drugs prevented him from intending to touch the victim. The Court
did, however, distinguish between deliberate touching and touching that is
accidental, which will not suffice whether the defendant was sober or drunk
at the relevant time[84]:

> "Because the offence is committed only by intentional touching, we agree that
> the Judge's direction that the touching must be deliberate was correct. To flail
> about, stumble or barge around in an unco-ordinated manner which results in an
> unintended touching, objectively sexual, is not this offence. If to do so when
> sober is not this offence, then nor is it this offence to do so when intoxicated. It
> is also possible that such an action would not be judged by the jury to be
> objectively sexual, on the basis that it was clearly accidental, but whether that is
> so or not, we are satisfied that in such a case this offence is not committed. The
> intoxication, in such a situation, has not impacted on intention. Intention is
> simply not in question. What is in question is impairment of control of the limbs
> . . . We would expect that in some cases where this was in issue the Judge might
> well find it useful to add to the previously-mentioned direction that 'a drunken
> intent is still an intent', the corollary that 'a drunken accident is still an accident'.
> To the limited, and largely theoretical, extent that a reckless sexual touching is
> possible the same would apply to that case also. Whether, when a defendant
> claims accident, he is doing so truthfully, or as a means of disguising the reality
> that he intended to touch, will be what the jury has to decide on the facts of each
> such case."

We suggest this passage is equally applicable in the context of s.9. On
intoxication, see further paras 2.81 and following, above.

It is a requirement of the offence, where B is 13, 14 or 15, that A does not   **4.66**
reasonably believe that B is 16 or over. If there is an issue as to whether A
held such a belief, it will be for the prosecution to prove that he did not, i.e.
either that he did not hold the belief or that it was not reasonable for him to
have done so. In considering whether the prosecution have discharged this
burden, the jury's task is not to consider whether the hypothetical reasonable
man would have believed B to be 16 or over, but whether A may actually have
believed that, and if so, whether the belief was reasonable. If they find that A
may have believed B to be 16 or over, then in determining whether the belief
was reasonable the jury should have regard to all the circumstances,
including what B told A about herself and B's appearance at the relevant

---

[82] *Heard* [2007] EWCA Crim 125, at [22].
[83] [2007] EWCA Crim 125.
[84] At [23].

time.[85] For the extent to which they should take into account any characteristics of A that may have predisposed him to that belief, see paras 1.382 and following, above.

CAUSING OR INCITING A CHILD TO ENGAGE IN SEXUAL ACTIVITY

DEFINITION

4.67 Section 10(1) of the Sexual Offences Act 2003 provides:

"A person aged 18 or over (A) commits an offence if—
(a) he intentionally causes or incites another person (B) to engage in an activity,
(b) the activity is sexual, and
(c) either—
(i) B is under 16 and A does not reasonably believe that B is 16 or over, or
(ii) B is under 13."

4.68 By analogy with *Walker*,[86] decided under s.8 of the 2003 Act, s.10 creates separate offences of intentionally causing and intentionally inciting a child under 16 to engage in sexual activity. It follows that a count alleging that the defendant "caused or incited" the complainant is in principle duplicitous and should be struck out or amended. Further, the effect of the decision in *Courtie*[87] is that the provision by s.10 of a higher maximum punishment where certain forms of penetration occur creates separate offences, one involving those forms of penetration and the other not. The combined effect of the two authorities is that s.10 creates four offences triable on indictment: causing penetrative sexual activity, causing non-penetrative sexual activity, inciting penetrative sexual activity and inciting non-penetrative sexual activity. It is important that indictments specify which of these offences is being charged. In practice, however, they often fail to do so: see the discussion of *Walker* in para.3.132, above.

4.69 The s.10 offences should be contrasted with those in s.8 of the 2003 Act (causing or inciting a child under 13 to engage in sexual activity). Section 8 covers the same conduct towards children under 13 as is caught by s.10. There is an ostensible difference between these offences, in that those in s.8 may be committed by anyone over the age of criminal responsibility whereas the offences in s.10 may be committed only by those aged 18 or over. However, a person under 18 who causes or incites a child under 16 to engage in sexual activity may in principle be convicted under s.13 of the 2003 Act read with s.10.[88] This has the effect that s.8 and s.10 both penalise the sexual touching of children under the age of 13. However, in any such case the

[85] cf. *Perry and Pledger* [1920] N.Z.L.R. 21, NZCA.
[86] [2006] EWCA Crim 1907.
[87] [1984] A.C. 463.
[88] For s.13, see paras 4.144 and following, below.

appropriate charge will be under s.8, which is specifically designed to protect children under 13 and, in cases involving penetration, carries a higher maximum penalty (life imprisonment) to reflect the fact that the child is particularly young and cannot legally consent to sexual activity.[89]

The following examples illustrate the possible application of s.10[90]:   **4.70**

- A, aged 25, urges B, a boy whom A knows to be 15, to masturbate himself. A commits the offence by inciting.
- A, aged 25, induces B, a boy whom he knows may be 15, to perform oral sex on a boy of 16. A commits the offence by causing.
- A, aged 18, encourages his 15-year-old girlfriend to perform a strip for him. If she declines, A commits the offence by inciting. If she strips, A commits the offence by causing.
- A and B are friends aged 18. A encourages B to try groping B's girlfriend, C, aged 15. If B declines, A commits the offence by inciting. If B does grope C, A commits the offence by causing and B commits the offence in s.9 of the 2003 Act (sexual activity with a child).
- A, aged 18, encourages B, aged 16, to grope B's girlfriend, C, aged 15. A commits no s.10 offence, whether or not B acts on his encouragement, as B is not under 16.
- A, aged 18, asks a 13 year-old girl to masturbate him. She claims to be 16 and A reasonably believes her. A does not commit the offence.
- A, aged 18, asks a 12 year-old girl to masturbate him. She claims to be 16 and A reasonably believes her. A commits the offence.

MODE OF TRIAL AND PUNISHMENT

Where the activity caused or incited involved any of the following, a s.10   **4.71**
offence is triable only on indictment and the maximum sentence is 14 years' imprisonment:

- penetration of B's anus or vagina,
- penetration of B's mouth with a person's penis,
- penetration of a person's anus or vagina with a part of B's body or by B with anything else, or
- penetration of a persons's mouth with B's penis.[91]

Otherwise, the offence is triable either way. The maximum sentence on conviction on indictment is 14 years' imprisonment and on summary conviction is six months' imprisonment or a fine, or both.[92] As from a day to

---

[89] See fn.9, above.
[90] In these examples, where A encourages B to engage in conduct with C that would constitute an offence on the part of B, then whether or not A commits a s.10 offence, he commits an offence under s.44 of the Serious Crime Act 2007 (intentionally encouraging an offence).
[91] s.10(2).
[92] s.10(3).

be appointed the maximum sentence of imprisonment on summary conviction will increase to 12 months.[93] The increase will have no application to offences committed before it takes effect.[94] Until recently, the maximum fine on summary conviction was a fine not exceeding the statutory maximum (i.e. £5,000). The effect of s.85 of the Legal Aid, Sentencing and Punishment of Offenders Act 2012 is that, from March 12, 2015, a fine of any amount may be imposed. A s.10 offence cannot be dealt with by way of a simple caution.[95]

4.72   For the purposes of listing, cases under s.10[96] fall within Class 2B, save for complex cases involving many complainants (often under age, in care or otherwise particularly vulnerable) and/or many defendants who are alleged to have systematically groomed and abused them, often over a long period of time, which fall within Class 1C. [97] Cases in Class 1C must be referred to the Resident Judge, and by the Resident Judge to a Presiding Judge. Cases in Class 2B must be similarly referred in certain specified circumstances, including where the case is unusually grave or complex or a novel and important point of law is to be raised; where the defendant is a police officer, a member of the legal profession or a high profile figure; or where for any reason the case is likely to attract exceptional media attention.

4.73   An offence under s.10 is a serious specified offence for the purposes of the dangerousness provisions of the Criminal Justice Act 2003.[98] A s.10 offence, whenever committed, may be made the subject of an extended sentence under s.226A of that Act.[99] The offence is also listed in Pt 1 of Sch.15B to the Criminal Justice Act 2003 for the purposes of s.224A of that Act (life sentence for a second listed offence).[100]

4.74   A person convicted under s.10, cautioned, found not guilty by reason of insanity or found to be under a disability and to have done the act charged, is automatically subject to the notification requirements in the Sexual Offences Act 2003.[101]

4.75   Amendments tabled in the House of Lords when the Sexual Offences Bill was before Parliament would have raised the maximum penalty to life imprisonment in cases involving penetration of or by a child under 13, to

---

[93] Criminal Justice Act 2003 s.282(2), (3).

[94] Criminal Justice Act 2003 s.282(4).

[95] Criminal Justice and Courts Act 2015 s.17(3), and the Criminal Justice and Courts Act 2015 (Simple Cautions) (Specification of Either-Way Offences) Order 2015 (SI 2015/790).

[96] And of soliciting, inciting, encouraging or assisting, attempting or conspiring to commit the offence or assisting an offender having committed the offence.

[97] *Consolidated Criminal Practice Directions*, Part XIII Listing B: CLASSIFICATION, available at *https://www.judiciary.gov.uk/wp-content/uploads/2015/09/crim-pd-2015.pdf* [Accessed April 30, 2016].

[98] Criminal Justice Act 2003 s.224 and Sch.15, Pt 2.

[99] Inserted by the Legal Aid, Sentencing and Punishment of Offenders Act 2012 s.124, brought into force on December 3, 2012, by SI 2012/2906.

[100] Inserted by the Legal Aid, Sentencing and Punishment of Offenders Act 2012 s.122, brought into force on December 3, 2012, by SI 2012/2906.

[101] s.80 and Sch.3, discussed in Ch.35, below.

bring it into line with the maximum for the offence under s.8.[102] The Government resisted the amendments on the basis that s.8, which is specifically designed to protect children under s.13, will normally be charged in such cases and so the desired maximum will be available.[103] A conviction under s.10 will occur only in exceptional cases, where a mistake has been made about the age of the child and it becomes apparent only during the proceedings, and too late to amend the indictment, that the child was under 13 at the relevant time. Also, raising the maximum to life imprisonment to ensure consistency with s.8 would raise questions about consistency with other sections of the Act which could be charged in cases involving penetration of or by a child under 13, e.g. the familial child sex and abuse of trust offences—though it was "very unlikely" that such charges would be brought in preference to a charge under s.8. These arguments are not very compelling. The fact that convictions under s.10 involving penetration of or by a child under 13 are likely to be rare does not make it any the less desirable that, when they occur, the maximum penalty should be that which Parliament sought fit to apply to such cases when prosecuted under s.8. It also seems of little importance that making the penalties consistent between that section and s.10 would give rise to possible inconsistencies with other offences which are "very unlikely" to be charged, and which are expected not to be charged.[104]

SENTENCING

For the Sentencing Council's guideline relating to the sentencing of sexual offences committed by offenders aged 18 and over, see Ch.33, below. A single guideline covers offences under both s.9 and s.10 of the 2003 Act and is considered at paras 4.32 and following, above.

4.76

Online or "cyber" offending

A welcome feature of the new guideline is that, unlike the SGC guideline that preceded it,[105] it has been designed to assist the courts in sentencing s.10 offences committed remotely over the internet, sometimes referred to as offences of "cyber sex", as well as offences involving physical contact. The SGC guideline for offences under ss.9 and 10 presupposed physical contact between the offender and the victim and so gave no guidance to a court required to sentence for offences committed online. As a result, different courts reached different conclusions as to how the sentencing of those cases

4.77

---

[102] *Hansard*, HL, vol.648, col.1098 (June 2, 2003); vol.649, col.679ff (June 17, 2003).
[103] *Hansard*, HL, vol.648, col.1101, Lord Falconer of Thoroton, (June 2, 2003); vol.649, col.680, Baroness Scotland of Asthal (June 17, 2003).
[104] See fn.9, above.
[105] cf. *Brocklebank* [2013] EWCA Crim 1813; *Shayne Prince* [2013] EWCA Crim 1768.

should be approached. In *Attorney General's Reference (No.24 of 2011)*,[106] the Vice-President, Hughes LJ, said that:

" . . . offences of 'cyber sex', serious as they are, are, in ordinary terms at least, likely to be less serious than physical contact offences. There are a number of reasons for that. The obvious ones include the greater freedom of activity for any child when connected only electronically; correspondingly the reduced opportunities for coercion or influence and of course the absence of health risks or pregnancy."

However, in *Attorney General's Reference (No.35 of 2013)*[107] the Court said it did not construe the earlier decision "as intending in any way to dilute the seriousness on their own facts of offences such as these". It added that whilst offences of cyber sex are in one sense less serious than physical contact offences, they are arguably more difficult to prevent; and contact offences could be readily envisaged which are less serious than some cyber sex offences, particularly where those offences are in number. Further, the long-term effect on a child confronting personal exposure to a stranger is likely to be severe.

4.78 The Sentencing Council designed the new guideline for ss.9 and 10 explicitly to cater for offences committed online. As the Council stated in the Preface to its consultation document[108]:

" . . . the Council has been mindful of the significant rise in sexual offences committed via the internet involving new and developing technologies, and has sought to tailor its approach to accommodate the factors and circumstances of a wide variety of offending behaviour."

Thus, the new guideline includes the statement: "This guideline also applies to offences committed remotely/online". We therefore suggest that in sentencing cyber offences the courts should focus on the terms of the guideline itself and be cautious in citing earlier judicial comment on the subject. The sentence for any particular cyber offence should turn, like that for a contact offence, on the application of the harm and culpability factors specified in the guideline; and the offence ought not to be regarded as mitigated (or aggravated) by reason only of the fact that it was committed online.

4.79 The new guideline was applied in relation to online activity in *Fagan*,[109] where the appellant (age not given) received a total sentence of three years' imprisonment after pleading guilty to four offences of attempting to incite a child to engage in sexual activity, one offence of attempting to cause a child to watch a sexual act and one of attempting to engage in sexual activity in the presence of a child. The offences were charged as attempts because three of the people contacted were untraced and so it could not be proved that they

---

[106] [2011] EWCA Crim 1960, at [8]. See also *Butcher* [2009] EWCA Crim 1458, in which the Court said that where, as in that case, the offender had no physical contact with the victim and the offending amounted to "no more than incitement" over the internet, there had to be a significant reduction in the starting point and sentencing range.

[107] [2013] EWCA Crim 1757.

[108] Sexual Offences Guideline Consultation, Dec 2012, p.5.

[109] [2014] EWCA Crim 2728.

were in fact children, while the fourth was a police officer purporting to be a child. In the four offences of attempted incitement, the appellant had encouraged the child to masturbate by vaginal penetration. When interviewed, he said that he had not believed that he had been speaking to underage girls; he believed that they were fake and was attempting to "out" them with his conversation. He abandoned this story at the preliminary hearing and admitted the offences. The sentencing judge described what the appellant had done in these terms:

> "Essentially what you did was to make contact with individuals on internet chat rooms believing the individuals to be 13 and 15 year old girls. What is clear from the downloaded material from your computer is that you systematically over a substantial period of time sought out individuals who you thought were young girls for the purpose of sexual gratification. You would chat to these individuals [and] give instructions to them to masturbate. You made it clear in your conversations with them that you were not in the least bit concerned they were 15 years or 13 years of age and you expressed the desire to have sex with them."

The judge considered that the offences of attempted incitement fell within category 1A, as the sexual activity involved the victim penetrating her vagina with an object, whilst culpability was raised by the grooming of the victims, the fact that the images were being recorded and retained and the significant disparity in age between the appellant and his victims. The starting point was therefore five years' imprisonment with a range of 4–10 years. As for the offence of attempting to engage in sexual activity in the presence of a child, this fell within category 2A as it involved masturbation with raised culpability by reason of grooming and a significant age disparity. The starting point was therefore two years' imprisonment with a range of 1–3 years. The judge sentenced the appellant as follows: for two of the offences of attempted incitement, two years' imprisonment concurrent; for the other two such offences, 12 months' imprisonment concurrent, but consecutive to the sentences imposed for the first two offences; and for the offences of attempting to cause a child to watch a sexual act and attempting to engage in sexual activity in the presence of a child, 12 months' concurrent, making a total of three years' imprisonment. On an appeal against sentence, the appellant's counsel referred the Court of Appeal to the comment on cyber offences made by the Vice-President in *Attorney General's Reference (No.24 of 2011)*, cited above. The Court accepted that in the absence of proof that any of the appellant's cyber contacts were in fact children, there was no evidence of actual harm. However, the appellant's conduct was directed to his contacts as if they were children, as they may have been, and offences of cyber sex are capable of having a serious and damaging effect on children, particularly if part of a sustained course of grooming. Nothing said by the Vice-President in *Attorney General's Reference (No.24 of 2011)* suggested otherwise or should be interpreted as minimising the seriousness of the appellant's offences. Internet conversations of this sort with children, or with people who the offender hoped and intended were children, were to be strongly discouraged. The Court was nonetheless persuaded that, taking into account the appellant's good character, remorse and shame and the personal consequences for him of conviction, the sentence passed was excessive. The appropriate course was to order that all the sentences should run concurrently, with the result that the overall total was reduced from three to two years' imprisonment.

4.80   In other cases, however, the Court of Appeal has shown itself unwilling to treat cyber or other remote offending as on a par with contact offending. In particular, in *Attorney General's Reference (No.94 of 2014)*[110] and *Buchanan*[111] it was not prepared to treat incitement to penetrative activity, where no sexual activity took place, as falling within category 1, apparently, on the basis that such incitement, without more, will not cause harm at a level for which that category was designed to cater. The Court in *Buchanan*, without citing the sentence "This guidance also applies to offences committed remotely/online", went so far as to say that it was "doubtful whether the guideline actually addressed this type of offending". As the implications of these decisions potentially extend beyond remote offending to offences of incitement committed face-to-face, they are discussed separately below.

Should offences of "incitement" attract a lower sentence than offences of "causing"?

4.81   There is nothing in the new guideline to suggest that a s.10 offence committed by way of inciting sexual activity, rather than causing it, should attract a lesser sentence because the sexual activity does not take place. If the Sentencing Council had intended such offences routinely to attract a lesser sentence, it would surely have said so. In fact, all it said was that an offence will be mitigated where "sexual activity was incited but no activity took place because the offender voluntarily desisted or intervened to prevent it". Although the mitigating factors specified in the guideline are not exhaustive, the implication of this wording is that if sexual activity was incited but did not take place for some *other* reason, e.g. the victim refused or the police intervened, the offender cannot for that reason alone expect a reduction in sentence. However, the Court of Appeal reached a contrary conclusion in *Attorney General's Reference (No.94 of 2014)*.[112] In that case the offender had pleaded guilty to one s.10 offence of inciting a child of 13 to engage in sexual activity. He had sent a message on WhatsApp to the victim, whom he knew, asking her in crude language to suck his penis. The girl found the message "cringey" and no sexual activity took place. The sentencing judge was concerned at the prosecution's suggestion that the guideline placed the offence in category 1A. In the event, he did not explain whether he accepted that categorisation or how the guideline assisted in the disposal of the case,

[110] [2014] EWCA Crim 2752.
[111] [2015] EWCA Crim 172.
[112] [2014] EWCA Crim 2752.

but in light of the various mitigating factors he passed a sentence of 180 days' imprisonment. The Attorney General referred the sentence to the Court of Appeal as unduly lenient, contending that the offence fell within category 1 because it involved penile penetration of the mouth by the victim. The Court rejected this contention in terms that are worth quoting in full:

"It is, of course, beyond argument that the offender did, in fact, incite the victim to suck his penis; the texts speak for themselves and, by his plea, he admitted the offence. The question is whether incitement to behave in that way, which does not involve anything more falls within the same category of harm as either penetration of the vagina or anus (using a body or object) or penile penetration of the mouth, deserving of similar sanction subject to culpability and such aggravating and mitigating circumstances as might otherwise exist.

On this basis, such incitement, which does not involve physical contact or exposure of any sort is more serious than a category 2 offence which involves touching or exposure of naked genitalia or naked breasts by or of the victim. To provide colour to this example, if the analysis is correct, it is more serious to incite a child as this offender did than had he actually persuaded her to undress before a web camera and expose to him her breasts or genitalia. It would equally be more serious than persuading a boy to masturbate in front of a web camera. In our judgment, that simply cannot be right.

[Counsel for the Attorney General] suggests the difficulty can be addressed by reference to the mitigating fact in Step 2 of the Guideline described as 'sexual activity was incited but no activity took place because the offender desisted or intervened to prevent it.' [I]t would then be possible in the interests of justice to reduce the sentence below the category range to avoid the anomaly to which we have referred. In other words it is to treat the activity which may not be uncommon as an exception to the operation of the guideline, the mitigating factor to which [counsel] is referring covering slightly different circumstances.

The answer however is to recognise that this guideline covers very different offending and that the language used within it must be construed by particular reference to the offence then under consideration. Thus, if over a web camera, a female child is incited to insert an object into her vagina and she does so, a category 1 offence is committed; if a child is persuaded to touch or expose his or her naked genitalia and does so, that is a category 2 offence. Similarly, if a child is incited to persuade someone else (whether or not the offender) actually to behave in that manner, the offence is correctly characterised as category 1 or 2 respectively. The harm is the impact on the victim of behaving as he or she has done, whether in the presence of the offender or remotely or on line.

To that extent, the offence of causing sexual activity is potentially more serious than inciting such activity because the actual activity is a necessary part of the offence. Incitement can lead to actual activity which can be categorised accordingly. But where the incitement does not lead the child to behave in the manner incited, although the culpability is likely to be identical, the harm is necessarily less: the same is so in relation to attempts.

. . .

In our judgment, what happened here did not fall within category 1 at all. In the circumstances, because the offending did not proceed beyond incitement, it was 'other sexual activity' within category 3. That accords not only with the judge's rejection of the suggestion that the offender's behaviour justified a starting point of 5 years but also provides appropriate headroom between the sexual suggestion and any actual activity without necessarily engaging upon the exceptional basis for departing from the Guideline.

> The offence was undeniably one of high culpability but as category 3 had a starting point of 26 weeks in custody and a range up to 3 years' imprisonment the sentence passed by the learned judge fell fairly and squarely within it."

In all the circumstances, the Court concluded that the sentence of 180 days' imprisonment was entirely appropriate.

4.82   To similar effect is *Buchanan*,[113] where the appellant (46) appealed against a sentence of 12 months' imprisonment imposed after he pleaded guilty to inciting a child to engage in sexual activity. He and the victim, a girl of 14, made contact over the internet. They sent each other sexually explicit messages in which the offender stated that he wanted to have unprotected intercourse with her and asked her to send him a picture of herself. The victim had sent the messages from a school computer. A teacher became aware and reported the matter to the police. The sentencing judge noted that, although there were features of the offence which placed it into category 1A, the five-year starting point for custody seemed excessive given that there had been no physical contact. The judge therefore placed the offence in category 2, with a three-year starting point and a range of two to six years. But he took as his starting point two years, i.e. the very bottom of the range, and after giving credit for the guilty plea, sentenced the offender to 12 months' imprisonment. The offender submitted that an immediate custodial sentence was excessive, and the 12-month sentence was manifestly excessive. The Court of Appeal agreed that it was too long. It said that the case, serious as it was, was not one where the appropriate sentencing range was 4–10 years with a five-year starting point. The judge faced difficulty in classifying the offence and it was doubtful whether the guideline actually addressed this type of offending. However, if the offence was to be categorised using the guideline, the most appropriate category was 3A, which had a sentencing range of a high level community order ranging to a three-year custodial sentence with a 26-week starting point.[114] In view of the significant disparity in age between the offender and the victim and the fact that he had solicited sexual images, the judge was right to conclude that an immediate custodial sentence was appropriate. The appropriate starting point was 18 months' imprisonment. There was significant mitigation: immediately following his arrest the offender undertook treatment and courses to prevent re-offending; he had never committed an offence prior to this one; and the pre-sentence report referred to difficulties that he had at the time of the offending. A just sentence before reduction for the guilty plea would have been 12 months' imprisonment. Applying the full discount for his plea, the appropriate sentence was eight months' imprisonment.

4.83   What is one to make of these decisions? It is difficult to contest the common sense assertion of the Court of Appeal in *Attorney General's Reference (No.94 of 2014)* that it "cannot be right" that inciting a child to

[113] [2015] EWCA Crim 172.
[114] Citing *Evans* [2012] EWCA Crim 2183.

suck the offender's penis, where there is no physical contact of any sort, falls within category 1 but causing a child to expose her breasts or genitalia or to masturbate falls within category 2. However, in order to avoid this conclusion the Court in both cases effectively rewrote the guideline so that incitement will only ever fall within category 3 (and in principle will be mitigated further where no activity took place because the offender voluntarily desisted or intervened to prevent it). Moreover, in *Attorney General's Reference (No.94 of 2014)*, which is the more closely reasoned of the two decisions, the Court of Appeal did not express itself in terms confined to cyber offending. It would seem to follow that if, in that case, the offender had exposed his penis to the victim in her presence and asked her to suck it, he would have committed a category 3 offence attracting a starting point of 26 weeks. One might comment that this also "cannot be right". What is the answer? It cannot be to accept the submission of counsel for the Attorney General in *Attorney General's Reference (No.94 of 2014)*, that the offence in that case could be mitigated by reference to the factor "sexual activity was incited but no activity took place because the offender desisted or intervened to prevent it". As noted above, this factor is clearly designed to cover the limited factual scenario in which sexual activity does not take place by reason of the offender's own conduct. This cannot justify a lesser sentence where sexual activity did not take place rather because the victim declined. This is not to suggest, however, that the offender in *Attorney General's Reference (No.94 of 2014)* should have been sentenced within the range for category 1. A case of this sort, where there is incitement to sexual activity by words alone unaccompanied by sexual activity on the part of the offender, clearly merits a lesser sentence than causing the same activity, or inciting it in circumstances in which the offender engages in sexual activity himself or exposes the victim to such activity. The real problem is that the guideline fails to deal head-on with the range of possible offending that s.10 can cover. As the Court of Appeal said in *Attorney General's Reference (No.94 of 2014)*, the harm of behaviour that offends against s.10 lies in the impact of that behaviour on the victim, whether it takes place in the offender's presence or on line. In that case, there appears to have been no evidence that the victim suffered any particular harm as a result of the offence: the judgment says only that the offender's messages made her feel "cringey". As noted above, the guideline is drafted on the basis that penetrative sexual activity is "generally" more harmful to the child than non-penetrative activity. But where penetrative sexual activity is incited in circumstances such as in this case, the harm may well be at a low level; and where this is so, a sentence significantly below the category range may be appropriate. It is regrettable that the guideline does not acknowledge this, but instead indicates that offences of incitement should be regarded as falling within the offence category that would have applied if the sexual activity incited had actually taken place. It is equally regrettable that, in order to avoid following this indication and to work justice in the particular case, the Court of Appeal was prepared to take an approach that in effect placed all offences of incitement in category 3.

Parties to the Offence

4.84 An offence under s.10 may be committed by and against persons of either sex. The defendant (A) must be 18 or over and the complainant (B) must be under 16. A person attains the age of 16 at the commencement of the sixteenth anniversary of his birth and the age of 18 at the commencement of its eighteenth anniversary.[115] For proof of age, see paras 3.73 and following, above. If A is under 18, the appropriate charge is under s.13 (child sex offences committed by children or young persons). As to whether a child under 16 may be convicted as an accessory to an offence of which they are the victim, see paras 4.57 and following, above.

Jurisdiction

4.85 By virtue of s.72 of and Sch.2 to the Sexual Offences Act 2003, as amended,[116] it is an offence under s.10 for a UK national to do an act in a country outside the UK which would constitute a s.10 offence if done in England and Wales. See further para.4.59, above.

"Causes or Incites Another Person"

4.86 For the meaning of "causing" and "inciting", see paras 2.98 and 3.158 and following, above. In *R. v M*,[117] the respondent approached a 13-year-old girl and handed her a note, telling her to keep it quiet. The note read:

> "Between me and you your beautiful and have a nice bum lol. Come round for some fun if you want to at 12. Please keep it quiet tho. If you don't that's fine. Come round the back if you do. x."

The respondent was charged under s.10 with inciting the girl to engage in sexual activity. At the close of the prosecution case the trial judge made a terminating ruling on the ground that, whilst the note contained an invitation to engage in sexual activity, it did not constitute incitement to do so. This ruling was reversed on appeal, the Court of Appeal stating that it had no doubt that the words used in the note were capable of amounting to incitement. The note was certainly a proposal or a request, and it sought to influence the mind of the girl by reference to a flattering description of her body and the prospect of having fun. It was open to the jury to conclude that by handing the note to the girl the respondent was inciting sexual activity in

---

[115] Family Law reform Act 1969 s.9(1).
[116] By the Criminal Justice and Immigration Act 2008 s.72, which came into force on July 14, 2008.
[117] Unreported, November 11, 2014.

that he was proposing, seeking to instigate and stimulating it. Neither was this inconsistent with the note being an invitation which the girl was at liberty to refuse, as it was a perfectly legitimate inference that the respondent wanted her to accept.

"TO ENGAGE IN AN ACTIVITY"

For the meaning of this term, see paras 2.99 and following and 3.164, above.   **4.87**

"THE ACTIVITY IS SEXUAL"

For the meaning of this term, see paras 2.66 and following and 3.165, above.   **4.88**

"PENETRATION"

For the meaning of this term, see paras 1.156 and following, above.   **4.89**

"VAGINA"

For the meaning of this term, see para.1.155, above.   **4.90**

CONSENT

Absence of consent is not an element of the s.10 offences. Accordingly, an offence is committed regardless of whether B agrees to engage in the sexual activity in question or goes along with A's incitement of it (as the case may be).   **4.91**

MENTAL ELEMENT

A must intentionally cause or incite B to engage in sexual activity. For the meaning of "intention" and the question whether A must intend to cause or incite activity which is sexual, see paras 2.78 and following, above. Recklessness will not suffice.[118] See further the discussion of *Heard*[119] in para.4.65, above, which is equally applicable in the context of s.10. On intoxication, see paras 2.81 and following, above.   **4.92**

As to the requirement, where B is 13, 14 or 15, that A does not reasonably believe that B is 16 or over, see para.4.66, above.   **4.93**

---

[118] *Heard* [2007] EWCA Crim 125, at [22].
[119] [2007] EWCA Crim 125.

Engaging in Sexual Activity in the Presence of a Child

Definition

4.94   Section 11(1) of the Sexual Offences Act 2003 provides:

> "A person aged 18 or over (A) commits an offence if—
> (a) he intentionally engages in an activity,
> (b) the activity is sexual,
> (c) for the purpose of obtaining sexual gratification, he engages in it—
>   (i) when another person (B) is present or is in a place from which A can be observed, and
>   (ii) knowing or believing that B is aware, or intending that B should be aware, that he is engaging in it, and
> (d) either—
>   (i) B is under 16 and A does not reasonably believe that B is 16 or over, or
>   (ii) B is under 13."

Mode of Trial and Punishment

4.95   The offence under s.11 is triable either way. The maximum sentence on conviction on indictment is 10 years' imprisonment. On summary conviction it is six months' imprisonment or a fine, or both.[120] As from a day to be appointed the maximum sentence of imprisonment on summary conviction will increase to 12 months.[121] The increase will have no application to offences committed before it takes effect.[122] Until recently, the maximum fine on summary conviction was a fine not exceeding the statutory maximum (i.e. £5,000). The effect of s.85 of the Legal Aid, Sentencing and Punishment of Offenders Act 2012 is that, from March 12, 2015, a fine of any amount may be imposed. The s.11 offence cannot be dealt with by way of a simple caution.[123]

4.96   For the purposes of listing, cases under s.11[124] fall within Class 2B, save for complex cases involving many complainants (often under age, in care or otherwise particularly vulnerable) and/or many defendants who are alleged to have systematically groomed and abused them, often over a long period of time, which fall within Class 1C.[125] Cases in Class 1C must be referred to the Resident Judge, and by the Resident Judge to a Presiding Judge. Cases in

---

[120] s.11(2).
[121] Criminal Justice Act 2003 s.282(2), (3).
[122] Criminal Justice Act 2003 s.282(4).
[123] Criminal Justice and Courts Act 2015 s.17(3), and the Criminal Justice and Courts Act 2015 (Simple Cautions) (Specification of Either-Way Offences) Order 2015 (SI 2015/790).
[124] And of soliciting, inciting, encouraging or assisting, attempting or conspiring to commit the offence or assisting an offender having committed the offence.
[125] *Consolidated Criminal Practice Directions*, Part XIII Listing B: CLASSIFICATION, available at *https://www.judiciary.gov.uk/wp-content/uploads/2015/09/crim-pd-2015.pdf* [Accessed April 30, 2016].

Class 2B must be similarly referred in certain specified circumstances, including where the case is unusually grave or complex or a novel and important point of law is to be raised; where the defendant is a police officer, a member of the legal profession or a high profile figure; or where for any reason the case is likely to attract exceptional media attention.

The offence under s.11 is a serious specified offence for the purposes of the **4.97** dangerousness provisions of the Criminal Justice Act 2003.[126] A s.11 offence, whenever committed, may be made the subject of an extended sentence under s.226A of that Act.[127] The offence is also listed in Pt 1 of Sch.15B to the Criminal Justice Act 2003 for the purposes of s.224A of that Act (life sentence for a second listed offence).[128]

A person convicted under s.11, cautioned, found not guilty by reason of **4.98** insanity or found to be under a disability and to have done the act charged, is automatically subject to the notification requirements in the Sexual Offences Act 2003.[129]

During the passage of the Sexual Offences Bill through Parliament, **4.99** amendments were tabled which would have made the s.11 offence triable only on indictment either in all cases or where B is under 13, on the basis that summary trial in such cases is inappropriate.[130] The Government resisted these amendments, which were not put to the vote, on the ground that the offence covers a wide range of offending behaviour and that trial in the Crown Court might not always be necessary.[131]

Sentencing

For the Sentencing Council guideline relating to the sentencing of sexual **4.100** offences committed by offenders aged 18 and over, see Ch.33, below. The previous guideline, issued in 2007 by the Sentencing Guidelines Council ("SGC"), treated separately the offences of engaging in sexual activity in the presence of a child (s.11) and causing a child to watch a sexual act (s.12 of the 2003 Act). In consulting on its draft guideline,[132] the Sentencing Council said that it proposed to deal with the offences in a single guideline, as they involve common offending behaviours, are equally harmful and share a statutory maximum of 10 years' imprisonment. Further, there is now increased

---

[126] Criminal Justice Act 2003 s.224 and Sch.15, Pt 2.
[127] Inserted by the Legal Aid, Sentencing and Punishment of Offenders Act 2012 s.124, brought into force on December 3, 2012, by SI 2012/2906.
[128] Inserted by the Legal Aid, Sentencing and Punishment of Offenders Act 2012 s.122, brought into force on December 3, 2012, by SI 2012/2906.
[129] s.80 and Sch.3, discussed in Ch.35, below.
[130] *Hansard*, HL, vol.646, col.1200 (April 1, 2003); vol.648, col.1099 (June 2, 2003); vol.649, col.679 (June 17, 2003).
[131] *Hansard*, HL, vol.646, col.1202, Lord Falconer of Thoroton (April 1, 2003); vol.648, col.1101, Lord Falconer of Thoroton (June 2, 2003); vol.649, col.681, Baroness Scotland of Asthal (June 17, 2003).
[132] *Sexual Offences Guideline: Consultation* (December 6, 2012). The consultation document is available on the Sentencing Council's website.

understanding of the ways in which children can be groomed and that the activities covered by both of these offences can be deployed by offenders to normalise and desensitise children to sexual activity. The Council duly followed the proposed approach in the published guideline.

Sentencing guideline

Step One—Harm and culpability

4.101   The guideline requires the sentencing court to go through a series of steps in order to determine the appropriate sentence. Step one involves determining the offence category by reference to the degree of harm caused and then the culpability level for the offence.

Harm

4.102   Severity of harm is determined in this guideline by the type of sexual activity viewed by the victim. The SGC guideline gave the highest starting point to images of consensual penetration and live sexual activity. However, the Sentencing Council believed that the highest starting point should relate to acts of sexual depravity and images portraying such acts, because of their distorting effect on the child's view of such activity. The harm factors for the offences in ss.11 and 12 of the 2003 Act are therefore as follows:

Harm	
Category 1	• Causing victim to view extreme pornography • Causing victim to view indecent/prohibited images of children • Engaging in, or causing a victim to view live, sexual activity involving sadism/violence/sexual activity with an animal/a child
Category 2	Engaging in, or causing a victim to view images of or view live, sexual activity involving: • penetration of vagina or anus (using body or object) • penile penetration of the mouth • masturbation
Category 3	Factor(s) in categories 1 and 2 not present

4.103   The term "extreme pornography" in category 1 is intended to refer to s.63 of the Criminal Justice and Immigration Act 2008,[133] which makes it an

---

[133] Amended by s.37 of the Criminal Justice and Courts Act 2015 with effect from April 13, 2015 (see SI 2015/778).

offence to possess an "extreme pornographic image". This offence had not been created when the SGC guideline was drafted and the Sentencing Council believed that its existence needed to be reflected in sentencing guidance for offences under ss.11 and 12. An image is "pornographic" for the purposes of s.63 if it is of such a nature that it must reasonably be assumed to have been produced solely or principally for the purpose of sexual arousal.[134] An image is "extreme" if it portrays, in an explicit and realistic way:

- an act which threatens a person's life;
- an act which results, or is likely to result, in serious injury to a person's anus, breasts or genitals;
- an act which involves sexual interference with a human corpse;
- a person performing an act of intercourse or oral sex with an animal (whether dead or alive);
- an act which involves the non-consensual penetration of a person's vagina, anus or mouth by another with the other person's penis; or
- an act which involves the non-consensual sexual penetration of a person's vagina or anus by another with a part of the other person's body or anything else,

where a reasonable person would think that any person or animal portrayed in the image was real, and the image is grossly offensive, disgusting or otherwise of an obscene character.[135] The offence covers any image falling within this definition, irrespective of whether the act portrayed is real, simulated or staged.

Category 2 deals with penetrative sexual activity and masturbation, **4.104** whether live or in the form of images. Causing a victim to view penetrative activity was the highest category of harm in the SGC guideline. As will be seen below, the Sentencing Council has retained similar sentence levels for causing a child to view this type of activity, but felt that the sorts of depravity covered by category 1 deserved even higher sentence starting points and ranges.

Culpability

As for culpability, the Sentencing Council noted that offenders can expose a **4.105** child to sexual imagery in order to desensitise them and so facilitate further sexual offending by the offender or others. It therefore considered that the culpability factors for offences under ss.11 and 12 of the 2003 Act should focus on whether there is evidence of such grooming or manipulation of the child. As a result, an offender's culpability will increase where, alongside the sexual gratification they gain by exposing the child to the sexual activity or

---

[134] s.63(3).
[135] s.63(5A), (7), (7A).

389

imagery, the offender deliberately tries to corrupt and desensitise the child. The culpability factors for these offences are:

CULPABILITY
A
• Significant degree of planning • Offender acts together with others in order to commit the offence • Use of alcohol/drugs on victim to facilitate the offence • Grooming behaviour used against victim • Abuse of trust • Use of threats (including blackmail) • Specific targeting of a particularly vulnerable child • Significant disparity in age • Commercial exploitation and/or motivation • Offence racially or religiously aggravated • Offence motivated by, or demonstrating, hostility to the victim based on his or her sexual orientation (or presumed sexual orientation) or transgender identity (or presumed transgender identity) • Offence motivated by, or demonstrating, hostility to the victim based on his or her disability (or presumed disability)
B
Factor(s) in category A not present

For discussion of the culpability A factors, see paras 4.36 and following, above. No factors are listed under culpability B, but the sentence starting points and ranges reflect the inherently abusive and corrupting behaviour that will always be present when an offender exposes a child to sexual imagery for the offender's sexual gratification.

Step Two—Starting point and category range

4.106   Once the court has determined the offence category and culpability level, at step two it should use the corresponding starting point specified in the guideline in order to reach a sentence within the category range. The starting point applies to all offenders irrespective of plea or previous convictions. Once the starting point has been determined, step two allows further adjustment for aggravating or mitigating features, as set out below. A case of particular gravity, reflected by multiple features of culpability or harm, could merit upward adjustment from the starting point before further adjustment for aggravating or mitigating features. Where there is a sufficient prospect of rehabilitation, a community order with a sex offender treatment programme requirement under s.202 of the Criminal Justice Act 2003 may be a proper alternative to a short or moderate length custodial sentence. The starting points and category ranges for offences under ss.11 and 12 of the Act are as follows:

	A	B
Category 1	Starting point 4 years' custody Category range 3–6 years' custody	Starting point 2 years' custody Category range 1–3 years' custody
Category 2	Starting point 2 years' custody Category range 1–3 years' custody	Starting point 1 year's custody Category range High level community order – 18 months' custody
Category 3	Starting point 26 weeks' custody Category range High level community order – 1 year's custody	Starting point Medium level community order Category range Low level community order – Medium level community order

The maximum sentences recommended in the SGC guideline were two years' imprisonment with a range of 1–4 years' imprisonment for sexual activity in the presence of a child involving consensual penetration, and 18 months' imprisonment with a range of 12 months–2 years' imprisonment for causing or inciting a child to watch a live sexual act. Both of these types of activity are now likely to fall within category 2, though with sentence levels similar to those under the SGC guideline. As explained above, the Council placed in category 1 activity that it regarded as more harmful to the child, for example, where the child is caused to watch sexual activity or pornography that involves sadism or is shown indecent images of children. The Council considered that the harm done to the child is increased in such cases by the extreme nature of the activity or imagery and that, where this is combined with manipulative and coercive behaviour on the part of the offender, so as to fall within culpability A, it should attract a custodial sentence higher than provided in the SGC guideline.

Aggravating and mitigating factors

4.107   After identifying the starting point and category range, the court should consider whether the presence of aggravating or mitigating factors should result in an upward or downward adjustment from the starting point or the imposition of a sentence outside the category range. In particular, relevant recent convictions are likely to result in an upward adjustment. When sentencing appropriate category 2 or 3 offences, the court should also consider whether the custody threshold has been passed; if so, whether a custodial sentence is unavoidable; and if it is, whether that sentence can be suspended. The non-exhaustive list of aggravating and mitigating factors for offences under ss.11 and 12 is as follows:

Aggravating factors
Statutory aggravating factors
• Previous convictions, having regard to a) the nature of the offence to which the conviction relates and its relevance to the current offence; and b) the time that has elapsed since the conviction • Offence committed whilst on bail
Other aggravating factors
• Location of offence • Timing of offence • Victim compelled to leave their home, school, etc. • Failure to comply with current court orders • Offence committed whilst on licence • Exploiting contact arrangements with a child to commit an offence • Presence of others, especially other children • Any steps taken to prevent the victim reporting an incident, obtaining assistance and/or from assisting or supporting the prosecution • Attempts to dispose of or conceal evidence • Failure of offender to respond to previous warnings • Commission of offence whilst under the influence of alcohol or drugs • Victim encouraged to recruit others

---

Mitigating factors

- No previous convictions **or** no relevant/recent convictions
- Remorse
- Previous good character and/or exemplary conduct*
- Age and/or lack of maturity where it affects the responsibility of the offender
- Mental disorder or learning disability, particularly where linked to the commission of the offence
- Demonstration of steps taken to address offending behaviour

---

* Previous good character/exemplary conduct is different from having no previous convictions. The more serious the offence, the less the weight which should normally be attributed to this factor. Where previous good character/exemplary conduct has been used to facilitate the offence, this mitigation should not normally be allowed and such conduct may constitute an aggravating factor.

For an example of possible additional aggravating factors, see *Buckingham*,[136] decided under the SGC guideline, where the court treated the offences as aggravated by the fact that they were part of a course of conduct lasting two or three days and involving extensive humiliation of the complainant.

Steps Three to Nine

The remaining steps cover the following points. At step three the court **4.108** should consider any factors which would indicate a reduction in sentence, e.g. assistance to the prosecution. At step four it should consider any reduction for a guilty plea. At step five the court should consider dangerousness, i.e. whether it would be appropriate to award a life sentence (s.224A of the Criminal Justice Act 2003) or an extended sentence (s.226A). Step six requires the court to consider whether the total sentence is just and proportionate to the offending behaviour. At step seven it should consider whether to make an ancillary order (e.g. a compensation order, a SHPO or a restraining order). Step eight requires the court to fulfil its duty under s.174 of the Criminal Justice Act 2003 to give reasons for, and explain the effect of, the sentence. Finally, at step nine the court should consider whether to give credit for time spent on bail in accordance with s.240A of that Act.

Sentencing example

In *Alderton*,[137] which concerned offences under s.11, the Court of Appeal **4.109** unfortunately failed to explain its reasoning by reference to the guideline, but instead adopted an impressionistic approach to the appeal focussed on

---

[136] [2012] EWCA Crim 1874.
[137] [2014] EWCA Crim 2204.

"totality". This reduces the decision's instructional value, though it does exemplify the likely attitude of the Court towards a not uncommon set of facts. The appellant (43) pleaded guilty at a plea and case management hearing to five offences of breaching a SOPO; two offences under s.11 of engaging in sexual activity in the presence of a child; one offence of attempting to engage in sexual activity in the presence of a child; and six offences of exposure contrary to s.66 of the 2003 Act. The appellant's offending involved him masturbating on camera after making contact with people online and asking them to watch. Some of the people he already knew, some he did not. They included young girls, one only eight years old. The appellant used different online identities and sometimes posed as a child. All the offences were committed while the appellant was subject to a community order imposed for three not dissimilar offences, namely, attempting to engage in sexual activity with a child, distributing an indecent photograph of a child and possessing indecent photographs of a child. When the community order was imposed the appellant had also been made subject to an indefinite SOPO, which prohibited him from using technology allowing access to the internet and having unsupervised contact with any female under the age of 18. He had no other convictions for sexual offences. In passing sentence, the judge described the appellant as a compulsive masturbator and exhibitionist who obtained sexual gratification completely oblivious to the impact he had on his victims. The offences were aggravated by the entrenched nature and persistence of the appellant's behaviour in defiance of earlier court orders, and the number and youth of his victims. The pre-sentence report assessed the appellant as being at very high risk of sexual re-offending. The judge sentenced the appellant to a total of seven years' imprisonment, made up of four years' imprisonment concurrent for each breach of the SOPO; four years concurrent for the offences under s.11 and the attempt to commit that offence; and 18 months for each offence of exposure, to run concurrently with each other but consecutively to the earlier sentences. The judge also revoked the community order and re-sentenced the appellant to 18 months' imprisonment for each of the three offences to which it related, to run concurrently with each other but consecutively to the other sentences. The total sentence was therefore seven years' imprisonment. On appeal, the appellant submitted that the total sentence passed was too long, given that it represented a starting point, before discount for the guilty pleas, in or approaching double figures. The Court of Appeal was in no doubt that a substantial sentence of imprisonment was merited in this case, but was persuaded that, having regard to the totality of the offending and to the guilty pleas, the sentence was manifestly excessive. The appropriate overall sentence should have been six years' imprisonment. In order to achieve a total sentence of that length, the Court quashed the sentences of four years' imprisonment imposed for each breach of the SOPO and for the offences under s.11 and the attempt to commit that offence and substituted concurrent terms of three years' imprisonment. It is worth noting that the s.11

offences involved causing children to view images of masturbation and so will have fallen within category 2, and the three-year sentences were at the top of the range for category 2A. It is therefore regrettable that the Court of Appeal did not identify the culpability A factors present in the case.

PARTIES TO THE OFFENCE

The offence under s.11 may be committed by and against persons of either **4.110** sex. The defendant (A) must be 18 or over and the complainant (B) must be under 16. A person attains the age of 16 at the commencement of the sixteenth anniversary of his birth and the age of 18 at the commencement of its eighteenth anniversary.[138] For proof of age, see paras 3.73 and following, above. If A is under 18, the appropriate charge is under s.13 (child sex offences committed by children or young persons) read with s.10. As to whether a child under 16 may be convicted as an accessory to an offence of which they are the victim, see paras 4.57 and following, above.

JURISDICTION

By virtue of s.72 of and Sch.2 to the Sexual Offences Act 2003, as **4.111** amended, it is an offence under s.11 for a UK national to do an act in a country outside the UK which would constitute a s.11 offence if done in England and Wales. See further para.4.59, above.

"ENGAGES IN AN ACTIVITY"

For the meaning of this term, see paras 2.99 and following and 3.163, **4.112** above.

"THE ACTIVITY IS SEXUAL"

For the meaning of this term, see paras 2.66 and following and 3.164, **4.113** above.

"PRESENT OR . . . IN A PLACE FROM WHICH A CAN BE OBSERVED"

If A engages in sexual activity when B is present, there is no requirement that **4.114** B must observe or be able to observe it, provided A intends, knows or believes that B is aware of it. So the offence will be committed where A and B are present together, A is masturbating, B cannot see the activity (e.g.

---

[138] Family Law Reform Act 1969 s.9(1).
[139] By the Criminal Justice and Immigration Act 2008 s.72, which came into force on July 14, 2008.

because he has covered his face or A is standing behind him), but A is describing to B what he is doing. Even if B is unaware of the activity, A may still be convicted if he intends or believes that B is aware of it.

4.115 Whether B is "present" when A engages in the relevant activity could raise difficult questions of fact and degree depending on the precise circumstances. If B is not present, A may nonetheless be convicted if B is in a place from which A can be observed. So an offence will be committed (provided the mental element can be established) if, for example, B is on a pier overlooking a beach on which A is openly masturbating, or is at the window of a house overlooking an adjoining garden in which A1 and A2 are having sexual intercourse. This is so even if B does not observe A, provided A can in fact be observed from that place. Section 79(7) provides that references to observation are to observation whether direct or by looking at an image. Observation by means of binoculars would seem to qualify as direct observation. By s.79(4), "image" means a moving or still image and includes an image produced by any means and, where the context permits, a three-dimensional image. These provisions ensure that s.11 covers the case where A sends B an image of himself engaging in sexual activity via a webcam or a photo messaging mobile phone, or where B can observe A on a CCTV screen. But it appears from the wording of the section that the sexual activity must be engaged in contemporaneously with B's ability to observe A. So there is no offence where B can observe A only by playing a recording of him engaging in the activity, e.g. by downloading and viewing an internet clip.

Consent

4.116 Absence of consent is not an element of the s.11 offence. Accordingly, the offence is committed regardless of whether the child agrees to the sexual activity taking place in their presence.

Mental Element

4.117 A must engage in the sexual activity intentionally. For the meaning of "intention" see paras 2.78 and following, above. A must also engage in the activity for the purpose of obtaining sexual gratification. It is not sufficient that A engages in it, for example, in order to shock B or simply by way of attention-seeking. A's purpose must be to obtain sexual gratification from B's presence or from being observed by B, rather than from the sexual activity itself.[140] The Home Office guidance on Pt 1 of the Act elaborates this point:

> "The offence is intended to cover the situation where someone seeks sexual gratification not from the sexual act itself but rather from the fact that he is

---

[140] *R. v W, T* [2005] EWCA Crim 2448, at [4] per Mitting J; *Ali and Ashraf* [2015] EWCA Crim 1279, at [76] per Fulford LJ.

performing that act in the presence or intended presence of a child. The motive of sexual gratification is a necessary safeguard intended to avoid capturing those who engage in sexual activity in front of a child for a legitimate reason. For example, a teacher who sexually kisses his partner just outside the school gates, could be deemed to be engaging in sexual activity intentionally in front of a child and might otherwise be caught by the offence.[141]

See further on this aspect para.5.98, below.

A must know or believe that B is aware, or intend that B should be aware, **4.118** that he is engaging in the activity. But there is no requirement that B must actually be aware: see para.4.114, above.

As to the requirement, where B is 13, 14 or 15, that A does not reasonably **4.119** believe that B is 16 or over, see para.4.66, above.

As to whether A is liable to conviction if he acts whilst in a state of **4.120** intoxication, see *Heard*,[142] discussed in paras 2.81 and following, above. In the light of that discussion, voluntary intoxication through drink or drugs will provide a defence to a charge under s.11 if it may have prevented the defendant forming the purpose of obtaining sexual gratification.

CAUSING A CHILD TO WATCH A SEXUAL ACT

DEFINITION

Section 12(1) of the Sexual Offences Act 2003 provides: **4.121**

"A person aged 18 or over (A) commits an offence if—
(a) for the purpose of obtaining sexual gratification, he intentionally causes another person (B) to watch a third person engaging in an activity, or to look at an image of any person engaging in an activity,
(b) the activity is sexual, and
(c) either—
(i) B is under 16 and A does not reasonably believe that B is 16 or over, or
(ii) B is under 13."

The better view is that s.12 creates one offence that can be committed in two **4.122** different ways, by causing another person to watch a third person engaging in a sexual activity or by causing another person to look at an image of any person engaging in sexual activity. The charge or indictment should make clear which variant of the offence is alleged. The s.12 offence is intended to protect children from exposure to pornographic material or to sexual activity engaged in by others. It has its genesis in concerns about the sexual grooming of children by paedophiles, which can begin with the exposure of children to pornography as a way of breaking down their inhibitions and accustoming them to sexual behaviour.

---

[141] H.O. Circular 21/2004: *Guidance on Part 1 of the Sexual Offences Act 2003*, para.62.
[142] [2007] EWCA Crim 125.

MODE OF TRIAL AND PUNISHMENT

4.123   The offence under s.12 is triable either way. The maximum sentence on conviction on indictment is 10 years' imprisonment. On summary conviction it is six months' imprisonment or a fine, or both.[143] As from a day to be appointed the maximum sentence of imprisonment on summary conviction will increase to 12 months.[144] The increase will have no application to offences committed before it takes effect.[145] Until recently, the maximum fine on summary conviction was a fine not exceeding the statutory maximum (i.e. £5,000). The effect of s.85 of the Legal Aid, Sentencing and Punishment of Offenders Act 2012 is that, from March 12, 2015, a fine of any amount may be imposed. The s.12 offence cannot be dealt with by way of a simple caution.[146]

4.124   For the purposes of listing, cases under s.12[147] fall within Class 2B, save for complex cases involving many complainants (often under age, in care or otherwise particularly vulnerable) and/or many defendants who are alleged to have systematically groomed and abused them, often over a long period of time, which fall within Class 1C.[148] Cases in Class 1C must be referred to the Resident Judge, and by the Resident Judge to a Presiding Judge. Cases in Class 2B must be similarly referred in certain specified circumstances, including where the case is unusually grave or complex or a novel and important point of law is to be raised; where the defendant is a police officer, a member of the legal profession or a high profile figure; or where for any reason the case is likely to attract exceptional media attention.

4.125   The offence under s.12 is a serious specified offence for the purposes of the dangerousness provisions of the Criminal Justice Act 2003.[149] Accordingly a s.12 offence, whenever committed, may be made the subject of an extended sentence under s.226A of that Act.[150] The offence is also listed in Pt 1 of Sch.15B to the Criminal Justice Act 2003 for the purposes of s.224A of that Act (life sentence for a second listed offence).[151]

---

[143] s.12(2).

[144] Criminal Justice Act 2003 s.282(2), (3).

[145] Criminal Justice Act 2003 s.282(4).

[146] Criminal Justice and Courts Act 2015 s.17(3), and the Criminal Justice and Courts Act 2015 (Simple Cautions) (Specification of Either-Way Offences) Order 2015 (SI 2015/790).

[147] And of soliciting, inciting, encouraging or assisting, attempting or conspiring to commit the offence or assisting an offender having committed the offence.

[148] *Consolidated Criminal Practice Directions*, Part XIII Listing B: CLASSIFICATION, available at *https://www.judiciary.gov.uk/wp-content/uploads/2015/09/crim-pd-2015.pdf* [Accessed April 30, 2016].

[149] Criminal Justice Act 2003 s.224 and Sch.15, Pt 2.

[150] Inserted by the Legal Aid, Sentencing and Punishment of Offenders Act 2012 s.124, brought into force on December 3, 2012, by SI 2012/2906.

[151] Inserted by the Legal Aid, Sentencing and Punishment of Offenders Act 2012 s.122, brought into force on December 3, 2012, by SI 2012/2906.

A person convicted under s.12, cautioned, found not guilty by reason of   **4.126**
insanity or found to be under a disability and to have done the act charged,
is automatically subject to the notification requirements in the Sexual
Offences Act 2003.[152]

During the passage of the Sexual Offences Bill through Parliament,   **4.127**
amendments were tabled which would have made the s.12 offence triable only
on indictment where B is under 13, on the basis that summary trial in such
cases is inappropriate.[153] The Government resisted these amendments, which
were not put to the vote, on the ground that the offence covers a wide range
of offending behaviour and that trial in the Crown Court might not always
be necessary.[154] In Committee, Lord Falconer of Thoroton gave as an
example of a case where summary trial might be appropriate, even when the
child is under 13, one where an 18-year-old causes a 12-year-old to watch a
pornographic film.[155] On Third Reading, Baroness Scotland of Asthal cited
as another possible example an 18-year-old showing a 12-year-old a photograph of two people kissing or sexually fondling.[156]

SENTENCING

For the Sentencing Council guideline relating to the sentencing of sexual   **4.128**
offences committed by offenders aged 18 and over, see Ch.33, below. A single
guideline covers the offences in ss.11 and 12 of the Act and is considered at
para.4.67 and following, above.

PARTIES TO THE OFFENCE

The offence under s.12 may be committed by and against persons of either   **4.129**
sex. The defendant (A) must be 18 or over and the child (B) must be under
16. A person attains the age of 16 at the commencement of the sixteenth
anniversary of her birth and the age of 18 at the commencement of its
eighteenth anniversary.[157] For proof of age, see para.3.73, above. If A is under
18, the appropriate charge is under s.13 (child sex offences committed by
children or young persons) read with s.11. As to whether a child under 16
may be convicted as an accessory to an offence of which they are the victim,
see paras 4.57 and following, above.

---

[152] s.80 and Sch.3, discussed in Ch.35, below.
[153] *Hansard*, HL, vol.648, col.1099 (June 2, 2003); vol.649, col.679 (June 17, 2003).
[154] *Hansard*, HL, vol.646, col.1202, Lord Falconer of Thoroton (April 1, 2003); vol.648, col.1101, Lord Falconer of Thoroton (June 2, 2003); vol.649, col.681, Baroness Scotland of Asthal (June 17, 2003).
[155] *Hansard*, HL, vol.646, col.1202 (April 1, 2003).
[156] *Hansard*, HL, vol.649, col.681 (June 17, 2003).
[157] Family Law Reform Act 1969 s.9(1).

JURISDICTION

4.130   By virtue of s.72 of and Sch.2 to the Sexual Offences Act 2003, as amended,[158] it is an offence under s.12 for a UK national to do an act in a country outside the UK which would constitute a s.12 offence if done in England and Wales. See further para.4.59, above.

ATTEMPT

4.131   *R. v K*[159] concerned an appeal against conviction of attempting to commit the s.12 offence. The appellant worked as a security guard in a residential tower block. He spoke to some children aged 13, 11 and 6 outside the entrance to the block and, according to the evidence of the 11-year-old, asked the 6-year-old if he would like to look at pornographic DVDs. The appellant's account was instead that it was the 6-year-old who asked if he could view girls on the internet. The judge directed the jury that they were entitled to draw an inference from the evidence that the appellant had a laptop in the concierge area of the block. He went on to direct them that in order to convict they had to be sure that the invitation had been made, and if they were sure of that, they then had to decide whether the invitation was mere preparation or an attempt. When the jury sought clarification, the judge directed them to the effect that if they were sure that the invitation had been issued and that there was a laptop in the concierge area that the appellant would use to show pornography, then they would have to consider whether the appellant's actions were more than merely preparatory. The ensuing conviction was quashed by the Court of Appeal on the ground that the invitation and the presence of a laptop were not in themselves sufficient to constitute an attempt.

4.132   The editors of *Blackstone's* considered the decision in *R. v K* likely to stimulate debate, since "if the child had accepted the invitation, all that would have remained for the full offence to be committed would be for the child to accompany the accused to the concierge area and then for the accused to show the pornography".[160] The decision does indeed seem borderline, given that by issuing the invitation to the child the appellant was taking perhaps the critical step towards committing the full offence. On the other hand, even if the child had accepted the invitation, the appellant would have committed the full offence only when he had accompanied the child to the concierge area and showed him pornography on the laptop. For that reason, it is understandable that the Court of Appeal held that the appellant had not gone beyond mere preparation, though clearly the preparation could

---

[158] By the Criminal Justice and Immigration Act 2008 s.72, which came into force on July 14, 2008.
[159] [2009] EWCA Crim 1931.
[160] Commentary in 2009 update to Blackstone's Criminal Practice, section B3.86.

be said to have been at an advanced stage. The editors of *Blackstone's* say the decision should be contrasted with *R. v R*,[161] discussed in para.4.173 and following, below, in which a man who asked a prostitute to find a girl of 12 or 13 for sex was convicted of attempting the offence under s.14 of the 2003 Act of arranging the commission of a child sexual offence. Why did the request in that case amount to an attempt, but the invitation in this one did not? The answer is that in *R. v R* the appellant had done all he needed to do to commit the full offence, since if the prostitute had responded positively to his request then the arrangement required by s.14 would have been made, with no need for any further action on the appellant's part. By contrast, the appellant in *R. v K* would have committed the full offence only if he had taken further steps after issuing the invitation.

"CAUSES"

For the meaning of "causes", see para.2.98, above. During the passage of the   **4.133** Sexual Offences Bill through Parliament, an amendment was tabled which would have extended the s.12 offence to cases where A "allows" B to watch sexual activity. The purpose was to catch someone who failed to take reasonable steps to prevent a child watching such activity. The Government argued against this amendment on the basis that it would extend the scope of the offence too far, e.g. to cover parents who consider it acceptable for their 15-year-old child to watch an X-rated film or to look at pornographic magazines, and allow him to do so.[162] This overlooks the point that in such cases the parents would not be acting "for the purpose of sexual gratification". If A, with that purpose, allows B to watch a pornographic film or read a pornographic magazine, it is certainly arguable that he should be liable to punishment in the same way as someone who causes B to undertake such activity. But that is not the law as enacted.

"TO WATCH A THIRD PERSON ENGAGING IN AN ACTIVITY, OR TO LOOK AT AN IMAGE OF ANY PERSON ENGAGING IN AN ACTIVITY"

The term "a third person" cannot include A, but the term "any person" can   **4.134** include him.[163] It follows that A does not commit the s.12 offence if he causes B to watch him (A) engaging in a sexual activity, but he does commit it if he causes B to look at an *image* of him engaging in the same activity, including a live image, i.e. one transmitted in real time.[164] The logic of this distinction is not obvious, though it may reflect the fact that, where A causes B to watch

---

[161] [2008] EWCA Crim 619.
[162] *Hansard*, HL, vol.646, col.1208, Lord Falconer of Thoroton (April 1, 2003).
[163] *Hansard*, HL, vol.646, col.1210, Lord Bassam of Brighton (April 1, 2003).
[164] See e.g. *Green* [2006] EWCA Crim 3294, where the offender caused a child of 12 to watch him masturbating via a webcam.

him (A) engaging in sexual activity, he is likely in any event to commit an offence under s.11 of the Act, discussed in paras 4.94 and following, above. For the meaning of "engaging in an activity", see paras 2.99 and following and 3.164, above.

4.135   Can A be charged under s.12 if, for the purpose of obtaining sexual gratification, he causes B to look at an image of his erect penis, e.g. by "sexting" her? We suggest that having an erection does not, without more, qualify as "engaging in an activity" for the purposes of the s.12 offence. It would be otherwise if, at the time the image was taken, A was masturbating. However, a man who, for the purpose of obtaining sexual gratification, sends a child an image of his erect penis will commit the offence of sexual communication with a child contrary to s.15A of the 2003 Act, discussed in paras 4.225 and following, below.

4.136   By s.79(4), "image" means a moving or still image and includes an image produced by any means and, where the context permits, a three-dimensional image. The term will therefore cover photographs and images produced by CCTV cameras, webcams and mobile phones. Section 79(5) provides that references to an image of a person include references to an image of an imaginary person. Accordingly, the term will cover pseudo-photographs within the meaning of the Protection of Children Act 1978[165] and also tracings, drawings and cartoons depicting sexual activity.

"THE ACTIVITY IS SEXUAL"

4.137   For the meaning of this term, see paras 2.66 and following and 3.165, above.

CONSENT

4.138   Absence of consent is not an element of the s.12 offence. Accordingly, the offence is committed regardless of whether the child agrees to watch the sexual activity or image.

MENTAL ELEMENT

4.139   A must cause B to watch, etc. intentionally and for the purpose of obtaining sexual gratification. For the meaning of "intention" see paras 2.78 and following, above. The meaning of "for the purpose of obtaining sexual gratification" was elucidated in *Abdullahi*,[166] where the appellant plied the 13-year-old victim with drink and drugs and caused him to watch pornographic films depicting heterosexual and homosexual activity. Later, he touched the victim's penis. He was convicted of offences under ss.9 and 12 of

[165] See paras 8.54 and following, below.
[166] [2006] EWCA Crim 2060.

the 2003 Act (sexual activity with a child and causing a child to watch a sexual act). In relation to the count under s.12, the trial judge directed the jury that they could convict if they were satisfied that the appellant did what he did "for the purpose of obtaining sexual gratification, either by enjoying seeing [the victim] looking at the images or with a view to getting [the victim] in the mood to provide sexual gratification to the defendant later". The appellant appealed, arguing that "for the purpose of obtaining sexual gratification" means for the purpose of obtaining *immediate* sexual gratification; that the judge had misdirected the jury that future gratification was sufficient; and that cases of future gratification or "putting the child in the mood" should be prosecuted instead under s.14 (arranging or facilitating the commission of a child sex offence). The Court of Appeal rejected this argument, holding that s.12 applies where the defendant's purpose is immediate gratification, or deferred gratification, or both immediate and deferred gratification. This is, with respect, an eminently sensible interpretation which avoids setting an evidential hurdle that prosecutors could often find impossible to surmount, in the form of a requirement to prove that the defendant's purpose was immediate rather than future sexual gratification. The decision does, however, have the effect of creating a significant overlap between the offences in ss.12 and 14.[167]

4.140　For the requirement, where B is 13, 14 or 15, that A does not reasonably believe that B is 16 or over, see para 4.66, above.

4.141　As to whether A is liable to conviction if he acts whilst in a state of intoxication, see the discussion of *Heard*[168] in paras 2.81 and following, above. In the light of that discussion, voluntary intoxication through drink or drugs will provide a defence to a charge under s.12 if it may have prevented the defendant forming the purpose of obtaining sexual gratification.

4.142　During the passage of the Sexual Offences Bill through Parliament, there were attempts to amend the offence so that it would be committed not only where A acted for the purpose of obtaining sexual gratification but also where he acted "for gain". The Government resisted these amendments, which were withdrawn, on the basis of their undesirable effects: they would, for example,have criminalised a film company which used an image of people kissing in an advert for a children's film, or a newspaper which printed pictures of models embracing in a state of undress, or even a teacher who was paid to deliver sex education lessons and distributed perfectly appropriate illustrated material or showed videos as part of the lessons.[169]

4.143　Amendments were also tabled, but not moved, which would have removed from the offence the word "intentionally" or added to them the words "or recklessly". The stated purpose was to catch the activity of paedophiles who may leave pornographic material lying around in the hope that children will

---

[167] See further the valuable commentary by Professor Ormerod at [2006] Crim. L.R. 185–6, and the articles cited therein.

[168] [2007] EWCA Crim 125.

[169] *Hansard*, HL, vol.646, vol.1205, Lord Falconer of Thoroton (April 1, 2003).

look at it. The Government argued against the amendments on the ground that they would extend the scope of the offence too far, so as to cover, for example, a who person accidentally or mistakenly leaves pornographic materials in a place where a child can and does find them.[170] Lord Falconer of Thoroton said that, while it is not unreasonable to expect adults to take care to keep sexually explicit material out of the reach of children, it would not be right to bring the full weight of the law against them in cases where a child finds and looks at such material.[171] Both sides to the debate seem to have overlooked the point that where a person acts accidentally or mistakenly, by definition he does not act "for the purpose of sexual gratification" and so the offence cannot in any event be committed.

CHILD SEX OFFENCES COMMITTED BY CHILDREN OR YOUNG PERSONS

DEFINITION

4.144   Section 13(1) of the Sexual Offences Act 2003 provides:

> "A person under 18 commits an offence if he does anything which would be an offence under any of sections 9 to 12 if he were aged 18."

4.145   The effect of this provision is to criminalise conduct by children and young people which falls within the scope of ss.9 to 12. However, it establishes a more lenient sentencing regime than applies to their adult counterparts, the maximum sentence on conviction on indictment being five years' imprisonment.[172]

4.146   Illustrations of the possible application of the s.13 offence are:

- A and B, boyfriend and girlfriend aged 15, kiss and caress each other. They both commit an offence if, as is likely, the jury consider their conduct "sexual" (conduct within s.9).
- A and B, girl and boy aged 13, meet at a party and kiss and caress each other. When they met, A told B that she was 16. She looks it, and he believed her. A knows that B is 13. B does not commit an offence but A does (conduct within s.9).
- A, aged 15, performs oral sex on B, his 15-year-old girlfriend. A's younger brother, C, knows that A intends to engage in such activity with B and agrees to keep watch to make sure their parents do not appear. A commits an offence (conduct within s.9) and C aids and abets it.
- A and B are 15-year-old boyfriend and girlfriend. A tries to persuade B to perform a strip for him. A commits an offence (conduct by

---

[170] The removal of the word "intentionally" would have had this effect, but the addition of the words "or recklessly" would require the defendant at least to realise that a child might see the material.

[171] *Hansard*, HL, vol.646, col.1209, Lord Falconer of Thoroton (April 1, 2003).

[172] s.14(2).

causing within s.10 if B strips or conduct by inciting within s.10 if she declines).

- A and B are friends aged 15. A encourages B to try groping B's girlfriend, C, also aged 15. If B refuses, A alone commits an offence (conduct by inciting within s.10). If B gropes C, A and B both commit an offence (A's conduct is within s.10 and B's within s.9).

MODE OF TRIAL AND PUNISHMENT

Offences under s.13 are triable either way. The maximum sentence on **4.147** conviction on indictment is five years' imprisonment. On summary conviction it is six months' imprisonment or a fine, or both. As from a day to be appointed the maximum sentence of imprisonment on summary conviction will increase to 12 months.[173] The increase will have no application to offences committed before it takes effect.[174] Until recently, the maximum fine on summary conviction was a fine not exceeding the statutory maximum (i.e. £5,000). The effect of s.85 of the Legal Aid, Sentencing and Punishment of Offenders Act 2012 is that, from March 12, 2015, a fine of any amount may be imposed.

For the purposes of listing, cases under s.13 that are tried in the Crown **4.148** Court fall within Class 2B, save for complex cases involving many complainants (often under age, in care or otherwise particularly vulnerable) and/or many defendants who are alleged to have systematically groomed and abused them, often over a long period of time, which fall within Class 1C.[175] Cases in Class 1C must be referred to the Resident Judge, and by the Resident Judge to a Presiding Judge. Cases in Class 2B must be similarly referred in certain specified circumstances, including where the case is unusually grave or complex or a novel and important point of law is to be raised; where the defendant is a police officer, a member of the legal profession or a high profile figure; or where for any reason the case is likely to attract exceptional media attention.

The offence under s.13 is a specified sexual offence for the purposes of the **4.149** Criminal Justice Act 2003.[176] The offence is also listed in Pt 1 of Sch.15B to that Act for the purposes of s.224A of the Act (life sentence for a second listed offence).[177]

A person convicted under s.13, cautioned, found not guilty by reason of **4.150** insanity or found to be under a disability and to have done the act charged,

---

[173] Criminal Justice Act 2003 s.282(2), (3).

[174] Criminal Justice Act 2003 s.282(4)

[175] *Consolidated Criminal Practice Directions*, Part XIII Listing B: CLASSIFICATION, available at *https://www.judiciary.gov.uk/wp-content/uploads/2015/09/crim-pd-2015.pdf* [Accessed April 30, 2016].

[176] s.224 and Sch.15, Pt 2.

[177] Inserted by the Legal Aid, Sentencing and Punishment of Offenders Act 2012 s.122, brought into force on December 3, 2012, by SI 2012/2906.

is automatically subject to the notification requirements in the Sexual Offences Act 2003.[178]

SENTENCING

4.151   For the Sentencing Council guideline relating to the sentencing of sexual offences committed by offenders aged 18 and over, see Ch.33, below. The previous guideline, issued in 2007 by the Sentencing Guidelines Council ("SGC"), contained (in Part 7) four separate but similar guidelines for young offenders convicted under s.13 read with ss.9–12. In consulting on its draft guideline,[179] the Sentencing Council proposed not to follow this model but instead to mirror the structure of the adult guidelines by adopting one guideline for s.13 read with ss.9–10 and another for s.13 read with ss.11–12.

4.152   Respondents to the consultation expressed mixed views about this approach. Some were concerned that replicating the adult guidelines for those under 18 would lead to wrong sentences or the need to ignore certain factors, and thought separate guidelines for offences under s.13 would be preferable in order to avoid treating children and young people who offend sexually as mini-adults. A number of respondents argued against the inclusion of any guidelines for the s.13 offences, suggesting that the issues should be covered instead in the review of the youth sentencing guidelines due to be commenced by the Sentencing Council in autumn 2014. Part of the Council's rationale for including guidelines for the s.13 offences was that they were covered by the SGC guideline and omitting them might create a sentencing "gap". However, these respondents did not feel that this was a significant risk given that sexual offences constitute a very small proportion of offences which come before the youth court.

4.153   In the event, the Council was persuaded that to include s.13 in its guideline, at that stage, was more likely to cause difficulties than to be of assistance. It appreciated that child sexual offences committed by young offenders can be very different in nature to those committed by adults, not least because of the use of social media. It was also concerned that producing guidelines for a very narrow range of serious youth offending, without considering the wider approach that should be adopted to the sentencing of those under 18, could cause problems when it came to review youth sentencing generally. Accordingly, the Council confined its guideline to adult offenders but issued an explanatory note to the effect that, when sentencing under s.13, sentencers should continue to follow Part 7 of the SGC guideline until such time as the Council produces new definitive guidelines for youth sentencing.[180] The

---

[178] s.80 and Sch.3, discussed in Ch.35, below.
[179] *Sexual Offences Guideline: Consultation* (December 6, 2012). The consultation document is available on the Sentencing Council's website.
[180] *Sexual offences—offenders under 18: Explanatory note.* The note is available on the Sentencing Council's website.

Council intended to consult on such guidelines in the course of 2015, but its consultation paper "Sentencing Youths - Overarching Principles and Offence Specific Guidelines for Sexual Offences and Robbery" was finally published in May 2016 (and can be found on the Council's website).

SGC guideline

Part 7 of the SGC guideline states a number of overarching principles which set out the key elements of the sentencing framework that applies to young offenders: **4.154**

> "7.9 The principal aim for all involved in the youth justice system is to prevent offending by children and young persons.[181]
>
> 7.10 A court imposing sentence on a youth must have regard to the welfare,[182] maturity, sexual development and intelligence of the youth. These are always important factors.
>
> 7.11 Where a young offender pleads guilty to one of these offences and it is the first offence of which they are convicted, a youth court may impose an absolute discharge, a mental health disposal, a custodial sentence, or make a referral order.
>
> 7.12 Except where the dangerous offender provisions apply:
>
> (i)   Where the young offender is aged 12, 13 or 14, a custodial sentence may only be imposed if the youth is a 'persistent offender' or has committed a 'grave crime' warranting detention for a period in excess of 2 years.[183]
>
> (ii)   Where a young offender is aged 10 or 11, no custodial sentence is available in the youth court.
>
> (iii)   Where a custodial sentence is imposed in the youth court, it must be a Detention and Training Order (DTO), which can only be for 4/6/8/10/12/18 or 24 months.
>
> (iv)   Where a custodial sentence is imposed in the Crown Court, it may be a DTO or it may be detention for a period up to the maximum for the offence."

Part 7 then specifies the starting points, sentencing ranges and aggravating and mitigating factors for offences under ss.9–12 as follows. They assume a first-time offender aged 17 who pleaded not guilty.   **4.155**

---

[181] Crime and Disorder Act 1998 s.37.
[182] Children and Young Persons Act 1933 s.44.
[183] Powers of Criminal Courts (Sentencing) Act 2000 s.100.

Section 9:

Type/nature of activity	Starting points	Sentencing ranges
Offence involving penetration where one or more aggravating factors exist or where there is a substantial age gap between the parties	Detention and Training Order 12 months	Detention and Training Order 6–24 months
CUSTODY THRESHOLD		
Any form of sexual activity (non-penetrative or penetrative) not involving any aggravating factors	Community order	An appropriate non-custodial sentence*

Additional aggravating factors	Additional mitigating factors
1.Background of intimidation or coercion. 2. Use of drugs, alcohol or other substance to facilitate the offence. 3. Threats to prevent victim reporting the incident. 4. Abduction or detention. 5. Offender aware that he or she is suffering from a sexually transmitted infection.	1. Relationship of genuine affection. 2. Youth and immaturity of offender.

Section 10:

Type/nature of activity	Starting points	Sentencing ranges
Offence involving penetration where one or more aggravating factors exist or where there is a substantial age gap between the parties	Detention and Training Order 12 months	Detention and Training Order 6–24 months

CUSTODY THRESHOLD		
Any form of sexual activity (non-penetrative or penetrative) not involving any aggravating factors	*Community order*	*An appropriate non-custodial sentence**

Additional aggravating factors	Additional mitigating factors
1. Background of intimidation or coercion. 2. Use of drugs, alcohol or other substance to facilitate the offence. 3. Threats to prevent victim reporting the incident. 4. Abduction or detention. 5. Offender aware that he or she is suffering from a sexually transmitted infection.	1. Relationship of genuine affection. 2. Offender intervenes to prevent incited offence from taking place. 3. Youth and immaturity of offender

Section 11:

Type/nature of activity	Starting points	Sentencing ranges
Offence involving penetration where one or more aggravating factors exist	*Detention and Training Order 12 months*	*Detention and Training Order 6–24 months*
CUSTODY THRESHOLD		
Any form of sexual activity (non-penetrative or penetrative) not involving any aggravating factors	*Community order*	*An appropriate non-custodial sentence**

Additional aggravating factors	Additional mitigating factors
1. Background of intimidation or coercion. 2. Use of drugs, alcohol or other substance to facilitate the offence. 3. Threats to prevent victim reporting the incident. 4. Abduction or detention.	1. Youth and immaturity of offender

Section 12:

Type/nature of activity	Starting points	Sentencing ranges
Live sexual activity	Detention and Training Order 8 months	Detention and Training Order 6–12 months
CUSTODY THRESHOLD		
Moving or still images of people engaged in sexual acts involving penetration	Community order	An appropriate non-custodial sentence*
Moving or still images of people engaged in sexual acts other than penetration	Community order	An appropriate non-custodial sentence*

Additional aggravating factors	Additional mitigating factors
1. Background of intimidation or coercion. 2. Use of drugs, alcohol or other substance to facilitate the offence. 3. Threats to prevent victim reporting the incident. 4. Abduction or detention. 5. Images of violent activity.	1. Youth and immaturity of offender*

*"Non-custodial sentence" in this context suggests a youth community order (as defined in the Criminal Justice Act 2003 s.147(2)) or a fine. In most instances, an offence will have crossed the threshold for a community order. However, in accordance with normal sentencing practice, a court is not precluded from imposing a financial penalty where that is determined to be the appropriate sentence.

Offender under 18 at time of offence but over 18 when sentenced

In *R. v C*,[184] the appellant appealed against a sentence of two years and six   **4.156**
months' detention in a young offender institution imposed following his
guilty plea to offences of sexual activity with a child (s.13 and s.9) and
inciting a child to engage in sexual activity (s.13 and s.10). The appellant had
been 17 at the time of the offences but 18 at the time of sentence. He had
contacted the victims, aged between 12 and 14, on social media. The online
relationships developed into sexual messages. The appellant then asked the
victims for naked photographs and to engage in sexual activity with him. One
of the victims began a consensual sexual relationship with the appellant. A
pre-sentence report stated that the appellant posed a high risk of serious
harm to children. The judge referred to the adult guideline for the offences
under ss.9 and 10 and found that there had been an element of grooming. He
sentenced the appellant to two years' detention for each of three offences of
sexual activity with a child, to run concurrently, and six months' detention
for each of three offences of incitement, to run concurrently, but consecutively to the sentences for the other offences. The appellant submitted that
the guideline contained no guidance on sentencing an offender who was
under 18 at the time of the offences but over 18 at the time of the sentencing
hearing, and that the judge should have sentenced him on the basis that he
was under 18 at that time. He also argued that his sentence was too high, as
there was considerable mitigation in that he was young and naïve with no
previous convictions. The Court of Appeal allowed the appeal in part. The
guideline did not deal with an offender who was under 18 at the time of the
offences but over 18 at the time of sentencing, so the judge had no direct
guidance to assist her. It was not right to be guided by an adult guideline
where the offender had turned 18 by the time of sentence. In the absence of
an applicable guideline, an offender should be sentenced on the basis that he
was a youth when the offences were committed. There were some aggravating
factors in this case such as the degree of planning, the disparity of age and
a degree of grooming, though grooming is not of such importance when
sentencing a youth as opposed to an adult offender. However, the Court
quashed the sentences for the first three offences on the basis that the starting
point should have been 18 months' detention which, following a discount for
the guilty plea, gave sentences of 12 months' detention for each of those
offences, to run concurrently. There was nothing wrong with the sentences
imposed for the other three offences, and the total sentence was therefore
reduced to 18 months' detention.

PARTIES TO THE OFFENCE

The offence under s.13 may be committed by and against persons of either   **4.157**
sex. The defendant must be under 18 and the complainant must be under 16.

[184] Unreported, September 10, 2014.

A person attains the age of 16 at the commencement of the sixteenth anniversary of her birth and the age of 18 at the commencement of its eighteenth anniversary.[185] For proof of age, see paras 3.73 and following, above. As to whether a child under 16 may be convicted as an accessory to a s.13 offence of which they are the victim, see paras 4.57 and following, above.

JURISDICTION

4.158 By virtue of s.72 of and Sch.2 to the Sexual Offences Act 2003, as amended,[186] it is an offence under s.13 for a UK national to do an act in a country outside the UK which would constitute a s.13 offence if done in England and Wales. See further para.4.59, above.

MENTAL ELEMENT

4.159 The requirement that the defendant must do something which would be an offence under any of ss.9 to 12 if he were aged 18 has the effect of introducing into this offence the elements of offences under those sections, including the mental element.

ARRANGING OR FACILITATING COMMISSION OF A CHILD SEX OFFENCE

DEFINITION

4.160 Section 14(1) of the Sexual Offences Act 2003 provides:

> "A person commits an offence if—
> (a) he intentionally arranges or facilitates something that he intends to do, intends another person to do, or believes that another person will do, in any part of the world, and
> (b) doing it will involve the commission of an offence under any of sections 9 to 13."

4.161 This provision makes it an offence to arrange or facilitate the commission of an offence under ss.9 to 13 of the Act. Much of the conduct that falls within the scope of the offence would be criminal in any event, because it would amount to encouraging or assisting an offence under ss.9–13, contrary to ss.44 to 46 of the Serious Crime Act 2007, or conspiring to commit or aiding and abetting such an offence. But the offence extends further, to catch a range of preparatory conduct that would not otherwise be criminal. It can be committed where a person arranges or facilitates child sex either for himself or for another, and wherever in the world the sex is intended to take place.

---

[185] Family Law Reform Act 1969 s.9(1).
[186] By the Criminal Justice and Immigration Act 2008 s.72, which came into force on July 14, 2008.

This last aspect was welcomed in Parliament as helping to protect children in poor countries overseas from sexual exploitation by paedophiles from the developed world who go there specifically to take advantage of them.[187]

By analogy with *Walker*,[188] decided under s.8 of the 2003 Act, s.14 creates   **4.162**
separate offences of intentionally arranging and intentionally facilitating a child sex offence. It follows that a count alleging that the defendant "arranged or facilitated" such an offence is in principle duplicitous and should be struck out or amended.

MODE OF TRIAL AND PUNISHMENT

Offences under s.14 are triable either way. The maximum sentence on   **4.163**
conviction on indictment is 14 years' imprisonment. On summary conviction it is six months' imprisonment or a fine, or both.[189] As from a day to be appointed the maximum sentence of imprisonment on summary conviction will increase to 12 months.[190] The increase will have no application to offences committed before it takes effect.[191] Until recently, the maximum fine on summary conviction was a fine not exceeding the statutory maximum (i.e. £5,000). The effect of s.85 of the Legal Aid, Sentencing and Punishment of Offenders Act 2012 is that, from March 12, 2015, a fine of any amount may be imposed. The s.14 offence cannot be dealt with by way of a simple caution.[192]

For the purposes of listing, cases under s.14[193] fall within Class 2B, save for   **4.164**
complex cases involving many complainants (often under age, in care or otherwise particularly vulnerable) and/or many defendants who are alleged to have systematically groomed and abused them, often over a long period of time, which fall within Class 1C.[194] Cases in Class 1C must be referred to the Resident Judge, and by the Resident Judge to a Presiding Judge. Cases in Class 2B must be similarly referred in certain specified circumstances, including where the case is unusually grave or complex or a novel and important point of law is to be raised; where the defendant is a police officer, a member of the legal profession or a high profile figure; or where for any reason the case is likely to attract exceptional media attention.

---

[187] See e.g. *Hansard*, HL, vol.646, cols 1233–1234, Lord Brennan (April 1, 2003).
[188] [2006] EWCA Crim 1907, discussed in para.3.132, above.
[189] s.14(4).
[190] Criminal Justice Act 2003 s.282(2), (3).
[191] Criminal Justice Act 2003 s.282(4).
[192] Criminal Justice and Courts Act 2015 s.17(3), and the Criminal Justice and Courts Act 2015 (Simple Cautions) (Specification of Either-Way Offences) Order 2015 (SI 2015/790).
[193] And of soliciting, inciting, encouraging or assisting, attempting or conspiring to commit a s.14 offence or assisting an offender having committed such an offence.
[194] *Consolidated Criminal Practice Directions*, Part XIII Listing B: CLASSIFICATION, available at *https://www.judiciary.gov.uk/wp-content/uploads/2015/09/crim-pd-2015.pdf* [Accessed April 30, 2016].

4.165   An offence under s.14 is a serious specified offence for the purposes of the dangerousness provisions of the Criminal Justice Act 2003.[195] Accordingly a s.14 offence, whenever committed, may be made the subject of an extended sentence under s.226A of that Act.[196] The offence is also listed in Pt 1 of Sch.15B to the Criminal Justice Act 2003 for the purposes of s.224A of that Act (life sentence for a second listed offence).[197]

4.166   A person convicted under s.14, cautioned, found not guilty by reason of insanity or found to be under a disability and to have done the act charged, is automatically subject to the notification requirements in the Sexual Offences Act 2003[198] if they were 18 or over at the time of the offence or they are sentenced to at least 12 months' imprisonment.

4.167   During the passage of the Sexual Offences Bill through Parliament, an amendment was tabled which would have made offences under s.14 triable only on indictment, on the basis that summary trial would never be appropriate.[199] The Government resisted the amendment on the ground that s.14 covers a wide range of offending behaviour and a Crown Court trial might not always be necessary. As an example of a case where summary trial might be appropriate, Lord Falconer of Thoroton cited a 15-year-old who arranges for his 17-year-old cousin to have sexual intercourse with a 15-year-old friend at his house while his parents are out.[200]

Sentencing

4.168   For the Sentencing Council guideline relating to the sentencing of sexual offences committed by offenders aged 18 and over, see Ch.33, below. By a curious omission, the Sentencing Council's draft guideline contained no guidance on sentencing offences under s.14. This was put right in the published guideline, which states:

> "Sentencers should refer to the guideline for the applicable, substantive offence of arranging or facilitating under sections 9 to 12.[201] The level of harm should be determined by reference to the type of activity arranged or facilitated. Sentences commensurate with the applicable starting point and range will ordinarily be appropriate. For offences involving substantial commercial exploitation and/or an international element, it may, in the interests of justice, be appropriate to increase a sentence to a point in excess of the category range. In exceptional cases, such as where a vulnerable offender performed a limited role, having been

---

[195] Criminal Justice Act 2003 s.224 and Sch.15, Pt 2.
[196] Inserted by the Legal Aid, Sentencing and Punishment of Offenders Act 2012 s.124, brought into force on December 3, 2012, by SI 2012/2906.
[197] Inserted by the Legal Aid, Sentencing and Punishment of Offenders Act 2012 s.122, brought into force on December 3, 2012, by SI 2012/2906.
[198] s.80 and Sch.3, discussed in Ch.35, below.
[199] *Hansard*, HL, vol.646, col.1201, Baroness Noakes (April 1, 2003).
[200] ibid., col.1202.
[201] The drafting of this sentence is inelegant but its meaning is tolerably clear, i.e.: "Sentencers should refer to the guideline for the substantive offence under sections 9 to 12 that the offender arranged or facilitated."

coerced or exploited by others, sentences below the starting point and range may be appropriate."

Sentencing examples

In *Collins*,[202] the appellant (51) made contact online with two women and made arrangements with them to have sex with an eight-year-old girl. The women were in fact undercover police officers and the child, purportedly the step-daughter of one of them, did not exist. Arrangements were also made for him to take indecent images and an indecent film of the girl. The appellant set off to hitchhike from Wales to Kent, where he believed the child to be, but was arrested en route. He was convicted of offences under s.14 and s.50 of the 2003 Act (arranging sexual exploitation of a child). In sentencing, the judge said in relation to the s.9 offence that there was a significant degree of planning and a considerable disparity of age between the appellant and the child. Also, the sex would have taken place in the presence of the girl's step-mother and so the trust between mother and child would have been breached. The intended offence fell within category 1A of the s.9 guideline. As for the s.50 offence, the intention to facilitate photographic activity either had to be regarded as an aggravating feature of the whole of the conduct or dealt with by way of separate sentence. That offence fell within category 1B of the s.50 guideline. The offences were predatory in nature and demonstrated a high degree of recklessness and a willingness to take significant risk to fulfil sexual urges. The appellant had a single-minded goal to use the internet to groom and facilitate situations in which he would be able to abuse a child for his own sexual gratification. The lengths to which he was willing to go to orchestrate the opportunity, such as trying to hitchhike to Kent for over 17 hours, demonstrated an alarming degree of single-mindedness and determination. The judge concluded that the appellant was dangerous to children. He imposed a 12-year extended determinate sentence (10 years with an extension period of two years) for the s.14 offence and six years concurrent for the s.50 offence. On appeal, the appellant did not challenge the finding that he was dangerous, the imposition of an extended determinate term, or the two year extension period. But he submitted that the total sentence was manifestly excessive, given that the relevant starting point for a category 1A s.9 offence involving penetration is five years' custody with a range extending to 10 years. Notwithstanding the seriousness of the offences in this case, the judge, he submitted, was not justified in imposing a custodial term right at the top of the range; it should have been closer to the starting point. The Court of Appeal held that the case was plainly in category 1 and culpability was of a very high order indeed, given the significant degree of planning, the significant disparity in age and the fact that the appellant acted

---

[202] [2015] EWCA Crim 915. Sentencing appeals under s.14 are rare, and so the few reported cases are all potentially instructive. For appeals decided by reference to the SGC guideline, see *Bayliss* [2012] EWCA Crim 269; *Jordan* [2007] 2 Cr. App. R.(S.) 189.

together with others to commit the putative offence. As for the judge's conclusion that the appellant's intention to have sex with the child in the presence of her step-mother constituted an abuse of trust, whether that was strictly correct was not relevant because if it were not an abuse of trust for the purposes of culpability, it would be an aggravating factor. Also the intended victim was only eight years old, and at that very young age would plainly be particularly vulnerable. The Court also had in mind that the appellant did not arrange just one act of sexual activity with a child, he planned to groom her and to engage in various and repeated sexual activities contrary to s.9, including penetration, that would have put the case in category 1A and indeed constituted rape of a child under 13. The combination of these many factors took the appellant's offending towards the very top of the range in the s.9 guideline. In addition, the offence of arranging child pornography, contrary to s.50 of the Act, could have attracted a substantial consecutive sentence. The relevant starting point in the guideline for that offence, standing alone, is eight years' custody with a range of six to 11 years. The judge's concurrent sentence of six years for this offence was at the very bottom of the range, but, as he explained, he had increased the sentence in respect of the s.14 offence to produce what he believed was a proportionate total sentence for the offending as a whole. The final sentence was at the top of the range in the guideline for the offence under s.14. However, given the seriousness of that offence, combined with the further offence under s.50, the Court was unable to accept that the custodial term imposed of 10 years was manifestly excessive.

PARTIES TO THE OFFENCE

4.170 Offences under s.14 may be committed by and against persons of either sex. The requirement that doing the thing arranged or facilitated will involve the commission of an offence under any of ss.9 to 13 has the effect of introducing into s.14 the elements of those offences, including the age requirements: see the discussion of ss.9–13, above. As to whether a child under 16 may be convicted as an accessory to a s.14 offence of which she is the victim, see paras 4.57 and following, above.

JURISDICTION

4.171 By virtue of s.72 of and Sch.2 to the Sexual Offences Act 2003, as amended,[203] it is an offence under s.14 for a UK national to do an act in a country outside the UK which would constitute a s.14 offence if done in England and Wales. See further para.4.59, above.

---

[203] By the Criminal Justice and Immigration Act 2008 s.72, which came into force on July 14, 2008.

"ARRANGES OR FACILITATES"

These terms are not defined in the Act. According to the New Shorter Oxford   **4.172**
English Dictionary, "arranging" something means planning it or settling
beforehand its details and "facilitating" something means making it easy or
easier, promoting it or moving it forward. Examples of "arranging" within
s.14 are where A agrees to procure a child for B to have sex with, or where
A, acting with a view to obtaining sexual gratification, persuades a child to
come round to his house later to view a pornographic film. The last example
indicates that s.14 is capable of catching aspects of the sexual grooming of
children. We discuss below whether the offence by "arranging" can be
committed by one person acting alone. Examples of "facilitating" within s.14
are where a person drives another person (X) to meet a child with whom he
knows or believes X is going to engage in sexual activity, or makes a room in
his house available to X for the same purpose.

The meaning of "arranges" was considered by the Court of Appeal in *R.*   **4.173**
v R.[204] The respondent (R) asked a prostitute, of whom he was a regular
client, to find a girl of 12 or 13 for sex. She gave him no reason to think she
would assist. He sent her two text messages repeating the request. She
reported him to the police and he was charged under s.14 with arranging
something the doing of which would amount to a child sex offence. At trial,
the judge made a terminating ruling on the ground that R had only made a
request of the prostitute that she had not agreed to carry out, and that of
itself could not constitute arranging or attempting to arrange a child sex
offence, but was at most an act preparatory to committing such an
offence.

The Court of Appeal reversed this ruling in part. It said that s.14 was   **4.174**
introduced in order to penalise steps preparatory to a child sex offence and
so enable individuals to be charged and punished for taking such steps before
a child suffered. As such, s.14 is wider than the law of criminal attempt. Nor
does it require an agreement or arrangement between two people, whether
formal or informal: "A defendant may take steps by way of a plan with the
criminal objective identified in the section without involving anyone else and
the mere fact that no-one else was involved would not necessarily mean that
no arrangement was made." As to whether a request can amount to
arranging something, where there is no proof that the person to whom it was
made agreed to or acquiesced in it, the Court found it unnecessary to decide
this. The Court was clear that, although s.14 penalises steps taken by way of
preparation, it is a substantive offence and so can be attempted.[205] On the
facts of the present case, the jury would be entitled to find that R had

---

[204] [2008] EWCA Crim 619. See also *Jordan* [2006] EWCA Crim 3311, an appeal against
sentence following conviction on facts similar to those in *R. v. R.*
[205] Citing *Chief Constable of Hampshire v Mace* (1987) 84 Cr. App. R. 40.

attempted to arrange a child sex offence. His request was not simply an act preparatory as he had done all that he needed to create the arrangement. The Court therefore ordered the resumption of the trial (which had been adjourned) on the basis of a charge of attempt.[206]

4.175   We respectfully agree with the Court of Appeal that a s.14 offence can be attempted, and that R's conduct in this case constituted an attempt given that he had done all he needed to do to arrange the commission by him of a child sex offence. However, it is difficult to see why the Court left open the possibility that the facts disclosed the full offence. The trial judge was surely right to rule that making a request cannot of itself constitute arranging something, since the essence of an arrangement is that it will, in due course, produce the desired result. The result of a request, on the other hand, must depend on whether the other person acts as requested; and unless they indicate that they will, nothing has been arranged. On that basis, the full offence was not committed in this case, since the prostitute had not indicated by words or conduct that she would act on R's request, i.e. nothing had been arranged.

4.176   What of the Court's statement that the offence of "arranging" in s.14 does not require an agreement or arrangement between two people, and that a person may commit the offence by arranging something by himself, without involving anyone else? We suggest that, while this statement may be correct as a matter of statutory construction, it is unlikely to have any practical application. The reason is that what is arranged must be something the doing of which will *itself* constitute a child sex offence. It is difficult to see how anything that would constitute such an offence can be arranged without the agreement or co-operation of at least one other person, either the child herself or someone else. The Court of Appeal seems to contemplate that "arranging" can cover the taking of steps with the intention of doing something that will constitute a child sex offence. If so, that is a misreading of the offence, since what A must arrange is something which, when done, will constitute such an offence. So arranging steps preparatory to a child sex offence is not sufficient, A must arrange the offence itself. Arranging preparatory steps could at most amount to an attempt to arrange. By way of illustration, suppose A agrees to baby-sit for some parents, his intention being to use the opportunity to sexually abuse the child. What he has arranged is the baby-sitting, not the sexual abuse. The fact that he intends to use the opportunity provided by the baby-sitting to commit the abuse does not mean he has arranged something the doing of which will *itself* constitute a sexual offence. He could have arranged that only if the parents and/or the child were aware of his intention and agreed to or acquiesced in it.

---

[206] The authors understand that at the resumed trial, the jury convicted of attempt within minutes. That conviction was later quashed because of a separate judicial misdirection: see *R. v JR* [2008] EWCA Crim 2912.

"IN ANY PART OF THE WORLD"

These words mean that an act of arranging or facilitating done in England   **4.177**
and Wales may constitute a s.14 offence regardless where the defendant
intends or believes that the thing arranged or facilitated will be done, whether
in England and Wales, elsewhere in the UK or overseas. Where the
arrangement or facilitation takes place overseas, it will constitute an offence
in England and Wales if the provisions of s.72 of the 2003 Act are satisfied:
see para.4.59, above.

"SECTIONS 9 TO 13"

The offence catches those who arrange or facilitate the commission of a child   **4.178**
sex offence under ss.9 to 13, but not those who arrange or facilitate an
offence against a child under 13 contrary to ss.5 to 8 of the 2003 Act. This
apparent anomaly was identified during the passage of the Bill[207] but was not
remedied. It is not fatal, as the offences in ss.9 to 13 protect *all* children under
16, including those under 13, and so it is possible to prosecute under s.14
even where the child victim was under that age, if there is no under-13 offence
available which fits the bill.[208] However, compare the position under s.14 with
the grooming offence under s.15, discussed below, which is committed where
A intends to commit against a child any offence under Pt 1 of the Act.

There is no requirement in s.14 that an offence under ss.9 to 13 must   **4.179**
actually be committed: it is sufficient that such an offence would be
committed if the thing arranged or facilitated is in fact done. Accordingly, if
the arrangement comes to nothing, e.g. it is disrupted by the police, those
involved may still be prosecuted.

EXCEPTION FOR ACTS DONE TO PROTECT THE CHILD

Section 14 is subject to an exception applicable where the person concerned   **4.180**
believes a child will engage in sexual activity with another person and does
something to protect her from the potential consequences, e.g. by providing
her with contraception or health advice, without intending the activity to
take place or causing or encouraging it. Section 14(2) and (3) provides:

> "(2) A person does not commit an offence under this section if—
>   (a) he arranges or facilitates something that he believes another person will
>   do, but that he does not intend to do or intend another person to do,
>   and
>   (b) any offence within subsection (1)(b) would be an offence against a child for
>   whose protection he acts.
> (3) For the purposes of subsection (2), a person acts for the protection of a child
> if he acts for the purpose of-

---

[207] cf. *Hansard*, HC, vol.409, col.233, Stephen Hesford MP (July 15, 2003).
[208] cf. *Collins* [2015] EWCA Crim 915, at [16]. *Collins* is discussed in para.4.169, above.

(a) protecting the child from sexually transmitted infection,
(b) protecting the physical safety of the child,
(c) preventing the child from becoming pregnant, or
(d) promoting the child's emotional well-being by the giving of advice,

and not for the purpose of obtaining sexual gratification or for the purpose of causing or encouraging the activity constituting the offence within subsection (1)(b) or the child's participation in it."

4.181   This exception was inserted by Government amendment during the passage of the Sexual Offences Bill in response to expressions of concern that s.14 would otherwise catch the legitimate work of doctors and others who seek to protect the health and welfare of young people. Under the previous law, doctors and other health professionals were not viewed as aiding and abetting a criminal offence provided they worked within professional or agreed policy guidelines. The point had arisen in the celebrated case of *Gillick v West Norfolk and Wisbech Area Health Authority*,[209] where one of the issues before the House of Lords was whether a doctor who provided contraceptive advice or treatment to a female patient under the age of 16 was liable to conviction as an accessory if a man later committed the offence of unlawful sexual intercourse with the girl (contrary to s.6 of the Sexual Offences Act 1956). A majority in the House held that the exercise by a doctor of his clinical judgment as to what he honestly believed to be necessary for the physical, mental and emotional health of his patient is a complete negation of the guilty mind which is essential for the commission of a criminal offence. Accordingly, a doctor who intended to act in the girl's best interests when giving contraceptive advice or treatment would not be,[210] or at least was unlikely to be,[211] criminally liable as an accessory to the unlawful sexual intercourse offence.

4.182   However, the introduction of the Sexual Offences Bill prompted expressions of concern from the medical profession about the security of the protection afforded them by *Gillick* in the light of the wide wording of what became s.14. Concern was also expressed about the potential for the new provision to deter people outside the medical profession from providing advice and assistance to children under 16, a vocal minority being the agony aunts who write for teenage magazines. The Government concluded that a statutory exception should be introduced to meet these concerns, both in relation to s.14 and more generally in relation to liability for aiding, abetting or counselling the offences of sexual activity with children (see s.73 of the Act, which is in the same terms as s.14(2)–(3)). Moreover, the exception

---

[209] [1986] A.C. 112. *Gillick* was followed in *R. (On the Application of Axon) v Secretary of State for Health* [2006] EWHC 37 (Admin) which concerned an unsuccessful challenge to Department of Health guidance to health professionals on giving advice and treatment on sexual matters to children under the age of 16. It was common ground between the parties that a medical professional who gives advice and treatment to a young person relating to contraception and sexual and reproductive health, including abortion, does not incur criminal liability.
[210] Per Lord Scarman and Lord Bridge of Harwich.
[211] Per Lord Fraser of Tullybelton.

needed to be more widely drawn than the principle in *Gillick* to ensure that it covered people other than doctors and other health professionals, such as parents, teachers and voluntary youth workers.[212]

The insertion of the exception was generally welcomed. However, initially   **4.183**
it did not include what became s.14(3)(d) (promoting the child's emotional well-being by the giving of advice), and it was forcefully argued that the exception was therefore too narrow.[213] The Government was sympathetic to this point and s.14(3)(d) was inserted on Third Reading.[214]

There was also a minority view that the exception was too wide, on the   **4.184**
ground that it could be relied upon by anyone claiming that he was giving sex education or advice on contraception or sexual health, even though he was not a health professional and even if he had a history of child sex offending.[215] An amendment moved by Baroness Blatch would have prevented registered sex offenders from relying on the exception.[216] The Government resisted this amendment on two grounds: it focused on a class of individuals defined by what they had done previously rather than by the purpose for which they acted on the particular occasion; and the class included individuals who had committed sexual offences which in no way involved children. The amendment was defeated on a vote.

MENTAL ELEMENT

The defendant must intentionally arrange or facilitate something that he   **4.185**
intends to do, intends another person to do or believes that another person will do. For the meaning of "intention", see paras 2.78 and following, above. The requirement that doing the thing arranged or facilitated will involve an offence under any of ss.9 to 13 has the effect of introducing into this offence the elements of the offences under those provisions, including the mental element.

MEETING A CHILD FOLLOWING SEXUAL GROOMING ETC.

DEFINITION

Section 15(1) of the Sexual Offences Act 2003[217] provides: **4.186**

"(1) A person aged 18 or over (A) commits an offence if—

---

[212] Hansard, HL, vol.646, col.1235, Lord Falconer of Thoroton (April 1, 2003).
[213] See ibid., col.1237, Baroness Walmsley and col.1242, Baroness Gould of Potternewton.
[214] Hansard, HL, vol.649, col.705, Baroness Scotland of Asthal (June 17, 2003).
[215] See *Hansard*, HL, vol.646, col.1238ff, Baroness Blatch (April 1, 2003).
[216] *Hansard*, HL, vol.649, col.692ff (June 17, 2003).
[217] As amended by the Criminal Justice and Immigration Act 2008 s.73 and Sch.15, para.1, with effect from July 14, 2008, and by the Criminal Justice and Courts Act 2015 s.36, with effect from April 13, 2015 (see SI 2015/778).

    (a) A has met or communicated with another person (B) on one or more occasions and subsequently—
      (i) A intentionally meets B,
      (ii) A travels with the intention of meeting B in any part of the world or arranges to meet B in any part of the world, or
      (iii) B travels with the intention of meeting A in any part of the world,
    (b) A intends to do anything to or in respect of B, during or after the meeting mentioned in paragraph (a)(i) to (iii) and in any part of the world, which if done will involve the commission by A of a relevant offence,
    (c) B is under 16, and
    (d) A does not reasonably believe that B is 16 or over."

A "relevant offence" is defined for the purposes of s.15(1)(b) to include any offence under Pt I of the 2003 Act, including the under-13 and child sex offences: see para.4.219, below.

4.187   As enacted, s.15 made it an offence for an adult, who had met or communicated with a child under the age of 16 at least twice and intended to commit a sexual offence against her, intentionally to meet the child or to travel with the intention of meeting her in any part of the world. The Criminal Justice and Immigration Act 2008 widened the offence to cover two further scenarios: where the adult arranges to meet the child, without taking steps to do so, or the child travels with the intention of meeting the adult. The Criminal Justice and Courts Act 2015 widened it further so that the offence applies where the adult meets or communicates with the child even on a single occasion before meeting her (etc.) with the requisite intent. The net result of these amendments is that it is now an offence if an adult, who has met or communicated with a child under the age of 16 at least once and intends to commit a sexual offence against her, subsequently meets or arranges to meet the child, or either the adult or the child travels to meet the other. However, in a case in which the adult met or communicated with the child only once before the subsequent meeting (etc.), the offence is committed only if that meeting or communication took place after the amendment made by the 2015 Act came into force, on April 13, 2015.[218]

4.188   The offence is intended to cover situations in which an adult establishes contact with a child, whether in person, online or by other means, with the intention of gaining the child's trust or confidence and then meeting the child in order to engage in sexual activity. For the purpose of the offence, communication between the adult and the child can take any form, but the offence will be committed only if the adult meets, travels to meet or arranges to meet the child, or the child travels to meet him, when he has the intention of committing a sexual offence against the child at the meeting or subsequently. There was previously no offence with which such a person could be charged (given their conduct would usually fall short of an attempt to commit the intended offence), and so s.15 enables earlier intervention that would otherwise be possible. It was generally welcomed in Parliament, but

---

[218] Criminal Justice and Courts Act 2015 s.36(2).

there were extra-Parliamentary expressions of concern. Liberty, in its briefing on the Sexual Offences Bill, warned the Government that in its "admirable desire to prioritise child protection, [it] should be careful of creating what is effectively 'thought crime'". But, even as widened by later amendment, the offence requires proof of more than just thought: A must be shown to have had contact with the child at least once and to have met or travelled to meet her (etc.) with the intention of committing a sexual offence against her.[219]

Finally, it should be noted that when s.15A of the 2003 Act comes into   **4.189** force, any communication by an adult with a child that is sexual in nature and engaged in for the purpose of the adult's sexual gratification will itself constitute a criminal offence. Section 15A is discussed in paras 4.225 and following, below.

Attempts

If A communicates with B, whom he believes to be a child but who is in fact,   **4.190** say, a police officer or a journalist, and then travels or arranges to meet B with the intention of committing a sexual offence against her at the meeting or subsequently, A may be convicted of attempting to commit the s.15 offence. In *Shivpuri*[220] the House of Lords held that a person may be convicted of an attempt if he does an act that is more than merely preparatory to a full offence, intending to commit that offence, notwithstanding the commission of the full offence is on the true facts impossible. In the scenario envisaged above, it is impossible for A to complete the offence because the person with whom he communicates, B, is not in fact aged under 16. In the light of *Shivpuri*, this impossibility does not preclude his conviction for an attempt. On this point, see also *Jones*,[221] discussed in paras 3.160 and following, above.

MODE OF TRIAL AND PUNISHMENT

The offence under s.15 is triable either way.[222] The maximum sentence on   **4.191** conviction on indictment is 10 years' imprisonment. On introduction, the Sexual Offences Bill set the maximum at five years' imprisonment. The maximum was subsequently raised by amendment to seven years[223] and then to 10 years. This was justified on the basis that the higher maximum would enable appropriate sentences to be passed in the most serious cases, e.g. where a paedophile with many previous and serious convictions repeatedly communicates with children on the internet, there is clear evidence that he

---

[219] *Hansard*, HL, vol.646, col.1258, Baroness Blatch (April 1, 2003). See generally on the s.15 offence, Alisdair A. Gillespie, *Tackling Grooming* Pol. J. 2004, 77(3), 239; Alasdair A. Gillespie, *Indecent Images, Grooming and the Law* [2006] Crim. L.R. 412.

[220] [1987] A.C. 1.

[221] [2007] EWCA Crim 1118.

[222] s.15(4).

[223] *Hansard*, HL, vol.646, col.1272.

intends to commit a violent sex act against one or more of them, and he sets off to meet one of the children. On summary conviction the maximum penalty is six months' imprisonment or a fine, or both.[224] As from a day to be appointed the maximum sentence of imprisonment on summary conviction will increase to 12 months.[225] The increase will have no application to offences committed before it takes effect.[226] Until recently, the maximum fine on summary conviction was a fine not exceeding the statutory maximum (i.e. £5,000). The effect of s.85 of the Legal Aid, Sentencing and Punishment of Offenders Act 2012 is that, from March 12, 2015, a fine of any amount may be imposed. A s.15 offence cannot be dealt with by way of a simple caution.[227]

4.192   For the purposes of listing, cases under s.15[228] fall within Class 2B, save for complex cases involving many complainants (often in care or otherwise particularly vulnerable) and/or many defendants who are alleged to have systematically groomed and abused them, often over a long period of time, which fall within Class 1C. [229] Cases in Class 1C must be referred to the Resident Judge, and by the Resident Judge to a Presiding Judge. Cases in Class 2B must be similarly referred in certain specified circumstances, including where the case is unusually grave or complex or a novel and important point of law is to be raised; where the defendant is a police officer, a member of the legal profession or a high profile figure; or where for any reason the case is likely to attract exceptional media attention.

4.193   The offence under s.15 is a serious specified offence for the purposes of the dangerousness provisions of the Criminal Justice Act 2003.[230] A s.15 offence, whenever committed, may be made the subject of an extended sentence under s.226A of that Act.[231] The offence is also listed in Pt 1 of Sch.15B to the Criminal Justice Act 2003 for the purposes of s.224A of that Act (life sentence for a second listed offence).[232]

4.194   A person convicted under s.15, cautioned, found not guilty by reason of insanity or found to be under a disability and to have done the act charged, is automatically subject to the notification requirements in the Sexual Offences Act 2003.[233]

---

[224] s.17(4).

[225] Criminal Justice Act 2003 s.282(2), (3).

[226] Criminal Justice Act 2003 s.282(4).

[227] Criminal Justice and Courts Act 2015 s.17(3), and the Criminal Justice and Courts Act 2015 (Simple Cautions) (Specification of Either-Way Offences) Order 2015 (SI 2015/790).

[228] And of soliciting, inciting, encouraging or assisting, attempting or conspiring to commit the offence or assisting an offender having committed the offence.

[229] *Consolidated Criminal Practice Directions*, Part XIII Listing B: CLASSIFICATION, available at *https://www.judiciary.gov.uk/wp-content/uploads/2015/09/crim-pd-2015.pdf* [Accessed April 30, 2016].

[230] Criminal Justice Act 2003 s.224 and Sch.15, Pt 2.

[231] Inserted by the Legal Aid, Sentencing and Punishment of Offenders Act 2012 s.124, brought into force on December 3, 2012, by SI 2012/2906.

[232] Inserted by the Legal Aid, Sentencing and Punishment of Offenders Act 2012 s.122, brought into force on December 3, 2012, by SI 2012/2906.

[233] s.80 and Sch.3, discussed in Ch.35, below.

During the passage of the Sexual Offences Bill, amendments were tabled   **4.195**
which would have made the s.15 offence triable only on indictment either in
all cases or at least where B was under 13 at the relevant time, on the basis
that summary trial in such cases is inappropriate.[234] The Government resisted
these amendments on the ground that the offence covers a wide range of
offending behaviour and that trial in the Crown Court might not always be
necessary.[235] In Committee, Lord Falconer of Thoroton conceded that the
vast majority of offences under the section will merit trial in the Crown
Court, but said there might be some for which summary trial is appropriate
and gave as a possible example the case where A is 19 and B is 15 years and
11 months.[236] On Third Reading, Baroness Scotland of Asthal, resisting an
amendment to make the offence indictable where the child was under 13,
gave as an example of a case that might conceivably merit summary trial one
in which a young adult meets or travels to meet a 12-year-old, with whom he
has communicated in a non-sexual way previously, in order to show her
photographs of two people sexually fondling.[237]

SENTENCING

For the Sentencing Council guideline relating to the sentencing of sexual   **4.196**
offences committed by offenders aged 18 and over, see Ch.33, below. In
consulting on its draft guideline,[238] the Council noted that the s.15 offence is
often referred to as "grooming", a term that can also be used to describe a
wide range of manipulative behaviour used by offenders to condition victims
in order to obtain their apparent acquiescence to sexual activity, e.g.
"on-street grooming" or "internet grooming". The Council emphasised the
importance of distinguishing this wider grooming activity from the more
limited range of conduct covered by the s.15 offence.

Sentencing guideline

Step One—Harm and culpability

The guideline requires the sentencing court to go through a series of steps in   **4.197**
order to determine the appropriate sentence. Step one involves determining
the offence category by reference to the degree of harm caused and then the
culpability level for the offence. The Sentencing Council noted that the s.15
offence differs from the other child sex offences in that it is essentially

[234] *Hansard*, HL, vol.646, col.1271 (April 1, 2003); vol.649, col.679 (June 17, 2003).
[235] *Hansard*, HL, vol.646, col.1202, Lord Falconer of Thoroton (April 1, 2003); vol.648, col.1101, Lord Falconer of Thoroton (June 2, 2003); vol.649, col.681, Baroness Scotland of Asthal (June 17, 2003).
[236] *Hansard*, HL, vol.646, col.1271 (April 1, 2003).
[237] *Hansard*, HL, vol.649, col.681 (June 17, 2003).
[238] *Sexual Offences Guideline: Consultation* (December 6, 2012). The consultation document is available on the Sentencing Council website.

preparatory, i.e. it is committed by persons who are preparing to commit another child sex offence. The offence is designed to enable early intervention, and harm and culpability may not have been fully realised at the time of intervention, so it is difficult to articulate them in the same way as for other sexual offences. For this reason, the guideline describes the offence categories for this offence as follows:

Category 1	Raised harm *and* raised culpability
Category 2	Raised harm *or* raised culpability
Category 3	Grooming *without* raised harm or culpability factors present

The previous guideline, issued in 2007 by the Sentencing Guidelines Council ("SGC"), identified just two categories of s.15 offence, the higher reserved for cases where the offender's intent was to commit rape or an assault by penetration and the lower applying where their intent was to coerce the child into another form of sexual activity. The new guideline articulates both harm and culpability in more detail than the SGC guideline. It provides that the court should determine the harm caused or intended and culpability by reference only to the factors listed below. It adds that where an offence does not fall squarely into an offence category, individual factors may require a degree of weighting before the sentencer makes an overall assessment of which category is appropriate.

Raised harm

4.198 The factors listed as raising harm in relation to the s.15 offence are:

Factors indicating raised harm
• Continued contact despite victim's attempts to terminate contact • Sexual images exchanged • Victim exposed to extreme sexual content for example, extreme pornography • Child is particularly vulnerable due to personal circumstances

In its consultation, the Sentencing Council said that "continued contact despite victim's attempts to terminate contact" is included because persistent contact of that sort is likely to induce a sense of menace in the victim and therefore increase the psychological harm to them. As for "sexual images exchanged", in other guidelines this is expressed as the culpability factor "sexual images of victim recorded, retained, solicited or shared". It is included as a feature of harm for the s.15 offence because of the damage caused by the victim's knowledge that the offender holds images which may be circulated and over which the victim has no control. "Victim exposed to extreme sexual content for example, extreme pornography" is included to reflect the fact that such exposure will have a harmful and corrupting effect on the child. "Child is particularly vulnerable due to personal circumstances" (which appeared in the consultation draft as "vulnerable victim targeted") is intended to cover vulnerability over and above the fact that the victim is a child, e.g. where they are living in care, particularly residential care, are excluded from mainstream school or are misusing drugs and alcohol.

Raised culpability

The following factors are listed as raising culpability for the s.15 offence: **4.199**

Factors indicating raised harm
• Offender acts together with others to commit the offence
• Communication indicates penetrative sexual activity is intended
• Offender lied about age/persona
• Use of threats (including blackmail), gifts or bribes
• Abuse of trust
• Specific targeting of a particularly vulnerable child
• Abduction/detention
• Commercial exploitation and/or motivation
• Offence racially or religiously aggravated
• Offence motivated by, or demonstrating, hostility to the victim based on his or her sexual orientation (or presumed sexual orientation) or transgender identity (or presumed transgender identity)
• Offence motivated by, or demonstrating, hostility to the victim based on his or her disability (or presumed disability)

The factor "communication indicates penetrative sexual activity is intended" must be taken to apply whether the communication indicates that the offender intended to penetrate the child or to be penetrated by them. In its consultation, the Sentencing Council said it included "offender lied about age/persona" because additional deception of that sort increases the offender's culpability. The Council accepted that not all offenders will disguise their identity and that some will exploit the fact that, for example, a young girl may be looking for an older, "grown up" boyfriend. Most importantly, it made clear that it did not intend an offender who was honest about their age and persona to be able to use this as mitigation.

Step Two—Starting point and category range

4.200   Once the court has determined the offence category and culpability level, at step two it should use the corresponding starting point specified in the guideline in order to reach a sentence within the category range. The starting point applies to all offenders irrespective of plea or previous convictions. Once the starting point has been determined, step two allows further adjustment for aggravating or mitigating features, as set out below. A case of particular gravity, reflected by multiple features of culpability or harm, could merit upward adjustment from the starting point before further adjustment for aggravating or mitigating features. The starting points and category ranges for the s.15 offence are as follows:

Category 1	*Starting point* 4 years' custody *Category range* 3–7 years' custody
Category 2	*Starting point* 2 years' custody *Category range* 1–4 years' custody
Category 3	*Starting point* 18 months' custody *Category range* 1 year–2 years 6 months' custody

Category 1 has the same starting point and range as the top range under the SGC guideline. However, that guideline had higher starting points and ranges for offences committed against those under the age of 13. The Sentencing Council felt this was inappropriate and proposed in its consultation that where there is raised harm and raised culpability, the highest sentence level and range should be available regardless of the child's age. The majority of respondents strongly supported removing the age distinction in this way. Accordingly, under the new guideline, the higher SGC starting point is available regardless of the age of the victim where raised harm and raised culpability are present.

Aggravating and mitigating factors

After identifying the starting point and category range, the court should **4.201** consider whether the presence of aggravating or mitigating factors should result in an upward or downward adjustment from the starting point or the imposition of a sentence outside the category range. In particular, relevant recent convictions are likely to result in an upward adjustment. The non-exhaustive list of aggravating and mitigating factors for offences under s.15 is as follows:

Aggravating factors
Statutory aggravating factors
• Previous convictions, having regard to a) the nature of the offence to which the conviction relates and its relevance to the current offence; and b) the time that has elapsed since the conviction • Offence committed whilst on bail
Other aggravating factors
• Failure to comply with current court orders • Offence committed whilst on licence • Any steps taken to prevent the victim reporting an incident, obtaining assistance and/or from assisting or supporting the prosecution • Attempts to dispose of or conceal evidence • Victim encouraged to recruit others

Mitigating factors
• No previous convictions **or** no relevant/recent convictions • Remorse • Previous good character and/or exemplary conduct* • Age and/or lack of maturity where it affects the responsibility of the offender • Mental disorder or learning disability, particularly where linked to the commission of the offence • Demonstration of steps taken to address offending behaviour

* Previous good character/exemplary conduct is different from having no previous convictions. The more serious the offence, the less the weight which should normally be attributed to this factor. Where previous good character/exemplary conduct has been used to facilitate the offence, this mitigation should not normally be allowed and such conduct may constitute an aggravating factor.

Steps Three to Nine

4.202 The remaining steps cover the following points. At step three the court should consider any factors which would indicate a reduction in sentence, e.g. assistance to the prosecution. At step four it should consider any reduction for a guilty plea. At step five the court should consider dangerousness, i.e. whether it would be appropriate to award a life sentence (s.224A of the Criminal Justice Act 2003) or an extended sentence (s.226A). Step six requires the court to consider whether the total sentence is just and proportionate to the offending behaviour. At step seven it should consider whether to make an ancillary order (e.g. a compensation order, a SHPO or a restraining order). Step eight requires the court to fulfil its duty under s.174 of the Criminal Justice Act 2003 to give reasons for, and explain the effect of, the sentence. Finally, at step nine the court should consider whether to give credit for time spent on bail in accordance with s.240A of that Act.

Grooming behaviour should not be double-counted for sentencing purposes

4.203 Where an offender is sentenced for a sexual offence committed against a child, in circumstances where his grooming of the child is taken into account as raising his culpability, and at the same time he is sentenced for a s.15 offence which preceded and provided the opportunity for him to commit the sexual offence, then, if the custody threshold is passed, a concurrent rather than a consecutive sentence should be imposed for the s.15 offence, since otherwise the grooming element of the offender's conduct will be taken into account twice for sentencing purposes. This point is illustrated by *Rees (Gareth)*,[239] where the appellant pleaded guilty to one s.15 offence and two offences under s.9 of sexual activity with a child. The victim was a 14-year-old girl whom the appellant met through his step-son, who was in a relationship with her for a while. When that relationship finished, the appellant kept in touch with the victim through Facebook. The content of their messages became sexual and they arranged to meet. The appellant drove the victim to a car park where consensual sexual activity took place involving digital penetration of the victim's vagina followed by sexual intercourse in the back of the car with the use of a condom. The appellant made full admissions in interview and indicated from the outset that he accepted his guilt and would plead guilty, which he did at the first opportunity. When in due course the case was sentenced, the judge made only passing reference to the guidelines relating to the s.9 and s.15 offences, saying simply that "This was a case of serious harm in accordance with the sentencing guidelines because you penetrated your victim's vagina [with your penis]". The appellant's counsel submitted that the appellant was entitled to full credit for his plea, but the judge made no reference to this in his

---

[239] [2014] EWCA Crim 2363.

sentencing remarks. The appellant was sentenced to a total of seven-and-a-half years' imprisonment, made up of sentences of four years and five-and-a-half years respectively for the two s.9 offences, to run concurrently, with a further sentence of two years' imprisonment for the s.15 offence to be served consecutively. If the judge gave full credit for the plea, his starting point must have been 11 years and three months' imprisonment. On appeal, the Court of Appeal was satisfied that the s.9 offences fell within category 1A due to the penetration, the grooming, the breach of trust and the planning. The correct starting point was therefore five years' custody. There were also aggravating features, including the psychological harm done to the victim, the ejaculation, albeit with use of a condom, and the very considerable age disparity. The mitigation was that the appellant was a man of good character and had shown real remorse. The Court considered that, when the mitigating and aggravating features were put into the scales, the appropriate sentence was six years' imprisonment, which, with a full discount for the early plea, was reduced to a term of four years. As for the grooming, this was part of the same criminality and one of the aggravating features of the s.9 offences, and so the court could see no proper basis for imposing a separate consecutive sentence for the s.15 offence. It therefore allowed the appeal and substituted a sentence of four years' imprisonment, made up of one year for the grooming offence, three years for the s.9 offence involving digital penetration and four years for the s.9 offence involving sexual intercourse, all the sentences to be served concurrently.

Offenders caught by a police or media "sting"

When an offender is convicted of attempting to commit the s.15 offence after   **4.204** being caught in a police or media "sting", should his sentence be mitigated to reflect the fact that there was never a risk to an identified child victim? We suggest that it should not, as this would enable an offender to benefit in sentencing terms from the mere accident that his efforts were targeted against someone who was not, as he had hoped and intended, a child. The Sentencing Council guideline is, however, silent on the point and the following cases, which were decided under the SGC guideline, are difficult to reconcile.

What we regard as the correct approach appears to have been taken in *R.*   **4.205** *v S,*[240] where the offender (27) had chatted on a social networking site with an undercover police officer posing as a 14-year-old girl. In an exchange of messages online and by text, which became sexual in nature, they arranged to

---

[240] [2008] EWCA Crim 600. See also *Warren* [2007] EWCA Crim 2733 (offender caught in sting by the *News of the World*); and *Lewis (Jeffrey)* [2016] EWCA Crim 304 (held, in relation to an offence under s.14 of the 2003 Act, that it was not relevant to culpability that the person whom the appellant arranged to meet was not a 15-year-old virgin, as he thought, but a man).

meet and the offender proposed that they "go all the way". He was arrested when he turned up at the agreed meeting place. He pleaded guilty at the first opportunity and was sentenced to 30 months' imprisonment. The Court of Appeal held that there was no justification for exceeding the recommended starting point of two years' custody. The girl's supposed age was 14, which put the offence in the middle of the relevant bracket in the guideline. The prompt guilty plea made it appropriate to move downwards from the starting point by one third. A term of 16 months' imprisonment was substituted. The Court said nothing about whether the sentence should be discounted because the offender had been trapped as the result of a police operation in which there was no actual victim, but the fact that it sentenced by reference to the girl's supposed age implies that this had no impact on its reasoning.

4.206   A less satisfactory case is *Barnett*,[241] where the offender (46) had joined an online chatroom for teenagers posing as a 17-year-old and had cultivated a friendship with a 12-year-old girl, Katie, who was in fact an investigative journalist. The offender sent Katie messages of a sexual nature and arranged a meeting with her. The girl he met was a young-looking colleague of the journalist. After the meeting he sent Katie further sexual messages, after which the newspaper exposed him. He pleaded guilty and was sentenced to 30 months' imprisonment. The Court of Appeal held that the sentence was manifestly excessive given that the offender was of previous good character, had been caught by a "sting" where there was no actual victim and had been subjected to very considerable humiliation as a result of exposure in the national press. It substituted a sentence of 18 months' imprisonment.

Parties to the Offence

4.207 The s.15 offence may be committed by and against persons of either sex. A must be 18 or over and B must be under 16. A person attains the age of 16 at the commencement of the sixteenth anniversary of her birth and the age of 18 at the commencement of its eighteenth anniversary.[242] For proof of age, see paras 3.73 and following, above. It follows that A does not commit the offence where the person whom he has been grooming online turns out to not to be a child, as A had believed, but, for example, a police officer or a journalist. But in those circumstances, A will be guilty of an attempt if he has done an act that is more than merely preparatory to committing the full offence.[243] As to whether a child under 16 may be convicted as an accessory to a s.15 offence of which she is the victim, see paras 4.57 and following, above.

---

[241] [2007] EWCA Crim 1625.
[242] Family Law Reform Act 1969 s.9(1).
[243] See para.4.190, above.

Jurisdiction

By virtue of s.72 of and Sch.2 to the Sexual Offences Act 2003, as   **4.208**
amended,[244] it is an offence under s.15 for a UK national to do an act in a
country outside the UK which would constitute a s.15 offence if done in
England and Wales. See further para.4.59, above.

"Has Met or Communicated"

Section 15(2)(a) provides that: **4.209**

> "the reference [in section 15(1)] to A having met or communicated with B is a
> reference to A having met B in any part of the world or having communicated
> with B by any means from, to or in any part of the world"

So if A and B are both, for example, in Thailand and meet or exchange
messages there, this is capable of being a "meeting" or "communication" for
the purposes of the section.

Communication may be "by any means" and so may be oral, written or in   **4.210**
the form of images. Online communication, e.g. by email or Skype, will
clearly qualify.

There is no requirement that the meeting or communication relied upon   **4.211**
must be proved to have been preparatory to a sexual offence, and it could
indeed have been perfectly innocent.[245] Some concern was expressed about
this during the passage of the Sexual Offences Bill on the ground that
innocent activities should not fall within the scope of the offence. The
Government argued in response that nobody can be convicted under s15
without proof that they met or travelled to meet the child[246] with the
intention of abusing her sexually, and it would therefore be unwise to limit
the nature of the prior meetings or communications upon which a conviction
could be founded to those involving a sexual element.[247] Nonetheless, a
number of amendments were tabled in the Lords with just this purpose. The
Government resisted these on the basis that they could operate to prevent
convictions in deserving cases, where A communicated with B on apparently
innocent matters but A was merely securing B's confidence with the intention
of making the relationship sexual later. As examples of prior communication
which would suffice for the purposes of the s.15 offence, the Home Office
guidance on the Act refers to cases where A gives B music lessons, or runs a

---

[244] By the Criminal Justice and Immigration Act 2008 s.72, which came into force on July 14,
2008.
[245] *Gaviria* [2010] EWCA Crim 1693 at [16] per Leveson LJ: "There is absolutely no
requirement that either communication must be sexual in nature."
[246] Or, now, that they arranged to meet the child or that the child travelled to meet them: see
para.4.187, above.
[247] *Hansard*, HL, vol.646, cols 1261–2, Lord Falconer of Thoroton (April 1, 2003). As
explained below, only one prior meeting or communication is now required.

youth club which B attends, or sells B sweets from a sweet shop.[248] In this connection it should be noted that when s.15A of the 2003 Act comes into force, any communication by an adult with a child that is sexual in nature and engaged in for the purpose of the adult's sexual gratification will itself constitute a criminal offence. Section 15A is discussed in paras 4.225 and following, below.

4.212   Another amendment proposed during the passage of the Sexual Offences Bill, based on a proposal by the Criminal Bar Association, would have required proof that at the time of the prior meeting or communication, A intended to commit a sexual offence against the child. Lord Falconer pointed out the difficulty this would create in prosecuting the offence, since it could be very difficult to obtain the necessary evidence of intention. He added:

> "It should not matter, when an adult travels to meet a child with an intention sexually to abuse that child, whether or not you can also prove that he had that sexual intention in previous communications with the child. It is enough that he has befriended that child and now travels to meet him with that intent."

On this reasoning, one could go further and ask why even the element of "befriending" should matter. Why should meeting (etc.) a child with the specified intention not be sufficient in itself for conviction? The short answer is that the offence was designed to deal with the menace of grooming, and a grooming element was therefore seen as an essential part of its formulation. The "befriending" element also provides the basis for the police to intervene well before contact offending takes place.

"ON ONE OR MORE OCCASIONS"

4.213 At least one meeting or communication must already have taken place for the s.15 offence to be committed. As enacted, the offence required two prior meetings or communications, with the result that A could not be convicted where he met or travelled to meet the child after only one meeting or communication, however compelling the evidence of his sexual intent. This was queried at Committee stage in the Lords, when Baroness Blatch asked why it should be necessary to prove two meetings or communications rather than one.[249] Lord Falconer of Thoroton, answering on behalf of the Government, said that the offence requires a course of conduct before A meets B, and the required course of conduct would not be established by just one meeting or communication.[250] We pointed out in previous editions of this work that Lord Falconer's formalistic answer did not address the point of substance underpinning Baroness Blatch's question, and that it remained to be seen whether this would prove a significant problem in practice. In fact

---

[248] H.O. Circular 21/2004: *Guidance on Part 1 of the Sexual Offences Act 2003*, para.88.
[249] *Hansard*, HL, vol.646, col.1261 (April 1, 2003).
[250] ibid., col.1262. See also Standing Committee B, September 16, 2003, col.196, Paul Goggins MP.

it did, and in consequence the Government was persuaded to insert a provision in what became the Criminal Justice and Courts Act 2015 so as to reduce from two to one the number of occasions on which, for the purposes of s.15, the defendant must meet or communicate with the child victim before meeting or travelling to meet them (etc.) with the required intent.[251] The amendment was prompted by the Report of a cross-party Parliamentary inquiry, chaired by Sarah Champion MP and supported by the charity Barnardo's, into the effectiveness of legislation for tackling child sexual exploitation.[252] In moving the amendment, Lord Faulks said that the s.15 offence was designed to tackle what in 2003 was a relatively new pattern of behaviour that was commonly thought of as grooming, the aim being to protect children who may be contacted by adults repeatedly over a period of time to build their trust with the intention of subjecting them to sexual abuse in future. However, the development of new technology and better, faster and simpler forms of communication, including chat rooms and social media sites, made it easier for offenders to make contact with their victims and build their trust relatively quickly. The Child Exploitation and Online Protection Centre ("CEOP") reported in 2013 that online child sexual exploitation had shifted in its nature, with the time between initial contact and offending behaviour often extremely short and characterised by rapid escalation to threats and intimidation.[253] CEOP described a "scattergun" approach taken by perpetrators, in which they target a large number of potential victims, are ignored by the vast majority and focus their efforts on the small number who respond positively. The Parliamentary inquiry had heard evidence that contact offending against a child can now occur following just one communication or meeting. Lord Faulks said that reducing the number of initial occasions on which the defendant must meet or communicate with the child in order to commit the s.15 offence from two to one would permit more effective intervention by the police, and in certain cases might prevent the contact element of the offence occurring. The amendment would also bring the offence in England and Wales into line with the equivalent Scottish offence, which requires only one initial contact.

We welcome this change in the law, our only regret being that the   **4.214** Government did not act on the point when Baroness Blatch raised it in 2003. There is no good reason why a second contact should ever have been required, given that, as noted by the Parliamentary inquiry, the offence is only committed where the adult meets or travels to meet a child (etc.) with the intention of abusing them sexually.

---

[251] *Hansard*, HL, col.960-1 (July 21, 2014).
[252] *Report of the Parliamentary inquiry into the effectiveness of legislation for tackling child sexual exploitation and trafficking within the UK* , which is available at *http://www.barnardos.org.uk/cse_parliamentary_inquiry_report.pdf* [Accessed April 30, 2016].
[253] Threat Assessment of Child Sexual Exploitation and Abuse 2013, available at *http://www.ceop.police.uk/Documents/ceopdocs/CEOP_TACSEA2013_240613%20FINAL.pdf* [Accessed April 30, 2016].

4.215   There is no limit on the period of time which may elapse between the initial meeting or communication and the later meeting arranged with B.

"TRAVELS WITH THE INTENTION OF MEETING . . . IN ANY PART OF THE WORLD"

4.216   The offence will be committed wherever in the world the meeting to which A or B travels is intended to take place.

"ARRANGES TO MEET"

4.217   For the meaning of "arranges", see paras 4.172 and following, above.

"DURING OR AFTER THE MEETING"

4.218   The offence may be committed where A intends to commit a sexual offence against the child, not at the meeting or intended meeting, but on some later occasion. An example might be where A meets and communicates with B over the internet, arranges to meet her for the first time in a public place, and sets off for that meeting intending to groom her further and meet her again in private on a later date in order to commit a sexual offence against her.

"RELEVANT OFFENCE"

4.219   Section 15(2)(b)[254] provides:

> "'relevant offence' means—
>   (i) an offence under this Part,
>   (ii) [. . .], or
>   (iii) anything done outside England and Wales which is not an offence within sub-paragraph (i) but would be an offence within sub-paragraph (i) if done in England and Wales."

For the purposes of this provision, an "offence under this Part" means an offence under ss.1 to 79 of the Act. The effect of s.15(2)(b)(iii) is that conduct prohibited by ss.1 to 79 of the 2003 Act in England and Wales will constitute a "relevant offence" if undertaken elsewhere in the world.

CONSENT

4.220   Absence of consent is not an element of the s.15 offence. Accordingly, the offence is committed regardless of whether B consents to the activity in question.

---

[254] As amended by the Sexual Offences (Northern Ireland Consequential Amendments) Order 2008 (SI 2008/1779) art.4.

MENTAL ELEMENT

At the time that A meets, travels to meet or arranges to meet B, or at the time   **4.221**
B is travelling to meet him, A must intend to do something to or in respect
of B, either at the meeting or later, which if done will involve the commission
by him of a relevant offence. It is not sufficient for the intention to arise at
a later stage. Accordingly, no s.15 offence is committed where, during a
meeting started without any such intention, A decides to take advantage of
the situation and commit a sexual offence against B.[255] In those circumstances, A should be prosecuted for any sexual offence that he commits; and
if he does an act that is more than merely preparatory to such an offence, he
should be prosecuted for attempt. For the meaning of "intention" see paras
2.78 and following, above.

There is no requirement in relation to the prior meeting or communication   **4.222**
that A must have planned or otherwise intended it to take place. So if A
meets B unexpectedly and without prior arrangement, e.g. by being introduced to her at a party, that will qualify as a prior meeting for the purposes
of the section.

As to the requirement that A does not reasonably believe that B is 16 or   **4.223**
over, see para.4.66, above. It could in principle be difficult for the prosecution
to establish that A did not have such a belief where A and B have not met and
only communicated by exchanging written messages online, especially if B
misled A as to her age. However, the issue of reasonable belief only rarely
arises in practice, no doubt partly because s.15 offenders are often keen to
establish that the person with whom they are in contact is indeed a child.

As to whether A is liable to conviction if he acts whilst in a state of   **4.224**
intoxication, see the discussion of *Heard*[256] in paras 2.81 and following,
above. In the light of that discussion, voluntary intoxication through drink or
drugs will provide a defence to a charge under s.15 if, at the relevant time, it
may have prevented A forming the intention to do something to or in respect
of B which would involve the commission of a relevant offence.

SEXUAL COMMUNICATION WITH A CHILD

DEFINITION

Section 15A(1) of the Sexual Offences Act 2003[257] provides: **4.225**

> "(1) A person aged 18 or over (A) commits an offence if—
> (a) for the purpose of obtaining sexual gratification, A intentionally commu-
>   nicates with another person (B),

---

[255] *Gaviria* [2010] EWCA Crim 1693.
[256] [2007] EWCA Crim 125.
[257] Inserted by the Serious Crime Act 2015 s.67, from a date to be appointed (the provision is
not in force as of April 29, 2016).

(b) the communication is sexual or is intended to encourage B to make (whether to A or to another) a communication that is sexual, and
(c) B is under 16 and A does not reasonably believe that B is 16 or over."

4.226 At the time of writing (January 15, 2016), this provision is not yet in force. When it is commenced, it will penalise an adult who, for the purpose of obtaining sexual gratification, communicates with a child under 16, whom he does not reasonably believe to be aged 16 or over, where the communication is sexual or intended to encourage the child to make a sexual communication. The offence is likely to be committed where an adult engages in sexual conversation with a child in an internet chatroom, sends a child sexually explicit text messages or invites a child to send such messages (whether or not the invitation is itself couched in sexual terms). The fact that the offence may be committed only by an adult who acts for the purpose of obtaining sexual gratification means that the provision does not criminalise ordinary social or educational interactions between children and adults nor communications between young people themselves.

4.227 Section 15A owes its origins to a campaign run in 2014 by the National Society for the Prevention of Cruelty to Children ("NSPCC") to promote the creation of an offence to target paedophiles who communicate sexually with a child.[258] In October 2014, Lord Harris of Haringey moved an amendment to insert such an offence into the Serious Crime Bill, which was at Report stage in the House of Lords.[259] Lord Bates, a Home Office minister, resisted the amendment on the ground that the Government was already considering the matter, though its preliminary view was that the behaviour targeted by the amendment was already covered by the criminal law. Lord Harris withdrew his amendment, but returned to the charge on Third Reading the following month.[260] On this occasion, Lord Bates conceded that there was a gap in the criminal law relating to contact between a predatory adult and his child victim where the messages are sexual in nature but where the victim is not being asked to respond in any particular way. He gave a strong hint that a Government amendment would be forthcoming when the Bill returned to the Commons, and on that basis Lord Harris again withdrew his amendment. Shortly afterwards, at the *We Protect Children Online* global summit held in London in December 2014, the Prime Minister announced the intention to create an offence of sexual communication with a child.[261] The following month what became s.15A was duly inserted into the Serious Crime Bill at Commons Committee stage.[262]

[258] *Flaw in the Law*: see *http://www.nspcc.org.uk/fighting-for-childhood/campaigns/flaw-law/* [Accessed April 30, 2016]; and see *http://www.publications.parliament.uk/pa/cm201415/cmpublic/seriouscrime/memo/sc01.htm* [Accessed April 30, 2016].
[259] *Hansard*, HL Report, Second Sitting (October 28, 2014), col.1110ff.
[260] *Hansard*, HL Third Reading (November 5, 2014), col.1622ff.
[261] *https://www.gov.uk/government/news/ending-online-child-sexual-exploitation-uk-leads-global-summit-in-london-weprotect-children-online* [Accessed April 30, 2016].
[262] *Hansard*, PBC (January 15, 2015), col.108ff.

The concern that drove the NSPCC to mount its campaign was that   4.228
children were inadequately protected from adults who send them sexual
messages, particularly online in the form of "sexualised chat". The fragmented nature of the existing law in this area, and the fact that it pre-dated
widespread use of the internet, made it hard for the police to deal with such
conduct appropriately, and as a result opportunities to stop abusers grooming young people online were being missed. The NSPCC was concerned that
the existing law did not enable the police to intervene sufficiently early in the
grooming process. If the adult had sent sexual messages but not as yet incited
the child to engage in sexual activity or made preparations to meet, then
there would be limited scope for the police to intervene based on an
apprehended offence under the Sexual Offences Act 2003. This was a
significant problem since in most cases of online grooming, the adult seeks to
flatter the child and attempt to gain their trust before inciting them to engage
in sexual activity. By the time such incitement occurs, a vital window of
opportunity to prevent abuse has been lost. If the adult sent messages that
were indecent or grossly offensive he might fall foul of s.1 of the Malicious
Communications Act 1988. But that offence requires an intent to cause
distress or anxiety, and when an adult is in the early stages of grooming a
child they are likely to send messages that flatter and compliment the child
rather than distress them or make them anxious. Also, sending a grossly
offensive, indecent, obscene or menacing message over the internet would fall
foul of s.127 of the Communications Act 2003. But again, in the early stages
of grooming an adult is unlikely to be sending grossly offensive or frightening
messages. Also, this offence is not a sexual offence and so does not
automatically attract sex offender registration. The NSPCC concluded that
an offence should be created to make clear that it is always illegal for an adult
to send a sexual message to a child. This would help protect children from
unwanted and distressing sexualised contact online, enable action to be taken
against offenders at an earlier stage of the grooming process, and help
prevent abuse escalating.

The NSPCC noted that the Sexual Offences (Scotland) Act 2009 contained   4.229
offences of sending or directing a sexual communication to a child. Drawing
on these provisions, it proposed the creation in England and Wales of a new
adult offence of intentionally sending a sexual message to a child. However,
the NSPCC identified shortcomings in the 2009 Act which it argued should
not be replicated here. First, the Scottish offences require that the offender's
purpose was either to obtain sexual gratification or to humiliate, alarm or
distress the victim. The NSPCC said that the reference to "humiliating,
distressing or alarming" failed to recognise that adults who groom children
aim to flatter and build trust with their victims rather than send them
distressing or offensive communications. The Government seems to have
agreed as this phrase does not appear in s.15A. As for the alternative purpose
of obtaining sexual gratification, the NSPCC understood from Scottish
police that this set a high threshold that had prevented prosecution in some

cases. This concern was raised by Seema Malhotra MP during Commons Committee stage of the Serious Crime Bill. In responding, the Solicitor-General, Robert Buckland MP, said that the concern was misplaced given the wide definition of "sexual gratification" as applied by the courts in relation to ss.11 and 12 of the 2003 Act.[263] It is true that case law under s.12 of the 2003 Act, relating to the offence of causing a child to watch a sexual act, establishes that an adult acts for the purpose of obtaining sexual gratification where his aim is to obtain such gratification immediately, or as part of a longer term plan, or both. In many cases where an adult has sent a child a sexual communication, the jury may readily be able to infer that his purpose must have been to obtain sexual gratification at some point. However, much is likely to turn on what other evidence is adduced and what explanation, if any, the defendant gives for his conduct. Accordingly, the Solicitor-General's response to Ms Malhotra perhaps misses the point of the NSPCC's concern, which was that the requirement to prove the purpose of sexual gratification, however that term is interpreted, is itself a potential obstacle to prosecution. It remains to be seen whether the requirement unduly limits the impact of the offence.

4.230   The second shortcoming that the NSPCC identified in the Scottish offences was that it was possible for a child to commit them. The NSPCC believed that prosecution would rarely be in the best interests of either the child offender or their victim, and so favoured confining the equivalent offence in England and Wales to adults. Section 15A is so confined. This limitation was, however, itself questioned at Commons Committee stage by Ann Coffey MP, who expressed concern about the exploitation of young people by other young people, giving as an example a 17-year-old who sends a sexual communication to a younger child of, say, 11. In response, the Solicitor-General referred to the need to be careful not to discourage the discussion of sexual matters between young children, and said that in the example cited by Ms Coffey, the 17-year-old would commit the offence under s.12 of the 2003 Act of causing a child to watch a sexual act. Again, this response rather misses the point, since the example given by Ms Coffey did not involve either a discussion of sexual matters or the watching of a sexual act; rather, she was concerned about an older child exploiting a younger one by communicating with them in a sexualised way. The fact is, the Government made a deliberate choice to confine the s.15A to adults, no doubt in recognition of the point made by the NSPCC that prosecution of young people for sending a sexual communication is unlikely to be in their interests or those of their victim. It is also the case that the offence of meeting a child following sexual grooming, contained in s.15 of the Act, can only be committed by adults. However, the child sex offences in ss.9–12 the 2003 Act can all be committed by children: see s.13, discussed in paras 4.144 and following, above.

---

[263] *Hansard*, PBC (January 15, 2015), col.112.

Attempts

If A communicates with B, whom he believes to be a child but who is in fact,   **4.231**
say, a police officer or a journalist, and the terms of the communication fall
within the scope of s.15A, A may be convicted of attempting to commit the
offence. In *Shivpuri*,[264] the House of Lords held that a person may be
convicted of an attempt if they do an act more than merely preparatory to a
full offence, intending to commit that offence, notwithstanding the commission of the full offence is on the true facts impossible. In the scenario
envisaged above, it is impossible for A to complete the offence because the
person with whom he communicates, B, is not in fact aged under 16. In the
light of *Shivpuri*, this impossibility does not preclude his conviction for an
attempt. See further *Jones*,[265] discussed in paras 3.160 and following,
above.

MODE OF TRIAL AND PUNISHMENT

The offence under s.15A is triable either way.[266] The maximum sentence on   **4.232**
conviction on indictment is two years' imprisonment. On summary convic-
tion the maximum penalty is six months' imprisonment or a fine, or both.[267]
As from a day to be appointed the maximum sentence on summary
conviction will increase to 12 months' imprisonment.[268] The increase will
have no application to offences committed before it takes effect.[269]

For the purposes of listing, cases of sexual communication with a child[270]   **4.233**
fall within Class 2B, save for complex cases involving many complainants
(often in care or otherwise particularly vulnerable) and/or many defendants
who are alleged to have systematically groomed and abused them, often over
a long period of time, which fall within Class 1C.[271] Cases in Class 1C must
be referred to the Resident Judge, and by the Resident Judge to a Presiding
Judge. Cases in Class 2B must be similarly referred in certain specified
circumstances, including where the case is unusually grave or complex or a
novel and important point of law is to be raised; where the defendant is a
police officer, a member of the legal profession or a high profile figure; or
where for any reason the case is likely to attract exceptional media attention.

---

[264] [1987] A.C. 1.
[265] [2007] EWCA Crim 1118.
[266] s.15A(3)(a).
[267] s.15A(3)(b) as read with the transitional provision in s.86(14).
[268] Criminal Justice Act 2003 s.282(2), (3).
[269] Criminal Justice Act 2003 s.282(4).
[270] And of soliciting, inciting, encouraging or assisting, attempting or conspiring to commit
the offence or assisting an offender having committed the offence.
[271] *Consolidated Criminal Practice Directions*, Part XIII Listing B: CLASSIFICATION,
available at *https://www.judiciary.gov.uk/wp-content/uploads/2015/09/crim-pd-2015.pdf* [Accessed
April 30, 2016].

4.234   The offence under s.15A is a specified sexual offence for the purposes of the Criminal Justice Act 2003.[272]

4.235   A person convicted under s.15A, cautioned, found not guilty by reason of insanity or found to be under a disability and to have done the act charged, is automatically subject to the notification requirements in the Sexual Offences Act 2003.[273]

Sentencing

4.236   The Sentencing Council guideline relating to the sentencing of sexual offences committed by offenders aged 18 and over, discussed in Ch.33, below, preceded the creation of the s.15A offence, and as such there is currently no sentencing guideline for the offence.

Parties to the Offence

4.237   The s.15A offence may be committed by and against persons of either sex. A must be 18 or over and B must be under 16. A person attains the age of 16 at the commencement of the sixteenth anniversary of her birth and the age of 18 at the commencement of its eighteenth anniversary.[274] For proof of age, see paras 3.73 and following, above. It follows that A does not commit the offence where the person with whom he has communicated on social media turns out not to be a child, as A had believed, but a police officer or a journalist. But in those circumstances, A will be guilty of an attempt if he has done an act that is more than merely preparatory to committing the full offence.[275] As to whether a child under 16 may be convicted as an accessory to a s.15A offence of which she is the victim, see para.4.57, above.

Jurisdiction

4.238   If A in England and Wales communicates in the prohibited terms with B in another jurisdiction, we suggest that he commits the s.15A offence in this jurisdiction on the basis that, in accordance with the test laid down in *Smith (Wallace Duncan) (No.4)*,[276] a substantial measure of his activities take place here. As for acts committed overseas, by virtue of s.72 of and Sch.2 to the Sexual Offences Act 2003 Act, as amended,[277] it is an offence under s.15A

---

[272] s.224 and Sch.15, Pt 2, as amended with effect from a date to be appointed by the Serious Crime Act 2015 s.85 and Sch.4, para.68(1), (2).

[273] s.80 and Sch.3, as amended with effect from a date to be appointed by the Serious Crime Act 2015 s.85 and Sch.4, para.66(1), (2). See further Ch.35, below.

[274] Family Law Reform Act 1969 s.9(1).

[275] See para.4.190, above.

[276] [2004] EWCA Crim 631.

[277] By the Criminal Justice and Immigration Act 2008 s.72, which came into force on July 14, 2008.

for a UK national to do an act in a country outside the UK which would constitute a s.15A offence if done in England and Wales. See further para.4.59, above. When the clause containing the s.15A offence was inserted into the Serious Crime Bill on Report in the Lords, it was accompanied by a provision the effect of which would have been to prevent s.72 applying to the new offence.[278] This provision was removed on a Government amendment following debate on the point in Committee.[279]

"For the Purpose of Sexual Gratification"

The fact that the offence may only be committed where the adult acts for the purpose of obtaining sexual gratification means that the offence does not criminalise ordinary social or educational interactions between children and adults. There is a similar requirement in the offences in ss.11 and 12 of the 2003 Act, which prohibit engaging in sexual activity in the presence of a child and causing a child to watch a sexual act. In *Abdullahi*,[280] the Court of Appeal held that the s.12 offence is committed whether the defendant's purpose was immediate gratification, or deferred gratification, or both. It is highly likely that the courts will apply the same construction to s.15A.   **4.239**

"Communicates"

The terms "communicates" and "communication" are not defined in the Act and therefore carry their ordinary meaning, which includes imparting or transmitting something intangible such as thought or feeling.[281] The terms are apt to cover any means of communication, whether oral, written or in the form of physical conduct or gesture. They will cover the sending of messages online, or by email or text.   **4.240**

   The requirement is that A communicates with B; there is no requirement that B responds in any way. However, A does not communicate with B unless A's communication actually reaches B. If for any reason it does not, A does not commit the full offence but, if the other requirements of the offence are met and A has done an act more than merely preparatory to communicating with B, he may be convicted of an attempt.   **4.241**

   Can A commit the offence by, say, posting online or writing on a lavatory wall a message in terms falling within the scope of s.15A, with the hope and intention that it will be read by a child under the age of 16? We suggest that in this scenario, assuming A acts for the purpose of obtaining sexual gratification, he will be guilty of the full offence as and when the message is   **4.242**

---

[278] HC Bill 160 2014–15, as amended in Public Bill Committee, Sch.4, para.59.
[279] *Hansard*, PBC (January 15, 2015), cols 107–116.
[280] [2006] EWCA Crim 2060.
[281] 6th edn (Oxford: Oxford University Press, 2007).

read by such a child. If no child reads the message, A may nonetheless be convicted of an attempt.[282]

"Sexual"

4.243 Section 15A(2) provides:

> "(2) For the purposes of this section, a communication is sexual if—
> (a) any part of it relates to sexual activity, or
> (b) a reasonable person would, in all the circumstances but regardless of any person's purpose, consider any part of the communication to be sexual;
> and in paragraph (a) "sexual activity" means an activity that a reasonable person would, in all the circumstances but regardless of any person's purpose, consider to be sexual.

Compare this provision with the definition of "sexual" in s.78 of the Act, which applies for all other purposes in Pt 1 save in relation to the offence in s.71. Section 78 is discussed in paras 2.66 and following, above. The effect of s.15A(2) is to focus attention on the content of the communication and the circumstances in which it is made. The purpose of those involved is to be disregarded. So if a reasonable person would, in all the circumstances, consider the communication to be possibly sexual depending on the purpose of the sender and recipient, it will not fall within the scope of the offence. In effect, s.15A(2) catches only communications that are explicitly or manifestly sexual. What if A communicates with B in code, so that their messages carry sexual connotations only because of what they have secretly agreed between themselves? Suppose, for example, A and B agree that A will email B page references from the *Kama Sutra* to indicate what he would like to do to her. Proof simply of the sending and receipt of those messages is unlikely to establish an offence on the part of A, since the messages do not on their face relate to sexual activity and it is improbable that a reasonable person would, regardless of the purpose of A and B, consider them to be sexual.[283] The position is likely to be otherwise, however, if the prosecution were able to prove the key to the code, i.e. the agreement by A and B to communicate by reference to the contents of the *Kama Sutra*, since if those circumstances were taken into account, it would be open to the jury to find, on the totality of the evidence, that the messages relate to sexual activity within the meaning of s.15A(2)(a).

4.244 In a trial for an offence under s.15A it will be a question of fact for the jury (or magistrates) whether the communication meets the requirements of s.15A(2). If the defence submit that no reasonable jury properly directed could find that it does, the judge will need to decide whether a reasonable

---

[282] See the discussion in in paras 3.159 and following, above.

[283] Cf. Karl Laird, *Parts 5 and 6 of the Serious Crime Act 2015—More than Merely Miscellany* [2015] Crim. L.R. 789 at p.792: " ... if a reasonable person would not consider the communication sexual because it seems innocuous, but D's purpose is a sexual one, it seems that D cannot be guilty".

person could, in all the circumstances as alleged by the prosecution, consider the communication to be sexual. If the judge concludes that a reasonable person could possibly answer that question adversely to the defendant, then the matter must be left to the jury.

CONSENT

Absence of consent is not an element of s.15A. Accordingly, the offence is committed regardless of how B reacts or responds to A's communication, and even if A sent it after being solicited to do so by B.   **4.245**

MENTAL ELEMENT

A must communicate with B intentionally and for the purpose of obtaining sexual gratification. For the meaning of "intention" see paras 2.78 and following, above. For the meaning of "for the purpose of obtaining sexual gratification", see paras 4.117 and 4.139, above. As to the requirement that A does not reasonably believe that B is 16 or over, see para.4.66, above. It could in principle be difficult for the prosecution to establish that A did not have such a belief where A and B have not met and have communicated only remotely, e.g. by exchanging written messages online, especially if B misled A as to her age. However, it can be anticipated that in practice the issue of reasonable belief will arise only rarely, as individuals who engage in the sort of behaviour that s.15A is designed to catch are likely to be keen to establish that the person with whom they are communicating is indeed a child.   **4.246**

As to whether A is liable to conviction if he acts whilst in a state of intoxication, see the discussion of *Heard*[284] in paras 2.81 and following, above. In the light of that discussion, voluntary intoxication through drink or drugs will provide a defence to a charge under s.15A if it may have prevented A forming the purpose of obtaining sexual gratification.   **4.247**

POSSESSION OF A PAEDOPHILE MANUAL

DEFINITION

Section 69(1) of the Serious Crime Act 2015 provides: **4.248**

> "(1) It is an offence to be in possession of any item that contains advice or guidance about abusing children sexually."

This section creates a new offence of possession of what is commonly referred to as a "paedophile manual". The offence owes its origins to increased awareness of the existence online, in particular, of material giving practical advice or guidance as to how to commit a sexual offence against a child.   **4.249**

---

[284] [2007] EWCA Crim 125.

Much of this material is deeply disturbing, giving detailed advice as to how to entrap or "groom" a child, where to find a child to abuse, and how to offend and escape capture. Although a number of criminal offences already penalised the creation, possession and distribution of indecent images of children, notably s.1 of the Protection of Children Act 1978 and s.160 of the Criminal Justice Act 1988 (for which see Ch.8, below), there was no offence that criminalised the possession of material of this sort. The Prime Minister announced in April 2014 that he intended to fill this gap[285]:

> "It's completely unacceptable that there's a loophole in the law which allows paedophiles to write and distribute these disgusting documents. I want to ensure we do everything we can to protect children—and that's why I'm making them illegal."

What became s.69 was duly included in the Serious Crime Bill on introduction in June 2014. The offence came into force on May 3, 2015.[286]

MODE OF TRIAL AND PUNISHMENT

4.250   The offence under s.69 is triable either way.[287] The maximum sentence on conviction on indictment is three years' imprisonment or a fine, or both.[288] On summary conviction the maximum penalty is six months' imprisonment or a fine, or both.[289] As from a day to be appointed the maximum sentence on summary conviction will increase to 12 months' imprisonment.[290] The increase will have no application to offences committed before it takes effect.[291]

4.251   For the purposes of listing, cases of possession of a paedophile manual[292] fall within Class 2B.[293] Cases in Class 2B must in certain circumstances be referred to the Resident Judge, and by the Resident Judge to a Presiding Judge, including where the case is unusually grave or complex or a novel and important point of law is to be raised; where the defendant is a police officer, a member of the legal profession or a high profile figure; or where for any reason the case is likely to attract exceptional media attention.

4.252   Where a justice of the peace is satisfied by information on oath, laid by or on behalf of the DPP or by a constable, that there is reasonable ground for suspecting that, in any premises, there is an item containing advice or

---

[285] http://www.telegraph.co.uk/news/politics/10791387/Cameron-to-close-legal-loophole-that-lets-paedophiles-download-child-grooming-manuals.html [Accessed April 30, 2016].

[286] See SI 2015/820.

[287] s.69(3).

[288] s.69(3)(c).

[289] s.69(3)(b) as read with the transitional provision in s.86(14).

[290] Criminal Justice Act 2003 s.282(2), (3).

[291] Criminal Justice Act 2003 s.282(4)

[292] And of soliciting, inciting, encouraging or assisting, attempting or conspiring to commit the offence or assisting an offender having committed the offence.

[293] Consolidated Criminal Practice Directions, Part XIII Listing B: CLASSIFICATION, available at https://www.judiciary.gov.uk/wp-content/uploads/2015/09/crim-pd-2015.pdf [Accessed April 30, 2016].

guidance about abusing children sexually, the justice may issue a warrant authorising a constable to enter (if need be by force) and search the premises and to seize and remove any articles which he believes (with reasonable cause) to be or include such items.[294] There is also provision for a magistrates' court to order the forfeiture of such items.[295] These provisions are additional to the powers of the courts to deprive an offender on conviction of property used or intended for use for the purposes of crime.[296]

A person convicted under s.69, cautioned, found not guilty by reason of insanity or found to be under a disability and to have done the act charged, is automatically subject to the notification requirements in the Sexual Offences Act 2003.[297]		**4.253**

Restriction on prosecution

By s.69(4)(a) of the 2015 Act, proceedings for an offence of possessing a paedophile manual may be brought in England and Wales only by or with the consent of the DPP. For the case law relating to an almost identical provision in s.1(3) of the Protection of Children Act 1978, relating to the prosecution of offences relating to indecent photographs of children, see paras 8.09 and following, below.		**4.254**

SENTENCING

The Sentencing Council's guideline on the sentencing of sexual offences committed by offenders aged 18 and over, discussed in Ch.33, below, preceded the creation of the s.69 offence, and as such there is currently no sentencing guideline for the offence.		**4.255**

PARTIES TO THE OFFENCE

The s.69 offence may be committed by persons of either sex and by companies. Under Sch.3 to the 2015 Act, internet service providers and other providers of "information society services", who are established in England and Wales or Northern Ireland, are covered by the new offence even when they are operating in other European Economic Area states. This provision is required to ensure that s.69 is consistent with the UK's obligations under the E-Commerce Directive.[298] However, Sch.3 exempts such providers from the s.69 offence in certain limited circumstances, i.e. where they are acting as		**4.256**

---

[294] s.69(5) as read with the Protection of Children Act 1978 s.4.
[295] s.69(5) as read with the Protection of Children Act 1978 s.5 and Sch.
[296] See s.143 of the Powers of Criminal Courts (Sentencing) Act 2000.
[297] s.80 and Sch.3, as amended with effect from May 3, 2015, by the Serious Crime Act 2015 s.85 and Sch.4, para.66(1), (3) (SI 2015/820). See further Ch.35, below.
[298] Dir.2000/31 EC.

mere conduits for such material, are simply caching it or are unwittingly hosting it.

JURISDICTION

4.257 The s.69 offence may be committed only in England and Wales. In the course of the passage of the Serious Crime Bill, Sir Paul Beresford MP moved an amendment to bring the offence within the scope of s.72 of the Sexual Offences Act 2003, which would have had the effect of making it an offence for a UK national to possess a paedophile manual in a country outside the UK. However, the Government resisted this extension of jurisdiction on two bases: that extra-territorial jurisdiction should be reserved for more serious offences, and that in any event a paedophile who travels overseas to abuse children and uses a manual in order to do so is likely to come into possession of the manual in some form before leaving this country, and will be liable to prosecution on that basis.[299] In light of the Government's stance, the amendment was not pressed to a vote.

"POSSESSION"

4.258 For the meaning of "possession" in the offences relating to indecent photographs of children, see paras 8.71, 8.96 and following and 8.135 and following, below. We anticipate that the courts will adopt a similar approach in construing the term in s.69.

"ITEM"

4.259 Section 69(8) provides:

> "(8) In this section—
> 'item' includes anything in which information of any description is recorded . . .
> "

This definition means that the term "item" is apt to include both paper documents and documents in digital form, e.g. emails or files downloaded to a computer or stored in the "cloud".

"ADVICE OR GUIDANCE"

4.260 The terms "advice" and "guidance" are not defined in the Act and therefore carry their ordinary meaning. The Shorter Oxford English Dictionary[300] states that "advice" means an opinion given or offered as to action, or

---

[299] *Hansard*, PBC (15 January 2015), cols 113–116; Commons Report stage (23 February 2015), col.89.
[300] 6th edn (2007).

counsel, and that "guidance" means the action of guiding, leadership or direction.

"ABUSING CHILDREN SEXUALLY"

Section 69(8) provides: **4.261**

> "In this section—
> 'abusing children sexually' means doing anything that constitutes—
> (a) an offence under Part 1 of the Sexual Offences Act 2003 ... against a person under 16, or
> (b) an offence under section 1 of the Protection of Children Act 1978 ... involving indecent photographs (but not pseudo-photographs),
> or doing anything outside England and Wales that would constitute such an offence if done in England and Wales ... "

The effect of the final words of this provision is that it is an offence under s.69 to possess an item that contains advice or guidance about committing acts in relation to children in another jurisdiction that would constitute an offence under Pt 1 of the 2003 Act or s.1 of the 1978 Act if committed in England and Wales.

DEFENCES TO CHARGES UNDER SECTION 69

Section 69(2) provides: **4.262**

> "(2) It is a defence for a person (D) charged with an offence under this section—
> (a) to prove that D had a legitimate reason for being in possession of the item;
> (b) to prove that—
>   (i) D had not read, viewed or (as appropriate) listened to the item, and
>   (ii) D did not know, and had no reason to suspect, that it contained advice or guidance about abusing children sexually; or
> (c) to prove that—
>   (i) the item was sent to D without any request made by D or on D's behalf, and
>   (ii) D did not keep it for an unreasonable time."

These defences are modelled on those provided for other, comparable   **4.263** offences, e.g. the possession of indecent images of children (s.160(2) of the Criminal Justice Act 1988) and the possession of extreme pornographic images (s.65 of the Criminal Justice and Immigration Act 2008). For s.160(2) of the 1988 Act, see para.8.144, below. The defences in s.69(2)(a), (b) are also very similar to those provided by s.1(4) of the Protection of Children Act 1978 in relation to the offences of distributing or showing indecent photographs or pseudo-photographs of a child or possessing such photographs etc. with a view to their being distributed or shown, contrary to s.1(1) of that Act. For the application of those defences, see paras 8.86 and following, below.

MENTAL ELEMENT

4.264 For the mental element required for "possession" in the offences relating to indecent photographs, see the cases discussed in paras 8.96 and following, below. We anticipate that the courts will follow these cases in relation to s.69.

CHAPTER 5

ABUSE OF POSITION OF TRUST

Introduction...............................	5.01	Abuse of Position of Trust:
Abuse of Position of Trust: Sexual		Engaging in Sexual Activity in
Activity with a Child...................	5.07	the Presence of a Child............... 5.75
Abuse of Position of Trust:		Abuse of Position of Trust:
Causing or Inciting a Child to		Causing a Child to Watch a
Engage in Sexual Activity............	5.51	Sexual Act................................... 5.103
		Abuse of Position of Trust: Acts
		Done in Scotland or Northern
		Ireland....................................... 5.126

INTRODUCTION

This chapter deals with the offences of abuse of position of trust contained 5.01
in the Sexual Offences Act 2003, which are as follows:

- abuse of position of trust: sexual activity with a child (s.16),
- abuse of position of trust: causing or inciting a child to engage in sexual activity (s.17),
- abuse of position of trust: sexual activity in the presence of a child (s.18),
- abuse of position of trust: causing a child to watch a sexual act (s.19),
- abuse of position of trust: acts done in Scotland or Northern Ireland (s.20).

The behaviour penalised by ss.16 to 20 is identical to that penalised by the 5.02
child sex offences in ss.9 to 12 of the Act, the essential difference being that
for the purposes of ss.16 to 20 there must be an abuse of a position of trust,
and the child victim may be 16 or 17.

These offences re-enact and extend the offence of abuse of a position of 5.03
trust created by the Sexual Offences (Amendment) Act 2000.[1] That Act was
introduced following the recommendations of an inter-departmental working

---

[1] Which came into force in January 2001.

group set up to identify additional safeguards needed to prevent unsuitable people from working with children, and to identify measures to protect young people from abuse by those in positions of trust. The Act made it an offence for a person aged 18 or over (A) to have vaginal or anal intercourse with, or to engage in any other sexual activity with or directed towards, a person aged under 18 (B) in relation to whom A was in a position of trust. The offence was triable either way and the maximum penalty on conviction on indictment was five years' imprisonment. The term "position of trust" was defined to cover a number of specified types of relationship, essentially those where B was in a residential institution of some sort or where A was in a particular position of influence in relation to B, such as a teacher. It was a defence that A did not know and could not reasonably have been expected to know that B was under 18 or that he (A) was in a position of trust with respect to B. There was also a defence where A and B were lawfully married, and an exception for sexual relationships which existed immediately before commencement of the Act.

5.04   The Bill that became the 2000 Act was still before Parliament when the Sexual Offences Review reported in *Setting the Boundaries*. The Review fully supported the introduction of the new offence.[2] It considered that any sexual relationship between adults in certain positions of trust and responsibility and children of 16 and 17 is so wrong and so inappropriate as to justify a criminal sanction.[3] The imbalance of power in such a relationship can be so great that it is difficult for the young person to deny the older person's sexual demands or to protest effectively about their actions. Consent will be either absent or obtained inappropriately. The Review thought that the combination of a recognised relationship of trust or care with a prohibition on sexual relations, as adopted in the 2000 Act, ought to be both fair and effective.[4]

5.05   In the subsequent White Paper, *Protecting the Public*, the Government proposed to re-enact the abuse of trust offence (the 2000 Act had by then become law) and to expand its scope to cover personal advisers and those who care for, advise, supervise or train young people in the community on a one-to-one basis pursuant to an order of a criminal court.[5] The Government also proposed that the maximum penalty for the offence should remain at five years' imprisonment.

5.06   The 2003 Act implements these proposals. There are two main differences between its provisions and those of the 2000 Act. First, the prohibited activities have been recast to match those prohibited by the child sex offences in ss.9 to 12 of the 2003 Act. Secondly, the types of relationship covered by the definition of "position of trust" have been expanded on the lines foreshadowed in *Protecting the Public*. Indeed, they were further expanded by Government amendment as the Bill received detailed scrutiny during the

[2] Para.3.11.1.
[3] Para.4.8.3.
[4] Para.4.8.11.
[5] Para.60.

Parliamentary process. However, as explained below, there remained some concern that the definition was insufficiently comprehensive.

ABUSE OF POSITION OF TRUST: SEXUAL ACTIVITY WITH A CHILD

DEFINITION

Section 16(1) of the Sexual Offences Act 2003 provides: **5.07**

> "A person aged 18 or over (A) commits an offence if—
> (a) he intentionally touches another person (B),
> (b) the touching is sexual,
> (c) A is in a position of trust in relation to B,
> (d) where subsection (2) applies, A knows or could reasonably be expected to know of the circumstances by virtue of which he is in a position of trust in relation to B, and
> (e) either—
>   (i) B is under 18 and A does not reasonably believe that B is 18 or over, or
>   (ii) B is under 13."

This offence should be compared with those in ss.5, 6, 7 and 9 of the Act   **5.08**
(rape, assault by penetration and sexual assault of a child under 13 and sexual activity with a child under 16). The offences overlap where A aged 18 or over sexually touches B aged under 16 or under 13 and A is in a position of trust in relation to B. Where the victim is a child under 16, an under-13 or the s.9 offence should normally be charged, as appropriate. See further para.5.13, below. However, the effect of the overlap is that if, in proceedings under s.16 in which A is charged with touching B aged 16 or 17, it becomes apparent that B was in fact under 16 at the material time, a conviction may nonetheless be obtained without any need to amend the indictment.

MODE OF TRIAL AND PUNISHMENT

The offence under s.16 is triable either way. The maximum sentence on   **5.09**
conviction on indictment is five years' imprisonment and on summary conviction is six months' imprisonment or a fine, or both.[6] As from a day to be appointed the maximum sentence of imprisonment on summary conviction will increase to 12 months.[7] The increase will have no application to offences committed before it takes effect.[8] Until recently, the maximum fine on summary conviction was a fine not exceeding the statutory maximum (i.e. £5,000). The effect of s.85 of the Legal Aid, Sentencing and Punishment of Offenders Act 2012 is that, from March 12, 2015, a fine of any amount may

---

[6] s.16(5).
[7] Criminal Justice Act 2003 s.282(2), (3).
[8] Criminal Justice Act 2003 s.282(4).

be imposed. An offence under s.16 cannot be dealt with by way of a simple caution.[9]

5.10   For the purposes of listing, cases under s.16[10] fall within Class 2B, save for complex cases involving many complainants (often under age, in care or otherwise particularly vulnerable) and/or many defendants who are alleged to have systematically groomed and abused them, often over a long period of time, which fall within Class 1C.[11] Cases in Class 1C must be referred to the Resident Judge, and by the Resident Judge to a Presiding Judge. Cases in Class 2B must be similarly referred in certain specified circumstances, including where the case is unusually grave or complex or a novel and important point of law is to be raised; where the defendant is a police officer, a member of the legal profession or a high profile figure; or where for any reason the case is likely to attract exceptional media attention.

5.11   For convictions on or after December 3, 2012,[12] an offence under s.16 is a specified offence for the purposes of s.226A of the Criminal Justice Act 2003 (extended sentence for certain violent or sexual offences), irrespective of the date of commission of the offence.

5.12   A person convicted under s.16, cautioned, found not guilty by reason of insanity or found to be under a disability and to have done the act charged, is automatically subject to the notification requirements in the Sexual Offences Act 2003[13] if, in respect of the offence, he is sentenced to a term of imprisonment, detained in a hospital or given a community sentence of at least 12 months.

5.13   During the passage of the Sexual Offences Bill, a Lords amendment was tabled that would have raised the maximum penalty on indictment to seven years' imprisonment.[14] The Government resisted the amendment on the basis that the primary purpose of the abuse of trust offences is to protect young people aged 16 and 17 from sexual exploitation by adults who hold a position of trust in their lives, and a maximum of five years' imprisonment was considered sufficiently severe for this purpose, given that the activity will be consensual[15] and the young person will be over the age of consent.[16] The Government pointed out that where an adult sexually exploits a child under 16, they will be charged with one of the offences specifically designed to

---

[9] Criminal Justice and Courts Act 2015 s.17(3), and the Criminal Justice and Courts Act 2015 (Simple Cautions) (Specification of Either-Way Offences) Order 2015 (SI 2015/790).

[10] And of soliciting, inciting, encouraging or assisting, attempting or conspiring to commit the offence or assisting an offender having committed the offence.

[11] *Consolidated Criminal Practice Directions*, Part XIII Listing B: CLASSIFICATION, available at *https://www.judiciary.gov.uk/wp-content/uploads/2015/09/crim-pd-2015.pdf* [Accessed April 30, 2016].

[12] When s.124 of the Legal Aid, Sentencing and Punishment of Offenders Act 2012 was brought into force by the Legal Aid etc Act 2012 (Commencement No.4 and Saving Provisions) Order 2012 (SI 2012/2906).

[13] s.80 and Sch.3, discussed in Ch.35, below.

[14] *Hansard*, HL, vol.646, col.1280ff (April 7, 2003).

[15] Otherwise, the defendant would be charged with one of the non-consensual offences in ss.1–4 of the Act.

[16] *Hansard*, HL, vol.646, cols 1280–1281, Lord Falconer of Thoroton.

protect such children, i.e. the offences under ss.5, 6, 7 and 9 of the Act, which attract a higher maximum penalty. In such cases there will be a conviction under s.16 only in exceptional circumstances, where a mistake has been made about the age of the child and it becomes apparent only in the course of the proceedings that the child was under 16 at the relevant time. This is a fair point, as it is certainly the case that convictions under the section involving child victims under the age of 16 are likely to be rare. However, we suggest it is nonetheless desirable that, when such convictions occur, the maximum penalty should be comparable to that which Parliament sought fit to apply to offences specifically designed to protect such children.

SENTENCING

For the Sentencing Council guideline applicable to sex offenders aged 18 or over who are sentenced on or after April 1, 2014, see Ch.33, below. In consulting on its draft guideline,[17] the Council proposed to follow the approach taken by the Sentencing Guidelines Council ("SGC") in 2007 by covering the offences in ss.16 and 17 of the 2003 Act in a single guideline, on the ground that harm and culpability are equally weighted in these offences and they have the same statutory maximum. It duly followed this course in the published guideline. For clarity, there is a text box at the start of the guideline stating "This guideline also applies to offences committed remotely/online".   **5.14**

Sentencing guideline

Step One–Harm and culpability

The guideline requires the sentencing court to go through a series of steps in order to determine the appropriate sentence. Step one involves determining the offence category by reference to the degree of harm caused and then the culpability level for the offence. The Sentencing Council adopted in this guideline the approach to harm taken in the guideline for the offence under s.9 of the 2003 Act (sexual activity with a child), discussed at para.4.34, above. As with that offence, the victim may believe him/herself to be in a relationship with the adult in the position of trust and may not be aware of the harm that is being done to them. Harm is therefore attributed based upon the nature of the sexual activity that has taken place. The harm and culpability factors for offences under ss.16 and 17 are as follows: **5.15**

---

[17] *Sexual Offences Guideline: Consultation* (December 6, 2012). The consultation document can be found on the Sentencing Council's website.

Harm	
Category 1	• Penetration of vagina or anus (using body or object) • Penile penetration of mouth in either case by, or of, the victim
Category 2	Touching, or exposure, of naked genitalia or naked breasts by, or of, the victim
Category 3	Factor(s) in categories 1 and 2 not present

CULPABILITY
A
• Significant degree of planning • Offender acts together with others in order to commit the offence • Use of alcohol/drugs on victim to facilitate the offence • Grooming behaviour used against victim • Use of threats (including blackmail) • Sexual images of victim recorded, retained, solicited or shared • Specific targeting of a particularly vulnerable child • Commercial exploitation and/or motivation • Offence racially or religiously aggravated • Offence motivated by, or demonstrating, hostility to the victim based on his or her sexual orientation (or presumed sexual orientation) or transgender identity (or presumed transgender identity) • Offence motivated by, or demonstrating, hostility to the victim based on his or her disability (or presumed disability)
B
Factor(s) in category A not present

This list omits some of the culpability factors in the s.9 guideline. "Abuse of trust" is omitted because such abuse is an essential feature of these offences.[18] "Offender lied about age" is dropped as deception about age is unlikely to be a principal factor in abuse of trust cases. Finally, "significant disparity in age'

---

[18] cf. *Cornwall* [2012] EWCA Crim 1227, discussed in para 5.20 below, in which the Court of Appeal criticised the sentencing judge for taking into account abuse of trust as an aggravating factor when it "is not an aggravating factor but is what makes otherwise lawful activity unlawful" (at 19).

is omitted as the Sentencing Council felt that the offender's age is not as significant a culpability factor as the position of trust the offender holds in relation to the child.

Step Two—Starting point and category range

Once the court has determined the offence category and culpability level, at step two it should use the corresponding starting point specified in the guideline in order to reach a sentence within the category range. The starting point applies to all offenders irrespective of plea or previous convictions. Once the starting point has been determined, step two allows further adjustment for aggravating or mitigating features, set out below. A case of particular gravity, reflected by multiple features of culpability or harm, could merit upward adjustment from the starting point before further adjustment for aggravating or mitigating features. Where there is a sufficient prospect of rehabilitation, a community order with a sex offender treatment programme requirement under s.202 of the Criminal Justice Act 2003 may be a proper alternative to a short or moderate length custodial sentence. The starting points and category ranges for offences under ss.16 and 17 of the Act are as follows:

5.16

	A	B
Category 1	*Starting point* 18 months' custody *Category range* 1–2 years' custody	*Starting point* 1 years' custody *Category range* 26 weeks'–18 months' custody
Category 2	*Starting point* 1 years' custody *Category range* 26 weeks'–18 months' custody	*Starting point* 26 weeks' custody *Category range* High level community order – 1 year's custody

	A	**B**
Category 3	*Starting point* 26 weeks' custody	*Starting point* Medium level community order
	Category range High level community order – 1 year's custody	*Category range* Low level community order – Medium level community order

Although similar factors are used to determine the offence categories in this guideline as in the guideline for the s.9 offence, the starting points and ranges are lower in order to reflect the fact that the statutory maximum for an offence under s.16 or s.17 is five years, as opposed to 14 years under s.9.

Aggravating and mitigating factors

5.17   After identifying the starting point and category range, the court should consider whether the presence of aggravating or mitigating factors should result in an upward or downward adjustment from the starting point or the imposition of a sentence outside the category range. In particular, relevant recent convictions are likely to result in an upward adjustment. When sentencing appropriate category 2 or 3 offences, the court should also consider whether the custody threshold has been passed; if so, whether a custodial sentence is unavoidable; and if it is, whether that sentence can be suspended. The non-exhaustive list of aggravating and mitigating factors for offences under ss.16 and 17 is as follows:

Aggravating factors
Statutory aggravating factors
• Previous convictions, having regard to a) the nature of the offence to which the conviction relates and its relevance to the current offence; and b) the time that has elapsed since the conviction • Offence committed whilst on bail

---

Other aggravating factors

- Ejaculation
- Pregnancy or STI as a consequence of offence
- Location of offence
- Timing of offence
- Victim compelled to leave their home, school, etc.
- Failure to comply with current court orders
- Offence committed whilst on licence
- Presence of others, especially other children
- Any steps taken to prevent the victim reporting an incident, obtaining assistance and/or from assisting or supporting the prosecution
- Attempts to dispose of or conceal evidence
- Failure of offender to respond to previous warnings
- Commission of offence whilst under the influence of alcohol or drugs
- Victim encouraged to recruit others

Mitigating factors

- No previous convictions **or** no relevant/recent convictions
- Remorse
- Previous good character and/or exemplary conduct*
- Age and/or lack of maturity where it affects the responsibility of the offender
- Mental disorder or learning disability, particularly where linked to the commission of the offence
- Sexual activity was incited but no activity took place because the offender voluntarily desisted or intervened to prevent it
- Demonstration of steps taken to address offending behaviour

---

* Previous good character/exemplary conduct is different from having no previous convictions. The more serious the offence, the less the weight which should normally be attributed to this factor. Where previous good character/exemplary conduct has been used to facilitate the offence, this mitigation should not normally be allowed and such conduct may constitute an aggravating factor.

As appears from its consultation, the Sentencing Council included "victim compelled to leave their home, school etc" as an aggravating factor because of the type of offenders likely to be charged with this offence. Where, for example, the victim has had to change schools because the offender was their teacher, the long-term effect of the disruption to their education should be reflected in an upward movement from the starting point. "Failure of offender to respond to previous warnings" is included to cover situations where, for example, a teacher has been warned by the school about becoming too close to a pupil and has then proceeded to engage in sexual activity with that pupil.

Steps Three to Nine

5.18 The remaining steps cover the following points. At step three the court should consider any factors which would indicate a reduction in sentence, e.g. assistance to the prosecution. At step four it should consider any reduction for a guilty plea. At step five the court should consider dangerousness, i.e. whether it would be appropriate to award an extended sentence (s.226A of the Criminal Justice Act 2003). Step six requires the court to consider whether the total sentence is just and proportionate to the offending behaviour. At step seven it should consider whether to make an ancillary order (e.g. a compensation order, a SHPO or a restraining order). Step eight requires the court to fulfil its duty under s.174 of the Criminal Justice Act 2003 to give reasons for, and explain the effect of, the sentence. Finally, at step nine the court should consider whether to give credit for time spent on bail in accordance with s.240A of that Act.

Sentencing examples

5.19 Sentencing appeals under ss.16 and 17 are rare beasts and as a result, cases decided by reference to the previous SGC guideline remain of instructive value.

5.20   Perhaps the most instructive is *Cornwall,*[19] where the appellant school-teacher (26) pleaded guilty to three offences under s.17 of causing or inciting a child to engage in sexual activity in abuse of a position of trust.[20] A pupil, aged 16, at the appellant's school who was not taught by him contacted him on Facebook. Over an eight-month period he sent her text messages that became increasingly explicit, describing the sexual activity he wanted to indulge in with her and asking her to send pictures of herself. She sent pictures of herself in a bikini and topless. Two months after contact with the first pupil ceased, the offender contacted another pupil, 14, on Facebook. Using that means and text messages he described the sexual activity he wanted to engage in with her and suggested they meet. She confided in a friend, who told the school. In sentencing, the judge treated the offences as falling within category 1 of the SGC guideline, with a starting point of 18 months' custody and a range of 12 months–2 years. He sentenced the appellant to 16 months' imprisonment concurrent on each count, with a

---

[19] [2012] EWCA Crim 1227.
[20] The reference to the charges is taken from the official transcript. However, if the appellant was indeed charged with "causing or inciting" then the indictment was duplicitous, as "causing" and "inciting" should be regarded for the purposes of s.17 as constituting two separate offences: see para.5.53, below. The point applies equally to the two other sentencing appeals discussed below.

SOPO and an order under s.28 of the Criminal Justice and Courts Services Act 2000 disqualifying him from working with children. On appeal against sentence, the Court of Appeal noted that the judge had treated the offences as aggravated by the prolonged nature of the offending, the fact that there was more than one victim and the abuse of trust. However, in the Court's view the judge had misjudged the appellant's activity. The offences were offences of inciting only, and no sexual activity actually took place (but as to the relevance of this point when sentencing under the current guideline, see paras 4.81 and following, above). One of the girls had instigated the contact. The judge should not have rejected the appellant's loss of career as a mitigating factor. This resulted in the judge pitching the offences at a level which was much higher in terms of seriousness than was justified by the facts of the case. In the Court's judgment, the appropriate sentence after trial would have been no more than six months. Giving the appellant credit for his early guilty plea, the Court substituted a sentence of four months concurrent on each count. It also set aside the SOPO as the appellant would never again be in a position of trust working with children, as the disqualification from working with children meant that he would be placed on the barred list by the Independent Safeguarding Authority (now the Disclosure and Barring Service).

The decision in *Cornwall* appears somewhat generous even by reference to the SGC guideline. The appellant's loss of his career certainly deserved to be treated as mitigation, and no doubt would be on similar facts today. However, the fact that the offences involved only incitement and that no actual sexual activity occurred appears to have been purely fortuitous, at least in the case of the second victim. Finally, although the Court treated as a mitigating factor the fact that one of the victims initiated contact, it appears from the transcript that contact was initially in non-sexual terms, and it was the appellant who introduced the sexual element. **5.21**

In *Howell*,[21] the appellant (35) was convicted of one offence under s.17 of causing or inciting a child to engage in sexual activity. He was sentenced to 12 months' imprisonment. Between May 2005 and January 2006 he sent text messages, some of which were of a sexually explicit nature, to one of his sixth form pupils. At the time he was head of the school music department. During the course of his conduct the school gave him a formal warning about texting a pupil. He denied sending the messages, claiming they had been sent maliciously by two of the girl's friends. On his appeal against sentence, the Court of Appeal said the case involved a serious breach of trust that was persisted in. But it was argued, first, that the evidence indicated the objectionable text messages did not start until October 2005 and that the complainant had reached her seventeenth birthday in November 2005. Secondly, her evidence was that the text messages made her feel uncomfortable, but the effect on her was not especially traumatic. Thirdly, on no **5.22**

---

[21] [2007] EWCA Crim 1863.

occasion did the appellant act on what was contained in the texts. Fourthly, at Christmas time the complainant had sent him a Christmas card thanking him for all he had helped her to achieve. Fifthly, the appellant was of previous good character, and lastly the conviction had been devastating to him and his family and had led to the loss of his teaching career. Reliance was placed on the suggestion in the SGC guideline that the starting points for an offence of this nature should be 18 months' custody for penile penetration of the vagina, anus or mouth and 26 weeks' custody for other forms of non-penetrative activity. In this case the offence was incitement and no act was in fact carried out at all (but as to the relevance of this point when sentencing under the current guideline, see paras 4.81 and following, above). The Court considered that the offence was of a comparatively modest nature, though it took place after warnings and was persistent. The sentence was manifestly excessive and the Court substituted one of six months' imprisonment.

5.23   In *Wilson*,[22] the appellant (31) pleaded guilty to an offence under s.17 of causing or inciting sexual activity with a girl aged 17. He was a student teacher at a college where the complainant was a pupil. An emotional relationship developed between them and progressed to the extent that they began a consensual sexual relationship. Sexual intercourse took place on at least five occasions. It was only subsequently that the appellant realised that he was acting unlawfully. The offence came to light during counselling sessions with the complainant for unrelated problems. The appellant was sentenced to 10 months' imprisonment. On appeal, it was noted that the appellant had been frank in interview and had accepted full responsibility for what had happened. He was remorseful and willing to participate in any programme designed to ensure that he did not re-offend. The pre-sentence report recommended a three-year community order with a requirement that the appellant attend a sex offender programme. It was submitted for the appellant that the sentence of 10 months' imprisonment was excessive, having regard in particular to his previous good character, his early admissions, the loss of his job as a teacher and his inability ever to work again with children. In the Court's view, the appellant should never have allowed his friendship with the complainant to develop in the way it did; he breached the trust placed in him by his employers, the complainant's parents and the complainant herself. But the appellant was not a sexual predator; he did not groom or corrupt the complainant, who was already sexually experienced. Given those factors, the Court took a merciful course and substituted a sentence of six months' imprisonment for the sentence imposed by the trial judge. The Court noted that the SGC guideline suggested a starting point of 18 months' imprisonment for this sort of offence, and a range of 12–30 months following a contested trial (cf. category 1B of the current guideline, which has a starting point of one year's custody and a range of 26 weeks–18 months). However

---

[22] [2007] EWCA Crim 2762.

the guideline was not rigid and a Court was entitled to depart from it in an appropriate case in order to do justice to a particular offender.

PARTIES TO THE OFFENCE

The s.16 offence may be committed by and against persons of either sex. The offender (A) must be 18 or over and B must be under 18. A person attains the age of 18 at the commencement of the eighteenth anniversary of his or her birth.[23] For proof of age, see paras 3.73 and following, above. **5.24**

The offence is principally designed to protect young people of 16 or 17, who do not fall within the scope of the under-13 or child sex offences, from sexual abuse by someone in a position of trust in relation to them. If B did not consent to the touching, then one of the non-consensual offences in ss.1–3 of the 2003 Act should be charged (rape, assault by penetration or sexual assault). Otherwise, if it is known on charging that B was under 13 at the material time, then in principle A should be charged under ss.5–7 of the Act rape, assault by penetration or sexual assault of a child under 13), which are specifically designed to protect children under that age and carry higher maximum penalties.[24] If it is known that B was 13, 14 or 15, the appropriate charge is under s.9 (sexual activity with a child under 16). But a charge under s.16 might be appropriate even in relation to a child aged 13, 14 or 15 in certain cases, e.g. where it is quite likely that A reasonably believed the child to be 16 or over, but unlikely that he reasonably believed her to be 18 or over.[25] If A is under 18 and B is under 16, the appropriate charge is under s.13 of the 2003 Act (child sex offence committed by child or young person) read with s.9. **5.25**

Child victims

If the child victim of the offence encourages or assists its commission are they liable to conviction as an accessory? This turns on the application of the principle in *Tyrrell*,[26] where it was held that a young girl could not be convicted as accessory to an offence of having unlawful carnal knowledge with a girl under 16 committed against herself, as the offence was created to protect girls against men and there was no indication in the statute of an intention to criminalise the girls themselves. The abuse of position of trust offences were clearly created to protect children under 18 from sexual **5.26**

---

[23] Family Law Reform Act 1969 s.9(1).
[24] See para.3.04, above.
[25] cf. H.O. Circular 21/2004: *Guidance on Part 1 of the Sexual Offences Act 2003*, para.101.
[26] [1894] 1 Q.B. 710; and see *DPP v Whitehouse* [1977] Q.B. 868. In *Gnango* [2011] UKSC 59, a majority of the Supreme Court said that *Tyrrell* is an illustration of a general rule, identified by Professor Glanville Williams in his article *Victims and other exempt parties in crime* (1990) 10 Legal Studies at p.245, that where legislation creates an offence that is intended to protect a class of persons, a member of that class cannot be convicted as an accessory to such an offence committed in respect of him.

exploitation by adults with whom they are in a relationship of trust, and there is nothing in the Act that indicates an intention to criminalise the children concerned. This strongly suggests that the principle in *Tyrrell* should apply in relation to s.16.

5.27   The point has been settled for all practical purposes by the decision in *Attorney General's Reference (No.53 of 2013) (Neil Wilson)*,[27] in which the offender pleaded guilty to one offence under s.9 of the 2003 Act (sexual activity with a child) committed against a girl aged 13 and was sentenced to eight months' imprisonment. The girl was sexually experienced and prosecuting counsel described her in the course of the sentencing hearing as "predatory", a term picked up by the judge in his sentencing remarks. On a reference by the Attorney General, the Court of Appeal held that the sentence was plainly unduly lenient. In doing so, it accepted the Attorney General's submission that the fact that the victim had initiated what had happened was an aggravating rather than a mitigating factor. Lord Thomas CJ said[28]:

> "It has been clear since at least the Offences Against the Person Act 1861, and subsequent nineteenth century legislation, that the purpose of Parliament in passing legislation to make it a crime punishable with imprisonment to have sexual relations with those under 16 was to protect those under 16. Indeed the Criminal Law Amendments [*sic*] Act 1885 makes it expressly clear that that was the purpose of the legislation. That can be seen from the preamble to the Act and was made clear by this court in *R. v Tyrrell* [1894] 1 QB 710.
>   That long-standing principle is well-known. The reduction of punishment on the basis that the person who needed protection encouraged the commission of an offence is therefore simply wrong. We agree with the submission of the Attorney General that an underage person who encourages sexual relations with her needs more protection, not less. Accepting that as the basis for sentencing for the reasons we have explained, the fact that the offender took advantage of what he asserted the victim did aggravated the offence."

Although his Lordship did not engage in elaborate legal analysis, his reference to *Tyrrell* clearly indicates that he considered the s.9 offence, and by inference all the other offences in the Act designed to protect children, to fall within the scope of the principle in that case, such that there can be no question of the child victim of such an offence being prosecuted for any part she may have played in encouraging it.

JURISDICTION

5.28   By virtue of s.72 of and Sch.2 to the Sexual Offences Act 2003, as amended,[29] it is an offence under s.16 for a UK national to do an act in a country outside the UK which would constitute a s.16 offence if done in England and Wales. The amendments, made in 2008, expanded the scope of s.72 in two respects.

---

[27] [2013] EWCA Crim 2544.
[28] At [19]–[20].
[29] By the Criminal Justice and Immigration Act 2008 s.72, with effect from July 14, 2008.

First, they removed the limitation on s.72 as enacted that it applied only to offences committed against victims aged under 16 (the relevant age is now 18). Secondly, they abolished, in respect of UK nationals, the "double criminality" requirement that the act must have been an offence in the country in which it was done. This requirement is, however, retained in respect of the prosecution of UK residents and those who become UK residents or nationals after the doing of the relevant act. For the purposes of s.72 a "country" includes a territory and a "United Kingdom national" means a British citizen, a British overseas territories citizen, a British National (Overseas), a British Overseas citizen, a person who under the British Nationality Act 1981 is a British subject, or a British protected person within the meaning of that Act.[30] An act is taken to be an offence in the country in which it was done unless the defendant serves a notice putting the prosecution to proof on the point.[31]

"Touches Another Person"

For the meaning of this term, see paras 2.63, above.   5.29

"The Touching is Sexual"

For the meaning of "sexual", see paras 2.66 and following, above.   5.30

"Position of Trust"

Section 21(1) of the 2003 Act provides: 5.31

> "For the purposes of sections 16 to 19, a person (A) is in a position of trust in relation to another person (B) if—
> (a) any of the following subsections applies, or
> (b) any condition specified in an order made by the Secretary of State is met."

No order under s.21(1)(b) has yet been made, and so the positions of trust recognised for the purposes of the section are those set out in s.21(2) to (13), as amended. In relation to England and Wales, they are as follows[32]:   5.32

- *A looks after persons under 18 who are detained in an institution by virtue of a court order or under an enactment, and B is so detained in that institution* (s.21(2)). This applies where, e.g. B is detained following conviction in a secure training centre or in a young offender institution. By s.22(2), a person "looks after" persons under 18 for the purposes of s.21 if he is "regularly involved in caring for, training, supervising or being in sole charge of such persons". The reference to

---

[30] s.72(9).
[31] s.72(6)–(8).
[32] The provisions are set out as amended.

"such persons" means that A need not be regularly involved in caring for, etc., B, provided he is regularly involved in caring for persons under 18. Indeed, A and B need not previously have even met. The word "regularly" is not defined. During the passage of the Sexual Offences Bill through Parliament, a number of amendments were tabled that would have removed the requirement of regularity, on the basis that it would wrongly exclude from the scope of the abuse of trust offences individuals who are involved in the care of young people and so have the opportunity to abuse them, purely because their involvement is not "regular".[33] The examples cited were supply teachers who fill in occasionally at a school or casual staff who work intermittently at a residential home. However, the Government of the day resisted pressure to remove the requirement, saying that what will constitute "regular" care etc. will depend on the particular circumstances, but that it is:

"expected to cover not only the full-time class teacher or matron in a children's home but, for example, the peripatetic teacher who takes a child for music lessons once a week; the supply teacher who provides cover during the maternity leave of the regular teacher; or the physiotherapist who treats a child daily during a short period of convalescence in hospital."[34]

In fact, these examples miss the point as they are all fairly clear cases of "regular" care. The concern relates to cases where the care is not regular, but still gives the adult the opportunity to commit abuse. The Government was, however, clear that removing the requirement of regularity would inappropriately widen the scope of the offences, so undermining their true purpose and weakening their credibility. The result, it said, would be to prohibit a sexual relationship between, for example, a 17-year-old and a supply teacher who teaches her class for one day while the regular teacher is off sick, or a nurse who looks after her for a day in hospital. But it is far from clear why the supply teacher or nurse in these examples ought not to be covered by the abuse of trust offences, for as long as the 17-year-old is in their care. Suppose, moreover, that they have the care of the 17-year-old not just for a day but on a frequent but irregular basis over a significant period, and use the contact to persuade her to begin a sexual relationship. There is surely a very strong argument that the offences ought to apply in those circumstances. At one point the Government seemed to think this sort of situation would satisfy the "regularity" requirement. At Third Reading, Baroness Scotland of Asthal said that regular contact:

---

[33] *Hansard*, HL, vol.646, col.1301, Baroness Blatch (April 1, 2003); vol.649, col.721, Baroness Blatch (June 17, 2003); HC, Standing Committee B, September 16, 2003, col.218ff, Sandra Gidley MP.
[34] *Hansard*, HL, vol.646, cols 1301–2, Lord Falconer of Thoroton (April 1, 2003); vol.648, col.724*ff*, Baroness Scotland of Asthal, June 2, 2003).

"may cover a long period of single days of contact such as a supply teacher who sees the child irregularly, but regularly over a period of time. The purpose of including the term 'regular' is to exclude one-off encounters which do not allow any sort of relationship of trust to have developed[35]".

It is, with respect, very difficult to see how irregular daily contact can ever amount to regular contact "over a period of time". This was apparently conceded by the Government during the Commons Standing Committee debate, when Paul Goggins MP said that to be "regular", contact "must have a pattern and be consistent".[36] This must be right, and it means that the legitimate concern discussed above is left unanswered. It would in our view have been best if the Act had provided that a person looks after another not only when they "regularly" care for them, but also where they do so "periodically" or "from time to time". Short of this, it would have been better to remove the requirement of regularity altogether, relying on prosecutorial discretion to ensure that the abuse of trust offences are not used inappropriately in relation to one-off or limited encounters between an adult and a young person. The Government was, after all, content to rely heavily on prosecutorial discretion in resisting attempts to remove teenage sexual experimentation from the scope of the child sex offences.[37]

- *A looks after persons under 18 who are resident in a home or other place in which accommodation and maintenance are provided by a local authority under s.22C(6) of the Children Act 1989[38] or accommodation is provided by a voluntary organisation under s.59(1) of that Act, and B is resident and provided with accommodation and maintenance or accommodation in that place* (s.21(3)). This covers a wide range of situations in which young people may be accommodated, including foster care, residential care (whether local authority, private or voluntary, including secure accommodation) and semi-independent accommodation. **5.33**

- *A looks after persons under 18 who are accommodated and cared for, and B is accommodated and cared for, in a hospital[39]; in Wales, an*

---

[35] *Hansard*, HL, vol.648, col.725 (June 17, 2003).
[36] *Hansard*, HC, Standing Committee B, September 16, 2003, col.220.
[37] See paras 4.10 and following, above.
[38] The reference to s.22C(6) of the 1989 Act was substituted (for a reference to s.23(2)) by the Children and Young Persons Act 2008 s.8(2) and Sch.1, para.15, which came into effect in England on April 1, 2011, by virtue of the Children and Young Persons Act 2008 (Commencement No.3, Saving and Transitional Provisions) Order 2010 (SI 2010/2981).
[39] Defined by s.22(5) in relation to England and Wales as a hospital as defined by s.275 of the National Health Service Act 2006 or s.206 of the National Health Service (Wales) Act 2006, or any other establishment in which in England any of the services specified in s.22(6) of the Act are provided or which in Wales is a hospital within the meaning given by s.2(3) of the Care Standards Act 2000.

independent clinic[40]; a care home[41]; a community home,[42] voluntary home[43] or children's home[44]; or a home provided under s.82(5) of the Children Act 1989 (s.21(4)). This provision covers places where young people with medical conditions, physical or learning disabilities, mental illness or behavioural problems might be accommodated, and includes NHS, private and voluntary sector accommodation.

5.34
- *A looks after persons under 18 who are receiving education at an educational institution and B is receiving, and A is not receiving, education at that institution* (s.21(5)). By s.22(4), a person receives education at an educational institution if he is registered or otherwise enrolled as a student or pupil at the institution, or he receives education at the institution under arrangements with another educational institution at which he is so registered or otherwise enrolled. It does not matter whether the student or pupil is in full-time or part-time education: he is covered by this provision in either case.[45] If both A and B are receiving education at the institution, A cannot be in a position of trust in relation to B for the purposes of the Act. This prevents, for example, the criminalisation of a sexual relationship between an 18-year-old head boy of a school and his 17-year-old girlfriend who attends the same school.[46]

- *A is engaged in the provision of services under, or pursuant to anything done under, ss.8 to 10 of the Employment and Training Act 1973 or s.68, 70(1)(b) or 74 of the Education and Skills Act 2008 and, in that capacity, looks after B on an individual basis* (s.21(7)). This provision will cover, for example, an adviser in the National Careers Service when providing one-to-one support for a young person with learning difficulties. Section 22(3) provides that a person (A) looks after another person (B) on an individual basis if A is regularly involved in caring for, training or supervising B and in the course of his involvement, A regularly has unsupervised contact with B (whether face-to-face or by other means). This provision contains a double requirement of regularity, i.e. regular involvement in the care etc. of B and regular unsupervised contact with B. The result is that the definition will not cover someone who has irregular involvement in a young person's care, or who has regular involvement in their care but

---

[40] By s.22(5), this term has the meaning given by s.2 of the Care Standards Act 2000.

[41] Defined by s.22(5) as an establishment which is a care home for the purposes of the Care Standards Act 2000.

[42] By s.22(5), this term has the meaning given by s.53 of the Children Act 1989.

[43] By s.22(5), this term has in relation to England and Wales the meaning given by s.60(3) of the Children Act 1989.

[44] By s.22(5), this term has in relation to England and Wales the meaning given by s.1 of the Care Standards Act 2000.

[45] cf. *Hansard*, HL, vol.646, cols 1298–1299, Baroness Blatch and Lord Falconer of Thoroton (April 1, 2003); vol.648, col.1146, Baroness Blatch and Lord Falconer of Thoroton (June 2, 2003).

[46] ibid., col.1299, Lord Falconer of Thoroton.

only irregular unsupervised contact. See further para.5.32, above. The reference in s.22(3) to unsupervised contact "by other means" is designed to cover those whose normal means of providing support is by telephone or online.

- *A regularly has unsupervised contact with B (whether face to face or by*   **5.35** *other means) in the exercise of functions of a local authority under s.20 or 21 of the Children Act 1989* (s.21(8)). This category covers people whose function it is to arrange accommodation for children who are not being looked after by those with parental responsibility and to check their welfare once accommodation has been found. This includes local authority staff such as social workers and family centre staff, who visit the accommodation in which a child has been placed in order to oversee the child's welfare. For criticism of the requirement of regularity, see para.5.32, above.

- *A, as a person who is to report to the court under s.7 of the Children Act 1989 on matters relating to the welfare of B, regularly has unsupervised contact with B (whether face to face or by other means)* (s.21(9)). This covers children and family reporters involved in family court proceedings which affect children's welfare. For criticism of the requirement of regularity, see para.5.32, above.

- *A is a personal adviser appointed for B under s.23B(2) of, or para.19C of Sch.2 to, the Children Act 1989 and, in that capacity, looks after B on an individual basis* (s.21(10)). These personal advisers generally provide help and support to children aged 16 or 17 who have left local authority care. For what it means to look after a person "on an individual basis", see para.5.34, above.

- *B is subject to a care order,[47] a supervision order[48] or an education*   **5.36** *supervision order,[49] and in the exercise of functions conferred by virtue of the order on an authorised person or the authority designated by the order, A looks after B on an individual basis* (s.21(11)). This provision covers persons who supervise children pursuant to a care order, supervision order or education supervision order. For what it means to look after a person "on an individual basis", see para.5.34, above.

- *A is an officer of the Service or Welsh family proceedings officer appointed for B under s.41(1) of the Children Act 1989, or is appointed a children's guardian of B under r.6 or r.18 of the Adoption Rules 1984,[50] or is appointed to be the guardian ad litem of B under r.9.5 of the Family*

---

[47] By s.22(5), this term has in relation to England and Wales the same meaning as in the Children Act 1989.

[48] By s.22(5), this term has in relation to England and Wales the meaning given by s.31(11) of the Children Act 1989.

[49] By s.22(5), this term has in relation to England and Wales the meaning given by s.36 of the Children Act 1989.

[50] SI 1984/265.

Proceedings Rules 1991,[51] *or is appointed to be the children's guardian of B under r.59 of the Family Procedure (Adoption) Rules 2005*[52] *or r.16.3(1)(ii) or r.16.4 of the Family Procedure Rules 2010*[53] *and, in that capacity, regularly has unsupervised contact with B (whether face to face or by any other means)* (s.21(12)[54]). This covers officers of the Children and Family Court Advisory and Support Service (CAF-CASS) when appointed to act as children's guardians under s.41(1) of the 1989 Act, and persons appointed to act as children's guardians in adoption proceedings and as children's guardians ad litem in private law Children Act 1989 and wardship proceedings. For criticism of the requirement of regularity, see para.5.32, above.

- *B is subject to requirements imposed by or under an enactment on his release from detention for a criminal offence, or is subject to requirements imposed by a court order made in criminal proceedings, and A looks after B on an individual basis in pursuance of those requirements* (s.21(13)). This applies to an adult supervising a child under bail supervision, or in connection with a community sentence such as a probation or attendance centre order, or after the child's release from detention following a criminal conviction (e.g. where the child is released on licence from a Young Offenders Institution). For what it means to look after a person "on an individual basis", see para.5.34, above.

5.37   The first four of these positions of trust were, with small variations, the positions of trust specified for the purposes of the Sexual Offences (Amendment) Act 2000. The remainder were introduced by the 2003 Act. Some were added during the passage of the Bill in response to expressions of concern, e.g. about supervisors under an education supervision order (s.21(11)) and guardians ad litem (s.21(12)). However, the Government resisted proposals to extend the list of positions of trust to cover a number of other persons, including voluntary workers in youth groups, such as the Scouts and Guides, registered sports coaches, registered child minders and ancillary workers and caretakers in institutions and homes.[55] It did so on the ground that the relationships such individuals have with young people do not meet any of the three criteria that it thought appropriate to determine the positions that merit intervention by the criminal law: that the young person is particularly vulnerable, e.g. by virtue of being on probation or in residential care; that their location and/or lack of access to other adults and the absence of countervailing influence make them particularly vulnerable; and that the

---

[51] SI 1991/1247.
[52] SI 2005/2795.
[53] SI 2010/2955.
[54] As amended with effect from April 6, 2013, by the Family Procedure (Modification of Enactments) Order 2011 (SI 2011/1045), art.15.
[55] *Hansard*, HL, vol.646, col.1288ff, Lord Falconer of Thoroton (April 1, 2003); vol.648, col.1147ff, Lord Falconer of Thoroton (June 2, 2003); vol.649, col 713ff, Baroness Scotland of Asthal (June 17, 2003).

adult in a position of special influence, i.e. the relationship is in loco parentis.[56]

It is, however, possible to conceive of circumstances in which some at least   **5.38** of the proposed additions might meet these criteria. An example given during Parliamentary debate on the Bill was of a voluntary worker in a youth group, who has weekly contact with young people in the group and who takes them away on a youth camp in the summer.[57] The Government response to this example was that even a short period in a camp might constitute "regular involvement in caring for" the young people, within the meaning of s.22(2).[58] But s.22(2) does not define a position of trust; it defines the meaning of the term "looks after" for the purposes of the positions of trust in s.21 in which that term is used. There is no position of trust in s.21 which would cover the example given. As to sports coaches, the Government acknowledged that they may sometimes act in loco parentis, e.g. where a talented young person is undergoing intensive training.[59] The difficulty, it said, lies in distinguishing this situation from others in which it would be inappropriate for the abuse of trust offences to apply, e.g. when an 18-year-old college student has a consensual sexual relationship with a 17-year-old member of the local netball team which he helps to coach one evening a week in his school holidays. The Government also noted the commitment of the Department of Culture, Media and Sport (DCMS) to introduce a national coaching certificate and an associated licensing regime, and believed that this was the more appropriate vehicle for dealing with the concerns raised about possible sexual exploitation by sports coaches. It did, however, say that if the DCMS initiative proved insufficient, sports coaches could be brought within the scope of the abuse of trust offences using the order-making power in s.21(1).[60] In 2005, the DCMS published a consultation paper seeking views on whether sports coaches should be brought within the scope of the offences.[61] It subsequently decided against extending the law in this way, on the ground that appropriate protection for young people with whom sports coaches work is now provided by the Safeguarding Vulnerable Groups Act 2006 (detailed consideration of which lies outside the scope of this book). However, the position of the NSPCC, and of the Child Protection in Sport Unit (established on a partnership basis by the NSPCC and Sport England,

---

[56] *Hansard*, HL, vol.646, cols 1294 and 1151, Lord Falconer of Thoroton (April 1, 2003).

[57] *Hansard*, HL, vol.649, col.720, Baroness Blatch (June 17, 2003).

[58] ibid., col.725, Baroness Scotland of Asthal.

[59] For an argument that sports coaches may in certain circumstances fall within the scope of the familial child sex offences in ss.25–29 of the 2003 Act, see below, Ch.6.

[60] *Hansard*, HL, vol.648, col.1153, Lord Falconer of Thoroton (June 2, 2003); vol.649, col.719, Baroness Scotland of Asthal, (June 17, 2003).

[61] *Consultation on the Scope and Implementation of the Sexual Offences Act 2003 in Relation to Sports Coaches* (DCMS, 2005). See generally Yvonne Williams, *Playing it safe* [2005] N.L.J. 234–5 (February 18, 2005).

Sport Northern Ireland and Sport Wales), is that sports coaches should be brought within the scope of the abuse of trust offences.[62]

"WHERE SUBSECTION (2) APPLIES"

5.39   Section 16(2) provides:

"This subsection applies where A—
(a) is in a position of trust in relation to B by virtue of circumstances within section 21(2), (3), (4) or (5), and
(b) is not in such a position of trust in relation to B by virtue of other circumstances."

The effect of this provision, read with s.16(1)(d), is that where A is in a position of trust in relation to B purely by virtue of circumstances falling within s.21(2) to (5),[63] it is an element of the offence that A knew or could reasonably have been expected to know of those circumstances. The rationale for this provision is that it is conceivable that persons in a position of trust by virtue of circumstances of that sort might reasonably be unaware of them: the Home Office guidance on Pt 1 of the Act gives as an example a teacher who meets in a bar, and subsequently has sex with, a sixth-form student who, unknown to him, attends the school at which he teaches.[64] However, in such cases there is an evidential presumption that A did know or could reasonably have been expected to know of the circumstances. This is the effect of s.16(4), which places an evidential burden on A to put the matter in issue. Section 16(4) provides:

"Where, in proceedings for an offence under this section—
(a) it is proved that the defendant was in a position of trust in relation to the other person by virtue of circumstances within section 21(2), (3), (4) or (5), and
(b) it is not proved that he was in such a position of trust by virtue of other circumstances,
it is to be taken that the defendant knew or could reasonably have been expected to know of the circumstances by virtue of which he was in such a position of trust unless sufficient evidence is adduced to raise an issue as to whether he knew or could reasonably have been expected to know of those circumstances."

EXCEPTION FOR MARRIAGE AND CIVIL PARTNERSHIP

5.40   Section 23 of the 2003 Act, as enacted, created a marriage exception from the abuse of trust offences. The exception was subsequently extended to cover civil partnerships.[65] Section 23(1) now provides that conduct by a person (A) which would otherwise be an offence under any of ss.16 to 19 against another

---

[62] *http://www.wru.co.uk/downloads/Abuse_of_positions_of_trust_within_sport_wdf81074.pdf* [Accessed April 30, 2016].
[63] See paras 5.32 and following, above.
[64] H.O. Circular 21/2004: *Guidance on Part 1 of the Sexual Offences Act 2003*, para.102.
[65] Civil Partnerships Act 2004 s.261(1) and Sch.27, para.173.

person (B) is not an offence under that section if, at the time, B is 16 or over and A and B are lawfully married or are civil partners of each other. By virtue of s.23(2), the burden of proving that the exception applies is on the defendant.

The exception is necessary in order to respect the right of married couples and those in a civil partnership to private and family life, as guaranteed by art.8 of the ECHR. In the case of marriage, the exception is capable of applying where B was under 16 at the time of the marriage, provided she is 16 or over at the time of the conduct in question.[66] These circumstances could of course apply only if the marriage took place in a foreign jurisdiction where marriages involving children under 16 are recognised as lawful, between people domiciled in that jurisdiction. Concerns were expressed during the passage of the Bill that this would create a loophole for predatory paedophiles, who could contract marriages overseas with one or more minors with the intention of bringing their wife or wives back to the UK, where they would be immune from the impact of the law. In response, the Government pointed out that as the legality of a marriage depends on the law of the parties' domicile, if an English man goes overseas, marries a child and brings her to this country, he would not be recognised as lawfully married to her for the purposes of English law unless he could discharge the difficult burden of proving that he had changed his domicile before the marriage ceremony took place.[67] The Solicitor General added that if the child is under the age of 16, the man could be prosecuted under s.9 of the 2003 Act (sexual activity with a child) or, if she was under 13, under ss.5–8 of the Act, to which there is no marriage exception.[68] The last point is open to the objection that, if the parties are indeed validly married for the purposes of domestic law, there is no obvious basis on which their right under art.8 ECHR to enjoy married life together, including sexual relations, can be denied them. See further on this point para.4.17, above. However, the Government seems to have considered it a bridge too far to extend the marriage exception to cases where one spouse is under 16 at the time of the relevant conduct.

5.41

SEXUAL RELATIONSHIPS WHICH PRE-DATE POSITION OF TRUST

Section 24 creates an exception for sexual relationships which pre-date the position of trust. Section 24(1) provides that conduct by a person (A) that would otherwise be an offence under s.16 against another person (B) is not an offence under the section if, immediately before the position of trust arose, a sexual relationship existed between A and B. In proceedings for an offence under s.16, the burden of proving that a sexual relationship existed at the

5.42

---

[66] Civil partnerships involving persons under 16 cannot be registered under UK law: Civil Partnerships Act 2004 ss.3, 215, 217.

[67] *Hansard*, HL, vol.654, col.1627, Baroness Scotland of Asthal (November 13, 2003).

[68] cf. *Hansard*, HC, Standing Committee B, September 16, 2003, col.182, the Solicitor General, Harriet Harman MP.

relevant time is placed on the defendant.[69] The reason the Government gave for this was that s.24 creates an exception to the offence, rather than a defence, and evidence of the relationship is within the defendant's particular knowledge, with the result that placing a legal burden on him is justified and proportionate.[70] The term "sexual relationship" is not defined in the Act. Whether such a relationship existed will be a question of fact for the jury or the magistrates. Section 24(2) provides that the exception does not apply if, immediately before the position of trust arose, sexual intercourse between A and B would have been unlawful. For this purpose "unlawful" must mean "criminal". The effect is that A cannot rely on the exception where, immediately before the position of trust arose, B was aged 13, 14 or 15 and A did not reasonably believe her to be 16 or over, since sexual intercourse between an adult and a child in those circumstances will always be unlawful under s.9 of the Act. However, the exception is capable of applying where, at the relevant time, B was 13, 14 or 15 but A reasonably believed her to be 16 or over, since in those circumstances A would commit no offence by having sexual intercourse with B. Further, the exception may apply where the sexual relationship began when B was under 16, provided that she was 16 or over immediately before the position of trust arose.

5.43   During the passage of the Bill, Baroness Blatch tabled amendments to remove this "outrageous" defence, which she said would give:

> "carte blanche to teachers and others in positions of trust to continue sexual relationships with young people in their care as long as they can produce evidence that the sexual relationship started prior to the position of care . . . The 'evidence' of the pre-existing relationship may be fabricated. It might be that a teacher begins a sexual relationship with a 16-year-old in his class and the two of them agree that, if they are ever asked, they will claim that the relationship started prior to the position of trust. That could become a standard technique. Even if the relationship really does begin prior to the position of trust, why should that justify the continuance of that sexual relationship during the time the child . . . is in the care of the other? Why should the teacher who begins his sexual relationship with a pupil a week after he starts his job be guilty of a criminal offence, but not the teacher who begins his sexual relationship a week before? That makes no sense. The person who takes up a position of trust over someone with whom he is in a sexual relationship ought simply to choose between the relationship and the job. To allow the relationship to continue without legal sanction eats away at the very trust on which professions such as teaching and caring are built."[71]

The Government resisted Baroness Blatch's amendments on the basis that the purpose of the offences in ss.16–19 is to protect young people from sexual exploitation by those in a position of trust in relation to them. If a young person, being over the age of consent, enters into a consensual sexual

---

[69] s.24(3).
[70] *Hansard*, HC, vol.412, col.599, the Solicitor General, Harriet Harman MP (November 3, 2003).
[71] *Hansard*, HL, vol.649, col.17 (June 2, 2003); and see vol.649, col.728 (June 17, 2003).

relationship with a person who is not in such a position in relation to them, the purpose of the offences is not brought into play and there can be no basis for interfering with the relationship.[72] This answer does not, however, address the possibility that, after the position of trust arises, the adult may pressurise the young person into continuing the sexual relationship when they would otherwise end it. It is legitimate to argue that, in order to prevent exploitation of this kind, the law should criminalise all sexual relationships involving those in a position of trust, regardless of whether the relationship began before or after the position of trust arose.

A further possible problem with this exception is that it will in principle be **5.44** available where A knows that he will, or foresees that he may, come into a position of trust in relation to B but nonetheless starts a sexual relationship with B before this happens. For example, A is a teacher at one school and B is a pupil at another, but they both know that B will be joining A's school next term. If A makes sexual advances to B, this knowledge could put B in an awkward position and influence her to agree to A's wishes.[73] An amendment to make the exception inapplicable in circumstances such as these was tabled on Third Reading in the Commons. The Government resisted it on the same basis as it had resisted Baroness Blatch's amendments, namely that the purpose of the abuse of trust offences is to protect young people from being manipulated into an exploitative relationship because of the imbalance of power that exists in a relationship of trust, and until that relationship of trust has been formed, such a causal link cannot be made.[74] This is, however, a very narrow approach to the issue: the example given above shows that a causal link can exist where the trust relationship is anticipated, as well as where it has already come into existence. It is, in our view, regrettable that the Government declined to accept this point and to amend the Bill accordingly.

The exception applies only if the couple have already started a sexual **5.45** relationship when the position of trust arises. This has the somewhat odd effect that an adult's exercise of self-restraint could place them at a disadvantage compared with one who engages in sexual activity with the child earlier in their relationship.

CONSENT

The offence is committed regardless of whether the child consents. **5.46**

---

[72] *Hansard*, HL, vol.649, col.19, Lord Falconer of Thoroton (June 2, 2003); vol.649, col.732, Baroness Scotland of Asthal (June 17, 2003).
[73] cf. *Hansard*, HC, Standing Committee B, September 16, 2003, col.224, Paul Goggins MP.
[74] *Hansard*, HC, vol.412, col.599, the Solicitor General, Harriet Harman MP (November 3, 2003).

MENTAL ELEMENT

5.47   The touching must be intentional. If A touches B accidentally or carelessly or recklessly, the offence is not committed. See further paras 2.78 and following, above.

5.48   Where s.16(2) applies, it is a requirement of the offence that A knew or could reasonably have been expected to know of the circumstances by virtue of which he was in a position of trust in relation to B. By virtue of s.16(4), where the prosecution prove the position of trust, it is taken that A knew or could reasonably have been expected to know of those circumstances unless sufficient evidence is adduced to put the matter in issue. If such evidence is adduced, the burden of proof falls on the prosecution in the normal way. It is a matter for the judge to consider (presumably at the close of the evidence) whether sufficient evidence has been adduced for the matter to be left to the jury, i.e. whether A's assertion that he did not know and could not reasonably have been expected to know of the relevant circumstances has some foundation in the evidence and is not merely fanciful.[75]

5.49   It is also a requirement of the offence, where B was aged between 13 and 17 (inclusive) at the material time, that A did not reasonably believe that B was 18 or over. By virtue of s.16(3), if the prosecution prove that B was under 18, A is taken not to have reasonably believed that B was 18 or over unless sufficient evidence is adduced to put the matter in issue. Again, it is for the judge to consider (presumably at the close of the evidence) whether sufficient evidence has been adduced for the matter to be left to the jury, i.e. whether there is some foundation in the evidence for the asserted belief and it is not merely fanciful to assert it.[76] If such evidence is adduced, the burden of proof falls on the prosecution in the normal way. The rationale for this provision is that adults in a position of trust in relation to a child should be expected to know the child's age and should carry the evidential burden of raising an issue as to whether they did.[77] There is no defence of reasonable belief where B was under 13 at the material time. If, however, it is known in advance of charge that B was under 13, or under 16, one of the offences under the 2003 Act specifically designed to protect such children should be charged: see para.5.08, above.

5.50   In the light of the decision in *Heard*,[78] a case of sexual assault for which an intentional touching is also required, it is not open to a defendant charged under s.16 to contend that voluntary intoxication through drink or drugs prevented him from intending to touch the child.

---

[75] cf. *White* [2010] EWCA Crim 1929.
[76] cf. *White* [2010] EWCA Crim 1929.
[77] *Hansard*, HC, Standing Committee B, September 16, 2003, col.210, Paul Goggins MP.
[78] [2007] EWCA Crim 125, discussed in paras 2.81 and following, above.

Abuse of Position of Trust: Causing or Inciting a Child to Engage in Sexual Activity

Definition

Section 17(1) of the Sexual Offences Act 2003 provides:

5.51

"A person aged 18 or over (A) commits an offence if—
(a) he intentionally causes or incites another person (B) to engage in an activity,
(b) the activity is sexual,
(c) A is in a position of trust in relation to B,
(d) where subsection (2) applies, A knows or could reasonably be expected to know of the circumstances by virtue of which he is in a position of trust in relation to B, and
(e) either—
(i) B is under 18 and A does not reasonably believe that B is 18 or over, or
(ii) B is under 13."

This offence should be compared with those in ss.8 and 10 of the Act **5.52** (causing or inciting a child under 13/under 16 to engage in sexual activity). The offences overlap where B is under 13/under 16 and A is 18 or over and in a position of trust in relation to B. Where the victim is a child under 16, the corresponding under-13 or child sex offence (s.8 or s.10) should normally be charged, as appropriate. See further para.5.13, above. However, the effect of the overlap is that if, in proceedings under s.17 charging A with causing or inciting B aged 16 or 17 to engage in sexual activity, it becomes apparent that B was in fact under 16 at the material time, a conviction may nonetheless be obtained without any need to amend the indictment.

By analogy with *Walker*,[79] decided under s.8 of the Act, s.17 creates two **5.53** offences, one of intentionally causing and one of intentionally inciting a person under 18 in relation to whom the inciter is in a position of trust to engage in sexual activity. It follows that a count alleging that the defendant "caused or incited" the complainant is in principle duplicitous and should be struck out or amended. See the discussion of *Walker* in paras 3.132 and following, above.

Mode of Trial and Punishment

Offences under s.17 are triable either way. The maximum sentence on **5.54** conviction on indictment is five years' imprisonment and on summary conviction is six months' imprisonment or a fine, or both.[80] As from a day to

[79] [2006] EWCA Crim 1907.
[80] s.17(5).

be appointed the maximum sentence of imprisonment on summary conviction will increase to 12 months.[81] The increase will have no application to offences committed before it takes effect.[82] Until recently, the maximum fine on summary conviction was a fine not exceeding the statutory maximum (i.e. £5,000). The effect of s.85 of the Legal Aid, Sentencing and Punishment of Offenders Act 2012 is that, from March 12, 2015, a fine of any amount may be imposed. An offence under s.17 cannot be dealt with by way of a simple caution.[83]

5.55 For the purposes of listing, cases under s.17[84] fall within Class 2B, save for complex cases involving many complainants (often under age, in care or otherwise particularly vulnerable) and/or many defendants who are alleged to have systematically groomed and abused them, often over a long period of time, which fall within Class 1C.[85] Cases in Class 1C must be referred to the Resident Judge, and by the Resident Judge to a Presiding Judge. Cases in Class 2B must be similarly referred in certain specified circumstances, including where the case is unusually grave or complex or a novel and important point of law is to be raised; where the defendant is a police officer, a member of the legal profession or a high profile figure; or where for any reason the case is likely to attract exceptional media attention.

5.56 For convictions on or after December 3, 2012,[86] an offence under s.17 is a specified offence for the purposes of s.226A of the Criminal Justice Act 2003 (extended sentence for certain violent or sexual offences), irrespective of the date of commission of the offence.

5.57 A person convicted under s.17, cautioned, found not guilty by reason of insanity or found to be under a disability and to have done the act charged, is automatically subject to the notification requirements in the Sexual Offences Act 2003[87] if, in respect of the offence, he is sentenced to a term of imprisonment, detained in a hospital or given a community sentence of at least 12 months.

SENTENCING

5.58 For the Sentencing Council guideline applicable to sex offenders aged 18 or over who are sentenced on or after April 1, 2014, see Ch.33, below. A single

---

[81] Criminal Justice Act 2003 s.282(2), (3).

[82] Criminal Justice Act 2003 s.282(4).

[83] Criminal Justice and Courts Act 2015 s.17(3), and the Criminal Justice and Courts Act 2015 (Simple Cautions) (Specification of Either-Way Offences) Order 2015 (SI 2015/790).

[84] And of soliciting, inciting, encouraging or assisting, attempting or conspiring to commit the offence or assisting an offender having committed the offence.

[85] *Consolidated Criminal Practice Directions*, Part XIII Listing B: CLASSIFICATION, available at *https://www.judiciary.gov.uk/wp-content/uploads/2015/09/crim-pd-2015.pdf* [Accessed April 30, 2016].

[86] When s.124 of the Legal Aid, Sentencing and Punishment of Offenders Act 2012 was brought into force by the Legal Aid etc Act 2012 (Commencement No. 4 and Saving Provisions) Order 2012 (SI 2012/2906).

[87] s.80 and Sch.3, discussed in Ch.35, below.

guideline covers the offences under ss.16 and 17 of the 2003 Act and is considered at para 5.14 and following, above.

Parties to the Offence

An offence under s.17 may be committed by and against persons of either **5.59** sex. A (the offender) must be 18 or over and B must be under 18. A person attains the age of 18 at the commencement of the eighteenth anniversary of his or her birth.[88] For proof of age see paras 3.73 and following, above.

The s.17 offences are principally designed to protect young people of 16 or **5.60** 17, who do not fall within the scope of the under-13 or child sex offences, from sexual abuse by someone in a position of trust in relation to them. If it is known on charging that B was under 13 at the material time, then in principle A should be charged under s.8 of the Act (causing or inciting a child under 13 to engage in sexual activity), which is specifically designed to protect children under that age and carries a higher maximum penalty.[89] If it is known that B was 13, 14 or 15, the appropriate charge is under s.10 (causing or inciting a child to engage in sexual activity). But a charge under s.17 might be appropriate even in relation to a child aged 13, 14 or 15 in certain cases, e.g. where it is quite likely that A reasonably believed the child to be 16 or over, but unlikely that he reasonably believed her to be 18 or over.[90] If A is under 18 and B is under 16, the appropriate charge is under s.13 of the 2003 Act (child sex offence committed by child or young person) read with s.10.

As to whether the child victim of a s.17 offence is liable to conviction as an **5.61** accessory if they encourage or assist the offence, see the discussion in paras 5.26 and following, above.

Jurisdiction

By virtue of s.72 of and Sch.2 to the Sexual Offences Act 2003, as amended,[91] **5.62** it is an offence under s.17 for a UK national to do an act in a country outside the UK which would constitute a s.17 offence if done in England and Wales. See further para.5.28, above.

"Causes or Incites Another Person . . . "

For the meaning of this term, see paras 2.98 and 3.158 and following, **5.63** above.

---

[88] Family Law Reform Act 1969 s.9(1).
[89] See para.3.04, above.
[90] cf. H.O. Circular 21/2004: *Guidance on Part 1 of the Sexual Offences Act 2003*, para.101.
[91] By the Criminal Justice and Immigration Act 2008 s.72, with effect from July 14, 2008.

"... to Engage in an Activity"

5.64 For the meaning of this term, see paras 2.99 and following, and 3.164, above.

"The Activity is Sexual"

5.65 For the meaning of "sexual", see paras 2.66 and following, above.

"Position of Trust"

5.66 For the meaning of this term, see paras 5.31 and following, above.

"Where Subsection (2) Applies"

5.67 Section 17(2) provides:

> "This subsection applies where A—
> (a) is in a position of trust in relation to B by virtue of circumstances within section 21(2), (3), (4) or (5), and
> (b) is not in such a position of trust in relation to B by virtue of other circumstances."

The effect of this provision, read with s.17(1)(d), is that where A is in a position of trust in relation to B purely by virtue of circumstances falling within s.21(2) to (5),[92] it is an element of the offence that A knew or could reasonably have been expected to know of those circumstances. The rationale for this provision is that it is conceivable that persons in a position of trust by virtue of circumstances of that sort might reasonably be unaware of them: the Home Office guidance on Pt 1 of the Act gives as an example a teacher who meets in a bar, and subsequently has sex with, a sixth-form student who, unknown to him, attends the school at which he teaches.[93] However, in such cases, there is an evidential presumption that A did know or could reasonably have been expected to know of the circumstances. This is the effect of s.17(4), which places an evidential burden on A in relation to this point. Section 17(4) provides:

> "Where, in proceedings for an offence under this section—
> (a) it is proved that the defendant was in a position of trust in relation to the other person by virtue of circumstances within section 21(2), (3), (4) or (5), and
> (b) it is not proved that he was in such a position of trust by virtue of other circumstances,
> it is to be taken that the defendant knew or could reasonably have been expected to know of the circumstances by virtue of which he was in such a position of trust

---

[92] See paras 5.32 and following, above.
[93] H.O. Circular 21/2004: *Guidance on Part 1 of the Sexual Offences Act 2003*, para.102.

unless sufficient evidence is adduced to raise an issue as to whether he knew or could reasonably have been expected to know of those circumstances."

EXCEPTION FOR MARRIAGE AND CIVIL PARTNERSHIP

Section 23 of the 2003 Act, as enacted, created a marriage exception from the abuse of trust offences. The exception was subsequently extended to cover civil partnerships.[94] Section 23(1) now provides that conduct by a person (A) which would otherwise be an offence under any of ss.16 to 19 against another person (B) is not an offence under that section if, at the time, B is 16 or over and A and B are lawfully married or are civil partners of each other. By virtue of s.23(2), the burden of proving that the exception applies is on the defendant. For further discussion see paras 5.40 and following, above. **5.68**

SEXUAL RELATIONSHIPS WHICH PRE-DATE POSITION OF TRUST

Section 24 creates an exception for sexual relationships which pre-date the position of trust. Section 24(1) provides that conduct by a person (A) that would otherwise be an offence under s.17 against another person (B) is not an offence under the section if, immediately before the position of trust arose, a sexual relationship existed between A and B. By virtue of s.24(3), the burden of proving that a sexual relationship existed at the relevant time is on the defendant. But s.24(2) provides that the exception does not apply if at that time sexual intercourse between A and B would have been unlawful. The effect is that A cannot rely on the exception where B was 13, 14 or 15 immediately before the position of trust arose and A did not reasonably believe B to be 16 or over, since sexual intercourse between an adult and a child in those circumstances will always be unlawful under s.9 of the Act. For further discussion see paras 5.42 and following, above. **5.69**

CONSENT

The offence is committed regardless of whether the child consents. **5.70**

MENTAL ELEMENT

A must intentionally cause or incite B to engage in sexual activity. For the meaning of "intention" see para.5.47, above. **5.71**

Where s.17(2) applies, it is a requirement of the offence that A knew or could reasonably have been expected to know of the circumstances by virtue of which he was in a position of trust in relation to B. By virtue of s.17(4), where the prosecution prove the position of trust, it is taken that A knew or **5.72**

---

[94] Civil Partnerships Act 2004 s.261(1) and Sch.27, para.173.

could reasonably have been expected to know of those circumstances unless sufficient evidence is adduced to put the matter in issue. If such evidence is adduced, the burden of proof falls on the prosecution in the normal way. It is a matter for the judge to consider (presumably at the close of the evidence) whether sufficient evidence has been adduced for the matter to be left to the jury, i.e. whether A's assertion that he did not know and could not reasonably have been expected to know of the relevant circumstances has some foundation in the evidence and is not merely fanciful.[95]

5.73   It is also a requirement of the offence, where B was aged between 13 and 17 (inclusive) at the material time, that A did not reasonably believe that B was 18 or over. By virtue of s.17(3), if the prosecution prove that B was under 18, A is taken not to have reasonably believed that B was 18 or over unless sufficient evidence is adduced to put the matter in issue. Again, it is for the judge to consider (presumably at the close of the evidence) whether sufficient evidence has been adduced for the matter to be left to the jury, i.e. whether there is some foundation in the evidence for the asserted belief and it is not merely fanciful to assert it.[96] If such evidence is adduced, the burden of proof falls on the prosecution in the normal way. The rationale for this provision is that adults in a position of trust in relation to a child should be expected to know the child's age and should carry the evidential burden of raising an issue as to whether they did.[97] There is no defence of reasonable belief where B was under 13 at the material time. If, however, it is known in advance of charge that B was under 13, or under 16, A should be charged under s.8 of the 2003 Act (causing or inciting a child under 13 to engage in sexual activity), or under s.10 (causing or inciting a child to engage in sexual activity) as these provisions are specifically designed to protect such children: see para.5.52, above.

5.74   In the light of the decision in *Heard*,[98] dealing with the requirement of intention in relation to the offence of sexual assault, it is not open to a defendant charged under s.17 to contend that voluntary intoxication through drink or drugs prevented him from forming the intention to cause or incite the child to engage in sexual activity.

ABUSE OF POSITION OF TRUST: ENGAGING IN SEXUAL ACTIVITY IN THE PRESENCE OF A CHILD

DEFINITION

5.75   Section 18(1) of the Sexual Offences Act 2003 provides:

"A person aged 18 or over (A) commits an offence if—
    (a) he intentionally engages in an activity,

---

[95] cf. *White* [2010] EWCA Crim 1929.
[96] cf. *White* [2010] EWCA Crim 1929.
[97] *Hansard*, HC, Standing Committee B, September 16, 2003, col.210, Paul Goggins MP.
[98] [2007] EWCA Crim 125, discussed in paras 2.81 and following, above.

    (b) the activity is sexual,

    (c) for the purpose of obtaining sexual gratification, he engages in it—

        (i) when another person (B) is present or is in a place from which A can be observed, and

        (ii) knowing or believing that B is aware, or intending that B should be aware, that he is engaging in it,

    (d) A is in a position of trust in relation to B,

    (e) where subsection (2) applies, A knows or could reasonably be expected to know of the circumstances by virtue of which he is in a position of trust in relation to B, and

    (f) either—

        (i) B is under 18 and A does not reasonably believe that B is 18 or over, or

        (ii) B is under 13."

5.76 This offence mirrors the offence in s.11 of the Act, discussed in paras 4.94 and following, above. The offences overlap where B is under 16 and A is in a position of trust in relation to B. The effect of the overlap is that if, in proceedings under s.18 charging A with engaging in sexual activity in the presence of B aged 16 or 17, it becomes apparent that B was in fact under 16 at the material time, a conviction may nonetheless be obtained without any need to amend the indictment. Where the victim is a child under 16, the s.11 offence should normally be charged. See further para.5.13, above.

MODE OF TRIAL AND PUNISHMENT

5.77 The offence under s.18 is triable either way. The maximum sentence on conviction on indictment is five years' imprisonment. On summary conviction it is six months' imprisonment or a fine, or both.[99] As from a day to be appointed the maximum sentence of imprisonment on summary conviction will increase to 12 months.[100] The increase will have no application to offences committed before it takes effect.[101] Until recently, the maximum fine on summary conviction was a fine not exceeding the statutory maximum (i.e. £5,000). The effect of s.85 of the Legal Aid, Sentencing and Punishment of Offenders Act 2012 is that, from March 12, 2015, a fine of any amount may be imposed. An offence under s.18 cannot be dealt with by way of a simple caution.[102]

5.78 For the purposes of listing, cases under s.18[103] fall within Class 2B, save for complex cases involving many complainants (often under age, in care or otherwise particularly vulnerable) and/or many defendants who are alleged to have systematically groomed and abused them, often over a long period of

---

[99] s.18(5).

[100] Criminal Justice Act 2003 s.282(2), (3).

[101] Criminal Justice Act 2003 s.282(4).

[102] Criminal Justice and Courts Act 2015 s.17(3), and the Criminal Justice and Courts Act 2015 (Simple Cautions) (Specification of Either-Way Offences) Order 2015 (SI 2015/790).

[103] And of soliciting, inciting, encouraging or assisting, attempting or conspiring to commit the offence or assisting an offender having committed the offence.

time, which fall within Class 1C.[104] Cases in Class 1C must be referred to the Resident Judge, and by the Resident Judge to a Presiding Judge. Cases in Class 2B must be similarly referred in certain specified circumstances, including where the case is unusually grave or complex or a novel and important point of law is to be raised; where the defendant is a police officer, a member of the legal profession or a high profile figure; or where for any reason the case is likely to attract exceptional media attention.

5.79   For convictions on or after December 3, 2012,[105] an offence under s.18 is a specified offence for the purposes of s.226A of the Criminal Justice Act 2003 (extended sentence for certain violent or sexual offences), irrespective of the date of commission of the offence.

5.80   A person convicted under s.18, cautioned, found not guilty by reason of insanity or found to be under a disability and to have done the act charged, is automatically subject to the notification requirements in the Sexual Offences Act 2003[106] if, in respect of the offence, he is sentenced to a term of imprisonment, detained in a hospital or given a community sentence of at least 12 months.

SENTENCING

5.81   For the Sentencing Council guideline applicable to sex offenders aged 18 or over who are sentenced on or after April 1, 2014, see Ch.33, below. In consulting on its draft guideline,[107] the Council noted that the offences in ss.18 and 19 of the 2003 Act mirror those in ss.11 and 12 of the Act and accordingly proposed to cover them in a single guideline. It duly followed this approach in the published guideline.

Sentencing guideline

Step One—Harm and culpability

5.82   The guideline requires the sentencing court to go through a series of steps in order to determine the appropriate sentence. Step one involves determining the offence category by reference to the degree of harm caused and then the culpability level for the offence. In this guideline, the Sentencing Council adopted the approach to harm and culpability that it took in the guideline for offences under ss.11 and 12 of the Act, discussed at para.4.100, above.

---

[104] *Consolidated Criminal Practice Directions*, Part XIII Listing B: CLASSIFICATION, available at *https://www.judiciary.gov.uk/wp-content/uploads/2015/09/crim-pd-2015.pdf* [Accessed April 30, 2016].

[105] When s.124 of the Legal Aid, Sentencing and Punishment of Offenders Act 2012 was brought into force by the Legal Aid etc Act 2012 (Commencement No. 4 and Saving Provisions) Order 2012 (SI 2012/2906).

[106] s.80 and Sch.3, discussed in Ch.35, below.

[107] *Sexual Offences Guideline: Consultation* (December 6, 2012). The consultation document can be found on the Sentencing Council's website.

The harm and culpability factors for offences under ss.18 and 19 are accordingly as follows:

Harm	
Category 1	• Causing victim to view extreme pornography • Causing victim to view indecent/prohibited images of children • Engaging in, or causing a victim to view live, sexual activity involving sadism/violence/sexual activity with an animal/a child
Category 2	Engaging in, or causing a victim to view images of or view live, sexual activity involving: • penetration of vagina or anus (using body or object) • penile penetration of the mouth • masturbation
Category 3	Factor(s) in categories 1 and 2 not present

CULPABILITY
A
• Significant degree of planning • Offender acts together with others in order to commit the offence • Use of alcohol/drugs on victim to facilitate the offence • Grooming behaviour used against victim • Use of threats (including blackmail) • Sexual images of victim recorded, retained, solicited or shared • Specific targeting of a particularly vulnerable child • Significant disparity in age • Commercial exploitation and/or motivation • Offence racially or religiously aggravated • Offence motivated by, or demonstrating, hostility to the victim based on his or her sexual orientation (or presumed sexual orientation) or transgender identity (or presumed transgender identity) • Offence motivated by, or demonstrating, hostility to the victim based on his or her disability (or presumed disability)
B
Factor(s) in category A not present

Step Two—Starting point and category range

5.83   Once the court has determined the offence category and culpability level, at step two it should use the corresponding starting point specified in the guideline in order to reach a sentence within the category range. The starting point applies to all offenders irrespective of plea or previous convictions. Once the starting point has been determined, step two allows further adjustment for aggravating or mitigating features, set out below. A case of particular gravity, reflected by multiple features of culpability or harm, could merit upward adjustment from the starting point before further adjustment for aggravating or mitigating features. Where there is a sufficient prospect of rehabilitation, a community order with a sex offender treatment programme requirement under s.202 of the Criminal Justice Act 2003 may be a proper alternative to a short or moderate length custodial sentence. The starting points and category ranges for offences under ss.18 and 19 of the Act are as follows:

	A	**B**
Category 1	*Starting point* 18 months' custody	*Starting point* 1 years' custody
	Category range 1–2 years' custody	*Category range* 26 weeks–18 months' custody
Category 2	*Starting point* 1 years' custody	*Starting point* 26 weeks's custody
	Category range 26 weeks–18 months' custody	*Category range* High level community order – 1 year's custody
Category 3	*Starting point* 26 weeks' custody	*Starting point* Medium level community order
	Category range High level community order – 1 year's custody	*Category range* Low level community order – Medium level community order

The factors used to determine the offence categories are very similar to those used in the guideline for offences under ss.11 and 12, but the starting points and ranges are lower in order to reflect the fact that the statutory maximum under ss.18 and s.19 is five years, as opposed to 10 years under ss.11 and 12. In the previous guideline, issued in 2007 by the Sentencing Guidelines Council, the starting point and ranges for an offender who had consensual intercourse in the presence of the victim, contrary to s.18, were higher (at two years and 1–4 years) than for an offender who had penetrative intercourse with the victim, contrary to s.16 (18 months and 1 year–2 years 6 months). The Sentencing Council accepted in its consultation that both forms of activity should have a custodial starting point but saw no justification for the difference between the two scenarios, and so the starting point and ranges are now the same in both cases.

Aggravating and mitigating factors

After identifying the starting point and category range, the court should   **5.84** consider whether the presence of aggravating or mitigating factors should result in an upward or downward adjustment from the starting point or the imposition of a sentence outside the category range. In particular, relevant recent convictions are likely to result in an upward adjustment. When sentencing appropriate category 2 or 3 offences, the court should also consider whether the custody threshold has been passed; if so, whether a custodial sentence is unavoidable; and if it is, whether that sentence can be suspended. The non-exhaustive list of aggravating and mitigating factors for offences under ss.18 and 19 is as follows:

Aggravating factors
Statutory aggravating factors
<ul><li>Previous convictions, having regard to a) the nature of the offence to which the conviction relates and its relevance to the current offence; and b) the time that has elapsed since the conviction</li><li>Offence committed whilst on bail</li></ul>
Other aggravating factors
<ul><li>Location of offence</li><li>Timing of offence</li><li>Victim compelled to leave their home, school, etc.</li><li>Failure to comply with current court orders</li><li>Offence committed whilst on licence</li><li>Exploiting contact arrangements with a child to commit an offence</li></ul>

- Presence of others, especially other children
- Any steps taken to prevent the victim reporting an incident, obtaining assistance and/or from assisting or supporting the prosecution
- Attempts to dispose of or conceal evidence
- Failure of offender to respond to previous warnings
- Commission of offence whilst under the influence of alcohol or drugs
- Victim encouraged to recruit others

Mitigating factors

- No previous convictions **or** no relevant/recent convictions
- Remorse
- Previous good character and/or exemplary conduct*
- Age and/or lack of maturity where it affects the responsibility of the offender
- Mental disorder or learning disability, particularly where linked to the commission of the offence
- Demonstration of steps taken to address offending behaviour

* Previous good character/exemplary conduct is different from having no previous convictions. The more serious the offence, the less the weight which should normally be attributed to this factor. Where previous good character/exemplary conduct has been used to facilitate the offence, this mitigation should not normally be allowed and such conduct may constitute an aggravating factor.

The non-statutory aggravating factors are the same as in the guideline for ss.16 and 17, discussed at paras 5.14 and following, above, except that "ejaculation" and "pregnancy or STI as a consequence of offence" are omitted as they are irrelevant to offences under ss.18 and 19, which involve causing a child to view, rather than to engage in, sexual activity.

Steps Three to Nine

5.85   The remaining steps cover the following points. At step three the court should consider any factors which would indicate a reduction in sentence, e.g. assistance to the prosecution. At step four it should consider any reduction for a guilty plea. At step five the court should consider dangerousness, i.e. whether it would be appropriate to award an extended sentence (s.226A of the Criminal Justice Act 2003). Step six requires the court to consider whether the total sentence is just and proportionate to the offending behaviour. At step seven it should consider whether to make an ancillary order (e.g. a compensation order, a SHPO or a restraining order). Step eight requires the court to fulfil its duty under s.174 of the Criminal Justice Act 2003 to give reasons for, and explain the effect of, the sentence. Finally, at step nine the court should consider whether to give credit for time spent on bail in accordance with s.240A of that Act.

PARTIES TO THE OFFENCE

The offence under s.18 may be committed by and against persons of either sex. A must be 18 or over and B must be under 18. A person attains the age of 18 at the commencement of the eighteenth anniversary of his or her birth.[108] For proof of age, see paras 3.73 and following, above.   **5.86**

The offence is principally designed to protect young people of 16 or 17, who do not fall within the scope of the under-13 or child sex offences, from sexual abuse by someone in a position of trust in relation to them. If it is known on charging that B was under 16 at the material time, then in principle A should be charged under s.11 of the Act (engaging in sexual activity in the presence of a child), which is specifically designed for the protection of children under that age and carries a higher maximum penalty.[109] But a charge under s.18 might be appropriate even in relation to a child aged 13, 14 or 15 in certain cases, e.g. where it is quite likely that A reasonably believed the child to be 16 or over, but unlikely that he reasonably believed her to be 18 or over.[110] If A is under 18 and B is under 16, the appropriate charge is under s.13 of the 2003 Act (child sex offence committed by child or young person) read with s.11.   **5.87**

As to whether the child victim of a s.18 offence is liable to conviction as an accessory if they encourage or assist the offence, see the discussion in paras 5.26 and following, above.   **5.88**

JURISDICTION

By virtue of s.72 of and Sch.2 to the Sexual Offences Act 2003, as amended,[111] it is an offence under s.18 for a UK national to do an act in a country outside the UK which would constitute an offence under s.18 if done in England and Wales. See further para.5.28, above.   **5.89**

"ENGAGES IN AN ACTIVITY"

For the meaning of this term, see paras 2.99 and following, and 3.164, above.   **5.90**

---

[108] Family Law Reform Act 1969 s.9(1).

[109] See para.3.04, above.

[110] cf. H.O. Circular 21/2004: *Guidance on Part 1 of the Sexual Offences Act 2003*, par-a.101.

[111] By the Criminal Justice and Immigration Act 2008 s.72, with effect from July 14, 2008.

"The Activity is Sexual"

5.91 For the meaning of "sexual", see paras 2.66 and following, above.

"Present or In a Place from which A can be Observed"

5.92 For the meaning of this term, see paras 4.114 and following, above.

"Position of Trust"

5.93 For the meaning of this term, see paras 5.31 and following, above.

"Where Subsection (2) Applies"

5.94 Section 18(2) provides:

> "This subsection applies where A—
> (a) is in a position of trust in relation to B by virtue of circumstances within section 21(2), (3), (4) or (5), and
> (b) is not in such a position of trust in relation to B by virtue of other circumstances."

The effect of this provision, read with s.18(1)(e), is that where A is in a position of trust in relation to B purely by virtue of circumstances falling within s.21(2) to (5),[112] it is an element of the offence that A knew or could reasonably have been expected to know of those circumstances. The rationale for this provision is that it is conceivable that persons in a position of trust by virtue of circumstances of that sort might reasonably be unaware of them: the Home Office guidance on Pt 1 of the Act gives as an example a teacher who meets in a bar, and subsequently has sex with, a sixth-form student who, unknown to him, attends the school at which he teaches.[113] However, in such cases there is an evidential presumption that A did know or could reasonably have been expected to know of the circumstances. This is the effect of s.18(4), which places an evidential burden on A in relation to this point. Section 18(4) provides:

> "Where, in proceedings for an offence under this section—
> (a) it is proved that the defendant was in a position of trust in relation to the other person by virtue of circumstances within section 21(2), (3), (4) or (5), and
> (b) it is not proved that he was in such a position of trust by virtue of other circumstances,
> it is to be taken that the defendant knew or could reasonably have been expected to know of the circumstances by virtue of which he was in such a position of trust unless sufficient evidence is adduced to raise an issue as to whether he knew or could reasonably have been expected to know of those circumstances."

---

[112] See paras 5.32 and following, above.
[113] H.O. Circular 21/2004: *Guidance on Part 1 of the Sexual Offences Act 2003*, para.102.

EXCEPTION FOR MARRIAGE AND CIVIL PARTNERSHIP

Section 23 of the 2003 Act, as enacted, created a marriage exception from the   **5.95**
abuse of trust offences. The exception was subsequently extended to cover
civil partnerships.[114] Section 23(1) now provides that conduct by a person (A)
which would otherwise be an offence under any of ss.16 to 19 against another
person (B) is not an offence under that section if, at the time, B is 16 or over
and A and B are lawfully married or are civil partners of each other. By
virtue of s.23(2), the burden of proving that the exception applies is on the
defendant. For further discussion see paras 5.40 and following, above.

SEXUAL RELATIONSHIPS WHICH PRE-DATE POSITION OF TRUST

Section 24 creates an exception for sexual relationships which pre-date the   **5.96**
position of trust. Section 24(1) provides that conduct by a person (A) that
would otherwise be an offence under s.18 against another person (B) is not
an offence under the section if, immediately before the position of trust arose,
a sexual relationship existed between A and B. By virtue of s.24(3), the
burden of proving that a sexual relationship existed at the relevant time is on
the defendant. But s.24(2) provides that the exception does not apply if at
that time sexual intercourse between A and B would have been unlawful. The
effect is that A cannot rely on the exception where B was 13, 14 or 15
immediately before the position of trust arose and A did not reasonably
believe B to be 16 or over, since sexual intercourse between an adult and a
child in those circumstances will always be unlawful under s.9 of the Act. For
further discussion see paras 5.42 and following, above.

CONSENT

The offence is committed regardless of whether the child consents.   **5.97**

MENTAL ELEMENT

A must engage in the activity intentionally. For the meaning of "intention"   **5.98**
see para.5.47, above. A must also engage in the activity for the purpose of
obtaining sexual gratification. It is not, therefore, sufficient that A engages in
it in order to shock B or simply by way of attention-seeking. During the
passage of the Bill the question was raised whether A's purpose must be to
obtain sexual gratification from the activity itself or from being observed by
B. On a natural reading, s.18(1)(c) requires the purpose of sexual gratification
to be related to the fact of observation, rather than to the sexual activity

---

[114] Civil Partnerships Act 2004 s.261(1) and Sch.27, para.173.

itself. This is supported by the Home Office guidance on Pt 1 of the Act, which states, in relation to the similarly-worded offence in s.11:

> "The offence is intended to cover the situation where someone seeks sexual gratification not from the sexual act itself but rather from the fact that he is performing that act in the presence or intended presence of a child. The motive of sexual gratification is a necessary safeguard intended to avoid capturing those who engage in sexual activity in front of a child for a legitimate reason. For example, a teacher who sexually kisses his partner just outside the school gates, could be deemed to be engaging in sexual activity intentionally in front of a child and might otherwise be caught by the offence."[115]

A similar example given in debate on the Bill was of a teacher accompanied on a school trip by his partner, with whom he shares a passionate kiss in front of the children: in the Government's view that would be inappropriate behaviour, but it would not constitute the s.18 offence.[116] However, this example led to discussion of a more difficult scenario, where a teacher and his partner take a party of 16-year-old schoolchildren to some woodland and, knowing but not caring that the children are watching, engage in sexual intercourse under a tree. Would this behaviour also fall outside the scope of the offence, on the basis that the teacher's purpose was to obtain sexual gratification from the sexual activity and not from being observed by the children? The Government expected that in these circumstances a jury would convict, on the basis that "the more outrageous the act, the more likely it is to be done in the knowledge that the children were watching and for sexual gratification purposes".[117] There is practical force in this observation. But if the teacher in the woodland was genuinely indifferent to the children's presence, or more accurately if the prosecution cannot prove otherwise, then in principle the offence will not be made out. See further the discussion in para.4.117, above, of the same element in the s.11 offence.

5.99   A must know or believe that B is aware, or intend that B should be aware, that he is engaging in the activity. But there is no requirement that B must actually be aware.

5.100   Where s.18(2) applies, it is a requirement of the offence that A knew or could reasonably have been expected to know of the circumstances by virtue of which he was in a position of trust in relation to B. By virtue of s.18(4), where the prosecution prove the position of trust, it is taken that A knew or could reasonably have been expected to know of those circumstances unless sufficient evidence is adduced to put the matter in issue. If such evidence is adduced, the burden of proof falls on the prosecution in the normal way. It is a matter for the judge to consider (presumably at the close of the evidence) whether sufficient evidence has been adduced for the matter to be left to the jury, i.e. whether A's assertion that he did not know and could not reasonably

---

[115] H.O. Circular 21/2004: *Guidance on Part 1 of the Sexual Offences Act 2003*, para.62.
[116] *Hansard* HC, Standing Committee B, September 16, 2003, col.212, Paul Goggins MP.
[117] *Hansard* HC, Standing Committee B, September 16, 2003, cols 213–4, Paul Goggins MP.

have been expected to know of the relevant circumstances has some foundation in the evidence and is not merely fanciful.[118]

It is also a requirement of the offence, where B was aged between 13 and 17 (inclusive) at the material time, that A did not reasonably believe that B was 18 or over. By virtue of s.18(3), if the prosecution prove that B was under 18, A is taken not to have reasonably believed that B was 18 or over unless sufficient evidence is adduced to put the matter in issue. Again, it is for the judge to consider (presumably at the close of the evidence) whether sufficient evidence has been adduced for the matter to be left to the jury, i.e. whether there is some foundation in the evidence for the asserted belief and it is not merely fanciful to assert it.[119] If such evidence is adduced, the burden of proof falls on the prosecution in the normal way. The rationale for this provision is that adults in a position of trust in relation to a child should be expected to know the child's age and should carry the evidential burden of raising an issue as to whether they did.[120] There is no defence of reasonable belief where B was under 13 at the material time. **5.101**

In the light of the decision in *Heard*,[121] discussed in paras 2.81 and following, above, the requirement that the defendant did the prohibited act for the purpose of obtaining sexual gratification makes the s.18 offence one of specific intent, such that voluntary intoxication through drink or drugs will provide a defence if it may have prevented the defendant forming that purpose. **5.102**

ABUSE OF POSITION OF TRUST: CAUSING A CHILD TO WATCH A SEXUAL ACT

DEFINITION

Section 19(1) of the Sexual Offences Act 2003 provides: **5.103**

"A person aged 18 or over (A) commits an offence if—
(a) for the purpose of obtaining sexual gratification, he intentionally causes another person (B) to watch a third person engaging in an activity, or to look at an image of any person engaging in an activity,
(b) the activity is sexual,
(c) A is in a position of trust in relation to B,
(d) where subsection (2) applies, A knows or could reasonably be expected to know of the circumstances by virtue of which he is in a position of trust in relation to B, and
(e) either—
   (i) B is under 18 and A does not reasonably believe that B is 18 or over, or
   (ii) B is under 13."

---

[118] cf. *White* [2010] EWCA Crim 1929.
[119] cf. *White* [2010] EWCA Crim 1929.
[120] *Hansard*, HC, Standing Committee B, September 16, 2003, col.210, Paul Goggins MP.
[121] [2007] EWCA Crim 125.

5.104   This provision mirrors s.12 of the Act, discussed in paras 4.121 and following, above. As with s.12, the better view is that s.19 creates one offence that can be committed in two different ways, by causing another person to watch a third person engaging in a sexual activity or by causing another person to look at an image of any person engaging in sexual activity. The charge or indictment should make clear which variant of the offence is alleged. The offences overlap where B is under 16 and A is in a position of trust in relation to B. The effect of the overlap is that if, in proceedings under s.19 charging A with causing B aged 16 or 17 to watch a sexual act, it becomes apparent that B was in fact under 16 at the material time, a conviction may nonetheless be obtained without any need to amend the indictment. Where the victim is a child under 16, the s.12 offence should normally be charged. See further para.5.13, above.

MODE OF TRIAL AND PUNISHMENT

5.105   The offence under s.19 is triable either way. The maximum sentence on conviction on indictment is five years' imprisonment. On summary conviction it is six months' imprisonment or a fine, or both.[122] As from a day to be appointed the maximum sentence of imprisonment on summary conviction will increase to 12 months.[123] The increase will have no application to offences committed before it takes effect.[124] Until recently, the maximum fine on summary conviction was a fine not exceeding the statutory maximum (i.e. £5,000). The effect of s.85 of the Legal Aid, Sentencing and Punishment of Offenders Act 2012 is that, from March 12, 2015, a fine of any amount may be imposed. An offence under s.19 cannot be dealt with by way of a simple caution.[125]

5.106   For the purposes of listing, cases under s.19[126] fall within Class 2B, save for complex cases involving many complainants (often under age, in care or otherwise particularly vulnerable) and/or many defendants who are alleged to have systematically groomed and abused them, often over a long period of time, which fall within Class 1C. [127] Cases in Class 1C must be referred to the Resident Judge, and by the Resident Judge to a Presiding Judge. Cases in Class 2B must be similarly referred in certain specified circumstances, including where the case is unusually grave or complex or a novel and important point of law is to be raised; where the defendant is a police officer,

---

[122] s.19(5).

[123] Criminal Justice Act 2003 s.282(2), (3).

[124] Criminal Justice Act 2003 s.282(4).

[125] Criminal Justice and Courts Act 2015 s.17(3), and the Criminal Justice and Courts Act 2015 (Simple Cautions) (Specification of Either-Way Offences) Order 2015 (SI 2015/790).

[126] And of soliciting, inciting, encouraging or assisting, attempting or conspiring to commit the offence or assisting an offender having committed the offence.

[127] *Consolidated Criminal Practice Directions*, Part XIII Listing B: CLASSIFICATION, available at *https://www.judiciary.gov.uk/wp-content/uploads/2015/09/crim-pd-2015.pdf* [Accessed April 30, 2016].

a member of the legal profession or a high profile figure; or where for any reason the case is likely to attract exceptional media attention.

For convictions on or after December 3, 2012,[128] an offence under s.19 is **5.107** a specified offence for the purposes of s.226A of the Criminal Justice Act 2003 (extended sentence for certain violent or sexual offences), irrespective of the date of commission of the offence.

A person convicted under s.19, cautioned, found not guilty by reason of **5.108** insanity or found to be under a disability and to have done the act charged, is automatically subject to the notification requirements in the Sexual Offences Act 2003[129] if, in respect of the offence, he is sentenced to a term of imprisonment, detained in a hospital or given a community sentence of at least 12 months.

SENTENCING

The Sentencing Council has issued a new guideline applicable to sex **5.109** offenders aged 18 or over who are sentenced on or after April 1, 2014, see Ch.33, below. A single guideline covers the offences in ss.18 and 19 of the 2003 Act and is considered at paras 5.81 and following, above.

PARTIES TO THE OFFENCE

The offence in s.19 may be committed by and against persons of either sex. **5.110** A must be 18 or over and B must be under 18. A person attains the age of 18 at the commencement of the eighteenth anniversary of his or her birth.[130] For proof of age see paras 3.73 and following, above.

The offence is principally designed to protect young people of 16 or 17, **5.111** who do not fall within the scope of the under-13 or child sex offences, from sexual abuse by someone in a position of trust in relation to them. If it is known on charging that B was under 16 at the material time, then in principle A should be charged under s.12 of the Act (causing a child to watch a sexual act), which is specifically designed for the protection of children under that age and carries a higher maximum penalty.[131] But a charge under s.19 might be appropriate even in relation to a child aged 13, 14 or 15 in certain cases, e.g. where it is quite likely that A reasonably believed the child to be 16 or over, but unlikely that he reasonably believed her to be 18 or over.[132] If A is

---

[128] When s.124 of the Legal Aid, Sentencing and Punishment of Offenders Act 2012 was brought into force by the Legal Aid etc Act 2012 (Commencement No. 4 and Saving Provisions) Order 2012 (SI 2012/2906).

[129] s.80 and Sch.3, discussed in Ch.35, below.

[130] Family Law Reform Act 1969 s.9(1).

[131] See para.3.04, above.

[132] cf. H.O. Circular 21/2004: *Guidance on Part 1 of the Sexual Offences Act 2003*, para.101.

under 18 and B is under 16, the appropriate charge is under s.13 of the 2003 Act (child sex offence committed by child or young person) read with s.12.

5.112   As to whether the child victim of a s.19 offence is liable to conviction as an accessory if they encourage or assist the offence, see the discussion in paras 5.26 and following, above.

JURISDICTION

5.113 By virtue of s.72 of and Sch.2 to the Sexual Offences Act 2003, as amended,[133] it is an offence under s.19 for a UK national to do an act in a country outside the UK which would constitute an offence under s.19 if done in England and Wales. See further para.5.28, above.

"CAUSES"

5.114 For the meaning of this term, see paras 2.98 and 3.158 and following, above.

"TO WATCH A THIRD PERSON ENGAGING IN AN ACTIVITY, OR TO LOOK AT AN IMAGE OF ANY PERSON ENGAGING IN AN ACTIVITY"

5.115 For the meaning of this term, see paras 4.134 and following, above.

"THE ACTIVITY IS SEXUAL"

5.116 For the meaning of "sexual", see paras 2.66 and following, above.

"POSITION OF TRUST"

5.117 For the meaning of this term, see paras 5.31 and following, above.

"WHERE SUBSECTION (2) APPLIES"

5.118 Section 19(2) provides:

> "This subsection applies where A—
>   (a) is in a position of trust in relation to B by virtue of circumstances within section 21(2), (3), (4) or (5), and
>   (b) is not in such a position of trust in relation to B by virtue of other circumstances."

The effect of this provision, read with s.19(1)(d), is that where A is in a position of trust in relation to B purely by virtue of circumstances falling

---

[133] By the Criminal Justice and Immigration Act 2008 s.72, with effect from July 14, 2008.

within s.21(2) to (5),[134] it is an element of the offence that A knew or could reasonably have been expected to know of those circumstances. The rationale for this provision is that it is conceivable that persons in a position of trust by virtue of those circumstances might reasonably be unaware of them: the Home Office guidance on Pt 1 of the Act gives as an example a teacher who meets in a bar, and subsequently has sex with, a sixth-form student who, unknown to him, attends the school at which he teaches.[135] However, in such cases there is an evidential presumption that A did know or could reasonably have been expected to know of the circumstances. This is the effect of s.19(4), which places an evidential burden on A in relation to this point. Section 19(4) provides:

> "Where, in proceedings for an offence under this section—
> (a) it is proved that the defendant was in a position of trust in relation to the other person by virtue of circumstances within section 21(2), (3), (4) or (5), and
> (b) it is not proved that he was in such a position of trust by virtue of other circumstances,
> it is to be taken that the defendant knew or could reasonably have been expected to know of the circumstances by virtue of which he was in such a position of trust unless sufficient evidence is adduced to raise an issue as to whether he knew or could reasonably have been expected to know of those circumstances."

EXCEPTION FOR MARRIAGE AND CIVIL PARTNERSHIP

Section 23 of the 2003 Act, as enacted, created a marriage exception from the   **5.119** abuse of trust offences. The exception was subsequently extended to cover civil partnerships.[136] Section 23(1) now provides that conduct by a person (A) which would otherwise be an offence under any of ss.16–19 against another person (B) is not an offence under that section if, at the time, B is 16 or over and A and B are lawfully married or are civil partners of each other. By virtue of s.23(2), the burden of proving that the exception applies is on the defendant. For further discussion see paras 5.40 and following, above.

SEXUAL RELATIONSHIPS WHICH PRE-DATE POSITION OF TRUST

Section 24 creates an exception for sexual relationships which pre-date the   **5.120** position of trust. Section 24(1) provides that conduct by a person (A) that would otherwise be an offence under s.19 against another person (B) is not an offence under the section if, immediately before the position of trust arose, a sexual relationship existed between A and B. By virtue of s.24(3), the burden of proving that a sexual relationship existed at the relevant time is on the defendant. But s.24(2) provides that the exception does not apply if at

---

[134] See paras 5.32 and following, above.
[135] H.O. Circular 21/2004: *Guidance on Part 1 of the Sexual Offences Act 2003*, para.102.
[136] Civil Partnerships Act 2004 s.261(1) and Sch.27, para.173.

that time sexual intercourse between A and B would have been unlawful. The effect is that A cannot rely on the exception where B was 13, 14 or 15 immediately before the position of trust arose and A did not reasonably believe B to be 16 or over, since sexual intercourse between and adult and a child in those circumstances will always be unlawful under s.9 of the Act. For further discussion see paras 5.42 and following, above.

Consent

5.121   The offence is committed regardless of whether the child consents.

Mental Element

5.122   A must cause B to watch etc. intentionally and for the purpose of obtaining sexual gratification. For the meaning of "intention" see para.5.47, above. For the purpose of obtaining sexual gratification, see para.5.98, above.

5.123   Where s.19(2) applies, it is a requirement of the offence that A knew or could reasonably have been expected to know of the circumstances by virtue of which he was in a position of trust in relation to B. By virtue of s.19(4), where the prosecution prove the position of trust, it is taken that A knew or could reasonably have been expected to know of those circumstances unless sufficient evidence is adduced to put the matter in issue. If such evidence is adduced, the burden of proof falls on the prosecution in the normal way. It is a matter for the judge to consider (presumably at the close of the evidence) whether sufficient evidence has been adduced for the matter to be left to the jury, i.e. whether A's assertion that he did not know and could not reasonably have been expected to know of the relevant circumstances has some foundation in the evidence and is not merely fanciful.[137]

5.124   It is also a requirement of the offence, where B was aged between 13 and 17 (inclusive) at the material time, that A did not reasonably believe that B was 18 or over. By virtue of s.19(3), if the prosecution prove that B was under 18, A is taken not to have reasonably believed that B was 18 or over unless sufficient evidence is adduced to put the matter in issue. Again, it is for the judge to consider (presumably at the close of the evidence) whether sufficient evidence has been adduced for the matter to be left to the jury, i.e. whether there is some foundation in the evidence for the asserted belief and it is not merely fanciful to assert it.[138] If such evidence is adduced, the burden of proof falls on the prosecution in the normal way. The rationale for this provision is that adults in a position of trust in relation to a child should be expected to know the child's age and should carry the evidential burden of

[137] cf. *White* [2010] EWCA Crim 1929.
[138] cf. *White* [2010] EWCA Crim 1929.

raising an issue as to whether they did.[139] There is no defence of reasonable belief where B was under 13 at the material time.

In the light of the decision in *Heard*,[140] discussed in para.2.81 and following, above, the requirement that the defendant did the prohibited act for the purpose of obtaining sexual gratification makes the s.19 offence one of specific intent, such that voluntary intoxication through drink or drugs will provide a defence if it may have prevented the defendant forming that purpose.   **5.125**

ABUSE OF POSITION OF TRUST: ACTS DONE IN SCOTLAND OR NORTHERN IRELAND

DEFINITION

Section 20 of the Sexual Offences Act 2003[141] provides: **5.126**

> "Anything which, if done in England and Wales, would constitute an offence under any of sections 16 to 19 also constitutes that offence if done in Scotland or Northern Ireland."

The effect of this section is that conduct carried out in Scotland or Northern Ireland which falls within the scope of the abuse of trust offences is triable in England and Wales as such an offence. It was originally enacted because of the intention on the part of the Scottish authorities to implement the abuse of trust offence in the Sexual Offences (Amendment) Act 2000 rather than the slightly wider offences in the 2003 Act. That gave rise to concern in Westminster that there might be a loophole in the 2003 Act, which would enable a person to avoid prosecution by going to Scotland to engage in conduct covered by the 2003 Act but not by the Scottish equivalent. Section 20 ensures that there is no such loophole: such conduct in Scotland or, by subsequent extension, in Northern Ireland will be prosecutable in England and Wales as if it was engaged in there.[142] A laudable effect of s.20 is therefore to prevent an English resident from avoiding criminal liability by the expedient of moving over the Scottish border to engage in conduct prohibited by ss.16–19 of the 2003 Act but not the equivalent Scottish provision. In such a case, the extra-territorial jurisdiction conferred by s.20 applies even if there is no relevant link to England and Wales. Indeed, in principle s.20 would permit an English court to try a case involving conduct prohibited by ss.16–19 that takes place in Scotland between Scottish residents, regardless of the fact that the conduct involved no breach of Scottish law. But it would be surprising if the CPS considered such a prosecution to be in the public interest.   **5.127**

---

[139] *Hansard*, HC, Standing Committee B, September 16, 2003, col.210, Paul Goggins MP.
[140] [2007] EWCA Crim 125.
[141] As amended by the Sexual Offences (Northern Ireland Consequential Amendments) Order 2008/1779 art.5.
[142] cf. *Hansard*, HL, vol.646, cols 1284–5, Lord Bassam of Brighton (April 1, 2003).

5.128   The extra-territorial jurisdiction conferred by s.20 on the courts of
England and Wales is concurrent with the jurisdiction of the courts of
Scotland and Northern Ireland (as the case may be) in so far as the
defendant's conduct falls within the scope of both the 2003 Act and the
corresponding provisions in Scotland or Northern Ireland.[143] In such
circumstances, i.e. where the defendant's conduct constitutes an offence in
both England and Wales and, say, Scotland, it will be triable in England and
Wales if the offence has a substantial connection with this jurisdiction unless
it can be argued, on a reasonable view, that the conduct ought to be dealt
with by the Scottish courts.[144]

---

[143] The law in Scotland is contained in the Sexual Offences (Scotland) Act 2009. For the law
of sexual offences in Northern Ireland, see Ch.32.
[144] *Smith (Wallace Duncan) (No.4)* [2004] EWCA Crim 631. See the CPS guidance on
Jurisdiction at *http://www.cps.gov.uk/legal/h_to_k/jurisdiction/* [Accessed April 30, 2016].

CHAPTER 6

FAMILIAL SEX OFFENCES

Introduction.................................... 6.01
Sexual Activity with a Child
    Family Member.......................... 6.12
Inciting a Child Family Member to
    Engage in Sexual Activity............ 6.54

Jurisdiction 6.63
Sex with an Adult Relative:
    Penetration 6.72
Sex with an Adult Relative:
    Consenting to Penetration............ 6.94

INTRODUCTION

Incest represents a fundamental social taboo in most societies. Nevertheless, apart from a brief period under the Commonwealth during the 1650s,[1] incest was not a crime in England and Wales until the enactment of the Punishment of Incest Act 1908. Consensual sexual relations between close family members were outside the confines of the criminal law and punishable only by the ecclesiastical courts,[2] although by the end of the nineteenth century such punishment was rare. The 1908 Act was passed against the background of an increasing awareness of the prevalence of incest and concern about its moral effects. The Act was repealed by the Sexual Offences Act 1956 which contained in ss.10 and 11 offences of incest by a man and incest by a woman. These offences were later supplemented by the creation, in s.54(1) of the Criminal Law Act 1977, of an offence of inciting a girl under 16 to have incestuous sexual intercourse. This provision was enacted following the controversial decision in *Whitehouse*,[3] in which a father's conviction of inciting his daughter to commit incest was quashed on the ground that, as the daughter was under 16, she could not commit the crime of incest and so her father could not commit the common law offence of inciting her to commit incest with him. These offences were all repealed by the Sexual

6.01

---

[1] During Cromwell's Protectorate in 1650 incest, together with adultery, was made a capital offence.

[2] It was dealt with by canon law and punishable with a penance: see *Setting the Boundaries: Reforming the law on sexual offences*, (Home Office, July 2000), p.81, fn.92.

[3] [1977] Q.B. 868.

Offences Act 2003 and replaced by the familial sex offences which are the subject of this chapter.

Sexual activity with a child family member

6.02   Under the old law of incest, the proscribed sexual behaviour was limited to vaginal sexual intercourse, and there had to be a close blood relationship between the parties. There were separate offences for men and women. There was an additional offence of inciting a girl under the age of 16 to have incestuous intercourse.[4] The 2003 Act repealed these offences and created two gender-neutral offences designed to capture the sexual abuse and exploitation of children within the "family" unit. Section 25 creates an offence of sexual activity with a child family member, and s.26 an offence of inciting a child family member to engage in sexual activity. The law in this area has been expanded in a number of ways: the Act widens the categories of family members who can commit offences, raises the maximum age of a child victim to 18, and increases the scope of the prohibited sexual behaviour to any form of sexual touching. The essence of the offences is intentional sexual touching (including penetration) which involves a family member under 18. The upper age of 18 was justified by the Sexual Offences Review on the ground that[5]:

> " . . . children up to the age of 18 deserve protection from abuse and exploitation in situations where they might not be able to make an informed and mature choice of sexual partner because of their dependence on members of the family. Children in a family are particularly vulnerable . . . until [18] they are still legally children and dependent in many ways on adult parents or guardians."

Related offences

6.03   The familial sex offences in ss.25 and 26 have a number of elements in common with other 2003 Act offences, in particular those in ss.9 and 10 (child sex offences) and ss.16 and 17 (abuse of position of trust). When considering the use of the familial sex offences to prosecute the sexual abuse or exploitation of family members under the age of 16, these offences may also be relevant. CPS guidance is that where the child is under 13, prosecutors should if appropriate charge the relevant under 13 offence under ss.5–8 of the Act, notwithstanding that ss.25 and 26 apply.[6] This reflects the fact that ss.5–8 are specifically designed to protect children under 13 and carry a higher maximum penalty to reflect the fact that the child is particularly young and cannot legally consent to sexual activity.[7] If there may

---

[4] s.54(1) of the Criminal Law Act 1977.
[5] *Setting the Boundaries,* 2000, para.5.5.7.
[6] *Legal Guidance: Rape and Sexual Offences* available at *http://www.cps.gov.uk/legal/p_to_r/rape_and_sexual_offences/soa_2003_and_soa_1956/£a32* [Accessed April 30, 2016].
[7] See para.4.07, above.

be difficulty in proving that the child was under 13 at the material time, then the guidance states that an offence under s.25 or s.26 should be charged, so long as the other elements of the offence can be proved. Where conduct falls within s.25 or s.26 and also within the scope of another 2003 Act offence which does not require proof of a familial relationship, such as s.9 or s.10, prosecutors should charge an offence under s.25 or s.26, as the case may be, if there is sufficient evidence to prove the family relationship, rather than the other offence.

The "family" unit

The prohibited family relationships are defined by s.27 of the 2003 Act. They   **6.04** extend beyond blood relationships of parent, grandparent, brother, sister, half-brother, half-sister, aunt or uncle to include adoptive relationships and past and present step-parent and foster-parent relationships. They also include relationships in which both parties live in the same household, and those where a person is regularly involved in caring for, training, supervising, or being in sole charge of the victim.

Sex with an adult relative

The 2003 Act also contains two offences of sex with an adult relative, which   **6.05** can be committed either by doing (s.64) or by consenting to (s.65) an act of sexual penetration. In contrast to the familial sex offences created by ss.25 and 26, these offences are committed when a person aged 16 or over sexually penetrates a relative aged 18 or over, or consents to sexual penetration by such a relative. In broad terms, then, sexual activity in a familial context will be prosecuted under ss.25 and 26 where it involves the abuse or exploitation of children and under ss.64 and 65 where it involves consensual activity between a child of at least 16 and an adult.

In respect of ss.64 and 65, penetration means penetration of another   **6.06** person's vagina or anus by any part of the defendant's body or anything else, and penetration of another person's mouth with his penis. The relationships caught by these offences include a limited circle of blood relationships, i.e. parent, grandparent, child, grandchild, brother, sister, half-brother, half-sister, uncle, aunt, nephew or niece. For the first time, uncles and aunts are included within the proscribed relationships. Adoptive relationships were specifically excluded, though as we will see the adoptive parent/child relationship is now expressly included. The maximum sentence is two years' imprisonment. These offences are designed to cover and extend those areas of the former law of incest which are not within the scope of ss.25 and 26. They are likely to be used primarily where there has been a history of abuse by a close blood or adoptive relative, which continues once the child becomes an adult.

The eugenic debate and the nature of the modern family

6.07   Eugenic considerations were not the fundamental reason for the 1908 legislation.[8] Whilst research does suggest that the offspring of blood unions run a significantly higher risk of developing certain diseases than the population at large,[9] the Sexual Offences Review recognised the dangers of basing the criminal law on any form of eugenic argument.[10] Moreover, this does not appear to have driven the preparation of the 2003 Act; the desire to ensure that the law provided protection for the family and in particular for children within the family was always regarded as much more significant. The NSPCC stated in its submission to the Sexual Offences Review:

> "With the rise in divorce and the increasingly diverse nature of modern families the offence of incest which outlaws sexual intercourse within the family should be a crime whether it is committed by a natural father or by a stepfather, by a natural sibling or by a stepsibling with no common genes. It is the protection of children within the family rather than the incestuous nature of the relationship, which is important. That fact should be recognized by the criminal law. There should be an offence which punishes the illegal sexual behaviour within the family and adds an extra penalty for the abuse of trust."[11]

The Review agreed with this approach, stating that "[t]he family unit is central to a healthy society and the protection of children in the family is vital to us all".[12] It considered that the scope of the criminal law should not only cover the existing offences of incest where the victim was under 18, but should extend protection for children so as to reflect the looser structure of modern families. It felt that the term "incest" was no longer appropriate. Research revealed that incest was generally understood as an offence of blood relations, and "carries a very heavy burden, not only for the offender but also for the victim/survivor who can be seen as complicit".[13] The 2003 Act duly brought certain informal and/or temporary family arrangements within the scope of the criminal law and the opportunity was taken to drop the term "incest" in favour of the "familial child sex offences".

---

[8] V. Bailey and S. Blackburn, *The Punishment of Incest Act 1908: A Case Study in Law Creation* [1979] Crim. L.R. 708. Despite the fact that the Act prohibits incest by reference to blood relations, the authors of this article take the view that eugenic considerations were by no means crucial to its passage. It is interesting to note that the Act was opposed by the then Lord Chancellor, the Earl of Halsbury, who felt it better that such matters should not be disclosed to the court.

[9] M.S. Adams and J.V. Neel, "Children of Incest", *Pediatrics*, Vol.40, No.1, July 1967, pp.55–62.

[10] The Sexual Offences Review put forward the powerful analogy: "Marriage between unrelated persons who carry genetic markers for various hereditary diseases such as Huntington's Chorea or Sickle Cell Anaemia is not proscribed, nor should it be." (*Setting the Boundaries*, 2000, para.5.1.6).

[11] NSPCC—Submission to the Sexual Offences Review, March 1999.

[12] *Setting the Boundaries*, 2000, para.5.1.9.

[13] *Setting the Boundaries*, 2000, para.5.5.5.

The proscribed sexual activity—ECHR considerations

The offence of incest was confined to cases where there was vaginal sexual **6.08**
intercourse. There had long been pressure to extend the law to cover other
sexual acts. In the 1970s, Sandra Butler wrote that where "the father is the
aggressor . . . the earliest sexual contact can begin when the child is as young
as 5 or 6, with genital fondling, mutual masturbation and oral-genital
contact . . . Explicit genital intercourse frequently does not begin until the
girl reaches puberty."[14] The Policy Advisory Committee wrote in 1984 that
"some indecent acts other than sexual intercourse, especially if repeated over
any length of time, can perhaps be as harmful as sexual intercourse, and . . .
they represent just as much an abuse of the familial relationship as acts of
sexual intercourse."[15]

If the law is intended to prevent the abuse of trust and power within the **6.09**
family, and the damaging effects of abuse on children, there is little
justification for confining it to acts of penile penetration of the vagina. The
White Paper *Protecting the Public* (2002) concluded: "the offence should . . .
protect children up to the age of 18 from any form of activity that a person
would consider to be sexual or indecent".[16] Accordingly, the two offences of
sexual activity with a child family member cover all sexual touching. In
contrast, the two offences of sex with an adult relative are confined to acts of
sexual penetration. These offences have attracted significant criticism, encapsulated in typically pithy fashion by Professor John Spencer[17]:

> "Fuelled by a mixture of political correctitude and moral panic, Parliament
> replaced the previous offence of incest, defined as vaginal intercourse between a
> limited range of blood relatives, with a new offence of 'sex with an adult relative',
> covering any act of penetrative sex between any of an extended range of adult
> relatives, and extending to 'homosexual incest' between related adult males. Even
> a weak utilitarian argument for this new offence would be difficult to find."

In light of this criticism, one might expect a Human Rights Act challenge to **6.10**
have been made to the adult offences, though this has not yet happened in the
12 years of their existence. Any such challenge would need to address the
decision in *Stubing v Germany*,[18] in which the European Court of Human
Rights considered whether the criminalisation of consensual sexual intercourse between adult siblings is compatible with art.8 ECHR. The complainant (S) was estranged from his natural family between the ages of 3 and 24.
When reunited, S and his sister (K), of whose existence he was previously
unaware, lived together for several years and had consensual sexual intercourse, producing four children. S was convicted three times of incest under
the German Criminal Code and jailed. K, who was found to be only partially

---

[14] J. Temkin, *Rape and the Legal Process*, 2nd edn (Oxford: Oxford University Press, 2002),
p.59.
[15] Cited in Criminal Law Revision Committee, Fifteenth Report, *Sexual Offences* (1984).
[16] Home Office, *Protecting the Public*, (HMSO, 2002), p.26.
[17] *Incest and article 8 of the European Convention on Human Rights (Case Comment)* C.L.J.
2013, 72(1), 5–7.
[18] [2013] 1 F.C.R. 107.

liable for her actions on account of a serious personality disorder and mild learning disabilities, was not sentenced. S contended that his convictions had violated his art.8 right to respect for his family life by preventing him from participating in the upbringing of his children and interfering with his sex life. The Strasbourg Court dismissed the complaint, holding that although S's conviction of incest interfered with his right to respect for his private life, which included his sex life, the interference was in accordance with the law and pursued a legitimate aim within the meaning of art.8(2), namely the protection of morals and of the rights of others. As to whether the interference was necessary in a democratic society, the Court noted the broad consensus in the contracting States that sexual relationships between siblings are accepted neither by the legal order nor by society as a whole, from which it followed that the domestic authorities enjoy a wide margin of appreciation in determining how to confront sexual relationships between consenting family members. The Federal Constitutional Court, having analysed the arguments put forward in favour of and against criminal liability, and relying on an expert opinion, had concluded that the imposition of criminal liability was justified by "a combination of objectives, including the protection of the family, self-determination and public health, set against the background of a common conviction that incest should be subject to criminal liability". The Court found these aims "not unreasonable" and also relevant to S's case, and accordingly concluded that his conviction corresponded to a pressing social need such that the German courts had acted within their margin of appreciation in convicting him.

6.11   The decision in *Stubing* relates to sexual intercourse between siblings and will not necessarily be determinative of an art.8 challenge by someone charged or convicted under s.64 or s.65 of the 2003 Act for engaging in penetrative sex with a more distant adult relative. HH Peter Bowsher QC has noted that the provisions of ss.64 and 65 are much wider than those of the German law regarding consensual adult familial sexual relationships in that they apply to both homosexual and heterosexual relationships and to sexual penetration in all forms, not just vaginal penetration, with the result that the law goes beyond incest as it is usually understood.[19] He concludes that "[b]ecause the law is wider in its scope than the German law, it might well be disapproved by the ECtHR without dissenting from its decision in *Stubing*". We respectfully agree.

SEXUAL ACTIVITY WITH A CHILD FAMILY MEMBER

DEFINITION

6.12   Section 25(1) of the Sexual Offences Act 2003 provides:

"A person (A) commits an offence if—

---

[19] *Incest—Should Incest between Consenting Adults be a Crime?* [2015] Crim. L.R. 3, 208–218.

(a) he intentionally touches another person (B),

(b) the touching is sexual,

(c) the relation of A to B is within section 27,

(d) A knows or could reasonably be expected to know that his relation to B is of a description falling within that section, and

(e) either—

    (i) B is under 18 and A does not reasonably believe that B is 18 or over, or

    (ii) B is under 13."

Mode of Trial and Punishment

The mode of trial of the s.25 offence depends on the age of the defendant and the type of sexual touching involved.[20] Where the defendant (A) was 18 or over at the time of the offence and the touching involved:

- penetration of B's anus or vagina with a part of A's body or anything else
- penetration of B's mouth with A's penis
- penetration of A's anus or vagina with part of B's body (but not with anything else), or
- penetration of A's mouth with B's penis,

6.13

the offence is triable on indictment only, with a maximum sentence of 14 years' imprisonment. Where A was 18 or over at the relevant time and the touching involved anything else, i.e. *not* penetration, the offence is triable either way, with a maximum sentence on indictment of 14 years' imprisonment and on summary conviction of six months' imprisonment or a fine, or both. The effect of the decision in *Courtie*[21] is that the provision by s.25 of a higher maximum punishment for adult offenders where certain forms of penetration occur is to create separate offences, one involving those forms of penetration and the other not. The indictment should be drafted so as to make clear which offence is being charged. Where A was under 18 at the relevant time, the offence is triable either way regardless of the nature of the touching. In these circumstances the maximum sentence on indictment is five years' imprisonment and on summary conviction is six months' imprisonment or a fine, or both.

As from a day to be appointed the maximum sentence of imprisonment on summary conviction for both adult and child offenders will increase to 12 months.[22] The increase will have no application to offences committed before it takes effect.[23] Until recently, the maximum fine on summary conviction for both adult and child offenders was a fine not exceeding the statutory maximum (i.e. £5,000). The effect of s.85 of the Legal Aid, Sentencing and Punishment of Offenders Act 2012 is that, from March 12, 2015, a fine of any

6.14

---

[20] s.25(4)–(6).

[21] [1984] A.C. 463.

[22] Criminal Justice Act 2003 s.282(2), (3).

[23] Criminal Justice Act 2003 s.282(4).

amount may be imposed. An either way offence under s.25 cannot be dealt with by way of a simple caution.[24]

6.15 For the purposes of listing, cases under s.25[25] fall within Class 2B, save for complex cases involving many complainants (often under age, in care or otherwise particularly vulnerable) and/or many defendants who are alleged to have systematically groomed and abused them, often over a long period of time, which fall within Class 1C.[26] Cases in Class 1C must be referred to the Resident Judge, and by the Resident Judge to a Presiding Judge. Cases in Class 2B must be similarly referred in certain specified circumstances, including where the case is unusually grave or complex or a novel and important point of law is to be raised; where the defendant is a police officer, a member of the legal profession or a high profile figure; or where for any reason the case is likely to attract exceptional media attention.

6.16 An offence under s.25 committed by an adult is a serious specified offence for the purposes of the dangerousness provisions of the Criminal Justice Act 2003.[27] Such an offence, whenever committed, may be made the subject of an extended sentence under s.226A of that Act (extended sentence for certain violent or sexual offences).[28] Section 25 is also listed in Pt 1 of Sch.15B to the Criminal Justice Act 2003 for the purposes of s.224A of that Act (life sentence for a second listed offence).[29]

6.17 A person convicted under s.25, cautioned, found not guilty by reason of insanity or found to be under a disability and to have done the act charged, who was aged 18 or over at the time of the offence or who is sentenced to at least 12 months' imprisonment, is automatically subject to the notification requirements in the Sexual Offences Act 2003.[30]

SENTENCING

Sentencing guideline

6.18 For the Sentencing Council's guideline applicable to sex offenders aged 18 or over who are sentenced on or after April 1, 2014, see Ch.33, below. A single guideline covers the offences in ss.25 and 26 of the 2003 Act.

---

[24] Criminal Justice and Courts Act 2015 s.17(3), and the Criminal Justice and Courts Act 2015 (Simple Cautions) (Specification of Either-Way Offences) Order 2015 (SI 2015/790).

[25] And of soliciting, inciting, encouraging or assisting, attempting or conspiring to commit the offence or assisting an offender having committed the offence.

[26] *Consolidated Criminal Practice Directions*, Part XIII Listing B: CLASSIFICATION, available at *https://www.judiciary.gov.uk/wp-content/uploads/2015/09/crim-pd-2015.pdf* [Accessed April 30, 2016].

[27] Criminal Justice Act 2003 s.224 and Sch.15, Pt 2.

[28] Inserted by the Legal Aid, Sentencing and Punishment of Offenders Act 2012 s.124, brought into force on December 3, 2012, by SI 2012/2906.

[29] Inserted by the Legal Aid, Sentencing and Punishment of Offenders Act 2012 s.122, brought into force on December 3, 2012, by SI 2012/2906.

[30] s.80 and Sch.3, discussed in Ch.35, below.

Step One—Harm and culpability

The guideline requires the sentencing court to go through a series of steps in   **6.19**
order to determine the appropriate sentence. Step one involves determining
the offence category by reference to the degree of harm caused and then the
culpability level for the offence. For offences under ss.25 and 26 of the 2003
Act, the court should determine which categories of harm and culpability the
offence falls into by reference only to the tables below. As these offences
involve those who have a family relationship with the victim, the court should
assume that the greater the abuse of trust within the relationship, the more
grave the offence. The harm and culpability factors in relation to ss.25 and 26
are as follows:

Harm	
Category 1	• Penetration of vagina or anus (using body or object) • Penile penetration of mouth in either case by, or of, the victim
Category 2	• Touching of naked genitalia or naked breasts by, or of, the victim Offender acts together with others to commit the offence
Category 3	Other sexual activity

Culpability
A
Significant degree of planning
Offender acts together with others to commit the offence
Use of alcohol/drugs on victim to facilitate the offence
Grooming behaviour used against the victim
Use of threats (including blackmail)
Sexual images of victim recorded, retained, solicited or shared
Specific targeting of a particularly vulnerable child
Significant disparity in age
Commercial exploitation and/or motivation
Offence racially or religiously aggravated

| Offence motivated by, or demonstrating, hostility to the victim based on his or her sexual orientation (or presumed sexual orientation) or transgender identity (or presumed transgender identity) |
| Offence motivated by, or demonstrating, hostility to the victim based on his or her disability (or presumed disability) |
| **B** |
| Factor(s) in category A not present |

Step Two—Starting point and category range

6.20 Having determined the offence category and culpability level, the court should then use the corresponding starting point specified in the guideline in order to reach a sentence within the category range. The starting point applies to all offenders irrespective of plea or previous convictions. Once the starting point has been determined, step two allows further adjustment for aggravating or mitigating features, as set out below. A case of particular gravity, reflected by multiple features of culpability or harm, could merit upward adjustment from the starting point before further adjustment for aggravating or mitigating features. Where there is a sufficient prospect of rehabilitation, a community order with a sex offender treatment programme requirement under s.202 of the Criminal Justice Act 2003 can be a proper alternative to a short or moderate length custodial sentence. The starting points and category ranges for offences under ss.25 and 26 are as follows:

	A	*B*
Category 1	*Starting point* 6 years' custody *Category range* 4–10 years' custody	*Starting point* 3 years' 6 months' custody *Category range* 2 years' 6 months'–5 years' custody

Category 2	Starting point 4 years' custody Category range 2–6 years' custody	Starting point 18 months' custody Category range 26 weeks'– 2 years' 6 months' custody
Category 3	Starting point 1 years' custody Category range High level community order –3 years' custody	Starting point Medium level community order Category range Low level community order–High level community order

Aggravating and mitigating factors

After identifying the starting point and category range, the court should **6.21** consider whether the presence of aggravating or mitigating factors should result in an upward or downward adjustment from the starting point or the imposition of a sentence outside the category range. In particular, relevant recent convictions are likely to result in an upward adjustment. When sentencing appropriate category 3 offences, the court should also consider whether the custody threshold has been passed; if so, whether a custodial sentence is unavoidable; and if it is, whether that sentence can be suspended. The non-exhaustive list of aggravating and mitigating factors for offences under ss.25 and 26 is as follows:

Aggravating factors
Statutory aggravating factors
Previous convictions, having regard to a) the nature of the offence to which the conviction relates and its relevance to the current offence; and b) the time that has elapsed since the conviction
Offence committed whilst on bail
Other aggravating factors
Severe psychological or physical harm
Ejaculation
Pregnancy or STI as a consequence of offence

Location of offence
Timing of offence
Victim compelled to leave their home, school etc
Failure to comply with current court orders
Offence committed whilst on licence
Exploiting contact arrangements with a child to commit an offence
Presence of others, especially other children
Any steps taken to prevent the victim reporting an incident, obtaining assistance and/or from assisting or supporting the prosecution
Attempts to dispose of or conceal evidence
Failure of offender to respond to previous warnings
Commission of offence whilst under the influence of alcohol or drugs
Victim encouraged to recruit others
Period over which offence committed

Mitigating factors
No previous convictions *or* no relevant/recent convictions
Remorse
Previous good character and/or exemplary conduct*
Age and/or lack of maturity where it affects the responsibility of the offender
Mental disorder or learning disability, particularly where linked to the commission of the offence
Sexual activity was incited but no activity took place because the offender voluntarily desisted or intervened to prevent it

* Previous good character/exemplary conduct is different from having no previous convictions. The more serious the offence, the less the weight which should normally be attributed to this factor. Where previous good character/exemplary conduct has been used to facilitate the offence, this mitigation should not normally be allowed and such conduct may constitute an aggravating factor.

In the context of this offence, previous good character/exemplary conduct should not normally be given any significant weight and will not normally justify a reduction in what would otherwise be the appropriate sentence.

Steps Three to Nine

The remaining steps cover the following points. At step three the court **6.22** should consider any factors which would indicate a reduction in sentence, e.g. assistance to the prosecution. At step four it should consider any reduction for a guilty plea. At step five the court should consider dangerousness, i.e. whether it would be appropriate to award a life sentence (s.224A of the Criminal Justice Act 2003) or an extended sentence (s.226A). Step six requires the court to consider whether the total sentence is just and proportionate to the offending behaviour. At step seven it should consider whether to make an ancillary order (e.g. a compensation order, a sexual harm prevention order ("SHPO") or a restraining order). Step eight requires the court to fulfil its duty under s.174 of the Criminal Justice Act 2003 to give reasons for, and explain the effect of, the sentence. Finally, at step nine the court should consider whether to give credit for time spent on bail in accordance with s.240A of that Act.

Offenders under 18

The Sentencing Council guideline does not cater for offences committed by **6.23** offenders under the age of 18. The guideline does however provide as follows as regards s.25 offences committed by offenders under the age of 18:

> "When sentencing offenders under 18, a court must in particular:
> - follow the definitive guideline *Overarching Principles—Sentencing Youths*;
> and have regard to:
> - the principal aim of the youth justice system (to prevent offending by children and young people); and
> - the welfare of the young offender."

The Council is currently preparing a new guideline for youth sentencing, on which it published a consultation document in May 2016. Meanwhile, the guideline *Overarching Principles—Sentencing Youths* can be found on the Council's website. See further paras 31.116 and following, below.

Attorney General's Reference (No.67 of 2009)[31] preceded the Sentencing **6.24** Council guideline but remains instructive. The Court of Appeal in that case upheld as not unduly lenient a total sentence of 12 months' detention imposed on a young offender (P) following early pleas of guilty to rape and a variety of sexual acts with his younger sister. The offences were committed when the offender was aged 14–16 and his sister 11–13. There was one incident of penile penetration that was sufficient to constitute rape though

[31] [2009] EWCA Crim 2221.

the penetration was as minimal as it could have been. P also penetrated V's vagina with his finger and tongue, masturbated and ejaculated in front of her and on one occasion ejaculated directly onto her. P made frank admissions in interview and pleaded guilty at the earliest opportunity. He stated that it had started out with them innocently playing but had become sexual. P pleaded guilty on the basis that only one incident had involved minimal penile penetration, which was not complete as he withdrew; although his sister was not enthusiastic and had not instigated the incidents she did not physically resist; when he was asked to stop he did; save on one occasion he did not ejaculate on her body. A pre-sentence report stated that P was emotionally damaged, extremely vulnerable and had self-harmed since he was 13. The sentencing judge took a starting point of three years but gave credit for a number of mitigating factors including P's guilty plea and frank admissions to the police and the fact that he was still very young. P was due to be released in about one month. The Court of Appeal held that it was understandable that the judge examined the sexual activity in total and he was not required to view the rape as an offence of much greater seriousness than the other offences which involved digital penetration. There was no background of intimidation, threats, coercion, misuse of drugs or alcohol and P was not suffering from a sexually transmitted infection. However, V was an innocent girl who had not reached puberty and had been subjected to systematic and persistent abuse. Custody was inevitable and appropriate. The sentence could have been longer but there were a number of other circumstances which needed to be addressed, namely the circumstances in which the horseplay gradually became sexual activity, P's age and lack of maturity when the offending began, the fact that he brought the offending to an end of his own volition, his frank interview and plea, and his upcoming release date. In light of those circumstances, the sentence could not be interfered with.

Abuse of trust

6.25　Abuse of trust is not specified in the guideline for ss.25 and 26 either as a factor in "culpability A" or as an aggravating factor. This reflects the view of the Sentencing Council, expressed in its consultation on the draft guideline, that abuse of trust is an "inherent feature" of these offences. A similar approach was evident in the pre-guideline case of *Attorney General's Reference (No.124 of 2010)*,[32] in which the Court of Appeal said that one must be very careful before treating a s.25 offence as aggravated by abuse of trust and authority, because the offence necessarily involves a close familial relationship and therefore, normally, a breach of trust. We respectfully agree, and suggest that a s.25 offence may properly be regarded as aggravated by

---

[32] [2011] EWCA Crim 337.

abuse of trust only if there is an element of such abuse which goes clearly beyond the abuse of trust inherent in the offence.

Sentencing examples

In *Attorney General's Reference (No.95 of 2014)*,[33] the Solicitor General   **6.26**
referred to the Court of Appeal as unduly lenient a sentence of nine months' imprisonment imposed on the offender (R) following his conviction under s.25 for sexual activity with a child family member. R (44), and his daughter, J (16), had been estranged for most of J's life. J had been taken into foster care as a result of her mother drinking heavily and suffering from depression. She made contact with R through social media and visited his home. On one occasion, lying clothed in bed, they watched lesbian pornography on R's mobile telephone. R massaged J's back, buttocks and touched her breasts under her bra before apologising. He later sent J texts saying that he knew that it was wrong, but that he wanted sexual intercourse. The texts ended when J and R argued and R apologised. J reported the matter to the police and R was arrested. He claimed to have accidentally brushed J's breast whilst massaging her back, but denied massaging her buttocks or sending her text messages of a sexual nature. R was sentenced under category 3A of the guideline. The Solicitor General submitted that the sentence failed adequately to reflect the seriousness of the offence and R's culpability, given the aggravating features which included R's abuse of a position of trust (as to which see para.6.25 above), J's vulnerability, R showing J pornography, and the sexualised texts. Relying on the fact that R had touched J's naked breasts and the significant age gap between them, he argued that the case properly fell within category 2A. R contended that the offence was mitigated by good character and the brevity of the incident. The Court allowed the reference, holding that the case was squarely within category 2A. R's behaviour had been elevated to category 2 by the fleeting contact with J's naked breasts. Accordingly, the Court quashed the sentence and substituted one of two years' imprisonment.

The decision in *Attorney General's Reference (No.124 of 2010)*[34] predates   **6.27**
the new guideline but is a useful example of the approach taken by the Court of Appeal under the previous guideline, issued by the Sentencing Guidelines Council ("SGC") in 2007 to common features of offending of this sort. The offender (F) pleaded guilty to one count of sexual activity with a child family member contrary to s.25 of the 2003 Act committed against his 17-year-old daughter. He had kissed, fondled the breasts and digitally penetrated the vagina of his daughter. It was F's birthday and he and the victim had been drinking at his house. He surrendered to the police and made full admissions in interview. Nothing like this incident had occurred before. The probation

[33] Unreported, November 12, 2014.
[34] [2011] EWCA Crim 337.

report opined that F sought to suggest that the victim was complicit in the
offence, but that he did show an awareness of the impact on the victim and
a genuine willingness to try and understand his offending behaviour. F was
assessed as a high risk of re-offending but a low risk of harm to the general
public. He had two previous convictions which tended to demonstrate
problems with alcohol but no offences of a sexual nature. F was sentenced to
40 weeks' imprisonment suspended for two years with a two-year supervision
order. On a reference, it was argued on behalf of the Attorney General that
the offence was aggravated by an abuse of trust and authority and the close
familial relationship. The Court said one must be very careful in classifying
these as aggravating features, because the offence itself is one that necessarily
involves a close familial relationship and therefore, normally, a breach of
trust. However it accepted that this case involved the closest possible familial
relationship, namely father and daughter. The offence was aggravated by the
fact that F was drinking with his 17-year-old daughter who was also, to his
knowledge, drinking heavily. Further, the victim expressed unwillingness to
become involved in F's activity and his failure to heed this was also an
aggravating factor. As to mitigation, the offender made full admissions to the
police at the earliest opportunity and followed that with the earliest possible
indication of an intention to plead guilty. He had shown remorse and the
victim was only two or three days off being 18 years old. The Court said that
the relevant category in the sentencing guideline was the first, involving
penetration of the vagina with another body part, albeit not penile penetration, which had a starting point of five years and a sentencing range of
four–eight years. It said that in view of the mitigating circumstances and in
particular the fact that the victim was very nearly 18, the proper starting
point was at the lower end, namely four years. With a deduction of a third to
represent the very early plea and remorse, the sentence came down to two
years eight months. Given that F had not been sentenced to custody and had
already completed a number of the requirements under the order that was
made, the right sentence was one of two years' imprisonment.

PARTIES TO THE OFFENCE

6.28   The law of incest was confined to close blood relationships: a man was
prohibited from having intercourse with his grand-daughter, daughter, sister
(including half-sister) or mother, whilst a woman was prohibited from having
intercourse with her grandfather, father, brother (including half-brother) or
son. Incest was always viewed as a fundamental breach of trust by one family
member against another, which raised issues about the extent of "the
family". In recommending changes to the law in this area, the Sexual
Offences Review wished "to increase protection within the family, including
looser and more informal arrangements than the traditional family. That
meant that the kind of definition linked only to bloodlines . . . was no longer

tenable on its own".[35] This increased protection, reflecting the looser structure of modern families, is achieved by s.27 of the Act, which extends the family relationships caught by the criminal law to relatively distant relatives and other people in a position of trust or control in relation to the child. The prohibited relationships are wider than the prohibited degrees of marriage under the Marriage Act 1949, under which someone aged 16 or over is legally capable of marrying not only a cousin, but also most of the other people within s.27. So A, who could legally marry B, can be liable for engaging in extra-marital sexual activity with B if he or she falls within the definition in s.27. An exception for sexual activity between spouses or civil partners in contained in s.28 of the Act, discussed in para.6.51, below.

Section 27[36] defines the new "family unit" for the purposes of ss.25 and 26   **6.29**
of the Act. Section 27(1) provides:

> "The relation of one person (A) to another person (B) is within this section if—
> (a) it is within any of subsections (2) to (4), or
> (b) it would be within one of those subsections but for section 39 of the Adoption Act 1976 or section 67 of the Adoption and Children Act 2002 (status conferred by adoption)."

To fall within the section, the relationship must be within one of the three   **6.30**
categories set out in ss.27(2)–(4). As for the reference in s.27(1)(b) to s.39 of the Adoption Act 1976 and s.67 of the Adoption and Children Act 2002, those sections provide that an adopted child is the child of their adoptive and not their biological parent. The Sexual Offences Review took the view that adoptive parents undertake a lifelong duty of trust and responsibility to the children they adopt and should be treated on a par with natural parents.[37] The effect of s.27(1)(b) is that for a child who is adopted, sexual contact is prohibited with both biological and adoptive relations falling within one of the three categories.

The first category

Section 27(2) provides: **6.31**

> "The relation of A to B is within this subsection if—
> (a) one of them is the other's parent, grandparent, brother, sister, half-brother, half-sister, aunt or uncle, or
> (b) A is or has been B's foster-parent."

The first category prohibits sexual contact between a child under 18 and their   **6.32**
blood relatives, with the addition of uncles and aunts[38] and present and past

---

[35] *Setting the Boundaries*, 2000, para.5.5.11.
[36] As amended by the Criminal Justice and Immigration Act 2008 s.73 and Sch.15, para.3, with effect from July 8, 2008, so as to make s.27(2)–(4) applicable to adoptions made before December 30, 2005.
[37] *Setting the Boundaries*, 2000, para.5.6.1.
[38] By s.27(5)(a), "aunt" means the sister or half-sister of a person's parent and uncle has the corresponding meaning.

foster-parents.[39] Notably, uncles and aunts by marriage and the partners of a child's blood aunt or uncle do not fall within s.27(2), but may be caught under s.27(4) if they live in the same household. People whose relationships fall within this first category will always be each other's family members for the purposes of ss.25 and 26. In this category, the proscribed relationships continue until the child is 18, even where the relationship is not one of blood and so can cease. It follows that even where A has ceased to be a child's foster-parent, A will commit an offence by having sexual contact with the child while the child is under 18.

The second category

6.33   Section 27(3) provides:

> "The relation of A to B is within this subsection if A and B live or have lived in the same household, or A is or has been regularly involved in caring for, training, supervising or being in sole charge of B, and—
> (a) one of them is or has been the other's step-parent,
> (b) A and B are cousins,
> (c) one of them is or has been the other's stepbrother or stepsister, or
> (d) the parent or present or former foster parent of one of them is or has been the other's foster parent."

6.34   Section 27(3) catches a wider category of relationships, where there is both a "familial bond" between A and B *and* A lives or has lived in the same household as B or has or has had a role in B's care. The familial bonds covered by this section include step-parents, cousins, step-siblings and foster-siblings. References to "step" relationships in s.27 are to be read as including relationships arising through civil partnership.[40] Step-parents include a parent's partner.[41] It follows that "stepbrother" and "stepsister" includes the child of a parent's partner. By s.27(5)(d), a person is another's partner (whether they are of different sexes or the same sex) if they live together as partners in an enduring family relationship. The courts are charged with determining what makes for an enduring family relationship but it is suggested that the phrase describes two people who are in a relationship analogous to marriage or civil partnership, i.e. cohabiting couples. The length of the relationship, the common intention underlying it and/or financial interdependency will be relevant to the court's assessment. For the meaning of "enduring family relationship" as the term is used in the Protection of Children Act 1978, see paras 8.78 and following, below.

---

[39] By s.27(5)(c), as amended by the Children and Young Persons Act 2008 s.8(2) and Sch.1, para.16, a person is a child's foster-parent if: (i) he is a person with whom the child has been placed under s.22C of the Children Act 1989 in a placement falling within subs.(6)(a) or (b) of that section (placement with local authority foster parent), (ia) he is a person with whom the child has been placed under s.59(1)(a) of that Act (placement by voluntary organisation), or (ii) he fosters the child privately, within the meaning given by s.66(1)(b) of that Act.

[40] Civil Partnership Act 2004 ss.246(1), 247(1) and Sch.21, para.61 (inserted by SI 2005/3137).

[41] s.27(5)(e).

As well as having a familial bond with B, A must have, or have had, a   6.35
prominent role in B's life, either by living in the same household as B or by
being involved in caring for, training, supervising or being in sole charge of
B. In family law, "household" refers to people held together by a particular
kind of tie, even if temporarily separated.[42] This implies that there must have
been a time when the parties lived under the same roof. There is no minimum
duration of time required for this purpose. A Law Commission report on
domestic violence took the view that people share a household "if they share
domestic chores and shopping, eat meals together or share the same living
room".[43] Sharing physical living space is deemed to be an alternative to
sharing domestic chores. In *G v F*,[44] it was held that the word "household"
should be interpreted purposively to give as much protection as possible to
victims of domestic violence. It is arguable that the same purposive construction should be given to the word in the context of s.27(3).

Whether the facts of a case fall within the scope of s.27 will be a matter for   6.36
the jury. An example of its application would be where a person (A) lives or
has lived in the same house as his first cousin who is under 18. If the cousins
had never lived in the same household, A would not commit this offence by
having a sexual relationship with the cousin. As with the first category, if the
relationship ceases (for example, A ceases to be the partner of B's mother),
the offence will still be committed as long as the child is under 18. Once the
relationship is established for the purposes of s 27(3), it continues as long as
B is under 18 even if A and B ceased to live in the same household or A
ceased to care, etc. for B, however long before the alleged offence.

The third category

Section 27(4) provides: 6.37

> "The relation of A to B is within this subsection if—
>   (a) A and B live in the same household, and
>   (b) A is regularly involved in caring for, training, supervising or being in sole
>   charge of B."

The third category draws in relationships where there is no familial bond   6.38
between A and B but they live in the same household and A plays a current
role in B's care. An example would be a nanny or au pair, who lives in the
same household and is regularly involved in caring for, training, supervising
or being in sole charge of B. This category of relationship differs from the
first two in that an offence will not be committed if A has sexual contact with
B after the relationship has ceased, even where the child is still under 18. So
if, for example, the nanny were to leave her job and move out of the house

---

[42] *Santos v Santos* [1972] Fam. 247 at 262, applied in *Gully v Dix* [2004] 1 W.L.R. 1399.
[43] *Domestic Violence and the Family Home*, Law Com. (1992), para.3.21.
[44] [2000] Fam. 186.

and/or to cease having any responsibility for the child, then the relationship would no longer be relevant for the purposes of ss.25 or 26.

6.39   The scope of this category is potentially very wide. It has been argued that it may encompass the relationship between a child and their sports coach, on the basis that close-knit relationships of this sort resemble those within the family unit.[45] In light of the discussion of the term "household" in para.6.35, it may be argued that a purposive construction should be given to the term in s.27(4) to provide as much protection as possible to children. On that basis a coach who is regularly involved in training the child may, depending on the circumstances, be part of and live in the same household for the purposes of the s.25 offence.

6.40   The offences in ss.25 and 26 are gender neutral and so apply equally if A is a man or a woman. They cover the sexual touching of a person of the same sex, thereby catching, for example, sexual behaviour between an uncle and his nephew or a foster-mother and foster-daughter.

The principle in *Tyrrell*

6.41   Neither s.25 nor s.26 requires A to have reached any particular age and accordingly the offences may in principle be committed by anyone who has reached the age of criminal responsibility. If a child victim of the offence has reached that age and encourages the commission of the offence, are they liable to conviction as an accessory? This turns on the application of the principle in *Tyrrell*,[46] where it was held that a young girl could not be convicted as accessory to an offence of having unlawful carnal knowledge with a girl under 16 committed against herself, as the offence was created to protect girls against men and there was no indication in the statute of an intention to criminalise the girls themselves. The offences in s.25 were clearly created to protect children under 18 from sexual exploitation in a family setting, and there is nothing in the Act that indicates an intention to criminalise the children concerned. This strongly suggests that the principle in *Tyrrell* should apply in relation to s.25.

6.42   The point has been settled for all practical purposes by the decision in *Attorney General's Reference (No.53 of 2013) (Neil Wilson)*,[47] in which the offender pleaded guilty to one offence under s.9 of the 2003 Act (sexual activity with a child) committed against a girl aged 13 and was sentenced to eight months' imprisonment. The girl was sexually experienced and prosecuting counsel described her in the course of the sentencing hearing as

---

[45] See *Incest in the "family" of sport*, N.L.J. February 16, 2004, 179.

[46] [1894] 1 Q.B. 710; and see *DPP v Whitehouse* [1977] Q.B. 868. In *Gnango* [2011] UKSC 59, a majority of the Supreme Court said that *Tyrrell* is an illustration of a general rule, identified by Professor Glanville Williams in his article *Victims and other exempt parties in crime* (1990) 10 Legal Studies at p.245, that where legislation creates an offence that is intended to protect a class of persons, a member of that class cannot be convicted as an accessory to such an offence committed in respect of him.

[47] [2013] EWCA Crim 2544.

"predatory", a term picked up by the judge in his sentencing remarks. On a reference by the Attorney General, the Court of Appeal held that the sentence was plainly unduly lenient. In doing so, it accepted the Attorney General's submission that the fact that the victim had initiated what had happened was an aggravating rather than a mitigating factor. Lord Thomas CJ said[48]:

> "It has been clear since at least the Offences Against the Person Act 1861, and subsequent nineteenth century legislation, that the purpose of Parliament in passing legislation to make it a crime punishable with imprisonment to have sexual relations with those under 16 was to protect those under 16. Indeed the Criminal Law Amendments [*sic*] Act 1885 makes it expressly clear that that was the purpose of the legislation. That can be seen from the preamble to the Act and was made clear by this court in *R. v Tyrrell* [1894] 1 QB 710.
>
> That long-standing principle is well-known. The reduction of punishment on the basis that the person who needed protection encouraged the commission of an offence is therefore simply wrong. We agree with the submission of the Attorney General that an underage person who encourages sexual relations with her needs more protection, not less. Accepting that as the basis for sentencing for the reasons we have explained, the fact that the offender took advantage of what he asserted the victim did aggravated the offence."

Although his Lordship did not engage in elaborate legal analysis, his reference to *Tyrrell* clearly indicates that he considered the offence in s.9, and by inference the other offences in the 2003 Act designed to protect children, to fall within the scope of the principle in that case, such that there can be no question of the child victim of such an offence being prosecuted for any part she may have played in encouraging it.

JURISDICTION

By virtue of s.72 of and Sch.2 to the Sexual Offences Act 2003, as amended,[49]   **6.43** it is an offence under s.25 for a UK national to do an act in a country outside the UK which would constitute a s.25 offence if done in England and Wales. The amendments, made in 2008, expanded the scope of s.72 in two respects. First, they removed the limitation on s.72 as enacted that it applied only to offences committed against victims aged under 16 (the relevant age is now 18). Secondly, they abolished, in respect of UK nationals, the "double criminality" requirement that the act must have been an offence in the country in which it was done. This requirement is, however, retained in respect of the prosecution of UK residents and those who become UK residents or nationals after the doing of the relevant act. For the purposes of s.72 a "country" includes a territory and a "United Kingdom national" means a British citizen, a British overseas territories citizen, a British National (Overseas), a British Overseas citizen, a person who under the British Nationality Act 1981 is a British subject, or a British protected person

---

[48] At [19]–[20].
[49] By the Criminal Justice and Immigration Act 2008 s.72, with effect from July 14, 2008.

within the meaning of that Act.[50] An act is taken to be an offence in the country in which it was done unless the defendant serves a notice putting the prosecution to proof on the point.[51]

"TOUCHES"

6.44   For the meaning of "touches", see paras 2.63 and following, above.

"SEXUAL"

6.45   For the meaning of "sexual", see paras 2.66 and following, above.

CONSENT

6.46   Children cannot consent to sexual activity with a family member for the purposes of ss.25 and 26. It follows that on a prosecution under those sections the issue of consent is irrelevant. As to the relevance of consent to sentence, see paras 3.50 and following, above. Whilst the age of consent is 16, the offences of sexual activity with a child family member protect children up to the age of 18. The rationale offered for this by the Sexual Offences Review was that "children up to the age of 18 deserve protection from abuse and exploitation in situations where they might not be able to make an informed and mature choice of sexual partner because of their dependence on members of the family".[52] These abusive relationships often reflect a long-term imbalance of power in the family, and a child who is brought up to think such behaviour is normal may not realise the true nature of the activity for many years. Such reactions are often thought to be the result of under-age grooming or sex, and as such a 16 or 17-year-old, who has been dominated by an adult in the family, cannot properly consent. Those under 18 are legally children and in many ways dependant on adult parents or guardians and "the responsibility and the criminal culpability always must lie with the adult".[53]

MENTAL ELEMENT

6.47   A's touching of B must be intentional. For the meaning of "intention" and the question whether A must intend the touching to be sexual, see paras 2.78 and following, above. Recklessness will not suffice.[54]

---

[50] s.72(9).
[51] s.72(6)–(8).
[52] *Setting the Boundaries*, 2000, para.5.5.7.
[53] *Setting the Boundaries*, 2000, para.5.5.7.
[54] *Heard* [2007] EWCA Crim 125, at [22].

Section 25(1)(d) requires the prosecution to prove that A knew or could   **6.48**
reasonably have been expected to know that his relation to B was of a
description falling within one of the s.27 categories. If it is established that A's
relation to B was of such a description, it is presumed that A knew or could
reasonably have been expected to know that B was his family member within
the meaning of s.27 unless sufficient evidence is adduced to put the point in
issue. This is the effect of 25(3), which provides:

> "Where in proceedings for an offence under this section it is proved that the
> relation of the defendant to the other person was of a description falling within
> section 27, it is to be taken that the defendant knew or could reasonably have
> been expected to know that his relation to the other person was of that
> description unless sufficient evidence is adduced to raise an issue as to whether
> he knew or could reasonably have been expected to know that it was."

This is accordingly an evidential rather than a legal presumption. The
presumption may be rebutted by reasonable inferences from the prosecution
evidence or by evidence given by the defendant himself. If the evidence is
merely speculative or fanciful, the judge will direct the jury in accordance
with s.25(3).[55]

By s.25(1)(e), the prosecution must prove either that B was under 18 and   **6.49**
A did not reasonably believe that B was 18 or over, or that B was under 13.
If B was under 13, it is immaterial whether the defendant knew or believed
that to be the case as the offence is one of strict liability as to age. If it is
proved that B was aged between 13 and 17, it is presumed that the defendant
believed that to be the case. The presumption can be rebutted if the
defendant adduces sufficient evidence to raise an issue as to whether he
reasonably believed B to be 18 or over.[56] This is the effect of s.25(2), which
provides:

> "Where in proceedings for an offence under this section it is proved that the other
> person was under 18, the defendant is to be taken not to have reasonably believed
> that the person was 18 or over unless sufficient evidence is adduced to raise an
> issue as to whether he reasonably believed it."

Again, the burden on A is evidential.

Intoxication

As to whether A is liable to conviction if he touches B whilst he (A) is in a   **6.50**
state of intoxication due to drink or drugs, see the discussion of *Heard*[57] in
paras 2.81 and following, above. In the light of that discussion, voluntary
intoxication through drink or drugs will provide no defence to a charge
under s.25.

---

[55] cf. *Gavin White* [2010] EWCA Crim 1929.
[56] s.25(2).
[57] [2007] EWCA Crim 125.

Exception for Spouses and Civil Partners

6.51 The offences under s.25 and s.26 are not committed if A and B were lawfully married or civil partners at the time the sexual touching took place, and B was 16 or over at the time. This is the effect of s.28,[58] which provides:

> "(1) Conduct by a person (A) which would otherwise be an offence under section 25 or 26 against another person (B) is not an offence under that section if at the time—
>
>   (a) B is 16 or over, and
>   (b) A and B are lawfully married or civil partners of each other.
>
> (2) In proceedings for such an offence it is for the defendant to prove that A and B were at the time lawfully married or civil partners of each other."

The legality of a marriage or civil partnership will depend upon the domicile of the parties at the time of the ceremony. Accordingly, this exception is most likely to be relevant where the parties have a foreign domicile and became lawful spouses or civil partners there when one of them was under 16. By virtue of s.28(2) there is a legal burden on the defendant to prove on a balance of probabilities that a lawful marriage was in existence at the time of the alleged offence.

Exception for Pre-Existing Sexual Relationships

6.52 Section 29[59] creates an exception from the offences in s.25 and s.26 if the defendant can establish that the sexual relationship immediately pre-dated the coming into existence of the family relationship. It provides:

> "(1) Conduct by a person (A) which would otherwise be an offence under section 25 or 26 against another person (B) is not an offence under that section if—
>
>   (a) the relation of A to B is not within subsection (2) of section 27,
>   (b) it would not be within that subsection if section 39 of the Adoption Act 1976 or section 67 of the Adoption and Children Act 2002 did not apply, and
>   (c) immediately before the relation of A to B first became such as to fall within section 27, a sexual relationship existed between A and B.
>
> (2) Subsection (1) does not apply if at the time referred to in subsection (1)(c) sexual intercourse between A and B would have been unlawful.
>
> (3) In proceedings for an offence under section 25 or 26 it is for the defendant to prove the matters mentioned in subsection (1)(a) to (c)."

A lapsed sexual relationship will not be sufficient for these purposes. Since the sexual relationship must be lawful, the child (B) must have been over 16 at the relevant time; or, if B was aged 13, 14 or 15, A must have reasonably believed B to be 16 or over. The Explanatory Notes to the Act give the following example: two divorced people meet because their respective 16 and

---

[58] As amended by the Civil Partnership Act 2004 s.261(1) and Sch.27, para.174(2), (3).
[59] As amended by the Criminal Justice and Immigration Act 2008 s.73 and Sch.15, para.4, with effect from July 8, 2008, so as to make s.29 applicable to adoptions made before December 30, 2005.

17-year old children are engaged in a sexual relationship and the parents decide to marry; if all four people move into the same household, the children would have a defence to a charge under s.25 or s.26 as their sexual relationship would have immediately predated the family relationship.[60] By virtue of s.29(3), there is a legal burden on the defendant to prove on a balance of possibilities that the exception applies.

The effect of s.29(1)(a) and (b) is that the exception can apply only where the   6.53
relationship between A and B is not considered to be permanent: it is, therefore, not available where A is the close blood relative, foster-parent (past or current)[61] or adoptive relative of B.

Inciting a Child Family Member to Engage in Sexual Activity

Definition

Section 26(1) of the Sexual Offences Act 2003 provides: 6.54

"A person (A) commits an offence if—
   (a) he intentionally incites another person (B) to touch, or allow himself to be touched by, A,
   (b) the touching is sexual,
   (c) the relation of A to B is within section 27,
   (d) A knows or could reasonably be expected to know that his relation to B is of a description falling within that section, and
   (e) either—
      (i) B is under 18 and A does not reasonably believe that B is 18 or over, or
      (ii) B is under 13."

A must incite B to touch A or allow himself to be touched by A. The offence   6.55
is narrower than the offences of causing or inciting sexual activity in ss.8, 10 and 17 of the Act, which cover the incitement of sexual activity with a third party. It is still an offence if the incitement does not succeed. If it does, the appropriate charge will be under s.25.

Mode of Trial and Punishment

Mode of trial and maximum sentences are the same for offences under s.26   6.56
as for those under s.25.[62] As with s.25, where the defendant (A) was 18 or over at the time of the offence and he incited or allowed touching that involved:

- penetration of B's anus or vagina with a part of A's body or anything else
- penetration of B's mouth with A's penis

[60] para.60.
[61] Relationships falling within s.27(2) of the Act.
[62] s.26(4)–(6).

- penetration of A's anus or vagina with part of B's body (but not with anything else), or
- penetration of A's mouth with B's penis,

the offence is triable on indictment only with a maximum sentence of 14 years' imprisonment. Where A was 18 or over at the relevant time and the touching took another form, the offence is triable either way, with a maximum sentence on indictment of 14 years' imprisonment and on summary conviction of six months' imprisonment or a fine, or both. The effect of the decision in *Courtie*[63] is that the provision by s.26 of a higher maximum punishment for adult offenders where certain forms of penetration occur is to create separate offences, one involving those forms of penetration and the other not. The indictment should be drafted so as to make clear which offence is being charged. Where A was under 18 at the relevant time, the offence is triable either way regardless of the nature of the touching. In these circumstances the maximum sentence on indictment is five years' imprisonment and on summary conviction is six months' imprisonment or a fine, or both.

6.57   As from a day to be appointed the maximum sentence of imprisonment on summary conviction for both adult and child offenders will increase to 12 months.[64] The increase will have no application to offences committed before it takes effect.[65] Until recently, the maximum fine on summary conviction for both adult and child offenders was a fine not exceeding the statutory maximum (i.e. £5,000). The effect of s.85 of the Legal Aid, Sentencing and Punishment of Offenders Act 2012 is that, from March 12, 2015, a fine of any amount may be imposed. An either way offence under s.26 cannot be dealt with by way of a simple caution.[66]

6.58   For the purposes of listing, cases under s.26[67] fall within Class 2B, save for complex cases involving many complainants (often under age, in care or otherwise particularly vulnerable) and/or many defendants who are alleged to have systematically groomed and abused them, often over a long period of time, which fall within Class 1C.[68] Cases in Class 1C must be referred to the Resident Judge, and by the Resident Judge to a Presiding Judge. Cases in Class 2B must be similarly referred in certain specified circumstances, including where the case is unusually grave or complex or a novel and important point of law is to be raised; where the defendant is a police officer, a member of the legal profession or a high profile figure; or where for any reason the case is likely to attract exceptional media attention.

---

[63] [1984] A.C. 463.
[64] Criminal Justice Act 2003 s.282(2), (3).
[65] Criminal Justice Act 2003 s.282(4).
[66] Criminal Justice and Courts Act 2015 s.17(3), and the Criminal Justice and Courts Act 2015 (Simple Cautions) (Specification of Either-Way Offences) Order 2015 (SI 2015/790).
[67] And of soliciting, inciting, encouraging or assisting, attempting or conspiring to commit the offence or assisting an offender having committed the offence.
[68] *Consolidated Criminal Practice Directions*, Part XIII Listing B: CLASSIFICATION, available at *https://www.judiciary.gov.uk/wp-content/uploads/2015/09/crim-pd-2015*.pdf [Accessed April 30, 2016].

An offence under s.26 committed by an adult is a serious specified offence   **6.59**
for the purposes of the dangerousness provisions of the Criminal Justice Act
2003.[69] Such an offence, whenever committed, may be made the subject of an
extended sentence under s.226A of that Act (extended sentence for certain
violent or sexual offences).[70] Section 26 is also listed in Pt 1 of Sch.15B to the
Criminal Justice Act 2003 for the purposes of s.224A of that Act (life
sentence for a second listed offence).[71]

A person convicted under s.26, cautioned, found not guilty by reason of   **6.60**
insanity or found to be under a disability and to have done the act charged,
who was aged 18 or over at the time of the offence or who is sentenced to at
least 12 months' imprisonment, is automatically subject to the notification
requirements in the Sexual Offences Act 2003.[72]

SENTENCING

For the Sentencing Council's guideline applicable to sex offenders aged 18 or   **6.61**
over who are sentenced on or after April 1, 2014, see Ch.33, below. A single
guideline covers the offences in ss.25 and 26 of the 2003 Act and is discussed
at paras 6.18 and following, above.

PARTIES TO THE OFFENCE

For the family relationships and other considerations which are relevant for   **6.62**
the purposes of s.26, see paras 6.28 and following, above. The offence
prohibits members of a child's family unit from encouraging the child to
engage in or perform sexual acts with them. It encompasses an inchoate
offence because it renders unlawful the intentional incitement to commit an
act, regardless of whether the act is ever performed. An example given in the
Explanatory Notes to the Act is where A encourages B to masturbate A, but
someone enters the room and so the act never takes place.[73] As the s.26
offence is committed whether or not the sexual touching takes place, in the
example given the offence is complete.

JURISDICTION

By virtue of s.72 of and Sch.2 to the Sexual Offences Act 2003, as   **6.63**
amended,[74] it is an offence under s.26 for a UK national to do an act in a

---

[69] Criminal Justice Act 2003 s.224 and Sch.15, Pt 2.
[70] Inserted by the Legal Aid, Sentencing and Punishment of Offenders Act 2012 s.124,
brought into force on December 3, 2012, by SI 2012/2906.
[71] Inserted by the Legal Aid, Sentencing and Punishment of Offenders Act 2012 s.122,
brought into force on December 3, 2012, by SI 2012/2906.
[72] s.80 and Sch.3, discussed in Ch.35, below.
[73] para.54.
[74] By the Criminal Justice and Immigration Act 2008 s.72, which came into force on July 14,
2008.

country outside the UK which would constitute a s.26 offence if done in England and Wales. See further para.6.43, above.

"INCITES"

6.64 For the meaning of "incites", see paras 3.158 and following, above.

"TOUCH"

6.65 For the meaning of "touches", see paras 2.63 and following, above.

"SEXUAL"

6.66 For the meaning of "sexual", see paras 2.66 and following, above.

CONSENT

6.67 As with s.25, it is irrelevant whether the child consents to the incitement or the activity being incited: see para.6.46, above.

MENTAL ELEMENT

6.68 In respect of the requirement on the prosecution to prove absence of a reasonable belief on the part of the defendant that B was 18 or over, and the defendant's knowledge, etc. that B was a family member, the same considerations apply as to s.25: see paras 6.47 and following, above.

Intoxication

6.69 As to whether A is liable to conviction if he incites B or allows B to touch him whilst he (A) is in a state of intoxication due to drink or drugs, see the discussion of *Heard*[75] in paras 2.81 and following, above. In the light of that discussion, voluntary intoxication through drink or drugs will provide no defence to a charge under s.26.

EXCEPTION FOR SPOUSES AND CIVIL PARTNERS

6.70 Section 28 creates an exception where A and B were lawfully married or civil partners at the relevant time: see para.6.51, above.

---

[75] [2007] EWCA Crim 125.

EXCEPTION FOR PRE-EXISTING SEXUAL RELATIONSHIPS

Section 29 creates an exception from the offence where A and B had a sexual   6.71
relationship which immediately pre-dated their family relationship: see paras
6.52 and following, above.

SEX WITH AN ADULT RELATIVE: PENETRATION

DEFINITION

Section 64(1) of the Sexual Offences Act 2003[76] provides: 6.72

"A person aged 16 or over (A) (subject to subsection (3A)) commits an offence
if—
   (a) he intentionally penetrates another person's vagina or anus with a part of
       his body or anything else, or penetrates another person's mouth with his
       penis,
   (b) the penetration is sexual,
   (c) the other person (B) is aged 18 or over,
   (d) A is related to B in a way mentioned in subsection (2), and
   (e) A knows, or could reasonably be expected to know that he is related to B
       in that way."

MODE OF TRIAL AND PUNISHMENT

An offence under s.64 is triable either way. The maximum sentence on   6.73
conviction on indictment is two years' imprisonment and on summary
conviction is six months' imprisonment or a fine, or both.[77] As from a day to
be appointed the maximum sentence of imprisonment on summary conviction will increase to 12 months.[78] The increase will have no application to
offences committed before it takes effect.[79] Until recently, the maximum fine
on summary conviction was a fine not exceeding the statutory maximum (i.e.
£5,000). The effect of s.85 of the Legal Aid, Sentencing and Punishment of
Offenders Act 2012 is that, from March 12, 2015, a fine of any amount may
be imposed.

For the purposes of listing, cases under s.64[80] fall within Class 2B.[81] In   6.74
certain specified circumstances cases in Class 2B must be referred to the
Resident Judge, and by the Resident Judge to a Presiding Judge, including
where the case is unusually grave or complex or a novel and important point

[76] As amended by the Criminal Justice and Immigration Act 2008 s.73 and Sch.15, para.5(2),
with effect from July 8, 2008.
[77] s.64(5).
[78] Criminal Justice Act 2003 s.282(2), (3).
[79] Criminal Justice Act 2003 s.282(4).
[80] And of soliciting, inciting, encouraging or assisting, attempting or conspiring to commit the
offence or assisting an offender having committed the offence.
[81] *Consolidated Criminal Practice Directions*, Part XIII Listing B: CLASSIFICATION,
available at *https://www.judiciary.gov.uk/wp-content/uploads/2015/09/crim-pd-2015.pdf* [Accessed
April 30, 2016].

of law is to be raised; where the defendant is a police officer, a member of the legal profession or a high profile figure; or where for any reason the case is likely to attract exceptional media attention.

6.75   An offence under s.64, whenever committed, may be made the subject of an extended sentence under s.226A of the Criminal Justice Act 2003 (extended sentence for certain violent or sexual offences).[82]

6.76   A person convicted under s.64, cautioned, found not guilty by reason of insanity or found to be under a disability and to have done the act charged is automatically subject to the notification requirements in the Sexual Offences Act 2003[83] if (a) where they were under 18 at the time of the offence, they are sentenced to a term of at least 12 months' imprisonment, or (b) in any other case, they are, in respect of the offence, sentenced to a term of imprisonment or detained in a hospital.

SENTENCING

Sentencing guideline

6.77   For the Sentencing Council's guideline applicable to sex offenders aged 18 or over who are sentenced on or after April 1, 2014, see Ch.33, below. A single guideline covers the offences in ss.64 and 65 of the 2003 Act.

Step One—Harm and culpability

6.78   The guideline requires the sentencing court to go through a series of steps in order to determine the appropriate sentence. Step one involves determining the offence category by reference to the degree of harm caused and then the culpability level for the offence. For offences under ss.64 and 65 of the 2003 Act, the court should determine the offence category using the tables below, which turn upon whether the harm caused or intended by the offence or the culpability of the offender, or both, are raised. Where an offence does not fall squarely into a category, individual factors may require a degree of weighting before making an overall assessment and determining the appropriate offence category. The categories and harm and culpability factors are as follows:

Harm	
Category 1	Raised harm **and** raised culpability
Category 2	Raised harm **or** raised culpability
Category 3	Sex with an adult relative **without** raised harm or culpability factors present

---

[82] Inserted by the Legal Aid, Sentencing and Punishment of Offenders Act 2012 s.124, brought into force on December 3, 2012, by SI 2012/2906.
[83] s.80 and Sch.3, discussed in Ch.35, below.

530

Factors indicating raised harm	*Factors indicating raised culpability*
Victim is particularly vulnerable due to personal circumstances Child conceived	Grooming behaviour used against victim Use of threats (including blackmail)

Step Two—Starting point and category range

Having determined the offence category and culpability level, the court **6.79** should then use the corresponding starting point specified in the guideline in order to reach a sentence within the category range. The starting point applies to all offenders irrespective of plea or previous convictions. Once the starting point has been determined, step two allows further adjustment for aggravating or mitigating features, as set out below. A case of particular gravity, reflected by multiple features of culpability or harm, could merit upward adjustment from the starting point before further adjustment for aggravating or mitigating features. Where there is a sufficient prospect of rehabilitation, a community order with a sex offender treatment programme requirement under s.202 of the Criminal Justice Act 2003 can be a proper alternative to a short or moderate length custodial sentence. The starting points and category ranges for offences under ss.64 and 65 are as follows:

Category 1	*Starting point* 1 years' custody *Category range* 26 weeks'–2 years' custody
Category 2	*Starting point* High level community order *Category range* Medium level community order–1 years' custody
Category 3	*Starting point* Medium level community order *Category range* Band A fine– High level community order

Aggravating and mitigating factors

6.80   After identifying the starting point and category range, the court should consider whether the presence of aggravating or mitigating factors should result in an upward or downward adjustment from the starting point or the imposition of a sentence outside the category range. In particular, relevant recent convictions are likely to result in an upward adjustment. When sentencing appropriate category 2 offences, the court should also consider whether the custody threshold has been passed; if so, whether a custodial sentence is unavoidable; and if it is, whether that sentence can be suspended. When sentencing category 3 offences, the court should consider whether the community order threshold has been passed. The non-exhaustive list of aggravating and mitigating factors for offences under ss.64 and 65 is as follows:

Aggravating factors
Statutory aggravating factors
<ul><li>Previous convictions, having regard to a) the nature of the offence to which the conviction relates and its relevance to the current offence; and b) the time that has elapsed since the conviction</li><li>Offence committed whilst on bail</li></ul>
Other aggravating factors
<ul><li>Failure to comply with current court orders</li><li>Offence committed whilst on licence</li><li>Failure of offender to respond to previous warnings</li><li>Any steps taken to prevent the victim reporting an incident, obtaining assistance and/or from assisting or supporting the prosecution</li><li>Attempts to dispose of or conceal evidence</li></ul>

Mitigating factors
<ul><li>No previous convictions **or** no relevant/recent convictions</li><li>Remorse</li><li>Previous good character and/or exemplary conduct*</li><li>Age and/or lack of maturity where it affects the responsibility of the offender</li><li>Mental disorder or learning disability, particularly where linked to the commission of the offence</li><li>Demonstration of steps taken to address offending behaviour</li></ul>

* Previous good character/exemplary conduct is different from having no previous convictions. The more serious the offence, the less the weight which should normally be attributed to this factor. Where previous good character/exemplary conduct has been used to facilitate the offence, this mitigation should not normally be allowed and such conduct may constitute an aggravating factor.

Steps Three to Nine

The remaining steps cover the following points. At step three the court   **6.81** should consider any factors which would indicate a reduction in sentence, e.g. assistance to the prosecution. At step four it should consider any reduction for a guilty plea. At step five the court should consider dangerousness, i.e. whether it would be appropriate to award an extended sentence (s.226A of the Criminal Justice Act 2003). Step six requires the court to consider whether the total sentence is just and proportionate to the offending behaviour. At step seven it should consider whether to make an ancillary order (e.g. a compensation order, a SHPO or a restraining order). Step eight requires the court to fulfil its duty under s.174 of the Criminal Justice Act 2003 to give reasons for, and explain the effect of, the sentence. Finally, at step nine the court should consider whether to give credit for time spent on bail in accordance with s.240A of that Act.

Sentencing example

The decision in *R. v B*[84] predates the Sentencing Council guideline but is a   **6.82** useful example of the approach taken to a particular factual scenario by the Court of Appeal under the previous guideline, issued by the Sentencing Guidelines Council in 2007. In that case the appellant (B), aged 72, pleaded guilty to six counts of indecent assault, two counts of sexual assault and four counts of penetrative sex with an adult relative. He appealed against his sentence of imprisonment for public protection with a minimum term of four years together with a concurrent determinate sentence of five years' imprisonment. The offences had been committed against his granddaughter (K); they began when she was 10 and ended when she was a young adult. They progressed from touching K's chest area to touching all parts of her body, including the vagina. B also inserted his finger into her vagina and there were four acts of oral sex. In imposing a sentence of imprisonment for public protection, the judge had regard to the pre-sentence report which stated that B showed "a distorted level of internal controls and moral understanding of appropriate behaviour" and that he posed a high risk of serious harm. The Court of Appeal allowed an appeal against sentence. While the judge had approached a difficult sentencing exercise with care, the draconian sanction of imprisonment for public protection was not necessary and appropriate

---

[84] [2012] EWCA Crim 328.

protection could be afforded by the imposition of an extended sentence, with a custodial term of eight years and an extended period of two years.

PARTIES TO THE OFFENCE

6.83   Sections 64 and 65 prohibit penetrative acts between family members, regardless of the gender or sexual orientation of the parties. The defendant (Λ) must be 16 or over and the victim (B) must be 18 or over. It follows that the offence may be committed where the defendant is a child and the victim an adult. The Home Office guidance on the Act states that there will be a presumption that criminal responsibility rests with the person who was adult at onset and that no criminal responsibility should attach to the younger party. However, this may not always be the case, as these offences have been specifically drafted to apply to defendants aged 16 or over to cover the kind of situation where, for example, a dominant brother aged 17 incites his submissive sister aged 18 into a sexual relationship, having groomed her for this purpose and with the expectation she will be held responsible because she is an adult.[85] The offence to be charged will depend on whether the abusive party was the penetrator or the penetrated. The fact that the other party may have committed an offence by being penetrated or by penetrating, as the case may be, may discourage her or him from coming forward to make a complaint.

6.84   Under s.64, A aged 16 or over will commit the offence if B, the victim, is 18 or over at the relevant time. If B is 16 or 17, A should be charged instead under ss.25 or 26 (if applicable). But in those circumstances, if A is 18 or over, B may himself be charged under s.65 for consenting to the penetration.

Adult relative

6.85   Section 64 covers the case where a person penetrates an adult relative. The prohibited relationships between the defendant and his victim are set out at s.64(2) and are: parent, grandparent, child, grandchild, brother, sister, half-brother, half-sister, uncle, aunt, nephew or niece.

6.86   The s.64 offence resembles the old law of incest in that it encompasses close blood relationships, but the new offence is broader as it includes blood uncles and aunts (but not their spouses or partners) and also adoptive parents. Section 64(3) and (3A) provide[86]:

---

[85] H.O. Circular 21/2004, *Guidance on Part 1 of the Sexual Offences Act 2003*, para.290. Where there is sexual penetration by a 17-year-old brother of his 18-year-old sister, the 17-year-old could be prosecuted under s.64 (sex with an adult relative), whilst the 18-year-old could be prosecuted under s.25 (sexual activity with a child family member). She could not be prosecuted under s.65 (sex with adult relative: consenting to penetration) as her brother was not an adult at the time.

[86] As amended by the Criminal Justice and Immigration Act 2008 s.73 and Sch.15, para.5(3), with effect from July 8, 2008.

"(3) In subsection (2)—
  (za) 'parent' includes an adoptive parent;
  (zb) 'child' includes an adopted person within the meaning of Chapter 4 of
      Part 1 of the Adoption and Children Act 2002;
  (a) 'uncle' means brother of a person's parent, and 'aunt' has a corresponding
      meaning;
  (b) 'nephew' means the child of a person's brother or sister, and 'niece' has a
      corresponding meaning.
(3A) Where subsection (1) applies in a case where A is related to B as B's child
by virtue of subsection (3)(zb), A does not commit an offence under this section
unless A is 18 or over."

When the Sexual Offences Bill was before Parliament there was considerable   **6.87**
debate as to whether uncles and aunts should be included within the
proscribed relationships. The Sexual Offences Review had stated that:

> "blood relatives are in a particular position of trust to their nieces and nephews;
> whatever the children may or may not know, the adults will understand the
> kinship and that any sexual relationship would be wrong. Accordingly . . . any
> new offence should explicitly mention aunts and uncles who are blood rela-
> tives".[87]

Research was cited suggesting that abuse by uncles was the most prevalent
form of abuse by relatives.[88] Nevertheless, the Bill as introduced did not
include uncles and aunts. An amendment to include them was defeated at
Third Reading in the Lords. In her argument resisting the amendment,
Baroness Scotland of Asthal stated: "we are content that the primary
motivation for the 'sex with an adult relative' offences should be concerned
with morality and eugenics . . . aunts and uncles have never been included in
the incest offences, and we can see no reason to make sexual activity between
such relatives an offence now".[89] However, after a process of further Home
Office consultation and Parliamentary discussion, uncles and aunts were
included within the proscribed relationship.

As for adoptive relatives, the 2003 Act originally excluded them from the   **6.88**
offences under ss.64 and 65. This was achieved by an amendment made to the
Adoption and Children Act 2002, to the effect that the provision in that Act
making an adopted child a child of the adoptive parents did not apply in
relation to these offences.[90] So, for example, it was not an offence under s.64
or s.65 for an adoptive brother and sister aged over 18 to have sexual
intercourse with each other. However, the effect of the amendments made to
those sections by the Criminal Justice and Immigration Act 2008, set out
above, is that the offences are committed where an adoptive parent has

---

[87] *Setting the Boundaries*, 2000, para.5.5.13.
[88] The Russell survey of 930 randomly selected adult female residents of San Francisco. See
Setting the Boundaries, 2000, para.5.5.12, citing D.J. West, *Sexual Victimisation* (1985) and
Professor Jennifer Temkin, *Do we need the crime of incest?* C.L.P. 1991 Vol.44.
[89] *Hansard*, HL Vol.649, col.742 (June 17, 2003).
[90] See the 2003 Act s.139 and Sch.6, para.47, which makes a consequential amendment to the
Adoption and Children Act 2002, to the effect that the provision in the 2002 Act that makes an
adoptive child a child of the adoptive parents does not apply in relation to these offences. See
also Explanatory Notes to the Act, para.124.

consensual sex with their adopted child aged 18 or over. But in such cases the adopted person does not commit the offence unless he or she is aged 18 or over. This limitation on criminal liability reflects the possibility that adopted children under 18 may have been subject to grooming by the adoptive parent. Finally, the 2008 Act also amends s.47(1) of the Adoption Act 1976, so that s.39 of that Act (status conferred by adoption) does not have effect for the purposes of ss.64 and 65 of the 2003 Act. The result is to make clear that adoptions preceding December 30, 2005, are treated in the same way for the purposes of ss.64 and 65 as subsequent adoptions.

"PENETRATES ANOTHER PERSON'S VAGINA OR ANUS . . . OR MOUTH"

6.89 For the meaning of an almost identical phrase in the context of rape, see paras 1.155 and following, above.

"SEXUAL"

6.90 For the meaning of "sexual", see paras 2.66 and following, above.

CONSENT

6.91 The s.64 offence is designed to catch consensual sexual penetration of an adult relative. If the adult does not consent to the penetration, the appropriate charge is likely to be rape or assault by penetration. The Sexual Offences Review said that it had been argued that the offence of incest should not apply to sexual activity between consenting adults, on the grounds that it is not harmful to society as a whole and that adults have the right to make decisions about their own sexual behaviour in private.[91] However, the Review noted research indicating that most adult familial relationships are not genuinely consensual as they are the result of long-term grooming and pressure from childhood by an older family member. In such situations, an adult's right to exercise sexual autonomy in their private life is not absolute and the criminal law needs to protect both the family as an institution and individuals within it from abuse.[92]

MENTAL ELEMENT

6.92 The prosecution must prove that A intended to penetrate B, and that he knew or could reasonably have been expected to know that he was related to B in the way alleged.[93] Section 64(4) provides:

[91] *Setting the Boundaries*, 2000, para.5.8.1.
[92] *Setting the Boundaries*, 2000, para.5.8.2; *Protecting the Public*, 2002, para.59.
[93] cf. H.O. Circular 21/2004, *Guidance as to Part 1 of the Sexual Offences Act* 2003, para.291: "Except in the most unusual circumstances, a person can reasonably be expected to be aware of such close familial ties."

"Where in proceedings for an offence under this section it is proved that the defendant was related to the other person in any of those ways, it is to be taken that the defendant knew or could reasonably have been expected to know that he was related in that way unless sufficient evidence is adduced to raise an issue as to whether he knew or could reasonably have been expected to know that he was."

The effect of s.64(4) is that, once the proscribed relationship is established, it will be presumed that A had the requisite knowledge, etc., unless he can point to sufficient evidence to raise an issue as to whether he knew, etc. that B was related to him as alleged. Evidence sufficient to raise an issue as to the defendant's knowledge may come from his own or from any other admissible evidence.

Intoxication

As to whether A is liable to conviction if he penetrates B whilst he (A) is in a state of intoxication due to drink or drugs, see the discussion of *Heard*[94] in paras 2.81 and following, above. In the light of that discussion, voluntary intoxication through drink or drugs will provide no defence to a charge under s.64.   **6.93**

SEX WITH AN ADULT RELATIVE: CONSENTING TO PENETRATION

DEFINITION

Section 65(1) of the Sexual Offences Act 2003[95] provides: **6.94**

"A person aged 16 or over (A) (subject to subsection (3A)) commits an offence if—
(a) another person (B) penetrates A's vagina or anus with a part of B's body or anything else, or penetrates A's mouth with B's penis,
(b) A consents to the penetration,
(c) the penetration is sexual,
(d) B is aged 18 or over,
(e) A is related to B in a way mentioned in subsection (2), and
(f) A knows or could reasonably be expected to know that he is related to B in that way."

MODE OF TRIAL AND PUNISHMENT

An offence under s.65 is triable either way. The maximum sentence on conviction on indictment is two years' imprisonment and on summary conviction is six months' imprisonment or a fine, or both.[96] As from a day to   **6.95**

---

[94] [2007] EWCA Crim 125.
[95] As amended by the Criminal Justice and Immigration Act 2008 s.73 and Sch.15, para.6(2), with effect from July 8, 2008.
[96] s.65(5).

be appointed the maximum sentence of imprisonment on summary conviction will increase to 12 months.[97] The increase will have no application to offences committed before it takes effect.[98] Until recently, the maximum fine on summary conviction was a fine not exceeding the statutory maximum (i.e. £5,000). The effect of s.85 of the Legal Aid, Sentencing and Punishment of Offenders Act 2012 is that, from March 12, 2015, a fine of any amount may be imposed.

6.96   For the purposes of listing, cases of sex with an adult relative: consenting to penetration[99] fall within Class 2B.[100] In certain specified circumstances cases in Class 2B must be referred to the Resident Judge, and by the Resident Judge to a Presiding Judge, including where the case is unusually grave or complex or a novel and important point of law is to be raised; where the defendant is a police officer, a member of the legal profession or a high profile figure; or where for any reason the case is likely to attract exceptional media attention.

6.97   An offence under s.65, whenever committed, may be made the subject of an extended sentence under s.226A of the Criminal Justice Act 2003 (extended sentence for certain violent or sexual offences).[101]

6.98   A person convicted under s.65, cautioned, found not guilty by reason of insanity or found to be under a disability and to have done the act charged is automatically subject to the notification requirements in the Sexual Offences Act 2003[102] if (a) where they were under 18 at the time of the offence, they are sentenced to a term of at least 12 months' imprisonment, or (b) in any other case, they are, in respect of the offence, sentenced to a term of imprisonment or detained in a hospital.

SENTENCING

6.99   For the Sentencing Council's guideline applicable to sex offenders aged 18 or over who are sentenced on or after April 1, 2014, see Ch.33, below. A single guideline covers offences under ss.64 and 65 of the 2003 Act and is discussed in paras 6.77 and following, above.

PARTIES TO THE OFFENCE

6.100   Section 65 mirrors s.64 in penalising those aged 16 or over who consent to penetration by an adult relative. The prosecution must prove that the

---

[97] Criminal Justice Act 2003 s.282(2), (3).

[98] Criminal Justice Act 2003 s.282(4).

[99] And of soliciting, inciting, encouraging or assisting, attempting or conspiring to commit the offence or assisting an offender having committed the offence.

[100] *Consolidated Criminal Practice Directions*, Part XIII Listing B: CLASSIFICATION, available at *https://www.judiciary.gov.uk/wp-content/uploads/2015/09/crim-pd-2015.pdf* [Accessed April 30, 2016].

[101] Inserted by the Legal Aid, Sentencing and Punishment of Offenders Act 2012 s.124, brought into force on December 3, 2012, by SI 2012/2906.

[102] s.80 and Sch.3, discussed in Ch.35, below.

defendant (A) is 16 or over, that the other person (B) is 18 or over and that the relationship between them is prohibited. The prohibited relationships covered by this section are set out in s.65(2) and are the same as for s.64.[103] See further paras 6.83 and following, above.

The s.65 offence resembles the old law of incest in that it encompasses close blood relationships, but the new offence is broader as it includes blood uncles and aunts (but not their spouses or partners) and also adoptive parents. Section 65(3) and (3A) provide[104]: **6.101**

"(3) In subsection (2)—
    (za) 'parent' includes an adoptive parent;
    (zb) 'child' includes an adopted person within the meaning of Chapter 4 of Part 1 of the Adoption and Children Act 2002;
    (a) 'uncle' means brother of a person's parent, and 'aunt' has a corresponding meaning;
    (b) 'nephew' means the child of a person's brother or sister, and 'niece' has a corresponding meaning.
(3A) Where subsection (1) applies in a case where A is related to B as B's child by virtue of subsection (3)(zb), A does not commit an offence under this section unless A is 18 or over."

"Penetrates A's Vagina or Anus . . . or Mouth"

For the meaning of an almost identical phrase in the context of rape, see paras 1.155 and following, above. **6.102**

"Sexual"

For the meaning of "sexual", see paras 2.66 and following, above. **6.103**

Consent

The prosecution must prove that the defendant consented to sexual penetration. For the meaning of consent in Pt 1 of the Act, see paras 1.169 and following, above. **6.104**

Mental Element

The prosecution must prove that A knew or could reasonably have been expected to know that he was related to B in a way that falls within s.65(2). Section 65(4) of the Act mirrors s.64(4), discussed in para.6.92. Its effect is that, once the proscribed relationship is established, it will be presumed that A had the requisite knowledge etc. unless he can point to sufficient evidence **6.105**

---

[103] cf. s.65(2).
[104] As amended by the Criminal Justice and Immigration Act 2008 s.73 and Sch.15, para.5(3), with effect from July 8, 2008.

to raise an issue as to whether he knew or could reasonably have been expected to know that B was related to him as alleged. Evidence sufficient to raise an issue as to the defendant's knowledge may come from his own or from any other admissible evidence.

Intoxication

6.106 As to whether A is liable to conviction if he consents to be penetrated by B whilst he (A) is in a state of intoxication due to drink or drugs, see the discussion of *Heard*[105] in paras 2.81 and following, above. In the light of that discussion, voluntary intoxication through drink or drugs will provide no defence to a charge under s.65.

---

[105] [2007] EWCA Crim 125.

CHAPTER 7

SEXUAL OFFENCES AGAINST THOSE WITH A MENTAL DISORDER*

Introduction...................................... 7.01
Overview of the Mental Disorder
Offences... 7.12
Overlap Between "Inability to
Refuse" and Absence of Consent. 7.29
Evidential Considerations in Cases
of Mental Disorder 7.35
Sexual Activity with a Person with
a Mental Disorder Impeding
Choice 7.47
"Unable to Refuse" 7.65
Causing or Inciting a Person, with
a Mental Disorder Impeding
Choice, to Engage in Sexual
Activity.. 7.91
Engaging in Sexual Activity in the
Presence of a Person with a
Mental Disorder Impeding
Choice 7.106
Causing a Person, with a Mental
Disorder Impeding Choice, to
Watch a Sexual Act...................... 7.126
Inducement, Threat or Deception
to Procure Sexual Activity with a
Person with a Mental Disorder.... 7.142

Causing a Person with a Mental
Disorder to Engage in or Agree
to Engage in Sexual Activity by
Inducement, Threat or Deception 7.160
Engaging in Sexual Activity in the
Presence, Procured by
Inducement, Threat or
Deception, of a Person with a
Mental Disorder............................ 7.173
Causing a Person with a Mental
Disorder to Watch a Sexual Act
by Inducement, Threat or
Deception 7.193
Offences Relating to Care Workers:
Sexual Activity with a Person
with a Mental Disorder................ 7.209
Care Workers: Causing or Inciting
Sexual Activity 7.237
Care Workers: Sexual Activity in
the Presence of a Person with a
Mental Disorder............................ 7.252
Care Workers: Causing a Person
with a Mental Disorder to Watch
a Sexual Act................................. 7.272

INTRODUCTION

Sections 30–41 of the Sexual Offences Act 2003 ("the 2003 Act") introduced **7.01** a range of sexual offences designed to protect those who suffer from mental disorder.

* The authors are indebted to Alexandra Ward, Barrister, who was the principal drafter of this chapter.

7.02   It has long been recognised that the criminal law should protect the mentally disordered from sexual abuse and exploitation, over and above the protection offered by other sexual offences. Research has consistently indicated that those with mental health issues are significantly more likely than other members of the population to suffer sexual abuse, and that offences committed against the mentally disordered are under-reported.[1] In its report *At Risk, Yet Dismissed*,[2] the charity and campaign organisation Mind confirmed the victimisation of those who suffer from mental illness. Their research showed that 40 per cent of female participants were victims of rape or attempted rape in adulthood and 10 per cent reported being a victim of sexual abuse in the year preceding the study. Those with a mental disorder remain reluctant to report the offences committed against them: 70 per cent of male victims of sexual assault did not disclose their experience. Interviewees felt "preyed upon" when unwell and targeted because of their vulnerability.

7.03   It is recognised that in common with other vulnerable groups (such as children), the mentally disordered may be at risk from those involved in their care. As in the studies carried out by Mind, a common reason given by those suffering from a mental disorder for not reporting offences committed against them is a worry that because of their disorder they will not be believed or considered credible. This fear is acute when the perpetrator is someone with responsibility for the victim's care, particularly in an inpatient environment when access to help could be denied. It has been suggested that abusers may deliberately seek employment within the care sector in order to abuse the vulnerable.[3] In addition, those interviewed by Mind in 2013 reported feeling vulnerable to sexual attacks from other inpatients. An earlier report also by Mind found that 18 per cent of inpatients had been sexually harassed and 1 in 20 sexually assaulted.[4]

7.04   There is a tension between the obligation to protect the mentally disordered from sexual abuse and unnecessary restriction of their sexual freedom.[5] Legislation that prevented adults capable of deciding whether to engage in sexual activity from enjoying sexual relationships could breach their rights under art.8 ECHR.[6] In determining whether an individual with

---

[1] Muccigrosso 1991, quoted in *Behind closed doors; preventing sexual abuse against adults with a learning disability*, Voice, Respond, Mencap, September 2001. Cf. *Hansard*, HC Vol.409, col.185, David Blunkett MP (July 15, 2003); *Hansard*, HL Vol.644, col.774, Lord Falconer of Thoroton (February 13, 2003).

[2] Mind (2013) (with Victim Support, the Institute of Psychiatry at King's College London, St George's University of London, Kingston University and University College London).

[3] *Behind closed doors: preventing sexual abuse against adults with a learning disability*, Voice, Respond, Mencap, September 2001, p.11.

[4] Mind, *Ward Watch: Mind's campaign to improve hospital conditions for mental health patients*, 2004.

[5] cf. submissions to the Criminal Law Revision Committee on its Working Paper on *Sexual Offences* (1980) by the Sexual Law Reform Society and the National Council for Civil Liberties; *Hansard*, HC Vol.409, col.228, Sandra Gidley MP (July 15, 2003).

[6] See further paras 7.42 and following, below.

a mental disorder has the capacity to consent to sexual relations, the law should not seek to prevent their engagement in sexual activity simply because such activity appears unwise. The decision-making process carried out on a daily basis by persons of capacity (who do not suffer from mental disorder) typically will not involve a refined analysis using and weighing all available information. In the context of human sexual relations, choices are generally made rather more by emotional drive and instinct than by rational choice. Human emotion and instinct may lead an individual with capacity to make misguided decisions.

There is accordingly a delicate balance to be struck such that the State **7.05** does not interfere unduly in an individual's sexual life but does discharge its responsibility to protect the individual from exploitation and abuse.[7] Evidently, Parliament's intention in enacting the 2003 Act was to protect the vulnerable by defending the interests of those denied choice because of their mental disorder, who as such are easy targets for abuse. Lord Rix stated that the intention was not to deny people who can make choices, the right to make choices about sex.[8] This includes the significant number of mentally disordered people likely to be engaging in sexual activity together.[9]

In the leading authority of *Cooper*,[10] Baroness Hale, in a powerful and **7.06** clear opinion, explained the development of the legislature's treatment of those with a mental disorder. In the second half of the twentieth century there was a sea change in the attitude of the law. Previously the mentally disordered had been segregated from the rest of society, detained in large institutions on the outskirts of town or deep in the countryside, and denied the benefits of close personal relationships. The policy introduced by the Mental Health Act 1959 provided that, so far as possible, the mentally disordered should be integrated into society, to be treated as much like anyone else as it was possible to do and enjoy the same rights as other people.

However, one area which remained restrictive was the rights of the **7.07** mentally disordered to engage in sexual relationships. The Sexual Offences Act 1956 protected only those with "severe" disability and so left unprotected those with a disability that was not severe but nevertheless impaired their capacity. The Act made it an offence for any man to have extra-marital sexual intercourse with a "defective", nor could such a woman or such a man give a valid consent to an indecent assault. The 1956 Act was therefore both over-protective and under-protective. It could be considered too restrictive in its application to those persons who, although suffering from mental disorder, were capable of making a genuine choice about their sexual partners and who would not be harmed by engaging in sexual activity. It denied them

---

[7] *X & Y v The Netherlands*, 8 E.H.R.R. 235.
[8] *Hansard*, HL Vol.644, col.792, Lord Rix (February 13, 2003).
[9] M.J. Gunn, *The Sexual Rights of the Mentally Handicapped*, in E. Alves (ed), *Issues in Criminological and Legal Psychology No 10: Mental Handicap and the Law* (1987), p.31.
[10] [2009] UKHL 42; [2010] 1 Cr. App. R. 7.

that sexual fulfilment which most people take for granted, solely on the basis of a status or diagnosis. However, the law left vulnerable those persons who were not considered "defective" but nonetheless suffered a mental disorder, which might well mean that they lacked the capacity to make a choice about their sexual relationships.

7.08   In three separate papers, the Law Commission and the then Government considered the mental capacity of those with a mental disorder,[11] and in due course the Mental Capacity Act 2005 was passed. The reports identified three approaches to capacity: "status", "outcome" and "functional". The "status" approach focuses upon diagnosis, irrespective of an individual's capacity to make a decision at a particular time. "Outcome" focuses upon the final content of the decision made and whether it was inconsistent with conventional values. Clearly, this approach would restrict the autonomy of those who are capable of making a decision, albeit one that might be seen as unwise and contrary to convention. The "functional" approach asks whether, at the time the decision had to be made, the person could understand its nature and effects. This approach recognises that capacity or incapacity is not a permanent state but may fluctuate. There may also be cases where a person can understand the nature and effects of a decision but the effects of their mental disorder prevent them from using that information in the decision-making process; a classic example would be that of an anorexic who decides not to eat.

7.09   The Law Commission recommended the functional approach in its Report on *Consent in sexual offences*, which was published as an appendix to the report of the Seuxal Offences Review *Setting the Boundaries: Reforming the law on sex offences.*[12] The functional approach now underpins the thinking behind the offences designed to protect those "unable to refuse" by reason of mental disorder in the 2003 Act. It strikes the balance between protection and sexual freedom by providing that a person did not have capacity to engage in sexual activity if, because of or for a reason related to their mental disorder, they were unable to understand or unable to decide on the material occasion. Sexual autonomy requires a person to be able to make a decision as to whether to engage in sexual activity with a particular person at a particular time. As Baroness Hale put it[13]:

---

[11] *Mental Incapacity,* Law Com No.231 (1995), *Who Decides? Making decisions on behalf of mentally incapacitated adults* (Cm 3803) (1997) and *Making Decisions* (Cm 4465) (1999).
[12] Home Office, July 2000.
[13] *Cooper (Gary Anthony)* [2009] UKHL 42; [2010] 1 Cr. App. R. 7 at [15]. Leveson LJ acknowledged in *IM v LM, AB, Liverpool City Council* [2014] EWCA Civ 37 that this was plainly right in the context of sexual offences where the focus of the criminal law will be upon a particular specific past event being evaluated in retrospect with respect to that singular event. He explained that this does not prevent a court such as the Court of Protection, when assessing capacity to make a general evaluation which is not tied down to a particular partner, time and place, and applying a test for capacity to consent to sexual relationships which is general and issue specific rather than person or event specific.

"Any particular choice to engage in sexual activity is, of course, both person-specific and occasion-specific: with you here and now, or not with you, (although possibly with some-one else), or not here, or not now."

The test of capacity in the criminal jurisdiction following the Mental Capacity Act 2005

The Mental Capacity Act 2005 made new provision relating to persons who   **7.10** lack capacity, defining capacity by reference to a functional test. The Court of Appeal has on a number of occasions stated that it is desirable that the test for capacity to consent to sexual relations should be the same in both the civil and criminal jurisdictions, or, at the very least, there should be a significant degree of conformity between the tests applied. In *R. v GA*[14] the Court of Appeal stated that the approach should be the same in both jurisdictions, necessarily informed by the definition and guidance contained in ss.2 and 3 of the Mental Capacity Act 2005 and focused upon whether the complainant had sufficient understanding of the nature or reasonably foreseeable consequences of what was being done.

An apparent conflict of judicial opinion at first instance in the Court of   **7.11** Protection on the issue of capacity to consent to sexual relations was explained in *IM v LM, AB and Liverpool City Council*,[15] as having arisen from two distinct and different contexts. The distinction is between the general capacity to give or withhold consent to sexual relations, which is the necessary forward-looking focus of the Court of Protection, and the person-specific, time and place-specific, occasion when that capacity is actually deployed and consent is either given or withheld, which is the focus of the criminal law and is illustrated by the approach of Baroness Hale in *Cooper*. In *IM*, Leveson LJ explained that the ability to use and weigh information is unlikely to loom large in the evaluation of capacity to consent to sexual relations. He acknowledged that the Mental Capacity Act 2005 mandates that the ability to use and weigh information should be taken into account, but warned that the notional process of using and weighing information attributed to the protected person should not involve a refined analysis of the sort which does not typically inform the decision to consent to sexual relations made by a person of full capacity. The Court approved the following comment made in graphic terms by Hedley J in *A NHS Trust v P*[16]:

"The intention of the Act is not to dress an incapacitous person in forensic cotton wool but to allow them as far as possible to make the same mistakes that all other human beings are at liberty to make and not infrequently do."

[14] [2014] EWCA Crim 299. See also *A Local Authority v H* [2012] EWHC 49 (COP); [2012] 1 F.C.R. 590; *D County Council v LS* [2010] EWHC 1544 (Fam).
[15] [2014] EWCA Civ 37.
[16] [2013] EWHC 50 (COP), approved in *IM* at [80]. See also Robert Sandland, *Sex and Capacity: The Management of Monsters?* [2013] 76(6) M.L.R. 981–1009.

Overview of the Mental Disorder Offences

The Three Categories

7.12 The Sexual Offence Act 2003 contains 12 offences designed to protect those with a mental disorder.[17] These offences fall into three categories, each of four offences dealing with a different exploitative context. The first category, in ss.30–33 of the Act, applies to cases where the complainant is "unable to refuse" sexual activity because of a mental disorder which impedes choice.[18]

7.13 The second category of offences, in ss.34–37, covers sexual activity in relation to a mentally disordered victim where agreement is obtained by inducement, threat or deception. The prosecution does not have to prove that the complainant was unable to refuse.

7.14 The third category, in ss.38–41, comprises sexual offences committed by care workers in respect of those suffering from mental disorder. Again the prosecution does not have to prove that the complainant was unable to refuse, and sexual activity between care worker and patient is prohibited regardless of consent. The purpose of these offences is to protect a person with a mental disorder who has the capacity to consent but who may be particularly vulnerable to exploitative behaviour and may agree to sexual activity because of dependence upon their carer.[19] The position of trust and responsibility enjoyed by a care worker is a feature of the offence, as opposed to simply an aggravating factor. It is not necessary for the prohibited conduct to have occurred in the place where care is provided: offences can be committed wherever the conduct took place and regardless of whether the complainant was an in or out patient.

Mental Element in Respect of the Three Categories

7.15 For offences under ss.30–33, the prosecution must prove that the defendant knew or could reasonably have been expected to know that the complainant had a mental disorder *and* because of or for a reason related to that disorder was likely to be unable to refuse their part in the sexual act alleged. For offences under ss.34–41, the prosecution must establish only that the defendant knew or could reasonably have been expected to know that the complainant had a mental disorder. For offences committed by care workers, it is presumed that the defendant knew or could reasonably have been expected to know that the complainant had a mental disorder unless sufficient evidence is adduced to raise an arguable case to the contrary.

---

[17] Sexual Offences Act 2003 ss.30–41.

[18] The prohibited sexual activity mirrors that in the four child offences in ss.9–12 of the Act and the four breach of trust offences in ss.16–19.

[19] *Hansard*, HL Vol.644, col.775, Lord Falconer of Thoroton (February 13, 2003).

In *Cooper*,[20] Baroness Hale expressed surprise that the appellant had not   7.16
been charged under s.34 as an alternative to the charge under s.30. The
appellant's offer to assist the complainant, combined with his giving her
crack cocaine, may well have induced her to engage in the sexual activity. The
complainant also gave evidence that she had feared the defendant and what
he, as a "crack-head", might do. If a charge had been brought under s.34, it
would have been sufficient for the prosecution to prove that the appellant
knew or could reasonably have been expected to know that the complainant
had a mental disorder. It would not have been necessary to prove that the
complainant was unable to refuse nor that the appellant knew or could
reasonably have been expected to know that she was unable to refuse because
of or for a reason related to her mental disorder. It would have been
necessary for the prosecution to include a count alleging the s.34 offence on
the indictment together with the s.30 offence, because an alternative verdict
is not possible.[21]

EXCEPTIONS RELATING TO CARE WORKERS

A care worker will not commit an offence under ss.38–41 if he proves that he   7.17
was lawfully married to, or in a civil partnership with, the complainant at the
relevant time and that the complainant was then over 16.[22] A similar
provision applies where a care worker proves that he had a lawful sexual
relationship with the complainant immediately before becoming involved in
the complainant's care.[23] These exceptions are vital given the breadth of the
definition of mental disorder as discussed below, e.g. to protect an individual
whose sexual partner develops dementia. There is no exception for those
undertaking what they believe to be legitimate sex education of the mentally
disordered, who could theoretically, in certain circumstances, be committing
offences under ss.38–41. Prosecutorial discretion may be required to avoid
the rigours of this category of offences where to prosecute would not be in
the public interest.

"UNABLE TO REFUSE"

Whilst, as with all the offences against the mentally disordered, the prosecu-   7.18
tion does not have to prove that the complainant did not consent to the
sexual activity, in respect of the first category of offences (ss.30–33) it must
establish to the criminal standard that the complainant was "unable to

---

[20] [2009] UKHL 42 at [32].
[21] A count alleging an offence under ss.30-33 will not expressly or impliedly include an
allegation under ss.34–37: cf. Criminal Law Act 1967 s.6(3), and *Wilson* [1984] A.C. 242.
[22] 2003 Act s.43.
[23] 2003 Act s.44.

refuse" because of or for a reason related to a mental disorder.[24] Section 30(2)[25] provides that the complainant (B) is "unable to refuse" if:

> "(a) he lacks the capacity to choose whether to agree to the touching (whether because he lacks sufficient understanding of the nature or reasonably foreseeable consequences of what is being done or for any other reason), or
> (b) he is unable to communicate such a choice to A."

7.19 The House of Lords considered the concept of "unable to refuse" in *Cooper*.[26] Baroness Hale held that the 2003 Act had made the position clear in relation to capacity to choose. She noted that by virtue of s.30(2)(a), a person is "unable to refuse" because of, or for a reason related to his mental disorder, if he lacks the capacity to choose whether to agree to the touching, whether because he lacks sufficient understanding of the nature or reasonably foreseeable consequences of what is being done "or for any other reason". The words "or for any other reason" should not be ignored. Baroness Hale explained that there is a wide range of circumstances in which a person's mental disorder might deny them the ability to make an autonomous choice as to whether to engage in the sexual activity, albeit that they may understand the nature of the act and its foreseeable consequences. She provided cogent examples (not necessarily in the context of sexual activity) of the compulsion from which mentally disordered persons may suffer which removes their autonomy of choice, for example, an anorexic who refused food, the delusions which drive a schizophrenic to believe that they must do something, or the phobia which leads a person to refuse a life-saving injection.[27] It is not sufficient that a person can understand the information relevant to making a decision; they must be able to weigh the information in the balance to arrive at a choice.[28]

7.20 Determining capacity in a criminal trial is necessarily retrospective in that the jury consider whether the complainant was "unable to refuse" at the time of the alleged offence. Baroness Hale acknowledged that a mentally disordered person's capacity to choose can fluctuate, and therefore the question which has to be asked is whether in the state the complainant was in on the particular day they were capable of choosing whether to consent. Capacity cannot be determined by considering the complainant's mental disorder in the abstract but must be considered within the context of whether the complainant had the capacity to consent to the particular sexual contact, at the particular time, with that particular person. Further, by virtue of s.30(2)(b), even if the complainant had the capacity to choose whether to agree to the touching, she or he is deemed to be "unable to refuse" if they were unable to communicate their choice to the defendant because of or for a reason related to mental disorder.

---

[24] *R. v A (G)* [2014] EWCA Crim 299; [2014] 2 Cr. App. R. 5.
[25] There are similar provisions in ss.31–34.
[26] [2009] UKHL 42.
[27] [2009] UKHL 42, at [25].
[28] [2009] UKHL 42 at [24], citing *Re C (adult: refusal of treatment)* [1994] 1 All E.R. 819, at 824.

It follows that there are three alternative routes to establishing that a   7.21
person is "unable to refuse":

- the complainant was incapable of choosing whether to agree to the particular sexual activity since they lacked sufficient understanding of the nature of the act etc. because of or for a reason related to their mental disorder.
- the complainant was incapable of choosing whether to agree to the particular sexual activity for any other reason because of or for a reason related to their mental disorder.
- the complainant was unable to communicate their choice to the defendant because of or for a reason related to their mental disorder.

In cases where a person has the capacity to choose whether to agree to the sexual activity but cannot communicate their choice to refuse because of a physical disability, the appropriate charge would be one of the offences in ss.1–4 of the Act. In such circumstances the prosecution may rely upon certain evidential presumptions: see s.75(1), (2)(e) of the 2003 Act, discussed in paras 1.263 and following, above.

The decision in *Cooper* is welcome because it protects a person who is   7.22
unable to refuse sexual activity because of or for a reason related to their
mental disorder, whilst allowing the mentally disordered their sexual autonomy. It recognises the complexity of mental disorder, which is not always
static, and that there may well be circumstances in which the same individual
will possess the capacity to choose in one situation but be unable to refuse in
another. Furthermore, it does not unduly restrict those with mental disorder
from engaging in sexual activity, as the 2003 Act offences are committed only
if the complainant comes within the definition of "unable to refuse."

Capacity and the burden and standard of proof

In *R. v A(G)*,[29] the appellant had been charged with sexual assault. Both he   7.23
and the complainant had learning difficulties and both had been students at
a special needs school. The appellant was deaf and had an IQ of 51. He was
classified as having a moderate learning difficulty, whilst the complainant was
diagnosed as having a mild learning disability. After a finding of disability
under s.4A of the Criminal Procedure (Insanity) Act 1964, a jury was
empanelled to decide whether the appellant had committed the act alleged.
Following the judge's direction to apply the civil standard of proof to the
issue of capacity, the jury found that he had done so.

Section 1(2) of the Mental Capacity Act 2005 provides: 7.24

"A person must be assumed to have capacity unless it is established that he lacks
capacity."

Section 2(4) provides:

[29] [2014] EWCA Crim 299 at [30].

"In proceedings under this Act or any other enactment, any question whether a person lacks capacity within the meaning of this Act must be decided on the balance of probabilities."

The Court of Appeal held that, notwithstanding these provisions, the judge had been in error to direct the jury to apply the civil standard of proof in respect of the complainant's capacity. Macur LJ, giving the judgment of the Court, observed that the similarity in the definition of "capacity" as between civil and criminal jurisprudence did not dictate the same standard of proof. She observed that the adjudications of the Court of Protection generally look towards the future, whilst the criminal law only looks retrospectively to specific acts in the past. She concluded that when capacity to consent is in issue in criminal proceedings, the burden of proving incapacity falls upon the party asserting it, which inevitably will be the prosecution. That burden must be discharged to a criminal standard. If the jury cannot be sure that the complainant lacked capacity, they must be directed to assume that he or she had it.

"MENTAL DISORDER"

7.25　The 2003 Act adopts the definition of "mental disorder" found in s.1 of the amended Mental Health Act 1983, as "any disorder or disability of the mind".[30] This is a wider definition than in the Sexual Offences Act 1956, whereby the prosecution had to prove the complainant was a "defective", i.e. suffering from a state of arrested or incomplete development of mind, including severe impairment of intelligence and social functioning.[31] The demise of the term "defective" is to be welcomed, not just because it was offensive and pejorative, but also because it led to terminological confusion and set too high a threshold by requiring severe impairment of intelligence and social functioning as minimum conditions. As a result, a person with a mental disorder that was significant, but not severe, was not protected by the 1956 Act.[32] Nor was a person whose mind had developed properly but who

---

[30] 2003 Act s.79(6), states that "mental disorder" has the meaning given by s.1 of the Mental Health Act 1983 (as amended by the Mental Health Act 2007).

[31] Sexual Offences Act 1956 s.45. There is no provision in this definition for "any other disability or disorder of mind" as appears in the 1983 Act.

[32] M.J. Gunn in *The Sexual Rights of the Mentally Handicapped*, in E. Alves (ed), *Issues in Criminological and Legal Psychology No 10: Mental Handicap and the Law* (1987), p.31, identified the three requirements to establish that a person was a "defective" under the old legislation. First, the person must be suffering from a state of arrested or incomplete development at a relatively early age, and any injury thereafter, such as a road traffic accident suffered at the age of 25, cannot fulfil this condition. Most mentally handicapped people, though, would fulfil it. Second, the person's intelligence must be severely impaired. Clearly IQ tests will be of some relevance to this issue. There is no legal indication of what IQ might amount to severe impairment and, in any case, the cultural biases of such tests and the possibility of training somebody to pass them cannot be ignored. Third, a person's social functioning must also be severely impaired. It could be claimed that if a person is capable of entering into a meaningful sexual relationship, that necessarily means that their social functioning cannot be impaired, however severely impaired their intelligence might be or however arrested or incomplete their development of mind is.

had subsequently suffered brain damage in an accident or had become an Alzheimer's victim. The revised definition means the 2003 Act applies to all mental disorders, it being recognised that psychiatry is not an exact science and that the classification of disorder is not easily to be equated with the underlying clinical diagnosis.[33] Practical examples of disorders covered by the definition are forms of personality disorder which would not previously have been considered to be "mental illness" and do not fall within the current definition of psychopathic disorder because they do not result in abnormally aggressive or seriously irresponsible conduct on the part of the person concerned. Other examples almost certainly include certain types of psychological dysfunction arising from brain injury or damage in adulthood. Examples of clinically recognised mental disorders include mental illnesses such as schizophrenia, bipolar disorder, anxiety or depression, as well as personality disorders, eating disorders and autistic spectrum disorders. Under the new definition, disorders or disabilities of the brain are not mental disorders unless (and only to the extent that) they give rise to a disability or disorder of the mind as well.[34] As Baroness Hale pointed out in *Cooper*, some physical disorders of the brain do give rise to disorders of the mind. Thus dependence on alcohol or drugs does not fall within the definition of mental disorder.[35]

"Learning disability" falls within the definition of "mental disorder" and   **7.26** is defined as "a state of arrested or incomplete development of the mind, which includes significant impairment of intelligence and social functioning."[36] Learning disability includes the presence of:

- a significantly reduced ability to understand new or complex information, to learn new skills (impaired intelligence), with
- a reduced ability to cope independently (impaired social functioning),
- which started before adulthood, with a lasting effect on development.[37]

Those suffering from a learning disability rendering them unable to choose   **7.27** whether to engage in the sexual activity in question, or to communicate their choice, should be protected by legislation.[38] It could be argued that the inclusion of learning disability within the definition has an overly restrictive effect in the criminal law, in that it extends the scope of ss.30–33 of the 2003 Act to those capable of making a choice about sexual partners who would

---

[33] *R. (B) v Ashworth Hospital Authority* [2005] A.C. 278 at [31], cited in P. Bowen, *Blackstone's Guide to The Mental Health Act 2007* (Oxford: Oxford University Press, 2007).

[34] Richard Card, Alisdair A. Gillespie and Michael Hirst, *Sexual Offences* (Bristol: Jordans, 2008), paras 9.11–9.12.

[35] Mental Health Act 1983 s.1(3), as substituted by the Mental Health Act 2007 s.3.

[36] Mental Health Act 1983 s.1(4), inserted by the Mental Health Act 2007 s.2(3).

[37] *Valuing People: A New Strategy for the 21st Century*, Cm.5086 (2001).

[38] Explanatory Notes to the 2003 Act, para.61; *Hansard*, HC Vol.412, col.602 (November 3, 2003); *Hansard*, HL Vol.646, col.402, Lord Falconer of Thoroton (April 10, 2003): "We [the Government] believe that 'learning disability' comes within the definition of 'mental disorder'. For that reason it does not need to be dealt with separately."

not be harmed by their sexual relationships, and so could deny proper sexual fulfilment.[39] However, it must be borne in mind that ss.30–33 will only be engaged if the complainant is "unable to refuse" because of or for a reason related to the particular learning disability. Many with learning disabilities will not meet this threshold.

7.28   In this connection it is worth noting that for the purpose of certain provisions of the 1983 Act, a person may not be considered to be suffering from a mental disorder simply as a result of having a learning disability, unless that disability is associated with abnormally aggressive or seriously irresponsible conduct on the part of the person concerned. The provisions in question include the criteria for detention and for the use of guardianship and guardianship orders. This tends to confirm that in other contexts, including the 2003 Act, a person with a learning disability *may* be considered to be suffering from a "mental disorder"; and there is certainly nothing in the 1983 Act to preclude this.

Overlap Between "Inability to Refuse" and Absence of Consent

7.29   The definition of "inability to refuse" includes cases where B lacks the capacity to choose, and thus there would be no consent under s.74. It follows that in such cases there is an overlap between the offences in ss.30–33 and the non-consensual offences in ss.1–4 of the Act. As Jo Miles has argued with some force:

> "But complainants who *do* fall within s.30 surely also do not consent—consent under s.74 entails capacity to choose—in which case again a charge could be brought under one of ss.1–4, rather than s.30. This leaves ss.30–33 with little, if any, independent sphere of operation."[40]

Miles contrasts ss.34–37 of the 2003 Act, which are concerned with inducements, threats or deceptions and which, as the general procurement offences in the 1956 Act have been repealed and not replaced, do fulfil a distinctive function in protecting vulnerable persons. Interestingly, Baroness Hale pointed out in *Cooper*[41] that on the facts of that case a charge under s.34 (intentional sexual touching with the agreement of the person touched, where the defendant has obtained that agreement by means of an inducement, threat or deception) could have been charged in the alternative to s.30. That would have avoided the need to address the meaning of "unable to refuse" in s.30, or the issue of consent as required by the non-consensual offences. She speculated that perhaps the view was taken that the evidence of lack of capacity was more robust than the evidence of any inducement, threat or deception.

---

[39] Smith and Hogan, *Criminal Law* 14th edn (Oxford: OUP, 2015), p.879.
[40] *Archbold News*, Issue 10, December 5, 2008.
[41] [2009] UKHL 42 at [32].

Miles takes the point about the lack of an independent sphere of operation   **7.30**
to its logical conclusion:

> "if the essence of the situations covered by s.30 is, and can only be, that the
> complainant lacked the capacity to consent at all, then—at least where the
> defendant is not subject to a similar disability—should we not simply recognise
> these cases as being non-consensual, and label and punish them as such?"

She notes that this was the approach taken in what became the Sexual
Offences (Scotland) Act 2009, s.17 of which provides that a person with a
mental disorder is incapable of giving consent for the purposes of the non-
consensual offences in the Act,[42] and there is no parallel in the Act to
ss.30–33. Miles was, however, writing before the House of Lords' decision in
Cooper, which gave a much wider interpretation to the phrase "unable to
refuse" than incapacity to consent. Section 30 does now have the potential
for an independent sphere of operation, particularly where a complainant is
able to make a choice but unable to communicate it because of or for a
reason related to mental disorder. In this connection it is notable that in
consulting on its draft Sentencing Guideline for sexual offences, the Sentencing Council drew an analogy between the non-consensual offences in the
2003 Act and the offences against mentally disordered complainants who are
"unable to refuse", and said that where a victim is unable to refuse, then in
practical, if not legal, terms this is likely to have a similar impact to lack of
consent in cases where the victim does not have a mental disorder.
Accordingly, in relation to offences where there is a mental disorder impeding
choice, the Sentencing Guideline follows a similar structure to the guidelines
for rape, assault by penetration and sexual assault (ss.1–3).

**Opting to charge or charging in the alternative a non-consensual offence
rather than under s.30**

Charging options in this area, where there is such an overlap between   **7.31**
offences, must be case specific. In certain cases there may be advantages for
the prosecutor in charging an offence under s.30 rather than a non-
consensual offence, particularly where there is compelling evidence of the
complainant's mental disorder:

- *Where the complainant is medically unfit to attend trial.* An example
  would be where doctors take the view that appearing in court will be
  positively harmful to the complainant's health. Section 116(2)(b) of
  the Criminal Justice Act 2003 would permit an ABE interview or
  earlier statement to be played in such circumstances, provided the
  witness was competent at the time of the interview or statement.

---

[42] Section 17 provides that for the purpose of the non-consensual offences in the Act, a
mentally disordered person is incapable of consenting to conduct where, by reason of mental
disorder, the person is unable to do one or more of the following: (a) understand what the
conduct is, (b) form a decision as to whether to engage in the conduct (or as to whether the
conduct should take place), (c) communicate any such decision.

However, the witness may not have been in a position to be interviewed or give a statement. In any event, for many cases under s.30 evidence from the complainant will not be essential.

- *Where it is thought desirable to avoid inquiry into actual consent and instead address the more general issue of inability to refuse.* Alzheimer's sufferers and bi-polar patients have been known to lose their sexual inhibitions, when clearly they do not have the capacity to choose under s.30.
- *Where the mental element under s.30 will be easier to establish.* In respect of the non-consensual offences (ss.1–4), the prosecution must prove that at the time of penetration the defendant did not reasonably believe that the complainant was consenting. In contrast, the mental element under s.30 is that the defendant knew or could reasonably have been expected to know that the complainant had a mental disorder and that because of it or for a reason related to it she was unlikely to be unable to refuse. In *Cooper*, Baroness Hale observed that the mental element in respect of s.30 puts a greater burden of restraint upon people who know or ought to know that a person's mental disorder is likely to affect her ability to choose, and that may have explained the decision in that case to charge under s.30. Whether there is advantage in opting for a charge under s.30 on this basis will depend on the facts of the particular case. There will be circumstances where there is such a stark choice between the defence and prosecution cases that there is no scope for a lesser mental element and the same outcome is likely whether the prosecution case is based on absence of consent or lack of capacity.
- *Where B is unable to communicate their choice by reason of a mental disorder.* "Inability to refuse" includes cases where B is unable to communicate their choice as a result of mental disorder, even though they may have the mental capacity to choose. In these cases, it may be difficult to establish absence of consent and the appropriate charge will be under ss.30–33.[43]

7.32   Depending on the circumstances, there may also be an absence of consent in these cases. When in *Cooper*[44] the Court of Appeal interpreted "unable to refuse" restrictively, it appeared that non-consensual offences would become an attractive alternative option for prosecutors, particularly in light of the potential width of the definition of consent in s.74. However, the House of Lords reversed the decision of the Court of Appeal, giving a far less restrictive interpretation to "unable to refuse". As a result there is likely to be less incentive for prosecutors to take the non-consensual option. But there will still be cases where a charge under s.1 (say) is as appropriate as a charge under s.30. A charge under s.1 has the advantage that the prosecution can put

---

[43] We are grateful to Professor David Ormerod QC for his analysis of the various possibilities set out in this paragraph: lecture at Criminal Bar Association conference, May 8, 2004.
[44] *R. v C* [2008] EWCA Crim 1155.

its case in the alternative in respect of that count. Section 74 provides that "a person consents if he agrees by choice, and has the freedom and capacity to make that choice". Capacity is therefore an integral part of the definition of consent, enabling the prosecution to put its case on alternative bases where a complainant has a mental disorder:

- the complainant never consented because they never agreed by choice, and
- in any event, the complainant never had the capacity to make that choice.

An example of when rape may be charged in the alternative is where there are some concerns as to the cogency of the evidence relating to inability to refuse because of a reason related to mental disorder, but the complainant was otherwise incapable through drink, for example, so that even without mental disorder they would not have been in a position to consent. A further example, not dependent upon s.74, could be where the defendant deceived the complainant as to the nature of the act, thereby enabling the prosecution to invoke the provisions of s.76 of the 2003 Act.[45]   **7.33**

If there is evidence that, because of a physical disability, the complainant would not have been able at the time to communicate to the defendant whether they consented, an evidential presumption may arise under s.75(2)(e) that the complainant did not consent.[46] However, it should be borne in mind that evidential presumptions arise very rarely in practice. Further, there may be cases where sufficient evidence can be adduced to displace the presumption, such as a defence claim that consent was communicated by other means. Also, where an inability to communicate derives from a mental rather than a physical disability, the issue of consent will be at large.   **7.34**

EVIDENTIAL CONSIDERATIONS IN CASES OF MENTAL DISORDER

The question of how to adduce evidence from a mentally disordered complainant is likely to require careful consideration by the prosecutor. "Special measures" and in particular intermediaries will be of particular relevance,[47] as will the statutory provisions enabling evidence to be presented from an absent complainant.[48] There will be cases where it will be unnecessary and inappropriate for a mentally disordered complainant to give evidence in court. There may also be an issue as to the complainant's competence to give evidence.   **7.35**

---

[45] Section 76 is discussed in paras 1.310 and following, above.
[46] In *Cooper*, Lord Rodger of Earlsferry (at [4]) gave the following example: B, who has the capacity to choose whether to agree to the sexual touching, chooses not to consent, but is unable to communicate her choice to A because of a "physical disability", and A does not reasonably believe that she consents, with the result that A is guilty of rape: see s.1 and s.75(2)(e). A person partly paralysed by a stroke but with full intellectual functioning would fall in this category.
[47] Special measures are considered in detail in Ch.27.
[48] Discussed below.

7.36 There is a general presumption that all witnesses are competent to give evidence.[49] A person is competent to give evidence in criminal proceedings unless they are unable to understand the questions put to them or give answers that can be understood.[50] It is for the party calling the witness to satisfy the court, on the balance of probabilities, that the witness is competent. In determining a witness's competence, the court shall treat the witness as having the benefit of any special measures direction the court has given or proposes to give. Expert evidence as to the witness's competence may be given.[51]

7.37 There may be difficulties on a practical level with a mentally disordered complainant giving coherent evidence. The special measure provisions for vulnerable witnesses (including intermediaries) will assist in cases where the complainant is fit enough to be cross-examined. Sometimes, however, it will either be detrimental to the health of the complainant for them to come to court, or their mental condition or memory will have so deteriorated by the date of the court hearing that they will no longer be competent or able to give useful evidence. An alternative which may be relied upon in certain circumstances is for the prosecutor to make an application under s.116 of the Criminal Justice Act 2003 that it is in the interests of justice to admit the written statement or video-recorded interview of a witness who, by the time of trial, is unable to testify through fear or physical or mental illness.[52] For a more detailed discussion see the discussion of hearsay in Ch.19.

7.38 An instructive case on this point is *R. v D*,[53] which concerned admissibility under the now repealed provisions of the Criminal Justice Act 1988. Similar considerations will apply under s.116, although it appears to be necessary to establish that the relevant person was person was competent at the time of the statement or interview.[54] *R. v D* involved an 81-year-old woman who was suffering from delusional problems and Alzheimer's disease. She complained of attempted rape and indecent assault. In the light of her mental condition, the decision was made to video-record her interview, which took place within 10 days of the alleged offence. It was evident at the time of the recording that

[49] Youth Justice and Criminal Evidence Act 1999 s.53(1); and see paras 27.143 and following, below.
[50] Youth Justice and Criminal Evidence Act 1999 s.53(3); and see paras 27.143 and following, below.
[51] Youth Justice and Criminal Evidence Act 1999 s.54(3), (5); and see paras 27.143 and following, below.
[52] *DPP v R* [2007] EWHC 1842 (Admin). Section 116(2)(b) is not concerned only with the ability of the prospective witness to get to court.
[53] [2002] EWCA Crim 990. See also *Sed (Ali Dahir)* [2004] EWCA Crim 1294; [2005] 1 Cr. App. R. 4, where the Court of Appeal followed the approach in *R. v D* in respect of the video interview of a complainant who was also suffering from Alzheimer's disease; *Watts* [2010] EWCA Crim 1824, in which a complainant's ABE interview was admitted under s.116 where after the interview but prior to the trial she suffered a stroke rendering her incapable of any form of communication.
[54] Competence is a pre-condition for admissibility under s.116 of the Criminal Justice Act 2003. For the test of "capability", see s.123 of that Act and *O'Leary* [2013] EWCA Crim 1371.

because of her degenerative mental state the complainant would not be able to give evidence at trial (whatever special measures were available) and at a preparatory hearing, the judge ruled that the video recording could be admitted. The Court of Appeal considered an interlocutory appeal against that ruling. The defence submitted that the video recording ought not to be admitted because the complainant would not have been competent to give live evidence at the time the recording was made and as such it would not be "in the interests of justice" to admit the recording within the meaning of s.26 of the 1988 Act. It was also argued that the video recording should be excluded under s.78 of the Police and Criminal Evidence Act 1984 and, further, that to admit it would breach the defendant's right to challenge the prosecution's evidence under art.6(3)(d) of the ECHR. The Court of Appeal held that the video was admissible under s.23 of the 1988 Act. It said that there was no requirement under that section for the witness to be competent at the time the document came into being. The issues for the court to consider when considering the admissibility of evidence under s.23 were those set out in s.26 of the Act. Whilst competence was a "highly material issue", it was not conclusive in determining admissibility. The Court dealt neatly with s.78 of the Police and Criminal Evidence Act 1984 and art.6(3)(d), holding that, provided the right approach was taken to ss.23 and 26, it would not be unfair to admit the evidence. This case demonstrates that, notwithstanding case law under art.6, the absence of the complainant at trial may not be an insurmountable obstacle to the prosecution of sexual offences, provided there is significant supporting evidence. In *R. v D*, there was evidence that the defendant's semen was on the back of the complainant's cardigan. The Court commented that the defendant would be able to challenge the complainant's account by adducing medical evidence of her unreliability, and by giving his own account. It should also be noted that in *R. v D*, the jury would have the advantage of being able to evaluate the complainant's account having seen and heard her on video. This is clearly of greater assistance to the jury than hearing the complainant's account second-hand through a police officer or care worker, or reading a statement signed by the complainant without seeing what questions were asked and how the complainant reacted. However, this option will now only be available where the witness was competent at the time of making the statement, as s.116 has narrowed the law in this regard.

Even if the narrative part of a video-recorded interview is not sufficiently   7.39
intelligible to be adduced in evidence, the rapport phase may be valuable evidence in that it may enable the jury to evaluate how the complainant must have appeared to the defendant at the time of the alleged offence. This underlines the importance not only of video-recording such interviews, but of doing so as close to the time of the allegation as reasonably practicable. There may be cases where it will be appropriate to rely upon such a video recording (or part of it) simply to demonstrate the complainant's condition and how at the relevant time he or she would not have had the capacity to agree by

choice or would have been "unable to refuse because of or for a reason related to a mental disorder". Here competence would not be an issue, as the video recording would not be adduced as evidence of the truth of its contents.

7.40   There may also be circumstances in which a witness's previous statement is admissible under s.120 of the Criminal Justice Act 2003. A mandatory requirement of s.120 is that, during the course of the witness's evidence, he indicates that to the best of his belief he made the statement, and that to the best of his belief it states the truth.[55] While s.116 would have to be relied upon in cases such as *R. v D*,[56] referred to above, s.120 may be of use when a witness's recollection is severely limited but nonetheless they are able to recall making what they believe to be a true statement. In those circumstances, provided that one of three further conditions is met, the statement is admissible.[57] The key condition in this context is that the statement was made by the witness when the matters stated were fresh in his memory but he does not remember them, and cannot reasonably be expected to remember them, well enough to give oral evidence of them in the proceedings. The other conditions are that the statement identifies or describes a person, object or place, or that it relates to a previous consistent complaint (for which see paras 19.72 and following, above).

SENTENCING IN CASES INVOLVING MENTALLY DISORDERED PERSONS

7.41   Although not applicable to offences committed under ss.30–41 of the Sexual Offences Act 2003, practitioners should nonetheless be aware of s.146 of the Criminal Justice Act 2003, which imposes a duty upon the courts to increase sentences for any offence aggravated by hostility towards a victim's actual or perceived disability. In the context of s.146, "disability" includes mental impairment. The sentencing of offences under ss.30–41 is discussed in the body of this chapter.

ARTICLE 8 OF THE ECHR: "RIGHT TO PRIVATE LIFE"

7.42   The European Court of Human Rights ("ECtHR") has considered the extent to which legislation should regulate and control the sexual activity of individuals. The starting point is that consensual sexual activity constitutes one of the most intimate aspects of an individual's private life, as guaranteed by art.8, and accordingly any interference with it by a public authority must be for a particularly serious reason. *Dudgeon v UK*[58] concerned the prohibition of homosexual activity in Northern Ireland. The ECtHR held that

---

[55] Criminal Justice Act 2003 s.120(4)(b).
[56] [2002] EWCA Crim 990.
[57] Criminal Justice Act 2003 s.120(4)(a), (5), (7).
[58] (1981) 4 E.H.R.R. 149.

prosecution for activity in breach of the prohibition constituted an interference with the individual's private life within the meaning of art.8(1), which was not justified under art.8(2). The ECtHR accepted that some degree of regulation of sexual conduct by means of the criminal law can be justified as "necessary in a democratic society" in accordance with art.8(2), and it cited the following extract from the Wolfenden Report[59]:

> "[the aim of the criminal law in this field is to . . .] preserve public order and decency, to protect the citizen from what is offensive or injurious, and to provide sufficient safeguards against the exploitation and corruption of others, particularly those who are especially vulnerable because they are young, weak in body or mind, inexperienced, or in a state of special physical, official or emotional dependence."

However, the ECtHR went on to say that regulation of private consensual sexual activity would only be justified under art.8(2) if there were "particularly serious reasons" for State interference.

The case of *X & Y v The Netherlands*[60] may assist when considering cases involving the mentally disordered, because it focuses on non-consensual sexual activity with a mentally disabled complainant and an alleged breach of art.8 by the State in failing to offer her sufficient redress against her attacker. The case involved a legal loophole, which resulted in a 16-year-old mentally disabled girl, who complained of a forced sexual assault, being prevented from prosecuting her alleged attacker. Under domestic law it was also the case that, as she had reached the age of 16, her father could not instigate proceedings on her behalf. The ECtHR interpreted art.8 not simply as compelling a State to abstain from interfering with an individual's private life but also as imposing a positive obligation on the State to adopt measures designed to secure respect for private life between individuals.[61] One way of achieving this would be to invoke the criminal law to protect an individual's private sexual life from being violated. Therefore, despite the Netherlands' concern not to be overly paternalistic in the protection of the physical integrity of the mentally disabled, the ECtHR held that the Government's failure to protect the complainant resulted in a breach of her rights under art.8. In doing so it stated[62]: **7.43**

> "This is a case where fundamental values and essential aspects of private life are at stake. Effective deterrence is indispensable in this area and it can be achieved only by criminal provisions."

It is evident that a delicate balance needs to be drawn in the context of art.8 **7.44** between protecting the vulnerable from sexual abuse and enabling them to seek sexual fulfilment; and in order that to strike that balance, the extent to which a person's mental disorder affects their ability to engage in sexual relations must be considered separately in respect of that individual and at

---

[59] 41 E.H.R.R. 149, at paras 17 and 49.
[60] 8 E.H.R.R. 235.
[61] 8 E.H.R.R. 235, at para.23.
[62] 8 E.H.R.R. 235, at para.27.

the time that the court is required to make the decision. In criminal cases this will necessarily involve looking back to a particular incident (or incidents), whereas the civil courts are more likely to consider whether an individual has the mental capacity to consent to sexual relations yet to occur. Moreover, as noted at para.7.11, the courts have interpreted "capacity" to engage in sexual relations so as not to impose upon the mentally disordered a more sophisticated decision-making process than that exercised by members of the population with full capacity. They have recognised that in the area of sexual relations, individuals even of full capacity do not necessarily analyse the consequences of their actions, and so when determining capacity the law does not demand an unrealistic or more stringent consideration of the consequences of engaging in sexual activity by the mentally disordered than that typically exercised by those of full capacity. In *R. v GA*[63] Macur LJ, giving the judgment of the Court, adopted the opinion of the Court of Appeal Civil Division in *IM v LM, AB and Liverpool City Council*,[64] that the decision to engage in sexual relations is "largely visceral rather than cerebral, and owes more to instinct and emotion rather than analysis".

7.45   The 2003 Act, at least in relation to defendants who are not care workers, appears to be sufficiently flexible not to infringe a mentally disordered person's right to engage in sexual activity unless it is necessary to do so. The inclusion of "capacity" within the definition of "unable to refuse" ensures that it is only those mentally disordered who are incapable of choosing whether to agree to sexual activity or of communicating their choice, and as such those who are unable to consent to such activity, that fall within the ambit of ss.30–33 of the Act. The mischief in offences contrary to ss.34–37 is in the inducement, threat or deception involved in "persuading" a mentally disordered person to become involved in the sexual activity. As such, any consent purportedly given by the complainant is justifiably considered not to be a valid consent. In those circumstances, State interference is likely to be considered necessary in order to protect a particularly vulnerable section of the population. The same flexibility is not apparent in the offences relating to care workers, where there is no requirement to prove that the complainant was unable to refuse (as in ss.30–33) or that the defendant obtained agreement by improper means (as in ss.34–37). The Act assumes that such relationships, even if consensual, will be exploitative and an abuse of the care worker's position.[65] This creates potential for prosecutions to be brought against the sexual partners of mentally disordered individuals who have the capacity to choose whether to participate in sexual activity. The restrictions

[63] [2014] EWCA Crim 299 at [30].
[64] [2014] EWCA Civ 37.
[65] *Hansard*, HL Vol.644, col.775, Lord Falconer of Thoroton (February 13, 2003): "The purpose of these provisions are to protect a person with a mental disorder who has the capacity to consent but may be particularly vulnerable to exploitative behaviour and may agree to sexual activity because of their dependence on their carer."

on the relationship between care worker and patient may well be the subject of a challenge under art.8.

Sexual activity between the mentally disordered is an especially sensitive   7.46
area. As noted in para.7.03, those interviewed by Mind for its report *At Risk, Yet Dismissed*[66] reported feeling vulnerable to sexual assault at the hands of other in-patients. Reliance must be placed upon the CPS to make sensible charging decisions in accordance with the Code for Crown Prosecutors so that activity between, e.g. two mentally disordered persons who are exploring their sexuality will not be prosecuted.[67] However, reliance on such discretion could be seen as an unsatisfactory means of avoiding the excessive rigour of particular laws.[68] This is especially so when there are examples of the discretion being inappropriately applied, as in *R. v GA*[69] where the Court of Appeal described as "astonishing" the decision to prosecute the defendant first with rape and then with sexual assault. The defendant was a deaf 22-year-old man of good character with a moderate learning disability. He had an IQ of 51 and was deemed to be unfit to plead in accordance with s.4A of the Criminal Procedure (Insanity) Act 1964. The complainant had a mild learning disability. They had been friends for some time, having met at a special needs school. It was accepted that there was a sexual encounter which involved the defendant removing the complainant's trousers and underwear, after which he removed his own, then laid on top of the complainant and rubbed his penis against her vagina before ejaculating on her underwear. The complainant reported that she and the defendant had had sex and that she had not wanted to and had said "no". The defendant told the police (in a statement prepared with the assistance of his solicitor) that they had cuddled and any touching was consensual. He did not think that penetration had occurred. The Court of Appeal taxed prosecuting counsel to explain the public interest said to be served in prosecuting the defendant, and said that the relative disability of the defendant compared to the complainant and the fact that he was a young man of good character ought to have weighed heavily in informing the appropriate outcome. The appeal was allowed due to a misdirection as to the standard of proof when determining capacity to consent. Macur LJ stated that the Court of Appeal[70]:

"would not wish our . . . disapprobation of the charging decision in this case to be seen as presenting any bar or obstacle to those cases which quite clearly have at their heart the intent to prosecute those who exploit the vulnerable and those of limited capacity."

---

[66] Mind (2013).
[67] *Hansard*, HL Vol.644, col.777, Baroness Noakes (February, 13 2003).
[68] A point made by M.J. Gunn in *Sexual Rights of the Mentally Handicapped*, in E. Alves (ed), *Issues in Criminological and Legal Psychology No 10: Mental Handicap and the Law* (1987), p.31.
[69] [2014] EWCA Crim 299.
[70] [2014] EWCA Crim 299 at [33].

Sexual Activity with A Person with A Mental Disorder Impeding Choice

Definition

7.47 Section 30(1) of the Sexual Offences Act 2003 provides:

"A person (A) commits an offence if:
  (a) he intentionally touches another person (B),
  (b) the touching is sexual,
  (c) B is unable to refuse because of or for a reason related to a mental disorder, and
  (d) A knows or could reasonably be expected to know that B has a mental disorder and that because of it or for a reason related to it B is likely to be unable to refuse."

Mode of Trial and Punishment

7.48 The mode of trial and punishment of an offence under s.30 depends upon the type of touching in question. If the touching involved any of the following, the offence is triable on indictment only, with a maximum penalty of life imprisonment:

- penetration of B's anus or vagina with a part of A's body or anything else,
- penetration of B's mouth with A's penis,
- penetration of A's anus or vagina with a part of B's body, or
- penetration of A's mouth with B's penis.[71]

Otherwise, the offence is triable either way. The maximum sentence on conviction on indictment is 14 years' imprisonment. On summary conviction it is six months' imprisonment or a fine, or both.[72] As from a day to be appointed the maximum sentence on summary conviction will increase to 12 months' imprisonment.[73] The increase will have no application to offences committed before it takes effect.[74] Until recently, the maximum fine on summary conviction was a fine not exceeding the statutory maximum (i.e. £5,000). The effect of s.85 of the Legal Aid, Sentencing and Punishment of Offenders Act 2012 is that, from March 12, 2015, a fine of any amount may be imposed.

7.49 For the purposes of listing, cases under s.30[75] fall within Class 2B, save for complex cases involving many complainants (in care or otherwise particularly vulnerable) and/or many defendants who are alleged to have systematically groomed and abused them, often over a long period of time, which

---

[71] s.30(3).
[72] s.30(4).
[73] Criminal Justice Act 2003 s.282(2), (3).
[74] Criminal Justice Act 2003 s.282(4).
[75] And of soliciting, inciting, encouraging or assisting, attempting or conspiring to commit the offence or assisting an offender having committed the offence.

fall within Class 1C.[76] Cases in Class 1C must be referred to the Resident Judge, and by the Resident Judge to a Presiding Judge. Cases in Class 2B must be similarly referred in certain specified circumstances, including where the case is unusually grave or complex or a novel and important point of law is to be raised; where the defendant is a police officer, a member of the legal profession or a high profile figure; or where for any reason the case is likely to attract exceptional media attention.

An offence under s.30 is a serious specified offence for the purposes of s.224 and, where the offence involved penetration, s.225(2) (life sentence for serious offences) of the Criminal Justice Act 2003.[77] A s.30 offence, whenever committed, may be made the subject of an extended sentence under s.226A of that Act.[78] The offence is also listed in Pt 1 of Sch.15B to the Criminal Justice Act 2003 for the purposes of s.224A of that Act (life sentence for a second listed offence).[79] **7.50**

A person convicted under s.30, cautioned, found not guilty by reason of insanity or found to be under a disability and to have done the act charged, is automatically subject to the notification requirements in the Sexual Offences Act 2003.[80] **7.51**

BAIL

Section 25 of the Criminal Justice and Public Order Act 1994[81] provides that a person charged with or convicted of certain offences who has a previous conviction for any such offence shall be granted bail only if the court, or as the case may be, the constable considering the grant of bail, is of the opinion that there are exceptional circumstances which justify it. The offences in question include offences under s.30 involving penetration as set out in para.7.48, above, and attempts to commit such an offence. For the full list of offences covered by s.25 of the 1994 Act, see para.1.24 and following, above. **7.52**

SENTENCING

For the Sentencing Council guideline relating to the sentencing of sexual offences committed by offenders aged 18 and over, see Ch.33. Where a victim **7.53**

---

[76] *Consolidated Criminal Practice Directions*, Part XIII Listing B: CLASSIFICATION, available at *https://www.judiciary.gov.uk/wp-content/uploads/2015/09/crim-pd-2015.pdf* [Accessed April 30, 2016].

[77] Criminal Justice Act 2003 s.224 and Sch.15, Pt 2.

[78] Inserted by the Legal Aid, Sentencing and Punishment of Offenders Act 2012 s.124, brought into force on December 3, 2012, by SI 2012/2906.

[79] Inserted by the Legal Aid, Sentencing and Punishment of Offenders Act 2012 s.122, brought into force on December 3, 2012, by SI 2012/2906. See Appendix A, below.

[80] s.80 and Sch.3, discussed in Ch.35, below.

[81] As amended with effect from December 3, 2012, by the Legal Aid, Sentencing and Punishment of Offenders Act 2012 s.90 and Sch.11 para.33.

is unable to refuse, then in practical, if not legal, terms this is likely to have a similar impact to lack of consent in cases where the victim does not have a mental disorder, and so the guidelines for offences where there is a mental disorder impeding choice follow a similar structure to the guidelines for rape, assault by penetration and sexual assault (ss.1–3 of the 2003 Act).

Sentencing guideline

Step One—Harm and culpability

7.54 A single guideline covers the offences in ss.30 and 31 of the 2003 Act (sexual activity with a person with a mental disorder impeding choice and causing or inciting such a person to engage in sexual activity). The guideline requires the sentencing court to go through a series of steps in order to determine the appropriate sentence. Step one involves determining the offence category by reference to the degree of harm caused and then the culpability level for the offence. The court should determine into which categories of harm and culpability the offence falls by reference to the tables below:

Harm	
Category 1	The extreme nature of one or more category 2 factors or the extreme impact caused by a combination of category 2 factors **may** elevate to category 1
Category 2	• Severe psychological or physical harm • Pregnancy or STI as a consequence of offence • Additional degradation/ humiliation • Abduction • Prolonged detention/sustained incident • Violence or threats of violence

Culpability
A
Significant degree of planning
Offender acts together with others to commit the offence
Use of alcohol/drugs on victim to facilitate the offence
Grooming behaviour used against the victim
Abuse of trust
Previous violence against victim
Offence committed in course of burglary
Sexual images of victim recorded, retained, solicited or shared
Deliberate isolation of victim

	• Forced/uninvited entry into victim's home	Commercial exploitation and/or motivation
		Offence racially or religiously aggravated
Category 3	Factor(s) in categories 1 and 2 not present	Offence motivated by, or demonstrating, hostility to the victim based on his or her sexual orientation (or presumed sexual orientation) or transgender identity (or presumed transgender identity)
		Offence motivated by, or demonstrating, hostility to the victim based on his or her disability (or presumed disability)
		B
		Factor(s) in category A not present

Step Two—Starting point and category range

Once the court has determined the offence category and culpability level, at step two it should use the corresponding starting point specified in the guideline in order to reach a sentence within the category range. The starting point applies to all offenders irrespective of plea or previous convictions. Once the starting point has been determined, step two allows further adjustment for aggravating or mitigating features, set out below. A case of particular gravity, reflected by multiple features of culpability or harm, could merit upward adjustment from the starting point before further adjustment for aggravating or mitigating features. Where there is a sufficient prospect of rehabilitation, a community order with a sex offender treatment programme requirement may be a proper alternative to a short or moderate length custodial sentence. The starting points and category ranges for offences under ss.30 and 31 of the Act differ according to whether the offence involves penetrative or non-penetrative activity, and are as follows:

7.55

Where offence involved penetration		
	A	B
Category 1	*Starting point* 16 years' custody	*Starting point* 13 years' custody
	Category range 13–19 years' custody	*Category range* 11–17 years' custody
Category 2	*Starting point* 13 years' custody	*Starting point* 10 years' custody
	Category range 11–17 years' custody	*Category range* 8–13 years' custody
Category 3	*Starting point* 10 years' custody	*Starting point* 8 years' custody
	Category range 8–13 years' custody	*Category range* 6–11 years' custody
Where offence did not involve penetration		
	A	B
Category 1	*Starting point* 6 years' custody	*Starting point* 4 years' custody
	Category range 4–9 years' custody	*Category range* 3–7 years' custody
Category 2	*Starting point* 4 years' custody	*Starting point* 2 years' custody
	Category range 3–7 years' custody	*Category range* 1–4 years' custody
Category 3	*Starting point* 1 years' custody	*Starting point* 26 weeks' custody
	Category range 26 weeks'–2 years' custody	*Category range* High level community order–1 years' custody

Aggravating and mitigating factors

After identifying the starting point and category range, the court should   7.56
consider whether the presence of aggravating or mitigating factors should
result in an upward or downward adjustment from the starting point or the
imposition of a sentence outside the category range. In particular, relevant
recent convictions are likely to result in an upward adjustment. In appropriate cases, the court should also consider whether the custody threshold
has been passed; if so, whether a custodial sentence is unavoidable; and if it
is, whether that sentence can be suspended. The non-exhaustive list of
aggravating and mitigating factors for offences under ss.30 and 31 is as
follows:

Aggravating factors
Statutory aggravating factors
Previous convictions, having regard to a) the nature of the offence to which the conviction relates and its relevance to the current offence; and b) the time that has elapsed since the conviction
Offence committed whilst on bail
Other aggravating factors
Ejaculation (where not taken into account at step one)
Blackmail or other threats made (where not taken into account at step one)
Location of offence
Timing of offence
Use of weapon or other item to frighten or injure
Victim compelled to leave their home (including victims of domestic violence)
Failure to comply with current court orders
Offence committed whilst on licence
Exploiting contact arrangements with a child to commit an offence
Presence of others, especially other children

Any steps taken to prevent the victim reporting an incident, obtaining assistance and/or from assisting or supporting the prosecution
Attempts to dispose of or conceal evidence
Commission of offence whilst under the influence of alcohol or drugs

Mitigating factors
No previous convictions *or* no relevant/recent convictions
Remorse
Previous good character and/or exemplary conduct*
Age and/or lack of maturity where it affects the responsibility of the offender
Mental disorder or learning disability, particularly where linked to the commission of the offence
Sexual activity was incited but no activity took place because the offender voluntarily desisted or intervened to prevent it

* Previous good character/exemplary conduct is different from having no previous convictions. The more serious the offence, the less the weight which should normally be attributed to this factor. Where previous good character/exemplary conduct has been used to facilitate the offence, this mitigation should not normally be allowed and such conduct may constitute an aggravating factor.

In the context of this offence, previous good character/exemplary conduct should not normally be given any significant weight and will not normally justify a reduction in what would otherwise be the appropriate sentence.

Steps Three to Nine

7.57   The remaining steps cover the following points. At step three the court should consider any factors, which would indicate a reduction in sentence, e.g. assistance to the prosecution. At step four it should consider any reduction for a guilty plea. At step five the court should consider dangerousness, i.e. whether it would be appropriate to award a life sentence (s.224A or s.225(2) of the Criminal Justice Act 2003) or an extended sentence (s.226A). Step six requires the court to consider whether the total sentence is just and proportionate to the offending behaviour. At step seven it should consider whether to make an ancillary order (e.g. a compensation order, a sexual harm prevention order ("SHPO") or a restraining order). Step eight requires the court to fulfil its duty under s.174 of the Criminal Justice Act 2003 to give reasons for, and explain the effect of, the sentence. Finally, at step nine the court should consider whether to give credit for time spent on bail in accordance with s.240A of that Act.

Sentencing examples

There remain few reported examples of sentencing for offences under this   7.58
Part of the 2003 Act. In 2011, 22 people were sentenced for offences contrary
to ss.30–33, no one was sentenced for offences contrary to ss.34–37 and eight
people were sentenced for offences contrary to ss.38–41.[82]

In *Attorney General's Reference (No.54 of 2014) (R. v Aiden Hill)*,[83] the   7.59
Court of Appeal increased from nine to 12 years' imprisonment the sentence
imposed on the offender following his conviction of four offences under s.30
and one under s.31 of the 2003 Act.[84] The offences spanned a two-year
period, during which the offender twice penetrated the victim's anus with his
penis (count 1), penetrated the victim's mouth with his penis on an
unspecified number of occasions (count 2), kissed the victim (count 3) and
touched the victim's penis (count 4). In respect of count 5, the offence under
s.31, the offender incited the victim to touch his (the offender's) penis. The
victim, who like the defendant was aged 27, suffered from cerebral palsy and
had very limited mobility. The offender had met the victim at college and
befriended him years later. Initially the victim welcomed the offender into his
home until the offender's behaviour became sexual. Thereafter the offender
forced his way into the victim's home on numerous occasions. A forensic
psychologist's report concluded that:

> " . . . [the victim] lacked capacity to make a decision in relation to the
> fundamental elements, in that he was not capable of processing what was
> proposed or its implications [before the alleged sexual activity]. Further . . . he
> was not able to exercise choice in relation to . . . sexual contact, although he
> maintains that he tried to refuse."

The sentencing judge identified the offending as falling within category 2B of
the guideline. The Court of Appeal noted that the repetitive nature of the
offender's visits could be described as "grooming" and so the offences could
have fallen within category 2A, but it did not reconsider the categorisation at
2B, and so for the offences involving penetration the starting point was 10
years' imprisonment with a range of 8–13 years. The Court noted that there
is no specific reference in the guideline which assists a sentencing judge with
how to approach a case of multiple offending. In such a case, ordinary
principles apply and require the sentencing court to impose a just and
proportionate sentence in respect of all the criminality involved. The Court
considered that a nine year sentence failed to reflect "the prolonged course of
serious sexual misconduct" and that the minimum sentence which could be
imposed was one of 12 years' imprisonment.

---

[82] *Sexual Offences Guideline: Consultation* (December 6, 2012). The consultation document is
available on the Sentencing Council's website.

[83] [2014] EWCA Crim 2999.

[84] The defendant had also been committed for sentence following pleas of guilty in the
magistrates' court to making and possessing indecent photographs of children.

7.60   In *R v P*,[85] the applicant made a renewed application before the Court of Appeal for leave to appeal a sentence of 13 years' imprisonment imposed following his conviction after trial under s.30. He was sentenced under the old guideline issued by the Sentencing Guidelines Council, but the single judge when refusing leave stated it would be a category 2 offence under the new guideline, with a starting point of 13 years. The victim suffered serious brain injury in her early 30s resulting in her being wheelchair-bound with little use of her arms and speech difficulties. She had lived in a care home for 10 years. The offence, described in the judgment as "truly horrific" and planned over a period of years, was committed by the applicant and the victim's step-father. The activity involved removing the victim's clothing and incontinence pad, penile penetration of her mouth, masturbation to the point of ejaculation over her breasts, and penetration of her vagina with a sex toy. She was told not to tell anyone. An additional aggravating feature was that the applicant had video-recorded the assault. The recording was played to the jury and the victim's childlike quality was apparent. In her ABE interview, the victim spoke of her "enjoyment" of the sexual activity. In dismissing the application, the Court held that comments as to their "enjoyment" or otherwise of what occurred, made by a victim who is assessed as incapable of consenting to sexual activity, are of "limited, if any, significance at all".

Parties to the Offence

7.61 Offences under s.30 may be committed by and against persons of either sex.

Jurisdiction

7.62 By virtue of s.72 of and Sch.2 to the Sexual Offences Act 2003, as amended,[86] it is an offence under s.30 for a UK national to do an act in a country outside the UK which would constitute a s.30 offence committed against a person aged under 18 if done in England and Wales. The amendments, made in 2008, expanded the scope of s.72 in two respects. First, they removed the limitation on s.72 as enacted that it applied only to offences committed against victims aged under 16 (the relevant age is now 18). Secondly, they abolished, in respect of UK nationals, the "double criminality" requirement that the act must have been an offence in the country in which it was done. This requirement is, however, retained in respect of the prosecution of UK residents and those who become UK residents or nationals after the doing of the relevant act. For the purposes of s.72 a "country" includes a territory and a "United Kingdom national" means a British citizen, a British overseas

---

[85] [2015] 2 Cr. App. R.(S.) 28.
[86] By the Criminal Justice and Immigration Act 2008 s.72, with effect from July 14, 2008.

territories citizen, a British National (Overseas), a British Overseas citizen, a person who under the British Nationality Act 1981 is a British subject, or a British protected person within the meaning of that Act.[87] An act is taken to be an offence in the country in which it was done unless the defendant serves a notice putting the prosecution to proof on the point.[88]

"TOUCHES ANOTHER PERSON"

For the meaning of "touches" see para.2.63 and following, above.   **7.63**

"THE TOUCHING IS SEXUAL"

For the meaning of "sexual", see para.2.66, above.   **7.64**

"UNABLE TO REFUSE"

Proving that the complainant was "unable to refuse" is an element common   **7.65**
to the offences under ss.30–33 of the Act. In relation to s.30, the complainant must be "unable to refuse" the sexual touching. Section 30(2) of the Act provides as follows:

> "B is unable to refuse if:
> (a) he lacks the capacity to choose whether to agree to the touching (whether because he lacks sufficient understanding of the nature or reasonably foreseeable consequences of what is being done, or for any other reason), or
> (b) he is unable to communicate such a choice to A."

The effect of s.30(2)(a) is that a person is unable to refuse is they lack the   **7.66**
capacity to choose whether to agree to sexual touching, whether because they lack sufficient understanding of the nature of the activity they are being approached to engage in, or of the reasonably foreseeable consequences of that activity, or for any other reason. Lord Falconer explained the then Government's understanding of the issue to be determined under s.30(2)(a) as being:

> "whether at that time they were able to understand enough of what was proposed to refuse if they did not want to engage in sexual activity. The clauses as drafted define the criminal behaviour in terms of it being committed against someone who is unable to refuse being subjected to it. That clearly defines the vulnerability of the victim in these cases and does so in straightforward language."[89]

The ability to choose whether to agree to sexual touching means that a   **7.67**
person must have the capacity to agree and not merely be able to refuse. To have capacity a person must be capable of deciding to agree to the touching.

---

[87] s.72(9).
[88] s.72(6)–(8).
[89] *Hansard*, HL Vol.646, col.397, Lord Falconer of Thoroton (April 10, 2003).

This approach moves firmly away from the heavily criticised and old-fashioned view that a mentally disordered person can legally consent to sexual activity if their "animal instincts" take over.[90]

7.68   In this respect, the Australian case of *Morgan*[91] is instructive. The defendant was charged with rape and the prosecution alleged that the 19-year-old complainant lacked the mental capacity to consent. It was held that a person has capacity to consent (to sexual intercourse) if they know or understand that the physical act involves penetration of their body by the male organ, and/or that the act of penetration is one of sexual connection as distinct from an act of a very different character. The complainant's knowledge must be sufficient for her to understand what the act comprises of and its character and make a judgment as to whether to withhold her consent.[92]

7.69   In *Morgan*, the court did not go so far as to rule that the complainant could only consent if she understood the potential physical consequences of the intercourse, such as pregnancy.[93] In the context of the 2003 Act, we suggest that in strict logic the phrase "reasonably foreseeable consequences" does refer to the complainant's understanding that the sexual activity could have implications for his or her sexual health and, in the case of women, could lead to pregnancy.[94] However, in determining whether an individual had the capacity to understand the "reasonably foreseeable consequences" at the time they engaged in sexual activity does not demand that the mentally disordered be capable of exercising a more stringent decision-making process than that carried out by persons of full capacity: see the discussion in paras 7.10 and following, above.

7.70   Whilst, as with all the offences against the mentally disordered, the prosecution does not have to prove that the complainant did not consent to the sexual activity, in respect of the offences in ss.30–33 it must establish to the criminal standard that they were "unable to refuse because of or for a reason related to a mental disorder".[95] The House of Lords considered the concepts of "capacity to choose" and "unable to refuse" in the case of *Cooper*,[96] in which the leading opinion was given by Baroness Hale, with whom their Lordships agreed. The complainant was a 28-year-old woman who suffered from a schizoaffective disorder, an emotionally unstable personality disorder, an IQ of less than 75 and a history of harmful alcohol use. The effects of the complainant's illness could come and go. When

---

[90] *Fletcher* (1884) 15 Cox C.C. 579.
[91] [1970] V.R. 337.
[92] [1970] V.R. 337, at pp.341–342.
[93] Jennifer Temkin, *Rape and the Legal Process*, 2nd edn (Oxford: Oxford University Press, 2002), p.113.
[94] See Tracey Elliott, *Capacity, sex and the mentally disordered, Archbold News*, 2008.
[95] "Inability to refuse" is defined in ss.30(2), 31(2), 32(2), and 33(2). See also paras 7.18 and following, above.
[96] [2009] UKHL 42.

suffering, she could experience delusions, hallucinations and severe disturbances of mood. An emotionally unstable personality disorder is an intrinsic
abnormality of mood, inability to interact with other people, and abnormal
thought processes and thinking style. A sufferer has a tendency to become
upset without rational cause, act impulsively, develop unstable relationships
and repeatedly self-harm. The complainant had had at least four admissions
to hospital, including three periods of detention under the Mental Health
Act 1983. On the day of the offence she had visited her community mental
health team and had dramatically left an appointment with a consultant
forensic psychiatrist in a distressed and agitated state. The psychiatrist had
recommended her compulsory admission to hospital. On leaving the
appointment, the complainant met the defendant in the car park outside the
centre. She told him that she had been in hospital for nine years and had
recently left. She said that she wanted to leave Croydon because she believed
people were after her. The defendant offered to help her and so the
complainant went with him to his friend's house. He sold her bicycle and
mobile telephone and gave her crack cocaine. She went to the bathroom but
the defendant came in and demanded that she give him a "blow job". The
complainant's evidence was that she was really panicky and afraid and had
wanted to leave. She was saying to herself, "these crack heads . . . they do
worse to you". She did not want to die so she just stayed there and just took
it all.

The complainant made a 999 call and at midnight the police found her   7.71
running around the street, screaming and saying, "They're going to kill me.
They're going to kill me." Psychiatric evidence was called to the effect that
she would not have had the ability to consent to sexual contact at the time of
the offence because of an irrational fear or confusion of mind arising from
her mental disorder.

The trial judge directed the jury as follows on the complainant's   7.72
capacity:

> "Now [the complainant] would be unable to refuse if she lacked the capacity to
> choose whether to agree to the touching, in other words the sexual activity, for
> any reason, for example an irrational fear arising from her mental disorder or
> such confusion of mind arising from her mental disorder, that she felt that she
> was unable to refuse any request the defendant made for sex. Alternatively, she
> would be unable to refuse if through her mental disorder she was unable to
> communicate such a choice to the defendants even though she was physically
> able to communicate with them."

The House of Lords eventually upheld the judge's direction on lack of   7.73
capacity. However, before it did so, the Court of Appeal allowed an appeal on
the basis that a lack of capacity to choose cannot be person or situation-
specific, and that an irrational fear that prevents the exercise of choice cannot
be equated with a lack of capacity to choose. The Court held that the relevant
test was whether the person concerned had sufficient knowledge of the sexual
character of the act to be able to give an informed consent to it. The effect
of the decision was to restrict the test of capacity so as to ignore the impact

a person's mental disorder may have on their ability to refuse to engage in sexual activity at a particular time. For example, a person with a mental disorder could well understand the nature and consequences of any act but yet be unable to refuse to engage in that activity because of a phobia or fear relating to their mental disorder.

7.74 The Court of Appeal agreed with Munby J[97] that "a woman either has capacity, for example, to consent to 'normal' penetrative vaginal intercourse, or she does not . . . Put shortly, capacity to consent to sexual relations is issue specific; it is not person specific." The Court also disagreed with the judge's direction that if the complainant was unable to say "no" because of an irrational fear, this was capable of amounting to an inability to communicate her choice.

7.75 The House of Lords overturned the Court of Appeal's decision. In Baroness Hale's view, the Court of Appeal had been led astray by their understandable reliance upon the view that capacity could not be situation-specific. She held that the 2003 Act had made the position in relation to ability and capacity to choose clear. Under s.30(2)(a), a person is unable to refuse if he lacks the capacity to choose whether to agree to the touching, whether because he lacks sufficient understanding of the nature or reasonably foreseeable consequences of what is being done "or for any other reason". The words "or for any other reason" should not be ignored. Her Ladyship stated that they were capable of encompassing a wide range of circumstances in which a person's mental disorder might rob them of the ability to make an autonomous choice as to whether to engage in the sexual activity, albeit that they may understand the nature of the act and its foreseeable consequences. She gave cogent examples of the compulsion from which mentally disordered persons may suffer which removes their autonomy of choice: an anorexic who refuses food, the delusions which drive a schizophrenic to believe that they must do something, or the phobia which leads a person to refuse a life-saving injection.[98] It is not sufficient that a person can understand the information relevant to making a decision; they must be able to weigh the information in the balance to arrive at a choice.[99] For instance, the complainant in *Cooper* knew what a blow job was, but was put in a vulnerable and terrifying situation by the defendant when she was in an aroused and agitated state. That may have robbed her of the ability to make a free choice.

7.76 Baroness Hale held that the test of capacity is neither "person-specific" nor "situation-specific". It is well accepted that a mentally disordered person's capacity to choose can fluctuate. They may be quite capable of exercising choice in one situation but not in another. The question to be

---

[97] See *X City Council v MB* [2006] EWHC 168 (Fam) and *Re M* [2007] EWHC 2003 (Fam).
[98] [2009] UKHL 42 at [25].
[99] [2009] UKHL 42 at [24], citing *Re C (adult: refusal of treatment)* [1994] 1 All E.R. 819, at 824.

asked was whether, in the state the complainant was in on the particular day, were they capable of choosing whether to consent? Capacity therefore cannot be determined by considering the complainant's mental disorder in the abstract but must be considered in the context of whether they had the capacity to consent to the particular sexual contact, at the particular time, with that particular person. As Baroness Hale put it with exemplary clarity: "It is difficult to think of an activity which is more person and situation specific than sexual relations". She went on to observe how this approach was entirely consistent with the respect for autonomy in matters of private life that is guaranteed by art.8 of the ECHR.

Inability to communicate choice

An inability to refuse can exist because the complainant is incapable of   7.77
choosing whether to agree to their involvement in the sexual activity or because they were unable to communicate their choice to the offender because of or for a reason related to their mental disorder. Baroness Hale in *Cooper* stressed that Parliament had in mind an inability to communicate which was the result of or associated with a disorder of the mind, and that there is no warrant for limiting it to a physical inability to communicate. She gave the example of a person with such a degree of learning difficulty they have never learnt the gift of speech, so that it is impossible to discover whether or not they can understand or make a choice. This category would also cover physical disorders of the brain, which lead to mental disorders when the cognitive and evaluative processes become impaired.

In *Hulme v DPP*,[100] the appellant, aged 73, was convicted under s.30 for   7.78
touching the private parts of the complainant, aged 27. She suffered from cerebral palsy and had a mental age well below her chronological age. On appeal, the appellant submitted that there was no evidence on which the justices could have concluded that the complainant was "unable to refuse" within the meaning of s.30(2). She was capable of both choosing and communicating her choice and, on the evidence, she did indeed make a choice: she chose not to consent to the appellant's activity, she communicated her choice and he overrode it. Effectively, the submission was that the appellant had been charged with an inappropriate offence and should have been charged instead with sexual assault under s.3 of the 2003 Act.

The Divisional Court, having analysed the justices' findings, held that they   7.79
had been entitled to conclude that the complainant was unable to refuse because of or for a reason related to a mental disorder. The Court interpreted the justices as essentially saying that, although the complainant did not want the appellant to act in the way that he did, she was unable effectively to communicate her choice to him. There was evidence capable of supporting this finding, in that the complainant had said that, when the appellant

---

[100] [2006] EWHC 1347 (Admin).

touched her private parts and pressed hard, she did not know what to do or say, although it made her feel sad, hurt and upset. If the justices accepted that she did not want him to continue but did not know what to say or do, that could only sensibly be because of her mental condition. The decision in *Hulme* is completely in line with the House of Lords' reasoning in *Cooper.*

"BECAUSE OF OR FOR A REASON RELATED TO A MENTAL DISORDER"

7.80   The complainant must be unable to refuse to engage in the activity because of or for a reason related to a "mental disorder". The 2003 Act relies upon the definition of "mental disorder" in s.1(2) of the Mental Health Act 1983, as amended by the Mental Health Act 2007.[101] The amendment simplified and extended the definition of the term, which is now defined simply as "any disorder or disability of the mind". See further the discussion in paras 7.25 and following, above.

7.81   The term "mental disorder" significantly widens the pool of potential complainants, compared to the previous legislation. Under s.7 of the Sexual Offences Act 1956, it had to be proved that the complainant was a "defective", i.e. that they were suffering from a state of arrested or incomplete development of mind, including severe impairment of intelligence and social functioning.[102] It follows that a complainant with a significant, but not severe, mental disorder was not protected.[103] Nor was a person whose mind had developed properly but who had subsequently suffered brain damage in an accident or had become an Alzheimer's victim.

7.82   The prosecution has to establish a causal link between the mental disorder and the inability to refuse. However, they are not required to prove that the mental disorder in isolation renders the complainant unable to refuse the sexual activity. The words "for a reason related to a mental disorder" enable the jury to consider the entirety of the circumstances surrounding the complainant's mental disorder when considering the issue of ability to refuse, as opposed to focusing solely upon their medical condition. For example, the jury may take into account such factors as the effects on the complainant of medication and institutionalisation (if they relate to a mental disorder).[104]

7.83   The effect of the words "for a reason related to" a mental disorder, used in addition to the words "because of" a mental disorder, is to widen the pool of potential complainants beyond those for whom there is a direct causal link

---

[101] 2003 Act s.79(6).

[102] Sexual Offences Act 1956 s.45. There is no provision in this definition for "any other disability or disorder of mind" as appears in the 1983 Act.

[103] M.J. Gunn in *Sexual Rights of the Mentally Handicapped*, in E. Alves (ed), *Issues in Criminological and Legal Psychology No 10: Mental Handicap and the Law* (1987), p.31, set out in fn.32, above.

[104] *Hansard*, HC Vol.412, col. 600, Harriet Harman QC, Solicitor-General (November 3, 2003).

between their disorder and the inability to refuse, to include those who are "unable to refuse" as an indirect result of mental disorder. For instance, a person who is "unable to refuse" because of the side-effects of medication administered to treat their mental disorder, or a patient who has become so institutionalised as a result of treatment for their mental disorder that they have become compliant when requests are made of them.[105]

Expert evidence

In most cases in which there is an issue as to whether the complainant lacks   **7.84** capacity due to a mental disorder, it will be necessary for the prosecution to call expert evidence of the complainant's intelligence and social functioning, as these are matters which would not be within the common experience of the jury.[106] Even if it is accepted that the complainant suffers from a mental disorder, expert medical evidence may be needed of the extent and degree of that disorder if the defence dispute that the complainant was unable to refuse, or assert that the defendant did not know, and could not reasonably have been expected to know, of the complainant's disorder. In rare cases, however, the jury may be able safely to assess the complainant's mental state from the evidence generally, without the assistance of a medical expert. In such cases it may be possible for the prosecution to establish that the complainant suffers from a mental disorder by inviting the jury to observe the behaviour and reactions of the complainant and to draw what they consider to be an appropriate inference. This point was graphically illustrated by Parker LJ in *Hall*[107] when dealing with the argument advanced on behalf of the appellant that the degree of impairment could only be proved by expert evidence:

> "We are unable to accept that a medical expert's opinion that a woman of say 30, with the intelligence of a girl of five is not severely impaired is of any real weight if indeed admissible at all. If, having heard such evidence, the jury observe the complainant happily playing with toys suitable for a child of five, unable to cope with toys for slightly older girls, and only able to converse like a child of five, the doctor's opinion cannot be regarded as being preferable to the observation of the jury."

Hall was followed in *Robbins*,[108] where there was an appeal against convic-   **7.85** tion on the ground that the judge had erred in allowing the issue of mental disorder to go before the jury without expert evidence from the prosecution to support it, and when experts consulted by the prosecution had expressly contradicted it. It was argued that as a result the jury's attention was diverted from the issue of consent, which should have been the sole issue. The appeal

---

[105] Paul Goggins MP, HC Deb, Vol. 412, col. 600. See also Card, Gillespie and Hirst, *Sexual Offences*, 2008, para.9.14.

[106] *R. v GA* [2014] EWCA Crim 299 at [30], where the Court said that it will "inevitably" be the case that such evidence is required.

[107] *Hall* (1988) 86 Cr. App. R. 159.

[108] [1988] Crim. L.R. 744.

was dismissed following the reasoning in *Hall* that medical evidence is unnecessary in order to establish a complainant's mental impairment.

7.86　　Judges must be careful to appraise the expertise and therefore competence of those called to give evidence as to capacity.[109] It is also vital that an expert called to address the issue of capacity, confines himself to that issue. In *R. v GA*[110] the expert exceeded her remit by articulating her own interpretation of the facts as to whether the complainant did or did not consent. The Court of Appeal said it was unfortunate that the witness was not adequately managed in the court process as a whole, and concluded that the evidence she gave was not fit for purpose to assist the jury on the issue of capacity.[111]

MENTAL ELEMENT

7.87　The touching must be intentional. If the touching is accidental, careless or even reckless, no offence will be committed. It will suffice if the defendant's act was deliberate.[112] In *Heard*,[113] dealing with the offence of sexual assault, for which an intentional touching is also required, the Court of Appeal upheld the trial judge's direction to the jury that it was not open to the defendant to contend that voluntary intoxication through drink or drugs prevented him from intending to touch the victim. We suggest that this must apply equally to the s.30 offence.

7.88　　It is also a requirement that the defendant knew or could reasonably have been expected to know that B had a mental disorder *and* that because of it or for a reason related to it, B was likely to be unable to refuse. This operates to restrain people who know or ought to know that a person's mental disorder is likely to affect their ability to choose. It is more restrictive than the mens rea for rape, which is that the defendant does not reasonably believe that the complainant consents.[114]

7.89　　To establish the defendant's awareness of B's mental disorder may be less problematic than proving that the defendant knew or could reasonably have been expected to know the impact B's disorder would have. In considering what the defendant could reasonably have been expected to know, it will be highly relevant for the jury to consider the extent and outward manifestation of the complainant's mental disorder, the relationship between the parties and the circumstances in which the conduct which is the subject of the proceedings occurred. The inclusion of the objective test of reasonableness is tempered by the fact that the focus is upon what the particular defendant could reasonably be expected to know. A defendant with a low IQ, or even an intelligent person with little or no experience of mental disorder, may have

[109] *R. v GA* [2014] EWCA Crim 299 at [27].
[110] [2014] EWCA Crim 299.
[111] [2014] EWCA Crim 299 at [30]–[31].
[112] *Heard* [2007] EWCA Crim 125, discussed in paras 2.78 and following, above.
[113] [2007] EWCA Crim 125, discussed in paras 2.81 and following, above.
[114] Sexual Offences Act 2003 s.1(1)(c).

difficulty recognising those sufferers whose symptoms are not obvious, but which still impact upon their ability to make decisions regarding the formation of sexual relationships. An appropriate test would be for the jury to consider what could reasonably be expected of a person of the particular defendant's age, IQ and other personal characteristics, which it would be unjust for the jury to ignore.

The fact that the prosecution must prove that the defendant knew or could   **7.90** reasonably have been expected to know of the complainant's mental disorder, and that (for ss.30–33) there is a causal link between the disorder and the complainant's inability to refuse, will not necessarily mean that the complainant will need to be called. Indeed, it is anticipated that these points may be proved by means of expert medical evidence.[115]

Causing or Inciting a Person, with a Mental Disorder Impeding Choice, to Engage in Sexual Activity

Section 31(1) of the Sexual Offences Act 2003 provides: **7.91**

"A person (A) commits an offence if:
  (a) he intentionally causes or incites another person (B) to engage in an activity,
  (b) the activity is sexual,
  (c) B is unable to refuse because of or for a reason related to a mental disorder, and
  (d) A knows or could reasonably be expected to know that B has a mental disorder and that because of it or for a reason related to it B is likely to be unable to refuse."

Mode of Trial and Punishment

The mode of trial and maximum sentence for an offence under s.31 depends   **7.92** upon the type of activity caused or incited. If the activity involved any of the following, the offence is triable on indictment only with a maximum penalty of life imprisonment:

- penetration of B's anus or vagina,
- penetration of B's mouth with a person's penis,
- penetration of a person's anus or vagina with a part of B's body or by B with anything else, or
- penetration of a person's mouth with B's penis.[116]

Otherwise, the offence is triable either way. The maximum sentence on conviction on indictment is 14 years' imprisonment. On summary conviction it is six months' imprisonment or a fine, or both.[117] As from a day to be appointed, the maximum term of imprisonment on summary conviction will

[115] *Hansard*, HL Vol.646, col.407 Lord Falconer of Thoroton (April 10, 2003). An alternative would be the admission of the video evidence of the complainant as a document under s.116 of the Criminal Justice Act 2003: see paras 7.37 and following, above.
[116] s.31(3).
[117] s.31(4).

increase to 12 months.[118] The increase will have no application to offences committed before it takes effect.[119] Until recently, the maximum fine on summary conviction was a fine not exceeding the statutory maximum (i.e. £5,000). The effect of s.85 of the Legal Aid, Sentencing and Punishment of Offenders Act 2012 is that, from March 12, 2015, a fine of any amount may be imposed.

7.93   For the purposes of listing, cases under s.31[120] fall within Class 2B, save for complex cases involving many complainants (in care or otherwise particularly vulnerable) and/or many defendants who are alleged to have systematically groomed and abused them, often over a long period of time, which fall within Class 1C.[121] Cases in Class 1C must be referred to the Resident Judge, and by the Resident Judge to a Presiding Judge. Cases in Class 2B must be similarly referred in certain specified circumstances, including where the case is unusually grave or complex or a novel and important point of law is to be raised; where the defendant is a police officer, a member of the legal profession or a high profile figure; or where for any reason the case is likely to attract exceptional media attention.

7.94   An offence under s.31 is a serious specified offence for the purposes of s.224 and, where the offence involved penetration, s.225(2) (life sentence for serious offences) of the Criminal Justice Act 2003.[122] A s.31 offence, whenever committed, may be made the subject of an extended sentence under s.226A of that Act.[123] The offence is also listed in Pt 1 of Sch.15B to the Criminal Justice Act 2003 for the purposes of s.224A of that Act (life sentence for a second listed offence).[124]

7.95   A person convicted under s.31, cautioned, found not guilty by reason of insanity or found to be under a disability and to have done the act charged, is automatically subject to the notification requirements in the Sexual Offences Act 2003.[125]

Bail

7.96 Section 25 of the Criminal Justice and Public Order Act 1994[126] provides that a person charged with or convicted of certain offences who has a previous

---

[118] Criminal Justice Act 2003 s.282(2), (3).

[119] Criminal Justice Act 2003 s.282(4).

[120] And of soliciting, inciting, encouraging or assisting, attempting or conspiring to commit the offence or assisting an offender having committed the offence.

[121] *Consolidated Criminal Practice Directions*, Part XIII Listing B: CLASSIFICATION, available *at https://www.judiciary.gov.uk/wp-content/uploads/2015/09/crim-pd-2015.pdf* [Accessed April 30, 2016].

[122] Criminal Justice Act 2003 s.224 and Sch.15, Pt 2.

[123] Inserted by the Legal Aid, Sentencing and Punishment of Offenders Act 2012 s.124, brought into force on December 3, 2012, by SI 2012/2906.

[124] Inserted by the Legal Aid, Sentencing and Punishment of Offenders Act 2012 s.122, brought into force on December 3, 2012, by SI 2012/2906. See Appendix A, below.

[125] s.80 and Sch.3, discussed in Ch.35, below.

[126] As amended with effect from December 3, 2012, by the Legal Aid, Sentencing and Punishment of Offenders Act 2012 s.90 and Sch.11 para.33.

conviction for any such offence shall be granted bail only if the court, or as the case may be, the constable considering the grant of bail, is of the opinion that there are exceptional circumstances which justify it. The offences in question include offences under s.31 involving penetration as set out in para.7.92, above, and attempts to commit such an offence. For the full list of offences covered by s.25 of the 1994 Act, see para.1.24 and following, above.

SENTENCING

For the Sentencing Council guideline relating to the sentencing of sexual offences committed by offenders aged 18 and over, see Ch.33. A single guideline covers the offences in s.30 and s.31 of the 2003 Act and is considered at paras 7.53 and following, above.   **7.97**

PARTIES TO THE OFFENCE

This offence may be committed by and against persons of either sex.   **7.98**

JURISDICTION

By virtue of s.72 of and Sch.2 to the Sexual Offences Act 2003, as amended,[127] it is an offence under s.31 for a UK national to do an act in a country outside the UK which would constitute a s.31 offence committed against a person aged under 18 if done in England and Wales. See further para.7.62, above.   **7.99**

"CAUSES OR INCITES ANOTHER PERSON . . . TO ENGAGE IN AN ACTIVITY"

For the meaning of those terms, see paras 2.98 and following, and 3.158 and following, above. The s.31 offence is complete once there has been incitement, even if the sexual activity does not take place.   **7.100**

"THE ACTIVITY IS SEXUAL"

The activity caused or incited must be "sexual". For the meaning of this term, see paras 2.66 and following, above. The sexual activity need not be with the defendant: the offence is committed where a person causes the   **7.101**

---

[127] By the Criminal Justice and Immigration Act 2008 s.72, with effect from July 14, 2008.

complainant to engage in sexual activity with another person, or incites the complainant to masturbate himself.

"Unable to Refuse"

7.102 The complainant must be "unable to refuse" to engage in the activity caused or incited. Section 31(2) of the Act provides:

> "B is unable to refuse if–
> (a) he lacks the capacity to choose whether to agree to engaging in the activity caused or incited (whether because he lacks sufficient understanding of the nature or reasonably foreseeable consequences of the activity, or for any other reason), or
> (b) he is unable to communicate such a choice to A."

For the effect of this provision, see paras 7.18 and following, and 7.65 and following, above.

"Because of or for a Reason Related to a Mental Disorder"

7.103 The complainant's inability to refuse must have been because of or for a reason related to a mental disorder. For the meaning and effect of this term, see paras 7.25 and following, and 7.80 and following, above.

Mental Element

7.104 The defendant (A) must intentionally cause or incite the complainant (B) to engage in sexual activity. Recklessness is insufficient. It will suffice if the defendant's act was deliberate.[128] In *Heard*,[129] dealing with the offence of sexual assault, for which an intentional touching is also required, the Court of Appeal upheld the trial judge's direction to the jury that it was not open to the defendant to contend that voluntary intoxication through drink or drugs prevented him from intending to touch the victim. We suggest that this must apply equally to the s.31 offence.

7.105 Additionally, it is a requirement that A knew or could reasonably have been expected to know that B had a mental disorder and that because of it or for a reason related to it B was likely to be unable to refuse. For discussion of an identical requirement in s.30 of the Act, see paras 7.88 and following, above.

---

[128] *Heard* [2007] EWCA Crim 125, discussed in paras 2.78 and following, above.
[129] [2007] EWCA Crim 125, discussed in paras 2.81 and following, above.

ENGAGING IN SEXUAL ACTIVITY IN THE PRESENCE OF A PERSON WITH A MENTAL DISORDER IMPEDING CHOICE

DEFINITION

Section 32(1) provides as follows: **7.106**

"A person (A) commits an offence if—
(a) he intentionally engages in an activity,
(b) the activity is sexual,
(c) for the purpose of obtaining sexual gratification, he engages in it—
    (i) when another person (B) is present or is in a place from which A can be observed, and
    (ii) knowing or believing that B is aware, or intending that B should be aware, that he is engaging in it,
(d) B is unable to refuse because of or for a reason related to a mental disorder, and
(e) A knows or could reasonably be expected to know that B has a mental disorder and that because of it or for a reason related to it B is likely to be unable to refuse."

MODE OF TRIAL AND PUNISHMENT

Offences under s.32 of the Sexual Offences Act 2003 are triable either way.   **7.107**
The maximum sentence on conviction on indictment is 10 years' imprisonment. The maximum on summary conviction is six months' imprisonment or a fine, or both.[130] As from a day to be appointed, the maximum term of imprisonment on summary conviction will increase to 12 months.[131] The increase will have no application to offences committed before it takes effect.[132] Until recently, the maximum fine on summary conviction was a fine not exceeding the statutory maximum (i.e. £5,000). The effect of s.85 of the Legal Aid, Sentencing and Punishment of Offenders Act 2012 is that, from March 12, 2015, a fine of any amount may be imposed.

For the purposes of listing, cases under s.32[133] fall within Class 2B, save for   **7.108**
complex cases involving many complainants (in care or otherwise particularly vulnerable) and/or many defendants who are alleged to have systematically groomed and abused them, often over a long period of time, which fall within Class 1C.[134] Cases in Class 1C must be referred to the Resident Judge, and by the Resident Judge to a Presiding Judge. Cases in Class 2B must be similarly referred in certain specified circumstances, including where

---

[130] s.32(4).
[131] Criminal Justice Act 2003 s.282(2), (3).
[132] Criminal Justice Act 2003 s.282(4).
[133] And of soliciting, inciting, encouraging or assisting, attempting or conspiring to commit the offence or assisting an offender having committed the offence.
[134] *Consolidated Criminal Practice Directions*, Part XIII Listing B: CLASSIFICATION, available at *https://www.judiciary.gov.uk/wp-content/uploads/2015/09/crim-pd-2015.pdf* [Accessed April 30, 2016].

the case is unusually grave or complex or a novel and important point of law is to be raised; where the defendant is a police officer, a member of the legal profession or a high profile figure; or where for any reason the case is likely to attract exceptional media attention.

7.109   An offence under s.32, whenever committed, is a specified offence for the purposes of s.226A of the Criminal Justice Act 2003 (extended sentence for certain violent or sexual offences).[135]

7.110   A person convicted under s.32, cautioned, found not guilty by reason of insanity or found to be under a disability and to have done the act charged, is automatically subject to the notification requirements in the Sexual Offences Act 2003.[136]

Sentencing

7.111   For the Sentencing Council guideline relating to the sentencing of sexual offences committed by offenders aged 18 and over, see Ch.33. Where a victim is unable to refuse, then in practical, if not legal, terms this is likely to have a similar impact to lack of consent in cases where the victim does not have a mental disorder, and so the guideline for offences where there is a mental disorder impeding choice follow a similar structure to the guidelines for rape, assault by penetration and sexual assault (ss.1–3 of the 2003 Act).

Sentencing Guideline

Step One—Harm and culpability

7.112   A single guideline covers the offences in ss.32 and 33 of the 2003 Act (engaging in sexual activity in the presence of a person with mental disorder impeding choice, and causing such a person to watch a sexual act). These offences replicate the offence behaviours covered by ss.11 and 12 of the Act (engaging in sexual activity in the presence of a child and causing or inciting a child to watch a sexual act), and the Sentencing Council's approach was to use the guideline for offences under those sections as a template for the offence categories and sentence levels for ss.32 and 33. As a result, harm is predicated on the extreme nature of the activity viewed by the victim and the culpability factors focus on exploitative and manipulative behaviour on the part of the offender. Under the guideline, the sentencing court must go through a series of steps in order to determine the appropriate sentence. Step one involves determining the offence category by reference to the degree of harm caused and then the culpability level for the offence. The court should

---

[135] Inserted by the Legal Aid, Sentencing and Punishment of Offenders Act 2012 s.124, brought into force on December 3, 2012, by SI 2012/2906.
[136] s.80 and Sch.3, discussed in Ch.35, below.

determine into which categories of harm and culpability the offence falls by
reference to the tables below:

Harm	
Category 1	• Causing victim to view extreme pornography • Causing victim to view indecent/ prohibited images of children • Engaging in, or causing a victim to view live, sexual activity involving sadism/violence/ sexual activity with an animal/a child
Category 2	Engaging in, or causing a victim to view live, sexual activity involving: • penetration of vagina or anus (using body or object) • penile penetration of mouth • masturbation
Category 3	Factor(s) in categories 1 and 2 not present

Culpability
A
Significant degree of planning
Offender acts together with others to commit the offence
Use of alcohol/drugs on victim to facilitate the offence
Grooming behaviour used against the victim
Abuse of trust
Previous violence against victim
Use of threats (including blackmail)
Commercial exploitation and/or motivation
Offence racially or religiously aggravated
Offence motivated by, or demonstrating, hostility to the victim based on his or her sexual orientation (or presumed sexual orientation) or transgender identity (or presumed transgender identity)
Offence motivated by, or demonstrating, hostility to the victim based on his or her disability (or presumed disability)
B
Factor(s) in category A not present

Step Two—Starting point and category range

7.113 Once the court has determined the offence category and culpability level, at step two it should use the corresponding starting point specified in the guideline in order to reach a sentence within the category range. The starting point applies to all offenders irrespective of plea or previous convictions. Once the starting point has been determined, step two allows further adjustment for aggravating or mitigating features, set out below. A case of particular gravity, reflected by multiple features of culpability or harm, could merit upward adjustment from the starting point before further adjustment for aggravating or mitigating features. Where there is a sufficient prospect of rehabilitation, a community order with a sex offender treatment programme requirement under s.202 of the CJA 2003 may be a proper alternative to a short or moderate length custodial sentence. The starting points and category ranges are as follows:

	A	B
Category 1	*Starting point* 4 years' custody *Category range* 3–6 years' custody	*Starting point* 2 years' custody *Category range* 1–3 years' custody
Category 2	*Starting point* 2 years' custody *Category range* 1–3 years' custody	*Starting point* 1 years' custody *Category range* High level community order–18 months' custody
Category 3	*Starting point* 26 weeks' custody *Category range* High level community order–1 years' custody	*Starting point* Medium level community order *Category range* Low level community order–Medium level community order

Aggravating and mitigating factors

7.114 After identifying the starting point and category range, the court should consider whether the presence of aggravating or mitigating factors should

result in an upward or downward adjustment from the starting point or the imposition of a sentence outside the category range. In particular, relevant recent convictions are likely to result in an upward adjustment. When sentencing appropriate category 2 or 3 offences, the court should also consider whether the custody threshold has been passed; if so, whether a custodial sentence is unavoidable; and if it is, whether that sentence can be suspended. The non-exhaustive list of aggravating and mitigating factors for offences under ss.32 and 33 is as follows:

Aggravating factors
Statutory aggravating factors
Previous convictions, having regard to a) the nature of the offence to which the conviction relates and its relevance to the current offence; and b) the time that has elapsed since the conviction
Offence committed whilst on bail
Other aggravating factors
Location of offence
Timing of offence
Failure to comply with current court orders
Offence committed whilst on licence
Any steps taken to prevent the victim reporting an incide~~r~~ ~~tr~~aining assistance and/or from assisting or supporting the prose~~cution~~
Attempts to dispose of or conceal evidence ~~ol~~ or drugs
Commission of offence whilst under the influence

Mitigating factors ~~o~~ns
No previous convictions *or* no relevant/rec~~ent~~
Remorse
Previous good character and/or exem~~plary~~ ~~r~~esponsibility of the
Age and/or lack of maturity where~~ particu~~arly where link~~ed~~ offender
~~M~~ental disorder or learni~~ng~~ ~~co~~mmission of the offenc~~e~~

> Demonstration of steps taken to address offending behaviour

* Previous good character/exemplary conduct is different from having no previous convictions. The more serious the offence, the less the weight which should normally be attributed to this factor. Where previous good character/exemplary conduct has been used to facilitate the offence, this mitigation should not normally be allowed and such conduct may constitute an aggravating factor.

Steps Three to Nine

7.115 The remaining steps cover the following points. At step three the court should consider any factors, which would indicate a reduction in sentence, e.g. assistance to the prosecution. At step four it should consider any reduction for a guilty plea. At step five the court should consider dangerousness, i.e. whether it would be appropriate to award an extended sentence (s.226A of the Criminal Justice Act 2003). Step six requires the court to consider whether the total sentence is just and proportionate to the offending behaviour. At step seven it should consider whether to make an ancillary order (e.g. a compensation order, a SHPO or a restraining order). Step eight requires the court to fulfil its duty under s.174 of the Criminal Justice Act 2003 to give reasons for, and explain the effect of, the sentence. Finally, at step nine the court should consider whether to give credit for time spent on bail in accordance with s.240A of that Act.

Parties to the Offence

7.116 This offence may be committed by and against persons of either sex.

Jurisdiction

7.117 By virtue of and Sch.2 to the Sexual Offences Act 2003, as amended,[12] it is an offence under s.32 for a UK national to do an act in a country outside the UK which would constitute a s.32 offence committed against a person under 18 if done in England and Wales. See further para.7.62, above.

"Engages in an Activity"

7.118 For the meaning of this phrase, see paras 2.99 and following, above.

"the Activity is Sexual"

7.119 For the meaning of "sexual", see paras 2.66 and following, above.

Act 2008 s.72, with effect from July 14, 2

result in an upward or downward adjustment from the starting point or the imposition of a sentence outside the category range. In particular, relevant recent convictions are likely to result in an upward adjustment. When sentencing appropriate category 2 or 3 offences, the court should also consider whether the custody threshold has been passed; if so, whether a custodial sentence is unavoidable; and if it is, whether that sentence can be suspended. The non-exhaustive list of aggravating and mitigating factors for offences under ss.32 and 33 is as follows:

Aggravating factors
Statutory aggravating factors
Previous convictions, having regard to a) the nature of the offence to which the conviction relates and its relevance to the current offence; and b) the time that has elapsed since the conviction
Offence committed whilst on bail
Other aggravating factors
Location of offence
Timing of offence
Failure to comply with current court orders
Offence committed whilst on licence
Any steps taken to prevent the victim reporting an incident, obtaining assistance and/or from assisting or supporting the prosecution
Attempts to dispose of or conceal evidence
Commission of offence whilst under the influence of alcohol or drugs

Mitigating factors
No previous convictions *or* no relevant/recent convictions
Remorse
Previous good character and/or exemplary conduct*
Age and/or lack of maturity where it affects the responsibility of the offender
Mental disorder or learning disability, particularly where linked to the commission of the offence

Demonstration of steps taken to address offending behaviour

* Previous good character/exemplary conduct is different from having no previous convictions. The more serious the offence, the less the weight which should normally be attributed to this factor. Where previous good character/exemplary conduct has been used to facilitate the offence, this mitigation should not normally be allowed and such conduct may constitute an aggravating factor.

Steps Three to Nine

7.115 The remaining steps cover the following points. At step three the court should consider any factors, which would indicate a reduction in sentence, e.g. assistance to the prosecution. At step four it should consider any reduction for a guilty plea. At step five the court should consider dangerousness, i.e. whether it would be appropriate to award an extended sentence (s.226A of the Criminal Justice Act 2003). Step six requires the court to consider whether the total sentence is just and proportionate to the offending behaviour. At step seven it should consider whether to make an ancillary order (e.g. a compensation order, a SHPO or a restraining order). Step eight requires the court to fulfil its duty under s.174 of the Criminal Justice Act 2003 to give reasons for, and explain the effect of, the sentence. Finally, at step nine the court should consider whether to give credit for time spent on bail in accordance with s.240A of that Act.

Parties to the Offence

7.116 This offence may be committed by and against persons of either sex.

Jurisdiction

7.117 By virtue of s.72 of and Sch.2 to the Sexual Offences Act 2003, as amended,[137] it is an offence under s.32 for a UK national to do an act in a country outside the UK which would constitute a s.32 offence committed against a person aged under 18 if done in England and Wales. See further para.7.62, above.

"Engages in an Activity"

7.118 For the meaning of this term, see paras 2.99 and following, above.

"The Activity is Sexual"

7.119 For the meaning of the term "sexual", see paras 2.66 and following, above.

[137] By the Criminal Justice and Immigration Act 2008 s.72, with effect from July 14, 2008.

"Present or . . . In a Place from which A can be Observed"

For the meaning of this phase, see paras 4.114 and following, above.   **7.120**

"Unable to Refuse"

The complainant must be "unable to refuse" to be present while the   **7.121**
defendant engages in the sexual activity. Section 32(2) of the Act provides:

> "B is unable to refuse if—
> (a) he lacks the capacity to choose whether to agree to being present (whether
>   because he lacks sufficient understanding of the nature of the activity, or
>   for any other reason), or
> (b) he is unable to communicate such a choice to A."

For the effect of this provision, see paras 7.18 and following, and 7.65 and
following, above.

"Because of or for a Reason Related to a Mental Disorder"

The complainant's inability to refuse to be present must be because of or for   **7.122**
a reason related to a mental disorder. For the meaning and effect of this term,
see paras 7.25 and following, and 7.80 and following, above.

Mental Element

The defendant (A) must engage in sexual activity intentionally. Moreover, for   **7.123**
the purpose of sexual gratification he must engage in it when B is present or
in a place from which A can be observed. The term "sexual" in this context
is undefined.[138] For discussion of this requirement, see para.5.98, above. This
requirement will safeguard those who engage in sexual activity in front of a
mentally disordered person for a legitimate reason.[139]

Additionally, it is a requirement that A knows or could reasonably be   **7.124**
expected to know that B has a mental disorder and that because of it or for
a reason related to it B is likely to be unable to refuse. For discussion of an
identical requirement in s.30 of the Act, see paras 7.88 and following,
above.

In the light of the decision in *Heard*[140] discussed in paras 2.81 and   **7.125**
following, the offence in s.32 appears to be one of basic intent, such that
voluntary intoxication through drink or drugs will provide no defence.

---

[138] s.78 of the 2003 Act defines "sexual" for the purposes of penetration, touching or any other activity.
[139] For example, two nurses kissing at a Christmas party at a care establishment.
[140] [2007] EWCA Crim 125.

Causing a Person, with a Mental Disorder Impeding Choice, to Watch a Sexual Act

Definition

7.126 Section 33(1) provides:

> "A person (A) commits an offence if:
> (a) for the purpose of obtaining sexual gratification, he intentionally causes another person (B) to watch a third person engaging in an activity, or to look at an image of any person engaging in an activity,
> (b) the activity is sexual,
> (c) B is unable to refuse because of or for a reason related to a mental disorder, and
> (d) A knows or could reasonably be expected to know that B has a mental disorder and that because of it or for a reason related to it B is likely to be unable to refuse."

Mode of Trial and Punishment

7.127 Offences under s.33 of the Sexual Offences Act 2003 are triable either way. The maximum sentence on conviction on indictment is 10 years' imprisonment. The maximum on summary conviction is six months' imprisonment or a fine, or both.[141] As from a day to be appointed, the maximum term of imprisonment on summary conviction will increase to 12 months.[142] The increase will have no application to offences committed before it takes effect.[143] Until recently, the maximum fine on summary conviction was a fine not exceeding the statutory maximum (i.e. £5,000). The effect of s.85 of the Legal Aid, Sentencing and Punishment of Offenders Act 2012 is that, from March 12, 2015, a fine of any amount may be imposed.

7.128 For the purposes of listing, cases under s.33[144] fall within Class 2B, save for complex cases involving many complainants (in care or otherwise particularly vulnerable) and/or many defendants who are alleged to have systematically groomed and abused them, often over a long period of time, which fall within Class 1C.[145] Cases in Class 1C must be referred to the Resident Judge, and by the Resident Judge to a Presiding Judge. Cases in Class 2B must be similarly referred in certain specified circumstances, including where the case is unusually grave or complex or a novel and important point of law is to be raised; where the defendant is a police officer, a member of the legal

---

[141] s.33(3).
[142] Criminal Justice Act 2003 s.282(2), (3).
[143] Criminal Justice Act 2003 s.282(4).
[144] And of soliciting, inciting, encouraging or assisting, attempting or conspiring to commit the offence or assisting an offender having committed the offence.
[145] *Consolidated Criminal Practice Directions*, Part XIII Listing B: CLASSIFICATION, available at *https://www.judiciary.gov.uk/wp-content/uploads/2015/09/crim-pd-2015.pdf* [Accessed April 30, 2016].

profession or a high profile figure; or where for any reason the case is likely to attract exceptional media attention.

An offence under s.33, whenever committed, is a specified offence for the 7.129 purposes of s.226A of the Criminal Justice Act 2003 (extended sentence for certain violent or sexual offences).[146]

A person convicted under s.33, cautioned, found not guilty by reason of 7.130 insanity or found to be under a disability and to have done the act charged, is automatically subject to the notification requirements in the Sexual Offences Act 2003.[147]

SENTENCING

For the Sentencing Council guideline relating to the sentencing of sexual 7.131 offences committed by offenders aged 18 and over, see Ch.33. A single guideline covers the offences in s.32 and s.33 of the 2003 Act and is considered at paras 7.112 and following, above.

PARTIES TO THE OFFENCE

This offence may be committed by and against persons of either sex. 7.132

JURISDICTION

By virtue of s.72 of and Sch.2 to the Sexual Offences Act 2003, as 7.133 amended,[148] it is an offence under s.33 for a UK national to do an act in a country outside the UK which would constitute a s.33 offence committed against a person aged under 18 if done in England and Wales. See further para.7.62, above.

"CAUSES"

For the meaning of this term, see paras 2.98 and following, above. 7.134

"TO WATCH A THIRD PERSON ENGAGING IN AN ACTIVITY, OR TO LOOK AT AN IMAGE OF ANY PERSON ENGAGING IN AN ACTIVITY"

For the meaning of this phrase, see paras 4.134 and following, above. The 7.135 offence covers such conduct as arranging for a mentally disordered person to watch live sexual activity or a pornographic film, or sending indecent images

---

[146] Inserted by the Legal Aid, Sentencing and Punishment of Offenders Act 2012 s.124, brought into force on December 3, 2012, by SI 2012/2906.
[147] s.80 and Sch.3, discussed in Ch.35, below.
[148] By the Criminal Justice and Immigration Act 2008 s.72, with effect from July 14, 2008.

to them in the post or by email. There must be a third party engaging in any sexual activity that is watched. In a case where the complainant is caused to look at an image, the image could be of the defendant or any other person, including the complainant.

"The Activity is Sexual"

7.136   For the meaning of "sexual", see paras 2.66 and following, above.

"Unable to Refuse"

7.137   The complainant must be "unable to refuse" to watch or look while the defendant engages in the sexual activity. Section 33(2) of the Act provides:

"B is unable to refuse if:
(a) he lacks the capacity to choose whether to agree to watching or looking (whether because he lacks sufficient understanding of the nature of the activity, or for any other reason), or
(b) he is unable to communicate such a choice to A."

For the effect of this provision, see paras 7.18 and following, and 7.65 and following, above.

"Because of or for a Reason Related to a Mental Disorder"

7.138   The complainant's inability to refuse to watch or look must be because of or for a reason related to a mental disorder. For the meaning and effect of this term, see paras 7.25 and following, and 7.80 and following, above.

Mental Element

7.139   The defendant (A) must act for the purpose of sexual gratification. It follows that if A shows B a video for the purpose of sex education, rather than sexual gratification, no offence is committed. The term "sexual" in this context is undefined.[149] For discussion of this requirement, see para.5.98, above.

7.140   Additionally, it is a requirement that A knows or could reasonably be expected to know that B has a mental disorder and that because of it or for a reason related to it B is likely to be unable to refuse. For discussion of an identical requirement in s.30 of the Act, see paras 7.88 and following, above.

7.141   In the light of the decision in *Heard*,[150] discussed in paras 2.81 and following, above, the offence in s.33 appears to be one of basic intent, such

---

[149] s.78 of the 2003 Act defines "sexual" for the purposes of penetration, touching or any other activity.
[150] [2007] EWCA Crim 125.

that voluntary intoxication through drink or drugs will provide no defence. It will suffice if the defendant's acts were deliberate. Recklessness is insufficient.

INDUCEMENT, THREAT OR DECEPTION TO PROCURE SEXUAL ACTIVITY WITH A PERSON WITH A MENTAL DISORDER

DEFINITION

Section 34(1) of the Sexual Offences Act 2003 provides as follows:　　　**7.142**

"A person (A) commits an offence if:
(a) with the agreement of another person (B) he intentionally touches that person,
(b) the touching is sexual,
(c) A obtains B's agreement by means of an inducement offered or given, a threat made or a deception practised by A for that purpose,
(d) B has a mental disorder, and
(e) A knows or could reasonably be expected to know that B has a mental disorder."

MODE OF TRIAL AND PUNISHMENT

The mode of trial and punishment of an offence under s.34 depends upon the　**7.143** type of "touching" in question. If the touching involved any of the following, the offence is triable on indictment only with a maximum penalty of life imprisonment:

- penetration of B's anus or vagina with a part of A's body or anything else,
- penetration of B's mouth with A's penis,
- penetration of A's anus or vagina with a part of B's body, or
- penetration of A's mouth with B's penis.[151]

Otherwise, the offence is triable either way. The maximum sentence on conviction on indictment is 14 years' imprisonment. On summary conviction it is six months' imprisonment or a fine, or both.[152] As from a day to be appointed, the maximum term of imprisonment on summary conviction will increase to 12 months.[153] The increase will have no application to offences committed before it takes effect.[154] Until recently, the maximum fine on summary conviction was a fine not exceeding the statutory maximum (i.e. £5,000). The effect of s.85 of the Legal Aid, Sentencing and Punishment of Offenders Act 2012 is that, from March 12, 2015, a fine of any amount may be imposed.

---

[151] s.34(2).
[152] s.34(3).
[153] Criminal Justice Act 2003 s.282(2), (3).
[154] Criminal Justice Act 2003 s.282(4).

7.144   For the purposes of listing, cases under s.34[155] fall within Class 2B, save for complex cases involving many complainants (in care or otherwise particularly vulnerable) and/or many defendants who are alleged to have systematically groomed and abused them, often over a long period of time, which fall within Class 1C.[156] Cases in Class 1C must be referred to the Resident Judge, and by the Resident Judge to a Presiding Judge. Cases in Class 2B must be similarly referred in certain specified circumstances, including where the case is unusually grave or complex or a novel and important point of law is to be raised; where the defendant is a police officer, a member of the legal profession or a high profile figure; or where for any reason the case is likely to attract exceptional media attention.

7.145   An offence under s.34 is a serious specified offence for the purposes of s.224 and, where the offence involved penetration, s.225(2) (life sentence for serious offences) of the Criminal Justice Act 2003.[157] A s.34 offence, whenever committed, may be made the subject of an extended sentence under s.226A of that Act.[158] An offence under s.34 involving penetration is also listed in Pt 1 of Sch.15B to the Criminal Justice Act 2003 for the purposes of s.224A of that Act (life sentence for a second listed offence).[159]

7.146   A person convicted under s.34, cautioned, found not guilty by reason of insanity or found to be under a disability and to have done the act charged, is automatically subject to the notification requirements in the Sexual Offences Act 2003.[160]

Sentencing

7.147   For the Sentencing Council guideline relating to the sentencing of sexual offences committed by offenders aged 18 and over, see Ch.33. A single guideline covers the offences in ss.34 and 35 of the 2003 Act (inducement, threat or deception to procure sexual activity with a person with a mental disorder, and causing such a person to engage in sexual activity by inducement, threat or deception). The guideline is modelled on the one for the offences in ss.9 and 10 of the Act of engaging in sexual activity with a child. In consulting on its draft guideline,[161] the Council explained that this

---

[155] And of soliciting, inciting, encouraging or assisting, attempting or conspiring to commit the offence or assisting an offender having committed the offence.

[156] *Consolidated Criminal Practice Directions*, Part XIII Listing B: CLASSIFICATION, available at *https://www.judiciary.gov.uk/wp-content/uploads/2015/09/crim-pd-2015.pdf* [Accessed April 30, 2016].

[157] Criminal Justice Act 2003 s.224 and Sch.15, Pt 2.

[158] Inserted by the Legal Aid, Sentencing and Punishment of Offenders Act 2012 s.124, brought into force on December 3, 2012, by SI 2012/2906.

[159] Inserted by the Legal Aid, Sentencing and Punishment of Offenders Act 2012 s.122, brought into force on December 3, 2012, by SI 2012/2906. See Appendix A, below

[160] s.80 and Sch.3, discussed in Ch.35, below.

[161] *Sexual Offences Guideline: Consultation* (December 6, 2012). The consultation document is available on the Sentencing Council's website.

is because the offences share a statutory maximum (14 years) and, in relation to all of them, the victim may appear to have acquiesced in sexual activity but only due to exploitation or manipulation by the offender.[162] In the guideline for ss.9 and 10, harm is linked to the sexual activity that has been engaged in (with penetrative sexual activity treated as the highest level of harm) whilst culpability concentrates on the exploitation and manipulation employed by the offender in order to procure the sexual activity. The same approach is taken in the guideline for ss.34 and 35, which also adopts the sentence starting points and ranges used in the guideline for ss.9 and 10. Like that guideline, the one for ss.34 and 35 contains at its head the statement "This guideline also applies to offences committed remotely/online".

Sentencing guideline

Step One—Harm and culpability

The sentencing court must go through a series of steps in order to determine the appropriate sentence. Step one involves determining the offence category by reference to the degree of harm caused and then the culpability level for the offence. The court should determine into which categories of harm and culpability the offence falls by reference to the tables below: **7.148**

Harm		Culpability
Category 1	• Penetration of vagina or anus (using body or object) • Penile penetration of mouth in either case by, or of, the victim	A
		Significant degree of planning
		Offender acts together with others to commit the offence
		Use of alcohol/drugs on victim to facilitate the offence
Category 2	• Touching, or exposure, of naked genitalia or naked breasts by, or of, the victim	Abuse of trust
		Sexual images of victim recorded, retained, solicited or shared
		Commercial exploitation and/or motivation
		Offence racially or religiously aggravated

---

[162] cf. *R. v P* [2015] 2 Cr. App. R. (S.) 28, discussed in para.7.60, above, in which the Court of Appeal stated that expressions of "enjoyment" by a complainant who had been medically assessed as incapable of giving consent would be of limited, if any, significance to the sentence.

Category 3	• Other sexual activity	Offence motivated by, or demonstrating, hostility to the victim based on his or her sexual orientation (or presumed sexual orientation) or transgender identity (or presumed transgender identity)
		Offence motivated by, or demonstrating, hostility to the victim based on his or her disability (or presumed disability)
		B
		Factor(s) in category A not present

Step Two—Starting point and category range

7.149 Once the court has determined the offence category and culpability level, at step two it should use the corresponding starting point specified in the guideline in order to reach a sentence within the category range. The starting point applies to all offenders irrespective of plea or previous convictions. Once the starting point has been determined, step two allows further adjustment for aggravating or mitigating features, set out below. A case of particular gravity, reflected by multiple features of culpability or harm, could merit upward adjustment from the starting point before further adjustment for aggravating or mitigating features. Where there is a sufficient prospect of rehabilitation, a community order with a sex offender treatment programme requirement under s.202 of the CJA 2003 may be a proper alternative to a short or moderate length custodial sentence. The starting points and category ranges for offences under ss.34 and 35 are as follows:

	A	*B*
Category 1	*Starting point* 5 years' custody	*Starting point* 1 years' custody
	Category range 4–10 years' custody	*Category range* High level community order–2 years' custody

| Category 2 | *Starting point*
3 years' custody

Category range
2–6 years' custody | *Starting point*
26 weeks' custody

Category range
High level community
order–1 years' custody |
| Category 3 | *Starting point*
26 weeks' custody

Category range
High level community
order–3 years' custody | *Starting point*
Medium level
community order

Category range
Low level community
order–High level
community order |

Aggravating and mitigating factors

After identifying the starting point and category range, the court should **7.150** consider whether the presence of aggravating or mitigating factors should result in an upward or downward adjustment from the starting point or the imposition of a sentence outside the category range. In particular, relevant recent convictions are likely to result in an upward adjustment. When sentencing appropriate category 2 or 3 offences, the court should also consider whether the custody threshold has been passed; if so, whether a custodial sentence is unavoidable; and if it is, whether that sentence can be suspended. The non-exhaustive list of aggravating and mitigating factors for offences under ss.34 and 35 is as follows:

Aggravating factors
Statutory aggravating factors
Previous convictions, having regard to a) the nature of the offence to which the conviction relates and its relevance to the current offence; and b) the time that has elapsed since the conviction
Offence committed whilst on bail
Other aggravating factors
Severe psychological or physical harm
Ejaculation

Pregnancy or STI as a consequence of offence
Location of offence
Timing of offence
Victim compelled to leave their home (including victims of domestic violence)
Failure to comply with current court orders
Offence committed whilst on licence
Any steps taken to prevent the victim reporting an incident, obtaining assistance and/or from assisting or supporting the prosecution
Attempts to dispose of or conceal evidence
Commission of offence whilst under the influence of alcohol or drugs

Mitigating factors
No previous convictions *or* no relevant/recent convictions
Remorse
Previous good character and/or exemplary conduct*
Age and/or lack of maturity where it affects the responsibility of the offender
Mental disorder or learning disability, particularly where linked to the commission of the offence

* Previous good character/exemplary conduct is different from having no previous convictions. The more serious the offence, the less the weight which should normally be attributed to this factor. Where previous good character/exemplary conduct has been used to facilitate the offence, this mitigation should not normally be allowed and such conduct may constitute an aggravating factor.

In the context of this offence, previous good character/exemplary conduct should not normally be given any significant weight and will not normally justify a reduction in what would otherwise be the appropriate sentence.

Steps Three to Nine

7.151 The remaining steps cover the following points. At step three the court should consider any factors which would indicate a reduction in sentence, e.g. assistance to the prosecution. At step four it should consider any reduction for a guilty plea. At step five the court should consider dangerousness, i.e.

whether it would be appropriate to award a life sentence (s.224A or s.225(2) of the Criminal Justice Act 2003) or an extended sentence (s.226A). Step six requires the court to consider whether the total sentence is just and proportionate to the offending behaviour. At step seven it should consider whether to make an ancillary order (e.g. a compensation order, a SHPO or a restraining order). Step eight requires the court to fulfil its duty under s.174 of the Criminal Justice Act 2003 to give reasons for, and explain the effect of, the sentence. Finally, at step nine the court should consider whether to give credit for time spent on bail in accordance with s.240A of that Act.

PARTIES TO THE OFFENCE

This offence may be committed by and against persons of either sex.   **7.152**

JURISDICTION

By virtue of s.72 of and Sch.2 to the Sexual Offences Act 2003, as amended,[163] it is an offence under s.34 for a UK national to do an act in a country outside the UK which would constitute a s.34 offence committed against a person aged under 18 if done in England and Wales. See further para.7.62, above.   **7.153**

"TOUCHES ANOTHER PERSON"

For the meaning of "touches", see paras 2.63 and following, above.   **7.154**

"THE TOUCHING IS SEXUAL"

The touching must be "sexual". For the meaning of this term, see paras 2.66 and following, above.   **7.155**

"INDUCEMENT, THREAT OR DECEPTION"

The complainant's agreement must be obtained by means of an inducement offered or given, a threat made or a deception practised by the defendant for the purpose of obtaining agreement to sexual touching. For this purpose an inducement may be, for example, the promise of sweets or a holiday; a threat may be to hurt a member of the complainant's family; and a deception may be telling the complainant that they will be in trouble if they refuse to take part or persuading him that it is expected that friends should engage in sexual activity.[164] There is no temporal limitation to the inducement, threat or   **7.156**

---

[163] By the Criminal Justice and Immigration Act 2008, s.72, with effect from July 14, 2008.
[164] cf. Explanatory Notes to the Act, para.67.

deception. It does not have to have taken place immediately before the "touching". Nor does the threat have to be capable of being carried out immediately. In *Cooper*,[165] where the defendant was charged under s.30, Baroness Hale remarked that he could have been charged in the alternative under s.34, on the basis that he had induced the complainant to take part in the sexual activity by offering her help and providing her with crack cocaine.

"Mental Disorder"

7.157 The complainant must have a "mental disorder" at the time of the touching. For the meaning of "mental disorder", see paras 7.25 and following, and 7.80 and following, above.

Mental Element

7.158 The defendant must intentionally touch the complainant and must obtain the complainant's agreement to the touching by means of an inducement offered, etc. for that purpose. For intentional touching, see the discussion in para.7.87, above.

7.159 Additionally, it is a requirement that the defendant knows or could reasonably be expected to know that the complainant has a mental disorder. For discussion of a similar requirement in s.30 of the Act, see paras 7.88 and following, above.

Causing a Person with a Mental Disorder to Engage in or Agree to Engage in Sexual Activity by Inducement, Threat or Deception

Definition

7.160 Section 35(1) of the Sexual Offences Act 2003 provides:

"A person (A) commits an offence if:
(a) by means of an inducement offered or given, a threat made or a deception practised by him for this purpose, he intentionally causes another person (B) to engage in, or to agree to engage in, an activity,
(b) the activity is sexual,
(c) B has a mental disorder, and
(d) A knows or could reasonably be expected to know that B has a mental disorder."

Mode of Trial and Punishment

7.161 The mode of trial and punishment for an offence under s.35 depends upon the type of activity the complainant engaged in or agreed to engage in. If it

---

[165] [2009] UKHL 42, discussed in para.7.70, above.

involved any of the following, the offence is triable on indictment only, with a maximum penalty of life imprisonment:

- penetration of B's anus or vagina,
- penetration of B's mouth with a person's penis,
- penetration of a person's anus or vagina with a part of B's body or by B with anything else, or
- penetration of a person's mouth with B's penis.[166]

Otherwise, the offence is triable either way. The maximum sentence on conviction on indictment is 14 years' imprisonment. On summary conviction it is six months' imprisonment or a fine, or both.[167] As from a day to be appointed, the maximum term of imprisonment on summary conviction will increase to 12 months.[168] The increase will have no application to offences committed before it takes effect.[169] Until recently, the maximum fine on summary conviction was a fine not exceeding the statutory maximum (i.e. £5,000). The effect of s.85 of the Legal Aid, Sentencing and Punishment of Offenders Act 2012 is that, from March 12, 2015, a fine of any amount may be imposed.

7.162   For the purposes of listing, cases under s.35[170] fall within Class 2B, save for complex cases involving many complainants (in care or otherwise particularly vulnerable) and/or many defendants who are alleged to have systematically groomed and abused them, often over a long period of time, which fall within Class 1C.[171] Cases in Class 1C must be referred to the Resident Judge, and by the Resident Judge to a Presiding Judge. Cases in Class 2B must be similarly referred in certain specified circumstances, including where the case is unusually grave or complex or a novel and important point of law is to be raised; where the defendant is a police officer, a member of the legal profession or a high profile figure; or where for any reason the case is likely to attract exceptional media attention.

7.163   An offence under s.35 is a serious specified offence for the purposes of s.224 and, where the offence involved penetration, s.225(2) (life sentence for serious offences) of the Criminal Justice Act 2003.[172] A s.35 offence, whenever committed, may be made the subject of an extended sentence under s.226A of that Act.[173] An offence under s.35 involving penetration is also listed in Pt 1 of Sch.15B to the Criminal Justice Act 2003 for the

---

[166] s.35(2).
[167] s.35(3).
[168] Criminal Justice Act 2003 s.282(2), (3).
[169] Criminal Justice Act 2003 s.282(4).
[170] And of soliciting, inciting, encouraging or assisting, attempting or conspiring to commit the offence or assisting an offender having committed the offence.
[171] *Consolidated Criminal Practice Directions*, Part XIII Listing B: CLASSIFICATION, available at *https://www.judiciary.gov.uk/wp-content/uploads/2015/09/crim-pd-2015.pdf* [Accessed April 30, 2016].
[172] Criminal Justice Act 2003 s.224 and Sch.15, Pt 2.
[173] Inserted by the Legal Aid, Sentencing and Punishment of Offenders Act 2012 s.124, brought into force on December 3, 2012, by SI 2012/2906.

purposes of s.224A of that Act (life sentence for a second listed offence).[174]

7.164 A person convicted under s.35, cautioned, found not guilty by reason of insanity or found to be under a disability and to have done the act charged, is automatically subject to the notification requirements in the Sexual Offences Act 2003.[175]

Sentencing

7.165 For the Sentencing Council guideline relating to the sentencing of sexual offences committed by offenders aged 18 and over, see Ch.33. A single guideline covers offences under both s.34 and s.35 of the 2003 Act and is considered at paras 7.147 and following, above.

Parties to the Offence

7.166 This offence may be committed by and against persons of either sex.

Jurisdiction

7.167 By virtue of s.72 of and Sch.2 to the Sexual Offences Act 2003, as amended,[176] it is an offence under s.35 for a UK national to do an act in a country outside the UK which would constitute a s.35 offence committed against a person aged under 18 if done in England and Wales. See further para.7.62, above.

"Inducement, Threat or Deception"

7.168 For discussion of the terms "inducement", "threat" and "deception", see para.7.156, above.

"Causes Another Person (B) to Engage in, or to Agree to Engage in"

7.169 This offence can be committed without any sexual activity taking place if the defendant has caused the complainant to agree to the sexual activity by means of an inducement etc.

---

[174] Inserted by the Legal Aid, Sentencing and Punishment of Offenders Act 2012 s.122, brought into force on December 3, 2012, by SI 2012/2906. See Appendix A, below.
[175] s.80 and Sch.3, discussed in Ch.35, below.
[176] By the Criminal Justice and Immigration Act 2008 s.72, with effect from July 14, 2008.

"The Activity is Sexual"

For the meaning of the term "sexual", see paras 2.66 and following, above. **7.170**
The offence under s.35 differs from that under s.34 in that the sexual activity
need not be with the defendant.

"Mental Disorder"

The complainant must have had a mental disorder at the time of the causing **7.171**
or inciting. For discussion of the definition of "mental disorder", see paras
7.25 and following, and 7.80 and following, above.

Mental Element

The prosecution must prove that the defendant intentionally caused the **7.172**
complainant to engage in, or to agree to engage in, sexual activity by means
of an inducement offered etc. for this purpose. Additionally, the prosecution
must establish that the defendant knew or could reasonably have been
expected to know that the complainant had a mental disorder. For discussion
of a similar requirement in s.30 of the Act, see paras 7.88 and following,
above.

Engaging in Sexual Activity in the Presence, Procured by Inducement, Threat or Deception, of a Person with a Mental Disorder

Definition

Section 36(1) of the Sexual Offences Act 2003 provides: **7.173**
"A person (A) commits an offence if:
(a) he intentionally engages in an activity,
(b) the activity is sexual,
(c) for the purposes of obtaining sexual gratification, he engages in it:
  (i) when another person (B) is present or is in a place from which A can
  be observed, and
  (ii) knowing or believing that B is aware, or intending that B should be
  aware, that he is engaging in it,
(d) B agrees to be present or in the place referred to in paragraph (c)(i)
because of an inducement offered or given, a threat made or a deception
practised by A for the purpose of obtaining that agreement,
(e) B has a mental disorder, and
(f) A knows or could reasonably be expected to know that B has a mental
disorder."

Mode of Trial and Punishment

Offences under s.36 of the 2003 Act are triable either way. The maximum **7.174**
sentence on conviction on indictment is 10 years' imprisonment. The

maximum on summary conviction is six months' imprisonment or a fine, or both.[177] As from a day to be appointed, the maximum term of imprisonment on summary conviction will increase to 12 months.[178] The increase will have no application to offences committed before it takes effect.[179] Until recently, the maximum fine on summary conviction was a fine not exceeding the statutory maximum (i.e. £5,000). The effect of s.85 of the Legal Aid, Sentencing and Punishment of Offenders Act 2012 is that, from March 12, 2015, a fine of any amount may be imposed.

7.175   For the purposes of listing, cases under s.36[180] fall within Class 2B, save for complex cases involving many complainants (in care or otherwise particularly vulnerable) and/or many defendants who are alleged to have systematically groomed and abused them, often over a long period of time, which fall within Class 1C.[181] Cases in Class 1C must be referred to the Resident Judge, and by the Resident Judge to a Presiding Judge. Cases in Class 2B must be similarly referred in certain specified circumstances, including where the case is unusually grave or complex or a novel and important point of law is to be raised; where the defendant is a police officer, a member of the legal profession or a high profile figure; or where for any reason the case is likely to attract exceptional media attention.

7.176   An offence under s.36 is a specified offence for the purposes of s.226A of the Criminal Justice Act 2003 (extended sentence for certain violent or sexual offences).[182]

7.177   A person convicted under s.36, cautioned, found not guilty by reason of insanity or found to be under a disability and to have done the act charged, is automatically subject to the notification requirements in the Sexual Offences Act 2003.[183]

SENTENCING

7.178   For the Sentencing Council guideline relating to the sentencing of sexual offences committed by offenders aged 18 and over, see Ch.33. A single guideline covers the offences in ss.36 and 37 of the 2003 Act (engaging in sexual activity in the presence, procured by inducement, threat or deception, of a person with a mental disorder, and causing such a person to watch a sexual act by inducement, threat or deception).

---

[177] s.36(2).
[178] Criminal Justice Act 2003 s.282(2), (3).
[179] Criminal Justice Act 2003 s.282(4).
[180] And of soliciting, inciting, encouraging or assisting, attempting or conspiring to commit the offence or assisting an offender having committed the offence.
[181] *Consolidated Criminal Practice Directions*, Part XIII Listing B: CLASSIFICATION, available at *https://www.judiciary.gov.uk/wp-content/uploads/2015/09/crim-pd-2015.pdf* [Accessed April 30, 2016].
[182] Inserted by the Legal Aid, Sentencing and Punishment of Offenders Act 2012 s.124, brought into force on December 3, 2012, by SI 2012/2906.
[183] s.80 and Sch.3, discussed in Ch.35, below.

Sentencing guideline

Step One—Harm and culpability

The sentencing court must go through a series of steps in order to determine the appropriate sentence. Step one involves determining the offence category by reference to the degree of harm caused and then the culpability level for the offence. The court should determine into which categories of harm and culpability the offence falls by reference only to the tables below: **7.179**

Harm	
Category 1	• Causing victim to view extreme pornography • Causing victim to view indecent/prohibited images of children • Engaging in, or causing a victim to view live, sexual activity involving sadism/violence/sexual activity with an animal/a child
Category 2	Engaging in, or causing a victim to view images of or view live, sexual activity involving: • penetration of vagina or anus (using body or object) • penile penetration of mouth • masturbation

Culpability
A
Significant degree of planning
Offender acts together with others to commit the offence
Use of alcohol/drugs on victim to facilitate the offence
Abuse of trust
Commercial exploitation and/or motivation
Offence racially or religiously aggravated
Offence motivated by, or demonstrating, hostility to the victim based on his or her sexual orientation (or presumed sexual orientation) or transgender identity (or presumed transgender identity)
Offence motivated by, or demonstrating, hostility to the victim based on his or her disability (or presumed disability)

Category 3	Factor(s) in categories 1 and 2 not present	B
		Factor(s) in category A not present

Step Two—Starting point and category range

7.180 Once the court has determined the offence category and culpability level, it should then use the corresponding starting point specified in the guideline in order to reach a sentence within the category range. The starting point applies to all offenders irrespective of plea or previous convictions. Once the starting point has been determined, step two allows further adjustment for aggravating or mitigating features, set out below. A case of particular gravity, reflected by multiple features of culpability or harm, could merit upward adjustment from the starting point before further adjustment for aggravating or mitigating features. Where there is a sufficient prospect of rehabilitation, a community order with a sex offender treatment programme requirement under s.202 of the Criminal Justice Act 2003 may be a proper alternative to a short or moderate length custodial sentence. The starting points and category ranges for offences under ss.36 and 37 are as follows:

	A	B
Category 1	Starting point 4 years' custody Category range 3–6 years' custody	Starting point 2 years' custody Category range 1–3 years' custody
Category 2	Starting point 2 years' custody Category range 1–3 years' custody	Starting point 1 years' custody Category range High level community order–18 months' custody
Category 3	Starting point 26 weeks' custody Category range High level community order– 1 years' custody	Starting point Medium level community order Category range Low level community order–Medium level community order

Aggravating and mitigating factors

After identifying the starting point and category range, the court should **7.181** consider whether the presence of aggravating or mitigating factors should result in an upward or downward adjustment from the starting point or the imposition of a sentence outside the category range. In particular, relevant recent convictions are likely to result in an upward adjustment. When sentencing appropriate category 2 or 3 offences, the court should also consider whether the custody threshold has been passed; if so, whether a custodial sentence is unavoidable; and if it is, whether that sentence can be suspended. The non-exhaustive list of aggravating and mitigating factors for offences under ss.36 and 37 is as follows:

Aggravating factors
Statutory aggravating factors
Previous convictions, having regard to a) the nature of the offence to which the conviction relates and its relevance to the current offence; and b) the time that has elapsed since the conviction
Offence committed whilst on bail
Other aggravating factors
Location of offence
Timing of offence
Failure to comply with current court orders
Offence committed whilst on licence
Any steps taken to prevent the victim reporting an incident, obtaining assistance and/or from assisting or supporting the prosecution
Attempts to dispose of or conceal evidence
Commission of offence whilst under the influence of alcohol or drugs

Mitigating factors
No previous convictions *or* no relevant/recent convictions
Remorse
Previous good character and/or exemplary conduct*

Age and/or lack of maturity where it affects the responsibility of the offender
Mental disorder or learning disability, particularly where linked to the commission of the offence
Demonstration of steps taken to address offending behaviour

* Previous good character/exemplary conduct is different from having no previous convictions. The more serious the offence, the less the weight which should normally be attributed to this factor. Where previous good character/exemplary conduct has been used to facilitate the offence, this mitigation should not normally be allowed and such conduct may constitute an aggravating factor.

Steps Three to Nine

7.182 The remaining steps cover the following points. At step three the court should consider any factors which would indicate a reduction in sentence, e.g. assistance to the prosecution. At step four it should consider any reduction for a guilty plea. At step five the court should consider dangerousness, i.e. whether it would be appropriate to award an extended sentence (s.226A of the Criminal Justice Act 2003). Step six requires the court to consider whether the total sentence is just and proportionate to the offending behaviour. At step seven it should consider whether to make an ancillary order (e.g. a compensation order, a SHPO or a restraining order). Step eight requires the court to fulfil its duty under s.174 of the Criminal Justice Act 2003 to give reasons for, and explain the effect of, the sentence. Finally, at step nine the court should consider whether to give credit for time spent on bail in accordance with s.240A of that Act.

Parties to the Offence

7.183 This offence may be committed by and against persons for either sex.

Jurisdiction

7.184 By virtue of s.72 of and Sch.2 to the Sexual Offences Act 2003, as amended,[184] it is an offence under s.36 for a UK national to do an act in a country outside the UK which would constitute a s.36 offence committed against a person aged under 18 if done in England and Wales. See further para.7.62, above.

"Engages in an Activity"

7.185 For the meaning of this term, see paras 2.99 and following, above.

[184] By the Criminal Justice and Immigration Act 2008 s.72, with effect from July 14, 200?

"THE ACTIVITY IS SEXUAL"

For the meaning of the term "sexual", see paras 2.66 and following, above. **7.186**

"PRESENT OR . . . IN A PLACE FROM WHICH A CAN BE OBSERVED"

For the meaning of this term, see paras 4.114 and following, above. **7.187**

"INDUCEMENT, THREAT OR DECEPTION"

The complainant must have agreed to be present or be in a place from which **7.188**
the defendant could be observed because of an inducement offered or given,
a threat made or a deception practised by the defendant for the purpose of
obtaining that agreement. For discussion of the terms "inducement",
"threat" and "deception", see para.7.156, above.

"MENTAL DISORDER"

The complainant must have had a "mental disorder" at the time they agreed **7.189**
to be present, etc. For discussion of the definition of "mental disorder", see
paras 7.25 and following, and 7.80 and following, above.

MENTAL ELEMENT

The prosecution must prove that the defendant intentionally engaged in the **7.190**
sexual activity. Moreover, for the purpose of sexual gratification he must
engage in it when B is present or in a place from which A can be observed.
The term "sexual" in this context is undefined.[185] For discussion of this
requirement, see para.5.98, above.

Additionally, the prosecution must establish that the defendant knew or **7.191**
could reasonably have been expected to know that B had a mental disorder.
For discussion of a similar requirement in s.30 of the Act, see paras 7.88 and
following, above.

In the light of the decision in *Heard*,[186] discussed in paras 2.81 and **7.192**
following, above, the requirement that the defendant did the prohibited act
for the purpose of obtaining sexual gratification makes the s.36 offence one
of specific intent, such that voluntary intoxication through drink or drugs
will provide a defence if it may have prevented the defendant forming that
purpose.

---

[185] s.78 of the 2003 Act defines "sexual" for the purposes of penetration, touching or any other
activity.
[186] [2007] EWCA Crim 125.

Causing a Person with a Mental Disorder to Watch a Sexual Act by Inducement, Threat or Deception

Definition

7.193   Section 37(1) of the Sexual Offences Act 2003 provides:

> "A person (A) commits an offence if:
> (a) for the purpose of obtaining sexual gratification, he intentionally causes another person (B) to watch a third person engaging in an activity, or to look at an image of any person engaging in an activity,
> (b) the activity is sexual,
> (c) B agrees to watch or look because of an inducement offered or given, a threat made or a deception practised by A for the purpose of obtaining that agreement,
> (d) B has a mental disorder, and
> (e) A knows or could reasonably be expected to know that B has a mental disorder."

Mode of Trial and Punishment

7.194   Offences under s.37 are triable either way. The maximum sentence on conviction on indictment is 10 years' imprisonment. The maximum on summary conviction is six months' imprisonment or a fine, or both.[187] As from a day to be appointed, the maximum term of imprisonment on summary conviction will increase to 12 months.[188] The increase will have no application to offences committed before it takes effect.[189] Until recently, the maximum fine on summary conviction was a fine not exceeding the statutory maximum (i.e. £5,000). The effect of s.85 of the Legal Aid, Sentencing and Punishment of Offenders Act 2012 is that, from March 12, 2015, a fine of any amount may be imposed.

7.195   For the purposes of listing, cases under s.37[190] fall within Class 2B, save for complex cases involving many complainants (in care or otherwise particularly vulnerable) and/or many defendants who are alleged to have systematically groomed and abused them, often over a long period of time, which fall within Class 1C.[191] Cases in Class 1C must be referred to the Resident Judge, and by the Resident Judge to a Presiding Judge. Cases in Class 2B must be similarly referred in certain specified circumstances, including where the case is unusually grave or complex or a novel and important point of law is to be raised; where the defendant is a police officer, a member of the legal

---

[187] s.37(2).

[188] Criminal Justice Act 2003 s.282(2), (3).

[189] Criminal Justice Act 2003 s.282(4).

[190] And of soliciting, inciting, encouraging or assisting, attempting or conspiring to commit the offence or assisting an offender having committed the offence.

[191] *Consolidated Criminal Practice Directions*, Part XIII Listing B: CLASSIFICATION, available at *https://www.judiciary.gov.uk/wp-content/uploads/2015/09/crim-pd-2015.pdf* [Accessed April 30, 2016].

profession or a high profile figure; or where for any reason the case is likely to attract exceptional media attention.

An offence under s.37 is a specified offence for the purposes of s.226A of the Criminal Justice Act 2003 (extended sentence for certain violent or sexual offences).[192]   **7.196**

A person convicted under s.37, cautioned, found not guilty by reason of insanity or found to be under a disability and to have done the act charged, is automatically subject to the notification requirements in the Sexual Offences Act 2003.[193]   **7.197**

SENTENCING

For the Sentencing Council guideline relating to the sentencing of sexual offences committed by offenders aged 18 and over, see Ch.33. A single guideline covers offences in s.36 and s.37 of the 2003 Act and is considered at paras 7.178 and following, above.   **7.198**

PARTIES TO THE OFFENCE

This offence may be committed by and against persons of either sex.   **7.199**

JURISDICTION

By virtue of s.72 of and Sch.2 to the Sexual Offences Act 2003, as amended,[194] it is an offence under s.37 for a UK national to do an act in a country outside the UK which would constitute a s.37 offence committed against a person aged under 18 if done in England and Wales. See further para.7.62, above.   **7.200**

"CAUSES"

For the meaning of this term, see paras 2.98 and following, above.   **7.201**

"TO WATCH A THIRD PERSON ENGAGING IN AN ACTIVITY, OR TO LOOK AT AN IMAGE OF ANY PERSON ENGAGING IN AN ACTIVITY"

For the meaning of this phrase, see paras 4.134 and following, and 7.135, above.   **7.202**

---

[192] Inserted by the Legal Aid, Sentencing and Punishment of Offenders Act 2012 s.124, brought into force on December 3, 2012, by SI 2012/2906.
[193] s.80 and Sch.3, discussed in Ch.35, below.
[194] By the Criminal Justice and Immigration Act 2008 s.72, with effect from July 14, 2008.

"The Activity is Sexual"

7.203 For the meaning of "sexual", see paras 2.66 and following, above.

"Inducement, Threat or Deception"

7.204 The complainant must agree to watch or look because of an inducement offered, a threat made, or a deception practised by the defendant. For discussion of the terms "inducement", "threat" and "deception", see para.7.156, above.

"Mental Disorder"

7.205 The complainant must have had a mental disorder at the time the defendant cause him to watch or look. For discussion of the definition of "mental disorder", see paras 7.25 and following, and 7.80 and following, above.

Mental Element

7.206 The prosecution must prove that "for the purpose of obtaining sexual gratification" the defendant intentionally caused the complainant to watch a third person engaging in a sexual activity, or to look at an image of any person engaging in sexual activity.

7.207 Additionally the prosecution must establish that the defendant knew or could reasonably have been expected to know that the complainant had a mental disorder. For discussion of a similar requirement in s.30 of the Act, see paras 7.88 and following, above.

7.208 In the light of the decision in *Heard*,[195] discussed in paras 2.81 and following, above, the requirement that the defendant did the prohibited act for the purpose of obtaining sexual gratification makes the s.37 offence one of specific intent, such that voluntary intoxication through drink or drugs will provide a defence if it may have prevented the defendant forming that purpose.

Offences Relating To Care Workers: Sexual Activity with a Person with a Mental Disorder

Definition

7.209 Section 38(1) of the Sexual Offences Act 2003 provides:

"A person (A) commits an offence if:

---

[195] [2007] EWCA Crim 125.

    (a) he intentionally touches another person (B),

    (b) the touching is sexual,

    (c) B has a mental disorder,

    (d) A knows or could reasonably be expected to know that B has a mental disorder, and

    (e) A is involved in B's care in a way which falls within section 42."

MODE OF TRIAL AND PUNISHMENT

The mode of trial and punishment for an offence under s.38 depends upon the type of "touching" in question. If the touching involved any of the following, the offence is triable on indictment only with a maximum penalty of 14 years' imprisonment: **7.210**

- penetration of B's anus or vagina with a part of A's body or anything else,
- penetration of B's mouth with A's penis,
- penetration of A's anus or vagina with a part of B's body, or
- penetration of A's mouth with B's penis.[196]

Otherwise, the offence is triable either way. The maximum sentence on conviction on indictment is 10 years' imprisonment. On summary conviction it is six months' imprisonment or a fine, or both.[197] As from a day to be appointed, the maximum term of imprisonment on summary conviction will increase to 12 months.[198] The increase will have no application to offences committed before it takes effect.[199] Until recently, the maximum fine on summary conviction was a fine not exceeding the statutory maximum (i.e. £5,000). The effect of s.85 of the Legal Aid, Sentencing and Punishment of Offenders Act 2012 is that, from March 12, 2015, a fine of any amount may be imposed.

For the purposes of listing, cases under s.38[200] fall within Class 2B, save for complex cases involving many complainants (in care or otherwise particularly vulnerable) and/or many defendants who are alleged to have systematically groomed and abused them, often over a long period of time, which fall within Class 1C.[201] Cases in Class 1C must be referred to the Resident Judge, and by the Resident Judge to a Presiding Judge. Cases in Class 2B must be similarly referred in certain specified circumstances, including where   **7.211**

---

[196] s.38(3).

[197] s.38(4).

[198] Criminal Justice Act 2003 s.282(2), (3).

[199] Criminal Justice Act 2003 s.282(4).

[200] And of soliciting, inciting, encouraging or assisting, attempting or conspiring to commit the offence or assisting an offender having committed the offence.

[201] *Consolidated Criminal Practice Directions*, Part XIII Listing B: CLASSIFICATION, available at *https://www.judiciary.gov.uk/wp-content/uploads/2015/09/crim-pd-2015.pdf* [Accessed April 30, 2016].

the case is unusually grave or complex or a novel and important point of law is to be raised; where the defendant is a police officer, a member of the legal profession or a high profile figure; or where for any reason the case is likely to attract exceptional media attention.

7.212 An offence under s.38 is a specified offence for the purposes of s.226A of the Criminal Justice Act 2003 (extended sentence for certain violent or sexual offences).[202]

7.213 A person convicted under s.38, cautioned, found not guilty by reason of insanity or found to be under a disability and to have done the act charged, is automatically subject to the notification requirements in the Sexual Offences Act 2003 if (a) where the offender was under 18 at the time of the offence, he is sentenced to at least 12 months' imprisonment, or (b) in any other case, the offender is, in respect of the offence, sentenced to a term of imprisonment, detained in a hospital or given a community sentence of at least 12 months.[203]

Sentencing

7.214 For the Sentencing Council guideline relating to the sentencing of sexual offences committed by offenders aged 18 and over, see Ch.33. A single guideline covers the offences in ss.38 and 39 of the 2003 Act (care workers: sexual activity with a person with a mental disorder and care workers: causing or inciting sexual activity by a person with a mental disorder). The guideline contains at its head the statement "This guideline also applies to offences committed remotely/online".

Sentencing guideline

Step One—Harm and culpability

7.215 The guideline requires the sentencing court to go through a series of steps in order to determine the appropriate sentence. Step one involves determining the offence category by reference to the degree of harm caused and then the culpability level for the offence. The court should determine which categories of harm and culpability the offence falls into by reference only to the tables below. The approach taken by the Sentencing Council is to identify the type of sexual activity which took place as determinative of the harm caused; this is because victims of these types of offences may be reluctant to articulate

---

[202] Inserted by the Legal Aid, Sentencing and Punishment of Offenders Act 2012 s.124, brought into force on December 3, 2012, by SI 2012/2906.
[203] s.80 and Sch.3, discussed in Ch.35, below.

harm or may regard themselves as in a genuine relationship with the offender.

Harm	
Category 1	• Penetration of vagina or anus (using body or object) • Penile penetration of mouth in either case by, or of, the victim
Category 2	Touching, or exposure, of naked genitalia or naked breasts by, or of, the victim
Category 3	Factor(s) in categories 1 and 2 not present

Culpability
A
Significant degree of planning
Offender acts together with others to commit the offence
Use of alcohol/drugs on victim to facilitate the offence
Grooming behaviour used against the victim
Use of threats (including blackmail)
Sexual images of victim recorded, retained, solicited or shared
Commercial exploitation and/or motivation
Offence racially or religiously aggravated
Offence motivated by, or demonstrating, hostility to the victim based on his or her sexual orientation (or presumed sexual orientation) or transgender identity (or presumed transgender identity)
Offence motivated by, or demonstrating, hostility to the victim based on his or her disability (or presumed disability)
B
Factor(s) in category A not present

Step Two—Starting point and category range

7.216 Once the court has determined the offence category and culpability level, it should then use the corresponding starting point specified in the guideline in order to reach a sentence within the category range. The starting point applies to all offenders irrespective of plea or previous convictions. Once the starting point has been determined, step two allows further adjustment for aggravating or mitigating features, set out below. A case of particular gravity, reflected by multiple features of culpability or harm, could merit upward adjustment from the starting point before further adjustment for aggravating or mitigating features. Where there is a sufficient prospect of rehabilitation, a community order with a sex offender treatment programme requirement under s.202 of the Criminal Justice Act 2003 may be a proper alternative to a short or moderate length custodial sentence. The starting points and category ranges for offences under ss.38 and 39 are as follows:

	A	*B*
Category 1	*Starting point* 5 years' custody *Category range* 4–10 years' custody	*Starting point* 18 months' custody *Category range* 1–2 years' custody
Category 2	*Starting point* 3 years' custody *Category range* 2–6 years' custody	*Starting point* 26 weeks' custody *Category range* Medium level community order–1 years' custody
Category 3	*Starting point* 26 weeks' custody *Category range* High level community order– 3 years' custody	*Starting point* Medium level community order *Category range* Low level community order–High level community order

The highest category, with a starting point of 5 years and a range of 4–10 years, is in line with the sentencing levels for exploitation cases under s.9 of the Act, and allows higher sentences to be imposed where vulnerable adults are groomed and exploited by care workers, whom they trust as they would a family member.

Aggravating and mitigating factors

After identifying the starting point and category range, the court should **7.217** consider whether the presence of aggravating or mitigating factors should result in an upward or downward adjustment from the starting point or the imposition of a sentence outside the category range. In particular, relevant recent convictions are likely to result in an upward adjustment. When sentencing appropriate category 2 or 3 offences, the court should also consider whether the custody threshold has been passed; if so, whether a custodial sentence is unavoidable; and if it is, whether that sentence can be suspended. The non-exhaustive list of aggravating and mitigating factors for offences under ss.38 and 39 is as follows:

Aggravating factors
Statutory aggravating factors
Previous convictions, having regard to a) the nature of the offence to which the conviction relates and its relevance to the current offence; and b) the time that has elapsed since the conviction
Offence committed whilst on bail
Other aggravating factors
Ejaculation (where not taken into account at step one)
Pregnancy or STI as a consequence of offence
Location of offence
Timing of offence
Victim compelled to leave their home or institution (including victims of domestic violence)
Failure to comply with current court orders
Offence committed whilst on licence
Any steps taken to prevent the victim reporting an incident, obtaining assistance and/or from assisting or supporting the prosecution
Attempts to dispose of or conceal evidence
Commission of offence whilst under the influence of alcohol or drugs

Mitigating factors
No previous convictions *or* no relevant/recent convictions
Remorse
Previous good character and/or exemplary conduct*
Age and/or lack of maturity where it affects the responsibility of the offender
Mental disorder or learning disability, particularly where linked to the commission of the offence
Sexual activity was incited but no activity took place because the offender voluntarily desisted or intervened to prevent it

* Previous good character/exemplary conduct is different from having no previous convictions. The more serious the offence, the less the weight which should normally be attributed to this factor. Where previous good character/exemplary conduct has been used to facilitate the offence, this mitigation should not normally be allowed and such conduct may constitute an aggravating factor.

In the context of this offence, previous good character/exemplary conduct should not normally be given any significant weight and will not normally justify a reduction in what would otherwise be the appropriate sentence.

Steps Three to Nine

7.218   The remaining steps cover the following points. At step three the court should consider any factors which would indicate a reduction in sentence, e.g. assistance to the prosecution. At step four it should consider any reduction for a guilty plea. At step five the court should consider dangerousness, i.e. whether it would be appropriate to award an extended sentence (s.226A of the Criminal Justice Act 2003). Step six requires the court to consider whether the total sentence is just and proportionate to the offending behaviour. At step seven it should consider whether to make an ancillary order (e.g. a compensation order, a SHPO or a restraining order). Step eight requires the court to fulfil its duty under s.174 of the Criminal Justice Act 2003 to give reasons for, and explain the effect of, the sentence. Finally, at step nine the court should consider whether to give credit for time spent on bail in accordance with s.240A of that Act.

Sentencing examples

7.219   There remain few reported cases. In *Taylor (Alan Edward)*,[204] the appellant was convicted of five charges under s.38, two relating to one victim and three

---

[204] [2015] EWCA Crim 322.

relating to another. The appellant worked as a care manager at a hospital, which provided in-patient care for people with learning disabilities, complicated by mental health problems. He sexually abused two patients, including by incidents of vaginal sexual intercourse over a two-year period. The appellant sexually abused one victim in his home in the grounds of the hospital. In relation to the other victim, the appellant had sexual intercourse with her in her locked hospital room, covering the observation window so that no one else could see what was happening in the room. He also took the victim cycling and had sexual intercourse with her. In 1999 the appellant was warned about inappropriate behaviour towards staff but retained his position as a care manager. In passing sentence, the judge placed the offending in category 1A. He said that there was a high degree of planning, an attempt to conceal evidence, a disregard for the earlier warning and repetitive and systematic offending against two separate victims. In mitigation, the appellant had been a man of good character, as a result of his offending he had lost his job and accommodation, he was married with a young family and there had been considerable delay on the part of the prosecution in deciding to charge him. The appellant was sentenced in relation to the first victim to six years' and two years' imprisonment concurrent, and in relation to the second victim, to six years and six months', five years' and two years' imprisonment concurrent, but consecutive to the sentences the first victim. The result was a total sentence of 12 years and 6 months' imprisonment. The Court of Appeal described the appellant's offending as an "appalling breach of trust" and commented that his victims were "extremely vulnerable, fragile individuals". The decision to impose consecutive sentences in respect of each victim was not criticised, but the Court of Appeal concluded that the judge had failed properly to account for totality and as such the overall sentence was manifestly excessive. The sentence of six years was reduced to four years and nine months, and the sentence of eight years was reduced to five years and three months, reducing the overall sentence from 12 to 10 years' imprisonment.

The following cases, decided under the previous guideline issued by the   **7.220** Sentencing Guidelines Council ("SGC"), remain instructive. In *Calver (Philip)*[205] the appellant was sentenced to 16 months' imprisonment after pleading guilty to a single offence under s.38. He had been employed as a support worker for the victim, who was a 25-year-old female with the mental age of a five-year-old. He had taken her to a woodland area, removed her top and kissed her mouth and breasts. The appellant was of previous good character. The Court of Appeal held that the judge's starting point of 24 months had been too high and the correct starting point was 15 months, which, when reduced by virtue of the guilty plea, resulted in a sentence of 10 months' imprisonment.

---

[205] Unreported, December 5, 2012.

7.221   In *Bennett*, one of the conjoined appeals in *Riat*,[206] the appellant was sentenced to two years' imprisonment following his conviction of one offence under s.38. He was a community psychiatric nurse and the Crown case was that he had had an on-going sexual relationship with a patient for some months. The complainant, 47, was, despite her mental disorder, capable of consenting. She gave a long, garrulous, and by no means always consistent account of a continuing sexual relationship between them. When the appellant was interviewed by the police, he at first denied any such relationship. However, it gradually became apparent that this first response was untruthful, and eventually he was confronted with a number of affectionate messages and cards which he had sent her, including a Valentine's card and a second card in which he had thanked her for "the great sex". At this, he broke down and gave the police a detailed account of a sexual relationship in which they had, he said, had intercourse on a number of occasions. Subsequently he faced disciplinary proceedings in his job. The Crown charged two offences, count one intended to be representative of vaginal intercourse and count two to reflect a specific occasion on which the complainant had said that the defendant penetrated her with his fingers without her consent. At trial the appellant did not deny having a continuing affectionate and sexual relationship with the patient but he contended that there had never been any successful penetration. The jury convicted him on count one but acquitted him on count two. In passing sentence, the judge observed that it was the greatest pity that the appellant had forfeited the mitigation which would have been afforded had he stood by the admissions which he had made. There were a number of impressive testimonials to his character, and his career of 15 years or more was ruined. Also, there was no element of offending against a woman who could not properly consent. But the sentence of two years was somewhat low in the range suggested in the SGC guideline for offences of this kind. There was the plainest breach of trust, and considerable actual and potential harm to a woman of fragile psyche. Accordingly, there was no basis for saying that the sentence was either manifestly excessive or wrong in principle.

Parties to the Offence

7.222   The offence may be committed by care workers of either sex against mentally disordered persons of either sex.

Jurisdiction

7.223   By virtue of s.72 of and Sch.2 to the Sexual Offences Act 2003, as amended,[207] it is an offence under s.38 for a UK national to do an act in a

---

[206] [2012] EWCA Crim 1509.
[207] By the Criminal Justice and Immigration Act 2008 s.72, with effect from July 14, 2008.

country outside the UK which would constitute a s.38 offence committed against a person aged under 18 if done in England and Wales. See further para.7.62, above.

"INVOLVED IN B'S CARE"

Section 42 of the 2003 Act[208] defines when a person is involved in the care of another for the purposes of ss.38–41. It provides:

7.224

"(1) For the purposes of sections 38 to 41, a person (A) is involved in the care of another person (B) in a way that falls within this section if any of subsections (2) to (4) applies.
(2) This subsection applies if—
  (a) B is accommodated and cared for in a care home, community home, voluntary home or children's home, and
  (b) A has functions to perform in the home in the course of employment which have brought him or are likely to bring him into regular face to face contact with B.
(3) This subsection applies if B is a patient for whom services are provided—
  (a) by a National Health Service body or an independent medical agency;
  (b) in an independent hospital; or
  (c) in Wales, in an independent clinic,
and A has functions to perform for the body or agency or in the hospital or clinic in the course of employment which have brought A or are likely to bring A into regular face to face contact with B.
(4) This subsection applies if A—
  (a) is, whether or not in the course of employment, a provider of care, assistance or services to B in connection with B's mental disorder, and
  (b) as such, has had or is likely to have regular face to face contact with B.
(5) In this section—
'care home' means an establishment which is a care home for the purposes of the Care Standards Act 2000;
'children's home' has the meaning given by section 1 of that Act;
'community home' has the meaning given by section 53 of the Children Act 1989;
'employment' means any employment, whether paid or unpaid and whether under a contract of service or apprenticeship, under a contract for service, or otherwise than under a contract;
'independent clinic' has the meaning given by section 2 of the Care Standards Act 2000;
'independent hospital'—
  (a) in England, means—
  (i) a hospital as defined by section 275 of the National Health Service Act 2006 that is not a health service hospital as defined by that section; or
  (ii) any other establishment in which any of the services listed in section 22(6) are provided and which is not a health service hospital as so defined; and
  (b) in Wales, has the meaning given by section 2 of the Care Standards Act 2000;

[208] As amended by SI 2007/961, art.3 and Sch., para.33; SI 2010/813, art.13(4); and the Health and Social Care Act 2012 s.55(2) and Sch.5, para.117.

621

'independent medical agency' means an undertaking (not being an independent hospital, or in Wales an independent clinic) which consists of or includes the provision of services by medical practitioners;
'National Health Service body' means—
  (a) a Local Health Board,
  (b) a National Health Service trust,
  (ba) the Secretary of State in relation to the exercise of functions under section 2A or 2B of, or paragraph 7C, 8 or 12 of Schedule 1 to, the National Health Service Act 2006,
  (bb) a local authority in relation to the exercise of functions under section 2B or 111 of, or any of paragraphs 1 to 7B, or 13 of Schedule 1 to, the National Health Service Act 2006,
  (c) [. . .], or
  (d) a Special Health Authority;
'voluntary home' has the meaning given by section 60(3) of the Children Act 1989.
  (6) In subsection (5), in the definition of 'independent medical agency', 'undertaking' includes any business or profession and—
  (a) in relation to a public or local authority, includes the exercise of any functions of that authority; and
  (b) in relation to any other body of persons, whether corporate or unincorporate, includes any of the activities of that body."

7.225 The care relationship is established if, in circumstances described in s.42(2)–(4), A is involved in the care of B and has functions to perform which bring him or are likely to bring him into "regular face to face contact" with B. The care relationship may arise whether the care is provided on a primary or ancillary level, and whether on a voluntary or paid basis. According to Home Office guidance,[209] such a relationship may arise not only with doctors, nursing staff and social workers, but also with receptionists, cleaning staff, advocates and voluntary helpers. The inclusion of functions "likely" to bring A into regular face to face contact with B suggests that a care relationship for the purposes of s.42 could be established at A and B's first meeting. It is, however, arguable that by limiting care workers to those with whom there is or is likely to be regular contact, vulnerable individuals will remain unprotected from those who care for them on an irregular or one-off basis, such as agency staff.[210]

7.226 Section 41(2) deals with the situation where the complainant is accommodated and cared for in a care home, community home, voluntary home or children's home. Section 41(3) relates to the situation where the complainant is a patient for whom services are provided by an NHS body or private medical agency, or an independent clinic or independent hospital. In both these situations, to be "involved in B's care" the defendant must have "functions to perform in the course of employment" which have brought him or are likely to bring him in regular face to face contact with B. This wording is wide enough to cover staff who are not providing medical or nursing care.

[209] H.O. Circular 21/2004: *Guidance on Part 1 of the Sexual Offences Act 2003*, para.181.
[210] See further on this aspect paras 5.32 and following, above.

Section 41(4) covers the situation where the defendant is a provider of care,   7.227
assistance or services to B in connection with B's mental disorder. To come
within this subsection, the defendant need not provide care etc. in the course
of employment, but he must have or be likely to have regular face to face
contact with B. There is no requirement that the offence is committed on
hospital premises or that the complainant is resident in an institution. The
complainant may be cared for at home. The Home Office guidance gives as
examples of care relationships within s.41(4) a voluntary care worker who
takes a mentally disordered person on weekly outings or visits him at home
to provide complimentary therapy.[211]

"TOUCHES ANOTHER PERSON"

For the meaning of "touches", see paras 2.63 and following, above.   7.228

"THE TOUCHING IS SEXUAL"

The touching must be "sexual". For the meaning of this term, see paras 2.66   7.229
and following, above.

"MENTAL DISORDER"

The complainant must have a mental disorder at the time of the touching.   7.230
For the definition of mental disorder, see paras 7.25 and following, and 7.80
and following, above.

MENTAL ELEMENT

The prosecution must prove that the defendant intended to touch the   7.231
complainant. For discussion of this requirement, see para.7.87, above
   Additionally, the prosecution must establish that the defendant knew or   7.232
could reasonably have been expected to know that the complainant had a
mental disorder. An important difference between the care worker offences
and the other offences in the Act relating to the mentally disordered is the
existence of an evidential presumption on this point in relation to care
workers. Section 38(2) of the Act provides:

> "Where in proceedings for an offence under this section it is proved that the other
> person had a mental disorder, it is to be taken that the defendant knew or could
> reasonably have been expected to know that that person had a mental disorder
> unless sufficient evidence is adduced to raise an issue as to whether he knew or
> could reasonably have been expected to know it."[212]

---

[211] H.O. Circular 21/2004: *Guidance on Part 1 of the Sexual Offences Act 2003*, para.182.
[212] Similar provisions are contained in ss.39(2), 40(2) and 41(2).

7.233   The effect of this provision is that offences committed by care workers are treated in a similar way to those committed by persons in a position of trust or in a familial relationship with the complainant, in that it is presumed that the defendant knew or could reasonably have been expected to know that the person had a mental disorder. First, the prosecution must prove that the complainant had a mental disorder. If they do so, then, unless sufficient evidence is adduced to raise an issue as to the defendant's knowledge, the defendant is taken to have known etc. that the complainant had a mental disorder. If sufficient evidence is adduced to put the point in issue, it falls to the prosecution to prove in the ordinary way that the defendant knew or could reasonably have been expected to know that the complainant had a mental disorder.[213]

7.234   In the light of the decision in *Heard*,[214] discussed in paras 2.81 and following, above, the additional requirement that the defendant did the prohibited act for the purpose of obtaining sexual gratification makes the s.38 offence one of specific intent, such that voluntary intoxication through drink or drugs will provide a defence if it may have prevented the defendant forming that purpose.

Exception for Spouses and Civil Partners

7.235   Section 43 of the 2003 Act creates an exception from the care worker offences for cases where the defendant proves that he and the complainant were lawfully married or in a civil partnership and that the complainant was aged 16 or over at the time of the alleged offence. It is for the defence to prove the elements of the exception on a balance of probabilities. Section 43[215] provides:

> "(1) Conduct by a person (A) which would otherwise be an offence under any of sections 38 to 41 against another person (B) is not an offence under that section if at the time:
>   (a) B is 16 or over, and
>   (b) A and B are lawfully married or civil partners of each other.
> (2) In proceedings for such an offence it is for the defendant to prove that A and B were lawfully married or civil partners of each other."

Pre-Existing Sexual Relationships

7.236   Section 44 of the Act creates an exception from the care worker offences when the defendant can prove on a balance of probabilities that a sexual relationship existed between him and the complainant immediately before he became the complainant's care worker. This exception does not apply if at the time of the pre-existing sexual relationship, sexual intercourse between the

---

[213] See *Hansard*, HL Vol.648, col.1142, Lord Thomas of Gresford (June 2, 2003).
[214] [2007] EWCA Crim 125.
[215] As amended by the Civil Partnership Act 2004 s.261(1) and Sch.27, para.175(2), (3).

two would have been unlawful. This would be the case if, for example, the complainant was suffering from a mental disorder and was "unable to refuse" during the earlier relationship. In those circumstances, the defendant would not be able to avail himself of the s.44 exception, and furthermore he is likely to have committed offences under ss.30–33. Section 44 provides:

> "(1) Conduct by a person (A) which would otherwise be an offence under any of sections 38 to 41 against another person (B) is not an offence under that section if, immediately before A became involved in B's care in a way that falls within section 42, a sexual relationship existed between A and B.
>
> (2) Subsection (1) does not apply if at that time sexual intercourse between A and B would have been unlawful.
>
> (3) In proceedings for an offence under any of sections 38 to 41 it is for the defendant to prove that such a relationship existed at that time."

CARE WORKERS: CAUSING OR INCITING SEXUAL ACTIVITY

DEFINITION

Section 39(1) of the Sexual Offences Act 2003 provides as follows: **7.237**

> "A person (A) commits an offence if:
> (a) he intentionally causes or incites another person (B) to engage in an activity,
> (b) the activity is sexual,
> (c) B has a mental disorder,
> (d) A knows or could reasonably be expected to know that B has a mental disorder, and
> (e) A is involved in B's care in a way which falls within section 42."

MODE OF TRIAL AND PUNISHMENT

The mode of trial and punishment for an offence under s.39 depends upon   **7.238**
the type of activity caused or incited. If it involved any of the following, the offence is triable on indictment only, with a maximum penalty of 14 years' imprisonment:

- penetration of B's anus or vagina,
- penetration of B's mouth with a person's penis,
- penetration of a person's anus or vagina with a part of B's body or by B with anything else, or
- penetration of a person's mouth with B's penis.[216]

Otherwise, the offence is triable either way. The maximum sentence on conviction on indictment is 10 years' imprisonment. On summary conviction it is six months' imprisonment or a fine, or both.[217] As from a day to be appointed, the maximum term of imprisonment on summary conviction will

[216] s.39(3).
[217] s.39(4).

increase to 12 months.[218] The increase will have no application to offences committed before it takes effect.[219] Until recently, the maximum fine on summary conviction was a fine not exceeding the statutory maximum (i.e. £5,000). The effect of s.85 of the Legal Aid, Sentencing and Punishment of Offenders Act 2012 is that, from March 12, 2015, a fine of any amount may be imposed.

7.239   For the purposes of listing, cases under s.39[220] fall within Class 2B, save for complex cases involving many complainants (in care or otherwise particularly vulnerable) and/or many defendants who are alleged to have systematically groomed and abused them, often over a long period of time, which fall within Class 1C.[221] Cases in Class 1C must be referred to the Resident Judge, and by the Resident Judge to a Presiding Judge. Cases in Class 2B must be similarly referred in certain specified circumstances, including where the case is unusually grave or complex or a novel and important point of law is to be raised; where the defendant is a police officer, a member of the legal profession or a high profile figure; or where for any reason the case is likely to attract exceptional media attention.

7.240   An offence under s.39 is a specified offence for the purposes of s.226A of the Criminal Justice Act 2003 (extended sentence for certain violent or sexual offences).[222]

7.241   A person convicted under s.39, cautioned, found not guilty by reason of insanity or found to be under a disability and to have done the act charged, is automatically subject to the notification requirements in the Sexual Offences Act 2003 if (a) where the offender was under 18 at the time of the offence, he is sentenced to at least 12 months' imprisonment, or (b) in any other case, the offender is, in respect of the offence, sentenced to a term of imprisonment, detained in a hospital or given a community sentence of at least 12 months.[223]

Sentencing

7.242   For the Sentencing Council guideline relating to the sentencing of sexual offences committed by offenders aged 18 and over, see Ch.33. A single guideline covers offences under both s.38 and s.39 of the 2003 Act and is considered at paras 7.215 and following, above.

---

[218] Criminal Justice Act 2003 s.282(2), (3).
[219] Criminal Justice Act 2003 s.282(4).
[220] And of soliciting, inciting, encouraging or assisting, attempting or conspiring to commit the offence or assisting an offender having committed the offence.
[221] *Consolidated Criminal Practice Directions*, Part XIII Listing B: CLASSIFICATION, available at *https://www.judiciary.gov.uk/wp-content/uploads/2015/09/crim-pd-2015.pdf* [Accessed April 30, 2016].
[222] Inserted by the Legal Aid, Sentencing and Punishment of Offenders Act 2012 s.124, brought into force on December 3, 2012, by SI 2012/2906.
[223] s.80 and Sch.3, discussed in Ch.35, below.

PARTIES TO THE OFFENCE

The offence may be committed by care workers of either sex against mentally   7.243
disordered persons of either sex.

JURISDICTION

By virtue of s.72 of and Sch.2 to the Sexual Offences Act 2003, as   7.244
amended,[224] it is an offence under s.39 for a UK national to do an act in a
country outside the UK which would constitute a s.39 offence committed
against a person aged under 18 if done in England and Wales. See further
para.7.62, above.

"CAUSES OR INCITES ANOTHER PERSON . . . TO ENGAGE IN AN ACTIVITY"

For the meaning of this term, see paras 2.98 and following, and 3.158 and   7.245
following, above. The s.39 offence is complete once there has been incitement,
even if the sexual activity does not take place.

"THE ACTIVITY IS SEXUAL"

The activity caused or incited must be "sexual". For the meaning of this   7.246
term, see paras 2.66 and following, above. The sexual activity need not be
with the defendant: the offence is committed where, e.g. a person causes the
complainant to engage in sexual activity with another person, or incites the
complainant to masturbate himself.

"MENTAL DISORDER"

The complainant must have had a mental disorder at the time of the   7.247
causing or inciting. For discussion of the definition of "mental disorder", see
paras 7.25 and following, and 7.80 and following, above.

MENTAL ELEMENT

The prosecution must prove that the defendant intended to cause or incite   7.248
the complainant to engage in sexual activity.

Additionally, the prosecution must establish that the defendant knew or   7.249
could reasonably have been expected to know that the complainant had a
mental disorder. However, s.39(2) provides that if the disorder is proved,
there is an evidential presumption that the defendant knew etc. of it, unless
sufficient evidence is adduced to put the point in issue. See further paras
7.232 and following, above.

[224] By the Criminal Justice and Immigration Act 2008 s.72, with effect from July 14, 2008.

7.250   In light of the decision in *Heard*,[225] discussed in paras 2.81 and following, above, the requirement that the defendant did the prohibited act for the purpose of obtaining sexual gratification makes the s.39 offence one of specific intent, such that voluntary intoxication through drink or drugs will provide a defence if it may have prevented the defendant forming an intent for that purpose.

Exceptions

7.251   The statutory exceptions in s.43 (spouses and civil partners) and s.44 (sexual relationships which pre-date care relationships) apply to offences under s.39. See paras 7.235 and following, above.

Care Workers: Sexual Activity in the Presence of a Person with a Mental Disorder

Definition

7.252   Section 40(1) of the Sexual Offences Act 2003 provides as follows:

"A person (A) commits an offence if:
(a) he intentionally engages in an activity,
(b) the activity is sexual
(c) for the purposes of obtaining sexual gratification, he engages in it:
  (i) when another person (B) is present or is in a place from which A can be observed, and
  (ii) knowing or believing that B is aware, or intending that B should be aware, that he is engaging in it,
(d) B has a mental disorder,
(e) A knows or could reasonably be expected to know that B has a mental disorder, and
(f) A is involved in B's care in a way that falls within section 42."

Mode of Trial and Punishment

7.253   Offences under s.40 of the Sexual Offences Act 2003 are triable either way. The maximum sentence on conviction on indictment is seven years' imprisonment. The maximum on summary conviction is six months' imprisonment or a fine, or both.[226] As from a day to be appointed, the maximum term of imprisonment on summary conviction will increase to 12 months.[227] The increase will have no application to offences committed before it takes effect.[228] Until recently, the maximum fine on summary conviction was a fine not exceeding the statutory maximum (i.e. £5,000). The effect of s.85 of the Legal Aid, Sentencing and Punishment of Offenders Act 2012 is that, from March 12, 2015, a fine of any amount may be imposed.

[225] [2007] EWCA Crim 125.
[226] s.40(3).
[227] Criminal Justice Act 2003 s.282(2), (3).
[228] Criminal Justice Act 2003 s.282(4).

For the purposes of listing, cases under s.40[229] fall within Class 2B, save for **7.254** complex cases involving many complainants (in care or otherwise particularly vulnerable) and/or many defendants who are alleged to have systematically groomed and abused them, often over a long period of time, which fall within Class 1C.[230] Cases in Class 1C must be referred to the Resident Judge, and by the Resident Judge to a Presiding Judge. Cases in Class 2B must be similarly referred in certain specified circumstances, including where the case is unusually grave or complex or a novel and important point of law is to be raised; where the defendant is a police officer, a member of the legal profession or a high profile figure; or where for any reason the case is likely to attract exceptional media attention.

An offence under s.40 is a specified offence for the purposes of s.226A of **7.255** the Criminal Justice Act 2003 (extended sentence for certain violent or sexual offences).[231]

A person convicted under s.40, cautioned, found not guilty by reason of **7.256** insanity or found to be under a disability and to have done the act charged, is automatically subject to the notification requirements in the Sexual Offences Act 2003 if (a) where the offender was under 18 at the time of the offence, he is sentenced to at least 12 months' imprisonment, or (b) in any other case, the offender is, in respect of the offence, sentenced to a term of imprisonment, detained in a hospital or given a community sentence of at least 12 months.[232]

SENTENCING

For the Sentencing Council guideline relating to the sentencing of sexual **7.257** offences committed by offenders aged 18 and over, see Ch.33. A single guideline covers the offences in ss.40 and 41 of the 2003 Act (care workers: sexual activity in the presence of a person with a mental disorder and care workers: causing a person with a mental disorder to watch a sexual act).

Sentencing guideline

Step One—Harm and culpability

The guideline requires the sentencing court to go through a series of steps in **7.258** order to determine the appropriate sentence. Step one involves determining the offence category by reference to the degree of harm caused and then the culpability level for the offence. The court should determine into which

---

[229] And of soliciting, inciting, encouraging or assisting, attempting or conspiring to commit the offence or assisting an offender having committed the offence.

[230] *Consolidated Criminal Practice Directions*, Part XIII Listing B: CLASSIFICATION, available at *https://www.judiciary.gov.uk/wp-content/uploads/2015/09/crim-pd-2015.pdf* [Accessed April 30, 2016].

[231] Inserted by the Legal Aid, Sentencing and Punishment of Offenders Act 2012 s.124, brought into force on December 3, 2012, by SI 2012/2906.

[232] s.80 and Sch.3, discussed in Ch.35, below.

categories of harm and culpability the offence falls by reference only to the tables below. The approach taken by the Sentencing Council is to identify the type of sexual activity which took place as determinative of the harm caused; this is because victims of these types of offences may be reluctant to articulate harm or may regard themselves as in a genuine relationship with the offender.

Harm		Culpability
Category 1	• Causing victim to view extreme pornography • Causing victim to view indecent/prohibited images of children • Engaging in, or causing a victim to view live, sexual activity involving sadism/violence/sexual activity with an animal/a child	A
		Significant degree of planning
		Offender acts together with others to commit the offence
		Use of alcohol/drugs on victim to facilitate the offence
		Grooming behaviour used against the victim
		Use of threats (including blackmail)
Category 2	Engaging in, or causing a victim to view images of or view live, sexual activity involving: • penetration of vagina or anus (using body or object) • penile penetration of mouth • masturbation	Commercial exploitation and/or motivation
		Offence racially or religiously aggravated
		Offence motivated by, or demonstrating, hostility to the victim based on his or her sexual orientation (or presumed sexual orientation) or transgender identity (or presumed transgender identity)
Category 3	Factor(s) in categories 1 and 2 not present	Offence motivated by, or demonstrating, hostility to the victim based on his or her disability (or presumed disability)
		B
		Factor(s) in category A not present

Step Two—Starting point and category range

Once the court has determined the offence category and culpability level, at   **7.259**
step two it should use the corresponding starting point specified in the
guideline in order to reach a sentence within the category range. The starting
point applies to all offenders irrespective of plea or previous convictions.
Once the starting point has been determined, step two allows further
adjustment for aggravating or mitigating features, set out below. A case of
particular gravity, reflected by multiple features of culpability or harm, could
merit upward adjustment from the starting point before further adjustment
for aggravating or mitigating features. Where there is a sufficient prospect of
rehabilitation, a community order with a sex offender treatment programme
requirement under s.202 of the Criminal Justice Act 2003 may be a proper
alternative to a short or moderate length custodial sentence. The starting
points and category ranges for offences under ss.40 and 41 are as follows:

	A	*B*
Category 1	*Starting point* 18 months' custody *Category range* 1–2 years' custody	*Starting point* 1 years' custody *Category range* 26 weeks'–18 months' custody
Category 2	*Starting point* 1 years' custody *Category range* 26 weeks'–18 months' custody	*Starting point* 26 weeks' custody *Category range* High level community order–1 year's custody
Category 3	*Starting point* 26 weeks' custody *Category range* High level community order– 1 year's custody	*Starting point* Medium level community order *Category range* Low level community order–High level community order

Aggravating and mitigating factors

After identifying the starting point and category range, the court should   **7.260**
consider whether the presence of aggravating or mitigating factors should

631

result in an upward or downward adjustment from the starting point or the imposition of a sentence outside the category range. In particular, relevant recent convictions are likely to result in an upward adjustment. When sentencing appropriate category 2 or 3 offences, the court should also consider whether the custody threshold has been passed; if so, whether a custodial sentence is unavoidable; and if it is, whether that sentence can be suspended. The non-exhaustive list of aggravating and mitigating factors for offences under ss.40 and 41 is as follows:

Aggravating factors
Statutory aggravating factors
Previous convictions, having regard to a) the nature of the offence to which the conviction relates and its relevance to the current offence; and b) the time that has elapsed since the conviction
Offence committed whilst on bail
Other aggravating factors
Location of offence
Timing of offence
Failure to comply with current court orders
Offence committed whilst on licence
Any steps taken to prevent the victim reporting an incident, obtaining assistance and/or from assisting or supporting the prosecution
Attempts to dispose of or conceal evidence
Failure of offender to respond to previous warnings
Commission of offence whilst under the influence of alcohol or drugs

Mitigating factors
No previous convictions *or* no relevant/recent convictions
Remorse
Previous good character and/or exemplary conduct*
Age and/or lack of maturity where it affects the responsibility of the offender

Mental disorder or learning disability, particularly where linked to the commission of the offence
Demonstration of steps taken to address offending behaviour

* Previous good character/exemplary conduct is different from having no previous convictions. The more serious the offence, the less the weight which should normally be attributed to this factor. Where previous good character/exemplary conduct has been used to facilitate the offence, this mitigation should not normally be allowed and such conduct may constitute an aggravating factor.

Steps Three to Nine

The remaining steps cover the following points. At step three the court   7.261
should consider any factors which would indicate a reduction in sentence, e.g. assistance to the prosecution. At step four it should consider any reduction for a guilty plea. At step five the court should consider dangerousness, i.e. whether it would be appropriate to award an extended sentence (s.226A of the Criminal Justice Act 2003). Step six requires the court to consider whether the total sentence is just and proportionate to the offending behaviour. At step seven it should consider whether to make an ancillary order (e.g. a compensation order, a SHPO or a restraining order). Step eight requires the court to fulfil its duty under s.174 of the Criminal Justice Act 2003 to give reasons for, and explain the effect of, the sentence. Finally, at step nine the court should consider whether to give credit for time spent on bail in accordance with s.240A of that Act.

PARTIES TO THE OFFENCE

The offence may be committed by care workers of either sex against mentally   7.262
disordered persons of either sex.

JURISDICTION

By virtue of s.72 of and Sch.2 to the Sexual Offences Act 2003, as   7.263
amended,[233] it is an offence under s.40 for a UK national to do an act in a country outside the UK which would constitute a s.40 offence committed against a person aged under 18 if done in England and Wales. See further para.7.62, above.

"ENGAGES IN AN ACTIVITY"

For the meaning of this term, see paras 2.99 and following, above.   7.264

---

[233] By the Criminal Justice and Immigration Act 2008 s.72, with effect from July 14, 2008.

"The Activity is Sexual"

7.265 For the meaning of the term "sexual", see paras 2.66 and following, above.

"Present or . . . In a Place from which A can be Observed"

7.266 For the meaning of this term, see paras 4.114 and following, above.

"Mental Disorder"

7.267 The complainant must have had a "mental disorder" at the relevant time. For discussion of the meaning of "mental disorder", see paras 7.25 and following, and 7.80 and following, above.

Mental Element

7.268 The defendant (A) must engage in sexual activity intentionally. Moreover, for the purpose of sexual gratification he must engage in it when B is present or in a place from which A can be observed. The term "sexual" in this context is undefined.[234] For discussion of this requirement, see para.5.98, above. This requirement will safeguard care workers who engage in sexual activity in front of a mentally disordered person for a legitimate reason.[235]

7.269 Additionally, the prosecution must establish that the defendant knew or could reasonably have been expected to know that the complainant had a mental disorder. However, s.40(2) provides that if the disorder is proved, there is an evidential presumption that the defendant knew etc. of it, unless sufficient evidence is adduced to put the point in issue. See further paras 7.232 and following, above.

7.270 In the light of the decision in *Heard*,[236] discussed in paras 2.81 and following, above, the requirement that the defendant did the prohibited act for the purpose of obtaining sexual gratification makes the s.40 offence one of specific intent, such that voluntary intoxication through drink or drugs will provide a defence if it may have prevented the defendant forming that purpose.

Exceptions

7.271 The statutory exceptions in s.43 (spouses and civil partners) and s.44 (sexual relationships which pre-date care relationships) apply to offences under s.40. See paras 7.235 and following, above

---

[234] s.78 of the 2003 Act defines "sexual" for the purposes of penetration, touching or any other activity.

[235] For example, two care workers kissing at a Christmas party at a care establishment.

[236] [2007] EWCA Crim 125.

CARE WORKERS: CAUSING A PERSON WITH A MENTAL DISORDER TO WATCH A SEXUAL ACT

DEFINITION

Section 41(1) of the Sexual Offences Act 2003 provides: 7.272

"A person (A) commits an offence if:
(a) for the purpose of obtaining sexual gratification, he intentionally causes another person (B) to watch a third person engaging in an activity, or to look at an image of any person engaging in an activity,
(b) the activity is sexual,
(c) B has a mental disorder,
(d) A knows or could reasonably be expected to know that B has a mental disorder, and
(e) A is involved in B's care in a way that falls within section 42."

MODE OF TRIAL AND PUNISHMENT

Offences under s.41 are triable either way. The maximum sentence on   7.273
conviction on indictment is seven years' imprisonment. The maximum on
summary conviction is six months' imprisonment or a fine, or both.[237] As
from a day to be appointed, the maximum term of imprisonment on
summary conviction will increase to 12 months.[238] The increase will have no
application to offences committed before it takes effect.[239] Until recently, the
maximum fine on summary conviction was a fine not exceeding the statutory
maximum (i.e. £5,000). The effect of s.85 of the Legal Aid, Sentencing and
Punishment of Offenders Act 2012 is that, from March 12, 2015, a fine of any
amount may be imposed.

For the purposes of listing, cases under s.41[240] fall within Class 2B, save for   7.274
complex cases involving many complainants (in care or otherwise particularly vulnerable) and/or many defendants who are alleged to have systematically groomed and abused them, often over a long period of time, which
fall within Class 1C.[241] Cases in Class 1C must be referred to the Resident
Judge, and by the Resident Judge to a Presiding Judge. Cases in Class 2B
must be similarly referred in certain specified circumstances, including where
the case is unusually grave or complex or a novel and important point of law
is to be raised; where the defendant is a police officer, a member of the legal

---

[237] s.41(3).
[238] Criminal Justice Act 2003 s.282(2), (3).
[239] Criminal Justice Act 2003 s.282(4).
[240] And of soliciting, inciting, encouraging or assisting, attempting or conspiring to commit the offence or assisting an offender having committed the offence.
[241] *Consolidated Criminal Practice Directions*, Part XIII Listing B: CLASSIFICATION, available at *https://www.judiciary.gov.uk/wp-content/uploads/2015/09/crim-pd-2015.pdf* [Accessed April 30, 2016].

profession or a high profile figure; or where for any reason the case is likely to attract exceptional media attention.

7.275   An offence under s.41 is a specified offence for the purposes of s.226A of the Criminal Justice Act 2003 (extended sentence for certain violent or sexual offences).[242]

7.276   A person convicted under s.41, cautioned, found not guilty by reason of insanity or found to be under a disability and to have done the act charged, is automatically subject to the notification requirements in the Sexual Offences Act 2003 if (a) where the offender was under 18 at the time of the offence, he is sentenced to at least 12 months' imprisonment, or (b) in any other case, the offender is, in respect of the offence, sentenced to a term of imprisonment, detained in a hospital or given a community sentence of at least 12 months.[243]

Sentencing

7.277   For the Sentencing Council guideline relating to the sentencing of sexual offences committed by offenders aged 18 and over, see Ch.33. A single guideline covers offences under both s.40 and s.41 of the 2003 Act and is considered at paras 7.257 and following, above.

Parties to the Offence

7.278   The offence may be committed by male or female care workers of either sex against mentally disordered persons of either sex.

Jurisdiction

7.279   By virtue of s.72 of and Sch.2 to the Sexual Offences Act 2003, as amended,[244] it is an offence under s.41 for a UK national to do an act in a country outside the UK which would constitute a s.41 offence committed against a person aged under 18 if done in England and Wales. See further para.7.62, above.

"Causes"

7.280   For the meaning of this term, see paras 2.98 and following, above.

---

[242] Inserted by the Legal Aid, Sentencing and Punishment of Offenders Act 2012 s.124, brought into force on December 3, 2012, by SI 2012/2906.
[243] s.80 and Sch.3, discussed in Ch.35, below.
[244] By the Criminal Justice and Immigration Act 2008 s.72, with effect from July 14, 2008.

"To Watch a Third Person Engaging in an Activity, or to Look at an Image of Any Person Engaging in an Activity"

For the meaning of this phrase, see paras 4.134 and following, and 7.135, above. **7.281**

"The Activity is Sexual"

For the meaning of "sexual", see paras 2.66 and following, above. **7.282**

"Mental Disorder"

The complainant must have had a mental disorder at the time the defendant **7.283**
caused him or her to watch or look. For discussion of the definition of
"mental disorder", see paras 7.25 and following, and 7.80 and following,
above.

Mental Element

The prosecution must prove that the defendant intentionally and for the **7.284**
purpose of obtaining sexual gratification caused the complainant to watch a
third person engaging in a sexual activity, or to look at an image of any
person engaging in sexual activity.

Additionally, the prosecution must establish that the defendant knew or **7.285**
could reasonably have been expected to know that the complainant had a
mental disorder. However, s.41(2) provides that if the disorder is proved,
there is an evidential presumption that the defendant knew etc. of it, unless
sufficient evidence is adduced to put the point in issue. See further paras
7.232 and following, above.

In the light of the decision in *Heard*,[245] discussed in paras 2.281 and **7.286**
following, above, the requirement that the defendant did the prohibited act
for the purpose of obtaining sexual gratification makes the s.41 offence one
of specific intent, such that voluntary intoxication through drink or drugs
will provide a defence if it may have prevented the defendant forming that
purpose.

Exceptions

The statutory exceptions under s.43 (spouses and civil partners) and s.44 **7.287**
(sexual relationships which pre-date care relationships) apply to offences
under s.41. See paras 7.235 and following, above.

---

[245] [2007] EWCA Crim 125.

CHAPTER 8

INDECENT PHOTOGRAPHS OF CHILDREN

Introduction...................................... 8.01   Possession of an Indecent
Taking (Etc.) an Indecent   Photograph or Pseudo-
  Photograph or Pseudo-   Photograph of A Child............... 8.119
  Photograph of a Child................. 8.03

INTRODUCTION

This chapter deals with the law relating to the exploitation of children **8.01** through the production, possession and dissemination of indecent images. The problem was first expressly addressed by the Protection of Children Act 1978.[1] Before that Act was passed, it was dealt with under a variety of provisions, including customs and excise legislation, the law of obscenity and the offences of indecent assault and gross indecency with children.[2] The 1978 Act made it an offence to take, show, distribute or publish indecent photographs of children under 16. Parliament later supplemented the Act by creating an offence, in s.160 of the Criminal Justice Act 1988,[3] of possession of an indecent photograph of a child. Further important changes in the law were driven by the development during the late 1980s and 1990s of computer technology and the internet, which facilitated the creation and dissemination of indecent images of children. This led Parliament, in the Criminal Justice and Public Order Act 1994,[4] to expand the offences under the earlier Acts to bring data stored on computer or by other electronic means within the definition of "photograph", to extend the scope of the offences to cover indecent "pseudo-photographs", i.e. computerised images purporting to be

---

[1] 1978 c.37.

[2] Interestingly, the Government view was that these various provisions were fairly effective in practice: during the passage of the Bill the Government spokesman in the House of Lords, Lord Harris of Greenwich, said: "We are assured by the D.P.P. . . . that it is very rare for an instance of this nature to come to light where charges in respect of one offence or another are not possible." He concluded that there was "no evidence" that the alleged problem was of "any significance" and that the value of the Act was "very much on the margins of the problem". How times change.

[3] 1988 c.33.

[4] 1994 c.33.

of real children, and to create an offence of "making" an indecent photograph (etc.) of a child alongside the offences of "taking" and "permitting to be taken". In 2001, the maximum penalties for the offences were substantially increased. The Sexual Offences Act 2003 further significantly extended the scope of the offences by amending the definition of "child" to cover those aged 16 and 17, subject to an exception where the parties are married or cohabiting at the material time. This extension was designed to implement the UK's international obligations to protect children up to the age of 18 from exploitation through pornography.[5] In 2008, the definition of "photograph" was further extended to cover tracings and other derivates from photographs.[6] The most recent legislative intervention is the creation in s.62 of the Coroners and Justice Act 2009 of an offence of possession of prohibited images of children. This offence[7] is targeted at non-photographic images, such as computer generated images, "cartoons" and drawings, and it specifically excludes indecent photographs or pseudo-photographs of children, as well as tracings or derivatives of photographs and pseudo-photographs, all of which are regulated by the 1978 and 1988 Acts. The offence is therefore best regarded as an aspect of the law of obscenity and as such falls outside the scope of this book.

8.02   This chapter considers separately the offences in the 1978 Act of taking etc. an indecent photograph or pseudo-photograph of a child and the offence in the 1988 Act of possession of such a photograph or pseudo-photograph.

TAKING (ETC.) AN INDECENT PHOTOGRAPH OR PSEUDO-PHOTOGRAPH OF A CHILD

DEFINITION

8.03   Section 1(1) of the Protection of Children Act 1978[8] provides:

"Subject to sections 1A and 1B,[9] it is an offence for a person—
  (a) to take, or permit to be taken or to make, an indecent photograph or pseudo-photograph of a child; or
  (b) to distribute or show such indecent photographs or pseudo-photographs; or

---

[5] See especially *Council Framework Decision 2004/68/JHA* and the *UN Convention on the Rights of the Child*, art.34. The Framework Decision has since been replaced: see *Directive 2011/93/EU of the European Parliament and of the Council of 13 December 2011 on combating the sexual abuse and sexual exploitation of children and child pornography, and replacing Council Framework Decision 2004/68/JHA*, as to which see para.10.09, below.

[6] See para.8.53, below.

[7] Which came into force on April 6, 2010.

[8] As amended by the Criminal Justice and Public Order Act 1994 s.84(1), (2), with effect from February 3, 1995 and by the Sexual Offences Act 2003 s.139 and Sch.6, para.24, with effect from May 1, 2004.

[9] For which see paras 8.75 and following, and 8.82 and following, below.

(c) to have in his possession such indecent photographs or pseudo-photographs, with a view to their being distributed or shown by himself or others; or

(d) to publish or cause to be published any advertisement likely to be understood as conveying that the advertiser distributes or shows such indecent photographs or pseudo-photographs or intends to do so."

MODE OF TRIAL AND PUNISHMENT

The offences in s.1(1) of the 1978 Act are triable either way.[10] On conviction   **8.04**
on indictment the maximum punishment is 10 years' imprisonment or a fine, or both.[11] On summary conviction, the maximum is six months' imprisonment or a fine, or both.[12] As from a day to be appointed the maximum sentence of imprisonment on summary conviction will increase to 12 months.[13] The increase will have no application to offences committed before it takes effect.[14] Until recently, the maximum fine on summary conviction was a fine not exceeding the prescribed sum (i.e. £5,000). The effect of s.85 of the Legal Aid, Sentencing and Punishment of Offenders Act 2012 is that, from March 12, 2015, a fine of any amount may be imposed. Fines will, however, continue to be set according to the seriousness of the offence and the means of the offender. An offence under s.1(1) cannot be dealt with by way of a simple caution.[15]

As regards listing, the Criminal Practice Directions 2015 ("CPD") are not   **8.05**
explicit as to whether indecent image offences[16] are to be treated as "sexual offences" within Class 2B (which must be heard before a judge authorised to hear such cases) or as offences within Class 3.[17] Where a case involves indecent image allegations and also allegations of one or more offences that clearly do fall within Class 2B, i.e. offences of physical sexual abuse, the case in its entirety will necessarily be listed before an authorised judge. What if the indecent image allegations stand alone? If a child victim of the offences is to

---

[10] 1978 Act s.6(1).

[11] 1978 Act s.6(2), as amended by the Criminal Justice and Court Services Act 2000 s.41(1), which was brought into force on January 11, 2001, by SI 2000/3302. The amendment raised the maximum sentence of imprisonment from three to 10 years. There is no transitional provision in the 2000 Act or SI 2002/3302, but the combined effect of s.3 of the Human Rights Act 1998 and art.7 of the European Convention on Human Rights is to require that the increased penalty applies only to offences committed on or after the commencement date.

[12] 1978 Act, s.6(3); Magistrates' Courts Act 1980 s.32 and Sch.1.

[13] Criminal Justice Act 2003 s.282(2), (3).

[14] Criminal Justice Act 2003 s.282(4).

[15] Criminal Justice and Courts Act 2015 s.17(3), and the Criminal Justice and Courts Act 2015 (Simple Cautions) (Specification of Either-Way Offences) Order 2015 (SI 2015/790).

[16] Including offences of soliciting, inciting, encouraging or assisting, attempting or conspiring to commit such an offence or assisting an offender having committed such an offence.

[17] See *Consolidated Criminal Practice Directions*, Part XIII Listing B: CLASSIFICATION, available at *https://www.judiciary.gov.uk/publications/criminal-practice-directions-2015/* [Accessed April 30, 2016].

give evidence, the better view is that the case should be treated as falling within Class 2B on the basis that the intention of the CPD is that any case in which a victim of sexual abuse is to give evidence of that abuse should be tried by an authorised judge. If indecent image allegations stand alone and the child victim is *not* to give evidence, the case may technically be regarded as falling within Class 3. However, the authors suggest it is better practice to treat such cases as within Class 2B, in the light of their potential sensitivity and the issues that are likely to arise. Accordingly, such cases should be listed wherever possible before an authorised judge, who will be familiar with the considerations that arise where a child has been sexually abused and with the sentencing options available on conviction. It is understood that the practice in certain List Offices, including the Old Bailey, is to treat such cases as falling within Class 2B. In certain circumstances cases in Class 2B must be referred to the Resident Judge, and by the Resident Judge to a Presiding Judge, including where the case is unusually grave or complex or a novel and important point of law is to be raised; where the defendant is a police officer, a member of the legal profession or a high profile figure; or where for any reason the case is likely to attract exceptional media attention.

8.06   A person convicted under s.1(1), cautioned, found not guilty by reason of insanity or found to be under a disability and to have done the act charged, is automatically subject to the notification requirements in the Sexual Offences Act 2003 if the images showed persons under 16 and the either the offender was 18 or over at the time of the offence or the offender is sentenced to at least 12 months' imprisonment.[18]

8.07   An offence under s.1(1), whenever committed, is a specified offence for the purposes of s.226A of the Criminal Justice Act 2003 (extended sentence for certain violent or sexual offences).[19] The offence is also listed in Pt 1 of Sch.15B to the Criminal Justice Act 2003 for the purposes of s.224A of that Act (life sentence for a second listed offence).[20]

8.08   Where a justice of the peace is satisfied by information on oath, laid by or on behalf of the DPP or by a constable, that there is reasonable ground for suspecting that, in any premises, there is an indecent photograph or pseudo-photograph of a child, the justice may issue a warrant authorising a constable to enter (if need be by force) and search the premises and to seize and remove any articles which he believes (with reasonable cause) to be or include such photographs or pseudo-photographs.[21] There is also provision for a magistrates' court to order the forfeiture of such items.[22]

---

[18] s.80 and Sch.3, discussed in Ch.35, below.
[19] Inserted by the Legal Aid, Sentencing and Punishment of Offenders Act 2012 s.124, brought into force on December 3, 2012, by SI 2012/2906.
[20] Inserted by the Legal Aid, Sentencing and Punishment of Offenders Act 2012 s.122, brought into force on December 3, 2012, by SI 2012/2906.
[21] 1978 Act s.4.
[22] 1978 Act s.5 and Sch.

Restriction on prosecution

Section 1(3) of the 1978 Act provides that proceedings for an offence under   **8.09**
the Act may not be instituted except by or with the consent of the DPP. For
this purpose, consent given by a Crown Prosecutor is to be treated as having
been given by the DPP.[23] It was held in *Jackson*[24] that the consent
requirement is met if the Crown Prosecutor reaches a conscious decision to
consent to the institution of proceedings after examining all the circumstances, and that the consent need not be in writing provided the Crown
Prosecutor has the need for it in mind when settling the indictment. The
decision in *R. v DM*[25] goes even further. There, a Crown Prosecutor
considered the case before charge and decided that the evidential and public
interest tests for prosecution were met, but on the relevant form he wrote
"not relevant" against the issue of the DPP's consent. This error was
corrected some months later when another Crown Prosecutor gave consent
before the PCMH, which was the first hearing of substance in the case. On
appeal against conviction, the appellant argued that these timings demonstrated that no proper consideration had been given to whether it was
appropriate to prosecute him, and that the later consent was no more than a
rubber stamp. The Court of Appeal rejected the appeal on the basis that the
first Crown Prosecutor had undertaken a proper scrutiny before deciding to
prosecute and, whilst as a matter of good practice he should have given
consent when deciding to charge, his failure to do so was rectified when
consent was later given by the second Crown Prosecutor before the appellant
was asked to answer the charge. The case differs somewhat from *Jackson*,
where the Crown Prosecutor did not give consent in writing but had the need
for it in mind when settling the indictment. Here, the first Crown Prosecutor
appears to have wholly overlooked the need for consent when deciding to
charge, but the later consent was held to be effective. This may be regarded
as somewhat generous to the prosecution, since s.1(3) provides that proceedings for an offence under the 1978 Act "shall not be instituted" except by or
with the DPP's consent. The Court was clearly of the view that proceedings
against the appellant were instituted when he was charged, at which time
there was no consent; and although consent was purportedly given before the
first hearing of substance, there is no provision in the Act that permits
consent to be given retrospectively.

What is the effect of a failure to obtain consent before proceedings are   **8.10**
instituted? It was long thought settled by the decision in *Angel*,[26] that in those
circumstances, the proceedings would be a nullity. But this position came

---

[23] Prosecution of Offences Act 1985 s.1(7).
[24] [1997] Crim. L.R. 293.
[25] [2011] EWCA Crim 2752.
[26] [1968] 1 W.L.R. 669 (decided under the Sexual Offences Act 1967 s.8); and see *Secretary of State for Defence v Warn* [1970] A.C. 394; *Pearce* [1981] Crim. L.R. 639.

under question following the decisions in *Sekhon*[27] and *Soneji*.[28] Those decisions rejected the traditional approach of classifying procedural requirements such as the one in s.1(3) of the 1978 Act as mandatory or directory, and treating non-compliance with a mandatory requirement as rendering the proceedings a nullity. Instead, they established that the court should ask what Parliament intended to be the result of non-compliance. The Court of Appeal in the later case of *Ashton*[29] regarded this development as marking a sea-change in the law relating to procedural failure. It held that in future a court required to determine the consequences of such a failure should focus on two things: first, the intention of Parliament (did it intend that a procedural failure should render the proceedings invalid?), and secondly, the interests of justice, in particular whether the procedural failure caused any prejudice to any of the parties such as to make it unjust to proceed further. Applying that approach, the Court in *Ashton* held that the absence in relation one of the appellants in that case of a signed bill of indictment did not invalidate the proceedings against him.

8.11   *Ashton* was applied in relation to s.1(3) by HH Judge Brown sitting at Lewes Crown Court in *R. v D*.[30] The defendant was charged with 20 offences of possession of indecent images of children, contrary to s.160(1) of the Criminal Justice Act 1988, in relation to images downloaded from the internet. Consent to prosecute was not obtained. The defendant was committed for trial and at the PCMH, an indictment was preferred charging him with 16 counts of "making" indecent images under s.1(1)(a) of the 1978 Act. The judge gave leave for the indictment to be signed out of time and the defendant gave notice of his intention to apply to quash it on the ground that proceedings had been instituted without the consent of the DPP. Prior to the hearing of the application, the purported consent of the DPP was given by a senior Crown Prosecutor.[31] The defendant argued that this consent was given too late and could not retrospectively authorise the institution of the proceedings. He relied on the decisions in *Angel* and *Pearce*,[32] which he contended had not been overruled by *Ashton* and were binding on the Crown Court. The learned judge rejected the application, holding that *Angel* and *Pearce* were distinguishable since in those cases there had at no point been a consent to the charges on which the defendants had been convicted. On the facts before him he went on to apply *Ashton*, holding that the failure to give prior consent under s.1(3) was a procedural failure that did not take away the

[27] [2002] EWCA Crim 2954.
[28] [2005] UKHL 49.
[29] [2006] EWCA Crim 794.
[30] [2007] Crim. L.R. 240.
[31] The case is therefore distinguishable from *R. v DM*, discussed in para.8.09, above, in which consent given *at* the PCMH was held to be effective. In *R. v D*, the consent was given only *after* the holding of the PCMH at which the judge gave leave for the indictment to be served out of time, and as such there was no scope even for the generous approach to s.1(3) taken by the Court in *R. v DM*.
[32] fn.26, above.

court's jurisdiction. Accordingly, he was required to consider the interests of justice generally and, in particular, whether if the case proceeded there was a real possibility of prejudice to either the prosecution or the defence. Although the maximum penalty for the "making" offences in the indictment was greater than for the "possession" offences with which the defendant had initially been charged, the "factual matrix" of the two sets of offences was the same, and the defendant was not taken by surprise by any change in the nature of the evidence against him. It was essential from the point of view of both the defendant and the public that the appropriate charges were brought and, if contested, decided on the evidence presented by both sides. The learned judge accordingly concluded that the interests of justice required that the Crown be allowed to proceed on the charges under the 1978 Act.

This reasoning is, with respect, convincing and the result consistent with **8.12** *Ashton*. However, in the subsequent case of *Clarke and McDaid*,[33] the House of Lords put the genie at least partly back in the bottle by downplaying the significance of *Sekhon* and *Soneji* and indicating disapproval of the reading given to them in *Ashton*. That case concerned the absence from a voluntary bill of indictment of the signature of "the proper officer of the court" as required by s.2(1) of the Administration of Justice (Miscellaneous Provisions) Act 1933. In the leading speech, Lord Bingham acknowledged that technicality is always distasteful when it appears to contradict the merits of a case, but said that the duty of the courts is to apply the law, which is sometimes technical, and that if the State exercises its coercive power to put a citizen on trial for serious crime, a certain degree of formality is not out of place. In relation to voluntary bills, it was inescapable that Parliament intended that a bill should not become an indictment unless and until it was duly signed by the proper officer, and that there could be no valid trial on indictment unless this was done. The decisions in *Sekhon* and *Soneji* were valuable and salutary, but they did not warrant a wholesale jettisoning of all rules affecting procedure irrespective of their legal effect.

Where does that leave the position as regards s.1(3)? The provision was not **8.13** referred to in *Clarke and McDaid*, though in the course of his speech Lord Brown of Eaton-under-Heywood mentioned the decision in *Angel* in apparently approving terms. We suggest, however, that the better view, in the light of *Clarke and McDaid*, is that a failure to comply with s.1(3) will be fatal to a prosecution and that *R. v D*, though persuasive and apparently consistent with case law as it stood at the time, was wrongly decided. This view derives some support from the recent decision of the Court of Appeal in *R. v CW and MM*,[34] which concerned s.4 of the Criminal Law Act 1977, a "consent" provision relating to offences of conspiracy that is in similar terms to s.1(3). In that case, the Court stated without prior analysis that proceedings for conspiracy instituted prior to consent being granted "would be a nullity",

---

[33] [2008] UKHL 8, followed in *Leeks* [2009] EWCA Crim 1612.
[34] [2015] EWCA Crim 906.

and went on to deprecate "the erosive effects of a cavalier attitude to statutory requirement".[35] The decision, which cited none of the authorities discussed above, suggests a return to simpler times in the Court of Appeal.

FORM OF CHARGE OR INDICTMENT

8.14   For the drafting of the indictment or information in proceedings under the 1978 Act, see *Thompson*,[36] discussed in para.8.124, below. The decision which relates to the offence of possession of an indecent image contrary to s.160(1) of the Criminal Justice Act 1988, but is equally applicable to charges under the 1978 Act.

SENTENCING

8.15   For the Sentencing Council guideline relating to the sentencing of sexual offences committed by offenders aged 18 and over, see Ch.33. In consulting on its draft guideline,[37] the Sentencing Council said that due to advances in technology, this area of offending, i.e. the making, etc. of indecent images of children, has changed since the offences were created and even since the Sentencing Guidelines Council ("SGC") issued the previous guideline in 2007. The ease with which images, including moving images, can be distributed and downloaded has increased the ability of offenders to share or trade in them; and advances in electronic storage capacity have also meant that offenders can retain a much larger volume of images than previously. These developments have shaped the way such offences are committed. Judicial understanding of the way in which offenders behave has also developed.

8.16   The guideline for offences relating to indecent images of children applies both to offences under s.1(1) of the 1978 Act and offences of possession under s.160(1) of the Criminal Justice Act 1988. It takes a different approach to the guidelines for other sexual offences, since the harm and culpability model used for those offences is not readily applicable here, often because there is no identified victim before the court because the victim in the image has not been identified or located. However, harm and culpability remain the focus of the guideline, albeit expressed in a different way. In relation to harm, the Council recognized that victims of these offences are harmed in several ways. First, there is the nature and level of harm caused by the abuse depicted in the indecent images. The victim is then subjected to further harm due to the images being recorded and viewed. There is yet further harm due to the

---

[35] At 14–15, 40, per Rafferty LJ.
[36] [2004] EWCA Crim 669.
[37] *Sexual Offences Guideline: Consultation* (December 6, 2012). The consultation document is available on the Sentencing Council's website.

fact that viewing creates a market and demand for such images and so leads to further abuse. In this connection the Council cited with approval the following passage in *Beaney*[38]:

> "The serious psychological injury which they [the children in the picture] would be at risk of being subjected to arises not merely from what they are being forced to do but also from their knowledge that what they are being forced to do would be viewed by others. It is not difficult to imagine the humiliation and lack of self-worth they are likely to feel. It is not simply the fact that without a market for these images the trade would not flourish. If people . . . continue to download and view images of this kind . . . the offences which they commit can properly be said to contribute to the psychological harm which the children in those images would suffer by virtue of the children's awareness that there were people . . . watching them forced to pose and behave in this way."

Sentencing guideline

Step One—Harm and culpability

The guideline requires the sentencing court to go through a series of steps in   8.17
order to determine the appropriate sentence. Step one involves determining the offence category by reference to the degree of harm caused and then the culpability level for the offence. The court's first task is to determine the offence category, which in other guidelines is done by reference to the degree of harm caused. However, in this context the Sentencing Council chose to determine the offence category by identifying the role of the offender (broadly reflecting culpability) and then by considering the severity of the image (broadly representing harm).

Role of the offender

The Council identified three categories of role: possession, distribution and   8.18
production/taking.

- *Possession*: An offender falls within this category if they possess images but there is no evidence of distributing, possession with a view to distributing, or involvement in the production of the image. For this purpose, the Sentencing Council considered that "making" an image by simple downloading should be treated for sentencing purposes as possession rather than as "production/taking", discussed below. This resolves an anomaly that existed under the previous SGC guideline, which drew a distinction between the deliberate saving of an image and the mere viewing of it, and treated mere viewing without storage as a mitigating factor. This failed to reflect the fact that indecent photographs which the user browses on the internet but does not deliberately save are nonetheless saved in the internet browser

---

[38] [2004] EWCA Crim 449, at 9, per Keith J.

cache as an automated function of the browser software. Where such images are recovered, the offender will commonly be charged with "making" the image contrary to s.1(1)(a) of the 1978 Act rather than "possession" of it contrary to s.160(1) of the 1988 Act. This is because the file data that is saved along with the offending image by the browser software will provide evidence of when the image was created, i.e. made. Ironically, given the disparity in maximum sentences between the making and possession offences, under the SGC guideline an offender would stand to receive a stiffer sentence for making an image recovered in this way from his browser than if he possessed the same image in a stored format. The Sentencing Council guideline resolves this issue by providing that both cases should be sentenced as possession.

- *Distribution*: This category includes both actual distribution and possession of images with a view to distributing them, showing them or sharing them with others (see s.1(1)(c) of the 1978 Act).
- *Production/taking*: This category includes involvement in the actual taking or making of an image at source, i.e. involvement in its production, and is the highest category for sentencing purposes.

Severity of the image

8.19   The SGC guideline identified five levels of prohibited image based on the levels originally set out in the judgment in *Oliver, Hartrey and Baldwin* (with 1 being the lowest level and 5 the highest)[39]:

Level 1	Images depicting erotic posing with no sexual activity;
Level 2	Non-penetrative sexual activity between children, or solo masturbation by a child;
Level 3	Non-penetrative sexual activity between adults and children;
Level 4	Penetrative sexual activity involving a child or children or both children and adults; and
Level 5	Sadism or penetration of, or by, an animal.

8.20   In consulting on the draft guideline, the Sentencing Council acknowledged that classification of images can be difficult and resource intensive for the police and prosecuting authorities, and that the images before the court may give only a partial indication of the abuse suffered by the victim and of the offender's behaviour. However, the court can only sentence on the basis of what is before it, and the Council believed that the severity of the sexual offence depicted in an image can be at least an initial guide to the harm that will have been suffered by the victim. It did, however, seek in the published guideline to simplify the levels of image by reducing them to three (category A being the highest level and category C the lowest):

[39] [2003] 1 Cr. App. R. 28.

Category A: *"Images involving penetrative sexual activity" and "images involving sexual activity with an animal or sadism"*. The Council thought that any image showing a child involved in penetrative sexual activity should be placed in the highest category. In line with the guidelines for the other child sex offences, it considered that "penetration" for this purpose should mean penetration of the vagina or anus (using body or object) and penile penetration of the mouth, in either case by, or of, the victim. It drew no distinction between penetrative activity involving an adult and a child and penetrative activity between children. Category A also includes images involving sexual activity with an animal or sadism. In the SGC guideline, "penetrative activity and sadism" and "penetration of, or by, an animal" were expressed as different levels of image (4 and 5 respectively), but they attracted the same sentence starting points and ranges, which the Council thought right, and it therefore placed both of them in category A. The Council also changed the wording "penetration of, or by, an animal" to "sexual activity with an animal" to ensure that it covers images involving non-penetrative activity such as a photograph showing an animal licking a child's sexual organs, which on a strict interpretation of the SGC guideline fell outside not only level 5 but also any level other than, conceivably, level 1.

Category B: *"Images involving non-penetrative sexual activity"*. This category combines the SGC's levels 2 and 3. The SGC guideline made a distinction between non-penetrative sexual activity between children (or involving a child on their own) and non-penetrative sexual activity between an adult and a child. However, the Sentencing Council considered that even if no adults appear in an image, this does not mean that an adult was not involved in making the image or otherwise exploiting the victim in order to generate it. In addition, the continuing victimisation of the child that flows from the image being recorded and viewed will be as great even if there is no adult in the picture. Taking into account the law enforcement resources needed to classify images, the Council believed that a distinction between images involving just children and those involving adults and children is not required for sentencing purposes, as both create similar levels of harm and culpability. Accordingly, all non-penetrative sexual activity is dealt with in Category B, and has the same starting points and category ranges.

Category C: *"Other indecent images not falling within categories A or B"*. In its consultation draft, the Council defined this category as "images of erotic posing". The term "erotic posing" was used in the SGC guideline, but the Council nonetheless thought it capable of misleading as there may be cases where an image that is not posed or "erotic" is still indecent, e.g. a picture of a naked child not engaged in sexual activity but with a focus on the child's genitals. The majority of respondents to the consultation agreed, the general view being that the term "erotic posing" was outdated and also inappropriate in that it indicated that responsibility for the nature of the posing lay with the victim rather than the offender. The Council accordingly dropped the term in the published guideline in favour of a neutral formulation referring to "other indecent images".

Responses to the consultation showed almost universal support for the Council's simplifying approach. The new levels are labelled A, B and C, rather than numbered, because the general scheme of the guideline is that offences in category 1 attract the highest starting points and ranges, whereas under the SGC grading system based on *Oliver*, category 1 images attracted the lowest starting point and range. That being so, the Council thought it would be confusing to retain numerical classification in relation to offences involving indecent images and that instead such offences should be categorised using the labels A, B and C.

Mixed levels of images

8.21 Most offenders have collections containing images at a mix of levels, which can cause difficulties for sentencers. The guideline resolves this by providing:

> "In most cases the intrinsic character of the most serious of the offending images will initially determine the appropriate category. If, however, the most serious images are unrepresentative of the offender's conduct a lower category may be appropriate. A lower category will not, however, be appropriate if the offender has produced or taken (for example photographed) images of a higher category."

8.22 An important difference from the SGC guideline is that the quantity of material is no longer used to determine the offence category. The SGC guideline determined sentence starting points and ranges for different levels of images by reference to whether there were a "small number" or a "large number" of images. These terms were not defined and this caused difficulties for sentencers in assessing what "small" or "large" meant in this context. The Council formed the view that the best indicator of the offender's culpability is what he has done with the images, rather than their number. For example, an offender who has produced even a small number of images should attract a higher starting point than one who is in possession of the same number. However, as a large volume of images may provide an additional indicator of increased culpability in some cases, it is included in the guideline as an aggravating feature, allowing the court to move up from the starting point as and when appropriate.

The offences categories

8.23 In light of these points, the offence categories for offences under s.1(1) of the 1978 Act and s.160(1) of the Criminal Justice Act 1988 are as follows:

	Possession	*Distribution**	*Production***
Category A	Possession of images involving penetrative sexual activity	Sharing images involving penetrative sexual activity	Creating images involving penetrative sexual activity
	Possession of images involving sexual activity with an animal or sadism	Sharing images involving sexual activity with an animal or sadism	Creating images involving sexual activity with an animal or sadism
Category B	Possession of images involving non-penetrative sexual activity	Sharing of images involving non-penetrative sexual activity	Creating images involving non-penetrative sexual activity
Category C	Possession of other indecent images not falling within categories A or B	Sharing of other indecent images not falling within categories A or B	Creating other indecent images not falling within categories A or B

* Distribution includes possession with a view to distributing or sharing images.
** Production includes the taking or making of any image at source, for instance the original image.

Making an image by simple downloading should be treated as possession for the purposes of sentencing.
In most cases the intrinsic character of the most serious of the offending images will initially determine the appropriate category. If, however, the most serious images are unrepresentative of the offender's conduct a lower category may be appropriate. A lower category will not, however, be appropriate if the offender has produced or taken (i.e. photographed) images of a higher category.

Step Two—Starting point and category range

Once the court has determined the offence category and culpability level, at   **8.24** step two it should use the corresponding starting point specified in the guideline in order to reach a sentence within the category range. The starting point applies to all offenders irrespective of plea or previous convictions. Once the starting point has been determined, step two allows further adjustment for aggravating or mitigating features, set out below. A case of particular gravity, reflected by multiple features of culpability or harm, could merit upward adjustment from the starting point before further adjustment for aggravating or mitigating features. Where there is a sufficient prospect of rehabilitation, a community order with a sex offender treatment programme requirement under s.202 of the Criminal Justice Act 2003 may be a proper alternative to a short or moderate length custodial sentence.

8.25   For the highest category of images (category A) a custodial option is recommended as a starting point in all cases whether the offender has been charged with possession, distribution or production. Where an offender has been involved in taking or making an image at source and this involves penetration, sadism or an animal, the recommended range goes towards the very top end of the 10-year statutory maximum and a starting point of six years' custody with a range of 4–9 years is recommended.

8.26   Category B images also attract a custodial starting point. The Council has moved away from the very short custodial sentences recommended in the SGC guideline under which, for example, four weeks was available in two of the categories. The Council said in its consultation that it did not believe that such short sentences are appropriate because of the very limited work the prison authorities can do in such a period to address the behaviour of the offender. A non-custodial starting point is recommended for possession and distribution of category C images and for possession of category B images. The Council added that there may be cases where the sentencer considers that a lengthy community order with a sexual offences treatment programme requirement will be more appropriate than a very short custodial sentence, on the basis that the offender's thinking and behaviour will be better addressed through treatment and the degree of risk they pose to the community can be closely monitored. It added that a Sexual Offences Prevention Order (now, a Sexual Harm Prevention Order) can provide a useful additional safeguard to a community order. However, it also deliberately included a custodial option as part of the sentencing range in every category to ensure that it is available to sentencers in appropriate cases. This is a change from the SGC guideline, under which possession of the lowest level of images attracted only a non-custodial option.

8.27   Accordingly, the sentence starting points and ranges for offences under s.1(1) of the 1978 Act and s.160(1) of the Criminal Justice Act 1988 are:

	Possession	Distribution*	Production**
Category A	Starting point 1 year's custody	Starting point 3 years' custody	Starting point 6 years' custody
	Category range 26 weeks–3 years' custody	Category range 2–5 years' custody	Category range 4–9 years' custody
Category B	Starting point 26 weeks' custody	Starting point 1 year's custody	Starting point 2 years' custody
	Category range High level community order–18 months' custody	Category range 26 weeks–2 years' custody	Category range 1–4 years' custody
Category C	Starting point High level community order	Starting point 13 weeks' custody	Starting point 18 months' custody
	Category range Medium level community order–26 weeks' custody	Category range High level community order–26 weeks' custody	Category range 1–3 years' custody

Aggravating and mitigating factors

After identifying the starting point and category range, the court should **8.28**
consider whether the presence of aggravating or mitigating factors should
result in an upward or downward adjustment from the starting point or the
imposition of a sentence outside the category range. In particular, relevant
recent convictions are likely to result in an upward adjustment. When
sentencing appropriate category 2 or 3 offences, the court should also
consider whether the custody threshold has been passed; if so, whether a
custodial sentence is unavoidable; and if it is, whether that sentence can be
suspended. The list of aggravating and mitigating factors is non-exhaustive:
the Council stated in its consultation that its intention was to set out factors
that are likely to be relatively common to offences relating to indecent images
of children to ensure that they are considered equally by all courts. The
factors are:

Aggravating factors
Statutory aggravating factors
<ul><li>Previous convictions, having regard to a) the nature of the offence to which the conviction relates and its relevance to the current offence; and b) the time that has elapsed since the conviction</li><li>Offence committed whilst on bail</li></ul>
Other aggravating factors
<ul><li>Failure to comply with current court orders</li><li>Offence committed whilst on licence</li><li>Age and/or vulnerability of the child depicted*</li><li>Discernable pain or distress suffered by child depicted</li><li>Period over which images were possessed, distributed or produced</li><li>High volume of images possessed, distributed or produced</li><li>Placing images where there is the potential for a high volume of viewers</li><li>Collection includes moving images</li><li>Attempts to dispose of or conceal evidence</li><li>Abuse of trust</li><li>Child depicted known to the offender</li><li>Active involvement in a network or process that facilitates or commissions the creation or sharing of indecent images of children</li><li>Commercial exploitation and/or motivation</li><li>Deliberate or systematic searching for images portraying young children, category A images or the portrayal of familial sexual abuse</li><li>Large number of different victims</li><li>Child depicted intoxicated or drugged</li></ul>

* Age and/or vulnerability of the child should be given significant weight. In cases where the actual age of the victim is difficult to determine sentencers should consider the development of the child (infant, pre-pubescent, post-pubescent)

Mitigating factors
<ul><li>No previous convictions *or* no relevant/recent convictions</li><li>Remorse</li><li>Previous good character and/or exemplary conduct*</li><li>Age and/or lack of maturity where it affects the responsibility of the offender</li><li>Mental disorder or learning disability, particularly where linked to the commission of the offence</li><li>Demonstration of steps taken to address offending behaviour</li></ul>

* Previous good character/exemplary conduct is different from having no previous convictions. The more serious the offence, the less the weight which should normally be attributed to this factor. Where previous good character/exemplary conduct has been used to facilitate the offence, this mitigation should not normally be allowed and such conduct may constitute an aggravating factor.

In the consultation that preceded the publication of the guideline, the **8.29** Sentencing Council explained as follows its reasons for including the various aggravating factors:

- "Age and/or vulnerability of the child depicted" should be given significant weight. The SGC guideline suggested that starting points should be higher where the subject of the photograph was under the age of 13. But the Sentencing Council recognised the difficulty for sentencers in ascribing an age to an unidentified victim and said it did not believe there should be a strict cut-off in age terms when assessing the harm caused to the victim, and that an assessment of the child's developmental stage will assist the sentencer more. Accordingly, in cases where the victim's actual age is difficult to determine, sentencers should consider their development (infant, pre-pubescent, post-pubescent).
- "Discernable pain or distress suffered by child depicted" was represented in the consultation draft as "visible physical pain suffered by the child depicted". The Council intended this factor to cover the increased harm demonstrated where the victim is visibly responding to physical pain. But it expanded the factor in the published guideline to "discernable pain or distress", in response to comments that the factor should apply equally where distress as opposed to pain is suffered and where the pain or distress is audible rather than visible.
- "Period over which the images were possessed, made or distributed" is included as it enables a more comprehensive picture to be formed of the offender's behaviour and may be relevant to risk. Where an offender has been involved with such images over a long period, sentencers may wish to take this into consideration in determining whether to give any weight to a claim of previous good character.
- "High volume of images possessed, distributed or produced" allows the sentencer to take into account the volume of images where this is a significant consideration. There will be cases when a high volume of images is a very significant aggravating factor especially where the material is being distributed or produced.
- "Placing images where there is the potential for a high volume of viewers" is intended to deal with the increased harm to the victim where an offender puts images in a place where, potentially, a large number of people could access them. It is intended to reflect the emotional distress caused to the victim by the potential for large numbers of unknown individuals to view them in a vulnerable state.

- "Collection includes moving images" is included because the Council felt that one moving image lasting, for example, 20 minutes does not equate directly with one still image, as more than one abusive incident may take place during that period and potentially hundreds of still images may be taken from one 20-minute film.
- "Attempts to dispose of or conceal evidence" is designed to address issues arising from the increasingly sophisticated efforts of offenders to prevent images being discovered. It will cover activity ranging from the mislabelling of computer files to give the impression that the content is lawful to advanced encryption techniques.
- "Abuse of trust" and "child depicted known to the offender" are aggravating factors because both indicate the close proximity of the offender to the commission of the offence. In very many cases the victim will not have been identified, but where the evidence establishes the offender's knowledge of the child or an abuse of trust it will demonstrate increased culpability due to the targeting or manipulation of the victim.
- "Active involvement in a network or process that facilitates or commissions the creation or sharing of indecent images of children" is included as this demonstrates a higher level of culpability on the part of the offender.
- "Deliberate or systematic searching for images portraying young children, category A images or the portrayal of familial sexual abuse", is intended to cater for cases where forensic examination of computers reveals that the offender has been searching for higher levels of image than those recovered. Whilst the offender can only be sentenced in relation to the images recovered, such searches can assist the court in assessing culpability.
- The factors "commercial exploitation and/or motivation", "large number of different victims" and "child depicted intoxicated or drugged" were all added in response to comments made on the draft guideline. The draft included as an aggravating factor "systematic storage of collection", on the basis that such storage may increase culpability by demonstrating the deliberate thought and effort invested by the offender in collecting indecent images. However, responses to the consultation questioned whether systematic storage not involving hiding or concealment should amount to an aggravating factor. The Council accepted that hiding or concealment is the greater aggravation and so retained "attempts to dispose or conceal evidence" but removed the reference to systematic storage.

Steps Three to Nine

8.30 The remaining steps cover the following points. At step three the court should consider any factors which would indicate a reduction in sentence, e.g.

assistance to the prosecution. At step four it should consider any reduction for a guilty plea. At step five the court should consider dangerousness, i.e. whether it would be appropriate to award an extended sentence (s.226A of the Criminal Justice Act 2003). Step six requires the court to consider whether the total sentence is just and proportionate to the offending behaviour. At step seven it should consider whether to make an ancillary order (e.g. a compensation order, a SHPO or a restraining order). Step eight requires the court to fulfil its duty under s.174 of the Criminal Justice Act 2003 to give reasons for, and explain the effect of, the sentence. Finally, at step nine the court should consider whether to give credit for time spent on bail in accordance with s.240A of that Act.

Viewing the images

In *Oliver, Hartrey and Baldwin*,[40] the Court of Appeal said that "it will   8.31
usually be desirable for sentencers to view for themselves the images involved, unless there is an agreed description of what those images depict". We suggest that, although it may be distressing, a sentencer should always view a good sample of the images before them, so that they can form their own impression of the seriousness of the offending and of the offender's proclivities.

"Dangerousness" provisions of Criminal Justice Act 2003

Offences under s.1(1) of the 1978 Act are specified sexual offences for the   8.32
purposes of the sentencing provisions of the Criminal Justice Act 2003 and so in principle the "dangerousness" provisions apply to them. However, the Court of Appeal has emphasised that those provisions do not apply where there might be indirect, small and uncertain harm occasioned by the repetition of offending behaviour. Thus in *Terrell*,[41] the Court quashed a sentence of imprisonment for public protection and imposed a determinate sentence for offences relating to simple downloading of indecent images of children, on the ground that the link between the downloading and the harm which might be occasioned to children as a result was too remote to satisfy the criteria relevant to determining the risk of serious harm that the offender posed. The relevant part of the judgment merits repetition in full[42]:

> " . . . in this case the Judge did not find that the offences which might be committed in the future were different from or graver than those which the Appellant had already committed. It was not suggested that the Appellant risked progressing to physical contact offences, or becoming a photographer of or commissioner of indecent images; there was no evidence that his role in perpetuating the market would become more significant or that he would play a

[40] [2003] 1 Cr. App. R. 28, at 10.
[41] [2007] EWCA Crim 3079. See also *Joy* [2007] EWCA Crim 3281.
[42] At [25]–[28], per Ouseley J.

more important role in a distribution network. There was no suggestion that the images he was interested in would become graver or contain a higher proportion of Levels 3, 4 or 5. There was no suggestion of greater frequency of offending . . . . . . The risk was of repetition of the same offence committed in the same way, albeit that that is a serious sexual offence.

The serious harm thus relied on here is the harm to children through the perpetuation of the market or distribution networks for indecent images. This puts children at risk of being forced to participate in the activities leading to such images, or causes psychological harm to a child who realises either at the time or later that images of him or her are being used as objects of perverted sexual gratification. There is no suggestion here however that the Appellant has any contact with children whom he might seek to photograph or to commission others to photograph, for himself, for sharing or for using as a means of gaining access to a network.

In all these circumstances, the re-offending which is at risk would make a direct but small contribution to the market or distribution of such indecent images; that in turn would make an indirect but small contribution to the risk that indecent images of children would be taken. A child groomed or made to participate in sexual acts for those purposes may suffer serious harm of one sort or another, depending on the activity. A child who becomes aware that he or she has been photographed for the sexual gratification of an adult, who may not even be known to them, may suffer serious psychological harm.

In our judgment it cannot reasonably be said . . . that there is a significant risk of this Appellant's re-offending occasioning harm to a child or children whether through perpetuating the market, or through further indecent images being taken, or through a child becoming aware of the indecent purposes to which photographs might be put. The link between the offending act of downloading these indecent images and the possible harm which might be done to children is too remote to satisfy the requirement that it be this Appellant's re-offending which causes the serious harm. At worst there would be an indirect and small contribution to a harm which might or might not occur, depending on whether further photographs were taken in part as a result of the Appellant's contribution to the market, or depending on whether a child found out about the uses to which they were put as a result. The imprisonment for public protection provisions of the CJA do not apply in the circumstances here, where simply as a matter of generalisation, a small, uncertain and indirect contribution to harm may be made by a repeat of this offender's offending. No significant risk of serious harm of the requisite gravity, occasioned by a repetition of the offending in this case by this offender can reasonably be said to exist."

8.33   Although *Terrell* was a case of simple downloading, this extract clearly indicates a number of matters which, had they been in evidence, might have justified a finding of dangerousness, including evidence of a risk that the appellant would progress to contact offending. The scope for a finding of dangerousness to be made in relation to an offender who has committed offences relating to indecent images of children is illustrated by *Cheshire*,[43] where the appellant (63) had persistently committed sexual offences involving children and child pornography over a very long period. In 2013 he was released on licence having served half of a three-year term of imprisonment

---

[43] [2014] EWCA Crim 627. The judgment is somewhat unsatisfactory as it contains no information about the offences of which the appellant had been convicted or whether he pleaded guilty or was convicted after a trial.

imposed for child pornography offences. Since 2011 he had been the subject of a Sexual Offences Prevention Order ("SOPO") which amongst other things prohibited him from owning equipment capable of accessing the internet. Almost immediately on his release he began to breach the terms of the SOPO, going to great lengths to hide what he was doing from the police. They nonetheless found concealed about his person a mobile telephone capable of accessing the internet and containing about 1,700 indecent images of children, which, on the categorisation in the SGC guideline, ranged from Level 1 through to Level 5 (with 55 at Level 4 and at least three at Level 5). These were only the most recent of a series of sex offences committed by the appellant over a period of 35 years. In 1978 he was imprisoned for nine months for indecently assaulting a man over 16. In 1995 he was imprisoned for three months for distributing indecent photographs of children. In 1998 he was convicted of three offences of inciting a child to commit acts of gross indecency. In 1999 he was made subject to a sex offender order for life after he had approached two children in a park. In 2000 he committed a number of breaches of the order by watching and following young children. In 2001 he was sentenced to a total of seven years' imprisonment for breaches of the sex offender order and making indecent photographs of children. In 2006, following his release from that sentence, he pleaded guilty to further child pornography offences and was sentenced to imprisonment for public protection. On appeal against that sentence, in 2009, the Court of Appeal concluded that on the evidence as it then was it could not be said that the appellant was dangerous within the meaning of the Criminal Justice Act 2003, because the link between his possession of indecent photographs and the risk of serious harm was too remote. The sentence of imprisonment for public protection was therefore quashed and replaced with a term of two years' imprisonment. In 2011 the appellant was sentenced to three years' imprisonment for further child pornography offences. Although the judge on that occasion concluded that the appellant presented a significant risk of serious harm, he decided that in line with the earlier Court of Appeal decision he could not impose either an extended sentence or an indeterminate sentence. The judge also made the SOPO which the appellant breached by committing the instant offences. It was argued on appeal, citing *Terrell*, that the appellant did not satisfy the dangerousness provisions. The Court of Appeal rejected this submission, holding that *Terrell* is more nuanced than the appellant suggested. It was a decisions on its own facts, and the judgment indicated matters which, had they been in evidence, may have justified a finding of dangerousness. It was clear that a finding of dangerousness may be appropriate if a significant risk of serious harm can properly be inferred from, for example, "a greater frequency of offending, a risk of contact offending or an escalation in the gravity of the relevant images". In the present case, there had been a significant escalation in the risk posed by the appellant since his case was last considered by the Court of Appeal in 2009, such that dangerousness could now properly be inferred. In particular, the

Court noted the sheer persistence and scale of the appellant's offending since 2009; the extreme lengths to which he was now prepared to go in order to conceal his offending from the police; and his wholesale failure to engage with the processes designed to help him overcome his criminality. As a result of these matters there was, in the Court's view, a clear risk that the appellant could revert to contact offences of the type he committed previously. Indeed, this risk had been explicitly flagged in the pre-sentence report. The Court concluded that this was the type of case that the Court in *Terrell* had in mind, where there has been an escalation, there is a risk of contact offences, and a finding of dangerousness can therefore be made out. The sentencing judge had accordingly been entitled to find that the appellant was dangerous within the meaning of the Criminal Justice Act 2003 and to pass an extended sentence.

Sentencing examples

Making images

8.34 In *Smith (Andrew)*,[44] the appellant (51) made indecent images of children spanning all three categories in the guideline by downloading them onto his computers. He pleaded guilty to nine specimen counts relating to a total of 462 images. Two of the counts related to a total of 28 images which fell within the most serious category, category A. As the offences related to the making of an image by downloading, the appellant fell to be sentenced pursuant to the guideline on the basis of possession. The judge sentenced him to a total of 34 months' imprisonment, made up of concurrent sentences of 16 months' imprisonment on the two counts relating to the category A images and consecutive sentences of various lengths on the other counts. The appellant was of effective good character. All the images were on deleted file space on his computers, which contained specialist erasing software. Although the appellant denied seeking out child pornography sites, his search history included such searches. He made an unsuccessful attempt to vacate his guilty pleas. The judge nonetheless said he would give a full one-third discount for plea. The Court of Appeal allowed an appeal against sentence. It said that in imposing consecutive sentences in relation to the different categories of image, the judge had paid insufficient regard to the principle of totality, since the overall sentence, although purportedly giving full credit for the guilty pleas, was only two months short of the top of the range for category A offences. Given the approach to mixed collections set out in the guideline, the offending was properly categorised within category A because of the 28 most serious images, which could not be said to be unrepresentative of the appellant's offences. However, this approach did not require consecutive sentences in relation to the lower category images. What was required in a

---

[44] [2014] EWCA Crim 2383.

case such as this, which involved multiple images spanning different levels of seriousness, was to impose a sentence on the most serious category of counts, which nonetheless took into account the overall totality of the offending and had regard to any of the aggravating and mitigating factors, before giving appropriate credit for any pleas of guilty, and thereafter to impose concurrent sentences on the remaining counts. The only mitigating factors in this case apart from the guilty pleas were the lack of relevant convictions, the appellant's effective previous good character, and the fact that there had been a delay in the matter coming before the court. However, there was no remorse. Aggravating factors were the overall volume of images, the possession of specialist software designed to dispose of or conceal evidence, and evidence of systematic searches for images of children. The proper starting point was two years' imprisonment. The appellant should not have had the full one-third discount for the guilty pleas, given his express attempt to renounce his pleas. The appropriate discount was no more than 20 per cent. In all the circumstances the proper sentence was 18 months' imprisonment on each of the level 4 counts, to run concurrently. The other sentences would be unchanged but ordered to run concurrently.

In *Prince (Ricky Ernest)*,[45] a search of the appellant's home found a total   8.35
of 12,020 indecent images of boys aged from five to 12. There were 12,012 images in category C of the guideline, five in category B and three in category A. A police investigation identified the appellant as a customer of a website that sold indecent images of children. In interview, the appellant admitted that he had looked at such images for around 14 years and gained sexual gratification from them. He pleaded guilty to five counts of making indecent images of a child and was sentenced to nine months' imprisonment. The judge took into account the guilty plea, but noted that the appellant had been caught red-handed. He identified as aggravating features the high volume of pictures, the large number of young and vulnerable victims, and the fact that many of the images showed children being assaulted. The judge expressed concern that the pictures included category A images and noted that the appellant's appetite to view such pictures fuelled the demand for them. He also noted the appellant's previous good character. On appeal, it was submitted that the judge had failed to apply the proper sentencing categories and that, had he done so, a community order would have been appropriate. The appeal was allowed. The Court noted that category A offences have a starting point of 12 months and category B offences a starting point of six months. According to the guideline, the character of the most serious images determines the category of offending unless those images are unrepresentative, in which case a lower category might be appropriate. Here there were three category A images, but the majority were category C. The volume and content of the images required a custodial sentence and a sentence of nine months' imprisonment after trial would have

[45] Unreported, May 6, 2015.

been appropriate. Applying full credit for the guilty plea, the Court quashed the sentence awarded by the judge and substituted one of six months' imprisonment.

Making images—prospect of rehabilitation made community order appropriate

8.36   In *Jones (David William)*,[46] the Court of Appeal quashed an immediate sentence of imprisonment and substituted a community order with a treatment requirement where it considered that there was a sufficient prospect of the appellant's rehabilitation and that treatment would better protect the public from him. The appellant appealed against concurrent sentences of two years' imprisonment imposed following guilty pleas to four counts of making indecent photographs of a child. A laptop seized from his home contained between 23 and 41 videos at levels 1 to 4 and six cartoons and images at level 5 (assessed by reference to the levels in the SGC guideline). The appellant, 64, had two previous convictions for 10 offences, the most significant being a series of convictions in 2006 for making, possessing and distributing indecent photographs of children, for which he had received a custodial sentence. A psychiatric report noted that the appellant had never engaged in sexual activity with a child and concluded that there was a low risk of his behaviour escalating to contact sexual offences in the future. The report referred to research indicating that sex offenders such as the appellant who received treatment had a lower sexual reconviction rate than those who did not and identified a number of treatment programmes which might be of benefit to the appellant, accessible both from within the prison system and also in the community. A pre-sentence report stated that the appellant accepted responsibility for his behaviour and demonstrated a good awareness of the impact of his offending on victims. It recommended that the appellant receive a suspended sentence and be required to engage with the Sex Offender Treatment Programme. In sentencing, the judge said that the appellant's case was in category A of the sentencing guideline, with a range of 26 weeks to three years' custody. He identified a number of aggravating features which in his view justified a sentence of three years' imprisonment after a trial, namely the 2006 convictions for the same or similar offences, the fact that the current offences were committed whilst the appellant was under supervision following the earlier offences, and that moving images were involved. Giving full credit for the appellant's guilty plea, he concluded that an immediate custodial sentence was unavoidable because of the previous convictions. The appellant

---

[46] [2014] EWCA Crim 1859. See also *Merritt (Kelvin James)* [2014] EWCA Crim 2384, where the Court of Appeal reduced a sentence from 21 to 16 months' imprisonment to reflect the exceptional mitigation that the appellant had voluntarily embarked upon rehabilitation to address his offending behaviour over an eight-month period before he was charged, with a reported degree of success.

submitted on appeal that, although his case fell within category A because of the level 4 and 5 images, the number of images was small and the judge had adopted too high a starting point by going immediately to the top of the range for category A. The judge had also been wrong to impose an immediate custodial sentence and should either have suspended it or taken the course indicated in the sentencing guideline of a community penalty. The appeal was allowed. The Court of Appeal held that the starting point for category A possession offences involving the kind of images in the instant case was one year, and there was no reason not to start there before considering the aggravating and mitigating features. The judge identified the aggravating features which would result in an upward adjustment from the starting point. He also observed unfairly that there was no evidence of remorse, as the author of the pre-sentence report considered that there was such evidence. Weighing all those features, the appropriate adjustment resulted in a notional sentence after trial of between 15 and 18 months. In those circumstances the starting point of three years adopted by the judge was manifestly excessive. As for the immediate custodial sentence, this had been imposed on the basis of the appellant's previous convictions. The judge had not expressly addressed the recommendations for treatment made in the pre-sentence report and the psychiatric report. The appellant had not had the benefit of treatment in the past. The sentencing guideline states that where there is sufficient prospect of rehabilitation, a community order with a sex offender treatment programme requirement could be a proper alternative to a short or moderate custodial sentence. Notwithstanding the aggravating features of the case, given the appellant's guilty plea and the content of the reports, the public would be better protected by a course that might prevent further offending rather than by a short sentence that was unlikely to have that result. The Court therefore quashed the sentence of two years' immediate imprisonment and substituted a 36-month community order with a supervision requirement and a sex offender treatment programme requirement.

Making images—impact of exceptionally large quantity

In *Nestoros (Costos)*,[47] the appellant (64) had downloaded 4.2 million   **8.37**
images over a period of two years, over 1.1 million of which were capable of being categorised, and 10,000 of which were actually categorised. These comprised 5,000 still images in Category A, 643 in category B and 2,009 in category C. In addition there were 463 Category B and 1,000 Category C moving images. In interview, the appellant admitted that he had obtained the images through peer-to-peer sites and that he had so many of them that it had become a matter of collecting. Once he started looking at one child he would try to get the whole collection of that child. He was sexually aroused

---

[47] [2015] EWCA Crim 1424.

by looking at the images and had tried to stop, attending counselling to help achieve that aim, but the urge and boredom would return and he would start looking again. The appellant pleaded guilty to six counts of making indecent images of children and two counts of possession of a prohibited image of a child, contrary to s.62 of the Coroners and Justice Act 2009. A pre-sentence report noted that the appellant acknowledged that, as a recipient of such material, he was complicit in helping to create a market for it but said that he had never passed any of the material on elsewhere. The author of the report felt that the appellant took full responsibility for his offending and, although he did not stop until he was arrested, he did not spare himself in his account of his activities and recognised the impact on the children used to create the images. The appellant had one previous conviction in 1989 for an offence of possession for showing or distributing a single indecent image of a child, for which he was fined £75. At the sentencing hearing for the instant offences, it was agreed that, as the offending was by simple downloading, the case fell to be treated as one of possession of category A images, with a starting point of 12 months and a range of six months to three years. The judge considered that the appellant was entitled to "maximum credit" because of the assistance that he had given to the police, the fact that he had pleaded guilty at the very first opportunity, expressing both contrition and remorse, and in the light of his candour as a whole. The judge considered that there was clearly a need for rehabilitation but also a need to protect children who might be at risk of being photographed. He concluded that, given the categories involved and the total amount of material, the case was well outside the guideline and he imposed a total sentence of five years' imprisonment. On appeal, the appellant submitted that the sentence was manifestly excessive having regard to the mitigation available to him. Specifically, he said that: (a) even in a case with such a large volume of images, particularly so many in category A, the judge was wrong to characterise the offences as sufficiently serious to justify such a significant departure from the guideline; (b) the images were downloaded for personal use but, because there were so many of them, it was difficult to see how they could be so used; (c) the appellant was an obsessive collector, who was now deeply remorseful for what had occurred; and (d) there was no indication of direct exploitation and no evidence of participation in a network facilitating or commissioning the creation or sharing of indecent images. It was held, allowing the appeal in part, that the judge's starting point must have been more than seven-and-a-half years, as he had acknowledged other features of the appellant's mitigation before giving full credit for the guilty plea. The reason why the judge took the starting point he did was because of the quantity of the images, particularly those in the most serious category. While he was fully entitled to treat the sheer quantity of images as taking the offending outside the range in the guideline, a starting point in the order of seven-and-a-half to eight years should usually be reserved for those who were involved in the production of such images. The appropriate starting point here was four years before taking into account the guilty plea. With maximum credit for the plea, the overall sentence should have been a term of two years and eight months.

Making images—aggravating and mitigating features cancelled each other out

In *White (Andrew Mark)*,[48] the Court of Appeal reduced a sentence of two   **8.38**
years' immediate imprisonment to 16 months where the sentencing judge had either taken too high a starting point, given that the aggravating and mitigating features of the case cancelled each other out, or had failed to give any or adequate discount for the appellant's guilty pleas. The appellant pleaded guilty to two offences of possessing indecent images of a child, two offences of making indecent images of a child and one of possessing prohibited images of children. The images were found on a hard drive and laptop at his home. The appellant was co-operative, made immediate admissions and appeared relieved to have been caught. The offences of possession of indecent images covered 54,008 still and moving images, the vast majority of which fell into the lowest category of indecency but of which 61 were at the highest level. Over 400,000 other images were found but these had not been graded. The "making" offences related to still and moving images which had previously been downloaded but a considerable proportion of which were likely to have been subsequently deleted, leaving behind a footprint in excess of 100,000 images. The vast majority were in the lowest category of indecency but 112 were in the highest. There was likely to be some overlap between the downloaded images and those which the applicant had retained and which were already accounted for by the possession offences. The offence of possession of prohibited images related to 10 indecent cartoons of children. The appellant (42 and of good character) was sentenced to two years' imprisonment for each of the first four offences and six months for the last offence, the sentences being concurrent and so making a total of two years. He appealed on the ground that the judge must have taken a starting point of three years before making a reduction of one-third for the guilty plea, so reaching a term of two years' imprisonment. That starting point was too high. The Court of Appeal noted that regrettably the judge had failed when sentencing to state that he had given any and, if so, what discount for the appellant's guilty plea. He did, however, rightly in the Court's view, place the offending within category A of the guideline, which has a starting point of one year's imprisonment and a range of between 26 weeks and three years' imprisonment. In deciding where to place the offending within this category the judge properly referred to the aggravating factors, namely the sheer volume of the indecent material and the period of five to 10 years over which the appellant had been accumulating it. On the

---

[48] [2015] EWCA Crim 98.

other hand, he also referred to the mitigating factors that the applicant was of good character, had shown genuine remorse for his conduct, was a sufferer from obsessive compulsive disorder, and had sought to address his behaviour by attending a course run by a child protection charity. The judge concluded that the aggravating and mitigating features effectively cancelled each other out. On balance, the Court considered that the enormous volume of material collated over a long period called for a condign sentence. Where it departed from the judge's approach was in his implicit choice of three years as the proper level of sentence before giving a discount for the appellant's plea. This would have been perfectly proper in the absence of the mitigating features he identified, but having reached a somewhat generous conclusion that these features were sufficient fully to offset the aggravating features, it was very difficult to justify pitching the level of sentencing at the very top of the category A range. In the absence of any further analysis in the sentencing remarks, the Court concluded that the judge had either taken too high a figure within the range or alternatively omitted to give any or adequate credit for the guilty plea. In any event, the resultant sentence was manifestly excessive. Balancing the aggravating features against the mitigating features justified a sentence of two years before a discount for the guilty plea. A reduction of one-third gave a sentence of 16 months, and the Court reduced the sentence accordingly.

PARTIES TO THE OFFENCE

8.39 The offences in s.1(1) of the 1978 Act may be committed as principal by persons of either sex and by corporations.[49] An indecent photograph or pseudo-photograph which is the subject of a charge must be of a child, meaning a person (male or female) under the age of 18: see further para.8.57 and following, below.

8.40   If the child who is photographed is a willing party or even encourages the offence, are they liable to conviction as an accessory? The short answer is, they are not: see the discussion in paras 4.59 and following, above, which is equally applicable to offences under s.1(1) of the 1978 Act.

JURISDICTION

8.41 By virtue of s.72 of and Sch.2 to the Sexual Offences Act 2003, as amended,[50] it is an offence under s.1(1) of the 1978 Act for a UK national to do an act in a country outside the UK which would constitute an offence under s.1(1) if done in England and Wales. The amendments, made in 2008, expanded the scope of s.72 in two respects. First, they removed the limitation on s.72 as enacted that it applied only to offences committed against victims aged under

---

[49] cf. 1978 Act s.3, considered in para.8.42, below.
[50] By the Criminal Justice and Immigration Act 2008 s.72, with effect from July 14, 2008.

16 (the relevant age is now 18). Secondly, they abolished, in respect of UK nationals, the "double criminality" requirement that the act must have been an offence in the country in which it was done. This requirement is, however, retained in respect of the prosecution of UK residents and those who become UK residents or nationals after the doing of the relevant act. For the purposes of s.72 a "country" includes a territory and a "United Kingdom national" means a British citizen, a British overseas territories citizen, a British National (Overseas), a British Overseas citizen, a person who under the British Nationality Act 1981 is a British subject, or a British protected person within the meaning of that Act.[51] An act is taken to be an offence in the country in which it was done unless the defendant serves a notice putting the prosecution to proof on the point.[52]

Officers of corporations

Section 3 of the 1978 Act provides: **8.42**

> "(1) Where a body corporate is guilty of an offence under this Act and it is proved that the offence occurred with the consent or connivance of, or was attributable to any neglect on the part of, any director, manager, secretary or other officer of the body, or any person who was purporting to act in any such capacity he, as well as the body corporate, shall be deemed to be guilty of that offence and shall be liable to be proceeded against and punished accordingly.
>
> (2) Where the affairs of a body corporate are managed by its members, subsection (1) shall apply in relation to the acts and defaults of a member in connection with his functions of management as if he were a director of the body corporate."

Provisions of this sort are not uncommon in modern legislation. Their purpose is to fix criminal liability on those in a position of real authority in a company, the decision-makers who have both the power and the responsibility to decide corporate policy and strategy.[53] Accordingly, a "manager" is a person who manages or has a governing role in the affairs of the company itself, and not someone who, for example, is responsible only for the day-to-day running of a shop or store belonging to the company.[54] Section 3(1) does not create a separate offence of "consent or connivance"; its effect is rather that the director, manager, secretary or other officer are guilty of the same offence under the Act as the company.[55] In this regard the provision probably adds little to the general law, as an officer who consents to or connives at an offence by the company is likely in any event to be liable to conviction as a secondary party or for encouraging or assisting the offence.

---

[51] s.72(9).
[52] s.72(6)–(8).
[53] *Boal* (1992) 95 Cr. App. R. 272 at 276, per Simon Brown J.
[54] *Boal* (1992) 95 Cr. App. R. 272 at 276, per Simon Brown J; and see *Tesco Supermarkets Ltd v Nattrass* [1972] A.C. 153 at 178, per Lord Morris of Borth-y-Gest.
[55] *Wilson* [2013] EWCA Crim 1780.

The reference to the officer's "neglect" clearly supposes a duty, the existence of which must be proved by the prosecution.[56]

8.43   The impact of s.3 is illustrated by the decision in *Chargot (t/a Contract Services)*.[57] The case concerned criminal proceedings under the Health and Safety at Work Act 1974, s.37 of which makes provision for the liability of a director, manager, secretary or other officer of a body corporate in terms almost identical to s.3 of the 1978 Act. The House of Lords held in that case that no fixed rule could be laid down as to what the prosecution must identify and prove in order to establish that a company officer's state of mind had been such as amounted to consent, connivance or neglect within the meaning of s.37. Where the officer's place of activity was remote from the workplace or what was done there was not under his immediate direction and control, it might require the leading of quite detailed evidence, of which fair notice might have to be given. Where the officer was in day-to-day contact with what was done at the workplace, very little more than establishing that the body corporate had committed an offence might be necessary. The question will always be whether the officer in question should have been put on enquiry so as to take steps to determine whether or not the appropriate safety features had been in place. The state of mind that connivance and neglect contemplated was one that could also be established by inference. Where it was shown that the body corporate failed to achieve or prevent the result contemplated by the 1974 Act, it would be a relatively short step for the inference to be drawn that there had been connivance or neglect on the part of the officer, if the circumstances under which the risk had arisen had been under his direction or control. The more remote his area of responsibility was from those circumstances, the harder it would be to draw that inference.

"Indecent"

8.44   In a trial under s.1(1), it is for the trier of fact, i.e. the jury or magistrates, to determine whether any photograph or pseudo-photograph is indecent. The word "indecent" is not defined in the Act and so carries its ordinary meaning. Accordingly, in directing a jury on the point, the judge should ask them to decide whether the image would be considered indecent according to "recognised standards of propriety" or "the standard of decency of ordinary, right-thinking members of the public".[58] In *Nicklass*,[59] the judge gave a lengthy direction to the jury in the course of which he invited them to consider whether the photographs were indecent by reference to "contemporary standards of modesty and privacy". The Court held that this reference was "out of place", but that the direction as a whole could have left the jury

[56] *Huckerby v Elliott* [1970] 1 All E.R. 189.
[57] [2008] UKHL 73.
[58] *Graham-Kerr* [1988] 1 W.L.R. 1098; *Smethurst* [2002] 1 Cr. App. R. 6; *Neal* [2011] EWCA Crim 461; *Miles* [2015] EWCA Crim 353.
[59] [2006] EWCA Crim 2613.

with no other impression than that the question they had to decide was whether the photographs were indecent, i.e. the statutory test, and the conviction was therefore safe.

A failure by the judge to direct the jury on the meaning of "indecency" will   **8.45**
not necessarily be fatal to a conviction if the point was not in issue in the case. Thus in *Steen (George)*,[60] the Court of Appeal declined to overturn a conviction where, in directing the jury on the element of indecency, the judge did not tell them that the test was objective and they had to consider whether the images were indecent according to "recognised standards of propriety". It was plain from the description of the photographs before the Court that they passed the test and this had not been in issue before the jury. In those circumstances, there had been no need for the judge to direct the jury on the technical legal question of what constitutes indecency. This is a somewhat generous decision. We recommend that a judge presiding over a trial relating to indecent images should always direct the jury on the test of indecency, unless the fact that the images pass the test is admitted by the defence.

The question whether images are indecent is not to be decided by reference   **8.46**
to the categories of image identified for sentencing purposes in the Sentencing Council guideline or in the preceding case of *Oliver, Hartrey and Baldwin*.[61] The categorisation of images is only useful for sentencing purposes once the jury have convicted the accused, having determined the images to be indecent in accordance with the test set out above.

What should the jury take into account in deciding whether an image was indecent?

It was held in *Owen*[62] that in deciding whether a photograph is indecent, the   **8.47**
jury are entitled to take into account the age of the child depicted in it. The appellant, a professional photographer, had taken photographs of a girl aged 14 who wished to become a model. Some of the photographs showed the girl bare-breasted and scantily clad. At the appellant's trial under s.1(1)(a) of the 1978 Act, the judge directed the jury that in deciding whether the photographs were indecent they were entitled to take into account not merely the girl's appearance in them, but also her age. This direction was upheld by the Court of Appeal. The Court emphasised that the word "indecent" in s.1(1)(a) qualifies the words "photograph of a child", not the words "to take or permit to be taken". In other words, it is not the defendant's conduct that the jury must find indecent but the photograph of a child which results from it, and in reaching its determination the age of the child is a relevant consideration. Moreover, said the Court, the jury will inevitably be aware of the child's age because it is a requirement of the offence that the subject of the photograph was under 16 (now, under 18) at the material time. That being so, a direction

---

[60] [2014] EWCA Crim 1390.
[61] *Dodd* [2013] EWCA Crim 660; *Miles* [2015] EWCA Crim 353.
[62] [1988] 1 W.L.R. 134.

telling them to disregard the child's age in deciding whether the photograph is indecent would create "an artificial situation" and "manifest difficulties".

8.48   It is implicit in *Owen* that knowledge of the child's age may materially affect the jury's conclusion on the question of indecency. Indeed, the Court expressly acknowledged the possibility that "a photograph [might] be held to be indecent by reason of such matters as the pose or the posture or the provocative position of the subject if it was a photograph of a child but not indecent if it was a photograph of an adult."[63] This reasoning was questioned by the late Professor Sir John Smith, on the ground that it is:

> "a little difficult to reconcile with the true construction of the section, as found by the court, because, *as photographs*, there is nothing to choose between the two. Any indecency there may be lies in the conduct of the photographer rather than in the photograph he takes."[64]

With respect, this criticism seems mistaken. The question for the jury, according to the Court of Appeal, is not simply whether the photograph is indecent *as a photograph* but whether it is indecent *as a photograph of a child*. It is of course a tenable view that the age of a photograph's subject should be immaterial to the question whether the photograph is indecent. But this is something on which people may legitimately differ, and on that basis, it seems that what separated Professor Smith from the Court of Appeal was an issue of morality rather than of law.

8.49   The Court in *Owen* declined to express any view on the prosecution's argument that, in deciding whether a photograph is indecent, the jury are entitled to have regard to "all the circumstances" and not merely to the child's appearance in the photograph and his or her age. This argument was, however, rejected by a differently constituted Court in *Graham-Kerr*.[65] The events in that case took place one evening when the child, who was aged seven, was at a public swimming pool with his parents. The family were naturists, and the general public were not admitted to the pool on that evening. Nude swimming took place, and while the boy was with his mother the appellant approached them and offered to help the boy to learn to swim. This offer was accepted and the appellant remained with the boy in the pool. He later took two photographs of the boy, in private and without the parents' permission, with a camera which he kept in the changing room. When interviewed by the police, the appellant said that he found the boy attractive and that he derived sexual gratification from taking or looking at such photographs. At trial, it was conceded that the appellant had taken the photographs and that they represented what it was he wanted to photograph; the sole issue was whether they were indecent. The appellant argued that the only items of prosecution evidence which should be put before the jury on

---

[63] At 138.
[64] [1988] Crim. L.R. 120.
[65] [1988] 1 W.L.R. 1098.

this issue were the photographs themselves. The judge disagreed. He purported to apply the decision of the Court of Appeal in the indecent assault case of *Court*,[66] that in deciding whether an assault that was capable of being considered indecent was in fact indecent, the jury were entitled to consider all the circumstances, including the defendant's motives in acting as he did. The appellant's conviction was quashed on appeal. The Court stated that the question:

> "whether or not a photograph is indecent cannot be related to the question whether or not an assault is indecent. An assault is an ephemeral matter, the mens rea of the offence being that of the person committing the assault. A photograph is a permanent matter. The question . . . is whether the photograph itself is indecent."[67]

It followed that the jury were to decide the issue of indecency without reference either to the circumstances in which the photographs were taken (e.g. whether overtly or covertly) or to the appellant's motives in taking them. The Court did, however, acknowledge that evidence of those matters could be relevant and admissible in relation to other issues, e.g. it could be used to rebut a defence that the photographs were taken accidentally or that the defendant had not been aware of the element of indecency when he released the shutter.

It would be possible to juxtapose passages from *Owen* and *Graham-Kerr* so   **8.50**
as to make the decisions seem inconsistent. For example, the Court in *Owen* firmly rejected the argument that, when the indecency of a photograph is in issue, the jury must consider "the photograph as it stands"; but in *Graham-Kerr* the Court said that "the only relevant evidence" on the issue of indecency comprises "the photographs themselves". In fact the decisions are entirely reconcilable, on the basis that in considering "the photograph itself" the jury should have regard to the age of the child depicted in it, but not to the circumstances in which the photograph was taken, including the motives of the defendant in taking it.

The decision in *Murray*[68] illustrates the need to direct the jury so that they   **8.51**
focus, when determining the issue of indecency, only on the images which are the subject of the charge. The case concerned a video which was in two parts, the first containing a TV programme in which a doctor examined the genitalia of a naked boy who suffered from a genital defect, accompanied by a commentary explaining what the doctor was doing, while the second part consisted of some of the earlier images, but without the commentary, slowed down and clearly focusing on the boy's penis and its manipulation. The appellant was charged with possessing an indecent photograph of a child. At trial, the defence argued that, because the prosecution had accepted that the first part of the video was not indecent, the images in the second part which

---

[66] [1987] Q.B. 156. The decision was affirmed on different grounds by the House of Lords: [1989] A.C. 28. See further para.2.66, above.
[67] [1988] 1 W.L.R. 1098 at 1104, per Stocker LJ.
[68] [2004] EWCA Crim 2211.

had been abstracted from it could not be indecent either, because they were merely the original programme slowed down. The judge held that the alterations made to the programme by removing the commentary, slowing it down and focusing on the manipulation of the penis, could make an image which the jury could find to be indecent. He directed the jury accordingly and they convicted. The Court of Appeal dismissed the appeal, holding that the jury were asked to look at a quite separate set of images from the images constituting the original programme, and were entitled to look at those images independently of the programme and to determine whether, objectively speaking, they were indecent, applying recognised standards of propriety. Accordingly, the judge had accurately directed the jury both that there were separate images which they were entitled to consider and as to their approach to the question of whether those images were indecent.

"PHOTOGRAPH"

8.52 Section 7(2) of the 1978 Act provides that references in the Act to an "indecent photograph" include an indecent film, a copy of an indecent photograph or film, and an indecent photograph comprised in a film. For this purpose, "film" includes any form of video recording. It is further provided by s.7(4)[69] that references to a "photograph" include the negative as well as the positive version and data stored on a computer disc or by other electronic means which is capable of conversion into a photograph.[70] The effect of this provision is that indecent images, whether still or moving, that are stored in the form of data on a computer hard drive, in the cloud or on a portable storage medium, all fall within the scope of the Act.
By s.7(3):[71]

> "Photographs (including those comprised in a film) shall, if they show children and are indecent, be treated for all purposes of this Act as indecent photographs of children and so as respects pseudo-photographs."

The Court of Appeal in *Owen* said that this provision:

> "would be apt to prohibit a photograph of . . . a highly indecent act being carried on by adults in which children appeared, albeit the children themselves were not photographed in any indecent manner."[72]

8.53 The meaning of "photograph" in the 1978 Act was extended by s.69 of the Criminal Justice and Immigration Act 2008, which inserted into the Act a new s.7(4A) as follows:

---

[69] As amended by the Criminal Justice and Public Order Act 1994 s.84(1), (3), with effect from February 3, 1995.

[70] cf. *Fellows and Arnold* [1997] 1 Cr. App. R. 244, holding that images stored in digital form on a computer disc were copies of photographs for the purposes of s.7(2) of the 1978 Act. The reasoning underpinning this decision has been superseded by the amendment made by the 1994 Act, which brought such images within the definition of a "photograph" in s.7(4).

[71] As amended by the Criminal Justice and Public Order Act 1994 s.84(1), (3), with effect from February 3, 1995.

[72] [1988] 1 W.L.R. 134 at 138.

"(4A) References to a photograph also include—
  (a) a tracing or other image, whether made by electronic or other means (of whatever nature)—
      (i) which is not itself a photograph or pseudo-photograph,[73] but
      (ii) which is derived from the whole or part of a photograph or pseudo-photograph (or a combination of either or both); and
  (b) data stored on a computer disc or by other electronic means which is capable of conversion into an image within paragraph (a);
and subsection (8)[74] applies in relation to such an image as it applies in relation to a pseudo-photograph."

The effect of this provision is that an offence under s.1(1) of the 1978 Act now covers derivatives of indecent photographs or pseudo-photographs alongside such photographs and pseudo-photographs themselves. These derivatives may include line-traced and computer-traced images, for example images made by pencil using tracing paper or computer-traced images of photographs taken on a mobile phone.

"PSEUDO-PHOTOGRAPH"

The 1978 Act originally covered only "photographs" and as time went on it proved difficult to apply this term to the increasingly sophisticated forms of computer pornography, and especially to composite and manipulated photographic images. A simple example is where an indecent photograph of an adult engaging in sexual activity and a photograph of a child are scanned into a computer, and the resulting data is manipulated so as to produce a composite image of the child's head and torso on the adult's lower body. It is doubtful whether such an image can be said to constitute an indecent photograph of a child, either because it is not a "photograph" (or a copy of one) or because the composite image is not an image of a child.   **8.54**

The provisions of the Act relating to pseudo-photographs[75] are designed to deal with this problem. Section 7(7) provides that "pseudo-photograph" means an image, whether made by computer-graphics or otherwise howsoever, which appears to be a photograph. By s.7(8), if the impression conveyed by a pseudo-photograph is that the person shown is a child, the pseudo-photograph is to be treated for all purposes of the Act as showing a child; and so is a pseudo-photograph where the predominant impression conveyed is that the person shown is a child, notwithstanding that some of the physical characteristics shown are those of an adult. Section 7(9)[76] provides that references to an "indecent pseudo-photograph" include a copy of such a pseudo-photograph and data stored on a computer disc or by other   **8.55**

---

[73] For pseudo-photographs, see paras 8.54 and following, below.
[74] For s.7(8) of the 1978 Act, see para.8.55, below.
[75] Introduced by the Criminal Justice and Public Order Act 1994 s.84(1), (3), with effect from February 3, 1995.
[76] As amended by the Criminal Justice and Immigration Act 2008 s.69(1), (4).

electronic means which is capable of conversion into an indecent pseudo-photograph.

8.56 It was held in *Atkins v DPP*[77] that an item consisting of parts of two different photographs Sellotaped together, so as to create the impression of a child's head over a naked adult torso, was not a "pseudo-photograph" within the meaning of s.7(7) as it did not appear to be "a photograph" but rather two photographs stuck together. However, the Court said that if such an item was photocopied, the result could well be a "pseudo-photograph" if the photocopy had the appearance of being a single photograph. We suggest that such an item would now constitute a "photograph" by reason of s.7(4A)(a), set out in para.8.53, above, in that it is an image made otherwise than by electronic means which is not itself a photograph or pseudo-photograph but is derived from a combination of parts of two photographs.

"CHILD"

8.57 A "child" was originally defined for the purposes of the 1978 Act as any person under the age of 16, but Sexual Offences Act 2003 extended the definition to any person under the age of 18.[78] A person attains the age of 18 at the commencement of the eighteenth anniversary of his or her birth.[79] On a charge under s.1(1)(a) the prosecution may rely on s.99(2) of the Children and Young Persons Act 1933, which enables the court to draw from the present appearance of the victim (i.e. the subject of the image) a rebuttable presumption that he was under 18 at the date of the alleged offence.[80] On a charge under s.1(1)(b), (c) or (d), s.99(2) is not available and the prosecution must therefore employ one of the other means of proving age set out in paras 3.74 and following, above.

8.58 A particular difficulty with many prosecutions under the 1978 Act is that the identity of the subject of the photograph is unknown, so that his or her age cannot be proved by any of the methods referred to above. In such a case, the jury must be asked to infer that the subject was under 18 at the time the photograph was taken from his or her appearance in it and from any other relevant evidence that may exist. Provision is made for this by s.2(3) of the Act,[81] which states:

> "In proceedings under this Act relating to indecent photographs of children a person is to be taken as having been a child at any material time if it appears from the evidence as a whole that he was then under the age of 18."

---

[77] [2000] 2 Cr. App. R. 248.
[78] See s.7(6) of the 1978 Act, as amended by the Sexual Offences Act 2003 s.45(2), with effect from May 1, 2004.
[79] Family Law Reform Act 1969 s.9(1).
[80] Children and Young Persons Act 1933 s.99(2) and Sch.1; 1978 Act, s.1(5).
[81] As amended by the Sexual Offences Act 2003 s.45(2), fn.78, above. For further provision in relation to pseudo-photographs, see s.7(8) of the 1978 Act, para.8.54, above.

The matter is one of fact for the jury alone, using their experience and judgment: paediatric or other expert evidence is inadmissible on the point.[82]

The extension of the definition of a "child" to include those aged 16 and 17 resulted in cases in which guilty pleas were tendered to offences involving indecent photographs of children on the basis that the subjects of the photographs were under 18 but not under 16. This was encouraged by the SGC guideline, which provided that offences relating to images of 16- and 17-years-olds were less serious than offences relating to images of those under 16, unless they were level 5 images. The current Sentencing Council guideline does not make such a stark distinction, though it acknowledges the (young) age of the child as an aggravating factor. In addition, offences involving images of 16- and 17-year-olds do not trigger the notification requirements under Pt 2 of the 2003 Act. Where a defendant pleads on the basis that the child was of or below a certain age, it will be for the judge to decide whether the images are of someone of or under that age.   **8.59**

Problems of proof of age of a different sort arise under s.1(1)(d). If an advertiser is prosecuted for offering indecent photographs of "young girls" or "Lolita photographs", the prosecution must satisfy the jury that the advertisement was likely to be understood as referring to photographs of children, as opposed to young-looking adults.   **8.60**

Section 1(1)(a)—"To Take . . . or to Make"

The words "take" and "make" in s.1(1)(a) of the 1978 Act must be given their natural and ordinary meaning. The most obvious way in which a person may "take" an indecent photograph is by taking a still or moving picture with a camera, including one in a mobile phone or other digital device.[83] The dictionary meaning of "make" is "to cause to exist; to produce by action; to bring about".[84] The following actions carried out in relation to digital images have all been held to involve "making" a photograph or pseudo-photograph: **8.61**

- downloading an image from the internet onto a computer screen,[85]
- opening an image attached to an e-mail,[86]
- downloading an image from the internet onto a disc,[87]

---

[82] *Land* [1998] 1 Cr. App. R. 301.

[83] In this regard, it is worth noting the concerns about "sexting" by teenagers, i.e. the taking and sending by mobile phone of indecent self-portraits: see *http://en.wikipedia.org/wiki/Sexting* and *http://www.nspcc.org.uk/preventing-abuse/keeping-children-safe/sexting/* [Accessed April 30, 2016]. For an analysis of the law as it applies to sexting, and whether, in the case of children, treating recipients as sex offenders risks unfairly stigmatising consensual sexual activity, see Felicity Gerry, *Sexting and the Criminal Law* (2010) C.L. & J. 174 (51/52), 786.

[84] *Atkins v DPP* [2000] 2 Cr. App. R. 248 at 258. The words "to make" have been given the same meaning in Scotland: *Smart v HM Advocate*, 2007 J.C. 119.

[85] *Smith and Jayson* [2002] EWCA Crim 683.

[86] *Smith and Jayson* [2002] EWCA Crim 683.

[87] *Bowden (Jonathan)* [2000] 1 Cr. App. R. 438.

- printing off an image downloaded from the internet,[88]
- storing such an image in a directory on the hard drive of a computer.[89]

8.62   In *Harrison*,[90] it was held that a person who accesses an adult pornographic website, knowing that the site will automatically generate "pop ups" that are likely to contain indecent images of children, commits the "making" offence each time such an image appears. Further, if he knows that the images he accesses on screen will be automatically copied to and stored on his computer hard drive, he also commits the "making" offence when an image is so copied; and thereafter he commits the "possession" offence for so long as the image, by virtue of being stored on the hard drive, remains in his custody and control.

Section 1(1)(a)—"permit to be taken"

8.63   The meaning of the word "permit" depends on the context in which it appears: it may mean "allow" or "authorise", in which case it covers a failure to forbid something that one is in a position to forbid,[91] or it may bear a wider meaning that includes failing to take reasonable steps to prevent.[92] As used in s.1(1)(a) the word is likely to bear the narrower meaning, so that a person only "permits" the taking of an indecent photograph of a child if he allows or authorises it to be taken, i.e. if he is in a position to forbid the taking of the photograph but does not do so.

Section 1(1)(b)—"distribute or show"

8.64   Section 1(2) of the 1978 Act provides:

> "For the purpose of this Act, a person is to be regarded as distributing an indecent photograph or pseudo-photograph if he parts with possession of it to, or exposes or offers it for acquisition by, another person."

For the meaning of "possession", see para.8.71, below. The reference to "exposing" for acquisition was inserted to accommodate the decision in *Fisher v Bell*,[93] in which it was held that the display of an article in a shop window was an invitation to treat and not an offer to sell. The use of the term "acquisition" means that the exposure or offer need not be made with a view to sale; an offer to rent images, for example, will be sufficient. The better view is that A "distributes" images to B for the purposes of s.1(2) only if his act

---

[88] *Bowden (Jonathan)* [2000] 1 Cr. App. R. 438.
[89] *Atkins v DPP* [2000] 2 Cr. App. R. 248.
[90] [2007] EWCA Crim 2976.
[91] cf. *Goodbarne v Buck* [1940] 1 K.B. 771; *Thompson v Lodwick* [1983] R.T.R. 76.
[92] *Vehicle Inspectorate v Nuttall* [1999] 1 W.L.R. 629, HL; and see *Barking and Dagenham LBC v Bass Taverns* [1993] C.O.D. 453.
[93] [1961] 1 Q.B. 394; and see J.C. Smith, *Civil Law Concepts in the Criminal Law* [1972B] C.L.J. 197 at pp.198–210.

in exposing or offering the images for acquisition makes them visible to or at least accessible by B. Thus there will be no distribution if A sends B a price list containing a description of what the images contain but without giving B a means to access the images directly. In those circumstances, the appropriate charge would be of possession with a view to distribution contrary to s.1(1)(c).

In *Fellows and Arnold*,[94] it was held that the appellants "distributed or showed" indecent images of children stored on a computer, within the meaning of s.1(1)(b), when they made the images accessible over the internet by other computer users who entered a password. The images in that case were stored on a computer in England and Wales. We suggest, however, that someone who in this jurisdiction uploads such images to a website commits an offence under s.1(1)(b) regardless of where the host server is located, even if it is in another jurisdiction. This proposition derives strong support from *Sheppard and Whittle*,[95] in which it was held that a person who had produced racially inflammatory material in England and Wales and posted it on a website hosted by a remote server in the USA could be tried in England and Wales for possessing, publishing and distributing racially inflammatory material contrary to s.19 of the Public Order Act 1986. W had written the material and S had uploaded it to a website, hosted by a server located in California, that he had set up for the purpose of disseminating what W had written. Once posted on the website, the material was available to be viewed and downloaded by those visiting the site, including people within the jurisdiction of England and Wales. At trial, the prosecution relied upon evidence from a police officer who had visited the site and downloaded the material. The judge, applying *Smith (Wallace Duncan) (No.4)*,[96] decided that the court had jurisdiction because a substantial measure of S and W's activities had taken place in the UK. The appellants submitted that the judge should not have applied the "substantial measure" test, as offences concerning publication on the internet could only be heard in the jurisdiction where the web server was located. The Court of Appeal dismissed that contention. In considering whether there was any basis for not applying the "substantial measure" test, the starting point was the terms of the 1986 Act. Section 42 provided that the Act's provisions extended to England and Wales, save for some limited exceptions which mainly related to Scotland and Northern Ireland. The section did not take the case outside the principle in *Smith*, as it did not restrict jurisdiction to England and Wales, but rather set out limitations as to the Act's extent, and so was not determinative of the jurisdiction of the court. Further, the "substantial measure" test not only

8.65

---

[94] [1997] 1 Cr. App. R. 244. See also *Taylor* [1995] 1 Cr. App. R. 131, where the owner of a photographic centre who developed prints depicting obscene acts from negatives submitted by customers and then passed the prints to the customers was held to have "distributed" the prints for the purposes of the offence of publishing an obscene article, contrary to s.2(1) of the Obscene Publications Act 1959.
[95] [2010] EWCA Crim 65.
[96] [2004] EWCA Crim 631.

accorded with the purpose of the relevant provisions of the Act, it also reflected the practicalities of the instant case, in which almost everything related to England and Wales, which was where the material was generated, edited, uploaded and controlled. The material was aimed primarily at the British public. The only foreign element was that the website was hosted by a server in California, but the use of the server was merely a stage in the transmission of the material. There was accordingly abundant evidence to satisfy the "substantial measure" test.

8.66   We suggest that this analysis applies equally to offences under the 1978 Act. The jurisdictional point reads across exactly, since s.9 of the 1978 Act, which describes the Act's extent, is materially identical in its terms to s.42 of the 1986 Act. As to the "substantial measure" test, this would seem equally applicable in the context of the 1978 Act. Whether the test is satisfied in any given case will of course depend upon the evidence, but if it is established that the defendant uploaded and controlled the indecent material in this jurisdiction, whether or not he generated or edited it, we suggest the test will be satisfied, regardless of where the host server is situated or where the material is primarily intended to be read.

8.67   A person "shows" an indecent photograph within the meaning of s.1(1)(b) only if he shows it to someone other than himself.[97] However, a person (A) may be convicted of conspiring with another person (B) to distribute indecent photographs of a child to himself. This is because s.1 of the Criminal Law Act 1977, under which such a conspiracy is charged, expressly contemplates that a conspiracy may involve the commission of a substantive offence by one or more, but not all, of the conspirators. It is therefore sufficient to found a charge that, if distribution takes place in accordance with the agreement, B will commit the substantive offence, although A will not. But it is important that in such a case the particulars of the offence correctly describe what is alleged. Particulars which simply state that A conspired with B to distribute indecent photographs imply that the distribution was to be to someone else, not to A or B, and a charge in those terms cannot be made out if the evidence is that the distribution was to be to one of the conspirators only. In order to found a conviction, the particulars must allege that A conspired with B to distribute indecent photographs to himself.[98]

8.68   In *DPP v Armstrong*,[99] it was held that the appellant could be convicted of inciting an undercover police officer (X) to distribute indecent photographs of children without proof that X intended actually to distribute the photographs; it was sufficient that A intended or believed that, if X acted as

[97] *R. v ET* [1999] Crim. L.R. 749, CA; *Fellows and Arnold* [1997] 1 Cr. App. R. 244. For a Scottish decision to the same effect as *Fellows and Arnold*, see *Peebles v HM Advocate* [2007] HCJAC 6. See further para.8.73, below.
[98] *Barker*, unreported, March 27, 1998, CA (No.9705014 Z5), as explained in *Drew* [2000] 1 Cr. App. R. 91.
[99] [2000] Crim. L.R. 379, CA, approved obiter in *R. v C* [2005] EWCA Crim 2827.

incited, he would do so with the fault required for the offence. It was also held that the appellant could not avoid conviction on the ground that the offence was impossible of completion since X had no intention of supplying any photographs. This was because X was in a position to fulfil the appellant's request by virtue of his access to indecent photographs in police custody. It would have been otherwise if X had not been in a position to commit the distribution offence, because he had no indecent photographs and no means of obtaining any. Although the offence of incitement has been abolished, it is clear that in circumstances such as those in *Armstrong* a defendant could now be convicted of the offence of intentionally encouraging X to commit the distribution offence, contrary to s.44 of the Serious Crime Act 2007, since he does an act capable of encouraging X to commit the offence, intending to encourage its commission. It remains the case, however, that a conviction will be possible in these circumstances only if X is in a position to commit the distribution offence, i.e. if he has access to indecent photographs that he could distribute if he chose to do so; otherwise, A's act is not capable of encouraging X to commit the offence.

In *R. v C*[100] the Court of Appeal held that the respondent had been   **8.69**
properly charged with inciting the distribution offence by subscribing to a website operated and controlled by a US company which sold child pornography. The Court of Appeal held that if a person carries out an act of incitement in this country to a person outside the jurisdiction, which amounts to an encouragement to that other person to commit an offence in this jurisdiction, then the courts of England and Wales have jurisdiction to try that offence on ordinary principles as the offence incited would be an attack on the Queen's peace. Since sending indecent photographs from a website abroad to a computer in this country constitutes an offence in this country under s.1(1)(b) of the 1978 Act (citing *Goldman*[101] and *Waddon*, unreported), it followed that the Crown Court had jurisdiction to entertain the charge. Professor Ormerod has commented that the Court was right to conclude that there would be a "distribution" by the US company under s.1(1)(b) if it sent images to the respondent, since s.1(2) provides that a person is to be regarded as distributing an image "if he parts with possession of it to, or exposes or offers it for acquisition by, another person".[102] In this case, the images on the internet were exposed for acquisition by the respondent in the UK and accordingly the offence the respondent had incited would, if completed, have been committed in the UK. Although the offence of incitement has since been abolished, it is clear that in circumstances such as those in *R. v C* a defendant could now be convicted of the offence of intentionally encouraging the commission of the distribution offence, contrary to s.44 of the Serious Crime Act 2007, in that he does an act capable of encouraging the US company to commit the offence, intending to encourage

---

[100] [2006] EWCA Crim 2132.
[101] [2001] EWCA Crim 1684, discussed below.
[102] [2007] Crim. L.R. 235, CA.

its commission, and the provisions on extra-territorial jurisdiction in the 2007 Act would on these facts be satisfied.

8.70   In *Goldman*,[103] in response to an advertisement published by X, the appellant sent a letter asking X to send him indecent images of children. It was held that he was rightly convicted of attempting to incite X to commit the distribution offence, and could not avoid conviction on the ground that his communication was merely a response to the offer made in X's advertisement. Although the offence of incitement has been abolished, on these facts a defendant could now be convicted of attempting to commit the offence under s.44 of the Serious Crime Act 2007, by intentionally encouraging the commission of the distribution offence. If it can be proved that the communication was received by the intended recipient, then it would be the appropriate to charge the s.44 offence rather than an attempt. It will be no defence to a charge of committing or attempting the s.44 offence in these circumstances that the communication was sent to a computer.[104] Although a computer cannot be encouraged, it is used to facilitate the business and there is a human mind lying behind it and it therefore does not matter that the entire process is automated.

SECTION 1(1)(c)—"HAVE IN HIS POSSESSION . . . WITH A VIEW TO THEIR BEING DISTRIBUTED OR SHOWN"

8.71   "Possession" involves both a physical and a mental element. The mental element is considered in paras 8.96 and following, below. The required physical element is custody or control over the item in question.[105] Possession which is originally lawful may become criminal because of a change of circumstances without any act by the defendant, but only after he has failed to divest himself of possession within a reasonable time.[106]

8.72   In *Porter*,[107] the Court of Appeal held that a person is in possession of an image in the form of a computer file if it is within his control, e.g. if he can produce it on his screen, make a hard copy of it or send it to someone else. In the case of a deleted image, if he cannot retrieve or access it in this way, he no longer has custody or control of it and so it is not within his possession. For detailed discussion of this case, see paras 8.135 and following, below.

---

[103] [2001] Crim. L.R. 822, CA.

[104] [2001] Crim. L.R. 822, CA.

[105] *Porter* [2006] EWCA Crim 560; and see *Bellerby v Carle* [1983] 2 A.C. 101; *Hussain* [1969] 2 Q.B. 567 (*held*, seaman not in possession of drugs simply because he allowed others to conceal them behind a bulkhead panel in his cabin).

[106] *Burns v Nowell* (1880) 5 Q.B.D. 444 at 454, per Baggallay LJ.

[107] [2006] EWCA Crim 560, applied in *Rowe* [2008] EWCA Crim 2712, where it was held that *Porter* applies whether the images have been deleted from a hard drive or a portable medium such as a floppy disc (as was the case in *Rowe*).

The word "shown" in s.1(1)(c) means shown to a third party, and so a   8.73
person does not commit an offence under the subsection if he is in possession
of an indecent photograph of a child with a view only to looking at it
himself.[108] The appropriate charge in such a case is one of possession
contrary to s.160 of the 1988 Act, discussed below. See further para.8.67,
above.

SECTION 1(1)(D)—"PUBLISH OR CAUSE TO BE PUBLISHED"

The term "publish" is not defined in the 1978 Act. In construing it, the courts   8.74
may have regard to s.1 of the Obscene Publications Act 1959, which defines
the term to include distributing, circulating, selling, letting, giving or lending
an article. It is clear that publication even to one person will constitute
"publication" for the purposes of that Act.[109] In other contexts it has been
held that a book is not published if it is circulated among friends gratuitously
or to pupils,[110] and that information is not published if it is circulated among
subscribers for their private use.[111] It is, however, highly unlikely that these
decisions will be followed in the context of s.1(1)(d), as this would tend to
encourage rather than address the mischief with which the provision is clearly
intended to deal. "Causes" requires proof of a positive act.[112] For the
question whether the word imports a requirement of mens rea, see
para.8.104, below.

EXCEPTIONS FOR CONSENT WITHIN MARRIAGE OR OTHER RELATIONSHIP

In extending the protection of the 1978 Act to children aged 16 and 17, the   8.75
Sexual Offences Act 2003 provided a limited defence of consent to certain
offences involving children of those ages. The defence, which is contained in
s.1A of the 1978 Act, applies if the child was 16 or 17 when the photograph
or pseudo-photograph[113] was taken or made, it shows the child alone or with
the defendant, and the child and the defendant were married,[114] in a civil

---

[108] *R. v ET* [1999] Crim. L.R. 749, CA.

[109] *Smith (Gavin)* [2015] EWCA Crim 398.

[110] *Prince Albert v Strange* (1849) 1 H. & T. 1; *Caird v Sime* (1887) 12 App. Cas. 326.

[111] *Exchange Telegraph Co v Central News* [1897] 2 Ch. 48.

[112] *Price v Cromack* [1975] 1 W.L.R. 988, DC; *Wychavon District Council v National Rivers Authority* [1993] 1 W.L.R. 125, DC; doubted in *Empress Car Company (Abertillery) Limited v National Rivers Authority* [1997] Env.L.R. 227. See also para.2.98, above.

[113] The provision was extended to pseudo-photographs by the Coroners and Justice Act 2009 s.69(1), with effect from April 6, 2010.

[114] The reference to marriage is to be read as including a reference to marriage of a same sex couple: Marriage (Same Sex Couples) Act 2013 s.11 and Sch.3, Pt 1 para.1, which was brought into force on March 13, 2014, by SI 2014/93.

partnership[115] or cohabiting at the time of the alleged offence. The section is unlikely to win an award from the Plain English Campaign, but its effects are as follows:

- In proceedings under s.1(1)(a) for taking or making an indecent photograph of a child, if (a) the defendant proves that the photograph was of the child aged 16 or 17 and that at the time it was taken or made he and the child were married, in a civil partnership or living together as partners in an "enduring family relationship", (b) sufficient evidence is adduced to raise an issue as to whether the child consented to the photograph being taken or made, or as to whether the defendant reasonably believed she consented, and (c) the photograph showed the child alone or with the defendant but nobody else, the defendant will be not guilty of the offence unless the prosecution proves that the child did not consent and that the defendant did not reasonably believe she did.

- In proceedings under s.1(1)(b) for distributing or showing an indecent photograph of a child, if (a) the defendant proves that the photograph was of the child aged 16 or 17 and that at the time he distributed, showed or obtained the photograph, he and the child were married, in a civil partnership or living together as partners in an "enduring family relationship" and (b) the photograph showed the child alone or with the defendant but nobody else, the defendant will be not guilty of the offence unless the prosecution proves that the showing or distribution was to a person other than the child.

- In proceedings under s.1(1)(c) for possessing an indecent photograph of a child with a view to its being distributed or shown, if (a) the defendant proves that the photograph was of the child aged 16 or 17 and that at the time he possessed or obtained the photograph, he and the child were married, in a civil partnership or living together as partners in an "enduring family relationship", (b) sufficient evidence is adduced to raise an issue as to both (i) whether the child consented to the defendant possessing the photograph, or whether the defendant reasonably believed she consented, and (ii) whether the defendant had the photograph in his possession with a view to its being distributed or shown to anyone other than the child, and (c) the photograph showed the child alone or with the defendant but nobody else, the defendant will be not guilty of the offence unless the prosecution proves either that the child did not consent and that the defendant did not reasonably believe she did, or that the defendant had the photograph in his possession with a view to its being distributed or shown to a person other than the child.

---

[115] The reference to civil partnership was added by the Civil Partnership Act 2004 s.261(1) and Sch.27 para.60, which came into force on December 5, 2005.

The section provides no defence of consent in proceedings for offences **8.76** under s.1(1)(a) of permitting an indecent photograph (etc.) to be taken or made, or offences under s.1(1)(d).

Section 1A's concoction of legal and evidential burdens may be difficult to **8.77** apply in practice.[116] Careful direction of the jury is essential. The defendant may be able to discharge the evidential burden as to consent by inviting the jury to draw an inference from the child's demeanour in the photograph, e.g. if she appears relaxed and happy.

As for proof that the defendant and child were in an "enduring family **8.78** relationship", this term is not defined and the Government envisaged that it will fall to be applied by the courts in the light of the circumstances of the particular case.[117] The term is intended to cover partners in relationships analogous to marriage, i.e. cohabiting couples. Clearly, the longer a relationship has lasted, the more likely it is to be held "enduring". This may pose a problem for at least some defendants who seek to rely upon the defence, since the operation of the age of consent means that a "family relationship" between an adult and a child of 16 or even 17 may not have lasted for any substantial period.

The limits of the s.1A defence were tested in *R. v DM*,[118] in which it was **8.79** held that the defence could not apply where the defendant and the child engaged in lawful and consensual sexual intercourse as a "one night stand" immediately before the photographs in question were taken. The complainant, 17, and the appellant, 23, had drunk alcohol and smoked cannabis together before having sex. Immediately afterwards, the appellant took intimate photographs of the complainant with his mobile phone. He was charged under s.1(1)(a) of the 1978 Act with making indecent photographs of a child. At the close of the evidence, the Recorder rejected an argument that, in order to give effect to the appellant's rights under art.8 (private and family life) and art.10 (freedom of expression) of the ECHR, the s.1A defence should be interpreted as applying to a brief sexual relationship or "one night stand" of the sort that had occurred in this case. The appellant was convicted and argued on appeal that the Recorder had erred in interpreting the defence as he had. Sexual relations between the complainant and the appellant had been consensual and therefore lawful. There was no evidence of an intention to distribute the photographs; indeed, such evidence as there was indicated than the appellant would probably have deleted them so that his girlfriend did not see them. The limitation of the s.1A defence to circumstances in which 16- and 17-year-olds were married or "living together as partners in an

---

[116] On the nature of the reverse burden imposed on the defendant by s.1A, see Alisdair A. Gillespie, *Child pornography: balancing substantive and evidential law to safeguard children effectively from abuse*, E. & P. 2005, 9(1), 29–49.

[117] *Hansard*, HC, Standing Committee B, col.251, Beverley Hughes MP (September 18, 2003).

[118] [2011] EWCA Crim 2752.

enduring family relationship" was arbitrary, unjustified and disproportionate, since it meant that an unmarried, non-cohabiting 16- or 17-year-old
has the capacity in law to consent to intercourse but not to the taking of
photographs during intercourse, whereas a married or cohabiting 16- or
17-year-old has the capacity to do both. The taking of an image with
consent, following consensual sexual relations, cannot require the imposition
of criminal liability so as to protect such children from sexual exploitation,
particularly in the light of the existence of the offences in s.1(1)(b)–(d) of the
Act, in relation to which no defence of consent arises. To argue that the
taking of such a photograph must be subject to criminal liability so as to
prevent future pornographic use was purely speculative. Accordingly, the
appellant argued, arts 8 and 10 were engaged; the interference with his rights
was not necessary in a democratic society for any of the legitimate aims listed
in art 8(2) or 10(2); and the Act's failure to make allowance for the private
lives of 16- and 17-year-olds who are sexually active whilst living with their
parents was accordingly a violation of those rights.

8.80   The Court of Appeal rejected what it called this "bold submission". It
noted the UK's obligations under international law[119] to take measures to
protect children from exploitation through pornography. It also noted the
decision in *Smethurst*,[120] decided when the 1978 Act protected children under
16, that s.1(1)(a) of the Act was compatible with arts 8 and 10. In the course
of its decision, the Court of Appeal in that case had rejected an argument
that s.1(1)(a) should apply only where the photographs were intended for
indecent purposes, on the basis that "once the photographs come into
existence, the harm may be done [as the] person in possession may circulate
them". The Court went on to consider the obligation placed on it by s.3 of
the Human Rights Act 1998, so far as possible to read and give effect to
legislation compatibly with Convention rights. But it concluded that s.1A was
drafted so as to provide effective protection for children whilst balancing
Convention rights. In prohibiting the taking of indecent photographs, the
Act did no more than was necessary to accomplish that objective. Parliament
had identified circumstances in which the taking of such a photograph
should *not* be criminalised, and without limiting those circumstances as it
had (i.e. to couples who were married, in a civil partnership or cohabiting)
there could not be the same degree of certainty about the genuine nature of
the commitment in a relationship, which can easily be terminated and may be
very short term. A statutory defence which included a brief sexual relationship would diminish the protection provided and risk introducing issues as to
the circumstances in which the photograph was taken and the motivation for

---

[119] art.34 of the UN Convention on the Rights of the Child and art.3 of the *Council
Framework Decision 2004/68/JHA*, since replaced by *Directive 2011/93/EU of the European
Parliament and of the Council of 13 December 2011 on combating the sexual abuse and sexual
exploitation of children and child pornography, and replacing Council Framework Decision
2004/68/JHA*, as to which see paras 10.07 and following, below.
[120] [2002] 1 Cr. App. R. 6.

taking it. In short, the limitation was necessary for the prevention of crime and the protection of morals, in particular the protection of children from being exploited, and struck the balance between keeping to a minimum the interference by the State in the private lives of individuals and maintaining the maximum protection of children from sexual abuse and exploitation.

This decision prompted James Turner QC to lambast: **8.81**

> " . . . the absurdity of a law that says a man may have sexual intercourse with a 17-year-old girl, but commits an offence if he takes a photograph of her in a state of undress even though she gives her wholehearted consent. If 16- and 17-year-olds need protection from persons who may wish to take photographs of them when undressed, they surely must be in much more urgent need of protection from predators who would like to take them to bed."[121]

Whatever the force of this comment, framed in those terms it is not so much a criticism of *R. v DM* as an argument for raising the age of consent, which is perhaps unlikely to gain much traction. Ashworth and Collins put the matter a little differently by asking "whether Parliament was being inconsistent when, given that the age of consent to sexual activity is 16, it raised the age of consent to being photographed in an indecent pose to 18".[122] In this respect the authors note that Parliament was not compelled by the UK's international obligations to increase the age limit for consent to 18, and that in English law 16 has long been the age of consent to sexual activity. Why, therefore, is a higher age of consent necessary in relation to indecent photographs? Why is it necessary to protect children from exploitation in the form of sexual activity until they are 16, but in the form of indecent photography until they are 18? These are good questions, to which there is no ready answer save that the Court of Appeal was clearly concerned by the risk that an adult who takes photographs in circumstances such as those in *R. v DM* may later use them in a way that harms and distresses the child, by circulating them to others or placing them on the internet. The Court's solution was to discourage the taking of such photographs in the first place. Arguably, its concern is now better addressed by the new offence contained in s.33 of the Criminal Justice and Courts Act 2015 of sending private sexual photographs and films with intent to cause distress. That as may be, the decision in *R. v DM* seems likely to have settled the scope of s.1A unless and until Parliament sees fit to reconsider it.

Exception for Criminal Proceedings and Investigations

Section 1B of the 1978 Act, introduced by the Sexual Offences Act 2003,[123]   **8.82** provides two defences to the s.1(1)(a) offence of making an indecent

---

[121] *Criminal Law Week*, Issue 34, 2012, p.2.
[122] [2012] Crim. L.R. 789 and 790–1.
[123] s.46, which was brought into force on May 1, 2004.

photograph or pseudo-photograph of a child. They apply where the defendant proves:

- that it was necessary for him to make the photograph or pseudo-photograph for the purposes of the prevention, detection or investigation of crime, or for the purposes of criminal proceedings, in any part of the world, or
- that at the time of the alleged offence he was a member of the Security Service (MI5), GCHQ (Government Communications Headquarters) or the Secret Intelligence Service (SIS)[124] and that it was necessary for him to make the photograph or pseudo-photograph for the exercise of the agency's functions.

8.83   The first of these defences ensures that police officers who investigate child sex offences and members of the CPS who prosecute such offences cannot be convicted of the s.1(1)(a) offence in relation to conduct necessarily undertaken in the course of their work, e.g. where they need to copy images for forensic purposes or in the course of a trial. It is, on the face of it, strange that this defence was created only in 2003, over 25 years after the 1978 Act was passed. The reason lies mainly in the expansion in recent years of the s.1(1)(a) offence, by statutory amendment and judicial interpretation, to cover a variety of computer-related activity of a sort which the police and prosecutors need to carry out in the course of their work: e.g. downloading images from a suspect's computer hard drive in order to gather and preserve evidence of his paedophile offences. The defence is not, however, confined to the law enforcement community and will also be available to individuals who provide the police with information about paedophile activity, so long as they do no more than necessary to enable the police to investigate the matter. So the defence could cover, e.g. an employee of an internet service provider who becomes aware that the company's services are being used to facilitate paedophile activity and who downloads or copies paedophile images for police inspection, provided the downloading or copying is genuinely necessary for that purpose. A Memorandum of Understanding concerning the defence has been agreed between the Crown Prosecution Service and the Association of Chief Police Officers.[125]

8.84   The separate defence for the security and intelligence agencies was introduced because members of those agencies may have to carry out activity within the scope of s.1(1)(a) in the course of their national security work, where information has been encrypted into an indecent photograph or image of a child and the agency needs to draw down the image in order to decode and deconstruct the information.[126]

---

[124] Section 1B as enacted applied only to members of MI5 and GCHQ. It was extended to members of SIS by the Criminal Justice and Immigration Act 2008 s.69(2).

[125] Available at *https://www.iwf.org.uk/assets/media/hotline/CPS%20ACPO%20S46%20-MoU%202014%202.pdf* [Accessed April 30, 2016].

[126] *Hansard*, HC, Standing Committee B, col.260, Beverley Hughes MP (September 18, 2003).

Finally, it is notable that s.1B, though described in the side-note as an   **8.85**
"exception", in fact creates defences which place the burden of proof on the
defendant. This no doubt reflects a wish to prevent paedophiles abusing the
crime-prevention defence by falsely claiming they were only doing what was
necessary to collect paedophile images to report to the police. If the provision
established a true exception, such individuals would be able to escape
conviction by simply raising an issue as to whether their claim was true.
Placing on defendants the burden of proof should significantly reduce the
risk of such claims succeeding.

Defences to Charges under Section 1(1)(b), (c)

Section 1(4) of the 1978 Act[127] provides: **8.86**

> "Where a person is charged with an offence under subsection (1)(b) or (c), it shall
> be a defence for him to prove—
> (a) that he had a legitimate reason for distributing or showing the photo-
> graphs or pseudo-photographs or (as the case may be) having them in his
> possession; or
> (b) that he had not himself seen the photographs or pseudo-photographs and
> did not know, nor had any cause to suspect, them to be indecent."

Section 1(4) imposes a legal rather than a mere evidential burden on the
defendant.[128]

Nothing turns on the use in s.1(4)(a) of the phrase "legitimate reason"   **8.87**
rather than the more common "lawful excuse" or "reasonable excuse".
Speaking in support of "legitimate reason" in debate on the Bill, Lord
Scarman urged his noble colleagues to "[g]et away from the old, hackneyed
phrases and use a phrase which means something to ordinary people".[129]
Examples given in the course of debate of a "legitimate reason" falling within
the scope of the defence were the use of indecent photographs for the
purposes of police training or clinical psychiatry and in the course of genuine
research. However, when construing the term "legitimate reason" in *Atkins v
DPP*[130] the Court of Appeal declined to consult the record of Parliamentary
discussions on the matter on the ground that the conditions for doing so
specified in *Pepper v Hart*[131] were not satisfied. This was presumably because
the Court considered the legislation not to be ambiguous or obscure.

The Court in *Atkins v DPP* went on to hold that what constitutes a   **8.88**
"legitimate reason" for the purposes of s.1(4)(a) is a pure question of fact in
each case. The Court said that where the defence is that the conduct was part

---

[127] As amended by the Criminal Justice and Public Order Act 1994 s.84(1), (2), with effect
from February 3, 1995.
[128] *Collier* [2004] EWCA Crim 1411, at.18. See further Alisdair A. Gillespie, *Child pornography: balancing substantive and evidential law to safeguard children effectively from abuse*, E. &
P. 2005, 9(1), 29–49.
[129] *Hansard*, HL Vol.392, col.546.
[130] [2000] 2 Cr. App. R. 248.
[131] [1993] A.C. 593.

of legitimate research, the central question will be whether the defendant is essentially a person with an unhealthy interest in the possession of indecent photographs in the pretence of undertaking research, or by contrast a genuine researcher with no alternative but to have this sort of unpleasant material in his possession. Cases in which other categories of "legitimate reason" are advanced must be considered on their own facts, and the courts "are plainly entitled to bring a measure of scepticism to bear upon such an enquiry: they should not too readily conclude that the defence has been made out."[132]

8.89   The defence in s.1(4)(b) is designed to protect people who innocently have photographs in their possession which they have not looked at and have no reason to suspect are indecent photographs of children. Read literally the defence would benefit only a defendant who proves that he did not know and had no cause to suspect that the photographs were indecent per se, and not one who knew the photographs were indecent but not that the subjects were children. But in *Collier*,[133] decided under the similar provision in s.160(2)(b) of the Criminal Justice Act 1988 (offence of possession of indecent images of children), the Court of Appeal held that Parliament must have intended the defence to be available to defendants in both categories. Accordingly, even if the prosecution proves that the defendant was knowingly in possession of an indecent photograph, the defence will be made out if he proves that he had not seen the photograph and did not know and had no reason to suspect it was of a child. In *Collier*, the appellant ordered CDs which he thought contained adult homosexual pornography. Unknown to him, there were four indecent images of children on the CDs. The Court of Appeal quashed his conviction on the basis that if he could prove that he had not seen the four images and did not know they were of children, he should be acquitted.

8.90   The effect of *Collier* is that on a charge in relation to which the statutory defence is available, i.e. under s.1(1)(b) or (c), where it is proved or admitted that the defendant knew the photograph was indecent, the prosecution need not prove that he knew it was a photograph of a child, since if that had to be proved the defence would never come into play. Instead, it will be for the defendant to prove that he did *not* know, or have cause to suspect, that the photograph was of a child. This is in contrast with the position where the statutory defence is unavailable because the charge is not under s.1(1)(b) or (c). Thus in *Smith and Jayson*,[134] it was held in relation to the offence of making or taking an indecent photograph of a child (s.1(1)(a) of the 1978 Act) that the prosecution must prove that the defendant knew the photograph was, or was likely to be, of a child. The Court of Appeal in *Collier*

---

[132] [2000] 2 Cr. App. R. 248, at 257.
[133] [2004] EWCA Crim 1411; and see *Land* [1998] 1 Cr. App. R. 301, para.8.98, below. *Matrix (Billy)* [1997] EWCA Crim 2058; [1997] Crim. L.R. 901, in which the opposite conclusion was reached in relation to s.1(4)(b). *Matrix* was not cited in *Collier* or *Land* and appears to have been generally overlooked.
[134] [2003] 1 Cr. App. R. 212, discussed in para.8.91, below.

pointed out that it follows "very ironically" that the prosecution has a heavier burden in the absence of the statutory defence.

MENTAL ELEMENT

Section 1(1)(a)—taking or making an indecent photograph or pseudo-photograph

It was held in *Smith and Jayson*[135] that the act of making or taking an   **8.91** indecent photograph or pseudo-photograph must be a deliberate and intentional act, done with knowledge that the image made is, or is likely to be, an indecent photograph or pseudo-photograph of a child. However, the prosecution is not required to prove that the defendant intended the photograph or pseudo-photograph to be for an indecent purpose.[136] It follows from *Smith and Jayson* that a person does not commit the "making" offence in the following cases:

- he downloads an indecent image believing that it is of an adult[137];
- he opens an attachment to an email without knowing that it contains an indecent image of a child[138];
- he accidentally takes a photograph of a child which, objectively viewed, is indecent[139];
- unknown to him, indecent images of children that he has been browsing on the internet are automatically downloaded by his browser onto the cache of his computer[140] (though it is now clear that in such a case he would be guilty of "making" the images when he downloads them from the internet onto his screen[141]).

In *Graham-Kerr*,[142] in the context of an image taken by camera, the Court   **8.92** said that "the photograph" means "the photograph of the subject as ultimately disclosed by the photograph produced." Proving that the defendant intended to take the indecent photograph actually taken could in principle be difficult in cases where the subject was moving at the relevant time. However, in the light of *Smith and Jayson* it should be sufficient to prove that the defendant knew the photograph he took was *likely* to be indecent, i.e. notwithstanding the subject might move between the time the shutter release was depressed and the moment the image was captured by the camera. This problem in fact arose before *Smith and Jayson* in the case of

---

[135] [2003] 1 Cr. App. R. 212, followed in *Smart v HM Advocate*, 2007 J.C. 119; and see *Graham-Kerr* [1988] 1 W.L.R. 1098, CA; *Atkins v DPP* [2000] 2 Cr. App. R. 248.

[136] *Smethhurst* [2002] 1 Cr. App. R. 6, rejecting an argument based on art.10 ECHR.

[137] *Steen (George)* [2011] EWCA Crim 461.

[138] *Smith and Jayson* [2003] 1 Cr. App. R. 212.

[139] *Graham-Kerr* [1988] 1 W.L.R. 1098 at 1106; *Smethhurst* [2002] 1 Cr. App. R. 6 at 21.

[140] *Atkins v DPP* [2000] 2 Cr. App. R. 248.

[141] *Smith and Jayson* [2003] 1 Cr. App. R. 212.

[142] [1988] 1 W.L.R. 1098 at 1105.

Fowler,[143] where HH Judge Rodwell QC declined to exclude a particular photograph on the ground that (as the prosecution expert accepted) the subject had moved whilst it was being taken. The judge's ruling was, with respect, correct, on the basis that there was evidence from which the jury could find that the defendant knew the child was moving at the time he depressed the shutter release and that he must have known that the resulting image was likely to be indecent. Any other approach would risk frustrating the purpose of s.1(1)(a) in a case where a paedophile randomly takes photographs of moving children, in circumstances in which he expects that some at least of the resulting photographs will be indecent.

8.93   Where there is material before the jury from which they could come to the conclusion that the defendant did not know at the time of making the images that they were or were likely to be of children, the judge should specifically direct the jury on this possibility. This is so even if the defendant does not give evidence on the point. Thus in *Steen (George)*[144] the appellant was prosecuted for making indecent images of children that had been found on his laptop. He claimed in interview that he thought all the images he had downloaded were of adult women. At trial he gave no evidence and called no witnesses. The Court of Appeal quashed his convictions on the basis that there was material which required the judge to deal with the possibility that he might have downloaded the images without knowing at that time that they involved children. Although the defence had not focused on this point, it was nonetheless a potential defence[145] and had to be left specifically for the jury to determine. Whilst the evidence very strongly suggested that they would have found that the requirement was satisfied, the Court was unable to say that they were bound so to have concluded.

Section 1(1)(a)—permitting an indecent photograph or pseudo-photograph to be taken

8.94   Although the courts have not been entirely consistent in their interpretation of the word "permit" where it appears in statute, they have frequently held that it imports a requirement of mens rea.[146] The better view is that this interpretation should be followed in relation to s.1(1)(a), so that a defendant may be convicted of permitting an indecent photograph of a child to be taken only if he knew or deliberately shut his eyes to the fact that the photograph was being taken.

---

[143] Unreported, September 20–27, 1994 (Luton Crown Ct. HH Judge Rodwell QC). The authors are indebted to Kate Mallison, barrister, for drawing the case to their attention.

[144] [2011] EWCA Crim 461.

[145] It was not, of course, strictly a potential defence; rather, the prosecution could not secure a conviction without disproving it.

[146] cf. *James & Son Ltd v Smee* [1955] 1 Q.B. 78; *Grays Haulage Co. Ltd v Arnold* [1966] 1 W.L.R. 534; *Souter* [1971] 1 W.L.R. 1187; and see Smith and Hogan, *Criminal Law* 14th edn, (Oxford: OUP, 2015), pp.184–185.

Section 1(1)(b)—distributing or showing indecent photographs or pseudo-photographs

It was held in *Price*[147] that the offence in s.1(1)(b) is one of strict liability, subject only to the statutory defences in s.1(4), discussed in paras 8.86 and following, above. Accordingly the prosecution need not prove that the defendant knowingly distributed or showed indecent photographs, only that he in fact did so; but the defendant will have a defence if he proves that he had not himself seen the photographs and did not know, nor had any cause to suspect, that they were indecent, or were indecent photographs of children.   **8.95**

Section 1(1)(c)—possession of indecent photographs or pseudo-photograph with a view to their being distributed or shown

"Possession" involves both a physical and a mental element. The physical element, addressed in para.8.71, above, constitutes custody or control. The mental element is knowledge,[148] and accordingly the defendant must knowingly have custody or control of the item before he can be said to possess it. What may constitute "knowledge" for this purpose? In *Matrix (Billy)*,[149] a sales assistant in a video shop who knew that the stock included sexually explicit material, but not that it depicted children, was held to have sufficient knowledge of the content of the relevant videos to be in "possession" of them for the purposes of s.1(1)(c). The Court said that whether a person is in possession of an item is a question of fact and degree for the jury. Citing cases decided under drugs legislation,[150] it said that a person does not possess something which has been "planted" on him, e.g. put into his pocket or his house without his knowledge. But a mere mistake as to the quality of a thing under his control is not enough to prevent him being in possession, e.g. where a person is in possession of heroin believing it to be cannabis or an aspirin. The present case was analogous to this example. The Court said that the difficult question of degree is at what point a difference in qualities amounts to a difference in kind, though this question did not arise on the facts before it.   **8.96**

A contrasting case is *Atkins v DPP*,[151] where A was held not to be in possession of indecent images which he had been viewing on the internet   **8.97**

---

[147] [2006] EWCA Crim 3363.
[148] *Atkins v DPP* [2000] 2 Cr. App. R. 248; *Porter* [2006] EWCA Crim 3363.
[149] [1997] EWCA Crim 2058; [1997] Crim. L.R. 901. For similar cases in the context of drugs offences see *Marriott* [1971] 1 W.L.R. 187; *Boyesen* [1982] A.C. 768.
[150] *Warner v Metropolitan Police Commissioner* [1969] 2 A.C. 256; *McNamara* (1988) 87 Cr. App. R. 246.
[151] [2000] 2 Cr. App. R. 248; and see Steele [1993] Crim. L.R. 298. For US authorities to the same effect as *Atkins v DPP*; *Goodland v DPP*, see *US v Kuchinski (John Charles)* (November 27, 2006) (9th Cir. (US)) and *US v Diodoro (Anthony)* (November 2, 2006) (Pennsylvania), discussed in C.T.L.R. 2007, 13(3), pp.63–4.

when, unknown to him, they were stored automatically by his browser on the cache of his computer. This is analogous to the "planting" example given in *Matrix (Billy)*. But the Court also held that in such a case, the transient downloading of the images onto the screen would be sufficient to constitute either possession or the "making" offence under s.1(1)(a).

8.98   As we have already seen, by virtue of s.1(4)(b) a person has a defence to the s.1(1)(c) offence if he had not seen the photograph and did not know, nor had any cause to suspect, that it was indecent, or that it was an indecent photograph of a child.[152] The existence of this defence necessarily means that a person may possess an indecent photograph for the purposes of s.1(1)(c) even if he has not looked at it and so does not know it is indecent, or is of a child; otherwise, the defence would be redundant.[153] In *Land*,[154] it was held that where the defence in s.1(4)(b) is not available because the defendant has seen the photograph, the prosecution may secure a conviction under s.1(1)(c) by proving that he knew he was in possession of an indecent photograph, without proof that he knew the photograph to be of a child. In other words, *Land* establishes that in cases where the defendant has seen the photograph, there is strict liability as to the age of the subject and the defendant carries the risk that the subject is a child. We question whether this is just. To impose strict liability as to age here appears inconsistent with the approach taken by the House of Lords to the same issue, albeit in a somewhat different context, in *B v DPP*.[155] We submit that if the defendant, having seen the photograph, honestly believes that it is of an adult, this should preclude his conviction.

8.99   A person does not cease to have possession of indecent photographs or pseudo-photographs because he forgets that he has them[156] or believes them to have been destroyed or disposed of, e.g. if he wrongly thinks he has permanently deleted them from his computer.[157]

8.100   The words "with a view to" in s.1(1)(c) involve an additional requirement of intention.[158] The meaning of these words was considered in *Dooley*,[159] in which the appellant had been a member of an internet file-sharing network, Kazaa, that enabled users to share any type of computer file. Users became

---

[152] *Collier* [2004] EWCA Crim 1411, discussed in para.8.89, above.

[153] The reasoning in this sentence provides a more direct route than was used in *Matrix (Billy)* [1997] EWCA Crim 2058, discussed in para.8.96, above, to establishing that a defendant who knows images are indecent, but not that they involve children, has possession of them for the purposes of s.1(1)(b). The reasoning was not used in *Matrix*, as the Court in that case held that the s.1(4)(b) defence was not available to the appellant. In this respect the decision is inconsistent with *Collier*, last note; and although it was not referred to in *Collier*, we suggest it should be regarded as unreliable as regards the availability of the defence.

[154] [1998] 1 Cr. App. R. 301, considered in *Collier* [2004] EWCA Crim 1411; and see *Arnott v McFadyen*, 2002 S.C.C.R. 96, HCJ Appeal.

[155] [2000] 1 All E.R. 833.

[156] cf. *Buswell* [1972] 1 W.L.R. 64; *Martindale* [1986] 1 W.L.R. 1042 (where the defendant forgot he had the item in his wallet).

[157] *Atkins v DPP* [2000] 2 Cr. App. R. 248 at 262.

[158] *Graham-Kerr* [1988] 1 W.L.R. 1098.

[159] [2005] EWCA Crim 3093.

part of the network by downloading the necessary software from the internet. All members had a "My Shared Folder", the files in which, when the computer was connected to the internet, could be accessed by any Kazaa member and downloaded to their own "My Shared Folder". A police search of the appellant's home found on his computer several thousand indecent images of children which had been obtained using Kazaa. Six images (to which the indictment related) were found in the appellant's "My Shared Folder", where they had been for 10 days. His case was that whenever he had downloaded images from the system, he had transferred them from his "My Shared Folder" to another part of his computer where they would not be accessible by others; and this had been his intention in relation to the six images that had remained in his "My Shared Folder", but he simply had not removed them by the time of the police search.

In a pre-trial ruling, the judge held that the words "with a view to" in **8.101** s.1(1)(c) required the prosecution to prove only that, when the appellant had downloaded a particular photograph, he had done so in the knowledge that it was likely to be seen by other members of the file-sharing system. The appellant's case that he had not intended to distribute or show the six images could therefore provide him only with mitigation. Following this ruling the appellant pleaded guilty. He appealed successfully to the Court of Appeal, which held that a person does X "with a view to" doing Y if one of his reasons for doing X is to do Y, even if it is not his primary reason. Thus, in a case such as *Dooley*, although it may be very important to examine the defendant's knowledge in the way the judge had done, the question for the jury is not whether it was likely that the images would be seen by others, but whether at least one of the reasons why the appellant had left the images in his "My Shared Folder" was so that others could have access to them. If, and only if, that were so would he be in possession of those images with a view to their being distributed or shown by himself.

The appellant in *Dooley* knew that the files in his "My Shared Folder" **8.102** were accessible by other members of the Kazaa network, as that was the way he had built up his own collection of images. This knowledge was powerful evidence from which the jury might properly infer that one of his reasons for keeping material in the folder was to distribute it to or share it with others. Also relevant in this context is *Peebles v HM Advocate*,[160] in which *Dooley* was cited with approval. The appellant in that case was convicted of the Scottish equivalent of the s.1(1)(c) offence, contained in s.52(1)(c) of the Civic Government (Scotland) Act 1982. He had also downloaded the Kazaa software from the internet and stored indecent images in his "My Shared Folder". There was evidence before the court that when installing the software, he had enabled the file-sharing function. One ground of appeal was

---

[160] [2007] HCJAC 6.

that there was no evidence of mens rea, but the appellant abandoned this ground during argument before the High Court of Justiciary. The Court observed that the evidence that the appellant had enabled the file-sharing function entitled the jury to infer that one of his reasons for so doing was to allow others to have access to the files in his "My Shared Folder". On that basis they could properly conclude that he held the files with a view to their being distributed or shown by himself.

8.103   The words "with a view to" comprise a mental element going beyond the prohibited act to the consequences of that act, and on the reasoning in *Heard*,[161] discussed in paras 2.81 and following, above, this serves to confirm that the s.1(1)(c) offence is one of specific intent. Accordingly, self-induced intoxication will provide a defence if it prevented the defendant forming an intention to distribute or share the images. Where intoxication may be an issue, a charge of simple possession under s.160(1) of the Criminal Justice Act 1988 should be brought instead.

Section 1(1)(d)—publishing or causing to be published an advertisement

8.104   It follows by analogy with the "making" offence under s.1(1)(a) of the 1978 Act that, on a charge under s.1(1)(d) of publishing an advertisement relating to indecent photographs or pseudo-photographs, the prosecution must prove that the defendant published the advertisement intentionally. On a charge of causing an advertisement to be published, it is unclear what mental element is required. In principle the word "causes" should be interpreted as importing a requirement of mens rea, but the law on this point is not settled.[162]

FORENSIC EVIDENCE

8.105   Many prosecutions under the 1978 Act depend upon the evidence produced by forensic analysis of computers and other digital devices. This is an area where specialist IT skills are vital if evidence is to be effectively secured: the mere act of switching on a computer to determine its ownership or the relevance of its contents may, for example, fatally compromise any prospect of obtaining evidence from it, since this act will change and overwrite many files. The deployment of an IT expert will not guarantee evidential integrity unless the expert undertakes the task in an appropriate manner. Although

---

[161] [2007] EWCA Crim 125.
[162] Compare *Lovelace v DPP* [1954] 1 W.L.R. 1468 (mens rea required) with *Sopp v Long* [1970] 1 Q.B. 518 (mens rea not required). In *Ross Hillman Ltd v Bond* [1974] Q.B. 435, DC, applied in *Cambridgeshire CC v Associated Lead Mills Ltd* [2005] EWHC 1627 (Admin), the Court said that *Lovelace* and *Sopp* are irreconcilable and that the former is to be preferred.

there are no nationally agreed or approved standards for specialist IT investigators called on to handle paedophile material, the Association of Chief Police Officers (ACPO) has produced guidelines for the police examination of digital evidence.[163] These guidelines remain in effect and are generally followed by independent analysts; any departure from them is likely to be a fruitful source of cross-examination.[164]

It was held in *R. (O) v Coventry Magistrates' Court*[165] that a computer **8.106** printout recording successful and unsuccessful attempts to enter a website containing commercial child pornography did not constitute hearsay and was admissible as real evidence. The claimant was charged with inciting and attempting to incite the distribution of indecent photographs of children. The computer printout was the principal evidence against him. The credit card details and home and email addresses in the printout were the same as the claimant's. The claimant argued that this was insufficient to connect him to the offence. It was held that in order to establish a prima facie case, what the prosecutor has to show is that there is evidence to prove the essential elements of the case. The prosecutor in this case had discharged that burden by adducing the printout. Once there was evidence to show that the credit card details were the claimant's, that was enough to justify an inference that he was the perpetrator.

In *Skinner*,[166] the Court of Appeal was required to consider whether **8.107** information copied from one website to another and adduced in the form of a printed screen image amounted to real evidence admissible under s.27 of the Criminal Justice Act 1988 (since replaced by s.133 of the Criminal Justice Act 2003). The appellant was convicted of possessing indecent images of children contrary to s.160(1) of the Criminal Justice Act 1988, the images having been found on CDs at his home. His defence was that he had found the discs but had been unable to open them and had not known or had cause to suspect that they contained indecent images of children. To rebut this defence, the Crown sought to adduce exhibit "SR1", which comprised printouts of screen images from the Kazaa website (for which see para.8.100, above). These showed that a user identifying himself as "Poloman@Kazaa" had offered for access by others on the website certain files with names indicative of child pornographic content. Superimposed on one of the screen

---

[163] *Good Practice Guide for Digital Evidence*, available at *http://www.digital-detective.net/acpo-good-practice-guide-for-digital-evidence/* [Accessed April 30, 2016]. For a discussion of the ACPO Guide and the issues which may arise when digital evidence is adduced in court, see Colin Smith, *Is Digital Evidence Really Forensic?*, *Counsel* magazine, January 2012, pp.27–28. More generally, see Micheál O'Floinn and David Ormerod, *Social Networking Material as Criminal Evidence* [2012] Crim. L.R. 486.

[164] See generally Phil Bowles, *An Expert Witness View on Access to Child Pornography*, *Criminal Bar Association Newsletter*, Issue 3, September 2003, pp.13–14.

[165] [2004] Crim. L.R. 948, DC.

[166] [2005] EWCA Crim 1439.

images was a smaller window containing material in DOS format, which revealed the internet protocol address of "Poloman@Kazaa". Inquiries of BT had identified the appellant as the offeror, and this prompted the search of his home.

8.108   The issue at trial was whether exhibit SR1 was admissible in evidence. On a *voir dire*, the police officer who printed out the screen images gave evidence that he had accessed them by entering a secure website, but he refused to identify the website, saying that there was a "source" involved; he did not know whether the source was an individual or a facility; he could not tell how the information was posted onto the secure website or whether one or a number of persons were involved; the information had been copied from a Word document, so he could not tell whether it had been altered; and he could not say whether the information had been received by another source and posted by a second or third person onto the website from which he had obtained it. The judge permitted SR1 to be adduced on the ground that it was real evidence and not hearsay. He considered s.27 of the Criminal Justice Act 1988, which provided that, where a statement contained in a document was admissible in evidence, it might be proved by production of the document or a copy thereof (or the material part of it) authenticated in such manner as the court may approve, it being irrelevant for this purpose how many removes there were between the copy and the original. The judge ruled that the original for these purposes was what appeared on the Kazaa site screen. It had been copied to a site that the prosecution declined to identify and then to a police computer and printed out. He held that this was entirely within the process contemplated by s.27.

8.109   The appellant was convicted and challenged his conviction on the basis that SR1 should not have been admitted, for two reasons: first, because copying the screen images electronically to another computer or website rendered them hearsay, and secondly, because there had been no evidence to explain the process by which the original screen image had come to be on the police computer, and no public interest immunity ruling to the effect that such an explanation need not be given. The Court of Appeal said that the screen images had probably (and it emphasised the word "probably") been real evidence rather than hearsay. This was so despite their being copied from the original website, because their content neither required nor acquired any human input other than that of a person responsible for the content of the website in the first place. As for s.27 of the 1988 Act, the case did not involve the straightforward use of a computer and the police officer did not give and was unable to give any proper explanation of the electronic process involved. That being the case, there had been no material upon which the judge could properly have concluded that the images were authentic in a manner which he might approve. The Court nonetheless went on to hold the appellant's conviction safe on the basis that the screen images could have had only a limited influence on the outcome of the trial, given the other evidence before the court.

The admissibility of copy documents is now regulated by s.133 of the   **8.110**
Criminal Justice Act 2003, which replaces s.27 of the 1988 Act and provides
as follows:

> "Where a statement in a document is admissible as evidence in criminal
> proceedings, the statement may be proved by producing either
>   (a) the document, or
>   (b) (whether or not the document exists) a copy of the document or of the
>   material part of it,
> authenticated in whatever way the court may approve."

Section 133 is intended to cover all forms of copying, including the use of
imaging technology.[167] Of course, even if the requirements of s.133 are met in
relation to a document copied in this way, the defendant may argue that the
evidence establishes a link with the relevant computer, but not with him, if
others may have had access to the machine.

Finally, where a party to criminal proceedings seeks to adduce in evidence   **8.111**
a representation of fact made otherwise than by a person, they must now
satisfy the accuracy safeguard introduced by s.129 of the Criminal Justice Act
2003:

> "(1) Where a representation of any fact—
>   (a) is made otherwise than by a person, but
>   (b) depends for its accuracy on information supplied (directly or indirectly) by
>   a person,
> the representation is not admissible in criminal proceedings as evidence of the
> fact unless it is proved that the information was accurate."

This safeguard will apply in relation to computer-generated evidence where
the accuracy of the evidence depends on information inputted by a person,
such as the date and time a file was created or sent. In such cases, compliance
with the safeguard in s.129 may be very difficult.

RECOVERY OF ENCRYPTED IMAGES

Suppose the police suspect an individual of holding indecent images of   **8.112**
children on a computer or other digital storage medium, but are unable to
gain access to the contents of the relevant files because they are protected by
a password or some form of encryption? In those circumstances, they may be
able to compel the individual to disclose the password or encryption key by
service of a notice under s.49 of the Regulation of Investigatory Powers Act
2000 ("RIPA").

Section 49 enables a properly authorised person, who may be a police   **8.113**
officer, to serve a notice on an individual or body requiring them to disclose
"protected information" in an intelligible form. Protected information is
defined as any electronic data which cannot, or cannot readily, be accessed or
put into an intelligible form without the key to the data. Section 49 applies

---

[167] Explanatory Notes, para.436.

inter alia where the police have come into possession of protected information in the exercise of a statutory power to seize, detain, inspect, search or otherwise to interfere with documents or other property, e.g. on the execution of a search warrant issued under the Police and Criminal Evidence Act 1984. In those circumstances an officer with the "appropriate permission" (as defined in Sch.2 to RIPA) may serve a s.49 notice requiring disclosure of protected information if he believes, on reasonable grounds:

- that the person on whom the notice is served has a key to the protected information in their possession;
- that the imposition of a disclosure requirement in respect of the protected information is necessary in the interests of national security, for the purpose of preventing or detecting crime, in the interests of the economic well-being of the UK, or for the purpose of securing the effective exercise or proper performance by a public authority of any statutory power or duty;
- that imposing a disclosure requirement is proportionate to what is sought to be achieved by doing so; and
- that it is not reasonably practicable to obtain the protected information in an intelligible form in any other way.
  A notice under s.49:
- must be given in writing or in a manner that produces a record of its having been given;
- must describe the protected information to which it relates;
- must specify the grounds on which the notice is given;
- must specify the office, rank or position held by the person giving it;
- must specify the office, rank or position of the person who granted permission for the notice to be given;
- must specify the time by which the notice is to be complied with;
- must set out the disclosure that is required by the notice and the form and manner in which it is to be made; and
- must allow a period for compliance which is reasonable in all the circumstances.

8.114   Section 50 of RIPA explains the effect of serving a notice. Where the recipient has, when the notice is served, possession of the protected information and a means of accessing it and of disclosing it in an intelligible form, the effect of the notice is that they may use any key in their possession (such as a password, code, algorithm or encryption key) to access the information or to put it into intelligible form and they must disclose the information in an intelligible form in accordance with the terms of the notice. Provision is made for a person who is required to disclose information in an intelligible form to instead disclose a relevant key if they so choose. Where the recipient of the notice does not have possession of the protected information, or of a key needed to access it, or the notice contains a direction (pursuant to s.51, below) that a key must be disclosed, the recipient must disclose any key to the information that is in their possession. The person giving the notice may allow the recipient access to the protected information in order to enable them to produce plain text rather than disclose a key. The recipient need only provide those keys which suffice to access the information and render it intelligible, and may choose which keys to provide to achieve that end. Where they no longer possess a key to the information, they must disclose all information in their possession that would facilitate the discovery of the key.

Section 51 sets out extra tests that are to be satisfied if a notice requires   **8.115** disclosure of a key rather than of protected information in an intelligible form. Such a notice may be given only if a direction to this effect has been given by the person giving permission for the notice to be served. A direction for the disclosure of a key must be authorised expressly by a person of the rank of chief officer of police or equivalent. A person may only give such a direction if he believes that there are special circumstances to the case making this necessary; and that giving such a direction is proportionate to what is sought to be achieved by doing so. In deciding whether it is proportionate to require that a key be disclosed, consideration must be given to the other sorts of information protected by the key in question and any potential adverse impact on a business that might result from requiring that a key be disclosed. Any direction to disclose a key given by the police must be notified, within seven days, to the Chief Surveillance Commissioner.

Section 53 of RIPA makes it an offence knowingly to fail to comply with   **8.116** the disclosure requirements contained in a s.49 notice. It is a defence for a person to show that it was not practicable to comply with the disclosure requirement placed upon him by the time he was required to do so, but that he did what was required as soon as was reasonably practicable. There is no maximum penalty on conviction on indictment, but on summary conviction the maximum is a fine of £5,000.

The service of a s.49 notice may be capable of engaging the recipient's   **8.117** privilege against self-incrimination. This issue arose for consideration in *Greater Manchester Police v Andrews*,[168] in which the respondent was arrested on suspicion of committing offences under s.1(1)(a) of the 1978 Act by making indecent images of children. His laptop was seized together with two pen drives. The laptop contained indecent images of children and the police wished to know what was on the pen drives, but they were unable to access the files contained in them. The respondent declined to provide any information as to the passwords and software applications that he had used to protect the files. The police therefore applied to a circuit judge for permission to serve on the respondent an order under s.49 of the Regulation of Investigatory Powers Act 2000 requiring him to disclose encryption keys to the pen drives. The judge refused permission on the ground that requiring the respondent to reveal the keys would be incompatible with his privilege

---

[168] [2011] EWHC 1966 (Admin), following *R. v S* [2008] EWCA Crim 2177.

against self-incrimination, since if by complying with the notice he revealed his knowledge of the keys, this would itself be an incriminating fact which had no existence independent of the recipient's will.[169] The Administrative Court allowed an appeal against this ruling, holding that an application for permission to serve a notice under s.49 engages the privilege against self-incrimination only to a very limited extent, and that in this case the interference with the privilege was entirely proportionate (within the meaning of s.49(2)(c) of the Act) to what the police were seeking to achieve, namely the protection of the public from crime. In reaching this decision the Court noted that at any trial following service of the notice, the judge would be empowered to exclude evidence of material discovered on the pen drives, of the keys or other means of access to the drives, and of the respondent's knowledge of those keys or means of access, as in the judge's discretion seemed appropriate in order to preserve the respondent's privilege against self-incrimination.

Perverting the Course of Justice by Deleting Indecent Images

8.118   In *T v R.*,[170] the appellant was charged with doing an act tending and intended to pervert the course of public justice on evidence that she had deleted files with titles indicative of child pornography from a memory stick belonging to her husband. The husband had been convicted some years before of downloading indecent images of children from the internet and was still a registered sex offender. The appellant's daughter was looking for a memory stick on which to download homework from her laptop. The appellant told her to look for one in a drawer where she (the daughter) found one. The appellant maintained that, when her daughter plugged the memory stick into her laptop, she had seen one file the title of which was something like "16 Sex". She had deleted it thinking it was adult pornography, so that her daughter would not see it. A computer expert later recovered from the memory stick three deleted files with titles indicative of child pornography, though the files did not contain any such material. The prosecution case was that the appellant had deleted these files with the intention of preventing a potential criminal investigation of her husband. The appellant was convicted and appealed on two grounds. First, the computer expert had been able to retrieve the names and contents of the deleted files, so there was no evidence that the appellant's deletion of the files tended to pervert the course of justice.

---

[169] cf. *Saunders v UK* (1996) 23 E.H.R.R. 313, where the European Court of Human Rights said (at 358) "[T]he right not to incriminate oneself . . . does not extend to the use in criminal proceedings of material which may be obtained from the accused through compulsory powers but which have an existence independent of the will of the suspect, such as, inter alia, documents acquired pursuant to a warrant, breath, blood and urine samples and bodily tissue for the purpose of DNA testing."

[170] [2011] EWCA Crim 729.

Secondly, given the inoffensive content of the files, there was insufficient evidence that their deletion did tend to pervert the course of justice. The appeal was dismissed. The Court of Appeal said that for the offence to be proved it must be established both that the defendant intended to pervert the course of justice and that the act in question tended to do so. In this case there was clear evidence that the appellant intended to pervert the course of justice by deleting the files, in order, as she must be taken to have thought, to render them unavailable to the police. The jury must be assumed to have found that she lied about the names of the files on the memory stick. Those lies, and the deletion of the files, were sufficient to justify the jury's finding of intent. As for the requirement that the act tended to pervert the course of justice, the Court said that it is not necessary to establish that the act did in fact affect the course of justice; it is sufficient that it created a serious risk that the course of justice would be affected. The course of justice includes the investigation by the police of a possible crime. An act that makes such an investigation more difficult, or which may mislead it, may tend to pervert the course of justice. Further, it is irrelevant that the act may be prejudicial to a potential defendant rather than to the police or the prosecuting authorities. For that reason, it did not matter that the files in this case, despite their titles, did not in fact contain child pornography. For similar reasons, the fact that the files were in the event recovered by a computer expert did not mean that their deletion could not be effective; in fact, if there had been sufficient use of the memory stick before the expert examined it, the files would have been overwritten and irrecoverable. For these reasons, the appellant had been rightly convicted.

POSSESSION OF AN INDECENT PHOTOGRAPH OR PSEUDO-PHOTOGRAPH OF A CHILD

DEFINITION

Section 160(1) of the Criminal Justice Act 1988[171] provides: **8.119**

"Subject to subsection (1A), it is an offence for a person to have any indecent photograph or pseudo-photograph of a child in his possession."

MODE OF TRIAL AND PUNISHMENT

The offence in s.160(1) was originally summary only, but became triable either way from January 11, 2001.[172] The maximum punishment on trial on **8.120**

---

[171] As amended by the Criminal Justice and Public Order Act 1994 s.84(1), (4), with effect from February 3, 1995 and by the Sexual Offences Act 2003 s.139 and Sch.6, para.29, with effect from May 1, 2004.
[172] See the Criminal Justice and Court Services Act 2000.

indictment is five years' imprisonment or a fine, or both.[173] The maximum punishment on summary conviction is six months' imprisonment or a fine, or both.[174] As from a day to be appointed the maximum sentence of imprisonment on summary conviction will increase to 12 months.[175] The increase will have no application to offences committed before it takes effect.[176] Until recently, the maximum fine on summary conviction was a fine not exceeding level 5 on the standard scale (i.e. £5,000). The effect of s.85 of the Legal Aid, Sentencing and Punishment of Offenders Act 2012 is that, from March 12, 2015, a fine of any amount may be imposed. Fines will, however, continue to be set according to the seriousness of the offence and the means of the offender. An offence under s.160(1) cannot be dealt with by way of a simple caution.[177]

8.121   A person convicted under s.160(1), cautioned, found not guilty by reason of insanity or found to be under a disability and to have done the act charged, is automatically subject to the notification requirements in the Sexual Offences Act 2003 if the images showed persons under 16 and the offender was 18 or over at the time of the offence or is sentenced to at least 12 months' imprisonment.[178]

8.122   Where a justice of the peace is satisfied by information on oath, laid by or on behalf of the DPP or by a constable, that there is reasonable ground for suspecting that, in any premises, there is an indecent photograph or pseudo-photograph of a child, the justice may issue a warrant authorising a constable to enter (if need be by force) and search the premises and to seize and remove any articles which he believes (with reasonable cause) to be or include such photographs or pseudo-photographs.[179] There is also provision for a magistrates' court to order the forfeiture of such items.[180]

Restriction on prosecution

8.123   Section 1(3) of the Protection of Children Act 1978, which provides that proceedings under the 1978 Act shall not be instituted except by or with the consent of the DPP, also has effect for the purposes of s.160(1) of the 1988 Act.[181] See further paras 8.09 and following, above.

---

[173] 1988 Act, s.160(2A), inserted by the Criminal Justice and Court Services Act 2000 s.41(3), which was brought into force on January 11, 2001, by SI 2000/3302. There is no transitional provision in the 2000 Act or SI 2000/3302, but the combined effect of s.3 of the Human Rights Act 1998 and art.7 of the ECHR is to require that the increased penalty applies only to offences committed on or after the commencement date.

[174] 1988 Act s.160(3), as amended by the Criminal Justice and Public Order Act 1994 s.86(1), with effect from February 3, 1995. The original maximum was a fine not exceeding level 5.

[175] Criminal Justice Act 2003 s.282(2), (3).

[176] Criminal Justice Act 2003 s.282(4).

[177] Criminal Justice and Courts Act 2015 s.17(3), and the Criminal Justice and Courts Act 2015 (Simple Cautions) (Specification of Either-Way Offences) Order 2015 (SI 2015/790).

[178] s.80 and Sch.3, discussed in Ch.35, below.

[179] 1978 Act s.4.

[180] 1978 Act s.5 and Sch.

[181] 1988 Act s.160(4).

Form of Charge or Indictment

In *Thompson*,[182] the Court of Appeal gave the following guidance as to the   **8.124**
drafting of the indictment (or information) in proceedings under s.160(1),
which is equally applicable to proceedings under the 1978 Act[183]:
   i) In cases where there are significant numbers of photographs, in
      addition to the specific counts, the inclusion of a comprehensive
      count covering the remainder is a practice that should be fol-
      lowed;
  ii) The photographs used in the specific counts should, if it is
      practicable, be selected so as to be broadly representative of the
      images in the comprehensive count. If agreement can then be
      reached between the parties that (say) 5 images in Category C, 10 in
      Category B, and 2 in Category C represent 500 Category C, 100
      Category B and 200 Category A images in the comprehensive count
      of 800 images, the need for the judge to view the entirety of the
      offending material may be avoided;
 iii) Where it is impractical to present the court with specific counts that
      are agreed to be representative of the comprehensive count, there
      must be available to the court an approximate breakdown of the
      number of images in each of the categories. This may best be
      achieved by the prosecution providing the defence with a schedule
      setting out the information and ensuring that the defence have an
      opportunity, well in advance of the sentencing hearing, of viewing
      the images and checking the accuracy of the schedule;
  iv) Each of the specific counts should, in accordance with what was
      stated by the Court in *Oliver, Hartrey and Baldwin*[184] make it clear
      whether the image in question is a real image or a pseudo-image;
      the same count should not charge both. As the Court pointed out
      in *Oliver, Hartrey and Baldwin* there may be a significant difference
      between the two and where there is a dispute, then there should be
      alternative counts. In the majority of cases there will be no doubt as

---

[182] [2004] EWCA Crim 669.

[183] The guidance in *Thompson* in fact refers to the old system under which indecent images were classified by reference to five levels of seriousness (1–5). That system was replaced in the Sentencing Council's sentencing guideline with a new system in which there are three categories of images (A–C), and in the text we have updated the *Thompson* guidance accordingly.

[184] [2003] 1 Cr. App. R. 28, at 15: "It will usually be desirable that a charge or count in an indictment specifies whether photographs or pseudo-photographs are involved." This statement reflected the Court's view that the making and possession of pseudo-photographs should generally be treated as being less serious than making or possessing photographic images of real children. Although there is nothing to this effect in the Sentencing Council guideline, which treats all images (whether photographs or pseudo-photographs) in the same way, there may nonetheless be cases in which it is appropriate for the court to regard an offence as mitigated by the fact that it involves a pseudo-photograph rather than a photograph. As such, we suggest that the guidance as to the drafting of charges and counts given in *Oliver, Hartrey and Baldwin* remains valid and should be followed.

to whether the image in question should be dealt with either as a
real image or a pseudo-image;

v) Each image charged in a specific count should be identified by
reference to its "jpg" or other reference so that it is clear with which
image the specific count is dealing;

vi) The estimated age range of the child shown in each of the images
should where possible be provided to the court.

8.125   There will be a natural desire in indecent photograph cases not to overload
the indictment and, as indicated in *Thompson*, this is likely to put a premium
on the use of specimen counts. However, care must be taken not to under-
weight the indictment; it is important that the defendant's full criminality is
adequately represented. The dangers in relying heavily on specimen counts
are illustrated by *Fox*.[185] The appellant had been convicted of, inter alia, two
counts of taking indecent photographs of a child contrary to s.1(1)(a) of the
Act. Two photographs had been specified in the particulars of the indictment
as sample counts. The jury was provided with a bundle of photographs
relating to each count. The trial judge directed the jury that they could
convict provided they were sure that at least one photograph in each bundle
was indecent. The Court of Appeal quashed the convictions on the ground
that the jury should have been directed that in order to convict on either
count, they had to be sure that the photograph specified in that count was
indecent. The trial judge's direction allowed for the possibility that different
jurors might have different views on which photograph they considered
indecent and it may have been that the jury did not consider the photograph
specified in the indictment to be indecent.

Sentencing

8.126   For the Sentencing Council guideline relating to the sentencing of sexual
offences committed by offenders aged 18 and over, see Ch.33. A single
guideline covers offences relating to indecent images of children and is
discussed in paras 8.15 and following, above.

Parties to the Offence

8.127   The offence may be committed as principal by persons of either sex and by
corporations.[186] The subject of the photograph or pseudo-photograph must
be a person under the age of 18; this requirement is considered in paras 8.57
and following, above. As to whether the child depicted in the photograph or
another child may be convicted as an accessory to the s.160(1) offence, see
para.8.40, above.

---

[185] [2009] EWCA Crim 653.
[186] For corporations, see below.

Jurisdiction

By virtue of s.72 of and Sch.2 to the Sexual Offences Act 2003, as amended,[187] it is an offence under s.160(1) for a UK national to do an act in a country outside the UK which would constitute an offence under s.160(1) if done in England and Wales. See further para.8.41, above.   **8.128**

Officers of corporations

Section 3 of the Protection of Children Act 1978, which makes provision for the officers of corporations convicted under that Act to be themselves proceeded against and punished, also has effect for the purposes of s.160(1). See further paras 8.42 and following, above.   **8.129**

"Indecent Photograph or Pseudo-photograph"

See paras 8.52 and following, above, discussing the meaning of these words in the Protection of Children Act 1978. Section 7 of the 1978 Act, which contains a partial definition of the phrase "indecent photograph" and a definition of the phrase "pseudo-photograph", also has effect for the purposes of s.160(1).[188]   **8.130**

"Child"

For the purposes of s.160(1), "child" carries the same meaning as in the 1978 Act, i.e. a person under the age of 18.[189] A person attains the age of 18 at the commencement of the eighteenth anniversary of his or her birth.[190] The prosecution are not permitted to prove that the child was under 18 at the time of the alleged offence by inferences drawn from his or her present appearance.[191] They must therefore rely upon one of the other methods of proving age, for which see paras 3.74 and following, above.   **8.131**

As explained in para.8.58, above, a particular difficulty with many prosecutions under the 1978 Act is that the identity of the subject of the photograph cannot be discovered, so that his or her age cannot be proved by any of the normal methods. The same problem is liable to arise under s.160. A partial solution is provided by s.2(3) of the 1978 Act, which enables the   **8.132**

---

[187] By the Criminal Justice and Immigration Act 2008 s.72, with effect from July 14, 2008.

[188] 1988 Act s.160(4).

[189] 1988 Act s.160(4), applying s.7(6) of the 1978 Act. The definition in s.7(6) was amended by the Sexual Offences Act 2003 s.45(2), with effect from May 1, 2004, so as extend the protection given by the Act from those aged under 16 to those aged under 18.

[190] cf. s.7(6) of the Protection of Children Act 1978, which by virtue of s.160(4) of the 1988 Act also has effect for the purposes of s.160.

[191] Family Law Reform Act 1969 s.9(1). The rebuttable presumption as to age which is provided for in s.99(2) of the Children and Young Persons Act 1933 applies only to the offences listed in Sch.1 to the Act, which do not include the offence under s.160.

jury to infer that the subject was at the time aged under 18 from his or her appearance in the photograph, and from any other relevant evidence which may exist. This provision also has effect for the purposes of s.160.[192]

8.133   The extension of the definition of a "child" by s.45 of the Sexual Offences Act 2003 to include those aged 16 and 17 resulted in cases in which guilty pleas were tendered to offences involving indecent photographs of children on the basis that the subjects of the photographs were under 18 but not under 16. This was encouraged by the SGC guideline, which provided that offences relating to images of 16- and 17-years-olds were less serious than offences relating to images of those under 16, unless they were level 5 images. The current Sentencing Council guideline does not make such a stark distinction, though it acknowledges the (young) age of the child as an aggravating factor. In addition, offences involving images of 16- and 17-year-olds do not trigger the notification requirements under Pt 2 of the 2003 Act. Where a defendant pleads on the basis that the child was of or below a certain age, it will be for the judge to decide whether the images are of someone of or under that age.

"POSSESSION"

8.134   For the meaning of "possession", see paras 8.71 and 8.96 and following, above.

8.135   In *Porter*,[193] the Court of Appeal held that a person is in possession of an image in the form of a computer file if it is within his control, e.g. if he can produce it on his screen, make a hard copy of it or send it to someone else. In the case of a deleted image, if he cannot retrieve or access it in this way, he no longer has custody or control of it and so it is not within his possession. The Court said[194]:

> "[T]he first question for the jury is whether the defendant in a case of this kind has possession of the image at the relevant time, in the sense of custody or control of the image at that time. If at the alleged time of possession the image is beyond his control, then . . . he will not possess it. If, however, at that time the image is within his control, for example, because he has the ability to produce it on his screen, to make a hard copy of it, or to send it to someone else, then he will possess it. It will be a matter for the jury to decide whether images are beyond the control of the defendant having regard to all the factors in the case, including his knowledge and particular circumstances. Thus, images which have been emptied from the recycle bin may be considered to be within the control of a defendant who is skilled in the use of computers and in fact owns the software necessary to retrieve such images; whereas such images may be considered not to

---

[192] 1988 Act s.160(4).
[193] [2006] EWCA Crim 560.
[194] At 20–28.

be within the control of a defendant who does not possess these skills and does not own such software.

We acknowledge that this introduces a subjective element into the concept of physical possession. But we note that the defences provided by section 160(2) import a consideration of the knowledge and behaviour of the particular defendant. Moreover, on any view, an important element of subjectivity is introduced by the requirement of knowledge. It follows that this is not an area where Parliament has enacted an absolute offence. In these circumstances, we see no objection to interpreting the word 'possession' in the particular context of the possession of images in a computer as referring to images that are within the defendant's control.

It will, therefore, be a matter for the jury to decide whether images on a hard disk drive are within the control of the defendant, and to do so having regard to all the circumstances of the case. Such is the speed at which computer technology is developing that what a jury may consider not to be within a defendant's control today may be considered by a jury to be within a defendant's control in the near future. Further, in the course of time more and more people will become skilled in the use of computers. This too will be a relevant factor for the jury to take into account."

Professor David Ormerod QC has questioned whether the approach to **8.136** "possession" taken in *Porter* might have the undesirable effect of rendering arbitrary the application of the s.160(1) offence in deletion cases, by making liability turn on the defendant's ability to retrieve the deleted images.[195] Why, he asks, should the "defence" of deletion be available only to the computer illiterate? One might respond that liability should fall only where it is merited, and the Court of Appeal in *Porter* made a convincing case that in relation to deleted images, it should fall on the person who has the software and computing skills to call up the images, but not on the one who does not. In other words, the computer illiterate ought to be able to defeat a charge of possession because, whilst it may remain possible in theory for them to call up the images, in practice they lack the necessary computing skills and software to do so. If there is a problem with the Court's approach, it is rather the evidential complexity that it generates in deletion cases. The prosecution may well find it difficult to establish that the defendant has the computing skills necessary for liability (note that the appellant in *Porter* himself worked in IT) and expert evidence is likely to be necessary to establish just how retrievable the images are.

The decision in *Porter* applies only to "deleted" images, and for this **8.137** purpose it does not matter whether the images have been deleted from a hard drive or from a portable storage medium such as a memory stick.[196] It will be very rare that images remaining within a computer, e.g. in its internet cache, will become inaccessible or irretrievable such that the requirement of "possession" ceases to be met.

---

[195] [2006] Crim. L.R. 748.
[196] *Rowe* [2008] EWCA Crim 2712 (floppy disks).

8.138   It should be noted that the Court in *Porter* said the problem it had to address would not have arisen if the appellant had been charged with possession during the period from the time when he viewed the images[197] until he deleted them. There will, however, often be a practical difficulty with this suggestion. When an image is emptied from the computer's recycle bin, the operating system places it in the unallocated disc space of the hard disc drive, where it will remain unless and until it is overwritten by the saving of further data to the disc drive or the wiping of the data using file eraser software. However, while an image that has not been overwritten remains retrievable from the disc drive by specialist software, the file data, in the form of the dates of file creation, last modification and last access, are not retained. Accordingly, in the absence of other evidence, it will not be possible for the prosecution in a charge of possession to aver when the image was created and when it was deleted.

8.139   Other evidence to this effect did exist in *Miller*.[198] That case was tried before the decision in *Porter* and so the judge did not have the benefit of the legal analysis in that case and did not direct the jury accordingly. The defendant was convicted, but after *Porter* was decided the Criminal Cases Review Commission referred his conviction to the Court of Appeal. The Court noted that no evidence had been adduced at trial that the defendant had access to the kind of specialist software which could enable him to access and control deleted material in the unallocated disc space of the computer's hard disc, and accordingly, following *Porter*, on the date the computer was seized he could not be said to have been in possession of the images. However, in order to rebut possible innocent explanations given by the defendant for the presence of the images on his computer, and his denial that the computer had ever been connected to the internet, the prosecution had led evidence showing that in March 2001 someone using the name D Miller had installed Windows 98 on the computer; that someone using the initials DM had re-installed Windows 98 in February 2002; that the defendant's email address, using his own name, was in use on the computer in January and February 2002; that in those same months the computer had been used to visit a large number of child pornography websites; and that in the same period a number of internet searches had been made on the computer using key words which were plainly used in order to find images of child pornography. This evidence was adduced at trial in order to prove the knowledge necessary for possession, and the Court of Appeal said that the jury's verdict meant they must have accepted it, i.e. they must have found that the defendant and not somebody else had searched for child pornography and accessed it many times in January and February 2002. On those facts,

---

[197] Or, as suggested in *Miller* [2010] EWCA Crim 2883, at 25, the time when he assumed control of the computer.
[198] [2010] EWCA Crim 2883.

unlike in *Porter*, there was evidence linking the defendant to the images beyond the simple fact of their presence on his computer.[199]

In the absence of such evidence, prosecutors who find themselves unable to   **8.140** identify the period in which the defendant had possession of a deleted image can avoid the problem, where there is evidence of internet browsing, by charging the defendant instead under s.1(1)(a) of the Protection of Children Act 1978 with "making" the images by downloading them from the internet.[200] Professor David Ormerod has pointed out that, by allowing deletion to operate as a "defence" to the s.160(1) charge, the Court of Appeal has increased the likelihood that individuals will be charged with the "making" offence, to which there is no defence either of quick disposal (as in s.160(2)(c) of the 1988 Act) or of deletion.[201] If it can be proved who deleted the images, then if all else fails it may be possible to charge that person with doing an act tending and intended to pervert the course of justice: see *T v R.*,[202] discussed in para.8.118, above.

Porter was cited with approval in the Scottish case *MacLennan v HM*   **8.141** *Advocate*,[203] in which the appellant was convicted of possessing indecent photographs or pseudo-photographs of a child contrary to s.52A(1) of the Civic Government (Scotland) Act 1982. The evidence related to images held on a laptop computer at his home. There were others in the house at the relevant time and the defence case was that one of them had been responsible for the images. The judge gave the jury no direction as to the meaning of "possession". The High Court of Justiciary quashed the conviction on the ground that the trial judge's omission to give the jury guidance as to the legal concept of possession, including the elements of knowledge and control, amounted to a miscarriage of justice. It said[204]:

> "Even if there had been no other occupant of the house who might have had access to the computer, we consider that the jury required guidance on the legal

---

[199] There was a potential problem in that the indictment charged the defendant with possession "on or before 20th November 2002", the date on which the computer was seized, and the Court of Appeal said the inclusion of the words "or before" was conventional drafting and had not been intended and was not apt to focus attention on the period January–February 2002. However, the Court went on to hold that as a matter of general law the date referred to in an indictment is not a material averment. Accordingly, it was not necessary for the Crown to prove that the defendant had the images in his possession on the date the computer was seized, and it was sufficient to prove that he had them in his possession *at some time*. This reasoning enabled the Court of Appeal to uphold a well-merited conviction despite a defect in the drafting of the indictment. However, in a future case in which there is evidence of possession relating to a period prior to the date of seizure of the computer, the appropriate course is to specify that period in the indictment.

[200] cf. *Smith and Jayson* [2003] 1 Cr. App. R. 212 (making by downloading onto screen); *Bowden* [2000] 1 Cr. App. R. 438 (making by downloading onto disc). Offences of "making" indecent images of children by downloading them fall to be sentenced in the same way as offences of possession of such images: see para.8.18, above.

[201] [2006] Crim. L.R. 748.

[202] [2011] EWCA Crim 729.

[203] [2012] HCJAC 94.

[204] [2012] HCJAC 94, at 19.

> concept of possession, including basic directions about the elements of knowledge and control: cf. the observations of Dyson L.J. in *R v Porter*. Such directions were required a fortiori in this case, where there were several people who might have had access to the computer, and where the accused disclaimed responsibility and raised questions about the responsibility of another."

We respectfully agree with these comments, and suggest that the right course is for the judge to direct the jury on the meaning of "possession" in any case in which the defendant raises, or the evidence is capable of raising, an issue as to whether he had the necessary knowledge and control of the images in question.

8.142   Finally, *Porter* was followed in *Leonard*,[205] which concerned deleted indecent images of children found in a temporary internet file on the appellant's computer. The files would have been accessible only to someone with specialist computer skills or specialist software, and there was no evidence that the appellant had either. The judge directed the jury on the meaning of "possession" but did not directly address the issue of the retrievability of the images. After some deliberation the jury sent her a note asking "If an image is stored on a computer but the user cannot actually retrieve it, could the image, in law, be said to be in a person's possession?". In the light of *Porter*, the appellant's counsel urged the judge to answer this question with a simple "No", but she instead directed the jury that there was no proof the appellant was a computer expert, indeed the evidence was to the contrary; and the images were not irretrievable, but in order to retrieve them special equipment was needed and no such equipment had been found. The Court of Appeal quashed the ensuing conviction on the basis that there was no sufficient evidence that the appellant was capable of retrieving the images so as to be in law in possession of them on the relevant date (which appears to have been the date on which the images were found). It said the jury should have been directed that for the appellant to be convicted, the prosecution had to prove that he was capable of retrieving the images or in a position to retrieve them; and, as the appellant's counsel had argued, the jury's question to the judge should have been answered with a simple "No". Indeed, though the Court did not say this, it seems clear that the evidence relating to retrievability was such that it would have been in order for the judge to withdraw the case from the jury at the close of the prosecution case.

EXCEPTION FOR CONSENT WITHIN MARRIAGE OR OTHER RELATIONSHIP

8.143   In extending the protection of s.160(1) to children aged 16 and 17, the Sexual Offences Act 2003 also provided a limited defence of consent in cases where the photograph was taken when the child was 16 or 17 and she and the

---

[205] [2012] EWCA Crim 277.

defendant were married,[206] in a civil partnership[207] or cohabiting at the time of the alleged offence. The effect of the provision, contained in s.160A, is that in proceedings for possessing an indecent photograph or pseudo-photograph[208] of a child, if:

- the defendant proves that the photograph was of the child aged 16 or 17 and that at the time he possessed or obtained it he and the child were married, in a civil partnership or living together as partners in an "enduring family relationship",
- sufficient evidence is adduced to raise an issue as to whether the child consented to the photograph being in the defendant's possession, or as to whether the defendant reasonably believed she consented, and
- the photograph showed the child alone or with the defendant but nobody else,

the defendant will be not guilty of the offence unless the prosecution proves that the child did not consent and that the defendant did not reasonably believe she did. One significant aspect of the defence is that it continues to apply even after the marriage or relationship between the defendant and the child (or former child) has broken down and she no longer consents to the defendant retaining possession of the photograph. See further paras 8.75 and following, above.

DEFENCES

Section 160(2) of the 1988 Act[209] provides: **8.144**

> "Where a person is charged with an offence under subsection (1) above, it shall be a defence for him to prove—
>
> (a) that he had a legitimate reason for having the photograph or pseudo-photograph in his possession; or
> (b) that he had not himself seen the photograph or pseudo-photograph and did not know, nor had any cause to suspect, it to be indecent; or
> (c) that the photograph or pseudo-photograph was sent to him without any prior request made by him or on his behalf and that he did not keep it for an unreasonable time."

For the application of these defences, see paras 8.86 and following, above.[210]

---

[206] The reference to marriage is to be read as including a reference to marriage of a same sex couple: Marriage (Same Sex Couples) Act 2013 s.11 and Sch.3, Pt 1 para.1, which was brought into force on March 13, 2014, by SI 2014/93.

[207] Civil reference to partnership was added by the Partnership Act 2004 s.261(1) and Sch.27 para.60, which came into force on December 5, 2005.

[208] The provision was extended to pseudo-photographs by the Coroners and Justice Act 2009 s.69(2), with effect from April 6, 2010.

[209] As amended by the Criminal Justice and Public Order Act 1994 s.84(1), (4), with effect from February 3, 1995.

[210] See also Dr Yaman Akdeniz, *Possession and dispossession: a critical assessment of defences in cases of possession of indecent photographs of children* [2007] Crim. L.R. 274.

Mental Element

8.145 For the mental element required for "possession", see paras 8.96 and
following, above.

CHAPTER 9

OFFENCES OF CHILD ABDUCTION

Introduction...................................... 9.01   Abduction of Child in Care 9.52
Child Abduction............................. 9.07   Mental Element 9.61

INTRODUCTION

In past times, the principal object of the law relating to abduction was to   **9.01**
protect young and unmarried girls from sexual and financial predators. The
paternalistic nature of the law was reflected in the requirement in the main
abduction offences that the girl should be taken out of the possession of her
parent or guardian against his will. The concept of parental possession was
fundamental to the offences, and whether the girl consented to go was
irrelevant.

The first offence of abduction of a woman appears to have entered the   **9.02**
statute book in 1275,[1] when Edward I ordained "that none do ravish, nor
take away by force, any maiden within age (neither by her own consent, nor
without) nor any wife or maiden of full age nor any woman against her will".
Henry VII later made abduction for the sake of "lucre" a capital felony if the
woman were married or ravished as a result of the abduction.[2] Then in
Wakefield's Case[3] the abduction of an heiress caused such a sensation that, in
the Offences Against the Person Act 1828,[4] forcible abduction of a woman on
account of her fortune and with intent to marry or defile her was made a
felony punishable with transportation for life. At the same time, unlawful
abduction of a girl under 16 from her parent or guardian was made a
misdemeanour punishable with a fine or imprisonment at the discretion of
the court.

The Sexual Offences Act 1956 contained five offences of abduction of   **9.03**
women: abduction of a woman by force or for the sake of her property (s.17),
abduction of a girl under 21, if she had property or expectation of property
and the abduction was by fraud and with intent that she should marry or

[1] 3 Edw. 1 c.13.
[2] 2 Hen. 7 c.2. See also 4 & 5 Phil. & Mar. c.8.
[3] (1827) 2 Lewin 1.
[4] 9 Geo. 4 c.31, ss.19 and 20.

have extra-marital intercourse (s.18, repealed by the Family Law Reform Act 1969 s.11(c)), abduction of an unmarried girl under 18 with intent that she should have extra-marital intercourse (s.19), abduction of an unmarried girl under 16 (s.20) and abduction of a female defective (s.21). These offences, which reflected an archaic picture of the social position of women, were finally swept away and not replaced by the Sexual Offences Act 2003.

9.04   The 2003 Act left unaffected, however, the important modern offence of abduction of a child under 16, contained in s.2 of the Child Abduction Act 1984.[5] This offence was enacted following recommendations by the Criminal Law Revision Committee (CLRC), which was concerned at the narrow scope of the offences of abduction in the 1956 Act and in particular at the requirement in those offences of a removal from "possession".[6] This concept had been narrowly interpreted in *Jones*[7] to require a "substantial interference with the possessory relationship" of parent and child. The defendant in that case had persuaded two young girls to agree to meet him for a walk, with the intention of performing indecent acts upon them. It was held that he could not be convicted of attempting to commit the offence of abduction of a girl under 16, contrary to s.20 of the 1956 Act, as the execution of his plan would not have involved taking the girls out of their parents' possession. In the light of this decision, the CLRC recommended the creation of a new offence of child abduction which would be committed by an act of interference with the "lawful control" of a child (whether a boy or a girl) rather than with "possession". The offence of child abduction in s.2 of the 1984 Act was enacted in the terms recommended by the CLRC.

9.05   In addition, s.49 of the Children Act 1989 contains a summary offence of abduction of a child who is in care pursuant to an order under Part IV of that Act, subject to an emergency protection order under s.43 of the Act or in police protection under s.46 of the Act. A "child" for these purposes means a person under the age of 18.

9.06   This chapter focuses on the offences of abduction and does not consider other offences which may be committed when a person abducts a child, e.g. kidnapping, false imprisonment and assault.

Child Abduction

Definition

9.07 Section 2(1) of the Child Abduction Act 1984 provides:

"Subject to subsection (3) below, a person, other than one mentioned in subsection (2) below, commits an offence if, without lawful authority or reasonable excuse, he takes or detains a child under the age of sixteen—

---

[5] 1994 c.37.
[6] Fourteenth Report, *Offences Against the Person*, Cmnd. 7844 (1980), para.242.
[7] [1973] Crim. L.R. 621, Stafford Crown Ct, Swanwick J.

(a) so as to remove him from the lawful control of any person having lawful control of the child; or

(b) so as to keep him out of the lawful control of any person entitled to lawful control of the child."

It was held in *Foster v DPP*[8] that s.2(1)(a) and (b) create two separate forms of the offence, neither of which is an alternative verdict for the other. It follows that an offence may be committed either by taking or detaining a child so as to remove her from the lawful control of any person having lawful control of the child (s.2(1)(a)), or by taking or detaining a child so as to keep her out of the lawful control of any person entitled to such control (s.2(1)(b)).

The Court in *Foster* went on to hold that if the child is already out of **9.08** lawful control, then any subsequent taking or detention could only have the effect of keeping the child out of the lawful control of someone entitled to it, so that the appropriate charge would be under s.2(1)(b) rather than s.2(1)(a). In that case the complainant, S, was aged 15 and living with foster parents, in whose control she lawfully was for the purposes of s.2 of the 1984 Act. On the afternoon of March 1, 2003, she met the second appellant, R, who took her to his home. He believed at this point that she was aged 16 or over. When S failed to return home that evening, her foster father reported her missing to the police. The police telephoned R's home at 1.30am the following day and told him that they were looking for S, who was under age and had been reported as missing. R passed on that information to the first appellant, F. At about 2am the police arrived at R's home. The appellants told them that S had been there, but had since left. That was a lie, as they knew S was hiding in the attic to avoid being found by the police. At 7am the police revisited R, found S in the living room and took her home. The appellants were charged with an offence contrary to ss.2(1)(a) and 4 of the Child Abduction Act 1984, the particulars of offence stating that "On 2nd March 2003 ... without lawful authority or reasonable excuse [they] detained S, a child under the age of 16, so as to remove her from the lawful control of ... a person having lawful control of the child ... ". Before the deputy district judge in the magistrates' court, the appellants submitted that S's foster parents had lost control of her on March 1 so that, if any offence was committed on March 2, it could only have been abduction contrary to s.2(1)(b) of the Act, namely keeping S out of the lawful control of any person entitled to lawful control of her, with which they were not charged and which was not an alternative to the charges laid. The deputy district judge found at the close of the prosecution case that an act of removal took place on March 2 when, knowing S's true age, the appellants took no steps to return her. The appellants appealed successfully by way of case stated.

The Court held that R's action in taking S to his home had the effect of **9.09** removing her from the control of her foster parents and F's complicit action

---

[8] [2004] EWHC 2955 (Admin); [2005] 1 W.L.R. 1402, at 7.

in detaining S at the house had the effect of removing or keeping her from the control of her foster parents. However, neither man was guilty of the offence of abduction on March 1, since at that point both believed S to be aged 16 or over. Had it not been for this belief, they would have been guilty of abduction on that day. The factual situation had however changed dramatically by 1.30am on March 2. The appellants had been told that S was 15, was missing from home and being sought by the police. Assuming, for the purposes of the appeal, that S did not wish to be restored to her foster parents and took advantage of the appellants' willingness to allow her to hide from the police and stay the night, then they detained her within the meaning of s.2(1), since that willingness constituted an inducement to stay with them, as contemplated by s.3(c) of the Act.[9] However, those acts of the appellants did not have the effect of removing S from the lawful control of her foster parents, since by the time they were committed, she had already left that control. The Court said it is clear from the wording of s.2 that Parliament intended a material distinction to be drawn between the two forms of the s.2 offence, which, when applied to facts such as those of the present case, is critical to guilt or innocence. Paragraph (a) uses the word "having" as the verb which qualifies or explains lawful control of the child, while paragraph (b) uses the words "entitled to lawful control of the child". From that two conclusions follow. The first is that the distinction between removal from a person having control, and keeping from a person entitled to control, is intended to reflect two materially different states of affairs. One requires the child to be in the lawful control of someone when taken or detained. The other requires only that the child is kept out of the lawful control of someone entitled to it when they are taken or detained. Paragraph (b) would cover a situation in which the child has run away from lawful control and is, whilst out of lawful control, detained unlawfully by the defendant. The second conclusion to be drawn from the distinction between removal from a person having lawful control and keeping from a person entitled to control is that, when laid in a charge, each is a material averment which alleges one of two separate forms of the s.2 offence. In the present case, by the time the appellants knew that their inducements to S were unlawful, she was no longer in the lawful custody of her foster parents. Accordingly, the offence charged under s.2(1)(a) was not proved.

Mode of Trial and Punishment

9.10   An offence under s.2(1) is triable either way[10] and for listing purposes falls within Class 3.[11] The maximum punishment on conviction on indictment is

---

[9] For which see para.9.37.
[10] 1984 Act s.4(1).
[11] *Consolidated Criminal Practice Directions*, Part XIII Listing B: CLASSIFICATION, available at *https://www.judiciary.gov.uk/wp-content/uploads/2015/09/crim-pd-2015.pdf* [Accessed April 30, 2016].

seven years' imprisonment.[12] The Law Commission has recommended raising this to 14 years, in order to avoid undesirable inconsistency between the most serious instances of the s.2(1) offence and kidnapping offences of a comparable level of seriousness.[13] The maximum punishment on summary conviction is six months' imprisonment or a fine, or both.[14] As from a day to be appointed the maximum sentence of imprisonment on summary conviction will increase to 12 months.[15] The increase will have no application to offences committed before it takes effect.[16] Until recently, the maximum fine on summary conviction was a fine not exceeding the statutory maximum (i.e. £5,000). The effect of s.85 of the Legal Aid, Sentencing and Punishment of Offenders Act 2012 is that, from March 12, 2015, a fine of any amount may be imposed. Fines will, however, continue to be set according to the seriousness of the offence and the means of the offender.

An offence under s.2(1) is not a specified offence for the purpose of the **9.11** dangerousness provisions of the Criminal Justice Act 2003.[17] Nor is the offence a "sexual offence" for the purposes of the power to impose longer than commensurate sentences contained in s.80(2)(b) of the Powers of Criminal Courts (Sentencing) Act 2000,[18] though it may, depending on the facts, be a "violent offence" for the purposes of that provision[19] (which is now applicable only to offences committed before April 4, 2005, when the sentencing regime in the Criminal Justice Act 2003 came into effect).

CHILD ABDUCTION WARNING NOTICES

Many police forces have adopted an administrative practice of issuing a **9.12** "child abduction warning notice", often referred to as a "CAWN", to warn an adult who associates with a child against the wishes of the child's parent or parents that he has no permission to do so, and that if he continues to associate with the child he may be arrested for an abduction offence, i.e. an offence under s.2(1) or, if the child is in care, under s.49 of the Children Act 1989. By making the recipient aware of the lack of parental consent, and of the child's age, a CAWN makes it easier to establish the mental element required for the relevant abduction offence should the recipient disregard the notice. CAWNs have proved to be a valuable measure for safeguarding children. They are of particular value in relation to children who do not recognise themselves as victims but whose families have identified that they are at risk of sexual exploitation, since a CAWN will be issued on the basis

---

[12] 1984 Act s.4(1)(b).
[13] *Simplification Of Criminal Law: Kidnapping And Related Offences*, Law Com 355 (2014), para.5.15.
[14] 1984 Act s.4(1)(a).
[15] Criminal Justice Act 2003 s.282(2), (3).
[16] Criminal Justice Act 2003 s.282(4).
[17] s.224 and Sch.15.
[18] *Wrench* [1996] 1 Cr. App. R.(S.) 145.
[19] *Newsome* [1997] 2 Cr. App. R.(S.) 69.

of a statement taken from the person with parental responsibility rather than the child. In *R. v G (Paul)*[20] the Court of Appeal referred with approval to the practice of issuing such notices.

9.13   However, CAWNs have no statutory basis and so to breach one is not in itself an offence. Law enforcement action can be taken only if the breach constitutes an abduction offence, which will be the case only if the recipient of the CAWN has subsequently taken or detained the child, and not if he is still in the process of grooming the child through mental or emotional manipulation, or the child goes to the recipient and remains with him of their own volition without any taking or detention on his part. For this reason, there has been some pressure on the Government to bring forward legislation to place such notices on a statutory footing and make it an offence to breach their conditions. In 2014, a cross-party inquiry into the effectiveness of legislation for tackling child sexual exploitation, chaired by Sarah Champion MP and supported by Barnardo's, the children's charity, argued that[21]:

> "[c]reating an offence of breaching a notice would [enable] the police to intervene earlier, rather than having to wait for a more serious offence and the associated harm to occur. There would also be less reliance on victims' evidence and their support for the prosecution, often required to prove the current abduction offence. Once it has got to that stage, it is further on in the grooming cycle and hence the victim is less likely to cooperate. An offence of breach of notice would only require evidence that the person on whom the notice is served breached the terms of the notice i.e. they were found to be with the young person . . . [T]he current approach has a further damaging effect, because it erodes victims' and their families' confidence in the police's ability to protect them when they see that their abuser has broken the terms of the notice and no action is taken. Plainly, this will have implications for their willingness to engage with the police and any potential prosecution in future. Creating an offence of breach of notice would therefore likely strengthen victims' confidence in seeking help and protection."

9.14   The inquiry was also concerned at the fact that CAWNs apply differently in relation to children in care and other children. This is because their availability mirrors the scope of the abduction offences, with the result that the police are able to issue CAWNs up to the age of 18 for children in local authority care but only up to age 16 for other children. The inquiry recommended that the police should be able to issue a notice in relation to 16- and 17-year-olds whether they are in care or not[22]:

> "While looked after children are particularly vulnerable and are disproportionately likely to be victims of [child sexual exploitation], the majority of victims are not in care . . . We consider it unacceptable that young people should not be afforded the same level of protection on the basis of whether they are living at

---

[20] [2012] EWCA Crim 1296.

[21] *Report of the Parliamentary inquiry into the effectiveness of legislation for tackling child sexual exploitation and trafficking within the UK* (April 2014), p.18. The Report is available at *http://www.barnardos.org.uk/cse_parliamentary_inquiry_report.pdf* [Accessed April 30, 2016].

[22] *Report of the Parliamentary inquiry into the effectiveness of legislation for tackling child sexual exploitation and trafficking within the UK* (April 2014), p.19. The Report is available at *http://www.barnardos.org.uk/cse_parliamentary_inquiry_report.pdf* [Accessed April 30, 2016].

home or are in the care of the State; there should be consistent provision for all children, regardless of their legal status."

During the passage of what became the Serious Crime Act 2015, amend- ments were laid that would have placed CAWNs on a statutory footing and made them applicable to all children under 18.[23] An alternative, more far-reaching amendment would have extended the s.2(1) abduction offence to protect 16- and 17-year-olds, so enabling CAWNs to be issued in relation to such children.[24] Neither amendment was adopted. At Commons Report, the Solicitor General, Robert Buckland MP, resisted them on the basis that they were unnecessary as their aims could be achieved through the use of Sexual Risks Orders ("SROs"),[25] breach of which carries a sentence of up to five years' imprisonment. Sarah Champion MP expressed concern that an SRO would not be available to protect a child from someone who has engaged in what she described as "low-level grooming activities", as SROs may be made only where an individual has done "an act of a sexual nature" as a result of which there is reasonable cause to believe that an SRO is necessary to protect the public or any particular member of it from harm. Ms Champion argued that, unless the police were given very specific guidance, they might not feel confident to apply for an SRO in relation, for example, to a 20-year-old who is hanging round with a 14-year-old. In response, the Solicitor General undertook that the Government would publish guidance on the use of SROs and would work with the police to review their effectiveness.

9.15

The guidance, which was published in March 2015, states that an SRO may be available to deter or prevent grooming behaviour whether that behaviour is sexual in nature, e.g. sending a child indecent images, or is rendered sexual because of the person's intentions, e.g. spending time with a child alone with the intention of committing a sexual offence against them.[26] It provides as follows[27]:

9.16

> "'Acts of a sexual nature' are not defined in legislation, and therefore will depend to a significant degree on the individual circumstances of the behaviour and its context. The term intentionally covers a broad range of behaviour. Such behaviour may, in other circumstances and contexts, have innocent intentions. It also covers acts that may not in themselves be sexual but which have a sexual motive and/or are intended to allow the perpetrator to move on to sexual abuse. As an indication, it is expected that examples of such behaviour might include the following:
>
> . . .
> - Acts which may be suggestive of grooming . . . , such as
>   ○ contacting a child via social media
>   ○ spending time with children alone . . . ".

---

[23] Lords Report stage (October 14, 2014), cols.161-165; Commons Report stage (February 23, 2015), cols 57–60, 77–89, 143–146.
[24] Commons Report stage (February 23, 2015), cols 76–78.
[25] See Ch.36.
[26] *Guidance on Part 2 of the Sexual Offences Act 2003* (Home Office, March 2015), p.45.
[27] *Guidance on Part 2 of the Sexual Offences Act 2003* (Home Office, March 2015), p.42.

In relation specifically to the relationship between SROs and CAWNs, the guidance states:

> "SROs and Child Abduction Warning Notices (CAWNs) are intended to be complementary. CAWNs are currently used by some forces as a deterrent for individuals thought to be grooming children. A CAWN states that the suspect has no permission to associate with the child and if they continue to do so they may be arrested for an abduction offence under the relevant legislation (section 2 of the Child Abduction Act 1984 and section 49 of the Children Act 1989).
> . . .
> A CAWN can be issued as an early intervention to deter an individual from progressing towards more harmful behaviour. If they fail to comply with a CAWN and are judged by the police to pose a risk of harm, the police may decide to apply for an SRO which would carry the added deterrent of criminal sanctions if breached. Under these circumstances the individual's failure to comply with the CAWN may be used as evidence in support of an application for an SRO."

9.17   In other words, SROs can be used to deter grooming behaviour and so to protect children from sexual exploitation, including in the form of an abduction offence. But the expectation is that they will be used by way of escalation when a person served with a CAWN fails to comply with it. The police can then apply for an SRO which will be designed to achieve the same deterrent effect as the CAWN, but with penalties in the event of a breach. As such, SROs seem capable of delivering the outcome sought by the cross-party inquiry, at least in relation to those children protected by the abduction offences. Although it remains the case that breaching a CAWN is not itself an offence, CAWNs remain available as a relatively swift and non-bureaucratic remedy for feared abduction cases. If a CAWN is breached, because the recipient continues to associate with the child, the police may then seek to enhance the deterrence by applying for an SRO. On the face of it, this does leave unaddressed the concern expressed by the inquiry in relation to 16- and 17-year-olds who are not in care and so are not currently within the scope of the CAWN regime. There is, however, a way to resolve this, namely by adapting the standard form of CAWN so that it puts the recipient on notice that, in the event of a breach, they may be subject *either* to prosecution for abduction *or* to an application for an SRO. By that means, the concerns of the inquiry may be addressed.

Alternative Verdict

9.18   A defendant indicted for child abduction may in appropriate circumstances be convicted in the alternative of common assault. This is perhaps surprising, since under s.6(3) of the Criminal Law Act 1967 a jury may bring in an alternative verdict only in relation to "another offence falling within the jurisdiction of the court of trial", and common assault, which used to be triable either way, was turned into a summary offence by s.39 of the Criminal

Justice Act 1988.[28] However, s.40 of the 1988 Act makes provision for a count charging common assault to be included on an indictment if it is founded on the same facts or evidence as a count charging an indictable offence. As a result, a count of common assault may be included as an alternative count on an indictment charging child abduction, where the alleged taking or detention involved the use or threat of force. Moreover, by virtue of subsequent changes to the 1967 Act, an alternative verdict of guilty of common assault may now be brought in if the prosecutor *could* have included a count of common assault on the indictment in accordance with s.40 of the 1988 Act, even if that was not in fact done.[29] However, if the jury convict of assault, the Crown Court may only deal with the offender for the offence in a manner in which a magistrates' court could have dealt with him. On a summary charge, the magistrates have no jurisdiction to find the defendant guilty of a lesser offence.[30]

SENTENCING

No sentencing guideline has been issued for the abduction offences, nor is   **9.19**
there any guideline case, though the following decisions are instructive.

In *Dean*,[31] the appellant (29) encountered a four-year-old boy who had   **9.20**
been sent on an errand by his mother. He told the boy to come to him and close his eyes and threatened to cut the boy's throat and to kill him. The boy's mother, who had been looking out for him, called his name. Though the appellant was holding his hand, the boy managed to break free and escape. The appellant ran to his car and drove off at speed but was subsequently arrested. In interview he denied the offence and said that he had not visited the area. He was convicted after a contested trial and sentenced to five years' imprisonment. It emerged at trial that when he was 19 he had been convicted of offences involving the transmission of indecent material of a homosexual nature to young boys relating to what he would like to do to them. Despite that background, the judge felt constrained to sentence on the basis that he did not know what the appellant's intention was in relation to the boy, and that it would be wrong to speculate about the matter. On appeal against sentence, the Court said that the circumstances of the offence and the background of the appellant's previous offending gave rise to grave concern. The appellant had offered no innocent explanation for his conduct nor at any time stated what his motive was. It was plain that he had been deliberately looking for a young child. He had also threatened violence. It was a matter

---

[28] cf. *Mearns* [1991] 1 Q.B. 82 (indictment for assault occasioning actual bodily harm); followed in *Burt* (1996) 161 J.P. 77; *Brownless*, Unreported, May 9, 2000; *Clifford*, *The Times*, December 5, 2003.

[29] 1967 Act s.6(3A), (3B), inserted by the Domestic Violence, Crime and Victims Act 2004 s.11.

[30] *Lawrence v Lawrence* [1968] 2 Q.B. 93.

[31] [2000] 2 Cr. App. R. 253.

of the greatest good fortune that the vigilance of the child's mother had brought the incident to an early end. The appellant had fought the case and lacked the mitigation of a plea. The sentence was a severe one, but one which the judge was entitled to impose for the protection of the public.

9.21   In *Oakes*,[32] the offender was a man of 44 with drink-related convictions, though none for sexual or violent offences. On the occasion in question, heavily intoxicated, he approached an 11-year-old boy who was waiting outside his school and said "Walk up here with us". He then put his arms around the back of the boy's neck and said "Fucking walk up here with us". They walked to the entrance to an alleyway where the offender tried to kiss and cuddle the boy, who was pinned against the wall. He succeeded in kissing the boy twice on the cheek. The boy was frightened. A teacher shouted at the offender to stop and the boy managed to slip away. The offender pleaded guilty to an offence under s.2(1)(b) of the 1984 Act and was sentenced to 32 months' imprisonment and made subject to an indefinite SOPO and a restraining order in relation to the boy, his mother, and the school. The sentence was upheld on appeal, the Court of Appeal commenting that the incident was short but was only stopped because of the teacher's intervention. Whilst both a psychiatrist and a probation officer were of the opinion that the offender was not a danger to children, the judge had been entitled to infer that his motivation had been sexual. There was no mitigation in the fact that the offender had been drunk, and the sentence was plainly within the appropriate range.

9.22   In *Wakeman*,[33] the offender was an educated man of previous good character who had become an alcoholic. He was sitting on a park bench with another man when two three-year-old girls passed nearby, pushing their buggies. The girls had been taken to the park by their mothers. The appellant took hold of the girls' hands and walked with them a distance of 20–30 metres, leaving the buggies by the bench. When confronted by the mothers he said he was going to show the girls a teddy bear in the window of a house overlooking the park. It was not in dispute at trial that such a bear existed and could be seen from an area not far from where the mothers confronted the offender. There was no evidence of any ulterior motive. The offender was convicted on two counts under s.2(1)(a) of the 1984 Act. The judge took the view that the offences were of the utmost severity and crossed the custody threshold, and he sentenced the offender to nine months' imprisonment concurrent on each count. The Court of Appeal disagreed that the custody threshold was crossed. The judge should, it said, have sentenced on the basis that the offender did not intend to remove the girls from the control of their mothers[34] and that his only intention was to show them the teddy bear. His

---

[32] [2011] 2 Cr. App. R.(S.) 588(102).
[33] [2011] EWCA Crim 1649.
[34] The decision clearly proceeds on the basis that a s.2 offence is committed even though the defendant does not intend to remove the child from lawful control, if that is the effect of his actions: see para.9.45, below.

intention and motive were highly relevant to sentence and, in the Court's view, a non-custodial sentence should have been passed. As the offender had already served the equivalent of a six-month sentence, it quashed the sentence of nine months' imprisonment and substituted a conditional discharge for one year.

In *Cash (Stephen)*,[35] the appellant (25) had met a 15-year-old girl who was troubled and was living with her grandmother. He told the grandmother that he was 18. The police later stopped the appellant with the girl in his car and took the girl home. They told the grandmother the appellant's true age, and that he had a criminal history and was a registered sex offender. The grandmother warned the girl not to see the appellant again. He subsequently came to the house in a van. The grandmother told him to leave and told the girl not to go with him. The girl pushed past her and got in the van. The appellant drove her to her friend's house. She returned home the next day. No complaint was made at the time, but the grandmother contacted the police a week later following another incident. The appellant pleaded guilty on the day of trial. The judge acknowledged that the abduction had lasted only a relatively short time. He sentenced the appellant to 24 months' imprisonment, reducing the sentence by 10 per cent to reflect the late guilty plea. The Court of Appeal held the sentence was excessive. The abduction had lasted only a few minutes before the appellant took the girl to her friend's house. Children had to be protected against themselves, but, equally, one could not entirely ignore that the victim in this case had been headstrong and made clear that she wished to be with the appellant. There was no question of the appellant having coerced her to go with him, although it was important to bear in mind that children at a vulnerable stage in their lives had to be protected from people such as the appellant. In all the circumstances, a starting point of around nine months would have been appropriate. With credit for the late plea, the Court substituted a sentence of eight months' imprisonment.

9.23

PARTIES TO THE OFFENCE

An offence of child abduction under s.2(1) may be committed by any person, male or female, other than the persons specified in s.2(2) of the Act. These are:

9.24

> "(a) where the father and mother of the child in question were married to each other at the time of his birth, the child's father and mother;
> (b) where the father and mother of the child in question were not married to each other at the time of his birth, the child's mother; and
> (c) any other person mentioned in section 1(2)(c) to (e) above."

Section 1(2)(c) to (e) of the Act mention a person who is a guardian or special guardian of the child, a person named in a child arrangements order

[35] [2014] EWCA Crim 1981.

as a person with whom the child is to live, and a person who has custody of the child. The effect of s.2(2) is therefore to exclude from the scope of the child abduction offences the child's mother, the child's father where he was married to the child's mother at the time of the child's birth, and certain persons standing in loco parentis to the child. In addition, s.2(1) does not apply in certain circumstances to voluntary homes, private children's homes or foster parents providing refuges for children at risk of harm.[36] In the case of a child born outside marriage, although only the mother is excluded from the scope of the offences, s.2(3)(a) of the Act makes it a defence for the defendant to prove that he is, or at the time of the alleged offence reasonably believed himself to be, the child's father.[37]

9.25   An offence of child abduction may be committed against any child under the age of 16: see para.9.41, below. An amendment that would have extended the protection of the law to 16- and 17-year-olds, for the purposes of enabling child abduction warning notices to be served on potential abductors of such children, was defeated during the passage of what became the Serious Crime Act 2015.[38]

Is the child victim liable to prosecution if she encouraged the offence?

9.26   It is inconceivable that a child victim who encouraged or assisted her own abduction would be prosecuted as an accessory to the offence. The long-standing principle in *Tyrrell*[39] is that where legislation creates an offence that is intended to protect a class of persons, a member of that class cannot be convicted as an accessory to such an offence committed in respect of him. The abduction offence is undoubtedly intended to protect children under 16 and so the principle in *Tyrrell* would prevent a child victim of the offence being convicted as an accessory. Further, the Court of Appeal in *Attorney General's Reference (No.53 of 2013) (R. v Wilson)*[40] held that where the victim of a child sex offence encouraged the offender to engage in sexual relations with her, her encouragement aggravated rather than mitigated his offence, since "an underage person who encourages sexual relations with her needs more protection, not less". The same logic applies in equal force to offences of child abduction; and if a child who colludes in her own abduction is more in need of the law's protection than other child victims, it must follow that there can be little or no public interest in prosecuting her for her role in events. See further the discussion in paras 4.57 and following, above, relating

---

[36] Children Act 1989 s.51.

[37] This provision applies only where D believes himself to be the father of the child actually abducted, and has no application where D takes a child, X, mistakenly believing X is Y, whose father D in fact is: *Berry* [1996] 2 Cr. App. R. 226. In such a case, the mistake may be relevant to whether the defendant acted "without lawful authority or reasonable excuse", for which see paras 9.27 and following.

[38] See para.9.15, above.

[39] [1894] 1 Q.B. 710.

[40] [2013] EWCA Crim 2544.

to the offence under s.9 of the 2003 Act (sexual activity with a child under 16).

"WITHOUT LAWFUL AUTHORITY OR REASONABLE EXCUSE"

In *Berry*,[41] it appears to have been common ground between the parties, and accepted by the Court of Appeal, that the prosecution carries the burden of proving absence of lawful authority or reasonable excuse. In *Re Owens*,[42] Simon Brown LJ (as he then was) stated obiter that it is for the prosecution to disprove what he termed "the 'defence' of reasonable excuse". However, given the practical difficulties which the prosecution may well face in discharging this burden, the better view must be that the defence carries an evidential burden to put the point in issue.   9.27

Lawful authority

The taking away or detention of a child will be with lawful authority where it is in implementation of a sentence passed by a court of law, in pursuance of a power of arrest or in the exercise of reasonable parental discipline. There are other, more specific powers which may be relevant, e.g. where a child is taken into local authority care or immigration detention pursuant to statute. A taking or detention will also be with lawful authority if it has the consent of the child's parent or guardian. The parent must, however, be in lawful control of the child.[43] Moreover, a consent will be ineffective for this purpose if it is induced by false representations made by the defendant as to his identity, the nature or quality of his act or, it seems, even as to his purpose in taking or detaining the child. This was so under s.20 of the 1956 Act, and comparable provisions elsewhere in the Commonwealth, and older cases on the point are likely to remain a good guide to the position under the 1984 Act. So in *Hopkins*,[44] there was held to be an offence where the defendant persuaded the girl's parents to consent to the taking by falsely representing that she was to go into employment in another town. In *Cox*,[45] a Canadian decision, there was an offence where the defendant obtained the mother's consent by falsely representing that he wanted the girl as a babysitter. An interesting case from New Zealand is *Lane*,[46] where the girl was resident in a hostel under the lawful charge of the matron. She was given general permission to go to places where the matron could not exercise control over   9.28

---

[41] [1996] 2 Cr. App. R. 226.
[42] [2000] 1 Cr. App. R. 195.
[43] cf. *Kingsbury* (1870) 9 S.C.R. (N.S.W.) 278, N.S.W. S.Ct. F.C. (*held*, in relation to an offence of abduction comparable to that in s.20 of the 1956 Act, that the consent of one parent would not avail the defendant if the girl was at the relevant time in the possession and under the care of the other parent).
[44] (1842) Car. & M. 254.
[45] (1968–1969) 5 C.R. (N.S.) 395, Ont. C.A.
[46] [1961] N.Z.L.R. 989.

her, so long as she returned to the hostel by a certain time. She was taken by the defendant while she was away from the hostel. It was held that, as the girl was expressly allowed to be at liberty, the taking was not without the matron's consent.

9.29   Of interest in this context is the old case of *Tinkler*,[47] where T took his orphaned niece from her guardian in fulfilment of a promise to her father that he would take care of her. He was acquitted of abducting the girl, contrary to the predecessor of s.20 of the 1956 Act, on a direction from Cockburn CJ in the following terms:

> "inasmuch as no improper motive was suggested on the part of the prosecution, it might very well be concluded, that the prisoner wished the child to live with him, and that he meant to discharge the promise which he alleged he had made to her father, and that he did not suppose he was breaking the law when he took the child away . . . if the jury should take that view of the case, and be of opinion that the prisoner honestly believed that he had a right to the custody of the child, then . . . he would be entitled to an acquittal."

The Court in the later case of *Tegerdine*[48] indicated that *Tinkler* was wrongly decided, as T had no lawful authority or lawful excuse for what he did, as required by s.20. But the Court's disapproval of the earlier decision was apparently based on the belief that T was acquitted simply because he acted from a "philanthropic motive", which it was established could not amount to lawful authority or lawful excuse.[49] This is not so. The essence of Cockburn CJ's direction was that T was innocent if he believed when he took the girl that he was entitled to custody of her. The case could therefore be seen as establishing that someone who took a child in the honest belief that he had a legal right to do so was entitled to be acquitted of the old abduction offence. If, however, this point were taken on a charge under s.2(1) of the 1984 Act, it would be highly likely to fail, since on a modern legal analysis, lawful authority either does or does not exist; and if it does not exist, a defendant cannot benefit from a mistaken belief that it does.[50] There would perhaps be more scope for securing an acquittal in such a case through reliance on the defence of reasonable excuse. A defendant will also be entitled to an acquittal if he had an honest but mistaken belief in a state of facts which, if true, would have made his conduct lawful.[51]

9.30   In *R. v S(C)*,[52] the Court of Appeal held that the defence of necessity is not available to a parent or guardian charged with removing a child from the jurisdiction contrary to s.1 of the 1984 Act. However, the s.1 offence, unlike the offences of child abduction in s.2(1), can be committed without proof of absence of lawful authority or reasonable excuse, s.1 instead being subject to

---

[47] (1859) 1 F. & F. 513.
[48] (1982) 75 Cr. App. R. 298.
[49] *Booth* (1872) 12 Cox C.C. 231; *Prince* (1875) L.R. 2 C.C.R. 154 at 174, per Bramwell B.
[50] *Cambridgeshire and Isle of Ely County Council v Rust* [1972] 2 Q.B. 426 (relating to a defence of "lawful excuse").
[51] *Cambridgeshire and Isle of Ely County Council v Rust* [1972] 2 Q.B. 426.
[52] [2012] EWCA Crim 389.

an exception based on consent. The better view, we suggest, is that the term "reasonable excuse" in s.2(1) is capable of covering those circumstances in which a defendant could otherwise run a defence of necessity.

Reasonable excuse

The term "reasonable excuse" must cover circumstances that excuse the defendant's conduct but fall short of providing lawful authority for it. It appears that an honest but mistaken belief that the child taken or detained is the defendant's son or daughter is capable of constituting a reasonable excuse for this purpose.[53] The provision may also be apt to cover cases of "good motive", as where a putative father takes the child from her mother in the belief that she is not being well cared for[54] or where a person takes a child in the belief that this is necessary to prevent the commission of an offence against her.[55] In *Foster v DPP*,[56] the Divisional Court referred to *Re Owens*[57] as a case in which a reasonable excuse plainly existed. The applicant was the nanny of two children of a US soldier serving in Germany. The children's mother had abandoned them. The father was killed in an accident and the applicant took the children to his funeral in the USA. On the day she flew back to Germany with the children, their grandmother was granted an ex parte order for temporary custody. Although the applicant knew that the grandmother intended to apply for custody, she was unaware that the application had been lodged and took the children back to Germany only after taking legal advice that it was permissible for her to do so. On arrival in the UK she was committed for extradition to the USA, where she had been indicted on kidnapping charges the equivalent of s.2(1) of the 1984 Act. She applied successfully for a writ of habeas corpus on the ground that there was no prima facie case against her. Although the argument in *Re Owens* turned on whether the applicant had the mens rea for a s.2(1) offence (for which see para.9.45, below), the court in *Foster* said that, had she been charged under s.2(1), it was difficult to see how the prosecutor could have established that she did not have a reasonable excuse for her actions.

9.31

---

[53] *Berry* [1996] 2 Cr. App. R. 226; and see *Re Owens* [2000] 1 Cr. App. R. 195. See also s.2(3)(a)(ii), which provides "In proceedings against any person for an offence under this section, it shall be a defence for that person to prove (a) where the father and mother of the child in question were not married to each other at the time of his birth (ii) that, at the time of the alleged offence, he believed, on reasonable grounds, that he was the child's father."

[54] cf. *Tegerdine* (1982) 75 Cr. App. R. 298 (decided under s.20 of the 1956 Act, where it was held that in such circumstances the father had no defence as his excuse was not "lawful", as required by that section).

[55] cf. *Tegerdine* (1982) 75 Cr. App. R. 298 at 300; and see *Prince* (1875) L.R. 2 C.C.R. 154 at 178, where Denman J suggested that there might be a lawful excuse for the purposes of the offence of abduction of a girl under 16 where the defendant acted "to prevent some illegal violence requiring forcible interference by way of protection".

[56] [2004] EWHC 2955 (Admin); [2005] 1 W.L.R. 1402, at 7.

[57] [2000] 1 Cr. App. R. 195.

9.32   In *Wakeman*,[58] the facts of which are set out in para.9.22, above, the sole issue for the jury was whether the appellant had a reasonable excuse for taking the girls out of the control of their mothers in the light of his evidence about why he took hold of their hands and walked with them, namely in order to show them a teddy bear in the window of a house overlooking the park. The jury convicted.

"Takes"

9.33   Section 3(a) of the 1984 Act provides:

> "For the purposes of this Part of this Act—
> (a) a person shall be regarded as taking a child if he causes or induces the child to accompany him or any other person or causes the child to be taken . . .".

9.34   It was held in *R. v A*[59] that there may be a "taking" for the purposes of s.3(a) even though the defendant's acts are not the sole cause of the child accompanying him. It is sufficient that his acts are an effective cause, and it is immaterial that there are also other causes, such as the child's wish to go with him. In that case, there was a history of the girl leaving home to be with the appellant. On each of the previous occasions he had "played his part to the full" to enable her to be with him. On the day in question he picked the girl up from her home in his car and drove her to London, where they lived together for the next nine days. It was held on appeal that the judge had been right to leave to the jury the question whether the appellant's acts had been a "more than peripheral or inconsequential" cause of the girl accompanying him. The Court said that "[o]n any ordinary meaning of the word, he took the girl away, albeit with her willing consent."

9.35   The reference in s.3(a) to the child being caused or induced to "accompany" the defendant (or other person) means there will be a "taking" only if the defendant is present.[60] So if the defendant phones the child at the parental home and induces her to join him in his car outside, and then drives them both to a place some miles away, the "taking" will occur not when the child leaves the house, but when she joins him in the car and he drives away. It is clear from the wording of s.3(a) there will be no "taking" if the child leaves the lawful control of her parents and comes to the defendant of her own free will, without any causative act or inducement on his part.[61] Moreover, the defendant will not "take" the child merely by allowing her

---

[58] [2011] EWCA Crim 1649.

[59] [2000] 2 All E.R. 177.

[60] cp. *Olifier* (1886) 10 Cox C.C. 402; *Manktelow* (1853) 6 Cox C.C. 143; *Robb* (1864) 4 F. & F. 59 (decided under what became s.20 of the 1956 Act).

[61] cf. *Olifier* (1866) 10 Cox C.C. 402; *Kauffman* (1904) 68 J.P. 189; *Alexander (Leon)* (1912) 107 L.T. 240; *Weinstein* (1916) 28 D.L.R. 327, Qc. Ct. of Sessions; *Leboe* (1965) 46 C.R. 375, B.C. Co.Ct (decided under what became s.20 of the 1956 Act).

secretly to stay with him and preventing her parents knowing her whereabouts.[62]

The better view is that an offence of "taking" is complete at the moment   9.36
when the child is caused or induced to accompany the defendant (or other
person), however long she stays with him thereafter. So in the example given
above, the "taking" is complete when the child joins the defendant in his car
outside the parental home and he drives away. The significance of this is that,
as discussed below, it is a defence under s.2(3)(b) of the 1984 Act if, at the
time of the offence, the defendant believed the child to be 16 or over. Where
a defendant is charged with "taking" a child, it may be important to know
precisely when the taking occurred in order to determine whether the
s.2(3)(b) defence may apply. In the example just given, suppose the defendant
initially believes, correctly, that the child is 15, but in the course of their car
journey she persuades him that she is really 16. If, as we suggest, the offence
is complete when she joins him in the car and he drives away, there is no
scope for the s.2(3)(b) defence to operate merely because he later comes to
believe she is 16. It should be noted that a contrary approach was taken in the
old case of *Packer*,[63] in which it was held that a "taking" could continue over
a substantial period of time. In that case, the child had her father's consent
to accompany the defendant to the theatre. While they were there, the
defendant persuaded her to accompany him to another town. On the way to
the station he asked her age and she falsely claimed to be 19. It was held that
the "taking" commenced when the couple left the theatre but did not end
until later, and was continuing when the girl misled the defendant about her
age. In those circumstances, the defendant was able to rely upon the statutory
exception which then applied where, at the time of the "taking", the
defendant reasonably believed the child to be 18 or over. The defendant in
Packer was perhaps fortunate not to have been found to have taken the child
when he induced her to accompany him from the theatre in order to go to
another town. In any event, we suggest that a court faced with similar facts
would be obliged by the wording of s.3(a) to regard the "taking" as complete
at that point, and to regard *Packer* as at most an historic curiosity. This view
derives support from *R. (Nicolaou) v Redbridge Magistrates' Court and
CPS*,[64] in which it was held that a parent does not commit an offence of child
abduction under s.1(1) of the 1984 Act where they have an effective consent
to remove the child from the UK for a defined period, but they keep the child
out of the UK after that period has expired and the consent no longer exists.
The Court held that it would be artificial and unnatural to treat "takes or
sends out of the United Kingdom" in s.1(1) as a continuing activity, such that
an initially lawful taking or sending out can become unlawful by reason of
the detention of the child outside the country after the consent has expired.

---

[62] cf. *Olifier* and *Alexander (Leon)*, last note. As to whether this might constitute "detaining"
the child, see paras 9.37 and following, below.
[63] (1886) 16 Cox C.C. 57.
[64] [2012] EWHC 1647 (Admin).

This approach is consistent with our view in relation to s.2(1), that a "taking" occurs at a point in time and is not a continuing activity.

"DETAINS"

9.37 Section 3(c) of the 1984 Act provides:

"For the purposes of this Part of this Act—
(c) a person shall be regarded as detaining a child if he causes the child to be detained or induces the child to remain with him or any other person . . . ".

9.38 In *Moore and Grazier*,[65] a Canadian decision on a provision comparable to the repealed offence under s.17 of the 1956 Act, of abduction of a woman by force or for the sake of her property, the Court said that "detain":

"has no special legal connotation and is used in its ordinary meaning that by some form of compulsion a person's liberty is restrained for a period, short or long, and either from moving away from, or staying in, a place."

We suggest that the first part of this dictum is equally applicable to the word "detain" as used in s.2(1) of the 1984 Act, i.e. the word is not used in any special sense but carries its ordinary meaning, and it is accordingly for the tribunal of fact to decide whether that meaning applies to the facts as proved.[66] However, there is nothing in the 1984 Act which suggests that detention necessarily involves an element of compulsion, and the better view, given the reference to "inducement" in s.3(c), is that a defendant may detain a child by persuading or deceiving the child into staying where she is. Accordingly, a person will "detain" a child for the purposes of s.3(c) not only if he were to keep her against her will but also if he were to induce her to remain with him by blandishments or simply by expressing willingness that she should stay, whether this is done by word or by deed (e.g. providing her with food or shelter).[67]

9.39 An instructive decision on the meaning of "detains" in s.2(1) is *Mortimore*,[68] in which the appellant (21) was convicted under s.2(1)(b) of detaining SR, aged 15, so as to keep her out of the lawful control of her mother. On a number of previous occasions SR had been found with the appellant after being reported missing by her mother. The appellant had previously pleaded guilty to an offence under s.2(1)(b) committed against SR and been served with a Child Abduction Warning Notice. On that occasion he had admitted SR into his home, where he lived with his family. When the police came to the address he told them SR was not there, but she was found hiding under a bed in an upstairs room. On the occasion which formed the basis of the charge,

---

[65] (1971) 1 Can.C.C. (2d) 521, at 537, B.C.C.A.
[66] *Brutus v Cozens* [1973] A.C. 854; *Moyna v Secretary of State for Work and Pensions* [2003] UKHL 44; *Evans* [2004] EWCA Crim 3102.
[67] *Foster v DPP* [2004] EWHC 2955 (Admin), at 30.
[68] [2013] EWCA Crim 1639.

SR had left home one morning to go to school but instead went to the appellant's house. When she was reported missing, the police went to the appellant's home. They found him sitting on his bed wearing boxer shorts and a T-shirt. SR was lying fully-clothed in the same bed under a duvet. The appellant was arrested and made no comment either then or in interview. At trial he did not give evidence and put forward no defence but simply challenged the prosecution to prove its case. The appellant appealed against conviction on a number of grounds, one of which was that there was no evidence upon which the jury could have found that he "detained" SR within the meaning of the 1984 Act. It was accepted for the purposes of this submission that SR had been in the appellant's company for some four-and-a-quarter hours. The Court of Appeal noted that, under s.3(c) of the Act, a person shall be regarded as detaining a child if he "induces the child to remain with him". The judge had accepted that the prosecution was required to prove that the appellant had, by his positive act, induced SR to remain at his home. Such an inducement could, the judge found, be by the provision of shelter, company or hospitality. It was also necessary for the prosecution to prove that the appellant's inducement was a cause of SR's continued presence in his house. These were matters, the judge said, for the jury to resolve and he directed them as follows:

> "A person shall be regarded as detaining a child if he causes her to be detained or induces the child to remain with him . . . The word 'detained' does not mean that the prosecution need to prove that it was against [SR's] will. It did does [*sic*] not matter so far as the offence is committed whether SR wanted to be there, consented to being in the defendant's company, although such things would be relevant to what sentence may be appropriate in due course. . . . On the facts of this case the defendant has, say the prosecution, caused her to be detained by allowing her to be there from, on one view of the evidence, 8 o'clock in the morning until 2.15 in the afternoon. He has, say the prosecution, permitted her to be there, provided hospitality to her, at least in form of shelter, allowing her to be in his house, in his bedroom, on his bed. He need not be, I direct you . . . the only cause of her being there, just one cause. The prosecution say that she would not have been there or been there for that length of time without some action on his part and that to suggest that his was in the circumstances of this case an entirely passive role, in her being in his room on this afternoon and morning would be absurd."

The Court of Appeal held that this direction as to the necessary constituents of the offence was correct. It accepted that there had been no direct evidence of inducement. The question for the jury was whether, as a matter of objective fact, the appellant had by his inducement to SR caused her to remain with him so as to keep her out of the lawful control of her mother. It was an inference plainly available to them that SR could not and would not have remained away from her home or school were it not for the appellant's preparedness to offer her shelter at his home. On that basis the Court upheld the conviction.

The better view is that an offence of "detaining" is complete at the **9.40** moment when the defendant induces the child to remain with him, although it may continue for as long as she does remain.[69] The significance of this is that, as discussed below, it is a defence under s.2(3)(b) of the 1984 Act if, at the time of the offence, the defendant believed the child to be 16 or over. Where a defendant is charged with "detaining" a child, it may be important to know precisely when the offence occurred in order to determine whether the s.2(3)(b) defence may apply. Suppose the defendant persuades a girl, whom he correctly believes to be 15, to stay with him overnight rather than go home to her parents. During the night she leads him to believe that she is 16. If, as we suggest, the offence is committed when the defendant persuades the girl to remain with him, there is no scope for the s.2(3)(b) defence to operate merely because he later comes to believe she is 16. It makes no odds for this purpose that the offence may have been continuing at that time. If, however, the defendant believes the girl is 16 at the outset, but during the night she reveals her true age, the s.2(3)(b) defence will be available until the point she does so. As the offence of "detaining" is a continuing one, the defendant will be liable to conviction from that point.

"Under the Age of Sixteen"

9.41 A child attains the age of 16 at the commencement of the sixteenth anniversary of his or her birth.[70] On a charge under s.2(1) the prosecution may rely on s.99(2) of the Children and Young Persons Act 1933, which enables the court to draw from the victim's present appearance a rebuttable presumption as to his or her age at the date of the alleged offence.[71]

"Remove from . . . Lawful Control"

9.42 The word "control" in s.2(1) requires no definition but is used in its ordinary meaning, and who has lawful control of a child is a question for the tribunal of fact.[72] In *Re Owens*[73] it was held that "lawful control" is not to be equated with "lawful custody". This, said the court, is plain from the language of s.2(1) itself, which speaks in para.(a) of someone "having lawful control" and in para.(b) of someone "entitled to lawful control". A person cannot be "entitled" to lawful custody: they either have it or they do not.

---

[69] *Hodgetts v Chiltern District Council* [1983] A.C. 120, at 127G per Lord Roskill: "It is not an essential characteristic of a criminal offence that any prohibited act or omission in order to constitute a single offence, should take place once and for all on a single day. It may take place, whether continuously or intermittently, over a period of time".

[70] Family Law Reform Act 1969 s.9(1).

[71] Children and Young Persons Act 1933 s.99(2) and Sch.1; Criminal Justice Act 1988 s.170(1) and Sch.15, para.9.

[72] *Mousir* [1987] Crim. L.R. 562 (where the Court of Appeal said that the concept of control may vary according to the person having control at the relevant time, whether it be a parent or a schoolmaster or a nanny); *Leather* (1994) 98 Cr. App. R. 179.

[73] [2000] 1 Cr. App. R. 195.

It was held in *Leather*[74] that the concept of "removal from lawful control" in s.2(1)(a) does not involve any geographical or spatial element. The appellant was charged with five counts of taking children so as to remove them from the lawful control of their parents and with two counts of attempt. In each case, the appellant persuaded or tried to persuade the child to accompany him in a search for a stolen bicycle. At no time did he try to touch any of the children or stop them from leaving. The children had all been on previous occasions, with the consent of their parents, to the places to which they went with the appellant. At the close of the prosecution case it was submitted that there was no case to answer as there was no evidence that the children had been removed from the control of their parents or, in relation to the counts of attempt, that the appellant had intended so to remove them. The appellant argued that the Crown had to prove not only that each child was, initially, in the lawful control of his parents and that he moved or was moved physically, but also that at the end of the movement the child was outside the geographical area of control. The judge rejected that submission and his ruling was upheld by the Court of Appeal, which held that the words "so as to remove him from the lawful control of any person having lawful control" does not have a necessary spatial element and therefore does not contemplate any geographical removal. The test in each case is whether the child was deflected, without lawful authority or reasonable excuse, by some action of the defendant from that which, with the consent of his parents or other person in lawful control, he would have been doing, to some activity induced by the defendant. *Leather* was cited with approval in *Foster v DPP*,[75] where the Divisional Court said "the word 'remove' is intended to convey a substitution of the authority by an accused for that of the person lawfully having it, and not the physical removal of the child from any particular place".[76]

9.43

Finally, in *Foster v DPP*[77] it was held that:

9.44

"there will be circumstances when a child may be removed from lawful control by detention rather than taking. The most obvious example is an occasion when the child is in the company of another with the agreement of his parent or guardian, but ceases to be so when knowingly detained beyond the period agreed. In [this] example, when consent knowingly expired, removal occurred."

MENTAL ELEMENT

In *Mousir*,[78] it appears to have been conceded by the defence, and accepted by the Court of Appeal, that the words "so as to" in s.2(1) are concerned with

9.45

[74] (1994) 98 Cr. App. R. 179.
[75] [2004] EWHC 2955 (Admin); [2005] 1 W.L.R. 1402. See also *Wakeman* [2011] EWCA Crim 1649.
[76] At 18.
[77] [2004] EWHC 2955 (Admin); [2005] 1 W.L.R. 1402, at 10.
[78] [1987] Crim. L.R. 562.

the objective consequence of the taking or detaining and not with the defendant's purpose in doing what he did. A contrary conclusion was reached in *Re Owens*,[79] where it was held that the words "so as to" are to be construed as meaning "with the intention of" rather than merely "with the effect of". The Court does not appear to have referred to *Mousir*, but the point was fully argued before it, and as no argument appears to have taken place in *Mousir* it might be thought that *Re Owens* is the preferable authority. However, in *Foster v DPP*[80] the Divisional Court considered the conflict between the two cases at length and concluded that *Mousir* is to be preferred. The Court noted that in *Mousir*, the Court of Appeal gave "emphatic" approval to the concession by the defence that the objective approach applies, and also that a direction to the jury in objective terms was subsequently approved in *Leather*[81] (albeit *Mousir* was not cited). It concluded that the mens rea of the abduction offence is "an intentional or reckless taking or detention of a child under the age of 16, the effect or objective consequence of which is to remove or to keep that child within the meaning of section 2(1)(a) or (b)." In other words, the defendant need not intend to remove or keep the child from lawful control, indeed he need not even know that another person has or is entitled to such control.

9.46   It also follows logically from the position reached in *Foster v DPP* that a mistaken belief on the part of the defendant that he had consent to take the child from a person entitled to lawful control of her will not prevent his conviction. There is a dictum in the old case of *Prince*[82] to the effect that a person charged with abduction contrary to the offence which preceded s.20 of the 1956 Act might escape conviction if he honestly believed on reasonable grounds that he had the consent of the girl's parent or guardian to the taking. Even if this dictum was correct when delivered, following *Foster v DPP* it cannot be regarded as accurately stating the law as regards s.2(1) of the 1984 Act. More consonant with the current position in England and Wales is the Australian decision in *Kennedy*,[83] in which it was held in relation to a comparable offence that a person who took a girl out of the possession of her parent or guardian did so at his peril as regards the parent's or guardian's will, and accordingly that a mistaken belief in consent was irrelevant.

9.47   The prosecution need not prove that the defendant knew the child to be under 16. This follows from s.2(3)(b) of the 1984 Act, which provides:

> "In proceedings against any person for an offence under this section, it shall be a defence for that person to prove—
>
> . . .
>
>   (b) that, at the time of the alleged offence, he believed that the child had attained the age of sixteen."

[79] [2000] 1 Cr. App. R. 195.
[80] [2004] EWHC 2955 (Admin); [2005] 1 W.L.R. 1402, cited with approval in *R. v X* [2010] EWCA Crim 2367 at [18], and *Wakeman* [2011] EWCA Crim 1649.
[81] *Leather* (1994) 98 Cr. App. R. 179.
[82] (1875) L.R. 2 C.C.R. 154 at 175, per Bramwell B.
[83] [1981] V.R. 565, Vict. S.Ct. F.C.

The availability of the defence in s.2(3)(b) may be contrasted with the   **9.48**
position that applied under s.20 of the Sexual Offences Act 1956, as settled
in *Prince*,[84] that a reasonable belief that the girl was 16 or over was not a
defence. Under s.2(3)(b), even an unreasonable belief that the child was 16 or
over will provide a defence. This is established by *Heys and Murtagh*,[85] in
which the Court of Appeal said[86]:

> "It is entirely clear . . . that this statutory defence does not require proof of a
> reasonable belief; only a honestly held subjective belief."

In that case, prosecution counsel had wrongly stated in his opening speech
that a reasonable belief was required. He corrected himself in closing. The
judge did not mention the error in summing up, but did mention various
objective factors which logically would be at least as relevant to a question of
reasonable belief as to a question of honest belief. The Court accepted that
the reasonableness of an asserted belief is material to the question whether it
is honestly held.[87] But it concluded that in this case, in the absence of a clear
statement by the judge that honesty and not reasonableness was the test,
there had been a "lively chance" that the jury had taken the judge's direction
as expressing a requirement of reasonable belief, and for that reason the
convictions were unsafe.

Although s.2(3)(b) requires the defendant to prove that he held the belief,   **9.49**
the better view is that the burden on him is an evidential rather than a legal
one, i.e. it should suffice for him to adduce sufficient evidence to put the point
in issue, whereupon the prosecution must prove that he did not hold the
asserted belief.

In a case where the defendant's belief as to the child's age changes over   **9.50**
time, the application of s.2(3)(b) will turn on when the taking or detaining
occurred, since it is the defendant's belief at the time of the offence, that is
critical. So if the defendant believes, correctly, when he takes the child that
she is 15, but is later persuaded by her that she is older, his change of belief
cannot prevent his conviction under s.2(1). An example of the reverse
situation is *Foster v DPP*,[88] where it was held that no offence had been
committed under s.2(1)(a) since, at the time of the taking, the appellants
believed the girl to be 16 or over, and it was only later that they became aware
that she was under that age.

An offence under s.2(1) is not a crime of specific intent,[89] and so a   **9.51**
defendant cannot avoid conviction by relying on his self-induced intoxication
to support a claim that he did not intend to take or detain the child.

---

[84] (1875) L.R. 2 C.C.R. 154.
[85] [2011] EWCA Crim 2112.
[86] At [6].
[87] Citing *Williams* (1984) 78 Cr. App. R. 276 and *Beckford* [1988] A.C. 130.
[88] [2004] EWHC 2955 (Admin); [2005] 1 W.L.R. 1402, discussed in paras 9.07 and following,
above.
[89] *Hunter (Sam Jordan)* [2015] EWCA 372.

Abduction of Child in Care

Definition

9.52   Section 49(1) of the Children Act 1989[90] provides:

> "A person shall be guilty of an offence if, knowingly and without lawful authority or reasonable excuse, he—
>   (a) takes a child to whom this section applies away from the responsible person;
>   (b) keeps such a child away from the responsible person; or
>   (c) induces, assists or incites such a child to run away or stay away from the responsible person."

In the light of *Foster v DPP*,[91] we suggest that s.49(1) creates three separate forms of the offence, neither of which is an alternative verdict for the other: taking a child to whom the section applies away from the responsible person; keeping such a child away from the responsible person; or inducing, assisting or inciting such a child to run away or stay away from the responsible person.

Mode of Trial and Punishment

9.53   An offence under s.2(1) is triable summarily and the maximum punishment is six months' imprisonment or a fine, or both.[92] As from a day to be appointed the maximum sentence of imprisonment will increase to 12 months.[93] The increase will have no application to offences committed before it takes effect.[94] Until recently, the maximum fine was a fine not exceeding level 5 on the standard scale (i.e. £5,000). The effect of s.85 of the Legal Aid, Sentencing and Punishment of Offenders Act 2012 is that, from March 12, 2015, a fine of any amount may be imposed. Fines will, however, continue to be set according to the seriousness of the offence and the means of the offender.

Child Abduction Warning Notices

9.54   See the discussion in paras 9.12 and following, above.

Parties to the Offence

9.55   An offence under s.49(1) may be committed by both males and females. By s.49(2), the offence may be committed only against a child who is the subject

---

[90] Which came wholly into force on October 14, 1991: see s.108(2), (3) of the Act and SI 1991/828, art.3(2).
[91] [2004] EWHC 2955 (Admin); [2005] 1 W.L.R. 1402, discussed in paras 9.07 and following, above.
[92] 1989 Act s.49(3).
[93] Criminal Justice Act 2003 s.282(2), (3).
[94] Criminal Justice Act 2003 s.282(4).

of a care order under Pt IV of the 1989 Act, the subject of an emergency protection order under s.43 of the Act or in police protection under s.46 of the Act. For this purpose, a "child" is a person under the age of 18.[95] A child attains the age of 18 at the commencement of the eighteenth anniversary of his or her birth.[96] As to whether the child may be convicted as an accessory to an offence of which they are the victim, see para.9.26, above.

"WITHOUT LAWFUL AUTHORITY OR REASONABLE EXCUSE"

For the meaning of these terms, see the discussion in paras 9.27 and following, above.   9.56

"TAKES ... AWAY"

For the meaning of this term, see the discussion of the word "takes" in paras 9.33 and following, above.   9.57

"KEEPS ... AWAY"

As explained in paras 9.37 and following, above, a person may "detain" a   9.58 child for the purposes of s.2(1) of the Child Abduction Act 1984 by keeping her against her will, by persuading or deceiving her into staying with him or simply by expressing willingness that she should stay, whether this is done by word or by deed (e.g. providing her with food or shelter). We suggest that the concept of "keeping away" in s.49(1)(b) should be construed in the same way.

"RUN AWAY OR STAY AWAY"

Given that s.49(1)(b) applies where a person keeps a child away from a   9.59 responsible person, s.49(1)(c) must apply where a person induces, assists or incites a child to run away or stay away but does not himself keep her away, e.g. where he pays for a train ticket to enable her to go to London or, having discovered that she has run away from care to be with her boyfriend, he persuades her to remain where she is.

"RESPONSIBLE PERSON"

Section 49(2) provides: 9.60

> " . . . in this section "the responsible person" means any person who for the time being has care of [the child] by virtue of the care order, the emergency protection order, or section 46, as the case may be."

For s.46, see para.9.55, above.

---

[95] 1989 Act s.105(1).
[96] Family Law Reform Act 1969 s.9(1).

Mental Element

9.61 The defendant must act "knowingly", i.e. he must know that the child is in care and intend to take her away (etc.) from the responsible person. There is some authority that "knowledge" in a criminal statute includes deliberately shutting one's eyes to the truth,[97] but the better view appears to be that this is a matter of evidence and that nothing short of actual knowledge will suffice.[98] May the defendant be convicted if he does not know the child is in care at the outset, but later learns that she is? This must turn on when the taking, etc., occurred and what the defendant's state of mind was at that point: see the discussion in paras 9.36, 9.40 and 9.50, above.

---

[97] *Warner v Metropolitan Police Commissioner* (1968) 52 Cr. App. R. 373 at 389, per Lord Reid; *Atwal v Massey* (1971) 56 Cr. App. R. 6.

[98] *Grainge* (1973) 59 Cr. App. R. 3; *Griffiths* (1974) 60 Cr. App. R. 14; *Moys* (1984) 79 Cr. App. R. 72; *Hall* (1985) 81 Cr. App. R. 260; *Westminster City Council v Croyalgrange Ltd* [1986] 1 W.L.R. 674 at 684, per Lord Bridge; *Sherif* [2008] EWCA Crim 2653 at [27].

CHAPTER 10

SEXUAL EXPLOITATION OF CHILDREN AND ADULTS

Introduction..................................... 10.01
Child Sexual Exploitation................ 10.03
Paying for Sexual Services of a
  Child.. 10.10
Causing or Inciting Sexual
  Exploitation of a Child 10.35
Controlling a Child in relation to
  Sexual Exploitation 10.69

Arranging or Facilitating Sexual
  Exploitation of a Child 10.88
Sexual Exploitation of Adults 10.105
Causing or Inciting Prostitution for
  Gain 10.111
Controlling Prostitution for Gain....10.143
Paying for Sexual Services of a
  Prostitute Subjected to Force etc. 10.163

INTRODUCTION

The offences in the Sexual Offences Act 2003 relating to the sexual **10.01** exploitation of children and adults have their origins in the Sexual Offences Review, which reported in 2000.[1] This chapter considers the offences under the following headings, which are taken from the Act:

- Sexual exploitation of children (ss.47–50 of the Act).
- Exploitation of prostitution (ss.52–53A).

It should be noted that the original heading to ss.47–50 was "Abuse of children through prostitution and pornography", and the offences all referred to child prostitution or pornography. In 2012, the Office of the Children's Commissioner for England recommended that:

"a review of all legislation and guidance which makes reference to children as 'prostitutes' or involved in prostitution should be initiated by the Government with the view to amending the wording to acknowledge children as sexually exploited, and where appropriate victimised through commercial sexual exploitation."[2]

This call was reiterated in the *Report of the Parliamentary inquiry into the effectiveness of legislation for tackling child sexual exploitation and trafficking*

---

[1] *Setting the Boundaries* (Home Office, July 2000), Ch.7. The report is available at *http://webarchive.nationalarchives.gov.uk/-/http://www.homeoffice.gov.uk/documents/vol1main.pdf?view=Binary* [Accessed April 30, 2015].

[2] *"I thought I was the only one. The only one in the world": Inquiry into Child Sexual Exploitation In Gangs and Groups,* Interim Report, The Office of the Children's Commissioner (November 2012). The Report is available on the Children's Commissioner website [Accessed April 30, 2016].

within the UK, produced by a cross-party group chaired by Sarah Champion MP and supported by the children's charity, Barnardo's.[3] The Report noted the concerns expressed to the inquiry about the impact of the existing terminology on attitudes towards victims, and in reinforcing misconceptions by implying an element of complicity with the offence. It called upon the Government to progress the removal of all legislative references to "child prostitution" as soon as possible. The Government responded by inserting amending provisions into what became the Serious Crime Act 2015. The key change for present purposes is the replacement of statutory references to "child prostitution" and "child pornography" in ss.48–51 of the 2003 Act with references to "sexual exploitation of children".[4] The rationale for the amendments was that "child prostitution" and "child pornography" were anachronistic terms and should be replaced by language that explicitly recognises the children concerned as victims. The amendments were not intended to widen or otherwise alter the scope of the offences,[5] and as such the definition of "sexual exploitation" in the Act is essentially a combination of the previous definitions of "prostitution" and "pornography".

10.02   The offences of slavery and trafficking for sexual exploitation are dealt with separately in Ch.11.

CHILD SEXUAL EXPLOITATION

OVERVIEW

10.03   The Sexual Offences Review, reporting in 2000, stated:[6]

> "We have all become far more aware of the extent of the commercial exploitation of children in recent years . . . The Government regards the children involved in prostitution as victims of others. The criminal law has an important role to play in ensuring that those who introduce, use and abuse children in prostitution can be dealt with appropriately."

10.04   The Review's members were unanimous that, in order to establish unambiguously that it is wrong for an adult to expect to buy or deal in the sexual services of a child, it was important to create a set of specific offences relating to the sexual exploitation of children under 18, rather than rely on the general offences of sexual exploitation. Further, the offences should cover the exploitation of children not only in prostitution but also in the production of commercial pornography,[7] and they should apply whether the child is recruited here for exploitation overseas or brought to this country

[3] The Report is available at *http://www.barnardos.org.uk/cse_parliamentary_inquiry_report.pdf* [Accessed April 30, 2016].
[4] See s.68 of the 2015 Act, which was brought into force on May 3, 2015, by SI 2015/820.
[5] cf. *Hansard*, Bill 160 2014–15, col.89, the Solicitor-General, Robert Buckland MP (February 23, 2015). But see the discussion in paras 10.63–64, below.
[6] *Setting the Boundaries* (Home Office, July 2000), para.7.6.1.
[7] The non-commercial sexual exploitation of children was dealt with by other of the Review's recommendations: see *Setting the Boundaries*, Chs 2 and 3 and Chs 3 and 4 of this work.

from overseas and exploited here. There should be no mistake of age defence, since the onus should be on the "buyer" of sexual services to ensure the child is over age.

The Review's recommendations were broadly adopted in the 2002 White **10.05** Paper *Protecting the Public*,[8] which stated the Government's intent to take effective action against those who sexually exploit children for gain by introducing a new offence, with severe penalties, of commercial exploitation of a child under 18. This offence would cover a range of activity, including buying the sexual services of a child, causing or encouraging a child into commercial sexual exploitation, facilitating the commercial sexual exploitation of a child, and controlling the activities of a child exploited by way of prostitution or pornography. This proposal made its way onto the statute book in the form of the following 2003 Act offences, which are set out as amended by the Serious Crime Act 2015:

- paying for sexual services of a child (s.47)
- causing or inciting sexual exploitation of a child (s.48)
- controlling a child in relation to sexual exploitation (s.49), and
- arranging or facilitating sexual exploitation of a child (s.50)

These were essentially new offences, although some of the prohibited **10.06** conduct was previously covered by the offence in s.28 of the Sexual Offences Act 1956 (causing prostitution of a girl under 16). The Sexual Offences Review regarded the offence under that section as inadequate as it applied only to the person in charge of the child and to children under 16. The new offences apply to anyone, regardless of their relationship with the child, and protect children under 18. The maximum penalties are also significantly higher than under s.28 of the 1956 Act. The offences are not committed if the defendant reasonably believes that the child is aged 18 or over. It is for the prosecution to prove that he did not reasonably believe this. Where the child is under 13, the offence is committed regardless of any belief the defendant may have had that the child was 18 or over.

The Government regards the 2003 Act as fulfilling the UK's international **10.07** obligations as regards the criminalisation of child sexual abuse and exploitation. Foremost among the international instruments operating in this area are the 2007 Council of Europe *Convention on the Protection of Children against Sexual Exploitation and Sexual Abuse*[9] and the 2011 EU *Directive on the sexual abuse, sexual exploitation of children and child pornography*.[10]

The Council of Europe Convention came into force on July 1, 2010, **10.08** following its fifth ratification. The UK signed the Convention on May 5, 2008

[8] *Protecting the Public: strengthening protection against sex offenders and reforming the law on sexual offences* (Cm 5668) (Nov 2002), Ch.5.

[9] CETS No. 201.

[10] *Directive 2011/93/EU of the European Parliament and of the Council of 13 December 2011 on combating the sexual abuse and sexual exploitation of children and child pornography, and replacing Council Framework Decision 2004/68/JHA.*

but has yet to ratify it. The Convention was the first international treaty to address all forms of sexual violence against children including child prostitution, child pornography, grooming and corruption of children through exposure to sexual content and activities. Its trademark is the "4 Ps" approach:

● Prevent and combat sexual exploitation and abuse of children,
● Protect the rights of child victims,
● Prosecute the perpetrators, and
● Promote appropriate policies and national and international co-operation against this phenomenon.

The Convention covers the following main topics: preventive and protective measures; assistance to child victims and their families; intervention programmes or measures for child sex offenders; criminal offences; child-friendly procedures for investigation and prosecution; recording and storing of data on convicted sex offenders; international co-operation; and a monitoring mechanism based on a body, the Committee of the Parties, composed of representatives of the parties to the Convention.

10.09   As for the EU, the 2004 *Framework Decision on combating the sexual exploitation of children and child pornography*[11] laid down a set of common minimum rules for EU States. In particular, it established common provisions on criminalisation, sanctions, aggravating circumstances, assistance to victims and jurisdiction. In order to enhance the level of protection for children from sexual exploitation, in March 2010 the Commission submitted a proposal for a new Directive on combating sexual abuse, sexual exploitation of children and child pornography to replace the 2004 Framework Decision. The UK opted in to the proposal in June 2010. The European Parliament and the Council agreed the text of the Directive in June 2011[12] and it came into force in December 2011. Member States had until December 2013 to implement the Directive, which contains provisions on the prosecution of offenders, the protection of victims and crime prevention. It was expected to have little, if any, impact on domestic criminal law, which the Government regarded as already compliant with its terms. Crispin Blunt MP, a minister in the Department of Justice, said in the Commons[13]:

> "As a leader in this field, we already comply with much of what is required by the directive, but by opting in, we have shown our support for the European Union's work in this area and we ensure that other member states will also have high standards in this field. The effect on our justice system will be minimal and we are developing co-operation mechanisms with other member states in seeking to ensure that all member states have common minimum standards of protection

---

[11] *Council Framework Decision 2004/68/JHA of 22 December 2003 on combating the sexual exploitation of children and child pornography.*
[12] *http://www.europa.eu/rapid/press-release_MEMO-11-474_en.htm* [Accessed April 30, 2015].
[13] H.C. (2010-11), European Committee B, April 26, 2011, col 18.

for children from sexual exploitation across Europe. We will seek to transpose by administrative measures, but some secondary legislation may be required."

For transposing regulations, see the Special Measures for Child Witnesses (Sexual Offences) Regulations 2013[14] and the Working with Children (Exchange of Criminal Conviction Information) (England and Wales and Northern Ireland) Regulations 2013.[15] The latter place an obligation upon the chief officer of a police force to comply with the information-sharing requirements of art.10(3) of the Directive; require the Secretary of State to identify a chief officer to implement those requirements; and allow that chief officer to obtain on request relevant information relating to disqualification from working with children from the Disclosure and Barring Service.

PAYING FOR SEXUAL SERVICES OF A CHILD

DEFINITION

Section 47(1) of the Sexual Offences Act 2003 provides: 10.10

"A person (A) commits an offence if—
(a) he intentionally obtains for himself the sexual services of another person (B),
(b) before obtaining those services, he has made or promised payment for those services to B or a third person, or knows that another person has made or promised such a payment, and
(c) either—
(i) B is under 18, and A does not reasonably believe that B is 18 or over, or
(ii) B is under 13."

MODE OF TRIAL AND PUNISHMENT

Offences under s.47 are triable and punishable as follows[16]:   10.11
- where B was under 13 at the material time and the offence involved:
  - penetration of B's anus or vagina with a part of A's body or anything else
  - penetration of B's mouth with A's penis
  - penetration of A's anus or vagina with a part of B's body or by B with anything else, or
  - penetration of A's mouth with B's penis,

---

[14] SI 2013/2971.
[15] SI 2013/2945.
[16] s.47(3)–(6).

the offence is triable on indictment and the maximum penalty is life imprisonment.

- where B was 13, 14 or 15 at the material time and the offence involved penetration as set out above, the offence is triable on indictment and the maximum penalty is 14 years' imprisonment.

- where B was 15 or younger at the material time and no penetration was involved, the offence is triable either way. The maximum penalty on conviction on indictment is 14 years' imprisonment. The maximum on summary conviction is six months' imprisonment or a fine, or both. As from a day to be appointed the maximum sentence of imprisonment on summary conviction will increase to 12 months' imprisonment.[17] The increase will have no application to offences committed before it takes effect.[18] Until recently, the maximum fine on summary conviction was a fine not exceeding the statutory maximum (i.e. £5,000). The effect of s.85 of the Legal Aid, Sentencing and Punishment of Offenders Act 2012 is that, from March 12, 2015, a fine of any amount may be imposed. An offence of this sort cannot be dealt with by way of a simple caution.[19]

- where B was 16 or 17 at the material time, then whether or not penetration was involved the offence is triable either way. The maximum penalty on conviction on indictment is seven years' imprisonment. The maximum on summary conviction is six months' imprisonment or a fine, or both. Again, as from a day to be appointed the maximum sentence of imprisonment on summary conviction will increase to 12 months' imprisonment.[20] The increase will have no application to offences committed before it takes effect.[21] Until recently, the maximum fine on summary conviction was a fine not exceeding the statutory maximum (i.e. £5,000). The effect of s.85 of the Legal Aid, Sentencing and Punishment of Offenders Act 2012 is that, from March 12, 2015, a fine of any amount may be imposed. An offence of this sort cannot be dealt with by way of a simple caution.[22]

10.12   The different maximum penalties are designed to reflect the different degrees of vulnerability of children at different ages and the seriousness of the sexual activity engaged in. In relation to children under 13, the CPS's guidance to prosecutors on the 2003 Act provides in relation to the offences in ss.47–50 that, where the child is under that age, the charge should be under

[17] Criminal Justice Act 2003 s.282(2), (3).
[18] Criminal Justice Act 2003 s.282(4).
[19] Criminal Justice and Courts Act 2015, s.17(3), and the Criminal Justice and Courts Act 2015 (Simple Cautions) (Specification of Either-Way Offences) Order 2015 (SI 2015/790).
[20] Criminal Justice Act 2003 s.282(2), (3).
[21] Criminal Justice Act 2003 s.282(4).
[22] Criminal Justice and Courts Act 2015 s.17(3), and the Criminal Justice and Courts Act 2015 (Simple Cautions) (Specification of Either-Way Offences) Order 2015 (SI 2015/790).

ss.5–8 of the Act.[23] In relation to children of 16 and 17, the lower maximum reflects the fact that the child is over the age of consent and so the gravamen of the offence rests in their exploitation rather than in the sexual activity itself.[24]

The effect of the decision in *Courtie*[25] is that the provision of different **10.13** maximum penalties creates distinct offences for each set of factual ingredients. It is accordingly important when settling an indictment to be clear which offence it is intended to charge and to specify all the material factual ingredients of that offence.[26]

For the purposes of listing, cases under s.47[27] fall within Class 2B, save for **10.14** complex cases involving many complainants (often under age, in care or otherwise particularly vulnerable) and/or many defendants who are alleged to have systematically groomed and abused them, often over a long period of time, which fall within Class 1C.[28] Cases in Class 1C must be referred to the Resident Judge, and by the Resident Judge to a Presiding Judge. Cases in Class 2B must be similarly referred in certain specified circumstances, including where the case is unusually grave or complex or a novel and important point of law is to be raised; where the defendant is a police officer, a member of the legal profession or a high profile figure; or where for any reason the case is likely to attract exceptional media attention.

An offence under s.47 is a specified offence for the purposes of the **10.15** dangerousness provisions of the Criminal Justice Act 2003.[29] It is a serious specified offence when committed against a child under 16. A s.47 offence, whenever committed, may be made the subject of an extended sentence under s.226A of that Act (extended sentence for certain violent or sexual offences).[30] An offence under s.47 committed against a child under 16 is also listed in Pt 1 of Sch.15B to the Criminal Justice Act 2003 for the purposes of s.224A of that Act (life sentence for a second listed offence).[31]

A person convicted under s.47, cautioned, found not guilty by reason of **10.16** insanity or found to be under a disability and to have done the act charged, is automatically subject to the notification requirements in the Sexual

---

[23] http://www.cps.gov.uk/legal/p_to_r/rape_and_sexual_offences/soa_2003_and_soa_1956/£a34 [Accessed April 30, 2016].

[24] *Hansard*, HL, vol.648, col.171, Lord Falconer of Thoroton (May 13, 2003); HC, Standing Committee B, September 18, 2003, col.265, Beverley Hughes MP.

[25] [1984] A.C. 463.

[26] cf. *R. v D* (1993) 14 Cr. App. R.(S.) 776.

[27] And of soliciting, inciting, encouraging or assisting, attempting or conspiring to commit the offence or assisting an offender having committed the offence.

[28] *Consolidated Criminal Practice Directions*, Part XIII Listing B: CLASSIFICATION, available at *https://www.judiciary.gov.uk/publications/criminal-practice-directions-2015/* [Accessed April 30, 2016].

[29] Criminal Justice Act 2003 s.224 and Sch.15, Pt 2.

[30] Inserted by the Legal Aid, Sentencing and Punishment of Offenders Act 2012 s.124, brought into force on December 3, 2012, by SI 2012/2906.

[31] Inserted by the Legal Aid, Sentencing and Punishment of Offenders Act 2012 s.122, brought into force on December 3, 2012, by SI 2012/2906.

Offences Act 2003,[32] if the victim or (as the case may be) other party was under 16 and the offender was 18 or over or is sentenced to at least 12 months' imprisonment.

Sentencing

10.17 For the Sentencing Council guideline relating to the sentencing of sexual offences committed by offenders aged 18 and over, see Ch.33, below. The previous guideline, issued in 2007 by the Sentencing Guidelines Council ("SGC"), was drafted on the basis that where the victim was under 16, the offender would be charged under ss.5–8 or s.9 of the 2003 Act (i.e. with an under-13 offence or an offence of sexual activity with a child). In the consultation on its draft guideline,[33] the Sentencing Council noted that since 2006, s.47 had been sentenced on 13 occasions, with four of these cases involving a child under 16. Given the low number of cases, the Council proposed that when sentencing for a s.47 offence committed in relation to a victim under the age of 16, the sentencer should follow the guidelines for offences under ss.5–8 (in the case of children under 13) or s.9 (children aged 13–15), with the sentence being increased to reflect the element of commercial exploitation. This approach, which was universally supported in responses to the consultation, has the result that the guideline for s.47 should be used only where the victim was aged 16 or 17.

10.18 An issue that was not directly covered in the consultation but on which the Sentencing Council received some of the strongest representations was the language used in relation to the child exploitation offences, including those in s.47: see further on this para.10.44, below.

Sentencing guideline

Step One—Harm and culpability

10.19 The guideline requires the sentencing court to go through a series of steps in order to determine the appropriate sentence. Step one involves determining the offence category by reference to the degree of harm caused and then the culpability level for the offence. As with offences of sexual activity with a child contrary to s.9 of the Act (for which see paras 4.31 and following, above), the guideline correlates harm to the sexual activity that has taken place. The harm and culpability factors for offences under s.47 are accordingly as follows:

---

[32] s.80 and Sch.3, discussed in Ch.35, below.
[33] *Sexual Offences Guideline: Consultation* (December 6, 2012). The consultation document is available on the Sentencing Council's website.

Harm	
Category 1	• Penetration of vagina or anus (using body or object) by, or of, victim • Penile penetration of mouth by, or of, victim • Violence or threats of violence • Victim subjected to unsafe/degrading sexual activity (beyond that which is inherent in the offence)
Category 2	Touching of naked genitalia or naked breasts by, or of, the victim
Category 3	Other sexual activity

CULPABILITY
A
• Abduction/detention • Sexual images of victim recorded, retained, solicited or shared • Offender acts together with others in order to commit the offence • Use of alcohol/drugs on victim to facilitate the offence • Abuse of trust • Previous violence against victim • Sexual images of victim recorded, retained, solicited or shared • Blackmail or other threats made (including to expose victim to the authorities, family/friends or others) • Offender aware that he has a sexually transmitted disease • Offender aware victim has been trafficked
B
Factor(s) in category A not present

In its consultation document, the Sentencing Council placed penetrative **10.20** activity within harm category 2, rather than category 1. It acknowledged that in other guidelines relating to sexual activity with children (e.g. the guideline for the offence in s.9 of the 2003 Act of sexual activity with a child), penetrative activity is placed in the highest category of harm. But those guidelines apply where the victim is under the age of consent, whereas the s.47 guideline is intended to apply only to victims aged 16 and 17. Ordinarily, it is lawful to engage in penetrative activity with someone aged 16 or 17; it is the fact that the offender is paying for sexual services that makes this an offence. In consequence, the Council considered that the fact of penetration should not of itself place the offence in the highest category of harm. A number of respondents took issue with this approach, arguing that penetrative activity should be within category 1 regardless of age because the element of commercial exploitation should carry more weight than the issue of the age of consent. The Council conceded this point and in the published guideline placed penetrative activity within category 1.

10.21   As regards culpability, the Council said:

- "Abduction/detention" is included within culpability A because any limitation of the victim's freedom will increase the culpability inherent in a s.47 offence, whether the offender was involved in the abduction or detention or simply knew of it.
- "Offender aware that he has a sexually transmitted disease" reflects the increased culpability where the offender deliberately exposes the victim to the risk of contracting such a disease.
- "Offender aware victim has been trafficked" is included as there may be cases where the child is trafficked before being subject to sexual exploitation for commercial purposes, and if the offender is aware of the trafficking this will increase their culpability.

Step Two—Starting point and category range

10.22   Once the court has determined the offence category and culpability level, at step two it should use the corresponding starting point specified in the guideline in order to reach a sentence within the category range. The starting point applies to all offenders irrespective of plea or previous convictions. Once the starting point has been determined, step two allows further adjustment for aggravating or mitigating features, set out below. A case of particular gravity, reflected by multiple features of culpability or harm, could merit upward adjustment from the starting point before further adjustment for aggravating or mitigating features. Where there is a sufficient prospect of rehabilitation, a community order with a sex offender treatment programme requirement under s.202 of the Criminal Justice Act 2003 may be a proper alternative to a short or moderate length custodial sentence. The starting points and category ranges for offences under s.47 where the victim is aged 16 or 17 are as follows:

	A	**B**
Category 1	*Starting point* 4 years' custody *Category range* 2–5 years' custody	*Starting point* 2 years' custody *Category range* 1–4 years' custody
Category 2	*Starting point* 3 years' custody *Category range* 1–4 years' custody	*Starting point* 1 year's custody *Category range* 26 weeks'–2 years' custody
Category 3	*Starting point* 1 years' custody *Category range* 26 weeks'–2 years' custody	*Starting point* 26 weeks' custody *Category range* High level community order – 1 years' custody

Aggravating and mitigating factors

After identifying the starting point and category range, the court should **10.23** consider whether the presence of aggravating or mitigating factors should result in an upward or downward adjustment from the starting point or the imposition of a sentence outside the category range. In particular, relevant recent convictions are likely to result in an upward adjustment. When sentencing appropriate category 3 offences, the court should also consider whether the custody threshold has been passed; if so, whether a custodial sentence is unavoidable; and if it is, whether that sentence can be suspended. The non-exhaustive list of aggravating and mitigating factors for offences under s.47 is as follows:

Aggravating factors
Statutory aggravating factors
<ul><li>Previous convictions, having regard to a) the nature of the offence to which the conviction relates and its relevance to the current offence; and b) the time that has elapsed since the conviction</li><li>Offence committed whilst on bail</li></ul>
Other aggravating factors
<ul><li>Ejaculation</li><li>Failure to comply with current court orders</li><li>Offence committed whilst on licence</li><li>Any steps taken to prevent the victim reporting an incident, obtaining assistance and/or from assisting or supporting the prosecution</li><li>Attempts to dispose of or conceal evidence</li></ul>

Mitigating factors
<ul><li>No previous convictions **or** no relevant/recent convictions</li><li>Remorse</li><li>Previous good character and/or exemplary conduct*</li><li>Age and/or lack of maturity where it affects the responsibility of the offender</li><li>Mental disorder or learning disability, particularly where linked to the commission of the offence</li><li>Demonstration of steps taken to address offending behaviour</li></ul>

* Previous good character/exemplary conduct is different from having no previous convictions. The more serious the offence, the less the weight which should normally be attributed to this factor. Where previous good character/exemplary conduct has been used to facilitate the offence, this mitigation should not normally be allowed and such conduct may constitute an aggravating factor.

Steps Three to Nine

10.24   The remaining steps cover the following points. At step three the court should consider any factors which would indicate a reduction in sentence, e.g. assistance to the prosecution. At step four it should consider any reduction for a guilty plea. At step five the court should consider dangerousness, i.e. whether it would be appropriate to award an extended sentence (s.226A of the Criminal Justice Act 2003). Step six requires the court to consider whether the total sentence is just and proportionate to the offending behaviour. At step seven it should consider whether to make an ancillary order (e.g. an SHPO or a restraining order). Step eight requires the court to fulfil its duty under s.174 of the Criminal Justice Act 2003 to give reasons for, and explain the effect of, the sentence. Finally, at step nine the court should consider whether to give credit for time spent on bail in accordance with s.240A of that Act.

PARTIES TO THE OFFENCE

Both the person who obtains the sexual services and the child victim may be **10.25** male or female. As to whether the child victim of a s.47 offence is liable to conviction as an accessory to the offence, see the discussion in paras 4.57 and following, above.

JURISDICTION

By virtue of s.72 of and Sch.2 to the Sexual Offences Act 2003, as amended,[34]   **10.26** it is an offence under s.47 for a UK national to do an act in a country outside the UK which would constitute a s.47 offence if done in England and Wales. The amendments, made in 2008, expanded the scope of s.72 in two respects. First, they removed the limitation on s.72 as enacted that it applied only to offences committed against victims aged under 16 (the relevant age is now 18). Secondly, they abolished, in respect of UK nationals, the "double criminality" requirement that the act must have been an offence in the country in which it was done. This requirement is, however, retained in respect of the prosecution of UK residents and those who become UK residents or nationals after the doing of the relevant act. For the purposes of s.72 a "country" includes a territory and a "United Kingdom national" means a British citizen, a British overseas territories citizen, a British National (Overseas), a British Overseas citizen, a person who under the British Nationality Act 1981 is a British subject, or a British protected person within the meaning of that Act.[35] An act is taken to be an offence in the country in which it was done unless the defendant serves a notice putting the prosecution to proof on the point.[36]

"OBTAINS FOR HIMSELF"

A s.47 offence is committed where a person obtains a child's sexual services   **10.27** for himself but not where he obtains them for another person. Depending on the circumstances, obtaining such services for another person could involve a range of other offences, including conspiracy to commit a s.47 offence; encouraging, assisting or aiding and abetting such an offence; causing or inciting child sexual exploitation (s.48); or arranging or facilitating child

---

[34] By the Criminal Justice and Immigration Act 2008 s.72, with effect from July 14, 2008.
[35] s.72(9).
[36] s.72(6)–(8).

sexual exploitation (s.50). It is clearly implicit in the requirement that A "intentionally obtains for himself" sexual services that there must be conduct on A's part which he intends to and does result in him obtaining sexual services, and that the mere receipt by him of such services without any conduct on his part would be insufficient. If Parliament had intended otherwise it might have been expected to make this explicit, e.g. by providing that A commits a s.47 offence where a child provides him with sexual services as well as (or instead of) where he "obtains" such services.

10.28   Sexual services are "obtained" only when they are actually provided. So, if A arranges with B (a child) that B will have sex with him for money that evening, he does not commit the s.47 offence until the sex takes place, though again, at the time the arrangement is made A may be guilty of the s.48 or 50 offence, or the offence under s.14 of the Act of arranging or facilitating child sexual activity.

"The Sexual Services of Another Person"

10.29   The term "sexual services" is not defined in the Act. We suggest that it should be interpreted by reference to the definition of the word "sexual" in s.78 of the Act.[37] That provision defines "sexual" in relation to "penetration, touching or any other activity". Whilst it does not refer specifically to "services", the provision of sexual services by B will inevitably involve "activity" of some sort. In any event, as the provisions appear in the same statute it is entirely proper for the courts to proceed by analogy with s.78 when considering the correct approach to the word "sexual" in s.47.

10.30   The application of s.78 may be important where the services provided by B are not obviously sexual in nature and the only sexual element is in A's head. This might be an issue where A is motivated by an obscure sexual fetish. Suppose, for example, that in order to obtain sexual gratification A pays B to read out to him supposed love letters from his (A's) girlfriend.[38] If one proceeds by reference to s.78, the admissibility of evidence of A's motive on the question whether the services he obtained from B were "sexual" will depend on whether a reasonable person, looking at the services and the circumstances in which they were provided, would consider them capable of being "sexual" services. If a reasonable person would think them so capable, but would want to know why A acted as he did before deciding, then evidence of A's purpose should be admissible. Otherwise, it should not.

10.31   Most cases that are considered for prosecution under s.47 will, of course, involve services that are manifestly sexual, involving intimate physical contact such as sexual intercourse or masturbation. If B's services take the form of sado-masochistic acts performed on A, the jury may convict if they consider the acts to be sexual in nature. What if the services involve no

---

[37] Discussed in paras 2.66 and following, above.
[38] cf. *May* (1990) 91 Cr. App. R. 157.

physical contact between A and B? This does not necessarily mean that A does not obtain "sexual" services. On the contrary, it seems clear that acts of a sexual nature that do not involve physical contact between the parties may nonetheless be capable of constituting sexual services, e.g. where B performs sexual acts on herself or a sexy strip in front of A for his pleasure.

"PAYMENT"

Section 47(2) provides: **10.32**

> "In this section, 'payment' means any financial advantage, including the discharge of an obligation to pay or the provision of goods or services (including sexual services) gratuitously or at a discount."

The reference to "any financial advantage" is sufficiently wide to bring within the definition any transaction that provides financial benefit of an indirect nature.[39] The definition has the effect that "payment" covers the satisfaction or remission of a debt and the provision of, for example, drugs or alcohol either free or at reduced cost. It also covers the case where A obtains a child's sexual services by providing other sexual services in return. This ensures that the s.47 offence catches the activities of paedophile rings whose members provide each other on a reciprocal basis with access to children to exploit sexually. It should be noted that there is no requirement to prove a causative link between the payment or promised payment and the obtaining of services, although of course ordinarily such a link will necessarily exist.

MENTAL ELEMENT

It must be proved that A "intentionally" obtained sexual services. For the   **10.33**
meaning of "intention", see paras 2.78 and following, above.

It is a requirement of the offence, where B is aged 13 to 17, that A did not   **10.34**
reasonably believe that B was 18 or over. The All-Party Parliamentary Group on Prostitution and the Global Sex Trade has called for this requirement to be removed in relation to children under the age of 16.[40] In contrast to the child sex offences, there is no evidential burden on A to put reasonable belief in issue. It is therefore for the prosecution to prove that he had no such belief. See further para.4.66, above.

---

[39] cf. *Jones* (1903) 6 O.L.R. 35, Ont. CA, where the appellant was held to have kept premises "for gain" where he allowed others to play poker in them, his only reward being the profit he made on cigar sales to the players. Osler JA said (at 38): "'Gain' is that which is acquired or comes as a benefit, profit or advantage, and it may be derived indirectly as well as directly."

[40] *Shifting the Burden: Inquiry to assess the operation of the current legal settlement on prostitution in England and Wales* (March 2014). The Report is available at *https://appgprostitution.files.wordpress.com/2014/04/shifting-the-burden1.pdf* [Accessed April 30, 2016].

Causing or Inciting Sexual Exploitation of a Child

Definition

10.35   Section 48(1) of the Sexual Offences Act 2003[41] provides:

> "A person (A) commits an offence if—
> (a) he intentionally causes or incites another person (B) to be sexually exploited in any part of the world, and
> (b) either—
>   (i) B is under 18, and A does not reasonably believe that B is 18 or over, or
>   (ii) B is under 13."

10.36   There is a significant overlap between this offence and the offences in ss.8 and 10 of the 2003 Act of causing or inciting a child under 13/under 16 to engage in sexual activity. The chief differences are that s.48 protects children under 18, and that in a prosecution under s.48 it must be shown that B was caused or incited not merely to engage in sexual activity but to be sexually exploited as defined in s.50, i.e. through payment for sexual services or the recording of an indecent image. The overlap between the offences means that prosecutors will need to decide whether to charge under s.8/s.10 or under s.48, as the differences between the offences are likely to make it inappropriate to include them as alternative counts on a single indictment.[42] When the Sexual Offences Bill was before Parliament, the Government expressed the view that whenever possible a person should be charged under s.10 rather than s.48, as s.10 is designed specifically to protect children under 16.[43] By implication this comment refers only to children aged 13, 14 or 15, so that where the child is under the age of 13 the charge should be under s.8 rather than under s.48. The CPS's guidance to prosecutors on the 2003 Act provides in relation to the offences in ss.47–50 that, where the child is under 13, the charge should be under ss.5–8 of the Act.[44] Although the guidance does not refer in this context to s.10, the better view is nonetheless that it should be used in preference to s.48 where the child is 13 or over.

10.37   By inference from *Walker*,[45] decided under s.8 of the Act, s.48 creates two offences, one of intentionally causing and one of intentionally inciting a child to be sexually exploited. Further, given that a child can be sexually exploited in two different ways, either by them offering or providing sexual services for

---

[41] As amended by the Serious Crime Act 2015 s.68(1), (3), with effect from May 3, 2015 (SI 2015/820).

[42] cf. *Hansard*, Standing Committee B, September 18, 2003, col.267, Dominic Grieve MP.

[43] ibid., col.269ff, Beverley Hughes MP. The maximum penalties under the two sections are the same.

[44] *http://www.cps.gov.uk/legal/p_to_r/rape_and_sexual_offences/soa_2003_and_soa_1956/£a34* [Accessed April 30, 2016].

[45] [2006] EWCA Crim 1907.

payment or by an indecent image of them being recorded, the better view is that s.48 creates distinct offences in relation to the two forms of activity. The net result is that s.48 creates four offences: causing a child to be sexually exploited by offering or providing sexual services for payment; inciting a child to be sexually exploited in that way; causing a child to be sexually exploited by an indecent image of them being recorded; and inciting a child to be sexually exploited by such an image being recorded. It is important that the charge or indictment makes clear which offence is being charged.

MODE OF TRIAL AND PUNISHMENT

Offences under s.48 are triable either way.[46] The maximum penalty on conviction on indictment is 14 years' imprisonment.[47] The maximum on summary conviction is six months' imprisonment or a fine, or both. As from a day to be appointed the maximum sentence of imprisonment on summary conviction will increase to 12 months' imprisonment.[48] The increase will have no application to offences committed before it takes effect.[49] Until recently, the maximum fine on summary conviction was a fine not exceeding the statutory maximum (i.e. £5,000). The effect of s.85 of the Legal Aid, Sentencing and Punishment of Offenders Act 2012 is that, from March 12, 2015, a fine of any amount may be imposed. Offences under s.48 cannot be dealt with by way of a simple caution.[50] **10.38**

For the purposes of listing, cases under s.48[51] fall within Class 2B, save for complex cases involving many complainants (often under age, in care or otherwise particularly vulnerable) and/or many defendants who are alleged to have systematically groomed and abused them, often over a long period of time, which fall within Class 1C.[52] Cases in Class 1C must be referred to the Resident Judge, and by the Resident Judge to a Presiding Judge. Cases in Class 2B must be similarly referred in certain specified circumstances, including where the case is unusually grave or complex or a novel and important point of law is to be raised; where the defendant is a police officer, a member of the legal profession or a high profile figure; or where for any reason the case is likely to attract exceptional media attention. **10.39**

---

[46] s.48(2).
[47] s.48(2).
[48] Criminal Justice Act 2003 s.282(2), (3).
[49] Criminal Justice Act 2003 s.282(4).
[50] Criminal Justice and Courts Act 2015 s.17(3), and the Criminal Justice and Courts Act 2015 (Simple Cautions) (Specification of Either-Way Offences) Order 2015 (SI 2015/790).
[51] And of soliciting, inciting, encouraging or assisting, attempting or conspiring to commit the offence or assisting an offender having committed the offence.
[52] *Consolidated Criminal Practice Directions*, Part XIII Listing B: CLASSIFICATION, available at *https://www.judiciary.gov.uk/publications/criminal-practice-directions-2015/* [Accessed April 30, 2016].

10.40   An offence under s.48 is a serious specified offence for the purposes of the dangerousness provisions of the Criminal Justice Act 2003.[53] A s.48 offence, whenever committed, may be made the subject of an extended sentence under s.226A of that Act (extended sentence for certain violent or sexual offences).[54] Section 48 is also listed in Pt 1 of Sch.15B to the Criminal Justice Act 2003 for the purposes of s.224A of that Act (life sentence for a second listed offence).[55]

10.41   A person convicted under s.48, cautioned, found not guilty by reason of insanity or found to be under a disability and to have done the act charged, is automatically subject to the notification requirements in the Sexual Offences Act 2003,[56] if he was 18 or over at the time of the offence or is sentenced to at least 12 months' imprisonment.

10.42   A s.48 offence is a "lifestyle" offence for the purposes of the Proceeds of Crime Act 2002.[57] Accordingly, a conviction for the offence may, if the other conditions set out in the 2002 Act are met, result in the court making a confiscation order in relation to the benefit the offender has derived from the offence or, if he has a general criminal lifestyle, from his general criminal conduct.

SENTENCING

10.43   For the Sentencing Council guideline relating to the sentencing of sexual offences committed by offenders aged 18 and over, see Ch.33, below. In its consultation on the draft guideline,[58] the Sentencing Council proposed to cover the offences in ss.48–50 of the 2003 Act in one guideline, given the commonality in the harm caused and in the culpability of the offender and the fact that the offences share a statutory maximum. It duly followed this approach in the guideline as published.

10.44   An issue not directly covered in the consultation but upon which the Sentencing Council received some of the strongest representations was the language used in relation to the exploitation offences. In particular, the very strong view of a substantial number of respondents was that using the terms "child prostitution" and "child pornography" was wholly inappropriate as they do not reflect the fact that the underlying criminal activity is child

---

[53] Criminal Justice Act 2003 s.224 and Sch.15, Pt 2.

[54] Inserted by the Legal Aid, Sentencing and Punishment of Offenders Act 2012 s.124, brought into force on December 3, 2012, by SI 2012/2906.

[55] Inserted by the Legal Aid, Sentencing and Punishment of Offenders Act 2012 s.122, brought into force on December 3, 2012, by SI 2012/2906.

[56] s.80 and Sch.3, discussed in Ch.35, below.

[57] 2002 Act Sch.2, as amended by the 2003 Act s.139 and Sch.6, para.46 and by the Serious Crime Act 2015 s.85 and Sch.4, para.58.

[58] *Sexual Offences Guideline: Consultation* (December 6, 2012). The consultation document is available on the Sentencing Commission website.

exploitation. The Council noted that the contested wording was taken directly from the legislation, but that in drafting the guideline it had been alive to sensitivities of language and so had referred where possible to "victims" rather than "child prostitutes". It also included the following statement on the title page of these offences: "The terms 'child prostitute', 'child prostitution' and 'child involved in pornography' are used in this guideline in accordance with the statutory language contained in the Sexual Offences Act 2003". The aim was to make it clear that the terminology was not intended to stigmatise the victims. The Council also committed to revise and update the guideline if and when statutory changes were made to the language of these offences. Those changes have since been made, with the terms "child prostitution" and "child pornography" as used in ss.47–50 of the 2003 Act replaced by references to "child sexual exploitation". In February 2016 the Sentencing Council published an updated version of the guideline to reflect these changes. This version is set out below.

Sentencing guideline

Step One—Harm and culpability

The guideline requires the sentencing court to go through a series of steps in order to determine the appropriate sentence. Step one involves determining the offence category by reference to the degree of harm caused and then the culpability level for the offence. The harm and culpability factors for offences under ss.48–50 are as follows: **10.45**

Harm	
Category 1	• Victims involved in penetrative sexual activity • Abduction/detention • Violence or threats of violence • Sustained and systematic psychological abuse • Victim(s) participated in unsafe/degrading sexual activity beyond that which is inherent in the offence • Victim(s) passed around by the offender to other "customers" and/or moved to other brothels
Category 2	Factor(s) in categories 1 not present

CULPABILITY		
A	*B*	*C*
• Directing or organising child prostitution or pornography on significant commercial basis • Expectation of significant financial or other gain • Expectation of significant financial or other gain • Abuse of trust • Exploitation of victim(s) known to be trafficked • Significant involvement in limiting the freedom of the victim(s) • Grooming of a victim to enter prostitution or pornography including through cultivation of a dependency on drugs or alcohol	• Close involvement with inciting, controlling, arranging or facilitating child prostitution or pornography (where offender's involvement is not as a result of coercion)	• Performs limited function under direction • Close involvement but engaged by coercion/ intimidation/ exploitation

10.46   Many of the harm factors for offences under ss.48–50 are adapted from the offences of sexual exploitation of adults (ss.52–53 of the 2003 Act) and are discussed in para.10.121, below. In its consultation, the Sentencing Council gave its reasons for including certain harm factors in category 1:
- "Victim involved in penetrative sexual activity" is included because, although the offender may have had no direct sexual contact with the victim, where penetrative activity takes place the offender's actions will have exposed the victim to a very high degree of harm.
- As to "victim(s) participated in unsafe/degrading sexual activity beyond that which is inherent in the offence", the Council said that any sexual activity that commercially exploits a child is degrading and

that this harm factor is intended to cover situations where there is additional degradation.

- In relation to "victim(s) passed around by the offender to other 'customers' and/or moved to other brothels", the Council thought that such "trading" of victims and their exposure to other offenders significantly increases the harm caused to them. One respondent to the consultation opposed the inclusion of this factor on the basis that it identifies behaviours that imply trafficking, which may in turn encourage the CPS to charge offenders under ss.48–50 instead of with the offence of human trafficking (for which see now s.2 of the Modern Slavery Act 2015, discussed in Ch.11, below), so encouraging the under-use of the trafficking offence. The Sentencing Council decided to retain the factor, saying that ss.48–50 are in practice sometimes used as alternative charges to human trafficking, and the guideline is drafted with the intention that, whichever offence is charged, where there is evidence of a child being passed between offenders, the increased harm should be reflected in the sentence starting point.

As for the culpability factors, the Council said in its consultation that **10.47** culpability A covers offenders with a high degree of influence and control:

- "Directing or organising sexual exploitation of child on significant commercial basis" and "expectation of significant financial or other gain" will apply to individuals who orchestrate activity for substantial commercial gain. The previous guideline, issued in 2007 by the Sentencing Guidelines Council, included "organised commercial exploitation" in the highest category of offence, but the new guideline widens this to cover situations where the activity may not be formally organised, so long as the commercial or financial element is "significant". As with the offences of sexual exploitation of adults (ss.52 and 53 of the 2003 Act), the Council wished to move away from placing a monetary value on the term "significant" in this context and so whether gain is sufficient will depend on the facts of the case.
- "Abuse of trust" is particularly relevant where an offender is involved in the exploitation of children and its presence demonstrates the highest level of culpability.
- As for "exploitation of victim(s) known to be trafficked", the Council said that where an offender knows that a child has been trafficked, this demonstrates the highest level of culpability due to the increased isolation and vulnerability of such children, whether they are trafficked into the UK from abroad or within the country.

As regards culpability C, the Council said that the specified factors are **10.48** intended to cover the offender who plays a peripheral role or who is engaged because they are exploited or coerced themselves. Nonetheless, as these offences concern the commercial sexual exploitation of children, even where the offender performs a limited role, a high level of culpability will exist which is reflected in the sentencing starting points and ranges.

Step Two—Starting point and category range

10.49   Once the court has determined the offence category and culpability level, at step two it should use the corresponding starting point specified in the guideline in order to reach a sentence within the category range. The guideline specifies different starting points and ranges for victims under 13, those aged 13–15 and those aged 16–17. The starting point applies to all offenders irrespective of plea or previous convictions. Once the starting point has been determined, step two allows further adjustment for aggravating or mitigating features, set out below. A case of particular gravity, reflected by multiple features of culpability or harm, could merit upward adjustment from the starting point before further adjustment for aggravating or mitigating features. Where there is a sufficient prospect of rehabilitation, a community order with a sex offender treatment programme requirement under s.202 of the Criminal Justice Act 2003 may be a proper alternative to a short or moderate length custodial sentence.

10.50   The starting points and category ranges for offences under ss.48—50 are as follows:

		A	*B*	*C*
Category 1	*U13*	*Starting point* 10 years' custody	*Starting point* 8 years' custody	*Starting point* 5 years' custody
		Category range 8–13 years' custody	*Category range* 6–11 years' custody	*Category range* 2–6 years' custody
	13–15	*Starting point* 8 years' custody	*Starting point* 5 years' custody	*Starting point* 2 years' 6 months' custody
		Category range 6–11 years' custody	*Category range* 4–8 years' custody	*Category range* 1–4 years' custody
	16–17	*Starting point* 4 years' custody	*Starting point* 2 years' custody	*Starting point* 1 years' custody
		Category range 3–7 years' custody	*Category range* 1–4 years' custody	*Category range* 26 weeks'–2 years' custody

Category 2		Starting point	Starting point	Starting point
	U13	8 years' custody	6 years' custody	2 years' custody
		Category range	Category range	Category range
		6–11 years' custody	4–9 years' custody	1–4 years' custody
	13–15	Starting point	Starting point	Starting point
		6 years' custody	3 years' custody	1 years' custody
		Range	Range	Category range
		4–9 years' custody	2–5 year's custody	26 weeks'–2 years' custody
	16–17	Starting point	Starting point	Starting point
		3 years' custody	1 years' custody	26 weeks' custody
		Range	Range	Range
		2–5 years' custody	26 weeks'–2 years' custody	High level community order– 1 year's custody

Aggravating and mitigating factors

After identifying the starting point and category range, the court should **10.51** consider whether the presence of aggravating or mitigating factors should result in an upward or downward adjustment from the starting point or the imposition of a sentence outside the range. In particular, relevant recent convictions are likely to result in an upward adjustment. When sentencing appropriate category 2 offences, the court should also consider whether the custody threshold has been passed; if so, whether a custodial sentence is unavoidable; and if it is, whether that sentence can be suspended. The non-exhaustive list of aggravating and mitigating factors for offences under ss.48-50 is:

Aggravating factors
Statutory aggravating factors
<ul><li>Previous convictions, having regard to a) the nature of the offence to which the conviction relates and its relevance to the current offence; and b) the time that has elapsed since the conviction</li><li>Offence committed whilst on bail</li></ul>
Other aggravating factors
<ul><li>Failure to comply with current court orders</li><li>Offence committed whilst on licence</li><li>Deliberate isolation of victim(s)</li><li>Vulnerability of victim(s)</li><li>Threats made to expose victim(s) to the authorities (for example, immigration or police), family/friends or others</li><li>Harm threatened against the family/friends of victim(s)</li><li>Passport/identity documents removed</li><li>Victim(s) prevented from seeking medical treatment</li><li>Victim(s) prevented from attending school</li><li>Food withheld</li><li>Earnings withheld/kept by offender or evidence of excessive wage reduction or debt bondage, inflated travel or living expenses or unreasonable interest rates</li><li>Any steps taken to prevent the victim reporting an incident, obtaining assistance and/or from assisting or supporting the prosecution</li><li>Attempts to dispose of or conceal evidence</li><li>Timescale over which the operation has been run</li></ul>

Mitigating factors
<ul><li>No previous convictions **or** no relevant/recent convictions</li><li>Remorse</li><li>Previous good character and/or exemplary conduct*</li><li>Age and/or lack of maturity where it affects the responsibility of the offender</li><li>Mental disorder or learning disability, particularly where linked to the commission of the offence</li></ul>

* Previous good character/exemplary conduct is different from having no previous convictions. The more serious the offence, the less the weight which should normally be attributed to this factor. Where previous good character/exemplary conduct has been used to facilitate the offence, this mitigation should not normally be allowed and such conduct may constitute an aggravating factor.

Steps Three to Nine

The remaining steps cover the following points. At step three the court   **10.52**
should consider any factors which would indicate a reduction in sentence, e.g.
assistance to the prosecution. At step four it should consider any reduction
for a guilty plea. At step five the court should consider dangerousness, i.e.
whether it would be appropriate to award a life sentence (s.224A of the
Criminal Justice Act 2003) or an extended sentence (s.226A). Step six
requires the court to consider whether the total sentence is just and
proportionate to the offending behaviour. At step seven it should consider
whether to make an ancillary order (e.g. a SHPO or a restraining order). Step
eight requires the court to fulfil its duty under s.174 of the Criminal Justice
Act 2003 to give reasons for, and explain the effect of, the sentence. Finally,
at step nine the court should consider whether to give credit for time spent on
bail in accordance with s.240A of that Act.

Sentencing examples

Where an offender is sentenced for both causing child sexual exploitation   **10.53**
contrary to s.48 and obtaining the sexual services of a child (contrary to s.47
of the Act) in relation to the same course of conduct, it is important for the
sentencer to pay due regard to the principle of totality and to avoid any
danger of double-counting. This point is illustrated by *Gribbin (Daniel
Peter)*,[59] in which the applicant was convicted under count 1 of causing or
inciting[60] child prostitution or pornography (s.48) and under counts two and
three of paying for the sexual services of a child (s.47). The applicant, 40, met
R, a girl aged 16, in an internet chatroom. He purported to be a 17-year-old
girl, saying he provided sexual services to men for money and asking R if she
wanted to get some money by selling her body. At the time R's mother was
ill and R was worried about her family going into debt, so she eventually
agreed to take a phone call from a man. The applicant, calling himself
"Dean", contacted R by telephone and arranged to meet her as a client. He
drove to her home town, met her and took her to a park where he gave her
£50 and they had sexual intercourse. He used a condom, but it split and he
gave her a further £20 to get the morning-after pill. They met again four days
later, when again he paid her money and they had sexual intercourse in the
park. The applicant was caught as a result of external monitoring of the
chatroom site. He had previously been cautioned for sending a letter
conveying an indecent or grossly offensive message, after he had texted a sex
worker and asked if she would help instruct his 13-year-old step-daughter in
the ways of sex and have sex with him and the step-daughter. There was in
fact no step-daughter. A pre-sentence report stated that the applicant

---

[59] [2015] EWCA Crim 736.
[60] If the indictment was in this form it was duplicitous: see para.10.37, above.

represented a high risk of re-offending. In passing sentence, the judge said that R was a complete stranger to the applicant, who knew that she was 16. R was vulnerable and in a desperately sad situation and the applicant made her into a prostitute and availed himself of her services with a considerable impact upon her. On count 1, the judge said that the s.48 offence fell into category 1A. He considered that there was planning and grooming to make R enter into prostitution. There were aggravating features in that R was vulnerable and the applicant had a previous caution. The judge said that counts 2 and 3 were separate and distinct offences and consecutive sentences could be passed. But having regard to totality, the sentences on counts 2 and 3 should run concurrently with each other, albeit consecutive to count 1. Taking into account mitigation, the judge imposed four years' imprisonment on count 1 and two years' imprisonment on each of counts 2 and 3, concurrent to each other but consecutive to the sentence on count 1, making six years in all. The grounds of appeal were that the judge was wrong to conclude that the offence in count 1 involved the highest level of culpability and so the sentence imposed on that count was too high; and he was also wrong to impose consecutive sentences, or should have substantially reduced the sentences on counts 2 and 3 to reflect the principle of totality. As regards count 1, the Court of Appeal held that one of the matters which put it into category 1 was the fact that there was penetrative sexual activity. So far as culpability was concerned, the Court accepted that what occurred here could be described as grooming, although it was very much at the lower end of the scale of grooming. The Court considered, however, that there was a real danger of double counting. If, as was appropriate, the judge took into account the fact that sexual intercourse occurred when addressing count 1, he could not take it into account again in treating counts 2 and 3 as requiring a consecutive sentence. Looking at the applicant's overall criminality, the appropriate sentence was one of four years' imprisonment, and the Court therefore made the sentences on counts 2 and 3 concurrent with the sentence on count 1, making four years in all.

10.54   The totality principle was also at the heart of the decision in *Arslan Khan*.[61] The appellant (19) was convicted of three offences: under count 1, of causing or inciting[62] child prostitution or pornography contrary to s.48; under count 2, of trafficking within the UK for sexual exploitation contrary to s.58 of the 2003 Act;[63] and under count 3, of causing or inciting a child to engage in sexual activity[64] contrary to s.10 of the 2003 Act. He was sentenced on count 1 to eight years' imprisonment; on count 2 to seven years' imprisonment; and on count 3 to five years' imprisonment, all the sentences to run concurrently. The appellant and his co-accused (W) met two 15-year-

---

[61] [2015] EWCA Crim 831.
[62] Again, if the indictment was in this form it was duplicitous: see para.10.37, above.
[63] See now s.2 of the Modern Slavery Act 2015, discussed in Ch.11, below.
[64] Again, if the indictment was in this form it was duplicitous: see para.4.68, above.

old girls, T and J, in Chesham. The two girls were invited into the appellant's car and willingly got into it. They were driven around Chesham for about two hours, but became concerned when the car was driven towards Watford. On the way the appellant said that he had a job for T working in his brothel. This was the basis of count 1. Count 2 reflected the driving of T from Chesham towards Watford. Once the car was in the Watford area it stopped and the appellant ordered T out of the car and told W have sex with her. This was to test T's suitability to work as a prostitute. T said that she got out of the car through fear, but accepted that she had consensual sexual intercourse with W. Those were the facts of count 3. The pre-sentence report found that the appellant showed no remorse, awareness or concern for the victim's welfare, and expressed the view that he posed a high risk of serious harm to children. In sentencing, the judge reminded herself of the principle of totality and imposed the eight year sentence on count 1 on the basis that the element of significant financial gain placed it in category 1A. On appeal, it was argued that the three offences were all part of one incident; that in respect of count 2 the higher sentencing range should not have applied because the trafficking was simply a journey from the Chesham area to Watford made whilst the appellant sought to persuade T to become a prostitute; and that the starting point for sentence should be that appropriate to count 3, because that was the gravamen of the offending. The Court of Appeal dismissed the last point on the basis that it failed to take into account the motivation behind the offending in relation to count 3, namely, to test T's suitability for prostitution. In the Court's opinion, the judge was right to start with the appropriate sentence in respect of counts 1 and 2. As for those counts, although the sentence fell outside the range specified in the guideline for offences under s.48, the case was aggravated because there were two young girls; the appellant knew that T was under 16 and was in awe of him; he was complicit in making T have sexual intercourse with W, albeit that it was consensual; he was prepared to intimidate and frighten T in order to get his own way; and he remained indifferent to her feelings. For those reasons, the Court held that there was nothing wrong in the total sentence imposed upon the appellant.

PARTIES TO THE OFFENCE

Both the person who causes or incites the sexual exploitation and the child **10.55**
victim may be male or female.

JURISDICTION

If A in England and Wales causes or incites the sexual exploitation of B in **10.56**
another jurisdiction, e.g. by activity conducted over the internet, he commits
a s.48 offence in England and Wales if, in accordance with the test laid down

in *Smith (Wallace Duncan) (No.4)*,[65] a substantial measure of A's activities take place within this jurisdiction. As for acts done overseas, by virtue of s.72 of and Sch.2 to the Sexual Offences Act 2003, as amended,[66] it is an offence under s.48 for a UK national to do an act in a country outside the UK which would constitute a s.48 offence if done in England and Wales. See further para.10.26, above.

"CAUSES OR INCITES"

10.57   For the meaning of these words, see paras 2.98 and 3.157 and following, above. A commits a s.48 offence where he causes or incites B to be sexually exploited, but not where he causes or incites C to sexually exploit B. In a case of that sort, the right course is to charge C with the appropriate substantive offence, e.g. sexual activity with a child under 16 (s.9 of the 2003 Act), taking an indecent photograph of a child (s.1(1)(a) of the Protection of Children Act 1978) or obtaining the sexual services of a child (s.47 of the 2003 Act), and A with encouraging, assisting or aiding and abetting that offence.

10.58   A's conduct must be shown to have caused or incited B to be sexually exploited, i.e. to offer or provide sexual services or to co-operate or acquiesce in the recording of an indecent image of himself. The "causing" offence will not be committed if B was a passive victim of the exploitation and unable to prevent or decline to participate in it, e.g. where an indecent image of him is recorded against his will whilst he under some form of sedation or restraint. In a case of this sort, however, it should be possible to prosecute A for another offence, e.g. encouraging or assisting the false imprisonment and/or sexual assault of B, or conspiracy to take an indecent photograph of a child.

"TO BE SEXUALLY EXPLOITED"

10.59   Section 51(2) of the 2003 Act[67] provides:

> "For the purposes of sections 48 to 50, a person (B) is sexually exploited if—
> (a) on at least one occasion and whether or not compelled to do so, B offers or provides sexual services to another person in return for payment or a promise of payment to B or a third person, or
> (b) an indecent image of B is recorded;
> and 'sexual exploitation' is to be interpreted accordingly."

---

[65] [2004] EWCA Crim 631.

[66] By the Criminal Justice and Immigration Act 2008 s.72, which came into force on July 14, 2008.

[67] As amended by the Serious Crime Act 2015 s.68(1), (6), with effect from May 3, 2015 (SI 2015/820).

Section 51(3) provides that "payment" in s.51(2) means: **10.60**

" . . . any financial advantage, including the discharge of an obligation to pay or the provision of goods or services (including sexual services) gratuitously or at a discount."

This provision is identical to s.47(2), discussed in para.10.32, above.

The language of s.51(2)(a) replicates the essential elements of the common   **10.61** law definition of a "prostitute" but without using that term.[68] It covers a child who is caused or incited to offer or provide any form of sexual services for payment, whether or not full intercourse is contemplated, e.g. where a 17-year-old is recruited to act as a "masseuse" in circumstances where she is required to masturbate clients on request. For the meaning of "sexual services", see paras 10.29 and following, above. Does A commit an offence under s.48 where he causes (or incites) B to provide sexual services to himself? There is an argument that he does not, on the basis that under s.51(2), B is "sexually exploited" only if he is caused to provide sexual services for payment to "another person", which should be taken to mean a person other than A. This leaves no gap in the law, since if A causes B to provide sexual services to himself for payment, he can be prosecuted under s.47 of the 2003 Act (paying for the sexual services of a child). We concede, however, that the courts may be reluctant to construe s.48 in this way, and may instead treat "another person" within s.51(2) as meaning any person other than B, i.e. as including A. An indication to this effect is provided by the sentencing case of *Gribbin (Peter Daniel)*,[69] in which the Court of Appeal appears to have seen no difficulty in the fact that the applicant was convicted under both s.48 and s.47 in relation to a course of conduct in which he persuaded a girl to provide sexual services to himself for payment. The Court did, however, make clear that, as the offences related to the same sexual services, the sentences needed to avoid double-counting, and indeed it made the sentences in that case concurrent rather than consecutive.

As for s.51(2)(b), the purpose of confining it to cases where an indecent   **10.62** image of B is "recorded" is to ensure that the scope of s.48 remains as it was before the statutory language was amended by the Serious Crime Act 2015, when A had to cause or incite B to be involved in "child pornography". The effect is that A does not commit a s.48 offence where he causes or incites B to transmit an indecent image of himself of which no recording is made, e.g. where A persuades B to expose his penis in the course of a Skype call. However, such conduct is likely to fall within the scope of other offences, such as causing or inciting a child to engage in sexual activity (s.8 or s.10 of the 2003 Act).

It is worth noting that, until the amendments made by the Serious Crime   **10.63** Act 2015, a s.48 offence was committed only if A caused or incited B "to

---

[68] See para.10.01, above, and paras 13.45 and following, below.
[69] [2015] EWCA Crim 736.

become" a prostitute or to be involved in pornography. It followed that A could not commit a s.48 offence by causing or inciting B to engage in prostitution if B was already a prostitute, since B could not be caused or incited to "become" what he already was.[70] In *Ubolcharoen and Thonarin*,[71] which concerned the similarly-worded offence in s.52 of the Act (discussed below), the Court of Appeal went further and said that no offence would be committed where B has previously acted anywhere in the world as a prostitute, even on a single occasion. In other words, for the purposes of s.52 the correct approach should be "once a prostitute, always a prostitute"; and the same must be true for s.48 in relation to its application to events taking place prior to its amendment. We argue below in relation to s.52 that this interpretation cannot be right, on the basis that if B has engaged in prostitution in the past but has since ceased to do so, it is logically possible for him to become a prostitute again. It would be highly unfortunate if he were to be denied the protection of the law because of past activities that he has put behind him. Accordingly, it ought in principle to be possible for A to commit a s.52 offence by causing or inciting B to become a prostitute even though B has previously been one, provided he is not one at the time of the causing or inciting. The Court in *Ubolcharoen* gave no reason for expressing a contrary view and appears not to have heard argument on the point. It may have been influenced by the definition of "prostitute" in s.51(2) of the Act as a person "who, on at least one occasion and whether or not compelled to do so, offers or provides sexual services" for payment. This could be read as having the effect that a person who on one occasion offered or provided sexual services for payment would thereafter remain a prostitute for the purposes of the Act. This would, we suggest, unduly narrow the scope of the law. The better view is that it must be possible for a person who in the past has acted as a prostitute by offering or providing sexual services for payment, but who has desisted from such conduct, to be regarded as no longer a prostitute for the purposes of s.52. If this issue should arise in a prosecution under s.48 for conduct predating May 3, 2015, we suggest it should be for the tribunal of fact to decide whether the circumstances were such that B had ceased to be a prostitute, such that he could be caused or incited to become one again.

10.64   This problem ought not to arise in relation to conduct engaged in on or after May 3, 2015, as s.48 now requires A intentionally to cause or incite B to "be" sexually exploited, rather than to "become" involved in prostitution, and as a result A may commit an offence under s.48 even if B has previously been sexually exploited through the provision of sexual services for payment.

---

[70] *Ubolcharoen and Thonarin* [2009] EWCA Crim 3263. For similar decisions under the previous law, see *Gold and Cohen* (1907) 71 J.P. 360; *Johnson* [1964] 2 Q.B. 404 at 408; *Broadfoot* [1976] 3 All E.R. 753 at 756. See also *Brown* (1985) 80 Cr. App. R. 36, where it was held that a defendant could not be convicted of attempting to procure a woman to become a common prostitute, contrary to s.22 of the Sexual Offences Act 1956, if he genuinely believed on reasonable grounds that she already was one: see further fn.132, below.
[71] [2009] EWCA Crim 3263 at [6].

There is, however, one potential wrinkle, in that the explanatory notes to the Serious Crime Act 2015, which made the relevant amendments, state that the changes "do not alter the scope of the relevant offences". Taken at face value, this might suggest that the amendments were not intended to remove the effect of the word "become" in s.51(2) as originally enacted, and that the s.48 offence should be construed accordingly. Explanatory notes are, however, admissible as an aid to construction only where a statutory provision is ambiguous or unclear.[72] It may be asserted that the current wording of s.48 is crystal clear. Further, a construction of the scope of s.48 based upon the explanatory notes would tend to frustrate the purpose of the statute to protect children from sexual exploitation. Against this, there is the ancient rule of statutory construction that a criminal provision should be strictly construed in favour of the defendant. We suggest there is certainly room for argument that, in the light of this rule of construction, it would be appropriate to have regard to the explanatory notes in construing the effect of the change from "become" to "be" in s.51(2), and that as a result the scope of s.48 should be regarded as unchanged. However, whilst such an argument might merit a hearing, the clarity of the amended s.51(2) and the important purpose served by the s.48 offences must mean that it is highly likely to fail.

"In any Part of the World"

The inclusion of these words means that s.48 is contravened wherever in world B is sexually exploited. **10.65**

Mental Element

It must be proved that A "intentionally" caused or incited B. For the meaning of "intention", see paras 2.78 and following, above. **10.66**

It is a requirement of the offence, where B was aged 13 to 17 (inclusive) at the relevant time, that A did not reasonably believe that B was 18 or over. Unlike with the child sex offences, there is no evidential burden on A to put this point in issue. It is therefore for the prosecution to prove that he had no such reasonable belief. See further para.4.66, above. If A may reasonably have believed B to be 18 or over, and it can be proved that he acted for or in the expectation of gain, he may be charged in the alternative with causing or inciting prostitution for gain (s.52). **10.67**

It is not necessary in proceedings under s.48 for the prosecution to prove that A acted for the purposes of gain. This was an element of the offences in ss.48–50 in the Sexual Offences Bill as introduced, but it was removed on Report in the Lords after earlier opposition.[73] Two points were made against **10.68**

---

[72] cf. *Montila* [2004] UKHL 50, at 35.
[73] *Hansard*, HL, vol.649, col.60 (June 9, 2003).

the requirement. First, the fact that A intentionally causes or incites a child to be sexually exploited should of itself be sufficient for a conviction, and adding a requirement that A must act for gain would therefore create an unnecessary hurdle which the prosecution might have difficulty in surmounting. Secondly, such a requirement would exclude from the scope of the offence certain conduct which ought properly to be within it, e.g. where A causes B to be sexually exploited not for financial gain but in order to trade the resulting indecent images with other paedophiles.[74] Despite these cogent objections, the Government at first clung to the "for gain" requirement, on the basis that its removal would criminalise certain conduct which should not be criminal. The only example given was of a mother who fails to persuade her 16-year-old daughter to stop selling her sexual services and, fearful for her daughter's safety, provides a room or flat in which she can work.[75] In the absence of a requirement that she acted for gain, this would in theory amount to the offence of facilitating child prostitution (s.50 of the Act). However, it would be surprising indeed if the CPS considered that in such a case the public interest required a prosecution. It is overwhelmingly likely that the efforts of the State would be focused on preventing the continued exploitation of the daughter, rather than on seeking to punish the mother for a misguided attempt to protect her child from physical harm.

Controlling a Child in Relation to Sexual Exploitation

Definition

10.69 Section 49(1) of the Sexual Offences Act 2003[76] provides:

"A person (A) commits an offence if—
(a) he intentionally controls any of the activities of another person (B) relating to B's sexual exploitation in any part of the world, and
(b) either—
(i) B is under 18, and A does not reasonably believe that B is 18 or over, or
(ii) B is under 13."

10.70   This offence is designed to penalise those involved in controlling child sexual exploitation at whatever level the control is exercised, i.e. not only pimps and others who are in actual contact with child victims but also those in the higher echelons of organised crime. However, the more remote from the child victim the individual is, the greater the evidential difficulties of proving the offence are likely to be, because of the need to establish that the individual knew what activities the child was engaged in and intended to control them.

---

[74] *Hansard*, HL, vol.648, col.176, Baroness Noakes (May 13, 2003).
[75] *Hansard*, HL, vol.648, col.179, Lord Falconer of Thoroton.
[76] As amended by the Serious Crime Act 2015 s.68(1), (4), with effect from May 3, 2015 (SI 2015/820).

The CPS's guidance to prosecutors on the 2003 Act provides in relation to the offences in ss.47–50 that, where the child is under 13, the charge should be under ss.5–8 of the Act.[77] See further para.10.36, above.

10.71

Mode of Trial and Punishment

The s.49 offence is triable either way.[78] The maximum penalty on conviction on indictment is 14 years' imprisonment.[79] The maximum on summary conviction is six months' imprisonment or a fine, or both. As from a day to be appointed the maximum sentence of imprisonment on summary conviction will increase to 12 months' imprisonment.[80] The increase will have no application to offences committed before it takes effect.[81] Until recently, the maximum fine on summary conviction was a fine not exceeding the statutory maximum (i.e. £5,000). The effect of s.85 of the Legal Aid, Sentencing and Punishment of Offenders Act 2012 is that, from March 12, 2015, a fine of any amount may be imposed. Offences under s.49 cannot be dealt with by way of a simple caution.[82]

10.72

For the purposes of listing, cases under s.49[83] fall within Class 2B, save for complex cases involving many complainants (often under age, in care or otherwise particularly vulnerable) and/or many defendants who are alleged to have systematically groomed and abused them, often over a long period of time, which fall within Class 1C.[84] Cases in Class 1C must be referred to the Resident Judge, and by the Resident Judge to a Presiding Judge. Cases in Class 2B must be similarly referred in certain specified circumstances, including where the case is unusually grave or complex or a novel and important point of law is to be raised; where the defendant is a police officer, a member of the legal profession or a high profile figure; or where for any reason the case is likely to attract exceptional media attention.

10.73

An offence under s.49 is a serious specified offence for the purposes of the dangerousness provisions of the Criminal Justice Act 2003.[85] A s.49 offence, whenever committed, may be made the subject of an extended sentence under s.226A of that Act (extended sentence for certain violent or sexual

10.74

---

[77] *http://www.cps.gov.uk/legal/p_to_r/rape_and_sexual_offences/soa_2003_and_soa_1956/£a34* [Accessed April 30, 2016].

[78] s.49(2).

[79] s.49(2).

[80] Criminal Justice Act 2003 s.282(2), (3).

[81] Criminal Justice Act 2003 s.282(4).

[82] Criminal Justice and Courts Act 2015 s.17(3), and the Criminal Justice and Courts Act 2015 (Simple Cautions) (Specification of Either-Way Offences) Order 2015 (SI 2015/790).

[83] And of soliciting, inciting, encouraging or assisting, attempting or conspiring to commit the offence or assisting an offender having committed the offence.

[84] *Consolidated Criminal Practice Directions*, Part XIII Listing B: CLASSIFICATION, available at *https://www.judiciary.gov.uk/publications/criminal-practice-directions-2015/* [Accessed April 30, 2016].

[85] Criminal Justice Act 2003, s.224 and Sch.15, Pt 2.

offences).[86] The offence is also listed in Pt 1 of Sch.15B to the Criminal Justice Act 2003 for the purposes of s.224A of that Act (life sentence for a second listed offence).[87]

10.75   A person convicted under s.49, cautioned, found not guilty by reason of insanity or found to be under a disability and to have done the act charged, is automatically subject to the notification requirements in the Sexual Offences Act 2003,[88] if he was 18 or over at the time of the offence or is sentenced to at least 12 months' imprisonment.

10.76   The s.49 offence is a "lifestyle" offence for the purposes of the Proceeds of Crime Act 2002.[89] Accordingly, a conviction for the offence may, if the other conditions set out in the 2002 Act are met, result in the court making a confiscation order in relation to the benefit the offender has derived from the offence or, if he has a general criminal lifestyle, from his general criminal conduct.

CHARGE OR INDICTMENT

10.77   There is nothing in s.49 to suggest that the control must last for any particular period. Accordingly, by analogy with the repealed offence of living off the earnings of prostitution (s.30 of the Sexual Offences Act 1956), a charge or indictment under s.49 may allege that the offence was committed on a single specified day; and where this is alleged, the prosecution may lead supporting evidence to show the nature of A's relations with B either before or after the specified day, as such evidence is clearly relevant to the issue.[90]

SENTENCING

10.78   For the Sentencing Council's guideline on the sentencing of sexual offences, see Ch.33, below. A single guideline covers offences under ss.48–50 of the 2003 Act and is discussed at paras 10.43 and following, above.

PARTIES TO THE OFFENCE

10.79   Both the person exercising the control and the child victim may be either male or female. As to whether the child victim of a s.49 offence is liable to conviction as an accessory to the offence, see the discussion in para.4.57 and following, above.

---

[86] Inserted by the Legal Aid, Sentencing and Punishment of Offenders Act 2012 s.124, brought into force on December 3, 2012, by SI 2012/2906.
[87] Inserted by the Legal Aid, Sentencing and Punishment of Offenders Act 2012 s.122, brought into force on December 3, 2012, by SI 2012/2906.
[88] s.80 and Sch.3, discussed in Ch.35, below.
[89] 2002 Act Sch.2, as amended by the 2003 Act s.139 and Sch.6, para.46 and by the Serious Crime Act 2015 s.85 and Sch.4, para.58.
[90] cf. *Hill and Churchman* [1914] 2 K.B. 386.

Jurisdiction

If A in England and Wales controls the activities of B relating to B's sexual exploitation anywhere else in the world, he commits the s.49 offence in England and Wales if, in accordance with the test laid down in *Smith (Wallace Duncan) (No.4)*,[91] a substantial measure of A's activities take place within this jurisdiction. As a result, the offence will be committed here where, e.g. A is in London and B is overseas, and A Skypes B or sends him a text in which he instructs B to provide C with sexual services in that country for payment, or to go to an address where indecent photographs will be taken of him. As for acts done overseas, by virtue of s.72 of and Sch.2 to the Sexual Offences Act 2003, as amended,[92] it is an offence under s.49 for a UK national to do an act in a country outside the UK which would constitute a s.49 offence if done in England and Wales. See further para.10.26, above. **10.80**

"Controls any of the Activities of Another Person (B) relating to B's Sexual Exploitation"

The offence under s.49 requires proof of "control", and accordingly if A profits from or is involved in B's sexual exploitation without controlling it in any way, he falls outside its scope. For the meaning of "controls", see paras 10.153 and following, below. **10.81**

It is sufficient for conviction that A controls any of B's activities relating to B's sexual exploitation. Examples of conduct covered by the offence would be where A tells B to charge a certain price for a particular sexual service and B complies, or where A directs B to pose for an indecent photograph or film. Indirect control will suffice, as where A exercises control of B's activities through another person. The words "activities... relating to B's sexual exploitation" mean that the offence applies not only where A controls B's sexual exploitation as such, but also where he controls any activity by B that relates to that exploitation, e.g. he arranges B's travel to and from places where he is to be exploited, directs B as to what clothes or make up he should wear, or tells B what to do with his earnings. **10.82**

"Sexual Exploitation"

For the meaning of this term, see paras 10.59 and following, above. **10.83**

"In any Part of the World"

The inclusion of these words means that s.49 is contravened wherever in world B is sexually exploited. **10.84**

[91] [2004] EWCA Crim 631.
[92] By the Criminal Justice and Immigration Act 2008 s.72, which came into force on July 14, 2008.

Mental Element

10.85 It must be proved that A "intentionally" controlled B's activities. For the meaning of "intention", see para.2.78 and following, above.

10.86 It is a requirement of the offence, where B was aged 13 to 17 (inclusive) at the relevant time, that A did not reasonably believe that B was 18 or over. Unlike with the child sex offences, there is no evidential burden on A to put this point in issue. It is therefore for the prosecution to prove that he had no such reasonable belief. See further para.4.66, above. If A may reasonably have believed B to be 18 or over, and it can be proved that he acted for or in the expectation of gain, he may be charged in the alternative with controlling prostitution for gain (s.53).

10.87 It is not necessary in proceedings under s.49 for the prosecution to prove that A acted for the purposes of gain. This was an element of the offence in the Sexual Offences Bill as introduced, but was dropped on Report in the Lords: see further para.10.68, above.

Arranging or Facilitating Sexual Exploitation of a Child

Definition

10.88 Section 50(1) of the Sexual Offences Act 2003[93] provides:

> "A person (A) commits an offence if—
> (a) he intentionally arranges or facilitates the sexual exploitation in any part of the world of another person (B), and
> (b) either—
>   (i) B is under 18, and A does not reasonably believe that B is 18 or over, or
>   (ii) B is under 13."

10.89 By inference from *Walker*,[94] decided under s.8 of the Act, s.50 creates separate offences of intentionally arranging and intentionally facilitating the sexual exploitation of a child. Further, given that a child can be sexually exploited in two different ways, either by them offering or providing sexual services for payment or by an indecent image of them being recorded, the better view is that s.50 creates distinct offences in relation to the two forms of activity. The net result is that s.50 creates four offences: arranging for a child to be sexually exploited by the offer or provision by the child of sexual services for payment; facilitating the sexual exploitation of a child in that way; arranging the sexual exploitation of a child by an indecent image of them being recorded; and facilitating the sexual exploitation of a child by such an image being recorded. It is important that the charge or indictment makes clear which offence is being charged.

---

[93] As amended by the Serious Crime Act 2015 s.68(1), (5), with effect from May 3, 2015 (SI 2015/820).
[94] [2006] EWCA Crim 1907.

The four offences are aimed at those who do not control the child's   **10.90**
exploitation but enable it to take place, e.g. by transporting the child to or
from a place where they will provide sexual services for payment or taking
"bookings" for the provision of sexual services. The CPS's guidance to
prosecutors on the 2003 Act provides in relation to the offences in ss.47–50
that, where the child is under 13, the charge should be under ss.5–8 of the
Act.[95] See further para.10.36, above.

MODE OF TRIAL AND PUNISHMENT

The offence under s.50 is triable either way.[96] The maximum punishment on   **10.91**
conviction on indictment is 14 years' imprisonment.[97] The maximum on
summary conviction is six months' imprisonment or a fine, or both. As from
a day to be appointed the maximum sentence of imprisonment on summary
conviction will increase to 12 months' imprisonment.[98] The increase will have
no application to offences committed before it takes effect.[99] Until recently,
the maximum fine on summary conviction was a fine not exceeding the
statutory maximum (i.e. £5,000). The effect of s.85 of the Legal Aid,
Sentencing and Punishment of Offenders Act 2012 is that, from March 12,
2015, a fine of any amount may be imposed. Offences under s.50 cannot be
dealt with by way of a simple caution.[100]

For the purposes of listing, cases under s.50[101] fall within Class 2B, save for   **10.92**
complex cases involving many complainants (often under age, in care or
otherwise particularly vulnerable) and/or many defendants who are alleged
to have systematically groomed and abused them, often over a long period of
time, which fall within Class 1C.[102] Cases in Class 1C must be referred to the
Resident Judge, and by the Resident Judge to a Presiding Judge. Cases in
Class 2B must be similarly referred in certain specified circumstances,
including where the case is unusually grave or complex or a novel and
important point of law is to be raised; where the defendant is a police officer,
a member of the legal profession or a high profile figure; or where for any
reason the case is likely to attract exceptional media attention.

---

[95] http://www.cps.gov.uk/legal/p_to_r/rape_and_sexual_offences/soa_2003_and_soa_1956/£a34 [Accessed April 30, 2016].

[96] s.49(2).

[97] s.49(2).

[98] Criminal Justice Act 2003 s.282(2), (3).

[99] Criminal Justice Act 2003 s.282(4).

[100] Criminal Justice and Courts Act 2015, s.17(3), and the Criminal Justice and Courts Act 2015 (Simple Cautions) (Specification of Either-Way Offences) Order 2015 (SI 2015/790).

[101] And of soliciting, inciting, encouraging or assisting, attempting or conspiring to commit the offence or assisting an offender having committed the offence.

[102] Consolidated Criminal Practice Directions, Part XIII Listing B: CLASSIFICATION, available at https://www.judiciary.gov.uk/publications/criminal-practice-directions-2015/ [Accessed April 30, 2016].

10.93   An offence under s.50 is a serious specified offence for the purposes of the dangerousness provisions of the Criminal Justice Act 2003.[103] Accordingly a s.50 offence, whenever committed, may be made the subject of an extended sentence under s.226A of that Act (extended sentence for certain violent or sexual offences).[104] The offence is also listed in Pt 1 of Sch.15B to the Criminal Justice Act 2003 for the purposes of s.224A of that Act (life sentence for a second listed offence).[105]

10.94   A person convicted under s.50, cautioned, found not guilty by reason of insanity or found to be under a disability and to have done the act charged, is automatically subject to the notification requirements in the Sexual Offences Act 2003,[106] if he was 18 or over at the time of the offence or is sentenced to at least 12 months' imprisonment.

10.95   An offence under s.50 is a "lifestyle" offence for the purposes of the Proceeds of Crime Act 2002.[107] Accordingly, a conviction for the offence may, if the other conditions set out in the 2002 Act are met, result in the court making a confiscation order in relation to the benefit the offender has derived from the offence or, if he has a general criminal lifestyle, from his general criminal conduct.

Sentencing

10.96   For the Sentencing Council guideline relating to the sentencing of sexual offences committed by offenders aged 18 and over, see Ch.33, below. A single guideline covers offences under ss.48–50 of the 2003 Act and is discussed at paras 10.43 and following, above.

Parties to the Offence

10.97   Both the person doing the arranging or facilitating and the child victim may be either male or female. As to whether the child victim of a s.50 offence is liable to conviction as an accessory to the offence, see the discussion in paras 4.57 and following, above. There is no reason in principle why in appropriate circumstances a child (C) could not be convicted as an accessory to a s.50 offence committed by A against another child, B. However, it will be rare for the prosecution of C in such a case to be in the public interest; it is much more likely that C will themselves be a victim of exploitation and so in need of the care and support of the State, rather than its condemnation.

---

[103] Criminal Justice Act 2003 s.224 and Sch.15, Pt 2.
[104] Inserted by the Legal Aid, Sentencing and Punishment of Offenders Act 2012 s.124, brought into force on December 3, 2012, by SI 2012/2906.
[105] Inserted by the Legal Aid, Sentencing and Punishment of Offenders Act 2012 s.122, brought into force on December 3, 2012, by SI 2012/2906.
[106] s.80 and Sch.3, discussed in Ch.35, below.
[107] 2002 Act Sch.2, as amended by the 2003 Act s.139 and Sch.6, para.46 and by the Serious Crime Act 2015 s.85 and Sch.4, para.58.

JURISDICTION

If A in England and Wales arranges or facilitates the sexual exploitation of **10.98**
B anywhere else in the world, he commits a s.50 offence in England and
Wales on the basis that, in accordance with the test laid down in *Smith
(Wallace Duncan) (No.4)*,[108] a substantial measure of A's activities take
place within this jurisdiction. As a result, the offence will be committed here
where, e.g. A in London emails permission to C in Thailand to use his
apartment there, knowing that C intends to use it to have sex with children
for payment (it is irrelevant that A is unaware of the identities of the victims),
or A in London makes arrangements online for an indecent recording to be
made of a child in the Philippines. As for acts done overseas, by virtue of s.72
of and Sch.2 to the Sexual Offences Act 2003, as amended,[109] it is an offence
under s.50 for a UK national to do an act in a country outside the UK which
would constitute a s.50 offence if done in England and Wales. See further
para.10.26, above.

"ARRANGES OR FACILITATES"

For the meaning of these words, see paras 4.172 and following, above. The **10.99**
scope of the s.50 offence is potentially very wide. The reference to "facilitation" would seem, for example, to make it an offence for A to allow B to use
his room to provide sexual services for payment, or give her a lift to a place
where she will provide such services, or even to babysit for her whilst she does
so. Indeed, any conduct falling short of the exercise of control, which enables
or assists a child's sexual exploitation, is likely to fall foul of s.50.

"SEXUAL EXPLOITATION"

For the meaning of this term, see paras 10.59 and following, above. **10.100**

"IN ANY PART OF THE WORLD"

The inclusion of these words means that s.50 is contravened wherever in **10.101**
world B is sexually exploited.

MENTAL ELEMENT

It must be proved that A "intentionally" controlled B's activities. For the **10.102**
meaning of "intention", see paras 2.78 and following, above.

---

[108] [2004] EWCA Crim 631.
[109] By the Criminal Justice and Immigration Act 2008 s.72, which came into force on July 14,
2008.

10.103   It is a requirement of the offence, where B was aged 13 to 17 (inclusive) at the relevant time, that A did not reasonably believe that B was 18 or over. Unlike with the child sex offences, there is no evidential burden on A to put this point in issue. It is therefore for the prosecution to prove that he had no such reasonable belief. See further para.4.66, above.

10.104   It is not necessary in proceedings under s.50 for the prosecution to prove that A acted for the purposes of gain. This was an element of the offence in the Sexual Offences Bill as introduced, but was dropped on Report in the Lords. See further para.10.68, above.

SEXUAL EXPLOITATION OF ADULTS

OVERVIEW

10.105   The key offences dealing with sexual exploitation of adults at the time of the Sexual Offences Review[110] in 2000 were those in ss.30 and 31 of the Sexual Offences Act 1956 (man living on the earnings of prostitution and woman exercising control over prostitute). The Review noted that views on those offences varied widely. Some considered that anyone who lives off the earnings of prostitution is a pimp and deserving of punishment, no matter what their relationship with the prostitute. Others were of the view that a prostitute who makes his or her own choice of work has a right to a private life with a partner, which the law as it stood denied them. The Review acknowledged that in some cases prostitutes earn money for partners or family, but said that in others the partner is actively exploiting the prostitute. It considered that the law had to cater for the latter case and so there could be no blanket exemption for partners; though in practice, it thought an investigation or prosecution of a partner was unlikely to take place in the absence of strong evidence of coercion. The Review concluded that there should be a set of gender-neutral offences penalising the sexual exploitation of others by abuse, pressure, force, deception or coercion. It accordingly recommended the creation of offences to cover exploiting others by receiving money or reward from prostitutes, managing or controlling the activities of prostitutes for money or reward, and recruiting men or women into prostitution, whether or not for reward or gain.

10.106   These proposals were adopted in the 2002 White Paper *Protecting the Public*,[111] which announced the Government's intention to introduce an offence of commercial sexual exploitation of adults. This led in due course to the creation in the Sexual Offences Act 2003 of the following offences:

- causing or inciting prostitution for gain (s.52) and

---

[110] *Setting the Boundaries* (Home Office, July 2000). The report is available at *http:/ /webarchive.nationalarchives.gov.uk/-/http:/www.homeoffice.gov.uk/documents/vol1main.pdf?view =Binary* [Accessed April 30, 2016].

[111] *Protecting the Public: strengthening protection against sex offenders and reforming the law on sexual offences* (Cm 5668) (Nov 2002), Ch.5.

- controlling prostitution for gain (s.53).

It is notable that the s.52 offence requires proof that the defendant acted   **10.107**
for gain. It therefore covers somewhat narrower ground than envisaged by
the Review, which recommended that recruiting into prostitution should be
an offence regardless of whether the act was done for reward or gain. The
offence will not, therefore, cover someone who causes or incites prostitution
for some other reason, e.g. to degrade the victim or obtain some perverted
sexual gratification.

To supplement the new offences, the 2003 Act also introduced into the   **10.108**
Sexual Offences Act 1956 a new s.33A, making it an offence, with a seven
year maximum penalty, to keep a brothel used for prostitution. This offence
is considered in Ch.12.

An important further offence has since been added to the 2003 Act, in a   **10.109**
new s.53A introduced by the Policing and Crime Act 2009,[112] which makes it
an offence to make or promise payment for the sexual services of a prostitute
who has been exploited for gain by a third person using force, threats,
coercion or deception. This offence was the main product of the review
Tackling the Demand for Prostitution, published by the Home Office in
2008.[113] The novelty of the offence is that it targets the client, not the
prostitute or the pimp. Moreover, the offence is one of strict liability as
regards the use of force, etc., in relation to the prostitute, so that it is
irrelevant whether the defendant (the client) knew, believed or suspected that
the prostitute was being exploited. In justifying the offence during the
passage of the 2009 Act, Lord West of Spithead, a Home Office minister,
said[114]:

> "Lest we forget, most prostitutes are more victims than volunteers . . . [T]o curb
> prostitution and tackle the most exploitative elements of prostitution, including
> trafficking, enforcement activity should be focused not just on those involved in
> the organisation of sexual exploitation but on those who contribute to the
> demand by paying for sex. This approach is supported by ACPO and a number
> of organisations working with victims of trafficking and campaigning on
> women's rights. In particular, Rights of Women, Eaves housing, the POPPY
> Project and Toynbee Hall support the approach that we are taking in Clause 13.
> That is why this Bill provides a new offence of paying for sex with a prostitute
> who has been subjected to force, threat or deception. There was much debate in
> the other place on ensuring that these measures do not inadvertently capture
> circumstances in which prostitutes are willingly in a voluntary business such as
> a relationship with a third party. That has never been our intention. Clause 13,
> following amendments in the other place, helps to clarify that by narrowing and
> tightening the scope of the offence."

Lord West's reference to "narrowing and tightening" amendments is sig-   **10.110**
nificant. In the Policing and Crime Bill as introduced, the offence referred to
prostitutes who were "controlled for gain" by a third person. This provoked

---

[112] s.14, which came into force on April 1, 2010.
[113] For further information see para.12.09, below.
[114] *Hansard*, HL, June 3, 2009, col.224 (Lords' Second Reading).

opposition on the ground that the offence was too broad and, in particular, did not require absence of free will on the part of the prostitute. The amendments introduced the concepts of force, threats, coercion and deception. Nonetheless, the absence of any required mental element as to those concepts remains controversial. There may be cases in which force, threats, coercion or deception has been used but even reasonable enquiries will not discover this: e.g. if the threats are so effective that the prostitute is terrified to admit to her situation, or the pimp has promised the prostitute something that he does not intend to provide. Indeed, in the latter case it is possible that at the relevant time even the prostitute is unaware of the deception. Is it appropriate to criminalise a client who does not know and has no reason to suspect that force etc. has been used? By doing so, will the law tend to drive prostitution underground so that it takes place in circumstances that are less likely to come to police attention and in which the prostitutes are more vulnerable? These questions take us to the heart of the current public debate about how the law relating to prostitution should be developed, i.e. whether it should remain the subject of criminal intervention but with the burden of the law shifted from the prostitute to the purchaser of their services, or whether the sale and purchase of sexual services should be de-criminalised and regulated. The merits of the debate lies beyond the scope of the book, but see the discussion of the *Honeyball Report* and the All-Party Parliamentary Group on Prostitution in paras 12.12 and following, below.

Causing or Inciting Prostitution for Gain

Definition

10.111   Section 52(1) of the Sexual Offences Act 2003 provides:

"A person commits an offence if—
(a) he intentionally causes or incites another person to become a prostitute in any part of the world, and
(b) he does so for or in the expectation of gain for himself or a third person."

10.112   By inference from *Walker*,[115] decided under s.8 of the 2003 Act, s.52 creates two offences, one of intentionally causing and one of intentionally inciting another person to become a prostitute. It is important that the charge or indictment makes clear which offence is being charged.

Mode of Trial and Punishment

10.113   Offences under s.52 are triable either way.[116] The maximum punishment on conviction on indictment is seven years' imprisonment.[117] The maximum on summary conviction is six months' imprisonment or a fine, or both. As from

[115] [2006] EWCA Crim 1907.
[116] s.52(2).
[117] s.52(2).

a day to be appointed the maximum sentence of imprisonment on summary conviction will increase to 12 months' imprisonment.[118] The increase will have no application to offences committed before it takes effect.[119] Until recently, the maximum fine on summary conviction was a fine not exceeding the statutory maximum (i.e. £5,000). The effect of s.85 of the Legal Aid, Sentencing and Punishment of Offenders Act 2012 is that, from March 12, 2015, a fine of any amount may be imposed. Fines will, however, continue to be set according to the seriousness of the offence and the means of the offender.

For the purposes of listing, cases under s.52[120] fall within Class 2B, save for **10.114** complex cases involving many complainants (often under age, in care or otherwise particularly vulnerable) and/or many defendants who are alleged to have systematically groomed and abused them, often over a long period of time, which fall within Class 1C.[121] Cases in Class 1C must be referred to the Resident Judge, and by the Resident Judge to a Presiding Judge. Cases in Class 2B must be similarly referred in certain specified circumstances, including where the case is unusually grave or complex or a novel and important point of law is to be raised; where the defendant is a police officer, a member of the legal profession or a high profile figure; or where for any reason the case is likely to attract exceptional media attention.

An offence under s.52, whenever committed, is a specified offence for the **10.115** purposes of s.226A of the Criminal Justice Act 2003 (extended sentence for certain violent and sexual offences).[122]

There is no provision for a person convicted under s.52 to be subject to the **10.116** notification requirements of the Sexual Offences Act 2003.

A s.52 offence is a "lifestyle" offence for the purposes of the Proceeds of **10.117** Crime Act 2002.[123] Accordingly, a conviction for the offence may, if the other conditions set out in the 2002 Act are met, result in the court making a confiscation order in relation to the benefit the offender has derived from the offence or, if he has a general criminal lifestyle, from his general criminal conduct.

SENTENCING

For the Sentencing Council guideline relating to the sentencing of sexual **10.118** offences committed by offenders aged 18 and over, see Ch.33, below. In its

[118] Criminal Justice Act 2003 s.282(2), (3).
[119] Criminal Justice Act 2003 s.282(4).
[120] And of soliciting, inciting, encouraging or assisting, attempting or conspiring to commit the offence or assisting an offender having committed the offence.
[121] *Consolidated Criminal Practice Directions*, Part XIII Listing B: CLASSIFICATION, available at *https://www.judiciary.gov.uk/publications/criminal-practice-directions-2015/* [Accessed April 30, 2016].
[122] Inserted by the Legal Aid, Sentencing and Punishment of Offenders Act 2012 s.124, brought into force on December 3, 2012, by SI 2012/2906.
[123] 2002 Act Sch.2, as amended by the 2003 Act s.139 and Sch.6, para.46 and by the Serious Crime Act 2015 s.85 and Sch.4, para.58.

consultation on the draft guideline,[124] the Sentencing Council proposed to deal with the offences of causing or inciting prostitution (s.52) and controlling prostitution (s.53) in the same guideline, as they have the same statutory maximum (seven years' imprisonment) and raise similar issues in relation to harm and culpability. It duly followed this approach in the guideline as published.

10.119   An issue not directly covered in the consultation but upon which the Sentencing Council received some of the strongest representations was the language used in relation to the exploitation offences. These representations focused on the offences of child exploitation in ss.47–50, but some respondents also expressed concern about the use in relation to the adult offences of the term "prostitute", which they regarded as loaded and pejorative. The suggested alternatives included "women in prostitution", "victim" and "those involved in prostitution". The Council considered carefully whether to adopt the last of these terms but felt that this could reduce clarity by making the language of the guideline wider than that of the Act. It also considered whether to use the term "victim", but noted some would take issue with the use of this term in relation to adults involved in prostitution. As an alternative, the Council decided, where possible and where clarity would not be affected, not to use the term "prostitute". This had the result that, e.g. "prostitute forced or coerced into seeing many customers" in the draft guideline became "individual(s) forced or coerced into seeing many customers" in the published version. In addition, the Council included in the title pages of the adult exploitation offences the statement: "The terms 'prostitute' and 'prostitution' are used in this guideline in accordance with the statutory language contained in the Sexual Offences Act 2003". The aim is to make it clear that the terminology is not intended to stigmatise but follows the language used in the Act. The Council also committed to revise and update the guideline if and when statutory changes are made to titles of these offences. These various measures indicate a curious defensiveness on the part of the Council in relation to the use of what are, after all, statutory terms reflecting common usage. The measures are also unlikely to satisfy those who object to the terms as a matter of principle.

Sentencing guideline

Step One—Harm

10.120   The guideline requires the sentencing court to go through a series of steps in order to determine the appropriate sentence. Step one involves determining the offence category by reference to the degree of harm caused and then the

---

[124] *Sexual Offences Guideline: Consultation* (December 6, 2012). The consultation document is available on the Sentencing Council website.

culpability level for the offence. The harm factors for the offences in ss.52 and 53 are:

Harm	
Category 1	• Abduction/detention • Violence or threats of violence • Sustained and systematic psychological abuse • Individual(s) forced or coerced to participate in unsafe/degrading sexual activity • Individual(s) forced or coerced into seeing many "customers" • Individual(s) forced/coerced/deceived into prostitution
Category 2	Factor(s) in categories 1 not present

In its consultation document, the Sentencing Council explained its reasons **10.121** for including the harm factors in category 1 as follows:

- "Abduction/detention" increases the harm suffered by the prostitute because they will be isolated from others and less able to seek help.
- As for "violence or threats of violence", the Council acknowledged that control and coercion can be exercised without the use of violence, and a lack of violence will not reduce the seriousness of the offence. But it also recognised that female prostitutes are often at risk of violent crime in the course of their work, in the form of both physical and sexual attacks, including rape, by violent clients or pimps, and the use of such violence should place the offence in the higher category.
- The same is true of "sustained and systematic psychological abuse", as psychological abuse may be a powerful weapon in controlling and exploiting prostitutes and can be as coercive and damaging as physical violence.
- "Individual(s) coerced or forced to participate in unsafe/degrading sexual activity" reflects the situation in which the offender coerces or forces a prostitute to have unprotected sex knowing that some clients will pay a premium for such activity. This increases the harm to the prostitute through exposing them to the risk of sexually transmitted infections and pregnancy. A prostitute may also be coerced or forced by the offender to undertake sexual activity with clients that the prostitute finds degrading. The harm results from the prostitute's lack of choice or control over the activity engaged in and the risk or humiliation they are exposed to as a consequence of the activity.
- "Individual(s) forced or coerced into seeing many 'customers'" again may increase the harm done to the prostitute as they will be coerced or forced into working in a way that they may not wish, over which they have little control and which increases their exposure to risk of physical and psychological harm.

- "Individual(s) forced/coerced/deceived into prostitution" reflects the fact that an offence under s.52 or s.53 will sometimes be charged instead of trafficking where an individual has been forced or deceived into entering into prostitution, e.g. they have willingly travelled to this country with the promise of a legitimate job and are then deceived into prostitution upon arrival, when they may be isolated and unable financially to support themselves. The harm to the individual in such cases is increased because of the lack of control they have over their situation.

Culpability

10.122   This guideline contains three levels of culpability, rather than two as in most other guidelines, in order to accommodate the wide range of culpability found in these offences. In particular, the element of "control" in s.53 is satisfied by the intentional control of *any* of the activities of another person relating to prostitution, and as a result may range from an offender with links to organised crime controlling a network of prostitutes, through to a former prostitute, who has been exploited, looking after the diary of another prostitute and involved in this work as a means of moving away from having to see clients. The previous guideline, issued in 2007 by the Sentencing Guidelines Council ("SGC"), dealt with the wide range of culpability by including "using employment as a route out of prostitution" and "coercion" as mitigating factors. The Sentencing Council thought it clearer and more transparent to set out the differing levels of culpability as part of step one. The three categories are as follows:

CULPABILITY		
A	*B*	*C*
• Causing, inciting or controlling prostitution on significant commercial basis • Expectation of significant financial or other gain • Abuse of trust • Exploitation of those known to be trafficked	• Close involvement with prostitute(s) e.g. control of finances, choice of clients, working conditions, etc (where offender's involvement is not as a result of coercion)	• Performs limited function under direction • Close involvement but engaged by coercion/ intimidation/ exploitation

• Significant involvement in limiting the freedom of prostitute(s) • Grooming of individual(s) to enter prostitution including through cultivation of a dependency on drugs or alcohol		

Culpability A includes factors which show a very high degree of culpability: **10.123**

- "Causing, inciting or controlling prostitution on significant commercial basis" is intended to cover offenders who deliberately engage in a role causing harm to a large number of people.
- In relation to "expectation of significant financial or other gain", the Sentencing Council decided not to place a monetary value on "significant gain" as what will qualify as "significant" depends on the circumstances of the offence and will vary over time. This is a change from the SGC guideline, which referred to "substantial gain" on which it placed a monetary value of £5,000.
- "Abuse of trust" will increase an offender's culpability even in the absence of commercial scale or significant financial gain because of the manipulation involved.
- "Exploitation of those known to be trafficked" is included because human trafficking for sexual exploitation fuels the market for prostitution in the UK, is a lucrative business and is often linked with other organised criminal activity such as immigration crime, violence, drug abuse and money laundering. Women may be vulnerable to exploitation because of their immigration status, economic situation or, more often, because they are subjected to abuse, coercion and violence.
- "Significant involvement in limiting the freedom of prostitute(s)" will increase an offender's culpability because it is an extreme example of control over the prostitute.
- "Grooming of individual(s) to enter prostitution including through cultivation of a dependency on drugs or alcohol" was introduced as a result of a response to the consultation: see para.10.131, below.

As to culpability B, the Council said that this will apply to cases where the   **10.124** offender has a close degree of control of the prostitute, and is, for example, exerting influence and making decisions on their behalf, e.g. controlling which clients they see. An offender will fall in this category if there is an absence of evidence that the prostitute was in any way coerced into involvement. The category could apply if the offender controls more than one prostitute, though if their activity is on a significant commercial scale it would, as noted above, fall within culpability A.

10.125   The Council said that culpability C applies to the offender who plays a relatively peripheral role, e.g. (in relation to the s.53 offence) by taking bookings on behalf of a prostitute or driving the prostitute around. This category may also apply if an offender has close involvement but are themselves exploited, intimidated or coerced.

Step Two–Starting point and category range

10.126   Once the court has determined the offence category and culpability level, at step two it should use the corresponding starting point specified in the guideline in order to reach a sentence within the category range. The starting point applies to all offenders irrespective of plea or previous convictions. Once the starting point has been determined, step two allows further adjustment for aggravating or mitigating features, set out below. A case of particular gravity, reflected by multiple features of culpability or harm, could merit upward adjustment from the starting point before further adjustment for aggravating or mitigating features. Where there is a sufficient prospect of rehabilitation, a community order with a sex offender treatment programme requirement under s.202 of the Criminal Justice Act 2003 can be a proper alternative to a short or moderate length custodial sentence.

10.127   In all category 1 cases where there is evidence of increased harm, a custodial starting point and range is recommended, in some cases near the statutory maximum. In category 2 cases there is a custodial starting point and range for offenders who demonstrate the highest level of culpability. Where the offender is shown to have been exploited themselves or has very limited involvement, and there are none of the category 1 harm factors present, the guideline envisages the most suitable disposal being a community order, which will deal with the underlying reasons why the offender has become involved and seek to avoid them re-offending. The starting points and category ranges for offences under ss.52 and 53 are as follows:

	A	*B*	*C*
Category 1	*Starting point* 4 years' custody	*Starting point* 2 years 6 months' custody	*Starting point* 1 year's custody
	Category range 3–6 years' custody	*Category range* 2–4 years' custody	*Category range* 26 weeks'–2 years' custody
Category 2	*Starting point* 2 years' 6 months' custody	*Starting point* 1 year's custody	*Starting point* Medium level community Order
	Category range 2–5 years' custody	*Category range* High level community order – 2 years' custody	*Category range* Low level community order – High level community order

Aggravating and mitigating factors

After identifying the starting point and category range, the court should **10.128** consider whether the presence of aggravating or mitigating factors should result in an upward or downward adjustment from the starting point or the imposition of a sentence outside the range. In particular, relevant recent convictions are likely to result in an upward adjustment. When sentencing appropriate category 2 offences, the court should also consider whether the custody threshold has been passed; if so, whether a custodial sentence is unavoidable; and if it is, whether that sentence can be suspended. The non-exhaustive list of aggravating and mitigating factors for offences under ss.52 and 53 is:

Aggravating factors
Statutory aggravating factors
• Previous convictions, having regard to a) the nature of the offence to which the conviction relates and its relevance to the current offence; and b) the time that has elapsed since the conviction • Offence committed whilst on bail

Other aggravating factors

- Failure to comply with current court orders
- Offence committed whilst on licence
- Deliberate isolation of victim(s)
- Vulnerability of victim(s)
- Threats made to expose victim(s) to the authorities (for example, immigration or police), family/friends or others
- Harm threatened against the family/friends of victim(s)
- Passport/identity documents removed
- Prostitute(s) prevented from seeking medical treatment
- Food withheld
- Earnings withheld/kept by offender or evidence of excessive wage reduction or debt bondage, inflated travel or living expenses or unreasonable interest rates
- Any steps taken to prevent the victim reporting an incident, obtaining assistance and/or from assisting or supporting the prosecution
- Attempts to dispose of or conceal evidence
- Prostitute(s) forced or coerced into pornography
- Timescale over which the operation has been run

Mitigating factors

- No previous convictions **or** no relevant/recent convictions
- Remorse
- Previous good character and/or exemplary conduct*
- Age and/or lack of maturity where it affects the responsibility of the offender
- Mental disorder or learning disability, particularly where linked to the commission of the offence
- Demonstration of steps taken to address offending behaviour

* Previous good character/exemplary conduct is different from having no previous convictions. The more serious the offence, the less the weight which should normally be attributed to this factor. Where previous good character/exemplary conduct has been used to facilitate the offence, this mitigation should not normally be allowed and such conduct may constitute an aggravating factor.

10.129   The Sentencing Council explained in its consultation document its reasons for including many of the aggravating factors:

- "Deliberate isolation of prostitute(s)" will aggravate the offence as it means that the offender can exert a greater degree of control over them. This will be particularly relevant if the prostitute is from another country and has been cut off from all social and family ties.

- "Threats made to expose prostitute(s) to the authorities (e.g. immigration or police), family/friends or others" is included as such threats are frequently used to control and coerce individuals involved in prostitution and are particularly effective where the prostitute has been brought into the country illegally and fears deportation. It was expanded in the light of responses to the consultation to cover threats of exposure to family/friends.
- "Harm threatened against the family/friends of prostitute(s)" covers another means by which an offender may control their victim. The victim's feelings of helplessness and fear are likely to increase where they know the offender has influence over or access to their family which could result in harm befalling family members.
- "Passport/identity documents removed" is included as this is a direct way of limiting the physical movement and freedom of the prostitute thereby placing them under the offender's control.
- "Prostitute(s) prevented from seeking medical treatment" demonstrates a high level of control that impacts upon the welfare and physical wellbeing of the individual.
- "Food withheld" and "earnings withheld/kept by offender or evidence of excessive wage reduction or debt bondage, inflated travel or living expenses or unreasonable interest rates" are further specific examples of how control can be exercised over prostitutes.

The Council of Circuit Judges submitted in response to the consultation **10.130** that many of the aggravating factors are simply means of committing the s.53 offence and so raised the risk of "double counting", with the result that almost every s.53 offence will be aggravated. The Sentencing Council rejected this point, saying that the controlling behaviours identified in the guideline are particularly severe examples which should be reflected in sentence, and that sentencers would be able to weigh up the facts to avoid any risk of double counting.

The draft guideline also contained the aggravating factor "use of drugs/ **10.131** alcohol or other substance to secure prostitute's compliance", in order to reflect the strong link between drug use and street prostitution. The Council said that where the offender has either assisted the prostitute to develop a dependency or exploited a pre-existing dependency in order to control and manipulate them, this will aggravate the offence. As a result of responses to the consultation, the reference to drugs and alcohol was moved to step one, where it appears in the harm factors as "grooming of individual(s) to enter prostitution including through cultivation of a dependency on drugs or alcohol".

Steps Three to Nine

The remaining steps cover the following points. At step three the court **10.132** should consider any factors which would indicate a reduction in sentence, e.g.

assistance to the prosecution. At step four it should consider any reduction for a guilty plea. At step five the court should consider dangerousness, i.e. whether it would be appropriate to award an extended sentence (s.226A of the Criminal Justice Act 2003). Step six requires the court to consider whether the total sentence is just and proportionate to the offending behaviour. At step seven it should consider whether to make an ancillary order (e.g. a SHPO or a restraining order). Step eight requires the court to fulfil its duty under s.174 of the Criminal Justice Act 2003 to give reasons for, and explain the effect of, the sentence. Finally, at step nine the court should consider whether to give credit for time spent on bail in accordance with s.240A of that Act.

Parties to the Offence

10.133   Both the person who causes or incites and the victim may be male or female. If the victim is a child, i.e. under the age of 18, the appropriate charge is under s.48 of the 2003 Act (causing or inciting child sexual exploitation). If, however, it may be difficult in proceedings under s.48 to establish that the defendant did not reasonably believe the child to be 18 or over, he may be charged instead or in the alternative under this section.

"Causes or Incites"

10.134   For the meaning of "causes" and "incites", see paras 2.98 and 3.158 and following, above.

10.135   A decision that remains illuminating despite the repeal of the relevant law is *Christian*,[125] decided under s.22 of the Sexual Offences Act 1956, which made it an offence to "procure" a woman to become a prostitute. The defendant was a brothel-keeper and the evidence showed that the girl who was alleged to have been "procured" had been introduced to her at the brothel by a third party. On her first visit the girl had willingly committed indecent acts in the presence of men, although she had done nothing of the kind before. Thereafter, on many occasions, she had gone to the brothel of her own free will and engaged in acts of prostitution. The Common Sergeant directed an acquittal, holding that there had been no procuration as the girl "wanted no procuring at all".[126] He said that the offence[127]:

---

[125] (1913) 23 Cox C.C. 541. See also *Broadfoot* [1976] 3 All E.R. 753, which is to similar effect.

[126] In *Pikos* [1967] V.R. 89, Vict. S.Ct., Smith J held that the statement that the girl "wanted no procuring" did not mean that it was necessary in such cases to establish that she "needed" to be procured, in the sense that because of her moral character or mental attitude she would be resistant to the idea of having illicit intercourse. The fact that the girl "wanted no procuring" was merely a part, though possibly a most important part, of the material to be weighed in deciding whether there was or was not a "real procuration".

[127] At 542.

"is aimed at people who get girls by some fraud or persuasion, or by inviting them to it if they cannot get money in any other way."

The courts are likely to take a similar approach to the "causing" offence in s.52. If A were to run a brothel where B performed acts of prostitution of his or her own volition, without invitation, persuasion or pressure on the part of A, this is unlikely without more to constitute a s.52 offence.

"To Become"

A s.52 offence is committed where a person (A) causes or incites another   **10.136**
person (B) "to become" a prostitute. It follows that A cannot commit a s.52 offence by causing or inciting B to engage in prostitution if B is already a prostitute, since B cannot be caused or incited to "become" what he already is.[128] In *Ubolcharoen and Thonarin*[129] the Court of Appeal went further and said that no offence is committed where B has previously acted anywhere in the world as a prostitute, even on a single occasion. In other words, for the purposes of s.52 the correct approach should be "once a prostitute, always a prostitute". We submit that this cannot be right, since if B has engaged in prostitution in the past but has since ceased to do so, it is logically possible for him to become a prostitute again. It would be highly unfortunate if he were to be denied the protection of s.52 because of past activities that he has put behind him. In principle it ought to be possible for A to commit an offence by causing or inciting B to become a prostitute even though B has previously been one, provided he is not one at the time of the alleged offence. The Court in *Ubolcharoen* gave no reason for expressing a contrary view and appears not to have heard argument on the point. It may have been influenced by the definition of "prostitute" in s.51(2) of the Act (discussed below) as a person "who, on at least one occasion and whether or not compelled to do so, offers or provides sexual services" for payment. This could be read as having the effect that a person who on one occasion offered or provided sexual services for payment would thereafter remain a prostitute for the purposes of the Act. This would, we suggest, unduly narrow the scope of s.52. The better view must be that a person who in the past has offered or provided sexual services for payment, but who has desisted from such conduct, is no longer to be regarded as a prostitute for the purposes of the Act.

"Prostitute"

Section 54(2) and (3) of the 2003 Act provide as follows: **10.137**

"(2) In sections 51A, 52, 53 and 53A 'prostitute' means a person (A) who, on at least one occasion and whether or not compelled to do so, offers or provides

---

[128] *Ubolcharoen and Thonarin* [2009] EWCA Crim 3263. For similar decisions under the previous law, see *Gold and Cohen* (1907) 71 J.P. 360; *Johnson* [1964] 2 Q.B. 404 at 408; *Broadfoot* [1976] 3 All E.R. 753 at 756.
[129] [2009] EWCA Crim 3263 at [6].

> sexual services to another person in return for payment or a promise of payment to A or a third person; and 'prostitution' is to be interpreted accordingly.
> (3) In subsection (2) and section 53A, 'payment' means any financial advantage, including the discharge of an obligation to pay or the provision of goods or services (including sexual services) gratuitously or at a discount."

For the meaning of "sexual services", see paras 10.29 and following, above. For the meaning of "payment", see para.10.32, above.

10.138   These provisions were substituted for the original s.54(2) by the Serious Crime Act 2015.[130] As enacted, s.54(2) provided simply that "prostitute" and "prostitution" had the meaning given by s.51(2) of the 2003 Act. Section 51(2), which applies for the purposes of the offences of child sexual exploitation in ss.48–50 of the Act, was itself amended by the 2015 Act so that references in it to "prostitution" were replaced by references to "child sexual exploitation". This change required a consequential amendment to s.54(2), which could no longer cross-refer to s.51(2) for a definition of "prostitution". The amendment has the effect of bringing into s.54(2) and (3) the definition of that term previously contained in s.51(2). As such, it does not change the law but retains the existing definition. The effect of that definition is that s.52 covers the full range of sexual services provided for payment, whether or not full intercourse is contemplated, e.g. the recruitment of women to act as "masseuses" in circumstances where they are required to masturbate clients on request.

"In Any Part of the World"

10.139   These words mean that s.52 is contravened wherever in the world a person is caused or incited to become a prostitute.

"For or in the Expectation of Gain"

10.140   Section 54(1) of the 2003 Act provides as follows:

> "In sections 52, 53 and 53A, 'gain' means—
> (a) any financial advantage, including the discharge of an obligation to pay or the provision of goods or services (including sexual services) gratuitously or at a discount; or
> (b) the goodwill of any person which is or appears likely, in time, to bring financial advantage."

10.141   For the scope of para.(a) of this definition, see para.10.32, above. The reference to "sexual services" means that A will commit a s.52 offence by causing or inciting someone to become a prostitute, in the expectation that they, or another prostitute, will then provide him with sexual favours free or at a discount. Paragraph (b) is intended to cover the situation in which one person causes or incites another to become a prostitute in the hope that it will

---

[130] s.85 and Sch.4, para.62, with effect from, May 3, 2015 (SI 2015/820).

please someone else who is likely in time to return the favour in a way that will bring financial advantage.[131] During the debates on the Sexual Offences Bill, Lord Falconer of Thoroton acknowledged the potential evidential difficulty of proving that the defendant was motivated by the hope or expectation of obtaining goodwill in this sense, but the Government resisted removing the provision because in some circumstances it might be possible to meet the evidential requirement, e.g. where the defendant told a third party why he acted as he did. It should be noted that there is no requirement that the expected gain must materialise.

MENTAL ELEMENT

It must be proved that A "intentionally" caused or incited B to become a   **10.142**
prostitute. For the meaning of "intention", see paras 2.78 and following, above. If A believes that B is already a prostitute, he cannot commit an offence of causing or inciting her to become one, since he cannot intend to cause or incite B to become something which he believes she already is.[132] If in any particular case A may have believed that B was already a prostitute, it may be appropriate to charge him in the alternative with attempting to control prostitution for gain (s.53 of the 2003 Act, discussed below). If B is already a prostitute but A believes she is *not*, he may be convicted of attempting to cause her to become a prostitute notwithstanding that it was impossible for him to commit the full offence.[133]

CONTROLLING PROSTITUTION FOR GAIN

DEFINITION

Section 53(1) of the Sexual Offences Act 2003 provides: **10.143**

"A person commits an offence if—
  (a) he intentionally controls any of the activities of another person relating to that person's prostitution in any part of the world, and
  (b) he does so for or in the expectation of gain for himself or a third person."

[131] *Hansard*, HL, vol.648, col.195 (May 13, 2003).
[132] cf. *Brown* (1985) 80 Cr. App. R. 36, where it was held that a defendant could not be convicted of attempting to procure a woman to become a common prostitute, contrary to s.22 of the Sexual Offences Act 1956, if he genuinely believed on reasonable grounds that she already was one. We suggest that in requiring the defendant's belief to be reasonable the court put the matter too high, as it is clear from subsequent decisions in other contexts that a genuine belief that the woman was already a prostitute should itself be sufficient to prevent a conviction, though of course the reasonableness of an asserted belief would bear upon the likelihood of it being genuinely held: see especially *B (A Minor) v DPP* [2000] 2 A.C. 428..
[133] cf. Criminal Attempts Act 1981 s.1(2), (3); *Shivpuri* [1987] A.C. 1.

Mode of Trial and Punishment

10.144   The offence under s.53 is triable either way.[134] The maximum punishment on conviction on indictment is seven years' imprisonment.[135] The maximum on summary conviction is six months' imprisonment or a fine, or both. As from a day to be appointed the maximum sentence of imprisonment on summary conviction will increase to 12 months' imprisonment.[136] The increase will have no application to offences committed before it takes effect.[137] Until recently, the maximum fine on summary conviction was a fine not exceeding the statutory maximum (i.e. £5,000). The effect of s.85 of the Legal Aid, Sentencing and Punishment of Offenders Act 2012 is that, from March 12, 2015, a fine of any amount may be imposed. Fines will, however, continue to be set according to the seriousness of the offence and the means of the offender.

10.145   For the purposes of listing, cases under s.53[138] fall within Class 2B, save for complex cases involving many complainants (often under age, in care or otherwise particularly vulnerable) and/or many defendants who are alleged to have systematically groomed and abused them, often over a long period of time, which fall within Class 1C.[139] Cases in Class 1C must be referred to the Resident Judge, and by the Resident Judge to a Presiding Judge. Cases in Class 2B must be similarly referred in certain specified circumstances, including where the case is unusually grave or complex or a novel and important point of law is to be raised; where the defendant is a police officer, a member of the legal profession or a high profile figure; or where for any reason the case is likely to attract exceptional media attention.

10.146   An offence under s.53, whenever committed, is a specified offence for the purposes of s.226A of the Criminal Justice Act 2003 (extended sentence for certain violent and sexual offences).[140]

10.147   There is no provision for a person convicted under s.53 to be subject to the notification requirements of the Sexual Offences Act 2003.

10.148   The s.53 offence is a "lifestyle" offence for the purposes of the Proceeds of Crime Act 2002.[141] Accordingly, a conviction for the offence may, if the other conditions set out in the 2002 Act are met, result in the court making a confiscation order in relation to the benefit the offender has derived from the

---

[134] s.53(2).

[135] s.53(2).

[136] Criminal Justice Act 2003 s.282(2), (3).

[137] Criminal Justice Act 2003 s.282(4).

[138] And of soliciting, inciting, encouraging or assisting, attempting or conspiring to commit the offence or assisting an offender having committed the offence.

[139] *Consolidated Criminal Practice Directions*, Part XIII Listing B: CLASSIFICATION, available at *https://www.judiciary.gov.uk/publications/criminal-practice-directions-2015/* [Accessed April 30, 2016].

[140] Inserted by the Legal Aid, Sentencing and Punishment of Offenders Act 2012 s.124, brought into force on December 3, 2012, by SI 2012/2906.

[141] 2002 Act Sch.2, as amended by the 2003 Act s.139 and Sch.6, para.46 and by the Serious Crime Act 2015 s.85 and Sch.4, para.58.

offence or, if he has a general criminal lifestyle, from his general criminal conduct.

CHARGE OR INDICTMENT

There is nothing in s.53 to suggest that control must last for any particular   **10.149**
period. Accordingly, by analogy with the repealed offence of living off the earnings of prostitution (s.30 of the Sexual Offences Act 1956), a charge or indictment under s.53 may allege that the offence was committed on a single specified day; and where this is alleged, the prosecution may lead supporting evidence to show the nature of A's relations with B either before or after the specified day, as such evidence is clearly relevant to the issue.[142]

SENTENCING

For the Sentencing Council guideline relating to the sentencing of sexual   **10.150**
offences committed by offenders aged 18 and over, see Ch.33, below. A single guideline covers offences under ss.52 and 53 of the 2003 Act and is discussed at paras 10.118 and following, above.

PARTIES TO THE OFFENCE

Both the person exercising control and the person whose activities are subject   **10.151**
to it may be male or female. If the person whose activities are controlled is under 18, the appropriate charge is under s.49 of the 2003 Act (controlling child sexual exploitation). If, however, it may be difficult in proceedings under s.49 to establish that the defendant did not reasonably believe the child to be 18 or over, he may be charged in the alternative under this section.

A prostitute who assists a person to control the activities of another   **10.152**
prostitute may be convicted as his accomplice.[143] She may also be charged with conspiring with him to commit the offence, unless they are spouses or civil partners.[144] But can the prostitute whose activities are controlled be convicted of aiding and abetting the s.53 offence? In *Congdon*,[145] HH Judge Addison ruled that a prostitute could not be convicted of aiding and abetting a man to live on her earnings, contrary to s.30 of the Sexual Offences Act 1956. As authority he cited the rule in *Tyrrell*,[146] that a person for whose

---

[142] cf. *Hill and Churchman* [1914] 2 K.B. 386.
[143] cf. *Stewart v DPP* (1986) 83 Cr. App. R. 327; and see *Reid (Lindsey) v HM Advocate*, 1999 J.C. 54, HCJ Appeal.
[144] Criminal Law Act 1977 ss.1(1), 2(2)(a).
[145] Unreported, Portsmouth Crown Court (discussed (1990) 140 N.L.J. 1221). cf. *Murphy and Bieneck* (1981) 21 C.R.(3d) 39, Alta. C.A., where it was held in relation to the offence of "living on the avails of prostitution of another person" that the law of accessories could not be construed so as to extend the scope of the offence to the prostitute herself.
[146] [1894] 1 Q.B. 710.

protection an offence has been enacted cannot be an accomplice to that offence committed against himself. It is, however, a moot point whether the s.30 offence was enacted in order to protect prostitutes, or rather to penalise pimps. In *Grizzle*,[147] another s.30 case where the prostitute gave evidence that the appellant had forced her into prostitution, it was assumed that she was at least technically his accomplice so that, as the law then stood, the judge was required to warn the jury of the danger of accepting her evidence without corroboration. The Court's willingness to treat the prostitute as an accomplice at least for this purpose tends to suggest that the approach taken in *Congdon* was wrong. But even if it was correct as regards the 1956 Act offence, we suggest that in appropriate circumstances a prostitute may properly be charged as an accomplice to a s.53 offence of which she is the subject. This is because the offence is directed at the exploitation of prostitution for gain, not at the exploitation of prostitutes per se, and as such it may be committed even where the prostitute accepts the control of her activities of her own free will: see para.10.156, below. In those circumstances there would seem to be no scope for regarding the offence as enacted for the prostitute's protection, so as to engage the rule in *Tyrrell*.

"Controls any of the Activities of Another Person relating to that Person's Prostitution"

10.153   The s.53 offence requires proof of "control", and accordingly an individual who profits from or is involved in the activities of a prostitute relating to prostitution but without controlling any of those activities falls outside its scope. It appears that the offence is considerably narrower than its main predecessor, the offence of living off the earnings of prostitution (s.30 of the Sexual Offences Act 1956). It will not, for example, cover the following activities, which were held to constitute the old offence:

- selling a directory of prostitutes in which prostitutes pay to have their details included,[148]
- providing prospective clients, for a fee, with information about the services offered by prostitutes,[149] and
- letting premises to prostitutes knowing they will be used for the purposes of prostitution, where the circumstances are such that the lessor and the prostitute are engaged in the business of prostitution together.[150]

In none of these examples does the relevant activity cause another person to "become" a prostitute, and so it cannot fall within the scope of the offence

---

[147] [1991] Crim. L.R. 553, decided before the abolition of the requirement of an "accomplice warning" by s.32 of the Criminal Justice and Public Order Act 1994. See also *Stewart v DPP* (1986) 83 Cr. App. R. 327 where a prostitute who paid some of her earnings to the appellant as rent and who collected for him rent from other prostitutes was regarded as an accomplice.

[148] *Shaw v DPP* [1962] A.C. 220.

[149] *Ansell* [1975] Q.B. 215.

[150] *Thomas* [1957] 1 W.L.R. 747 and *Stewart v DPP* (1986) 83 Cr. App. R. 327.

of causing or inciting prostitution for gain (s.52 of the 2003 Act). However, if any of the prostitutes in such a case is under 18, then the relevant activity might well constitute an offence of arranging or facilitating child sexual exploitation (s.50 of the 2003 Act).

It is sufficient for a conviction that the defendant controls any of the **10.154** activities of another person relating to that person's prostitution. Examples of conduct covered by the offence would be where the defendant controls the price charged by a prostitute for different sexual services, the places where she works or the number of clients she services every night. Indirect control should suffice, as where A exercises control of B's activities through another person. The words "relating to that person's prostitution" mean that the offence applies not only where the defendant controls the prostitute's activities as such but also where, e.g. he controls the prostitute's diary or travel arrangements, takes bookings by telephone or completes her tax return. An amendment tabled by Lord Lucas when the Sexual Offences Bill was on Report in the Lords would have confined the s.53 offence to cases where the defendant controls activity "directly" relating to prostitution. In resisting this amendment, which was withdrawn, Lord Falconer of Thoroton said on behalf of the Government:

> "We want control of activities that relate to prostitution to be caught. That would include, for example, telling a prostitute which street corner to stand on, telling her what to wear when she works, or controlling her supply of drugs so that she is obliged to sell herself to get the drugs. We know that pimps are engaged in doing all of those things. Including the word 'directly' in the offence would throw doubt on whether all those examples would be covered.
>
> The amendment would narrow the scope so that the control of activities that were only indirectly related to the person's prostitution would not be covered. In Committee, the noble Lord raised his concern to ensure that the partners of prostitutes were not caught by the provisions. . . . However, such individuals will not be caught. If, for example, a partner drives a prostitute to her place of work and collects her from it, that would not be caught, even if the money that she derived from prostitution benefited both of them, unless he directed or otherwise exerted control, so that she was required to be at that place for the purposes of prostitution.
>
> [The] amendment stems from a desire to ensure that people who, for gain, provide services to prostitutes that may assist them in their prostitution—a travel agent, a taxi driver or a hairdresser—are not covered by the offence. . . . If a taxi driver or a hairdresser is hired by the prostitute herself for their services, no control is exerted, and they would not be liable for the offence. If a taxi driver, a hairdresser or a travel agent is hired by a pimp to provide their services to a prostitute, it is the pimp who directs the activities relating to prostitution who is exerting the control, not the service provider. If it can be proven that the partner of a prostitute or someone providing a service to her exerts control over activities related to prostitution, it is right that he is liable to be charged in connection with the offence."

It was held in *Massey*[151] that "control" does not require proof of coercion **10.155** and may even be present where the prostitute acts of her own free will. D,

---

[151] [2007] EWCA Crim 2664.

then 19, met the appellant, then 35, when she was already working as a prostitute. She told him of her troubled background, i.e. she had been taken into care when she was two years old, had committed various offences and had developed an addiction to drugs. Their relationship developed and D went to live with the appellant. The relationship was turbulent. During it, D continued to work as a prostitute. After 10 years she left the appellant and complained to the police that he had forced her to work as a prostitute and had lived on her earnings. The appellant denied the allegations. He was charged under s.53 with controlling prostitution for gain and (for the period prior to the commencement of the 2003 Act) with living on the earnings of prostitution. At trial, D said that the appellant took all her money, set up a website for her to advertise her services and kept a log of the work she did. The appellant was domineering and violent, and she did what he wanted because she felt intimidated. The appellant said that he had taken her in through pity, had not liked her working as a prostitute and had tried to convince her to stop. The judge directed the jury to the effect that "control" required D to have acted under compulsion and not of her own free will, but did not require proof that the appellant had forced her into prostitution. The appellant contended that this was a misdirection and that the jury should have been told that coercion is an essential element of "control" under s.53. The Court of Appeal rejected this argument, saying[152]:

> "In our judgment, 'control' includes but is not limited to one who forces another to carry out the relevant activity. 'Control' may be exercised in a variety of ways. It is not necessary or appropriate for us to seek to lay down a comprehensive definition of an ordinary English word. It is certainly enough if a defendant instructs or directs the other person to carry out the relevant activity or do it in a particular way. There may be a variety of reasons why the other person does as instructed. It may be because of physical violence or threats of violence. It may be because of emotional blackmail, for example, being told that 'if you really loved me, you would do this for me'. It may be because the defendant has a dominating personality and the woman who acts under his direction is psychologically damaged and fragile. It may be because the defendant is an older person, and the other person is emotionally immature. It may be because the defendant holds out the lure of gain, or the hope of a better life. Or there may be other reasons."

In the present case, although the judge's direction put the matter too high in saying that the woman must have acted under compulsion, nonetheless his direction as a whole could not have led the jury to underestimate what the prosecution had to prove and the appellant's conviction was therefore safe.

10.156   The Court in *Massey* also made it clear that the s.53 offence is committed even if the prostitute accepts direction or instruction of her own free will. It said[153]:

> "Exploitation of prostitution for financial gain is the broad mischief against which section 53 is aimed, whether or not it involves intimidation of the

---

[152] At 20.
[153] At 21.

prostitute or prostitutes concerned. At one stage it was suggested by [counsel for the appellant] that some degree of absence of free will on the part of the prostitute is an essential ingredient of control. But on reflection he withdrew that submission and, in our judgment, he was right to do so. If, for example, a group recruits young women from overseas and puts them to work in organised prostitution in the United Kingdom, we do not see any ground for saying that the prosecution would have to prove absence of free will in order to be able to show that the organisers were controlling the activities of the women for gain."

Also instructive on the meaning of "control" in s.53 is *Drew*,[154] where HH **10.157** Judge Rivlin QC ruled that the word is a simple everyday one the meaning of which may embrace compulsion, as one of its more extreme manifestations, but also any one of a number of situations involving the power to exert influence over another person's behaviour in connection with a particular activity. Thus, "control" could well include a person ordering, directing, instructing or requiring a prostitute either to do or not to do something in connection with any of her activities in that capacity, in circumstances in which she is expected, and feels obliged, to comply. The learned judge rejected the suggestion by one defendant that he had not controlled the prostitutes in question but merely "managed" them, stating that in dictionary after dictionary the definitions of the word "manage" include the word "control". He went on to hold[155] that s.53 may cover, for example, controlling the prostitute's days and hours of employment, where she should work, the price to be charged by her, the commission to be paid to the agency, the services which she shall or shall not render, or the clothing she should or should not wear in the course of her work. The fact that a prostitute may be willing to work on these terms, and be subject to one kind of control or another, cannot affect the issue of criminal responsibility, although it may amount to a mitigating circumstance. The learned judge went on to hold that in the case before him there was sufficient evidence of control to go before the jury: although there was no evidence of compulsion or coercion, there was evidence, including documentary evidence, that the prostitutes were subject to control as to their working times, the services they should offer, the items they were to have with them whilst working, their charges and the arrangements for payment. Although the ruling in *Drew* was given before the decision in *Massey*, we respectfully suggest that it is both consistent with that decision and correct.

If the control exercised by a person over a prostitute involves physical **10.158** restraint, a charge of false imprisonment may be appropriate.[156]

"PROSTITUTION"

For the meaning of "prostitution", see s.54(2) and (3) of the 2003 Act, set out **10.159** in paras 10.137 and following, above. This definition ensures that the offence

---

[154] Unreported, Southwark Crown Court, December 2006. The case resulted in acquittals.
[155] Citing with approval pp.309–311 of the 3rd edition of this work.
[156] cf. *Neville and Bailey* (1995) 16 Cr. App. R.(S.) 647.

under s.53 catches someone who controls activities relating to the full range of sexual services provided for payment, whether or not full intercourse is contemplated, e.g. the control of women employed to act as "masseuses" in circumstances where they are required to masturbate clients on request. To prove an offence under s.53 it is, of course, necessary to establish that the person whose activities were controlled was at the relevant time engaged in prostitution.[157]

"In any Part of the World"

10.160   These words mean that s.53 is contravened when a person in England and Wales controls any of the activities of a prostitute relating to her prostitution, regardless whether the prostitution takes place in that jurisdiction or elsewhere in the UK or overseas.

"For or in the Expectation of Gain"

10.161   For the meaning of these words, see paras 10.140 and following, above. The defendant will act for or in the expectation of "gain" where, e.g. he lives with a prostitute whose activities he controls and takes all or part of her earnings for himself,[158] or the prostitute pays some or all of his rent, or buys his food, drink or drugs. In a case where the defendant takes a prostitute's earnings, it will not matter for this purpose whether he receives the earnings from the prostitute herself or directly from the client.[159] In *Drew*,[160] HH Judge Rivlin sitting at Southwark Crown Court rejected the proposition advanced on behalf of some of the defendants that a charge under s.53 requires proof that the prostitute concerned was exploited by the defendant, as opposed to an equal partner in the business. He said that the section requires only that the defendant acted in the expectation of gain, and the absence of exploitation, whilst it may go to mitigation, cannot extinguish criminal liability. With respect, this must be correct.

Mental Element

10.162   It must be proved that the defendant "intentionally" controlled the prostitute's activities. For the meaning of "intention" see paras 2.78 and following, above. It follows that an essential element of the offence will be lacking if the defendant does not know that the other person is a prostitute or that the activities he controls relate to her prostitution.[161] So if a person controls a

---

[157] cf. *Wilson (D.T.)* (1984) 78 Cr. App. R. 247; *Grizzle* [1991] Crim. L.R. 553 (both decided under s.30 of the 1956 Act).
[158] cf. *Stewart v DPP* (1986) 83 Cr. App. R. 327, at 332.
[159] cf. *Ansell* [1975] Q.B. 215 (decided under s.30 of the 1956 Act).
[160] Unreported, Southwark Crown Court, December 2006.
[161] cf. *Wilson (D.T.)* (1984) 78 Cr. App. R. 247.

prostitute's appointments in the expectation of payment, whilst mistakenly believing that she is an escort or a stripagram artist, he commits no offence. The same is true if he knows she is a prostitute but wrongly thinks that the activities he controls relate to something other than her prostitution.

PAYING FOR SEXUAL SERVICES OF A PROSTITUTE SUBJECTED TO FORCE ETC

DEFINITION

Section 53A of the Sexual Offences Act 2003, inserted by s.14 of the Policing   **10.163** and Crime Act 2009 with effect from April 1, 2010, provides:

> (1) A person (A) commits an offence if—
>   (a) A makes or promises payment for the sexual services of a prostitute (B),
>   (b) a third person (C) has engaged in exploitative conduct of a kind likely to induce or encourage B to provide the sexual services for which A has made or promised payment, and
>   (c) C engaged in that conduct for or in the expectation of gain for C or another person (apart from A or B).
> (2) The following are irrelevant—
>   (a) where in the world the sexual services are to be provided and whether those services are provided,
>   (b) whether A is, or ought to be, aware that C has engaged in exploitative conduct."

MODE OF TRIAL AND PUNISHMENT

Offences under s.53A are summary only and the maximum punishment on   **10.164** conviction is a fine not exceeding level 3 on the standard scale (currently £1000).[162] There is no provision for a person convicted under s.52 to be subject to the notification requirements of the 2003 Act.

SENTENCING

The offence is not the subject of a sentencing guideline issued by the   **10.165** Sentencing Council or a guideline judgment handed down by the Court of Appeal.

PARTIES TO THE OFFENCE

Both the person who makes or promises payment and the prostitute may be   **10.166** either male or female.

---

[162] s.53A(4).

"Payment"

10.167   See s.54(3) of the 2003 Act, set out in para.10.137, above.

"Sexual Services of a Prostitute"

10.168   See 54(2) of the 2003 Act, set out in para.10.137, above. This definition ensures that the offence under s.52 covers the full range of sexual services provided for payment, whether or not full intercourse is contemplated, e.g. the recruitment of women to act as "masseuses" in circumstances where they are required to masturbate clients on request. It is immaterial whether the sexual services are actually provided, or whether they are provided or intended for A or a third party. So long as A makes or promises payment in England and Wales, it does not matter where in the world the sexual services are provided or intended to be provided.

"Exploitative Conduct"

10.169   Section 53A(3) provides:

> "C engages in exploitative conduct if—
>   (a) C uses force, threats (whether or not relating to violence) or any other form of coercion, or
>   (b) C practises any form of deception."

The use of physical violence falls clearly within the scope of the section, but s.53A(3) is potentially very wide in its application and will cover any form of threat, coercion or deception by C of a kind likely to induce or encourage B to provide sexual services (in accordance with s.53A(2)). Examples of the sorts of threat that could fall within the scope of the provision are where C threatens to report B to the immigration authorities or the police; to restrict B's access to children, family and friends; to withdraw B's accommodation, financial support or other basic necessities; to stop supplying B with drugs and/or alcohol; to end a relationship with B or withdraw love or affection; to take action that would make B feel guilty or responsible, e.g. threatening to commit suicide or threats relating to the effect on C of being unable to buy drugs and/or alcohol; to restrict B's movements or other personal freedom; to tell family, friends or community about B's involvement in prostitution or some other fact about B that would damage B's reputation or embarrass B; or to harm B's family or someone close to B.[163] As for "any form of coercion", this is intended to cover dominating or unequal relationships in which C induces or encourages B to provide sexual services by using his

---

[163] Examples taken from Home Office Circular 006/2010, titled *Provisions in the Policing and Crime Act 2009 that relate to prostitution (sections 14 to 21)* and published on 29 March, 2010, which can be found at *https://www.gov.uk/government/publications/provisions-in-the-policing-and-crime-act-2009-that-relate-to-prostitution-sections-14-to-21* [Accessed April 30, 2016].

influence over B or by exploiting B's vulnerabilities, such as B's youth; physical or mental incapacity, illness or disability; drug or alcohol dependency; history of experienced violence or abuse; economic disadvantage, social status or social exclusion; or immigration status.[164] Finally, "any form of deception" could cover deception as to such matters as the financial or other rewards promised to B if B provides sexual services, the terms on which the sexual services will be provided, or the identity of the person who is to receive them.

"FOR OR IN THE EXPECTATION OF GAIN"

Section 54(1) of the 2003 Act,[165] provides as follows: **10.170**

"In sections 52, 53 and 53A, 'gain' means—
 (a) any financial advantage, including the discharge of an obligation to pay or the provision of goods or services (including sexual services) gratuitously or at a discount; or
 (b) the goodwill of any person which is or appears likely, in time, to bring financial advantage."

For the scope of this definition, see paras 10.32 and 10.140 and following, above.

MENTAL ELEMENT

Section 53A(2)(b) makes clear that the defendant may be convicted whether   **10.171** or not he knew or ought to have known that the prostitute had been exploited. In other words, the offence is one of strict liability as regards this element.

ibid., para.20.
[165] As amended by the Policing and Crime Act 2009 ss.112(1), 116(1) and Sch. 7, para.24(d).

CHAPTER 11

MODERN SLAVERY AND TRAFFICKING

By Riel Karmy-Jones QC and Robert Ward QC

Introduction 11.01
Prosecution of the Victims of
  Trafficking 11.22
Modern Slavery Act 2015 .... 11.44
Slavery, Servitude and Forced
  Compulsory Labour 11.59

Human Trafficking 11.72
Committing an Offence with Intent
  to Commit a Human Trafficking
  Offence 11.114
Powers Available Under the
  Modern Slavery Act 2015 ....11.117

INTRODUCTION

Kevin Hyland OBE, the first Independent Anti-Slavery Commissioner, has written[1]:   **11.01**

> "In 2014 the Home Office estimated that there were between 10,000 and 13,000 potential victims of modern slavery in the UK. This trade in human misery is taking place in cities, towns and rural communities across the nation on a shameful scale. Sexual exploitation is the most common form of modern slavery currently reported by potential victims in the UK, followed by labour exploitation, forced criminal exploitation, and domestic servitude."

Early international measures

The European Convention on Human Rights, which was drafted in 1950 by   **11.02**
the newly formed Council of Europe and entered into force on September 3, 1953, contains in art.4 a prohibition on slavery and forced labour:

> "1. No one shall be held in slavery or servitude.
> 2. No one shall be required to perform forced or compulsory labour.
> 3. For the purpose of this article the term 'forced or compulsory labour' shall not include:

---

[1] Strategic Plan 2015–17 (October 2015), p.1.

  a. any work required to be done in the ordinary course of detention imposed
  b. according to the provisions of Article 5 of this Convention or during conditional release from such detention;
  c. any service of a military character or, in case of conscientious objectors in countries where they are recognised, service exacted instead of compulsory military service;
  d. any service exacted in case of an emergency or calamity threatening the life or well-being of the community;
  e. any work or service which forms part of normal civic obligations."

It has been held that trafficking falls within the scope of art.4.[2] It was not, however, until the 1990s that the international dimension of the problem of trafficking, specifically for the purposes of sexual exploitation, began to be recognised. In 1996 the Agenda for Action of the Stockholm World Congress on the Sexual Exploitation of Children[3] required all signatories to develop a National Plan to combat the sexual exploitation of children, including by a review of their laws. The following year, the EU Joint Action on Trafficking in Human Beings and the Sexual Exploitation of Children called on Member States to review their laws on the sexual exploitation of children and on trafficking.

11.03   In 2000, the Protocol to Suppress, Prevent and Punish Trafficking in Persons was added to the UN Convention against Transnational Organised Crime. Known as the Palermo protocol, this provided the first internationally recognised definition of human trafficking. The UK signed the Protocol on December 14, 2000, and ratified it on February 9, 2006. Article 3 defines trafficking as follows:

"(a) 'Trafficking in persons' shall mean the recruitment, transportation, transfer, harbouring or receipt of persons, by means of the threat or use of force or other forms of coercion, of abduction, of fraud, of deception, of the abuse of power or of a position of vulnerability or of the giving or receiving of payments or benefits to achieve the consent of a person having control over another person, for the purpose of exploitation. Exploitation shall include, at a minimum, the exploitation of the prostitution of others or other forms of sexual exploitation, forced labour or services, slavery or practices similar to slavery, servitude or the removal of organs;

(b) The consent of a victim of trafficking in persons to the intended exploitation set forth in subparagraph (a) of this article shall be irrelevant where any of the means set forth in subparagraph (a) have been used;

(c) The recruitment, transportation, transfer, harbouring or receipt of a child for the purpose of exploitation shall be considered 'trafficking in persons' even if this does not involve any of the means set forth in subparagraph (a) of this article;

(d) 'Child' shall mean any person under eighteen years of age."

---

[2] *Rantsev v Cyprus* (App. No. 25965/04) [2010] ECHR 25965/04.
[3] Which was followed by World Congress II held in Yokohama in December 2001 and World Congress III held in Rio de Janeiro in November 2008.

In the European context, the EU Joint Action was superseded in 2002 by **11.04** the EU Framework Decision on Combating Trafficking in Human Beings.[4] This provided for measures aimed at ensuring approximation of national penal legislation concerning the definition of offences, penalties, jurisdiction and prosecution, protection and assistance to victims.

Sexual Offences Act 2003

The growing interest in the problem of trafficking on the international plane **11.05** was mirrored in the domestic context. In 2000, the report of the Sexual Offences Review referred to the rapid growth in the sex industry world-wide, the increasing involvement of organised crime, the significant problem posed by associated people trafficking, and an increasing awareness in the UK of the use of children in prostitution.[5] It acknowledged that UK law was deficient in addressing these problems. At that time there was no specific offence of trafficking a person in to (or out of) the UK. There were a number of offences in the Sexual Offences Act 1956 that could be used against traffickers who sexually exploited those they were trafficking, such as ss.30 and 31 (man living on the earnings of prostitution and woman exercising control over prostitute), s.22 (causing prostitution of women), s.24 (detention of a woman in a brothel) and s.28 (causing prostitution of a girl under 16). However, there were mixed views as to the effectiveness of these offences, which were complex and tended to result in low sentences even where large criminal organisations were involved. Furthermore, the offences were rarely used, largely because of the difficulty of persuading those affected to give evidence and because of the low maximum penalties.

The Review concluded that the nature and scale of the problem were such **11.06** that there should be a specific offence of trafficking, to stand alongside other offences of sexual exploitation. It acknowledged that the effectiveness of such an offence could be reduced if victims proved unwilling to testify, but nonetheless saw it as a potentially valuable tool for the police. It suggested that the offence should involve bringing a person, or enabling a person to

---

[4] 2002/629/JHA (O.J. 2002/L, 203/1, 1.8.2002). See also the Council Directive 2004/81/EC of April 29, 2004 on the residence permit issued to third-country nationals who are victims of trafficking in human beings or who have been the subject of an action to facilitate illegal immigration, who cooperate with the competent authorities (O.J. 2004/L, 261, 6.8.2004), which places an obligation on Member States to provide victims of trafficking with a reflection period and residence status, with related assistance and support measures. The Council EU plan on best practices, standards and procedures for combating and preventing trafficking in human beings (OJ 2005/C, 311/1, 9.12.2005) provides for Member States, the Commission and other EU bodies to take steps for the coordination of EU action on preventing trafficking, reducing demand, investigating and prosecuting, protecting and supporting victims of trafficking, returns and reintegration and external relations.

[5] Setting the Boundaries, *Reforming the Law on Sexual Offences* (Home Office, July 2000), Ch.7.

move (e.g. by facilitating transportation), from one place to another for the purposes of commercial sexual exploitation, for reward. Evidence of deception, coercion or force should add to the seriousness of the offence. In order to reflect the fact that trafficking is frequently organised as part of major international operations, the penalties for the offence should be substantial.

11.07   This recommendation was adopted in the White Paper *Protecting the Public* which set out proposals for reform of the law of sexual offences. In it, the Government announced an intention to make it an offence to traffic people for commercial sexual exploitation to cover those who recruit, harbour and facilitate the movement of another person for such purposes. In the event, the Sexual Offences Act 2003 contained three complementary offences of trafficking:

- trafficking into the UK for sexual exploitation (s.57)
- trafficking within the UK for sexual exploitation (s.58), and
- trafficking out of the UK for sexual exploitation (s.59).

11.08   These offences, which covered trafficking within the UK as well as across international borders, were intended to implement the Government's commitments under the Palermo Protocol and the EU Framework Decision on Combating Trafficking in Human Beings. In fact, before the 2003 Act was passed Parliament had already created an offence of trafficking into the UK for prostitution, in s.145 of the Nationality, Asylum and Immigration Act 2002. But the Government saw this as a "stop gap" measure that did not take account of the changes to the law on sexual exploitation announced in the White Paper. Accordingly the offence was repealed by the 2003 Act and replaced by the offences in ss.57–59. During the passage of the Bill, Lord Falconer gave the following graphic and depressing explanation of the problem that those offences sought to tackle:

> "We are all aware that some of those who are trafficked are often very vulnerable to intimidation and threats against themselves, or their families in their country of origin; and, indeed, to deception by the promise of good earnings, a better life, and greater opportunity. However, the actual conditions under which they are expected to work are very different from those that they are led to believe will be the case.
>
> In the destination country, those who are trafficked may often be unable to speak the language, know no one and may be without legal immigration status. Their freedom of movement can be severely curtailed by the trafficker, their earnings and passports can be taken away, and they can be subject to debt bondage. They may be forced to service many men, have unprotected sex, or engage in perverse sexual practices once at their destination or even en route. There are considerable reports of violence and rape being used to subdue and control such victims.
>
> Of those trafficked domestically, many are young, kept isolated from their friends and family, and misled by their trafficker into believing that they are earning money to build a future life together. When they become aware of the reality of their exploitation, fear of violence and the sense of stigma that derives from being a prostitute often inhibit their coming forward to report their

situation. They are therefore potentially more vulnerable to exploitative practices."[6]

The Council of Europe Trafficking Convention

In 2005, the Council of Europe agreed the Convention on Action against Trafficking in Human Beings (the "Trafficking Convention").[7] This was the first European treaty to deal with the prevention of trafficking, the prosecution of traffickers and the protection and support of their victims. It entered into force on February 1, 2008, and was ratified by the UK on December 17, 2008. Article 4 provides: **11.09**

> "4(a) 'Trafficking in human beings' shall mean the recruitment, transportation, transfer, harbouring or receipt of persons, by means of the threat or use of force or other forms of coercion, of abduction, of fraud, of deception, of the abuse of power or of a position of vulnerability or of the giving or receiving of payments or benefits to achieve the consent of a person having control over another person, for the purpose of exploitation. Exploitation shall include, at a minimum, the exploitation of the prostitution of others or other forms of sexual exploitation, forced labour or services, slavery or practices similar to slavery, servitude or the removal of organs;
>
> (b) The consent of a victim of 'trafficking in human beings' to the intended exploitation set forth in subparagraph (a) of this article shall be irrelevant where any of the means set forth in subparagraph (a) have been used;
>
> (c) The recruitment, transportation, transfer, harbouring or receipt of a child for the purpose of exploitation shall be considered 'trafficking in human beings' even if this does not involve any of the means set forth in subparagraph (a) of this article;
>
> (d) 'Child' shall mean any person under eighteen years of age;
>
> (e) 'Victim' shall mean any natural person who is subject to trafficking in human beings as defined in this article."

Article 10 of the Convention places the State under an obligation to identify victims of trafficking and to ensure that different authorities collaborate and co-operate in order to do so. Article 18 emphasises the rights of victims, including their right to be provided with assistance and support as soon as there are reasonable grounds for believing that they have been trafficked. Article 26 requires signatories to "provide for the possibility of not imposing penalties on victims for their involvement in unlawful activities to the extent that they have been compelled to do so". This provision led eventually to the creation of the defence now enshrined in s.45 of the Modern Slavery Act 2015, discussed at paras.11.37 and following, below. **11.10**

The UK signed the Trafficking Convention on March 23, 2007, but did not ratify it for almost another two years. The catalyst that caused the Government to react was the landmark case of *R v O*,[8] the first appeal to challenge the prosecution of a victim of trafficking. In that case, in a caustic judgment **11.11**

---

[6] *Hansard*, HC, Vol.648 col.204 (May 13, 2003).
[7] Council of Europe Treaty Series (CETS) 197/1975.
[8] [2008] EWCA Crim 2835.

given by Laws LJ, the Court of Appeal held that despite the fact that the Convention had not been ratified it nonetheless governed the case and gave rise to rights under art.6 of the ECHR. The Court accordingly quashed the conviction of a young Nigerian woman for possessing a false identity card in circumstances where no consideration had been given before or at trial to the possibility that she might have been trafficked. The judgment, given on September 2, 2008, was fundamental and caused the UK finally to ratify the Convention later that year. It entered into force in respect of the UK on April 1, 2009. On the same date the National Referral Mechanism ("NRM")[9] was set up to give effect to art.10 of the Convention by acting as a mechanism for identifying and supporting victims of trafficking in the UK.

11.12   Thereafter a series of domestic appeals considered art.26 of the Convention and the rights of victims: *R v LM*,[10] *R v N and Le*[11] and *L v R*,[12] considered at paras 11.22 and following, below.

EU Directive on Trafficking in Human Beings

11.13   In March 2010, the European Commission issued a proposal for a new anti-trafficking Directive which would build on the Council of Europe Trafficking Convention and supersede the 2002 EU Framework Decision. The EU Directive on Trafficking in Human Beings ("the Trafficking Directive") came into force on April 15, 2011. It covers action on several fronts, relating to criminal law and the prosecution of offenders; victims' rights in criminal proceedings and victim support; prevention; and monitoring.[13]

11.14   In August 2010 the UK Government indicated that it would not at that stage be opting in to the proposed Directive, on the grounds that doing so would make very little difference to the way the problem of human trafficking was tackled by the UK, and it would be better to review the position when the Directive was agreed.[14]

---

[9] The NRM is a framework for identifying victims of human trafficking and ensuring they receive the appropriate protection and support. It encourages the sharing of information between agencies with a view to ensuring an appropriate safeguarding response. It is also the mechanism through which the UK Human Trafficking Centre ("UKHTC") collects data about victims. This information aims to help build a clearer picture about the scope of human trafficking in the UK, which in turn helps to shape policy and can aid police investigations into trafficking.

[10] [2010] EWCA Crim 2327.

[11] [2012] EWCA Crim 189.

[12] [2013] EWCA Crim 991.

[13] Europa press release MEMO/10/108, *Proposal for a Directive on preventing and combating trafficking in human beings and protecting victims, repealing Framework Decision 2002/629/JHA*, 29 March 2010. For the full text of the proposal, see European Commission, COM(2010)95 final, 2010/0065 (COD), *Proposal for a Directive of the European Parliament and of the Council on preventing and combating trafficking in human beings, and protecting victims, repealing Framework Decision 2002/629/JHA*, 29 March 2010.

[14] Home Office press release, *Home Office defends position on human trafficking*, August 31, 2010.

The final text of the Directive was adopted by the Council of Ministers on **11.15**
March 21, 2011 and was subsequently issued as *Directive 2011/36/EU of the*
European Parliament and of the Council of 5 April 2011 on preventing and
combating trafficking in human beings and protecting its victims, and replacing
Council Framework Decision 2002/629/JHA. On March 22, 2011, the day
after the Directive's adoption, the Government announced that, subject to
parliamentary scrutiny, the UK would after all be opting in to the measure.
Home Office minister Damian Green MP said:

> "In June [2010], the Government took the decision not to opt in at the outset to
> the proposal for a directive to combat human trafficking but undertook to review
> the position when there was a finalised text. We have now carefully considered
> the finalised text. The main risk associated with the text has now been overcome:
> by waiting to apply to opt in, we have a text that has been finalised and we have
> avoided being bound by measures that are against the UK's interests.
>
> The new text still does not contain any measures that would significantly
> change the way the UK fights trafficking. However, the UK has always been a
> world leader in fighting trafficking and has a strong international reputation in
> this field. Applying to opt in to the directive would continue to send a powerful
> message to traffickers that the UK is not a soft touch, and that we are supportive
> of international efforts to tackle this crime."[15]

The UK duly opted in to the Directive in July 2011. Member States were
required to implement it by April 6, 2013.[16]

Implementation of the Trafficking Directive: the 2003 Act offences

In July 2011, the Government published *Human Trafficking: The Govern-* **11.16**
ment's Strategy, one of the main objectives of which included working to
implement the Trafficking Directive by the deadline of April 6, 2013. As part
of this work, the Government undertook to review by the end of 2011
whether current legislation supported the effective prosecution of traffickers.
In May 2012, the *Report on the Internal Review of Human Trafficking*
Legislation identified three areas for action. The first and second involved
expanding the territorial extent of the trafficking offences in the Sexual
Offences Act 2003 and the Asylum and Immigration (Treatment of Claimants, etc) Act 2004. In relation to the 2003 Act this was achieved by the
Protection of Freedoms Act 2012, which replaced the three offences created
by ss.57–59 of the 2003 Act with a single offence of trafficking for the
purposes of sexual exploitation, contained in a new s.59A of the 2003 Act.[17]
Section 59A covered the same sorts of conduct as had been penalised by
ss.57–59 but extended the scope of the law so that a UK national could be
prosecuted regardless of where the arrangement or facilitation of the
trafficking took place or where in the world the trafficking occurred or was

---

[15] HC Deb March 22, 2011 c52WS.
[16] art.22.1.
[17] Created by s.109(1), (2), brought into force on April 6, 2013, by SI 2013/470.

intended to occur. When the new clauses were introduced at Lords Committee Stage, Home Office minister Lord Henley said:

> "Under Sections 57 to 59 of the Sexual Offences Act 2003, it is already an offence to traffic a person into, within or out of the United Kingdom for the purposes of sexual exploitation. In the interests of clarity, Amendment 152B proceeds by consolidating these existing trafficking offences into new Section 59A and also adding the necessary additional provisions to ensure extra-territorial application of the offences where a UK national commits a trafficking offence anywhere in the world . . . These provisions will apply to England and Wales only. We have been advised by the Scottish Government that, following the enactment of provisions in the Criminal Justice and Licensing (Scotland) Act 2010, the criminal law in Scotland already satisfies the criminal law requirements of the directive. The Northern Ireland Administration intend to bring forward separate legislation in the Northern Ireland Assembly to achieve a similar effect.
>
> The Government are committed to implementing the rest of the EU directive on human trafficking. These amendments deal with those points of the directive that require primary legislation. The rest we will implement through secondary legislation or by other appropriate means."[18]

The clause inserting s.59A into the 2003 Act was passed without a division and was enacted as s.109 of the Protection of Freedoms Act 2012, which came into force on April 6, 2013.

11.17 Section 59A also incorporated a change that had been made to s.57 by the UK Borders Act 2007,[19] whereby the offence was expanded to cover arranging or facilitating entry into, as well as arrival in, the UK for the purposes of sexual exploitation. This ensured that the s.57 offence covered acts of facilitation done after the victim had arrived at a UK port or airport with a designated immigration area, but before they had been granted entry by an immigration officer, i.e. in the secure areas of our major ports and airports.[20] At the Commons Committee stage of the UK Borders Bill, the Parliamentary Under-Secretary of State for the Home Department, Joan Ryan MP, said in relation to a similar amendment made to the Immigration Act offence of helping an asylum seeker to enter the UK[21]:

> "A person is said to have arrived in the United Kingdom upon disembarkation. That is distinct from his or her entry into the United Kingdom, which takes place at border control. At some ports there can be a considerable distance between. I am thinking that, after stepping off the plane at Heathrow, it can be some time and distance before one gets to the point where one meets the immigration officer and has one's passport checked. That physical and legal gap is exploited by facilitators, who use the opportunity to carry out acts such as the destruction or disposal of false passports. Even though such acts are often captured on CCTV or witnessed by surveillance officers, they cannot currently be taken into account

---

[18] HL Deb January 12, 2012 ccGC61-2.

[19] s.31(3).

[20] For the distinction between arrival and entry, see *Nailie* [1993] A.C. 674, decided under s.25 of the Immigration Act 1971 (facilitating illegal entry); *Javaherifard* [2005] EWCA Crim 3231 (which makes clear that "entry" in the context of immigration law is an ordinary word and will take place on arrival in the UK elsewhere than at a port or airport with a designated immigration area).

[21] *Hansard*, Public Bill Committee, March 15, 2007, cols 394–5.

as evidence of facilitation because they have occurred after a person has disembarked or arrived."

The third area for action identified in the *Report on the Internal Review of* **11.18** *Human Trafficking Legislation* involved extending the regime for unduly lenient sentences so that the Attorney General could refer sentences for trafficking offences to the Court of Appeal where the trafficking was for non-sexual exploitation, as well as where it was for sexual exploitation. This was achieved by the Criminal Justice Act 1988 (Reviews of Sentencing) (Amendment) Order 2012.[22]

Implementation of the Trafficking Directive: secondary legislation

As well as expanding the scope of the criminal law, the Government also **11.19** considered what secondary legislation was needed in order to achieve compliance with the Trafficking Directive.[23] It went on to make the Trafficking People for Exploitation Regulations 2013,[24] which came into force on the same day as the Trafficking Directive and s.59A of the 2003 Act, i.e. April 6, 2013, and contain specific measures in relation to child complainants. The aim of the Regulations is to prevent "secondary victim-isation" of the complainant through unnecessary repetition of interviews, unnecessary questioning about private life, and visual contact with the accused. They also provide that every victim of a human trafficking offence should be eligible for special measures under the Youth Justice and Criminal Evidence Act 1999 when giving evidence in criminal proceedings. The Regulations have since been amended so as to define a "human trafficking offence" to include an offence under s.2 of the Modern Slavery Act 2015, i.e. an offence of trafficking for exploitation.[25]

Regulations 3 and 4 apply where there is a police investigation into a **11.20** human trafficking offence, and set out measures aimed at the protection of complainants. The measures in reg.3 apply in relation to all complainants, and reg.4 contains specific measures in relation to child complainants. The two regulations provide as follows:

> "*Protection of complainants in criminal investigations*
>
> **3.** Without prejudice to the rights of the accused, and in accordance with an individualised assessment of the personal circumstances of the complainant, the relevant chief officer of police shall ensure that the complainant receives specific treatment aimed at preventing secondary victimisation by avoiding, as far as possible, during an investigation of a human trafficking offence—
>   (a) unnecessary repetition of interviews;

[22] SI 2012/1833.
[23] cf. Letter from Lord Henley to Lord McColl of Dulwich re *Protection of Freedoms Bill: Human Trafficking*, February 1, 2012, DEP2012-0194.
[24] SI 2013/554.
[25] Modern Slavery Act 2015 (Consequential Amendments) Regulations 2015 (SI 2015/1472).

(b) visual contact between the complainant and the accused, using appropriate means including communication technologies;

(c) unnecessary questioning concerning the complainant's private life.

Protection of child complainants in criminal investigations

4.—(1) This regulation applies where the complainant is under the age of 18 and without prejudice to regulation 3.

(2) Without prejudice to the rights of the accused, during an investigation of a human trafficking offence, the relevant chief officer of police shall ensure that—

(a) interviews with the complainant take place without unjustified delay after the facts have been reported;

(b) interviews with the complainant take place, where necessary, in premises designed or adapted for the purpose;

(c) interviews with the complainant are carried out, where necessary, by or through professionals trained for the purpose;

(d) if possible and where appropriate, the same persons conduct all the interviews with the complainant;

(e) the number of interviews with the complainant is as limited as possible and interviews are carried out only where strictly necessary for the purposes of the investigation;

(f) the complainant may be accompanied by an adult of the complainant's choice, unless a reasoned decision has been made to the contrary in respect of that adult."

Regulation 6 requires the Secretary of State to review the operation and effect of the Regulations and publish a report within five years after they come into force, and every five years after that. Following a review, it will fall to the Secretary of State to consider whether the Regulations should remain as they are, or be revoked or amended.

Modern Slavery Act 2015

11.21   Matters did not rest there. On August 25, 2013, shortly after the measures described above came into effect, the Home Secretary announced the Government's intention to introduce a Modern Slavery Bill to overhaul the laws on human trafficking in an attempt to eradicate an "evil in our midst".[26] A Parliamentary Joint Select Committee chaired by Frank Field MP was set up to scrutinise the draft Bill. The Committee held a series of evidence-gathering sessions in which it took evidence from many sources, including judges, barristers, solicitors, academics, police and non-governmental organisations. One of the points of focus in the Committee's deliberations was the question whether, and to what extent, victims should be protected from prosecution for crimes they were forced to commit while enslaved or under the control of their traffickers. The Committee published its report and a revised draft Bill in April 2014.[27] The Government's revised draft Bill was

[26] *http://www.theguardian.com/law/2013/aug/25/modern-slavery-bill-human-trafficking* [Accessed January 30, 2016].

[27] Report of the Joint Committee on the Draft Modern Slavery Bill, Session 2013–14, HL Paper 166/Hc 1019: Draft Modern Slavery Bill, para.1.

introduced in June 2014. As the Modern Slavery Act, it received the Royal Assent in March 2015 and came into force on July 31, 2015. The Act contains wide ranging provisions, but in terms of the criminal law it consolidates and simplifies the pre-existing offences of slavery, servitude and forced compulsory labour in s.71 of the Coroners and Justice Act 2009 and the trafficking offence in s.59A of the 2003 Act,[28] which are replaced by two new offence provisions, one dealing with slavery, servitude and forced compulsory labour (s.1) and the other with human trafficking (s.2). Both provisions are considered below. At this early stage in its history, the new Act has not yet begun to make its full effect known. As a consequence, although in this chapter we provide an analysis of the Act, we have also included a review of the background to it, as this is likely to be relevant to any application of the new provisions.

PROSECUTION OF THE VICTIMS OF TRAFFICKING

Given the history set out above, including the decision in *R v O*,[29] it may not   **11.22** be surprising that the protection of victims forms a large part of the new legislation, albeit not all provisions are as yet in force. The background to this victim-focused approach is set out below, along with the new statutory defence provided for by s.45 of the Modern Slavery Act 2015.

Article 26 of the Trafficking Convention

In what circumstances is it appropriate to prosecute the victims of trafficking   **11.23** for unlawful activities in which they engage after they have been trafficked and that are connected to their trafficked status? This important practical question is addressed in art.26 of the Trafficking Convention, which requires signatories to:

> "provide for the possibility of not imposing penalties on victims for their involvement in unlawful activities to the extent that they have been compelled to do so".

In *R. v LM*,[30] the Court of Appeal (Hughes LJ presiding) said that in   **11.24** England and Wales the implementation of art.26 is achieved through three mechanisms: the common law defences of duress and necessity; the guidance given to CPS prosecutors as to whether charges should be brought against those who are or may be victims of trafficking, and, lastly, if the duty laid on prosecutors to exercise judgment is not properly discharged, the power of the court to stay the prosecution for abuse of process. To these mechanisms must now be added a fourth, the new defence in s.45 of the 2015 Act, though as we

---

[28] s.57(1) and Sch.5(1), para.5(2). The commencement of these provisions was effected by SI 2015/1476. Transitional provisions and savings are specified in SI 2015/1476, art.3.

[29] [2008] EWCA Crim 2835, referred to in para.11.11, above.

[30] [2010] EWCA Crim 2327.

shall see, the new defence is if anything narrower in its application than the defences of duress and necessity.

Prosecutorial discretion

11.25   The Court in *R. v LM* noted that the guidance given to prosecutors requires them to undertake a three-stage exercise of judgment. First, they must decide whether there is reason to believe that the person has been trafficked. The Court said that this first step is not limited to reacting to any assertion of trafficking, since by art.10 of the Convention, States must take active steps to consider the question whenever it is a realistic possibility. This is because one of the consequences of trafficking, especially far from home, may be to inhibit the victim from complaining. Secondly, if there is reason to believe the person has been trafficked, the prosecutor must consider whether there is clear evidence of a credible common law (or, now, statutory) defence. If there is, the case will not proceed on evidential grounds. Thirdly, even if there is no such defence, if the offence may have been committed as a result of compulsion arising from the trafficking, then the prosecutor must consider whether the public interest lies in proceeding to prosecute or not. The Court went on to give the following guidance as to the application of art.26[31]:

> "Article 26 . . . does not say that no trafficked victim should be prosecuted, whatever offence has been committed. It does not say that no trafficked victim should be prosecuted when the offence is in some way connected with or arises out of trafficking. It does not provide a defence which may be advanced before a jury. What it says is no more, but no less, than that careful consideration must be given to whether public policy calls for a prosecution and punishment when the defendant is a trafficked victim and the crime has been committed when he or she was in some manner compelled (in the broad sense) to commit it. Article 26 does not require a blanket immunity from prosecution for trafficked victims.
>
> It follows that the application of Article 26 is fact-sensitive in every case. We attempt no exhaustive analysis of the factual scenarios which may arise in future. Some general propositions can perhaps be ventured.
>
> i) If there is evidence on which a common law defence of duress or necessity is likely to succeed, the case will no doubt not be proceeded with on ordinary evidential grounds independent of the convention, but additionally there are likely to be public policy grounds under the convention leading to the same conclusion.
>
> ii) But cases in which it is not in the public interest to prosecute are not limited to these . . .
>
> iii) It may be reasonable to prosecute if the defendant's assertion that she was trafficked meets the reasonable grounds [for being treated as a victim of trafficking] test, but has been properly considered and rejected by the Crown for good evidential reason. The fact that a person passes the threshold test as a person of whom there are reasonable grounds to believe she has been trafficked is not conclusive that she has. Conversely, it may well be that in other cases that

---

[31] At [13]–[14].

[*sic*] the real possibility of trafficking and a nexus of compulsion (in the broad sense) means that public policy points against prosecution.

iv) There is normally no reason not to prosecute, even if the defendant has previously been a trafficked victim, if the offence appears to have been committed out with any reasonable nexus of compulsion (in the broad sense) occasioned by the trafficking, and hence is outside Article 26.

v) A more difficult judgment is involved if the victim has been a trafficked victim and retains some nexus with the trafficking, but has committed an offence which arguably calls, in the public interest, for prosecution in court. Some of these may be cases of a cycle of abuse. It is well known that one tool of those in charge of trafficking operations is to turn those who were trafficked and exploited in the past into assistants in the exploitation of others. Such a cycle of abuse is not uncommon in this field, as in other fields, for example that of abuse of children. In such a case, the question which must be actively confronted by the prosecutor is whether or not the offence committed is serious enough, despite any nexus with trafficking, to call for prosecution. That will depend on all the circumstances of the case, and normally no doubt particularly on the gravity of the offence alleged, the degree of continuing compulsion, and the alternatives reasonably available to the defendant."

The Court of Appeal again considered the application of art.26 in *R. v N*   **11.26**
and Le.[32] The decision concerned two unconnected cases in which the defendants (aged 16 and 17 respectively) had been sentenced to detention after pleading guilty to being concerned in the production of cannabis. Before the Court, they argued that they had been victims of child trafficking for labour exploitation, and the prosecution ought therefore to have been discontinued or stayed as an abuse of process pursuant to the UK's obligation under art.26. The Court, in a judgment given by Lord Judge CJ, said that art.26 does not provide trafficked victims with blanket immunity from prosecution or preclude the imposition of penalties upon them in a broad general way, but provides for the possibility of not imposing penalties where the victims were compelled to participate in criminal activities and the defence of duress was unavailable to them. It referred with approval to *R. v LM* and went on[33]:

"Summarising the essential principles, the implementation of the United Kingdom's Convention obligation is normally achieved by the proper exercise of the long established prosecutorial discretion which enables the Crown Prosecution Service, however strong the evidence may be, to decide that it would be inappropriate to proceed or to continue with the prosecution of a defendant who is unable to advance duress as a defence but who falls within the protective ambit of Article 26. This requires a judgment to be made by the CPS in the individual case in the light of all the available evidence. That responsibility is vested not in the court but in the prosecuting authority. The court may intervene in an individual case if its process is abused by using the 'ultimate sanction' of a stay

---

[32] [2012] EWCA Crim 189. These cases are now the subject of an application to the European Court of Human Rights. See also *Dao* [2012] EWCA Crim 1717, citing both *R. v LM and others* and *R. v N and Le* in approving terms and expressing a strong disinclination to accept the proposition that a threat of false imprisonment suffices for the defence of duress, without an accompanying threat of death or serious injury.
[33] At 21.

of the proceedings. The burden of showing that the process is being or has been abused on the basis of the improper exercise of the prosecutorial discretion rests on the defendant. The limitations on this jurisdiction are clearly underlined in *R v LM*. The fact that it arises for consideration in the context of the proper implementation of the United Kingdom's Convention obligation does not involve the creation of new principles. Rather, well established principles apply in the specific context of the Article 26 obligation, no more, and no less. Apart from the specific jurisdiction to stay proceedings where the process is abused, the court may also, if it thinks appropriate in the exercise of its sentencing responsibilities implement the Article 26 obligation in the language of the article itself, by dealing with the defendant in a way which does not constitute punishment, by ordering an absolute or a conditional discharge."

In N's case, the Court said that there had been no evidence before the Crown Court, or for that matter the CPS or indeed the defence, which suggested that N had been trafficked into the UK or fell within the protective ambit of art.26. Rather, the effect of the evidence was that he was a volunteer, "smuggled" into this country to make a better life for himself, and that he had a home with a family member to which he could have gone and where he would have been welcome.[34] He was very young, and in a vulnerable position as an illegal immigrant, and in his short time working in the cannabis factory he had been exploited by others. All that provided real mitigation, but in the light of the facts as they appeared to be, and on the basis of the CPS guidance then current, there was nothing before the Court to justify the conclusion that N's prosecution constituted an abuse of process on the basis of a breach of art.26. The Court reached a similar conclusion in Le's case.

11.27   Laura Hoyano criticised *R. v N and Le* for its "anaemic" approach to art.26, which (she argued) served to undermine efforts by anti-trafficking agencies and charities to encourage reporting, since the threat of prosecution, regardless of the likely sentence, gives the trafficker an additional weapon with which to entrap his victim into silent compliance.[35] For this reason she welcomed the provision in art.8 of the Trafficking Directive (discussed above) that Member States "are *entitled not to prosecute* or impose penalties on victims of trafficking for their involvement in criminal activities which they have been compelled to commit as a direct result" of the prohibited acts (emphasis added). This language marked a step forward from the somewhat ambiguous provision in art.26 of the Trafficking Convention, which requires signatories to "provide for the *possibility of not imposing penalties* on victims for their involvement in unlawful activities to the extent that they have been compelled to do so". The specific reference in the Directive to the non-prosecution of victims, as well as their non-punishment, seems to have been

---

[34] Laura Hoyano has pointed out that the Court's emphasis on the fact that N was "smuggled" rather than " 'trafficked" into the UK was misplaced, as the Trafficking Convention is not restricted to cases of cross-border migration but applies also to exploitation of willingly smuggled immigrants: see [2012] Crim L.R. 964.

[35] See [2012] Crim L.R. 960ff; and see Michelle Brewer, *The Prosecution of Child Victims of Trafficking*, Archbold Review, Issue 4, May 17, 2013.

a response to criticism of the narrowness of art.26, and Hoyano expressed the hope "that the CPS and the British courts will take account of this . . . evinced intention" when construing and applying art.8.

It was indeed clear, following *R. v N and Le*, that the content and **11.28** application of the CPS's guidance to prosecutors would be key to the UK's ability to comply with this aspect of the Directive. The point is forcefully made in a passage of the judgment in which, noting that it had examined "a vast bundle of post-conviction evidence, much of which is, on analysis repetitive [and] numerous publications", the Court concluded that:

> "in future the only publication likely to be relevant to an inquiry into an alleged abuse of process in the context of Convention obligations is the CPS Guidance in force at the time when the relevant decisions were made. It should normally be assumed that the contemporaneous CPS Guidance will have taken account of all the relevant material to be found in all the guidance offered by different authorities with responsibilities in this area, and indeed that it will be updated in the light of any new information. Unless it is to be argued that the CPS Guidance itself is inadequate and open to question because it has failed to keep itself regularly updated in the light of developing knowledge, for the purposes of the court considering an abuse of process for which the prosecutorial authority is responsible, it is the CPS Guidance which should be the starting point, and in the overwhelming majority of cases, the finishing point for any argument of alleged non-compliance with Article 26."[36]

The Court added that it had not been assisted in determining the case by the substantial body of expert evidence adduced before it, and expressed great reservations about the value of expert evidence which is said to bear upon the abuse of process issue. It concluded:

> "in making its decisions in future, save to the extent that its own Guidance may make provision for it, we do not anticipate that the CPS would normally be required to seek evidence of the expert nature deployed in these appeals."[37]

Stays of prosecution on grounds of abuse of process

In the conjoined appeals of *L v R*,[38] the Court of Appeal provided guidance **11.29** as to how courts should approach the interests of those who are or may be victims of human trafficking, in particular children, who become enmeshed in criminal activities in consequence, after criminal proceedings against them have begun. In a judgment again delivered by Lord Judge CJ, the Court had the benefit of written submissions not only from the appellants and the prosecution, but also from the Children's Commissioner for England and the Equality and Human Rights Commission. It was also provided with "a multiplicity of reports and papers, protocols and conventions in which, using

---

[36] [2012] EWCA Crim 189, at [86(b)].
[37] ibid.
[38] [2013] EWCA Crim 991.

different language to the same effect, the evils of trafficking . . . are simultaneously highlighted and condemned".[39] The Court annexed a list of these documents to its judgment, but commented that in reality "despite lengthy repetition, the principles to be applied are not complicated, and we shall endeavour to encapsulate them in this judgment. Henceforth it will rarely be necessary for them, or even a substantial proportion of them, to be copied and repeated in proceedings where these and similar issues arise."[40]

11.30   The Court went on to provide the following guidance as to how, where a defendant claims to be the victim of trafficking, the court should approach issues relating to the defendant's age, whether they were indeed trafficked, and whether the alleged offending was an aspect of their exploitation[41]:

> " . . . when there is evidence that victims of trafficking have been involved in criminal activities, the investigation and the decision whether there should be a prosecution, and, if so, any subsequent proceedings require to be approached with the greatest sensitivity. The reasoning is not always spelled out, and perhaps we should do so now. The criminality, or putting it another way, the culpability, of any victim of trafficking may be significantly diminished, and in some cases effectively extinguished, not merely because of age (always a relevant factor in the case of a child defendant) but because no realistic alternative was available to the exploited victim but to comply with the dominant force of another individual, or group of individuals.
>
> In the context of a prosecution of a defendant aged under 18 years of age, the best interests of the victim are not and cannot be the only relevant consideration, but they represent a primary consideration. These defendants are not safeguarded from prosecution or punishment for offences which were unconnected with the fact that they were being or have been trafficked, although we do not overlook that the fact that they have been trafficked may sometimes provide substantial mitigation. What, however, is required in the context of the prosecutorial decision to proceed is a level of protection from prosecution or punishment for trafficked victims who have been compelled to commit criminal offences. These arrangements should follow the 'basic principles' of our legal system. In this jurisdiction that protection is provided by the exercise by the 'abuse of process' jurisdiction.
>
> It was submitted, particularly, on behalf of L and T, that the courts' obligation to safeguard a trafficked victim's rights was independent of any review of the prosecutor's decision to bring or continue a prosecution . . . It was argued that the court should afford the protection required by the Directive and Convention by exercising what was described as a 'primary role'. The submission was based on the Supreme Court's consideration of the need to ensure that confiscation orders are proportionate in order to safeguard a defendant's rights under A1P1 of the ECHR in *R v Waya* [2012] UKSC 51, [2013] 1 AC 294:
>
>> 'But the safeguard of the defendant's Convention right under A1P1 not to be the object of a disproportionate order does not, and must not, depend on prosecutorial discretion, nor on the very limited jurisdiction of the High Court to review the exercise of such discretion by way of judicial review' [19].
>
> *Waya* is not analogous. In that case the Supreme Court was seeking to ensure that the order of the court adequately protected the rights of a defendant against

---

[39] At [10].
[40] ibid.
[41] At [13]–[18].

whom an order of confiscation was sought. The court is the primary decision-maker as to whether a confiscation order should be made. In contrast, the prosecution is and remains responsible for deciding whether to prosecute or not. In any case, where it is necessary to do so, whether issues of trafficking or other questions arise, the court reviews the decision to prosecute through the exercise of the jurisdiction to stay. The court protects the rights of a victim of trafficking by overseeing the decision of the prosecutor and refusing to countenance any prosecution which fails to acknowledge and address the victim's subservient situation, and the international obligations to which the United Kingdom is a party. The role of the court replicates its role in relation to *agents provocateurs*. It stands between the prosecution and the victim of trafficking where the crimes are committed as an aspect of the victim's exploitation (see *R v Loosely A-G's Ref (No.3 of 2000)* [2001] UKHL, [2002] 1 Cr. App. R.29).

It may be that the submissions advanced in erroneous reliance on *Waya* stem from a fear that the court will do no more than review the prosecutor's decision on traditional *Wednesbury* grounds and decline to interfere, even though its own conclusion would be that the offences were a manifestation of the exploitation of a victim of trafficking. For the reasons we have already given, no such danger exists. In the context of an abuse of process argument on behalf of an alleged victim of trafficking, the court will reach its own decision on the basis of the material advanced in support of and against the continuation of the prosecution. Where a court considers issues relevant to age, trafficking and exploitation, the prosecution will be stayed if the court disagrees with the decision to prosecute. The fears that the exercise of the jurisdiction to stay will be inadequate are groundless.

If issues relating to the age of the victim arise, and questions whether the defendant is or was a victim of trafficking, or whether the alleged offences were an aspect of the victim's exploitation, have reached the Crown Court, or a magistrates court, they must be resolved by the exercise of the jurisdiction to stay a prosecution. In accordance with the process endorsed in *M(L)* (15-19) and *N* (86) that remains the correct procedure for determining such issues even after the EU Directive 2011/36/EU became directly effective. This provides sufficient vindication for the rights enshrined in the EU Directive as well as the Anti-Trafficking Convention, and indeed in Articles 4, 6 and 8 of the European Convention of Human Rights . . . ".

As regards the age of the defendant, the Court suggested that any issue should be addressed head on at the first appearance before the court and the documentation accompanying the defendant to court should record their date of birth, either as asserted by them or as best known to the prosecution, or both.[42] Alternatively, the issue should be raised at the PCMH (now the PTPH). As for the resolution of an issue as to the defendant's age, the Court said that this[43]:

> " . . . requires much more than superficial observation of the defendant in court or in the dock to enable the judge to make an appropriate age assessment. The facial features of the defendant may provide a clue or two, but experience has shown that this is very soft evidence indeed and liable to mislead. What we do know is that young people mature at different ages, and that their early life experiences can sometimes leave them with a misleading appearance. We also

11.31

---

[42] At [31].
[43] At [22]–[25].

appreciate that young people from an ethnic group with which the court is unfamiliar may seem older, or indeed younger, than those from ethnic groups with which the court has greater experience. Therefore when an age issue arises, the court must be provided with all the relevant evidence which bears on it. Although the court may adjourn proceedings for further investigations to be conducted, these have to be undertaken by one or other or both sides, or by the relevant social services. The court is not vested with any jurisdiction, and is not provided with the resources to conduct its own investigations into the age of a potential defendant until after the investigation has completed its course, and the individual in question is brought before the court.

In this context we repeat the observations of this court in *R v Steed* [1990] 12 Cr. App. R(S) 230, where the question of the appellant's age was significant to the different methods of the disposal of the case on sentence, and therefore went to the legality of the sentence,

'It may often be right, indeed might usually be right, for the matter to be adjourned, if there is any real doubt about it, so that it may be more satisfactorily determined'.

More recently, this approach was underlined in *R v O* [2008] EWCA Crim 2835 where the court emphasised that:

'(W)here there is doubt about the age of a defendant who is a possible victim of trafficking, proper enquiries must be made, indeed statute so required.'

The Children's Commissioner invites us to consider the impact of Article 10(3) of the Anti-Trafficking Convention which provides:

'When the age of the victim is uncertain and there are reasons to believe that the victim is a child, he or she shall presume to be a child and shall be accorded special protection measures pending verification of his/her age'.

The explanatory report to the Anti-Trafficking Convention also refers to a requirement that the parties should 'presume that a victim is a child if there are reasons for believing that to be so and if there is uncertainty about their age.' In our judgment Article 10(3) addresses evidential issues. Where there are reasons to believe that the defendant is a child, then he should be treated as a child. In other words it is not possible for the court to brush aside evidence which suggest that the defendant may be a child. The issue must be addressed head on. If at the end of an examination of the available evidence, the question remains in doubt, the presumption applies and the defendant must be treated as a child. There is therefore no relevant difference between the approach required by Article 10(3) of the Anti-Trafficking Convention and the Guidance provided by the Director of Public Prosecutions."

11.32 As to the issue of whether the defendant is a victim of trafficking, the Court said[44]:

"The National Referral Mechanism (NRM) was set up on 1 April 2009 to give effect in the United Kingdom to Article 10 of the Council of Europe Anti-Trafficking Convention. Enough is now known about people who are trafficked into and within the United Kingdom for all those involved in the criminal justice process to recognise the need to consider at an early stage whether the defendant (child or adult) is in fact a victim of trafficking. The NRM establishes a three stage process for this purpose:

i) An initial referral of a potential victim of trafficking by a first responder[45] to a competent authority. At present there are two competent authorities.

---

[44] At [26]–[28].
[45] First responders for this purpose include UKBA, the UK Human Trafficking Centre, local authorities, UK police forces, NSPCC/CTAC, Barnados and the Salvation Army.

They are UKBA and the United Kingdom Human Trafficking Centre (UKHTC), a multidisciplinary organisation led by SOCA (The Serious and Organised Crime Agency). In the present appeals we are concerned only with UKBA because the potentially trafficked individuals were subject to immigration control. We note that where the potential victim of trafficking is a child his consent is not necessary before the referral is made, but where he is an adult consent is required.

ii) An UKBA official decides whether the person referred might have been a victim of trafficking. This is known as a 'reasonable grounds' decision, for which UKBA have a target of five days. We are told that the average time is nine days. If and when a favourable reasonable grounds decision has been made the first responder is notified, and, in effect that decision allows for a period of forty five days[46] during which the final stage of the NRM process continues, leading to

iii) consideration by UKBA whether the evidence is sufficient to confirm conclusively that the individual has been trafficked.

. . . .

Neither the appellants nor the interveners accept that the conclusive decision of UKBA (or whichever department becomes a competent authority for these purposes) is determinative of the question whether or not an individual has been trafficked. They, of course, are concerned with the impact of a decision adverse to the individual. We are asked to note that the number of concluded decisions in favour of victims of trafficking is relatively low, and it seems unlikely that a prosecutor will challenge or seem to disregard a concluded decision that an individual has been trafficked, but that possibility may arise. Whether the concluded decision of the competent authority is favourable or adverse to the individual it will have been made by an authority vested with the responsibility for investigating these issues, and although the court is not bound by the decision, unless there is evidence to contradict it, or significant evidence that was not considered, it is likely that the criminal courts will abide by it."

The Court concluded that where it is found that a defendant is a victim of **11.33** trafficking, it is necessary to assess his culpability for the offence charged having regard to the exploitation that he has suffered[47]:

"As we have already explained the distinct question for decision once it is found that the defendant is a victim of trafficking is the extent to which the offences with which he is charged, or of which he has been found guilty are integral to or consequent on the exploitation of which he was the victim. We cannot be prescriptive. In some cases the facts will indeed show that he was under levels of compulsion which mean that in reality culpability was extinguished. If so when such cases are prosecuted, an abuse of process submission is likely to succeed. That is the test we have applied in these appeals. In other cases, more likely in the case of a defendant who is no longer a child, culpability may be diminished but nevertheless be significant. For these individuals prosecution may well be appropriate, with due allowance to be made in the sentencing decision for their diminished culpability. In yet other cases, the fact that the defendant was a victim of trafficking will provide no more than a colourable excuse for criminality which

---

[46] This is a "reflection and recovery" period during which the individual can access services such as those provided by children's services, the Poppy Project, the Salvation Army and Migrant Help.

[47] At [33].

is unconnected to and does not arise from their victimisation. In such cases an abuse of process submission would fail."

11.34   Applying these principles to the four appeals before it, the Court allowed all of them on the basis that there was evidence that the appellants had been victims of trafficking whose criminal activities were part and parcel of the circumstances of their trafficking. In each case, the Court said that if that evidence had been available at an earlier stage, either the appellant would not have been prosecuted or the prosecution would have been stopped by the court, which "protects the rights of a victim of trafficking by overseeing the decision of the prosecutor and refusing to countenance any prosecution which fails to acknowledge and address the victim's subservient situation, and the international obligations to which the United Kingdom is a party".

11.35   The difficulty with the judgment in the case of *L v R.* is that, although the Court raised the prospect of a challenge being made to a decision to prosecute, it failed to provide clarity as to how this should be done. The Court plainly suggests both some form of abuse of process argument and a variation of judicial review, but fails to give guidance either on what procedure should be adopted, or how to deploy it. This has been criticised as a "serious omission",[48] and was certainly a missed opportunity.

CPS guidance on prosecuting victims of trafficking

11.36   The CPS's Legal Guidance on Human Trafficking and Smuggling[49] has been a key document in a number of subsequent cases in which art.26 and/or art.8 have been considered. The guidance is presently under revision to accommodate the Modern Slavery Act 2015 but at the time of writing, it provides as follows:

> *"Suspects in a criminal case who might be victims of trafficking or slavery*
>
> This part of the guidance applies to victims of trafficking who are also suspects in a criminal offence, but when dealing with cases involving a child, prosecutors must consider the additional requirements set out below in the section 'Suspects who may be children'. Victims of slavery, including forced labour and servitude, are also covered by this part of the guidance (see below), if they are suspected of committing a criminal offence, but the trafficking element is not always relevant in every such case.
>
> *Indicators of trafficking*
>
> Prosecutors should be alert to the particular circumstances or situations where someone suspected of committing a criminal offence might also be a trafficked victim, e.g. an unaccompanied foreign national child who is in the UK but committing offences such as pickpocketing or cultivation of cannabis or in the case of adults, crimes involving immigration document offences when fleeing

---

[48] Peter Carter QC, Peer Review.
[49] *http://www.cps.gov.uk/legal/h_to_k/human_trafficking_and_smuggling/* [Accessed May 4, 2016]. We understand that the guidance is being further reviewed and may change again.

their situation or controlling prostitution offences. However, these are examples of offences most frequently committed and is not an exhaustive list. [*A hyperlink is here provided within the CPS Guidance, but the linked document has now been archived and is no longer accessible*].

Awareness of the prosecutor's obligations

When considering whether to proceed with prosecuting a suspect who might be a victim of trafficking, prosecutors should be aware of the clear obligations imposed to consider *whether to not prosecute* where the suspect has been compelled to commit a criminal offence as a direct consequence of being trafficked.

The prosecutor's obligations

These obligations arise under:

- Article 4 of ECHR which prohibits slavery and forced labour.
- Article 26 of the Council of Europe Anti-Trafficking Convention which requires the United Kingdom to: ' . . . provide for the possibility of not imposing penalties on victims [of trafficking] for their involvement in unlawful activities, to the extent that they have been compelled to do so'.
- Article 8 of EU Anti-Trafficking Directive 2011/36/EU whereby 'national authorities are *entitled* not to prosecute or impose penalties on victims of trafficking human beings for their involvement in criminal activities which they have been *compelled to commit* as a direct consequence of being subjected to trafficking'.

A three-stage approach to the prosecution decision

In addition to applying the Full Code Test in the Code for Crown Prosecutors, prosecutors should adopt the following three stage assessment:

1. is there a reason to believe that the person has been trafficked? if so,
2. if there is clear evidence of a credible common law defence of duress, the case should be discontinued on evidential grounds; but
3. even where there is no clear evidence of duress, but the offence may have been committed as a result of compulsion arising from trafficking, prosecutors should consider whether the public interest lies in proceeding to prosecute or not. (See the judgment in *LM & Ors* [2010] EWCA Crim 2327)

The duty to make proper enquiries and to refer through the National Referral Mechanism (NRM)

In considering whether a suspect might be a victim of trafficking, as required in the first stage of the assessment, prosecutors should have regard to the following:

1. the duty of the prosecutor to make proper enquiries in criminal prosecutions involving individuals who may be victims of trafficking.
2. The enquiries should be made by:
   - advising the law enforcement agency which investigated the original offence that it must investigate the suspect's trafficking situation; and
   - advising that the suspect is referred through the NRM for victim identification. All law enforcement officers are able to refer potential victims of trafficking through the NRM. Referral forms can be found at *http://www.nationalcrimeagency.gov.uk/*. Further information concerning the NRM can be found on the Council of Europe Convention on Action against Trafficking in Human Beings.

- If an adult suspect does not consent to their referral, the charging decision should be made on whatever other information might be available, without the benefit of the Competent Authority's (CA) decision on their victim status (See below for explanation of the CA).
- These steps *must be done* regardless of what has been advised by the investigator or whether there is an indication of a guilty plea by the suspect's legal representative (see the section 'Early guilty plea' below). It should be noted that adults must consent to have their case referred through the NRM.

Referral through the NRM and the Competent Authority decision

- Following the NRM referral, the Competent Authority (CA) will first make a 'reasonable grounds' decision. In the United Kingdom, the CA is either the Home Office or the UK Human Trafficking Centre (UKHTC) depending on the victim's immigration status. A positive reasonable grounds decision is made when there are reasonable grounds to believe the individual is a potential victim of human trafficking. This decision should take 5 days. The trafficked victim will then be eligible for government funded support during a recovery and reflection period for 45 days.
- During the 45 day period, the CA gathers further information about the victim; and this additional information is used to make a conclusive decision on whether the referred person is a victim of human trafficking.
- A conclusive decision is whether on the balance of probability it is more likely than not that the individual is a victim of human trafficking.
- Prosecutors should take account of the CA decision (reasonable grounds or conclusive grounds) of the identification and status of the suspect as a victim of trafficking when considering the decision to prosecute.

Where there is credible evidence of trafficking (a positive CA decision)

- Prosecutors should consider whether or not there is clear evidence of a credible common law defence of duress, as required in the second stage of the assessment. If so the case should be discontinued on evidential grounds.
- If not consider whether or not the trafficking victim was compelled to commit the offence.

Has the victim been compelled to commit an offence?

The following guidance on considering whether a victim has been compelled, as required in the third stage of the assessment, applies to adults only and does not apply to child victims of trafficking (see the section below 'Children and 'the means of trafficking'').

'Compulsion' includes all the means of trafficking defined by the United Nations Protocol on Trafficking (The United Nations Convention against Transnational Organised Crime 2000 supplemented by the Protocol to Prevent, Suppress and Punish Trafficking in Persons.): threats, use of force, fraud and deception, inducement, abuse of power or of a position of vulnerability, or use of debt bondage. It does not require physical force or constraint.

In considering whether a trafficked victim has been compelled to commit a crime, prosecutors should consider whether any of these means has been employed so that the victim has effectively lost the ability to consent to his / her actions or to act with free will.

The means of trafficking used in an individual case may not be sufficient to give rise to a defence of duress, but how the person was trafficked will be relevant when considering whether the public interest is met in deciding to prosecute or proceed with a prosecution.

In assessing whether the victim was compelled to commit the offence, prosecutors should consider whether:

- the offence committed was a direct consequence of, or in the course of trafficking and whether the criminality is significantly diminished or effectively extinguished because no realistic alternative was available but to comply with the dominant force of another.

Where a victim has been compelled to commit the offence, but not to a degree where duress is made out, it will generally not be in the public interest to prosecute unless the offence is so serious or there are other aggravating factors.

If the defendant has previously been a trafficked victim but the offence has been committed without reasonable compulsion occasioned by the trafficking, there are no particular trafficking related public interest considerations, and the Full Code Test should be applied in the usual way.

Early guilty plea indicated

Where there is (1) an indication of an early guilty plea, (2) a full investigation has not been carried out and (3) the circumstances are such that there is suspicion of trafficking: at the first hearing prosecutors should request an adjournment for further investigation and ask that a plea is not formally entered.

Credible evidence of trafficking post-charge

In cases where a decision has already been taken to charge and prosecute a suspect, but further information or evidence comes to light, or the status of a suspect as a possible credible victim of trafficking is raised post-conviction, for example in mitigation or through a pre-sentence report, then prosecutors should seek relevant adjournments and ensure that the steps outlined in the section 'The duty to make proper enquiries and to refer through the NRM' above are carried out.

Suspects who may be children—Additional requirements

Assessing age and trafficking status

In cases where the defendant may be a child victim of trafficking, two linked questions must be addressed:

1. what is the defendant's age?
2. what evidence is there to suggest that the defendant has been trafficked?

If the defendant is a child victim of trafficking, the extent to which the crime alleged against him was consequent on and integral to his / her exploitation must be considered. In some cases the criminal offence is a manifestation of the exploitation. This might also arise in the case of an adult victim: see paragraph 20 of *L, HVN, THN and T* [2013] EWCA Crim 991.

Due enquiry as to age

Section 99(1) of the Children and Young Persons' Act 1933 directs the court to 'make due inquiry' about the defendant's age and 'take such evidence as may be forthcoming at the hearing of the case' for this purpose. Similar provisions require the court addressing the age question to consider 'any available evidence'

(Section150 of the Magistrates Court Act 1980; Section 1(6) of the Criminal Justice Act 1982; and Section 305(2) of the Criminal Justice Act 2003).

Where any issue as to the age of a defendant arises, it must be addressed at the first court appearance. The documentation accompanying the defendant to court should record his date of birth, whether as asserted by him, or as best known to the prosecution, or indeed both.

If age becomes or remains an issue at the Plea and Case Management Hearing in court, prosecutors should ensure that the appropriate age-assessment enquiries are carried out. This may require a request for an adjournment to the court.

Prosecutors should consider the separate *CPS guidance concerning age assessment*. See paragraphs 31 and 32 of *L, HVN, THN and T* [2013] EWCA Crim 991.

Presumption that a victim is a child

Article 10(3) of the Council of Europe Anti-Trafficking Convention provides: 'When the age of the victim is uncertain and there are reasons to believe that the victim is a child, he or she shall presume to be a child and shall be accorded special protection measures pending verification of his/her age'. If at the end of a 'due enquiry' into age the age of the defendant remains in doubt s/he must be treated as a child. See paragraph 25 of *L, HVN, THN and T* [2013] EWCA Crim 991.

Referring children through the NRM

In the case of suspects who are (or appear to be) children, the NRM referral should be made through the relevant social services department.

Children and 'the means of trafficking'

In determining whether a child is a victim of trafficking, his or her consent to being trafficked is irrelevant and the means by which they are trafficked is also irrelevant. Therefore it is not necessary for any of the following to be present: threats, use of force, fraud and deception, inducement, abuse of power or of a position of vulnerability, or use of debt bondage.

When considering whether to prosecute a child victim of trafficking, prosecutors will only need to consider whether or not the offence is committed as a direct consequence of, or in the course of trafficking.

Guidance has been issued to police and Immigration authorities on identification of victims and the indicators that might suggest that someone is a trafficked victim. However, all decisions in the case remain the responsibility of the prosecutor.

Victims of slavery including forced labour and servitude

Prosecutors should also be alert to situations where a person suspected of having committed a criminal offence is also a victim of slavery, including forced labour and servitude. The victim may have been trafficked but this may not always be the case with victims of slavery. Where the victim has been trafficked the 3 stage approach set out above should be followed. However, if there is no evidence that the victim has been trafficked, but there is evidence they have been held as a slave and subject to forced labour or servitude, the prosecutor should consider whether the criminal offence the victim is suspected of committing may be directly related to their position and checks must be made as to whether the offence was committed under duress or other form of compulsion. Where there is clear evidence of duress or compulsion, it will generally not be in the public interest to prosecute unless the offence is so serious or there are other aggravating factors."

New statutory defence in s.45 of the Modern Slavery Act 2015

The most recent development in this sphere is the creation in s.45 of the 2015   **11.37**
Act of a defence for victims of slavery and trafficking. It builds upon the CPS guidance, with the purpose of encouraging victims to come forward and give evidence without fear of being convicted of offences connected to their own slavery or trafficking situation, since the fear of conviction is something that is often used by offenders as a means through which to ensure their victims' compliance.[50] The defence does not supersede the CPS guidance nor remove the requirement for the proper exercise of prosecutorial discretion before proceedings are brought against a possible victim of slavery or trafficking. Indeed, close adherence to the guidance is vital to avoid any risk of prosecutors paying less regard to the UK's obligations under the Trafficking Convention and Directive on the basis that the statutory defence is now available at trial. This point is all the more important given the limitations on the scope of the defence.

Section 45(1) states that a person aged 18 or over is not guilty of an offence   **11.38**
if he did the act constituting the offence because he was compelled to do so, the compulsion is attributable to slavery or to "relevant exploitation" and a reasonable person in the same situation and having the person's "relevant characteristics" would have had no realistic alternative to doing the act. The statutory language is closely analogous to the defence of duress. For the purposes of the statutory defence, a person may be compelled to do something by another person or by their own circumstances.[51] The compulsion is attributable to slavery or to relevant exploitation only if it is, or is part of, conduct that constitutes an offence under s.1 or relevant exploitation, or it is a direct consequence of a person being, or having been, a victim of slavery or relevant exploitation.[52] A person's "relevant characteristics" means their age, sex and any physical or mental illness or disability.[53] The term "relevant exploitation" is defined as exploitation (as defined in s.3 of the Act) that is attributable to the person being or having been a victim of human trafficking.[54] The term "direct consequence" is not defined, or explained in the Explanatory Notes to the Act. This has been hotly criticised and it is anticipated that the absence of a definition may lead to some difficulty in the future.

Section 45(4) makes similar provision for persons under the age of 18,   **11.39**
though the test is different as the element of compulsion is absent from it.

---

[50] Explanatory Notes, para.218.
[51] s.45(2).
[52] s.45(3).
[53] s.45(5).
[54] s.45(5).

This is because it is recognised that children under 18 can be particularly vulnerable to being influenced into committing criminal offences. Thus, for a person under the age of 18, the test is simply whether they did the act as a direct consequence of being, or having been, a victim of slavery or relevant exploitation, and a reasonable person in the same situation as them and having their relevant characteristics would do the act.

11.40   The defence is limited, however, as s.45(7) specifies that it is not applicable to any of the offences in the extensive list in Sch.4 to the Act, which includes those offences that are generally considered the most serious in the calendar of crime, including murder, manslaughter, false imprisonment, perverting the course of justice, various offences against the person, offences against children, firearms and serious theft offences, sexual offences, terrorism, and slavery and trafficking offences, amongst others. This significant restriction of the scope of the defence also includes the ancillary offences of attempt, conspiracy, aiding and abetting, counselling or procuring, and offences under Pt 2 of the Serious Crime Act 2007 (encouraging or assisting).[55]

11.41   The defence is likely to place only an evidential burden on the defendant, so that once the defence is in issue it will be for the prosecution to disprove it. But the defendant will need to give or call evidence, including possibly expert evidence, in order to put the prosecution to proof.

11.42   The defence has been the subject of much criticism for its complexity and restrictiveness, and for requiring more of the trafficked defendant than the Convention and Directive would require.[56] Indeed, some have suggested that it may leave the UK non-compliant with art.8 of the Trafficking Directive, entitled "Non-prosecution or non-application of penalties to the victim", which states:

> "Member States shall, in accordance with the basic principles of their legal systems, take the necessary measures to ensure that competent national authorities are entitled not to prosecute or impose penalties on victims of trafficking in human beings for their involvement in criminal activities which they have been compelled to commit as a direct consequence of being subjected to any of the acts referred to in Article 2."

11.43   It is interesting to note that other jurisdictions have gone further than the UK. For example, s.31 of the Trinidad and Tobago Trafficking in Persons Act 2011 provides an absolute defence to any criminal charge if the accused committed the act because they were compelled as a direct result of being trafficked. This may be seen as demonstrating the commitment of these jurisdictions to eradicating trafficking, and their view that the best means by which to do so is to protect victims and encourage them to come forward to testify without fear.

---

[55] s.45(7) and Sch.4, paras 1–37.
[56] See e.g. Steven Bird and Philippa Southwell, *Does the new "slavery" defence offer victims of trafficking any greater protection?*, Archbold Review, 2015, 9, 7–9.

Modern Slavery Act 2015

Introduction

On August 25, 2013, the Home Secretary announced the Government's **11.44**
intention to introduce a Modern Slavery Bill. The Bill was published in April
2014 and the Modern Slavery Act received Royal Assent on March 26,
2015.

The Explanatory Notes to the Act describe modern slavery as: **11.45**

> "a brutal form of organised crime in which people are treated as commodities
> and exploited for criminal gain. The true extent of modern slavery in the United
> Kingdom, and indeed globally, is unknown. Modern Slavery, in particular
> human trafficking, is an international problem and victims may have entered the
> United Kingdom legally, on forged documentation, or clandestinely, or they may
> be British citizens living in the United Kingdom. Modern slavery takes a number
> of forms, including sexual exploitation, forced labour and domestic servitude,
> and victims come from all walks of life. Victims are often unwilling to come
> forward to law enforcement or public protection agencies, not seeing themselves
> as victims, or fearing further reprisals from their abusers, In particular, there may
> be particular social and cultural barriers to men identifying themselves as
> victims, Victims may also not always be recognised as victims of Modern Slavery
> by those who come into contact with them."

The Home Office Circular accompanying the Act states[57]: **11.46**

> "The 2015 Act will ensure that the National Crime Agency, the police and other
> law enforcement agencies have the powers they need to pursue, disrupt and bring
> to justice those engaged in human trafficking and slavery, servitude and forced or
> compulsory labour. The 2015 Act also introduces measures to enhance the
> protection of victims of slavery and trafficking."

Prior to the Act, the offences used to prosecute cases of slavery and **11.47**
trafficking tended to be:

- Sexual Offences Act 2003 ss.57–59, and subsequently s.59A (trafficking into, out of and within the UK for the purposes of sexual exploitation)
- Asylum and Immigration (Treatment of Claimants) Act 2004 s.4 (trafficking people for exploitation as defined by art.4 of the ECHR)
- Coroners and Justice Act 2009 s.71 (holding a person in slavery or requiring another person to perform forced or compulsory labour)
- Immigration Act 1971 s.25 (facilitating unlawful immigration), and
- Gangmasters (Licensing) Act 2004.

The effects of the Modern Slavery Act are: **11.48**

- To consolidate the hitherto disparate law around slavery and trafficking offences

---

[57] Circular 24/2015.

- To bring the UK into line with international instruments on human trafficking and slavery, servitude and forced compulsory labour
- To enhance the prospects of eradicating slavery, servitude, trafficking and exploitation (both work and sexual)
- To rescue and protect victims of modern slavery (both trafficking and exploitation), and
- To provide measures so as to encourage victims of these offences to come forward.

11.49   In order to meet these aims, the Act includes provisions for the establishment of the role of an Anti-Slavery Commissioner, an independent office-holder appointed by the Secretary of State (in practice the Home Secretary). The Commissioner's role is "to encourage good practice in the prevention, detection, investigation, and prosecution of slavery and human trafficking offences, as well as the identification of victims of those offences".[58] The Act places a duty on public authorities to co-operate with the Commissioner if requested to do so.[59]

11.50   The Act is in seven parts:

- Part 1 consolidates and clarifies the existing offences of slavery and human trafficking, and increases the maximum penalties
- Part 2 provides for two new civil preventative orders, the Slavery and Trafficking Prevention Order and the Slavery and Trafficking Risk Order
- Part 3 provides for new maritime enforcement powers in relation to ships
- Part 4 establishes the office of Independent Anti-slavery Commissioner and sets out the functions of the Commissioner
- Part 5 introduces a number of measures focused on supporting and protecting victims, including a statutory defence for slavery or trafficking victims and special measures for witnesses in criminal proceedings
- Part 6 requires certain businesses to disclose what activity they are undertaking to eliminate slavery and trafficking from their supply chains and their own business
- Part 7 requires the Secretary of State to publish a paper on the role of the Gangmasters Licensing Authority and otherwise relates to general matters such as consequential provision and commencement.

Overlap of offences and alternative/additional charges

11.51   This book relates to the law of sexual offences, but the manner in which the Act is drafted necessitates an examination of the provisions relating to slavery and servitude, as well as those relating to human trafficking for the

---

[58] See Explanatory Notes, paras 192–193, and Home Office Circular 45/2015 (July 2015).
[59] s.43 of and Sch.3.

purposes of exploitation, as there is an obvious potential overlap between the offences. Section 1 (slavery/servitude) does not exclude sexual exploitation, and the Explanatory Notes recognise that slavery may encompass sexual exploitation, as has been seen in highly publicised cases in recent years. As HHJ Martin Edmunds QC said when giving evidence to the Joint Select Committee[60]:

> "Experience shows that when a person is trafficked they are commonly exploited in a number of ways; whatever advantages the trafficker. Thus a person who is in forced labour may also be required to work in controlled prostitution. This is a very common scenario."

Further, as will be seen below, the definition in s.3 of "exploitation" for the 11.52 purposes of the human trafficking offence (s.2) encompasses the possibility of exploitation in the sense of conduct penalised by s.1 or s.2. Consequently, both sections are considered below.

It goes without saying that cases of slavery and trafficking are difficult 11.53 both to investigate and to prosecute, so when considering charges under the Modern Slavery Act 2015 it is sensible also to consider other possible charges, such as conspiracy, controlling prostitution and joint enterprise rape. Consideration should also be given to charges which may help to disrupt the criminal activity, e.g. participating in the activities of an organised criminal network (s.45 of the Serious Organised Crime Act 2015), fraud by false representation, money laundering and tax avoidance. For an example of addressing trafficking issues by prosecuting other offences, see *Valujevs and Mezals*,[61] involving fraud by abuse of position by unlicensed gangmasters contrary to s.4 of the Fraud Act 2006.

It is also worth considering the inclusion in an indictment of a charge 11.54 under s.25 of the Immigration Act 1971 (assisting unlawful immigration to a Member State), which need not be charged in the alternative to the primary trafficking offence but may be a stand-alone charge in its own right. In *Suchy and Sana*,[62] the Court of Appeal endorsed the giving of consecutive sentences in relation to a trafficking offence and a s.25 offence that were founded upon largely the same facts, stating that such an approach was appropriate as it reflected the two different and distinct victims: the individual who has been trafficked and the State.

Territorial extent

Whilst the Act mainly applies to England and Wales, some provisions, such 11.55 as those in respect of the Independent Anti-Slavery Commissioner and the powers to pursue, intercept and board ships (see below), also apply to Scotland and Northern Ireland.[63]

---

[60] See Report on Draft Modern Slavery Bill (April 2014), para 20.
[61] [2014] EWCA Crim 2888.
[62] [2014] EWCA Crim 1245.
[63] ss.36–39 and Sch.2, Pts 2 and 3.

Commencement and transitional provisions

11.56   The provisions of the Act relating to the offences in ss. 1–4, prevention orders, the independent slavery commissioner, a defence for slavery and trafficking victims who commit certain offences, and special measures for witnesses in criminal proceedings, were brought into force on July 31, 2015.[64] The offences in ss. 1–4 apply to conduct which takes place from that date. Conduct that pre-dates July 31, 2015, may be prosecuted under the old slavery and trafficking offences.[65] Where conduct straddles that date, transitional provisions allow for a prosecution under the pre-commencement legislation.[66] For the pre-commencement offences of trafficking for the purpose of sexual exploitation, see paras 11.07 and 11.16, above, and previous editions of this work.

Where next?

11.57   The Act has, however, been criticised not only for being something of a cut-and-paste job of the legislation it replaces and purports to consolidate, and also for not going far enough. Anthony Steen, chair of the Human Trafficking Foundation, said it was a "missed opportunity" that had "yawning gaps".[67] Parosha Chandran[68] called it the "starting point" for further legislation[69] and suggested the need for the following additional measures[70]:

- Statutory provisions (as opposed to policy) for a reformed National Referral Mechanism so as better identify and protect trafficked victims
- A criminal defence for trafficked victims that is in line with the UK's EU and international legal obligations
- The right of Overseas Domestic Workers to switch their employers
- The right of victims to bring civil claims for damages against their traffickers and enslavers for trafficking, forced labour and slavery
- Extra-territorial jurisdiction over the crimes of slavery, trafficking and forced labour

---

[64] Modern Slavery Act (Commencement No.1, Saving and Transitional Provisions Regulations) 2015 (SI 2015/1476).

[65] Modern Slavery Act 2015 (Commencement No.1, Saving and Transitional Provisions) Regulations 2015 (SI 2015/1476).

[66] Modern Slavery Act 2015 (Commencement No.1, Saving and Transitional Provisions) Regulations 2015 (SI 2015/1476); and see Home Office Circular 45/2015, para.25.

[67] *http://www.theguardian.com/law/2014/nov/03/modern-slavery-bill-lost-opportunity-human-trafficking-adviser* [Accessed January 30, 2016].

[68] General Editor of and Specialist Contributor to *The Human Trafficking Handbook: Recognising Trafficking and Modern-Day Slavery in the UK* (LexisNexis, October 2011).

[69] *http://www.ibtimes.co.uk/men-trafficked-vietnam-grow-marijuana-uk-failed-by-system-says-top-human-rights-lawyer-1513575* [Accessed January 30, 2016].

[70] Parosha Chandran, Lexis Nexis Webinar, May 7, 2015.

- An obligation on companies to report on the supply chains of their wholly owned subsidiaries and on all their supply chains, including those which produce goods which are consumed only abroad or use services (e.g. labour) overseas.

Also said to be missing are stand-alone offences of exploitation, specifically one directed towards child victims. This point is discussed at para.11.105, below.   **11.58**

SLAVERY, SERVITUDE AND FORCED COMPULSORY LABOUR

Section 1 of the Modern Slavery Act 2015 provides as follows: **11.59**

"(1) A person commits an offence if—
  (a) the person holds another person in slavery or servitude and the circumstances are such that the person knows or ought to know that the other person is held in slavery or servitude, or
  (b) the person requires another person to perform forced or compulsory labour and the circumstances are such that the person knows or ought to know that the other person is being required to perform forced or compulsory labour.
(2) In subsection (1) the references to holding a person in slavery or servitude or requiring a person to perform forced or compulsory labour are to be construed in accordance with Article 4 of the Human Rights Convention.[71]
(3) In determining whether a person is being held in slavery or servitude or required to perform forced or compulsory labour, regard may be had to all the circumstances.
(4) For example, regard may be had—
  (a) to any of the person's personal circumstances (such as the person being a child, the person's family relationships, and any mental or physical illness) which may make the person more vulnerable than other persons;
  (b) to any work or services provided by the person, including work or services provided in circumstances which constitute exploitation within section 3(3) to (6).
(5) The consent of a person (whether an adult or a child) to any of the acts alleged to constitute holding the person in slavery or servitude, or requiring the person to perform forced or compulsory labour, does not preclude a determination that the person is being held in slavery or servitude, or required to perform forced or compulsory labour."

Section 1 is intended to replace s.71 of the Coroners and Justice Act 2009, which was repealed by the 2015 Act.

MODE OF TRIAL AND PUNISHMENT

An offence under s.1 is triable either way.[72] The maximum sentence on conviction on indictment is life imprisonment.[73] This compares with the 14-year maximum under the previous legislation. There is also a power to   **11.60**

---

[71] See para.11.02, above.
[72] s.5(1).
[73] s.5(1)(a).

impose a fine as determined by s.163 of the Criminal Justice Act 2003 (general power of the Crown Court to fine offender convicted on indictment). On summary conviction, the maximum sentence is six months' imprisonment or an unlimited fine, or both. The maximum sentence of imprisonment will increase to 12 months when s.154(1) of the Criminal Justice Act 2003 comes into force.[74]

11.61   The s.1 offence is a specified violent offence for the purposes of the dangerousness provisions of the Criminal Justice Act 2003.[75] A s.1 offence, whenever committed, may be made the subject of an extended sentence under s.226A of that Act (extended sentence for certain violent or sexual offences).[76] The offence is also listed in Pt 1 of Sch.15B to the Criminal Justice Act 2003 for the purposes of s.224A of that Act (life sentence for a second listed offence).[77]

11.62   An offender who is sentenced to imprisonment for a term of 12 months or more will also be subject to management by Multi-Agency Public Protection Arrangements ("MAPPA").[78] The offender will automatically be allocated to the National Probation Service rather than one of the Community Rehabilitation Companies, and such allocation will take place at the court immediately following the sentence.

11.63   In exceptional circumstances, and with the agreement of an Inspector, a person who has committed a s.1 offence may be dealt with by way of a caution.[79]

11.64   Section 7 to the 2015 Act amends Sch.2 to the Proceeds of Crime Act 2002 so that offences under s.1 are "lifestyle" offences for the purposes of the 2002 Act.[80] Accordingly a conviction may, if the other conditions set out in the 2002 Act are met, result in the court making a confiscation order after conviction in relation to the benefit the offender has derived from the offence or, if he has a general criminal lifestyle, from his general criminal conduct.[81] The Explanatory Notes to the 2015 Act state that the purpose of the amendments to Sch.2 are to ensure "that defendants convicted will be

---

[74] s.5(1)(b), (4). Section 154(1) of the 2003 Act is not in force as of January 30, 2016. For offences committed before the commencement date, the reference in s.5(1)(b) to 12 months' imprisonment on summary conviction is to be read as a reference to six months.

[75] s.6(1), (2), amending the 2003 Act so as to insert s.1 into the list of offences in Sch. 15, Pt 1.

[76] Inserted by the Legal Aid, Sentencing and Punishment of Offenders Act 2012 s.124, brought into force on December 3, 2012, by SI 2012/2906.

[77] Inserted by the Legal Aid, Sentencing and Punishment of Offenders Act 2012 s.122, brought into force on December 3, 2012, by SI 2012/2906.

[78] These are a framework of statutory arrangements operated by criminal justice and social care agencies that seek to manage and reduce the risk presented by sexual and violent offenders in order to reduce re-offending and protect the public. This is done by the sharing of information and establishing a coordinated risk-management plan that will allow offenders to be effectively managed: see Home Office Circular on the 2015Act (24/2015), para.24.

[79] By amendment of the Criminal Justice and Courts Act 2015 (Simple Cautions) (Specification of Either-Way Offences) Order 2015 (SI 2015/790): see the Modern Slavery Act 2015 (Consequential Amendments) Regulations 2015 (SI 2015/1472), regs 20, 21.

[80] s.7 of the 2015 Act.

[81] s.10 contains supplementary provisions relating to confiscation.

deemed to have a criminal lifestyle and will therefore be subject to the toughest regime in respect of calculating confiscation orders under the 2002 Act."[82]

SENTENCING

At the time of writing there are no published authorities in respect of **11.65** sentencing under s.1 of the 2015 Act. As the subject of this book is sexual offences, we do not summarise the old authorities in relation to cases of slavery, forced compulsory labour or servitude, but for reference, the leading case under the old legislation is *Attorney General's References (Nos.37, 38 and 65 of 2010) (Khan)*,[83] which was followed in *Attorney General's References (Nos 2, 3, 4 and 5 of 2013) (Connors)*.[84]

"ALL THE CIRCUMSTANCES"

Section 1(3) provides that in determining whether a person is being held in **11.66** slavery or servitude or required to perform forced or compulsory labour, the court may have regard to "all the circumstances". As examples, s.1(4)(a) cites any personal circumstances that make the person more vulnerable than others, such as being a child, family relationships or mental or physical illness. The listed circumstances are non-exhaustive. This provision seeks to address the common situation where a victim has been chosen specifically because of their individual vulnerability. As the Helen Bamber Foundation said in evidence to the Joint Select Committee[85]:

> "vulnerability is often complex and multi-faceted rather than definable by one single element. It is also cumulative, and increases as victims are sold, exploited and trafficked on. Crucial factors [are] for example socio-economic deprivation, adversity, change of familial or political circumstances . . . "

Section 1(4)(b) gives as examples of potentially relevant circumstances any work or services provided by the person, which may cover a broad range of activities from begging and pick-pocketing to prostitution. Such activities may also amount to exploitation for the purposes of s.2 of the Act, and s.1(4)(b) expressly provides that regard may be had to work or services provided in circumstances which constitute exploitation as defined in s.3(3)–(6) of the Act, for which see paras 11.101 and following, below. By incorporating the exploitation principles into s.1, the Act avoids a potential loophole.[86]

---

[82] See Explanatory Notes, para.47.
[83] [2010] EWCA Crim 2880; [2011] 2 Cr. App. R.(S.) 31.
[84] [2013] EWCA Crim 324.
[85] See Report on Draft Modern Slavery Bill (April 2014), para.24.
[86] See Peter Carter QC and Riel Karmy-Jones QC, Lexis Nexis interview, May 5, 2015, available at *http://redlionchambers.com/pdf/Modern%20slavery%20Act%20New%20Of-fences%20by%20Carter%20&%20Karmy-Jones.pdf* [Accessed January 30, 2016].

CONSENT

11.67   Section 1(5) provides that the consent of a person (whether an adult or a child) to any act alleged to constitute an offence under the section does not prevent the court from finding that they are being held in slavery or servitude or being required to perform forced or compulsory labour. This is not a change from the law as previously established by the authorities, but for it now to be incorporated into the legislation is a significant advance.

VICTIM SUPPORT

Special measures

11.68   Although trafficked victims were previously eligible for special measures, s.46 of the Act amends the Youth Justice and Criminal Evidence Act 1999 so as to extend special measures provisions to all victims of s.1 and s.2 offences who now include victims of slavery, servitude and forced compulsory labour.

Independent child trafficking advocates

11.69   At the time of writing,[87] s.48 is not yet in force. It requires the Secretary of State to make such arrangements as considered necessary to enable "independent child trafficking advocates" to be available to support children who there are reasonable grounds to believe may be victims of human trafficking. At the time the Act came into force these arrangements were being trialled, and the commencement provisions were tailored to allow the trial to conclude and be evaluated. The Secretary of State was required report on the steps proposed to be taken and the success or otherwise of the trials to Parliament no later than nine months after the day the Act was passed, on March 26, 2015. The report, which is in broadly positive terms, was published in December 2015.[88]

Other measures of support

11.70   Sections 49–54 of the Act, which (except for s.50) came into force in late 2015, contain further measures for identifying and supporting victims, create presumptions as to age, impose upon public authorities a duty to notify the Secretary of State (or, if regulations so require, a public authority) if they

[87] January 30, 2016.
[88] Ravi K.S. Kohli, Patricia Hynes, Helen Connolly, Angela Thurnham, David Westlake and Kate D'Arcy (University of Bedfordshire),*Evaluation of Independent Child Trafficking Advocates trial: Final Report* (Research Report 86), Home Office, December 2015. The report is available at *https://www.gov.uk/government/uploads/system/uploads/attachment_data/file/486138/icta-horr86.pdf* [Accessed January 30, 2016].

have reasonable grounds to believe that a person may be a victim of slavery or human trafficking, and make provision for overseas domestic workers who are determined to be victims of slavery or trafficking to be granted leave to remain in the UK.

Mental Element

It must be proved that A knew or ought to have known that B was held in slavery or servitude, or was being required to perform forced or compulsory labour.[89] For the meaning of "knowledge", see para.12.63, below.

11.71

Human Trafficking

Section 2 of The Modern Slavery Act 2015 provides as follows:

11.72

"(1) A person commits an offence if the person arranges or facilitates the travel of another person ("V") with a view to V being exploited.

(2) It is irrelevant whether V consents to the travel (whether V is an adult or a child).

(3) A person may in particular arrange or facilitate V's travel by recruiting V, transporting or transferring V, harbouring or receiving V, or transferring or exchanging control over V.

(4) A person arranges or facilitates V's travel with a view to V being exploited only if—

(a) the person intends to exploit V (in any part of the world) during or after the travel, or

(b) the person knows or ought to know that another person is likely to exploit V (in any part of the world) during or after the travel.

(5) "Travel" means—

(a) arriving in, or entering, any country,

(b) departing from any country,

(c) travelling within any country.

(6) A person who is a UK national commits an offence under this section regardless of—

(a) where the arranging or facilitating takes place, or

(b) where the travel takes place.

(7) A person who is not a UK national commits an offence under this section if—

(a) any part of the arranging or facilitating takes place in the United Kingdom, or

(b) the travel consists of arrival in or entry into, departure from, or travel within, the United Kingdom."

Section 2 replaces both s.59A of the Sexual Offences Act 2003 and s.4 of the Asylum and Immigration (Treatment of Claimants, etc.) Act 2004,[90] and provides for a single offence of human trafficking to cover both sexual and non-sexual exploitation. The purpose was to make it administratively simpler

---

[89] s.1(a), (b).
[90] Both repealed by s.57 and Sch.5.

for investigators and prosecutors to bring forward human trafficking prosecutions.[91]

11.73   By analogy with *Walker*,[92] decided under s.8 of the Sexual Offences Act 2003, s.2 creates separate offences of arranging and facilitating human trafficking. It follows that a count alleging that the defendant "arranged or facilitated" such an offence is in principle duplicitous and should be struck out or amended.

MODE OF TRIAL AND PUNISHMENT

11.74   An offence under s.2 is triable either way.[93] The maximum sentence on conviction on indictment is life imprisonment.[94] This compares with the 14-year maximum under the previous legislation. There is also a power to impose a fine as determined by s.163 of the Criminal Justice Act 2003 (general power of the Crown Court to fine offender convicted on indictment). On summary conviction, the maximum sentence is six months' imprisonment or an unlimited fine, or both. The maximum sentence of imprisonment will increase to 12 months when s.154(1) of the Criminal Justice Act 2003 comes into force.[95]

11.75   A s.2 offence is a specified offence for the purposes of the dangerousness provisions of the Criminal Justice Act 2003, either a specified violent offence if it is not committed with a view to sexual exploitation or a specified sexual offence if it is so committed.[96] A s.2 offence, whenever committed, may be made the subject of an extended sentence under s.226A of that Act. (extended sentence for certain violent or sexual offences).[97] Consequently, where a s.2 offence is committed for the purpose of sexual exploitation, if an extended determinate sentence is imposed, an extended licence period of up to eight years may be included. Where the offence is not committed for the purpose of sexual exploitation, it is treated as a violent offence for which, if an extended determinate sentence is imposed, an extended licence period of up to five years may be included. The offence is also listed in Pt 1 of Sch.15B to the Criminal Justice Act 2003 for the purposes of s.224A of that Act (life sentence for a second listed offence).[98] The effect of this provision is that

---

[91] See Explanatory Notes, para.23.
[92] [2006] EWCA Crim 1907, discussed in para.3.131, above.
[93] s.5(1).
[94] s.5(1)(a).
[95] s.5(1)(b), (4). Section 154(1) of the 2003 Act is not in force as of January 30, 2016. For offences committed before the commencement date, the reference in s.5(1)(b) to 12 months' imprisonment on summary conviction is to be read as a reference to six months.
[96] s.6(1)–(3), amending Sch.15 to the 2003 Act.
[97] Inserted by the Legal Aid, Sentencing and Punishment of Offenders Act 2012 s.124, brought into force on December 3, 2012, by SI 2012/2906.
[98] Inserted by the Legal Aid, Sentencing and Punishment of Offenders Act 2012 s.122, brought into force on December 3, 2012, by SI 2012/2906.

adults with a previous conviction for a very serious violent or sexual offence that is listed in Sch.15B face an automatic life sentence.

An offender who is sentenced to imprisonment for a term of 12 months or more will also be subject to management by MAPPA.[99] The offender will automatically be allocated to the National Probation Service rather than one of the Community Rehabilitation Companies, and such allocation will take place at the court immediately following the sentence. **11.76**

In exceptional circumstances, and with the agreement of an Inspector, a person who has committed a s.1 offence may be dealt with by way of a caution.[100] **11.77**

Section 7 to the 2015 Act amends Sch.2 to the Proceeds of Crime Act 2002 so that offences under s.2 are "lifestyle" offences for the purposes of the 2002 Act.[101] Accordingly a conviction may, if the other conditions set out in the 2002 Act are met, result in the court making a confiscation order after conviction in relation to the benefit the offender has derived from the offence or, if he has a general criminal lifestyle, from his general criminal conduct.[102] The Explanatory Notes to the 2015 Act state that the purpose of the amendments to Sch.2 are to ensure "that defendants convicted will be deemed to have a criminal lifestyle and will therefore be subject to the toughest regime in respect of calculating confiscation orders under the 2002 Act."[103] **11.78**

SENTENCING

For the Sentencing Council guideline relating to the sentencing of sexual offences committed by sexual offenders aged 18 or over after April 1, 2014, see Ch.33, below. The guideline covers the now repealed s.59A of the 2003 Act and has not been updated to take account of the Modern Slavery Act 2015. However, we set out the s.59A guideline here since its content, and the Council's consultation document,[104] help explain how sentencing may be approached under the 2015 Act. Many of the principles underpinning the **11.79**

---

[99] These are a framework of statutory arrangements operated by criminal justice and social care agencies that seek to manage and reduce the risk presented by sexual and violent offenders in order to reduce re-offending and protect the public. This is done by the sharing of information and establishing a coordinated risk-management plan that will allow offenders to be effectively managed: see Home Office Circular on the 2015Act (24/2015), para.24.

[100] By amendment of the Criminal Justice and Courts Act 2015 (Simple Cautions) (Specification of Either-Way Offences) Order 2015 (SI 2015/790): see the Modern Slavery Act 2015 (Consequential Amendments) Regulations 2015 (SI 2015/1472), regs 20, 21.

[101] s.7 of the 2015 Act.

[102] s.10 contains supplementary provisions relating to confiscation.

[103] See Explanatory Notes, para.47.

[104] *Sexual Offences Guideline: Consultation* (December 6, 2012). As will be plain from the date, this consultation dealt with the old s.57–59 of the 2003 Act; however, the guideline being contemplated by the Council was identical to the s.59A guideline discussed here.

s.59A guideline remain valid and it will undoubtedly form the basis of a new guideline in due course, though the starting points and ranges for the s.2 offence will no doubt be higher to take account of the increase in the maximum sentence from 14 years' to life imprisonment under the 2015 Act. Further, the s.59A guideline remains applicable to conduct taking place before July 31, 2015.

Sentencing Guideline

Step One—Harm

11.80   The guideline requires the sentencing court to go through a series of steps in order to determine the appropriate sentence. Step one involves determining the offence category by reference to the degree of harm caused and then the culpability level for the offence. The harm factors for offences under s.59A are:

Harm	
Category 1	• Abduction/detention • iolence or threats of violence • Sustained and systematic psychological abuse • Victim(s) under 18 • Victim(s) forced or coerced to participate in unsafe/degrading sexual activity • Victim(s) forced/coerced into prostitution • Victim(s) tricked/deceived as to purpose of visit
Category 2	Factor(s) in categories 1 not present

The Sentencing Council explained in its consultation document that "abduction/detention" is included because the harm caused by the offence is increased by reason of the fear and loss of control the victim will have experienced. "Victim(s) under 18" is included because harm is increased by virtue of the corrupting effect on a young victim's emotional development. As for "victim(s) forced/coerced into prostitution" and "victim(s) tricked/deceived as to purpose of visit", these are included because the use of force or deception increases the harm to the victim flowing from the offence.

11.81   In responding to the consultation, the CPS suggested extending the factor "victim tricked/deceived as to purpose of visit" to cover instances where the victim knew they were coming to the UK to work as a prostitute but on arrival were tricked and exploited as to the nature and conditions of the work. The Council thought this might over-complicate the factor at step one, but noted that it is open to prosecutors to rely on deception of this sort as an aggravating factor at step two, given that the list of aggravating factors is non-exhaustive.

Culpability

The s.59A guideline contains three levels of culpability. The Sentencing   **11.82** Council explained that this reflects the fact that the court may be faced with offenders who have played various roles, from directing and organising a trafficking chain to limited involvement through pressure, exploitation or coercion. The categories of culpability, with culpability A being the most serious, are as follows:

CULPABILITY		
A	*B*	*C*
• Directing or organising trafficking on significant commercial basis • Expectation of significant financial or other gain • Significant influence over others in trafficking organisation/ hierarchy • Abuse of trust	• Operational or management function within hierarchy • Involves others in operation whether by coercion/ intimidation/ exploitation or reward (and offender's involvement is not as a result of coercion)	• Performs limited function under direction • Close involvement but engaged by coercion/ intimidation/ exploitation

In its consultation document, the Sentencing Council said that the factor   **11.83** which appears in the published guideline as "directing or organising trafficking on significant commercial basis" would encompass an offender who was at the top of an organised trafficking chain. Such offenders have high levels of influence and control and therefore their lack of interaction with individual victims should not decrease their culpability. It is the power and influence they exert in directing the operation that are significant. As for culpability B, the Council said that "operational or management function within hierarchy" and "involves others in operation whether by coercion/ intimidation/exploitation or reward (and offender's involvement is not as a result of coercion)" would apply to an offender who has more than a peripheral role and is responsible for engaging others in the trafficking operation or has a degree of oversight or control over the trafficking activity. Culpability C is intended to apply to offenders who play a peripheral role and have not directed, controlled or managed any activity, along with those whose involvement is as a result of their own exploitation or trafficked status.

Step Two—Starting point and category range

11.84 Once it has determined the offence category and culpability level, the court should then use the corresponding starting point specified in the guideline in order to reach a sentence within the category range. The starting point applies to all offenders irrespective of plea or previous convictions. Once the starting point has been determined, step two allows further adjustment for aggravating or mitigating features, set out below. A case of particular gravity, reflected by multiple features of culpability or harm, could merit upward adjustment from the starting point before further adjustment for aggravating or mitigating features. Where there is a sufficient prospect of rehabilitation, a community order with a sex offender treatment programme requirement under s.202 of the Criminal Justice Act 2003 can be a proper alternative to a short or moderate length custodial sentence.

11.85   The starting points and category ranges for offences under s.59A are as follows:

	A	*B*	*C*
Category 1	*Starting point* 8 years' custody	*Starting point* 6 years' custody	*Starting point* 18 months' custody
	Category range 6–12 years' custody	*Category range* 4–8 years' custody	*Category range* 26 weeks'–2 years' custody
Category 2	*Starting point* 6 years' custody	*Starting point* 4 years' custody	*Starting point* 26 weeks' custody
	Category range 4–8 years' custody	*Category range* 2–6 years' custody	*Category range* High level community order – 18 months' custody

As noted above, when the guideline is updated to refer to the offences in s.2 of the 2015 Act, it is likely that the starting point and sentence range will be increased to reflect the increase in the maximum sentence to life imprisonment.

Aggravating and mitigating factors

After identifying the starting point and category range, the court should   **11.86**
consider whether the presence of aggravating or mitigating factors should
result in an upward or downward adjustment from the starting point or the
imposition of a sentence outside the category range. In particular, relevant
recent convictions are likely to result in an upward adjustment. When
sentencing appropriate category 2 offences, the court should also consider
whether the custody threshold has been passed; if so, whether a custodial
sentence is unavoidable; and if it is, whether that sentence can be suspended.
The non-exhaustive list of aggravating and mitigating factors for offences
under s.59A is:

Aggravating factors
Statutory aggravating factors
<ul><li>Previous convictions, having regard to a) the nature of the offence to which the conviction relates and its relevance to the current offence; and b) the time that has elapsed since the conviction</li><li>Offence committed whilst on bail</li></ul>
Other aggravating factors
<ul><li>Failure to comply with current court orders</li><li>Offence committed whilst on licence</li><li>Deliberate isolation of victim(s)</li><li>Children of victim(s) left in home country due to trafficking</li><li>Threats made to expose victim(s) to the authorities (for example, immigration or police), family/friends or others</li><li>Harm threatened against the family/friends of victim(s)</li><li>Exploiting of victim(s) from particularly vulnerable backgrounds</li><li>Victim(s) previously trafficked/sold/passed around</li><li>Passport/identity documents removed</li><li>Food withheld</li><li>Use of drugs/alcohol or other substance to secure victim's compliance</li><li>Earnings withheld/kept by offender or evidence of excessive wage reduction or debt bondage, inflated travel or living expenses or unreasonable interest rates</li><li>Any steps taken to prevent the victim reporting an incident, obtaining assistance and/or from assisting or supporting the prosecution</li><li>Attempts to dispose of or conceal evidence</li><li>Timescale over which the operation has been run</li></ul>

Mitigating factors
• No previous convictions **or** no relevant/recent convictions • Remorse • Previous good character and/or exemplary conduct* • Age and/or lack of maturity where it affects the responsibility of the offender • Mental disorder or learning disability, particularly where linked to the commission of the offence

* Previous good character/exemplary conduct is different from having no previous convictions. The more serious the offence, the less the weight which should normally be attributed to this factor. Where previous good character/exemplary conduct has been used to facilitate the offence, this mitigation should not normally be allowed and such conduct may constitute an aggravating factor.

In the context of this offence, previous good character/exemplary conduct should not normally be given any significant weight and will not normally justify a reduction in what would otherwise be the appropriate sentence.

11.87   The Sentencing Council explained in its consultation document the reasons for the inclusion of many of the aggravating factors:

• In relation to "deliberate isolation of victim(s)" it was recognised that a degree of isolation is an inevitable consequence of the victim being in a different country or area of the UK, but felt that the seriousness of the offence is increased where the victim is then denied access to any form of communication with family/friends or is deliberately separated from people they have travelled with.

• "Children of victim(s) left in home country due to trafficking" was included as this situation is likely to cause considerable further anguish to the victim and additional harm to the children left behind. Where the motivation for travelling is improved prospects for the victim's family, this may make them susceptible to being trafficked and the harmful consequences for such victims are also greater.

• As for "exploitation of victim(s) from particularly vulnerable backgrounds", the Council said that all victims of trafficking are likely to be vulnerable in some way, but the exploitation of particularly vulnerable groups, e.g. children in care or from dysfunctional backgrounds, increases the severity of the offence.

• "Harm threatened against the family/friends of victim" is included since this means of controlling the victim is likely to increase their feelings of helplessness and fear.

• "Victim(s) previously trafficked/sold/passed around" increases the seriousness of the offence as there is continuing damage and harm to the victim.

• Finally, "passport/identity documents removed", "victim(s) prevented from seeking medical treatment", "use of drugs/alcohol or other substance to secure victim's compliance", "food withheld" and "earnings of victim(s) withheld/kept by offender or evidence of excessive wage reduction, debt bondage, inflated travel or living expenses, unreasonable interest rates" are included as they are all common means by which offenders exert control over their victims.

As for the mitigating factors, the Council said that where offenders have **11.88** previously been exploited or trafficked themselves, this should be dealt with by placing them in the lowest category of offending rather than by treating previous exploitation as mitigation, and this is the approach followed in the guideline. On this aspect, see the discussion of the prosecution of victims in paras 11.22 and following, above.

Steps Three to Nine

The remaining steps cover the following points. At step three the court **11.89** should consider any factors which would indicate a reduction in sentence, e.g. assistance to the prosecution. At step four it should consider any reduction for a guilty plea. At step five the court should consider dangerousness, i.e. whether it would be appropriate to award an extended sentence (s.226A of the Criminal Justice Act 2003). Step six requires the court to consider whether the total sentence is just and proportionate to the offending behaviour. At step seven it should consider whether to make an ancillary order (e.g. a SHPO or a restraining order). Step eight requires the court to fulfil its duty under s.174 of the Criminal Justice Act 2003 to give reasons for, and explain the effect of, the sentence. Finally, at step nine the court should consider whether to give credit for time spent on bail in accordance with s.240A of that Act.

Sentencing examples

There are, at time of writing, no reported sentencing appeals relating to s.2 of **11.90** the 2015 Act. It is likely that sentencing decisions under ss.57–59 and s.59A of the Sexual Offences Act 2003 will remain instructive, especially where a case pre-dates July 31, 2015 and so is prosecuted under the latter provision. For cases prosecuted under the new Act, the earlier authorities must be approached with caution given the increase in the maximum sentence from 14 years' to life imprisonment. Some of the more useful authorities under the 2003 Act are set out below.

The decision in *Attorney General's Reference (No.126 of 2014) (Omar* **11.91** *Jumale and Said Zakaria)*,[105] illustrates the importance of the sentencing exercise properly addressing an offence of trafficking that is charged with other sexual offences. The Attorney General referred as unduly lenient Z's sentence of 11 years' imprisonment for two counts of engaging in sexual activity with a child, two counts of rape and one of trafficking. The judge had

---

[105] [2015] EWCA Crim 128. See also *Arslan Khan* [2015] EWCA Crim 831, discussed in para.10.54, above.

not imposed a separate sentence for the trafficking offence. That offence had involved taking the 13-year-old victim first to a flat and then to a hotel room for the purpose of making her available to other men to sexually abuse. It was argued that the 11-year sentence failed to reflect the gravity of Z's offending, his high degree of culpability and the effect his offending had had on the victim. In particular, it was submitted that the trafficking offence represented a serious case of exploitation, and as such warranted a separate sentence. The Court held that although the sentencing judge had to consider totality, he had erred in failing to reflect the trafficking offence at all in his sentencing. The trafficking offence was particularly serious: a substantive sentence of five years' imprisonment would have been justified for it, and the total 11-year sentence was unduly lenient. Accordingly the Court imposed a five-year sentence for the trafficking offence to run consecutively to the original 11 years, resulting in a total sentence of 16 years' imprisonment.

11.92   *Ali (Yasir)*[106] concerned offences of sexual activity against children, rape, making indecent photographs of a child, intimidation and trafficking within the UK for sexual exploitation. The Crown's case was that D1 and D2 had targeted young girls, often from troubled backgrounds, and groomed them for sexual purposes. The victims were usually driven to out-of-town locations and given alcohol before being sexually assaulted or raped. Hotel rooms had been booked on two occasions for overnight stays with a number of girls, and sexual activity was said to have occurred in the presence of a 14-year-old girl. D1 had applied unsuccessfully at half-time for the seven trafficking charges brought against him to be dismissed on the basis that relatively short, ad hoc, car journeys were not covered by the offence in s.58 of the 2003 Act: on this aspect see para.11.100, below. On conviction D1 was sentenced to an extended sentence comprising 20 years' imprisonment and a five-year extended licence period. As regards the trafficking offences, the judge determined that these fell within category 1 of the guideline because, for the purposes of harm, the victims were under 18 and they were deceived as to the purpose of the trips. D1's role was best described as an operational or management function within the hierarchy, so placing the offences in category B as regards culpability. The aggravating factors included the exploitation of girls from particularly vulnerable backgrounds, the use of alcohol and the steps that D1 took to ensure that the offences were not reported to the authorities. The judge expressly reminded himself that he had to bear in mind the overlap between these offences and the individual sexual offences relating to each of the complainants. On their own, the trafficking offences came within the bracket which provided a starting point of six years and a range of 4–8 years before any uplift to reflect the aggravating factors. The judge imposed concurrent sentences of four years' imprisonment on the

---

[106] [2015] EWCA Crim 1279. See also *Bassam Karrar and Others* [2015] EWCA Crim 850, discussed at paras 1.124 and following, above.

seven trafficking counts. The Court of Appeal dismissed D1's appeal against sentence.

In *Brusch and Horvat*,[107] the appellants each appealed against total **11.93** sentences of 10 years' imprisonment imposed following their pleas of guilty to trafficking women for sexual exploitation. B and H, who were Czech citizens, had trafficked two women (Z and G) from the Czech Republic. Z was 19, suffered from a serious illness, had a drug problem and had left her parental home after a disagreement. She was clearly vulnerable. G was 37, a drug addict, and had worked as a prostitute in the past. B's role was to get the women abroad and he persuaded them to go with him to the Republic of Ireland to take part in bogus marriages. Once there they met H, whose role was to enforce their sexual exploitation. They were coerced into having sex with a number of men. From Ireland all four travelled to the UK where Z and G were again coerced into having sex with a number of men. They were threatened with violence and their phones were removed. The offending came to an end only when they managed to escape. In a personal impact statement, Z said she had been hospitalised for three weeks following her escape. Her internal organs had been damaged, she suffered from night-mares, was frightened to have a relationship with a man and felt dirty and degraded. G described herself as having been mentally tortured and bru-talised into submission. Both B and H had previous convictions in the Czech Republic. In sentencing, the judge considered the guideline issued by the Sentencing Guidelines Council in 2007 (now replaced by the Sentencing Council's guideline). He identified the previous convictions as an aggravating factor. B and H submitted there was nothing to take the case outside the guideline range of four to nine years' imprisonment, and nothing to warrant the sentence being much above the six-year starting point. Their appeals were allowed. In considering the guideline it was important to bear in mind that each appellant had previous convictions, though not for offences of the instant kind, and that each had been involved in dealing with more than one woman. The offences were not single offences. What happened in Ireland aggravated the offences, showing a continued course of conduct which lengthened and intensified the ordeal to which the victims had been subjected in the UK. It was important to remember that there were two victims and a significant degree of coercion. Z and G were vulnerable women who had been detained, kept isolated, degraded and forced to engage in sexual intercourse. However, given that the maximum sentence for each offence was 14 years' imprisonment, the 10-year sentence was too high. The sentences were therefore quashed and replaced with total sentences of eight years' imprisonment.

In *Dunkova*[108] the appellant, a prostitute, had brought a 15-year-old girl **11.94** (P) to the UK from Slovakia and, in league with her brother and husband,

---

[107] [2011] EWCA Crim 1554.
[108] [2010] EWCA Crim 1318.

forced her to work as a prostitute. P gave all her earnings to the appellant, who gave them to her husband. He inflicted violence on P and, with the appellant's brother, threatened to kill her should she run away. The appellant was convicted on two counts of trafficking for sexual exploitation, one of causing child prostitution and one of controlling a child prostitute. She was given consecutive sentences of eight years' imprisonment for the trafficking and eight for the controlling, making 16 years in all. Her brother and husband were each sentenced to 17 years' imprisonment. The appellant submitted that her sentence failed to reflect the essential disparity between her and the other two defendants' involvement. Her appeal was allowed. Although the appellant's role had been substantial from start to finish, it had been subordinate to that of the two males. Whilst she had fetched P from Slovakia and supervised her, they had organised the transit and threatened and falsely imprisoned P. She had essentially minded P on their behalf. The justice of the case could be met by quashing the appellant's two sentences of eight years' imprisonment and substituting sentences of seven years, giving a total sentence of 14 years' imprisonment.

Jurisdiction

11.95   The offences in s.2 are extra-territorial in their reach in relation to UK nationals, who may commit a human trafficking offence regardless of where in the world the arranging or facilitating or the travel takes place.[109] For example, a UK national may be prosecuted under s.2 in England and Wales for trafficking a person within the Far East. A non-UK national, however, will only commit a s.2 offence if some part of the arranging or facilitating takes place in the UK or the travel consists of arrival in or entry into, departure from or travel within the UK.[110]

"Arranges or Facilitates"

11.96   Section 2, like the repealed offences, is dependent on the arrangement or facilitation of the travel of a victim from one place to another with the intention of exploiting them,[111] with travel being defined as arriving in, entering, departing from or travelling within any country.[112]

11.97   For the meaning of the terms "arranges" and "facilitates", see paras.4.172 and following, above. Section 2(3) provides that a person may in particular arrange or facilitate a victim's travel by recruiting them, transporting or transferring them, harbouring or receiving them, or transferring or exchanging control over them. These examples are largely drawn from international

---

[109] s.2(6) and Explanatory Notes, para.28.
[110] s.2(7).
[111] s.2(1), (4).
[112] s.2(5).

instruments such as the Palermo Protocol. It should be noted that there is no requirement that the thing arranged or facilitated must actually occur; it is sufficient that the act of arrangement or facilitation is committed.[113]

During the passage of what became the Sexual Offences Act 2003 through **11.98** Parliament, Lord Falconer said that the predecessor offence in s.57 of that Act (trafficking into the UK for sexual exploitation) would, for example, catch someone who facilitated a victim's arrival in the UK by providing him with an airline or ferry ticket, or false immigration papers, believing that someone else was likely post-arrival to commit a relevant offence against him (i.e. exploit him).[114] Lord Falconer also suggested that the offence would be committed if someone provided a victim with food and water for his journey to the UK. It is, however, difficult to see that the provision of food and water could of itself facilitate a victim's arrival in the UK, unless the circumstances were such that the victim would not have made the journey, or could not have survived, without it. Otherwise, the provision of food and water will at most facilitate the victim's arrival in a better state of health than might otherwise have been the case. This proposition derives support from a dictum of Ouseley J, giving the judgment of the Court of Appeal in *Javaherifard*[115] (which concerned the offence of facilitating a breach of immigration law contrary to s.25 of the Immigration Act 1971):

> "If someone provides food, money or accommodation to an illegal entrant, knowing or having reasonable cause for believing[116] that such acts facilitate him being in the country *as an illegal entrant*, he would be guilty of an offence and we see no reason why that should not be so. If food, money or accommodation is supplied to someone known to the provider to be an illegal immigrant, but is not supplied with the knowledge that it will assist his presence *as an illegal entrant* but instead is supplied knowing that it will assist him simply as a human being e.g. to avoid degradation or destitution, there would be no offence."

The better view is that it is possible to facilitate a person's arrival or entry **11.99** in a country by an act which occurs close to but after the person's actual arrival or entry, if the act is necessary for the arrival or entry to be effective and is closely related to it in place and time. The Court of Appeal so held in *Javaherifard*,[117] which concerned the offence of facilitating a breach of immigration law (contrary to s.25 of the Immigration Act 1971). The Court referred with approval to *Singh and Meeuwsen*,[118] in which the appellants had assisted some illegal entrants to get away from a trailer, in which they had been concealed, after it left the port area. They had not been involved in bringing the trailer into the UK. The Court of Appeal rejected the argument

[113] cf. *Ali (Yasir)* [2015] EWCA Crim 1279, at [79].
[114] cf. *Hansard,* Vol.648, col.210 (May 13, 2003).
[115] [2005] EWCA Crim 3231, at [50].
[116] The offences in s.2 are crimes of intention; it is not sufficient to know or have reasonable cause to believe that the act in question will facilitate (etc). See further paras 11.110 and following, below.
[117] [2005] EWCA Crim 3231, at [25]–[29].
[118] [1972] 1 W.L.R. 1600.

that they could not be guilty of an offence of facilitating entry on the ground that the individuals had already entered by the time they were released. The Court reasoned that those who wish to enter illegally have no wish to be discovered as soon as they disembark, and effective plans for their illegal entry would involve plans for their getting away from the port, undiscovered, as soon as possible. No doubt the same analysis will be applied in relation to the offences in s.2 of the 2015 Act.

<h3 style="text-align:center">"TRAVEL"</h3>

11.100   Travel is defined for the purposes of s.2 as arriving in, entering, departing from or travelling within any country.[119] In *Ali (Yasir)*,[120] the Court of Appeal had to consider whether, applying the *de minimis* principle, a very short car journey was sufficient to constitute "travel" for the purposes of the repealed trafficking offence in s.58 of the Sexual Offences Act 2003. The Court said[121]:

> "In our view the key factor in the present context is that travel—a journey—is contemplated and the fact that it may be short does not affect whether or not the offence is committed. The judge correctly observed that the appellant was the driver of the car on each occasion, and in that sense there was clear evidence that he intentionally arranged or facilitated travel. It is self-evident that walking, for instance, between adjacent rooms, or other journeys involving truly minimal distances (for instance of a few feet or yards) may well be outside the ambit of this provision because there is a clear geographical element to this offence; but in the present case, substantive journeys took place involving a number of miles. The legislation does not specify a minimum distance or duration for the travel or journey, no doubt because victims can be 'trafficked' within or across a small area or locality. The cases before our courts indicate that victims are exploited in this way within small, tight-knit communities, and it would unjustifiably undermine the reach of this statutory provision to introduce a requirement that journeys over a specified distance or time need to be contemplated or covered before a person is 'trafficked' for the purposes of sexual exploitation. It would lead to absurdity to try to stipulate, for instance, a minimum number of miles, or that the journey must be planned with a clear destination, before the provision is engaged. On the evidence, this count was properly left to the jury."

<h3 style="text-align:center">"EXPLOITATION"</h3>

11.101   Section 3 of the Modern Slavery Act 2015 defines "exploitation" for the purposes of s.2 as follows:

> "(1) For the purposes of section 2 a person is exploited only if one or more of the following subsections apply in relation to the person.

---

[119] s.2(5).
[120] [2015] EWCA Crim 1279.
[121] At [80] per Fulford LJ.

Slavery, servitude and forced or compulsory labour

(2) The person is the victim of behaviour—
  (a) which involves the commission of an offence under section 1, or
  (b) which would involve the commission of an offence under that section if it took place in England and Wales.

Sexual exploitation

(3) Something is done to or in respect of the person—
  (a) which involves the commission of an offence under—
    (i) section 1(1)(a) of the Protection of Children Act 1978 (indecent photographs of children), or
    (ii) Part 1 of the Sexual Offences Act 2003 (sexual offences), as it has effect in England and Wales, or
  (b) which would involve the commission of such an offence if it were done in England and Wales.

Removal of organs etc

(4) The person is encouraged, required or expected to do anything—
  (a) which involves the commission, by him or her or another person, of an offence under section 32 or 33 of the Human Tissue Act 2004 (prohibition of commercial dealings in organs and restrictions on use of live donors) as it has effect in England and Wales, or
  (b) which would involve the commission of such an offence, by him or her or another person, if it were done in England and Wales.

Securing services etc by force, threats or deception

(5) The person is subjected to force, threats or deception designed to induce him or her—
  (a) to provide services of any kind,
  (b) to provide another person with benefits of any kind, or
  (c) to enable another person to acquire benefits of any kind.

Securing services etc from children and vulnerable persons

(6) Another person uses or attempts to use the person for a purpose within paragraph (a), (b) or (c) of subsection (5), having chosen him or her for that purpose on the grounds that—
  (a) he or she is a child, is mentally or physically ill or disabled, or has a family relationship with a particular person, and
  (b) an adult, or a person without the illness, disability, or family relationship, would be likely to refuse to be used for that purpose."

Accordingly, for the purpose of s.2 a person is to be regarded as having been **11.102** "exploited" if and only if one of the five subsections applies, namely slavery, servitude or forced compulsory labour; sexual exploitation; removal of organs; the use of force, threats or deception to induce them to provide services; or in the case of a child or a person vulnerable by reason of age, disability or family relationship, their use to provide services where someone without that vulnerability would be likely to refuse. Exploitation by the securing of services expressly covers services of any kind and also the provision of benefits of any kind to another or enabling another to acquire such benefits, provided the services are secured by use of force, threats or deception or from a child or vulnerable person. It is irrelevant whether the provision of the services in itself constitutes a criminal offence.

11.103   Consequently, the offence of human trafficking for the purpose of sexual exploitation is committed pursuant to s.2 read with s.3(3). Sexual exploitation is defined as something done to or in respect of the victim which involves an offence of taking, permitting to take or making an indecent photograph of a child, or an offence within Pt 1 of the Sexual Offences Act 2003, which includes rape, the child sex offences, and the offences of child sexual exploitation and of adult prostitution. Section 3(3)(b) provides that conduct of this sort that takes place outside England and Wales also constitutes sexual exploitation for this purpose, although for jurisdictional reasons the index offence could not be prosecuted in England and Wales. So a rape intended to be committed outside the jurisdiction may be taken into account as sexual exploitation for the purposes of the human trafficking offence, despite it not being possible to prosecute the rape itself here.

11.104   The overlap between the s.1 and s.2 offences is clearly indicated in s.3, which appears to define "exploitation" only for the purposes of s.2 (human trafficking) but in doing so makes reference back to s.1 (slavery etc.). A concern has been raised that by restricting the definition of exploitation to the s.2 offences, the Act creates a loophole as far as s.1 is concerned. As observed above, however, this point is dealt with by s.1(4), which expressly provides that in determining whether a person is being held in slavery or servitude etc., regard may be had to circumstances that constitute exploitation under s.3(3) to (6). It is nonetheless fair comment that the end result is perhaps a little cumbersome.

11.105   Peter Carter QC and Riel Karmy-Jones QC have observed that "it seems a little anomalous that the Act does not make 'exploitation' an offence in its own right", given that the gravamen of the offences under ss.1 and 2 really lies in the nature of the treatment of the victim and the exploitation to which they are subjected. The fact that there is no stand-alone offence of exploitation has been said to be serious flaw, especially in relation to trafficking cases where the transportation of the victim may be difficult to evidence, perhaps because it took place a long time ago or the victim has no clear memory of it—as may be the case with a child—even though the exploitation element can be proven. Indeed, the Act has come under particular attack from those specifically concerned with the welfare of children, who fought for the creation of a specific offence of child exploitation even if one was not created for adults. The difficulty with creating a child exploitation offence lies in confining the scope of the offence to activity that can properly be described as criminal, rather than as falling within the scope of other areas of law such as family law. There would also be a risk that different judges and juries could reach inconsistent conclusions as to what conditions are sufficiently serious to amount to criminal "exploitation", resulting in conflicting decisions that could bring the law into disrepute. Further, there is already a series of offences that deal with different factual scenarios that might amount to child exploitation, e.g. the offences of wilful neglect and cruelty under the Children and Young Persons Act 1933, the offences in the Offences Against the Person Act 1861 and begging offences.[122]

The question of whether an offence of exploitation is necessary or feasible **11.106** was considered by the Joint Select Committee on the Modern Slavery Bill and raised by others in Parliament during debates on the Bill. The complexity of the question was recognised, as were the difficulties in defining the proper extent of any such offence, the fact that it would cross different areas of law and the fact that legislation was already in place to deal with the main scenarios envisaged. In all the circumstances, it was decided that there was no need for such an offence. The reasons are understandable, but the point may require further consideration in the future. Modern slavery and trafficking is a form of offending that is constantly evolving, and this aspect of it is particularly important where it relates to those who are especially vulnerable, for example by reason of their age or mental ability/incapacity.[123]

"IN ANY PART OF THE WORLD"

It is irrelevant where in the world the person arranging or facilitating the **11.107** travel intends the exploitation to take place.[124]

CONSENT

Section 2(2) provides that it is irrelevant whether the victim consents to their **11.108** travel. As with the similar provision in s.1, this is not a change from the law as previously established by the authorities, but its incorporation into the legislation is a significant advance. It must however be recognised that there is sometimes an overlap between the questions of the victim's consent and the defendant's intention, so consent may nonetheless become an issue at trial. See para.11.111, below.

VICTIM SUPPORT

For special measures and other mechanisms to support victims, see paras **11.109** 11.68 and following, above.

MENTAL ELEMENT

The defendant must engage in the prohibited conduct "with a view to V **11.110** being exploited". The mental element of the previous offence under s.59A of

---

[122] Peter Carter QC and Riel Karmy-Jones QC, Lexis Nexis interview, May 14, 2015.
[123] Peter Carter QC and Riel Karmy-Jones QC, Lexis Nexis interview, May 14, 2015.
[124] s.2(4).

the Sexual Offences Act 2003 was expressed as a requirement that the defendant acted intentionally. The change of wording in the new Act is unlikely to have any practical impact.[125] This proposition derives support from a direction given to the jury by HHJ Topolski QC in a recent human trafficking case tried under s.59A at the Central Criminal Court[126]:

> "trafficking involves the transportation of a person into the UK, intending that at the time of doing so, that is at the time of their arrival, they should be exploited. It is not a form of kidnapping. The victim may want to come to the UK and indeed may agree to do so. Therefore, the agreement or consent of the trafficked person is irrelevant. At the heart of the definition of trafficking is that it is something that is done *with the intention* of exploitation."

11.111   Whilst the complainant's consent is irrelevant to the question whether or not they have been trafficked for the purposes of s.2, it is nonetheless something that may go to the question of the defendant's intent: i.e. if the defendant believes that the complainant is consenting to the travel and subsequent work that they are made to undertake, can it be said that he is acting with a view to exploiting them? The Court of Appeal considered the issue of consent in *Ali (Yasir)*[127] when dismissing an appeal against conviction for sexual offences committed against children, including rape and trafficking within the UK for sexual exploitation contrary to s.59A of the 2003 Act. It held that where a vulnerable or immature individual had allegedly been subjected to grooming for sexual purposes, the question of whether real or proper consent had been given will usually be for the jury to decide, unless the evidence clearly indicated that proper consent had been given.

11.112   In the unreported case of *Mohammed Khubaib*, charged under s.59A, there was an application to dismiss at half-time on the question of the defendants' intention to commit a relevant offence.[128] It was common ground that the actus reus of the offence was arranging or facilitating travel, and that there must be an intention to commit a relevant offence at the time of arranging or facilitating as opposed to an intention formed later, for example when an opportunity presented itself after the journey.[129] It was argued by the defence that the trafficking offence does not permit what is described as a "conditional intention", namely an intention to commit an offence "if the opportunity arose". Rather, it was suggested that the travel must have a particular purpose, namely as the necessary precursor to the commission of

---

[125] cf. *Graham-Kerr* [1988] 1 W.L.R. 1098, holding that the words "with a view to" in s.1(1)(c) of the Protection of Children Act 1978 involve a requirement of intention.
[126] *Suchy, Sana, Sanova, Ziga, Ziga and Boros*, CCC, June 2015. The reference in the direction to trafficking involving the transportation of a person "into the UK" reflects the facts of the case rather than the scope of the law, which is of course much wider.
[127] [2015] EWCA Crim 1279, discussed in paras 1.194 and following, above.
[128] In that case, an offence under s.9 or s.10 of the Sexual Offences Act 2003.
[129] Consideration was given to *Gaviria* [2010] EWCA Crim 1693, relating to the elements of the grooming offence under s.15 of the Sexual Offences Act 2003: see para.4.221, above. But that simply underlined that for the purposes of s.15 the mens rea must coincide with actus reus, and so an intent formed only when an opportunity arose would not be sufficient.

a sexual offence, not as a precursor to creating the possibility of committing an offence. The prosecution contended that nothing in the 2003 Act prevented the interpretation of the requisite intention as being "an intention to commit a relevant offence should the occasion arise", which, it was submitted, was in line with the approach taken in other areas of the criminal law such as s.16 of the Firearms Act 1968, the law of offensive weapons and burglary. In his ruling, HHJ Rook QC held that the better view was the approach suggested by the prosecution, provided that intent is established at the time of the arranging. He also found that there is no reason why the normal rules as to secondary liability should not apply. Thus where two defendants, X and Y, are both charged with trafficking a particular person on the same occasion, X can be guilty either if he intended to commit a relevant offence or if he knew Y intended to commit a relevant offence and he intended to assist or encourage Y to do so.

It is not necessary for the prosecution to prove that a person charged under s.2 acted for the purposes of gain. **11.113**

COMMITTING AN OFFENCE WITH INTENT TO COMMIT A HUMAN TRAFFICKING OFFENCE

Section 4 of the Modern Slavery Act 2015 provides as follows: **11.114**

> "A person commits an offence under this section if the person commits any offence with the intention of committing an offence under section 2 (including an offence committed by aiding, abetting, counselling or procuring an offence under that section)."

Section 4 brings within the ambit of the Act the commission of any offence in furtherance of the commission of an offence under s.2, which for this purpose includes an offence of aiding, abetting, counselling or procuring such an offence. By way of example, this means that a comparatively minor offence, such as the theft of a motor vehicle, will be caught by s.4 if it is committed with the intention that the vehicle will be used to traffic a victim. The effect is that the court will have the power to impose the higher sentence in s.5 for that offence.

MODE OF TRIAL AND PUNISHMENT

The s.4 offence is triable either way. It carries a maximum sentence of 10 years' imprisonment on conviction on indictment except where it is committed by kidnapping or false imprisonment, when the maximum sentence is increased to imprisonment for life.[130] Like the offences in ss.1 and 2 of the Act, it is punishable on summary conviction by six months' imprisonment or a fine, or both. The maximum sentence of imprisonment will increase to 12 **11.115**

---

[130] s.5(3).

months when s.154(1) of the Criminal Justice Act 2003 comes into force.[131]

MENTAL ELEMENT

11.116   The offender must commit the index offence with the intention of committing a human trafficking offence under s.2 of the Act. Section 4 is not engaged if he intends that a s.2 offence will be committed by someone else.

POWERS AVAILABLE UNDER THE MODERN SLAVERY ACT 2015

SLAVERY AND TRAFFICKING REPARATION ORDERS

11.117   Although ss.130–134 of the Powers of Criminal Courts (Sentencing) Act 2000 already provide for the making of compensation orders, it was noted by the drafters of the 2015 Act that those powers have rarely been used in human trafficking cases. Sections 8 to 10 of the Act provide that a court may make a slavery and trafficking reparation order (in effect a compensation order[132]) against a person convicted under s.1, 2 or 4 of the Act if a confiscation order under s.6 of the Proceeds of Crime Act 2002 is made in respect of the relevant offence.[133] This enables the court to order specific reparation in respect of the exploitation and degradation suffered by the victim.[134] The court must consider making a reparation order in any case where it has the power to make one, even where an application is not made.[135] If the court considers that it is not appropriate to make such an order, it must give reasons.[136] In deciding whether to make such an order, and in what amount to make it, the court must have regard to the offender's means.[137] If the court considers that it would be appropriate to impose both a fine and a reparation order, but the defendant has insufficient funds, priority is to be given to the reparation order.[138] A reparation order may be made after sentence is imposed, and there is a power to amend a sentence in order to make a reparation order.[139] However, if the reparation order is made as against someone who has already been sentenced, the date of the person's sentence is to be regarded as the date the reparation order was imposed for the purpose of any relevant appeal time limits.[140]

[131] s.5(2), (4).
[132] s.9.
[133] s.8(8)(b) and (c).
[134] See Explanatory Notes, para.48.
[135] s.8(7)(a).
[136] s.8(7)(b).
[137] s.8(5).
[138] ss.8(6) and 9(5).
[139] s.8(3).
[140] s.10(2).

Forfeiture and Detention of Land Vehicles, Ships and Aircraft

Under s.11 of the 2015 Act, where a person is convicted of a s.2 offence of **11.118** human trafficking, the court may in certain circumstances order the forfeiture of any land vehicle, ship or aircraft used or intended to be used in connection with the offence.[141] Section 12 provides for the detention of the same on a person's arrest pursuant to s.2. Where a person claims to have an interest in a vehicle etc. that is the subject of the application, the court must give them an opportunity to be heard before ordering forfeiture.

It should be noted that although the Act devotes a considerable amount of **11.119** legislative space to the subject of marine enforcement, it says nothing about crossing the Channel by tunnel or entering the country by air. The effectiveness of the maritime provision will depend on the resources made available for enforcement and a qualitative assessment as to whether invoking the powers is proportionate and worth the expenditure in each case. It must be remembered that trafficking persons under the 2015 Act is not the same as smuggling people or refugees into the country so as to avoid immigration, and to date cases of mass trafficking as defined by the Act are rare, bordering on non-existent.[142]

Slavery and Trafficking Prevention Orders

Although there is no provision for a person convicted under s.2 to be subject **11.120** to the notification requirements of Pt 2 of the Sexual Offences Act 2003, the Act makes provision (in ss.14–22 and Sch.1) for the court to impose a new form of order, a slavery and trafficking prevention order ("STPO") upon those convicted of a s.1 or s.2 offence. An STPO may be made where the court is satisfied that there is a risk that the offender may commit further such offences, and it is necessary to make the order for the purpose of protecting persons generally, or particular persons, from the physical or psychological harm which would be likely to occur if the defendant committed such an offence.[143] In addition to prohibiting an offender from doing certain things, an STPO may also impose a positive requirement on the offender to provide their name and address to a person specified in the order.[144] The Home Office Circular published in advance of the Act stated that the purpose of these orders is to prevent, restrict or disrupt a person's involvement in slavery or human trafficking offences.[145] The Explanatory Notes to the Act state that the rationale for creating the orders is to enable law enforcement bodies and the courts to take tougher action against those

[141] s.11.
[142] Peter Carter QC and Riel Karmy-Jones QC, Lexis Nexis Interview, May 14, 2015.
[143] s.14.
[144] s.19.
[145] Home Office Circular 24/2015, para.38.

involved in trafficking, and to protect individuals from the harm caused by slavery or trafficking by preventing further offending.[146]

11.121   An STPO may be imposed on sentence for a slavery or human trafficking offence[147] or on application by a chief officer of police in respect of an offender who lives in the officer's area or who the officer believes is in the area or intending to come to it.[148] Application may also be made by an immigration officer or the Director General of the National Crime Agency,[149] who must give notice of the application to the chief of police for a relevant police area.[150]

11.122   The effect of an STPO is to prohibit the offender from doing anything described in the order.[151] The only prohibitions that may be included are those which the court is satisfied are necessary for the purpose of protecting persons generally, or particular persons, from the physical or psychological harm which would be likely to occur if the defendant committed a slavery or human trafficking offence.[152] The potential ambit of such an order is intentionally wide. It may include such prohibitions as preventing a person from participating in a particular type of business, working in a particular type of job, visiting a particular place, working with children, or travelling to a specified country.[153] An STPO can prohibit a defendant from doing things not only in the UK, but anywhere in the world, including by prohibiting travel in an area outside the jurisdiction.[154] An order may have effect for a fixed period of at least five years or until further order.[155] Different prohibitions may specify different time periods.[156] An order can be made against an offender who is under the age of 18. In such a case, the application will be heard in the youth court.

11.123   Section 18 provides that there may be a specific prohibition on foreign travel outside the UK for a fixed period of not more than five years. The prohibition may be on travelling to any country outside the UK named or described in the order; travelling to any country outside the UK other than a country so named or described; or travelling to any other country whatsoever. The five year period may be extended under s.20, which allows for an STPO to be varied, renewed or discharged on application. If a prohibition on travelling to any other country is imposed, the court must also require the offender to surrender all passports in their possession to the

---

[146] Explanatory Notes para.69.
[147] s.14. The relevant offences are listed in Sch.1 to the Act, and include offences under the repealed legislation.
[148] s.15(4).
[149] s.15.
[150] s.15(7). The term "relevant police area" is defined in s.15(8).
[151] s.17(1).
[152] s.17(2).
[153] See Explanatory Notes, para.80.
[154] *Suchy, Ziga, Ziga and Boros*, CCC, January 16, 2016: see para.11.127, below.
[155] s.17(3), (4).
[156] s.17(5).

police.[157] Section 19 provides that the court may also include a requirement that the offender notify a specified person of his name and address, and any changes to these within the specified period, within three days of such order being made. Application may be made for variation, renewal or discharge of a prevention order under s.20, and the court must not discharge an order before the five year period is concluded without the consent of the defendant and the chief officer of police of the area where the defendant lives,[158] unless the discharge relates to a prohibition on travel.[159] Section 22 of the Act confers a right of appeal against such an order to the Crown Court or the Court of Appeal, depending on which court made the STPO.

Where an application for an STPO has yet to be determined, an interim order may be made against a defendant prohibiting him from doing anything described in the order, within or outside the UK, and may also impose notification requirements upon the defendant in accordance with s.19. The court may make such an order before the main application is dealt with where it considers it necessary for the purpose of protecting a person from immediate harm pending the full determination of the application for the order, and it is just to do so.[160] **11.124**

Under s.30, a person who, without reasonable excuse, does anything that they are prohibited from doing by an STPO, including failing to notify as required, commits an either way offence. The maximum punishment on indictment is five years' imprisonment and on summary conviction is imprisonment for six months or a fine, or both. **11.125**

The Home Office has issued guidance on STPOs accompanied by pro-forma applications. These are available at *https://www.gov.uk/government/ publications/slavery-and-trafficking-prevention-and-risk-orders*. **11.126**

It will be interesting to see how STPOs work in practice. Bearing in mind the international dimension of many trafficking offences, it may well be challenging to draft prohibitive measures that are not only reasonable and proportionate, but also capable of being policed and prosecuted if breached. Few such orders have as yet been made. Extra-territorial prohibitions were first imposed at the Central Criminal Court in January 2016 in *Suchy, Ziga, Ziga, and Boros*. In a carefully reasoned judgment, HHJ Topolski QC concluded: **11.127**

> "(i) There is no doubt that the powers conferred by sec. 14 of The Modern Slavery Act are draconian and they are clearly intended to be so. It would I suspect surprise many to be told that this court is now possessed of a power to exclude a foreign national from a part of his home town at the conclusion of a prison sentence served in this country. It is clear that the rationale behind the creation of these new orders is to enable law enforcement bodies and courts to take tougher action against those involved in trafficking people. It is in my judgment equally clear that the purpose of these orders is to prevent slavery and

[157] s.18(4)–(6).
[158] s.19(6).
[159] s.19(7).
[160] s.21.

human trafficking offences being committed by people who have already committed such offences and indeed punished for them.

(ii) The despicable trade in human beings is a source of very considerable national and international attention and anxiety. Legislators across Europe have created a set of international obligations, and no doubt as part of that developing concern, the UK Parliament has enacted the 2015 Act and introduced the provision under which this court is invited to make the orders in relation to these defendants.

. . .

(vi) Each of these defendants in my judgment poses a serious risk of reoffending and consequently I find that there is a risk that each of them may commit slavery or human trafficking offences in the future.

(vii) I am also entirely satisfied that it is necessary to make orders for the purpose of protecting not just their known victims but also persons generally, that is to say, other potential victims, from the physical or psychological harm which would be likely to occur if any or all of these defendants committed a slavery or human trafficking offence in the future.

(viii) As regards the extra territorial nature of the proposed orders. I am satisfied that this is not a disproportionate response. The Act provides that an order may prohibit a defendant from doing things in any part of the UK and anywhere outside the UK. I accept the submission that an STPO is particularly appropriate where, as here, a particular area in a town in a foreign jurisdiction has been one where these defendants have operated to recruit their victims. I accept the evidence I have read provided by a victim who gave evidence, when she speaks of her genuine fear at the prospect of even seeing a member of the Suchy or Ziga family.

(ix) I do not accept that the Article 8 rights of Tibor Suchy or Josef Ziga will be infringed. The law permits limitations to be placed upon this very important right where it is appropriate, proportionate and necessary. Tibor Suchy has effectively conceded that he would be willing and able to locate elsewhere and so not return to Lunic 9. Josef Ziga can easily see his estranged child and its mother wherever he wishes but will not be able to do so within the confines of what is in effect a single housing estate on the edge of town. Given the evidence of the activities of this criminal enterprise in other parts of Kosice it may be said that the application to restrict these defendants just from Lunic 9 is generous.

(x) I do not find that the issue of so called proof of enforceability and the associated issue of extradition are, taken separately or together, prerequisites for the making of any order, still less are they determinative of these applications. The Act is silent on enforceability. It expressly permits that the reach of an order can be extra territorial, provided that the court finds that the making of the order is necessary and that its terms are proportionate and reasonable. The guidance provided makes it perfectly clear that the nature of any prohibition is a matter for the court to determine, once of course the criteria are satisfied.

(xi) If I am wrong about that and enforceability is a prerequisite, I am satisfied that the prosecution have clearly demonstrated that the order would indeed be enforceable and that extradition proceedings would be available in the event of a breach. I find therefore that a sec. 30 offence under the 2015 Act would be an extraditable offence.

(xii) Finally, as to enforceability, I am satisfied based upon all the material before me that it is appropriate for this court to proceed upon the basis that it can assume that the Republic of Slovakia can and will, as it has demonstrated in this case already, fulfil its international obligations.

(xiii) In reaching the clear conclusion that it is appropriate to grant the orders sought in the case of each defendant, I have sought to follow an approach that gives effect to this new legislation. I find that the intention of the Modern Slavery Act and the terms in which it is expressed is clear, and provides this court with the power to impose the extra territorial restrictions upon these defendants that are sought in the applications which are therefore granted in each case."

SLAVERY AND TRAFFICKING RISK ORDERS

Sections 23–29 provide that on application by a chief officer of police, an immigration officer or the Director General of the National Crime Agency, a magistrates' court may make a slavery and trafficking risk order ("STRO") against a defendant who has not yet been convicted.[161] The court must be satisfied that the defendant has acted in a way which means that there is a risk that they will commit a slavery or human trafficking offence, and that it is necessary to make the order for the purpose of protecting persons generally, or particular persons, from the physical or psychological harm which would be likely to occur if the defendant committed such an offence.[162] An STRO may place prohibitions on the defendant for at least two years or until further order,[163] and may also include a prohibition on foreign travel of up to five years,[164] similar in effect to the provisions in respect of slavery and trafficking prevention orders. Applications to vary, renew or discharge STROs may be made pursuant to s.27, and s.29 confers a right of appeal to the Crown Court. **11.128**

Under s.30, a person who, without reasonable excuse, does anything that they are prohibited from doing by an STRO, including failing to notify as required, commits an either way offence. The maximum punishment on indictment is five years' imprisonment and on summary conviction is imprisonment for six months or a fine, or both. **11.129**

The Home Office has issued guidance on STROs accompanied by pro-forma applications. These are available at *https://www.gov.uk/government/publications/slavery-and-trafficking-prevention-and-risk-orders*. **11.130**

STROs could be put to good effect as a warning system in cases where there is some evidence of involvement in slavery or trafficking but it is insufficient to prosecute, for example in cases of sexual exploitation where a victim makes an initial complaint but is unwilling to make formal allegations, or to engage with criminal proceedings. They could also be made against individuals who appear to be using either their own or other children as part of a begging network. In terms of process, the Explanatory Notes state[165]: **11.131**

> "Consideration of the application is a two stage process (although both can take place at the same hearing). Firstly, the Court must be satisfied so that it is sure that behaviour giving rise to the application took place. This means that the enhanced civil standard of proof, which is akin to the criminal standard of being

[161] s.23(1).
[162] s.23(2).
[163] s.24(1), (4) MSA '15.
[164] s.25(1).
[165] Para.5.2.5; see also para.3.3.5.

sure beyond reasonable doubt, applies. If a person has previously been convicted of one or more offences, the Court will normally accept proof of these convictions as evidence of the behaviour which formed the basis of those convictions. If not, then evidence of the alleged behaviour will need to be put before the Court. Once the Court has decided that the relevant behaviour has taken place, the Court must be satisfied that it is necessary to make the Order applied for to protect persons or a person from harm. For the second part of this process exercises its judgment *and is not applying a particular standard of proof* (see *R v Manchester Crown Court ex parte McCann* [2002] UKHL 39, as per Lord Steyn at paragraph 37)".

11.132   One possible failing in the legislation is that there is no power for a Crown Court judge who has tried a case to make an STRO in respect of a defendant who has been acquitted of a trafficking charge but convicted of an ancillary charge such as an offence under s.25 of the Immigration Act 1971. The judge may therefore be satisfied that the offender has acted in a way which means that there is a risk that they will commit a human trafficking offence in the future, but unable to impose an order so as to seek to prevent this.

CHAPTER 12

BROTHEL KEEPING AND RELATED OFFENCES

Introduction...................................... 12.01	Tenant Permitting Premises to Be	
Keeping a Brothel............................. 12.21	Used for Prostitution 12.76	
Keeping a Brothel used for	Keeping a Disorderly House 12.85	
Prostitution.................................... 12.42	Allowing a Person under 16 to Be	
Landlord Letting Premises for Use	in a Brothel 12.97	
as a Brothel.................................. 12.57	Knowingly Permitting Prostitutes	
Tenant Permitting Premises to Be	to Meet and Remain in House of	
Used as a Brothel......................... 12.65	Refreshment 12.104	

INTRODUCTION

The law relating to brothels, or the provision of sexual services in a building **12.01** or other premises, is one of the least-reformed areas of the law of sexual offences. It comprises a rag-bag of archaic offences that proceed on the basis that brothels, or perhaps more accurately their functioning, are an offensive nuisance that needs to be suppressed. As it is not an offence to engage in prostitution or, as yet, to seek the services of a prostitute, the law focuses on those who run or manage a brothel or allow premises to be used as one.

DEVELOPMENT OF THE LAW

Sexual Offences Act 1956

The law relating to brothels is still regulated by the Sexual Offences Act 1956, **12.02** which makes it an offence:
- for any person to keep, manage or act or assist in the management of a brothel (s.33),
- for any person to keep, manage or act or assist in the management of a brothel to which people resort for practices involving prostitution (s.33A),
- for a landlord to let premises to be used as a brothel, or to be wilfully a party to such use continuing (s.34),

865

- for a tenant knowingly to permit premises to be used as a brothel (s.35), and
- for a tenant knowingly to permit premises to be used for the purposes of habitual prostitution (s.36).

12.03 The notable feature of this scheme is the significant overlap between the brothel keeping offences in s.33 and s.33A. The offences are of very different gravity. Section 33 creates a purely summary offence punishable on first conviction with a fine of up to £1,000 and, on a subsequent conviction, with up to six months' imprisonment. By contrast, s.33A creates an "either way" offence with a maximum penalty of seven years' imprisonment on indictment. The explanation of the overlap between the offences lies in the history of the Sexual Offences Act 2003, by which s.33A was introduced.[1] The then Government's original intention was simply to increase the maximum penalty for the s.33 offence to bring it into line with the penalties for the offences relating to exploitation of adult prostitution created in ss.52 and 53 of the 2003 Act. The driver for the change was concern expressed by the police that it might not be possible to prove the elements of those offences, particularly the "control" required by s.53, in a case where the owner of a brothel exploits prostitutes at the premises but puts himself at a distance from the actual running of the establishment. The Government's plan was accordingly to raise the maximum penalty for the s.33 offence, to ensure that another serious offence was available for use against those who exploit prostitutes in this way.[2] Shortly before the Bill's enactment, however, the Government decided instead to create the offence in s.33A and leave s.33 unaffected. The reason for the change of tack was that the term "brothel" is not, as we shall see, confined to cases where prostitution takes place but is also capable of covering premises where people go for non-commercial sexual encounters, such as certain saunas and adult clubs. The Government's policy intention was limited to places where prostitution takes place, and so it decided to create the s.33A offence to cover such places and to leave s.33 for use in cases where the brothel is not used for prostitution.[3]

Other offences

12.04 There are, in addition to the offences in the 1956 Act, a number of offences of more limited application that are relevant in this context:
- the common law offence of keeping a disorderly house. This does not require proof that the premises were a "brothel", and so the activities even of a single prostitute may fall within its scope,
- the offence of allowing a person under 16 to be in a brothel, contrary to s.3 of the Children and Young Persons Act 1933, and

[1] See s.55 of the 2003 Act, which came into force on May 1, 2004.
[2] *Hansard*, HC Vol.412, col.545 (November 3, 2003), Paul Goggins MP.
[3] *Hansard*, HL Vol.654, col.1638 (November 13, 2003), Baroness Scotland of Asthal.

- the summary offences applicable only in London of permitting prostitutes to meet and remain in a house of refreshment, contrary to s.44 of the Metropolitan Police Act 1839 and s.28 of the City of London Police Act 1839.

The London-focused offences mentioned in the last paragraph were **12.05** principally designed to prevent prostitutes from congregating in licensed premises. They penalise the keeper of the premises, not the prostitutes. Further, the prostitutes need not be present for the purpose of prostitution or soliciting; it is sufficient that they congregate on the premises. Until quite recently there were a number of other summary offences to similar effect, the application of which was not confined to London.[4] The Wolfenden Report recommended the retention of these offences[5] and subsequent legislation increased the maximum penalties for them.[6] But Wolfenden also suggested that the offences should be enforced only where the prostitutes' presence gave offence to other users of the premises or to neighbouring residents, since the presence of prostitutes in pubs and cafés known to be their haunt reduced the problem of prostitution on the streets. The offences were repealed by the Licensing Act 2003,[7] which reformed the licensing regime for liquor, entertainment, night cafés, late night refreshment houses, theatres and cinemas. The Act created no successor offence relating directly to prostitution, though it does contain (in s.140) an offence of knowingly allowing disorderly conduct on licensed premises. That offence falls outside the scope of this work and is not considered here.

A Coordinated Prostitution Strategy (2006)

The Sexual Offences Review, which reported in 2000, made recommenda- **12.06** tions for changes to the law of sexual offences that were substantially implemented by the Sexual Offences Act 2003. In the course of its work the Review heard a range of evidence on the law relating to prostitution, including from groups that argued for radical reform through decriminalisation and/or moving the law's focus from the providers of sexual services to the purchasers. The Review considered that the important issues of social policy raised by this evidence fell outside its remit, and accordingly confined itself to recommending that there should be a further review of the law on prostitution.[8] In the 2002 White Paper, *Protecting the Public*, the Government said it would examine the scope for a review of the issues surrounding prostitution and associated exploitation, organised criminality and class "A"

[4] Licensing Act 1964 ss.175, 176; Town Police Clauses Act 1847 s.35; Late Night Refreshment Houses Act 1969 s.9(1).
[5] Cmnd. 247 (1957), para.351.
[6] Street Offences Act 1959 s.3.
[7] s.199 and Sch.7. The repeals took effect on November 24, 2005.
[8] *Setting the Boundaries* (Home Office, July 2000), para.7.8. The report is available at *http://webarchive.nationalarchives.gov.uk/-/http://www.homeoffice.gov.uk/documents/vol1main.pdf?view=Binary* [Accessed April 30, 2016].

drug abuse.[9] Accordingly, in July 2004, the Home Office published *Paying the Price: a Consultation Paper on Prostitution*, which was intended to be "the starting point for the development of a realistic and coherent strategy to deal with prostitution".[10] It was in relation to off-street prostitution that the responses to *Paying the Price* were most divided. The essential question posed in the paper was: should the off-street market be managed or policed? Some respondents argued for decriminalisation and others for regimes of licensing or registration, but the majority were sceptical of the ability of such regimes to reduce violence and exploitation. There were concerns based on evidence from overseas that providers of sexual services who were unwilling or unable to comply with such a regime would be driven into an illegal sector or onto the streets, where it would be harder to address the issues represented by their activities. There were also fears that, if licensing or registration were introduced, both the legal and illegal sectors would grow as a result of an increasing acceptance of prostitution.

12.07   Against that background, the Government decided broadly to maintain the current legal regime relating to off-street prostitution. But in the paper published following the consultation, *A Coordinated Prostitution Strategy*,[11] it announced the intention to make one significant change. This was to address a concern that the current definition of a "brothel" as premises where two or more women work together, gives an incentive to prostitutes to work in isolation, which in turn inhibits their ability to protect themselves from violence. The Government noted significant support from respondents for a change in the law to allow two or three women to work together without the premises becoming a "brothel", and it undertook to bring forward legislation to effect this change.

12.08   This proposal is an important one given the vulnerability of women working alone to offences of violence, including robbery. It is, however, at least potentially in tension with two of the key objectives of the *Strategy*, namely to "reduce all forms of criminal sexual exploitation" and to "improve the quality of life of communities". Amending the law on brothel keeping so as exclude from the definition of a "brothel" premises in which two or three prostitutes sell sexual services would necessarily create greater scope for the commercial exploitation of the individuals concerned. As for the quality of life of communities, this is affected by nuisance behaviour, and it is inevitable that such behaviour is more likely to be associated with premises where two or three prostitutes work than those where one prostitute works alone. Fiona Mactaggart, the Home Office minister who announced the strategy, was quoted as saying that there would have to be more consultation over how to

[9] *Protecting the Public: strengthening protection against sex offenders and reforming the law on sexual offences* (Cm 5668) (Nov 2002), para.73.

[10] Home Secretary's Foreword, p.5. For discussion, see Belinda Brooks-Gordon, *Clients and Commercial Sex: Reflections on Paying the Price: a Consultation Paper on Prostitution* [2005] Crim. L.R. 425.

[11] January 2006 (Home Office). See *http://www.popcenter.org/problems/street_prostitution/PDFs/Home%20Office_prostitution_2006.pdf* [Accessed April 30, 2016].

prevent adverse effects on neighbourhoods: "I'm not trying, by having a clear strategy in the street sex market, to move it from the streets to a series of pairs of women working out of flats and causing a nuisance to their neighbours. But I do think that very small-scale operations can operate in a way which is not disruptive to neighbours."[12] Matters have rested there, and legislation to narrow the definition of a "brothel" is yet to be introduced.

Tackling the Demand for Prostitution: A Review (2008)

In 2008, the Home Office launched a six month review to explore what **12.09** further action could be taken to reduce the demand for prostitution. It reported in November that year in *Tackling the Demand for Prostitution: A Review*. Its most significant recommendation was that the Government should consider creating a new offence to criminalise those who pay for sex, where the sex provider is being controlled against their wishes for someone else's gain. This recommendation was implemented by the Policing and Crime Act 2009, which inserted into the Sexual Offences Act 2003 a new offence (s.53A) of paying for the sexual services of a prostitute subjected to force. That offence is considered in Ch.10, above.

Since the publication of *Tackling the Demand for Prostitution*, the Govern- **12.10** ment's focus has been on practical approaches rather than on the law itself. Thus, in 2011 the Coalition Government published *A Review of Effective Practice in Responding to Prostitution*,[13] encouraging local authorities and community safety partnerships "to develop a response to prostitution that aims to improve the outcomes for the community and particularly those involved in prostitution". In relation to the policing response to off-street prostitution, the Review provides[14]:

> "While the approach to policing off-street prostitution may be different from that for street prostitution, it is important that an effective response is developed. In this respect a number of areas focus on the premises where sexual services are sold and that present a nuisance, or where exploitation, trafficking or the involvement of children is suspected. This highlights the need for areas to develop a definition of exploitation and a way of identifying and responding to it, including ensuring that support is in place for victims identified."

In December 2011, the Home Office launched a national "Ugly Mugs" **12.11** pilot scheme, run by the UK Network of Sex Work Projects ("UKNSWP"), to help protect sex workers from violent and abusive individuals. The

---

[12] *Times*, January 18, 2006.

[13] October 2011. See *https://www.gov.uk/government/uploads/system/uploads/attachment_data/file/97778/responding-to-prostitution.pdf* [Accessed April 30, 2016].

[14] paras 7.9–7.10. See also the *ACPO Strategy & Supporting Operational Guidance for Policing Prostitution and Sexual Exploitation* (November 2011), the purpose of which is to provide a framework for the policing of this area of the law. The Guidance is available at *http://www.npcc.police.uk/documents/crime/2011/20111102%20CBA%20Policing%20Prostitution%20and%20%20Sexual%20Exploitation%20Strategy_Website_October%202011.pdf* [Accessed April 30, 2016].

12-month pilot included establishing a national online network to bring together and support locally-run "Ugly Mug" schemes. These local "Ugly Mug" or "dodgy punter" schemes have been running for some years and have proved useful in passing on warnings to sex workers about dangerous people, as well as helping to increase the reporting and detection of crimes. Following the success of the pilot, UKNSWP was able to find funding to enable the scheme to continue: details can be found on the UKNSWP website.[15]

Where next? The Honeyball Report and the All-Party Parliamentary Group on Prostitution

12.12 At the time of writing, *Tackling the Demand for Prostitution* was the last major Government consideration of the law relating to prostitution. Further impetus towards law reform in this area has, however, been provided by two reports issued in early 2014. First, the Committee on Women's Rights and Gender Equality of the European Parliament published a *Report on sexual exploitation and prostitution and its impact on gender equality*, known as the *Honeyball Report*, which was approved by the European Parliament on February 3, 2014.[16] Secondly, in March 2014 the All-Party Parliamentary Group on Prostitution and the Global Sex Trade ("APPG") published a report on the law of prostitution.[17] Both reports are wide-ranging, covering child as well as adult prostitution and human trafficking for sexual purposes. In terms of the relationship between prostitution and the law, the reports both reject the model currently applied in the UK of primarily criminalising prostitutes rather than their clients. As the APPG report puts it:

> "those who sell sexual services carry the burden of criminality despite being those who are most vulnerable to coercion and violence."

The APPG called on all political parties, ahead of the 2015 election, to commit to a review of the law with a view to reducing the demand for sexual services, by transferring the burden of criminality from those selling sexual services onto those who facilitate or create the demand for their sale. It recommended a number of legislative changes, the key one being the abolition of the offences of soliciting and their replacement with a general offence of purchasing sexual services.

12.13 The APPG's approach chimes with the recommendation of the *Honeyball Report* in favour of what is often referred to as the "Nordic Model", under which the law criminalises the purchaser of sexual services but not the provider. The Report referred to the change made to Swedish law in 1999 so as to prohibit the purchase of sex and decriminalise the prostitute:

---

[15] *https://uknswp.org/uml* [Accessed April 30, 2016].
[16] 2013/2103(INI).
[17] *Shifting the Burden: Inquiry to assess the operation of the current legal settlement on prostitution in England and Wales* (March 2014). The Report is available at *https://appgprostitution.files.wordpress.com/2014/04/shifting-the-burden1.pdf* [Accessed April 30, 2016].

"Sweden's prostituted population is one-tenth of neighbouring Denmark's where sex purchase is legal and has [*sic*] a smaller population . . . The evidence of the effectiveness of the Nordic Model in reducing prostitution and trafficking of women and girls and thereby promoting gender equality is growing all the time."

Neither Report favours the third possible approach to the issue, namely decriminalisation and regulation of the adult sex trade while continuing to criminalise sex trafficking and child prostitution. Variations of this model may be found in Germany, the Netherlands and Denmark. The German Government reported in 2007 that decriminalisation had not led to improvements in the protection or operating conditions of sex workers.[18] The *Honeyball Report* states[19] that since decriminalisation the Netherlands has become a prime destination for human trafficking. But there remain strong voices in favour of decriminalisation. Most notably, in mid-2015 the human rights group Amnesty International, after a period of extensive research, came out in favour of the complete decriminalisation of consensual sex work.[20] The group's position attracted immediate criticism from those who favour for the Nordic model.[21]

At the time of writing there has been no formal response from Westminster   **12.14**
to these developments.

THE CANADIAN EXPERIENCE

Canada (Attorney General) v Bedford

The Canadian experience is of particular interest given the similarity between   **12.15**
the laws relating to prostitution in Canada and in England and Wales before the celebrated decision in *Canada (Attorney General) v Bedford*.[22] In that case, the Supreme Court of Canada struck down as unconstitutional the criminal prohibitions on bawdy-houses, living on the avails of prostitution and public communication for purposes of prostitution, on the ground that they violated the safety of prostitutes contrary to s.7 of the Charter of Fundamental Rights and Freedoms (which provides that the State cannot deny a person's right to life, liberty or security of the person except in accordance with the principles of fundamental justice). The unanimous (9–0) decision was suspended for one year to allow time for the Canadian

---

[18] C. MacKinnon, *Trafficking, Prostitution and Inequality* (2011) 46 Harvard Civil Rights-Civil Liberties Review 271, 304–6.

[19] pp.16–17.

[20] See *https://www.amnesty.org/en/latest/news/2015/08/global-movement-votes-to-adopt-policy-to-protect-human-rights-of-sex-workers/* [Accessed April 30, 2016]. For criticism by sex workers of the APPG report, see *http://prostitutescollective.net/2014/03/19/objections-from-the-ecp-to-the-methodology-content-of-the-report-from-the-appg-on-prostitution/* [Accessed April 30, 2016].

[21] See e.g. *http://www.theguardian.com/society/2015/jul/28/actors-streep-winslet-thompson-dunham-amnesty-decriminalisation-sex-trade* [Accessed April 30, 2016].

[22] [2013] SCC 72.

Parliament to devise another way to regulate the sex trade if it chose to do so.

12.16 The case was brought by one current and two former prostitutes who argued that sex workers would be safer if they were allowed to screen clients, or "johns", and operate in brothels with bodyguards if they chose. The safety of prostitutes became a high-profile issue in Canada following the conviction in 2007 of serial killer Robert Pickton, who preyed on prostitutes and other women in Vancouver's Downtown Eastside. Against that background, the Supreme Court found the existing prohibitions overly broad or grossly out of proportion to the law's goals. Beverley McLachlin CJ said that a law that banned what she called "safe havens" for prostitutes exposed them to risks from predators. She said many prostitutes had no choice but to work in the sex trade, and the law should not make their work more dangerous[23]:

> "The prohibitions at issue do not merely impose conditions on how prostitutes operate. They go a critical step further, by imposing *dangerous* conditions on prostitution; they prevent people engaged in a risky—but legal—activity from taking steps to protect themselves from the risks."

12.17 In relation to the prohibition on bawdy-houses, McLachlin CJ said[24]:

> "It is not an offence to sell sex for money. The bawdy-house provisions, however, make it an offence to do so in any 'place' that is 'kept or occupied' or 'resorted to' for the purpose of prostitution . . .
>
> The practical effect . . . is to confine lawful prostitution to two categories: street prostitution and out-calls . . . In-calls, where the john comes to the prostitute's residence, are prohibited. Out-calls, where the prostitute goes out and meets the client at a designated location, such as the client's home, are allowed. Working on the street is also permitted, though the practice of street prostitution is significantly limited by the prohibition on communicating in public . . .
>
> The application judge found, on a balance of probabilities, that the safest form of prostitution is working independently from a fixed location . . . She concluded that indoor work is far less dangerous than street prostitution—a finding that the evidence amply supports. She also concluded that out-call work is not as safe as in-call work, particularly under the current regime where prostitutes are precluded by virtue of the living on the avails provision from hiring a driver or security guard. Since the bawdy-house provision makes the safety-enhancing method of in-call prostitution illegal, the application judge concluded that the bawdy-house prohibition materially increased the risk prostitutes face under the present regime. I agree.
>
> First, the prohibition prevents prostitutes from working in a fixed indoor location, which would be safer than working on the streets or meeting clients at different locations, especially given the current prohibition on hiring drivers or security guards. This, in turn, prevents prostitutes from having a regular clientele and from setting up indoor safeguards like receptionists, assistants, bodyguards and audio room monitoring, which would reduce risks . . . Second, it interferes with provision of health checks and preventive health measures. Finally—a point developed in argument before us—the bawdy-house prohibition prevents resort to safe houses, to which prostitutes working on the street can take clients. In Vancouver, for example, 'Grandma's House' was established to support street

---

[23] At 60.
[24] At 61–65.

workers in the Downtown Eastside, at about the same time as fears were growing that a serial killer was prowling the streets—fears which materialized in the notorious Robert Pickton. Street prostitutes—who the application judge found are largely the most vulnerable class of prostitutes, and who face an alarming amount of violence—were able to bring clients to Grandma's House. However, charges were laid under [the bawdy-house provision] and although the charges were eventually stayed . . . Grandma's House was shut down . . . For some prostitutes, particularly those who are destitute, safe houses such as Grandma's House may be critical. For these people, the ability to work in brothels or hire security, even if those activities were lawful, may be illusory.

I conclude, therefore, that the bawdy-house provision negatively impacts the security of the person of prostitutes and engages s. 7 of the *Charter*."

As to the purpose of the prohibition, McLachlin CJ held that it was not directed at the mischief of prostitution per se but rather at the harm to the community in which prostitution is carried on in a notorious and habitual manner. But the harm imposed by the prohibition, as set out above, was grossly disproportionate to this purpose and accordingly the relevant provisions were unconstitutional. In so holding, McLachlin CJ dismissed the Canadian Government's argument that it is the prostitute's choice to engage in prostitution, rather than the laws that govern the activity, that puts the prostitute at risk[25]:

12.18

"First, while some prostitutes may fit the description of persons who freely choose (or at one time chose) to engage in the risky economic activity of prostitution, many prostitutes have no meaningful choice but to do so . . .

Second, even accepting that there are those who freely choose to engage in prostitution, it must be remembered that prostitution—the exchange of sex for money—is not illegal. The causal question is whether the impugned laws make this lawful activity more dangerous. An analogy could be drawn to a law preventing a cyclist from wearing a helmet. That the cyclist chooses to ride her bike does not diminish the causal role of the law in making that activity riskier. The challenged laws relating to prostitution are no different.

. . . It makes no difference that the conduct of pimps and johns is the immediate source of the harms suffered by prostitutes. The impugned laws deprive people engaged in a risky, but legal, activity of the means to protect themselves against those risks. The violence of a john does not diminish the role of the state in making a prostitute more vulnerable to that violence."

Finally, in explaining why the Court suspended the effect of its decision for a year, McLachlin CJ said[26]:

"Parliament is [not] precluded from imposing limits on where and how prostitution may be conducted. Prohibitions on keeping a bawdy-house, living on the avails of prostitution and communication related to prostitution are intertwined. They impact on each other. Greater latitude in one measure—for example, permitting prostitutes to obtain the assistance of security personnel—might impact on the constitutionality of another measure—for example, forbidding the nuisances associated with keeping a bawdy-house. The regulation of prostitution is a complex and delicate matter. It will be for Parliament, should it choose to do

---

[25] At 86–89.
[26] At 165.

so, to devise a new approach, reflecting different elements of the existing regime."

12.19   The question arises whether the arguments accepted by the Canadian Supreme Court in *Bedford* could be run successfully in this jurisdiction. We suggest not. It is true that the language of s.7 of the Canadian Charter, guaranteeing a person's right to "security of the person", is mirrored in the right to "liberty and security of person" conferred by art.5 of the ECHR. However, the better view is that the focus of art.5 is the protection of liberty in its classic sense of personal freedom, and that "liberty and security of person" are best considered as one concept, with "security" meaning freedom from arrest or detention rather than "safety".[27] That said, the ECHR is not a static instrument and so it is possible that the arguments canvassed in *Bedford* will at some point be given an airing before a UK court.

Protection of Communities and Exploited Persons Act

12.20   As noted above, in recognition that the regulation of prostitution is "a complex and delicate matter",[28] the Supreme Court suspended the effect of its decision for a year in order that the Canadian Parliament could, if it chose, devise a new approach. The result, following a period of research and consultation, was Bill C-36, the Protection of Communities and Exploited Persons Act,[29] which came into force on December 6, 2014. The Act is notable for adopting the Nordic model of regulation by recognising that the primary victims of prostitution are those who sell their sexual services, and that it is the purchasers of sexual services and the third parties who benefit economically from the sale of those services who cause and perpetuate prostitution's harms and so deserve to be the focus of the criminal law.

Keeping a Brothel

Definition

12.21   Section 33 of the Sexual Offences Act 1956 provides:

"It is an offence for a person to keep a brothel, or to manage, or act or assist in the management of, a brothel."

---

[27] See e.g. *Guide on Article 5—Right to Liberty and Security: Article 5 of the Convention* (Council of Europe/European Court of Human Rights, 2012), available at *http://www.echr .coe.int/Documents/COUREDH-2012-Guide_on_article_5_ENG.pdf* [Accessed April 30, 2016], para.17 of which says: "The key purpose of Article 5 is to prevent arbitrary or unjustified deprivations of liberty."
[28] At 165.
[29] S.C. 2014, c.25.

The structure of the section indicates that it creates three offences: keeping a brothel, managing a brothel, and acting or assisting in the management of a brothel.[30]

MODE OF TRIAL AND PUNISHMENT

Offences under s.33 are triable summarily.[31] The maximum punishment on first conviction is three months' imprisonment or a fine not exceeding level 3 on the standard scale (currently £1,000), or both. For an offence committed after a previous conviction, it is six months' imprisonment or a fine not exceeding level 4 (currently £2,500), or both.[32] The higher maxima also apply on first conviction under the section if the offender has a previous conviction under s.34, 35 or 36 of the 1956 Act. A convicted offender may be deprived of the financial benefit obtained as a result of his criminal conduct by means of a confiscation order made under the Proceeds of Crime Act 2002.[33]   **12.22**

Until April 13, 2015, a s.33 offence was a specified offence for the purposes   **12.23** of the provisions of the Criminal Justice Act 2003 relating to the sentencing of dangerous offenders.[34] On that date, the reference to s.33 in Sch.15 to that Act was replaced by a reference to s.33A, discussed below. This change, made by the Criminal Justice and Courts Act 2015,[35] was described in Parliament as a "minor technical correction to ensure that the correct form of the offence of brothel keeping under the Sexual Offences Act 1956 is on the schedule".[36]

CHARGE

Brothel-keeping is a continuing offence, and for this reason it was held in   **12.24** *Anderton v Cooper* [37] that an information is not bad for duplicity where it charges the defendant with keeping a brothel on specified non-consecutive dates within a specified period. In that case, the information charged that the defendant "on Friday February 13, 1979 and other days between that date and Thursday March 15, 1979, did manage a brothel . . . ". It was held that those words charged a single continuing transaction. Whilst it might have been better if the words "on other days" had been omitted, their inclusion

---

[30] cf. *Walker* [2006] EWCA Crim 1907, discussed in para.3.131, above.
[31] 1956 Act s.37 and Sch.2, para.33.
[32] 1956 Act s.37 and Sch.2, para.33; Criminal Justice Act 1982 s.46. The enhanced penalties were expressly preserved by the 1982 Act s.35(3).
[33] cf. *Worrall* [2012] EWCA Crim 1150 (order wrongly based on brothel's turnover rather than on the benefit obtained).
[34] Criminal Justice Act 2003 s.224 and Sch.15, Pt 2.
[35] s.2(1), (5), (6).
[36] HC, Public Bill Committee, March 18, 2014, col 166 (Parliamentary Under-Secretary of State for Justice, Jeremy Wright MP).
[37] (1981) 72 Cr. App. R. 232, following *Ex p. Burnby* [1901] 2 K.B. 458.

did not make the charge bad for duplicity. It is clear from *Anderton v Cooper* that the s.33 offence may continue over a long period of time.[38]

Parties to the Offence

12.25 An offence under s.33 may be committed as principal by both males and females. On the question whether a prostitute working in the brothel may be convicted under s.33, see para.12.39, below.

"To Keep"

12.26 It was held in New Zealand in relation to a similar provision that "keeping" a brothel involves having "conduct of the business accommodated therein"[39] or "control or a share of control over the brothel."[40] See further the discussion in paras 12.88 and following, below, of the meaning of "keeping" a disorderly house.

"Brothel"

12.27 Whether premises are being used as a brothel is a question of fact and degree.[41] The term "brothel" is not defined by the 1956 Act and its meaning is therefore a matter of common law. The leading modern authority is *Gorman v Standen*,[42] where Lord Parker CJ, after reviewing earlier decisions, defined a "brothel" as:

> "a house resorted to or used by more than one woman for the purposes of fornication."[43]

This definition contains three elements, namely:

- "a house"
- "resorted to or used by more than one woman"
- "for the purposes of fornication".

"A house"

12.28 It is clear that a brothel need not comprise an entire house or other building. So in *Stevens v Christy*,[44] Watkins LJ cited with approval Sir Leslie Stephen's definition of a brothel as:

---

[38] See also *Pritchett* [2008] Crim. L.R. 214, discussed in para.12.45, below.

[39] *Mickle* [1978] 1 N.Z.L.R. 720 at 723, per Bain, J, N.Z.S.C.

[40] *Barrie* [1978] 2 N.Z.L.R. 78 at 81, per Cooke, J, N.Z.C.A.

[41] *Stevens v Christy* (1987) 85 Cr. App. R. 249.

[42] [1964] 1 Q.B. 294.

[43] At 303; and see *JJ. of Parts of Holland, Lincolnshire* (1882) 46 J.P. 312 at 312, per Grove, J; *Singleton v Ellison* [1895] 1 Q.B. 607 at 608, per Wills, J.

[44] (1987) 85 Cr. App. R. 249 at 251.

"a house or room, or set of rooms in any house kept for the purpose of prostitution."[45]

It has sometimes proved difficult to apply the definition of "brothel" to
buildings in multiple occupation, where prostitutes occupy different parts of
the building under separate lettings. One of the earliest such cases was *Durose
v Wilson*,[46] which concerned a large building divided into 18 flats, each self-
contained and each let to a different tenant. There was one street door which
gave access to a common staircase. Among the tenants were 12 prostitutes.
The magistrates found that the building as a whole constituted one set of
premises which were properly described as a brothel. This finding was upheld
by the Divisional Court, which rejected the appellant's argument that the
relevant premises was not the building as a whole but the individual flats,
none of which was used by more than one woman.

The leading authority is now *Donovan v Gavin*,[47] which establishes that the   **12.29**
letting of individual rooms in a house under separate tenancies to different
prostitutes does not necessarily preclude the house, or the relevant parts of it,
from being a brothel. In that case the appellant owned a large house in which
he occupied a self-contained flat on the ground floor. Three further rooms on
the ground floor had been let to three different women, each of whom had a
key to her own room and to the front door. Their respective tenancies had
come into existence separately and at different times. The women were
common prostitutes who solicited from within or near the house, two of them
doing so in concert, and who used their rooms for the purposes of
prostitution. The Divisional Court held that the mere fact that the rooms
were originally let as separate units under separate tenancies did not preclude
the finding that the house, or part of it, was a brothel. Nor was it necessary
for the prosecution to establish that the original lettings were a subterfuge to
escape the effect of the Act. Sachs J, in a vivid turn of phrase that may be
offensive to modern ears, said that individual rooms in a single house may
together constitute a brothel if they:

> "are sufficiently close to each other to constitute in effect what might be called
> a nest of prostitutes, be that nest large or small."[48]

A contrasting decision is *Strath v Foxon*,[49] where the respondent let the   **12.30**
first and second floors of a building to one prostitute and the third floor to
another. The premises shared a kitchen on the second floor, a street door and
a staircase. On the staircase, a substantial door fitted with a Yale lock divided
the third floor from the lower floors and thereby made it entirely self-
contained. The appellant, relying on *Durose v Wilson*, contended that the
premises should be considered in their entirety as a brothel. The Divisional

---

[45] Stephen, p.142.
[46] (1907) 96 L.T. 645, followed in *Abbott v Smith* [1965] 2 Q.B. 662, Liverpool Crown Court
(HH Judge Chapman).
[47] [1965] 2 Q.B. 648.
[48] At 659.
[49] [1956] 1 Q.B. 67.

Court held that there was evidence to support the magistrate's findings that there existed two separate lettings of two separate flats and no common user other than joint user of the kitchen. On those facts, the Court reluctantly concluded that the premises did not constitute a brothel. The decision was distinguished in *Donovan v Gavin* on the basis that it involved separate flats on separate floors; that even so the Court said no more than that there was evidence to justify the magistrate's decision; and that moreover the Court did not throw doubt on the correctness of the decision of *Durose v Wilson*. These points of distinction are unconvincing, whether taken singly or together, and indicate that the Court in *Donovan v Gavin* was less than fully enamoured of the earlier decision.

"Resorted to or used by more than one woman"

12.31   In *Singleton v Ellison*,[50] it was held that the term "brothel" is not appropriate to describe a place where a single prostitute plies her trade, however numerous her clients may be. This decision was followed in *Caldwell v Leach*,[51] where the respondent let to her sister a room in premises where she lived with her husband, and the sister used the room to work as a prostitute. The premises were held not to be a brothel, as only one woman was using them for the purposes of prostitution. It was held in *Stevens v Christy*,[52] however, that a small terraced house used by a team of prostitutes was properly described as a brothel, although there was only one prostitute working on the premises on any particular day. Watkins LJ (as he then was) said[53]:

> "where more than one woman resorts to premises for the purpose of prostitution then those premises are a brothel if there is a joint use of them as a team."

Furthermore, if two women are bringing men to the premises for the purposes of prostitution, the fact that one of the women is the tenant and occupier does not prevent the premises from being a brothel.[54]

12.32   Finally, although the term "brothel" is usually defined at common law to cover premises resorted to or used by more than one "woman", it is clear that the definition applies equally to premises used by male prostitutes, and that it does not matter whether the services provided there are heterosexual or homosexual in nature. This is the effect of s.6 of the Sexual Offences Act 1967, which provides:

> "Premises shall be treated for the purposes of sections 33 to 35 of the Act of 1956 as a brothel if people resort to it for the purpose of lewd homosexual practices

---

[50] [1895] 1 Q.B. 607.
[51] (1913–1914) 109 L.T. 188.
[52] (1987) 85 Cr. App. R. 249, followed in *Krausky* (1989) 45 A.Crim.R. 41, Qd. CCA.
[53] At 254.
[54] *Gorman v Standen* [1964] 1 Q.B. 294.

in circumstances in which resort thereto for lewd heterosexual practices would have led to its being treated as a brothel for the purposes of those sections."

"For the purposes of fornication"

It is striking that in defining a "brothel" in *Gorman v Standen*, Lord Parker **12.33** CJ described it as a house used for the purpose of "fornication", rather than "prostitution". The explanation for this is to be found in the decision in *Winter v Woolfe*,[55] which is a striking example of judicial moralism in action. A charge was laid against the occupier of dance rooms near Cambridge which were open on Sunday afternoons for dancing and teas, and in which lewd and improper acts were alleged to have taken place between male undergraduates and women of "the working class type". The magistrates dismissed the charge on the grounds that acts of gross indecency and fornication did not amount to prostitution, the women were not known prostitutes and there was no evidence that they were paid for the acts they committed. In the Divisional Court, Avory J held that the magistrates had given too restrictive a meaning to the term "brothel"[56]:

> "There was evidence . . . that . . . men were resorting to those premises for the purpose of committing fornication with women who resorted there for the same purpose . . . That of itself is quite sufficient to justify the inference that these premises were being used for the purposes of prostitution."

This conclusion is clearly inconsistent with the definition of "prostitution" **12.34** developed by the courts,[57] which requires that the sexual activity takes place for reward. The effect is to expand the meaning of "brothel" beyond the common understanding of the term to cover premises where sexual activity takes place otherwise than for payment. *Winter v Woolfe* has been described as "an extraordinary case which contradicts the usual supposition that non-commercial sex is not the concern of the criminal law".[58] It was, however, cited with approval in *Kelly v Purvis*.[59] The respondent had been charged with assisting in the management of a brothel, namely a licensed massage parlour. The prosecution had adduced evidence that, during the massage, the masseuse offered extra services involving masturbation of the client for an additional fee. The additional fee was usually paid direct to the masseuse and there was no evidence that it was treated as part of the parlour's takings, nor that full sexual intercourse was offered. The magistrate dismissed the information on the basis that, as there was no evidence that sexual intercourse took place on the premises, they did not constitute a brothel and so the prosecution had failed to establish an essential element of the offence.

[55] [1931] 1 K.B. 549.
[56] At 554–555.
[57] See paras 13.45 and following, below.
[58] A.A. Sion, *Prostitution and the Law* (London: Faber & Faber, 1977), p.132. The author must be understood as using the term "non-commercial sex" to refer to otherwise lawful sexual activity between adults not undertaken for reward.
[59] [1983] 1 All E.R. 525, DC.

On appeal by the prosecutor, it was common ground that the premises were used for the purpose of prostitution.[60] The issue was whether that was sufficient for them to qualify as a brothel, or whether the prosecution had to establish that sexual intercourse took place there with the women who used the premises. Having reviewed the authorities, Ackner LJ (as he then was) said that *Winter v Woolfe*[61]:

> "demonstrates that to constitute premises as a brothel it is not essential to show that they are in fact used for the purpose of prostitution, which involves payment for services rendered. A brothel is also constituted where the women . . . do not charge for sexual intercourse."

He concluded that on a charge under s.33:[62]

> "it is not essential that there be evidence that normal sexual intercourse is provided in the premises. It is sufficient to prove that more than one woman offers herself as a participant in physical acts of indecency for the sexual gratification of men."

12.35   The sexual activity undertaken in *Kelly v Purvis* undoubtedly constituted prostitution, rather than simply "fornication", and the *ratio* of the case is accordingly that premises may be used as a brothel although sexual activity falling short of full sexual intercourse takes place there. It follows that Ackner LJ's approving reference to *Winter v Wolfe* is only a *dictum*. On the basis of the case law alone, it might therefore be possible to argue that *Winter v Wolfe* is a decision of dubious authority which should not be followed, and that the definition of "brothel" should instead be linked expressly to the concept of prostitution. However, the scope for running this argument has been greatly reduced by the insertion into the 1956 Act of the offences in s.33A of keeping (etc.) a brothel used for prostitution. The genesis of s.33A was considered in para.12.03, above, but its enactment constitutes Parliamentary recognition that premises may be a brothel even if they are not used for prostitution, and so has the effect of embedding the decision in *Winter v Wolfe* in the law. It follows that, as matters stand, the brothel-keeping offences in s.33 are capable of covering a range of premises used for the purpose of sexual activity not amounting to prostitution, e.g. saunas and adult clubs to which people resort for consensual sexual activity which takes place without reward. If premises are used for prostitution, one would expect an offence under s.33A to be charged.

"TO MANAGE"

12.36   In *Abbott v Smith*,[63] HHJ Chapman said that on a charge of "managing" a brothel there must be:

---

[60] cf. *Webb* [1964] 1 Q.B. 357, discussed in para.13.47, below.
[61] At 528.
[62] At 529.
[63] [1964] 3 All E.R. 762 at 765–766; approved in *Jones and Wood v DPP* (1993) 96 Cr. App. R. 130, discussed in para.12.38, below.

"some sort of evidence indicating the taking of an active part in the running of the business as a business, something suggesting control . . . there must . . . be something 'a cut above' purely menial or routine duties, such as cleaning the stairs or answering the door."

"TO ACT OR ASSIST IN THE MANAGEMENT"

In *Gorman v Standen*,[64] Lord Parker CJ said: **12.37**

"the mere fact that a woman participates in the activities being conducted in a brothel does not make her a person assisting in the management of a brothel. 'Assisting in the management of a brothel' seems to me to contemplate in the ordinary way the case of a man who runs a brothel not living there himself; he keeps and manages it but he has on the premises a woman who assists in the management."

One of the appellants in *Gorman v Standen* actually kept the brothel; the other, her step-daughter, was proved to have had "a part, at any rate, of the say of what goes on at [the] house."[65] Lord Parker CJ concluded that, although this was some way from the ordinary case contemplated by the section, it was just possible on the evidence to uphold the finding that the step-daughter was assisting in the brothel's management.

The point was further examined in *Jones and Wood v DPP*.[66] The **12.38** appellants lived with a male prostitute (K) who operated a brothel at other premises. They had on numerous occasions placed advertisements for the brothel in local newsagents, sometimes paying for them with their own money. Both had visited the brothel frequently and carried out odd jobs for K, often when customers were on the premises. Both had also frequently given K a lift to the brothel in the morning and driven him on shopping and other expeditions. Further, they had both been at all times ready, willing and able to assist K in any way necessary, short of actually providing sexual services themselves, in the successful operation of the brothel. Their roles were not limited to menial or routine duties and the brothel was in fact a joint enterprise of all three. They were convicted of assisting in the management of the brothel, but appealed on the ground that they did not exercise any control over the business. This argument was rejected by the Court of Appeal. Beldam LJ said:[67]

"a person assists in the management of a brothel if he gives help to a person in the management of the brothel . . . [I]t is not a necessary condition of the offence of assisting in the management that the person has to exercise some sort of control over the management. That is the requirement of managing. Equally it seems to me it is not necessary to show that there was a specific act of management for that would be acting in the management. Assisting is a wider concept. No doubt not everyone who carries out some menial task at a brothel,

[64] [1964] 1 Q.B. 294 at 303.
[65] [1964] 1 Q.B. 294 at 303.
[66] (1993) 96 Cr. App. R. 130.
[67] At 132.

like cleaning the stairs as a daily woman, would be said to be assisting in the management but that was not this case. In my judgment, it was a question of fact for the Crown Court. There was sufficient substance in the acts which they found proved to support the holding that the appellants were 'assisting in the management of a brothel.'"

12.39   In the light of these decisions, it is tolerably clear that prostitutes who provide sexual services at a brothel will not, without more, commit an offence under s.33. But everything turns on the precise activities undertaken and if the prostitutes do more than provide sexual services they may well commit the offence. So in *Elliott v DPP*[68] it was held that six women who performed lewd acts in massage parlours were guilty of assisting in the management of a brothel because they negotiated the nature and extent of the lewd acts they performed in addition to receiving payment for their services. The Court was satisfied that the acts went considerably beyond the menial tasks, such as cleaning the premises and removing the rubbish, which could be done without taking part in the management. Given the negotiations carried out by the women, the fact that there had been a receptionist at one of the premises made no difference.

Problems of Proof

12.40   The difficulty of obtaining direct proof of the use of premises as a brothel means that many police investigations involve the deployment of undercover police officers. It was held in *Woodhouse v Hall*[69] that, in order to show the purpose for which the premises were used, police officers may give evidence of conversations in which, in the absence of the defendant, a masseuse employed there offered to perform sexual services. Such evidence is not hearsay, as the truth of the alleged statements is not in point; the evidence is relevant to show simply that the offers were made. To similar effect is *Roberts v DPP*,[70] in which the appellant was convicted of assisting in the management of a brothel at "Loughton Health Spa". Evidence was given that two women had already been convicted of the offence in relation to the premises. A police surveillance operation showed that the appellant had entered the premises on one occasion. Documents were found at his home which linked him with the premises, including a repair bill, a gas bill and handwritten accounts described as daily record sheets relating to the premises. In addition, a magazine sales consultant produced in evidence a request purportedly signed by the appellant to place an advertisement referring to "Many Stunning Masseuses". The appellant appealed against conviction on the ground that the magistrates had relied on the documents found in his possession as evidence of the truth of their contents and had thus infringed the rule against hearsay. The Court rejected this argument, holding that the prosecution had

[68] *The Times*, January 19, 1989; and see *DPP v Curley and Farrelly* [1991] C.O.D. 186.
[69] (1981) 72 Cr. App. R. 39.
[70] [1994] Crim. L.R. 926.

relied not on the truth of the contents of the documents but on the fact that the documents were in the appellant's possession, from which it could be inferred that he was concerned in the management of the premises. On the evidence, that inference was irresistible. As to the appellant's knowledge that the premises were a brothel, that was an easy inference from the fact that he had been seen to visit the premises and from the terms of what the magistrates could infer was his written request for the insertion of the advertisement in the magazine.

In *Korie*,[71] it was held that evidence of visits to the premises by known **12.41** prostitutes was admissible to prove that the premises were a brothel. HHJ Chapman said:

> "It is hardly to be expected that visual observation will be possible of what takes place between a man and a woman in a particular room in a particular house. It must therefore be a matter of inference from the general surrounding circumstances what the purpose of a visit or a succession of visits is. Among these surrounding circumstances it seems to me highly relevant and probative if it can be shown that a woman concerned follows the trade, calling or profession of prostitute."

KEEPING A BROTHEL USED FOR PROSTITUTION

DEFINITION

Section 33A of the Sexual Offences Act 1956[72] provides: **12.42**

> "It is an offence for a person to keep, or to manage, or act or assist in the management of, a brothel to which people resort for practices involving prostitution (whether or not also for other practices)."

The structure of the section indicates that it creates three offences: keeping a brothel to which people resort for practices involving prostitution, managing such a brothel, and acting or assisting in the management of such a brothel.[73] The overlap between the offences in s.33A and s.33 is discussed in para.12.03, above.

MODE OF TRIAL AND PUNISHMENT

Offences under s.33A are triable either way.[74] The maximum punishment on **12.43** conviction on indictment is seven years' imprisonment. On summary conviction it is six months' imprisonment or a fine, or both. As from a day to be appointed the maximum sentence of imprisonment on summary conviction will increase to 12 months' imprisonment.[75] The increase will have no

---

[71] [1966] 1 All E.R. 50 at 51 (Liverpool Crown Court).
[72] Inserted by s.55 of the Sexual Offences Act 2003, which came into force on May 1, 2004.
[73] cf. *Walker* [2006] EWCA Crim 1907, discussed in para.3.132, above.
[74] 1956 Act s.37 and Sch.2, para.33A.
[75] Criminal Justice Act 2003 s.282(2), (3).

application to offences committed before it takes effect.[76] Until recently, the maximum fine on summary conviction was a fine not exceeding the statutory maximum (i.e. £5,000). The effect of s.85 of the Legal Aid, Sentencing and Punishment of Offenders Act 2012 is that, from March 12, 2015, a fine of any amount may be imposed. Fines will, however, continue to be set according to the seriousness of the offence and the means of the offender. A convicted offender may be deprived of the financial benefit obtained as a result of his criminal conduct by means of a confiscation order made under the Proceeds of Crime Act 2002.[77]

12.44   Before April 13, 2015, an offence under s.33A was not a specified offence for the purposes of the provisions of the Criminal Justice Act 2003 relating to the sentencing of dangerous offenders.[78] On that date, the reference to s.33 (discussed above) in Sch.15 to that Act was replaced by a reference to s.33A. This change, made by the Criminal Justice and Courts Act 2015,[79] was described in Parliament as a "minor technical correction to ensure that the correct form of the offence of brothel keeping under the Sexual Offences Act 1956 is on the schedule".[80]

Charge

12.45   See para.12.24, above. In *Pritchett*,[81] the indictment alleged a contravention of s.33A over a period that commenced before May 1, 2004, the date when the section came into force. The Court of Appeal held that this defect did not render the indictment a nullity. An offence under s.33A is a continuing one and the prosecution in this case did not have to prove that it continued throughout the period alleged in the indictment; it was sufficient for them to prove the commission of the offence in the period from May 1, 2004, onwards.

Sentencing

Sentencing Council Guideline

12.46   For the Sentencing Council guideline relating to the sentencing of sexual offences committed by offenders aged 18 and over, see Ch.33, below. The guideline covers the offences in s.33A as follows.

---

[76] Criminal Justice Act 2003 s.282(4).
[77] cf. *Worrall* [2012] EWCA Crim 1150 (order wrongly based on brothel's turnover rather than on the benefit obtained).
[78] Criminal Justice Act 2003 s.224 and Sch.15, Pt 2.
[79] s.2(1), (5), (6).
[80] HC, Public Bill Committee, March 18, 2014, col 166 (Parliamentary Under-Secretary of State for Justice, Jeremy Wright MP).
[81] [2008] Crim. L.R. 214.

Step One—Harm and culpability

As with other offences, the guideline requires the sentencing court to go   12.47
through a series of steps in order to determine the appropriate sentence. Step
one involves determining the offence category by reference to the degree of
harm caused and then the culpability level for the offence. The harm factors
for offences under s.33A are:

Harm	
Category 1	• Under 18 year olds working in brothel • Abduction/detention • Violence or threats of violence • Sustained and systematic psychological abuse • Those working in brothel forced or coerced to participate in unsafe/degrading sexual activity • Those working in brothel forced or coerced into seeing many "customers" • Those working in brothel forced/coerced/deceived into prostitution • Established evidence of community impact
Category 2	Factor(s) in categories 1 not present

In consulting on the draft guideline,[82] the Sentencing Council said that it had
focused on factors that increase the harm to prostitutes working within the
brothel. This focus is not, however, exclusive, as the harm factors for category
1 include "established evidence of community impact". The Council included
this factor to take account of cases where the brothel has an impact on the
local area; for example, it is located near a school and there are clients going
in and out frequently, or it is in a residential area and the presence of clients
is intimidating for residents at night. Many of the other harm factors also
appear in the guideline for the offences of causing or inciting prostitution for
gain (s.52 of the Sexual Offences Act 2003) and controlling prostitution for
gain (s.53) and are discussed in Ch.10.

As for culpability, the Sentencing Council said that the main focus of s.33A   12.48
is the role played by the offender and the level of deliberate exploitation and
corruption of those working in the brothel. As the provision penalises those
who keep, manage or act or assist in the management of a brothel, it covers
a wide range of involvement and of culpability. The culpability factors
therefore seek to distinguish between those who have genuine power and
influence in relation to the brothel and those who have a minor role or are
coerced or exploited themselves. The factors are:

[82] *Sexual Offences Guideline: Consultation* (December 6, 2012). The consultation document is
available on the Sentencing Council's website.

CULPABILITY		
A	*B*	*C*
• Keeping brothel on significant commercial basis • Involvement in keeping a number of brothels • Expectation of significant financial or other gain • Abuse of trust • Exploitation of those known to be trafficked • Significant involvement in limiting freedom of those working in brothel • Grooming of a person to work in the brothel including through cultivation of a dependency on drugs or alcohol	• Keeping/managing premises • Close involvement with those working in brothel e.g. control of finances, choice of clients, working conditions, etc. (where offender's involvement is not as a result of coercion)	• Performs limited function under direction • Close involvement but engaged by coercion/ intimidation/ exploitation

A number of these factors appear in the guideline for ss.52 and 53 of the 2003 Act and are discussed at paras 10.121 and following, above. In its consultation document, the Sentencing Council said that "keeping brothel on significant commercial basis" and "involvement in keeping a number of brothels" are at culpability A to reflect the fact that the offender will be directing and involving a large number of people in the operation of brothels. "Keeping/managing premises" is at culpability B to reflect the level of culpability of those who undertake a management role with a degree of day-to-day responsibility for the running of the brothel. "Close involvement with those working in brothel e.g. control of finances, choice of clients, working conditions, etc. (where offender's involvement is not as a result of coercion)" is intended to reflect situations where the offender has a degree of control and autonomy in the running of the brothel. As for culpability C, the factors "performs limited function under direction" and "close involvement but engaged by coercion/intimidation/exploitation" would apply in this context to "maids" who may help look after the other women in the brothel or have a limited role such as answering the door and letting in clients, and to those helping run the brothel but who are doing so due to coercion or exploitation.

Step Two—Starting point and category range

Once the court has determined the offence category and culpability level, at step two it should use the corresponding starting point specified in the guideline in order to reach a sentence within the category range. The starting point applies to all offenders irrespective of plea or previous convictions. Once the starting point has been determined, step two allows further adjustment for aggravating or mitigating features, set out below. A case of particular gravity, reflected by multiple features of culpability or harm, could merit upward adjustment from the starting point before further adjustment for aggravating or mitigating features. Where there is a sufficient prospect of rehabilitation, a community order with a sex offender treatment programme requirement under s.202 of the Criminal Justice Act 2003 may be a proper alternative to a short or moderate length custodial sentence. The starting points and category ranges for offences under s.33A are as follows:

12.49

	A	B	C
Category 1	*Starting point* 5 years' custody	*Starting point* 3 years' custody	*Starting point* 1 year's custody
	Category range 3–6 years' custody	*Category range* 2–5 years' custody	*Category range* High level community order – 18 months' custody
Category 2	*Starting point* 3 years' custody	*Starting point* 12 months' custody	*Starting point* Medium level community order
	Category range 2–5 years' custody	*Category range* 26 weeks' – 2 years' custody	*Category range* Low level community order – High level community order

At the top level, the starting point and range are higher than in the previous guideline, issued in 2007 by the Sentencing Guidelines Council, which had at its top level a starting point of 2 years' custody with a range of 1–4 years. The highest category under that guideline was for an offence where the offender was the keeper of the brothel and had made profits in the region of £5,000 and upwards. The top category in the new guideline has a starting point of 5 years' custody with a range of 3–6 years. In its consultation document, the Sentencing Council said this category will apply where, e.g. the offender has been involved in serious exploitation or the brothel used child prostitutes, and in addition there is a degree of larger scale management of the brothel and either an abuse of trust or an element of limiting the freedom of the prostitute. At the other end of the offending scale, where the offender has had minimal involvement and there are no signs of exploitation of prostitutes working in the brothel, a community order is proposed. Such a disposal would be designed to address the reasons the offender has become involved in assisting at the brothel.

Aggravating and mitigating factors

12.50 The court should next consider whether the presence of aggravating or mitigating factors should result in an upward or downward adjustment from the starting point or the imposition of a sentence outside the category range. In particular, relevant recent convictions are likely to result in an upward adjustment. When sentencing appropriate category 1 offences, the court should also consider whether the custody threshold has been passed; if so, whether a custodial sentence is unavoidable; and if it is, whether that sentence can be suspended. The non-exhaustive list of aggravating and mitigating factors for offences under s.33A is:

Aggravating factors
Statutory aggravating factors
• Previous convictions, having regard to a) the nature of the offence to which the conviction relates and its relevance to the current offence; and b) the time that has elapsed since the conviction
• Offence committed whilst on bail
Other aggravating factors
• Failure to comply with current court orders • Offence committed whilst on licence • Deliberate isolation of victim(s) • Threats made to expose victim(s) to the authorities (for example, immigration or police), family/friends or others • Harm threatened against the family/friends of victim(s) • Passport/identity documents removed

- Those working in brothel prevented from seeking medical treatment
- Food withheld
- Those working in brothel passed around by offender and moved to other brothels
- Earnings withheld/kept by offender or evidence of excessive wage reduction or debt bondage, inflated travel or living expenses or unreasonable interest rates
- Any steps taken to prevent the victim reporting an incident, obtaining assistance and/or from assisting or supporting the prosecution
- Attempts to dispose of or conceal evidence
- Those working in brothel forced or coerced into pornography
- Timescale over which the operation has been run

Mitigating factors

- No previous convictions **or** no relevant/recent convictions
- Remorse
- Previous good character and/or exemplary conduct*
- Age and/or lack of maturity where it affects the responsibility of the offender
- Mental disorder or learning disability, particularly where linked to the commission of the offence
- Demonstration of steps taken to address offending behaviour

* Previous good character/exemplary conduct is different from having no previous convictions. The more serious the offence, the less the weight which should normally be attributed to this factor. Where previous good character/exemplary conduct has been used to facilitate the offence, this mitigation should not normally be allowed and such conduct may constitute an aggravating factor.

A number of these factors appear in the guideline for ss.52 and 53 of the Act and are discussed at para.10.129, above.

Steps Three to Eight

The remaining steps cover the following points. At step three the court **12.51** should consider any factors which would indicate a reduction in sentence, e.g. assistance to the prosecution. At step four it should consider any reduction for a guilty plea. Step five requires the court to consider whether the total sentence is just and proportionate to the offending behaviour. At step six it should consider whether to make an ancillary order (e.g. a confiscation order, a Serious Crime Prevention Order or a restraining order). Step seven requires the court to fulfil its duty under s.174 of the Criminal Justice Act 2003 to give reasons for, and explain the effect of, the sentence. Finally, at step eight the court should consider whether to give credit for time spent on bail in accordance with s.240A of that Act.

Parties to the Offence

12.52 An offence under s.33A may be committed as principal by both males and females. On the question whether a prostitute working in the brothel may be convicted under s.33A, see para.12.39, above.

"To Keep. . . to Manage, or Act or Assist in the Management"

12.53 See the discussion of these terms in paras 12.26 and 12.36 and following, above.

"Brothel"

12.54 For the meaning of "brothel", see paras 12.27 and following, above.

"Prostitution"

12.55 Offences under s.33A may be committed only in relation to a brothel to which people resort for practices involving "prostitution". Accordingly, s.33A does not cover the keeping (etc.) of premises that qualify as a "brothel" only because of non-commercial sexual encounters that take place there, as in *Winter v Wolfe*,[83] discussed in paras 12.33 and following, above. Section 33A(2) provides that "prostitution" in s.33A has the meaning given by s.51(2) of the Sexual Offences Act 2003. Section 51(2) is discussed in paras 10.59 and following, above. The definition essentially replicates the common law, which is considered in paras 13.45 and following, below.

Defence of Necessity

12.56 In 2010, Claire Finch was tried under s.33A at Luton Crown Court, the Crown's evidence being that she had kept a brothel at her home in Bedfordshire where she worked with up to four other women. Ms Finch ran a defence of necessity, telling the jury that she wanted to work with other women for the sake of "safety" and "camaraderie". Her legal representative said Ms Finch had used her home in this way because of concern for the safety of herself and the other women, and referred to 18 incidents of serious violence against sex workers in Bedfordshire over a four-year period, which she said was the "tip of the iceberg". Ms Finch was acquitted.[84]

---

[83] [1931] 1 K.B. 549.

[84] *Finch (Claire)*, unreported, April 29, 2010 (Luton Crown Court). For further information see *http://news.bbc.co.uk/1/hi/england/beds/bucks/herts/8652533.stm* [Accessed April 30, 2016]. See also Anna Morris, *Happy ending*, Soc. L. 2010, 55(Jul), 21, considering whether the law should recognise the collective organisation of sex workers in a safe environment as an exception to the offence of brothel keeping.

LANDLORD LETTING PREMISES FOR USE AS A BROTHEL

DEFINITION

Section 34 of the Sexual Offences Act 1956 provides: 12.57

> "It is an offence for the lessor or landlord of any premises or his agent to let the whole or part of the premises with the knowledge that it is to be used, in whole or in part, as a brothel, or, where the whole or part of the premises is used as a brothel, to be wilfully a party to that use continuing."

The section creates two offences: one of letting premises knowing that they are to be used as a brothel, the other of being wilfully a party to the continuing use of leased premises as a brothel.[85]

MODE OF TRIAL AND PUNISHMENT

Offences under s.34 are triable summarily.[86] The maximum punishment on 12.58 first conviction is three months' imprisonment or a fine not exceeding level 3 on the standard scale (currently £1,000), or both. For an offence committed after a previous conviction, it is six months' imprisonment or a fine not exceeding level 4 (currently £2,500), or both.[87] The higher maxima also apply on first conviction under the section if the offender has a previous conviction under s.33, 35 or 36 of the Act.

PARTIES TO THE OFFENCE

An offence under s.34 may be committed as principal by both males and 12.59 females and by companies.

"LESSOR OR LANDLORD . . . OR HIS AGENT"

The appellant in *Durose v Wilson*[88] was a porter employed by the owner of 12.60 a building divided into 18 flats, of which 12 were let to prostitutes. He resided on the premises and was in charge of them, and though he did not collect the rents, it was part of his duty to evict undesirable tenants. He closed the building's street door at midnight and from then until 2 a.m. he would wait in the street and admit the women and their clients by unlocking the door. When couples left after midnight he called cabs for them and received tips from the men. He was convicted under the forerunner of s.34 in that, as the agent of the landlord, he had been wilfully a party to the use of the premises

---

[85] *Donovan v Gavin* [1965] 2 Q.B. 648 at 657, per Sachs, LJ.
[86] 1956 Act s.37 and Sch.2, para.34.
[87] 1956 Act s.37 and Sch.2, para.34; Criminal Justice Act 1982 s.46. The enhanced penalties were expressly preserved by the 1982 Act s.35(3).
[88] (1907) 96 L.T. 645.

as a brothel continuing. He appealed, arguing that the premises were not a brothel, but his conviction was upheld.

12.61   The respondent in *Strath v Foxon*[89] was also the lessor's agent, being employed as a negotiator by a firm of estate agents who were instructed to act for the lessor in letting the premises. It does not appear from the report why only the respondent was charged, but it was presumably because she alone had the requisite knowledge that the premises were to be used by prostitutes.

"Brothel"

12.62   For the meaning of "brothel", and the application of the definition to cases in which prostitutes occupy different parts of a building under separate lettings, see paras 12.27 and following, above.

"With the Knowledge that it is to be Used"

12.63   There is some authority that "knowledge" in a criminal statute includes deliberately shutting one's eyes to the truth,[90] but the better view appears to be that this is a matter of evidence and that nothing short of actual knowledge will suffice.[91]

"To be Wilfully a Party to that Use Continuing"

12.64   In *Donovan v Gavin*,[92] Lord Parker CJ said that in determining whether a person has committed the s.34 offence of being wilfully a party to the use of premises as a brothel continuing:

> "*prima facie* the terms of the original lettings, whether they were independent or separate lettings, is an immaterial matter. One has to look at the position at the relevant time and say: is any part of the premises being used as a brothel, and if so, was the defendant wilfully a party to that use continuing?"

One possible interpretation of this element of s.34 is that a lessor becomes wilfully a party to the use of premises as a brothel continuing if, having power to give notice to quit, he abstains from giving such notice as soon as he learns with reasonable certainty of the criminal user.[93] To use demised premises as

---

[89] [1956] 1 Q.B. 67.
[90] *Warner v Metropolitan Police Commissioner* (1968) 52 Cr. App. R. 373 at 389, per Lord Reid; *Atwal v Massey* (1971) 56 Cr. App. R. 6.
[91] *Grainge* (1973) 59 Cr. App. R. 3; *Griffiths* (1974) 60 Cr. App. R. 14; *Moys* (1984) 79 Cr. App. R. 72; *Hall* (1985) 81 Cr. App. R. 260; *Westminster City Council v Croyalgrange Ltd* [1986] 1 W.L.R. 674 at 684, per Lord Bridge; *Sherif* [2008] EWCA Crim 2653, at 27; *Corrigan (Patrick)* [2014] NICA 85 (N.I.C.A.), at 37.
[92] [1965] 2 Q.B. 648 at 661.
[93] This was formerly the view expressed in *Woodfall's Law of Landlord and Tenant*, which is now silent on the point. The suggestion derives some tacit support from *Donovan v Gavin*.

a brothel will invariably be a breach of an express covenant against immoral user, justifying notice to quit, though there is no implied covenant against such user.[94] But the better view is probably that expressed in *Stone's*, that a positive act on the part of the lessor is required and that mere acquiescence will not suffice.[95] The word "wilfully" requires that the defendant either was intentionally a party to the use of the premises as a brothel or was at least reckless as to whether that use was continuing, i.e. he knew that it might be but did nothing to stop it.[96]

TENANT PERMITTING PREMISES TO BE USED AS A BROTHEL

DEFINITION

Section 35(1) of the Sexual Offences Act 1956 provides: 12.65

> "It is an offence for the tenant or occupier, or person in charge, of any premises knowingly to permit the whole or part of the premises to be used as a brothel."

MODE OF TRIAL AND PUNISHMENT

Section 35(1) creates a purely summary offence.[97] The maximum punishment   12.66
on first conviction is three months' imprisonment or a fine not exceeding level 3 on the standard scale (currently £1,000), or both. For an offence committed after a previous conviction, it is six months' imprisonment or a fine not exceeding level 4 (currently £2,500), or both.[98] The higher maxima also apply on first conviction under the section if the offender has a previous conviction under s.33, 34 or 36 of the Act.

PARTIES TO THE OFFENCE

The offence under s.35(1) may be committed as principal by both males and   12.67
females and by companies.

---

[94] The court has a discretion to grant relief from forfeiture even where the tenant is in breach of a covenant against immoral user: *Central Estates (Belgravia) v Woolgar (No.2)* [1972] 1 W.L.R. 1048. But it will do so only in very exceptional circumstances: *GMS Syndicate Ltd v Gary Elliott Ltd* [1982] Ch 1 at 10, per Nourse J; *Ropemaker Properties Ltd v Noonhaven Ltd* [1989] 2 E.G.L.R. 50 at 56, per Millett J; *Patel v K&J Restaurants Ltd* [2010] EWCA Civ 1211 at 82, per Lloyd LJ.
[95] Stone's Justices' Manual 2015, para.7–10511, citing *Bell v Alfred Franks & Bartlett Co Ltd* [1980] 1 All E.R. 356; and see *Re Maidstone Building Provisions Ltd* [1971] 1 W.L.R. 1085.
[96] *Sheppard* [1981] A.C. 394; *Attorney General's Reference (No.3 of 2003)* [2004] 2 Cr. App. R. 366; and see *Turbill (Maxine)* [2013] EWCA Crim 1422.
[97] 1956 Act s.37 and Sch.2, para.35.
[98] 1956 Act s.37 and Sch.2, para.35; Criminal Justice Act 1982 s.46. The enhanced penalties were expressly preserved by the 1982 Act s.35(3).

"Tenant or Occupier or Person in Charge"

12.68   For the meaning of the word "tenant" in this section, see *Siviour v Napolitano*,[99] discussed in para.12.79, below. There is no decision on the meaning of the word "occupier" in this context. An indication of its possible scope can be gleaned from *Tao*,[100] decided in relation to the offence in s.8 of the Misuse of Drugs Act 1971 of knowingly permitting the use of premises for drug-related activities. The appellant was an undergraduate who lived in a furnished room at a college hostel, for the use of which he paid the college. The Court of Appeal held that he was the "occupier" of the room for the purposes of s.8 of the 1971 Act. It was irrelevant whether the appellant was a tenant with legal possession of the premises or merely a licensee with exclusive possession:[101] the crucial question was whether he had sufficient control of the premises to exclude from them persons who might otherwise use them for purposes forbidden by s.8. The Court went on to indicate that someone who takes a room in a hotel is its "occupier" for the purposes of s.8, as is a passenger with a cabin on a ship, and a squatter in unlawful physical occupation of a house or part of a house. This last suggestion is borne out by the Scottish decision *Christison v Hogg*.[102]

12.69   Another instructive case is *Mogford*,[103] the decision in which, though not the reasoning, was approved in *Tao*. Two sisters (aged 15 and 20) who lived at their parents' home were charged that, while their parents were away on holiday, they permitted the premises to be used for the purpose of smoking cannabis, contrary to s.5 of the Dangerous Drugs Act 1965. Nield J ruled that the sisters were not at that time "occupiers" of the premises within the meaning of s.5, as they were neither in legal possession of the premises nor in control of them while their parents were away. Mere power to invite guests to the house, he said, did not amount to control of the nature and measure required by the Act. The Court of Appeal in *Tao* approved Nield J's ruling but criticised his reasoning, in particular because, as we have seen, it considered that a person without legal possession may nonetheless be an "occupier" of premises. But the parts of the ruling in which Nield J held that the girls were not occupiers because they lacked sufficient control of the house would appear to remain authoritative. This is borne out by the later ruling of HHJ Oddie in *Campbell and Campbell*.[104] In that case, S and G were left in charge of their mother's house, where S lived. S arranged a party,

---

[99] [1931] 1 K.B. 636.

[100] [1976] 3 All E.R. 65.

[101] This distinction has been undermined by subsequent developments in the law of leasehold property, under which exclusive possession is now treated as one of the indicators of a tenancy: *Street v Mountford* [1985] A.C. 809.

[102] 1974 J.C. 55. See also *Read v DPP* [1997] C.L.Y. 1202; *Coid* [1998] Crim. L.R. 199, which establish that a person may be an "occupier" for the purposes of s.8 of the 1971 Act although he does not have the legal right to exclude others from the premises.

[103] [1970] 1 W.L.R. 988.

[104] [1982] Crim. L.R. 595.

which G attended, at which cannabis was smoked by guests. S and G were charged with permitting the premises to be used for smoking cannabis, contrary to s.8 of the 1971 Act. The learned judge held that for S and G to be "occupiers" of the premises within the meaning of that Act, they had to have such exclusive possession of the premises as to enable them to prevent the smoking of cannabis in them. Not every transient use of premises or physical ability to remove others amounted to occupation, and on the facts of the present case, the mother remained the occupier of the house.

These decisions should, however, be approached with a degree of caution when construing s.35(1), given the very different statutory context in which they were decided. Thus an offence under s.8 of the 1971 Act may be committed by a person who is the "occupier or concerned in the management of any premises", whereas the s.35(1) offence may be committed by the "tenant or occupier, or person in charge" of any premises. The use of the term "tenant" might well lead the courts to construe an "occupier" for the purposes of s.35(1) as a person who is in lawful occupation otherwise than under a tenancy, i.e. under a licence. The term "person in charge" would be apt to cover a person who, whilst neither a tenant nor a licensee, nonetheless has sufficient control of the premises to exclude prostitutes from them, for example, depending on the circumstances, a concierge or key-holder.   **12.70**

"Knowingly"

For the meaning of the word "knowingly", see para.12.63, above.   **12.71**

"Permit"

For the meaning of "permit", see para.12.82, below.   **12.72**

"Brothel"

For the meaning of "brothel", see paras 12.27 and following, above.   **12.73**

Position of Lessor or Landlord where Tenant or Occupier is Convicted under Section 35(1)

Section 35(2) of the 1956 Act as amended provides: **12.74**

> "Where the tenant or occupier of any premises is convicted of knowingly permitting the whole or part of the premises to be used as a brothel, the First Schedule to the Act shall apply to enlarge the rights of the lessor or landlord with respect to the assignment or determination of the lease or other contract under which the premises are held by the person convicted."

The First Schedule entitles the lessor or landlord, in addition to any rights he may have under the lease or contract, to require the tenant to assign the lease or contract to some person approved by the lessor or landlord; and, if the tenant fails to do so within three months, to determine the lease or contract. Section 35(3) of the Act provides:

> "Where the tenant or occupier of any premises is so convicted . . . and either—
>
>   (a) the lessor or landlord, after having the conviction brought to his notice, fails . . . to exercise his statutory rights in relation to the lease or contract under which the premises are . . . held by the person convicted; or
>
>   (b) the lessor or landlord, after exercising his statutory rights so as to determine that lease or contract, grants . . . a new lease or enters . . . into a new contract of tenancy of the premises to, with or for the benefit of the same person, without having all reasonable provisions to prevent the recurrence of the offence inserted in the new lease or contract;
>
> then, if subsequently an offence under this section is committed in respect of the premises during the subsistence of the lease or contract referred to in paragraph (a) of this subsection or (where paragraph (b) applies) during the subsistence of the new lease or contract, the lessor or landlord shall be deemed to be a party to that offence unless he shows that he took all reasonable steps to prevent the recurrence of the offence.
>
> References in this subsection to the statutory rights of a lessor or landlord refer to his rights under the First Schedule to this Act".

12.75   It is anomalous that these provisions apply only where a tenant or occupier is convicted under s.35(1) of permitting premises to be used as a brothel, and not where a tenant is convicted of brothel keeping (s.33 or s.33A) or permitting premises to be used for habitual prostitution (s.36). The provisions were criticised by the Criminal Law Revision Committee[105] on the ground that they run counter both to the principle that the landlord is merely a reversioner and to the ordinary principles of the criminal law relating to accessories. The Committee also thought it odd to require the tenant to assign his interest, rather than forfeit it (as would be the case with a breach of covenant), and pointed out the lack of machinery for inquiring into the suitability of the assignee.

Tenant Permitting Premises to Be Used for Prostitution

Definition

12.76   Section 36 of the Sexual Offences Act 1956[106] provides:

> "It is an offence for the tenant or occupier of any premises knowingly to permit the whole or part of the premises to be used for the purposes of habitual prostitution (whether any prostitute involved is male or female)."

---

[105] Working Paper, *Offences relating to Prostitution and Allied Offences* (1982), para.2.42.
[106] As amended by the Sexual Offences Act 2003 s.56 and Sch.1, para.1.

Mode of Trial and Punishment

Section 36 creates a purely summary offence.[107] The maximum punishment   **12.77**
on first conviction is three months' imprisonment or a fine not exceeding
level 3 on the standard scale (currently £1,000), or both. For an offence
committed after a previous conviction, it is six months' imprisonment or a
fine not exceeding level 4 (currently £2,500), or both.[108] The higher maxima
also apply on first conviction under the section if the offender has a previous
conviction under s.33, 34 or 35 of the Act.

Parties to the Offence

The offence under s.36 may be committed as principal by both males and   **12.78**
females and by companies.

"Tenant or Occupier"

The leading case on the meaning of "tenant" in s.36 is *Siviour v Napoli-*   **12.79**
tano.[109] The appellant, a tailor, was the lessee of premises consisting of four
floors and a basement. He used the ground floor and basement for his
business and sub-let two of the upper floors to women whom he knew to be
prostitutes. The upper floors were entirely separate from each other and from
the retained floors. An information was laid against him, as the "lessee" of
the premises, under the forerunner of s.36. The charge was dismissed and the
decision was upheld on appeal. Avory J approved the following statement of
the magistrate:

> "Only those who had immediate control of the premises were responsible.
> 'Lessee' must be construed . . . as meaning 'lessee in occupation'."

It would seem to follow that a tenant who sublets the entirety of the demised
premises cannot commit an offence under the section, though he might be
liable to conviction under s.34 (landlord letting premises for use as a
brothel).[110] It would be otherwise if the tenant were merely to allow a licensee
to use the premises, retaining exclusive possession: he could then be
convicted under the section even if he did not himself use the premises in any
way.

For the meaning of the word "occupier", see paras 12.68 and following,   **12.80**
above. Unlike the offence in s.35(1), the s.36 offence cannot be committed by
a "person in charge" of premises. There is no authority on the effect of this
difference, but it is unlikely that the courts would construe the word

---

[107] 1956 Act s.37 and Sch.2, para.36.
[108] 1956 Act s.37 and Sch.2, para.36; Criminal Justice Act 1982 s.46. The enhanced penalties
were expressly preserved by the 1982 Act s.35(3).
[109] [1931] 1 K.B. 636.
[110] At 642, per Avory, J.

"occupier" differently in the two sections. On that basis, the better view may be that the s.36 offence can be committed only by a tenant or a licensee, and not by someone who, without having a lease or a licence, nonetheless has sufficient control of premises to exclude prostitutes from them.

"Knowingly"

12.81   For the meaning of the word "knowingly", see para.12.63, above.

"Permit"

12.82   For the meaning of "permit", see para.8.63, above. Given the range of persons by whom the s.35(1) offence may be committed, the word "permit" is likely in this context to bear the meaning "fail to take reasonable steps to prevent", rather than a narrower meaning referable to a failure to exercise a power to forbid the use of the premises for prostitution. This proposition derives some support from *Brock and Wyner*,[111] where the Court of Appeal held that the offence in s.8 of the Misuse of Drugs Act 1971 of knowingly permitting the use of premises for drug-related activities requires proof of unwillingness to prevent the prohibited activity, which may be inferred from a failure to take reasonable steps readily available to prevent it.

12.83   It was held in *Mattison v Johnson*[112] that a female tenant or occupier who herself uses the premises for prostitution cannot be convicted under s.36. Only if she permits another prostitute to use the premises might she be convicted. In the words of Lord Reading CJ[113]:

> "You do not use the word 'permit' when speaking of the person who himself does an act."

To similar effect is the Scottish decision in *Girgawy v Strathern*.[114] The two appellants jointly occupied a flat in Glasgow for about six weeks, using it for the purpose of engaging in acts of prostitution with women who came there habitually either at the appellants' invitation or on their own initiative. The appellants also allowed friends of theirs to use the flat for the same purpose. Their convictions under the forerunner of s.36 were upheld, but the court drew a distinction between acts of prostitution in which the appellants had participated and acts engaged in by their friends. Instances within the former category did not constitute an offence, as the appellants could not be said to have permitted themselves to use the premises for habitual prostitution. Further, the fact that they were in joint occupation was irrelevant, as it could not be maintained that each was permitting the other to use the premises. But

---

[111] [2001] 1 W.L.R. 1159.
[112] (1916) 85 L.J.K.B. 741.
[113] At 743.
[114] 1925 S.L.T. 84, HCJ.

instances within the second category did, on the evidence, fall within the scope of the offence.

"FOR THE PURPOSES OF HABITUAL PROSTITUTION"

The reference to use of the premises "for the purposes of habitual prostitu- **12.84** tion", rather than "as a brothel", means that the s.36 offence may be committed where a tenant or occupier permits a single prostitute to use the premises for her work.[115] Compare s.34 of the 1956 Act, under which a lessor or landlord commits an offence only if he lets premises to be used "as a brothel". The word "habitual" implies regular and/or frequent use of the premises for the purposes of prostitution. It is a question of fact and degree when prostitution may properly be described as "habitual". In *Dias v O'Sullivan*,[116] Mayo J said:

> "A habit results from a condition of mind that has become stereotyped. In terms of conduct its presence is demonstrated by the frequency of acts that by repetition have acquired the characteristics of being customary or usual: behaviour that is to be regarded as almost inevitable when the appropriate conditions are present. The tendency will ordinarily be required to be demonstrated by numerous instances of reiteration."

It has been held in Australia that premises may be used "for purposes of prostitution" if they are used to arrange acts of prostitution to be carried out elsewhere.[117] It is irrelevant that no acts of prostitution take place on the premises, or that the parties who are to be involved in those acts do not meet or even communicate there. Although there is no decision on the point, there is in principle no reason why the same interpretation should not apply to the s.36 offence.

KEEPING A DISORDERLY HOUSE

It is an offence at common law to keep a disorderly house.[118] The offence was **12.85** used in the past to deal with cases of brothel-keeping, but such cases are now normally prosecuted under s.33 or s.33A of the 1956 Act. The current use of the common law offence is mainly to prosecute cases in which premises are used by a single prostitute for the purposes of prostitution (and so do not constitute a "brothel") or for indecent or offensive activity of a sexual nature

---

[115] There is support for this construction in Australian cases: cf. *Storey v Wick* [1977] W.A.R. 47; *Samuels v Bosch* (1972) 127 C.L.R. 517, H.Ct.Aust. However, it was held in Queensland that the offence of keeping premises "for purposes of prostitution" involves proof that the premises were kept as a brothel: *Thick* [1907] Q.S.R. 198, Qd. S.C.F.C.; *Parker v Jeffrey Ex p. Parker* [1963] Q.W.N., Qd. S.C.F.C.; *Ferricks v Guzikowski* (1990) 51 A.Crim.R. 78, Qd. S.C.F.C.

[116] [1949] A.L.R. 586 at 589.

[117] *Ferricks v Guzikowski* (1990) 51 A.Crim.R. 78, Qd. S.C.F.C.; *Samuels v Bosch* (1972) 127 C.L.R. 517, H.Ct.Aust. (office of escort agency, arrangements with customers and girls made by telephone).

[118] 3 Co. Inst. 205; *Higginson* (1762) 2 Burr. 1272; *Tan* [1983] Q.B. 1053 at 1059.

not involving prostitution, such as premises where sado-masochistic services are offered.

MODE OF TRIAL AND PUNISHMENT

12.86 The common law offence of keeping a disorderly house is triable on indictment and the maximum punishment is imprisonment or a fine at the discretion of the court, or both, although the sentence imposed must not be inordinate.[119] A convicted offender may be deprived of the financial benefit obtained as a result of his criminal conduct by means of a confiscation order made under the Proceeds of Crime Act 2002. The offence is not a specified offence for the purpose of the provisions of the Criminal Justice Act 2003 relating to dangerous offenders.[120]

SENTENCING

12.87 In *Payne*,[121] the notorious "Madame Cyn", the late Cynthia Payne, was initially sentenced to 18 months' imprisonment for an offence of keeping a disorderly house. The term was reduced on appeal to six months, the Court stating that the facts disclosed a bad case of brothel-keeping, an offence under s.33 of the 1956 Act for which the maximum sentence (after a previous conviction) is six months, and that it was difficult to see why a longer term should be imposed in the present case. This would suggest that where the facts disclose a simple offence of brothel-keeping, the Court should follow sentencing practice under s.33 of the 1956 Act. *Payne* was decided before the introduction of s.33A of the 1956 Act, which penalises brothel-keeping for the purposes of prostitution and for which the maximum sentence is seven years' imprisonment. Accordingly, if the common law offence is prosecuted in a case involving the use of what amounts to a brothel for prostitution, the approach taken in *Payne* might indicate that the sentencer should have regard to the provisions of the definitive guideline relating to sentencing under s.33A. In *Court and Gu*,[122] discussed below, which involved keeping a disorderly house for the purposes of prostitution, the appellants were sentenced on conviction at trial to short sentences of imprisonment, suspended for 12 months, with a curfew requirement.

---

[119] *Morris* [1951] 1 K.B. 394. There used to be an argument, based on a provision in the Magistrates' Courts Act 1980, that the offence was triable either way: see the 3rd edition of this work, para.11.66. The argument is no longer tenable as the relevant provision has been repealed.

[120] Criminal Justice Act 2003 s.224 and Sch.15, Pt 2.

[121] (1980) 2 Cr. App. R.(S.) 161.

[122] [2012] EWCA Crim 133. For an approving consideration of the decision, see Dermot Keating, *An Orderly House?*, C.L. & J., Vol.176, pp.233–4, April 21, 2012. The case involved two properties, neither of which constituted a brothel since only one prostitute worked in them at any one time.

"KEEP"

One may "keep" a disorderly house without owning the relevant premises. By **12.88** the same token, one may own premises which constitute a disorderly house without "keeping" them as such. Thus in *Stannard*,[123] the owner of a house let rooms to women tenants on a weekly basis, knowing and assenting that their rooms would be used for prostitution. He retained no part of the premises for himself, and he derived no advantage from and exercised no control over the use made of the premises by the women. He was held not to be the keeper of a disorderly house. A similar case is *Barrett*,[124] where the owner of a house let it to a weekly tenant who used it for prostitution. The owner obtained no increase in rent by reason of the nature of the occupation, but had notice of the use to which the house was being put and took no steps to put an end to the nuisance. It was held that he could not be convicted of keeping a bawdy house (for which see para.12.96, below).

In *Moores v DPP*,[125] the Court of Appeal held that "keeping" a disorderly **12.89** house involves some persistent or habitual keeping of the premises for disorderly purposes. In that case, the requirement of persistency was not satisfied where a male exotic dancer gave a single indecent performance, in the course of which one female member of the audience rubbed oil on the man's penis behind a towel and the man walked naked round the audience and stood over another woman, causing her embarrassment. Bingham LJ (as he then was) said[126]:

> "It seems to me that a house does not acquire the legal character of disorderliness because disorder occurs there on one occasion . . . [T]he mischief at which the common law is aimed is the mischief of keeping a house to which members of the public resort for purposes of the disorderly recreation—if one can so describe it—which is available there . . . The essence of the mischief is the continuity which exists where the use of premises for a given unlawful purpose becomes notorious."

The Court held that the element of persistency was not supplied by the persistent indecency of the dancer's conduct throughout the performance. Bingham LJ said[127]:

> "persistency is not established because there was a performance of given length which was wholly indecent on a single occasion".

However, it was established in *Brady and Ram*[128] that the prosecution may **12.90** call evidence, or rely upon evidence called by the defence, to show that what happened on the occasion in question was merely the continuation of a prior

---

[123] (1863) 9 Cox C.C. 405.
[124] (1863) Le. & Ca. 263.
[125] (1992) 94 Cr. App. R. 173.
[126] At 178.
[127] At 177. An earlier performance by the dancer that same evening, while "not of the most tasteful", had not been capable of being considered indecent.
[128] [1964] 3 All E.R. 616.

user. In that case, the appellants were convicted of keeping a disorderly house on July 25, 1962, and on other days between that date and August 6, 1962. Evidence was adduced of strip-tease performances given in that period and of the fact that on August 1, 1962, one of the performers sang an indecent song immediately before the strip-tease. The jury were directed that in considering the nature of the entertainment provided by the appellants, they were entitled to have regard to the whole of the evidence relating to the singing of the song, including evidence of occasions when it had been sung outside the period specified in the indictment. It was held on appeal that this direction had been correct.

12.91 See further para.12.26, above, on the meaning of "keeping" a brothel.

"Disorderly House"

12.92 There is no statutory definition of the term "disorderly house". The common law defines the expression in general terms as a house which is not regulated by the restraints of morality and which is so conducted as to violate law and good order.[129] There must be an element of keeping open house, although the house need not be open to the public at large.[130] Misbehaviour or illegality on the part of persons resorting to the alleged disorderly house is not essential, nor is the creation of a common nuisance.[131] In *Quinn and Bloom*,[132] the Court of Criminal Appeal said that where indecent performances or exhibitions are alleged, a "disorderly house" is:

> "a house conducted contrary to law and good order in that matters are performed or exhibited of such a character that their performance or exhibition in a place of common resort (a) amounts to an outrage of public decency or (b) tends to corrupt or deprave or (c) is otherwise calculated to injure the public interest so as to call for condemnation and punishment."

The Court added that these elements are not mutually exclusive, and that a particular performance or exhibition may well fall within all three.

Charge based on the Provision of Sexual Services

12.93 A single prostitute who provides sexual services in private premises to one client at a time without spectators may be convicted in appropriate circumstances of keeping a disorderly house, even though the provision of the services may not itself amount to an offence.[133] This is settled by the decision

---

[129] *Berg* (1927) 20 Cr. App. R. 38.

[130] *Berg* (1927) 20 Cr. App. R. 38; *Rogier* (1823) 2 Dow. & Ry 431, cited with approval by Hawkins J in *Jenks v Turpin* (1884) 13 Q.B.D. 505.

[131] *Quinn and Bloom* [1962] 2 Q.B. 245.

[132] At 255.

[133] If the premises are used by more than one prostitute, they will constitute a brothel and anyone who manages or acts or assists in their management will be liable to conviction under s.33 or s.33A of the 1956 Act.

in *Tan*.[134] The two appellants, operating at separate premises and with the aid of a mass of equipment, some manual (such as whips and chains), some mechanical and some electrical, had subjected clients, at their own wish and with their full consent, to various forms of humiliation, flagellation, bondage and torture, often accompanied by masturbation. They had advertised extensively in contact magazines the fact that they provided these services at the premises. It was argued on their behalf that law and good order had not been violated, since what took place between the appellants and each client was not a criminal offence and there was "no element of open house". Parker J (as he then was), giving the judgment of the Court of Appeal, held that the public invitation by advertisement to resort to the premises was sufficient to supply the element of open house, and that there was authority for the view that lawful activities could become unlawful if carried to excess, it being for the jury to set the standard. He said that if the argument for the appellants was correct, the results would fly in the face of common sense: premises would be incapable of being a disorderly house if, e.g. there was a large notice in neon light over the door containing an open invitation to be whipped or subjected to any form of perversion, with the tariff set out. He concluded that whilst it might be novel to charge conduct of this nature as keeping a disorderly house, the circumstances "fall squarely within the scope of an existing offence".[135] Parker J also said that it is "both undesirable and impossible" to provide a universal yet precise definition of the offence. But where the basis of the charge is that premises were used for the provision of sexual services, the judge should give a direction along the following lines[136]:

> "In order to convict, the jury must be satisfied that the services provided are open to those members of the public who wish to partake of them and are of such a character and are conducted in such a manner (whether by advertisement or otherwise) that their provision amounts to an outrage of public decency or is otherwise calculated to injure the public interest to such an extent as to call for condemnation and punishment. They should further be directed that the fact, if it be a fact, that the services are provided by a single prostitute to one client at a time and without spectators does not prevent the house being a disorderly house."

The decision in *Tan* does not necessarily leave every prostitute operating within private premises liable to a charge of keeping a disorderly house. It was significant that the services provided in that case were "of a particularly revolting and perverted kind. Straightforward sexual intercourse was not provided at all."[137]

The suggestion that the offence of keeping a disorderly house is not apt to   **12.94** penalise the provision of "straightforward sexual intercourse" is borne out

---

[134] [1983] Q.B. 1053, CA.
[135] At 1062.
[136] At 1062–1063.
[137] At 1058.

by *Court and Gu*.[138] The appellants in that case rented two properties in which sexual services were provided. They placed two "commonplace, unremarkable and non-descript" advertisements in the personal services section of the local newspaper. When police officers called the mobile phone numbers given in the advertisements, they were offered sexual services. When the properties were searched a scantily dressed woman was found in one and a large number of condoms in both. In one property a vibrator was found, but no other devices or instruments. No customers were found at either property and no customers and no women offering services were observed going to or from the properties. The case proceeded on the basis that only one woman was ever offering sexual services at any one time, that only one customer at a time was ever present at either property, and that the sexual services on offer did not go further than "normal sexual intercourse". No complaint had been received and no concern had been expressed by people living in either neighbourhood. The appellants were first charged with acting or assisting in the management of a brothel, contrary to s.33A of the 1956 Act. However, the prosecution concluded that they could not establish that the premises were a brothel for the purposes of that provision. The appropriate charge should have been that, as tenants, the appellants knowingly permitted the premises to be used for the purposes of habitual prostitution, contrary to s.36 of the Sexual Offences Act 1956. But that is a summary offence and the usual six-month limitation period had expired. For that reason, the indictment was amended to charge the appellants with keeping a disorderly house. They were convicted by the jury but the convictions were quashed on appeal. Lord Judge CJ, giving the judgment of the Court, said[139]:

> "In the context of such detailed statutory provisions relating to sexual crime in its many different manifestations, an ancient common law offence should not normally be expanded beyond well-established parameters by judicial decision. The reality is that on the evidence available in this case the conviction of the appellants represented a significant widening of the ambit of the ancient offence.
> Our attention was focused on *R v Tan and others* [1983] QB 1053. Tan and others were accused of keeping a disorderly house. The difference between the facts of that case and the present are encapsulated in the advertisements, of which one example in *Tan* read:
> 'Humiliation enthusiast, my favourite past time is humiliating and disciplining mature male submissives, in strict bondage, lovely tan coloured mistress invites humble applicants, T.V., C.P., B.D. and rubber wear. . . . '
> Services of this kind were indeed provided. According to the judgment, they were 'of a particularly revolting and perverted kind . . . with the aid of a mass of

---

[138] [2012] EWCA Crim 133. For an approving consideration of the decision, see Dermot Keating, *An Orderly House?*, C.L. & J., Vol.176, pp.233–4, April 21, 2012. See also *DPP v Curley and Farrelly* [1991] C.O.D. 186, where the Divisional Court held that the justices were entitled to conclude that the prosecution had failed to establish a prime facie case that the appellants kept a disorderly house, since the services they provided did not outrage public decency or otherwise injure the public interest so as to call for condemnation and punishment.

[139] At 8–15.

equipment, some manual (such as whips and chains), some mechanical and some electrical, clients were subjected at their own wish and with their full consent, to a variety of forms of humiliation, flagellation, bondage and torture . . . '.

In one of the earlier cases referred to in the judgment, *R v Berg and Others* [1927] 20 Cr. App. R 38, the activities in the disorderly house involved exhibitions of a perverted nature, and in *R v Quinn and Others* [1962] 2 QB 245 the premises were used for the performance of acts which were 'seriously indecent and, in some respects, revolting', and the public was invited to resort to the premises for indulging in 'perverted and revolting practices'.

In *R v Tan* itself the court indicated that before a defendant could be convicted the jury had to be satisfied that the services provided were open to members of the public who wished to partake of them, and were 'of such a character and conducted in such a manner (whether by advertisement or otherwise) that their provision amounts to an outrage of public decency, or is otherwise calculated to injure the public interest to such an extent as to call for condemnation and punishment'. The entire judgment proceeds on the basis that the provision of what was described as 'straightforward sexual intercourse' would not be sufficient to constitute this offence.

The researches of counsel have not found anything in the old books which suggest any case where, on facts remotely similar to those present in this case, there has ever been a prosecution, let alone a conviction for the offence of keeping a disorderly house.

We have reached the unhesitating conclusion that the circumstances described here, taken at their highest, were not capable of falling within the scope of the common law offence. The criminality which should have been alleged was that the appellants allowed the premises of which they were tenants to be used for prostitution. That however cannot be an appropriate basis for upholding the use of the common law charge."

MENTAL ELEMENT

It must be proved that the house was kept for disorderly purposes with the defendant's knowledge.[140] For the meaning of "knowledge", see para.12.63, above.   **12.95**

KEEPING A COMMON BAWDY HOUSE

There is at common law a distinct offence of keeping a common bawdy house.[141] The term "common bawdy house" is convertible with the term "brothel" and means a house or room, or set of rooms in any house, kept for purposes of prostitution.[142] There are no reported prosecutions in modern times for the offence of keeping a common bawdy house. Where the elements of the offence are present, a prosecution will be brought today under ss.33 to 36 of the Sexual Offences Act 1956 or for the offence of keeping a disorderly house.   **12.96**

[140] *Moores v DPP* (1992) 94 Cr. App. R. 173.
[141] cf. *Barrett* (1863) Le. & Ca. 263.
[142] *Singleton v Ellison* [1895] 1 Q.B. 607.

Allowing a Person under 16 to Be in a Brothel

Definition

12.97 Section 3(1) of the Children and Young Persons Act 1933[143] makes it an offence:

> "If any person having the responsibility for a child or young person who has attained the age of four years and is under the age of sixteen years, allows that child or young person to reside in or to frequent a brothel . . . ".

Mode of Trial and Punishment

12.98 Section 3(1) creates a purely summary offence, the maximum punishment for which is six months' imprisonment or a fine not exceeding level 2 on the standard scale (currently £500), or both.[144]

Parties to the Offence

12.99 The offence may be committed as principal by both males and females.

"Responsibility for"

12. 100 Section 17 of the 1933 Act[145] provides:

> "(1) For the purposes of this Part of this Act, the following shall be presumed to have responsibility for a child or young person—
> (a) any person who—
> > (i) has parental responsibility for him (within the meaning of the Children Act 1989), or
> > (ii) is otherwise legally liable to maintain him; and
> (b) any person who has care of him.
> (2) A person who is presumed to be responsible for a child or young person by virtue of subsection (1)(a) shall not be taken to have ceased to be responsible for him by reason only that he does not have care of him."

For the meaning of "parental responsibility", see s.3 of the Children Act 1989.[146] On a charge under s.3 of the 1933 Act, the question whether a person has "responsibility for" a child within the meaning of s.17 is a question of fact for the magistrates.[147]

---

[143] 23 & 24 Geo. 5 c.12 as amended by the Children Act 1989 s.108(5) and Sch.13, para.3.
[144] s.3(1), as amended by the Children Act 1989 s.108(5) and Sch.13, para.5.
[145] As substituted by the Children Act 1989 s.108(5) and Sch.13, para.5.
[146] Not printed in this work.
[147] cf. *Liverpool Society for the Prevention of Cruelty to Children v Jones* [1914] 3 K.B. 813.

"Has Attained the Age of Four Years and is Under the Age of Sixteen Years"

A person attains the ages of four and 16, respectively, at the commencement   **12.101**
of the fourth and sixteenth anniversaries of his or her birth.[148] On a charge
under s.3(1) the prosecution may rely on s.99(2) of the 1933 Act, which
enables the court to draw from the victim's present appearance a rebuttable
presumption that he was between four and 16 at the date of the alleged
offence.[149] Alternatively, they may employ one of the other means of proving
age set out in paras 3.73 and following, above.

"Allows"

For the meaning of "allows", see para.8.63, above.   **12.102**

"Brothel"

For the meaning of "brothel", see paras 12.27 and following, above.   **12.103**

Knowingly Permitting Prostitutes to Meet and Remain in House of Refreshment

Definition

Section 44 of the Metropolitan Police Act 1839[150] provides that: **12.104**

> " . . . Every person who shall have or keep any house, shop, room, or place of
> public resort within the metropolitan police district, wherein provisions, liquors,
> or refreshments of any kind shall be sold or consumed, (whether the same shall
> be kept and retailed therein or procured elsewhere) and who shall . . . knowingly
> permit or suffer prostitutes or persons of notoriously bad character to meet
> together and remain therein, shall for every such offence be liable to a penalty . . .
> ".

This offence may be committed only within the Metropolitan Police District,
i.e. Greater London, excluding the City of London, Inner Temple and
Middle Temple.[151] An exactly similar provision relating to premises situated
in the City is contained is s.28 of the City of London Police Act 1839.[152]

---

[148] Family Law Reform Act 1969 s.9(1).
[149] 1933 Act s.99(2) and Sch.1.
[150] 2 & 3 Vict. c.47.
[151] For which see the London Government Act 1963 s.76(1).
[152] 2 & 3 Vict. c.94.

Mode of Trial and Punishment

12.105 Section 44 creates a purely summary offence, the maximum punishment for which is a fine not exceeding level 1 on the standard scale (currently £200).[153]

"Place of Public Resort"

12.106 A public house was held to be a "place of public resort for the sale or consumption of refreshments of any kind" within the meaning of s.35 of the Town Police Clauses Act 1847 (now repealed).[154]

"Knowingly"

12.107 The defendant must be proved to have known the character of the women resorting to his premises.[155] Where the premises are licensed and the licensee delegates the conduct of the business to a servant, the knowledge of the servant will be imputed to the licensee.[156] In the case of a joint licence where one licensee has the conduct of the business, his knowledge will be imputed to his co-licensee.[157] On the meaning of "knowingly", see further para.12.63, above.

"Permit or Suffer"

12.108 For the meaning of "permit", see paras 8.63 and 12.82, above. The word "suffer" normally carries the same meaning as "permit",[158] but this is unlikely to be the case where, as in s.44, both words are used together. It may be that the courts will interpret "permit" in this section as covering the case where the defendant positively allows or authorises prostitutes to meet and remain in his premises and "suffer" as covering the case where they meet and remain there and he does not bar or remove them.[159] There is no authority on the point.

"Prostitute"

12.109 For the meaning of "prostitute", see paras 13.45 and following, below.

[153] 2 & 3 Vict. c.94; Criminal Justice Act 1982 ss.38, 46.
[154] *Cole v Coulton* (1860) 24 J.P. 596.
[155] *Somerset v Wade* [1894] 1 Q.B. 574.
[156] *Allen v Whitehead* [1930] 1 K.B. 211; *Howker v Robinson* [1973] Q.B. 178.
[157] *Linnett v Metropolitan Police Commissioner* [1946] K.B. 280.
[158] *Bond v Evans* (1888) 21 Q.B.D. 249 at 257, per Stephen J; *Somerset v Wade* [1894] 1 Q.B. 574 at 576, per Matthew, J. Cp. *Rochford RDC v Port of London Authority* [1914] 2 K.B. 916 at 924, per Darling, J.
[159] In *Rochford RDC v Port of London Authority* [1914] 2 K.B. 916 at 924, Darling J defined "suffer" in broadly this way, as failing to prevent something that one is in a position to prevent without committing a legal wrong.

CHAPTER 13

STREET PROSTITUTION

Introduction...................................... 13.01
Loitering or Soliciting for the
  Purpose of Prostitution............... 13.25
Advertising by or on Behalf of
  Prostitutes.................................... 13.54

Soliciting for the Purpose of
  Obtaining the Sexual Services of
  a Prostitute.................................. 13.60
Anti-social Behaviour: IPNAs and
  CBOs... 13.73
Binding Over 13.83

INTRODUCTION

The law relating to street prostitution concentrates on suppressing offensive **13.01** or nuisance behaviour by prostitutes and their would-be clients and on encouraging the rehabilitation of those who have become involved in prostitution. In particular, whilst it is not an offence to engage in prostitution or, as yet, to seek the services of a prostitute per se, a person will fall foul of the criminal law if they solicit in public for the purpose of prostitution or for the purpose of obtaining the sexual services of a prostitute.

DEVELOPMENT OF THE LAW

The Wolfenden Committee

Until 1959, prostitutes who loitered or solicited in the street might be **13.02** prosecuted under a number of different provisions,[1] the most important in practice being s.3 of the Vagrancy Act 1824,[2] which made it an offence for a "common prostitute" to engage in "riotous or indecent behaviour" while wandering in a public street or place of public resort. There were also several local Acts, all of which required proof of "annoyance" to residents or passers-by, and other enactments which, while not specifically directed at

[1] For details, see the *Report of the Wolfenden Committee*, Cmnd. 247 (1957), paras 234–241.
[2] 5 Geo. 4 c.83.

909

prostitutes, were used on occasion to prosecute them for soliciting in such a manner as to cause nuisance or annoyance. Finally, there were numerous byelaws for the prevention and suppression of nuisances not otherwise punishable which were used to control offensive behaviour by prostitutes.

13.03   This statutory regime was fragmented and ineffective, and in the early 1950s concern began to mount about the visible and obvious presence of large numbers of prostitutes working in the streets of some parts of London and a few provincial towns. In response, the Government appointed a departmental committee under the chairmanship of Sir John Wolfenden, with a brief that included considering the law and practice relating to prostitution and solicitation for immoral purposes. The Wolfenden Committee, which reported in 1957, took the view that prostitution itself should not be made a criminal offence, as "no amount of legislation directed towards its abolition will abolish it."[3] But the Committee considered that:

> "What the law can and should do is to ensure that the streets of London and our big provincial cities should be freed from what is offensive and injurious and made tolerable for the ordinary citizen who lives in them or passes through them."[4]

The Committee accordingly recommended that the law relating to street offences should be reformulated to make it of general application and to eliminate the requirement of "annoyance". It also recommended that consideration be given to the wider introduction of the formal cautioning system functioning in Edinburgh and Glasgow, which kept prostitutes out of the courts until they had been cautioned for soliciting on two previous occasions. Finally, the Committee considered that the system of repeatedly bringing prostitutes before the courts and fining them a small sum, which they regarded as "an indirect and not very onerous form of taxation or licence", was making a farce of the criminal law, and it therefore recommended the introduction of a system of progressively higher penalties culminating in imprisonment for a term not exceeding three months.

Street Offences Act 1959

13.04   The Committee's main recommendations were implemented in the Street Offences Act 1959,[5] which made it an offence for a "common prostitute" to loiter or solicit in a street or public place for the purpose of prostitution. This, coupled with the repeal of the existing local Acts, gave the law on soliciting much greater uniformity than before. The Act did leave in place the offence of "riotous or indecent behaviour" in s.3 of the Vagrancy Act 1824, but that was belatedly repealed in 1989.[6] In accordance with the Wolfenden

---

[3] Above, fn.1, para.225.
[4] para.285.
[5] 7 & 8 Eliz. 2 c.57.
[6] By the Statute Law (Repeals) Act 1989 s.1 and Sch.1.

Committee's recommendations, the maximum sentence for a third or sub-sequent offence under the Act was set at three months' imprisonment, though the custody option was later removed.[7] On the Act's commencement, a cautioning system was introduced nationally on the lines recommended by the Committee.

One problem with the 1959 Act was that it covered only female and not male prostitutes.[8] This gap was partially plugged by the offence in s.32 of the Sexual Offences Act 1956 of persistent soliciting by a man for immoral purposes, which could be used to prosecute a male prostitute who touted for business in public. However, the Sexual Offences Review, reporting in 2000, considered that the s.32 offence should be abolished, as it was too broadly drawn and had been used to regulate conduct by men that amounted to no more than "chatting up" other men.[9] The Review did, though, recognise that soliciting by male prostitutes can cause distress for local residents and accordingly recommended that consideration be given to bringing soliciting by male prostitutes within the scope of the Street Offences Act 1959. This recommendation was implemented by the Sexual Offences Act 2003.[10]   **13.05**

Sexual Offences Act 1985

The 1959 Act dealt with soliciting by prostitutes, but not by would-be clients. It used to be thought that a man who solicited women for sexual purposes could be prosecuted for the offence in s.32 of the 1956 Act of persistent soliciting for immoral purposes.[11] But in *Crook v Edmondson*[12] it was held as a matter of law that a man who persistently solicited women for the purpose of having sexual intercourse with them was not soliciting for an "immoral purpose" within the meaning of s.32. This decision left the criminal law in the unhappy state of penalising the female prostitute who solicited prospective clients, but not the prospective client who solicited women for prostitution. Leaving aside the inequity of the situation, there was no specific offence to cater for the nuisance caused by persistent male soliciting of women for prostitution, which was endemic in certain urban areas.   **13.06**

A particularly offensive form of this nuisance is kerb crawling, whereby a motorist (typically male) drives slowly past a female pedestrian and invites her into his car. The Wolfenden Committee regarded this as a serious   **13.07**

---

[7] By the Criminal Justice Act 1982 s.71.

[8] *DPP v Bull* [1995] 1 Cr. App. R. 413, CA.

[9] *Setting the Boundaries* (Home Office, July 2000), paras 6.6.12ff.

[10] s.56 and Sch.1, which came into force on May 1, 2004.

[11] See e.g. the *Wolfenden Report*, above, fn.1, para.238.

[12] [1966] 2 Q.B. 81, DC. The courts later moved away from *Crook v Edmondson* by treating the meaning of "immoral purposes" in s.32 of the 1956 Act not as a question of law but as a question of fact for the jury. The result was that the s.32 offence became capable of catching at least some male soliciting of women. In particular, it was held in *Goddard* (1991) 92 Cr. App. R. 185 that the offence could be committed by a man who persistently solicited women for sexual purposes in a way that was "unpleasant, offensive and disturbing" to the victims.

nuisance,[13] but felt that if it were made an offence, difficulties of proof would be considerable and there would be the possibility of a very damaging charge being levelled at innocent motorists. The Committee felt unable to make any positive recommendation, other than that the problem should be kept under review. The Criminal Law Revision Committee, reporting in 1984, concluded that the nuisance caused by kerb crawling was sufficiently serious to justify legislative intervention.[14] It accordingly recommended the creation of an offence specifically to deal with the solicitation of women from or from the immediate vicinity of a motor vehicle. The Committee recognised that if the law merely penalised kerb crawlers, many men would simply park their vehicles and solicit on foot; in fact, there was already considerable evidence of such soliciting even without a prohibition on kerb crawling. The Committee thought that the making on foot of an unwelcome sexual advance should not of itself give rise to the possibility of a criminal conviction, but regarded it as an "acceptable compromise" that such advances should be penalised if there is an element of persistence. Accordingly, it recommended that it should also be an offence for a man persistently to solicit a woman or women in a street or public place for the purpose of prostitution.

13.08   The Committee's recommendations were implemented, with one important change, by the Sexual Offences Act 1985.[15] The change was that the offence of kerb crawling was limited by a requirement that the solicitation must either be "persistent" or conducted in such a manner or in such circumstances as to be likely to cause annoyance to those solicited or nuisance to others. The resulting offence proved controversial, mainly because of the evidential difficulties created by the requirement of "persistence" and the low level of average fines. An unsuccessful attempt to remove the need for persistence was made by the Sexual Offences Bill 1990, which failed to complete its passage through Parliament.

Sexual Offences Review: Setting the Boundaries (2000)

13.09   The Sexual Offences Review spent some time considering issues relating to prostitution. We have already mentioned its recommendation that s.32 of the 1956 Act should be repealed and the 1959 Act extended to cover soliciting by male prostitutes. The Review's main focus in this area was in fact on commercial sexual exploitation and the associated trafficking of adults and children, topics covered in Chs.10 and 11, above. But it also heard a range of evidence on other aspects of the law of prostitution, including from groups who favoured radical change in the law's approach to the subject, some proposing that prostitution should be decriminalised and regulated, and others that the burden of the criminal law should be from prostitutes to the purchasers of their services. This evidence raised major and important issues

---

[13] Above, fn.1, para.267.
[14] Sixteenth Report, *Prostitution in the Street*, Cmnd. 9329 (1984).
[15] 1985 c.44.

of social policy falling outside the Review's remit and in response it confined itself to recommending that there should be a further review of the law on prostitution.[16] In the ensuing White Paper, *Protecting the Public*, the Government said it would examine the scope for a review of the issues surrounding prostitution and associated exploitation, organised criminality and class "A" drug abuse.[17]

A Coordinated Prostitution Strategy (2006)

In 2006, following a consultation process,[18] the then Labour Government **13.10** published *A Coordinated Prostitution Strategy*.[19] The four key objectives of the Strategy were to challenge the view that street prostitution is inevitable and here to stay; to achieve an overall reduction in street prostitution; to improve the safety and quality of life of communities affected by prostitution, including those directly involved in street sex markets; and to reduce all forms of commercial sexual exploitation.[20] Changes to the law formed a relatively limited part of the package, with greater emphasis being placed on methods of preventing individuals becoming involved in prostitution, developing routes out for those already involved and tackling demand by deterring would-be clients. In the latter context the Strategy considered, but rejected, the Swedish (often referred to as the "Nordic") model of decriminalising prostitution and instead making it an offence to purchase sexual services. Many respondents to the consultation supported the principles underpinning this model and the shift of enforcement away from prostitutes onto those who create a demand for their services.[21] The Government was unpersuaded, citing the differences between the size and nature of the problem in the two countries (1,500 prostitutes in Sweden when the law was changed, an estimated 80,000 in the UK, many of whom, unlike in Sweden, suffer from severe addiction problems). However, as explained below, it subsequently performed a significant about-turn as regards the criminalisation of clients.

Some respondents to the consultation favoured repealing the offence of **13.11** loitering or soliciting in the street by a common prostitute (s.1 of the Street Offences Act 1959), to reduce the stigmatisation of prostitutes and the inhibition they may feel in seeking help and support. The Strategy accepted that enforcement alone has no long-term effect on street prostitution and tends simply to displace it to other areas or to other forms of criminal activity. But it also said that decriminalisation would send out the wrong

[16] *Setting the Boundaries*, 2000, para.7.8.
[17] *Protecting the Public: strengthening protection against sex offenders and reforming the law on sexual offences* (Cm 5668) (Nov 2002), para.73.
[18] Initiated by the publication of *Paying the Price: a Consultation Paper on Prostitution* (Home Office, 2004).
[19] Home Office, January 2006.
[20] Executive Summary.
[21] For argument in favour of criminalising the use of prostitutes, see M. Madden Dempsey, *Rethinking Wolfenden: Prostitute-use, Criminal law and remote harm* [2005] Crim. L.R. 444.

message about the acceptability of street prostitution, and make it harder to control the nuisance associated with the street sex trade. So it proposed that the loitering and soliciting offence should be retained, but that the available penalties should be better tailored to meet the needs of prostitutes and to address the factors that keep them on the streets. The Strategy noted that the offence is a low-level one and at present the courts will usually only consider a fine, which leads to a "revolving door" syndrome as prostitutes go back onto the streets in order to fund their fines. It therefore proposed the introduction of a more rehabilitative approach, allowing the courts to order an "appropriate package of interventions" to address the causes of persistent offending behaviour. Part of the reform would involve removing the outdated and offensive term "common prostitute", which was first recommended by the Criminal Law Revision Committee as long ago as 1984.[22]

13.12   The Strategy also declared an intention to use Anti-Social Behaviour Orders to address nuisance activity by prostitutes. It admitted that many respondents to the consultation criticised the effectiveness of ASBOs, some saying that they tended to displace prostitution to other geographical areas and so drive the women away from local support services, others that they failed to address the underlying reasons for the women's involvement in prostitution. The English Collective of Prostitutes stated that ASBOs had operated essentially to re-introduce prison sentences for the offence of loitering and soliciting, some 20 years after they were abolished by the Criminal Justice Act 1982. Despite this criticism, the Strategy concluded that ASBOs had a role to play in addressing the nuisance to communities associated with street prostitution, as part of a package of measures designed to encourage prostitutes to engage with support services. It said the Government would be issuing guidance on the subject, which would include advice on how ASBOs could be used effectively as part of an overall strategy designed to help those involved in prostitution to get out of it, and advice on drafting prohibitions that did not prevent women accessing support services.[23]

13.13   As regards young people involved in prostitution, there was a wide consensus amongst respondents to the consultation in favour of taking those under 18 outside the scope of the offences of loitering and soliciting, on the basis that criminalisation tends to undermine the message that they are victims of child abuse. The Strategy noted that the *Guidance on Safeguarding Children Involved in Prostitution* (published in 2000) required young people involved in prostitution to be treated primarily as victims of abuse, and that since its issue the numbers of cautions and prosecutions of those under 18 had dropped dramatically. Against that background, the Strategy's favoured approach was not decriminalisation for under 18s but, as with adults, encouraging the law to operate in a way that provided opportunities for

---

[22] Sixteenth Report, Prostitution in the Street, Cmnd. 9329 (1984), para.17.
[23] See   *http://webarchive.nationalarchives.gov.uk/20100413151441/http://www.crimereduction. homeoffice.gov.uk/antisocialbehaviour/antisocialbehaviour058.htm* [Accessed April 30, 2016].

diversion into contact with support services that would help young people to get out of prostitution. To this end, it announced an intention to re-emphasise that the criminal law was not to be used against children save in the most exceptional circumstances and as a last resort. This remained the position for a further decade, until under 18s were finally taken outside the scope of the 1959 Act by the Serious Crime Act 2015.

The responses to the Strategy were mixed. It was welcomed by ACPO and   **13.14** by organisations working with children, including the Children's Society and Barnardo's. The Conservative Party criticised it, its spokesman saying:

> "policy cannot simply focus on demand . . . We need to focus on the underlying social problems which force men, women and children into prostitution, such as family breakdown, drug misuse, child abuse, domestic violence and debt."

This criticism was a little unfair, as the theme running through the Strategy was the need to address underlying issues. The Lib Dems adopted a more regretful tone, calling the Strategy a "missed opportunity" and saying it would do "very little to reduce the number of prostitutes on the street, to improve the appalling conditions they work in, or to tackle health problems". They favoured the piloting of "managed zones" in designated city areas, a possibility which the Strategy considered but rejected. The English Collective of Prostitutes, on the other hand, was outraged, calling the proposals "a brutality" and stating that "clamping down on clients does not make women safer, it makes the lives of women more dangerous". In terms of its overall approach, the Collective appeared to share the view of the Conservative Party that the Strategy did not deal with the fundamental issue that "poverty and debt and drug misuse are sending women into the sex industry".

Policing and Crime Act 2009

In 2008, the Home Office launched a review to explore what further action   **13.15** could be taken to reduce the demand for prostitution. It reported in November that year in *Tackling the Demand for Prostitution: A Review*. In an about-turn from *A Coordinated Prostitution Strategy*, it concluded that there was evidence to support the creation of a new offence to criminalise those who pay for sex, where the sex provider is being controlled against their wishes for someone else's gain. This proposal was implemented by the Policing and Crime Act 2009, which inserted into the Sexual Offences Act 2003 a new offence (s.53A) of paying for the sexual services of a prostitute subjected to force. That offence is considered in Ch.10. The review made a number of further recommendations, including that the Government should consider amending the offences of kerb crawling and persistent soliciting under the Sexual Offences Act 1985 to remove the requirement of "persistence", so allowing a person to be prosecuted the first time they undertake the proscribed activity.

13.16   The 2009 Act also made a number of other legislative changes foreshadowed in *A Coordinated Prostitution Strategy*:

- It removed the concept of "common prostitute"[24] from s.1 of the Street Offences Act 1959 Act and introduced in its place a requirement of persistence, which captures the essence of the epithet "common" but without the offensive overtones.
- The Act also removed the little-used provisions of the 1959 Act by which a person who was unjustly cautioned for the offence could apply to a magistrates' court for an order that the caution should not be recorded or that the record of it should be expunged. It is not clear why the provisions were so little used, whether because the police were so circumspect in their use of the cautioning system that few people had cause for complaint, or because those who were unjustly cautioned were unaware of their rights under s.2 or unwilling to face a court appearance, even *in camera*. In any event, the provisions have not been missed.
- The Act also made provision for the courts to deal with persons convicted of the loitering and soliciting offence by way of a new form of order, dubbed an "engagement and support order", the objective of which is to promote rehabilitation. These orders require the offender to attend three meetings with a suitably qualified person ("the supervisor"), the aim being to assist them to address the causes of their offending behaviour and find ways to cease engaging in it.
- Finally, the Act repealed the Sexual Offences Act 1985 in its entirety and replaced the offences of kerb crawling and persistent soliciting with a single offence (contained in a new s.51A inserted into the Sexual Offences Act 2003) of soliciting a person in a street or public place for the purpose of obtaining their sexual services as a prostitute. The effect of this change was to remove the 1985 Act's requirement of "persistence" or, in the case of the kerb crawling offence, the requirement that the behaviour was likely to cause annoyance to the person solicited or others in the neighbourhood. As a result, the police are now able to prosecute a person on the first occasion on which they are found to be kerb crawling or otherwise soliciting for sexual services.[25]

Where next? The Honeyball Report and the All-Party Parliamentary Group on Prostitution

13.17   At the time of writing, *Tackling the Demand for Prostitution* remains the last major Government consideration of the law relating to prostitution. Since it was published, the focus has been on practical approaches to prostitution

---

[24] For which see paras 13.46 and following, below.
[25] See Lord Brett, *Hansard*, HL, col. 453 (July 6, 2009). An attempt to prosecute a single act of soliciting as a public nuisance failed in *DPP v Fearon* [2010] EWHC 340 (Admin).

rather than on the law.[26] Further impetus towards law reform in this area has, however, been provided by two reports issued in early 2014. First, the Committee on Women's Rights and Gender Equality of the European Parliament published a *Report on sexual exploitation and prostitution and its impact on gender equality*, known as the *Honeyball Report*, which was approved by the European Parliament on February 3, 2014.[27] Secondly, the All-Party Parliamentary Group on Prostitution and the Global Sex Trade ("APPG") published its report on the law of prostitution.[28] Both reports are wide ranging, covering child as well as adult prostitution and human trafficking for sexual purposes. In terms of the relationship between prostitution and the law, both reports reject the model currently applied in the UK of placing the burden of criminality on prostitutes rather than the purchasers of their services. As the APPG report puts it:

> "those who sell sexual services carry the burden of criminality despite being those who are most vulnerable to coercion and violence."

The APPG called on all political parties, ahead of the 2015 election, to commit to a review of the law with a view to reducing the demand for sexual services, by transferring the burden of criminality from those selling such services onto those who facilitate or create the demand for their sale. It recommended a number of legislative changes, the key one being the abolition of the offences of soliciting and their replacement with a general offence of purchasing sexual services.

This accords with the recommendation of the *Honeyball Report* in favour   **13.18**
of the "Nordic model", which criminalises the purchaser of sexual services and not the provider. The Report referred to the change made to Swedish law in 1999 so as to prohibit the purchase of sex and decriminalise the prostitute:

> "Sweden's prostituted population is one-tenth of neighbouring Denmark's where sex purchase is legal and has a smaller population . . . The evidence of the effectiveness of the Nordic Model in reducing prostitution and trafficking of women and girls and thereby promoting gender equality is growing all the time."

Neither Report favours the third possible approach to the issue, namely decriminalisation of the adult sex trade while continuing to criminalise

---

[26] See *A Review of Effective Practice in Responding to Prostitution* (Home Office, October 2011), encouraging local authorities and community safety partnerships "to develop a response to prostitution that aims to improve the outcomes for the community and particularly those involved in prostitution"; the *ACPO Strategy & Supporting Operational Guidance for Policing Prostitution and Sexual Exploitation* (November 2011), which provides a framework for the policing of this area of the law; and the national "Ugly Mugs" scheme launched by the Home Office and run by the UK Network of Sex Work Projects, which is intended to help protect sex workers from violent and abusive individuals (details of the scheme can be found on the UKNSWP website).

[27] 2013/2103(INI).

[28] *Shifting the Burden: Inquiry to assess the operation of the current legal settlement on prostitution in England and Wales* (March 2014). The Report is available at *https://appgprostitution.files.wordpress.com/2014/04/shifting-the-burden1.pdf* [Accessed April 30, 2016].

human trafficking and child prostitution. Variations of this model may be found in Germany, the Netherlands and Denmark. The German Government reported in 2007 that decriminalisation had not led to improvements in the protection or operating conditions of sex workers.[29] The *Honeyball Report* states[30] that since decriminalisation the Netherlands has become a prime destination for human trafficking. However, there remain strong voices in favour of decriminalisation.[31] Most notably, in mid-2015 the human rights group Amnesty International, after a period of extensive research, came out in favour of the complete decriminalisation of consensual sex work.[32] The group's position attracted immediate criticism from those who favour for the Nordic model.[33]

13.19   At the time of writing there has been no formal Government response to either Report.

THE CANADIAN EXPERIENCE

Canada (Attorney General) v Bedford

13.20   The Canadian experience is of particular interest given the similarity between the laws relating to prostitution in Canada and in England and Wales before the celebrated decision in *Canada (Attorney General) v Bedford*.[34] In that case the Supreme Court of Canada struck down as unconstitutional the criminal prohibitions on bawdy-houses, living on the avails of prostitution and public communication for purposes of prostitution. It did so on the ground that the offences violated the safety of prostitutes in breach of s.7 of the Charter of Fundamental Rights and Freedoms, which provides that the State cannot deny the right to life, liberty or security of the person except in accordance with the principles of fundamental justice. The unanimous decision (9–0) was suspended for one year to allow time for the Canadian Parliament to devise another way to regulate the sex trade if it chose to do so.

---

[29] C. MacKinnon, *Trafficking, Prostitution and Inequality* (2011) 46 Harvard Civil Rights-Civil Liberties Review 271, 304–6.

[30] pp.16–17.

[31] See   e.g.   *http://www.independent.co.uk/life-style/health-and-families/decriminalise-prostitution-top-medical-journal-lancet-calls-for-global-action-to-protect-sex-workers-from-hiv-9620273.html*;   *http://www.telegraph.co.uk/women/sex/11036096/Sex-work-in-the-UK-Just-what-would-decriminalising-prostitution-mean.html* [Accessed April 30, 2016].

[32] See   *https://www.amnesty.org/en/latest/news/2015/08/global-movement-votes-to-adopt-policy-to-protect-human-rights-of-sex-workers/ [Accessed April 30, 2016]. For criticism by sex workers of the APPG report, see http://prostitutescollective.net/2014/03/19/objections-from-the-ecp-to-the-methodology-content-of-the-report-from-the-appg-on-prostitution/* [Accessed April 30, 2016].

[33] See   e.g.   *http://www.theguardian.com/society/2015/jul/28/actors-streep-winslet-thompson-dunham-amnesty-decriminalisation-sex-trade* [Accessed April 30, 2016].

[34] [2013] SCC 72.

The case was brought by one current and two former prostitutes who **13.21** argued that sex workers would be safer if they were allowed to screen clients, or "johns", and operate in brothels with bodyguards if they chose. The safety of prostitutes became a high-profile issue in Canada following the conviction in 2007 of serial killer Robert Pickton, who preyed on prostitutes and other women in Vancouver's Downtown Eastside. Against that background the Supreme Court found the prohibitions overly broad or grossly out of proportion to the law's goals. Beverley McLachlin CJ said that a law that banned what she called "safe havens" for prostitutes exposed them to risks from predators. She said many prostitutes had no choice but to work in the sex trade, and the law should not make their work more dangerous[35]:

> "The prohibitions at issue do not merely impose conditions on how prostitutes operate. They go a critical step further, by imposing *dangerous* conditions on prostitution; they prevent people engaged in a risky—but legal—activity from taking steps to protect themselves from the risks."

In relation to the prohibition on communicating for the purpose of prostitution, which was analogous to the offence in England and Wales of soliciting for the purpose of prostitution, McLachlin CJ said[36]:

> "The application judge found that face-to-face communication is an 'essential tool' in enhancing street prostitutes' safety . . . Such communication, which the law prohibits, allows prostitutes to screen prospective clients for intoxication or propensity to violence, which can reduce the risks they face . . . The application judge also found that the communicating law has had the effect of displacing prostitutes from familiar areas, where they may be supported by friends and regular customers, to more isolated areas, thereby making them more vulnerable . . . By prohibiting communicating in public for the purpose of prostitution, the law prevents prostitutes from screening clients and setting terms for the use of condoms or safe houses. In these ways, it significantly increases the risks they face."

The purpose of the prohibition was not to eliminate street prostitution for **13.22** its own sake, but to take prostitution "off the streets and out of public view" in order to prevent the nuisances that street prostitution can cause. McLachlin CJ held that the harm imposed by the prohibition was grossly disproportionate to this purpose and that the prohibition was therefore unconstitutional. In so holding, she dismissed the Canadian Government's argument that it is the prostitute's choice to engage in prostitution, rather than the laws that govern the activity, that puts the prostitute at risk[37]:

> "First, while some prostitutes may fit the description of persons who freely choose (or at one time chose) to engage in the risky economic activity of prostitution, many prostitutes have no meaningful choice but to do so . . . As the application judge found, street prostitutes, with some exceptions, are a particularly marginalized population . . . Whether because of financial desperation, drug addictions, mental illness, or compulsion from pimps, they often have little

[35] At 60.
[36] At 68–71.
[37] At 86–89.

choice but to sell their bodies for money. Realistically, while they may retain some minimal power of choice—what the Attorney General of Canada called 'constrained choice' . . . these are not people who can be said to be truly 'choosing' a risky line of business . . .

Second, even accepting that there are those who freely choose to engage in prostitution, it must be remembered that prostitution—the exchange of sex for money—is not illegal. The causal question is whether the impugned laws make this lawful activity more dangerous.

. . . It makes no difference that the conduct of pimps and johns is the immediate source of the harms suffered by prostitutes. The impugned laws deprive people engaged in a risky, but legal, activity of the means to protect themselves against those risks. The violence of a john does not diminish the role of the state in making a prostitute more vulnerable to that violence."

13.23   The question arises whether the arguments accepted by the Canadian Supreme Court in *Bedford* could be run successfully in this jurisdiction. We suggest not. It is true that the language of s.7 of the Canadian Charter, guaranteeing a person's right to "security of the person", is mirrored in the right to "liberty and security of person" conferred by art.5 of the ECHR. However, the better view is that the focus of art.5 is the protection of liberty in its classic sense of personal freedom, and that "liberty and security of person" are best considered as one concept, with "security" meaning freedom from arrest or detention rather than "safety".[38] That said, the ECHR is not a static instrument and so it is possible that the arguments canvassed in *Bedford* will at some point be given an airing before a UK court.

Protection of Communities and Exploited Persons Act

13.24   As noted above, in recognition that the regulation of prostitution is "a complex and delicate matter",[39] the Supreme Court suspended the effect of its decision for a year in order that the Canadian Parliament could, if it chose, devise a new approach. The result, following a period of research and consultation, was Bill C-36, the Protection of Communities and Exploited Persons Act,[40] which came into force on December 6, 2014. The Act is notable for adopting the Nordic model of regulation by recognising that the primary victims of prostitution are those who sell their sexual services, and that it is the purchasers of those services and the third parties who benefit economically from their sale who cause and perpetuate prostitution's harms. Accordingly, the aims of the Act are to protect those who sell their sexual services from exploitation, protect communities from the harms caused by

---

[38] See e.g. *Guide on Article 5—Right to Liberty and Security: Article 5 of the Convention* (Council of Europe/European Court of Human Rights, 2012), available at *http://www.echr.coe.int/Documents/COUREDH-2012-Guide_on_article_5_ENG.pdf* [Accessed April 30, 2016], para.17 of which says: "The key purpose of Article 5 is to prevent arbitrary or unjustified deprivations of liberty."
[39] At 165.
[40] S.C. 2014, c.25.

prostitution and reduce the demand for sexual services. To that end it creates offences of purchasing sexual services and receiving a material benefit from the commission of the purchasing offence. The Act also provides that an individual cannot be prosecuted for selling their own sexual services, wherever their conduct takes place.

LOITERING OR SOLICITING FOR THE PURPOSE OF PROSTITUTION

DEFINITION

Section 1(1) of the Street Offences Act 1959[41] provides: **13.25**

> "It shall be an offence for a person aged 18 or over (whether male or female) persistently to loiter or solicit in a street or public place for the purpose of prostitution."

The section creates two offences, one of loitering and the other of soliciting.[42]

MODE OF TRIAL AND PUNISHMENT

Section 1(1) creates summary-only offences the maximum punishment for   **13.26**
which is a fine not exceeding level 2 on the standard scale (currently £500) or, for an offence committed after a previous conviction, a fine not exceeding level 3 on that scale (currently £1,000).[43] A second offence committed before conviction for the first offence is not committed "after a previous conviction".[44]

The Policing and Crime Act 2009[45] inserted into the 1959 Act provisions   **13.27**
empowering the courts to make a new form of order, the Engagement and Support Order, to promote the rehabilitation of persons convicted of an offence of loitering or soliciting instead of imposing any form of punishment. Under these provisions (contained in ss.1(2A)–(2D) and s.1A of the 1959 Act), the court may deal with a person convicted of an offence under s.1(1) by making an order requiring them to attend three meetings with a specified person ("the supervisor") or such other person as the supervisor may direct. The purpose of such an order is to assist the offender, through attendance at the meetings, to address the causes of the conduct constituting the offence and find ways to cease engaging in such conduct in the future. If the court

---

[41] As amended by the Sexual Offences Act 2003 s.56 and Sch.1, with effect from May 1, 2004; the Policing and Crime Act 2009 s.16, with effect from April 1, 2010 (SI 2010/507); and the Serious Crime Act 2015 s.68(1), (7), with effect from May 3, 2015 (SI 2015/820).

[42] cf. *Walker* [2006] EWCA Crim 1907, discussed in para.3.132, above.

[43] s.1(2), as substituted by the Criminal Justice Act 1982 s.71. Before the amendment made by the 1982 Act, a prostitute could be imprisoned for up to three months for a third or subsequent conviction under the section. See generally Roger Leng, *Imprisonment for Prostitutes* (1992) 142 N.L.J. 270.

[44] *South Shields Licensing JJ* [1911] 2 K.B. 1.

[45] s.17, which came into force on April 1, 2010 (SI 2010/507).

makes an Engagement and Support Order, it may not impose any other penalty in respect of the offence. The order ceases to be in force (unless revoked earlier) at the end of the day on which the supervisor notifies the court that it has been complied with, or at the end of the day specified in the order, whichever occurs first. Detailed provision is made relating to breaches of Engagement and Support Orders and the revocation and amendment of orders.

13.28   The rehabilitation period applicable to an Engagement and Support Order is six months beginning on the date of conviction and ending on the day provided for by or under the order as the last day on which the order is to have effect.[46]

PARTIES TO THE OFFENCE

13.29 In *DPP v Bull*[47] it was held that an offence under s.1(1) of the 1959 Act as enacted could be committed only by women. This decision was reversed by the Sexual Offences Act 2003,[48] which inserted into the provision the words "(whether male or female)".

13.30   The words "aged 18 or over" were inserted by the Serious Crime Act 2015[49] and have the effect that the offences of loitering and soliciting for the purpose of prostitution may be committed only by adults. Previously, Home Office guidance was that children under 18 who were engaged in prostitution should be treated as victims and prosecuted only as a last resort when all other options had failed.[50] In addition, guidance issued by the Department for Children, Schools and Families[51] stated that the criminal law was rarely an effective or appropriate response to children and young people under the age of 18 found loitering or soliciting for the purposes of prostitution, and that responsibility for the sexual exploitation of children or young people lies with the abuser, i.e. the person who pays for sex with the child or who grooms

[46] Rehabilitation of Offenders Act 1974 s.5(2)–(8), as substituted by the Legal Aid, Sentencing and Punishment of Offenders Act 2012 ss.139, 141 and Sch.25, Pt 2, which were brought into force on March 10, 2014, by SI 2014/423.

[47] [1995] 1 Cr. App. R. 413, CA.

[48] s.56 and Sch.1, which came into force on May 1, 2004.

[49] s.68(7), which came into effect on May 3, 2015 (SI 2015/820). This amendment does not apply in the case of an offence for which proceedings started before that date: 2015 Act s.86(11).

[50] H.O. Circular 006/2010, *Provisions in the Policing and Crime Act 2009 that relate to prostitution (sections 14 to 21)* (March 29, 2010), paras 53–55. The Circular is available at *http://webarchive.nationalarchives.gov.uk/-/http://www.homeoffice.gov.uk/about-us/home-office-circulars/circulars-2010/006-2010/* [Accessed April 30, 2016].

[51] *Safeguarding Children and Young People from Sexual Exploitation: Supplementary Guidance* (August 2009), pp.15.75. The guidance is available at *https://www.gov.uk/government/uploads/system/uploads/attachment_data/file/278849/Safeguarding_Children_and_Young_People_from_Sexual_Exploitation.pdf* [Accessed April 30, 2016].

the child and/or organises their exploitation. However, in 2012 the Office of the Children's Commissioner for England recommended that[52]:

"a review of all legislation and guidance which makes reference to children as 'prostitutes' or involved in prostitution should be initiated by the Government with the view to amending the wording to acknowledge children as sexually exploited, and where appropriate victimised through commercial sexual exploitation."

This call was repeated in the *Report of the Parliamentary inquiry into the effectiveness of legislation for tackling child sexual exploitation and trafficking within the UK*,[53] produced by a cross-party group chaired by Sarah Champion MP and supported by the children's charity, Barnardo's, which urged the Government to remove all legislative references to "child prostitution" as soon as possible. The Government responded by inserting amending provisions into what became the Serious Crime Act 2015, amongst them one that confines the offences in s.1(1) of the 1959 Act to adults, in order explicitly to recognise that children whose sexual services are purchased are victims of exploitation and not deserving of criminal punishment.

"PERSISTENTLY"

Section 1(4)(a) of the 1959 Act[54] provides that: 13.31

"conduct is persistent if it takes place on two or more occasions in any period of three months;"

This sets the threshold for "persistence" very low and as a result should avoid problems of proof, of the sort that acted as a significant limitation on the effectiveness of the repealed kerb crawling offence in s.1(1) of the Sexual Offences Act 1985.

Cautions issued to prostitutes under the informal cautioning scheme   13.32
explained in para.13.51, below, may be used to demonstrate "persistence", just as they were previously used to establish that a defendant was a "common prostitute".[55]

"LOITER"

The loitering offence appears to cover a wider range of behaviour than the   13.33
offence of soliciting and is more commonly charged. There is no authority on

---

[52] *"I thought I was the only one. The only one in the world": Inquiry into Child Sexual Exploitation In Gangs and Groups,* Interim Report, The Office of the Children's Commissioner (November 2012). The Report is available at *http://www.childrenscommissioner.gov.uk/content/ publications/content_636* [Accessed April 30, 2016].

[53] The Report is available at *http://www.barnardos.org.uk/cse_parliamentary_inquiry_report.pdf* [Accessed April 30, 2016].

[54] Inserted by the Policing and Crime Act 2009 s.16(1), (3), with effect from April 1, 2010 (SI 2010/507).

[55] H.O. Circular 006/2010, *Provisions in the Policing and Crime Act 2009 that relate to prostitution (sections 14 to 21)* (March 29, 2010), para.46. For web reference, see fn.50, above.

the meaning of "loiter" in s.1(1), but there is an instructive Scottish decision on the meaning of the word in another statute. *Williamson v Wright*[56] involved an appeal against conviction for loitering in a street for the purpose of betting, contrary to what is now s.8(1) of the Betting, Gaming and Lotteries Act 1963. Lord Alness, the Lord Justice-Clerk, stated that loitering connotes the idea of "lingering".[57] Lord Anderson said that loitering "is just travelling indolently and with frequent pauses"[58] and involves an idea of a certain persistence or repetition. But the Court was unanimous in holding that no offence was committed where a car slowed down on a single occasion to pick up betting slips. If these dicta are followed in the present context, a prostitute will "loiter" for the purposes of the 1959 Act if she lingers in a street or public place, or walks slowly up and down it. She need not actively solicit clients; simply standing around in the hope that clients will approach is enough.

"SOLICIT"

13.34 "Soliciting" can be accomplished by physical movements alone and does not require use of the spoken word. One can, therefore, solicit by a smile or a wink, by wriggling the body or by some other gesture or signal. Moreover, soliciting can occur even if the invitation does not reach the mind of the intended recipient or is not understood by him. Both points are settled by *Horton v Mead*,[59] a case of persistent male soliciting decided under what became s.32 of the Sexual Offences Act 1956 (now repealed). The appellant, who had artificially reddened his face and lips, was seen by two police officers to enter certain public lavatories in the West End of London and remain a few minutes in each. While in the lavatories and also while in the street he smiled at men, pursed his lips and wriggled his body. He did not speak to or touch anybody, and nobody complained about his conduct or alleged that they had been solicited. It was held that the appellant's conduct amounted to soliciting, and (by a majority) that it was not necessary for the prosecution to prove that the solicitation reached the mind of the persons intended to be solicited so as to attract their notice.

13.35 In *Weisz v Monahan*,[60] it was held that a prostitute who displays in a street or public place an advertisement indicating by some well-known euphemism that she is available as a prostitute between certain hours to anybody who desires her services, but who is not herself physically present, does not

---

[56] 1924 S.L.T. 363, HCJ, followed in *Rawlings v Smith* [1938] 1 K.B. 675 (a decision on the offence of loitering with intent to commit a felony, contrary to s.4 of the Vagrancy Act 1824).
[57] At 366.
[58] At 365.
[59] [1913] 1 K.B. 154; see also *Field v Chapman* [1953] C.L.Y. 787.
[60] [1962] 1 All E.R. 664, DC, followed in *Burge v DPP* [1962] 1 All E.R. 666, DC.

"solicit" within the meaning of the 1959 Act. Lord Parker CJ said that in this context:

> "soliciting . . . involves the physical presence of the prostitute and conduct on her part amounting to an importuning of prospective customers."[61]

The advertisement in *Weisz v Monahan* was displayed in a case outside a small shop, but it follows from the decision that a prostitute commits no offence under the section if she advertises her services by, e.g. placing advertisements online or in the press, putting cards in phone boxes or displaying on her premises a "model" sign, a red light or a doll.

Weisz v Monahan was distinguished in *Behrendt v Burridge*,[62] in which the **13.36** respondent had seated herself on a stool in the downstairs bay window of a house in order to advertise her services to passers-by. The window was illuminated by a red light and the respondent was dressed in a low-cut top and a mini skirt. The respondent did not actively seek to communicate in any way with anybody in the street. During the time she was sitting in the window, two men were seen to enter the house and one was proved to have paid for sexual intercourse. The magistrates held that the respondent's conduct could not be regarded as anything more than an explicit form of advertising and that therefore she had not been "soliciting" within the meaning of the section. On appeal by the prosecution, it was held that although the respondent had not made any active approach to prospective clients by way of word or gesture, her presence at the window was sufficient in the circumstances to constitute "soliciting", in the sense that she was tempting or alluring prospective clients to come in for the purpose of prostitution. Lord Widgery CJ said that soliciting and advertising are not mutually exclusive but can easily overlap to a considerable extent.[63]

"Street"

Section 1(4) of the 1959 Act provides as follows: **13.37**

> "For the purposes of this section 'street' includes any bridge, road, lane, footway, subway, square, court, alley or passage, whether a thoroughfare or not, which is for the time being open to the public; and the doorways and entrances of premises abutting on a street (as hereinbefore defined), and any ground adjoining and open to a street, shall be treated as forming part of the street."

The use of the word "includes" indicates that this does not purport to be an exhaustive definition. Bridges, roads, lanes, etc. are included in the definition even if they are privately owned, in so far as the public has access to them. Premises "abut" on a street if they actually touch the street and form part of

---

[61] At 665.
[62] [1976] 3 All E.R. 285, DC.
[63] At 288.

its boundary.[64] In some contexts it has been held that land "adjoins" other land only if the two parcels actually touch, while in others it has been held enough that they are "near" or "in close proximity" to each other.[65] In the context of s.1(4) the narrower meaning is most likely to be the correct one, given the need for the ground not only to adjoin the street but also to be "open to" it.

13.38   A particular question that has been addressed by the courts is whether s.1(1) penalises soliciting conducted from a window or balcony overlooking the street. One difficulty with holding that it does is that the words "in a street" seem to govern the location of the prostitute rather than of the person solicited. Moreover, s.1(4) expressly includes in the definition of street "doorways and entrances of premises abutting on a street", so Parliament has arguably addressed itself to the issue of how far the street may extend in relation to buildings with street frontages. Nonetheless, in order to meet the mischief at which the Act is aimed, the courts have stretched the meaning of "street" so as to catch such soliciting. The leading case is *Smith v Hughes*,[66] which involved six charges relating to two prostitutes who plied their trade at a house at 39 Curzon Street in London. On one occasion the first appellant had solicited passing males from the first floor balcony, which was some eight to 10 feet above pavement level. She attracted the men's attention by tapping on the balcony railing with a metal object and by hissing at them and, having attracted their attention, talked to them and invited them into the premises, indicating the correct door. On another occasion the same appellant had solicited by tapping the pane of a closed ground floor window and, having attracted the attention of men, invited them in for a price which she indicated by extending three fingers of her hand, and once again indicated the correct door. The other appellant had solicited male passers-by from a half-open ground floor window at the same address. She leaned out of the window towards the men as they passed in front of her and then talked to them, giving them a price. She also tapped the pane of a closed window and then smiled and indicated the correct door. On another occasion she solicited from a partly-open first floor window. The Divisional Court upheld the convictions. It took the view that the object of the Act is to enable people to walk along the streets without being molested or solicited by prostitutes, and for that purpose it mattered little whether the prostitute was soliciting while in the street or while standing in a doorway, or on a balcony, or at a window,

[64] *Barnett v Covell* (1903) 68 J.P. 93 at 94, per Lord Alverstone CJ; *R. (on the prosecution of Lambeth BC) v S.E. Rly. Co* (1910) 74 J.P. 137 at 139, per Kennedy LJ; *Buckinghamshire County Council v Trigg* [1963] 1 All E.R. 403 at 406, per Lord Parker CJ.
[65] The broader approach was taken in *Wakefield Local Board of Health v Lee* (1876) 1 Ex. D 336 at 342, per Cleasby B and *Lightbound v Higher Bebington Local Board* (1885) 16 Q.B.D. 577 at 584, per Bowen LJ. The narrower approach was taken in *New Plymouth BC v Taranaki Electric Power Board* [1933] A.C. 680 at 682, per Lord Macmillan; *Re Ecclesiastical Commissioners for England's Conveyance* [1936] Ch. 430 at 440, per Luxmoore J; *Buckinghamshire County Council v Trigg*, last note.
[66] [1960] 1 W.L.R. 830.

or whether the window was shut or half-open, since in each case the solicitation was projected to and addressed to someone walking in the street.

A similar case is *Behrendt v Burridge*,[67] in which a prostitute sat on a stool **13.39** in a downstairs bay window of a house in order to advertise her services to passers-by. As we have seen,[68] her presence at the window in those circumstances was held to be sufficient to constitute soliciting, in the sense that she was tempting or alluring prospective clients to come in for the purpose of prostitution. It was not an objection that she was not physically present in the street.

In light of the decision in *Horton v Mead*,[69] the prostitute in *Behrendt v* **13.40** *Burridge* would have been guilty of soliciting even if she had failed to attract the attention of any passers-by. But in *Smith v Hughes*, Hilbery J said in relation to the activities of the prostitutes in that case[70]:

> "[The] signals were intended to solicit men passing by in the street. They did effect solicitation of the men when they reached those men. At that moment the person in the street to whom the signal was addressed was solicited ... ".

In short, his Lordship seems to have considered an act of solicitation to be complete only when the prostitute succeeds in attracting the attention of the person solicited. This point was not, however, in issue in the case, nor was *Horton v Mead* cited to the Court. For those reasons we suggest that the dicta of Hilbery J ought not to be followed.

"PUBLIC PLACE"

It is a question of fact and degree whether a place is a public place, though **13.41** whether the material for consideration suffices to support one view or the other is a matter of law.[71] The phrase "public place" is not defined in the 1959 Act, nor is there any common law definition of the term in relation to the activities of prostitutes. The phrase should be interpreted *eiusdem generis* with "street".[72] Guidance as to its meaning can be derived from decisions relating to the meaning of "public place" in other offences, although these must be read in the context of the mischief which the particular offence is intended to avert.[73] A frequently cited dictum is that of Grove J in *Wellard*, a case of indecent exposure:

> "a public place is one where the public go, no matter whether they have a right to go or not."[74]

---

[67] [1977] 1 W.L.R. 29.
[68] para.13.36, above.
[69] para.13.34, above.
[70] [1960] 1 W.L.R. 830 at 832–3.
[71] *DPP v Vivier* [1991] R.T.R. 205 at 209, DC.
[72] cf. *Collinson* (1931) 23 Cr. App. R. 49; *Elkins v Cartlidge* [1947] 1 All E.R. 829.
[73] *Woods v Lindsay*, 1910 J.C. 88.
[74] (1884) 14 Q.B.D. 66 at 66–67.

Also helpful are decisions under the old law of affray. In *Kane*,[75] Barry J summed up to the jury in the following terms:

> "A 'public place' is a place to which the public can and do have access... It matters not whether they come to that place at the invitation of the occupier or whether they come to it merely with his permission; ... it matters not whether some payment, or indeed, the performance of some small formality such as the signing of a visitor's book, is required before they are allowed access. The real question is whether... access... is restricted to a particular class of the public ... it would be a private place and not a public place if access to it was restricted to members of the club or their guests."

13.42   In *Waters*,[76] it was held that a place may be a "public place" within the meaning of the Road Traffic Act 1960 even though there is a right to exclude particular members or a particular class of the public. So if only a restricted class of persons is permitted or invited to have access, the place is a private place; but if only a restricted class is excluded, it may be a public place. In *DPP v Vivier*,[77] a decision on the meaning of "public place" in the Road Traffic Act 1988, Simon Brown J (as he was then) said:

> "How then, in cases where some particular road or place is used by an identifiable category of people, should justices decide whether that category is 'special' or 'restricted' or 'particular' such as to distinguish it from the public at large? What, in short, is the touchstone by which to recognise a special class of people from members of the general public?... [O]ne asks whether there is about those who obtain permission to enter 'some reason personal to them for their admittance'. If people come to a private house as guests, postmen or meter readers, they come for reasons personal to themselves, to serve the purposes of the occupier.
>
> But what of the rather different type of case such as the present where those seeking entry are doing so for their own, rather than the occupier's purposes and yet are screened in the sense of having to satisfy certain conditions for admission. Does the screening process operate [to] endow those passing through with some special characteristic whereby they lose their identity as members of the general public and become instead a special class?
>
> Our approach would be as follows. By the same token that one asks in the earlier type of case whether permission is being granted for a reason personal to the user, in these screening cases one must ask: do those admitted pass through the screening process for a reason, or on account of some characteristic, personal to themselves? Or are they in truth merely members of the public who are being admitted as such and processed simply so as to make them subject to payment and whatever other conditions the landowner chooses to impose?"

13.43   A public place can become a private place if there is evidence to show that after a certain hour or at a particular point of time some physical obstruction has to be overcome in order to enter the place, so that entry thereafter is in defiance of an express or implied prohibition. Thus, it was suggested by Paull

---

[75] [1965] 1 All E.R. 705, at 708.
[76] (1963) 47 Cr. App. R. 149.
[77] [1991] R.T.R. 205 at 212–3, DC. See also *Planton v DPP* [2001] EWHC 450 (Admin); *May v DPP* [2005] EWHC 1280 (Admin).

J in *Mapstone*[78] that a public house ceases to be a public place not at the end of "drinking-up time", but when the public have actually drunk up and gone home and the licensee has locked the door.

Prostitutes who solicit otherwise than on the street naturally tend to do so in busy places where there is a greater chance of them finding potential clients, such as night clubs,[79] hotel bars and cinema foyers. Such venues are highly likely to be "public places": they are places to which members of the public are admitted as such, and any processing of those given admittance is merely to extract the price of entry or to apply such other conditions as the owner or occupier of the premises may require, e.g. a dress code or a registration requirement. A pub or bar is, however, unlikely to be a public place if it has been hired exclusively, e.g. for a wedding reception or a stag party. The same applies if a hotel is closed to non-residents. **13.44**

"FOR THE PURPOSE OF PROSTITUTION"

Section 1(4)(b) of the 1959 Act[80] provides: **13.45**

> "any reference to a person loitering or soliciting for the purposes [*sic*] of prostitution is a reference to a person loitering or soliciting for the purposes of offering services as a prostitute."

The term "prostitute" is not defined in the Act, but there are numerous decisions as to its meaning in this and other statutes.

Some of those decisions relate to the term "common prostitute", which appeared in s.1(1) of the 1959 Act until the word "common" was repealed by the Policing and Crime Act 2009. That word was not mere surplusage. In *Morris-Lowe*,[81] the Court of Appeal said that whether or not the performance by a woman of a single act of lewdness with a man on one occasion for reward is sufficient to make her a prostitute, it did not make her a "common" prostitute, which means a woman: **13.46**

> "who is prepared for reward to engage in acts of lewdness with all and sundry, or with anyone who may hire her for that purpose."[82]

It is, of course, highly unlikely that a person will persistently loiter or solicit in a street etc. for the purpose of engaging in a single act of lewdness with a man on one occasion, and so the question left open by the Court of Appeal, i.e. whether such an act would suffice to make the woman a prostitute, will not in practice arise in the context of the 1959 Act. However, despite the repeal of the word "common", in principle such a limited purpose ought not to suffice for the purposes of s.1(1). The repeal was motivated by a desire to

---

[78] [1963] 3 All E.R. 930 at 932.
[79] cf. *Morris* (1963) 47 Cr. App. R. 202 (dance hall).
[80] Inserted by the Policing and Crime Act 2009 s.16(1), (3), with effect from April 1, 2010 (SI 2010/507).
[81] [1985] 1 All E.R. 400.
[82] At 402, per Lord Lane CJ.

remove an offensive epithet, and not to widen the scope of the offence. We therefore suggest that the term "prostitute" should be interpreted to require that the purpose of the person loitering etc. is to engage in acts of lewdness with anyone who may hire them.

13.47   In *de Munck*,[83] the Court of Criminal Appeal held that a woman could be a "common prostitute" by engaging for reward in sexual activity falling short of sexual intercourse. Darling J stated it was sufficient to make a woman a common prostitute that she "offers her body commonly for lewdness for payment in return".[84] In *Webb*,[85] it was held that the term "common prostitute" is not confined to persons who offer their body in a passive way or submit to something being done to them, but extends to those who take an active role, e.g. by whipping or masturbating the client. The appellant, who ran an institute of massage for men, was convicted of a number of offences relating to prostitution. Three young women, all former masseuses at the institute, gave evidence that they had understood it to be part of their job to masturbate male clients who asked them to do so and one of the women stated that she had in fact masturbated clients. The appellant denied instructing the women to act in that way and contended that, if they had, they had done so of their own accord. The judge directed the jury that prostitution was the offering by a woman of her body commonly for lewdness in return for payment and that, if the girls had done the alleged acts, they had acted as common prostitutes. On appeal against conviction, the appellant argued that the concept of prostitution does not include acts of indecency carried out by the woman herself. The Court rejected this argument, holding that it was artificial to draw a distinction between cases in which the woman takes a passive role and those where her role is active. Lord Parker CJ said:

> "It cannot matter whether she whips the man or the man whips her: it cannot matter whether he masturbates himself or she masturbates him. In our judgment, the expression used by Darling J. 'a woman offers her body commonly for lewdness', means no more and was intended to mean no more than offers herself, and it includes, at any rate, such a case as this where a woman offers herself as a participant in physical acts of indecency for the sexual gratification of men."[86]

13.48   For there to be an act of prostitution there must, however, be physical contact between the prostitute and the client. In *Armhouse Lee Ltd v Chappell*,[87] it was held that engaging in telephone sex conversations for reward did not constitute prostitution. Simon Brown LJ (as he then was) said

---

[83] [1918] 1 K.B. 635.

[84] [1918] 1 K.B. 635 at 637. The judicial comments cited in this section all refer to prostitutes as female, no doubt reflecting the particular facts before the court and the reality that most sex workers are indeed female. As a matter of law, however, a person may be a prostitute whatever their gender.

[85] [1964] 1 Q.B. 357.

[86] At 366.

[87] *The Independent*, July 26, 1996, DC.

that prostitution requires at the very least both that the putative prostitute is at some stage in her client's presence, and that her offer, whether intended to be fulfilled or not, is of some direct physical contact of a sexual nature between them. It must follow that a woman who offers to carry out sexual acts on herself or on another for a paying voyeur is not a prostitute.

The key feature of prostitution is the making of an offer of sexual services **13.49** for reward. It was held in *McFarlane*[88] that a woman who acts as a "clipper" by offering such services and taking the reward in advance, never intending to provide the services, is nonetheless acting as a prostitute. The Court declined to draw a distinction for this purpose between "clippers" and "hookers", i.e. women who intend to provide the services they offer. The case involved a charge of living on the earnings of prostitution, but the Court was influenced by the effect of a contrary decision on the statutory offences aimed at soliciting by prostitutes:

> "If it were a defence to soliciting for prostitution under section 1 of the [Street Offences Act 1959] that the accused woman was acting as a 'clipper' and not as a 'hooker', proof of such offences would be extremely difficult. It would be necessary to prove not merely the offer of sexual services in a public place, but that the services were actually provided, or were at the time of the offering intended to be provided. The mischief being simply the harassment and nuisance to members of the public on the streets, the distinction between 'clippers' and 'hookers' is immaterial."[89]

It was held in *Knight v Fryer*[90] that the purpose of the loitering or soliciting **13.50** may be inferred from the circumstances. The respondent, a prostitute, had spent an afternoon standing in the doorway of a café in a red light area. From time to time she walked to the kerb, looked into cars driven by lone male drivers and then returned to the café doorway. The magistrates dismissed a charge under s.1(1) on the ground that there was no proof that the respondent had been loitering for the purpose of prostitution. The prosecutor appealed successfully to the Divisional Court, which held that it had been open to the magistrates to infer from the circumstances that the respondent's purpose had been prostitution.

THE CAUTIONING SYSTEM

The Wolfenden Committee, reporting in 1957, was impressed by the caution- **13.51** ing system operated by the police in Edinburgh and Glasgow, under which prostitutes were not brought to court for the first time until they had been twice cautioned for soliciting. It recommended that consideration should be given to the possibility of introducing this system more widely, in order to divert those who were just embarking on a career of prostitution from that

---

[88] (1994) 99 Cr. App. R. 8. *McFarlane* was distinguished in *Armhouse Lee Ltd v Chappell*, last note.
[89] (1994) 99 Cr. App. R. 8 at 12, per Lord Taylor CJ.
[90] [1976] Crim. L.R. 322.

way of life. The system was subsequently introduced nationally at the same
time as the bringing into force of the 1959 Act. It has no statutory basis, but
is derived from an undertaking by the Metropolitan Police Commissioner
and the chief officers of the provincial police forces. The effect of the system
is that prostitutes who have not previously been convicted of an offence
under s.1(1) will not be charged with such an offence until they have been
twice cautioned under the section by two police officers who have witnessed
the activity. Details of cautions are recorded at the local police station[91] and
this practice should be followed in relation to the non-statutory prostitutes'
caution. There is no right of appeal against such a caution and any challenge
would need to be made by way of an application for judicial review. In the
event of a prosecution under s.1(1) of the 1959 Act, the fact that the
individual has received such a caution on previous occasions may be adduced
as evidence that he or she has persistently solicited. The cautioning system is
described in Home Office guidance as follows[92]:

> "Current practice, as established by the 1959 Home Office Circular,[93] is to use a
> non-statutory 'prostitutes' caution' to demonstrate that a person is involved in
> prostitution and offenders are not prosecuted until at least 2 cautions have been
> given. It is expected that prostitutes' cautions will continue to be used to
> demonstrate 'persistence' under the amended legislation [*sc.* s.1(1) of the Street
> Offences Act 1959].
>
> Two officers would need to witness the activity and administer the caution.
> Details of these 'prostitutes' cautions' are recorded at the local police station.
> However there are two respects in which prostitutes' cautions differ from
> ordinary police cautions:
> * The behaviour leading to a caution may not itself be evidence of a
>   criminal offence for which the prostitute could be prosecuted.
> * There is no requirement for a woman to admit guilt before she may be
>   given a 'prostitutes caution', unlike an ordinary police caution.
> The caution is not a formal pre-requisite of conviction but it has become the way
> in which evidence is adduced to prove that an individual charged for the first time
> is a 'common prostitute.' It is expected that 'prostitutes' cautions' will continue
> to be used to adduce evidence of persistence."

13.52   The Criminal Justice and Courts Act 2015 provides, in s.17(4), that a
constable may not give a simple caution for a summary offence if the person
has, in the two years before the commission of the current offence, received
a caution or conviction for a similar offence, unless there are exceptional
circumstances. Whether there are exceptional circumstances and whether a
previous offence is similar to the current offence are not to be determined by

[91] Convictions, cautions, reprimands and warnings for the s.1(1) offence are recordable in
national police records: see the National Police Records (Recordable Offences) Regulations 2000
(SI 2000/1139).
[92] H.O. Circular 006/2010, *Provisions in the Policing and Crime Act 2009 that relate to
prostitution (sections 14 to 21)* (March 29, 2010), paras 46–48. For web reference, see fn.50,
above.
[93] H.O. Circular No.109/1959.

a police officer below the rank of inspector.[94] A determination must be made in accordance with guidance issued by the Secretary of State.[95] The guidance, *Simple Cautions for Adult Offenders*,[96] does not indicate whether the introduction of the statutory restrictions affects the use of the "prostitute's caution". We suggest that it does not, on the basis that this form of caution falls outside the intended scope of the restrictions. Any other interpretation would be likely to hamper significantly the effectiveness of the non-statutory scheme in keeping prostitutes out of the courts until their third offence.

Power of Arrest

The 1959 Act, as enacted, empowered a constable to arrest without warrant **13.53** anyone he found in a street or public place and suspected, with reasonable cause, to be committing an offence under s.1(1).[97] This power was repealed by the Serious Organised Crime and Police Act 2005.[98] The general police powers of arrest are set out in s.24 of the Police and Criminal Evidence Act 1984, as substituted by s.110 of the 2005 Act. They empower a constable to arrest a person if the constable has reasonable grounds for believing that the arrest is necessary inter alia to prevent the person committing an offence against public decency, but only where members of the public going about their normal business cannot reasonably be expected to avoid the person.[99] There is no power to stop and detain a prostitute for the purpose of cautioning her for loitering or soliciting, and a constable may therefore use only that degree of physical force which is lawful between two ordinary citizens.[100] It follows that the successful operation of the cautioning system explained above depends upon the co-operation of the individual in providing their name and address, so that the police can check whether any cautions have been previously recorded against them.

Advertising by or on Behalf of Prostitutes

We have already seen that a prostitute does not "solicit" within the meaning **13.54** of s.1(1) of the Street Offences Act 1959 if she advertises her services by placing advertisements online or in the press, putting a card in a phone box or on a newsagent's board, or by displaying on premises a "model" sign, a red light or a doll. But *Behrendt v Burridge* makes clear that advertising and

---

[94] 2015 Act s.17(5); Criminal Justice and Courts Act 2015 (Simple Cautions) (Specification of Police Ranks) Order 2015 (SI 2015/830).

[95] 2015 Act s.17(6).

[96] MoJ (2015), available at *https://www.gov.uk/government/uploads/system/uploads/attachment_data/file/416068/cautions-guidance-2015.pdf* [Accessed April 30, 2016].

[97] s.1(3) of the 1959 Act. This power of arrest was expressly preserved by the Police and Criminal Evidence Act 1984 s.26 and Sch.2.

[98] s.111 and Sch.7, Pt I, para.14, which came into force on January 1, 2006.

[99] s.24(4), (5)(c)(iv) and (6).

[100] *Collins v Wilcock* [1984] 3 All E.R. 374.

soliciting are not mutually exclusive activities, and that a prostitute who, in a street or in premises visible from a street, advertises her services by her dress and demeanour may be soliciting. Advertising by third parties on a prostitute's behalf may amount to a conspiracy to corrupt public morals[101] or a conspiracy to outrage public decency.[102] Depending on the content, advertising a prostitute's services may also contravene the Obscene Publications Act 1959 or the Indecent Displays (Control) Act 1981.[103]

13.55   The 1981 Act was designed to check the publication of pornographic material in bookstalls and shop windows. Section 1(1) provides that if any indecent matter is publicly displayed, the person making the display and any person causing or permitting the display to be made shall be guilty of an offence. For this purpose, any matter which is displayed in, or so as to be visible from, any public place is deemed to be publicly displayed.[104] The term "public place" in this context is defined to mean any place to which the public have or are permitted to have access (whether on payment or otherwise) while the matter is displayed.[105] The word "indecent" is not defined by the Act, and so in every case it will be for the jury to decide whether the matter displayed is indecent. The word does however represent a significant practical limitation on the application of the offence to advertisements by or on behalf of prostitutes. In particular, prostitutes' advertisements are usually suggestive or euphemistic rather than indecent and as such will not fall foul of the offence. "Matter" is defined to include anything capable of being displayed, except that it does not include an actual human body or any part thereof; and in determining for the purposes of the section whether any displayed matter is indecent, any part of that matter which is not exposed to view shall be disregarded, and account may be taken of the effect of juxtaposing one thing with another.[106] There are exceptions from the offence for matter included in a television broadcasting service or other television programme service, a display in an art gallery or museum where the matter is visible only from within the gallery or museum, a performance of a play or an exhibition of a film; and for matter displayed by or with the authority of, and visible only from within a building occupied by, the Crown or any local authority.[107]

13.56   The offence under s.1(1) of the 1981 Act is triable either way. The maximum punishment on summary conviction is a fine. On conviction on indictment it is two years' imprisonment or a fine, or both. Until recently, the

---

[101] *Shaw v DPP* [1962] A.C. 220.
[102] *Knuller v DPP* [1973] A.C. 435.
[103] 1981 c.42.
[104] s.1(2).
[105] s.1(3). There is an exception for places to which the public are permitted to have access only on payment which is or includes payment for the display, and for shops or parts of shops to which the public can only gain access by passing beyond an adequate warning notice (as defined in s.1(6)). The exceptions apply only where persons under 18 are not permitted to enter while the display is continuing.
[106] s.1(5).
[107] s.1(4).

maximum fine on summary conviction was a fine not exceeding level 5 on the standard scale (i.e. £5,000). The effect of s.85 of the Legal Aid, Sentencing and Punishment of Offenders Act 2012 is that, from March 12, 2015, a fine of any amount may be imposed. Fines will, however, continue to be set according to the seriousness of the offence and the means of the offender.

In the 1990s and early 2000s a particular nuisance was caused in urban   **13.57**
areas by the placement of prostitutes' advertising cards in phone boxes. The activities of those involved in the business of "carding" were often prolific: for example, in 1999 BT estimated that they removed some 150,000 cards from their 700 central London phone boxes each week.[108] The nuisance created by this phenomenon was addressed in the Criminal Justice and Police Act 2001, s.46(1) of which makes it an offence to place on, or in the immediate vicinity of, a public telephone an advertisement relating to prostitution with the intention that the advertisement should come to the attention of any other person or persons.[109] For this purpose an advertisement relates to prostitution if it is for the services of a prostitute, whether male or female, or indicates that premises are premises at which such services are offered.[110] Moreover, in proceedings for an offence under the section, any advertisement which a reasonable person would consider to be an advertisement relating to prostitution is presumed to be such an advertisement unless it is shown not to be.[111] For the purposes of the section a "public telephone" means any telephone located in a public place and made available for use by the public, or a section of the public, and includes any kiosk, booth, acoustic hood, shelter or other structure in or on which such a telephone is located or to which it is attached.[112] For this purpose, a "public place" means any place to which the public have or are permitted to have access, whether on payment or otherwise, other than a place to which children under the age of 16 are not permitted to have access, whether by law or otherwise, and any premises which are wholly or mainly used for residential purposes. The effect of this is that an adult-only club or a student hall of residence will fall outside the scope of the offence. A person guilty of the offence under s.46(1) is liable on summary conviction to imprisonment for a term not exceeding six months (a surprisingly high maximum considering the nature of the offence) or a fine.[113] As from a day to be appointed the maximum sentence on summary conviction will increase to 12 months' imprisonment.[114] The increase will

---

[108] cf. *New Measures to Control Prostitutes' Cards in Phone Boxes* (Home Office Consultation Paper, May 18, 1999), para.6.

[109] Before the enactment of this offence there were attempts to prosecute "carders" with the littering offence under s.87 of the Environmental Protection Act 1990. In the case of enclosed telephone boxes, these prosecutions ran into the difficulty that such boxes are neither a public open space nor a covered place open to the air on at least one side, as required by s.87: cf. *Felix v DPP* [1998] Crim. L.R. 657.

[110] s.46(2).

[111] s.46(3).

[112] s.46(5).

[113] s.46(4).

[114] Criminal Justice Act 2003 s.282(2), (3).

have no application to offences committed before it takes effect.[115] Until recently, the maximum fine was a fine not exceeding level 5 on the standard scale (i.e. £5,000). The effect of s.85 of the Legal Aid, Sentencing and Punishment of Offenders Act 2012 is that, from March 12, 2015, a fine of any amount may be imposed.

13.58   By s.47(1) of the 2001 Act, the Secretary of State may by order provide for s.46 to apply in relation to any public structure of a description specified in the order. For this purpose, "public structure" means any structure that is provided as an amenity for the use of the public or a section of the public and is located in a public place.[116] No order has yet been made under the section.

13.59   In recent years, the growth of the internet and the ubiquity of smartphones have led to a significant decline in both the number of phone boxes in our communities and their use to advertise sexual services, as sex workers have increasingly turned to online advertising, including through the use of social media such as Facebook and Twitter. As a result, the offence in s.46(1) of the Criminal Justice and Police Act 2001 has an increasingly archaic flavour. The statistics show a dramatic decline in the number of convictions for this offence over recent years[117]:

2007–2008: 330
2008–2009: 349
2009–2010: 457
2010–2011: 331
2011–2012: 149
2012–2013: 80
2013–2014: 91
2014–2015: 37

There is little or no policing interest in the online advertising of sexual services, primarily because, unlike advertising in a public place which may offend passers-by, advertising through social media is perceived as essentially victimless and thus commands no law enforcement priority. Some concern has, however, been expressed about the phenomenon and in particular the risk that on-line advertising of sexual services may be too readily accessed by children.[118]

---

[115] Criminal Justice Act 2003 s.282(4).
[116] s.47(2).
[117] *http://www.cps.gov.uk/data/violence_against_women/prostitution_key_findings_14_15/ prostitution_table_4_advertising_prostitution_offences_0809_1415.csv* [Accessed April 30, 2016].
[118] See *http://www.telegraph.co.uk/technology/facebook/9836358/Prostitutes-advertising-on-Facebook-and-Twitter.html* and *http://www.dailymail.co.uk/femail/article-2296576/How-Twitter-Facebook-expose-children-websites-prostitutes-Vice-girl-ads-illegal-phone-boxes-social-media.html* [Accessed April 30, 2016].

SOLICITING FOR THE PURPOSE OF OBTAINING THE SEXUAL SERVICES OF A PROSTITUTE

DEFINITION

Section 51A of the Sexual Offences Act 2003[119] provides: **13.60**

> "It is an offence for a person in a street or public place to solicit another (B) for the purpose of obtaining B's sexual services as a prostitute."

This offence replaced the offences in the Sexual Offences Act 1985 of kerb   **13.61**
crawling (s.1(1)) and persistent soliciting (s.2(1)) with a single offence of soliciting. The effect of this change was to remove the 1985 Act's requirement that the soliciting was "persistent" or, in the case of the kerb crawling offence, that the behaviour was likely to cause annoyance to the person solicited or others in the neighbourhood. As a result, the police are now able to prosecute a person on the first occasion on which they are found to be kerb crawling or otherwise soliciting for sexual services.

The 1985 Act offences overlapped in cases where the defendant persistently   **13.62**
solicited from a motor vehicle or in the immediate vicinity of a motor vehicle that he had just got out of or off. The Criminal Law Revision Committee anticipated this overlap when recommending the creation of the two offences[120] and suggested that there might be circumstances in which it would be desirable to charge both offences. However, this suggestion was rarely acted upon: charging both offences would generally be over-kill and, as the offences attracted the same maximum penalty, the prosecution normally had little to gain by it. The replacement of the 1985 Act offences by s.51A has the welcome effect of removing the overlap and so injecting greater clarity into the application of the law in this area.

MODE OF TRIAL AND PUNISHMENT

Section 51A creates a purely summary offence, the maximum punishment for   **13.63**
which is a fine not exceeding level 3 on the standard scale (currently £1,000).[121]

PARTIES TO THE OFFENCE

The offence under s.51A may be committed as principal by males or females.   **13.64**
The person solicited may be male or female.

---

[119] Inserted by the Policing and Crime Act 2009 s.19, with effect from April 1, 2010 (SI 2010/507).
[120] Sixteenth Report, *Prostitution in the Street*, Cmnd. 9329 (1984), para.49.
[121] s.51A(3).

"Street"

13.65 Section 51A(4) provides that the word "street" in s.51A has the meaning given by s.1(4) of the Street Offences Act 1959, discussed in paras 13.37 and following, above. In addition, s.51A(2) provides:

> "The reference to a person in a street or public place includes a person in a vehicle in a street or public place."

This provision makes clear that the s.51A offence may be committed by kerb crawling. Although kerb crawling is usually carried out from a motor vehicle, as a matter of law there is no requirement that the vehicle is motorised or otherwise mechanically propelled.[122] The vehicle may be moving or stationary at the relevant time. It must be in a street or public place, so soliciting from a vehicle on private land is not caught by the offence.

"Public Place"

13.66 For the meaning of this phrase in s.1(1) of the Street Offences Act 1959, see paras 13.41 and following, above. See also s.51A(2), set out in the last paragraph.

"Solicit"

13.67 See the discussion of the meaning of "solicit" in s.1(1) of the Street Offences Act 1959, in paras 13.34 and following, above. Two decisions relating to the repealed offences in the Sexual Offences Act 1985 are instructive.

13.68 In *DPP v Ollerenshaw*,[123] which related to the offence of kerb crawling in s.1(1) of the 1985 Act, the woman allegedly solicited by the appellant had called out to him, offering her services as a prostitute. He had accepted and invited her into his car. His conviction was quashed on the ground that "soliciting" implies begging a favour, an element of importuning or asking. Given the existing agreement between them for sexual intercourse, the appellant's act of inviting the woman into his car was not soliciting. But the Court said its decision did not mean that if the prostitute makes the first approach, the man cannot be guilty of soliciting thereafter. Provided there is some importuning or asking on his part, he may be convicted of the offence.

13.69 In *Darroch v DPP*,[124] the appellant was convicted of persistent soliciting contrary to s.2(1) of the 1985 Act on evidence that he had driven round and round a red light area and at one point had beckoned a prostitute towards him. It was held on appeal that the driving did not constitute "soliciting" in

---

[122] cf. the Road Traffic Act 1988 s.185(1), which defines a "motor vehicle" as "a mechanically propelled vehicle intended or adapted for use on roads".
[123] *The Independent*, January 6, 1992, DC (No.CO/2197/90).
[124] (1990) 91 Cr. App. R. 378, CA.

the absence of evidence that the appellant had given some indication, by act or word, to a prostitute that he required her services. As for the beckoning of the prostitute, it was argued on the appellant's behalf that the justices had been wrong to treat this as an act of soliciting, as he might only have been calling over an unknown woman to ask for directions. The Court rejected this "unreal submission" on the ground that the justices had heard evidence that four days earlier the appellant had been found in the same area with a prostitute in a stationary car, and they were entitled to use that evidence to counter the innocent explanation proffered for the later incident. The Court nonetheless went on to quash the conviction for want of evidence that the soliciting was "persistent".

Section 51A makes it an offence for "a person in a street or public place   **13.70** to solicit another (B)". Must B also be in the street or public place when they are solicited, or may they be elsewhere, e.g. on private land adjoining the street? The section is not clear on this point. This might lead the courts to construe it narrowly, in order not to penalise conduct that Parliament has not explicitly prohibited. Soliciting is, however, equally offensive wherever the person at whom it is directed happens to be. We therefore suggest that the courts are more likely to adopt a purposive construction of the section, in order to curb the mischief at which it is aimed. On that basis, the better view is that whilst the defendant must be in a street or public place when he solicits B, it is not a requirement that B is also in the street or public place at the relevant time.

There is no requirement that the offence is committed face-to-face and so   **13.71** it may in principle be committed where A in a street or public place solicits B by remote means such as "bluejacking" (the sending of unsolicited messages to Bluetooth-enabled devices).

"FOR THE PURPOSE OF OBTAINING B'S SEXUAL SERVICES AS A PROSTITUTE"

A must solicit B "for the purpose of obtaining B's sexual services as a   **13.72** prostitute". Accordingly, asking a person to obtain the services of another person as a prostitute will not amount to an offence under the Act, nor will asking a prostitute to perform services which are not sexual. For the meaning of "prostitute", see paras 13.45 and following, above. As to what the concept of "sexual services" might cover, see para.10.14, above. The purpose of A's soliciting may no doubt be inferred from the circumstances, as it may under s.1(1) of the Street Offences Act 1959: see para.13.50, above. As with the repealed 1985 Act offences, most prosecutions under s.51A are likely to be brought against men who approach prostitutes, but the person approached need not be proved to be a prostitute. Part of the mischief the section is designed to prevent is the harassment of people who are innocently walking in the street.

ANTI-SOCIAL BEHAVIOUR: INJUNCTIONS TO PREVENT NUISANCE AND ANNOYANCE AND CRIMINAL BEHAVIOUR ORDERS

13.73 The Anti-Social Behaviour, Crime and Policing Act 2014 Pt 1, which came into force on March 23, 2015,[125] reforms the tools for dealing with anti-social behaviour. In short, the Act abolishes the anti-social behaviour order ("ASBO") provided for by the Crime and Disorder Act 1998, both the order made on application and the order ancillary to a criminal conviction (commonly referred to as a "CRASBO"), and replaces them respectively with a new form of injunctive relief called the Injunction to Prevent Nuisance and Annoyance ("IPNA") and a new Criminal Behaviour Order ("CBO").[126] One potential application of the new orders is to control the activities of prostitutes and the would-be purchasers of their services, in much the same way that police forces round the country used the ASBO.[127] This use of the ASBO did, however, attract powerful criticism, on the ground that it was both ineffective as a means of deterring street prostitution without recourse to the criminal courts (in accordance with the policy underpinning the ASBO) and discriminatory in its application to street prostitutes.[128] This criticism is likely to apply equally to the IPNA and CBO, if used in the same way, as their operation is very similar to that of the ASBO.

13.74 The Injunction to Prevent Nuisance and Annoyance is dealt with ss.1–21 of the 2014 Act. Section 1 provides that a court, which in the case of an adult will be the county court, may grant an IPNA against a person aged 10 or over ("the respondent") if two conditions are met. The first condition is that the court is satisfied, on the balance of probabilities, that the respondent has engaged or is threatening to engage in anti-social behaviour. The Act defines "anti-social behaviour" as "conduct that has caused, or is likely to cause, harassment, alarm or distress to any person". This is very similar to the definition that applied for the purposes of the ASBO. The terms "harassment", "alarm" and "distress" are to be treated as ordinary words, the meaning of which is to be determined as a question of fact by the court.[129] It was held in relation to the definition of anti-social behaviour applicable to

---

[125] Anti-social Behaviour, Crime and Policing Act 2014 (Commencement No.8, Saving and Transitional Provisions) Order 2015 (SI 2015/373). For guidance on the Pt 1 powers, see *Anti-social Behaviour, Crime and Policing Act 2014: Reform of anti-social behaviour powers—Statutory guidance for frontline professionals* (Home Office, July 2014), available at *https://www.gov.uk/government/uploads/system/uploads/attachment_data/file/352562/ASB_Guidance_v8_July2014_final__2_.pdf* [Accessed April 30, 2016].

[126] For discussion, see Nigel Law, *Courts enjoy greater powers to grant injunctions* (2015) 159(21) S.J. 27; Stavros Demetriou, *Replacing the ASBO with the IPNA*, 179 C.L. & J. 407.

[127] For examples, see *http://www.yorkshireeveningpost.co.uk/news/Leeds-prostitutes-handed-Asbos-in.6074842.jp* and *http://www.statewatch.org/asbo/asbowatch-puborder.htm*; *http://www.hulldailymail.co.uk/ORDERED-HESSLE-ROAD-Prostitutes-banned/story-26189385-detail/story.html* [Accessed April 30, 2016].

[128] See, e.g. Helen Jones and Tracey Sagar, *Crime and Disorder Act 1998: Prostitution and the Anti-social behaviour order* [2001] Crim. L.R. 873.

[129] cf. para.14.136, below.

ASBOs that "likely" meant "more probable than not"[130] and the same is almost certain to apply here. The use of the alternative formulation "has caused, *or is likely to cause*" (our italics) means that evidence need not be produced from an actual victim of harassment etc.; evidence of the respondent's conduct may be given instead by, e.g. a police or local authority officer. This minimises the risk of the provisions being nullified in their effect by witness intimidation.

The second condition for the grant of an IPNA is that the court considers **13.75** it just and convenient to grant the injunction. Determining whether this condition is met is an exercise of judgment or evaluation not involving a standard of proof.[131]

An IPNA may include prohibitions and/or requirements that assist in the **13.76** prevention of future anti-social behaviour. ASBOs made against prostitutes often prohibited the respondent from entering a particular area or building, and the same will no doubt be true of the IPNA. Any requirement included in an injunction must be designed to deal with the underlying causes of the respondent's anti-social behaviour. By s.3 of the Act, where an injunction imposes a requirement, it must specify the person (an individual or an organisation) responsible for supervising compliance, e.g. the local authority or social services, and the court must receive evidence on the suitability and enforceability of the requirement from this person. An injunction must specify the period for which it has effect or state that it has effect until further order. By s.8, a court may vary or discharge an injunction upon application by the original applicant or respondent. A variation may take a number of forms, including the addition of a new prohibition or requirement or the removal of an existing one, the extension or reduction of the duration of an existing prohibition or requirement, or the attachment of a power of arrest. Breach of an injunction by an adult is a contempt of court, punishable in the usual way by the county court by a term of imprisonment of up to two years or an unlimited fine. A decision of the county court is appealable to the High Court.

As for the Criminal Behaviour Order, s.22 of the Act provides that where **13.77** a person is convicted of an offence the court may make such an order, on the application of the prosecution, if two conditions are met. The first condition is that the court is satisfied beyond reasonable doubt (i.e. to the criminal standard) that the offender has engaged in behaviour that caused, or was likely to cause, harassment, alarm or distress to any person. The words "was likely to cause" do not require proof that the offending behaviour was actually witnessed; it is sufficient if there were people in the vicinity at the relevant time. The offender's behaviour must therefore have taken place in

---

[130] *Chief Constable of Lancashire v Potter* [2003] EWHC 2272 (Admin), DC.
[131] *R. (McCann) v Manchester Crown Court* [2002] 3 W.L.R. 1313, HL; *Chief Constable of Lancashire v Potter* [2003] EWHC 2272 (Admin), DC (ASBO cases); *DPP v Bulmer* [2015] EWHC 2323 (Admin) (CBO case, referred to below).

circumstances where it was likely to be witnessed and, if witnessed, likely to cause harassment, alarm or distress.[132]

13.78   The second condition is that the court considers that making the order will help in preventing the offender from engaging in such behaviour, i.e. behaviour that is likely to cause harassment, alarm or distress. There is no burden of proof upon the prosecution to establish that this condition is met. While the court hearing an application for a CBO should proceed with caution and circumspection, because such orders are not to be imposed lightly, determining whether the condition is met is an evaluative exercise and satisfaction to the criminal standard is not required.[133]

13.79   A CBO may be made only when an offender has been sentenced for an offence or given a conditional discharge, and not where they have been given an absolute discharge or simply bound over to keep the peace. By s.23(2), the court can consider evidence which was inadmissible in the criminal proceedings, such as hearsay or bad character evidence. A prosecutor will normally apply for a CBO at the instigation of the police or local authority and, unlike with the ASBO, a local authority may make a request directly to the prosecution without approaching the police first. However, a court may not make a CBO of its own volition. A CBO may impose prohibitions and/or positive requirements that assist in preventing the offender from engaging in behaviour that is likely to cause harassment, alarm or distress in the future. Orders must be tailor-made for the individual offender and the terms must be proportionate, that is, commensurate with the risk to be guarded against.[134] If a CBO includes a requirement, then, as with the IPNA, it must specify the person responsible for supervising compliance and must receive evidence as to the enforceability and suitability of the requirement from that person.

13.80   By s.25, where a CBO is made against an adult, it must be made either for a fixed period of two years or more, or for an indefinite duration. By s.27, a court may vary or discharge an order upon the application of the offender or the prosecution. However, where a previous such application has been dismissed, that party cannot make a further application to vary or discharge the order without the consent of the court or the agreement of the other party. On an appeal against a CBO, the court should not interfere with the order unless it concludes that the lower court plainly erred in some way, either in its assessment of the facts or in applying the wrong test, or in leaving out of account matters that it was required to take into account.[135]

13.81   By s.30, breach of a CBO without reasonable excuse is an either way offence, punishable on indictment with a maximum of five years' imprisonment or a fine, or both, and on summary conviction with a maximum of six months' imprisonment or a fine, or both. A person convicted under s.30 may

---

[132] *Hashi* [2015] 1 Cr. App. R.(S.) 135(17), considering *R. (Gosport BC) v. Fareham Magistrates' Court* [2007] 1 W.L.R. 634.
[133] *DPP v Bulmer* [2015] EWHC 2323 (Admin).
[134] *Boness and Bebbington* [2005] EWCA Crim 2395; [2006] Crim. L.R. 160 (an ASBO case).
[135] *DPP v Bulmer* [2015] EWHC 2323 (Admin).

not be conditionally discharged. There is an evidential burden on the defendant to raise the issue of reasonable excuse but the burden of proving the absence of such an excuse is then on the prosecution.[136]

As a matter of law, there is no reason why the IPNA and CBO should not **13.82** be used in the same way as the ASBO and CRASBO to deal with anti-social behaviour on the part of prostitutes or would-be purchasers of their services, e.g. kerb crawlers. The availability of an ASBO to address the impact of prostitution was confirmed in *Chief Constable of Lancashire v Potter*,[137] which involved an application for such an order against the respondent arising out of her activities as a street prostitute in certain residential areas of Preston. The magistrates had found that there was a "substantial problem" caused by the activities of prostitutes in the relevant areas, to which the respondent's conduct had contributed. But they held that her conduct could not be aggregated with the conduct of the other prostitutes when considering whether she had caused or been likely to cause harassment, alarm or distress, and that it had not been proved that her conduct, considered on its own, had caused or been likely to cause those effects. The Chief Constable's appeal was successful. The Divisional Court held that street prostitution in residential areas was capable, when considered as a whole and depending on the circumstances, including the number, regularity and degree of concentration of the activity, of causing or being likely to cause harassment, alarm or distress to others in the area within the meaning of the ASBO provisions. It was a question of fact whether any individual prostitute, by her contribution to that activity and its overall effect, had caused a problem caught by the provisions. But the Court emphasised that not all street prostitution in residential areas would fall within those provisions, e.g. where the conduct upon which the applicant relied was of one prostitute or a small number or where, however few or many there were, there was no significant concentration of their activities in a particular area to mark it out as a red light district.

BINDING OVER

A person coming before a magistrates' court may be bound over to be of **13.83** good behaviour under the court's common law powers or under the Justices of the Peace Act 1361.[138] The powers are exercisable in relation to anyone

---

[136] cf. *Charles* [2010] Crim. L.R. 303 (an ASBO case decided under the similar provision in s.1(10) of the Crime and Disorder Act 1998).

[137] [2003] EWHC 2272 (Admin), DC. For an example of an ASBO being made against a purchaser of the services of prostitutes, see *http://swns.com/news/pensioner-69-asbo-caught-hookers-times-night-30924/* [Accessed April 30, 2016].

[138] By virtue of s.1(7) of the Justices of the Peace Act 1968, the bind over power under the 1361 Act may be exercised by any court of record having a criminal jurisdiction, e.g. the Crown Court. The common law power is to bind over to "prevent conduct which is contrary to a good way of life": *Percy v DPP* [1995] 3 All E.R. 124 at 129; *DPP v Speede*; *R. v Liverpool JJ Ex p. Collins*; *R. v Liverpool JJ Ex p. Santos* [1998] 2 Cr. App. R. 108 at 113. In addition, the Magistrates' Court Act 1980 s.115, empowers a magistrates' court on the complaint of any person to bind over any other person to be of good behaviour towards the complainant.

who is before the court, whether they are there in answer to a complaint or for any other reason, with the result that a court may bind over an acquitted defendant or a witness who has given evidence (including a complainant). Bind overs have been used in the past to control soliciting by prostitutes and kerb crawlers. However, as explained below, the powers now appear to be of limited application in this context.

13.84   A person can be bound over to be of good behaviour if their conduct on a particular occasion was *"contra bonos mores"* and the magistrates have cause to believe that without a bind over the conduct might be repeated.[139] The bind over power was used in *Hughes v Holley*,[140] a case of kerb crawling in which the relevant events took place shortly before the Sexual Offences Act 1985 became law. The appellant drove his car slowly past a woman police officer who was dressed in civilian clothes and walking on the pavement in the red light area of Leicester. He stopped a little way in front of her and, when she drew level, solicited her to have sex with him. A complaint was laid against him under the Act of 1361 and the magistrates bound him over to be of good behaviour for 12 months, holding that his conduct had been offensive and contrary to general standards of decent behaviour. On appeal, the appellant argued that as his conduct had not amounted to "soliciting for immoral purposes" within the meaning of s.32 of the Sexual Offences Act 1956 (now repealed),[141] it could not have been *contra bonos mores*. The Court dismissed this argument, stating that *contra bonos mores* means simply "contrary to a good way of life" and denotes conduct which has the property of being wrong rather than right in the judgment of contemporary fellow citizens. It also held that the magistrates had been right, in deciding whether the appellant's conduct had been *contra bonos mores,* to admit evidence that respectable women living in the area were frequently accosted, to their annoyance and frustration, by men seeking sex.

13.85   However, the decision in *Hughes v Holley* subsequently fell foul of the European Convention on Human Rights. In *Hashman and Harrup v UK*,[142] the applicants were hunt saboteurs who had disturbed a meet of the Portman Hunt by blowing a horn and shouting at the hounds. They were bound over by the magistrates to keep the peace and be of good behaviour for 12 months. On appeal, the Crown Court acknowledged that there had been no use or threat of violence and no breach of the peace, but dismissed the appeal on the ground that the applicants had behaved *contra bonos mores* and would repeat their conduct unless bound over. The applicants complained to Strasbourg, arguing that the order violated their Convention rights including their right under art.10 (freedom of expression). The Court upheld their complaint by

---

[139] *R. v Aubrey-Fletcher Ex p. Thompson* [1969] 2 All E.R. 846.

[140] (1988) 86 Cr. App. R. 130, DC; applied in *Percy v DPP* [1995] 3 All E.R. 124.

[141] Citing *Crook v Edmondson* [1966] 2 Q.B. 81, for which see para.13.06, above.

[142] [1999] E.H.R.L.R. 342. The decision was no surprise: the Law Commission had warned that the *contra bonos mores* power was contrary to the Convention in its report *Binding Over* (Law. Com. No.222 (1994)), para.4.34.

a majority of 16–1. It found that the applicants had indeed been exercising their right to freedom of expression by their non-violent protest. It also held that, whilst that right may be interfered with in circumstances set out in art.10(2), the interference must be "prescribed by law", which requires amongst other things that the law is formulated with sufficient precision to enable the citizen to regulate his conduct. The Court found that the expression *contra bonos mores*, as defined in *Hughes v Holley*, failed the "prescribed by law" test as it was too imprecise and so the bind over order did not give the applicants sufficiently clear guidance as to how they should behave in future.

The Court did, however, recognise that certainty in the law can make for   **13.86** excessive rigidity, and held that the degree of certainty required by the Convention will depend to some extent on the context. It went on to consider some examples of laws that meet the certainty requirement, including the Austrian offence of "causing a breach of the peace by conduct likely to cause annoyance" considered in *Chorherr v Austria*.[143] The Court said that this offence is sufficiently certain because "likely to cause annoyance" indicates the type of conduct penalised.[144] It would seem to follow that, even after *Hashman*, an order binding over a kerb crawler to be of good behaviour would be consistent with art.10, provided the order specified with sufficient certainty what the subject was required to do or refrain from doing, e.g. not visit a defined area at all or during particular hours. This was certainly the view of the CPS and the Home Office.[145] However, the *Criminal Practice Directions* have gone a step further in providing that, in the light of *Hashman*, courts should no longer bind an individual over "to be of good behaviour" or to "keep the peace" in general terms, but should identify the specific conduct or activity from which the individual must refrain.[146]

There is, however, a more fundamental obstacle to the use of bind overs in   **13.87** this context, namely that, again to take account of *Hashman*, the *Criminal Practice Directions* also provide that, before imposing a binding over order, the court must be satisfied so that it is sure that a breach of the peace involving violence, or an imminent threat of violence, has occurred or that there is a real risk of violence in the future.[147] It will be unusual for these requirements to be met in a case involving soliciting for prostitution, and accordingly bind overs to regulate this aspect of the conduct of prostitutes and their clients are likely now to be rare creatures.

---

[143] (1994) 17 E.H.R.R. 358.

[144] *Chorherr* was followed in *Tabernacle v Secretary of State for Defence* [2008] EWHC 416 (Admin), in relation to a prohibition on acting "in any way likely to cause annoyance" in the Atomic Weapons Establishment (AWE) Aldermaston Byelaws 2007.

[145] cf. Bulletin (CPS) 06/2000: *Bind Overs and the European Convention on Human Rights*, para.13; *Bind Overs: A Power for the 21st Century* (Home Office, 2003).

[146] CPD VII Sentencing J: Binding Over Orders and Conditional Discharges, J.3.

[147] CPD VII Sentencing J: Binding Over Orders and Conditional Discharges, J.2.

CHAPTER 14

PREPARATORY OFFENCES

Introduction.................................... 14.01
Administering a Substance with
  Intent to Stupefy or Overpower... 14.08

Committing an Offence with Intent
  to Commit a Sexual Offence........ 14.37
Trespass with Intent to Commit a
  Sexual Offence............................. 14.51

INTRODUCTION

This chapter covers three preparatory offences created by the Sexual Offences   **14.01**
Act 2003:
- administering a substance with intent to stupefy or overpower the victim so as to enable any person to engage in sexual activity with them (s.61),
- committing an offence with intent to commit a relevant sexual offence (s.62), and
- trespass with intent to commit a relevant sexual offence (s.63).

It also briefly considers, in para.14.06, below, the status of the old common   **14.02**
law offence of assault with intent to rape.

Administering a substance with intent to stupefy or overpower

Section 4 of the Sexual Offences Act 1956 made it an offence to apply or   **14.03**
administer to, or cause to be taken by, a woman any drug, matter or thing
with intent to stupefy or overpower her so as to enable any man to have
unlawful sexual intercourse with her. The Sexual Offences Review, reporting
in 2000, described s.4 as an "important offence", which caught the "cold-
blooded administration of a knock-out substance in order to exploit and take
advantage of another".[1] Given the level of concern about the use of drugs
and alcohol to facilitate rape, the Review recommended that the offence be
retained, in gender-neutral form and drafted so as to catch any new method

---

[1] *Setting the Boundaries*, (Home Office, 2000), para.2.19.

of mental or psychological control that might be developed. This recommendation was taken up in the White Paper *Protecting the Public*, where the Government announced its intention to create an offence of administering drugs or other substances with intent to stupefy a victim in order that they can be subjected to an indecent act without their consent.[2] This proposal was implemented by s.61 of the 2003 Act, which replaced the s.4 offence. The s.62 offence overlaps to a certain extent with the offence in s.22 of the Offences Against the Person Act 1861, of using chloroform, laudanum or other stupefying or overpowering drug, matter or thing to commit or assist in the committing of any indictable offence. Where the substance is administered with the intent that someone else shall engage in sexual activity with the victim, there will be a substantial overlap with the offences in ss.44–46 of the Serious Crime Act 2007 of encouraging and assisting an offence: see the discussion of those offences in paras 1.411 and following, below.

Committing an offence with intent to commit a sexual offence

14.04   Section 62 of the 2003 Act penalises the commission of an offence with the intention of committing an offence under Pt 1 of the 2003 Act (which includes all the major sexual offences). The potential impact of this provision is remarkably wide and it was criticised during the passage of the Bill as creating "thought crime". It had its genesis in the recommendation of the Sexual Offences Review for the creation of two new statutory offences to fill perceived gaps in the criminal law: an offence of assault with intent to commit rape or assault by penetration, and an offence of abduction with intent to commit rape, assault by penetration, sexual assault or adult sexual abuse of a child.[3] In *Protecting the Public*, the Government favoured creating one, broader offence of committing a criminal offence with intent to commit a sex offence. This was justified on the basis that the criminal law should fully recognise an offender's sexual motivation, i.e. he should be charged with an offence reflecting that motivation and, if found guilty, managed as a sex offender.[4] There is, however, provision in s.62 for a higher maximum penalty where the offence committed is kidnapping or false imprisonment.

14.05   The s.62 offence may be used to prosecute individuals who are highly deserving of conviction and punishment as sex offenders, including a person who assaults or abducts another with the intention of committing rape or another serious sexual assault on them. But it is also capable of producing some surprising results, especially where the preliminary offence is minor and the individual's conduct falls some way short of an attempt to commit the intended Pt 1 offence. For example, s.62 will in principle cover someone who steals a door key with the intention at some future date of entering the house

---

[2] *Protecting the Public: strengthening protection against sex offenders and reforming the law on sexual offences* (Cm 5668) (Nov 2002), para.43.
[3] *Setting the Boundaries*, 2000, paras 2.15 and 2.17.
[4] *Protecting the Public*, 2002, para.47.

and committing a sexual offence against its occupant, or who smashes a street light and lays in wait in the dark with the intention of sexually assaulting a passer-by.[5] In some cases, the s.62 offence may expose individuals to much more serious punishment than they would otherwise receive, purely on the basis of their intention. So if A drives slowly round a red light area soliciting women for prostitution, with the intention of committing rape, he will be prosecutable either under s.51A of the 2003 Act for soliciting for prostitution (maximum penalty a fine of £1,000) or, if his intention can be proved, under s.62 (maximum penalty 10 years' imprisonment).[6] These examples show how significant the offence could be, if used to its fullest extent. In practice, however, the need to prove the intention to commit a Pt 1 offence will limit the offence's impact. This is not least because, the more remote A's conduct is from the commission of a Pt 1 offence, the harder it is likely to be to prove that he intended to commit such an offence. The courts may also be expected to restrict the scope of s.62 by interpreting it so as to require a purposive link between the offence actually committed and the intended Pt 1 offence. This point draws support from the fact that s.62 appears in the 2003 Act under the cross-heading "Preparatory offences",[7] the inference being that the offence that A actually commits must be preparatory to, and carried out for the purpose of facilitating, the relevant sexual offence. So, for example, A would not commit the s.62 offence by driving without insurance merely because at the same time he has the intention to commit a sexual assault. It is only when his offence has a purposive nexus with his intention that he should fall foul of s.62: for example, where he drives the wrong way up a one-way street in order to reach his intended victim. As yet, there has been no case in which this point has arisen for determination.

Old offence of assault with intent to rape

There used to be an ancient common law offence of "assault with intent to   **14.06** murder, ravish or commit other felonies or high misdemeanours".[8] Even before the enactment of s.62 of the 2003 Act, there was considerable doubt as to whether it remained possible to charge an offence of assault with intent to rape. The last case to consider the question was *R. v P,*[9] in which Pill J (as he then was) quashed a count charging the offence on the ground that it was no longer known to the law. The Sexual Offences Review said that the offence

---

[5] See also *Jones* [2007] EWCA Crim 1118, referred to in para.14.47, below.
[6] But see the sentencing guideline for this offence, set out in para.14.44, below, which states that the starting point and sentence range should be commensurate with that for the preliminary offence actually committed, with an enhancement to reflect the nature and seriousness of the intended sexual offence, with two years' imprisonment suggested as a suitable enhancement where the intent was to commit rape or assault by penetration.
[7] For the permissibility of using cross-headings as aids to construction, see *Montila* [2004] UKHL 50.
[8] East P.C. 406–7. For an example see *Gisson* (1847) 2 C. & K. 781.
[9] [1990] Crim. L.R. 323.

"has become unusable because of arguments about its status, and . . . has to all intents and purposes ceased to exist".[10] The Review considered that this left a real gap in the protection afforded by the law to women, who can be left deeply affected by an assault carried out with intent to rape but falling short of an attempt. It recommended the creation of a statutory offence of assault with intent to commit rape or assault by penetration and, as explained above, this led in due course to the creation of the s.62 offence. There is accordingly no longer any need to consider prosecuting the common law offence.

Trespass with intent to commit a sexual offence

14.07 The Sexual Offences Review noted the existence of the offence of aggravated burglary under s.9(1)(a) of the Theft Act 1968, committed where a person enters a building or part of a building as a trespasser with intent to rape, and punishable with a maximum of 14 years' imprisonment.[11] The Review considered that as the essence of this offence was the sexual intent, rather than the burglary, it should be regarded as a sexual offence. Further, it thought there was a risk that the offence could be overlooked, being tucked away in the Theft Act, and noted that it did not carry a requirement to register as a sex offender. The Review accordingly recommended the repeal of the Theft Act offence and its replacement in a new law of sexual offences by an offence of trespass with intent to commit a serious sexual offence, i.e. rape, assault by penetration, sexual assault or adult sexual abuse of a child. In *Protecting the Public*, the Government developed this recommendation by announcing an intention to create an offence of trespass with intent to commit any sexual offence.[12] The same justification was given for this offence as for what became s.62, i.e. a person trespassing in these circumstances should be charged with a criminal offence reflecting his motivation and, if found guilty, managed as a sex offender. The Government's intention was implemented in s.63 of the 2003 Act.

ADMINISTERING A SUBSTANCE WITH INTENT TO STUPEFY OR OVERPOWER

DEFINITION

14.08 Section 61(1) of the Sexual Offences Act 2003 provides:

"A person commits an offence if he intentionally administers a substance to, or causes a substance to be taken by, another person (B)—
(a) knowing that B does not consent, and
(b) with the intention of stupefying or overpowering B, so as to enable any person to engage in a sexual activity that involves B."

---

[10] *Setting the Boundaries*, 2000, para.2.15.1.
[11] *Setting the Boundaries*, 2000, para.2.16.
[12] para.47.

MODE OF TRIAL AND PUNISHMENT

The offence under s.61 is triable either way.[13] The maximum punishment on **14.09**
conviction on indictment is 10 years' imprisonment. The maximum on
summary conviction is six months' imprisonment or a fine, or both. As from
a day to be appointed the maximum sentence of imprisonment on summary
conviction will increase to 12 months.[14] The increase will have no application
to offences committed before it takes effect.[15] Until recently, the maximum
fine on summary conviction was a fine not exceeding the statutory maximum
(i.e. £5,000). The effect of s.85 of the Legal Aid, Sentencing and Punishment
of Offenders Act 2012 is that, from March 12, 2015, a fine of any amount
may be imposed. Fines will, however, continue to be set according to the
seriousness of the offence and the means of the offender.

For the purposes of listing, cases under s.61[16] fall within Class 2B.[17] Cases **14.10**
in Class 2B must be referred to the Resident Judge, and by the Resident
Judge to a Presiding Judge, in certain specified circumstances, including
where the case is unusually grave or complex or a novel and important point
of law is to be raised; where the defendant is a police officer, a member of the
legal profession or a high profile figure; or where for any reason the case is
likely to attract exceptional media attention.

The offence under s.61 is a specified offence for the purposes of s.226A **14.11**
(extended sentence for certain violent or sexual offences) of the Criminal
Justice Act 2003.[18]

A person convicted under s.61, cautioned, found not guilty by reason of **14.12**
insanity or found to be under a disability and to have done the act charged,
is automatically subject to the notification requirements in the Sexual
Offences Act 2003.[19]

SENTENCING

For the Sentencing Council guideline relating to the sentencing of sexual **14.13**
offences committed by offenders aged 18 and over, see Ch.33. The guideline
for offences under s.61 of the 2003 Act adopts the same harm and culpability
factors as those for offences of exposure (s.66) and voyeurism (s.67), which
are discussed in Ch.15, below.

---

[13] s.62(2).
[14] Criminal Justice Act 2003 s.282(2), (3).
[15] Criminal Justice Act 2003 s.282(4).
[16] And of soliciting, inciting, encouraging or assisting, attempting or conspiring to commit the offence or assisting an offender having committed the offence.
[17] *Consolidated Criminal Practice Directions*, Part XIII Listing B: CLASSIFICATION, available at *https://www.judiciary.gov.uk/wp-content/uploads/2015/09/crim-pd-2015.pdf* [Accessed April 30, 2016].
[18] Inserted by the Legal Aid, Sentencing and Punishment of Offenders Act 2012 s.124, brought into force on December 3, 2012, by SI 2012/2906.
[19] s.80 and Sch.3, discussed in Ch.35, below.

Sentencing guideline

Step One—Harm and culpability

14.14   The guideline requires the sentencing court to go through a series of steps in order to determine the appropriate sentence. Step one involves determining the offence category. The categories are defined by reference to whether the harm to the victim and the culpability of the offender are raised. As this offence is a preparatory one, harm and culpability are unlikely to have been fully realised at the time of commission. Accordingly, the Sentencing Council found it difficult to articulate harm and culpability in the same way as for other sexual offences[20] and so specified the offence categories for offences under s.61 as follows:

Category 1	Raised harm *and* raised culpability
Category 2	Raised harm *or* raised culpability
Category 3	Administering a substance with intent **without** raised harm or culpability factors present

14.15   The previous guideline, issued in 2007 by the Sentencing Guidelines Council ("SGC"), distinguished between s.61 offences by reference to the nature of the offence that was to be committed; for example, an intention to carry out a rape or assault by penetration would result in the offender being placed in the highest category. The Sentencing Council considered that, whilst intention is an important factor, there are other factors which should also be taken into consideration as indicating raised harm. The guideline accordingly identifies the following factors as raising the harm caused by the offence:

Factors indicating raised harm
• Severe psychological or physical harm
• Prolonged detention/sustained incident
• Additional degradation/humiliation

14.16   As for culpability, the Council specified the following factors as raising culpability under s.61:

---

[20] *Sexual Offences Guideline: Consultation* (December 6, 2012). The consultation document is available on the Sentencing Council's website.

Factors indicating raised culpability
• Significant degree of planning
• Specific targeting of a particularly vulnerable victim
• Intended sexual offence carries a statutory maximum of life
• Abuse of trust
• Recording of offence
• Offender acts together with others to commit the offence
• Commercial exploitation and/or motivation
• Offence racially or religiously aggravated
• Offence motivated by, or demonstrating, hostility to the victim based on his or her sexual orientation (or presumed sexual orientation) or transgender identity (or presumed transgender identity)
• Offence motivated by, or demonstrating, hostility to the victim based on his or her disability (or presumed disability)

The guideline provides that the sentencing court should determine culpability   **14.17**
and harm caused or intended by reference *only* to the specified factors. Where
an offence does not fall squarely into a category, individual factors may
require a degree of weighting before making an overall assessment and
determining the appropriate offence category. The guideline also states that
where no substantive sexual offence has been committed, the main consideration for the court will be the offender's conduct as a whole, including,
but not exclusively, their intention. This statement was included in the
published guideline on the request of the senior judges following the decision
in *Watson*,[21] discussed in para.14.24, below, in order to provide guidance to
sentencers when dealing with offenders who, after committing the preparatory offence in s.61, have *not* then gone on to commit a sexual offence.

Step Two—Starting point and category range

Once the court has determined the offence category, at step two it should use   **14.18**
the corresponding starting point specified in the guideline in order to reach
a sentence within the category range. The starting point applies to all
offenders irrespective of plea or previous convictions. Once the starting point
has been determined, step two allows further adjustment for aggravating or
mitigating features, set out below. A case of particular gravity, reflected by
multiple features of culpability or harm, could merit upward adjustment

---

[21] Unreported, October 17, 2013, CA.

from the starting point before further adjustment for aggravating or mitigating features. The starting points and category ranges for offences under s.61 are as follows:

Category 1	*Starting point* 6 years' custody *Category range* 4–9 years' custody
Category 2	*Starting point* 4 years' custody *Category range* 3–7 years' custody
Category 3	*Starting point* 2 years' custody *Category range* 1–5 years' custody

Aggravating and mitigating factors

14.19 After identifying the starting point and category range, the court should consider whether the presence of aggravating or mitigating factors should result in an upward or downward adjustment from the starting point or the imposition of a sentence outside the range. In particular, relevant recent convictions are likely to result in an upward adjustment. The non-exhaustive list of aggravating and mitigating factors for offences under s.61 is:

Aggravating factors
Statutory aggravating factors
• Previous convictions, having regard to a) the nature of the offence to which the conviction relates and its relevance to the current offence; and b) the time that has elapsed since the conviction   • Offence committed whilst on bail

Other aggravating factors
• Location of offence • Timing of offence • Any steps taken to prevent the victim reporting an incident, obtaining assistance and/or from assisting or supporting the prosecution • Attempts to dispose of or conceal evidence • Failure of offender to respond to previous warnings • Offence committed whilst on licence

Mitigating factors
• No previous convictions **or** no relevant/recent convictions • Remorse • Previous good character and/or exemplary conduct* • Age and/or lack of maturity where it affects the responsibility of the offender • Mental disorder or learning disability, particularly where linked to the commission of the offence • Demonstration of steps taken to address offending behaviour

* Previous good character/exemplary conduct is different from having no previous convictions. The more serious the offence, the less the weight which should normally be attributed to this factor. Where previous good character/exemplary conduct has been used to facilitate the offence, this mitigation should not normally be allowed and such conduct may constitute an aggravating factor.

Steps Three to Nine

The remaining steps cover the following points. At step three the court **14.20** should consider any factors which would indicate a reduction in sentence, e.g. assistance to the prosecution. At step four it should consider any reduction for a guilty plea. At step five the court should consider dangerousness, i.e. whether it would be appropriate to award an extended sentence (s.226A of the Criminal Justice Act 2003). Step six requires the court to consider whether the total sentence is just and proportionate to the offending behaviour. At step seven it should consider whether to make an ancillary order (e.g. a SHPO or a restraining order). Step eight requires the court to fulfil its duty under s.174 of the Criminal Justice Act 2003 to give reasons for, and explain the effect of, the sentence. Finally, at step nine the court should consider whether to give credit for time spent on bail in accordance with s.240A of that Act.

Sentencing examples

14.21 The following decisions pre-date the Sentencing Council guideline, but, given the scarcity of reported sentencing appeals relating to s.61, they are useful illustrations of the approach taken by the Court of Appeal to different factual scenarios.

14.22 In *Wright*[22] the appellant (W) was sentenced to five years' imprisonment following his conviction under s.61. He met the complainant whilst working as a doorman at a bar. She was out for an evening with friends and left the bar to make a phone call. They agreed to go for a drink at another bar, and whilst there he spiked her drink with the drug GHB. They then returned to the first bar, where the complainant became unwell, collapsed and was taken to hospital by ambulance. W was present while she was carried out but told nobody about the spiking of her drink. The Court of Appeal noted that under the SGC guideline (which was not in place at the time W was sentenced), the starting point for this offence was four years' imprisonment. There were, however, aggravating features. First, there was a breach of trust, in that W was employed as a doorman to ensure that the premises were conducted within the law, yet was actively engaged in breaking it. Secondly, W had administered a significant overdose of the drug. Thirdly, he had failed to take action by calling an ambulance when the complainant became unwell or by indicating when the ambulance arrived what had transpired. In all the circumstances, the Court held that the sentence of five years' imprisonment was entirely appropriate.

14.23 In *Attorney General's Reference (No.31 of 2006)*,[23] the Solicitor General referred to the Court of Appeal as unduly lenient a sentence of two years' imprisonment imposed following a conviction under s.61. The offender arranged to meet the complainant for a drink. He took her in his chauffeur-driven car to a restaurant where he was known to the staff. He had been drinking and kept trying to kiss the complainant, who refused. While they were waiting to be seated at the restaurant, the offender told a waiter that he wanted to "fuck" the complainant. When they were at the table, he asked the waiter to keep bringing her more drink whether she ordered it or not, and asked for "something special" to "knock her out". The complainant eventually said she would need to leave to catch a train home. She declined an invitation to stay at the offender's address. When she left the table to go to the lavatory, the waiter and the chef saw the offender take something from his pocket and put it into her glass of wine. The waiter alerted the complainant and she asked him to call the police. She saw that her glass contained a tablet, and took a sip of it before walking away. On analysis the tablet turned out to be a strong sedative, but not one that could commonly be described as a "date rape" drug. In sentencing, the judge noted that the

---

[22] [2006] EWCA Crim 2672.
[23] [2007] EWCA Crim 1623.

tablet was a sedative, that the offender was thwarted by the quick wittedness of the restaurant staff, that the complainant was not sexually interfered with in any way, and that it was uncertain what would have been the outcome if the offender's activities had remained undetected. He also took into account the offender's good character and the effect of the offence on the complainant, as set out in the victim impact statement. The Court of Appeal held that the sentence of two years' imprisonment was unduly lenient. It regarded four features of the case as particularly relevant. First, the case proceeded as a trial, so there could be no discount for a guilty plea. Secondly, the offender made persistent efforts to persuade and cajole the complainant to participate in sexual activity with him and administered the drug when he was thwarted by her adamant refusal. Thirdly, the impact on the complainant was serious. Fourthly, there was considerable public concern about the administration of drugs to young women who do not wish to participate in sexual activity, in order to make them amenable or unable to resist. Giving due weight to those features, the Court substituted a sentence of three-and-a-half years' imprisonment. Unfortunately it did not indicate what sentence it would have considered appropriate in the absence of the element of "double jeopardy" inherent in a reference.

In *Watson*,[24] the appellant (W), 38 and effectively of good character, was convicted of one offence under s.61 and acquitted of rape. He was sentenced to eight years' imprisonment. W and the victim had been together for eight years and had had a child together, but the victim had ended the relationship. W was desperate to continue it. One day he persuaded the victim to drink from an opened can of Red Bull which he had laced with ecstasy. She became nauseous and he helped put her on her bed. She lay there unable to move her limbs and struggling to speak. He had sexual intercourse with her to ejaculation. She then became so ill that she suffered a seizure and an ambulance was called. W did not tell the paramedics or hospital staff about the ecstasy he had administered, but this was revealed by medical tests. In prepared statements W claimed the intercourse was consensual and denied administering the drug. In sentencing, the judge observed that W had turned to foul means to rekindle his relationship with the victim, giving her ecstasy to enable him to have sexual intercourse with her without resistance. She observed that in convicting W under s.61 the jury must have disbelieved his denial of having administered the ecstasy, but that in acquitting him of rape they must have concluded that he may have reasonably believed the victim was consenting. However, on the evidence the judge was sure that the victim had not consented but was unable to convey that or resist because of the effects of the drug. There were many aggravating features, in particular W had planned the offence and it was a gross breach of trust, committed against the mother of his child, in her own home. The Court of Appeal agreed that there were serious aspects to the case and that the judge had been entitled to

14.24

---

[24] Unreported, October 17, 2013, CA.

make the findings she did, including that the jury must have concluded that W may reasonably have believed the victim was consenting to sexual intercourse. The judge had faced a difficult sentencing exercise since the s.61 offence may be committed where the offender's intention is to engage in consensual sexual activity, but the SGC guideline did not contemplate a case in which no sexual offence was intended. In such circumstances, the Court considered the vital considerations to be the culpability involved in the offender's overall conduct and the harm caused by it. In this case, the exceptional facts did not fit neatly into either category in the SGC guideline, both of which assumed that a sexual offence was intended. In the event, the judge took the view that the case fell within the higher category as W's intention was to have sexual intercourse rather than some lesser sexual activity. In the Court's view, the guideline was of limited assistance in this case since it focused upon a completed sexual offence. The judge had placed the case in the higher category on the basis that the category was reserved for penetrative sex, but a significant allowance should have been made for the fact that, on the basis of the jury verdicts, no non-consensual activity was intended and that it was not unreasonable for W to have believed the victim was consenting. In the circumstances, the Court considered that the eight-year sentence was manifestly excessive and it substituted one of four-and-a-half years.

14.25   As noted above, as the result of a request made to the Sentencing Council by the senior judges following *Watson*, the Council's guideline for s.61 states that where no substantive sexual offence has been committed, the main consideration for the court will be the offender's conduct as a whole, including, but not exclusively, their intention. This statement was included in order to provide guidance to sentencers when dealing with offenders such as the one in *Watson* who, after committing the preparatory offence in s.61, do *not* then go on to commit a sexual offence. A similar statement appears in the guideline for s.63.

JURISDICTION

14.26   By virtue of s.72 of and Sch.2 to the Sexual Offences Act 2003, as amended,[25] it is an offence under s.61 for a UK national to do an act in a country outside the UK which would constitute a s.61 offence if done in England and Wales. The amendments, made in 2008, expanded the scope of s.72 in two respects. First, they removed the limitation on s.72 as enacted that it applied only to offences committed against victims aged under 16 (the relevant age is now 18). Secondly, they abolished, in respect of UK nationals, the "double criminality" requirement that the act must have been an offence in the country in which it was done. This requirement is, however, retained in respect of the prosecution of UK residents and those who become UK

---

[25] By the Criminal Justice and Immigration Act 2008 s.72, with effect from July 14, 2008.

residents or nationals after the doing of the relevant act. For the purposes of s.72 a "country" includes a territory and a "United Kingdom national" means a British citizen, a British overseas territories citizen, a British National (Overseas), a British Overseas citizen, a person who under the British Nationality Act 1981 is a British subject, or a British protected person within the meaning of that Act.[26] An act is taken to be an offence in the country in which it was done unless the defendant serves a notice putting the prosecution to proof on the point.[27]

"ADMINISTERS A SUBSTANCE TO, OR CAUSES A SUBSTANCE TO BE TAKEN BY"

The term "substance" is undefined but will clearly include alcohol and drugs   **14.27** (including so-called "date-rape" drugs such as rohypnol or GHB). The specification of alternative ways of committing the offence, by administering or causing to be taken, covers the main possibilities whereby the substance might take effect upon the victim, i.e. by being swallowed, inhaled (as where a chloroform-impregnated cloth is held over the mouth and nose) or injected.

Cases decided under similarly worded provisions in the Offences against   **14.28** the Person Act 1861 are helpful in indicating the likely scope of the s.61 offence.[28] In *Gillard*,[29] it was held that the word "administer" in s.24 of the 1861 Act (administering etc. any poison or other destructive or noxious thing with intent to injure, aggrieve or annoy) does not postulate any form of entry to the body, whether through an orifice or by absorption, but covers conduct which, not being the application of direct force, nonetheless brings the noxious thing into contact with the victim's body. Accordingly, the word covered the spraying of the victim with a noxious fluid or vapour (in that case, CS gas). In *Kennedy (No.2)*,[30] a decision under s.23 of the 1861 Act (administering etc. any poison or other destructive or noxious thing so as thereby to endanger life), the House of Lords held that the offence of administering is committed where "D administers the noxious thing directly to V, as by injecting V with the noxious thing, holding a glass containing the noxious thing to V's lips, or (as in *Gillard*) spraying the noxious thing in V's face".

In *Gillard*, it was held that the word "taken" in the phrase "cause to be   **14.29** taken" in s.24 of the 1861 Act postulates some ingestion by the victim and for

---

[26] s.72(9).

[27] s.72(6)–(8).

[28] See s.23 (administering etc. any poison or other destructive or noxious thing so as thereby to endanger life), s.24 (administering etc. any poison or other destructive or noxious thing with intent to injure, aggrieve or annoy), s.58 (administering any poison or other noxious thing with intent to procure a miscarriage).

[29] (1988) 87 Cr. App. R. 189, disapproving *Dones* [1987] Crim. L.R. 682.

[30] [2007] UKHL 38, at 10.

this purpose "ingest" should bear its natural meaning of intake into the digestive system. In *Kennedy (No.2)*, the House held that, for the purposes of the s.23 offence, D causes a noxious thing to be taken if he "causes the noxious thing to be taken by V and V does not make a voluntary and informed decision to take it. If D puts a noxious thing in food which V is about to eat and V, ignorant of the presence of the noxious thing, eats it, D commits [the offence]."[31] It appears that for the purpose of s.58 of the 1861 Act (administering or causing to be taken any poison or other noxious thing with intent to procure a miscarriage), A may cause something to be taken by B where he leaves the substance for B to take, and he need not actually deliver it by hand to B.[32] It would seem to follow that A may cause B to take a substance by acting through an innocent intermediary, as where A, who wishes to have sex with B, gives C a knock-out drug to administer to B, telling C it is cough medicine; or where he persuades C, who knows B socially, to spike B's drink for him. If the intermediary is not innocent but is aware of A's intention, then the intermediary himself commits the s.61 offence and A may be guilty of encouraging or assisting the offence, aiding and abetting it, or conspiring to commit it.

"Sexual Activity"

14.30   As to when an activity is "sexual", see paras 2.66 and following, above.

Consent

14.31   It is an element of the s.61 offence that B does not consent to the administration or taking of the substance. For this purpose s.74 of the 2003 Act applies and so B consents if she agrees by choice and has the freedom and capacity to make that choice.[33] However, the presumptions as to absence of consent in ss.75 and 76 of the Act do not apply to this offence. On consent, see further paras 1.169 and following, above.

14.32   The effect of the requirement of absence of consent is that the person administering etc. the substance (A) does not commit the offence if B knows what she is taking and takes it voluntarily, even if she is unaware that A intends to engage in sexual activity with her once she is stupefied or overpowered. So to wine and dine a woman in the hope that the alcohol will make her more readily agree to sexual intercourse does not constitute the offence, provided the woman knows what she is drinking and drinks it of her own free will. It would seem this is so even if B is mistaken as to the quantity of the substance administered (unless the mistake is because A has misled her), or if she underestimates its likely effects upon her. But if B is unaware

---

[31] At 12.
[32] *Harley* (1830) 4 C. & P. 369.
[33] s.74 of the Act, discussed in paras 1.179 and following, above.

of the administration (e.g. her drink is spiked or the substance is administered to her while she is asleep or insensible), she does not consent to it. Moreover, if B consents to the administration, but becomes so affected by the substance that she lacks the capacity to choose whether to agree to sexual activity or to resist, and A or another person engages in such activity with her, they may commit a non-consensual sexual offence such as rape or sexual assault.[34]

MENTAL ELEMENT

There are three aspects to the mental element of the offence. First, the defendant must intentionally administer the substance to, or cause it to be taken by, B. Secondly, he must know that B does not consent. Thirdly, he must have the intention of stupefying or overpowering B so as to enable any person (himself or another) to engage in a sexual activity involving B. To "stupefy" means "to make stupid or torpid; to deprive of apprehension, feeling or sensibility; to benumb, deaden".[35] Although it is arguable that the contrast between "with the intention of" and "so as to enable" suggests that intention need not be proved in relation to the element of sexual activity, the better view is that the prosecution must prove that A had the intention that some person would be enabled to engage in sexual activity with B.[36] **14.33**

Is a person liable to conviction under the section if he administered, etc., the substance to B whilst in a state of intoxication due to drink or drugs? Not if his intoxication was involuntary, e.g. it was the result of his drinks being spiked.[37] What if it was self-induced? It is an express requirement of the s.61 offence that the administration is intentional, and also that A has the intention of stupefying or overpowering B. If, despite his condition, the defendant was able to and did form the required intention, it is no defence that he did so only because of loss of self-control or disinhibition caused by intoxication.[38] However, in the light of *Heard*,[39] discussed in paras 2.81 and following, above, the requirement that the defendant did the prohibited act (the administration, etc.) with the intention of stupefying or overpowering B, so as to enable any person to engage in a sexual activity that involves B, makes the s.61 offence one of specific intent, such that voluntary intoxication through drink or drugs will provide a defence if it may have prevented him forming that intention. **14.34**

---

[34] cf. *Lang* (1975) 62 Cr. App. R. 50.

[35] *Oxford English Dictionary*, 2nd edn (Oxford: Oxford University Press), vol.XVI, p.999.

[36] cf. *Utting* (1988) 86 Cr. App. R. 164; *Tobierre* (1987) 82 Cr. App. R. 212, decided under the Forgery and Counterfeiting Act 1981. Contrast the Offences Against the Person Act 1861 s.23, considered in *Cato* [1976] 1 All E.R. 260.

[37] *Kingston* [1995] 2 A.C. 355, HL.

[38] *Sheehan and Moore* (1975) 60 Cr. App. R. 308, at 312 ("A drunken intent is nevertheless an intent").

[39] [2007] EWCA Crim 125.

14.35   The offence is complete once the substance has been administered, etc., with the required intent. The essence of the offence is the administration, and it is not necessary to prove that sexual activity took place. Nor is it necessary to prove that the substance administered was capable of stupefying or overpowering B, whether in the quantity administered or at all.

14.36   Where there is only one administration, there can be only one offence, even though the intention of the administration is to enable more than one man to engage in sexual activity with B. In *Shillingford and Vanderwall*,[40] S was convicted of two offences under s.4 of the 1956 Act in relation to the same administration of a barbiturate to a French au-pair girl. The first offence charged administration, etc., to enable him to have unlawful sexual intercourse and the second charged administration to enable V to have unlawful sexual intercourse. The Court of Appeal held that the second count ought not to have been preferred because there had been only one administration.

COMMITTING AN OFFENCE WITH INTENT TO COMMIT A SEXUAL OFFENCE

DEFINITION

14.37   Section 62(1) of the Sexual Offences Act 2003 provides:

> "A person commits an offence under this section if he commits any offence with the intention of committing a relevant sexual offence."

A "relevant sexual offence" is defined by s.62(2) to mean any offence under Pt 1 of the Act (ss.1–79), including an offence of aiding, abetting, counselling or procuring such an offence.

Section 62 must be taken to cover the case where the defendant intended to commit a specific "relevant sexual offence", and cases where the prosecution allege that it is obvious from all the circumstances that the defendant intended to commit such an offence, but it is impossible to specify precisely which one and upon whom: see the discussion in para.14.52A, below, which is equally applicable to s.62.

14.38   It should be noted that s.21 of the Offences against the Person Act 1861 makes it an offence, carrying a maximum of life imprisonment, for a person to attempt to choke, suffocate, or strangle another person with intent to enable himself or any other person to commit, or to assist any other person in committing, an indictable offence. This offence may be charged instead of s.62 where a person attempts to choke etc. another with intent to rape them or commit another form of serious sexual assault: see e.g. *Clark*.[41]

---

[40] [1968] 2 All E.R. 200.
[41] [2014] EWCA Crim 1891.

MODE OF TRIAL AND PUNISHMENT

An offence under s.62 committed by kidnapping or false imprisonment is **14.39** triable on indictment and is punishable by a maximum of life imprisonment.[42] Other offences under the section are triable either way[43] and the maximum punishment on conviction on indictment is 10 years' imprisonment and the maximum on summary conviction is six months' imprisonment or a fine, or both. The provision of a higher maximum punishment where particular factual ingredients are proved (kidnapping or false imprisonment) has the effect that s.62 creates two offences, one with those ingredients and one without.[44] It is important that any indictment makes clear which offence is being charged. As from a day to be appointed the maximum sentence of imprisonment on summary conviction will increase to 12 months.[45] The increase will have no application to offences committed before it takes effect.[46] Until recently, the maximum fine on summary conviction was a fine not exceeding the statutory maximum (i.e. £5,000). The effect of s.85 of the Legal Aid, Sentencing and Punishment of Offenders Act 2012 is that, from March 12, 2015, a fine of any amount may be imposed. Fines will, however, continue to be set according to the seriousness of the offence and the means of the offender.

For the purposes of listing, cases under s.62[47] fall within Class 2B.[48] Cases **14.40** in Class 2B must be referred to the Resident Judge, and by the Resident Judge to a Presiding Judge, in certain specified circumstances, including where the case is unusually grave or complex or a novel and important point of law is to be raised; where the defendant is a police officer, a member of the legal profession or a high profile figure; or where for any reason the case is likely to attract exceptional media attention.

An offence under s.62 is a serious specified offence for the purposes of **14.41** s.224 and, where the offence was committed by kidnapping or false imprisonment, s.225(2) (life imprisonment for serious offences) of the Criminal Justice Act 2003.[49] Accordingly a s.62 offence, whenever committed, may be made the subject of an extended sentence under s.226A of that Act.[50] An offence under s.62 committed by kidnapping or false imprisonment is also listed in Pt

---

[42] s.63(3). The Government's original intention was to make life imprisonment the maximum for the offence in all circumstances: *Protecting the Public*, 2002, para.47.
[43] s.63(4).
[44] *Courtie* [1984] A.C. 463.
[45] Criminal Justice Act 2003 s.282(2), (3).
[46] Criminal Justice Act 2003 s.282(4).
[47] And of soliciting, inciting, encouraging or assisting, attempting or conspiring to commit the offence or assisting an offender having committed the offence.
[48] *Consolidated Criminal Practice Directions*, Part XIII Listing B: CLASSIFICATION, available at *https://www.judiciary.gov.uk/wp-content/uploads/2015/09/crim-pd-2015.pdf* [Accessed April 30, 2016].
[49] Criminal Justice Act 2003 s.224 and Sch.15, Pt 2.
[50] Inserted by the Legal Aid, Sentencing and Punishment of Offenders Act 2012 s.124, brought into force on December 3, 2012, by SI 2012/2906.

1 of Sch.15B to the Criminal Justice Act 2003 for the purposes of s.224A of that Act (life sentence for a second listed offence).[51]

14.42 A person convicted under s.62, found not guilty by reason of insanity or found to be under a disability and to have done the act charged, is automatically subject to the notification requirements in the Sexual Offences Act 2003,[52] if (a) he was under 18 at the time of the offence, he is sentenced to at least 12 months' imprisonment, or (b) in any other case, the intended victim was under 18 and the offender is, in respect of the offence, sentenced to a term of imprisonment, detained in a hospital or given a community sentence of at least 12 months.

Alternative Verdict

14.43 A defendant indicted under s.62 may, if the requisite intent is not proved, be acquitted of the offence charged and convicted in the alternative of the offence actually committed if that offence falls within the jurisdiction of the Crown Court. On a summary charge, the magistrates have no jurisdiction to find the defendant guilty of a lesser offence.[53]

Sentencing

14.44 For the Sentencing Council guideline relating to the sentencing of sexual offences committed by offenders aged 18 and over, see Ch.33. The previous guideline, issued in 2007 by the Sentencing Guidelines Council, took the approach that the starting point and sentencing range for offences under s.62 should be commensurate with that for the preliminary offence actually committed, but with an enhancement to reflect the intention to commit a sexual offence, which should vary depending on the nature and the seriousness of the intended offence. It suggested two years as a suitable enhancement where the intent was to commit rape or an assault by penetration. The Council followed this approach in the new guideline, which provides:

> "The starting point and range should be commensurate with that for the preliminary offence actually committed, but with an enhancement to reflect the intention to commit a sexual offence.
> The enhancement will vary depending on the nature and seriousness of the intended sexual offence, but 2 years is suggested as a suitable enhancement where the intent was to commit rape or assault by penetration."

14.45 A useful sentencing example is *O'Conner (Daniel)*,[54] in which the appellant, 28, pleaded guilty to one count under s.62 and two counts of common assault, one relating to the victim and one to her boyfriend. He had accosted

---

[51] Inserted by the Legal Aid, Sentencing and Punishment of Offenders Act 2012 s.122, brought into force on December 3, 2012, by SI 2012/2906.
[52] s.80 and Sch.3, discussed in Ch.35, below.
[53] *Lawrence v Lawrence* [1968] 2 Q.B. 93.
[54] [2015] EWCA Crim 515.

a young woman as she was leaving a cubicle in a town centre public toilet. The appellant grabbed the victim's face, put his hand over her mouth and pushed her backwards into the cubicle, banging her head against the wall. He managed to close the door behind him and moved his hand from her mouth, when she screamed and shouted. Her boyfriend then came into the toilet. He and the appellant fought and the appellant ran off, but was later detained. In interview he said it had all been a big misunderstanding. The appellant had previous convictions for burglary with intent to commit rape and an indecent assault on an elderly victim, for which he was sentenced to six years in a young offender institution with an extension period of three years. He was on licence for those offences when he committed the present ones. The pre-sentence report said that he denied his motive was sexual intimidation and a forced violent sexual attack, but admitted that he would have "grabbed her tits" if the victim had not screamed sufficiently to achieve his aim of alerting the police, because he wanted to get arrested and recalled to prison where he felt safer. He had entered a guilty plea because he did not want to put the victim through any more trauma. He wished he had not done it and would rather kill himself than put anyone else through this again. It was assessed that he took minimal responsibility for the offence, blamed a variety of causes for his actions and was in denial about his real motivation. He had failed to complete the relapse prevention module of a sex offender group programme whilst on licence in the community, and his engagement with the sessions which he did attend had been poor. It was assessed that he posed a very high risk of sexual re-conviction. In sentencing, the Recorder concluded that the appellant was dangerous within the meaning of the dangerousness provisions of the Criminal Justice Act 2003, so that an extended sentence should be passed. This conclusion was not challenged on appeal. The Recorder imposed an extended sentence under s.226A of that Act for the s.62 offence, with a custodial term of three years and five months and an extension period of three years, and sentences of five months' imprisonment concurrent for each of the common assaults, with the sentence for the assault on the boyfriend being consecutive to the extended sentence. On appeal against sentence, the Court of Appeal noted that the sentencing guideline for the s.62 offence states that the starting point should be commensurate with that for the preliminary offence actually committed, but with an enhance-ment to reflect the intention to commit a sexual offence. The enhancement will vary depending on the nature and seriousness of the intended sexual offence but two years is suggested as a suitable enhancement where the intent was to commit rape or assault by penetration. The Recorder had recognised that he could not say that the appellant's intention was to commit rape and so had approached the question of sexual intent on the basis of what the appellant said in interview, that he might have grabbed the victim's breasts. The Recorder had imposed a sentence of five months for the common assault on the victim and added an enhancement of three years for the intent to commit a sexual offence. He recognised this was in excess of the guideline figure of two years, but did not explain how he arrived at it. The Court of Appeal accepted that in light of various aggravating features a sentence of five months or perhaps more would have been justified for the common assault after a contested hearing. But some credit had to be given for the guilty plea at PCMH; and the Recorder appeared to have given only small credit because he thought the appellant should have been charged with a more serious preliminary offence, such as false imprisonment. The Court agreed that a more serious preliminary offence should have been charged, but held that this was an unprincipled basis for disallowing the appropriate credit. The appropriate sentence for both common assaults, giving credit for the guilty plea, was four months. As for the enhancement to reflect sexual intent, the figure of three years could not be justified. On any view the sexual intent was less than an intent to commit rape, as the Recorder recognised, so the enhancement must be less than two years. Nevertheless, this was a serious and violent attack, and given the circumstances and location together with the appellant's previous conviction he clearly intended to commit a sexual assault. The Court was sceptical whether this would have been limited to grabbing the victim's breasts, as the appellant had claimed, given the nature of his previous offending. Furthermore, the attack had had a devastating psychological impact on the victim. In the Court's judgment, the enhancement should be 18 months, and it therefore reduced the custodial term of the sentence from three years five months to 22 months. The Court reached that conclusion with the utmost reluctance since it considered the seriousness of this offending merited a more severe sentence. However, the three year extended licence period remained. That left the question of whether the sentence for the assault on the boyfriend should have been made to run consecutively to the extended sentence for the s.62 offence. As this assault was separate from the attack on the victim, in principle a consecutive sentence was justified. The Court ordered the sentence for that offence to be served before the custodial term of the extended sentence and the concurrent four month sentence on count 2, followed by the extended licence period.

JURISDICTION

14.46   By virtue of s.72 of and Sch.2 to the Sexual Offences Act 2003, as amended,[55] it is an offence under s.62 for a UK national to do an act in a country outside the UK which would constitute a s.62 offence if done in England and Wales, where the intended victim was under 18 at the time of the offence. See further para.14.26, above.

---

[55] By the Criminal Justice and Immigration Act 2008 s.72, which came into force on July 14, 2008.

"ANY OFFENCE"

The term "offence" as it appears in the phrase "any offence" is not defined **14.47** in the Act. It is likely to cover any offence punishable by criminal proceedings, including crimes of negligence, offences of strict liability and offences against byelaws. It should follow that a person may be convicted under s.62 if, for example, he commits an offence of careless driving whilst trying to get near a pedestrian against whom he intends to commit a Pt 1 offence, or he parks illegally with the intention of exposing himself to a passer-by. Examples of the potential application of s.62 given in the Home Office guidance on the Act are where A kidnaps B so that he can rape him but is caught by the police before he commits the rape, or where A detains B in his flat with this intention, or assaults B to subdue him so that he can more easily rape him.[56] In these examples the preliminary offence is committed against the intended victim of the sexual offence, but this is not a requirement of s.62. Thus the offence will be committed where A assaults C in order to make off with C's child, B, against whom he intends to commit a Pt 1 offence; or where A breaks the window of C's house in order to be able to get in and sexually assault C's lodger, B. The width of the s.62 offence is demonstrated by *Jones*,[57] where the appellant was convicted of criminal damage with intent to commit a sexual offence after he left graffiti messages on toilet doors in trains and stations seeking girls aged 8–13 for sex and giving a mobile telephone number.

MENTAL ELEMENT

There are two aspects to the mental element of the s.62 offence. First, the **14.48** defendant must have whatever mental element is required for the preliminary offence, i.e. the one actually committed. Secondly, he must have the intention of committing a relevant sexual offence, i.e. the intention to engage in conduct which would, if carried out, constitute such an offence.

Is a person liable to conviction under s.62 if he acts whilst in a state of **14.49** intoxication due to drink or drugs? Not if his intoxication was involuntary, e.g. it was the result of his drinks being spiked.[58] What if it was self-induced? Let us assume for this purpose that the preliminary offence is itself one of basic intent and so can be committed by someone in a state of self-induced intoxication.[59] It is an express requirement of the s.62 offence that the defendant committed the preliminary offence with the intention of committing a relevant sexual offence. If, despite his intoxicated condition, at the time he committed the preliminary offence the defendant had such an intention,

---

[56] Home Office Circular 21/2004, *Guidance on Part 1 of the Sexual Offences Act 2003*, para. 121.

[57] [2007] EWCA Crim 1118, discussed in paras 3.160 and following, above.

[58] *Kingston* [1995] 2 A.C. 355 HL.

[59] cf. *DPP v Majewski* [1977] A.C. 443

it is no defence that he had it only because of loss of self-control or disinhibition caused by his intoxication.[60] But in the light of *Heard*,[61] discussed in paras 21.81 and following, above, the requirement that the defendant did the prohibited act (i.e. committed the preliminary offence) with the intention of committing a relevant sexual offence makes the s.62 offence one of specific intent, such that voluntary intoxication through drink or drugs will provide a defence if it prevented or may have prevented him forming that intention.

14.50   The offence is complete once the preliminary offence is committed, if at that point the defendant has the required intent. If he goes on to commit the intended sexual offence, he can and should be prosecuted for that offence rather than under s.62.

Trespass with Intent to Commit a Sexual Offence

Definition

14.51 Section 63(1) of the Sexual Offences Act 2003 provides:

"A person commits an offence if—
(a) he is a trespasser on any premises,
(b) he intends to commit a relevant sexual offence on the premises, and
(c) he knows that, or is reckless as to whether, he is a trespasser."

14.52   Section 63(2) provides that "relevant sexual offence" has the same meaning as in s.62, i.e. any offence under Pt 1 of the Act (ss.1–79), including an offence of aiding, abetting, counselling or procuring such an offence.

It was held in *Pacurar*[61a] that while there will be many cases under s.63 that point to a specific sexual offence having been intended, there will be others where (as in that case) the prosecution allege that it is obvious from all the circumstances that the defendant intended to commit a sexual offence, but it is impossible to specify precisely which one and upon whom. Parliament must have intended s.63 to cover both situations, and accordingly a count was not bad for lack of particularity that merely stated that the defendant had "intended to commit a relevant sexual offence". There might have been more reason for concern if the prosecution had put their case on the basis that the defendant intended to commit any of the very many offences created in Part 1 of the 2003 Act against any one of a number of people in the area, but here they had at trial narrowed down the possible offences to ss.1 to 3 and 5 to 7 of the Act, against specified individuals at an identified time and place. The conviction was therefore safe, thought the Court said that other prosecutors may wish to put more details into the particulars in future. It

---

[60] *Sheehan and Moore* (1975) 60 Cr. App. R. 308, at 312 ("A drunken intent is nevertheless an intent").
[61] [2007] EWCA Crim 125.
[61a] (2016) 160(19) S.J. 37.

also held that the case did not call for a *Brown* direction,[61b] requiring the jury to be unanimous on the basis upon which they found the defendant guilty, as it would not matter that some jurors were satisfied that the defendant intended to commit an assault on the victim, while others were satisfied that he intended to commit a more serious offence, provided that they were all agreed that the ingredients of the offence charged were made out, namely trespass with intent to commit a sexual offence.

MODE OF TRIAL AND PUNISHMENT

The s.63 offence is triable either way.[62] On conviction on indictment the **14.53**
maximum punishment is 10 years' imprisonment. The maximum on summary conviction is six months' imprisonment or a fine, or both. As from a
day to be appointed the maximum sentence of imprisonment on summary
conviction will increase to 12 months.[63] The increase will have no application
to offences committed before it takes effect.[64] Until recently, the maximum
fine on summary conviction was a fine not exceeding the statutory maximum
(i.e. £5,000). The effect of s.85 of the Legal Aid, Sentencing and Punishment
of Offenders Act 2012 is that, from March 12, 2015, a fine of any amount
may be imposed. Fines will, however, continue to be set according to the
seriousness of the offence and the means of the offender.

For the purposes of listing, cases under s.63[65] fall within Class 2B.[66] Cases **14.54**
in Class 2B must be referred to the Resident Judge, and by the Resident
Judge to a Presiding Judge, in certain specified circumstances, including
where the case is unusually grave or complex or a novel and important point
of law is to be raised; where the defendant is a police officer, a member of the
legal profession or a high profile figure; or where for any reason the case is
likely to attract exceptional media attention.

The offence under s.63 is a specified offence for the purposes of s.226A **14.55**
(extended sentence for certain violent or sexual offences) of the Criminal
Justice Act 2003.[67]

A person convicted under s.63, found not guilty by reason of insanity or **14.56**
found to be under a disability and to have done the act charged, is
automatically subject to the notification requirements in the 2003 Act[68] if (a)
where he was under 18 at the time of the offence, he is sentenced to at least

---

[61b] *Brown (Kevin)* (1984) 79 Cr.App.R. 115, discussed in para.1.26, above.
[62] s.64(3).
[63] Criminal Justice Act 2003 s.282(2), (3).
[64] Criminal Justice Act 2003 s.282(4).
[65] And of soliciting, inciting, encouraging or assisting, attempting or conspiring to commit the offence or assisting an offender having committed the offence.
[66] *Consolidated Criminal Practice Directions*, Part XIII Listing B: CLASSIFICATION, available at *https://www.judiciary.gov.uk/wp-content/uploads/2015/09/crim-pd-2015.pdf* [Accessed April 30, 2016].
[67] Inserted by the Legal Aid, Sentencing and Punishment of Offenders Act 2012 s.124, brought into force on December 3, 2012, by SI 2012/2906.
[68] s.80 and Sch.3, discussed in Ch.35, below.

12 months' imprisonment or (b) in any other case, the intended victim was under 18 and the offender is, in respect of the offence, sentenced to a term of imprisonment, detained in a hospital or given a community sentence of at least 12 months.

SENTENCING

14.57 For the Sentencing Council guideline relating to the sentencing of sexual offences committed by offenders aged 18 and over, see Ch.33. The guideline for offences under s.63 of the 2003 Act adopts a similar approach to the guideline for s.61, discussed in paras 14.14 and following, above.

Sentencing guideline

Step One—Harm and culpability

14.58 The guideline requires the sentencing court to go through a series of steps in order to determine the appropriate sentence. Step one involves determining the offence category. The categories are defined by reference to whether the harm to the victim and the culpability of the offender are raised. As this offence is a preparatory one, harm and culpability are unlikely to have been fully realised at the time of commission. Accordingly, the Sentencing Council found it difficult to articulate harm and culpability in the same way as for other sexual offences[69] and so specified the offence categories for offences under s.63 as follows:

Category 1	Raised harm **and** raised culpability
Category 2	Raised harm **or** raised culpability
Category 3	Trespass with intent to commit a sexual offence **without** raised harm or culpability factors present

14.59 The previous guideline issued in 2007 by the Sentencing Guidelines Council distinguished between s.63 offences by reference to the nature of the offence that was to be committed; for example, an intention to carry out a rape or assault by penetration would result in the offender being placed in the highest category. In its consultation document, the Sentencing Council considered that, whilst intention is an important factor, there are other factors that should also be taken into consideration as indicating greater harm. The guideline accordingly identifies the following factors as raising the harm caused by the offence:

[69] See *Sexual Offences Guideline: Consultation* (December 6, 2012). The consultation document is available on the Sentencing Council's website.

Factors indicating raised harm
• Prolonged detention/sustained incident
• Additional degradation/humiliation
• Offence committed in victim's home

As regards "offence committed in victim's home", the Sentencing Council noted that while the s.63 offence requires trespass, the trespass may be on any premises and does not require forced entry but rather entry without consent. But it thought that, where the trespass does involve forced entry into the victim's home, this may increase the psychological harm done to the victim and so should indicate raised harm. The harm factor "forced entry into victim's home" was therefore included in the consultation draft. However, in responding to the consultation, the Criminal Bar Association pointed out that harm may equally be raised where the entry into the victim's home is *unforced*. In acknowledgment of this, the Council amended the factor in the published guideline to "offence committed in victim's home".

As for culpability, the Council specified the following factors as raising **14.60** culpability under s.63:

Factors indicating raised culpability
• Significant degree of planning
• Specific targeting of a particularly vulnerable victim
• Intended sexual offence attracts a statutory maximum of life imprisonment
• Possession of weapon or other item to frighten or injure
• Abuse of trust
• Offender acts together with others to commit the offence
• Commercial exploitation and/or motivation
• Offence racially or religiously aggravated
• Offence motivated by, or demonstrating, hostility to the victim based on his or her sexual orientation (or presumed sexual orientation) or transgender identity (or presumed transgender identity)
• Offence motivated by, or demonstrating, hostility to the victim based on his or her disability (or presumed disability)

The guideline provides that the sentencing court should determine culpa- **14.61** bility and harm caused or intended by reference only to the specified factors.

Where an offence does not fall squarely into a category, individual factors may require a degree of weighting before making an overall assessment and determining the appropriate offence category. The guideline also states that where no substantive sexual offence has been committed, the main consideration for the court will be the offender's conduct as a whole, including, but not exclusively, their intention. This statement was included in the published guideline on the request of the senior judges following the decision in *Watson*,[70] discussed in para.14.24, above, in order to provide guidance to sentencers when dealing with offenders who, after committing the preparatory offence in s.63, have not then gone on to commit a sexual offence.

Step Two—Starting point and category range

14.62   Once the court has determined the offence category, at step two it should use the corresponding starting point specified in the guideline in order to reach a sentence within the category range. The starting point applies to all offenders irrespective of plea or previous convictions. Once the starting point has been determined, step two allows further adjustment for aggravating or mitigating features, set out below. A case of particular gravity, reflected by multiple features of culpability or harm, could merit upward adjustment from the starting point before further adjustment for aggravating or mitigating features. The starting points and category ranges for offences under s.63 are as follows:

Category 1	*Starting point*
	6 years' custody
	Category range
	4–9 years' custody
Category 2	*Starting point*
	4 years' custody
	Category range
	3–7 years' custody
Category 3	*Starting point*
	2 years' custody
	Category range
	1–5 years' custody

[70] Unreported, October 17, 2013, CA.

Aggravating and mitigating factors

After identifying the starting point and category range, the court should   **14.63**
consider whether the presence of aggravating or mitigating factors should
result in an upward or downward adjustment from the starting point or the
imposition of a sentence outside the range. In particular, relevant recent
convictions are likely to result in an upward adjustment. The non-exhaustive
list of aggravating and mitigating factors for offences under s.63 is:

Aggravating factors
Statutory aggravating factors
<ul><li>Previous convictions, having regard to a) the nature of the offence to which the conviction relates and its relevance to the current offence; and b) the time that has elapsed since the conviction</li><li>Offence committed whilst on bail</li></ul>
Other aggravating factors
<ul><li>Location of offence</li><li>Timing of offence</li><li>Any steps taken to prevent the victim reporting an incident, obtaining assistance and/or from assisting or supporting the prosecution</li><li>Attempts to dispose of or conceal evidence</li><li>Failure of offender to respond to previous warnings</li><li>Offence committed whilst on licence</li></ul>

Mitigating factors
<ul><li>No previous convictions **or** no relevant/recent convictions</li><li>Remorse</li><li>Previous good character and/or exemplary conduct*</li><li>Age and/or lack of maturity where it affects the responsibility of the offender</li><li>Mental disorder or learning disability, particularly where linked to the commission of the offence</li><li>Demonstration of steps taken to address offending behaviour</li></ul>

* Previous good character/exemplary conduct is different from having no previous
convictions. The more serious the offence, the less the weight which should normally be
attributed to this factor. Where previous good character/exemplary conduct has been used to
facilitate the offence, this mitigation should not normally be allowed and such conduct may
constitute an aggravating factor.

Steps Three to Nine

14.64 The remaining steps cover the following points. At step three the court should consider any factors which would indicate a reduction in sentence, e.g. assistance to the prosecution. At step four it should consider any reduction for a guilty plea. At step five the court should consider dangerousness, i.e. whether it would be appropriate to award an extended sentence (s.226A of the Criminal Justice Act 2003). Step six requires the court to consider whether the total sentence is just and proportionate to the offending behaviour. At step seven it should consider whether to make an ancillary order (e.g. a SHPO or a restraining order). Step eight requires the court to fulfil its duty under s.174 of the Criminal Justice Act 2003 to give reasons for, and explain the effect of, the sentence. Finally, at step nine the court should consider whether to give credit for time spent on bail in accordance with s.240A of that Act.

Sentencing where offender goes on to commit the intended offence

14.65 A person who commits a s.63 offence by trespassing in someone's home intending to commit a sexual offence, and who does commit a sexual offence there, may be charged both under s.63 and with the relevant sexual offence. In such cases, it will be important to avoid effectively penalising the offender twice for the same conduct. Accordingly, if the sentencer enhances the sentence for the sexual offence to reflect the element of trespass, by treating the trespass as an aggravating factor, the better course will be to impose no separate sentence for the s.63 offence[71] or a concurrent sentence which avoids double-counting and respects the totality principle.[72]

Sentencing example

14.66 In *Miah*,[73] the appellant, 33, who was under the influence of alcohol and drugs, followed a woman into her home at about 7:40 a.m., put his arms around her and held a knife to her cheek. She fought back and he moved the knife to her throat, then made towards the door, pushed her away and fled. When approached by the police shortly afterwards, he said he had just tried to rape someone. He pleaded guilty to one offence under s.63 and one of having a bladed article, contrary to the Criminal Justice Act 1988 s.139(1). The judge sentenced the offender to six years' imprisonment for the s.63 offence and three years concurrent for the 1988 Act offence. On appeal, the Court of Appeal identified as aggravating features the violation of the victim's home, the carrying and use of a knife, the terrifying nature of the attack and the grave psychological harm caused. This was a serious category

[71] cf. *Barclay* [2012] EWCA Crim 2375.
[72] cf. *Taylor* [2012] EWCA Crim 1326.
[73] [2016] 1 Cr. App. R.(S.) 168(27).

1 offence and the use of the knife, in particular, justified an increase in the starting point of six years recommended in the Sentencing Council's guideline. However, the judge's starting point, before discount for plea, was too high, having regard to the appellant's previous good character, and immediate admission and plea at the earliest opportunity, which had relieved the complainant of having to give evidence. The Court therefore substituted a sentence of five years' imprisonment. We would make two comments on this case. First, the violation of the victim's home was the single factor that made the case one of "raised harm" so as to bring it within category 1. The Court should not, therefore, have cited the violation as a factor that aggravated the seriousness of the offence, as this amounted to double-counting. Secondly, the appellant was perhaps fortunate not to have been charged also under s.62 of the 2003 Act with assaulting the complainant with intent to commit a sexual offence. The s.63 charge reflected the violation of the victim's home, but the serious assault on her could properly have formed the basis of a separate count under s.62.[74]

JURISDICTION

By virtue of s.72 of and Sch.2 to the Sexual Offences Act 2003, as amended,[75] **14.67** it is an offence under s.63 for a UK national to do an act in a country outside the UK which would constitute a s.63 offence if done in England and Wales, where the intended victim was under 18 at the time of the offence. See further para.14.26, above.

"TRESPASSER"

The word "trespasser" is not defined in the Act. It is likely to bear its civil law **14.68** meaning, as it does in the offence of burglary (s.9 of the Theft Act 1968), i.e. it will cover anyone who intentionally, recklessly or negligently enters into premises in the possession of another person who does not consent to the entry.[76] However, the scope of the s.63 offence is limited by s.63(1)(c), which requires that the defendant must trespass knowingly or recklessly, with the result that a person who trespasses negligently will not be liable to conviction.[77] The requirement of absence of consent means that if a person enters premises pursuant to an effective invitation, he is not a trespasser. Someone other than the owner, tenant or occupier of premises may in

---

[74] cf. James Richardson QC, *Criminal Law Week*, Issue 7, February 22, 2016, p.15.
[75] By the Criminal Justice and Immigration Act 2008 s.72, which came into force on July 14, 2008.
[76] *Archbold* (London: Sweet & Maxwell, 2015), para.21–116.
[77] The position is the same in relation to burglary: *Collins* [1973] Q.B. 100; *Smith and Jones* (1976) 63 Cr. App. R. 47 at 52, per James LJ.

appropriate circumstances give an effective invitation.[78] But the better view is that a person will trespass if he enters premises in response to an invitation that he knows or suspects was given without authority or in excess of a limited authority.[79]

14.69   There is an important difference between the offence of burglary and the s.63 offence, in that burglary requires a person to "enter" as a trespasser, whereas under s.63 it is sufficient that he "is" a trespasser. So a person who enters a building pursuant to an effective invitation does not become a burglar if he remains there after the invitation is withdrawn (unless he subsequently enters another part of the building as a trespasser). But he may commit the s.63 offence if, after the invitation has been withdrawn, he decides to commit a sexual offence against someone in the building. This difference could be significant: suppose, for example, B invites A back to her flat for coffee, A becomes amorous, B asks him to leave, A refuses and says he will rape B and B runs out of the flat. In those circumstances A will not be a burglar and may not commit rape or even attempted rape, depending on exactly what passes between him and B in the flat, but he may well commit the s.63 offence.

14.70   A person commits trespass if he has a right of entry onto another's land for a specific purpose but enters for another purpose.[80] It follows that if a person obtains permission to enter premises by fraud, claiming that he wishes to enter for one purpose but secretly intending another, he will be a trespasser. So if A gains entry to B's premises by falsely claiming that he wishes to read the electricity meter, but he secretly intends to commit a sexual offence against B, he will be liable to conviction under s.63.

"PREMISES"

14.71   The s.63 offence requires the defendant to be a trespasser on "any premises". It is therefore wider, in this respect, than the offence of burglary, which requires the defendant to enter as a trespasser "any building or part of a building". Section 63(2) of the Act provides that "premises" includes "a structure or part of a structure", and that "structure" includes a tent, vehicle or vessel or other temporary or movable structure. This is not an exhaustive definition. The word "premises" is sometimes used in a popular sense to mean buildings, or buildings with land immediately adjoining them, but its legal meaning is anything which may form the subject matter of the habendum of a lease, and this may include land without buildings on it, so

---

[78] *Collins*, last note (invitation by occupier's daughter was effective to prevent the appellant being trespasser).

[79] cf. *Archbold*, (London: Sweet & Maxwell, 2015), para.21–116.

[80] *Taylor v Jackson* (1898) 78 L.T. 555; *Hillen and Pettigrew v ICI (Alkali) Ltd* [1936] A.C. 65; *Farrington v Thomson and Bridgland* [1959] V.R. 286; *Strong v Russell* (1904) 24 N.Z.L.R. 916; *Barker v R.* (1986) 153 C.L.R. 338 (H.Ct.Aust).

long as it has defined boundaries.[81] We suggest that this wider, legal meaning should be applied to s.63, given in particular that Parliament chose to use the word "premises" rather than "building", as in the offence of burglary, and that the mischief at which the provision is aimed is the same whether the trespasser is in a building or on open land. It follows from this that the s.63 offence may be committed where a person trespasses on premises which comprise a building or part of a building, or some other structure, or even no structure at all, e.g. a private garden or yard.

Mental Element

There are two aspects to the mental element of the offence. First, the defendant must know that, or be reckless as to whether, he is a trespasser. Secondly, he must intend to commit a relevant sexual offence on the premises.   **14.72**

Is a person liable to conviction under s.63 if he acts whilst in a state of intoxication due to drink or drugs? Not if his intoxication was involuntary, e.g. it was the result of his drinks being spiked.[82] What if it was self-induced? As recklessness as to the lawfulness of entry will suffice for the element of trespass, it follows that someone in a state of self-induced intoxication may be a trespasser for the purposes of s.63.[83] It is, however, an express requirement of the offence that at the time he trespassed, the defendant intended to commit a relevant sexual offence. If, despite his intoxicated condition, he was able to and did form the required intention, it is no defence that he did so only because of loss of self-control or disinhibition caused by his intoxication.[84] But in the light of *Heard*,[85] discussed in paras 2.81 and following, above, the requirement that the defendant did the prohibited act (i.e. trespassed) with the intention of committing a relevant sexual offence makes the s.63 offence one of specific intent, such that voluntary intoxication through drink or drugs will provide a defence if it prevented or may have prevented him forming that intention.   **14.73**

The offence is complete once the defendant knowingly or recklessly trespasses on the premises with the required intent. If he goes on to commit the intended sexual offence, he can and should be prosecuted for that offence rather than under s.63.   **14.74**

---

[81] *Whitley v Stumbles* [1930] A.C. 544; *Bracey v Read* [1963] Ch. 88.
[82] *Kingston* [1995] 2 A.C. 355.
[83] cf. *DPP v Majewski* [1977] A.C. 443
[84] *Sheehan and Moore* (1975) 60 Cr. App. R. 308, at 312 ("A drunken intent is nevertheless an intent").
[85] [2007] EWCA Crim 125.

CHAPTER 15

OFFENCES AGAINST PUBLIC DECENCY

Introduction....................................... 15.01
Outraging Public Decency 15.26
Exposure.. 15.69
Voyeurism 15.90
Intercourse with an Animal.............15.126
Sexual Penetration of a Corpse 15.145
Sexual Activity in a Public
    Lavatory 15.156
Insulting Behaviour under Section
    4 of the Public Order Act 1986....15.163
Insulting Behaviour with Intent to
    Harass, Alarm or Distress under
    Section 4A of the Public Order
    Act 1986 ....15.171
Abusive or Disorderly Behaviour
    under Section 5 of the Public
    Order Act 1986............................15.179
Other Relevant Offences 15.199

INTRODUCTION

The indecent acts which may be committed in public are many and varied   **15.01**
and the offences covered in this chapter accordingly have a miscellaneous
character. The widest-ranging is the common law offence of outraging public
decency, which was originally triable only on indictment but was made an
either way offence by the Criminal Justice Act 2003.[1] The background to this
change is of some importance and we explain it below.

The Sexual Offences Act 2003 implemented a general modernisation of the   **15.02**
statutory offences in this area. In brief, it abolished the old offences of
bestiality and male indecent exposure[2] and created new offences of:

- exposure of the genitals (s.66),
- voyeurism (s.67),
- intercourse with an animal (s.69),
- sexual penetration of a corpse (s.70), and
- sexual activity in a public lavatory (s.71).

These offences, particularly exposure of the genitals and voyeurism, are   **15.03**
available for use in circumstances that in the past would have been prosecuted

---

[1] s.320(1), which was brought into force on January 20, 2004, by SI 2004/81. Offences
committed before that date remain indictable only: s.320(2).
[2] Vagrancy Act 1824 s.4, and Town Police Clauses Act 1847 s.28.

as outraging public decency. In the event of an overlap, the better practice is to charge the statutory offence, unless, exceptionally, the case is of such seriousness that the common law offence should be deployed in order to make available the higher maximum penalty. In *Rimmington and Goldstein*,[3] the House of Lords held, in relation to the common law offence of public nuisance, that where conduct covered by the offence has been made the subject of a statutory offence, any prosecution should be brought under the statute unless there is good reason for doing otherwise. Lord Bingham said[4]:

> "Where Parliament has defined the ingredients of an offence, perhaps stipulating what shall and shall not be a defence, and has prescribed a mode of trial and a maximum penalty, it must ordinarily be proper that conduct falling within that definition should be prosecuted for the statutory offence and not for a common law offence which may or may not provide the same defences and for which the potential penalty is unlimited . . . It cannot in the ordinary way be a reason for resorting to the common law offence that the prosecutor is freed from mandatory time limits or restrictions on penalty. It must rather be assumed that Parliament imposed the restrictions which it did having considered and weighed up what the protection of the public reasonably demanded. I would not go to the length of holding that conduct may never be lawfully prosecuted as a generally-expressed common law crime where it falls within the terms of a specific statutory provision, but good practice and respect for the primacy of statute do in my judgment require that conduct falling within the terms of a specific statutory provision should be prosecuted under that provision unless there is good reason for doing otherwise."

15.04   The reasoning of the House is no doubt equally applicable to the common law offence of outraging public decency. The courts do, however, remain surprisingly ready to tolerate the use of that offence in circumstances that would be capable of prosecution under the 2003 Act, in particular as an exposure of the genitals contrary to s.66 of that Act.[5] We suggest that in cases of exposure where there is evidence that the defendant intended to cause alarm or distress, s.66 should be charged. That said, there may be cases where a prosecution for outraging public decency may remain appropriate. In *Hardy*,[6] for example, the appellant was convicted of that offence for exposing his penis in public where, judging from the transcript, no evidence was led at trial that he intended someone to see what he was doing and be caused alarm or distress.[7] The appellant's conduct was nonetheless clearly deserving of criminal punishment and a prosecution for the common law offence was perfectly proper since, notwithstanding the enactment of s.66, the need to

---

[3] [2005] UKHL 63.
[4] At [30].
[5] See the cases considered in para.15.36, below.
[6] [2013] EWCA Crim 2125.
[7] cf. *Cosco* [2005] EWCA Crim 207, a case preceding the enactment of s.66, where the appellant exposed his penis on a crowded beach but there was evidence that he had been trying to hide what he was doing with a rolled-up newspaper, indicating that he did not intend anyone to see his penis, let alone be alarmed or distressed.

discourage such behaviour supplied the "good reason" required by *Rimmington and Goldstein*. It is however worth noting that the Court of Appeal disposed of the appeal against sentence by reference to the sentencing guideline for the s.66 offence, which it said "mirrored" the criminality of the appellant's offence.

Finally, those who commit indecent acts in public may in appropriate   **15.05** circumstances be prosecuted for an offence of "insulting behaviour" contrary to s.4 or s.4A of the Public Order Act 1986,[8] for an offence of "abusive" or "disorderly" behaviour contrary to s.5 of that Act, or under local Acts or bye-laws. These possibilities are considered at the end of this chapter.

Outraging public decency

The report of the Sexual Offences Review, published in 2000, spent some time   **15.06** considering the proper application of the criminal law to sexual activity in public.[9] It thought that such activity, whether heterosexual or same-sex, is essentially a problem of public decency, the real nuisance being not sexual activity as such, but sexual activity that is seen by others in circumstances where it is likely to cause distress or offence. The Review saw a clear need to protect members of the public from being unwilling witnesses to such activity, or harassed or intimidated by it in their use of public space and facilities. It also identified a number of existing offences that were used to deal with the problem.[10] Some—buggery, gross indecency between men and soliciting by men—were used to prosecute cottaging and overt sex between males and were marked for abolition by the Review on the grounds of their discriminatory content. The other offences most often used in this context were insulting behaviour likely to cause harassment, alarm or distress (s.5 of the Public Order Act 1986) and the common law offences of outraging public decency and public nuisance.

The Review noted that outraging public decency was prosecuted in about   **15.07** 60 cases a year, typically involving couples having sexual intercourse in public places, prostitutes "advertising" from windows or men masturbating in public view. As these examples illustrated, the offence was flexible and capable of use in a wide variety of circumstances. But the Review thought its very width and flexibility made it an "uncertain" offence which lacked the clarity required of modern criminal law. Rather than rely on this and the other existing offences, the Review's preferred response to the problem of sexual activity in public was to introduce a new offence, modelled on s.5 of the Public Order Act 1986, penalising sexual behaviour that a person knew

---

[8] 1986 c.64.

[9] *Setting the Boundaries* (Home Office, July 2000), para.8.4. The report is available at *http://webarchive.nationalarchives.gov.uk/-/http://www.homeoffice.gov.uk/documents/vol1main.pdf?view=Binary* [Accessed April 30, 2016].

[10] ss.12, 13 and 32 of the Sexual Offences Act 1956.

or should have known was likely to cause distress, alarm or offence to others in a public place.

15.08   The Government rejected this recommendation. Instead it proposed, in the White Paper *Protecting the Public*,[11] to introduce an offence of sexual activity in a public place targeted at specified sexual acts. The Sexual Offences Bill duly contained a clause creating two offences along these lines, one covering sexual activity in a public place and the other sexual activity outside a dwelling but visible from a public place. The clause was, however, mercilessly savaged both in Parliament and elsewhere because of its odd and unsatisfactory impact. It was pointed out, for example, that a couple having sexual intercourse in their garden would commit an offence if they knew that someone in a public place might see them, e.g. because there were slats missing from the fence which separated the garden from the pavement on one side of the house, but not if they knew that their neighbour on the other side might see them from his first floor window. Again, the provision would criminalise sexual activity in a public place only if it could be seen, and it was therefore suggested that activity carried out in a cubicle in a public lavatory would be prohibited if the cubicle door was open but not if it were closed.

15.09   In the light of these and other criticisms, the Government undertook to reconsider the clause.[12] Having done so, it elected to withdraw it altogether and instead proposed that sexual activity in public should be prosecuted either as the offence of outraging public decency or as insulting behaviour under s.5 of the Public Order Act 1986. Moreover, to ensure that the common law offence was up to the task, the Government said it would introduce an amendment to the Criminal Justice Bill then before Parliament (which became the Criminal Justice Act 2003) to make the offence triable either way rather than only on indictment.[13]

15.10   This change of tack did not, however, satisfy Parliamentary concern, which came to focus particularly on the need for sexual activity in a public lavatory to be effectively penalised.[14] Members of the Lords were not convinced that the offence of outraging public decency and s.5 of the 1986 Act were up to the challenge. The perceived problem with the common law offence lay in the requirement that two people must have seen or been able to see the activity, which, it was argued, would perpetuate the problem of the closed cubicle door. As to s.5, there was no confidence that sexual activity in a public lavatory would necessarily be regarded as "insulting" behaviour. Amendments were accordingly tabled to resolve the matter by introducing a new offence of sexual activity in a public lavatory.[15] The Government resisted

---

[11] *Protecting the Public: strengthening protection against sex offenders and reforming the law on sexual offences* (Cm 5668) (Nov 2002), para.77.

[12] *Hansard*, HL Vol.644, col.876, Lord Falconer of Thoroton (February 13, 2003).

[13] *Hansard*, HL Vol.648, col.585 et seq., Lord Falconer of Thoroton (May 19, 2003). See fn.1 above.

[14] *Hansard*, HL Vol.648, col.576 et seq., Lord Falconer of Thoroton (May 19, 2003).

[15] *Hansard*, HL Vol.648, col.576 et seq. (May 19, 2003); vol.649, col.64 (June 9, 2003).

this development, but was defeated on a vote at Report.[16] At that point it decided to drop its opposition and to concentrate instead on making the new offence workable. The result is s.71 of the Sexual Offences Act 2003. The promised amendment to the Criminal Justice Bill was pursued in parallel, so that the offence of outraging public decency may now be prosecuted in the magistrates' court.

The common law offence was considered most recently by the Law **15.11** Commission in a report issued as part of its programme of simplification of the criminal law.[17] After an extensive review of the authorities, the Commission recommended that the offence should be replaced by a statutory offence which should continue to cover any act or display of an obscene or disgusting nature sufficient to outrage contemporary standards of decency, which occurs in a place which is accessible to or within view of the public; however, there should be no requirement that two persons should be present. The mental element should be intention or recklessness as to the constituent elements of the offence, but a defendant should not be guilty if their conduct was reasonable in the circumstances as they knew or reasonably believed them to be. We support these recommendations.

Exposure of the genitals

The Sexual Offences Review noted that the problem of male indecent **15.12** exposure was often referred to "flashing", a term with connotations of pathetic and inadequate men who need not be taken seriously.[18] But research showed that exposure of the penis may have a serious impact on those who witness it, and that some men engage in it as part of a wider pattern of sexual offending, some of it very serious. The relevant law was archaic, being largely set out in two nineteenth century statutes, the Vagrancy Act 1824 and the Town Police Clauses Act 1847, which quaintly described the prohibited activity as "exposure of the person". The common law offence of outraging public decency could also be used. The Review noted that these offences did not penalise any exposure of the penis, but only exposure that caused offence. It also noted that not all public exposures of the penis are intended to threaten or are targeted at a particular victim, and cited as examples the enjoyment by naturists of their preferred lifestyle and the activities of streakers and other exhibitionists who strip off in public for fun or in order to shock.

The Review considered that, whilst the courts should be able to deal with **15.13** exhibitionist behaviour as a social nuisance, there was a need for a more serious sexual offence to replace the old offences of exposure of the person. It therefore recommended the creation of an offence of indecent exposure of

[16] *Hansard*, HL Vol.648, col.585 et seq. (May 19, 2003); vol.649, col.79 (June 9, 2003).
[17] *Simplification of Criminal Law: Public Nuisance and Outraging Public Decency* (Law Com No.358) (June 2015).
[18] *Setting the Boundaries*, 2000, para.8.2.

the penis in circumstances where the defendant knew or should have known that he might cause fear, alarm or distress to another person. This should be capable of covering exposure to another man or boy, as this could be as threatening or frightening as exposure to a woman. But the Review concluded that on balance there was no need to cover exposure of the female genitalia, as this is not common, does not carry the same degree of threat and can be satisfactorily dealt through the law of public nuisance or public order.

15.14   The Government accepted the recommendation to create a new offence, but not that it should be confined to males. In *Protecting the Public* it announced its intention to introduce a gender-neutral offence of exposure of the genitalia where the defendant intended to cause or it was reasonably likely that their behaviour would cause alarm or distress.[19] In fact, the offence introduced in the Sexual Offences Bill went somewhat wider than this, covering intentional exposure of the genitals, knowing or intending that someone would see them and knowing or intending that, or being reckless whether, someone who saw them would be caused alarm or distress. A limited exception was created for cases of recklessness where the defendant was in a dwelling and did not know or intend that their genitals would be seen by a child under 16.

15.15   The proposed offence encountered widespread opposition. Naturists, in particular, were deeply concerned that it could be committed recklessly. It is inevitable that naturists going about their normal business will sometimes be seen by other people, as naturist beaches and campsites are often visible or poorly screened from other areas. A public opinion survey conducted by British Naturism in 2001 revealed that, while the vast majority of the public regarded naturism as harmless, 7 per cent considered it disgusting. The naturist community was therefore concerned that they might commit the offence in circumstances where they knew they would be seen by other people, and knew there was a risk that one or more of the people who saw them would be among the 7 per cent and would be alarmed or distressed by what they saw. The Government purported to regard this concern as unfounded, but at the Lords' Committee stage it nonetheless introduced an amendment to remove the reference to recklessness from the offence.[20] This concession failed, however, wholly to satisfy the naturist lobby, which continued to express concern about the impact of the offence on naturist activities.[21] Finally, the Government introduced a further amendment to restrict the offence to cases where the individual intentionally exposes his genitals intending someone to see them and be caused alarm or distress.[22] It was in this amended form that the offence passed into law.

---

[19] para.76.
[20] *Hansard*, HL Vol.648, col.555 (May 19, 2003).
[21] See the debate in Standing Committee B, col.300 et seq. (September 9, 2003).
[22] *Hansard*, HL Vol.654, Col.560 (November 3, 2003).

Voyeurism

Cases of voyeurism reported to the Sexual Offences Review included   **15.16**
landlords creating spyholes into their tenant's bathrooms; covert observation
in changing rooms in shops, market stalls and schools; hidden cameras used
to film in public changing areas and on beaches; and the classic "Peeping
Tom" activity of looking into the windows of private houses.[23] The Review
considered that, rather like "flashing", the traditional attitude to such
activity has been to regard it as an unpleasant nuisance rather than as
criminal conduct.[24] However, the Review was impressed by evidence linking
voyeurism to a range of offending behaviour, including the most serious sex
offences. It thought there was a genuine problem in the secret observation of
people in circumstances where they could reasonably expect privacy and
where the watcher acted for the purpose of sexual gratification. The
experience of victims, particularly those observed in their own homes, was
that not only their privacy but also their personal integrity and safety had
been violated. A number of other jurisdictions had introduced offences to
deal with this sort of behaviour and the Review considered that one should
be introduced here, too.

The first element of the offence should, it said, be that the observation   **15.17**
took place where there was a reasonable expectation of privacy. If, for
example, there was a notice in a changing room stating that video surveillance was in use, there could be no such expectation, but if there was no such
notice an expectation of privacy could arise. The Review also thought it
would be sensible to limit the offence to observation of a person in a building
or other structure, on the somewhat dubious basis that someone in the open,
even in a private garden, will not have an expectation of privacy. As to
whether there should be a requirement that the observation be for the
purpose of sexual gratification, the Review thought this could be difficult to
prove and also that observation in violation of privacy, and the fear and
distress its discovery could cause the victim, was sufficient of itself to justify
the offence. But the Review recognised that the absence of a sexual element
would risk impeding the work of the investigative press and it therefore
sought views on this aspect. Subject to resolution of this point, it recommended the creation of an offence of voyeurism to apply where a person in
the interior of a building or other structure has a reasonable expectation of
privacy and is observed without their knowledge or consent, including by
remote or mechanical means.

---

[23] *Setting the Boundaries*, 2000, para.8.3.
[24] There were in fact reported examples of the use of the criminal law to penalise voyeuristic
activity: see, e.g. *Choi* [1999] EWCA Crim 1279, para.15.39, below (conviction for outraging
public decency); *Vigon v DPP* [1998] Crim. L.R. 289, DC, para.15.181, below (conviction for
insulting behaviour under s.5(1) of the Public Order Act 1986).

15.18   In the White Paper *Protecting the Public*[25] the Government adopted the main thrust of this recommendation, but it departed from the Review in announcing that the new offence would apply only where the voyeur acted for their own or another's sexual gratification. It added that it would want the courts to treat as particularly serious those cases in which a person takes indecent photographs of another person without their consent and publicises them by, for example, posting them on the internet or placing them in a pornographic magazine. The Sexual Offences Bill as introduced contained a clause designed to implement the Government's proposal. The clause proved uncontroversial, though it was substantially revised by Government amendments during the Bill's passage.[26] One significant and welcome amendment was the expansion of the offence so that it is not limited to "structures" but covers the observation of another person doing a private act in any "place" in which there is a reasonable expectation of privacy. The offence as so amended became s.67 of the 2003 Act.

Intercourse with an animal

15.19   Section 69 of the Sexual Offences Act 2003 creates two offences of intercourse with an animal, one committed by penetrating the anus or vagina of a living animal and one committed by being penetrated by the penis of a living animal. These offences replace the offence of buggery with an animal under s.12 of the Sexual Offences Act 1956.

15.20   This change was a long time coming. As far back as 1984, the Criminal Law Revision Committee ("CLRC") took the view that the maximum penalty of life imprisonment under s.12 was too harsh and proposed that bestiality should instead be a summary offence punishable with a maximum of six months' imprisonment.[27] In recognition of the fact that those who procure acts of bestiality are often more deserving of punishment than those who actually commit them, the CLRC also proposed that there should be a separate statutory offence of procuring bestiality, triable either way and punishable with a maximum of five years' imprisonment. These proposals were reflected in clauses 118 and 119 of the draft Law Commission's Criminal Code Bill.[28]

15.21   In the Commentary which accompanied the draft Bill, the Law Commission stated that some of its members disagreed with the CLRC on the need to retain an offence of bestiality at all (as opposed to an offence of procuring bestiality), on the ground that it was outdated and that conduct falling within its scope was punishable under the law of criminal damage and cruelty to animals.[29] The Sexual Offences Review considered this point and concluded

[25] para.78.
[26] *Hansard*, HL Vol.648, col.570 et seq (May 19, 2003).
[27] Fifteenth Report on *Sexual Offences*, Cmnd. 9213 (1984), paras 12.7–12.9.
[28] Law Com. No.177 (1989).
[29] Law Com. No.177 (1989), Vol.2 (Commentary), para.15.53.

that the behaviour covered by the offence should continue to be criminal, on the grounds that it was an affront to the dignity of animals and of people and profoundly abhorrent to society.[30] Moreover, the offence was primarily a sexual offence: it constituted profoundly disturbed behaviour and there was evidence of linkage between abuse of animals and other forms of sexual offending. The Review did, however, share the view of the CLRC that the maximum penalty should be much reduced.

The Review's recommendations were adopted in *Protecting the Public*, **15.22** where the Government proposed the creation of an offence covering those who sexually penetrate animals and those who allow an animal to penetrate them.[31] The maximum penalty in both cases was to be two years' imprisonment. This proposal led directly to the creation of the two offences of intercourse with an animal in s.69 of the 2003 Act.

Sexual penetration of a corpse

One of the issues considered by the Sexual Offences Review was whether the **15.23** law should prohibit sexual interference with human remains.[32] Most members were surprised to find that necrophilia was not an offence under the existing law. The Review considered that, though necrophilia is rare, the activity is sufficiently serious that it should be criminalised. The main arguments for this were that the families of those who have died have every right to expect the deceased's remains to be treated with respect and propriety, and that most people would expect necrophilia to be penalised by the law. The Review accordingly recommended that interference with human remains should be made an offence.

This recommendation was adopted in *Protecting the Public*, where the **15.24** Government said:

> "Although there is no indication that such activity is anything but extremely rare, we believe that this behaviour is so deviant as to warrant the intervention of the criminal law."[33]

The result is s.70 of the Sexual Offences Act 2003, which makes it an offence intentionally to penetrate, with part of the body or anything else, part of the body of a dead person.

The White Paper also made the point that where a defendant is suspected of **15.25** killing their victim and sexually penetrating their body after death, the priority will be to charge them with murder or manslaughter, but the sexual deviance of the offending behaviour should also be recognised by a separate count under s.70. If the defendant is found guilty on both charges, this will

---

[30] *Setting the Boundaries*, 2000, para.8.5.
[31] para.79.
[32] *Setting the Boundaries*, 2000, para.8.6.
[33] para.80.

ensure that he is sentenced accordingly and treated and monitored as a sex offender both in prison and after release.

Outraging Public Decency

Definition

15.26 It is an offence at common law to do in public any act of a lewd, obscene or disgusting nature which outrages public decency.[34] Although the scope of the offence is very wide,[35] it appears to be sufficiently certain to comply with art.10 of the ECHR.[36] Most cases involve indecent exposure of the human body and this is reflected in the following discussion.

15.27 The creation by the Sexual Offences Act 2003 of offences of exposure of the genitals, voyeurism and sexual activity in a public lavatory has served to limit the use to which the common law offence is put. If conduct falls within the scope of one of the statutory offences, the better practice is to charge that offence, unless there is good reason to do otherwise; and the mere fact that the common law offence carries a higher maximum penalty will not of itself supply such a reason: see *Rimmington and Goldstein,*[37] discussed in para.15.03, above. In *May,*[38] the appellant was convicted on an indictment containing three counts of the common law offence and one of gross indecency with a child (contrary to s.1(1) of the Indecency with Children Act 1960, since repealed). He appealed against conviction on the common law counts, arguing that it had been improper to charge him with the common law offence when the facts alleged in each count fell within the scope of the

---

[34] 2 Russ. Cr. 1423; 1 East P.C. 3; 1 Hawk. c.5; *Sidley* (1663) 1 Sid. 168 (reported *sub nom. Sedley* 17 St. Tr. 155n.); *Rowed* (1824) 3 Q.B. 180; *Mayling* [1963] 2 Q.B. 717; *Knuller (Publishing, Printing and Promotions) Ltd v DPP* [1973] A.C. 435; *May* (1990) 91 Cr. App. R. 157; *Gibson and Sylveire* (1990) 91 Cr. App. R. 341; *Hamilton* [2007] EWCA Crim 2062.

[35] It has been held to cover disinterring a corpse (*Lynn* (1788) 2 Durn. & E. 733); selling a wife (cited in *Delaval* (1763) 3 Burr. 1434 at 1438); exhibiting a deformed child (*Herring v Walround* (1681) 2 Ch. Cass. 110); exhibiting a picture of sores (*Grey* (1864) 4 F. & F. 73); exhibiting earrings made from freeze-dried human foetuses (*Gibson and Sylveire* (1990) 91 Cr. App. R. 341); simulating sexual intercourse in a solo performance on a desk-top (*May* (1990) 91 Cr. App. R. 157); having sexual intercourse and oral sex in an airport car park (*Curran* [1998] EWCA Crim. 3048); secretly video filming a woman urinating in a supermarket lavatory (*Choi* [1999] EWCA Crim. 1279); taking photographs up women's skirts (*Hamilton* [2007] EWCA Crim 2062); physically abusing and urinating on a dying woman in the street (*Anderson* [2008] EWCA Crim 12); and urinating on a poppy wreath on a war memorial (*Laing*, Sheffield Magistrates' Court, November 4, 2009, reported in *The Times*, November 5, 2009, p.24).

[36] See *Simplification of Criminal Law: Public Nuisance and Outraging Public Decency*, Law Com Consultation Paper No.193 (2010), para.4.29 and following. See also *S and G v United Kingdom* (App No.17634/91), in which the European Commission on Human Rights declined to allow an application to proceed that had been lodged by the convicted defendants in *Gibson and Sylveire*, last note, on the basis that the restriction on their freedom of expression was "prescribed by law" and pursued a "legitimate aim", namely the protection of morality.

[37] [2005] UKHL 63.

[38] (1990) 91 Cr. App. R. 157.

gross indecency offence, under which the maximum penalty is only two years' imprisonment. The Court of Appeal rejected this argument, holding that the availability of charges under the 1960 Act did not make reliance upon the common law offence any the less appropriate. We suggest that *May* is consistent with *Rimmington and Goldstein*, since the 1960 Act offence was expressed in general terms and in creating it Parliament was not making express provision for the sort of conduct engaged in by the appellant. Accordingly, there was no reason of good practice to require a charge to be brought under the 1960 Act if the prosecutor judged that the appellant's criminality was better reflected by a charge of the common law offence.

MODE OF TRIAL AND PUNISHMENT

The offence is triable either way.[39] An offender convicted on indictment may be fined or imprisoned, or both. There is no maximum punishment, but the sentence imposed must not be inordinate.[40] On summary conviction the maximum sentence is six months' imprisonment or a fine.[41] As from a day to be appointed the maximum period of imprisonment will increase to 12 months.[42] The increase will have no application to offences committed before it takes effect.[43] Until recently, the maximum fine on summary conviction was a fine not exceeding the prescribed sum (i.e. £5,000). The effect of s.85 of the Legal Aid, Sentencing and Punishment of Offenders Act 2012 is that, from March 12, 2015, a fine of any amount may be imposed. Fines will, however, continue to be set according to the seriousness of the offence and the means of the offender.   **15.28**

The common law offence is not a serious specified offence for the purpose of the dangerousness provisions of the Criminal Justice Act 2003.[44]   **15.29**

For the purposes of listing, cases which qualify as a sexual offence will fall within Class 2B; otherwise, they will fall within Class 3.[45] Cases in Class 2B must be referred to the Resident Judge, and by the Resident Judge to a Presiding Judge, in specified circumstances, including where a novel and important point of law is to be raised; where the defendant is a police officer, a member of the legal profession or a high profile figure; or where for any reason the case is likely to attract exceptional media attention.   **15.30**

---

[39] The offence was indictable only until January 20, 2004: see fn.1 above.

[40] *Morris* [1951] 1 K.B. 394.

[41] Magistrates' Courts Act 1980 s.32(1).

[42] Criminal Justice Act 2003 s.282(2), (3).

[43] Criminal Justice Act 2003 s.282(4).

[44] s.224 and Sch.15, Pt 2.

[45] *Consolidated Criminal Practice Directions*, Part XIII Listing B: CLASSIFICATION, available at *https://www.judiciary.gov.uk/wp-content/uploads/2015/09/crim-pd-2015.pdf* [Accessed April 30, 2016].

Charge or Indictment

15.31   A charge or indictment will be defective if it does not contain an averment of indecency.[46] It has also been common practice to aver that the defendant's act was done "to the great disgust and annoyance of divers of Her Majesty's subjects", though it has been doubted whether this is strictly necessary[47] and in modern times the practice has not been followed.[48] For proof of this averment, see para.15.51, below.

Sentencing

15.32   There is no sentencing guideline for the common law offence, nor any guideline judgment.

Sentencing examples

15.33   In *May*,[49] the appellant ordered two boys to command him to simulate sexual intercourse with a desk in a classroom, with the door open, and then obeyed the command. He was sentenced to 15 months' imprisonment concurrent for three offences of outraging public decency. The Court of Appeal reduced the sentences to nine months' concurrent. It counted against the appellant that the offences had all involved young boys, his behaviour had been "disgusting" and a breach of trust, and there had been no guilty plea; but there had also been no physical contact, and the Court doubted whether the boys had suffered or would suffer any lasting damage.

15.34   In *Vaiculevicius*[50] the applicant, 30, sought leave to appeal a sentence of six months' imprisonment imposed after he pleaded guilty to outraging public decency in relation to an incident when he and a woman, both heavily intoxicated, had consensual sexual intercourse in a public park on a Sunday afternoon. They made no attempt to conceal their activity and were visible to others in the park, including young children who were playing there. They had removed their lower clothing. They stopped only when spoken to by police officers. The applicant admitted the offence in interview and said that he was disgusted by his own behaviour. Before the Court of Appeal, the applicant argued that this sentence was wrong in principle or manifestly excessive given that the other persons were some distance away in the park, that his genitals and those of the woman were not deliberately exposed to view and that the offence did not involve any element of exhibitionism or

---

[46] *Clifford* [1988] 8 C.L. 86 (Maidstone Crown Ct.; leave to amend refused and jury directed to acquit). In *May* (1990) 91 Cr. App. R. 157, one count alleged that the appellant had committed the offence by "behaving in an indecent manner with a desk".
[47] *Mayling* [1963] 2 Q.B. 717, at 725.
[48] cf. *Curran* [1998] EWCA Crim 3048.
[49] (1990) 91 Cr. App. R. 157.
[50] [2013] EWCA Crim 185.

even knowledge that others might see the sexual activity. The Court of Appeal noted that the applicant had previous convictions for a total of 30 offences, mainly involving dishonesty and none involving any form of sexual activity. A feature of his record was a repeated disregard for court orders. The Court also noted that the sentence for the offence of outraging public decency is at large and there is no sentencing guideline directly applicable to it, though it was relevant to consider the guidelines for the offences of exposure (s.66 of the 2003 Act) and sexual activity in a public lavatory (s.71). The applicant placed particular reliance upon the guideline for the s.66 offence, though he acknowledged that it did not provide a perfect analogy to his case. The Court of Appeal accepted that there were no reported cases involving broadly similar facts, though, as the learned judge had said in the court below, such guidance as can be obtained confirms that "[t]he courts take this type of activity rather seriously". The Court said it could well understand why the judge came to that conclusion, but the reality was that there was only very limited guidance to be obtained as to the appropriate sentence from either guidelines or reported decisions of the courts. It went on to identify the following aggravating features in this case: (i) the offence was committed in public, with a complete disregard for the shock or distress that it was likely to cause anyone who witnessed it; (ii) young children were present nearby, and whether or not the applicant realised this, it was readily foreseeable that children would be playing in the park on a Sunday afternoon; (iii) the applicant's intoxication; and (iv) his previous convictions, albeit they were for different types of offence, and the fact that he had very recently been released from prison. For all these reasons, despite this being the first such offence that the applicant had committed, the learned judge had been entitled to view the case as serious. The Court rejected the submission that a sentence of immediate imprisonment was wrong in principle: the judge had been entitled to conclude that this offence passed the custody threshold and that only an immediate sentence of imprisonment would suffice. However, the judge had taken a starting point of nine months before giving full credit for the prompt guilty plea. The Court was persuaded that the resulting sentence of six months' imprisonment was manifestly excessive. Having regard to all relevant factors, including the guilty plea, the appropriate sentence here would have been three months' imprisonment, and accordingly the Court quashed the sentence imposed below and substituted a term of that length.

In *Carton*[51] the appellant (C) appealed against a sentence of 14 months' **15.35** imprisonment imposed after he pleaded guilty to five offences of outraging public decency relating to incidents in which he had used his mobile phone to take photographs or videos up women's skirts. Upon his arrest his mobile phone was found to have 48 clips of various women on it. The women had been unaware of C's actions. He admitted the offences. A pre-sentence report

[51] [2012] EWCA Crim 3199.

considered that he posed a low risk of re-offending and a medium risk to women, and recommended a community order with a supervision requirement and attendance on a sex offender programme. The sentencing judge concluded that C should be sentenced upon the totality of his offending. He took a 20-month starting point and reduced it to 14 months to take account of C's early plea and mitigation. He also imposed an anti-social behaviour order prohibiting C from having in his possession in a public place a mobile phone with a video or photographic function. C submitted that the starting point was too high. The appeal was allowed. The Court of Appeal said that the judge had been required to sentence C for a very large number of offences of a kind that could not be regarded as commonplace. The sentencing guideline for voyeurism dealt with offences that were rather more serious than the instant offence, although the guideline for the basic offence of spying through a hole in a changing room wall was of some assistance. For a single offence of that kind, the guideline then in force suggested a community sentence. C's offending behaviour had persisted for some months but there was no evidence to suggest that he showed any of his films to anyone else. He had already taken steps to reduce his ability to re-offend by obtaining a mobile phone that did not have a camera and ceasing to be connected to the internet. However, it was also important not to minimise the effect of this type of offending. Those who became aware of what C had done were understandably shocked and distressed. But the interests of the public, and women in particular, would be best served by requiring C to undergo therapy to assist him in changing his attitude and urges. The recommendation in the pre-sentence report was realistic and was more likely to lead to C's rehabilitation than a custodial sentence. C had already spent two-and-a-half months in custody, which would serve as both punishment and a reminder of what awaited him if he offended in that way again. The Court quashed C's sentence and replaced it with a community order for three years, comprising a supervision requirement and a requirement to attend a community sex offence group work programme. The ASBO was not altered.

15.36   The following decisions are instructive on sentencing where a man commits the common law offence by indecent exposure. In *Cosco*,[52] the appellant was convicted on three counts of outraging public decency relating to acts of indecent exposure committed near children on a crowded beach. He had a long history of similar offending. No treatment or cure was available and the appellant continued to deny committing the offences. He was sentenced to 18 months' imprisonment on each count to run consecutively, making a total of four-and-a-half years. The Court of Appeal said that some guidance as to sentencing in such cases may be derived from the fact that in s.66 of the 2003 Act (which was not then in force), Parliament fixed a maximum sentence of two years' imprisonment for exposure of the genitals. Here, the appellant could have had no complaint if the sentences

---

[52] [2005] EWCA Crim 207.

imposed upon him had been made concurrent rather than consecutive and the Court substituted sentences to that effect. It pointed out that this reflected the fact that the offences were in truth aspects of a single course of conduct on one afternoon. In *Birch*,[53] the appellant pleaded guilty to outraging public decency in relation to an incident in which he had followed a woman through a city centre in the early hours of the morning with his penis exposed and masturbating. He was seen on CCTV and the police were able to intervene before the woman became aware of his presence. He had a long history of similar offending. He was sentenced to three years' imprisonment, which was ordered to run consecutively to an unserved licence period of 489 days. The Court of Appeal held that a sentence of three years on top of the existing sentence was unnecessarily long. But this was a serious offence and the appellant was a real risk to women, and in those circumstances the Court substituted a sentence of 18 months' imprisonment. In *Miah*,[54] the appellant pleaded guilty to outraging public decency, common assault and using racially aggravated threatening behaviour. A woman collected her 13-year-old daughter from a dance class. The daughter and her friends were giving a demonstration of what they had learned when the appellant, who was drunk, began to spit at the children. He exposed himself to them and the woman. He was also racially abusive. There was mitigation in his early plea, repentance and personal circumstances. He was sentenced to three years' imprisonment for outraging public decency and 15 months concurrent for racially aggravated threatening behaviour. On appeal it was held that the offence was serious, but the appellant had not used violence, nor touched or attempted to touch anyone and, in view of the mitigation, the proper sentence for the common law offence was two years' imprisonment.

PARTIES TO THE OFFENCE

The offence may be committed as principal by both males and females.[55] In cases involving indecent exposure, the exposure need not be to persons of the opposite sex.[56]   **15.37**

"A LEWD, OBSCENE OR DISGUSTING ACT"

The defendant must be proved to have done a lewd, obscene or disgusting act. The meaning of "obscenity" is illuminated by the Scottish case   **15.38**

---

[53] [2007] EWCA Crim 1008.
[54] [2006] EWCA Crim 132.
[55] cf. *Elliot and White* (1861) Le. & Ca. 103; and see also *Clark* (1883) 15 Cox C.C. 171.
[56] cf. *Mayling* [1963] 2 Q.B. 717; *May* (1990) 91 Cr. App. R. 157.

McGowan v Longmuir,[57] where Lord Parker said, in relation to the offence of keeping for sale indecent or obscene prints:

> "I do not think the words 'indecent' and 'obscene' are synonymous. The one may shade into the other, but there is a difference of meaning. It is easier to illustrate than to define . . . for a male bather to enter the water nude in the presence of ladies would be indecent,[58] it would not necessarily be obscene. But if he directed the attention of the ladies to a certain member of his body his conduct would certainly be obscene."

A similar approach was taken in *Stanley,*[59] where Lord Parker CJ said that the words "indecent or obscene" in s.11 of the Post Office Act 1953 (prohibition on sending certain articles by post):

> "convey one idea, namely offending against the recognised standards of propriety, indecent being at the lower end of the scale and obscene at the upper end of the scale."

We suggest that in directing a jury on the meaning of an "obscene" act for the purposes of the common law offence, a judge should do so in the terms used by Lord Parker CJ. The Court of Appeal did, however, take a different approach in *Kirk,*[60] in holding that the words "indecent" and "obscene" in s.85(4) of the Postal Services Act 2000 (offence of sending a postal packet on which there are words etc. of an indecent or obscene character) are ordinary words that would be readily understood by members of a jury, and so it is unnecessary and potentially misleading to give the jury any interpretation of them, using other words which might narrow or enlarge their meaning. A simple direction using the words "indecent" and "obscene" will instead be sufficient, and it will be for the jury to set the standard. The Court did not refer to the statement of Lord Parker CJ in *Stanley*. After *Kirk,* the right course for a judge directing a jury on s.85(4) of the 2000 Act is to avoid elaborating in any way the meaning of "indecent" and "obscene". We nonetheless suggest that the decision has no necessary application in other contexts and that, given the archaic framing of the offence of outraging public decency, it remains appropriate to rely on the statement in *Stanley* when directing a jury in relation to the meaning of an "obscene" act for the purposes of that offence.

15.39   As for the word "disgusting", it was stated in *Choi*[61] that a disgusting act is an act "which fills the onlooker with loathing or extreme distaste or causes the onlooker extreme annoyance". In that case, the appellant was convicted of outraging public decency on evidence that he had used a camcorder to film a woman while she was urinating in a supermarket lavatory. It was argued on appeal that his use of the camcorder, viewed objectively and without

[57] 1931 S.C.(J.) 10 at 13.
[58] Unless, presumably, he does so on a nudist beach: see paras 15.62 and following, below.
[59] [1965] 2 Q.B. 327.
[60] [2006] EWCA Crim 725; [2006] Crim. L.R. 850.
[61] [1999] EWCA Crim 1279.

reference to his motive,[62] was not lewd, obscene or disgusting. The Court rejected this argument, holding that the jury could properly have concluded that the appellant's conduct was disgusting.

In *May*,[63] the appellant, a schoolmaster, was alleged in one count to have   **15.40** committed the offence "by inducing H a male pupil to complete an indecent questionnaire." The evidence on this count was that the appellant had handed H a letter and told him to open it and ask the appellant the questions contained inside. The questions related to the appellant's sexual relationship with his girlfriend, and were couched in rude language. No point was taken at trial as to whether the appellant's conduct amounted to a lewd or obscene act. On appeal, the Court said the wording of the count and the facts on which it was based raised questions which required a careful direction to the jury: but as nobody had taken the point, no such direction had been given. In those circumstances the conviction was unsafe and it was quashed.

It was held in *Rowley*[64] that if the defendant's act is not lewd, obscene or   **15.41** disgusting, it cannot be made so by virtue of his intention or motive in carrying it out. In that case, the appellant wrote notes offering money to boys for being his "pretended son" or for delivering secret messages, and left them in public places. He was convicted on a direction to the jury that in deciding whether the notes were lewd, obscene or disgusting they were entitled to look at the purpose behind them, as evidenced by entries from the appellant's diary in which he indicated his desire for sexual activity with boys. This was held on appeal to be a misdirection. Taylor LJ (as he then was) said:

> "Although the ultimate intention of the actor and his motive for his act may be the subsequent performance of lewd, obscene or disgusting acts, his intention and motive cannot supply lewdness or obscenity to the act if the act itself lacks those qualities."[65]

However, we suggest that evidence of intention or motive will be relevant and should be admissible if the act is *capable* of being lewd, obscene or disgusting, but members of the public would wish to know why the defendant had done it before deciding whether it was in fact lewd, obscene or disgusting. This would be consistent with the approach taken to the definition of "sexual" in s.78(b) of the Sexual Offences Act 2003, under which an activity which a reasonable person would consider may be sexual may be shown to be so by evidence of the purpose of the person undertaking it, or another person: see paras 2.66 and following, above.[66]

---

[62] See *Rowley* (1992) 94 Cr. App. R. 94, discussed in para.15.41, below.
[63] (1990) 91 Cr. App. R. 157.
[64] (1992) 94 Cr. App. R. 94.
[65] At 99.
[66] See also *Court* [1989] A.C. 28, a decision on indecent assault in which it was held that where the defendant's conduct is ambiguous, evidence of his motive may be admitted to show that the assault was in fact indecent and that he intended it to be so. This aspect of the decision is reflected in s.78(b) of the 2003 Act.

"Outrage to Public Decency"

15.42   A lewd, obscene or disgusting act will not fall within the scope of the offence unless it outrages public decency, i.e. is so indecent that it would outrage ordinary members of the public.[67] Whether the act has this effect is a question of fact for the jury. In *Knuller (Publishing, Printing and Promotions) Ltd v DPP*,[68] where one of the charges was conspiracy to outrage public decency, Lord Reid, referring to the law of indecent exhibitions, said:

> "'indecency' is not confined to sexual indecency; . . . it includes anything which an ordinary decent man or woman would find to be shocking, disgusting and revolting."[69]

Again, in the indecent assault case of *Court*[70] the House of Lords said that the question of indecency should be left to the jury by asking them to decide whether "right-minded persons would consider the conduct indecent or not". See also *Stanley*,[71] discussed in para.15.38, above. Similar but slightly differing approaches to the meaning of "indecency" have been taken elsewhere in the Commonwealth. The Australian courts have used a test of whether the conduct in question would offend the ordinary modesty of the average person.[72] In Canada, the decency or otherwise of a defendant's conduct has been judged by reference to the "standard of community tolerance".[73]

15.43   As for the requirements of an "outrage" to public decency, Lord Reid indicated in *Knuller* that "outraged" means "utterly disgusted".[74] Lord Simon said:

> "'outrage' . . . is a very strong word. 'Outraging public decency' goes considerably beyond offending the susceptibilities of, or even shocking, reasonable people."[75]

In *Curran*,[76] where the appellant had engaged in sexual intercourse and oral sex in the short-term car park at Heathrow's Terminal 4, the judge told the jury that the word "outraging" spoke for itself and did not require definition. It was held on appeal that it would have been better if he had cited Lord Simon's words from *Knuller*, though the appellant's conviction was nonetheless upheld as safe.

---

[67] *Knuller (Publishing, Printing and Promotions) Ltd v DPP* [1973] A.C. 435 at 458A, B, per Lord Reid; at 467H–468A, 469B, C, per Lord Morris of Borth-y-Gest.

[68] [1973] A.C. 435.

[69] At 458C; and see the cases cited in paras 15.38 and following, above.

[70] [1989] A.C. 28 at 42C, per Lord Ackner.

[71] [1965] 2 Q.B. 327.

[72] *Moloney v Mercer* [1971] 2 N.S.W.L.R. 207.

[73] *Hecker* (1981) 58 Can.C.C. (2d) 66, Yukon T. Ct.; *Gray* (1982) 65 Can.C.C. (2d) 353, Ont. H.Ct.; *Giambalvo* (1983) 70 Can.C.C. (2d) 324, Ont. C.A.

[74] [1973] A.C. 435 at 457G.

[75] At 495C.

[76] [1998] EWCA Crim. 3048.

Whether an act is indecent to such a degree that it would outrage ordinary **15.44** members of the public is a relative rather than an absolute question: the same act may outrage public decency in one context but not in another.[77] Accordingly, the jury should be directed that, in deciding whether the defendant's act amounted to an outrage to public decency, they should have regard not only to the nature of the act, but also to the circumstances in which it was done: the location, the time, the duration of the act and so on.[78] They should also take into account the consent or lack of consent of the witnesses to it.[79]

Context is particularly important where the alleged act involved exposure **15.45** of the genitals.[80] A person who exposes their genitals with the intention of causing another person alarm or distress should ordinarily be prosecuted for the offence of exposure under s.66 of the Sexual Offences Act 2003. However, genitals may be exposed for other reasons and in such cases a prosecution may be brought for the common law offence. In the last century, any such exposure appears to have been treated, almost without argument, as outraging public decency.[81] But standards of decency change over time[82] and conduct of this sort may sometimes now be socially acceptable, e.g. where it takes place on a theatre stage or a nudist beach. In short, public exposure of the genitals may or may not be indecent, depending on the circumstances in which it occurs. This point can be illustrated by contrasting two Canadian cases in which the question was whether a "streaker" had committed an "indecent act" within s.173 of the Criminal Code.[83] In *Niman*,[84] the defendant had streaked through the streets of Toronto, naked except for a red scarf around his neck. When apprehended, he said he was on his way to an off-licence. Swabey Prov. J held that an act was indecent if it was done "in a base or shameful manner" and with a degree of "moral turpitude". The defendant was convicted on the ground that his conduct fell below the standards of decency generally prevalent in the community. This decision should be compared with *Springer*,[85] where the defendant had streaked on a

---

[77] *Clifford* [1988] 8 C.L. 86; *Stanley* [1965] 2 Q.B. 327 at 333, per Lord Parker CJ, approving *McGovern v Langmuir*, 1931 S.C. (J.) 10 at 13, per Lord Sands; *Hecker* (1981) 58 Can.C.C. (2d) 66 at 71, per Stuart, CJ, Yukon T. Ct.

[78] cf. *Moloney v Mercer* [1971] 2 N.S.W.L.R. 207; *Bennett* (1976) 29 Can.C.C. (2d) 403; *Balazsy* (1981) 54 Can.C.C. (2d) 346, Ont. Prov. Ct.; *Giambalvo* (1983) 70 Can.C.C. (2d) 324, Ont. C.A.

[79] cf. *Gray* (1982) 65 Can.C.C. (2d) 353, Ont. H.Ct.; *S. v K.* 1983 (1) S.A. 65 at 70, per van den Heever J, Cape Prov. Div. See further on consent paras 15.62 and following, below.

[80] There are no reported cases in which sexual intercourse or other acts of sexual intimacy in public have been held *not* to outrage to public decency, though it is always possible that a jury might acquit on appropriate facts.

[81] cf. *Crunden* (1809) 2 Camp. 89; *Reed* (1871) 12 Cox C.C. 1 (both cases of naked bathing); *McKenzie v Whyte* (1864) 4 Irv. 570 at 573, per Lord Neave; at 576, per Inglis CJ.

[82] *Knuller (Publishing, Printing and Promotions) Ltd v DPP* [1973] A.C. 435 at 468G–H, per Lord Morris of Borth-y-Gest; at 495 C–D, per Lord Simon of Glaisdale.

[83] R.S. 1985, c. C–46.

[84] (1975) 31 C.R. (N.S.) 51, Ont. Prov. Ct.

[85] (1975) 31 C.R. (N.S.) 48, Sask. Dist. Ct.

football field in the course of a match. McIntyre CJ declined to hold that the defendant's conduct had been indecent. There was, he said, no moral turpitude in streaking, and no sexual deviation or exploitation. The phenomenon was viewed by the great majority of people "with amused tolerance", and media coverage had turned it into "a sport and a ritual".[86]

15.46   Depending on the context, the exposure of parts of the body other than the genitals may constitute an outrage to public decency. The obvious potential candidates are a woman's exposure of her breasts and "mooning", i.e. the public display of bare buttocks.

15.47   Exposure of the breasts was considered in the Canadian case of *Jacob*,[87] where a woman who had gone topless in public was convicted of the offence of engaging in an indecent act contrary to s.173 of the Criminal Code. On a very hot and humid day, the appellant had strolled along several urban streets and sat on the porch of a house with no top on. She was seen by a number of people and complaints were made to the police. When arrested, she said that men were permitted to appear in public with their chests uncovered and she had a constitutional right to do likewise. In quashing her conviction, Osborne JA said:

> "There was nothing degrading or dehumanizing in what the appellant did. The scope of her activity was limited and was entirely non-commercial. No one who was offended was forced to continue looking at her. I cannot conclude that what the appellant did exceeded the community standard of tolerance when all of the relevant circumstances are taken into account. It follows that what the appellant did . . . did not constitute an indecent act."

The fact that Jacob's acts had no commercial motivation was clearly integral to the decision, as was the fact that she did not behave in a lewd or degrading manner.[88] It was perhaps for these reasons that in *Gowan*[89] a known sex worker, under the impression that after *Jacob* it was lawful to expose her breasts in public, was convicted of engaging in an indecent act after she had

---

[86] See also the acquittal of public nuisance of Vincent Bethell, the pro-nudity campaigner, in respect of five incidents in which he had gone naked in public: *The Times*, January 11, 2001 (p.5). This was apparently the first prosecution for causing a public nuisance by being naked since 1871. *The Times* reported that Mr Bethell "emerged from the courtroom defiantly wearing only a broad grin . . . [b]ut after a few minutes the cold weather did what the full force of Her Majesty's Government could not: make a man put some clothes on." But cf. *Gough v DPP* [2013] EWHC 3267 Admin, discussed in paras 15.186 and following, below, in which another pro-nudity campaigner, Stephen Gough, was held to have been properly convicted of disorderly behaviour contrary to s.5 of the Public Order Act 1986 after he had walked naked through Halifax town centre.

[87] 142 DLR (4th) 411; 112 CCC (3d) 1.

[88] cf. David Pannick QC, *If Men Can Go Topless, So Can Women, The Times*, September 13, 1994 (discussing a decision of the New York Court of Appeals in 1992 in which the majority held that a law prohibiting exposure of the female breast did not apply in circumstances that were neither "commercial" nor "lewd". The minority went further, holding the law to be in breach of the constitutional right to equal protection. Pannick records that following the decision, the New York Transit Authority conceded that women, like men, had a right to travel topless on the New York subway).

[89] March 3, 1998; Doc. Ottawa 97-20544 (Ontario Court of Justice, Provincial Division).

solicited clients at an intersection, motioned to her naked breasts and called out "Do you want to fuck?".

As for mooning, it is instructive to compare two Canadian cases in both of **15.48** which the defendant was charged with the "indecent act" offence in s.173 of the Criminal Code. The first was *Balazsy*,[90] where the defendant had mooned outside a crowded restaurant for two or three minutes, accompanying his act with verbal and physical abuse, his intention being to provoke some of the restaurant's patrons. Nosanchuk Prov. Ct. J held that the defendant had committed an indecent act. The opposite conclusion was reached in *Hecker*,[91] where the defendant mooned at some friends during the course of a curling match. Stuart J said:

> "A 'moon' is in some situations no more or less than a bad joke. In other situations it may be an indecent act."[92]

He went on to hold that the present case fell within the first category. The important considerations were that the act had taken place at 4am, when few people were present; that the defendant had had reasonable grounds for believing that only his friends would see it; that he had intended it only as a joke; that he had not accompanied it with any verbal or physical abuse; and that his trousers had been down for only a few seconds. The distinction between mooning as an act of offensive indecency and as simple bad taste is further illustrated by the Australian case of Liam Warriner, an anti-monarchist Sydney bartender who pleaded guilty to public nuisance and was fined $750 after mooning the Queen, with an Australian flag between his buttock cheeks, during her visit to Queensland in October 2011.[93] It was suggested in mitigation that if Warriner had carried out his actions in front of the New South Wales team bus prior to a State of Origin match (i.e. one of the annual best-of-three rugby league matches played between Queensland and New South Wales), it would not have raised an eyebrow.

In certain circumstances, a partial immunity from prosecution for the **15.49** common law offence is conferred by legislation. Section 2(4) of the Theatres Act 1968[94] provides that no person shall be proceeded against in respect of anything done in the course of a performance of a play for any offence at common law where it is of the essence of the offence that what was done was "obscene, indecent, offensive, disgusting or injurious to morality". For this purpose, a "play" is defined as "any dramatic piece . . . in which the whole or a major proportion . . . involves the playing of a role".[95] An immunity in

---

[90] (1981) 54 Can.C.C. (2d) 346, Ont. Prov. Ct. See also *Ferguson (Mark Brandon)* [2008] EWCA Crim 2940, in which, on not dissimilar facts, the appellant pleaded guilty to outraging public decency.

[91] (1981) 58 Can.C.C. (2d) 66, Yukon T. Ct.

[92] At 69.

[93] *http://www.theguardian.com/world/2012/feb/14/man-who-mooned-queen-fined*   [Accessed April 30, 2016].

[94] 1968 c. 54.

[95] s.18(1).

similar terms is provided for television or radio broadcasts by the Broadcasting Act 1990.[96] Important as these immunities are, they clearly do not extend to every sort of public entertainment.

15.50 The application of the immunities provided by the 1968 and 1990 Acts is illustrated by *R. (On the application of Green) v City of Westminster Magistrates' Court*.[97] The claimant, a member of the organisation Christian Voice, sought to bring a private prosecution for blasphemous libel in relation to the theatrical work *Jerry Springer: the Opera*, which had been performed in various theatres and a recording of a live performance of which had been broadcast by the BBC. The claimant sought magistrates' court summonses against the producer of the stage play and the Director General of the BBC. The District Judge refused to issue the summonses, inter alia because the prosecution was prevented by s.2(4) of the Theatres Act 1968. The Administrative Court refused the claimant's application for judicial review of the District Judge's decision. In doing so, it held in relation to the Theatres Act 1968 that a "play" is defined by s.18 of that Act in terms which mean, in effect, a live performance and that the District Judge had been correct to hold that s.2(4) of the Act prevented the prosecution which the claimant sought to bring at least so far as the live performances were concerned. It went on to hold that the Theatres Act did not apply to the BBC broadcast because it was not within the definition of a "play", in that it was not a live performance given to the viewer by persons present and performing. However, the provisions of the Broadcasting Act 1990 applicable to broadcasts are couched in terms identical to those of s.2(4) as it applies to plays. Although the District Judge had not been referred to that Act, her reasoning in relation to the Theatres Act applied equally to it, and accordingly she had been right to refuse to issue the summonses.

"To the Great Disgust and Annoyance of Divers of Her Majesty's Subjects"

15.51 It has been common practice to aver that the act alleged to constitute the common law offence was done "to the great disgust and annoyance of divers of Her Majesty's subjects".[98] This averment may be proved by evidence that the act was calculated or likely to disgust and annoy, and it is not necessary for the prosecution to show that anyone was in fact disgusted and annoyed.[99] The better view is that the act must be likely to disgust and annoy members

---

[96] Sch.15, para.6.

[97] [2007] EWHC 2785 (Admin).

[98] See para.15.31, above. The Law Commission has tentatively suggested that it may be preferable for prosecutors not to use these words: *Simplification of Criminal Law: Public Nuisance and Outraging Public Decency*, Law Com Consultation Paper No.193 (2010), para.3.35. The safer course, though, is to continue to do so until such time as the courts indicate they are no longer required.

[99] *Mayling* [1963] 2 Q.B. 717; *May* (1990) 91 Cr. App. R. 157; *Lunderbech* [1991] Crim. L.R. 784. But cp. *Cheeseman v DPP* (1991) 93 Cr. App. R. 145.

of the public generally, rather than those who actually saw it.[100] Thus in *May*,[101] the appellant's conviction was upheld although the witnesses had not been disgusted and annoyed by his conduct, and at times might have enjoyed what was going on. Similarly, it is settled that a defendant may be convicted where the only witnesses to his act were police officers, who do not say that they were disgusted and annoyed and are unlikely to have been so.[102] As a practical matter, if the jury are satisfied that the act outraged public decency they will probably also be satisfied that it was likely to disgust and annoy.[103]

THE "TWO PERSON" RULE

It is a necessary ingredient of the offence that at least two people saw the **15.52** defendant's act or were able to see it.[104] It is not entirely clear when a person will be regarded as "able to see" an act for this purpose. On one view, a person qualifies only if they are actually present at the time of the act and would be able to see it if they happened to look. The alternative view is that it is sufficient that a person might reasonably have been expected to come upon the scene who would have been able to see the act if they had looked. The authorities tend to suggest that actual presence is required.[105] The issue has been squarely raised in only one case, *Elliot and White*,[106] and in that the judges were in disagreement. The court ordered a rehearing but later intimated that it was "not desirable to have the case re-argued", and therefore no judgment was delivered.

In *Hamilton*,[107] the Court of Appeal held that the "two person" rule is **15.53** satisfied "if there are two or more people present who are capable of seeing the nature of the act, even if they did not actually see it". It is tempting to regard this as settling the issue left unresolved in *Elliot and White*, i.e. that two people must actually be present who either see the defendant's act or

---

[100] Or were able to see it: see para.15.52, below.

[101] (1990) 91 Cr. App. R. 157.

[102] See the cases cited in fn.99, above.

[103] cf. *Mayling* [1963] 2 Q.B. 717 at 726–7.

[104] *Watson* (1847) 2 Cox C.C. 376; *Webb* (1848) 1 Den. 338; *Rouverard* (1830), referred to in *Webb*, at 344, per Parke B (the case name appears only in the short report of *Webb* in 2 Car. & K. 933 at 936); *Farrell* (1862) 9 Cox C.C. 446, C.C.A. Ir.; *May* (1990) 91 Cr. App. R. 157.

[105] *Webb* 2 Car. & K. 933 at pp.343–4, per Pollock CB; at 344, per Parke B; *Farrell* (1862) 9 Cox C.C. 446 at pp.447–8, per Monaghan CJ; *Mayling* [1963] 2 Q.B. 717 at 724; *May* (1990) 91 Cr. App. R. 157. This interpretation would certainly help to differentiate the "two person" rule from the requirement of "publicity", discussed in paras 15.58 and following, below. The Law Commission also takes the view that two people must be present and capable of seeing the act: *Simplification of Criminal Law: Public Nuisance and Outraging Public Decency* (Law Com No.358) (June 2015), para.2.50, citing *Hamilton* [2007] EWCA Crim 2062 and *R. v F* [2010] EWCA Crim 2243, discussed below. However we believe, with respect, that this is an over-interpretation of those decisions.

[106] (1861) Le. & Ca. 103.

[107] [2007] EWCA Crim 2062. See Alisdair A. Gillespie, *'Up-skirts' and 'down-blouses': Voyeurism and the law* [2008] Crim. L.R. 370.

would be able to see it if they happened to look. However, that point did not arise for the decision in *Hamilton*, and anything said by the Court that appears to bear upon it must therefore be treated with caution. The appellant admitted "up-skirting" in supermarkets, i.e. taking video footage up the skirts of women shoppers using a camera positioned in a rucksack. Neither the women he filmed nor anyone else had ever noticed what he was doing, and on that basis the appellant argued that his conduct lacked the public element required for the offence to be committed. The trial judge rejected this argument and directed the jury that it was sufficient if there was a real possibility, when the appellant carried out the filming, that at least two people would have been able to see it if they had looked. The arguments were rehearsed before the Court of Appeal, which exhaustively analysed the case law and concluded as follows:[108]

> "In our view it is necessary to have regard to the purpose of the two person rule; it goes solely to the necessity that there be a public element in the sense of more than one being present and capable of being affected by it. There is in our view no reason to confine the requirement more restrictively and require actual sight or sound of the nature of the act. The public element in the offence is satisfied if the act is done where persons are present and the nature of what is being done is capable of being seen; the principle is that the public are to be protected from acts of a lewd, obscene or disgusting act which are of a nature that outrages public decency and which are capable of being seen in public. As was pointed out in *Bunyan and Morgan*, a person committing such an act may wish as much privacy as possible, if there is a possibility of them being discovered in public, it would nonetheless be an offence. Looking therefore at the purpose of the two person rule, it can, in our view, be satisfied if there are two or more persons present who are capable of seeing the nature of the act, even if they did not actually see it . . .
>
> Thus in the present case, although no one saw the appellant filming, there was evidence from the videos that there were others present. But was what the appellant was in fact doing capable of being seen, even though no one actually did? It cannot be said . . . that this type of filming is incapable of being seen. Whether on the facts of this case the way in which the appellant filmed up the skirts of the women was capable of being seen was a question for the jury. As is clear from the passage in the summing up which we have set out at paragraph 13, this was an issue expressly left to the jury by the judge. By their verdict of guilty the jury must have concluded that the way the appellant filmed was capable of being seen by those in the supermarket."

The Court's assertion that there must be "two or more people present" was made in the context of a decision that the "two person" rule does not require that at least two people actually witness the act: it was held sufficient if at least two people are present and able to see it. It is possible that, on appropriate facts, the courts would go a step further and, given the purpose of the rule, find it sufficient that, although the defendant is alone when he commits the act, there is a real possibility that at least two people could happen upon him and see what he is doing. For example, D films himself

---

[108] At [39]–[40]; and see [2007] EWCA Crim 2062 at [21].

masturbating in broad daylight in a corner of a public park, which happens to be empty at the time, but is generally well-used so that there is a real chance that he could be caught *in flagrante* by members of the public. We suggest that in those circumstances, the fact that nobody (other than D) is actually present when the act is committed ought not to preclude a conviction based upon the evidence of the film, and there is nothing in *Hamilton* which would have this effect. In short, the point in *Elliot and White* remains open.[109]

In *Rose v DPP*,[110] the Administrative Court considered whether the **15.54** offence may be committed where the defendant's act is viewed, not in real time, but through the playing of a CCTV recording. The appellant was recorded by a CCTV camera having an act of oral sex performed upon him by a female, in the foyer of a bank containing ATM machines to which the public had access. The next morning, the manageress of the bank, as part of her normal duties, viewed the CCTV recording on which the act was captured. The time on the CCTV was 00:54. The manageress reported the matter to the police and the appellant was charged with outraging public decency. At trial, the appellant did not dispute the factual basis of the allegation, but contended that his act could not have outraged public decency as it was not witnessed at the time it was committed, there having been no passers-by at that time in the morning who might have witnessed it. The judge ruled that the witnessing of the event by the manageress satisfied the requirements of the offence. On appeal, the Divisional Court re-iterated that the offence of outraging public decency is not committed where the act is seen by only one person other than the participants in it: there must be at least two witnesses for the required public element to be established. In this case, the only evidence of anyone else seeing the act was from the manageress, and on the authorities that was insufficient. The conviction was therefore quashed. The Court added obiter that there was considerable force in the appellant's alternative submission that the private viewing of a private recording of an act which had not previously been seen by anyone is insufficient to constitute the offence. That is because "the offence is committed when it is committed", and it would be curious if the offence was completed by a private viewing of a recording, and if it could make a difference, for example, whether the manageress was in the company of somebody else or not when she saw the video, or whether she showed it to someone else afterwards or not. No court has previously considered whether the relevant act must be witnessed by a person's own unaided senses, or whether it is sufficient that it is witnessed through some visual or other medium. We respectfully suggest that the Court was right to doubt that the offence may be committed by the replaying of a CCTV recording. However, viewing of the product of a camera ought to be sufficient where the viewing

---

[109] For a similar point arising in the very different context of s.5(1) of the Public Order Act 1986, see paras 15.193 and following, below.

[110] [2006] EWHC 852 (Admin); [2006] Crim. L.R. 993.

takes place in real-time, e.g. where the product is broadcast over the internet or on live-feed CCTV.[110a]

15.55   The "two person" rule will often generate an issue of evidential sufficiency in cases where there is only one complainant, as in *Rose v DPP*, or where there are none and the defendant's act is evidenced by a recording or photograph, as in *Hamilton*. In accordance with ordinary principle, the court should allow such a case to proceed only if there is sufficient evidence to put before the jury to establish that the "two person" rule is satisfied. An instructive decision in this respect is *R. v F*,[111] where the prosecution and the defence agreed to invite the judge to make a pre-trial ruling in relation to the application of the rule. As presented to the judge, the question was whether, on the assumption that the sole prosecution witness gave evidence in accordance with her witness statement, the case would get past a half-time submission. The statement described an incident in which the defendant, over a period of about 10 minutes, masturbated in his car which was parked adjacent to local playing fields on which children were playing football, but that he covered himself up and ceased to masturbate whenever anybody came into view. The judge, applying the law as most recently expounded in *Hamilton*, ruled that on those facts the "two person" rule was not satisfied:

> " . . . it is perfectly plain from the evidence of [the witness], which is the only evidence which the Crown have, that when people other than herself were seen to be present by her, on each occasion that that occurred the defendant stopped indulging in the act and covered himself with a sheet of paper that was clearly placed on the seat next to him for that purpose. And it seems plain to me that

---

[110a] The suggestion in the text was not followed in the case of *Danielle Smith* (Shrewsbury Crown Court, February 2, 2016). The case turned on the question whether a security guard watching the defendant on live CCTV could count as one of the persons necessary to satisfy the "two person" rule. In dismissing the case, HH Judge Barrie found persuasive authority in the reference in *Hamilton* by Thomas LJ (as he then was) to persons "actually" present ([2007] EWCA Crim 2062, at [31]). The learned Judge held that the purpose of the two person rule is to prohibit outrageous behaviour in public, which it achieves by requiring that at least two other people are present. As the person engaging in the behaviour cannot tell whether or not they are being observed by CCTV, it would introduce uncertainty and significantly extend the scope of the common law offence if a person viewing events live on CCTV were to be treated as a person who is present. We are grateful to HH Judge Barrie for drawing this case to our attention, and make two comments on it. First, we argue above that *Hamilton* should be understood by reference its facts and as such does not necessarily establish that the "two person" rule requires the actual presence of two people at the relevant time. On the contrary, we suggest that the rule may be satisfied on appropriate facts if there is a real possibility that two people could happen upon the person engaging in the outrageous behaviour and see what they are doing. If that is right, then HH Judge Barrie's point about the uncertainty engendered where a person cannot tell that they are being observed by CCTV becomes less persuasive. It should be sufficient for conviction if the person engages in their behaviour in a place and in circumstances in which there is real possibility that two people will observe them, by whatever means including live CCTV, provided that they have the required mental element, i.e. they are at least reckless as to whether their behaviour will be seen, or be capable of being seen, by two or more persons (see para.15.67, below). Secondly, if the learned Judge's analysis were correct it would have provided a much shorter route to judgment for the Divisional Court in *Rose v DPP*. We respectfully suggest that, as the Court did not adopt that route, the inference can be drawn that the analysis is wrong.
[111] [2010] EWCA Crim 2243, applying *Hamilton* [2007] EWCA Crim 2062.

although these people were present, they were not capable of seeing the act in which he was indulging because on each of the occasions that they were observed to be present by [the witness], he ceased the act in which he was engaged and covered himself up. So . . . the evidence available, therefore, does not in my view satisfy the requirement that at least two people are present and capable of seeing the nature of the act and being affected by it."

The Court of Appeal upheld the judge's ruling, though it conceded that there was "an element of unreality to the suggestion that nobody else could have seen the defendant masturbating". For the Court to go behind the agreed facts by saying that there must have been a possibility of other people seeing the defendant masturbating would be impermissible speculation. However, their Lordships also said that they themselves would not, in the particular circumstances of this case, have necessarily "gone down the route taken by the judge", given that the question whether or not passers-by might have seen what the defendant was doing was quintessentially a question for the jury. This is a clear indication that the Court thought the matter should have gone to trial. We respectfully disagree. The evidence that the sole prosecution witness was expected to give was incapable of satisfying the "two person" rule and indeed was inconsistent with the requirements of that rule. Whilst it is conceivable that in the course of giving oral evidence she might have been less definitive as to the effectiveness of the defendant's actions in covering himself up when people passed by, that can only be a matter of speculation and as such, in our view, could not in itself justify allowing the case to proceed. Similarly, the fact that the witness had been able to see the defendant's conduct could not in itself justify the inference that one or more other people would have been able to do likewise, without some evidence from which that inference could properly be drawn.

A defendant may be convicted of the offence where the only witnesses to **15.56** his act were police officers.[112] The fact that police officers may, as part of their duty, have to see indecent behaviour does not mean that their presence must be discounted for the purposes of the "two person" rule.

The "two person" rule as traditionally expressed appears to require the **15.57** defendant's act to be seen rather than experienced in some other way, e.g. by being heard. This point received some attention in Parliament during the passage of the Sexual Offences Bill, when the Government was resisting the creation of an offence of sexual activity in a public lavatory on the basis that such behaviour could be prosecuted as outraging public decency. Some scepticism was expressed in the Lords as to the availability of the common law offence where the act in question takes place behind the closed door of a lavatory cubicle and so is heard but not seen.[113] Lord Falconer, speaking on behalf of the Government, thought the common law was sufficiently flexible to cover this scenario and that an act would be covered if it was witnessed or

---

[112] *Mayling* [1963] 2 Q.B. 717; *Lunderbech* [1991] Crim. L.R. 784, distinguishing *Cheeseman v DPP* (1991) 93 Cr. App. R. 145.
[113] *Hansard,* HL Vol.648, cols 581–2, Baroness Blatch (May 19, 2003).

capable of being witnessed, whether by being seen or heard.[114] We respectfully agree.[115]

Requirement of "Publicity"

15.58   In addition to the need for at least two people to have seen or been able to see the defendant's act, there is a further requirement that the act must have been done in a public place, i.e. a place where there existed a real possibility that members of the general public might witness it. This requirement was affirmed in *Walker*,[116] where the appellant had exposed himself to two young girls in the living room of his house. While the "two person" rule was clearly satisfied, the appellant's conviction of outraging public decency was quashed on the basis that there was no possibility of his act being witnessed by the general public. The Court emphasised that the requirement of "publicity" does not mean that the spot where the act is done must be a place of public resort. It must, however, be a place where the public are able to see what takes place there.[117]

15.59   *Walker* in fact represents a significant restriction of the scope of the offence as it had come to be understood in modern times. The early cases on outraging public decency established that the defendant's act must be done in a public place.[118] But in the later nineteenth century this requirement began to fall into disfavour and was liberally applied. In *Thallman*,[119] for example, the conviction was upheld of a man who had exposed himself on the roof of a private house, where he could be seen only from the back windows of other private houses. In a number of cases, eminent judges expressly doubted whether the requirement for the act to be done in a public place formed any part of the offence.[120] This trend culminated in *Mayling*,[121] where the Court of Criminal Appeal stated obiter that the requirement of "publicity" is satisfied by proof that at least two people saw or were able to see the defendant's act.[122] *Walker* represents a swinging-back of the pendulum, with the requirement given a content of its own quite distinct from the "two person" rule. The decision places the law at variance with that in certain

---

[114] *Hansard,* HL Vol.648, cols 585–6.
[115] The second part of this paragraph (beginning "Some scepticism . . . ") was cited with approval by the Court of Appeal in *Hamilton* [2007] EWCA Crim 2062, at [33]–[34].
[116] [1996] 1 Cr. App. R. 111; and see *Hamilton* [2007] EWCA Crim 2062 at [21].
[117] *Watson* (1847) 2 Cox C.C. 376.
[118] *Orchard and Thurtle* (1848) 3 Cox C.C. 248; *Holmes* (1853) 3 Car. & K. 360.
[119] (1863) 9 Cox C.C. 388.
[120] (1863) 9 Cox C.C. 388, at 390, per Erle CJ; *Watson* (1847) 2 Cox C.C. 376 at 377, per Lord Denman CJ; *Harris* (1871) 11 Cox C.C. 659 at 661, per Willes J; *Wellard* (1884) 15 Cox C.C. 559 at 562, per Lord Coleridge CJ; at 563, per Huddleston B.
[121] [1963] 2 Q.B. 717 at 724–725; and see *May* (1990) 91 Cr. App. R. 157.
[122] But the events in that case took place in a public lavatory, which is clearly a place which satisfies the requirement of "publicity" identified in *Walker*.

other jurisdictions, where the courts have followed to its logical conclusion the trend identified in the earlier English cases.[123]

Is the internet a "public place" for this purpose?

There is no English authority on this point, but it has been considered in **15.60** Hong Kong. In *HKSAR v Chan Yau Hei*,[124] the appellant posted a message on an online forum inciting the bombing of the Hong Kong Liaison Office of the Central People's Government.[125]. The Hong Kong Court of Final Appeal accepted that the content of the message might have been such as to cause outrage. But it held that the offence of outraging public decency must be committed in a physical, tangible space which is accessible to or within view of the public, and that an online forum does not qualify for this purpose, as the internet is not a place in any physical or actual sense but is instead properly to be regarded as a medium of communication. It is in the actual places, public or private, where people access or download the relevant webpage that their sense of decency may be outraged, not in some virtual place. It is similarly a fiction to regard persons who access an internet discussion forum as being in the same position as people who venture out physically in public, and who are entitled to protection against having their sense of decency outraged. Though they may be physically outdoors at the time, those who surf the internet are not in fact venturing out anywhere and are instead only virtually visiting a place. The Court did, however, say that it remains a possibility that a message posted to a discussion forum will be seen in a physical place to which the public has access, or where what is done is capable of public view, in which case the offence may be committed: e.g. if a computer hacker interferes with a public computer display, such as an airport's flight information display, to project an outrageous message, or a person uses a mobile device to access obscene material in a physical place, such as a bus, to which the public have access. In that case the offence would be committed by the person who projected or showed the image, rather than the person who originally posted it (if different).

If a person posts online a recording or photograph of an indecent act being **15.61** done in a public place, then (assuming *Chan Yau Hei* is followed in this jurisdiction) the act of posting the material will not itself constitute the common law offence. However, the material will be evidence of such an offence and, depending on the circumstances depicted, could be sufficient in itself to found a prosecution of the actor.

---

[123] cf. *Madercine* (1899) 20 N.S.W. Law Rep. 36, followed in *Black* (1921) 21 S.R. (N.S.W.) 748 (the facts of which were very similar to those in *Walker*) and approved in *Reinsch* [1978] 1 N.S.W.L.R. 483 at 485, per Street CJ; *R. v B* 1955 (3) S.A. 494.

[124] [2014] HKCFA 18.

[125] This was a notably wide application of the offence, which is unlikely to be regarded as appropriate in this jurisdiction.

Consent

15.62 It has been suggested that the common law offence cannot be committed by an indecent exposure to which the witnesses consent, on the ground that their consent negatives the outraging of decency.[126] This suggestion, if correct, cannot be confined to indecent exposure, but must apply to any act falling within the scope of the offence. But it must also be said that there is no authority which expressly decides that the offence is non-consensual, and the indications are that it is not.[127] The most significant indicator is the requirement of "publicity", discussed in paras 15.58 and following, above, whereby the prosecution must show that there was a real possibility that members of the general public might witness the defendant's act. If such a possibility existed, then, given the purpose of the offence, the fact that those who actually witnessed the act were not outraged and consented to it ought not to be determinative of liability.[128]

15.63 At a practical level the arguments for and against allowing consent to negative the offence are fairly evenly balanced. It would certainly be a useful means of protecting nudists, some of the more provocative artists and any legitimate public entertainers who fall outside the scope of the immunities in the Theatres Act 1968 and the Broadcasting Act 1990. The fact that it would also benefit strippers and lap dancers might be a small price to pay in order to protect more worthy activities. On the other hand, there might be objections to allowing the defendant to rely on consent in cases where the witnesses were or included children or people who were vulnerable for other reasons.[129] This might create a difficulty in the case of nudist camps and beaches, which may contain people of all ages. Also, the operation of consent could be erratic. Artists and entertainers, in particular, would be at the mercy of their public. If an exhibit in an art gallery were to fall within the scope of the offence, it would require only two persons to react with disgust to deny the gallery owner the right to plead consent. Meanwhile, less socially beneficial activities would be relatively secure; strippers, for example, normally perform to receptive audiences and would therefore have a virtual immunity from conviction.

15.64 The fact that consent cannot and should not negate the outraging of decency does not mean, however, that it is wholly irrelevant. The point has

---

[126] Smith and Hogan, *Criminal Law,* 10th edn (Oxford: Oxford University Press, 2002), p.491. This suggestion is not made in the current (14th) edition.

[127] See *Wollaston* (1872) 12 Cox C.C. 180 at 182, per Kelly CB; *May* (1990) 91 Cr. App. R. 157, discussed in para.15.51, above; *Lunderbech* [1991] Crim. L.R. 784. In *Moloney v Mercer* [1971] 2 N.S.W.L.R. 207, it was held that the statutory offence of indecent exposure had been committed by a stripper in front of an appreciative audience of paying customers.

[128] Smith and Hogan acknowledged (10th edn) that consent could not operate if the relevant act might have been observed by others, had they happened to look: fn.126, above.

[129] cf. *May* (1990) 91 Cr. App. R. 157, discussed in para.15.51, above. There would be no valid consent if the children did not understand the nature of the defendant's act: cf. *Burrell v Harmer* [1967] Crim. L.R. 169.

already been made that it is a question of fact whether or not a particular act outrages public indecency, and in answering that question the trier of fact is entitled to take into account all the circumstances, including the consent or lack of consent of the witnesses.[130] There is no necessary reason why, say, an exposure of the genitals should necessarily fall within the scope of the offence if it is done in circumstances that make it socially acceptable; and in determining whether this is the case, the trier of fact must be entitled to have regard to the reactions of those who witnessed it. This may not be a very secure means of protecting nudists and legitimate public entertainers, in that its efficacy depends upon the view taken by the trier of fact in the particular case, but for the same reason it is perhaps free from the drawbacks associated with a requirement of lack of consent.

A related question is whether the offence is committed where the only   **15.65** witnesses to the defendant's act are also participants in it. The point was argued but not decided in *May*,[131] where the appellant, a schoolmaster, was convicted on two counts of the common law offence on evidence that he had induced male pupils to order him to simulate sexual intercourse on a desk. It was argued that the convictions could not be maintained, as the only witnesses to the acts had been the pupils, who had also participated in them. The Court of Appeal declined to decide the point, holding that the boys had not truly been participants; the appellant's acts had been "solo perform- ances", to which the boys had contributed only their presence and the commands that they had been induced to give, which apparently added zest to the appellant's enjoyment. However, the suggestion that the willing participation of the witnesses may negative the offence is open to the same objection as discussed above in respect of consent, namely that it cuts across the requirement of "publicity". If the prosecution must and does prove that there was a real possibility that members of the general public might witness the defendant's act, then, given the purpose of the offence, the fact that those who actually witnessed it also willingly participated in the act ought not to be determinative of liability.

MENTAL ELEMENT

It was held in *Gibson and Sylveire*[132] that the prosecution need not prove that   **15.66** the defendant intended to outrage public decency, or even that he was reckless in the sense that he appreciated there was a risk of outrage but determined nevertheless to run it. A deliberate act which the jury finds to have outraged public decency is sufficient for a conviction. To the same effect is *Crunden*,[133] where it was held that the prosecution need prove no sexual motive on the part of the defendant, nor any intention to insult or annoy. The

---

[130] See the cases cited in fn.79, above.
[131] (1990) 91 Cr. App. R. 157.
[132] (1990) 91 Cr. App. R. 341.
[133] (1809) 2 Camp. 89.

defendant in that case undressed on the beach opposite the East Cliff at Brighton and swam naked in the sea. This had been common practice at that spot for many years. Unfortunately for him, houses had recently been built on the cliff and his actions were witnessed from their windows. His conviction was upheld, the Court holding it irrelevant that his intention had been simply "to promote health, and enjoy a favourite recreation".

15.67 Notwithstanding the statement in *Gibson and Sylveire* that all that is required is a deliberate act which outrages public decency, the prosecution must in principle prove that the defendant was at least reckless as to whether his act would be seen, or be capable of being seen, by two or more persons, and as to whether there was a real possibility that members of the general public might witness it.[134] In fact, the only authority that addresses this point suggests that negligence may suffice. In *Bunyan and Morgan*,[135] two men sought privacy for indecent acts by locking themselves in the parlour of a public house. Unknown to them, they were watched by several persons through the window of another room in the building. Holding that there was sufficient evidence to go before the jury, the recorder said:

> "It cannot be necessary to prove that the parties intended that the public should detect them; they would always seek as much privacy as they could conveniently obtain; but was this such a situation that there was no reasonable probability of their being so discovered?"[136]

This is an old case, and it is hoped that when the point arises again it will not be followed.

15.68 In the light of the decision in *Heard*,[137] discussed in paras 2.81 and following, above, the offence of outraging public decency appears to be one of basic intent, such that voluntary intoxication through drink or drugs will provide no defence.

Exposure

Definition

15.69 Section 66(1) of the Sexual Offences Act 2003 provides that:

> "A person commits an offence if—
>   (a) he intentionally exposes his genitals, and

---

[134] cf. Smith and Hogan, *Criminal Law,* 10th edn, (2002) p.491 (the point is not addressed in the current edition (14th), and see *Usai v Russell*, 2000 J.C. 144 (*held*, the mens rea of the offence of shameless indecency may be inferred where the likelihood was that there would be persons who would observe the defendant's conduct and the defendant was recklessly indifferent as to whether or not he was observed). In [1991] Crim. L.R. 786, the late Professor Sir John Smith argued that where the jury's decision is to be based not only on the nature of the defendant's act but also on the circumstances in which it was done, they can convict only if the defendant was aware of the relevant circumstances.

[135] (1844) 1 Cox C.C. 74.

[136] At 75.

[137] [2007] EWCA Crim 125.

(b) he intends that someone will see them and be caused alarm or distress."

MODE OF TRIAL AND PUNISHMENT

The offence under s.66(1) is triable either way.[138] The maximum punishment **15.70** on conviction on indictment is two years' imprisonment. The maximum on summary conviction is six months' imprisonment or a fine, or both. As from a day to be appointed, the maximum period of imprisonment on summary conviction will increase to 12 months.[139] The increase will have no application to offences committed before it takes effect.[140] Until recently, the maximum fine on summary conviction was a fine not exceeding the statutory maximum (i.e. £5,000). The effect of s.85 of the Legal Aid, Sentencing and Punishment of Offenders Act 2012 is that, from March 12, 2015, a fine of any amount may be imposed. Fines will, however, continue to be set according to the seriousness of the offence and the means of the offender.

An offence under s.66 is a specified offence for the purposes of s.226A of **15.71** the Criminal Justice Act 2003[141] (extended sentence for certain violent or sexual offences), irrespective of the date of commission of the offence.

A person convicted under s.66, cautioned, found not guilty by reason of **15.72** insanity or found to be under a disability and to have done the act charged, is automatically subject to the notification requirements in the Sexual Offences Act 2003[142] where (a) he was under 18 at the time of the offence and is sentenced to at least 12 months' imprisonment or (b) in any other case, the victim was under 18 or the offender is, in respect of the offence, sentenced to a term of imprisonment, detained in a hospital or given a community sentence of at least 12 months.

For the purposes of listing, cases under s.66 fall within Class 2B.[143] Cases **15.73** in Class 2B must be referred to the Resident Judge, and by the Resident Judge to a Presiding Judge, in specified circumstances, including where a novel and important point of law is to be raised; where the defendant is a police officer, a member of the legal profession or a high profile figure; or where for any reason the case is likely to attract exceptional media attention.

PARTIES TO THE OFFENCE

The offence may be committed as principal by males and females.   **15.74**

---

[138] s.66(2).

[139] Criminal Justice Act 2003 s.282(2), (3).

[140] Criminal Justice Act 2003 s.282(4).

[141] Inserted by the Legal Aid, Sentencing and Punishment of Offenders Act 2012 s.124, brought into force on December 3, 2012, by SI 2012/2906.

[142] s.80 and Sch.3, discussed in Ch.35, below.

[143] *Consolidated Criminal Practice Directions*, Part XIII Listing B: CLASSIFICATION, available at *https://www.judiciary.gov.uk/wp-content/uploads/2015/09/crim-pd-2015.pdf* [Accessed April 30, 2016].

SENTENCING

15.75   For the Sentencing Council guideline relating to the sentencing of sexual offences committed by offenders aged 18 and over, see Ch.33. The guideline for exposure adopts the same approach as the guideline for voyeurism (s.67, discussed in paras 15.103 and following, below), i.e. the categorisation of the offence, and so the starting points and sentencing ranges, depend upon whether there are factors indicating raised harm and/or raised culpability.

Sentencing guideline

Step One—Harm and culpability

15.76   The guideline requires the sentencing court to go through a series of steps in order to determine the appropriate sentence. Step one involves determining the offence category. The categories are defined by reference to whether the harm to the victim and the culpability of the offender are raised. The court should determine harm and culpability by reference only to the factors set out in the guideline (below). Where an offence does not fall squarely into a category, individual factors may require a degree of weighting before making an overall assessment and determining the appropriate offence category. The offence categories for offences under s.66 are as follows:

Category 1	Raised harm *and* raised culpability
Category 2	Raised harm *or* raised culpability
Category 3	Exposure *without* raised harm or culpability factors present

15.77   The guideline identifies the following factors as raising the harm caused by the offence:

Factors indicating raised harm
• Victim followed/pursued
• Offender masturbated

In consulting on its draft guideline,[144] the Sentencing Council said that following or pursuit increases the harm to the victim as it will increase the sense of fear and menace they experience. This is no doubt true, but there are other forms of offender behaviour which could also increase the victim's

---

[144] *Sexual Offences Guideline: Consultation* (December 6, 2012). The consultation document is available on the Sentencing Council's website.

sense of fear or menace, e.g. where an offender moves towards or confronts the victim with their genitalia exposed,[145] or where they expose their genitalia in circumstances in which the victim has difficulty in escaping, e.g. by sitting in the aisle seat on a bus when the victim is in the window seat and so is effectively trapped in place.[146] The focus in the new guideline on following or pursuit seems to indicate that such scenarios do not indicate raised harm. We expect, however, that the courts will feel free to enhance a sentence in such cases by regarding the offender's behaviour as aggravating the offence (aggravating factors are considered below). As for "offender masturbated", the Council said that where the offender masturbates in front of the victim in addition to exposing their genitalia, this is likely to increase the shock and disgust felt by the victim.

The guideline identifies the following factors as raising culpability for the **15.78** offence:

Factors indicating raised harm
• Specific or previous targeting of a particularly vulnerable victim
• Abuse of trust
• Use of threats (including blackmail)
• Offence racially or religiously aggravated
• Offence motivated by, or demonstrating, hostility to the victim based on his or her sexual orientation (or presumed sexual orientation) or transgender identity (or presumed transgender identity)
• Offence motivated by, or demonstrating, hostility to the victim based on his or her disability (or presumed disability)

In the Council's consultation draft, the factor "specific or previous targeting of a particularly vulnerable victim" appeared as "vulnerable victim targeted". It was included on the basis that the offender's culpability will be increased where they have deliberately sought out someone who may be less able to deal with, or more affected by, their actions because of, for example, youth, old age or disability. Some respondents to the consultation suggested adding as a further factor "multiple offences against the same victim". However, the Council noted that the s.66 offence is normally committed against strangers and so, rather than adopting this suggestion, it decided to

---

[145] See, e.g. *Jones* [2013] EWCA Crim 145, in which the offender walked towards complainant in an alleyway at night with his penis exposed, leaving her disgusted, angry and shaken; and *Ashford* [2013] EWCA Crim 720, in which the offender exposed his penis to a 17-year-old girl at a bus stop, manipulating it as he did so. She turned away in shock and the offender moved to stand directly in front of her, then sat next to her on the seat at the bus stop. She realised he was wearing a mask or stocking to conceal his mouth and nose. She was terrified.

[146] cf. *Mailer* [2006] EWCA Crim 665.

cover the point by amending the factor to the published wording. As for "abuse of trust", the Council thought that culpability is increased, as with other offences, where the offender has exploited a relationship of trust in order to commit an offence. "Use of threats (including blackmail)" is included because, whilst the offence of exposure is inherently upsetting, the Council thought that an offender increases his culpability if he uses deliberately or explicitly threatening language to further intimidate or frighten the victim.

Step Two—Starting point and category range

15.79   Once it has determined the offence category by considering these harm and culpability factors, at step two the court should use the corresponding starting point specified in the guideline in order to reach a sentence within the category range. The starting point applies to all offenders irrespective of plea or previous convictions. Once the starting point has been determined, step two allows further adjustment for aggravating or mitigating features, set out below. A case of particular gravity, reflected by multiple features of culpability or harm, could merit upward adjustment from the starting point before further adjustment for aggravating or mitigating features. Where there is a sufficient prospect of rehabilitation, a community order with a sex offender treatment programme requirement under s.202 of the Criminal Justice Act 2003 can be a proper alternative to a short or moderate length custodial sentence. The starting points and category ranges for offences under s.66 are as follows:

Category 1	*Starting point*
	26 weeks' custody
	Category range
	12 weeks'–1 years' custody
Category 2	*Starting point*
	High level community order
	Category range
	Medium level community order–26 weeks' custody

Category 3	*Starting point*
	Medium level community order
	Category range
	Band A fine–High level community order

The previous guideline, issued in 2007 by the Sentencing Guidelines Council, had two categories, "basic offence" and "repeat offender", with the latter carrying a 12-week custodial starting point and a 4–26 week range. In its consultation the Sentencing Council noted that in 2011, 6.8 per cent of offenders were sentenced above the ranges. The Council considered that there are some offences for which a sentence longer than 26 weeks may need to be available as an option, for example where there are vulnerable victims or there is targeting of children. It therefore increased the highest starting point (for category 1 offences) to a 26 weeks' custody with a range of 12 weeks to 1 year.

Aggravating and mitigating factors

After identifying the starting point and category range, the court should **15.80** consider whether the presence of aggravating or mitigating factors should result in an upward or downward adjustment from the starting point or the imposition of a sentence outside the category range. In particular, relevant recent convictions are likely to result in an upward adjustment. When sentencing a category 2 offence, the court should also consider whether the custody threshold has been passed; if so, whether a custodial sentence is unavoidable; and if so, whether that sentence can be suspended. When sentencing a category 3 offence, the court should also consider whether the community order threshold has been passed. The non-exhaustive list of aggravating and mitigating factors for offences under s.66 is as follows:

Aggravating factors
Statutory aggravating factors
• Previous convictions, having regard to a) the nature of the offence to which the conviction relates and its relevance to the current offence; and b) the time that has elapsed since the conviction   • Offence committed whilst on bail

Other aggravating factors

- Location of offence
- Timing of offence
- Any steps taken to prevent the victim reporting an incident, obtaining assistance and/or from assisting or supporting the prosecution
- Failure of offender to respond to previous warnings
- Offence committed whilst on licence
- Commission of offence whilst under the influence of alcohol or drugs
- Presence of others, especially children

Mitigating factors

- No previous convictions **or** no relevant/recent convictions
- Remorse
- Previous good character and/or exemplary conduct*
- Age and/or lack of maturity where it affects the responsibility of the offender
- Mental disorder or learning disability, particularly where linked to the commission of the offence
- Demonstration of steps taken to address offending behaviour

* Previous good character/exemplary conduct is different from having no previous convictions. The more serious the offence, the less the weight which should normally be attributed to this factor. Where previous good character/exemplary conduct has been used to facilitate the offence, this mitigation should not normally be allowed and such conduct may constitute an aggravating factor.

Steps Three to Nine

15.81   The remaining steps cover the following points. At step three the court should consider any factors which would indicate a reduction in sentence, e.g. assistance to the prosecution. At step four it should consider any reduction for a guilty plea. At step five the court should consider dangerousness, i.e. whether it would be appropriate to award an extended sentence (s.226A of the Criminal Justice Act 2003). Step six requires the court to consider whether the total sentence is just and proportionate to the offending behaviour. At step seven it should consider whether to make an ancillary order (e.g. a SHPO or a restraining order). Step eight requires the court to fulfil its duty under s.174 of the Criminal Justice Act 2003 to give reasons for, and explain the effect of, the sentence. Finally, at step nine the court should consider whether to give credit for time spent on bail in accordance with s.240A of that Act.

Sentencing examples

In *Ketteridge*,[147] the appellant, 45, with no previous convictions, was driving   **15.82**
on a motorway when, in slow-moving traffic, he drew up alongside a school
minibus, and, whilst staring at the pupils inside (aged 17 and 18), masturbated his exposed penis. Five months later, and three days after being
committed for trial, he committed a similar offence whilst repeatedly driving
past girls aged 13 to 16 who were standing at the side of the road. On pleas
of guilty, he was sentenced to a total of nine months' imprisonment, made up
of sentences of 5 months and 4 months, and disqualified from driving for 12
months under the Powers of Criminal Courts (Sentencing) Act 2000 s.147
(vehicle used for purposes of crime). The judge placed the offences in
category 1 of the sentencing guideline, although no indicator of raised
culpability was present, due to the aggravating factors—the appellant had
recently been cautioned for similar offending, the second offence was
committed when he was on bail for the first, the offences were committed in
daylight on the open road, and the victims of the second offence were
comparatively young. On appeal against sentence, the Court of Appeal
treated the offences as falling within category 2 but noted that aggravating
factors might take the appropriate sentence for each offence outside the
range for that category. Where a judge reflects repetitive offending in
consecutive sentences, however, he should be careful not to double-count any
aggravating factor so as to sentence outside the appropriate range for each
offence. Here, in the result, the judge did not fall into this error. The case was
not so obviously one for a community order that a sentence of imprisonment
was wrong in principle or manifestly excessive. Further, as the upper limit of
the range for a category 2 offence was six months' imprisonment, the
sentences were both within the range, and were neither wrong in principle
nor manifestly excessive. In relation to the disqualification, the power under
s.147 of the 2000 Act arose where the court was satisfied that a vehicle was
used for the purpose of committing or facilitating the commission of an
offence punishable on conviction on indictment with a term of imprisonment
of two years or more. That was the case here with both offences, and so the
judge had been entitled to disqualify the appellant under s.147 on that
ground alone. Further, when deciding on the length of the disqualification,
the judge was not bound to ignore the undeniable circumstances of the
driving, including the obvious danger to other road users, notwithstanding
that there had been no charge of dangerous or careless driving.

"Exposes"

It was established in *Hunt v DPP*,[148] decided under the repealed offence of   **15.83**
male exposure in s.4 of the Vagrancy Act 1824, that a defendant may be

[147] [2015] R.T.R. 40(5).
[148] [1990] Crim. L.R. 812, DC.

proved to have "exposed" his penis without evidence that anyone actually saw it. This decision is likely to be regarded as relevant to s.66 but we respectfully suggest that it ought not to be followed in relation to that offence. The appellant was seen by a police officer standing at his front window, naked except for his trousers which were half way between his knees and thighs. He had pulled back the curtain with his left hand and was moving his right hand backwards and forwards in the area of his penis. The justices found that he had been masturbating and that he knew his actions could be seen by passers-by. It was held on appeal that they had been fully entitled, on those findings, to draw the inference that the appellant's penis had been exposed. This decision was, however, doubted by the late Professor Sir John Smith QC, on the ground that a penis is "exposed" only if it is capable of being seen by others, and in the present case the only witness had been unable to see it, despite (presumably) trying to do so. The finding that the appellant knew his actions could be seen by passers-by could not justify the inference that his penis was exposed if, in fact, nobody could see it.[149] Sir John's logic is impeccable and we share his view that *Hunt* is not a reliable authority.

15.84   Compare the decision in *Mohammed Rakib*.[150] The complainant, 17, was walking along a footpath one morning when she heard music coming from an area of bushes nearby. She turned and saw a man standing in the bushes with his trousers and boxer shorts round his ankles, masturbating his naked erect penis with his left hand. She walked off but did not report the incident to the police. Some weeks later, at about the same time of day, she was again walking along the footpath when she heard music and turned to see the same man, standing in the same location as before. She looked him in the face before walking off. On this occasion she did not look towards his genitals but, from the motion of his left arm, which she did see, she said he was "doing the same thing" and that his arm was making motions as if he were masturbating. On this occasion she complained to the police and the appellant was subsequently arrested and charged with two offences of exposure contrary to s.66 of the 2003 Act. He was convicted by a jury and appealed on two grounds which essentially turned on the same point. First, it was submitted on his behalf that the judge had erred in rejecting the submission at the close of the prosecution case that the count relating to the second incident should be withdrawn from the jury because, as the complainant did not suggest that she actually saw the appellant's penis on that occasion, the jury could not safely conclude that it had been exposed merely because the complainant said that his left arm was moving in the same way as on the first occasion as if he was masturbating. The appellant could, it was submitted, have been masturbating under his clothing without exposing his private parts, or could simply have been engaged in some preparatory acts without any exposure having taken place. Secondly, the judge had been

---

[149] [1990] Crim. L.R. 813.
[150] [2011] EWCA Crim 870.

wrong to direct the jury that they were entitled to take into account that there had been exposure of the penis during the first incident when deciding whether they were sure that there had been exposure during the second. The Court of Appeal rejected both grounds. As to the first, it was clearly implicit in the jury's verdict in relation to the first incident that they were satisfied on the basis of the complainant's evidence that on that occasion the appellant was masturbating his exposed penis, with music playing, with the intent that someone should be attracted to see him and with the intent that alarm or distress should be caused thereby. This was patently relevant to the question whether he was exposing himself on the second occasion. Given the similarity of the arm movements that the complainant saw, and the similar circumstances in which she saw them, it was clearly open to the jury to be satisfied that, on the second occasion as on the first, the appellant was masturbating his naked penis. Simply because there might possibly have been another, innocent interpretation did not mean that the matter had to be withdrawn from the jury, and it would have been inappropriate for the judge to withdraw it, since whether the appellant was exposing himself was a matter for the jury to consider on all the evidence. As for the second ground, the judge had taken an unimpeachable approach in directing the jury to the effect that they could and should take into account any exposure they found to have taken place on the first occasion when considering whether exposure had also taken place on the second. He had directed them to the effect that the incidents were so similar that they were entitled to find that it would be beyond coincidence if the appellant was not doing on the second occasion what he was doing on the first, i.e. masturbating his naked penis. The direction, taken overall, was at the very least adequate, and no further or more complex direction was required.

15.85 *Rakib* is not vulnerable to the criticism made above of *Hunt*, where no evidence was given that anyone had seen or could have seen the appellant's exposed penis, which makes it exceedingly difficult to see how his penis could be found to have been "exposed". In *Rakib*, by contrast, the complainant had seen the appellant's exposed penis on the first occasion and she would undoubtedly have been able to see it on the second, if it had then been exposed and if she had looked towards it. The question was rather whether, given the fact of exposure on the first occasion and the similarity of circumstance between the two incidents, the fact of exposure could also be inferred on the second. We suggest the Court of Appeal's decision on that point is correct.

"GENITALS"

15.86 The term "genitals" is not defined in the Act but its natural meaning covers the external male and female genitalia,[151] i.e. the male penis and testicles and the female vulva. For what comprises the vulva, see para.21.31, below.

---

[151] cf. *Hansard*, HL Vol.648, col.558, Lord Falconer of Thoroton (May 19, 2003).

"Alarm or Distress"

15.87 These terms are borrowed from the law of public order. For their meaning, see para.15.196, below.

Mental Element

15.88 The defendant must expose his genitals intentionally and intend that someone will see them and be caused alarm or distress. It is not sufficient if his purpose is simply to obtain sexual gratification: in those circumstances, the common law offence of outraging public decency may properly be charged (see para.15.04, above). It is not enough that the defendant suspects that someone will see his exposed genitals: he must intend someone to see them. And even if he intends someone to see them, it is not enough that he suspects that that person will be caused alarm or distress: he must intend that alarm or distress will be caused. These limitations ensure that a naturist cannot commit the offence merely because he suspects that someone will see his exposed genitals and experience unreasonable alarm or distress in consequence.

15.89 In the light of the decision in *Heard*,[152] discussed in paras 2.81 and following, above, the requirement that the defendant did the prohibited act with the intention that someone would see his genitals and be caused alarm or distress makes the s.66 offence one of specific intent, such that voluntary intoxication through drink or drugs will provide a defence if it may have prevented the defendant forming that intention.

Voyeurism

Definition

15.90 Section 67 of the Sexual Offences Act 2003 creates four offences of voyeurism. It provides:

> "(1) A person commits an offence if—
>   (a) for the purpose of obtaining sexual gratification, he observes another person doing a private act, and
>   (b) he knows that the other person does not consent to being observed for his sexual gratification.
> (2) A person commits an offence if—
>   (a) he operates equipment with the intention of enabling another person to observe, for the purpose of obtaining sexual gratification, a third person (B) doing a private act, and
>   (b) he knows that B does not consent to his operating equipment with that intention.
> (3) A person commits an offence if—

---

[152] [2007] EWCA Crim 125.

(a) he records another person (B) doing a private act,
(b) he does so with the intention that he or a third person will, for the purpose of obtaining sexual gratification, look at an image of B doing the act, and
(c) he knows that B does not consent to his recording the act with that intention.
(4) A person commits an offence if he installs equipment, or constructs or adapts a structure or part of a structure, with the intention of enabling himself or another person to commit an offence under subsection (1)."

The following examples illustrate the potential application of the s.67 **15.91** offences:

- A, in order to obtain sexual gratification, looks from outside a house through a chink in the curtains to spy on B and C having sexual intercourse, knowing they do not consent to him doing so: offence under s.67(1). What if the curtains are open? It will be a question of fact whether, in the circumstances, the room would reasonably be expected to provide privacy: see paras 15.113 and following, below.

- A, a landlord, operates a webcam in the bedroom of his tenant, B, to enable people visiting a pornographic website on the internet to view, for their sexual gratification, live images of B getting undressed, where A knows that B does not consent to being observed: offence under s.67(2). People viewing the images will not commit the offence, nor will the internet service provider. However, depending on the circumstances they might commit other offences, e.g. relating to indecent photographs of children or to obscenity.

- A, B's boyfriend, secretly photographs B masturbating in her bedroom, with the intention of distributing the images to others for their sexual gratification by posting them on a pornographic website or sending them to a pornographic magazine: offence under s.67(3). Again, people viewing the image would not commit the offence, nor would the internet service provider or the magazine publisher, but depending on the circumstances they might commit other offences. It is important to note that in the example given, A will not commit the offence if his intention when taking the photographs is to distribute them in order to humiliate or embarrass B, rather than in order to enable others to obtain sexual gratification from looking at them. Also, A will not commit the offence if he forms the intention of enabling others to look at the images for the purposes of sexual gratification only after he has recorded them, e.g. on the ending of his relationship with B.[153]

- A, a landlord, drills a spyhole or installs a two-way mirror in his house with the intention of spying on his tenant, B, for sexual gratification, or allowing others to do so: offence under s.67(4). The

[153] But see now the offence of "revenge porn" in the Criminal Justice and Courts Act 2015 s.33.

offence will be committed even if the spyhole or mirror is discovered before it is used. Note that s.67(4) does not cover a person who installs equipment with the aim of enabling another person to commit an offence under s.67(2) or (3). But in such circumstances the installer may be guilty of conspiring to commit a s.67(2) or (3) offence, encouraging or assisting such an offence contrary to ss.44–46 of the Serious Crime Act 2007, or aiding and abetting such an offence.

Mode of Trial and Punishment

15.92   The offences in s.67 are triable either way.[154] The maximum punishment on conviction on indictment is two years' imprisonment. The maximum on summary conviction is six months' imprisonment or a fine, or both. As from a day to be appointed, the maximum period of imprisonment on summary conviction will increase to 12 months.[155] The increase will have no application to offences committed before it takes effect.[156] Until recently, the maximum fine on summary conviction was a fine not exceeding the statutory maximum (i.e. £5,000). The effect of s.85 of the Legal Aid, Sentencing and Punishment of Offenders Act 2012 is that, from March 12, 2015, a fine of any amount may be imposed. Fines will, however, continue to be set according to the seriousness of the offence and the means of the offender.

15.93   An offence under s.67 is a specified offence for the purposes of s.226A of the Criminal Justice Act 2003 (extended sentence for certain violent or sexual offences),[157] irrespective of the date of commission of the offence.

15.94   A person convicted under s.67, cautioned, found not guilty by reason of insanity or found to be under a disability and to have done the act charged, is automatically subject to the notification requirements in the Sexual Offences Act 2003[158] where (a) he was under 18 at the time of the offence and is sentenced to at least 12 months' imprisonment or (b) in any other case, the victim was under 18 or the offender is, in respect of the offence, sentenced to a term of imprisonment, detained in a hospital or given a community sentence of at least 12 months.

15.95   For the purposes of listing, cases under s.67 fall within Class 2B.[159] Cases in Class 2B must be referred to the Resident Judge, and by the Resident Judge to a Presiding Judge, in specified circumstances, including where a novel and important point of law is to be raised; where the defendant is a police officer, a member of the legal profession or a high profile figure; or

---

[154] s.67(5).
[155] Criminal Justice Act 2003 s.282(2), (3).
[156] Criminal Justice Act 2003 s.282(4).
[157] Inserted by the Legal Aid, Sentencing and Punishment of Offenders Act 2012 s.124, brought into force on December 3, 2012, by SI 2012/2906.
[158] s.80 and Sch.3, discussed in Ch.35, below.
[159] *Consolidated Criminal Practice Directions*, Part XIII Listing B: CLASSIFICATION, available at *https://www.judiciary.gov.uk/wp-content/uploads/2015/09/crim-pd-2015.pdf* [Accessed April 30, 2016].

where for any reason the case is likely to attract exceptional media attention.

Fitness to plead

The issue of fitness to plead arose in *R. v B*,[160] where the appellant was   **15.96**
charged with two counts of voyeurism contrary to s.67(1) after two incidents
at a sports centre in which he was alleged to have looked under partitions
into cubicles in which two young boys were changing. It became clear at an
early stage that the appellant suffered from a learning disability and autistic
spectrum disorder. When the matter came before the Crown Court, the judge
considered psychiatric reports and ruled that the appellant was unfit to plead
and stand trial by reason of disability, pursuant to the Criminal Procedure
(Insanity) Act 1964 s.4(5), (6). In the light of that ruling, s.4A(2) of the 1964
Act required the jury to decide whether they were satisfied that the appellant
had committed "the act . . . charged against him as the offence". The judge
invited submissions as to what matters the jury should consider in order to
reach a decision on this point. The prosecution submitted that they had only
to decide whether the appellant had observed each of the two boys doing a
private act. The defence submission was that, given the serious consequences
for the appellant, the jury had also to decide whether he had observed the
boys "for the purpose of sexual gratification". The judge ruled in favour of
the prosecution, and the jury decided that the appellant had observed one of
the boys as alleged. On appeal, it was argued that the judge's ruling had been
in error and that, in relation to the offence of voyeurism in s.67(1) of the 2003
Act, the jury can be satisfied that the appellant did "the act . . . charged
against him as the offence" for the purposes of s.4A(2) of the 1964 Act only
if they are satisfied that he acted for the purpose of sexual gratification, since
this purpose forms part of the "act" charged and cannot be divorced from it
as being an independent mental element. The Court of Appeal accepted this
argument.

It began by considering *Antoine*,[161] in which the House of Lords con-   **15.97**
sidered obiter the question whether a jury that has to determine, pursuant to
s.4A(2) of the 1964 Act, whether the accused did the act charged against him
as the offence need only be satisfied as to the actus reus of the offence or
whether it must also be satisfied as to mens rea. Lord Hutton, in the only
reasoned speech, with which the other members of the House agreed, said
that the jury need only be satisfied as to the actus reus.[162] In doing so, he said
that the purpose of s.4A(2) is[163]:

> " . . . to strike a fair balance between the need to protect a defendant who has,
> in fact, done nothing wrong and is unfit to plead at his trial and the need to

[160] [2012] EWCA Crim 770, applied in *Wells* [2015] EWCA Crim 2.
[161] [2001] 1 A.C. 340.
[162] Approving *Attorney General's Reference (No.3 of 1998)* [2000] Q.B. 401, C.A.
[163] [2001] 1 A.C. 340, at 376A.

protect the public from a defendant who has committed an injurious act which would constitute a crime if done with the requisite *mens rea* . . . ".

Lord Hutton considered that the provision strikes this balance by distinguishing between "a person who has not carried out the *actus reus* of the crime charged against him and a person who has carried out an act (or made an omission) which would constitute a crime if done (or made) with the requisite *mens rea*". The Court in *R. v B* said that in the light of this analysis, the problem in any given case lies in discerning what elements of the offence with which the person is charged constitutes the "injurious act" (in the words of Lord Hutton) and what constitutes the mental element.

15.98   Turning to the case before it, the Court said that as a preliminary, despite the widespread use in other cases of the Latin tag "actus reus" in order to isolate and define what, for a particular offence, constitutes the "act" charged, for the purposes of s.4A(2) of the 1964 Act, it preferred not to do so. The statute uses ordinary English words and their meaning is a matter of interpretation; substituting imprecise terms in a foreign language did not facilitate the resolution of the problem. Secondly, it seemed to the Court that in s.67(1) of the 2003 Act the link between deliberate observation and the purpose of sexual gratification of the observer is central to the offence. It accepted that enquiring into someone's purpose for doing something is to enquire into their state of mind when they did it. However, a person's state of mind is just as much a fact as the "outward act" of deliberate observation and, in this case at least, the creation of the state of mind must be the result of a positive thought process by the observer. For the offence of voyeurism, these two actions, the one aimed at the outside world and the other going on in the consciousness of the observer, have to go together; the deliberate observation must be done simultaneously with the specific, albeit subjective, purpose of obtaining sexual gratification. That being so, then in the case of an offence of voyeurism under s.67(1) of the 2003 Act, the "act charged as the offence" for the purposes of s.4A(2) is the act of deliberate observation of another doing a private act where the observer's specific purpose is the obtaining of sexual gratification. That omnibus activity is the "injurious act". Although the activity has two components, deliberate observation and the purpose of obtaining sexual gratification, they are indissoluble and together comprise the relevant "act". The other element in the offence, namely the observer's knowledge that the person observed does not consent to being observed for the purpose of the observer's sexual gratification, is not directly linked to the outward component of the "act". It refers to the state of mind that the observer must have, but it is not the reason for the observation, and so is not part of the "act charged" for the purposes of s.4A(2).

15.99   The Court considered this conclusion to be consistent with the social purpose of s.4A of the 1964 Act. If all that a jury had to determine was whether a person deliberately observed another doing a private act, then the consequence would be that the person would have to be dealt with in accordance with s.5 of the 1964 Act and so could be subject to a hospital order, with or without a restriction order; he would have to register as a sex offender (s.80(1)(c) of the 2003 Act); and he could be made the subject of a Sexual Offences Prevention Order (now, a Sexual Harm Prevention Order). In the Court's view, although a person observing another doing a private act can be regarded as an unpleasant nuisance, there is not the same pressing social need to protect the public from him as there would be if it were proved that the observation was done for the specific purpose of his sexual gratification. It followed that the judge's ruling that the jury need determine only whether the appellant deliberately observed each of the two boys doing a private act was wrong as a matter of law, as was his direction to the jury to the same effect. Accordingly, the determination of the jury on what had been count two was unsafe and the appeal had to be allowed.

This is an unsatisfactory decision. The essence of Lord Hutton's analysis **15.100** in *Antoine* was that "the act" for the purposes of s.4A(2) of the 1964 Act means the actus reus of the offence charged and not the mens rea. It is true that towards the end of his speech Lord Hutton noted that a number of learned authors have commented that it is difficult in some cases to distinguish precisely between the actus reus and the mens rea and that the actus reus can include a mental element.[164] He concluded that nevertheless, actus reus and mens rea are useful terms. He also said that:

> "[W]here a person is unfit to be tried in the normal way because of his mental state, it would be unrealistic and contradictory that in carrying out the determination under s.4A(2) the jury should have to consider what intention that person had in his mind at the time of the alleged offence. I consider that . . . by using the word "act" and not the word "offence" in [s.4A(2)] Parliament made it clear that the jury was not to consider the mental ingredients of the offence."

Accordingly, there is nothing in Lord Hutton's speech to suggest that an element which is part of the mens rea of the offence needs to be proved for the purposes of s.4A(2), indeed to the contrary. The element of the s.67(1) offence that requires the defendant's observation of the complainant to be for the purpose of his, i.e. the defendant's, sexual gratification must surely be a matter of mens rea, since it is part of the defendant's state of mind that must be proved for the offence to be established, and is separate from any element of deliberation that may be required as part of the act of observation itself. The purpose of sexual gratification cannot be said to be part of the actus reus merely because, as the Court said, its existence is an objective fact or because it is the result of "positive thought processes" by the observer. The Court sought to sidestep these difficulties by avoiding the terms "actus reus" and "mens rea" and by focusing rather on the question what was the "injurious act" that had to be proved, picking up a passing reference to that term in

---

[164] [2001] 1 A.C. 340, at 376C.

Lord Hutton's speech. This sleight of hand enabled it to reach the opposite conclusion to the one to which that speech ought to have driven it.

15.101   This might not matter if its conclusion was the right one, but we doubt that it was. First, it produced the "unrealistic and contradictory" situation which Lord Hutton sought to avoid through his comments in *Antoine*, whereby the jury were required to consider the appellant's state of mind at the time of the alleged offence despite the fact that his mental state made him unfit to be tried. It would surely also have been unfair to the appellant for the jury to be asked to determine his purpose in observing the boys, since this would put him at risk of an adverse finding when the jury's decision on the point would have to be reached without the evidence of the person best placed to enlighten them, i.e. the appellant. Secondly, the "injurious act" in s.67(1) is the act of observing another person doing a private act and, from the perspective of the person being observed, the injury is done by the observation itself, regardless of the purpose with which it is done. It is true, as the Court said, that a finding that the appellant did "the act" charged would have put him at risk of a hospital order and a SOPO and would have involved his registration as a sex offender. But it would also have enabled the court to make a supervision and treatment order. The result achieved by the court was that none of these options was available to it and the appellant was acquitted, so that he did not have the opportunity to benefit from any of the orders which might have been made. The Court, acknowledging the possibility of public concern about the outcome of the appeal, emphasised that, even on the limited directions of the judge, the jury were not satisfied that the appellant deliberately observed one of the two boys; that there was no finding that the appellant observed the other boy for the purpose of sexual gratification; that neither the authors of the psychiatric reports nor the judge considered the appellant to be in any way a sexual predator, indeed the judge went out of his way to say the opposite; and that the appellant had and continued to have a good character. But the fact remains that the appellant was found to have observed a young boy under the partition of a changing cubicle, and the Court's conclusion precluded the imposition of any treatment or restriction that might have prevented him doing the same again. For these reasons, the decision is to be regretted.

Parties to the Offence

15.102   The offence may be committed as principal by males and females.

Sentencing

15.103   For the Sentencing Council guideline relating to the sentencing of sexual offences committed by offenders aged 18 and over, see Ch.33. The guideline for offences of voyeurism adopts the same approach as the guideline for exposure (s.66, discussed in paras 15.75 and following, above), i.e. the categorisation of the offence, and so the starting points and sentencing ranges, depend upon whether there are factors indicating raised harm and/or raised culpability.

Sentencing guideline

Step One—Harm and culpability

The guideline requires the sentencing court to go through a series of steps in order to determine the appropriate sentence. Step one involves determining the offence category. The categories are defined by reference to whether the harm to the victim and the culpability of the offender are raised. The court should determine harm and culpability by reference only to the factors set out in the guideline (below). Where an offence does not fall squarely into a category, individual factors may require a degree of weighting before making an overall assessment and determining the appropriate offence category. The offence categories for offences under s.67 are as follows: **15.104**

Category 1	Raised harm *and* raised culpability
Category 2	Raised harm *or* raised culpability
Category 3	Voyeurism *without* raised harm or culpability factors present

The guideline identifies the following factors as raising the harm caused by the offence: **15.105**

Factors indicating raised harm
• Image(s) available to be viewed by others
• Victim observed or recorded in their own home or residence

In consulting on its draft guideline,[165] the Sentencing Council said that it included "image(s) available to be viewed by others" because where a permanent record of the image has been made, the victim will be subject to ongoing humiliation and anxiety about others viewing and accessing the image, thereby increasing the harm caused by the offence. As for "victim observed or recorded in their own home or residence", this factor is designed to deal with the increased harm caused by the victim no longer feeling safe in their own home and having the knowledge of intrusion.

---

[165] *Sexual Offences Guideline: Consultation* (December 6, 2012). The consultation document is available on the Sentencing Council's website.

15.106　　The Sentencing Council identified the following factors as raising culpability for the offence:

Factors indicating raised culpability
• Significant degree of planning
• Image(s) recorded
• Abuse of trust
• Specific or previous targeting of a particularly vulnerable victim
• Commercial exploitation and/or motivation
• Offence racially or religiously aggravated
• Offence motivated by, or demonstrating, hostility to the victim based on his or her sexual orientation (or presumed sexual orientation) or transgender identity (or presumed transgender identity)
• Offence motivated by, or demonstrating, hostility to the victim based on his or her disability (or presumed disability)

In its consultation, the Sentencing Council said it included "image(s) recorded" to reflect the increased culpability of an offender who records (rather than simply views) images of the victim. "Abuse of trust" is included to reflect the increased culpability of an offender who has abused their position in order to observe or record people, e.g. a manager of a leisure centre who sets up recording equipment in the female changing rooms, or a step-father who sets up recording equipment in the home to spy on a step-child. As for "significant degree of planning", this reflects the increased culpability of the offender who has put forethought into how to observe their victim(s) and who may also have been involved in setting up recording equipment.

Step Two—Starting point and category range

15.107　Once it has determined the offence category by considering these harm and culpability factors, at step two the court should use the corresponding starting point specified in the guideline in order to reach a sentence within the category range. The starting point applies to all offenders irrespective of plea or previous convictions. Once the starting point has been determined, step two allows further adjustment for aggravating or mitigating features, set out below. A case of particular gravity, reflected by multiple features of culpability or harm, could merit upward adjustment from the starting point before further adjustment for aggravating or mitigating features. Where there is a sufficient prospect of rehabilitation, a community order with a sex offender treatment programme requirement under s.202 of the Criminal Justice Act 2003 can be a proper alternative to a short or moderate length custodial sentence. The starting points and category ranges for offences under s.67 are as follows:

Category 1	Starting point 26 weeks' custody Category range 12 weeks' – 18 months' custody
Category 2	Starting point High level community order Category range Medium level community order – 26 weeks' custody
Category 3	Starting point Medium level community order Category range Band A fine – High level community order

The proposed sentence levels are very similar to those for offences of exposure under s.66 of the 2003 Act, for which see para.15.79, above. However, the top of the range for category 1 is higher than for that offence, as the Council said in its consultation that it felt a higher sanction should be available where an offence of voyeurism has involved the aggravating factors of recording and/or distribution of images.

Aggravating and mitigating factors

After identifying the starting point and category range, the court should consider whether the presence of aggravating or mitigating factors should result in an upward or downward adjustment from the starting point or the imposition of a sentence outside the category range. In particular, relevant recent convictions are likely to result in an upward adjustment. When sentencing a category 2 offence, the court should also consider whether the custody threshold has been passed; if so, whether a custodial sentence is

15.108

unavoidable; and if so, whether that sentence can be suspended. When sentencing a category 3 offence, the court should also consider whether the community order threshold has been passed. The non-exhaustive list of aggravating and mitigating factors for offences under s.67 is as follows:

Aggravating factors
Statutory aggravating factors
• Previous convictions, having regard to a) the nature of the offence to which the conviction relates and its relevance to the current offence; and b) the time that has elapsed since the conviction • Offence committed whilst on bail
Other aggravating factors
• Location of offence • Timing of offence • Failure to comply with current court orders • Offence committed whilst on licence • Distribution of images, whether or not for gain • Placing images where there is the potential for a high volume of viewers • Period over which victim observed • Period over which images were made or distributed • Any steps taken to prevent the victim reporting an incident, obtaining assistance and/or from assisting or supporting the prosecution • Attempts to dispose of or conceal evidence

Mitigating factors
• No previous convictions **or** no relevant/recent convictions • Remorse • Previous good character and/or exemplary conduct* • Age and/or lack of maturity where it affects the responsibility of the offender • Mental disorder or learning disability, particularly where linked to the commission of the offence • Demonstration of steps taken to address offending behaviour

* Previous good character/exemplary conduct is different from having no previous convictions. The more serious the offence, the less the weight which should normally be attributed to this factor. Where previous good character/exemplary conduct has been used to facilitate the offence, this mitigation should not normally be allowed and such conduct may constitute an aggravating factor.

In its consultation, the Sentencing Council said that "placing images where there is the potential for a high volume of viewers" does not rely on establishing how many people actually saw the images but is based on the potential for them to be viewed, e.g. where the offender places them on a website or a social networking site which has a high volume of access. Although the guideline refers here to "images" rather than "image(s)", we suggest that placing even one image where there is potential for a high volume of viewers should trigger this aggravating factor. "Period over which images were made or distributed" covers the case where there is a pattern of offending on the part of the offender. Some respondents to the consultation submitted that the factor "observed in own home" in the consultation draft was too narrowly drawn and should be expanded to cover other private settings similar to a home. In light of these representations, the Council amended this factor to "victim observed or recorded in their home or residence" in order to cover situations where, for example, the victim resides at a care home or other institution.

Steps Three to Nine

The remaining steps cover the following points. At step three the court should consider any factors which would indicate a reduction in sentence, e.g. assistance to the prosecution. At step four it should consider any reduction for a guilty plea. At step five the court should consider dangerousness, i.e. whether it would be appropriate to award an extended sentence (s.226A of the Criminal Justice Act 2003). Step six requires the court to consider whether the total sentence is just and proportionate to the offending behaviour. At step seven it should consider whether to make an ancillary order (e.g. a SHPO or a restraining order). Step eight requires the court to fulfil its duty under s.174 of the Criminal Justice Act 2003 to give reasons for, and explain the effect of, the sentence. Finally, at step nine the court should consider whether to give credit for time spent on bail in accordance with s.240A of that Act. **15.109**

Sentencing examples

In *Adams (John)*[166] the appellant (J) appealed against a total sentence of 28 months' imprisonment, imposed after he pleaded guilty to voyeurism and making indecent images of children. J had concealed a camera in the public lavatory of a hospital and over a period of three years had filmed footage of at least 50 unidentified people using the toilet. Three of the subjects were girls between the ages of 10 and 14. The footage of those three girls had been isolated and saved separately, and formed the basis of the indecent image counts. J was 54, of previously good character and pleaded guilty at the first **15.110**

---

[166] [2014] EWCA Crim 1898.

opportunity. He suffered from Parkinson's disease. A pre-sentence report indicated that he posed a medium risk of reconviction for sexual offences and recommended a community order with supervision and a sex offender treatment programme. J received concurrent sentences of 16 months' imprisonment in respect of each of six counts of voyeurism. He also received sentences of 12 months' in respect of each of three counts of making indecent photographs of children, to run concurrently with each other but consecutively to the 16-month sentences. J submitted that the judge, despite accepting that the offences fell within category 2 of the guideline, had exceeded the category range and imposed a sentence which was the maximum for the offence. His appeal was allowed. The aggravating features of the case were that the voyeurism persisted for many years and was effectively a campaign, during which at least 50 people were filmed, including young girls with their genitals exposed. The offence involved a significant degree of planning and J had filmed hospital outpatients who might have been vulnerable or unwell and had been entitled to feel entirely safe. Those features justified the conclusion that the offences involved higher culpability and higher harm than those envisaged as falling within category 2. The case was properly to be regarded as a serious category 1 case with a starting point of 18 months' custody. The judge's conclusion that only immediate imprisonment could be justified was not wrong in principle, but the mitigating factors meant that 28 months was manifestly excessive. The consecutive sentences were wrong in principle and ought to have been concurrent as they related to a single course of conduct. The overall totality of the term of imprisonment had to be appropriate, and the serious but concurrent element of indecent image production had to be reflected in the voyeurism sentence. Though the maximum sentence for voyeurism was two years, there were six counts and so it would have been open to the judge to impose consecutive sentences on more than one count. Adopting that course and taking account of all of the aggravating features, but making allowance for the mitigation, it was appropriate to impose an overall sentence of 27 months, reduced to 18 months to reflect the guilty plea. The existing voyeurism sentences were quashed and concurrent sentences of 18 months' imprisonment imposed on each count. The existing 12-month sentences for the indecent images offences remained, but were ordered to run concurrently with each other and with the 18-month voyeurism sentence.

"Observes"

15.111   Section 79(7) of the Act provides that for the purposes of Pt 1, which includes s.67, references to observation (however expressed) are to observation whether direct or by looking at an image. An "image" is defined by s.79(4) as a moving or still image and as including an image produced by any means and, where the context permits, a three-dimensional image. Observation will therefore cover looking at an image produced by a digital or CCTV camera, a web cam or a mobile phone messaging service. Direct observation is likely to cover observation by the naked eye, whether or not aided by the use of, e.g. binoculars or a telescope. Observing a person by watching them in a mirror will constitute observing their image rather than observing them directly,[167] but in any event will clearly constitute observation for the purposes of the section.

In *R. v B*,[168] when considering the elements of the s.67(1) offence, the Court of Appeal said: **15.112**

> "The verb 'observes' is not further defined in the SOA but we think it must connote a deliberate decision on the part of the defendant to look at someone doing a 'private act', as opposed to an accidental perception of someone doing a 'private act'. 'Observes' must also exclude a careless and, we think, reckless perception."

This is surely correct. It chimes with the construction given by the Court in *Heard*[169] to the verb "touches" in the offence of sexual assault (s.3 of the 2003 Act), i.e. that the required touching must be deliberate and that a reckless, careless or accidental touching will not suffice. This is strictly speaking, of course, an aspect of mens rea rather than actus reus, though the Court in *R. v B* may have been led to blur the distinction by the context in which it was analysing the matter: see paras 15.96 and following, above.

"DOING A PRIVATE ACT"

Section 68(1) provides that for the purposes of s.67 a person is doing a private   **15.113** act if the person is in a place which, in the circumstances, would reasonably be expected to provide privacy and:

    (a) the person's genitals, buttocks or breasts are exposed or covered only with underwear,

    (b) the person is using a lavatory, or

    (c) the person is doing a sexual act that is not of a kind ordinarily done in public.

In *R. v B*,[170] when considering the provision in s.68(1) that a person is   **15.114** doing a private act if they are in a place which, in the circumstances, would reasonably be expected to provide privacy, the Court of Appeal said: "Whether a particular place is such would appear to be an objective test". With respect, this must be so, given that the expectation of privacy must be a reasonable one, i.e. an expectation which a reasonable person could hold, as opposed to one which was in fact held by the person concerned, which would constitute a subjective test. As the Court said in *Bassett*,[171] the

---

[167] cf. *Hansard*, Vol.648, col.571, Lord Falconer of Thoroton (May 19, 2003).
[168] [2012] EWCA Crim 770, at [59].
[169] [2007] EWCA Crim 125, discussed in paras 2.78 and following, above.
[170] [2012] EWCA Crim 770, at [59].
[171] [2008] EWCA Crim 1174.

question whether the complainant had a reasonable expectation of privacy is one for the jury (or magistrates) in each case.

15.115   The place in which the act is done need not be a building or other structure; indeed, the word "place" was substituted by Government amendment for the word "structure" during the passage of the Sexual Offences Bill. It follows that any place will qualify provided that, in the circumstances, it would reasonably be expected to provide privacy. This might be capable of covering, e.g. an enclosed garden or a private beach or a remote rural location.

15.116   For the meaning of "genitals" see para.15.86, above.

15.117   It was held in *Bassett*[172] that the term "breasts" in s.68(1) does not include the male chest. The appellant took a concealed video camera into the men's changing room at a public swimming pool. He was seen watching and filming or intending to film a man taking a shower and washing the hair of his three-year-old daughter with whom he had been swimming. The man was wearing trunks. It seems that the appellant's object was in fact to film the man rather than the child. He was convicted of voyeurism. The question on appeal was whether the man observed was doing a "private act" as defined by s.68. The issues on the appeal were (1) whether the man was in a place and in circumstances which would reasonably be expected to provide privacy and, if so, (2) whether "breasts" were exposed within the meaning of s.68. The Court of Appeal allowed the appeal by reference to the second issue, holding that the intention of Parliament in enacting s.68 was to bring within the meaning of "private act" those parts of the body for which people conventionally expect privacy, and accordingly "breasts" means female breasts and not the exposed male chest. The Court did not decide the first issue, but it did say that a person may have a reasonable expectation of privacy without being wholly enclosed or sheltered from the possibility of being seen.[173] Accordingly, the judge had rightly directed the jury that the fact that there was no door on the shower cubicle did not mean that the man observed by the appellant had no reasonable expectation of privacy. Further, it said that the question whether a person had a reasonable expectation of privacy from observation is one for the jury in each case; that in many cases the question will turn on the nature of the observing; but the *purpose* of the observing will not be relevant, so the fact that it is done for the purpose of sexual gratification does not of itself mean that the observation is one from which there is a reasonable expectation of privacy. In *Barrett*, the judge had directed the jury that in a changing room the expectation is that one will be seen only by people who are there for a similar purpose, i.e. swimming and changing beforehand and afterwards, and that one would be entitled to expect privacy from people looking for sexual gratification. The Court of Appeal said that

---

[172] [2008] EWCA Crim 1174.
[173] Citing *Swyer* [2007] EWCA Crim 204 in which marathon runners who had gone behind a hedge to urinate were held to have an expectation of privacy from being pursued and watched.

this direction needed to be qualified by a reminder that the mere deriving of sexual gratification from the act of observation could not create an expectation of privacy, but that the *nature* of the observation, i.e. observation aided by a hidden camera, as opposed to its *purpose*, might be relevant in determining whether such an expectation existed. Given its decision on the second issue, the Court did not decide whether this misdirection rendered the conviction unsafe. Professor David Ormerod has commented that the effect of the Court's comments on the relevance of the nature of the observation would appear to be that "a casual glance from which D derives a sexual thrill is not enough [to amount to observation from which there is a reasonable expectation of privacy], but determined ogling might be".[174] He adds that if a person (V) does have an expectation of privacy, it will not excuse D that V impliedly consented to being viewed in a state of nakedness in a place in which privacy would be expected, as V has not consented to being observed *for the purpose of sexual gratification*.

In *Police Service for Northern Ireland v MacRitchie*[175] it was held that "underwear" in s.68 does not include bikini bottoms worn as such. The defendant, who was in a changing cubicle in a public swimming pool, had twice placed his mobile phone under the wall of an adjoining cubicle and made video recordings with the camera facility. The adjoining cubicle was occupied by the complainant, a young woman. She saw the phone and kicked it away. The recordings showed that the complainant had been wearing her bikini at the time they were made. Before noticing the camera she had changed into her underwear, but this was not captured on the recordings. The Court of Appeal in Northern Ireland (Kerr LCJ presiding) held that the cubicle was a place that would reasonably be expected to provide privacy, within the meaning of s.68. However, at the time the recordings were made the complainant was not doing a private act, since at that time she was wearing her bikini and not her underwear. The Court said that in its normal connotation, "underwear" means clothing worn next to the skin under outer clothes. Swimwear, in its normal function, is not underwear, although the Court commented that if a person chose to wear, for instance, bikini bottoms as underpants, they would constitute underwear for the purposes of s.68 whilst being so worn. The magistrate was therefore right to find there was no case to answer on a charge of voyeurism. However, as the magistrate had found there was prima facie evidence that the defendant had made the recordings intentionally for the purpose of sexual gratification, there was sufficient evidence for the case to proceed as an attempt. If it was the defendant's intention to record the complainant in a state of undress (as the evidence unmistakably indicated it was), and if his actions were more than merely preparatory to doing so (as his counsel accepted they were), the fact that a recording of the complainant in a state of undress could not be made

15.118

---

[174] [2008] Crim. L.R. 998, at p.1001.
[175] [2010] NICA 26.

would not prevent his conviction for attempting to commit an offence of voyeurism.

"Consent"

15.119   For the meaning of consent in the 2003 Act, see paras 1.79 and following, above.

"Image"

15.120   For the meaning of this word, see para.15.111, above.

"Structure"

15.121   Section 68(2) provides that in s.67, "structure" includes a tent, vehicle or vessel or other temporary or movable structure.

Mental Element

15.122   All four offences in s.67 are defined to require proof of purpose, intention and/or knowledge. In *R. v B*[176] the Court of Appeal said that it is clear from the use of the words "he" and "his" in s.67(1)(b) that the s.67(1) offence requires the defendant's purpose in observing the complainant's private act to be his own sexual gratification, and not that of someone else. This conclusion is surely correct, though it is Parliament's use of the words "obtaining" in s.67(1)(a) and "his" in s.67(1)(b), both preceding the words "sexual gratification", that most clearly indicate this interpretation. By way of contrast, the offence in s.67(2) requires the defendant to have acted for the purpose of enabling another person to obtain sexual gratification, and the offence in s.67(3) requires him to have acted for the purpose of either obtaining or enabling another person to obtain such gratification.

15.123   The Court of Appeal in *R. v B* went on to say[177] that the word "purpose" in s.67(1)(a) must refer to the defendant's subjective thought process and that it is irrelevant whether he actually obtained any sexual gratification, although proof that he did would be evidence of his purpose.

15.124   Lastly, the Court said[178] that the requirement in s.67(1)(b) that the defendant "knows that the other person does not consent to being observed for his sexual gratification" involves proof of a specific state of mind on the part of the defendant, i.e. actual knowledge that the other person does not consent to being observed by the defendant for the purpose of the defendant obtaining sexual gratification from that observation. As noted in para.12.63,

---

[176] [2012] EWCA Crim 770, at [60].
[177] [2012] EWCA Crim 770, at [60].
[178] [2012] EWCA Crim 770, at [61].

above, there is some authority that "knowledge" in a criminal statute includes deliberately shutting one's eyes to the truth, but the better view appears to be that this is a matter of evidence and that, as indicated by the Court of Appeal in *R. v B*, nothing short of actual knowledge will suffice.

In the light of the decision in *Heard*,[179] discussed in paras 2.81 and **15.125** following, above, the requirement that the defendant did the prohibited act for the purpose of obtaining or enabling another to obtain sexual gratification means that the offences under s.67 are offences of specific intent, such that voluntary intoxication through drink or drugs will provide a defence if it may have prevented the defendant forming that purpose. In relation to the offences in s.67(2) and (3), the requirement that the defendant acted for the purpose of obtaining or enabling another to obtain sexual gratification has the effect that the offences will not be committed where the defendant acts with some other intention, for example, to humiliate or embarrass B. This is potentially an unfortunate limitation on the scope of the offences, which as a result does not cover, for example, A who makes a recording of B engaging in private sexual activity and then places it on the internet with the sole object of making B a laughing stock. In this respect, the equivalent Scottish offences in s.9 of the Sexual Offences (Scotland) Act 2009 are preferable, as they require that the defendant acted for the purpose either of obtaining sexual gratification or of humiliating, distressing or alarming the victim.[180]

INTERCOURSE WITH AN ANIMAL

DEFINITION

Section 69 of the Sexual Offences Act 2003 creates two offences of **15.126** intercourse with an animal.[181] It provides:

"(1) A person commits an offence if—
  (a) he intentionally performs an act of penetration with his penis,
  (b) what is penetrated is the vagina or anus of a living animal, and
  (c) he knows that, or is reckless as to whether, that is what is penetrated.
(2) A person (A) commits an offence if—
  (a) A intentionally causes, or allows, A's vagina or anus to be penetrated,
  (b) the penetration is by the penis of a living animal, and
  (c) A knows that, or is reckless as to whether, that is what A is being penetrated by."

It should be noted that s.63 of the Criminal Justice and Immigration Act **15.127** 2008 makes it an offence to possess an extreme pornographic image.[182] An

---

[179] [2007] EWCA Crim 125.
[180] But see now the offence of "revenge porn" in the Criminal Justice and Courts Act 2015 s.33.
[181] For criticism of the conceptual basis of s.69, see Imogen Jones, *A beastly provision: why the offence of "intercourse with an animal" must be butchered*, 75 J. Crim. L. 528.
[182] For a critical discussion of the s.63 offence, see Erika Rackley and Clare McGlynn, *Prosecuting the Possession of Extreme Pornography: a Misunderstood and Misused Law* [2013] Crim. L.R. 400.

"extreme image" is defined to include an image which portrays, in an explicit and realistic way, a person performing an act of intercourse or oral sex with an animal (whether dead or alive), where a reasonable person looking at the image would think the person and animal portrayed in it were real, and the image is grossly offensive, disgusting or otherwise of an obscene character.[183] An image is "pornographic" for this purpose if it is of such a nature that it must reasonably be assumed to have been produced solely or principally for the purpose of sexual arousal.[184] By s.67 of the 2008 Act, the offence is triable either way with a maximum punishment on indictment of two years' imprisonment where the image is of an act of this sort.

Mode of Trial and Punishment

15.128 The offences in s.69 are triable either way.[185] The maximum punishment on conviction on indictment is two years' imprisonment. The maximum on summary conviction is six months' imprisonment or a fine, or both. As from a day to be appointed, the maximum period of imprisonment on summary conviction will increase to 12 months.[186] The increase will have no application to offences committed before it takes effect.[187] Until recently, the maximum fine on summary conviction was a fine not exceeding the statutory maximum (i.e. £5,000). The effect of s.85 of the Legal Aid, Sentencing and Punishment of Offenders Act 2012 is that, from March 12, 2015, a fine of any amount may be imposed. Fines will, however, continue to be set according to the seriousness of the offence and the means of the offender.

15.129 A person convicted under s.69, cautioned, found not guilty by reason of insanity or found to be under a disability and to have done the act charged, is automatically subject to the notification requirements in the Sexual Offences Act 2003[188] where (a) he was under 18 at the time of the offence and is sentenced to at least 12 months' imprisonment or (b) in any other case, he is, in respect of the offence, sentenced to a term of imprisonment or detained in a hospital.

15.130 For the purposes of listing, cases under s.69 fall within Class 2B.[189] Cases in Class 2B must be referred to the Resident Judge, and by the Resident Judge to a Presiding Judge, in specified circumstances, including where a novel and important point of law is to be raised; where the defendant is a police officer, a member of the legal profession or a high profile figure; or

[183] s.63(5A), (7).
[184] s.63(3).
[185] s.69(3).
[186] Criminal Justice Act 2003 s.282(2), (3).
[187] Criminal Justice Act 2003 s.282(4).
[188] s.80 and Sch.3, discussed in Ch.35, below.
[189] *Consolidated Criminal Practice Directions*, Part XIII Listing B: CLASSIFICATION, available at *https://www.judiciary.gov.uk/wp-content/uploads/2015/09/crim-pd-2015.pdf* [Accessed April 30, 2016].

where for any reason the case is likely to attract exceptional media attention.

PARTIES TO THE OFFENCE

The s.69(1) offence may be committed as principal only by males. The s.69(2)   **15.131**
offence may be committed as principal by males and females.

SENTENCING

The Sentencing Council guideline relating to the sentencing of sexual   **15.132**
offences committed by offenders aged 18 and over, discussed in Ch.33, does
not cover the offences in ss.69–71 of the 2003 Act. In consulting on its draft
guideline,[190] the Sentencing Council explained:

> "Given that these are very low volume offences with low maximum sentences
> available, the Council has taken the view that sentencing guidance is not needed
> for these offences."

In the absence of any guidance as to the sentencing of these offences, there
is a risk that sentencing courts will adopt inconsistent approaches. To
mitigate this risk we suggest that, although the Sentencing Council guideline
formally replaced the one issued by the Sentencing Guidelines Council in
2007, it may nonetheless be appropriate for a court to take the content of that
guideline into account when sentencing an offence under s.69. Under the
2007 guideline the recommended starting point, assuming no aggravating or
mitigating features, was a community order and the sentencing range was an
appropriate non-custodial sentence, which in this context suggested a
community order (which would be the appropriate sentence in most
instances) or a fine. The guideline also specified as an aggravating factor the
recording of the activity and/or circulating pictures or videos of it, and as a
mitigating factor that the activity was a symptom of isolation rather than
depravity.

In addition, sentencing decisions relating to the pre-2003 Act offence of   **15.133**
buggery with an animal remain instructive, despite the much longer maximum punishment that was available for that offence (life imprisonment, as
opposed to two years on indictment under s.69). The object of sentencing in
cases of buggery with an animal was considered in *Higson*,[191] where the
Court of Appeal quashed a two-year prison sentence and substituted a two-
year probation order for an offence of attempted buggery with a Pyrenean
Mountain bitch. Leggatt J stated that the object of the sentence in such

---

[190] *Sexual Offences Guideline: Consultation* (December 6, 2012). The consultation document
is available on the Sentencing Council's website.
[191] *The Times*, January 21, 1984. See also *P (Pamela Jean)* (1992) 13 Cr. App. R.(S.) 369;
Williams [1974] Crim. L.R. 558.

circumstances should be to avoid so far as possible any recurrence of the offence:

> "When all is said and done, it is the appellant and indeed his wife, and not the dog, who need help. That is best afforded by making a probation order."

15.134   *Higson* was distinguished in *Tierney*,[192] where the appellant had persuaded his ex-wife to commit buggery with an Alsatian dog. He took photographs of the incident, and later took the film to a public laboratory for processing. The staff at the laboratory alerted the police. He was charged with the buggery offence, pleaded guilty and was sentenced to nine months' imprisonment. On appeal against sentence, the Court noted the view expressed in *Higson* that it is desirable that help should be available for the offender who may be unhappy, distressed and not sexually orientated in the normal way. However, Beldam LJ pointed out that in the present case:

> "[t]he appellant, . . . whilst sorry for the fact that he had committed the offence and accepted [*sic*] responsibility for it did not consider that he was a person who is in any way deviant or in need of psycho/sexual counselling. It seems to this Court quite clear that this appellant was a person who would enjoy or obtain satisfaction from this form of unnatural sexual behaviour and was probably the sort of person who would by looking at the photographs continue to derive satisfaction from this type of activity. In our opinion, those facts, the fact that he involved his former wife in this behaviour and the fact that he caused others to see these photographs, distinguishes the conduct in this case from the conduct in the case of *Higson*.[193] We consider that a sentence of imprisonment was entirely appropriate in this case."[194]

The Court did however conclude that a shorter sentence would have served to mark the disgust which ordinary people would feel at the appellant's behaviour, and so it reduced his sentence to three months' imprisonment.

"PENETRATION"

15.135   For the meaning of this word, see paras 1.155 and following, above. The s.69(2) offence is committed where a person causes or allows her vagina or his or her anus to be penetrated by the penis of a living animal. For the meaning of "cause", see paras 2.98 and 8.104, above. For the meaning of "allow", see para.8.63, above. As s.69(2) requires penetration by an animal's penis, it does not cover the practice of "felching", which involves inserting a whole animal (e.g. a hamster or gerbil) into the vagina or anus for purposes of sexual gratification.[195] If A inserts an animal into the vagina or anus of B without B's consent, he may commit the offence of assault by penetration (s.2 of the 2003 Act). It is a moot point whether any purported consent to such activity

---

[192] (1990) 12 Cr. App. R.(S.) 216.
[193] The appellant in *Higson* had also involved his wife in his behaviour, although it is not clear from the report in what way.
[194] At 217.
[195] cf. *Hansard*, Vol.648, col.574, Lord Lucas (May 19, 2003); Vol.649, col.81, Lord Lucas (June 9, 2003).

would be recognised by the law: see the discussion of consent and public policy in paras 2.109 and following, above. In any event, if B is under 13 then, regardless of whether B purportedly consents, A will commit the offence of assault of a child under 13 by penetration (s.6 of the Act).

"Vagina or Anus"

Section 79(9) of the Act provides that "vagina" includes vulva. Section **15.136** 79(10) provides that, in relation to an animal, references to the vagina or anus include references to any similar part. It is not clear what lies behind this provision, i.e. what animal might be involved in the s.69(1) offence that does not have a vagina or anus but has a "similar part".[196]

"Living Animal"

The s.69 offences cannot be committed if the animal is dead. Under the **15.137** repealed offence of buggery with an animal, the word "animal" was held to include domestic fowl.[197]

Consent and Coercion

In *Bourne*[198] the appellant had forced his wife on two occasions to submit to **15.138** the insertion into her vagina of a dog's penis. He was charged with aiding and abetting her to commit buggery. His wife gave evidence that she had been terrorised into committing the acts, which were entirely against her will. The appellant argued that he could be convicted of aiding and abetting only if his wife could have been convicted as principal, which was not possible as she had acted under his coercion. In the face of this argument, the trial judge left two questions to the jury: had the appellant caused his wife to have carnal knowledge of a dog and were they satisfied that she did not consent? The jury answered both questions in the affirmative and the appellant was duly convicted.

The necessary inference from the questions left to the jury is that the judge **15.139** rejected the appellant's argument, and that coercion, or absence of consent on the part of his wife, could not prevent him from being an aider and

[196] There is an anecdote to the effect that when the Bill was before Parliament, a learned academic criminal lawyer, having pondered this provision for some time, telephoned the Home Office to ask what animal they had in mind. After mature deliberation, they called him back with the answer "a lobster". We have been unable to confirm the truth of this story.
[197] *Brown* (1889) 24 Q.B.D. 357; and see *Reynolds* (1881) 1 L.R. (N.S.W.) 129, N.S.W. S.Ct. Note the practice of avisodomy, which involves breaking the neck of a hen or other bird immediately before penetrating it, so as to derive sexual stimulus from the spasms which the bird then undergoes: *Hansard*, HL Vol.649, col.81, Lord Lucas (June 9, 2003). Whether this practice constitutes an offence under s.69 will turn on whether the bird is dead when penetration occurs.
[198] (1952) 36 Cr. App. R. 125.

abettor. But in that case, why did the judge ask for a jury verdict on the issue of consent? The only plausible explanation is that he must have believed the law to be the very opposite of the appellant's contention, i.e. if the wife had consented (rather than if she had been coerced), there would have been no offence for the appellant to aid and abet. If this was indeed the judge's view, it was firmly rejected by the Court of Criminal Appeal when the appellant appealed unsuccessfully against his conviction. Lord Goddard CJ, delivering the judgment of the Court, said that it had been unnecessary for the trial judge to require the special verdict, as the question whether the offence of buggery was committed "does not depend upon consent; it depends on the act". The same is no doubt true as regards s.69(2), which contains no defence of consent.

15.140   The Court in *Bourne* was, however, prepared to assume that, if the wife had been charged with buggery, she would have had a defence of duress. This again must be equally true in relation to charges under s.69(2). In an appropriate case, it would no doubt also be a defence that the defendant participated in the relevant acts only because of physical compulsion.

ACCOMPLICES

15.141   A person may be convicted as an accomplice to a s.69 offence if, e.g. he arranges the performance of acts falling within the scope of the provision as part of a live sex show or to be filmed for some other form of pornographic display, or if, without any motive of financial gain, he encourages others to perform such acts. In those circumstances he is also liable to conviction for encouraging or assisting a s.69 offence contrary to ss.44–46 of the Serious Crime Act 2007.

15.142   In *Bourne*, considered above, the Court of Criminal Appeal assumed that the wife would have been entitled to an acquittal on the ground of duress, but nonetheless held that the appellant had been properly indicted as a principal in the second degree to the commission of buggery. Opinions differ over the correct explanation of this decision, which will be equally applicable to offences under s.69. On one view, which was clearly that of the Court itself,[199] the wife had committed the actus reus of buggery but because of the defence of duress she lacked mens rea; and therefore the case demonstrates that one may be guilty as an accomplice by aiding and abetting merely the actus reus of an offence. On another view,[200] the wife had committed the actus reus of buggery with the requisite mens rea, but was excused from criminal liability by the duress defence, and accordingly the case illuminates the operation of

---

[199] At 128 per Lord Goddard, CJ; and see *Millward* [1994] Crim. L.R. 527; *DPP v K and B* [1997] 1 Cr. App. R. 36.

[200] cf. R. Cross, *Duress and Aiding and Abetting (A Reply)* (1953) 69 L.Q.R. 354; I. Dennis, *Duress, Murder and Criminal Responsibility* (1980) 96 L.Q.R. 208 at 222 et seq.; *DPP for Northern Ireland v Lynch* [1975] A.C. 653 at 710–11, per Lord Edmund Davies; Smith and Hogan, *Criminal Law*, 14th edn, (Oxford: OUP, 2015), p.265.

that defence rather than the law of accomplices. Whichever analysis is correct, the result is clear and the case has been generally approved.[201]

MENTAL ELEMENT

It must be proved that the defendant intentionally performed the act of penetration (in the case of the s.69(1) offence) or intentionally caused or allowed the penetration (in the case of the s.69(2) offence). It must also be proved that he knew or was reckless as to the circumstance that the penetration was of the vagina or anus (s.69(1)) or by the penis (s.69(2)) of a living animal. The meaning of "reckless" in s.70 is likely to be that identified in *R. v G*,[202] i.e. the defendant will be reckless if he perceived a risk that the relevant circumstance existed.

15.143

In the light of the decision in *Heard*,[203] discussed in paras 2.81 and following, above, the offences in s.69 appear to be offences of basic intent, such that voluntary intoxication through drink or drugs will provide no defence.

15.144

SEXUAL PENETRATION OF A CORPSE

DEFINITION

Section 70(1) of the 2003 Act provides:

15.145

"A person commits an offence if—
(a) he intentionally performs an act of penetration with a part of his body or anything else,
(b) what is penetrated is a part of the body of a dead person,
(c) he knows that, or is reckless as to whether, that is what is penetrated, and
(d) the penetration is sexual."

It should be noted that s.63 of the Criminal Justice and Immigration Act 2008 makes it an offence to possess an extreme pornographic image.[204] An "extreme image" is defined to include an image which portrays, in an explicit and realistic way, an act which involves sexual interference with a human corpse, where a reasonable person looking at the image would think that the corpse was real, and the image is grossly offensive, disgusting or otherwise of

15.146

---

[201] Smith and Hogan described it as "just and logical", *Criminal Law*, 7th edn, (Oxford: Oxford University Press, 1992), p.153, Williams, as "desirable": Glanville Williams, *Textbook of Criminal Law*, 2nd edn (London: Stevens & Sons Ltd, 1983), p.372.
[202] [2003] UKHL 50 HL; and see *Attorney General's Reference (No.3 of 2003)* [2004] 2 Cr. App. R. 367.
[203] [2007] EWCA Crim 125.
[204] For a critical discussion of the s.63 offence, see Erika Rackley and Clare McGlynn, *Prosecuting the Possession of Extreme Pornography: a Misunderstood and Misused Law* [2013] Crim. L.R. 400.

an obscene character.[205] An image is "pornographic" for this purpose if it is of such a nature that it must reasonably be assumed to have been produced solely or principally for the purpose of sexual arousal.[206] By s.67 of the 2008 Act, the offence is triable either way with a maximum punishment on indictment of two years' imprisonment where the image is of an act of this sort.

Mode of Trial and Punishment

15.147   The offence under s.70 is triable either way.[207] The maximum punishment on conviction on indictment is two years' imprisonment. The maximum on summary conviction is six months' imprisonment or a fine, or both. As from a day to be appointed, the maximum period of imprisonment on summary conviction will increase to 12 months.[208] The increase will have no application to offences committed before it takes effect.[209] Until recently, the maximum fine on summary conviction was a fine not exceeding the statutory maximum (i.e. £5,000). The effect of s.85 of the Legal Aid, Sentencing and Punishment of Offenders Act 2012 is that, from March 12, 2015, a fine of any amount may be imposed. Fines will, however, continue to be set according to the seriousness of the offence and the means of the offender.

15.148   A person convicted under s.70, cautioned, found not guilty by reason of insanity or found to be under a disability and to have done the act charged, is automatically subject to the notification requirements in the Sexual Offences Act 2003[210] where (a) he was under 18 at the time of the offence and is sentenced to at least 12 months' imprisonment or (b) in any other case, he is, in respect of the offence, sentenced to a term of imprisonment or detained in a hospital.

15.149   For the purposes of listing, cases under s.70 fall within Class 2B.[211] Cases in Class 2B must be referred to the Resident Judge, and by the Resident Judge to a Presiding Judge, in specified circumstances, including where a novel and important point of law is to be raised; where the defendant is a police officer, a member of the legal profession or a high profile figure; or where for any reason the case is likely to attract exceptional media attention.

Parties to the Offence

15.150   The offence may be committed as principal by males and females.

---

[205] s.63(5A), (7).
[206] s.63(3).
[207] s.70(2).
[208] Criminal Justice Act 2003 s.282(2), (3).
[209] Criminal Justice Act 2003 s.282(4).
[210] s.80 and Sch.3, discussed in Ch.35, below.
[211] *Consolidated Criminal Practice Directions*, Part XIII Listing B: CLASSIFICATION, available at *https://www.judiciary.gov.uk/wp-content/uploads/2015/09/crim-pd-2015.pdf* [Accessed April 30, 2016].

Sentencing

The Sentencing Council guideline relating to the sentencing of sexual **15.151** offences committed by offenders aged 18 and over, discussed in Ch.33, does not cover the offences in ss.69–71 of the 2003 Act. In consulting on its draft guideline,[212] the Sentencing Council explained:

> "Given that these are very low volume offences with low maximum sentences available, the Council has taken the view that sentencing guidance is not needed for these offences."

Clearly, in the absence of any guidance as to the sentencing of these offences, there is a risk that sentencing courts will adopt inconsistent approaches. To mitigate this risk we suggest that, although the new guideline has formally replaced the one issued by the Sentencing Guidelines Council in 2007, it will nonetheless be appropriate for a court to consult that guideline when sentencing an offence under s.70. Under the 2007 guideline, the recommended starting point, assuming no aggravating or mitigating features, was a community order and the sentencing range was an appropriate non-custodial sentence, which in this context suggested a community order (which would be the appropriate sentence in most instances) or a fine. The guideline also specified as aggravating factors distress caused to relatives or friends of the deceased; physical damage caused to the body of the deceased; whether the corpse was that of a child; or whether the offence was committed in a funeral home or mortuary. The authors suggest that recording the activity and/or distributing pictures or videos of it will also aggravate the offence.

"Penetration"

For the meaning of this word, see paras 1.55 and following, above. The **15.152** penetration may be with a part of the body (e.g. the penis, finger, tongue or hand) or anything else. The parts most likely to be penetrated in a way that is sexual are the vagina, anus or mouth, but the offence is not so confined.

"Sexual"

For the meaning of this word, see paras 2.66 and following, above. The **15.153** requirement that the penetration is "sexual" excludes from the offence legitimate penetration of a dead body, e.g. during a post-mortem examination.[213]

---

[212] *Sexual Offences Guideline: Consultation* (December 6, 2012). The consultation document is available on the Sentencing Council's website.
[213] Explanatory Notes to the Act, para.133.

Mental Element

15.154 The act of penetration must be performed intentionally and the defendant must know or be reckless as to the circumstance that what is penetrated is a part of the body of a dead person. The meaning of "reckless" in s.70 is likely to be that identified in *R. v G*,[214] i.e. the defendant will be reckless if he perceived a risk that this circumstance existed. So the offence will be committed where a person (A) intentionally penetrates part of the body of a dead person (B) if A suspects B may be dead, even if he does not know that to be the case, or if he could not care less whether B is alive or dead. The offence will not, however, be committed where A penetrates B believing B is alive, though B is in fact dead. Nor will it be committed where B unexpectedly dies during intercourse with A.[215] In that case, the better view is that A does not commit the offence by continuing to penetrate B after B's death, despite the provision in s.79(2) that penetration is a continuing act from entry to withdrawal. This is because s.70 requires that the offender "intentionally performs an act of penetration" of the body of a dead person, and in this example the "act of penetration" is performed when A initially penetrates B, i.e. when B is still alive, even if it continues thereafter.

15.155 In the light of the decision in *Heard*,[216] discussed in paras 2.81 and following, above, the offence in s.70 appears to be one of basic intent, such that voluntary intoxication through drink or drugs will provide no defence.

Sexual Activity in a Public Lavatory

Definition

15.156 Section 71(1) of the Sexual Offences Act 2003 provides:

> "A person commits an offence if—
> (a) he is in a lavatory to which the public or a section of the public has or is permitted to have access, whether on payment or otherwise,
> (b) he intentionally engages in an activity, and
> (c) the activity is sexual."

Mode of Trial and Punishment

15.157 The offence under s.71(1) is summary only.[217] The maximum sentence on summary conviction is six months' imprisonment or a fine, or both. Until recently, the maximum fine was a fine not exceeding level 5 on the standard

---

[214] [2003] UKHL 50, HL; and see *Attorney General's Reference (No.3 of 2003)* [2004] 2 Cr. App. R. 367.
[215] Explanatory Notes to the Act, para.133.
[216] [2007] EWCA Crim 125.
[217] s.71(3).

scale (i.e. £5,000). The effect of s.85 of the Legal Aid, Sentencing and Punishment of Offenders Act 2012 is that, from March 12, 2015, a fine of any amount may be imposed. Fines will, however, continue to be set according to the seriousness of the offence and the means of the offender.

PARTIES TO THE OFFENCE

The offence may be committed as principal by males and females.   **15.158**

SENTENCING

The Sentencing Council guideline relating to the sentencing of sexual   **15.159** offences committed by offenders aged 18 and over, discussed in Ch.33, does not cover the offences in ss.69–71 of the 2003 Act. In consulting on its draft guideline,[218] the Sentencing Council explained:

> "Given that these are very low volume offences with low maximum sentences available, the Council has taken the view that sentencing guidance is not needed for these offences."

This statement is, however, highly misleading, as sentencing guidance for the s.71 offence remains in effect in the Magistrates' Court Sentencing Guidelines.[219] That guidance is taken from the previous sexual offences guideline, issued by the Sentencing Guidelines Council ("SGC") in 2007. Whilst the Magistrates' Court Sentencing Guidelines have been updated in relation to other offences under the Sexual Offences Act 2003 to reflect the replacement of the SGC guideline by the new one, this is not the case in relation to the entry for the s.71 offence, which continues to refer to the SGC guideline. Accordingly, the sentencing starting point and range for a first time offender pleading not guilty, where there are no aggravating or mitigating factors, is a Band C fine. Where there are aggravating factors, the starting point is a low level community order and the range a Band C fine to a medium level community order. For a repeat offender, the starting point is a low level community order and the range a Band C fine to a medium level community order. Two aggravating factors are identified: intimidating behaviour/threats of violence to member(s) of the public and blatant behaviour. The presence of these or other aggravating factors may suggest that a sentence above the range is appropriate.

---

[218] *Sexual Offences Guideline: Consultation* (December 6, 2012). The consultation document is available on the Sentencing Council's website.
[219] p.92. The Guidelines are available at *http://www.sentencingcouncil.org.uk/wp-content/uploads/Final-MCSG-April-2016.pdf* [Accessed April 30, 2016].

"Lavatory to which the Public or a Section of the Public has or is Permitted to have Access, whether on Payment or Otherwise"

15.160 The offence applies to lavatories to which all members of the public have access and also to those to which only a "section" of the public has access. For the meaning of this phrase, see the cases discussed in paras 13.41 and following, above. The offence will therefore be capable of covering lavatories in e.g. a student hall of residence or a sports stadium.

"Sexual"

15.161 Section 71(2) provides:

> "For the purposes of the section, an activity is sexual if a reasonable person would, in all the circumstances but regardless of any person's purpose, consider it to be sexual."

Compare the definition of "sexual" in s.78, which applies for all other purposes in Pt 1 of the Act (save in relation to the offence in s.15A). Section 78 is discussed in paras 2.66 and following, above. The effect of s.71(2) is to focus attention on the nature of the activity and the circumstances in which it is carried out. The purpose of those involved is to be disregarded. So if a reasonable person, looking at the activity and the circumstances, would regard it as possibly sexual, depending on the purpose of the participants, it will not fall within the scope of the offence. In short, only manifestly sexual activity will be caught.

Mental Element

15.162 The defendant must intentionally engage in the relevant activity. In the light of the decision in *Heard*,[220] discussed in paras 2.81 and following, above, the offence in s.71 appears to be one of basic intent, such that voluntary intoxication through drink or drugs will provide no defence.

Insulting Behaviour under Section 4 of the Public Order Act 1986

Definition

15.163 Section 4(1) of the 1986 Act provides that:

> "A person is guilty of an offence if he ... uses towards another person threatening, abusive or insulting ... behaviour ... with intent to cause that person to believe that immediate unlawful violence will be used against him or another ... or to provoke the immediate use of unlawful violence by that person

---

[220] [2007] EWCA Crim 125.

or another, or whereby that person is likely to believe that such violence will be used or it is likely that such violence will be provoked."

In appropriate cases, a person doing an indecent act in public may be charged under this section with using threatening, abusive or insulting behaviour likely to provoke unlawful violence. The offence might, for example, be used in appropriate circumstances to prosecute someone who "moons" at another person or exposes his penis to them.[221] The section creates one offence that may be committed in four different ways.[222] The offence may be committed in both public and private places, but not if both parties are in a dwelling (even if they are in different dwellings).[223]

MODE OF TRIAL AND PUNISHMENT

The offence under s.4(1) of the 1986 Act is triable summarily. The maximum sentence is six months' imprisonment or a fine, or both.[224] Until recently, the maximum fine was a fine not exceeding level 5 on the standard scale (i.e. £5,000). The effect of s.85 of the Legal Aid, Sentencing and Punishment of Offenders Act 2012 is that, from March 12, 2015, a fine of any amount may be imposed. Fines will, however, continue to be set according to the seriousness of the offence and the means of the offender.   **15.164**

"USES TOWARDS ANOTHER PERSON"

The behaviour in question must be "used towards another person". The other person must be physically present in order to perceive the defendant's behaviour.[225] It is not essential for him to give evidence that he was present and perceived the behaviour; in appropriate circumstances this can be inferred from the other evidence.[226] The words "uses towards" suggests that the defendant's behaviour must be directed towards another person. It is, however, possible that the defendant may commit the offence if he knows or intends that his behaviour will be witnessed by another, even if he is not directing the behaviour towards that person. But the offence will not be committed if the defendant believes that nobody is witnessing his behaviour.   **15.165**

---

[221] The CPS's Legal Guidance on Public Order Offences does not address the issue of whether and in what circumstances it is appropriate for s.4 to be used in this way: see *http://www.cps.gov.uk/legal/p_to_r/public_order_offences/* [Accessed April 30, 2016].

[222] *Winn v DPP* (1992) 156 J.P. 881.

[223] s.4(2). A common landing in a block of flats is not part of a "dwelling" for this purpose: *Rukwira v DPP* [1993] Crim. L.R. 882.

[224] s.4(4).

[225] *Atkin v DPP* (1989) 89 Cr. App. R. 199, DC.

[226] *Swanston v DPP* (1997) 161 J.P. 203, DC (inference drawn from proximity of defendant and victim that the latter must have heard what defendant did and said).

"INSULTING BEHAVIOUR"

15.166 "Insulting" is an ordinary word, the meaning of which is to be determined as a question of fact by the magistrates.[227] This does not give them carte blanche to interpret the word as they will: the Divisional Court may overturn a conviction on appeal if it considers that no bench of magistrates acquainted with the use of language could reasonably find the defendant's behaviour to be insulting.[228] *Parkin v Norman*,[229] decided under s.5 of the Public Order Act 1936, the predecessor of s.4, remains instructive on the possible application of the term "insulting behaviour". But it must be emphasised that the decision turns on its particular facts and no doubt reflects societal attitudes at the time it was decided, so it is no more than illustrative of the possible scope of the s.4(1) offence. In that case, the appellant masturbated in a public lavatory in sight of another man, who was in fact a plain clothes detective. The question before the Court was whether the appellant could reasonably have been found to have insulted the police officer. The Court said there was a difference between insulting behaviour and behaviour that might offend, disgust or cause anger. However, the appellant's behaviour was tantamount to a statement that he believed the police officer to be homosexual, something "which the average heterosexual would surely regard as insulting". It did not matter that the officer was not in fact insulted: the appellant's behaviour was "potentially insulting" and that was sufficient to justify the magistrates' findings.[230]

15.167 Similar reasoning was used to uphold the convictions of the appellants in *Masterson v Holden*,[231] which was also decided under s.5 of the 1936 Act but is highly unlikely to be a reliable guide to the modern application of the s.4(1) offence. The appellants engaged in overt homosexual behaviour, kissing and fondling one another, in the early hours of the morning in Oxford Street. Their activities were witnessed by two young men and two young women, who voiced their objections. The Court held that the appellants' conduct could reasonably be found to be insulting, on the basis that it suggested that the witnesses would find such conduct in public acceptable. Glidewell LJ said:

> "Overt homosexual conduct in a public street, indeed overt heterosexual conduct in a public street, may well be considered by many persons to be objectionable, to be conduct which ought to be confined to a private place."

---

[227] *Brutus v Cozens* [1973] A.C. 854; *DPP v Clarke* (1992) 94 Cr. App. R. 359. See also *Chambers and Edwards v DPP* [1995] Crim. L.R. 896; *Hammond v DPP* [2004] EWHC 69 (Admin); *Bright v Secretary of State for Justice* [2014] EWCA Civ 1628 at [37].

[228] *Brutus v Cozens* [1973] A.C. 854; *Bryan v Robinson* [1960] 1 W.L.R. 506; *Ambrose* (1973) 57 Cr. App. R. 538 (in which it was held that words which are rude and offensive are not necessarily insulting).

[229] [1983] Q.B. 92.

[230] cf. *Cheeseman v DPP* (1991) 93 Cr. App. R. 145; *DPP v Orum* [1988] 3 All E.R. 449, discussed in para.15.193, below; and see para.15.56, above.

[231] [1986] 1 W.L.R. 1017.

As that might have been the magistrates' reasoning, the Court refused to set aside the convictions. It should be noted, however, that the decision pre-dates the Human Rights Act 1998. The prosecution of two homosexuals in similar circumstances would be likely now to offend that Act since it would be an unjustified and discriminatory interference with their private lives, given that, despite the words of Glidewell LJ quoted above, a heterosexual couple in similar circumstances would be most unlikely to be prosecuted. There is also the technical point that under s.4, unlike under s.5 of the 1936 Act, the insulting behaviour must be "used towards another". It is doubtful whether this requirement would have been satisfied on the facts of *Masterson v Holden*, where the magistrates had found that "the appellants appeared wholly unaware of other persons in the vicinity".

"IMMEDIATE UNLAWFUL VIOLENCE"

"Violence" is defined in s.8 of the 1986 Act as "any violent conduct",   **15.168** including violent conduct towards property as well as towards persons. The violence which the defendant intends to be feared or provoked, or which is likely to be feared or provoked, must be "unlawful". The use of force against persons or property may be lawful if, for example, it is justified or excused by the common law rules on self-defence, self-help, duress or necessity, or by the provision in s.3(1) of the Criminal Law Act 1967 permitting the use of reasonable force in the prevention of crime. The unlawful violence must also be "immediate". This does not mean "instantaneous", and violence is immediate for the purposes of s.4(1) if it results within a relatively short period of time and without any other intervening occurrence.[232]

"WHEREBY IT IS LIKELY THAT SUCH VIOLENCE WILL BE PROVOKED"

In *Parkin v Norman*, the Court said of s.5(1) of the 1936 Act: **15.169**

> "It is to be noted that the words of the statute are 'whereby a breach of the peace is likely to be occasioned' and not 'whereby a breach of the peace is liable to be occasioned'. This is a penal measure and the courts must take care to see that the former expression is not treated as if it were the latter."[233]

A similar approach will no doubt be taken to s.4(1) of the 1986 Act. This could create a difficulty for the prosecution in cases where the insulting behaviour is used towards a police officer, as police officers do not commonly resort to violence merely because they are insulted. If the defendant does not intend violence to be feared or provoked, and the likely consequence of his conduct is simply that he will be questioned and possibly arrested by the

---

[232] *R. v Horseferry Road Magistrates' Court, Ex p. Siadatan* (1991) 92 Cr. App. R. 257. See also *DPP v Ramos* [2000] Crim. L.R. 768.

[233] [1983] Q.B. 92 at 100. See also *Chief Constable of Lancashire v Potter* [2003] EWHC 2272 (Admin), DC, at [32], discussed in para.13.82, above.

police officer, then logically there can be no conviction.[234] A conviction was, however, obtained under s.5 of the 1936 Act in precisely these circumstances in *Parkin v Norman*. Also, a conviction will be possible if the prosecution can show that the defendant intended the officer to fear or to be provoked to violence, even though he was unlikely to succeed in his intention; or that the defendant's behaviour was likely to cause the officer to believe that violence would be used against him or another. Alternatively, it may be possible to bring a charge under s.5 of the 1986 Act.[235] It has been held that the words "such violence" mean "immediate unlawful violence".[236]

Mental Element

15.170   Section 6(3) of the Act provides that a person is guilty of an offence under s.4(1) only if he intends his behaviour to be threatening, abusive or insulting, or is aware that it may be.[237] Section 6(5) further provides that a person whose awareness is impaired by intoxication shall be taken to be aware of that of which he would have been aware if not intoxicated, unless he shows either that his intoxication was not self-induced or that it was caused solely by the taking or administration of a substance in the course of medical treatment.

Insulting Behaviour with Intent to Harass, Alarm or Distress under Section 4A of the Public Order Act 1986

Definition

15.171   Section 4A(1)(a) of the Public Order Act 1986[238] provides that:

> "A person is guilty of an offence if, with intent to cause a person harassment, alarm or distress, he . . . uses threatening, abusive or insulting words or behaviour, or disorderly behaviour, . . . thereby causing that or another person harassment, alarm or distress."

In appropriate cases, a person who does an indecent act in public may be charged under this section with using threatening, abusive or insulting behaviour that is intended to and causes another person harassment, alarm

---

[234] cf. *Marsh v Arscott* (1982) 75 Cr. App. R. 211; *Parkin v Norman* [1983] Q.B. 92; *Read v Jones* (1983) 77 Cr. App. R. 246; *Nicholson v Gage* (1984) 80 Cr. App. R. 40.

[235] See *DPP v Orum*, discussed para.15.193, below.

[236] *DPP v Clarke* (1992) 94 Cr. App. R. 359.

[237] The question whether the person had the requisite intention or awareness is to be answered subjectively by reference to the person's state of mind: *DPP v Clarke* (1992) 94 Cr. App. R. 359.

[238] Inserted by the Criminal Justice and Public Order Act 1994 s.154, with effect from February 3, 1995.

or distress. The offence might, for example, be used in appropriate circumstances to prosecute someone who "moons" at that person or exposes his penis to them.[239]

The offence may be committed in both public and private places, but it   **15.172** cannot be committed when both parties are inside a dwelling (even if they are in different dwellings).[240]

MODE OF TRIAL AND PUNISHMENT

The offence under s.4A(1)(a) of the 1986 Act is triable summarily. The   **15.173** maximum sentence is six months' imprisonment or a fine, or both.[241] Until recently, the maximum fine was a fine not exceeding level 5 on the standard scale (i.e. £5,000). The effect of s.85 of the Legal Aid, Sentencing and Punishment of Offenders Act 2012 is that, from March 12, 2015, a fine of any amount may be imposed. Fines will, however, continue to be set according to the seriousness of the offence and the means of the offender.

"INSULTING BEHAVIOUR"

For the meaning of "insulting", see paras 15.166 and following, above.   **15.174**

"ABUSIVE OR DISORDERLY BEHAVIOUR"

For the meaning of "abusive" and "disorderly", see paras 15.185 and   **15.175** following, below.

"HARASSMENT, ALARM OR DISTRESS"

For the meaning of "harassment, alarm or distress", see para.15.196,   **15.176** below.

DEFENCES

It is a defence under s.4A(3) for the defendant to prove that he was inside a   **15.177** dwelling and had no reason to believe that his behaviour would be seen by a

---

[239] The CPS's Legal Guidance on Public Order Offences does not address the issue of whether and in what circumstances it is appropriate for s.4A to be used in this way: see *http://www.cps.gov.uk/legal/p_to_r/public_order_offences/* [Accessed April 30, 2016].
[240] 1986 Act s.4A(2). Cp. *Rukwira v DPP* [1993] Crim. L.R. 882.
[241] s.4A(5).

person outside that or any other dwelling; or that his conduct was reason-able.[242] The defendant bears the burden of proving these defences on a balance of probabilities.[243]

Mental Element

15.178 The defendant must intend to cause a person harassment, alarm or distress. He may be convicted if he causes harassment, etc., whether to the person to whom he intended to cause it or to another person. So if, for example, the defendant moons at a police officer, who takes it in her stride, but the defendant's behaviour is witnessed by a member of the public who is alarmed or distressed by it, then the offence is committed.

Abusive or Disorderly Behaviour under Section 5 of the Public Order Act 1986

Definition

15.179 Section 5(1) of the Public Order Act 1986 [244] creates an offence of abusive or disorderly behaviour, of lesser gravity than the offence in s.4(1) of the Act. It provides:

> "A person is guilty of an offence if he ... uses threatening or abusive ... behaviour, or disorderly behaviour, ... within the ... sight of a person likely to be caused harassment, alarm or distress thereby."[245]

15.180 The offence was also used to penalise "insulting" behaviour, and as such was sometimes used to penalise indecent acts in public. The word "insulting" was repealed by the Crime and Courts Act 2013 and, as a result, the potential for s.5(1) to be used to penalise indecent acts has greatly reduced. The repeal was the result of increasing criticism of the "insulting behaviour" offence by civil liberties and faith groups, who were concerned by its potential to suppress freedom of expression. These concerns resonated with the Coalition Government, which came to power in 2010 and was committed to restoring rights to non-violent protest. To that end, in October 2011 the Home Office published

---

[242] The question whether the defendant's conduct was reasonable is to be answered by reference to objective standards of reasonableness: *DPP v Clarke* (1992) 94 Cr. App. R. 359.

[243] cf. *Hunt* [1987] A.C. 352, HL. The shifting of the burden of proof may be open to challenge under the Human Rights Act 1998 as being incompatible with art.6(2) ECHR (presumption of innocence): cf. *R. v DPP, Ex p. Kebilene* [2000] 2 A.C. 326, HL; *Lambert* [2002] 2 A.C. 545, HL; *Johnstone* [2003] 1 W.L.R. 1736, HL; *Attorney General's Reference (No.4 of 2004)* [2004] UKHL 43, HL. We suggest that the argument ought to fail, given that the offence is a minor one, the defence is likely to be easy for a defendant to prove, and there is little risk that the reverse burden will lead to the conviction of the innocent. However, there is as yet no reported case on the point.

[244] As amended by the Crime and Courts Act 2013 s.57, with effect from February 1, 2014.

[245] See also s.4A of the Act, inserted by the Criminal Justice and Public Order Act 1994 s.154, which creates an offence of intentional harassment, harm or distress.

a consultation paper seeking views on three areas of police powers which the Government was committed to reviewing, the first being the effect of the word "insulting" in s.5(1) of the 1986 Act.[246] The consultation questions sought to understand the significance of the word "insulting" in s.5(1), the protection it offered to groups targeted by hate crime, and the potential impact of removing the word on the ability of the police to deal with disorder, particularly behaviour such as swearing at police officers and burning poppy wreaths on Remembrance Day. This part of the consultation attracted nearly 3,000 responses, the vast majority supporting the removal of the word "insulting" from the s.5 offence, mostly because of its impact on freedom of expression.[247] Some concern about the removal of the word was expressed by the police and judicial authorities, but the CPS were unable to identify any "insulting" behaviour that could not be characterised also as "abusive", and the DPP was therefore of the view that "insulting" could safely be removed without undermining the ability of the CPS to bring prosecutions. Meanwhile, in December 2012, the House of Lords stole a march on the Government by voting in favour of an amendment to what became the Crime and Courts Act 2013, s.57 of which repealed the word "insulting" from s.5(1). The Government, having considered the responses to the consultation, the advice of the DPP and the views expressed in Parliament, decided not to reverse the amendment. The Home Secretary explained the position as follows during the Second Reading of the Crime and Courts Bill[248]:

> "Let me now deal with [the clause] which would remove the word 'insulting' from the offence of using threatening, abusive or insulting words or behaviour in section 5 of the Public Order Act 1986. This was added to the Bill in the other place. I respect the view taken by their lordships, who had concerns that I know are shared by some in this House about section 5 encroaching upon freedom of expression. On the other hand, the view expressed by many in the police is that section 5, including the word 'insulting', is a valuable tool in helping them to keep the peace and maintain public order.
>
> There is always a careful balance to be struck between protecting our proud tradition of free speech and taking action against those who cause widespread offence with their actions. The Government support the retention of section 5 as it currently stands, because we believe that the police should be able to take action when they are sworn at, when protesters burn poppies on Armistice day and in similar scenarios. We have always recognised that there are strong views in both Houses. Looking at past cases, the Director of Public Prosecutions could not identify any where the behaviour leading to a conviction could not be described as 'abusive' as well as 'insulting'. He has stated that 'the word

[246] *Consultation on police powers to promote and maintain public order* (Home Office, October 2011), available at *https://www.gov.uk/government/uploads/system/uploads/attachment_data/file/157869/consultation-document.pdf* [Accessed April 30, 2016].
[247] *Police powers to promote and maintain public order, Section 5 of the Public Order Act 1986: Summary of consultation responses and Government response* (Home Office, January 2013), available at *https://www.gov.uk/government/uploads/system/uploads/attachment_data/file/157871/consultation-responses-summary.pdf* [Accessed April 30, 2016].
[248] *Hansard*, January 14. 2013, col 642.

'insulting' could safely be removed without the risk of undermining the ability of the CPS to bring prosecutions.' On that basis, the Government are not minded to challenge the amendment made in the other place. We will issue guidance to the police on the range of powers that remain available to them to deploy in the kind of situation I described, but the word 'insulting' should be removed from section 5."

15.181   We entertain some doubt about the blanket assurance conveyed by the DPP's advice. The fact is that the "insulting behaviour" offence was used in the past to penalise some forms of indecent behaviour which may not have been perceived as abusive or, still less, disorderly. Take for example *Vigon v DPP*,[249] in which a market trader covertly filmed customers trying on swimwear in the changing area of his stall. He was convicted of insulting behaviour contrary to s.5(1). It was argued on appeal that his behaviour was not within the ambit of the section, which (it was said) is concerned with the creation of disturbances, the shouting of abuse or obscenities and rowdy behaviour generally. The Divisional Court disagreed, saying that s.5 need not be so limited. The Court accordingly held that the appellant's conduct in setting up the camera, switching it on and letting it run amounted to insulting behaviour within the section. It is easy to see how what was done in that case could be regarded as insulting of the customers. It is more difficult to see that it was abusive, let alone disorderly. What the appellant did undoubtedly involved an abuse of position, but that surely cannot be within the scope of the offence, since otherwise it would criminalise all sharp practice and bullying. However, even if the DPP's advice was mistaken, this is unlikely to mean that indecent behaviour formerly prosecutable under s.5(1) is now not prosecutable at all. Facts such as those in *Vigon* would be prosecutable as voyeurism under s.67 of the 2003 Act, or possibly as an offence of outraging public decency.[250] As for instances of indecent exposure charged as insulting behaviour under s.5(1),[251] such cases are likely now to be prosecuted as offences of exposure under s.66 of the 2003 Act, or again, conceivably, as offences of outraging public decency.[252]

15.182   We nonetheless continue to cover the offence given the possibility that it could be used to prosecute some forms of behaviour that members of the public might consider indecent. The discussion is also relevant to the offence under s.4A(1)(a) of the 1986 Act, discussed above, which creates an offence of using threatening, abusive or insulting words or behaviour, or disorderly behaviour, with intent to cause a person harassment, harm or distress. This offence might be committed where, e.g., a person "moons" another whilst using abusive words or gestures towards them.

---

[249] [1998] Crim. L.R. 289, DC.
[250] cf. *Choi* [1999] EWCA Crim 1279, discussed in para.15.39, above.
[251] cf. *Andrew M*, unreported, January 27, 2000 (No.99/6651/Y3), CA.
[252] cf. *Hardy* [2013] EWCA Crim 2125, discussed in para.15.04, above.

Relationship between s.5 and art.10 ECHR

In *Abdul v DPP*,[253] the Administrative Court said that s.5 is to be read **15.183** together with art.10 of the ECHR and so, at the close of the Crown's case, the judge is required to have regard to art.10 as well as to s.5(1) and s.6(4). The Court said that the principles governing the relationship between s.5 and art.10 could be summarised as follows. The starting point was the importance of the right to freedom of expression, but it was to be recognised that legitimate protest could be offensive, at least to some. The justification for interference had to be convincingly established and the restrictions in art.10(2) were to be construed narrowly. The justification for invoking the criminal law was the threat to public order and was for the Crown to establish. In striking the right balance when determining whether speech was threatening or abusive, the focus on minority rights is not to result in overlooking the rights of the majority. If the line between legitimate freedom of expression and a threat to public order is crossed, freedom of speech will not be impaired by "ruling out" threatening or abusive speech. Finally, the decision is one for the judge and is not to be overturned unless the judge is shown to have been plainly wrong.

MODE OF TRIAL AND PUNISHMENT

An offence under s.5(1) of the 1986 Act is triable summarily and punishable **15.184** by a fine not exceeding level 3 on the standard scale (currently £1,000).[254]

"ABUSIVE OR DISORDERLY BEHAVIOUR"

The words "abusive" and "disorderly" are not defined in the Act. They are **15.185** to be treated as ordinary words in everyday use and given their normal meaning, and the question whether behaviour on any occasion is properly characterised as "abusive" or "disorderly" is to be determined as a question of fact by the magistrates.[255]

Going naked in public

In *Gough v DPP*[256] the well-known pro-nudity campaigner Stephen Gough, **15.186** appealed unsuccessfully against his conviction under s.5(1) after he had walked through Halifax town centre wearing only a hat, socks and walking

---

[253] [2011] EWHC 247 (Admin).
[254] s.5(6).
[255] *Brutus v Cozens* [1973] A.C. 854; *Chambers and Edwards v DPP* [1995] Crim. L.R. 896; *Southard v DPP* [2006] EWHC 3449 (Admin); *Harvey v DPP* [2011] EWHC 3992 (Admin). For the control exercised over magistrates by the Divisional Court, see para.15.166, above.
[256] [2013] EWHC 3267 (Admin).

boots. The decision throws light on the scope for prosecuting authorities to use s.5 to penalise public displays of nudity, whatever their motivation.

15.187   Evidence was adduced at trial that two women were "alarmed and distressed" and "disgusted" at seeing the appellant naked. The district judge, citing authority,[257] held that the appellant's behaviour had caused alarm or distress to members of the public and that the appellant had foreseen that, and at least been aware that his behaviour could have been threatening, abusive, insulting or disorderly. In his defence, the appellant argued that his conduct had been reasonable within the meaning of s.5(3)(c) of the 1986 Act, given that his right to express himself was guaranteed by art.10 ECHR. The judge considered reports from two experts submitted by the appellant, relating to changing public attitudes to nudity and the reactions of children to male nudity, but held that the issues to be determined were for the court and did not require expert evidence. He accepted that art.10 was engaged, on the basis that being naked in public was a form of expression, but held that there was a pressing social need for the restriction of the appellant's right to be naked in the context of this case. The restriction imposed by s.5, under which the maximum penalty was a fine, was a proportionate response to that social need. The judge observed that although public nudity was not, of itself, a criminal offence, s.5(1) was sufficiently clear and accessible, and Parliament had left it to the courts to consider the context of particular facts: "[W]hether behaviour does or does not 'cross the line' is heavily fact dependent and not best criminalised on a 'catch-all' basis". Although the appellant's minority view had to be respected, it did not entitle him to "trample roughshod" over the rights of the majority "to enjoy a shared public space without being caused distress and upset". Accordingly, the appellant could not avail himself of the defence in s.5(3)(c).

15.188   On appeal, it was submitted on the appellant's behalf that he had posed no threat to the public and was not abusive or insulting. The reaction of those whom he passed was temporary and unlikely to reach such a level of emotional significance as to satisfy the threshold of harassment, alarm or distress. Reference was made to naked bike rides and nudist beaches, which were legal and not deemed offensive. It was further submitted that the appellant's behaviour could not be categorised as disorderly: he did no more than walk in his natural state without interfering with others, promoting what he does or challenging those who disagreed.

15.189   In considering whether the elements of the offence were made out, the Administrative Court held that it was not necessary to decide whether the district judge had been right to conclude that the appellant's conduct had been threatening, abusive or insulting; he had been entitled to conclude that, by walking naked through a town centre, the appellant had engaged in disorderly behaviour by contributing "to a breakdown of peaceful and law-

---

[257] *Vigon v DPP* [1998] Crim. L.R. 289, DC, and *Hammond v DPP* [2004] EWHC 69 (Admin).

abiding behaviour as evidenced by the reactions of the public". The appellant had known full well that many members of the public would be alarmed and distressed by sight of his naked body, whether or not others would take a more benign view and whatever the origins or psychological reasons for that alarm and distress. The existence of nudist colonies and naturist beaches were not to the point: they are in areas marked out, clearly identifiable and thus avoidable. Nor was the existence of naked cycle rides determinative. Each case is fact sensitive and must be considered on its merits. In relation to the appellant's intention, on the evidence accepted by the district judge it was beyond argument that, at the very least, the appellant had been aware that his behaviour could be disorderly, which was sufficient for the purposes of s.5(1).

15.190 The appellant renewed before the Administrative Court the argument that his conduct had been reasonable within the meaning of s.5(3)(c), given that his right to freedom of expression is guaranteed by art.10. He argued that public nudity is a form of expression; there was no pressing need to restrict it in pursuit of the aims set out in art.10(2); and criminal sanctions were in any event a disproportionate means of addressing any social need that did exists. The Crown was not prepared to concede that art.10 was engaged, as the appellant's conviction did not regulate or interfere with his right to express his views, to hold opinions or to receive or impart information and ideas. However, it noted that the point was before the European Court of Human Rights in relation to an earlier incident involving Mr Gough[258] and so was prepared, for the purposes of this case only, to proceed on the premise that art.10 was engaged. That being so, the Crown's position was that the appellant was not prevented from being naked in public contexts where nudity is expected or tolerated, but that the adults and children in Halifax town centre on the day in question had no expectation of seeing him naked and so no opportunity to avoid him until it was too late. For that reason the restriction imposed by s.5 corresponded to a pressing social need and, given that s.5 is a summary-only offence with a maximum penalty of a fine at level 3, the prosecution was a proportionate response to the appellant's behaviour. The Court accepted the Crown's submissions, holding that the district judge's analysis of the evidence and the law could not properly be challenged. It had been open to him to reach the conclusions he had and, given the evidence, it was difficult to see how he could have decided otherwise.

15.191 When the Strasbourg Court gave judgment on Mr Gough's application,[259] it held that his repeated arrest, prosecution, conviction and imprisonment for public order offences on account of his being naked in public did not violate his rights under either art.10 or art.8 (right to private and family life). As regards art.10, Mr Gough's public nudity could be seen as a form of expression, and his arrest, prosecution, conviction and detention constituted

[258] *Gough v United Kingdom* (application no.49327/11), October 28, 2014.
[259] *Gough v United Kingdom* (application no.49327/11), October 28, 2014.

repressive measures taken in reaction to that form of expression, so there had been an interference with his exercise of his art.10 rights. However, that interference was justified under art.10(2), as it was the consequence of Mr Gough's repeated violation of the criminal law in full knowledge of the consequences, through conduct which he knew full well, not only went against the standards of accepted public behaviour in any modern democratic society, but also was liable to be alarming and morally and otherwise offensive to other, un-warned members of the public going about their ordinary business. The measures adopted by the police, the prosecuting authorities and the courts met a pressing social need in response to Mr Gough's repeated anti-social conduct and, even if considered cumulatively, were not disproportionate to the legitimate aim being pursued, namely the prevention of disorder and crime. Article 10 does not go so far as to enable individuals, even those sincerely convinced of the virtue of their own beliefs, repeatedly to impose their anti-social conduct on other, unwilling members of society and then, when brought before the courts, to claim a disproportionate interference with their freedom of expression by the state. As for art.8, this cannot be taken to protect every conceivable personal choice by an individual as to his desired appearance in public. There must be a de minimis level of seriousness as to the choice of desired appearance in question, and it was doubtful whether the requisite level of seriousness had been reached in relation to Mr Gough's choice to appear fully naked on all occasions in all public places without distinction, having regard to the absence of support for such a choice in any known democratic society in the world. In any event, even if art.8 were taken to be applicable, the circumstances were not such as to disclose a violation of that provision on the part of the public authorities. Any interference with Mr Gough's right to respect for his private life was justified under art.8(2) for essentially the same reasons as applied in relation to art.10.

15.192   It is notable that Mr Gough was prosecuted in respect of his promenade through Halifax under s.5(1) rather than under s.66 of the 2003 Act (exposure of the genitals), doubtless because his conduct was, rightly, perceived to be a public order matter rather than a form of sex offending.[260] That said, Mr Gough did intentionally expose his genitals with the intention that other people would see them; and whilst he may not have desired to cause those people alarm or distress (indeed, quite the opposite), given the reactions that he had provoked on previous occasions he was virtually certain to alarm or distress someone who saw him, and must have known this to be the case, such that he could be said to have intended that result.[261] In other words, there may well have been an evidential basis for a conviction under s.66 had such a charge been brought.

---

[260] For the CPS guidance on prosecuting nudity in public, see *http://www.cps.gov.uk/legal/l_to_o/nudity_in_public/* [Accessed April 30, 2016].
[261] *Woollin* [1999] 1 A.C. 82.

"WITHIN THE SIGHT OF A PERSON LIKELY TO BE CAUSED"

Section 5, unlike s.4, does not require the abusive or disorderly behaviour to **15.193** be "used towards another person". However, it must occur within the sight of a person likely to be caused harassment, alarm or distress thereby. Evidence from a witness that he or she was harassed, alarmed or distressed will not necessarily be conclusive of this point, as the crucial question is whether the act occurred within the sight of a person who was *likely* to be so affected.[262] Thus in *Harvey v DPP*,[263] which involved the use of swear words in public, the conviction was quashed as there was no evidence that anyone had experienced harassment, alarm or distress as a result and no basis for inferring that anyone within earshot had been likely to experience such a reaction. What if the conduct is witnessed by a police officer? It was held in *DPP v Orum*[264] that a police officer may be a person likely to be caused harassment, alarm or distress within the meaning of s.5(1). However, the Court said this did not mean that every police officer who witnesses behaviour within the scope of s.5(1) would be likely to be harassed, alarmed or distressed by it. The question whether the behaviour had the effect described in the section is one of fact to be determined by the magistrates.[265]

In *Norwood v DPP*,[266] the Divisional Court held that it is not necessary **15.194** that the behaviour was actually seen by someone who was likely to be caused harassment, alarm or distress; it is sufficient that the behaviour was plainly capable of causing harassment, etc., to persons passing by who might see it. The case concerned a poster offensive to Muslims which the appellant, a member of the BNP, placed in the window of his home. The thrust of the decision is that he could be convicted without proof that the poster had actually been seen by someone of that faith. A similar issue arose in *Holloway v DPP*,[267] in which *Norwood* was not cited. In that case, the appellant had filmed himself naked in a rural location, with schoolchildren playing on a sports field in the background. There was an express finding that no one actually saw the appellant's behaviour. His appeal against conviction was allowed. Collins J (as he then was) said:

> "[I]t is not sufficient that someone might have come on the scene and therefore might have seen what the individual who is charged was doing . . . What, in my view, is required is that there is at least evidence that there was someone who

[262] cf. *Chief Constable of Lancashire v Potter* [2003] EWHC 2272 (Admin), at [34].
[263] [2011] EWHC 3992 (Admin).
[264] [1988] 3 All E.R. 449, DC. See also *Taylor v DPP* and *R. v DPP*, discussed below.
[265] cf. *Southard v DPP* [2006] EWHC 3449 (Admin); *Cheeseman v DPP* (1991) 93 Cr. App. R. 145; *Parkin v Norman* [1983] Q.B. 92, discussed in para.15.166, above; and see para.15.56, above.
[266] [2003] EWHC 1564 (Admin); [2003] Crim. L.R. 888; and see *Norwood v UK* (2005) 40 E.H.R.R. SE11 (application to the European Court of Human Rights claiming a breach of art.10 declared inadmissible).
[267] [2004] EWHC 2621 (Admin).

could see, or could hear, at the material time, what the individual was doing."[268]

He added:

"It may be that what I am saying goes to the evidence which has to be called in order to establish this offence because I do not believe it to be necessary that the prosecution call a person or persons who can say that they did see what was happening. The evidence must be sufficient, so that the court can draw the inference, having regard to the criminal standard, that what he was doing was visible or audible to people who were in the vicinity at the relevant time."[269]

In *Taylor v DPP*,[270] a third Divisional Court said that in *Holloway*, Collins J was right to say that there must be evidence that someone was able to see or hear the defendant's conduct, and that the prosecution does not have to call evidence from a person who did see or hear it. But it is not enough to establish that someone might have come on the scene and observed what was going on. This is, with respect, a persuasive analysis which also ensures there is no air-gap between *Norwood* and *Holloway*. In the former, it was plain on the evidence that the poster was freely visible to passers-by, some of whom were likely to find it offensive; whereas in the latter, the most that could be said was that there was a possibility that someone could have stumbled on the scene.

15.195   The s.5(1) offence may be committed in both public and private places, but it cannot be committed when both parties are inside a dwelling (even if they are in different dwellings).[271]

"Harassment, Alarm or Distress"

15.196   The Act contains no definition of "harassment", "alarm" or "distress". They are likely to be treated as ordinary words, the meaning of which is to be determined as a question of fact by the magistrates.[272] It was held in *Lodge v DPP*[273] that "alarm" in s.5 is not confined to alarm for oneself, but extends to alarm felt for the safety of an unconnected third party. In other words, it is an offence under the section for X to use abusive or disorderly behaviour within the sight of Y, if the behaviour is likely to cause Y to be alarmed for the safety of Z, who is unknown to Y. In *R. v DPP*[274] the Divisional Court held that "harassment, alarm or distress" are "relatively strong words" and that "distress" requires "real emotional disturbance or upset".

---

[268] paras 28–29.
[269] para.32.
[270] [2006] EWHC 1202 (Admin).
[271] 1986 Act s.5(2). Cp. *Rukwira v DPP* [1993] Crim. L.R. 882.
[272] cf. *Chambers and Edwards v DPP* [1995] Crim. L.R.896. For the control exercised over magistrates by the Divisional Court, see para.15.166, above. For the meaning of "harassment" in s.4(1) of the Protection from Harassment Act 1997, see *Curtis* [2010] EWCA Crim 123.
[273] *The Times*, October 26, 1988, DC.
[274] [2006] EWHC 1375 (Admin), a decision relating to the more serious offence in s.4A(1) of the 1986 Act.

DEFENCES

It is a defence under s.5(3) for the defendant to prove that he had no reason   **15.197**
to believe there was any person within sight who was likely to be caused
harassment, alarm or distress; or that he was inside a dwelling and had no
reason to believe that his behaviour would be seen by a person outside that
or any other dwelling; or that his conduct was reasonable.[275] The first of these
grounds of defence ensures that, if the defendant engaged in conduct before
people who he thought were *not* likely to be harassed etc. by it, but he
miscalculated and one of the witnesses was in fact harassed, he should be
able to avoid conviction. The defendant bears the burden of proving these
defences on a balance of probabilities.[276]

MENTAL ELEMENT

Section 6(4) of the Act[277] provides that a person is guilty of an offence under   **15.198**
s.5 only if he intends his behaviour to be abusive or disorderly, or is aware
that it may be.[278] It is further provided by s.6(5) that a person whose
awareness is impaired by intoxication shall be taken to be aware of that of
which he would have been aware if not intoxicated, unless he shows either
that his intoxication was not self-induced or that it was caused solely by the
taking or administration of a substance in the course of medical treatment.

OTHER RELEVANT OFFENCES

It used to be common for local Acts and bye-laws to contain offences relating   **15.199**
to indecent behaviour in public. Section 231(1)(d) of the Public Health Act
1936[279] provided that a local authority may make bye-laws with respect to
public bathing and may by such byelaws regulate, so far as decency requires,
the costumes to be worn by bathers. The provision was repealed by the Local
Government and Public Involvement in Health Act 2007 with effect from

---

[275] The question whether the defendant's conduct was reasonable is to be answered by
reference to objective standards of reasonableness: *DPP v Clarke* (1992) 94 Cr. App. R. 359.
[276] cf. *Hunt* [1987] A.C. 352, HL. The shifting of the burden of proof may be open to challenge
under the Human Rights Act 1998 as being incompatible with art.6(2) ECHR (presumption of
innocence): cf. *R. v DPP, Ex p. Kebilene* [2000] 2 A.C. 326, HL; *Lambert* [2002] 2 A.C. 545, HL;
Johnstone [2003] 1 W.L.R. 1736, HL; *Sheldrake v DPP* [2004] UKHL 43, HL. We suggest that
the argument ought to fail, given that the offence is a minor one, the defence is likely to be easy
for a defendant to prove, and there is little risk that the reverse burden will lead to the conviction
of the innocent. However, there is as yet no reported case on the point.
[277] As amended by s.57 of the Crime and Courts Act 2013, with effect from February 1,
2014.
[278] The question whether the defendant had the requisite intention or awareness is to be
answered subjectively by reference to the defendant's state of mind: *DPP v Clarke* (1992) 94 Cr.
App. R. 359.
[279] 26 Geo. 5 & 1 Edw. 8 c. 49.

January 27, 2010.[280] However, s.235 of the Local Government Act 1972[281] empowers district and London borough councils to make byelaws for good rule and government and for the suppression of nuisances.[282] Among the model form of Good Rule and Government Byelaws that used to be issued by the Home Office for the guidance of such councils was a byelaw relating to indecent bathing, which provided that no person should within 200 yards of any street or public place, bathe from the bank or strand of any water, or from any boat thereon, without wearing a dress or covering sufficient to prevent indecent exposure of the person. This provision no longer appears in the model Byelaw now issued by the Department for Communities and Local Government;[283] but this does not mean that a byelaw in these terms could no longer be made, nor that existing byelaws in these terms are no longer valid.

15.200 Section 235(3) of the 1972 Act provides that byelaws shall not be made for a purpose for which provision is made by another enactment. This provision was considered in *Owen v DPP*,[284] where the appellant had engaged in mutual masturbation with another man and was convicted of an offence of indecency with another person in a public place, contrary to Byelaw 16 of the London Borough of Ealing Byelaws. He contended on appeal that Byelaw 16 was invalid by virtue of s.235(3), as the conduct falling within it was proscribed by a number of other enactments, i.e. s.28 of the Town Police Clauses Act 1847 (indecent exposure), s.13 of the Sexual Offences Act 1956 (gross indecency between men) and s.5 of the Public Order Act 1986 (insulting or disorderly behaviour). His appeal was dismissed, the Divisional Court holding that the range of conduct covered by Byelaw 16 and its purpose were sufficiently different from the enactments cited by the appellant to avoid offending against s.235(3). The presence of some overlap with the general law did not render the Byelaw invalid.

15.201 In *DPP v Gawecki and Bazar*[285] the respondents had allegedly engaged in similar behaviour to the appellant in *Owen*. Informations were laid charging them with committing an act of indecency being an offence which was not already punishable "in a summary manner" by virtue of an Act of Parliament, contrary to Byelaw 23 of the City of Westminster Byelaws for Good Rule and Government. They were acquitted on the ground that their

---

[280] Local Government and Public Involvement in Health Act 2007 ss.135, 241 and Schs 6, para.2(c), and 18, Pt 7. For commencement, see SI 2010/112.

[281] 1972 c.70.

[282] For the equivalent power in Wales, which is conferred on county and county borough councils, see the Local Government Byelaws (Wales) Act 2012 s.2, which was brought into force on March 31, 2015, by SI 2015/1025 (W.74). Prior to that date the power in s.235 of the Local Government Act 1972 extended to councils of principal areas in Wales. The power was limited to English councils by a consequential amendment made by the 2012 Act s.20 and Sch.2, para.9(1), (2).

[283] See *https://www.gov.uk/government/publications/good-rule-and-government-model-byelaw-8* [Accessed April 30, 2016].

[284] [1994] Crim. L.R. 192.

[285] [1993] Crim. L.R. 202.

conduct was covered by the offence in s.13 of the Sexual Offences Act 1956 of gross indecency between men, which was triable either way and so, the magistrate held, was punishable in a summary manner. On appeal by the prosecution, the Divisional Court held that an offence is punishable in a summary manner if, when committed by an adult, it is triable only summarily, so that there was no clash between Byelaw 23 and the gross indecency offence.

It is an offence under s.2 of the Ecclesiastical Courts Jurisdiction Act 1860[286] to use "riotous, violent or indecent behaviour" in a place of religious worship. It has been held that the word "indecent" in this provision has no sexual connotation and that the offence relates to the creation of a disturbance in a sacred place.[287] Nonetheless, in *Blake and Austin v DPP*[288] the appellants were convicted under s.2 for masturbating in a churchyard.   **15.202**

---

[286] 23 & 24 Vict. c. 32.
[287] *Abrahams v Cavey* [1968] 1 Q.B. 479; *Farrant* [1973] Crim. L.R. 240. A similar limitation applies to the offences of violent or indecent behaviour in a police office or police station house, contrary to the Metropolitan Police Act 1839 s.58, and the Town Police Clauses Act 1847 s.29.
[288] [1993] 97 Cr. App. R. 169; [1993] Crim. L.R. 283.

CHAPTER 16

POLICE INVESTIGATION OF RAPE AND SERIOUS SEXUAL
OFFENCES

By Assistant Commissioner Martin Hewitt QPM,
Metropolitan Police Service*

Introduction.................................... 16.01   Primary Guidance Documents 16.11
The Structure of Police Rape   The Investigative Process................. 16.12
  Investigations.............................. 16.07   Conclusion..................................... 16.35

INTRODUCTION

Rape and other serious sexual offences are among the most serious and **16.01**
damaging offences that the police deal with, and present unique investigative
and prosecution challenges. The legal framework is covered in detail
elsewhere in this work; the purpose of this chapter is to explore the practical
application of the law by the police, and to describe the key considerations
that will be in the mind of an investigating officer.

The fact that rape, and other sexual offences, are, in essence, the coming **16.02**
together of some form of power and some form of vulnerability present real
complexity in the effective management of both victim and suspect. Furthermore, the challenge is exacerbated by the backdrop against which
investigations take place. That backdrop has a number of elements, and they
are worth briefly describing in order to set the context.

First, there is a moral ambiguity in society about sexual offending where **16.03**
both victims and suspects are variously demonised depending on the
perspective of the commentator. Even the use of the term "victim", which is
entirely uncontroversial in all other crime types, is strongly opposed in some
quarters, where the preferred term would be "survivor". From an opposing
perspective, there continues to be a use of language that implies some form
of culpability on the part of the victim. Such a position has no foundation,

---

* National Policing Lead for Adult Sexual Offences.

but yet it persists, and forms part of what are referred to in this chapter as "rape myths and stereotypes".

16.04   Secondly, the history and narrative of the police investigation of rape is both challenging and very resistant to change. Going as far back as the infamous rape episode in Roger Graef's ground-breaking fly-on-the-wall documentary made with Thames Valley Police in 1984, the media focus has been on inadequate recording practices, insensitive handling of victims, missed investigative opportunities and failed trials. Undoubtedly, there have been significant failings in the past and, indeed, some contemporary cases will not meet the standard that is set. But the service has learned and developed policy and practice, and continues to do so. This chapter will give a brief description of the current thinking and approach that is taken.

16.05   Finally, it is important to note that the investigation of rape can only achieve success through the effective collaboration of a number of agencies, groups and individuals. This is driven primarily by the fact that the complex and individual needs of victims, which extend well beyond those traditionally seen within the criminal justice system, must be met if each victim is to become a survivor. Players in this collaboration include police officers, support workers from groups such as Rape Crisis and Survivors Trust, Independent Sexual Violence Advisors ("ISVAs"), various medical practitioners, and lawyers and advocates.

16.06   The purpose of this brief introduction has been to give a sense of the complex environment in which rape investigation by the police takes place, and to convey some of the real pressures that are faced by investigators, supervisors and managers.

THE STRUCTURE OF POLICE RAPE INVESTIGATIONS

16.07   The National Police Chief's Council ("NPCC") has a chief officer that undertakes the lead role for Adult Sexual Offences. The purpose of the role is to represent the NPCC on matters relating to such offences, to provide operational direction and co-ordination, to be the national liaison with other interested organisations, and to work closely with the College of Policing in the formulation of policy and guidance. As this role only specifically covers offences where the victim is an adult, there is a close working relationship with the chief officer who has the NPCC lead for Child Sexual Offences. This has become particularly important in recent years with the significant rise in the reporting of rape and other sexual offences, and especially in circumstances when an adult makes a complaint about non-recent offending that occurred when they were a child. Due to the prevalence of rape offences in a domestic or relationship setting, there is similar close working with the chief officer lead for Domestic Abuse. The NPCC lead for Adult Sexual Offences works in conjunction with the Director of Public Prosecutions ("DPP"), and they are both signatories to the April 2015 *Joint CPS and*

Police Action Plan on Rape.[1] That plan seeks to address current gaps in the response to rape and will be discussed in more detail below.

The NPCC lead chairs a national working group that brings together the **16.08** full spectrum of parties with an interest in the process of rape investigation and prosecution (police, CPS, support groups, NHS, Sexual Assault Referral Centre representatives, Home Office, Her Majesty's Inspectorate of Constabulary and the College of Policing). This group is supported by regional meetings that are chaired by the deputy lead. Each force in England and Wales retains operational independence and configures its resources to deal with rape in line with its overall deployment plan. All forces have officers trained and accredited to deal with rape offences, and many forces have dedicated specialist teams who have this as their sole function.

In each police area there will be Sexual Assault Referral Centres **16.09** ("SARCs") which provide a medical environment in which to support victims, and which undertake the forensic retrieval processes that will often be critical to an investigation. These centres are staffed by a range of medical practitioners who provide emotional, psychological and physical care. The lack of consistency in geographic coverage, range of capabilities and quality of service in the SARCs is a challenge that is being addressed at a national level. In support of this statutory care, local police will all have relationships with the range of support groups that exist across the country. These groups are vital in providing additional and ongoing support to victims, whether or not they have reported an offence to the police.

A key partnership in every police area will be with the Crown Prosecution **16.10** Service. In each CPS area there is a Rape and Serious Sexual Offences Unit ("RASSO") that handles all prosecutions of rape and other serious sexual offences. The RASSOs have recently been reviewed in order to improve consistency. Once again, there are geographic variations not only in the make-up of the units, but also in the way in which they work with police. Models range from entirely separate to entirely co-located, dependent on local circumstances and decision-making.

PRIMARY GUIDANCE DOCUMENTS

As noted above, recent work has been undertaken to identify and address the **16.11** gaps in the police investigation of rape. Joint work between all parties, but particularly the police, the CPS and the College of Policing, has produced a range of guidance documentation to assist practitioners in the application of the law and in the discharge of their particular responsibilities in the process of taking a rape allegation from report to trial. It is useful to give a brief description of each of these documents:

---

[1] Available at *http://www.cps.gov.uk/publications/equality/vaw/rape_action_plan_april_2015.pdf* [Accessed April 30, 2016].

Authorised Professional Practice (APP) Rape and Sexual Offences—Currently under revision by the College of Policing in conjunction with the NPCC lead, this document provides the definitive description of investigative practice for rape.

Protocol between the police service and Crown Prosecution Service in the investigation and prosecution of rape[2]—This document reflects national police and CPS policy and demonstrates a commitment to work together in order to improve consistency, performance, service to victims, and public confidence in the response to rape.

Police investigators toolkit for addressing consent and associated myths in rape cases—Produced in response to the Joint CPS and Police Action Plan on Rape, this document covers a range of investigative considerations that are associated with the issue of consent in rape allegations.

Toolkit for police supervisors and managers addressing consent and associated myths in rape investigations and prosecutions—Covers the same issues as the investigators toolkit, and then goes on to discuss the decision making process for No Further Action (NFA), and risk assessment and exit strategy processes at the end of an investigation.

Rape cases—police referral to the Crown Prosecution Service for early investigative and other advice—Provides clarity on Early Investigative Advice and the criteria for charging advice.

Toolkit for addressing consent and associated myths for reviewing lawyers in rape cases—Building on the police documents above, this toolkit guides the lawyer in preparing papers for prosecuting advocates.

Toolkit for addressing consent and associated myths for prosecuting advocates—contains guidance in case preparation for rape trials with an emphasis on dealing with consent.

Whilst this chapter will not cover each of these documents in detail, they do demonstrate the degree of joint working between police and CPS and the centrality of dealing effectively with the issue of consent in rape cases.

THE INVESTIGATIVE PROCESS

16.12 In this section, we outline the key considerations for investigators as they progress a rape case. For many years there has, quite properly, been a clear drive to conduct "victim focused" investigations. This has partly been in response to criticism of insensitive handling of victims, but is also a result of ever greater appreciation of the needs of those that have been victims of these crimes. The outcome has been a number of practice developments. The primary one, from a policing perspective, has been the introduction of specially trained officers to take the victim through the investigative process

---

[2] Available at *https://www.cps.gov.uk/publications/agencies/cps_acpo_rape_protocol_v2-1.pdf* [Accessed April 30, 2016].

from shortly after the point of reporting. Such officers are accredited for the role, and combine the challenging requirements of providing support to the victim whilst gathering best evidence to assist building the case. As referred to above, much of the early phase of support and evidence retrieval should take place at a SARC. These are medical facilities and are staffed with medical practitioners. Their primary function is to meet the emotional, psychological and physical medical needs of the victim, with the secondary function being the provision of a suitable environment in which the police can undertake the initial evidence gathering processes. This will include taking accounts from the victim and retrieving appropriate evidence through the forensic medical examination.

It is very important to stress that attendance at the SARC, and submitting **16.13** to all the processes therein, is an entirely voluntary action on the part of the victim. The offence of rape is one in which the loss of power and control by the victim plays a significant part, and this must not be exacerbated by the investigation making the victim feel that once again they have no control. The pace and the extent of the process must be led by the victim, and the evidential consequences have to be accepted.

Adopting a "victim focused" approach has had many benefits and has **16.14** undoubtedly contributed to an increase in confidence amongst victims that they will be treated sensitively and professionally if they report an offence to the police. This has played some part in the significant year-on-year increases in reported offences that have been seen since 2012. More recently, however, there has been a growing realisation that investigative practice needed to re-balance, and whilst continuing to ensure that an effective response is maintained for victims, greater attention needed to be paid to the offender in constructing a case. This seeks to take the process away from being an examination focused on the credibility of the victim, to one that is an examination of the credibility of all the surrounding facts and circumstances.

We will now work through the elements of the investigation to explain the **16.15** key considerations in the mind of the investigator.

Identifying risk factors—suspect and victim

It is essential that risk factors are identified at the earliest opportunity. This **16.16** will not only uncover potential evidence, but may also be critical from a safeguarding perspective. It will be a priority to understand any particular and ongoing vulnerability on the part of the victim, and it must be ascertained whether the suspect, particularly if unidentified at that point, presents an ongoing threat to either the victim or others.

In relation to potential suspects, understanding their actions in the **16.17** reported offence and building up a picture of previous behaviour will be critical in building an "offender centric" case.

If the suspect is not identified at this stage, patterns of other offending may **16.18** assist identification. As the knowledge of the psychology of sexual offending has developed, it has become possible to use previous offending history to add supporting context to the current behaviour, or lead to the identification of potential suspects. Previous violence, particularly with the use of a weapon, and previous sexual offences are clearly of interest. Additionally, prowling type offences are often a precursor to substantive sexual offences, as can be burglary offences that do not appear to have had any sexual connection.

16.19   As stated above, in the majority of rape cases there will be some form of vulnerability present in the victim that has been exploited by the offender. This may, in some cases, be a vulnerability that has some degree of permanence and renders the individual vulnerable in a more general sense, such as being a child or having some form of mental impairment. In other cases, the vulnerability can be temporary and very much circumstantial. This is an extremely important point to understand in building a case and a prosecution. In some cases, the victim will be an individual who would not in any ordinary circumstances be viewed as a vulnerable person. Indeed, they can often be powerful and assertive people. But at a particular point in time, due to particular circumstances, there was a vulnerability that the offender exploited. Proving this by evidence, and presenting it at trial, is the essential challenge of rape investigation and prosecution.

16.20   The specially trained officers who support victims through the process have the responsibility to identify risk factors, and to build an understanding of how vulnerability played a role in the offender's selection of the victim. There are many possible factors that may play a part, and some victims may be subject to multiple vulnerability factors simultaneously. It is critical to allow victims to articulate their own perception of risk, and particularly any concerns that they may have about future harm. This is vital from a safeguarding perspective, but also for the continued engagement of the victim with the criminal justice process. Disability, incapacity, location and opportunity are all self-evident vulnerability factors. It is also a fact that certain social behaviours and occupations place someone at a statistically higher chance of becoming a victim of a sexual offence. Sex workers, for example, are a highly victimised group who often present multiple vulnerability factors. Indeed, the very fact that they are a cohort that has very low reporting rates to the police provides yet another vulnerability factor that will make them a target group for predatory offenders.

Prioritised forensic opportunities

16.21   In dealing with a victim, the priority is to deal with any urgent medical requirements. Once this has been done, a forensic medical examination should take place. Both the specially trained officer and the forensic physician have a responsibility to explain the process in as much detail as possible to the victim. As has already been said, this process must be conducted at the pace determined by the victim. Conducting what is by

necessity a medico-legal procedure in the hours immediately after a traumatic emotional and physical assault requires considerable skill and sensitivity, and the role of the forensic physician is at all times both therapeutic and
forensic. Relevant samples will be collected and injuries will be recorded.
These may become particularly important in case building, and non-intimate
injuries may be photographed by a Crime Scene Investigator ("CSI"). The
forensic medical examination process must also record any treatment and
arrange any further or ongoing treatment that may be required.

Evidential opportunities associated with specific types of cases

To "categorise" rape offences is an approach that brings with it significant **16.22**
difficulties. It can cause an investigator to restrict their thinking, it can create
expectations of behaviour on the part of both victim and offender and, most
damagingly, it can lead to some rape offences being seen as "more serious"
than others. All of these consequences must be avoided if possible. That said,
the context in which particular offences are committed may clearly be
relevant in terms of evidential requirements and opportunities. For example,
in a domestic or relationship rape, understanding the nature and history of
the relationship will be critical in assessing the control and vulnerability
factors. It will also be very important from a safeguarding perspective to try
to establish whether the offence has taken place within the context of broader
domestic abuse. Acquaintance rape will require specific evidence of how
victim and offender came to be in contact, and communication both before
and after the alleged offence will be critical evidence. This is especially
relevant in the age of social media and internet dating, where such
communication will have a key role in supporting or undermining consent.
Drug assisted offences will present particular challenges and opportunities
from a forensic perspective, and where a rape is committed by multiple
offenders, building a picture of the broader context in which the offence
occurred will often be critical. But to reiterate, categorising offences must be
done to assist in thinking through the investigative and evidential requirements, and not in any way to place them in some form of hierarchy. Each
offence is individual and unique.

General evidential considerations

As with any serious crime investigation, the expectation is that the inves- **16.23**
tigator will exhaust all opportunities to gather relevant evidence. It would be
neither fruitful nor appropriate to cover all such opportunities in any detail
here. Suffice to say that witness evidence, CCTV, communications evidence,
Automatic Number Plate Recognition ("ANPR"), covert techniques, financial investigation and searches of various types may all be legitimate lines of
enquiry, depending on the circumstances of the offence. This is in addition to
the evidence gathered through the victim interview and forensic medical

examination. Wherever possible, the victim interview will be video-recorded and will be undertaken in accordance with the Achieving Best Evidence ("ABE") guidance.[3] The nature of ABE interviews and their presentation at court is a subject of considerable debate, and following the publication of a joint report by Her Majesty's Inspectorate of Constabulary and Her Majesty's Crown Prosecution Service Inspectorate, a response is being prepared by the NPCC lead for Investigative Interviewing. One of the key issues in relation to the victim interview is appreciating that it may be necessary to deal with inconsistencies between the account given and subsequent independent evidence that is gathered. On this basis, it is not uncommon for victims to undertake a number of interviews during the course of an investigation. Because of the nature of rape as an offence, and the psychological affect that it can have, there may be many reasons for such inconsistencies.

16.24   Guidance concerning suspect interviews is found primarily in the *Authorised Professional Practice (APP) on Investigative Interviewing*. Such interviews in large part follow standard processes. There are, however, a number of particular aspects to rape suspect interviews that are worthy of note. First, in most forces the practice is that the specially trained officer who supports the victim and undertakes much of the evidence retrieval from the victim is not the actual investigating officer. This requires a high degree of liaison between the two officers to ensure that the investigative plan is as comprehensive as it can be and that the investigating officer has a thorough grasp of all the contextual detail discussed above. Secondly, in rape cases there are usually three lines of potential defence: that the victim has fabricated the offence, that there was consent to the act(s), or that the police have identified the wrong person. The interview plan must be able to address each of these defences. Finally, there is a growing body of research on the psychology of sex offenders that is beginning to point to different approaches to suspect interviews that will better allow police to gather the key evidence to meet the challenge of the issue of consent.

The issue of consent

16.25   Consent sits at the heart of every rape investigation and prosecution. The legal definition of consent and the case law that explains it are covered in Ch.1. In the research that led to the 2015 *Joint CPS and Police Action Plan on Rape*, it became clear that there was a lack of understanding of consent amongst both police officers and lawyers that was leading to inadequate investigations and court presentation. In one sense, this lack of clarity reflects the wider societal confusion that exists about consent in rape. Any scan of the media at the time of notable rape cases will illustrate that even among

---

[3] Available   at   *https://www.cps.gov.uk/publications/docs/best_evidence_in_criminal_proceedings.pdf* [Accessed April 30, 2016].

intelligent and well-informed commentators, the range of diametrically opposed views on the consent is both remarkable and concerning. If such ambiguity exists in the relatively sterile environment of the court, it presents a considerable challenge for potential victims and potential suspects at the point where sexual feelings are aroused. And, as one is bound to conclude, if this lack of clarity exists in society as a whole, then it exists in police officers, lawyers and juries as well.

Much is being done to raise awareness and understanding of the consent **16.26** issue, and to challenge the "rape myths" that have persisted over time as society has struggled to develop its understanding of sexual violence. Specifically, within the *Joint Action Plan* is a commitment to produce clear and practical guidance for police officers and lawyers that not only gives them a sound understanding of the legal definition on consent contained in s.74 of the Sexual Offences Act 2003, but also guides them as to the evidence required to rebut defences and the way in which such evidence should be presented at court. These guidance documents are identified above. It is worth giving a brief description of the evidential issues and the investigative considerations that are laid out for police officers.

In the first instance, broader contextual issues have to be considered and **16.27** understood. The victim's age, maturity and level of understanding are all critical to their capacity to consent. The relationship history between the parties, if one exists, is of significance, particularly if it conveys some sort of position of power on the part of the offender. Additionally, especially in the case of younger victims, any evidence of grooming activity such as the provision of gifts, lifestyle changes and insincere gestures of affection, will be important contextual evidence of the motivation of both victim and offender. This has become particularly significant as our understanding of the nature and extent of child sexual exploitation has developed over the last few years.

The guidance then focuses on four key areas for consideration: *capacity to* **16.28** *consent, freedom to choose, steps taken to obtain consent* and *reasonable belief in consent*. In each area the investigator is pointed towards the key questions to ask. In *capacity to consent*, the focus is on self-evident vulnerability factors such as the influence of alcohol, drugs or an incapacitating medical condition. It asks whether the victim suffers from a learning or physical disability, has a mental health issue or was actually asleep or unconscious at the time of the incident. In *freedom to choose*, the focus shifts more towards coercive or controlling factors such as the application of drugs or alcohol, the impact of an abuse of power or a domestic abuse scenario, or some other form of deception by the offender. *Steps taken to obtain consent* is a critical evidence-gathering exercise that will either support or undermine the accounts of the parties. Consent is given, not taken, and all the circumstances must be examined to ascertain the actions of the suspect in this regard. Finally, *reasonable belief in consent* challenges whether the suspect's belief that consent had been given was reasonable when considered in the context of all the surrounding circumstances. This section also asks the investigator to consider whether any of the six rebuttable presumptions of absence of consent, as laid down by s.75 of the Sexual Offences Act 2003, apply in the circumstances.

16.29   The guidance then goes on to address a number of additional areas that support the initial analysis and also assist the investigator in challenging some of the "rape myths and stereotypes" that are often used by the defence to undermine the credibility of a victim and their account. The clothing that the victim was wearing may well have contributed to the reasons why they were targeted by the offender, but it has no impact on the issue of consent. Equally, there can be no standard response to a rape. Victims will display very different responses to the trauma of an offence that can range from being vocal to being entirely withdrawn. Neither is right or wrong, and neither signifies a greater or lesser veracity to the complaint. Additionally, the impact of trauma can lead to memory loss and inconsistency that do not necessarily undermine the truth of an account. Finally, there is the issue of how a victim defends themselves. A lack of overt and physical resistance is often portrayed as in some way representing consent. This must be challenged evidentially as academic research shows that most victims do not fight. In many cases, defence is through dissociation and this must be thoroughly covered in both victim and suspect interviews.

16.30   The objective of all this investigative activity is to build a case with a clear narrative to help advocates challenge assumptions about consent and the associated victim-blaming myths and stereotypes that are still prevalent. In doing so, it will set out a case theory, centred on the issue of consent, that demonstrates how the suspect made choices as to how they would commit the offence in a way that was hoped to prevent or limit the likelihood of being caught and convicted.

Police disposal decision-making

16.31   The issue of the police taking a decision that No Further Action ("NFA") is warranted is worthy of brief discussion as it is very significant in terms of public confidence in rape investigation. Such a decision can only be authorised by an officer holding the substantive rank of Inspector. The decision must be based solely on the evidential test and must not rely on public interest considerations. The decision should apply only to cases that cannot and will not be able to meet the appropriate evidential standard (full code or threshold test). NFA will only be authorised when all lines of enquiry have been exhausted and there is no prospect of improving the evidential case. The decision in such cases must be based on facts alone, and not on opinion. Of particular importance is that such a decision must never be based on an assessment of the credibility of victims or witnesses. Where such a decision is taken, it must be formally recorded with a clear articulation of the facts on which it is based. It is critical that the decision is appropriately and sensitively communicated to the victim. This should be done by the specially trained officer who has been working with them, who should clearly explain the victim's right to have the decision reviewed.

Both the individual and broader implications of NFA are well understood, **16.32** and in most force areas Joint Scrutiny Panels have been established to dip-sample NFA decisions in order to provide reassurance and feedback. Typically, the panels are made up of police, CPS and third sector representatives.

The decision to NFA requires the completion of risk assessments on both **16.33** victim and suspect and the construction of an exit strategy that identifies any forward looking actions that are required to mitigate the risk identified in that process. In relation to the victim, this exercise is very much about ensuring ongoing support and assisting their progress towards becoming a survivor. In relation to the suspect, this is a public protection activity. First, consideration must be given to submitting details of the offence to the National Crime Agency Serious Crime Analysis Section for comparison with other predatory sexual offences. It must then be considered whether an application should be made to a court for the suspect to be made subject of one of the two preventive orders provided for in Pt 2 of the Sexual Offences Act 2003, i.e. a Sexual Harm Prevention Order related if the suspect has been cautioned, or a Sexual Risk Order, which is available in relation to any individual sufficient against whom sufficient evidence exists to convince a magistrate that the individual poses a risk of sexual harm.

Early Investigative Advice

The final area to be covered from the investigative perspective is liaison with **16.34** the CPS, particularly in relation to the provision of Early Investigative Advice ("EIA"). A lack of consistency in this area was identified in the research that led to the *Joint CPS and Police Action Plan on Rape*, and the guidance is now clear. Work within both agencies is under way to ensure that guidelines are followed and that the required capability and capacity exists to support the provision of timely and effective advice. Cases of rape or other serious sexual offences should be referred by the police supervisor to a prosecutor as soon as a suspect is identified, or when it becomes apparent that the continuing investigation will provide evidence upon which a charging decision may be made. Additionally, a case may be forwarded for EIA to ensure early development of a joint strategy for prosecution where the expertise of a lawyer will assist in directing investigative activity in order to meet all the evidential requirements set out above.

CONCLUSION

The effective investigation of rape is one of the greatest challenges that **16.35** policing faces. Cases are often highly complex and will invariably present vulnerability factors in the victim that would be unusual in other crime types. These factors are challenging to manage effectively in the course of an investigation, and even more so in the prosecution and trial processes. The position is further complicated by the fact that offenders are often predatory and extremely devious in the way that they identify and target their victims with the very objective of frustrating a potential investigation and prosecution.

16.36   All of this takes place against a media and public backdrop that indicates ever-developing attitudes to sexual behaviour and an ambiguity about sexual offending that pervades all elements of society. Most significantly, the degree of confusion that exists about the legal concept of consent presents the single greatest challenge to the work, and this is why providing clarity to police and prosecutors on this point is at the heart of the 2015 *Joint CPS and Police Action Plan on Rape.*

CHAPTER 17

PROSECUTING RAPE AND SERIOUS SEXUAL OFFENCES—
CPS POLICY AND DECISION-MAKING

By Alison Levitt QC* and Tim Thompson**

Introduction..................................... 17.01
The Full Code Test.......................... 17.03
The Evidential Stage: Common
  Myths and Stereotypes and the
  "Merits-Based" Approach............ 17.06
Withdrawal of Allegations............... 17.17
Cases Involving Children................. 17.21

Abuse of Process, Reconsideration
  of Decisions Not to Prosecute
  and the Victims' Right to Review
  Scheme 17.28
The Public Interest Stage of the
  Full Code Test............................. 17.35
False Rape Allegations 17.48
Breaches of the Non-Reporting
  Provisions.................................... 17.66

INTRODUCTION

Crown Prosecution Service ("CPS") decisions as to whether to prosecute are **17.01**
governed by the *Code for Crown Prosecutors*.[1] This requires prosecutors to
apply the test set out in section 4, known as the "Full Code Test",[2] which is
described in the paragraphs which follow. Decisions in cases involving
allegations of rape or other serious sexual offences are made on the same
basis as those made in relation to all other kinds of crime, from fraud to road
traffic, and involve the application of the same criteria. There is no different
standard.

---

* Partner, Mishcon de Reya, Principal Legal Advisor to the Director of Public Prosecutions
2009–2014.
** Managing Associate, Mishcon de Reya, Deputy Chief Crown Prosecutor CPS until
2015.
[1] See *www.cps.gov.uk/publications/code_for_crown_prosecutors* [Accessed April 30, 2016]. The
Code is issued by the Director of Public Prosecutions under the Prosecution of Offences Act
1985 s.10. The current edition is the seventh, issued in January 2013.
[2] The Full Code Test is applied when the investigation is complete. Occasionally a prosecutor
is required to apply the "threshold test" in cases where the evidence is incomplete, but this is of
limited relevance in cases involving sexual offences.

17.02   Sitting beneath the Code are a number of pieces of published Legal Guidance and policy.[3] These are issued sporadically by the CPS and have two distinct but related purposes. The first is to provide guidance to prosecutors to help them to apply the law in particular situations and in a consistent fashion. The second is to allow the public to see the basis upon which prosecutorial decisions are made: the guidance provides both transparency and accountability, in that the public can see the way in which decisions are reached, and victims[4] may be able to hold the CPS accountable, through the mechanism of judicial review, should prosecutors fail to apply it properly. There are a number of pieces of CPS Legal Guidance which are either directly or tangentially relevant to the prosecution of rape; some of these are considered in this chapter.

THE FULL CODE TEST

17.03   The test set out in the Code consists of two stages: an evidential sufficiency stage followed by a public interest stage. These must be applied sequentially. As a consequence, if there is insufficient evidence a prosecution will not take place, irrespective of such public interest factors as the seriousness of the allegation, the sensitivity of the case or the wishes of the complainant. As the *Policy on Prosecuting Cases of Rape*[5] makes clear, whilst the views and interests of the victim are important, they cannot be the final word on the subject of a CPS prosecution.

17.04   At the evidential sufficiency stage, the prosecutor is required to make an objective assessment as to whether there is a realistic prospect of conviction.[6] This means that he or she must conclude that " . . . an objective, impartial and reasonable jury or bench of magistrates or judge hearing the case alone, properly directed and acting in accordance with the law, is more likely than not to convict the defendant of the charge alleged".[7] This is a higher standard than that applied by a judge when considering the state of the evidence at the conclusion of the prosecution case (that is to say, whether there is a case to answer), but is lower than the standard of proof required before the tribunal of fact can convict.

17.05   In considering whether the tribunal of fact is more likely than not to convict, the prosecutor should judge the available evidence according to its

---

[3] The Code, para 2.6, requires prosecutors to have regard to CPS policy and legal guidance.

[4] Most CPS policy and legal guidance uses the word "victim" rather than the less controversial "complainant". In common with the practice generally adopted in this book, we have tended to use "complainant" when referring to individual cases but "victim" when speaking generically.

[5] "the Rape Policy", available at: *www.cps.gov.uk/publications/docs/rape_policy_2012.pdf* [Accessed April 30, 2016].

[6] This is not uncontroversial. Some are strongly of the view that, provided there is sufficient evidence to establish a case to answer, the case should go before a court for determination rather than it being left to the judgement of an individual prosecutor as to the likely outcome.

[7] The Code para.4.5.

admissibility, reliability and credibility.[8] He or she must also take into account what is known about the defence case, including any evidence or other information provided on behalf of the suspect. This may involve more than simply considering what (if anything) has been said by the suspect in interview: for example, it is not uncommon for a suspect's legal representatives to write to the CPS at the pre-charge stage either drawing the prosecutor's attention to particular material or making representations as to the application of the Full Code Test. The Code requires prosecutors to give these representations proper, objective consideration.[9]

THE EVIDENTIAL STAGE: COMMON MYTHS AND STEREOTYPES AND THE "MERIT-BASED" APPROACH

In rape cases, the evaluation of the reliability and credibility of evidence can give rise to particular difficulty. It is axiomatic that rape rarely takes place in front of witnesses, so that in the majority of cases the evidence consists of no more than the complainant's account. Because of concern about the risk of false allegations, investigators, prosecutors and juries may feel uneasy about the prospect of convicting on the basis of one person's word against another's. In some cases this has led to the burden of proof being interpreted as meaning that some supporting evidence (that is to say, evidence which, objectively considered, reinforces the truth of the complainant's allegation) is required before it is safe to convict. However, whilst taking a cautious approach is understandable and even superficially attractive, there can be little doubt that if it is followed to its logical conclusion many true complaints of rape would never be prosecuted. The Legal Guidance[10] and the Rape Policy make it explicit that, Parliament having abolished the requirement for corroboration,[11] the CPS must be careful not to reintroduce it by the back door, for example by deciding that there is no realistic prospect of conviction simply because there is no supporting evidence. | 17.06

An inevitable consequence of this is that where the prosecution case consists solely of the complainant's account, with no supporting evidence, the prosecutor is faced with the difficult task of assessing how a jury will resolve the conflict in the evidence. In the absence of any independent material capable of acting as a barometer, the jury will have little option but to consider whether the complaint is inherently believable or whether there are features either of the complaint itself or aspects of the complainant's behaviour which make it less likely to be true. | 17.07

Whilst this is unavoidable, experience has shown that the use of "common sense" as the touchstone of reliability and credibility should be approached | 17.08

---

[8] The Code para.4.6.
[9] The Code para.4.5.
[10] http://www.cps.gov.uk/legal/p_to_r/rape_and_sexual_offences/ [Accessed April 30, 2016].
[11] See paras 19.106 and following, below.

with caution. As the psycho-legal analysis of violent sexual offences has evolved and become more sophisticated, it has revealed that many people —not just jurors, but lawyers and judges too—hold deeply-rooted beliefs about rape which are in fact wholly without scientific or other foundation. These assumptions, which are known collectively as "rape myths and stereotypes", continue to present obstacles to the successful prosecution of rape.[12] Some of them may have been consigned to history but there are others which undoubtedly have currency. For example, it is unlikely that evidence of the way a woman dresses would, these days, be seen as having any relevance to the issue of whether or not she consented to sexual activity. Thus a defendant who sought to argue that he believed that the complainant would consent to intercourse solely on the basis of her appearance would be unlikely to be acquitted. But that can be contrasted with the prevalent belief that rapists are likely to be inadequate and unattractive; thus those who are seen as having no "need" to rape (such as a good-looking man or a man who is married and whose wife gives evidence about the frequency with which they have sex) may be less likely to be convicted. Another frequently-encountered myth is that rape will usually result in some form of physical trauma, with the concomitant risk that if there is no evidence of injury the jury may treat that as proof that the complainant consented.

17.09   A further example of a prevalent myth is that a genuine victim of rape would be likely to make immediate complaint (a relic of the old rule about raising the hue and cry). The corollary is the belief that an allegation which is not reported straightaway is unlikely, or less likely, to be true. However, research has shown that many truthful complainants hesitate before telling anyone about what has happened to them, so that evidence of delay in making the complaint is likely, in the majority of cases, to be neutral (in the sense that in and of itself it is not a reliable indicator as to where the truth lies). Yet prosecutors continue to be confronted with evidence that investigators, as well as the public at large, consider delay in complaining to be a factor which weakens the allegation.

17.10   Issues such as these present a dilemma for the prosecutor, who is required by the Code to assess whether a jury is more likely than not to convict. Experience has taught many of those involved in the criminal justice system that, in what may be perceived as "difficult" cases, such as where there has been delay in reporting or the complainant has been drinking, juries have proved reluctant to convict. Yet to decline to charge on the basis of factors that are known to be without substance is not only intellectually unsatisfactory but may actively contribute to the problem, in that it reinforces some of these unfounded beliefs.

17.11   In 2009, the Administrative Court heard the case of *R. (FB) v DPP*.[13] Although the case concerned a physical rather than a sexual assault, the

---

[12] *http://www.cps.gov.uk/legal/p_to_r/rape_and_sexual_offences/societal_myths/*   [Accessed April 30, 2016].
[13] [2009] EWHC 106 (Admin).

issues considered are of direct relevance to the decisions which prosecutors are required to make in rape cases. In *FB*, the prosecution had decided to offer no evidence on the basis that the complainant's mental health condition made him an inherently unreliable witness. Toulson J (as he then was), in a judgment which repays reading, said:

> "There was also discussion whether in applying the 'realistic prospect of conviction test' a prosecutor should adopt a 'bookmaker's approach' (as it was referred to in argument) or should imagine himself to be the fact finder and ask himself whether, on balance, the evidence was sufficient to merit a conviction taking into account what he knew about the defence case. In many cases it would make no difference, but in some it might . . .
>
> There are some types of case where it is notorious that convictions are hard to obtain, even though the officer in the case and the crown prosecutor may believe that the complainant is truthful and reliable. So-called 'date rape' cases are an obvious example. If the crown prosecutor were to apply a purely predictive approach based on past experience of similar cases (the bookmaker's approach), he might well feel unable to conclude that a jury was more likely than not to convict the defendant. But for a crown prosecutor effectively to adopt a corroboration requirement in such cases, which Parliament has abolished, would be wrong. On the alternative 'merits based' approach, the question whether the evidential test was satisfied would not depend on statistical guesswork."

It is this which has come to be known as the "merits-based approach". In **17.12** the context of sexual offences, what this means is that even though past experience might tell a prosecutor that juries have been unwilling to convict in cases where, for example, the complainant has mental health issues or learning difficulties, factors of this sort should be treated with caution when deciding whether or not there is a realistic prospect of conviction. The prosecutor should proceed on the basis of a notional jury which is wholly unaffected by any myths or stereotypes, which will act in a rational way and will faithfully follow directions on the law.[14] Examples of the judicial directions on the way a jury should approach issues such as delay, consumption of alcohol, lack of injury, withdrawal of consent in long relationships and so on, are to be found elsewhere in this work.

Taking a merits-based approach is not uncontroversial. There has been **17.13** criticism of the CPS attitude, on the basis that requiring prosecutors to charge cases in defiance of what is seen as common sense and experience of real life has a number of undesirable consequences. It is said that the complainant is unnecessarily exposed to the experience of being cross-examined before the inevitable acquittal, the defendant is put through the anxiety, expense and publicity of a trial, and scarce public resources are expended on prosecutions which are highly unlikely to succeed.

The CPS counters that to decline to prosecute a case on the basis that a **17.14** jury may be ignorant, irrational or prejudiced, or will refuse to apply the directions on the law which it is given, is in fact to apply a different standard to rape cases from that which would be applied in any other. For example,

---

[14] CPS Rape Policy.

were a black lesbian to be a victim of a street robbery, no prosecutor would decline to prosecute on the off-chance that the jury might prove to be racist or homophobic. In addition, predictions as to the outcome of a trial based on past experience are inescapably flawed, because a jury does not give reasons for its decision. Thus although the judge, lawyers or police may believe that the jury acquitted because of the existence of a factor such as delay in reporting, they may be mistaken. This would be a fragile foundation upon which to build a prosecutorial policy.

17.15   The CPS argues that in addition to the logic of not basing prosecutorial decisions on an intellectually flawed analysis, there are sound policy reasons for adopting the merits-based approach. Research has shown that many rapists seek out vulnerable people, such as those with mental health issues or physical disabilities, on the basis that it is easier to commit offences against them, they are less likely to report the behaviour and less likely to be believed if they do. A system which does not seek justice for the vulnerable not only offends against the provisions of the Human Rights Act 1998 but also runs counter to the beliefs and values of those who work within it and is plainly difficult either to justify or to explain. There is, too, evidence of success in the application of the merits-based approach, which has on occasion resulted in convictions being achieved in cases which would previously have been unimaginable, for example those where the victims have had physical disabilities, such as cerebral palsy, or learning difficulties.[15]

17.16   It is now settled that the merits-based approach will be adopted by prosecutors in all cases. Decisions in rape cases are made by specialist prosecutors who operate in Rape and Serious Sexual Offences units ("RAS-SOs") and have received extensive training on how to eliminate the so-called myths and stereotypes from their analysis of the evidence. That being said, there is evidence that some degree of oversteering may have taken place since the judgment in *FB*. Some prosecutors appear to have interpreted the guidance as meaning that all complaints should result in prosecution even when this involves ignoring obvious flaws in the case. As a result, further guidance has been issued[16] which reminds prosecutors that the merits-based approach does not require them to suspend logic or judgment, but merely to make decisions which are fair and reasonable. The prosecutor needs to be able to distinguish between a difficult case and one which is evidentially weak.

Withdrawal of Allegations

17.17   It is a common feature of allegations of sexual offences that the complainant may reconsider having made the allegation and say that he or she no longer wishes to give evidence. The issue for the prosecutor is whether that decision

[15] See, e.g. *Watts (James Michael)* [2010] EWCA Crim 1824.
[16] *http://www.cps.gov.uk/legal/l_to_o/merits_based_approach/* [Accessed April 30, 2016].

should be accepted unquestioningly and the prosecution brought to an end, or whether more can or should be done. A related—and unresolved—issue is whether, where the prosecution is halted because of the complainant's wishes, this is an evidential decision or a matter for prosecutorial discretion at the public interest stage. This may matter little in the majority of cases but is likely to become important in the event that the decision is challenged.[17]

There is a distinction to be drawn between a complainant who is said no **17.18** longer to "support" the prosecution and one who actually refuses to give evidence. Police and prosecutors sometimes treat these expressions as being interchangeable, but this is a mistake, as they give rise to different considerations. The first question a prosecutor should ask is whether the complainant is saying that, given the choice, he or she would rather a prosecution didn't take place, or whether he or she is in fact refusing to come to court. As far as the former is concerned, the Code makes it plain that whilst the views of victims are important, a prosecution is not a private matter between complainant and defendant, and so the victim's views cannot be determinative of whether a prosecution should or should not take place. Conversely, a complainant who refuses to come to court to give evidence may make a prosecution difficult or indeed impossible. But even then, the *CPS Rape Policy* makes it plain that the fact that the victim does not want to give evidence should not, without more, be treated as conclusive[18]:

> "We know that some victims will find it very difficult to give evidence and may need practical and emotional support . . . Sometimes a victim may withdraw support for a prosecution and may no longer wish to give evidence. This does not mean that the case will automatically be stopped."

The *Policy* and the CPS Legal Guidance require that the prosecutor should **17.19** approach the case by, first, considering the reasons given as to why the complainant does not wish to "support" the prosecution, and, secondly, seeing whether there are any special measures or other steps which could be taken to allay the concerns. If not, then consideration should be given to whether it is possible to continue the prosecution without the complainant's evidence, for example by obtaining other evidence or by use of the rules permitting hearsay evidence to be given. If this proves impossible then the prosecutor should consider whether to continue with the prosecution against the complainant's wishes by compelling him or her to attend court. Usually the means of compulsion will involve the obtaining of a witness summons, but real difficulties will arise if the complainant still declines to attend court as the next step will be to obtain a warrant for his or her arrest. Plainly, this would be an exceptional course to take because of the obvious risk that the complainant may see this as compounding the harm caused by the original

---

[17] It is suggested that the better view is that it is a public interest decision, unless there are factors which make the evidence unreliable or it actually becomes impossible to call the complainant, for example because he or she can no longer be put forward as a witness of truth.

[18] CPS Rape Policy paras 5.7–5.20.

offence, but the prosecutor's duty to the public at large requires that consideration should at least be given to this possibility.

17.20   In a small but nevertheless significant number of cases, the complainant not only declines to cooperate with the police but seeks to bring the investigation or prosecution to an end by asserting that the allegation was in fact untrue. Predominantly this occurs in situations where the complainant and suspect are married or in a relationship. This particular form of adamancy presents the prosecutor with real difficulty: he or she is required to form a judgment as to whether the original complaint was genuine and it is the retraction which is a lie, or vice versa. In some of these cases the prosecutor has concluded that, irrespective of the complainant's current attitude, the evidence remains sufficiently strong for there to be a realistic prospect of conviction in relation to the original charge. In the majority of cases, however, it is impossible to continue with the prosecution of the original allegation; where that is the case, the prosecutor must take care not to fall into the trap of concluding that, without more, the original allegation is necessarily false and thus could found a charge of perverting the course of justice. This aspect is considered in greater detail under the heading 'False rape allegations', below.

Cases Involving Children

17.21   Allegations of rape and sexual assaults against children are some of the most difficult cases with which prosecutors deal. Whilst the test for a prosecution is the same, the decisions as to reliability and credibility of evidence can be even more complex than those involving adult complainants. For example, it is a common characteristic of these offences that victims may feel unable to tell anyone for many years and the prosecutor will then have to consider the effect of the passage of time, with its attendant difficulties such as loss of documents, on the prospects of successfully prosecuting the case to conviction.

17.22   Where the victim complains close to the time of the commission of the offence and is thus still a child at the time of the trial, this brings further complications. Children often struggle to give their account in a conventional "linear" way, or may have difficulty in giving a coherent account of the time when the offence took place; factors such as these may make the complaint appear unreliable to adult eyes. In addition, it is now known that some children give their account piecemeal, often holding back the most serious allegations. Adults may be inclined to treat this as evidence of unreliability, but there is a psychological explanation for this behaviour: that the child may be testing the adults to see whether they believe him or her before giving the full story. It is not uncommon for a child to make an allegation of sexual touching which is then followed up some time later by a far more serious allegation of oral or vaginal rape. It is particularly important in such cases that the prosecutor does not allow him- or herself to fall into the trap of believing that if the child were telling the truth, he or she would necessarily have made the most serious allegations at the first available opportunity.

Recent cases have shown that police and prosecutors have not always got   **17.23**
the decisions right. In 2013, the CPS was driven to conclude that when the late Jimmy Savile was still alive, it had made the wrong decision not to prosecute him for allegations of sexual assault on girls. Similar conclusions were reached about the failure to prosecute in cases involving the grooming of vulnerable children in the Rotherham and Rochdale cases. Although the issues were different, a common theme emerged from these cases: that in order to guard against false allegations, police and prosecutors had approached complaints of sexual offences with excessive caution. This reflects the concern of society at large, namely that there is a real and prevalent risk that someone will make a false allegation that a suspect will find impossible to disprove. In the Savile case, this manifested itself in a police decision not to tell each complainant that there were others, with the consequence that each believed that she was the only one and was thus understandably nervous about making a complaint against such a famous and powerful man. In the grooming cases, a similarly equivocal approach informed the assessment of the complainants and their lifestyles. Frequently, great weight was placed upon the fact that the complainants were in care, took drugs, drank to excess or had a history of making complaints and then retracting them. These factors were seen as making their allegations inherently unreliable. Whilst superficially understandable, this ignored the reality that many victims are preyed upon precisely because their lifestyles or personal difficulties make them susceptible to abuse. To decline to prosecute such cases risks leaving vulnerable children unprotected by the criminal law. It is also unlawful.[19]

Following the conclusion of the Savile investigation, the then Director of   **17.24**
Public Prosecutions, Sir Keir Starmer QC, expressed his intention that this should be a watershed moment. He announced a raft of measures intended to improve the handling of sexual abuse cases, including the issuing of new guidelines on child sexual abuse. The interim guidelines were published in June 2013 following extensive consultation with the police, and informed by a series of round-table discussions attended by front-line investigators, lawyers, victims' representatives, academics, social services, the judiciary, and others with an interest or expertise in criminal justice. The interim guidelines were put out for public consultation, the result of which indicated broad endorsement of the new approach. The final guidelines were published in October 2013[20] and apply to all allegations of sexual assaults on children, regardless of whether the complainant is still a child or is now an adult. Cases where the allegations relate to a period some time earlier are generically described by police and CPS as "non-recent", as the expression "historic" is

---

[19] *R. (FB) v Director of Public Prosecutions* [2009] EWHC 106 (Admin).
[20] *www.cps.gov.uk/legal/a_to_c/child_sexual_abuse* [Accessed April 30, 2016].

disliked by victim groups on the ground that it suggests the harm and damage caused is confined to the past.

17.25   Fundamental to the new guidelines is the approach to be taken when assessing the complainant's evidence: police and prosecutors are reminded that they are required to focus on the credibility of the allegation rather than forming value judgements about the personal characteristics or lifestyle of the person making it. It is emphasised that the complainant's circumstances or experiences may influence his or her choices and behaviour and prosecutors need to have an understanding of these issues. By way of example, victims of grooming may themselves have committed criminal offences; this should not be seen as inevitably fatal to the prospects of a successful prosecution. It is recognised too that groomed children frequently return to the suspect, mistaking the attention given for genuine love and concern: they often do not see themselves as victims, instead believing that they are in authentic loving relationships. In situations such as these, both police and prosecutors need to have a sophisticated and informed attitude to the issue of consent.

17.26   The need to challenge canards such as these does not end with the CPS and police. The prevalence of myths and stereotypes has caused prosecutions to fail at trial. The CPS Legal Guidance requires that prosecuting advocates should be instructed to present the case in a way which addresses and neutralises any false assumptions, should they arise. They should consider the directions which appear at Ch.17 of the *Crown Court Bench Book* and, where appropriate, invite the trial judge to give them.

17.27   An unsatisfactory feature of investigations into the sexual abuse of children has been the haphazard approach taken to material in the possession of social services, schools and other organisations not party to the criminal trial process. All too frequently it has been left to individual resident judges to issue local practice directions which would determine whether or not it was possible to gain access to those files even for the preliminary purpose of assessing their content for relevance. This had obvious potential for injustice. In an effort to address this, the CPS has published a joint *Protocol and Good Practice Model*[21] governing disclosure of information in cases of alleged child abuse and linked criminal and family proceedings, the intention being that the approach to so-called third-party disclosure in such cases will be both streamlined and consistent across England and Wales. The *Protocol* deals with how material can, and should, be exchanged from the outset of a police investigation and from the stage when Family Court proceedings are contemplated by a local authority. It is, though, a matter for each local authority to decide whether to adopt the *Protocol*. The *Protocol* is considered in Ch.18.

---

[21] Published October 2013 and available at *http://www.cps.gov.uk/publications/docs/third_party_protocol_2013.pdf* [Accessed April 30, 2016].

Abuse of Process, Reconsideration of Decisions not to Prosecute and the Victims' Right to Review Scheme

It should be noted that the CPS Legal Guidance on Abuse of Process[22] **17.28** appears not to have been updated for some time and as a result should be approached with caution. One important point of principle which should be borne in mind is this: the fact that there is a potential abuse of process argument rarely provides a proper basis for not prosecuting or not continuing with an existing prosecution. *R. (on the application of Guest) v DPP*[23] is authority for the proposition that, in a case which would otherwise have gone ahead, prosecutors should decide not to charge on the basis of a possible abuse of process application only where it is clear that the application would succeed. The majority of cases should be put before a court for the decision to be made.

There is a discrete aspect of the abuse of process jurisprudence which can **17.29** properly to be considered in this context, which is the CPS approach to reconsidering an earlier decision not to prosecute. Section 10 of the Code provides as follows:

> "People should be able to rely on decisions taken by the CPS. Normally, if the CPS tells a suspect or defendant that there will not be a prosecution, or that the prosecution has been stopped, the case will not start again. But occasionally there are reasons why the CPS will overturn a decision not to prosecute or to deal with the case by way of an out-of-court disposal or when it will restart the prosecution, particularly if the case is serious."

Section 10 gives four examples of situations in which a decision not to **17.30** prosecute might be reversed, the most significant of which in this context is where:

> "a new look at the original decision shows that it was wrong and, in order to maintain confidence in the criminal justice system, a prosecution should be brought despite the original decision".

The CPS has given anxious consideration to what is meant by a decision which is "wrong". Some have taken the view that a decision not to prosecute should only be overturned where it fails the *Wednesbury* test, that is to say, it was a decision which no reasonable prosecutor could have made. The previous DPP took the view that such a restrictive test was neither fair to complainants nor conducive to public confidence and the test should be simply whether, on consideration of the Code Test, the decision was "wrong". Thus under the present system, the views of the most senior prosecutor involved in the chain of decision-making will prevail.

Such cases are sometimes characterised as the CPS "going back on a **17.31** decision" not to prosecute. The limits as to when this is permissible were

---

[22] *http://www.cps.gov.uk/legal/a_to_c/abuse_of_process/* [Accessed April 30, 2016].
[23] [2009] EWHC 5494 (Admin).

considered in *Abu Hamza*,[24] in which it was held that reconsideration by the prosecution was unlikely to constitute an abuse of process unless there has been both an unequivocal representation by those charged with the conduct of the investigation or prosecution of a case that the defendant would not be prosecuted, and the defendant has acted on that representation to his or her detriment.

17.32   *Abu Hamza* was applied in *Killick*,[25] in which three adult men with cerebral palsy had made allegations of rape against the defendant. The defendant had been told on more than one occasion that he would not be prosecuted; nevertheless (following a complaint from the victims) the decision was found by the CPS to have been wrong. The defendant was charged and subsequently convicted on two of three counts, the convictions being upheld by the Court of Appeal. The Court held that victims have a right to a review in circumstances such as these but should not have to seek recourse to judicial review. It invited the CPS to put in place a clearer procedure compatible with art.10 of European Union Directive 2012/29/EU, which establishes minimum standards as to the rights, support and protection of victims of crime.

17.33   As a result the CPS introduced the Victims' Right to Review ("VRR") scheme.[26] The scheme provides a mechanism whereby a victim is able to seek a review of a decision not to charge, to discontinue or otherwise to terminate proceedings. A "victim" is defined, for the purposes of complaints made on or after December 10, 2013, as "a person who has suffered harm, including physical, mental or emotional harm or economic loss which was directly caused by criminal conduct". This includes bereaved relatives and parents of children under 18. The scheme has two stages: a review at local level, followed, if the complainant remains unsatisfied, by a further review at either Chief Crown Prosecutor[27] level or within the Appeals and Review Unit. Perhaps understandably, there have been suggestions that the lawyers involved in the Appeals and Review Unit will be unlikely to overturn decisions made elsewhere in the CPS. This scepticism is not borne out by the decisions made by the Unit which, at least on an anecdotal basis, displays an admirable independence and has reversed a number of decisions not to prosecute.

17.34   In October 2015, in *S v CPS*,[28] the Administrative Court considered an application for permission to apply for judicial review of a decision taken under the VRR scheme. The case concerned an allegation of rape and the issue was the complainant's capacity to consent to intercourse in the light of the amount of alcohol she had consumed. The principal submissions were, first, that the suspect should have been notified that the review was taking place and given the right to make representations and, secondly, that in order

---

[24] [2007] 1 Cr. App. R. 27.
[25] (2011) EWCA Crim 1608.
[26] *http://www.cps.gov.uk/victims_witnesses/victims_right_to_review/* [Accessed April 30, 2016].
[27] Or Head of Division.
[28] [2015] EWHC 2868 (Admin).

to prosecute the suspect at this stage, the CPS needed to prove to the criminal standard that the original decision was *Wednesbury* unreasonable. Those arguments were roundly rejected by Sir Brian Leveson P. Although the VRR scheme guidance provided that a suspect was not to be made aware of a victim's request for a review during the review process, which meant that the suspect could not make representations to the reviewing prosecutor, that did not mean it was contrary to natural justice. The guidance required the reviewing prosecutor to take account only of information available at the time of the decision under review, which would include any explanation the suspect provided during the preceding investigation. Natural justice did not require a decision-maker who was assessing only pre-existing material, and who was prohibited from taking into account new evidence or information from the person seeking the review, to invite a response from a third party who might be effected by the result of the review. As for the claimant's argument relating to the *Wednesbury* test, this would impose a duty on the CPS to prove its case in judicial review proceedings, whereas the function of the review was to provide a mechanism for a fresh reconsideration of the facts. In the present case, the reviewing prosecutor considered the available evidence fully and properly, correctly identified evidence from which a penetrative sexual act could be inferred, and properly approached the law which required the issue of capacity to consent to fall within the province of the jury. Since there was sufficient evidence to demonstrate that the complainant lacked capacity to give consent to sexual intercourse, there was evidence to demonstrate lack of consent. On that basis, the reviewer concluded that the case should be tried. Axiomatically, she considered that the approach of the original decision-makers was wrong, and was entitled to conclude that the instant case was one in which maintenance of public confidence in the criminal justice system required a prosecution. It was not remotely arguable that her decision was irrational or unreasonable. The Court took the opportunity to restate the general principles governing the role of the court in the superintendence by judicial review of prosecutorial decisions: future applications for judicial review will depend on the reasonableness of the VRR decision which is being impugned.

The Public Interest Stage of the Full Code Test

It has never been the rule that simply because there is sufficient evidence to bring a prosecution, one will automatically take place. In every case, once the prosecutor has determined that there is a realistic prospect of conviction, he or she must then go on to consider whether the public interest requires a prosecution to take place. That being said, in a case in which there is sufficient evidence, a prosecution will generally take place unless the prosecutor determines that there are public interest factors tending against prosecution which outweigh those tending in favour.[29] It must be emphasised

17.35

---

[29] The Code para.4.8.

that this is not simply a question of adding up the factors on each side: each case is fact-sensitive and a single factor may be of such significance that it outweighs a number on the other side. In all cases, prosecutors are required to consider whether the case should go ahead and the judge invited to consider any public interest factors in the suspect's favour as mitigation when determining the sentence.

17.36   The Code lists seven factors which should be considered at the public interest stage but stresses that these are not exhaustive. The factors are: the seriousness of the offence, the culpability of the offender, the harm caused to the victim, the victim's circumstances (for example whether he or she was especially vulnerable, or whether the offence involved a breach of trust), whether the suspect is under 18, community impact, proportionality and the protection of confidential sources.

17.37   In the majority of cases involving sexual offences, the allegations are so serious that it is likely that a prosecution will be required, irrespective of the public interest factors tending against. There are two exceptions to this general rule: where the suspect is a child and where the offence alleged took place a very long time ago and a nominal penalty appears likely, particularly if the suspect is now in poor health.

Where the suspect is a child

17.38   In all cases, the Code requires prosecutors to address with particular care the question whether to prosecute a suspect who is under the age of 18. The starting point is, as in every case, the evidential stage of the full Code test: if there is no realistic prospect of conviction then the consideration of the public interest does not arise. If there is sufficient evidence, then the age of the suspect is a factor which requires specific and explicit consideration in relation to the public interest in prosecuting. There is extensive CPS Legal Guidance on the topic of prosecuting children, both generally and in relation to sexual offences.[30] Decisions to prosecute children must only be taken or approved by prosecutors who are designated "youth specialists". The prosecutor must consider a range of factors including the views of the alleged victim, the interests of the child suspect, the views of expert agencies concerned in the welfare of children, the need to divert children away from the criminal justice system where possible and the potential need for positive action.

17.39   Where the alleged victim was under 13 at the relevant time, CPS Guidance states that the appropriate charge will be under ss.5–8 of the Act and that prosecutors should not charge under ss.1–4. In cases where the alleged victim was 13, 14 or 15 at the relevant time, the appropriate charge will be under ss.9–12 of the Act, but will be charged as an offence contrary to section 13. See further paras 4.144 and following, above.

---

[30] *www.cps.gov.uk/legal/p_to_r/rape_and_sexual_offences/youths/* [Accessed April 30, 2016].

A common feature of cases involving child suspects is that the suspect asserts that the alleged victim consented or indeed actively participated in the behaviour complained of. However, the law does not permit a defence of consent where the alleged victim was under the age of 16. Thus the arguably absurd position is reached where each child is in law the "victim" of the behaviour of the other and the designation as suspect or victim is dictated solely by whose parents or carers go to the police first. In these cases it is particularly important to assess factors which in the majority of cases involving an adult suspect would be largely irrelevant. These include the relative ages of the suspect and the alleged victim, their sexual and emotional maturity, the existence and nature of any relationship between them, any element of seduction or exploitation, and the impact of a prosecution on each child involved. In some cases it may be clear that a serious sexual offence has been committed, but the prosecutor must be cautious about jumping to conclusions that one child was the victim of the other, when that may not have been the case. Often parents and carers of the alleged victim find it impossible to accept that their child may have been a willing participant or even the instigator, particularly if the sexual activity includes some form of penetration. The investigator must be encouraged to obtain material such as internet searches or social media exchanges, which may provide evidence of the true nature of the relationship or the relative degree of involvement of each child. As Lord Thomas CJ said in *R. v DS, TS*[31] (albeit in a different context):

> "[investigators should appreciate] given the widespread use of social media, that it is likely that in many cases of sexual offending which arise contemporaneously that what is contained on social media is likely to be relevant and sometimes of great importance".

Additional guidance is provided to prosecutors in cases where the children involved are siblings, with the emphasis on considering alternatives to prosecution where the activity was wholly consensual.

Non-recent cases in which a nominal penalty is likely

17.41
In some cases it is clear from an early stage in the investigation that a nominal penalty is likely in the event of conviction. Two situations in which this is likely to arise are:

- Where the suspect has been already been prosecuted, convicted and sentenced for offending which is in effect part of the same conduct; and
- Where the suspect is unfit to plead but would not be made subject to a mental health disposal in the event of a finding of fact, so that an absolute discharge is the only likely outcome.

[31] [2015] EWCA Crim 662 at [51].

17.42   However, even in situations such as these, it is by no means certain that no
prosecution should take place. Often it is far from automatic that there will
in fact be a "nominal penalty". Whilst consideration should be given to the
guidance on "Minor Offences",[32] it is emphasised that some offences would
now be viewed more seriously than they may have been in the past.
Prosecutors are also reminded to consider possible ancillary orders such as
Sexual Harm Prevention Orders (where they are available given the date of
the alleged offence).

17.43   Even where it is concluded that a nominal penalty is likely, there may still
be legitimate reasons why a prosecution is in the public interest. Prosecutors
are reminded that punishment is only one of the reasons for prosecuting:
others include rehabilitation of the offender (for example, if restorative
justice measures are available), deterrence of others, justice for victims,
encouragement to others to report similar offences and public confidence in
the administration of justice.

17.44   In the section headed "Offender's culpability in hiding the offending",[33]
the guidance indicates that particular consideration should be given to the
question whether the suspect has failed to take an earlier opportunity to
admit the offences now under consideration, or to have them taken into
consideration by an earlier sentencing court.

17.45   The guidance deals in some detail with the need for the prosecutor to take
the views of the complainant into account. But it reminds prosecutors that
these views should be weighed against the likely outcome, and that the
prosecutor must not treat himself or herself as being bound by them.

17.46   By their nature, many non-recent cases may involve suspects who are
elderly. As people are living longer, dementia is becoming more common
amongst elderly persons and, as a result, some suspects may not be fit to
plead. Such suspects are unlikely to be suitable for a mental health disposal,
as there is no treatment that will cure dementia. They would therefore be
likely to receive an absolute discharge (a nominal penalty). The guidance
states that where the suspect is unfit to plead, "where a mental health
disposal is not available or not appropriate, in some circumstances this may
mean that it is less likely that a prosecution is required". The fact that this
single sentence contains three qualifications ("some", "may" and "less
likely") is an indication of the difficulties these cases present. Prosecutors are
referred to the Legal Guidance on Mentally Disordered Offenders,[34]
para.4.12 of the Code; the public interest factors in the specific guidance, and
two additional principles, namely that the seriousness of the disorder should
be evaluated against the seriousness of the offence and the risk of reoffending, and that criminal proceedings should be a proportionate response in all
the circumstances of the case.

[32] *www.cps.gov.uk/legal/l_to_o/non-recent_cases/* [Accessed April 30, 2016].
[33] The heading suggests a wider range of potential factors than does the text which follows.
[34] *www.cps.gov.uk/legal/l_to_o/mentally_disordered_offenders/* [Accessed April 30, 2016].

In cases in which a suspect has been told by the police or the CPS that he   **17.47**
or she will not be prosecuted the guidance on "Reconsidering a Prosecution
Decision"[35] will also need to be applied.

False Rape Allegations

It is sometimes believed that the CPS is reluctant to prosecute cases where a   **17.48**
false allegation of rape has been made. In fact, the CPS recognises that such
an allegation not only has a devastating impact on the person wrongly
accused, but also makes it commensurately more difficult successfully to
prosecute truthful complaints to conviction.

That is not to say that prosecuting allegedly false rape allegations is easy: **17.49**
the existence of assumptions about human sexual behaviour (the so-called
myths and stereotypes) can make it as difficult to identify cases which are
demonstrably false as it can be to prosecute a genuine case of rape. Were a
prosecutor to make the wrong decision, he or she risks both criminalising
someone who is in fact a victim of rape and discouraging other victims from
coming forward.

The case of *R. v A*[36] prompted the issue of guidance in this area. A had   **17.50**
reported to the police that she had been raped on three occasions by her
husband; this was against a background of other domestic violence. As a
result of her complaint, her husband was arrested and charged. Some weeks
later, A told the police that, whilst what she had said about the rapes was
true, she and her husband were reconciled and she wished to retract her
allegations. After consideration, the CPS decided that the prosecution should
continue, on the ground that cases involving a serious allegation such as rape
are not a private matter between the parties.

Upon being told that the case would continue, A then said that she had   **17.51**
lied in her statements and that her husband had never raped or otherwise
assaulted her. The reviewing lawyer decided that, in light of the fact that she
appeared to be untruthful by her own admission, there was no longer a
realistic prospect of conviction and offered no evidence. A's husband, who
had been in custody for some months, was released. Following this, a
decision was made to charge A with perverting the course of justice on the
basis that she had made false allegations against her husband.

After she was charged, A said that she had not perverted the course of   **17.52**
justice, because the original allegations of rape had been true and she had
only withdrawn them because she and her husband were trying to rebuild
their marriage.

A situation such as this (which is far from uncommon in rape cases where   **17.53**
the allegation arises in the context of other domestic violence) has come to

---

[35] *www.cps.gov.uk/legal/p_to_r/reconsidering_a_prosecution_decision/*   [Accessed   April   30,
2016].
[36] [2012] EWCA Crim 434; [2012] 2 Cr. App. R. 8.

be known as a "double retraction". In *R. v A*, the CPS reviewing lawyer considered that it was not possible to distinguish between A's two versions of what had happened. Given that she was, by her own admission, undoubtedly guilty on one or other basis, the indictment was drafted so that it contained two mutually inconsistent counts of perverting the course of justice: the first alleging that she had done so by making a false allegation of rape and the second that she had done so by falsely saying that a truthful allegation of rape was a lie. A pleaded guilty to the count which averred that the original rape allegation was true and she had lied when retracting it; no evidence was offered on the alternative count. It follows as a matter of logic that A had been prosecuted for retracting what the prosecutor accepted was a truthful complaint of rape. Her status as a genuine rape victim notwithstanding, she was sentenced at the Crown Court to eight months' imprisonment.[37]

17.54   This case caused the CPS to consider how the Full Code Test should be applied in difficult circumstances such as these. The first question is whether the evidential stage is met when the prosecution has evidence which leads to one of two mutually exclusive conclusions but finds itself unable to choose between them. However much common sense might revolt at the idea that the defendant should escape punishment entirely, if the prosecution is wholly unable to say which version is correct, then the case cannot meet the criminal standard of proof.[38] In such a situation, the Legal Guidance accepts that it is wrong in law to charge mutually contradictory counts and simply invite the jury to choose which it prefers.[39]

17.55   Further, when the prosecution accepts a plea on the factual basis that the complainant had lied when he or she withdrew a truthful allegation of rape, then the reviewing lawyer must go on to consider whether the decision to prosecute is in the public interest, given that the only logical inference will be that he or she was a victim of rape.

17.56   As a result of A's case, and following a period of public consultation, CPS Legal Guidance on how to approach such cases was published in July 2011.[40] It seeks to strike a balance between ensuring that genuine victims who retract truthful allegations (often as a result of emotional pressure or violence) are not prosecuted, whilst recognising the need to protect the innocent against false allegations of rape or domestic violence.

17.57   Because the then DPP wished to ensure that the Guidance was being applied in a consistent manner, he personally approved all charging decisions[41] in these cases from January 2011 to May 2013. During that 17-month

[37] This was reduced by the Court of Appeal to a community order: see [2010] EWCA Crim 2913.
[38] See, by analogy, the line of authority dealing with offences committed by a closed group where there is no evidence of common purpose and the prosecution is unable to choose between the suspects, e.g. *Abbot* [1955] 2 Q.B. 497.
[39] *Tsang Ping-Nam v R* (1982) 74 Cr. App. R. 139.
[40] The current, updated guidance is to be found at *www.cps.gov.uk/legal/p_to_r/perverting_the_course_of_justice_-_rape_and_dv_allegations/* [Accessed April 30, 2016].
[41] The expression "charging decision" is used within the CPS to mean the decision whether to charge or not, and thus encompasses cases in which no further action is taken.

period the CPS made 159 decisions involving allegedly false complaints of rape and domestic violence. Those decisions were analysed and became the foundation for a report which was published in March 2013.[42] One of the things that emerged from the analysis was that only a very small proportion of the complaints of rape and domestic violence investigated by the police and referred to the CPS for a charging decision could be shown to be demonstrably false to the criminal standard. In the other cases, it had to be accepted that the original allegation of rape might have been true. These figures have to be treated with some caution because the way the data was collected does not permit a direct comparison to be made,[43] but the overall comparison makes an arguably sound point: during the period of the review there were 5,651 prosecutions for rape and 111,891 for domestic violence, compared with 35 prosecutions for false allegations of rape, six for false allegations of domestic violence and three for false allegations involving both.

CPS Charging Standards

False allegations can be prosecuted either as perverting the course of justice   **17.58**
or wasting police time.[44] Usually the less serious charge of wasting police time is used when there has been a generalised complaint of rape rather than one made against a specific person. Charges of perverting the course of justice are usually reserved for cases where an identifiable person was in jeopardy of being arrested or tried for the offence,[45] the allegation was persisted in for a long period of time, other evidence was manufactured, or the complaint could fairly be described as not merely false but malicious.

Wasting police time is a summary-only offence. In some cases, by the time   **17.59**
the investigation has concluded it is clear that the proper charge would have been wasting police time, but the statutory time limit has expired, leaving the choice of charging the more serious but less appropriate offence or taking no further action. This is not an unusual situation: it arises most commonly in relation to allegations of assault. The CPS Charging Standards for assaults[46] state that:

> "From time to time, there may be exceptional circumstances where a case would ordinarily be considered more suitable for being charged as Common Assault under this Charging Standard, but more than six months has passed since the incident complained of. In such circumstances, it may be appropriate (where the

[42] www.cps.gov.uk/publications/research/perverting_course_of_justice_march_2013.pdf [Accessed April 30, 2016].
[43] Not least because in some of the cases which did not result in prosecution, this may have been for public interest reasons.
[44] s.5(2) of the Criminal Law Act 1967.
[45] See *Rowell* (1977) 65 Cr. App. R. 174 at p.179.
[46] http://www.cps.gov.uk/legal/l_to_o/offences_against_the_person/#a23 [Accessed April 30, 2016].

injuries were more than 'transient and trifling') to charge an offence of ABH, but great care must be taken in making such a decision.

Such a course of action may be argued as being an abuse of process, and it is therefore necessary to clearly establish [sic] the reason for not bringing summary proceedings within six months (or laying a protective information within that time). Issues around the nature and complexity of the investigation will be relevant, as will be the stage at which the case was referred by the police. In determining whether the preferring of a charge of ABH in these circumstances is manifestly an abuse of process, or whether in fact it would be regarded as an affront to justice for proceedings not to be brought, reference should be had to the Legal Guidance chapter on Abuse of Process"

Thus where, following an investigation, it appears that a false rape allegation would more usually be prosecuted as wasting police time but the statutory time limit has elapsed, the reviewing lawyer will need to determine whether the case should be dealt with as perverting the course of justice, if the alternative is that otherwise the suspect would escape justice entirely. One of the factors which the reviewing lawyer should take into account is that, in the event of a conviction, the trial judge will be able to reflect the mitigating factors in sentence.

Difficult issues

17.60   The Legal Guidance reminds prosecutors that the Crown will need to be able to prove to the criminal standard that the suspect[47] has made a clear and unambiguous complaint. It is a feature of many investigations that complaints to the police can be made by persons other than the alleged victim, for example, the parents of teenagers. In a surprising number of cases the suspect had made an allegation of rape but had failed to appreciate that the fact that he or she did not actually want to have intercourse did not mean that he or she did not consent to it. In addition, there is some evidence that the police may occasionally conclude that the complainant is alleging rape when there is no clear evidence that this is what was in fact said.[48] Particular care needs to be taken in cases in which the suspect is young, has mental health issues or learning difficulties.

17.61   It may be felt that there should be few problems in the requirement that the prosecution prove that the complaint was in fact false, but in practice this may present considerable difficulty. The fact that the original rape allegation did not meet the test for a prosecution, or that the complainant withdrew the allegation or the jury acquitted the alleged rapist, does not necessarily mean

---

[47] There are some difficulties with the terminology. In this context "suspect" is used to mean the person who has made the allegedly false complaint.

[48] For example, in one case, careful analysis of the original complaint to the police revealed that what the suspect had in fact said was that she "felt" that she had been "taken advantage of", but that she could not remember exactly what had happened because of the amount of alcohol she had had to drink. It became clear that at no stage had she said explicitly that she was raped, rather it was the police who had drawn the conclusion that this was what she was alleging.

that the complaint was untrue. This is particularly complicated when the alleged victim has made allegations in the past which he or she has either withdrawn or which have not resulted in prosecution. "Common sense" might suggest that this indicates a history of making false allegations (the "lightning doesn't strike twice" principle), but this is in fact another example of how common sense can prove to be an unreliable touchstone: there is some evidence to show that victims may have been subjected to other sexual and other violent offences, possibly as a result of their vulnerability. This is characterised as "repeat victimisation". There is a risk that a circular kind of logic can develop: a complaint is not believed because the complainant has a history of making allegations which have not resulted in prosecution or conviction, then that complaint itself joins the list so that were he or she to make another allegation, that too would not be taken seriously. In light of this, prosecutors are reminded that a previous allegation is of no significance unless there is evidence to show that that allegation was itself provably false; and even then, a previous false allegation will rarely be conclusive.

Prosecutors should also be careful not to conclude that the allegation was **17.62** false solely on the basis of the so-called "myths and stereotypes". Examples of flawed decision-making have, in the past, included a case in which the reviewing lawyer concluded that because the complainant had no injuries, this in itself amounted to evidence that it was a false allegation.

The Legal Guidance reminds prosecutors that in these cases the principle **17.63** that it is generally safe to rely on an admission of guilt (as being a declaration against interest) may not in fact apply. An example of this is provided by "double retraction" cases such as that of *R. v A*[49] where the relationship between the parties, in addition to other factors such as their having children, may lead to the withdrawal of a truthful allegation. As the Court said in *R. v A*[50]:

> "Experience shows that the withdrawal of a truthful complaint of crime committed in a domestic environment usually stems from pressures, sometimes direct, sometimes indirect, sometimes immensely subtle, which are consequent on the nature of the individual relationship and the characters of the people who are involved in it."

The Legal Guidance sets out a number of factors which prosecutors **17.64** should bear in mind, such as whether there is any other evidence which tends to support one version of events over the other.

A further example of the difficulties which may confront prosecutors is **17.65** where the alleged rape victim has lied or manufactured evidence[51] to support an allegation which otherwise appears to be true, or where there is clear evidence of violent assaults on other occasions. In such cases although it would be possible as a matter of law to charge him or her with perverting the

---

[49] [2012] EWCA Crim 434; [2012] 2 Cr. App. R. 8, discussed in paras 17.50 and following, above.
[50] At [5].
[51] In one case a false diary entry.

course of justice, careful consideration needs to be given to the public interest. Examples of public interest considerations in this context are to be found in the Guidance.

BREACHES OF THE NON-REPORTING PROVISIONS

17.66 Most allegations involving sexual offences carry with them so-called "anonymity" for the victim, by virtue of the Sexual Offences (Amendment) Act 1992. This subject is fully discussed in Ch.29, below. Although the Act uses the expression "anonymity" in the section headings, the actual protection conferred is from publication of matters likely to lead members of the public to identify the person concerned. This is not to be confused with "anonymity" in the sense provided for in the Coroners and Justice Act 2009: in almost every case the complainant's identity will be disclosed to the suspect and his or her name will be given in open court.

17.67 The 1992 Act provisions are akin to reporting restrictions but their effect is not limited to the media: individuals may be prosecuted for publishing information. The advent of widespread use of social media has increased the speed and ease with which such information may be distributed. It has also had a profound effect on the impact it may have. The rape conviction in 2012 of a footballer, Ched Evans,[51a] was followed by extensive comment on social media, in some of which the victim's identity was deliberately and maliciously revealed to the public at large. A number of those who published such comments were prosecuted under the 1992 Act. Similar prosecutions have taken place in other cases but the extent of the impact on the victim in that case has been of particular concern and has been widely reported.

17.68 Proceedings for an offence under the 1992 Act may be instituted only with the consent of the Attorney General[52] and thus the public interest decision in such cases falls to the Law Officers to make rather than the CPS, although the prosecutor will make recommendations. The CPS Legal Guidance sets out the procedure for submitting these cases to the Attorney General's Office.[53] Recommendations on the public interest stage are likely to reflect the circumstances in which the alleged offence occurred, which may range from inadvertent publication[54] (where a prosecution is less likely to be considered necessary) to malicious publication where the clear intention was to victimise, or further victimise, the person concerned, in which case a prosecution is more likely to be required, subject to other factors specific to the individual

---

[51a] The conviction was recently quashed and a retrial ordered: see *http://www.independent. co.uk/news/uk/crime/ched-evans-wins-appeal-against-rape-conviction-and-faces-retrial-a6993966.html* [Accessed April 30, 2016].

[52] Or the Solicitor General by virtue of the Law Officers Act 1997.

[53] *www.cps.gov.uk/legal/a_to_c/contempt_of_court/£a19* [Accessed April 30, 2016].

[54] For example, where someone commenting, critically, on one act of publication accidentally re-publishes that on which they are commenting.

concerned. It is of note that the protection is limited in that the offence only carries a financial penalty.

The protection of the Act is automatic (that is to say, it is not dependent on the judge making an order) and extends throughout the lifetime of the person concerned, though they can, if over 16, waive the entitlement by written consent. However, s.1(4) provides that:

> "nothing in this section prohibits the inclusion in a publication of matter consisting only of a report of criminal proceedings other than proceedings at, or intended to lead to, or on an appeal arising out of, a trial at which the accused is charged with the offence."

17.69

The Judicial College guidance *Reporting restrictions in the Criminal Courts*[55] includes this comment, annotated by reference to s.1(4):

> "the media is free to report the victim's identity in the event of criminal proceedings other than the actual trial or appeal in relation to the sexual offence e.g. if the complainant were to be prosecuted for perjury in separate proceedings."

It is by no means clear that the wording of s.1(4) actually provides a basis for the example contended for in the guidance, but the point has not yet been tested. If the example is right, then it follows that those accused of making a false allegation lose the protection of the 1992 Act merely as a result of being prosecuted, potentially in proceedings launched by a private prosecutor, and while still presumed in law to be innocent.

[55] *www.judiciary.gov.uk/publications/reporting-restrictions-in-the-criminal-courts/* [Accessed April 16, 2016].

CHAPTER 18

DISCLOSURE

By H.H. Judge Johannah Cutts QC

Introduction	18.01	Documents Not Held by the
Prosecution Duty to Disclose	18.10	Family Court ... 18.67
Material in the Hands of Third		Article 8 ECHR and Issues of
Parties	18.32	Confidentiality ... 18.92
Documents Held by the Family		Conclusion ... 18.99
Court	18.39	

INTRODUCTION

The rules of disclosure set out in the Criminal Procedure and Investigations Act 1996 ("CPIA"), as amended by the Criminal Justice Act 2003, apply to proceedings for sexual offences as to all other criminal proceedings. Material held by the prosecution must be disclosed in such proceedings in accordance with the principles laid down in those Acts. **18.01**

In proceedings for sexual offences, the issue that rears its head time and again is that of disclosure of material held not by the prosecution but by third parties. Typically this material consists of records held by, amongst others, social services, doctors, counsellors and schools. In many allegations of a sexual nature, especially those of child sexual abuse, this material may be crucial to a defendant at his trial where the jury are confronted with acts taking place in private and, in consequence, with one person's word against another. **18.02**

Disclosure in general, and third party disclosure in particular, has historically caused many problems in the criminal courts and continues to do so. In recent years there has been a plethora of protocols and guidelines intended to eradicate the cost and delay of misplaced applications and those made without a proper adherence to the rules. As the *Judicial Protocol on the* **18.03**

Disclosure of Unused Material in Criminal Cases[1] ("the Judicial Protocol") states[2]:

> "Disclosure remains one of the most important—as well as one of the most misunderstood and abused—of the procedures relating to criminal trials. . . . Applications by the parties or decisions based on misconceptions of the law or a general laxity of approach (however well-intentioned) which result in an improper application of the disclosure regime have, time and again, proved unnecessarily costly and have obstructed justice."

The answer provided by the Judicial Protocol, together with the Criminal Procedure Rules, the *Attorney General's Guidelines on Disclosure*[3] and the *2013 Protocol and Good Practice Model: Disclosure of information in cases of alleged child abuse and linked criminal and care directions hearings*[4] ("the 2013 Protocol") is for judges to insist on a rigid adherence to the rules, both in substance and time.

18.04   The emphasis is on early identification of issues and material potentially held by third parties relevant to those issues. Prosecutors are expected to lead the disclosure process and their own guidance points to the need in allegations of child sexual abuse to seek third party material at an early stage "preferably pre charge".[5]

18.05   For pre-charge applications local authorities must comply with the Data Protection Act 1998. However, s.29(1)(b) of the Act provides an exemption from the general principles of that Act if personal data is processed for "the apprehension or prosecution of offenders".[6] The 2013 Protocol states[7]:

> "the law permits the disclosure of confidential information where a counter-vailing public interest can be identified. Such a public interest will include the administration of justice, the prevention of wrongdoing and enabling another public body to perform its public duty (*R v Chief Constable of North Wales Police ex parte Thorpe* [1996] QB 396). In these circumstances the exchange of relevant

---

[1] Published December 2013 and available at *https://www.judiciary.gov.uk/publications/protocol-unused-material-criminal-cases/* [Accessed April 30, 2016].

[2] Paras 1, 3.

[3] Available at *https://www.gov.uk/government/publications/attorney-generals-guidelines-on-disclosure-2013* [Accessed April 30, 2016].

[4] Published October 2013 and available at *http://www.cps.gov.uk/publications/docs/third_party_protocol_2013.pdf* [Accessed April 30, 2016].

[5] CPS *Guidelines on prosecuting cases of child sexual abuse* (2013), para.118. The Guidelines are available at *http://www.cps.gov.uk/legal/a_to_c/child_sexual_abuse/* [Accessed April 30, 2016]. Paragraph 118 states that sufficient time should be set aside to receive and process third party material, particularly in large and complex cases. It reminds prosecutors that the material may contain information that could enhance or strengthen the prosecution case. This is a welcome recognition which needs to be applied in practice rather than the prosecution seeking only disclosure of that which would strengthen the defence case or undermine their own.

[6] Although s.29(1)(b) and the 2013 Protocol make it clear that local authorities do not offend against the Data Protection Act by the provision of such material pre-charge, it has come to the attention of the author that some local authorities are wary of providing the material sought at this stage for fear they may do so. Those seeking such information at this point should be prepared to direct a local authority to the relevant provisions in order to allay their fears.

[7] para.10.7, fn.15.

material with the police and CPS is not restricted under Data Protection Act 1998."

It is expected that by the pre-trial preparation hearing at the Crown Court, **18.06** the prosecution will have identified third party material issues and the defence will have engaged and assisted in the early identification of the real issues in the case.[8] If disclosure has not yet taken place, the judge at that hearing is required to set down a timetable to ensure that it takes place expeditiously and well before any trial.[9]

Between them the above documents provide guidance and set down **18.07** procedures for how and when to make disclosure applications. There can be no doubt that all are expected to know and follow the rules to the letter.

This is particularly important in those cases involving child witnesses **18.08** under the age of 10 years. A protocol now exists for such cases, which applies to all cases charged on or after April 1, 2015.[10] The timescales set down in the protocol prior to the first hearing are the same as those being used by the three Crown Court areas currently piloting the pre-trial cross-examination of child witnesses under s.28 of the Youth Justice and Criminal Evidence Act 1999.[11] The protocol envisages that the investigator, disclosure officer and prosecutor should be proactive in identifying and seeking access to relevant third party material prior to the decision to charge, wherever possible. It states that trials involving child witnesses under 10 should be listed no longer than eight weeks from the pre-trial preparation hearing. The prosecution should have sought third party disclosure before that hearing. The defence must be astute in obtaining any additional material they seek in order to be ready for the trial. The protocol recognises that the nature and complexity of some investigations, for example those involving "significant" third party disclosure, may be such that charge cannot take place within the timescales set down, but this should not be commonplace.[12]

This chapter briefly sets out the duty of disclosure and looks in more detail **18.09** at the issues facing practitioners dealing with issues of disclosure of information held by third parties, where the law differs depending on whether or not the material is held by the Family Court. It is not an exhaustive

---

[8] The Judicial Protocol, para.16, states that a constructive approach to disclosure is a necessary part of professional best practice for the prosecution and the defence. This does not undermine the defendant's legitimate interest, it accords with his or her obligations under the Rules and it ensures that all the relevant material is provided.

[9] See the Judicial Protocol, paras 8 and 9.

[10] *A Protocol between the Association of Chief Police Officers, the Crown Prosecution Service and Her Majesty's Courts & Tribunals Service to Expedite Cases Involving Witnesses under 10 Years* (March 2015). The Protocol is available at *https://www.judiciary.gov.uk/wp-content/uploads/2015/03/police-cps-hmcts-ywi-protocol.pdf* [Accessed April 30, 2016].

[11] For which see paras 27.43 and following, below.

[12] Para 6.9. See, too, the *Judicial Protocol on the Implementation of section 28 of the Youth Justice and Criminal Evidence Act 1999 Pre-recording of cross-examination and re-examination* (September 2014). This Protocol came into existence for the pilot run by Leeds, Liverpool and Kingston Crown Courts on the implementation of s.28. At PTPH orders should be made regarding disclosure of third party material in these cases.

analysis of the problems but is rather intended as a starting point for busy practitioners.

PROSECUTION DUTY TO DISCLOSE

CRIMINAL PROCEDURE AND INVESTIGATIONS ACT 1996

18.10 For all cases where the investigation commenced on or after April 4, 2005, the disclosure regime to be followed is that set down in the CPIA as amended by Pt V of the Criminal Justice Act 2003.

18.11 In making decisions on disclosure, the prosecutor must have regard to the *Attorney General's Guidelines on disclosure*, most recently published in 2013. These do not have the force of law. However the foreword to the Judicial Protocol states that given that all those in the disclosure process have separate constitutional roles, the judiciary and the Attorney General have worked together to produce complementary guidance that is shorter than the previous iterations but remains comprehensive. The two documents are similarly structured and should be read together.

18.12 Additionally the prosecutor must have regard to the CPS Disclosure Manual,[13] the CPS Rape and Sexual Offences Guidance,[14] the CPS Guidelines on Prosecuting Cases of Child Sexual Abuse,[15] the Judicial Protocol[16] and the 2013 Protocol,[17] and must comply with the procedure set down by Pt 15 of the Criminal Procedure Rules 2015.

18.13 Under the CPIA the prosecutor must first disclose any material which might reasonably be considered capable of undermining the case for the prosecution or of assisting the case for the defence.[18] It is important to note that material for this purpose is that which came into the prosecutor's possession in connection with the case for the prosecution or "which, in pursuance of a code operative under Part II [of the CPIA] he has inspected in connection with the case for the prosecution against the accused".[19]

---

[13] Available at *https://www.cps.gov.uk/legal/d_to_g/disclosure_manual* [Accessed April 30, 2016].

[14] Available at *https://www.cps.gov.uk/legal/p_to_r/rape_and_sexual_offences* [Accessed April 30, 2016].

[15] Available at *https://www.cps.gov.uk/legal/a_to_c/child_sexual_abuse* [Accessed April 30, 2016].

[16] See fn.1, above.

[17] See fn.4, above.

[18] CPIA ss.3, 7.

[19] CPIA s.3(2), See also the Code of Practice under the Act, para.5, which imposes on the officer in charge of an investigation a duty to record and retain material "relevant to the investigation." As paras 4.9 and 4.15 of the CPS Disclosure Manual point out, if material comes to the knowledge of the investigator which is obtained from a third party it will become unused material or information within the Codes of Practice. This applies particularly to relevant information conveyed verbally by a third party. Any such material must be recorded in a retrievable form. If relevant material held by third parties is inspected by the police but not retained, a record of its contents must be made. This must then be placed on the relevant schedule.

The Judicial Protocol emphasises that only that material which satisfies the 18.14
test should be disclosed.[20] It reminds judges that they should not allow the
prosecution to avoid their statutory responsibility for reviewing the unused
material by the expedient of permitting the defence to have access to, or
copies of, the material listed in the schedules of non-sensitive unused
material, irrespective of whether it satisfies the test.[21] The larger and more
complex the case, the more important it is for the prosecution to adhere to
the overarching principle and ensure that sufficient attention and resources
are allocated to the task. Handing the defence the "keys to the warehouse"
has been the cause of many gross abuses in the past, resulting in considerable
expenditure by the defence without any material benefit to the course of
justice.

By Rule 15.2 of the Criminal Procedure Rules 2015 ("CPR 2015") the 18.15
prosecution must, inter alia, inform the court of compliance with the initial
duty to disclose.

The CPIA places on the prosecutor a continuing duty to keep under review 18.16
the question whether at any given time (and particularly after receipt of the
defence statement) there is prosecution material which might reasonably be
considered capable of undermining the case for the prosecution or of
assisting the case for the defence.[22] If there is, the prosecutor must disclose
it.

The Act also enables the defence to apply to the court for a disclosure 18.17
order where there is reasonable cause to believe that there is material in
existence, not yet disclosed, which might reasonably be considered capable of
undermining the prosecution case or assisting the defence case.[23] The judge
at PCMH or, where no such hearing is held, at the pre-trial preparation
hearing should set down a date by which any application for disclosure (if
there is to be one) is to be made.

An important provision in relation to trials of sexual offences is paragraph 18.18
3.6 of the CPIA Code of Practice, which states that if the officer in charge of
the investigation believes that other persons (third parties) may be in
possession of material that may be relevant to the investigation, he should
ask the disclosure officer to inform them of the existence of the investigation
and to invite them to retain the material in case they receive a request for its
disclosure.[24] The disclosure officer should inform the prosecutor that the

---

[20] Para.3.
[21] Paras 13–14.
[22] CPIA s.7A(2), (3).
[23] CPIA s.8.
[24] Chapter 4 of the CPS Disclosure Manual, chapter 15 of the CPS Rape and Sexual Offences
Guidance and para.116 of the CPS Guidelines on Prosecuting Cases of Child Sexual Abuse all
remind investigators that they are under a duty to pursue all reasonable lines of enquiry whether
they point towards or away from the suspect. This may include enquiries as to the existence of
relevant material in the possession of third parties such as a local authority.

third person may have such material. The officer in charge of the investigation is not, however, required to make speculative enquiries of other persons. There must be some reason to believe that the third person may have relevant material. In practice an officer investigating a case where social services have been involved with the complainant or other important witness should make enquiry of the relevant social services department as to whether records exist and, if so, whether there is likely to be material of relevance within them. Once an officer is aware that records do exist, any request for disclosure must be focused to the likely issues in the case. Blanket or vague requests should not be entertained.

18.19   Paragraph 6.14 of the Code requires the disclosure officer to list on a sensitive schedule any material "the disclosure of which he believes would give rise to a real risk of serious prejudice to an important public interest and the reason for that belief." Paragraph 6.15 includes in a list of examples of material which should be included in such a schedule, material supplied to an investigator during a criminal investigation which relates to a child or young person and which has been generated by a local authority social services department, an Area Child Protection Committee or other party contacted by an investigator during the investigation, and material relating to the private life of a witness (this must include medical records).

18.20   The responsibilities imposed by the CPIA and the *Attorney General's Guidelines* cannot be sidestepped by not making an enquiry. A police officer who believes that a person may have information which might undermine the case for the prosecution or assist the case for the suspect or defendant cannot decline to make enquiries of that person in order to avoid the need to disclose what they might say.[25]

18.21   The CPIA makes no special provision in relation to material held by individuals or companies overseas or by foreign governmental authorities, or material that may be examined overseas in the course of the investigation. The *Attorney General's Guidelines*[26] and the Judicial Protocol[27] apply to this material in the same way as they apply to material within the jurisdiction. In *Flook*,[28] the Court of Appeal said that although the provisions of the Code under the CPIA and the *Attorney General's Guidelines* are expressed in a domestic context, they make clear the obligations of the Crown to pursue reasonable lines of enquiry in relation to material that may be held overseas. The power of the Crown to obtain this information is limited if disclosure is declined. For these reasons there cannot be any absolute obligation on the Crown to disclose relevant material held overseas by entities not subject to

---

[25] See *Joof* [2012] EWCA Crim 1475. The defendants were charged with murder. The prosecution case rested substantially on the evidence of a witness, T. The police decided not to investigate complaints made by T about an officer as they were concerned that any investigation could undermine his evidence, making it disclosable to the defence.
[26] paras 59–64
[27] paras 51–53.
[28] [2009] EWCA Crim 682.

the jurisdiction of the court of English and Wales. The obligation is to take reasonable steps. The position in such a case should be set out clearly in writing so the court and defence know what the position is.

PUBLIC INTEREST IMMUNITY

Although the "golden rule" is that full disclosure should be made of material   **18.22** held by the prosecution which weakens its case or strengthens that of the defence,[29] the duty to disclose is not absolute. The CPIA provides that material must not be disclosed to the extent that the court, on an application by the prosecutor, concludes that it is not in the public interest to disclose it.[30] The common law relating to public interest immunity is expressly preserved by the Act.[31] The principles to be applied are laid down by the House of Lords decision in *R. v H; R. v C.*[32]

Rule 15.3 of the CPR 2015[33] requires a prosecutor who wishes the court to   **18.23** decide whether it would be in the public interest for material to be disclosed to make an application in writing. This should be served on the court, any person who the prosecutor thinks would be directly affected by disclosure of the material and the defendant, to the extent that it does not disclose that which the prosecution seeks to withhold.[34] The application must describe the material and explain why the prosecutor thinks that it is material that the prosecutor would ordinarily have to disclose, the grounds upon which the prosecutor asserts it would not be in the public interest to do so and why no measure such as the disclosure of an edited copy could be taken.

The CPR 2015 lay down a format for the hearing which must be followed   **18.24** unless the court directs otherwise. The general rule is that the defence will have notice of the application. Applications without notice should be confined to those rare cases where the prosecutor apprehends that it may not be in the public interest to disclose even the existence of the material in question. If the defence are present (and it is for the court to decide if they should be absent), the prosecutor first makes representations in their presence. He is then followed by any other person served with the application. The defence then has the opportunity to make representations before the prosecutor (and any other person served with the application) makes further representations ex parte.[35]

---

[29] *R. v H; R. v C* [2004] 2 A.C. 134, at 147.
[30] ss.3(6), 7A(8), 8(5).
[31] s.21(2).
[32] [2004] 2 A.C. 134. See also the Judicial Protocol, paras 54–55, in which the procedure laid down in Pt 15 of the Criminal Procedure Rules 2015 is endorsed and further guidance given.
[33] SI 2015/1490.
[34] Rule 15.3(2)(b).
[35] Rule 15.3(7).

18.25   The 2013 Protocol deals directly with issues of public interest immunity in applications for disclosure of material held by third parties. For that reason this topic is dealt with later in this chapter: see paras 18.67 and following, below.

Limiting the Distribution of Material Relating to Sexual Offences

18.26   The Sexual Offences Act 1997 received Royal Assent on March 21, 1997. It has not yet been brought into force. As it has been on the statute book for over 18 years it is unlikely to be implemented and almost certainly not in its current form. If it were to be implemented, the prosecution duty of disclosure set out in CPIA would be subject to s.3 of the Act, which regulates the people to whom disclosure can be made.

18.27   The Act is designed to ensure that the defendant and others unrelated to the proceedings do not have copies of "protected material" in relation to proceedings for a sexual offence. "Protected material" is defined as statements relating to that or any other sexual offence made by any victim of the offence (whether in written or any other form), a photograph or pseudo-photograph of any such victim or the report of a medical examination of the physical condition of any such victim.[36] It follows that the Act does not relate solely to unused material but covers much of the prosecution case in trials of sexual offences. The idea is to prevent distribution of such material and, indeed, the opportunities for such material to be mislaid or left unattended so that others may see it.

18.28   If the defendant is represented, his legal adviser will receive the material upon undertakings not to leave the defendant alone with it or to provide copies to any other person unless he is of the view that it is necessary to do so in connection with the proceedings or for the purpose of assessment or treatment of the accused.[37]

18.29   If the defendant is unrepresented and is in custody, the prosecution should give a copy of the material to the governor or any other person nominated by him. If the defendant is on bail, a copy should be given to the officer in charge of a suitable police station to enable the defendant to have access to the material. This person is to take all reasonable steps to ensure the defendant is supervised when viewing it, is given access to it as he reasonably requires and that no other person sees or takes a copy of it.

18.30   Although this Act is not yet in force, there are understandable concerns to ensure that only those concerned with the case see certain material, particularly indecent photographs of children. Nonetheless arrangements

---

[36] s.1(1).
[37] s.4(2)(b).

must be made for defence lawyers to view such images with a defendant in circumstances where they can give advice and take instructions. If this is not done, a case may be stayed for abuse of process.

An instructive decision in this context is *CPS v LR*.[38] D was charged with 18.31 possession of indecent photographs of children. His defence was that in at least some of them the subjects were over the age of 18. He denied that he was responsible for any of the images saying that someone else must have used his computer and credit card. The defence wanted copies of the images in order to take instructions and prepare for trial. The prosecution refused to provide them, claiming they would be committing an offence if they copied them at all. Arrangements for the photographs to be viewed only at court with an officer outside the room were unsatisfactory as the conference rooms had glass walls and discussions could be heard outside. The judge made orders for service of papers with which the CPS did not comply. The judge then stayed the indictment. The Court of Appeal lamented the lack of mutual co-operation. It held the prosecution could not commit a criminal offence by supplying copies of such images to the defence in compliance with a court order, and must propose satisfactory arrangements to enable D to have a sensible and confidential discussion with his lawyers with, in the event of disagreement, the judge deciding whether they are sufficient. In the absence of such proposals there was nothing wrong with the stay. The Court said that lawyers and jurors must be trusted to act in good faith unless and until there is some reason to suggest they are deficient in any respect. No further hard or digital copies beyond those necessary for the purpose of the conference or trial should be made and all copies should be returned to the CPS when the relevant trial has concluded.

MATERIAL IN THE HANDS OF THIRD PARTIES

As already indicated, in proceedings for sexual offences disclosure is 18.32 frequently sought of records or other documents in the hands of third parties. It is not uncommon, for example, in allegations of child sexual abuse for social services to have been involved with the family or with the child who has made the complaint. As is their duty, social workers will have made records of their contact with the child concerned. Their files may contain records of meetings with other professionals and of child protection conferences. The existence of such files is not restricted to children. Now that more vulnerable adults are giving evidence there are more cases before the courts where social services or other authorities hold files on complainants in proceedings for sexual offences, particularly where the complainant is mentally ill or suffering from a degree of learning disability.

---

[38] [2010] EWCA Crim 924.

18.33   In many cases, disclosure of third party material is crucial to the issues in the case. A good example is *North (Mark)*.[39] North was convicted in 2001 of sexual offences committed in relation to two boys. He was sentenced to a term of five years' imprisonment. His appeal in 2004 failed. In 2011 the Criminal Cases Review Commission ("CCRC") referred his case once more to the Court of Appeal. There had been no application for third party material at his trial.[40] The CCRC obtained such material which formed the basis of the successful appeal. One of the complainants (AW) had been ABE interviewed several times. He was inconsistent on occasions. During cross-examination he resolutely denied that there had been any discussion between himself and the other complainant (SS) after SS's first interview and before his own first interview. He denied that he had colluded with SS to give false evidence against North. He said they had ceased to see each other regularly in September 1999. Social services records revealed this to be a lie. They showed that the two boys had been truanting together as late as December 1999. The records suggested that they were involved in "running" drugs for dealers between October and December 1999 having been supplied with mobile phones for this purpose. AW was also asked in cross-examination if anyone had told him that he could make some money out of complaining. He said that no one had told him about that. Social services records showed that AW had made a successful claim to the Criminal Injuries Compensation Authority ("CICA") in 1993. Enquiries of the Authority revealed that a substantial award was made to him in respect of an alleged sexual assault by his stepfather when he was aged about two years. It was accepted to be a proper award. It was held in trust until AW's eighteenth birthday. Social services records revealed that in July, October and November 1999, AW was seeking an interim payment from the award in order to repay money he had stolen from his foster parents. In August 2000 he wanted an advance to buy a computer and scooter. In February 2001 his social worker agreed to look into his request for an advance to buy a computer. The Court of Appeal held that AW's answer to the question at trial of whether anyone had told him of his ability to claim money may have been literally true. However it deliberately or unconsciously concealed the fact that AW knew from previous experience of the existence of the CICA and of his ability to make a claim. Furthermore he had been expressing his anxiety to obtain an advance from the award already made. Had counsel been aware of the true position, AW's already fragile credibility would have been further undermined. In allowing the appeal, the Court stated that these were facts which would have come to the attention of trial counsel had an application for third party material been made. The evidence would have been admissible, subject to the trial judge's

---

[39] [2011] EWCA Crim 88.
[40] No explanation for this failure was forthcoming at the appeal. It may have been that it was as a result of the extremely restrictive disclosure regime operated by many courts in the late 1990s and early 2000s, when defence counsel making applications were often threatened with wasted costs orders being made against them personally.

power to admit it, under s.100 of the Criminal Justice Act 2003. The Court had little doubt leave would have been given.[41]

PROCEDURE

Third parties are under no duty of disclosure. In the context of allegations of a sexual nature the information they hold is likely to be sensitive. If either the prosecution or defence seek disclosure of such documents, applications must be made in the proper way.   **18.34**

The procedure to be adopted depends on whether the material is held by the Family Court and relates to family proceedings. This may often be the case where a child who has complained to the police of sexual or other abuse has been or is also the subject of care proceedings. Any material held by the Family Court is confidential to the parties and their representatives in those proceedings unless leave to disclose is granted by the Family Court Judge. It may be that the defendant in a criminal trial was party to the family proceedings and will therefore be aware of the existence and content of the documents used in them. This does not permit him to disclose the documents to his lawyers in the criminal trial. Should he seek to do so his criminal lawyers should not accept the documents but should instead apply for leave to the civil court for their disclosure.   **18.35**

If the material is held otherwise than by a civil court the normal rules applying to third party documents apply and a witness summons to produce documents may have to be served.   **18.36**

The Family Procedure Rules 2010 ("FPR")[42] and the Criminal Procedure Rules 2015 ("CPR")[43] each set out the procedure for applying for disclosure.   **18.37**

---

[41] It is not the case that failure to disclose social services records in an historical case will always result in a successful appeal. Newly disclosed material has to be considered against the test of whether it renders the conviction unsafe or raises a reasonable doubt as to the guilt of the accused. It is also important in examining the records to do so with an eye to the very different approach to victims of sexual abuse and the likely impact on their lives 25 years ago. In this context, see *Butler (Carl)* [2015] EWCA Crim 854, in which the CCRC uncovered records showing that prior to the appellant's conviction in 1998, the complainant had made allegations of sexual misconduct against other men. There were notes on file showing the police and Social Services were of the view she had problems distinguishing fact from fantasy. It was clear from the records that a number of her sexual allegations were not believed by professionals who dealt with her. The Court of Appeal stated that the opinion of such professionals as to the truthfulness of a complaint was not admissible as a basis for challenging the complaint's veracity. The Court also analysed the basis for the opinions on the records and found them to be unfounded. They were largely based on the complainant's retraction of a complaint against her father when she was 10 years of age, without consideration of why she might have retracted it and in spite of medical evidence of abuse. The Court said that whatever comments the professionals of the time made, the fact that the complainant was a victim of sexual abuse and the vulnerability that results both from the clear evidence of sexual abuse and the approach of the police and others did not undermine her ability to tell the truth.

[42] SI 2010/2955, Part 12.73.

[43] SI 2015/1490, Part 17.

These are vital tools ensuring that such applications are made in good time and appropriately. They should now be considered together with the *2013 Protocol and Good Practice Model; Disclosure of information in cases of alleged child abuse and linked criminal and care directions hearings*[44] ("the 2013 Protocol"). The principles set out in this document should have been enshrined in local protocols and in use by January 1, 2014.[45] The Protocol does not replace the procedure rules in either jurisdiction. It does, however, set out a streamlined procedure with scope for more agreement and voluntary disclosure than has previously been the case, reducing the need for formal applications in many, if not most, cases. It (or a local protocol set up enshrining its terms) must be followed by anyone concerned in third party material applications. It applies to cases involving criminal investigations into alleged child abuse (child victims who were 17 or under at the time of the alleged offending)[46] and/or Family Court proceedings concerning a child of the same age. It states amongst its aims:

- Subject to the FPR (and relevant practice direction[47]), the CPR[48] and the common law duty of confidentiality, to facilitate timely and consistent disclosure of information and documents from the family justice system to the police and/or CPS.
- To provide a timely, expeditious process for a local authority to respond to a request from the police for material held by the local authority which would assist a criminal investigation.
- To provide for a timely consultation between the CPS and the local authority where local authority material satisfies the test in the CPIA for disclosure to the defence.
- To provide a streamlined and standard process for applications by the police and/or the CPS for the permission of the Family Court for disclosure of material relating to Family Court proceedings.

18.38 The regime for the disclosure of documents held by third parties differs according to whether the documents are or are not held by the Family Court, and we go on to look at these two categories in turn.

---

[44] Published October 2013 and available at *http://www.cps.gov.uk/publications/docs/third_party_protocol_2013.pdf* [Accessed April 30, 2016].

[45] Not all court centres yet have their own protocols in place. There is huge variance throughout the country. Although once the Protocol is up and running the procedure for obtaining third party material is much simplified and less problematic, there is no denying that it has taken a large amount of work to put it together. Resident and Designated Family Judges have had to work together at the same time that the timetable for dealing with family cases has halved. Stretched local authorities have also had to agree to a new document. This has not proved straightforward in some areas.

[46] Local protocols should deal with similar applications made in relation to vulnerable adults. The procedure laid down in the Protocol could be easily used in such applications.

[47] In particular PD12G.

[48] The reference is to the CPR 2013 but this should be taken as referring to the CPR 2015, which came into force on October 5, 2015.

Documents Held by the Family Court

the Family Procedure Rules

Rule 27.10 of the FPR states that proceedings under the Children Act 1989   **18.39**
are to be held in private except where statute or regulation provides otherwise
or where the court directs otherwise. Section 12 of the Administration of
Justice Act 1960 provides that it is a contempt of court to publicise
information relating to proceedings that:

- relate to the exercise of the inherent jurisdiction of the High Court
  with respect to minors,
- are brought under the Children Act 1989, or
- otherwise relate wholly or mainly to the maintenance or upbringing of
  a minor.

Section 98 of the Children Act 1989 provides that no person shall be   **18.40**
excused from giving evidence on any matter or from answering questions put
to him in the course of giving evidence on the ground that doing so may
incriminate him or his spouse of an offence. Section 98(2) provides that a
statement or admission made in such proceedings shall not be admissible in
evidence against the person making it or his spouse in proceedings for an
offence other than perjury.

That is not to say that disclosure of material cannot be made from family   **18.41**
proceedings to a party to criminal proceedings. The current rules concerning
disclosure of information are contained in Chapter 7 of Part 12 of the FPR,
supplemented by Practice Direction 12G.[49] Rule 12.73(1) of the FPR provides:

> "(1) For the purposes of the law relating to contempt of court, information
> relating to proceedings held in private (whether or not contained in a document
> filed with the court) may be communicated—
>   a.   Where the communication is to—
>   i. a party;
>   ii. the legal representative of a party;
>   iii. a professional legal adviser;
>   iv. an officer of the service or a Welsh family proceedings officer;
>   v. the welfare officer;
>   vi. the director of legal casework within the meaning of the Legal Aid
>   Sentencing and Punishment of Offenders Act 2012;
>   vii. an expert whose instruction by a party has been authorised by the
>   court for the purposes of the proceedings;
>   viii. a professional acting in furtherance of the protection of children;
>   ix. an independent reviewing officer appointed in respect of a child
>   who is, or has been, subject to proceedings to which this rule
>   applies.

---

[49] The FPR relax further the restrictions on disclosure imposed by previous Family Procedure
Rules, but the provisions governing disclosure into the criminal arena remain substantially the
same as before, i.e. under the 1991 Rules as amended in 2005 (and discussed in previous editions
of this work).

b.   Where the court gives permission; or
c.   Subject to any direction of the court, in accordance with rule 12.75 and Practice Direction 12G."

"Information relating to proceedings held in private (whether or not contained in a document filed with the court)"

18.42   Rule 4.23 of the FPR 1991 related to disclosure of "documents held by the court", a narrower definition than now applies. The Court of Appeal held in *Re G (a minor) (Social Worker: Disclosure)*[50] that rule 4.23 placed no bar on the disclosure by social services to the police, without leave of the court, of information given orally to social workers, recorded in case notes and never put before the court. That was so even if the documents were created for the purpose of proceedings and were intended to be filed with the court.[51] The Court noted that, save for the limited scope of rule 4.23, there was no bar to the exchange of information between those engaged in the investigation and prevention of child abuse, which should be encouraged.

18.43   The change in wording to "information relating to proceedings (whether or not in a document filed with the court)", which was effected by the FPR 2005, means that the Rules now allow for the disclosure of information held in documents contained within social services files to a child protection officer, whether the documents are filed with the court or not. Even copying the documents on the court file is permissible. There is no need to obtain the court's permission. This is for the purposes of child protection. However, information contained in documents filed with the court cannot be used for any other purpose without the court's express permission.[52] In the *Reading Borough Council* case, Sumner J pointed out that disclosure of such documents to the police in accordance with this rule does not remove their confidentiality.[53] The Rules merely make it clear that if a local authority, for instance, wishes to pass to the police information that is already in a document filed with the court, there is no need for it to obtain the court's permission. Thus the current Rules create a far wider regime of disclosure

---

[50] [1996] 1 W.L.R 1407.

[51] At 1415.

[52] *Reading Borough Council v D (Angela) (Chief Constable intervening)* [2006] EWHC 1465 (Fam). This was a decision on r.10.20A of the FPR 1991, as inserted by the Family Proceedings (Amendment No 4) Rules 2005 (SI 2005/1976), but the wording remains the same. In this case the local authority properly disclosed two medical reports on injuries sustained by one of the children and their causation (these were already on the court file), an undated and unsigned statement from the mother blaming the father for the injuries, a signed statement from the father prepared for the care proceedings in which he accepted being violent to the mother but denied causing the injuries (these were destined for the court file but had not yet reached it) and a letter unsigned and undated from the father in which he withdrew a confession of liability for the child's injuries, stating he had confessed under pressure from the child's mother and grandmother.

[53] The information remains confidential but once known to the police it is subject to the CPIA disclosure regime. The police would need to obtain the consent of the Family Court before disclosing the material to the defence.

without leave than the FPR 1991.[54] Any decision in cases before the introduction of the change in FPR 2005 is therefore unlikely to be helpful.

If an unopposed application is subsequently made by the police to use such   18.44 documents, the application should be considered on paper and without a hearing, unless the court decides one is necessary.[55] This is subject to the court subsequently requiring an oral hearing.

"A professional legal adviser"

In the *Reading Borough Council* case, Sumner J held that the term "pro-   18.45 fessional legal adviser" does not include the representatives of a defendant in a criminal trial who is also a party to family proceedings. He interpreted the term more narrowly, as covering a party to family proceedings who seeks legal advice to assist in those proceedings.

Bodey J held completely the opposite in *B (A child: Disclosure of evidence*   18.46 *in care proceedings)*[56] when he stated that the phrase "professional legal adviser" covers a solicitor instructed in parallel or subsequent proceedings. No leave of the Family Court is therefore necessary before disclosure to such a solicitor can take place.[57] This decision is to be welcomed. There can be no reason why the term "professional legal adviser" should be defined as narrowly as in the *Reading Borough Council* case. As Baker J observed in *A Local Authority v A Mother, A Father, X and Y (by their guardian)*,[58] the cloak of confidentiality surrounding care proceedings has been significantly lifted in the last 17 years by the successive relaxation of the rules. Yet the definition adopted in the *Reading Borough Council* case would, if correct, leave the position of legal representatives akin to that which prevailed before the process of relaxation began, and would do little to explain the purpose of the FPR 2005 in introducing the "professional legal adviser" as a category of potential recipient of such communications.

---

[54] Expressly stated by the Court of Appeal in *Re H (Children)* [2009] EWCA Civ 704.

[55] See the *Reading Borough Council* case [2006] EWHC 1465 (Fam) at 90.

[56] [2012] 1 F.L.R. 142.

[57] In that case the parents had made partial admissions in the care proceedings in respect of failing to protect their baby. The Chief Constable applied for disclosure of the transcripts of their evidence. He sought a delay before such was disclosed to each parent as the police wished to interview each before he or she had sight of what had been said by the other. The court granted the application for disclosure. However, on a proper construction of r.12.73(1)(a)(iii) the application for delayed disclosure to the parents had to fail. The guiding principle was one of fairness and disclosure was to be authorised on such terms as to achieve a proper balance between the competing rights and interests referred to in *Re C (A minor)* [1997] Fam 76. Each parent had heard the evidence of the other and had discussed it with their family law teams. Their learning disabilities compounded their difficulty in remembering and telling their criminal defence teams about it. The fairest outcome was for both sets of defence solicitors to have both sets of transcripts with no court imposed delay.

[58] [2014] EWHC 278 (Fam) at [36].

Practice Direction 12G

18.47 Practice Direction 12G, referred to in rule 12.73(1)(c) of the FPR, provides inter alia:

> "Subject to any direction of the court information may be communicated for the purposes of the law relating to contempt in accordance with paragraph 2.1 . . . "

Paragraph 2.1 contains a table in which certain specified persons are given permission to communicate specified information to other specified people for specified purposes. The two aspects of most relevance to the trial of criminal offences relating to the sexual (or indeed physical) abuse of children are, first, that a party to care proceedings may disclose to a police officer the text or summary of the whole or part of a judgment for the purposes of a criminal investigation,[59] and secondly, that a party or person lawfully in receipt of information may communicate the text or summary of the whole or part of a judgment given in the proceedings to a member of the CPS to enable that service to discharge its functions under any enactment.

18.48 The current rules therefore state that communication of information relating to care proceedings falls into three categories:

  a. Communications which, under rule 12.73(1)(a), may be made as a matter of right;

  b. Communications which, under rule 12.73(1)(c) and Practice Direction 12G, may be made subject to any direction of the Family Court, including in appropriate circumstances a direction that they should not be made; and

  c. Other communications which, under rule 12.73(1)(b), may only be made with the court's permission.

When Disclosure should be Ordered

18.49 When an application for disclosure is made to the family court, the judge has to perform a balancing exercise between the importance of maintaining confidentiality in family cases and the public interest in making material information available for the purposes of a criminal trial. In doing so the judge should take into account the purpose for which the information is required, its weight and significance, the importance of the child witness and the gravity of the offence.[60]

---

[59] "Criminal investigation" is defined (in para.6(1) of the Practice Direction) as meaning "an investigation conducted by police officers with a view to it being ascertained (a) whether a person should be charged with an offence or (b) whether a person charged with an offence is guilty of it".

[60] *Re A (Criminal Proceedings: Disclosure)* [1996] 1 F.L.R 221, at 224 per Butler-Sloss LJ.

In *Re H*,[61] the Court of Appeal observed: 18.50

"... these cases inevitably involve a fine balance. This is so especially (a) where a parent has made a confession within what I will call the confines of the family court, with all the consequential benefits within the family justice system and (b) where there is the ongoing possibility of rehabilitation, which might be impeded or harmed by further criminal investigations: but at the same time (c) where there is still, inevitably, a strong public interest in the investigation and prosecution of serious crime."

The Court of Appeal in *Re C (A Minor)*[62] identified the following among   18.51
the matters for a judge to consider when deciding whether to order disclosure:

"(1) The welfare and interests of the child or children concerned in the care proceedings. If the child is likely to be adversely affected by the order in any serious way, this will be a very important factor.[63]

(2) The welfare and interests of other children generally.

(3) The maintenance of confidentiality in children cases.

(4) The importance of encouraging frankness in children's cases. All parties to this appeal agree that this is a very important factor and is likely to be of particular importance in a case to which section 98(2) applies. The underlying purpose of section 98 is to encourage people to tell the truth in cases concerning children, and the incentive is that any admission will not be admissible in evidence in a criminal trial. Consequently, it is important in this case. However, the added incentive of guaranteed confidentiality is not given by the words of the section and cannot be given.

(5) The public interest in the administration of justice. Barriers should not be erected between one branch of the judicature and another because this may be inimical to the overall interests of justice.

(6) The public interest in the prosecution of serious crime and the punishment of offenders, including the public interest in convicting those who have been guilty of violent or sexual offences against children. There is a strong public interest in making available material to the police which is relevant to a criminal trial. In many cases, this is likely to be a very important factor.

(7) The gravity of the alleged offence and the relevance of the evidence to it. If the evidence has little or no bearing on the investigation or the trial, this will militate against a disclosure order.

(8) The desirability of co-operation between various agencies concerned with the welfare of children, including the social services departments, the police service, medical practitioners, health visitors, schools, etc. This is partic- ularly important in cases concerning children.

(9) In a case to which section 98(2) applies, the terms of the section itself, namely that the witness was not excused from answering incriminating

---

[61] *Re H (Children)* [2009] EWCA Civ 704.
[62] [1997] Fam 76, at 85. This case was decided under the FPR 1991, but the guidelines set down in it were held still to be applicable by Baker J in *A Local Authority v A Mother, A Father, X and Y (by their guardian)* [2014] EWHC 278 (Fam).
[63] See *Re X (Children)* [2007] EHWC 1719 (Fam), at 37, where Munby J (as he then was) ordered disclosure of a father's evidence in which he admitted to seven instances of incest for use in the criminal trial where he was charged with only one instance (the only evidence before the court coming from the fact his daughter was pregnant by him). The daughter refused to co-operate. The father pleaded guilty and the information was held to be relevant to the victim impact statement. It was held that the children have a direct and important interest in ensuring there is no miscarriage of justice in the criminal trial and ensuring the truth comes out.

questions, and that any statement of admission would not be admissible against him in criminal proceedings. Fairness to the person who has incriminated himself and any others affected by the incriminating statement and any danger of oppression would also be relevant considerations.

(10) Any other material disclosure which has already taken place."

It should be remembered that *Re C* was decided before the implementation of the Human Rights Act. As a result of that Act, a court when deciding whether to order disclosure is now also called upon to consider arts 6 and 8 of the ECHR. The art.8 rights of the child are likely to be infringed in many instances where disclosure is sought. One example is *London Borough of Lewisham v D*,[64] in which there were concurrent care proceedings and a police investigation. The maternity of some of the children was in dispute. The police had a DNA sample from the putative mother as a result of her arrest on allegations of assault and child cruelty. They sought access from the family court to the results of the DNA tests performed upon the children. The judge found that the art.8 rights of the children would be infringed by such disclosure, but he decided that disclosure was nonetheless justified under art.8(2) as being necessary for the prevention of crime or for the protection of the rights and freedoms of others and also proportionate for those purposes.

18.52   An extremely useful analysis of the current law and the principles to be applied can be found in the first instance decision of Baker J in *A Local Authority v A Mother, A Father, X and Y (by their guardian)*.[65] Care proceedings began when child Y was found to have sustained serious injuries. After the initial hearing the judge found that neither parent had told the truth about how the injuries were sustained; the injuries were sustained when the child was in the care of one or both of the parents; it was not possible to say whether the injuries were sustained in one or more than one incident nor to identify which parent was responsible; it was probable that one parent was the perpetrator and the other lied to protect him or her. At the end of the hearing the judge urged both parents to be more frank with the court about what had happened to Y, so that the court and professionals could work with them to ensure both children were safe in the future. Two days later the father (F) confessed to being the perpetrator. The parents separated. A further fact finding hearing took place. F in a detailed statement set out the circumstances by which he had come to hurt the child. Experts confirmed the injuries could have been caused in that way. The judge ordered the children to be returned to the mother. F had supervised contact. The police had earlier opened a file on the case but it was closed as they could not prove which parent had inflicted the injuries. Following the hearing, the police applied for disclosure of any information that had come to light indicating the perpetrator of the injuries "in order that the decision to prosecute that person can be taken". F, the mother and the guardian opposed disclosure.

[64] [2010] EWHC 1238 (Fam).
[65] [2014] EWHC 278 (Fam).

The local authority argued for it. Baker J stated that in the 17 years since *Re C* was decided, the cloak of confidentiality surrounding care proceedings had been significantly lifted by the successive relaxation of the rules. In this case, the fact that no warning had been given to F when he gave his evidence in the family proceedings that in certain circumstances any confession could be disclosed to the police was a factor in his decision whether or not to order disclosure of his judgment, but was only one factor in the balancing exercise. Baker J concluded that the balance in the case clearly fell in favour of disclosure to the police and CPS, subject to clear directions restricting further disclosure of the judgment or any information contained therein without permission of the court. He concluded[66]:

> "The assaults inflicted on Y by the father were serious. The amendments [of] the rules have been carefully crafted to enable the police to be informed of the judge's findings and reasons, but to preclude any further use of the information in the judgment without the further permission of the family court. The public interest in the sharing of information between the agencies involved in child protection, and the removal of barriers between different branches of the justice system, have been recognised by the terms of Practice Direction 12G and are underlined by the terms of the 2013 Protocol. There may be cases where other factors outweigh this public interest. In my judgment, this case does not fall into that category. The welfare of the children will not be significantly affected simply by the disclosure of the judgment, provided the police and the CPS are precluded from disclosing it, or any information contained in it, to any person without the court's permission. Indeed in so far as the judgment completes the exoneration of the mother, it may indeed buttress the children's placement in her care and therefore perhaps improve their emotional security . . . The purpose of disclosing the judgment is to inform the police of the outcome of the fact-finding process in the care proceedings so that they can decide whether to pursue their investigation and make a further application for disclosure."

PRIVILEGE AGAINST SELF-INCRIMINATION

Although s.98(2) of the Children Act 1989 makes an admission of guilt by a parent in proceedings brought under that Act inadmissible in criminal proceedings for any offence other than perjury, the section does not prohibit the use of the admission in other ways: **18.53**

- As seen in *A Local Authority v A Mother, A Father, X and Y (by their guardian)*, discussed above, the fact of it can be disclosed to the police to be used as a pointer in their investigation;
- Putting inconsistent statements to a witness in a criminal trial in order to challenge their evidence or attack their credibility has been held not to amount to using their evidence "against" them.[67]

---

[66] At [56], [59].

[67] *Re L (care: confidentiality)* [1999] 1 F.L.R. 165 (*held*, a statement made in care proceedings could be used to cross-examine a witness by the prosecution and co-defendants. Further, any injunction made to try to afford absolute protection to a witness in care proceedings might fall foul of art.6 of the ECHR).

- In one case,[68] it was held that an admission of guilt by a mother to doctors in care proceedings that she had inflicted fatal injuries on her child should be disclosed to the police and the Crown Court judge in later criminal; proceedings against her, in order to prevent the "peddling of a bogus defence". A summary account of how the injuries were caused could be disclosed to medical experts instructed for the criminal trial, though her admission of guilt should not.

- Similarly, it has been held that the disclosure of a father's confession in family proceedings that he had committed incest with his daughter on seven occasions should be disclosed in a victim impact statement where the father had pleaded guilty to one offence of incest.[69] This was "necessary in order to ensure that the defendant is properly, fairly and justly sentenced for this particularly wicked crime; in particular to ensure that he is not able to escape his just deserts by peddling a false account in mitigation." This did not offend against s.98, as the material was to be used by the prosecution not in order to make its case against the defendant, but to challenge any account he sought to put forward at trail that was inconsistent with his evidence in the family proceedings. Disclosure was also ordered to the Criminal Injuries Compensation Authority. Munby J (as he then was) found it relevant to the issue of disclosure that the father had not engaged frankly with the Family Court. There was a marked absence of co-operation. The father was obliged to admit the extent of his wrongdoing because of an unintended slip of the tongue when he referred to the occasions (plural) on which sexual intercourse had taken place. Had he engaged frankly, the judge said his conclusion might have been different. The defendant received a sentence of imprisonment two years longer than may otherwise have been the case.

Legal Professional Privilege

18.54   A client can claim legal professional privilege for two types of communication.[70] First, communications between him and his lawyer made for the purposes of obtaining and giving legal advice. A document intended to be a communication between solicitor and client is privileged even if it is never communicated.[71] In this regard the privilege is absolute and any document protected by it is immune from production in the absence of waiver by the

---

[68] *A District Council v M (West Yorkshire Police as interveners)* [2007] EWHC 3471 (Fam).
[69] *Re X children* [2008] EWHC 242 (Fam).
[70] The history, case law and present day scope of each form of the privilege were extensively reviewed in *Three Rivers DC v Governor and Company of the Bank of England (No.5)* [2003] Q.B. 1556 (CA) and *Three Rivers DC v Governor and Company of the Bank of England (No.6)* [2005] 1 A.C. 610.
[71] See *Three Rivers (No.5)*, last note.

holder of it. In *R. v Derby Magistrates' Court Ex p. B*,[72] the House of Lords held that legal professional privilege is a fundamental condition on which the administration of justice as a whole rests. No question of a balance of competing interests arises and no exception should be allowed to the absolute nature of the privilege, once established.

This aspect of the *Derby* decision could result in serious miscarriages of   **18.55**
justice. It is difficult to envisage a more obvious example of the need for disclosure than the facts of that very case. The witness had himself been charged with (and acquitted of) the murder with which the defendant, his step-father, was later charged. At first he denied the murder, but he subsequently admitted being solely responsible for the killing. Thereafter he made a statement alleging that his step-father had killed the girl and said that although he (the witness) was present and took some part, he did so under duress. At his trial he successfully relied on his second account. It is perhaps unsurprising that the magistrate at the step-father's committal proceedings described documents held by the witness's solicitors as "very material to the conduct of the defence". Nonetheless, legal professional privilege was described as absolute. It follows that the proof of a co-defendant who at the eleventh hour pleads guilty and then gives evidence for the prosecution against his co-defendants will not be disclosable, even if it is highly material and wholly inconsistent with his evidence. In light of the decision in *Derby Magistrates' Court,* disclosure is simply impossible unless the privilege is voluntarily waived. In practice, the defence advocate is confined to asking the witness to waive privilege and commenting upon any refusal in his final speech. In certain extreme cases, for example where the case against a defendant rests wholly on the evidence of the witness who has refused to waive privilege, the only course open to the defence is to seek to mount an abuse of process argument and/or raise an objection to the calling of the evidence on the basis that it would be impossible for the defendant to have a fair trial as guaranteed by art.6 of the ECHR.

The second type of communication for which a client can claim privilege   **18.56**
is communications between him, his lawyer and third parties with the dominant purpose of preparation for contemplated or pending litigation. In *Re L*,[73] the House of Lords held that an expert's report obtained in care proceedings with the leave of the court is not the subject of this "litigation privilege" and has to be disclosed to the other parties in the proceedings, whether or not it is favourable to the case of the party who has obtained it. Justification for litigation privilege arises from the nature of the adversarial process. As proceedings under Pt IV of the Children Act 1989 are essentially non-adversarial in nature, litigation privilege has no place in relation to reports which could not have been obtained without the leave of the court. It

---

[72] [1996] A.C. 487.
[73] [1996] 2 W.L.R. 395.

is not a case of the court overriding litigation privilege. In these circumstances it simply does not exist.[74] However similar reports prepared for criminal proceedings, which are obviously adversarial in nature, are protected from disclosure in family or any other proceedings.[75]

THE 2013 PROTOCOL

18.57 Part A of the Protocol lays down detailed rules about the procedure for disclosure into the family justice system by the police and/or CPS. Part B is of more direct relevance to criminal courts concerned with the trial of sexual offences, as it concerns disclosure from the local authority/family justice system into the criminal justice system. The key provisions of Part B insofar as it concerns documents relating to family proceedings are[76]:

- As soon as is reasonably practicable, and in any event on the issue of proceedings, the local authority will provide notice to the police of the contemplation or existence of Family Court proceedings, including, where proceedings have been instituted, the details of all parties and legal representatives. Where criminal proceedings are contemplated or have been instituted, the police will forward this information to the CPS who will give due priority to making charging decisions in cases involving Family Court proceedings.
- An application by the police and/or CPS to the Family Court for disclosure must be in form C2, must (in the case of the police) contain details of the named officer to whom release is sought and must specify the purpose and use to which the material is intended to be put. The application should seek leave to disclose the material to the CPS or police (as appropriate) and the defence and (subject to s.98(2) of the Children Act 1989) to use it in evidence in criminal proceedings. The application must be served on all parties to the Family Court proceedings.[77]
- The application will be determined at a hearing at the Family Court. The CPS and police will not attend unless directed by the court to do so. Where practicable the police/CPS should seek prior written consent from all the parties and make a written application for a

---

[74] See *Vernon v Bosley (No.2)* [1997] 1 All E.R. 614. The ratio of *R v L* is not confined to wardship and care proceedings. If reports are obtained from experts in Children Act proceedings they are not privileged. That position does not change if they are then used in other civil proceedings. Leave of the Family Court would however be required. Reports obtained without leave will not be privileged where leave ought first to have been obtained.

[75] *S County Council v B* [2000] Fam. 76, at 102.

[76] It must be remembered that local protocols should be in place enshrining these principles. The wording and order may therefore not be the same as in the original protocol.

[77] There is no reference in the Protocol to how the defence should make any application they might wish. This may be because it is envisaged that all necessary disclosure will be applied for by the police/CPS. If this is the rationale, it may be naïve. If the defence do seek disclosure the same procedure for applications can and probably should be followed. Local protocols should deal with defence applications.

a

consent order to the Family Court. Alternatively and wherever possible, the police and/or CPS will ask the local authority lawyer to request that the Family Court considers the issue of disclosure to the police and/or CPS at the next hearing. In this way the Family Court will be able to make any orders that appear appropriate without the need for an application to the court. If such a request is made, the local authority must put the other parties to the Family Court proceedings on notice and provide the court with details of the officer to whom disclosure is to be made and the purpose for which it is to be made.[78]

- In rare cases where it considers it appropriate to do so, the Family Court should make orders for disclosure to the police and/or CPS without application having been made.
- The local authority will forward to the CPS copies of relevant Family Court judgments in their possession. If necessary, these will be appropriately redacted. If not in possession of such a judgment, the local authority will notify the CPS so that the CPS can obtain the judgment direct from the Family Court. In these circumstances no formal application needs to be made. Where it appears to a local authority that a judgment will be relevant to criminal proceedings, the authority will request the Family Court to expedite the preparation of the judgment for release to the CPS. Alternatively this will be considered at a linked directions hearing.
- All material obtained from the local authority, including the list of material not disclosed by the authority, will be listed on the sensitive disclosure schedule MG6D. The police will reveal the existence of material obtained in accordance with rule 12.73(1)(a)(viii) of the FPR 2010 without describing it on this schedule. As appropriate, the CPS will seek the permission of the Family Court to access this material.
- Where material has been obtained following an application to the Family Court, the police must indicate to the CPS whether the court has given permission for the material to be shared with the CPS and defence. Further application may have to be made to the court by the police/CPS as appropriate.

Linked Directions Hearings

Part C of the 2013 Protocol, dealing with linked directions hearings, applies where a person connected with the child who is the subject of the care **18.58**

[78] There is sense in a procedure which reduces the number of hearings at the Family Court and in this all being resolved at the same time. Some local authorities, however, have refused to include this provision in local protocols on the ground that this will hamper their already strained relationship with the parties. Courts in these areas may like to consider whether the police/CPS could, on notice to all parties, in writing invite the Family Court to consider the question of disclosure at the next hearing.

proceedings or the child himself is to be tried at the Crown Court for a violent or sexual offence or for an offence of child cruelty against the child, or any other child or any person connected with the child, and either:

- The local authority ("LA"), CPS or any party to the care proceedings (including the child's guardian) considers that the care and criminal proceedings do, or may, impinge on one another, or
- In any public law proceedings in the High Court or County Court or in any proceedings in the Crown Court, a judge is satisfied that the protocol does, or may, apply.

18.59 If the allocated case management judge ("ACMJ") in the Family Court considers a linked directions hearing may be appropriate, he/she shall liaise with the Resident Judge ("RJ") to invite him/her to nominate a judge to be responsible for the management of the criminal case. If that is the case:

- In the care proceedings the ACMJ will issue directions for the linked hearing spelling out the respective parties' obligations, which may include but will not be limited to recordings and orders in the form at Annex I to the Protocol (use of which by the Family Court is mandatory).[79] At the same time, the ACMJ will consider giving permission to the LA to serve its case summary on the CPS and the Crown Court. This will state:
  - ○ The basis of the LA's application;
  - ○ Its contentions in respect of findings sought in relation to the "threshold criteria"[80];
  - ○ The current position in respect of the child;
  - ○ Details of the proposed assessments and/or expert assessments being undertaken and the time scales for the same;
  - ○ The timetable, if any, set for the proceedings within the Family Court.[81]
- Once a judge has been nominated to manage the criminal proceedings, the RJ shall direct the listing officer to liaise with family listing to agree the listing of the criminal and care cases for a linked directions hearing before the nominated criminal judge and the ACMJ. In appropriate cases, the RJ may agree to the ACMJ undertaking the responsibility for the management of the criminal

---

[79] This is in the form of an order. This includes a police disclosure order. The CPS will seek disclosure of papers from the family proceedings and documents held by the LA on its Social Services files. It contains a request that the RJ nominates a judge to be responsible for the management of the case with a view to listing a linked directions hearing.

[80] These are the criteria set out in s.31(2) of the Children Act 1989 which must be met before the Family Court can make a care or supervision order. The LA in making such an application must satisfy the judge that "(a) the child is suffering or is likely to suffer significant harm and (b) that harm or likelihood of harm is attributable to (i) the care given to a child or likely to be given to him if the order were not made, not being what it would be reasonable to expect a parent to give to him; or (ii) the child being beyond parental control". The threshold document sets out the allegations made against the parent, i.e. what the parent is alleged to be doing to affect the wellbeing of the child.

[81] 2013 Protocol, para.16.6.

case where he/she is authorised to try criminal cases and, where appropriate, serious sexual offence cases.

If at a preliminary or other pre-trial hearing listed before the Crown Court the judge is satisfied that the 2013 Protocol does or may apply but no reference has yet been made by the ACMJ for consideration of a linked directions hearing, the judge shall notify the Designated Family Judge accordingly who shall consider with the RJ and ACMJ whether a linked directions hearing is required. If there is a need for such a hearing the RJ shall nominate a judge to be responsible for the management of the criminal case and arrangements made for the linked directions hearing. The respective court files will be cross referenced and clearly marked as "linked cases". **18.60**

The criminal case will be listed before the judge at the Crown Court in public, with the linked directions hearing appointment in the care proceedings listed for hearing in private immediately thereafter. Subject to specific objections raised by the parties, the advocates appearing in the criminal case may be invited to remain during the directions appointment in the care proceedings. **18.61**

The LA's legal representative and the CPS shall agree a schedule of issues identifying those matters which are likely to be considered at the linked directions hearing. The LA must circulate that schedule to the other parties in the criminal and care proceedings by 16.00 no less than two working days prior to the linked directions hearing. On the day of the hearing, the advocates in each set of proceedings shall meet no later than one hour prior to the time fixed for the hearing to discuss the schedule of issues with a view to identifying what directions may be required with particular reference to the trial timetable, disclosure and expert evidence.[82] **18.62**

The directions hearing will be linked but not wholly combined, because of the different parties and different procedural rules which apply. The judge will determine whether it is appropriate for some or all of the directions to be issued at a joint hearing or separately and the order of any directions to be issued. **18.63**

At the conclusion of the hearing in the criminal case, counsel for the Crown will be invited to draw the minute of order, to be agreed with the defence, which will be submitted to the judge on the day of hearing for his/her approval.[83] This will be copied to the parties in the care proceedings. With the permission of the family court, the order made in the care proceedings will be copied by the LA to the CPS and defence lawyers in the criminal proceedings. **18.64**

---

[82] There may be practical difficulties in achieving this. Family practitioners will be accustomed to the court requiring them to attend at a stated time before the actual hearing time. Those legally aided will be paid for those additional hours. There are no such provisions for criminal practitioners who will be paid a set fee for the hearing. Criminal practitioners are likely to have other hearings within the court centre to make the day economically viable for them. The ideal of all dedicating the time needed for an effective discussion and hearing may in those circumstances be difficult to achieve.

[83] It may be that the judge will type the directions as they are made and distribute them. As long as there is a record which cannot be disputed it matters not how it is achieved.

18.65 Any adjourned linked directions hearing shall be listed before the same judge (unless the judge otherwise directs), but the judge who is the ACMJ shall not preside over the trial in the criminal proceedings or pass sentence if there is a guilty plea nor shall the judge give a *Goodyear* indication. The judge who presides over the criminal trial or who passes sentence if there is a guilty plea shall notify the ACMJ of the outcome.

18.66 The following are to be considered at the linked directions hearing:

- The timetabling of both the criminal and care proceedings to coordinate such as to ensure the most appropriate order of trial and that each case is heard as expeditiously as possible;
- Disclosure of evidence with particular reference to disclosure from one set of proceedings to the other with such permission as may be required by the relevant procedural rules;
- Expert evidence with particular reference to the identification of expert witnesses, their willingness to act within the court timetable and the requirements of the Practice Direction concerning the instruction of experts, their availability and role in the criminal and care proceedings;
- Any directions to be given in relation to issues of PII and for any witness summonses required for third party disclosure (Part 17 of the CPR 2015);
- Arrangements for the interviewing of children in care for the purpose of the criminal proceedings and any arrangement for the child to give evidence at any criminal or family hearing;
- Ensuring where appropriate that a transcript of relevant evidence or judgment in the trial heard first in time is available in the subsequent proceedings;
- Issues relating to any question of assessment or therapeutic input required by any child involved in the proceedings;
- Issues in relation to restrictions on publicity which it is considered may be required;
- Issues in relation to any relevant material which may be pertinent to the issue of bad character (in respect of previous convictions or other alleged "reprehensible behaviour"), whether of defendants or non-defendants;
- Other legal or social work related steps in the Family Court.

Documents Not Held by The Family Court

The 2013 Protocol

18.67 Until relatively recently, most local authorities would not voluntarily disclose the documents most likely to be of relevance to a criminal trial. They felt under a duty to claim public interest immunity for records such as those held by social services. This has changed. As the 2013 Protocol states:

"PII applications in the criminal court will be rare. Local Authority material relating to a child is no longer a 'class' of material to which PII applies."[84]

The Protocol sets down a procedure based on proper and timely requests for disclosure in compliance with the Rules which are expected to be met in a spirit of co-operation. Annexes to the Protocol contain forms to be used at various points in the application process. Part B deals with requests made of local authorities for material in documents not held by the civil court.[85]

The Protocol envisages that in cases involving children, applications for third party material (largely social services documents) from the LA will be made by the police or CPS at an early stage, preferably pre-charge. Part B states: **18.68**

- Following the commencement of a criminal investigation into alleged child abuse, the police will provide to the LA the form at Annex C of the Protocol. This will involve requests for material which must be as prescriptive and detailed as possible and necessary for the pursuit of reasonable lines of enquiry. The form will include reasonable time-scales, but the presumption is that the LA will deal with any request from the police as expeditiously as possible so as not to jeopardise the criminal investigation.[86]

- Upon receipt of the form at Annex C from the police, the LA will identify and collate relevant material from Children's Services or other files as appropriate. The LA single point of contact ("SPOC")[87] will liaise with relevant departments in the collation of such material for the police to assist the criminal investigation.[88]

- The LA will identify for the police the school(s) attended by the child/children subject to the investigation. This will enable the police to approach the schools directly. If it is practicable to do so, the LA will obtain and collate relevant educational files for police examination.[89]

---

[84] Para.14.1. While this wording is technically correct, i.e. Local Authority material relating to a child is no longer a "class" of material to which PII applies, that is not to say that PII never applies to Local Authority material relating to a child. The principle is that the documents should not be subject to PII merely because they are such material; instead, the contents should be examined. PII may apply to individual pieces of such material when assessed in relation to their contents. That said, the Protocol clearly intends that such applications should be rare.

[85] It must be remembered that the 2013 Protocol only applies to documents held by local authorities about children who were 17 or under at the time of the alleged criminality. Local protocols should address the procedure for those held on vulnerable adults or by other third parties such as schools. The Protocol is not, however, binding on local authorities and some areas have found it more difficult than others to draft acceptable local protocols.

[86] Para.9.2. This is where in practice many applications are deficient. The police often make blanket requests for disclosure with little attempt, if any, to give the detail needed by local authority lawyers to enable them to comply with their disclosure responsibilities. Note also the need for the local authorities to comply with the Data Protection Act 1998: see para.18.05, above.

[87] This person will have been identified and contact details given in each local protocol.

[88] Para.10.1.

[89] Para.10.2.

- Subject to occasions when the LA can disclose to the police documents relating to Family Court proceedings without the consent of the court, the LA will ensure that documents relating to Family Court proceedings are not included in the files to be examined by the police. Where there are such documents, the LA will provide a list (e.g. by providing a redacted copy of the court index) of the material without describing what it is, in order for the police and/or CPS, if appropriate, to apply to the Family Court for disclosure.[90]
- Where, in exceptional circumstances, the LA is not able to include other material (not relating to Family Court proceedings) in the files to be examined by the police, the LA will notify the police in writing of the existence of the material, including the reason why the material is not being made available to them. Such a course should be exceptional because the LA recognises that the material will be regarded as sensitive by the police and the CPS. It will not be disclosed without further consultation with the LA or by order of the court.[91]
- Within the timescales set out in the Annex C request (or otherwise agreed between the police and the LA), the police will examine and review the material collated by the LA. This will usually take place on LA premises but may be elsewhere by agreement. The police may make notes and take copies of the material. The material will not be disclosed to the defence without further consultation with the LA or order of the court.[92]
- The LA will notify the police and/or CPS if further relevant material comes to light to arrange further examination.[93]
- Where new issues arise in the criminal case (e.g. following submission of a defence case statement), the police will submit a further Annex C form requesting access to material not previously examined.[94]
- The CPS will review the material in accordance with its duties under the CPIA and under the *Attorney General's Guidelines on Disclosure*. Blanket disclosure must not be made to the defence—only material which might undermine the prosecution case or assist the defence case will fall to be disclosed.[95]

[90] Para.10.3.
[91] Para.10.7. This does not mean that the police or CPS are absolved of their duties under the CPIA. Paras 13.9–13.11 deal with the procedure before disclosure to the defence is made.
[92] Para.10.8.
[93] Para.10.9.
[94] Para.10.10.
[95] Para.13.6. Para.13.2 states that PII applications to the criminal court for the withholding of sensitive material should be rare. Fairness ordinarily requires that all material which weakens the prosecution case or strengthens that of the defence should be disclosed. There is no basis for making a PII application except where the prosecutor has identified material which fulfils the disclosure test, disclosure of which would create a real risk of serious prejudice to an important public interest. The Protocol cites *R. v H and C* [2004] 2 A.C. 134.

- Where the LA has not made a document available to the police on the basis of confidentiality (e.g. consent has not been obtained from the person to whom the document relates), the CPS will consider whether it is appropriate to seek access to such material by means of a witness summons under s.2 of the Criminal Procedure (Attendance of Witnesses) Act 1965 in the Crown Court.[96]
- If application is made by the CPS for such a summons, the CPS will serve the application on the criminal court and the LA, identifying the LA SPOC as the person required to produce the documents. In addition, where the Crown Court so directs, the CPS will serve the application on the person to whom the confidential document relates.[97]
- Where any LA material falls to be disclosed under the CPIA, the CPS will notify the LA of that decision and the reasons for it within two days of the review, whenever possible. The CPS will provide proposals for editing or summarising material for the purposes of disclosure to the defence. Where no material falls to be disclosed, the CPS will inform the LA that is the case.[98]
- Within five working days the LA will be given an opportunity to make any written representations to the CPS regarding disclosure. Where exceptionally the LA cannot meet the five working day timetable, the LA will communicate with the CPS to seek an extended timetable.[99]

THE DUTY TO OBTAIN THIRD PARTY MATERIAL IN A CRIMINAL TRIAL

The 2013 Protocol clearly places the duty to obtain third party material in cases involving allegations against children at the door of the prosecution and, as stated above, envisages that this will take place at an early stage of the investigation.   **18.69**

Paragraphs 53–55 of the *Attorney General's Guidelines on Disclosure* stress that where the investigator, disclosure officer or prosecutor believes that a third party has material which might reasonably be considered as undermining the prosecution case or assisting the case of the defence, the investigator, disclosure officer or prosecutor should take whatever steps are reasonable in the particular case to obtain it. The matter should not be left   **18.70**

---

[96] Para.13.7.

[97] Para.13.8. This is in accordance with r.17.5(3) of the CPR 2015.

[98] Para.13.9. The form at Annex E to the Protocol is to be used where it has been decided that material falls to be disclosed.

[99] Paras 13.10 and 13.11. Again there are no provisions for the defence to obtain disclosure. This will have to be done by means of the procedure set out in r.17 of the CPR 2015. Local protocols should state how and when this should be done and whether it is possible to include defence requests in prosecution applications following defence case statements or even earlier, possibly within 14 days of the preliminary hearing. This will avoid the need for the LA to go through its files too many times.

if the third party refuses disclosure. If it is felt that the disclosure test in s.2 of the Criminal Procedure (Attendance of Witnesses) Act 1965 is met, the prosecutor or investigator should apply for a witness summons.

18.71　The duty of the prosecution in obtaining third party disclosure is also contained in CPS guidelines:

- Chapter 4 of the CPS Disclosure Manual;
- Chapter 15 of the Rape and Sexual Offences Guidance;
- Paragraphs 114–118 of the Guidelines on Prosecuting Cases of Child Sexual Abuse.[100]

18.72　It does not follow that the prosecution must take steps to obtain disclosure in every case where there may be material held by a third party. Documents sought must be relevant to the issues in the trial.[101] However the *Attorney General's Guidelines*, CPS guidance and 2013 Protocol are all clear that the prosecution cannot sit back in a case where information exists in the hands of a third party and wait for the defence to obtain it on the grounds that it is more likely to assist them. This is not to say that the defence play no part in this process. The prosecution should have considered third party disclosure pre-charge in most cases. It will fall to be considered afresh once the issues are known. Judges should identify issues and make directions about third party disclosure at the preliminary hearing.[102] This will be particularly necessary in cases involving pre-trial cross examination of children under s.28 of the Youth Justice and Criminal Evidence Act 1999 and for trials involving witnesses under 10.[103]

Non-voluntary Disclosure of Third Party Material

18.73　It can be seen that the 2013 Protocol envisages early co-operation between the police and the local authority to obtain relevant material. The emphasis is on voluntary disclosure of relevant material with controlled onward disclosure only in prescribed circumstances. There are circumstances, however, when more formal applications will have to be made following the procedure set out in Part 17 of the CPR 2015:

---

[100] For references, see para.18.12, above.

[101] See *Alibhai* [2004] EWCA Crim 681, in which the Court of Appeal said that before taking steps to obtain third party material it must be shown that there was not only a suspicion that the third party had relevant material but also a suspicion that the material held by the third party was likely to satisfy the disclosure test. Even if there is the necessary suspicion, the prosecution has "a margin of consideration" as to what steps to take in any particular case and is thus not under an absolute obligation to obtain material that is suspected to satisfy the disclosure test.

[102] Para.9 of the Judicial Protocol, for which see para.18.03, above.

[103] Local Authorities frequently have but one legal adviser. They need as much notice as possible to look at third party requests and multiple requests should be avoided. One way to achieve this would be for a direction at the preliminary hearing that the prosecution serves its list of focused requests, whether already made or intended to be made, of the third party on the defence within 14 days. The defence should add any focused requests of their own (setting out the issues in the case and why such requested material is relevant) and serve upon the prosecution 14 days thereafter. The joint request is then to be served by the prosecution on the third party.

- When the LA refuses to make voluntary disclosure to the prosecution following a request to them for disclosure from Social Services files;
- When the police/CPS seek disclosure from other third parties such as medical practitioners or counsellors who are not willing to make voluntary disclosure[104];
- Defence applications to a third party where the prosecution have indicated they are not prepared to pursue the disclosure sought by the defence.

THE CRIMINAL PROCEDURE RULES

Applications for non-voluntary third party disclosure must comply with Part 17 of the CPR 2015, which provides: **18.74**

"**17.3.**—(1) A party who wants the court to issue a witness summons, warrant or order must apply as soon as practicable after becoming aware of the grounds for doing so.
(2) The party applying must—
    (a) identify the proposed witness;
    (b) explain—
        (i) what evidence the proposed witness can give or produce,
        (ii) why it is likely to be material evidence, and
        (iii) why it would be in the interests of justice to issue a summons, order or warrant as appropriate.
(3) The application may be made orally unless—
    (a) rule 17.5 applies; or
    (b) the court otherwise directs.
17.4.—(1) An application in writing under rule 17.3 must be in the form set out in the Practice Direction, containing the same declaration of truth as a witness statement.
(2) The party applying must serve the application—
    (a) in every case, on the court officer and as directed by the court; and
    (b) as required by rule 17.5, if that rule applies.
17.5.—(1) This rule applies to an application under rule 17.3 for a witness summons requiring the proposed witness—
    (a) to produce in evidence a document or thing; or
    (b) to give evidence about information apparently held in confidence,
that relates to another person.
(2) The application must be in writing in the form required by rule 17.4.
(3) The party applying must serve the application-
    (a) on the proposed witness, unless the court otherwise directs; and
    (b) on one or more of the following if the court so directs—
        (i) a person to whom the proposed evidence relates,
        (ii) another party.

---

[104] The 2013 Protocol does not cover material held by bodies other than the local authority. Local protocols should cater for this and, it is suggested, in so far as is possible adopt the procedure set out in the 2013 model.

(4) The court must not issue a witness summons where this rule applies unless—

(a) everyone served with the application has had at least 14 days in which to make representations, including representations about whether there should be a hearing of the application before the summons is issued; and

(b) the court is satisfied that it has been able to take adequate account of the duties and rights, including rights of confidentiality, of the proposed witness and of any person to whom the proposed evidence relates."

18.75 Rule 17.6 provides for the person in receipt of the summons to object to the production of the material sought on the grounds that it is not likely to be material evidence or, if it is, the duties and rights (including rights of confidentiality) of the proposed witness or of any person to whom the document or thing relates, outweigh the reasons for issuing a summons. The court may require the proposed witness to make the material available for the objection to be assessed, and may invite the proposed witness or any person to whom the document or thing relates or any representative of such a person to help the court assess the objection.

SECTION 2 OF THE CRIMINAL PROCEDURE (ATTENDANCE OF WITNESSES) ACT 1965

18.76 Applicants must satisfy the court that they have met the test set out in s.2(1) of the Criminal Procedure (Attendance of Witnesses) Act 1965 before disclosure can be made:

"**2.—Issue of witness summons on application to Crown Court.**

(1) This section applies where the Crown Court is satisfied that—

(a) a person is likely to be able to give evidence likely to be material evidence, or produce any document or thing likely to be material evidence, for the purpose of any criminal proceedings before the Crown Court, and

(b) it is in the interests of justice to issue a summons under this section to secure the attendance of that person to give evidence or to produce the document or thing."

It is made clear in s.2(3) that the court may refuse to issue a summons if any requirement relating to the application is not fulfilled. Section 2(5) requires that the application must be made as soon as is reasonably practicable after the transfer of the case to the Crown Court and it must comply with the Criminal Procedure Rules.

"Likely to be material evidence"

18.77 It can be seen that a wholly separate disclosure regime is in existence for disclosure from third parties. An applicant for such material must satisfy the court that the material sought is "likely to be material evidence". For these purposes "likely" means a real possibility, not necessarily a probability.[105] The test is neither whether the material is relevant (although it would have to   **18.78** be relevant to be admissible) nor whether it is helpful to the person seeking it. The applicant has to show that the document sought is itself admissible in evidence. The material would not fall to be disclosed if:

- it is desired merely for the purposes of cross-examination. Documents used for this purpose are not admissible in evidence and therefore not likely to be material evidence.[106]
- it would be inadmissible without interpretation by an expert.[107] The most likely way in which a document may be admissible per se is if it is a business record and so falls within s.117 of the Criminal Justice Act 2003. Records held by social services and other agencies are likely to be business records within the meaning of s.117 in that they are "created or received by a person in the course of a trade, business, profession or other occupation, or as the holder of an unpaid office", and "the person who supplied the information contained in the statement had or may reasonably be supposed to have had personal knowledge of the matters dealt with". Note that s.117(1)(a) states that "a statement contained in a document is admissible if oral evidence given in the proceedings would be admissible as evidence of that matter". Opinion is therefore largely inadmissible.[108]

"In the interests of justice to issue a summons"

Section 2(1)(b) of the 1965 Act requires a judge to be satisfied that it is in the   **18.79** interests of justice for a summons to be issued. Rule 17.3(2)(b) of the CPR 2015 requires an applicant for third party material to state why the document requested is likely to be material evidence and why it is in the interests of

---

[105] *R. v Reading Justices, Ex p. Berkshire County Council* [1996] 1 Cr. App. R.239. In that case a wasted costs order was made against an advocate personally who was found not to have made a proper application. This may partly explain why counsel were reluctant in the immediate aftermath of the case to make any application for third party disclosure even in appropriate cases such as *North (Mark)* [2011] EWCA Crim 88, discussed in para.18.33, above.

[106] *North (Mark)* [2011] EWCA Crim 88 at 34. See also *R. v Derby Magistrates' Court Ex p. B* [1996] A.C. 487, at 500, where the House of Lords held that s.4 of the Criminal Procedure Act 1865 contemplates the cross-examiner having the inconsistent statement in his hand so that the procedure which might culminate in the document being admissible can begin. Section 97 of the Magistrates Courts Act 1980 (similar to s.2 of the Criminal Procedure (Attendance of Witnesses) Act 1965) contemplates the production by a witness of documents which are immediately admissible per se without more.

[107] *R. (on the application of Cunliffe) v West London Magistrates Court* [2006] EWHC 2081 (Admin), concerning an application for engineers' reports and calibration service sheets, the engineer's standing operation procedures and complete unedited F11 settings in relation to breath testing machines where D sought to argue he was not over the legal limit for driving and the machine must therefore be at fault. This was held to be a fishing expedition in any event.

[108] See *Butler (Carl)* [2015] EWCA Crim 854, fn.41, above.

justice in the particular case for a summons to be issued. This will necessarily involve the applicant setting out the reasons why the material sought is of importance to his case.

18.80 It is not permissible for an applicant to embark speculatively on an application for disclosure in the hope that something helpful may emerge—i.e. to embark on a fishing expedition.[109] It is impermissible therefore to call for the entirety of a file or files held by a local authority in cases where it is known there is a social services background. It does not, however, offend the spirit or the letter of s.2 of the 1965 Act to issue a witness summons seeking production of such documents with the motive of discovering both the precise nature of the contents of documents and, if they are helpful, adducing them in evidence.[110]

18.81 Strict compliance with the criminal procedure rules should enable an applicant to avoid the accusation that he is "fishing". If the application is properly made and the material sought of importance to the person making it, then the judge is likely to find that it is in the interests of justice to issue the summons and more likely to find in the applicant's favour when considering the material in question.[111]

WHERE A SUMMONS IS SERVED

18.82 Once the third party is in receipt of the summons, it is for him to form an initial judgment as to whether the test in s.2 of the 1965 Act is met and whether the files contain anything even potentially admissible in the trial. If the third party considers there is no such material, the applicant may still proceed with the application but is at risk as to costs if the application should fail.[112]

18.83 The decision whether the files contain anything even potentially admissible must necessarily involve questions of relevance. In *R. v W(G) and W(E)*,[113] the Court of Appeal held that the question of relevance is initially a decision for the possessor of the documents to make. He is entitled to claim that all

---

[109] See *R. v Reading Justices, Ex p. Berkshire County Council* [1996] 1 Cr. App. R.239; and see the Judicial Protocol, para.44, which states that "speculative enquiries without any proper basis in relation to third party material—whether by the prosecution or the defence—are to be discouraged and, in appropriate cases, the court will consider making an order for costs where an application is clearly unmeritorious and misconceived".

[110] *Clowes* (1992) 95 Cr. App. R 440 at 449.

[111] It is clear from recent judgments (e.g. *North (Mark)* [2011] EWCA Crim 88, discussed in para.18.33, above) that in recent years a more liberal approach has been taken to the question of third party disclosure. Fishing expeditions and general non-specific applications are still not allowed, but the restrictive regime following the *Reading Justices* case has been significantly relaxed. Many of the cases now coming before the Court of Appeal date from the period c.1996-2000, when there is little doubt that practitioners fought shy of making clearly appropriate applications for fear of wasted costs orders being made against them personally.

[112] *R. v H(L)* [1997] 1 Cr. App. R 176, at 178. Applications have to be carefully considered and, if appropriate, made notwithstanding this decision. It is applicable to applications under s.2 but dates from the more restrictive regime of the late 1990s.

[113] [1997] 1 Cr. App. R 166.

or some of the documents are irrelevant and should give his reasons for doing so. The next stage is for the judge, in the exercise of his or her discretion, to either accept the assertion of the possessor of the documents or to look at the documents himself. If the possessor's claim that the documents are irrelevant is suspect or implausible, the judge will wish to look at them. On the other hand he may regard an assurance from an independent and competent member of the Bar as sufficient reason for treating the documents as irrelevant. It is for the judge to give directions, impose conditions and monitor the process as he thinks fit. In *R. v W(G) and W(E)*, the defence had sought a large number of social services records. The judge directed that the local authority should appoint separate counsel to sort the documents for relevance. The Court of Appeal was keen to ensure that the judge was assisted in his task and not just dumped with the material for his decision. Again, this authority is from the late 1990s as the courts sought to impose some sort of structure on third party applications which were often made in an unfocused way and culminated in local authorities simply delivering their files for the judge to read. The CPR now impose the regime to be followed on applications. Local authorities are used to receiving more focused applications and should have looked through the material at an early stage at the request of the police or CPS in compliance with the 2013 Protocol. If there is an application for material previously refused, they will flag that within the files for the judge's attention. Local practices may vary, but in many areas the files are sent to the court with the local authority content to abide by the judge's decision without the need for oral argument.

It is vital that whoever considers the files must do so diligently with the   **18.84**
issues in the case well in mind. In this respect, see *The Queen on the Application of JRP v The Crown Prosecution Service*,[114] which Hooper LJ said provided a "salutary lesson to all charged with the responsibility of carrying out this task as to how grave the consequences can be if this task is not carried out diligently". The Court of Appeal in that case allowed an appeal following a referral from the CCRC. P was convicted in 2002 on 15 counts of indecent assault, buggery, incest and rape committed against three of his daughters when they were children. The local authority was asked pre-trial to review any material held on the complainants. Prosecution counsel was instructed to look at the files. She identified two and a quarter pages out of 284 that were relevant. The judge ordered the disclosure of those pages. The Court of Appeal accepted that considerably more should have been disclosed. There was material to refute the contention of two of the complainants that they had not wanted to see or live with their father following the period when they claimed to have been abused; there was considerable material to support the defence contention (denied by them) that they were taken into care not because of any sexual or physical abuse but

---

[114] [2010] EWCA Crim 2438.

because they had been out of control and their father had been concerned about them; and there was material to show that social services had investigated the sexual behaviour of two of the complainants that led to proceedings being taken against two other males. They had ample opportunity to complain about sexual abuse at the hands of their father in the course of that investigation, but had not done so. Hooper LJ said that the Protocol now in existence should mean that the sorry history of this case should not be repeated.

18.85   If the third party considers there is material that is relevant and admissible per se, then he must form a view as to whether he is prepared to make voluntary disclosure or will seek to claim public interest immunity. The question of PII is considered in the 2013 Protocol. This deals exclusively with disclosure by the local authority to the prosecution. It recognises that once disclosure has been made, the prosecution may be under a duty to disclose such material to the defence under the CPIA. It provides that the local authority is to be consulted before this takes place. The clear expectation in the Protocol is that the local authority will agree, subject to the sensitivity of the material, that the public interest in the prosecution of crime overrides the interests of confidentiality.[115]

18.86   Paragraph 13.2 of the 2013 Protocol states:

> "PII applications to the criminal court for the withholding of sensitive material should be rare. Fairness ordinarily requires that all material which weakens the prosecution case or strengthens that of the defence should be disclosed. There is no basis for making a PII application except where the prosecutor has identified material that fulfils the disclosure test, disclosure of which would create a real risk of serious prejudice to an important public interest."

Paragraph 14.1 acknowledges that disclosure can be made in edited form or by summarising in another document the issues arising in the material which may remove the sensitivity. It states:

> "PII applications in the criminal court will be rare. Local Authority material relating to a child is no longer a 'class' of material to which PII applies."[116]

18.87   Paragraph 14.1 states that, if the local authority does not agree to disclosure to the defence even in summary or edited form, then in "highly exceptional" cases, the CPS may need to make disclosure without the

---

[115] Para 14.1 and *R. v Chief Constable of West Midlands, Ex p. Wiley* [1995] 1 A.C. 274.

[116] Although this paragraph deals specifically with disclosure by the prosecution of material obtained from the local authority pursuant to its duties under the CPIA, this observation will be of use to defence counsel seeking disclosure directly from the local authority itself. It is to be hoped that if the Protocol is followed by the police/CPS there will be little need for such applications to take place. The Protocol only relates to proceedings concerning children and records from the local authority. Applications will need to be made by prosecution and defence of other third parties. In practice, those organisations are unlikely to claim PII to withhold documents and more likely to focus on the art.8 rights of the person whose records they are.

authority's consent.[117] If a PII application is appropriate in cases where the prosecution wish to disclose material to the defence in pursuance of their duty under the CPIA, the CPS should make application to the criminal court as soon as is reasonably practicable.[118] The CPS should notify the local authority of the date and venue of the application and inform the local authority of their right to make representations to the criminal court.

Where PII is sought on the basis of lack of consent to disclose, rule   **18.88** 15.3(2)(b)(ii) of the CPR 2015 states that the CPS must serve the application on any person the prosecutor thinks would be directly affected by disclosure of the material. The application must explain why the prosecutor thinks it is material the prosecutor would have to disclose, why it would not be in the public interest to disclose it and why no measure such as a summary or redaction would adequately protect both the public interest and the defendant's right to a fair trial.[119]

Test to be Applied

If the third party has refused to disclose the requested material on public   **18.89** interest grounds, the test to be applied is that approved in *Brushett*.[120] In that case the Court of Appeal approved the test set out by Butler-Sloss LJ in *Re M*[121] in which she said that, when it came to disclosure of social work records, the judge had to decide whether the public interest in protecting such records overrides the public interest in the party to the proceedings obtaining the information which he or she is seeking in order to get legal redress. The decision in *Re M* followed the decision of the same court in *Higgins*,[122] in which it was held that in such applications the judge has to decide as a balancing exercise whether the public interest in maintaining the confidentiality of the documents and the public interest in seeing that justice is done, particularly in a criminal case involving the liberty of the subject, requires that the documents be withheld or disclosed.

If the third party material is already in the hands of the prosecution, it is   **18.90** for the prosecution to consider whether it should be disclosed under the more liberal test for prosecution disclosure set out in the CPIA. As indicated above, the 2013 Protocol specifies that where any local authority material

---

[117] The Protocol is silent about the types of cases which may fall into the "highly exceptional" category of cases which would warrant disclosure to the defence of the edited or summarised document without the consent of the local authority. In practice, it is hard to foresee any case in which the CPS would make such disclosure without an order of the court. A court would give the local authority an opportunity to be heard. This must be the preferred course in just about every case.

[118] Para 14.2 of the 2013 Protocol.

[119] See also para 14.3 of the 2013 Protocol.

[120] [2001] Crim. L.R 471. The full report would be of considerable assistance to any judge faced with such an application (No 99/7712). The decision and approach was cited with approval in *Niwar Doski v R.* [2011] EWCA Crim 987.

[121] [1990] 2 F.L.R. 36, at 43.

[122] [1996] 1 F.L.R. 137.

viewed by the CPS falls within the statutory disclosure test the CPS will notify the local authority of that within two working days of review, setting out the reasons why the material falls to be disclosed and informing them of that decision.[123] The form at Annex E is to be used for this purpose. The CPS will provide to the local authority proposals for editing or summarising the material for the purposes of disclosure to the defence. Within five working days of receipt of that notification, the local authority shall be given the opportunity to make any representations in writing to the CPS on the issues of disclosure, including the fact that the person to whom the disclosure relates has not consented. This is by use of the form at Annex F. The timescale can be extended by agreement.

18.91   Some cases may involve third party material from more than one local authority, each of whom takes a different view on disclosure. The trial judge in *Brushett*[124] was faced with that situation. The prosecution were in possession of some of the documents (CPIA test to be applied) and other local authorities refused to disclose other documents (third party test of materiality to be applied). The Court of Appeal approved the course followed by the trial judge in adopting only the CPIA/PII test in relation to all the documents, on the basis that it would be unfair to the defence to have to satisfy the materiality defence as some of the documents were already held by the prosecution. His decision included the following:

- The court should define materiality in accordance with the *Reading Justices* case, but if circumstances arise where it would be unjust not to allow disclosure of certain other material, so that a defendant would not receive a fair trial in the sense that he could not establish his innocence where he might otherwise do so, then that material must be disclosed.
- The balancing act does not envisage endless cross examination as to credit on very peripheral matters.[125]

ARTICLE 8 ECHR AND ISSUES OF CONFIDENTIALITY

18.92   Any disclosure of confidential records by bodies such as social services, medical practitioners and counsellors will infringe the right to respect for the private life of the person concerned afforded by art.8 ECHR. This right cannot be subject to interference by a public authority:

"except such as is in accordance with the law and is necessary[126] in a democratic society in the interests of national security, public safety or the economic well-

---

[123] Part B, paras 13.9 and 13.10.

[124] [2001] Crim. L.R 471.

[125] The Court of Appeal have approved and followed *Brushett* more recently in looking at the test to be applied under s.23(1) of the Criminal Appeal Act granting the court the power to order the production of documents for the purposes of the appeal: *Doski v R.* [2011] EWCA Crim 987.

[126] The word "necessary" implies a pressing social need for the interference: *Sunday Times v UK* 2 EHRR 245.

being of the country, for the prevention of disorder or crime, for the protection of health and morals, or for the protection of the rights and freedom of others."

A criminal prosecution constitutes an "interference by a public authority" for the purposes of art.8.[127]

Paragraph 47 of the Judicial Protocol[128] states: 18.93

"Applications for third party disclosure must identify the documents that are sought and provide full details of why they are discloseable [*sic*]. This is particularly relevant when access is sought to the medical records of those who allege that they are victims of crime. It should be appreciated that a duty to assert confidentiality may arise when a third party receives a request for disclosure, or the right to privacy may be claimed under article 8 of the ECHR (see in particular Crim PR Part 28.6). Victims do not waive the confidentiality of their medical records or their right to privacy under article 8 of the ECHR by making a complaint against the accused. The court as a public authority must ensure that any interference with the right to privacy under article 8 is in accordance with the law and is necessary in pursuit of a legitimate public interest."[129]

Rules 17.5(3)(b)(i) and 17.6(3)(b) of the CPR 2015 require that in every   18.94 application for third party disclosure where such is not to be provided voluntarily,[130] the court must decide whether the person to whom the material relates should be given notice of it and an opportunity to make representations. There is also a specific requirement in rule 17.5(4)(b) for the court to be satisfied that it has been able to take adequate account of the duties and rights, including rights of confidentiality, of any person to whom the information relates before issuing a witness summons.

The rules were amended to this effect following the case of *R. (TB) v The*   18.95 *Combined Court at Stafford*.[131] TB, a 14-year-old girl, had made allegations of a sexual nature. She had been receiving psychiatric treatment and had attempted suicide by overdose on three separate occasions. The defence wanted access to her medical and hospital records on the grounds that a history of self-harm and mental illness might undermine her credibility as a witness. Application was made in the usual way. The NHS Trust resisted disclosure and a hearing took place following which the judge ordered disclosure of 23 pages of her psychiatric records. The Trust informed the Official Solicitor who asked the judge to state a case for the consideration of the High Court. The judicial review form asked for a declaration that TB was entitled to service of the application for disclosure and to make representations as to what order should be made. The court held that right of privacy

---

[127] *Dudgeon v UK* 4 EHRR 149.
[128] See fn.1, above.
[129] The paragraph goes on to reiterate that general and unspecified requests to trawl through such records should be refused.
[130] It is unlikely that voluntary disclosure will be made without the consent of the person to whom the records relate. In many cases this is obtained by the local authority or other body. The court will be called upon to rule in cases where such consent has been withheld.
[131] [2006] EWHC 1645 (Admin).

in relation to these records belonged to TB, not to the Trust, and as such she should have had an opportunity to make representations.

18.96 Rule 17 now complies with this decision. Every trial judge to whom an application for disclosure is made must consider the position of the person whose records are sought. It would seem that in every case where medical, educational and social services records are sought and voluntary disclosure is refused, a court is likely to require the person whose records they are to be told of the application and given a chance to make representations. Indeed, the 2013 Protocol makes provision for just that: it requires the CPS, in cases where PII is sought on the basis of lack of consent from the person to whom the confidential material relates, to notify that person of the date and venue of the PII application and that person's right to make representations to the court.[132] In this way the art.8 rights of the individual are protected.

18.97 Some difficulties arise however in practice:

- Under the CPR the applicant for third party material is required to make his application in writing specifying what he wants and why he wants it. Disclosure of the application will alert the witness to the issues likely to arise at trial;
- Although the court may order that the witness is told of his or her right to representation there are no provisions in place within the legal aid provisions for the advocate to be remunerated. Someone in TB's position—14 and with mental health issues—should not, if at all possible, represent herself at any hearing. There seems no other option at the current time. This places a considerable burden on the judge of explaining what is required, why it is relevant and the implications of a decision that it would be necessary to disclose documents. It places a very difficult burden on a vulnerable witness already concerned about having to give evidence.

18.98 If an invasion of privacy is deemed necessary, it should be reduced to the minimum so that no unnecessary disclosure of intimate information is made.[133]

Conclusion

18.99 The Judicial Protocol concludes:

"Historically, disclosure was viewed essentially as being a matter to be resolved between the parties, and the court only became engaged if a particular issue or complaint was raised. That perception is now wholly out of date. The regime

---

[132] Para.14.3.

[133] A recent report on disclosure of medical records and counselling notes following an inspection by HM CPS Inspectorate identified that in too many cases the CPS were "over disclosing". This was an apparent breach of the complainant's right to private and family life under art.8 ECHR, as consent to disclosure is generally to material which meets the test under the CPIA: *Disclosure of medical records and counselling notes* (July 2013), available *at http:/ /www.justiceinspectorates.gov.uk/crown-prosecution-service/wp-content/uploads/sites/ 3/2014/04/DOMRACN_thm_Jul13_rpt.pdf* [Accessed April 30, 2016].

established under the Criminal Justice Act 2003 and the Criminal Procedure Rules gives judges the power—indeed, it imposes a duty on the judiciary —actively to manage disclosure in every case. The efficient, effective and timely resolution of these issues is a critical element in meeting the overriding objective of the Criminal Procedure Rules of dealing with cases justly."[134]

The duties and obligations of the parties concerning third party disclosure and the rules to be applied in such applications have never been clearer. There are signs that most third parties involved in the disclosure process are willing to co-operate as they never have before. In these circumstances, there can be no conceivable reason for disclosure not to take place at the very earliest opportunity or for trials, often involving the most vulnerable in society, to be adjourned through lack of disclosure. Yet this does not often represent the reality in many courts up and down the country.

The Protocols, rules, guidelines and procedures can only ensure best **18.100** practice if they are known about, understood and applied appropriately. Just as with the most modern computer, these provisions can only do their job if the operator gets it right. In many parts of the country there is a woeful lack of understanding by the police about what to request of local authorities and how to go about it. There is little, if any, consultation between them and the CPS at an early stage to identify issues and areas of possible third party material to request. Local authorities, with stretched resources, are inundated with wide or blanket requests for disclosure with no attempt made to state what would be relevant and why. The defence give too little information about the real issues in the case and often fail to liaise with the prosecutors at an early stage on the question of third party material.[135]

The result? All too often advocates at trial, finally coming to grips with the **18.101** issues in the case, say they do not have what they need, causing delay for witnesses while making late and urgent applications to local authorities.

Judges must be assiduous in overseeing third party disclosure. In austere **18.102** times, advocates must be alive to potential issues of third party disclosure by the time of the pre-trial preparation hearing and be in a position to assist the court. There must be greater out-of-court communication, to clarify the issues in the case as time moves on and make real attempts to resolve problems. Failure to do so will result in many more pre-trial hearings, as the

---

[134] Para.56.

[135] [2015] EWCA Crim 662, in which a woeful lack of disclosure resulted in the trial judge staying the case for abuse of process. He said that in his many years as an advocate and a judge he had never encountered a case where there had been "such a total and abject failure to deal with disclosure". He described what happened as "a charade which made a mockery of the judicial system. Public money was squandered because of the abject failure of the CPS to organise disclosure at any stage prior to trial". The Court of Appeal lifted the stay, having concluded that having regard to the gravity of the allegations there was a very strong public interest in the offences being tried and the complainants having their allegations determined at trial. The Court noted there had also been significant defence failings before trial. The Lord Chief Justice stated "We trust that the judgments of this court in *Boardman* [[2015] EWCA Crim 175] and in this case will receive the closest study by all Chief Crown Prosecutors and all Chief Constables. There should be no recurrence of failures of this kind by either the CPS or any police force." The Court emphasised the need for adequate training of police officers on disclosure.

judge complies with his or her duty to manage disclosure and pulls the parties back to court to force them to comply with theirs.

18.103   Failure to comply with the rules may be met in future not only with further hearings and frustrated judges. In *R. v DS*,[136] the Lord Chief Justice said:

> "[Given] the fact this this is the second occasion within two months that prosecution appeals have been brought to this court arising out of a failure to provide materials, the adequacy of the sanction needs greater consideration. As the failure relates to a failure in criminal procedure, we will ask the Criminal Procedure Rule Committee to consider whether any other sanctions can be imposed through new Rules on those charged with the prosecution of a case and, in the absence of any power to provide for sanctions through new Rules, to set out whether any other steps or sanctions they consider should be taken to ensure compliance with the Rules."

There can be no doubt that all concerned with disclosure must comply with their obligations. If those responsible for making such disclosure do not, they may in the future face more serious sanctions. Of course, the most serious consequence of all may be that an innocent defendant spends many years in prison for a crime he did not commit.

---

[136] [2015] EWCA Crim 662 at 71.

CHAPTER 19

EVIDENCE: GENERAL

Introduction...................................... 19.01   Complainant's Evidence 19.67
Joinder and Severance .... 19.04   Consistent Statements—Evidence
Multiple Offending: Count   of Earlier Complaints by the
   Charging More than One   Complainant............................... 19.72
   Incident .... 19.22   Collateral Questions and the Rule
Hearsay Evidence .... 19.28   of Finality 19.91
The Approach to the Statutory   Corroboration and Warnings about
   Scheme Governing Hearsay .... 19.35   Reliance on a Complainant's
Inconsistent Statements: s.119 of   Evidence....................................... 19.106
   the CJA 2003............................... 19.64   Evidence of Defendant's Spouse or
                                                        Civil Partner................................. 19.123

INTRODUCTION

Evidential considerations are of such importance in trials of sexual offences   **19.01**
that no book on the substantive law can be considered complete unless it
pays due attention to the key rules of evidence. The aim of this chapter is not
to state the rules exhaustively, but to explain them in concise terms, to
illustrate their application and to point out some of the difficulties to which
they may give rise. Those who require more extensive treatment of particular
topics should refer to one of the specialist works on the subject.

The chapter deals with evidential rules of general application. Some areas   **19.02**
merit discrete coverage in separate chapters. For instance, the bad character
regime in the Criminal Justice Act 2003 ("CJA 2003") features so frequently
in the trial of sexual offences we have covered it separately in Ch.20. The law
relating to the restrictions upon evidence or questions about a complainant's
sexual history (s.41 of the Youth Justice and Criminal Evidence Act 1999) is
an important and complex subject warranting separate treatment and is dealt
with in Ch.26. Similarly, special measures for vulnerable witnesses are
commonplace in sex cases. These are considered in Ch.28. The principles
governing expert evidence are addressed in Ch.25.

We begin this chapter by dealing with issues relating to the indictment in   **19.03**
trials of sexual offences, namely joinder and severance. We then move on to
deal with evidential issues not covered elsewhere in this work.

Joinder and Severance

Joinder

19.04   Joinder of other offences in an indictment charging rape is considered at paras 1.146 and following, above. This chapter covers the general principles in respect of joinder and severance, using Court of Appeal decisions in sex cases to illustrate their application. The position on joinder is now governed by r.10.2(3) of the Criminal Procedure Rules 2015, which is the successor to the provision formerly contained in r.9 of the Indictment Rules 1971[1] and is drafted in similar terms:

> "An indictment may contain more than one count if all the offences charged—
> (a) are founded on the same facts; or
> (b) form or are a part of a series of offences of the same or a similar character."

Cross-admissibility of evidence between different counts in the indictment is a separate question from that of joinder. There are two separate regimes, one governing the joinder and severance of counts in an indictment, and the other governing cross-admissibility as between counts.[2] As will be seen below, this does not mean that cross-admissibility will not be relevant to joinder. It is not, however, an essential pre-condition of the joinder of counts. We cover the rules governing cross-admissibility in Ch.21, as they engage the bad character regime established by ss.101 and 103 of the Criminal Justice Act 2003.

19.05   An indictment which contains counts which are not linked in either of the ways specified in r.10.2(3) will be invalid. The cases on the application of r.9 are still relevant. For the purpose of r.10.2(3), two offences may form a "series".[3] Furthermore, where incidents of the commission of an offence amount to a course of conduct, having regard to the time, place and purpose of commission, they may properly be included in one count following the revision of the rule against duplicity by the Criminal Procedure (Amendment Rules) 2007: see now r.10.2(2) of the Criminal Procedure Rules 2015, discussed in paras 19.22 and following, below.

19.06   The courts have held that the propriety of joinder depends on whether the offences are linked by a sufficiently close nexus, meaning a feature of similarity which in all the circumstances enables the offences to be described as a series.[4] This requirement is liberally interpreted. So in *Baird*,[5] it was held that counts charging indecent assaults on two boys nine years apart had been properly regarded as a "series" for the purposes of r.9. The Court said that

[1] SI 1971/1253.
[2] *Powell* [2014] EWCA Crim 642 at [35] per Jackson LJ.
[3] *Ludlow v Metropolitan Police Commissioner* [1971] A.C. 29.
[4] *Ludlow v Metropolitan Police Commissioner* [1971] A.C. 29; *Blackstock* (1980) 70 Cr. App. R. 34.
[5] (1993) 97 Cr. App. R. 308.

the similarities between the offences were "truly remarkable": in each case the appellant had built upon a casual encounter with a young boy in the street to cultivate a friendship and to gain the confidence of the boy's parents, and in each case the friendship led to physical contact in the form of play-fighting. Although there was no coincidence in time or place, the prosecution case could well be described as one of history repeating itself in the methods by which and the motives with which the appellant built up a degree of familiarity with the boys, which resulted in the alleged offences. The judge had therefore been entitled to hold that the counts could be joined in one indictment, and to refuse to order severance.

Baird was followed in *R. v C*,[6] where counts charging the appellant with the **19.07** rape and attempted rape of his daughter were held to have been properly joined in one indictment, although the incidents had occurred 11 years apart. The Court of Appeal said that where two or more offences alleged against a defendant are of a broadly similar character and there is a single complainant, not only will it generally be permissible to join the counts in a single indictment but, additionally, it will seldom be appropriate for the judge to order severance of the indictment. But it noted, without expressing a final view, that r.9 might have been stretched towards its limits to accommodate the counts against the appellant, given the separation in time between them. The Court also said that quite different considerations arise in a case where there are two or more complainants, since the jury could well be prejudiced by such complaints being heard together. This was a very proper note of caution, but it is clear that joinder in cases involving more than one complainant is not necessarily to be treated more strictly. An example of a liberal approach being taken in this context is *Carman (Philip)*,[7] where a GP was charged with indecently assaulting seven different women patients between 1983 and 2002. Three of the women alleged that he had masturbated them, two that he had pressed his groin against them during examination and two that he had touched their breasts. On appeal, it was argued that the wide difference between the nature and time of the offences meant that they should not have been joined together. This argument was rejected, the Court holding that the charges could properly form part of a single indictment. Although it did not say so expressly, it is likely that it was the context in which the offences were allegedly committed, i.e. by the defendant GP in the course of examining female patients, that enabled them properly to be regarded as a "series".

A contrasting case is *R. v TB*,[8] where the appellant was convicted on an **19.08** indictment containing 12 counts charging sexual offences against four different complainants. The offences charged in counts 1–9 were said to have been committed in 1996–97 and those in counts 10–12 in 1977–79. The two groups of offences had no common factual origin and there was no evidence

[6] *The Times*, February 4, 1993.
[7] [2004] EWCA Crim 540.
[8] Unreported, November 11, 1999 (No.99/1447/Y2).

interlinking them. The prosecution argued that joinder was justified because the victim of the earlier offences (DC) had only complained of those offences when, many years later, she learned of the complaints made by her niece, who was the victim of the later offences. A fair trial, it was argued, could not have taken place without this information being before the jury, because if they had no explanation for DC suddenly making a complaint after 20 years, they might well have formed an adverse view of her credibility. The Court observed in response that cases frequently arise in which complaints are made after long periods of time, and it is possible to devise a formula which will satisfy the jury and avoid them forming an adverse view on credibility. In the circumstances, it was held that the offences in counts 10–12 did not form part of a series with those in counts 1–9 and that there was no sufficient nexus between the offences such as to justify their joinder. The Court was, however, careful to add that its judgment should not be regarded as authority for the proposition that offences 20 years apart can never form part of a "series" within the meaning of r.9. It was subsequently affirmed in *O'Brien*[9] that events widely separated in time are capable of being a "series" for the purposes of r.9, although the longer the time gap, the clearer the required nexus between them needs to be. In that case, it was held that the similarities between sexual offences allegedly committed by a school headmaster against pupils in the 1970s and 1990s were insufficient to justify their joinder in one indictment.

19.09   *R. v AB*[10] is a relatively recent example of case in which the Court of Appeal decided that two sets of sexual offences had not been properly joined. All the offences involved females who were in some way related to the appellant, albeit the later complainants were not related by blood. The first set of alleged offences had begun when the appellant was a young man and involved children. The nature of the second set of alleged offences was different. It involved older women and comprised individual drunken episodes committed by an alcoholic middle-aged man. Furthermore, something in the order of 30 years had elapsed between the two sets of offences. Having regard to those features, the Court of Appeal held that it was stretching language too far to describe the different sets of allegations as a series or part of a series of offences of the same or a similar character. It followed that the counts were not properly joined.

SEVERANCE

19.10   Where there has been a proper joinder, the court nonetheless has the power to order the separate trial of an accused or of offences. Section 5(3) of the Indictments Act 1915 provides:

> "Where, before trial, or at any stage of a trial, the court is of opinion that a
> person accused may be prejudiced or embarrassed in his defence by reason of

[9] [2000] Crim. L.R. 863.
[10] [2011] EWCA Crim 3331.

being charged with more than one offence in the same indictment, or that for any other reason it is desirable to direct that the person should be tried separately for any one or more offences charged in an indictment, the court may order a separate trial of any count or counts of such indictment."

Where two or more counts are properly joined in an indictment, it will **19.11** usually be appropriate for them to be tried jointly if the evidence relating to one count is admissible in relation to the other. This will prevent the evidence having to be given twice and considered by two different juries, who may come to different conclusions upon it. If the evidence relating to one count is not admissible in relation to another, the question of severance is likely to be raised, on the ground that the jury will have to perform impossible "mental gymnastics"[11] in keeping the evidence of the various counts separate in their minds.

Substantial differences between categories of offences such as time, the **19.12** nature of the complainant and the activity may weigh heavily in favour of severance. In *R. v SW*[12] the complainants included the appellant's younger sister, her daughters, and his second wife's sister's four daughters. The first three counts alleged rape when the appellant was aged at least 39 and the complainant was aged between nine and 14. Other counts alleged indecencies beginning with the touching of a 12 or 13-year-old by the appellant aged 15–16. There were striking temporal gaps of 32 and 20 years. The gulf in terms of harm, culpability, and date between the rapes and the remaining allegations was wide. The Court of Appeal revealed its surprise that the Crown considered the rapes ought to be prosecuted with the balance of the indictment, indicating that each member of the Court would unhesitatingly have ordered severance of the rape counts.

There may be compelling case management reasons in favour of severance **19.13** even though counts are properly joined. In *R. v JM*[13] a 96-year-old man faced a 50 count indictment with charges of sexual abuse (including rapes) during 1954–57, 1957–60, and 1975–79. The complainants were his daughters and people who had been pupils at a special school he ran. The judge, who found M fit to stand trial, indicated that a series of shorter linked trials might be more practical than a lengthy single trial. At a preparatory hearing the judge severed the counts involving M's daughters, ordered that they be tried first and ruled that, to ensure the trials were practicable given M's age, no trial should involve more than six complainants. The prosecution appealed this decision under s.35 of the CPIA 1996. The Court of Appeal regarded the judge's decision to sever so that the "family only" allegations were tried separately as a matter of effective case management that he was best placed to decide and it was a "logical and consistent approach to the trials of the daughters, relating to domestic abuse, separately from cases involving the school pupils. The cross-over in evidence was relatively limited."

[11] *DPP v Boardman* [1975] A.C. 421 at 459, per Lord Cross.
[12] [2011] EWCA Crim 2463.
[13] [2015] EWCA Crim 1928.

Cross-admissibility is not an essential pre-condition for court to refuse severance

19.14   As seen above, s.5(3) of the Indictments Act 1915 gives a court a discretion to direct separate trials where it is of the opinion that the accused may be prejudiced or embarrassed in his defence by reason of being charged with more than one offence in the same indictment or where for any other reason it is desirable to order severance.[14] In the past, where an indictment charged multiple sexual offences against children, and the evidence in respect of each complainant's allegations was not cross-admissible under principles relating to similar fact evidence, it was common for the judge to exercise his discretion under s.5(3) to direct separate trials.[15] Indeed, in *DPP v P*[16] Lord Mackay appeared to treat the question of severance in such cases as consequential on the application of the similar fact principles.

19.15   Following the implementation of the bad character regime contained in the Criminal Justice Act 2003, separate allegations are more likely to be cross-admissible. However, in *Christou*[17] the House of Lords rejected the argument that in cases of sexual abuse of children, where the evidence of one child is not admissible in support of allegations by another child, the judge's discretion should always be exercised in favour of severance. Lord Taylor CJ, giving the leading speech, said that any such requirement would fetter the statutory discretion conferred on judges by the 1915 Act. His Lordship said that cases involving the sexual abuse of children can vary greatly, and the factors the judge should consider in reaching a decision on severance will therefore vary from case to case, but the essential criterion is the achievement of a fair resolution of the issues. That requires fairness to the accused but also to the prosecution and those involved in it. Some of the factors which might need to be considered are: how discrete or inter-related are the facts giving rise to the counts; the impact of ordering two or more trials on the defendant and his family, on the victims and their families and on press publicity; and, importantly, whether directions the judge can give to the jury will suffice to secure a fair trial if the counts are all tried together. Approaching the question of severance in this way, judges will often consider it right to order separate trials, but his Lordship said that there is no requirement that they should do so either generally or in respect of any class of case. It is a matter for the judge's discretion, and the Court of Appeal will not interfere with his decision unless he has failed to exercise his discretion properly by taking into

---

[14] Where the discretion is exercised it is almost always upon application by the defence. There may be cases in which no application is made and the right course is for the court to order severance of its own motion, but this will be appropriate only in highly unusual circumstances: cf. *Cannan* (1991) 92 Cr. App. R. 16; *R. v SW* [2011] EWCA Crim 2463 at [28].

[15] cf. *DPP v Boardman* [1975] A.C. 421; *Novac* (1976) 65 Cr. App. R. 107; *Scarrott* [1978] Q.B. 1016; *Beggs* (1990) 90 Cr. App. R. 430.

[16] [1991] 2 A.C. 447; and see *Channing* [1994] Crim. L.R. 924.

[17] [1996] 2 Cr. App. R. 360, applying *Cannan* (1991) 92 Cr. App. R. 16; and see *R. v F* [1996] Crim. L.R. 257.

account everything he should and not taking into account anything he should not.[18]

A pre-Criminal Justice Act 2003 case which neatly illustrates the interplay   **19.16** of the rules relating to joinder and severance is *R. v F.*[19] Charges of buggery, rape, assault and cruelty to a child were all joined in one indictment. The victims were the appellant's daughters, wife and mistress. The prosecution case was that the appellant ruled the victims by fear and violence. The judge rejected a submission that the offences of violence should be severed from the sexual offences, and a similar submission that the counts relating to each victim should be severed. These rulings were upheld on appeal. The Court said that there was a sufficient nexus for the counts to be joined. If and in so far as the charges were not founded on the same facts, they plainly formed or were part of a series of offences of the same or a similar character. The reality was that the charges all arose from a history of domination by violence and threats of violence for sexual purposes by the male head of an unusual family, consisting of two adult women and their female children, who submitted to the man's sexual demands because of the domination that he exercised. As for severance, the judge had applied his mind to the relevant principles and had decided that the counts were properly triable together, even if the evidence in relation to one was not admissible as similar fact evidence in relation to the others. Having done so, he had directed the jury to consider the counts separately and had warned them of the risk of collusion. In those circumstances there was no substance in the argument that the judge ought to have severed the counts as suggested.

In cases of this sort, where offences are tried together but the evidence on   **19.17** particular counts is not mutually supportive, it may be appropriate for the judge to direct the jury on how to approach the evidence in relation to each count. However, such a direction is not required as a matter of law. Everything depends on the facts of the particular case, and the danger that the jury might seek to use the evidence of one complainant as evidence of a defendant's guilt on counts concerned only with another complainant.[20]

---

[18] And see *Scarrott* [1978] Q.B. 1016 at 1028, per Scarman LJ.

[19] [1996] Crim. L.R. 257; and see *Alderson*, unreported, May 6, 1988 (No.97/4008/22); *Milton Brown*, unreported, May 6, 1998 (No.97/8393/Z4); *Panayiotou*, unreported, June 19, 1998 (No.97/5500/W2).

[20] See para.20.134, below. In *R. v F* [2005] EWCA Crim 3217, Scott Baker LJ stated that the judge's direction to treat all the charges in respect of two complainants separately was adequate. There was no need, where there is no cross-relationship between the complainants' evidence, to go further and give a more detailed direction. See also *R. v H* [2011] EWCA Crim 2344 where the Court of Appeal traced the history of the argument that a judge should give a non-cross-admissibility direction over and above the traditional direction to give each count separate treatment. The appellant relied on *R. v D* [2003] EWCA Crim 2424; [2004] 1 Cr. App. R.(S.) 19, where the Court considered that an adequate direction "sufficiently clear to bring home to the jury the absolute need for them to treat the evidence in relation to each set of allegations separately" had not been given and therefore the convictions were unsafe. Having considered subsequent jurisprudence, Rix LJ observed that the suggested non-cross-admissibility direction has not fared well as a ground of appeal. See also *Wall* [2005] EWCA Crim 3251.

Indictments that straddle the implementation date of the Sexual Offences Act 2003—can severance ever be justified?

19.18   The Sexual Offences Act 2003 came into force on May 1, 2004. Section 141 of the Act empowered the Secretary of State to make transitional provisions, but no such provisions were made. It followed that, if there was doubt as to whether an offence occurred before or after the coming into force of the Act, the proceedings would fail because the prosecution would not have proved whether a statutory offence was committed under the old or the new law.[21] This lacuna in the law was filled by s.55 of the Violent Crime Reduction Act 2006, a deeming provision which came into force on February 12, 2007. It covers the situation where a defendant is charged in respect of the same conduct both with an offence under the 2003 Act and with an offence under the old law, and the only thing preventing him being found guilty of either offence is the fact that it has not been proved beyond a reasonable doubt that the time when the conduct took place was either after the coming into force of the 2003 Act offence or before the repeal of the old law, as the case may be. In such circumstances, for the purposes of determining guilt, it shall be conclusively presumed that the time when the conduct took place was when the old law applied, if the old offence attracted a lesser maximum penalty; otherwise, it will be presumed the conduct took place after the implementation of the new law. If the penalties are the same, then it will be conclusively presumed that the conduct took place after the commencement of the 2003 Act.

19.19   The question nonetheless arises whether severance will ever be justified where the allegations in an indictment relate to a course of conduct extending both before and after the commencement date of the 2003 Act, i.e. May 1, 2004. In some cases, factually similar conduct occurring before and after commencement will constitute different offences. For example, the 2003 Act redefines rape to include penile penetration of another person's mouth without their consent, which was formerly indecent assault. It follows that such conduct committed before and after commencement will constitute different offences.

19.20   There have also been fundamental changes in the law relating to the meaning of "consent" and the mechanisms for proving its absence. Further, in relation to non-consensual offences, the subjective *Morgan* test in relation to the mental element has been replaced by a more objective test. These changes may complicate trials for non-consensual offences straddling the implementation date, as the jury will need to be directed differently on the consent issues arising in respect of the earlier and later offences.

19.21   It is, however, doubtful whether these considerations will ever provide good grounds for an application by the defence to sever the indictment.

---

[21] *A (Prosecutor's Appeal)* [2006] 1 Cr. App. R. 433 sometimes referred to as *R. v C* [2005] EWCA Crim 3533; *Newbon* [2005] Crim. L.R. 738.

Severance may be ordered where the court is of the opinion that trying the counts together may prejudice the defence. It is unlikely that prejudice will ever be made out simply on the basis that the jury have to be directed to consider different counts by reference to different legal and/or evidential tests. Even in a very complicated case, any difficulty the jury might have in following and applying different directions on the "old" and "new" counts should be capable of being resolved by the use of clear written directions.

MULTIPLE OFFENDING: COUNT CHARGING MORE THAN ONE INCIDENT—RULE 10.2(2) OF THE CRIMINAL PROCEDURE RULES 2015—REVISION OF THE RULE AGAINST DUPLICITY[22]

Rule 10.2(2) of the Criminal Procedure Rules 2015 provides for more than one incident of the commission of an offence to be included in a count if those incidents taken together amount to a course of conduct having regard to the time, place or purpose of commission. This provision was introduced into the Rules by the Criminal Procedure (Amendment) Rules 2007, with effect from April 2, 2007. For cases sent, transferred or committed to the Crown Court prior to that date, the Indictment Rules 1971 applied. The 2007 Rules revoked the Indictment Rules 1971 and consolidated them with the procedural rules about indictments, which were already included in the Criminal Procedure Rules. What is now Pt 10 of the 2015 Rules was intended to revise and simplify the rules about the service, form and content of indictments. **19.22**

The most important change made in 2007 was to the rule against particularising a series of like offences within a single count, with the result that it is no longer essential for a count to relate to a single act. This has had a significant impact on the ways indictments are drafted in cases involving allegations of repeated sexual abuse, in order to reflect a continuing course of conduct. It is now proper to charge one count covering a period over which a number of offences have occurred, instead of charging a number of specimen counts divided up by reference to time and type of assault. **19.23**

The Criminal Procedure Rules Committee has stated that the facility to charge more than one incident of the commission of an offence in a single count may be used: "when, for example, a defendant is alleged to have repeatedly assaulted the same victim in the same way over a period of time".[23] The Committee's intention in creating the new rule was to take account, amongst other things, of the potential under the old rules for there to be a perceived unfairness to a victim of multiple offending where, out of many alleged offences, only a few were prosecuted as examples, giving the **19.24**

---

[22] For full discussion drafting of indictments in sexual cases and the revision of the old rule against duplicity, see Eleanor Laws QC and HHJ Patricia Lees, *The Sexual Offences Referencer: A Practitioner's Guide to Indictment and Sentencing*, 2nd edn (Oxford: Oxford University Press, 2015), Ch.1.
[23] See guidance to the Rules, dated March 27, 2007.

impression that the victim's distress had been underestimated or that he or she had not been believed.[24]

19.25   To be effective, multiple incident counts need to cover the extent, seriousness and time span of a defendant's offending. When the prosecution fail to specify a sufficient minimum number of occasions within the count or counts, they are not making proper use of the procedure. In cases of sustained abuse, it will often be unhelpful to draft counts as representing, potentially, no more than two incidents; otherwise the sentencing judge may be deprived of a solid basis upon which to decide the ambit of the jury's verdict. It is important to bear in mind the cardinal rule that a judge may sentence only for those offences of which an accused has been convicted or which he has asked to be taken into consideration, which applies to sentencing "multiple incident" counts just as it applies to specimen counts. The point is illustrated by *A v R*,[25] where the appellant was convicted on two multiple incident counts, one alleging rape and the other alleging sexual assault by penetration. He was married to the complainant, who maintained that the marriage had deteriorated over time. The appellant had begun behaving violently towards her, raping her every few days. He also assaulted her by penetration on a number of occasions. Although the complainant gave some particulars of the occasions when, and the circumstances in which she was raped or sexually assaulted, in the main the allegations were broadly similar in nature, albeit she set out in considerable detail the various ways in which her husband repeatedly mistreated her. Therefore, the incidents of rape and sexual assault by penetration constituted more of a pattern of behaviour on the part of the appellant, as opposed to clearly identifiable individual incidents. In respect of the multiple incident counts, the judge directed the jury that they must be sure that the defendant carried out the alleged activity on more than one occasion during the period specified in the count. It followed that following conviction, the judge should have sentenced on the basis that the appellant had committed two offences of rape and two of sexual assault by penetration.

19.26   Good practice will continue to develop in respect of the drafting of such counts. It may not be appropriate for a count to cover a period of a number of years. It may still be necessary to include separate counts where significantly different forms of sexual activity are alleged to enable the sentencer properly to evaluate the gravity of the offender's conduct. The purpose underpinning multiple counts is to enable the prosecution to reflect the defendant's alleged criminality when the offences are so similar and numerous that it is inappropriate to indict each occasion, or a large number of different occasions, in separate charges.

---

[24] Taken from a note prepared by the Secretariat to the Committee dated March 27, 2007 and published with the guidance, above.
[25] [2015] EWCA Crim 1177.

Criminal Practice Directions 2015

Part 10 of the 2015 Rules is supplemented by provisions in the Criminal   **19.27**
Practice Directions 2015 giving guidance on when a "multiple incidents"
count under r.10.2(2) may be appropriate. The following is the relevant
extract:

"CPD II Preliminary Proceedings 14A: Settling the Indictment

Multiple offending: count charging more than one incident

10A.10 CrimPR 10.2(2) allows a single count to allege more than one incident
of the commission of an offence in certain circumstances. Each incident must be
of the same offence. The circumstances in which such a count may be appropriate
include, but are not limited to, the following:
   (a) the victim on each occasion was the same . . . ;
   (b) the alleged incidents involved a marked degree of repetition in the method
       employed or in their location, or both;
   (c) the alleged incidents took place over a clearly defined period, typically (but
       not necessarily) no more than about a year;
   (d) in any event, the defence is such as to apply to every alleged incident
       without differentiation. Where what is in issue differs between different
       incidents, a single "multiple incidents" count will not be appropriate,
       though it may be appropriate to use two or more such counts according to
       the circumstances and to the issues raised by the defence.
   . . .
10A.12 For some offences, particularly sexual offences, the penalty for the
offence may have changed during the period over which the alleged incidents
took place. In such a case, additional 'multiple incidents' counts should be used
so that each count only alleges incidents to which the same maximum penalty
applies.
10A.13 In other cases, such as sexual or physical abuse, a complainant may be
in a position only to give evidence of a series of similar incidents without being
able to specify when or the precise circumstances in which they occurred. In these
cases, a 'multiple incidents' count may be desirable. If on the other hand, the
complainant is able to identify particular incidents of the offence by reference to
a date or other specific event, but alleges that in addition there were other
incidents which the complainant is unable to specify, then it may be desirable to
include separate counts for the identified incidents and a 'multiple incidents'
count or counts alleging that incidents of the same offence occurred 'many'
times. Using a 'multiple incidents' count may be an appropriate alternative to
using 'specimen' counts in some cases where repeated sexual or physical abuse is
alleged. The choice of count will depend on the particular circumstances of the
case and should be determined bearing in mind the implications for sentencing
set out in *R v Canavan; R v Kidd; R v Shaw* [1998] 1 W.L.R. 604, [1998] 1 Cr. App.
R. 79, [1998] 1 Cr. App. R. (S.) 243."

HEARSAY EVIDENCE

The admissibility of hearsay evidence is now governed by the Pt 11 of the   **19.28**
Criminal Justice Act 2003 ("CJA 2003"). This chapter does not attempt a
comprehensive analysis of the relevant law. We have focused upon the areas
we consider most likely to be of assistance to those involved in trials of sexual

offences.[26] There have been significant developments in the law governing the admissibility of hearsay evidence during the last five years that will be of relevance to such trials, particularly where the prosecution seeks to rely upon the untested statement of an absent complainant or upon previous consistent or inconsistent statements made by a complainant who is available to give evidence. We commend above all the case of *Riat*[27] as providing not only a clear exposition of the statutory framework governing hearsay evidence, with a step-by-step approach to its application, but also three instructive examples illustrating the application of the law.

IDENTIFYING HEARSAY

19.29 The conjoined appeals of *Twist*[28] provide helpful guidance when difficulties arise as to the application of the definition of hearsay to a statement in a communication. Hughes LJ, as he then was, suggested the following approach:

(a) Identify the relevant fact (matter) it is sought to prove.

(b) Ask whether there is a statement of *that matter* in the communication. If there is not, the issue of hearsay simply does not arise whatever other matters may be contained in the communication.

(c) If there is a statement of the matter, ask whether it was one of the purposes (not necessarily the only or dominant purpose) of the maker of the communication that the recipient, or any other person, should believe *that matter* or act upon it as true? If this was one of the purposes, the statement is hearsay. If it was not, the statement falls outside the definition of hearsay.

The problem of implied assertions

19.30 The Court of Appeal in *Twist* also suggested that references to "implied assertions" should be avoided. However, problems may still linger where the maker's purpose may have been to cause someone to believe the matter in question by the use of such assertions.[29]

19.31 In many cases the approach set out by Hughes LJ will be easy to apply. In *Lowe,* which was one of the conjoined appeals in *Twist*, it was held that text

---

[26] We are deeply indebted to Professor David Ormerod QC for his highly instructive lectures on the hearsay provisions and their application to the trial of sex cases, delivered to the Judicial College Serious Sexual Offences Seminar between 2006 and 2016. For an excellent section-by-section commentary on all the relevant provisions, see Professor John Spencer QC, *Hearsay Evidence in Criminal Proceedings*, 2nd edn (Oxford: Hart Publishing, 2014).

[27] [2012] EWCA 1509.

[28] [2011] EWCA 1143.

[29] See Professor Ormerod's commentary on *Twist* [2011] Crim. L.R. 793. For an example where the Court of Appeal failed to resolve the issue as it was clear that the text should be excluded under s.78 PACE, see *Andrade* [2015] EWCA Crim 1722.

messages from the appellant to his victim in which he had made incriminating statements, and which had been copied out from the victim's phone by the Deputy Head of her school, did not amount to hearsay. The prosecution alleged that some of them amounted to confessions to, and apologies for, the rape. The Court of Appeal held that the trial judge had been correct to rule that the texts were not hearsay since the appellant was not intending to cause the victim to believe or act on the statements he made. She knew what had happened. In any event, the messages amounted to statements contrary to interest by the appellant himself and as such were admissible, even if they were hearsay, under ss.114(1)(b) and 118 of the CJA 2003 (preservation of common law).

There will be cases where, in the absence of the maker of the statement at trial, it is virtually impossible to decide what the maker's likely purpose (whether express or implied) was when making the statement. As always, s.78 will provide an important safeguard in cases where the maker's purpose is less than clear and where for a jury to make a judgment about that purpose and the true meaning of the text would be entirely speculative.[30] In borderline cases, it may be appropriate to consider admissibility in the alternative under s.114(1)(d) of the CJA 2003 (interests of justice).[31] **19.32**

Personal diaries

Personal diaries often feature in evidence in cases where it is alleged that children have been sexually abused. If it is established that a child wrote a private diary not intending it to be read by anyone, then relevant entries are direct or real evidence and not hearsay within the definition in s.115 of the CJA 2003. In *R. v N(K)*,[32] it was held that it was not the child's purpose in making the entries "to cause another person to believe the matter". If, on the other hand, she had been making assertive statements for her friends to see and believe, the entries would have been excluded by the hearsay rule. **19.33**

Similarly, there will be cases where text messages with strong sexual overtones from children who are not to be called to give evidence at trial, will not involve hearsay. In *Ahdel Ali and Mubarek Ali*,[33] the principal allegation was that the two appellants, significantly older than the girl complainants, groomed and controlled them. The Court of Appeal held that texts of a highly sexualised nature from these girls (who were not complainants) were **19.34**

---

[30] Cf. *Andrade* [2015] EWCA Crim 1722, a rape case where the defence was consent and the prosecution had sought to rely on two text messages from a friend of the appellant to the complainant saying "Sorry about that" and "RU mad at me". Whilst the friend had not been charged with aiding and abetting the rape, it was the prosecution's case that he had facilitated it. The friend was not called by either side. The jury may have treated the texts as important evidence supporting the prosecution case. The Court of Appeal decided, whatever their proper classification, they should have been excluded under s.78.
[31] *Isiecha* [2006] EWCA Crim 1815.
[32] [2006] EWCA Crim 3309; 171 JP 158.
[33] [2014] EWCA Crim 140.

not relevant as to the truth, or otherwise, of their contents; they were relevant as to the fact they were sent. Furthermore, it was a matter for the judge's discretion whether they should be excluded as unduly prejudicial.

THE APPROACH TO THE STATUTORY SCHEME GOVERNING HEARSAY AS RECOMMENDED IN RIAT

19.35 There is no over-arching rule, either in domestic law or under the ECHR, that hearsay evidence which is "sole or decisive" is automatically inadmissible. The Supreme Court held in *Horncastle*[34] that there is nothing in English law to prevent a conviction being based solely or decisively on hearsay, provided appropriate safeguards are in place and due caution is adopted. Nor does hearsay evidence have to be independently verified, as that would be to re-introduce the abolished rules for corroboration

19.36 The CJA 2003 provides a code for admissibility which, approached properly, secures a fair trial. In *Al Khawaja and Tahery v UK*[35] the European Court of Human Rights, in a Grand Chamber decision, had held that a conviction based solely or decisively on untested hearsay evidence can be compatible with art.6(3)(d) where the accused has not caused the witness's absence, the absence is for a good reason and there are sufficient safeguards in place. In so far as the decision of the Grand Chamber may be inconsistent with the approach of the Supreme Court, courts must, absent wholly exceptional circumstances, follow faithfully the decision of the latter.[36]

19.37 The importance of the hearsay evidence to the case against the defendant is, however, central to the various matters that have to be considered. A number of cases have stressed that, notwithstanding the decision of the Grand Chamber in *Al Khawaja*, the admissibility of evidence which is the sole or decisive evidence against the accused must be approached with great care. Notably, the Court of Appeal took the opportunity in *Riat*[37] to consider the correct approach in English law to cases involving the admission of hearsay evidence after the Supreme Court decision in *Horncastle*, read, as Lord Phillips explained that it must be, together with the judgment of the Court of Appeal in the same case.[38] We commend *Riat* as the clearest resumé of the law as it now stands. It is of particular importance to sex cases, as three of the conjoined appeals (*Riat, Clare* and *Bennett*) involved sexual allegations based upon hearsay evidence. We consider these appeals below as they provide excellent examples of the appropriate application of the hearsay rules

---

[34] [2009] UKSC 14.
[35] [2009] 49 EHRR 1.
[36] *Ibrahim* [2012] EWCA Crim 837; *R. (RJM) v Secretary of State for Work and Pensions (Equality and Human Rights Commissioner Intervening)* [2008] UKHL 63, at [64] per Lord Neuburger.
[37] [2012] EWCA Crim 1509.
[38] [2009] EWCA Crim 964.

in sex cases. In *Riat* the Court of Appeal cited *Ibrahim*,[39] another case involving allegations of sexual offences, as a good illustration of the working of the statutory framework governing the admission of hearsay. For this reason we also set out the facts of *Ibrahim* below.

Hughes LJ (as he then was) explained in *Riat* that in working through the statutory framework in a hearsay case, the court is concerned at several stages with both (i) the extent of the risk of unreliability and (ii) the extent to which the reliability of the evidence can safely be tested and assessed. It is clear that hearsay evidence must not be "nodded through". A focused decision must be made as to whether it is to be admitted or not. His Lordship set out the statutory framework for hearsay evidence under the CJA 2003 in terms of six successive steps: **19.38**

  (i) Is there a specific statutory justification (or "gateway") permitting the admission of hearsay evidence (ss.116–118)? The general principle is that the necessity to resort to second-hand evidence must be demonstrated under one or other of the statutory exceptions.

 (ii) What material is there which can help to test or assess the hearsay (s.124)? The court should always consider the vital linked questions of the apparent reliability of the evidence and the practicality of the jury testing and assessing its reliability. In the Court of Appeal's view, the judge will often not be able to make the decision as to whether the hearsay evidence should be admitted unless he considers first, as well as the importance of the evidence and its apparent strengths and weaknesses, what material is available to help test and assess it.

(iii) Is there a specific "interests of justice" test at the admissibility stage?

 (iv) If there is no other justification or gateway, should the evidence nonetheless be considered for admission on the ground that admission is, despite the difficulties, in the interests of justice (s.114(1)(d))? Section 114(1)(d) contains a general residual power to admit hearsay evidence which does not otherwise pass a statutory gateway, if the judge is satisfied that it is in the interests of justice for it to be admitted. If this gateway is invoked, the judge is specifically directed to have regard to the (non-exhaustive) considerations set out in s.114(2). As the Court emphasised in *R. v D(E)*,[40] s.114(1)(d) cannot be used routinely to avoid the statutory conditions for the admission of evidence which properly falls to be considered under ss.116–118.

  (v) Even if prima facie admissible, ought the evidence to be ruled inadmissible under s.78 of the Police and Criminal Evidence Act

---

[39] [2012] EWCA Crim 837.
[40] [2010] EWCA Crim 1213.

1984 and/or s.126 of the CJA 2003? The non-exhaustive considerations listed in s.114(2) are useful aides memoires for any judge considering the admissibility of hearsay evidence, whether under that subsection or under s.78 of the 1984 Act or otherwise. Section 126 provides a free-standing jurisdiction to refuse to admit hearsay evidence. If the evidence is tendered by the Crown, it stands in parallel to the general jurisdiction under s.78 of the 1984 Act, but it goes further than s.78 because it applies also to evidence tendered by a defendant, which might be targeted either at refuting Crown evidence or at inculpating a co-accused.

  (vi) If the evidence is admitted, then should the case subsequently be stopped under s.125 on the ground that the evidence is so unconvincing that a conviction would be unsafe? That provision is an important safeguard against unfairness. In a non-hearsay case, the jury must be left to assess the evidence. It is not for the judge to do so. Under the rule in *Galbraith*,[41] the judge's power to stop the case upon a submission of no case to answer is limited to doing so if the necessary minimum evidence does not exist upon which a jury, properly directed, could convict the defendant. It is essential to understand that the rule is different for hearsay cases. There, the judge is required by s.125 to look to see whether the hearsay evidence is so unconvincing that, considering its importance to the prosecution case, any conviction would be unsafe. That means looking at its strengths and weaknesses, at the tools available to the jury for testing it, and at its importance to the case as a whole.

Ibrahim: Where the untested hearsay evidence is critical

19.39 In *Ibrahim*[42] the appellant was convicted of three rapes. The allegations of rape and of a separate wounding were contained in statements made by a complainant, a drug addict who was working at the time as a street prostitute and who had subsequently died. The trial judge, pursuant to s.116 of the CJA 2003 (unavailability of witness), allowed the prosecution to admit three statements that the complainant had made to the police. The Court of Appeal identified four questions that had to be answered:

  (i) Was there proper justification for admitting the untested hearsay? Here the conditions in s.116(1) and (2)(a) were met, subject to the issue of counterbalancing measures.

  (ii) How important were the three untested hearsay statements in relation to the prosecution's case? Did they amount to the "central

---

[41] [1981] 1 W.L.R. 1039.
[42] [2012] EWCA Crim 837.

corpus of evidence"[43] without which the case could not proceed? The Court of Appeal had no doubt the statements were central.

(iii) How demonstrably reliable were those statements? As a drug user, the complainant belonged to a category of potentially very unreliable witnesses. She had made a false allegation of rape and then withdrawn it. She had been prepared to make this false allegation in a statement under s.9 of the Criminal Justice Act 1967. Further, there had been a two-and-a-half year delay in making the key statement. The Court concluded that on the central issue of whether the appellant had non-consensual sexual intercourse with her, it could not be shown that the complainant's statements were reliable.

(iv) Were the counterbalancing safeguards inherent in the common law, the CJA 2003 and s.78 of the 1984 Act properly applied in this case? The Court concluded that they were not, observing that the trial judge had not invited the jury to scrutinise the hearsay evidence with care nor drawn their attention to the specific risks of relying upon the evidence, such as the discrepancies between the complainant's statements.

The Court of Appeal held that the hearsay statements were so flawed, so   **19.40**
central to the case, and so difficult to assess, that it was unfair for them to be left to the jury. The Court rejected the prosecution submission that the question of the reliability and credibility of the complainant's evidence should have been left to the jury. Aitkens LJ, analysing the effect of the judgments of the Court of Appeal and Supreme Court in *Horncastle,* concluded that it is a pre-condition of the admission of untested hearsay evidence that it is shown to be "potentially safely reliable" before it is admitted. A trial judge should rule on this issue either at the admission stage or after the close of the prosecution case pursuant to s.125 of the CJA 2003. Hughes LJ explained in the later case of *Riat* that the critical word is "potentially"[44]:

> "The job of the judge is not to look for independent complete verification. It is to ensure that the hearsay can *safely* be held to be reliable. That means looking . . . at its strengths and weaknesses, at the tools available to the jury for testing it, and at its importance to the case as a whole."

Riat: Hearsay statement by a complaint who has subsequently died

The appellant in *Riat* was a karate instructor in his forties who was charged   **19.41**
with 10 sexual offences committed against one of his pupils when she was aged 13 or 14. She had died before the trial, so the statutory gateway under

---

[43] This phrase was used by Professor John Spencer in an article in *Archbold Review*, February 16, 2012, p.7.
[44] [2012] EWCA Crim 1509, at [33].

s.116(2)(a) was passed, and the prosecution successfully applied to adduce her several detailed statements and video-interviews as hearsay evidence. The issue in the case was whether there was any sexual relationship at all between the appellant and his pupil. The prosecution case was that there had been an active sexual relationship lasting about 14 months. The jury convicted the appellant of the eight offences in relation to which consent was not an issue but acquitted of the two non-consensual counts of rape. On appeal, it was submitted that the hearsay evidence was central to the case and was not reliable because the complainant could be shown to have lied on some occasions. The Court of Appeal held that the evidence had been rightly admitted for the following reasons:

(i) The central allegation had its origins in frequent spontaneous statements which were separately proved and which were made in circumstances redolent of truth. Several of the complainant's friends gave evidence that she made no secret to them, contemporaneously, of her relationship with her instructor. The first time the relationship came to the attention of anyone in any authority strongly suggested reliability and was not sensibly explainable away as either bragging or fantasy. The complainant had made a visit to the school nurse and had confided her fear that she might be pregnant, telling the nurse in detail about her relationship with her karate instructor. When the nurse said she would have to report the matter, the complainant immediately asserted that the man in question was not her instructor after all, but a boy of 18 about whom she gave no information apart from a first name. The complainant then attempted suicide and was accommodated, when recovering, in a supervised psychiatric rehabilitation unit for young people. There she told her head of house that the man in question was the appellant and not the 18-year-old.

(ii) Two of the complainant's friends gave evidence of the relationship independent of the complainant.

(iii) When resident at the supervised unit, the complainant had asked for permission to contact the appellant.

(iv) Although there could be no questioning of the complainant, the jury was able to see her since her evidence had been video-recorded.

(v) There was a great deal of material by which the evidence of the complainant could be tested and assessed.

The complainant's hearsay evidence was strongly supported and did not stand as a bare, untestable allegation. It could be safely assessed by the jury. The jury acquitted of the two counts of non-consensual activity, which did depend wholly upon the unsupported evidence of the complainant, which showed that it applied itself realistically and responsibly to the assessment of her evidence. The overwhelming likelihood, on the evidence as a whole, was that the consensual, but abusive, relationship had indeed existed, and that the complainant had done her best from time to time to avoid getting the appellant into trouble.

Clare: Hearsay statement by a young child

The appellant in *Clare* had been convicted of a single offence of sexual   19.42
assault upon a child aged three-and-a-half. On a summer's day he was a
visitor at the home of the child's family. He had been drinking for some of the
day. There was a tent in the garden and in the early evening he was in it with
the little girl. The child told her mother that the appellant had licked her
private parts. By the time the mother had decided what to do and had called
the police, the appellant had left without saying anything by way of farewell.
The child was never a potential witness.

The medical evidence was neutral. The appellant was arrested the same   19.43
evening and interviewed the next day. In the course of his arrest he told one
of the officers not to look at him as if he were a paedophile, before the officers
had said anything to suggest they were enquiring into indecency with a child.
In interview, the appellant said that it was possible that his DNA would be
found on the girl's knickers and gave an unlikely explanation suggesting that
his face had been pressed up against her groin when he had been attempting
to swat a wasp and remove a sticky sweet from her knickers. In the event,
there was no scientific evidence of matchable DNA on the knickers. There
was both a full female profile and a contribution from a male.

The prosecution applied to adduce the child's complaint to her mother   19.44
under the "interests of justice" gateway in s.114(1)(d). The judge worked his
way carefully through the s.114(2) factors. He concluded, and the Court of
Appeal agreed, that the case depended substantially on the girl's statement,
which was admitted.

On appeal it was submitted on behalf of the appellant that no assessment   19.45
had been undertaken of the ability of the little girl to be interviewed under
ABE conditions. The Court of Appeal agreed that, if that had not been done
when it should have been done, it might have been a material consideration
when confronting under s.78 of the 1984 Act the question of fairness in
relation to the admission of evidence. But the Court was quite satisfied that
the judge had correctly concluded that the police had approached the
question responsibly and reached a proper answer. On any view, the child was
near the bottom of the age range in which an ABE interview might be
achievable. Her strong reaction to any examination or enquiry was a
powerful reason not to trouble her further, and more enquiry of her risked
being abusive.

If the girl's one-line statement to her mother had stood alone, it would   19.46
have been wrong to admit it. Children of three-and-a-half vary a good deal.
The jury could have had no opportunity to assess her, nor could she have
been asked any questions. However, the girl's statement did not stand alone.
It was powerfully supported by (i) the appellant leaving the house without a

word, (ii) his remark to the officer about paedophiles, and (iii) the remarkable story about the wasp and the sweet. There was sufficient support for the girl's statement to her mother, which was also spontaneous, unprompted and made originally not by way of complaint but simply by way of request for cream.

Bennett: Hearsay statement by patient with mental disorder who was too ill to give evidence[45]

19.47 The appellant in *Bennett*, a community psychiatric nurse, was convicted of sexual activity with a person with mental disorder. The prosecution case was that he had had an ongoing sexual relationship with his patient for some months. There was no doubt that the complainant was, despite her mental disorder, capable of consenting. She had given very long interviews to the police which had been video-recorded and were available to the jury. By the time of trial she was plainly too ill to give oral evidence, and that was not in dispute. Accordingly, the trial judge, on the application of the prosecution, admitted the complainant's recorded interviews as hearsay under the s.116(2)(b) gateway (person unfit to be a witness because of bodily or mental condition). In the interviews, the complainant gave a long, garrulous and by no means always consistent account of a continuing sexual relationship. When interviewed, the appellant initially denied any kind of affectionate or sexual relationship with the patient. Later, he broke down and gave a detailed account of their sexual relationship. At trial, the appellant, whilst accepting a sexual relationship, denied any penetration.

19.48 The Court of Appeal was satisfied that the judge had been correct to admit the evidence of the interviews with the patient. The case could be proved against the appellant without the complainant's evidence, by relying on messages and cards which he had sent her, his initial lies to the police and then his explicit confessions. Furthermore, there was ample material which enabled the reliability of the complainant to be tested. She was internally inconsistent. She could be shown to have asserted that she suffered from serious medical conditions when her doctor gave evidence that she did not. She had subsequently made another complaint against a second erstwhile boyfriend, whose virtues she had in the interviews repeatedly contrasted with what she said were the appellant's demerits; there was a clear basis for concern that she was prone first to profess great affection and then rapidly to turn to wounded resentment. She had made non-sexual complaints against neighbours and could be shown to have threatened to set fire to some property. It was impossible that any juror could have thought her wholly reliable.

---

[45] See also paras 7.35 and following, above.

Frightened witnesses: Admission through gateway s.116(2)(e)—The 12 steps

In *Shabir*[46] Aitkens LJ, drawing upon the decisions of the Supreme Court   **19.49**
and Court of Appeal in *Horncastle,* and of the Court of Appeal in *Ibrahim*
and *Riat,* gave a very clear exposition of the law governing the admissibility
of hearsay evidence when reliance is placed upon s.116(2)(e). We set out
below the 12 steps that he identified, with references to recent cases. When it
is sought to admit a hearsay statement through the gateway of s.116(2)(e),
because it is said that the witness will not give oral evidence at the trial
"through fear", the framework is as follows[47]:

(1) The "default" position is that hearsay evidence is not admissible.
(2) It is a pre-condition to the admission of a hearsay statement that the
     witness concerned is identified: s.116(1)(b).
(3) The necessity to resort to second-hand evidence must be clearly
     demonstrated. The more central the evidence, the greater the
     scrutiny that has to be undertaken.
(4) Although "fear" is to be widely construed in accordance with
     s.116(3) and, specifically, fear on the part of a witness does not have
     to be attributed to the defendant, a court has to be satisfied to a
     criminal standard that the proposed witness will not give evidence
     (either at all or in connection with the subject matter of the relevant
     statement) "through fear". Thus a causative link between the fear
     and the failure or refusal to give evidence must be proved.
(5) How it is proved that a witness will not give evidence "through fear"
     depends upon the background together with the history and the
     circumstances of the particular case. Every effort must be made to
     get the witness to court to test the issue of his "fear". The witness
     alleging "fear" may be cross-examined by the defence (if needs be in
     a *voir dire*), using "special measures" to assist the witness where
     necessary. However, Aitkens LJ acknowledged that whilst that
     procedure may be possible, in certain cases it may not be appro-
     priate. Subsequent cases have illustrated this.

For instance, in *Adeojo*[48] a *voir dire* was held in which the witness
indicated he would refuse to answer questions from the defence, but
no questions were put to the witness on the issue of the genuineness
of his fear either by defence counsel or the judge. The judge
subsequently concluded that there was an abundance of material
which satisfied him that the witness was genuinely in fear for himself
and his family. He considered s.78 of the 1984 Act by examining the
s.114(2) factors and concluded that it was in the interests of justice
to admit the statement. He gave an appropriate warning to the jury

---

[46] [2012] EWCA Crim 2564.
[47] At [64]–[65] per Aitkens LJ.
[48] [2013] EWCA Crim 41.

in his summing up. The Court of Appeal concluded that the verdicts of the jury were safe.

In *Jabbar*,[49] the appellant's counsel sought to criticise the trial judge for not explaining to the witness, who was available for a *voir dire*, that it was the witness's public duty to give evidence. It was contended that might have produced a change of heart. Treacy LJ stated:

> "Although *Riat* encourages the court to take all possible steps to enable a fearful witness to give evidence, notwithstanding his or her apprehension, it has to be recognised that the factual situation will vary from case to case, as will the steps a judge should take in any given circumstances. Given the judge's finding that Tahir's fears were genuine and that he attended court, explained his position after meeting prosecuting counsel and had been cross-examined as to credibility, we do not find any failure in the way *Tahir* was handled which could avail the appellant on his challenge to the admissibility of the evidence."

Further, in *Fagan*[50] the Court of Appeal stated that, whilst it would have been wise to ensure the witness was brought to court, nevertheless, in the circumstances of that case the failure to do so was nowhere near fatal to the judge's conclusion that the witness was in a state of extreme fear.

(6) If testing by the defence is properly refused (after consideration) then "it is incumbent on the judge to take responsibility vigorously to test the evidence of fear and to investigate all the possibilities of the witness giving oral evidence in the proceedings". The manner in which that should be done will depend on the circumstances of the case and upon the witness and will necessarily involve discussions with counsel as to the approach and questions to be asked. For example, if a court cannot hear from a witness, a tape recording or video of an interview on the question of his "fear" should, if possible, be made available. The critical thing is that "every effort is made to get the witness to court".

In *Clarke*,[51] it was alleged that the victim had given the name of his attacker "off the record" to a police officer. In evidence the victim denied that he had told the officer the identity of the attacker but in all other respects he was co-operative. The trial judge accepted that the victim was plainly in fear and ruled that it was in the interests of justice that the officer should give evidence of the hearsay "off the record" statement. Hallett LJ observed that it is clear from the wording of s.116(2)(e), which applies where a person does not give or "does not continue to give" evidence, that the provision may apply where a witness is available. In that case there

[49] [2013] EWCA Crim 801.
[50] [2012] EWCA Crim 2248.
[51] [2012] EWCA Crim 2354.

was sufficient evidence to justify the finding that the witness was in genuine and substantial fear of the appellant. This came not only from the circumstances of the attack upon him, but also from the evidence of the appellant's background.

(7) In relation to the gateway in s.116(2)(e), leave to admit the statement will only be given if the conditions for passing through a specific "secondary gateway" are satisfied. These are set out in s.116(4). Overall, a court will only admit a statement under s.116(2)(e) if it considers that it is "in the interests of justice" to do so. In that respect, the court has to have specific regard to the matters set out in s.116(4)(a)–(c).

(8) When a court considers s.116(4)(c), it should take all possible steps to enable a fearful witness to give evidence notwithstanding his apprehension: "A degree of (properly supported) fortitude can legitimately be expected in the fight against crime". A court must therefore have regard to whether (in an appropriate case) a witness would give evidence if a direction for "special measures" were to be made under s.19 of the Youth Justice and Criminal Evidence Act 1999.

(9) In this regard it is important that, before the court has ruled on the application to admit under s.116(2)(e), no indication, let alone assurance, is given to a potential witness that his evidence will or may be read if he says he is afraid, because that can only give rise to an expectation that this will, indeed, happen. Thomas LJ (as he then was) in *Horncastle* had enunciated a general prohibition on such assurances. Aitken LJ, following this lead in *Shabir*, went so far as to indicate that if such assurances are given then the statement will have been admitted on an improper basis; the impact of the evidence will be diminished and that may have further conse- quences, e.g. an application to the judge under s.125 at the end of the prosecution case to stop the case. However, the subsequent decision in *Abdulle*[52] illustrates that these outcomes are necessarily fact-dependent. In that case, a young witness was given an assur- ance before a second ABE interview that he would not have to testify. This was held not to be fatal to the interview's admissibility under s.114(1)(d). The judge had made express reference to all the points in *Horncastle* and had explained his reasoning in a very full ruling at the outset of the trial. The judge had carefully considered the whole issue of reliability. He had found that it was under- standable in the circumstances that the assurance had been given. In summing-up, he had highlighted the potential disadvantage to the defence in not being able to cross-examine the witness and had

[52] [2013] EWCA Crim 1069.

stressed the need for caution. Overall, he had exercised his discretion in a proper manner and his ruling could not be criticised.

(10) When a judge considers the "interests of justice" test under s.116(4), although he or she is not obliged to consider all the factors set out in s.114(2)(a)–(i), those factors may be a convenient check list for the judge to consider.

(11) Once the judge has concluded that the specific secondary gateways set out in s.116(4) have been satisfied, the court must consider the vital linked questions of (a) the apparent reliability of the evidence sought to be adduced as hearsay and (b) the practicality of the jury testing and assessing its reliability. In this regard, s.124 (which permits a wide range of material going to the credibility of the witness to be adduced as evidence) is vital.

(12) In many cases, a judge will not be able to make a decision as to whether to admit an item of hearsay evidence unless he has considered not only the importance of the evidence and its apparent strengths and weaknesses, but also what material is available to help test and assess it, in particular what evidence could be admitted as to the credibility of the witness and the hearsay evidence under s.124. The judge is entitled to expect that "very full" enquiries as to witness credibility will have been made if it is the prosecution that wishes to put in the hearsay evidence, and if it is the defence, they too must undertake proper checks.

19.50 *Ali (Yasir)*[53] is a recent case in which the Court of Appeal took the view that the trial judge had been wholly correct to permit a complainant's statement to be read in a rape case pursuant to s.116(2)(e) because it had been established that she was in fear, most particularly of having to confront the events of a night at a hotel. Her account was that that night was the worst in her life, and she had wanted to be able to forget about what had occurred. There was evidence before the jury from a social worker that at the time of the trial, she was emotionally traumatised by what had occurred, and was unable to answer questions about it. There was an accurate record of the ABE interview. Pursuant to s.124, the appellant had had a wide-ranging opportunity to challenge the contents of her statement on the basis of other evidence in the case, including the witness's first account. The judge had been right to conclude that this evidence had considerable probative value against the appellant, and would assist the jury in their evaluation of other evidence in the case. There was no reason for the judge to conclude, applying s.125, that her statement was so unconvincing that the conviction of the appellant would be unsafe, bearing in mind it was of critical importance against him. Her statement was a credible account by someone who had been intimidated and had not given proper consent. The contradictions between her earlier and later accounts were explicable, as with many witnesses in situations of

[53] [2015] EWCA Crim 1279.

this kind, on the basis that initially she was reluctant to disclose what had occurred.

Statement of witness admitted where s.116 criteria fulfilled

Under s.116 of the CJA 2003 (cases where a witness is unavailable), first hand   19.51
hearsay evidence, whether oral or documentary, is admissible without leave
provided certain criteria are met (witness dead, ill, absent abroad, lost, or in
fear). However, in all cases under s.116 it is necessary to establish that the
relevant person was competent[54] at the time of making the relevant
statement. Section 123(1) of the 2003 Act provides:

> "Nothing in section 116, 119 or 120 makes a statement admissible as evidence if
> it was made by a person who did not have the required capability at the time
> when he made the statement."

Section 123 bases the test of a person's capability on (a) understanding
questions put to him about matters stated, and (b) giving answers to such
questions which can be understood. A *voir dire* may be held and expert
evidence called if necessary. The inclusion of the requirement of competence
appears, somewhat surprisingly, to have narrowed the law at a time when
Parliament was adopting a far more inclusive approach to the admissibility
of evidence. Under the pre-2003 Act provisions, the Court of Appeal in *Ali
Sed*[55] held that the video interview of an Alzheimer's sufferer (who was a
complainant in case of attempted rape) was rightly admitted under s.23 of the
Criminal Justice Act 1988, even though the complainant was not available to
give evidence. *Ali Sed* followed *R. v D*,[56] where it was held in an attempted
rape case that the video interview of another Alzheimer's victim was rightly
admitted under s.23, and, in particular, there was no requirement for
admission under s.23 that the witness be competent.

When deciding whether to admit a statement in evidence where the   19.52
defendant has not had an opportunity to examine the witness, there is only
one governing criterion: is the admission of the evidence compatible with a
fair trial? In *Konrad Cole and Rocky Keet*,[57] Lord Phillips LCJ, as he then
was, stated[58]:

> "There are many reasons why it may be impossible to call a witness. Where the
> defendant is himself responsible for that fact, he is in no position to complain
> that he has been denied a fair trial if a statement from that witness has been
> admitted. Where the witness is dead, or cannot be called for some other reason,
> the question of whether the admission of a statement from that witness will

---

[54] The age of a child witness is not determinative of its competence or its ability to give
truthful and accurate evidence: *Barker* [2010] EWCA Crim 4. Ability to remember is not the
same as competence: *DPP v R.* [2007] EWHC 1842 (Admin).
[55] [2004] Crim. L.R. 1036. For the present position, see *DPP v R.* [2007] EWHC 1842
(Admin).
[56] [2002] 2 Cr. App. R. 601. In both *Ali Sed* and *R. v D* there was supporting evidence.
[57] [2007] EWCA Crim 1924.
[58] At [21].

impair the fairness of the trial will depend on the facts of the particular case. Factors that will be likely to be of concern to the court are identified in s.114(2) of the Act."

He went on to point out that the s.114(2) list of factors relevant to the interests of justice does not state expressly which way each individual factor is intended to cut. The Court considered that the inference is that the more important and the more reliable the statement appears to be, the stronger the case for its admission. When the factors in s.114(2) are considered in respect of several statements, the correct approach is not to consider each statement on its own, but to consider each in context. Each statement may be part of a wider picture that is coherent and compelling. The Court also endorsed the trial judge's remarks that s.116 and its predecessors provide an important weapon in the prosecution armoury in respect of offences alleged to have been aimed at the elderly and vulnerable.

Statement admitted in the interests of justice under s.114(1)(d) of the Criminal Justice Act 2003

19.53　Section 114(1)(d) is not a route to be invoked only when none of the other hearsay gateways apply. Section 114(2) contains a list of matters that it is mandatory for the court to take into account when deciding whether to admit hearsay evidence under s.114(1). Although the judge must take these factors into account, he need not express a conclusion on each factor. The courts have been known to give the provision a relatively wide interpretation. In *R. v SJ*,[59] at a trial for assault by penetration of a child under 13 (the defendant's step-daughter aged 30 months), it was held that the trial judge had been right to allow a mother to report statements made by the child about what had happened to her shortly after the time of the allegation. The Court of Appeal commented that s.114 was a safety-valve to deal with this kind of case.

19.54　However, it is necessary to approach s.114(1)(d) with caution, particularly where a party is seeking to adduce hearsay evidence from a witness who is not being called, but whose absence is not within the reasons listed in s.116.

Earlier disclosures by very young children unconfirmed in evidence

19.55　What is the situation where the witness is called but has no recollection of making an earlier disclosure or of the events described in it? This is not an uncommon feature of cases where there are allegations of long-term abuse. A complainant may have little or no recollection of a contemporaneous report to a police officer or a social worker. Earlier disclosures may be relevant to rebut allegations of fabrication (see paras 19.88 and following, below). It may

---

[59] [2009] EWCA Crim 1869.

also be in the interests of justice for the jury to hear a contemporaneous account by a witness given during the grooming process.

MH v R.[60] provides some assistance as to how to approach earlier **19.56** disclosures unconfirmed by a complainant in evidence. In that case, it was held that unconfirmed disclosures made by a small child were admissible in the interests of justice under s.114(1)(d). The respondent's counsel sought to counter the suggestion that admitting such evidence would infringe the prohibition against "self-corroboration". He submitted that there was a material difference between an adult, or an older child, making repeated allegations of sexual misconduct (with the risk that mere repetition may provide spurious self-support) and a child aged three who did not possess the sophistication required to manipulate such opportunities to his own advantage, consciously or sub-consciously. The child's repeated and unsolicited references, in an unchallenging domestic context, to the appellant's conduct towards him provided cogent evidence of the child's truthfulness and reliability. It was in the interests of justice for such evidence to be considered by the jury both for its capacity to demonstrate the truth of the witness's evidence and, on account of its inherent reliability, because it was evidence of the appellant's conduct. The Court of Appeal, whilst acknowledging that the trial judge had not been asked to exercise his discretion under s.114(1)(d) and so had not addressed these issues, concluded that there would have been no prospect of successfully resisting the prosecution's wish to adduce the evidence. The circumstances were overwhelmingly in favour of the admission of the hearsay evidence in the interests of justice, whether or not it was capable of admission under s.120(2) to rebut a suggestion of fabrication.

To similar effect is *Strotten*,[61] where the appellant (then aged 23) was **19.57** arrested in connection with an allegation of sexually touching a boy, RG (then aged three years). It was alleged that he had sexually assaulted RG when alone with him and told him not to tell anyone as it was their "big secret" and that he (RG) would get into trouble if he did so. RG exhibited behaviour consistent with having been sexualised by an adult while at nursery school. RG, born in May 2009, was interviewed in accordance with ABE guidelines on April 5, 2013, when he was aged three, and in June and July 2013 when he was aged four. In the interviews, RG stated that the appellant had never done anything to his (RG's) penis. When put to him that he had told his mother that the appellant had touched his penis, he replied, "No, that didn't happen".

---

[60] [2012] EWCA Crim 2725. See also *R. v SJ* [2009] EWCA Crim 1869, considered in para.19.53, above, where the victim of sexual assault was a child aged 30 months who was not competent to give an ABE interview. There was a strong circumstantial case against the appellant. The child's responses to questions asked by her mother and on one occasion by a social worker were held to have been properly admitted under s.114(1)(d). The Court in *MH v R.* derived from *R. v SJ* the proposition that, whilst care must be exercised, there may be circumstances in which the interests of justice demand the admission of hearsay evidence, even if it is of critical importance to the main issue in case.

[61] [2015] EWCA Crim 1101.

19.58   RG's mother gave evidence that the appellant would run errands for her and look after RG when he was a toddler which would include helping her to change RG's nappy and playing together in the communal gardens. She went on to say that RG, when two-and-a-half years' old, told her and her partner that the appellant had been "playing with RG's willy". There was a further occasion when RG told her that the appellant had been "playing with his willy". RG has also told her that the appellant liked to put RG's penis into his mouth and suck it. RG's mother also stated that after RG had been interviewed by the police, he had told her that he had not been forthcoming in his ABE interview as he was frightened, and would feel bad if others got into trouble. The appellant gave evidence that he had not touched RG's penis.

19.59   The sole ground of appeal concerned the admission by the trial judge of the hearsay evidence of RG's mother and partner as to the complaints which RG made, but which he did not repeat in ABE interview. It was argued that RG, who was available to give evidence at the trial, had failed to substantiate the allegations and that, as a result, the application to admit the hearsay evidence could not be brought within s.114(1)(d) of the Criminal Justice Act 2003.

19.60   The respondent referred the Court to other potentially supporting evidence. The remarks by RG spanned 18 months and were consistent. They were supported by observations that RG had made to his mother and her partner, and by evidence of sexualised incidents at the nursery. The respondents also relied upon a similar fact allegation made by another boy entirely unconnected with RG. The Court of Appeal was satisfied that these circumstances were sufficient to permit the judge to admit the evidence. The Court added that an argument could have been advanced that RG's reported remarks were admissible as part of the *res gestae*. Sir Brian Leveson stated[62]:

> "In that regard, the possibility of concoction or distortion in relation to that allegation alone is capable of being discounted, not only because the appellant was there accepting that he was touching the boy RG, albeit not, as he asserted it, sexually, and by the immediacy of the circumstances."

19.61   Nevertheless, earlier Court of Appeal decisions suggest a move to limit the scope of s.114, particularly where no s.116 conditions are satisfied and the witness is unwilling to attend. For instance, in *R. v Z*[63] the Court of Appeal

---

[62] At [26].

[63] [2009] EWCA Crim 20; [2009] 1 Cr. App. R. 34. See also *O'Hare* [2006] EWCA Crim 2512, where the Court of Appeal pointed out that s.114(1)(d) should not be applied so as to render s.116 nugatory; *Khan* [2009] EWCA Crim 86, where the Court of Appeal upheld the decision of the trial judge to refuse an application to adduce the evidence of a prostitute under s.114(1)(d) in a case where the witness was available to be called as a witness; and *Warnick* [2013] EWCA Crim 2320, where the Court of Appeal stated that the judge was wrong to admit evidence under s.114(1)(d), when he had concluded that one of the conditions for admitting evidence under s.116 was not satisfied. In *R. v ED* [2010] Crim. L.R. 862, the Court of Appeal suggested that s.114(1)(d) is subordinate to the other exceptions.

quashed convictions of historical offences of indecent assault and rape where the trial judge had given the Crown leave under the hearsay provisions to adduce bad character evidence relating to two complainants in respect of alleged rapes and sexual abuse. One of the complainants was the appellant's former wife. She was dead and so the test under s.116(2)(a) was satisfied. However, the judge had failed to direct the jury that they had to be sure of the allegation before they could take it into account. The position in respect of the other complainant is more significant in that it sheds light on the proper approach where a hearsay application is made in respect of a complainant who is unwilling to give evidence for no apparent good reason. She was unwilling to give evidence and had explained why to the Crown. The Court held that her reluctance or apparent but untested unwillingness to testify did not justify the admission of her hearsay evidence. This was a case in which the conditions on the admission of hearsay in s.116, none of which applied to her, were being circumvented. The Court added that s.114(1)(d) should be cautiously applied[64] since otherwise the conditions laid down by Parliament in s.116 would be avoided, although s.114(1)(d) should not be so narrowly applied that it had no effect, and there would be cases where hearsay evidence might be admitted under s.114(1)(d) in which it could not be admitted under s.116. In *Riat*,[65] Hughes LJ observed that the power to admit evidence under section 114(1)(d) in the interests of justice should not be used so as to circumvent the conditions laid down in s.116.

Statement admitted under the preserved common law rule of *res gestae*: s.118(1) of the Criminal Justice Act 2003

The *res gestae* rule is specifically preserved by s.118(1), the relevant part of which reads: **19.62**

> "(1) The following rules are preserved.
> . . .
> *Res gestae*
> (4) Any rule of law under which in criminal proceedings a statement is admissible as evidence of any matter stated if—
> (a) the statement was made by a person so emotionally overpowered by an event that the possibility of concoction or distortion can be disregarded,
> (b) the statement accompanied an act which can be properly evaluated as evidence only if considered in conjunction with the statement, or
> (c) the statement relates to a physical sensation or a mental state (such as intention or emotion)."[66]

The *res gestae* rule might apply where a complainant manages to **19.63** communicate with the emergency services during the course of or immediately after a sexual attack. Where s.118(1) applies, the prosecution do not

---

[64] The importance of a cautious approach in these circumstances was stressed in *R. v C* [2010] Crim. L.R. 858.

[65] [2013] 1 Cr. App. R. 2 at [20].

[66] There is no need to serve a notice to introduce hearsay evidence that is admitted through s.118(1), (4).

have to apply to introduce the evidence under s.114(1)(d). The guiding authority is *Andrews*[67] where Lord Ackner strongly cautioned against attempting to use the *res gestae* principle as a device to avoid calling the maker of the statement if he or she is available. It is now clear that there are exceptions. In *Barnaby v DPP*[68] the Divisional Court held in an assault case that the admission of the evidence of emergency 999 telephone calls, together with conversations with the police officers that occurred shortly after an attack by a boyfriend, fell well within the *res gestae* principle even though the maker of the statement, the alleged victim, was available but was not called to give evidence. Immediately after the incident the victim had expressed fears as to the likely consequences if the appellant discovered that she had co-operated with the police, and particularly that she had provided information against him. Fulford LJ stated[69]:

> "Although the court has a cardinal responsibility to ensure the defendant receives a fair trial, careful decisions need to be taken in situations of this kind if there is a real risk that a victim of domestic abuse may suffer harm following her co-operation with the prosecution authorities. Here, the prosecution authority was aware from the outset that Ms X was frightened that providing a witness statement might provoke a violent reaction from the appellant. This was not a situation in which the prosecution was seeking to resort to unfair tactics in order to avoid introducing evidence that was potentially inconsistent with the case against the defendant, or it simply anticipated that there was a risk the witness might give an untruthful account. The Crown's stance was a seemingly sensible recognition of the potentially dangerous position in which Ms X had been placed. Given these facts, it was appropriate to admit this *res gestae* evidence notwithstanding, in a strict sense, Ms X was available as a witness if the court had issued a witness summons."

Inconsistent Statements: Section 119 of the Criminal Justice Act 2003

Inconsistent statements now evidence of the truth

19.64   Section 119(1) of the Criminal Justice Act 2003 makes a person's previous inconsistent statement, once admitted, "evidence of any matter stated of which oral evidence by him would be admissible". The effect is that a previous inconsistent statement related to the subject matter of the indictment is capable of being evidence of the truth of any matter stated if the witness admits making the statement or is proved to have made it. It follows that this provision has potentially a significant impact in respect of the evidence of complainants of a sexual offence.[70] If it is not established that the witness made the inconsistent statement, s.119 does not apply. If the witness

---

[67] [1987] A.C. 281.
[68] [2015] EWHC 232 (Admin) at [32]ff per Fulford LJ.
[69] At [34].
[70] For a strong example of s.119 in operation, see *Joyce and Joyce* [2005] EWCA Crim 1785, where two eye-witnesses in respect of a firearms offence became hostile at trial.

adopts his earlier statement or could reasonably be understood to be endorsing it, then s.119 does not apply.[71]

Hostile witnesses

If the witness is hostile and the statement is proved to be inconsistent, then 19.65 s.119 applies. There is no bar to calling a witness, expecting them to resile from what they said before, and then applying to make them hostile.[72] It follows that a previous consistent statement of a hostile witness, who admits making the statement, is admissible to prove the facts stated in it.[73] However, there may be very compelling reasons why it would be wholly inappropriate to call a complainant in a sex case when it is known that she retracts her original statement and does not want to give evidence.[74] For instance, where there is a continuing close relationship between the complainant and defendant, the situation may call for particular sensitivity. However, this very much depends upon the facts of a particular case, and the public interest in continuing to prosecute. Where a complainant's hostility is the result, for example, of fear or parental coercion, there may be strong arguments for calling the complainant, and, if necessary, applying to make them hostile.

The principle that an inconsistent statement by a witness becomes evidence 19.66 of the truth of its contents is not, of course, confined to hostile witnesses. However, the witness needs to give some oral evidence and to admit making the previous inconsistent statement. A good example is *Leach*,[75] where the Court of Appeal upheld a conviction of sexual assault where the first complaint of a 14-year-old to her mother was that the appellant had kissed her. In subsequent interviews, she alleged that he had touched her beneath her underwear. This inconsistent statement became evidence of the truth of her complaint as well as material which, if the jury thought the inconsistency was significant, could be used to cast doubt upon the truth of what she said. Arguably, judges should be astute to remind juries of any important inconsistencies in a complainant's previous statement, as the jury would be entitled to act upon a previous inconsistent statement as evidence of the truth.[76] It is likely that prosecutors will seek to rely more on the previous statements of complainants who have retracted their statements, particularly

---

[71] *R. v M* [2011] EWCA Crim 1458.
[72] *Osborne* [2010] EWCA Crim 1981.
[73] *Joyce and Joyce* [2005] EWCA Crim 1785; *Bennett* [2008] EWCA Crim 248; *Osborne* [2010] EWCA Crim 1981.
[74] See e.g. *R. v C* [2007] EWCA Crim 3463 where, in a domestic violence case, the Court of Appeal recommended relying on other available evidence rather than calling the complainant and making her hostile, thereby only exacerbating the wretched situation in which she found herself.
[75] [2005] EWCA Crim 58.
[76] *R. v Keith D* [2005] EWCA Crim 3043 (obiter).

where there is other evidence in the case supporting the previous state-ment.[77]

COMPLAINANT'S EVIDENCE

Reluctant complainants

19.67   It happens not infrequently in sex cases that a complainant refuses to give evidence or to continue to give evidence. When such a situation arises, it will usually be necessary for the judge to tell the witness that, as a witness in a court of law, he or she is under an obligation to answer questions and does not have a choice in the matter. The situation requires a blend of sensitivity and fairness which may involve giving the witness time to reflect. If the witness maintains their refusal, the judge may point out that, in the event of a continued refusal, the witness would be in contempt of court and there is a power to punish the witness. Whether or not there is evidence to suggest that the refusal is attributable to fear, a court may grant legal representation to such a witness, who has come to court as a result of a summons or warrant but is steadfastly refusing to give evidence. The court-appointed lawyer will not be able to discuss the witness's evidence with them, but will be able to explain the implications of failing to give evidence, which may amount to a contempt of court. We are firmly of the view that the court-appointed lawyer should have appropriate experience of sex cases in order that they are in a position to give proper advice in these highly sensitive cases. In sensitive situations, it may be better for the judge to leave it to the court-appointed lawyer to explain the repercussions of continued refusal.

No rule that there cannot be a conviction for rape without oral evidence from the complainant

19.68   Generally speaking, a complainant in a sex case, if available, will be expected to testify if their evidence is in dispute. There are, however, exceptional circumstances in which a complainant's statement might be properly admissible under the hearsay provisions. These will include cases in which the complainant has subsequently become seriously ill. Whilst the circumstances are limited in which a complainant's disputed evidence can be put before a jury under the hearsay provisions, there is no principle preventing such

---

[77] In *Crown Prosecution Service v CE* [2006] EWCA Crim 1410, the Court of Appeal upheld the trial judge's ruling not to admit a complainant's video evidence in a rape case even though two of the criteria under s.116 of the Criminal Justice Act 2003 were satisfied. The hearsay evidence was the sole or decisive evidence against the accused. The complainant was "potentially a completely flawed witness" and the defendant would be deprived of the opportunity of cross-examining her on a large numbers of issues relating to consent. Cf. two cases under s.23 of the Criminal Justice Act 1988, where the Court of Appeal held that the complainant's video was properly admitted: *Ali Sed* [2004] Crim. L.R.1036; *R. v D* [2002] 2 Cr. App. R. 601.

evidence being admitted if the appropriate criteria are satisfied. As Sir Igor Judge LJ, as he then was, observed in *Coates*[78]:

"A conviction for rape may, of course, be returned without the oral testimony of the complainant. As examples, after giving a detailed statement of the incident, the complainant may suffer a justified fear of serious repercussions if she were to give evidence, or she may suffer an accident with head injury[79] and loss of memory. The written statement would almost certainly be admitted. Again, the complainant may have been unconscious at the time of intercourse, or so inebriated as to have no memory of the precise circumstances, but others may have witnessed it. In other words a positive case may be mounted by the prosecution without the complainant giving oral evidence."

Where complainant disavows an earlier account

If the witness admits making the previous statement but does not repeat it at trial, or denies its contents, and the statement is proved to be "inconsistent" with his present testimony,[80] then, as seen above, the statement is potentially admissible under s.119 of the CJA 2003 (previous inconsistent statements).[81] It may also be admissible in the interest of justice under s.114(1)(d) of the Act. See paras 19.53 and following, above.   **19.69**

However, the effect of a disavowal in evidence by a complainant of an earlier account will depend upon the case. Where there is evidence that a vulnerable witness or a child has retracted an earlier allegation as a result of fear or coercion, the earlier allegation may still carry significant evidential weight. That was not the position in *Coates*[82] where the complainant had completely rejected her first account and there was no suggestion of any such pressure. This led to the conviction being quashed by the Court of Appeal as the tribunal had taken an impermissible route to conviction. The complainant had given evidence in which she rejected her own first account of and statement about the incident in which she alleged rape. Unusually, and because this was a Court-Martial, the factual basis on which the conviction was returned is known. The Board convicted the appellant on the basis of the first of the complainant's four statements, notwithstanding their rejection of her oral evidence. During the trial, defence counsel had put the first statement to the complainant during the course of her evidence. This was to establish significant inconsistencies with her evidence that her fourth statement was the true account so as to demonstrate her general unreliability. The   **19.70**

---

[78] [2007] EWCA Crim 1471; [2007] Crim. L.R. 887.

[79] Presumably this would include a complainant who made an ABE interview whilst competent, but subsequently was not fit to give evidence because of a degenerative condition such as dementia: see *Ali Sed* [2004] Crim. L.R. 1036; *R. v D* [2002] 2 Cr. App. R. 601.

[80] *Chinn* [2012] EWCA Crim 501, where s.119 was held not to apply where there was no suggestion that the witness was making an inconsistent statement. However, a claim to have no recollection may lead to a clear inference of inconsistency: see *Bennett* [2008] EWCA Crim 248.

[81] *R. v B* [2008] EWCA Crim 365.

[82] See *Coates* [2007] EWCA Crim 1471; [2007] Crim. L.R. 887.

fourth statement was made after later consultations and therapy with a doctor of clinical psychology, who was an accredited consultant in Eye Movement Desensitisation and Reprocessing. The Court of Appeal accepted that, on a strict application of the language of s.119(1), the statutory conditions governing admissibility of an inconsistent statement were fulfilled. However, the complainant, in her evidence, did not support any version of events which she had given before she saw the clinical psychologist. Defence counsel had introduced the first statement as a direct consequence of the prosecution proceeding on the fourth statement. The Court held that in those circumstances, notwithstanding the provisions of s.119, the issue of exclusion under s.78 of the Police and Criminal Evidence Act 1984 should have been addressed and, as a matter of discretion and overall fairness, the first statement should not have been treated as admissible evidence sufficient to form the basis of a conviction for a rape disavowed by the complainant herself.

Complainant's testimony at previous trial admitted at re-trial

19.71   On a re-trial, the transcript of the witness's testimony may be admissible under s.114(1)(d) or s.116 of the CJA 2003 where the defence have had a full opportunity to cross-examine and test the evidence at the previous trial. This may apply whether the testimony is the evidence of the complainant in respect of the allegation or of witnesses adduced under s.101(1)(d) of the bad character provisions.[83] Here, the argument in favour of admission is at its most compelling as the defence will already have had an opportunity to challenge and test the evidence. Often there will be an ABE interview, which, if admitted, will assist the jury in assessing the witness's demeanour, albeit not during cross-examination. In *Sadiq*[84] the Court of Appeal approved the admission of a complainant's testimony from a first trial at a re-trial under s.114(1)(d) in "some very exceptional circumstances". The complainant had been the victim of a shooting which had left him paralysed and unable to speak. At the first trial he had given important identification evidence by pointing to letters on an alphabet board. He then refused to give evidence at the re-trial. The Court of Appeal approved this course, but went out of its way to make clear that it was not normally in the interests of justice that an important witness's evidence should be given under the hearsay provisions when the witness simply refuses to testify and will not provide a good reason for the refusal. The judge, however, had been entitled to take into account a very relevant factor, namely that the jury would gain little assistance from the witness's demeanour at the re-trial.

[83] See Professor David Ormerod's discussion as to hearsay possibilities if there had been a re-trial in *O'Dowd* [2009] Crim. L.R. 827; but see *R. v Z* [2009] EWCA Crim 20; [2009] 1 Cr. App. R. 34.
[84] [2009] EWCA Crim 712.

CONSISTENT STATEMENTS—EVIDENCE OF EARLIER COMPLAINTS BY THE COMPLAINANT

Section 120 of the CJA 2003 specifies six gateways under which previous   19.72
consistent statements can become admissible as evidence of the truth. The
following paragraphs focus on two of those gateways: earlier complaints (in
the past commonly described as evidence of recent complaint) (s.120(4)–(7))
and evidence to rebut suggestion of fabrication (s.120(2)). The scope
provided by the Act for previous consistent statements to be admitted and
used as evidence of the truth represents a major shift from the common law
position.

History of evidence of earlier complaints

In the Middle Ages, suspicion of the veracity of any claim of rape led to the   19.73
imposition of a requirement on the woman to prove that, while the offence
was still recent, she raised "hue and cry" in the neighbouring towns and
showed her injuries and clothing.[85] By the eighteenth century, this requirement had evolved into a strong presumption against the victim of an alleged
rape if she made no complaint within a reasonable time of the offence.[86] This
presumption itself withered away, but a complaint made within a reasonable
time by the victim of an alleged rape remained admissible, contrary to the
general rule against the admission of previous consistent statements. Indeed,
recent complaints were recognised to be of such potential evidential significance that the rules relating to them were extended to all sexual
offences.

At common law, the prosecution in a trial for a sexual offence could, as   19.74
part of its case, call evidence that the victim had made a voluntary complaint
at the first reasonable opportunity after the commission of the offence.[87] The
complaint was not admissible as evidence as to the truth of the facts
complained of[88] but as evidence of the consistency of the victim's conduct
with her story in the witness box, and as tending to negative her consent.[89]

---

[85] Bracton, *De Corona* lib. iii. fol. 147; 1 Hale 633.
[86] 1 Hawk. c.41.
[87] *Lillyman* [1896] 2 Q.B. 167; *Osborne* [1905] 1 K.B. 551; *Camelleri* [1922] 2 K.B. 122; *Lovell* (1923) 17 Cr. App. R. 163; *Coulthread* (1934) 24 Cr. App. R. 44; *Evans* (1924) 18 Cr. App. R. 123; *Wannell* (1923) 17 Cr.App.R. 53; *Valentine* [1996] 2 Cr. App. R. 213. The rule was initially applied in respect of sexual offences against females; its application to offences against males was settled in *Camelleri*.
[88] Though a complaint may be admitted for this purpose if it was made in the presence of the defendant in circumstances where his response amounted to an admission or formed part of the res gestae: see Sir Rupert Cross and Colin Tapper, *Cross & Tapper on Evidence*, 9th edn (London: LexisNexis, 1999), pp.547 and following and 558 and following.
[89] *Lillyman*, above fn.87, at 170 per Hawkins J; *Osborne*, above fn.87; *Wallwork* (1958) 42 Cr. App. R. 153; *Redpath* (1962) 46 Cr. App. R. 319.

It was essential for the trial judge to direct the jury on the limited effect of the evidence.[90]

19.75   The common law on recent complaint was superseded by the provisions of s.120 of the CJA 2003 with effect from April 4, 2005. The provisions are founded on recommendations by the Law Commission[91] that the common law should be codified, subject to two highly important modifications. First, the Commission saw no justification for limiting the exception to sexual offences and recommended that it should apply to all offences. Secondly, the Commission regarded as "unrealistic" the common law requirement that the jury must be directed that evidence of recent complaint serves only to show that the victim is now telling the truth, and may not be taken as evidence of what happened. It took the view that, where a previous complaint is admissible at all, it should be treated as evidence of the truth of its contents and not merely as providing support to the witness's credibility.

19.76   The Law Commission noted that the temporal straitjacket represented by the "first reasonable opportunity" requirement was open to objection as being based on the idea that the natural reaction of any genuine victim of a sexual offence is to tell someone immediately. Research clearly showed, on the contrary, that most victims are too embarrassed to tell anyone, let alone to do so spontaneously and early. Nevertheless, s.120(7)(d) of the CJA 2003 as enacted required a complaint to be made as soon as could reasonably be expected after the alleged conduct. This anachronism was finally swept away by s.112 of the Coroners and Justice Act 2009,[92] which repealed s.120(7)(d). This means that, subject to the other s.120 requirements being fulfilled, *all* complaints in sex cases are admissible, regardless of when they are made. Evidence as to the terms of the first complaint or complaints and what motivated them can be very illuminating, and the removal of any temporal restriction on their admission is to be welcomed.

Earlier statement is "evidence of any matter stated of which oral evidence by [the complainant] would be admissible" but is not independent confirmation of the complainant's evidence

19.77   The major change brought about by s.120 in respect of evidence of earlier complaints is that they become evidence of the truth of the complaints, and their relevance is not confined to consistency as it was in the past. This should be explained to the jury, but it is important that the jury are reminded

---

[90] *Islam* [1999] 1 Cr. App. R.(S.) 22; *Wright and Ormerod* (1990) 90 Cr. App. R. 91; *R. v L(GB)*, unreported, November 28, 2000 (No.00/1697/21). Cp. *Akin*, unreported, September 23, 1996 (No.96/1196/W3), where it was held that the direction was not required as the circumstances were such that the limited effect of the evidence must have been obvious to the jury. It is nonetheless suggested that the safer course for a trial judge is to give the direction rather than omit it, even if in the particular case it amounts to a statement of the obvious.

[91] *Evidence in Criminal Proceedings: Hearsay and Related Topics* (Cm 245).

[92] Which came into force on February 1, 2010.

that the evidence of the earlier complaint does not come from an independent source. In *R. v AA*[93] the Court of Appeal stated[94]:

"... in deciding the weight such a statement should bear, the jury should have in mind the fact that it comes from the same person who now makes the complaint in the witness box and not from some independent source."

In that case the Court of Appeal quashed a rape conviction where the judge had not directed the jury that a statement from a friend of the complainant in respect of a complaint made by her the day after the incident was not independent of the complainant's evidence and so could not constitute independent confirmation of her evidence.

However, whilst such a direction should be routinely given, an omission to **19.78** give it will not necessarily be fatal to a conviction.[95] It is after all self-evident that complaint evidence does not come from an independent source. The Court of Appeal has also indicated that there may be cases where an independence warning is not necessary at all. *R. v H(J)*[96] concerned the historic abuse by the appellant of his three step-sons. Two of them had reported the abuse to their mother. The Court held that the failure to give an independence direction in relation to this complaint did not render the appellant's convictions unsafe. The trial judge had not been asked by defence (or Crown) counsel to give such a direction. Much had to be allowed for the feel of the case which the judge and counsel would have had. The defence case was that the boys were fabricating. In circumstances where it was the defence rather than, or as much as, the prosecution which was relying on the evidence of complaint, there was a danger in overcomplicating matters. It was clear from the trial as a whole and the judge's fair and helpful directions that the jury had to decide whether the truth was to be found in the complainants' allegations or in the defence, but that the burden lay on the prosecution. The judge emphasised that the reliability of the complainants was the critical question. In the circumstances, the Court inclined to the conclusion that there had been no misdirection at all. In any event, the case was distinguishable from *R. v AA*, above, where a single and prompt complaint to a friend following a single act of what was either rape or consensual intercourse was of special significance. By contrast, the allegations in *R. v H(J)* were of an ongoing course of conduct, both before and after the complaint, and the appellant relied on the evidence of the complaint for his own purposes as being part of the fabrication of which he complained.

As *R. v H(J)* indicates, there will be cases where the defence, rather than **19.79** the prosecution, wish to introduce an earlier statement so that they can rely upon inconsistencies as demonstrating the unreliability of the witness.

---

[93] [2007] EWCA Crim 1779.
[94] At [17].
[95] *Amrani* [2011] EWCA Crim 1517; *R. v A* [2011] EWCA Crim 1943.
[96] [2011] EWCA Crim 2344.

Classically, earlier statements may contain passages some of which are consistent with the present allegation and some of which are inconsistent. Even if introduced by the defence, such a statement becomes evidence of the truth of its contents. Technically, this will be so even if the witness admits making the earlier statement but rejects the truth of its contents. In those circumstances, notwithstanding its admission at the behest of the defence, it may be necessary to invoke s.78 of PACE so that the jury do not treat the earlier statement as evidence of its truth.[97] In respect of mixed earlier statements (both consistent and inconsistent), it is important that the jury are reminded of any significant inconsistencies in the context of their consideration of the reliability of the witness.

Pre-condition that witness indicates he/she made the earlier statement and it represents the truth

19.80   Section 120(4) of the 2003 Act provides that a previous statement by a witness called to give oral evidence in criminal proceedings is admissible as evidence of any matter stated of which oral evidence by the witness would be admissible, if one of a number of conditions are met and if, while giving evidence, the witness indicates that, to the best of his belief, he made the statement and it represents the truth. This is a pre-condition for evidence of an earlier complaint to be admissible under s.120(7). Section 120(4) is frequently overlooked by prosecutors. In *R. v AA*,[98] the Court of Appeal observed that if evidence to this effect is available it should be plainly and clearly stated that the statement has been given and to the best of the complainant witness's belief it states the truth. It follows that if a complainant only complains of one incident, a complaint to a friend about a further incident will not be admissible under s.120(7) as the s.120(4) pre-condition will not have been satisfied.[99]

19.81   For this reason, a previous complaint was not admissible in *MH v R*.[100] In that case, a father was convicted of various sexual offences committed against his very young son. The child gave evidence, but was not asked to confirm that he had described the appellant's conduct to his mother or that the description he had given her was true. The Court of Appeal observed that, despite the warnings in *R. v AA* and *Athwal*,[101] "complaints" continue to be admitted as if the former common law still applied. In those circumstances, the prosecution's only route to admissibility may be to satisfy the criteria for the admissibility of hearsay under the safety-valve provision of s.114(2).[102]

---

[97] *Coates* [2007] EWCA Crim 1471; [2007] Crim. L.R. 887.
[98] [2007] EWCA Crim 1779.
[99] *Avery* [2007] EWCA Crim 1830.
[100] [2012] EWCA Crim 2725.
[101] [2009] EWCA 789.
[102] *Gilloley* [2009] EWCA Crim 671.

The "third condition"

If s.120(4) is satisfied, then admissibility of complaint evidence will depend   **19.82**
upon whether the "third condition" set out in s.120(7)[103] can be established.
The third condition is that:

> "(a) the witness claims to be a person against whom an offence has been
>   committed;
> (b) the offence is one to which the proceedings relate;
> (c) the statement consists of a complaint made by the witness (whether to a
>   person in authority or not) about conduct which would, if proved,
>   constitute the offence or part of the offence;
> [(d) the complaint was made as soon as could reasonably be expected after the
>   alleged conduct;] *This requirement was repealed with effect from February 1,*
>   *2010.*
> (e) the complaint was not made as a result of a threat or a promise; and
> (f) before the statement is adduced the witness gives oral evidence in connec-
>   tion with its subject matter."

The Court of Appeal gave consideration to the use of s.120(7) soon after its   **19.83**
implementation in *Xhabri*.[104] The complainant, a 17-year-old Latvian,
alleged that she had been kidnapped, raped and forced to work as a
prostitute. She made telephone calls to her parents and others alleging that
she was being detained against her will. At trial the complainant gave
evidence of those calls without any objection. The Court of Appeal held that
the trial judge had been correct to allow the recipients' evidence to be
received as evidence of recent complaint under s.120(7) of the Act. All the
criteria of the third condition had been satisfied. The Court also indicated
that the evidence could have been admitted under s.114(1)(d). No issue arose
in respect of s.120(7)(d) in *Xhabri* as to the time the complaints were made as
they were made when the conduct was continuing.

Section 120(7)(b)—"the offence is one to which the proceedings relate"

Section 120(7) does not provide a route to admissibility unless the offence   **19.84**
alleged in the complaint relates to the current proceedings. This precludes the
use of s.120(7) where the complaint relates to some other matter or evidence
of it is called as bad character evidence.[105]

No limit as to the number of complaints that may be admitted

As was the position under the common law,[106] the Act places no limitation   **19.85**
on the number of complaints that may be admitted.[107] In *R. v O*[108] the Court

---

[103] So described because s.120(4) is the gateway for two other routes to admissibility, i.e. under
s.120(5) and s.120(6), and not because there are three conditions for admissibility of complaint
evidence.
[104] [2006] 1 Cr. App. R. 26, Lord Phillips CJ presiding.
[105] See dicta to this effect in *Trewin* [2008] EWCA Crim 484.
[106] *Lee* (1912) 7 Cr. App. R. 31; *Wilbourne* (1917) 12 Cr. App. R. 280.
[107] *R. v O* [2006] 2 Cr. App. R. 405.
[108] [2006] 2 Cr. App. R. 405.

of Appeal observed that there is obviously a need to restrict evidence of "complaint upon complaint". In practice, the law of diminishing returns may apply.

Section 120(7)(e)—"the complaint was not made as a result of a threat or a promise"

19.86 Section 120(7)(e) requires that the complaint was not made as a result of a threat or a promise. For this purpose, s.120(8) provides that the fact that a complaint was elicited, e.g. by a leading question, is irrelevant unless a threat or a promise was involved. This is on the face of it a narrower exclusion than applied at common law, under which evidence of recent complaint was admissible only if the judge was satisfied that the complaint was "spontaneous", in the sense of being an unassisted and unvarnished statement of what happened.[109] This requirement was explained by Ridley J in *Osborne*[110] as meaning that a complaint would be admitted only if it was not elicited by questions of a "leading and inducing or intimidating character". He added that the mere fact that the statement was made in answer to a question was not of itself sufficient to make it inadmissible as a complaint, giving as examples questions such as "What is the matter?" or "Why are you crying?", put by a parent or other relative or friend. He continued[111]:

> "in each case the decision on the character of the question put, as well as other circumstances, such as the relationship of the questioner and the complainant, must be left to the discretion of the presiding judge. If the circumstances indicate that, but for the questioning, there probably would have been no voluntary complaint, the answer is inadmissible. If the question merely anticipates a statement which the complainant was about to make, it is not rendered inadmissible by the fact that the questioner happens to speak first."

The statutory bar is less restrictive than this. A statement elicited from the victim by leading questions or reluctantly[112] will be admissible as a complaint, unless it is the result of a threat or promise (either explicit or implicit).

Section 120(7)(f)—"before the statement is adduced the witness gives oral evidence in connection with its subject matter"

19.87 Section 120(7)(f) requires that before the statement is adduced the witness gives oral evidence "in connection with" its subject matter. There is no express requirement that the statement must be consistent with the oral

---

[109] *Osborne* [1905] 1 K.B. 551; *Norcott* [1917] 1 K.B. 347 at 350, per Lord Reading CJ.
[110] [1905] 1 K.B. 551.
[111] At 556.
[112] cf. *Squirrel*, unreported, January 22, 1998 (No.97/3618/Z4), where a complaint made by a Royal Navy petty officer to the Warrant Officer Master at Arms was held inadmissible since it was made reluctantly, as the petty officer did not want to get the offender into trouble.

evidence, as was required at common law.[113] This is because the effect of evidence of recent complaint under s.120 has changed. At common law it was admissible only to demonstrate the consistency of the victim's story, and without such consistency there was no point in admitting it. Under the Act, a complaint may be admitted not just to show consistency but also as evidence of the facts stated. It follows that it may be admitted for the latter purpose, on behalf of either prosecution or defence, whether it is consistent or inconsistent with the victim's evidence in the box.

Evidence to rebut a suggestion that oral evidence has been fabricated

In the past, a previous consistent statement by the complainant, even if **19.88** inadmissible as a recent complaint because of lapse of time before it was made, was admissible to rebut a suggestion of recent fabrication.[114] At common law, if a suggestion of recent fabrication is made in cross-examination of a witness, evidence of a previous consistent statement is admissible in re-examination to negative the suggestion and confirm the witness's credibility. The widening of the scope of the admissibility of previous complaints by s.120 of the CJA 2003 means there is less resort now to the admission of previous statements on this basis. Many complaints will be admissible under both s.120(4) and (7), as well as under the common law in order to rebut recent fabrication.

Section 120(2) provides: **19.89**

> "If a previous statement is admitted to rebut a suggestion that his oral evidence has been fabricated, that statement is admissible as evidence of any matter stated of which oral evidence by the witness would be admissible."

Section 120(2) is not in itself a gateway to admissibility.[115] Rather, it regulates the use to which the evidence can be put once it has been admitted. However, the wording of s.120(2) differs from the common law in that s.120(2) makes no reference to *recent* fabrication. As was made clear by the Court of Appeal in *Athwal*,[116] the common law of recent fabrication is not to be confined within a temporal straitjacket. The Court went on to clarify that "recent" is an elastic description, the purpose of which is to assist in the identification of circumstances in which the traditional rule against self-corroboration should not extend to the exclusion of a previous consistent statement, where there is a rational and potentially cogent basis for its use as a tool for deciding where the truth lies. The touchstone is whether the evidence may fairly assist the jury in ascertaining where the truth lies. Once admitted, it can be relied upon as evidence of the truth, and not merely of consistency. In *R. v PK*,[117] an early ruling admitting previous complaints was approved by the

[113] See para.19.69, above.
[114] *Tyndale* [1999] Crim. L.R. 320.
[115] *Trewin* [2008] EWCA 484.
[116] [2009] EWCA Crim 789.
[117] [2008] EWCA Crim 434.

Court of Appeal in circumstances where the defence of fabrication could properly be anticipated.

19.90 The evidence of early disclosures in *MH v R.*,[118] although not admissible under s.120(4) and (7), was potentially admissible on two other bases. First, the fact that the disclosure was made tended to disprove the accusation of coaching and so was relevant evidence. However, that would not make the disclosure admissible as proof of its contents. Secondly, it was admissible under s.120(2) to rebut the accusation of fabrication, and as such was admissible as proof of its contents and not merely as evidence going to the issue of consistency.[119]

COLLATERAL QUESTIONS AND THE RULE OF FINALITY

19.91 The general rule, designed to keep trials within manageable limits, is that evidence may be adduced only if it is relevant to an issue in the case.[120] This means that answers given during cross-examination to questions going not to an issue but only to the creditworthiness of the witness must generally be regarded as final. The answers to such "collateral questions" may be believed or disbelieved by the jury, but, subject to certain exceptions not covered here, evidence cannot be called to contradict them.[121] However, the common law developed an exception to the general rule in trials for rape and indecent assault where consent was in issue. In such cases, the defence were permitted to adduce evidence to rebut denials by the complainant in cross-examination relating to her sexual history, on the ground that such questions might be highly relevant not merely to credit but to the issue of consent.[122] The common law rules have been superseded in relation to all sexual offences by s.41 of the Youth Justice and Criminal Evidence Act 1999, which severely restricts the asking of questions and the calling of evidence about the complainant's sexual history.[123] No question may be asked (or evidence adduced) about the sexual behaviour of the complainant without leave of the court. Furthermore, any questions in cross-examination as to a witness's bad character are only permissible if they come within one of the specified categories of admissibility set out in s.100 of the Criminal Justice Act 2003 (non-defendant's bad character).[124] Otherwise, the general rule continues to apply in trials for sexual offences as in all other trials. Its effect is particularly

---

[118] [2012] EWCA Crim 2725.
[119] *Athwal* [2009] EWCA Crim 789; *R. v T* [2008] EWCA Crim 484, at [18] per David Clarke J.
[120] *Attorney General v Hitchcock* (1847) 1 Ex. 91; *Funderburk* (1990) 90 Cr. App. R. 467; *R. v N*, unreported, April 8, 1998 (No.97/6290/Z3).
[121] *Harris v Tippett* (1811) 2 Camp. 637; *Attorney General v Hitchcock* (1847) 1 Ex. 91; *Cracknell* (1866) 10 Cox C.C. 408; *Holmes* (1871) L.R. 1 C.C.R. 334.
[122] *Barker* (1829) 3 C. & P. 589; *Clay* (1851) 5 Cox C.C. 146; *Holmes* (1871) L.R. 1 C.C.R. 334; *Riley* (1887) 18 Q.B.D. 481; *Turner* [1944] K.B. 463; *Bashir* [1969] 1 W.L.R. 1303; *Krausz* (1973) 57 Cr. App. R. 466.
[123] See Ch.26, below.
[124] See Ch.20, below.

important where the defence wish to call evidence to rebut a denial by the complainant that she has previously said something inconsistent with her evidence or made false sexual allegations against persons other than the defendant. The courts' response to this situation is considered below. The cases arc citcd to illustrate the principles, but it must be borne in mind that some pre-date the regimes under s.41 of the Youth Justice and Criminal evidence Act 1999 (previous sexual history) and s.100 of the Criminal Justice Act 2003 (non-defendant's bad character).

IDENTIFYING COLLATERAL QUESTIONS: FUNDERBURK

In *Funderburk*[125] the Court of Appeal acknowledged the difficulty of distinguishing collateral questions from questions going to the issue, where the issue is a sexual encounter between two people in private. The appellant had been charged with three counts of having unlawful sexual intercourse with the complainant, a girl of 13. The girl gave evidence that she had had a crush on the appellant and described in detail the acts of intercourse which she said had taken place. Although she did not say expressly that she had been a virgin at the time of the first incident, her evidence clearly implied that she had. The defence case was that the complainant had been both experienced and sexually interested, and that she had transposed to the appellant experiences that she had had with others and/or fantasised about her experience with the appellant. In support of that defence, counsel wished to put to the complainant that she had told P, a potential defence witness, that she had had sexual intercourse with two married men and that consequently she wanted to take a pregnancy test. The judge refused to allow these questions to be put, or to allow P to give evidence of the alleged conversation. Those rulings were challenged on appeal.   **19.92**

The first issue was whether the disputed questions should have been permitted, as going either to an issue or to the credibility of the complainant. On this, the Court adopted the test set out by Lawton J in *Sweet-Escott*[126] as to whether questions should be admitted as going to credit: **19.93**

> "What, then, is the principle upon which the judge should draw the line? It seems to me that it is this. Since the purpose of cross-examination as to credit is to show that the witness ought not to be believed on oath, the matters about which he is questioned must relate to his likely standing after cross-examination with the tribunal which is trying him or listening to his evidence."

The Court considered that the jury, having heard a graphic account from the complainant as to how she had lost her virginity, might reasonably have wished to re-appraise her evidence and her credibility if they had heard that on another occasion she had spoken of experiences which, if true, would indicate that she could not have been a virgin at the time of the incident. In

---

[125] (1990) 90 Cr. App. R. 467.
[126] (1971) 55 Cr. App. R. 316 at 320.

short, if the disputed questions had been put, her standing as a witness might well have been reduced. It followed that the judge had been wrong to disallow them.

19.94   A similar conclusion was reached in *Lloyd*,[127] where the judge prevented the defence from questioning the complainant in cross-examination about previous complaints of sexual abuse made by her against others. The ensuing conviction was quashed on appeal, the Court of Appeal citing with approval the following comment by the late Professor Sir John Smith:[128]

> "The fact that a complainant has made false allegations against a third party similar to those made against the defendant seems obviously relevant to her credibility and therefore it must be possible to put it to her in cross-examination that she has made such false allegations."

19.95   A final example of a question relevant to credit is provided by *R. v AB*,[129] which concerned the widespread and well-established practice of prosecution counsel asking the defendant whether he can offer any explanation why the complainant might make allegations against him and then commenting on the absence of an explanation. The Court confirmed the propriety of this practice, saying that the question was[130]:

> " . . . admissible because it was relevant. If there was anything known to the defendant, which provided a reason for the complainant to lie, this would tend to undermine her credibility. The fact that a negative answer was anticipated by counsel as likely cannot, as it seems to us, determine the admissibility of the question. If the defendant, unexpectedly, had given a positive answer, this would obviously have been relevant to his credibility and might have required further exploration. The prosecution, as it seems to us, were entitled by the question to seek to close, with finality, an avenue which was open to the defence."

The Court rejected the argument that the effect of the question was to reverse the onus of proof, saying that the evidential effect of the defendant's answer, in the context of the burden of proof, was a matter for summing-up, with a direction tailored to the circumstances of the case.

19.96   The second issue that arose in *Funderburk* was whether, if the disputed questions had been put and the complainant had denied speaking to P as alleged, her answers would have been final, or whether P could have been called to contradict her. P could have been called only if the questions went not just to credit, but to an issue in the case.[131] The Court noted that the complainant's evidence had been a "clear and pathetically moving account of the loss of virginity". It seemed very likely that this detailed account would be the most vivid picture the jury took with them into their retiring room. Unchallenged, the descriptive details could give the account the stamp of

[127] Unreported, February 18, 2000 (No.99/7714/Z1).
[128] Commentary on *R. v S* [1992] Crim. L.R. 309, discussed in para.19.95, below.
[129] [2003] EWCA Crim 951.
[130] At [41]–[42].
[131] See s.4 of the Criminal Procedure Act 1865 (which allows proof of previous inconsistent statements relative to the subject-matter of an indictment which are not admitted by a witness under cross-examination).

truth; but if details of such significance are successfully challenged, it can destroy both the account and the credit of the witness who gave it. On that basis, the appellant submitted that the disputed questions went not merely to credit but directly to the issue. Henry J, giving the judgment of the Court, cited the following extract from *Cross on Evidence*:

> "It has been remarked that sexual intercourse, whether or not consensual, most often takes place in private, and leaves few visible traces of having occurred. Evidence is often effectively limited to that of the parties, and much is likely to depend on the balance of credibility between them. This has important effects for the law of evidence since it is capable of reducing the difference between questions going to credit and questions going to the issue to vanishing point."

His Lordship said the answer to the question whether a fact is or is not collateral is an instinctive one, based on the prosecutor's and the court's sense of fair play rather than any philosophic or analytic process.[132] The prosecution had rightly accepted in argument that if the defence had had medical evidence that the complainant was not a virgin before the date on which she gave her account of losing her virginity, they would have been allowed to call it. Otherwise, there would be a danger that the jury would make their decision as to credit on an account of the original incident in which the most emotive, memorable and potentially persuasive fact was, to the knowledge of all in the case save the jury, false. In fact there was no such medical evidence, but there were the complainant's conflicting statements. Henry J concluded that, on the way the prosecution had presented its case, the challenge to the loss of virginity not only might have affected the jury's view on the central question of credit, but was sufficiently closely related to the subject matter of the indictment for justice to require investigation of the basis of the challenge. Consequently, if the disputed questions had been put and had elicited a denial from the complainant, the evidence of P could have been called.

IDENTIFYING COLLATERAL QUESTIONS: ILLUSTRATIVE CASES

The statement in *Funderburk* that "fair play", rather than any "philosophic   **19.97** or analytic process", is the key to identifying collateral questions makes it clear that decisions in this area will turn on their facts, as the courts strive to do justice in the particular circumstances of each case. If that is so, consistency between decisions may be at a premium, and a comparison of the cases tends to bear this out.

First, three cases in which evidence was held to have been rightly excluded   **19.98** on grounds that it went to a collateral issue. In *R. v S*,[133] the appellant was charged with committing sexual offences against the complainant. Under

---

[132] cp. *R. v N*, unreported, April 8, 1998 (No.97/6290/Z3), where the Court said that the test of relevance to an issue does involve an analytical process: the starting point is to define the issues in the case and then "logic and common sense" come into play.

[133] [1992] Crim. L.R. 307.

cross-examination the complainant admitted that she had previously made similar allegations against B and D. The defence wished to call D to testify that the allegations against him were untrue.[134] The judge refused to admit D's evidence and this ruling was upheld on appeal. The Court said that if the evidence had been admitted, the jury would have had to determine the entire issue of whether the complainant's or D's version of events was correct. That would not have been a confined issue but would have meant the jury embarking on an extremely difficult and complex task, and the Crown would have had to consider whether to call yet further evidence in rebuttal. Moreover, the jury would have had to be directed that, whatever they concluded (and the strong probability was that they would have been unable to come to a clear conclusion), it was not determinative of the real issue they had to decide. D's evidence would only have been relevant to the complainant's creditworthiness. In the circumstances the judge had come to the right conclusion, given the need to keep criminal trials within bounds and not distract the jury from the principal issue by involving them in other issues that were unsuitable for determination in the forum of the trial taking place.

19.99   In *Rackham*,[135] the appellant was convicted of a number of sexual offences committed against his two step-daughters. One of the complainants was asked in cross-examination why she had left a previous job, and she said she had left voluntarily. The defence sought to call evidence that the true reason for her leaving was that she had made a false allegation that she had been the subject of sexual interference. The judge refused to allow this evidence to be given and on appeal it was held that he had been right to do so, as the evidence would have introduced "what would plainly have been a collateral issue". To similar effect is *R. v W*,[136] where the complainant, a child, gave evidence that a telephone call had been made at a particular time to the house in which he claimed to have been indecently assaulted. The judge admitted evidence from the telephone company showing that the child's evidence as to the timing of the call was inaccurate, and directed the jury that the inaccuracy of the child's recollection could be relevant to the truthfulness of his account of the indecent assault. On appeal it was held, quashing the conviction, that the accuracy of the child's evidence in this respect was irrelevant to the main issue, and that the evidence from the telephone company accordingly went to a collateral questions and should not have been allowed in.

---

[134] They did not seek to call B, as they accepted the truth of the allegations against him and instead asserted that the complainant had fantasised and transported to S conduct which had in fact occurred between her and B.

[135] [1997] 2 Cr. App. R. 222; and see *Ahmed and Khan* [1994] Crim. L.R. 669; *R. v N*, Unreported, April 8, 1998 (No.97/6290/Z3); *Fernandes* [2002] EWCA Crim. 1773; *Colwill* [2002] EWCA Crim. 1320; *R. v AD* [2002] EWCA Crim 1789.

[136] Unreported, March 25, 1997 (No.97/0806/Y3).

Compare these cases with *Nagrecha*,[137] where the complainant alleged that   **19.100**
the appellant had indecently assaulted her at the restaurant which he owned
and where she was working for the first time on the evening in question. The
defence had a statement from L, a manager at the complainant's previous
place of work, stating that she had made "allegations of a sexual nature"
against him when he reprimanded her about her performance, and that she
made sexual allegations to her work colleagues, which no one believed, about
a taxi driver and about building workers. When the contents of L's statement
were put to the complainant she denied them, admitting only that she had
complained about L's "aggressive behaviour" towards her. The defence
sought to call L's evidence, but the judge excluded it as it did not go to an
issue in the case. On appeal it was held that this ruling had been wrong, and
that L's evidence went not merely to credit but to the heart of the case, as it
bore upon the crucial issue of whether or not there had been any indecent
assault. As to that, only the complainant and the appellant were able to give
evidence and, that being so, the judge ought to have allowed L's evidence to
be called, as it might well have led the jury to take a different view of the
complainant's evidence.

The court in *Nagrecha* distinguished *R. v S* on two grounds. First, in that   **19.101**
case the complainant had admitted making the complaint against another
whereas here the complainant denied doing so. Secondly, in *R. v S* the
admission of the evidence would necessarily have led to a lengthy exploration
of irrelevant and peripheral issues as to the falsity or otherwise of the earlier
complaint, whereas here there would have been no such exploration. These
grounds of distinction are unpersuasive. The admission of evidence relating
to a previous complaint cannot depend on whether the individual admits or
denies making the complaint. This would be an arbitrary and illogical basis
for determining whether a complaint goes to the issue or to credit. One
certainly cannot assume that the exploration of a previous complaint will
necessarily be kept within manageable limits merely because the complaint is
admitted rather than denied, at least where the complainant maintains that
the complaint was true. As to the need to avoid lengthy exploration of
irrelevant issues, it is difficult to see how this was less compelling in *Nagrecha*
than in *R. v S.* As Professor Birch commented[138]:

> "to have admitted L's evidence would have started a debate about what [the
> complainant] understood by 'aggressive behaviour' and what L meant by
> 'allegations of a sexual nature' in order to even begin to substantiate the
> allegation that [the complainant] lied on oath. This would seem to be precisely
> the sort of debate which the rule of finality exists to prevent, for, whatever the
> answer, the cost of discovering it is likely to be out of all proportion to the benefit
> to the jury in deciding what went on behind closed doors between [the
> complainant and the appellant]."

---

[137] [1997] 2 Cr. App. R. 401.
[138] [1998] Crim. L.R. 65–7. See also Stephen Seabrooke, *The Vanishing Trick—Blurring the
Line between Credit and Issue* [1999] Crim. L.R. 387, criticising the reasoning in *Nagrecha* but
agreeing with the decision on the merits.

19.102   In *Nagrecha*, as in *Funderburk*, the Court cited the statement contained in *Cross and Tapper on Evidence*, that the distinction between credit and the issue is often reduced to vanishing point in cases where the only issue for the jury is whether to believe the complainant or the accused. This statement is undoubtedly true, but it cannot mean that any evidence connected with the witness's credit, however remotely, must bear on the issue of guilt. There is, however, a risk that in a hard case a court may lean in this direction, so as to permit rebuttal evidence to be adduced which ought properly to be excluded. An example is *Gibson*,[139] where the appellant was convicted of rape. The incident occurred after some horseplay between the complainant and a group of boys, one of whom was the appellant. The sole issue at trial was consent. When the complainant gave evidence, the judge asked her why she had not complained of rape for two weeks after the incident, when she had complained much earlier about the boys pushing her into the bushes where the alleged rape occurred. She said she was frightened of the boys. However, a teacher at the school had interviewed her on the afternoon of the incident and asked her whether she was frightened of what the boys would do if she identified them, to which the complainant had answered "No". In cross-examination the complainant denied having given that answer, so the defence sought to call the teacher. The judge ruled that the evidence was inadmissible as it would go only to credit, and in cross-examination as to credit the witness's answers are final. The ensuing conviction was quashed on appeal. The Court accepted that in so far as the complainant told the judge that the reason she had not complained was fear, that did not go directly to the issue in the case but might be said to have gone only to her credit on that issue. On the other hand, that was the first occasion that any suggestion of fear was introduced into the case. Their Lordships cited *Funderburk*, which they understood to say that in sexual cases one cannot draw too fine a line between what goes to an issue and what goes only to credit. In the circumstances, the judge should have allowed the teacher's evidence to be given, although there was considerable doubt as to what effect, if any, it would have had on the jury. This error was insufficient by itself to justify interfering with the conviction, but when combined with a number of other matters raised on the appeal, it created a doubt sufficient to require the conviction to be overturned. The decision drew the following comment from Professor Birch[140]:

> "The best that the defence could have hoped for had the teacher been called was to establish the appearance of inconsistency in the complainant as to her reason for not disclosing the alleged rape earlier. To gain this slender advantage it was necessary to persuade the court that what the girl had said on the matter went to

[139] [1993] Crim. L.R. 453; and see *R. v W*, unreported, December 13, 1999 (No.98/7675/W3).
[140] [1993] Crim. L.R. 453, pp.454–5.

the issues in the case . . . Given that the complaint itself was not evidence that she had not consented,[141] it is rather hard to see how the possible falsity of her reason for delay in making disclosure could in any sense be evidence that she did. It is all so very remote from the issue of what happened between the boy and the girl in the bushes that it makes one wonder whether since *Funderburk* . . . there is such a thing as a collateral issue in a sexual case."

These decisions demonstrate that collateral issues do of course still exist in **19.103** such cases. But *Funderburk* has certainly blurred the line between credit and the issue in a way that enables a court to reason creatively to achieve what seems the right result in the case before it. This is further illustrated by an interesting and potentially important decision relating to the admission of evidence showing a complainant's character in a positive light. It is settled that, subject to exceptions relating to recent complaint and distress,[142] such evidence is inadmissible on the basis that it goes solely to bolster the complainant's credibility and so is "oath-helping".[143] The theory underpinning this exclusionary rule is that the jury ought to be able to decide for themselves whether the witness is telling the truth, unswayed by evidence that suggests she is. This contrasts starkly with the position of the defendant, who may call evidence designed to show himself in a good light for the purpose of assisting his own credibility.[144] This can work an apparent injustice in cases where the defendant makes full use of his freedom to call character evidence. However, the possible beginnings of a shift in the law are discernable in *Tobin*.[145] The appellant was convicted of two offences of indecent assault committed against a girl of 16. It was alleged that the assaults had been committed whilst the girl, who had been drinking excessively, was a passenger in his car. His defence was that the girl initiated the sexual activity. He gave evidence that he was a married man of 36 with three children, and that he had previous convictions but none for sexual offences. He called five character witnesses who described him as "decent, trustworthy, hard working and honest". The judge permitted the prosecution to call evidence from the complainant's mother, in which she said that she had never had any problems with the complainant, who had done really well at school, got on well with her brothers and sisters, was very polite and quiet and had been brought up to respect people.

On appeal, the appellant submitted that this evidence had no probative **19.104** value in relation to any issue in the case but rather was "oath-helping" and so inadmissible. The Court accepted that the evidence did go to boost the

---

[141] This is no longer the case: see the discussion of s.120 of the Criminal Justice Act 2003 in paras 19.72 and following, above.

[142] See paras 19.72 and following, above, and paras 19.119 and following, below.

[143] *Robinson* (1994) 98 Cr. App. R. 370; *Hamilton, The Times*, July 25, 1998; *Kyselka* (1962) 133 C.C.C. 103, Ont. C.A.

[144] *Aziz* [1996] A.C. 41.

[145] [2003] Crim. L.R. 408; and see *Amado-Taylor* [2003].

girl's credibility, but held that it was nonetheless admissible. It acknowledged that evidence is not admissible merely to show that the complainant is not the type of person who would conduct herself in the manner alleged by the defendant. But it also recognised the force of the observation of Henry J in *Funderburk*, adopting *Cross on Evidence*, that in sexual cases much is likely to depend on the balance of credibility between the parties and the difference between questions going to credit and questions going to the issue may be reduced to vanishing point. The Court also noted that, in such circumstances, the decision as to the admissibility of evidence of the sort given by the mother is an instinctive one based on the prosecutor's and the Court's sense of fair play. In the present case very full evidence had been given about the appellant's character and background, and in those circumstances the court's sense of fair play was not offended but rather affirmed by the admission of the very limited evidence given by the mother about the girl's character and previous conduct. The evidence did not render the trial unfair nor offend the rule against "oath-helping", nor was it to be excluded for lack of relevance. Given the jury's vital task of deciding whether the events in the car were as described by the girl or as described by the appellant, the prosecution had been entitled to adduce the evidence they did.

19.105   The blurring in *Funderburk* of the difference between credit and the issue clearly provided the means by which the court in *Tobin* could reach what feels like the right conclusion on the facts of the case. But there is an element of sleight of hand in the elevation of evidence of the complainant's character from "mere" evidence of credibility to evidence relevant to the central issue in the case. A more direct route to the same end would have been for the Court to rest its decision on the indication in the last part of its judgment that, as the appellant's character had been put in "in the round", it was "fair play" to admit the limited evidence given about the girl's character. This aspect of the decision at least indicates a possible path that the Court may feel able to take in another case. As Professor Birch has commented, *Tobin* does not quite get us to the point where evidence to bolster the complainant's credibility can be admitted because the defendant is making full use of the rules allowing him to bolster his own, but there is certainly scope for such a development to take place.[146]

Corroboration and Warnings about Reliance on a Complainant's Evidence

19.106   There used to be a rule of practice at common law which required the judge to warn the jury of the danger of accepting without corroboration the

---

[146] [2003] Crim. L.R. 408, at 410. See also Sir Richard Buxton, *Victims as witnesses in trial of sexual offences: Towards equality of arms* [2015] Crim. L.R. 679.

evidence of the complainant of a sexual offence.[147] The reason for the rule was stated as follows by Salmon LJ in *Henry*:[148]

> "Human experience has shown that in these courts girls and women do sometimes tell an entirely false story which is very easy to fabricate, but extremely difficult to refute. Such stores are fabricated for all sorts of reasons... and sometimes for no reason at all."

The full corroboration warning was technical and cumbersome. The judge was required to tell the jury that it would be dangerous to convict on the uncorroborated evidence of the complainant, to explain the reason why (preferably using the words of Salmon LJ quoted above), to explain what "corroboration" meant, to identify the evidence which was and was not capable of being corroboration, and to explain that it was the jury's role to decide whether to accept that evidence and, if they did accept it, whether it did corroborate the complainant.

It is not surprising that these requirements were a fruitful source of appeals, and were much criticised for their complexity and because of the difficulty of directing juries upon them.[149] More importantly, they were criticised as casting a particular and unwarranted slur on women. Furthermore, the rule was attacked because a full warning was required in every case regardless of the particular circumstances of the case, however compelling the complainant's evidence. In 1991, the Law Commission recommended the abolition of the rule of practice.[150] This recommendation was implemented by ss.32 and 33 of the Criminal Justice and Public Order Act 1994.[151] Section 32(1) of the Act provides: **19.107**

> "Any requirement whereby at a trial on indictment it is obligatory for the court to give the jury a warning about convicting the accused on the uncorroborated evidence of a person merely because that person is—
> (a) [*not printed*];
> (b) where the offence charged is a sexual offence, the person in respect of whom it is alleged to have been committed, is hereby abrogated."

Similar provision is made by s.32(3) for summary trials.

---

[147] *Rudge* (1924) 17 Cr. App. R. 113; *Berry* (1924) 18 Cr. App. R. 65; *Killick* (1924) 18 Cr. App. R. 120; *Marshall* (1924) 18 Cr. App. R. 164; *Jones* (1925) 19 Cr. App. R. 40; *Freebody* (1935) 25 Cr. App. R. 69; *Winfield* [1939] 4 All E.R. 164; *Dent* (1943) 29 Cr. App. R. 120; *Mitchell* (1952) 36 Cr. App. R. 79; *Burgess* (1956) 40 Cr. App. R. 144; *O'Reilly* [1967] 2 Q.B. 722; *Henry* (1968) 53 Cr. App. R. 150; *Spencer* [1987] A.C. 128; *Chance* [1988] Q.B. 932. There was in addition a statutory requirement of corroboration in respect of a number of offences in the Sexual Offences Act 1956 as originally enacted.

[148] *Henry* (1968) 53 Cr. App. R. 150, at 153. Despite the reference to "girls and women", the corroboration warning was also required in the case of male complainants: *Burgess*, above; *Gammon* (1959) 43 Cr. App. R. 155.

[149] cf. *Cheema* [1994] 1 W.L.R. 147 at 158, per Lord Taylor CJ, describing the rules as "arcane, technical and difficult to convey".

[150] Law Com. No.202 (1991), *Corroboration of Evidence in Criminal Trials*. These recommendations were endorsed by the Royal Commission on Criminal Justice, Cmd. 2263 (1993), Ch.8, para.35.

[151] Which came into force on February 3, 1995: SI 1995/127.

THE DECISION IN MAKANJUOLA AND EASTON

19.108 The impact of s.32(1) on the practice of the courts fell to be determined by the Court of Appeal in *Makanjuola and Easton*.[152] The decision involved two conjoined cases, in both of which there was an application for leave to appeal against a conviction of indecent assault. No warning had been given to the jury in either case about the complainant's evidence. The applicants argued that although the requirement to give a corroboration warning had been abrogated by s.32(1), the judge should still in his discretion warn the jury that it is dangerous to convict on the uncorroborated evidence of the complainant in a sexual case. The Court rejected this argument. Lord Taylor CJ said that if it were right, Parliament would have enacted s.32(1) in vain: practice would continue unchanged. He went on[153]:

> "It is clear that the judge does have a discretion to warn the jury if he thinks it necessary, but the use of the word 'merely' in the subsection shows that Parliament does not envisage such a warning being given just because a witness complains of a sexual offence . . . "

Lord Taylor said that if a warning is to be given, there must be an evidential basis for suggesting that the evidence of the witness may be unreliable, and for this purpose mere suggestions by counsel during cross-examination will not be sufficient. Moreover, if the judge decides that a warning is necessary, he need not give the old-style direction on corroboration. It was "partly to escape from this tortuous exercise, which juries must have found more bewildering than illuminating, that Parliament enacted section 32".[154] Lord Taylor went on to give guidance as to the circumstances in which a judge should urge the jury to caution in regard to a particular witness, and the terms in which that should be done[155]:

> "Whether, as a matter of discretion, a judge should give any warning and if so its strength and terms must depend upon the content and manner of the witness's evidence, the circumstances of the case and the issues raised. The judge will often consider that no special warning is required at all. Where, however, the witness has been shown to be unreliable, he or she may consider it necessary to urge caution. In a more extreme case, if the witness is shown to have lied, to have made previous false complaints, or to bear the defendant some grudge, a stronger warning may be thought appropriate and the judge may suggest it would be wise to look for some supporting material before acting on the impugned witness's evidence. We stress the these observations are merely illustrative of some, not all, of the factors which judges may take into account in measuring where a witness stands in the scale of reliability and what response they should make at that level in their directions to the jury."

---

[152] [1995] 2 Cr. App. R. 469. See also *Hickmet* [1996] Crim. L.R. 588; *R. v R* [1996] Crim. L.R. 815.

[153] At 471.

[154] [1995] 2 Cr. App. R. 469; and see *Doheny and Adams* [1997] 1 Cr. App. R. 369 at 386–7.

[155] at 472.

His Lordship added that if any question arises as to whether the judge should give a warning in respect of a witness, it is desirable for the question to be resolved by discussion with counsel in the absence of the jury before final speeches. A warning should be given as part of the judge's review of the evidence and his comments as to how the jury should evaluate it, rather than as a set-piece legal direction. Finally, his Lordship said that the Court of Appeal will be disinclined to interfere with the exercise of discretion by a trial judge, who has the advantage of assessing the manner in which the witness's evidence is given as well as its content, save where that exercise is unreasonable in the *Wednesbury* sense.[156]

In neither of the cases before it did the Court see any need for a warning **19.109** about the witness's evidence. In the first, the complainant had been challenged in cross-examination on the basis that there had been no assault and that she had made up the allegation because she was angry with the applicant. But the applicant did not give evidence to that effect, and there was accordingly no evidential basis, as opposed to submissions from counsel, to throw doubt upon the complainant's story. In the second case, the complainant was a girl of 16 who had been asleep or dozing in bed immediately before the alleged assault. The applicant submitted that in those circumstances the judge should have given a warning in the exercise of his discretion. Lord Taylor said that, in effect, the applicant's case was that the judge should have given the time-honoured direction that complainants of sexual offences may be prone to fantasise or dream or fabricate untrue complaints. The Court rejected the applicant's submission, holding once again that there was no evidential basis for regarding the complainant as an inherently unreliable witness.

In cases which depend upon the credibility of the complainant, there will **19.110** frequently be evidence of (i) contemporary lies, (ii) late disclosure, (iii) significant inconsistencies between accounts and (iv) particularly in cases where sexual abuse is alleged over a substantial period, allegations raised for the first time when the complainant gives evidence at trial. Where any of these issues are of significance to the complainant's reliability and credibility, the trial judge should properly expose them in his summing up. It does not, however, follow that in such cases a *Makanjuola* warning is necessary. The critical issue is that the jury is reminded of the lies, inconsistencies and late disclosures and any explanations for them, so that the jury can properly evaluate the evidence.

This point is illustrated by *Udaykamaur Joshi*,[157] where the Court of **19.111** Appeal for Northern Ireland, in a judgment by Lord Morgan CJ, considered the application of the principles set out by Lord Taylor CJ in *Makanjuola* when considering an appeal against conviction on two counts of buggery and one of indecent assault committed against a "minor" in 1979. It was alleged

---

[156] *Crown Court Compendium* 2016, ch.10, para.2. See Appendix G, below.
[157] [2012] NICA 56.

that the appellant had committed the offences whilst he had been employed as a professional at a cricket club of which the complainant's father was a member. The principal ground advanced on behalf of the appellant was that the trial judge had failed to give a warning to the jury that they should exercise caution before acting on the evidence of the complainant. At trial, the appellant had raised the issue of the need to give the jury such a warning in advance of speeches. The submission, which was opposed by the prosecution, was that the jury should be told that it would be unwise to convict on the unsupported evidence of the complainant. Lord Morgan went through the process of identifying those factors which pointed towards the need for a *Makanjoula* warning of some kind and then examining how they were dealt with by the judge. The complainant had admitted that on two occasions he had lied about the allegations. First, he had lied in the account he gave a year after the incident when he had said that he had resisted the appellant and had fought him off with a shoe. In evidence he said that he had been ashamed to admit that he had not tried to resist the appellant. This was also his explanation for late disclosure. Secondly, the complainant had told his therapist that the appellant had leant over him and clasped his arm in order to get him into the appellant's bedroom. In evidence he explained that he had gone into the bedroom quietly as he did not want his grandmother to be wakened and the events of the previous week to be discovered. Lord Morgan stated[158]:

> " . . . it is clear from Lord Taylor's guidance that the nature of any warning that a judge decides to give in relation to a witness should be woven into the review of the evidence and the language used should reflect the strength of the warning considered appropriate by the judge."

Having regard to the nature of the lies admitted and the explanations provided (which were all covered by the judge in her summing up), the Court did not consider that the judge could be criticised for taking the view that this was not one of those cases where the lies called for the need for supporting material before relying on the evidence of the complainant. There were a number of inconsistencies in the complainant's evidence, most notably between his accounts to his therapist and his evidence. The complainant's explanation in evidence was that in some cases it was too painful to give a full account, in other cases the issues were irrelevant and on some occasions he merely gave a summary because the purpose of the therapy was not to investigate the detail of the attacks. All these inconsistencies were put before the jury by the trial judge on the basis that they were material to the issue of who the jury should believe. The Court concluded that the appellant's case was fully explored by the judge who had properly dealt with the issues in the complainant's case which touched on his reliability and credibility. It was a paradigm case for a decision by the jury. There was no basis upon which to

[158] At [32].

interfere with the jury's decision and the Court was not left with any sense of unease about the verdict.

SUBSEQUENT CASES

There are, however, a number of cases decided since *Makanjuola* in which the **19.112** Court of Appeal has held that a warning should have been given about the evidence of a prosecution witness. The following four examples are instructive.

In *Walker*,[159] the appellant was convicted on two counts of raping his **19.113** cohabitee's daughter, who was 11 or 12 when the alleged incidents occurred. He was acquitted on a third count of raping her. His defence was a complete denial, and he suggested that the girl had invented the allegations in order to have him ousted from the family home in the hope of securing the return of her real father. While the appellant was awaiting trial, the girl wrote to the police saying that she had lied about the allegations. She subsequently made a statement consistent with that letter. Five days later she went to the police station and said that her original complaint was true. At that stage the appellant, who was on bail, had returned to the family home. In summing up to the jury, the judge made no mention of the retraction letter, the statement or the withdrawal of the retraction, nor did he warn the jury about the dangers of the girl as a witness. It was held on appeal that he should have done so. The retraction and its withdrawal were important and relevant to the credibility of the girl, whose evidence was unsupported.

In *Hopkins*,[160] the appellant, a social worker, was convicted of indecently **19.114** assaulting two vulnerable women clients, H and R. The defence in each case was a complete denial. H's evidence at trial was variable and contradictory and on crucial issues was difficult to follow. There were also concerns about the intrinsic weight of R's account, in that she had made no complaint to anyone about the appellant until she went to the police after proceedings were commenced in respect of the alleged assault on H; she gave no explanation for the delay in complaining; and the allegations she made were extreme in terms of behaviour and recklessness and were, therefore, "against the probabilities". Both witnesses were "potentially incredible" and in those circumstances the jury should have been directed that it was wise to look for some supporting material before relying on the evidence of either. No such direction had been given and accordingly the appellant's convictions were quashed.

In *Adey*,[161] the appellant was convicted of raping a woman he had met at **19.115** a nightclub. She accompanied him home and they had consensual sex. Shortly afterwards, the appellant accused the woman of attempting to steal

---

[159] [1996] Crim. L.R. 742.
[160] Unreported, February 16, 1998 (No.97/5836/Y3).
[161] Unreported, March 3, 1998 (No.97/5306/Y3).

his wallet. He went on to assault her and subject her to deeply humiliating treatment in front of his housemates, conduct which he admitted. The woman alleged that he then raped her. After the incident, when the woman told her sister and two separate police officers what had happened, she did not say anything about the consensual sex. When she saw a doctor, he specifically asked whether she had had consensual intercourse and she denied it. It was held that in the circumstances the jury should have been warned of the dangers of convicting without any evidence that supported the rape allegation. The woman had been shown to be unreliable and to have lied, and there was also a possibility that she bore a grudge against the appellant because of his assault and humiliating treatment of her in front of his housemates. The Court gave as a further reason the fact that the jury had heard highly prejudicial evidence about the appellant's treatment of the woman, and it was necessary to warn them not to let this colour their view as to whether the rape allegation had been proved. It is, with respect, surely right that such a warning should have been given, but the need for it does not derive from *Makanjuola*: it would be a warning not about the potential unreliability of the woman as a witness, but rather that evidence from others about the defendant's conduct should not sway the jury on the central allegation, to which it was not relevant.

19.116   Finally, the decision in *Blasiak*[162] illustrates that, even where there is an issue as to the reliability of a prosecution witness's evidence, a specific warning need not be given provided the issue is properly addressed in some way. The appellant in that case appealed against his conviction of raping a 15-year-old girl who was an in-patient at a psychiatric unit and had been diagnosed with a complex post-traumatic stress disorder and an attachment disorder. There was evidence from a psychiatrist concerning her unreliability. It was contended that the judge had been wrong not to give a direction that caution had to be exercised before convicting on the complainant's uncorroborated evidence. The Court of Appeal rejected this argument, holding that the issue of the complainant's unreliability had been brought to the jury's attention and there had been no need for a specific direction, as the judge had already said enough about the complainant's unreliability.

FORM OF MAKANJUOLA WARNING

19.117 In giving a *Makanjuola* warning, the trial judge is not necessarily required to warn the jury to look for supporting evidence in respect of every element of the offence. In *Doheny and Adams*,[163] the appellant A was convicted of buggery of the complainant, a psychologically disturbed woman. She said she had spoken to him when she phoned the Samaritans, where he was a

---

[162] [2010] EWCA Crim 2620. See also the *Crown Court Compendium* 2016, Ch.10.2: Corroboration and the special need for caution.
[163] [1997] 1 Cr. App. R. 369.

volunteer, and that he had later visited her in her house where the offence was committed. His defence was a complete denial. Evidence was given by a forensic expert that the DNA in a semen stain found at the complainant's house matched the appellant's. In the light of the complainant's psycho-logical state the judge gave a *Makanjuola* warning, and told the jury that the semen stain, if they found it was the appellant's, was capable of corroborating her evidence. On appeal it was objected that, while the stain was potentially corroborative of the complainant's evidence that the appellant had engaged in sexual activity with her, it was not corroborative of her allegation that the activity amounted to buggery. It was further argued, citing cases on the old corroboration requirement, that where the elements of a sexual offence are in issue the judge should direct the jury as to the desirability of corroboration of each element. These arguments were rejected. The Court of Appeal said that even under the old law, it had been held that corroboration which went to the heart of the disputed issue of consent made it unnecessary to warn the jury about the need for corroboration in relation to the other elements of the offence. In this case, the DNA evidence strongly corroborated the woman in respect of most of her evidence and, in particular, the central issue of whether the appellant had visited her and engaged in sexual activity. Stripping away the technicalities of the old law, the Court emphatically concluded that the judge's failure to give a fuller direction on corroboration did not make the conviction unsafe.

However, where supporting evidence is required the judge must be careful **19.118** to identify for the jury any that exists.[164] Furthermore, it is vital to identify the critical issues in the case, and whether the particular evidence is truly supporting evidence. An earlier complaint by the complainant is not independent[165] and so, even with its enhanced evidential status under the Criminal Justice Act 2003, it is submitted that it has no value as supporting evidence. Similarly, neutral medical evidence consistent with consensual vaginal penetration does not implicate the defendant or negative con-sent.[166]

THE COMPLAINANT'S APPARENT DISTRESS

One important question is whether the complainant's apparent distress at the **19.119** time of or following the alleged incident can provide support for her evidence. The issue of the correct approach to evidence of the complainant's apparent distress arises in many cases. In most cases, the jury will no longer be required to look for supporting evidence. Where distress is observed shortly after the time of the allegation and there is nothing to suggest it was feigned,[167] it is likely to carry more weight than in circumstances where there

[164] *B (MT)* [2000] Crim. L.R. 181.
[165] *Whitehead* [1929] 1 KB 99.
[166] *James v R.* [1970] 55 Cr. App. R. 299.
[167] *Redpath* [1962] 46 Cr. App. R. 319; *Dowley* [1983] Crim. L.R. 168.

is evidence of an alternative explanation. This question was considered in *Romeo*,[168] where the Court was invited to follow authorities decided under the old law of corroboration to the effect that juries should be warned to attach little weight to evidence of distress. The Court preferred the following statement of the law from the case of *Chauhan*[169]:

> "In normal cases, however, the weight to be given to distress varies infinitely, and juries should be warned that, although it may amount to corroboration they must be fully satisfied that there is no question of it having been feigned."

In *Romeo*, the appellant was convicted of indecently assaulting the complainant by forcing her to have oral sex. Afterwards the complainant went round to a neighbour, who gave evidence that the complainant had been upset and distressed. The sole issue at trial was consent. In relation to the neighbour's evidence, the judge directed the jury that they should ask themselves what had happened to reduce the complainant to apparent extreme distress, drew their attention to the fact that it could have arisen as a result of a variety of circumstances and asked them to consider carefully whether it might have been feigned. On appeal, this was held to be an entirely adequate direction in the circumstances of the case.

19.120   It is important to recognise the principles that have emerged during the era since the abolition of the corroboration warning. Juries should be warned that they must only act on evidence of contemporary distress if they are sure it was genuine and not feigned or attributable to some other circumstance. To be supporting evidence, it must be independent and not come from the complainant's own evidence. In *Zala*,[170] the appellant, a retired general practitioner, was convicted of 10 counts of indecent assault committed against three of his patients between 1985 and 1991. The judge gave the correct warning that the jury should first decide if the evidence of complainant distress was genuine, but failed to point out that they could not regard evidence from the complainants themselves as potential supporting evidence because it was not independent. The Court of Appeal observed that evidence of long-term psychological effects and distress should be treated differently from evidence of distress at the time. For example, in the circumstances of *Zala* it was difficult to see how evidence of distress displayed by a complainant when interviewed many years later provided much material assistance.

19.121   In *Keast*,[171] the Court of Appeal was of the view that in a case concerning charges of indecent assault and indecency on a young girl, evidence from the

---

[168] [2004] Crim. L.R. 302 where Professor Di Birch noted the potential importance of evidence of complainant demeanour "now that we have emerged from the shadow of corroboration." In a case, such as *Romeo,* where it is one person's word against another, the jury might find evidence of demeanour particularly important. Once the judge has drawn attention to the possibility that the complainant was acting, it was up to the jury to give such weight as to the evidence of distress as they thought fit.

[169] (1981) 73 Cr. App. R. 232 at 235.

[170] [2014] EWCA Crim 2181.

[171] [1998] Crim. L.R. 748.

girl's father and step-father as to the child's "withdrawal and cowed demeanour" fell into a completely different category from evidence of contemporary complainant distress. In *Keast* the Court felt that there was no "concrete basis" for regarding demeanour and states of mind described by the witness as confirming or disproving that sexual abuse has occurred:

> " . . . when incidents of child abuse have come to light it is sometimes said that the warning signs apparent from the demeanour or the behaviour of the victims ought to have been noticed, but we think it would be dangerous to infer from this that any generalised dejected demeanour in a child or young person could be regarded as indicative that sexual abuse has occurred. We do not think that such evidence is likely to assist a jury in concluding whether the complainant is telling the truth any more than evidence of an apparently happy disposition suggests that the complainant must be lying."

The reasoning in *Keast* was adopted in *Abdal Miah*,[172] where the Court of Appeal considered that evidence of a complainant's reaction to the alleged offence was unlikely to be of any material assistance to a jury. In the overwhelming majority of cases such evidence, though technically admissible or relevant, is likely to be of such tenuous relevance that it would not be right to admit it bearing in mind (1) the very different causes that can give rise to a reaction and (2) the difficulties that will arise if evidence has to be called as to a complainant's reaction.[173] The Court also observed that such evidence would lead to the calling of collateral witnesses to explain the reaction of the alleged victim.

Whilst the general approach to evidence of distress shown significantly **19.122** after the time of the allegation is settled, the position is not always clear cut. In cases where there are multiple allegations over a significant period, evidence such as a complainant's chaotic lifestyle, anti-social behaviour and serial absconding from schools and/or homes, may be important background evidence which is inextricably linked to the allegations. This evidence might, for instance, include a sudden drop in school performance. In any event, the defence may well wish to raise any subsequent psychological condition as a reason for the fabrication of the allegations. In those circumstances, it is arguable that, as in Canada, the prosecution should be able to call rehabilitative opinion evidence to show the condition may be a consequence of the abuse. Clearly these matters may well go beyond those such as late reporting and numb presentation, which can properly be covered by judicial comment to prevent false assumptions. This is a controversial area. The

---

[172] [2014] EWCA Crim 938.
[173] The Court did however hold that in *Abdal Miah* such evidence was admissible. The case involved the alleged kidnapping of a 14-year-old. The defence was that he had invented his own fake kidnapping. If the defence was true, then on the victim's mother's evidence, the victim would have to have faked for a considerable time a reaction to the kidnapping. This provided (in the language used in *Keast*) a "concrete basis" as to why the evidence would be relevant and helpful to the jury in deciding whether the kidnapping was indeed fake.

position in Canada is described by Laura Hoyano and Caroline Keenan[174]:

> " . . . evidence of the spectrum of behaviours often exhibited by child abuse victims, drawing upon the patterns identified by such clinical child abuse experts, can serve to educate the jury in evaluating defence attempts to use a child's troubled personality to discredit her testimony, by explaining how the apparent indicia of unreliability may be the product of the offence rather than the source of false allegations."

Hoyano and Keenan observe how courts have been concerned as to the ability of mental health professionals to diagnose sexual abuse, considering that their diagnoses rely upon subjective assessment of a vague symptomology with unquantifiable results which cannot be tested effectively in cross-examination.[175] However, to the extent that the defence place reliance upon such matters as aberrant behaviour as undermining a complainant's credibility, Canadian jurisprudence[176] suggests that it is open to the prosecution to rebut that evidence by showing that very behaviour could well be the product of the alleged sexual abuse. Evidence may be admitted to show that certain behaviour, symptoms or psychological conditions could be consistent with sexual abuse. A classic example would be PTSD. The permissible purpose would be to support the complainant's statements, not to show that the complainant is a truthful witness.[177] It remains to be seen if the English courts will review the position in light of a growing understanding of the effects of sexual abuse.

EVIDENCE OF DEFENDANT'S SPOUSE OR CIVIL PARTNER

19.123   The compellability of the defendant's spouse or civil partner is dealt with in s.80 of the Police and Criminal Evidence Act 1984.[178] The basic rule is that the defendant's spouse or civil partner is a compellable witness for the defendant in all cases, and a compellable witness for the prosecution and for any co-defendant in respect of any "specified offence" charged in the proceedings.[179] An offence is a "specified offence" if:

> "(a) it involves an assault on, or injury or a threat of injury to, the spouse or civil partner or a person who was at the material time under the age of 16;
> (b) it is a sexual offence alleged to have been committed in respect of a person who was at the material time under that age; or

---

[174] Laura Hoyano and Caroline Keenan, *Child Abuse Law and Policy across Boundaries* (Oxford: Oxford University Press, 2010), p.887. See *Llorenz* (2000) 145 CCC (3d) 535 (Ontario CA); *R. v C(G)* (1997) 8 CR (5th) 21 (Ontario Gen Div) 44. We are very grateful to Laura Hoyano for bringing this point to our attention.

[175] Hoyano and Keenan cite *Hellstrom v Commonwealth* 825 SW 2d 612 (Kentucky Supreme Ct, 1992); *New Jersey v JQ* 617 A 2d 1196 (New Jersey Supreme Ct, 1993).

[176] *R. v F(DS)*, 1999 Can L II 3704 (Ont CA); 43 O.R. (3d) 609.

[177] *Burns* (1994) Can LII 127 (SCC); (1994) 1 S.C.R. 656.

[178] As amended by the Youth Justice and Criminal Evidence Act 1999 s.67(1) and Sch.4, para.13, and the Civil Partnership Act 2004 ss.261(1), 263 and Sch.27, para.97.

[179] s.80(2), (2A).

(c) it consists of attempting or conspiring to commit, or of aiding, abetting, counselling, procuring or inciting the commission of, an offence falling within paragraph (a) or (b) above."[180]

A "sexual offence" for the purposes of para.(b) means an offence under the Protection of Children Act 1978 or Pt 1 of the Sexual Offences Act 2003.[181] The term therefore does not cover the offence of child abduction under s.2 of the Child Abduction Act 1984, the common law offence of outraging public decency or the offence of possession of an indecent photograph or pseudo-photograph of a child under 18 under s.160 of the Criminal Justice Act 1988. For the purposes of paragraphs (a) and (b), a person's age at the material time shall be deemed to be or to have been that which appears to the court to be or to have been his age at that time.[182]

It was held in *R. v BA*[183] that the decision whether an offence is one in respect of which the defendant's spouse or civil partner can be compelled to give evidence under s.80(3)(a) of the 1984 Act, on the ground that it involves "an assault on, or injury or threat of injury to" the spouse or a child under 16, has to be taken by reference to the legal nature of the charged offence and not the factual circumstances surrounding the offence.   **19.124**

The basic rule on compellability set out above does not apply if the spouse or civil partner is charged in the proceedings, unless the spouse or civil partner is not, or is no longer, liable to be convicted of any offence, whether as a result of pleading guilty or for any other reason (e.g. the charges against them are dropped).[184]   **19.125**

The prosecution are barred from commenting on the failure of the defendant's spouse or civil partner to give evidence in the proceedings.[185]   **19.126**

A former spouse or civil partner is compellable in any proceedings to give evidence as if he or she and the defendant had never been married or civil partners.[186] For this purpose, a former spouse or civil partner may give evidence about events that occurred even before s.80 came into force, on January 1, 1986.[187]   **19.127**

If a spouse or civil partner who is not compellable is called as a prosecution witness at her spouse's or civil partner's trial, the judge should explain to her, in the absence of the jury and before she takes the oath, that she has a right to refuse to give evidence but that if she chooses to give it she may be treated like any other witness.[188]   **19.128**

---

[180] s.80(3).
[181] s.80(7), as amended by the Sexual Offences Act 2003 s.139 and Sch.6, para.28, which came into force on May 1, 2004.
[182] s.80(6).
[183] [2012] EWCA Crim 1529.
[184] s.80(4), (4A).
[185] s.80A.
[186] s.80(5), (5A).
[187] *Cruttenden* (1991) 93 Cr. App. R. 119.
[188] *Pitt* (1983) 75 Cr. App. R. 254.

19.129   In *R. v L*,[189] the prosecution were permitted to admit a wife's statement under s.114(1)(d) of the Criminal Justice Act 2003 in the appellant's trial for the rape and indecent assault of his teenage daughter, even though the judge had held that she was not a compellable witness under s.80 of the Police and Criminal Evidence Act 1984 as her evidence related to when the daughter was aged 19. Arguably this undermines the purpose of s.80. On appeal it was submitted that the wife's statement should not have been admitted in evidence. However, the Court of Appeal held that there were no grounds for saying that the appellant's conviction was unsafe and that it was permissible to call hearsay evidence of a spouse's voluntary statement incriminating her husband. The Court took the view that there is no requirement to tell a spouse (or civil partner) that they are a non-compellable witness before interviewing them about a crime of which their spouse is accused. But it did acknowledge that in some cases the police would be well-advised to make it plain that a person need not make a statement that implicated their spouse.

---

[189] [2008] EWCA Crim 973. For a critique, see Janice Brabyn, *A Criminal Defendant's Spouse as a Prosecution Witness* [2007] Crim. L.R. 613.

CHAPTER 20

EVIDENCE OF BAD CHARACTER

The Criminal Justice Act 2003 .... 20.01
Notice Requirements 20.03
Proving the Details of a Previous
    Sexual Offence............................. 20.07
The Definition of "Bad Character". 20.13
The Gateways 20.24
Exclusionary Discretion under
    Section 101(3)............................. 20.92

Jury Direction..................................20.109
Cross-Admissibility and Bad
    Character....................................20.111
Non-Defendant's Bad Character 20.139
Overlap Between Section 100 of the
    Criminal Justice Act 2003 and
    Section 41 of the Youth Justice
    and Criminal Evidence Act 1999 .20.151

THE CRIMINAL JUSTICE ACT 2003

This chapter does not seek to be a substitute for a specialist textbook on **20.01**
this topic.[1] However, it does seek to set out the general principles of the bad
character regime, with illustrations of the provisions in operation by
reference to a significant number of Court of Appeal decisions and practical
examples on bad character issues in sex offences. The last few years have seen
a great number of appeals to the Court of Appeal in respect of sexual
offences in which bad character issues have been involved. Most do not
involve points of principle. We have included them only if either they have
clarified how a certain category of bad character evidence should be treated,
as in *R. v D, P and U*,[2] or they provide instructive examples of how bad
character evidence should be approached in sex cases. In addition, some
appeals relating to other criminal offences have shed valuable light on the
proper approach to this area of evidence.

The bad character regime introduced by the Criminal Justice Act 2003 **20.02**
represented a sea change in the basis for the admissibility of evidence of the
defendant's previous convictions and other misconduct. The 2003 Act
established a statutory scheme regulating the admissibility of evidence of the

---

[1] There can be no substitute for Professor John Spencer's excellent *Evidence of Bad Character*,
2nd edn (Oxford: Hart Publishing, 2009).
[2] [2011] EWCA Crim 1474.

bad character of both defendants and non-defendant witnesses. It reversed the pre-existing general rule that such evidence was generally inadmissible subject to exceptions.[3] Now, such evidence is admissible if certain criteria are satisfied. The criteria are set out in the "gateways" listed in s.101(1)(a)–(g) of the Act. The bad character provisions came into force in December 2004 and apply in trials that began on or after December 15, 2004, irrespective of when the prosecution was instituted.[4] Court of Appeal decisions have helped to ensure that convictions are based on truly relevant evidence and not on prejudice. Inevitably the issue of the defendant's bad character arises frequently in the trial of sexual offences, where previous sexual mores and predilection can be important if truly relevant to the issues in the case.

Notice Requirements

20.03 It is important that there is compliance with the notice requirements set out in Pt 35 of the Criminal Procedure Rules 2015 ("CPR"). However, it does not follow that non-compliance by the prosecution will lead to an application to introduce bad character evidence being refused.[5] In *Dalby*[6] the Court of Appeal described the late bad character application advanced at trial in oral form as "unfortunate". The Court underlined the importance of following the practice set out in the CPR. Applications should be made in proper form and on time so that there is an adequate opportunity for them to be considered. Whilst the courts have taken the position that a culture of non-compliance should not be allowed to take root, the higher courts will not interfere with a conviction unless the appellant can demonstrate prejudice. The main considerations will be (a) the reason for the failure to comply with the rules and (b) whether the other party was prejudiced by the failure. The trial judge's discretion to allow late applications is not limited by the principle that it is only to be exercised in exceptional circumstances.[7] Furthermore, a perceived need to discipline the Crown Prosecution Service is not the overriding consideration.[8]

20.04 A late application may mean that the defence do not have sufficient time to investigate important matters. In *R.(O) v Central Criminal Court*[9] the Divisional Court gave the warning that prosecuting authorities need to be aware of the consequences of late applications, in that they may lead to additional complexity and delay which may have repercussions on custody

---

[3] See Lord Herschell in *Makin v Attorney General for New South Wales* [1894] A.C. 57.
[4] *Bradley* [2005] 1 Cr. App. R. 24.
[5] *Delay (Timothy)* [2006] EWCA Crim 1110, where the Court of Appeal held that the Recorder's decision that the defendant had not suffered any prejudice was not unreasonable even though the application was made at the end of the prosecution case. See also *Hassett* [2008] EWCA Crim 1634.
[6] [2012] EWCA Crim 701.
[7] *R. (Robinson) v Sutton Coldfield Magistrates' Court* [2006] 2 Cr. App. R. 13.
[8] *Moran* [2007] EWCA Crim 2947.
[9] [2006] EWHC 3542 (Admin).

time limits and the issue as to whether the prosecution has proceeded with due expedition.

A good example of a case where a late application led to clear prejudice is **20.05** *R. v M*,[10] where the Court of Appeal quashed the conviction of a 17-year-old for rape. At trial, just before the end of its case, the prosecution applied to admit evidence of two previous allegations of sexual assault against the appellant, dating back to when he was 14, as evidence capable of showing a propensity to commit offences of the kind with which he was charged. The Court of Appeal held that, on the facts of the case, the late application had put undue pressure on the appellant and the judge. The judge had originally rejected the application, but later changed his mind, limiting the evidence that could be called in respect of the two previous allegations to the complainants (and the appellant, if he chose to do so). The judge ruled that no other live evidence could be called as to the earlier allegations, even though the appellant denied them. It followed that the appellant had been unable to examine a witness to the first incident to confirm that his acts of oral sex with the complainant had been consensual. Nor could he call the first complainant's doctor to give evidence about the scratches on her breast, which were alleged to have occurred at that time.

The Court of Appeal stated that the time limits in the 2003 Act should be **20.06** observed. If not, there was a risk of unfairness. A defendant might be reluctant to apply for an adjournment if he and the complainant had already given evidence, and judges might be reluctant to grant an adjournment in such circumstances. The appellant in the instant case had had no opportunity to make any investigations into important matters such as the medical evidence with regard to the scratches, or letters from the complainant describing consensual conduct. There can be real practical problems when the defence need to investigate the facts of previous convictions, and these are likely to be compounded when an application is made late in the day. However, where the prosecution has properly carried out its duties of disclosure, and the defence are in a position to make their own enquiries, a speculative application for further particulars is unlikely to succeed.[11]

Proving the Details of a Previous Sexual Offence

In some cases it will not be necessary to prove the details of the previous **20.07** offence, and a mere list of convictions will be sufficient. For instance, for the purposes of s.101(1)(g), the gateway for admissibility where the defendant has made an attack on another person's character, the details are likely to be unnecessary as the relevance of the previous conviction will be to "character" in a broad sense.[12] However, there will be cases where the prosecution will

---

[10] [2006] EWCA Crim 1509.
[11] *Alobayadi* [2007] EWCA Crim 2984. See also *R. v K* [2007] EWCA Crim 911.
[12] *Lamaletie* [2008] EWCA Crim 314.

wish, and will be entitled, to prove more than the fact of conviction. Whilst s.117 of the Criminal Justice Act 2003 can be used to prove the fact of a previous conviction, it cannot be used to establish the circumstances of the offence.[13] The prosecution must decide whether they need any more evidence to achieve the purpose for which they want the evidence to be admitted, i.e. more than the evidence of conviction and the matters that can be formally established. They must ensure that they have available the necessary evidence to support what they require.

20.08   Where evidence of bad character is admitted, and is challenged, there may be circumstances in which the judge has to give the jury both a full good character direction and a full bad character direction, depending upon the jury's factual finding. In *Olu*[14] the judge admitted evidence of the appellant's acceptance of a caution for possession of a flick knife, which contained an admission that the offence had occurred, as evidence of propensity to possess a knife in a public place. The admission was challenged in evidence by the appellant. Apart from the caution, the appellant was a young man of good character. The Court of Appeal held that the jury should have been directed that, if they were not sure that the appellant had committed the caution offence, they should treat him as a person of good character.

20.09   Often the details of the modus operandi of the previous sexual offending can only be established by the evidence of the complainant.[15] In *Ainscough*[16] the Court of Appeal stressed that it is important for courts to avoid the proliferation of satellite issues, particularly where there is a short trial on a simple issue. It may be possible, in appropriate cases, to prove previous facts by relying on s.116 of the 2003 Act (admission of statement where witness unavailable) if any of the conditions in s.116(2) is met, or on s.114(1)(d)[17] (admission of hearsay in the interests of justice) where the court has had regard to the factors set out in s.114(2). Clearly, "bad character" includes foreign convictions, which may be admissible under the Act in precisely the same way as domestic convictions. Propensity is unlikely to be affected by the jurisdiction in which the offences were committed. Section 103 of the 2003 Act, as amended,[18] puts beyond doubt that previous convictions in any other country can be admitted as evidence of propensity under gateway (d) to the same extent as previous convictions in England and Wales, provided the foreign offence would also be an offence in England and Wales if it were done

---

[13] *Humphris* [2005] EWCA Crim 2030.
[14] [2010] EWCA Crim 2975. Not only was the application late, but it involved a harassment notice based upon the complaint of a witness whose identity remained anonymous. The harassment warning did not involve an admission of culpability, but there was underlying material capable of constituting bad character evidence.
[15] *Ainscough* [2006] EWCA Crim 694; *Woodhouse* [2009] EWCA Crim 498.
[16] [2006] EWCA Crim 694.
[17] *R. v S* [2007] EWCA Crim 335.
[18] By the Coroners and Justice Act 2009 s.144 and Sch.17, which implemented the Council of the European Union Framework Decision 2008/675/JHA.

here at the time of the trial. The fact of a foreign conviction may be proved under s.7 of the Evidence Act 1851.[19]

In *Hanson*,[20] the Vice President, Rose LJ said[21] that he contemplated that applications under the Act would be dealt with by admission, and observed that there is an obligation of frankness upon both the Crown and the defence, reinforced by the general obligation contained in the Criminal Procedure Rules to give active assistance to the court in its case management. Often admissions can be made, but there will be cases where the defence, for whatever reason, are unable to do so. Where the relevance of the previous conviction derives, not so much from the conviction, but more from the way the offence was committed, the prosecution may be placed in the situation where they have little choice but to seek to call the complainant. This may be problematic, particularly when the earlier conviction was for an offence some years before. However, where there are close and relatively unusual similarities, this may justify the prosecution calling an earlier complainant, provided (i) this does not deflect the jury from the critical issues in the case and spawn satellite issues that cannot be properly contained and (ii) there was no agreed basis of plea which was inconsistent with the alleged similarities. In *Woodhouse*,[22] the defendant, a farm worker, had been cautioned in 1995 when he admitted touching the penis of a 13-year-old boy on the farm. At his trial over 10 years later for an offence of sexual activity with a child aged 13, the prosecution successfully applied to adduce evidence of the caution as evidence of propensity under s.101(1)(d). The allegation at trial was that the defendant had asked the complainant boy to help him find a lock and chain. During the search, he had put his arm around the boy and touched his penis. The paperwork in respect of the caution had been lost so that it had been difficult for a form of admission to be agreed. The appellant suffered from severe dyslexia and lack of long-term memory so his counsel lacked assistance as to the circumstances of the earlier offence. Despite the appellant having an opportunity to consider the witness statement of the complainant involved in the 1995 incident, it was submitted that he was put in the very disadvantageous situation where he was unable, by agreeing some form of written admission, to prevent evidence being led by the Crown from the man who had been involved, as a boy, in the previous incident. Further, there was a need to ensure that the trial did not give rise to satellite issues. The Court of Appeal declined to say that the trial judge had exercised his discretion wrongly in allowing the application and permitting the prosecution to call the earlier complainant. The judge had addressed the matters raised by the appellant's counsel, and the appellant and his legal advisers did have the

[19] *Kordasinski* [2007] 1 Cr. App. R. 17 (evidence of the appellant's convictions in Poland for rape and kidnapping were admissible for the purpose of proving that he did in fact commit the rape and false imprisonment alleged within this jurisdiction). See also *Corriera de Oliveira* [2009] EWCA Crim 378.

[20] [2005] EWCA Crim 824; [2005] 2 Cr. App. R. 21 (299).

[21] At 17.

[22] [2009] EWCA Crim 498.

opportunity to consider their attitude to the Crown's application with reference to the witness statement about the 1903 incident.

20.11   Another example might be a rape case, where the allegation is that the complainant, after a heavy day's drinking, awoke to find herself being penetrated by the defendant's penis. The defendant's previous conviction for sexual assault in similar circumstances, where the then victim had woken up to find the defendant uninvited in her bed preparing himself for penetrative sex, might well be relevant under s.101(1)(d). Its relevance would derive from the similarity of the circumstances. Even if the defendant had pleaded guilty in respect of the earlier matter, if he now claimed that this plea had been equivocal, the prosecution would have to call the earlier complainant to establish the similarities, unless the hearsay provisions could properly be invoked.

20.12   The bad character regime has not changed the approach to the admissibility of convictions of a co-accused under s.74 of the Police and Criminal Evidence Act 1984.[23]

The Definition of "Bad Character"

20.13   "Bad character" is defined by s.98 of the Criminal Justice Act 2003, which provides:

> "References in this Chapter to evidence of 'bad character' are to evidence of, or of a disposition towards, misconduct on his part, other than evidence which—
> (a) has to do with the alleged facts of the offence with which the defendant is charged, or
> (b) is evidence of misconduct in connection with the investigation or prosecution of that offence."

Section 99 of the Act provides:

> "(1) the common law rules governing the admissibility of evidence of bad character in criminal proceedings are abolished.
> (2) Subsection (1) is subject to section 118(1) in so far as it preserves the rule under which a person's reputation is admissible for the purposes of proving his bad character."

The term "misconduct" is defined in s.112(1), which provides:

> "'Misconduct' means the commission of an offence or other reprehensible behaviour."

20.14   The result of these provisions is to exclude from the "bad character" regime the central facts of the case. This would appear to encompass offences committed at the same time as the offence alleged and offences committed in preparation for it. It should be remembered that it does not follow that merely because evidence fails to come within the s.101 gateways, it will be

---

[23] *R. v S* [2007] EWCA Crim 2105; *Greaves* [2007] EWCA Crim 1348.

inadmissible. Where the exclusions in s.98 are applicable, and the evidence is relevant, it will be admissible without further ado.[24]

This may lead to an overlap between the central facts of the case, evidence of which is admissible outside the bad character regime, and evidence that is admissible as "important explanatory evidence" under the gateway in s.101(1)(c). In *McKintosh*,[25] evidence that the appellant had shown the complainant a firearm some months before the alleged rape was held to be part of the alleged facts of the case, in that it explained why she had not complained earlier. Professor Ormerod has argued that in such circumstances, s.101(1)(c) would be a safer route to admissibility.[26] He suggests that counter-intuitive thinking is necessary, as the wider the definition of bad character, the greater the protection for the defendant (as bad character evidence is admissible only if one of the gateways is open). In the subsequent case of *Tirnaveau*[27] the Court of Appeal held that the exclusion in s.98(a) must be related to evidence of misconduct where there is some nexus in time between the offence with which the defendant is charged and the misconduct. Clearly, this temporal constraint can apply to events that occurred either before or after the offence alleged, provided they were reasonably contemporaneous with and closely associated with the alleged facts.[28] It is important to remember that it does not necessarily follow that because evidence is relevant to the alleged offence, then it "has to do with the alleged facts of the offence" so that s.98(a) will apply.[29] If that were the case, all the restrictions contained in the bad character regime in the Criminal Justice Act 2003 would be rendered redundant.[30]   **20.15**

It is not unknown for juries to convict a defendant of an offence of violence that occurred at the same time as an alleged sexual offence, such as rape, on which the jury then fail to agree. On a retrial for the alleged rape, the earlier conviction for violence may well be within s.98(a) in that it "has to do with" the sexual allegation because it occurred during the same incident. It will then fall outside the definition of "bad character", but be admissible at common law as going to the issue whether the defendant had been violent to the complainant in the context of the rape allegation.[31] An example of a retrial of a sexual offence where a conviction of another offence was held to have been properly admitted is *Brand*[32] where, on a retrial of charges of rape   **20.16**

---

[24] *Edwards and Rowlands* [2005] EWCA Crim 3244.
[25] [2006] EWCA Crim 193.
[26] In a lecture to the Judicial Studies Board Serious Sexual Offences Seminar, July 2007.
[27] [2007] EWCA Crim 1239.
[28] *McNeill* [2007] EWCA Crim 2927. See also *Haigh* [2010] Crim 90.
[29] *Sullivan* [2015] EWCA Crim 1565. Incorrect admission under s.98 meant that no bad character warning was given, rendering the conviction unsafe.
[30] *Loftus* [2009] EWCA Crim 2688 at [25].
[31] See *R. v W* [2006] EWCA Crim 2308, where the Court of Appeal concluded that a conviction of assault occasioning actual bodily harm was admissible on a retrial of the rape on the basis of common law relevance rather than under gateway s.101(1)(d).
[32] [2009] EWCA Crim 2878.

and kidnapping, the appellant's conviction of the theft of the complainant's handbag was properly treated as "having to do with the offence".

20.17   A harassment warning, like a penalty notice, does not involve an admission of culpability and so will not, on its own, ordinarily be capable of constituting bad character evidence.[33] However, the underlying material may be capable of doing so.

20.18   What constitutes "reprehensible behaviour" in a sexual context, within the meaning of s.112(1) of the Act, can provoke lively debate.[34] In *Renda*[35] the Court of Appeal accepted that the word "reprehensible" carries with it some element of culpability or blameworthiness. A definition using such a subjective term means that much will depend on the facts of the particular case. If the prosecution seeks to place an interpretation upon behaviour that amounts to treating it as evidence of bad character, the bad character regime is likely to be engaged. In *Rossi*[36] the appellant had been charged with voyeurism. The Court of Appeal held that the trial judge had been correct to allow the prosecution to adduce evidence under s.101(1)(d) of earlier occasions when the appellant had been seen loitering around and following boys into toilets as evidence of his propensity to loiter outside toilets, on which the prosecution could rely to rebut his case that he was outside the toilets for innocent reasons. The defence argument that this was not reprehensible behaviour was rejected. In any event, a broader interpretation of "reprehensible behaviour" provides greater protection for the defendant.

20.19   Drinking to excess and taking illegal drugs constitutes reprehensible behaviour,[37] but self-harming should not be so characterised.[38] Homosexual behaviour between consenting adults cannot properly be described in 2015 as "reprehensible behaviour". Engaging in consensual sado-masochistic sexual behaviour amounts to the commission of a criminal offence where injury is caused,[39] and so it is not necessary to consider whether the behaviour is "reprehensible". What of conduct involving a sexual relationship with someone significantly younger than the defendant? In *Manister*[40] the Court of Appeal held that the trial judge was wrong to conclude that an earlier sexual relationship between the appellant (aged 36) and a girl of 16 was

---

[33] *Dalby* [2012] EWCA Crim 701.

[34] Roderick Munday, *What constitutes "other reprehensible behaviour" under the bad character provisions of the Criminal Justice Act 2003?* [2005] Crim. L.R. 24. Dr Munday believes that the definition is dangerously vague and "will prove a nightmare of interpretation".

[35] [2006] 1 Cr. App. R. 24; and see *Osbourne* [2007] EWCA Crim 481, where it was held that "reprehensible behaviour" did not include shouting and being aggressive towards a partner over the care of an infant.

[36] [2009] EWCA Crim 2406.

[37] *R. v AJC* [2006] EWCA Crim 284.

[38] By analogy with the decision in *Hall-Chung* [2007] EWCA Crim 3429. See commentary on *R. v M* by Professor David Ormerod [2014] Crim. L.R. 823.

[39] In *Marsh* [2009] EWCA Crim 2696 the Court of Appeal felt that this was arguable. But see *Brown* [1994] A.C. 212, discussed in paras 2.114 and following, above.

[40] [2005] EWCA Crim 2866; [2006] 1 Cr. App. R. 19 (a consolidated appeal with *Weir*).

reprehensible behaviour. Evidence of the relationship was nonetheless admissible at common law, in the particular circumstances of the case, because it was relevant to the issue of whether the appellant had a sexual interest in the complainant, in that it was capable of demonstrating that he had a sexual interest in early or mid-teenage girls much younger than himself. However, it should be borne in mind that often evidence of sexual taste will be evidence of bad character and so the bad character regime will be engaged.

It is important that the nature of the evidence sought to be adduced is   **20.20** considered with care so that the judge can apply the appropriate test. There will be cases where some of the evidence falls to be considered under the bad character regime, whilst other parts do not amount to evidence of bad character, and so the common law applies. This is particularly likely where there are photographs and material relating to pre-pubescent, pubescent and post-pubescent girls. It does not necessarily follow that all the evidence will fall in the same category. Following categorisation of the evidence, the judge should decide which route it is appropriate to follow in respect of each category. First, the judge should decide whether it should be admitted as evidence of bad character, and if so, give his reasons as required by s.110 of the Criminal Justice Act 2003. Secondly, if the evidence does not qualify as evidence of bad character, the judge should decide whether it should be admitted at common law as in *Manister*. It is then incumbent on the judge when summing up to the jury to explain with care in respect of each aspect of the evidence how the jury should approach it and what it might or might not prove.

Fox[41] is an instructive case illustrating the difficulties that can sometimes   **20.21** arise in determining whether evidence amounts to evidence of bad character. It is a useful guide as to the appropriate approach to adopt, although the Court of Appeal's own categorisations in *Fox* are in some instances open to question. The appellant had been convicted on two counts of causing a child under 13 to engage in sexual activity (s.8(1) of the Sexual Offences Act 2003) and two counts of taking an indecent photograph of a child (s.1(1)(a) of the Protection of Children Act 1978). It was alleged that he held himself out to be a photographer and took indecent photographs of girls aged six or seven for his own sexual gratification. It was further alleged that in choreographing the girls to strike poses for the photographs, he caused them to engage in sexual activity. It was the defence case that the appellant was embarking upon an artistic project and he did not obtain sexual gratification from what he had done.

The appellant was arrested and the contents of his van (in which he lived)   **20.22** were seized. Among the contents were photographs, clothing and a notebook which were said to be relevant to his state of mind. It was alleged that certain poses struck by the girls were the same as those in which he photographed grown women. It was said that he was obsessed with young girls to the extent

---

[41] [2009] EWCA Crim 653.

of going so far as to collect their clothing, including their underclothes. The trial judge followed *Manister* in concluding that evidence in relation to the older girls, the notebook, and the contents of the van could be admitted either at common law or as bad character evidence. The Court of Appeal held that the judge had fallen into error by adopting this approach. The evidence fell into three categories:

(i) evidence in relation to the older girls

The photographs were of a higher order of indecency than those that were the subject matter of the counts. Taking an indecent photograph of a person aged under 18 is a criminal offence. The prosecution's case was that the photographs were indecent and taken for the appellant's sexual gratification. The Court of Appeal took the view that the girls' evidence and the production of the photographs fell for consideration as bad character evidence under gateway (d) or (f).

(ii) the notebook

The notebook contained references to such matters as smelling teenage girls' well-worn knickers, school girls' furry pubic nests and looking up girls' skirts, as well as apparent memories or fantasies going back many years. The judge concluded that there were extensive entries that showed an interest in pubescent and pre-pubescent girls. The notebook, although it contained many "dirty" sexual thoughts, was a private document which the appellant had no reason to expect would see the light of day. The Court of Appeal took the view that keeping a private document expressing the author's thoughts could not properly be described as a disposition towards reprehensible behaviour, and thus it fell outside the bad character regime. Professor Ormerod has, however, pointed out[42] that the definition of misconduct is not confined to disposition towards reprehensible behaviour. Misconduct is defined by s.112 as "commission of another offence or other reprehensible behaviour." He puts forward the compelling argument that keeping a diary of sexual fantasies about pre-pubescent girls amounts to reprehensible behaviour.

(iii) the contents of the van

These included photographs of girls in various stages of undress, some of which were designed to make the girls look younger (i.e. they were wearing schoolgirl uniforms). The Court of Appeal considered that photographs showing young women in blatantly sexual poses were

---

[42] See commentary on *Fox* at [2009] Crim. L.R. 12, 881–886.

admissible as similar fact evidence at common law and were probative of the deliberate and intentionally sexual nature of posing. Here, arguably, depending upon the nature of the photographs and the age of the girls, the bad character regime was engaged and so the common law did not apply.[43]

Where there has been an acquittal, or proceedings have been stayed as an abuse of process, the prosecution may still produce evidence at a later trial to show that the defendant was in fact guilty.[44] Where the prosecution seek to rely upon an allegation where there has been an acquittal, the jury may need to be told of the previous acquittal so they have the full picture.[45] Where there has been a favourable basis of plea agreed by the prosecution at the time in respect of a previous conviction, a jury may be entitled to revisit that basis of plea if on the evidence it is open to a different interpretation.[46] In *Smith*[47] the Court of Appeal held that the trial judge had properly admitted allegations of sexual offences which had been stayed as an abuse of process because the defendant had had a legitimate expectation of non-prosecution. **20.23**

THE GATEWAYS

Section 101(1)(a)—"all parties to the proceedings agree to the evidence being admissible"

Agreement for this purpose can be express or tacit.[48] Judges need to know why the evidence is being admitted, so that they are able to direct the jury appropriately when summing up and/or prevent misuse of the evidence by counsel.[49] **20.24**

Section 101(1)(b)—"the evidence is adduced by the defendant himself or is given in answer to a question asked by him in cross-examination and intended to elicit it"

This does not encompass the accidental eliciting of evidence. Once evidence is admitted through gateway (b), the judge must still direct the jury as to its potential relevance and how they should approach it.[50] **20.25**

---

[43] ibid.

[44] *R. v Z* [2000] 2 A.C. 483.

[45] *R. v W* [2015] All E.R. (D) 46 Feb.

[46] *Wynes* [2014] EWCA Crim 2585. The basis of plea was that the appellant had inadvertently downloaded a 49-minute child pornography film entitled "Daughter in Pleasure Lessons" while attempting to download a Dr Who television programme. In deciding that the jury was entitled to go behind the basis of plea, the Court followed the principle in *R. v Z* [2000] 2 A.C. 483 in respect of the admissibility of previous acquittals.

[47] [2005] EWCA Crim 3244.

[48] *Marsh* [2009] EWCA Crim 2696.

[49] *R. v DJ* [2010] EWCA Crim 385.

[50] *Edwards and Rowlands* [2005] EWCA Crim 3244; *Enright and Gray* [2005] EWCA Crim 3244.

Section 101(1)(c)—"important explanatory evidence"

20.26   To be admissible under this gateway the evidence must be both important and explanatory.[51] Whilst the Court of Appeal has been prepared to give a wide interpretation to gateway (c),[52] it is clear that the gateway needs to be kept within proper bounds and not used to smuggle in evidence whose admissibility should properly be considered under gateway (d), i.e. whether it is relevant to an important matter in issue between the defendant and the prosecution, including propensity. In *Davis*[53] the Court of Appeal recognised that the safeguards are more stringent under gateway (d) than under gateway (c), and that there is a danger of admitting evidence as merely explanatory evidence, when it is really intended to use it as evidence of propensity. In *Pronick*[54] the Court held that evidence of a previous rape of the complainant by the appellant was properly admissible as explanatory evidence under this gateway.

20.27   However, it should be remembered that gateway (c) does not apply if the evidence in the case is readily understandable without the evidence of bad character.[55] In *R. v D, P and U*[56] the Court of Appeal observed that gateway (c) is open to misuse. It is designed to deal with the situation in which a jury cannot properly understand the case without hearing evidence which amounts to or includes evidence of bad character. In that case, the Court held that the possession of child pornography could not amount to important explanatory evidence in respect of an allegation of physical child abuse, as the jury could properly understand the allegations without that evidence. The trial judge in *D* had been correct not to admit the evidence under gateway (c). In *Smith*,[57] where the appellant had been charged with sexual offences against children, the Court of Appeal approved the approach of the trial judge, who had rejected the submission that evidence of other sexual assaults upon children by the appellant was admissible through gateway (c), but had concluded that it was evidence of propensity under gateway (d).

20.28   In *Lee*,[58] Hughes LJ, as he then was, took the opportunity further to underline the importance of reading gateway (c) with s.102 of the Act, and

---

[51] Section 102 provides that evidence is important explanatory evidence for the purposes of s.101(1)(c) if (a) without it, the court or jury would find it impossible or difficult properly to understand other evidence in the case, and (b) its value for understanding the case as a whole is substantial.

[52] *McKintosh* [2006] EWCA Crim 193.

[53] [2008] EWCA Crim 1156. See *Haigh* [2010] EWCA Crim 90 for a graphic example of where an erroneous admission under gateway (c) led to significant prejudice. See also *Saint* [2010] EWCA Crim 1924.

[54] [2006] EWCA Crim 2517.

[55] *Beverley* [2006] EWCA Crim 1287. The Court noted that gateway (c) does not apply where the evidence requires "no footnote or lexicon" to be readily understandable. For a classic example of where evidence was properly admitted under this gateway, see *Chohan*, an appeal consolidated with *Edwards* [2006] 1 Cr. App. R. 3.

[56] [2011] EWCA Crim 1474.

[57] [2005] EWCA Crim 3244 (an appeal consolidated with *Edwards and Rowlands*).

[58] [2012] EWCA Crim 316.

for counsel and the judge to focus on the exact basis upon which evidence has been admitted. Section 102 states that evidence will be important explanatory evidence if, first, without it the court or jury would find it impossible or difficult properly to understand other evidence in the case and, second, its value for understanding the case as a whole is substantial. To say that evidence fills out the picture is not the same as saying the rest of the picture is either impossible or difficult to see without it. In *Lee*, the appellant appealed against a single conviction for indecent assault committed on a friend of his step-daughter, S. He was acquitted of other charges. The trial judge had allowed the prosecution to adduce under gateway (c) evidence of two occurrences which S alleged had taken place after the incidents which gave rise to the charges. First, the appellant had placed a camcorder in the bathroom to allow him to watch S bathing. Secondly, after she had left home, S returned to babysit for her younger brother and discovered on the family computer indecent photographs of pubescent children, which it was suggested the appellant had uploaded. The trial judge ruled that evidence of these two occurrences amounted to important explanatory evidence on the grounds (i) that it explained how events progressed and it was the trigger behind S's decision to leave the house at the age of 16, (ii) that to exclude it would leave a lacuna as to what happened, and (iii) that S's reaction to the appellant's behaviour was an important part of the evidence and was necessary to enable the jury to understand why events moved on in the way that they did and, in particular, to address the delay in allegations being made over a number of years. The Court of Appeal acknowledged that these observations may well have been true. However, the first condition was not met in this case: S's evidence was perfectly comprehensible without her evidence about the camcorder and computer incidents. The computer evidence of the appellant taking an unhealthy interest in pubescent children was potentially admissible through gateway (d): see *R. v D, P and U*, discussed below. However, the judge had not been invited to rule on that basis, and had not given the jury the appropriate direction as to how to approach evidence of propensity. In those circumstances, it was impossible to exclude the possibility that some members of the jury may have relied on the two additional pieces of evidence when arriving at a verdict on the single count on which the appellant was convicted, and so that conviction was simply not safe.

When a defendant is tried for a breach of a sexual offences prevention **20.29** order ("SOPO"), it is unlikely that the conviction of the sexual offence that led to the imposition of the order will be admissible under s.101(1)(c) as important explanatory evidence. The judge should tell the jury that they are not concerned as to the reason why the order was imposed and they should simply accept that it was and then focus on whether or not it had been infringed. In *Sabir Sheikh*[59] the appellant was charged with two counts of

---

[59] [2013] EWCA Crim 907.

breach of a SOPO contrary to s.113(1) of the Sexual Offences Act 2003. It was alleged that on two occasions he held himself out to be a taxi driver. The prosecution sought to put in evidence as important explanatory evidence his conviction in 2005 of the rape on the back seat of his taxi of a woman passenger he had picked up from outside a nightclub. The terms of the SOPO were:

"The defendant is prohibited from:
  1. Being a taxi driver licensed or unlicensed.
  2. Hackney Carriage Driver.
  3. Private hire driver unless two passengers are on board."

The Recorder ruled that the conviction for rape was important explanatory evidence since if the jury were unaware of it, it was difficult to see how they could understand how the appellant could be subject to the SOPO in the terms of that order. He also considered that it was important explanatory evidence for the jury to be told that the rape took place in the back of a car. Otherwise, he felt that it was hard to see how the jury could understand the specific prohibition on being a taxi driver, hackney carriage driver or private hire driver unless they were made aware that the offence which gave rise to the order being made was one involving a motor vehicle driven by the appellant. The Court of Appeal rejected the Recorder's reasoning. While the jury might have speculated as to the reason for the making of the order, that was not a proper basis for adducing the evidence of the rape conviction under gateway (c). The sole issue was whether the appellant had breached the order.

20.30   Evidence of bad character that amounts to an explanation for an apparently late disclosure by the complainant may be admissible as "important explanatory evidence". In *R. v S*[60] the Court of Appeal held that a caution for indecent assault in 2003 was properly admitted as "important explanatory evidence" as to why the appellant's two sisters had then, for the first time, made allegations that he had raped them 20 years before.

Section 101(1)(d)—evidence "relevant to an important matter in issue between the defendant and the prosecution"

20.31   Under s.101(1)(d), all that is required is that the bad character is relevant to an "important matter in issue between the prosecution and the defence". An important matter in issue between the prosecution and the defence is defined by s.112(1) as "a matter of substantial importance in the context of the case as a whole". The threshold for admissibility is not an enhanced one, as it was under the old similar fact rule, even in its more liberal later form as set out in *DPP v P*.[61] In *Somanathan*[62] the Court of Appeal held that if the evidence

---

[60] [2006] EWCA Crim 756. For an example under the old law see *R. v TMG* [2000] 2 Cr. App. R. 266, following the principle in *Pettman*, Court of Appeal, May 5, 1985.
[61] [1991] 2 A.C. 447; 93 Cr. App. R. 267.
[62] [2005] EWCA Crim 2866 (a conjoined appeal with *Weir*).

of a defendant's bad character is relevant to an important issue between the prosecution and the defence, then, unless there is an application to exclude the evidence, it is admissible. Leave is not required. The previous one-stage test, which balanced probative value against prejudicial effect, is obsolete.

It is vital to appreciate that gateway (d) is not confined to propensity. The **20.32** important matters in issue in the particular case must be identified, and then it must be determined whether the evidence is truly relevant to the issue or issues. Relevance is likely to depend on the defence advanced.[63] A stark example where relevance was established is *Watson*,[64] where the defendant ran an alibi defence in a rape case. A conviction for another offence committed at the same time and place was powerful evidence to disprove his alibi defence. Essentially, gateway (d) codifies the principle that where evidence is relevant to a disputed issue in the case, it is admissible. It follows that this includes cases where the bad character evidence supports the truth of the present allegation because of the similar nature of the allegations, thereby rebutting any suggestion of coincidence or innocent association.[65] *R. v M (Donald Gordon)*[66] provides a further good example in the context of sexual offences. A father was alleged to have raped his daughter and penetrated her digitally. She stated that she awoke to find her father lying next to her. The appellant claimed to have been absolutely oblivious of any such act and that he had been involuntarily drugged. During a prison visit, a prison officer had seen the appellant kissing his daughter on the lips at inappropriate length, toying habitually with her hair and stroking her leg. He had also sent her letters from prison containing protestations of love and romantic sentimental poems about her. Both the conduct with her in the prison and the letters were capable of demonstrating inappropriate sexual interest which was capable of rebutting the defence. Effectively his defence was innocent association in that he claimed that, although he shared a bed with her, nothing inappropriate had occurred.

Indecent photographs

The issue of the admissibility of indecent photographs found in a defendant's **20.33** possession often arises in trials of sexual offences. The evidence may be directly relevant to a complainant's account. For instance, where a young male complainant alleges as part of his account that the defendant used to show him pictures of child pornography, evidence of the existence of indecent photographs of children including boys on the defendant's computer may be admissible independently of the bad character provisions to support the

---

[63] [2008] EWCA Crim 4 (where conviction no real relevance as propensity to behave violently when drunk accepted).
[64] [2006] EWCA Crim 2308.
[65] See *Freeman and Crawford* [2008] EWCA Crim 1863; *McAlister* [2009] 1 Cr. App. R. 10; *Wallace* [2007] 2 Cr. App. R. 30.
[66] [2006] EWCA Crim 3388.

complainant's evidence of being shown pornography.[67] In such circumstances, the evidence is not bad character evidence by virtue of s.98(a) of the Criminal Justice Act 2003 in that it has to do with the alleged facts of the offence.

20.34   What if the viewing of child pornography by the defendant is not to do with any of the alleged facts of the offence or offences charged? Not infrequently in a case of alleged child sexual abuse there will be evidence that the defendant had viewed and/or made indecent photographs of children. Where the defendant denies any sexual contact with the complainant(s), it is likely that the prosecution will seek to adduce evidence of the indecent photographs as bad character evidence under s.101(1) of the 2003 Act. In *R. v D, P and U*[68] the Court of Appeal, dealing with three conjoined appeals, held that if a defendant is charged with the sexual abuse of a child, evidence of his possession of indecent photographs of children is capable of being admitted by way of bad character evidence under gateway (d) on the ground that evidence of a sexual interest in children is relevant to an important matter in issue between the defendant and the prosecution. Hughes LJ, as he then was, giving the judgment of the Court, did however stress that such evidence is not automatically admissible. An exercise of judgment is required, and there may be a sufficient difference between what has been viewed and what is alleged to have been done for there to be no plausible link. Further, the conclusion that the evidence is capable of admission under gateway (d) is only the first part of the exercise for the court. It must also direct its attention to whether it is unfair to admit the evidence, and in some cases it might be particularly so where the probative value of the evidence is marginal.

20.35   The Court of Appeal in *R. v D, P and U* observed that evidence that a defendant collects or views child pornography is by itself evidence of the commission of a criminal offence. That offence is not itself one involving sexual assault or abuse or indeed any sexual activity which is prohibited. It is obvious that it does not necessarily follow that a person who enjoys viewing such pictures will act out in real life the kind of activity which is depicted in them by abusing children. Accordingly, evidence of the possession of such photographs is not evidence that the defendant has demonstrated a practice of committing offences of sexual abuse or assault. However, the critical question is whether the evidence is relevant to demonstrate that the defendant exhibited a sexual interest in children. The Court of Appeal held that such evidence can indeed be relevant.[69] A sexual interest in small

---

[67] See the appeal of *P*, one of the conjoined appeals in *R. v D, P and U* [2011] EWCA Crim 1474.

[68] Last note.

[69] See also *Wynes* [2014] EWCA Crim 2585 where a previous conviction for downloading a 49 minute video file of girls aged seven to 11 being penetrated was held to have been properly admitted at a subsequent trial for the rape of young girls. When sentenced in respect of the file, the appellant had claimed he had downloaded the file accidentally when trying to download Dr Who. He was conditionally discharged. The jury at the rape trial would have been entitled to reassess the evidence and use it as evidence demonstrating a sexual interest in prepubescent girls.

children or pubescent girls is a relatively unusual character trait. The case against a defendant charged with the sexual abuse of children is that in addition to this character trait, he has translated the interest into active abuse of a child. The evidence of his interest tends to prove the first part of the case. In such cases it is important that juries should be reminded that they cannot proceed directly from possession of photographs to active sexual abuse.[70] The relevance of the indecent photographs is limited to demonstrating a sexual interest in children. The extra step does not necessarily follow. They must ask themselves whether this further step is proved so that they are sure.

The Court also recommended that judges should consider including a **20.36** warning to juries, in a case where there is such a risk, not to allow any revulsion at the use of child pornography to overcome their duty as jurors to examine carefully the question whether the evidence shows that the interest has been translated beyond actual viewing and into active abuse. It is a sensible practice to avoid the jury seeing the photographs so as to avoid the risk of the effects of distaste. It is likely that in most cases a suitable description of the general contents of the photographs, which should be as neutral and dispassionate as possible, can be agreed and presented to the jury. The Court suggested that it is better for such a description to be linked to the photographs actually found, rather than to generalised descriptions of categories such as the Copine scale. Where it is in issue whether the images were indecent, it is for the jury to evaluate them rather for the matter to be resolved by any pre-conceived categorisation of images into various levels.[71] When dealing with the appeal of *D*, the Court pointed out that the evidence of both the internet searches for child pornography and the product of those searches would have been admissible, and the judge had been wrong to exclude the bulk of the photographic evidence.

The Court in *R. v D, P and U* observed that in *R. v A*[72] the trial judge had **20.37** limited the bad character evidence to photographs, films and the like demonstrating a particular interest in incestuous relationships, so the Court of Appeal did not have to decide whether the collection of child pornography falling short of a particular interest in incest would also be admissible. However, the tenor of the trial judge's decision as approved by the Court plainly demonstrates that it could. The judge had said that:

> "[A] reasonable jury would be entitled to consider the complainant's independent complaint and assess it in the light of the complainant's subsequent computer misuse, and conclude that the proposition that the complainant should make her complaints against an innocent man who just happened later in life to develop peculiar sexual preoccupations consistent with the complainant's complaint is profoundly unlikely."

---

[70] See *Miles* [2015] EWCA Crim 353 where the trial judge went further than the prosecution case and suggested that the images, if indecent, were evidence of a propensity to engage in sexual contact defending.

[71] *Miles* [2015] EWCA Crim 353 the Court of Appeal pointed out that categorisation into various levels is only useful for sentencing levels once the jury have convicted the accused.

[72] [2009] EWCA Crim 513.

20.38   Hughes LJ noted that this brief expression of principle was approved by the Court of Appeal and would apply mutatis mutandis to a demonstrated sexual interest in young children. The principle has been given a wide interpretation. In *Latham*,[73] the appellant was convicted of indecent assault of the complainant when he was aged 17 or 18. The trial judge had allowed the prosecution to adduce evidence of the appellant's nine previous convictions of making or possessing indecent images of children, even though there were no details of the age of the children involved in the images or their gender. On appeal, it was argued that as the complainant was most probably 18, proof of an interest in children was irrelevant. Reliance was placed on Hughes LJ's general conclusion in *R. v D, P and U*[74]:

> "Possession of child pornography may, depending upon the facts of the case, demonstrate a sexual interest in children which can be admissible through gateway D upon trial for offences of sexual abuse of children. It will not always be so. There may be sufficient difference between what is viewed and what is alleged to have been done for there to be no plausible link."

The Court decided that, as sparse as the details were, they were sufficient to be capable of establishing a propensity to have a sexual interest in children. Although the complainant was technically an adult, he was an immature teenager the appellant had known since he was nine years old. The appellant must have looked upon him as a child. A sexual interest in children was, therefore, potentially relevant and admissible.

Generalised history as opposed to unusual form of sexual interest

20.39   The line of cases dealing with child pornography is to be contrasted with cases where the evidence sought to be adduced shows nothing more than a generalised history of exceeding sexual boundaries. In *Clements*,[75] the appellant had been charged with two sexual assaults upon adults. He had a previous conviction for consensual sexual behaviour, apparently amounting to kissing, involving a 14-year-old girl. The Court of Appeal held that the previous conviction should not have been admitted. Whilst it could be said to demonstrate an inability to recognise, or perhaps a willingness to disregard, the normal boundaries of sexual propriety, the dividing line between consensual and non-consensual behaviour in sexual matters is very significant and the circumstances of the previous offence and the offences for which the appellant was being tried were very different. In the Court's view, the previous conviction was not probative of a propensity on the part of the appellant to commit sexual assaults of the kind under consideration, and to the extent that it could be said to be probative of a general inability to

---

[73] [2014] EWCA Crim 207. The Court also found that the evidence was undoubtedly admissible under gateway (g) as the appellant had made a significant attack upon the character of witnesses.
[74] [2011] EWCA Crim 1474 at [19].
[75] [2009] EWCA Crim 2726.

recognise the normal boundaries of sexual propensity its probative force was, at best, weak. On the other hand, the prejudicial effect of admitting the conviction was likely to be very significant. Furthermore, in that case the previous incident did not show any unusual form of sexual interest which was relevant to the charges before the Court.

Clements should be compared with *R. v P,*[76] in which the applicant, 56, was   **20.40** convicted of 13 counts of sexual assault upon his god-daughter when she was aged 10. He was caught on CCTV with his hand up her skirt. When interviewed, she disclosed extensive abuse by him over a number of years. It was the applicant's case that the complainant was fabricating or mistaken. At trial the judge had admitted as bad character evidence emails sent by the applicant to three other young girls in which he had pretended to be 16. He had told one of the girls that he looked good and another that he loved her. In a renewed application for leave to appeal, it was submitted that the admissibility of online communication with other children depended upon the prosecution being able to show that the applicant had an unusual sexual interest in children. The prosecution had been able to go no further than to show he had an "odd" but non-sexual relationship with children and so the emails should not have been admitted. The Court of Appeal refused the application for leave and accepted the prosecution's submission that the evidence of the emails supported the complainant's account that the applicant had an unhealthy interest in girls. The computer contact between him and the three girls was capable of showing a propensity to get close to and have non-innocent relationships with girls. It was not necessary to show a propensity to commit offences such as those charged. The Court also held that, although the trial judge had not made specific reference to s.101(3) of the 2003 Act (under which evidence must not be admitted under gateway (d) or (g) if its admission would have such an adverse effect on the fairness of the proceedings that the court ought not to admit it), he had been entitled to conclude that the prejudice caused by admission of the evidence was not such as to require its exclusion.

Propensity

The scope of gateway (d) is expanded by s.103(1)(a). Section 103 provides: **20.41**

"(1) For the purposes of section 101(1)(d) the matters in issue between the defendant and the prosecution include—
   (a) the question whether the defendant has a propensity to commit offences of the kind with which he is charged, except where his having such a propensity makes it no more likely that he is guilty of the offence;
   (b) the question whether the defendant has a propensity to be untruthful, except where it is not suggested that the defendant's case in untruthful in any respect.

[76] [2013] EWCA Crim 913.

(2) Where subsection (1)(a) applies, a defendant's propensity to commit offences of the kind with which he is charged may (without prejudice to any other way of doing so) be established by evidence that he has been convicted of—

    (a) an offence of the same description as the one with which he is charged, or

    (b) an offence of the same category as the one with which he is charged."

20.42 Evidence of propensity can be very significant in sex cases. In the leading case of *Hanson*,[77] the Court of Appeal stated that where propensity to commit an offence is relied upon, there are essentially three questions to be considered:

    (i) Does the history of conviction(s) establish a propensity to commit offences of the kind charged?

    (ii) Does that propensity make it more likely that the defendant committed the offence charged?

    (iii) Is it unjust to rely on the conviction(s) of the same description or category; and, in any event, will the proceedings be unfair if they are admitted?

20.43 The Court adopted what Professor Spencer describes as an "expansive" as opposed to a "restrictive" construction of s.103.[78] It held that the reference in s.103(2) to offences of the same description or category is not exhaustive of the types of conviction which might be relied upon to show evidence of propensity to commit offences of the kind charged. Nor is it necessarily sufficient, in order to show such propensity, that a conviction should be of the same description or category as that charged.[79] Furthermore, the Court of Appeal pointed out that a single previous conviction of an offence of the same description will often not show propensity. Whilst circumstances demonstrating probative force are not confined to those sharing a striking similarity, if the modus operandi has significant features shared by the offence, it may be more likely to show propensity, and so evidence of the detail of the offence may be necessary.

20.44 It does not follow that there is a minimum number of events necessary to demonstrate propensity. Whilst, generally speaking, the fewer the number of convictions, the weaker the evidence of propensity is likely to be, certain sexual behaviour may, in appropriate circumstances, provide an exception to this general proposition. In *Hanson*, the Court of Appeal observed that a single previous conviction may show propensity where, for example, it shows a tendency to unusual behaviour or where its circumstances demonstrate probative force in relation to the crime charged. The Court suggested child sexual abuse or fire-setting as comparatively clear examples, but declined to provide an exhaustive list.

---

[77] [2005] EWCA Crim 824.

[78] Professor John Spencer, *Evidence of Bad Character*, 2nd edn (Oxford: Hart Publishing, 2009), paras 4.46–4.49.

[79] *Hanson, Gilmore and P* [2005] 2 Cr. App. R. 21.

It follows that the provisions are significantly wider than the old similar **20.45** fact rules. As Smith LJ explained in *Tully*,[80] the similarities do not have to be striking in the way similar fact evidence has to be, but there must be a degree of similarity. However, admissibility of evidence of bad character to establish propensity is not necessarily confined to conduct of a similar description or category. The Criminal Justice Act 2003 (Categories of Offences) Order 2004[81] contains lists of offences which are of the same category for the purposes of s.103. The category covering "sexual offences (persons under the age of 16)" does not include offences in relation to indecent photographs or offences where the complainant was 16 or over. However in *Weir*,[82] where the appellant had been on trial for sexually assaulting a 10-year-old child, the Court of Appeal held that the trial judge had been right to admit in evidence under gateway (d) that the appellant had been cautioned for taking an indecent photograph of a child contrary to s.1 of the Protection of Children Act 1978.

Clearly, depending on the facts, a previous conviction for rape might show **20.46** a propensity to rape in the circumstances alleged at a rape trial. It is important to consider whether the conviction or convictions shared sufficient similar and unusual features with the allegation. In *R. v B (Richard William)*,[83] the Court of Appeal held that a defendant's rape convictions were, in principle, admissible to prove his propensity to rape. Further examples might be where a previous conviction shows a defendant's particular sexual taste, such as a tendency to force victims to give him oral sex[84] or to take advantage of women who are asleep, unconscious and/or incapable through drink or drugs. In *Burdess*,[85] a propensity to embark on non-consensual sexual activity in circumstances where there was an acute risk of discovery was held to be a sufficiently distinctive and unusual feature for a previous conviction for rape to be admissible as evidence of propensity in a case where the rape alleged at trial occurred in the defendant's bedroom separated only by a single wall from his mother's bedroom. Similarly, in *R. v MD*,[86] the Court of Appeal held that two convictions for rape were safe where a judge had allowed the prosecution to adduce evidence of the appellant's conviction for sexual assault upon a teacher. The offender aged 17 had been convicted of the rape of two girls, aged 13 and 14. Both rapes took place at homes where a number of young people had met. In the first

---

[80] [2006] EWCA Crim 2270.
[81] SI 2004/3346.
[82] [2006] 1 Cr. App. R. 19.
[83] [2008] EWCA Crim 1850. The appeal against the rape conviction was allowed for a different reason. For a recent example, see *Miller* [2010] EWCA 1578, where the Court of Appeal held that the defendant's conviction of a gang rape of a 15-year-old when he was 16 was properly admitted as evidence of propensity on a rape charge where the defendant was 23. The allegation on trial was that he had crept into his 11-year-old niece's room at night and raped her.
[84] *R. v H* [2006] EWCA Crim 2898.
[85] [2014] EWCA Crim 270.
[86] [2015] EWCA Crim 818.

incident, the appellant entered the bedroom where the victim was, turned off the light and raped her. She told him to stop and screamed. He withdrew, took a knife and threatened her with it, before he penetrated her again. In the second incident, he followed the victim into the bathroom and attempted to force his way in. She told him to leave. Later the victim woke up to find the appellant pulling down her clothing and raping her. The previous conviction had involved the appellant grabbing a teacher's bottom. She had flinched but he had persisted rubbing his penis against her through her clothing. On appeal it was argued that this was very different from the facts of the instant offences. However, the Court of Appeal held that the judge had not erred in admitting the conviction. The three offences had all involved audacity, persistence after initial rebuffs and carelessness as to the victims' consent. In addition, all had been committed while other people were around. The three offences established features sufficiently unusual to enable the judge to allow the previous conviction to be admitted.

20.47   Evidence of controlling behaviour towards partners culminating in non-consensual sexual activity frequently arises in rape cases, and it may establish a relevant propensity. For instance, in *Balazs*[87] it was held that the trial judge had properly admitted a conviction for rape which, taken together with convictions for violence and harassment, was evidence of the appellant's propensity to engage in violent, threatening and sexual behaviour to assert his control over his partner within the relationship or after the relationship has ended. The Lord Thomas CJ said that the single unifying characteristic in respect of four offences admitted under gateway (d) was such behaviour in relation to a girlfriend or former girlfriend during or after a relationship had ended. It was on that basis that, although 22 years old, the rape conviction was admissible. This was one of those rare cases identified in *Hanson* where a single conviction was capable of showing propensity.

20.48   The Court of Appeal has resolved a number of issues which may have a significant impact on the trial of sexual offences. Evidence of propensity may be admissible irrespective of whether the defendant's case in relation to an allegation of sexual assault is one of complete denial or one of innocent explanation.[88] Evidence of propensity can support identification evidence.[89] There is no rule that because the previous offences are unpleasant, the detail of them should not be admitted.[90] The prosecution may cross-examine a defendant about evidence of his bad character as adduced under gateway (d). The prosecution may well wish to explore the extent of the similarities to bolster its case.

---

[87] [2014] EWCA Crim 937.
[88] *Wilkinson* [2006] EWCA Crim 1332.
[89] *Heath Randall* [2006] EWCA Crim 1413; *Blake* [2006] All E.R. (D) 361; *Eastlake and Eastlake* [2007] EWCA Crim 603.
[90] *Smith* [2006] All E.R. (D) 280.

Age of previous convictions/allegations

By virtue of s.103(3), s.103(2) does not apply in the case of a particular **20.49** defendant if the court is satisfied, by reason of the length of time since the conviction or for any other reason, that it would be unjust for it to apply in his case. Furthermore, when the court comes to consider its discretion to exclude under s.101(3), by virtue of s.101(4) it must have regard, in particular, to the length of time between matters when considering whether to exercise the discretion to exclude.[91] This has been stressed by the Court of Appeal in a number of cases.

In *Michael Murphy*,[92] the Court of Appeal considered the proposition put **20.50** forward in *Hanson* that a single conviction might show a tendency to unusual behaviour even where there has been significant passage of time. Where the conviction is relatively stale, much will depend upon similarities, particularly unusual and distinctive features, that the old offence and the present allegation have in common. Keene LJ stated:

> " . . . it is the combination of only one previous conviction being relied upon to show propensity and the passage of time since that conviction that must cause concern. There may be cases where the factual circumstances of just one conviction, even as long ago as 20 years earlier, might be relevant to show propensity, but we would expect such cases to be rare and to be ones where the earlier conviction showed some very special and distinctive feature, such as predilection on the part of the defendant for a highly unusual form of sexual activity, or some arcane or highly specialised knowledge relevant to the present offence. In cases with less distinctive features in common, one would require some evidence of propensity manifesting itself during the intervening period to render the earlier evidence admissible as evidence of a continuing propensity."

However, evidence of previous sexual offences has been held rightly **20.51** admitted, even where they related to matters that took place many years before.[93] In *Pickstone*, one of the appeals conjoined with *Hanson*, the prosecution sought to have the applicant's 1993 conviction for indecent

---

[91] See *Dhooper* [2008] EWCA Crim 2892, where a conviction for manslaughter (when intoxicated) was quashed when a conviction for violence (when intoxicated) over 13 years before had been introduced without any reference by the judge to s.101(4) and the effect of passage of time on the significance and probative value of the earlier offence *or* the greater difficulty for the defendant in explaining or dealing with the circumstances of the previous offence. Note also the words of Lord Hope in the Privy Council case of *DS v Her Majesty's Advocate* [2007] UKPC D1 at [49], when looking at an "interests of justice" test in the context of the admissibility of a defendant's previous convictions for sexual offences in a trial of a sex case: "The test needs to be exacting in proceedings on indictment, in view of the risk that the jury may attach a significance to the conviction which, due to its age or other factors, it cannot properly bear."

[92] [2006] EWCA Crim 3408. The case related to the admissibility of a firearms offence committed 20 years earlier at a trial for further firearms offences. The Court found itself unable to accept that one isolated instance of possession of a firearm without a licence when the appellant was 24 was capable of establishing a propensity to commit firearms offences when he was 48.

[93] *Cox* [2007] EWCA Crim 3365; *Woodhouse* [2009] EWCA Crim 498; *R. v A* [2009] EWCA Crim 513; *Jasionis* [2010] EWCA Crim 2981. See also *Balazs* [2014] EWCA Crim 937, where a 22-year-old rape conviction was held to have been properly admitted.

assault on an 11-year-old girl put in evidence under gateway (d), as showing propensity and so making it more likely that he committed offences of rape and indecent assault on his step-daughter (born in May 1996), who made the revelations to her foster mother in March 2004. The earlier offence had taken place over 10 years before. The trial judge concluded that the earlier offence was of the same description and the same category, within the meaning of the Criminal Justice Act 2003 (Categories of Offences) Order 2004,[94] as the offences charged. He expressly took into account the length of time since the previous offence and observed that "a defendant's sexual mores and motivations are not necessarily affected by the passage of time". He concluded that the passage of time was not here sufficient to make the admission of the evidence unjust. The evidence had significant probative value, and its admission would not adversely affect the fairness of the proceedings.[95] The Court of Appeal described the judge's conclusion as "unassailable."

20.52   The case of *Woodhouse*,[96] as the Court of Appeal acknowledged, raised a classic point about the admission of bad character evidence relating to an old offence with distinctive similarities. The appellant had been convicted of a single count of sexual activity with a child. The allegation was that in November 2006 he had asked for the help of a boy aged 13 to assist him in the search for a chain and lock that had disappeared from a gate in circumstances where it was thought that the boy might know where the chain was. The boy found the chain between two barbed wire fences and began to pass it under one of the fences to the appellant. The appellant was then said to have put his arm around the complainant's shoulder, whisper something in his ear and to have deliberately put his hand on the boy's penis over his clothing. The defence case was that the touching had been accidental. The prosecution sought to rely upon evidence from a young man who, back in 1995, when he was 13 himself, had complained that the appellant had touched his penis. He had been allowed to share the driving seat of a tractor with the appellant. The boy had steered whilst the appellant sat behind him operating the pedals. The boy alleged that the appellant had put his hands on top of and underneath his trousers and grabbed his penis. The appellant had been cautioned for the 1995 matter, which he admitted. The prosecution argued that the earlier offence was capable of rebutting the defence of accidental touching as well as establishing a propensity to commit similar offences. The trial judge allowed the application, stating that he was quite satisfied that the evidence was capable of showing a propensity to commit the type of offence with which the appellant was charged. The two incidents had similarities and the propensity was relevant to a matter in issue, namely whether the touching was intentional. There were distinctive features in the

---

[94] SI 2004/3346.
[95] The judge also admitted this evidence under gateway (g) on the basis that what the defendant had said in interview was a false allegation giving rise to an attack on the complainant's character within s.106(1)(c)(i).
[96] [2009] EWCA Crim 498.

touching of a 13-year-old boy's penis and putting an arm around him. On appeal, the appellant sought to rely upon Keene LJ's words in *Murphy*[97] and submitted that this was not "a highly unusual form of activity". The Court of Appeal concluded[98]:

> "In our judgement, however, we consider that a propensity to touch the penis of a 13-year-old boy in this setting, accompanied by the other feature of putting an arm around the boy is a matter, even though arising on only one occasion, at some distance, which the jury could reasonably consider to be evidence of propensity which would assist them in the issue in the case of accidental touching. Indeed such a case is not unfamiliar to the common law even before the 2003 Act."

The same point arose in *Sully*,[99] where the convictions dated back to 1968 and 1974. However, they related to the unusual sexual practice of touching girls under their skirts at fairground rides, so their similarity and potential probative force was high enough to justify admission in evidence in respect of a similar, more recent allegation. In contrast, in *Leaver*,[100] on a charge of rape, it was held that an old conviction for indecent exposure was not evidence of propensity, nor did it go to the appellant's credibility. The appellant had been on trial for rape and grievous bodily harm with intent. It was common ground between the prosecution and the defence that the sex had begun as consensual sex. It was alleged that the appellant had become violent during the sex, and had refused to stop when asked to do so. He had ended up breaking the complainant's jaw. The issues in the case were whether the complainant had consented throughout the sex and whether the appellant had intended to cause her really serious harm. It is difficult to see how a conviction for indecent exposure could have been relevant to either of these issues. **20.53**

Incidents following date of allegation being tried

Propensity can be proved by relying on incidents which have occurred since the incident which is the subject matter of the trial.[101] This issue is likely to arise from time to time in the trial of sexual offences. Take the case of a schoolmaster who is alleged to have sexually assaulted some of the boys at the school where he teaches. After his arrest for those offences, he is re-arrested because child pornography has been found on his computer, and it is clear that it had been downloaded after the alleged earlier offences. His **20.54**

---

[97] [2006] EWCA Crim 3408.

[98] At [15].

[99] [2008] EWCA Crim 2556.

[100] [2006] EWCA Crim 2988. See also *Bullen* [2008] 2 Cr. App. R. 25 (364), where the Court of Appeal discussed *Leaver* and suggested that, in respect of the rape count, there would have been no difficulty if the judge had adopted the formula agreed between counsel limiting the previous conviction's relevance to whether the defendant had a propensity to degrade and insult women for his own gratification. *Quaere* whether a single conviction of indecent exposure would be enough to establish this.

[101] *Adenusi* [2006] EWCA Crim 1059; *R. v M (Donald Gordon)* [2006] EWCA Crim 3388.

subsequent possession of the child pornography is likely to be admissible in respect of the earlier sexual assaults.

20.55   A graphic example can be found in *R. v A (Alec Edward)*[102] where the defendant was tried for offences of rape and indecent assault of his daughter between 1981 and 1992 when she was aged between seven and 17. The bad character offences were committed between 2005 and 2008, some 14 years or so after the last and most serious of the offences against his daughter, the rape. They related to 65,858 indecent images of children found on his computer. The material included images between levels 1 and 5. There were "chat logs" where the appellant had posed as a 20-year-old female exchanging indecent images with an incest-related theme and expressing a desire to become involved in father/daughter incest. It was clear that the appellant had visited incest-related websites. There were 34 folders on the hard disc, each containing between eight and 115 incest-related pictures. There were story-book images where the appellant had obtained a generic image of child pornography and had overwritten it with a storyline with an incestuous theme. The trial judge took the view that the bad character evidence was relevant because it supported the proposition that the appellant had a tendency to offend in the manner set out in the indictment, in that that he had developed an entrenched, persistent and sustained interest in sexual offending against children, with a particular pre-occupation with father/daughter incestuous sexual activity. He said that in his judgement, a reasonable jury would be entitled to consider the complainant's independent complaint and assess it in the light of the appellant's subsequent computer misuse, and conclude that the proposition that the complainant had made her complaints against an innocent man who just happened in later life to develop peculiar sexual preoccupations consistent with the complainant's complaint, was profoundly unlikely. He considered the potential adverse effect on the proceedings through lapse of time, and concluded that the evidence was highly relevant and powerful such as to justify its admission notwithstanding the prejudicial effect.

20.56   On appeal, it was submitted that the passage of time is even more important when the bad character material post-dates rather than pre-dates the allegations being tried by the jury. If the complainant had reported matters promptly, the bad character offences would not have been committed by the time they were dealt with. In effect, the appellant was prejudiced twice over: by the delay in the complaint and by the passage of time before the bad character material came into existence. It was observed that the material proved voyeurism and aberrant fantasy, but did not include or depict any physical act on the part of the appellant. The Court of Appeal, in dismissing the appeal, readily accepted that in many cases a gap in time of this duration,

---

[102] [2009] EWCA Crim 513. Contrast *Wright* [1990] 90 Cr. App. R. 325 where, under the old law, a headmaster's convictions for buggery of young male pupils were quashed on the basis that the trial judge had wrongly admitted evidence of his possession of homosexual pornography and a guide to homosexual brothels in Paris.

coupled with this order of events, might militate against admitting evidence of bad character. However, the Court noted that incestuous rape is no ordinary offence. It can only be committed by an abnormal offender against a very limited number of victims and usually for a relatively short period of time. In particular, an allegation of incestuous rape is more likely to be true when made against a man with an obvious interest in deriving sexual satisfaction from material depicting incestuous rape, even many years later, than against a man with no such provable interest.

Past heterosexual offences where present allegation is a homosexual offence

In *Morgan*,[103] the prosecution submitted that the appellant's previous **20.57** convictions established a propensity to seek sexual gratification by attacking vulnerable children at a time when he was in a position of trust. J, the complainant, was a four-year-old boy. The appellant was a friend of his parents. The prosecution case was that the appellant raped the boy when he babysat him in April 2008 and, again, twice in May 2008. The prosecution sought to rely upon the appellant's convictions in 2000 for historic sexual offences, including two offences of rape and nine of indecent assault committed against girls. The offences had been committed some 20 years earlier. They were of the same kind and description as the offences charged. They were committed against children, although somewhat older than J, who had been temporarily in the appellant's care and so they were committed in breach of trust. In opposing the application, it was submitted on behalf of the appellant inter alia that the earlier offences were committed against girls and so involved heterosexual rather than homosexual abuse. The Court of Appeal took the view that the trial judge's ruling, allowing the application, could not be faulted. He had observed that the offences were of the same description. He had pointed out that the 2003 Act made no distinction between male and female in the way that it lays down the prescribed criminal behaviour. In his judgment, the appellant had demonstrated a propensity to commit offences against vulnerable children to whom and with whom he was in a position of trust. He could see no valid distinction to be drawn based on the gender of the alleged victims.

The admissibility of evidence of homosexual disposition

Where a male defendant is alleged to have committed sexual offences against **20.58** male children, is evidence that the defendant is not purely heterosexual, has bisexual interests or has had consensual sexual relations with other men relevant and admissible? As noted earlier, where the evidence is not evidence of bad character, admissibility will depend upon the common law rules as to

---

[103] [2009] EWCA Crim 2705.

relevance. Otherwise, it will be admissible only if one of the gateways in the bad character regime is open.

20.59   The admissibility of evidence of homosexual disposition has received recent attention from the Court of Appeal,[104] which has emphasised the vast difference between an interest in consensual sex with an adult male partner and an interest in paedophilic sex with boys. A mutually agreed sexual relationship between adults, without more, does not show a propensity to commit sexual offences against children within the scope of gateway (d). Normally such evidence will not be relevant and admissible. However, there may be cases where a defendant makes his sexual disposition an issue in the case such that gateway (f) applies, and the evidence is admitted to correct a false impression given by the defendant. In these circumstances, the jury should be given a powerful warning as to the limits of the relevance of such evidence.[105]

20.60   In addressing such questions it is always vitally important to identify what matters are in issue in the particular case and whether the bad character evidence that the prosecution seeks to adduce is truly relevant to those issues and complies with the bad character regime criteria. For example, the fact that the defendant has had consensual sexual relations with males over the present-day age of consent on other occasions is not germane to the question whether he has committed violent paedophile offences. Problems have arisen when the prosecution has sought to argue (i) that the defendant's homo-sexual disposition is relevant because it shows an unusual sexual interest, or (ii) that the defendant's apparent heterosexuality demonstrated by his marriage or by other acts consistent with heterosexuality risks giving the jury a false impression. This is a difficult area. Given the potential pitfalls and the obvious scope for significant prejudice, even in 2016, both lines of reasoning need to be scrutinised with great care before such evidence is admitted. Three recent cases are highly instructive. What they make clear is that, in the event of such evidence being relevant and admissible, a powerful direction is called for to prevent juries adopting an illegitimate line of reasoning.[106]

20.61   *Laws-Chapman*[107] is a strong example of a case in which the bad character evidence did not have any real relevance to the matters in issue and its admission would inevitably have been highly prejudicial. The issue on appeal was whether, in the context of two historic sexual offences alleged to have been committed in 1978,[108] which involved an allegation of violent paedo-phile behaviour against the will of the victim (who was aged 12 or 13 at the

---

[104] *Laws-Chapman* [2013] EWCA 1851, discussed in paras 20.61 and following, below.

[105] *R. v IJ*[2011] EWCA Crim 2734, discussed in paras 20.67 and following, below.

[106] *R. v IJ* [2011] EWCA Crim 2734 at [29] and [44] per Pitchford LJ. See also *R. v B (Peter)* [2012] EWCA Crim 1659.

[107] [2013] EWCA Crim 1851. The decision was strongly criticised by James Richardson QC in *Criminal Law Week*, Issue 46, December 16, 2013, pp.2–4.

[108] Gross indecency with a child under 14, contrary to s.1(1) of the Indecency with Children Act 1960, and buggery of a person under the age of 21, contrary to s.12 of the Sexual Offences Act 1956.

time), the trial judge had been right to admit in evidence a single conviction for buggery in 1985, involving a 17-year-old, where the buggery may well have been consensual and when the court had no details relating to the offending apart from the identity of the victim and the location of the offence.

The applicant denied the entirety of the sexual allegations made by the complainant. In interview, when asked whether he had ever touched any boys inappropriately, he answered "No, definitely no". When the allegations were put in more detail he stated, "I should never think I would want to do that sort of thing" and "When you're a married man why the hell do you want to do a thing like that?" The defence case was that the principal witness was mistaken in his identification. The applicant did not give evidence.   **20.62**

The judge allowed the prosecution's application to admit the 1985 conviction on the basis that it provided evidence from which the jury could properly conclude that the applicant had a sexual interest in boys and was inclined towards buggery. He concluded that the fact that it was an isolated conviction would not preclude the jury properly concluding that the applicant had the relevant propensity. The judge also considered that the assertion by the defence that the complainant had mistakenly identified the applicant, and that the more likely candidate was an identified individual who had convictions for child sex abuse, meant that the application was properly made out under gateway (g) on the basis of an attack on the character of another. Further, the judge suggested that the evidence served to contradict the impression created in interview by the applicant that he would never have acted as alleged towards the victim in the present case and "was not that way inclined."   **20.63**

In summing up, the judge directed the jury that the principal reason why they had heard about the offence was because the prosecution said that it contradicted the impression the jury might think the applicant gave during interview, when he had suggested he was not the sort of person to do something like that. He continued: **20.64**

> "The Crown say, on the contrary, his conviction demonstrates that he was someone with a particular side to his character, which included having a sexual interest in boys and being inclined to act pursuant to that interest, even to the extent of buggery . . . ".

The judge then left the 1985 conviction for the jury's consideration in two further issues: if the applicant did have that side to his character, it potentially made it more likely that he committed the 1978 offences, and it was also relevant to whether the identified man with convictions for child sexual abuse was the perpetrator rather than the applicant.

The Court of Appeal observed that the 1978 allegations being tried by the jury were that the applicant committed violent, paedophile offences against the will of a 12 or 13-year-old victim, and none of those features formed part of the 1985 incident. Fulford LJ, giving the judgment of the Court, explained why the judge's directions involved flawed reasoning: **20.65**

"During the course of oral submissions—in order to explore the relevance of the 1985 conviction—these overall circumstances were notionally transposed into a heterosexual context, and the Crown accepted that it is inconceivable that an attempt would be made to introduce the fact that a male defendant, at some stage in his past, had had lawful, consensual sexual intercourse with a female——however great the age difference between them—in support of a prosecution for violent and paedophile offences, committed against an unwilling young victim. Lawful and consensual sexual activity would simply be irrelevant in this context, regardless of whether the offender is a homosexual or heterosexual. Put otherwise, mutually agreed sexual relations between individuals over the age of consent do not, certainly without more, tend to prove that the older participant is a paedophile, who has a propensity to commit violent crimes against children."

20.66   The Court added that the applicant's assertion in interview that he had never had sexual intercourse with a man was irrelevant and could have been excluded from the interview transcripts put before the jury. Further, the 1985 conviction was of no legitimate use to the jury when assessing whether the other identified man, as opposed to the applicant, was the perpetrator.

20.67   The argument against admission was particularly strong in the case of *Laws-Chapman*. The issues are not always so clear-cut, as for example in *R. vIJ*,[109] where the Court of Appeal held that controversial evidence of a consensual homosexual affair had been properly admitted and no improper prejudice had resulted. The evidence had relevance in the light of the way the case had been run and the appellant's own evidence. The Court of Appeal acknowledged the need for an adequate direction containing powerful words to the jury designed to prevent them from using the evidence for an inadmissible or prejudicial purpose.

20.68   The appellant in that case had been convicted of sexual offences against two boys (his own son when aged between five and seven and his wife's son over a period of over 12 years between the ages of four and 17). During the course of the appellant's interview with the police, he was asked about his sexuality. He told them that in about 1998 or 1999 he was using homosexual internet chatrooms. This had lasted in all for some two years. As a result, he had arranged a sexual encounter with a 20-year-old man with whom he had an "affair" for "some time". As a result, he left the family home for about a year.

20.69   The defence case at trial was that there never had been inappropriate physical contact between the appellant and the two boys. The prosecution sought the admission of the unexpurgated contents of the interview. It was submitted that these were relevant to the issue whether the appellant was a man who, despite being married with children, had a sexual interest in males. It was relevant that, at the time covered by the indictment, when his step-son was aged 16 to 19, he admitted having an affair with a man aged 20. It was further submitted that the jury should hear the evidence in case they were otherwise left with a mistaken impression that the appellant was by reason of

---

[109] [2011] EWCA Crim 2734.

his long-term marriage exclusively heterosexual. The appellant's counsel opposed the admission of the unexpurgated interview on the grounds that it was irrelevant, or of marginal relevance, and plainly prejudicial.

The trial judge made it clear that the evidence could not go to propensity, **20.70** but he ruled that it was highly relevant to prevent the jury from forming a false impression of the appellant's family life and the background against which the complaints were made. The jury ought to know that the appellant was a man with dual sexual interests, particularly as the last counts related to when the complainant was a young adult, and the appellant was having a consensual relationship with an adult at the time. Otherwise they would be likely to deal with the matter on a false basis.

The evidential picture changed after the judge's ruling. When the appellant **20.71** gave evidence, contrary to the summary of his interview, he suggested that both his sons knew that he was bisexual before one of them made the complaint to the police. An argument was put forward on the appellant's behalf that it was that knowledge which became the cause of or a contributory factor leading to malicious complaints. In cross-examination, prosecution counsel challenged the appellant's assertion that he became interested in a homosexual affair only because he thought his wife was having an affair. He suggested that the appellant was in fact a closet homosexual and must have known for some years about his attraction towards the male sex.

On appeal, it was argued that this cross-examination demonstrated the **20.72** extent of the prejudice which was risked by the admission of this evidence before the jury. Secondly, the suggestion that the appellant had not been entirely truthful about his homosexual activity, subject to a *Lucas* direction, could go to his credibility. The judge had added:

> "The most important thing to remember is that the fact of the defendant's homosexual activity does not affect his credibility as a witness and does not show he has a propensity to commit the offences against him.
>
> He admits to consensual homosexual activity with a 20 year old man, that is sexual activity to which they both consented. That does not show that he had a sexual interest in boys, or unwanted or forced sexual activity with boys or young men. Not every heterosexual man has an interest in young girls. Not every homosexual man has an interest in boys."

The Court of Appeal accepted that evidence of a consensual sexual **20.73** relationship with a 20-year-old was not reprehensible behaviour and so the bad character regime did not apply. It followed that the issue was whether it amounted to relevant evidence under the common law. The Court followed the same line of reasoning as in *Manister*[110] in holding that a sexual attraction by one male for another is still sufficiently unusual to make that disposition relevant to the question whether the appellant had an innocent or a sexual association with his own male children. Nevertheless, the evidence should not have been admitted if its prejudicial effect would have outweighed

---

[110] [2005] EWCA Crim 2866.

its probable value. The Court accepted that the probative value of the evidence in this case was modest. However, it did not conclude that the judge's decision was wrong. At the time when he decided to admit the evidence, he had been correct to conclude that it was relevant. But the Court did not agree that at that time the evidence was admissible in order to counteract any false impression which the appellant attempted to give merely by asserting in the course of his interview that he had been married for a period of 15 years.

20.74   As can happen, by the time of the summing-up the evidence was different from that anticipated at the time of the earlier ruling. By that stage, it *was* the prosecution case that the appellant had attempted to give a false picture to the jury about his committed family life, only interrupted, on his own account, by his wife's infidelity. Secondly, the prosecution said that he had attempted to turn the fact of his own sexuality into an argument that it was for this reason that false complaints had been made against him. The Court of Appeal concluded that once the evidence had been admitted, prosecution counsel was not prevented from challenging the appellant upon the terms in which he dealt with it in his own evidence-in-chief. By mounting such a challenge, prosecuting counsel was in no sense bringing about prejudice to the appellant which outweighed the relevance of the evidence.

20.75   The judge had also added that it was a matter for the jury to make a judgment whether the appellant had told the truth about the reason for his homosexual interest. If they concluded he had lied, that lie was relevant to the question whether he had given truthful evidence generally. The Court of Appeal acknowledged that a risk of prejudice must have been present without adequate directions from the judge. However, the powerful direction quoted above, which was designed to prevent the jury from using the evidence for an inadmissible or prejudicial purpose, would have drawn the sting save for the strictly limited purposes which the judge identified.

20.76   A similar point arose in *Bullas*[111] where the applicant, a trainer with St. John's Ambulance, was convicted of offences involving sexual abuse of five young boys who attended training sessions. The applicant denied the offences in interview, stating that he knew the complainants but nothing had occurred. He denied being homosexual and said the thought of the acts made him sick. At trial the prosecution adduced evidence from CW, a male, to the effect that when he was 17 he had a consensual relationship with the applicant when the latter was 21. One of the complainants also gave evidence that he had been with the applicant to a gay bar. The Court of Appeal rejected the argument that evidence tending to show that the applicant had a homosexual disposition was irrelevant as the applicant himself had put his sexual disposition in issue. The jury was entitled to hear evidence to contradict the applicant's denial in interview and at trial that he had any

---

[111] [2012] EWCA Crim 1659.

homosexual disposition and that he engaged in any homosexual acts with young boys, as the complainants had alleged. The position would be no different with a heterosexual male who, for example, sought to bolster his defence that he had not engaged in sexual intercourse with an under-age girl by asserting falsely that he had chosen to live a wholly celibate life, or because of some physical or psychological disability he was incapable of having such sexual relations with any female.

The Court of Appeal did however grant leave on the ground that the trial 20.77 judge should have given a direction on the lines of the strong direction approved by the Court in *R. v IJ*.[112] The Court identified a risk of prejudice only if the jury would be likely to draw an inference that evidence of homosexual disposition tended to show, by reason of that fact alone, that a defendant has a disposition to abuse young boys. The Court accepted that homosexuals have suffered historic prejudice where perhaps illogical inferences have been drawn. Kenneth Parker J said:

> "The question arises whether in 2012 there remains a real risk that such illogical and discriminatory inferences would be drawn."

The Court accepted that in the light of *R. v IJ* it appeared that it was at least arguable that to avoid a risk of unfair prejudice, a more extensive direction should have been given.

The Court that heard the full appeal[113] concurred with Kenneth Parker J's 20.78 encapsulation of the issue. The Court considered that there may be circumstances such as in *R. v IJ* when, to avoid prejudice arising from the admission of the evidence, it will be necessary to provide the jury with an explanation of the use to which the evidence can be put and to warn them against using it for a purpose which is unfairly prejudicial or not logically open to them. However, the Court considered that there was no risk of unfair prejudice in *Bullas*. It regarded the possibility that the jury might have jumped to the conclusion that the appellant was guilty of sexual abuse of children solely upon their finding that he was a homosexual who had been in a close and loving relationship with CW as highly improbable. There had been no scope for misunderstanding. The jury well knew, because they were so directed, that the evidence of CW was admitted to rebut the assertion as to the appellant's sexual preference which the prosecution said was false. The trial judge had made the distinction between inferences which might be drawn from a proved lie on an important issue in the case and propensity to commit sexual offences against young boys. The evidence of CW was only mentioned in connection with the lies issue, and the judge explicitly identified the need to concentrate not on the question whether the appellant was homosexual, but on the issue whether he had committed offences against the complainants.

[112] [2011] EWCA Crim 2734 at [44] per Pitchford LJ.
[113] [2012] EWCA Crim 2451.

Propensity for untruthfulness

20.79   This arises far less than propensity to commit the type of offence charged, and will be relatively rare in the trial of a sexual offence. First, in *Hanson* it was pointed out that propensity to untruthfulness is not the same as propensity to dishonesty. Previous convictions for dishonesty are not necessarily evidence of propensity for untruthfulness. It is confined to lies told by the defendant when committing an offence or when accounting for his behaviour. Secondly, as was explained by the then Lord Chief Justice, Lord Phillips, in *Campbell*,[114] untruthfulness is only likely to be an important matter in issue if telling lies or deception is an element of the offence charged, such as perjury or fraud. However, Lord Phillips did not say it could never apply in other circumstances and there remains some scope for propensity for untruthfulness where a defendant has given a series of false accounts in interview or on oath in respect of earlier occasions, particularly if there is a similar pattern of response to allegations. Where the prosecution are given leave to adduce evidence of untruthfulness, it is essential that the judge directs the jury as to the limited use to which such evidence may be put, and the fact that untruthfulness on one occasion does not necessarily mean untruthfulness on another.

Section 101(1)(e)—evidence of "substantial probative value in relation to an important matter in issue"

20.80   Section 101(1)(e) provides that evidence of the defendant's bad character is admissible if:

> "it has substantial probative value in relation to an important matter in issue between the defendant and co-defendant."

This is more restrictive than s.101(1)(d), as the evidence has to have substantial probative value in relation to an important issue, as opposed to relevance to an important matter. If evidence of bad character is only marginally probative or only probative in relation to a minor matter, it should not be admitted.[115] In *Edwards and Rowlands*,[116] the Court of Appeal made it clear that simply because an application is made by a co-defendant, the judge is not bound to admit the evidence. The gateway in s.101(1)(e) must be gone through, and marginally relevant matters should not be admitted through it. In determining an application under s.101(1)(e), analysis with a fine-tooth comb is unlikely to be helpful; it is the context of the case as a whole that matters.

---

[114] *Ellis* [2010] EWCA Crim 163.
[115] *Edwards and Rowlands* [2006] 2 Cr. App. R. 4.
[116] [2006] 2 Cr. App. R. 4.

Although gateway (e) is more restrictive, a defendant whose defence has **20.81** been undermined by a co-defendant may use it to adduce evidence of that co-defendant's bad character, if the evidence has substantial probative value. It cannot be excluded under s.78 of the Police and Criminal Evidence Act 1984 or s.101(3) of the Criminal Justice Act 2003 (under which evidence must not be admitted under gateway (d) or (g) if its admission would have such an adverse effect on the fairness of the proceedings that the court ought not to admit it).[117] The jury is entitled to consider evidence of a co-defendant's bad character when considering the case against that co-defendant, even though the evidence is adduced by another defendant and not by the prosecution. However, the prosecution should not refer to such "windfall" evidence in their closing speech unless it is, in any event, admissible at the prosecution's behest.[118] In *Lawson*,[119] the Court of Appeal held that a co-defendant's previous conviction had been properly admitted under gateway (e) even though its relevance was confined to the co-defendant's truthfulness/credibility, and the conviction was not for an offence which necessarily involved untruthfulness. The appellant had been convicted of manslaughter. The principal defendant pushed the victim into a lake and the victim did not surface. The principal defendant pleaded guilty. The prosecution case was that the appellant and a third defendant encouraged him. These two defendants ran cut-throat defences, although it did not follow that one or the other was guilty. Co-defending counsel put the appellant's conviction for wounding to the appellant in cross-examination. This was done without notice, which was reprehensible because it went against established rules and principles of advocacy and the unannounced cross-examination put the judge in a very difficult position. However, the judge was entitled to admit such evidence under gateway (e) in that it was of substantial probative value to an important matter in issue between the accused. The conduct of the appellant's defence had undermined the co-defendant's defence. The issue of who was telling the truth was of substantial importance to the case as a whole. The conviction was properly before the jury on the issue of truthfulness/credibility. The Court of Appeal did, however, observe that not every conviction or episode of bad character on the part of a witness whose truthfulness or credibility is in issue will be capable of having probative value on that question. The approach adopted in *Lawson*, focusing upon conduct of a co-defendant relevant to his unreliability as a witness, was confirmed in *Rosato*.[120]

[117] But see the surprising but practical decision in *Musone* [2007] EWCA Crim 1237, where it was held that there are limited circumstances where relevant evidence can be excluded after non-compliance with the Criminal Procedure Rules.
[118] *Robinson* [2005] EWCA Crim 3233; [2006] 1 Cr. App. R. 32.
[119] [2006] EWCA Crim 2572.
[120] [2008] EWCA Crim 1243.

Section 101(1)(f)—evidence to correct a false impression given by the defendant

20.82   Gateway (f) applies relatively rarely.[121] In *R. v D, P and U*[122] the Court of Appeal observed that in their Lordships' experience, gateway (f) is "too often invoked". First, a defendant who has on proper analysis done no more than deny the offence is not by doing so giving a false impression to the court for the purposes of gateway (f). If that were true, virtually every defendant would be within the gateway. Gateway (f) and s.105 of the Criminal Justice Act 2003 (which elaborates when gateway (f) applies) are in broad terms concerned with attempts to mislead the court in a way which goes beyond denying the offence, even if the offence subsequently be proved. The Court held that the judge in *D* had been wrong to admit evidence of the appellant's internet searches for child pornography on the basis that the appellant's denial that he had an interest in teenage girls and his claim that his relationship with his niece was honourable had created a false impression which needed to be corrected.

20.83   Furthermore, the false impression must be one which is given *to the court*: see s.105(1)(a). It may be given via a police interview, but only if that interview is given in evidence: see s.105(2)(b). If, however, the defendant withdraws the impression or dissociates himself from it, gateway (f) ceases to apply: see s.105(3). In *P*, the trial judge had ignored the effect of s.105(1)(a) and (3) in that she had been invited on the appellant's behalf to edit the passage in the interview where the appellant had stated that he preferred females. This would have withdrawn any false impression. The judge overlooked the fact that a defendant is entitled to disassociate himself from what he said earlier in interview.

20.84   A good example of gateway (f) being opened by a defendant's answers in interview is *Somanathan*.[123] The appellant was charged with twice raping a woman who attended a Hindu Temple where he was a priest. The trial judge acceded to a prosecution application under s.101(1)(f) to call a witness who was involved in the running of a Hindu Temple where the appellant had previously worked. The appellant had told the police that he had left his employment at that Temple of his own accord. The witness gave evidence that the appellant had been dismissed from his post because he had lied and because his behaviour towards women had given cause for concern. The Court of Appeal held that the gateway had been opened, and the prosecution was entitled to adduce from the witness a full account of what, according to the witness, brought the contract to an end. Part of the false impression given

---

[121] For a clear cut case where gateway (f) applied, see *Verdol* [2015] EWCA Crim 502 where the defendant, on trial for numerous sex offences, had claimed that, apart from breaching immigration rules, he was otherwise a "God-fearing and law-abiding" man. He also claimed his mobile phones would support his alibi. When examined, they revealed class A drug dealing.
[122] [2011] EWCA Crim 1474 at [21] per Hughes LJ.
[123] [2006] 1 Cr. App. R. 19.

by the appellant in interview and, as it turned out later, by calling seven character witnesses, was that he was a priest who had never behaved inappropriately towards female worshippers at his Temple.

However, the prosecution should be careful about leading evidence of **20.85** assertions or denials by the defendant in interview with the police, with a view to setting up an application under gateway (f). In *R. v B (Richard William)*[124] the appellant, in answer to a question, had denied in interview that he had ever been interested in children in a sexual way. The prosecution deliberately led this evidence at trial so as to enable them to apply under gateway (f) to adduce evidence that the appellant had shown a child a dirty book. The Court of Appeal expressly disapproved of this tactic.

If evidence is admissible only under gateway (f) and not also under **20.86** gateway (d), considerable care is required in summing up because the jury must be warned that the evidence is not capable of being used as evidence of propensity. See also cases on the relevance of homosexual sexual disposition, discussed in paras 20.58 and following, above.

Section 101(1)(g)—the defendant has made an attack on another person's character[125]

This gateway is wider than that formerly contained in s.1(f)(ii) of the **20.87** Criminal Evidence Act 1898, as it encompasses an attack on "any person", not necessarily a witness or a victim. However, the Court of Appeal has said that it would be unusual for evidence to be admitted through this gateway where the attack is on the character of a person who is not a witness or a victim, particularly where the allegation was made in interview and not pursued at trial.[126] Another contrast to the previous law is that this gateway, as with gateway (f), is opened even if the defendant does not give evidence.[127] In *Ball*,[128] the Court of Appeal accepted that the defendant's use in interview of the epithet "slag" to describe the complainant was sufficient to trigger s.101(1)(g) in a case where two violent rapes were alleged and the defence was consensual intercourse after heavy alcohol consumption. In interview, the appellant had told the police that most of the men in the local public house had had sexual intercourse with the complainant. He criticised her sexual promiscuity in very disparaging terms, stating "She's a bag really, you know what I mean, a slag". The judge took the view that this amounted to an attack on the complainant's character for the purposes of s.101(1)(g), as that concept is explained and expanded in s.106. The Court of Appeal held that the answers given by the appellant in interview purported to be exculpatory

[124] [2008] EWCA Crim 1850.
[125] s.106 of the Act elaborates on the application of this gateway.
[126] cp. *Nelson* [2006] EWCA Crim 3412 (suggestion that neighbour was a drug user in interview would not have been sufficient to justify admission of defendant's bad character under gateway (g)).
[127] cf. *Butterwasser* [1948] 1 K.B. 4.
[128] [2005] EWCA Crim 2826 (an appeal consolidated with *Renda*).

in nature (there was no rape: it was consent) but were said by the Crown, with every justification, to provide evidence which indicated an attitude to the complainant which carried with it the implication that the appellant believed that she would have agreed to sexual intercourse with him, and any other man, at any time and in any circumstances, and that if and when she purported to be unwilling to have sexual intercourse, any such refusal should be disregarded as quite meaningless. In reality, answers which might have been treated as exculpatory, and possibly not admissible on that basis, properly formed part of the prosecution case and were "evidence given of an imputation" under the terms of s.106(1)(c).

20.88   In *R. v D, P, and U*,[129] the appellant *D* had asserted to the police, and maintained at trial, that far from abusing his niece, he had to discourage her when she made inappropriate approaches to him. The issue arose as to whether the judge had properly admitted evidence of child pornography on the ground that the appellant had made an attack upon another's character. The Court of Appeal was satisfied that gateway (g) had been opened. The judge did not direct the jury on this gateway but, as he had explained the potential relevance of the evidence under gateway (d), that omission was of no assistance to the appellant.

20.89   If this gateway is engaged, it can lead to admission of general evidence of bad character.[130] A classic example of the gateway in operation is where there is an allegation that the police have conspired to set up a defendant. In *Williams*,[131] the Court of Appeal held that such an allegation was sufficient to justify the admission of the appellant's bad character in respect of his trial for breach of a sexual offences prevention order. Where complainant and defendant give two widely divergent accounts, effectively attacking each other's characters, the courts will be inclined to take the view that it is only right and fair that the defendant should not be able to besmirch the complainant's character whilst presenting himself by implication as a person of good character. This time-hallowed rule, preserved in gateway (g), can apply even where a judge has refused to admit a similar conviction under s.101(1)(d), and accordingly must warn the jury not to treat the conviction as evidence of propensity. This occurred in *Lewis* where the judge had allowed the prosecution to adduce evidence of the appellant's conviction of gross indecency 20 years before, after the appellant had attacked the character of the complainant, a 14-year-old boy, by claiming that the only sexual misconduct had been by the boy. There is clear authority that in such circumstances, where the bad character evidence is admissible under gateway (g) and not gateway (d), the jury should be directed that the relevance of the evidence is restricted to the defendant's credibility, and that they should not consider it as showing propensity.[132]

[129] [2011] EWCA Crim 1474.
[130] *Singh* [2008] EWCA Crim 2140.
[131] [2007] EWCA Crim 1951.
[132] *Lafayette* [2008] EWCA Crim 3238.

Is the suggestion in a non-consensual sex case that the complainant consented "an attack upon a person's character"?

Before the implementation of the Criminal Justice Act 2003, it was settled   **20.90**
law that a defendant advancing the defence that a complainant consented
would not have been making an "imputation" on the complainant's character, even if that consent amounted to demeaning behaviour. The authority for
this proposition was *Turner*,[133] which survived intact even when considered
by the House of Lords in *Selvey v DPP*.[134] In *Selvey* the House of Lords,
whilst holding that "imputation" included imputations which were necessarily part of a defence, still managed to approve *Turner*. Could it be that this
anomaly[135] has survived the implementation of the new regime governing
evidence of a defendant's bad character?

The trial judge in *Ball*,[136] in a ruling given after the implementation of the   **20.91**
2003 Act, refused to admit the evidence of bad character on the basis,
advanced by the prosecution, that the appellant had made a direct attack
upon the credibility of the complainant based on the appellant's instructions
that the allegations of rape were fabricated. The Court of Appeal held that
the judge's approach to this part of the case was impeccable. But this was not
the ratio of the decision and the point was not closely scrutinised by the
Court of Appeal. We submit that the rule in *Turner* has gone, and that a
suggestion that the complainant consented *may* amount to an attack on her
character for the purposes of gateway (g). Much will depend on the
circumstances in which it is contended that consent was given. Many consent
defences will necessarily involve an attack upon the character of the
complainant. By putting an alternative scenario based upon the defendant's
instructions, a defence advocate, consistent with their duty, will in reality by
necessary implication be making a strong imputation against the complainant. A good recent example is *Craig Pedley*.[137] The applicant had been
convicted of two rapes. The trial judge had allowed the prosecution to adduce
the applicant's convictions for wounding and domestic burglaries under
gateway (g), having taken the view the applicant's case was, in reality, that the
complainant had lied when she alleged that he had raped her and that other
aspects of her account were also untrue. He concluded that this was a direct
attack upon her character. In his judgment the jury was entitled to know the
character of the man who was alleging she had fabricated her evidence. The

---

[133] (1945) 30 Cr. App. R. 9.
[134] [1970] A.C. 304.
[135] So described by Professor John Spencer, *Evidence of Bad Character*, 2nd edn (Oxford: Hart Publishing, 2009), para.4.122. Professor Spencer provides an extreme example, *Hutchinson* (1986) 82 Cr. App. R. 51, where a defendant accused of rape claimed that the daughter of the house consented to sex with him when shortly before, she had overheard her parents and her brother being killed by an intruder. Under the old law this was not an imputation upon her character!
[136] [2005] EWCA Crim 2826.
[137] [2014] EWCA Crim 848.

Court of Appeal rejected the submission on behalf of the applicant that this was no more than an emphatic denial. It was by implication an allegation of fabrication. The Court observed that in *Hanson* the Court of Appeal had indicated that the pre-2003 authorities would continue to apply when assessing whether an attack has been made on another person's character to the extent that they are compatible with s.106 of the 2003 Act. The Court then referred to *Jones*[138] and *Alan Carl Owen*[139] which make it clear this is the proper approach whether the attack on an important witness's character is explicit or by implication.

Exclusionary Discretion under Section 101(3)

20.92 Section 101(3) provides:

"The court must not admit evidence under subsection (1)(d) or (g) if, on an application by the defendant to exclude it, it appears to the court that the admission of the evidence would have such an adverse effect on the fairness of the proceedings that the court ought not to admit it."

In *Hanson,* which focused upon admissibility on the basis of propensity, the Court of Appeal identified a non-exhaustive list of factors that a judge might take into account when considering under s.101(3) the fairness of the proceedings:

(i) the degree of similarity between the previous conviction and the offence charged;

(ii) the respective gravity of the past and present offences; and

(iii) the strength of the prosecution case. If there is no or very little other evidence against a defendant, it is unlikely to be just to admit previous convictions, whatever they are. Previous convictions cannot be used to bolster a weak case.

It follows that the strength of the rest of the prosecution case is always a highly relevant factor.[140] The strength of the prosecution case may be difficult to evaluate until some of the prosecution witnesses have given their evidence. In those circumstances, it may be wise for the trial judge to postpone his ruling.[141]

20.93   Whilst the judge must weigh up the respective gravity of the previous convictions compared to the current allegation when considering the fairness of the proceedings, it does not follow that the admission in evidence of convictions of a very grave offence or offences will render a fair trial

---

[138] (1924) Cr. App. Rep. 17 at p.117, where the Lord Chief Justice stated that it was one thing for the applicant to deny that he had acted as alleged, but another thing entirely to suggest that the whole allegation against him was a deliberate and elaborate concoction on the part of the principal witness.

[139] (1986) 83 Cr. App. R. 104.

[140] *Brima*[2007] 1 Cr. App. R. 24.

[141] *Giyma*[2007] EWCA Crim 429. The Court of Appeal declined the invitation to set out hard and fast rules in *R. v HSD* [2006] EWCA Crim 1703.

impossible. Highly probative evidence is bound to be prejudicial in the popular sense of the word. The issue is whether the evidence would be unfairly prejudicial. The judge has to consider the fairness of the trial, not only from the point of view of the defendant, but also from the point of view of the prosecution. There will be cases where there is no reason why the jury should be deprived of critical and cogent evidence of a defendant's propensity to behave in just the way alleged by the prosecution in respect of the allegations in the trial. *Witty*[142] was such a case. The applicant had been convicted of three counts of rape of three different women. Some 14 months earlier the applicant had been convicted of three further rapes and a sexual assault committed against different women. At trial, the defence did not dispute that the convictions were admissible under gateway (d) as they amounted to evidence of propensity to engage in sexual intercourse or other sexual activity without consent. However, reliance was placed on s.101(3). In particular, it was contended that the prejudicial impact upon the applicant's case would be so extreme that it would be totally unrealistic to expect the jury to approach the current allegations with open minds. It was submitted that if the jury was informed of the number and nature of the earlier convictions the result of the trial would be a foregone conclusion. It was inconceivable to expect the jury in those circumstances (even if properly and robustly directed by the judge) to fairly and impartially consider the current allegations on their merits. The Court of Appeal held this argument to be wholly misconceived. It agreed with the judge's analysis that to have excluded the evidence of the previous convictions would, in the circumstances of the case, have made the trial unfair. The safeguard was the clarity and prominence of the directions which the judge gave.

In *Witty*, the probative value of the previous convictions was extremely **20.94** powerful given the nature of the defence which was being advanced: in the case of two complainants, that the incident never took place and had been invented; in the third case, that intercourse took place and was consensual. In contrast, *Benabbou*[143] provides an example of a case where, although the evidence of a previous offence of rape was technically admissible, the Court of Appeal held that it should not have been admitted in evidence as its admission must have been highly prejudicial to the fairness of the proceedings. Reliance was placed upon s.101(3). In *Benabbou* the appellant was tried in respect of offences of sexual assault and assault by penetration. The allegations related to wholly separate episodes and different complainants. The first alleged offence was said to have occurred after an impromptu party at a flat where the complainant was sleeping. The second allegation related to events at a flat after the appellant had played "truth or dare" with the complainant and her partner. His defence to the first allegation was that nothing had happened between him and the complainant and he was the

---

[142] [2014] EWCA Crim 2333 (non-counsel application, Spencer J giving the judgment of the court).
[143] [2012] EWCA Crim 1256.

victim of a false identification. His defence to the second was that nothing had happened between himself and the complainant and the allegation was being made by the complainant and her partner because they had stolen £100 in cash and his mobile phone.

20.95   At trial, the prosecution applied successfully to adduce evidence that in 2002 the appellant had been convicted of rape, in order to demonstrate a propensity on his part to commit offences of the kind with which he was now charged. The victim on that occasion, described as a drunk lesbian female, was stopped in the street by two offenders, one being the appellant. She was pulled into a car and driven to a house where she was raped in turn by the two offenders whilst a third person held her down.

20.96   The defence had submitted that the rape conviction should not be admitted. It was a single offence committed some eight years before the two offences now being tried. The circumstances of the rape were markedly different. On the earlier occasion the appellant had not been acting alone but as one of three offenders. The victim had been a complete stranger. She had been encountered in the street and taken in a vehicle to a place in which she had been raped not once but twice and with the co-operation of a third party. The only truly common feature was that the earlier rape constituted an assault of a sexual nature. The prosecution contended that there were similarities between the earlier rape and the alleged offences in that each was an opportunistic offence committed at night in relation to a young woman who was vulnerable because she was either drunk or asleep.

20.97   The judge concluded that there was sufficient similarity between the earlier rape and the current offences, in particular the assault by penetration, to render evidence of it admissible. Maddison J, giving the judgment of the Court of Appeal, stated that, though the rape bore some similarities to the current offences, they were limited and there were also dissimilarities. It followed that the probative value of the earlier rape in establishing propensity was limited. Although it was technically admissible under gateway (d), the admission of the evidence must have had a highly prejudicial effect upon the fairness of the trial. The circumstances of the offence, involving as it did participation in a multiple rape of a vulnerable stranger picked up in a street, was in the Court's view such as potentially to distract the jury from considering and indeed blind them to the issues in the case.

20.98   The Court of Appeal's conclusion in *Benabbou* was, as Maddison J pointed out, very much a decision on the particular facts of that case involving questions of fact and degree. As Rose LJ stated in *Hanson*, circumstances demonstrating probative force are not confined to those showing striking similarity. The decision is, however, a reminder of the potential prejudice of admitting evidence of a previous offence of a more serious nature than the allegations at the trial.

20.99   Section 101(4) of the Act provides that when a court is determining whether to exclude evidence of bad character under s.101(3), it must have regard in particular to the length of time between the events said to constitute the bad character evidence and the offences with which the defendant is charged. In *Imiela*[144] the Court of Appeal upheld convictions of rape, indecent assault and buggery which were alleged to have occurred on Christmas Day 1987. In March 2003 the applicant was convicted of a number of offences of rape which had occurred in 2001 or 2002. As a consequence of his conviction of these rapes, the applicant's DNA was obtained and retained upon a police database. Some years went by, and after a cold case review it was discovered that the DNA in the semen taken from the 1987 complainant's vagina and anus matched the applicant's DNA. The match probability was one in a billion. When in 2010 the applicant was first interviewed under caution about this matter, after comprehensive disclosure, he declined to answer any questions put to him. In the applicant's defence statement, he admitted for the first time that he had engaged in vaginal and oral intercourse with the complainant, but claimed it was consensual. In the same statement he denied that anal intercourse had taken place.

At trial, the prosecution applied under s.101(1)(d) to adduce evidence of   **20.100** the applicant's 2003 convictions for rape on the basis that it showed he had a propensity to commit such crimes. The prosecution also alleged that the circumstances of the offences leading to the rape convictions bore strong similarities to those surrounding the alleged attack upon the 1987 complainant. The evidence was relevant to the issue of consent. The prosecution also submitted that it was relevant to rebut the suggestion that the buggery had not taken place.

The applicant's counsel sought leave to appeal from the full Court of   **20.101** Appeal on the basis of the time that had elapsed between 1987 (the time of the allegation) and 2001 or 2002 (the time of the rape convictions). The Court held that the evidence of the later convictions was properly admitted, and the admission of the convictions would not have had such an adverse effect upon the fairness of the trial that they ought to have been excluded. In particular, the Court acknowledged that the intervening years amounted to a significant period, but observed that the applicant had been in prison serving sentences for serious offences for some of that time, which drew some of the sting from the point made by the applicant that a long time had lapsed between the relevant offences. There could not be any criticism of the summing-up whatsoever. The trial judge had given directions about the probative value of the convictions and the caution with which the jury should proceed in relation to those convictions in trenchant terms.

In written grounds of appeal, reliance had been placed upon the fact that   **20.102** the evidence relating to the convictions for rape in 2003 was presented to the jury by adducing witness statements of the complainants in those cases. The judge declined a defence request that the witnesses should be brought to court for cross-examination. The Court of Appeal gave this point short shrift. In the applicant's trial in 2003 there was no dispute but that each of the

---

[144] [2013] EWCA Crim 2171.

complainants had been raped. The defence was mistaken identity. The Court was unable to see why the complainants from the 2003 case were necessary live witnesses to describe events about which essentially there was no dispute.

The risk of satellite litigation

20.103   Another important factor, in considering the exclusionary discretion under s.101(3), is the risk that the bad character evidence might spawn unnecessarily complicating collateral issues. There is always a need to ensure that the bad character evidence will not deflect the jury from focusing upon the critical issues in the case. In *McKenzie*,[145] Toulson LJ identified these problems and added the warning that "if allegations of previous misconduct are few in number, they may well fail to show propensity even if they are true, but the greater the plethora of collateral allegations, the greater the risk of the trial losing its proper focus."

20.104   It follows that it may be necessary to evaluate the potential nature and complexity of the bad character evidence so as to be able to decide whether it might distract the jury. Clearly, the length of time that the evidence will take may be a significant factor. In *O'Dowd*,[146] the appellant was convicted of rape, sexual assault, false imprisonment, threatening to kill and poisoning in respect of one complainant after a trial at the Central Criminal Court that lasted six-and-a-half months. The bad character evidence (evidence of three previous allegations of rape), which was disputed by the appellant, took up 38 per cent of the trial days on which evidence was heard. There were strong similarities between the three earlier allegations (an acquittal in 1983, a conviction in 1988 and a case which had been stayed as an abuse of process) and all three allegations were admissible under s.101(1)(d), both so as to negative the coincidence of four similar independent allegations and as evidence of propensity to rape. There was no proper criticism on appeal of the trial judge's decision that the s.101(1)(d) criteria had been satisfied and that all the allegations were cross-admissible, or of his directions to the jury on how to approach the bad character evidence. Indeed, there was a powerful argument that to see the appellant's repeated conduct in its proper light so as to be able properly to assess whether it negatived coincidence, the jury should hear evidence in respect of all three earlier allegations. They contained strikingly similar features, such as repulsed sexual advances, detention against the victims' will and claims that the allegations were made up to cover up the victims' own misconduct. The fact that the previous allegations were admissible as highly relevant evidence without recourse to propensity enhanced their probative value and reduced the risk of any prejudice.

---

[145] [2008] EWCA Crim 758 (a case of death by dangerous driving).
[146] [2009] EWCA Crim 905.

The appeal focused rather on the matters that must be taken into account   20.105
under s.101(3). The Court of Appeal concluded that the trial judge had not
given adequate consideration to "the cumulative effect of the introduction of
three separate contested issues into the trial on its overall length and on the
jury, or how the evidence might be timetabled or truncated" and that "if ever
there was a case to illustrate the dangers of satellite litigation this is it". On
hearing that the estimate of the length of trial was four months, the judge
should have taken steps to limit or exclude the bad character evidence, such
as picking the best of the three allegations, setting a firmer timetable and
using s.74(3) of PACE (conviction as evidence of commission of offence). The
Court also criticised the judge for failing to direct the jury adequately as to
the weaknesses in the bad character evidence.

O'Dowd was a case on unusual facts which are most unlikely to be   20.106
repeated. It would have been impossible to predict all the matters that
contrived to prolong the trial. The length of the trial was due to special
circumstances, some of which were not foreseeable at the outset. In particular, time was lost due to changes in counsel, the appellant seeking to
represent himself and then re-instructing counsel. Further time was also lost
because the appellant had health problems and underwent surgery. A juror
who had a pre-booked holiday had to be accommodated. This length of trial
was highly undesirable. However, presumably, this was not a case where the
previous allegations had become difficult to follow or where collateral
allegations had lost their potential probative value so that the trial risked
losing its proper focus.

Furthermore, it must be borne in mind that there is a real danger that a   20.107
manipulative and unco-operative defendant will seek to abuse the system so
as to try and make a case as unmanageable as possible. A premium should
not be place upon conduct such as sacking counsel and claiming illness. In
the event, the prosecution did not apply for a re-trial.[147]

Section 78 of the Police and Criminal evidence Act 1984

It would appear that s.78 of PACE applies to bad character evidence adduced   20.108
by the prosecution, although its application may not add significantly to
s.101(3).[148] Where the prosecution seek to adduce bad character evidence in

---

[147] In his illuminating commentary upon *O'Dowd* at [2009] Crim. L.R. 828, Professor
Ormerod, when observing that the Court of Appeal was clearly determined to express a strong
message regarding case management, expressed the view that is debatable whether it had chosen
the right case in which to do it, taking into account the conduct of the accused. On the
assumption that the CPS did not apply for a retrial because of concerns about the complainants
undergoing a harrowing ordeal yet again, he suggests that if similar circumstances were to recur,
consideration should be given to using the hearsay provisions in s.114(1)(d) of the Criminal
Justice Act 2003.

[148] *Highton* [2005] EWCA Crim 1985.

respect of a co-defendant, s.78 (or severance) may be the only remedy to which the defendant can resort.[149]

JURY DIRECTION

20.109   Once evidence is admitted through one gateway, it may transpire that it is also relevant in respect of another. For instance, it may be relevant not only to credibility but also to propensity.[150] However, there will be cases where there is a risk that the jury will follow a line of reasoning which is not applicable in that particular case. A classic example is where a jury might seek to use bad character evidence as evidence as propensity, where its only basis of admissibility is another gateway, such as (g). In such a case the jury should be specifically warned not to take that route.[151]

20.110   A jury warning along the lines suggested in *Hanson*,[152] as modified by *Campbell*,[153] is crucial. In particular, the jury should be warned not only of the relevance of bad character evidence to the case and the limits as how they can use that evidence, but also against attaching too much weight to it, let alone concluding that the defendant is guilty simply because of his bad character. On the assumption that the judge has given the correct warnings, the Court of Appeal will only interfere if the trial judge's decision-making has been *Wednesbury* unreasonable.[154]

CROSS-ADMISSIBILITY AND BAD CHARACTER

20.111   The cross-admissibility of evidence between different counts in an indictment is a separate question from that of joinder. There are separate statutory regimes, one governing the joinder and severance of counts in an indictment, and the other, derived from ss.101 and 103 of the Criminal Justice Act 2003, governing cross-admissibility between counts.[155] *Ludlow v Metropolitan Commissioner*[156] remains the leading authority on severance. Nevertheless, bad character evidence is, of course, highly relevant to issues of (a) joinder and severance, (b) cross-admissibility, and (c) the risk of collusion and/or contamination. A number of Court of Appeal decisions have underlined the need for the judge and counsel to address these issues before closing

---

[149] *R. v B* [2009] EWCA Crim 1690.
[150] *Highton* [2005] EWCA Crim 1985.
[151] *Lafayette* [2008] EWCA Crim 3238.
[152] [2005] EWCA Crim 824; [2005] 2 Cr. App. R. 21 (299).
[153] [2007] EWCA Crim 1472, where Lord Phillips CJ questioned the desirability of the judge identifying the gateway or gateways through which the bad character evidence has been admitted by reference to the wording of the Act.
[154] *Cushing* [2006] All E.R. (D.) 22; *Chand* [2007] EWHC 90 (Admin).
[155] *Powell* [2014] EWCA Crim 642 at [35] per Jackson LJ.
[156] [1971] A.C. 29.

speeches.[157] It will assist the jury if they are provided with a written direction on these issues.

The question frequently arises in sex cases as to whether the evidence of one complainant can be used by the jury in support of allegations made by another or other complainants. Section 112(2) of the Criminal Justice Act 2003 provides: **20.112**

> "Where a defendant is charged with two or more offences in the same criminal proceedings, this Chapter (except section 101(3)) has effect as if each offence were charged in separate proceedings; and references to the offence with which the defendant is charged are to be read accordingly."

It follows that evidence in relation to one count in an indictment is capable of being admitted as bad character evidence in relation to any other count in the indictment *if* it meets any of the criteria or gateways in s.101(1) of the 2003 Act. However, that is a pre-condition for cross-admissibility. Normally, cross-admissibility will depend on whether the evidence of each complainant is relevant to an important matter in issue between the prosecution and the defence in respect of the allegations. It follows that cross-admissibility will usually depend upon gateway (d) and will turn on propensity and/or the unlikelihood of coincidence.

The decision in Chopra

The issue of cross-admissibility arose in *Chopra*,[158] where the Court of Appeal stated that s.112(2) must be followed and that the criteria in s.101(1)(d) had been met in that case. The appellant was a dentist who was tried on an indictment which alleged indecent touching of three teenage patients over a period spanning 10 years. In each case, the complainant alleged that the appellant had deliberately placed his hand on her breast and squeezed it. The appellant denied he had done any such thing and maintained that nothing resembling in any way a deliberate squeezing of the breast had occurred.   **20.113**

The trial judge, without reference to the bad character regime, held that the evidence of the several complainants was cross-admissible provided collusion or contamination between them could be excluded. On appeal, it was submitted that the jury should not have been permitted to treat the evidence of one complainant as supportive of the evidence of another. The Court of Appeal was, however, satisfied that the evidence in respect of each allegation was, as the trial judge ruled, available to the jury to support the other allegations if the jury accepted it and if collusion and contamination were excluded.   **20.114**

The evidence of the several complainants was cross-admissible if, but only if, it was relevant to an important matter in issue between the defendant and   **20.115**

---

[157] *R. v SW* [2011] EWCA Crim 2463; *R. v AT* [2013] EWCA Crim 1850.
[158] [2006] EWCA Crim 2133.

the prosecution. The present case was one in which quite clearly, if the evidence did establish a propensity in the defendant occasionally to molest young female patients in the course of dental examination, that did make it more likely that he committed the several offences charged. It followed that the jury could treat the evidence of one complainant as being supportive of another if they were sure the evidence of that first complainant was true.

20.116 The Court held that in determining admissibility, the common law rules relating to propensity and similar fact evidence no longer apply. The judgment then focused principally upon whether the evidence on each count was capable of establishing propensity. This led the Court to an assumption that it would be necessary for the jury to be sure in respect of one count before they could bring it to bear in respect of another count (the sequential approach). This assumption appears to have been made on the basis of a misunderstanding of the width of gateway (d), which is not confined to propensity, but encompasses all evidence relevant to an important matter in issue between the defendant and the prosecution. If the Court's assumption were correct, pooling of evidence could no longer take place even where there were wholly independent similar allegations with no evidence of collusion or innocent contamination (the pooling approach). Could it be that the bad character provisions, in abolishing the old common law similar fact rules, prevented the prosecution from submitting that the jury could, if they were able to exclude the possibility of contamination and/or collusion, take the view that it would be an affront to common sense to conclude that several complainants had independently made similar false allegations? The point derives its strength from the fact of several independent complaints rather than from the fact that a particular allegation, once proved, can support another.

20.117 Subsequent cases in the Court of Appeal served to underline the point that s.101(1)(d) is not confined to propensity. For instance, there may be strong circumstantial evidence that the offences were committed by the same person, and that the defendant is that person. In *Wallace*[159] the evidence adduced by the prosecution in relation to a series of robberies was such as to show that they must have been committed by the same person or persons. It followed that the evidence in respect of each robbery was bad character evidence for the purposes of s.98, and could only be admitted in relation to the other counts if it met the criteria in one of the s.101 gateways. At trial, the issue of bad character did not see the light of day. The Court of Appeal took the view that where there was evidence of such similarities, then inevitably the evidence was admissible under s.101(1)(d). Scott Baker LJ, in distinguishing between propensity and other legitimate lines of reasoning under s.101(1)(d), said:

> " . . . the important matter in issue was not whether the appellant had a propensity to commit offences or to be untruthful but whether the circumstantial

---

[159] [2007] EWCA Crim 1760.

evidence linking him to the robberies, when viewed as a whole, pointed to his participation in and guilt of each offence."

Freeman and Crawford

The uncertainty engendered by *Chopra* was ended by the welcome decision of   **20.118**
the Court of Appeal in *Freeman and Crawford*.[160] It remains the case that the jury must approach each count in a sequential manner if cross-admissibility depends only upon propensity, but where the evidence is relevant and admissible in itself as evidence to support the truth of other allegations, the jury will be entitled to consider that evidence together with the other evidence. It follows that, in those circumstances, pooling is the appropriate approach. Latham LJ explained this as follows:

> "In some of the judgements since *Hanson*, the impression may have been given that the jury, in its decision making process in cross-admissibility cases should first determine whether it is satisfied on the evidence in relation to one of the counts of the defendant's guilt before it can move on to using the evidence in relation to that count in dealing with any other count in the indictment. A good example is the judgement of this court in *R v S*.[161] We consider that this is too restrictive an approach. Whilst the jury must be reminded that it has to reach a verdict on each count separately, it is entitled, in determining guilt in respect of any count, to have regard to the evidence in regard to any other count, or any other bad character evidence if that evidence is admissible and relevant in the way we have described. It may be that in some cases the jury will find it easier to decide the guilt of a defendant on the evidence relating to that count alone. That does not mean that it cannot, in other cases, use the evidence in relation to the other count or counts to help it decide on the defendant's guilt in respect of the count that it is considering. To do otherwise would fail to give proper effect to the decision on admissibility."

Where the evidence is capable of being probative in relation to another   **20.119**
count, in the sense that it supports the truth of the other allegation because of its similarities, it is not always helpful to concentrate on propensity. This is well illustrated by the case of *Freeman*, where the appellant had been charged with sexual offences committed on separate occasions against two young girls. In the wake of *Chopra*, the trial judge had unsurprisingly directed the jury to adopt the sequential approach and had told them that they could consider one complaint as providing support for the other *only* if they were satisfied that it was proved. In the Court of Appeal's view, the evidence given by each child was sufficiently similar for it to be capable of

---

[160] [2008] EWCA Crim 1863; [2009] 1 Cr. App. R. 11. For a very clear analysis of the position following *Freeman and Crawford* and *McAllister,* see Professor Ormerod's commentary on *Freeman and Crawford* in [2009] Crim. L.R. 104.

[161] [2008] EWCA Crim 544. See also *Field* [2016] EWCA Crim 385 where, in respect of a trial on four counts of engaging in sexual activity in the presence of a child (s.11 SOA 2003) and one of exposure, the Court of Appeal concluded that where identity was in issue the judge should have directed the jury that they needed to be sure that the appellant was the person involved in at least one alleged incident of misconduct before they could rely on the other evidence as cross-admissible.

supporting the evidence of the other. It followed that admissibility under s.101(1)(d) was not confined to propensity and that was an unnecessarily restrictive approach. The principle clarified in *Freeman* is now well-established, although it is on occasions overlooked.[162]

Chopra revisited and recategorised

20.120   Differently constituted Courts of Appeal have taken the opportunity to reconsider *Chopra* and have reached the same conclusion, namely that it was not primarily a propensity case but a classic case of separate sexual allegations by wholly independent complainants. Moses LJ pointed out in *McAllister*,[163] when considering *Chopra*, that (i) the prosecution was not seeking to show propensity, (ii) the trial judge had correctly directed the jury that absent evidence that the witnesses had colluded, or that their evidence had been contaminated by gossip, they were entitled to deploy the fact that a number of different complainants had made similar accusations, and (iii) *Chopra* demonstrates the danger of attaching a wrong label to a case. If a case is categorised as a propensity type case, *Hanson* directions[164] have to be given (the sequential approach) and the jury have to be sure in respect of one allegation before they can deploy it in relation to another. *Chopra* was not such a case. It was a case where the complaint in one allegation strengthened the cogency of the evidence in relation to the other offences.

What if the evidence on each count is cross-admissible both on the basis that it strengthens the cogency of the other allegations and as evidence of propensity?

20.121   This situation will arise with regularity in sex cases where there are separate allegations by different complainants. Indeed, arguably *Chopra* and *Freeman* are examples where the evidence was cross-admissible on both bases, but where the more appropriate course was a general direction on cross-admissibility as was in fact given by the trial judge in *Chopra,* and no propensity direction. A jury direction on both will be complicated, and will involve covering both the pooling approach and the sequential approach. Experience has shown that that where there is little to choose between the strength of the evidence supporting each of the counts, the propensity direction may only serve to confuse because (i) the direction, if given, will be burdened with conditional clauses and (ii) in any event, the real question for

---

[162] *O'Leary* [2013] EWCA Crim 1371, where evidence of the circumstances of the appellant's transactions in respect of two separate victims of dementia was admissible on the issue as to whether he was acting dishonestly towards either of them, provided the jury were sure of the pattern of conduct.
[163] [2008] EWCA Crim 1544.
[164] See para.20.110, above; and see also the Crown Court Compendium 2016, Chapter 12: Bad Character. Chapter 13: Cross-admissibility is reproduced in Appendix G, below.

the jury in such a case is whether the evidence supporting each count tends to strengthen the prosecution case on the others.

In contrast, where the evidence on one count is independently compelling, **20.122** the propensity direction should be given. Furthermore, where the real issue is propensity, the defendant must have the protection of the sequential direction.

Cross-admissibility and the danger of collusion and/or unconscious influence

Where the bad character provisions make the evidence on each count cross- **20.123** admissible on the others, it can be important for the judge to direct the jury carefully about the dangers of innocent contamination as well as guilty collusion. This will apply to all cases where the potential strength of the prosecution point on cross-admissibility derives from the fact that the complaints were truly independent of one another. Such a direction will be necessary unless it is clear that there is no evidence of collusion or innocent contamination whatsoever.

In *N(H) v R.*,[165] the Court of Appeal considered the necessity for the jury **20.124** to exclude collusion or innocent contamination as an explanation for the similarity of complaints in any case where the evidence of the complainants is treated as cross-admissible, before they can assess the force of the argument that they are unlikely to be the product of coincidence. The Court concluded that, save in an obvious case, in which the evidence has plainly excluded the risk of collusion and innocent contamination and no point is taken on behalf of the defendant, a direction to the jury will be required. Where, however, the evidence is not treated as cross–admissible, the need to provide the jury with guidance upon the risk of collusion and/or contamination will depend upon the particular circumstances of the case.

Where there is no evidence from which a jury could reasonably conclude **20.125** that innocent contamination could be an explanation for the complaints, there is no necessity for a warning, as there is no duty upon a judge to address the jury about hypothetical possibilities. In *N(H) v R.*, the Court examined in detail the evidence given at trial and the conduct of the defence. The appeal did not concern allegations of historic abuse which, in con-sequence of possible repetition in the household, or by other innocent means, could have become the learned memory of the complainants. The case put to the complainants was that S's evidence was lies, driven not by a wish to tell the truth but by misplaced loyalty to her mother, and the evidence of L and A was solely motivated by dishonest support for S. It was a case where, as the lines were drawn between the prosecution and the defence, there was no room for innocent contamination. Furthermore, this was not a case where there was a risk of collusion between the witnesses which may have become obscured by the passage of time. The appellant's counsel was unable to

---

[165] [2011] EWCA Crim 730.

demonstrate to the Court a route by which the jury could have sensibly concluded that, while the witnesses had not deliberately put their heads together, they may innocently have learned the complaints they each made shortly afterwards.

20.126   To similar effect is *R. v K*,[166] a case concerning allegations of abuse dating back to the 1970s by two brothers who were neighbours of the appellant. In that case the battleground was drawn between honest attempted recollection by mature adults of incidents many years past in their teenage years, and deliberate dishonesty, said to be at the behest of an ex-partner. The judge had directed the jury to consider each allegation separately without directing them on cross-admissibility. The Court of Appeal held that issue of innocent collusion or contamination did not arise and so there was no merit in the argument that the judge had failed properly to direct the jury of the risk surrounding possible contamination.

20.127   In *R. v AT*,[167] which involved allegations made by two sisters against their father, the Court of Appeal analysed how the case had been put and concluded that innocent contamination was not, realistically, a feature arising in the case; accordingly, no direction on innocent contamination had been necessary. Again, *Coull*[168] is an example of a sex case with multiple complainants where close analysis of the evidence revealed that the appellant had never suggested deliberate or innocent contamination. The judge's directions on cross-admissibility had dealt with the possibility of contamination and had focused upon the critical issue whether the complaints made by the women were truly independent of each other. However, in *R. v P*,[169] a conviction was quashed where, following a trial at which there had been no evidence as to the risk of apparent collusion, it was discovered that a witness had overheard one of the complainants persuading the other to complain.

20.128   In many cases involving family or friends, it is inevitable that the complainants will have had the opportunity to discuss their respective allegations, and they may indeed have done so. However, the fact that complainants are close and know each other well does not mean that their complaints are not independent of each other. As Davis LJ put it in *R. v AT*[170]:

> "It is not the position in sex abuse cases that where two (or more) siblings have had the opportunity to discuss matters (and, indeed, have discussed matters) between themselves, then necessarily their evidence never can be pooled or treated as supportive, the one of the other."

20.129   In *R. v PR*[171] the appellant had been convicted on 24 counts relating to sexual offences (indecent assault and incest) committed against his two

---

[166] [2008] EWCA Crim 3301; [2009] Crim. L.R. 517.
[167] [2013] EWCA Crim 1850.
[168] [2012] EWCA Crim 2893.
[169] [2009] EWCA Crim 1327.
[170] [2013] EWCA Crim 1850 at [91].
[171] [2010] EWCA Crim 2741.

daughters. The judge had given a conventional direction on cross-admissibility explaining the extent to which the evidence of one complainant could support the evidence of the other. He asked the jury to bear in mind that the mere fact that some discussion had taken place or might have taken place between the sisters, or that they might have heard of the nature of the other's complaint, did not automatically mean that the complaints could not be regarded as independent of each other. On appeal, it was submitted on behalf of the appellant that it was not open to the jury in this particular case to find that the complaints were independent, and that the direction on cross-admissibility should not have been given at all. The Court of Appeal rejected this argument, stating that it did not accept that the family context and the fact there had been discussions between the daughters, and between them and their mother, precluded a finding that the complaints were independent of each other. The judge's findings accorded with common sense. It was for the jury to decide whether the discussions that took place amounted to or may have amounted to collusion.

In *Lamb*[172] the appellant, a teacher, had been convicted of sexual activity **20.130** in breach of trust with two 17-year-old girl pupils whom he taught at his school. The Court of Appeal took the view that there was a clear possibility that the two complainants had been consciously or unconsciously influenced in their complaints or their evidence about them by hearing of, and discussing with one another, the circumstances of their respective incidents. The trial judge had directed the jury on dishonest collusion, but had failed to warn the jury that they must take the possibilities of conscious or unconscious influence into account when assessing the weight of the complainants' evidence. Furthermore, the appellant's counsel argued that the judge had over-emphasised the similarities between the incidents, making no allowance for the dissimilarities. The Court of Appeal acknowledged that it is necessary for the judge to give a balanced and accurate account of similarities, as the level of similarity is relevant to the issue of likelihood or unlikelihood of innocent coincidence.

Cross-admissibility—need for counsel and trial judge to consider the issue before summing up

An examination of recent Court of Appeal judgments in sex cases involving **20.131** multiple allegations and/or defendants reveals that in a number, the issue of cross-admissibility was not properly addressed before speeches. In *R. v SW*[173] the Court of Appeal expressed surprise and disappointment that the prosecution considered that the rape allegations ought to be tried with the balance of the indictment when the gulf between the rape and the other allegations was very wide in terms of harm, of culpability and of intervening

---

[172] [2007] EWCA Crim 1766.
[173] [2011] EWCA Crim 2463.

period. Rafferty LJ, giving the judgment of the Court, indicated that each member of the Court would unhesitatingly have ordered severance of the rape counts. The trial judge had been confronted with an apparent agreement between counsel. There had been no detailed discussion of the issue of cross-admissibility, and the judge had given a direction on cross-admissibility in its widest possible form without giving the jury particular guidance as to how to treat the evidence of the various complainants on the various counts. Furthermore, he had not stressed the great gulf in seriousness between the first three counts (the rape allegations) and the remaining counts. The Court of Appeal concluded that the verdicts were unsafe, as the judge's directions did not give the jury proper assistance on the all-important issue of cross-admissibility.

20.132   There may be cases where, because of the strong similarity between the allegations made by separate complainants, there is a significant risk that the jury will treat the allegations as cross-admissible even in the face of a direction to give each count separate consideration. Although, at first blush, a direction to give separate consideration would seem in these circumstances to be overly favourable to the defence, there may be a risk that otherwise the jury will treat the allegations as cross-admissible without the protection of a direction as to the appropriate approach. It will depend upon the circumstances whether such a direction should be given.[174]

20.133   In *R. v AT*,[175] the Court of Appeal stated that it was unsatisfactory that the relatively brief discussion between judge and counsel before speeches meant that there could not have been proper consideration of the appropriate directions to be given on matters such as (in particular) cross-admissibility. The two complainants, who were sisters, had made allegations of sexual abuse against their father, the applicant. The abuse was alleged to have occurred between 1975 and 1983 when J was aged between six and 13 and V between seven and 12. Each alleged that during this period their father would frequently summon them to his bedroom when his wife was away. It was alleged that he would require each of them to take her clothes off and masturbate him to ejaculation. These allegations were covered by specimen counts, counts 1 and 4, alleging indecency with a child contrary to s.1(1) of the Indecency with Children Act 1960. The judge gave a separate treatment direction, but his invitation to "deal with counts one and four first" was suggestive of a cross-admissibility approach. Furthermore, the prosecution had adopted a similar stance in their closing speech. The Court decided, given such circumstances, that it would be appropriate for them to approach matters on the footing that the jury would have pooled the evidence of J and V, at least in considering counts 1 and 4. It is plain that the Court considered

---

[174] *R. v H* [2011] EWCA Crim 2344.
[175] [2013] EWCA Crim 1850, discussed in para.20.127, above. See also *Suleiman (Omar Mohammed)* [2012] EWCA Crim 1569 (not a sex case) in which the Court of Appeal expressed regret that there was no discussion before speeches as to the judge's directions on the admissibility of bad character evidence.

the similarities between the complainants' allegations meant that they were cross-admissible, and the applicant's counsel did not argue otherwise. In a sense, the lack of an express cross-admissibility direction potentially told against the prosecution and not the defence. However, the fact that the jury may have pooled the complainants' evidence inexorably led to the issue of collusion/contamination. On that point, the trial judge's closing remarks in the summing up had encapsulated the central issue in the case, i.e. whether J and V may have discussed matters by way of deliberate collusion so as to fabricate the allegations. Whilst conventionally, the direction might have come earlier in the summing up, it was not necessarily diminished by reason of being placed at the very end, and the convictions were accordingly held to be safe.

Where there is more than one complainant, and the complainants' **20.134** evidence is not cross-admissible, there is no rule of law that the judge must direct the jury that the evidence of one complainant cannot be treated as proof of an allegation against the defendant made by another complainant.[176] The supposed need for such a direction derived from the approach adopted in *R. v D*[177] in the early days of the cross-admissibility jurisprudence. However, the principles and subsequent authorities were reviewed fully by the Court of Appeal in *R. v H*[178] where the Court of Appeal observed that the absence of the suggested direction in *R. v D* has not fared well as a ground of appeal. No complaint could be made about the giving of such a direction, but it is not required as a rule of law. Everything depends on the facts of the particular case, and the danger that the jury might seek to use the evidence of one complainant as evidence of a defendant's guilt on counts concerned only with another complainant.

Cross-admissibility—whether statistical assessment of unlikelihood of coincidence required

Nicholson[179] is a classic case in which a direction on cross-admissibility based **20.135** upon the unlikelihood of coincidence was appropriate. In that case a precondition for such a direction was expert evidence as to the unlikelihood of a number of victims suffering from false memory. However, it is not the law that statistical value must be placed upon the unlikelihood of coincidence before such a direction is appropriate, although any evidence capable of narrowing a range of relevant possibilities is likely to be admissible.

The facts are instructive. The appellant was a nurse who was convicted of **20.136** three counts of sexual assault upon three patients in his care whilst they were

---

[176] *R v F* [2005] EWCA Crim 3217, at [22] per Scott Baker LJ.
[177] [2004] 1 Cr. App. R. 19.
[178] [2011] EWCA Crim 2344, at [31] per Rix LJ; see also the judgment of Spencer J in the case of *Sanderson* [2013] EWCA Crim 2037, an application for leave to appeal in which the Court of Appeal took the view that such a direction could not have been usefully given without causing confusion and potentially undermining the force of the defence case.
[179] [2012] EWCA Crim 1568.

coming round from a general anaesthetic. At trial, there had been an issue as to whether the three complainants were suffering from false memories as a side effect of anaesthesia. Expert evidence was called and it was agreed that such false memories are very rare.

20.137   On appeal, an argument was mounted based on *Norris*[180] that, since proof that one complainant was not suffering from false memories did not make it statistically less likely that the next complainant was, the rarity of false memory in recovering patients, and the unlikelihood of coincidence of false memory in these four patients, should have been treated as inadmissible by the judge to support (i) the proposition that any of the patients were not subject to false memory, or (ii) the proposition that all four were not subject to it. The Court of Appeal held that *Norris* only supported the second proposition, and the defence argument defied experience. Coincidence may be unlikely in a variety of circumstances. One was that the four independent complainants were suffering from the rare phenomenon of false memory of sexual assault. The jury was just as entitled, when considering the evidence of any of the complainants, to have regard to the unlikelihood of a cluster of false memories as they would have been entitled, if the appellant's assertion had been that they had been lying, to have regard to the unlikelihood of the coincidence that they were all liars.

20.138   Before the jury could be entitled to have regard to the unlikelihood of a cluster of victims of false memory, there would have to be, as there was in this case, expert evidence that the coincidence was indeed unlikely, because the jury would not have experience of that matter. What the jury could not do was, on the basis of coincidence, leap to the conclusion that all four complainants were giving true accounts rather than false memories. What was required was an examination of the evidence relevant to each count separately and a separate conclusion upon the reliability of each complainant's memory. In reaching that conclusion upon the evidence relevant to each count, the jury was entitled to have in mind the rarity of false memory and, if they so concluded, the unlikelihood of the coincidence. It followed that the judge had not been wrong to direct the jury that when assessing the evidence of each complainant in order to determine whether they were suffering from false memory, they could have regard to the evidence of the other complainants (and a similar incident admitted as bad character evidence), on the basis that they could consider the unlikelihood of coincidence that four women should each have had false memories of sexual interference in the same hospital in similar circumstances in the relevant period. The judge had made it clear to the jury that that, while the evidence of one complainant might be treated as supportive of another, they were not entitled to lump the evidence together to reach a blanket conclusion on all the counts. Following the judge's direction, there was no prospect that the jury might have fallen into the trap of reasoning improperly so as to reach the conclusion that the rarity

---

[180] [2009] EWCA Crim 2697.

of the coincidence disproved the defence on all three counts, without examining the evidence on each count separately.

NON-DEFENDANT'S BAD CHARACTER

With the exponential rise in the number of prosecutions of sexual cases and the greater focus on the nature of the offending alleged rather than the character of the complainant, an increasing number of complainants will have histories of "misconduct" within the meaning of the bad character provisions, and often may have undergone a disturbed adolescence. Frequently the complainant's credibility will be central to the case, and the defence will wish to cross-examine the complainant about any evidence of misbehaviour in their past in order to undermine their creditworthiness.

20.139

Section 100 of the Criminal Justice Act 2003 regulates the admissibility of evidence of bad character against non-defendants in criminal trials, whether they be witnesses or strangers to the proceedings. The misconduct need not relate to an earlier occasion.[181] The provision is designed to protect the feelings and reputations of witnesses, as well as to prevent fact-finders in trials from being distracted by satellite issues. The test for admissibility is stricter and more rigorous than the test under the old common law.[182] If the evidence has to "do with the alleged facts of the offence", s.100 is not engaged.[183]

20.140

It must be borne in mind that even if the evidence does not constitute bad character evidence, a judge has the power to prevent cross-examination about a subject which can only go to the credit of a witness if the truth of the matters suggested would not, in his opinion, affect the credibility of the witness concerned.[184]

20.141

Unless all parties to the proceedings agree to the evidence being admitted, such evidence is admissible only if (a) it is important explanatory evidence or (b) it has substantial probative value in relation to a matter which (i) is a matter in issue in the proceedings, and (ii) is of substantial importance in the context of the case as a whole. Evidence may be admitted under s.100 if it is directly relevant to an issue in the proceedings or if it bears upon the credibility of a witness who gives evidence about such an issue.[185]

20.142

The case law has made clear that s.100(1)(b) sets a high threshold. In this context, the word "substantial" must mean that the evidence concerned has more than trivial probative value but it is not necessarily of conclusive

20.143

---

[181] See, e.g., *R. v A* [2009] EWCA Crim 513.

[182] *Goddard* [2007] EWCA Crim 3134; *R. v M* [2014] EWCA Crim 1457 (where Beatson LJ analyses the relevant case law).

[183] See s.98 of the Criminal Justice Act 2003.

[184] See *Scott* [2009] EWCA Crim 2457 at [41]; *Sweet-Escott* (1971)55 Cr. App. R. 316; *Funderburk* (1990)90 Cr. App. R. 466. For further discussion, see paras 19.92 and following, above.

[185] *Yaxley-Lennon* [2006] 1 Cr. App. R. 19. See also the Explanatory Notes to the Criminal Justice Act 2003.

probative value.[186] In *Phillips*,[187] the Court of Appeal concluded that the term "substantial probative value" must mean that the bad character evidence has an enhanced quality of proving or disproving a matter in issue. Lord Justice Pitchford observed:

> "What evidence is of substantial probative value should be judged in a fact-sensitive manner in the context of the trial as it appears at the time the application is made."

Section 100(3) stipulates that the court must have regard to the factors set out in paragraphs (a) to (d) of that subsection and any other relevant factors, in assessing the probative value of the evidence for the purposes of s.100(1)(b). The decision whether to admit "non-defendant bad character evidence" is a matter of judgment, taking into account all the relevant factors, rather than a matter of discretion.[188]

Credibility of the complainant

20.144   It is now well-established that a previous conviction or other evidence of bad character may be relevant to credibility even though it does not necessarily show a propensity to be untruthful, provided it is of substantial probative value. In *Hanson*,[189] the Court of Appeal made the observation that dishonesty is not the same as untruthfulness. In *Stephenson*,[190] Hughes LJ said that it did not follow from this that previous convictions that do not involve either the making of false statements or the giving of false evidence are incapable of having substantial probative value in relation to the credibility of a non-defendant under s.100. If the evidence has substantial probative value in relation to a matter in issue in the proceedings and is of substantial importance in the context of the case as a whole, the judge has no discretion and must allow the s.100 application. This principle was demonstrated in *Riley*,[191] where the appellant was charged with wounding contrary to s.18 of the Offences Against the Person Act 1861. His defence was self-defence. The complainant was due to stand trial in respect of an allegation of actual bodily harm on the appellant himself. The appellant applied to cross-

---

[186] *Scott* [2009] EWCA Crim 2457 is a highly instructive case where the Court of Appeal reviewed the case law in respect of the various issues that need to be resolved in respect of s.100 applications where there is evidence of a false complaint against another man on another occasion. See also *Braithwaite* [2010] Crim. L.R. 855, where police crime reports (CRIS reports) indicating that some third party had made an allegation against the witness or that the witness had been investigated in respect of some offence were held to have been correctly not admitted under s.100. They were no more than evidence that a complaint or allegation had been made.

[187] [2011] EWCA Crim 2935 at [44]. See also *Braithwaite*, last note, at [44] per Hughes LJ.

[188] Cf. *Scott*, last note, at [45] where Aikens LJ preferred to characterise the judge's exercise as one of judgment as opposed to Dyson LJ's view in *Carr* [2008] EWCA Crim 1283 that it is an exercise of discretion.

[189] [2005] EWCA Crim 824; [2005] 2 Cr. App. R. 21 (299).

[190] [2006] EWCA Crim 2325. cf. *Garnham* [2008] EWCA Crim 266 where the Court of Appeal surprisingly took a different view.

[191] [2006] EWCA Crim 2030.

examine the complainant about this, on the basis that it was important explanatory evidence which went to the issue of appellant's propensity to violence. The trial judge refused leave on the basis that the application raised an unhelpful satellite issue. The Court of Appeal held that this decision had been wrong. The evidence was capable of showing that the complainant was the aggressor and was therefore important explanatory evidence.

It follows that an issue as to the creditworthiness of a witness, including a **20.145** complainant, is within the scope of the words "matter in issue in the proceedings" in s.100(1)(b)(i). *R. v S (Andrew)*[192] is a good illustration. The complainant was a prostitute. She had previous convictions for theft. She complained that the appellant had raped her. The appellant claimed that she had agreed to the sexual act in return for £10. When afterwards he refused her demand for more money, she threatened to accuse him of rape and tried to grab hold of the gold chain he was wearing. At trial, the judge refused the appellant's application for leave to cross-examine the complainant pursuant to s.100 in relation to convictions for theft, handling and burglary. The Court of Appeal stated that the convictions did not demonstrate a propensity to untruthfulness, as asserted by the appellant, but they did demonstrate the complainant's propensity to act in the way asserted, in short to act dishonestly. Section 100 does not spell this out by providing gateways, as s.101 does in the case of a defendant's bad character, but clearly the convictions for dishonesty were relevant to an important matter in issue between the appellant and the prosecution. To similar effect is *Hussain*,[193] where the complainant's convictions were so numerous, varied and recent, the Court of Appeal held they were of substantial probative value in relation to the complainant's credibility. The appellant was convicted of raping the complainant at a house party they attended. The prosecution and defence cases were diametrically opposed. Central to the appellant's case was that the complainant had lied in alleging sexual intercourse, and saying that she did not make sexual advances towards him and did not sexually assault him by masturbating him to ejaculation. The Court of Appeal stated that after correctly ruling that the complainant's general creditworthiness was central to the case, her numerous previous convictions for assault, robbery, dangerous driving, taking motor vehicles without consent, shoplifting and burglary were of substantial probative value on the issue of whether her accusation against the appellant was worthy of belief.

Where it is contended that the material is of substantial probative value in **20.146** respect of the credibility of a witness, including the complainant, the relevant test is that established in *Brewster*,[194] where Pitchford LJ held:

---

[192] [2006] EWCA Crim 1303; [2006] 2 Cr. App. R. 31. cf. *Ul-Haq* [2010] EWCA Crim 1683, where the credibility of a witness was important, but the convictions were too historical and did not satisfy the criteria of being of sufficient "probative value".
[193] [2015] EWCA Crim 383.
[194] [2010] EWCA Crim 1194 at [22].

"The question is whether the evidence of previous convictions, or bad behaviour, is sufficiently persuasive to be worthy of consideration by a fair minded tribunal upon the issue of creditworthiness."

He added that the Court did not consider that the conviction must, in order to qualify for admission in evidence, demonstrate any tendency towards dishonesty or untruthfulness:

"The question is whether a fair-minded tribunal would regard them as affecting the worth of the witness's evidence."

20.147   *R v M*[195] is a case where background material was considered to be too peripheral to amount to evidence of a "disposition towards misconduct" of a nature that would have satisfied s.100(1)(b). The appellant was convicted of engaging in sexual activity with a child under 16. The complainant had alleged that he touched her vagina on one occasion and, when she protested, said it was "only a bit of fun". At other times he had touched her breasts. The appellant, upon the basis of material that had been disclosed from social services files in relation to the complainant, applied to adduce evidence of her background and/or bad character as being admissible to show her motive in making the allegations and thus undermine her credibility. The material included a history of self-harming, drinking to excess and drug-taking, and cautions, reprimands and warnings (drunk and disorderly and public order offences). The Court of Appeal held that the evidence of misconduct did not satisfy the test in s.100(1)(b). The Court stressed that satellite litigation needed to be controlled and the jury would have been overwhelmed by trying issues from her disturbed adolescence. Similarly, the Court of Appeal in *Barlow*[196]regarded it as a proper exercise of the trial judge's discretion to refuse to admit evidence that a 17-year-old complainant had been excluded from school on a number of occasions for infringements of school rules, including truancy and smoking cannabis, as it did not affect the worth of the witness's evidence.

Allegations

20.148   It will rarely be possible to adduce evidence of mere allegations (as opposed to convictions or cautions), since it is unlikely to be of "substantial probative value".[197] In assessing whether evidence has substantial probative value the court has to evaluate the nature and sources of the evidence. For instance, largely unsubstantiated items of intelligence are unlikely to satisfy the test of

[195] [2014] EWCA Crim 1457.
[196] [2013] EWCA Crim 920.
[197] *Braithwaite* [2010] EWCA Crim 1082; *Miller* [2010] EWCA Crim 809. For a recent example of the correct approach where the prosecution failed to disclose that a critical witness was under investigation for defrauding her clients at the time of the trial, see *Kelly* [2015] EWCA Crim 817.

having substantial probative value.[198] An unsupported assertion of an unknown associate will rarely satisfy s.100.[199]One relevant factor will be whether or not the evidence is hearsay, although the mere fact that it is hearsay cannot be determinative.[200]

The position as regards allegations is unaffected by s.109 of the Criminal **20.149** Justice Act 2003, which contains an assumption as to the truth of the evidence for the purposes of determining admissibility. This is because the s.109 assumption is not determinative of the admissibility question, but provides the context in which the admissibility decision falls to be made. The bare fact of an allegation (even if assumed to be true) is not necessarily conclusive of the question whether it constitutes evidence of substantial probative value or evidence of substantial importance in the context of the case as a whole (the s.100 criteria). If evidence sought to be introduced at trial about the bad character of a witness requires investigation of a nature which may be liable to distract the attention of the jury from the crucial issue, which is whether the case against the defendant has been proved, that may be a relevant consideration bearing on the assessment of the probative value of the evidence and its importance in the overall context of the case. When the court is assessing the probative value of evidence of the bad character of a witness in accordance with the s.100 criteria, among the factors relevant to the admissibility judgment, it should reflect on whether the admission of the evidence might make it more difficult for the jury to understand the remainder of the evidence, and whether its understanding of the case as a whole might be diminished. In such cases the conclusion may be that the evidence is not of substantial probative value in establishing the propensity or lack of creditworthiness of the witness, or that the evidence is not of substantial importance in the context of the case as a whole, or both. If so, the pre-conditions to admissibility will not be established.

As with s.101, the court when making its judgment under s.100 is entitled **20.150** to take into account the danger of the proliferation of satellite issues,[201] provided it is recognised that once the statutory test is satisfied, leave must be given.[202] In *Dizaei*[203] the question arose as to whether, in the context of the bad character of a non-defendant, there is an exclusionary discretion to avoid satellite litigation. Lord Judge CJ, giving the judgment of the Court, made it clear that if the judge is satisfied that the pre-conditions of admissibility are satisfied, there is no such discretion.[204] In deciding whether those pre-conditions are met, the court is entitled to consider the cumulative effect of

[198] *Braithwaite* [2010] EWCA Crim 1082.
[199] *Abbas v Crown Prosecution Service* [2015] EWHC 579 (Admin).
[200] *Matthews* [2013] EWCA Crim 2238.
[201] *Bovell and Dowds* [2005] 2 Cr. App. R. 242; *Carr* [2008] EWCA Crim 1283; *R. v AJC* [2006] EWCA Crim 284.
[202] *Riley* [2006] EWCA Crim 2030.
[203] [2013] EWCA Crim 88.
[204] At [35].

a variety of different allegations upon the complainant's credibility,[205] and must be careful not to adopt too restrictive an approach. This occurred in *Griffiths*[206] where the Court of Appeal held that the trial judge had been wrong to refuse leave to cross-examine the complainant about the fact that she had been on LSD and glue-sniffing at the time she made the allegation of sex abuse.

Overlap between Section 100 of the Criminal Justice Act 2003 and Section 41 of the Youth Justice and Criminal Evidence Act 1999

20.151   The restriction in s.100 operates cumulatively with the prohibition on adducing evidence of the complainant's previous sexual behaviour imposed by s.41 of the Youth Justice and Criminal Evidence Act 1999. This means that when a defendant wishes to cross-examine a complainant in a sex case, they face a double hurdle, which may be very difficult to surmount. However, evidence that the complainant has made false allegations against someone, particularly if the allegations were of sexual misconduct, even if not against the defendant at trial, can (if properly admissible, consistent with s.41 of the 1999 Act) often be powerful material in a trial of alleged sexual offences in which the key issue is the parties' credibility. For instance, the Court of Appeal concluded in *Scott*,[207] a rape case, that evidence of false complaints by the complainant of relatively minor "sexual advances"[208] by her son's martial arts teacher towards the complainant herself and of him leaving faeces on her doorstep, did have substantial "probative value in relation to a matter which is of substantial importance in the context of the case as a whole".

20.152   If the material might fall foul of s.41, an application must be made under that section. Crane J observed in *R. v V*[209] that obtaining a ruling under s.41 permitting cross-examination and the introduction of evidence concerning a false allegation of sexual misconduct may be a "more formidable obstacle" than obtaining leave pursuant to s.100 of the Criminal Justice Act 2003. However, if, as the Court of Appeal decided on the facts in *Scott,* there is a sufficient evidential basis in accordance with the principles set out in *R. v BT and MH*[210] and *R. v AM*[211] that the complainant has made false allegations on another occasion, s.41 is not engaged.

---

[205] *R. v NK* [2009] EWCA Crim 2425. The Lord Chief Justice expressed the view that the trial had gone wrong when only a limited amount of material in respect of the complainant's bad character had gone before the jury in an historic sex case. The convictions were quashed and a retrial was ordered. The defendant was subsequently re-convicted of some, but not all counts.
[206] [2007] EWCA Crim 2468.
[207] [2009] EWCA Crim 2457.
[208] The advances were in the form of "undressing her with his eyes and licking his lips".
[209] [2006] EWCA Crim 1901.
[210] [2002] 1 W.L.R. 633, see para.26.154, below.
[211] [2009] EWCA Crim 618, see para.26.156, below.

For the purposes of s.41, the term "complainant" is limited to the   **20.153**
complainant of the offence that is the subject of the trial. This means that a
complainant in a matter of which evidence is admitted under the bad
character provisions does not enjoy the protection of s.41.[212] However, such
a complainant might be protected by s.100, and even if not so protected, will
be protected by the general rules as to common law relevance as informed by
the principles underpinning s.41. These principles are designed to outlaw
irrelevant and illegitimate lines of reasoning based on the Canadian "twin
myths": for detailed discussion of these, see Ch.26.

---

[212] *R. v M* [2006] EWCA Crim 1509.

CHAPTER 21

MEDICAL EVIDENCE: ADULTS

By Dr Catherine White*

Introduction .... 21.01   Forensic Samples 21.37
Prevalence .... 21.04   Drug-facilitated Sexual Assault 21.40
Presentation .... 21.12   Aftercare 21.41
SARCs .... 21.16   Psychological Sequelae of Sexual
Forensic Medical Examination .... 21.18   Violence 21.55

INTRODUCTION

Whilst not all doctors will have knowingly dealt with a victim of sexual **21.01** assault or rape, given the prevalence of the problem, all will have done so to better or less effect. The forensic medical examination is a complex process, addressing forensic aspects for the criminal justice system and also the medical and psychological needs of the person. This should be done in a dedicated unit by staff with the requisite qualifications, knowledge, experience, skills and attitudes. In the UK, this would usually be in a SARC ("Sexual Assault Referral Centre").

The Faculty of Forensic and Legal Medicine ("FFLM"), is recognised by **21.02** the Home Office[1] as being responsible for advising on the standards to be expected from all healthcare professionals involved in custody healthcare and forensic examination, and has developed a wide set of standard documents. Further guidance confirmed the role of both the Forensic Science Regulator and the FFLM in setting standards.[2] The FFLM has set out Quality

---

* Clinical Director of the Sexual Assault Referral Centre, St Mary's Hospital, Manchester; author of Sexual Assault, A Forensic Physician's Guide (Manchester, St Mary's SARC, 2010).
    [1] Hansard, March 18, 2009, col.1164W.
    [2] *Responding to violence against women and children—the role of the NHS*: The Report of the Taskforce on the Health Aspects of Violence Against Women and Children (March 2010), recommendation 21.

Standards in Forensic Medicine which covers the standards required of the doctors working in this field.[3]

21.03   Terminology is important. In the criminal justice process, the terms "complainant" and "victim" are used. As this chapter is dealing with the medical aspects of sexual assault, the term "patient" will be used. Whilst it is often said by those reporting sexual assault that what is very important to them is to be believed, equally it is vital that the forensic physician, whilst still being caring and respectful, remains alert to the need to be objective and independent so they are best able to assist the court.[4] Also in this chapter the feminine will be used (she, woman) as although it is acknowledged that men and boys are also victims of sexual violence, the majority of victims are female.

PREVALENCE

21.04   The accurate prevalence of sexual violence in any particular society is difficult to determine as, for a variety of reasons, under-reporting is an issue. It is estimated that for England and Wales, only approximately 15 per cent of victims of the most serious sexual offences reported the incident to the police. The Office for National Statistics report *Crime in England and Wales, Year Ending June 2015*,[5] published in October 2015, gave the following information:

> "Police recorded crime figures showed an increase of 41% in all sexual offences for the year ending June 2015 compared with the previous year (up from 67,880 to 95,482 . . .). This is the highest level recorded, and the largest annual percentage increase, since the introduction of the National Crime Recording Standard (NCRS) in April 2002. Increases in recorded offences against both adults and children have contributed to this rise. Increases were seen in all but one territorial police force areas . . .
>
>   The rises in the volume of sexual offences recorded by the police should be seen in the context of a number of high-profile reports and inquiries which is thought to have resulted in police forces reviewing and improving their recording processes. These include:
>
> - the investigation by Her Majesty's Inspectorate of Constabulary (HMIC) and HM Crown Prosecution Service Inspectorate (HMCPSI) in 2012, which highlighted the need to improve the recording and investigation of sexual offences

---

[3] *Quality Standards in Forensic Medicine: General Forensic Medicine (GFM) and Sexual Offence Medicine (SOM)* (July 2013), available at *http://www.fflm.ac.uk/wp-content/uploads/documentstore/1378397186.pdf* [Accessed April 30, 2016].

[4] *The Role of the Independent Forensic Physician* (FFLM, January 2014), available at *http://fflm.ac.uk/publications/the-role-of-the-independent-forensic-physician/* [Accessed April 30, 2016].

[5] *Crime in England and Wales, Year Ending June 2015* (ONS, October 2015), available at *http://www.ons.gov.uk/ons/rel/crime-stats/crime-statistics/year-ending-june-2015/stb-crime-ye-june-2015.html£tab-Sexual-offences* [Accessed April 30, 2016].

- concerns about the recording of sexual offences, for example in evidence presented to the Public Administration Select Committee (PASC) inquiry into crime statistics and arising from other high profile cases
- the creation of the 'Independent Panel Inquiry into Child Sexual Abuse', which was set up to consider whether, and the extent to which, public bodies and other non-state institutions have taken seriously their duty of care to protect children from sexual abuse in England and Wales."

Around one in 20 females (aged 16 to 59) reported being a victim of a most **21.05** serious sexual offence since the age of 16. Extending this to include other sexual offences such as sexual threats, unwanted touching or indecent exposure, increased the figure to one in five females reporting being a victim since the age of 16.[6]

The Crime Survey of England and Wales 2013 recorded that 2 per cent of **21.06** women and 0.5 per cent of men had experienced some form of sexual assault (including attempts) in the previous year.

Around 90 per cent of victims of the most serious sexual offences in the **21.07** previous year knew the perpetrator, compared with less than half for other sexual offences.[7]

Whilst for some victims the sexual violence will be an isolated and one-off **21.08** event, for many there will be an overlap with other types of abuse, such as domestic abuse or emotional abuse, and unfortunately this will form part of an ongoing situation.

Men

There is much evidence that the prevalence of sexual violence against males **21.09** is greatly underestimated. As is the case for women, there will be many barriers to disclosing and reporting. It has been argued that the social construction of masculinity, and the central role of the male in a patriarchal society, stifles the reporting of male-on-male sexual assaults to a greater degree than male-on-female.[8] In the year 2014–15, 11 per cent of the 1,632 cases seen at St Mary's SARC, Manchester, were male.

During a sexual assault of a male, direct penile stimulation or stimulation **21.10** of the prostate during anal penetration may result in a physiological response in the victim. This physiological response may result in an erection and subsequent ejaculation.[9] This response is involuntary and should not be seen as proof of consent or enjoyment, although it often adds to the difficulties a male victim has when deciding whether or not to report.

---

[6] *An Overview of Sexual Offending in England and Wales* (MoJ, Home Office, ONS, January 2013), available at *https://www.gov.uk/government/uploads/system/uploads/attachment_data/file/ 214970/sexual-offending-overview-jan-2013.pd* [Accessed April 30, 2016].
[7] ibid.
[8] McLean, I., Balding, V. and White, C., (2005) *Further aspects of male-on-male rape and sexual assault in Greater Manchester*, Medicine, Science and the Law, 45(3), 225–232.
[9] Levin RJ, van Berlo W. (2004), Sexual arousal and orgasm in subjects who experience forced or non-consensual sexual stimulation—a review. J Clin Forensic Med;11(2):82–8.

Learning Difficulties

21.11 People with learning disabilities are at greater risk of sexual assault than the rest of the population.[10] Research shows that every year in the United Kingdom there will be almost 1,400 new cases of reported sexual abuse of people who have a learning disability.[11] More than 90 per cent of people with a learning disability will experience sexual abuse at some point in their lives, and 49 per cent will experience 10 or more abusive incidents.[12] Additional to this higher risk are the difficulties they may face in disclosing the abuse and then getting appropriate medical and psychological help, and also in terms of access to justice. Many professionals are not skilled at identifying that a person has a learning disability or communicating effectively with them. Use of intermediaries at an early stage should assist, but this is dependent upon resources being made available.

PRESENTATION

21.12 As noted above, many patients who have been victims of abuse will never disclose the abuse. They may still present with medical issues that are directly related to the abuse and may do so either directly or indirectly:

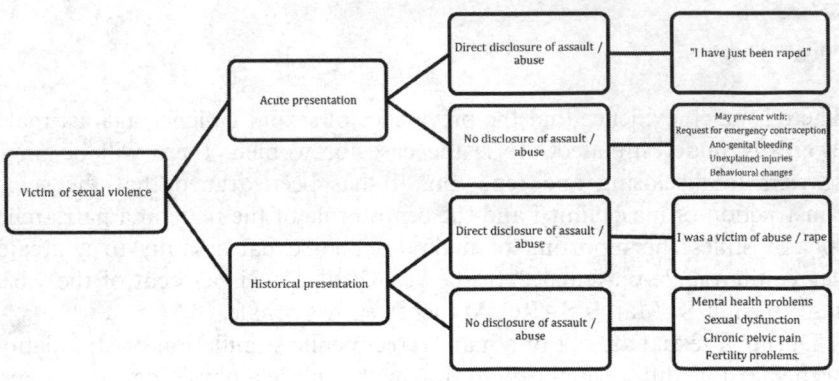

21.13 The degree to which a patient may discuss past events will be dependent upon issues particular to them, the setting and the degree of confidence they have in the clinician and the system, to respond appropriately to the information.

[10] Bernert, D.J. and Ogletree, R.J., (2013). *Women with intellectual disabilities talk about their perceptions of sex,* Journal of Intellectual Disability Research. 57:3: 240-249. doi: 10.1111/j.1365—2788.2011.01529.x

[11] *Behind Closed Doors,* Mencap, Respond and Voice UK 2001.

[12] Valenti-Hein and Schwartz, 1995.

Where a person has made a disclosure, for example directly to the police, 21.14 or the clinician has a high degree of suspicion that something has happened, a number of issues must be considered:

- What needs the patient may have:
  - Medical
  - Forensic
  - Psychological
  - Social/Practical
  - Safeguarding
- What legal/statutory duties the clinician may have such as:
  - Safeguarding referrals
  - Female Genital Mutilation reporting.
- What are the options for the patient and what are their ideas, concerns and expectations.
- What resources are available to assist (the patient and the clinician) and how they might be accessed.

Many of these cases can be complex, and are often made even more so by 21.15 the high level of emotion that they can generate. Ideally patients should be referred to a SARC which should have the staff, including forensic physicians, with the knowledge, experiences and skills to deal with these cases, and provide a holistic response with ongoing support. That said, all clinicians need to be able to provide a safe initial response.

SARCs

The delivery aim of a SARC, as set out in NHS England's guide to 21.16 commissioners,[13] is that it should provide clients with:

- Acute healthcare and support in age-appropriate settings.
- Comprehensive forensic medical examination.
- Follow up services which address the client's medical, psychosocial and on-going needs.
- Direct access or referral to an Independent Sexual Violence Advisor ("ISVA").

Self-Referrals

Most SARCs will be able to accept "self-referrals" as well as police referrals. 21.17 With the former, the patient should receive the same choice of services with the option of having forensic samples stored at the SARC for a fixed length of time while they decide whether or not they wish to go on to make a report to the police. Self-referrals may generate ethical issues and duties such as

---

[13] *Commissioning Framework for Adult and Paediatric Sexual Assault Referral Centres (SARC) Services* (NHS England, August 2015), available at *http://www.england.nhs.uk/commissioning/wp-content/uploads/sites/12/2013/05/SARCs-service-spec-contract-template-and-paed-framework.pdf* [Accessed April 30, 2016].

disclosure in the public interest or safeguarding referrals; the SARC would have to consider these on a case-by-case basis, working closely with the individual patient.

FORENSIC MEDICAL EXAMINATION

21.18 The role of the forensic clinician is twofold: to attend to the therapeutic needs and also the forensic needs of the patient.

Capacity, consent and confidentiality

21.19 When a patient discloses that they have been a victim, the doctor must consider what duty they have to maintain confidentiality, balanced against any requirements to share information. The sharing of information may be in order to protect the patient from future abuse or to protect others. Sexual violence is about control. During the assault, the victim has no control over what happens to them. An important element of aiding recovery is to offer back control as soon as possible.

21.20   With both police and self-referrals, the initial duty of the forensic clinician is to assess the capacity of the patient to provide consent for the forensic medical examination. The definition of, assessment of and responsibilities in relation to capacity (also known as mental capacity) in England and Wales are set out in the Mental Capacity Act ("MCA") 2005 and it applies to all adults aged over 16. The MCA 2005 defines capacity as the ability to make a decision. It relates to the *process* of making a decision and not to the *outcome* of the decision. It is not limited to medical decisions, but can apply to any decision-making process. Capacity is task specific. A person may be capable of deciding one issue but not another. Capacity is also time specific. A person's capacity may alter with time.

21.21   Many victims of sexual violence may have impaired capacity. The clinician will have to determine whether this is temporary, e.g. due to intoxication, or permanent, and whether the examination should be postponed or continue on the basis that it is in the patient's best interest. The FFLM has produced guidelines to aid clinicians when they are dealing with a patient who may have been assaulted and seems to not have full capacity.[14]

Disclosure

21.22 As part of the medical and forensic assessment it is likely that the clinician will be gathering a large amount of sensitive information. Much of this will be disclosable during any subsequent police investigation and criminal justice

---

[14] *Consent from patients who may have been seriously assaulted* (FFLM, July 2011), available at   *http://lfflm.ac.uk/publications/recommendations-consent-from-patients-who-may-have-been-seriously-assaulted/* [Accessed April 30, 2016].

process and it is incumbent upon the clinician to ensure that the patient understands this.

History taking

Although in theory the history taking precedes the physical examination, in reality, as with any other medical encounter, the examination starts as soon as the doctor and patient meet. With sexual violence this is no different. The level of detail of the history will be dependent upon what is to be achieved by it. The doctor must be mindful of any immediate emergency medical needs. With an acute police referral, the norm would be for the forensic clinician to first obtain details of the allegations from the attending police officer prior to obtaining a history from the patient.

21.23

History taking and record keeping:

21.24

- Should be accurate, clear and contemporaneous.
- Consider what questions to ask and why. How might any information gained be relevant to the task at hand?
- Use open ended rather than closed questions as much as possible and record responses verbatim.
- Be clear about who gave a piece of information and who was present when they did so.
- Go at the pace of the patient.
- Use language that the patient can understand.
- Be non-judgmental.

There are a number of proformae that have been developed by various bodies to act as an aide memoire and assist with the history and examination, bearing in mind that there is a real prospect of these notes becoming crucial in a subsequent trial with the liberty of a person at stake. These examinations have a dual purpose, medical and forensic, and will include a variety of risk assessments to cover the medical and psychological needs of the individual, the gathering of forensic evidence as well as the discharge of safeguarding duties.

21.25

Table: History taking in sexual assault cases	
In broad terms questions will cover	*Examples of some of the reasons why they should be asked:*
What has happened?	The nature of the assault will influence: • Assessing need for emergency contraception

	• Prophylaxis in terms of blood borne viruses such as HIV and Hepatitis B • Where injuries may be found • Where forensic samples may be sought • Sites for screening for sexually transmitted infections • Subsequent criminal charges
When did it happen?	Again this will influence medical treatments such as emergency contraception, PEP (post-exposure prophylaxis), the need for forensic samples and the interpretation of subsequent results. Information regarding actions post assault, such as washing, changing clothing etc. should therefore be gathered.
Who was involved?	This will be of relevance to the criminal justice process. For example where the abuser is alleged to be a child the history taking is likely to be approached differently than in the case of an adult suspect, especially an adult in a position of custody, care or control. It will also influence the risk assessment of the need for HIV and Hepatitis B PEP, for example a suspect who is known to be from an area with a high endemic level of HIV.
Where did it happen?	This may assist in the criminal investigation. It may assist in the interpretation of injuries (or absence of injuries), for example, a recent assault in a wooded area, or the importance of fibres detected on clothing.

How did it happen?	This may include details such as threatened or actual violence and may assist in the interpretation of injuries (or absence of injury). Was this a drug-facilitated assault? Was there a particular MO (modus operendi) that may assist investigations?

In addition to the above, the history must be tailored on a case by case basis to cover social aspects, past and current medical history, drug history, family history etc., again recording who gave the information and who else was present at the time.

The forensic examination

An independent chaperone should always be used. In SARCs, this will often be a crisis worker. Some patients may indicate a desire to have a family member or friend with them, but it is worth discreetly checking that it is truly the wish of the patient and that there is still an opportunity for the patient to speak in confidence. In some areas a police officer will be present during the examination, but it is widely considered best practice for this not to be the case.   21.26

The forensic examination should follow a careful structure but be flexible so as to accommodate the needs of the individual patient. As a minimum it should: 21.27

- Go at the patient's pace, with regular checks regarding consent and understanding of the process.
- Be undertaken in an examination room that is fit for purpose, minimising the risk of forensic contamination.
- Have a good light source and magnification as necessary.
- Entail a head-to-toe examination.
- Consider the use of video colposcopy for the ano-genital examination.
- Record all negative as well as positive findings.

Where positive findings occur consider: 21.28

- Is this abnormal or a normal variation?
- Is it related to a pre-existing condition, e.g. lichen sclerosis atrophicus?
- Is it due to trauma and, if yes, could it be accidental or non-accidental?
- Are there signs such that may assist with ageing, such as scab formation?

- Is there any evidence of the patient being more susceptible than normal to trauma (e.g. on steroids, concurrent skin infection, abnormal clotting)?

21.29   One needs to consider the detail of the allegations, the time that has past etc., the general health of the patient, medication that may affect bruising tendency, skin conditions etc. when interpreting any findings. It goes without saying that an appreciation of "normal" is vital in order to determine what might be "abnormal". Most sexual assaults will either cause no injuries or injuries that are small and likely to heal quickly leaving no trace. Therefore the absence of injury does not necessarily negate the allegation. Contrary to popular opinion, most patients following an allegation of sexual violence will not have any ano-genital injuries. The forensic examination should include a thorough examination of this area.

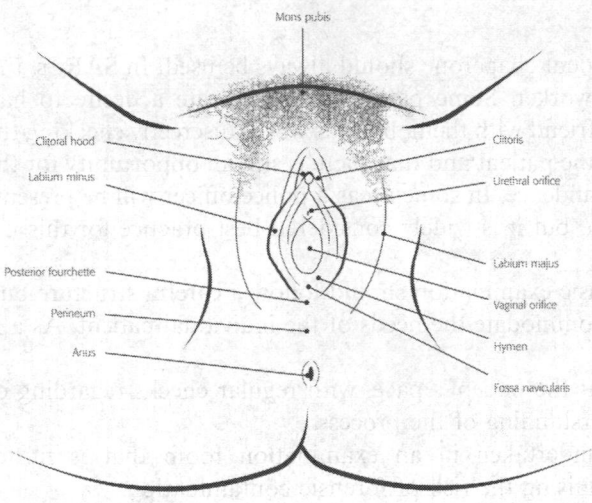

Figure 1 Adult female.[15]

Anatomical Terms

21.30   That there are different medical and legal definitions for the term "vagina" may give rise to confusion and error. In medicine, the vagina is defined as a muscular tube which has the cervix (neck of the womb) at its upper end and

---

[15] Illustration taken from Dr Catherine White, *Sexual Assault, A Forensic Physician's Practice Guide* (Feb 2010), ISBN 978-0-9564737-0-7.

the hymen (or hymenal remnants) at its outer end. The legal definition, in s.79(9) of the Sexual Offences Act 2003, has the outer end of the vagina starting with the vulva, i.e. between the labia, and so in a legal sense, penetration of the vagina does not have to involve penetration of the hymen.

There are several medical glossaries for ano-genital anatomy terms, **21.31** however most utilise medical terms throughout and so can be unhelpful for the lay person. The following is a list of the most frequently used terms:

Anal Canal	End part of the large intestine from the rectum to the anal opening.
Cervix	Neck of the womb.
Hymen	A tissue surrounding the vaginal opening and partially covering it.
Labia Majora	Large lips surrounding the vagina.
Labia Minora	Small lips surrounding the vagina and lying between the labia majora.
Posterior Fourchette	Area where the labia minora meet in the middle at the back of the vaginal opening.
Vestibule	The innermost part of the vulva surrounding the vaginal and urethral openings.
Vulva	The external female genitalia which includes the labia majora and minora, the mons pubis, clitoris, vestibule, vaginal and urethral openings.

Documenting Injuries

Body charts as well as written notes should be used. Photography and video **21.32** colposcopy should be considered, with the caveats that correct consent is obtained, and they are done to an adequate standard with suitable security of the images afterwards. The FFLM has produced guidance on images taken in these circumstances.[16]

Documentation of an injury should include: **21.33**
- Classification of the injury type
  - Abrasion
  - Bruise
  - Laceration
  - Incision
  - Heat, chemical or electrical injury
- Size, shape, position, pattern,
- Associated features e.g. tenderness and swelling

---

[16] *Guidance for best practice for the management of intimate images that may become evidence in court* (FFLM, May 2014), available at *http://www.fflm.ac.uk/publications/guidance-for-best-practice-for-the-management-of-intimate-images-that-may-become-evidence-in-court-2/* [Accessed April 30, 2016].

21.34   Bite marks, whilst fairly common in sexual violence, may be easy to miss. Swabbing for saliva and DNA is recommended for acute bites. The interpretation of bite marks should be left to forensic odontologists. They will require specialist photography, so it is best to seek their advice as soon as possible bite marks are identified.

Ano-genital Injuries

21.35   The likelihood of sustaining an injury during non-consensual sexual activity will be determined by many factors, including the type of activity, force used, lubrication, hormonal status, medical condition that predisposes to injury such as those affecting tissue friability etc.[17] Whilst ano-genital injuries can occur as a result of non-consensual sexual activity, they are not the norm and seldom are they marked. This is true even with first time intercourse, making the concept of virginity-testing a nonsense.[18]

21.36   Absence of injuries can have several explanations:
- No injuries were sustained during the assault.
- Any injury sustained has healed in the time that has elapsed from assault to examination.
- Injuries are not visible at time of examination, especially if seen quickly.
- Some pigmented skin does not show injuries very easily.
- The allegation is false.

It also should be remembered that genital injuries can be sustained during consensual sexual activity, although this is unusual and the injuries tend to be minor.

FORENSIC SAMPLES

21.37   Where appropriate, and providing that the patient, or where applicable their guardian, has provided informed consent, the taking of forensic samples should be considered. With police cases, an Early Evidence Kit may already have been obtained.

21.38   Forensic samples can take various forms. For any given case one must consider what is suitable, based on various factors such as:
- The nature of the alleged assault.
- Time passed since alleged assault.
- Actions subsequent to the alleged assault.

Recommendations as to what forensic samples to take, with brief guidance on how to take them and how to store them, can be found on the website of

---

[17] White C., *Genital injuries in adults*, Best Practice & Research Clinical Obstetrics and Gynaecology (2012), available at *http://www.dx.doi.org/10.1016/j.bpobgyn.2012.08.011* [Accessed April 30, 2016].

[18] Kellog N., Menard S. and Santos A., *Genital Anatomy in Pregnant Adolescents: "Normal" Does Not Mean "Nothing Happened"*, Pediatrics 2004: 113: 67-69.

the Royal College of Physicians Faculty of Forensic and Legal Medicine (*http://www.ffl.ac.uk*). These recommendations are reviewed and updated as necessary every six months. For the persistence of trace evidence, see para.22.19, below.

Forensic samples must be taken in the prescribed way and order to ensure   21.39
the correct interpretation of the results by the forensic scientist. With the advancements in forensic science and increased sensitivity of techniques such as DNA 17,[19] it is vital that the risk of contamination of samples is minimised. The Forensic Science Regulator is currently in the process of producing, as part of the Codes of Practice and Conduct, standards for the forensic medical examination of adult and child sexual assault complainants; it is anticipated that these will be available in summer 2016.[20] These standards will include processes designed to reduce the risk of forensic contamination and potential miscarriages of justice as a consequence. There are guidelines on the labelling of forensic samples and on ensuring due regard for the chain of custody.[21]

DRUG-FACILITATED SEXUAL ASSAULT

Misuse of alcohol and drugs, such as cannabis, may be an issue and should   21.40
be considered. Medical staff should be aware of the symptoms of the common drugs of abuse, and the signs of intoxication and withdrawal. In addition, the phenomenon of drug-facilitated sexual assault is widespread throughout the world to varying degrees. The UN Office on Drugs and Crime defines drug-facilitated sexual assault as:

> "Drug-facilitated sexual assault (DFSA), which is a subset of drug-facilitated crimes, occurs when a person (male or female) is subjected to sexual act(s) while they are incapacitated or unconscious due to the effect(s) of ethanol, a drug and/ or other intoxicating substance, and as a result unable to resist or consent to such acts. Substances may be administered covertly to an intended victim or victims, or a perpetrator may take advantage of a victim after voluntary ingestion of the substance."[22]

AFTERCARE

The therapeutic aspects of the forensic medical examination will include risk   21.41
assessments for:

---

[19] *Allele frequency databases and reporting guidance for the DNA-17 profiling* (Sept 2014), available at *https://www.gov.uk/government/publications/allele-frequency-databases-and-reporting-guidance-for-the-dna-17-profiling* [Accessed April 30, 2016].
[20] *https://www.gov.uk/government/organisations/forensic-science-regulator* [Accessed April 30, 2016].
[21] *Labelling Forensic Samples* (FFLM, 2013), available at *http://fflm.ac.uk/publications/recommendations-labelling-forensic-samples/* [Accessed April 30, 2016].
[22] *Guidelines for the Forensic analysis of drugs facilitating sexual assault and other criminal act* (UNODC, 2011), available at *https://www.unodc.org/documents/scientific/forensic_analy of_drugs_facilitating_sexual_assault_and_other_criminal_acts.pdf* [Accessed April 30, 2016].

- Pregnancy and emergency contraception.
- Screening for sexually transmitted infections.
- Post-exposure prophylaxis ("PEP") for HIV and Hepatitis B.
- Self-harm and suicide.
- Domestic violence.
- Safeguarding—child and vulnerable adults.

Emergency Contraception

21.42   Although the risk of pregnancy following rape is low, prevention of a pregnancy after non-consensual sexual activity is a key concern for many attending for a forensic examination. In the UK there are three methods of emergency contraception currently available:
- Copper–containing intrauterine device (Cu-IUCD).
- Progestogen–levonorgestrel (LNG) 1.5mg.
- Progesterone receptor modulator–ulipristal acetate 30mg.

The risk of conception and the suitability of method will need to be assessed on a case-by-case basis. Appropriate follow up care and advice needs to be given.[23]

Pregnancy

21.43   If it is considered a possibility that the patient is already pregnant as a result of the assault, then it would be good practice to perform a pregnancy test. Prior to doing so:
- Ensure consent for test and explain accuracy and any limitations of the test used.
- Ensure that you can respond appropriately to a positive test.

If there is a pregnancy following a sexual assault there are two potential options:
- Termination of the pregnancy
- Continuation of the pregnancy

The patient will need practical and emotional support either way.

21.44   There may be an opportunity for identification of the alleged assailant by means of paternity analysis carried out on the products of conception, foetus or infant. The ethics and legalities of this process are complex and advice should be sought. The Forensic Science Service has produced guidelines on practicalities of this process.[24]

---

[23] Your guide to emergency contraception. FPA. 2014. ISBN 978-1-908249-56-2.
[24] *ACPO/FSS/FFLM Guidance in Criminal Paternity Cases*, available at *http://www.fflm.ac.uk/ 'ications/acpo-fss-fflm-guidance-in-criminal-paternity-cases/* [Accessed April 30, 2016].

Sexually transmitted infections

Sexual violence may lead to the patient acquiring a sexually transmitted   **21.45**
infection ("STI"), including blood borne viruses such as Hepatitis B and
HIV. If the patient is seen soon enough after the assault, then post-exposure
prophylaxis ("PEP") should be considered. Up-to-date advice on HIV,
Hepatitis B PEP and STI screening can be obtained from the British
Association for Sexual Health and HIV at *http://www.bashh.org*. In all cases
screening for infection at the relevant time frames should be considered.

HIV Post-exposure Prophylaxis

A risk assessment should be undertaken to see if HIV PEP is warranted. The   **21.46**
risk is calculated as follows:

   Risk of transmission = risk that source is positive x risk of exposure.

Therefore in assessing risk, details of the alleged perpetrator are important.
Often their HIV status is unknown, so factors such as whether they are
thought to be from a high-prevalence area or group (geographical area such
as sub-Saharan Africa, a male who has sex with men (MSM) etc) need to be
evaluated. Time is of the essence as commencing HIV PEP is not generally
recommended more than 72 hours after the assault. Advice from a HIV
physician should be sought where there is any uncertainty or complicating
factors such as the patient is a child, pregnant or breast-feeding.

Hepatitis B Prophylaxis

Again, a risk assessment is required. Here the time frame for commencing the   **21.47**
assessment is a more generous six weeks. Usually an accelerated or a super-
accelerated course is recommended. In cases where the assailant is known to
be Hepatitis B positive, then Hepatitis B immunoglobulin may be offered.

Bacterial STI prophylaxis

There are mixed views on the efficacy of antibiotics as prophylaxis against   **21.48**
infections such as gonorrhoea and chlamydia immediately after an assault.
Proponents advise that in high risk cases who are unlikely to return for
follow-up, a suitable regime of antibiotics should be provided at the acute
examination. Others believe that such action will only treat previously
acquired infections and not protect the patient from infection from the acute
assault, resulting in the patient having a false sense of security and at risk of
harbouring untreated infection and possible complications associated with
such.

Screening for infection post assault

21.49 As a general rule, the usual advice for screening timeframes is:

Bacterial infections   two weeks
Blood borne viruses   three months

However, in some areas more sensitive tests may be available which can be done sooner, so it is important to check what is available locally. In the meantime, it will be important to advise against unprotected sexual intercourse. In certain situations, including child cases, the screening should be done bearing in mind the chain of evidence so that results may be admissible in any subsequent criminal proceedings.

Suicide risk and Psychological issues

21.50 Patients with mental health problems are susceptible to sexual assault, and also patients who have been sexually assaulted may be at risk of mental health problems. Consequently the clinician must screen for such in both the history and examination, including a risk assessment for imminent self-harm/ suicide. Robust referral pathways for those deemed at risk need to be in place.

21.51 Sexual assault, regardless of the degree of violence associated with it, is a traumatic event for most people. It is normal for patients to be affected by it and they should be reassured that they are not mentally unwell if they are. That said, for some, such disturbance can go on to become persistent, and problems such as post-traumatic stress disorder ("PTSD") may develop. The risks of PTSD developing will be dependent upon factors such as the patient's previous background and support systems, the circumstances of the assault and the response the patient receives from others, including professionals such as doctors and police, when they disclose. Treating patients in a non-judgmental manner, with respect and dignity, will never do them harm and is likely to be very beneficial to them in both the short and long term. Of course there will always be examples of false allegations, but the doctor must remain objective as, luckily for them, they do not have to be judge or jury.

Safeguarding

21.52 All forensic medical examinations should screen for safeguarding issues. That is, medical examiners should look for vulnerabilities pertinent to the patient in front of them, as well as considering vulnerable dependents such as children or adults who may be at risk. In some instances, for example where sexual violence occurs in the context of domestic violence, urgent referrals to social services may need to be made. All SARCs should have in place robust assessment processes and referral pathways. In some instances there may be a tension between the wants of the patient and of the SARC staff as to limiting the sharing of information between professionals. Whilst this should be covered in the initial consent process, there may still be situations where there will be a conflict between confidentiality for the patient and safe-guarding.[25]

Domestic Violence

In March 2013, the Home Office made changes to the definition of domestic violence and abuse. It was widened to include young people aged 16 to 17 who exhibited coercive control, a pattern of controlling behaviour. The new definition of domestic violence is[26]:

21.53

> "any incident or pattern of incidents of controlling, coercive, threatening behaviour, violence or abuse between those aged 16 or over who are, or have been, intimate partners or family members regardless of gender or sexuality. The abuse can encompass, but is not limited to:
> * psychological
> * physical
> * sexual
> * financial
> * emotional".

All patients undergoing a forensic medical examination for sexual violence should be screened for domestic violence, no matter who the alleged perpetrator is. Positive disclosures should then lead to more in-depth risk assessment.

A risk assessment is required when domestic violence is identified:
* Is the victim at immediate risk of harm?
* Are there any children or other dependents that may be at risk of harm?
* Does the victim have a safety plan?
* What services are available?

21.54

There are a variety of risk identification checklists that can be used which can help health care workers identify high-risk cases, for example the CAADA-DASH Risk Identification Checklist.[27] Those deemed at higher risk are referred on appropriately, for example to a Multi-Agency Risk Assessment Conference ("MARAC") or, in some situations, as an immediate referral to social care.

---

[25] *Protecting children and young people. The responsibilities of all doctors* (GMC), available at *http://www.gmc-uk.org/guidance/ethical_guidance/13257.asp* [Accessed April 30, 2016] and *Vulnerable adults and the disclosure of confidential information* (BMA), available at *http://bma. org.uk/support-at-work/ethics/mental-capacity/vulnerable-adults-and-confidentiality* [Accessed April 30, 2016].

[26] *Domestic Violence and Abuse*, available at *https://www.gov.uk/guidance/domestic-violence-and-abuse£history* [Accessed April 30, 2016].

[27] See *http://www.dashriskchecklist.co.uk/uploads/pdfs/DASH%202009.pdf* [Accessed April 30, 2016].

PSYCHOLOGICAL SEQUELAE OF SEXUAL VIOLENCE

21.55   The psychological effects of sexual violence are considered in Ch.23. Two topics deserve mention here.

Independent Sexual Violence Advisors (ISVAs)

21.56   ISVAs are victim-focused advocates who work with people who have reported sexual violence to enable them to access the services they need. Most SARCs and some voluntary organisations will have access to ISVAs. Many will see people in cases where the police are not involved. They will be able to support the person with practical issues and through the criminal justice process. Should counselling be required, they will be able to facilitate this. ISVAs should have an understanding of the criminal justice process and their role within it. Similar roles, such as Young Person's advocates, exist for younger age groups.

Vicarious trauma

21.57   Staff working with traumatised patients can pay a personal price. In their care of the patient, staff will develop empathy, i.e. "the ability to sense and understand someone else's feelings as if they were one's own".[28] It is believed that professionals who work with traumatised children and their families take on some of the physiological, psychological and emotional consequences of the abuse.[29] Terms used to describe this phenomenon are vicarious trauma, secondary trauma, compassion fatigue and burnout. It can come on gradually after chronic exposure to cases or suddenly after one particular case. The effects will vary but include:

- Emotional numbing, cynicism, social withdrawal.
- Loss of confidence, physical symptoms such as headaches, nausea, insomnia.

There are several strategies to protect against vicarious trauma:

- Adequate levels of managerial supervision with recognition that it is a risk.
- Peer review.
- Positive reinforcement of the value of the job.
- Avoidance of a "blame culture" when cases have poor outcomes.
- Encourage and support staff to strengthen and maintain their emotional wellbeing and encourage resilience-promoting behaviours.[30]

---

[28] The Collins Dictionary 1995.

[29] Tehrani, N. (ed.), *Managing trauma in the workplace: supporting workers and organisations.* (London: Routledge, 2011).

[30] *http://www.headington-institute.org/files/going-the-distance–article_15919.pdf*   [Accessed April 30, 2016]; Christian Pross, MD, *Burnout, vicarious traumatization and its prevention. What is burnout, what is vicarious traumatization? http://www.irct.org/Files/Filer/TortureJournal/16_1_2006/page_1-9.pdf* [Accessed April 30, 2016].

CHAPTER 22

MEDICAL EVIDENCE: CHILDREN

By Dr Catherine White*

Introduction..................................... 22.01
The Medical Response to an
  Allegation or Suspicion of Child
  Sexual Abuse................................ 22.04
The Medical Examination 22.25
Interpretation of Ano-Genital
  Findings 22.42

Sexually Transmitted Infections....... 22.67
Female Genital Mutilation 22.68
Child Sexual Exploitation................ 22.75
Learning Disability and Sexual
  Exploitation................................. 22.78
Conclusion...................................... 22.79

INTRODUCTION

There has been a marked increase over recent years in the number of police   **22.01**
reported cases of child sexual abuse. Childline saw an increase of 8 per cent
in calls relating to sexual abuse in the 12 months between 2013/14 and
2014/15.[1] In the last five years there has been a 128 per cent increase in
contacts to the NSPCC helpline where child sexual abuse was given as the
reason (3,867 in 2009/10 rising to 8,805 contacts in 2014/15).[2]

In 2000 the NSPCC published a paper by Cawson et al that looked at   **22.02**
prevalence of childhood abuse based on a household survey of 2,869 young
adults' memories of such abuse.[3] In 2011 the NSPCC published a second
review of prevalence.[4] The study involved household interviews by a

---

* Clinical Director of the Sexual Assault Referral Centre, St Mary's Hospital, Manchester;
author of *Sexual Assault, A Forensic Physician's Guide* (Manchester, St Mary's SARC,
2010).

[1] *Always There When I Need You*, Childline Review: What's affected children in April
2014-March 2015 (NSPCC), available at *http://www.nspcc.org.uk/globalassets/documents/annual-
reports/childline-annual-review-always-there-2014-2015.pdf* [Accessed April 30, 2016].

[2] How safe are our children? (NSPCC, 2015), available at *http://www.nspcc.org.uk/services-and-
resources/research-and-resources/how-safe-are-our-children-2015/* [Accessed April 30, 2016].

[3] Cawson P., Wattam C., Brooker S. and Kelly G., *Child Maltreatment in the United Kingdom:
a study of the prevalence of child abuse and neglect.* (London: NSPCC, 2000).

[4] Radford, L. et al., *Child abuse and neglect in the UK today* (London: NSPCC, 2011).

market research company using computer-assisted self-interviewing. The response rate was 60.4 per cent and interviews were completed with 2,160 parents or guardians of children and young people under 11 years of age, 2,275 young people aged between 11 and 17, with additional information provided by their parents or guardians, and lastly 1,761 young adults aged between 18 and 24. The results showed that:

- 1 in 20 children in the UK have been sexually abused.
- 0.5 per cent of under 11s, 4.8 per cent of 11–17 year olds and 11.3 per cent of 18–24 year olds had reported contact sexual abuse as defined by the criminal law at some point in childhood.
- 65.9 per cent of the contact sexual abuse reported by children and young people (0–17s) was perpetrated by other children and young people under the age of 18.
- 1.2 per cent of under 11s, 16.5 per cent of 11–17s and 24.1 per cent of 18–24s had experienced sexual abuse, including non-contact offences, by an adult or by a peer at some point in childhood.
- 0.6 per cent of under 11s and 9.4 per cent of 11–17s had experienced sexual abuse including non-contact offences in the past year.
- Teenage girls aged between 15 and 17 reported the highest past-year rates of sexual abuse.
- The majority of perpetrators of sexual abuse were males, either adults or other young people, who were known to the child or young person.
- In 34 per cent of cases of sexual assault by an adult and 82.7 per cent of cases of sexual assault by a peer, nobody else knew about it.

22.03   In 2012 a WHO-funded systematic review in 2012[5] indicated that children with disabilities are 3.7 times more likely than non-disabled children to be victims of any sort of violence, 3.6 times more likely to be victims of physical violence, and 2.9 times more likely to be victims of sexual violence. Children with mental or intellectual impairments appear to be among the most vulnerable, with 4.6 times the risk of sexual violence than their non-disabled peers.

THE MEDICAL RESPONSE TO AN ALLEGATION OR SUSPICION OF CHILD
SEXUAL ABUSE

22.04   The correct management of allegations of child sexual abuse or assault requires skill, sensitivity and good interagency communication and co-operation. Effective safeguarding systems are child-centred. Failings in safeguarding systems are too often the result of losing sight of the needs and

---

[5] Jones L, Bellis M et al, *Prevalence and risk of violence against children with disabilities: a systematic review and meta-analysis of observational studies*, published online, July 12, 2012, at *http://www.dx.doi.org/10.1016/S0140-6736(12)60692-8* [Accessed April 30, 2016].

views of the children within them, or placing the interests of adults ahead of the needs of children.[6] Factors to be considered by the clinicians include:

- Is a medical examination required?
- Who should do the examination?
- Where should the examination be done?
- When should it be done?
- How should it be done?

THE PURPOSES OF THE MEDICAL EXAMINATION

As with adult cases, there may be forensic as well therapeutic aspects to any examination. The best interests of the child should be the foremost consideration. The assessment should take into account the nature of the allegations bearing in mind the individual's medical, social and family history. It is important that sexual abuse should not be considered in isolation from other forms of physical and emotional abuse and neglect.   **22.05**

The medical or therapeutic aspects may include: **22.06**

- Assessment and treatment of injuries.
- Emergency contraception.
- Screening and treating of sexually transmitted infections.
- Post-cxposure prophylaxis (e.g. for HIV or Hepatitis B).
- Psychological or psychiatric needs.
- Reassurance (of child and/or carers).
- Overall medical assessment.
- Child protection issues including screening for risk of child sexual exploitation.

The forensic aspects may include: **22.07**

- Documentation of injuries (including negative findings).
- Gathering of forensic samples.

WHO SHOULD DO THE MEDICAL EXAMINATION?

Forensic physician qualifications

The General Medical Council ("GMC") sets the standards for doctors working in the UK. For the individual doctor providing care, the GMC is clear that the doctor must recognise and work within the limits of his/her competence.[7]   **22.08**

---

[6] *Working together to safeguard children: A guide to inter-agency working to safeguard and promote the welfare of children* (March 2015).
[7] *Good Medical Practice. Working with doctors, Working for Patients* (GMC, March 2013, updated April 2014; ISBN 978-0-901458-60-5).

22.09   The Royal College of Paediatrics and Child Health ("RCPCH") has stipulated that assessments for children up until their sixteenth birthday, and ideally children up to their eighteenth birthday must be undertaken by a qualified medical practitioner with appropriate competences.[8] A key aspect of this is that it is specifying a doctor rather than a nurse as the clinician.

22.10   The Faculty of Forensic and Legal Medicine ("FFLM") has produced Quality Standards for doctors undertaking paediatric sexual offence medicine.[9] These include the recommendation that all trainees should complete the Licentiate of the FFLM (Sexual Offences Medicine) ("FFLM (SOM)") (formerly the Diploma in the Forensic and Clinical Aspects of Sexual Assault ("DFCASA")) or Membership of the FFLM (SOM). All doctors who wish to practice independently in paediatric sexual offence medicine will need to pass the MFFLM (SOM) or MRCPCH plus LFFLM (SOM).

Two doctors or one?

22.11   There has been much confusion over the years regarding who should conduct the examination. It has become a widespread, but mistaken, belief that a two-doctor examination is the recommended best practice. The Royal College of Paediatrics and Child Health and the Faculty of Forensic and Legal Medicine produced updated guidance on this matter in October 2012.[10] This guidance defines a "child" as being under the age of 16 years. It urges:

> "that any doctor who undertakes a forensic assessment of a child who may have been subjected to sexual abuse must have particular skills. The child or young person must be assessed fully but appropriately dependent on the age and gender of the child, and the suspected nature and timing of possible abuse."

The Guidance goes on to discuss whether or not the examination should be a single or joint examination. It states:

> "A single doctor examination may take place provided the doctor concerned has the necessary knowledge, skills and experience for the particular case. When a doctor does not have all the necessary knowledge, skills and experience for a particular paediatric forensic examination two doctors with *complementary skills* should conduct a joint examination."

It goes on to say

> "If two professionals are involved they need to determine in advance of the assessment what skills they bring to the examination and who will conduct which component of the examination."

---

[8] *Service specification for the clinical evaluation of children and young people who may have been sexually abused* (RCPCH, September 2015), available at *http://www.rcpch.ac.uk/news/rcpch-has-published-revised-%E2%80%98service-specification-clinical-evaluation-children-and-young-who-m* [Accessed April 30, 2016].
[9] *Quality Standards for Doctors Undertaking paediatric Sexual Offence Medicine (PSOM)* (FFLM, February 2014), available on the FFLM website.
[10] *Guidelines on Paediatric Forensic Examinations in Relation to Possible Child Sexual Abuse* (FFLM, RCPCH, October 2012), available on the FFGM website.

Peer review

As part of the process of ensuring good clinical standards, it is important   **22.12**
that the clinicians take part in regular peer review. Peer review is the
evaluation of work or performance by colleagues in the same field in order to
maintain or enhance the quality of the work or performance in that field. The
word "peer" is often defined as a person of equal standing. However, in the
context of peer review, it is generally used in a broader sense to refer to
people in the same profession who are of the same or higher ranking. Peer
review has become an accepted aspect of clinical governance and is
encouraged by the General Medical Council.

The aim of peer review is to provide a proactive culture of learning where   **22.13**
clinicians and Sexual Assault Referral Centre ("SARC") staff can review
cases and discuss procedures, process and evidence bases underpinning
diagnosis, and in doing so provide a supportive environment to debrief cases
with peers undertaking similar work. In turn this will help prevent professional isolation and aid sharing of best practice. The fact that a clinician
regularly attends effective peer review may help reassure the courts as to the
quality of their work. It will also contribute to the evidence collected by a
clinician for the purposes of annual appraisal and revalidation.

It should be noted that the case discussion in peer review tends to be in   **22.14**
broad terms, rather than addressing fine detail, and therefore opinions
proffered by members should be viewed in this context. The aim of the case
discussion is not to generate either a second opinion or an expert opinion.

As part of the process of ensuring good clinical standards, it is important   **22.15**
that the clinicians take part in regular peer review. Following some unease
within the legal community regarding the application of the law of disclosure
to the process of peer review and its conclusions in relation to cases going
through the criminal justice system, the FFLM has produced recommendations around the process.[11]

WHERE SHOULD AN EXAMINATION BE DONE?

The RCPCH guidance states that the preferred overall model for paediatric   **22.16**
sexual abuse referral services is a "hub and spoke", with a central hub, a
paediatric SARC or equivalent, seeing all acute forensic cases.[12]

WHEN SHOULD AN EXAMINATION BE DONE?

The decision as to when to undertake a forensic examination is a complex   **22.17**
one and requires evaluation of numerous factors. Using guidance originally

---

[11] *Recommendations Peer Review in Sexual Offences including Child Sexual Abuse cases and the
implications for the disclosure of Unused Material in criminal investigations and prosecutions*
(April 2014), available on the FFLM website [Accessed April 30, 2016].
[12] See fn.8, above.

devised by St Mary's SARC, Manchester, in May 2013, the FFLM published a *Guide to establishing urgency of sexual offence examination*[13] which comprises two flowcharts, one for pre-pubertal children and the other for post-pubertal children and adults. This guidance aims to encourage decision makers (primarily the clinician but in discussion with others such as police and social services) to consider the therapeutic and forensic aspects of the case as well as issues such as safeguarding risks.

22.18   When considerable time has elapsed since the last alleged activity, then there will be no urgency to setting up an immediate examination. Where the last alleged activity is more recent, then consideration needs to be given to forensic matters (e.g. opportunities for recovery of forensic trace material such as semen, presence of injuries) and also medical considerations. The benefits of an early forensic examination need to be balanced against the doctor seeing the child before all details of the allegations and important background information about the child are known. Often the initial details can be incomplete. This makes decisions on the extent of the forensic examination (e.g. the necessity to take rectal swabs) difficult for the doctor, who will be keen to maximise forensic recovery whilst minimalising the trauma to the child of the medical examination. It must be remembered that it is not unusual for a child to disclose the nature and extent of the abuse in stages.

22.19   Knowledge of persistence of trace evidence is therefore crucial. The current timescales are given in the following table.[14] The recommendations from which this data is extracted are updated every six months by the Forensic Science Committee of the FFLM.

Persistence of trace evidence*		
Assault type	*Pre pubertal*	*Post pubertal*
Vaginal penetration	3 days	7 days
Anal penetration	3 days	3 days
Oral	2 days	2 days
Digital penetration (vaginal or anal)	48 hours	48 hours
Skin contact	2 days (but up to 7 if not washed)	2 days (but up to 7 if not washed)

[13] *Guide to establishing urgency of sexual offence examination* (FFLM, May 2013), available at the FFLM website.

[14] Table from data given in *Recommendations for the collection of forensic specimens from complainants and suspect* (FFLM, January 2016), available on the FFLM website.

Toxicology	Blood samples up to 3 days Urine samples up to 5 days (but up to 14 days if drug facilitated sexual assault suspected) Hair samples may be of use up to 6 months later.	Blood samples up to 3 days Urine samples up to 5 days (but up to 14 days if drug facilitated sexual assault suspected) Hair samples may be of use up to 6 months later.

*These timescales indicate possible upper limits. This is not the *expected* time to have positive forensic results. This expected time is much shorter. Also the likelihood of detecting trace evidence will depend on a number of factors, e.g. whether or not the alleged assailant ejaculated, used a condom, the child washed, changed their clothes, opened their bowels etc since the incident.

CONSENT AND PARENTAL RESPONSIBILITY

The doctor will need to gain informed consent for the examination prior to commencing it. For child cases, the doctor should be familiar with GMC documents such as *0–18 years; guidance for all doctors (2007)*.[15] The consent process should cover issues such as the nature and purpose of the examination, and who will have access to any medical records, including any photo-documentation. The latter point is crucial as the photo-documentation may include images of the ano-genital examination. The FFLM together with the RCPCH have updated guidance for clinicians on the issue regarding disclosure of highly sensitive images.[16]   **22.20**

When considering the management of a child, the best interests of the child should always be the paramount consideration. Where it would seem that parents are not acting in the child's best interests and the child is not *Gillick* competent, a court can be approached to gain alternative proxy consent.   **22.21**

GILLICK AND FRASER COMPETENCE

Children become adults for medical, i.e. therapeutic, purposes at the age of 16 years, when they are then able to consent to their own medical treatment. Children under the age of 16 may have the capacity to consent to medical treatment if they have sufficient understanding and intelligence to enable them to understand fully what is involved in the proposed intervention. This is sometimes described as being "*Gillick* competent", by reference to the decision of the House of Lords in *Gillick v West Norfolk and Wisbech Area*   **22.22**

[15] ISBN 978-0-901458-29-2, available on the GMC website.
[16] *Guidance for best practice for the management of intimate images that may become evidence in court* (May 2014), available on the FFLM website.

Health Authority.[17] Although there is no legal decision on the point, it is reasonable to assume that young people aged 16 and 17 have the capacity to consent to a forensic examination just as they do a therapeutic examination.[18] The term "Fraser competent" is sometimes erroneously used rather than "*Gillick* competent". This is reference to the speech of Lord Fraser in *Gillick*, and relates solely to the steps a clinician must take when deciding whether or not to provide contraception to a patient under the age of 16 years.[19]

HISTORY TAKING

22.23   The history taking should be comprehensive and recorded contemporaneously. It should be in sufficient depth so that a holistic assessment of the child's well-being can be made. It should be tailored so as to incorporate relevant information that may assist in interpreting any examination findings. For example, certain medical conditions or medications may affect bruising tendency. Knowledge of the physiological development of a child, such as onset of puberty, may have an effect on the likelihood of them sustaining genital injuries from certain sexual activities. It should be clear in the records who has given any information to the doctor and who else is present when that information is divulged. Any questions directed to the child should be open. Use of leading questions is to be avoided. If direct questions must be employed, then both the question and the answer should be recorded verbatim. Where possible, the forensic examination should be done after the police have carried out their video-recorded interview. In some acute forensic cases this will not be possible. Where forensic samples are taken, the history should encompass information that will help in the interpretation of the results. For example, has the child or young person bathed, changed their clothing, and cleaned their teeth etc. since the assault.

CHILD SEXUAL ABUSE ACCOMMODATION SYNDROME

22.24   The disclosure of sexual abuse may be very traumatic for a child. Children under pressure may retract their disclosure. A retraction per se does not mean that the original disclosure was untrue. Children can display a variety of behaviours following sexual abuse. These include: secrecy, helplessness, entrapment and accommodation, delayed and unconvincing disclosure and retraction. This has been called the Child Sexual Abuse Accommodation Syndrome.[20]

---

[17] [1986] A.C. 112, discussed in paras 4.181 and following, above.
[18] *Consent from children and young people in police custody in England and Wales* (March 2008), available on the FFLM website.
[19] Robert Wheeler, *Gillick or Fraser? A plea for consistency over competence in children*, BMJ 2006; 332:807.
[20] Summit R.C. (1983), *The Child Sexual Abuse Accommodation Syndrome. Child Abuse & Neglect*, 7, 177-193.

THE MEDICAL EXAMINATION

THE PROCESS

An age-appropriate setting should be used. If forensic trace evidence is a   **22.25**
consideration, then the forensic sterility of the examination suite must be
such that it minimises the risk of cross-contamination. The Forensic Science
Regulator is currently in the process of producing, as part of the Codes of
Practice and Conduct, standards for the forensic medical examination of
adult and child sexual assault complainants and these are anticipated to be
available in summer 2016.[21] In keeping with a comprehensive holistic
assessment of the child, a thorough top-to-toe examination should be
conducted. This will involve assessing all body surfaces, general demeanour,
height, weight, examination of the mouth, interaction with carers, physiological development etc.[22] Notes should be contemporaneous. Body charts
should be utilised as well as the written notes to document injuries, and
photo-documentation of injuries should be considered. If photographs are
taken, this should be done by someone suitably trained. The contemporaneous notes should state whether or not body charts or photographs,
including colposcopic images (see below), have been produced. Negative
examination findings as well as positive findings should be documented. This
not only helps to demonstrate impartiality but also is a clear indication of the
extent and nature of the examination.

Most examinations for child sexual abuse will not reveal injuries. Few   **22.26**
children (no more than 15 per cent) who have been or are being abused will
show physical evidence of the abuse.[23] Where they do, it is important that the
clinician records certain key information about any individual injury. This
will include a clear description of what type of injury it is, the size of the
injury, and the position of the injury on the child's body. Information which
may assist in determining the age and mechanism of the injury is vital, e.g.
the presence or not of fresh bleeding, scab formation, swelling etc. Any
disclosure of the causation should be noted verbatim.

THE GENITAL EXAMINATION

There are several purposes to the genital examination. In the main it is to   **22.27**
identify injuries, if there are any, and deal with them as necessary, to take
forensic samples if appropriate, to take swabs in order to screen for sexually

---

[21] See *https://www.gov.uk/government/organisations/forensic-science-regulator* [Accessed April
30, 2016].

[22] Dr. Catherine White, *Sexual Assault, A Forensic Physician's Practice Guide* (February 2010,
ISBN 978-0-9564737-0-7).

[23] *Report from the Child Sexual Abuse sub-group. Taskforce on the Health Aspects of Violence
Against Women and Children* (March 2010), available at *http://www.health.org.uk/sites/default/
files/RespondingtoViolenceAgainstWomenAndChildrenTheRoleofTheNHS_guide.pdf* [Accessed
April 30, 2016].

transmitted infections, to identify any condition that may be mistaken for an injury and hence have raised the suspicion of assault, and finally to reassure the child and the carer.

22.28   Good lighting is essential, as is having the child or young person as relaxed as possible. A piece of medical equipment called a colposcope will often be used. Basically this is a bright, cool light source which allows magnification and also the option of making a recording of the examination.

22.29   The ano-genital examination is done after a general body examination has been conducted. A general assessment will consider the child's physiological development (Tanner stage) and the overall health of the tissues, e.g. if there is any evidence of infection, inflammation or poor hygiene which may either mimic injury or make the tissues more susceptible to damage when subjected to trauma.

22.30   The genital examination can be done with the child in several positions. The ability to see a particular injury may depend on the examination position and technique. It is therefore important that the positions and techniques employed are stated in the notes. Research has shown that certain hymenal findings that may initially appear to be suggestive of injury, may in fact be artefacts, and if the child is examined in a different anatomical position then the "abnormality" disappears. For example, with a girl lying on her back, the lower part of the hymen may appear reduced. If the girl was to roll over into the knee-chest position, the hymen may appear completely normal. This is because gravity is now allowing the whole depth of the hymen to be seen. Hence, particularly with pre-pubertal examinations, it is considered best practice to always utilise more than one position especially if there is suspicion of an abnormal finding of the hymen.

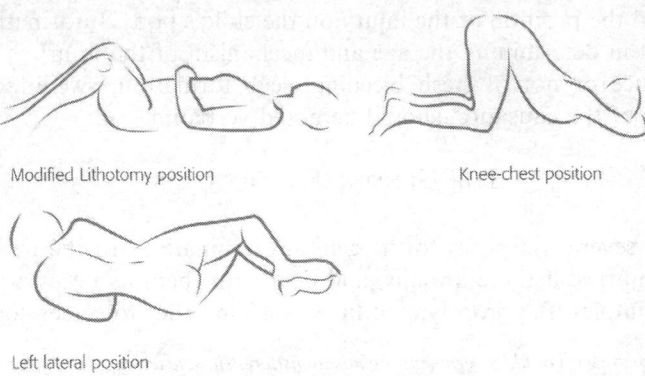

Modified Lithotomy position   Knee-chest position

Left lateral position

Figure 1: Images taken from *Sexual Assault, A Forensic Physician's Practice Guide.*

22.31   In a post-pubertal girl, the edges of the hymen may be examined using the moistened tip of a swab or a Foley catheter. If vaginal forensic samples are to be taken, this should be done prior to the insertion of the catheter in order to minimise the chances of contaminating the evidence.

BACKGROUND INFORMATION ON THE GENITALIA

Females

Pre-pubertal female anatomy

A good understanding of female genital anatomy and the effects that age and   **22.32** hormones have on these structures is essential.

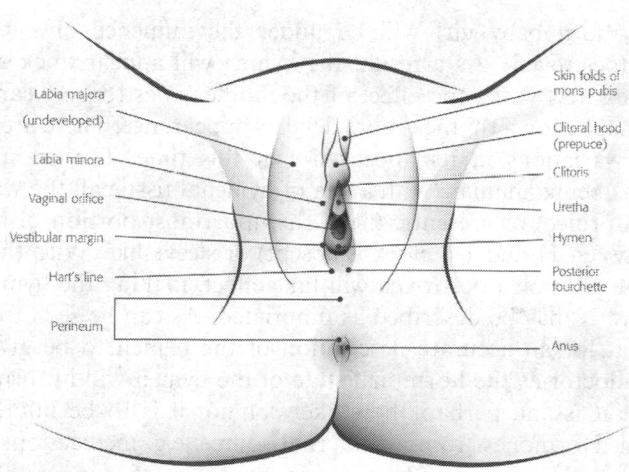

Figure 2: Pre-pubertal female
Image taken from *Sexual Assault, A Forensic Physician's Practice Guide.*

The face of a clock is often used to help denote anatomical positions. With   **22.33** a child lying on their back, the centre of the clock would be the centre of the hymenal orifice, 12 o'clock would indicate the area nearest the abdomen, 6 o'clock would be that nearest the bed etc. The same exercise can be used when commenting on anal findings. Note that as the child changes position, e.g. if lying on their side, the face of the clock changes with them, so that 12 o'clock would still refer to that closest to the abdomen, etc.

Figure 3: Image taken from *Sexual Assault, A Forensic Physician's Practice Guide.*

22.34   The new-born baby girl will be under the influence of her mother's hormones (oestrogen). As a result, the hymen will appear thick and fleshy. Over the next few years, the effect of the mother's oestrogen wears off. The hymen then takes on a thinner, more delicate appearance. There are a number of normal variations in its appearance at this time. The main ones are described as being annular (with a rim of hymenal tissue all the way around the vaginal orifice) or cresentic (here, the uppermost portion of the hymen usually between 11 and 1 o'clock is absent) or sleeve-like. With the onset of puberty, the girl's own oestrogen will take effect, making the hymen thicker and stretchy. It may be described as fimbriated. As can be seen from this, it is important for an accurate description of the hymen to be given by the examining doctor as the hormonal state of the hymen will in turn influence how elastic it is and perhaps how likely or not it is to be injured by any penetration. Hormones from an external source, e.g. medication, may have an effect on the tissues. There is no evidence of congenitally absent hymen.[24]

The legal vagina versus the medical vagina

22.35   That the definition of the vagina has a different medical definition to the legal definition may give rise to confusion and error. The medical definition defines the vagina as a muscular tube which has the cervix (neck of the womb) at its upper end and the hymen (or hymenal remnants) at its outer end. The legal definition of the "vagina", as used in s.79(9) the Sexual Offences Act 2003, has the outer end of the vagina starting with the vulva, i.e. between the labia. Therefore in a legal sense, penetration of the vagina does not have to involve penetration of the hymen.

[24] Jenny C., Kuhns M.L., Arakawa F., *Hymens in newborn female infants.* Pediatrics 1987;80(3):399-400.

Males

The appearance of the male genitalia as it is influenced by hormonal changes 22.36
during puberty is described in the Tanner stages. Of importance is that the
male erection can occur as a result of physical stimulation and in itself does
not necessarily indicate either consent to or enjoyment of said physical
stimulus.

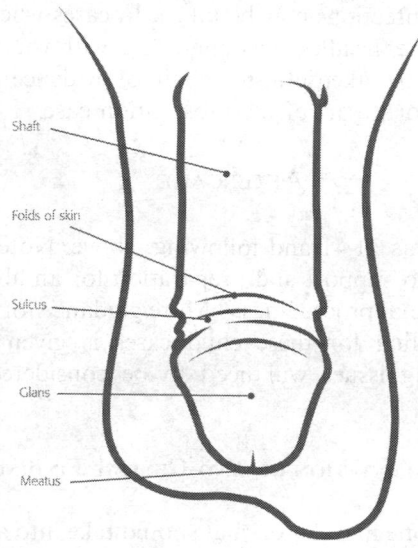

Figure 4: Image taken from *Sexual Assault, A Forensic Physician's Practice Guide.*

Tanner stages

Tanner was a paediatrician who documented the changes of the secondary 22.37
sexual characteristics as a child went through puberty. There are stages 1 to
5 for breast, pubic hair and male genital development. The stages refer to
physiological age and should not be used to determine the chronological age
of the child.

Anal anatomy

The anal canal is the end or terminal part of the large intestine. It extends 22.38
from the rectum to the anal orifice. The peri anal area is defined as the
external area which encircles the anal orifice to a diameter (in adults) of 3 cm.
The anal orifice is usually closed. This is due to two sets of muscles, the
internal sphincter which encircles the anal canal and the external sphincter,
a muscle under voluntary control at the anal verge.

Forensic Samples

22.39 These should be taken, assuming consent, as necessary in accordance with the latest guidelines (see Ch.21). It is important to be mindful of maintaining a chain of evidence which will allow any results to be admissible in court. With a pre-pubertal girl, penetration of the hymen with instruments such as a speculum should not be done, other than in exceptional circumstances such as a surgical repair of injuries in theatre.

22.40 Dependent upon the nature of the alleged abuse, screening tests for sexually transmitted infections may be taken. In cases where the only sexual contact is thought to be the alleged assailant, e.g. with younger children, then these samples should be taken utilising chain of evidence procedures as any positive results may form part of the prosecution case.

Aftercare

22.41 For aftercare, see paras 21.41 and following, above. Note that for children there is guidance as to support and preparation for an abused child who is also a witness in criminal proceedings.[25] More guidance for lawyers regarding therapy and counselling for these child cases is given in updated CPS advice.[26] Safeguarding issues will need to be considered in all of these cases.

Interpretation of Ano-Genital Findings

22.42 This must never be done in isolation, but should take into account the details and nature of the alleged assault and the overall assessment of the child, including the medical, social and family history. This will allow the findings to be put into context.

22.43 Normal ano-genital examination is the norm for most examinations. There are numerous possible explanations that need to be considered: that the allegations are unfounded; that the assault took place but did not cause any injury; that it took place causing injury which has since healed. Another explanation, coined by Dr Raine Roberts, is the "honest mistake". Here a sexually naïve child alleges penetration, as to them it may have felt like penetration (of vagina or anus) when in fact what they were feeling was pressure against the orifice but not actual penetration.

22.44 Unfortunately there are many misconceptions about the frequency that trauma is sustained, the degree of said trauma, residual evidence in the way of scarring and general misinterpretation of ano-genital findings. Much

---

[25] *Safeguarding Children as Victims and Witnesses* (CPS, Nov 2014), available at *http://www.cps.gov.uk/legal/v_to_z/safeguarding_children_as_victims_and_witnesses/index.html* [Accessed April 30, 2016].
[26] *Guidelines on Prosecuting Cases of Child Sexual Abuse* (CPS, Nov 2009), available at *http://www.cps.gov.uk/legal/a_to_c/child_sexual_abuse/* [Accessed April 30, 2016].

emphasis is often erroneously placed on whether or not the hymen is "intact". There is plenty of evidence demonstrating that penetration of the hymen can occur without causing any damage to the hymen.[27]

In 2008 the Royal College of Paediatrics and Child Health, in collabora-   **22.45** tion with the Faculty of Forensic and Legal Medicine, published the book *The Physical Signs of Child Sexual Abuse*. The updated 2nd edition, written this time in collaboration with both the FFLM and the American Academy of Pediatrics, was published in May 2015.[28] The book's aim is to set out both the strengths and limitations of the research evidence behind the most important clinical signs in children. Some of the key points are summarised below. These summaries are brief and the reader is strongly urged to consider the full text for more comprehensive discussion and information.

As a result of the publication of *The Physical Signs of Child Sexual Abuse*,   **22.46** it became clear that diagnostic criteria for such abuse have changed over the years. This resulted in a number of appeals seeking to rely upon fresh evidence to challenge convictions.[29] The most notable of these is *S, B, C and R v R.*,[30] in which the Court of Appeal allowed three of four conjoined appeals all of which turned upon fresh medical evidence. The Court noted that its role in such appeals is to evaluate the importance of the fresh evidence in the context of the remainder of the evidence in the case, the question being whether, in light of the fresh evidence, the conviction is safe, not what effect the fresh evidence would have had on the mind of the jury.[31] Further, when assessing the impact of fresh evidence, the Court should assume that the jury was faithful to the directions of law.[32]

GENITAL SIGNS OF SEXUAL ABUSE IN GIRLS

Erythema (redness): This is a non specific sign. If a result of trauma, it may   **22.47** disappear quickly, so early examinations are required. It may be due to other causes. In pigmented skin it may be more difficult to detect.

Oedema (swelling): This may occur after trauma and is likely to disappear   **22.48** quickly afterwards. Causes such as inflammation or infection need to be considered. The evidence base for determining the significance of oedema is weak.

---

[27] Kellog N., Menard S. and Santos A, *Genital Anatomy in Pregnant Adolescents: "Normal" Does Not Mean "Nothing Happened"*. Pediatrics 2004;113;67–69. White C. and McLean I., *Adolescent complainants of sexual assault; Injury patterns in virgin and non-virgin groups*. Journal of Clinical Forensic Medicine 13 (2006) 172–180.

[28] *The Physical Signs of Child Sexual Abuse. An evidence–based review and guidance for best practice* (RCPCH, May 2015).

[29] It is, of course, open to the Crown in such cases to adduce fresh evidence in response.

[30] [2012] EWCA Crim 1433. See also *R. v PF* [2009] EWCA Crim 1086.

[31] See also *R. v PF* [2009] EWCA Crim 1086, at [3], citing *Pendleton* [2002] 1 Cr. App. R. 34; *Hakala* [2002] EWCA Crim 730; *Dial and another v State of Trinidad and Tobago* [2005] 1 WLR 1660; *Noye* [2011] EWCA Crim 650.

[32] *Christou* [1996] 2 Cr. App. R. 360, at 371 per Lord Taylor CJ.

22.49   *Bruising*: This happens when there is damage to blood vessels allowing blood to leak into the surrounding tissues. Bruises sustained simultaneously may resolve at different rates. Therefore it is very difficult to age a bruise by colour and general appearance. As well as trauma, a bruise may be caused by a haematological condition. There are also other medical conditions that may be confused with bruises. Bruises may be more difficult to see in pigmented skin. Following trauma, a bruise is more likely to be found if the girl is examined quickly. Penetrative abuse can occur without causing bruising. Bruises will eventually fade leaving no trace. Small bruises such as petechiae may disappear within a couple of days. It is unusual to bruise the genital area accidentally and one would expect a clear history to explain such an injury. More information on interpretation of bruises can be found at *http://www.core-info.cf.ac.uk*.

22.50   *Abrasions*: This is a superficial injury involving only the outer layers of the skin/mucous membrane that does not extend to the full thickness of the epidermis. Lay terms include scratch or graze. If an injury is very small it may be difficult to distinguish an abrasion from a laceration. An abrasion can be caused by scratching by the child as well as by trauma, accidental or otherwise. In the studies reviewed, abrasions were noted in some pre-pubertal girls with a history of vaginal penetration. In pubertal girls, the one study suggests that genital abrasions are seen in a proportion of girls who allege penile penetration and are examined within 72 hours after the abuse. Abrasions tend to heal quickly so early examination is more likely to detect them. Abrasions will heal without leaving any scars.

22.51   *Lacerations*: This is defined as an injury caused by blunt force splitting the full thickness of the skin. Where the genitalia are concerned, it can be confusing as other terms are often used. These include "splits", "tears" or "transections". In *The Physical Signs of Child Sexual Abuse*, the term "laceration" refers to the fresh injury made by tearing through the skin, mucous membrane or deeper structures. This acute injury may be associated with bleeding and bruising. A laceration to the hymen may be partial or complete. An incomplete laceration of the hymen is an injury that does not involve the full thickness of the hymen. It may heal to form a notch (which may be superficial or deep). With regards to hymenal lacerations, in the pre-pubertal girl they are associated with a history of vaginal penetration/fondling. Lacerations tend to heal quickly. Most will heal without leaving a scar. Lacerations are seen more often to the posterior fourchette/fossa navicularis than any other genital tissue in abused girls, including the hymen. When lacerations are found on the genitalia, unless there is a convincing history of penetrating accidental injury, then sexual abuse should be strongly suspected. Scars of the genitalia are not commonly seen. They are however associated with sexual abuse, although other possible explanations should be sought. Some normal variants such as a median raphe may sometimes be mistaken for a scar. Lacerations and tears can heal without causing scar formation. Scars cannot be accurately aged.

Hymenal transections: A full thickness laceration of the hymen will heal (the raw edges) to form a transection. Here the defect of the hymen extends through to the base. The term "transection" should not be used for acute (fresh) injuries but reserved to describe non-acute injury to the hymen where the defect extends the full width of the hymen to the base (and this defect has been confirmed by examination in more than one position or with different techniques). As noted above, a transection of the hymen (a laceration through the full thickness of the hymen to the base) will not heal completely. Most pre-pubertal girls, where there is a history of penetration, do not have evidence of such injury to the hymen in the way of a transection. Where a transection was seen there was usually a history of penetration.   22.52

Clefts and notches of the hymen: These are defined as indentations of the hymen not extending to its base. A superficial notch is defined as one that is less than 50 per cent of the width of the hymenal membrane. A deep notch is more than 50 per cent of the width of the hymenal membrane (but not the full width as it then becomes a transection). In summary: 22.53

- Less than 50 per cent of the width of the hymenal membrane = a superficial notch.
- More than 50 per cent but less than 100 per cent of the width of the hymenal membrane = a deep notch.
- Full thickness of the hymenal membrane = transection.
- Acute hymenal lacerations can heal to leave a notch.
- Superficial notches in the posterior hymen have been seen in pre-pubertal girls with a history of vaginal penetration and also in pre-pubertal girls with no history of penetration.
- Notches in the anterior hymen (that is between 9 to 3 o'clock using the face of the clock) have been described in new-borns and pre-pubertal sexually abused and non abused girls.
- Deep notches in the posterior portion of the hymen (between 4 and 8 o'clock) were only seen in pre-pubertal girls with a history of vaginal penetration and not in pre-pubertal girls selected for non-abuse.
- In pubertal girls with a history of vaginal penetration deep notches were seen in 25 per cent.
- In pubertal girls, posterior deep notches or transections were reported more often in girls with a history of consensual sexual intercourse (33 per cent) than girls denying sexual intercourse (7 per cent).
- Where a hymenal defect is noted during the examination, it should be confirmed by examination in another position (e.g. supine and prone) or where appropriate by use of a swab or catheter.

Hymenal bumps or mounds: These are solid localised rounded or thickened area of tissue on the edge of the hymen. They can be a normal variant. They   22.54

have been reported in newborns, girls selected for non abuse as well as girls examined following abuse.

22.55   *Size of hymenal orifice*: There is substantial overlap in the range of hymenal diameters between prepubertal sexually abused girls and girls selected for non-abuse, therefore it is non-discriminatory for sexual abuse. Measurement of the hymenal orifice is not recommended.

22.56   *Hymenal width*: Studies have looked at the significance of the width of the hymenal rim. Terms such as attenuation, have been used in the past. This was thought to signify "wearing away" of the tissue due to abuse. Implicit is the suggestion that the changes are due to trauma and that there has been a change to the width as a result. So unless the appearance of the hymen has been documented previously, then these terms should not be used. In reality it is very difficult to measure the width of the tissue. The apparent width will depend upon such factors as the examination position, age and ethnicity of the girl. Particularly with an apparently narrow or absent posterior hymen seen with the girl on her back, she should be re-examined in the knee chest position as the findings may then be very different. Overall measurement of the width of the hymen is considered imprecise and not recommended.

22.57   *Labial fusion*: This is seen when there is adherence of adjacent mucosal surfaces of the labia minora (small lips of the vagina). There are a number of causes including local inflammation, vaginitis and poor hygiene. This makes it difficult to determine the significance of it in the child where sexual abuse is suspected. It is seen in younger children and tends to resolve sponta- neously. It can make the examination of other structures, such as the hymen, difficult if the fusion is marked.

Genital Signs of Sexual Abuse in Boys

22.58   There is very little published research on this subject. Indications from that research are that genital injuries in sexually abused boys occur predominantly to the penis. They occur in a small proportion of boys who have been abused. Testicular or scrotal injuries are more frequently associated with accidental injury than sexual abuse, although there are also injuries to these anatomical areas in cases of abuse. Early examinations (within 72 hours) are more likely to detect genital injuries in boys.

Anal Signs of Sexual Abuse

22.59   *Anal and perianal erythema* (redness): This is a non-specific finding. It may be seen in children subject to abuse, especially if examined soon afterwards. However it is also seen in children where there has been no abuse.

Perianal venous congestion: This describes the pooling of venous blood in the   **22.60**
veins of the area. It should be distinguished from bruising (where blood has
come out of the blood vessel into the surrounding tissues). It is a non-specific
sign in that it has been described in children where there has been an
allegation of abuse and also seen in children selected for non-abuse.

Anal, perianal bruising: Studies have shown that anal and/or perianal   **22.61**
bruising is occasionally seen in anally abused children. It has not been
reported in children selected for non-abuse. Bruising is an indication of
trauma. It will disappear over time without leaving any scar.

Acute breaks in the perianal skin—lacerations: Lacerations, tears and fissures   **22.62**
in the skin are due to blunt force splitting the full thickness of skin or mucous
membrane. There has been some confusion regarding terminology in this
area. The 2015 edition of *The Physical Signs of Child Sexual Abuse* proposes
that the term "laceration" is used to include fissures, tears and lacerations
and that the term "fissure" is dropped from use when describing signs around
the anus.

Care must be given to not confuse variants such as congenital failure of   **22.63**
midline fusion with a laceration. Some lacerations will heal resulting in scars,
but this is not the rule. Whilst perianal lacerations may be a result of sexual
abuse, consideration must also be given to other possible causes such as
constipation with the passage of large hard stools and bowel and skin disorders.

Anal scars and tags: Healing of a laceration in the anal verge skin can result   **22.64**
in the formation of a scar. An anal skin tag is a protrusion of anal verge tissue
and may be a marker of a past injury. Tags have also been noted in new-born
babies. Fleshy skin tags are also noted in Crohn's disease.

Anal dilatation: The 2015 edition of *The Physical Signs of Child Sexual*   **22.65**
Abuse covers the area of anal signs such as anal dilatation, reflex anal
dilatation, gaping, laxity, funnelling etc. in great detail, trying to bring
together the various definitions and papers on these matters. The reader is
advised to read the full text for a comprehensive picture of the current
thinking on these matters. Some key messages from the text are that:
  • There is a lack of good quality comparative studies in this area.
  • Reflex anal dilatation can occur in both abused and non-abused
    children although it may be more frequent in the former.
  • Certain terms should no longer be used including: gaping, laxity,
    funnelling, twitching and winking.
Finally, many children will have a normal examination and this may be   **22.66**
determined by such factors such as the type of abuse, the force used and the
time between abuse and examination. Equally where positive findings are
seen there needs to be consideration as to whether the findings are as a result

of accidental trauma, a disease process or even a normal variant. They must be placed into context of the history provided by the child and will be one part of the jigsaw.

SEXUALLY TRANSMITTED INFECTIONS

22.67 Part of the therapeutic care of a child being assessed for possible sexual abuse is a risk assessment as to the need to screen for sexually transmitted infections. This will depend partly on the nature of the abuse, if known, and details regarding the alleged assailant. For some conditions, such as ano-genital warts, there may be alternative explanations for a positive diagnosis, such as vertical transmission. For older, sexually active young people, an infection may have been acquired from unrelated "consensual" sexual activity. In some circumstances, such as with young children, a positive diagnosis may have forensic implications and so there should be consideration as to how any screening samples are taken, in order that any results may be admissible as evidence in a legal process.

FEMALE GENITAL MUTILATION

22.68 Female genital mutilation ("FGM") is defined as all procedures involving partial or total removal of the external female genitalia or other injury to the female genital organs, whether for cultural or other non-therapeutic reasons. In England, Wales and Northern Ireland, FGM is illegal under the Female Genital Mutilation Act 2003 (this offence captures mutilation of a female's labia majora, labia minora or clitoris). In Scotland it is illegal under the Prohibition of Female Genital Mutilation (Scotland) Act 2005.

22.69 Under the 2003 Act, a person is guilty of an offence if they excise, infibulate or otherwise mutilate the whole or any part of a girl's or woman's labia majora, labia minora or clitoris, except for necessary operations performed by a registered medical practitioner on physical and mental health grounds; or an operation performed by a registered medical practitioner or midwife (or a person undergoing training with a view to becoming a medical practitioner or midwife) on a woman who is in labour or has just given birth, for purposes connected with the labour or birth (these exceptions are set out in s.1(2) and (3) of the Act).

22.70 Under the 2003 Act it is an offence for any person (regardless of their nationality or residence status) to perform FGM (s.1) or to assist a girl to carry out FGM on herself (s.2). It is also an offence to assist (from England, Wales or Northern Ireland) a non-UK national or resident to carry out FGM outside the UK on a UK national or permanent UK resident (s.3).

22.71 Section 4 extends ss.1–3 to extra-territorial acts, so that it is also an offence for a UK national or permanent UK resident to perform FGM abroad; to assist a girl to perform FGM on herself outside the UK; or to assist (from

outside the UK) a non-UK national or resident to carry out FGM outside
the UK on a UK national or permanent UK resident.

Section 70(1) of the Serious Crime Act 2015 amends s.4 of the 2003 Act so   22.72
that the extra-territorial jurisdiction extends to prohibited acts done outside
the UK *by* a UK national or a person who is resident in the UK. Consistent
with that change, s.70(1) also amends s.3 of the 2003 Act (offence of assisting
a non-UK person to mutilate overseas a girl's genitalia) so it extends to acts
of FGM done *to* a UK national or a person who is resident in the UK.

For these purposes "UK resident" is defined as an individual who is   22.73
habitually resident in the UK. The term habitually resident covers a person's
ordinary residence, as opposed to a short, temporary stay in a country.

All cases should be dealt with under existing safeguarding frameworks,   22.74
which for children under 18 who have undergone FGM would mean a
referral to Children's Social Care and/or the police as appropriate.

CHILD SEXUAL EXPLOITATION

Child sexual exploitation is a phenomenon that has doubtless been a problem   22.75
for many years but has recently become much more widely recognised.[33] The
sexual exploitation of children and young people under the age of 18 has
been defined as that which:

> "involves exploitative situations, contexts and relationships where young people
> (or a third person or persons) receive 'something' (e.g. food, accommodation,
> drugs, alcohol, cigarettes, affection, gifts, money) as a result of them performing,
> and/or another or others performing on them, sexual activities. Child sexual
> exploitation can occur through the use of technology without the child's
> immediate recognition; for example being persuaded to post sexual images on
> the Internet/mobile phones without immediate payment or gain. In all cases,
> those exploiting the child/young person have power over them by virtue of their
> age, gender, intellect, physical strength and/or economic or other resources.
> Violence, coercion and intimidation are common, involvement in exploitative
> relationships being characterised in the main by the child or young person's
> limited availability of choice resulting from their social/economic and/or emo-
> tional vulnerability".[34]

One of the difficulties with some cases of child sexual exploitation is that   22.76
the vulnerability of these children, that makes them a target for predators,
can also mean that they are seen as "poor" witnesses by the criminal justice
system. In June 2013, the Director of Public Prosecutions produced *Interim
Guidelines on Prosecuting Cases of Child Sexual Abuse*[35] which covers some

---

[33] See *I thought I was the only one. The only one in the world*, The Office of the Children's
Commissioner's Inquiry into Child Sexual Exploitation in Gangs and Groups, Interim report
(Nov 2012), available on the Commissioner's website.
[34] *Tackling Child Sexual Exploitation: National Action Plan Progress Report* (Department for
Education, 2012).
[35] *https://www.cps.gov.uk/consultations/csa_consultation_index.html* [Accessed April 30,
2016].

of these issues, including assessing the credibility of child abuse allegations and the credibility or reliability of a child or young person.

22.77   In 2012, the Office of the Children's Commissioner in England ("OCCE") began an enquiry into child sexual exploitation in gangs and groups. The interim report of this enquiry[36] outlines a list of vulnerabilities which may be present in children prior to abuse and a further list of signs and behaviours generally seen in children who are already being sexually exploited. Prosecutors should consider whether the victim whose evidence they are considering demonstrates any of these factors. Whilst the absence of any of these characteristics does not mean that an allegation is unlikely to be true, their presence may assist the prosecutor in forming an overall view of the case. The OCCE list is as follows:

Child Sexual Exploitation	
Typical vulnerabilities in children prior to abuse:	The following signs and behaviour are generally seen in children who are already being sexually exploited:
• Living in a chaotic or dysfunctional household (including parental substance use, domestic violence, parental mental health issues, parental criminality); • history of abuse (including familial child sexual abuse, risk of forced marriage, risk of "honour"-based violence, physical and emotional abuse and neglect); • recent bereavement or loss; • gang association either through relatives, peers or intimate relationships (in cases of gang associated CSE only); • attending school with young people who are sexually exploited; • learning disabilities;	• Missing from home or care; • physical injuries; • drug or alcohol misuse; • involvement in offending; • repeat sexually-transmitted infections, pregnancy and terminations; • absent from school; • change in physical appearance; • evidence of sexual bullying and/or vulnerability through the internet and/or social networking sites; • estranged from their family; • receipt of gifts from unknown sources; • recruiting others into exploitative situations; • poor mental health; • self-harm; • thoughts of or attempts at suicide

---

[36] Above fn.34.

Child Sexual Exploitation	
<ul><li>unsure about their sexual orientation or unable to disclose sexual orientation to their families;</li><li>friends with young people who are sexually exploited;</li><li>homeless;</li><li>lacking friends from the same age group;</li><li>living in a gang neighbourhood;</li><li>living in residential care;</li><li>living in hostel, bed and breakfast accommodation or a foyer;</li><li>low self-esteem or self-confidence;</li><li>young carer.</li></ul>	

LEARNING DISABILITY AND SEXUAL EXPLOITATION

Recent research[37] shows that there is evidence that children with a learning **22.78** difficulty are at increased risk of becoming a victim of child sexual exploitation. The authors conclude that the reasons for this are multi-factorial but include issues such as:

- capacity issues making it difficult to appreciate risk.
- societal treatment of young people with learning disabilities, including over-protection, disempowerment, isolation and not seeing them as sexual beings, leading to little attention being given to informing them about healthy sexual relationships.
- a lack of knowledge, understanding and awareness of the sexual exploitation of young people with learning disabilities among professionals, parents and carers, and the wider community.
- a lack of identification of learning disabilities, and focus being placed on behavioural issues at the expense of identifying exploitation or learning needs.
- a lack of understanding of capacity to consent and of the abilities of professionals to assess this.
- the lack of training received by professionals concerning child sexual exploitation and learning disabilities.

---

[37] Anita Franklin, Phil Raws and Emilie Smeaton, *Unprotected, overprotected: meeting the needs of young people with learning disabilities who experience, or are at risk of, sexual exploitation* (Barnardo's, 2015).

- the low priority generally given to young people with learning disabilities by service providers and policymakers.

CONCLUSION

22.79   As can be seen, child sexual abuse is a common, though frequently unreported phenomenon. The medical evaluation is often complex, requiring consideration of the ongoing medical and psychological needs of the child, any child protection issues, as well as the gathering of forensic evidence which may assist a court in determining the veracity of an allegation or suspicion of abuse. The evidence base is in need of further work. There are many myths held both by the public and those involved in this work regarding likely medical findings. It is incumbent on clinicians working in this field to produce the evidence base to dispel these beliefs. It should be remembered that the medical examination findings are just one part of the overall assessment of a case, that the history taken from the child should be given due weight and that the needs of the child should remain paramount.

CHAPTER 23

PSYCHOLOGICAL EFFECTS OF RAPE AND SERIOUS SEXUAL ASSAULT

By Professor Fiona Mason MB BS FRCPsych DFPDr,
Paula Murphy MBChB MRCPsych MSc

Introduction...................................... 23.01
Myths and stereotypes..................... 23.18
Psychological reactions during rape
  and serious sexual assault 23.32
Psychological reactions following
  sexual assault............................... 23.36
Legal implications............................ 23.59
Late reporting.................................. 23.73
Re-traumatisation 23.76
Inconsistencies and lies.................... 23.78
The trial... 23.80
What do victims need?..................... 23.83

INTRODUCTION

The links between traumatic experience and psychological distress have been **23.01** reflected in art and literature for centuries. However, our scientific understanding of these links and the reactions of victims have only developed over the last century. Victims (or survivors, as many would prefer to be known) are just that; people who have experienced an adverse circumstance and have lived through in spite of the adversity. Victims of rape and serious sexual assault can be of either sex, and of any age, but the majority are women; therefore, whilst not forgetting child victims or male survivors, this chapter is written from the perspective of the majority. Reference will also be made to both rape and serious sexual assault; much of the research has focused on the former, however many of the difficulties seen in rape victims are equally applicable to those subject to other forms of serious sexual assault.

Recent years have seen significant changes in attitudes towards sexual **23.02** crimes. There has been an increased recognition of the psychological effects of sexual offences on victims. The low conviction rate of these types of offences has been recognised and the inadequate handling of these offences by the police has been highlighted. There has been a plethora of new victim-focused guidance, for police,[1] CPS prosecutors,[2] Sexual Offence Examiners/ Practitioners, Sexual Assault Referral Centres[3] and other professionals who come into contact with rape complainants,[4] but implementation remains patchy. Recent developments, however, indicate a cultural shift; there have been changes in the way rape is dealt with by the police, prosecutors and judiciary and the number of convictions is slowly rising, with official figures showing an increase from 1,778 in 2006/07 to 2,021 in 2008/09.[5] More recently, there has been a focus on the arrest and prosecution of high profile offenders, particularly in relation to historic child sexual abuse cases.

23.03   However, the fact remains that sexual violence continues to be a significant global problem and the full extent of the problem remains largely unknown. It is estimated that the lifetime risk of attempted or completed rape is up to 20 per cent for women, and men and children are also often sexually assaulted.[6]

23.04   In England and Wales, sexual crime statistics, alongside other crime statistics, are generated from both the Crime Survey for England and Wales ("CSEW") (previously known as the British Crime Survey) and police recorded crime. Whilst both provide a basic estimate of crime over time, neither can offer a complete picture. This is due to a number of reasons. First, the CSEW is a face-to-face survey of household residents in England and Wales where respondents (adults aged 16 and over) are questioned about their experiences of a selected number of offences in the 12 months prior to the interview. It does not include those living in group residences (for example, hospitals, prisons, care homes or student halls of residence), or crimes against commercial or public sector bodies. It relies therefore on interviewees reporting being victim to crime, which they may or may not have reported to the police.

23.05   Secondly, police recorded crime figures include selected offences, which have been reported to and recorded by the police, therefore crimes that have not been reported cannot be accounted for.

23.06   Thirdly, doubt has recently been cast on the quality and reliability of police recorded crimes following an assessment of the Office of National Statistics ("ONS") crime statistics by the UK Statistics Authority, published in January 2014, where the statistics based on police recorded crime data were

---

[1] *An assessment of the viability of the dedicated team approach to rape investigation* (Association of Chief Police Officers, 2008); *Guidance on investigating and prosecuting rape* (Association of Chief Police Officers and CPS, 2009).

[2] *Policy for prosecuting cases of rape* (CPS, 2009).

[3] *Revised national service guide: a resource* (Department of Health, Home Office and Association of Chief Police Officers, 2009).

[4] *Responding to violence against women and children—the role of the NHS. The report of the violence against women taskforce* (Department of Health, 2010).

[5] The Stern Review, *A report by Baroness Vivien Stern CBE of an independent review into how rape complaints are handled by public authorities in England and Wales* (Government Equalities Office and Home Office, 2010).

[6] R. Jewkes, C. Garcia-Moren, and P. Sen, *Sexual Violence in World Report on Violence & Health* (Geneva: World Health Organisation, 2002) 149–81.

found not to meet the required standard for designation as National
Statistics.[7] This led to an investigation by Her Majesty's Inspectorate of
Constabulary ("HMIC"), who conducted a national inspection of crime data
integrity by auditing a large sample of records. In their report, *Crime-
recording: making the victim count,*[8] published on November 18, 2014, HMIC
concluded that, across England and Wales, an estimated 1 in 5 offences (19
per cent) that should have been recorded as crimes were not, with 26 per cent
of sexual offences being under-recorded. It also found that there were poor
systems in place in some police forces for recording such crimes.

Finally, to obscure the figures further, sexual offences in particular are   **23.07**
known to be underreported[9] and therefore extremely difficult to obtain
reliable data on.

It can therefore be concluded with some certainty that the figures that   **23.08**
follow are by no means inclusive and merely representative of the actual
problem.

According to the CSEW for the year ending June 2015,[10] there were an   **23.09**
estimated 6.5 million incidents of crime against households and resident
adults. This was an 8 per cent decrease compared to the previous year. This
is the lowest recorded figure since the CSEW's inception in 1981. However, in
contrast to this, police recorded crime increased by 5 per cent as compared
with the previous year, with 4.3 million offences recorded in the year ending
June 2015.

Sexual offences in particular saw the largest increase since the introduction   **23.10**
of the National Crime Recording Standard ("NCRS") in 2002/03. Sexual
offences were reported to rise by 41 per cent compared with the previous
year, to a total of 95,482 across England and Wales in the year ending June
2015. Rape offences increased by 43 per cent to 31,621 offences and "other
sexual offences" increased by 40 per cent to 63,861 offences.

It is believed that these increases are most likely the result of a combination **23.11**
of improvements in the recording of crime by the police and victims being
more willing to report these types of crimes, rather than any real increase in
these types of offences. A number of high profile historic sexual abuse cases
and the commencement of Operation Yewtree in 2012 were shown to have
contributed to the previous year's increase in the number of sexual offences
reported to the police. Both current and historic offences continue to rise in

---

[7] *Crime in England and Wales, Year Ending June 2015* (ONS, October 2015), available at *http:/
/www.ons.gov.uk/ons/rel/crime-stats/crime-statistics/year-ending-june-2015/stb-crime–ye-june-
2015.html£tab-Sexual-offences* [Accessed April 30, 2016].

[8] *Crime recording: making the victim count. The final report of an inspection of crime data
integrity in police forces in England and Wales* Her Majesty's Inspectorate of Constabulary
(2014), available at *https://www.justiceinspectorates.gov.uk/hmic/publications/crime-recording-
making-the-victim-count/* [Accessed April 30, 2016].

[9] *Crime in England and Wales, Year Ending December 2014* (ONS, 2014), available at *http:/
/www.ons.gov.uk/ons/rel/crime-stats/crime-statistics/focus-on-violent-crime-and-sexual-offences–
2013-14/rpt-chapter-4.html* [Accessed April 30, 2016].

[10] fn.7, above.

the year ending June 2015 compared with the previous year, although the major contribution is believed to be from current offences.

23.12   Figures from the self-completion section of CSEW in the year ending March 2015 show little change in the number of adults reporting being victim to sexual assault or attempted sexual assault in the previous year with 1.7 per cent reporting such offences as compared to 1.5 per cent in the year ending March 2014. Detailed findings from the 2014/15 survey are not due to be released until February 2016 and so the statistics that follow are based on the estimates from the 2013/14 CSEW[11]:

- 19.9 per cent of women and 3.6 per cent of men reported sexual assault (including attempts) since the age of 16.
- Women were more likely than men to have been a victim in the last year (8.5 per cent or 1.4 million female victims compared with 4.5 per cent or 700,000 male victims). These figures are consistent with the lifetime prevalence (28.3 per cent compared with 14.7 per cent).
- 2.2 per cent women and 0.7 per cent men had experienced some form of sexual assault (including attempts) in the last year. The majority of these were less serious assaults, including indecent exposure and unwanted sexual touching.
- 0.7 per cent women and 0.1 per cent men had experienced serious sexual assault (including attempts).
- 0.4 per cent of women and less than 0.1 per cent of men had experienced serous sexual assault (excluding attempts).
- Women in the youngest age category (aged 16 to 19) were more likely to have experienced any sexual abuse in the last year (6.7 per cent) as compared with all older age groups (for example 2 per cent of women aged between 25 and 34). Similarly, women who were single were more likely to be victims of sexual assault (4.1 per cent) compared with women who were married (1.0 per cent), cohabiting (1.6 per cent), divorced (2.6 per cent) or widowed (0.3 per cent). Relationship status was believed to be strongly linked to age.
- With regard to the relationship of the victim to the offender, recorded as any abuse experienced since the age of 16, 56 per cent of female victims had experienced at least one incident of serious sexual assault by a partner/ex-partner since the age of 16, whereas 23.8 per cent had experienced at least one incident of less serious sexual assault where a partner/ex-partner was the offender. 16 per cent of female victims of serious sexual assault reported the offender as a stranger. It should be noted that the new questions do not allow for the establishment of all types of abuse for each participant. For example, if someone has been abused by a partner/ex-partner or family member, the survey does not

[11] *Crime in England and Wales, Year Ending December 2014* (ONS, 2014), available at *http:/ /www.ons.gov.uk/ons/rel/crime-stats/crime-statistics/focus-on-violent-crime-and-sexual-offences– 2013-14/rpt-chapter-4.html* [Accessed April 30, 2016].

allow for reporting other abuse by someone else, such as by a stranger.

A recent US study[12] notes that rape affects one in seven women in the   23.13
USA. The authors investigated the prevalence of reporting rape among a national sample of 3,001 women, and examined concerns, barriers and predictors about reporting. Results demonstrated that the overall prevalence of reporting (15.8 per cent) had not significantly increased since the 1990s. Differences were found between rape types, with those involving drug or alcohol incapacitation or facilitation being less likely to be reported than forcible rapes. The authors advocate the need to conduct further research into identification of barriers to reporting that will inform recommendations.

Rape and other serious sexual assaults are deeply damaging, serious   23.14
crimes, and as mentioned previously, whilst many new policies and practices have been developed to assist victims, implementation has been patchy.[13] Baroness Stern argued in her 2010 review that:

" . . . it is time to take a broader approach to measuring success in dealing with rape. The conviction rate, however measured, has taken over the debate to the detriment of other important outcomes for victims. We do not say that prosecuting and convicting in rape cases is in any way unimportant. Far from it. It is important, and necessary. But in dealing with rape there is a range of priorities that needs to be balanced. Support and care for victims should be a higher priority. The obligations the State has to those who have suffered a violent crime, and a crime that strikes at the whole concept of human dignity and bodily integrity, are much wider than working for the conviction of a perpetrator."

Notwithstanding this, it is essential for those victims who choose to   23.15
become complainants that those interacting with them through the criminal justice process understand the significant physical and psychological consequences resulting from issues such as sexually transmitted infections, depression, anxiety and post-traumatic stress disorder; conditions which can have a long-lasting impact on people's well-being and future functioning.[14]

People with mental health problems are particularly vulnerable to being   23.16
victim of crime as compared to the general population.[15] An analysis of the

---

[12] K.B. Wolitzky-Taylor, H.S. Resnick, J.L. McCauley, A.B. Amstadter, D.G. Kilpatrick and K.J. Ruggiero, *Is reporting of rape on the rise? A comparison of women with reported versus unreported rape experiences in the national women's study-replication*, Journal of Interpersonal Violence, Vol./is. 26/4 (807-832) (2011).

[13] fn.5, above.

[14] J. Welch and F. Mason, "Rape and Sexual Assault". *British Medical Journal* 2007, 334 (7604) 1154–1158.

[15] Pettitt B, Greenhead S, Khalifeh H, et al. (2013) *At Risk Yet Dismissed: The Criminal Victimisation of People with Mental Health Problems*. London: Victim Support/Mind; Khalifeh H, Howard LM, Osborn D, et al. (2013) *Violence against people with disability in England and Wales: Findings from a national cross-sectional survey*. PLoS ONE 8(2). Available at: *http://www.plosone.org/article/info%3Adoi%2F10.1371%2Fjournal.pone.0055952* [Accessed April 30, 2016].

2009/10 British Crime Survey by Khalifeh et al (2013)[16] using multivariate logistic regression estimated the relative odds of being a victim of violence in the past year (physical/sexual domestic or non-domestic violence) in people with disability compared to those without, after adjusting for socio-demographics, behavioural and area confounders. Of the sample, 2.4 per cent of participants had one or more disabilities including mental illness and 13.9 per cent had one or more disabilities excluding mental illness. Participants with mental illness had an adjusted relative odds ("aOR") of 3.0 (95 per cent confidence interval (CI) 2.3–3.8) of being a victim of violence in the past year as compared with the non-disabled; i.e. their relative risk was three times higher; whilst participants with non-mental disability had an aOR of 1.8 (95 per cent CI: 1.5–2.2) (with similar relative odds for domestic and non-domestic violence). In addition, disabled victims were more likely to suffer mental ill health as a result of violence than non-disabled victims.

23.17   A recently published report, *At risk, yet dismissed* (2013),[17] examined the victimisation of people with mental health problems and their experiences of engagement with the criminal justice system. A random sample of 361 people with severe mental illness who were using community mental health services were surveyed using a modified version of the CSEW. The findings from this sample were compared with those from the general population who took part in the CSEW survey over the same time period in London. The researchers found very high rates of being victim to a sexual offence, with 40 per cent of women reporting being a victim of rape or attempted rape in adulthood, and 10 per cent being a victim of sexual assault in the past year.

Myths and Stereotypes

23.18   Myths and stereotypes about rape persist in society, despite available data outlining the reality. Myths can have a significant impact on those affected by rape, as well as on those involved in the judicial system, and it is important to tackle such myths and barriers.

23.19   Research indicates that rape myths differ with time and within different societies and cultural settings, with higher acceptance of rape myths being noted in societies with a culture of hostility towards women. Awareness is needed if such myths are to be challenged.

23.20   For many people, the word "rape" will conjure up an image of a stranger attacking a woman at knife point in a dark public place. In reality this situation is extremely rare. Most rapes and other sexual assaults are committed by someone known to the victim. Common categories of perpetrators include current and former husbands and partners, recent

---

[16] Available at: *http://www.plosone.org/article/info%3Adoi%2F10.1371%2Fjournal.pone. 0055952* [Accessed April 30, 2016].
[17] fn.15, above.

acquaintances, colleagues and people in positions of trust.[18] This in turn means that many assaults take place in private—including in the victim's home, in the perpetrator's home, in workplaces—and in the context of daily lives. And yet, for some, including the victims themselves,[19] such encounters are not always seen as rape, and indeed, it was not until 1991 that rape within marriage was criminalised.

A joint publication by the Ministry of Justice, Home Office and the Office   **23.21** for National statistics, *An Overview of Sexual Offending in England and Wales*,[20] reported that around 90 per cent of victims of the most serious sexual offences in the previous year knew the perpetrator, compared with less than half for other sexual offences. This contradicts the commonly held belief that rapes are most frequently perpetrated by strangers.

The issue of force is another area around which myths abound. Force is   **23.22** not an essential element of the offence of rape and many rapes do not involve additional physical assault or threat going beyond the act of penetration. Often victims do not resist and many are not physically injured.[21] However, if the basic assumption made is that anyone being raped would fight back, and/or be injured, this will cloud the judgments made about whether an incident was or was not rape.

Anyone can be the victim of rape and all have the same rights to protection   **23.23** under the law. Women of all ages, sizes and appearances are raped and rapists can be attractive, successful and having regular sex. Particularly vulnerable women, such as those with, for example, a history of childhood sexual abuse, mental health problems, or learning disability, have the same rights as others. These women, who are some of the most vulnerable in our society, are in fact more likely to be subject to repeat victimisation,[22] and yet multiple reports of rape or sexual assault by an individual can be used to suggest that they are lying; that they are a serial complainant; that they are attention-seeking; or that they are hysterical, deluded or victims of unscrupulous therapists who implant false memories.

[18] fn.14 above; H. McGee, R. Garavan, M. de Barra, J. Byrne and R. Conroy, *The SAVI Report: Sexual Abuse & Violence in Ireland—a national study of Irish experiences, beliefs and attitudes concerning sexual violence* (Dublin: The Liffey Press, 2002); E.K. Martin, C.T. Taft and P.A. Resick, "A review of marital rape". *Aggression and Violent Behaviour* 2007, 12(3), 329–347.
[19] A. Myhill and J. Allen, *Rape and sexual assault of women: Findings from the British Crime Survey* (Home Office Findings 159, 2002).
[20] *An overview of sexual offending in England and Wales* (Ministry of Justice, Home Office and the Office for National Statistics, 2013).
[21] N.F. Sugar, D.N. Fine and L.O. Eckert, "Physical injury after sexual assault; findings of a large case series", *American Journal of Obstetrics and Gynecology* 2004, 190(1) 71–6.
[22] C.C. Classen, O. Palesh and R. Aggarwal, *Sexual revictimisation: A review of the empirical literature*, Trauma, Violence & Abuse, Vol.6, No.2, 103–129 (2005); N.N. Sarkar and R. Sarkar, *Sexual assault on woman: Its impact on her life and living in society*, Sexual & Relationship Therapy, 20(4), 407–419 (2005); J. Read, J. van Os, A. Morrison and C. Ross, *Childhood trauma, psychosis and schizophrenia: A literature review with theoretical and clinical implications*, Acta Psychiatrica Scandinavia, 112 pp.330–350 (2005). D. Finkelhor and K. Yllo, *License to Rape: Sexual abuse of wives*, (NY: Holt, Rinehart and Winston, 1985).

23.24   It is important to emphasise that women who have engaged in behaviour which may be perceived as risky, for example, accepting a lift home, walking alone or getting intoxicated, are also entitled to protection under the law. However, we know from published survey data that people make judgments about responsibility based on such factors. This was illustrated in a 2005 report by Amnesty International[23] and a 2010 survey[24] which indicated that over half (56 per cent) of those surveyed thought that there were some circumstances where a person should accept responsibility for being raped. For those people the circumstances were:

- Performing another sexual act on the rapist (73 per cent).
- Getting into bed with them (66 per cent).
- Drinking to excess/blackout (64 per cent).
- Going back to theirs for a drink (29 per cent).
- Dressing provocatively (28 per cent).
- Dancing in a sexy way with a man at a night club or bar (22 per cent).
- Acting flirtatiously (21 per cent).
- Kissing them (14 per cent).
- Accepting a drink and engaging in a conversation at a bar (13 per cent).

It cannot reasonably be assumed that a woman is consenting to sex from the way in which she is dressed, from her reputation, from her previous agreement to levels of intimacy, or even to consensual sex with the accused on another occasion, and yet it seems that many of the general public believe that such behaviours make women responsible for being raped. This is clearly at odds with the law as it stands.

23.25   A number of studies utilise data from surveys of US college students to examine attitudes and beliefs among a "normal" population. A meta-analysis of the correlates of rape myth acceptance ("RMA") was published in 2010.[25] Continuing the results of 37 studies, the findings indicated that men displayed a significantly higher endorsement of RMA than women. Such acceptance was also strongly associated with hostile attitudes and behaviours toward women, thus supporting the feminist premise that sexism perpetuates RMA. It was also found to be correlated with other "isms", such as racism, heterosexism, classism and ageism. A study published in 2013 highlighted that RMA was positively correlated with psychopathy.[26] Myths transferring responsibility to victims were related to Factor 1 psychopathy (i.e. callous

---

[23] ICM (2005) *Sexual Assault research: Summary Report. Prepared for Amnesty International UK.*
[24] Opinion Matters (2010). *Wake Up To Rape Research Summary Report.* Prepared for the Havens (Sexual Assault Referral Centres).
[25] E. Suarez and T.M. Gadalla, *Stop blaming the victim: A meta-analysis on rape myths*, Journal of Interpersonal Violence, Vol./is. 25/11 (2010–2035) (2010).
[26] E.R. Mouilso and K.S. Calhoun, *The role of rape myth acceptance and psychopathy in sexual assault perpetration*, Journal of Aggression, Maltreatment and Trauma, Vol./is. 22/2 (159–174) (2013).

and manipulative traits). The myth that "rape is trivial" was associated with both Factor 1 and Factor 2 (i.e. impulsive and antisocial behaviour), suggesting it bears relation to a wider tendency to excuse aggressive behaviour.

A 2012 study examined the antecedents of RMA, in which 237 students were surveyed. Knowledge, social norms regarding sexual behaviour, future time perspective and RMA were examined.[27] The majority of the sample was female. Forty-one per cent believed that a woman who was raped while drunk was responsible. Limited sexual knowledge was associated with high levels of RMA among men.

23.26

A more recent US study (2014) examined three common rape myths, that sexual assault victims: (1) immediately report the crime, (2) experience severe physical and/or anogenital injury and (3) forcefully resist their assailant.[28] A total of 317 subjects victim to sexual assaults were reviewed. Of these, 12 (4 per cent) experienced physical injury requiring medical intervention and 34 (11 per cent) acquired anogenital injuries; 253 (81 per cent) did not actively resist at some point during the assault with 178 (57 per cent) never actively resisting; and 129 (43 per cent) did not attend the emergency department for 12 or more hours from the time of the assault.

23.27

Compared with the US, there are relatively few European studies concerning this issue. A preliminary study in Italy[29] comprised surveys of 210 participants who were asked to express their opinions on two scenarios of sexual assault (a forced rape and an acquaintance rape). Only 48 per cent of the participants thought that acquaintance rape should be tried in a criminal court.

23.28

In England and Wales, the CSEW (2013/14)[30] included questions aimed at gauging public attitudes towards victims of sexual violence. It found that 1 in 11 people thought that the victim is "completely" or "mostly" responsible for a sexual assault or rape by someone they have been flirting with heavily beforehand (9 per cent), or when they are under the influence of drugs (8 per cent) or drink (6 per cent).

23.29

These results demonstrate that the misplaced beliefs commonly held by members of the general public, who make up the jury, remain prevalent today.

23.30

[27] T. Aronowitz, C.A. Lambert and S. Davidoff, *The Role of Rape Myth Acceptance in the Social Norms Regarding Sexual Behaviour Among College Students*, Journal of Community Health Nursing, Vol./is. 29/3 (173–182) (2012).

[28] Carr, M. Thomas, A.J. Atwood, D. Muhar, A. Jarvis, K. Wewerka, S.S. (2014) *Debunking three rape myths*. International Association of Forensic Nurses. 1 October 2014, vol/is. 10/4 (217-225).

[29] I. Sarmiento, *Rape stereotypes and labelling: Awareness of victimization and trauma*, Psychological Reports, Vol./is. 108/1 (141–148) (2011).

[30] C.C. Classen, O. Palesh and R. Aggarwal, *Sexual revictimisation: A review of the empirical literature*, Trauma, Violence & Abuse, Vol.6, No.2, 103–129 (2005); N.N. Sarkar and R. Sarkar, *Sexual assault on woman: Its impact on her life and living in society*, Sexual & Relationship Therapy, 20(4), 407–419 (2005); J. Read, J. van Os, A. Morrison and C. Ross, *Childhood trauma, psychosis and schizophrenia: A literature review with theoretical and clinical implications*, Acta Psychiatrica Scandinavia, 112 pp.330–350 (2005).

23.31   Men who are raped, and men who rape men, are often assumed to be homosexual. On the contrary, both the perpetrators and victims of male rape are frequently heterosexual.[31] The impact of such ignorance is profound, leaving male victims with feelings of shame, confusion and a sense of isolation. Children are also victims of this crime, although detailed consideration of childhood sexual assault and abuse lies outside the scope of this chapter.

Psychological Reactions During Rape and Serious Sexual Assault

23.32   Issues of behaviour during rape were addressed in a 2012 article which reported two studies that examined qualitatively the behaviour of female rape victims during sexual assaults.[32] The first study was an analysis of 78 stranger sexual assaults, committed in the UK, by male offenders. The second study was an analysis of 89 allegations of stranger rape, again from the UK, perpetrated by multiple male suspects. Information about victim behaviour was extracted from victims' accounts given to the police. More than 100 different victim behaviours were identified in each study, and more than 80 behaviours were common across studies. Myth-congruent behaviours were present in the sample, however, the behaviours displayed by victims were complex and diverse. Indirect and face-saving communications were used by victims and they discussed their ordeal in terms of expectations regarding victim behaviour and rape stereotypes. The implications of the findings for training legal professionals, educating jurors and counselling victims were discussed.

23.33   What are the mental processes which might impact on a victim during the assault? It is important to understand that it is the perception of threat, not the actual threat, which governs individuals' responses. Most will be profoundly affected; fearful, disorientated, and helpless. Victims may be constantly re-evaluating their situation during the attack and changing their behaviour accordingly. Others, particularly where repeat victimisation is a factor, may cut off, dissociating from reality. Some women may submit to sexual intercourse from fear of what might happen if they were to resist, or even merely to protest. Lodrick[33] has argued that the human system broadly responds in one (or more) of five predictable ways when threatened: "fight,

---

[31] N. Abdullah-Kahn, *Male rape: The emergence of a social and legal issue* (Hampshire: Palgrave MacMillan, 2008); A.N. Groth, H.J. Birnbaum, *Men who rape: the psychology of the offender* (New York: Plenum Press, 1979).

[32] J. Woodhams, C.R. Hollin, R. Bull and C. Cooke, *Behaviour displayed by female victims during rapes committed by lone and multiple perpetrators,* Psychology, Public Policy and Law, Vol./is. 18/3 (415–452) (2012).

[33] Z. Lodrick, (2007) "Psychological trauma—what every trauma worker should know", *The British Journal of Psychotherapy Integration,* Vol. 4(2).

flight and freeze" (well documented responses to threat), and "friend" and "flop". It is Lodrick's contention that the survival strategy adopted in any given situation will depend on a number of factors, namely:

- What is most likely to ensure survival (and also maintain vital attachments)?
- What worked in the past?
- What was unsuccessful in the past?

These processes mean that some women resist, run away or cry for help, whilst others will take a far more passive approach; indeed they may appear frozen and unable to act.[34] Submission or adopting a passive stance is not however the same as consent and yet people might wrongly assume that if there is no injury, torn clothing, struggle or cries for help, then an assault was not committed.

Mechanisms such as de-realisation (a sense that the world around them is not real), de-personalisation (a sense that it is not happening to them, it is happening to some other person) and dissociation (a sense of being cut off from the actual situation) can result from extreme fear. Other features of dissociation occurring at the time of the trauma include: **23.34**

- losing track of what was going on,
- doing things that they later realise they had not actively decided to do,
- a sense that time was altered, e.g. things seemed to be happening in slow motion, or at speed,
- sensory disturbances, e.g. moments when their body seemed distorted or changed.[35]

These mechanisms may severely impair the victim's ability to recall details of the assault and recall may change over time. Memories of the traumatic event are often initially experienced as fragmented. They are more likely to be stored predominantly as "implicit memory", which is emotional, sensory, less adaptable and context-free, as opposed to normal "explicit memory", which is autobiographical, organised by language, adaptable, contextualised and subject to conscious organisation and recall. Thus sensory components, feelings and emotions may be more easily recalled whilst a detailed narrative cannot be given. Questions should thus focus on the victim's perceptions (what did you feel/smell/hear? etc.). With further questioning and processing of the event (for example talking it though with a friend or support worker) more of the narrative component may become accessible, and the victim's account will change. **23.35**

---

[34] P. Levine with A. Frederick, *Waking the tiger: healing trauma* (Berkley, California: North Atlantic Books, 1997).

[35] C.R. Marmar, D.S. Weiss, W.E. Schlenger, J.A. Fairbank, K. Jordan, R.A. Kulka and P.L. Hough, "Peritraumatic dissociation and posttraumatic stress in male Vietnam theater veterans", *American Journal of Psychiatry* 1994, 151, 902–907.

Psychological Reactions Following Sexual Assault

23.36 Many factors will affect an individual's response to trauma; resilience and psychological reactions vary greatly between individuals. Personal meaning is likely to be very significant, a fact that is illustrated by the differences between stranger and acquaintance rape. It might be assumed that the former would be far more traumatic, but this is often not the case and research has shown that rape victims have similar levels of depression and greater difficulty re-establishing intimate relationships following acquaintance rape.[36]

23.37 Other elements that also contribute significantly to post-traumatic responses include perception of life threat, actual injury and being the victim of a completed, as opposed to an attempted rape.[37] Other variables are also important as listed below:

- Pre-existing individual variables; age, prior psychiatric history, previous exposure to trauma and preparedness.
- Stressor variables; unpredictability, suddenness, receiving intentional harm, relationship to perpetrator.
- Responses of external world; lack of support, victim blaming.
- Specific experiences of the individual; captivity, a sense of hopelessness, cultural beliefs, repeat traumatisation interrupting the recovery process.

23.38 Emotions will vary following rape and should be viewed as a normal reaction to an abnormal event. Individuals may be expressive and tearful, quiet and controlled, distressed, shocked or in denial. Other early symptoms experienced may include anxiety, shame, physical revulsion and helplessness. Self-blame may serve as a means of warding off fears of unpredictability and uncontrollability. In the weeks that follow, anxiety, increased arousal and hyper-vigilance, depression, disturbed sleep and appetite, avoidance, poor concentration, intrusive imagery, irritability, guilt, self-blame and psychosomatic complaints may be seen. Most women will experience extreme distress and disruption in many areas of their lives.

23.39 A more recent study identified that high levels of distress were evident in nearly all participants (119 female sexual assault survivors) at one month post-assault. The results of the study suggested that theoretical models of post-trauma response positing resilience as the modal outcome may not generalise to all cases of sexual assault.[38]

[36] S.E. Ullman and J.M. Siegel, "Victim-Offender relationship and sexual assault", *Violence and Victims* 1993, Vol. 8, No. 2, pp.121–134(14).

[37] D.G. Kilpatrick, B.E. Saunders, A. Amick-McMullan, C.L. Best, L.J. Veronen and H.S. Resnick, "Victim and crime factors associated with the development of crime-related post-traumatic stress disorder, *Behavior Therapy* 1989, 20: 199–214.

[38] M.M. Steenkamp, B.D. Dickstein, K. Slaters-Pedneault, S.G. Hofmann, B.D. Dickstein and B.T. Litz, *Trajectories of PTSD symptoms following sexual assault: Is resilience the modal outcome?* Journal of Traumatic Stress, Vol./is. 25/4 (469–474) (2012).

Research indicates that the majority of women recover from the acute   **23.40**
effects of the attack at between three and four months. Originally described
as "rape trauma syndrome" by Burgess and Holmstrom,[39] many of the more
persistent psychological symptoms seen following rape are now recognised as
being compatible with a diagnosis of post-traumatic stress disorder
("PTSD").[40]

Rothbaum et al[41] found that soon after the crime (mean 12.64 days) 94 per   **23.41**
cent of their sample met symptomatic criteria for PTSD, but at 94 days
(mean) post-assault only 47 per cent continued to do so. However, many will
experience more prolonged distress and develop difficulties such as persistent
PTSD, substance abuse, anxiety, irritability and anger and depression.
Kilpatrick et al[42] found that 51 per cent of completed rape victims had
developed PTSD sometime after the assault and 16.5 per cent still had PTSD
when re-assessed some years later. This condition is described in more detail
below, given the high rates seen in those who have been raped.

There are four broad symptom groups in PTSD: re-experiencing; persis-   **23.42**
tent avoidance of stimuli associated with the trauma; negative alterations in
cognitions and mood; and persistent symptoms of increased arousal. For a
formal diagnosis to be made the symptoms must last for more than one
month and lead to clinically significant distress or impairment in social,
occupational or other important areas of functioning.

In order to make a diagnosis of PTSD, the onset of symptoms must follow   **23.43**
a traumatic incident. The American classification system, *Diagnostic and
Statistical Manual of Mental Disorder 5th edition*[43] ("DSM-V"), published in
May 2013, revised the classification of PTSD to include the specific addition
of sexual assault as a traumatic event. It also added a sub-type called *PTSD
Dissociative Subtype*. This subtype of PSTD is chosen when PTSD is seen
with prominent dissociative symptoms which can be either experiences of
feeling detached from one's own mind or body, or experiences in which the
world seems unreal, dreamlike or distorted. Traumas of a sexual nature may
have a central role in the development of a dissociative-PTSD group
according to previous research studies.[44] Similarly, the British Classification

---

[39] A.W. Burgess and L.L. Holmstrom, "Rape Trauma Syndrome", *American Journal of Psychiatry* 1974, 131, 981–986.
[40] American Psychiatric Association, *Diagnostic and statistical manual of mental disorders: Fourth edition—text revision (DSM-IV-TR)* (Washington DC: American Psychiatric Association, 2000).
[41] B.O. Rothbaum, E. Foa, D.S. Riggs, T. Murdock and W. Walsh, "A prospective examination of post-traumatic stress disorder in rape victims", *Journal of Traumatic Stress* 1992, 5 (3), 455–475.
[42] D.G. Kilpatrick, B.E. Saunders, L.J. Veronen, L. et al, "Criminal victimisation: lifetime prevalence, reporting to the police and psychological impact", *Crime and Delinquency* 1987, 33, 479–489.
[43] American Psychiatric Association. (2013) *Diagnostic and Statistical Manual of Mental Disorder 5th edition*. Washington. DC.
[44] Armour, C. Elkit, A. Lauterbach, D. Elhai J.D. *The DSM-5 dissociative-PTSD subtype: Can levels of depression, anxiety, hotility and sleeping difficulties differentiate between dissociative-*

system, *International Classification of Disease—Version 10* ("ICD-10")[45] recognises the onset of the condition:

> "following a stressful event or situation (either short—or long-lasting) of an exceptionally threatening or catastrophic nature, which is likely to cause pervasive distress in almost anyone (e.g. natural or man-made disaster, combat, serious accident, witnessing the violent death of others, or being the victim of torture, terrorism, rape, or other crime)."

23.44 PTSD can be an extremely distressing and disabling condition. Intrusive symptoms such as flashbacks, nightmares and feeling as though the assault is reoccurring are profoundly distressing to individuals who experience them. Their psychological response is often to become avoidant of thoughts, feelings, places and other reminders of the assault. This in turn will mean that individuals with PTSD will not want to talk about what has happened to them; they may also forget important aspects of the events in question. Some individuals present with significant levels of numbing and detachment, a presentation which can lead those observing them to believe that they are not at all distressed, when in fact these symptoms are characteristic of PTSD. PTSD sufferers also experience increased levels of arousal with difficulty sleeping, poor concentration, anger and irritability, jumpiness and an exaggerated startle response. As a result of these symptoms many with PTSD (up to 30 per cent) will utilise substances in order to cope with the unpleasant feelings; characteristically depressant drugs such as alcohol, marijuana or prescribed benzodiazepines are used. The difficulties experienced by complainants with PTSD should be understood, so that their presentation is contextualised. It should also be remembered that some individuals will have significant post traumatic responses without a formal diagnosis being merited, although they may still be profoundly affected by these symptoms.

23.45 A longitudinal study from Sweden (2014)[46] involving 317 female victims of rape who sought help at an Emergency Clinic for Raped Women ("ECRW") identified the following risk factors for developing PTSD: having been sexually assaulted by more than one person; suffering from acute stress disorder shortly after the assault; having been exposed to several acts during the assault; having been injured; having co-morbid depression; and having a history of more than two earlier traumas. It also found that one in five women had pre-existing PTSD at the time of the assault. The authors conclude that this is not surprising given the well-documented research

---

PTSD and PTSD in rape and sexual assault victims? Journal of Anxiety Disorders. 28 (2014) 418–426.

[45] World Health Organisation. (1992). ICD-10 Classifications of Mental and Behavioural Disorder: Clinical Descriptions and Diagnostic Guidelines. Geneva. World Health Organisation.

[46] Möller, A.T. Bäckström, T. Söndergaard, H. P. Helström, L. *Identifying Risk Factors for PTSD in Women Seeking Medical Help after Rape.* Plos One. October 2014. Vol 9. Issue 10.

finding that earlier trauma substantially increases the risk of re-victimisation. The clinical implications of establishing the risk factors for PTSD were highlighted, particularly that identifying victims at highest risk of developing PTSD could aid in reducing incidence through early interventions.

Other authors have examined social reactions as a predictor of PTSD.[47]   **23.46** Using a longitudinal design, the authors examined the course of PTSD in a group of recent rape survivors. They found four distinct PTSD symptom trajectories that were labelled resilience, recovery, moderate chronicity and high chronicity. Sixty-nine sexual assault survivors completed online questionnaires monthly for the first four months following the assault. These included the Social Reactions Questionnaire,[48] which assesses seven types of positive and negative reactions to sexual assault disclosure (emotional support, treat differently, distraction, take control, informational support, victim blame and egocentric). PTSD symptom severity was assessed using the PTSD Checklist.[49] An analysis of variance indicated that the moderate chronic group reported significantly more negative reactions than both the recovery and resilience groups. Specifically, negative reactions where the person treated the survivor differently or took control of the situation distinguished between the moderate chronic and the recovery/resilience groups. Blaming the victim or making the situation about the person instead of the survivor distinguished between the moderate chronic and the resilience groups. This study therefore confirmed that, consistent with previous studies, negative social reactions to assault disclosure were associated with greater PTSD symptom severity. The study also demonstrated that social reactions after sexual assault predicted distinct PTSD trajectories, with negative reactions predicting a chronic PTSD symptom course. This suggests that reactions of mental health providers, criminal justice workers, friends and family may affect PTSD symptom trajectories in survivors and has implications for improving social reactions to sexual assault disclosure. Thus, in addition to interventions directly targeting survivors' distress and PTSD symptoms after sexual assault, it may be helpful to educate others on the impact of negative social reactions after sexual assault disclosure.

In addition, negative social reactions towards rape victims can strongly   **23.47** affect whether or how survivors blame themselves for a sexual assault. A negative response from others reinforces the self-blame that survivors often experience and leads to poorer recovery.[50] Recent research from Chicago

---

[47] L.E. Rosebrock, T.M. Au, B.D. Dickstein, M. Steenkamp, B.T. Litz, *Social reactions as a predictor of PTSD symptom trajectories following sexual assault*, Comprehensive Psychiatry, Vol./is. 52/6 (E13–E14) (2011).

[48] S.E. Ullman, *Social reactions questionnaire* (2000).

[49] F.W. Weathers, B.T. Litz, D.S. Herman, J.A. Huska and T.M. Keane, *PTSD Checklist PCL-C* (1993).

[50] Sigurvinsdottir, R. Ullman, S. E. (2014) *Social reactions, Self-blame, and Problem Drinking in adult sexual assault survivors.* Psychology of Violence, Aug 2014 (Aug 11, 2014) 2152-0828.

(2014)[51] found that specific negative social reactions such as infantalising the victim (i.e. patronising them, treating them as if they were irresponsible) led to less perceived control by the victim over their recovery. This was in turn related to more PTSD and problem drinking in victims.

23.48   Mason and Lodrick outlined the psychological reactions to serious sexual assault and rape, including development of PTSD, in an article published in 2013.[52] Other publications of relevance have addressed a variety of related issues, as summarised below.

23.49   Many studies have documented associations between sexual victimisation, PTSD symptoms and alcohol use. A study published in 2012[53] evaluated the effect of sexual victimisation on the longitudinal trajectory of PTSD symptoms and binge drinking among adolescent girls, a population already known to have high rates of sexual victimisation and alcohol use. Interviews were conducted with 1,808 participants regarding PTSD symptoms, binge drinking and sexual victimisation experiences over approximately three years. Multilevel modelling revealed decreases in PTSD symptoms over the course of the study; however, compared with non-victims, adolescents who were sexually victimised reported greater PTSD symptoms at initial interview and maintained higher levels of PTSD symptoms over the course of the study after controlling for age. Sexual victimisation reported during the study also predicted an acute increase in PTSD symptoms at that occasion. Binge drinking increased significantly over the course of the study; however, sexual victimisation did not predict initial binge drinking or increases over time. Sexual victimisation reported during the study was associated with acute increases in binge drinking at that occasion, although this effect diminished when participants reporting substance-involved rape were excluded. Sexual victimisation was associated with immediate and long-lasting elevations in PTSD symptoms, but not with initial or lasting elevations in binge drinking over time, suggesting that adolescent victims have yet to develop problematic patterns of alcohol use to cope with sexual victimisation. However, sexual victimisation was associated with acute increases in PTSD symptoms and binge drinking, suggesting a need for binge drinking interventions to reduce alcohol-related sexual victimisation.

23.50   Whilst there have been many studies reporting the short term effects of rape,[54] fewer exist on the longer term effects which persist into older adult

---

[51] Peter-Hagene, L.C. Ullman, S. (2014) *Social Reactions to Sexual Assault Disclosure and Problem Drinking: Mediating Effects of Perceived Control and PTSD*. Journal of Interpersonal Violence. Vol 29(8) 1418-1437.

[52] F. Mason and Z. Lodrick, *Psychological Consequences of Sexual Assault*, Best Practice and Research: Clinical Obstetrics and Gynaecology, Vol./is.27/1 (27–37) (2013).

[53] K. Walsh, C.K. Danielson, J. McCauley, R.R. Hanson, D.W. Smith, H.S. Resnick, B.E. Saunders and D.G. Kilpatrick, *Longitudinal trajectories of posttraumatic stress disorder symptoms and binge drinking among adolescent girls: The role of sexual victimization*, Journal of Adolescent Health, Vol./is. 50/1 (54–59) (2012).

[54] Elkit, A. Christiansen, D.M. (2010) *ASD and PTSD in rape victims*. Journal of Interpersonal Violence 25(8), 1470-1488.

life. A US cross sectional study published in 2014[55] examined the association between a history of rape and current psychological and health functioning. The study looked at pre-existing data for 1,228 females from the National Social Life, Health, and Aging Project ("NSHAP"), which interviewed respondents aged between 57 and 85. The respondents were questioned on whether they had experienced forced sexual contact since the age of 18. A modularised questionnaire was used to obtain measures of psychological health, (e.g. scales of depression, anxiety and loneliness), the presence or absence of serious health problems and self-esteem. Of the sample population, 7 per cent reported being victim to rape in adulthood, which occurred on average 36 years previously. Through structural equation modelling, rape was found to be significantly associated with lower self-esteem, and lower physical and psychological health functioning. Self-esteem was found to partially mediate the relationship between rape and psychological functioning. It is of note that this study design allows only for observations of associations rather than causality. The authors concluded that professionals and older survivors might not associate current symptoms with traumatic events, which occurred in the past, and might instead relate them to more proximal issues and the aging process. Recommendations were made for treatments aimed at treating traumatic memories and self-blame, and increasing coping and resilience.

Other long-term difficulties seen include generalised and phobic anxiety, depression, difficulties with social adjustment and sexual functioning. Kilpatrick et al[56] reported that of the 507 victims of rape surveyed, 30 per cent had experienced at least one episode of major depression and 21 per cent were depressed at the time of the survey. In contrast, only 10 per cent of women who had never been raped had ever experienced major depression and only 6 per cent were depressed at the time of survey. Feelings of shame and humiliation are commonly described, often persist and clearly contribute to loss of self-esteem and depression. The level of suicidal ideation and attempts among rape victims is notable. Kilpatrick et al[57] found that 33 per cent of rape victims had ever contemplated suicide as opposed to 8 per cent non-victims, whereas 13 per cent of rape victims had made a suicide attempt as opposed to only 1 per cent of non-victims.   **23.51**

Burgess and Holmstrom[58] found 78 per cent of their sample had been sexually active at the time of rape but of these 38 per cent gave up sex for at   **23.52**

---

[55] Sachs-Ericsson, N. Kendall-Tackett. K. A. Sheffler, J. Arce, D. Rushing, N.C. Corsentino, E. (2014) *The influence of prior rape on the psychological and physical health functioning of older adults.* Aging and Mental Health. Vol 18, No. 6, 717-730.

[56] D.G. Kilpatrick, L.J. Veronen and C.L. Best, "Factors predicting psychological distress among rape victims" in *Trauma and its Wake* (ed C.E. Figley), (New York: Brunner, 1985).

[57] D.G. Kilpatrick, C.L. Best, L.J. Veronen, A.E. Amick, L.A. Villeponteaux and G.A. Ruff, "Mental health correlates of criminal victimization: a random community survey", *Journal of Consulting and Clinical Psychology*, 1985, 53, 866–873.

[58] A.W. Burgess and L.L. Holmstrom, "Rape Trauma Syndrome", *American Journal of Psychiatry* 1974, 131, 981–986.

least 6 months and 33 per cent decreased their frequency of sexual activity following rape. Studies comparing sexual satisfaction of rape victims with non-victims all report that rape survivors experience less sexual satisfaction. Given that defence counsel may seek to introduce evidence about the victim's behaviour (and potentially use this to undermine the victim), such figures are useful as they demonstrate that rape victims are more often than not sexually active prior to the rape, and may return to sexual activity following the rape.

23.53   A study by Hester et al[59] (2012) found that:

> "[V]ictim/survivors stressed the long term psychological impact of being the victim of a sexual offence. The offence may have caused injury and alarm at the time it occurred and the survivor may have experienced numerous episodes of sexual abuse or violence. Survivors identified post-traumatic stress disorder, depression, anxiety, inability to sleep and other effects such as physical disability, as the long term effects they directly attributed to the offence. These had the secondary effect of reducing their ability to work or study, to forge new relationships or maintain positive relationships with family and friends, or their ability to care for others, such as their children. Suicide attempts were also reported."

The same study found that whilst the public acknowledged that sexual offences were harmful to the victim, they had:

> " . . . monolithic views of the type of harm the offence may have to victims, relating it to the immediate details and aftermath—the fear and distress the victim would feel, the injuries sustained due to violence—rather than the long term harm that victim/survivors described and ensuing effect on their day to day life. However, public perception tended to focus on any immediate harm (such as physical injury) or broader harm to society (such as increased fear of crime) rather than the long term impact that victim/survivors themselves described."

23.54 As reported previously, women who have been sexually abused in childhood are at significantly higher risk of re-victimisation in adolescence and adulthood. Re-victimisation is associated with a raft of adverse mental and physical health outcomes, and understanding why victims of childhood sexual abuse are more vulnerable to later sexual assaults has critical implications for their development. In their paper, Noll and Grych noted the hypothesis that sexual abuse in childhood resulted in reduced ability to recognise and/or respond effectively to sexual threats later in life, but, as they reported, studies examining these ideas have produced inconsistent results.[60] Further, this research failed to incorporate the powerful physiological reaction elicited by threats of imminent harm to the self, which has the potential to disrupt cognitive processing and coping behaviour. The authors proposed a model of re-victimisation that integrated contemporary theory and research on the biological stress response with cognitive, affective and

---

[59] M. Hester, *Attitudes to Sentencing Sexual Offences, Sentencing Council Research Series 01/12* (2012).
[60] J.G. Noll and J.H. Grych, *Read-react-respond: An integrative model for understanding sexual revictimization*, Psychology of Violence, Vol./is. 1/3 (202–215) (2011).

behavioural factors believed to be involved in adaptive responses to sexual threats. The model provides a conceptual guide to understanding why females with a history of sexual abuse are more vulnerable to re-victimisation and offers ideas for improving prevention programmes designed to strengthen females' ability to resist sexual coercion.

Najdowski and Ullman[61] surveyed 555 women twice, with a one-year **23.55** interval between the two. Path analyses, controlling for baseline coping and depression, revealed that those who were re-victimised during the study reported using more maladaptive and adaptive coping strategies than those who were not re-victimised. Further, women who were re-victimised reported more depression than others. This effect was explained in part by re-victimised women's increased maladaptive coping. Results are consistent with other research showing that all traumatic experiences must be taken into consideration to understand fully how sexual assault influences coping and recovery.

Whilst mental health problems are prevalent following the trauma of a **23.56** sexual assault, many victims already have pre-existing mental health disorders at the time of the assault.[62] Sexual Assault Referral Centres ("SARCs") in England and Wales, first established in 1986 in response to problems victims encountered within the medical and criminal justice system, aim to provide a "one stop location" for victims, where they can receive healthcare assessments, counselling and support throughout the prosecution stage.[63] It is expected that mental health risk assessments be undertaken as part of the healthcare assessment, in accordance with the 2013 service specification outlined by NHS England. A study published in 2015 surveyed all 37 SARCs in England, of which a total of 25 responded (68 per cent response rate). The survey results estimated that SARCs had around 400 contacts a year and that 40 per cent of clients were already known to mental health services. The authors note such figures are very similar to findings in both Holland and the US. Clearly, those with pre-existing mental health problems are at risk of worsening of their psychiatric symptoms following an attack. It is of note however that only 11 centres (49 per cent) routinely performed a mental health risk assessment as part of the assessment whilst 83 per cent included substance misuse history.

Research has revealed that victims with serious mental illness ("SMI") at **23.57** the time of the assault have been found to be more likely to suffer social, psychological and physical adverse effects as a result of the crime compared

---

[61] C.J. Najdowski and S.E. Ullman, *The effects of revictimization on coping and depression in female sexual assault victims*, Journal of Traumatic Stress, April 2011, Vol./is. 24/2 (218–221) (2011).

[62] Brooker, C. Durnmaz E. (2015) *Mental Health, sexual violence and the work of Sexual Assault Referral Centres (SARCs) in England*. Journal of Forensic and Legal Medicine. 31. 47-51.

[63] Department of Health and Home Office. National Service Guidelines for Developing Sexual Assault Referral Centres (SARCs). October 2005.

to victims who do not have SMI.[64] The same study found that the domestic or sexual violence had particularly detrimental effects with 40 per cent of women and 25 per cent of men attempting suicide as a result of experiencing these crimes.

23.58   There have been few studies of men, however Mezey and King[65] demonstrated that the reactions of men following sexual assault appear to parallel the responses of women. It is noteworthy that men may experience particular issues such as a loss of a sense of masculinity, confusion over sexuality and fear of disbelief. Men may also find that there are fewer services available to support them when they seek help.

Legal Implications

23.59   It is important to remember that rape and serious sexual assault can affect many areas of an individual's life for many months, if not years, following the attack. In addition to experiencing psychological difficulties, the survivor may suffer ongoing physical problems, may resort to alcohol or drug abuse, may alter their day-to-day behaviour and find that their thought processes are very different. When a complaint is made, the understanding of potential psychological reactions to sexual assault and its aftermath is important for a number of reasons. When a victim turns to anyone and discloses what has happened, that individual (and society's) response is important, and one determinant of the victim's future psychological well-being.[66] If the victim has chosen to disclose to the police and thus become a complainant, they are often aware that a series of events and interactions will follow. Those that they subsequently encounter through the judicial process will make judgments based on their own belief systems. Attitudes might affect questioning, evidential acquisition, victim response, decisions about proceeding and juror deliberations. So beliefs held, when myth rather than reality, may have a crucial role to play both in terms of well-being and achieving justice.

23.60   Phenomena occurring at the time of the trauma, as described earlier, can impact on the survivor's ability to give a coherent, consistent account of their experiences, and yet a change in the account may be viewed as evidence that they cannot be believed. Post-traumatic symptoms will also potentially affect recall and consistency, and indeed an inability to recall aspects of the event is one characteristic symptom of PTSD. Victims experience feelings of shame

[64] Pettitt B, Greenhead S, Khalifeh H, et al. (2013) *At Risk Yet Dismissed: The Criminal Victimisation of People with Mental Health Problems*. London: Victim Support/Mind.
[65] G.C. Mezey and M. King, "The effects of sexual assault on men—a survey of 22 subjects" *Psychological Medicine* 1989, 19, 205–209.
[66] R. Campbell and S. Raja, "Secondary victimization of rape victims: insights from mental health professionals who treat survivors of violence", *Violence Vict* 1999, 14(3): 261–75. J. Briere and C. Scott, *Principles of trauma therapy: a guide to symptoms, evaluation and treatment* (Thousand Oaks, California: Sage, 2006).

and self-blame[67] and this may lead them to give an incomplete or inaccurate account of the circumstances surrounding the rape. Cultural issues may have a significant impact.

Depression and anxiety associated with sexual assault may lead to   **23.61** insomnia and eating disturbance. The survivor will often experience an increase in somatic complaints such as headaches, muscle tension and stomach upsets, and research has demonstrated that rape survivors visit their doctors more frequently for such complaints. It may be hard for the individual who has been assaulted to do anything that reminds them of the circumstances of the assault and simple tasks may become impossible. They may be unable to go to certain areas and may avoid social contact. Home security may be enhanced and they may be unable to confide in those who love them most. Their ability to access and benefit from support may therefore be limited. These factors may lead complainants to seem avoidant, and that avoidance may be wrongly interpreted as indicating that their account was false. For those with symptoms of numbing, their presentation may also be misinterpreted, and their complaint taken less seriously as a result.

There is a growing body of research examining issues relating to the   **23.62** disclosure of sexual assault. Survivors differ in how they disclose, to whom they disclose, and the types of reactions they receive during disclosure. A study published in 2010[68] sought to provide a more comprehensive view, identifying patterns of disclosure and how these related to physical and mental health outcomes among a sample of 103 female sexual assault survivors. Results revealed four distinct patterns: non-disclosers, slow starters, crisis disclosers and ongoing disclosers. Assault characteristics and rape acknowledgment distinguished non-disclosers and slow starters from the other two disclosure groups. Slow starters were also less likely to disclose to police and medical personnel, and received fewer negative reactions, while non-disclosers experienced more symptoms of depression and PTSD than other groups.

The Government's Office for Criminal Justice Reform Consultation paper,   **23.63** *Convicting Rapists and protecting Victims—Justice for Victims of Rape*,[69] aimed to improve the outcome of rape cases through "further strengthening the existing legal framework and improving our care for victims and witnesses". This stemmed from the belief that complainants were being evaluated "without juries appreciating the potential effects of the trauma of serious assault and how it might affect a victim's evidence". As described in the Consultation paper:

---

[67] S. Dahl, "Acute response to rape—a PTSD variant", *Acta Psychiatrica Scandinavica* 1989, 80, 56–62.

[68] C.E. Ahrens, J. Stansell, A. Jennings, *To tell or not to tell: the impact of disclosure on sexual assault survivors' recovery*, Violence and victims, Vol./is. 25/5 (631–648) (2010).

[69] Criminal Justice Reform Consultation paper, *Convicting Rapists and protecting Victims —Justice for Victims of Rape* (2006).

"we want to ensure that stronger cases are presented to the courts, witnesses are given greater assistance in providing their evidence and courts hear evidence from experts that will better inform juries about the realities of rape and the psychological impact of sexual offences upon victims and address certain myths and stereotypes concerning how a victim might be expected to behave"

23.64   Given the public misconceptions about the victims of rape and the aftermath of its effects, one has to question the fairness of trials in rape cases. The Crown Court Bench Book (2010), *Directing the Jury*,[70] used by judges as a point of reference when preparing legal directions for summing up, provides particular guidance in this area. It lists the factors which may lead to unjustified stereotyping by juries in rape cases:

- The complainant wore provocative clothing; therefore he/she must have wanted sex.
- The complainant got drunk in male company; therefore he/she must have been prepared for sex.
- An attractive male does not need to have sex without consent.
- A complainant in a relationship with the alleged attacker is likely to have consented.
- Rape takes place between strangers.
- Rape does not take place without physical resistance from the victim.
- If it is rape there must be injuries.
- A person who has been sexually assaulted reports it as soon as possible.
- A person who has been sexually assaulted remembers events consistently.

23.65   Over recent years there has been increasing recognition of the vulnerability of many of those reporting rape and serious sexual assaults, making them more likely to be a victim and less likely to report it to the police. The CPS acknowledges that "barriers exist, which mean that some people are less likely to report offences . . . People with learning difficulties or mental health problems may feel that they will not be believed if they report being raped."[71]

23.66   The Stern Review (2010) identified that:

"[A] pervading theme throughout the evidence was the vulnerability of many of those reporting rape. Their vulnerability means they have less capacity to consent. Many of those who are particularly vulnerable will not be one-off victims, but will experience rape and sexual assault on multiple occasions. Such 'repeat victims' may have mental health problems or learning disabilities which make them vulnerable to being taken advantage of."[72]

---

[70] Judicial Studies Board. Crown Court Bench Book. Directing the Jury Ch.17, p.353.

[71] Crown Prosecution Service, *CPS Policy for prosecuting cases of rape* (2012), p.3. The policy can be found at *http://www.cps.gov.uk/publications/docs/rape_policy_2012.pdf* [Accessed April 30, 2016].

[72] The Stern Review, *A report by Baroness Vivien Stern CBE of an independent review into how rape complaints are handled by public authorities in England and Wales* (Government Equalities Office and Home Office, 2010).

Issues relating to victim responsibility and credibility have been further   23.67
examined in a simulated case.[73] In this study, Weiner's attribution model was
applied to understand why victim blame impacts credibility and verdict.
Weiner's model posits that perceptions of a target's responsibility will lead to
less sympathy and therefore reduced willingness to help the target. In line
with this model, it was hypothesised that sympathy for a rape victim mediates
the relationship between perceptions of victim responsibility, willingness to
help the victim, credibility and verdict. Participants read a 1,000-word
transcript of a rape trial and made judgments regarding the victim's
responsibility for the rape, their sympathy for the victim, willingness to help
the victim, perceived witness credibility and verdict. The statement was
manipulated between subjects to give differing impressions of responsibility.
The hypotheses were supported that sympathy mediated the relationships
between perceived victim responsibility and their willingness to help the
victim, credibility and verdict.

The high levels of attrition in rape cases have received much attention over   23.68
recent years and have led to the development of specific policy and guidance
in this area.[74] Research has found that attrition rates are higher for cases
involving victims with psychosocial disabilities than those without psychosocial disabilities.[75]

There has been concern raised about how the police handle allegations of   23.69
sexual assault made by people with mental health problems or disabilities, a
concern consolidated in HMIC's inspection, *Crime-recording: making the
victim count.*

Low conviction rates also result from rape myths.[76] Expert witness   23.70
testimony to combat rape myths and educate jurors is therefore crucial. In
the US, this precedence was set in case law in in *State v Obeta* (2011) where
the Minnesota Supreme Court ruled that "in cases of criminal sexual contact
where consent is an issue, district courts are given discretion to admit expert
opinion evidence on the typicality of delayed reporting, lack of physical
injuries and 'submissive conduct' by sexual assault victims".[77] Research
studies have shown that expert witness testimony results in higher convictions
rates and greater sentiment for victims amongst jurors.

Amnesia for some or all the event can be a particular problem for victims   23.71
of sexual assault. One of the mechanisms behind this is dissociation during
threat, which can lead to victims being unable to consciously integrate

---

[73] K. Sperry and J. T. Siegel, *Victim responsibility, credibility, and verdict in a simulated rape
case: Application of Weiner's attribution model,* Legal and Criminological Psychology, Vol./is.
18/1 (16–29) (2013).

[74] The Stern Review, fn.73, above.

[75] Pettitt B, Greenhead S, Khalifeh H, et al. (2013) *At Risk Yet Dismissed: The Criminal
Victimisation of People with Mental Health Problems.* London: Victim Support/Mind.

[76] Carr, M. Thomas, A.J. Atwood, D. Muhar, A. Jarvis, K. Wewerka, S.S. (2014) *Debunking
three rape myths.* International Association of Forensic Nurses. 1 October 2014, vol/is. 10/4
(217-225).

[77] Last note.

traumatic experiences, which in turn interferes with their ability to provide a statement during police questioning. Later recall of memory during the trial stage can lead to perceived inconsistencies in the victim's account, hence allowing questions to be raised regarding the victim's reliability and credibility.

23.72   Memory can also be affected, however, by some of the newer pharmacological treatment used for PTSD, which can have an impact on victims during the prosecution stage. Whilst the usual recommended pharmacological treatment for PTSD is antidepressant medication, other classes of drugs are being explored.[78] As described by Chandler et al (2013),[79] one of the etiological theories for PTSD is that the traumatic experience leads to the overstimulation of stress hormones, which enforce conditioned fear responses to stimuli which are frightening. Drugs that block the conditioning effect of stress hormones, such as beta adrenergic blockers, have therefore been explored as a potential way to prevent the development of PTSD. Chandler et al. (2013) highlight the effects of the beta-adrenergic blocker, propranolol, or "what has come to be called memory dampening treatment", and report on several studies which have found promising results in treating established PTSD by using propranolol to disrupt the reconsolidation of traumatic memories. The authors discuss the ethico-legal issues that this treatment raises, and particularly the impact it could have on the victim's testimony "given recently published results suggesting that this treatment may affect factual recall of a traumatic event as well as the emotional qualities of the memory". They raise concern that a woman's credibility might be adversely affected if her memory and emotional response to the traumatic memory are dampened. They conclude by suggesting "general ethical analyses to be tested in specific cases before general conclusions are made about the ethical appropriateness of novel treatments for PTSD".

Late Reporting

23.73   The timing of reporting has historically influenced conviction rates, and it is important to understand why women may not report immediately. One study has shown that if the woman made an immediate complaint, then there was a 73 per cent chance of conviction. However, immediate in this context meant within 24 hours of the rape. Late reporting (i.e. one day to three months after the event) resulted in a 38 per cent conviction rate.[80]

23.74   In the previously mentioned report, *At risk, yet dismissed*,[81] qualitative interviewing of participants with mental problems revealed the factors which

---

[78] Chandler, J.A. Mogyoros, A. Rubio, T.M. Racine, E. (2013) *Another look at the Legal and Ethical Consequences of Pharmacological Memory Dampening: The Case of Sexual Assault.* Human Right and Disability. Winter 2013.
[79] Last note.
[80] Z. Adler, *Rape on Trial* (Routledge, 1987).
[81] fn.76, above.

made them reluctant to report crimes to the police. These included fearing a negative response from the police, worrying that their mental problems would be used against them to discredit them or not believe them, fear of being sectioned, feelings of shame and embarrassment, and being distressed or overwhelmed or confused following the assault.

Complainants are usually aware that in reporting a rape they face the risk of not being believed, of being blamed and of having their behaviour exposed and scrutinised. Many will feel ashamed. In rape, the lines between appropriate trust and carelessness or failure to protect oneself are difficult to draw and the victim may well battle with her own thoughts and feelings for some time before reporting the crime that has been committed against them. Women may fail to report immediately for simple, practical reasons: they may have childcare responsibilities and little social support, they may not have transport, or they may have to remain in the home with the perpetrator. If they have developed PTSD symptoms they will also be battling against powerful avoidance symptomatology. **23.75**

RE-TRAUMATISATION

Requiring the complainant, especially if they have developed PTSD, to confront her traumatic history during interviews and courtroom testimonies thwarts characteristic efforts at avoidance and predictably results in the resurgence of intrusive ideation and increased arousal. The wish to avoid such distress may lead women to avoid court by retracting or altering their account, or not disclosing the full extent of their experiences. On the other hand, it may only be during times of high arousal that the complainant is able to access the traumatic memories in detail. Thus it is important that a balance is struck, that the woman is given the time and support that she needs in order to give her account and that her reactions in court are dealt with appropriately. **23.76**

The nature of the court process pits the complainant against the defendant, whom the survivor already sees as the enemy. They will then be faced with counsel for the defendant, who is likely to attempt to discredit their experience and to try to persuade the jury that they are not to be believed. The defence may also attempt to shift responsibility on to the complainant and blame her for their client's conduct. Women often complain that it is they who feel as though they are on trial and that they, unlike the accused, are merely a witness and as such are not assigned counsel. It could be argued that the rape prosecutor acts as that counsel, however the complainant will only believe this if that prosecutor looks at their case positively and starts with a belief in the woman and her account. Corroboration must be actively sought and inconsistencies or lies must be dealt with rather than wished away. An informed prosecutor, who offers respect to the complainant and who understands the issues outlined in this chapter, is far more likely to secure the **23.77** best evidence possible from the complainant who is, after all, a key witness.

INCONSISTENCIES AND LIES

23.78 Trauma can lead to extremes of retention and forgetting. Terrifying experiences may be remembered with extreme vividness or may be totally inaccessible, and amnesia for all or part of a traumatic experience is not uncommon. As noted earlier, the victim may dissociate when faced with overwhelming threat and will then be unable to integrate the totality of their experience into consciousness. This in turn will hamper her ability to provide a detailed, temporally accurate statement. Individuals are more likely to access somatosensory information (that relating to sensory stimuli from the skin, internal organs and other deep tissues) than narrative. An understanding of these issues is vital, in that it is only by asking appropriate questions that memories will be accessed. It must also be remembered that victims may "fill in the gaps", without any conscious attempt to deceive, and if narrative memory subsequently returns (as is often the case) this may lead to inconsistency. Difficulties with altered accounts and variable recall will be familiar to those in the criminal justice system and previously assumptions have been made that such inconsistencies equated to lying. This is not necessarily the case.

23.79 Women may also consciously alter parts of their account so as to avoid shame, humiliation or possible consequences of their actions. Thus, the woman who has, for example, taken illicit substances, may fabricate elements of her account so as to avoid having to disclose her illegal activity. Unless dealt with, such deception may create a false impression in court, in that the victim will be seen as lying in all aspects of the account that they gave.

THE TRIAL

23.80 Research supports the assumption that jurors are not familiar with typical reactions of rape survivors[82] and hold a number of attributional beliefs about the complainant's responsibility. Jurors tend to identify with a complainant (or defendant) and may have trouble understanding how that person could have felt or acted any differently to how they themselves would have felt or acted in the same situation. Yet their judgment in this regard will be flawed, unless they understand the issues described.

23.81 Ellison and Munro[83] conducted a study in which volunteers observed one of nine mini rape trial reconstructions and were asked to deliberate as a

[82] P. Frazier and E. Borgida, "Juror common understanding and the admissibility of rape trauma syndrome in court", *Law and Human Behaviour* 1998, 12, 101–122.
[83] L. Ellison and V.E. Munro, "Reacting to Rape Exploring Mock Jurors' Assessments of Complainant Credibility", *British Journal of Criminology* 2008, Vol. 49, No. 2, 202–219.

group towards a verdict. These deliberations were analysed to better understand what goes on behind the closed doors of the jury room in rape cases. While previous research has established that jurors are often influenced by extra-legal factors relating to the complainant's behaviour before an alleged attack, this study explored the impact of complainant conduct during and after the assault on assessments of credibility. More specifically, it examined the effects of (1) lack of physical resistance, (2) delayed reporting and (3) calm emotional demeanour. Many jurors were influenced by expectations regarding the instinct to fight back, the compulsion to report immediately and the inability to control one's emotions. Many jurors harboured unrealistic expectations regarding the association of sexual assault and physical injury. Jurors who received educational guidance were less likely to consider the fact of a three-day delay before reporting or a calm demeanour as necessarily problematic. However, jurors often failed to connect the guidance on the feasibility of a freezing response with non-stranger rape scenarios, and no impact could be discerned as a result of education in terms of expectations of complainant resistance and or injury. The authors concluded that concerns regarding the limits of current public understanding as to what constitutes a normal reaction to sexual victim-isation appeared to be merited.

23.82 If the case proceeds, the trial will often take place while the complainant is still experiencing psychological symptoms. Research has shown that under ordinary conditions people with PTSD often have fairly good psychosocial adjustment; however, they do not respond to stress the way other people do. Under pressure (such as at interview, or in court) they may act or feel as if they were being traumatised all over again. This high state of arousal may facilitate memory retrieval and therefore should not necessarily be avoided, although significant explanation and support will be needed. During the attack the survivor was overpowered and helpless. She needs to feel that she has control over her life again. She can be helped if she is allowed to make decisions, where possible. Simple techniques such as enabling her to decide if she needs a break during her testimony can be helpful. This will not only empower her, but will also prevent the compassionate judge rising just at the point when arousal is positively impacting on accessing memories.

WHAT DO VICTIMS NEED?

23.83 Following rape, services should ideally be available at one place and time, in a safe and private environment. Female staff should be available if possible. Models of service provision[84] include sexual assault health services, specialist services providing 24/7 forensic examinations, other medical and psycho-logical services and aftercare in a secure and sensitive setting.

---

[84] World Health Organisation, *Guidelines for medico-legal care for victims of sexual violence* (Geneva: World Health Organisation, 2003).

23.84   Staff must have a good understanding of the victim's possible reactions, as it is likely that the victim will want answers to impossible questions, in addition to needing answers to questions that can be answered, by informed, understanding individuals. It is therefore vital to understand some of the psychological processes that the individual experienced during the attack, in addition to having knowledge of what they might expect over the coming weeks and months. Further information, such as available help and support, can also be provided both to the victim and to those who will be involved with them over a longer time period.

23. 85   Care given must be guided by the individual's wishes and needs. It should be provided sensitively, in a coordinated and timely fashion, to avoid the individual having to attend multiple different services, reliving the assault each time it has to be recounted. Considerations after a recent assault include treatment of injuries, evidence preservation, prevention of unwanted pregnancy and sexually transmitted infections and psychosocial support. These matters are considered in Chs 21 and 22.

23.86   Each woman will have individual feelings, attitudes and emotions about the attack as described earlier. She should be enabled to show how she is feeling, to cry, shout or be quiet. She should not be told "don't cry" or "forget it", as such suggestions are asking the impossible of her.

23.87   The general principles of early intervention are to be educational, offer support, offer a space to ventilate and explore anger, and to reduce shame and guilt. Recent evidence indicates that emotional debriefing may do harm rather than good.[85] Help may however be needed to reduce problematic coping mechanisms, deal with sexual matters and assist in establishing social support and integration, as individuals who report greater social support tend to have lower levels of psychological difficulties. The approach should be holistic and written information can be of great help. Support and help in a safe environment can be provided by, for example, victim support and rape crisis services, general practitioners, and family, friends and partners.

23.88   Ongoing treatment is essential following the development of clinically significant psychopathology and the general practitioner has an important role in identifying those who require formal treatment and ensuring active follow up, given the risks outlined above and the avoidance symptoms associated with PTSD. Clear guidance for the management of PTSD has now been published[86] and indicates that all PTSD suffers should be offered a course of trauma-focused psychological treatment (cognitive-behavioural therapy or eye movement desensitisation and reprocessing). These treatments

---

[85] M.S. Andij, M. Olff, J.B. Rietisma, I.V.E. Carlier and B.J.R. Gersons, "Emotional or educational debriefing after psychological trauma", *British Journal of Psychiatry* 2006: 189: 150–5. S. Wessely, R. Rose and J. Bisson, "Brief psychological interventions (debriefing) for trauma related symptoms and the prevention of post traumatic stress disorder", *Cochrane Database System Reviews* 2001; (3).

[86] National Clinical Practice Guidelines No. 26 (2005), *The Management of PTSD in Adults and Children in Primary and Secondary Care*, commissioned by the National Institute for Clinical Excellence, Gaskell and the British Psychological Society.

should normally be provided on an individual outpatient basis, and should be offered regardless of the time that has elapsed since the trauma. For PTSD suffers who have no or only limited improvement with such treatment, healthcare professionals should consider an alternative form of trauma-focused psychological treatment and/or the augmentation of psychological treatment with a course of pharmacological treatment. The use of anti-depressant medication is particularly indicated where depressive symptoms are prominent. Given hyperarousal, short-term use of hypnotics and anxiolytics may be of benefit in the immediate aftermath of a rape, but should not be continued for a prolonged period. Treatment requirements may be more complex in individuals with a history of repeat traumatisation, when referral to an appropriate specialist centre should be considered.

CHAPTER 24

EXPERT EVIDENCE

Introduction...................................... 24.01
Expert Evidence.............................. 24.02
What Counts as "Expertise"?.......... 24.07
When is Expert Evidence
    Sufficiently Reliable to be
    Admitted?.................................... 24.08
The Duties of an Expert.................. 24.16
General Considerations as regards
    Expert Evidence in Sex Cases...... 24.20

Expert Evidence of the
    Psychological Effects of Serious
    Sexual Assault on Victims............ 24.23
Expert Evidence as to Memory....... 24.31
The Mental Condition of the
    Victim.. 24.49
The Mental Condition of the
    Defendant.................................... 24.50

INTRODUCTION

Expert evidence is frequently adduced in trials of sexual offences. The nature   **24.01**
of the expertise sought to be relied on, whether by the prosecution or the
defence, can range significantly, from readily understood descriptions of
injuries observed by a physician and drawn from medical orthodoxy, to ideas
at the edge of accepted medical or psychological science. The admissibility of
the evidence of experts is limited by principles of law, and not all asserted
expertise will be recognised as admissible evidence for forensic consideration.
This Chapter provides an overview of the general legal principles governing
the admission of expert evidence, and then considers their application to
some difficult areas in which expertise may be proffered in cases of alleged
sexual offences. Expert evidence of DNA analysis is dealt with separately in
Ch.25.

EXPERT EVIDENCE

The general rule at common law is that witnesses may not give evidence as to   **24.02**
their opinions; rather they are limited to recounting facts that are within their

own knowledge.[1] The evidence of experts usually involves both the recounting of facts, not always from first-hand knowledge,[2] and explaining the opinions based on those facts that their specialist expertise has led them to form. The law therefore provides an exception to the general rule against opinion evidence in order to accommodate expert testimony.

24.03   The key consideration governing the admission of expert evidence is the need to preserve the role of the jury as the ultimate arbiter of the facts on which guilt or innocence is decided. This necessarily limits the ability of the parties to call an expert to advance an opinion on any matter that is central to the case. The task of the expert, as Kay LJ said in *R. v Bernard V*,[3] is only:

> "to inform the jury of experience of a scientific and medical kind of which they might be unaware, which they ought to take into account when they assess the evidence in the case in order to decide whether they can be sure about the reliability of a particular witness."

The operating principle is that no expert witness should pronounce on the "ultimate issue" and thereby usurp the function of the jury.[4] This principle is amply demonstrated by the authorities considered later in this chapter.

24.04   The leading English authority on the admissibility of expert evidence is *Turner*,[5] in which Lawton LJ said[6]:

> "An expert's opinion is admissible to furnish the Court with scientific information which is likely to be outside the experience and knowledge of a judge or jury. If on the proven facts a judge or jury can form their own conclusions without help, then the opinion of an expert is unnecessary. In such a case, if it is given dressed up in scientific jargon, it may make judgment more difficult. The fact that an expert witness has impressive scientific qualifications does not by that fact alone make his opinion on matters of human nature and behaviour within the limits of normality any more helpful than that of the jurors themselves; but there is a danger that they may think it does."

24.05   It follows that the first criterion of admissibility is necessity, i.e. the jury need expert assistance in order to understand fully an issue that is likely to be outside their knowledge and experience. In addition, it is generally accepted that there are two further conditions for the admissibility of expert evidence.[7] First, the witness must possess the relevant expertise. Secondly, the

---

[1] *Carter v Boehm* (1766) 3 Burr 1905.

[2] In a case where the expert bases an opinion of facts outwith their own experience, those facts must be proven satisfactorily as a condition precedent for of the expert's opinion: *Somers* [1963] 1 W.L.R. 1306. Also, if an expert is to introduce what amounts to hearsay evidence, direct evidence of the same must be given by another witness in the proceedings: *Jackson* [1996] 2 Cr. App. R. 420. The common law rules in relation to hearsay and expert evidence were specifically preserved by s.118(8) of the Criminal Justice Act 2003.

[3] [2003] EWCA Crim 3917 at [29].

[4] *R. v E* [2009] EWCA Crim 1370 at [40]–[41] (see para.24.39, below); *Pora v R.* [2015] UKPC 9, at 24.

[5] [1975] Q.B. 834.

[6] [1975] Q.B. 834, at p.60F.

[7] Expressed as this three-stage test first in overseas jurisdictions (*Bonython* (1984) 38 S.A.S.R. 45)) and approved in, for example, *Gilfoyle* [2001] 2 Cr. App. R. 57.

subject matter and nature of the expertise must be of sufficient standing to be reliable as evidence. As the Court of Appeal said in *Dlugosz*[8]:

> "It is essential to recall the principle which is applicable, namely in determining the issue of admissibility, the court must be satisfied that there is a sufficiently reliable scientific basis for the evidence to be admitted. If there is then the court leaves the opposing views to be tested before the jury."

As will be seen below, the requirement that expert evidence must be **24.06** sufficiently reliable to be admitted has been a source of difficulty for the courts. Its practical impact is illustrated by *Cannings*,[9] which concerned the conviction of Angela Cannings for the murder of two of her children who had died when aged six and 13 weeks respectively. The prosecution case was that she must have smothered them; her defence was that, albeit the deaths were unexplained, the infants had both died from natural causes in the form of "Sudden Infant Death Syndrome". Judge LJ, as he then was, described the understanding of the causes of Sudden Infant Death Syndrome as at the "frontiers of knowledge" and indicated that prosecutions should not be commenced, in the absence of additional evidence, when there is disagreement as to the cause of death between reputable experts, and a body of reasonable expert opinion maintains that a natural cause of death is a reasonable possibility.[10] Whilst in terms of their facts cases of this sort are outside of the purview of this work, they illustrate the dangers of over-reliance on the opinion of experts, especially where the subject matter of the expertise is the subject of debate or controversy. Plainly, where the state of scientific understanding exhibits a significant lack of consensus, the third criterion is not met. This topic is considered further below.

WHAT COUNTS AS "EXPERTISE"?

In practice there is a close link between an individual's qualifications and the **24.07** question whether their purported area of expertise is sufficiently established or accepted to pass the *Turner* test. There is no single overarching definition of expertise by which the sufficiency of a purported expert's knowledge and understanding of the relevant specialism may be conveniently assessed. Only rarely does statute provide minimum criteria. The sufficiency of an individual's qualifications and expertise is a decision for the court[11] and, if necessary, will be the subject of a *voir dire*. In practice, experts on a very wide range of subject areas can be located through their entries in expert witness directories.

---

[8] [2013] EWCA Crim 2, at 11. See also the Rt Hon Sir Brian Leveson, President of the QBD, *Review of Efficiency in Criminal Proceedings* (Jan 2015), at 228. The Review is available at *https://www.judiciary.gov.uk/wp-content/uploads/2015/01/review-of-efficiency-in-criminal-proceedings-2015I.pdf* [Accessed April 30, 2016].

[9] [2004] EWCA Crim 1; see also *Clarke* [2003] EWCA Crim 1020; *R. v I* [2012] EWCA Crim 1288 (relating to a test for establishing whether or not animal protein is present in blood).

[10] [2004] EWCA Crim 1, at 178 per Judge LJ.

[11] *R. v G* [2004] Cr. App. R. 638.

WHEN IS EXPERT EVIDENCE SUFFICIENTLY RELIABLE TO BE ADMITTED?

24.08   In 2011 the Law Commission, reporting on the admissibility of expert evidence in criminal trials in England and Wales,[12] criticised the laissez faire approach that had developed at common law to the admission of expert opinion evidence without sufficient regard to whether it was sufficiently reliable to be considered by a jury. In the Commission's view, the problem was exacerbated by two factors. First, expert evidence is often technical and complex, and jurors lack the experience to assess its reliability properly. Secondly, there is no clear legal test to safeguard the reliability of expert evidence. The Commission recommended the introduction of a new reliability-based test of admissibility for expert evidence in criminal proceedings, with a view to excluding unreliable evidence, and it published a draft Bill alongside its report. But the Government declined to legislate, citing financial constraints.[13] The common law therefore remains the source of the criteria by reference to which the courts must assess admissibility.

24.09   The matter has not, however, rested there. In an important development, after the Government announced its decision not to legislate, the Rule Committee sought to fill the gap by adopting as many of the Law Commission's recommendations as it could in the Criminal Procedure Rules.[14] Thus, the 2015 Rules now list those matters which must be covered in an expert's report to enable the court to conduct an assessment of its reliability. In particular rule 19.4 provides that an expert's report must:

> "(a) give details of the expert's qualifications, relevant experience and accreditation;
>
> (b) give details of any literature or other information which the expert relied on in making the report;
>
> (c) contain a statement setting out the substance of all facts given to the expert which are material to the opinions expressed in the report or on which those opinions are based;
>
> (d) make clear which of the facts stated in the report are within the expert's own knowledge;
>
> (e) say who carried out any examination, measurement, test or experiment which the expert has used for the report and:
>
> > (i) give the qualifications, relevant experience and accreditation of that person,

---

[12] *Expert Evidence in Criminal Proceedings in England and Wales*, March 22, 2011 (Law Com 325), which is available at *http://www.lawcom.gov.uk/wp-content/uploads/2015/03/lc325_Expert_Evidence_Report.pdf* [Accessed April 30, 2016]. For an example of a more rigorous approach being taken in another jurisdiction, see *Honeysett v The Queen* [2014] HCA 29.

[13] *The Government's response to the Law Commission report: "Expert evidence in criminal proceedings in England and Wales" (Law Com No.325)*, MoJ, 2013, available at *https://www.gov.uk/government/uploads/system/uploads/attachment_data/file/260369/govt-resp-experts-evidence.pdf* [Accessed April 30, 2016].

[14] Criminal Procedure Rules 2015 (SI 2015/1490), which came into force on October 5, 2015.

       (ii) say whether or not the examination, measurement, test or experiment was carried out under the expert's supervision, and

       (iii) summarise the findings on which the expert relies;

   (f) where there is a range of opinion on the matters dealt with in the report:

       (i) summarise the range of opinion, and

       (ii) give reasons for the expert's own opinion;

   (g) if the expert is not able to give his opinion without qualification, state the qualification;

   (h) include such information as the court may need to decide whether the expert's opinion is sufficiently reliable to be admissible in evidence;

   (i) contain a summary of the conclusions reached;

   (j) contain a statement that the expert understands his duty to the court, and has complied and will continue to comply with that duty; and

   (k) contain the same declaration of truth as a witness statement."

In addition, the Criminal Practice Directions 2015 now list the factors the court may take into account in determining the reliability of expert opinion.[15] CPD 19A.4 states: **24.10**

> "Nothing at common law precludes assessment by the court of the reliability of an expert opinion by reference to substantially similar factors to those the Law Commission recommended as conditions of admissibility, and courts are encouraged actively to enquire into such factors."

The factors that the court may take into account for this purpose are listed in CPD 19A.5 as follows:

> "(a) the extent and quality of the data on which the expert's opinion is based, and the validity of the methods by which they were obtained;
>
> (b) if the expert's opinion relies on an inference from any findings, whether the opinion properly explains how safe or unsafe the inference is (whether by reference to statistical significance or in other appropriate terms);
>
> (c) if the expert's opinion relies on the results of the use of any method (for instance, a test, measurement or survey), whether the opinion takes proper account of matters, such as the degree of precision or margin of uncertainty, affecting the accuracy or reliability of those results;
>
> (d) the extent to which any material upon which the expert's opinion is based has been reviewed by others with relevant expertise (for instance, in peer-reviewed publications), and the views of those others on that material;
>
> (e) the extent to which the expert's opinion is based on material falling outside the expert's own field of expertise;
>
> (f) the completeness of the information which was available to the expert, and whether the expert took account of all relevant information in arriving at the opinion (including information as to the context of any facts to which the opinion relates);
>
> (g) if there is a range of expert opinion on the matter in question, where in the range the expert's own opinion lies and whether the expert's preference has been properly explained;
>
> (h) whether the expert's methods followed established practice in the field and, if they did not, whether the reason for the divergence has been properly explained."

---

[15] CPD V (Evidence) 19A. The Criminal Practice Directions are available at *https://www. judiciary.gov.uk/wp-content/uploads/2015/09/crim-pd-2015.pdf* [Accessed April 30, 2016].

24.11 In particular, CPD 19A.6 states that in considering reliability, especially of expert scientific opinion, the court should be astute to identify potential flaws which detract from the opinion's reliability, such as:

> "(a) being based on a hypothesis which has not been subjected to sufficient scrutiny (including, where appropriate, experimental or other testing), or which has failed to stand up to scrutiny;
>
> (b) being based on an unjustifiable assumption;
>
> (c) being based on flawed data;
>
> (d) relying on an examination, technique, method or process which was not properly carried out or applied, or was not appropriate for use in the particular case; or
>
> (e) relying on an inference or conclusion which has not been properly reached."

24.12 It is also significant that the Criminal Procedure Rules encourage discussion between the parties in advance of trial, where more than one party wishes to introduce expert evidence, and enable the court to direct that the experts meet and, if possible, produce a report setting out the areas where they agree and disagree.[16] In this way, the issues to be put to the jury may be narrowed to those where there is disagreement. Sir Brian Leveson, in his *Review of Efficiency in Criminal Proceedings*, commented[17]:

> "Juries cannot and should not be expected to understand and interpret complex scientific concepts. This is important for several reasons, but certainly in order to avoid unnecessary use of limited court resources, and in order to prevent juries reaching perverse decisions which might contribute to a loss of confidence not only in specific scientific areas but more fundamentally in the system of trial by jury. This is not to say that opposing scientific views should not be placed before the jury. Instead, this should be restricted to only those circumstances where it genuinely is an issue, and efforts made to minimise the number of contentious scientific questions in relation to which a jury is asked to make a decision. It is rare to have a case where a large part of the complex technical or scientific evidence is not common ground."

Sir Brian went on to say[18]:

> "Courts must use more frequently their power . . . to direct a discussion between experts and jointly agree at the earliest possible stage before trial those issues on which they agree and those on which they do not, and to prepare a joint statement for use in evidence indicating the measure of their agreement and a summary of the reasons for their disagreement."

24.13 These changes, taken in combination, should encourage and facilitate a more careful scrutiny of proposed expert evidence. In *Hamilton v R.*,[19] which dealt with evidence of memory formation, Leveson P said[20]:

---

[16] SI 2015/1490, r.19.6.

[17] The Rt Hon Sir Brian Leveson, President of the QBD, *Review of Efficiency in Criminal Proceedings* (Jan 2015), at 234-5. The Review is available at *https://www.judiciary.gov.uk/wp-content/uploads/2015/01/review-of-efficiency-in-criminal-proceedings-20151.pdf*   [Accessed April 30, 2016].

[18] The Rt Hon Sir Brian Leveson, President of the QBD, *Review of Efficiency in Criminal Proceedings* (Jan 2015), at 236.

[19] [2014] EWCA Crim 1555, discussed in paras 20.46 and following, below.

[20] At [43]–[44].

"Whilst legislative reform has not been taken forward, following the Law Commission Report on Expert Evidence in Criminal Proceedings, there is real concern about the use of unreliable or inappropriate expert evidence. As a result, Part [19] of the Criminal Procedure Rules has been revised . . . and a new Practice Direction [incorporates] the reliability factors recommended by the Law Commission for the admission of expert evidence. The Advocacy Training Council, also, is in the course of preparing a 'tool kit' for advocates to use when considering expert evidence and its admissibility, itself based upon the recommendations in the Law Commission Report. [Following these changes] a new and more rigorous approach on the part of advocates and the courts to the handling of expert evidence must be adopted. That should avoid misunderstandings about what is (and what is not) appropriately included in an expert's report and so either avoid, or at least render far more straightforward, submissions on admissibility such as those made in this case."

The extent of rule 19.4's beneficial impact will, of course, depend upon the willingness of the courts to insist on its requirements being met. In this respect, the Court of Appeal has given an encouraging early lead. *Berberi*[21] was a drugs case in which the prosecution alleged that a large amount of money found in the possession of the appellant, an Albanian, was criminal property. To rebut this assertion, the defence applied to call an expert witness from the London School of Economics to say that Albanians have a history of mistrust of financial institutions and so hold their money not in banks but at home in cash. The judge refused the application on the ground that the expert's report was not relevant to the issues the jury had to decide. The Court of Appeal upheld this ruling, but before doing so it also severely criticised the content of the report. The Court set out the essential requirements of rule 19.4 and continued[22]:

24.14

"[The expert's] report did not begin to comply with these requirements, and, on reading it, it is easy to understand why: it was not in fact an expert report at all but an academic research note, dealing with the historical position over the last 20 years; it did not give details of [the expert's] qualification or experience; it gave no details of the information he had relied on in order to form his opinion; it did not make clear which of the facts set out were within his own knowledge, nor did it include any information which would enable the court to assess whether his opinion was sufficiently reliable to be admissible as expert evidence; it contained no statement that [the expert] knew anything about the facts of the case, nor that he understood his duty to the court; it was unsigned and undated. Those are not matters of form but of substance. As the Practice Direction to CPR [19] makes clear, Rule [19].4 lists these matters with which an expert's report must deal so the court can assess the admissibility and weight of such evidence.

We are told that no point was taken on [the] defaults we have mentioned, and the contest between the parties on admissibility related only to [the report's] relevance. This was inexcusably casual, in our view. Expert evidence can be potent evidence. The Rules provide the structure for the admission of such evidence, but they also ensure that expert opinion evidence is of the highest quality, that it is balanced and that it is well researched. None of the criteria by which the court or the jury for that matter could assess those factors were present in this case."

---

[21] [2014] EWCA Crim 2961.
[22] At [17]–[18], per Sharp LJ.

24.15   Finally, the requirement for expert evidence to be reliable is closely related to the issue of regulation. The role of the Forensic Science Regulator, established in 2008, is to ensure that the provision of forensic science across the criminal justice system is subject to an appropriate regime of scientific standards. The Regulator has published *Codes of Practice and Conduct*[23] for forensic service providers, outlining the requirements for method validation and intended to help ensure the reliability of expert evidence. The introduction states the Regulator's belief that "adherence to the validation and accreditation requirements [of the *Codes*] will go a long way towards satisfying the amendment to the Criminal Practice Directions". However, the Regulator currently lacks any powers of enforcement. In his *Review of Efficiency in Criminal Proceedings*, Sir Brian Leveson expressed the view that it is now necessary for the Forensic Science Regulator to have statutory powers to ensure, and if necessary enforce, compliance with quality standards.[24] For the role of the Regulator, see further paras 25.60 and following, below.

The Duties of an Expert

24.16   In criminal cases the evidence of an expert may be relied on by either the prosecution or the defence, but irrespective of who instructs them, the expert owes an overriding duty to the court to assist in the fair and just resolution of the case. Thus Rule 19.2 of the Criminal Procedure Rules[25] provides:

> "(1) An expert must help the court to achieve the overriding objective by giving opinion which is—
> (a) objective and unbiased; and
> (b) within the expert's area or areas of expertise . . .
> (2) This duty overrides any obligation to the person from whom the expert receives instructions or by whom the expert is paid."

In practical terms, this means that any report prepared and evidence given should be the expert's own unbiased opinion, informed by their expertise alone and unaffected by the interests of the party on whose behalf they may be instructed.[26]

24.17   What are the duties of experts when their opinions differ? In *Re AB (Child Abuse: Expert Witnesses)*,[27] a case in the Family Division of the High Court, Wall J (as he then was) noted that there will be cases in which there is a

---

[23] Available at *https://www.gov.uk/government/collections/forensic-science-providers-codes-of-practice-and-conduct* [Accessed April 30, 2016].
[24] The Rt Hon Sir Brian Leveson, President of the QBD, *Review of Efficiency in Criminal Proceedings* (Jan 2015), at 229.
[25] See also the Rules' overriding objective.
[26] See also the *Ikarian Reefer* case [1993] 2 Lloyds Rep. 68, at 81, per Cresswell J. For consideration of the importance of impartiality and whether it is sufficiently met in practice, see The Rt Hon Sir Brian Leveson, President of the QBD, *Review of Efficiency in Criminal Proceedings* (Jan 2015), at 238ff.
[27] *Re AB (Child Abuse: Expert Witnesses)* [1995] 1 F.L.R. 181.

genuine disagreement on a scientific or medical issue, or where it is necessary for a party to advance a particular hypothesis to explain a given set of facts. He went on:

> "Where that occurs, the judge will have to resolve the issue which is raised. Two points must be made. In my view, the expert who advances such a hypothesis owes a very heavy duty to explain to the court that what he is advancing is a hypothesis, that it is controversial (if it is) and place before the court all material which contradicts the hypothesis. Secondly, he must make all his material available to the other experts in the case. It is the common experience of the courts that the better the experts the more limited their areas of disagreement, and in the forensic context of a contested case relating to children, the objective of the lawyers and the experts should always be to limit the ambit of disagreement on medical issues to the minimum."

While this was a family case, the overriding duty of experts to the court is not materially different in the criminal context and the same principles therefore apply, except that in a criminal case it is the jury rather than the judge that will have to resolve the issue raised by the disagreement of the experts.[28]

The duties of experts as regards the disclosure of material are set out in **24.18** *Disclosure: Experts' Evidence, Case Management and Unused Material: A Guidance Booklet for Experts,*[29] which was initially produced by the Attorney General in response to a review of Shaken Baby Syndrome cases. The Guidance deals with the obligations of experts instructed by the prosecution in relation to unused material, and focuses on the retention of material, record-keeping and revelation to the prosecution.

Finally, those who are responsible for the conduct of criminal cases should **24.19** have in mind their duties in respect of service of experts' reports.[30]

General Considerations as regards Expert Evidence in Sex Cases

Expert witnesses, those who instruct them and counsel who adduce or **24.20** challenge their evidence should approach the question of admissibility in a way which acknowledges its status as an exception. The proposed evidence of an expert may consist of a number of observations, of which some may not satisfy the *Turner* criteria; experts themselves cannot always be expected to appreciate nuances in this area of the law. The point is illustrated by *Ugoh*,[31] a rape case in which the complainant had been inebriated at the relevant time and had no recollection of the incident. The prosecution called a psycho-pharmacologist to give evidence that the complainant would have lacked the ability to give informed consent, but the witness went beyond this, stating that in his opinion the complainant's inability to consent would have been

---

[28] cf. *Harris and others* [2005] EWCA Crim 1980, at 272–3 per Gage LJ.
[29] Current version published May 2010 and available at *http://www.cps.gov.uk/legal/d_to_g/disclosure_manual/annex_k_disclosure_manual/* [Accessed April 30, 2016].
[30] Criminal Procedure Rules 2015 r.19.3–5.
[31] [2001] EWCA Crim 1587.

obvious to the defendant. The Court of Appeal quashed the ensuing conviction, holding that the jury did not require assistance in order to decide whether it had been clear to the defendant that the victim had been incapable of giving informed consent, and it had been inappropriate for that evidence to be admitted.

24.21   Practical guidance on the deployment of expert evidence was provided in *Henderson*,[32] linked appeals which concerned Shaken Baby Syndrome. In general remarks towards the end of the judgment of the Court of Appeal, Moses LJ identified the following lessons in relation to case management and summing-up in prosecutions which depend solely on medical report evidence, all of which may be relevant in sex cases[33]:

- Where there is a conflict of opinion between reputable experts, it is for the jury to evaluate the expert evidence.
- In those circumstances, proper and robust pre-trial management is essential, in order to identify the real medical issues.
- The process of identifying the medical issues is also vital to the judge's ability to determine whether all aspects of an expert's report meet the criteria of admissibility.
- Experts who are in clinical practice may provide a more reliable source of evidence than those who have ceased to practice or have an exclusively academic interest, as clinical practice affords the opportunity to maintain and develop experience and to learn from new cases.
- The jury should be directed as to how they should approach conflicting expert evidence, and given pointers as to the basis for identifying reliable evidence and evidence which should be rejected:

  "If the issue arises, a jury should be asked to judge whether the expert has, in the course of his evidence, assumed the role of an advocate, influenced by the side whose cause he seeks to advance. If it arises, the jury should be asked to judge whether the witness has gone outside his area of expertise. The jury should examine the basis of the opinion. Can the witness point to a recognised, peer-reviewed, source for the opinion? Is the clinical experience of the witness up-to-date and equal to the experience of others whose evidence he seeks to contradict?"

24.22   Finally, it is vital for all concerned in a trial for a sexual offence to understand that expert evidence relating to the physical state of the victim is not necessarily probative. Specifically, the absence of vaginal, anal or oral injuries, or indeed any other injuries that may be associated with physical violence or restraint, may not suggest one way or another whether an offence was committed. Depending on the circumstances of the alleged offence there may be no medical reason to expect injuries to be present. Plainly, for example, not all rapes involve the physical overpowering of the victim in a way that results in injury. Where the victim does not consent but is physically compliant through, for example, fear, no injuries would be expected. It would

---

[32] Linked cases reported as [2010] EWCA Crim 1269.
[33] At 200ff.

be misleading in such a case to suggest that the absence of injuries indicates that no assault took place, and such a suggestion should not be made or, if made, should not be allowed to go uncorrected. As for the medical aspects of sexual assault for adults and children, see Ch.21 and Ch.22 of this work.

EXPERT EVIDENCE OF THE PSYCHOLOGICAL EFFECTS OF SERIOUS SEXUAL ASSAULT ON VICTIMS

A substantial amount of research has been conducted into the psychological   **24.23** effects of rape and other serious sexual assault on victims. A detailed account of this subject is provided by Professor Fiona Mason in Chapter 23 of this work.[34] There is clear potential for evidence of these psychological effects to be adduced in evidence by the prosecution in order to explain the behaviour of victims, for example late reporting or uncharacteristic conduct, and so to help counter "rape myths", i.e. to negate any assumptions that may be held by jurors that the victims of serious sexual assaults will behave in a certain way, such that, if the complainant did not behave in that way, their credibility is undermined. Indeed, a complainant's account could gain credibility if evidence were adduced to show that their behaviour is consistent with, or shares similarities with, a pattern of emotional, psychiatric and behavioural reactions exhibited by victims generally. However, the general position is that evidence of this type is inadmissible.

There are two preliminary objections to its admission. First, it is not   **24.24** generally accepted that jurors require expert evidence of the emotional and psychological aftermath of sexual assault, either to understand how ordinary people react to this unusual and traumatic event or in order to assess the veracity of a complaint. Put another way, the first of the criteria in *Turner*, that of necessity, is not automatically satisfied. Secondly, there is the principle that evidence may not be called which has the specific purpose of bolstering the credibility of a witness, so-called "oath-helping". In *Turner*, Lawton LJ stated that: "in general evidence can be called to impugn the credibility of a witness, but cannot be led in chief to bolster it up".[35] It is suggested that both of these objections are open to serious question. The research into public attitudes in this area shows that many myths persist. There is arguably, therefore, just the sort of deficit in general understanding that would ordinarily signify the need for expert assistance. As for the second objection, this could be addressed if the admissibility of such evidence were based on its educative function, to counter any misapprehension and prejudice on the part of jurors, rather than on any suggestion that it fortifies the evidence of the particular complainant.

---

[34] An overview of rape trauma syndrome and post-traumatic stress disorder is provided in Philip N. Rumney and Martin M. Taylor, *The use of syndrome evidence in rape trials*, 2002 Criminal Law Forum 471.
[35] [1975] Q.B. 834, at p.75A.

24.25   Until recently there was little authority on the admissibility of this type of evidence. The most instructive decision was *Doody*,[36] in which the complainant alleged that the appellant had raped her on a number of occasions over a period of months while they were co-habiting. The appellant alleged that the complainant had invented the allegations because she wanted him to leave their shared home. In cross-examination, the complainant said that she had not complained earlier because she felt ashamed. The judge, in summing up, made comments about the reasons why a woman in a relationship might delay complaining to the police of forced sexual intercourse. In appealing against conviction, the appellant argued that the judge's comments had been seriously unfair to him. The Solicitor General submitted in response that the comments had merely underlined to the jury something that was clearly relevant to their considerations, and had not gone beyond what was permissible. She referred the Court to material which was made available to judges and recorders at the Judicial Studies Board seminars on trials in serious sexual cases, which included material relating to the psychological effects of serious sexual assaults collated by (now Professor) Dr Fiona Mason. Latham LJ, giving the judgment of the Court, said that where a defendant raises the issue of delay as undermining the complainant's credibility, the judge is entitled to make comments as to the way the evidence is to be approached in order to ensure fairness to the complainant, so long as any comment is uncontroversial. He continued[37]:

> "It is no part of the judge's task to put before the jury Dr Mason's learning without her having been called as a witness."

Although the judgment did not specifically address the admissibility of expert evidence as to late reporting, it was taken to indicate that the Court would be unreceptive to attempts to introduce such evidence.[38] The Court clearly preferred to leave comments on late reporting to the good sense of the trial judge, and the direction given by the judge in *Doody* and the possible explanations of late reporting suggested by Latham LJ in that case are, indeed, now encouraged by the Judicial College.[39]

24.26   The issue of admissibility was firmly resolved in *R. v ER*.[40] The case concerned multiple counts of historic indecent assault on a child, which were alleged to have occurred around 30 years prior to the report to the police. At trial, the Crown relied on evidence of a psychotherapist who had extensive experience of counselling individuals who had suffered intra-familial sexual abuse. She was not medically qualified, nor did she have a notable academic background. The issue, however, was not the quality of her expertise, but

---

[36] [2008] EWCA Crim 2557, discussed in paras 1.356 and following, above.
[37] At 11.
[38] See e.g. Neil Kibble, *R. v D: Rape: rape within a relationship—delayed allegations—summing up* [2009] Crim. L.R. 590–597.
[39] See *Crown Court Compendium* 2016, Pt.1, Ch.20 Sexual offences – The dangers of assumptions. See paras 1.354 and following, above.
[40] [2010] EWCA Crim 2522.

whether her evidence was properly admitted. The stated purpose of this evidence was twofold. First, to counter any inference that might be drawn from the delay in reporting the allegations to the police. Secondly, to counter the defendant's assertion that continued relations between the complainant and the appellant within the family setting, in particular during a period when the complainant lived with the appellant and his wife (the complainant's sister), were inconsistent with the alleged sexual abuse having taken place. The complainant explained the delay and her continued normal relations with the appellant by stating that she was concerned for her sister's marriage and for the well-being and normality of family relations, and because she had been disbelieved when she had mentioned the allegations to family members in the past. Hughes LJ, giving the judgment of the Court, acknowledged that not all jurors will have experience of the kind of familial abuse allegedly suffered by the complainant and the jury will need some assistance and warning when confronted with the kind of issue that the passage of time posed in this case. But he went on: "The remedy for that need, however, is, and is now well understood to be, judicial warning and direction." His Lordship said that once such a warning has been given, the jury's general experience will mean they have no difficulty in focusing on the issues. He identified three further reasons for excluding expert evidence as to the possible reasons for late reporting. First, expert testimony, as opposed to neutral judicial warning, may appear to the jury to lend weight to the complainant's explanation, which it is properly for the jury alone to evaluate. Secondly, the evidence of an expert may lack the balance that a judicial direction would have, and particularly may fail to take account of the position of the defendant. Finally, if expert evidence were to be called routinely by the prosecution, it is likely that the defence would wish to instruct their own expert, which would add to the complexity and difficulty of trials and focus the attention of the jury away from the central issues. Hughes LJ concluded:

> "All that, we are satisfied, is reason enough to say that expert evidence of this kind is simply unnecessary. It should not be employed unless there is something very unusual which really does mean that the evidence is directed to something which is quite outside both the experience of the jury and the ability of the judge to explain common understanding and common patterns of behaviour."

R. v ER removes any doubt that expert evidence addressing the reasons for late reporting is inadmissible. More generally, the decision takes a highly restrictive approach to the circumstances in which expert evidence may properly be given of the possible impact of serious sexual offences on victims generally.

R. v ER was followed in *C v R.*,[41] which concerned sexual offences **24.27** allegedly committed by the appellant some years earlier against his daughter and step-son. At trial, evidence was adduced from an art therapist and a

---

[41] [2012] EWCA Crim 1478.

psychodynamic counsellor with the aim of establishing the circumstances in which the daughter originally complained and how the complaints came to light. However, during the course of their evidence, the witnesses were asked and gave their opinions on the truth of the daughter's complaint. The art therapist said "I felt that in my experience, the way she was speaking was a genuine distress, and hence I made the immediate referral to social services." The counsellor said she found the complainant to be "quite insightful, intelligent, angry" and she "felt she was genuine". At the close of the counsellor's evidence, the jury asked whether she thought that the complainant was avoiding disclosing information relating to her family. The witness responded that people sometimes are not ready to talk about something buried deep inside for a long time. The jury also asked whether the witness felt there was "an underlying problem" during the therapy sessions, and the witness replied that the complainant's disclosure of the sexual abuse explained all the anger. In summing up, the judge explicitly invited the jury to use the witnesses' opinions in reaching their conclusion. The Court of Appeal quashed the ensuing convictions and ordered a retrial. It said that evidence given by an expert that tended to convey to the jury the expert's opinion of the truth or otherwise of the complaint was clearly inadmissible. *R. v ER* established that the truth and reliability of the evidence was a matter for the jury, not for the expert. In this case, the judge had misdirected the jury and there was a real risk that they had founded their conclusion in part upon the views of the experts. As such, the verdicts were not safe in respect of the daughter. Further, that evidence might have influenced the jury in their decision in relation to the appellant's step-son, and accordingly the convictions in relation to both complainants had to be quashed.

24.28   These authorities deal with the admissibility of expert evidence as to the psychological effects of rape and serious sexual assault on victims in general; they do not necessarily preclude the calling of expert evidence as to the impact of alleged sexual offences on the particular complainant, where that evidence is relevant to an issue in the case. Thus, prior to *Doody* and *R. v ER*, dicta of the Court of Appeal in *Zubair Anwar*[42] appeared to contemplate the use of expert evidence in a rape case to explain that the complainant was suffering from post-traumatic stress disorder. The complainant in that case was aged 14 when the sexual intercourse occurred. The defence was that intercourse was consensual and the defendant believed the complainant was aged 16. Following conviction, the prosecution disclosed to the defence that, subsequent to the date of the rape, the complainant had made three further accusations of rape which she subsequently withdrew, and had written two letters to the police accepting that past allegations had been untrue, one of which related to the appellant. The appellant argued that this was fresh evidence which warranted the quashing of his conviction. The Crown sought to maintain the conviction, referring to expert evidence that the complainant

---

[42] [2007] EWCA Crim 3226.

was suffering from post-traumatic stress disorder and that the complainant's behaviour was consistent with this condition. The Court dismissed this argument and ordered a retrial, Gage LJ stating[43]:

> "In our judgment, the question of whether or not it is so consistent and whether or not [the complainant] is telling the truth is one for a jury to decide, having heard, if it is admitted, the evidence of psychiatrists and [the complainant] give evidence. The jury can judge her evidence against the background of such psychiatric evidence as is called."

It appears that the Court of Appeal here was prepared to countenance the possibility of expert evidence being adduced as to the psychiatric condition of a complainant of rape, where this may assist the jury in determining the credibility of her evidence.

Also relevant in this context is *Coates*,[44] an appeal from a Court Martial **24.29** at which a senior naval rating was found guilty of raping a female colleague. The complainant, having made three written statements and several oral complaints, underwent therapy and consultations with a doctor of clinical psychology, after which she made a fourth written statement which was materially different from the earlier complaints, in that it alleged she had been forcibly raped while offering physical resistance. At trial, the Judge Advocate General held that the process by which the clinical psychologist had facilitated what was called "pre-memory recall" was inappropriate in the circumstances, but the evidence contained in the fourth statement was admissible nonetheless. In evidence, the complainant explained that after the consultations she had remembered additional and different details. Expert evidence was called before the Board to the effect that, of the versions given, the first was most likely to be accurate. In deciding an abuse of process argument, the Judge Advocate General decided that the fourth statement, and the evidence given to the same effect, was unreliable; he did not, however, direct the Board to ignore it. Ultimately, the appellant was convicted on a factual basis in line with the first statement and the appeal was allowed on the basis that that statement should not have been admitted. For present purposes, this case is of note in that no criticism was made of the calling of expert evidence as to which of the accounts was most reliable. While the content of that expert evidence is not summarised in the judgment, it must have touched upon the emotional state of the complainant and the point at which she was at her most reliable. However, it is difficult to place any reliance on this authority as the appeal was resolved without the need to refer to the expert evidence and without any point being taken on it.

The decision in *R. v ER* may be criticised for unduly limiting the **24.30** prosecution's ability to adduce expert evidence to counter juror misconceptions, on the basis "that if myths and stereotypes are to be articulated and confronted, as they should be, it is important that they be articulated and

[43] At [18].
[44] [2007] EWCA Crim 1471.

confronted with precision otherwise the old myths will simply be replaced by new myths."[45] But the effect of the decision is that intervention by Parliament is likely to be necessary before the understanding of experts as to the possible effects of serious sexual assault on victims, when given by way of evidence rather than judicial direction, is anything other than an exceptional feature of trials for sexual offences. That said, there is validity to the point made in *R. v ER* that a potential drawback of allowing the prosecution to adduce such evidence is that the defence are likely to wish to call their own expert in response. It is accepted that there is no classic reaction to sexual assault and that responses vary considerably between individuals. That being so, strong judicial management would be required to minimise the risk of conflicting expert evidence becoming a dominant and distracting issue in the case, causing difficulties in trial management and focusing the attention of the jury away from the key issues.

Expert Evidence as to Memory

24.31   There is now a significant body of research into the operation and functioning of human memory. Clearly, there is potential for such research to be used in a criminal case either to challenge or to bolster the evidence of a witness who claims to recall events from the past, especially an adult recounting events that they say happened in childhood. The area of sexual offences gives particular scope for the application of this science, in relation to both the recollection of events from childhood and the quality of memories formed of traumatic events.

24.32   As explained above, however, the need to preserve the jury's exclusive role in deciding factual issues means that expert evidence will not normally be admissible to analyse the reliability or otherwise of statements made by a witness. Any distinction between commenting on or analysing the quality or accuracy of a witness' evidence, and addressing whether the witness is to be believed, is so fine as to be illusory and admitting any such comment or analysis will inevitably usurp the jury's function. Furthermore, the state of the "very difficult science" [46] of memory research is such that there are currently strict limits on the admissibility of evidence based upon it. The Court of Appeal in *Snell and Wilson*[47] stated that, except where there is evidence that the witness suffers from mental disability or learning difficulties, attempts to persuade the court to admit such evidence should be scrutinised with great care. The Court pointed out the dangers inherent in the general deployment of evidence of this area of expertise. An expert's statement based on an analysis of the accuracy of a complainant's evidence

---

[45] Neil Kibble, fn.38, above.
[46] *Snell and Wilson* [2006] EWCA Crim 1404 at [17], per Hallett LJ.
[47] [2006] EWCA Crim 1404.

will be read as an indication of the expert's view of the truthfulness of that evidence.

The position is different where a witness suffers from a disease, defect or abnormality of the mind, including learning difficulties. It was established in *Toohey v Metropolitan Police Commissioner*[48] that expert evidence is admissible to show that the witness may be unreliable as a consequence of a condition of this sort. In *Toohey*, the issue was whether evidence of a doctor describing the hysterical condition of a youth who claimed to have been assaulted was admissible in order to challenge the youth's credibility. Lord Pearce, with whom the other Law Lords concurred, stated that "when a witness through physical (in which I include mental) disease or abnormality is not capable of giving a true or reliable account to the jury, it must surely be allowable for medical science to reveal this vital hidden fact to them".   24.33

Memory formation and childhood memories

Although expert evidence as to the operation and deficiencies of human memory is not normally admissible, it has been suggested that there is a strong argument for providing jurors with expert guidance regarding the way in which memories are formed and subsequently constructed in acts of remembering. In *Guidelines on Memory and the Law*,[49] the British Psychological Society states that memories of childhood events have special features that are unlikely to be commonly known by a non-expert. Relying on uninformed evaluations of memory can only lead to unreliable judgments. The Society rejects the proposition that juries know enough about memory from the experience of their own memories to make reliable evaluations of accounts put forward as memories by others.   24.34

The Society's suggestion has not, as yet, had a discernible impact on the law. The admissibility of this type of evidence reached its high watermark in *R. v JH and TG*,[50] which involved evidence from an academic psychologist, Professor Martin Conway, described as an expert in the field of memory formation and development.[51] The Court of Appeal admitted Professor Conway's evidence in order to determine whether it amounted to expert evidence which would, if available, have been admissible at the trial of JH and whether its relevance to the issues in the case was such that it might afford grounds for allowing the appeal. The gist of the evidence was that memories   24.35

---

[48] [1965] A.C. 595; see also *R. v D*, unreported, Court of Appeal, November 3, 1995; *Pora v R.* [2015] UKPC 9 (unreliability of confession). For a comprehensive analysis of this subject, including comparisons with overseas jurisdictions, see Laura Hoyano and Caroline Keenan, *Child Abuse: Law and Policy across Boundaries* (Oxford: OUP, 2010), Ch.11.

[49] British Psychological Society, first published June 2008 and revised April 2010. The *Guidelines* are available to members of the Society on its website.

[50] [2005] EWCA Crim 1828; [2006] 1 Cr. App. R. 10.

[51] Professor Conway was also chair of the Working Party of the Research Board of the British Psychological Society that produced the *Guidelines on Memory and the Law*, referred to above.

of early childhood are qualitatively different from memories of later events; that adults cannot usually remember events of early childhood so as to be able to give a coherent narrative account, the recall being fragmentary, disjointed and idiosyncratic; and that the period in early childhood of which the adult will have an impoverished memory—the "period of childhood amnesia"—lasts until about the age of seven. Hence, Professor Conway considered that a narrative account of an event said to have occurred during the years of childhood amnesia should be treated with caution, especially if it contained details that were extraneous to the central event, since the account might well appear credible but nonetheless be unreliable. The Court concluded that Professor Conway's evidence was true expert evidence, suitable for admission at trial, in that it provided information likely to be outside the knowledge and experience of the jury. Further, in the exceptional circumstances of the case before it, where JH had provided remarkably detailed accounts of events which she claimed had taken place at the ages of 3, 4 and 5, his evidence was relevant and capable of affording a ground for allowing the appeal, in that it might affect a jury's view of JH's reliability as a witness.

24.36   A number of subsequent cases have seen the Court of Appeal draw increasingly further back from the position adopted in *R. v JH and TG*, stressing the very limited admissibility of this category of evidence given the current limitations of this "very difficult science"[52].

24.37   In *Snell and Wilson*,[53] which again concerned an attempt to adduce fresh evidence from Professor Conway on appeal, the Court said that the admission of evidence of the sort considered in *R. v JH and TG* was confined to "exceptional cases" in which "an adult claimed very detailed memory of events said to have taken place when the adult was very young indeed". The Court added that "save where there is evidence of mental disability or learning difficulties, attempts to persuade the court to admit such evidence should be scrutinised with very great care". As for the cases before the Court, in *Snell* there was nothing to suggest that the complainant's mental capacity and maturity did not reflect his actual age and so Professor Conway's evidence was not admissible on the basis identified in *R v JH and TG*. In *Wilson*, the essence of the complaint was of a pattern of sexual abuse which the complainant estimated began when she was about three and a half years old, though she could not remember precisely when, and went on until she was about 13. Professor Conway's concern was the absence of specific memories of abuse at or before seven years of age, which he found "extraordinary". In the Court's judgment, his evidence could not properly be tendered to establish a justifiable criticism of an adult witness who says that she suffered abuse throughout her childhood, which must have begun at too early an age for her to remember the first occasion. Further, the concerns in

---

[52] *Snell and Wilson* [2006] EWCA Crim 1404 at [17] per Hallett LJ.
[53] [2006] EWCA Crim 1404.

this case were the opposite of the concerns which troubled the court in *R v JH and TG*, i.e. the presence of highly specific details of abuse at such an early age, and it was this area of expertise which was regarded as admissible, not, as suggested here, the contrary. Finally, the issue of the reliability of the complainant's evidence as to when the abuse started was explicitly addressed at trial by both counsel for the applicant and the judge, and so the jury would not have been assisted by expert evidence on the point. Having examined Professor Conway's evidence closely, the Court concluded that it would not have been admissible at either trial, neither of which fell anywhere near the category of "exceptional case" referred to in *R v JH and TG*.

In *Bowman*,[54] the Court of Appeal again considered evidence from **24.38** Professor Conway that, as a memory researcher, he would not rely on the accuracy of memories laid down between the ages of five and seven unless there was additional, independent, corroborating evidence. Professor Conway also said that childhood memories are likely to be accurate in their theme but may be coloured by inaccuracies. In the Court's judgment the Professor's evidence was "on the very borderline of admissibility", and essentially went little further than is common sense and well within normal human experience. It noted that he accepted that a traumatic event occurring when a person is under the age of seven may be recalled by that person in adulthood. The Court was satisfied that if Professor Conway's evidence had been given at trial it would not have affected the verdicts and that it afforded no ground for allowing the appeal.

In *R. v E*,[55] another attempt was made on appeal to adduce fresh evidence **24.39** from Professor Conway. Hallett LJ, having considered both *Snell and Wilson* and *R. v JH and TG*, stated[56]:

> "In our judgement, absent exceptional circumstances, the question of the plausibility of a child's account and the extent of detail he or she provides are all matters for a jury. Experts should not be used so as to usurp the function of a jury. A jury will decide where the truth lies, subject to the overriding safeguard that the prosecution must make the jury sure of guilt before convicting."

The case before the Court was not truly exceptional and the Court declined to admit Professor Conway's evidence:

> "There was no evidence of any particular difficulty as far as the children were concerned. There was no evidence of mental disability and no evidence of learning difficulties. There was no reason to doubt their reliability on medical grounds. Some may think that the nature of the evidence put before us, in the final analysis, comes to little more than common sense. There was no reason to burden the jury, in our view, with conflicting evidence from experts on how much detail might be expected from a child of 10 trying to remember what happened when she was aged 4, 5, 6, 7 and 8."

[54] [2006] EWCA Crim 417.
[55] [2009] EWCA Crim 1370; followed in *McCalmont and Wade* [2010] NICA 27.
[56] At [40]–[41].

24.40 In *R. v H*[57] the appellant had been convicted of sexual offences committed against his three step-sons. One of the step-sons, D, was between five and eight years' old during the period when the abuse was said to have occurred. One argument advanced in support of an appeal against conviction related to the evidence of D, whose earliest recollection took him back to the age of 3 or 4 years' old. It was submitted that the judge ought to have warned the jury about the dangers and unreliability of purported memories of early childhood. The Court was again referred to expert evidence from Professor Conway on the unreliability of detailed early childhood memories, to the effect that there is childhood amnesia until about the age of six or seven, before which childhood memory is disjointed and patchy, so that detailed recollection should be regarded as unreliable. Rix LJ, giving the judgment of the Court, stated[58]:

> "such evidence has come to be regarded as unsatisfactory in itself: see *R. v [Snell and Wilson]* [2006] EWCA Crim 1404, [2007] 2 All ER 974; *R v E* [2009] EWCA Crim 1370. At most this controversial evidence, now sceptically regarded, could in any event relate only to counts 1 and 2 on the indictment . . . Moreover, D did not purport to remember early matters in any suspicious detail. [Counsel for the appellant] suggested that the jury should have been warned that even an honest and apparently credible witness, speaking of his extreme childhood, may be mistaken and then led astray by false recollection: as though this was the constant experience of the courts, as a sort of analogy to a *Turnbull* identification direction . . . We disagree. The difficulties of recollection of our early childhood are familiar to us all: although perhaps it is only those who have suffered abuse at an early age who can really understand the extent to which the abuse may be known even if the details of the surrounding circumstances are not. In any event the judge did warn the jury, in more traditional terms, of the problem of delay, the danger of prejudice to a defendant, and that this must be in the jury's mind when deciding whether the prosecution had made them sure of the defendant's guilt. He also cautioned them that the passage of time 'may play tricks on memories'; and asked them to 'Look at all of the evidence fairly and apply your collective knowledge of life in deciding where the truth lies'. In our judgment these were entirely satisfactory directions."

24.41 Most recently, in *Anderson*,[59] expert evidence from Professor Conway was used as the basis for an appeal against a conviction from 16 years earlier. The appellant was a former schoolteacher and the complainant of sexual abuse was one of his former pupils. Giving the judgment of the Court of Appeal, Hallett LJ stated[60]:

> "[Professor Conway's] reports are controversial. Only once to our knowledge, in an 'unusual' case, has this court accepted his evidence (see *R. v JH and R. v TG* [2006] 1 Cr App R 10). However, the court was unaware at that time of significant criticisms of Professor Conway's methodology which have led to the courts declining to receive his evidence (see *R. v [Snell and Wilson]* [2006] EWCA Crim 1404, *R. v E* [2009] EWCA Crim 1370 and *R. v H* [2011] EWCA Crim 2344). In

[57] [2011] EWCA Crim 2344.
[58] At [40]–[41].
[59] [2012] EWCA Crim 1785.
[60] At [9].

the light of those decisions, we have our doubts as to whether *JH and TG*, which was restricted very much to a specific set of facts, would be decided the same way today."

She added[61]:

"[i]t is also highly unlikely, given the state of medical opinion, that this court will receive evidence of the kind put forward by Professor Conway in the near future."

The combined effect of these Court of Appeal decisions is that evidence of **24.42** research into the functioning of human memory is most unlikely to be admitted in a trial for sexual offences, unless the evidence is necessary to illuminate for the jury some particular factor that bears upon the reliability of the particular complainant. The decision in *R. v JH and TG* is explicable on the basis of the highly unusual facts: the victim, aged 21 at the time she gave evidence, offered a particularly detailed account of abuse which she said began before she was aged three years, and included details of her emotional response. In those circumstances the Court of Appeal held that the expert evidence should be admitted, as it might affect the jury's evaluation of the reliability of that account. The contrary view would be that it is just this kind of case that ought to be left to the judgment and experience of the jury; and this thought no doubt underlies subsequent judicial discomfort with the decision. In any event, as matters stand it seems certain that *R. v JH and TG* will not be followed except, perhaps, on facts that are materially identical. The guiding principle in all cases would seem to be that, if evidence of memory research would in all material respects accord with the experience of the jury, it will be unnecessary to admit it.

Recovered memories and false memory syndrome

Some psychiatrists and psychologists assert that it is possible, by the use of **24.43** certain therapeutic processes and methods, to "recover" memories of abuse that have been suppressed due to trauma. The scientific basis of what is sometimes referred to as "recovered memory therapy" is weak and the subject is surrounded in controversy. In 1998, the Royal College of Psychiatrists Working Group on Reported Recovered Memories of Sexual Abuse stated[62]:

"No evidence exists for the repression and recovery of verified, severely traumatic events, and their role in symptom formation has yet to be proved. There is also striking absence in the literature of well-corroborated cases of such repressed memories recovered through psychotherapy. Given the prevalence of childhood sexual abuse, even if only a small proportion are repressed and only some of them are subsequently recovered, there should be a significant number of corroborated cases. In fact there are none."

---

[61] At [18].
[62] Brandon S, Boakes J, Glaser D & Green R (1998). *Recovered memories of childhood sexual abuse: implications for clinical practice. British Journal of Psychiatry* 172: 296–307.

24.44   The term "false memory syndrome" is often used to describe what are asserted to be the false memories created by these therapeutic processes and methods. It is not an officially recognised diagnosis. Evidence of false memory syndrome is sometimes sought to be admitted on behalf of defendants charged with offences relating to the historic sexual abuse of children. The admissibility of such evidence was first considered by the Court of Appeal in *R. v Richard W.*[63] The Court, presided over by Judge LJ (as he then was), had to determine the admissibility in evidence of a report by Dr Janet Boakes, a consultant psychiatrist and psychotherapist and one of the members of the Royal College of Psychiatrists Working Group referred to above. In fact it was unnecessary for the Court to consider this matter in detail, because of its conclusions about other aspects of the case, but it nonetheless provided a clear statement of the principles under which such evidence is admissible[64]:

> "Dealing with it broadly, evidence from expert witnesses is designed to inform a jury of what they might not know of their own collective experience of life. There is therefore, we perceive, a distinction between evidence that a condition has been identified by experts in this particular field which may explain that the memory of an apparently truthful witness may, in fact, be false (which we describe as the syndrome) and evidence from an expert witness based on a study of identical or virtually identical material to that available to the jury which directly (or much more likely, indirectly) informs the jury of the expert's opinion whether the witness in question was or was not to be believed (which we identify as credibility). If the Crown were to call an expert to give testimony which bore on the credibility issue, the defence would rightly object. In our judgment, the defence is in the same position, no better and no worse, when it seeks to call such evidence. The primacy of the jury on issues of credibility has to be maintained. If, however, the trial judge is persuaded in a particular case that the jury would be better able to perform their duties on credibility issues by hearing evidence of the existence and nature of the syndrome, such evidence is in principle admissible. If admitted, trial judges have to be careful not to permit evidence about the syndrome to develop into comment, direct or indirect, on credibility. There will inevitably be grey areas, and questions whether and where in a particular case the appropriate line should be drawn. In our judgment, those decisions can safely be left to the judgment of the trial judge."

24.45   This statement was endorsed by Kay LJ giving the judgment of the Court of Appeal in *R. v Bernard V.*[65] In that case, a post-conviction report had been obtained from Dr Boakes which dealt with the evidence in the case and gave information about false memory syndrome. The appellant argued that if the report had been available before trial, he would have been able to call evidence in accordance with it that might well have had an impact upon the jury's consideration. The first question for the Court was whether it should admit the new evidence. It found that Dr Boakes' report contained material in both of the two categories referred to by Judge LJ in *R. v. Richard W.*

---

[63] [2003] EWCA Crim 3490.
[64] At [24].
[65] [2003] EWCA Crim 3917.

Much of it comprised a review of the evidence in the case and indicated Dr Boakes' conclusions about the extent to which various factors may have influenced the witnesses. This material went to the credibility of the witnesses, a matter exclusively for the jury, and as such the Court declined to admit it on the basis that it would not have been admissible at trial. The Court did admit in evidence the part of the report dealing with false memory syndrome, on the basis that its purpose was[66]:

> "to inform the jury of experience of a scientific and medical kind of which they might be unaware, which they ought to take into account when they assess the evidence in the case in order to decide whether they can be sure about the reliability of a particular witness."

However, having examined this part of the report, the Court concluded that it would do very little to advance the ordinary understanding of a jury about the issues that arose in the case. It accepted that there are circumstances in which a jury may not appreciate the danger of memories suddenly materialising; and the evidence referred to the possibility of an idea occurring to somebody for the first time during the course of counselling or therapy sessions. If, in this case, any of the witnesses had indicated that during the course of a therapy session with one of their counsellors they had suddenly had a revelation for the first time that they had been abused, then the evidence would have been highly relevant and the jury probably ought to have had the advantage of at least understanding that there is a body of opinion that such memories can be and frequently are false. However, the allegations had not been produced by the counselling, which was rather the response to allegations that had already been made in a domestic setting. The case was of a sort that the courts frequently encounter, in which jurors have to make up their own minds as to the extent to which outside influences may have brought about a situation in which someone honestly believes that something has occurred many years before when that is not so. The evidence about false memory syndrome that had been placed before it would be unlikely to have any significant impact upon a jury's consideration of such issues.

The most recent appellate consideration of this subject was in *Hamilton v R.*,[67] in which the trial judge had refused to admit evidence from Dr Boakes that the complainant, who had a history of mental illness, was suffering from false memory syndrome. Dr Boakes' thesis was that the complainant, the applicant's daughter, had a delusional belief as a result of "recovered memories" and had filled in gaps in her memory to make a coherent narrative; and that such recovered memories could not be relied upon in the absence of independent confirmatory information. The judge, having carefully considered the evidence in the case, concluded that it provided no sound basis for Dr Boakes' conclusions; on the contrary, it clearly demonstrated

24.46

---

[66] At [29].
[67] [2014] EWCA Crim 1555.

that the complainant had a continuous memory throughout the relevant period of the way that the applicant had treated her. In his ruling, the judge considered a number of authorities including *R. v Richard W* and *R. v Bernard V.* He added that Dr Boakes' reports in this case were littered with wholly inappropriate, adverse comments on the credibility and reliability of the complainant, and that she had assumed the role of advocate for the defence, forcefully carrying out what amounted to a deconstruction, if not demolition, of the complainant's reliability. The applicant's principal ground before the Court of Appeal was that, as a result of the judge's ruling, the jury had had to reach their decisions without the assistance of any expert evidence as to how the complainant's mental illness may have affected the reliability of her allegations. The Court rejected this argument, Sir Brian Leveson, President of the QBD, saying[68]:

> "The fact of mental ill health . . . does not mean that the witness . . . cannot accurately be describing what has happened to her or that it would prevent her from (or make her incapable of) being reliable in her account. These issues of fact are not for resolution by doctors but are to be determined by the jury."

Here, the judge had approached the task of evaluating the evidence with consummate care and by reference to the applicable principles, including the entitlement of the defence in appropriate cases to call expert evidence on a subject outside the knowledge and experience of the jury and which might assist them in the task of assessing credibility and reliability. The obstacle to admitting Dr Boakes' evidence lay in the way in which she had formulated her opinion, which required the judge to untangle what was of assistance to the jury and what was confusing and inadmissible comment. As a result, to admit her evidence would have had the effect of focusing the jury away from assessing the complainant and towards resolving conflicting evidence of diagnosis. As such, the judge had not erred in refusing to admit it.

24.47   The clear inference to be drawn from these comments is that, if the expert's report had been confined to an account of false memory syndrome alone, without commenting on the evidence in the case, it would have been admissible. This is somewhat difficult to reconcile with the Court's approval of the judge's conclusion that there was "no basis whatsoever" for admitting the evidence of false memory syndrome, since on the evidence the jury could not make a sound finding that the complainant had "recovered" her memories during her treatment for mental ill health. That being so it is surely likely that, even if the evidence had been presented in wholly neutral terms, the Court of Appeal would have declined to interfere with the judge's ruling.

24.48   A final area which warrants consideration under this heading is the use of hypnotherapy, a device sometimes used in psycho-therapeutic counselling sessions. It is not unknown for allegations of sexual abuse, particularly in

---

[68] [2014] EWCA Crim 1555 at [26].

childhood, to be made following such treatment. Where this is the case, expert evidence may be admissible on a number of issues, including the quality of the hypnotherapeutic techniques used, the effect of hypnotherapy on the reliability of memory and the possibility of the creation of false memories. In *Clark*,[69] the trial judge refused to admit the evidence of an expert on hypnotherapy where the allegations were made by a claimant who had undergone such therapy. The Court of Appeal held that the report contained evidence outside the knowledge and experience of the ordinary juror, in that it explained how during hypnotherapy a susceptible person could come to form false memories, and it criticised the techniques used in relation to the complainant. That the jury were deprived of hearing this evidence was held to be a sufficient reason to allow the appeal.

THE MENTAL CONDITION OF THE VICTIM

Expert evidence may sometimes be required in the prosecution of offences specifically designed to protect individuals who, owing to a mental condition, are unable to give valid consent. There is no requirement in ss.30-33 of the Sexual Offences Act 2003 that "inability to refuse" is proved through expert evidence. There may, however, be cases in which the precise extent of an individual's mental impairment is unclear, or their condition is not within the common experience of the jury, when expert evidence will be necessary in order to establish the point. If this course is followed, it is vitally important that such evidence deals only with the matter in issue, namely capacity, and that the expert does not express their own opinion as to whether or not the complainant consented, which is the very matter that the jury must decide.[70] The case of *R. v D*[71] is instructive. The facts, briefly, were that an elderly woman with Alzheimer's disease complained of attempted rape and indecent assault. Her interview by the police was video-recorded. At the time of trial she was unable to give evidence and the video recording was played to the jury having been admitted as hearsay. A pre-condition of the admissibility of such evidence under s.116 of the Criminal Justice Act 2003 is the competence of the maker of the hearsay statement at the time it was made; in this sort of case it may well be necessary to call expert evidence to prove that an individual was or would have been competent at the relevant time. Additionally, the Court of Appeal remarked that the defendant would be able to call expert evidence to impugn the reliability of the complainant owing to the effects of disease.[72] See Ch.7 for a fuller examination of this subject.

24.49

---

[69] [2006] EWCA Crim 231.
[70] *R. v A(G)* [2014] EWCA Crim 299 at [30], per Macur LJ.
[71] [2002] EWCA Crim 990.
[72] See also *Sed (Ali)* [2004] EWCA Crim 1294.

The Mental Condition of the Defendant

24.50   As noted above, the case of *Toohey v Metropolitan Police Commissioner*[73] established that expert evidence is admissible to show that a witness may be unreliable as a consequence of a medical condition. Lord Pearce stated[74]:

> "Medical evidence is admissible to show that a witness suffers from some disease or defect or abnormality of mind that affects the reliability of his evidence. Such evidence is not confined to a general opinion of the unreliability of the witness, but may give all the matters necessary to show not only the foundation of and reasons for the diagnosis but also the extent to which the credibility of the witness is affected."

However, as a matter of principle medical evidence is admissible not only where it goes to credibility but also when it is relevant to the jury's consideration of any other issue in a case, which may include whether the defendant had the mental element required for the offence. An illustration is *Tipu Sultan*,[75] which concerned an individual who was convicted of rape and subsequently diagnosed as suffering from Asperger's Syndrome, a severe form of autism. The relevance of this diagnosis was that it may have meant he lacked the mental element for rape.[76] The Court of Appeal quashed his conviction and ordered a retrial, at which it was anticipated that experts would give evidence as to how the defendant's condition would have affected his perception of whether the sexual intercourse was consensual.

24.51   In a prosecution for one of the non-consensual offences contained in the Sexual Offences Act 2003, the defendant's state of mind as regards the complainant's consent may be the crucial issue for the jury. In such cases the defendant will avoid conviction if he had an honest and reasonable belief that the complainant was consenting: see paras 1.374 and following, above. In some circumstances expert evidence as to a defendant's mental condition may be admissible on the basis of its relevance to this issue. Indeed, other medical conditions may be similarly relevant to the issue of honest and reasonable belief, though two related points must always be borne in mind. First, in all cases the evidence must meet the requirements for admissibility discussed in this chapter. Secondly, the condition must be capable of giving rise to a reasonable belief in consent, as opposed to an honest but unreasonable belief. There is a range of conditions which may affect a defendant's understanding but, it is suggested, are incapable of supporting a defence of reasonable belief on the basis that, owing to their delusional character, any belief in consent to which they may have given rise would not be reasonable.[77] If that is the position, then expert evidence of the condition will be inadmissible as it does not meet the condition of relevance.

---

[73] fn.48, above.
[74] At p.163.
[75] [2008] EWCA Crim 6; and see *Thompson v R.* [2014] EWCA Crim 836.
[76] The case pre-dated the Sexual Offences Act 2003 and was decided when an honest belief in consent would preclude a conviction, even if the belief was unreasonable.
[77] See paras 1.382 and following, above.

CHAPTER 25

DNA EVIDENCE

By Jonathan Rees QC

Introduction 25.01
The Nature of DNA Evidence 25.02
Admissibility of DNA Evidence 25.24
Criminal Procedure Rules 2015 .... 25.29
Assessing the Weight of DNA
   Evidence 25.39

Low Template DNA 25.46
Evaluation of Mixed Samples 25.56
The Forensic Science Regulator 25.60
The National DNA Database 25.63
Preparing for a Case involving
   DNA Evidence 25.67

INTRODUCTION

The contents of this chapter are directed at identifying the main issues that   **25.01**
the practitioner is likely to encounter when conducting a case that involves
DNA evidence. Much of the material is taken from the corresponding
chapter in the 4th edition of this work, by Graham Cooke, together with
material in the Supplement to the 4th edition, by Victoria Oakes. In addition,
a section has been added which provides an outline of the nature of DNA
evidence, knowledge of which is key to understanding the various grounds on
which a challenge to DNA evidence may be advanced. Recent developments
in relation to the analysis of complex profiles are dealt with in the section
concerning the evaluation of mixed samples, and the increasing importance
of the Forensic Science Regulator is acknowledged. The section on the
admissibility of DNA evidence has been updated to take account of the
Criminal Procedure Rules 2015.

THE NATURE OF DNA EVIDENCE

In *Dlugosz, Pickering and MDS*,[1] the Court of Appeal observed that in cases   **25.02**
involving DNA evidence it should be general practice for a written, and non-

---

[1] [2013] EWCA Crim 2; [2013] 1 Cr. App. R. 32 (p.425).

controversial, presentation explaining the basic science of DNA to be handed to the jury. Practitioners will readily appreciate that the detail into which one has to descend when explaining the nature of DNA profiling will very much depend on the particular case and the extent of any challenge to the evidence. In some cases, the effect of the DNA evidence can be reduced to simple and clear admissions which make no reference to the underlying science; in others one may not need to go beyond the standard paragraphs that are routinely included in the reporting scientist's statement. However, in cases where there is a significant challenge to the DNA evidence, the judge or jury will simply not be able to get to grips with the issues that need to be decided unless they have an understanding of the key principles underpinning the science. In this last group of cases, it will be necessary for the evidence to include an explanation of the basic science of DNA. Similarly, in order to identify important issues that may arise in a case which features DNA evidence, the practitioner will need to have an understanding of the basic science and the key factors that might affect the cogency of that evidence in the context of a criminal trial. Accordingly, the purpose of this section is to provide an outline of the nature of DNA evidence. The outline is, to a large extent, extracted from the introductory presentations that are often produced by reporting forensic scientists when giving evidence in cases where elements of the DNA evidence are challenged. Many of these key principles were identified by the Court of Appeal in *Reed and Reed*,[2] the judgment in which includes a very helpful "primer" or guide to the basic science of DNA profiling.

What is DNA?

25.03   DNA (Deoxyribonucleic Acid) is a complex chemical found in most of the cells of the human body. In almost all instances, each individual's DNA is the same in all of these cells, so DNA in the blood cells will be the same as DNA from the cells in hair roots, skin, saliva and semen. The DNA carries genetic information that determines the physical characteristics of an individual and controls the functioning of their body. The information is carried in coded form and half is inherited from each parent. Except for identical twins, each person's total DNA complement is unique.

DNA profiling

25.04   Current DNA profiling techniques used in casework do not enable the scientist to analyse every part of an individual's DNA. Instead, DNA profiling targets certain areas of the DNA which are known to vary considerably between individuals. These areas contain short sequences of DNA which are repeated and the variation is found in the number of repeats.

---

[2] [2009] EWCA Crim 2698; [2010] 1 Cr. App. R. 23 (p.310).

Over recent years, the standard DNA profiling technique used in the UK has been SGM Plus, which is a form of STR (short tandem repeat) profiling. The system examines 11 different areas (loci) of the DNA. Ten of these areas contain STR regions, each of which has a name (e.g. D3, D16, THO1 etc.). For each region there are two STRs, one inherited from each parent. The eleventh area, called AMG, indicates the sex of the individual (XY for male and XX for female). However, since July 2014, a new and more sensitive system has been introduced called DNA-17 which has been used to produce DNA profiles loaded to the National DNA Database ("NDNAD"). DNA-17 targets 16 STR areas, the 10 areas targeted by SGM Plus as well as a further six areas, in addition to AMG.

Together, the results from these regions are referred to as the STR profile **25.05** of an individual and are produced in graphical form known as an electro-phoretogram (epg) comprising a series of peaks. In respect of the STR regions, the position of the peak on the x-axis indicates the number of short tandem repeats present at a particular region, and the height of the peak on the y-axis indicates the amount of DNA. Leaving aside the area that indicates the sex of the donor, a person's full STR profile produced using SGM Plus might consist of 20 peaks; two peaks for each of the 10 STR regions, one from each parent. However, in some cases a full STR profile will consist of less than 20 separate peaks because the individual is homozygous at one or more of the STR regions; in other words, the individual has inherited the same number of short tandem repeats from each parent. Where this occurs, the result will show a single peak at the particular region(s).

Conventionally, DNA results are presented in tabular form, setting out the **25.06** STRs found at each region. Therefore, a person's full STR profile produced using SGM Plus will comprise a table containing 20 components (alleles), with a further two where the sex marker is included. Each component is a number indicating the number of STRs. Where the individual has inherited the same number of STRs from his parents at a particular region, this will be shown by two components of the same value for that region. The following table provides an example of a typical full DNA profile for a male produced using SGM Plus:

REGION:	D3	VWA	D16	D2	AMG	D8	D21	D18	D19	THO1	FGA
COMPONENTS:	14,16	17,18	10,13	24,25	X,Y	12,13	30,31	16,16	13,16	7,8	19,23

Note: This particular male is homozygous at D18, i.e. he has inherited the same number of STRs, namely 16, from his mother and father.

The electrophoretogram requires careful interpretation by the scientist, **25.07** who will be governed by the laboratory's reporting guidelines. These will determine, amongst other things, whether a component was strong enough to be confirmed. Often, scientists refer to unconfirmed or possible components where a peak is present but does not cross the reporting threshold.

Additionally, as the Court of Appeal noted in *Reed and Reed*,[3] the scientist may need to identify features of the electrophoretogram, known as "arte-facts", which are a consequence of the process itself rather than the DNA being analysed. One of the most commonly encountered is "stutter", which arises from a miscopying of the DNA in the amplification process (see below) and typically manifests itself as a peak indicating an STR one unit fewer than the true value. Where the scientist is relying on his or her expertise to determine whether a peak is a true peak or a false peak there may be room for disagreement between experts.

25.08   Although less frequently encountered in casework, there are other types of DNA analysis. Y-STR analysis targets regions on the male (Y) chromosome which vary significantly between individuals and mitochondrial DNA analysis targets two hypervariable regions. Mitochondrial DNA analysis is typically used in connection with materials with little DNA (teeth, dry bone etc.) and where the sample is severely degraded.

DNA samples

25.09   In the course of a criminal investigation, forensic scientists will routinely seek to obtain samples connected to the crime in the expectation that the samples may contain body fluids or other cellular material suitable for DNA analysis. Such samples may be collected by swabbing, scraping, taping or cutting. STR profiling can be used to analyse DNA contained in material connected to a criminal offence such as, for example, semen on a vaginal swab, blood on a knife, skin cells on the handle of a gun, or saliva on a cigarette deposited at the scene. In summary, the profiling process will involve the following stages:

    (i) extracting and purifying the DNA from the sample;
    (ii) quantification—estimating the amount of DNA present;
    (iii) amplification—making copies of the targeted areas of DNA;
    (iv) measurement—separating the pieces of DNA in order of size (which will depend on the number of short tandem repeats); analysing and representing the results.

The quantification stage is important because the amount of DNA present will inform the scientist as to the appropriate profiling system to be used and will affect the interpretation of the profile, particularly if very small amounts of DNA are involved (see the discussion of low template DNA at para.25.46). The amplification stage involves a process known as polymerase chain reaction (PCR), which exponentially amplifies the areas of interest. It is this stage that makes STR profiling such a sensitive technique, enabling DNA profiles to be produced from very small quantities of DNA.

---

[3] [2009] EWCA Crim 2698; [2010] 1 Cr. App. R. 23 (p.310).

"Conventional" crime sample profile

Where DNA analysis of a crime sample has been carried out, the question of 25.10 interest is usually: "What is the evidence that the suspect/victim has contributed DNA to the crime sample?" This will involve comparing the DNA profile obtained from the crime sample with the reference DNA profile from the individual of interest. The most straightforward case is where the crime sample contains sufficient DNA of good quality and yields a strong, full profile from a single individual. This is sometimes called a conventional profile. This profile can be compared to the reference profile. Some of the components can be expected to be shared between individuals by chance. However, if the profiles do not match across all of the components in the profiles, then the suspect cannot have been the source of the DNA. On the other hand, if the profiles match, then it means that the source of the DNA was either the suspect or someone else who shared the same profile as the suspect.

Statistical evaluation

In a case where a match can be shown, statistical evaluation can provide 25.11 important evidence of the significance of the match. In the straightforward case under consideration, where these is a match between a conventional profile and a reference profile, the statistical evaluation involves calculating the probability that another, unrelated, person would have the DNA profile observed. This depends on how common or rare the profile is in the population (sometimes referred to as the random occurrence ratio[4]). This is calculated by estimating the frequency of occurrence of each component in the DNA profile within a population and using a formula based on the product rule to multiply these frequencies together. As people who are related are more likely to have similar profiles than unrelated people, the calculation makes a generous allowance, known as an FST adjustment, for "general relatedness" between people.

Estimates of the frequency of occurrence of a particular component of a 25.12 DNA profile are derived from databases containing details of large numbers of individuals. There are three databases used by the forensic service providers in the UK, composed of profiles from people in this country described as Caucasian, Afro-Caribbean and Indo-Pakistani. Where the racial origin of the individual who was the source of the DNA in a crime sample is unknown, the most common of the estimates obtained from the various databases is quoted in order to produce a conservative figure. Changing the database can have a significant impact on the end statistic.

---

[4] This term was used by the Court of Appeal in the course of the judgment in *Doheny and Adams* [1997] 1 Cr. App. R. 369.

The match probability

25.13   Although scientists have employed more than one way of expressing the statistical significance of finding a match, in the straightforward case involving a match between a single, full profile obtained from a crime sample and a reference profile, the significance is often expressed in terms of the "match probability". This is the probability of obtaining the match if the DNA came, not from the suspect, but from an unknown person, unrelated to the suspect, who shares the same profile. Thus, the practitioner will be familiar with statistical conclusions expressed in the following terms: "*If the DNA did not come from the suspect, then the profiles must match by chance. It has been estimated that the probability of obtaining matching profiles if the DNA came from someone other than, and unrelated to, the suspect is the order of one in a billion*". The figure of one in a billion is the match probability. It means that the scientist would expect approximately one in every billion of the particular population to have the particular profile. This figure is often quoted in witness statements made by the reporting forensic scientist because for full matching profiles using SGM Plus, the match probability has been shown to be of this order.[5] However, it is important to note that this does not mean that the chance of the DNA having come from someone other than the suspect is one in a billion. To express the effect of the statistical analysis in this way is to commit "the prosecutor's fallacy". The relationship between the statistical analysis and the weight of the evidence is an important topic and the subject of further discussion below.

Close relatives

25.14   In some cases it may be important to calculate the probability that the DNA has come from someone who is related to the person of interest. This probability will be less than the match probability calculated by reference to a population database because, as DNA is inherited, two people are more likely to have the same DNA profile if they are related than if they are unrelated.[6] The probability that related individuals will have matching full SGM Plus profiles can easily be calculated. For example, the probability that siblings will share the same full profile is 1 in 10,000. This is significantly greater than the figure of one in a billion (in the sense that it is a higher probability). That is why in some cases, where it is suggested that a sibling of a suspect could have been the source of the DNA in a crime sample, the police will seek to obtain a DNA sample from the sibling for exclusion purposes.

---

[5] The new DNA-17 system provides even better discrimination and lower match probabilities.

[6] The term "related" used in this context is to be distinguished from the term "general relatedness" used in para.25.11.

Partial profiles

Not every crime sample yields a single, strong, complete DNA profile. **25.15** Sometimes the results provide a weak and incomplete (i.e. partial) profile. In other words, the peaks on the electrophoretogram are relatively low and some peaks are missing or unconfirmed. This result may be because there is insufficient DNA or the DNA has degraded. Furthermore, there may have been problems in the amplification process. Where only one peak is seen at a particular STR region in an incomplete (partial) profile, it may be difficult to say whether the peak represents a single component or two of the same component. In such a situation, the result becomes open to expert inter-pretation and potential disagreement. Where such a result is obtained using SGM Plus, the sample can be submitted for more sensitive low template DNA analysis (see below) to see if more information can be obtained. Where a partial profile has been produced, a match probability can be calculated using conventional statistical analysis if the scientist concludes that the partial profile has been produced from a single individual's DNA, although the match probability will be higher because there are fewer matching components.

Mixed profiles

DNA analysis of a crime sample may produce a mixed profile because DNA **25.16** from more than one person is present in the sample. A mixed profile is indicated by more than two peaks at one of the STR regions. In a mixed profile with no more than four peaks at any one of the STR regions, it can be said that *at least* two people contributed DNA to the sample. By the same token, in a mixed profile where there are no more than six peaks at any one of the STR regions, it can be said that *at least* three people contributed DNA to the sample. Expressing the number of contributors in this way allows for the possibility that components from an additional individual may be being "masked" because of the large number of components contained in the profile. Put another way, it is possible that the components of a further contributor are being hidden because, where different contributors have components in common, they will not appear as separate peaks.

In some mixed profiles, the height of the peaks will enable the scientist to **25.17** identify a single, major profile within a mixture of major and minor components, where one individual has contributed more DNA to the sample than others. Where this result is obtained, a match probability can be calculated in the usual way. Additionally, where all of the components of a reference profile are represented in a mixed profile and the evidence indicates no more than two contributors, conventional statistical analysis can be used to calculate a "likelihood ratio" even though the profile cannot be separated into major and minor contributions. In general terms, a likelihood ratio compares the likelihood of two competing hypotheses that are chosen because they are relevant to the issues in the case. For example, in a case of sexual assault where a mixture of DNA is found on the complainant's knickers, the two hypotheses that reflect the competing contentions of the prosecution (P) and the defence (D) might be:

H(P): the DNA in the mixture came from the victim and the suspect.

H(D): the DNA came from the victim and another, unknown person.

The result is expressed in terms which indicate that the DNA profile of the crime sample is x times more likely under one hypothesis than the other and, like a match probability, can be used by the jury to assess the strength of the DNA evidence in the case.

25.18   Sometimes, not all of the components of a reference profile will be detected in a mixed profile from a crime sample. However, this does not necessarily mean that the suspect's DNA is not present in the sample. As was noted in the context of partial profiles, it may be that some of the components were not detected because of the low amounts of DNA present. This is another area of reporting where the expertise of the scientist may be required to interpret the result and say whether the suspect could have contributed to the sample, even though the conclusion may not be capable of statistical analysis.

25.19   It is common for crime samples to produce profiles indicating the presence of DNA from more than two individuals. Accordingly, the DNA profile may contain a large number of components, increasing the chances of a match with the components from a reference profile merely by chance. Again, the reporting scientist may only be able to comment on whether a person could have contributed DNA to the sample. However, the evidential significance of finding all of the components of a reference profile in a profile obtained from a mixed sample will be virtually nil where the profile from the crime sample contains a large number of components from a large number of contributors. The extent to which such crime samples can be statistically evaluated is an important topic and is dealt with in paras 25.56 and following, below.

Other topics typically dealt with by the reporting scientist

25.20   As well as giving evidence regarding the composition of DNA profiles and the results of any statistical analysis, the reporting scientist may well give evidence relating to a variety of linked topics that could potentially have a significant bearing on the weight to be attached to the DNA evidence. For example, the scientist may be able to provide an opinion on whether a DNA profile can be attributed to a detectable body fluid such as blood, semen or saliva, especially where a sample from a large stain produces a clear, strong profile. However, the scientist may be less willing to provide such an opinion where the stain is small and weak, and there is a real possibility that the DNA profile is derived not from the stain but from another source of DNA present in the sample. In some cases it may be possible to draw an inference as to the likely source of the DNA because of the location from where the sample was taken. For example, it may be likely that DNA extracted from a sample taken from the filter end of a cigarette has come from saliva. The evidential consequences of being able to attribute a DNA profile to a particular body fluid might be very important in some cases. Consider a case where the victim has been stabbed and the defendant is claiming that he acted in self-defence using the knife that the victim had produced. If the evidence indicates that the victim's DNA is on the knife, the question whether it came from the victim's blood as opposed to, say, his skin cells may be very significant. In this regard, it is important to clarify where precisely the samples were taken from as it is often the case that samples taken from different areas of an object or surface are combined before the DNA is extracted.

"Touch DNA" is a term often used to describe DNA, presumed to be from   **25.21**
skin cells, which have been transferred to an object, such as a gun, knife or glass, by directly touching it. Plainly, in some cases it will be important for the jury to consider whether the DNA was deposited on an item as a result of direct, "primary", transfer or otherwise. In such cases it is commonplace for scientists to be asked to comment on the possibility that an individual's DNA could have been deposited on an item through secondary or even tertiary transfer. So, for example, if A shakes hands with B and then B picks up a glass, it is possible that A's skin cells may have been transferred on to the surface of the glass by B. This is an example of secondary transfer. The likelihood of secondary, or even tertiary, transfer in a particular scenario may depend on a large variety of factors, including whether the source of the DNA is a good/poor "shedder" of skin cells. The issue whether DNA has come to be deposited on a surface by primary transfer or otherwise is not restricted to touch DNA. The possibility of secondary transfer etc. may also need to be considered where the apparent source of DNA is, for example, blood or semen.

In some case it might be important to attribute an item of clothing to an   **25.22**
individual. In this context, the scientist may give evidence about "wearer's DNA", i.e. the results of DNA analysis of samples taken from areas of the item of clothing (such as a cuff, collar or headband) which might be expected to rub against the skin and collect skin cells. It is important to note that the absence of DNA on an object does not necessarily mean that the item was not touched or worn by a specified individual.

Two important issues that often arise in criminal cases involving incrimi-   **25.23**
natory DNA evidence are how and when the DNA was deposited. In general terms, it will be difficult for the expert to comment on these matters, although if the DNA can be attributed to a body fluid then some comment might be possible, depending on the other evidence in the case. However, because DNA can potentially remain on a surface indefinitely, it may be very difficult to address these issues unless, for example, there is some other evidence that a surface had been thoroughly cleaned on a particular date, indicating that the DNA must have been deposited after that date. In *Reed and Reed*,[7] the

---

[7] [2009] EWCA Crim 2698; [2010] 1 Cr. App. R. 23 (p.310).

Court of Appeal considered the extent to which an expert could express an opinion on how DNA came to be present at a particular location. The Court noted that scientific knowledge on the transferability of DNA from unidentified biological material was incomplete but held that the underlying science was sufficiently reliable (where the profile was derived from a quantity of DNA above 200pg) for a forensic science officer with scenes of crime experience properly to use knowledge of the scene of the crime and the other agreed circumstances (including the quality of the profile) to set out the possible explanations for the presence of DNA, and to evaluate those possibilities. The Court emphasised that care would need to be taken to avoid any such evaluation being tainted with the verisimilitude of scientific certainty.

ADMISSIBILITY OF DNA EVIDENCE

25.24   In practice, where DNA evidence is thought to advance the prosecution case and the statistical analysis is routine, it has become commonplace for the prosecution to serve a single statement from a reporting forensic scientist employed by the police who will rely on DNA profiling results produced by an independent forensic service provider. The statement will usually contain a section relating to evidential issues which will include a few paragraphs explaining no more than the essential elements of DNA profiling and the significance of the results of the analysis. This may be sufficient in a case where there is no challenge to the reliability of the DNA evidence, but in cases where a challenge is mounted, statements may also be required from the lead scientist who produced the DNA profiles and (if a different person) the expert who carried out the statistical analysis. The admissibility of such statements is governed by the rules and provisions relating to the admissibility of expert evidence. In contrast to the general rule, it is permissible for such experts to give opinion evidence where it relates to matters which are likely to be outside the knowledge and experience of the judge or jury. It is well established that expert opinion evidence is permissible in relation to the production, interpretation and statistical analysis of DNA profiles. The expertise of the scientist or statistician in the particular field will need to be established. This is a question for the judge but rarely arises in practice.

25.25   In *Reed and Reed*,[8] conjoined appeals which involved a consideration of the reliability and evidential value of low template DNA evidence, the Court of Appeal identified the three relevant principles relating to the admissibility of expert evidence of a scientific nature. In summary:

    (i) expert evidence of a scientific nature is not admissible where the scientific basis on which it is advanced is insufficiently reliable;

    (ii) the evidence is not admissible unless it is within the scope of evidence an expert can properly give; and

---

[8] [2009] EWCA Crim 2698; [2010] 1 Cr. App. R. 23 (p.310).

(iii) where admissibility is challenged, the burden of establishing admissibility rests on the party seeking to rely on the evidence; where there is no challenge to admissibility the evidence will be admitted.

As to the first of these principles, the Court of Appeal, drawing on other authorities, gave further guidance as to what constitutes a sufficiently reliable scientific basis[9]:

(i) the subject matter of the evidence must be part of a body of knowledge or experience which is sufficiently organised or recognised to be accepted as a reliable body of knowledge or experience;

(ii) the better and now more widely accepted view is that so long as the field is sufficiently well established to pass the ordinary tests of reliability and relevance, then no enhanced test of admissibility should be applied, but the weight of the evidence should be established by the same adversarial forensic techniques applicable elsewhere;

(iii) the policy of the English courts has been to be flexible in admitting expert evidence and to enjoy the advantages to be gained from new techniques and new advances in science.

Thus, if the scientist has made use of new or unfamiliar techniques or   **25.26** technology, the court may require to be satisfied that such techniques or technology have a sufficiently reliable scientific basis before the results are admitted in evidence. The process by which a technique or technology is shown to have a sufficiently reliable scientific basis is known as "validation". In *Trochym v The Queen*,[10] the Supreme Court of Canada held that whilst a party wishing to rely on novel scientific evidence must first establish that the underlying science is sufficiently reliable to be admitted in a court of law, the same applies to the application of a scientific technique to the testimony of a lay witness; and reliability is to be evaluated according to (a) whether the technique can be and has been tested, (b) whether it has been subjected to peer review and publication, (c) the known or potential rate of error, and (d) whether the theory or technique has been generally accepted. Thus, there is always scope for challenging the admissibility of DNA evidence where, for example, it is reasonably arguable that a new process involved in the extraction, detection or statistical analysis of DNA is insufficiently validated for the resulting evidence to be relied upon.

It is open to the judge to allow the prosecution to call evidence regarding   **25.27** expert evaluation of DNA evidence, even though there may exist genuine and real differences as to the appropriate interpretational approach within the scientific community. In the conjoined appeals of *Hookway and Noakes*[11] the appellants sought to argue that their convictions for robbery were unsafe

[9] At 111.
[10] 216 C.C.C.(3d) 225.
[11] [2011] EWCA Crim 1989.

since experts had disagreed as to their evaluation of DNA found in a stolen vehicle used in connection with the robbery. The prosecution called an expert who stated that the DNA evidence provided extremely strong scientific support connecting the appellants with the vehicle. The defence expert stated that the evidence provided some support for the assertion that the appellants had contributed to the sample, but that it was not appropriate to give a statistical evaluation of the evidence. Each expert accepted that the other's interpretation was accepted within the scientific community. On appeal, it was argued on behalf of the appellants that, relying on *Cannings (Angela)*,[12] the DNA evidence should have been withdrawn from the jury because the outcome of the trial had depended on the resolution of a serious disagreement between experts which the jury could not have resolved. The Court of Appeal dismissed this argument. The case differed significantly from *Cannings* in that the prosecution in the instant case did not depend "exclusively or almost exclusively" on the disputed DNA evidence; the disagreement was not as to whether there was any DNA evidence, but merely as to its strength; and, finally and significantly, the defendants had accepted that they might have been in the getaway car (although for innocent purposes). The evidence of the prosecution expert had not been criticised as being unscientific or based on any misconception. Each expert had disagreed with the other, without stating that the other was wrong. It had therefore been open to the jury to consider the expert evidence and to place what they considered to be the appropriate weight on each expert's opinion.

25.28   In 2011, the Law Commission reported on the admissibility of expert evidence in criminal trials in England and Wales.[13] It criticised the laissez faire approach that had developed at common law to the admission of expert opinion evidence without sufficient regard to whether it was sufficiently reliable to be considered by a jury. In the Commission's view, this problem was exacerbated by two factors. First, expert evidence is often technical and complex, and jurors lack the experience to assess its reliability properly. Secondly, there is no clear legal test to safeguard the reliability of expert evidence. The Commission recommended the introduction of a new reliability-based test of admissibility for expert evidence in criminal proceedings, with a view to excluding unreliable evidence. In his 2014 Kalisher Lecture to the Criminal Bar Association on expert evidence,[14] the Lord Chief Justice observed that the Government response in November 2013 rejected the recommendations for primary legislation on this aspect. However, the Lord Chief Justice also noted that the Rule Committee had adopted as many of the recommendations as it could adopt through the Rules, and these had been

---

[12] [2004] EWCA Crim 1.
[13] *Expert Evidence in Criminal Proceedings in England and Wales*, March 22, 2011 (Law Com 325).
[14] *https://www.judiciary.gov.uk/wp-content/uploads/2014/10/kalisher-lecture-expert-evidence-oct-14.pdf* [Accessed April 30, 2016].

accompanied by the Practice Directions.[15] Thus, although the common law remains the source of the criteria by reference to which the court must assess admissibility, the Rules simply list those matters which must be covered in the experts' report so that the court can conduct such an assessment. Additionally, the Forensic Science Regulator ("FSR") has published a consultation paper on validation.[16] The consultation concluded on June 10, 2015, and the responses were taken into account when redrafting the revised codes of practice and conduct issued for forensic service providers and practitioners in the criminal justice system. The role of the FSR is further considered at para.25.60, below.

CRIMINAL PROCEDURE RULES 2015

Section 81 of the Police and Criminal Evidence Act 1984 provides for the making of rules requiring a party to proceedings before the Crown Court to give advance notice of any expert evidence he proposes to adduce, and prohibiting a party from adducing such evidence if he does not make the necessary advance disclosure, except with the leave of the court. The current rules are to be found in Part 19 of the Criminal Procedure Rules 2015.[17]   25.29

Rule 19.2(1) of the Criminal Procedure Rules 2015 provides that an expert must help the court to achieve the overriding objective by giving objective, unbiased opinion on matters within his expertise. Rule 19.3(3) contains provisions relating to the introduction of expert evidence otherwise than as an admitted fact. These provisions require, amongst other things, that the party must serve a report by the expert on the court officer and each other party which complies with rule 19.4, the rule that governs the content of an expert's report. Failure to comply with rule 19.3(3) will mean that a party may not introduce expert evidence unless the parties otherwise agree or the court directs.   25.30

By virtue of rule 19.4, an expert's report must: 25.31

"(a) give details of the expert's qualifications, relevant experience and accreditation;
(b) give details of any literature or other information which the expert relied on in making the report;
(c) contain a statement setting out the substance of all facts given to the expert which are material to the opinions expressed in the report or on which those opinions are based;[18]
(d) make clear which of the facts stated in the report are within the expert's own knowledge;

---

[15] Crim PD 33A.5.
[16] Forensic Science Regulator, *Guidance: Validation Consultation Draft* (August 2013), available at *https://www.gov.uk/government/uploads/system/uploads/attachment_data/file/229944/fsr-validation-guidance-consulation-2013.pdf* [Accessed April 30, 2016].
[17] SI 2015/1490, which came into force on October 5, 2015.
[18] See the discussion in para.25.35, below, of s.127 of the Criminal Justice Act 2003, relating to hearsay.

    (e) say who carried out any examination, measurement, test or experiment which the expert has used for the report and:

        (i) give the qualifications, relevant experience and accreditation of that person,

        (ii) say whether or not the examination, measurement, test or experiment was carried out under the expert's supervision, and

        (iii) summarise the findings on which the expert relies;

    (f) where there is a range of opinion on the matters dealt with in the report:

        (i) summarise the range of opinion, and

        (ii) give reasons for the expert's own opinion;

    (g) if the expert is not able to give his opinion without qualification, state the qualification;

    (h) include such information as the court may need to decide whether the expert's opinion is sufficiently reliable to be admissible in evidence;

    (i) contain a summary of the conclusions reached;

    (j) contain a statement that the expert understands his duty to the court, and has complied and will continue to comply with that duty; and

    (k) contain the same declaration of truth as a witness statement."

25.32   Rule 19.6 is an important rule which applies where more than one party seeks to introduce expert evidence. Pursuant to this rule, the court may direct the experts to discuss the expert issues in the proceedings and prepare a statement for the court setting out the matters on which they agree and disagree, giving their reasons. In suitable cases, such a statement can greatly assist in presenting the evidence to the jury. Matters about which there is no dispute may be placed before the jury as a series of agreed facts leaving the jury to concentrate on the key areas of dispute. In *Reed and Reed*,[19] the Court of Appeal stressed the importance of observing the obligations (under the 2005 rules) and bringing to the attention of the court any disagreements between experts. Where there was no good reason for the failure to comply with an order as to the provision of a joint statement, the judge should consider whether to exercise the power to refuse permission to the party whose expert is in default to call that expert to give evidence. The Court indicated that a failure to find time for a meeting because of commitments to other matters is not to be treated as a good reason.

25.33   It is trite law that an expert has an overriding duty to the court, which overrides any obligation to the person by whom he is paid. *Cleobury (Dean Charles)*[20] illustrates the application of this rule in the context of expert evidence provided in support of an appeal.[21] The case concerned an application for leave to appeal against a rape conviction. At trial there had been no substantial disagreement between the two experts in relation to DNA evidence. However, following his conviction the appellant instructed another expert to compile a report on the DNA evidence given at trial for the purpose of informing his decision whether to appeal. The report was highly

---

[19] [2009] EWCA Crim 2698; [2010] 1 Cr. App. R. 23 (p.310).

[20] [2012] EWCA Crim 17.

[21] A summary of the other points to note in the case can be found in Roberts, A., *R v Cleobury: fresh evidence—DNA evidence given by the Crown and defence experts at rape trial* [2012] Crim. L.R. 8, at [615]–[618].

critical of the expert who gave evidence at trial, the conduct of defence counsel and the judge's summing up of the evidence. The Single Judge refused leave to appeal, but the application was renewed before the full Court of Appeal. The Court expressed the view that the Single Judge had been right to refuse leave as "there was strong evidence, quite apart from the DNA evidence, which made the conviction unarguably safe".[22] Although it was unnecessary to do so, the Court went on to explain the role of an expert on appeal in terms that were highly critical of the report placed before it[23]:

> "It has become not uncommon to try to persuade this court to reconsider the DNA evidence given at trial by adducing a new report. There are occasions when this is justified where there has, for example, been an advance in DNA science; there may be other cases where it is in the interests of justice for the court to receive fresh evidence. However, as this court has said on many previous occasions, it is for the defence to call their expert evidence at trial. It is not the function of this court to permit expert evidence to be re-litigated on appeal.
>
> In the present case, there was not a shred of evidence to suggest that [the experts at trial] were not competent experts who had set about their task for the Crown and the defence in an entirely professional and proper manner. In accordance with Rule 33 [now 19] of the Criminal Procedure Rules, the experts had discussed the issues. The evidence that they gave was clear; the difference in emphasis that they placed on the issues left to the jury reflects two experts acting as experts should in narrowing the issues, giving explanations to the jury that were helpful and highlighting their differences of opinion.
>
> It may, of course, be the case that after the trial there is some new scientific discovery or other matter which, despite the exercise of due diligence by lawyers for the defence and the work of a competent expert, make it in the interests of justice for this court to consider fresh evidence. That is not the position in this appeal, as would have been apparent if the new expert instructed in this case . . . had properly discharged his duty to the court by confining his report to matters within his sphere of expertise, namely the DNA evidence.
>
> When an expert is asked to consider a case after a trial, it is essential that the expert presents his report as evidence within his sphere of expertise and not as an advocate's critique of what happened at the trial. If there are issues properly within the province of an expert, then the expert should write a report in relation to those issues. If the report in this case has been written in such a way . . . it would have been readily apparent that the grounds advanced were in fact, as the single judge observed, unarguable."

R. v C[24] illustrates the importance of compliance with the procedure set out in Part 19 of the Criminal Procedure Rules if expert evidence is to be admissible. The appeal focused on the admissibility of low template DNA evidence. One of the points that arose on the appeal concerned the proper approach to determining the admissibility of DNA evidence. The appellant in that case sought to exclude the evidence under s.78 of the Police and Criminal Evidence Act 1984 on the basis that it was so unreliable that it should not be admitted. The Court of Appeal emphasised the importance of strict adherence to what is now Part 19 of the Criminal Procedure Rules and

25.34

---

[22] At [14].
[23] At [15]–[18].
[24] [2010] EWCA Crim 2578; [2011] 3 All E.R. 509.

to the guidance given by the Court in *Reed and Reed*.[25] It said that if the rules and guidance are properly observed, there are likely to be few cases where a *voir dire* will be necessary to determine whether the Crown's expert evidence in relation to DNA should be excluded under s.78 of the 1984 Act. The Court continued[26]:

> "It is clear that an expert instructed for the defence who disputes the evidence in relation to DNA given by the Crown's expert must set out his reasoning and conclusions in proper detail in a witness statement, duly signed and containing a declaration of truth ... The court will then order the opposing experts to prepare a statement for the court of the matters on which they agree and disagree, giving their reasons ... If, after such a meeting, the defence expert maintains his view that the overall deficiencies in the way the process has been followed or the conclusions reached are so extensive that the evidence is so unreliable that it should not be admitted, he must make a duly signed and verified statement identifying the shortcomings in the methodology and results of the Crown's expert, and the reasons for asserting that such shortcomings fundamentally undermine the reliability of the Crown's DNA evidence to the point that it should be excluded. It would not be proper for an advocate for a defendant to embark on an application under s.78 of this kind without such a statement from a duly qualified expert which has been provided to the court and to the Crown. At the hearing on admissibility under s.78, the judge will manage the hearing so that it is confined within defined issues and during which both experts would be expected to give evidence. We recognise that sometimes, despite the best efforts of the parties and their experts, points may arise in evidence on a voir dire which have not been foreseen, through non-disclosure or otherwise, but the judge will be astute to manage the hearing so that it does not become the type of protracted hearing that occurred in this case. Furthermore such hearings are not to be used for the ulterior purpose of cross examining experts in advance of the trial; the court must ensure that this does not happen."

Hearsay issue and section 127 of the Criminal Justice Act 2003

25.35　It is usual for prosecution experts (whether in relation to DNA evidence or other scientific evidence) to base an opinion on findings of fact produced by other scientists not working under the "reporting" expert's control. In the past, this situation led to attempts to exclude the opinion of the reporting expert on the ground that the expert's opinion was based on inadmissible hearsay. The position is now governed by s.127 of Criminal Justice Act 2003, which provides that an expert may base an opinion or inference on a statement prepared for the purposes of a criminal investigation by someone who had or may reasonably be supposed to have had personal knowledge of the matters stated. The section does not apply if the court, on an application by a party to the proceedings, orders that it is not in the interests of justice that it should apply. Section 127 requires notice to be given that the expert will be giving evidence based on such a statement, together with details of the person who prepared the statement and the nature of the matter stated. It is

[25] [2009] EWCA Crim 2698; [2010] 1 Cr. App. R. 23.
[26] At [40].

submitted that the safest course is to read Part 19 of the Criminal Procedure Rules 2015 so as to include these requirements.

Rule 19.4 requires an expert who relies on any literature or other **25.36** information in the making of the report to list those sources. In this regard, it is to be noted that an expert is entitled to rely upon published work or data which is generally accepted and not seriously challenged.[27] Secondly, an expert who has established the primary facts by admissible evidence can rely upon the unpublished work of others in order to arrive at a conclusion.[28] In *Weller (Peter)*,[29] the Court of Appeal approved the practice whereby a trial court, faced with determining whether there was a sufficiently reliable scientific basis for expert evidence to be given, examined unpublished papers and the experience of experts. The appellant in that case had been convicted of sexual assault by penetration and sentenced to 3 years' imprisonment. He applied for leave to appeal out of time on the basis of fresh evidence relating to the DNA evidence provided at trial, the possibilities of the transfer of DNA material and the ability of experts to evaluate it. In the course of evidence the Court examined a number of scientific papers, one of which remained unpublished. That paper was relied upon by the prosecution expert, Dr Clayton, a highly experienced scientist working on DNA matters at the Forensic Science Service. His interpretation of the paper was contested by the defence expert, Dr Bader, a scholar who lacked practical experience of working with DNA. The Court of Appeal said[30]:

> "The question therefore arises as to whether we are entitled to take into account an unpublished paper and unpublished field experience that Dr Clayton has relied upon. It seems to us there are two clear answers to that question.
>
> First . . . it is unrealistic to examine a field of science of this kind only by reference to published sources. A court in determining whether there is a sufficiently reliable scientific basis for expert evidence to be given and a jury in evaluating evidence will be entitled to take into account the experience of experts and, if their experience is challenged, to test that. If the evidence upon which they rely for the basis of their experience is challenged, then that can be evaluated by cross-examination.
>
> Secondly, each of our long experience of dealing with expert witnesses in different fields is that experts often rely of necessity on unpublished papers and on their own experience and experiments. As long ago as 1982 in the case of *R. v Abadom* 76 Cr. App. R., 48, the question arose as to whether an expert could rely on the work of others. Kerr L.J., who had enormous experience of expert evidence in many areas of the law, gave the judgment of the court which included the following passage at page 52:
>
> > 'Once the primary facts on which their opinion is based have been proved by admissible evidence, they are entitled to draw on the work of others as part of the process of arriving at their conclusion. However, where they have done so, they should refer to this material in their evidence so that the cogency and

---

[27] *Somers* (1963) 48 Cr. App. R. 11.
[28] *Abadom* (1983) 76 Cr. App. R. 48.
[29] [2010] EWCA Crim 1085.
[30] At [36]–[38].

probative value of their conclusion can be tested and evaluated by reference to it.'

What is said by [counsel for the appellant] in this case is that the experience and evidence upon which Dr Clayton relies is not publicly available and was not available to Dr Bader. But the real problem was that Dr Bader was a scholar not a person who had experience of this form of science.

It is clear that there are many competitor providers of expert evidence in DNA science and many individuals of great experience who can draw on their own practical experience. Dr Bader was at the distinct disadvantage that he had none. He therefore could not bring to bear any experience of his own which could challenge the logical cogency and clarity of the evidence given by Dr Clayton."

Partial profiles

25.37   In *Bates*,[31] the Court of Appeal thoroughly examined the issues involved in the use of partial profiles. The judgment merits thorough reading by anybody dealing with a "partial profile" case. In relation to the admissibility of such profiles, the Court said:

"We can see no reason why partial profile DNA evidence should not be admissible provided that the jury are made aware of its inherent limitations and are given a sufficient explanation so as to evaluate it. There may be cases where the match probability in relation to all the samples tested is so great that the judge may consider its probative value to be minimal and decides to exclude the evidence in the exercise of his discretion, but this gives rise to no new question of principle and can be left for decision on a case by case basis. However the fact that there exists in the case of all partial profiles evidence that a 'missing allele' might exculpate the accused altogether does not provide sufficient grounds for rejecting such evidence. In many cases there is a possibility (at least in theory) that evidence exists which would assist the accused and perhaps even exculpate him altogether, but that does not provide grounds for excluding relevant evidence that is available and otherwise admissible, though it does make it important to ensure that the jury are given sufficient information to enable them to evaluate the evidence properly."[32]

Blood samples given in confidence

25.38   In *R. v R*,[33] the appellant (A) had been charged with six counts of indecent assault, rape and incest. At the request of his solicitors, he had provided a sample of blood to his GP which was then forwarded to a scientist to carry out DNA tests. During the prosecution case, the trial judge permitted representatives of the CPS to interview the scientist and subsequently ruled that the evidence of the scientist, who had been subpoenaed as an expert witness for the prosecution, was admissible against A. The scientist duly gave evidence in relation to the count of incest, on which A was later convicted.

[31] [2006] EWCA Crim 1395.
[32] At [32].
[33] [1995] 1 Cr. App. R. 183.

A appealed against conviction on the ground that the scientist's evidence in respect of the blood sample was inadmissible because the sample had been given to his solicitors in confidence and was thus subject to legal privilege within s.10(1) of the Police and Criminal Evidence Act 1984. The Crown contended that s.10 was limited to items which were "made" in connection with legal proceedings and that a blood sample could not be said to have been so "made". The Court of Appeal held, applying the proviso to the Criminal Appeal Act 1968 s.2, and dismissing the appeal, that (1) a sample of blood provided by a defendant to his GP at the request of his solicitors and for the purposes of his defence in criminal proceedings was clearly given in circumstances of confidence, and s.10 of the 1984 Act accordingly applied to enable the defendant to object to the blood sample being produced in evidence or to oral evidence of opinion based on it, since the sample constituted an item "made" in the general sense of "brought into existence" for the purposes of legal proceedings; (2) the Court was, however, satisfied that no miscarriage of justice had occurred since there was ample evidence of the appellant's guilt quite apart from the weight which the jury might have placed on the scientist's expert evidence.

ASSESSING THE WEIGHT OF DNA EVIDENCE

In the first section of this chapter, it was noted how a match probability of one in a billion was regularly quoted when there was a match between a reference profile and a single, full, profile obtained from a crime sample. The match probability, based on estimated frequencies of components in a population, provides a jury with evidence about the frequency with which a particular profile is estimated to occur within the relevant population. It is important to note that it is only an estimate and not the true figure; the true figure may be higher or lower. It is one piece of circumstantial evidence which can help a jury decide whether the DNA in the crime sample came from the individual who provided the reference profile or some other, unrelated, individual.

25.39

A match probability can, in many cases, provide powerful evidence that the DNA in a crime sample came from a particular individual whose reference profile is available. However, it is vital that a judge or jury does not wrongly accord too much weight to the match probability by falling foul of "the prosecutor's fallacy". Take, by way of example, a case where using SGM Plus there is a match between the reference profile of the suspect and a single, full, DNA profile obtained from the handle of a knife that had been used to threaten a victim. Whereas it would be correct to say (a) "It has been estimated that the probability of obtaining matching profiles if the DNA on the handle came from someone else, unrelated to the suspect, is the order of one in a billion", it would be incorrect to say (b) "The probability of the DNA having come from someone other than the suspect is one in a billion." The statement at (b) is an example of "the prosecutor's fallacy".

25.40

25.41   The fallacious logic underpinning such a statement can be demonstrated by the following illustration:

(a) A crime is committed by an adult Caucasian male. There are about 20 million such males in the population of which the suspect is one.

(b) The single DNA profile produced from the crime sample matches the DNA profile of the suspect. For the purposes of this example, the match probability is estimated to be one in a million.

(c) This would mean that the suspect is one of an estimated 20 men in the relevant population who share the same profile and, therefore, could have been the source of the DNA in the crime sample.

(d) In the absence of any other evidence regarding the source of the DNA in the crime sample, the probability that the suspect was the source is estimated to be one in 20.

(e) Thus, to say that the probability that the DNA came from an adult Caucasian male other than the suspect is one in a million is grossly inaccurate.

25.42   In *Doheny and Adams*,[34] the Court of Appeal highlighted the dangers of "the prosecutor's fallacy" and made some general comments about the manner in which conclusions based on DNA analysis should be presented to the jury. In particular, the Court stated that the expert should not be asked his opinion on the likelihood that it was the defendant who had contributed DNA to the crime stain. It is this part of the judgment which commonly results in brackets being put around certain passages within an expert's statement which are considered to offend against this principle. The Court indicated that once the expert had explained the nature of the match and the results of the statistical analysis, it was then for the jury to decide, having regard to all of the relevant evidence, whether they were sure that it was the defendant who left the crime stain, or whether it is possible that it was left by someone else with matching DNA characteristics. In this regard, the Court observed:

> "The significance of the DNA evidence will depend critically upon what else is known about the suspect. If he has a convincing alibi at the other end of England at the time of the crime, it will appear highly improbable that he can have been responsible for the crime, despite his matching DNA profile. If, however, he was near the scene of the crime when it was committed, or has been identified as a suspect because of other evidence which suggests that he may have been responsible for the crime, the DNA evidence becomes very significant."

The Court commented that the judge should explain to the jury the relevance of the statistical analysis (random occurrence ratio) in arriving at their verdict and draw attention to the extraneous evidence which provides the context which gives the random occurrence ratio its significance, and to that

---

[34] [1997] 1 Cr. App. R. 369.

which conflicts with the conclusion that the defendant was responsible for the crime stain.

Therefore, the significance of the match probability, like any piece of circumstantial evidence, will depend on the other evidence in the case, including evidence about the size of the pool of people who could reasonably have had the opportunity to contribute DNA to the crime sample. In a case where the match probability is low and the pool of potential contributors is small, the DNA evidence is likely to be compelling. In the context of how a jury assesses the weight of various pieces of evidence, some of which may be statistical and others not, it is important to note the Court of Appeal's disapproval of the application of Bayes Theorem to non-scientific evidence in a jury trial, save in exceptional circumstances, see *Adams (Denis John) (Nos.1 and 2)*.[35] 25.43

Cases based wholly or primarily on DNA evidence

In *R. v FNC*,[36] the Court of Appeal considered a terminatory ruling that there was no case to answer in a case where the prosecution had relied wholly on DNA evidence. Unusually, the submission was determined before any evidence had been adduced. The case concerned a sexual assault that had occurred approximately 10 years earlier. The allegation was that the defendant had masturbated against a woman while both were on a crowded underground train, and that he had ejaculated over the back of her trousers. The prosecution case depended on the match between the defendant's DNA profile and the profile obtained from the semen on the trousers. The match probability was in the order of one in a billion. Whereas the complainant described a white man with brown hair, the defendant was of middle-eastern origin with what was described as an "olive skin" appearance. When interviewed, the defendant advanced a prepared statement in which he denied being the person responsible for the assault, adding that he could not say where he was at the relevant time. The prosecution had no evidence as to when the defendant had entered the UK, where he was living at the time of the offence, or whether he had any brothers. The Court of Appeal held that the decision of the recorder was wrong in law; the DNA was deposited in the course of the commission of the offence by the person who committed the offence. As the match with the defendant was one in a billion, there was plainly a case for the defendant to answer. It would be open to the defence to call evidence that the defendant had a brother or adduce other evidence to show that he was not in London at the relevant time. The jury would then have to consider all the evidence, including the difference in description. 25.44

The judgment in *R. v FNC* contains a review of a number of earlier cases in which the Court of Appeal was required to consider the issue of sufficiency 25.45

---

[35] *Adams (Denis John) (No.1)* [1996] 2 Cr. App. R. 467; *Adams (Denis John) (No.2)* [1998] 1 Cr. App. R. 377.
[36] [2015] EWCA Crim 1732.

of evidence where the prosecution relied wholly or primarily on DNA evidence. It is recommended reading for any practitioner who is involved in such a case. A detailed analysis of each case reviewed is beyond the scope of this chapter. However, the key principles and observations would appear to include the following:

(a) There is nothing inherent in the nature of DNA evidence which justifies a special, unique rule, that evidence falling into such a category cannot found a conviction in the absence of other evidence. In every case, the probative effect of a particular piece of evidence depends on its quality individually and in relation to all of the other evidence.[37]

(b) The significance of the DNA evidence will depend critically upon what else is known about the suspect (see paras 25.42 and 25.43).[38]

(c) As the authorities stand, there is a clear distinction to be drawn between cases where DNA is directly deposited in the course of the commission of the offence by the offender (e.g. *Sampson and Kelly*[39]) and cases where DNA was deposited on an article left at the crime scene (e.g. *Lashley,*[40] *Grant*[41] and *Ogden*[42]). In the first category, a low match probability will be sufficient to raise a case for the defendant to answer, even in cases where there is no other evidence implicating the defendant.[43]

(d) The factors that might support a conclusion that the DNA evidence alone was insufficient to found a case in the second category of cases referred to in (c), above, include:

- DNA from more than one person on the article;
- the possibility that DNA has been deposited on the article prior to the article being taken to the crime scene;
- uncertainty as to the mechanism by which DNA has been deposited on the article.

However, where there is some other evidence capable of supporting the DNA evidence in this category of case, there may be sufficient evidence to found a conviction.[44]

(e) It is open to question whether the decisions in *Lashley, Grant* and *Ogden* were correctly decided. It is important to bear in mind that the analysis and techniques of DNA have improved markedly in the past decade. Thus, the fact that the DNA was on an article left at the

---

[37] *Adams (Denis John) (No.1)* [1996] 2 Cr. App. R. 467.
[38] *Doheny and Adams* [1997] 1 Cr. App. R. 369.
[39] [2014] EWCA Crim 1968.
[40] Unreported, February 8, 2000.
[41] [2008] EWCA Crim 1890.
[42] [2013] EWCA Crim 1294.
[43] *R. v FNC* [2015] EWCA Crim 1732, at [27].
[44] e.g. *Byron* [2015] EWCA Crim 997, where the appellant had a relevant previous conviction.

scene of the crime (as distinct from DNA being directly deposited in the course of the commission of the offence by the offender) may be sufficient to raise a case to answer where the match is in the order of one in a billion.[45]

Low Template DNA

The term "Low Template DNA" (LTDNA) is a term generally used to refer to samples where the amount of DNA present is very small, typically <100–200 picograms (pg), a picogram being one millionth of a millionth of a gram (which is roughly equivalent to one ten millionth of a grain of salt). Sometimes, the phrase "Low Copy Number DNA" is used to mean the same thing, although historically it was used to describe a particular enhancement technique used to increase the sensitivity of DNA profiling where small amounts of DNA were present. In broad terms, the threshold of 100–200pg (referred to as "the stochastic threshold" for reasons explained below) has been used to identify "sub-optimal" samples where it might be appropriate to use an enhanced method of DNA analysis to obtain a profile. This is because SGM Plus is designed optimally to produce a profile with 1 nanogram of DNA, (i.e. one billionth of a gram), although it can be used with smaller quantities. However, it should be noted that the quantification process generally does not evaluate the amount of DNA from individual contributors and so in a mixed sample, it may be that the total amount of DNA is above the threshold but a particular contributor's DNA is sub-optimal and may exhibit the stochastic effects associated with such small amounts.   **25.46**

LTDNA samples require DNA profiling techniques that are more sensitive than SGM Plus. In general terms, these techniques work either by increasing the number of amplification cycles (from 28 to 34) or by removing "impurities" and thus enhancing the profile. Indeed, enhancements in sensitivity now allow DNA profiles to be produced from only tens of picograms of DNA, which equates to only a few cells. It is of note that the new DNA-17 system is far more sensitive than SGM Plus and therefore its use is likely to result in the production of more mixed DNA profiles.   **25.47**

The threshold of <100-200pg is often referred to as the "stochastic threshold" because of the stochastic (random) effects that are typically encountered when producing profiles from such small quantities of DNA. With LTDNA analysis, there is increased variability in the profiling process due to random effects which leads to greater variability in peak heights. This may result in stochastic effects such as "allelic drop-out", where components/ alleles are missing from the profile, and "heterozygote imbalance", where there is a variation in peak heights relating to the components inherited from mother and father. Other effects associated with LTDNA analysis are   **25.48**

---

[45] *R. v FNC* [2015] EWCA Crim 1732, at [30].

"stutter", which is a small artefact peak at a position that is generally one unit below the true STR value, and "allelic drop-in", which is a term used to describe one or two "foreign" components/alleles in a profile which originate from random fragmented sources of DNA. Partial profiles, which can be observed with conventional and LTDNA analysis, are examples of the effect of allelic drop-out. Indeed, whereas these stochastic effects are more frequently encountered where there is LTDNA, they are not eliminated with higher levels of DNA. Due to the increased likelihood of stochastic effects when analysing LTDNA, repeat tests are undertaken to ensure the validity of the results. In order to report a DNA component it must be seen in at least two separate tests of the sample.

25.49   The vast majority of LTDNA samples will be taken from surfaces which are very likely to have been in contact with more than one person. So, for example, one might find that LTDNA analysis will be used where a very small amount of body fluid is found on a piece of clothing or a sample has been taken from an item, such as a doorbell, which can be expected to have been touched by numerous people. The increased sensitivity of LTDNA analysis means that such samples often produce weak, partial, mixed profiles which may not be capable of statistical analysis. Moreover, as the number of components in the sample profile increases, so does the probability of seeing all or most of the components of the reference profile. In some cases, there may be so many components in the profile obtained from the crime sample that any number of individuals could have contributed DNA, making the evidence to be obtained from a comparison with a reference profile virtually worthless.

25.50   Furthermore, where a sample has been obtained from a surface which has, for example, a very small amount of blood or semen on it, the scientist may not be able to say whether any DNA detected came for the body fluid or the underlying surface which already had cellular material on it. It will often be very difficult to say how the DNA came to be present in the crime sample, and secondary or tertiary transfer should always be considered as a possible explanation. In this regard, it is important to note that as with other sources of DNA, so semen can be transferred directly and indirectly, although the likelihood of secondary transfer might depend on the amount of semen in the crime sample.

25.51   In *Reed and Reed*,[46] the Court of Appeal examined the difficulties associated with LTDNA analysis. In particular, the Court noted that analysis of samples where the total amount of DNA was below "the stochastic threshold", which was accepted to be between 100–200pg, can produce statistically random ("stochastic") effects. These include:

(a) "drop-out", where a DNA component (allele) that is present is not seen, thus giving a false negative; and

---

[46] [2009] EWCA Crim 2698; [2010] 1 Cr. App. R. 23 (p.310).

(b) "drop-in", where one or two "spurious" additional components (alleles) are seen, thus giving false positives (this phenomenon is to be distinguished from gross contamination, where a partial or complete profile is introduced as a result of a contamination event).

When addressing the reliability of LTDNA evidence, the Court observed that, in the absence of new scientific evidence, a challenge to the validity of the method of analysing Low Template DNA should no longer be permitted at trials where the quantity of DNA analysed is above the stochastic threshold of 100–200pg.[47] However, the Court acknowledged that there may be differences between experts when it comes to interpretation of the results. As to cases where reliance is placed on a profile obtained where the quantity of DNA analysed is within the range of 100–200pg, the Court stated that expert evidence must be given as to whether, in the particular case, a reliable interpretation can be made. Earlier in the judgment,[48] it had noted that even with a sample below the stochastic threshold, it is possible to produce reliable profiles capable of expert interpretation where, for example, there is reproducibility between two runs.

The guidance given in *Reed and Reed* regarding analysis of LTDNA fell to   **25.52** be considered in *R. v C.*[49] The complainant had been raped in the 1980s. Swabs were taken from her vagina at the time, but attempts to retrieve DNA profiles from the swabs had been unsuccessful. Years later, the Forensic Science Service carried out further analysis using, at first, the SGM Plus system. This produced a major profile and a minor profile. It was ascertained that the major profile came from the complainant, and the minor profile was then compared with DNA profiles held on the national database. There were three possible matches: two were eliminated and the third was the appellant. The sample from the appellant was then subjected to the "LCN method" in the manner described in *Reed and Reed*. The minor profile was said by the FSS expert to show a match probability of one in over three million. After the analysis of the further swab taken from the victim and an analysis made combining the SGM Plus and LCN results, the match probability of the minor profile to that of the appellant was one in over 50 million. In each of the SGM Plus and LCN processes, more than one run was made. In all runs, the results were compared with one another for stochastic effects and reproducibility. In accordance with the Criminal Procedure Rules, a pre-trial meeting took place between the two experts. There were the following areas of disagreement:

(i) Whether the quantity of the minor profile was such that stochastic variations had been sufficiently taken into account.
(ii) Whether there were more than two contributors.

---

[47] At [74].
[48] At [48].
[49] [2010] EWCA Crim 2578; [2011] 3 All E.R. 509.

    (iii) Whether the way in which the process of analysis was carried out had properly followed the applicable protocols.

    (iv) Whether the samples had been handled, stored and recorded correctly.

    (v) The reproducibility of the runs.

    (vi) The match probability calculation.

    (vii) The applicable statistics.

The appellant's expert was of the view that the cumulative effect of the points of disagreement was such that the DNA evidence was unreliable. On that basis, an application was made to the trial judge for the evidence to be excluded under s.78 of the Police and Criminal Evidence Act 1984. The application was heard at a pre-trial *voir dire*, in which the Crown's expert was cross-examined for three days, prior to the court hearing legal argument on admissibility. Of particular note in relation to the LCN method was the appellant's submission that if the amount of the minor profile was 50pg (as he contended), the profile was inadmissible because it fell below the stochastic threshold set out in *Reed and Reed* of 100–200pg. The prosecution submitted that the appellant had misunderstood *Reed and Reed*, and that there could be cases in which the quantities of DNA were below the stochastic threshold but the evidence remained admissible. Furthermore, it was the reliability of the profile that determined admissibility and there was no lower limit below which the DNA evidence was inadmissible. At the conclusion of the hearing the judge gave an ex tempore ruling. He held that the FSS expert had not been undermined in such a way that the DNA evidence should be excluded under s.78 of the 1984 Act. It was the total amount of DNA that mattered, rather than the ratio of the profiles, and it was the quality and reliability of the DNA that mattered rather than the quantity.

25.53   The single ground of appeal was that the learned trial judge had wrongly ruled that the DNA evidence was sufficiently reliable to be admitted. The Court of Appeal resoundingly upheld the ruling. It said that its earlier decision in *Broughton*,[50] which had not been available to the judge or the parties at the *voir dire*, made clear that the submissions advanced by the Crown in this case were entirely correct. In *Broughton,* where the DNA profiles had been derived from unquantified samples of DNA of less than 100pg, the Court had said[51]:

> "At these very low levels of DNA, the dangers presented by the possibility of stochastic effects, including allelic drop-out, drop-in and stutter are very real and must be fully appreciated, but they may often be addressed by repeating the process a number of times, as [the Crown's expert] recognised.
>
> There will of course be occasions where profiles generated from less than 200pg are wholly and obviously unreliable. We anticipate that the Crown would never seek to adduce such profiles in evidence. If it put forward such a profile,

[50] [2010] EWCA Crim 549.
[51] At [34]–[37].

then the unreliability would be pointed out in the report of the defence expert and, if not accepted by the Crown's expert in the exchange that must take place under Part 34 of the Criminal Procedure Rules, the judge would have to consider the dispute; if they were unreliable, he would exclude them.

There will be other occasions where the probative value of the profiles is more debatable. In such cases the evidence may properly be adduced and it must then be addressed and its weight established by adversarial forensic techniques. But we do not accept that these are reasons for ruling out LTDNA evidence altogether. In our judgment, the science of LTDNA is sufficiently well established to pass the ordinary tests of reliability and relevance and it would be wrong to wholly deprive the justice system of the benefits to be gained from the new techniques and advances which it embodies, in cases where there is clear evidence (adduced in the manner discussed) that the profiles are sufficiently reliable."

On this basis, the Court in *R. v C* held that counsel for the appellant[52]:

" . . . was wrong in his view that a 'knockout blow' could be achieved if he persuaded the judge that the amount of DNA in the minor male profile was below 100–200 picograms. The sole question was whether, despite the low quantity, a reliable profile could be produced."

It went on to add[53]:

"Although that is sufficient to affirm that the judge adopted the correct approach, we would add one further observation. In *Reed & Reed* there was no express consideration by the experts who gave evidence in that case as to whether the stochastic threshold of 100–200 picograms related to the amount subject to analysis or, where mixed profiles were obtained, the particular profile. However, it is clear from the whole of that decision that the court was referring to the total quantity of DNA in its reference to the stochastic threshold. Of course if, in the case of a mixed profile, the DNA relating to a particular profile comprises less than 200 picograms, problems may arise. But as was made clear in *Reed & Reed* and in *Broughton*, profiles obtained from less than 200 picograms can be reliable. It is reliability that is the issue, not the quantity, though plainly the quantity is relevant (as has been made clear) to the consideration of stochastic effects."

Contamination

Another issue that has been brought into sharper focus as a result of the   25.54
sensitivity of LTDNA analysis is the issue of contamination. Plainly, in the absence of appropriate anti-contamination procedures, there is potential for introducing extraneous, post-incident DNA at various points such as the collection of the sample, the examination of the sample, and when subjecting the sample to the DNA profiling process. If contamination occurs, then it may be reflected in the DNA profile, thereby resulting in misleading evidence. This is why such care is taken when collecting and packaging DNA samples intended for analysis, and why laboratories have rigorous anti-contamination procedures and protocols directed towards avoiding cross-contamination. It explains why laboratories are regularly cleaned and why surfaces and

[52] At [26].
[53] At [27].

equipment are tested to ascertain levels of environmental DNA. The DNA annex to the Codes of Practice and Conduct issued by the Forensic Science Regulator in September 2014[54] contains various requirements expected of the service providers aimed at addressing issues of contamination, including the maintenance of local databases to detect staff contamination. However, in years gone past, the procedures to avoid contamination were not as strict as they are now because the methods of DNA analysis were not so sensitive. Accordingly, when involved in a case where contemporary methods of DNA analysis are applied to historic cases, it is always prudent to examine the evidential chain to identify opportunities for contamination. This may involve close scrutiny of documentation relating to each link in the chain of continuity.

25.55 In the 2007 prosecution of *Sean Hoey*, a suspect in the Omagh bombing, the trial judge was very critical of the LTDNA analysis that was used by the prosecution. The criticism focused on the lack of continuity and inappropriate anti-contamination procedures, as well as the validity of the technique itself. The resulting publicity led to an investigation into the use of the new "technique" by Professor Caddy. His report concluded that, with proper safeguards, the technique could properly be used.[55]

EVALUATION OF MIXED SAMPLES

25.56 It has been noted how conventional statistical analysis may be used in respect of crime samples that produce a single profile or a single major profile, and mixed samples where there is no evidence of more than two contributors and all of the components of the reference profile are seen in the profile from the crime sample. Until recently, however, there was no accepted method of evaluating the likelihood that a particular individual had contributed DNA to a sample where analysis of the sample produced a complex profile, where stochastic effects may be in play and where there may be more than one contributor. There have been two important developments in this area. The first is the use of computer software to produce a statistical evaluation of such profiles, and the second is an acknowledgment by the Court of Appeal that, in principle, it is permissible for a suitably qualified expert to express an evaluative opinion as to whether a particular individual has contributed DNA to a sample that has produced a mixed profile, even if there is no statistical basis for the opinion.

Computer software

25.57 In recent years, experts from different countries have developed computer software that can be used to analyse complex DNA profiles, including mixed

---

[54] This document is available on the FSR's website: *https://www.gov.uk/government/organisations/forensic-science-regulator* [Accessed April 30, 2016].

[55] The report is at *http://www.homeoffice.gov.uk/publications/police/operational-policing/Review_of_Low_Template_DNA_1.pdf* [Accessed April 30, 2016].

profiles where there are at least four contributors. The software can be used to perform calculations to measure the relative strengths (likelihoods) of two alternative hypotheses in order to explain the profile obtained from the crime sample. The hypotheses are chosen to represent the prosecution and the defence contentions. The result may be expressed as a likelihood ratio in the following terms: "The DNA profiling results are about x times more likely under hypothesis (P) than under hypothesis (D)." In this jurisdiction, Professor Balding developed a programme called "likeLTD" during his tenure as Professor of Statistical Genetics at UCL, and it has been used in casework since 2010. The programme uses information about the number of contributors, as well as information as to the components of the reference profile(s) and the crime sample profile. Additionally, the programme is designed to estimate effects such as allelic drop-out and allelic drop-in. The likelihood ratios produced are approximations designed to provide a fair reflection of the relative strength of the alternative hypotheses which can be considered in the context of the other evidence in the case. The mathematics involved are relatively complicated, although the programme is open-source and therefore the underlying algorithms are available for scrutiny by the wider scientific community. Furthermore, the programme has been described in various publications including the prestigious American journal, *Proceedings of the National Academy of Science*.[56] There have been challenges in criminal cases to the admissibility of such evidence based on the reliability of the assumptions inherent in the programme and whether the programme had been sufficiently validated. In this connection, it is noteworthy that Cellmark adopted the programme for use in casework after carrying out its own validation studies in 2014 and other forensic service providers have developed their own software. However, the use of computer software to analyse complex profiles is a relatively recent innovation and there remain distinguished scientists who take the view that such programmes have been insufficiently validated for use in criminal casework.

Non-statistical evaluative opinion

In *Dlugosz, Pickering and MDS*,[57] the Court of Appeal heard three conjoined appeals in respect of cases in which the judge was asked by the Crown to admit expert opinion evidence which supported the proposition that the appellant had contributed DNA to a mixed sample to which at least two or three individuals had contributed. In each case, the evidence suggested that 19 or 20 of the components of the appellant's DNA had been present in the mixture. The experts were unable to give a statistical basis for their opinion; instead they drew upon their experience of interpreting and comparing DNA profiles in order to provide an evaluation of the DNA evidence using various   25.58

---

[56] *PNAS* 2013 110(3) 1241-12246.
[57] [2013] EWCA Crim 2; [2013] 1 Cr. App. R. 32 (p.425). See also Brewis, B. and Stockdale, M., *Admissibility of low template DNA evidence*, J. Crim. L. 2013, 77(2), 115–118.

verbal expressions to convey the strength of the evidence. The experts who gave evidence in the cases of Dlugosz and Pickering were not prepared to express their evaluations with reference to the sliding scale of expressions, (ranging from "lends no support" to "lends powerful support"), used in other areas of expert evidence such as facial mapping and handwriting. The judge's decision to admit the evidence was the main issue in each of the appeals. The Court of Appeal held that an expert evaluative opinion as to whether a defendant or another person had contributed DNA is, in principle, admissible, even if it has not been possible to provide a statistical basis in support of the opinion. In determining the issue of admissibility, the court must be satisfied that there is a sufficiently reliable scientific basis for the evidence to be admitted. If such a basis exists, then the court leaves the opposing views to be tested before the jury. The experience of the scientist could provide such a basis. In such cases, conclusions from the analysis of a mixed profile should be supported by detailed evidence in the form of a report of the experience the expert is relying upon and the particular features of the mixed profile that make it possible to give an evaluative opinion in the particular case. In order to prevent undue weight being attached to the opinion evidence, it must be made clear to the jury that the evaluation has no statistical basis, that the opinion expressed is quite different from the usual DNA evidence based on statistical match probability, and that it is only of more limited assistance. If there is a danger that the jury might attach a false or misleading significance to such an opinion, the court should decline to admit the evidence, but generally there will not be such a danger provided the court sufficiently explains the basis of the opinion and its limitations. The Court further held that an expert is not bound to express an evaluative opinion by reference to a hierarchy or sliding scale of support, like that set out in *Atkins and Atkins*; the expert is entitled to use other phrases. The real significance of the expert's inability to use the hierarchy might be that it is indicative of the lack of a proper basis on which to express an opinion. It can be no more than that. It is a matter to be taken into account in an assessment of whether there is a sufficiently reliable scientific basis for such an evaluative opinion to be given. In the course of the judgment, the Court of Appeal expressed the view that the experience of the reporting scientists must be the subject of detailed study and evaluation as soon as possible by the commercial providers, making all of their data available for critical independent examination under the superintendence of the Forensic Science Regulator.[58]

25.59   The way in which a non-statistical evaluative opinion may be expressed can be illustrated by reference to part of the evidence given by the expert called by the prosecution in *MDS*. The case involved an allegation of murder. One of the issues for the jury to consider was whether the victim's blood was on

---

[58] For a critical analysis of the judgment in this case, see the commentary by Andrew Roberts in [2013] Crim. L.R. 8, 684-686.

the blade of a knife said by the prosecution to be the murder weapon. Swabs taken from the blade of the knife were subjected to DNA SenCE profiling (a sensitive technique used in relation to LTDNA). The result comprised a mixed STR profile with contributions of DNA from at least two individuals with unconfirmed indications of DNA from a third. The profile was not suitable for conventional DNA analysis. It was not possible to separate the components into the STR profiles of the contributors. However, all of the more prominent components in this mixed profile matched the corresponding components in the STR profile of the victim. In order to assess this finding the scientist considered the following hypotheses:

H(1): the victim has contributed a portion of his DNA to the result;
H(2): the victim has not contributed a portion of his DNA to the result and the matching components observed are due to coincidental matches from another unrelated person or persons.

The scientist stated that, based on her experience (the detail of which was the subject of a detailed statement), the observation of the more prominent components matching those in the victim's profile is what she would have expected under H(1). However, she considered the result "very unlikely" under H(2) and that all of the victim's components matched all of the more prominent components in the result by chance alone. Therefore, the expert concluded that, using the sliding scale, the results provided strong support for the view that the victim had contributed DNA to the crime sample rather than the view he had not.

THE FORENSIC SCIENCE REGULATOR

In December 2010, the Government announced that the Forensic Science **25.60** Service ("FSS") was to be wound down by March 2012. On July 1, 2011, the House of Commons Science and Technology Committee published a report on the FSS,[59] citing dire financial straits as the reason for closure. Consequently, the police use forensic service providers in the private sector to provide DNA profiling results, which has meant that the role of the Forensic Science Regulator has become increasingly important. This post was established in 2008 with the remit "to ensure that the provision of forensic science services across the criminal justice system is subject to an appropriate regime of scientific quality standards". The Regulator is a public appointee, sponsored by the Home Office but operating independently on behalf of the criminal justice system as a whole. At the time of writing, the Regulator does not have any statutory powers, although at the end of 2013, the Government

---

[59] The Forensic Science Service, Seventh Report of Session 2010–12, available at *http://www.publications.parliament.uk/pa/cm201012/cmselect/cmsctech/855/855.pdf* [Accessed April 30, 2016].

ran a consultation on whether such powers should be provided.[60] The Regulator has issued various publications relating to DNA evidence which are available on the Regulator's website[61] and has established a number of specialist working groups, including a DNA Analysis Specialist Group. The Group's remit is to review the standards in place as they apply to the National DNA Database (for which see para.25.62, below) and forensic DNA analysis more generally. The publications that can be accessed on the website include notes of meetings of the DNA Analysis Specialist Group and reports relating to complaints about the performance of forensic service providers in certain cases. In particular, the Regulator commissioned a report relating to the interpretation of DNA evidence (including low-template DNA) which was published in July 2012, and in September 2014, the Regulator issued an appendix to the Codes of Practice and Conduct relating specifically to DNA analysis. The appendix deals with issues such as anti-contamination procedures, the use of validated methodologies and the maintenance of local databases to detect contamination events. Alongside the Regulator, the United Kingdom Accreditation Service accredits private providers against the International Organisation for Standardisation, including the requirements of ISO 17025 (accreditation for laboratory based work), in order to ensure the competency of individuals working within forensic science and the systems and processes being used. Compliance with the requirements set out in the DNA appendix to the Codes of Practice is required for ISO 17025 accreditation of DNA for forensic use.

25.61   The Court in *Dlugosz, Pickering and MDS*[62] observed that in two of the cases before it the DNA evidence had been presented at trial through the use of a written presentation handed to the jury explaining the basic science of DNA. It noted that this is now general practice and expressed the hope that, unless there are unusual circumstances, such written material will always be provided to juries. The Court also saw great advantage in the Forensic Science Regulator, in conjunction with the Royal Society and the Royal Statistical Society, developing standardised material for this purpose in a format that is understandable by a jury and not open to debate.

25.62   Against a background of concerns regarding the effects that budget cuts have had on the depth and rigour of the scientific analysis carried out by the prosecution in particular cases, it seems inevitable that the importance of the role played by the Regulator in superintending the quality of the forensic science services offered by the prosecution will continue to increase. Indeed, it was reported recently in the national press that the current Regulator, Dr Gillian Tully, has ordered a review of sexual assault cases following concerns

---

[60] *Consultation on new statutory powers for the forensic science regulator* (Home Office, Nov 2013), which is available at *https://www.gov.uk/government/consultations/new-statutory-powers-for-the-forensic-science-regulator* [Accessed April 30, 2016]. The consultation closed on January 3, 2014.

[61] Website address: *https://www.gov.uk/government/organisations/forensic-science-regulator.*

[62] [2013] EWCA Crim 2, at [29].

raised about poor practice.[63] Dr Tully explained that her review had been prompted by a number of cases where she had been told that the scientific opportunities did not appear to have been maximised. These included examples where scientific analysis was not carried out at all. Dr Tully was quoted as saying "I am aiming to find out whether there are occasional examples of poor practice or whether there are more systematic issues".

THE NATIONAL DNA DATABASE

Since October 1, 2012, the National DNA Database ("NDNAD") has been   **25.63**
controlled and run by the Home Office on behalf of UK police forces. Prior
to that, it had been under the control of the National Policing Improvement
Agency. The operation of the NDNAD is overseen by a Strategy Board
which publishes annual reports on the operation of the database. The annual
report for 2013–14 was presented to Parliament in December 2014.[64] As of
March 31, 2014, the NDNAD held 5,716,085 DNA profiles from individuals
and 456,856 DNA profiles from crime scenes.[65] This figure takes account of
1,352,356 profiles that were deleted from the NDNAD during 2013–14
pursuant to provisions in the Protection of Freedoms Act 2012 ("PoFA") that
came into force on October 31, 2013. The 2012 Act changed the law to
prevent the permanent retention of DNA profiles from innocent people. The
NDNAD holds profiles from all UK police forces including England and
Wales, Scotland and Northern Ireland, but only the profiles belonging to
England and Wales forces are subject to the Act. In addition to the deletions,
PoFA has resulted in the destruction of 7,753,000 DNA samples. Despite the
reduction in the number of profiles on the NDNAD, it is noted in the
ministerial foreword to the 2013–14 report, written by Lord Bates, Lords
Minister and Minister for Criminal Information, that there had not been a
reduction in the number of matches that the database has produced. "In the
quarter from 1st April to 30th June 2014, the database produced 37 matches
to murder, 127 to rapes and 6,111 to other crime scenes... We have
transformed it from a database that infringed the privacy of innocent citizens
to one that is proportionate and still effective."

The 2012 Act introduced a new regime for the destruction, retention and   **25.64**
use of, amongst other things, DNA profiles taken from the DNA samples of
arrested persons. The new regime was amended by provisions in the Anti-
Social Behaviour, Crime and Policing Act 2014, which came into effect on
May 13, 2014. Sections 1–17 of the 2012 Act inserted new ss.63D–63U into
the Police and Criminal Evidence Act 1984. Under these provisions, DNA
profiles falling within s.63D of the 1984 Act must be destroyed if it appears
to the responsible chief officer of police that the taking of the material from

---

[63] *The Guardian*, September 18, 2015.
[64] *https://www.gov.uk/government/publications/national-dna-database-annual-report-2013-to-2014* [Accessed April 30, 2016].
[65] National DNA Database, Strategy Board Annual Report 2013–14, Pt 1.2.

which the DNA profile was derived was unlawful, or the sample was taken as a result of an arrest based on mistaken identity. Otherwise, the material should be destroyed unless it is retained under any of the powers conferred by ss.63E–63O of the 1984 Act, or any other power of retention that applies to it.[66] By virtue of s.63T of the 1984 Act, where material is required to be destroyed, it must not at any time thereafter be used as evidence against the person from whom it was taken or for the purpose of a criminal investigation, subject to the material being relevant material for the purposes of the Criminal Procedure and Investigations Act 1996. It should be noted that the retention of DNA samples, as opposed to the profiles derived from those samples, is governed by s.63R of the 1984 Act. A sample taken in the same circumstances as material falling within s.63D must be destroyed before the end of the period of six months beginning with the date on which it was taken, or, if sooner, as soon as a DNA profile has been derived from the sample.[67] However, the responsible chief officer of police may apply to a District Judge for an order to retain a sample beyond this date if the sample is, for example, likely to be needed in any proceedings for an offence, or disclosure to, or use by, a defendant. Section 63T specifies the uses to which material retained under ss.63D and 63R may be put. It cannot be used in evidence against the person to whom it relates, or for the purposes of the investigation into any offence at any time after it is required to be destroyed. Section 63U (as amended) excludes some aspects of the provisions where other specified regimes apply.

25.65   The National DNA Database Strategy Board Annual Report 2013–14 recorded that significant work had been undertaken to prepare for the introduction of more sensitive DNA systems to replace SGM Plus, which is currently used to generate DNA profiles for loading on the NDNAD. The DNA-17 system targets 16 STR areas (the 10 areas targeted by SGM Plus as well as a further six areas), in addition to gender. The use of the new system will increase the discriminating power of DNA matches on the NDNAD and enable profiles to be obtained from crime scenes where DNA evidence has been degraded or is present only in very small quantities. The report states that DNA profiles using the new system have been loaded to the NDNAD since July 2014 following development of new NDNAD software, including a thorough testing, validation and implementation programme. The NDNAD Unit works with the United Kingdom Accreditation Service in the preparation and assessment processes for forensic laboratories, and on ensuring compliance with the Forensic Science Regulator's Code of Practice.

25.66   The main provisions relating to the taking of intimate and non-intimate samples are contained in PACE, ss.62, 63, 63A and Sch.2A. In *R. (on the application of R) v A Chief Constable*,[68] the Divisional Court held that it was

---

[66] Police and Criminal Evidence Act 1984 s.63D(3)–(4).
[67] Police and Criminal Evidence Act 1984 s.63R(4).
[68] [2013] EWHC 2864 (Admin); [2014] 1 Cr. App. R. (16).

lawful to require a man convicted of offences of manslaughter and kidnap about 20 years earlier to provide a non-intimate DNA sample so that it could be compared with samples for unsolved crimes. Although the requirement breached the offender's right to respect for private and family life, the interference with that right was in the interests of solving crime and was proportionate.

PREPARING FOR A CASE INVOLVING DNA EVIDENCE

It follows from the preceding paragraphs that, depending on the degree to which the DNA evidence is disputed, the practitioner should be alive to the following questions when preparing for a case involving DNA evidence: **25.67**

   (i) Does the expert have the requisite expertise?

   (ii) Does the expert have any quality accreditation?

   (iii) Has the expert complied with the relevant Criminal Procedure Rules?

   (iv) Has the way in which the sample was collected or subsequently examined created the possibility of a gross contamination event?

   (v) Is it possible that DNA which had been deposited on the surface or item of interest prior to sampling has been transferred to other locations on the item/surface during the sampling or examination process?

   (vi) Have the correct anti-contamination procedures observed?

   vii) Has the continuity been established?

   viii) Were the correct procedural steps observed when taking samples?[69]

   (ix) Has the scientist taken and submitted representative samples? Would the samples be expected to yield a profile?

   (x) Are there other items/samples that should have been taken and/or submitted for analysis given the likely issues in the case?[70]

   (xi) Was the correct profiling technique chosen given the information about the amount of DNA present?

   (xii) Has the scientist correctly interpreted the electrophoretogram? Have any stochastic effects been identified? Is there any scope for reasonable disagreement?

---

[69] See *Cooke* [1995] 1 Cr. App. R. 318, where the question was whether the proper steps under the Police and Criminal Evidence Act 1984 (PACE) had been followed in taking a hair sample, and *Nathaniel* [1995] 2 Cr. App. R. 565, where an appeal was allowed because, under PACE, earlier samples should have been destroyed. In *Willoughby*, unreported, November 11, 1996, the Court of Appeal upheld a ruling of the trial judge rejecting a defence submission that a DNA frequency derived from a "frequency" database was inadmissible. The rejected defence argument was that the profile results contained in the frequency database were being used, wrongly, for the "purposes of investigation" (contrary to PACE s.64, as amended by the Criminal Justice and Public Order Act 1994 s.57).

[70] This type of question has arguably become more important in the light of the budget constraints that limit the amount of work that forensic service providers are able to carry out.

(xiii) Do the procedures involved in producing the profile accord with the FSR's Codes of Practice?

(xiv) Has the scientist made reasonable statements with regard to how and when the DNA was deposited, and whether the DNA came from a particular body fluid or other cellular material? Are there alternative explanations that could explain the results?

(xv) Has the comparison between any reference profile and the profile from the crime sample been conducted correctly?

(xvi) Has the profile from the crime sample been compared against all relevant reference profiles? Have all hits on the NDNAD been adequately investigated?

(xvii) Have profiles obtained from crime samples that don't fit the party's case been properly investigated?

(xviii) Have all reasonable hypotheses been considered when evaluating the profile obtained from the crime sample?

(xix) Is the statistical analysis correct?

(xx) Have any new methods of statistical analysis been sufficiently validated?

(xxi) Are the evaluations of the DNA evidence misleading? If non-statistical, is there a sufficiently reliable scientific basis for the evaluation?

(xxii) Has the judge/jury been provided with materials that adequately explain the basic science underlying DNA evidence?

CHAPTER 26

RESTRICTIONS ON EVIDENCE OR QUESTIONS ABOUT THE
COMPLAINANT'S SEXUAL HISTORY

Introduction.................................... 26.01
Sections 41 to 43 of the Youth
    Justice and Criminal Evidence
    Act 1999....................................... 26.21
Scope and Application of Section
    41... 26.22
The Application for Leave.............. 26.45
The Position of the Prosecution 26.49
The Four Gateways and Two
    Restrictions................................. 26.50
The First Gateway—Section
    41(3)—Issue Other than Consent. 26.54

The Second Gateway—Section
    41(3)—Consent and
    Contemporaneity......................... 26.80
The Third Gateway—Section
    41(3)—Consent and Similarity..... 26.83
The Fourth Gateway—Section
    41(5)—the Rebuttal Gateway 26.117
The Court's Overriding Duty under
    Section 41(2)...............................26.127
The Two Restrictions......................26.139
Evidence that the Complainant has
    made False Complaints................26.151
The Canadian Experience...............26.168
The Future of Section 41 ....26.177

INTRODUCTION

Whilst no one can describe ss.41 to 43 of the Youth Justice and Criminal   **26.01**
Evidence Act 1999 as an example of model parliamentary drafting, after 17
years the courts and the majority of practitioners have become accustomed
to the regime governing the admissibility of the previous sexual history of
complainants.

A clear understanding by advocates of the restrictions set out in s.41, as   **26.02**
explained in *R. v A (No.2)*,[1] and the principles that underpin them is critical
to the smooth running of trials of sexual offences. A close scrutiny by judges
of all applications is essential in order to tease out the real issues. The
requirement that all applications for leave must be in writing has the virtue
of focusing applicant, respondent and the court upon the appropriate
gateway or gateways and what is truly relevant.

---

[1] [2002] 1 A.C. 45.

26.03   Under the s.41 regime a complainant's sexual experiences with third parties will rarely be relevant. Yet the courts are still frequently faced with wholly unmeritorious applications and appeals which reveal a failure to understand the gateways to admissibility. It should be borne in mind that many s.41 applications will have great difficulty in surmounting the credibility restriction in s.41(4) (evidence may not be adduced nor question asked if the purpose would be to impugn the complainant's credibility as a witness) and meeting the test set out in s.41(2)(b) (court must be satisfied that refusal of leave might render unsafe a conclusion of the jury on a relevant issue in the case).

Background

26.04   The issue of the relevance and admissibility of evidence of previous sexual history has often provoked controversy. It has led to debates on the role of judicial discretion in this area, on the extent to which the courts can use the interpretative power conferred by s.3 of the Human Rights Act 1998, and above all on how best to resolve in a proportionate manner the natural tension between protecting the complainant's privacy and dignity and the accused's right to a fair trial. Many jurisdictions have adopted "rape shield" legislation[2] designed both to protect complainants from unnecessary humiliation and distress when giving evidence and to prevent the trial process being distorted by the "twin myths" line of reasoning. The "twin myths", as described in Canadian jurisprudence,[3] are: "that unchaste women were more likely to consent to intercourse and, in any event, were less worthy of belief." There is an increasing acceptance that the scope for such improper lines of reasoning should be eradicated.[4] There is less of a consensus as to the legislative model most appropriate to achieve the right balance between protection of the complainant and a defendant's right to a fair trial.

26.05   The present restrictions enshrined in s.41 of the Youth Justice and Criminal Evidence Act 1999 are a result of the dissatisfaction of the Home Office, informed by a powerful body of academic opinion, with the operation by the courts of the previous regime under s.2 of the Sexual Offences (Amendment) Act 1976. The wording and structure of s.41 suggest close attention was paid to the Canadian and Scottish models. However, there are very significant differences. On the face of the legislation there is no residual discretion for the trial judge to admit evidence that would otherwise be

---

[2] For discussion of different models of rape-shield legislation, see Neil Kibble, *The Sexual History Provisions: Charting a Course between Inflexible Legislative Rules and Wholly Untrammelled Judicial Discretion?* [2000] Crim. L.R. 274, 279.

[3] *Seaboyer* (1991) 83 D.L.R. (4th) 193, 258, 278C, per McLachlin J.

[4] cf. *R. v A (No.2)* [2002] 1 A.C. 45, at [27] per Lord Steyn: "Such generalised, stereotyped and unfounded prejudices ought to have no place in our legal system."

excluded.[5] In *R. v A (No.2)*,[6] when the new provisions were considered by the House of Lords within a few months of implementation, Lord Steyn stated:

> "Whilst the statute pursued desirable goals, the methods adopted amounted to legislative overkill."

R. v A (No.2) provided an opportunity for the House of Lords to consider **26.06** the excessive breadth of the new provisions and to loosen the straitjacket that the s.41 regime had imposed upon judges. The virtual blanket exclusion of evidence of previous sexual history between the complainant and the accused under s.41(1), subject to narrow categories of exception, has, as a result of the House of Lord's intervention, given way to the admission in trials, where appropriate, of logically relevant sexual experiences between the complainant and the accused.[7] This is a highly welcome development. Whilst evidence of the previous, or subsequent, sexual behaviour of the complainant with third parties is irrelevant in most cases,[8] far more cases than ever before are now being prosecuted where there has been a previous sexual relationship between the complainant and the accused. To reconstruct the parties in the eyes of the jury as strangers or people who have never enjoyed consensual intimacy together would in many cases arbitrarily exclude key matters from the jury's consideration and, worse still, would positively mislead juries.

The decision in *R. v A (No.2)* has not, however, heralded an effective **26.07** return to the old s.2 regime. Section 41 has led judges and practitioners alike to adopt a clinical, structured approach, where true relevance to an issue in the case is properly and carefully analysed. This process requires the defence to seek to enter the narrow gateways and surmount the hurdles of the s.41 regime. In many cases that regime, whilst unnecessarily over-elaborate, does not pose problems in its operation, and truly relevant evidence will be admitted. However, s.41 continues to spawn problems in the trial of some sexual offences, where the credibility of complainant and accused is often all-important. The present regime for regulating the admission of this evidence, with its "categories approach", still risks the exclusion of relevant evidence. Predicting relevance and then creating narrow, pre-ordained exceptions risks arbitrariness. It would be far better to have a regulatory regime which prohibited illegitimate lines of reasoning, and thus excluded evidence with no true relevance to an issue in the case, whilst avoiding the arbitrary exclusion which stems from a categories approach.

---

[5] In *R. v A (No2)*, last note, Lord Hope sets out (at [100]–[103]) the four American models and the Canadian and Scottish models, and notes how s.41 has departed in significant ways from the Canadian and Scottish models by reducing the element of discretion to a bare minimum.

[6] [2002] 1 A.C. 45, at [43].

[7] This was described by Professor Andrew Ashworth as "probably the high water-mark of the interpretive power in the first year of the Human Rights Act": *Criminal Proceedings After The Human Rights Act: The First Year* [2001] Crim. L.R. 855, at p.869.

[8] For the exceptions identified by Lord Hope in *R. v A (No.2)*, see paras 26.55 and following, below.

Position at common law

26.08   The previous sexual history of complainants in sex cases was usually admissible at common law on two bases. First, it might be admissible as being relevant to the issue of the complainant's credibility. A woman who had had sexual experience before marriage, or a married woman who had had sexual experience outside marriage, was considered potentially unreliable and untruthful as a witness. Secondly, it might be admissible if the complainant was a prostitute or of notoriously immoral character, as being relevant to the issue of consent. In cases other than those involving complainants of a notoriously immoral character, evidence of previous sexual experience was generally inadmissible unless it related to sexual intimacy with the defendant himself, and so sexual behaviour on other occasions with third parties was not usually relevant to consent.[9]

26.09   Whether the common law was being applied properly or not, it is clear that before the implementation of s.2 of the Sexual Offences (Amendment) Act 1976, unnecessary and irrelevant cross-examination of complainants on the basis of their previous sexual history occurred frequently. This was embarked upon to test their credibility, but at times was also underpinned by the line of reasoning that a woman's sexual experience was indicative of a general willingness to consent. On occasions, a complainant's evidence would be undermined without justification by cross-examination on irrelevant matters. There was a powerful case for at the very least imposing a leave requirement in respect of evidence of previous sexual history with third parties. Lord Steyn in *R. v A (No.2)*[10] noted that, even in the very recent past, defensive strategies playing upon generalised, stereotyped and unfounded prejudices were habitually employed.

The Heilbron Committee

26.10   In December 1975 the Heilbron Committee, which had been set up to give urgent consideration to the law of rape in the wake of the House of Lords' decision in *DPP v Morgan*,[11] recommended that some curtailment of unnecessary cross-examination of the complainant as to her sexual history was one of the most important and urgent reforms required. The Heilbron Report stated[12]:

> "Much of the criticism we have received is directed not so much against the substantive law of rape or the particular decision in *Morgan* as against practice and procedure in rape cases.

---

[9] *Riley* (1887) 18 Q.B.D. 481, at 485 per Lord Coleridge CJ; *Clay* (1851) 5 Cox C.C. 146; *Greatbanks* [1959] Crim. L.R. 450; *Holmes* (1871) L.R. 1; *Bashir and Manzur* [1969] 3 All E.R. 692.

[10] [2002] 1 A.C. 45, at para.27.

[11] [1976] A.C. 182.

[12] Cmnd 6352 (1975), paras 85–86.

Thus it is said that attitudes towards a woman who complains that she has been raped are not always as sympathetic or understanding as they might be—unless she has been subjected to obvious brutality. Complaint is also made that the laws of evidence, and the procedures and practice of the courts, subject women to searching, irrelevant cross-examination, resulting in unnecessary and hurtful revelation of their private life."

The Committee reached the conclusion that the previous sexual history of **26.11** the alleged victim with third parties is of no significance as far as credibility is concerned, and is only rarely likely to be relevant to issues directly before the jury. It said[13]:

"In contemporary society sexual relationships outside marriage, both steady and of a more casual manner, are fairly widespread, and it now seems that a woman's sexual experience with partners of her choice, are neither indicative of untruthfulness nor of a general willingness to consent. There exists, in our view, a gap between the assumptions underlying the law, and those public views and attitudes which exist today which ought to influence today's law."

The Heilbron Committee drew a clear distinction between a complainant's **26.12** previous relationship with the accused and a complainant's relationship with third parties. It did not recommend any curtailment of evidence of a previous sexual relationship between the complainant and the defendant himself.[14]

The Committee recommended that the trial judge's decision should be **26.13** guided by and based on principles set out in legislation with relevance clearly defined.[15] There was considerable opposition to this from some politicians and judges.

Section 2 of the Sexual Offences (Amendment) Act 1976

Section 2 of the Sexual Offences (Amendment) Act 1976, whilst leading to **26.14** some curtailment, left trial judges to decide the relevance of a complainant's previous sexual behaviour with third parties without specific guidance. It did, however, bring all such evidence within a new regulatory regime whereby it could not be adduced without leave of the trial judge. Section 2 provided[16]:

"(1) If at a trial any person is for the time being charged with a rape offence to which he pleads not guilty, then except with the leave of the judge, no evidence and no question in cross-examination shall be adduced or asked at trial, by or on

---

[13] Cmnd 6352 (1975), para.131.
[14] Evidence of previous relationship with the accused was not regulated because the common law of relevance was regarded as providing an adequate filter, when combined with the trial judge's duty to curtail oppressive and inappropriate questioning as to the detail of the relevant matters: see Professor Di Birch, *Rethinking Sexual History Evidence: Proposals for Fairer Trials* [2002] Crim. L.R. 531, p.543.
[15] In the event, the Heilbron Committee recommendation that the test for admissibility should be one of "striking similarity" was rejected.
[16] s.2(4) of the 1976 Act made it clear that any evidence adduced or question to be asked must first satisfy the test of admissibility at common law.

behalf of any defendant at the trial, about any sexual experience of a complainant with a person other than that defendant.

(2) The judge shall not give leave in pursuance of the preceding subsection for any evidence or question except on an application made to him in the absence of the jury by or on behalf of the defendant; and on such an application the judge shall give leave if and only if he is satisfied that it would be unfair to that defendant to refuse to allow the evidence to be adduced or the question asked."

The operation of section 2

26.15   Under s.2, if the proposed questions were relevant in accordance with common law principles, the next step was for the trial judge to decide if he was satisfied that it would be unfair to the defendant not to allow him to put them. In *Lawrence,*[17] when considering an application under s.2, May J said:

> "In my judgment before a judge is satisfied or may be said to be satisfied that to refuse to allow a particular question or series of questions in cross-examination would be unfair to the defendant, he must take the view that it is more likely than not that the particular question or line of cross-examination, if allowed, might reasonably lead the jury, properly directed in the summing-up, to take a different view of the complainant's evidence from that which they might take if the question or series of questions was or were not allowed."

This approach was subsequently endorsed by the Court of Appeal *Mills (Leroy).*[18]

26.16   In *Viola,*[19] Lord Lane CJ, whilst refraining from laying down any hard and fast rule, set out some useful guidelines. Generally speaking, if the proposed questions merely sought to establish that the complainant had had sexual experience with other men to whom she was not married, so as to suggest that she ought not to be believed on oath, the judge should exclude the evidence as the questions simply went to credit. If, on the other hand, the questions were relevant to an issue in the trial in the light of the way the case was being run, such as consent, as opposed merely to credit, they were likely to be admitted, as to exclude such questions would mean the jury were being prevented from hearing something which might cause them to change their minds about the complainant's evidence. The Court of Appeal acknowledged the existence of a grey area between relevance to credit and relevance to an issue in the case. Lord Lane CJ continued[20]:

> "On one hand evidence of sexual promiscuity may be so strong or so closely contemporaneous in time to the event in issue so as to come near to, or indeed to reach the border between mere credit and an issue in the case. Conversely, the relevance of the evidence to an issue in the case may be so slight as to lead the judge to the conclusion that he is far from satisfied that the exclusion of the

---

[17] [1977] Crim. L.R. 492 (Nottingham Crown Court).
[18] (1978) 68 Cr. App. R. 327.
[19] [1982] 3 All E.R. 73.
[20] [1982] 3 All E.R. 73, at 77.

evidence or the question from the consideration of the jury would be unfair to the defendant."

Academic criticism of the operation of section 2

The 1980s and 1990s saw substantial academic criticism of the operation of **26.17**
the 1976 Act. In the vanguard of the critics was Professor Temkin, whose
view was that s.2 had not had the effect intended by the Heilbron Committee
and that the previous sexual history of complainants was still being given
undue significance in rape trials.[21] Suzanna Adler argued that the previous
sexual history of complainants was often introduced to play on the jury's
prejudices and widely held myths regarding the role of the alleged victim in
sexual assaults.[22] Professor McColgan felt that s.2 was having little effect on
the admission of sexual history evidence and that it was being used
improperly to secure undeserved acquittals.[23]

This wave of criticism was directed at s.2, which regulated evidence of **26.18**
previous sexual history with third parties.[24] It follows that it was not focused
on previous sexual history with the defendant.[25] However, it undoubtedly
provided the impetus for the repeal of s.2 and the enactment of s.41 of the
1999 Act.

A new regime: sections 41 to 43 of the Youth Justice and Criminal Evidence Act 1999

The Interdepartmental Working Group on Vulnerable or Intimidated Wit- **26.19**
nesses was established by the Home Secretary to take forward a Government
manifesto commitment to provide greater protection for victims in rape and
serious sexual offence trials. In its report *Speaking up for Justice*, published
in June 1998, the Working Group concluded that s.2 was unsatisfactory and
not achieving its purpose. It recommended that in cases of sexual offences
"the law should be amended to provide a more structured approach to
decision taking and to set out more clearly when evidence of previous sexual
history can be admitted". No clear indication was given in the report that
there was to be a major departure from s.2 in that evidence of the

---

[21] Professor J Temkin, *Rape and the Legal Process* (Oxford: Oxford University Press, 2002); J. Temkin *Sexual History Evidence—the Ravishment of Section 2* [1993] Crim. L.R. 3.

[22] *Relevance of Sexual History in Rape* [1985] Crim. L.R. 769.

[23] *Common Law and the Relevance of Sexual History Evidence* (1996) 16 Oxford Journal of Legal Studies 275.

[24] Lord Steyn felt that it created too broad an inclusionary discretion: *R. v A (No.2)* [2002] 1 A.C. 45, at [28].

[25] In *The Admissibility of Prior Sexual History with the Defendant in Sexual Offence Cases* (University of Wales, Aberystwyth, Feb 2001), Neil Kibble observes (at p.23) that the literature was concerned almost exclusively with the problems surrounding previous sexual history with third parties and that little systematic attention had been paid to the question of the relevance and admissibility of prior sexual history with the accused.

complainant's relationship with the accused was to be brought within the new regulatory regime.[26]

26.20   Some of the senior judiciary came to the defence of s.2. For instance, Lord Bingham argued[27]:

> "That [the old section 2] strikes one as a good and well designed provision. What more is needed? . . . the consultation paper 'Speaking up for Justice' states that the working group reported overwhelming evidence that the present practice in the courts is unsatisfactory and the existing law is not achieving its purpose. If there is such overwhelming evidence, the consultation paper is noticeably reticent in giving the details. It refers to some research carried out nearly 10 years ago which shows that 75% of applications made under that section succeed. That may mean applications are lightly made and lightly granted, but it may equally mean that applications are cautiously and prudently made, and properly granted, in the main."

However, the opponents of the new regulatory regime for *all* previous sexual history evidence failed to persuade the Government that it was essential to retain a significant measure of judicial discretion. The Youth Justice and Criminal Evidence Act 1999 received the Royal Assent on July 27, 1999, and on December 4, 2000, the old s.2 was repealed and ss.41–43 of the new Act were implemented. The s.2 case law, including the cases of *Viola*,[28] *R. v SMS*[29] and *Brown*,[30] was accordingly overturned.

Sections 41 to 43 of the Youth Justice and Criminal Evidence Act 1999

The General Prohibition

26.21   Sections 41–43 of the 1999 Act impose wide restrictions on evidence and questioning about a complainant's sexual history. There is a general prohibition on the admission of previous sexual history evidence and on questions about previous sexual history *unless* the court gives leave. Section 41(1) provides that:

> "If at a trial a person is charged with a sexual offence, then, except with the leave of the court—
> (a) no evidence may be adduced, and
> (b) no question may be asked in cross-examination,
> by or on behalf of any accused at the trial, about any sexual behaviour of the complainant."

---

[26] Professor Di Birch describes this omission as damning and culpable, and laments the failure to debate the merits of regulation: *Rethinking Sexual History Evidence: Proposals for Fairer Trials* [2002] Crim. L.R. 531, at p.544.
[27] *Hansard*, HL Vol.595, Col.1272 (December 15, 1998).
[28] [1982] 3 All E.R. 73.
[29] [1992] Crim. L.R. 310.
[30] [1988] Crim. L.R. 828.

SCOPE AND APPLICATION OF SECTION 41

Wider scope than section 2 of the Sexual Offences (Amendment) Act 1976

Section 41(1) applies to "sexual offences", as defined in s.62 of the 1999 Act.   26.22
When enacted, this referred to offences under the Sexual Offences Act 1956.
Unlike the 1976 Act, s.41(1) is not restricted to "rape offences". Under the
1976 Act, "rape offence" had been defined as rape, attempted rape, aiding,
abetting, counselling and procuring rape or attempted rape, and incitement
to rape. It was subsequently extended to conspiracy to rape and burglary
with intent to rape. Section 62 of the 1999 Act gave "sexual offence" a much
wider definition. As enacted it provided:

> "(1) In this Part 'sexual offence' means—
> (a) rape, or burglary with intent to rape;
> (b) an offence under any of sections 2 to 12 and 14 to 17 of the Sexual
> Offences Act 1956 (unlawful intercourse, indecent assault, forcible abduc-
> tion etc.);
> (c) an offence under section 128 of the Mental Health Act 1959 (unlawful
> intercourse with person receiving treatment for mental disorder by
> member of hospital staff etc.);
> (d) an offence under section 1 of the Indecency with Children Act 1960
> (indecent conduct towards a child under 14);
> (e) an offence under section 54 of the Criminal Law Act 1977 (incitement of
> a child under 16 to commit incest).
> (2) In this Part any reference (including a reference having effect by virtue of
> this subsection) to an offence of any description ('the substantive offence') is to
> be taken to include a reference to an offence which consists of attempting or
> conspiring to commit, or of aiding, abetting, counselling, procuring or inciting
> the commission of, the substantive offence."

Application of section 41 to offences under the Sexual Offences Act 2003 and the lack of provision for pre-2003 Act cases

Section 62(1) was replaced as follows with effect from May 1, 2004 by the   26.23
Sexual Offences Act 2003[31]:

> "(1) In this Part 'sexual offence' means any offence under Part 1 of the Sexual
> Offences Act 2003."

It seems that in making this change, the draftsman overlooked the fact that
sexual offences committed before May 1, 2004, would continue to be charged
under the old law. The point was taken in *Warner*[32] whether a complainant
should enjoy the protection of s.41 where the defendant is charged with an
offence pre-dating the Sexual Offences Act 2003. HH Judge Morrison QC
ruled that it was not within the competence of the Crown Court to repair the
gap left by the failure of the then Secretary of State to make the appropriate

---

[31] s.139 and Sch.6, para.41.
[32] Birmingham Crown Court, June 5, 2007.

transitional provisions and/or of the parliamentary draftsman to secure the position in the wording of the statute. Shortly afterwards, in *Cartwright*,[33] the Court of Appeal resolved this important point of statutory construction by deciding that s.41 does apply to the "old regime", i.e. to pre-Sexual Offences Act 2003 cases.

26.24   The trial in *Cartwright* had proceeded upon the assumption that s.41 applied to offences pre-dating the implementation of the 2003 Act, and the jurisdiction point had not been taken. The alleged offences had taken place before May 1, 2004, when the Sexual Offences Act 2003 came into force, but no complaint had been made until after that date. The appellant submitted that it was perfectly clear from a literal reading that the amendment brought about by the 2003 Act had had the effect of dis-applying s.41 in respect of the "old regime" pre-2003 Act offences. The Court of Appeal observed that if this submission was right, then something extraordinary had happened. A "minor" or "consequential" amendment had, by substituting the definition of "sexual offences" in s.62(1) of the 1999 Act, brought about absurd consequences. It was necessary to consider whether there was legislative incoherence,[34] which, based on an analysis of the legislative context and structure, produced a result which contradicted the clear intention of Parliament and defeated its legislative purpose. The Court distinguished *R. v A*,[35] which related to the failure of the 2003 Act to make transitional provisions when it repealed the old law of sexual offences. Correcting that oversight by the draftsman would have effected a radical extension of the substantive law relating to criminal liability. In contrast, s.41 was procedural or evidential, representing further development of a statutory process begun in 1976 by extending the restrictions upon admissibility of the previous sexual history of complainants in sex cases. There had been an omission by the draftsman, which could easily have been covered by a short saving provision, expressly preserving protection for old offences. The resulting vacuum was wholly unintended and was contrary to the intention of Parliament. The virtually universally discredited common law rules relating to cross-examination in this class of case were not resuscitated merely because of adventitious discrepancy between the date when the offences were committed and the trial. The Court of Appeal stated that, despite its careful reasoning, it was not able to follow the judgment of Judge Morrison in *Warner* and held that s.41 did apply. Technical amendments in the Criminal Justice and Immigration Act 2008 have given statutory effect to the Court of Appeal judgement in *Cartwright* so that pre-SOA 2003 sexual offences are

---

[33] [2007] EWCA Crim 2581. Section 41 now applies to all offences under Pt 1 of the SOA 2003 and any relevant superseded offence as now defined in s.62(1A) of the YJCEA 1999. Section 62 also now includes an offence under s.2 of the Modern Slavery Act 2015 that consists of or includes behaviour within s.3(3) of that Act (sexual exploitation).
[34] cf. *Inco Europe Ltd v First Choice Distribution (a firm)* [2000] 1 W.L.R. 586.
[35] Sometimes referred to as *R. v C* [2005] EWCA Crim 3533.

included. The amendments are deemed to have effect from May 1, 2004 when SOA 2003 came into force.

When is section 41 in play?

A subsisting charge of a sexual offence against any person brings s.41 into play.[36] Section 41(7) provides: **26.25**

> "Where this section applies in relation to a trial by virtue of the fact that one or more of a number persons charged in the proceedings is or are charged with a sexual offence—
> (a) it shall cease to apply in relation to the trial if the prosecutor decides not to proceed with the case against that person or those persons in respect of that charge; but
> (b) it shall not cease to do so in the event of that person or those persons pleading guilty to, or being convicted of, that charge."

"any sexual behaviour"

Section 41(1) of the 1999 Act covers evidence or questions about "any sexual behaviour".[37] Section 2 of the 1976 Act applied to evidence or questions about "any sexual experience". Section 42(1)(c) of the 1999 Act provides: **26.26**

> "'sexual behaviour' means any sexual behaviour or other sexual experience, whether or not involving any accused or other person, but excluding (except in section 41(3)(c)(i) and (5)(a)) anything alleged to have taken place as part of the event which is the subject matter of the charge against the accused".

The exclusion means that sexual foreplay, alleged by the defendant to have taken place immediately before the sexual activity which forms the subject matter of the charge against him, is excluded from the definition of "sexual behaviour". It appears that the exclusion is not limited to anything alleged by the *prosecution* to have taken place as part of the event. It follows that since words on their own can amount to sexual behaviour,[38] where the sexual foreplay included the complainant's descriptions of sexual activities with others and personal preferences for particular types of activity, such conversation may fall outside the ambit of s.41 regime provided it is alleged to have taken part as part of the event which is the subject matter of the charge against the accused.   **26.27**

The Explanatory Notes to the 1999 Act state that the provisions do not limit the meaning of "evidence" in this context and it is therefore to be understood to include secondary evidence of sexual behaviour, such as   **26.28**

---

[36] Section 41 has been applied to proceedings in the Court Martial, the Service Civilian Court and the Court Martial Appeal Court: see the Youth Justice and Criminal Evidence Act 1999 (Application to Service Courts) Order 2009 (SI 2009/2083), art.7.

[37] For the distinction drawn by the Court of Appeal between questions about "any sexual behaviour" of the complainant and questions about statements about such behaviour, see paras 26.151 and following, below.

[38] See *Grout* [2011] EWCA Crim 299.

abortions and paternity suits. It is submitted that this is correct if the purpose of introducing the evidence is to establish sexual behaviour by inference. In *R v. P(R)*[39] the court recognised that a question about an abortion might in some cases be away of asking about a person's sexual history in which case it would be a question about sexual behaviour. In *R. v K(P) and K(T)*,[40] the Court of Appeal did not find it necessary to decide whether s.41 applies to cross-examination concerning an abortion. At trial one of the appellants had unsuccessfully sought leave to cross-examine a complainant about an abortion that had taken place long after the dates of the alleged indecent assaults. It was proposed to put to the complainant that there had been an argument about whether she should have an abortion and she had asked the appellant to take her to the clinic. She had already accepted in cross-examination that she had seen this appellant after the alleged abuse had ended and that she had felt "fine" around him. Pill LJ, giving the judgement of the court, ruled that the trial judge was entitled to exclude the proposed cross-examination, whether s.41 applied or not. Whether or not what the appellant proposed to put to the complainant was true, it was likely to cause the complainant considerable distress. Its very limited significance did not justify its admission in circumstances in which other contacts between the defendant and complainant had been proved. He continued[41]:

> "The claimed significance of the questions, to demonstrate that the witness had visited an abortion clinic, underlines the overall fairness of excluding it. Unlike *R. v F* [2005] 1 WLR 2848, this was not a case in which sexual relations between the defendant and the complainant had resumed when the complainant was an adult. That might well throw light on the conduct in earlier years. Evidence that, some time after the alleged abuse, a complainant was prepared to ask her alleged abuser to accompany him to an abortion clinic, barely supports a case that she was prepared to lie, and join . . . a conspiracy to lie, about events many years before."

26.29   It is at least in part an objective test as to whether conduct amounts to "sexual behaviour or other sexual experience". In *Etches*[42] the Court of Appeal held that cross-examination of very young girls (aged four and six), on behalf of a father charged with abusing them, as to similar allegations against other family members, was caught by the s.41 regime. The girls were not too young to have had a "sexual experience" even if they had no appreciation that what had occurred was sexual.

26.30   The parameters of the definition of "sexual behaviour" are not entirely clear. In *Mukadi*,[43] which involved an appeal against a conviction for rape, Sir Edwin Jowitt stated:

---

[39] [2013] EWCA Crim 2331 at [33].
[40] [2008] EWCA Crim 434.
[41] At [73]ff.
[42] [2004] EWCA Crim 1313.
[43] [2003] EWCA Crim 3765; [2004] Crim. L.R. 373. See in particular criticism of the decision in commentary by Professor Di Birch at [2004] Crim. L.R. 374.

"The learned judge took the view that the complainant's act in getting into the car was sexual behaviour. In many cases it will be very easy to say what is or is not sexual behaviour, but there are obviously borderline cases in which the sexuality of what happens may not be so apparent. It would not be possible to try to define sexual behaviour further. Indeed, it probably would be foolish to do so. It is really a matter of impression and common sense. The judge, as we have said, took the view that this was sexual behaviour."

In that case the complainant, a 23-year-old woman, attracted the attention of the appellant whilst she was in a supermarket where he worked as a security guard. He was about to finish work, and the woman agreed to go out with him. They drank some wine together and then went to the appellant's flat. The complainant accepted that sexual activity between them was consensual up until intercourse. The appeal turned on the trial judge's refusal to permit cross-examination of the complainant about an incident which had happened shortly before the complainant had gone into the supermarket. She had been on the pavement in Oxford Street when a large, expensive looking car driven by a man a good deal older than her had pulled up alongside her. The man accosted the complainant who got into the car. He then drove her to a filling station. After a while the complainant left after exchanging telephone numbers. In the judgment of the Court of Appeal, it would have been a possible and proper inference for the jury to conclude that when the complainant accepted this man's invitation and got into his car, what she had in mind was that there might follow some form of sexual activity. The Court disposed of the appeal without deciding if the incident in the car amounted to sexual behaviour, taking the view that if the jury had heard the evidence of the incident, it might have led them to take a different view of the complainant's evidence on the issue of consent. Since the Court felt that it was a proper inference that the car incident amounted to soliciting and the incident's relevance depended on that inference being drawn, we suggest that the episode was within the definition of "sexual behaviour".[44] Professor Temkin and colleagues have noted that *Mukadi* raises the question whether the complainant's purpose should be taken into account when considering whether ambiguous behaviour is sexual or not. They note that s.78 of the Sexual Offences Act 2003 provides a way of determining whether conduct was "sexual" which might be of use in the context of s.41.[45] Provided the conduct, when viewed objectively, *might* be sexual, it should be permissible to consider whether there was a reasonable inference that the complainant's

26.31

---

[44] Presumably, as the incident related to consent, the appropriate gateway was thought to have been s.41(3)(b), in that the incident occurred "at or about the same time" that the complainant met the appellant. However, the fact that the incident was "at or about the same time" does not necessarily mean that the evidence of sexual behaviour related to the issue of consent. As Professor Di Birch puts it in her commentary on the decision (last note, p.375): " . . . the defence have to get over the hurdle posed by the (rather obvious) objection that preparedness to consent is not generally a transferable commodity."

[45] L. Kelly, J. Temkin and S. Griffiths, *Section 41: an evaluation of new legislation limiting sexual history evidence in rape trials* (Home Office, 2006).

purpose was in fact "sexual". If so, that would lead to the inevitable conclusion that her conduct was "sexual".

Where the issue relates to the genuineness of entries in documents and not "sexual behaviour"

26.32   In *Lloyd*,[46] the appellant was convicted on 10 counts of indecent assault committed against four young women, who at the time were all working with him at a supermarket where he was a trainee manager. The defence case was that there had been no indecent assaults, that the complainants had fabricated their evidence and that they were acting in collusion with one employee (not a complainant) whose work the appellant had criticised. In order to rebut the defence of recent fabrication, the prosecution introduced into evidence a diary entry which one of the complainants said she had made on the same day as the assaults (June 12, 2002). The relevant page was put before the jury. The diary entry read: "James abused me (sexual) in cake shop." The defence sought to cross-examine the complainant about an entry for June 14 on the opposite page of the same diary, which had been deleted but which could still be read. It read as follows: "I had 10-inch cock in my mouth today mmm." The complainant stated in a witness statement that the entry had been made by a friend as a joke and that she had crossed it out when she saw it. In a witness statement, disclosed in the unused material, the friend denied all knowledge of the diary.

26.33   The trial judge refused to permit cross-examination on the diary entry for June 14. He ruled that the entry related to "sexual behaviour" and thus cross-examination was prohibited under s.41. Furthermore, such cross-examination would go only to credit, and could not be relevant to the issue of fabrication of the allegations. The Court of Appeal held that defence counsel's proposed questions in respect of the June 14 diary entry were intended to highlight the potential untruthfulness of the complainant as to the authorship of an entry in the diary, and not to assert that the entry in the diary, although having a sexual content, was true. The proposed cross-examination went to the accuracy and veracity of the pages in the diary as a record. Although the content in relation to June 14 was sexual in nature, the cross-examination would not be about sexual activity. Instead it would have been directed to the disputed explanation for the appearance of the entry in the diary. The cross-examination would have been carried out to show that the complainant's account as to how the entry came to be in her diary was untrue. The trial judge had failed to focus on the real issue of relevance, the genuineness of the diary entry.[47]

---

[46] [2005] EWCA Crim 1111.
[47] If the complainant had denied stating that a friend had made the entry, the defence would have been entitled to call the friend to contradict her under s.4 of Criminal Procedure Act 1865: See *R. v V* [2006] EWCA Crim 1901.

Posting entries on social networking sites

Micheal O'Floinn[48] has pointed out that the sheer volume and nature of the material available about individuals on Social Networking Sites ("SNS") poses unique challenges for the application of rules of relevancy and those which seek to limit the admissibility of a complainant's sexual behaviour. He stresses that whilst care must be taken not to attribute excessive importance to SNS communications, they cannot simply be ignored as mere "SNS waffle". Some helpful guidance has now emerged on this point. It is clear from *Ben-Rejab*[49] that sexually provocative postings on Facebook may amount to "sexual behaviour" and will engage the s.41 regime. Applications to adduce such material are likely to fall foul of the credibility restriction in s.41(4). In any event, whether s.41 is engaged or not, where there is no direct connection to the allegation, such postings are likely to be of little or no relevance to the issues in the case. The words "any sexual behaviour or experience" in s.42(1)(c) are extremely wide in their ambit and have been given a wide meaning by the Court of Appeal. Words alone can amount to sexual behaviour.[50] The behaviour or experience need not necessarily involve another person. In *Ben-Rejab* the Court of Appeal took the view that the expression is plainly wide enough to embrace the activity of viewing pornography or engaging in sexually-charged messaging over a live internet connection. It followed that it included answering questions in a sexually explicit quiz. The Court had little difficulty in rejecting the submission that activity by the complainant (C) in entering such quizzes and posting this fact on a publicly available website page amounted to relevant and admissible evidence.   **26.34**

The appellant in that case was charged with two rapes, sexual assault by penetration and sexual assault of C. It was alleged that C had been subjected to a sexual ordeal by the appellant and two others in October 2008 after meeting the appellant at a nightclub. C was a Facebook user who regularly made entries on her own page and uploaded photographs to it. In February 2010 she made a victim impact statement in which she described how she had become a changed person as a result of the ordeal. She did not socialise any more. She rarely went to town because of fear of seeing the appellant and his associates. She had not been clubbing since the incident happened. She had flash-backs and panic attacks. She had undergone counselling and had been prescribed anti-depressants and sleeping tablets. Her entries on Facebook tended to demonstrate that her victim impact statement was untrue or exaggerated. The trial judge gave leave for C to be cross-examined about this suggested inconsistency. She maintained that she had been changed by the   **26.35**

[48] Lecturer in Cyber-Security Law, University of Southampton, at the Judicial College's Serious Sexual Offences Seminar, July 2015.
[49] [2011] EWCA Crim 1136.
[50] cf. *Grout* [2011] EWCA Crim 299, discussed in para.3.113, above, relating to the meaning of "sexual activity" in s.8 of the 2003 Act.

experience but conceded she had been out socialising on a number of occasions, contrary to the impression she had given in her victim impact statement.

26.36   However, the appellant's counsel wished to go further and ask C about other entries she had posted on her Facebook page. On December 18, 2008, she posted:

"[C] is having sex! Click here to see more or try it yourself!"

On or about February 9, 2009, the following further entries appeared:

"[C] just took the Best Places to have Sex Around the House quiz. See your match score!"

"[C] took How good are you in bed? Quiz and the result is Incredible Lover. Click to compare your results or try other quizzes."

"[C] took Whats your sex style? Quiz and the result is YOU ARE FIERCE. Click here to compare your results or try other quizzes."

On January 12, 2010, the following entries appeared:

"[C] Answered some questions on some weird questionnaire where you get fined for ceetain [sic] sexual encounters!!! Lol xxxx"

"[C] My fine is . . . wait for it . . . £660.60!!!! oops! Apparently I'v [sic] been a naughty girl!!!!"

26.37   The judge refused leave to ask C about these Facebook entries. He took the view that questions concerning these entries would inevitably be about C's sexual behaviour on other occasions and so were caught by s.41. The purpose of the questions was, the judge concluded, to undermine C's credibility as a witness. It followed that, even if one of the gateways in s.41(3) was satisfied, the purpose of the questions prohibited their admission. In the alternative, if s.41(3) or the rebuttal gateway in s.41(5) applied, it could not be said, as required by s.41(2)(b), that a refusal of leave might have the result of rendering unsafe a conclusion of the jury on any relevant issue.

26.38   On appeal, the Court of Appeal rejected the appellant's submission that C's participation in the quizzes was not sexual behaviour. Pitchford LJ posed the question: What motive can there have been when engaging in the activity of answering sexually explicit questions unless it was to obtain sexual pleasure from it? It was certainly the purpose for which the judge concluded the defence sought to ask these questions. The questions had no purpose unless the jury was being invited to conclude that C was the sort of person who would engage in consensual foursome sexual activity and was not the sort of person who had recently been the victim of rape. Furthermore, the Court stated that even if it was wrong about that, since the proposed questions all related to activity which took place two months or so after the time of the allegation, they would have been of minimal value to the jury's task.

26.39   *R. v D*[51] is a further illustration of the difficulties likely to be encountered by those wishing to adduce evidence of a complainant's social network

---

[51] [2011] EWCA Crim 2305.

postings. On an application for leave to appeal against his conviction of rape, the applicant wished to introduce fresh evidence under s.23 of the Criminal Appeal Act 1968. The "fresh" material consisted of 57 pages of Facebook printouts taken from the 13-year-old complainant's profile. Apart from one which was posted a day or so before the alleged rape, all the other postings post-dated the event and the trial. They contained pictures of the complainant posing provocatively, boasting about how much she drank and her interest in having sexual intercourse. Mackay J commented:

> "The complex mixture of motives which impels people, especially young people, to post messages on such sites includes, the court suspects, the desire to attract attention, admiration from peers and to provoke the interest of others in the person posting the material. We suspect the objective truth and the dissemination of factual evidence comes low on the list. In this instance the complainant's postings can be summarised as her saying outrageous or provocative things or claiming daring behaviour on her part. There are many entries, for example, boasting about how much she drank and the great hangovers she suffered as a result. In addition, there are claims of interest in sexual matters. These come later in the postings and are to be found at the time of trial. By the following August she was posting photographs of herself and of herself with other girls. All the pictures are of the girls clothed, but provocatively so, no doubt in a way perceived by her and by them sexually attractive. Choosing our words with care, they are images not dissimilar in content and presentation to what can be seen travelling many an underground escalator, albeit the model in question here is a girl in her early teens rather than a grown woman. None of these postings lays claim to direct sexual activity on the part of the complainant, though three or four of them indicate that she thinks quite a lot about her sexuality and indeed about having sexual intercourse."

26.40 The Court of Appeal had to consider whether, had the material been available at trial, it would have been admissible, and whether its introduction would have required an application under s.41. The applicant's counsel submitted that no application under s.41 was necessary and the jury might have taken a different view about the complainant had they known that such thoughts as these were in her mind and such boasts or claims about her activity were being made, if not to the world at large, at least to the world that visits Facebook. The Court reacted in a similar way as in *Ben-Rejab*. First, the so-called "fresh evidence" was of a non-existent value and not relevant to the issues the jury had to decide. The complainant had never been put forward as a "complete innocent". Secondly, if the Court's leave was required under s.41, there were immovable barriers to the introduction of the evidence. No gateway had been opened. The evidence would have fallen foul of the credibility restriction in s.41(4).

26.41 In an instructive analysis of social networking sites as criminal evidence, Michael O'Floinn and Professor David Ormerod observe that the most likely admissibility route for evidence of sexual behaviour in a posting on a social networking site is as rebuttal evidence under s.41(5).[52] This could arise where

---

[52] *Social networking material as criminal evidence* [2012] Crim. L.R. 501.

a complainant has given evidence suggesting that she is monogamous, sexually modest or, in the words of Mackay J in *R. v D*, a "complete innocent". O'Floinn and Ormerod refer to a case reported to them in which a complainant had given evidence that "she did not go in for one night stands" and "did not go prepared with condoms". In such circumstances, reference to a specific instance or instances of previous or subsequent sexual behaviour in a Facebook posting which rebut this assertion might be admissible under the rebuttal gateway. However, in *R. v ED*[53] the Court of Appeal decided that sexting[54] by the complainant the day before the alleged rape suggesting that she would be prepared to engage in a threesome was "sexual behaviour" and engaged s.41. Once s.41 was engaged, there was no gateway available to admissibility.

Complainant's false denial of previous sexual experience

26.42 The s.41 regime applies in the case of evidence or questions about a complainant's false denial of a previous sexual experience. A complainant's false assertion that she was a virgin at the time of the alleged allegation, when earlier that day she had had sexual intercourse with someone other than the accused, relates to her "sexual behaviour."[55] Whilst a truly false complaint is not "sexual behaviour" if there was no sexual activity, it is of paramount importance to distinguish between such complaints and allegedly false complaints relating to a complainant's previous sexual history: see paras 26.151 and following, below.

Sexual behaviour with the defendant

26.43 Section 41(1) of the 1999 Act, unlike s.2 of the 1976 Act, does not include the words "with a person other than that defendant". Section 41 therefore takes the same exclusionary approach to a complainant's sexual experience with the accused as to her experience with other men.[56] Parliament made this change without any significant intellectual debate, although very different considerations apply to the two scenarios.[57] Virtually all academic criticism since Heilbron had related to the admission of evidence of a complainant's

---

[53] [2015] EWCA Crim 1092. The defendant did not see the sexting. Even if he had, there could have been no meritorious argument under s.41 as it could not have founded a reasonable belief.

[54] Defined by Wikipedia as sending or receiving sexually explicit messages, primarily between mobile phones.

[55] *R. v S* [2003] EWCA Crim 485.

[56] Even the most restrictive of the American rape-shield models, the Michigan model, permits evidence of prior sexual behaviour between the complainant and the defendant.

[57] Professor Di Birch has vigorously criticised s.41 for extending the regulatory machinery to include evidence of a previous relationship between the parties themselves: *Re-thinking Sexual History Evidence: Proposals for Fairer Trials* [2002] Crim. L.R. 531; *Untangling Sexual History Evidence—A Rejoinder to Professor Temkin* [2003] Crim. L.R. 370.

sexual relationship with third parties.[58] The correct approach in respect of sexual behaviour with the defendant on other occasions has now been clarified by the House of Lords in *R. v A (No.2)*.[59] Although Lord Steyn felt that the breadth of the new provisions was "legislative overkill", he also took the view that wholly unregulated questioning about sexual experience between the complainant and the defendant, even if remote in time and context, was a serious mischief that needed to be corrected.[60]

PROCEEDINGS TO WHICH SECTION 41 APPLIES

The provisions of s.41 apply equally to trials in the Crown Court and   **26.44** magistrates' courts, committals, applications to dismiss following a notice of transfer, *Newton* hearings and the hearing of appeals. Section 42(3) of the 1999 Act provides:

> "Section 41 applies in relation to the following proceedings as it applies to a trial, namely—
> (a) proceedings before a magistrates' court inquiring into an offence as examining justices,
> (b) the hearing of an application under paragraph 5(1) of Schedule 6 to the Criminal Justice Act 1991 (application to dismiss charge following notice of transfer of case to Crown Court),
> (c) the hearing of an application under paragraph 2(1) of Schedule 3 to the Crime and Disorder Act 1998 (application to dismiss charge by person sent for trial under section 51 of that Act),
> (d) any hearing held, between conviction and sentencing, for the purpose of determining matters relevant to the court's decision as to how the accused is to be dealt with, and
> (e) the hearing of an appeal,
> and references (in section 41 or this section) to a person charged with an offence accordingly include a person convicted of an offence."

THE APPLICATION FOR LEAVE

The court may give leave under s.41 in relation to any evidence or question   **26.45** *only* on an application made by or on behalf of an accused.[61] The application must be heard in private and in the absence of the complainant. When such an application has been determined, the court must state in open court its reasons for giving or refusing leave and, if it gives leave, the extent to which evidence may be adduced or questions asked. This is the result of s.43 of the 1999 Act, which provides:

[58] For a balanced review of the voluminous critical literature, see Neil Kibble in *Cambrian Law Review*, vol.32, pp.27–63, which was extensively cited pre-publication in *R. v A (No.2)*.
[59] [2002] 1 A.C. 45 at [28].
[60] See Professor Di Birch, *Untangling Sexual History Evidence—A Rejoinder to Professor Temkin* [2003] Crim. L.R. 370, at p.376.
[61] s.41(2) of the Youth Justice and Criminal Evidence Act 1999.

"(1) An application for leave shall be heard in private and in the absence of the complainant.

In this section 'leave' means leave under section 41.

(2) Where such an application has been determined, the court must state in open court (but in the absence of the jury, if there is one)—

(a) its reasons for giving, or refusing, leave, and

(b) if it gives leave, the extent to which evidence may be adduced or questions asked in pursuance of the leave,

and, if it is a magistrates' court, must cause those matters to be entered in the register of proceedings."

If an error has occurred, and an application has been made in public revealing sexual history evidence, there could be difficulties in making a reporting direction under s.46 of the 1999 Act because the criteria for such an order may well not have been met. For a s.46 order to be made, it must be established that the order will be likely to improve the quality of the witness's evidence or the level of co-operation given by the witness to any party to the proceedings in connection with that party's preparation of its case. It follows that once the witness has given evidence, then neither of the s.46 criteria can be established.

Procedure

26.46 Section 43(3) of the 1999 Act provides:

"Rules of court may make provision—

(a) requiring applications for leave to specify, in relation to each item of evidence or question to which they relate, particulars of the grounds on which it is asserted that leave should be given by virtue of subsection (3) or (5) of section 41;

(b) enabling the court to request a party to the proceedings to provide the court with information which it considers would assist it in determining an application for leave;

(c) for the manner in which confidential or sensitive information is to be treated in connection with such an application, and in particular as to its being disclosed to, or withheld from, parties to the proceedings."

26.47 The procedure to be followed on applications for leave under s.41 is contained in Pt 22 of the Criminal Procedure Rules 2015. The Court of Appeal has underlined that there should be rigorous compliance with the rules.[62] The Rules provide in particular:

"(a) that every application must be in writing,

(b) the timetable for such applications and replies to such applications (not more than 28 days after the prosecutor has complied or purported to comply with s.3 of the Criminal Procedure and Investigations Act 1996), with a requirement for a party who wants to make representations about such an application to do so in writing within 14 days of receiving it indicating whether an application is opposed, and if so, giving reasons,

---

[62] *McKendrick* [2004] EWCA Crim 1393.

(c) requirements as to the contents of such applications (to identify the issue to which the defendant says the complainant's sexual behaviour is relevant, to give particulars of any evidence the defendant wants to introduce and questions he wants to ask, and to identify the exception to the s.41 general prohibition on which the defendant relies.)"

Although the rules are designed to encourage applications to be made at an early stage if at all possible, the court has the power to vary the time limits or to hear an application out of time. It is important to note that there is no power to waive the requirement that the application should be in writing. It follows that even if for good reason the issue arises out of time during the trial, the application must still be in writing. The mandatory requirement that the application must be in writing is still frequently overlooked.[63]

Part 22 of the Rules provides: 26.48

"**22.1** This Part applies in magistrates' courts and in the Crown Court where a defendant wants to—
(a) introduce evidence; or
(b) cross-examine a witness,
about a complainant's sexual behaviour despite the prohibition in section 41 of the Youth Justice and Criminal Evidence Act 1999.

Application for permission to introduce evidence or cross-examine

22.2 The defendant must apply for permission to do so—
(a) in writing; and
(b) not more than 28 days after the prosecutor has complied or purported to comply with section 3 of the Criminal Procedure and Investigations Act 1996 (disclosure by prosecutor).

Content of application

22.3 The application must—
(a) identify the issue to which the defendant says the complainant's sexual behaviour is relevant;
(b) give particulars of—
    (i) any evidence that the defendant wants to introduce, and
    (ii) any questions that the defendant wants to ask;
(c) identify the exception to the prohibition in section 41 of the Youth Justice and Criminal Evidence Acon which the defendant relies; and
(d) give the name and date of birth of any witness whose evidence about the complainant's sexual behaviour the defendant wants to introduce.

Service of the application

22.4 The defendant must serve the application on the court officer and all other parties.

Reply to application

22.5 A party who wants to make representations about an application under rule 22.2 must—
(a) do so in writing not more than 14 days after receiving it; and
(b) serve those representations on the court officer and all other parties.

---

[63] *Ogbodo* [2011] EWCA Crim 564; *Andrade* [2015] EWCA Crim 1722.

Application for special measures

22.6 If the court allows an application under rule 22.2 then—

    (a) a party may apply not more than 14 days later for a special measures direction or for the variation of an existing special measures direction; and

    (b) the court may shorten the time for opposing that application.

Court's power to vary requirements under this Part

22.7 The court may shorten or extend (even after it has expired) a time limit under this Part."

The Position of the Prosecution

26.49 The prosecution are not covered by the exclusionary rule in s.41, although they will be expected to follow the spirit of the legislation. In certain cases they may well adduce evidence suggesting an ongoing or past sexual relationship between the defendant and the complainant as essential background, for instance where the parties are married or living together. There may be exceptional cases where evidence of the medical examination of the complainant can only be properly evaluated if sexual history evidence is adduced. There may also be cases where the prosecution take the view that evidence of the complainant's previous sexual history underlines the non-consensual nature of the sexual activity alleged against the defendant, and they wish to adduce that evidence. In *Soroya*[64] it was argued that the prohibitions in s.41 should embrace the prosecution, and, as they do not, the process is unbalanced adversely to the defendant. The Court of Appeal rejected this argument, holding that s.78 of the Police and Criminal Evidence Act 1984 is perfectly apt to be deployed in an appropriate case where the impact of s.41 might produce an adverse effect upon the fairness of the proceedings. The appellant's argument involved a broad forensic attack on the impact of s.41 of the 1999 Act and its compatibility with art.6 of the ECHR. It was submitted that the evidence of the appellant's previous sexual history had been wrongly introduced by the prosecution at trial in circumstances that would not have been permitted to the defence. This, it was said, constituted a breach of the appellant's right to a fair trial, and infringed the requirement that there should be "equality of arms" between prosecution and defence. The Court of Appeal took the view that the prosecution had properly introduced the complainant's evidence that in order to try to avoid being raped she had made an untruthful claim that she was a virgin. It was an integral part of the incident and was important evidence bearing upon consent. It explained how the complainant had reacted, and what she had said, to avoid the dreadful incident unfolding.

[64] [2006] EWCA Crim 1884.

The Four Gateways and Two Restrictions

Section 41(2)–(6) reads: 26.50

"(2) The court may give leave in relation to any evidence or question only on an application made by or on behalf of an accused, and may not give such leave unless it is satisfied—
   (a) that subsection (3) or (5) applies, and
   (b) that a refusal of leave might have the result of rendering unsafe a conclusion of the jury or (as the case may be) the court on any relevant issue in the case.
(3) This subsection applies if the evidence or question relates to a relevant issue in the case and either—
   (a) that issue is not an issue of consent; or
   (b) it is an issue of consent and the sexual behaviour of the complainant to which the evidence or question relates is alleged to have taken place at or about the same time as the event which is the subject matter of the charge against the accused; or
   (c) it is an issue of consent and the sexual behaviour of the complainant to which the evidence or question relates is alleged to have been, in any respect, so similar—
      (i) to any sexual behaviour of the complainant which (according to evidence adduced or to be adduced by or on behalf of the accused) took place as part of the event which is the subject matter of the charge against the accused, or
      (ii) to any other sexual behaviour of the complainant which (according to such evidence) took place at or about the same time as that event,
   that the similarity cannot reasonably be explained as a coincidence.
(4) For the purposes of subsection (3) no evidence or question shall be regarded as relating to a relevant issue in the case if it appears to the court to be reasonable to assume that the purpose (or main purpose) for which it would be adduced or asked is to establish or elicit material impugning the credibility of the complainant as a witness.
(5) This subsection applies if the evidence or question—
   (a) relates to any evidence adduced by the prosecution about any sexual behaviour of the complainant; and
   (b) in the opinion of the court, would go no further than is necessary to enable evidence adduced by the prosecution to be rebutted or explained by or on behalf of the accused.
(6) For the purposes of subsections (3) and (5) the evidence or question must relate to a specific instance (or specific instances) of alleged sexual behaviour on the part of the complainant (and accordingly nothing in those subsections is capable of applying in relation to the evidence or question to the extent that it does not so relate)."

It follows that an application by or on behalf of an accused at trial can only   26.51
succeed if the court is satisfied of two matters:
   (1) that one of the four "gateways" applies:
         s.41(3)(a) (evidence or question relates to an issue which is not an issue of consent),
         s.41(3)(b) (relates to consent and the sexual behaviour is alleged to have taken place "at or about the same time as" the event in issue),

s.41(3)(c) (relates to consent and the sexual behaviour to which the evidence or question relates is so similar to behaviour which, according to the evidence, took place as part of the event or other behaviour by the complainant at about that time that the similarity cannot reasonably be explained as a coincidence), or

s.41(5) (relates to and rebuts evidence adduced by the prosecution about the complainant's sexual behaviour); and

(2)   that a refusal of leave might have the effect of rendering unsafe a conclusion of the jury or (as the case may be) the court on any relevant issue in the case.[65]

26.52   Even if there is an appropriate gateway available, and the court is satisfied that a refusal might have the effect of rendering unsafe a conclusion of the jury, two more hurdles have to be surmounted. In all cases the evidence or question must relate to a "specific instance (or specific instances)" of alleged sexual behaviour.[66] Furthermore, where the gateway is s.41(3)(a), (b) or (c), no evidence or question shall be regarded as relating to a relevant issue in the case if the primary purpose is to impugn the credibility of the complainant as a witness.[67] The four gateways and two hurdles will be examined in further detail below.

26.53   It should be remembered that even if there is sufficient evidence to open a particular gateway, the judge must still consider whether the test in s.41(2)(b) is satisfied, i.e. whether exclusion of the evidence might render unsafe a conclusion of the jury on a relevant issue in the case. However, where the evidence relates to a relevant issue in the case, and the criteria for admissibility are established, then, subject to s.41(4), the court lacks any discretion to refuse to admit the evidence, or to limit its admission. Once the criteria are established, all the evidence relevant to the issues may be adduced. As Judge LJ, as he then was, put it in *R. v F*[68]:

> "It is sometimes loosely suggested that the operation of s.41 involves the exercise of judicial discretion. In reality, the trial judge is making a judgement whether to admit or refuse evidence which is relevant, or asserted by the defence to be relevant. If the evidence is not relevant, on elementary principles, it is not admissible . . . As part of his control over the case, the judge is required to ensure that that a complainant is not unnecessarily humiliated or cross-examined with inappropriate aggression, or treated otherwise than with proper courtesy. All that is elementary, but his obligation to see that the complainant's interests are protected throughout the trial process does not permit him by way of general discretion, to prevent the proper deployment of evidence which falls within the ambit permitted by statute merely because, as here, it comes in a stark uncompromising form."

[65] s.41(2)(b).
[66] s.41(6).
[67] s.41(4).
[68] [2005] 2 Cr. App. R. 13.

THE FIRST GATEWAY—SECTION 41(3)—ISSUE OTHER THAN CONSENT

Section 41(3)(a) applies where the evidence or question relates to a relevant   26.54
issue in the case and that issue is not an issue of consent. By virtue of
s.42(1)(a), a "relevant issue in the case" means any issue falling to be proved
by the prosecution or defence in the trial of the accused.

In *R. v A (No.2)*,[69] Lord Hope gave four examples of issues which fall   26.55
within this paragraph because evidence is proffered for specific reasons
pointing to guilt or innocence as opposed to impermissible generalisations
about consent:

The defendant believed the complainant was consenting

The first example given by Lord Hope was: 26.56

> "the defence of honest belief, which McLachlin J [in *Seaboyer*] defined for the
> purposes of her examination of the Canadian legislation as resting on the
> concept—which I consider to be consistent with that described in *Director of
> Public Prosecutions v Morgan* . . . —that the accused may honestly but mis-
> takenly (but not necessarily reasonably) have believed that the complainant was
> consenting to the sexual act".

The scope for evidence of a complainant's sexual history to be relevant to   26.57
the issue of a defendant's belief that the complainant was consenting has
narrowed significantly now that, under the Sexual Offences Act 2003, such a
belief has to be reasonable to provide a defence in respect of the non-
consensual offences. As Lord Woolf CJ observed in *Bahadoor*[70]: "Honest
belief and reasonable belief are very different things." In *Bahadoor* the
appellant had been charged with indecent assault. It was his contention that
he genuinely believed the complainant was consenting because he had seen
her earlier that evening in a night-club take part in a competition which
involved her exposing her breasts and simulating oral sex. The Court felt
compelled to conclude that since the appellant's defence was based upon
honest belief, it was difficult to say that what he contended had taken place
on stage could not have been relevant, but it gave the strongest possible hint
that it would not have been relevant under the new law. In any event, the
extent to which a complainant may be cross-examined about her previous
sexual history for the purposes of the defence of honest belief will be subject
at all times to control by the court under s.41(2)(b). For instance, in
Bahadoor, the Court of Appeal held that the exclusion of the evidence did not
render unsafe the conclusion of the jury that the appellant was guilty of the
offence of which he was convicted, and the evidence had been properly
excluded under s.41(2)(b).

---

[69] [2002] 1 A.C. 45 at [79].
[70] [2005] EWCA Crim 396.

26.58   Notwithstanding the introduction of an objective element into the concept
of belief in consent, a measure of subjectivity remains, in that the jury may
take into account relevant characteristics of the defendant in assessing the
reasonableness of his belief. This is because s.1(2) of the 2003 Act provides
that whether a belief is reasonable is to be determined having regard to *all* the
circumstances, including any steps A has taken to ascertain whether B
consents. Ministerial statements in Parliament suggested that the reference to
"all the circumstances" would allow juries to take into account, where
necessary and subject to any directions of the judge, any relevant characteristics of the defendant in determining whether it was reasonable for him to
have had the belief he claims to have held.[71] Whilst relevant characteristics
might include learning difficulties, youth and possibly sexual inexperience,
they could never include the defendant's voluntary intoxication through
drink or drugs.[72] It is also now clear that evidence of a psychiatric condition
giving rise to delusional beliefs can never be a relevant defendant characteristic, but the Court of Appeal has left open the possible relevance of autism
or Asperger's syndrome.[73] If material about the complainant's previous
sexual history may have had a bearing on whether the defendant, with any
relevant characteristics, had a reasonable belief, it could come within the
s.41(3)(a) gateway. It was argued at the time the 2003 Act was passed that,
notwithstanding the Government's avowed purpose to make the previous
sexual history of the complainant less relevant,[74] the adoption of an objective
element in relation to belief in consent may have little impact on the
admissibility of previous sexual history evidence.[75] These fears have proved
unfounded and experience has shown otherwise as there has been a general
acceptance that the complainant's previous sexual history with third parties
is very rarely admissible on the basis that it is relevant to a defendant's
reasonable belief.

26.59   One possible exception is where a defendant contends that the complainant told him of her sexual activities with a person other than her normal

[71] *Hansard*, HL Vol.648, col.1073, Lord Falconer of Thoroton (June 2, 2003); Vol.649,
col.677, Baroness Scotland of Asthal (June 17, 2003). See the discussion of absence of reasonable
belief in consent in paras 1.374 and following, above.
[72] See *Grewal* [2010] EWCA Crim 2448, at [30] per Elias LJ.
[73] *B. v The Queen* [2013] EWCA Crim 3. For discussion, see paras 1.388 and following,
above.
[74] *Hansard*, HC, Standing Committee B, col.21, Beverley Hughes MP (September 9, 2003).
One of the reasons advanced by the Sexual Offences Review against the preservation of the
defence of honest but mistaken belief was that it opened the door to the element of previous
sexual history as part of the defence: *Setting the Boundaries*, (Home Office, 2002) para.2.13.7.
[75] See Professors Jennifer Temkin and Andrew Ashworth, *The Sexual Offences Act 2003: (1)
Rape, Sexual Assaults and the Problems of Consent* [2004] Crim. L.R. 328 at p.342, where the
authors argue that the reference to "all the circumstances" is an invitation to the jury to
scrutinise the complainant's behaviour to determine whether there was anything about it which
could have induced a reasonable belief in consent. The authors fear that the 2003 Act contains
no challenge to society's norms and stereotypes about either the relationship between men and
women or other sexual situations, and leaves open the possibility that those stereotypes will
determine assessments of reasonableness.

partner with a view to giving him a "green light". What if the reference to another relationship was designed to encourage the defendant to make sexual advances? This argument was advanced by the defence without success in *Winter*.[76] The defence wished to elicit the fact that earlier that evening, in the course of flirtatious behaviour with the defendant, the complainant had told him she was having a relationship with another man, "S". It was argued that this gave the defendant a reasonable basis for the belief that she was consenting to sex with him. The trial judge decided that evidence of the complainant's relationship with S and what she said about it to the defendant was nothing to do with her flirtatiousness with the defendant and refused that limb of the application. The Court of Appeal held that the "green light" argument in this case ran counter to the first of the Canadian twin myths and amounted to the very mischief to which s.41 is directed. The judge was entitled to conclude that it would be unreal to distinguish evidence that the complainant was having an affair with S from the fact that the affair existed. A true statement that the complainant was having an affair with S fell into the category of relationships with other men and was thus more similar to the area of flirting with other men rather than the allowable area of flirtation with the defendant. The Court also concluded that even if the reference to the affair with S could be seen as part of the allowable area of flirtation with the defendant, it added little in that particular case. Nevertheless, situations can be envisaged where a complainant tells a defendant of another relationship in such a manner as to be tantamount to an invitation to him to have sex with her. In such a case, the complainant's descriptions of her behaviour with the other person are likely to be evidence of "sexual behaviour" and the "green light" argument would have a much greater prospect of success.

It should be borne in mind that, even under the old s.2 regime, at a time **26.60** when an honest belief in consent did not have to be reasonable, the defendant was not entitled as of right to put before a jury any matter which he claimed persuaded him to believe that the complainant was consenting. The Court of Appeal in *Barton*[77] stated that, when considering the effect of the complainant's past sexual activities upon the defendant's alleged belief that she was consenting, the judge must reach his decision in the context of the facts of the case. A belief, based on a complainant's previous conduct with others, that she might welcome the defendant's advances is quite different to a belief that the complainant was in fact consenting during the act of intercourse. O'Connor LJ put it succinctly[78]:

> "It must be remembered that there is a difference between believing that a woman is consenting to intercourse, and believing that a woman will consent if advances are made to her."

---

[76] [2008] EWCA Crim 3.
[77] (1987) 65 Cr. App. R. 5.
[78] At 13.

26.61   In many cases there will be strongly diverging evidence as to what happened, with the prosecution and defence cases diametrically opposed. In these cases, there may be little scope for a defence of belief in consent and evidence of belief may be of marginal relevance to the real issue in the case, which will often be whether the complainant or the defendant has given a truthful account. This point is well illustrated by *Miah and Uddin,*[79] where the Court of Appeal held that the trial judge had been right to refuse the defence permission to call a third man, whom the defence claimed had had consensual sex with the complainant at a party (three months before the incident) when he had never previously met her, and only a short while after she had performed oral sex on one of the accused, with whom she had also not previously been sexually involved. Miah and Uddin were convicted of kidnap and indecent assault arising out of activity said to have taken place in Miah's car in which Uddin was a passenger. The complainant said that Miah had offered her a lift, that they had refused to let her leave the car and that they had sexually assaulted her. Miah and Uddin denied that the sexual assaults alleged by the complainant ever happened, saying that the sexual activity was limited to kissing the complainant and touching her breasts over her clothing, and was consensual. Given the strongly opposed accounts of what happened in the car, the real issue was whether the jury accepted the complainant's account or whether they thought the appellants' account might be true. In the circumstances, evidence of the appellants' beliefs was of marginal relevance.

26.62   It follows that, quite apart from the repercussions that flow from the stricter test under the Sexual Offences Act 2003, in many trials the defence of belief in consent will not in practice be available. Often there will be no scope on the facts for separate and different findings on the issues of consent and honest and reasonable belief. The issues will stand or fall together. In Canadian and Californian cases, there is a requirement that there be evidence of equivocal conduct from the complainant—something which could have caused the accused to make a mistake as to consent. Jenny McEwan argues that the judgement in *R. v A (No.2)* has set courts in England some way along this road.[80] Certainly, in cases where the facts are diametrically opposed, there is unlikely to be any scope for a separate defence of reasonableness of purported belief, and, in such circumstances, this defence cannot be used as a basis for admission of evidence of previous sexual history.

26.63   Since the enactment of s.41 and the implementation of the Sexual Offences Act 2003, there have been numerous cases in which the Court of Appeal has

---

[79] [2006] EWCA Crim 1168.

[80] For an illuminating discussion, see Jenny McEwan, *"I thought She Consented": Defeat of the Rape Shield or the Defence that Should Not Run?*[2006] Crim. L.R. 969. See also *Esau* [1997] 2 S.C.R. 443 and *The People v Williams,* 841 P.2d 961 (1992), for a Canadian and a Californian example of the principle that a defendant cannot plead both defences absent significant evidence of equivocal conduct explaining how it could be that the defendant believed consent existed where it did not.

upheld a trial judge's decision to refuse leave to admit the complainant's previous sexual history with a third party, on the basis that the evidence did not go to the defendant's belief and was precisely the kind of evidence s.41 was designed to exclude, as it laid the ground for the inadmissible submission that, because the complainant had had consensual sex with the third party, she was likely to have had consensual sex with the defendant. In *Harrison*[81] the Court of Appeal held that the trial judge's decision not to admit the fact that the complainant had had consensual sexual intercourse with a third party three hours before the incident not only was right, but had been compelled by s.41.

Conversations with third parties about the complainant's previous sexual behaviour

A belief in consent must be both honest and reasonable to provide a defence, **26.64** and in normal circumstances a belief based on the word of a third party will not be reasonable. For instance, it would be difficult to argue that it was reasonable to accept the word of the complainant's partner that any protestations she might make simply meant that she was enjoying herself. Furthermore such evidence may well fall foul of the prohibition on evidence of reputation, i.e. the "specific instance" requirement contained in s.41(6).

In *Gjoni*,[82] the Court of Appeal did, however, acknowledge that it might **26.65** well be that there would be circumstances in which evidence of a conversation between a defendant and a person other than a complainant will have probative value in relation to an honest and reasonable belief in consent. This statement should be approached with some care as the Court of Appeal appear to have been placing reliance upon obiter dicta in *Bahador*,[83] which was decided when the relevant test was confined to honest belief. In reality, the circumstances in which such a conversation will have probative value are likely to be extremely rare, as to be admissible such evidence must be relevant not just to honest but also to *reasonable* belief. Given that the focus must be on the stricter test if the prosecution is for a non-consensual offence under the Sexual Offences Act 2003, it is difficult to envisage circumstances where it could be properly argued that a defendant could reasonably believe consent could be given by proxy.

In her insightful commentary on *Gjoni*[84] Laura Hoyano expressed dismay **26.66** that 15 years after s.41 was enacted, the argument could be deployed that a discussion between third parties, of which the complainant had no knowledge, could give rise to an honest and *reasonable* belief that she would

[81] [2006] EWCA Crim 1543.
[82] [2014] EWCA Crim 691.
[83] [2005] EWCA Crim 396 In her commentary on *Gjoni* at [2014] Crim. L.R 765, Laura Hoyano described the citation of the *Bahador* as illustrating how "obiter dicta of this kind tend to have a toxic half-life" (p.768). She argues with some force that the fact that the defence argument in *Gjoni* did not prevail is of little reassurance.
[84] [2014] Crim. L.R 765, at pp.767–768.

consent to sexual intercourse with a stranger on their first encounter. Hoyano writes:

> "The hypothesis ventured in *Gjoni* trips the trap of stripping the complainant of her human rights to sexual autonomy and bodily integrity, because of a third party had chosen a sexual partner for her. It is difficult to see how this could be forestalled by judicial direction to the jury—which is why the admissibility structures were imposed by the 1999 Act in the first place. It invites a similar defence contention in reliance upon assurances of a pimp where the victim is subject to forced sexual exploitation."

26.67   In *Gjoni*, the third party had stated to the appellant that he had had sexual intercourse with the complainant on at least one occasion a week or so earlier. Whilst the Court stressed that each application must be decided according to its own circumstances, it was clearly of the view that this conversation was of no probative value. The line of reasoning required was exactly that prohibited by s.41(4): that a woman who consents to intercourse with one comparative stranger will, a week later, and in different circumstances, consent to have intercourse with another. The trial judge had ruled that (i) it was permissible for the appellant to say in evidence that he entered the bedroom believing, as a result of what he had been told, that the complainant would be willing to have sex with him, but (ii) it was not permissible for him to relate to the jury the content of the conversation since to do so would introduce evidence of the complainant's previous sexual behaviour. The Court of Appeal agreed that the content of the conversation should not have gone before the jury. In particular, the Court entertained considerable doubt that allowing the appellant to report the full content of the conversation with a third party who he claimed had told him he had had sexual intercourse with the complainant on a previous occasion could have amounted to any justification for any belief that the complainant would consent to sexual intercourse with him when she had, only hours before, explicitly rejected him.

26.68   Laura Hoyano takes the view that the Court in *Gjoni* should have gone further[85]:

> "The Court of Appeal should have ruled that a reasonable belief in consent must be grounded on evidence of the defendant's direct observation and (mis)perception of the complainant's actual communicative conduct towards him indicating that she did (not would) consent[86] . . . Evidence of androcentric gossip between the defendant and a third party about the complainant's unchastity and/or purported willingness to engage in sexual activity with the defendant or anyone else should not be relevant to the inquiry into the qualities of the defendant's claimed belief, because it is incapable of giving the defence the necessary 'air of reality' (a phrase borrowed from the Supreme Court of Canada in *Pappajohn* [1980] 2 S.C.R. 120 by Lord Steyn in *A (No.2)*)."

---

[85] [2014] Crim. L.R. 765, at p.768.
[86] Citing *Park* [1995] 2 S.C.R. 836 at [44], per L'Heureux-Dubé J; *Ewanchuck* [1999] 1 S.C.R. 330 at [64], per Major J; *Barton* (1987) 65 Cr. App. R. 5 at 13, per O'Connor LJ.

Where defendant autistic or suffering from learning disability

Not only is the test of "honest and reasonable belief" not entirely objective,   26.69
but during the passage of the Sexual Offences Bill through the House of
Lords, the Government agreed to remove the circumstance "where agreement is expressed by a third party not the victim" from the list of evidential
presumptions in respect of absence of consent. It did so because it accepted
that there may be defendants with learning difficulties who would be unfairly
treated by such a rule. Obviously, free agreement is an issue between sexual
partners and cannot be given by others, whether a husband, partner or
someone in authority over the complainant. However, assertions by a third
party about the previous sexual behaviour and the likely response of a
complainant to, e.g. a young defendant with a low IQ might *conceivably* be
relevant as to whether he had an honest and reasonable belief in consent. For
instance, a statement by a third party to such a defendant, when combined
with the fact that the defendant was suffering from a mental condition which
leads him genuinely to misinterpret social signals, might circumvent the
prohibitions imposed by s.41. However, it is unlikely a defendant's low
intelligence on its own could ever make an assertion by a third party relevant
to the defence of honest and reasonable belief.

**The complainant was biased against the accused or had a motive to fabricate
the evidence**

Whilst Lord Hope recognised in *R. v A (No.2)*[87] that bias or a motive to   26.70
fabricate would fall within the qualifying condition, it is not necessarily an
easy gateway to admissibility. In *Mokrecovas*,[88] the trial judge ruled that it
was not open to the defence to cross-examine the complainant about an
allegation that she had consensual intercourse with the defendant's brother
on two occasions, one some 12 hours before the alleged rape and the other
two hours before it. It was argued by the appellant that the motive to lie was
a distinct issue from the issue of consent. The complainant had stayed away
from home at the brothers' flat without her parents' permission; she had
drunk excessively; and returned late the following morning in a condition
such that she had immediately to go to bed. It was argued that she wished to
deflect blame from herself by making an allegation of rape. In the view of the
Court of Appeal, the question of whether sexual intercourse took place
added nothing to the foundations for the allegation that the complainant had
a motive for telling untruths. Lord Woolf CJ added:

> "We also bear in mind that if [counsel for the appellant] is right, the language of
> section 43(1)(a) could be used to drive a coach and horses through the desirable
> policy reflected in section 41(4) of the Act. It would elicit material by the
> backdoor to impugn the credibility of the complainant as a witness."

[87] [2002] 1 A.C. 45 at [79].
[88] [2002] 1 Cr. App. R. 20.

26.71   The Court of Appeal in *Mokrecovas* did not rule that evidence of motive to
fabricate could never provide a proper foundation for admissibility, or that
such evidence would always fall foul of s.41(4). Courts are frequently
confronted with suggestions from step-fathers or mothers' partners that
children have been motivated to fabricate allegations of sexual abuse against
them because of disciplining for sexual promiscuity. There may be cases
where, as in *Mokrevocas*, the defence case can properly be put and evaluated
without any need to refer to sexual behaviour. However, there may be others
where to eliminate all reference to sexual behaviour would unfairly deprive
the defence allegation of all credibility. Extracting a story from its historical
context may have fatal consequences for that story and a profound effect on
the fairness of the trial. De-contextualisation may prevent a proper consideration of the defence case. The jury may find a complainant's spiteful
motive to fabricate difficult to accept if they do not know of the sexual
context. In the unusual case of *R. v MH*,[89] the complainant had a sexual
relationship with the police officer who had escorted her to court, and
subsequently, when she discovered that he had a permanent girlfriend,
reported the relationship to the officer in charge of the case. The trial judge
ruled that he would not allow questions as to the sexual behaviour of the
complainant, but he was content with an alternative formula that allowed
cross-examination on the issue of spite without reference to sexual behaviour.
The Court of Appeal stated that they were inclined to the view that it would
have been preferable if the formula had referred in terms to consensual sex
taking place between the complainant and the police officer (although in the
circumstances of this case it was inconceivable that the jury did not know
what the formula encompassed).

26.72   In *R. v RT, R. v MH*,[90] Keene LJ contemplated a situation where
significant and relevant evidence of motive to fabricate might on normal
principles of interpretation be excluded by s.41(4) on the basis that the
purpose of adducing it was to impugn the complainant's credibility. He
said[91]:

> "Since the 1999 Act has come into force, in *R. v A. (No.2)* Lord Hope of
> Craighead has indicated that questions about the sexual behaviour of a
> complainant could be admissible if they went to show that the complainant had
> a motive to fabricate the evidence, despite the ban in section 41(4) on questions
> as to credibility. This is a matter which needs to be borne in mind by trial judges.
> If one finds on normal principles of interpretation that relevant and significant
> evidence would be excluded by section 41, then it might be that a court would
> need to go on and consider section 3 of the Human Rights Act 1998 and to
> adopt the approach suggested by Lord Hope of Craighead in *R. v A. (No.2)* and
> also by Lord Steyn. In appropriate cases, that could lead to a restrictive
> interpretation of section 41(4) because of the provisions of section 3 of the

---

[89] [2003] EWCA Crim 1066.
[90] [2001] EWCA Crim 1877; [2002] 1 W.L.R. 633.
[91] At [29].

Human Rights Act and to a narrow definition of credibility as used in section 41(4)."

Notwithstanding the possibility of a restrictive approach to s.41(4), the **26.73** problem remains that the evidence or question must relate to "a relevant issue in the case".[92] By virtue of s.42(1)(a), a "relevant issue in the case" means any issue falling to be proved by the prosecution or defence in the trial of the accused. A complainant's motive to fabricate is not an issue that has to be resolved in the trial. In *Darnell*[93] the appellant's counsel sought to argue that s.42(1)(a) must be given a wide interpretation, and Lord Hope must have contemplated a definition which is very broad in scope. It should be approached on the basis that, in any given case, the nature of the prosecution case or the proper conduct of the defence may be such as to erect into an issue falling to be proved by the prosecution a particular proposition or factual circumstance, which does not in the ordinary way amount to an issue required to be proved by the prosecution as an ingredient of the offence. Although not deciding the issue, Potter LJ was somewhat sceptical when dismissing the appeal on the basis that the defence had not satisfied the "specific instance" requirement of s.41(6):

> "That is an argument which may have considerable force as a general proposition. However it is not one which we are obliged to explore in this case. We would however pause to observe that, in paragraph 79 of his speech, Lord Hope did not refer to, and therefore it is difficult to know how far he had in mind, the definition of a 'relevant issue in the case' set out in section 42(1)(a). Nor does the passage reveal how the particular example given by him may be reconciled in any given case with the provision of section 41(4) which forbids evidence or questioning as to sexual behaviour, the main purpose of which is to establish or elicit material for impugning the credibility of the complainant as a witness."

Professor Temkin, whilst supporting the view that motive to fabricate can **26.74** provide a gateway, applauded Lord Woolf CJ for being commendably firm about a dubious claim of motive to fabricate in *Mokrecovas*.[94] In her rejoinder to Professor Temkin, Professor Di Birch has written that it is not clear that it is permissible to rely on the common law test of relevance in this context, given the statutory definition of a "relevant issue in the case" for the purposes of s.41 as a matter "falling to be proved" by the prosecution or defence.[95] However, Professor Temkin believes that "any issue falling to be proved" is potentially capable of broad construction. She derives support not only from Keene LJ in *R. v RT, R. v MH*,[96] but also from the old s.2 case of *Viola*,[97] where Lord Lane CJ said that evidence of sexual history could be

---

[92] s.41(3).
[93] [2002] EWCA Crim 176.
[94] *Sexual History Evidence—Beware the Backlash* [2003] Crim. L.R. 217 at p.228.
[95] *Untangling Sexual History Evidence: A Rejoinder to Professor Temkin* [2003] Crim. L.R. 370 at p.380.
[96] [2001] EWCA Crim 1877; [2002] 1 W.L.R. 633.
[97] [1982] 3 All E.R. 73. *Viola* was the subject of much criticism and was reversed by s.41. Nevertheless, it is arguable that its approach to relevance based on how the case is being run has not been disapproved.

admitted if it was "relevant to an issue in the trial in the light of the way the case is being run".

26.75   Despite the academic debate, there remains a compelling argument that where there is significant and relevant, as opposed to dubious, evidence of bias/motive to fabricate, which realistically cannot be properly advanced or evaluated without reference to sexual behaviour of the complainant, then to ensure a fair trial the court may need to give a wide construction to "relevant issue in the case", and at the same time interpret s.41(4) restrictively. Indeed, without this potential gateway, there will be cases where the main thrust of the defence case will never be properly considered by the jury.[98] An example of a case where evidence that was truly relevant to motive to fabricate should have been admitted without limitation, notwithstanding its stark and uncompromising form, is *R. v F.*[99] It was alleged that the complainant had been subjected to systematic sexual abuse and repeatedly raped by the appellant, her step-father, starting when she was about seven years old and continuing throughout her childhood and puberty until she was 16. The appellant denied that any form of sexual activity had taken place during the appellant's childhood or adolescence. It was, however, common ground that they lived together and shared a consensual relationship for four or five years, when the complainant was aged between 18 or 19 and 24 years, and the appellant between 30 and 36 years. It was the appellant's case that the complainant had made false allegations motivated by malice following his decision to end the adult relationship. The trial judge had allowed the defence to ask questions about the appellant's adult relationship with the complainant, on the basis that otherwise he would be unable to advance a crucial element of his defence which was that the complaint of childhood abuse was motivated by his action in ending the adult relationship. However, the trial judge refused to allow evidence to be adduced or questions to be asked concerning photographs and videotapes made during the course of the adult relationship. The material showed the complainant posing in a pornographic manner.

26.76   The Court of Appeal allowed the appeal. The photographs and videotapes were relevant to (i) whether the complaint of childhood abuse had been motivated by a desire for revenge, and (ii) in the light of the critical dispute as to how the adult relationship started and its nature, whether the childhood abuse occurred at all. Where evidence of sexual behaviour relates to a relevant issue in the case, and the criteria for admissibility are established, and it is not caught by s.41(4), the trial judge has no discretion to exclude it

---

[98] cf. *Martin* [2004] EWCA Crim 916 for a case where the Court of Appeal held that evidence of sexual behaviour between the appellant and complainant should have been admitted as it went to the issue of the complainant's motive to fabricate and strengthened the defence case. The Court does not appear to have been constrained by Potter LJ's scepticism in *Darnell* about Lord Hope's approach in *R. v A (No.2)* to the definition of a "relevant issue in the case". Furthermore, the evidence did not fall foul of s.41(4). See para.26.143, below, for further discussion in respect of the important case of *Martin*.

[99] [2005] 2 Cr. App. R. 13.

or limit its admission because it is in stark and uncompromising form such as the pornographic videos. The case illustrates that, while due regard must be had to the need to protect the complainant from indignity and from humiliating questions, there may be cases where that protection must give way to some extent if the defence case is to be put properly. However, if the evidence sought to be adduced had been of only minimal relevance, then presumably the judge would have been obliged to exclude it under s.41(2)(b).

There is an alternative explanation for the physical conditions on which the Crown relies to establish that intercourse took place

Where the prosecution choose to rely on injuries sustained by the complain-   **26.77** ant, evidence of sexual behaviour which might explain those injuries is likely to be relevant. Where a doctor concludes from medical examination of a child that there has been penetration by an object the size of a penis, evidence of other sexual behaviour that explains the child's physical condition will be relevant. For instance, where the prosecution asserted that the medical evidence of hymenal penetration resulted from rape by the appellant when the complainant was a teenager, evidence that she had previously been raped by her landlord in Nigeria when she was five was relevant as an explanation for the hymenal damage.[100] It effectively neutralised the medical evidence in all the known circumstances. Similarly, evidence of previous sexual liaison with a third party which might explain why the complainant contracted a sexually transmitted disease which the prosecution rely on as evidence of penetration by the defendant would be relevant to an issue in the case which is not an issue of consent. Where the presence of semen is discovered, but not its origin, recent sexual activity with another may provide an explanation for its presence. Similarly, where there is evidence of a complainant's pregnancy and/or a "pregnancy scare" following a disputed penetration, evidence of sexual intercourse with another which might explain the pregnancy is likely to be relevant.[101]

Especially in the case of young complainants, the detail of their account must have come from some other sexual activity before or after the event which provides an explanation for their knowledge of that activity

This issue could arise in cases where the prosecution is seeking to argue, or   **26.78** the jury might otherwise form the view, that the complainant would only be able to describe the particular sexual activity alleged if they had experienced it with the defendant. Much will depend upon the age of the complainant, his or her level of sophistication, and whether the sexual activity alleged is

---

[100] *R. v L* [2015] EWCA Crim 741.
[101] *R. v F* [2008] EWCA Crim 2859 at [22]; *R. v DGF* [2008] EWCA Crim 2859.

unusual or something a jury might reasonably expect the complainant to know of. In the Scottish case of *Love v HM Advocate*,[102] which was cited by Lord Hope, the appellant was tried on an indictment including a charge of "shameless indecency and sodomy" against A at a time when A was between 10 and 14 years old (A being aged 15 at the time of trial). A gave detailed evidence of the appellant's behaviour. The prosecution also adduced medical evidence which described injuries consistent with penile penetration of his anus. The appellant's counsel applied to be allowed to cross-examine A on an alleged sexual relationship with another named person which had started when he was 12, the purpose of the cross-examination being to explain A's knowledge of the matters to which he had spoken in evidence. The trial judge refused the application on the ground that the proposed evidence related to matters which occurred two years after the abuse, which was the subject of the charge, had allegedly started. In his speech the advocate-depute asked rhetorically what possible reason there could be for A to make up such serious allegations. The appeal was allowed in part on the basis that the proposed line of questioning might have afforded an alternative explanation for the explicit and detailed evidence given by A in examination-in-chief and, in particular, his ability to give such evidence at the age of 15.

26.79   However, this issue is only likely to arise in exceptional cases. Children may gain knowledge of sexual practices from a variety of sources, for instance, in the playground or from sex education at school. In *R. v MF*[103] the Court of Appeal stressed that Lord Hope had referred to the issue arising when the detail of a child's account "must" have come from some other sexual activity which provides an explanation for their knowledge. At trial, the defence had sought leave to cross-examine the complainant as to whether she had told a doctor that she had had penile intercourse with a boy from school. This was on the basis that this showed she had been sexually active before she had complained to the police about the appellant, and this activity provided a source of knowledge of the explicit details given in her account, other than the alleged acts of the appellant. The trial judge refused the application on the ground that, being 14, the complainant fell outside the scope of young complainants who could only have acquired their knowledge of sexual activity through the alleged acts that formed the subject matter of the trial. The judge also indicated that the complainant's account to the police went beyond penile intercourse, and that the proposed question could not provide an explanation for her knowledge of the matters she described to them which did not involve any penile penetration. The Court of Appeal upheld the judge's decision, stating that the reasons the judge had given were "obviously correct." It was "almost inevitable" that a 14-year-old would be able to describe acts of masturbation and sexual intercourse. The defence were

---

[102] 1999 S.C.C.R. 783.
[103] [2005] EWCA Crim 3376.

rightly denied the opportunity to cross-examine the complainant about what she had told the doctor.

THE SECOND GATEWAY—SECTION 41(3)—CONSENT AND CONTEMPORANEITY

Where there is an issue of consent, on the face of the legislation there are two narrow gateways. Although clearly designed to cater for very limited categories of cases, it is significant that the legislation recognises two areas where the sexual behaviour of the complainant may be relevant to the issue of consent. The first, set out in s.41(3)(b), is where the evidence or question relates to:

> "an issue of consent and the sexual behaviour of the complainant to which the evidence or question relates is alleged to have taken place at or about the same time as the event which is the subject matter of the charge against the accused."

26.80

It should be noted that even if the behaviour is alleged to have taken place at or about the same time as the event which is the subject matter of the charge against the accused, it does not necessarily follow that it relates to an issue of consent or that the judge will be satisfied for the purposes of s.41(3)(b) that a refusal might leave unsafe a decision of the jury.[104] The decision in *Mukadi*,[105] discussed in para.26.30, above, has been widely criticised and we submit that it should not be followed as an example of how this gateway should operate. It is out of kilter with the approach adopted in the vast majority of Court of Appeal decisions on s.41. Both Professor Birch[106] and Professor Temkin and colleagues[107] consider that the trial judge was wholly correct in his refusal of leave to cross-examine the complainant about an incident that took place earlier on the same day as the alleged rape.

In the Parliamentary debates on the Bill, it was suggested that this gateway would be interpreted no more widely than 24 hours before or after the alleged offence.[108] Other jurisdictions have rape shield legislation with "reasonably contemporaneous" exceptions. In *State of Missouri v Kevin Murray*,[109] the Missouri Court of Appeal had to consider the requirement that prior instances of consensual sexual intercourse between the defendant and victim are only admissible when reasonably contemporaneous with the charged incident. The Court held that the defendant's right to due process and a fair

26.81

---

[104] *R. v GM* [2004] EWCA Crim 1393.

[105] [2003] EWCA Crim 3765.

[106] [2004] Crim. L.R. 373, where Professor Birch points out that "consent is not a transferrable commodity".

[107] L. Kelly, J. Temkin and S. Griffiths, *Section 41: an evaluation of new legislation limiting sexual history evidence in rape trials* (Home Office, 2006), at p.16.

[108] The first draft of the Youth Justice and Criminal Evidence Bill confined the period within which relevant sexual behaviour had to take place to the 24 hours before and after the event which is the subject matter of the charge.

[109] 842 S.W. Reporter (2d) 122.

trial required the admission of evidence of prior consensual intercourse three-and-a-half months and six-and-a-half months before the events in question.

26.82   Any time limitation risks being arbitrary. Closeness in time will be a factor when considering relevance, but the parties might have an intimate relationship and see each other only occasionally.[110] Nevertheless, it would appear that in practice the courts are interpreting this subsection relatively restrictively. In *R. v A*[111] in the Court of Appeal it was submitted on behalf of the appellant that s.43(1)(b) should be construed as applying to sexual behaviour "sufficiently close in time to be relevant to the issue of consent". Relevance could not be decided by use of a clock and calendar. An unyielding time limit is artificial when considering the relevance of circumstances. The subsection should be given the widest possible construction to give effect to Convention rights. The proposed interpretation would ensure that the section is applied in a just, less arbitrary and more proportionate manner. It would ensure that its application was confined to truly relevant circumstances, thereby meeting the objective of the section. However, Rose LJ found it impossible to construe the words "at or about the same time" as applying to events months, weeks or even days prior to the events said to give rise to the rape. The same argument was considered by the House of Lords in *R. v A (No.2)*. Lord Slynn[112] stated that he was initially tempted to think that the words "at or about the same time as the event" could be given a wide meaning—certainly a few hours, and perhaps a few days when a couple were continuously together. But upon reflection he felt that, even if read with art.6, they must be a given a narrow meaning and would not allow evidence of sexual behaviour to be adduced other than in cases where the acts relied on were really contemporaneous.

THE THIRD GATEWAY—SECTION 41(3)—CONSENT AND SIMILARITY

26.83   The third gateway applies where there is an issue as to consent and the sexual behaviour of the complainant to which the evidence or question relates is:

> "so similar—
> (i) to any sexual behaviour of the complainant which (according to evidence adduced or to be adduced by or on behalf of the accused) took place as part of the event which is the subject matter of the charge against the accused, or
> (ii) to any other sexual behaviour of the complainant which (according to such evidence) took place at or about the same time as that event,
> that the similarity cannot reasonably be explained as a coincidence."

---

[110] For the argument that time is only one of a totality of circumstances, see Clifford Fishman: *Consent, Credibility and the Constitution: Evidence relating to a Sex Offence Complainant's Past Sexual Behaviour*, Catholic University Law Review [Vol.44: 709 1995] at p.709.

[111] [2001] EWCA Crim 4; [2001] Crim. L.R. 389.

[112] [2002] 1 A.C. 45, at [55].

This provision was introduced in response to the "Romeo and Juliet" 26.84
scenario recounted by Baroness Mallalieu during a House of Lords debate.
The complainant alleged she had been raped by a man who had climbed up
onto her balcony into her bedroom. Both before and after the alleged rape
she had asked men to re-enact the Romeo and Juliet balcony scene before
having sexual intercourse with her.

This subsection, unlike s.41(3)(b), is not subject to a temporal constraint. 26.85
It permits comparison between the instance of sexual behaviour of the
complainant which the defendant wishes to raise and *either* sexual behaviour
that took place as part of the event which is the subject matter of the charge
or any other sexual behaviour of the complainant which took place at or
about the same time as that event. The gateway opens (subject to the other
restrictions imposed by the section) if the instance in question is so similar
"that the similarity cannot reasonably be explained as a coincidence" either
to sexual behaviour which is the subject matter of the charge (where there is
no time constraint)[113] or to sexual behaviour which is relevant and admissible
under s.41(3)(b).[114] In *R. v T*[115] the trial judge, when faced by an application
on behalf of T in respect of evidence that T and the complainant had had
consensual sex in the same triangular frame in a similar position three weeks
prior to the alleged rape, referred to s.41(3)(c)(ii), and excluded the evidence
on the basis it was not sufficiently contemporaneous. The Court of Appeal
pointed out that the judge should have been referred to s.41(3)(c)(i) of the
Act, which has no time constraint. He might then have ruled that the
evidence was admissible and accordingly the conviction could not be
regarded as safe.

On the face of it the gateway appears to be a narrow one, although its very 26.86
existence calls into question the coherence of the Government's position on
the relevance of evidence of previous sexual behaviour.[116] The way the
subsection deals with other similar conduct can be compared with the
approach of the courts to the admission of similar fact evidence. The
subsection appears closer in spirit to *DPP v Boardman*,[117] where the House
of Lords held that the admission of similar fact evidence required a strong
degree of probative force, than to the later decision in *DPP v P*,[118] where the
House held that evidence of similar fact was admissible if its probative force
was so great that it was just to admit it. The subsection does not, however, go
so far as to adopt the *Boardman* test of "striking similarity", where "the
similarity would have to be so unique or striking that common sense makes
it inexplicable on the basis of coincidence".[119] Moreover, the purpose of

[113] s.41(3)(c)(i).
[114] s.41(3)(c)(ii).
[115] [2004] EWCA Crim 1220.
[116] Neil Kibble, *The Sexual History Provisions: Charting a course between inflexible legislative rules and wholly untrammelled judicial discretion?* [2000] Crim. L.R. 274, at p.285.
[117] [1975] A.C. 421.
[118] [1991] 2 A.C. 447.
[119] [1975] A.C. 421 at 462, per Lord Salmon.

admitting previous sexual history evidence under this gateway is to fortify the proposition that the complainant was consenting, rather than to establish that the defendant committed the offence as in the case of similar fact evidence. As Lord Clyde put it in *R. v A (No.2)*[120]:

> "The context and the purpose of the evidence is not so much to show from past events that history has been repeated, as to indicate a state of mind on the part of the complainant towards the defendant which is potentially highly relevant to her state of mind on the occasion in question."

26.87   Nevertheless, the requirement that the similarity cannot reasonably be explained as a coincidence imposes a much tighter restriction than under the rule in *DPP v P*. Lord Hutton in *R. v A (No.2)*[121] stressed that some weight must be given to the fact that "similar" in the subsection is qualified by the word "so", which he thought was intended to emphasise that mere similarity was not sufficient, and accordingly other sexual behaviour with the same man would not of itself come within the section following ordinary principles of construction. The similarity can be "in any respect". However, identity alone is clearly insufficient as a non-coincidental factor. Lord Clyde in *R. v A (No.2)*[122] considered the extent of similarity necessary to come within the section:

> "What must be found is a similarity in some other or additional respect. Further the similarity must be such as cannot reasonably be explained as a coincidence. To my mind that does not necessitate that the similarity has to be in some rare or bizarre conduct. So long as the particular factor is of a significance which goes beyond the realm of what could reasonably be explained as a coincidence it should suffice. Something about the sexual behaviour of the complainant on each of the occasions, such as something said or done by him or her which is not so unremarkable as to be reasonably explained as a coincidence has to be found. I would not attempt any kind of definition and in any event it is the words of the statute which matter, but the language seems to me to be looking for some characteristic or incident of the complainant's behaviour which can reasonably be seen to have a significance beyond the fact that it is contemporaneous with the behaviour and which bears some kind of connection or relationship with the behaviour which on a reasonable view is not a mere matter of chance. The task for the judge is to examine the evidence proposed to be led and see if such a similarity in some respect can be found."

26.88   It follows that mere similarity is not sufficient to open this gateway. The behaviour of the complainant must be so similar to the allegation that the similarity cannot reasonably be explained as a coincidence. Furthermore, the similarity must be relevant similarity. In *R. v MM*[123] the Court of Appeal held that the trial judge had been right to reject the argument that this gateway was opened by the complainant's sexual behaviour on two earlier occasions four months and three months respectively before the time of the

---

[120] [2002] 1 A.C. 45, at [133].
[121] [2002] 1 A.C. 45, at [159].
[122] [2002] 1 A.C. 45, at [135]. Evidence of similar unusual sexual conduct such as sadomasochistic sexual behaviour on a previous occasion might be sufficiently similar.
[123] [2011] EWCA Crim 1291.

allegation. At the appellant's trial for vaginal, anal and oral rape, it was an admitted fact that the complainant and the appellant had engaged in full sexual relations, including anal intercourse, before the complainant ended the relationship. The complainant's evidence was that she was simply not prepared to engage in sexual activity in the circumstances in which the appellant was demanding it. The Court held that the behaviour alleged on the earlier occasions was not so similar that it could not be explained as coincidence. The "parallels" to which the appellant referred were (i) the complainant's willingness to engage in fellatio in a public place (oral sex performed by the complainant upon the appellant in a cinema), and (ii) her willingness to engage in sexual intercourse in her own bedroom (anal and vaginal sexual intercourse with the appellant in the complainant's bedroom after sending her younger brother out of the house). The material feature of the alleged sexual behaviour of the complainant at the time of the alleged rapes was not the fact of intercourse of any particular type, which was not in issue, but the circumstances in which it occurred, namely at 07.00 in a bedroom adjoining the complainant's mother's bedroom and with her sister, brother and friend moving about outside the room. In its environmental circumstances this behaviour was not so similar that it might support a conclusion that coincidence could be excluded, nor was it probative on the issue of consent. Nor was there any sufficient chronological nexus between the events to render the previous behaviour in any sense probative of the issue the jury had to resolve.

The tightness of the requirement is also well illustrated by *Hamadi*.[124] The   **26.89** defence identified similarities between the circumstances in which "D" described having sexual intercourse with the complainant and the circum- stances in which the applicant said he had intercourse with her: the complainant herself instigated sexual activity; the activities took place outside in relatively public places; they took place in winter; and they took place whilst she was involved in a relationship with her boyfriend. The Court of Appeal did not think that such similarities could reasonably be described as not a coincidence.

Harris[125] provides a good illustration of the range of judgment open to a   **26.90** judge when evaluating similarities to assess if they open the gateway under s.41(3)(c). It also demonstrates the narrowness of the interpretation of this gateway by the courts. The appellant was convicted of rape, false imprison- ment and assault. The complainant was a teacher. On her way home after drinking heavily in July 2006, she had met the appellant on the street and invited him back to her flat. They also invited a Polish man, previously unknown to them both, to join them after a chance encounter. The complainant's account was that at her flat the appellant had attacked her and raped her violently. He also tied up the Polish man. The appellant did not

---

[124] [2007] EWCA Crim 3048.
[125] [2009] EWCA Crim 434.

give evidence. However, in interview, he had said that all the sexual activity had been consensual and any assault by him was in response to being attacked by her after the sex. In cross-examination the complainant denied that she had consented to sexual intercourse with the appellant. She said that she had led an openly homosexual lifestyle since she was 21. She had never previously invited strangers to her flat. She accepted that she had been taking anti-depressants and that she had in the past drunk excessively.

26.91   At trial, application was made under s.41(3)(c) to cross-examine the complainant on the basis of two documents that had been disclosed from the psychiatric and medical records relating to her which showed a history of depressive episodes and self-harm dating back to 2004. The complainant was recorded by a senior clinical nurse on a visit to A & E in December 2005 as having stated:

> "She described life choices involving behaviours which potentially put her at risk of abuse from others, i.e. casual sex with illegal taxi drivers, excessive alcohol intake, etc. She reported awareness of the dangers of the behaviour and also described a wish to punish herself."

Also, in April 2006 her general practitioner had written a letter of referral to a Hospital Psychiatric Department, which stated:

> "She presents today with increased anxiety, low esteem and thoughts of self harm. My opinion accords with that of the clinical nurse. [The complainant] for some reason punishes herself with excess alcohol and risky sexual liaisons."

26.92   Counsel for the appellant sought to cross-examine the complainant as to the source of the information contained in the documents, to ask for details and about her attitude to risk. It was contended that the casual sex and risky sexual encounters when in drink referred to in the documents were a similar course of conduct to the events out of which the charges against the appellant had arisen. It would not be general cross-examination, but cross-examination directed at specific instances. The submission was that the similarity lay in the risky sexual encounter in which the complainant had had sexual intercourse with a stranger; it had been made clear in *R. v A (No.2)*[126] that striking similarity was not required.

26.93   Two statements were subsequently taken from the complainant about the documents. She said that she had been engaged in a heterosexual relationship several years ago. In the summer of 2005, she had had heterosexual intercourse with a cab driver whom she knew, but since then had lived an entirely homosexual lifestyle. The notes taken in A & E can only have referred to what happened with the cab driver on one occasion; the reference to casual sex was a reference to sex with women she knew. The notes had misinterpreted what she had said.

26.94   The trial judge refused the application, concluding that there was no similarity within the meaning of s.41(3)(c). To allow such cross-examination would have been tantamount to saying that the complainant was a person

---

[126] [2002] 1 A.C. 45, at [133].

who engaged in casual sex in the past and therefore would have been likely to do so on the occasion she was with the appellant. Even if there had been a similarity, refusal of leave was not such that it would have had the effect of rendering the verdict unsafe.

The Court of Appeal upheld the conviction for rape on the basis that the **26.95** material in the medical documents was not sufficiently similar to what the complainant alleged had happened on the night in issue. The Court considered that the trial judge adopted a view on similarity which it was open to him to adopt within the margin of judgment open to a decision-maker. He was also entitled to conclude that cross-examination on the basis of what was set out in the two documents would have brought into play matters in relation to the complainant's general sexual behaviour and not the similarity of the two occasions.

Two further points arise from *Harris*. First, if there had been sufficient **26.96** similarity, presumably the application would have been granted even though the complainant claimed the contents of the documents were incorrect, as the documents amounted to evidence supporting the allegation. Secondly, the chances of a successful application might have been enhanced if steps had been taken to see if the complainant's explanation for what appeared in the documents was accepted by the nurse and the GP. No such steps had been taken. It followed that, if the application had been granted, there would have been no other evidence to contradict the complainant's explanation. In those circumstances, the Court of Appeal stated that it would be difficult to see how it could have been asserted that there was any similarity, without the principal purpose of cross-examination conducted in that way being to impugn the complainant's credibility.

Evidence that the complainant had worked as a prostitute

Can evidence of specific instances of the complainant working as a prostitute **26.97** amount to evidence of a similar non-coincidental event? Applying Lord Clyde's test, circumstances can be envisaged which might come within this exception where the defendant alleges that he paid the complainant for consensual sex and seeks to adduce evidence that she had acted as a prostitute on previous occasions. However, evidence that the complainant has been a prostitute is likely to fall foul of s.41(6), which precludes the admission of evidence of reputation by requiring that the evidence or questions must relate to a specific instance, or specific instances, of the complainant's behaviour. Professor Birch has suggested that the section would (perhaps) allow the admission of evidence that the complainant was picking up clients as a prostitute (if it was the defendant's evidence that he was so picked up).[127] Clearly there would have to be at least one specific instance, which might be provided by a conviction for soliciting.

[127] Professor Di Birch, *A Better Deal for Vulnerable Witnesses?* [2000] Crim. L.R. 223 at 248–9.

26.98   In *White*,[128] the Court of Appeal held that the trial judge had been correct to refuse to allow evidence of, or cross-examination as to, the fact that the complainant had worked for 19 years as a prostitute. The complainant alleged that she had met the appellant in a public house, and that they had gone back to her flat where he raped her. The appellant's case was that consensual sexual intercourse had occurred, but the complainant had asked for money, which he had refused, and that after intercourse had taken place he had awoken to find her with his wallet, whereupon there was a struggle, following which he had left. Importantly, it was not the defence case that this was an act of prostitution or that the appellant was one of the complainant's clients. The Court of Appeal held that there could be no contention that the bare fact that the victim was a prostitute could be relevant to consent. It could not be accepted that information contained in a list of previous convictions for prostitution was capable of fulfilling the requirements of s.41(6); to decide otherwise would be tantamount to saying that any encounter could come within the provision if it could be given a time and date. The Court considered there were great difficulties in fitting the case within any of the provisions contained in s.41(3). The material in respect of the complainant's life as a prostitute was in too general terms for it to be asserted that any of her acts were sufficiently contemporaneous with the alleged rape to engage s.41(3)(b), and there was nothing of sufficient similarity between those acts and the alleged rape for the purposes of s.41(3)(c).[129]

The interpretative obligation under section 3 of the Human Rights Act 1998 as applied to section 41(3)(c) by the House of Lords in R. v A (No.2)

26.99   Lord Steyn in *R. v A (No.2)*[130] gave this exception more flexibility in relation to prior sexual experience between an accused and the complainant:

> "45. In my view section 3 requires the court to subordinate the niceties of the language of section 41(3)(c), and in particular the touchstone of coincidence, to broader considerations of relevance judged by logical and common sense criteria of time and circumstances. After all, it is realistic to proceed on the basis that the legislature would not, if alerted to the problem, have wished to deny the right to an accused to put forward a full and complete defence by advancing truly probative material. It is therefore possible under section 3 to read section 41, and

---

[128] [2004] EWCA Crim 946, CA; *Criminal Law Week*, Issue 11, March 15, 2004.

[129] For a robust criticism of the decision, see James Richardson in *Criminal Law Week*, Issue 11, March 15, 2004. It is contended that s.41(3)(c)(i) might have been engaged in that evidence of previous requests for money could not reasonably be explained as a coincidence and, if admitted, might have led the jury to a different conclusion when resolving the conflict between the complainant's and the defendant's evidence in respect of the wallet episode. Instances (particularly if recent) of the complainant's other professional activities had a direct bearing on whether she was consenting on the basis that she had expected payment. Whilst the mere fact that she had convictions for prostitution offences, of course, does not mean she was consenting on this occasion, the evidence had a tendency to support the contention that she consented on this occasion in return for payment.

[130] [2002] 1 A.C. 45, at 45–46.

in particular section 41(3)(c), as subject to the implied provision that evidence or questioning which is required to ensure a fair trial under Article 6 of the Convention should not be treated as inadmissible. The result of such a reading would be that sometimes logically relevant sexual experiences between a complainant and an accused will be irrelevant, e.g. an isolated episode distant in time and circumstances. Where the line is to be drawn must be left to the judgment of trial judges. On this basis a declaration of incompatibility can be avoided. If this approach is adopted, section 41 will have achieved a major part of its objective but its excessive reach will have been attenuated in accordance with the will of Parliament as reflected in section 3 of the 1998 Act. That is the approach which I would adopt.

46. It is of supreme importance that the effect of the speeches today should be clear to trial judges who have to deal with problems of the admissibility of questioning and evidence on alleged prior sexual experience between an accused and a complainant. The effect of the decision today is that under section 41(3)(c) of the 1999 Act, construed where necessary by applying the interpretative obligation under section 3 of the Human Rights Act 1998, and due regard always being paid to the importance of seeking to protect the complainant from indignity and from humiliating questions, the test of admissibility is whether the evidence (and questioning in relation to it) is nevertheless so relevant to the issue of consent that to exclude it would endanger the fairness of the trial under Article 6 of the convention. If this test is satisfied the evidence should not be excluded."

Whatever differences the Law Lords may have had over the relevance of **26.100** previous sexual history evidence to the defence of consent, there was a consensus as to this guidance for trial judges. Professor Birch has pointed out that the "if" in the last sentence cited above was a much bigger "if" for some of their Lordships than for others.[131] In *R. v R*[132] the Court of Appeal allowed an appeal on the basis of the decision in *R. v A (No.2)*. The facts are instructive. Counsel for the appellant had applied to the trial judge for leave to cross-examine the complainant on three matters:

(a) that the complainant and the appellant had had a consensual sexual relationship,
(b) that in April 2000 (approximately four months before the date of the alleged rape) the complainant had had consensual intercourse at the appellant's home, and
(c) that she had had consensual intercourse with the appellant in around July 2001 (almost a year after the alleged rape).

The trial judge allowed the application only in respect of (a), on the ground **26.101** that it was relevant to the appellant's belief. Mantell LJ stated that on a strict interpretation of the Act, the evidence of both the previous and the post-complaint sexual relationship between the appellant and the complainant had to be excluded. The only cross-examination and evidence admissible under the Act was as to the April 2000 incident, which was so similar to the alleged rape that it could not reasonably be explained as a coincidence.

[131] Professor Di Birch, *Rethinking Sexual History Evidence: Proposals for Fairer Trials* [2002] Crim. L.R. 531.
[132] [2003] EWCA Crim 2754.

However, applying the test proposed by Lord Steyn in *R. v A (No.2)*, the evidence of the previous and the post-complaint sexual relationship as alleged was so relevant to the issue of consent that its exclusion deprived the appellant of a fair trial. In respect of the April 2000 episode, there was no logical reason for excluding the fact (if it was found to be so by the jury) that the last act of sexual intercourse prior to the alleged rape in August 2000 occurred in April 2000. A jury might take the view that the closer to the date of the alleged rape the last act of consensual intercourse was, the more cogent the evidence. In respect of the subsequent consensual intercourse, a reasonable jury could take the view that it was highly unlikely that a girl or woman who had been raped in the circumstances alleged in this case, would volunteer to have sexual intercourse with the man subsequently. Accordingly, cross-examination should also have been permitted in respect of (b) and (c).

Relevance to the issue of consent of the complainant's previous (and subsequent) sexual behaviour with the defendant

26.102   Given that the House of Lords' decision in *R. v A (No.2)* made the gateway in s.41(3)(c) more accessible in respect of previous sexual behaviour between the complainant and the defendant, the relevance of such evidence to the issue of consent is discussed at this stage. In the light of the new departure represented by s.41 in bringing such evidence within the regulatory regime, it was inevitable that soon after implementation there would be a serious challenge to the new blanket prohibition (with very narrow exceptions) on the basis that truly relevant evidence was being excluded on an arbitrary basis. Within days of implementation of the new legislation, HH Judge Goldstein in a preparatory hearing at the Central Criminal Court in the case that became *R. v A (No.2)*, ruled that s.41 prohibited cross-examination of the complainant as to her alleged previous sexual activity with the defendant who was charged with rape. It was the defendant's case that, on the occasion of the alleged rape on June 14, 2000, the complainant initiated consensual sexual intercourse and that this was part of a continuing sexual relationship. The consensual sexual relationship covered a period of approximately three weeks prior to June 14, 2000; and in particular he had consensual sexual relations with her, including sexual intercourse, at his flat on occasions between May 26, 2000, and June 14, 2000. The last instance was approximately one week before June 14, 2000.

26.103   It was argued at an interlocutory appeal that, depending upon the facts of the case, in particular the passage of time and the nature of the relationship, evidence of a pre-existing (or subsequent) consensual sexual relationship between the complainant and the defendant may be relevant in deciding whether there was consent in a particular case. This is not inconsistent with the fact that each party to consensual sexual behaviour gives consent afresh on each occasion. Furthermore, it would be wrong for the jury to evaluate the evidence of what will otherwise appear to them to be a first encounter without knowing the background and understanding the history of the sexual relationship.[133]

The Court of Appeal in *R. v A (No.2)* had little difficulty in deciding the   **26.104**
potential relevance of such evidence:

> "In our judgment, provisional though we emphasise it is, it is not mythical but common sense that a person, whether male or female, who has previously had consensual intercourse with another, particularly in recent weeks or months may, on the occasion in dispute have been more likely to consent to intercourse with that other than if that other were a stranger or one with whom no previous sexual familiarity had occurred. We do not accept, on the basis of the matter as we presently understand it, that such an approach stems from 'sexist beliefs about women which distort the trial process'. On the contrary, it seems to us to reflect human nature regardless of sex. The trial process would be unfairly distorted if a jury were precluded from knowing, if it be the case, that the complainant and defendant had recently engaged in consensual sexual activity with each other."

The interlocutory appeal was allowed to the extent that it was held that   **26.105**
questions and evidence about the alleged previous sexual history between the defendant and the complainant were admissible under s.41(3)(a) (honest belief in consent). However, the Court of Appeal took the view that the trial judge was correct to conclude that such cross-examination and evidence were impermissible under s.41(3)(b). This would have meant that evidence that the Court of Appeal considered was relevant and admissible could not be adduced in support of the defence of consent. As Rose LJ put it:

> "As will be apparent from what we have already said, it may be that a fair trial will not be possible if there cannot be adduced, in support of the defence of consent, evidence as to the complainant's recent consensual sexual activity with the defendant."

The prospect of trial judges being forced by the new legislation to exclude   **26.106**
evidence that the Court of Appeal considered was truly relevant to the issue of consent led the prosecution to seek leave to appeal. The Court of Appeal granted leave to appeal to the House of Lords on the following question of law:

> "May a sexual relationship between a defendant and a complainant be relevant to the issue of consent so as to render its exclusion under section 41 of the Youth

---

[133] This argument is well expressed in *Pettman* (unreported, May 2, 1985), CA, per Purchas LJ: "In *R. v Campbell* (unreported) this court upheld a ruling by the trial judge that the evidence relating to an incident some six months earlier than the date of the offence charged was necessary in order to give a continuous and intelligible account of the relationship between an appellant and the victim. In a case such as this, which depends upon the relationship between the parties as part of a continuum, the excision of one isolated part of the history would, in our judgment, inevitably have caused distortions of the account placed before the jury and would have prevented them from being in a position to judge the actions of the appellant in or about the early days of October in their true setting." Professor Di Birch argues that the evidence in *R. v A (No.2)* was relevant as background evidence and suggests that "important explanatory evidence" of sexual history should be admissible: *Untangling Sexual History Evidence: A Rejoinder to Professor Temkin* [2003] Crim. L.R. 370, at p.381.

Justice and Criminal Evidence Act 1999 a contravention of the defendant's right to a fair trial?"

26.107   In his speech Lord Steyn dealt with the issue of relevance of such evidence[134]:

"As a matter of common sense, a prior sexual relationship between the complainant and the accused may, depending on the circumstances, be relevant to the issue of consent. It is a species of prospectant evidence which may throw light on the complainant's state of mind. It cannot, of course, prove that she consented on the occasion in question. Relevance and sufficiency of proof are different things. The fact that an accused a week before an alleged murder threatened to kill the deceased does not prove an intent to kill on the day in question. But it is logically relevant to that issue. After all, to be relevant the evidence need merely have some tendency in logic and common sense to advance the proposition in issue. It is true that each decision to engage in sexual activity is always made afresh. On the other hand, the mind does not usually blot out all memories. What one has been engaged on in the past may influence what choice one makes on a future occasion. Accordingly, a prior sexual relationship between a complainant and an accused may sometimes be relevant to what decision was made on a particular occasion."

26.108   Lord Hutton agreed that such evidence may be relevant[135]:

"The second observation is that whilst there can be no dispute that the Minister of State was correct to say... 'The fact that a complainant has consented previously does not mean that she will consent again', it does not follow, in my opinion, where there has been a recent affectionate relationship between a woman and a man, that one cannot say that the fact that she has consented previously is relevant in deciding whether she consented when there was intercourse with the same man a relatively short time later. I consider there is much force in the statement of Professor Galvin, at p.807 of her article,[136] that
    'Even the most ardent reformers acknowledged the high probative value of past sexual conduct in at least two instances. The first is when the defendant claims consent and establishes prior consensual relations between himself and the complainant ... although the evidence is offered to prove consent, its probative value rests on the nature of the complainant's specific mindset towards the accused rather than on her general unchaste character.'
In my opinion there will be some cases where evidence of previous consensual intercourse between the complainant and the defendant would be clearly relevant, but there will also be cases where such evidence would not be relevant. Where there has been a recent close and affectionate relationship between the complainant and the defendant it is probable that the evidence will be relevant, not to advance the bare assertion that because she consented in the past she consented on the occasion in question, but for the reason given by Professor Galvin, which is that evidence of such a relationship will show the complainant's specific mindset towards the defendant, namely her affection for him. In relation to this point Professor Galvin, at p.786, cites the opinion of Dean Wigmore that such evidence shows: 'an emotion towards the particular defendant tending to allow him to repeat the liberty.' But where there had only been some isolated acts

---

[134] [2002] 1 A.C. 45, at [31].
[135] [2002] 1 A.C. 45, at [151].
[136] Professor Harriet Galvin, *Shielding Rape Victims in the State and Federal Courts: A Proposal for the Second Decade* (1986) 70 Minn. L. Rev. 763.

of intercourse, even if fairly recently, without the background of an affectionate relationship, it is probable that the evidence will not be relevant. But beyond stating that the test is that of relevance, I think that it is not possible to state with precision where the dividing line is to be drawn—it will depend on the facts of the individual case as assessed by the trial judge."

Even if there was no affectionate relationship, if there was a history of physical attraction, presumably the same approach would apply.

The majority of the House of Lords agreed the potential relevance of such **26.109** evidence, but left it for the trial judge to determine the issue on the specific facts of the case, applying the test set out in Lord Steyn's speech (set out in para.26.99, above). Lord Clyde stated that he was not able to affirm that the evidence in question may not fall within the scope of s.41(3)(c). It would depend upon a careful assessment by the trial judge of the presence or absence of similarity beyond coincidence between the previous and critical occasions.[137] The consensus of the speeches was that evidence of previous sexual history between the defendant and the complainant may be relevant to the issue of consent. In each case it will be necessary to consider the circumstances, including the nature of the relationship and its closeness in time to the episode in issue.[138]

Sexual behaviour between the complainant and the defendant after the **26.110** date of the allegation may also be relevant, and is now potentially admissible under s.41(3)(c). As Mantell LJ stated in *R. v R*[139]:

"Evidence of complaint and of distress following rape is admissible to prove consistency in the complainant's conduct. Equally, evidence of lack of distress and a failure to complain when a reasonable opportunity to do so arises is admissible as conduct which may not be consistent with the allegation of rape. Evidence that the complainant was friendly with the appellant after the alleged rape and was content to spend time in his company must be relevant for the same reason.

This reasoning must equally apply to an act of consensual intercourse. It is but an extreme example of such evidence. A reasonable jury could take the view that it was highly unlikely that a girl or woman who had been raped in such circumstances as alleged here, would volunteer to have sexual intercourse with him subsequently."

In the Australian case of *Bannister*,[140] it had been alleged that the **26.111** complainant had made a statement to the accused at the surf club some six days after some of the offences charged were alleged to have taken place. The

[137] [2002] 1 A.C. 45, at 137.
[138] cf. *Dickson* [1994] 1 S.C.R. 153 and *Crosby* [1995] 2 S.C.R. 912, decisions of the Supreme Court of Canada that evidence of a complainant's previous sexual history with the accused is not admissible without some further compelling justification. See also *Darrach* (1998) 38 O.R. (3d) 1, Ont. CA. cf. *R. v M(M)* in the Ontario Superior Court of Justice, where Langdon J stated: "To say that the sexual character of a prior intimate relationship between the accused and the complainant is not relevant to the issue of consent is to invite the court to take judicial notice that all complainants are so promiscuous that it is equally likely that they will agree to sexual activity with a perfect stranger as with their intimate partners."
[139] [2003] EWCA Crim 2754, at [20].
[140] (1993) 10 W.A.R. 484; approved in *Bull v The Queen* [2000] H.C.A. 24, May 11, 2000.

complainant allegedly said to the accused: "Any hope?" This was accepted as referring to a hope of sexual activity with the accused. Kennedy J stated:

> "In my view, the evidence sought to be called went beyond a mere matter of credibility and went to the issue of whether the events of which the complainant gave evidence had occurred. It would have raised for the jury, if they accepted the evidence for the defence, the unlikelihood that the complainant, having suffered, would sexually proposition the appellant six days later."

Subsequent decisions in respect of sexual behaviour with the defendant

26.112   It is instructive to consider the approach the courts have adopted to the admission of evidence of sexual behaviour with the defendant in the years following the House of Lords' decision in *R. v A (No.2)*. In *Ogbodo*[141] the Court of Appeal held that the trial judge had correctly distinguished between the admissibility of alleged previous sexual behaviour of the complainant with the applicant and her alleged previous sexual behaviour with third parties. The prosecution case was that the applicant lured the complainant to a flat on the false pretence of there being some emergency but with the real purpose of committing rape. Once at the flat, he locked her in and detained her against her will. The applicant held a knife to her throat and threatened to burn her eyes out with a burning cigarette if she did not comply. He then forcibly chewed her nipples and anally raped her twice. He also orally raped her after he had anally raped her.

26.113   The defence case was that all the sexual activity was consensual. The parties had met that day for the purpose of having sex. They had previously engaged in sex on over 30 occasions and had known each other for a number of years. The judge allowed the applicant's counsel to explore the question of previous sexual relations between the complainant and the applicant, but refused an application in relation to allegations about the complainant's sexual behaviour with other persons. There was no suggestion that anyone other than the applicant and the complainant was present at the time of the incident that the jury had to consider. Previous group sex was, on the face of it, irrelevant. The Court of Appeal held that the judge had not unduly limited the complainant's cross-examination.

26.114   It is not to be thought that, merely because there has been a previous sexual relationship between the complainant and the defendant, the date of the last act of sexual intercourse between them is necessarily admissible. In *R. v S*[142] the appellant had been convicted of a single count of rape of his wife. It was alleged that on December 15, 2008, he had gone to his wife's flat and committed a particularly violent rape. It was argued on appeal that the trial judge had wrongly refused leave under s.41 to cross-examine the complainant about consensual sex with the appellant that had occurred just days before the alleged rape, on December 6, 2008. It was conceded by the appellant's

[141] [2011] EWCA Crim 564.
[142] [2010] EWCA Crim 1579.

counsel that this evidence did not fall within the provisions of s.41(3)(c) if literally interpreted. However, it was argued that the judge should have adopted the permissive construction of the section which the House of Lords approved in the speech of Lord Steyn in *R v A (No.2)*, i.e. he should have admitted the evidence on the basis that it was so relevant to the issue of consent that to exclude it would endanger the fairness of the trial.[143] It was submitted that, without the knowledge that the complainant and appellant had sexual intercourse together on December 6, the jury may have been under the mistaken impression that there had been no sexual intercourse for a period of six months during which the complainant said in interview she had been very unhappy.

In the Court of Appeal's view it was perfectly clear to the jury that **26.115** unhappiness had caused the separation but that in November there had been a resumption of normal co-habitation between husband and wife. It was also clear that the complainant was describing a sexually active relationship which was, nevertheless, a source of unhappiness for her. Furthermore there was no logical connection between the last act of consensual intercourse between husband and wife and the event of the alleged rape.

As for the responsibility of trial judges, in accordance with the speech of **26.116** Lord Steyn in *R. v A (No.2)*, to admit evidence that is so relevant to the issue of consent that to exclude it would endanger the fairness of the trial, the judgment of fairness is fact-sensitive and will depend upon the detail of the issues which arise in the case. In the view of the Court of Appeal in *R. v S*, it was of no particular moment in the jury's assessment of the issue of consent in that case whether the last act of intercourse occurred on December 6 or a few days or a week or more earlier. What mattered to the jury was the nature of the relationship after December 7 when, it was common ground, the deterioration became terminal. The question was whether the admitted contact between the parties can only have confirmed to the appellant that the complainant meant what she said, and clearly the jury found that she did.

THE FOURTH GATEWAY—SECTION 41(5)—THE REBUTTAL GATEWAY

Section 41(5) of the 1999 Act provides: **26.117**

"This subsection applies if the evidence or question—
(a) relates to any evidence adduced by the prosecution about any sexual behaviour of the complainant; and
(b) in the opinion of the court, would go no further than is necessary to enable the evidence adduced by the prosecution to be rebutted or explained by or on behalf of the accused."

For discussion of rebuttal evidence arising from postings on social networking sites, see paras 26.34 and following, above.

---

[143] [2002] 1 A.C. 45, at [46].

26.118   This provision is subject to s.41(6), so that the evidence or questioning must relate to a specific instance or instances of sexual behaviour. However, it is not restricted by the credibility restriction set out in s.41(4).[144] A classic example of the subsection in operation is *R. v F*,[145] where the complainant's evidence was that as a consequence of an alleged rape she had become pregnant, and so evidence of medical records showing that she had informed her general practitioner that she thought she was pregnant as a result of a condom accident with her boyfriend would have been admissible under s.41(5). It is important to note that s.41(5)(b) provides that the questioning by the defence must "go no further than is necessary to enable the evidence adduced by the prosecution to be rebutted or explained". This enables the judge to restrict the ambit of such evidence if elements are wholly unnecessary for the purposes of rebuttal or explanation. However, even if the proposed questioning does fall within s.41(5), the judge still has to consider the court's overriding duty under s.41(2)(b) and should refuse leave if not satisfied that such a refusal would have the result of rendering unsafe a conclusion of the jury. See further para.26.127, below.

"Evidence adduced by the prosecution"

26.119   By restricting rebuttal to "evidence adduced by the prosecution", the s.41(5) gateway is arguably narrower than similar provisions in other jurisdictions, which allow the defence to rebut inferences that may reasonably be drawn from the way in which the prosecution case is presented or from the circumstances of the case.[146]

26.120   In *Hamadi*,[147] the Court of Appeal took a restrictive view of the expression "adduced by the prosecution". The expression naturally refers in this context to evidence placed before the jury by prosecution witnesses in the course of their evidence-in-chief and by other witnesses in the course of cross-examination by prosecuting counsel. It does not naturally extend to evidence obtained from prosecution witnesses by the defence in the course of cross-examination. However, the Court did acknowledge that in order to ensure a fair trial there may be cases in which the accused ought to be allowed to call evidence to explain or rebut something said by a prosecution witness in cross-examination about the complainant's sexual behaviour, where it was not deliberately elicited by defence counsel and was potentially damaging to the accused's case. The Court was therefore accepting that s.41(5) would have to be read in a broader sense than its language might otherwise suggest in order to accommodate such cases. However, even on this more liberal interpretation of s.41(5), the Court was unable to accept that what was said by the

---

[144] See paras 26.139 and following, below.
[145] [2008] EWCA Crim 2859.
[146] cf. Neil Kibble, *The Sexual History Provisions: Charting a course between inflexible legislative rules and wholly untrammelled judicial discretion?* [2000] Crim. L.R. 274, at p.278.
[147] [2007] EWCA Crim 3048.

complainant under cross-examination in that case was evidence adduced by the prosecution which would trigger the rebuttal provisions.

The appellant in *Hamadi* was convicted of rape. The complainant had   **26.121** maintained that she was in a steady relationship with her boyfriend, Lee, at the relevant time and had stopped kissing the appellant because "that was not what she wanted". The trial judge rejected a defence application to adduce evidence from another man, "D", of a sexual relationship with the complainant approximately two months before the incident, during the time she was living with Lee. The application arose out of the following exchange between the complainant and counsel for the appellant in the course of cross-examination:

> "Q: What do you mean, realised that was not what you wanted?
> A: Well, I don't want sex with a stranger. I have got a—I had a boy—I've got a boy—well, I finished him, but I know that me and Lee would a'getten back together straight way. I loved him, he loved him [sic], we were starting a family.
> . . .
> Q: Because of that?
> A: Well, I wouldn't go with any stranger.
> Q: Or anybody, apart from Lee?
> A: Or anybody—anybody at all."

At trial the defence sought leave to adduce evidence from D to rebut the   **26.122** complainant's assertion that she would not have had sexual intercourse with anyone else whilst she was in a steady relationship with Lee. The judge rejected that application on the grounds that the evidence had no probative value and allowing it in would drive a coach and horses through the provisions of s.41. On appeal, it was submitted that the complainant's assertion in cross-examination that she would not have had sexual intercourse with anyone other than Lee came within the terms of s.41(5), and D's evidence ought to have been admitted because without it the jury would have been misled about the complainant's sexual inclinations. Not only did the Court of Appeal take the view that the complainant's assertion was not "adduced by the prosecution", but it also stated that the case could not be brought within the scope of s.41(2)(b). The evidence tended to show that the complainant had a promiscuous nature among quite a wide circle of friends, but there was nothing in it to suggest that she was prepared to pick up strangers from the street as alleged by the defence.

Professor Ormerod has pointed out[148] that the complainant in *Hamadi*   **26.123** said twice that she did not want sex with a stranger in answer to questions from the defence. The evidence from D that the defence sought to admit in rebuttal would not in fact rebut the complainant's evidence on this point, because D was not a stranger to the complainant when they had a relationship. It was only when defence counsel elicited the answer "Or

---

[148] Lecture Notes, *Recent Developments on s.41*, Judicial Studies Board Serious Sexual Offences Seminar 2010, July 2010, p.42.

anybody, apart from Lee" that the complainant finally agreed to a description of her state of mind which rendered her susceptible to rebuttal evidence from D. Professor Ormerod contrasts this with the complainant who says without repeated prompting that she was not prepared to have sex with anyone other than her boyfriend. This assertion makes it less likely that she consented to sex with the defendant. It follows that in those circumstances the rebuttal evidence should be admitted. It would be unfair to the defendant to refuse to allow evidence to rebut a statement which is probative of non-consent.

26.124   Section 41(5) received some consideration by the House of Lords in *R. v A (No.2)*. The prosecution had suggested that to enable the defence to adduce truly relevant evidence and avoid the straitjacket of s.41, the prosecution could lead evidence which would in turn enable the defence to lead evidence of sexual evidence in rebuttal. Lord Steyn[149] felt that this was not a coherent or satisfactory solution. It depended on the goodwill and co-operation of the prosecutor. Since the defendant has the right in a criminal trial to offer a full and complete defence, he rejected the suggested solution.

26.125   Nevertheless, it will often be in the hands of the prosecution (which is not subject to the s.41 prohibition) to decide whether to lead evidence which may open the rebuttal gateway. In sexual cases, prosecution evidence of the complainant's background and characteristics does not necessarily offend the rule against oath-helping. For instance, where consent is in issue, the prosecution is entitled under the common law to adduce evidence about the lack of previous sexual experience of a complainant, and about her attitudes and religious beliefs that intercourse before marriage is wrong. Such evidence is capable of being relevant to the issue of consent and therefore admissible even though it may bolster the complainant's credibility.[150] In *Amado-Taylor*[151] it was held that s.41 did not affect the admissibility of such evidence. In enacting the section, Parliament appears to have proceeded on the basis that the prosecution could adduce such evidence by providing in s.41(5)(a) that, if the prosecution did so, the defence could cross-examine on it and adduce evidence to contradict it. In *Tobin*[152] it was held that very limited evidence from the complainant's mother that she never had any problems with the complainant, who had done really well at school, got on well with her brothers and sisters, was very polite and quiet and had been brought up to respect people, did not render the trial unfair. Similarly, in a number of cases it has been accepted that the prosecution may adduce evidence that the complainant had been a virgin before the act of intercourse

---

[149] [2002] 1 A.C. 45, at [41].

[150] Colin Tapper, *Cross and Tapper on Evidence*, 12th edn (Oxford: Oxford University Press, 2010), at p.330: " . . . rape is rare in being a crime where the state of mind of the complainant is important; in evidential terms her disposition may be relevant to the question of whether or not she consented."

[151] [2001] EWCA Crim 1898.

[152] [2003] Crim. L.R. 408.

in question because it is relevant to the issue of consent.[153] Clearly, if the prosecution do call such evidence, the defence may obtain leave to rebut under s.41(5)(a).[154]

In his commentary on *Beedall*,[155] Neil Kibble has raised the issue of whether in a same-sex rape, the prosecution should be allowed to anticipate or respond to suggestions, express or implied, that the complainant is a homosexual or prepared to engage in homosexual activity by calling evidence that the complainant would never have engaged in such activity. Following the approach adopted in *Amado-Taylor*,[156] such evidence would appear to be admissible. Once admitted, the evidence would open the rebuttal gateway.[157]   **26.126**

THE COURT'S OVERRIDING DUTY UNDER SECTION 41(2)

Section 41(2)(b) of the 1999 Act requires the court to be satisfied: **26.127**

> "(b)   that a refusal of leave might have the result of rendering unsafe a conclusion of the jury or (as the case may be) the court on any relevant issue in the case."

Even if one of the four gateways is opened, because the judge is satisfied that "subsection (3) or (5) applies",[158] the defence still have to satisfy the judge that a refusal of leave might have the effect of rendering unsafe a conclusion on a relevant issue in the case. Evidence of marginal relevance, even if technically capable of passing through a gateway, will not surmount this hurdle. The evidence must be so significant that its exclusion would render the jury's conclusion unsafe. The House of Lords in *R. v A (No.2)* recognised that this overriding duty would filter out cases where the evidence was not truly probative.[159] For this purpose, "relevant issue in the case" in

---

[153] *R. v SMS* [1992] Crim. L.R. 310; *Redguard* [1991] Crim. L.R. 213. See also the Australian case of *Byczko* [1997] 16 S.A.S.R. 506, where Hogarth J took the view that such evidence was relevant to the likelihood of consent to having intercourse with a stranger.

[154] In *Singh (Gulab)* [2003] EWCA Crim 485 it was held that on a retrial, the rebuttal provision is not triggered by evidence given at an earlier trial that the complainant was a virgin at the time of the alleged rape. In those circumstances, evidence that the claim as to virginity in the first trial was a lie fell foul of s.41(4). cf. *McKendrick* [2004] EWCA Crim 1393, where the defence did not make an application under s.41(5) at trial.

[155] [2007] EWCA Crim 23, discussed in para.26.147, below.

[156] [2000] 2 Cr. App. R. 189.

[157] See Kramer, *When men are victims: applying rape shield laws to male same-sex rape* (1998) 73 N.Y.U.L. Rev. 293, where it is argued that the prosecution should not be allowed to use past sexual history or orientation evidence to show absence of consent. Kramer claims that for the prosecution to lead such evidence is unfair to the defendant and may open the door to "humiliating testimony about the victim" being introduced in rebuttal. See the American case of *Murphy* (1996) 919 P.2d, where the prosecution's emphasis on the complainant having been married and having children to show that he would not consent to same-sex activity led to the introduction of expert evidence to the effect that married men may nevertheless be homosexual. Whilst such evidence would not be admissible in this jurisdiction, issues in respect of a complainant's family life may become live.

[158] s.41(2)(a).

[159] [2002] 1 A.C. 45, at [71], per Lord Hope.

s.41(2)(b) is to be read in accordance with the definition of "relevant issue" in s.42(1)(a), i.e. "any issue falling to be proved by the prosecution or defence in the trial of the accused".

26.128   The application of the provision is well illustrated by *R. v DB*,[160] in which the appellant was convicted at a retrial of six counts of rape and two counts of assault by penetration of his daughter over a period of over a year when she was aged 13 or 14. At trial the appellant categorically denied all the sexual abuse offences.

26.129   The complainant had undergone two abortions. She said that the appellant was the "father" of the terminated pregnancies. She ran away on August 22 alleging she had been raped on that day, and she was taken into police protection five days later. She was examined medically on August 27 and at the time she said that she had only had intercourse with her father. She repeated this in her ABE interview the following day; indeed, she said that, but for her father, she still would have been a virgin. In fact, endocervical swabs identified the presence of male DNA which was not the appellant's. The medical assessment was that it would have been deposited some three or four days before the examination. It was found to belong to a 41-year-old Asian man referred to by the court as X.

26.130   Later, the complainant admitted that she had had intercourse with her boyfriend on three occasions when her father was away on holiday. This was before the last occasion on which she was raped. Notwithstanding the evidence about the DNA, she denied ever having intercourse with the Asian male X.

26.131   The prosecution conceded that the appellant ought to be allowed to cross-examine the complainant with respect to her boyfriend. This was because it was evidence of sexual intercourse occurring during the period of the abortions and the complainant had been secretive about the relationship, so the prosecution accepted it was potentially relevant to the appellant's contention that he was not the father.

26.132   However, the trial judge rejected an application under s.41 in relation to X. The basis of the application was that the appellant had lied about her relationship with X. It was submitted that this was potentially relevant to the question whether she was lying about having intercourse with her father, and also the evidence provided a potential motive for her leaving home. She might have wanted to leave home in order to have a sexual relationship with X rather than, as claimed, to escape the clutches of a father who had just raped her. Section 41(4) was not engaged as the primary reason for seeking to adduce the evidence was to demonstrate her motive in leaving the house.

26.133   The judge expressly adopted the prosecution's reasoning. The evidence in respect of X concerned sexual activity which had occurred outside the relevant period when the alleged sexual involvement with the appellant had occurred. It cast no light on what might have happened during that period;

[160] [2012] EWCA Crim 1235.

it was wholly collateral to any issue in the case. The aim was to show that the complainant had lied about not having had a relationship with anyone other than her father. That went to credit and was outlawed by s.41(4). In any event, there was already evidence before the jury that she had lied about having sex only with her father, because she had admitted in evidence having sex with her boyfriend. It followed that the refusal would not render unsafe a conclusion of the jury on any relevant issue in the case.

The Court of Appeal accepted that, to the extent that the existence of a   **26.134** relationship with X might have provided a motive for the complainant to leave home other than the reason she gave, it would not be an entirely collateral issue because of its relevance to the last allegation of rape. However, even in relation to that count, the judge had been right for a number of reasons to reject the application in relation to X.

First, s.42(1)(a) defines a "relevant issue in the case" as "any issue falling   **26.135** to be proved by the prosecution or defence in the trial of the accused". It was highly questionable whether an issue of motive can be said to constitute an issue in the case as so defined. Elias LJ accepted that the concept of "an issue in the case" will sometimes have to be stretched in order to ensure that a trial is art.6 compliant.[161] Too rigid a construction of the subsection might, in some cases, exclude evidence of motive which it would be unfair to exclude. However, the Court did not believe this was such a case. Even if it were the case that the complainant had wanted to leave home in order to continue her relationship with X, that did not explain why she would make sexual abuse allegations against her father. The allegations of physical abuse established at the first trial would have been sufficient to provide cover for her actions. It was pure speculation to suppose she would need to have fabricated such an extravagant claim in order to create a false reason to leave the house.

Secondly, s.41(2)(b) did not begin to be satisfied in this case. The Court of   **26.136** Appeal could not see how the failure to leave to the jury the possibility of this particular motive could have led them to reach an unsafe conclusion on any relevant issue in the case. In any event, a range of other possible explanations, unconnected with any alleged rape, as to why the complainant wanted to leave the house that morning had been deployed in evidence. Furthermore, given the weakness and essentially wholly peripheral nature of this allegation, the only reason left for wanting to adduce this evidence would be to challenge the credit of the complainant, and that would be unambiguously barred by s.41(4).

The Court also rejected the submission that the identity of X should have   **26.137** been revealed, since then he could have been interviewed and he may have admitted to a longstanding relationship with the complainant, which could have explained how it was that she became pregnant. The Court said that this submission faced insurmountable practical difficulties and was based on

---

[161] Citing (at [45]) the observations of Keene LJ in *R. v RT, R. v MH* [2001] EWCA Crim 1877, for which see paras 26.153 and following, below.

wholly speculative contentions. Further, there was no evidence to suggest that the relationship with X had existed for that lengthy period of time.

26.138   Finally, even if, at the time of an unsuccessful application, the evidence was capable of passing through a gateway and at that time a refusal of leave might have had the result of rendering the jury's conclusion unsafe, it does not follow that the Court of Appeal will allow an appeal if it considers in the light of all the evidence that the conviction was in fact safe.[162]

THE TWO RESTRICTIONS

The credibility restriction—section 41(4)

26.139 Section 41(4) provides:

> "For the purposes of subsection (3) no evidence or question shall be regarded as relating to a relevant issue in the case if it appears to the court to be reasonable to assume that the purpose (or main purpose) for which it would be adduced or asked is to establish or elicit material for impugning the credibility of the complainant as a witness."

26.140   This further restriction is designed both to protect the complainant from humiliating and irrelevant cross-examination and to prevent the impermissible line of reasoning known as the second of the twin myths, "that unchaste women are less worthy of belief".[163] It is not permissible to adduce evidence on the basis of ostensible relevance to consent when the real purpose is to discredit the complainant.[164] This restriction does not apply to rebuttal evidence admitted under s.41(5). However well-intentioned the subsection, problems arise because many serious sex cases turn on the credibility of the complainant and the defendant. As the Court of Appeal said in *Funderburk*,[165] "where the disputed issue is a sexual one between two persons in private the difference between questions going to credit and questions going to the issue is reduced to vanishing point".

26.141   Lord Clyde expressed the same sentiment in *R. v A (No.2)*[166] when considering s.41(4):

> "It seems to me that [subsection (4)] will require a very fine analysis in its practical application. Issues of consent and issues of credibility may well run so close to each other as almost to coincide. A very sharp knife may be required to separate what may be admitted from what may not."

26.142   Even if the defence can establish that the evidence is relevant to an issue in the case, the hurdle represented by s.41(4) still has to be surmounted. The

---

[162] *Rooney* [2001] EWCA Crim 2844.
[163] See *Seaboyer* (1991) 83 D.L.R. (4th) 193, p.537.
[164] For a graphic example of where a trial judge felt that the real purpose of the evidence was to discredit the complainant, see *Mukadi* [2004] Crim. L.R. 373, discussed in para.26.30, above. The Court of Appeal disagreed and allowed the appeal.
[165] (1990) 90 Cr. App. R. 467. See also *R. v T* [2002] 1 W.L.R. 632 at 638.
[166] [2003] Crim. L.R. 4908.

potential height of the hurdle can be illustrated in *Singh (Gulab)*,[167] where the Court of Appeal held that questions at a retrial designed to show that the complainant had lied on oath at the first trial about being a virgin at the time of the alleged rape had rightly been excluded. The only purpose of the cross-examination would have been to impugn the credibility of the complainant as a witness and this is impermissible, notwithstanding the likely impact on a jury of a lie on oath. In *Darnell*,[168] evidence of a third party's semen on the complainant's knickers was held to fall foul of s.41(4).[169] The defendant was convicted of counts arising from an allegation of a pattern of escalating physical assaults and abuse including rape and indecent assault. The original allegation of false imprisonment had not been pursued and the question whether or not the complainant had had intercourse with someone else over the nine-day period of the offences was irrelevant to an issue in the case and thus inevitably failed the test under s.41(4). For the tension between evidence of the complainant's bias/motive to fabricate and this subsection, see para.26.70, above.[170]

It is not, however, fatal to an application for leave that one purpose of the questions may be to impugn the credibility of the complainant, provided it is not the sole or main purpose. In *Martin*[171] the appellant was convicted of indecent assault in respect of an act of forced oral sex. His defence was that he was elsewhere at the time and the complainant had fabricated the incident because he had rejected her advances two days before, after she had performed an act of oral sex upon him. The trial judge allowed cross-examination in respect of the alleged rejection of sexual advances but refused to permit any reference to the oral sex before the rejection. The Court of Appeal considered that whilst one purpose of the proposed questions was to impugn the credibility of the complainant, another was to strengthen the defence case. Arguably the rejection could have been said to be more hurtful if she had performed an act of oral sex upon him and then been rejected. The Court clearly considered that the evidence related to a relevant issue in the case and the issue was an issue which was not an issue of consent, namely that the complainant was biased against the appellant or had a motive to fabricate the evidence, and so the first gateway (s.41(3)(a)) was entered.[172] Crane J stated:[173]

26.143

[167] [2003] EWCA Crim 485. See also commentary in *Criminal Law Week*, Issue 16, 2003, p.4. Counsel for the appellant, for undisclosed reasons, did not feel it appropriate to argue that the questions were not "about sexual behaviour".

[168] [2002] EWCA Crim 176.

[169] And probably s.41(6). Nor was the evidence relevant to an issue within the meaning of s.42(1)(a).

[170] And see in particular *Mokrecovas* [2002] 1 Cr. App. R. 20, but note the judgment of Keene LJ in *R. v RT, R. v MH* [2001] EWCA Crim 1877, at [29].

[171] [2004] EWCA Crim 916, cited in *R. v F* [2005] EWCA Crim 493.

[172] See *R. v A (No.2)* [2002] 1 A.C. 45, at [79] per Lord Hope.

[173] [2004] EWCA Crim 916, at [37]–[38].

"We conclude that, on ordinary principles of interpretation, it was one purpose but not 'the purpose' or the 'main purpose' of the questions to impugn the credibility of the complainant."

He added:

"Had we not reached that conclusion, it would have been necessary to consider whether the provisions of subsection (4) should be read down to ensure a fair trial. In our judgment, that might have been done by interpreting the word 'impugned' as implying the initiation of an attack on the appellant's credibility rather than including any questions or evidence going to the issue of the complainant's credibility. It is not in fact necessary to rely on a reading down of subsection (4)."

The "specific instance" restriction—section 41(6)

26.144   Section 41(6) provides:

"For the purposes of subsections (3) and (5) the evidence or question must relate to a specific instance (or specific instances) of alleged sexual behaviour on the part of the complainant (and accordingly nothing in those subsections is capable of applying in relation to the evidence or question to the extent that it does not so relate)."

26.145   Since the evidence or questioning must relate to a specific instance or instances of sexual behaviour, evidence of general reputation is excluded.[174] This provision outlaws once and for all the common law rule that a woman's previous sexual experiences might be admissible if she was a prostitute or of notoriously immoral character. If the complainant is a prostitute, then quite apart from the problem of opening one of the gateways, evidence of specific instances of prostitution (such as convictions for soliciting) will be necessary to surmount this hurdle.[175]

Evidence as to sexual orientation and/or sexual preference

26.146   It is submitted that evidence of sexual orientation is suggestive of sexual activity and should be regarded as subject to the s.41 restrictions. Its compass is wider than evidence of sexual behaviour because it may include marital status and paternity. Evidence of preference for particular sexual practices may well flout s.41(6). Even if there is a specific instance, it will be excluded by the general s.41 regime unless it is of such an unusual nature that it cannot reasonably be explained away as a coincidence so as to come within s.41(1)(c). It follows that in a rape case, where the defence case was that the

---

[174] cf. *Bogie* [1992] Crim. L.R. 301; *Howes* [1996] 2 Cr. App. R. 490.

[175] But see *White* [2004] EWCA Crim 946, where the Court of Appeal stated that s.41(6) only possesses intellectual coherence if it is taken to require that there must be something about the circumstances of a specific episode of alleged sexual conduct by a complainant which has potential probative force. Arguably, this interpretation gives s.41(6) attributes that belong to other subsections. See also commentary on *White* in *Criminal Law Week*, Issue 11, March 15, 2004.

complainant consented to oral sex with the defendant because she enjoyed it whilst her boyfriend did not, an application to question the complainant about this sexual preference is likely to fall foul of s.41(6). Furthermore, even if there was a specific instance, s.41(3)(c) would not be engaged as oral sex cannot be regarded as sufficiently unusual.

Evidence of sexual orientation in same-sex cases

Normally the evidence of a complainant's sexual orientation is neutral and does not provide a proper basis for cross-examination save where the rebuttal provisions are triggered by the prosecution adducing evidence of sexual orientation to bolster its case on absence of consent (see paras 26.125 and following, above). There is no difference in substance between questioning a female complainant about her suggested sexual habits, promiscuity or frequency of casual sexual engagement, and questioning a male about his suggested homosexuality and casual homosexual encounters, since both cases are predicated on the basis that previous consent is evidence supporting present consent. This would apply equally to evidence of previous sexual partners or habitual association with places where homosexual encounters take place. In *Beedall*[176] the appellant had been convicted of homosexual rape and associated sexual assaults. At trial, defence counsel had been refused leave to ask the complainant whether he was homosexual. On appeal, the submission was renewed based on medical findings that following the rape the complainant did not appear to have suffered any anal trauma and that his anus was unusually lax, capacious and patulous, although the report made it clear that this did not necessarily mean that the complainant had engaged in previous homosexual activity. The Court of Appeal dismissed the appeal, holding that the question was precluded by s.41(6) unless *R. v A (No.2)* applied. The Court stated that the inconclusive medical evidence, had it been admissible, would have entitled the jury to conclude that the complainant had previous homosexual experience. If he had no interest in men, then, on the face of it, he would have been less likely to have consented. Conversely, if he did have a sexual interest in men, it is possible to argue that he was more likely to have consented, although the issue of whether he had actually consented on the occasion in question remained open. However, the purpose of the 1999 Act was to eliminate the perpetuation of that myth, as well as the myth that a promiscuous complainant is less credible. It followed that the evidence as to sexual orientation was designed to provide a foundation for an illegitimate line of reasoning. If it is possible for there to be a fair trial without such evidence in the case of an allegedly promiscuous female complainant, it has to be equally possible for there to be a fair trial in relation to a homosexual male complainant. If the Court had held that the evidence of sexual orientation was relevant and admissible, it would have led

26.147

---

[176] [2007] EWCA Crim 23.

to the argument that a complainant's bisexuality or homosexuality was a proper basis for arguing that he was more likely to be willing to engage in casual sex with another man.

26.148   Neil Kibble points out[177] that whilst the decision in *Beedall* broadly reflects the position in the USA,[178] academic literature contains arguments to the contrary. He rephrases the Court's question, whether there is a sufficient distinction between male and female complainants to warrant a different outcome, as follows: "Is there a difference in substance between questions of a female complainant about her sexuality in an opposite-sex rape and questions of a male complainant about his sexuality in a same sex rape?" He notes that the question of heterosexuality is not usually engaged in opposite-sex rape. In most cases there will be an assumption that the complainant is heterosexual, whereas in same-sex rape, the question of sexual orientation is engaged. Kibble suggests that it is less than clear that the answer to his rephrased question should be a resounding "No", as it was to the Court's actual question.

Alternative explanation for penetration when no evidence as to specific instance

26.149   Where on a charge of rape the defence is denial of penetration but there is medical evidence to show penetration of the vagina of the complainant by an object the size of a penis, s.41(6) may restrict the extent to which an alternative explanation for the medical evidence can be properly explored by the defence. On the face of the legislation, where a defendant has no evidence beyond a bare denial, he would not be permitted to allege an alternative sexual experience to explain the medical evidence, albeit that is a logical extension of his case. There would be no evidence of "a specific instance" upon which to found an application for leave. It remains to be seen whether in these circumstances the courts can be persuaded to adopt a "purposive" construction of s.41(6), so as to restrict its ambit on the basis that the subsection is designed to prevent general reputation evidence and general fishing expeditions.[179] It is arguable that the defendant should at least be allowed to put his case to the complainant, namely to ask if the medical evidence could be explained by a sexual experience with another person, even though he does not have the biographical details to support it. Otherwise the defence are placed in a very difficult position, particularly in relation to young complainants. The jury will have no opportunity to hear the question

---

[177] Commentary at [1997] Crim. L R. 911.

[178] *Hackett* 365 NW 2d 120 (1984) and *Whaley* 1993 WL 167342.

[179] We are grateful to Neil Kibble for this point, which emerged from his discussions with judges when conducting his research into the operation of s.41 (see fn.217 and para.26.179, below).

and evaluate the answer.[180] Neil Kibble has argued[181] that s.41(6) should be read as outlawing questions or evidence as to reputation as well as fishing expeditions, but not the simple, single question as to whether the physical condition was brought about by sex with another.

No Residual Discretion

The s.41 regime gives the trial judge no residual discretion to admit otherwise   **26.150** excluded evidence. There is no "catch all" provision that allows the judge to admit evidence, or questioning, as to the complainant's previous sexual behaviour where the court is satisfied that it would be contrary to the interests of justice to exclude it. In relation to the issue of consent, relevance is confined to certain very specific categories of evidence. This could have led to the exclusion on a very arbitrary basis of truly relevant evidence in respect of previous sexual relationships between complainants and accused. As a result of *R. v A (No.2)*, and in particular Lord Steyn's test of admissibility referring to art.6 of the ECHR, s.41(3)(c) has become a far less narrow gateway. The House of Lords has given trial judges the scope to prevent unfair trials, principally in cases where the previous (or subsequent) sexual behaviour relates to the defendant as opposed to third parties.

Evidence that the Complainant has made False Complaints

If it is alleged by the defendant that the complainant has made previous false   **26.151** complaints of sexual behaviour, is questioning or evidence relating to this allegation caught by the general prohibition under s.41? It has been recognised from the time of implementation that s.41 is not engaged if a past complaint is truly false. Difficulties have arisen as to the extent that there must be evidence to demonstrate falsity.

The Explanatory Notes to the Act correctly state that false complaints are   **26.152** not caught by s.41 as they relate to untruthful conduct on prior occasions. If the complaint was false in that there was no sexual behaviour, no problem should arise. If the allegation of false complaint is established, such evidence

---

[180] Unless the prosecution ask the complainant whether she has had any other sexual experience which might explain the medical evidence. Clearly it is desirable that the complainant be asked this, as otherwise the medical evidence will not be evaluated in its proper context.

[181] In a lecture to the Judicial Studies Board Serious Sexual Offences Seminar in July 2007, Kibble criticised the Court of Appeal in *White* [2004] EWCA Crim 946 for adopting a very narrow reading of s.41(6). Section 41(6) is simply one of the hurdles that must be negotiated if evidence is to be allowed, and does not have an added requirement of potential probative force. He concludes that it is wrong to read that requirement into s.41(6), the purpose of which is to ensure that reputation evidence is no longer admissible and to put an end to fishing expeditions. See also Kibble, *Judicial perspectives on the operation of s.41, and the relevance and admissibility of prior sexual history evidence: Four scenarios* [2005] Crim. L.R. 190 at p.202 and following, from which it appears that the majority of judges would have allowed the one question in relation to sexual penetration by a third party, but not any further questions.

would be clearly relevant.[182] It would not simply go to credit but also to the issue as to whether there was a sexual assault at all.[183] But, what if the complainant denies that it was a false complaint? The defence will normally be bound by that answer,[184] and yet in some cases the damage to the complainant's reputation may already be done. What if the defence wish to adduce evidence of the complainant's previous consensual sexual behaviour in order to establish that there is a history of false complaints of non-consensual sexual assault? Furthermore, would such a line of evidence/cross-examination fall foul of s.41(4) in that its purpose would be to impugn the credibility of the complainant?

26.153   The Court of Appeal addressed some of these issues in the leading case of *R. v RT, R. v MH*,[185] in allowing the defendants' interlocutory appeals in two separate cases where trial judges had refused to allow certain lines of cross-examination of the complainants. The Court, being satisfied as to the proper evidential basis for the questions the defence sought to put, held that (i) a past fabricated allegation by a complainant was relevant, and (ii) a complainant's failure to mention the current allegation when being questioned about other sexual matters was also relevant. In relation to both these matters, the Court drew a distinction between questions "about any sexual behaviour" of the complainant and questions about statements about such behaviour.[186] Questions in the above two categories were about past statements[187] or a failure to complain, and *not* about any sexual behaviour of the complainant. Accordingly, the s.41 regime did not apply. This distinction would appear to apply even if the falsity of the complaint related to consent rather than the sexual behaviour itself, even though that would mean the jury would hear of previous sexual behaviour with the complainant.[188] However, even where such a line of questioning is clearly relevant, a judge, as a matter of trial management, is under a duty to curtail lengthy and/or inappropriate cross-examination. For instance, in *Ahdel Ali and Mubarek Ali*[189] the Court of Appeal held that where a complainant was in significant distress giving evidence and had accepted that she had made a false complaint of a sexual assault by her brother, it was open to the trial judge to restrict cross-examination on this issue, which she had admitted, and to direct that the

---

[182] *Nagrecha* [1997] 2 Cr. App. R. 401. *R. v V* [2006] EWCA Crim 1901.

[183] *Gibson* [1993] Crim. L.R. 453.

[184] *R. v S* [1992] Crim. L.R. 307.

[185] [2001] EWCA Crim 1877; [2002] 1 W.L.R. 633, followed in *Warren* [2005] EWCA Crim 659 where disclosure of a false allegation after the trial led to the conviction being quashed. See, however, *Michael S* [2016] EWCA Crim 242, where the complainant's failure to make an allegation against the applicant when making an allegation against another was held to be of no relevance to the issues the jury had to decide.

[186] See *Cox (David)* (1986) 84 Cr. App. R. 132.

[187] In *Guled Yusuf* [2010] EWCA Crim 359 the Court of Appeal observed that the courts in the earlier cases, such as *R. v RT, R v MH*, were not giving some formal meaning to "statement". An allegation made to police officers or a doctor would be sufficient.

[188] Professor Birch, *Untangling Sexual History Evidence: A Rejoinder to Professor Temkin* [2003] Crim. L.R. 370 at p.382.

[189] [2014] EWCA Crim 140 at [14]–[15].

details of the false complaint be reduced into writing and placed before the jury as admissions.

In *R. v RT, R. v MH*, the Court was concerned that there should not be   **26.154** abuses of the system. The defence, wishing to put questions about *any* alleged previous false complaints, must seek a ruling from the judge that s.41 does not exclude them. It would be professionally improper for those representing the defendant to put such questions in order to elicit evidence about the complainant's past behaviour as such under the guise of false complaints. The defence must have a proper evidential basis for asserting that any previous false complaint was (a) made and (b) untrue. If those requirements are not met, the questions would not be about lies but would be "about any sexual behaviour of the complainant" within the meaning of s.41(1). The trial judge is entitled to seek assurances from the defence that it has a proper basis for its assertions that the complaint was made and was untrue.[190]

Professor Birch[191] has called for previous false complaints to be brought   **26.155** within some form of regulatory regime, whilst Professor Temkin and colleagues in their report for the Home Office[192] recommended that only demonstrably false accusations should be admissible. In practice, it is commonplace for the defence to suggest that a complaint is false if the matter has not proceeded to trial, even though there may have been any number of reasons why the case was dropped, and the falsity of the complaint has not been established. In such circumstances, the jury may unfairly draw an adverse inference against the complainant. It is now clear that where there is no evidential basis for asserting that a previous complaint was false, it is not open to an advocate to ask the question in the hope of receiving an answer that it was true and to follow that up with a question as to why it had not led to charges being pursued. In *Abdelrahman*,[193] the Court of Appeal noted that s.41 is not just designed to "preserve the sexual reputation of the complainant, it is to protect her from having to relive previous experiences and ordeals in the witness box save to the extent permitted by the section."

---

[190] See Neil Kibble, *The Sexual History Provisions: Charting a course between inflexible legislative rules and wholly untrammelled judicial discretion?* [2000] Crim. L.R. 275. See also *Etches* [2004] EWCA Crim 1313; [2005] Crim. L.R. 227, for an example where the Court of Appeal held that the requirements set down in *R. v RT, R. v MH* had not been met. The defence wished to cross-examine two child complainants about a series of allegations of sexual abuse they had made against other people on the basis that it was wholly implausible that they had been abused by so many people. The Court pointed out that because none of the later allegations had been investigated, there was no evidence that they were untrue. If the cross-examination elicited assertions by the complainants that the subsequent complaints had been true, then the court would be faced with the dilemma of either letting those allegations stand unanswered, or descending into factual enquiries with no obvious limit and wholly collateral to the issue in the case.

[191] See *Untangling Sexual History Evidence: A Rejoinder to Professor Temkin* [2003] Crim. L.R. 370 at p.382.

[192] L. Kelly, J. Temkin, S. Griffiths, *Section 41: an evaluation of new legislation limiting sexual history evidence in rape trials* (Home Office, 2006), p.76.

[193] [2005] EWCA Crim 1367.

Proper evidential foundation, not strong factual foundation

26.156   The critical test for the defence to satisfy is that a reasonable inference can be drawn from the evidence that the previous complaint was false. This does not require every possible alternative inference to be eliminated. It is vital for the trial judge to ask himself whether the jury could be satisfied on the basis of the evidence that the previous allegation was untrue. In *R. v AM*,[194] the Court of Appeal observed that it was a striking feature of that case that the judge had not asked himself this critical question. The Court identified a number of features which, when taken together, could have led the jury to the conclusion that the previous complaint was false: (i) there was a four month interval between the date of the alleged rape and the date of reporting it to the police; (ii) aspects of the complaint were puzzling and caused the police to be sceptical; (iii) the complainant did not follow through with her complaint and would not allow a police investigation; and (iv) the complainant was only willing to give the police sufficient information to allow her to be re-housed. Her desire to be re-housed was her motivation for reporting. The Court held that the judge's refusal to allow cross-examination had deprived the defendant of a valuable line of reasoning. In particular, the Court explained that a proper evidential foundation is less than a strong factual foundation, but there must be some material from which it could be properly concluded that the previous complaint was false. It is a matter for the judge to decide on which side of the line any particular case falls. It is not a matter of discretion, rather it is a matter for the judge to evaluate on the basis of all the relevant material.

26.157   There may be a tendency to regard *R. v AM* as representing a change in the law. However, the Court of Appeal in *Evans (Stephen)*[195] doubted whether there is in reality any significant distinction between the tests formulated in *R. v RT, R. v MH* and *R. v AM*. It remains important that allegations of previous false complaint should be rigorously scrutinised. There must be material that, at the very least, is capable of founding an inference that the previous complaint was false. In its absence, a suggestion that the complaint was false is merely a matter of speculation.[196] An acquittal of the alleged offender in respect of a previous complaint does not, by itself, make that complaint false. All it shows is that the prosecution did not satisfy the criminal burden of proof.[197] Similarly, the fact that an earlier complaint has not been prosecuted does not provide a proper evidential basis for asserting that it was false, even if the police decided there was insufficient evidence to prosecute. The views of the CPS or the police are simply expressions of opinion and are irrelevant to the issue. Inconsistencies in a complainant's

---

[194] [2009] EWCA Crim 618.
[195] [2009] EWCA Crim 2668.
[196] [2009] EWCA Crim 2668.
[197] *R. v BD* [2007] EWCA Crim 4.

account in respect of an earlier complaint may be due to the trauma of the sexual assault.

The fact that there is evidence of more than one unpursued allegation does **26.158** not necessarily provide the appropriate evidential foundation. In *Salaam David All-Hilly*[198] the Court of Appeal rejected the appellant's contention that the circumstances revealed an inherent unlikelihood of unpursued allegations of sexual abuse against a number of men being true. Treacy LJ stated[199]:

> "The Courts should be ready to deploy a degree of understanding of those who have made sexual allegations. Failure to pursue the complaint does not of necessity show that it is untrue. A rather closer examination of the circumstances is required."

The Court then examined the individual matters separately and concluded that none of them began to provide a basis for an inference or conclusion of a false complaint. In those circumstances, there was no advantage to the appellant in seeking to rely on an accumulation of negative results. The fact that there was no instance which began to show falsity could not be converted into evidence of falsity by the fact that complaints had been raised more than once.

Care must be taken to ensure that the suggestion of falsity is not being **26.159** overstated. The facts of *Stephenson*[200] are instructive. The Court of Appeal concluded that the defence case statement, in which it had been suggested that the complainant had accused every adult male with whom she had had significant contact of abusing her, was "grossly overstated". The suggestion that the complainant had accused her natural father of abusing her was based on a single and subsequently retracted suggestion she made to a counsellor in the course of counselling, when she said, "I don't know, but my father may have abused me." In relation to an old man she was said to have accused of being a paedophile, the complainant had merely repeated gossip that she had heard the man was a paedophile, but she made no allegation against him whatsoever.

In *R. v AM*, the Court felt that in applying the test of whether the jury **26.160** could be satisfied on the basis of the evidence that the previous allegation was untrue, judges would not be assisted by an examination of the facts of other cases. The application of the test is fact sensitive, and the cases simply provide examples of the Court of Appeal's view as to which side of the boundary the evidence in a particular case fell. A recurring theme in the cases is the failure by a complainant to co-operate with the police. Clearly, there may be a multitude of reasons why a complainant would not wish to see through a complaint, and there is now a much greater understanding of the feelings of shame and embarrassment that may be suffered by a complainant that may

---

[198] [2014] EWCA Crim 1614.
[199] At [19].
[200] [2006] EWCA Crim 2325.

lead them not to pursue a complaint. Care should be taken not to make any unjustified assumptions merely from the fact of non-co-operation. Nevertheless, in some cases, when taken with other evidence, the Court of Appeal has held that a failure to co-operate has provided a sufficient evidential basis to found an allegation of falsity. In *Shino Garaxo,*[201] the Court of Appeal concluded that the material was such that the judge should have permitted cross-examination regarding two previous complaints:

> "It seems to us that the material was such that, depending upon answers given by Miss B, the jury could have been satisfied that these two previous allegations were untrue. The reference by Miss B, in the first complaint, to getting a crime reference number for the 'Social' seems to us at least capable of implying an improper motive for making the complaint . . . and the refusal to co-operate with the police, in our judgment, is also capable of providing or founding an inference that the complaint is untruthful, particularly when the complainant was, as the note of her complaint makes clear, under the influence of drugs at the time."

Garaxo[202] is very much a decision upon its own facts, and is not an authority for the proposition that an inference that a previous complaint was false can be drawn from the mere fact of withdrawal of the complaint. In *R. v V,*[203] the Court of Appeal, having been referred to *Garaxo,* expressed the view (obiter) that "a failure to co-operate may or may not justify a conclusion that an allegation is false, depending upon the circumstances".

26.161   Recent decisions illustrate the principles in operation. However, the courts continue to stress that the exercise for the judge is fact-sensitive and so is unlikely to be assisted to any great extent by other cases.[204] Judges need to evaluate the matter on the basis of all the relevant material. The ultimate question is whether the material is at the very least capable of leading to the conclusion that the previous complaint was false. Context is all-important and it should be borne in mind that reports as to what a complainant has said about other sexual experiences may reflect her then understanding of certain sexual terms. In *R. v L,*[205] the Court of Appeal pointed out that no one had asked the complainant for her interpretation of the term "rape", and, given the widening of the scope of "rape" under the Sexual Offences Act 2003, the opportunity for misapprehension was great.

26.162   First, the judge must consider the evidence in order to decide whether there was in fact an earlier complaint. For example, an analysis of the four alleged false complaints in *Lefeuvre*[206] revealed there had either been no complaint of sexual assault, or nothing to suggest it was a false complaint, or no complaint had been made. The Court of Appeal held that the judge had been correct to refuse to allow the defence to cross-examine the

---

[201] [2005] EWCA Crim 1170.
[202] Louise Ellison criticised the decision in her commentary in [2005] Crim. L.R. 883, on the basis that a safe inference could not be drawn from the fact of withdrawal.
[203] [2006] EWCA Crim 1901.
[204] *Salaam David All-Hilly* [2014] EWCA Crim 1614.
[205] [2015] EWCA Crim 741.
[206] [2011] EWCA Crim 1253.

complainant about each of these matters. In *Knight*,[207] where the appellant had been convicted of rape of his 16-year-old step-daughter, it was argued on appeal that he had wrongly been prevented from adducing at trial evidence that, when aged 14, the complainant had made a false allegation of rape against a boy at school, in a 999 call in which she stated that the boy "basically forced her to do it". She made a statement the following day saying that the sexual intercourse had been consensual and that she had gone along with it as she had not wished to hurt the boy's feelings. The trial judge accepted that the complainant had never made an allegation of rape, false or otherwise, and the evidence in relation to that incident was irrelevant. The Court of Appeal agreed.

Secondly, if there was an earlier false complaint, the court must then focus upon whether there is a proper evidential foundation for inferring or concluding that it was false, i.e. the jury could have been satisfied on the evidence that it was untrue (not that there was a strong factual foundation for such a conclusion). Suggestions of false complaint must not be used as a device to avoid the s.41 restrictions on evidence about sexual behaviour.[208]   **26.163**

In *R. v MC*,[209] it was held that where it is contended on appeal that there was a proper evidential foundation for the conclusion that a complaint was false, the appellant has to show that the judge reached a conclusion that was not reasonably open to him in his evaluation of materials relied upon in support of the s.41 application.   **26.164**

Overlap between section 41 and section 100 of the Criminal Justice Act 2003

There has been a tendency for the courts and counsel to overlook the fact that, if there is an application to cross-examine a complainant on the basis that she has made a previous (or subsequent) false complaint of a sexual offence, this engages s.100 of the Criminal Justice Act 2003, which regulates the admissibility of evidence of bad character against non-defendants. For the principles underpinning s.100, see Ch.20. An application to cross-examine the complainant on the basis that she has made a previous false complaint is likely to engage s.100 of the Criminal Justice Act 2003, in that the making of false complaints will amount to evidence of her bad character. *Guled Yusuf*[210] is a compelling example where there was held to be ample evidence of misconduct within the definition of s.98 of the Criminal Justice Act 2003, and so by implication of the falsity of a rape allegation made four years earlier. There was evidence that the complainant had set in motion a substantial investigation, had identified three suspects and then had declined to produce her knickers. She had not told the investigating officer that the   **26.165**

---

[207] [2013] EWCA Crim 2486.
[208] *R. v KJC* [2012] EWCA Crim 1669.
[209] [2012] EWCA Crim 213.
[210] [2010] EWCA Crim 359.

blood on her clothing and her vagina was, or was likely to be, menstrual. She had not attended ABE interviews and had made herself scarce so police resources were wasted. The Court of Appeal noted that the trial judge had made no reference to s.100 of the Criminal Justice Act 2003 in her ruling, and that, if she had done so, it was difficult to believe that she would not have found that the provisions of s.100(1)(b) were satisfied, i.e. that evidence was of substantial probative value in relation to a matter that was in issue in the proceedings and of substantial importance in the context of the case as a whole. The Court quashed the conviction for rape on the basis that the appellant had been denied the opportunity to cross-examine the complainant about this earlier allegation.

Deployment of s.4 of the Criminal Procedure Act 1865

26.166   If there are proper grounds for asserting a previous complaint was untrue, cross-examination is not prohibited by s.41 and the test for leave under s.100 is likely to be satisfied. If the complainant then denies that she told a witness that the previous complaint was untrue, that denial would be a denial "relative to the subject matter or proceeding" within the meaning of s.4 of the 1865 Act. In those circumstances, s.4 would be engaged and the witness could be called to prove the previous inconsistent statement. In *R. v V*,[211] it was held that the trial judge had been wrong to rule that, in such circumstances, s.4 did not permit the witness to be called to prove the inconsistent statement. Notwithstanding this, the conviction was upheld as safe in light of all the evidence.

26.167   Even though s.4 may be engaged, if questioning is permitted as to false complaints, care must be taken not to allow contradiction of the complainant's denial to become protracted and to lead to an exploration of irrelevant materials[212]

The Canadian Experience

An Example of The Demise of a Blanket Exclusion

26.168   In 1976 the Canadian Parliament enacted a provision designed to limit the virtually unrestricted inquiry into a complainant's previous sexual history allowed at common law. The provision in question, s.142 of the Criminal Code, was in broadly similar terms to s.2 of the 1976 Act. However, judicial interpretation of s.142 was perceived to have limited the protection afforded to the complainant and so the section was repealed and replaced by ss.276 and 277 of the Criminal Code. Section 276 prohibited the use of prior sexual

---

[211] [2006] EWCA Crim 1901.
[212] *R. v B (Lee)* [2005] EWCA Crim 3146; and see *R. v S* [2003] EWCA Crim 485.

history evidence and allowed only three specific exceptions. The relevant part of s.276 was in the following terms:

"(1) In proceedings in respect [of certain sexual offences], no evidence shall be adduced by or on behalf of the accused concerning the sexual activity of the complainant with any person other than the accused unless:
  (a) it is evidence that rebuts evidence of the complainant's sexual activity or absence thereof that was previously adduced by the prosecution;
  (b) it is evidence of specific instances of the complainant's sexual activity tending to establish the identity of the person who had sexual contact with the complainant on the occasion set out in the charge;
  (c) it is evidence of sexual activity that took place on the same occasion as the sexual activity that forms the subject matter of the charge, where that evidence relates to the consent that the accused alleges he believed was given by the complainant."

Section 277 provided: 26.169

"In proceedings in respect of [certain sexual offences], evidence of sexual reputation, whether general or specific, is not admissible for the purpose of challenging or supporting the credibility of the complainant."

In *Seaboyer*,[213] the Supreme Court of Canada was asked to consider   26.170
whether ss.276 and 277 infringed the right to a fair trial found in the Canadian Charter of Rights and Freedoms. The majority, whose opinion was delivered by McLachlin J, as she then was, held that s.276 infringed the right to a fair trial because it amounted to a blanket prohibition on evidence of sexual activity, regardless of whether the evidence was tendered for an illegitimate purpose or a valid one. This "pigeon-hole approach" was incapable of dealing adequately with the problem of determining whether or not evidence was relevant. Section 277 was held not to infringe the right to a fair trial.

The "Twin Myths"

Although s.276 was struck down, it was held that this did not have the effect   26.171
of reviving the old common law rules of evidence. The Court recognised that the illegitimate use of past sexual conduct evidence should be avoided. McLachlin J summarised the applicable principles as follows:

"1. On a trial for a sexual offence, evidence that the complainant has engaged in consensual sexual conduct on other occasions (including past sexual conduct with the accused) is not admissible solely to support the inference that the complainant is by reason of such conduct:
  (a) more likely to have consented to the sexual conduct at issue in the trial;
  (b) less worthy of belief as a witness.
2. Evidence of consensual sexual conduct on the part of the complainant may be admissible for purposes other than an inference relating to the consent or credibility of the complainant where it possesses probative value on an issue in

---

[213] (1991) 83 D.L.R. (4th) 193; [1991] 2 S.C.R. 577.

the trial and where that probative value is not substantially outweighed by the danger of unfair prejudice flowing from the evidence.

3. By way of illustration only, and not by way of limitation, the following are examples of admissible evidence:

(A) Evidence of specific instances of sexual conduct tending to prove that a person other than the accused caused the physical consequences of the rape alleged by the prosecution;

(B) Evidence of sexual conduct tending to prove bias or motive to fabricate on the part of the complainant;

(C) Evidence of prior sexual conduct, known to the accused at the time of the act charged, tending to prove that the accused believed that the complainant was consenting to the act charged (without laying down absolute rules, normally one would expect some proximity in time between the conduct that is alleged to have given rise to an honest belief and the conduct charged);

(D) Evidence of prior sexual conduct which meets the requirements for the reception of similar fact evidence, bearing in mind that such evidence cannot be used illegitimately merely to show that the complainant consented or is an unreliable witness;

(E) Evidence tending to rebut proof introduced by the prosecution regarding the complainant's sexual conduct. . . .

4. Where evidence that the complainant has engaged in sexual conduct on other occasions is admitted on a jury trial, the judge should warn the jury against inferring from the evidence of the conduct itself, either that the complainant might have consented to the act alleged, or that the complainant is less worthy of credit."

26.172   McLachlin J noted that s.276 factored past sexual conduct with the accused into the exclusion with no apparent intellectual debate on the subject and its possible repercussions. She made this comment: "I question whether evidence of other sexual conduct with the accused should automatically be admissible in all cases; sometimes the value of such evidence might be little or none." *Seaboyer* certainly does not justify the breadth of the exclusionary provisions of s.41.

The New Section 276

26.173   Following the decision in *Seaboyer*, s.276 was amended to read as follows:

"(1) In proceedings in respect of [certain sexual offences], evidence that the complainant has engaged in sexual activity, whether with the accused or with any other person, is not admissible to support an inference that, by reason of the sexual nature of that activity, the complainant:

(a) is more likely to have consented to the sexual activity that forms the subject-matter of the charge; or

(b) is less worthy of belief.

(2) In proceeding in respect of an offence referred to in subsection (1), no evidence shall be adduced by or on behalf of the accused that the complainant has engaged in sexual activity other than the sexual activity that forms the subject-matter of the charge, whether with the accused or with any other person, unless the judge, provincial court judge or justice determines . . . that the evidence:

(a) is of specific instances of sexual activity;

(b) is relevant to an issue at trial; and

(c) has significant probative value that is not substantially outweighed by the danger of prejudice to the proper administration of justice.

(3) In determining whether evidence is admissible under subsection (2), the judge, provincial court judge or justice shall take into account:

(a) the interests of justice, including the right of the accused to make a full answer and defence;

(b) society's interest in encouraging the reporting of sexual assault offences;

(c) whether there is a reasonable prospect that the evidence will assist in arriving at a just determination in the case;

(d) the need to remove from the fact-finding process any discriminating belief or bias;

(e) the risk that the evidence may unduly arouse sentiments of prejudice, sympathy or hostility in the jury;

(f) the potential prejudice to the complainant's personal dignity and the right to privacy;

(g) the right of the complainant and of every individual to personal security and to the full protection and benefit of the law; and

(h) any other factor that the judge, provincial court judge or justice considers relevant."

THE DECISION IN DARRACH

A constitutional challenge to the amended provision was considered by the **26.174** Supreme Court in *Darrach*.[214] Gonthier J, delivering the unanimous opinion of the Court, stated:

"The accused objects to the exclusionary rule itself in section 276(1) on the grounds that it is a 'blanket exclusion' that prevents him from adducing evidence necessary to make full answer and defence as guaranteed by the Charter. He is mistaken in his characterization of the rule. Far from being a 'blanket exclusion', section 276(1) only prohibits the use of evidence of past sexual activity when it is offered to support two specific illegitimate inferences. These are known as the 'twin myths', namely that a complainant is more likely to have consented or that she is less worthy of belief 'by reason of the sexual nature of the activity' she once engaged in.

This section gives effect to McLachlin J's finding in *Seaboyer* that the 'twin myths' are simply not relevant at trial. They are not probative of consent or credibility and can severely distort the trial process. The Criminal Code excludes all discriminatory generalisations about a complainant's disposition to consent or about her credibility based on the sexual nature of her past sexual activity on the grounds that these are improper lines of reasoning. This was the import of the Court's findings in *Seaboyer* about how sexist beliefs about women distort the trial process. The text of the exclusionary rule in section 276(1) diverges very little from the guidelines in *Seaboyer*. The mere fact that the wording differs between the Court's guidelines and Parliament's enactment is itself immaterial . . . In this case, the legislation follows the Court's suggestions very closely."

---

[214] [2000] S.C.R. 46.

The Relevance of the Canadian Experience

26.175 The new s.276 sets out:
- (a) a general prohibition on illegitimate uses of prior sexual history evidence (the so-called twin myths),
- (b) pre-conditions that must be satisfied before the evidence may be admissible, and
- (c) factors to be taken into account by judges so as to guide their exercise of discretion.

26.176   Whilst the Canadian experience clearly influenced the s.41 regime, the Court of Appeal in *R. v A*[215] found *Darrach* of limited assistance on the issue of relevance of a complainant's previous sexual history with the defendant to the issue of actual consent. The Court pointed out that the Canadian legislation is very different in structure to the s.41 regime, s.276(2) and (3) preserving considerable judicial discretion. The House of Lords also found that the Canadian model was substantially less restrictive than s.41, and noted that Commonwealth developments did not support the breadth of the exclusionary provisions of that section in respect of the potential relevance of the sexual experience of the complainant with an accused.[216]

The Future of Section 41

26.177 There has been a significant change in cultural values since 1976 when the Heilbron Committee's recommendations were watered down in the face of judicial and political resistance. The approach of advocates and the judiciary to the issue of relevance in this field will ultimately determine the success of this legislation. The s.41 regime is now rigorously applied with the Judicial College placing strong emphasis on a strict application of the rules. Any suggestion that this is not so both misrepresents the true position and risks doing a disservice to complainants, who deserve the reassurance that their previous sexual histories are most unlikely to be ventilated in court.

26.178   Although the route has been tortuous, in the majority of cases the courts have been able satisfactorily to regulate the admissibility of previous sexual history evidence to strike the appropriate balance between the protection of the complainant and the guarantee of a fair trial. However, the "credibility"

---

[215] [2001] EWCA Crim 4.
[216] See the reports of the New Zealand Law Commission (1997) and the New South Wales Law Reform Commission (1998) (No.87), where flexible approaches are advocated in respect of complainant/defendant evidence. There remains no provision in New Zealand law that deals with previous sexual experiences between the complainant and the defendant: see s.44 of the Evidence Act 2006. In Australia, evidence about the complainant's sexual experience prior to the offence charged is restricted in all the States and Territories. However, the nature and extent of the protection of the law differs across jurisdictions. The rape shield in all states except the Northern Territory and the Australian Capital Territory covers all sexual history including that with the accused, meaning that such evidence is presumed to be inadmissible in the first instance.

(s.41(4)) and "specific instance" (s.41(6)) restrictions are rocks lurking beneath the surface, which have the capability to threaten the fairness of trials.

Research was undertaken into the operation of s.41 by the courts during   **26.179** the immediate post-*R. v A (No.2)* era.[217] Writing after his research,[218] Neil Kibble put forward three options as appearing to merit careful investigation:

    (i) Leave the section alone, now that *R. v A (No.2)* has introduced a measure of judicial discretion.

   (ii) Add further exceptions to s.41—for example, to provide for motive to fabricate, prior false allegations and evidence of prior sexual history with the defendant.

  (iii) Adopt the Canadian "twin myths" model, as amended by the New South Wales Law Reform Commission.

However, Kibble stresses that any reform must first give proper consideration to the primary and fundamental question of judicial discretion and should recognise that a reasonable measure of judicial discretion should be preserved. He states that open-ended rules are not the answer, neither are rules which allow of only mechanical application and do not permit judges to exercise judgment.

Jennifer Temkin and colleagues have argued that *R. v A (No.2)* has   **26.180** engendered uncertainty, and judges tend to interpret it more broadly than was intended. They made a number of recommendations for changes to the legislation in a report produced for the Home Office[219]:

    (i) Both "sexual behaviour" and "sexual experience" should be defined.

   (ii) The embargo on sexual behaviour evidence should also apply to the prosecution, as is the case in some jurisdictions.

  (iii) Consideration should be given to amending and substantially curtailing s.42(1)(b) (the belief in consent exception) to reflect both the Sexual Offences Act 2003 and the fact that it is not generally reasonable to formulate a belief in consent on the basis of past history.

  (iv) A new exception to the rule of exclusion should be inserted into s.41, allowing the admission of evidence of previous or subsequent sexual behaviour with the accused. The exception could have a time duration.

---

[217] The Criminal Bar Association together with the University of Wales also sponsored research into this area by Neil Kibble, who interviewed many judges who try serious sex cases. His research report *Judicial Perspectives on Section 41 of the Youth Justice and Criminal Evidence Act 1999* was published in 2004. Kibble has reproduced much of the report in two articles in the Criminal Law Review: [2005] Crim. L.R. 190, 263.

[218] [2005] Crim. L.R. 263, at p.274.

[219] L. Kelly, J. Temkin, S. Griffiths, *Section 41: an evaluation of new legislation limiting sexual history evidence in rape trials* (Home Office, 2006), p.76.

26.180
(v) There should be a clear statement in the legislation that sexual behaviour evidence is not to be admitted other than in the exceptional circumstances set out there.

26.181   Seventeen years after *R. v A (No.2)*, there is little evidence to suggest that the feared uncertainty has materialised. It is accepted by Bar and Bench that the twin myths are illegitimate lines of reasoning and that it is *not* permissible to argue that, by virtue of a complainant's sexual experiences with other partners, he or she is less credible or more likely to have consented. *R. v A (No.2)* has *not* opened the floodgates and heralded a return to the old s.2, but it has, by redesigning the similar fact gateway (s.41(3)(c)), unshackled judges from a legislative straitjacket that might otherwise have led them to exclude truly relevant evidence on an arbitrary basis (principally in the context of sexual relationships between defendants and complainants).[220] In any case, the scope of *R. v A (No.2)* should not be exaggerated. In the case of sexual relationships with third parties, the position remains that it will only be in rare cases that the trial judge will grant leave in relation to the issue of consent. But the safety-valve of Lord Steyn's test is now there, should an exceptional factual situation arise. It is to be noted that in *White*[221] Laws LJ, giving the judgment of the Court of Appeal, made it clear that *R. v A (No.2)* is not authority for a wider reading of s.41 by force of s.3 of the Human Rights Act 1998, in a case where sexual acts of the complainant with men other than the appellant are sought to be adduced, than is justified by the application of conventional canons of construction.

26.182   Furthermore, the rigorous regime imposed by s.41 is now reinforced by the Criminal Procedure Rules, that require those defending in such cases to submit coherent written argument as to why the previous sexual history evidence in question is truly relevant and to spell out in terms the questions that are proposed.

26.183   There remain compelling arguments that the structure of the exclusionary regime is flawed,[222] although there is disagreement as to the nature of those flaws and how best to eradicate them. History shows that in the vast majority of cases where jurisdictions have adopted a non-discretionary approach, to

---

[220] Professor Temkin has argued that, strictly speaking, the rule of precedent which the House of Lords has tacked on to s.41(3)(c) applies only in the case of a previous relationship with the accused: *Sexual History Evidence—Beware the Backlash* [2003] Crim. L.R. 217 at p.240.

[221] [2004] EWCA Crim 946 at [35].

[222] Professor Di Birch, *Rethinking Sexual History Evidence: Proposals for Fairer Trials* [2002] Crim. L.R. 539. Professor Birch concludes that s.41 is theoretically flawed and inconsistent with good evidence doctrine. In *Sexual History Evidence—Beware the Backlash* [2003] Crim. L.R.217, Professor Temkin expresses concern that *R. v A (No.2)* will engender uncertainty. She concludes that the Home Office has drawn upon the experience of rape shield legislation here and elsewhere to produce a fair (perhaps too fair to the accused) and balanced attempt to control the use of sexual history evidence. cp. *Untangling Sexual History Evidence: A Rejoinder to Professor Temkin* [2003] Crim. L.R. 370, where Professor Birch concludes: "For the future we need to think of ways of taking the jury into the light rather than deliberately keeping them in the dark."

ensure a fair trial the courts have either had to read down the legislation[223] or declare a blanket exclusion unconstitutional.[224] This demonstrates that rape shield models that entirely eliminate judicial discretion tend to be unworkable in practice. The major flaw lies in an attempt to predict relevance in advance. Where courts have to strain statutory interpretation to its limits so as to shoehorn truly relevant evidence into pre-determined categories in order to avoid arbitrary exclusion, there remains a high risk of uneven, unsatisfactory and potentially unfair application of the rape shield.

The words of McLachlin J (as she then was) in *Seaboyer*, when the Supreme Court of Canada was considering whether the then Canadian rape shield provisions infringed the right to a fair trial found in the Canadian Charter of Rights and Freedoms, should be heeded before any significant change to s.41 is introduced: **26.184**

> "In achieving its purpose—the abolition of outmoded, sexist based use of sexual conduct evidence—it overshoots the mark and renders inadmissible evidence which may be essential to the presentation of legitimate defences and hence to a fair trial. In exchange for the elimination of the possibility that the judge and jury may draw illegitimate inferences from the evidence, it exacts as a price the real risk that an innocent person may be convicted. The price is too great in relation to benefits secured, and cannot be tolerated in a society that does no[t] countenance in any form the conviction of the innocent."

---

[223] See, e.g. the decision of the Supreme Court of Michigan in *People v Hackett*, 365 N.W. 2d 120 (1984) and, of course, *R. v A (No.2)*. See also *White* [2004] EWCA Crim 946, referred to in para.26.181, above. But cf. *Martin* [2004] EWCA Crim 916 at [38] per Crane J, where the Court of Appeal indicated a willingness to consider reading down s.41(4) if the Court had not found a way to circumvent the provision on the basis that one purpose of the proposed questions was to strengthen the defence case.

[224] *Seaboyer* (1991) 83 D.L.R. (4th) 193; [1991] 2 S.C.R. 577.

CHAPTER 27

VULNERABLE WITNESSES, "SPECIAL MEASURES" AND
RELATED MATTERS

By Alexandra Ward, Barrister

Introduction...................................... 27.01
Vulnerable Witnesses and "Special
    Measures" 27.12
Types of Special Measures............... 27.55
Procedural Matters 27.116

Vulnerable Witnesses: Practicalities .27.125
Competence to Give Evidence.........27.143
Prohibition on Cross-Examination
    by the Defendant in Person 27.157

INTRODUCTION

Approximately 40 per cent of Crown Court trials involve sexual offences.[1] As   **27.01**
a result, the criminal justice system cannot ignore the issue of vulnerable
witnesses. There is a growing understanding of the difficulties that many
witnesses may have in giving best evidence. *The Bercow report: A Review of
Services for Children and Young People (0–19) with Speech, Language and
Communication Needs*[2] found that 7 per cent of five-year-old children
entering school in England have significant difficulties with speech or
language; those with good speech sounds and poor language skills are most
at risk of being missed; and approximately 50 per cent in some socio-
economically disadvantaged populations have speech and language skills that
are significantly lower than those of other children of the same age. In
addition, 10 per cent of children in Britain aged 5–16 have a clinically
recognisable mental disorder, and rates of childhood autism are thought to
be around 1 per cent (higher than previous estimates).[3] Also of concern is the

---

[1] Sir Brian Leveson, *Review of Efficiency in Criminal Proceedings* (Jan 2015), available at
https://www.judiciary.gov.uk/publications/review-of-efficiency-in-criminal-proceedings-final-report/
[Accessed April 30, 2016].
[2] Department for Children, Schools and Families (2008), p.13.
[3] See materials cited in *European Commission Communication on the Rights of the Child
2011–2014: Contribution by the Bar Council of England & Wales*, para.8. The Contribution is
available at *http://ec.europa.eu/justice/news/consulting_public/0009/contributions/unregistered_
organisations/127_bar_council_england_wales_sept10.pdf* [Accessed April 30, 2016].

finding that chronic childhood trauma interferes with neurobiological development and questions reminding child victims of the trauma may cause them to "freeze" and shut down their ability to respond.[4] Fortunately, "special measures" designed to assist witnesses deemed vulnerable due to the nature of the offence, youth or disability, or who are reluctant to come forward and give evidence due to fear or intimidation, are now commonplace.[5]

Speaking Up for Justice

27.02   The main special measures are provided for by Pt II of the Youth Justice and Criminal Evidence Act 1999 ("YJCEA 1999"). Part II derives from *Speaking Up for Justice*,[6] the report of an interdepartmental working group established to identify improvements that could be made in the treatment of vulnerable witnesses and those likely to be subject to intimidation, at every stage of the criminal justice process. The report reflected a concern, particularly amongst victims' groups, that certain witnesses do not come forward because of their disability, or worse, that those within the criminal justice system such as police officers and prosecutors were excluding vulnerable witnesses because they were perceived to be unreliable. The objective of the working group was to encourage such witnesses to give evidence of crime and enable them to give their best evidence in court. The group's remit included identifying the categories of witness that should be classified as vulnerable. In broad terms, the group concluded that vulnerability should be defined by reference to age (youth), mental disorder, and learning and physical disability. Vulnerability should also include those suffering from fear and distress in relation to giving evidence. The report identified a range of special measures which it recommended should be available to defence witnesses; but it considered that the defendant should be excluded from the proposed regime.

27.03   Many of the report's recommendations were implemented in Pt II of the YJCEA 1999. The Coroners and Justice Act 2009 took matters further, extending eligibility for special measures by reason of age from children aged under 17 to those aged under 18, increasing the number of offences for which a witness is eligible for special measures and making the special measures available to child witnesses more flexible. In addition, guidance was issued to the various agencies likely to be involved with vulnerable witnesses. The third edition of *Achieving Best Evidence: Guidance on Interviewing Victims and Witnesses, and Guidance on using Special Measures*[7] ("the ABE guidance") was published in March 2011.[8] In addition, the College of Policing provides

---

[4] Ibid.
[5] Pt II of the Youth Justice and Criminal Evidence Act 1999. For commencement, see SIs 2002/1739 and 2004/299.
[6] *Speaking Up for Justice*, Report of the Home Office Interdepartmental Working Group on the Treatment of Vulnerable or Intimidated Witnesses in the Criminal Justice System (1998).
[7] *http://www.cps.gov.uk/publications/docs/best_evidence_in_criminal_proceedings.pdf* [Accessed April 30, 2016].
[8] Ministry of Justice Circular 2011/03.

guidance on working with victims and witnesses.[9] Also useful is ACPO's *Advice on the Structure of Visually Recorded Witness Interviews* (October, 2013),[10] which provides guidance to police on how to interview victims and witnesses effectively. Practitioners and investigators will recognise the necessity for such guidance in light of the problems often encountered with the sound, visual quality and length of video-recorded interviews.

Measuring Up?

Whilst these statutory and other interventions have done much to assist vulnerable witnesses to give evidence, there remains concern that special measures are not being used in every case where they would be appropriate or are being under-used in others. One cause of this is the failure to identify vulnerable witnesses at an early stage, thereby denying them the assistance for which they are eligible under Pt II of the YJCEA 1999.[11] The difficulty in achieving early identification of vulnerability has been known for some time in the context of the police's ability to identify accurately vulnerable suspects at the stage of their detention or interview under caution.[12] It clearly would not be practical to train all police officers in sophisticated methods of identifying witnesses with mild mental disorder or learning difficulties. That said, a series of screening questions before the taking of a witness statement might assist to identify more vulnerable witnesses than is currently the case. Research indicates that 9 per cent of witnesses are identified at an early stage as being potentially vulnerable, but that following a screening questionnaire, as many as 54 per cent of witnesses are found to be potentially vulnerable.[13] If all of these witnesses are in fact vulnerable, it should mean that giving evidence with the assistance of special measures should be the norm in criminal courts as opposed to the exception. Worryingly, the research also identified cases where, although the witness fulfilled the eligibility criteria, they were not considered vulnerable because of social or cultural factors (the examples given are a 16-year-old soldier and a 16-year-old prostitute). A report by the mental health charity, Mind, found that complainants with mental health problems did not feel that they were receiving equal access to justice.[14]

27.04

[9] *https://www.app.college.police.uk/app-content/investigations/victims-and-witnesses/* [Accessed April 30, 2016]

[10] *http://library.college.police.uk/docs/APPREF/ACPO-Witness-Interview-Structure-2013.pdf* [Accessed April 30, 2016].

[11] M. Burton, R. Evans and A. Sanders, *Implementing special measures for vulnerable and intimidated witnesses: The problem of identification* [2006] Crim. L.R. 229.

[12] G. Gudjonsson, I. Clare, S. Rutter and J. Pearse, *Persons at Risk during Interviews in Police Custody: the Identification of Vulnerabilities,* Royal Commission on Criminal Justice Research Study No.12, (London: HMSO, 1993).

[13] M. Burton, R. Evans and A. Sanders, *Implementing special measures for vulnerable and intimidated witnesses: The problem of identification* [2006] Crim. L.R. 229.

[14] Mind, *Another Assault; Mind's campaign for equal access to justice for people with mental health problems* (2007). This report is discussed in greater detail in Ch.7.

27.05   A major review of the implementation of the Government's pledges regarding young witnesses, undertaken jointly by the NSPCC and The Nuffield Foundation, resulted in the 2009 report *Measuring Up? Evaluating implementation of Government commitments to young witnesses in criminal proceedings.*[15] The report found that much more needed to be done to assist vulnerable witnesses to give their best evidence at trial.[16] It was critical of participants in the criminal justice system who fail to recognise the needs of vulnerable witnesses, including advocates who could do more to ensure that there is effective communication between themselves and the witness. Moreover, the report cautioned that the vulnerability of eligible witnesses should not be taken advantage of by advocates or their evidence dismissed by the police, CPS or judiciary. Of real concern was that half the children spoken to stated that they had not understood all the questions that were put to them in court, and there appeared to be an unrealistic expectation from the judiciary and advocates that the witness would tell the court that they were experiencing difficulties in understanding the questions being put. The report also concluded that intermediaries were being woefully underused. It suggested that 70 per cent of the children involved in the study ought to have been assessed by an intermediary; in fact, only two children had been so assessed. *Measuring Up* contains *Good practice guidance in managing young witness cases and questioning children,* see Ch.28. Also of concern is the finding that chronic childhood trauma interferes with neurobiological development and questions reminding child victims of the trauma may cause them to "freeze" and shut down their ability to respond.[17]

27.06   In *Young Witnesses in Criminal Proceedings: A Progress Report on Measuring Up?* (2009),[18] Joyce Plotnikoff and Richard Woolfson provided an update on the position as regards the treatment of child witnesses. They recorded that progress has been made in some areas and note the steps taken by the CPS, Association of Chief Police Officers and HM Courts and Tribunals Service in reviewing and improving guidance on how to approach young witnesses throughout the court process. They concluded, however, that action was still needed in relation to how young witnesses were treated at court. In this area, ensuring appropriate questioning and avoiding long delays at court remained key priorities, particularly in light of the increasing

---

[15] The full report was published in July 2009 and is available on the NSPCC website [Accessed April 30, 2016].

[16] Researchers interviewed 182 children aged 5–19, parents (of 172 of those children) and professionals from 52 Witness Service teams and seven young witness support schemes. 157 of the children were witnesses in cases involving violent or sexual offences. 172 of the interviewees gave evidence at courts in England, Wales and Northern Ireland (30 Crown Courts, 26 magistrates' courts and 23 youth courts).

[17] See materials cited in *European Commission Communication on the Rights of the Child 2011–2014: Contribution by the Bar Council of England & Wales,* para.8. The web reference for the report is given at fn.3, above.

[18] Nuffield Foundation, June 2011, available at *http://www.nuffieldfoundation.org/sites/default/files/files/Young%20witnesses%20in%20criminal%20proceedings_a%20progress%20report%2-0on%20Measuring%20up_v_FINAL.pdf* [Accessed April 30, 2016].

number of children giving evidence in proceedings. Whilst there were no official figures for the number of children who gave evidence, around 48,000 were called to court in 2008/9, compared to around 30,000 in 2006/7, an increase of 60 per cent.

Subsequent developments

Developments in the last few years have ensured that there is now much greater focus within the criminal justice system on considering how witnesses can best give evidence. There is widespread acceptance that a witness should no longer be expected to cope within the confines of a traditional system, and instead that the courts and those practising within them should respond to the witness's needs. The Criminal Procedure Rules 2015 impose a duty on the court to identify the needs of witnesses at an early stage and may require the parties to identify arrangements to facilitate their giving of evidence and participation in the trial.[19] In all but very exceptional circumstances, the court should hold a "Ground Rules Hearing" to set the parameters of the treatment of vulnerable witnesses, such as type and length of questioning, location of giving evidence and the availability of other special measures.[20] Decisions of the Court of Appeal, such as *Lubemba*,[21] and the *Equal Treatment Bench Book* (November 2013) reinforce the obligations of the judiciary in this regard. The *Bench Book* includes advice on dealing with witnesses with specific learning difficulties where only some areas of functioning are affected.[22] It provides assistance for judges in recognising learning difficulties and identifying the consequential effect on court proceedings. A judge is duty-bound to take every reasonable step to encourage and facilitate the attendance of vulnerable witnesses and their participation in the trial process. As *Lubemba* makes clear, this includes a duty to control the questioning of a witness, to set reasonable time limits and interrupt inappropriate questioning.

27.07

Following a series of high profile cases, there has been much debate as to how child and other witnesses of sexual offences should give evidence. Intermediaries are now valued as participants throughout the criminal justice process. The possibility that a witness may require the assistance of an intermediary should be considered at the outset of the investigation. Once assessed by an intermediary, the intermediary can assist the investigators to plan the ABE interview, conduct identification procedures and help the

27.08

---

[19] CPR 2015 rr.3.2(2)(b), 3.11(c)(iv) and (v); Criminal Practice Directions 2015, 3D.3.
[20] *Lubemba* [2014] EWCA Crim 2064; [2015] 1 Cr. App. R. 12, discussed in paras 28.16 and following, below.
[21] *Lubemba* [2014] EWCA Crim 2064; [2015] 1 Cr. App. R. 12.
[22] Available at *http://www.judiciary.gov.uk/publications-and-reports/judicial-college/2013/equal-treatment-bench-book* [Accessed April 30, 2016].

witness to understand the trial process.[23] The automatic assessment of young witnesses is now discouraged because of the limited number of available intermediaries.[23a] Further, the acceptance that the very young or those with severe communication difficulties are competent to give evidence has led to a reassessment by advocates and the judiciary of their own methods of communication. The prevailing approach is now that a witness should not be denied the opportunity to give their best evidence due to their inability to comprehend an old-fashioned style of complex questioning, but rather that questioning should be tailored to the witness's understanding. In this respect the Advocacy Training Council has provided invaluable "toolkits" for practitioners, which are freely available through its website *http://www.theadvoacatesgateway.org*.[24] Many practitioners acknowledge the new approach and recognise that the principles of a fair trial are undermined when an advocate seeks to take advantage of a witness's vulnerability. We consider the sea-change in the questioning of the young and vulnerable in Ch.28.

27.09   However, there remains a strong perception that some advocates do not comply with the guidance set out by the Court of Appeal and maintain an out-dated approach to the questioning and treatment of vulnerable witnesses. This has led to calls to require both prosecution and defence advocates to undertake compulsory training in this area. There is also more to be done in terms of the measures themselves. Section 33BA of the YJCEA 1999, which provides for intermediaries for defendants, is not yet in force. Also, pre-recorded cross-examination under s.28 was piloted only recently.[25] The pilots have been regarded as a success: once technical difficulties were ironed-out, use of pre-recorded cross-examination led to less waiting time for young witnesses and a more efficient trial process. There is now an appetite amongst the judiciary for full implementation of s.28. In his *Review of Efficiency in Criminal Proceedings*, Sir Brian Leveson champions the use of two recorded interviews with a vulnerable witness, the first as an investigative tool and the second as a source of evidence. We welcome this proposal as a means of enabling an investigator to obtain as full account of events as possible, without needing to worry about whether matters are admissible or are being divulged in a comprehensible narrative. The second recorded interview should be a focused examination-in-chief.

---

[23] For a detailed discussion of this topic, see Joyce Plotnikoff and Richard Woolfson, *Intermediaries in the criminal justice system* (Policy Press, 2015), in particular Ch.3, *Behind the scenes: planning to assess the witness,* and Ch. 6, *Contributing to the effectiveness of the police interview.*

[23a] See para.3F.5 of the Criminal Practice Directions 2015 Amendment No. 1 [2016] EWCA Crim 97.

[24] See also Appendix F, below, for Toolkits related to; Ground Rules Hearings & the Treatment of Vulnerable People in Court (1), Planning to Question a Child or Young Person (6); Children Under 7 (7), Effective Participation Young Defendants (8), Identifying Vulnerability in Witnesses and Defendants (10), General Principles When Questioning Witnesses and Defendants with Mental Disorder (12) and Intermediaries.

[25] At Kingston-Upon-Thames, Liverpool and Leeds Crown Court.

An application for special measures should be considered before a party 27.10
who is calling a witness makes an application to adduce the witness's
evidence as hearsay under the Criminal Justice Act 2003 due to their illness,
trauma or fear. This is because, whatever their condition when the statement
was taken, the witness may now be in a position to give their evidence in
person with the benefit of special measures. The use of special measures such
as pre-recorded examination-in-chief and live link cross-examination within
the context of the YJCEA 1999 is no doubt preferable from the point of view
of the defendant to the presentation of the witness's evidence under s.116 of
the 2003 Act. However, the availability of special measures will not eradicate
the need for s.116 applications in all cases. In *R. v D*,[26] which was a case of
attempted rape and indecent assault on a person suffering from a degenerative condition, namely Alzheimer's, it was held that there was unlikely to
be a breach of the defendant's right to examine witnesses under art.6(3)(d)
ECHR if video evidence from the complainant was admitted under s.23 of
the Criminal Justice Act 1988. The Court had a difficult decision to make in
that, because of the complainant's condition, the admission of the video was
the only way in which the Crown could advance its case at trial. In *Watts*[27]
a complainant's ABE interview was admitted under s.116 (and its admission
not challenged on appeal) where, after the interview but prior to the trial, she
suffered a stroke rendering her incapable of any form of communication. For
discussion of the hearsay provisions, see Ch.19.

The main part of this chapter considers in some detail the special measures 27.11
introduced by the YJCEA 1999 and the associated practical matters to be
addressed in cases involving a vulnerable witness. At the end of the chapter
we consider two important related matters: the law governing competence,
particularly in relation to young witnesses, and the prohibitions on a
defendant cross-examining a witness in person.

VULNERABLE WITNESSES AND "SPECIAL MEASURES"

THE LEGISLATION

Part II of the YJCEA 1999 (ss.16–30) provides a statutory umbrella over all 27.12
special measures available for children and other vulnerable or intimidated
witnesses, other than defendants. Previously, practitioners had to rely upon
a mixture of various statutory and common law powers.[28] As for defendants,
the only statutory special measures available to them are contained in ss.33A
(live link) and 33BA (intermediaries) of the YJCEA 1999, and the eligibility

---

[26] [2002] 2 Cr. App. R. 601, discussed in para.7.35, above. See also *R. v Ali Sed* [2004] EWCA
Crim 1294; [2005] 1 Cr. App. R. 4.
[27] [2010] EWCA Crim 1824.
[28] Much of the movement for reform derived from the "needless complexity" of previous
measures to assist witnesses: J.R. Spencer, *Orality and Evidence of Absent Witnesses* [1994] Crim.
L.R. 628, 632.

criteria are different from those applied to other witnesses.[29] The provisions in respect of intermediaries for defendants are not yet in force and it is necessary for the courts to rely upon the common law. Special measures for defendants are considered at paras 18.27 and following, above.

Eligibility

27.13   There are three categories of eligibility created by ss.16 and 17:
- child witnesses;
- those eligible because of mental disorder, significantly impaired social functioning or intelligence or physical disability or disorder;
- those eligible through fear, distress or intimidation.

27.14   Eligibility for special measures depends upon whether a witness is vulnerable because they fall into one or more of these categories, and not necessarily upon the nature of the alleged offence. However, there are certain presumptions in relation to the type of special measure to be directed in particular circumstances: for example, the primary rule is that child witnesses will give all their evidence-in-chief by way of video recording and that other evidence will be given by live link.[30] The presumption will not apply if the witness informs the court that they wish to give evidence through another means, provided the court is satisfied that the disapplication of the primary rule would not diminish the quality of the witness' evidence.[31]

Child witnesses

27.15   By s.16(1)(a) of the YJCEA 1999, child witnesses (those under 18 at the time of the special measures directions hearing) are automatically deemed vulnerable and consequently eligible for special measures. The court is not required to consider whether the witness's vulnerability is likely to affect the quality of the evidence they will give.[32] A complainant of a "relevant offence" whose age is uncertain will be presumed to be under the age of 18 if there are reasons to believe they are under that age.[33] For this purpose a "relevant offence" is defined to mean an offence under Pt 1 of the Sexual Offences Act 2003,[34] an offence under s.1 of the Protection of Children Act 1978, an offence under s.160 of the Criminal Justice Act 1988 and an offence under s.1

---

[29] Inserted by the Coroners and Justice Act 2009 s.104(1).

[30] s.21(3) of the YJCEA 1999. The term "sexual offence" for this purpose is an offence within s.35(3)(a) of the Act, i.e. an offence under the Sexual Offences Act 1956, the Indecency with Children Act 1960, the Sexual Offences Act 1967 s.54 of the Criminal Law Act 1977, the Protection of Children Act 1978 or Pt 1 of the Sexual Offences Act 2003.

[31] s.21 of the YJCEA 1999, as amended by the Coroners and Justice Act 2009 s.100(6).

[32] s.16(1)(a) of the YJCEA 1999.

[33] s.33(5) of the YJCEA 1999, as amended by the Special Measures for Child Witnesses (Sexual Offences) Regulations 2013 (SI 2013/2971), reg.2 (b), with effect from December 18, 2013.

[34] s.62 of the YJCEA 1999, as amended.

or s.2 of the Modern Slavery Act 2015.[35] The effect is that the complainant of such an offence will be eligible for "special measures" under s.16(1) of the YJCEA 1999.

The YJCEA 1999 makes provision for "qualifying witnesses", i.e. young   **27.16** witnesses who have reached the age of 18 at the date of the special measures directions, but who were under 18 at the date of the video recording of the *Achieving Best Evidence* interview.[36] All "qualifying witnesses" will have the benefit of the video recording standing as their evidence-in-chief. However, they will not automatically be cross-examined over the live link.[37]

Adult witnesses eligible because of mental disorder or physical disability

The second category of eligibility, in s.16(1)(b) of the YJCEA 1999, covers   **27.17** witnesses with a mental disorder or other significant impairment of intelligence and social functioning, or witnesses with a physical disability or disorder.[38] "Mental disorder" is defined by reference to s.1 of the Mental Health Act 1983 (as amended).[39] Section 1(2) of the 1983 Act provides[40]:

> "'mental disorder' means any disorder or disability of the mind; and mentally disordered shall be construed accordingly."

A court may consider expert evidence when determining whether a witness   **27.18** is eligible for special measures under s.16(1)(b). Such evidence could be heard at a contested special measures directions hearing if a party to the proceedings has indicated that they dispute the witness's eligibility. In order to determine eligibility within this category, the court is under a further duty to consider the witness's views and whether the "quality of the evidence" given will be diminished by their vulnerability.[41] The "quality" of evidence refers to its completeness, accuracy and coherence. "Coherence" is further defined as a witness's ability to give answers which address the questions put to him or her and can be understood both individually and collectively.[42] For a discussion of "mental disorder" see Ch.7.

Adult witnesses eligible through fear, distress or intimidation

Witnesses whose quality of evidence is likely to be diminished because of fear,   **27.19** distress or intimidation suffered in connection with giving evidence in the

---

[35] s.33(6) of the YJCEA 1999, as amended by Modern Slavery Act 2015 s.46(4) with effect from July 31, 2015 (SI 2015/1476).
[36] s.22(1)(a) of the YJCEA 1999.
[37] s.22(2)(a).
[38] s.16(1)(b), (2) of the YJCEA 1999.
[39] The definition was amended by the Mental Health Act 2007. For a detailed discussion of "mental disorder", see Ch.7.
[40] The term "disability of the mind" is not defined.
[41] s.16(4), (5) of the YJCEA 1999.
[42] s.16(5).

proceedings are eligible for special measures under s.17.[43] Complainants of sexual offences or offences of slavery or human trafficking under s.1 or 2 of the Modern Slavery Act 2015 are automatically eligible under this provision, unless they inform the court that they do not wish a special measures direction to be made.[44] This shortcut to eligibility is also available to witnesses in proceedings involving Sch.1A specified offences involving knives or firearms.[45] For other adult witnesses, s.17(2) requires the court to determine eligibility by considering the nature and alleged circumstances of the offence; the witness's age; if considered relevant, the witness's social, cultural and ethnic background, domestic and employment circumstances, religious beliefs or political opinions; and any behaviour towards the witness on the part of the accused, members of the family or associates of the accused and any other person likely to be an accused or a witness in the proceedings. The court is obliged to take into account the views of the witness.[46] Special measures are an established and uncontroversial feature of our criminal court system and the practical reality seems to be that judges will grant special measures for adult witnesses who express fear or distress at the prospect of giving evidence, without finding it necessary to consider in detail the criteria set out in s.17(2).

SPECIAL MEASURES AND THE DEFENDANT

27.20 Although an application for special measures can be made on behalf of any vulnerable defence witness, a defendant is not equally eligible for statutory special measures, even when giving evidence as a witness in his own case. As we explain below, with the exception, in certain limited circumstances, of live link, statutory special measures remain unavailable to child or vulnerable defendants. In *R. (on the application of D) v Camberwell Green Youth Court*,[47] the House of Lords rejected a challenge to the YJCEA 1999 scheme under art.6 ECHR based upon inequality of arms, in so far as the scheme does not apply to defendants. Baroness Hale, with whom the other members of the House agreed, recognised the real difficulties that exist in the Youth Court, where child defendants are often among the most disadvantaged and the least able to give a good account of themselves. However, the answer to these problems was not to deprive the court of the best evidence available from other child witnesses merely because the YJCEA 1999 scheme does not also apply to the accused. Baroness Hale held that the defendant is excluded from the statutory scheme because it would be "clearly inappropriate" to apply the whole scheme to him. There were obvious difficulties identified by

---

[43] cf. *Brown and Grant* [2004] EWCA Crim 1620.
[44] s.17(4) of the YJCEA 1999, as amended by the Modern Slavery Act 2015 s.46(2), with effect from July 31, 2015.
[45] s.17(5), as amended by the Coroners and Justice Act 2009 s.99(1), (2).
[46] s.17(3).
[47] [2005] UKHL 4; [2005] 1 W.L.R. 393; [2005] 2 Cr. App. R. 1.

Baroness Hale about admitting a video-recorded interview as the defendant's evidence-in-chief. For example who would conduct it, and how? What safeguards could there be against repeated interviews? There are also difficulties in applying binding advance presumptions about how a defendant's evidence should be given, if indeed it is to be given at all, when the defence is ordinarily free to make such decisions in the light of events as they unfold.

Sadly, as one may anticipate, children with communication difficulties and low IQs are over-represented in the court system, yet the fact that such difficulties are familiar does not mean that the courts should do nothing to address them.[48] To some extent the potential unfairness caused by the statutory scheme not applying to defendants has been addressed by the courts using their inherent powers to grant equivalent special measures to defendants. But the pragmatic filling of gaps in this way will still fail to ensure that all vulnerable defendants receive the assistance they need to participate in the proceedings and give their best evidence. As Professor McEwan notes, a fundamental difficulty is the identification of vulnerable defendants.[49] Vulnerabilities may go unnoticed at the police station. At court, many defendants are unrepresented and the pressure to progress cases means that even an experienced representative is unlikely to have sufficient time to assess whether their client is able to participate effectively in the proceedings. Efforts are, however, being made to address these challenges. The Advocacy Training Council has provided guidance on identifying vulnerability in witnesses and defendants in their Toolkit 10[50] and as to the effective participation of young defendants in their own trial in Toolkit 8.[51] In the Crown Court, judges at early hearings should be alive to any vulnerability of the defendant. The Court is required by r.3.9(3)(b) of the Criminal Procedure Rules 2015, to "take every reasonable step . . . to facilitate the participation of . . . the defendant". Under r.3.9(6), the Court may give directions for the appropriate treatment and questioning of the defendant and direct that such questioning is to be conducting through an intermediary.

In addition, the Criminal Practice Directions 2015 provide (at 3D.2 and 3G.9) detailed direction as to how vulnerable defendants should be treated and require the judiciary to ensure by any appropriate means that defendants understand the proceedings.[52] Matters for consideration include whether a vulnerable defendant should be part of what would otherwise be a joint trial; whether a court familiarisation visit is necessary; ensuring, subject to security considerations, that a child can sit with their family or supporter throughout

27.21

27.22

---

[48] See *R. (on the application of AS) v Great Yarmouth Youth Court* [2011] EWHC 2059 (Admin); [2012] Crim. L.R. 478.

[49] *Vulnerable defendants and the fairness of trials* [2013] Crim. L.R. (2) 100–113.

[50] Dated 10 July 2014 and available at *www.theadvocatesgateway.org* [Accessed April 30, 2016].

[51] Dated 21 October 2013 and available at *www.theadvocatesgateway.org* [Accessed April 30, 2016].

[52] [2015] EWCA Crim 1567.

the proceedings as opposed to being seated in the dock; and timetabling the trial so that it is conducted at a pace at which the defendant can follow and maintain concentration. In the Crown Court, robes and wigs should not be worn without good reason, security guards should not be in uniform and consideration should be given to restricting the members of the public and press who are permitted access to the courtroom (it may, for example, be preferable for the press to report from another room to which proceedings are live-streamed by video). Any adaptations for a vulnerable defendant should be explained to the jury so as to not prejudice the defendant. The *Equal Treatment Bench Book*[53] also provides practical examples of methods that have been utilised to assist vulnerable defendants. Examples include seating a visually impaired defendant close to the jury during empanelment, seating a defendant with a hearing problem within the body of the court, agreeing that a defendant with mental health issues should be given brief pauses during cross examination, and permitting an autistic defendant comforting objects in the dock in order to help his concentration.

27.23   Professor McEwan cites an example of a jury disapproving of the behaviour of a young defendant with a short attention span who would talk throughout the proceedings to the social worker seated next to them. The judge should be alert to the defendant's behaviour and in such circumstances should either increase the number of breaks or explain to the jury why the defendant is seated in the well of the court together with the reason why frequent communication with their social worker is permitted. We discuss in Ch.28 the questioning of vulnerable witnesses and submit that the same approach should be adopted when questioning vulnerable defendants. Prosecutors should be no more tempted to try to "catch-out" a vulnerable defendant by asking confusing questions which are likely to obtain unreliable answers than defence counsel should be tempted to try to trick a vulnerable complainant. The training video *A Question of Practice* prepared by the CBA and others illustrates this point very well.[54]

27.24   Practitioners should also refer to the excellent information pack, *Mental health and learning disabilities in the criminal courts: Information for magistrates, district judges and court staff*, prepared by Polly McConnell and Jenny Talbot on behalf of the Prison Reform Trust and Rethink Mental Illness.[55] The pack addresses the difficulty in identifying a vulnerable defendant and reinforces how alienating an appearance in a criminal court can be for someone with a mental health condition or learning disability. It gives practical advice as to how the courts might obtain assistance from other agencies at various stages of the process. An overview is also provided of fitness to plead, bail, sentencing and mental health disposals.

---

[53] Available at *http://www.judiciary.gov.uk/publications-and-reports/judicial-college/2013/equal-treatment-bench-book* [Accessed April 30, 2016].

[54] Available at *http://www.theadvocatesgateway.org/* [Accessed April 30, 2016].

[55] Available at *http://www.mhldcc.org.uk* [Accessed April 30, 2016].

Limited provision for defendants: live link and intermediaries

The statutory denial of special measures to the accused led initially to the   **27.25**
courts using their inherent powers to ensure a fair trial[56] and latterly to
legislative amendment. Statute now provides for defendants to give evidence
by live link in certain circumstances and, when the relevant provisions are in
force, to give evidence with the assistance of an intermediary.[57]

Live link

Parliament responded to the *Camberwell*[58] by enacting s.33A of the YJCEA   **27.26**
1999, which provides that a vulnerable defendant may apply to give evidence
by live link in the Crown Court and magistrates' court where certain criteria
are met.[59] The criteria are more restrictive for defendants than for other
vulnerable witnesses there is and an additional requirement that the court is
satisfied that it is in the interests of justice to grant the defendant's
application.[60] As with other witnesses, eligibility depends upon age.

Where a defendant has not reached the age of 18 at the date of his   **27.27**
application, he will be eligible if his ability to participate effectively in the
proceedings as a witness is compromised by his level of intellectual ability or
social functioning and the use of the live link would enable him to participate
effectively in the proceedings.[61] In *Rahman*,[62] the Court of Appeal stated that
the fact that a defendant has a temper and does not like being challenged by
authority figures is not a characteristic that Parliament had in mind when it
referred to "social functioning" in this context. The Court in that case held
that, while an expert report is not required to support a live link application
by a defendant under the age of 18, the judge had not misdirected himself by
observing that if reliance was placed upon a claimed impairment of social
functioning, the usual means of establishing this would be by an expert or
somebody skilled or experienced in communicating with young people. A
statement from someone as obviously partisan as the defendant's mother was
unlikely to be sufficient.

Where a defendant has attained the age of 18 at the date of the application,   **27.28**
he will be eligible if he suffers from a mental disorder or otherwise has a
significant impairment of intelligence or social function[63] and because of his

---

[56] See *R. v H* [2003] EWCA Crim 1209 and *R. (on the application of C) v Sevenoaks Youth Court* [2009] EWHC 3088 (Admin), D.C.

[57] ss.33A–C (live link) were inserted by the Police Justice Act 2006 s.47, which came into came into force on January 5, 2007 (SI 2008/617) and ss.33BA–BC (intermediaries) were inserted by the Coroners and Justice Act 2009 s.104(1) (not in force).

[58] [2005] UKHL 4; [2005] 2 Cr. App. R. 1.

[59] Inserted by s.47 of the Police and Justice Act 2006, which came into force on January 5, 2007 (SI 2008/617).

[60] s.33A(2)(b) of the YJCEA 1999.

[61] s.33A(4)(a), (b).

[62] [2015] 1 Cr. App. R. 457(30).

[63] s.33A(5)(a).

mental disorder or impairment of intelligence or social function he is unable
to participate effectively as a witness in the proceedings, but the use of the live
link would enable him to participate effectively.[64]

27.29   A live link direction may be varied or discharged but whilst it is in effect
the defendant may only give evidence via the live link.[65]

27.30   The question arises whether the courts have inherent power to allow the
use of the live link in cases falling outside the scope of the statutory scheme.
In *R. (on the application of S) v Waltham Forest Youth Court*,[66] the
Divisional Court held that there was no such power. In the *R. (on the
application of D) v Camberwell Green Youth Court*[67] Baroness Hale clearly
had some difficulty with this decision, but as the point was not before the
House, she left open whether the case had been correctly decided. Then in
Ukpabio,[68] decided after s.33A came into force, the Court of Appeal held that
s.33A is an exhaustive list of the circumstances in which a live link may be
used when a defendant gives evidence. The statutory scheme means that
evidence should be given by a witness present in court, subject to such
measures short of video-link as are appropriate to ensure that the witness is
able to give evidence properly and fully and, in particular, without fear. The
Court went on to say that there may be exceptional circumstances in which
it is appropriate for a defendant, on his own application, not to be present in
court for all or part of his trial, provided that he can participate effectively by
live link or in some other way. Although not determining the point, the Court
appeared to agree with submissions that live link would not be available to a
defendant who suffered health difficulties but was not mental disordered.[69]

Intermediaries

27.31   A further example of the court using its inherent powers, in a somewhat
different context, is the case of *R. v H*,[70] where the Court of Appeal held that
the trial judge's inherent power to ensure a fair trial could lead to the
provision of an interpreter for a defendant with severe learning difficulties,
regular breaks in the court day and reliance in the witness box on a detailed
defence statement or leading questions based upon it.[71]

27.32   An application for an intermediary to assist a defendant must be made in
accordance with Pt 18 of the Criminal Procedure Rules and, where available,
the intermediary report must be provided with the application. The Criminal
Practice Directions (at 3F.6–3F.26) set out the approach the court should
take when determining whether to appoint an intermediary to assist a

[64] s.33A(5)(b), (c).
[65] s.33A(6), (7).
[66] [2004] EWHC 715 (Admin).
[67] [2005] UKHL 4; [2005] 2 Cr. App. R. 1.
[68] [2007] EWCA Crim 2108; [2008] 1 Cr. App. R. 6.
[69] *R. (on the application of Hamberger) v CPS* [2014] EWHC 2814; [2015] MHLR 439.
[70] [2003] EWCA Crim 1209.
[71] *R. v H (Special Measures)*, *The Times*, April 15, 2003.

defendant. Due to the scarcity of available intermediaries, there is no longer a presumption that children under 11 will be assessed. Intermediary assessment should be considered for witnesses and defendants under 18 who seem liable to misunderstand questions or to experience difficulty expressing answers, including those who seem unlikely to be able to recognise a problematic question, or if able to do so, may be reluctant to say so to a questioner in a position of authority. The statutory provisions for defendant intermediaries were only inserted into Pt II of the YJCEA 1999 in 2009 and are still not in force. The courts have sought to plug this gap through use of common law powers to ensure a fair trial, though the Criminal Practice Directions now make clear that there is no presumption that a vulnerable defendant will be assisted by an intermediary and even when an intermediary would improve the trial process, their appointment is not mandatory.[72] In *R. (on the application of C) v Sevenoaks Youth Court*[73] it was held, following *R. v H* and *SC v United Kingdom*,[74] that the courts have a common law duty to appoint an intermediary to help a child defendant to follow the proceedings where this was necessary to ensure a fair trial. C was a 12-year-old boy due to stand trial with a 15-year-old on charges of assault with intent to rob and theft. He had been diagnosed by a clinical psychologist and also by a consultant forensic neuro-psychiatrist with Autistic Spectrum Disorder with Asperger's Syndrome. Openshaw J concluded that whilst there was no statutory power under the YJCEA 1999 to order the use of an intermediary, an order could be made under the court's inherent powers, given that the Criminal Procedure Rules provide that the overriding objective is to deal with cases justly, the court must consider a defendant's rights under art.6 of the ECHR, and the court's case management powers require it to consider what arrangements are necessary to facilitate the participation of any person in the trial. In *R. (on the application of AS) v Great Yarmouth Youth Court*[75] Mitting J held that "[t]here was a right, which might in certain circumstances amount to a duty, to appoint a registered intermediary to assist the defendant to follow the proceedings and give evidence if without assistance he would not be able to have a fair trial". Penny Cooper and David Wurtzel compare the position of a defendant who needs an intermediary in order to understand and be understood with a non-English speaking defendant who requires an interpreter.[76] They develop the powerful argument that the absence of an interpreter for a non-English speaking defendant would constitute a violation of the defendant's right to a fair hearing under art.6 of the ECHR, and that the absence of an intermediary for a vulnerable defendant would constitute the same violation.

---

[72] See para.3F.5 of the Criminal Practice Directions 2015 Amendment No. 1 [2016] EWCA Crim. 97.

[73] [2009] EWHC 3088 (Admin), DC; see also *Archbold Review*, Issue 3, April 2, 2010.

[74] (2005) 40 E.H.R.R. 10.

[75] [2011] EWHC 2059 (Admin); [2012] Crim. L.R. 478.

[76] *A day late and a dollar short: in search of an intermediary scheme for vulnerable defendants in England and Wales* [2013] Crim. L.R. 1, 4–22.

27.33   The issue of intermediaries for defendants was considered by the Court of Appeal, Lord Judge CJ presiding, in *Cox*.[77] The appellant suffered from complex psychiatric difficulties and at a special measures hearing the trial judge, relying upon his common law powers in accordance with *R. (on the application of C) v Sevenoaks Youth Court*,[78] made a direction for an intermediary to assist the appellant at trial. Unfortunately an intermediary could not be identified for whom funding was available. The judge refused to stay the prosecution on the basis that absent an intermediary the appellant could not have a fair trial. He applied the test set out in *R. (TP) v West London Youth Court*,[79] namely "Taking into account the steps that can be taken in the [youth] court will the claimant be able effectively to participate in his trial?" The judge answered this question in the affirmative as there would be regular breaks (every 20 minutes), evidence would be adduced by simply phrased questions, witnesses would be asked to express their answers in short sentences, and the video of the appellant's police interview under caution would be played to enable the jury to become accustomed to his patterns of speech. Also, an admission would be made as to the appellant's complex learning difficulties and the extent of his understanding. Throughout the trial the judge kept matters under review and revisited his ruling prior to closing speeches. In upholding the conviction, the Court held that ultimately the judge retains overall responsibility for the fairness of a trial. Even if the presence of an intermediary is desirable, where one is not available the judge must make an informed assessment of whether the absence of an intermediary would make the proposed trial unfair or whether fairness can be safeguarded by modifications to the trial process. It will be most unusual for a defendant who is fit to plead to be found to be so disadvantaged by his condition that a properly brought prosecution would be stayed.

27.34   In outlining the history of the case, the Court of Appeal in *Cox* referred to funding difficulties in respect of intermediaries for defendants; the judgment is silent, however, on whether the unavailability of an intermediary in this case was ultimately due to a lack of funding or the particular communication needs of the appellant. If a lack of funding was the problem in *Cox*, this is most regrettable; it seems clear that the presence of an intermediary would have enabled the Court to be assured that the appellant was able to participate effectively in his trial. Instead, the money that may have been saved by not paying for an intermediary was no doubt spent several times over in the form of court delays and the abuse of process application. The Criminal Practice Directions set out (at para.3F.16) the procedure for funding. Where a defendant is publicly funded, application should be made to the Legal Aid Agency to fund a pre-trial assessment. If the LAA refuse, then application may be made to the court.

---

[77] [2012] EWCA Crim 549.
[78] [2009] EWHC 3088 (Admin), discussed at para.27.32, above.
[79] [2005] EWHC 2583 (Admin).

The process of finding a defendant intermediary carries its own problems.   **27.35**
The Witness Intermediary Service ("WIS") does not identify intermediaries
for a defendant.[80] In *R (OP) v Secretary of State for Justice*,[81] the Divisional
Court quashed a decision by the MoJ not to provide a Registered Intermediary to a defendant who had significant learning disabilities and suffered from
Asperger's Syndrome. There was no issue that the defendant, who faced a
summary charge of dishonestly receiving a motorcycle, would be granted a
non-registered intermediary. But the Court noted the protections offered by
the Registered Intermediary scheme which cannot be guaranteed with non-
registered intermediaries, i.e. a six-module training course, a rigorous
assessment and accreditation process, and regulation by reference to Codes
of Practice and Ethics. Rafferty LJ said that at the point that a defendant
goes into the witness box, the system should offer him the best opportunity
to do himself justice. The scheme currently operated would allow a witness
for the prosecution to be supported by a Registered Intermediary matched by
the Witness Intermediary Scheme, but the offender against whom he gave
evidence would be denied one under the same scheme, which would puzzle
the intelligent observer. The disparity created a risk of unfairness or, at the
least, a perceived risk of unfairness. The Court therefore held that, pending
the commencement of s.33BA of the YJCEA 1999 (discussed below), when
a request is received from the defence for a Registered Intermediary,
consideration should be given to granting the request but limiting it to the
stage when the defendant gives evidence. For the remainder of the proceedings, appointment of a suitable non-registered intermediary would be sufficient.

The decision in effect pre-empts the commencement of s.33BA which,   **27.36**
when in force, will empower a court to direct that a defendant is assisted by
a Registered Intermediary during the course of their evidence. The application should be made by the defence and in addition to the meeting of
specified criteria, as explained below, it will be necessary to show that
without an intermediary the defendant would not receive a fair trial. The
provision will be available in both magistrates' courts and the Crown Court.
The statutory restriction on the role of the intermediary to when the
defendant gives evidence is of concern, as is the recent amendment of the
Criminal Practice Directions to state (in para.3F.13) that there is "no
illogicality in restricting the appointment to the defendant's evidence . . .
when the most pressing need arises. Directions to appoint an intermediary
for a defendant's evidence will thus be rare, but for the entire trial extremely
rare." However, in the majority of cases when a defendant needs an
intermediary when giving evidence, they may require assistance to provide
instructions to their legal team, understand the advice received and follow
the evidence of other witnesses. The restriction of the intermediary's role to

---

[80] See para.3F.15 of the Criminal Practice Directions 2015 Amendment No.1 [2016] EWCA
Crim. 97.
[81] [2015] 1 Cr. App. R. 7.

when the defendant gives evidence also goes against the recognition in the *Sevenoaks* case that the duty to assist a defendant may well exist before the trial in order to enable him to prepare effectively and understand all aspects of the trial process. The court pointed out what is known in relation to other witnesses, namely that a defendant must have confidence in the intermediary, and to help achieve this, the defendant and intermediary should meet before the first day of the trial.

27.37   On an application for the use of an intermediary by a defendant aged under 18 at the date of the application, there is a requirement for the applicant to show that the defendant's intellectual ability or social functioning compromises his ability to participate effectively in the proceedings as a witness giving oral evidence.[82] The responsibility for identifying these needs may in reality fall to the defence lawyer who is unlikely to have any form of mental health training. For an adult defendant to be eligible, they must be suffering from a mental disorder or otherwise have significantly impaired intelligence or social function and unable because of their mental disorder or impaired intelligence or social functioning to participate effectively in the proceedings as a witness giving oral evidence in court.[83] For obvious reasons, any evidence given by a defendant with the assistance of an intermediary must be given in such a way that the judge or justices (or indeed both on appeal) are able to see and hear the defendant and communicate with the intermediary. Moreover, the jury and any co-defendant (together with their legal representatives) must be able to see and hear the examination of the defendant.[84] As with intermediaries appointed under s.30, discussed below, an intermediary appointed under s.33BA must make a solemn declaration and s.1 of the Perjury Act 1911 will apply.[85] Section 33BB provides that a court may discharge a direction made under s.33BA if it considers that the direction is no longer necessary or vary a direction if it appears that variation is necessary to ensure a fair trial.[86] For the question whether the courts will have inherent power to order the use of an intermediary in cases falling outside the statutory scheme, once it is in force, see the discussion in paras 27.62 and following, above, above about the live link provisions.

27.38   Despite the limited extension of special measures to defendants, it seems clear that Parliament is determined that fewer special measures should be available to young defendants than to other young witnesses. This is so even though there are no practical difficulties in using the live link. For example the statutory provisions regarding live link do not cover a defendant who is vulnerable through fear or distress. Consequently, concern remains for the defendant who becomes distressed due to the intimidating surroundings of

---

[82] s.33BA(5) of the YJCEA 1999 (as inserted by s.104 of the Coroners and Justice Act 2009, not yet in force).
[83] s.33BA(6) (as inserted by s.104 of the Coroners and Justice Act 2009, not yet in force).
[84] s.33BA(7) (as inserted by s.104 of the Coroners and Justice Act 2009, not yet in force).
[85] s.33BA(9), (10) (as inserted by s.104 of the Coroners and Justice Act 2009, not yet in force).
[86] s.33BB(2) (as inserted by s.104 of the Coroners and Justice Act 2009, not yet in force).

the courtroom or who is fearful of giving evidence in the presence of co-defendants.

Certain special measures would create obvious difficulties for the defence. 27.39 For example, pre-recorded examination-in-chief may give rise to practical problems, such as the need to find a suitable interviewer who is independent of the police but capable of interviewing child or vulnerable witnesses in accordance with the appropriate guidance. One can, therefore, identify reasons why certain special measures should not be extended to defendants.

The question for any court is whether denying a defendant a particular 27.40 special measure will deny him a fair trial. In relation to child defendants, it is important to remember that in order to protect their art.6 rights they must be able to participate effectively in their trial and such participation may be achieved by the use of special measures. It must also be remembered that the disparity between the statutory provision of special measures for defendants and witnesses was considered by the House of Lords in *R. (on the application of D) v Camberwell Green Youth Court*,[87] where the House ruled that such disparity did not of itself breach an accused's art.6 rights; the issue will always be whether an accused had a fair trial.

AVAILABILITY OF SPECIAL MEASURES

All the special measures provided for in ss.23–27, 29 and 30 of the YJCEA 27.41 1999 are available.[88] As discussed above, pre-recorded cross-examination (s.28) has not yet been implemented. Prior to the decision in *R. v R*,[89] it was considered necessary for the Secretary of State to notify (usually by Home Office Circular) when particular special measures became available.[90] In *R. v R* the appellant appealed his conviction for rape. The main evidence against him had been the complainant's ABE interview which took place in July 2004. Two years earlier, on July 24, 2002, the provisions relating to video-recorded evidence-in-chief (s.27 of the YJCEA 1999) had been brought into force, but no notification letter had been sent to the relevant Crown Court informing it that pre-recorded evidence-in-chief was available in adult rape cases. The appellant argued that in those circumstances there had been no power for the Crown Court to admit the ABE interview. That evidence was the primary evidence in the case and without it his conviction was unsafe. In rejecting his appeal, the Court of Appeal held that as there was no geographical restriction on the availability of special measures in the commencement order, special measures had been available across the whole

[87] [2005] UKHL 4; [2005] 1 W.L.R. 393; [2005] 2 Cr. App. R. 1.
[88] Ministry of Justice Circular 2010/09.
[89] [2008] EWCA Crim 678.
[90] The following Circulars were issued pursuant to s.18(2) of the YJCEA 1999: H.O. Circulars 6/2002, 35/2002, 58/2003, 12/2004, 31/2004, 48/2004, 39/2005 and Ministry of Justice Circular 25/06/2007.

of England and Wales since commencement, regardless of the date of notification. Consequently, notification was an administrative procedure upon which the availability of special measures within a particular area did not depend.

27.42   *R. v R* is a welcome and convenient decision. Whatever the correct interpretation of the legislation, it seems clear the Home Office and latterly the Ministry of Justice had sought to achieve phased implementation of special measures and in their circulars had stated that certain special measures were specifically not yet available. In relation to s.27, at the time of R's trial the relevant Circular (58/2003) expressly stated that pre-recorded evidence-in-chief was only available to child witnesses in need of special protection and was not available to adult rape victims; the delay in implementation had been deliberate due to there being insufficient resources for transcribing ABE interviews.

PRE-RECORDED CROSS-EXAMINATION

27.43   The Government brought into force s.28 of the YJCEA 1999 for the purposes of a pilot scheme run from December 30, 2013, in the Crown Court at Kingston-upon-Thames, Leeds and Liverpool, under which the cross-examination and re-examination of witnesses under the age of 16 and vulnerable adult witnesses was pre-recorded for later admission in court.[91] The Ministry of Justice said the scheme would allow children and vulnerable adults to "escape being grilled in court, in front of an audience, by recording their cross-examination away from the highly charged court environment".[92] If the pilot was a success, the MoJ planned to roll out the scheme across England and Wales.

27.44   In his *Review of Efficiency in Criminal Proceedings*, Sir Brian Leveson comments that "technological problems aside" the pilot proved to be a "huge success".[93] We welcome this development, given the trauma that may be suffered by a child or vulnerable witness who has to give evidence about alleged events several months, or longer, after they have been reported to the police and they have given their account in an ABE interview. In cases involving several defendants there can be considerable delay before trial. However, even if pre-recorded cross-examination becomes the norm, safeguards will have to be included to ensure that further questions may be asked if they are justified (although this has not yet proved necessary during the Liverpool pilot). Pre-recorded cross-examination will put pressure upon the courts to ensure that the trial judge is available during the recording of the cross-examination; this will require early allocation. In order to ensure the

---

[91] SI 2013/3236.
[92] *https://www.gov.uk/government/news/victims-to-be-spared-from-harrowing-court-cases* [Accessed April 30, 2016].
[93] (Jan 2015), para.259.

availability of the same advocate, cases will also have to be fixed rather than placed in the warned list. Functioning technology will have to be in place. Crucially, the prosecution will need to comply with disclosure obligations (and consider third party disclosure) at a much earlier stage than is current practice. The defence must have all the material required to conduct the cross-examination in order to ensure a fair trial. Delays in disclosure could lead to the appointed day for pre-recorded cross-examination being adjourned, no doubt causing distress to the witness and all parties involved. We also suggest that cases involving pre-recorded cross-examination will justify the allocation of a reviewing lawyer and assigned caseworker by the Crown Prosecution Service, although this will involve additional resources. Provided the defence have received disclosure, we do not see how there can be an argument against the pre-recording of cross-examination. It may have benefits to the defence who will know in advance of the trial the main evidence against them and will have the luxury of time to address any unexpected matters raised by the witness. The judge will also be able to manage the case more effectively. The recording of cross-examination will be played, without the need for the court to break to accommodate the witness and, as with pre-recorded evidence-in-chief, the recording may also be edited to remove irrelevant or inadmissible passages.

The use of pre-recorded cross-examination by reference to experience in **27.45** different jurisdictions is examined in *Children and Cross-Examination: Time to Change the Rules?*[94] On the same theme is the article, *Pre-recording children's evidence: the Western Australian experience.*[95] The pre-recording of children's evidence has been the norm in Western Australia (which operates an adversarial system) since the early 1990s. After studying its advantages and disadvantages, the authors conclude:

> "In Western Australia, both the judiciary and advocates believe that pre-recording children's entire evidence carries significant advantages, not only in the reduction of children's stress and improvement in their recovery prospects but also the improved quality of their evidence and advantages to the trial process itself. These include the ability to edit the recording of pre-judicial material, to shorten the time juries spend watching the child's evidence, and the advantages to both counsel of knowing the strength and content of the complainant's evidence before trial, raising the prospect of cutting weaker cases from the court waiting list, whether by a guilty plea or prosecutorial withdrawal.
>
> Most importantly Western Australian defence counsel do not believe that pre-recording disadvantages the defence or threatens the defendant's right to a fair trial. In fact, many consider it to have, in one Western Australian judge's words, 'distinct advantages to defence counsel'."

---

[94] Professors J.R. Spencer QC and Michael E. Lamb (eds), *Children and Cross-Examination: Time to Change the Rules?* (Oxford: Hart Publishing, 2012).
[95] E. Henderson, K. Hanna and E. Davies, *Pre-recording children's evidence: the Western Australian experience* [2012] Crim. L.R. 3.

27.46   The authors' reference to stress is significant given that research by Plotnikoff and Woolfson[96] revealed that 123 of the 144 witnesses sampled had experienced signs of pre-trial stress, including self-harming, panic attacks, bed-wetting, loss of concentration, loss of confidence and flashbacks of the offence.

27.47   Professor J.R. Spencer has argued that the defence should be permitted to put their questions to the child in an informal manner shortly after the child has given their ABE interview.[97] This would be compliant with art.6. Professor Spencer considers that unless material later came to light about which the defence needed to ask further questions of the child, the child would then be able to drop out of the proceedings and begin to put the matter behind them.[98] This would assist the child to concentrate on their recovery from the allegation by way of therapy or counselling, as opposed to having to focus upon giving evidence at a future date. Professor Spencer also argues that pre-trial cross-examination may be required in order to comply with European Law. Referring to the *Framework Decision on the Rights of Victims* (2001), in 2005 the European Court of Justice found that Italy had failed to implement its obligation under EU law because it had no mechanism to take the evidence of young children before trial.[99] Professor Spencer argues that the same criticism could be made of the system in England and Wales.

27.48   Professor Spencer expressed his continued support for pre-recorded evidence from children in *Child Witnesses and Cross-examination at Trial: Must it Continue?*[100] He has the support of Lord Judge, the former Lord Chief Justice, who, in delivering the Bar Council's 2013 law reform lecture, *The Evidence of Child Victims: the Next Stage*, said that the requirement for the physical presence of a child witness or victim in the court building should be seen as an "antediluvian hangover from laughable far off days of the quill pen and the ink well".[101] See also *Child Q, England's Youngest Witness*,[102] about a case of child abuse where the three-year-old victim gave evidence, in which prosecution counsel Caroline Wigin is supportive of pre-recorded cross-examination. The child, when aged two, was caused life-threatening injuries by being kicked in the stomach by his mother's cohabitee. There was a delay of one year before the ABE interview and thereafter a further delay

---

[96] *Evaluation of Young Witness Support* (2005), cited in Laura Hoyano, *The Child Witness Review: Much Ado about too Little* [2007] Crim. L.R. 849. See also the conclusion of Laura Hoyano, *Coroners and Justice Act 2009: (3) Special Measures Directions Take Two: Entrenching Unequal Access to Justice* [2010] Crim. L.R. 345.

[97] Professor J.R. Spencer, *Children's Evidence; the Barker Case and the case for Pigot*, *Archbold Review*, Issue 3, April 2, 2010, p.5; *Barker* [2010] EWCA Crim 4 discussed at paras 27.149 and following, below.

[98] Professor J.R. Spencer, last note.

[99] *Criminal Proceedings Against Pupino*, Case C-105/03.

[100] *Archbold Review*, Issue 3, April 3, 2011, pp.7–9.

[101] The lecture is available at *http://www.barcouncil.org.uk/media/241783/annual_law_reform_lecture_rt_hon_the_lord_judge_speech_2013.pdf* [Accessed April 30, 2016].

[102] Caroline Wigin, *Counsel Magazine*, July 2012, pp.24–5.

of eight months before trial. It was inevitably traumatic for the child to relive the experience many months later. Pre-recorded cross-examination could have taken place much earlier around a table with the judge, counsel and the intermediary present; as it was, the first occasion on which the defence were able to put their case was on the live link video.

DETERMINATION OF THE APPROPRIATE SPECIAL MEASURE

In relation to adult witnesses, once it is determined that the witness is eligible for special measures under either s.16 or s.17, the court must determine whether any of the special measures would be likely to improve the quality of the witness's evidence and, if so, must direct the use of the measure or combination of measures which in its opinion is likely to maximise the quality of the evidence.[103] To determine this, the court must consider all the circumstances of the case, including the views of the witness and whether the measure(s) "might tend to inhibit such evidence being tested by a third party to the proceedings".[104] In undertaking this task, the court will need to give detailed consideration to the range of special measures available to adult vulnerable witnesses, some of which are dependent on the witness's particular vulnerability or the nature of the alleged offence. For example, evidence may be given in private (with the exception of a nominated media representative) only if the nature of the offence is sexual or the witness is vulnerable due to intimidation.[105] Intermediaries and communication aids are available only to adult witnesses who are eligible by virtue of their mental or physical impairment (children eligible under s.16 can apply for an intermediary). The other available special measures may be provided to all adult vulnerable witnesses.   27.49

THE "PRIMARY RULE" FOR CHILD WITNESSES: VIDEO-RECORDED EVIDENCE-IN-CHIEF AND LIVE LINK

The issue of eligibility is made simpler now that all witnesses under the age of 18 are within the scope of the "primary rule", that child witnesses give evidence-in-chief by video-recorded statement and any further evidence by live link. An option is preserved whereby the witness can inform the court that they wish the rule to be dis-applied.[106] If, as a result of the witness opting out of the primary rule, they are to give evidence in court (and not via live link), the default position is that their evidence will be given from behind a screen.[107] The court need not order the witness to give evidence from behind   27.50

[103] s.19(2)(a), (b) of the YJCEA 1999.
[104] s.19(3)(a), (b).
[105] s.25(4)(a).
[106] 2009 Act s.100(4)(ba).
[107] s.21(4A) of the YJCEA 1999, inserted by s.100(1), (5) of the Coroners and Justice Act 2009.

a screen if to do so would not maximise their evidence.[108] Again, however, the witness can opt out of this special measure provided the court is satisfied that not complying would not diminish the quality of the witness's evidence.[109] In determining whether the child witness may opt out of the primary rule, the court must consider the following factors relating to the witness: age and maturity, ability to understand the consequences of giving evidence in court rather than by video-recorded statement, any relationship between the witness and the accused, the witness's social, cultural and ethnic background, and the nature and circumstances of the offence being tried, as well as any other factors the court considers relevant.[110] The same provisions apply for qualifying witnesses.[111] The court must then consider whether the special measures available in relation to the witness would be likely to improve the quality of their evidence and, if so, which measures would be likely to maximise the quality of their evidence.[112]

27.51   In *R. (on the application of D) v Camberwell Green Youth Court*,[113] the defence argued that to secure the defendant's right under art.6(3)(d) to examine witnesses, the court was required to consider the circumstances of every case as opposed to applying a generic rule. The House of Lords held that the court must start from the statutory presumption that there is nothing intrinsically unfair to defendants in child witnesses giving evidence in accordance with the primary rule. As for art.6, nothing in the provisions of the YJCEA 1999 is inconsistent with its principles, because all the evidence is produced at trial in the presence of the accused who can see and hear it and has every opportunity to challenge and question the witnesses against him. The only element missing is a face-to-face confrontation, which is not guaranteed by the Convention. The courts are entitled to apply the special measures scheme without showing special justification in every case because Parliament had decided that the scheme is justified for good policy reasons. Baroness Hale noted that after a live link direction has been made, the court may give permission under s.24(3) of the YJCEA 1999 for the witness to give evidence in some other way, if this appears to be in the interests of justice. The appropriate time to consider these matters will usually be at trial, when the trial judge will be in the best position to consider the matter in the round. Possible circumstances in which permission may be given under s.24(3) are where the live link equipment is not working properly, or where the child is positively anxious to give evidence in court rather than via the live link, or where the alleged abuse involved video recording of the witness. Similarly, circumstances may arise in which the court may, in the exercise of its discretion under s.27(2) of the Act,[114] exclude the video-recorded interview as

---

[108] s.21(4B)(b), inserted by s.100(1), (5) of the Coroners and Justice Act 2009.
[109] s.21(4B)(a), inserted by s.100(1), (5) of the Coroners and Justice Act 2009.
[110] s.21(4C), inserted by s.100(1), (6) of the Coroners and Justice Act 2009.
[111] s.22(2), amended by s.100(8), (5) of the Coroners and Justice Act 2009.
[112] ss.21(2), 19(2).
[113] [2005] UKHL 4; [2005] 1 W.L.R. 393; [2005] 2 Cr. App. R. 1.
[114] Discussed in paras 27.82 and following, below.

the child's evidence-in-chief, on the ground that it would not be in the interests of justice for it to be admitted.

The presumption that the primary rule will apply creates certainty and a   **27.52**
degree of reassurance for the majority of witnesses who will know in advance how their evidence will be presented. Contrast with this the position under s.32A of the Criminal Justice Act 1988 (the previous legislation relating to the admissibility of video-recorded evidence of children) as construed by the Divisional Court in *R. v Redbridge Youth Court*.[115] The Court (in a judgment by Latham LJ) held that Parliament had provided that a video interview was the primary method of presenting the evidence of a child witness where there had been such an interview. The wording of s.32A(3)(c) made clear that leave had to be granted for the video recording to be admitted, unless, having regard to all the circumstances of the case, it was not in the interests of justice for it to be admitted. The Court held that where s.32A(3)(c) was at issue, the court was required to consider whether there would be any arguable injustice in admitting the video. It would be for the defendant to establish that any prejudice to him displaced Parliament's intention in making the video interview the primary method of presenting the child's evidence. If the injustice alleged was simply the fact that the child would not be giving live evidence, it was unlikely that could ever prevail if there was material which established that the child could be upset, intimidated or traumatised by appearing in court, as a result of which there was a real risk that the quality of the child's evidence would be affected or that no evidence would be forthcoming. Accordingly, the court was required to consider on the one hand the extent to which the child's evidence would be affected if the video recording was not admitted in evidence, and on the other the prejudice to the defendant if the recording was admitted. In short, the Court interpreted s.32A(3)(c) as requiring the court to carry out a balancing exercise between the interests of the child witness and the defendant. But the suggestion that the party calling the child witness should demonstrate that the child would suffer some upset or intimidation if they gave live evidence in court was open to criticism as erecting a hurdle to the admission of video evidence which Parliament had not intended. By contrast, the mandatory nature of the primary rule in the 1999 Act appears to make such an interpretation impossible.

It is, however, submitted that the advocate should consider the best means   **27.53**
of presenting the witness' evidence. Even before the commencement of the YJCEA 1999, research commissioned by the Home Office saw value in giving prosecuting counsel greater latitude in determining the use to be made of video-recorded evidence in the presentation of the case,[116] but the decision was made that certainty for the witness was of paramount importance. Those responsible for witnesses will need to support the child witness in making

---

[115] [2001] Crim. L.R. 473, DC.
[116] Davis et al, *An Assessment of the Admissibility and Sufficiency of Evidence in Child Abuse Prosecutions*, Home Office (1999).

their decision as to how they would prefer to give evidence. It may be difficult to explain to a young child the differences between giving evidence in court or by video recording and via the video-link, and time will have to be spent properly consulting with the witness. Moreover, if in a particular instance the use of pre-recorded evidence-in-chief were to contravene the defendant's art.6 right to a fair trial, it is inconceivable that the video would be admitted. In terms of the legislative scheme, admission of the video evidence in those circumstances would be contrary to the interests of justice and would therefore fall within the exception in s.27(2).

Video-Recorded Examination-in-Chief and Supplementary Questions

27.54   The ability of the party calling the witness to remedy any perceived difficulty with the video recording is constrained by the extent to which they are allowed to ask the witness supplementary questions.[117] If a matter has not been dealt with at all in the interview, it is inferred that questions may be asked in relation to it as of right. However, there is no right to examine a witness on matters that have been dealt with adequately in the video interview.[118] Where matters have been dealt with inadequately in the interview, the court may grant leave to ask supplementary questions either of its own motion or on application by a party to the proceedings.[119] In either case, the court must be satisfied that asking the questions is in the interests of justice. The court may also be able to exercise a discretion to permit supplementary questions of its own motion if it considers it to be in the interests of justice.

Types of Special Measures

27.55   Section 22A of the YJCEA 1999[120] provides that adult complainants in trials for sexual offences in the Crown Court (but not in magistrates' courts) may give evidence-in-chief by way of video-recorded statement under s.27 of the YJCEA 1999, unless this would not be in the interests of justice or would not maximise the quality of the complainant's evidence. In the case of other vulnerable adult witnesses, the court must consider which type of special measures direction is likely to maximise the quality of their evidence. As for child witnesses, once the court has gone through the detailed procedures set out in ss.21 and 22 of the YJCEA 1999, described above, it must then consider in accordance with s.19(2) whether any additional special measures are likely to further improve the quality of the witness's evidence. Pt 18 of the

[117] s.27(5) of the YJCEA 1999.
[118] s.27(5)(b)(i).
[119] s.27(5)(b)(ii).
[120] Inserted by s.101 of the Coroners and Justice Act 2009 as from June 27, 2011 (SI 2011/1452).

Criminal Procedure Rules 2015 set out the correct procedure for applying for special measures directions and certain requirements as to intermediaries and editing of pre-recorded evidence.

With the exception of pre-recorded cross-examination and re-examination **27.56** all special measures have been implemented.

SCREENS

Section 23 of the YJCEA 1999 provides for the use of screens in court.   **27.57**

It may be impossible to assess but practitioners have often expressed the **27.58** view that the impact of a witness's evidence upon a jury or fact-finder is increased by the use of screens and diminished by the use of live link. However, with the use today in most court centres of good quality, large screens (as opposed to small table-top monitors) it may well be that such comments are no longer valid.[121] The screens enable everyone in the courtroom to see the witness, and so it may be an additional reassurance to the witness who gives evidence from behind a screen that the accused and the public gallery cannot see them. This in itself causes concern, because the usual course would be for a defendant to see each witness who gives evidence against them. It should only be in exceptional cases that a defendant does not see those who accuse him.[122] All too often screens are simply agreed by the parties and sanctioned by the court without full consideration being given to the defendant's right to see the witness. Juries are often reminded that in assessing a witness's evidence they should consider not just what the witness said, but also their demeanour. If the witness's demeanour is important to the tribunal of fact, the defendant should not be denied the same opportunity to assess the witness.[123] The Privy Council has held that an individual can have a fair trial even though the witnesses are shielded from him and, unless being directly questioned by them, from the defendant's counsel. Lords Brown and Roger dissented, on the ground that it is essential that the defendant's representatives and the prosecution should be in a position to see the witness during the entirety of their evidence.[124]

---

[121] That said, in many courts the large screens are on the opposite wall some distance away from the jury box. It may be harder for the jury to assess the witness's demeanour compared to that of the witness who gives evidence directly opposite and focused upon them.

[122] *Taylor* [1995] Crim. L.R. 253, CA; *R. v Watford Magistrates' Court Ex p. Lenman* [1993] Crim. L.R. 388, CA.

[123] Laura Hoyano, *The Child Witness Review: Much Ado about too Little* [2008] Crim. L.R., p.859. See also *Van Mechelen v Netherlands* (1987) 25 E.H.R.R. 647 at [50], ECtHR; *Hols v Netherlands* App. No.25206/94 ruled inadmissible, October 19, 1995 at [7], EComHR; *Stanford v United Kingdom* [1994] E.C.H.R. 16757/90 at [26], ECtHR and Ms Hoyano's article, *Striking a Balance between the Rights of Defendants and Vulnerable Witnesses: will Special Measures Directions Contravene Guarantees of a Fair Trial?* [2001] Crim. L.R. 948, p.963.

[124] *Attorney General for the Sovereign Base Areas of Akrotiri and Dhekelia v Steinhoff* [2005] UKPC 31.

27.59   For many years supporters have been able to accompanying a screened witness.[125] Amendments made to the YJCEA 1999 by the Coroners and Justice Act 2009 provided that a supporter may accompany the witness in the live link room, but there is no equivalent provision that expressly permits a screened witness to be supported. Nonetheless, we submit that witnesses should be provided with the support they need whether they give evidence from behind a screen or in a live link room. Any supporter, whether they are with a screened witness or in the live link room, must act with care to ensure that they do nothing to encourage the witness to give anything other than truthful evidence.[126] It is suggested that they should say nothing at all and, if they do speak, should do so audibly.[127]

27.60   The fact that a bench of magistrates are asked to consider an application for screens will not necessarily preclude them from hearing the case.[128] In a trial on indictment, the jury should be directed that no adverse inference should be drawn against the accused from the use of the screen, but the absence of such a direction is not necessary fatal to a conviction.[129]

27.61   Finally, it was held in *Brown and Grant* that the fact that one witness elects to give evidence without screens does not require that all other witnesses do so as well.[130]

LIVE LINK

27.62   Whilst the use of the live link is not uncommon in the Crown Court, its use is extended by s.24 of the YJCEA 1999 to all child witnesses and eligible adult witnesses. A supporter may also accompany the witness whilst giving evidence in the live link room in order to provide emotional support and reduce anxiety. In determining who may accompany the witness, the court must have regard to the witness's wishes.[131] For example, whilst a young child might be reassured by the presence of an older supporter, a teenager may feel uncomfortable giving evidence about personal sexual matters in the presence of such a person. Also, it should not be assumed that the witness would prefer the support of an individual of the same gender.

27.63   Until recently, the supporter was required to be someone completely independent of the witness or his or her family, as well as without knowledge

---

[125] *R. v X* (1990) 91 Cr. App. R. 36 (child witnesses); *Cooper and Schaub* [1994] Crim. L.R. 531; *Foster* [1995] Crim. L.R. 333; *Nicholas,* unreported, December 13, 1994, CA; *Best,* unreported, December 7, 1999 (No.98/6932/X5) (adult witnesses).

[126] *R. v X* (1990) 91 Cr. App. R. 36.

[127] *Smith* [1994] Crim. L.R. 458.

[128] *KL and LK v DPP,* 166 J.P. 369, QBD (Richards, J.).

[129] *Ghani,* Unreported, October 25, 1999, CA (No.99/04599/Z4); *Brown and Grant* [2004] EWCA Crim 1620.

[130] [2004] EWCA Crim 1620.

[131] s.24(1A), (1B) of the YJCEA 1999, inserted by s.102 of the Coroners and Justice Act 2009 with effect from June 27, 2011 (SI 2011/1452).

of or personal involvement in the case. The Criminal Practice Directions 2015 now provide[132]:

> "An increased degree of flexibility is appropriate as to who can act as supporter. This can be anyone known to and trusted by the witness who is not a party to the proceedings and has no detailed knowledge of the evidence in the case. The supporter may be a member of the Witness Service but need not be an usher or court official. Someone else may be appropriate."

In practice, if the supporter is not an usher, they will often be a representative of the Witness Service. A supporter from the Witness Service does not assume the responsibilities of the usher in the live link room, and as such the usher should continue to be available to assist the witness and the supporter and to ensure that the judge's requirements are properly complied with in the room.[133]

It is important to be flexible and to understand the needs of a vulnerable   **27.64** witness; the usual way of eliciting evidence may not in fact enable that particular witness to give their best evidence. David Wurtzel cites an example where a five-year-old (aged four at the date of the incident) was to give evidence.[134] The intermediary had identified that the child's communication was most effective when she was face-to-face with the person asking her questions. Before trial the child had practiced communicating through the live link, but her communication was less effective and she found it more difficult to concentrate. It is no surprise that children (and indeed adults) may find answering questions to a screen disengaging. The suggestion at the "ground rules" meeting was that the advocates join the witness in the live link room. This was permitted by the judge and had the advantage of visual aids being in the same room as the advocate and the witness. Counsel noted that the proximity between him and the witness made it easier for him to adjust his tone and pace when appropriate. The Criminal Practice Directions 2015 suggest that witnesses should be afforded the opportunity to practice with the live link equipment as opposed to simply being shown the live link room.[135]

With the approval of the Recorder of Durham, Judge Christopher Price   **27.65** and the Ministry of Justice, Durham Police are currently piloting a scheme whereby complainants who allege sexual assaults give their evidence from a Sexual Assault Referral Centre ("SARC") located away from the court. Reports indicate that the first case involved a young complainant who was cross-examined for less than five minutes following a ground rules hearing in which the judge approved the defence questions. A significant advantage of the complainant giving evidence some distance from the court building is that it removes the risk of an accidental encounter between the complainant

---

[132] CPD 18B.2.
[133] CPD 18B.5, 3F.29 and 3G.2 [2016] EWCA Crim 97.
[134] *Time to Change the Rules, Counsel Magazine,* November 2012, pp.32–34.
[135] CPD 18B.4.

and defendants. Such an encounter may be stressful for both parties.[136] Sir Brian Leveson anticipated such an approach and that with the correct technological support evidence from vulnerable witnesses could be obtained outside of the court setting.[137]

Gɪᴠɪɴɢ Eᴠɪᴅᴇɴᴄᴇ ɪɴ Pʀɪᴠᴀᴛᴇ

27.66 Section 25 of the YJCEA 1999 provides that proceedings may take place in private if they relate to a sexual offence or where there are reasonable grounds to believe that a person other than the accused has intimidated, or will seek to intimidate, the witness in connection with giving evidence.[138] The accused, his legal representatives or any appointed interpreter may not be excluded.[139] Despite the provision that justice should be seen to be done, a properly considered direction that evidence be given in private is unlikely to breach the defendant's right to a fair trial.[140]

Rᴇᴍᴏᴠᴀʟ ᴏғ Wɪɢs ᴀɴᴅ Gᴏᴡɴs

27.67 Section 26 of the YJCEA provides a statutory basis for the uncontroversial procedure of removing wigs and gowns.

Vɪᴅᴇᴏ-Rᴇᴄᴏʀᴅᴇᴅ Eᴠɪᴅᴇɴᴄᴇ-ɪɴ-Cʜɪᴇғ

27.68 Section 27 provides for the evidence-in-chief of any eligible witness to be pre-recorded. An advantage of pre-recorded evidence-in-chief is the avoidance of memory loss in the period between the alleged incident and the trial. Moreover, in the case of a young witness it assists the jury in assessing the witness's maturity level closer to the time of the alleged incident, rather than at trial when their cognitive functioning may have developed considerably.

27.69 Current guidance for interviewers is found in *Achieving Best Evidence in Criminal Proceedings: Guidance on Interviewing Victims and Witnesses and Guidance on Using Special Measures*[141] ("the ABE guidance") and ACPO's *Advice on the Structure of Visually Recorded Witness Interviews.*[142] It is, though, important to recognise the challenges presented by the fact that ABE interviews serve two distinct purposes: investigative and evidential. Those conducting the interviews are required simultaneously to investigate an offence and consider how to take a witness through their evidence-in-chief. In

---

[136] *The Northern Echo*, October 10, 2015.
[137] *Review of Efficiency in Criminal Proceedings* (Jan 2015), para.259.
[138] s.25(4) of the YJCEA 1999.
[139] s.25(2).
[140] *Richards* 163 J.P. 246, CA.
[141] MoJ, November 2011, available at *https://www.cps.gov.uk/publications/docs/best_evidence_in_criminal_proceedings.pdf* [Accessed April 30, 2016].
[142] 2nd edition, October 2013.

cases where a relatively straightforward allegation has been made against a single individual, this may not prove too difficult a task but in many cases the investigating officer will not know the full details of the allegation prior to the interview. In cases involving human trafficking or so-called sex-rings, it is a very difficult task to obtain an account from a witness, let alone a coherent and chronological account that will assist the jury to determine the issues in the case. We therefore welcome the recommendation of Sir Brian Leveson that two interviews (conducted in accordance with Achieving Best Evidence guidance) should take place,[143] a general investigative interview followed by a shorter interview, which is presented chronologically and directed only at the relevant material. The second interview would be presented as evidence-in-chief. This approach will enable the investigating officer to explore matters fully with the witness without needing to consider whether they are admissible in criminal proceedings. In human trafficking cases, for example, investigators are keen for intelligence material to identify suspects and trafficking routes. They cannot limit or even compartmentalise the interview they conduct. The second interview could focus upon the proposed charges.

It is, however, important to acknowledge that the impact of a witness's **27.70** evidence may be reduced when their ABE interview is played as evidence-in-chief. In respect of an adult witness, therefore, consideration should always be given as to whether they would be prepared to provide a witness statement and give their evidence-in-chief live before the jury, with screens if appropriate. This will of course be a matter for the individual witness, but simply because a witness meets the eligibility criteria for a particular special measure does not mean inflexibility as to how the prosecution case is presented.

We understand that new digital video-recording equipment is being **27.71** installed in certain ABE suites, which should improve the quality of recordings. Officers interviewing vulnerable witnesses must ensure that the camera is in the best position to maximise the impact of the evidence. The camera is often positioned at ceiling height in the corner of the room. As the sensitive nature of the subject matter may mean that the witness looks down when speaking, this can result in the jury seeing only the top of the witness's head throughout the entire interview. This is disengaging and the impact of the evidence may be lost. Also, the camera lens is all too often focused some distance from the witness, leaving a jury in a large courtroom unable to see facial expressions and demeanour. It is not a question of putting the camera physically close to the witness, but of zooming in to the witness's face so that the jury are afforded the best possible view. The assistant interviewer who watches the interview from a separate room should be aware of such matters and intervene if the witness cannot be seen properly on the screen. Best practice is for the camera to clearly show the witness's head, face and upper body.

---

[143] *Review of Efficiency in Criminal Proceedings* (Jan 2015), para.250.

27.72   When planning an interview it may be necessary for the child to be assessed. While such an assessment is unlikely to be video-recorded, a full written record must be kept, referred to in a witness statement relating to the interview and submitted to the CPS.[144]

27.73   The ABE guidance suggests brevity in respect of neutral topics and at the rapport stage. If extensive rapport is needed, this can be dealt with prior to the recorded interview. Moreover, there is no requirement for interviewers to summarise throughout the interview everything the witness says. Continued repetition by the interviewing officer may discourage the witness from giving their best evidence and the evidence is likely to have less impact in front of the jury.

27.74   The case of *R. v MH*[145] involved a four-year-old giving evidence at a trial held 15 months after the recording of his ABE interview. The appellant was critical of the interview, which did not strictly comply with the ABE guidance in three respects: the child had not been asked about truth and lies; the allegation followed a leading question ("Can you remember what happened to your winky?"); and the child had been praised at the end of the interview as "a very good boy". The appeal was dismissed. The Court of Appeal said that the leading question did not suggest what the boy's answer should be and could have prompted a comment which accorded with the appellant's case. In fact the boy's response, "Daddy sucked it", was "immediate, unguarded, direct and clear". It was not essential for a child of such an age to be confronted with the concepts of truth and lies, and the praise at the end of the interview was insignificant.

27.75   In *Davies*,[146] the appellant was convicted of six counts of indecent assault (contrary to s.14 of the Sexual Offences Act 1956) which took place over a period of two-and-a-half years between 1985 and 1988 when the complainant was aged 8–11 years old. At trial, the defence objected to the ABE interview being played as the complainant's evidence-in-chief because it potentially deprived them of the ability to cross-examine on any differences between the account provided by the complainant in her ABE interview and what she might say if she gave live evidence before the jury. The appeal was allowed on other grounds, but Roderick Evans J, delivering the judgment of the Court of Appeal, said that when a witness is eligible for special measures under s.19(2) of the YJEA 1999, it is for the judge to determine whether any of the available special measures would be likely to improve the quality of the witness's evidence by considering all the circumstances of the case, including the views of the witness and whether the special measure requested would inhibit the effective testing of the evidence by the defendant. The speculative possibility that a witness might say something when giving evidence that is different to the account given during the ABE interview is not, in itself, an

[144] ABE guidance, paras 2.47 and following.
[145] [2012] EWCA Crim 2725; [2013] Crim. L.R. 10, 849–853 (with commentary by Laura Hoyano).
[146] [2011] EWCA Crim 1177.

adequate reason for the ABE interview not to stand as the witness's evidence-in-chief. Laura Hoyano has remarked that, had this ground of appeal succeeded, the legislation would have been eviscerated.[147]

Arguments of injustice based solely upon the fact that the witness is not giving "live" evidence are unlikely ever to succeed, nor will the absence of live evidence breach a defendant's right to examine witnesses under art.6(3)(d) ECHR.[148] Also, the court has a duty to further the overriding objective to deal with cases justly,[149] which includes not only dealing with the prosecution and defence fairly but also respecting the interests of witnesses.[150] It has been recognised that whilst witnesses are not protected by art.6, other protections guaranteed by the Convention may be affected when they give evidence, for example, the right to private life guaranteed by art.8. The principles of a fair trial accordingly require that in appropriate cases a balance is struck between the interests of a defendant and the interests of the witness called to give evidence on behalf of the State.[151] 27.76

The fact that an account is provided in a video-recorded interview does not make admissible any inadmissible evidence contained within the recording.[152] It is important that any inadmissible passages are agreed or ruled upon well in advance of the trial so that the video recording can be appropriately edited. It was held in *R. v B(K)*[153] that answers given during the "rapport" stage at the beginning of the interview, although not strictly relevant to the issues at trial, were unobjectionable and did not need to be excluded. In the same case a social worker had commented during the interview that the complainant was "doing really well". The jury ought to have been directed not to take the social worker's comment into account but there was no need to edit the comment from the video. 27.77

In *R. v M(A)*,[154] the Court of Appeal underlined the importance of securing agreement or a judicial ruling on edits in advance of trial, and held that the parties are entitled to rely upon edited passages not being admitted into evidence. In that case the trial judge, in response to a question from the jury, adduced evidence of recent complaint which, somewhat surprisingly, had been edited by agreement from the complainant's ABE interview. The witness was then recalled. The Court of Appeal allowed an appeal against conviction on the ground that the appellant had been caused unfair prejudice. An agreement as to edits was generally binding, though not absolute, and whilst it was important to answer questions from the jury 27.78

---

[147] See commentary at [2011] Crim. L.R. 732.
[148] *R. v Redbridge Youth Court* [2001] Crim. L.R. 473, DC and *R. (D) v Camberwell Green Youth Court* [2005] UKHL 4; [2005] 1 W.L.R. 393; [2005] 2 Cr. App. R. 1.
[149] Criminal Procedure Rules 2015 r.1.1.
[150] Criminal Procedure Rules 2015 r.1.1(2)(b) and (d).
[151] *Doorson v Netherlands* 22 E.H.R.R. 330 (a drugs case).
[152] *R. (on the application of CPS Harrow) v Brentford Youth Court* [2003] EWHC 2409 (Admin).
[153] [2002] EWCA Crim 2140.
[154] [2012] EWCA Crim 899; [2013] 1 Cr. App. R. 245.

accurately and without in any way misleading them, it should be remembered that the trial process was adversarial, not inquisitorial. The Court said it was of crucial importance that there had been no criticism in this case of how the defence had conducted their case, and in particular they had not sought to ambush the prosecution with their line of questioning, such as would have entitled the prosecution to revisit the agreement over editing. The Criminal Practice Direction provides that the party applying to adduce the video-recorded evidence is obliged to edit the video in accordance with any direction made by the court and serve edited copies on the court and other parties.[155] Failure to prepare a correctly edited copy could lead to an adjournment and the appropriate award of costs.[156] Video recordings should be produced into evidence by the interviewer or an individual present at the interview.

27.79   The court may also exclude the video where the witness is unavailable for cross-examination and the parties have not agreed that there is no need for the witness to be so available.[157]

27.80   It should be noted that s.119 of the Criminal Justice Act 2003 provides for the admission of previous inconsistent statements as evidence of the truth of their contents, thereby providing an additional vehicle, in appropriate circumstances, for the admission of video-recorded interviews. In *Crown Prosecution Service v CE*,[158] it was held that video evidence given by a complainant of rape and tendered as hearsay under s.116 of the 2003 Act was fairly excluded by the trial judge where the complainant refused to attend court to be cross-examined through fear, which had not been induced by the defendant. The Court of Appeal said that the admission of the evidence would have infringed art.6 (3) of the ECHR, and that if the defendant had been convicted on the basis of hearsay evidence, which had not been subject to cross-examination, he would have been likely to succeed in an appeal against conviction. For discussion of the hearsay provisions, see Ch.19.

27.81   Finally, regardless of whether the video recording has been admitted as their evidence-in-chief, a witness is entitled to refresh their memory by watching the video provided the criteria set out in s.139 of the Criminal Justice Act 2003 are met. The witness may accordingly refresh their memory provided they state in oral evidence that the video records their recollection of the events and that at the time that it was recorded their recollection was significantly better than at the time of giving oral evidence. Where a transcript of the recording has been made, the witness may refresh their memory by reference to the transcript. What is not necessary is for the witness to watch their ABE recording at the same time as the jury.[159] In many

---

[155] CPD 2015, 16B.2: see Amendment No.1 [2016] EWCA Crim. 97.
[156] CPD 2015, 16B.4: see Amendment No.1 [2016] EWCA Crim. 97.
[157] s.27(4) of the YJCEA 1999.
[158] [2006] EWCA Crim 1410.
[159] *Equal Treatment Bench Book* (November 2013), para.5; Criminal Practice Directions Amendment No.1 [2016] EWCA Crim. 97, 18C.

cases it will be far better for the witness to have watched their ABE recording away from the court setting and a day or two before they attend court for cross-examination. Consideration should be given to: (i) the venue for watching the ABE recording; (ii) monitoring of the viewing by the officer in the case, who will note any comments; (iii) advice from the intermediary as to whether the witness should watch the video recording more than once; (iv) if the witness does not watch the video recording at the same time as the jury, arrangements for them to watch it shortly before being cross-examined.

Exclusion of video-recorded interview in the interests of justice

The fact that an eligible witness has been video-interviewed does not   **27.82**
necessarily mean that their evidence will be admitted at trial in that format. Witnesses must be made aware that the court retains a discretion (under s.27(2) of the YJCEA 1999) to exclude the video recording, in whole or in part, if it considers that it is not in the interests of justice to admit it.[160] The consideration for the court is whether any prejudice to the defendant which might result from the admission of the recording is outweighed by the desirability of showing the whole, or substantially the whole, of the recorded interview.[161]

Where an application is made to exclude a video recording on the grounds   **27.83**
of the interests of justice because there have been breaches of the guidelines for conducting such interviews, the court should ask itself whether a reasonable jury properly directed could be sure that the witness has given a credible and accurate account on the video recording, notwithstanding any breaches.[162] If the answer is "yes", the breaches are a matter for the jury. If "no", the interview should be ruled inadmissible. *Howard K*[163] concerned an allegation that the appellant had indecently assaulted his daughter. Three video-recorded interviews were conducted when the child was six years old, and it was only in the third that she implicated the appellant. The interviews had been conducted in breach of the ABE guidance[164] because the complainant's mother had been present and had participated. At one point, she said to her daughter: "You have to tell the truth, then we can go." Shortly afterwards, the complainant gave the evidence that implicated the appellant. In deciding whether to admit that evidence, the trial judge considered whether the evidence given on the video recording could be relied upon by

[160] s.27(2), s.21(4)(b) of the YJCEA 1999.
[161] s.27(3).
[162] *Howard K* [2006] 2 Cr. App. R. 10, citing with approval *Hanton* [2005] EWCA Crim 2009. The passages to which objection is taken should be identified in advance for the judge to consider, along with the comments of the applicant and the Crown either presented side-by-side in an accompanying schedule or written on photocopies of the relevant parts of the transcript: *Aboulkadir* [2009] EWCA Crim 956 at [23].
[163] [2006] 2 Cr. App. R. 10.
[164] See now *Achieving Best Evidence in Criminal Proceedings: Guidance on Interviewing Victims and Witnesses, and Using Special Measures*, available at *https://www.cps.gov.uk/publications/docs/best_evidence_in_criminal_proceedings.pdf* [Accessed April 30, 2016].

reference to other supporting evidence. The Court of Appeal held that the primary consideration should be the reliability of the video-recorded evidence, which will normally be assessed by reference to the interview itself, the conditions under which it was held, the age of the child and the nature and extent of any breach of the guidelines. There might be cases where other evidence demonstrated that the breaches had not had the effect of undermining the credibility or accuracy of the video interview, but any reference to other evidence should be made with considerable caution. Although in *Howard K* the judge had not addressed the appropriate test in terms, it was plain that he had in fact considered whether the jury could properly rely on the video and the Court declined to allow the appeal on that basis.[165] In the course of its judgment the Court considered the earlier case of *G v DPP*,[166] where it was held not to be in the interests of justice to admit a video recording (under the previous provision in s.32A of the Criminal Justice Act 1988) because the interview had been conducted in breach of the Memorandum of Good Practice on interviewing vulnerable witnesses.[167] The Court said that whether or not to admit a video recording will depend upon the degree of likelihood that the evidence is reliable. In *G v DPP* it was noted that an application to edit the video would not necessarily be determined by reference to the nature and extent of the breaches but would depend upon the extent to which the tainted passages were supported by other passages of which no complaint could be made.

27.84   A decision as to whether to exclude the entirety of the video may depend upon other evidence in the case. In *Howard K,* the Court stressed that the primary consideration is the reliability of the video-recorded evidence and not the existence of corroborative evidence. This point was reiterated in *Krezolek; Luczak*,[168] where the Court said that it is not the modern approach to subject the accounts of children to the same kind of forensic analysis as that sometimes applied to adult witnesses; allowance must be made for the fact that children may well have certain difficulties (such as in the present case, where the child struggled to place things in the correct chronological order), but that does not render their evidence unreliable. This test of whether, despite leading questions, a reasonable jury could conclude that a mentally disordered victim had given a credible account was applied in *Boxer*.[169] In dismissing the appeal, the Court concluded that the victim had given his central account in response to open questions and had given clear and direct answers. Consequently the absence of an intermediary during the interview and a series of leading questions did not render the entire video inadmissible.

---

[165] Although the appeal was allowed on another ground. See also cases relating to competence, discussed at paras 27.143 and following, below.
[166] [1997] 2 Cr. App. R. 78.
[167] [1997] 2 Cr. App. R. 78 (decided in relation to the 1992 *Memorandum of Good Practice on Video Recorded Interviews for Child Witnesses for Criminal Proceedings*).
[168] [2015] Crim. L.R. 628.
[169] *Boxer* [2015] EWCA Crim 1684.

Video recordings have been excluded where a witness subsequently   27.85
retracted the evidence given in the recording[170] and where the video only
showed the child in profile.[171] Video-recorded evidence has been admissible
when the interview occurred some years before trial[172] and where another
complainant had been present whilst the interview was being conducted.[173]

Exclusion of video-recorded interview: witness retraction

Video-recorded interviews may be excluded in the interests of justice when   27.86
the witness has subsequently indicated that they wish to change the evidence
given in the interview. In *Hawkins*[174] the appellant was convicted on four
counts of indecent assault on K, a girl of 13. It was proposed that the
evidence of K and another child witness (R) should be given by way of video-
recordings under s.32A of the Criminal Justice Act 1988. Before leave was
given to admit the recordings, R indicated that she wished to change what she
had said in her interview, particularly on one count. It now appeared that the
incident she described was no more than a playful argument. The appellant
argued at trial that the video recording of R's interview should not be
admitted, since the evidence it contained was no longer the evidence which R
was prepared to give. The judge rejected that argument and made it plain that
he thought R might have been exposed to some improper influence. At trial,
R's evidence was given by video recording and she was cross-examined about
her change of mind, which she confirmed. The appellant was convicted. On
appeal, the Court of Appeal said that where a young witness later gives a
different account to that which is contained in her video-recorded interview,
it is a matter for the judge's discretion whether to permit the video evidence
to be given or to require the child to be examined afresh. In the present case,
the judge had properly taken into account that the object of s.32A was to
spare a child the trauma of giving evidence, in so far as that could be done.
He also had in mind that the defence were in possession of R's later statement
and were in a position to cross-examine her upon the changed account.
Finally, he had directed the jury only to have regard to R's evidence on the
particular count in so far as they considered that it helped the appellant. In
those circumstances, the judge's exercise of his discretion was far from being
plainly wrong and the attack upon it failed.

A contrasting case is *Parker*,[175] where the appellant was charged with   27.87
committing sexual offences against a number of boys. It became known that
one of the boys (B) had retracted the allegations made in his video-recorded
interview and was a reluctant witness. In those circumstances, it was held that

---

[170] This issue is discussed at paras 29.86 and following, below.
[171] *PI* [1998] C.Law.
[172] *Best*, Unreported, December 7, 1999 (No.98/6932/X5).
[173] *D (Michael) and S (Anthony)* 2002 166 J.P. 792.
[174] (1995) C.L.Y. 946; February 20, 1995, CA (No.94/5793/X4).
[175] [1996] Crim. L.R. 511.

the judge should have excluded the recording and that B should have given his evidence-in-chief before the jury (possibly by means of the live link). The Court said that this would have prevented the tainting of the jury's deliberations, which was inevitable, despite the directions given by the judge, if the video recording was admitted.[176]

27.88   European case law suggests that where evidence that has subsequently been retracted is relied upon, this will not necessarily make the trial unfair. In *Doorson v Netherlands*[177] it was held not to be improper for the witness to be cross-examined on his previous statement and for the court to compare the statement he gave to the police with the evidence he gave to the court and reach its own conclusion as to which account, if any, to believe.

Replaying the video

27.89   A further question of great practical importance is whether, once the video has been played as the witness's evidence-in-chief, it may be replayed to the jury. Evidence given by video captures not merely the witness's words but also their demeanour and vocal inflection, which is also likely to be of vital importance in the case. In those circumstances, it is not surprising that juries sometimes ask to re-view a video after they have retired to consider their verdict. Clearly, had the witness given live evidence such repetition would not be possible. The courts have consistently taken the view that replaying of the video should be discouraged, as it departs from the normal course of events in a criminal trial and arguably provides the prosecution with a second bite of the evidential cherry.[178]

27.90   The leading case is *Rawlings and Broadbent*,[179] where the prosecution had relied upon the child complainant's video interview to stand as their evidence-in-chief. While considering their verdict, the jury asked to re-view the video, a request to which the judge agreed. It was argued on appeal that a video should not be replayed as to do so would give undue weight to the witness's evidence-in-chief in the absence of recorded cross-examination to redress the balance. The Court of Appeal held that that it was a matter for the judge's discretion whether a video should be replayed. In exercising that discretion, the potential unfairness of replaying only the complainant's evidence-in-chief and no other evidence should be borne in mind. The judge should clarify with the jury whether they wished to be reminded of *what* the witness said or *how* the witness said it. If the jury needed to be reminded of what was said, this could usually be done by reference to the judge's note. But if the judge in his discretion allowed the video or the relevant part to be replayed, he should comply with the following three requirements:

[176] See also *Riby*, Unreported, February 6, 1995, CA (No.94/4933/Y5).
[177] 22 E.H.R.R. 330, at 349 (76–77).
[178] *R. v John M* [1996] 2 Cr. App. R. 56; *Mullen* [2004] EWCA Crim 602.
[179] [1995] 2 Cr. App. R. 222, applied in *R. v P (G)* [2006] EWCA Crim 1980.

- the video should be replayed in court with judge, counsel and defendant present;
- the judge should warn the jury that because they are hearing the evidence-in-chief of the complainant repeated a second time well after all the other evidence, they should guard against the risk of giving it disproportionate weight simply for that reason and should bear well in mind the other evidence in the case; and
- to assist in maintaining a fair balance, after the replay of the video the judge should remind the jury of the cross-examination and re-examination of the complainant from his notes.[180]

Although the Court described these as "requirements", subsequent decisions have injected an element of flexibility by treating them as guidance as to good practice, with the result that convictions may be allowed to stand where the *Rawlings and Broadbent* procedure is not strictly followed but the nature of the departure is not such as to produce imbalance or unfairness in the trial.[181] The wisest course is nonetheless for the judge to follow the procedure as closely as possible, as this will minimise the chances of a departure leading to an unsafe conviction. **27.91**

The approach adopted in *Rawlings and Broadbent*[182] was affirmed in *R. v W*[183] in which Rix LJ, giving the judgment of the Court of Appeal, said that if the video evidence is replayed or the jury are reminded of passages from the transcript it is incumbent upon the judge to warn them not to give disproportionate weight to the evidence because it is repeated after all of the evidence has been given. The judge should also remind the jury of cross-examination, re-examination and any relevant defence evidence. **27.92**

The scope for error is considerable, as the following decisions show. In *R. v John M*[184] an appeal was upheld where the trial judge had allowed the video to be replayed immediately before counsel made their closing speeches. The jury had not made any request in relation to the video but the judge was concerned that they had been unable to follow detailed cross-examination of the police officer who conducted the video interview. The Court of Appeal held that in normal circumstances it is inappropriate for the video to be replayed without a specific request from the jury, and that replaying should generally be discouraged and not undertaken without an exceptional reason. In this case there was no such reason, as there was nothing raised in the course of cross-examination which demanded that the whole video be replayed. The Court said that there may be circumstances in which part of a video needs to be replayed during cross-examination, so that the witness and the jury can understand the nature of the question being put, but this was not **27.93**

---

[180] [1995] 2 Cr. App. R. 222, at 227–228.
[181] See, e.g. *Horley* [1999] Crim. L.R. 488; *R. v MR*, Unreported, February 21, 2000 (No.98/6035/W5).
[182] [1995] 2 Cr. App. R. 222.
[183] [2011] EWCA Crim 1142.
[184] [1996] 2 Cr. App. R. 56.

such a case. In *McQuiston*,[185] where the jury asked for the complainant's video evidence to be replayed to remind them of what the complainant had said and how he had said it, the judge decided that, rather than replay the video, he would remind the jury of the complainant's evidence by slowly reading a lengthy passage from the transcript; indeed, he read so slowly that many of the jury could be seen taking a verbatim note. The Court of Appeal upheld the appellant's appeal on the basis that no reference was made by the judge to the cross-examination, to contradictions in the complainant's evidence-in-chief or to the defendant's account. In *R. v B (K)*[186] it was confirmed that the re-viewing of a video by the jury is a departure from normal practice which should only be undertaken in exceptional cases. The Court said that it had been wrong for the judge in that case, when summing up, effectively to encourage the jury to think that re-viewing of the video is a standard exercise and not to identify with them what was exceptional about the case that justified them in re-viewing it. Simply identifying that the jury were interested in both the words the witness used and the way she gave her answers was insufficient. Finally, the judge in *Wilson*,[187] perhaps taking the strictures of *Rawlings and Broadbent* a little too far, said while summing up that the jury should not ask to see the video-recordings replayed as that would simply be asking for a repeat of the prosecution evidence. The Court said that, while video-recordings should be replayed only exceptionally and the judge's inclination to discourage a jury request was understandable, the better practice is not to announce in advance that any such request will be refused.

27. 94   Jury requests to review the pre-recorded evidence of a witness are not limited to the evidence of the complainant but may apply to any witness. The same careful approach should be applied to a jury request to review any witness's video evidence.[188]

27.95   The defence are equally restricted in applying for a video interview to be replayed. In *Eldridge and Salmon*[189] the complainant had been interviewed three times. In the first interview no allegations were made, in the second the complainant made allegations against the defendant E but not against S, but the allegations were the result of leading questions, and in the third interview allegations were made against both E and S. The Crown relied upon the video of the last interview as the complainant's evidence-in-chief. The jury were shown the second video at the end of the Crown's opening but were told that the Crown did not rely upon it. When addressing the jury, counsel for E

---

[185] [1998] 1 Cr. App. R. 139, applied in *R. v C (Brian William)* [2005] EWCA Crim 3121; *Horley* [1999] Crim. L.R. 488, not following *McQuiston*; but as the commentary by Professor Birch points out, there is no real conflict between the decisions on the basis that in *McQuiston* the procedure adopted by the judge had left the jury with an unbalanced picture whereas in *Horley* it had not.

[186] [2002] EWCA Crim 2140 at [32].

[187] Unreported October 6, 1998 (No.98/1938/Y4).

[188] *Mullen* [2004] EWCA Crim 602.

[189] [1999] Crim. L.R. 166.

asked for parts of the second video to be replayed. The trial judge was held to have acted correctly in refusing this request, relying on *Rawlings and Broadbent*. The jury had seen the video once and were aware of the inconsistent accounts given by the complainant, and counsel could remind the jury of the comments made in the video and, if he deemed fit, could quote from the transcript. The judge had reminded the jury of what counsel had said and told them that they could ask to see the video again. In those circumstances E's conviction was not unsafe.

Jury access to video transcripts

Similar issues may arise in relation to jury access to the transcripts of video recordings. It is necessary to distinguish between the use of transcripts to help the jury follow what is said in a recording whilst it is being played, and their later use as a reminder of what was said. In *Welstead*,[190] the Court of Appeal held that the trial judge is entitled to allow the jury to have a copy of the transcript of a video recording whilst it is being played, provided: **27.96**

- the transcript is likely to assist the jury in following the witness's evidence,[191]
- the judge makes clear to the jury that the transcript is being made available to them only for that limited purpose and that they should concentrate primarily on the oral evidence, and
- that the judge gives the jury such directions, both at the time and in summing-up, as are likely to be effective safeguards against the risk of them giving the transcript disproportionate weight.

The position is rather different if the jury wish to have access to the transcript after they have retired, as a reminder of what was said. The issues here are analogous to those raised by a jury request to re-view a video recording. In *Coshall*,[192] the Court of Appeal held that the judge had erred in allowing the jury to keep the transcript even after they had retired to consider their verdict. The Court said that the need to maintain the fair balance referred to in *Rawlings and Broadbent* applies equally to the supply to the jury of a transcript as to the replaying of the recording itself. Where both the prosecution and defence agree, there can be no objection to the jury having a transcript, provided they are reminded of the other evidence and the status of the transcript in the context of the evidence as a whole. In the face of defence objections, it will generally be inappropriate for the jury to be supplied with a transcript after their retirement, because of the serious risk **27.97**

---

[190] [1996] 1 Cr. App. R. 59. See also *Springer* [1996] Crim. L.R. 903. *Welstead* was approved in *R. v SW* [2004] EWCA Crim 2979.
[191] The value of a transcript in any particular case will depend upon a variety of factors, including the quality of the sound and visual recording and any difficulty which the jury may have in hearing and comprehending what the witness is saying: ibid. at 69, per Auld J. For observations on the need to ensure that the costs of transcription are incurred only where there is proper justification, see [1996] 1 Cr. App. R. 59.
[192] *The Times*, February 17, 1995; and see *Morris* [1998] Crim. L.R. 416.

of them attaching disproportionate weight to its contents. As was suggested in *Rawlings and Broadbent*, the better way to deal with such a request, if it answers the jury's need, is for the judge to remind the jury of what was said from his own note.

27.98   The earlier cases were reviewed in *Popescu*,[193] where Aikens LJ gave the following guidance on jury access to transcripts:

"35. First, the general rule must be that great care must be taken before a jury is given transcripts of an ABE interview at all, even whilst the video is being shown. It should only be given to the jury after there has been discussion of the issue between the judge and counsel in the absence of the jury, and it should only be done if there is a very good reason for it, e.g. the evidence would be difficult to follow on the screen or the audio quality is very poor.

36. Secondly, if the transcripts are given to the jury, we suggest, first, that the judge must warn the jury then and there to take care to examine the video as it is shown, not least because of the importance of the demeanour of the witness in giving evidence. Thirdly, the transcript should, save perhaps in very exceptional circumstances, be withdrawn from the jury once the ABE video evidence in chief has been given. Again, if the jury is to retain the transcripts during the cross-examination, this possibility must be given positive thought before it is done, and should, if possible, be discussed in the jury's absence before the start of the evidence in chief, if practicable. If the jury are to retain the transcripts, the reasons why the jury are being permitted to do so should be explained to them.

37. Fourthly, if the transcripts are retained during cross-examination, then they should be recovered once the witness had finished his or her evidence. The general rule must be that the jury should not thereafter have the transcripts again.

38. Fifthly however, it must be for a very good reason. It must be discussed with counsel in the jury's absence and the judge should give a ruling on it. Sixthly, the jury should not, except perhaps in exceptional circumstances, be permitted to retire with the transcripts. Those exceptional circumstances will usually only be present if the defence positively wants the jury to have the transcript and the judge is satisfied that there are very good reasons why the jury should retire with the transcripts.

39. If the jury is to do so, it must again be the subject of discussions with counsel and a specific ruling from the judge. The judge must explain to the jury, in the course of his summing-up, why they are being allowed the transcripts and the limited use to which they must put them, viz. to aid them to understand the evidence in chief of the relevant witness and, if it be the case, that the defence wants the jury to retain the transcripts. If this course is adopted, then it is incumbent upon the judge to ensure that the cross-examination and re-examination of the witness is fully summed up to the jury, and the jury must be specifically reminded that they must take all that evidence into consideration in their deliberations, and must not be over-reliant upon the evidence in chief."

27.99   Judge Roderick Denyer QC has summarised the correct approach as follows[194]:

- Transcripts should only be provided to the jury if there is good reason, they should not be provided as a matter of routine.

---

[193] [2010] EWCA Crim 1230.
[194] *Showing Video Transcripts to the Jury,* 176 C.L. & J., 235.

- The judge should direct the jury, when they are provided with the transcript, that they should concentrate on the recording rather than the transcript so that they are able to observe the demeanour of the witness.
- Save in "very exceptional circumstances" the transcript should be taken back from the jury when the recording has finished being played.
- If the judge considers that the jury should keep the transcript through cross-examination he should explain to the jury the reason for his or her decision.
- The transcript should only remain with the jury after the witness has given evidence if the judge rules that there is "a very good reason".
- It would only be in exceptional circumstances that a jury would retire with the transcript.
- Where a jury has kept a transcript during their retirement, the judge should direct them as to the limited use they may make of it (i.e. to assist them to understand the witness's evidence-in-chief) and must warn them against over reliance on the document. In such circumstances any cross-examination must be summed up in detail.

Popescu concerned a gang rape of a Romanian female. She spoke English **27.100**
to a reasonable standard but with quite a strong accent. Her evidence-in-chief took the form of video-recordings of her two ABE interviews. At some stage during the playing of the recordings, the jury were given transcripts of the interviews. None of the counsel who appeared at the trial could recall why this was done, but it was presumably so that the jury could better follow what the complainant was saying in the videos. Counsel for the appellant, and counsel for some of his co-defendants, used the transcripts in cross-examining the complainant. The transcripts were not retrieved from the jury after the complainant had finished her evidence. In closing, counsel for the appellant, and counsel for some of his co-defendants, drew the jury's attention to passages in the transcripts. The judge also drew on the contents of the transcripts in summing up. He also directed the jury not to regard the transcripts in isolation from the other evidence in the case. The jury took the transcripts with them into the jury room. On appeal, it was argued for the appellant that the jury should not have been allowed to keep the transcripts after the complainant's evidence-in-chief had been given or, alternatively, that the judge should have given the jury a clear explanation of why they were being permitted to keep the transcripts and a warning not to give them disproportionate weight. The Court of Appeal began by saying that it suspected, and hoped, that the course of events followed in this case were most unusual. However, it was satisfied that the jury had had the transcripts principally because the appellant and his co-accused wanted the jury to have them. The appellant's counsel wished to use the transcripts in order to make points that were thought to be advantageous to the appellant, both in cross-examination of the complainant and in his closing speech. It was clear that

other defence counsel had taken the same view. Further, the points counsel made would have been difficult, if not impossible, for the jury to follow without the transcripts. As for the judge, he had used the transcripts in his summing up only to identify the points in the complainant's evidence-in-chief with which the jury had to deal on retirement. He did so without any objection from defence counsel. He also gave the jury a careful warning about not looking at the transcripts in isolation from the other evidence, and a full and proper summary of the complainant's cross-examination and re-examination and of the responses of the accused to her evidence. In those circumstances, the Court was satisfied that the appellant had had a fair trial. It added that the case against him was very strong. No doubt this factor, coupled with the appellant's attempts to have his cake and eat it by using the transcripts with the jury and then claiming that the jury's retention of them had prejudiced him, helps to explain why the regrettable course followed in this case did not lead to the quashing of the conviction.

27.101   It is clear from *Watts*[195] that permitting the jury to retain transcripts of evidence will be acceptable if a summary of the evidence would not accurately reflect the way in which the evidence was given. That case involved two witnesses who suffered from profound cerebral palsy. One of them gave evidence using an electronic communication device mounted onto her wheelchair. It took the form of a tablet computer onto which had been programmed a number of pages relating to different topics. Each page took the form of a grid on which were drawings, picture or symbols and a square for "Yes" or "No". Though the witness could not read, save to a limited extent, there was text added to each square. An illuminated cursor ran along the rows. When the cursor reached the row in which her desired answer lay she activated a switch in her headrest by touching or bumping the side of her head against it. The cursor would then run down the columns and when it reached the correct column she would activate the switch again. Where the two intersected, an electronic "voice" would speak the written text. A summary of the evidence would create the impression that it was given smoothly. The Court of Appeal described the process as "tortuous and lengthy" and almost painful to watch. It endorsed the "wise" decision of the trial judge to leave the jury with the transcripts from which to reach their conclusions. The Court recognised that this was an unusual step, but it was a sensible one in the circumstances. It should be noted that the course adopted by the judge had been agreed by both trial counsel and that no ground of appeal was advanced in relation to it. Moreover, the defence counsel did not cross-examine the complainant (a decision described as understandable by the trial judge), so the transcript contained the entirety of her evidence and there was no additional evidence from her of which the jury should have been reminded.

---

[195] [2010] EWCA Crim 1824.

Finally, on the question whether the jury should be provided with the transcripts of the ABE interview was also considered in *Sardar*.[196] In that case the Court of Appeal, applying *Popescu*,[197] overturned a rape conviction where the transcript was provided to the jury and remained with them during cross-examination, defence closing submissions and their retirement. The judge did not warn the jury as to the dangers of giving the transcript undue weight. The Court of Appeal held that the fact that the defence consented to the jury being provided with the transcript and that the jury had a transcript of the defendant's police interview under caution did not justify the provision of the ABE transcript. The danger was that the jury would have paid disproportionate attention to what was written in the ABE transcript rather than concentrate on "their impression of the witness and their assessment of that witness as she gives her evidence, both in the form of a video recording and during cross-examination".

27.102

Video-Recorded Cross-Examination and Re-Examination (where Examination-in-Chief is Recorded)

Whilst the pilot of s.28 is being appraised,[198] pre-recorded cross-examination remains unavailable and so those witnesses who have made a recording suitable for use as evidence-in-chief must still attend court to be cross-examined (ordinarily by live link), unless the parties agree to the admission of the evidence[199] or their evidence can be admitted in statement form under the hearsay provisions of the Criminal Justice Act 2003.[200]

27.103

When brought into force, pre-recorded cross-examination and re-examination will become a possible special measures direction in all cases where examination-in-chief is being provided by means of video recording.[201] The recording must be made in the absence of the defendant but in circumstances where he can see and hear the witness being examined and communicate with his legal representative.[202] Once the witness has been cross-examined, they may not be called back for further cross-examination without leave of the court.[203] Leave may be granted only if a new matter has arisen which the party seeking further cross-examination could not have discovered with reasonable diligence before the original recording, or if for some other reason the proposed cross-examination is in the interests of justice.[204]

27.104

---

[196] [2012] EWCA Crim 134.
[197] [2010] EWCA Crim 1230.
[198] See paras 27.43 and following, above.
[199] s.27(4)(ii) of the YJCEA 1999.
[200] For examples, see *Duffy* [1999] 1 Cr. App. R. 307; *R. v D* [2002] 2 Cr. App. R. 36. In *Crown Prosecution Service v CE* [2006] EWCA Crim 1410 the Court of Appeal held that such evidence had been properly excluded whereby the witness would not attend court due to fear (not attributable to the defendant).
[201] s.28(1) of the YJCEA 1999.
[202] s.28(2).
[203] s.28(5).
[204] s.28(6)(a) or (b).

Intermediaries

27.105   Section 29 of the YJCEA 1999 provides for questions to be put to a witness through an intermediary.[205] It is perhaps this area, together with the adaptation of cross-examination style for vulnerable witnesses, that has effected the most radical change in the criminal justice system over the past decade. In his foreword to Joyce Plotnikoff and Richard Woolfson's excellent text *Intermediaries in the Criminal Justice System*, Lord Thomas CJ remarks:

> "It is a truism that change is not just about having a new framework and new legislation in place, but about the change in culture necessary to make the new legislation and framework a reality. It is evident in 2015 that some of the ideas that would have seemed radical at the outset of the intermediary pilot have been absorbed into the culture of criminal proceedings. There have been tangible advances in the way advocates and judges deal with vulnerable witnesses and, while there is much yet to be done, I do believe that we have achieved real change."

A great part of this change is the result of the use of intermediaries.

27.106   Witnesses under 18 at the date of the application hearing are eligible for the assistance of an intermediary as of right. Adults are eligible if they have a mental disorder, significant impairment of intelligence and social functioning or physical disorder or disability and the court considers that the quality of their evidence is likely to be diminished.[206] Intermediaries are not available to those who are considered vulnerable because of distress or fear.[207] The function of an intermediary is to facilitate communication between the questioner and the witness.[208] As all children are eligible for assistance from an intermediary, consideration should be given as to whether any child witness would benefit from this special measure. It is not necessary for the child to have learning difficulties, all that is required is that they need help to understand questions or convey answers. The NSPCC report, *Measuring Up* recorded that witnesses as old as 17 remarked that they were denied the opportunity to ask for time to answer the question or request that the question be repeated; witnesses felt that they were being put under pressure to give the answer straightaway. Of course, counsel must ensure that they tailor their "lawyerly language"[209] to suit children, but intermediaries provide an additional means of facilitating communication and it may well be that currently intermediaries are being under-used in the criminal justice

---

[205] The section came into force on February 23, 2004: SI 2004/299.

[206] See Joyce Plotnikoff and Richard Woolfson, *Making Best Use of the Intermediary Special Measure at Trial* [2008] Crim. L.R. 91.

[207] s.18(1) of the YJCEA 1999.

[208] Expressed as: "to communicate to the witness, questions put to the witness, and to any person asking such questions, the answers given by the witness in reply to them, and to explain such questions or answers so far as necessary to enable them to be understood by the witness or person in question" (s.29(2) YJCEA 1999).

[209] So described by one of the witnesses in the study.

system.[210] There is, however, a scarcity of intermediaries which, as noted above, has led the Lord Chief Justice to amend the Criminal Practice Directions so that the appropriateness of intermediary assessment is decided with care in order that intermediaries are available for those witnesses and defendants who are "most in need". Applications for intermediaries will usually be made by the prosecution (although intermediaries are available to defence witnesses), but the judiciary should also be proactive in seeking to identify cases which might benefit from an intermediary. Intermediaries are tools not only for the Crown but for all parties to assist the tribunal of fact in understanding the witness's evidence.

The use of an intermediary should be considered at the very early stages of **27.107** an investigation. An evaluation of the pilot areas in which intermediaries were used found that in certain cases, which resulted in a conviction, the investigation would have stopped before the witness was ABE interviewed had an intermediary not been available to the witness.[211] It is therefore best practice to consider whether an intermediary is needed before the ABE interview takes place. That said, the absence of an intermediary during the ABE interview is no bar to one being appointed for the trial.

An intermediary will assess the witness and then assist the parties, or the **27.108** police during the ABE video-recorded interview or identification procedures, to communicate with the witness. One of the intermediary's functions is to establish what types of question the witness will experience difficulty comprehending, the length of time it may take a witness to answer a question and the frequency of breaks that the witness will require. Intermediaries' consideration of how best a witness can communicate goes beyond advising as to questioning style. An intermediary will consider a range of methods to enable the witness to give their best evidence. Examples include: that advocates question the witness from within the live link room, allowing children to pause without leaving the live link room or taking a full break, allowing a child to take "time-out" by going behind a curtain or under a blanket.[212] Other examples include allowing a witness (and Registered Intermediary) to answer questions with their backs to the camera, allocating a female judge and female counsel in respect of a witness who would not discuss the case with a man, letting a man with autism spectrum disorder give evidence wearing a lion's tail (his "comforter" in daily life).

The intermediary will prepare a report for the court detailing the witness's **27.109** needs and any arrangements that need to be made to meet them. Where necessary, the report will set out examples of types of questions which the witness may find difficult it to answer so that advocates can avoid questioning

---

[210] *Measuring Up?* found that 70 per cent of children may have benefitted from having their communication skills assessed by an intermediary.

[211] Joyce Plotnikoff and Richard Woolfson, *The "Go-Between": Evaluation of Intermediary Pathfinder Projects* (2007).

[212] Useful examples are found in the *Equal Treatment Bench Book* (November 2013), and for a detailed analysis see Joyce Plotnikoff and Richard Woolfson, *Intermediaries in the Criminal Justice System* (Policy Press, 2015).

the witness in a style or manner which is likely to confuse. These issues must be agreed between the parties or dealt with by the judge at the "Ground Rules Hearing" listed before the trial date. As a general rule the role of the intermediary should be explained to the jury. Ground Rules Hearings are discussed in Ch.28.

27.110   The presence of the intermediary does not relieve the judge of his responsibility to ensure that the witness is not subjected to inappropriate questioning. However, where an intermediary is of the view that a witness could not understand or has not understood the question asked, their role is to ask counsel to rephrase the question, and if counsel is unable to do so satisfactorily, the intermediary will "interpret" the question for the witness. The intermediary's role is also to communicate the answers given by the witness; guidance requires that the intermediary does this, however illogical the answer may appear to be. The intermediary should not alter the witness's answers for the purpose of shielding or protecting them. However, if the intermediary considers that the witness will not understand a particular question as phrased, it is preferable for them to identify this before the answer is given, rather than wait until the witness has given an answer, which the intermediary then seeks to correct. Failure to intervene at the appropriate time may lead the questioner to believe that their question was suitable but that the intermediary is seeking to assist the witness to give an answer, which "fits" the witness's story.[213]

27.111   The National Crime Agency hosts the Witness Intermediary Scheme, which provides a "matching-service" to pair a Registered Intermediary with the needs of the witness. Unfortunately, the Witness Intermediary Scheme is currently only available for witnesses, though in *R. (OP) v Secretary of State for Justice*, the Divisional Court ruled the refusal of the MoJ to provide a defendant with a registered intermediary unlawful.[214] At the end of 2014, there were 98 Registered Intermediaries, with 3,332 requests of which 83 were not matched.[215] Registered Intermediaries are recruited, trained, registered and regulated by the MoJ and their duty is to the Court. Under r.18.7 of the Criminal Procedure Rules 2015, they make a solemn declaration to the Court prior to the video interview and examination of a witness.[216] Procedural guidance for intermediaries has been issued by the MoJ, which sets out the Principles of Registered Intermediary Practice.[217] Under those principles the intermediary is required to keep full records of their involvement including

---

[213] Joyce Plotnikoff and Richard Woolfson, *Making Best Use of the Intermediary Special Measure at Trial* [2008] Crim. L.R. 91.

[214] [2014] EWHC 1944 (Admin); [2015] 1 Cr. App. R. 7.

[215] Joyce Plotnikoff and Richard Woolfson, *Intermediaries in the criminal justice system* (Policy Press, 2015). See also the Advocates Gateway at *http://www.theadvocatesgateway.org/ intermediaries* [Accessed April 30, 2016].

[216] "*I solemnly, sincerely and truly declare [or I swear by Almighty God] that I will well and faithfully communicate questions and answers and make true explanation of all matters and things as shall be required of me according to the best of my skill and understanding.*"

[217] *Registered Intermediary Procedural Guidance Manual* (February 2012), available via the Advocates Gateway website.

notes of the assessments, and in respect of prosecution witnesses, they must inform the officer in charge of the case of anything of which they become aware that might undermine the case for the prosecution or assist the case for the accused. When assisting a defence witness the intermediary must not disclose anything about the defence case or what has been said to them without the defendant's (i.e. defence solicitor's) express consent. Intermediaries should not express an opinion about the truth or reliability of what the witness has said, neither should they express or offer an opinion on the guilt or otherwise of the accused.

Killick[218] is a case in which conscientious pre-trial preparation and a   **27.112** flexible approach on the part of the court enabled witnesses who, according to the trial judge, would not have given evidence half a generation ago, to give their accounts to the jury. The accused, who was himself physically disabled, was convicted of sexual assaults committed against three disabled victims. In her article about the case in *Counsel* magazine,[219] Elizabeth Smaller describes how the complainants suffered with cerebral palsy and severe speech difficulties, which made it impossible for them to give evidence in the conventional way. They were unable to move, dress or feed themselves and every action required assistance (they all had personal assistants). The main issue at trial was the witnesses' severe speech difficulties and how their answers could be given in a manner intelligible to the jury. One witness ("A") could speak but his answers were intelligible only to those who were very experienced in speaking with him. The other two complainants relied upon Voice Output Communication Aids, or "VOCA". One operated his VOCA by hand (a painfully slow process), the other through a pressure pad on his wheelchair at the back of his head; the vocabulary was limited to 900 pre-programmed words. Early special measures meetings were held with each complainant. They all wanted to give evidence in court from behind a screen and to be given sufficient time to give their evidence. The vocabulary on the VOCAs was prepared ahead of trial, but preparations were also made to add further words if necessary. A Registered Intermediary explained to the jury how VOCAs operate and that the mechanical voice meant that it would be impossible for the jury to judge the complainants from their inflections or choice of words. During the course of A's evidence it became apparent that the quality of his evidence would be maximised if his personal assistant acted as his intermediary; this provided greater flexibility than the use of a Registered Intermediary and so enabled the time A spent giving evidence to be kept to a minimum.

The judge and parties in *Killick* are to be commended for doing everything   **27.113** possible to ensure that the complainants were able to give their best evidence. All those involved understood the need to adapt their questioning of the complainants and the court timetable to accommodate the complainants'

---

[218] [2011] EWCA Crim 1608. For the complex pre-trial history of this case, see para.30.69 and following, below.
[219] Elizabeth Smaller (now HH Judge Smaller), Counsel for the Prosecution, January 2012.

requirements. Also, the evidence given by the intermediary before the complainants were called no doubt demystified the disability they suffered, so ensuring that the jury were best placed to focus on assessing the evidence.

27.114   A further example of intermediaries playing a key role in trial preparation is the case of Child Q, discussed in para.27.48, above. When assessing the child's competence to give evidence, the trial judge had the benefit of the intermediary's initial assessment, the ABE interview (at which the intermediary was present), an intermediary report following the ABE interview and a further report considering the impact of the delay awaiting trial. The intermediary also assisted at the "ground rules" meeting with respect to how questions should be asked and Child Q's likely period of concentration.[220] In yet another case, following a recommendation from the intermediary, both trial counsel joined the witness in the live link room throughout cross-examination and re-examination.[221]

PROVIDING AIDS TO COMMUNICATION

27.115   The special measure relating to aids to communication, set out in s.30 of the YJCEA 1999, is available to witnesses who are eligible by virtue of s.16.[222] The purpose of the measure is to enable a witness who suffers from a disability or disorder to be provided with an appropriate "device" to assist them to answer questions.

PROCEDURAL MATTERS

PROCEDURE FOR APPLYING FOR, OR OPPOSING, SPECIAL MEASURES

27.116   The procedure for applying for special measures under s.19 of the YJCEA 1999 is governed by Pt 18 of the Criminal Procedure Rules 2015. The same rules apply in the Crown Court and magistrates' courts. The court may make a direction for special measures on its own initiative.[223] If a party intends to make an application for special measures it must do so in writing and within 28 days of the defendant entering a not guilty plea in the magistrates' court or within 14 days in the Crown Court.[224] The application must be served on the court and each other party.[225] The application form for special measures is scheduled to the Criminal Procedure Rules, but the court may allow an

---

[220] Caroline Wigin, *Child Q, England's Youngest Witness*, *Counsel Magazine*, July 2012, pp.24–25.
[221] cf. David Wurtzel, *Time to Change the Rules*, *Counsel Magazine*, November 2012, pp.32–34.
[222] s.18(1)(a) of the YJCEA 1999.
[223] CPR 2015 r.18.1(1)(a).
[224] r.18.3(a).
[225] r.18.3(b).

application to be made in a different form or orally, and may vary the time limit for the application.[226] The provision for an oral hearing and variation of the time limit means that special measures applications may be dealt with efficiently at an early stage in the proceedings. There is no reason why, if the parties are in agreement, an oral application could not be made and granted at the Pre-Trial Preparation Hearing ("PTPH") in the Crown Court or on the first appearance in the magistrates' court (if the matter is to be dealt with summarily).

The Criminal Procedure Rules set out what information is required in a   27.117
special measures application, which varies depending upon the type of witness. Where the application concerns a young witness to whom the primary rule applies, the party calling the witness should, as soon as is reasonably practicable, notify the court of the witness's eligibility and provide the court with any information which could assist it to assess the witness's views if the witness does not want the primary rule to apply. The court should also be supplied with the video-recorded interview.[227] For other witnesses, the application should set out the following: why the witness is eligible; why special measures are likely to improve the quality of the witness's evidence; and a proposal for the appropriate special measures and the witness's views as to their eligibility and how the special measures would assist their evidence. If use of the live link is proposed and it is intended that the witness should be accompanied whilst giving evidence over the live link, the application should identify who will accompany the witness. If it is proposed that the witness's video-recorded interview is played, the application should identify the date of the recording and which part of it is to be adduced into evidence, if it is not intended to rely upon the entire recording.[228]

An opposing party has 14 days from service of the application to   27.118
respond.[229] Representations against special measures must set out why the witness is not eligible for assistance or why any special measure or the proposed special measure is unlikely to improve the quality of the witness's evidence, or why the proposed special measure might tend to inhibit the effective testing of the witness's evidence.[230]

There has been concern that witnesses who are the subject of an   27.119
application for special measures are sometimes not notified of the court's decision until they attend court for the trial. When one considers that an aim of many of the special measures is to put witnesses at ease, any delay in communicating the court's decision to the person arguably most affected by it is unfortunate. It is now a procedural rule that the party making the special measures application must inform the witness of the court's decision as soon

[226] r.18.5.
[227] r.18.9.
[228] r.18.10.
[229] r.18.13.
[230] r.18.13(4).

as is reasonably practicable, and must also explain to the witness the arrangements for them giving evidence.[231] The court's decision and reasons must also be announced at a public hearing before the witness gives evidence.[232]

27.120   Applications may be made in private or without disclosing information to another party where the application includes information that the applicant thinks ought not to be revealed to that party.[233] Such an application would be appropriate where the defence wish to be reassured that their witnesses will be afforded special measures at an early stage in the proceedings without having to reveal to the prosecution the witnesses' identities or the nature of any pre-recorded evidence. It also offers an appropriate means for the prosecution to make an application which contains sensitive information.

27.121   Any special measures direction may be discharged or varied on written application to the court.[234] The application, which must set out each material change of circumstance upon which the application is based, should be sent to the appropriate officer of the Crown Court and other parties as soon as is reasonably practicable after the material change in circumstances occurs. Other parties have a right to oppose the application and should make representations explaining why the special measures order should not be varied or discharged.[235] There is no express provision in the Criminal Procedure Rules 2015 for renewed special measures applications, but where there has been a material change of circumstances since the date of a previous unsuccessful application, the overriding objective must permit the application to be renewed.

27.122   Any party seeking to rely upon expert evidence should serve that evidence as soon as is practicable and in any event should serve it with the special measures application. The court may extend the time allowed for service.[236]

Revocation or Variance of Special Measures Directions

27.123   Once a special measures direction has been given, it is binding until the proceedings are determined or abandoned.[237] An exception applies where the direction was made in respect of a child who was eligible only because of their age and who attains the age of 18 before giving evidence, unless the direction was to admit a recording of a child's evidence-in-chief or cross-examination.[238] Despite its binding status, an application can be made to

---

[231] r.18.4(1).
[232] r.18.4(2).
[233] r.18.12.
[234] r.18.11.
[235] r.18.13(5).
[236] r.19.9.
[237] s.20(1) of the YJCEA 1999.
[238] s.21(8), (9) of the YJCEA 1999.

discharge or vary a special measures direction in the interests of justice.[239] The court may exercise this power of its own motion, or on an application by a party to the proceedings if there has been a material change of circumstances since the direction was given or a previous application for discharge or variance was made.[240]

RESTRICTIONS ON REPORTING SPECIAL MEASURES DIRECTIONS

Section 47(1) of the YJCEA 1999 provides that, except as provided by the section, no publication shall include a report of a special measures direction, or of an order varying or discharging such a direction, or of proceedings on an application for such a direction or order, or where the court of its own motion determines whether to give such a direction or order. The restrictions do not apply to evidence given by witnesses in the case or to the identity of witnesses.[241] The court may by order dis-apply s.47(1) in whole or in part.[242] Where the defendant or, in a multi-handed case, one or more of the defendants objects to the making of such an order, the court may only make the order if satisfied, after hearing representations from the defendant, that it is in the interests of justice to do so.[243] Section 47(1) does not apply to reports after the proceedings are determined (by acquittal, conviction or otherwise) or abandoned in relation to the accused or, where there is more than one, all of them.[244] Publication in breach of s.47(1) is a summary offence punishable with a fine.[245] Until recently, the maximum was a fine not exceeding level 5 on the standard scale (i.e. £5,000). The effect of s.85 of the Legal Aid, Sentencing and Punishment of Offenders Act 2012 is that, from March 12, 2015, a fine of any amount may be imposed. Fines will, however, continue to be set according to the seriousness of the offence and the means of the offender. A prosecution may be brought only by or with the consent of the Attorney General in England or Wales, or in Northern Ireland, the Attorney General for Northern Ireland.[246]

27.124

VULNERABLE WITNESSES: PRACTICALITIES

The wide range of possible special measures means that considerable pre-trial planning is required if they are to be used effectively. This is best done at the Ground Rules Hearing, considered in Ch.28. The CPS and police should jointly approach the issue of special measures in relation to prosecution witnesses from an early stage. It is particularly important that police officers

27.125

---

[239] s.20(2) of the YJCEA 1999.
[240] s.20(2)(a),(b).
[241] For protection of the identity of witnesses, see Ch.29.
[242] s.47(3) of the YJCEA 1999.
[243] s.47(4), (5).
[244] s.47(6).
[245] s.49 of the YJCEA 1999.
[246] s.49(6).

clearly communicate information concerning special measures to witnesses, taking care not to raise their expectations and not making promises, which may turn out to be misleading given that it is for the court to decide what, if any, special measures are necessary. The ABE guidance notes that early identification of a vulnerable or intimidated witness by the police and discussion with the CPS prosecutor will enable the prosecutor to make informed decisions about special measures at an early stage, e.g. in relation to the appointment of an intermediary. Early identification can also assist the police to record the witness's statement in a format designed to achieve best evidence. All special measures options should be explained to the witness. The prosecution may well be able to play an adult complainant's ABE interview as their evidence-in-chief, but the prosecutor should ask themselves whether that particular interview maximises the quality of the evidence. If the recording is of poor quality or the interview was not conducted particularly well by the interviewer, the evidence may be more effective given direct to the jury, either from a live link room or from behind a screen. The witness should not of course be placed under any pressure, but all options should be explored. The guidance emphasises that witnesses must be informed that the final decision regarding special measures rests with the court and not the prosecution team.

27.126   Any special measures direction is bound to impact upon the practicalities of running a trial; for example, video facilities may need to be available or breaks incorporated into the court day for the comfort of a vulnerable witness. Applications for special measures should therefore be submitted as early as possible. Part 18 of the Criminal Procedure Rules 2015 sets out when applications can be dealt with in writing and when an oral hearing is required.[247] Whilst the Rules do not require special measures applications to be made until 14 days after a not guilty plea has been entered, it makes sense for applications to be made early, and at the PTPH if possible. Certainly, it is desirable for advocates at the PTPH to know what special measures applications are to be made and their likely impact on managing the trial. For that reason, the advocate instructed in relation to setting the trial date should be apprised of any witness requirements in order that the necessary logistics can be arranged and a realistic time estimate for the trial put forward.

27.127   In appropriate cases, the prosecution should arrange an "early special measures meeting" between the investigating police officer and the CPS in order to discuss the needs of any prosecution witness who may be vulnerable or intimidated. It is desirable for prosecuting counsel also to attend that meeting. It may also be appropriate for an expert who can provide information on a particular disability to attend in order to assist in the identification of appropriate special measures. There is no bar to a witness being present at an early special measures meeting, although the decision as

---

[247] See para.27.116, above.

to who should attend rests with the prosecution. However, if the witness is absent, their views on special measures should be obtained prior to the meeting in order that they may be taken into account. The witness must also be kept informed of any decisions made. If there is any issue in relation to a witness's competence, it should be discussed at this meeting. Any matter discussed or decision taken in relation to special measures must be recorded and the record may be liable to disclosure in accordance with the Criminal Procedure and Investigations Act 1996.[248]

JUDICIAL "TICKETING"

Under the Criminal Practice Directions, Judges (other than High Court Judges) must be authorised by the Lord Chief Justice before they may hear sexual offences cases in Class 1C or 2B.[249] Any judge previously granted a "Class 2" or "serious sex offences" authorisation is so authorised. The authorisation does not take effect until the judge has attended the relevant Judicial College course, and the Resident Judge should check that newly authorised judges have attended that course. Judges who have been previously authorised to try such cases should make every effort to ensure their training is up-to-date and maintained by attending the Serious Sexual Offences Seminar at least once every three years. **27.128**

MEETINGS BETWEEN ADVOCATES, JUDGES AND WITNESSES

The *Witness Charter* states that, where practicable, the relevant lawyer will introduce themselves and seek to answer any practical questions from the witness.[250] The guidance encourages such meetings in order to establish a link between the CPS and the witness and to reassure the witness that their needs will be taken into account. During the meeting, the prosecutor should explain which special measures will be available or are to be applied for. The evidence must not be discussed, and should there be more than one vulnerable witness, separate meetings will need to be held. A contemporaneous written record of the meeting must be kept and retained on the CPS file and, in the absence of sensitive material, the record should be disclosed to the defence as a matter of course.[251] It follows that the defence must be informed that the meeting has taken place.[252] **27.129**

---

[248] *Early Special Measures Meetings between the Police and the Crown Prosecution Service and Meetings between the Crown Prosecution Service and Vulnerable or Intimidated Witnesses: Practice Guidance* (Home Office, CPS, ACPO, 2001), para.39.

[249] CPD XIII Listing D: Authorisation of Judges.

[250] *The Witness Charter: Standards of care for witnesses in the Criminal Justice System* OCJR, December 2013.

[251] *Early Special Measures Meetings between the Police and the Crown Prosecution Service and Meetings between the Crown Prosecution Service and Vulnerable or Intimidated Witnesses: Practice Guidance* (Home Office, CPS, ACPO, 2001), paras 57–60.

[252] *Early Special Measures Meetings between the Police and the Crown Prosecution Service and Meetings between the Crown Prosecution Service and Vulnerable or Intimidated Witnesses: Practice Guidance* (Home Office, CPS, ACPO, 2001), para.62.

27.130   The Law Society and Criminal Bar Association have recognised that it can be of benefit for advocates (both prosecution and defence) to meet with child witnesses before they give evidence. This may help to demystify the court process.[253] For the same reason it is sensible for the judge to introduce himself to the witness in the presence of the advocates, or over the live link. It is inadvisable for the judge to see the witness alone. This happened in *R. v P(J)*,[254] where the judge saw the witness following the playing of her ABE interview and decided, without any intermediary assessment or providing either advocate with the opportunity to ask a few questions, that the witness should not be cross-examined. The Court of Appeal quashed the conviction and ordered a retrial.

PRE-TRIAL THERAPY FOR WITNESSES

27.131   Vulnerable or intimidated witnesses may receive therapy after the commission of the alleged offence and before giving evidence. Both parties must, however, be aware of the implications such treatment could have for the criminal process. Guidance has now been issued relating to the provision of therapy for both child and adult witnesses.[255] This guidance recognises that the criminal process should not prevent therapy from taking place and neither should the prosecutor seek to prevent such therapy simply because it may damage the Crown's case.[256] However, if possible, therapy should not be conducted before the witness is video-interviewed and should not involve any discussion of the evidence the witness is likely to give in criminal proceedings.[257]

27.132   Where a witness receives therapy, this may assist the party calling the witness to determine which special measures may be required. This could extend to the provision of expert evidence on the level of the witness's cognitive functioning or the need for an intermediary.[258]

27.133   Prosecutors are under a duty to ensure that they are aware of the content of any therapy sessions and it must be confirmed that during them the witness did not say anything inconsistent with their statement or video recording.[259] Clearly, any inconsistent statement should be disclosed to the

[253] See *Achieving Best Evidence in Criminal Proceedings: Guidance on Interviewing Victims and Witnesses, and Using Special Measures*, point 5.
[254] [2014] EWCA Crim 2064; [2015] 1 Cr. App. R. 12.
[255] *Provision of Therapy for Vulnerable or Intimidated Witnesses Prior to a Criminal Trial: Practical Guidance* (Home Office, CPS, DoH, 2001) and *Provision of Therapy for Child Witnesses Prior to a Criminal Trial: Practical Guidance* (CPS and DoH, with Home Office, 2001).
[256] *Provision of Therapy for Vulnerable or Intimidated Witnesses Prior to a Criminal Trial: Practical Guidance*, last note, paras 4.5–4.6.
[257] *Provision of Therapy for Vulnerable or Intimidated Witnesses Prior to a Criminal Trial: Practical Guidance*, paras 6.2, 1.5.
[258] *Provision of Therapy for Vulnerable or Intimidated Witnesses Prior to a Criminal Trial: Practical Guidance*, paras 9.1–9.4.
[259] *Provision of Therapy for Vulnerable or Intimidated Witnesses Prior to a Criminal Trial: Practical Guidance*, para.11.5.

defence if the prosecution is to continue. Furthermore, the defence may in any event apply for third party disclosure of the records of any therapy session. The witness must therefore be made aware that the confidentiality of such sessions cannot be guaranteed.

PRE-TRIAL COURT FAMILIARISATION VISITS

It is now commonplace for a witness to attend a pre-trial court familiarisa-   27.134
tion visit before the day on which they are to give evidence. An intermediary or supporter may accompany the witnesses during the visit. The visit should enable the witness to practise using the live link that is to be used. Witnesses (prosecution and defence) should also be shown an explanatory DVD on going to court as a witness, which is available from the Ministry of Justice (and also available online[260]). The Criminal Practice Directions 2015 suggest (at 3F.29) that a policy is developed regarding the photography of court facilities to assist witnesses with court familiarisation.

LISTING

The Court Service is under an obligation to give priority to cases involving   27.135
vulnerable witnesses, including child witnesses, and the prosecution should remind the court of the need for priority listing.[261] The need for early listing may mean that cases involving vulnerable witnesses are not listed for a fixed date but are put in a "warned list", meaning that the case could be listed for any day within a two-to-three week period, depending on the court centre. The warned list system is not ideal for any participant in the trial and is likely to increase stress and anxiety for all involved, including witnesses. Another difficulty encountered is the "floating trial," when parties attend in the expectation that a courtroom will become available during the course of the court day. Cases listed as "floaters" are unlikely to meet the target of a maximum waiting time for all witnesses of two hours in the Crown Court.[262] In fact, it is highly unlikely that even the first witness will be heard within this time. Particularly stressful are courts where floating trials can be moved (on the same day) to a different court building. The Court Service does not provide facilities to transport witnesses and if the officer in the case does not have access to a police car, witnesses will have to make their own way to a different court building at very short notice, having already travelled to one court building that day. This situation is most unsatisfactory and it is submitted should never occur when vulnerable witnesses are involved,

---

[260] *https://www.youtube.com/watch?v=jNTcsRy3FTU&list=PL5g5tPp-sxrh07dok-pOspQvL1WA_DD_jW&index=1* [Accessed April 30, 2016].

[261] *Witness Charter: Standards of care for witnesses in the Criminal Justice System*, December 2013.

[262] *Witness Charter: Standards of care for witnesses in the Criminal Justice System*, December 2013.

whatever pressure this may put on court targets to have cases listed. The *Equal Treatment Bench Book* (November 2013) recognises that cases involving young witnesses should be fixed and not listed as floating trials. Other matters being listed in the same court as a trial can also cause delays. Short hearings should not be listed if they will delay the start of a trial. The Criminal Practice Directions provide (3F.28) that where the court has directed an intermediary to attend the trial, their dates of availability should be provided to the court. It is preferable for cases involving an intermediary to be listed as a fixture and not placed in a warned list.

At Trial

27.136   The court should consider safety at court for all witnesses and facilitate different entrance and exit routes for witnesses to avoid contact between them and the defendant.[263] In addition, s.31 of the Children and Young Persons Act 1933 requires arrangements to be made to prevent the association of young persons with adult defendants, unless they are a relative and/or jointly charged. The terms of s.31 apply to any child witness, although provision is usually in place through witness services to ensure that young witnesses do not come into contact with adult defendants. In *R.(T) v Secretary of State for Justice*[264] the Ministry of Justice was held to have breached s.31 when a 13-year-old boy (with severe impairment of mental functioning, autism and attention deficit hyperactivity disorder) was detained, following his arrest for breach of bail, in the same area as adult defendants at a magistrates' court. The custody area for young persons was unavailable due to refurbishment. The young person was detained where he could see the custody desk, had transitory contact with at least two adult prisoners in the corridor and could hear other prisoners shouting at him.

27.137   The target of a maximum waiting time of two hours, which applies to all witnesses, is commendable.[265] However, it has implications for listing and the order in which witnesses are called, and for the current practice in shorter trials of requiring all witnesses to attend on the first day of trial. When it is anticipated that the first witness will take longer than one-and-a-half hours, consideration should be given to warning the other witnesses for later in the day. However, in many cases this will cause difficulties. It is not always known whether all witnesses, including the proposed first witness, will attend the trial to give evidence, and there may well be matters that need to be clarified with a witness before any evidence can be called. Moreover, if witnesses are not required until part way through the court day, it will not be practical for counsel to comply with other requirements of the *Witness Charter*, e.g. to

[263] *Witness Charter: Standards of care for witnesses in the Criminal Justice System*, December 2013.
[264] [2013] EWHC 1119 (Admin).
[265] *Witness Charter: Standards of care for witnesses in the Criminal Justice System* December 2013.

introduce themselves to the witness before their evidence is called, because to do so would interrupt the court day and the flow of evidence.

The quality of a witness's evidence may be adversely affected by lengthy   **27.138** waiting times. The impact of a long wait before giving evidence may affect school-age children most. A useful guideline for such children (without any particular learning or concentration difficulties) is the timetable of the school day. Put simply, there is a common-sense reason why primary school children have mathematics classes in the morning and art and sport in the afternoon. The court day should reflect this and not call on very young witnesses to be cross-examined late in the afternoon. Consideration should be given to frequent breaks and to the possibility of an earlier lunch-break. The replaying of the ABE interview in the presence of the witness just before the witness gives their evidence is not necessary, and there is no reason why, if the trial is not ready to watch the witness's ABE video-recorded interview, the witness could not watch it earlier. This may avoid the witness being kept waiting whilst legal argument is concluded, the jury sworn and the case opened, only to watch a video that they could have watched earlier in the day and then gone home. The jury can watch the ABE interview at the appropriate time and the witness can be called first thing the next morning to answer questions. This procedure has the added advantage of ensuring that when the child gives evidence they will be fresher and more alert than if they watched the (possibly protracted) ABE interview until lunchtime before giving evidence in the afternoon. It is essential that the witness is accompanied whilst watching the video by a court officer who can note any comment made by the witness, which should then be disclosed to all parties.

In cases involving young witnesses or witnesses eligible by virtue of   **27.139** s.16(1)(b) of the YJCEA 1999, it is important that planned breaks are honoured. There was criticism in one study of a case where the intermediary's report indicated that the witness would be able to concentrate for up to 20 minutes, yet he gave evidence for one hour on the first day and 50 minutes on the second before breaks were taken.[266] The understandable temptation to avoid interruptions by "seeing how the witness gets on" should be resisted.

Pre-recorded cross-examination will of course obviate any problem over   **27.140** witness waiting times, as will playing the witness's pre-recorded evidence-in-chief to the jury in the witness's absence.

LIVE LINK ROOM

A simple point often overlooked is that the live link room may be some   **27.141** distance from the courtroom where the trial is taking place, and indeed in a different building altogether. If it is necessary to ask a witness to examine a

---

[266] Joyce Plotnikoff and Richard Woolfson, *Making Best Use of Intermediary Special Measures* [2008] Crim. L.R. 91.

particular physical exhibit, counsel should ensure that the exhibit is in the live link room before the witness begins their evidence. This avoids delay and awkwardness whilst waiting for the exhibit to be taken to the room. The position of the camera in the live link room when a witness is giving evidence is as important as its position when recording the ABE interview, for which see para.27.73, above. The camera should be focused on the witness so as to pick up facial expressions and demeanour, thereby ensuring that the impact of their evidence is not lost.

27.142   There is no reason why questioning the witness cannot occur within the live link room itself. In one case this approach was adopted in respect of a five-year old witness who struggled to communicate over the live link.[267]

Competence to Give Evidence

Competence

27.143   Section 53(1) of the YJCEA 1999 establishes a general rule that at every stage in criminal proceedings all persons, whatever their age, are competent to give evidence. There are two exceptions to this rule. The first is that a person is not competent if it appears to the court that the person is not able to understand questions put to him as a witness and give answers to them, which can be understood.[268] The second is that a defendant is not competent to give evidence for the prosecution (unless he has ceased to be liable to conviction, e.g. because he has pleaded guilty).[269] Section 54 of the 1999 Act provides that if any question is raised as to the competence of a witness, whether by a party to the proceedings or by the court of its own motion, it is for the party calling the witness to satisfy the court, on a balance of probabilities, that the witness is competent. In deciding this question, the court is to treat the witness as having the benefit of any special measures direction under s.19 of the Act which the court has given, or proposes to give, in relation to the witness.[270] Any proceedings held to decide the question of competence must be heard in the absence of the jury and expert evidence may be called.[271] If the court considers it necessary for the witness to be questioned, the questioning is to be conducted by the court in the presence of the parties.[272] Whilst the issue of competence should normally be determined before the witness is sworn, usually as a preliminary issue, it may be reviewed by the trial judge at the end of the witness's evidence; at that point the judge must not address credibility but restrict his or her consideration to competence.[273]

---

[267] *Equal Treatment Bench Book* (November 2013).
[268] s.53(3) of the YJCEA 1999.
[269] s.53(4), (5).
[270] s.54(3).
[271] s.54(4), (5).
[272] s.54(6).
[273] *MacPherson* [2005] EWCA Crim 3605; *Barker* [2010] EWCA Crim 4.

The purpose behind s.53 of the YJCEA 1999 was to remove the old 27.144 misconceptions that a witness's very young age may prevent them from giving truthful and reliable evidence.[274] Those misconceptions meant that the evidence of very young children was not being heard; justice was being denied and criminals who targeted such children were able to do so with impunity.[275] The effect of s.53 is that, whilst a witness's age may go to the weight a tribunal of fact attaches to their evidence, very young age alone will not mean that the witness is incompetent.

It is important to remember that, whilst the issue of competence has arisen 27.145 most recently in relation to particularly young witnesses, it may also arise in cases involving adult witnesses with severe learning difficulties or mental disorder, or those suffering from dementia. In those cases it will fall to be determined in the same way.

The test of competence is one of intelligibility, namely whether the witness 27.146 can understand the questions asked of him in court and give answers that the jury can understand.[276] Where a party is seeking to call at trial a witness who has been ABE interviewed, competence should be considered both at the time of the ABE interview and when the witness is called upon to give evidence in court.[277] If it proves impossible to cross-examine the witness, then the ABE interview ought to be retrospectively excluded.[278] When the party seeking to rely upon the witness's evidence is of the view that they were competent during the ABE interview but are no longer competent by the date of trial, then an application could be made to admit the ABE interview as hearsay pursuant to s.116 of the Criminal Justice Act 2003.[279] If the witness lacked capability at the time that the witness statement was taken, then their statement cannot be adduced in accordance with the hearsay provisions. The test of capability is the same as competence and the burden of proof lies on the party seeking to adduce the statement. Whether a witness was capable of providing a witness statement should be determined in the absence of the jury and the court can hear expert evidence.[280] In *O'Leary*[281] the defendant successfully resisted a prosecution application to adduce the witness statement of a dementia sufferer as hearsay on the basis that at the time the witness made the statement he lacked capability within the meaning of s.123 of the Criminal Justice Act 2003. In the course of his evidence the defendant alleged that the CPS and police had conspired to keep the witness's evidence

[274] *Barker*, last note, referring to Spencer and Flin, *The Evidence of Children, the Law and the Psychology*, 2nd edn (London: Blackstone Press, 1993).
[275] Professor J.R. Spencer, *Children's Evidence: the Barker Case, and the Case for Pigot, Archbold Review*, Issue 3, April 2, 2010.
[276] *Barker* [2010] EWCA Crim 4; *Malicki* [2009] EWCA Crim 365; *Powell* [2006] 1 Cr. App. R. 31; *MacPherson* [2005] EWCA Crim 3605; *Sed (Ali Dahir)* [2005] 2 Cr. App. R. 4; *R. v D* [2002] 2 Cr. App. R. 36.
[277] *DPP v R* (2007) EWHC 1842 (Admin), confirmed in *Barker*, last note.
[278] *Barker* [2010] EWCA Crim 4.
[279] *R. v D* [2002] 2 Cr. App. R. 36.
[280] Criminal Justice Act 2003 s.123.
[281] [2013] EWCA Crim 1371.

from the jury. The Court of Appeal held that in those limited circumstances it was open to the judge to inform the jury that the witness's evidence had been ruled inadmissible. Ordinarily, however, it would be inappropriate to inform the jury of a ruling as to admissibility following a voir dire without the agreement of the parties.

27.147   In *R. v F*[282] the Court of Appeal stressed the importance of a trial judge, when determining competence, having the benefit of a full assessment by an intermediary to assist them to understand the witness's capability (with the benefit of special measures). The complainant in that case was profoundly deaf and suffered mild learning difficulties. Two intermediaries assessed her as able to give evidence. The prosecution proposed to rely upon her ABE interview as evidence-in-chief. An intermediary and British sign language ("BSL") interpreter would be present. The judge watched a short extract of the ABE interview and prosecution counsel then asked the complainant a series of questions, including asking her to point to different parts of her body. As a result, it became apparent that the BSL interpreter would have to point to a part of the body to ask the question, so in part leading the witness. The BSL interpreter could not use finger-spelling to see whether the complainant could understand the name of the body part because he was unprepared for that type of questioning. The intermediary's suggestion of drawings or pictures was not taken up. The prosecutor asked no more questions. The judge then asked questions dealing with the concept of time and abstract matters, topics which had not been covered in the intermediaries' assessments. Thereafter it appears that, outside court, the complainant was shown anatomical drawings and indicated animatedly that she could point to places where she could recall being touched. The judge nonetheless gave a terminating ruling that the complainant was not competent to give evidence, on the basis that there were difficulties asking her about body parts in a non-leading way and she had difficulty dealing with abstract concepts and concepts of time. The prosecution successfully appealed the ruling under s.58 of the Criminal Justice Act 2003. The Court of Appeal reviewed the ABE interview and transcript and concluded that with "time and patience", and the assistance of a BSL interpreter, the complainant was able to give a comprehensible account of the alleged offences. The difficulties in this case arose out of the questioner's inability to ask questions appropriately for this particular witness, as opposed to the witness's lack of comprehension. The competence hearing did not fully and fairly explore the complainant's ability to communicate. There was "a lack of preparation and a lack of ability to respond flexibly to the difficulties which arose". The Court recognised that the questioning of vulnerable witnesses requires "not only training, flexibility and sensitivity but time and patience". It approved the guidance in *Barker* and drew attention to the further guidance offered in the Crown Court Bench Book and the Advocacy Training Council's report

[282] [2013] EWCA Crim 424.

Raising the Bar: the Handling of Vulnerable Witnesses, Victims and Defendants in Court.[283] In allowing the prosecution appeal, the Court of Appeal held that whilst the judge had identified the correct test, she had substituted the issue of the interpreter's difficulties for the test of whether the witness could understand questions and give intelligible answers. With the right assistance from a BSL interpreter, the witness could understand and be understood. Clearly the judge remains under a continuing duty to keep the issue of competence under review and the Court of Appeal reiterated that careful consideration should be given before deciding that a competence hearing is required at the beginning of a case.

In *MacPherson*,[284] the child was four-and-a-half years old when she **27.148** alleged she had been indecently assaulted. The trial took place six months later. The Court of Appeal dismissed an appeal against conviction argued on the basis that the child had not been competent. Forbes J stated that a young child who is capable of speaking and understanding basic English with strangers would be competent. The child witness in *MacPherson* was plainly capable of understanding the questions she was being asked and was able to provide clear and intelligible answers. Moreover, in clear demonstration of her understanding the witness accompanied her verbal answers with "careful and graphic" illustrations of what had occurred.

The case of *Barker*[285] is instructive as to how judges should approach s.53. **27.149** *Barker* involved an allegation of anal rape of the complainant, who was four-and-a-half years old when she gave evidence about matters which occurred when she was three. The child had made an unprompted disclosure of the offences to a foster mother and a few months later to a child psychiatrist. During the course of her meeting with the psychiatrist, the child demonstrated the position of her body and the appellant's using a girl doll and a boy doll. When aged three-and-a-half, an ABE interview was conducted, during the course of which she demonstrated what had happened by laying on her stomach. During the interview the child was able to describe how the appellant "put his willy in her" and pointed to her bottom. The trial did not take place until over a year later because the appellant was also facing trial for the murder of the complainant's brother, known as "Baby P". During the trial the complainant's ABE interview was played and she was then cross-examined by a QC. Amongst other matters, cross-examination related to whether the child knew the difference between the truth and a lie and whether she told fibs. It was also put to the child that she was being untruthful because one or both of her sisters had put her up to making up allegations against the appellant. The child was asked about what she remembered of her ABE interview. In general she responded in monosyllabic

---

[283] Final Report of the Advocacy Training Council Working Group on Vulnerable Witness Handling, *Raising the Bar: The Handling of Vulnerable Witnesses, Victims and Defendants in Court* (Advocacy Training Council, 2011).

[284] (2006) 1 Cr. App. R. 30 at [27]–[28].

[285] [2010] EWCA Crim 4.

answers or by shaking her head. On some occasions the child would respond to a question by answering the previous question. The child was also cross-examined by co-defendant's counsel, who asked short and simple questions; it was conceded that the witness could understand these questions and give answers which were understood. At the conclusion of the complainant's evidence the judge was invited to reconsider the issue of competence. In rejecting the defence application to exclude the complaint's ABE interview under s.78 of the Police and Criminal Evidence Act 1984, the judge ruled that "when simple questions were asked, the defence were able to put their cases sufficiently to ensure that the defendants have a fair trial." The judge correctly identified that matters of credibility and reliability were not matters of competence. In dismissing an appeal against conviction, the Court of Appeal made plain that the question to be asked is whether the particular witness is competent to give evidence in the particular trial; in broad terms, can the witness understand the questions put to him and can he provide understandable answers? It is not necessary for the witness to be able to understand every single question or give a readily understood answer to each question, neither need the witness be aware of their status as a witness, nor understand the special importance that the truth should be told in court. The Court of Appeal made welcome comments that the age of a witness is not determinative of her or his ability to give truthful and accurate evidence, and that a child will begin their evidence on the basis of equality with every other witness. The Court emphasised the importance of making allowances for the fact that children are children and cannot be judged by adult standards. The trial process must adapt and cater for the child's needs to enable them to give the best evidence of which they are capable; the process must make allowance for the fact that children will have a shorter attention span than most adults and the courts should make good use of intermediaries. The Lord Chief Justice also commented that the forensic techniques of the advocate may have to adapt when dealing with a child witness.[286]

27.150   *Barker* confirms that competence may be reviewed at the end of the child's evidence and that the ability of the trial judge to reconsider competence is an important element of the defendant's right to a fair trial. If the witness cannot provide competent answers in cross-examination, then the defendant has been denied the opportunity to challenge the allegations against him and in effect the first decision on competence is proved wrong.[287] If that were to be the case, the ABE interview could be retrospectively excluded under s.78 of the Police and Criminal Evidence Act 1984.[288] *Barker* also emphasises that when assessing competence a judge makes a decision as to whether the witness fulfils the statutory criteria, and at no point is he exercising discretion.

---

[286] At [42]. See further Ch.28.
[287] *Barker* [2010] EWCA Crim 4, at [43].
[288] At [43].

Barker is a welcome decision, which recognises the change brought about   27.151
by the introduction of s.53. However, in this difficult and sensitive area,
judges and advocates must remain alert to the risk of falling into error. In *R.
v P(J)*[289] (the conjoined appeal with *Lubemba*), the appellant's conviction
was overturned because, having visited the eight-year-old complainant alone,
the judge decided that she should not be cross-examined. Hallett LJ
described the judge's approach as "wrong in a number of respects", before
going on to set out the correct procedure where a judge has concerns over
whether a vulnerable witness should be cross-examined. In accordance with
s.54(6) of the YJCEA 1999, any judicial assessment of a witness's competence
must take place in the presence of the parties (including via live link). The
judge should also consider whether any further special measures, including
an intermediary, might assist the witness (s.54(3)) and it is also open to the
judge to seek expert assistance (s.54(5)). It was not clear that the judge in *R.
v P(J)* had determined that the witness lacked competence, but if he had, he
should have reconsidered the admissibility of the ABE interview in accordance with s.27(5) of the YJCEA 1999. In addition, the judge failed to give
sufficient consideration to the fairness of the trial when the defence were
prohibited from testing the evidence of the main prosecution witness.

Impact of delay in case coming to trial

Prior to *Barker* there was concern that children who witnessed or were   27.152
victims of crime were being denied justice because of delays in the criminal
justice system. In the case of *Powell*[290] the witness, aged three-and-a-half, had
complained to her mother that the appellant had licked her private parts. The
witness was not ABE interviewed until nine weeks after the allegation and
the case took nine months to reach trial. The Court of Appeal expressed
concern about this unfortunate elapse of time and described it as "completely
unacceptable" that the appellant should have been tried for an offence, proof
of which relied upon the evidence of a three-and-a-half year old, when the
trial did not take place until nine months had passed from the date of the
alleged offence. One might add that it was also wholly unsatisfactory that, by
reason of the delay, the child was denied the opportunity to give her best
evidence of the incident that led to the charge. Whilst even very young
children may be capable of giving reliable evidence, cases need to be fast-
tracked to assist them to so do. The decision in *Powell* added voice to those
in favour of the introduction of pre-recorded cross-examination for very
young witnesses. The later case of *Malicki*[291] caused concern that trials
involving very young witnesses would not be able to take place at all. The
complaint was four years and eight months old at the date of the alleged
incident. The ABE interview was conducted in good time but unfortunately

---

[289] [2014] EWCA Crim 2064; [2015] 1 Cr. App. R. 12, at [48]–[50].
[290] [2006] 1 Cr. App. R. 31.
[291] [2009] EWCA Crim 365.

the trial did not take place until 14 months after the alleged incident. In that case the Court of Appeal held that, at the point of cross-examination, it was impossible to discern whether the complainant was recalling events or simply recalling what she had said in the ABE interview. This is an unfortunate decision, since in matters of recollection child witnesses are not in a special category and cross-examination ought to be capable of exposing when a witness has no recollection of events. The Court in *Malicki* also doubted that a child as young as the one in that case would have any accurate recollection of events which took place 14 months earlier. The decision arguably came close to creating a special sub-category of abuse of process based on delay and reserved for cases involving children. *Barker* underlined "the importance to the trial and investigative process of keeping any delay involving a child complainant to an irreducible minimum" as stated in *Powell* and *Malicki* but emphasised that those decisions are not authority for any unspecified limitation period or that an application under s.78 was bound to succeed. Accordingly, delay does not of itself prevent or stop the evidence of a child witness from being considered by the jury. No doubt any jury would consider the effect that delay may have had on the reliability of the witness's evidence.

27.153   *R. v MH*[292] involved a four-year-old giving evidence at a trial for sexual abuse 15 months after the recording of the ABE interview. The reason for the delay was to allow the forensic examination of the appellant's computer. The Court of Appeal confirmed that delay of itself will not necessarily render a very young witness incompetent to give evidence, but the passage of time may affect the child's ability to give intelligible answers about the incident. It follows that where a child is, despite the passage of time, able to give intelligible answers they will be competent. The trial judge should, of course, direct the jury to consider any disadvantage to the defendant because of the delay.

27.154   However, all of these decisions relating to competence should serve to underline for practitioners and others within the criminal justice system the importance of early listing of cases involving very young witnesses, or adult witnesses with mental disorder or learning difficulties.

Sworn and Unsworn Evidence

27.155   Section 55 of the YJCEA 1999 provides that a witness may not be sworn for the purpose of giving evidence on oath in criminal proceedings unless he has reached the age of 14 and has sufficient appreciation of the solemnity of the occasion and of the particular responsibility to tell the truth which is involved in taking an oath.[293] If the witness is able to give intelligible

---

[292] [2012] EWCA Crim 2725, also reported at [2013] Crim. L.R. 10, 849–853 with commentary by Laura Hoyano.
[293] s.55(2) of the YJCEA 1999.

testimony, i.e. he is able to understand questions put to him as a witness and give answers, which can be understood, he is presumed to have sufficient appreciation of these matters if no evidence is adduced by any party which tends to show the contrary.[294] If such evidence is adduced, it is for the party seeking to have the witness sworn to satisfy the court, on a balance of probabilities, that the witness meets the requirements for being sworn.[295] For this purpose, the witness's age is taken as that which it appears to the court to be after considering any available evidence.[296] Any proceedings held to decide this question shall be heard in the absence of the jury, expert evidence may be called and, if the court considers questioning of the witness to be necessary, the questioning is to be conducted by the court in the presence of the parties.[297]

A person who is competent to give evidence within the meaning of s.53 of **27.156** the YJCEA 1999, but who cannot be sworn because he does not fulfil the requirements of s.55, must give his evidence unsworn.[298] Further, a deposition of unsworn evidence given by the person may be taken and received by the court as if that evidence had been given on oath.[299] If it subsequently turns out that the witness did in fact fulfil the s.55 requirements and so should have been sworn, this will not affect the safety of the conviction.[300]

PROHIBITION ON CROSS-EXAMINATION BY THE DEFENDANT IN PERSON

The YJCEA 1999 restricts cross-examination by the defendant, in person, of **27.157** complainants, children and other vulnerable witnesses in trials for sexual offences.

Section 34 of the YJCEA 1999 provides that a person charged with a **27.158** sexual offence may not in any criminal proceedings[301] cross-examine in person the complainant in connection with either the offence or any other offence with which he is charged in the proceedings.

Section 35(1) provides that a person charged with an offence to which that **27.159** section applies may not in any criminal proceedings cross-examine in person a "protected witness" in connection with either the offence or any other offence with which he is charged in the proceedings. A "protected witness" is defined as the complainant or a witness to the offence, who either is a child or falls to be cross-examined after giving evidence-in-chief by means of a

---

[294] s.55(3), (8).
[295] s.55(4).
[296] s.65(3).
[297] s.55(5)–(7).
[298] s.56(1), (2), (4).
[299] s.56(3), (4).
[300] s.56(5).
[301] i.e. not only those relating to the sexual offence.

video recording (or other means) made when he was a child.[302] By s.35(3),[303] the offences to which the section applies are:

    (a) the Protection of Children Act 1978, Pt 1 of the Sexual Offences Act 2003, any offence under the Sexual Offences Act 1956, the Indecency with Children Act 1960, the Sexual Offences Act 1967, s.54 of the Criminal Law Act 1977, or,

    (b) kidnapping, false imprisonment or an offence under s.1 or 2 of the Child Abduction Act 1984,

    (c) any offence under s.1 of the Children and Young Persons Act 1933, and

    (d) any offence (not within paragraphs (a) to (c)) which involves an assault on, or injury or threat of injury to, any person."

Where the offence falls within s.35(3)(a), a "child" for the purposes of the section means someone under the age of 18.[304] Where the offence falls within s.35(3)(b) to (d), it means a person under the age of 14.[305] There appears to be no sensible reason for the lower age limit in relation to offences of kidnap, false imprisonment or physical abuse.[306]

27.160   Section 36 of the YJCEA 1999 enables a prosecutor to apply, in circumstances other than those provided for in ss.34 and 35, to prevent an accused from cross-examining a particular witness.[307]

27.161   Section 38 of the YJCEA 1999 provides that, where the defendant is prohibited by s.34, s.35 or s.36 from cross-examining a witness in person, the court must invite him to arrange for a legal representative to act for him for the purpose of cross-examining the witness and must require him to notify the court within a specified period whether he has done so.[308] If the defendant notifies the court that no legal representative is to act for him for this purpose, or it so appears to the court at the end of the specified period, the court must consider whether it is necessary in the interests of justice for the witness to be cross-examined by a legal representative appointed to represent the defendant's interests.[309] If so, the court must appoint a qualified legal representative to conduct the cross-examination.[310] The person

---

[302] s.35(2).

[303] As amended by the Criminal Justice and Immigration Act 2008 Sch.26, para.36. The amendments were generated by concerns that by virtue of legislative oversight, complainants of sexual offences pre-dating the 2003 Act were denied the protection of ss.34 and 35 of the YJCEA 1999. This was initially resolved in *Cartwright* [2007] EWCA Crim 2581. Parliament corrected matters in the 2008 Act.

[304] Raised from 17 by the Coroners and Justice Act 2009 s.105, with effect from June 27, 2011 (SI 2011/1452).

[305] s.35(4).

[306] Laura Hoyano describes the different age limits as "perplexing" in her article *Coroners and Justice Act 2009: (3) Special Measures Directions Take Two: Entrenching Unequal Access to Justice* [2010] Crim. L.R. 345.

[307] s.36(1) of the YJCEA 1999.

[308] s.38(1), (2).

[309] s.38(3).

[310] s.38(4).

appointed is to act in the defendant's interests but is not responsible to the defendant.[311] Unfortunately it is unclear whether funding is available for the appointed representative to attend pre-trial hearings. In *Abbas v CPS*[312] the appointed advocate was not funded to attend any pre-trial hearings and was therefore in the unfortunate position of seeking disclosure and making a non-defendant bad character application on the day of trial. The Divisional Court commented that matters that were genuinely part of an advocate's duty to cross-examine should be funded. In view of Hallett LJ's judgment in *Lubemba*,[313] funding ought to be extended to enable an advocate appointed under s.38 to attend the Ground Rules Hearing, which should occur in all but the most exceptional of cases. The Court in *Abbas* confirmed that the role of a s.38 advocate ends once cross-examination is complete. They do not have a free-ranging remit to conduct the trial on the accused's behalf. But the Court said that if, at the conclusion of the cross-examination, the advocate is prepared to stay and to act pro bono, there is no reason why the court should oblige them to leave.

Part 23 of the Criminal Procedure Rules 2015 sets out the procedure to be followed where a person is prohibited by s.34, s.35 or s.36 from cross-examining in person.[314] **27.162**

Finally, s.39 provides that where, on trial on indictment, a defendant is barred by ss.34, 35 or 36 from cross-examining a witness in person, the judge must give the jury such warning (if any) as the judge considers necessary to ensure that the defendant is not prejudiced: **27.163**

    (a) by inferences that might be drawn from the fact that the defendant has been prevented from cross-examining in person and,

    (b) where the cross-examination was conducted by a legal representative appointed by the court, by the fact that it was carried out by such a representative and not by the defendant's own representative.

---

[311] s.38(5).

[312] [2015] 2 Cr. App. R. 11.

[313] [2014] EWCA Crim 2064; [2015] 1 Cr. App. R. 12, discussed in paras 28.16 and following, below.

[314] Criminal Procedure Rules 2015 r.23.2(4)(b).

CHAPTER 28

ADVOCACY AND THE VULNERABLE

By H.H. Judge Peter Rook QC, Angela Rafferty QC
and Alexandra Ward, Barrister

Introduction 28.01
The Correct
  Approach—Adaptation 28.10
Confrontation—Putting the Case 28.22

Case Management—Ground Rules
  Hearing 28.31
Questioning—Practical Suggestions 28.41

INTRODUCTION

There is now widespread recognition that the questioning of children and **28.01** other vulnerable persons is a specialist skill. It is also widely recognised that the traditional style of cross-examination does not achieve best evidence from a vulnerable witness. It is unfit for the task of enabling a jury to assess the credibility and the accuracy of the witness's evidence. This recognition, together with the availability of special measures (discussed in Ch.27), has led to a sea change in the questioning of vulnerable witnesses and defendants. There is no place for entrenched behaviour simply because it is how things have always been done. As Dr Emily Henderson comments:

> "processes are to be judged not by their antiquity but by their efficiency in enabling us to protect what matters most."[1]

Hallett LJ set out the correct approach in her judgment in *Lubemba*[2]: **28.02**

> "it is now generally accepted that if justice is to be done to the vulnerable witness and also to the accused, a radical departure from the traditional style of advocacy will be necessary. Advocates must adapt to the witness, not the other way round."

---

[1] Dr. Emily Henderson, *Judges as Cross-Examiners: the Starmer v Grieve Debate*, Archbold Review 2014, 5, 3–4.
[2] [2014] EWCA Crim 2064; [2015] 1 Cr. App. R. 12 at [45].

28.03 What matters most is the principle of a fair trial. Recent developments in questioning of the vulnerable do not infringe that fundamental principle; the role of the judge is to protect a vulnerable witness from unnecessary and oppressive questioning, but not at the expense of a fair trial for the defendant.[3]

28.04 Every practitioner in this area must be aware of relevant developments and training. Some advocates have already acquired the necessary specialist skill but there remain justified concerns that advocacy has not evolved to ensure best practice is universally adopted in respect of the handling and questioning of vulnerable witnesses and defendants. Questioning which ignores the principles designed to obtain accurate information from a witness and exploits his or her developmental limitations is not only wholly inconsistent with a fair trial but also contravenes the advocate's Code of Conduct. Moreover, repetitive questioning on the same point by multiple advocates may produce unreliable answers and should be discouraged.[4]

28.05 Most acknowledge that it will only be a matter of time before every criminal and family law advocate will have to be a specialist at handling the vulnerable as part of their basic training.[5] To that end, the Advocacy Training Council ("ATC"), which was renamed the College of Advocacy from May 1, 2016, has established a pan-disciplinary working group under the chairmanship of HHJ Rook QC to design and build a specialist training course for all advocates engaged in criminal cases involving vulnerable witnesses. The aim is to promote consistent standards across the legal profession, including consistency with the training currently provided to judges who deal with such cases. A course to teach advocates the key principles relating to the proper treatment of the vulnerable has now been devised. It is expected that this training will be mandatory for those who practise in this area.

28.06 There is a plethora of appellate authority which will assist the advocate to question such a witness properly whilst still protecting the interests of their client.[6] In addition, practical guidance published by professional organisations is readily available. Leading the field in this respect is the Advocacy Training Council ("ATC") through the first-class toolkits provided on its Advocates Gateway.[7] The Criminal Bar Association ("CBA") and the Crown

---

[3] Dr. Emily Henderson *All the proper protections—the Court of Appeal rewrites the rules for the cross-examination of vulnerable witnesses* [2014] Crim. L.R. 93.

[4] *Jonas* [2015] EWCA Crim 562; [2015] Crim. L.R. 742.

[5] See Penny Cooper, *Ticketing Talk Gets Serious, Counsel Magazine*, Nov 2014, pp.24–5.

[6] See *Lubemba* [2014] EWCA Crim 2064; [2015] 1 Cr App R. 12; *Barker* [2010] EWCA Crim 4; *R v IA* [2013] EWCA Crim 1308; *R. v E* [2011] EWCA Crim 3028; *Wills* [2011] EWCA Crim 1938; Lord Judge CJ, *Toulmin Lecture in Law and Psychiatry* (King's College London, March 20, 2013, accessible at *http://www.judiciary.gov.uk/media/speeches/2013/lcj-speech-toulmin-lecture* [Accessed April 30, 2016]; Criminal Bar Association, Advocate's Gateway Toolkits; Advocacy Training Council, CPS and NSPCC training video *A Question of Practice* (2013), accessible at *http://www.theadvocatesgateway.org/* [Accessed April 30, 2016].

[7] See Appendix F. The authors are grateful to the College of Advocacy and Professor Penny Cooper for permission to publish these.

Prosecution Service deliver training (the CPS online portal will soon be made available to its graded Panel Advocates). The CBA video, *A Question of Practice,* and all of the Advocates Gateway toolkits are readily accessible online. The Criminal Procedure Rules 2015, Criminal Practice Direction 2015, Bench Checklist for young witness cases[8] and Equal Treatment Bench Book 2013 all reinforce the role of the judiciary in this area.

Effective case management plays a vital role in protecting the vulnerable **28.07** within the court process. Just as advocates must re-train and perhaps alter an advocacy style developed over many years, so must the judiciary accept their responsibility to control the nature and length of the advocate's questioning. This necessarily involves setting clear ground rules before trial, at a Ground Rules Hearing, and the enforcement of those rules during proceedings.

The modern approach to cross-examination of vulnerable witnesses **28.08** applies equally to vulnerable defendants. It follows that prosecutors have the same obligation not to exploit a defendant's communicative and psychological vulnerability and a judge has the same responsibility to protect a defendant from inappropriate questioning.

This chapter discusses the correct approach to the cross-examination of **28.09** the vulnerable as set out by the Court of Appeal; Ground Rules Hearings; and some practical suggestions for questioning vulnerable witnesses.

THE CORRECT APPROACH—ADAPTATION

The role of the court is to ensure a fair trial and "[the] purpose of the trial **28.10** process is to identify the evidence which is reliable and that which is not, whether it comes from an adult or a child."[9] However, a convention has arisen where cross-examination is used to create an impression of the witness's evidence considered favourable to the case being advanced. The objective of cross-examination in such cases is not necessarily, therefore, to communicate with the witness but rather to communicate with the jury.

Traditionally, with this style of advocacy, advocates are taught to cross- **28.11** examine in such a way as to control the witness, it being assumed that their evidence will be hostile. In recent decisions, the Court of Appeal has placed greater emphasis on obtaining reliable and truthful answers to the questions asked. This process, more akin to forensic examination, is alien to many advocates and in stark contrast to the conventional approach of aiming to control the witness.[10]

It is recognised that advocates will need to adjust their style of cross- **28.12** examination for witnesses who are vulnerable young age or other reasons. As

---

[8] *http://www.judiciary.gov.uk/publications-and-reports/guidance/2012/jc-bench-checklist-young-wit-cases* [Accessed April 30, 2016].

[9] *Barker* [2010] EWCA Crim 4.

[10] Dr. Emily Henderson, *All the proper protections—the Court of Appeal rewrites the rules for the cross-examination of vulnerable witnesses* [2014] Crim. L.R. 93.

HHJ Peter Collier QC states on the training video *A Question of Practice*, produced by the CBA and others:

> "Many advocates have quite a journey to make to achieve changes in habits of questioning that have been learned over many years and often have become deeply entrenched but which are not appropriate for the examination of children and vulnerable witnesses."

28.13   The Court of Appeal has made plain in a series of cases (considered below) that a style of questioning will be required which enables effective communication with the witness. No longer will questioning be permitted that prevents the witness from effective participation in the trial process. This does not conflict with an accused's right to a fair trial under art.6 of the ECHR. An advocate cannot complain that their client has been denied a fair trial if they are prevented from cross-examining in a way that is liable to elicit false or unreliable evidence from a confused witness.

28.14   The Court of Appeal has stated in the plainest of terms that the approach to cross-examination of children and vulnerable witnesses[11] should be markedly different from the approach to non-vulnerable adults. In light of those authorities, the advocate must now adapt their cross-examination to the witness.[12] The aim is to obtain reliable evidence whilst remaining fair to the defendant.

28.15   In a recent article,[13] Dr Emily Henderson considers whether the approach of the Court of Appeal has undermined the accused's right to a fair trial. Dr Henderson identifies three main aspects of traditional questioning techniques which have undergone radical reform in respect of vulnerable witnesses. First, miscommunication with the witness through the use of developmentally inappropriate language. Secondly, suggestive questions resulting in unreliable answers. Thirdly, the requirement to put the defence case (i.e. to confront the witness with the defence version of events or case theory). We would add a fourth, namely cross-examination on the same topic by multiple advocates.

28.16   In *Lubemba*,[14] the Court of Appeal expressly considered what measures a trial judge might take to protect a vulnerable witness, without undermining the defendant's right to a fair trial. In giving judgment, Hallett LJ summarised some of the key steps:

> "The court is required to take every reasonable step to encourage and facilitate the attendance of vulnerable witnesses and their participation in the trial process. To that end, judges are taught, in accordance with the Criminal Practice Directions, that it is best practice to hold hearings in advance of the trial to

---

[11] *Dixon* [2013] EWCA Crim 465.
[12] *Barker* [2010] EWCA Crim 4; *R. v W and M* [2010] EWCA Crim 1926; *Wills* [2011] EWCA Crim 1938; *R. v E* [2012] EWCA Crim 563, *Lubemba* [2014] EWCA Crim 2064; [2015] 1 Cr. App. R. 12.
[13] *All the proper protections—the Court of Appeal rewrites the rules for the cross-examination of vulnerable witnesses* [2014] Crim. L.R. 93.
[14] [2014] EWCA Crim 2064; [2015] 1 Cr. App. R. 12. See also *Jonas* [2015] EWCA Crim 562.

ensure the smooth running of the trial, to give any special measures directions and to set the ground rules for the treatment of a vulnerable witness. We would expect a ground rules hearing in every case involving a vulnerable witness, save in very exceptional circumstances. If there are any doubts on how to proceed, guidance should be sought from those who have the responsibility for looking after the witness and or an expert.

In general, experts recommend that the trial judge should introduce him or herself to the witness in person before any questioning, preferably in the presence of the parties. This seems to us to be an entirely reasonable step to take to put the witness at their ease where possible. The ground rules hearing should cover, amongst other matters, the general care of the witness, if, when and where the witness is to be shown their video interview, when, where and how the parties (and the judge if identified) intend to introduce themselves to the witness, the length of questioning and frequency of breaks and the nature of the questions to be asked. So as to avoid any unfortunate misunderstanding at trial, it would be an entirely reasonable step for a judge at the ground rules hearing to invite defence advocates to reduce their questions to writing in advance.

The judge has a duty to intervene, therefore, if an advocate's questioning is confusing or inappropriate.

It is now generally accepted that if justice is to be done to the vulnerable witness and also to the accused, a radical departure from the traditional style of advocacy will be necessary. Advocates must adapt to the witness, not the other way round. They cannot insist upon any supposed right 'to put one's case' or previous inconsistent statements to a vulnerable witness. If there is a right to 'put one's case' (about which we have our doubts) it must be modified for young or vulnerable witnesses. It is perfectly possible to ensure the jury are made aware of the defence case and of significant inconsistencies without intimidation or distressing a witness (see for example paragraph 3E.4 of the Criminal Practice Directions)."

In *Barker*,[15] the then Lord Chief Justice considered the circumstances in which very small children might give evidence in criminal trials. The Court acknowledged that the trial process must cater for the needs of child witnesses and that forensic techniques have to be adapted to enable the child to give the best evidence of which he or she is capable, but that the defendant's right to a fair trial remained sacrosanct. Lord Judge CJ added: **28.17**

"At the same time the right of the defendant to a fair trial must be undiminished. When the issue is whether the child is lying or mistaken in claiming that the defendant behaved indecently towards him or her, it should not be over-problematic for the advocate to formulate short, simple questions which put the essential elements of the defendant's case to the witness, and fully to ventilate before the jury the areas of evidence which bear on the child's credibility. Aspects of evidence which undermine or are believed to undermine the child's credibility must, of course, be revealed to the jury, but it is not necessarily appropriate for them to form the subject matter of detailed cross-examination of the child and the advocate may have to forego much of the kind of contemporary cross-examination which consists of no more than comment on matters which will be before the jury in any event from different sources. Notwithstanding some of the difficulties, when all is said and done, the witness whose cross-examination is in

---

[15] [2010] EWCA Crim 4.

contemplation is a child, sometimes very young, and it should not take very lengthy cross-examination to demonstrate, when it is the case, that the child may indeed be fabricating, or fantasising, or imagining, or reciting a well rehearsed untruthful script, learned by rote, or simply just suggestible, or contaminated by or in collusion with others to make false allegations, or making assertions in language which is beyond his or her level of comprehension, and therefore likely to be derived from another source. Comment on the evidence, including comment on evidence which may bear adversely on the credibility of the child, should be addressed after the child has finished giving evidence."

The dangers of suggestive questioning

28.18 The case of *R. v W and M*[16] involved two 10-year-old defendants alleged to have raped an eight-year-old girl. Somewhat surprisingly, there was no intermediary to assist either the witness or the defendants. Following suggestive questioning, the girl had agreed to propositions put to her under cross-examination that the boys had not attempted to penetrate or actually penetrated her. The Court of Appeal held that the jury could conclude that a child witness who contradicted her original allegations during cross-examination was not actually agreeing in any meaningful way to what was being suggested to her. When questioning was framed with direct suggestions with an indication of the answer sought, a vulnerable witness may agree simply in order to bring the questioning to an end rather than take the more difficult course of disagreeing. The trial judge was also concerned that the witness was getting tired.

28.19 The Court of Appeal emphasised the importance of avoiding "tag" questions[17]:

> "It is particularly important in the case of a child witness to keep a question short, and even more important than it is with an adult witness where it also matters to avoid questions which are rolled up and contain, inadvertently, two or three at once. It is generally recognized that particularly with child witnesses short and untagged questions are best at eliciting the evidence. By untagged we mean questions that do not contain a statement of the answer which is sought."

This is the definition of a leading question, which indicates the changes many defence advocates will have to make to their "usual" style of cross-examination.[18]

28.20 The Court in *R. v W and M* also noted that during the cross-examination in that case the judge had been conscious that the child was showing signs of getting tired. The Court gave no guidance specifically on this point. It may be felt that there are competing interests between finishing the child's evidence so as to avoid them needing to return the next day or insisting that a break is taken. Effective case management and Ground Rules Hearings should

---

[16] [2010] EWCA Crim 1926.
[17] At [30].
[18] *Advocacy Focus, Counsel Magazine*, January 2011, pp.40–42.

enable the witness' needs to be accommodated so that they are not tired when giving evidence. For example, a young witness should have watched their ABE interview recently, not be kept waiting at court and only be cross-examined for a reasonable time. However, if the judge assesses that a witness is too tired to deal with appropriate questioning by an advocate, their evidence should be stopped and resumed following an opportunity to rest. It is not fair to the witness if they are too tired to cope with such questioning, nor is it fair to the defendant, since the jury may attribute any retraction to the witness's tiredness as opposed to a genuine intention to retract the allegation. The defence ought not to be denied a proper opportunity to explore that possibility because the witness is exhausted.

Often cross-examination is a method used by the advocate to comment **28.21** upon the evidence. Such comment, which does not seek to elicit useful evidence for the tribunal of fact, is impermissible. In short, a vulnerable witness should be asked questions they are capable of responding to in a meaningful way, no more and no less. Challenge through complicated language or tag questions, which merely disrupt the child's ability to respond, will be impermissible.

CONFRONTATION—PUTTING THE CASE

Advocates have traditionally been taught that they are required to "put" **28.22** their client's case to any relevant witness. This requirement pre-dates the right of defence counsel to open or close their client's case. It usually involves a set of questions (or quite often comments with questions at the end) designed to reveal what is disputed on essential matters. This "putting of the case" is in fact founded on fairness to the witness and not the defendant. It was designed to allow the witness an opportunity of answering the case. It can be highly confusing for a vulnerable person to have the case "put" to them in the traditional way. However, it should be noted that most witnesses can cope if the questions are framed correctly and are based on the ground rules.

The experience of the s.28 pilots in Liverpool and Leeds suggests that most **28.22A** vulnerable witnesses, even very small children, are able to deal with the defendant's version of events if this is correctly formulated in appropriate questions. The tone and language of such challenges will be very different from the "traditional" approach. Similarly, it will be done briefly and gently. However, it should be possible to draft simple and direct questions, which comply with the ground rules and allow the witness fairly to deal with what is being said by the accused. The presence of the intermediary at the Ground Rules Hearing should assist with this.

A suggestion that they are lying is often a difficult subject for a vulnerable **28.22B** witness to deal with by way of direct challenge. There are a variety of ways in which the witness can be asked about disputed evidence, which makes it clear to them that they are being challenged without the need for the use of emotive or potentially counter-productive language and tone. In the majority of cases, a way can be found.

28.23   Following *Barker*,[19] it was accepted by the Court of Appeal that cases may arise where it is no longer be necessary for defence counsel to "put their case" to a very young witness. The Court of Appeal has made clear that the traditional approach of the advocate putting their case in stark terms may be neither necessary nor appropriate. It may instead be proper for an advocate to explain to the jury prior to the complainant's evidence that the allegation is denied and to set out the fundamental aspects of the defence (i.e. the complainant is lying and seeking attention).

28.24   However, the Criminal Practice Directions 2015 ("CPD") recognise, at CPD 3E.4, that when a witness is young or vulnerable the court *may* dispense with the normal practice and impose restrictions on the advocate "putting his case". This could be where there is a risk of a young or vulnerable witness failing to understand, becoming distressed or acquiescing to leading questions.[20]

28.25   Important guidance was provided in *Lubemba*,[21] where the Court of Appeal approved the guidance given in *Barker* and considered what measures a trial judge may legitimately take to protect a vulnerable witness, without impacting adversely on the right of an accused to a fair trial. In respect of "putting one's case" the Court doubted that such a right existed and stated:

> "If there is a right to 'put one's case' (about which we have our doubts) it must be modified for young or vulnerable witnesses. It is perfectly possible to ensure the jury are made aware of the defence case and of significant inconsistencies without intimidation or distressing a witness (see for example paragraph 3E.4 of the Criminal Practice Directions)."

In *Lubemba*, the trial judge had restricted cross-examination to 45 minutes, interrupted when the advocate's questions were unclear or inappropriate and had prevented the advocate from putting the defence case to the complainant.

28.26   The general guidance given in *Barker* was also approved in *Wills*,[22] where the Court considered that in many cases it will be perfectly possible for a defence advocate to contradict the evidence of a child or vulnerable witness by reference to other evidence rather than by "putting their case" directly to the witness. Such contradictory material may be found in first complaints or in records held by social services or education departments. Therefore, important inconsistencies can be adduced for example in schedules, or agreed facts or read statements, and the witness does not necessarily have to be asked about them. Even if external evidence is not available, the advocate

---

[19] [2010] EWCA Crim 4.
[20] Rule.3.9(7)(b)(i) of the Criminal Procedure Rules 2015; Criminal Practice Directions 2015 3E.4.
[21] [2014] EWCA Crim 2064; [2015] 1 Cr. App. R. 12 at [45].
[22] [2011] EWCA Crim 1938.

may still be able to outline to the jury the basis of their defence and the elements of dispute with the witness before the witness gives evidence, to avoid putting to the witness that they have lied. This is in circumstances where it is considered the witness cannot deal with allegation of lying.

In the earlier case of *R. v E*,[23] the appellant was convicted of child cruelty **28.27** by punching his five-year-old step-daughter, C. The jury were made aware throughout the trial that he denied punching her. The trial judge prevented defence counsel from putting this assertion directly to C, but specifically directed the jury to make allowances for the difficulties faced by the defence when questioning her.[24] The appellant appealed on the basis that his counsel had been unduly restricted in his cross-examination. In dismissing the appeal, the Court of Appeal stated[25]:

> "The real complaint here, in our view, is that the defence was deprived of the opportunity to confront C in what we might venture to call 'the traditional way'. It is common, in the trial of an adult, to hear, once the nursery slopes of cross-examination have been skied, the assertion: 'You were never punched, hit, kicked as you have suggested, were you?' It was precisely that the judge was anxious to avoid and, in our view, rightly. It would have risked confusion in the mind of the witness whose evidence was bound to take centre stage, and it is difficult to see how it could have been helpful. Putting the same thing a different way, we struggle to understand how the defendant's right to a fair trial was in any way compromised simply because [his counsel] was not allowed to ask: 'S did not punch you in the tummy, did he?'"

The Court of Appeal was clear that not permitting counsel to "put their **28.28** case" had not infringed the defendant's right to a fair trial. The Court of Appeal also commented: "it is difficult to see that the Appellant could with greater skill have been represented or his interests better served". Defence counsel showed real skill in putting the defence's alternative hypotheses to account for C's injuries with courtesy and gentleness. Tag questions were occasionally used, and with the advantage of being able to analyse the transcript after the conclusion of the trial process, it is possible to see how such questions might have been avoided. With the benefit of pre-recorded examination-in-chief for child witnesses, it is possible for an advocate to plan their cross-examination in some detail and there is an advantage in these types of cases in writing out questions in full before they are asked.

The authors stress that such restrictions should only apply where it is **28.29** necessary. It is not to be assumed that an advocate can avoid putting their case in respect of every young or vulnerable witness. An opposing version of events should be put to the witness if it can be achieved through questions which the witness can understand and which do not apply unfair pressure. The presence of the intermediary at the Ground Rules Hearing should assist with this. The intermediary may provide valuable assistance in drafting

---

[23] [2011] EWCA Crim 3028.
[24] For the appropriateness of such directions, see Adrian Keane, *Towards a Principled Approach to the Cross-Examination of Vulnerable Witnesses* [2012] Crim. L.R. 407.
[25] At [28].

questions that can be understood. Witnesses who can cope with short, simple, direct questions should be asked them. If the advocate chooses not to put such questions then the judge or prosecutor may do so.

28.30   Where advocates are restricted from putting their case in cross-examination, they can use their right to make an opening submission or a statement to the jury as to the matters they would have put if the witness were not vulnerable. If such opportunities are taken, the jury will have the defendant's case well in mind. Where restrictions are imposed, the judge should explain to the jury the reasons for them and remind the jury after the witness has finished giving evidence of important inconsistencies upon which the defence rely.[26] So in *Edwards*,[27] the judge made clear to the jury the difficulty the defendant faced by reason of the limits on cross-examination:

> "The jury knew that the defendant disputed the evidence of [the victim]. The judge clearly explained his decision as to cross-examination technique and why he had taken it. In addition, the jury was specifically directed 'to make proper fair allowances for the difficulties faced by the defence in asking questions about this'."

CASE MANAGEMENT—GROUND RULES HEARINGS

28.31   Cases involving the vulnerable require effective case management from the outset. Any restrictions, and the means by which an advocate intends to challenge the witness's account without putting their case directly to the witness, should be considered in advance at a Ground Rules Hearing. There must be full compliance with the ground rules that are set. It may frequently be necessary and appropriate for the trial judge to control the style, length and content of cross-examination. This may involve the defence being ordered to reduce proposed questions to writing enabling the judge to consider them in advance.

28.32   Ground Rules Hearings are an essential part of the pre-trial process in cases involving vulnerable witnesses and should take place in all but the most exceptional of cases.[28] We emphasise pre-trial, because experience has shown that Ground Rules Hearings which occur on the day of trial are perfunctory in nature and less likely to achieve their objectives. Their value in facilitating the participation of the vulnerable is recognised by r.3.9(7) of the Criminal Procedure Rules 2015, which provides that the court must:

    (a) invite representations by the parties and by any intermediary; and

    (b) set ground rules for the conduct of the questioning, which rules may include—

---

[26] *Wills* [2011] EWCA Crim 1938; CPD 3E.4.

[27] [2011] EWCA Crim 3028.

[28] *Lubemba* [2014] EWCA Crim 2064; [2015] 1 Cr. App. R. 12; Sir Brian Leveson, *Review of Efficiency in Criminal Proceedings* (January 2015), para.8.3.1.

    (i) a direction relieving a party of any duty to put that party's case to a witness or a defendant in its entirety,[28a]

    (ii) directions about the manner of questioning,

    (iii) directions about the duration of questioning,

    (iv) if necessary, directions about the questions that may or may not be asked,

    (v) where there is more than one defendant, the allocation among them of the topics about which a witness may be asked, and

    (vi) directions about the use of models, plans, body maps or similar aids to help communicate a question or an answer.

28.33 Ground Rules Hearings provide an invaluable opportunity to identify the scope and length of the cross-examination, following which the judge can manage a timetable fair to all parties. When there is detailed consideration of how cross-examination will be conducted before trial, the parties can, if needs be, adapt their cross-examination accordingly.

28.34 What is required are clearly defined rules tailored for the particular vulnerable witness, but a judge could expect to cover the following topics[29]:

- Proposed questions for cross-examination of the vulnerable witness (questions prepared in advance of the Ground Rules Hearing and provided to the judge).
- Length of time permitted to question a vulnerable witness.
- If limitation is to be put on cross-examination, how the jury will be directed.
- Whether there will be an intermediary at trial and, if so, their role (including whether the advocates have shown the intermediary their proposed questions, where the intermediary (for a defendant) will sit during the trial, use of communication aids).
- In multi-handed cases, how repetitive questioning by more than one advocate will be avoided.
- When the witness will watch the DVD of their ABE interview.
- Trial timetable (including any scheduled breaks).
- How the witness wishes to be addressed and other practical arrangements specific to the witness.

28.35 Criminal Practice Direction ("CPD") 3E.3 refers to the usefulness of a "trial practice note" of the boundaries set at the Ground Rules Hearing. Advocates must expect to provide a list of cross-examination questions to the judge at the Ground Rules Hearing and that these will be shared with the intermediary. The witness must not be informed of the questions in advance,

---

[28a] But such cases are likely to be rare: see paras 28.22 and following, above.

[29] See the ATC checklist, *Ground Rules Hearings*, and toolkit 1, *Ground Rules Hearings and the Fair Treatment of Vulnerable People in Court* on the Advocate's Gateway (dated March 6, 2015); Penny Cooper, Paula Backen and Ruth Marchment, *Getting to grips with ground rules hearings: a checklist for judges, advocates and intermediaries to promote the fair treatment of vulnerable people in court* [2015] Crim. L.R. 420.

and it may be inappropriate to share the questions with the prosecutor and co-defending advocates in the event of a cut-throat defence.

28.36   Ground Rules Hearings have the additional purpose in multi-handed cases of identifying the topics of cross-examination and so enabling the judge to ensure that the witness is treated fairly overall and not asked questions on the same topics, to the same end, by each and every advocate. The judge must ensure that questioning of the witness is controlled such that repetitive cross-examination is stopped.[30] CPD 3E.5 states:

> "If there is more than one defendant, the judge should not permit each advocate to repeat the questioning of a vulnerable witness. In advance of trial, the advocates should divide the topics between them, with the advocate for the first defendant leading the questioning, and the advocate(s) for the other defendant(s) asking only ancillary questions relevant to their client's case, without repeating the questioning that has already taken place on behalf of the other defendant(s)."

28.37   In practical terms, this means that a structured timetable for cross-examination should be agreed at the Ground Rules Hearing. Absent a conflict on the particular topic or a cut-throat defence relevant to the witness being questioned, advocates should assume that they will not be permitted to ask questions on the same topic without leave. In *Jonas*,[31] Hallett LJ made plain that:

> "Advocates must accept that the courts will no longer allow them the freedom to conduct their own cross-examination where it involves simply repeating what others have asked before, or exploring precisely the same territory. For these purposes defence advocates will now be treated as a group and, if necessary issues divided amongst them, provide, of course, there is no unfairness in so doing."

28.38   Limitations on cross-examination, properly applied, will not prevent the defence advocate from eliciting necessary evidence. What will be required is the use of a less confrontational, confusing or complex style of questioning than the "traditional" approach. It is the responsibility of the trial judge to ensure that if restrictions are imposed in order to avoid "over-rigorous or repetitive" cross-examination, the advocate keeps within them.[32] This will ensure the fairness of the trial to all parties by enabling a vulnerable witness to give the best evidence of which they are capable. The judge must ensure that the tenor, tone, language and duration of the questioning is developmentally appropriate to the particular child; prevent questioning that is irrelevant, repetitive, oppressive or intimidating; and be alert to possible difficulties in understanding. See also in this regard the informative training materials and guidance issued by the CBA and the ATC.[33] Advocates who persistently flout ground rules can place the trial judge in a difficult position,

---

[30] [2015] EWCA Crim 562.
[31] [2015] EWCA Crim 562 at [34].
[32] CPD 3E.1.
[33] See the Advocate's Gateway Toolkits and the training video *A Question of Practice*, available at *http://www.theadvocatesgateway.org/* [Accessed April 30, 2016].

as frequent intervention from the Bench disrupts the flow of the evidence and risks confusing witness and jury alike. If those rules are wrong, the Court of Appeal may examine the safety of the conviction.[34]

In this respect an illuminating decision is *Wills*.[35] The appellant and his   28.39
co-defendant, who was separately represented, were both charged with and acquitted of one count of sexual activity with a child. The appellant was convicted of a further 13 serious sexual offences committed against young girls. It therefore appears that the jury could not be sure that the offence alleged against both men occurred. The trial judge imposed strict limitations on how the eight young witnesses could be questioned; in particular counsel were not to challenge the witnesses or put to them their inconsistent statements. Counsel representing the appellant observed the limitations, using short questions, which he did not tag with a comment. By contrast, counsel for the co-defendant paid the judge's directions only passing regard. The judge found it necessary to intervene throughout the cross-examination because counsel for the co-defendant asked long questions and made inappropriate comment in order to prompt an answer. In summing-up, the judge directed the jury that it was necessary to tailor the style of cross-examination of vulnerable witnesses to their age and maturity and that the different styles of the two advocates did not reflect the strengths or weaknesses of either case.

The appellant appealed against conviction, arguing that the fact that his   28.40
counsel observed the limitations set by the judge when cross-examining, whilst counsel for his co-defendant adopted a less constrained and more traditional approach, rendered the trial so unfair that the judge ought to have discharged the jury. The Court of Appeal rejected this argument. Whilst the cross-examination by counsel for the co-defendant failed to comply with the proper limitations imposed by the judge, and to that extent differed from the cross-examination by the appellant's counsel, the Court did not consider that this led to any unfairness in the way in which the trial was conducted from the point of view of the appellant. The form of direction given by the judge properly dealt with any unfairness. However, the Court went on to make the following observations[36]:

> "First, we consider that in cases where it is necessary and appropriate to have limitations on the way in which the advocate conducts cross-examination, there is a duty on the judge to ensure that those limitations are complied with. This is important to ensure that vulnerable witnesses are able to give the best evidence of which they are capable. Where appropriate the judge, in fairness to defendants, should explain the limitations to the jury and the reasons for them. It is also important that defendants do not perceive, whatever the true position, that the cross-examination by their advocate was less effective than that of another advocate in eliciting evidence to defend them on allegations such as those raised in the present case.

[34] *Farooqi* [2013] EWCA Crim 1649.
[35] [2011] EWCA Crim 1938.
[36] At [36]–[39].

This means that the limitations must be clearly defined. One way of achieving this, as suggested in the Advocacy Training Counsel's report,[37] is for a practice note or protocol to be drafted for use by advocates and the trial judge containing the relevant matters set out in paragraph 15 of part 5 of that Report.

Secondly, we observe that if there is some lapse by counsel in failing to comply with the limitations on cross-examination, it is important that the judge gives a relevant direction to the jury when that occurs, both for the benefit of the jury and any other defendant. To leave that direction until the summing up will in many cases mean that it is much less effective than a direction given at the time.

Thirdly, this case highlights that, for vulnerable witnesses, the traditional style of cross-examination where comment is made on inconsistencies during cross-examination must be replaced by a system where those inconsistencies can be drawn to the jury at or about the time when the evidence is being given and not, in long or complex cases, for that comment to have to await the closing speeches at the end of the trial. One solution would be for important inconsistencies to be pointed out, after the vulnerable witness has finished giving evidence, either by the advocate or by the judge, after the necessary discussion with the advocates."

Questioning—Practical Suggestions

28.41   The Toolkits available on the Advocates Gateway are compulsory reading for any advocate who is to question a vulnerable witness. They are an invaluable guide. Fact-finders will only be assisted if witnesses are questioned in a developmentally appropriate way. The question, *"X never touched you with his willy, did he?"* requires seven stages of reasoning to answer. Many young witnesses would struggle to answer it. It is now considered bad practice to ask "tag" questions of young witnesses, such as in this example.

28.42   There are certain points which should be borne in mind by all advocates questioning vulnerable witnesses. Many of these are taken from the very helpful guidance provided in the NSPCC report *Measuring Up? Evaluating implementation of Government commitments to young witnesses in criminal proceedings*[38] and on the Advocate's Gateway:

    a. Use simple, common words and phrases.

    b. Deal with one issue at a time.

    c. Ask one question at a time.

    d. Repeat names and places often.

    e. Be alert to literal interpretation by younger children and those with autistic spectrum disorders; for example a witness who is asked

---

[37] Final Report of the Advocacy Training Council Working Group on Vulnerable Witness Handling, *Raising the Bar: The Handling of Vulnerable Witnesses, Victims and Defendants in Court* (Advocacy Training Council, 2011), accessible at *http://www.advocacytrainingcouncil.org/ images/word/raisingthebar.pdf* [Accessed April 30, 2016].

[38] *Good practice guidance in managing young witness cases and questioning children* (Annex A, pp.9–12) (NSPCC).

"describe the geography of your bedroom" may well respond that they are not very good at geography.

f. Children may have difficulty responding to conceptual questions, such as "how did you feel?" or "why didn't you . . . ".

g. Young witnesses or witnesses with learning difficulties are assisted by questions being asked in a chronological sequence. Children find it more difficult to answer questions about events which are taken out of order.

h. The structure should be sign-posted, so that the witness knows when they are going to be asked about a new topic.

i. Be consistent in the name used for the same individual. For example, if the child knows the ABE interviewing officer by a particular name (e.g. "blonde Susan", use that name throughout as opposed to interchanging with "Susan" or the "lady police officer").

j. Avoid using negatives in questions.

k. Avoid using phrases such as, "I suggest to you that . . . "; "I believe you told us . . . "; "Isn't it a fact that . . . ".

l. Avoid starting questions with "Do you remember . . . ?".

m. Use names rather than pronouns.

n. Adapt questions to child's developmental stage, enabling *this* child's "best evidence".

o. Follow a logical sequence.

p. Ask questions at an appropriate pace.

q. Signpost a change of subject.

r. Do not rapidly change subjects.

s. Allow full opportunity to answer (at least six seconds).

t. Do not ask children to give their address aloud unless for a specific reason.

u. Never assume that the witness (particularly if a teenager) will tell you that they do not understand the question, the court is intimidating and run by adults.[39]

v. Avoid intimidating or distracting body language.

w. Ask a question and do not make a statement which poses as a question simply by intonation.

x. Instead of, "You didn't do it did you?" and "You weren't there were you", aim for the simple and straightforward, "Did you do it?" and "Were you there?"

y. Calling a child witness a liar will often cause the child to become visibly distressed and evoke reluctance in them to answer further questions; in effect they clam-up. It is recognised that often the defence case is that the witness is lying. However, it is rarely

[39] It may also be the case that "robust" adults will not seek clarification of cross-examiner's language: *Farooqi and others* [2013] EWCA Crim 1649; Dr. Emily Henderson *"Did you see the broken headlight?" Questioning the cross-examination of robust adult witnesses*, Archbold Review 2014, 10, 4–6.

necessary for the case to be put in strong terms direct to the witness, rather matters can be left for comment.

Practicalities

28.43 When a witness is giving evidence via live link, the advocate should face the camera. Eye contact is as important over the live link as in face-to-face questioning to reduce the witness's feeling of alienation from the proceedings.

28.44 Rule 3.9(7) of the Criminal Procedure Rules 2015 outlaws requests that a child demonstrate intimate touching on their body, or mimic sexual actions. If it is necessary to ask to the witness to demonstrate how or where they were touched, the witness should be provided with a gender-neutral diagram or doll.

28.45 Finally, advocates should remember that the process of giving evidence in sexual cases can be stressful and distressing for all witnesses. Those with vulnerabilities are often affected even more acutely. Respect, consideration and politeness to the witness should be maintained as well as the appropriate questioning techniques.

CHAPTER 29

ANONYMITY IN SEX CASES AND REPORTING RESTRICTIONS
RELATING TO CHILDREN AND YOUNG PERSONS

Introduction..................................... 29.01
Anonymity of Complainants in Sex
   Cases 29.12
Anonymity and the Defendant........ 29.33
Reporting Restrictions Relating to
   Children and Young Persons........ 29.58
Lifetime Reporting Restrictions
   Relating to Witnesses and
   Victims under 18.........................29.108
Reporting Restrictions Relating to
   Adult Witnesses............................29.123

INTRODUCTION

This chapter covers two separate but related subjects: the law relating to the   **29.01**
anonymity of complainants and defendants in sex cases, and the statutory
provisions enabling a criminal court to restrict publication of the identity of
a child or young person or of an eligible adult witness.

Anonymity of complainants in sex cases

Section 4(1) of the Sexual Offences (Amendment) Act 1976 established a   **29.02**
general rule protecting the anonymity of the complainant of a rape offence.
The rationale for the rule is that, without a guarantee of anonymity, the
victim of a rape offence may not be prepared to report it or to give evidence
against the perpetrator at court. The Sexual Offences (Amendment) Act 1992
later replicated the general rule in relation to complainants of other sex
offences. This resulted in two parallel statutory regimes dealing with the
anonymity of complainants of sex offences. The Youth Justice and Criminal
Evidence Act 1999[1] unified the two regimes with effect from October 7, 2004,
by extending the 1992 Act to cover all sex offences, including rape offences,
and repealing the relevant provisions of the 1976 Act.

---

[1] s.67 and Sch.6, brought into force on October 7, 2004, by the Youth Justice and Criminal
Evidence Act 1999 (Commencement No. 10) (England and Wales) Order 2004 (SI
2004/2428).

29.03   At the same time, the 1992 Act was amended so as to bring it into line with ss.44 and 45 of the 1999 Act, discussed below, which deal with protection of the identity of persons under 18 who are involved in criminal investigations or criminal proceedings. The amendments ensure that the regimes for protecting the identities of complainants of sex offences and of children and young persons are broadly similar.

Anonymity and the defendant

29.04   What of the anonymity of defendants in sex cases? The 1976 Act protected not only the anonymity of the complainant of a rape offence, but also that of the defendant, until the point of conviction. Defendant anonymity was, however, controversial and was abolished in 1988. It also never applied beyond rape cases. The justification for the divergent treatment of complainants and defendants has been the subject of periodic debate since then, including during the passage of the Sexual Offences Act 2003. It came as something of a surprise that the coalition Government, on taking office in 2010, committed itself to re-introducing anonymity for rape defendants, given that this had not been a manifesto commitment of either the Conservatives or the Lib Dems. But the proposal attracted considerable criticism and was quietly shelved. We look below at the arguments for and against defendant anonymity in sex cases, whether pre- or post-charge. We also consider the related subject of police practice and guidance relating to the naming of suspects.

29.05   Finally, we look at two statutory interventions that place restrictions on the reporting of alleged criminal offences in order to protect the identity of the alleged offender. The first is a provision in the Education Act 2002 that restricts the identification of a teacher alleged to have committed an offence against a pupil. This provision is intended to protect teachers from malicious allegations. The second, which is more far-reaching in its impact but is not yet in force, is s.44 of the Youth Justice and Criminal Evidence Act 1999, which, when commenced, will restrict the reporting of offences allegedly committed by under-18s once a criminal investigation has begun and until proceedings are commenced. Both provisions are explained below.

Reporting restrictions relating to children and young persons

29.06   The Youth Justice and Criminal Evidence Act 1999 contains provisions that restrict the identification of persons under 18 concerned in criminal proceedings and enable the restrictions to be extended for the life of the person concerned. In each case, there is a procedure for the restriction to be lifted or varied on application.

29.07   The power of the courts to restrict publication of the identity of a child or young person concerned in legal proceedings was until recently found in s.39 of the Children and Young Persons Act 1933. However, since April 13, 2015, subject to some transitional arrangements explained below, s.39 is restricted to civil and family proceedings and proceedings in respect of civil orders dealing with anti-social behaviour, including Injunctions to Prevent Nuisance and Annoyance and Criminal Behaviour Orders.[2] The role of s.39 in relation to criminal proceedings is now fulfilled by s.45 of the 1999 Act, under which a court may impose reporting restrictions in relation to a child or young person concerned in criminal proceedings who is under the age of 18.[3] The restrictions last, like those under s.39, until the child or young person reaches the age of 18. The power does not apply to proceedings that take place in or on appeal from the Youth Court, where s.49 of the Children and Young Persons Act 1933 (discussed in Ch.31) continues to provide automatic anonymity.

In addition, criminal courts (including the Youth Court) and service courts   **29.08** have a new power under s.45A of the 1999 Act to impose lifetime reporting restrictions in relation to witnesses and victims under the age of 18. The introduction of this power, by the Criminal Justice and Courts Act 2015, brings the law for under-18s into line with that for adult witnesses, as set out in s.46 of the 1999 Act. However, consistently with the law relating to adult defendants, s.45A does not enable a court to impose lifetime restrictions in relation to defendants under 18. The provisions of ss.45 and 45A are considered below.

The background to these changes is that, prior to the Criminal Justice and   **29.09** Courts Act 2015, reporting restrictions applying specifically to under-18s ended automatically when the individual who was the subject of the restriction reached their eighteenth birthday.[4] In *JC and RT v the Central Criminal Court*,[5] Sir Brian Leveson P commented that it was "truly remarkable" that legislation provided for discretionary lifetime reporting restrictions for adult witnesses, but that reporting restrictions for under-18s ended at the age of 18. He went on to say that "victims and witnesses need individual and tailor-made protection within the criminal justice system" and that "it is for Parliament to fashion a solution: the problem requires to be addressed as a matter of real urgency." In response, the Government used the opportunity of the 2015 Act to introduce s.45A, so that witnesses or victims under the age of 18 may be the subject of lifetime reporting restrictions in circumstances similar to those applying to adult witnesses.

We also consider below the circumstances in which the High Court, in the   **29.10** exercise of its inherent jurisdiction, may make an order prohibiting the

---

[2] See the Criminal Justice and Courts Act 2015 s.79; the Criminal Justice and Courts Act 2015 (Commencement Order No.1 and Saving and Transitional Provisions) Order 2015 (SI 2015/778); and the Youth Justice and Criminal Evidence Act 1999 (Commencement No.14) (England and Wales) Order 2015 (SI 2015/818).

[3] For criticism of the differences between the regimes for civil and criminal proceedings, see *Aitken v DPP* [2015] EWHC 1079 (Admin).

[4] *JC and RT v the Central Criminal Court* [2014] EWHC 1041 (Admin) (s.39 of the CYPA 1933); *T v DPP & North East Press* [2003] EWHC 2408 (Admin) (s.49 of the CYPA 1933).

[5] [2014] EWHC 1041, at [12], [37].

publication of information about criminal proceedings in order to protect the rights of a child under art.8 ECHR, in circumstances where s.45 of the 1999 Act cannot be used as the child is not "concerned in" the proceedings.

Reporting restrictions relating to adult witnesses

29.11   The Youth Justice and Criminal Evidence Act 1999 also contains in s.46 provisions enabling criminal courts to restrict the identification of adult witnesses concerned in criminal proceedings. These provisions apply where the quality of the witness's evidence or the level of their co-operation with any party to the proceedings in that party's preparation of their case is likely to be diminished by reason of the witness's fear or distress in connection with being publicly identified as a witness in the proceedings. A reporting direction under s.46 lasts for the lifetime of the witness, unless removed or relaxed by the court or on appeal.

Anonymity of Complainants in Sex Cases

29.12   The Heilbron Committee, reporting in 1975 on the law of rape,[6] recommended the creation of a general rule protecting the anonymity of the complainant in a rape case. The Committee stated:[7]

> "Public knowledge of the indignity which [the complainant] has suffered in being raped may be extremely disturbing and even positively harmful, and the risk of such positive knowledge can operate as a severe deterrent to bring proceedings"

It recommended that, to be fully effective, anonymity should commence from the making of a complaint to the police or, in the case of a private prosecution, when proceedings are formally started by complaint to a magistrate.[8]

29.13   In response, Parliament enacted s.4(1) of the Sexual Offences (Amendment) Act 1976, which created a general rule restricting publication of the identity of a complainant of a "rape offence" together with a strong presumption against lifting the restriction. A "rape offence" was defined to cover rape, attempted rape, aiding, abetting, counselling and procuring rape or attempted rape, and incitement to rape. Parliament subsequently enacted provisions in the Sexual Offences (Amendment) Act 1992 which extended the statutory protection of anonymity to complainants of most other sexual offences. This had the effect of creating two parallel regimes dealing with anonymity in sex cases. To address this, provisions were included in the Youth Justice and Criminal Evidence Act 1999 extending the 1992 Act to all sex offences, including rape, and repealing the 1976 Act. However, these provisions were not immediately brought into force. Before they were, the

---

[6] Report on the Advisory Group on the Law of Rape, Cmnd. 6352 (1975), para.163.
[7] ibid. paras 153–157.
[8] ibid. para.166.

scope of the 1976 and 1992 Acts was significantly amended by the Sexual Offences Act 2003, with effect from May 1, 2004. That Act amended the definition of "a rape offence" in the 1976 Act to cover all the offences of rape and penetration created by the 2003 Act itself. But it also amended the scope of the 1992 Act to cover almost all the sexual offences created by Pt 1 of the 2003 Act, including the offences of rape and penetration.[9] The effect was to create a substantial overlap between the two regimes dealing with anonymity in sex cases. This untidy situation was resolved on October 7, 2004, when the provisions of the Youth Justice and Criminal Evidence Act 1999 were brought into force, extending the 1992 Act to all sex offences (with some exceptions, discussed below) and repealing the 1976 Act. Accordingly, as matters stand, the anonymity of complainants of sex offences, including offences of rape and penetration, is secured by the 1992 Act.

The 1999 Act[10] also brought the provisions of the 1992 Act relating to   **29.14** protection of the identity of complainants of sex offences into line with those on protection of the identity of persons under 18, contained in s.45 of the 1999 Act.[11] The changes included:

- the addition to the 1992 Act of a provision (s.1(3A)) specifying that the restrictions apply in particular to the complainant's name, address, school or educational establishment, place of work and any still or moving picture of them,
- the expansion of the list of offences to which the Act applies (set out in s.2(1)) to include aiding, abetting, counselling or procuring an offence in the list, and
- the provision of a defence to criminal proceedings for breach of the restrictions where the defendant is able to prove that he was not aware, and neither suspected nor had reason to suspect, that the allegation in question had been made.

THE SEXUAL OFFENCES (AMENDMENT) ACT 1992

Section 1 of the 1992 Act provides that once an allegation of a sex offence has   **29.15** been made, and until a person has been accused of the offence, there is a prohibition on the publication of material that is likely to lead to the identification of the complainant, in particular their name, address, place of education or work and any still or moving picture of them. Once someone has been accused of the offence, no material likely to identify the complainant may be published unless the court so directs.

Section 1 of the 1992 Act[12] provides as follows: **29.16**

"(1) Where an allegation has been made that an offence to which this Act applies has been committed against a person, no matter relating to that person shall

---

[9] 2003 Act s.139 and Sch.6, paras 20, 31.
[10] See s.48 and Sch.2.
[11] Discussed in paras 29.64 and following, below.
[12] As amended by the Youth Justice and Criminal Evidence Act 1999 ss.48(d), 67(3), (4) and Schs 2, paras 6–14 and 6.

during that person's lifetime be included in any publication if it is likely to lead members of the public to identify that person as the person against whom the offence is alleged to have been committed.

(2) Where a person is accused of an offence to which this Act applies, no matter likely to lead members of the public to identify a person as the person against whom the offence is alleged to have been committed ('the complainant') shall during the complainant's lifetime be included in any publication.

(3) This section—

    (a) does not apply in relation to a person by virtue of subsection (1) at any time after a person has been accused of the offence, and

    (b) in its application in relation to a person by virtue of subsection (2), has effect subject to any direction given under section 3.

(3A) The matters relating to a person in relation to which the restrictions imposed by subsection (1) or (2) apply (if their inclusion in any publication is likely to have the result mentioned in that subsection) include in particular—

    (a) the person's name,

    (b) the person's address,

    (c) the identity of any school or other educational establishment attended by the person,

    (d) the identity of any place of work, and

    (e) any still or moving picture of the person.

(4) Nothing in this section prohibits the inclusion in a publication of matter consisting only of a report of criminal proceedings other than proceedings at, or intended to lead to, or on an appeal arising out of, a trial at which the accused is charged with the offence."

29.17   The 1992 Act protects the alleged victims of sexual offences. Once a person has been accused of an offence, the alleged victim is referred to for the purposes of the Act as the "complainant". It is important to note that the complainant's identity will be automatically protected even if they have not in fact made any complaint, and even if they deny that the offence was committed (as might be the case e.g. in some cases of alleged familial abuse). The Act does not, however, protect the identity of a witness who supports the prosecution by giving evidence of a similar offence which they say was committed against them.

29.18   In *R. (Press Association) v Cambridge Crown Court*,[13] the Court of Appeal said that s.1:

> "encompasses publication of prohibited material by anyone by whatever means publication occurs, and extends to bloggers and twitterers [*sic*] or any other commentators."

29.19   The inclusion in a publication of matters relating to a complainant will be "likely to lead" to their identification within the meaning of s.1(2) if there is a real risk, real danger or real chance that it may do so.[14]

---

[13] [2012] EWCA Crim 2434.

[14] *O'Riordan v DPP* [2005] EWHC 1240 (Admin), citing Dame Elizabeth Butler Sloss in *Attorney General v Greater Manchester Newspapers Ltd* (2002) 99(6) L.S.G. 30 QBD. See further *R. (on the application of Gazette Media Co Ltd) v Teesside Crown Court* [2005] EWCA Crim 1983; [2006] Crim. L.R. 157, discussed in para.29.92, below.

The list of offences to which the Act applies is set out in s.2(1)[15]:   **29.20**

"This Act applies to the following offences against the law of England and Wales—
(aa) rape;
(ab) burglary with intent to rape;
(a) any offence under any of the provisions of the Sexual Offences Act 1956 mentioned in subsection (2);
(b) any offence under section 128 of the Mental Health Act 1959 (intercourse with mentally handicapped person by hospital staff etc.);
(c) any offence under section 1 of the Indecency with Children Act 1960 (indecent conduct towards young child);
(d) any offence under section 54 of the Criminal Law Act 1977 (incitement by man of his grand-daughter, daughter or sister under the age of 16 to commit incest with him);
(da) any offence under any of the provisions of Part 1 of the Sexual Offences Act 2003 except section 64, 65, 69 or 71;
(db) any offence under section 2 of the Modern Slavery Act 2015 (human trafficking);
(e) any attempt to commit any of the offences mentioned in paragraphs (aa) to (db);
(f) any conspiracy to commit any of those offences;
(g) any incitement of another to commit any of those offences;[16]
(h) aiding, abetting, counselling or procuring the commission of any of the offences mentioned in paragraphs (aa) to (e) and (g)."

For the purposes of s.2(1)(a), s.2(2) specifies the offences under ss.2 to 7, 9 to 12 and 14 to 17 of the 1956 Act.

The 1992 Act does not apply to the offences relating to indecent **29.21** photographs and pseudo-photographs of children contained in the Protection of Children Act 1978 and s.160(1) of the Criminal Justice Act 1988.[17] For the purpose of those offences, a "child" is defined as a person under 18: see para.8.57, above. Where an offence under those provisions is charged, an order under s.45 of the Youth Justice and Criminal Evidence Act 1999 may be necessary to protect the identity of anyone under that age who is concerned in the proceedings.

The anonymity conferred by s.1 lasts for the complainant's lifetime[18] and **29.22** so it ceases when they die. This no doubt reflects the fact that the primary purpose of according anonymity is to spare the victim the indignity and potential harm of being identified as such, and the risk that this could deter them from coming forward. It might be argued that this rationale no longer applies once the victim is deceased. However, it is conceivable that in some

---

[15] As amended by the Criminal Justice and Public Order Act 1994 s.168(1) and Sch.9, para.52(2); the Sexual Offences Act 2003 s.42 and Sch.6, para 31; the Youth Justice and Criminal Evidence Act 1999 ss.48(d), 67(3), (4) and Schs 2, paras 6–14, and 6; and the Modern Slavery Act 2015 s.57(1) and Sch.5, para.4.

[16] The reference to incitement has effect as a reference to the offences under Pt 2 of the Serious Crime Act 2007: the Serious Crime Act 2007, s.63(1) and Sch.6, para.20(a).

[17] *R. (on the application of Gazette Media Co Ltd) v Teesside Crown Court* [2005] EWCA Crim 1983; [2006] Crim. L.R. 157.

[18] Unless lifted earlier by the court: see para.29.25, below.

circumstances knowledge that they would forfeit their anonymity on death could deter victims from coming forward, most obviously if they have reason to believe that they may not have long to live. The naming of a deceased victim may also be distressing for their family. This was the position in the case of Delroy Grant, the "Night Stalker", who was tried and convicted at Woolwich Crown Court in 2011 for a series of rapes and indecent assaults committed against elderly victims, a significant number of whom had died by the time of the trial. There was serious concern that the families of these victims would suffer considerable distress as a result of them being named. Whilst the anonymity conferred by s.1 had ceased by reason of the victims' deaths, the trial judge (His Honour Judge Rook QC) allowed the victims to be anonymised during the trial as their statements were not in dispute. The issue in the case was identity, not the fact that there had been a series of rapes and indecent assaults. In many cases, however, this practical solution will not be available. The answer to these points must be to make anonymity permanent. This would be a modest adjustment to the law that would not cause significant additional prejudice to the public interest in open justice, and we urge Parliament to make it when the opportunity next arises.

29.23   Section 1 confers a right to anonymity on the complainant of a sex offence, but does not empower a court to make an order enforcing that right. In *R. (Press Association) v Cambridge Crown Court*,[19] the trial judge purported to make an order under s.1(2) imposing an indefinite prohibition on the publication of "anything relating to the name of the defendant which could lead to the identification of the complainant". On appeal by the Press Association, the Court of Appeal held that the Act gives the courts no power to make an order restricting publication of the defendant's name in order to protect or enforce a complainant's right to anonymity. Indeed, there is no need for any such power since a contravention of the complainant's right to anonymity involves the commission of a criminal offence. The Court noted that the absence of a judicial power to restrict publication provides a clear demarcation of responsibility, in that decisions about what should or should not be published in the media are left to editors and reporters. In the present case, it was for the press to decide how to report the proceedings so as to ensure the anonymity of the complainant: it was not for the court to instruct them how to do so by making an order which in effect imposed a blanket prohibition against publication of the defendant's name.

29.24   The Court in the *Cambridge* case went on, however, to dismiss the Press Association's submission that for the judge to give any guidance to the press risked usurpation of the editor's discretion about what and how to publish:

> "The judge is entitled to express concerns as to the possible consequences of publication, and indeed to engage in a discussion with representatives of the press present in court about these issues, whether on his own initiative, or in a response to a request from them. The judge is in charge of the court, and if he

[19] [2012] EWCA Crim 2434.

thinks it appropriate to offer comment, we anticipate that a responsible editor would carefully consider it before deciding what should be published. The essential point is that whatever discussions may take place, the judicial observations cannot constitute an order binding on the editor or the reporter."

In practice, it is often helpful for a judge to indicate whether in his or her view a category or piece of evidence would be likely to lead to identification. The media often seek such guidance and the judge may, for example, be able to identify evidence which could lead to "jigsaw identification".[20] If judicial guidance is given, it will then be a matter for the editor or reporter whether to follow it. A reporter will need to exercise particular care if communicating from court by social media, e.g. on Twitter.[21] It is good practice for the court clerk to have a list of the reporters present in court so that action can be taken swiftly if there is a problem.

The protection of s.1 is not absolute, as s.3 of the Act contains a power for **29.25** the court to disapply the section by a direction given either before or at trial. Before the trial commences, a person charged with a sex offence may apply to a judge of the Crown Court for a direction that s.1 shall not apply in relation to the complainant.[22] Such a direction must be given if the applicant satisfies the judge that it is required for the purpose of inducing witnesses to come forward and that the conduct of the applicant's defence at trial is otherwise likely to be substantially prejudiced. In addition, if, at the trial, the judge is satisfied that the effect of s.1 is to impose a substantial and unreasonable restriction upon the reporting of proceedings, and that it is in the public interest to remove or relax the restriction, he must direct that s.1 shall not apply to such matter as is specified in the direction.[23] Such a direction cannot be given by reason only of the outcome of the trial. A direction that s.1 shall not apply may be sought from an appellate court where a person has been convicted of an offence and has given notice of appeal against conviction, or notice of an application for leave so to appeal. The appellate court must give the requested direction if it is satisfied both that the direction is required for the purpose of obtaining evidence in support of the appeal, and that the applicant is likely to suffer substantial injustice if the direction is not given.[24]

In *R. (Press Association) v Cambridge Crown Court*,[25] the Court of Appeal **29.26** rejected the submission that what is now r.6.1 of the Criminal Procedure Rules 2015 confers a general power to vary the protection conferred by s.1 of the 1992 Act. The submission turned on the language of r.6.1, which states

---

[20] For a discussion of "jigsaw identification" see Professor Jenny Temkin, *Rape and the Legal Process*, 2nd edn, (Oxford: OUP, 2002), p.88; and see para.29.91, below.

[21] In accordance with CPD I General matters 6C: Use of live text-based forms of communication (including Twitter) from court for the purposes of fair and accurate reporting.

[22] 1992 Act s.3(1).

[23] 1992 Act s.3(2). By s.3(7) of the Act, if a new trial is ordered for a sex offence (for instance after a jury disagree on a verdict), the commencement of any previous trial is to be disregarded for the purposes of s.3(1).

[24] 1992 Act s.3(4).

[25] [2012] EWCA Crim 2434.

that Part 6 of the Rules, dealing with reporting restrictions, applies "where the court can . . . vary or remove a reporting . . . restriction that is imposed by legislation". The Court of Appeal held that this provision cannot be read as providing the court with a power not conferred on it by primary legislation.

29.27   Section 5 of the 1992 Act makes it a summary offence punishable by a fine to publish in breach of s.1. The maximum penalty was until recently a fine not exceeding level 5 on the standard scale (i.e. £5,000). The effect of s.85 of the Legal Aid, Sentencing and Punishment of Offenders Act 2012 is that, from March 12, 2015, the maximum is a fine of any amount. Fines will, however, continue to be set according to the seriousness of the offence and the means of the offender. In *R. (Press Association) v Cambridge Crown Court*,[26] the Court of Appeal noted that the offence attracts only a financial penalty and commented:

> "Whether this is always a sufficient punishment for those who deliberately breach the anonymity of the victim of sexual crime appears to us to require urgent reconsideration."

There is indeed a case for particularly egregious breaches of s.1 to be punishable by imprisonment, especially in the internet age when publication to a mass audience is so easy to achieve. The authors hope that an early opportunity will be found for Parliament to amend the law to make this possible.

29.28   Proceedings may not be instituted under s.5 except by or with the consent of the Attorney General.[27] A defence is available if the defendant can establish on a balance of probabilities that at the time of the alleged offence he was not aware, and neither suspected nor had reason to suspect, that the publication was of or included the matter in question.[28] It is also a defence to establish on a balance of probabilities that the complainant gave written consent to the appearance of the matter in issue.[29] Written consent does not provide a defence if it is proved that any person interfered unreasonably with the complainant's peace or comfort with intent to obtain it.[30] Where the s.5 offence has been committed by a company and it is proved that it was committed with the consent or connivance of, or to be attributable to, any neglect on the part of any director, manager, secretary or other similar officer of the company, or any person purporting to act in such a capacity, that person as well as the company is guilty of the offence.[31] The offence under s.5, though one of strict liability, does not offend against art.10 ECHR.[32]

---

[26] ibid.
[27] 1992 Act s.5(4).
[28] 1992 Act s.5(5).
[29] 1992 Act s.5(2).
[30] 1992 Act s.5(3).
[31] 1992 Act s.5(6). Section 5(7) provides: "In relation to a body corporate whose affairs are managed by its members 'director', in subsection (6), means a member of the body corporate." For offences by companies, see *Chargot (t/a Contract Services)* [2008] UKHL 73, discussed at para.8.43, above.
[32] *O'Riordan v DPP* [2005] EWHC 1240 (Admin).

SECTION 4(2) OF THE CONTEMPT OF COURT ACT 1981

An order may be made under s.4(2) of the Contempt of Court Act 1981 **29.29**
postponing (rather than prohibiting altogether) the publication of a defendant's identity where this is necessary to avoid prejudice to his trial or to
other pending proceedings. It is important to note that an order cannot be
made under s.4(2) simply for the purpose of protecting the identity of a
complainant of a sex offence.

Section 4(2) provides that: **29.30**

> "In any [legal proceedings held in public] the court may, where it appears
> necessary for avoiding a substantial risk of prejudice to the administration of
> justice in those proceedings, or in any other proceedings pending or imminent,
> order that the publication of any report of the proceedings, or any part of the
> proceedings, be postponed for such period as the court thinks necessary for that
> purpose."

The provision was misused in a purported attempt to protect a complainant's
identity in *R. (Press Association) v Cambridge Crown Court*.[33] In that case,
after prosecuting counsel expressed concern at the sentencing hearing that
reporting of the defendant's name would compromise the complainant's
anonymity, the trial judge initially purported to make an order under s.4(2)
imposing an indefinite prohibition on the publication of "anything relating to
the name of the defendant which could lead to the identification of the
complainant". Shortly afterwards, he was persuaded by a representative of
the local press that s.4(2) did not apply and he purported instead to make an
order in similar terms under s.1(2) of the Sexual Offences (Amendment) Act
1992, as to which see para.29.16, above. On appeal by the Press Association
against both orders, the Court of Appeal held that orders under s.4(2) are
intended to avoid "a substantial risk of prejudice" to the proceedings in
which they are made, or to linked or related proceedings, such as a
subsequent trial involving the same defendants or witnesses. It said that
examples of the use of the power in s.4(2) can be found in prohibitions
against the publication of evidence or argument before the judge in the
absence of the jury and, after a successful appeal against conviction, when a
new trial is ordered so as to avoid prejudice to any retrial. In the *Cambridge*
case, at the time the order was made, the defendant had been tried, convicted
and sentenced in public, with no order restricting publication of his identity,
and there were no pending proceedings which might be prejudiced by the
publication of his name. The pre-conditions for making an order under s.4(2)
therefore did not exist. Further, as its wording suggests, s.4(2) is aimed at
postponing publication rather than banning it altogether. An order prohibiting publication for an indefinite period carries with it the natural inference
that publication has not simply been postponed, but permanently banned.

---

[33] [2012] EWCA Crim 2434.

Accordingly, as the judge had swiftly recognised, s.4(2) provided no basis for making the initial order.

SECTION 11 OF THE CONTEMPT OF COURT ACT 1981

29.31 Finally, it is important to note the limited effect in this context of s.11 of the Contempt of Court Act 1981, which provides:

> "In any case where a court (having the power to do so) allows a name or other matter to be withheld from the public in proceedings before the court, the court may give such directions prohibiting the publication of that name or matter in connection with the proceedings as appear to the court to be necessary for the purpose for which it was so withheld."

As will be immediately apparent, the section does not itself confer any power upon courts to allow "a name or other matter to be withheld from the public in proceedings before the court", but applies in circumstances where such a power has been exercised.[34] The purpose of s.11 is to support the exercise of that power by enabling the court to give ancillary directions prohibiting the publication, in connection with the proceedings, of the name or matter which has been withheld from the public in the proceedings themselves. The directions which the court is permitted to give are such as appear to the court to be necessary for the purpose for which the name or matter was withheld.

29.32 Thus in *R. (Press Association) v Cambridge Crown Court*,[35] discussed above, the Court of Appeal said that s.11 plainly could not have provided the foundation for the trial judge's order purportedly imposing an indefinite prohibition on the publication of "anything relating to the name of the defendant which could lead to the identification of the complainant". This is because s.11 does not arise for consideration unless the court, having the power to do so, withholds the name or other matter from the public in the proceedings before it. It followed that an order such as that made by the trial judge in that case could only be made on the basis of s.11 if the name of the defendant had already been properly withheld by order of the court, e.g. an order under s.4(2) of the 1981 Act, discussed above.

ANONYMITY AND THE DEFENDANT

29.33 Unlike complainants, defendants do not currently enjoy the benefit of statutory anonymity in sex cases. As matters stand, therefore, defendants accused of rape or any other sex offence may be named unless naming them would be unlawful for some other reason; for example, the name of the defendant may not be made known if it would be likely to reveal the identity

---

[34] *A v British Broadcasting Corporation* [2014] UKSC 25, at [59].
[35] [2012] EWCA Crim 2434, citing *R. v Arundel Justices Ex p. Westminster Press Limited* [1985] 1 W.L.R. 708 and *Re Trinity Mirror Plc* [2008] Q.B. 770.

of the complainant and thereby contravene s.1(1) of the 1992 Act (as it would e.g. in a case of alleged marital rape), or if it would infringe a reporting restriction imposed under s.45 of the Youth Justice and Criminal Evidence Act 1999, discussed below. In *R. (Press Association) v Cambridge Crown Court*,[36] the Court of Appeal suggested that there are two limited circumstances in which the Crown Court has power to order at the outset of proceedings that the defendant should not be named: where this is required in order to counter a significant threat to the interests of justice, and where the court is satisfied that there is a real and immediate risk to the life or safety of the defendant or his family. It will be very rare for either of these circumstances to apply in the context of a sex case. It is clear from the judgment that the power to accord anonymity can never be exercised simply in order to protect the defendant from the indignity and humiliation of being named.

The subject of defendant anonymity in sex cases has a long and somewhat   29.34
tortured history. Although the Heilbron Committee did not recommend introducing it,[37] s.6(1) of the Sexual Offences (Amendment) Act 1976 nonetheless gave defendants in rape cases an entitlement to anonymity from the time they were accused up to the moment of conviction.[38] This protection from publicity was, however, short-lived. In certain cases the prohibition on the identification of alleged rapists was said to be hampering police investigations because they could not publish details or pictures of suspects. It was accordingly abolished after a little over a decade by the Criminal Justice Act 1988.[39]

Defendant anonymity has, however, remained the subject of debate. The   29.35
Home Affairs Select Committee, when investigating cases of historic abuse in children's homes, became convinced of the "potentially ruinous impact of publicity on those accused of past sexual abuse on children"[40] and accordingly suggested that anonymity should be extended to the defendant in those cases. In the 2002 White Paper *Protecting the Public*, the Government stated that it was not minded to change the existing arrangements as "the criminal justice system operates on the principle of openness, which is a vital ingredient in maintaining public confidence, and in encouraging witnesses to come forward."[41] However, it was "still prepared to listen to arguments of those who feel strongly on the matter".[42]

---

[36] [2012] EWCA Crim 2434, at [18].

[37] *Report of the Advisory Group on the Law of Rape*, Cmnd. 6352 (1975), paras 175–8.

[38] The restriction was introduced as a concessionary Government amendment after the Standing Committee voted by a large majority to extend anonymity to both complainants and defendants.

[39] s.158(5).

[40] Fourth Report of Session 2001–2002, *The Conduct of Investigations into Past Cases of Sexual Abuse in Children's Homes*, HC 836–1, paras 98–99.

[41] *Protecting the Public*, HMSO, November 2002 (cm 5668), p.19.

[42] *Protecting the Public*, HMSO, November 2002 (cm 5668), p.20. See also Home Affairs Select Committee, Criminal Justice Bill, Second Report of Session 2002–2003, HC83 Q 440 (Lord Falconer of Thoroton, Minister of State, Home Office).

29.36   During the passage of the Bill that became the Sexual Offences Act 2003, there was sustained support from some quarters for extending anonymity to defendants in sex cases.[43] It was argued that there should be equality in the law as between defendants and complainants, and that acquitted defendants need protection from the social stigma of the allegation, which often remain for life, notwithstanding an acquittal.[44] Further, it was envisaged that equality as between defendants and complainants would not mean absolute protection for the former, as the courts could be empowered to lift the restriction in appropriate circumstances.[45]

29.37   Opponents of such an exension argued that the general principle of open justice meant that anonymity should be the exception rather than the rule and that, in contrast to the position of complainants, there is no strong public policy reason for granting anonymity to defendants in sex cases.[46] Moreover, there was said to be no justification for treating defendants in sex cases any differently from those in other cases, where the allegation may also leave a stigma. On a practical level, it was suggested that anonymity for defendants would inhibit police investigations, in that other victims might come forward if a defendant's identity is publicised.

29.38   The matter was put to a vote in the House of Lords[47] and an amendment was passed to the Bill inserting in it a new clause 2, providing:

> "The defendant in rape etc. cases shall enjoy the same right to anonymity as is enjoyed by the complainant."

29.39   The Home Affairs Select Committee, in its report on the Sexual Offences Bill published after the insertion of clause 2, supported the case for defendant anonymity. The Committee concluded that the stigma attaching to sex offences, particularly those involving children, is enormous, and the accusation alone can be devastating. If the individual is never charged, there is no possibility of them being publicly vindicated by acquittal.[48] The Committee concluded that there should be anonymity for the defendant "for a limited period between allegation and charge", on the ground that "this strikes an appropriate balance between the need to protect potentially innocent suspects from damaging publicity and the wider public interest in retaining free and full reporting of criminal proceedings".[49]

---

[43] The Metropolitan Police supported a limited anonymity provision in cases involving children, pointing to research showing that between 5 per cent and 7 per cent of those arrested for child abuse related offences commit suicide.

[44] cf. House of Commons Home Affairs Select Committee, Sexual Offences Bill, Fifth Report of Session 2002–2003, HC 639, para.69.

[45] cf. para.29.25, above.

[46] House of Commons Home Affairs Select Committee, Sexual Offences Bill, Fifth Report of Session 2002–2003, HC 639, para.72ff.

[47] Hansard, HL, vol.648, cols 1084–1097 (June 2, 2003).

[48] House of Commons Home Affairs Select Committee, Sexual Offences Bill, Fifth Report of Session 2002–2003, HC 639, para.76.

[49] ibid., para.80. Current guidance and practice as regards pre-charge anonymity is discussed below.

However, the then Government opposed clause 2 and it was removed in **29.40**
the Commons.[50] As a result, there is no provision in the 2003 Act for the
anonymity of a defendant at any stage of proceedings for a sexual offence, or
before charge.

Although the re-introduction of defendant anonymity in rape cases had **29.41**
been Lib Dem policy since 2006, the issue did not feature in any of the
manifestos published before the 2010 General Election. It was therefore a
surprise when the coalition Government published in the Coalition Agreement a commitment to extend anonymity to rape defendants. This commitment came under sustained criticism, which led the Prime Minister to clarify
the position in June 2010 by stating that he supported the conclusion of the
Home Affairs Select Committee in 2003 that there should be a "limited
extension" of the law to cover the period between arrest and charge.[51] This
did little to damp things down, and in a Commons debate on the issue in July
2010, the Justice Minister, Crispin Blunt MP, said that the Government had
asked the Director of Analytical Services at the Ministry of Justice to
produce "an independent assessment of the current research and statistics on
defendant anonymity in rape cases".[52] The resulting report, published in
November 2010,[53] drew on official statistics and findings from primary
research studies conducted in the UK and, in some cases, North America, as
well as other evidence reviews. The headline conclusion was that there was
insufficient reliable empirical evidence on which to base an informed decision
as to the value of anonymity for rape defendants. Announcing the report's
publication, Mr Blunt said:

> "Evidence is lacking in a number of key areas, in particular, whether the inability
> to publicise a person's identity will prevent further witnesses to a known offence
> from coming forward, or further unknown offences by the same person from
> coming to light. The coalition Government made it clear from the outset that
> they would proceed with defendant anonymity in rape cases only if the evidence
> justifying it was clear and sound, and in the absence of any such finding they
> have reached the conclusion that the proposal does not stand on its merits. It will
> not, therefore, be proceeded with further."[54]

Opponents of defendant anonymity tend now to draw support from the **29.42**
infamous cases investigated under Operation Yewtree and related police
investigations,[55] in which celebrities such as the broadcasters Jimmy Savile,

[50] *Hansard* HC, vol.412, col.562ff (November 3, 2003).
[51] cf. *http://www.bbc.co.uk/news/10219053* and *www.bbc.co.uk/news/uk-politics-10760239*
[Accessed April 30, 2016].
[52] *Hansard* HC July 8, 2010, c.559.
[53] *Providing anonymity to those accused of rape: an assessment of evidence*, Ministry of Justice
Research Series 20/10, available at *http://www.justice.gov.uk/downloads/publications/research-and-
analysis/moj-research/anonymity-rape-research-report.pdf* [Accessed April 30, 2016]. For a discussion of the report, see Philip N.S. Rumsey and Rachel Anne Fenton, *Rape, defendant anonymity
and evidence-based policy making*, M.L.R. 2013, 76(1), 109-133.
[54] *Hansard* HC Deb November 12, 2010, cols.27-28WS.
[55] For the background to these investigations, see *https://en.wikipedia.org/wiki/Operation_
Yewtree* [Accessed April 30, 2016].

Stuart Hall and Rolf Harris abused their positions over many years to commit sexual offences against vulnerable women and girls, but a significant number of their victims came forward only after publicity was given to other allegations.[56] Against this, the proponents of anonymity refer to the significant number of cases in which celebrities and other public figures have been acquitted of alleged sexual offences and have gone on to complain of the injustice done to them by the trashing of their reputations.[57] As a result of cases such as these, defendant anonymity in sex cases still has powerful proponents. Thus in 2013, Maura McGowan QC, then Chairman of the Bar Council, said in a radio interview that defendants should have the same anonymity as complainants as charges of sexual offences carry "such a stigma".[58] Her comments provoked strong rebuttals,[59] demonstrating that the subject remains contentious.

29.43   Most recently, in March 2015, the Home Affairs Select Committee repeated the call it made in 2003 for a pre-charge right of anonymity for persons accused of sexual offences, unless there are "public safety" reasons for naming them.[60] The Committee's stance was underpinned by two considerations: the reputational damage caused by high profile arrests when the individual is not then prosecuted or is acquitted; and the advent of social media, which facilitates the public discussion of these matters in a way that is unprecedented and has the potential to amplify the reputational damage done by naming a suspect. The Committee cited in support of its recommendation evidence given to it by the Commissioner of the Metropolitan Police, Sir Bernard Hogan-Howe.[61] Its Report was published shortly before

[56] See e.g. *http://liberalconspiracy.org/2013/05/10/the-stuart-hall-case-ends-the-debate-on-anonymity-for-rape-defendants/* and *http://www.telegraph.co.uk/women/womens-politics/10765589/Nigel-Evans-is-categorically-wrong-about-rape-defendants-needing-anonymity.html* [Accessed April 30, 2016].

[57] See e.g. *http://metro.co.uk/2013/09/17/michael-le-vell-cleared-of-rape-do-defendants-deserve-anonymity-too-4027181/* and *http://www.theopinionsite.org/reintroduce-anonymity-for-defendants-sex-cases/* [Accessed April 30, 2016].

[58] *http://www.bbc.co.uk/news/uk-21487266* [Accessed April 30, 2016]. See also *http://www.guardian.co.uk/media/2013/apr/21/press-intrusion-name-suspects* [Accessed April 30, 2016], quoting to similar effect the Conservative MP Robert Buckland (now Solicitor General) and Frances Crook, Chief Executive of the Howard League for Penal Reform.

[59] See e.g. *http://www.politics.co.uk/comment-analysis/2013/02/19/comment-anonymity-for-rape-defendants-is-a-tired-argument-th* (by Holly Dustin, Director of the End Violence Against Women Coalition) and *https://www.facebook.com/Vera.Baird.QC/posts/537442576290368* (by Vera Baird QC, Police and Crime Commissioner for Northumbria [Accessed April 30, 2016].

[60] *Police Bail*, Seventeenth Report of the Home Affairs Select Committee, March 20, 2015, available at *http://www.publications.parliament.uk/pa/cm201415/cmselect/cmhaff/962/96204.htm* [Accessed April 30, 2016]. The Committee also called for a 28-day limit on police bail, subject to review by a senior officer. The Government subsequently committed itself to this course: See *https://www.gov.uk/government/news/home-secretary-announces-time-limits-for-police-bail* [Accessed April 30, 2016].

[61] Sir Bernard subsequently repeated his position in an appearance before the Committee in October 2015: see *http://www.independent.co.uk/news/uk/crime/scotland-yard-chief-calls-for-ban-on-publicly-naming-suspects-in-any-police-inquiry-a6697511.html* [Accessed April 30, 2016].

the 2015 General Election that saw the return of a majority Conservative administration, which has yet to set out its position on the subject.[62]

Two Legislative Interventions

Although there is no consensus on the merits of defendant anonymity for those accused of sexual offences, Parliament has twice legislated to grant pre-charge anonymity to two categories of individual: teachers and those under the age of 18. The provisions relating to under-18s, however, are not yet in force.   29.44

Restrictions on reporting allegations against teachers

Section 141F of the Education Act 2002[63] contains an automatic reporting restriction which prevents the identification of any teacher who is alleged by a pupil at the same school, or by someone on the pupil's behalf, to have committed a criminal offence against the pupil. The provision, which applies in England and Wales, fulfils a White Paper commitment made by the coalition Government after taking office in 2010 to protect teachers from malicious allegations, as part of an effort to improve behaviour in schools.[64] The provision applies to allegations against any teacher who works at a school, including supply and peripatetic teachers. The effect of the restriction is that no matter relating to the teacher is to be included in any publication if it is likely to lead members of the public to identify the teacher as the subject of the allegation. A "publication" for this purpose is defined to include any communication which is addressed to the public at large or any section of the public, and so includes communications via the internet. The definition of publication does not include documents prepared in connection with legal proceedings or documents published by a professional regulatory body in the course of disciplinary proceedings against the individual.   29.45

The restriction imposed by s.141F may be varied or lifted by a magistrates' court on the application of any person, if the court is satisfied that it is in the interests of justice to do so having regard to the welfare of the teacher and of the victim of the offence. Provision is made for appeals to the Crown Court. Otherwise, the restriction remains in place unless or until the Secretary of State or the General Teaching Council for Wales publishes information about an investigation or decision in a disciplinary case arising from the allegation, or proceedings for the offence are instituted. The restriction also   29.46

---

[62] See further on this topic Clare McGlynn, *Rape, Defendant Anonymity and Human Rights: Adopting a "Wider Perspective"* [2011] Crim. L.R. 199, and David Wolchover and Anthony Heaton-Armstrong, *Rape Defendant Anonymity*, 176 C.L. & J. 5 and 24.

[63] Inserted by the Education Act 2011 s.13(1).

[64] *The Importance of Teaching: The Schools White Paper 2010* (Cm.7980, DfE, Nov 2010), para.3.14. The White Paper is available at *https://www.gov.uk/government/uploads/system/uploads/attachment_data/file/175429/CM-7980.pdf* [Accessed April 30, 2016].

ceases to apply if the teacher publishes their side of the story or gives written consent for someone else to do so. Under s.141G of the 2002 Act, publication in breach of such a restriction is a summary offence. The maximum penalty was until recently a fine not exceeding level 5 of the standard scale (i.e. £5,000). The effect of s.85 of the Legal Aid, Sentencing and Punishment of Offenders Act 2012 is that, from March 12, 2015, the maximum is a fine of any amount. Fines will, however, continue to be set according to the seriousness of the offence and the means of the offender. It is a defence for a person to prove that, at the time of the alleged offence, they were not aware, and neither suspected nor had reason to suspect, that the publication included the matter in question, or that they were not aware, and neither suspected nor had reason to suspect, that the allegation had been made.

Restrictions on reporting alleged offences by persons under 18

29.47   Section 44 of the Youth Justice and Criminal Evidence Act 1999, which is not yet in force, provides that where a criminal investigation has begun into an alleged offence against the law of England and Wales or Northern Ireland, no information shall be published relating to the alleged offender if he is aged under 18 and the information is likely to lead members of the public to identify him.[65] Unless made lifelong under s.45A of the Act, the restrictions apply until the individual reaches the age of 18 or until the institution of criminal proceedings, when s.45, discussed below, comes into play.[66] The section also empowers the Secretary of State by order to impose restrictions on the publication of information likely to lead to the identification of persons under 18 who are alleged to have been the victims of, or witnesses to, a criminal offence.[67] These restrictions can only be commenced through the draft affirmative resolution procedure, i.e. both Houses of Parliament must agree that they should be brought into force.[68] The matters to which the restrictions imposed by s.44 apply include in particular the person's name, his address, the identity of any school or other educational establishment attended by him, the identity of any place of work, and any still or moving picture of him.[69] But reporting of any information, even the items listed in the section, is not restricted if it is not likely to lead to the person's identification. A court with jurisdiction in or in relation to any criminal proceedings may make an order lifting the restrictions, to an extent specified in the order, if satisfied that it is necessary in the interests of justice to do so.[70] In deciding whether to make such an order, the court must have regard to the welfare of the person concerned.[71] There is a right of appeal to the Crown

[65] 1999 Act s.44(1), (2).
[66] 1999 Act s.44(3).
[67] 1999 Act s.44(4), (5).
[68] 1999 Act s.64(3).
[69] 1999 Act s.44(6).
[70] 1999 Act s.44(7), (9).
[71] 1999 Act s.44(8).

Court against a decision of a magistrates' court making or refusing to make such an order.[72]

Section 44[73] provides:

"**44.**—(1) This section applies (subject to subsection (3)) where a criminal investigation has begun in respect of—

(a) an alleged offence against the law of—

(i) England and Wales, or

(ii) Northern Ireland; or

(b) an alleged civil offence (other than an offence falling within paragraph (a)) committed (whether or not in the United Kingdom) by a person subject to service law.

(2) No matter relating to any person involved in the offence shall while he is under the age of 18 be included in any publication if it is likely to lead members of the public to identify him as a person involved in the offence.

(3) The restrictions imposed by subsection (2) cease to apply once there are proceedings in a court (whether a court in England and Wales, a service court or a court in Northern Ireland) in respect of the offence.

(4) For the purposes of subsection (2) any reference to a person involved in the offence is to—

(a) a person by whom the offence is alleged to have been committed; or

(b) if this paragraph applies to the publication in question by virtue of subsection (5)—

(i) a person against or in respect of whom the offence is alleged to have been committed, or

(ii) a person who is alleged to have been a witness to the commission of the offence;

except that paragraph (b)(i) does not include a person in relation to whom section 1 of the Sexual Offences (Amendment) Act 1992 (anonymity of victims of certain sexual offences) applies in connection with the offence.

(5) Subsection (4)(b) applies to a publication if—

(a) where it is a relevant programme, it is transmitted, or

(b) in the case of any other publication, it is published,

on or after such date as may be specified in an order made by the Secretary of State.

(5A) In the application of this section to Northern Ireland, the reference in subsection (5) to the Secretary of State shall be construed as a reference to the Department of Justice in Northern Ireland.

(6) The matters relating to a person in relation to which the restrictions imposed by subsection (2) apply (if their inclusion in any publication is likely to have the result mentioned in that subsection) include in particular—

(a) his name,

(b) his address,

(c) the identity of any school or other educational establishment attended by him,

(d) the identity of any place of work, and

(e) any still or moving picture of him.

(7) Any appropriate criminal court may by order dispense, to any extent specified in the order, with the restrictions imposed by subsection (2) in relation

---

[72] 1999 Act s.44(11), (12).

[73] As amended by the Courts Act 2003 s.109(1) and Sch.8, para.386; SI 2003/1247, Sch.1, para.23; the Armed Forces Act 2006 s.378 and Sch.16, para.158; and SI 2010/976, Sch.14, para.43.

to a person if it is satisfied that it is necessary in the interests of justice to do so.

(8) However, when deciding whether to make such an order dispensing (to any extent) with the restrictions imposed by subsection (2) in relation to a person, the court shall have regard to the welfare of that person.

(9) In subsection (7) 'appropriate criminal court' means—
(a) in a case where this section applies by virtue of subsection (1)(a)(i) or (ii), any court in England and Wales or (as the case may be) in Northern Ireland which has any jurisdiction in, or in relation to, any criminal proceedings (but not a service court unless the offence is alleged to have been committed by a person subject to service law);
(b) in a case where this section applies by virtue of subsection (1)(b), any court falling within paragraph (a) or a service court.

(10) The power under subsection (7) of a magistrates' court in England and Wales may be exercised by a single justice.

(11) In the case of a decision of a magistrates' court in England and Wales, or a court of summary jurisdiction in Northern Ireland, to make or refuse to make an order under subsection (7), the following persons, namely—
(a) any person who was a party to the proceedings on the application for the order, and
(b) with the leave of the Crown Court, or in Northern Ireland a county court, any other person,
may, in accordance with Criminal Procedure Rules in England and Wales, or rules of court in Northern Ireland, appeal to the Crown Court, or in Northern Ireland a county court, against that decision or appear or be represented at the hearing of such an appeal.

(12) On such an appeal the Crown Court or in Northern Ireland a county court—
(a) may make such order as is necessary to give effect to its determination of the appeal; and
(b) may also make such incidental or consequential orders as appear to it to be just.

(13) In this section—
(a) 'civil offence' means an act or omission which, if committed in England and Wales, would be an offence against the law of England and Wales;
(b) any reference to a criminal investigation, in relation to an alleged offence, is to an investigation conducted by police officers, or other persons charged with the duty of investigating offences, with a view to it being ascertained whether a person should be charged with the offence;
(c) any reference to a person subject to service law is to—
(i) a person subject to service law within the meaning of the Armed Forces Act 2006, or
(ii) a civilian subject to service discipline within the meaning of that Act."

29.49   In s.44(1)(b) and (9), the references to "a person subject to service law" include a person who, at the time of the alleged offence, was subject to military law or air-force law or to the Naval Discipline Act 1957, or was a civilian subject to the Army Act 1955, the Air Force Act 1955 or the Naval Discipline Act 1957.[74]

---

[74] Armed Forces Act 2006 (Transitional Provisions etc.) Order 2009 (SI 2009/1059), art.205 and Sch.1, para.44(1).

It is a summary offence under s.49 of the 1999 Act to publish in   **29.50**
contravention of the restrictions imposed by s.44. The maximum penalty was
until recently a fine not exceeding level 5 on the standard scale (i.e. £5,000).[75]
The effect of s.85 of the Legal Aid, Sentencing and Punishment of Offenders
Act 2012 is that, from March 12, 2015, the maximum is a fine of any amount.
Fines will, however, continue to be set according to the seriousness of the
offence and the means of the offender.

The s.49 offence may be committed in Scotland as well as in England,   **29.51**
Wales and Northern Ireland.[76] Where the publication is in a newspaper or
periodical, the offence is committed by the proprietor, the editor and the
publisher. Where it is in a programme included in a programme service
within the meaning of the Broadcasting Act 1990, e.g. on TV or the radio, it
is committed by the body corporate or Scottish partnership providing the
service and by any person having functions in relation to the programme
corresponding to those of a newspaper editor. In the case of any other
publication, the offence is committed by the person publishing it. Where a
s.49 offence committed by a body corporate is proved to have been
committed with the consent or connivance of, or to be attributable to any
neglect on the part of, an officer of the body, the officer is also guilty of the
offence and may be prosecuted and punished accordingly.[77] Proceedings
under s.49 may not be instituted in England and Wales otherwise than by or
with the consent of the Attorney General, or in Northern Ireland otherwise
than by or with the consent of the Attorney General for Northern Ireland.[78]

It is a defence for a person charged under s.49 with breaching the   **29.52**
restrictions in s.44 to prove that he was not aware, and neither suspected nor
had any reason to suspect, that the publication included the restricted
matter.[79] There is also a defence in three further situations:

- where the defendant can prove that he was not aware, and neither
  suspected nor had any reason to suspect, that the criminal investigation had begun.[80]
- where the defendant can satisfy the court, where the publication
  related to a suspected victim or a witness to any alleged offence other
  than a sex offence, that the publication was in the public interest on
  the ground that the restrictions imposed a substantial and unreasonable restriction on the reporting of matters connected with the
  offence.[81] For the factors to which the court must have regard in
  considering whether publication was in the public interest, see

[75] 1999 Act s.49.
[76] 1999 Act s.68(6).
[77] 1999 Act s.51. For offences by companies, see *Chargot (t/a Contract Services)* [2008] UKHL
73, discussed at para.8.43, above.
[78] 1999 Act s.49(2).
[79] 1999 Act s.50(1).
[80] 1999 Act s.50(2).
[81] 1999 Act s.50(3).

para.29.67, below. Where a case exists for publication in the public interest, the safer course will be to apply under s.44(7) for an order dispensing with the restrictions to the desired extent, rather than to publish and be damned and then seek to rely on this defence.

- where the defendant can prove that written consent had been given to publication.[82] Consent cannot be given by the alleged offender, or by a witness to an alleged sexual offence who is under 16. Otherwise, consent can be given by the person concerned if they are aged 16 or 17, or by an appropriate person on their behalf if they are under 16. However, written consent is not a defence if it is proved that any person interfered with the peace or comfort of the person giving it, or of the appropriate person, with intent to obtain it.[83]

POLICE GUIDANCE AND PRACTICE RELATING TO ANONYMITY BETWEEN ARREST AND CHARGE

29.53 It is important in this context to say something about the guidance and practice followed by the police in relation to the identification of arrested individuals before charge. In recent years there has been heated debate about the varying approaches taken to this issue by different police forces, which has been fuelled by the naming in the media of well-known individuals arrested on suspicion of committing sexual offences against children. Perhaps the most marked controversy was in August 2014, when, following an allegation made against the singer Sir Cliff Richard, the BBC were tipped off in advance about a police search of Sir Cliff's Berkshire apartment and were able to film the event. In fact, the guidance issued by the Association of Chief Police Officers (now the National Police Chiefs' Council) had for some years been that individuals should be anonymous before charge.[84] This guidance was, however, frequently disregarded. There was also disagreement as to whether the guidance was sound. In its 2012 consultation on the law of contempt, the Law Commission proposed, contrary to the ACPO guidance, that suspects should generally be identified following a media request.[85] It said:

> "We propose that the Home Office request that the Association of Chief Police Officers issue guidance, for dissemination to police forces, which would encourage the police to adopt consistent decision-making about whether to release information about arrestees following a request from the media to identify the arrestee. We consider that such policy should establish that, generally, the names of arrestees will be released, but that appropriate safeguards will need to be put in place to ensure that some names are withheld, for example, where it would

---

[82] 1999 Act s.50(6), (8)–(14).
[83] 1999 Act s.50(8).
[84] cf. *Hansard*, HL, vol.648, cols 1092, Lord Falconer of Thoroton (June 2, 2003).
[85] *Contempt of Court*, Law Commission Consultation Paper No. 209 (TSO, 2012), para.2.20. See *http://lawcommission.justice.gov.uk/docs/cp209_contempt_of_court.pdf* [Accessed April 30, 2016].

lead to the unlawful identification of a complainant, where the arrestee is a youth or where an ongoing investigation may be hampered."

Shortly afterwards, the orthodox approach was robustly affirmed in the Leveson Report[86]:

"the current guidance in this area needs to be strengthened. For example, I think that it should be made abundantly clear that save in exceptional and clearly identified circumstances (for example, where there may be an immediate risk to the public), the names or identifying details of those who are arrested or suspected of a crime should not be released to the press nor the public."

In responding to the Law Commission's consultation, the senior judiciary (Treacy LJ and Tugendhat J) drew on Sir Brian Leveson's comments in expressing a preference for withholding the identification of those arrested save in exceptional circumstances.[87] They commented[88]:

"If there were a policy that the police should consistently publish the fact that a person has been arrested, in many cases that information would attract substantial publicity, causing irremediable damage to the person's reputation."

Given these differences of view and inconsistent police practice in applying the existing guidance, in May 2013 the Home Secretary wrote to the College of Policing stating her belief that there should be a right to anonymity before charge, save in highly unusual circumstances where the public interest requires an arrested person to be named, and inviting the College to work up new guidance to make the position clear.[89] Shortly afterwards, the College published *Guidance on Relationships with the Media*.[90] This states that "[t]here is nothing to prevent police forces from naming an arrested person where there is a policing purpose for doing so".[91] It continues[92]:   **29.54**

"Decisions must be made on a case-by-case basis but, save in clearly identified circumstances, or where legal restrictions apply, the names or identifying details of those who are arrested or suspected of a crime should not be released by police forces to the press or the public. Such circumstances include a threat to life, the prevention or detection of crime or a matter of public interest and confidence. This approach aims to support consistency and avoid undesirable variance which can confuse press and public."

In the context of alleged sexual offences, the reference to the "detection of crime" is key. Its effect is that the police may properly release the name of an arrested person if they have good reason to believe that, by doing so, they

---

[86] *Leveson Inquiry: Culture, Practice and Ethics of the Press* (TSO, 2013) at G, Ch 3, para.2.39. The report is available at *http://www.official-documents.gov.uk/document/hc1213/hc07/0780/0780.asp* [Accessed April 30, 2016].

[87] *Contempt of Court: A Judicial response to Law Commission Consultation Paper No. 209* (March 4, 2013). See h*ttp://www.judiciary.gov.uk/Resources/JCO/Documents/Consultations/sen-judiciary-response-to-law-comm-on-contempt-court.pdf* [Accessed April 30, 2016].

[88] At para.5.

[89] See *http://www.bbc.co.uk/news/uk-22548065* [Accessed April 30, 2016].

[90] May 20, 2013, Available at *http://www.npcc.police.uk/documents/reports/2013/201305-cop-media-rels.pdf* [Accessed April 30, 2016].

[91] para.3.5.1.

[92] para.3.5.2.

may encourage further complainants to come forward with information about other offences committed by that person. But what constitutes "good reason" for this purpose? We suggest that the Guidance should not be read as encouraging speculative "tree-shaking" by the police, i.e. the release of an arrested person's name in order to see whether other complainants come forward. Such tactics are to be deprecated. In order for the release to be justified there should be something in the nature or context of the offending for which the person has been arrested that justifies the police in thinking that there may be other complainants who may be loath to reveal themselves without the encouragement of knowing about the arrest. For example, naming may be justified where the offender boasted to the complainant of the index offence that he had exploited other children; or he threatened her in order to secure her silence, and so may have done the same to other victims; or there are two or more complainants whose stories indicate that the suspect may be an opportunistic serial offender who could have committed other offences. The Guidance goes on to state that at the point of charge, where no legal restrictions apply, the release of information can include the name, address, occupation and charge details for an adult.[93]

29.55   An important practical question is whether the College of Policing's Guidance applies only where the police are deciding whether themselves to release a name, or whether it should also be followed when they are approached by the media for confirmation that a named person has been arrested. Prior to the issue of the Guidance, it was common police practice to give media representatives who came to them with the name of an arrested person an "off the record steer" that the name was correct.[94] It was assumed that the Guidance would put an end to this practice, but days before it was issued the Home Secretary wrote in an article in *The Sun* that when the media put a correct name to the police, they ought to confirm it.[95] The Guidance does not address this point explicitly, but states[96]:

> "The ability to converse informally and frankly on an unattributable basis where appropriate is generally uncontroversial. For example, the Chatham House Rule is used by a range of organisations to allow speaker anonymity, encourage openness and information sharing. There will be occasions when it may be appropriate for police officers or staff to speak on these terms to clarify or illustrate a point, for example, to guide media away from an inaccurate story. Any such occasions should be authorised and recorded. The principle that police

---

[93] para.3.5.5.

[94] Martin Evans, *Secret arrest plans in disarray*, *Daily Telegraph*, May 27, 2013, available at *http://www.telegraph.co.uk/news/10064781/Secret-arrest-plans-in-disarray.html* [Accessed April 30, 2016].

[95] May 17, 2013: see *http://www.bbc.co.uk/news/uk-22565675* [Accessed April 30, 2016]. Shortly afterwards the then Attorney General, Dominic Grieve MP, said that, whilst the police should not be subject to "fishing expeditions" by the media, where the name of an arrested person becomes known, it would be right for them to confirm it: see *http://www.theguardian.com/politics/2013/jun/04/secret-arrests-police-dominic-grieve* [Accessed April 30, 2016].

[96] para.3.4.4.

officers and staff should speak on matters for which they are responsible and
where there is a policing purpose for doing so should apply."

The effect of this passage is that, if a journalist comes to the police with a
name which is wrong, it may be appropriate for the police to say so. But if the
name is correct, then the elements of the Guidance cited above mean that
unless exceptional circumstances apply, they should not confirm it. There is
an obvious problem here, since if the police comment only on inaccurate
names, then their silence is likely to be taken as indicating that the name put
to them is correct. This is an unsatisfactory state of affairs, as it undermines
the protection otherwise given by the Guidance to arrested persons and,
incidentally, acts as an incentive to those in the know to leak names to the
media. We suggest that it would be far preferable for the Guidance to require
the police to make no comment on the correctness of names put to them
unless there is a proper policing reason to do so.

It is worth adding here that the Guidance deals with the release of   **29.56**
information by police forces and not with its leaking by individual officers
acting on their own account. Accordingly, it provides that a decision to
release the name of an arrested person should be made at chief officer level
and a record made of the reason for releasing it.[97] By contrast, leaks are
frowned upon. In March 2015, in its Report on *Police Bail*,[98] the Home
Affairs Select Committee, having considered the cases of Sir Cliff Richard
and the broadcaster Paul Gambaccini, stated:

> "The police should not release information on a suspect to the media in an
> informal, unattributed way . . . It is in the interests of the police to demonstrate,
> post-Leveson, that there is zero tolerance for informal leaks to the press. Police
> forces need to monitor and publish the number of instances where the identity of
> a suspect in their area has found its way into the public domain without an
> attributed source."

Such a leak will constitute grounds for disciplinary proceedings against the
officer concerned and may, depending on the circumstances, result in
prosecution for the offence of misfeasance in public office.

In light of the College of Policing's Guidance, might an arrested person   **29.57**
secure an injunction to prevent the media from publishing their name unless
and until they are charged? This is certainly possible in the right circumstances. In *PNM v Times Newspapers Ltd*,[99] the Court of Appeal said that if
an arrested person is to obtain an injunction preserving their anonymity
pending charge, it must be on the basis of an application of the principles set
out in *Re S (a child) (identification: restriction on publication)*.[100] These

---

[97] para.3.5.3.
[98] Seventeenth Report of the Home Affairs Select Committee, March 20, 2015, paras 14–15.
The report is available at *http://www.publications.parliament.uk/pa/cm201415/cmselect/cmhaff/
962/96204.htm* [Accessed April 30, 2016].
[99] [2014] EWCA Civ 1132.
[100] [2004] UKHL 47, discussed in paras 29.98 and following, below.

principles relate to the interaction between art.8 and art.10 ECHR, dealing respectively with the right to private life and the right to freedom of expression, the balancing of which is now a familiar exercise for the courts. The applicant in that case applied for an interim non-disclosure order, or "privacy injunction", to prevent publication of the fact of his arrest on suspicion of committing serious sexual offences against children, and associated information which would lead to his identification as the person so arrested, because of the damage that publication might cause to him and his family, including his own children. The relevant information had been referred to on a number of occasions in open court in earlier criminal proceedings to which the appellant was not a party, but publication of it had been temporarily postponed by orders made at the appellant's request under s.4(2) of the Contempt of Court Act 1981. The application for a privacy injunction was made in the expectation that those orders would be lifted. Tugendhat J refused to grant the injunction, on the basis that the general public interest in publishing a report of the court proceedings which identified the applicant and any normally reportable details of the proceedings outweighed any resulting curtailment of the rights of the applicant and his family to respect for their private and family life. In upholding this decision, the Court of Appeal referred to the strength of the principle of open justice, and continued[101]:

> "[Counsel for the appellant] has also drawn our attention to some recent material, which considers whether the police should publish the name of someone who has simply been arrested. I accept this material provides some support for the proposition that there should be a more careful consideration of such a person's rights than there might have been in the past: see for example, the Judicial Response to Law Commission's Consultation Paper on Contempt of Court at paragraph 5 . . . and the 2013 College of Policing *Guidance on Relations with the Media*, where it is said that consideration must be given to an individual's right to respect for a private and family life, the right of publishers to freedom of expression and the right of defendants to a fair trial. The Guidance goes on to say that save in clearly identified circumstances the names or identifying details of those who are arrested or suspected of crime should not be released by police forces to the press or the public.
>
> The appellant is not, however, someone who has simply been arrested. The fact of his arrest and other associated information has been extensively referred to in open court, including in public rulings given at the criminal trial, and the respondents want to report this. It was this which gave rise to the many factors bearing on the rights engaged which the judge correctly identified and carefully considered."

The last paragraph might be taken to indicate that, had the applicant's arrest not already been extensively revealed in open court, his application might have had much better prospects of success.

---

[101] At [41]–[42].

REPORTING RESTRICTIONS RELATING TO CHILDREN AND YOUNG PERSONS

The Youth Justice and Criminal Evidence Act 1999 contains provisions **29.58** restricting the identification of persons under 18 concerned in legal proceedings and enabling those restrictions to be extended forward for the lifetime of the person concerned. Restrictions imposed by courts in England and Wales or Northern Ireland are effective throughout the UK, including in Scotland.

Until recently this subject was primarily dealt with in s.39 of the Children **29.59** and Young Persons Act 1933. However, as from April 13, 2015, s.39 has been restricted to civil and family proceedings and proceedings in respect of civil orders dealing with anti-social behaviour, including Injunctions to Prevent Nuisance and Annoyance and Criminal Behaviour Orders. Since that date, its role in relation to criminal proceedings has been performed by s.45 of the Youth Justice and Criminal Evidence Act 1999,[102] which empowers a court to impose reporting restrictions in relation to persons under the age of 18 who are concerned in criminal proceedings as defendant, complainant or witness. It is important to note that the similarities between the terms of s.39 of the 1933 Act and s.45 of the 1999 Act are such that the case law built up under s.39 continues to provide appropriate guidance as to the principles and practice to be followed on applications under s.45.[103] In addition, s.45A of the 1999 Act, which came into force on the same date, creates a new power for the courts to impose lifetime reporting restrictions relating to persons under the age of 18 who are complainants or witnesses (but not defendants). Finally, the High Court has inherent jurisdiction to make an order prohibiting the publication of information about criminal proceedings in order to protect the rights of a child under art.8 ECHR, in circumstances where s.45 cannot be used as the child is not "concerned in" the proceedings.

It is also important to note s.44 of the Youth Justice and Criminal **29.60** Evidence Act 1999, which is not yet in force but which provides that where a criminal investigation has begun into an alleged offence against the law of England and Wales or Northern Ireland, and until proceedings are commenced in respect of the offence, no information shall be published relating to the alleged offender if he is aged under 18 and the information is likely to lead members of the public to identify him. This provision is considered in paras 29.45 and following, above.

Transitional arrangements on the coming into force of s.45 and s.45A of the 1999 Act

For the purpose of what follows, criminal proceedings commence when an **29.61** information is laid before a justice of the peace, a public prosecutor issues a

---

[102] But s.39 continues to apply to proceedings commenced before its repeal.
[103] *R. v H* [2015] EWCA Crim 1579 at [8], per Treacy LJ.

written charge and requisition for an offence, a person is charged with an offence after being taken into custody without a warrant or a bill of indictment is preferred.[104] Criminal proceedings conclude once all appellate proceedings have concluded.

29.62   Where criminal proceedings were ongoing at the date of commencement of s.45 and s.45A of the 1999 Act, i.e. April 13, 2015, the court may exercise its discretion under s.45A to impose a lifetime reporting restriction on or after that date. The power under s.45 to impose reporting restrictions in relation to a person under 18 does not apply to proceedings instituted before the commencement date.[105] However, s.39 of the Children and Young Persons Act 1933 continues to operate in relation to criminal proceedings instituted before that date.[106] Accordingly, where criminal proceedings are ongoing on April 13, 2015 and a reporting restriction order under s.39 of the Children and Young Persons Act 1933 has previously been made, s.39 continues to apply until the proceedings conclude or the reporting restriction order expires. The wider definition of "publication" inserted into s.39 by the Criminal Justice and Courts Act 2015 s.79, will not apply to that order. However, the court may make a new order under s.39 (as amended by the 2015 Act) on or after the date of commencement. Where this happens, any previous publication of information that falls within the wider definition of "publication" (e.g. publication online rather than in print or broadcast media) will not constitute a breach of the order. However, the order may be breached by the subsequent publication or re-publication of information online.

29.63   Where criminal proceedings are ongoing at the date of commencement and no order under s.39 of the 1933 Act has previously been made, the court may make an order under the amended s.39 on or after the date of commencement. The wider definition of "publication" inserted into s.39 will apply to such orders.

REPORTING RESTRICTIONS RELATING TO UNDER-18S WHO ARE
"CONCERNED IN" CRIMINAL PROCEEDINGS

29.64   Section 45 of the 1999 Act empowers criminal courts in England and Wales and Northern Ireland and service courts to direct that no matter relating to any person "concerned in" the proceedings shall while he is under the age of 18 be included in any publication if it is likely to lead members of the public to identify him.[107] For the meaning of "likely to lead" in this context, see para.29.19, above. The person may be concerned in the proceedings as a victim, witness or defendant.[108] Directions made under s.45 apply until the

[104] Prosecution of Offences Act 1985 s.15(2).
[105] Youth Justice and Criminal Evidence Act 1999 s.67 and Sch.7, para.6(3).
[106] Criminal Justice and Courts Act 2015 s.79(12).
[107] 1999 Act s.45(1), (3).
[108] 1999 Act s.45 (7).

person reaches the age of 18 or until they are otherwise lifted before that date. However, the court now has the power if certain conditions are met to impose lifetime reporting restrictions under s.45A of the 1999 Act in relation to an under-18 who is a witness or victim (but not one who is a defendant): see paras.29.108 and following, below. Section 45 does not apply to proceedings in or on appeal from the Youth Court, where s.49 of the Children and Young Persons Act 1933 (discussed in Ch.31) continues to provide automatic anonymity.

For the purposes of s.45, a "publication" includes any speech, writing, **29.65** programme included in a programme service or other communication in whatever form, which is addressed to the public at large or any section of it, but does not include an indictment or other document prepared for use in particular legal proceedings.[109] The reference to "any . . . other communication in whatever form" means that s.45 is effective to restrict publication not only in print or broadcast media but also online, e.g. on social media sites or micro-blogging sites such as Twitter.

The court has a discretion whether or not to make a direction under s.45 **29.66** and, if it makes one, as to its terms. It is the duty of prosecuting counsel to remind the judge to consider making a direction under the section.[110] When deciding whether to make a direction, the court must have regard to the welfare of the person to which it will relate.[111] If a direction is made, the restrictions apply in particular to the person's name, address, school or other educational establishment, place of work and any still or moving picture of him, if their inclusion in any publication is likely to lead members of the public to identify him.[112] But any information, even relating to these matters, may be reported if it is not likely to lead to the person's identification.

A direction may be revoked by the court or an appellate court.[113] Further, **29.67** the court or an appellate court may make an "excepting direction" dispensing with reporting restrictions imposed under s.45, to any extent specified in the excepting direction, if satisfied that doing so is in the interests of justice or that the restrictions impose a substantial and unreasonable restriction on the reporting of the proceedings and it is in the public interest to remove or relax them.[114] In deciding whether removal or relaxation is in the public interest, the court must have regard, in particular, to the following matters, so far as relevant: the interest in the open reporting of crime, the interest in the open reporting of matters relating to human health or safety, the interest in the prevention and exposure of miscarriages of justice, the welfare of the child or young person, and any views expressed by the child or young person or, if they are under 16, by an appropriate person on their behalf, so long as

[109] 1999 Act s.63(1).
[110] *R. v Central Criminal Court Ex p. Crook and Godwin* [1995] 2 Cr. App. R. 212 (relating to s.39 of the CYPA 1933).
[111] 1999 Act s.45(6).
[112] 1999 Act s.45(8).
[113] 1999 Act s.45(9).
[114] 1999 Act s.45(4), (5).

that person is not the accused.[115] An excepting direction may not be made on public interest grounds purely by reason of the fact that the proceedings have been concluded or abandoned, though this may be a relevant factor.[116] A court or an appellate court deciding whether to make an excepting direction must have regard to the welfare of the child or young person.[117] An excepting direction may be given at the time the reporting restriction is made or subsequently and may be varied or revoked by the court or an appellate court. [118] For the purposes of s.45, an appellate court means a court dealing with an appeal (including an appeal by way of case stated) arising out of the proceedings or with any further appeal.[119]

29.68   Section 45 provides:

"**45.**—(1) This section applies (subject to subsection (2)) in relation to—
    (a) any criminal proceedings in any court (other than a service court) in England and Wales or Northern Ireland; and
    (b) any proceedings (whether in the United Kingdom or elsewhere) in any service court.

(2) This section does not apply in relation to any proceedings to which section 49 of the Children and Young Persons Act 1933 applies.

(3) The court may direct that no matter relating to any person concerned in the proceedings shall while he is under the age of 18 be included in any publication if it is likely to lead members of the public to identify him as a person concerned in the proceedings.

(4) The court or an appellate court may by direction ('an excepting direction') dispense, to any extent specified in the excepting direction, with the restrictions imposed by a direction under subsection (3) if it is satisfied that it is necessary in the interests of justice to do so.

(5) The court or an appellate court may also by direction ('an excepting direction') dispense, to any extent specified in the excepting direction, with the restrictions imposed by a direction under subsection (3) if it is satisfied—
    (a) that their effect is to impose a substantial and unreasonable restriction on the reporting of the proceedings, and
    (b) that it is in the public interest to remove or relax that restriction;
but no excepting direction shall be given under this subsection by reason only of the fact that the proceedings have been determined in any way or have been abandoned.

(6) When deciding whether to make—
    (a) a direction under subsection (3) in relation to a person, or
    (b) an excepting direction under subsection (4) or (5) by virtue of which the restrictions imposed by a direction under subsection (3) would be dispensed with (to any extent) in relation to a person,
the court or (as the case may be) the appellate court shall have regard to the welfare of that person.

(7) For the purposes of subsection (3) any reference to a person concerned in the proceedings is to a person—
    (a) against or in respect of whom the proceedings are taken, or

---

[115] 1999 Act s.52.
[116] 1999 Act s.45(5).
[117] 1999 Act s.45(6).
[118] 1999 Act s.45(10).
[119] 1999 Act s.45(11).

(b) who is a witness in the proceedings.

(8) The matters relating to a person in relation to which the restrictions imposed by a direction under subsection (3) apply (if their inclusion in any publication is likely to have the result mentioned in that subsection) include in particular—

(a) his name,

(b) his address,

(c) the identity of any school or other educational establishment attended by him,

(d) the identity of any place of work, and

(e) any still or moving picture of him.

(9) A direction under subsection (3) may be revoked by the court or an appellate court.

(10) An excepting direction—

(a) may be given at the time the direction under subsection (3) is given or subsequently; and

(b) may be varied or revoked by the court or an appellate court.

(11) In this section 'appellate court', in relation to any proceedings in a court, means a court dealing with an appeal (including an appeal by way of case stated) arising out of the proceedings or with any further appeal."

For modifications of s.45 in relation to the Court Martial, the Service Civilian Court and the Court Martial Appeal Court, see the Youth Justice and Criminal Evidence Act 1999 (Application to Service Courts) Order 2009.[120]   **29.69**

Offence to contravene a direction under s.45

It is a summary offence under s.49 of the 1999 Act to publish in contravention of a direction imposed under s.45. The maximum penalty was until recently a fine not exceeding level 5 on the standard scale (i.e. £5,000).[121] The effect of s.85 of the Legal Aid, Sentencing and Punishment of Offenders Act 2012 is that, from March 12, 2015, the maximum is a fine of any amount. Fines will, however, continue to be set according to the seriousness of the offence and the means of the offender.   **29.70**

The s.49 offence may be committed in Scotland as well as in England, Wales and Northern Ireland.[122] Where the publication is in a newspaper or periodical, the offence is committed by the proprietor, the editor and the publisher. Where it is in a programme included in a programme service within the meaning of the Broadcasting Act 1990, e.g. on TV or the radio, it is committed by the body corporate or Scottish partnership providing the service and by any person having functions in relation to the programme corresponding to those of a newspaper editor. In the case of any other publication, the offence is committed by the person publishing it. Where a s.49 offence committed by a body corporate is proved to have been   **29.71**

---

[120] SI 2009/2083, as amended. See also the Court Martial and Service Civilian Court (Youth Justice and Criminal Evidence Act 1999) Rules 2009 (SI 2009/2100).

[121] 1999 Act s.49.

[122] 1999 Act s.68(6).

committed with the consent or connivance of, or to be attributable to any neglect on the part of, an officer of the body, the officer is also guilty of the offence and may be prosecuted and punished accordingly.[123] Proceedings under s.49 may not be instituted in England and Wales otherwise than by or with the consent of the Attorney General, or in Northern Ireland otherwise than by or with the consent of the Attorney General for Northern Ireland.[124] Where there has been an alleged breach of a direction under s.45, the better course is for the court to report the matter for consideration as to whether there should be a prosecution rather than to deal with it as an alleged contempt.[125]

29.72   By virtue of the Electronic Commerce (EC Directive) Regulations 2002,[126] which transpose the EU's E-Commerce Directive, a provider of "information society services", which include social media and search engines, is not liable for any criminal sanction by reason of acting as a mere "conduit" or providing "caching" or "hosting" services, if certain specified conditions are met. The effect is that a provider of such services may not, in those circumstances, be convicted of breaching a reporting direction made under s.45.

29.73   It is a defence for a person charged under s.49 with breaching a direction under s.45 to prove that he was not aware, and neither suspected nor had any reason to suspect, that the publication included the restricted matter.[127]

Burden of proof on an application for a direction under s.45

29.74   In *R. (on the application of Y) v Aylesbury Crown Court, CPS, Newsquest Media Group Limited*,[128] the Administrative Court said that a defendant applying for an order under s.39 of the Children and Young Person Act 1933:

> "will have to satisfy the court that there is a good reason to impose it. This is probably an evaluative exercise and would not involve the application of any burden or standard of proof (unless perhaps there is a factual dispute) . . . ".

The same will be true of an application for a direction under s.45.[129] It would seem to follow that, if a court is considering whether to discharge or vary a direction already made, then the party who obtained the direction must satisfy the court that there remains a good reason not to discharge or vary it.

---

[123] 1999 Act s.51. For offences by companies, see *Chargot (t/a Contract Services)* [2008] UKHL 73, discussed at para.8.43, above.

[124] 1999 Act s.49(2).

[125] *R. v Tyne Tees Television Ltd* [1997] EWCA Crim 2395 (relating to breach of an order made under s.39 of the CYPA 1933).

[126] SI 2002/2013, reg.17.

[127] 1999 Act s.50(1).

[128] [2012] EWHC 1140 (Admin), citing *Lee* (1993) 96 Cr. App. R. 188.

[129] *R. v H* [2015] EWCA Crim 1579 at [8], per Treacy LJ.

Principles governing the decision whether to make a direction or an excepting direction under s.45

Section 45(6) requires that, in deciding whether to make a direction or an   **29.75** excepting direction in relation to a person, the court is to have regard to the person's welfare. In this respect, the position is the same under s.45 as it was under s.39 of the Children and Young Persons Act 1933, since s.44 of the 1933 Act required the court to have regard to the welfare of the child or young person when deciding an application under that section. However, neither statute is drafted to make the person's welfare the sole consideration. Indeed, the effect of the Human Rights Act 1998 is that in many cases the court's decision is likely to turn on the balance between the child's welfare, as an aspect of their right to private and family life under art.8 ECHR, [130] and the freedom of the media under art.10 to report proceedings.[131] The latter freedom is particularly treasured by the courts. Thus, the guidance published by the Judicial College[132] states that before making a direction under s.45:

> "the court must be satisfied that, on the facts of the case, the welfare of the child outweighs the strong public interest in open justice."

As noted above, given the similarities between the terms of s.39 of the 1933   **29.76** Act and s.45 of the 1999 Act, the case law built up under s.39 continues to provide appropriate guidance as to the principles and practice to be followed in relation to applications under s.45.[133] Accordingly, when a court is deciding whether to make a direction or an excepting direction under s.45 in relation to a defendant, it should follow the principles that applied in relation to the imposition or lifting of restrictions under s.39. In *R. v Winchester CC Ex p. B*,[134] Simon Brown LJ (as he then was) set out those principles as follows:

> "i) In deciding whether to impose or thereafter to lift reporting restrictions, the court will consider whether there are good reasons for naming the defendant;
>
> ii) In reaching that decision, the court will give considerable weight to the age of the offender and to the potential damage to any young person of public identification as a criminal before the offender has the benefit or burden of adulthood;

---

[130] In *R. (on the application of Y) v Aylesbury Crown Court, CPS, Newsquest Media Group Limited* [2012] EWHC 1140 (Admin) the Administrative Court said that, having regard to the mandatory requirement in s.44 of the 1933 Act for the court to have regard to the welfare of the child when deciding a s.39 application, it is probably unnecessary to consider art.8.

[131] cf. *R. v. Croydon Crown Court Ex p. Trinity Mirror Plc and others* [2008] EWCA Crim 50 at [25].

[132] *https://www.judiciary.gov.uk/publications/reporting-restrictions-in-the-criminal-courts/* [Accessed April 30, 2016]. See further para.29.79, below.

[133] *R. v H* [2015] EWCA Crim 1579 at [8], per Treacy LJ.

[134] [2000] 1 Cr. App. R. 11, cited with approval in *R. (A) v St Albans Crown Court Ex p. T* [2002] EWHC 1129 (Admin), at 20, and *R. (on the application of Y) v Aylesbury Crown Court, CPS, Newsquest Media Group Limited* [2012] EWHC 1140 (Admin), at 26. See also *R. v Central Criminal Court Ex p. Simpkins* [1999] Crim. L.R. 159; *R. v Inner London Crown Court Ex p. B* [1996] C.O.D. 17, DC; *R. v Central Criminal Court Ex p. W, B and C* [2001] 1 Cr. App. R. 2, DC.

iii) By virtue of section 44 of the 1933 Act, the court must 'have regard to the welfare of the child or young person';

iv) The prospect of being named in court with the accompanying disgrace is a powerful deterrent and the naming of a defendant in the context of his punishment serves as a deterrent to others. These deterrents are proper objectives for the court to seek;

v) There is a strong public interest in open justice and in the public knowing as much as possible about what has happened in court, including the identity of those who have committed crime;

vi) The weight to be attributed to the different factors may shift at different stages of the proceedings and, in particular, after the defendant has been found, or pleads, guilty and is sentenced. It may then be appropriate to place greater weight on the interest of the public in knowing the identity of those who have committed crimes, particularly serious and detestable crimes;

vii) The fact that an appeal has been made may be a material consideration."

29.77   In *R. (on the application of Y) v Aylesbury Crown Court, CPS, Newsquest Media Group Limited*,[135] the Administrative Court described the way in which a court should approach an application by a defendant for an order under s.39:

"The defendant will have to satisfy the court that there is a good reason to impose it. This is probably an evaluative exercise and would not involve the application of any burden or standard of proof (unless perhaps there is a factual dispute) . . .

In most cases the good reason upon which the defendant child or young person will rely is his or her welfare . . .

Because the defendant is a child or young person and not an adult, his or her future progress may well be assisted by restricting publication. Publication could well have a significant effect on the prospects and opportunities of the young person, and, therefore, on the likelihood of effective integration into society. Identifying a defendant in the media may constitute an additional and disproportionate punishment on the child or young person. In rare cases (and not in this case) the child or young person may be at serious personal risk if identified.

In reaching the decision upon an application by a defendant to restrict publication under section 39, the court must, in addition to having regard to the welfare of the child, have regard to the public interest and to Article 10 of the ECHR.

Amongst the possible public interests is the public interest in knowing the outcome of proceedings in court and the public interest in the valuable deterrent effect that the identification of those guilty of at least serious crimes may have on others.

In so far as Article 10 is concerned . . . any order restricting publication must be necessary, proportionate and there must be a pressing social need for it.

The court must thus balance the welfare of the child or young person which is likely to favour a restriction on publication with the public interest and the requirements of Article 10 which are likely to favour no restriction on publication. Prior to conviction the welfare of the child or young person is likely to take precedence over the public interest. After conviction, the age of the defendant and the seriousness of the crime of which he or she has been convicted will be particularly relevant.

[135] [2012] EWHC 1140 (Admin) at [39]–[48].

What the court should do is to identify the factors which would favour restriction on publication and the factors which would favour no restriction. The court may also decide, as the judge did in this case, to permit the publication of some details but not all.

If having conducted the balancing exercise between the welfare of the child or young person, on the one hand, and the public interest and the requirements of Article 10 on the other, the factors favouring a restriction on publication and the factors favouring publication are very evenly balanced, then it seems to us . . . that a court should make an order restricting publication."

In the *Aylesbury* case, the claimant (16) pleaded guilty to one offence of arson   **29.78**
and was sentenced to an eight months' detention and training order. His adult co-defendant also pleaded guilty. The prosecution offered no evidence in relation to other alleged arsons which, if proved, would have shown, on the prosecution's case, a serious campaign of "revenge arson" against a number of individuals. The claimant's identity was protected by an order made earlier under s.39. Following sentence, the publishers of the local newspaper and the police applied to the trial judge to lift that order. The trial judge acceded to the application in part by varying the order so as to permit the publication of the claimant's name and address, but not a photograph or other description of him. The judge gave two reasons for this decision: the defendant's identity was already known to local people, and the limited publication of his name and address together with the fact that he had pleaded guilty to and been sentenced for one arson would give him, on his release, some protection from those who thought him to have been involved in more arsons. The Administrative Court said that neither of these reasons was satisfactory. The fact that the defendant's identity was already known to some people in the locality was not a good reason for letting a very large number of others know about it. It was also doubtful on the facts of the case whether it was permissible to allow publication in order, in some way, to help the claimant, particularly whilst at the same time letting many people know his name and address. In any event the judge did not, as he should have done, apply the relevant principles (as set out above) and so the Court quashed his decision and proceeded to consider the matter itself. The publishers and the police had contended that it was in the public interest to publish the claimant's name and address for the following reasons:

(i) it would deter others from committing such a grave offence;

(ii) it would be an additional necessary punishment for him;

(iii) the naming of both offenders would demonstrate to the community that the police had done all that they could do in the face of a serious problem of gang-related arson and intimidation and so would restore the confidence of the community in the criminal justice system;

(iv) the naming of both offenders would encourage victims of arson attacks and other individuals, who were frightened of the repercussions of coming forward, to feel confident about coming forward and give information about some 100 other arsons.

Having considered these reasons, the Court said that if the claimant had been convicted of offences which showed that he was a party to a serious campaign of revenge arson, it would not have been appropriate to place a restriction on publication. However, he had pleaded guilty to one count of simple arson committed when he was 16. That being so, on the facts of the case, the public interest in publication did not take precedence over the claimant's welfare.[136]

29.79   For practical guidance as to the application of the above principles, see para.4.2 of *Reporting Restrictions in the Criminal Courts*, published by the Judicial College in May 2015, and adopted by the Media Lawyers' Association, the News Media Association and the Society of Editors.[137]

Representations by the media

29.80   Reporting restrictions are dealt with in r.6 of the Criminal Procedure Rules 2015,[138] which determine the way a case is managed as it progresses through the criminal courts in England and Wales. Rule 6.2 provides:

> "**6.2.**—(1) When exercising a power to which this Part applies, as well as furthering the overriding objective, in accordance with rule 1.3, the court must have regard to the importance of—
> (a) dealing with criminal cases in public; and
> (b) allowing a public hearing to be reported to the public.
> (2) The court may determine an application or appeal under this Part—
> (a) at a hearing, in public or in private; or
> (b) without a hearing.
> (3) But the court must not exercise a power to which this Part applies unless each party and any other person directly affected—
> (a) is present; or
> (b) has had an opportunity—
> (i) to attend, or
> (ii) to make representations."

The term "any other person directly affected" in r.6.2(3) covers members of the media. This is reinforced by the guidance *Reporting Restrictions in the Criminal Courts*, referred to in para.29.79, above, which states in para.4.1:

> "The imposition of a reporting restriction directly engages the media's interests, affecting its ability to report on matters of public interest. For this reason the court should not impose any reporting restrictions without first giving the media an opportunity to attend or to make representations, or, if the Court is persuaded

---

[136] For another, much publicised example of the application of the principles in the *Winchester* and *Aylesbury* cases, see *Cornick* [2014] EWHC 3623 (QB), in which Coulson J declined to extend a s.39 order post-conviction so as to protect the identity of a 16-year-old convicted of the murder of his schoolteacher.

[137] *https://www.judiciary.gov.uk/publications/reporting-restrictions-in-the-criminal-courts/* [Accessed April 30, 2016]. A previous version of para.4.2 was quoted extensively and described as "helpful" in *R. (on the application of Y) v Aylesbury Crown Court, CPS, Newsquest Media Group Limited* [2012] EWHC 1140 (Admin) at [29]–[31].

[138] See *http://www.legislation.gov.uk/uksi/2015/1490/article/6.2/made* [Accessed April 30, 2016].

that there is an urgent need for at least a temporary restraint, as soon as practicable after they have been made. The media bring a different perspective to that of the parties to the proceedings. They have a particular expertise in reporting restrictions and are well placed to represent the wider public interest in open justice on behalf of the general public. Because of the importance attached to contemporaneous court reporting and the perishable nature of news, courts should act swiftly to give the media the opportunity to make representations."

It is clear from *R. v Jolleys (Robert), Ex p. Press Association*[139] that if the   **29.81**
media are not given an opportunity to make representations in accordance with r.6.2(3)(b)(ii) before a direction is made under s.45, this will be a serious procedural defect that could lead to the overturning of the direction. In that case, the Court of Appeal said[140]:

"The requirements of open justice demand that judges are fully mindful of the underlying principles which this judgment has sought to elucidate. In most cases, the application of the law is obvious and nobody will contend to the contrary. The fact that an order has been or may be made under section 39 of the Act and is so identified in the court list is more than enough notice to the press should any reporter wish to make representations or challenge a subsisting order.

Where, however, there is the slightest doubt, or any novel approach is suggested, it should be identified in good time and notice provided as required by the Criminal Procedure Rules so that the press can also consider the matter in good time. Even then, judges cannot expect local reporters to be in a position to instruct lawyers or argue the principles in depth, and in any event counsel should be required to research and develop the arguments to assist the court in a balanced way. That is not in any way to limit the right of reporters or their lawyers to advance argument on their own behalf."

As a practical matter, the absence of a definitive list of directions made   **29.82**
under s.45 creates an obvious hazard for the media. The Law Commission has recommended the adoption in England and Wales of a publicly available online list of orders under s.4(2) of the Contempt of Court Act 1981 (postponement of reporting of proceedings), similar to the one already operating in Scotland, whereby information about orders is posted online with a facility to register for electronic alerts of any new orders.[141] The Commission has also recommended that the list of orders be supplemented by an additional restricted database which would contain the terms of s.4(2) orders themselves. The Commission reported strong support from some consultees for increasing the scope of the proposed online list to cover other types of reporting restrictions, including those under s.39 of the Children and Young Persons Act 1933 (now replaced, in relation to criminal proceedings, by s.45 of the 1999 Act). However, given the concerns expressed by other consultees about the practicality and cost of maintaining the online list, the Commission recommended limiting it in the first instance to s.4(2) orders; if,

---

[139] [2013] EWCA Crim 1135, decided in relation to s.39 of the CYPA 1933.
[140] At [16], [20]–[21] per Leveson LJ (as he then was).
[141] *Contempt of Court (2): Court Reporting*, Law Com No. 344 (March 25, 2014), available at *http://lawcommission.justice.gov.uk/docs/lc344_contempt_of_court_court_reporting.pdf* [Accessed April 30, 2016].

as the Commission anticipated, the list worked well, it could be treated as a pilot scheme for a more ambitious system for publicising all reporting restrictions. The Commission also noted that publication of court reporting restrictions was currently under consideration by HMCTS as part of wider plans to replace Court Service IT systems[142]:

> "Under the planned replacement, which HMCTS intends to roll out across the courts of England and Wales in the medium term, data, including information regarding all reporting restrictions, would be automatically available for interested parties when such information is first recorded on case management systems. An automated system of this kind would be extremely welcome, and would clearly be more comprehensive and efficient in various respects than the limited system discussed in this report, which is dependent on a person uploading the information about the order that has been emailed from the court centre.
>
> For the reasons set out above, and in light of the reassuring results of our pilot scheme, we consider that this system of uploading material for publicising section 4(2) orders remains a valuable interim measure in the short term. Such a system could be set up very quickly, and would provide a valuable resource for prospective publishers in discovering their legal obligations. In the longer term, the system proposed here could represent an important stepping stone towards a more comprehensive system for the publication of all court reporting restrictions, which would clearly be a desirable final outcome."

The Government welcomed the recommendations in the Law Commission's report, on the basis that it supports proposals encouraging transparency and openness in the criminal justice system, and it undertook to consider how an online reporting restriction database could be taken forward as existing technology is replaced and updated.[143]

Framing of a direction under s.45

29.83   The guidance *Reporting Restrictions in the Criminal Courts*, referred to in para.29.79, above, states in para 4.1:

> "Any reporting restriction imposes potential criminal liability on media organisations, journalists or editors who breach it. If a breach occurs, media organisations and their employees may face unlimited fines. For these reasons, it is essential that any reporting restriction should be reduced to writing as soon as possible, clear and precise in its terms and drawn up as a court order as soon as practicable. Once orders have been made, they should be drawn to the attention of the media by being shown on the court list and on the door of the court and wherever possible sent to relevant local and/or national media organisations. Court staff should respond positively to media organisations' requests for assistance in relation to the existence or terms of reporting restriction orders."

---

[142] Paras 5.44–5.45.
[143] *Report on the implementation of Law Commission proposals* (MoJ, March 2015), para.77. The Report is available at *https://www.gov.uk/government/uploads/system/uploads/attachment_data/file/410228/report-on-implementation-of-law-commission-proposals.pdf* [Accessed April 30, 2016].

In addition, the guidance as to the procedure to be followed on the making   **29.84**
of an order under s.39 of the Children and Young Persons Act 1933, given by
the Court of Appeal in *R. v Central Criminal Court Ex p. Crook and
Godwin*,[144] remains valid in relation to s.45 of the 1999 Act:

(1) the judge should make clear what the terms of the order are. It will
     suffice to use the words of the section, or a suitable adaptation, and
     to relate the order to, e.g. "the child/children named in the charge/
     indictment". But if there is possible doubt as to the child or children
     to which the order relates, the judge should identify the relevant
     child or children with clarity;

(2) a written copy of the order should be drawn as soon as possible
     after the order has been made orally.[145] There should be available in
     every court a pro forma on which the necessary details can be
     entered and which can be amended as necessary to meet an unusual
     case. The written order, or a copy of it, should be made available in
     the court office for representatives of the press to inspect;

(3) the fact that an order has been made should be communicated to
     those who were not present when it was made. This is best done by
     means of a short notice in the daily list. Words such as "Order made
     under the C and YP Act 1933 s.39", appended to the name of the
     case, should suffice.[146]

In relation to the wording of a s.45 direction, the guidance *Reporting*   **29.85**
Restrictions in the Criminal Courts states in para 4.2:

"Section 45 orders should be carefully framed, to prevent them from having an
overbroad effect. The purpose of a s.45 order is not to prevent the publication of
the name, address or other details of the child or young person per se; what a s.45
order seeks to do is to prevent their identification as a victim, witness or
defendant in criminal proceedings. For this reason, when making an order under
s.45, courts should track the language of s.45(3) YJCEA and make sure to
include the qualifying words in italics 'if it is likely to lead members of the public
to identify him *as a person concerned in the proceedings*'. Adopting this language
prevents media reports of unrelated matters e.g. the same child winning a prize
at school, being caught by the restriction."

**How can the making, variation or revocation of a direction under s.45 be
challenged?**

Those aggrieved by the making or extension of a direction under s.45 (most   **29.86**
commonly the media) have a remedy by way of appeal, with leave, to the
Court of Appeal (Criminal Division) under s.159 of the Criminal Justice Act
1988.[147] However, this provision does not enable a person to appeal against

[144] [1995] 2 Cr. App. R. 212.
[145] cf. *R. v Stafford Crown Court Ex p. BBC Litigation Dept* [2002] EWCA Crim 962.
[146] The words "reporting restrictions applied" were held too vague to constitute a basis for
prosecuting for breach of an order made under s.39 of the CYPA 1933: *Briffet v DPP* [2001]
EWCA Admin 841, DC.
[147] See *R. v Winchester Crown Court Ex p. B* [2000] 1 Cr. App. R. 11, DC.

the refusal to make such a direction, the revocation of one previously made or a variation of a direction that has the effect of permitting publication. What recourse does such a person have, other than by asking the court to reconsider its decision?

29.87   One might expect a remedy by way of judicial review to be ruled out by s.29(3) of the Senior Courts Act 1981, which provides that the Crown Court is not subject to judicial review "in matters relating to trial on indictment". However, in relation to orders under s.39 of the Children and Young Persons Act 1933 the weight of authority was that judicial review was available to challenge the making, variation or discharge by the Crown Court of such an order,[148] provided the application was made after verdict and sentence.[149] The central reason is that, as the Divisional Court said in *Wang Yam*,[150] "the application may be said to arise out of a trial on indictment but it is not a matter relating to trial on indictment since the trial has concluded". This is almost certain to remain the position now that s.45 of the 1999 Act is in force, although the point must remain open to argument on appeal.

29.88   It was held in *Lee*[151] that the Court of Appeal had no original jurisdiction to make an order under s.39 of the 1933 Act restricting the publication of proceedings in the Crown Court: the only court which could make such an order was the Crown Court itself. We suggest that this must, again, remain the position under s.45. The Court went on to give the following guidance on challenges by the media to the making, or by the defendant to the withholding or discharge, of an order under s.39 by the Crown Court:

(1)   a member of the media who is aggrieved by the making of such an order should go back to the Crown Court in the event of any change in circumstances, or should appeal to the Court of Appeal under s.159 of the Criminal Justice Act 1988;

(2)   a defendant aggrieved by the withholding or discharge of an order under the section should go back to the Crown Court in the event of any change in circumstances, or should challenge the validity of the order by proceedings for judicial review;

(3)   if the defendant indicates that he is intending to apply for judicial review, the Crown Court may, in its discretion, give a temporary

---

[148] *R. v Leicester Crown Court Ex p. S* [1993] 1 W.L.R. 111, DC; *Lee* (1993) 96 Cr. App. R. 188; *R. v Harrow Crown Court Ex p. Perkins* (1998) 162 J.P. 527, DC; *R. v St Albans Crown Court, Ex p. T* [2002] EWHC 1129 (Admin); *R. (on the application of Y) v Aylesbury Crown Court, CPS, Newsquest Media Group Limited* [2012] EWHC 1140 (Admin); *JC, RT v The Central Criminal Court v Crown Prosecution Service, British Broadcasting Corporation, Just for Kids Law* [2014] EWHC 1041 (Admin); and see *R. (on the application of Wang Yam) v Central Criminal Court* [2015] 1 Cr. App. R. 10. Cp. *R. v Winchester Crown Court Ex p. B* [2000] 1 Cr. App. R. 11, DC.
[149] *R. v Manchester Crown Court Ex p. H and D* [2000] 1 Cr. App. R. 262, DC, considering the earlier authorities; and see *R. v Central Criminal Court Ex p. W, B and C* [2001] 1 Cr. App. R. 2, DC.
[150] *R. (on the application of Wang Yam) v Central Criminal Court* [2015] 1 Cr. App. R. 10, DC, at [13] per Elias LJ, citing Ouseley J.
[151] (1993) 96 Cr. App. R. 188.

direction under the section or may grant a stay on the order discharging the direction pending such an application;

(4) an application to restrain the publication of proceedings in the Court of Appeal should be made in the ordinary way to the Court of Appeal.

Can a direction under s.45 expressly prohibit the identification of an adult concerned in the proceedings in order to protect the anonymity of a child or young person?

Section 45 does not empower a court to direct in terms that the name etc. of **29.89** an adult concerned in the proceedings, e.g. as defendant, should not be published, though this may be the practical effect where publication of the adult's name is "likely to lead" to the identification of the child or young person whom the direction was made to protect.[152]

The guidance *Reporting Restrictions in the Criminal Courts*, referred to in **29.90** para.29.79, above, states in Appendix 1, in relation to s.39 of Children and Young Persons Act 1933, that:

"there is no power [under s.39] to prohibit the publication of the names of adults involved in the proceedings . . . The court may, however, give guidance to the media if it considers that the naming of an adult defendant would be likely to identify a child. Such guidance is not binding. The media may, for instance, be able to name a defendant without infringing the order, if the relationship of the victim to the defendant is omitted[153] or the nature of the offence is blurred (e.g. 'a sexual offence' rather than incest)."

It is not clear why the guidance does not repeat this statement in relation to s.45, to which in principle it is equally applicable.

Also relevant here is para.5.9 of the guidance, which, under the heading **29.91** "Jigsaw identification", provides:

"Jigsaw identification refers to the phenomenon whereby the identity of a person protected by a reporting restriction order may be inadvertently disclosed as a result of different media reports, none of which breach the terms of any order or statutory provision, but which taken together enable the protected person to be identified. In most cases this is not an issue, but particular difficulties arise in relation to sex offences within the same family. For example, where one report refers to an unnamed defendant convicted of raping his daughter and another refers to the name of the defendant, the daughter will be identifiable to the public in breach of the automatic prohibition protecting victims of sexual offences.

In recognition of these potential difficulties the newspapers and broadcasters have aligned their respective codes so that the media adopts a common approach when reporting sexual offences. Typically the media will name the defendant but not name the victim (this would breach the statutory prohibition) or give any details of his or her relationship with the defendant. It is routine for in-house

---

[152] cf. *R. v Crown Court at Southwark Ex p. Godwin* (1992) 94 Cr. App. R. 34.
[153] But see *R. (on the application of Gazette Media Co Ltd) v Teesside Crown Court* [2005] EWCA Crim 1983; [2006] Crim. L.R. 157, discussed in para.29.92, below.

lawyers to check what information is already in the public domain before advising on whether a report of court proceedings is likely to breach any legal requirement, so even in non-sex cases in practice the media often ends up adopting a common approach."

29.92   In *R. (on the application of Gazette Media Co Ltd) v Teesside Crown Court*,[154] the Court of Appeal quashed an order purportedly made under s.39 of the Children and Young Persons Act 1933 that explicitly prohibited the identification of a defendant by name. The defendants, S and L, were charged on an indictment containing one count of conspiracy to rape and a number of counts under s.1 of the Protection of Children Act 1978. The complainant was S's daughter, who had been the subject of indecent photographs and also an agreement between the defendants to commit further offences against her. While the conspiracy count fell within the scope of the anonymity provisions of the Sexual Offences (Amendment) Act 1992, the 1978 Act counts did not. The trial judge therefore made an order under s.39, which prohibited inter alia the identification by name of S. Three media companies appealed successfully against the order. The Attorney General submitted on the appeal that the prohibition on the naming of S was necessary in order to give effect to the daughter's right to respect for her private life under art.8 ECHR. The Court of Appeal rejected this argument, holding that there was no scope for restricting the right to freedom of expression guaranteed by art.10 ECHR, beyond what was provided by s.39. The balance between the two articles was struck by the primary legislation. The Court accordingly quashed the order and substituted one that did not prohibit the identification of S. However, it added that it was not axiomatic that reporting that identified S by name, and referred to the complainant as "an 11-year-old schoolgirl", would comply with a proper order under s.39 or avoid a breach of s.1 of the 1992 Act. Offences of the kind in question were often committed by fathers and step-fathers. In this case, the history of photography and the planning of further offences were indicative of a close relationship between the defendant and the complainant. Were a defendant to be named and the complainant described as an 11-year-old schoolgirl, in circumstances in which the defendant had an 11-year-old daughter, it would be at least arguable that the composite picture embraced "particulars calculated to lead to the identification" of the complainant within the meaning of s.39. These comments are fairly made and are likely to have had a chilling effect on the media's desire to identify S, even under the revised order.

29.93   Publication of the identity of an adult concerned in criminal proceedings may, however, be expressly prohibited by an order made in the exercise of the High Court's inherent jurisdiction if this is necessary to protect the art.8 rights of a child; this possibility is explained below.

---

[154] [2005] EWCA Crim 1983; [2006] Crim. L.R. 157.

IS THERE ANY MEANS OF PROTECTING THE IDENTITY OF A CHILD WHO IS NOT A COMPLAINANT OR WITNESS IN CRIMINAL PROCEEDINGS BUT MAY NONETHELESS BE ADVERSELY AFFECTED BY THEM?

The full reporting of criminal proceedings may be capable of damaging the   **29.94**
interests of a child who is not directly involved in them as complainant or
witness. One possible example is where a father is prosecuted for serious
sexual offences, not committed against his own child and to which the child
was not a witness, but the reporting of the proceedings may lead to the child
being bullied or harmed in some other way. Do the courts have power to
make an order in such cases restricting the reporting of the proceedings to
the extent necessary to protect the child's identity?

Application of section 45

In *R. v Jolleys (Robert), Ex p. Press Association*,[155] it was held that an order   **29.95**
could not be made under s.39 of the Children and Young Persons Act 1933
to protect the identity of a child who might be adversely affected by criminal
proceedings but who was not concerned in them in one of the ways specified
in the section. Leveson LJ, giving the judgment of the Court of Appeal, said
of s.39[156]:

> "The phrase 'concerned in the proceedings' is defined and limited by the words
> that follow 'the person by or against, or in respect of whom proceedings are
> taken, or as being a witness therein'. It does not extend to children or young
> persons simply on the basis that they may be concerned in the more general sense
> of being affected thereby."

The same analysis must apply to s.45, the wording of which is materially the
same.

It is, however, worth noting that a child will be "concerned in" criminal   **29.96**
proceedings for the purposes of the section, even though they are not a
complainant or a witness, if the proceedings are taken "in respect of" them.
A good example of such proceedings is *R. (on the application of A) v
Lowestoft Magistrates' Court*,[157] in which A was charged with being found
drunk in a public place while having the charge of a child apparently under
the age of seven years, contrary to s.2(1) of the Licensing Act 1902. The
Administrative Court held that the proceedings were taken "in respect of"
the child referred to in the charge, who was therefore "concerned in the

---

[155] [2013] EWCA Crim 1135. See also *C v CPS* [2008] EWHC 854 (Admin); *R. v Croydon
Crown Court Ex p. Trinity Mirror Plc* [2008] EWCA Crim 50 at [25]; *Re S (a child)
(identification: restriction on publication)* [2004] UKHL 47 at [21], per Lord Steyn; *Z v News
Group Newspapers Ltd* [2013] EWHC 1150 and 1371 (Fam).
[156] At [13].
[157] [2013] EWHC 659 (Admin). Cp. *Z v News Group Newspapers Ltd* [2013] EWHC 1150 and
1371 (Fam), discussed in para.29.103, below.

proceedings" for the purposes of s.39 of the 1933 Act. Kenneth Parker J, giving the leading judgment, said[158]:

> "In a strictly formal sense, it might be argued that the only two parties to criminal proceedings are the prosecution and the defendant, and that criminal proceedings are not taken 'in respect of' any other person. However, it is plain that the legislature in enacting section 39 sought to capture, in wide language, at least the central participants in proceedings, whether civil or criminal, who would for that very reason be likely to be the focus of any report of the proceedings; and a narrow interpretation of section 39 would tend to defeat the main objective of protecting, where appropriate, the identity of a child or young person in that position. It is notable that section 39 extends in terms to a child or young person as a witness in proceedings, even if in a particular case the child or young person may have a relatively insignificant part in the proceedings. A broad interpretation of section 39 would now also be supported by article 8 of the European Convention of Human Rights ('ECHR') and the jurisprudence emphasising the best interests of children as a primary consideration, to which I shall turn later. Where in any event someone is prosecuted on a charge of violently or sexually assaulting a child or young person, or of inflicting cruelty on a child, it has never been seriously doubted that the putative victim of such conduct is a person 'in respect of whom' the criminal proceedings are brought.
>
> A here stood charged with 'being drunk in a public place while having the charge of a child under the age of 7 years', contrary to section 2(1) of the Licensing Act 1902. Under section 2(1) it is unnecessary to show that the defendant positively inflicted physical or psychological harm on the young child, or even that the defendant in the particular circumstances was likely to do so. In that strict sense the child might not be considered a victim as in the case of a violent or sexual assault, or of child cruelty. However, whatever the original intent of section 2(1), I am prepared to give it an interpretation that would best promote public policy in modern conditions, namely, that it is intended, among other things, to promote the welfare of small children who could be at risk of physical or psychological harm, because the person responsible for that welfare is intoxicated. Accordingly, the child that is specifically referred to in any charge under section 2(1) is in a real sense a subject of the criminal proceedings, and these proceedings on any sensible construction of section 39 of the CYP Act 1933 are taken 'in respect of', and thus 'concern', that child."

Inherent jurisdiction of the High Court

29.97 There is, however, one other possible means of securing the anonymity of a child who is not within the scope of s.45. This derives from the inherent jurisdiction of the High Court to make an order protecting the identity of a child or an incapacitated adult, whether in relation to particular court proceedings or otherwise. Whatever the scope of the inherent jurisdiction in earlier times, since the coming into force of the Human Rights Act 1998 the courts have treated it as derived from the ECHR, and if an order is made in relation to a child, it will be to prevent a breach of the child's rights under art.8.

---

[158] At [8]–[9].

The leading modern authority on the jurisdiction is *Re S (a child)*   **29.98**
(identification: restriction on publication).[159] The mother of S, the child, was
charged with the murder of her other child, DS. Care proceedings had been
commenced in relation to S, and he applied successfully through his guardian
under the High Court's inherent jurisdiction for an injunction to prohibit the
publication of information that might lead to his identification, including the
names of his mother and DS. There was psychiatric evidence before the court
that, if S was bullied and teased at school as a result of media publicity once
his mother's identity became known, he would suffer increased trauma and
a risk of mental illness. The injunction was challenged by certain newspapers,
which accepted that they should not identify S but wished to report the
mother's trial and the names of the mother and DS. After hearing argument,
the judge modified the order so as to permit them to publish what transpired
at the trial. S appealed unsuccessfully to the Court of Appeal and to the
House of Lords, asserting that his art.8 right to private and family life
required the State to protect him from harmful publicity about his family
that could damage his health and well-being. Lord Steyn, giving the leading
speech, held that the appeal turned on the interaction of art.8, and art.10,
which guarantees the right to freedom of expression. His Lordship
approached that interaction on the basis of four propositions.[160] First,
neither article has precedence over the other. Secondly, where the values
under the two articles are in conflict, an intense focus on the comparative
importance of the specific rights being claimed in the individual case is
necessary. Thirdly, the justifications for interfering with or restricting each
right must be taken into account. Finally, the proportionality test must be
applied to each. Lord Steyn readily accepted that this case engaged art.8 and
that the trial of S's mother for murder would be "dreadfully painful" for him.
But the impact of the trial upon S would be essentially indirect: he would not
be involved in it as a witness or otherwise, it would not be necessary to refer
to him or his upbringing, and no photograph of him would be published. As
for art.10, Lord Steyn noted the importance of the media's ability to report
criminal trials, which ensures that trials are properly conducted, permits
informed public debate and promotes public confidence in the administration
of justice and the rule of law. His Lordship noted in particular that from the
media's point of view, a sensational trial would be "disembodied" if reported
in such a way as not to reveal the identity of the defendant. It was likely that
readers would be less interested in such reports and so editors would be less
likely to give them prominence, with the result that informed debate about
criminal justice would suffer. Lord Steyn concluded that, in the circumstances of this case, the force of the argument under art.10 outweighed the
argument based on the rights of the child under art.8.

[159] [2004] UKHL 47. See also *C v CPS* [2008] EWHC 854 (Admin); *R. v Croydon Crown Court
Ex p. Trinity Mirror Plc* [2008] EWCA Crim 50, at [22].
[160] Derived from the opinions in *Campbell v Mirror Group Newspapers Ltd* [2004] UKHL
22.

29.99   The clear implication of *Re S* is that the tussle between art.8 and art.10, where the art.8 rights are those of a child not "concerned in" the proceedings within the meaning of s.45, the rights of the media and the public under art.10 are likely to prevail unless the apprehended harm to the child is real and well evidenced.[161] This also emerges from comments made by a five-judge Court of Appeal in *R. v. Croydon Crown Court Ex p. Trinity Mirror Plc*.[162] In that case the Crown Court made an order purporting to restrain the media from identifying a man convicted of child pornography offences in order to protect his children, who were neither victims nor witnesses in the proceedings. The order was held to have been made without jurisdiction, for reasons explained in para.29.107, below. But the Court went on to say that in any event the judge had incorrectly resolved the balance between the rights of the children under art.8 and those of the media and public under art.10 in favour of the former. Sir Igor (now Lord) Judge, then President of the QBD, giving the judgment of the Court, said[163]:

> "In our judgment it is impossible to over-emphasise the importance to be attached to the ability of the media to report criminal trials. In simple terms this represents the embodiment of the principle of open justice in a free country. An important aspect of the public interest in the administration of criminal justice is that the identity of those convicted and sentenced for criminal offences should not be concealed. Uncomfortable though it may frequently be for the defendant that is a normal consequence of his crime. Moreover the principle protects his interests too, by helping to secure the fair trial which, in Lord Bingham of Cornhill's memorable epithet, is the defendant's 'birthright'. From time to time occasions will arise where restrictions on this principle are considered appropriate, but they depend on express legislation, and, where the Court is vested with a discretion to exercise such powers, on the absolute necessity for doing so in the individual case.
>
> It is sad, but true, that the criminal activities of a parent can bring misery, shame, and disadvantage to their innocent children. Innocent parents suffer from the criminal activities of their sons and daughters. Husbands and wives and partners all suffer in the same way. All this represents the further consequences of crime, adding to the list of its victims. Everyone appreciates the risk that innocent children may suffer prejudice and damage when a parent is convicted of a serious offence. Among the consequences, the parent will disappear from home when he or she is sentenced to imprisonment, and indeed, depending on the crime but as happened in this case, there is always a possibility of the breakdown of the relationship between their parents. However . . . there is nothing in this case to distinguish the plight of the defendant's children from that of a massive group of children of persons convicted of offences relating to child pornography.

---

[161] cp. *K v News Group Newspapers Ltd* [2011] EWCA Civ 439, where Ward LJ said (at [19]): "where the court is deciding where the balance lies between the Article 10 rights of the media and the Article 8 rights of those whose privacy would be invaded by publication, it should accord particular weight to the Article 8 rights of any children likely to be affected by the publication, if that would be likely to harm their interests." In *PNM v Times Newspapers Ltd* [2014] EWCA Civ 1132, the Court of Appeal found it unnecessary on the facts to decide whether there is any tension between the approach of Ward LJ and that of Lord Steyn in *Re S* and, if so, how it should be resolved.

[162] [2008] EWCA Crim 50. See also *C v CPS* [2008] EWHC 854, esp. at [31]–[32].

[163] At [32]–[33].

If the court were to uphold this ruling so as to protect the rights of the defendant's children under Article 8, it would be countenancing a substantial erosion of the principle of open justice, to the overwhelming disadvantage of public confidence in the criminal justice system, the free reporting of criminal trials and the proper identification of those convicted and sentenced in them. Such an order cannot begin to be contemplated unless the circumstances are indeed properly to be described as exceptional."

Although orders under the High Court's inherent jurisdiction are excep-   **29.100**
tional, in appropriate cases they will be made, and it is instructive to give some examples of how the balance has been struck between art.8 and art.10 in particular cases[164]:

- In *A Local Authority v W*[165] Sir Mark Potter, then President of the   **29.101**
  Family Division, made an order restraining publication of the identity
  of a woman charged under s.20 of the Offences against the Person Act
  1861 with knowingly infecting her former partner with the HIV virus.
  He did so on the application of a local authority in order to protect
  the privacy of the children of the relationship, who were not witnesses
  or otherwise involved in the trial but were the subject of care
  proceedings. His Lordship distinguished the facts from those in *Re S*
  on a number of grounds. First, in *Re S* there had, at the time of the
  application, already been widespread press reporting of the matter
  that named the parents, DS and S, and identified their home and S's
  school. Accordingly, the order in that case offered no real hope of
  isolating S from the fall-out of publicity from the trial. By way of
  contrast, in *Re W* there had been no previous publicity and, if the
  injunction was granted, there was a good prospect that the children,
  who were too young to be aware of the existence or significance of
  their mother's trial, would be largely isolated from its fall-out.
  Secondly, the application in *Re S* was made at the final hearing in S's
  care proceedings, when a care order had been made and there was no
  suggestion that the refusal of the application would have any adverse
  effect on the placement, upon which S's future in a secure and happy
  family life would depend. But in *Re W,* the children's situation
  remained unresolved and the refusal of an injunction could place real
  difficulties in the way of providing a suitable placement for them.
  Finally, in *Re W* the case for an injunction was not put on the basis
  of the damage likely to be caused to the children by the widespread
  knowledge that their mother was or might be a criminal, an experience which regrettably many children have to bear, but on the basis
  that an injunction would protect them from personal attribution of

---

[164] See also *A (A Minor)* [2011] EWHC 1764 (Fam); *North Somerset Council v LW* [2014] EWHC 1670 Fam); *City and County of Swansea v XZ and YZ* [2014] EWHC 212 (Fam); *Birmingham City Council v Riaz* [2014] EWHC 4247 (Fam); *Surrey County Council v ME* [2014] EWHC 489 (Fam); *PNM v Times Newspapers Ltd* [2014] EWCA Civ 1132.
[165] [2005] EWHC 1564 (Fam).

HIV infection, with all the stigma and damaging long-term consequences that such attribution would bring. However, his Lordship
said that these points of distinction had to be balanced against the
public interest in the free reporting of criminal proceedings and in the
identity of the mother being published. He did not find it easy to
determine where the balance lay between these "two powerful and
emotive competing interests":

> "On the one hand, the freedom of the press in relation to the open
> reporting of criminal proceedings, coupled with what Munby J has
> described as the 'clear and compelling interest' of the media and the public
> in the publication of the photograph of a person convicted of a serious
> crime so as to 'put a face on the man' (see *F v Newsquest Limited and others*
> [2004] EWHC 762 (Fam), [2004] EMLR 607 at para 98); on the other hand
> the need to protect the privacy of the children caught up in a situation over
> which they have no control and where they are in a delicate and vulnerable
> state and the subject of care proceedings of uncertain outcome. As to the
> former, the interference with the Convention right is certain and clear cut.
> As to the latter, it is more problematic in two respects. First, what is the
> likelihood of interference if the injunction is withheld? Second, if the
> injunction is granted how effective will it be to prevent or reduce the
> interference against which protection is sought? In these respects, when
> having regard to proportionality, it is necessary to consider not only the
> extent of harm which has already occurred, but the likelihood that the
> harm sought to be avoided will occur in any event."[166]

After careful consideration, his Lordship granted the injunction. He
accepted, so far as art.10 was concerned, that there was high media
and public interest in the case, and that suppression of the identity of
the parents would result to that extent in what Lord Steyn in *Re S* had
called a "disembodied trial". However, what made the case of high
interest was the issues involved in it, and his Lordship did not
consider that reporting or discussion of those issues would be
significantly inhibited if the injunction was granted. Also, publication
of the identity of the mother was bound to have an adverse effect
upon the children in a manner that was likely to inflict substantial
damage on their art.8 rights. Although the children's age was such
that they would not be conscious of the nature of the proceedings, this
did not mean there was no immediate threat to their health or well-
being if the injunction was refused. His Lordship was persuaded by
the evidence that, if the order was not made, the children and the
families concerned or potentially concerned in their care were likely to
be the focus of attention, pressure and harassment of a far higher
profile and more intense degree than would otherwise be the case.

29.102　　● In *A Council v M (Judgment 3: Reporting Restrictions)*,[167] a mother
(M) had adopted three children (A, B and C) from different countries.

---

[166] At [71].
[167] [2012] EWHC 2038 (Fam).

M purchased donor sperm and made A impregnate herself in order that she might have a child which M could bring up as her own. A became pregnant and miscarried at the age of 14. She became pregnant at the age of 16 and gave birth to a baby boy. M's behaviour in hospital caused serious concern to the midwives who alerted social services. Care proceedings were commenced. At the time of the care proceedings there were criminal proceedings pending relating to child cruelty and abuse. B was still residing with M but C was in long-term foster care, as were A and her son, D. This judgment concerned the reporting restrictions in respect of the criminal proceedings. Peter Jackson J considered the decision in *Re S*,[168] which he said was authority that it will be "highly exceptional, though not beyond contemplation" for the art.8 rights of individuals to prevail over the art.10 rights of the public so as to restrict the reporting of criminal proceedings. He said[169]:

> "The resolution of this conflict of legitimate interests can only be achieved by close attention to the circumstances that actually exist in the individual case. As Sir Mark Potter has said,[170] the approach must be hard-headed and even, from the point of view of this jurisdiction, hard-hearted. Rights arising under Art. 8 on the one hand and Art. 10 on the other are different in quality. Art. 8 rights are by their nature of crucial importance to a few, while Art. 10 rights are typically of general importance to many. The decided cases, together with s.12(4) HRA, act as a strong reminder that the rights of the many should not be undervalued and incrementally eroded in response to a series of hard cases of individual misfortune. On the other hand, there is no hierarchy of rights in this context and there are cases where individual rights must prevail. In highly exceptional cases this can even include making inroads into the fundamental right to report criminal proceedings, but only where that is absolutely necessary."

On the evidence before him, Jackson J found that the children were highly vulnerable to exploitation and that their identification would "at best be harmful and at worst disastrous" to them. The reporting restrictions sought, by contrast, were not absolute. Accordingly, he ordered that in reporting the care proceedings and the criminal proceedings, nothing should be published which might compromise the identity of the children. The order would last until D was 18 years old.

- In *Z v News Group Newspapers Ltd.*[171] a mother of eight was on trial   **29.103**
  in the Crown Court for serious benefit fraud arising from claims she had made in relation to the children's supposed multiple complex disabilities and needs. An order for reporting restrictions had been made earlier in the criminal proceedings under s.39 of the Children

---

[168] fn.159, above.
[169] At [82]–[84].
[170] *A Local Authority v W* [2005] EWHC 1564 (Fam) at [72].
[171] [2013] EWHC 1150 and 1371 (Fam).

and Young Persons Act 1933, but News Group Newspapers Ltd ("NGN") had successfully challenged this on the basis that s.39 applied only to children "concerned in" the proceedings and, in this case, whilst the children's medical and other conditions would be the subject of lengthy and detailed analysis in the course of the proceedings, they were not within the scope of the Act. The father of the five younger children then applied to the High Court for an injunction to preserve their anonymity. In determining the application, Cobb J noted that the inherent jurisdiction enabled the court to conduct the exercise of balancing the competing ECHR rights under arts 8 and 10. He considered *Re S*, s.12(4) of the Human Rights Act 1998 and earlier case law. He said he bore in mind the importance to democratic society of reporting such trials; the need to guard against the "instinctive desire to extend a protective wing to shield the children of parents who are accused of criminal activity"; that press freedom should only be displaced in exceptional circumstances; and that the burden of proof lay with the applicant. Cobb J found that the balance of the arguments was "exquisitely finely poised" but that the applicant had discharged the heavy burden of proof required for the making of the reporting restriction. He gave four specific reasons for imposing the restriction;

- The central role of the children in the case, which would involve "constant" references to their private lives and upbringing.
- The trial was about to focus on detailed examination of the children's medical records which would constitute a serious intrusion into their private lives and was therefore a powerful art.8 consideration.
- When considering the art.8 rights of the children the court must have regard to their "unusual stated vulnerabilities".
- In terms of proportionality: (i) the order would be a considerable interference with art.10, (ii) while there was a "hierarchy" amongst the children in respect of the need for protection, it was necessary and proportionate to protect the art.8 rights of the most vulnerable to preclude the identification of all the family, and (iii) the balancing exercise he had conducted pertained to the particular point reached in the criminal trial.

Cobb J then considered the impact that a conviction might have upon the balancing exercise he had conducted, observing that in such circumstances there should probably not be "reporting restraint". He therefore invited further representations at the point at which the trial judge started summing up, so that he could make a further decision in time for the verdict. When the matter was restored, no party sought a variation of the order if the mother were to be acquitted, but NGN sought a variation in the event of conviction. Cobb J gave a short judgment focusing on whether or not art.10 should prevail in such circumstances. His Lordship reminded himself of the need to guard against an assumption that reporting would be "sensational" and of the duty on the media (of which they hardly needed reminding) to maintain the highest professional standards. Whilst regretting that the consequence of naming the defendant would identify the children, who were wholly innocent, he concluded that the "marginal re-weighting of factors in the event of a conviction would tilt the balance in favour of freedom of expression". However, while the balance had tipped in favour of allowing reporting, the art.8 rights of the children were not eradicated, and so Cobb J varied the order so as to ban the publication of photographs and the forenames of the children and their father, and information about the children's medical conditions or disabilities. He concluded by noting that, in the event of a conviction leading to the variation of the reporting restriction, the "misery, shame and disadvantage" caused to the children would be the mother's sole responsibility as it was "the inevitable cause of her offending".

HH Judge Denyer QC has commented that, in the light of previous authority emphasising the importance of the general principle of open justice and the need for exceptional circumstances before it is departed from, Cobb J's decision to grant an injunction in this case "comes as a bit of a surprise"[172]:

> "Of course, cases turn on their own facts. Given the particular circumstances and that the health of the children was a central issue, there is some force in the argument that the position was analogous to that dealt with by s.39. In other words, it may truly be regarded as 'exceptional'. It is to be hoped that it is not perceived as a green light for the more general granting of injunctions restraining press freedom."

It is certainly to be hoped that injunctions of this sort continue to be granted only where exceptional circumstances give rise to a pressing need to protect art.8 rights. But the carefully reasoned decision of Cobb J in *Z v News Group Newspapers Ltd* seems to us to fall the right side of a line that is inevitably very difficult to draw in practice.

- Finally, in *Waltham Forest LBC v AD*[173] it was alleged that the father   **29.104** of a three-year-old girl (E) had stabbed E's mother to death in E's presence. E was placed in foster care. At the father's trial for murder, the local authority sought an order under s.39 of the Children and Young Persons Act 1933, but that was refused as E did not come within the scope of the section. The local authority then applied to the High Court for a reporting restriction order. It argued that identifying E as the child involved in the case would thwart the therapeutic process in which she was engaged; any coverage on the internet would

---

[172] *Restrictions on reporting the name of a defendant*, *Archbold News*, Issue 8, September 11, 2013, pp.3–5.
[173] [2014] EWHC 1985 (Fam).

be there for the rest of her life, and if she or someone she knew were to come across her name in relation to her mother's death, that would undo the benefits of the therapy. Keehan J refused the application. He said the question was whether there was sufficient evidence of harm to E if she was named, which, when balanced against the media's rights to freedom of expression under art.10 ECHR, made it an absolute necessity to make the order. E faced a very difficult future, emotionally and psychologically. There was a possibility that if she was named in the media, particularly on the internet, she could come across such coverage in future, or other people could come across it and mention it to her, and it could distress her. However, there was no clear or cogent evidence that that risk would either thwart her therapy or undo its benefits. The potential risks of further harm to E were speculative. Even if that was wrong, the risks of further harm did not overcome the high hurdle required for the granting of an order. If the court was solely concerned with E's best interests, it could be that it would want to take the course of least harm to her and make an order. However, it had to balance E's art.8 rights with the media's art.10 rights. The risks to E were not so clear or compelling that they justified placing a restriction on the media in the manner in which they reported the father's trial. The naming of E had to be left to the good sense and professionalism of the media. Keehan J added that local authorities should give very careful thought to alternative means of achieving their aim in cases such as these, e.g. by writing to the media, inviting them not to name the child in connection with a particular story and setting out clearly the reasons in support of the request. That course should be considered before an application for a reporting restriction order is launched.

Applying for a High Court order

29.105 Applications for an order under the High Court's inherent jurisdiction should be made to the Family Division following the procedure set out in *Practice Direction 12I—Applications for Reporting Restriction Orders*, which can be found on the HMCTS website.[174] *Practice Direction 12I* also states that applicants should follow the Practice Note issued on March 18, 2005, by the Official Solicitor and the Deputy Director of Legal Services, CAF-CASS.[175]

---

[174] *http://www.justice.gov.uk/courts/procedure-rules/family/practice_directions/pd_part_12i* [Accessed April 30, 2016].
[175] [2005] 2 F.L.R. 120. The text of the Practice Note is available at *http://www.medialawyer-.press.net/courtapplications/practicenote.jsp* [Accessed April 30, 2016].

Interests of the media

Practice Direction 121 states that s.12(2) of the Human Rights Act 1998   **29.106**
means that an injunction restricting the exercise of the right to freedom of
expression must not be granted where the person against whom the
application is made is neither present nor represented unless the court is
satisfied (a) that the applicant has taken all practicable steps to notify the
respondent, or (b) that there are compelling reasons why the respondent
should not be notified. It states that the norm as regards service of
applications for reporting restriction orders on the national media is to use
the Press Association's CopyDirect service, to which national newspapers
and broadcasters subscribe as a means of receiving notice of such applications. The Practice Direction also states that the court will bear in mind that
legal advisers to the media are used to participating in hearings at very short
notice where necessary, and are able to differentiate between information
provided for legal purposes and information for editorial use. Nonetheless, it
is clear that the Family Division will be exceedingly slow to grant an order
against the media unless there has been an opportunity for proper argument.
In *Waltham Forest LBC v AD*,[176] Keehan J said that local authorities or
others applying for reporting restriction orders must give "proper and
adequate notice" to the media. In that case the media had been given just a
few hours' notice, which was "wholly unacceptable".

Can the Crown Court make an order under the inherent jurisdiction?

The Crown Court is a creature of statute and so has no inherent jurisdiction   **29.107**
of its own to make an order protecting a child's identity. However, under
s.45(4) of the Senior Courts Act 1981, the Crown Court has the powers of the
High Court in relation to all matters "incidental to its jurisdiction". Might
this provision operate to confer on the Crown Court the inherent jurisdiction
of the High Court in relation to proceedings before it, so enabling it to
prohibit the publication of information in order to protect the art.8 rights of
children not "concerned in" those proceedings? The point arose for decision
in *R. v Croydon Crown Court Ex p. Trinity Mirror Plc*,[177] where the Crown
Court purported to make an order restraining the media from identifying the
defendant and his convictions for offences of child pornography in order to
protect the interests of his children, who were neither victims of the offences
nor witnesses at the trial. The Court of Appeal held that for the purposes of
s.45(4) matters are "incidental to" the jurisdiction of the Crown Court only
when the powers to be exercised relate to the proper dispatch of the business
before the Court. The order in this case was not incidental to the defendant's
trial, conviction and sentence, and the Crown Court therefore lacked

---

[176] [2014] EWHC 1985 (Fam), at [26].
[177] [2008] EWCA Crim 50.

jurisdiction to make it. The power of the Crown Court to order the anonymity of a defendant is limited to the circumstances noted in paras 29.44 and following, above.

LIFETIME REPORTING RESTRICTIONS RELATING TO WITNESSES AND VICTIMS UNDER 18

29.108   With effect from April 13, 2015, the Criminal Justice and Courts Act 2015 s.78, inserted into the Youth Justice and Criminal Evidence Act 1999 a new s.45A, which makes provision in respect of lifetime reporting restrictions for witnesses and victims under the age of 18 involved in criminal proceedings or proceedings before a service court. The new power is additional to the power under s.45 of the Act to impose reporting restrictions relating to under-18s in criminal proceedings.

29.109   Under the new provision the court may, at any time during criminal proceedings, and provided the statutory test is met, make a "reporting direction".[178] Such a direction can apply to:

- a witness other than an accused in the proceedings, and/or
- a victim, i.e. a person against whom the offence, which is the subject of the criminal proceedings, is alleged to have been committed.[179]

A reporting direction applies for the lifetime of the witness or victim, so that no matter relating to them may be included in any publication if it is likely to lead to them being identified by members of the public as being concerned in the criminal proceedings. Such matters or information might include, e.g. the name of the witness or victim, their address, the identity of their school, educational establishment or place of work, or any still or moving picture.[180] For the meaning of "likely to lead" in this context, see para.29.19, above.

29.110   A court may make a reporting direction under s.45A if it is satisfied that fear or distress on the part of the witness or victim in connection with being identified by members of the public as a person concerned in the proceedings is likely to diminish the quality of their evidence or the level of co-operation they give to any party to the proceedings in connection with that party's presentation of its case.[181] This is similar to the test for making a reporting restrictions direction in respect of an adult witness set out in s.46 of the Act, discussed in paras 29.123 and following, below. When considering this test, the court must in particular take into account:

- the nature and alleged circumstances of the offence to which the proceedings relate;
- the age of the witness or victim;

---

[178] 1999 Act s.45A(2).
[179] 1999 Act s.45A(3).
[180] 1999 Act s.45A(4).
[181] 1999 Act s.45A(5).

- the social and cultural background and ethnic origins of the witness or victim if they appear relevant to the court;
- the domestic, educational and employment circumstances of the witness or victim if they appear relevant to the court;
- any religious beliefs or political opinions of the witness or victim if they appear relevant to the court;
- any behaviour towards the witness or victim on the part of an accused, members of the family or associates of an accused, or any other person who is likely to be an accused or witness in the proceedings; and
- any views expressed by the witness or victim or, where they are under the age of 16, by an "appropriate person" (who cannot be the accused). An appropriate person may be the parent or guardian of the witness or victim, i.e. someone with parental responsibility for them. If the witness or victim is under 16 and is looked after by a local authority, the appropriate person may be a representative of that authority or a parent or guardian with whom the witness or victim is allowed to live.[182]

The court must also have regard to the welfare of the witness or victim, whether it would be in the interest of justice to make the reporting direction and the public interest in avoiding the imposition of a substantial and unreasonable restriction on the reporting of proceedings.

The court or appellate court may make an "excepting direction" dispens- **29.111** ing, to any extent specified, with the restrictions imposed by a reporting direction, if is satisfied that it is necessary in the interests of justice to make the excepting direction or that the effect of the reporting direction is to impose a substantial and unreasonable restriction on the reporting of the proceedings and it is in the public interest to remove or relax the restriction[183] In determining whether to make an excepting direction the court must have regard to the welfare of the victim or witness.[184] The excepting direction may be given at the time the reporting direction is given or subsequently and the excepting direction may be varied or revoked by the court or an appellate court.[185] No excepting direction can be given by reason only of the fact that the proceedings have been determined in any way or abandoned.

When considering the "public interest" for the purposes of s.45A, the **29.112** court must have regard, in particular, to the following matters, so far as relevant: the interest in the open reporting of crime, the interest in the open reporting of matters relating to human health or safety, the interest in the prevention and exposure of miscarriages of justice, the welfare of the victim or witness, and any views expressed by the witness or victim or, if the witness

---

[182] 1999 Act s.45A(6), (7).
[183] 1999 Act s.45A(10), (11).
[184] 1999 Act s.45A(13).
[185] 1999 Act s.45A(14).

or victim is under 16, by the appropriate person on their behalf, so long as that person is not the accused.[186]

29.113   Section 45A provides:

"45A. (1) This section applies in relation to—
(a) any criminal proceedings in any court (other than a service court) in England and Wales, and
(b) any proceedings (whether in the United Kingdom or elsewhere) in any service court.

(2) The court may make a direction ('a reporting direction') that no matter relating to a person mentioned in subsection (3) shall during that person's lifetime be included in any publication if it is likely to lead members of the public to identify that person as being concerned in the proceedings.

(3) A reporting direction may be made only in respect of a person who is under the age of 18 when the proceedings commence and who is—
(a) a witness, other than an accused, in the proceedings;
(b) a person against whom the offence, which is the subject of the proceedings, is alleged to have been committed.

(4) For the purposes of subsection (2), matters relating to a person in respect of whom the reporting direction is made include—
(a) the person's name,
(b) the person's address,
(c) the identity of any school or other educational establishment attended by the person,
(d) the identity of any place of work of the person, and
(e) any still or moving picture of the person.

(5) The court may make a reporting direction in respect of a person only if it is satisfied that—
(a) the quality of any evidence given by the person, or
(b) the level of co-operation given by the person to any party to the proceedings in connection with that party's preparation of its case,
is likely to be diminished by reason of fear or distress on the part of the person in connection with being identified by members of the public as a person concerned in the proceedings.

(6) In determining whether subsection (5) is satisfied, the court must in particular take into account—
(a) the nature and alleged circumstances of the offence to which the proceedings relate;
(b) the age of the person;
(c) such of the following as appear to the court to be relevant—
(i) the social and cultural background and ethnic origins of the person,
(ii) the domestic, educational and employment circumstances of the person, and
(iii) any religious beliefs or political opinions of the person;
(d) any behaviour towards the person on the part of—
(i) an accused,
(ii) members of the family or associates of an accused, or
(iii) any other person who is likely to be an accused or a witness in the proceedings.

---

[186] 1999 Act s.52.

(7) In determining that question the court must in addition consider any views expressed—

(a) by the person in respect of whom the reporting restriction may be made, and

(b) where that person is under the age of 16, by an appropriate person other than an accused.

(8) In determining whether to make a reporting direction in respect of a person, the court must have regard to—

(a) the welfare of that person,

(b) whether it would be in the interests of justice to make the direction, and

(c) the public interest in avoiding the imposition of a substantial and unreasonable restriction on the reporting of the proceedings.

(9) A reporting direction may be revoked by the court or an appellate court.

(10) The court or an appellate court may by direction ("an excepting direction") dispense, to any extent specified in the excepting direction, with the restrictions imposed by a reporting direction.

(11) The court or an appellate court may only make an excepting direction if—

(a) it is satisfied that it is necessary in the interests of justice to do so, or

(b) it is satisfied that—

(i) the effect of the reporting direction is to impose a substantial and unreasonable restriction on the reporting of the proceedings, and

(ii) it is in the public interest to remove or relax that restriction.

(12) No excepting direction shall be given under subsection (11)(b) by reason only of the fact that the proceedings have been determined in any way or have been abandoned.

(13) In determining whether to make an excepting direction in respect of a person, the court or the appellate court must have regard to the welfare of that person.

(14) An excepting direction—

(a) may be given at the time the reporting direction is given or subsequently, and

(b) may be varied or revoked by the court or an appellate court.

(15) For the purposes of this section—

(a) criminal proceedings in a court other than a service court commence when proceedings are instituted for the purposes of Part 1 of the Prosecution of Offences Act 1985, in accordance with section 15(2) of that Act;

(b) proceedings in a service court commence when the charge is brought under section 122 of the Armed Forces Act 2006.

(16) In this section—

(a) 'appellate court', in relation to any proceedings in a court, means a court dealing with an appeal (including an appeal by way of case stated) arising out of the proceedings or with any further appeal;

(b) 'appropriate person' has the same meaning as in section 50;

(c) references to the quality of evidence given by a person are to its quality in terms of completeness, coherence and accuracy (and for this purpose 'coherence' refers to a person's ability in giving evidence to give answers which address the questions put to the person and can be understood both individually and collectively);

(d) references to the preparation of the case of a party to any proceedings include, where the party is the prosecution, the carrying out of investigations into any offence at any time charged in the proceedings."

29.114   For the purposes of s.45A, a "publication" includes any speech, writing, programme included in a programme service or other communication in whatever form, which is addressed to the public at large or any section of it, but does not include an indictment or other document prepared for use in particular legal proceedings.[187] The reference to "any . . . other communication in whatever form" means that s.45A is effective to restrict publication not only in print or broadcast media but also online, e.g. on social media sites or micro-blogging sites such as Twitter.

29.115   For modifications of s.45A in relation to the Court Martial, the Service Civilian Court and the Court Martial Appeal Court, see the Youth Justice and Criminal Evidence Act 1999 (Application to Service Courts) Order 2009.[188]

Offence to contravene a direction under s.45A

29.116   It is a summary offence under s.49 of the 1999 Act to publish in contravention of a direction made under s.45A. The maximum penalty was until recently a fine not exceeding level 5 on the standard scale (i.e. £5,000).[189] The effect of s.85 of the Legal Aid, Sentencing and Punishment of Offenders Act 2012 is that, from March 12, 2015, the maximum is a fine of any amount. Fines will, however, continue to be set according to the seriousness of the offence and the means of the offender.

29.117   Where the direction was made by a service court, the s.49 offence may be committed in England and Wales, Scotland and Northern Ireland; otherwise, it may be committed only in England and Wales.[190] Where the publication is in a newspaper or periodical, the offence is committed by the proprietor, the editor and the publisher. Where it is in a programme included in a programme service within the meaning of the Broadcasting Act 1990, e.g. on TV or the radio, it is committed by the body corporate providing the service and by any person having functions in relation to the programme corresponding to those of a newspaper editor. In the case of any other publication, the offence is committed by the person publishing it. Where a s.49 offence committed by a body corporate is proved to have been committed with the consent or connivance of, or to be attributable to any neglect on the part of, an officer of the body, the officer is also guilty of the offence and may be prosecuted and punished accordingly.[191] Proceedings under s.49 may not be instituted in England and Wales otherwise than by or with the consent of the

[187] 1999 Act s.63(1).
[188] SI 2009/2083, as amended. See also the Court Martial and Service Civilian Court (Youth Justice and Criminal Evidence Act 1999) Rules 2009. (SI 2009/2100)
[189] 1999 Act s.49.
[190] 1999 Act s.49(1A).
[191] 1999 Act s.51. For offences by companies, see *Chargot (t/a Contract Services)* [2008] UKHL 73, discussed at para.8.43, above.

Attorney General, or in Northern Ireland otherwise than by or with the consent of the Attorney General for Northern Ireland.[192]

Schedule 2A to the 1999 Act[193] transposes parts of the EU's E-Commerce **29.118** Directive dealing with breaches of domestic law (in this case, breach of lifetime reporting directions made under s.45A), by providers of "information society services", which include social media and search engines. In summary, the new Schedule:

- makes a provider established in England and Wales, Scotland or Northern Ireland liable to prosecution under s.49 of the 1999 Act for breaching a lifetime reporting direction in respect of a matter published in an EEA state other than the UK, and permits the proceedings to be brought, in the case of a direction made by a service court, in England and Wales, Scotland or Northern Ireland, and in the case of a direction made by any other court, in England and Wales.

- provides that proceedings under s.49 for breach of a lifetime reporting direction cannot be taken against a service provider established in an EEA state other than the UK in respect of anything done in the course of providing information society services, unless the proceedings are necessary for the pursuit of public policy, they relate to an information society service that prejudices or presents a serious and grave risk of prejudice to the pursuit of public policy, and the institution of proceedings is proportionate to the pursuit of public policy.

- provides that a service provider is not guilty of an offence under s.49 in relation to the breach of a lifetime reporting direction if at the relevant time it was acting as a mere "conduit" or providing "caching" or "hosting" services, and certain specified conditions are met.

It is a defence for a person charged under s.49 with contravening a **29.119** direction made under s.45A to prove that he was not aware, and neither suspected nor had any reason to suspect, that the publication included the restricted matter.[194] It is also a defence to prove that the person in relation to whom the direction was given had given written consent to publication.[195] Written consent cannot be effective for this purpose if given when the person is under 18 years of age or if it is proved that anyone interfered with their peace or comfort with that of the appropriate person with the intent of obtaining it.[196]

[192] 1999 Act s.49(2).
[193] Inserted by the Criminal Justice and Courts Act 2015 s.80 and Sch.15, with effect from April 13, 2015.
[194] 1999 Act s.50(1).
[195] 1999 Act s.50(6A).
[196] 1999 Act s.50(6B), (8).

Representations by the media

29.120   The comments at para.29.80, above, apply equally to reporting directions under s.45A.[197]

Framing of a direction under s.45A

29.121   The guidance *Reporting Restrictions in the Criminal Courts*, referred to in para.29.83, above, states in para 4.1:

> "Any reporting restriction imposes potential criminal liability on media organisations, journalists or editors who breach it. If a breach occurs, media organisations and their employees may face unlimited fines. For these reasons, it is essential that any reporting restriction should be reduced to writing as soon as possible, clear and precise in its terms and drawn up as a court order as soon as practicable. Once orders have been made, they should be drawn to the attention of the media by being shown on the court list and on the door of the court and wherever possible sent to relevant local and/or national media organisations. Court staff should respond positively to media organisations' requests for assistance in relation to the existence or terms of reporting restriction orders."

How can the making, variation or revocation of a direction under s.45A be challenged?

29.122   See the discussion at para.29.86, above.

REPORTING RESTRICTIONS RELATING TO ADULT WITNESSES

29.123   Section 46 of the Youth Justice and Criminal Evidence Act 1999 empowers the court in any criminal proceedings to make a direction, on the application of any party to the proceedings, restricting reporting about eligible adult witnesses (other than the accused). For this purpose a reporting direction in relation to a witness is a direction that no matter relating to the witness shall during the witness's lifetime be included in a publication if it is likely to lead members of the public to identify him as being a witness in the proceedings. The matters in relation to which the restrictions imposed by a reporting direction apply include in particular the witness's name, address, educational establishment, place of work and any still or moving picture of the witness, if their inclusion in a publication is likely to lead to the witness's identification. For the meaning of "likely to lead" in this context, see para.29.19, above. A reporting direction under s.46 may also restrict the identification of children where this is likely to lead to the identification of the adult in question, provided the eligibility requirements for a direction are met.[198]

---

[197] See the guidance published by the Judicial College, para.4.1. The guidance is available at *https://www.judiciary.gov.uk/publications/reporting-restrictions-in-the-criminal-courts/*   [Accessed April 30, 2016].

[198] *ITN News* [2013] EWCA Crim 773 at [29].

An adult witness is eligible for protection by a reporting direction under   **29.124**
s.46 if the court is satisfied that the quality of their evidence or the level of
their co-operation with any party to the proceedings in that party's preparation of their case is likely to be diminished by reason of the witness's fear or
distress in connection with being publicly identified as a witness in the
proceedings. The applicant for a reporting direction must explain why the
direction would improve the quality of the witness' evidence or level of
co-operation.[199] Quality of evidence relates to its quality in terms of
completeness, coherence and accuracy. In determining a witness's eligibility
for this purpose, the court must take into account in particular the nature
and alleged circumstances of the offence; the age of the witness; the witness's
social and cultural background and ethnic origins, domestic and employment
circumstances and religious beliefs or political opinions (if these appear
relevant); any behaviour towards the witness by the accused or his family or
associates; and any views expressed by the witness.[200] The court must also
consider whether the making of a reporting direction would be in the
interests of justice and the public interest in avoiding the imposition of a
substantial and unreasonable restriction on the reporting of proceedings.[201]
The fact that a special measures direction has been made under the 1999 Act
does not of itself justify the making of a reporting direction under s.46, and
a reporting direction should not automatically follow the making of such an
order.[202] Section 46 provides a distinct power which may be exercised
alongside a special measures direction, but also separately from it.

The court or an appellate court may at any time make an "excepting   **29.125**
direction" dispensing with the restrictions imposed by a reporting direction
under s.46 if satisfied either that it is in the interests of justice to do so or that
the restrictions impose a substantial and unreasonable restriction on the
reporting of the proceedings and that it is in the public interest to remove or
relax them.[203] The fact that the proceedings have been determined or
abandoned does not in itself provide sufficient reason to dispense with the
restrictions, though it may well be a relevant consideration.

When considering the "public interest" for the purposes of s.46, the court   **29.126**
must have regard, in particular, to the following matters, so far as relevant:
the interest in the open reporting of crime, the interest in the open reporting
of matters relating to human health or safety, the interest in the prevention
and exposure of miscarriages of justice, the welfare of the witness, and any
views expressed by the witness or, if the witness is under 16, by the
appropriate person on their behalf, so long as that person is not the
accused.[204]

---

[199] Criminal Procedure Rules 2015 r.6.4(3)(e).
[200] 1999 Act s.46(4), (5).
[201] 1999 Act s.46(8).
[202] *ITN News* [2013] EWCA Crim 773 at [29].
[203] 1999 Act s.46(9).
[204] 1999 Act s.52.

29.127   In *ITN News*,[205] the Court of Appeal rejected a submission that s.46 applies only in those cases where the witness is anonymous. It said that in the overwhelming majority of cases the "identity" of every witness is known, so limiting the application of s.46 in that way would confine it to very rare cases. However, anonymity is an entirely distinct and extreme form of special measure for which a separate statutory system is in place. Accordingly, under s.46(7), a still or moving picture of a witness may be prohibited if the "eligibility" test is satisfied, whether or not the name and identity of the witness is otherwise known. That conclusion was reinforced by analysis of the wide-ranging provision for an "excepting direction" in s.46(9), which showed that a reporting restriction could be much wider than the mere naming of the witness and could impose substantial restrictions that could be considered unreasonable from a public interest perspective.

29.128   Section 46 provides:

> "46(1) This section applies where—
>   (a) in any criminal proceedings in any court (other than a service court) in England and Wales or Northern Ireland, or
>   (b) in any proceedings (whether in the United Kingdom or elsewhere) in any service court,
> a party to the proceedings makes an application for the court to give a reporting direction in relation to a witness in the proceedings (other than the accused) who has attained the age of 18.
>   In this section "reporting direction" has the meaning given by subsection (6).
>   (2) If the court determines—
>   (a) that the witness is eligible for protection, and
>   (b) that giving a reporting direction in relation to the witness is likely to improve—
>   (i) the quality of evidence given by the witness, or
>   (ii) the level of co-operation given by the witness to any party to the proceedings in connection with that party's preparation of its case,
> the court may give a reporting direction in relation to the witness.
>   (3) For the purposes of this section a witness is eligible for protection if the court is satisfied—
>   (a) that the quality of evidence given by the witness, or
>   (b) the level of co-operation given by the witness to any party to the proceedings in connection with that party's preparation of its case,
> is likely to be diminished by reason of fear or distress on the part of the witness in connection with being identified by members of the public as a witness in the proceedings.
>   (4) In determining whether a witness is eligible for protection the court must take into account, in particular—
>   (a) the nature and alleged circumstances of the offence to which the proceedings relate;
>   (b) the age of the witness;
>   (c) such of the following matters as appear to the court to be relevant, namely—

---

[205] [2013] EWCA Crim 773.

    (i) the social and cultural background and ethnic origins of the witness,

    (ii) the domestic and employment circumstances of the witness, and

    (iii) any religious beliefs or political opinions of the witness;

(d) any behaviour towards the witness on the part of—

    (i) the accused,

    (ii) members of the family or associates of the accused, or

    (iii) any other person who is likely to be an accused or a witness in the proceedings.

(5) In determining that question the court must in addition consider any views expressed by the witness.

(6) For the purposes of this section a reporting direction in relation to a witness is a direction that no matter relating to the witness shall during the witness's lifetime be included in any publication if it is likely to lead members of the public to identify him as being a witness in the proceedings.

(7) The matters relating to a witness in relation to which the restrictions imposed by a reporting direction apply (if their inclusion in any publication is likely to have the result mentioned in subsection (6)) include in particular—

(a) the witness's name,

(b) the witness's address,

(c) the identity of any educational establishment attended by the witness,

(d) the identity of any place of work, and

(e) any still or moving picture of the witness.

(8) In determining whether to give a reporting direction the court shall consider—

(a) whether it would be in the interests of justice to do so, and

(b) the public interest in avoiding the imposition of a substantial and unreasonable restriction on the reporting of the proceedings.

(9) The court or an appellate court may by direction ("an excepting direction") dispense, to any extent specified in the excepting direction, with the restrictions imposed by a reporting direction if—

(a) it is satisfied that it is necessary in the interests of justice to do so, or

(b) it is satisfied—

    (i) that the effect of those restrictions is to impose a substantial and unreasonable restriction on the reporting of the proceedings, and

    (ii) that it is in the public interest to remove or relax that restriction;

but no excepting direction shall be given under paragraph (b) by reason only of the fact that the proceedings have been determined in any way or have been abandoned.

(10) A reporting direction may be revoked by the court or an appellate court.

(11) An excepting direction—

(a) may be given at the time the reporting direction is given or subsequently; and

(b) may be varied or revoked by the court or an appellate court.

(12) In this section—

(a) 'appellate court', in relation to any proceedings in a court, means a court dealing with an appeal (including an appeal by way of case stated) arising out of the proceedings or with any further appeal;

(b) references to the quality of a witness's evidence are to its quality in terms of completeness, coherence and accuracy (and for this purpose 'coherence' refers to a witness's ability in giving evidence to give answers which address the questions put to the witness and can be understood both individually and collectively);

(c) references to the preparation of the case of a party to any proceedings include, where the party is the prosecution, the carrying out of investigations into any offence at any time charged in the proceedings."

29.129   For modifications of s.45 in relation to the Court Martial, the Service Civilian Court and the Court Martial Appeal Court, see the Youth Justice and Criminal Evidence Act 1999 (Application to Service Courts) Order 2009.[206]

Offence to contravene a direction under s.46

29.130   It is a summary offence under s.49 of the 1999 Act to publish in contravention of a reporting direction made under s.46. The maximum penalty was until recently a fine not exceeding level 5 on the standard scale (i.e. £5,000).[207] The effect of s.85 of the Legal Aid, Sentencing and Punishment of Offenders Act 2012 is that, from March 12, 2015, the maximum is a fine of any amount. Fines will, however, continue to be set according to the seriousness of the offence and the means of the offender.

29.131   The offence may be committed in Scotland as well as in England, Wales and Northern Ireland.[208] Where the publication is in a newspaper or periodical, the offence is committed by the proprietor, the editor and the publisher. Where it is in a programme included in a programme service within the meaning of the Broadcasting Act 1990, e.g. on TV or the radio, it is committed by the body corporate or Scottish partnership providing the service and by any person having functions in relation to the programme corresponding to those of a newspaper editor. In the case of any other publication, the offence is committed by the person publishing it. Where a s.49 offence committed by a body corporate is proved to have been committed with the consent or connivance of, or to be attributable to any neglect on the part of, an officer of the body, the officer is also guilty of the offence and may be prosecuted and punished accordingly.[209] Proceedings under s.49 may not be instituted in England and Wales otherwise than by or with the consent of the Attorney General, or in Northern Ireland otherwise than by or with the consent of the Attorney General for Northern Ireland.[210]

29.132   By virtue of the Electronic Commerce (EC Directive) Regulations 2002,[211] which transpose the EU's E-Commerce Directive, a provider of "information society services", which include social media and search engines, is not liable for any criminal sanction by reason of acting as a mere "conduit" or

---

[206] SI 2009/2083, as amended. See also the Court Martial and Service Civilian Court (Youth Justice and Criminal Evidence Act 1999) Rules 2009 (SI 2009/2100).

[207] 1999 Act s.49.

[208] 1999 Act s.68(6).

[209] 1999 Act s.51. For offences by companies, see *Chargot (t/a Contract Services)* [2008] UKHL 73, discussed at para.8.43, above.

[210] 1999 Act s.49(2).

[211] SI 2002/2013, reg.17.

providing "caching" or "hosting" services, if certain specified conditions are met. The effect is that a provider of such services may not, in those circumstances, be convicted of breaching a reporting direction made under s.46.

It is a defence for a person charged under s.49 with breaching a reporting   29.133
direction under s.46 to prove that he was not aware, and neither suspected nor had any reason to suspect, that the publication included the restricted matter.[212] It is also a defence to prove that the witness or, if they are under 16, an appropriate person had given written consent to publication.[213] However, written consent is not a defence if it is proved that any person interfered with the peace or comfort of the witness, or the appropriate person, with intent to obtain it.[214]

Representations by the media

The comments at para.29.80, above, apply equally to reporting directions   29.134
under s.46.[215]

Framing of a reporting direction under s.46

The guidance *Reporting Restrictions in the Criminal Courts*, referred to in   29.135
para.29.83, above, states in para 4.1:

> "Any reporting restriction imposes potential criminal liability on media organisa-
> tions, journalists or editors who breach it. If a breach occurs, media organisa-
> tions and their employees may face unlimited fines. For these reasons, it is
> essential that any reporting restriction should be reduced to writing as soon as
> possible, clear and precise in its terms and drawn up as a court order as soon as
> practicable. Once orders have been made, they should be drawn to the attention
> of the media by being shown on the court list and on the door of the court and
> wherever possible sent to relevant local and/or national media organisations.
> Court staff should respond positively to media organisations' requests for
> assistance in relation to the existence or terms of reporting restriction orders."

How can the making, variation or revocation of a reporting direction under s.46 be challenged?

See the discussion at para.29.86, above. It was held in *ITN News*[216] that a   29.136
reporting direction under s.46 falls within the ambit of s.159(1)(c) of the

---

[212] 1999 Act s.50(1).
[213] 1999 Act s.50(7)–(14).
[214] 1999 Act s.50(8).
[215] See the guidance published by the Judicial College, para.4.1. The guidance is available at *https://www.judiciary.gov.uk/publications/reporting-restrictions-in-the-criminal-courts/* [Accessed April 30, 2016].
[216] *ITN News* [2013] EWCA Crim 773 at [29].

Criminal Justice Act 1988, even when the restriction is confined to photographs or film, and as such the media may, with leave, appeal against such a direction to the Court of Appeal. In the event of an appeal against conviction or sentence (or indeed a Reference by the Attorney General), then, in accordance with s.46(12), the jurisdiction of the Court of Appeal to revoke any reporting or excepting direction is immediately engaged.

CHAPTER 30

HISTORIC CASES

Introduction.................................... 30.01
Historic Sexual Abuse where the
    Defendant was or may have been
    Aged between 10 and 14 at the
    Relevant Time 30.12
The Indictment 30.15
Continuing Course of Conduct 30.18
Disclosure 30.24

Abuse of Process............................ 30.26
Previous Police Investigations and
    Promises not to Prosecute............ 30.66
Directions 30.83
"Late" Complaint...........................30.102
Sentencing.....................................30.109
The Approach to Sentencing
    Historic Sexual Offence................30.110

INTRODUCTION

Today, well into the second decade of the twenty-first century, far more **30.01**
prosecutions of sexual offending are being brought than ever before relating
to events that occurred years ago.[1] Some involve incidents that are alleged to
have taken place several decades ago.[2] These have been described as
"historic" sex cases. Our use of that descriptor (rather than an alternative
such as "non-recent") is not intended in any way to detract from the
seriousness of the cases and the continuing nature of their impact, or the

---

[1] See the Joint Statistical Bulletin published by the Ministry of Justice, the Home Office and
the Office of National Statistics, *An Overview of Sexual Offending in England and Wales*, January
10, 2013, which is available at *https://www.gov.uk/government/publications/an-overview-of-sexual-
offending-in-england-and-wales* [Accessed April 30, 2016]. For current trends see Crime Survey
for England and Wales (CSEW). Crime in England and Wales, Year Ending March 2015
(ONS.).
[2] For a recent example see *R. v PS* [2013] EWCA Crim 992, where the allegations related to
events that had occurred 34 years before. See also *R. v RD* [2013] EWCA Crim 1592, where the
Court of Appeal upheld convictions where the time span in respect of the allegations by four
female complainants ranged from 39 to 63 years ago, and *Taylor* [2013] EWCA Crim 2398 where
the Court of Appeal upheld convictions in relation to allegations that the appellant had acted
as a sexual predator 33 years ago.

need to investigate and prosecute them. In respect of historic cases, whilst many complainants may take matters to their grave without revealing abuse they endured when they were young, in the wake of high profile investigations such as Operation Yewtree[3] there is evidence of greater disclosure. Whilst this is a complex subject and over-simplification should be avoided, it is clear that there are a number of reasons for these developments:

    (i) an ever increasing awareness of the depth of psychological harm caused by sexual abuse and its continuing nature, which has been matched by an increase in sentence lengths;

    (ii) an increase in reporting against the background of a change in social attitudes, reflecting a more sympathetic environment with a greater understanding of the scale of historic abuse and the reasons for late reporting;

    (iii) Parliament's removal in 1994 of the common law requirement of corroboration of the evidence of the complainant of a sexual offence,[4] so that defendants on trial in respect of pre-1994 matters can no longer rely on the absence of corroboration in order to defeat the allegations[5];

    (iv) the timely ending in *R. v R*[6] of the anachronism that a woman could not in law refuse sexual intercourse with her husband, following which there has been a steady increase of prosecutions where the parties were or had been in a spousal relationship;

    (v) a change in prosecution policy whereby the focus is upon the alleged offending rather than the credibility of the complainant.

The response of the courts

30.02   The law governing the trial of historic sexual offending has developed in a haphazard way, with different constitutions of the Court of Appeal adopting different approaches to both applications to stay for abuse of process on grounds of delay, and sentencing. This left judges and counsel to undertake these trials against the background of contradictory guidance. The period since our 4th edition in December 2010 has seen welcome intervention in both these areas by the Court of Appeal, with a powerful lead being given by the last Lord Chief Justice.

---

[3] The police investigation into sexual abuse allegations, predominantly the abuse of children, against British media personality Jimmy Savile (who died in 2011) and others: see the joint Metropolitan Police Service and NSPCC report *Giving victims a voice* (January 2013), available at *https://www.nspcc.org.uk/news-and-views/our-news/child-protection-news/13-01-11-yewtree-report/yewtree-report-pdf_wdf93652.pdf* [Accessed April 30, 2016].

[4] Criminal Justice and Public Order Act 1994 ss.32(1)(b), 33: see para.30.106, below.

[5] *R. v B* [2003] 2 Cr. App. R. 13.

[6] [1992] 1 A.C. 599.

First, the five-judge Court of Appeal in *R. v F(S)*[7] gave clear guidance as   30.03
to the approach to be taken to an application for a stay due to delay. This
guidance included assistance as to the appropriate time for such an application, a series of propositions to be followed in determining such applications,
and positive discouragement to the courts from trawling through old Court
of Appeal authorities when hearing them.

Secondly, the Court of Appeal revisited the sentencing of historic cases in   30.04
R. v H(J).[8] Until that case, in which the then Lord Chief Justice set out the
principles underpinning the correct approach, the courts had faced various
difficulties when it came to sentencing such cases. In some, the statutory
maximum had been increased since the time of the offence. The 2003 Act also
introduced some very broad changes in the statutory identification of
different forms of sexual crime. In respect of many sexual offences, the
Sentencing Guidance Council's Definitive Guideline[9] suggested higher sentences than would have been awarded in the past. In *Millberry*[10] Lord Woolf
CJ had stated that the same starting points should apply to historic cases as
to other cases.

In *R. v H(J)*, the Lord Judge CJ identified two critical issues on which   30.05
conflicting approaches by the Court of Appeal in its past decisions on
sentencing were discernible and upon which specific guidance was
required:

    (i) the extent, if any, to which the court passing sentence should reflect
        the levels of sentence which were likely to have been imposed if the
        defendant had been convicted at a trial shortly after the offences
        were committed; and

    (ii) the extent to which events during the long period between the
        commission of the crime and the sentencing decision may be rele-
        vant.

He then set out the principles to be derived from statute,[11] the authorities   30.06
which purport to provide guidance, and fact-specific decisions. The Court
suggested that with the exception of *Millberry*, and the current sentencing
guideline (used in a measured way), reference to earlier decisions is unlikely
to be helpful and is to be discouraged. Sentencers should adopt the modern
approach[12] to be found in the current Sentencing Council guideline when
evaluating the gravity of historic cases, provided that any individual sentence

---

[7] [2011] EWCA Crim 1844, discussed in paras 30.30 and following, below.
[8] [2011] EWCA Crim 2753, discussed in paras 30.111 and following, below.
[9] Which, by reason if s.125 of the Coroners and Justice Act 2009, every court, when sentencing
an offender, was required to follow unless satisfied that to do so would be contrary to the
interests of justice. The guideline applies to the sentencing of offenders convicted of any sexual
offences covered by the guideline on or after May 14, 2007.
[10] [2003] 2 Cr. App. R.(S.) 31.
[11] [2011] EWCA Crim 2753 at [46]–[47].
[12] *Clifford* [2014] EWCA Crim 2245 at [40] per Treacy LJ.

reflects any lower maximum sentence applicable at the time.[13] Courts should not interpret "measured" as meaning that they should calculate a notional scale reflecting the maximum sentences at the time.[14] Sentencers are entitled to pass consecutive sentences so that the overall sentence reflects the gravity of the overall criminality.[15]

30.07   Notwithstanding the important guidance in *R. v H(J)*, judges frequently face difficult sentencing exercises in historic sex cases. There have been an increasing number of Attorney General's References in this area. In one of these, *Attorney General's Reference (No.38 of 2013) (R. v Stuart Hall)*,[16] the Court acknowledged that there are public concerns about sexual crimes against children and young victims which for very good reason have been heightened by our increasing understanding of the criminality involved and the serious consequences to the victims, however minor (in the legal sense) the offence may seem to be. Greater awareness of this harm underpins the higher sentences set out in the guidelines issued by the Sentencing Council with effect from April 1, 2014.

No limitation period

30.08   In contrast with the position at civil law, there is no limitation period to prevent the prosecution of stale offences that are alleged to have taken place many years before. It is not appropriate to conclude that a fair trial is no longer possible simply because of passage of time. In *R. v RD*[17] a conviction was upheld even though the earliest allegation related to events in 1949 as many as 63 years earlier. It is not unknown for defendants in sexual cases to be in their eighties or to have reached their nineties[18].

30.09   Where specimens have been preserved, advances in forensic science have led to the prosecution of serious sexual and violent cases many years after the offences were committed. However, many historic sex cases involve recent

---

[13] Lyndon Harris and Dan Bunting, *Has the approach to sentencing historical offences changed?*, *Archbold Review*, Issue 4, May 11, 2015. The authors suggest that the use of the imprecise concept of "measured reference" has led the Court of Appeal subtly to change its approach over the years since *R. v H(J)*. Presently, the courts tend to focus more upon the equivalent modern offence and the applicable sentence (having applied the relevant sentencing guideline). They contend that this starting point will be the end point unless the sentence required under the current guideline could not lawfully have been passed (because of the maximum sentence which pertained at the time of the offence). The only "discount" upon the inflationary effect of the new guidelines is the limitation upon the sentencing process by adherence to the maximum sentence. This "limitation" is far more forceful where a defendant is charged with only one offence. They point out that CPS charging practice becomes highly relevant, as the court is entitled to re-structure the overall sentence using consecutive sentences with reductions for totality.
[14] *Attorney General's Reference (No.27 of 2015)* [2015] EWCA Crim 1538.
[15] *Clifford* [2014] EWCA Crim 2245.
[16] [2013] EWCA Crim 1450, for which see paras 30.127 and following, below.
[17] [2013] EWCA Crim 1592.
[18] *R. v AB* [2015] EWCA Crim 1042 (appellant aged 90).

disclosure by a mature adult of events that occurred in their childhood or youth.

Classically, historic cases will involve "late" reporting of abuse within the **30.10** "family" setting or by those who have been in care and, in particular, resident in care homes. Not only are these cases difficult to investigate,[19] they are also very demanding to prosecute, creating significant challenges to the criminal justice system. It is now well understood that children who have been abused within the family or whilst resident in institutions may not complain about the abuse until they confide in some adult outside the family with whom they have a close relationship or even well into adulthood. Judges are encouraged to direct juries in appropriate cases that "late" reporting does not necessarily mean that the allegation is false,[20] and there may be a variety of reasons, such as embarrassment, self-blame and fear of the calamitous fall-out that such a disclosure may cause, which may explain why a true complaint is disclosed "late".

Recognition of the phenomenon of "late" reporting needs to be counter- **30.11** balanced by the criminal justice system ensuring that defendants prosecuted for an historic allegation after a "late" report receive a fair trial. This natural tension has been recognised by Barlow and Newby[21]:

> "Whilst attitudes to and awareness of sexual abuse have significantly changed over the last decade, the 'conspiracy of silence' of family sexual abuse has been a long standing feature within the law, with many abusers maintaining dominance over their victims for years, 'secrets' being taken to the grave. But this position should not be used as a vehicle to deny those accused the fundamental right to a fair hearing. This is a difficult issue and the law struggles to maintain these two but conflicting needs of protecting the accused whilst bringing justice for the abused."

HISTORIC SEXUAL ABUSE WHERE THE DEFENDANT WAS OR MAY HAVE BEEN AGED BETWEEN 10 AND 14 AT THE RELEVANT TIME

Doli incapax

The rebuttable presumption at common law that a child of not less than 10 **30.12** but under 14 years of age was doli incapax (i.e. incapable of committing a crime) still applies to historic abuse cases relating to events that preceded the presumption's abolition on September 30, 1998.[22] The presumption was rebutted only if the prosecution proved beyond reasonable doubt, not only that the child caused the actus reus with the appropriate mens rea, but also

---

[19] cf. Home Affairs Select Committee, Fourth Report, *The Conduct of Investigations into Past Cases of Abuse in Children's Homes*, October 22, 2002 (criticism of trawling). See also *Mayberry* [2003] EWCA Crim 782.

[20] *Doody* [2008] EWCA Crim 2557.

[21] Mark Barlow and Mark Newby, *The Challenges of Historic Allegations of Past Sexual Abuse*, February 16, 2009.

[22] *Fethney* [2010] EWCA Crim 3096.

that he knew that the particular act was "seriously wrong" and not merely naughty or mischievous.

30.13   However, since the presumption is rebuttable by evidence that the child knew its actions were "seriously wrong", there may be features in the evidence which will lead the Court of Appeal to conclude, even in the absence of the appropriate direction, that there was no prospect that the jury would not have been convinced that the appellant had known his actions to be seriously wrong. *Bevan*[23] is a case where there was abundant evidence to rebut the presumption. The Court of Appeal was obliged to quash a conviction for rape alleged to have been committed by the appellant when he may have been aged under 14, thereby engaging the irrebuttable presumption of penetrative incapacity (for which see para.30.14, below). However, the Court of Appeal held that the other convictions, which did not involve penetrative activity, were safe. The evidence was that at no time during the relevant period was the appellant less than 12 years old. His own description of himself as a young teenager was that he was difficult to control, he was streetwise, he truanted from school, and he described himself at the ages of 13 and 14 as "a nasty piece of work". The complainant described how her attacker would threaten her with the consequences if she revealed what she was doing to her: "He would say that mum would get hurt if I said anything and no one would believe me." The activity only happened when both the complainant and the appellant were clothed, so that they could re-adjust themselves if they were interrupted. The appellant would use language towards the complainant about her mother such as "slag" and "whore". The nature of the acts was such as to be inconsistent with the mere sexual curiosity of an immature boy or a game.

Presumption that a boy under 14 was incapable of vaginal or anal intercourse

30.14   The anomalous common law presumption that a boy under the age of 14 was incapable of vaginal or anal intercourse was abolished by s.1 of the Sexual Offences Act 1993, which came into force on September 20, 1993. However, it was not abolished retrospectively. It follows that, whatever the circumstances, a defendant cannot be convicted of rape where the relevant events occurred before September 20, 1993, and at that time he was under 14.[24] However, in those circumstances evidence of penetration can be adduced and the case can be dealt with as an indecent assault.

---

[23] [2011] EWCA Crim 654.
[24] *Fethney* [2010] EWCA Crim 3096. See also *Claydon* [2006] 1 Cr. App. R. 20 (p.339), where a conviction for buggery was quashed on a retrospective basis because the appellant would have been under 14 at the time. See also *R. v C* [2005] EWCA Crim 2827.

THE INDICTMENT

Historic cases may well include allegations of sexual misconduct over a **30.15**
number of years. Sometimes the nature of the allegations will go through
phases, such as grooming, sexual assault and then rape. Sometimes there may
be several complainants, such as in the classic step-father case where the
misconduct starts with the onset of each complainant's puberty. Whilst the
indictment should properly reflect the criminality alleged, it should ensure
that the case is manageable for the jury. This can be achieved by properly
setting out the offences in the indictment. Where there are several counts in
an indictment alleging a course of sexual misconduct, the prosecution should
particularise each count so as to identify the incident, if specific, or the form
of misconduct.[25] To prevent the prosecution's natural tendency towards
overloading the indictment, sample counts or multiple incident counts[26] may
be used. It is important that the indictment is framed in such a way as to
assist the judge in interpreting the jury's verdicts, as well as to provide
adequate sentencing powers in the event of conviction.

Where an indictment straddles periods covered by the Sexual Offences Act **30.16**
1956 and the 2003 Act, it is important to check that each count is drafted
under the right Act. In *R. v MC*[27] the appellant was charged with sexual
offences committed against his natural daughter. The offences were alleged
to have occurred some time ago and an additional count of indecent assault,
contrary to s.14(1) of the Sexual Offences Act 1956, was added by a late
amendment to the indictment. The count was defective as the particulars
alleged that the offence had taken place at a time when the Sexual Offences
Act 1956 had long since been repealed and replaced by the 2003 Act. On
appeal, it was submitted by the Crown that it was open to the Court to
substitute for the jury's verdict on the defective count a conviction of sexual
activity with a child, contrary to s.9 of the 2003 Act. The Court of Appeal
found a difficulty with this argument because it did not pay sufficient
attention to the requirement in s.3 of the Criminal Appeal Act 1968 that the
jury could on the indictment have found the appellant guilty of some other
offence. The words "on the indictment" were important because in order to
find a person guilty of an alternative offence, the allegations in the indictment
had to amount to or include an allegation of that other offence.[28] The Court
concluded that s.3 of the Criminal Appeal Act 1968 did not allow it to
substitute a verdict under s.9 of the 2003 Act.

The situation in *R. v MC* can be contrasted with that in *Stewart*,[29] where **30.17**
it was held in relation to an indictment charging a specimen count of rape by
reference to the 2003 Act, that it did not matter that the particulars of the

[25] See *Rackham* [1997] 2 Cr. App. R. 22.
[26] Discussed below.
[27] [2012] EWCA Crim 213.
[28] *Graham* [1997] 1 Cr. App. R.(S.) 302.
[29] *The Times,* May 21, 2012.

offence specified a period beginning some weeks before, and continuing some
weeks beyond, the coming into force of that Act. On the evidence, the jury
must have been sure that there had been regular, continuing rapes, and the
case was not analogous with those in which there was a single offence which
might have been committed before, or after, the coming into force of the
Act.

Continuing Course of Conduct

30.18   A series of like offences can now be tried in a single count without that count
being bad for duplicity. This radical change applies to all cases sent,
transferred, or committed to the Crown Court on or after April 2, 2007,
when the Criminal Procedure (Amendment) Rules 2007[30] were implemented.
Rule 10.2(2) of the Criminal Procedure Rules 2015[31] allows, in certain
circumstances, a single count to allege more than one incident of the same
offence. The circumstances in which such a count may be appropriate
include, but are not limited to, the following:

- The victim on each occasion is the same;
- The alleged incidents involved a marked degree of repetition in the
  method employed and/or the location, or both;
- The alleged offences took place over a clearly defined period typically
  (but not necessarily) no more than about a year; or
- In any event, the defence is such as to apply to every alleged incident
  without differentiation. Where what is in issue differs between
  different incidents, a single "multiple incidents" count will not be
  appropriate, though it may be appropriate to use two or more such
  counts according to the circumstances and to the issues raised by the
  defence.

30.19   The intention of the Criminal Rules Committee in creating this new rule
was to take account, among other things, of the potential under the old rules
for a perceived unfairness to a victim of multiple offending where, out of
many alleged offences, only a few are prosecuted as samples, giving the
impression that the victim's distress has been underestimated or that he or
she has not been believed.[32]

30.20   The introduction of "multiple incidents" counts is likely to make prosecutors less inclined to adopt the old practice of drafting a series of specimen
counts reflecting different periods and different types of proscribed sexual
activity. It will still be necessary to draft separate counts where different types
of sexual activity are alleged and to ensure that the alleged criminality is
properly reflected so that the judge has adequate sentencing powers upon

---

[30] SI 2007/699.
[31] SI 2015/1490.
[32] Note prepared by the Secretariat of the Committee and published with the Guide to the
Rules.

conviction. "Multiple incidents" counts should not straddle different sentencing regimes.

For some offences, particularly sexual offences, the maximum penalty for **30.21** the offence may have changed during the period over which the alleged incidents took place. In such a case, additional "multiple incidents" counts should be used so that each count only alleges incidents to which the same maximum penalty applies. Failure to do this may result in the court being restricted to the lower statutory maximum, unless the evidence unequivocally establishes that one or more offences occurred after the implementation of the new legislation.[33]

It is important to consider whether there is a realistic possibility of **30.22** different verdicts in respect of the conduct sought to be brought within one "multiple incidents" count. Where there are significant differences in the evidence as to the proscribed activity, particularly where the defences are likely to be different, such a count would be inappropriate. Where, however, a complainant makes a broad allegation as to repeated similar abuse over a period, such a count may be justified. This is summarised by the Criminal Practice Directions 2015 at 10A.13:

> "In other cases, such as sexual or physical abuse, a complainant may be in a position only to give evidence of a series of similar incidents without being able to specify when or the precise circumstances in which they occurred. In these cases, a 'multiple incidents' count may be desirable. If on the other hand, the complainant is able to identify particular incidents of the offence by reference to a date or other specific event, but alleges that in addition there were other incidents which the complainant is unable to specify, then it may be desirable to include separate counts for the identified incidents and a 'multiple incidents' count or counts alleging that incidents of the same offence occurred 'many' times. Using a 'multiple incidents' count may be an appropriate alternative to using 'specimen' counts in some cases where repeated sexual or physical abuse is alleged. The choice of count will depend on the particular circumstances of the case and should be determined bearing in mind the implications for sentencing set out in *R v Canavan; R v Kidd; R v Shaw* [1998] 1 W.L.R. 604, [1998] 1 Cr. App. R. 79, [1998] 1 Cr. App. R. (S.) 243."[34]

The decision in *Canavan, Kidd and Shaw* sets out the cardinal rule that the **30.23** judge may sentence only for those offences in respect of which the accused has been convicted, or which he has asked to be taken into consideration. The prosecution must bear this rule in mind when formulating a charging strategy designed to reflect an accused's overall criminality. Whilst a multiple incidents count may, where offences are very similar and numerous, enable the prosecution to reflect offending in a single count rather than a number of specimen counts, if the prosecution fails to specify a sufficient minimum number of occasions within the count, they are not making proper use of the

---

[33] *R. v R (Paul Brian)* [1993] Crim. L.R. 541; and see *Harries* [2008] 1 Cr. App. R.(S.) 255 for cases where a count straddled the Criminal Justice Act 2003 implementation date (April 4, 2005).

[34] [1998] 1 Cr. App. R. 79.

procedure.[35] If a supposed multiple incidents count specifies no more than that the defendant carried out the activity on more than one occasion, the only fair approach is for him to be sentenced for two offences. It follows that in cases of sustained abuse, it will often be unhelpful to draft the count as representing, potentially, no more than two incidents.[36]

DISCLOSURE

30.24 As in all cases, there should be rigorous observance of disclosure obligations under the regime created by the Criminal Procedure and Investigations Act 1996 (discussed in Ch.18). A Defence Statement as required by s.5 of the Act may alert the police to the importance of following certain lines of inquiry. If the police fail to do so, the defence can then apply under s.8 of the Act for specific disclosure.[37]

30.25 Inevitably there will be occasions when significant material cannot be discovered or no longer exists. The extent to which there can be disclosure of contemporaneous documents is likely to have a bearing upon abuse of process applications which often arise from death, illness, memory loss, disappearance of witnesses and/or loss or destruction of records (medical, social services, school, housing, employment). The disclosure process may lead to the disclosure of social services files, which may include material which is admissible under the bad character or hearsay provisions of the Criminal Justice Act 2003. Such material should not be put before a jury without a clear ruling from the trial judge upon the matter.[38]

ABUSE OF PROCESS

PROCEDURE

30.26 The procedure for making an abuse of process application is set out in the Criminal Practice Directions 2015 as follows:

---

[35] See *R. v A* [2015] EWCA Crim 1177 at [47] per Fulford LJ.

[36] In *R. v A* [2015] EWCA Crim 1177 the judge directed the jury that they could convict if they were sure that the defendant carried out the activity in the count on at least one occasion. It followed that the defendant could only be sentenced on the basis that he had done so on two occasions.

[37] See *Bryan* [2009] EWCA Crim 2291 for a graphic example of how a failure to seize and interrogate the complainant's phone at the time of the allegation of rape ultimately led the Court of Appeal to quash a conviction. If a certain number had been stored on the phone, it would have established that the complainant and the appellant were not strangers and the complainant's allegation of stranger-rape would have been fatally undermined. Cf. *Lamont* [2010] EWCA Crim 2144 where there had been a failure to investigate a rape complainant's phone records at the time of the original allegation in 2002. The argument on appeal that this should have led to a stay was rejected. The Court had regard to the criteria in *Ebrahim v Feltham Magistrates' Court* [2001] 1 W.L.R. 1293 and concluded it was not unreasonable in the circumstances for the police to fail to pursue the relevant lines of enquiry. The evidence, if it had been obtained, would have related to a peripheral matter.

[38] *R. v DJ* [2010] EWCA Crim 385.

"3C.1 In all cases where a defendant in the Crown Court proposes to make an application to stay an indictment on the grounds of abuse of process, written notice of such application must be given to the prosecuting authority and to any co-defendant as soon as practicable after the defendant becomes aware of the grounds for doing so and not later than 14 days before the date fixed or warned for trial ("the relevant date"). Such notice must:

(a) give the name of the case and the indictment number;

(b) state the fixed date or the warned date as appropriate;

(c) specify the nature of the application;

(d) set out in numbered sub-paragraphs the grounds upon which the application is to be made;

(e) be copied to the chief listing officer at the court centre where the case is due to be heard.

3C.2 Any co-defendant who wishes to make a like application must give a like notice not later than seven days before the relevant date, setting out any additional grounds relied upon.

3C.3 In relation to such applications, the following automatic directions shall apply:

(a) the advocate for the applicant(s) must lodge with the court and serve on all other parties a skeleton argument in support of the application, at least five clear working days before the relevant date. If reference is to be made to any document not in the existing trial documents, a paginated and indexed bundle of such documents is to be provided with the skeleton argument;

(b) the advocate for the prosecution must lodge with the court and serve on all other parties a responsive skeleton argument at least two clear working days before the relevant date, together with a supplementary bundle if appropriate.

3C.4 All skeleton arguments must specify any propositions of law to be advanced (together with the authorities relied upon in support, with paragraph references to passages relied upon) and, where appropriate, include a chronology of events and a list of dramatis personae. In all instances where reference is made to a document, the reference in the trial documents or supplementary bundle is to be given.

3C.5 The above time limits are minimum time limits. In appropriate cases, the court will order longer lead times. To this end, in all cases where defence advocates are, at the time of the preliminary hearing or as soon as practicable after the case has been sent, considering the possibility of an abuse of process application, this must be raised with the judge dealing with the matter, who will order a different timetable if appropriate, and may wish, in any event, to give additional directions about the conduct of the application. If the trial judge has not been identified, the matter should be raised with the Resident Judge."

The Court of Appeal has said that beyond emphasising the need for **30.27** careful scrutiny, it is impossible to lay down clear principles according to which a judge should decide whether or not it is safe to leave a case to the jury. In *Robson*,[39] Moses LJ stated that it would be undesirable for any principle to be established, as that would be liable to provide far too rigid a process of determination. The issue must be left to the good judgment of the judge. Some general guidance can nonetheless be found in the decisions of the Court of Appeal on delay, some of which, whilst not laying down any

[39] [2006] EWCA Crim 2754.

principle, are instructive examples of the way historic cases should be approached.

The Correct Approach

Authorities preceding *R. v F(S)*

30.28   In what used to be the leading case of *Stephen Paul S*,[40] Rose LJ, Vice-President, explained that the discretionary decision whether or not to grant a stay on grounds of abuse of process, because of delay, is an exercise in judicial assessment dependent on judgment rather than on any conclusion as to fact based on evidence. The judge should bear in mind the following general propositions:
    (i) Even where delay is unjustifiable, a permanent stay should be the exception rather than the rule;
    (ii) Where there is no fault on the part of a complainant or the prosecution, it will be very rare for a stay to be granted; In particular, as the trial judge in *MacKreth (deceased)*[41] noted, when distilling propositions of law from the authorities, where the delay results from the reticence of an alleged victim in reporting an allegation of sexual abuse, one is entitled to adopt an understanding attitude towards the difficulties that can be encountered by such witnesses in making complaints about sexual abuse;
    (iii) No stay should be granted in the absence of serious prejudice to the defence so that no fair trial can be held. A judge may stay the whole indictment or individual counts;
    (iv) When assessing possible serious prejudice, the judge should bear in mind his or her power to regulate the admissibility of evidence and the trial process itself should ensure that all relevant factual issues arising from delay will be placed before the jury for their consideration in accordance with appropriate directions from the judge about the difficulties which the delay has presented to the defence;
    (v) If having considered all these factors, a judge's assessment is that a fair trial will be possible, a stay should not be granted, and it will be in the public interest for such a case to be tried.

30.29   To these principles should be added a further proposition identified by the trial judge in *MacKreth (deceased)*, namely that judges may take into account the extent to which a prosecution case depends upon contemporaneous documents. The more it does so, the more difficult it will be for a defendant to establish that an indictment should be stayed. The absence of

[40] [2006] EWCA Crim 756.
[41] [2009] EWCA Crim 1849.

contemporaneous evidence will be of far greater importance where it bears on real conflicts of evidence on which it would have been decisive.[42]

R. v F(S)—the facts

The leading case is now *R. v F(S)*,[43] in which the Court of Appeal took the opportunity to carry out a comprehensive review of all the authorities concerning applications for a stay of criminal proceedings on the grounds of delay. The then Lord Chief Justice, Lord Judge, said the review had revealed that the decisions of the Court of Appeal on this issue had not always been consistent, and that some of the jurisprudence about long delays in sexual cases appeared to have become disconnected from the well-known principles in *Galbraith*[44] and to have obscured those principles by eliding the distinct concepts of abuse of process and withdrawal of the case from the jury on evidential grounds. The Lord Chief Justice distilled the principles to be applied in such cases and stressed that applications to stay an indictment for abuse of process must not be elided with submissions of no case to answer. **30.30**

In *R. v F(S)*, it was alleged that on three occasions in 1992 or 1993, when he was aged about 16, the defendant had abused the complainant, his step-brother, who was aged about six. It was common ground that at the time the boys shared sleeping accommodation in a caravan in the garden of the family home. No complaint was made until autumn 2008. **30.31**

At the outset of the trial, the defendant gave notice of an application for a stay of the proceedings on the grounds of abuse of process. The judge, following *Smolinski*,[45] declined to rule on the application at the start of the trial, which then proceeded. During the course of his evidence, the complainant explained why the complaint was delayed and was cross-examined about it. At the conclusion of the prosecution case, the judge considered the application and acceded to it. Since it was a terminating ruling, the prosecution appealed under s.58 of the Criminal Justice Act 2003 with the leave of the Court of Appeal. **30.32**

Although the application was advanced to the judge as an application to stay, and was granted in those terms, the argument in support of the application ranged widely over what were submitted to be weaknesses in the Crown's case. These included: (i) the fact that the case depended entirely upon the unsupported word of the complainant; (ii) that it concerned events which, if they occurred, had happened some 16 years before any report of them was made and the defendant had any opportunity to deal with them; (iii) that there was no satisfactory explanation for the failure to report the **30.33**

---

[42] *Anver Daud Sheikh* [2006] EWCA Crim 2625; *Joynson* [2008] EWCA Crim 3049.
[43] [2011] EWCA Crim 1844.
[44] [1981] 73 Cr. App. R. 124; [1981] 1 W.L.R. 1039.
[45] [2004] EWCA Crim 1270. This approach was endorsed by Hooper LJ in *Burke* [2005] EWCA Crim 29, but did not find favour with the Court of Appeal in *R. v F(S)*.

matter, not at the age of six, but when the complainant realised what had happened was seriously wrong, as he clearly had by his mid-teens. He had opportunities to report it when he was receiving counselling for anger management when aged 14, but had failed to do so; (iv) that his initial disclosures, which were partial and limited, were made to his wife in 2008 when he had collapsed apparently suffering from stress; (v) that there was a possibility that what he now said was in part the result of suggestions made by the complainant's mother when, on the following day, he spoke to her; (vi) that the complaint was recorded by way of witness statement rather than by way of ABE interview; (vii) that the explanations offered by the complainant in evidence both as to when he had realised what had happened was wrong, and as to why he had not reported it, were inconsistent and unsatisfactory; (viii) that the notes of the counsellor had been long destroyed; (ix) that if the allegations had been made contemporaneously, the defendant could not have been convicted because as the law then stood the absence of corroboration would have been fatal; and (x) that it had been unfair that the defendant should face trial as an adult rather than as a youth, which he had been when the offences were said to have been committed.

30.34   The trial judge approached her decision on the basis of five propositions identified in the then most recent case of *R. v F(TB)*.[46] She quoted in full the fifth of Jackson LJ's propositions from that case:

> "That a complainant's delay in coming forward was so unjustified, is relevant to the question whether it is fair to try the defendant so long after the events in issue. In determining whether the complainant's delay is justified, it must be firmly borne in mind that victims of sexual abuse are often unwilling to reveal or talk about their experiences for some time and for good reason."

The Lord Chief Justice pointed out that this passage suggests that the judge should embark upon a fact-finding decision during the course of the trial in relation to the issue of the credibility of the complainant, which is pre-eminently for the jury's decision.

30.35   The judge ruled that on the evidence, a jury properly directed could not safely return a verdict of guilty. This ruling proceeded on the basis that no specific prejudice had been established other than the potential prejudice inherent in any prolonged delay. However, the judge explained that the absence of justification for the delay was her principal concern, and the basis for her decision was the absence of any "real satisfactory explanation" for the complainant's failure to take advantage of a number of opportunities to report what had happened to him. The Lord Chief Justice observed that the argument advanced by the defendant, and perhaps in consequence the ruling, represented an amalgam of two distinct questions:

    (i) Should the prosecution be stayed for "abuse of process" on the
        grounds that the defendant could not receive a fair trial?

---

[46] [2011] EWCA Crim 726.

(ii) Should the case be withdrawn from the jury on the grounds that the evidence was such that a conviction would be unsafe?

The Court of Appeal allowed the prosecution appeal on the ground that **30.36** the judge had applied the wrong test. She had been led into thinking that the crux of her decision was the presence or absence of justification for the delayed complaint. She had taken into account matters which went to the issue of whether the offences alleged were proved or not. These matters were capable of exploration at trial, and had been explored. They did not provide any reason on abuse of process grounds for preventing the trial from taking place or continuing to its normal end.

R. v F(S)—the Postscript: Guidance to be derived from the authorities

As is clear from Rose LJ's propositions in *Stephen Paul S*,[47] cited above, even **30.37** before *R. v F(S)* it was generally acknowledged that an application to stay a case where there are allegations of historic sexual abuse will be resolved on its own facts. Citation of the authorities is unlikely to help resolve the issues, although some Court of Appeal cases in the last decade provided useful illustrations of the governing principles in operation. In giving judgment in September 2009 in *MacKreth (deceased)*,[48] when reaching the conclusion that the relevant principles had not changed, Rix LJ reviewed eight authorities dating from 2000 to 2008. He observed that the cases on the whole had been sparing of citation of authority; they all emphasise how much they each turn on their own special facts. Furthermore, the Court of Appeal will not interfere lightly with a judgment reached by a trial judge on an application for a stay because of alleged abuse of process founded on delay, so long as the judge has correctly addressed himself on the law to be applied.[49]

The Lord Chief Justice set the governing principles in stone in a postscript **30.38** to his judgment in *R. v F(S)*.[50] He made it clear that when abuse of process submissions on the grounds of delay are advanced, provided the principles articulated in *Galbraith* and *Attorney General's Reference (No.1 of 1990)*[51] are clearly understood, it will no longer be necessary or appropriate for reference to be made to any Court of Appeal decisions except *Stephen Paul S*[52] and the decision in *R. v F(S)*. These four authorities contain all the necessary discussion about the applicable principles. Their application is fact-specific, and, unless the Court of Appeal in any subsequent judgment expressly indicates to the contrary, is to be regarded as a fact-specific decision

---

[47] [2006] EWCA Crim 756.
[48] [2009] EWCA Crim 1849.
[49] *Joynson* [2008] EWCA Crim 3049.
[50] At [47]–[49].
[51] [1992] Q.B. 630.
[52] [2006] EWCA Crim 756.

rather than an elaboration of or an amendment to the governing principles. Lord Judge then drew together the headlines to the Court of Appeal's principal conclusions:

   (i) An application to stay for abuse of process on grounds of delay and a submission of "no case to answer" are two distinct matters. They must receive distinct and separate consideration.

  (ii) An application to stay for abuse of process on grounds of delay must be determined in accordance with *Attorney General's Reference (No.1 of 1990)*. It cannot succeed unless, exceptionally, a fair trial is no longer possible owing to the prejudice occasioned by the delay which cannot fairly be addressed in the normal trial process. The presence or absence of explanation or justification for the delay is relevant only insofar as it bears on that question.

 (iii) An application to stop the case on the grounds that there is no case to answer must be determined in accordance with *Galbraith*. For the reasons there explained, it is dangerous to ask the question in terms of whether a conviction would be safe, or the jury can safely convict, because that invites the judge to evaluate the weight and reliability of the evidence, which is the task of the jury. The question is whether the evidence, viewed overall, is such that the jury could properly convict.

  (iv) There is no different *Galbraith* test for offences which are alleged to have been committed some years ago, whether or not they are sexual offences.

   (v) In general, an application to stay for abuse of process ought ordinarily to be heard and determined at the outset of the case, and before the evidence is heard, unless there is a specific reason to defer it because prejudice and fair trial can better be determined at a later stage. It follows that applications should be preliminary to the trial process unless there is a specific reason for deferment, such as the evaluation of the significance of long-lost evidence, for example institutional records. The practice of deferment that had developed since *Smolinski*[53] will only be appropriate in such cases.

After *R. v F(S)*—Instructive examples of the application of the principles

30.39   The relatively recent case of *R. v RD*[54] is a highly instructive example in which the principles in *R. v F(S)* were held to have been properly applied. The Court of Appeal there upheld convictions relating to the sexual abuse of four complainants, notwithstanding exceptionally long delay amounting to

---

[53] [2004] EWCA Crim 1270.
[54] [2013] EWCA Crim 1592.

as much as 63 years in the case of one complainant. The case sheds light on the proper approach to issues arising from the combined effect of delay and missing documents and exhibits.

The allegations, looked at comprehensively, covered the period between **30.40** 1949 at the outset of the events described by the different complainants and 1973 at their conclusion. The Court of Appeal acknowledged that this level of delay was extreme even by the standards of courts in this jurisdiction, which are used to trying allegations of historical sexual abuse. The first complainant's allegations spanned the years 1949–1956, covering a period when she was aged 8 or 9, up until a time when she was aged about 14. At that stage the appellant was aged between 15 and 22. The offences were alleged to have occurred at the complainant's maternal grandparent's home in South Wales which was also the home address of the appellant. The second complainant's allegations related to the years 1953–1957 when she would have been aged between 10 and 14. It was alleged that sexual abuse occurred when she spent holidays at the home of the appellant's parents. The third complainant was the biological daughter of the appellant. Her complaints related to the period between 1965 and 1971, by which time the appellant had married and was living with his present wife. The final complainant was a niece. Her complaint was confined to a single incident.

Prior to the trial, the appellant had applied to stay the proceedings as an **30.41** abuse of process on the ground that the delay had caused him serious prejudice, with the result that a fair trial could not take place. The judge rejected the application. On appeal against conviction, it was submitted that the cumulative effect of all the missing evidence was that the appellant could not have a fair trial. The judge had wrongly concluded that the trial process could fairly address the issues arising from the delay and the deficits in potential evidence. In particular, it was contended that the judge had wrongly focused on the credibility of the witnesses as a central issue and had failed properly to assess the impact of the missing evidence upon the appellant's ability to mount a defence. It was asserted that the appellant's defence was not merely one of denial, but also raised an alibi which the appellant could not make good. He was prevented from positively attacking the prosecution's case, which he might well have been able to do had the missing evidence been available.

The Court of Appeal accepted that, in summing up, the judge had given **30.42** appropriate directions about delay and its potential impact upon the ability of the appellant to raise a defence, and had left those issues clearly and fairly to the jury. However, the Court felt that it was right to go on and assess the impact of the missing evidence for itself. The approach it adopted in undertaking this task is instructive.

The Court observed that in considering the question of prejudice to the **30.43** defence, it was necessary to distinguish between mere speculation about what missing documents or witnesses might show, and missing evidence which represents a significant and demonstrable chance of amounting to decisive or strongly supportive evidence emerging on a specific issue in the case.[55] The Court needed to consider what evidence directly relevant to the appellant's case had been lost by reason of passage of time. It would then need to go on to consider the importance of the missing evidence in the context of the case as a whole and the issues before the jury. The Court would have to identify what prejudice, if any, had been caused to the appellant by the delay and whether judicial directions would be sufficient to compensate for such prejudice as may have been caused or whether in truth a fair trial could not properly be afforded to the appellant.

30.44   In carrying out this exercise the Court felt that some of the submissions on behalf of the appellant were overstated, in that it felt unable to accept the assumption that the missing evidence would necessarily have supported his case. Moreover, the complaints were not date specific but were couched in general terms of sexual abuse occurring on very many occasions during visits during school holidays, with wide periods identified in the indictment. Accordingly, an alibi in its true sense was not the issue before the jury. The issue was in reality whether or not the jury could be sure the abuse had taken place. It was not in dispute in relation to each of the premises at which the offences were alleged to have taken place that the appellant was present on occasions so that the opportunity to do what was alleged undoubtedly existed. Fuller evidence about shift patterns at work, or about dates of leave from the army, school holiday records or evidence from family witnesses or military friends would not have taken the matter much further, and was not of a degree of cogency to amount to a finding of serious prejudice in its absence. The question for the jury was to consider whether they were sure the appellant had availed himself of the acknowledged opportunities which existed to commit the offences.

30.45   Nonetheless, the Court accepted that there was detriment to the appellant's case by reason of delay and that it needed to evaluate the extent and effect of that detriment. The Court accepted that this matter required careful scrutiny because of the very substantial delay in this case. However, having evaluated the impact of the delay and missing documents and witnesses for itself, it was satisfied that the judge had been correct in her assessment that the trial process could properly cope with the difficulties faced by the appellant, and that there would be and indeed was no prejudice of a type which would mean he could not and did not get a fair trial. On an analysis of the missing material and the evidence given at trial and the issues before the jury, the Court was satisfied that the appellant received a fair trial, and was not disadvantaged in a way that could properly be described as amounting to serious prejudice to his ability to mount a proper defence to the allegations brought against him.

---

[55] This reasoning was adopted by the Court of Appeal in *Halahan (Maxwell Crosby)* [2014] EWCA Crim 2079 where there was no doubt that contemporaneous documents were missing, principally children's home records, but it could not be accepted that those documents would necessarily cast light on the reliability of the complainant's present evidence.

It is desirable that any application for a stay for abuse of process and any **30.46** unfitness to plead argument should be heard by the same judge, and ideally the trial judge. In *Hayford*[56] the appellant, then aged 84, was to be tried on four counts of indecent assault. An application was made that the indictment should be stayed on three grounds: delay, loss of evidence, and the appellant's ill-health. A judge determined this issue for the good reason that he did not want witnesses to fly from Canada unnecessarily, but had insufficient time to hear the fitness to plead argument. Another judge, the trial judge, considered the application to stay because the appellant was unfit to plead. The Court of Appeal took the view, with hindsight, that it would have been better for both issues to have been dealt with together by the trial judge.

When cases are likely to be so fact specific, it is quite impossible to isolate **30.47** particular features which will necessarily found a meritorious application for a stay on the grounds of abuse of process. The court will look at the cumulative effect of the loss of material evidence and balance that against the extent to which an appropriate judicial direction will cure any prejudice following from that loss. Nevertheless, we endeavour in the following paragraphs to categorise features that frequently arise with illustrations as to how the courts have approached the particular problems they throw up. These cases must be read bearing in mind that *R. v F(S)* has now settled the principles to be applied, and many of these cases pre-date that decision.

LENGTH OF THE DELAY

There is no statement of principle that the passage of any particular period **30.48** of time should be regarded as determinative of an application to stay on the grounds of abuse of process by reason of delay. It is apparent from the authorities that delay is but one of the factors to be considered.[57] There has, however, been a sea-change in the Court of Appeal's approach to delay following the decision in *R. v F(S)* in 2011. In *Joynson*,[58] in 2008, the Court described a delay of 35 years as being by any standards exceptional. The Court was troubled by the very great delay and its particular consequences in the context of the specific allegations in that case, and reached the conclusion that the convictions were unsafe. The complainants in that case gave evidence about events alleged to have occurred during their childhood, in one instance when the complainant was as young as eight. The Court held that the surprising apparent powers of recall of witnesses 35 years after the event did not lessen the importance of the absence of contemporaneous evidence by which to test the degree to which the recall was true. However, in 2013, the Court in *R. v RD*,[59] following the principles in *R. v F(S)*, upheld convictions

---

[56] [2015] EWCA Crim 782.
[57] *Hooper* [2003] EWCA Crim 2427; *R. v E(T)* [2004] 2 Cr. App. R. 36.
[58] [2008] EWCA Crim 3049.
[59] [2013] EWCA Crim 1592.

for historic sexual abuse notwithstanding exceptionally long delay amounting to 63 years in the case of one complainant.

Significant Inconsistencies

30.49 Before *R. v F(S)*[60] in 2011, the Court of Appeal in cases such as *Robson*[61] suggested that when dealing with an abuse of process application in a historic case, the trial judge should not ignore significant inconsistencies in the evidence. *R. v F(S)* clarified that the courts in the past had on occasion fallen into the trap of eliding the two distinct concepts of abuse of process and the withdrawal of a case from the jury on evidential grounds. Matters going to the credibility of the complainant are capable of exploration at trial and are pre-eminently for a jury. In *Robson*, Moses LJ had suggested that, on an application for abuse of process, the trial judge's scrutiny of the evidence should include consideration of not only the nature and quality of the evidence, but also inconsistencies, either within the evidence of one witness or between a number of witnesses. The approach suggested in *Robson* must now be adapted so as to comply with the principles in *R. v F(S)*. It is not for the judge to assess weight and reliability, which are entirely for the jury. The judge must focus not on the safety of any conviction based upon evidence to be called at trial, but rather on whether the defendant can have a fair trial.

Decisions by Civil Courts

30.50 A decision in care proceedings cannot determine the outcome of criminal proceedings. No question of autrefois acquit, issue estoppel or double jeopardy can arise. The position was addressed in *R. v L*,[62] where it was submitted that the judge's decisions and findings in proceedings under the Children Act 1989 were conclusive of the criminal proceedings, and that the indictment should therefore be stayed as an abuse of process. In the family court, Hedley J had made certain crucial findings, including that he was quite unable to say on the evidence whether one parent was more likely to have inflicted the injuries than the other. This was overall a grave failure of parenting for which both must bear responsibility. Nearly a year after Hedley J's judgment, the appellant (the father) was tried for murder of the child, and was convicted of manslaughter and other offences in respect of the child. The mother gave evidence for the prosecution. The Court of Appeal rejected the appellant's submission that the indictment should have been stayed as an abuse of process and, in so doing, took the opportunity to review the authorities. The care proceedings had been brought to establish where and

---

[60] [2011] EWCA Crim 1844.
[61] [2006] EWCA Crim 2754.
[62] [2007] 1 Cr. App. R. 1.

with whom the child should live and arrangements for his future welfare. The proceedings were brought and conducted by the local authority, the prosecution had taken no part and the family court had had no jurisdiction to convict or acquit the appellant of a criminal offence. In those circumstances, the Crown's decision to continue with the prosecution of the appellant and the eventual verdict of the jury could not reasonably be regarded as an affront to the administration of justice.

The principle in *R. v L* is not confined to proceedings under the Children **30.51** Act 1989 but applies to civil cases generally. For instance, the fact that a jury's verdict of guilty would be inconsistent with a High Court judge's conclusion in a civil case is not a ground for staying an indictment.[63] Until relatively recently it was thought that, if the facts of an individual case might give rise to a criminal prosecution, the prosecution should be concluded before any care or equivalent proceedings took place, reflecting a former rule of law that civil proceedings could not be pursued until the conclusion of criminal proceedings. However, the position has changed since the advent of the Children Act 1989, with its emphasis on the paramountcy of the welfare of the child and the consequent need for expedition in the disposal of care proceedings. In *Re TB (Minors) (Care Proceedings: Criminal Trial)*,[64] Butler-Sloss LJ observed that the existence of criminal proceedings is not a reason to adjourn care proceedings. There must be some detriment to the children in the broadest terms if care proceedings are not to be brought on, because delay is detrimental generally to the children. In *R. v L*, the Court of Appeal emphasised that, because procedural and evidential difficulties can arise where there are in existence parallel care proceedings in respect of a child and criminal proceedings against a person connected with that child in respect of a serious offence against the child (or any person connected with the child), it is essential that there should be close liaison between the local social services authority conducting the care proceedings and the Crown Prosecution Service. Wherever possible, linked criminal and care directions hearings should take place as cases progress, in order to deal with issues such as timetabling and disclosure.

MISSING DOCUMENTS

Whilst we have continued to include in this chapter some Court of Appeal **30.52** cases decided before 2011, they must be read with the principles underpinning *R. v F(S)* in mind. It remains the position that where missing documents would settle the matter one way or other, a fair trial may not be possible. However, where the missing documents would merely have been further evidence in the case, their absence will not render the trial unfair,

---

[63] See *R. v L*, last note, at [54] and [62], where *Steidl and Baxendale-Walker* (June 27, 2002, Southwark Crown Court) and *Stocker* (November 23, 2004, Central Criminal Court) were held to have been wrongly decided.
[64] [1995] 2 F.L.R. 801.

especially if the judge gives the jury a strong warning about possible prejudice to the defendant within the delay direction. This must be a free-standing, self-contained direction and not be diluted by interweaving with directions dealing with other aspects of the consequences of delay such as witness memory.[65] The mere absence of documents which, speculatively, might have thrown up material for cross-examination, does not render a trial unfair in the context of historic allegations of abuse.[66] It is often the case that the absence of documents cuts both ways: had they been available, they would have had the potential to assist the defence but also to damage it.[67]

30.53   Much will depend upon how important the missing documents would have been. This necessitates a careful analysis of the consequences of the documents' absence. In this context, *Anver Daud Sheikh*[68] is a highly instructive case illustrating the importance of evaluating the particular difficulties arising from the missing documents. It demonstrates that, even if significant contemporaneous material still exists, this may only offset the difficulties created by the absence of other material if the existing documents shed no light on the critical issue. In *Sheikh* the appellant had been convicted of three counts of indecent assault upon a male and two counts of buggery. It was alleged that the offences had been committed over 20 years before, in 1980, when the appellant, then aged 30, had been a member of the care staff at St. Camilla's Community Home. His duties had included night-time care work. It was alleged that two of the offences had taken place when the appellant had been on duty at night and had taken the complainant MG to another room for "safety". This had occurred after the complainant had told the appellant that he was being bullied. The matter was not reported until the complainant went to the police after watching a Crimewatch programme. He had received £11,000 compensation from the State and was in the process of bringing a civil action against Catholic Care. It emerged at trial that the only possible time when there was an opportunity for the offences to have occurred was the weekend starting Friday, August 29, 1980. MG agreed that, on his account, he must have met the appellant on a number of occasions during August to build up the necessary trust to tell him about the bullying. At trial, it was submitted on behalf of the appellant that certain crucial documents were missing, namely the day book, which would have shown who was on duty, and the personnel records/staff records, the absence of which meant that it was impossible to say when the appellant took leave. The very existence of those documents, it was said, would have provided the appellant with the means by which he could establish his alibi. There could not be a clearer example of prejudice to a defendant as a result of missing documents. The trial judge rejected this submission without addressing defence counsel's point, simply stating that at no stage during the trial had he

[65] *R. v PS* [2013] EWCA Crim 992.
[66] *MacKreth (deceased)* [2009] EWCA Crim 1849 at [45].
[67] *Hooper* [2003] EWCA Crim 2427; *Joynson* [2008] EWCA Crim 3049.
[68] [2006] EWCA Crim 2625.

said to himself that the trial was unfair because of the absence of these documents. He pointed out that there had been proper disclosure. Defence counsel had been the author of his own misfortune in that "his cross-examination was consummate, detailed, very compelling and understandable to a jury, and he has brought all those matters to the jury's attention". The issue was re-visited during the jury's deliberations in the light of the recently published decision of the Court of Appeal in *Burke* (discussed below). However, the trial judge stated that that decision had not changed his view one iota.

On appeal, Hooper LJ, giving the judgment of the Court, stated: 30.54

"In our view the missing documents, in particular the staff rota and the personnel records, were likely to be highly relevant to two issues in this case. First, whether the appellant would have come into contact with MG so as to have the opportunity to win his trust as MG alleged he had; secondly, whether the appellant had the opportunity to commit these offences as against MG.

The likely relevance is intensified by the following considerations:
i) The appellant and MG were both present at the Home only during a specific and limited period, 1st–31st August 1980.
ii) The offences were shown to have been committed within a very narrow time frame on 29th or 30th August 1980.
iii) On the evidence of MG the appellant was on duty during the evening preceding the alleged offences.
iv) The particular circumstances of the termination of the appellant's employment gave rise to a real possibility that he was on leave at the time of the offences.
v) It had been demonstrated by reference to other documents which survived (day books etc.) that the missing documents would have been likely to include information directly bearing on opportunity or the lack of it."

The Court allowed the appeal, expressing grave doubts as to whether a judge who properly analysed the consequences of the missing documents would have concluded that the trial was fair.

Burke[69] is another instructive example of an historic sex case where the   30.55 Court of Appeal felt it had to allow an appeal against conviction on one count because of the absence of critical records. The appellant had been convicted of buggery of a boy committed whilst he was working as a temporary teacher at a remand home The complaint was one of a number made after four complainants were contacted in 1999 and 2000 by police officers conducting an investigation into schools, children's homes and remand centres in South Wales. The offence was alleged to have taken place some 30 years earlier in 1971 when the appellant was in his twenties. It was alleged that the appellant had buggered the complainant during the early hours of the morning in the staff bathroom after he had absconded and been returned by the police. Documents which would have existed and would have recorded serious incidents, such as boys absconding or punishments imposed, had long disappeared, as also had staff rotas, medical records and

[69] [2005] EWCA Crim 29.

similar documents. The only document relating to the home at the critical period to have survived was the register.

30.56   Contemporary social service files confirmed that the complainant had absconded during the relevant period (more than once) but it was not possible to tie down the exact date of absconding. The complainant's antecedents did not assist with this. Furthermore, even if that date were known, the documentation that would have shown whether the appellant was on night duty on that date was missing. It followed that the jury was deprived of evidence that might either have powerfully supported the complainant's evidence or have fatally undermined it. As a consequence of the absence of these crucial documents, the Court of Appeal held that the appellant was prevented from having a fair trial on this count. The Court, did, however, uphold the other convictions. The staff rotas did not have the same critical importance in respect of the other complainants. Furthermore, it was too speculative to say that the absence of potential witnesses prevented the appellant from having a fair trial.

30.57   *Joynson*[70] is another case in which there were real conflicts of evidence on which missing contemporaneous evidence would have been decisive. The decision shows that when missing documents could have seriously compromised the credibility of the complainant, this is a factor which should be taken into account in assessing whether or not a fair trial is possible. The trial in *Joynson*, which took place in 2007, concerned allegations made by five complainants against the appellant, who had been housemaster at a special needs boarding school from 1969 until 1972. The trial was complicated by the fact that the headmaster of the school, Eagles, had himself been convicted of abusing boys at a trial in 1999, this being relevant to the appellant's defence that any abuse at school was not his (the appellant's) responsibility. There were no extant records from the school except for a register which had turned up in the headmaster's home when the police had investigated his activities. There was evidence from one of the complainants (PF) about the appellant's comments about another boy (DC), who, it could be established, had not come to the school until *after* the appellant said he had left. In the absence of the school's other records, the appellant could not establish other than by his evidence when he had left. In addition to the issue whether or not the appellant had already left the school at the relevant time, there was a separate issue going to the credibility of PF. His mother had given evidence about a contemporaneous complaint by her son to her about a person who was not the appellant. At the time of the trial she was still certain that her son had complained about Eagles, not about the appellant. PF disagreed and maintained that he had complained about the appellant. The mother had immediately gone to the social services to inform them about the complaint, but the documents containing her original statement were no longer

---

[70] [2008] EWCA Crim 3049, considered in *MacKreth (deceased)* [2009] EWCA Crim 1849 at [39].

available. This was a very direct contradiction between the complainant and his mother. There was no objective evidence to show that PF was wrong. Without the missing material, the effectiveness of any cross-examination was bound to be reduced.

On the special facts of the case, the Court of Appeal identified significant prejudice. Toulson LJ said:[71]   **30.58**

> " . . . we must consider whether the case was so strong and/or whether there were sufficient safeguards that the convictions may nevertheless be regarded as safe, despite such prejudice . . . For example, if contemporaneous documents had shown that as a schoolboy PF complained about Eagles, not the appellant, and that his evidence about the appellant's references to DC were an instance of his memory playing him false, the case would inevitably have appeared less strong than otherwise . . . In relation to PF, the defence . . . had available to it the contradiction between PF and his mother. It also had the evidence of the appellant himself that he had left the school before DC arrived. In relation to those issues the jury was left with the word of one witness against another. They lacked the contemporaneous evidence that would have settled those points . . . ".

The Court was troubled by the very great delay and its particular consequences in the context of the specific allegations in this case. It reached the conclusion that it could not regard the convictions as safe.

Missing documents in respect of an earlier police investigation

The destruction of documents relating to an earlier allegation by the same   **30.59**
complainant may cause problems that cannot be remedied by any direction of law or control over evidence, if the destroyed documents would have gone to the heart of the issues in the case. Once the governing principles are ascertained, each case will turn on its own facts and so citation of authority is likely to be of limited assistance to the court. Nevertheless, some cases are useful illustrations of the principles in operation. In *R. v B*,[72] the prosecution appealed against a terminating ruling by the trial judge in April 2008 in respect of a count alleging abduction of a child in 1995 (count 1). A second count on the same indictment related to a similar offence in June 2007. The defendant had been charged in 1995 in respect of count 1. He made several appearances in the magistrates' court. Eventually, however, the prosecution discontinued the proceedings against him. The issue when the matter came to trial in February 2008 was identification. The prosecution file from 1995 was no longer in existence. The judge was concerned about three matters. First, there was no video or transcript of the complainant's account made at the relevant time when she was the victim of this incident. That made it virtually impossible to challenge her evidence as to the identity of the vehicle allegedly driven by the defendant. Secondly, the E-fit prepared by the complainant of

---

[71] At [31].
[72] [2008] EWCA Crim 1114.

the man who was seeking to abduct her was no longer available. The prosecution's evidence from the investigating officer as to the similarities between the E-fit and the defendant was of dubious admissibility. Thirdly, the defendant's original interviews were no longer available. The documents relating to the identification parade where the complainant did not identify the defendant had also gone. Sir Igor Judge P, giving the judgment of the Court of Appeal, observed that many abuse of process arguments, up and down the land in the Crown Court, are ill founded and unjustified, but this argument was not. The Court took the view that the missing documentation was critical and it was not unreasonable for the judge to have exercised his discretion in stopping the case.

30.60   *O'Dell*[73] concerned allegations of sexual abuse dating back to the period 1972–77 when the defendant had been a young residential case assistant in a children's home. There were six complainants at the 1999 trial, who as children had been residents at the home. Three of the complainants had complained to parents and to staff at the home in 1976, the defendant had been arrested and interviewed, but the DPP had decided not to prosecute. The 1999 trial stemmed from the renewed complaint of one of the complainants. The summing up was commended by the Court of Appeal as a model of fairness, but the papers from the 1976 investigation had been lost, local authority files were unavailable and the appellant had difficulty tracing witnesses. The Court of Appeal, in a judgment given by Laws LJ, concluded that, whilst the decision was "wholly dependent on the special facts", the appellant had been caused such prejudice as to make a fair trial impossible and render the convictions unsafe.

30.61   In *Turner (Michael John)*,[74] the Court of Appeal observed, when holding that a fair trial had not been possible, that missing police files relating to an earlier police investigation into a complaint made against the appellant by the same individual, had gone to the heart of the case so creating difficulties that could not be repaired by judicial case management. The Court recommended that, given the tendency of allegations of sexual offences to have a long gestation period, police forces should keep documents relating to complaints of sexual offences for considerably longer than three years.[75] In the case before it, the difficulties caused by the absence of earlier police files were compounded by the problem that old complaints may have been prompted by the contemporary complaints, and without the police records this issue could not be determined. It would appear that the difficulties were particularly acute here because the earlier complaint related to the same individual and the same period as alleged in the present indictment.

[73] November 10, 2000.
[74] [2000] Crim. L.R 832. For recent analysis of this case, see *MacKreth (deceased)* [2009] EWCA 1849 at [33].
[75] Since 2006, under MoPI guidelines, where police receive a report involving a sexual incident the information is retained for 10 years in all cases. It is then reviewed under national retention assessment criteria (NRAC) every 10 years and according to the severity can then be retained up to 100 years.

The appellant in *Turner* had been convicted of sexually abusing his niece **30.62**
(D) and half-niece (C) 15 to 17 years previously. The first rape of D was said
to have occurred between 1975 and 1978, the second in 1980. The offences
against C were alleged to have occurred in the period 1984–86. She had gone
to the police and made a complaint in 1985 or 1986, after, it appeared, all but
the last two offences relating to her had allegedly been committed. As a
result, a single count of indecent assault was laid, but no evidence was offered
and the appellant had been discharged. The police file, including the witness
statements, the police report, the record of interview and any correspondence
with the defence, had been destroyed as a matter of routine after three years.
The only surviving police record indicated that the indecent assault consisted
of undescribed sexual acts, not including intercourse. C's current account was
that she had told the police everything she now claimed happened, including
rape (except one incident which occasioned counts of rape, buggery and false
imprisonment).

In 1997, E, the appellant's 12-year-old daughter by P, made a complaint of **30.63**
indecent assault, with which he was charged. Some time after, police visited
C and asked her if she wanted to "re-do" her statement. Her 1985–86
statement would have been destroyed by 1997. E then withdrew her
allegations. The following day D made her statement. D said that she had
talked to C about C's 1985–86 allegations.

On appeal, it was argued that the indictment should have been stayed. **30.64**
Great reliance was placed upon the missing documents relating to the
1985–86 complaint, the difficulties caused to the defence by the withdrawal
of allegations by E and P, and their relationship with the complaints made by
C and D. Counsel could not explore this in front of the jury without revealing
the allegations made by E and P. The defence also identified six potential
witnesses who could not be called because of the delay.

The Court of Appeal was very concerned about the effect of the missing **30.65**
1985–86 documents. It was difficult to reconcile C's account at trial of what
happened at the time of the earlier complaint with what was known. The
appellant had faced just one count of indecent assault. Either C complained
of rape at the time and the police did not believe her, or she did not complain,
which would affect her credibility. The documents would have clarified what
had happened, but they had been destroyed by the police. A potentially
crucial plank in the appellant's defence would have been any discrepancy
between what she had said at trial and what she had alleged 12 years before.
The Court did not consider that the result was neutral with a "we must do
our best with the remaining evidence" conclusion. The destruction of the
documents raised the twin possibilities of serious prejudice to the defendant
and positive advantage to the prosecution. It gave C a free hand to say what
she wished, confident that she could not be contradicted by the 1985–86
documents. Those documents would have been crucial to the case, and a trial
without them could not be as fair as a trial with them. The prejudice to the
appellant was obvious and substantial.

Previous Police Investigations and Promises not to Prosecute

30.66   A promise not to prosecute may provide a basis for an abuse argument. We have included some paragraphs on recent developments in this area as it is not uncommon for this issue to be raised in abuse applications in respect of historic cases.

30.67   To succeed with such an argument, the defence must establish that there has been an unequivocal representation by the CPS upon which the defendant has acted to his detriment.[76] However, even then there may be circumstances in which it would not be an abuse of process to proceed. In *Abu Hamza*,[77] the Court of Appeal held that if facts come to light which were not known when the representation was made, those facts may justify proceeding despite the representation.

30.68   Representations by the CPS must be seen in the context of a victim's right to seek a review of a decision not to prosecute. The procedure is now set out in the Victims' Right to Review scheme.[78] In sexual cases it is not unusual for victims to exercise their right to a review. In determining whether in particular circumstances there was an abuse of process, regard must be had to the right of the complainant to have the decision reviewed. The review should be conducted within a reasonable time, but inevitably may contribute to or compound the delay before a case comes to trial. Once a review is sought, it is then for the independent prosecutor to reach a decision impartially. In reviewing a decision not to prosecute, the CPS is responding appropriately to the rights of complainants in the prosecution process. It is an integral part of the exercise of prosecutorial discretion. The right of a complainant to a review has nothing to do with complaints about the level of service provided by the CPS.

30.69   Although the right of a victim to judicially review a decision not to prosecute is well-established, the Court of Appeal in 2011 clarified the position in *Killick*,[79] concluding that as a decision not to prosecute is in reality a final decision for a victim, there must be a right to seek a review of such a decision, particularly as the police have such a right under the charging guidance. As an independent prosecutor, the CPS has a duty to respond to a request made by a complainant for a review of a decision not to prosecute. The Court of Appeal pointed out that it would be disproportionate for a public authority not to have a system of review without recourse to court proceedings. In considering whether to prosecute, the prosecutor has to take into account the interests of the State, the defendant and the victim.[80] The Court of Appeal explained that the complainants in *Killick* were

---

[76] See *Abu Hamza* [2006] EWCA Crim 2918.
[77] [2006] EWCA Crim 2918.
[78] See paras 17.28 and following, above.
[79] [2011] EWCA Crim 1608.
[80] cf. *R. v B* [2003] 2 Cr. App. R. 197, at [27] per Lord Woolf CJ.

exercising their right to seek a review of the prosecutor's decision. That right under the law and procedure of England and Wales is in essence the same as the right expressed in what is now art.11 of Directive 2012/29/EU on establishing minimum standards on the rights, support and protection of victims of crime.

Killick is an instructive case in which the Court of Appeal held that a prosecution brought in 2010 after the CPS reversed their earlier decision taken in 2007 not to prosecute, following a series of complaints and the threat of judicial review, did not amount to an abuse of process. **30.70**

The three complainants had made serious sexual allegations to the police in 2006. The first allegation dated back to the early 1990s. The complainants all suffered from cerebral palsy. The appellant also suffered from cerebral palsy, although less severely than the complainants. Although the appellant was arrested in April 2006, within a relatively short period of the making of the complaints, the decision on whether to prosecute was not made until June 2007, a year later, when the CPS decided that the appellant should not be prosecuted. **30.71**

A "complaint"[81] was then made about that decision in accordance with the then CPS complaints procedure. Solicitors acting for the complainants advised that there should be an application for judicial review of the decision not to prosecute and sent a pre-action protocol letter to the CPS in August 2007. This complaint led to a decision to conduct a completely fresh review of the case by one of the CPS Special Casework Lawyers. The review took almost two years, in part because the CPS sought the advice of an independent QC experienced in the prosecution of sexual offences. The QC advised that the decision not to prosecute took into account all the relevant considerations and was wholly reasonable. **30.72**

The CPS wrote to the complainants' solicitors stating that on the basis of the review, the decision not to prosecute had been correct. This led to the solicitors writing a further pre-action protocol letter indicating their intention to commence judicial review proceedings on the basis that the decision not to prosecute was irrational and on other grounds, including that the decision was arrived at unlawfully by taking into account the complainants' status as disabled persons. The CPS responded to this by initiating a third tier review which was carried out expeditiously by Miss Alison Levitt QC, the then Principal Legal Adviser to the Director of Public Prosecutions. She considered the matter afresh. She concluded that the earlier decisions were wrong (though not unreasonable), that there was a realistic prospect of conviction and that it was in the public interest that there should be a prosecution. **30.73**

---

[81] Thomas LJ (as he then was) explained (at [23]) that this was not in fact a "complaint" but a request for a review. The use of the term "complaint" can lead to suggestions that the prosecutor is influenced by a complaint, when the CPS is duty bound to carry out an impartial review.

30.74   It follows that the decision to prosecute was not made until December 9, 2009, three-and-a-half years after the arrest. In the meantime, the appellant had been told he would not be prosecuted in an email to his solicitors in June 2007. The email, which was sent by the police, had not followed the usual CPS practice[82] of including an explanation that the decision was subject to some form of qualification.[83] In November 2007 the appellant's solicitors were informed that, following the request for a further review, the CPS was conducting such a review in accordance with the Code for Crown Prosecutors. In May 2009, an Inspector in the Metropolitan Police wrote to an MP, following his intervention on behalf the appellant, explaining that no further action would be taken. This was a reference to the earlier decision, as the Inspector was unaware of the review then taking place within the CPS. The appellant was subsequently informed following the third tier review that he would be prosecuted when he was summonsed to appear at the magistrates' court in February 2010.

30.75   Before the trial, the judge heard an application on behalf of the appellant that the proceedings should be stayed for abuse of process. It was contended that the decision of the Divisional Court in *Croydon Justices Ex p. Dean*[84] made clear that the prosecution of a person to whom it has been represented that he would not be prosecuted would generally amount to an abuse of process. The judge concluded that there was a strong public interest that the case should be tried, particularly as the complainants were very vulnerable, subject to the appellant being able to have a fair trial. In his view, it would have been an affront to justice for the case not to proceed. He dismissed the application, and after the prosecution evidence he affirmed his decision. On appeal, it was submitted that the judge's decision to allow the matter to proceed and to dismiss the application for a stay for abuse of process was wrong. The Court of Appeal held that the trial judge had been correct in his conclusions. There had been no unequivocal representation. Furthermore, whilst accepting there was clear strain upon the appellant, the delay in itself did not amount to an abuse of process or cause prejudice or detriment.

30.76   There will be historic cases in which there will have been earlier decisions not to prosecute. To prosecute after such a decision where there has been no manipulation of the process of the court, will not without more amount to an abuse. In any event, often the earlier decision will be understandable in the light of the application of the rules of evidence and/or the landscape of criminal justice at that time.[85]

---

[82] See Phillips LJ in *Burk*, Unreported, December 12, 1996, CO/2286/96.

[83] In *Killick*, the Court of Appeal concluded (at [22]) that, notwithstanding the absence of the usual qualification, the appellant's solicitor must be taken to have been aware of the usual rights of review.

[84] [1993] Q.B. 769.

[85] See *Taylor* [2013] EWCA Crim 2398, in which Treasury Counsel had advised that the case should not be prosecuted in 1980. The Court of Appeal was satisfied that the trial judge had been correct to reject an application for abuse of process.

WHERE CHALLENGES IN RESPECT OF DELAYED COMPLAINTS RISK REVELATION OF EARLIER OR LATER WITHDRAWN COMPLAINTS

The defence may face the dilemma of whether or not to explore matters   **30.77**
relating to an earlier trial in which the defendant was acquitted, and the
investigations that led to that trial. If the complainant in the current trial
alleges different offences to the ones of which the defendant was acquitted,
and the current charges are not based on the same or substantially the same
facts as the original allegations, then without more, an application to stay is
unlikely to succeed. In those circumstances it will be for the defence to make
the kind of tactical decision that frequently arises in trials. This situation
arose in *MacKreth (deceased)*,[86] where neither the prosecution nor the
defence faced any impediment in leaving the events relating to the earlier trial
and investigation unmentioned. The Court of Appeal took the view that it
was plainly the defence's calculation that there was no mileage in opening up
the issue and that it represented unacceptable dangers.

The Court in *Turner (Michael John)*[87] also took account of the defence's   **30.78**
forensic dilemma brought about by the delay. A proper investigation of the
reasons for the delayed complaints risked the revelation of the withdrawn
complaints. The appellant was therefore impeded in the way he could
conduct his defence. Here, a fair trial was jeopardised because the dilemma
was the product of extreme delay combined with the absence of crucial
documents. The Court felt that, standing alone, the absence of the potential
witnesses would not have led it to quash the conviction. The judge had
summed up as to the effect their evidence might have had. However, taken
cumulatively with the other aspects of the case, a fair trial was not possible.

COMPLAINANTS SEEKING FINANCIAL COMPENSATION

A complainant's application to the Criminal Injuries Compensation Author-   **30.79**
ity ("CICA") for financial compensation may be significant if the details of
the application show significant inconsistencies with the complainant's
evidence. Whilst the loss of an application form is unlikely, on its own, to lead
to a finding of abuse, it was the major factor in leading the Court of Appeal
in *Ali and Altaf*[88] to conclude that the loss of evidence could not be cured by
judicial direction. The trial, for offences of rape and false imprisonment, had
taken place just over 10 years after the date of the allegations. Both
complainants, who were friends, had made applications to the CICA after
they had complained to the police. The application in respect of complainant

---

[86] [2009] EWCA Crim 1849.

[87] [2000] Crim. L.R 832. For recent analysis of this case, see *MacKreth (deceased)* [2009]
EWCA 1849 at [33].

[88] [2007] EWCA Crim 691. There was also an "unsatisfactory initiation of complaints" and an
important officer's notebook had been destroyed.

S existed and was admitted by S to be false in significant respects. The complainant T's application was no longer available. No one could know whether she had falsified her account to the CICA. Delay had removed any opportunity for the defence to investigate whether she adopted the same approach as her friend. When giving his ruling, the trial judge had stated: "It is inconceivable, in my judgment, that a jury reading S's claim will not say 'there is a real risk here that not one but both these girls are lying about what happened'." When directing the jury he said " . . . we do not know what was in T's application to the CICA. If it contained lies, like S's did, the defendants have been disadvantaged by its loss. Although you must not speculate as to the detail it contained, if you think that it is a disadvantage to the defendants you must bear that in mind when considering whether the prosecution have made you sure of his guilt." In the Court of Appeal, Moses LJ accepted that the judge was attempting to assist the appellants and mitigate any prejudice caused by the missing document, but pointed out the contradiction between the direction not to speculate and the fact that he was leaving to the jury the question whether the absence of the document caused the appellants any disadvantage. Effectively the judge was enjoining the jury not to make any assumption that the missing document contained a falsehood. The only way the prejudice caused by such a loss could have been cured was by directing the jury to assume that T's application was as mendacious as that of S, in line with the judge's earlier conclusion in his ruling. The Court held that the absence of the document and the way the jury were directed gave them grave cause for concern as to the safety of the verdicts.

30.80 There will be cases where complainants make applications for compensation after the outcome of the trial or deliberately defer an application until its conclusion. During the trial, it is a perfectly acceptable tactic on the part of the defence to suggest that a complainant may be motivated by the prospect of compensation and that such motive may make the complainant's evidence unreliable. However, the Court of Appeal has stated that it does not see it as unacceptable for complainants to defer (or for their solicitors to advise them to defer) making a final decision on whether to claim compensation until after the conclusion of the trial.[89]

30.81 In *MacKreth (deceased)*,[90] one of the grounds of appeal related to the danger that the complainants were motivated by the lure of compensation to such an extent that they gave perjured evidence, and to a complaint that non-disclosure by the prosecution denied the jury a proper appreciation of that danger. This was an historic abuse case dating back to when Mr MacKreth was the superintendent or deputy of Derwent House, a residential care home for young persons aged between 12 and 16. By the time of the appeal it was known that the majority of complainants at least had made compensation claims after the trial, either to the CICA or in the courts, and some had made

---

[89] *Sutton* [2005] EWCA Crim 190.
[90] [2009] EWCA Crim 1849.

both. The Court of Appeal was unimpressed by this ground, observing that it must have been obvious to the jury that compensation in one form or another would be available to the complainants if Mr MacKreth was convicted. This is likely to be the position in many historic sex cases.

NATURE OF THE INVESTIGATION—TRAWLING OR DIP SAMPLING

In a report in 2002,[91] the Home Affairs Select Committee identified the fact **30.82** that in many cases relating to allegations of sexual abuse in residential homes the evidence is produced by trawling for witnesses, often by "dip sampling", which carries with it the risk of instilling into those who are providing the information, in effect, the indication that certain answers may be expected by those making the enquiries. This practice is unlikely to found a meritorious application for a stay, since the defence can explore with witnesses the way in which they first made their allegations. However, in *Mayberry*,[92] Latham LJ, after referring to the practice of trawling for witnesses, acknowledged that it is not easy to make a proper inquiry into the way in which the evidence has ultimately emerged so as to enable a court to evaluate the quality of the evidence satisfactorily. He observed that the court has various control mechanisms, which include ensuring that the jury is directed adequately as to the way in which the defendant may be prejudiced, both generally and in relation to particular allegations, by the way in which the evidence has emerged, so ensuring that the defendant's case in respect of individual complainants is adequately presented to the jury. This requires the judge to be scrupulous about putting the defendant's case to the jury in summing up.

DIRECTIONS

INCONSISTENCIES AND SUMMING UP WHERE THERE ARE MULTIPLE COUNTS

In relation to each count, it is necessary to summarise the evidence which **30.83** goes to that count and any significant disputes that arise upon that evidence, so that such discrepancies as arise from each witness whose evidence goes to that count are disclosed. It will only confuse a jury if the judge outlines the evidence of one witness in relation to several events and then, possibly a day later, turns to another witness's evidence in relation to the same events. Only by a summary focused upon a particular count can assistance be given to a jury faced with numbers of counts relating to different events. This was the

---

[91] Fourth Report, *The Conduct of Investigations into Past Cases of Abuse in Children's Homes*, October 22, 2002. See also the Government's reply to the Fourth Report 2002 (2003).
[92] [2003] EWCA Crim 782 at [36].

approach advocated by the Court of Appeal in *Robson.*[93] The Court went on to say[94]:

> "We would again suggest, without intending to be prescriptive, that the best way of coping with the task is to take time after the end of the evidence, either before or after speeches, to consider with counsel on both sides how the evidence is to be summarised focused on the relevant counts and issues . . . we suggest in cases . . . posing complicated factual counts arising out of historical events, time would be well spent in seeking assistance of counsel as to which pieces of evidence go to which counts and the significant controversies that arise out of that evidence. By such means a judge, with the assistance of counsel, can give directions as to fact to the jury which do, in reality, assist them to focus on the significant issues which arise under the separate counts. If this process takes time and causes delay before the jury's consideration, it is, we suggest, time well spent."

DELAY

30.84   The courts have decided that even very considerable delays before prosecution can, save exceptionally,[95] be managed within the trial process. The point is often (though not necessarily always) best addressed by a short, self-contained direction that focuses on the defendant rather than one that amalgamates this aspect with other aspects of the relevance of delay, for instance its impact on the complainant's ability to recall events. As with the direction on the burden and standard of proof, the direction regarding delay as it affects the defendant is designed to ensure the trial is fair. Whilst it is appropriate to deal with other aspects of the consequences of delay, these should be dealt with separately so as not to dilute the impact of the direction that is designed to protect the defendant from the potential consequences of delay. It is desirable for the direction to identify the possible difficulties which the defence have encountered as result of the delay. For instance, quite apart from difficulties for a defendant in remembering events many years ago, significant lines of inquiry may have been closed for the defence in that records may have been lost or destroyed, whilst witnesses who are of potential importance may have died or become untraceable.

30.85   In *R. v PS*,[96] the Court of Appeal had to consider the adequacy of a judge's directions to the jury on the approach they should take to a delay of 34 years before the alleged events were brought to trial. The complainant V came from a family of devout Buddhists from Sri Lanka. Every fortnight whilst she was a child her family travelled from Birmingham to attend services at a temple in West London, which the appellant had joined as a junior monk in February 1978. The allegation against the appellant was that in 1978 he

---

[93] [2006] EWCA Crim 2754.
[94] At [11].
[95] See para.30.95, below.
[96] [2013] EWCA Crim 992.

committed four sexual assaults upon V when she was approximately nine, on three occasions in his bedroom and once in the shrine at the Temple. V told no one at the time, but over the years she told a friend, a man with whom she had a long term relationship, her sister, her husband and her mother. V's evidence was that the birth of her child in 2010 provided the catalyst for informing the police about these offences and her sister confirmed that V once again started to talk about these events.

The appellant denied the allegations. He stated that he abided by the **30.86** Buddhist principle that monks must not touch women. He suggested a nine-year-old child would not have been in the shrine room on a Saturday or Sunday and that there were many visitors to the temple (about 400 people during the course of a day). The appellant did accept that he took sweets to the appellant.

The Court of Appeal rejected the criticism that the judge had erred when **30.87** he directed the jury that identity was the issue in the case, as his approach to this issue reflected the clear reality of the trial and he correctly left identity as the determinative factor that the jury needed to resolve.

However, it was submitted that the direction on delay regarding identity **30.88** was wholly insufficient and that the jury should have been told there was a substantial need for caution or "conscientious concern", or an expression to like effect. The judge ought to have focused on the defendant's position alone and he should not—at that stage—have dealt with other issues linked to the issue of delay. For instance, whilst it was entirely appropriate for the judge to address delay in the context of the complainant's evidence, it was contended that wider considerations of this kind required distinct and separate treatment clearly delineated from the effect of delay upon the accused's case.

When dealing with the consequences of delay, the judge had described in **30.89** some detail the reasons V gave for the delay and suggested some of the questions that might have influenced V. Whilst the judge had directed the jury that effluxion of time can affect memory, he did so when reminding the jury that V and the appellant had been able to remember a substantial amount of the detail of what had occurred. Thereafter, in suggesting that delay may have acted to the appellant's disadvantage because "lines of enquiry which might have been open to him have been closed", particularly as regards the medical evidence for the last of the allegations (the shrine room incident), the judge then made the observation that if records had been available they may have assisted the prosecution, and he commented that this particular contention was in any event dependent upon a nine-year-old girl having made a complaint that would have led to a medical inspection.

The Court of Appeal took the view that, given the facts of this case, the **30.90** direction to the jury on delay should have included the following elements:

    (i) delay can place a defendant at a material disadvantage in challenging allegations arising out of events that occurred many years before, and this was particularly so in this case where the defence was essentially a simple denial;

(ii) the longer the delay, the more difficult meeting the allegation often becomes because of fading memories and evidence that is no longer available—indeed it may be unclear what has been lost;

(iii) when considering the central question whether the prosecution has proved the defendant's guilt, it is necessary to bear in mind the prejudice delay can occasion; and

(iv) a summary of the main elements of prejudice that were identified during the trial.

30.91   Whilst the Court accepted that the judge's direction, when considered globally, contained all the essential elements he needed to include when directing the jury on the issue of delay, it did not consider it was structured in the right way given the circumstances of the case. The Court felt that in most cases the correct approach would be a self–contained direction that focuses upon the potential consequences of delay for the accused. Fulford LJ explained[97]:

> "The risk of combining and interweaving the potential consequences of delay for the accused with other delay-related considerations ('putting the other side of the coin') is that the direction, as the principle means of protecting the defendant, is diluted and its force is diminished."

30.92   However, although the Court would have favoured a different approach to this aspect of the summing up, it did not consider what the judge had said amounted to a misdirection. He had addressed all matters relevant to this issue and had made it clear that the problems consequent upon delay were directly related to the burden and standard of proof. This case turned on the central question of the reliability of V's identification of the appellant 34 years after the events in question and it was inconceivable that the jury did not understand the potential difficulties this posed for the defence. The Court was confident that the convictions were safe.

30.93   *R. v MC*[98] is a classic example of a trial judge in an historic sex case "interweaving the potential consequences of delay for the accused with other delay related considerations" and failing to give a self-contained direction that focuses on the defendant. The appellant was convicted of a series of sexual offences on his daughter which were said to have been committed between 1981 and 1995, when she was aged between three and 15 years old. It was submitted on appeal that the trial judge had failed to give any adequate direction as to the consequences for the trial of the long lapse of time since the events in issue, and particularly failed to give a proper direction as to the potential for prejudice to the appellant in seeking to advance a defence after such a delay. The trial judge gave his direction on delay embedded in the middle of a long passage dealing with the delay in the emergence of the complainant's allegations and its effect on the complainant's evidence. The Court of Appeal agreed with the submission made by the appellant's counsel that the judge should have emphasised the fact that the

[97] At [37].
[98] [2015] EWCA Crim 717.

appellant may well have been deprived of the opportunity of lending reasonable colour to a mere denial of allegations made.

The origin of the delay direction is to be found in *Percival*,[99] where the   **30.94** Court of Appeal observed that prolonged delay must threaten the fairness of proceedings, particularly when the prosecution depend upon oral testimony as to events that occurred many years before and there has been a late complaint. Before a conviction could be regarded as safe in those circumstances, the Court would need to be satisfied that the judge had addressed in his directions the impact of delay both on the preparation and conduct of the defence and on the prosecution's discharge of the burden and standard of proof. Simply reciting the arguments of counsel is not enough, nor is it appropriate to diminish the impact of the delay by implying that there are disadvantages to both sides. However, in *R. v M (Brian)*[100] the Court of Appeal made it clear that *Percival* is not a blueprint. What is required is a direction tailored to the circumstances of the case. It needs to give a clear warning as to the impact of delay on the presentation of the defence case and any potential prejudice to the defence as a result of delay. In *R. v H (Henry)*,[101] Potter LJ, after reviewing the authorities in respect of the trial judge's obligation to refer to delay, stated that such a direction is not invariably required except where some significant difficulty or aspect of prejudice is aired or otherwise becomes apparent to the judge in the course of the trial. In particular, he stressed that the direction should be given in any case where it is necessary for the purposes of being even-handed as between complainant and defendant. In *R. v H (Henry)*, the appellant had been convicted of committing sexual offences against his daughter who was aged 25 by the time of the trial. The offences were alleged to have occurred when she aged between five and 17. She first made a complaint five years after the last act of abuse. On appeal, it was contended that the judge had erred in failing to refer to the difficulties faced by the defence in responding to the stale and uncorroborated allegations of the complainant. The Court of Appeal concluded that in this particular case the jury were well aware of the age of the case and the problems it raised, and the verdict was not unsafe. The evidence of the complainant was cogent in circumstances where the question of credibility was clearly underlined to the jury.

By way of contrast, *Dutton*[102] is an example of a case in which it was   **30.95** incumbent upon the judge, having decided not to stay the proceedings, to point out to the jury that what was said by the defendant about the possible prejudice to the defence as a result of the delay was a matter to which they should have proper regard. The case involved uncorroborated allegations relating to a period of between 14 and 20 years before the complaint was made. In the meantime a number of witnesses had died who realistically

[99] (1998) 95(27) L.S.G. 25.
[100] [2000] 1 Cr. App. R. 49.
[101] [1998] 2 Cr. App. R. 161.
[102] [1994] Crim. L.R. 910.

could have been expected assist the defence. *R. v E (John)*[103] is another powerful example of a case where the trial judge should have given directions as to the difficulties in which the defence found themselves. The complaints were made following a family disagreement. The allegations related to events that took place between 17 and 23 years before the trial. The appellant's brothers could have given crucial evidence, but they had died. Lord Taylor CJ said that the Court was not saying that as a matter of invariable practice the judge must give directions as to the difficulties in which the defence find themselves as a result of delay. But he went on to conclude:

> "We consider that in a case of this antiquity, with the evidence of the complainant totally uncorroborated, it was appropriate for the judge to give a direction of the kind we have indicated. His failure to do so in the circumstances we consider was a misdirection. It is upon that basis that we allow the appeal."

It follows that in cases of substantial delay, a direction should usually be given to the jury on possible difficulties with which the defence may have been faced as a result.

Irremediable prejudice

30.96 Whilst abuse of process remains an exceptional remedy in any circumstances, and the length of the delay is not of itself determinative of the need for a stay, rare cases do arise in which a jury direction is incapable of addressing the prejudice. The Court of Appeal regarded *R v JM*[104] as such a case in respect of certain counts that appeared on the indictment. The defendant was aged 96 and faced an indictment of 50 counts alleging sexual abuse in the 1950s and 1970s. The contemporaneous records of those complaints, which had not been sufficient to lead to charges at the time, were no longer available, depriving the defendant of the opportunity to explore discrepancies between the present allegations and those originally made. The judge stayed some of the counts as an abuse of process. The Court of Appeal rejected the prosecution's appeal against the terminating ruling. It was not a case where it was speculative whether the absence of materials might prejudice the defendant. The judge was entitled to assess the missing statements and investigations as fundamental and to rule that the prejudice arising to the defence not only was very real but also could not be adequately remedied by instruction to the jury.

Memory

30.97 Where appropriate, the jury should be directed as to how the passage of time is likely to affect memory. The impact on a witness's ability to recall detail

---

[103] [1996] 1 Cr. App. R. 88.
[104] [2015] EWCA Crim 1928.

applies equally to prosecution and defence witnesses, but it is of course the prosecution that bears the burden of proof. The jury may be troubled by the absence of circumstantial detail which, but for the delay, they would expect to be available. Conversely, they may be troubled by a witness's claim to recall a degree of detail which is unlikely after such a prolonged passage of time.[105] In this connection, the Court of Appeal in *Joynson*[106] referred to the "surprising apparent powers of recall" of witnesses in that case, relating to events 35 years and more before the trial.

Normally, expert evidence on the reliability of memory will not be   **30.98** admissible where the purpose of seeking to adduce it is to analyse the accuracy or otherwise of a statement made by a witness about distant childhood events, since such questions are for the jury to determine upon careful reflection on the evidence. Furthermore, the state of this difficult science means that currently there are strict limits on the admissibility of evidence based on memory research. This subject is discussed in paras 24.31 and following, above.

SPECIFIC LINES OF INQUIRY THAT HAVE BEEN CLOSED TO THE DEFENCE

A direction to the jury on the potential effect of delay on the defendant   **30.99** should be tailored to the particular case. The disadvantages that the delay presents should be identified and explained by reference to the burden of proof.[107] The disadvantages might be: (i) how an early report of rape might have led to a medical or forensic examination,[108] (ii) the difficulty in putting forward an alibi defence where dates are imprecise or events happened so long ago, (iii) the death of and/or inability to trace witnesses, and (iv) the loss or destruction of contemporaneous documents. In *MacKreth (deceased)*[109] the Court of Appeal quoted with approval the trial judge's summing up to the jury:

> "What you should have well in mind is that the documents which are no longer available may have enabled the defence to challenge the character, reliability and credibility of the complainants in ways not open now to the defence."

The judge then went on to discuss the specific effect certain pieces of missing evidence might have had upon the defendant's ability to challenge the prosecution's case. He ended with the strong warning that: "you must

---

[105] But see *Crown Court Compendium* 2016, Ch.20.1, Sexual offences —The danger of assumptions. Example 2: Complaint made for the first time when giving evidence.

[106] [2008] EWCA Crim 3049, cited in the *Crown Court Bench Book* 2010.

[107] *Crown Court Compendium* 2016, Ch.20.2, Sexual offences —Historical allegations; *R. v PS* [2013] EWCA Crim 992.

[108] In assessing whether there is prejudice one should bear in mind that such examinations do not always produce evidence helpful to the defence but equally may produce evidence that is very damaging to the defendant.

[109] [2009] EWCA Crim 1849.

have well in mind, when considering whether or not the prosecution have proved their case, the various points I have made to you about the delay in general terms and about the absence of documents specifically."

30.100   A defendant of good character will be able to assert that the absence of any further and similar allegation is significant. It follows that a defendant who faces an historic allegation of a sexual offence against a child may rely upon the fact that he has lived a family life for many years surrounded by children without any further such allegations being made.

30.101   Where, during the time since which has elapsed since the alleged offence, a defendant has not committed any offence, let alone one involving sexual abuse, the normal propensity direction should be tailored to include this. In *GJB v R.*,[110] it was held that such a direction is particularly apt where delay since the date of the alleged offence renders it more difficult for a defendant to defend himself. The jury in that case should have been directed that the fact that the appellant had been convicted of no similar offence during the intervening 10 years was an aspect of his character to which they should have had specific regard.

"Late" Complaint

30.102   Frequently, evidence of when and how the complaint was first made will be before the jury. In historic cases there will be occasions when the complainant did complain to someone at the time, but the matter did not lead to a prosecution. If a voluntary complaint was made shortly after the alleged offence, the prosecution may wish to rely upon the evidence of the person to whom the complaint was made, not just to show consistency, but also as evidence of the truth of the complaint where the criteria for admitting evidence of recent complaint are met under s.120(4) and (7) of the Criminal Justice Act 2003, discussed in paras 19.72 and following, above.

30.103   The common law required that the complaint must have been made at the first reasonable opportunity. The 2003 Act required (in s.120(7)(d)) that it must have been made "as soon as could reasonably be expected after the alleged conduct". But the courts soon began to give a broad interpretation to those words, in light of the increased understanding that early non-disclosure by a child, vulnerable witness or other complainant of a sexual offence will not necessarily have been unreasonable in the circumstances prevailing at the time.[111] Parliament took this trend to its natural conclusion by enacting s.112 of the Coroners and Justice Act 2009, which abolished the requirement that the complaint be made "as soon as could reasonably be expected" with effect from February 1, 2010. It follows that complaints, whenever made, are now admissible as evidence of their truth, and not merely as evidence of consistency, provided the s.120 criteria are met. It is important that juries are

---

[110] [2011] EWCA Crim 867.
[111] cf. *Openshaw* [2006] EWCA Crim 556.

directed that the evidence of a consistent complaint comes from the same person who now makes the complaint in the witness box and not from some independent source.[112]

The defence will frequently wish to bring out the fact that the complaint   **30.104** was made long after the time of the allegation, and will rely upon the lateness of the complaint to support a defence case of fabrication. Often there will be a catalyst that leads to the late revelation, e.g. the complainant family member forming an intimate relationship with a boyfriend, or the discovery that the defendant has abused another or others. In such cases the timing and nature of the disclosure will be instructive. Alternatively, the complainant may only recently have felt sufficiently confident to disclose the allegation.

Now that the phenomenon of 'late' reporting is better understood, it is   **30.105** acceptable for a trial judge to warn a jury about the dangers of making false assumptions because a complaint has been made at such a late stage, provided the direction is balanced and even-handed.[113] The judge can assist the jury with the common experience of the court in dealing routinely with such offences. A judge is entitled to make measured comments in a summing up as to the reasons why it might take time for young complainants to make allegations of abuse, in a case where late disclosure is relied on as supporting a defence of fabrication. In *R. v MM*,[114] the appellant was the step-father of the two complainants. He had moved in with the family. The prosecution case was that he had repeatedly raped one step-daughter over a three-year period when she was aged between eight and 10, and indecently assaulted an older step-daughter when she was aged between 11 and 13. The girls did not report what happened until some years later, significantly after the appellant had left the family home. One of the grounds of appeal was that the summing up was unfair and slanted towards the prosecution and against the defence in that the judge took it upon himself to give evidence to the jury about the reasons why the girls might not report incidents that had happened. After giving the appropriate direction to the jury as to how they should be alive to the possible prejudice to the defendant because of delay, the judge giving the following direction:

> "You are entitled to consider why these matters did not come to light sooner. The defence say it is because they are not true. The allegations are fabricated. Had they been true, they say, you would have expected a complaint to be made earlier and certainly when the defendant was out of the way. The prosecution say that it is not as simple as that. When children are abused, whether these two girls were abused is what you have to decide, they are often confused about what is happening to them and why it is happening. They are children. That is something you should have in the forefront of your mind when considering this. They might have some inkling that what is going on is wrong. Sometimes children even blame

---

[112] *R. v AA* [2007] EWCA Crim 1779.
[113] *Doody* [2008] EWCA Crim 2557; *Miller* [2010] EWCA Crim 1578. See also directions in the *Crown Court Compendium* 2016, Ch.20.1, Sexual offences —The danger of assumptions: see Directions, example 1: see Appendix G, below.
[114] [2007] EWCA Crim 1558.

themselves when there is obviously no need for them to do so. A child can be inhibited for a variety of reasons from speaking out. They might be fearful that they may not be believed, a child's word against a mature adult, or they might be scared of the consequences, or fearful of the effect upon relationships which they have come to know. The difficulties, you may think, are compounded in the family situation where they involve a family member for whom the feelings of the child may be ambivalent. The child might not like the abuse but there may be aspects of the abuser that causes the child to view them with some degree of affection. The fallout from disclosures can be unpredictable and sometimes calamitous. So, if a child or children are abused, they are often subject to very mixed emotions, and that can be the case particularly where there is an imposing adult in the household of whom they are perhaps afraid and who has overborne them and has power over them and warned them if they tell.

Whether any of that applies here is a matter for you. Equally, there are sometimes in lives, sometimes earlier, sometime later, when there is a trigger or the need arises to disclose, speak out. No easy thing to do, you may think, and it takes some courage to do so.

Ladies and gentleman, I make clear to you that I offer these matters to you not by way of direction in law but as things which in common sense and with knowledge of the world you might like to consider in assessing whether you find that there is a reason for the delay here and of course it also affects the honesty and truthfulness of the two girls.

You have heard explanations and it is entirely a matter for you but you may think that some of the things they said on the video and to you, K 'He told me I would get the blame. It's our secret', R, 'I didn't know whether they would believe me or him', both of them scared to an extent. 'I was worried about what would happen. I was worried about his reaction, what people might say.' It is a matter for you but you may think some of those reactions, if they are true, mirror some of the matters I have just been speaking about."

The Court of Appeal said that this passage, slightly elaborate as it was, did not go beyond the bounds of permissible comment on the part of a judge. The defence was fabrication, the jury were aware of it and in the Court's judgment did need some assistance as to the reasons why it might take time for girls to make allegations of this nature. The judge was entitled to give the measured comment he did. The Court also said that it took the view that this was a fair, and not a biased, summing up.

Corroboration

30.106 Since the implementation of s.32(1)(b) of the Criminal Justice and Public Order Act 1994, it has been unnecessary to warn a jury about the dangers of convicting a defendant on the uncorroborated evidence of a complainant merely because he or she has alleged a sexual offence. Guidance as to whether a judge should give a jury a warning and, if so, the nature of any such warning was given in *Makanjuola*.[115] It is a matter for the trial judge's discretion whether or not to give a warning to the jury in respect of the

---

[115] [1995] 2 Cr. App. R. 469, discussed in paras 19.106 and following, above. See also *Crown Court Compendium* 2016, Ch.10.2 (in Appendix G, below).

unsupported evidence of a complainant in a sexual case. To carry on giving "discretionary warnings" generally and in the same terms as were previously obligatory would be contrary to the policy and purpose of the 1994 Act. The nature of the warning and whether or not to give it will depend upon the circumstances of the case, the issues raised and the quality of the witness's evidence. There would need to be an evidential basis for suggesting that the evidence of a witness is unreliable, which does not include mere suggestions by cross-examining counsel. Where some warning is required, it will be for the judge to decide the strength and terms of the warning; it does not need to be invested with the florid regime of the old corroboration rules. Where a witness has been shown to be unreliable in their evidence, as distinct from this merely being suggested in cross-examination, the trial judge may consider that the jury should be warned to approach the evidence with caution; however, such a warning may not be necessary.[116] There is no rule that in all cases of historic abuse it is necessary for judges to direct the jury on the need for corroboration; and the *Makanjuola* guidance applies to historic cases as it does to all others. The decision whether to give a direction on the special need for caution is a matter for the discretion of the trial judge, depending upon the evidence and the issues.

COLLUSION

Frequently in historic abuse cases there are allegations by more than one   **30.107**
complainant, e.g. allegations of sexual abuse made by former pupils or residents of an institution where the defendant used to work, or allegations of sexual abuse of children within the family. In these cases, assuming that severance is not appropriate, the issue of cross-admissibility will need to be addressed. For this subject, see paras 19.02 and following, above.

Where the allegations are cross-admissible, it is important for the judge to   **30.108**
direct the jury carefully about the dangers of innocent contamination[117] if there is any reasonable possibility that it may have occurred.[118] In *Lamb*,[119] the appellant, a teacher, had been convicted of engaging in sexual activity in breach of trust with two 17-year-old pupils he had taught at school. The Court of Appeal took the view that there was a clear possibility that the two complainants had been consciously or unconsciously influenced in their complaints, or their evidence about them, by hearing of and discussing with one another, the circumstances of their respective incidents. The trial judge had directed the jury on the dangers of dishonest collusion, but had failed to warn the jury that they must take into account the possibility of conscious or

---

[116] *Jobe* [2004] EWCA Crim 3155.

[117] Described in the standard JSB direction as conscious or unconscious influence.

[118] See *Lee* [2007] EWCA Crim 764 for a case in which the Court of Appeal considered that no direction on unconscious influence was necessary. See also *Ryder* (1994) 98 Cr. App. R. 242.

[119] [2007] EWCA Crim 1766.

unconscious influence when assessing the weight of the complainant's evidence. Furthermore, the appellant's counsel argued that the judge had over-emphasised the similarities between the incidents, making no allowance for the dissimilarities. The Court of Appeal acknowledged that it is necessary for the judge to give a balanced and accurate account of similarities, as the level of similarity is relevant to the issue of likelihood or unlikelihood of innocent coincidence.

Sentencing

30.109   Any offence committed before May 1, 2004, when the Sexual offences Act 2003 came into force, will be subject to the sentencing provisions of the applicable statute, e.g. the Sexual Offences Act 1956. We set out towards the end of this section the main offences under the pre-2003 Act regime, their maximum penalties and important points to bear in mind when sentencing these old offences. One such point is that all offences committed on or after April 4, 2005, will be the subject to the sentencing provisions of the Criminal Justice Act 2003, including the dangerousness provisions. If the offence was committed between May 1, 2004, and April 3, 2005, inclusive, the offence will be contrary to the Sexual Offences Act 2003 but the pre-Criminal Justice Act sentencing regime will apply. However, before looking at sentencing options, we first explain the general approach to the sentencing of historic sexual offences.

The Approach to Sentencing Historic Sexual Offences

30.110   The Sentencing Council guideline must be followed in relation to all offenders aged 18 and older when sentencing sexual offences on or after April 1, 2014, whenever the offence was committed. Further, Court of Appeal guidance on sentencing which is not compliant with the guideline should be disregarded.

30.111   In *R. v H(J)*,[120] the then Lord Chief Justice, Lord Judge, reviewed numerous Court of Appeal sentencing decisions in the context of sexual offences committed many years ago but only recently brought to conviction. He found that the Court of Appeal had at different times adopted conflicting approaches to the critical sentencing issues. He identified that specific guidance was required as to the extent, if any, to which the court passing sentence should reflect the levels of sentence which are likely to have been imposed if the defendant had been convicted at a trial shortly after the offences were committed and, by contrast, the extent to which the events during the long period between the commission of the crime and the sentencing decision may be relevant.

---

[120] [2011] EWCA Crim 2753. See Appendix B, below.

The approach was complicated not only by the way the substantive law and sentencing provisions have changed over the years, but also by the variety of sentencing regimes that have been in force over the same period. 30.112

In terms of principle, the Lord Chief Justice found it impossible to reconcile all the authorities. However, he summarised as follows the principles to be derived from statute, the authorities which purport to provide guidance, and fact-specific decisions[121]: 30.113

> "We suggest that with the exception of *Millberry and others*,[122] and the definitive sentencing guideline (used in the measured way we shall suggest) the following considerations should be treated as guidance. We further suggest that reference to earlier decisions is unlikely to be helpful, and, again dealing with it generally, to be discouraged. Subsequent decisions of this court which do not expressly state they are intended to amend or amplify this guidance should be treated as fact-specific decisions, and therefore unlikely to be of assistance to a court.
>
> (a) Sentence will be imposed at the date of the sentencing hearing, on the basis of the legislative provisions then current, and by measured reference to any definitive sentencing guidelines relevant to the situation revealed by established facts.
>
> (b) Although sentence must be limited to the maximum sentence at the date when the offence was committed, it is wholly unrealistic to attempt an assessment of sentence by seeking to identify in 2011 what the sentence for the individual offence was likely to have been if the offence had come to light at or shortly after the date when it was committed.[123]
>
> (c) As always, the particular circumstances in which the offence was committed and its seriousness must be the main focus. Due allowance for the passage of time may be appropriate. The date may have a considerable bearing on the offender's culpability. If, for example, the offender was very young and immature at the time when the case was committed, that remains a continuing feature of the sentencing decision.[124] Similarly if the allegations had come to light many years earlier, and when confronted with them, the defendant had admitted them, but for whatever reason, the complaint had not been drawn to the attention of, or investigated by, the police, or had been investigated and not then pursued to trial, these too would be relevant features.
>
> (d) In some cases it may be safe to assume that the fact that, notwithstanding the passage of years, the victim has chosen spontaneously to report what happened to him or her in his or her childhood or younger years would be an indication of continuing inner turmoil. However the circumstances in which the facts come to light varies, and careful judgment of the harm done to the victim is always a critical feature of the sentencing decision.

---

[121] At [46]–[47].

[122] [2003] 1 W.L.R. 546.

[123] In *R. v S (Paul Martin)* [2012] EWCA Crim 2668, the judge erred in sentencing on the basis of authorities existing at the time of the offence in 2000. However, the sentence under the current regime would not have been significantly different so it was not massively excessive.

[124] It follows that the historic nature of the case is not necessarily irrelevant to the sentencing decision. *R. v O*, Unreported, December 4, 2012, CA) is good example of a case where the appellant's mental age of eight at the time when he had raped his 17-year-old sister in 1977 was of relevance to the sentencing decision. The offender was 82 at the time of the appeal. The Court of Appeal, in reducing the sentence from seven to five-and-a-half years' imprisonment, also took into account the impact of imprisonment upon the appellant's wife who also had mental health difficulties. See also *Clarke (Robert)* [2012] EWCA Crim 9.

Simultaneously, equal care needs to be taken to assess the true extent of the defendant's criminality by reference to what he actually did and the circumstances in which he did it.

(e) The passing of the years may demonstrate aggravating features if, for example, the defendant has continued to commit sexual crime or he represents a continuing risk to the public. On the other hand, mitigation may be found in an unblemished life over the years since the offences were committed, particularly if accompanied by evidence of positive good character.

(f) Early admissions and a guilty plea are of particular importance in historic cases. Just because they relate to facts which are long passed, the defendant will inevitably be tempted to lie his way out of the allegations. It is greatly to his credit if he makes early admissions. Even more powerful mitigation is available to the offender who out of a sense of guilt and remorse reports himself to the authorities. Considerations like these provide the victim with vindication, often a feature of great importance to them."

It follows from (a) above that when passing sentence for an offence committed before April 6, 2010, the sentencer has a duty to have regard to the SGC guideline.[125] To apply a current guideline to an offence committed before it came into force does not offend the rule against retrospectivity as enshrined in art.7 ECHR.[126] That article prevents a sentence being imposed which could not have been passed at the time because the maximum was lower. In historic cases, provided sentences fall within or do not exceed the maximum sentence which could lawfully have been imposed at the date when the offence was committed, neither the retrospectivity principle nor art.7 is contravened.[127]

"Measured reference to any definitive sentencing guidelines relevant to the situation revealed by established facts"

30.114 The use by Lord Judge of the expression "measured reference" does not mean that the court should create a notional guideline, scaling down the starting point to a figure in the middle of the sentencing range that would have been available at the time the defendant committed these offences. The judge must follow the clear and structured decision-making process set out the in the current guideline whenever the offence was committed and reflect modern attitudes to historic offences.[128] In *Attorney General's Reference*

---

[125] s.172 of the Criminal Justice Act 2003. This provision was repealed by s.125(1) of the Coroners and Justice Act 2009, which requires the court to follow the relevant guideline unless it is not in the interests of justice to do so. However, it remains in force for offences committed before April 6, 2010.

[126] *Bao* [2007] EWCA Crim 2781.

[127] *R. v H(J)* [2011] EWCA Crim 2753 at [17]ff; *Flynn v HM Advocate* [2004] UKPC D 1; *R. (on the application of Uttley) v Secretary of State for the Home Department* [2004] UKHL 38.

[128] *Clifford* [2014] EWCA Crim 2245. In *Attorney General's Reference (No.1 of 2016) (GG)* [2016] EWCA Crim 62, Lord Thomas C.J. expressed the hope that in future courts will follow the Sentencing Council guideline (see Appendix B, below) and the judgment of Treacy LJ in *Clifford*.

(No.27 of 2015),[129] the defendant had been convicted of seven counts of indecent assault contrary to s.14(1) of the Sexual Offence Act 1956. The first four counts spanned a period between 1998 and 2004. It was alleged that he had subjected his niece to extensive sexual abuse over a number of years from the time she was aged five. The last three counts related to events in 1996 when it was alleged he abused a nine-year-old friend of one of his sisters. The judge reminded herself that the maximum sentence under s.14(1) was 10 years' imprisonment. She observed that the current equivalent offence is assault by penetration, which carries a maximum of life imprisonment and for which under the sentencing guideline there is an overall custody range of two to 19 years imprisonment and a starting-point of 11 years in the middle of the range. She then compared this to the position under 1956 Act, where the maximum was 10 years, which led her to re-calculate the sentencing range as four to seven years with a starting-point of five-and-a-half years, in the middle of that range. The Court of Appeal held that this approach of constructing an alternative notional sentencing guideline had been wrong.[130]

Youth/immaturity of the offender at the time of the offences

Lord Judge CJ in the leading authority of *R. v H(J)* made it plain that the court should not seek to establish the likely sentence had the offender been convicted shortly after the offence. The court should have regard to any applicable sentencing guidelines under the Sexual Offences Act 2003. However, the principle that an offender must be sentenced according to the sentencing regime applicable to his or her age at the time of sentence can produce acute difficulties when sentencing an offender who has committed offences many years earlier when a youth or a child. In *R. v H(J)*, Lord Judge also stated[131]:

> "As always, the particular circumstances in which the offence was committed and its seriousness must be the main focus. Due allowance for the passage of time may be appropriate. The date may have a considerable bearing on the offender's culpability. If, for example, the offender was very young and immature at the time

30.115

---

[129] [2015] EWCA Crim 1538 the overall sentence was increased from nine to 13 years.

[130] For strong criticism of this approach to "measured reference", see Lyndon Harris and Dan Bunting, *Has the approach to sentencing historical offences changed?*, *Archbold Review*, Issue 4, May 11, 2015. The authors point out that the impact upon sentencing levels of this apparent change in focus—now centred on the current sentencing levels for the modern equivalent offence—is to sentence historical offences as if they were current offences, subject to the maximum sentence which pertained at the time. In many cases lower maximum sentences will not limit sentence since, where a defendant falls to be sentenced for multiple offences, consecutive sentences are of course permissible, subject to a reduction for totality. See *Clifford* [2014] EWCA Crim 2245. The authors observe that the main exception to this would appear to be "single incident" cases, where the lower maximum sentences may provide an actual constraint on the sentencing powers of the Court. The nature of the historical sexual offences means these cases will be few and far between.

[131] At [47(c)].

when the case was committed, that remains a continuing feature of the sentencing decision."

It follows that there can be no doubt that culpability has to be assessed by reference to the age and maturity of the offender at the time of the offending.[132] The assessment of an offender's maturity and the situation many years earlier that led to the offending is often far from straightforward. As Macur LJ acknowledged in *Attorney General's Reference (No 121 of 2015) (Jonathan R)*,[133] when stating that it was not possible to derive any sentencing principles from that case:

"... a collection of scenarios involving far more varied circumstances and ages would have to be before the court to gain any meaningful baseline, if it is at all possible to do so in the face of multi factor considerations in the nuances of an individual's maturity and the nature of the offending involved."

30.116 In the Sentencing Council's recently-published consultation paper *Sentencing Youths – Overarching Principles and Offence Specific Guidelines for Sexual Offences and Robbery*,[134] it is observed that it is important to bear in mind any factors that may diminish the culpability of a young offender. They have not attained full maturity and as such may not fully appreciate the effect their actions can have on other people. They may not be capable of fully understanding the distress and pain they cause to the victims of their crimes. They are also likely to be susceptible to peer pressure and other external influences. It is important to consider the extent to which the offender acted impulsively, and to which their conduct was affected by inexperience, emotional volatility or negative influences. The draft *Sexual Offences Guideline* in the consultation paper begins with a short narrative that provides a good illustration of the myriad circumstances in which offending by the young can arise:

"Young people are less emotionally developed than adults; offending can arise through inappropriate sexual experimentation; confusion about sexual identity or orientation; gang or peer group pressure to engage in sexual activity; or a lack of understanding regarding consent, exploitation and coercion.
Background factors may also play a part:
–   Offender is or has been the victim of abuse (sexual, physical or emotional)
–   Exposure to pornography or materials which are unsuitable to the age of the offender
–   Involvement in gangs associated with child sexual exploitation
–   Unstable living or educational arrangements
–   A trigger event such as the death of a close relative or a family breakdown."

---

[132] See the *SGC Guideline – Overarching Principles – Sentencing Youths*, para.24. See also the judgment of Hallett VP in *Attorney General's Reference (No 32 of 2016)*, unreported, April 7, 2016.
[133] [2016] EWCA Crim 173.
[134] p.9. The consultation paper, which was published in May 2016, can be found on the Council's website.

More guidance is required in terms of the appropriate reduction for 30.117
offences committed during an adult offender's minority and, in particular,
how the court should balance the seriousness of the offending against the
offender's immaturity at the time. Recent cases shed light on the extreme
difficulty of these sentencing exercises. Unresolved issues include the extent
to which reliance should be placed upon (i) the Sentencing Guidelines
Council's *Definitive Guideline – Overarching Principles – Sentencing Youths*,
and (ii) Part 7 of the SGC's definitive guideline, dealing with sentencing of
youth offenders for offences with a lower statutory maximum when committed by a person under the age of 18. In *Attorney General's Reference
(No.121 of 2015) (Jonathan R)*,[134a] the trial judge, when sentencing a man
aged 49 for one count of rape of his sister when he was aged 14 and she was
five, and four counts of indecent assault of another sister when she was three
or four, made reference to the SGC's youth guideline. In particular, the judge
referred to the principles governing sentences of long-term detention for
offenders aged 14 or less, and the guidance on scaling down sentence for
young offenders aged between 14 and 17 on the basis of immaturity. She
made reference to cases where it may be appropriate to consider a starting
point from half to three quarters of that applicable to an adult offender. She
said:

> "I have to consider you as a 14-year-old and if we roll back the years and you
> were standing in front of me, aged 14, having committed these offences and
> having come from the background that you did, it seems unlikely I would have
> passed a sentence of detention...I would be saying this is a young boy who needs
> some serious help and intervention, as did all his siblings to get them out of the
> terrible family situation that they were living in."

The Court of Appeal took the view that the judge had departed from the
basic tenets of *R. v H* and had not sentenced in accordance with the
offender's age at the time of sentence. It therefore quashed a two-year
suspended sentence and imposed an immediate custodial sentence of three
years. In particular, the Court was concerned by the interplay given by the
judge to the sentencing guideline in respect of sexual offences now in force
and applicable to the case, and the youth guideline. The Court stated that the
narrative of the youth guideline will be significant and helpful in identifying
the appropriate principles to be applied in considering the impact on
culpability in an individual case. What is of less, if any, import in such a case
as this is what sentence would have been imposed if the offender was 14, 15,
16 or 17, appearing before the court at date of sentence. It follows that the
Court was expressly not adopting the 75 per cent reduction derived by the
judge from the youth sentencing guideline.

However, it has been suggested in other cases that weight should be given 30.118
to the reductions envisaged in the SGC's youth guideline. In *Attorney
General's Reference (No.61 of 2014) (R. v GJH)*,[134b] the Court of Appeal

[134a] [2016] EWCA Crim 173.
[134b] [2014] EWCA Crim 1933; [2015] 1 Cr. App. R.(S.) 25.

acknowledged that, when considering whether a sentence passed in an historic case was unduly lenient, the offender's youth and immaturity at the time of the offences must be highly relevant to an assessment of culpability, even though the Court found it hard to conceive that a 14, 15, or 16-year-old youth of sufficient intelligence subsequently to become a teacher, could regard the sort of repeated conduct which he inflicted on two very young children over a protracted period as anything other than seriously wrong. The Court acknowledged that the Attorney General's concession that the age of the offender operated significantly to reduce sentence was correct in the light of the SGC's youth guideline. The Court observed that for someone of the offender's age at the time of the offending, that guideline would envisage a reduction of around 50 per cent from the appropriate sentence to reflect the youth and immaturity inherent in the offender's age.

30.118A   A further issue has emerged. In relation to offences which carry a lower statutory maximum for young offenders, and which might have been charged had the offender been under 18, the issue arises as to the extent that a sentencing court should have regard to Pt 7 of the SGC's definitive guideline, which has not been superseded by the Sentencing Council's adult guideline. This begs the question of whether the equivalent offence under the Sexual Offences Act 2003 would have been the adult offence or the offence (under s.13, 25 or 26 of the Act) that carries a lower maximum for youths, i.e. (i) sexual activity with a child; (ii) causing or inciting a child to engage in sexual activity; (iii) engaging in sexual activity in the presence of a child; (iv) causing a child to watch a sexual act; (v) sexual activity with a child family member; or (vi) inciting a child family member to engage in sexual activity. The maximum sentence in all these cases is limited to five years. A reference to Pt 7 would be likely to lead to significant reductions in sentence.

30.118B   The Court of Appeal in *R. v GB*[134c] took the view that Pt 7 should have been applied. The judge at first instance had been significantly misled in that he had not been referred to either Pt 7 of the SGC guideline or the SGC's *Overarching Principles – Sentencing Youths*. The appellant, aged 67 when sentenced, received a total sentence of 15 months' imprisonment for one offence of incest and two of indecent assault committed upon his sister when he was 14–15 and she was 13–14. The Court of Appeal had regard to Pt 7 of the SGC guideline in respect of offences involving penetration where one or more aggravating features were present[134d]: *Sentencing Youths* and s.41(1)

[134c] [2015] EWCA Crim 1501 (the judgment was given by Goss J sitting with Hallett VP and Baker J).

[134d] The modern equivalent offences would be s.25 of the SOA 2003 (sexual activity with a family member), to which s.91 of the Powers of Criminal Courts (Sentencing) Act 2000 applies, setting a maximum for an offender aged under 18 of five years' custody. Part 7 of the SGC guideline provides a starting-point of a Detention and Training Order of 18 months for a first-time offender who pleads not guilty for an offence involving penetration where one or more aggravating features is present with a range of a Detention and Training Order of six to 24 months. In cases in which there are no aggravating features, the starting point is a community order with a range of an appropriate non-custodial sentence.

of the Children and Young Persons Act 1933. In particular, the Court of Appeal observed that regard had to be had to the welfare of the offender. It was common ground that if the offences had occurred and were brought to the attention of the authorities the day of the appeal, in the absence of any of the aggravating features referred to in the guidelines, a 15-year-old boy who offended in this way might well be made the subject of a non-custodial sentence in order to educate, repair damage and effect rehabilitation rather than retribution. The Court then asked itself whether the judge had been justified in passing a sentence on the appellant far harsher than would be imposed if he were a 15-year-old boy. It was noted that this was not a case where the appellant's behaviour had added to the complainant's reasons for not revealing what happened. Further, as an adult, the appellant had led an honest and industrious life for 50 years. He had been of considerable assistance to all his family, including the complainant and her immediate family. He was remorseful, had acknowledged what he did and been punished for it. The Court concluded that, in the circumstances, to impose a custodial sentence was wrong in principle and it substituted a community sentence.

Similarly, in *R. v PK*[134e] the Court of Appeal, without making direct reference to Pt 7 of the SGC guideline, when dealing with an appeal against sentence by an appellant, aged 53, in respect of indecent assaults committed upon his two younger siblings when he was aged between 11 and 14, noted the existence of the equivalent child sex offence under s.13 of the Sexual Offences Act 2003 and the need to consider SGC's *Overarching Principles – Sentencing Youths* if a person was aged under 18. The Court concluded that, in applying the modern adult guideline, the judge had failed to give sufficient weight to the factors of exceptional mitigation upon which the appellant could properly rely. In particular, the Court stressed the appellant's very young age at the time he committed the offences and his evident immaturity. **30.118C**

It remains to be seen whether the Court of Appeal will continue to take the view that s.13 (or ss.25 or 26, as the case may be) is the modern equivalent offence, on the basis that the offence was committed by a person under the age of 18, *or* whether the view will be taken that this approach falls foul of the principle enunciated in *R. v H*, that the court should not seek to establish the likely sentence had the offender been convicted shortly after the date of the offence. Furthermore, following a consultation period, it is likely that Pt 7 of the SGC guideline will be replaced by a new youth guideline as part of wider work by the Sentencing Council on the issue of youth sentencing. In particular, the proposed offence-specific guideline on sexual offences will cover *all* sexual offences committed by a person under 18, rather than just those offences which have a lower maximum penalty when committed by a person under that age. Arguably, they will be of great relevance to the **30.118D**

[134e] [2015] EWCA Crim 648.

assessment of culpability when offenders are sentenced for sexual offences committed when they were very young.

30.118E   On any view, the focus of these difficult sentencing exercises should be on assessing culpability on the basis of the offender's young age and maturity at the time of the offending. There may also be mitigation in the absence of further offending over a long period of time, especially when combined with evidence of good character.[134f] Whilst rehabilitation will not be of such importance when a mature adult is being sentenced, it may be illogical to pass a higher sentence when a person has in fact rehabilitated himself. Passage of time since the offence, the age of the offender at the time he committed an offence, and the fact that an offender has not been convicted of any offence since the offending, are all factors which are relevant to sentencing and to the question of suspension.[134g]

Elderly offenders/declining health

30.119   There are an increasing number of elderly offenders who have to be sentenced for offences involving sexual abuse committed even 50 or 60 years ago. Some are in their eighties. There have been and will likely continue to be offenders who have reached the age of 90. Many of them will not have offended for many decades. It is well recognised that these cases pose difficult questions for sentencers. Advanced age often accompanied by severe health problems are factors that have to be taken into account. However, in serious cases they will have only limited effect.

30.120   In *R. v AM and MG*,[135] the Court of Appeal, when dealing with an appeal against sentence by an appellant aged 81 at the time of sentence, reviewed appeal cases dealing with offenders who were elderly at the time of sentence. The Court acknowledged that whilst there appeared to be little in the way of

---

[134f] The passage of time may aggravate the seriousness of the offence where the offender has continued to commit sexual offences against the victim or others, or has continued to prevent the victim from reporting.

[134g] See *Attorney General's Reference (No.32 of 2016)*, unreported, April 7, 2016, per Hallett VP, for discussion of factors relevant to suspension. In that case, the Court refused leave to the Solicitor General to refer the sentences on the basis they were unduly lenient. The offender had been convicted of two counts under s.15 of the SOA 1956. The first offence was committed when the offender was 11 and the victim was three. The offender committed the second offence when he was 14 and that victim was five. Arguably, the equivalent offences under the SOA 2003 would have been s.5 (rape (oral) of a child under 13). In February 2016, following a trial, the judge passed concurrent sentences of two years' imprisonment suspended for two years. The offender was in his mid-forties at the time. In refusing leave, Hallett VP indicated that there is no principle of sentencing that all offences of this kind must be met by immediate terms of imprisonment whatever the circumstances. The Court also rejected the argument that the judge would not have been entitled to suspend sentence upon the basis of exceptional circumstances. In particular, *Attorney General's Reference (No.61 of 2014)* [2014] EWCA Crim 1933; [2015] 1 Cr. App. R.(S.) 25 was a case on its own facts, and does not lay down any principle that the passage of time can never amount to an exceptional circumstance so as to justify suspension under the Powers of Criminal Courts (Sentencing) Act 2000, which applies to cases before the implementation of the CJA 2003.

[135] [2014] EWCA Crim 1970.

general principle laid down in the cases, it is clear that old age and infirmity are factors to be taken into account in setting the sentence, in particular because prison will often be a greater punishment for someone of advanced years suffering from infirmity. The Court referred to Hughes LJ's observation in *Attorney General's Reference (No.65 of 2011)*[136] that the impact of prison is likely to be greater upon a frail man in his eighties than it would be on a younger person.

30.121 However, the starting points in the sentencing guideline must not be overlooked. Furthermore, it should be borne in mind that a decline in sexual urge[137] in advancing years is more a matter that goes to whether the court should invoke the dangerousness provisions of the Criminal Justice Act 2003 and pass an indeterminate sentence rather than to the length of a determinate sentence.

30.122 In *R. v C*,[138] the Court of Appeal upheld sentences totalling eight years' imprisonment on a man aged 79 for a series of sexual offences committed against his grandchildren, the last of which was committed 10 years earlier. Lord Taylor CJ stated:

> "Had this appellant been of younger years, we have no doubt that the appropriate sentence would have been in the region of 12 years. As it is the learned Judge was very conscious of the age of the appellant, and the fact that he suffered from certain illnesses . . . We consider that the reduction that the learned Judge made here was as great a reduction as these appalling circumstances could permit."

He added:

> "If we were to reduce it by one, two, three or four years, the point could still be made that the appellant, at the age of very nearly 80, might well not be able to live any part of his life in the community again."

30.123 In *Symmons*,[139] Hallett LJ observed:

> "The inevitable consequence of a 62 year old man committing a murder, for which the agreed starting-point is a minimum term of 15 years' imprisonment (to serve) is that he is going to grow old if not die in prison. His age, therefore, cannot be determinative of the finishing point; it is but one factor to be borne in mind in the sentencing process."

30.124 It is clear from *R. v C* and *Symmons* that there is no principle that the term of imprisonment must seek to avoid the likelihood that the defendant will die in prison. Lloyd Jones LJ noted in *R. v AM and MG*[140] that inevitably if there is a substantial delay in investigating and prosecuting historic sexual offences, the mere passage of time is going to increase the risk that, when prosecuted to conviction, elderly offenders are going to spend much of their declining years in prison and may die there.

---

[136] [2011] EWCA Crim 2277 at [14].
[137] A factor taken into account in *Hutchinson* (1988) 10 Cr. App. R.(S) 50.
[138] (1992) 14 Cr. App. R.(S.) 562.
[139] [2009] EWCA Crim 1304, at [21].
[140] At [39].

30.125   In *R. v AB*[141] the appellant, aged 90, had pleaded guilty to 14 counts of indecent assault. All counts were multiple incidents counts pursuant to what is now r.10.2(2) of the Criminal Procedure Rules 2015, each representing a different type of indecent behaviour. The victims were the appellant's own daughters by different wives. The offences were committed over 30 years earlier, between 1970 and 1984. Although the appellant's offending behaviour had been known within the family for many years, it was not until January 2014 that the police investigation began. One of the complainants had visited the appellant's home and confronted him about the abuse. She appeared drunk. There was an altercation and the appellant called the police. When officers arrived to investigate the incident, the appellant told them that he had sexually abused the complainant when she was a child and she had called to confront him about it. He said he could not take any more so he had called the police. In interview he admitted most of the offending. He was sentenced to a total of four years' imprisonment in December 2014. On appeal, it was argued that given his extreme age and poor health an immediate custodial sentence should have been avoided and a suspended sentence was appropriate given the pleas of guilty, previous good character and personal mitigation. The sentences were upheld. There were three significant aggravating features. First, there was the length of the offending; it was against his two daughters with successive periods of seven years in relation to each. There had been very grave impact on his victims. The appellant had tried to minimise his offending. The Recorder of Leeds, His Honour Judge Collier QC, giving the judgment of the Court, stated[142]:

> "A phrase that falls from the lips of a mitigator from time to time is that a judge in passing sentence should not deprive the defendant of the prospect of some light at the end of the tunnel. It is a factor, but another factor is the blighted lives that this appellant has caused to two of his own daughters. The course of their lives can properly be described as a long and dark tunnel with no light at its end, even though the offences have now been admitted. The damage done those years ago was too great. The appellant's health, his age, the prospect of his dying in prison were all factors to be taken into account in the sentencing. The judge took them into account. In our judgment the sentence of four years for the totality of offending cannot be said to be either wrong in principle or manifestly excessive. This appeal is therefore dismissed."

30.126   In *R. v AM and MG*,[143] the appellant was 81 at the time of sentence. He was frail and had declining faculties. He had a history of diabetes, anxiety, and osteoarthritis He suffered from falls and his mobility was severely impaired. Between 1981 and 1992, he had abused his step-daughter on a regular basis from when she was seven until she was 18. The abuse, described by the Court of Appeal as an appallingly cruel catalogue of offending, had culminated in the step-daughter bearing two of his children and continued until she fled the family home and went to live in a women's refuge. The

---

[141] [2015] EWCA Crim 1042.
[142] At [25].
[143] [2014] EWCA Crim 1970.

Court, whilst noting that the trial judge had not indicated how much allowance she was making for age and infirmity, concluded that the starting point would have been 25 years had the defendant been sentenced when he was 50 with no considerations as to age or infirmity. It followed that the judge did in fact make an appropriate reduction, from a starting point of 25 years to 20 years, in order to take into account these factors.

Abuse of celebrity status

In *Attorney General's Reference (No.38 of 2013) (R. v Stuart Hall)*,[144] the **30.127** Court of Appeal had to consider whether concurrent terms of imprisonment totalling 15 months for 14 counts of indecent assault upon children or teenage girls amounted to an unduly lenient sentence. The offender was aged 83 at the time of sentence. He had no previous convictions. For those with no idea of his criminal activities, he was highly regarded. At the time of the offences he had become a well-known television personality, and a popular and successful public figure. The indecent assaults upon 13 female victims took place over a period of almost 20 years between 1967 and 1985–6. The ages of the victims ranged from 9 to 17.

A significant, damaging effect of the offending was that it had caused **30.128** difficulties between the victims and their parents. For instance, one of the victims, aged 16, had told her parents and grandparents at the time, but the family had decided not to report the matter to the authorities. The victim's initial feelings of shock and humiliation had turned to anger because of her family's decision that she should try and forget about it as there was "no point in reporting it as Mr Hall was rich and famous and we were nobody. After that my anger stayed with me. I had no way to express it and no one I could tell".

Giving the judgment of the Court, the then Lord Chief Justice, Lord **30.129** Judge, observed[145]:

> "We reject the submission made to the trial judge that somehow the fact that the adults did not report these incidents when the children told their parents or grandparents (or whoever it may have been) provides an indication that they could not have taken the allegations seriously. We know why two families did not formally complain: they could not take on the famous celebrity. The offender's successful career provides no mitigation. On the contrary, it was the career that put him in a position of trust which he was then able to exploit and which contributed to his image as a cheerful, fun-loving, fundamentally decent man. This contributed to the view he could be trusted; and second, if he could not be trusted, effectively he was untouchable. It is true that he had no previous convictions of any kind. It is true that he has behaved decently on occasions and deserves credit for that. But we now know, as the world at large knows, that since the mid-60's he molested children and growing girls and therefore that he lived

[144] [2013] EWCA Crim 1450.
[145] At [75].

a lie—a lie for more than half his life; a lie repeated on the steps of the magistrates' court for the benefit of the accompanying media."

30.130   The Lord Chief Justice went on to explain that the offender's proclamation of innocence on the steps of the magistrates' court was a seriously aggravating feature.[146] The Court concluded that he was hoping to escape justice and was attempting to manipulate the media for the purpose of possibly influencing jurors. He was traducing 13 adult women who had been sexually assaulted by him in different ways 20–30 years before. Consistent with current sentencing practice, it was appropriate to reflect this aggravating feature in the assessment of sentence and then discount from it to allow for the guilty plea.

30.131   Taken in isolation, some of the offences would not have required a custodial sentence. Some, as time went by and the offender escaped detection, seemed to the Court to be marked with an increasing degree of thought and premeditation. The result of the offending taken as a whole was that a multiplicity of young girls were sexually molested over an 18-year period, some when they were very young, all when they were in one way or another vulnerable, and all when the offender was in a position to misbehave as he did just because of who he was, which meant he was trusted. All the offences were real assaults and not just technical assaults because the victims were too young to have consented in law. There was no question of any of the victims consenting to anything.

30.132   The Court concluded, making every allowance that could reasonably be made for the matters of mitigation, the sentence was inadequate, and increased it to 30 months' imprisonment. The double jeopardy principle did not apply. The appellant was in custody; he had been sentenced to an immediate custodial term. He had known that the Attorney General proposed to refer the sentence to the Court of Appeal.

The impact of exceptional circumstances where current guidelines suggest immediate custodial sentences are appropriate

30.133   Whilst all cases are fact-specific, recent Attorney General's References suggest that even wholly exceptional circumstances, including age and poor health, will not necessarily entitle a judge to depart from following current guidelines which indicate that an immediate custodial sentence is appropriate. In *Attorney General's Reference (No.1 of 2016)*,[146a] Lord Thomas C.J. stated that a judge, when sentencing historical sexual offences, should follow the approach in *R. v H(J)* and should guard against any temptation that,

---

[146] In *Clifford* [2014] EWCA Crim 2245 the Court of Appeal took the view that the appellant's statements to reporters were not comparable to Hall's public denouncement of his victims in particularly virulent terms. Treacy LJ stated that great care needs to be taken by sentencing courts not to elevate denials, albeit vehement, into something deserving of further punishment in the absence of some more explicit traducing of the victim.
[146a] [2016] EWCA Crim 62.

because of what happened in the intervening years, an appropriate sentence (here significantly in excess of two years) can be reduced and suspended. The trial judge had correctly identified the sentence of the modern equivalent offence as having a starting point of some eight years' custody with a range of 5-10 years, and then passed a suspended sentence on the basis of "exceptional mitigating factors". In *Attorney General's Reference (No.21 of 2015)*,[147] the 77-year old offender pleaded guilty to 10 specimen counts of indecent assault in respect of two female children aged 7–15 in circumstances where he had admitted to the offences when confronted by one victim, admitted them to his wife, the police and then the court. When the police called at his home in November 2014, he commented to them: "I have waited 40 years for this call." The Court of Appeal recognised that these were exceptional features. Rarely would an offender admit what he had done when confronted by his victim, and then confess to others including his wife. Even more rarely would an offender volunteer that he had abused not just one, but two victims. It had to help the offender's two victims to know that he had accepted, both in private and in public, the suffering he had inflicted upon them. Neither woman had to endure going into the witness box. It followed that the offender was entitled to a very considerable degree of credit. Furthermore the offender was suffering from a number of debilitating conditions and had led a blameless life since then. Nevertheless the court concluded that, in the particular circumstances, the judge had made too great an allowance for the powerful mitigation and paid too little attention to the seriousness of the offending. The aggravating features were (i) the age of the victims; (ii) the fact that there were two victims; (iii) the duration and frequency of the offending; (iv) that the offender would abuse one victim in the presence of the other and witnessed by her on occasion; (v) that there was a breach of trust involved; (vi) that the offending occurred in the victim's home; and (vii) that significant psychological damage was suffered by both victims. The Recorder had sentenced the offender to a total of two years' imprisonment suspended for two years. The Court of Appeal held that a sentence of significantly greater length should have been imposed. The Court was prepared to show a degree of mercy, but felt it had no alternative but to lift the suspension and order that the two years should be served as an immediate custodial term.

Similarly, in *Attorney General's Reference (No.14 of 2015) (R. v H)*[148] the **30.134** Court of Appeal held that a suspended sentence of two years' imprisonment imposed upon a 90-year-old offender in respect of historical sexual offences had been unduly lenient. The offences had been committed against two of his male relatives, the first when he was in his 30's and the complainant was between nine and 16, the second when he was in his 70's and the complainant was under 14. The offender had a dementing illness as well as significant

---

[147] [2015] EWCA Crim 953; [2015] 2 Cr. App. R.(S.) 41.
[148] [2015] EWCA Crim 949.

health problems. His prognosis was poor and he was completely dependent upon his wife to function properly, but the medical evidence was not such that it could not be managed in a custodial setting. The Court imposed a total sentence of five years' imprisonment to be served immediately.

30.135   Cases are always fact-specific and it does not follow from the cases cited above that a suspended sentence can never be appropriate in an historic case where children have been sexually abused, although such a case is likely to be rare. In *Attorney General's Reference (No.61 of 2014) (R. v H)*[149] the offender, when aged 15 and 16, had abused his step-brother aged five and step-sister aged six, when he had been "left in charge". The offences were committed over a period of 12–18 months and ended when the offender left the family home to join the army. Subsequently both victims received counselling and the judge found that the offences had had a profound effect upon them. Over two decades later, the offender's former wife made a complaint to the police and the offences came to light. In 2010, the offender pleaded guilty to taking a child without lawful authority and meeting a child following sexual grooming. He had become a teacher and head of the IT department whilst the victim was a 15-year-old female pupil. He was sentenced to 10 months' imprisonment for that offence and was made the subject of a sexual offences prevention order ("SOPO"). In January 2013, he admitted being in breach of the SOPO and received a three-year community order. The breach related to the continued contact with the female pupil. Subsequently, the SOPO was varied to permit contact between the offender and the pupil, who by then had become an adult and formed a relationship with the offender. The community order included a sex-offender treatment programme requirement which remained in force at the date of the Court of Appeal hearing.

30.136   At the time of sentence for the sexual abuse of his step-siblings, the offender was engaged in the sex-offender treatment programme. There was evidence of a shift in his level of denial to some form of acceptance of guilt, albeit not a whole-hearted one. The pre-sentence report stated that a custodial sentence would be unlikely to be of sufficient length to enable sex offender work to be undertaken with the offender in custody so as to reduce the risk of harm that he posed to others, and recommended a suspended sentence with an unpaid work requirement. The judge considered the breach of trust element but concluded that, because of the offender's age at the time, there was no significant breach of trust. The offender was sentenced to 18 months' imprisonment suspended for two years.

---

[149] [2014] EWCA Crim 1933; [2015] 1 Cr. App. R.(S.) 25. See also *Attorney General's Reference (No.32 of 2016)*, unreported, April 7, 2016, where Hallett VP, when dealing with two historic offences where the equivalent modern offence would have been rape of a child under 13 (s.5 of the SOA 2003) committed when the offender was aged 11 and 14 some 30 years earlier, stated that the passage of time, the age of an offender at the time he committed the offence, and the fact that an offender has not been convicted of any offence since the offending, may be relevant to the question of suspension. She made it clear that there is no principle of sentencing that all offences of this kind must be met by immediate sentences of imprisonment.

The Attorney General accepted that, whatever the appropriate starting point, the offender's age at the time ought significantly to reduce his sentence. The guideline *Overarching Principles—Sentencing Youths* envisaged a reduction of approximately 50 per cent for someone of the offender's then age (15 to 16). 30.137

The Court of Appeal concluded that whilst the 2010 conviction was an aggravating factor, research demonstrated that non-completion, or partial treatment, could increase the risk of re-offending. The effect of the judge's sentence would be to enable the sex-offender treatment programme currently in play to continue and be completed. To bring that programme to an end by substituting an immediate term of custody would not only frustrate such work as had been done but could actually exacerbate the situation. Two of the purposes of sentencing to which the court must have regard pursuant to s.142 of the Criminal Justice Act 2003 were the reduction in crime and the rehabilitation of offenders. To substitute an immediate term of imprisonment would be to run counter to those objectives, notwithstanding the objective of punishing an offender for serious offending which had done significant harm to others. Whilst the passage of time since the offending could not amount to an exceptional circumstance, the interruption of the sex-offender programme, with its concomitant potential exacerbation of the situation, could amount to an exceptional circumstance[149a] which would justify the suspension of the sentence under s.118 of the Powers of Criminal Courts (Sentencing) Act 2000. 30.138

Adequacy of the Medical Treatment Available When in Custody

In *Qazi*,[150] it was made clear that when passing sentence, the court ought not to concern itself with the adequacy of arrangements for the medical needs of the offender in prison. The medical needs of prisoners are well understood in the administration of prisons. It is only in circumstances where the very fact of imprisonment itself might expose the individual to a real risk of a breach of art.3 ECHR that the court will be called upon to enquire into whether sentencing a person to custody will mean a breach of that provision. The Court in *Qazi* was doubtful whether this situation would ever arise. This is not inconsistent with the general position set out by Rose LJ in *Bernard*,[151] that an offender's serious medical condition may enable a court to impose a lesser sentence as an act of mercy in the exceptional circumstances of a particular case rather than by virtue of any general principle of law. 30.139

[149a] Now see *Attorney General's Reference (No.32 of 2016)*, unreported, April 7, 2016, where the view was taken that *Attorney General's Reference (No.61 of 2014)* did not lay down any general principle that the passage of time can never amount to an exceptional circumstance.
[150] [2010] EWCA Crim 2579.
[151] [1997] 1 Cr. App. R.(S.) 135.

30.140   A medical condition which may at some unidentifiable future date affect either life expectancy or the prison's ability to treat a prisoner satisfactorily may call into operation the Home Secretary's power of release, but is not a reason for the Court of Appeal to interfere with an otherwise appropriate sentence. The fact that an offender is HIV positive, or has a reduced life expectancy, should not generally affect the sentence.

Good character since the offending

30.141   As Lord Judge acknowledged in *R. v H(J)*,[152] good character since the offending may be a mitigating factor. A recent example is *R. v PK*,[153] where one of the factors of exceptional mitigation was the fact that the appellant showed qualities of positive good character and excellent family background between the time when he sexually abused his younger siblings, when he was aged between 11 and 14, to his current age of 53. However, a judge must be careful not to make too great an allowance for powerful mitigating factors such a as a respectable life since the offending combined with poor health. These are only relevant to a degree in the face of serious offences with significant aggravating features.[154]

Relevance of change in licensing regime

30.142   Under the Criminal Justice Act 1991, an offender was entitled to automatic release only after serving two-thirds of his sentence, although he was eligible to apply for parole after serving a half. In contrast, following the implementation of the sentencing provisions in the Criminal Justice Act 2003, an offender who has served half his sentence is entitled to release, but subject to more stringent licensing conditions than before.[155] Sentences should follow appropriate principle and authority without regard to the practical effect of the licensing regime in force at the time of the commission of the offences. The difference in the release provisions does not justify a downwards adjustment in sentence.[156] It follows that it is not appropriate to make a reduction in an otherwise appropriate sentence because since the time of the offence the early release provisions have been changed and/or the licensing system made more severe.[157] Furthermore, a mis-statement by the judge of

[152] [2011] EWCA Crim 2753.
[153] [2015] EWCA Crim 648.
[154] *Attorney General's Reference (No.21 of 2015)* [2015] EWCA Crim 953; [2015] 2 Cr. App. R.(S.) 41, discussed in para.30.133, above.
[155] See *Whittle* [2007] EWCA Crim 539, where Stanley Burnton J (as he then was) described the benefits and disadvantages to an offender of the change as "more or less in balance."
[156] *R. v G (Raymond)* [2008] EWCA Crim 3123, where MacDuff J, giving the judgment of the Court, stated that they could see no reason why the appellant should benefit, if benefit it be, merely because his offences did not come to light until many years later.
[157] *Matthews (Alex Joseph)* [2011] EWCA Crim 3110; *Round, Dunn* [2009] EWCA Crim 2667; [2010] 2 Cr. App. R.(S.) 45 (p.292), referred in *R. v H(J)* [2011] EWCA Crim 2753 at [19].

the appropriate licensing regime does not necessarily mean that the judge has been wrongly influenced by the mistake.[158]

MAXIMUM SENTENCES FOR SEXUAL OFFENCES BEFORE THE SEXUAL OFFENCES ACT 2003

In the late 1990s and early 2000s, much greater public awareness of the nature **30.143** and effect of sexual assaults and other sex crime combined with an increase in reporting meant that the issue has steadily climbed the political agenda. It was increasingly apparent that the Sexual Offences Act 1956 failed to reflect present day morality and sexual practices. Following a comprehensive review of the law, the Government responded by enacting the Sexual Offences Act 2003, which came into force on May 1, 2004. The Act overhauled the legislation governing sexual offences, introducing many new offences and re-defining others. It abolished much of the old law. However, that law still applies to offences committed before May 1, 2004.[159] Accordingly, for many years to come, the courts will have to deal with offences committed before the 2003 Act came into force, or defendants will face indictments alleging offences that straddle the Act's commencement date.

Sentences are imposed on the basis of the legislative provisions in force at **30.144** the time of the offence, and it follows that when sentencing historic sex cases, it is important to have two critical dates in mind: (i) May 1, 2004, when the 2003 Act came into force, and (ii) April 4, 2005, when the sentencing provisions of the Criminal Justice Act 2003 ("CJA 2003") came into force. As there were a number of statutes governing the law of sexual offences before the 2003 Act, some of which were themselves amended as to the maximum sentence, it is essential to check what was the maximum sentence at the relevant time, as well as the nature of the sentences then available. The Court should then make the appropriate "measured reference"[160] to the current sentencing guideline.

"Measured reference" to the current sentencing guideline

"Measured reference" as required by *R. v H(J)* has not been interpreted as **30.145** meaning that there should be some form of pro rata discount because of the disparity between the maximum sentence at the time the offence was committed and the maximum sentence today.[161] Courts have applied the

---

[158] *Bright* [2008] EWCA Crim 462; *Giga* [2008] EWCA Crim 703; *Round and Dunn* [2009] EWCA Crim 2667; *Rhule* [2010] EWCA Crim 2177.

[159] For analysis of the law governing sexual offences before the implementation of the Sexual Offences Act 2003, see *Rook and Ward on Sexual Offences*, 2nd edn (London: Sweet and Maxwell, 1997). See also HHJ Patricia Lees and Eleanor Laws QC, *The Sexual Offences Referencer, A Practitioner's Guide to Indictments and Sentencing*, 2nd edn (Oxford: Oxford University Press, 2014).

[160] *R. v H(J)* [2011] EWCA Crim 2753 at [47(a)].

[161] *Attorney General's Reference (No.27 of 2015)* [2015] EWCA Crim 1538.

current guideline as if the offence or offences had been committed recently. The only limitation that is placed upon sentencers is that required by the existence of a lower maximum sentence. In practice, that may only limit sentences when there is a single count on the indictment. Where there are multiple counts, even with limitations upon particular counts, a judge is entitled to pass consecutive sentences so as to structure a sentence which would reflect the overall criminality involved according to modern standards and attitudes[162]. For more discussion on the approach to sentencing historic sex cases, see para 30.110, above.

Most commonly charged sexual offences pre-dating the Sexual Offences 2003

Rape

30.146 The core of the old law was the Sexual Offences Act 1956, itself a consolidating Act, but the four decades that followed its enactment saw a succession of legislation designed to deal with perceived problems, with incremental changes responding to particular political imperatives. Some of the most important offences were amended or their maximum sentences were increased over the years. The main offences were as follows.

30.147 Rape, contrary to s.1(1) of the Sexual Offence Act 1956–January 1, 1957 until December 21, 1976. Rape, contrary to s.1(1) of the Sexual Offences Act 1956 as amended by the Sexual Offences (Amendment) Act 1976–December 22, 1976 until April 30, 2004.
Maximum sentence–life.

Attempted rape

30.148 Maximum sentence–seven years' imprisonment until 1985 when increased to life by the Sexual Offences Act 1985.

30.149 The case of one appellant, P, in *R. v H(J)*[163] illustrates the difficulty that arises where a court is called upon to sentence for attempted rape committed before September 16, 1985. In January 1978, P had attacked an 18-year-old girl who was waiting for a bus. He told her he had a knife and would kill her. After pushing his erect penis between her legs and ejaculating over her inner thighs and clothing, he forced her to perform oral sex upon him. The effect upon the victim was particularly traumatic. Shortly after the attack she discovered she was pregnant. She was terrified that this could have resulted from P ejaculating over her inner thighs. She went through pregnancy in a state of turmoil, although it later transpired that her husband was the father of her child.

---

[162] *Clifford* [2014] EWCA Crim 2245 at [35] per Treacy LJ.
[163] [2011] EWCA Crim 2753, at [116]–[129].

P was arrested after a "cold case review" in 2009. In January 2010 he was   **30.150**
convicted by a jury of attempted rape and indecent assault, which reflected
the only way in which in 1978 it was possible to indict for oral rape. P had
convictions for sexual offences he had committed both before and after the
offences of which he was convicted. In February 2010 he was sentenced to life
imprisonment for attempted rape and two years' imprisonment concurrent
for indecent assault. The minimum specified term was seven years and six
months.

The Court of Appeal concluded that if the sentencing court had had the   **30.151**
necessary jurisdiction, the sentence would have been entirely appropriate.
However, by operation of the Attempted Rape Act 1948 and the Sexual
Offences Act 1956 s.37(3) and Sch.II, para.(1)(b), the maximum sentence for
an offence of attempted rape in 1978 was seven years' imprisonment. The
maximum was increased to life imprisonment for offences committed after
September 16, 1985, as a result of ss.3 and 5(5) of the Sexual Offences Act
1985. None of this was affected by the coming into force of the Criminal
Attempts Act 1981. The Court therefore quashed the sentence of life
imprisonment for the attempted rape and substituted one of seven years'
imprisonment, i.e. the statutory maximum, with the two-year sentence for
indecent assault to run consecutively. It said[164]:

> "This is a most unfortunate case. The sentence imposed, although fully justified,
> was unlawful. It must be quashed. The reasonable understanding of the victim of
> the crime, that the life sentence was fully justified, has been dashed. That should
> not have happened. Without any consideration beyond the aggravating and
> mitigating features of the individual offence or offences, the sentencing decision
> in cases like these is never straightforward. It is made more complicated because
> of the variations in the maximum sentences lawfully available in historic cases . . .
> Particular care is therefore needed to ensure that before the sentencing hearing
> begins, the parameters of sentence in force at the time when the offence was
> committed are identified.
>
> Justice will not appear to the victim to have been done, and for what it is
> worth, we do not think that the sentence which we must now impose appro-
> priately represents this appellant's criminality. Nevertheless the decision is
> unavoidable. It is a consequence of the legislation in force at the time, which we
> are bound to apply. Fortunately that has now been changed, and for such a crime
> committed today, the sentence imposed on this appellant would have been
> upheld."

Indecent assault

Indecent assault on a woman, contrary to s.14 of the Sexual Offences Act   **30.152**
1956–November 1, 1957 until April 30, 2004.
Maximum sentence–for offences committed before September 16, 1985, the
maximum sentence was two years' imprisonment, or five years after January
1, 1961, if the complainant was a girl under 13 and that fact was averred in

---

[164] At [124]–[125].

the indictment.[165] For offences committed on or after September 16, 1985, the maximum was 10 years regardless of the age of the victim.[166]

Indecent assault on a man, contrary to s.15 of the Sexual Offences Act 1956–November 1, 1957 until April 30, 2004.

Maximum sentence–10 years' imprisonment.

30.153 Indecent assault includes conduct which today would be prosecuted as rape (penetration of the complainant's mouth with the defendant's penis) or assault by penetration (digital penetration of the vagina). When a defendant is convicted of indecent assault in circumstances such as these, it may pose a sentencing problem because the statutory maximum at the time was significantly lower than the suggested starting point in the Sentencing Council guideline. However, where there are a number of counts, provided each individual sentence is below the statutory maximum, a judge is entitled to structure the sentence using consecutive sentences subject to the principle of totality so as to reflect the overall criminality involved according to modern standards and attitudes. A stark example is *Clifford*,[167] where it was argued that the judge should not have approached two counts of indecent assault involving the performing of oral sex as being the equivalent of rape offences as they are now understood. Under the guideline such conduct now carries a severe sentence, with an available maximum of life imprisonment. It was submitted that the effect of this was unfair and disproportionate because of the very large disparity between the maximum sentence available at the time of the commission of the offence and the maximum sentence available for rape in modern times.

30.154 The Court of Appeal held that the judge was entitled in the course of his sentencing remarks to observe that some of the offending would now be charged as offences as serious as rape or assault by penetration. In so doing he was drawing attention to the gravity of this offending by modern standards. The Court did acknowledge that the judge might more profitably have drawn attention to the starting points for a single offence of sexual assault or sexual activity with a child, which, on the facts of this case, would under the guideline have starting points of four and five years respectively, again substantially above the maximum available at the relevant time.

30.155 It is important to remember that there is a significant difference between indecent assault under the 1956 Act and sexual assault under the Sexual Offences Act 2003. Sexual assault is confined to cases where a touching takes place and so does not extend to cases where a victim is put in fear of being touched. However, whilst a sexual assault must be deliberate, there need be no hostile intent. In 1951, in *Fairclough v Whipp*,[168] the Divisional Court decided that where a man exposed himself to a nine-year-old girl and invited

---

[165] Sexual Offences Act 1956 s.37 and Sch.2, amended by the Indecency with Children Act 1960 s.2.
[166] Sexual Offences Act 1956 s.37 and Sch.2, amended by the Sexual Offences Act 1985 s.3.
[167] [2014] EWCA Crim 2245.
[168] 35 Cr. App. R. 138.

her to touch his penis, the invitation to touch the man could not amount to an assault on the girl. Whilst the distinction between the defendant touching the complainant and vice versa may appear highly technical, when Parliament enacted the Indecency with Children Act 1960 it proceeded on the basis that *Fairclough v Whipp* was correctly decided. It follows that when charging indecent assault in these circumstances it should be borne in mind that there is no indecent assault without some form of threat or show of force to the victim. In 2015 in *Dunn*,[169] the Court of Appeal allowed an appeal against conviction for indecent assault when the allegation was that between March 1999 and March 2000 the appellant had indecently assaulted a 15-year-old girl by causing her to masturbate him. In fact, a charge under s.1(1) of the Indecency with Children Act 1960 would not have been appropriate either, as the protection of that provision was only extended to children aged 14 and 15 from January 12, 2001.

Sexual intercourse with a girl under 13/a girl under 16

Sexual intercourse with a girl under 13, contrary to s.5 of the Sexual Offences Act 1956.   **30.156**
Maximum sentence–Life (attempt seven years).
Sexual intercourse with a girl under 16, contrary to s.6 of the Sexual Offences Act 1956.
Maximum sentence–two years' imprisonment.

  A prosecution under s.6 of the 1956 Act, or for an attempt to commit the   **30.157** offence, could not be brought more than 12 months after the offence was committed.[170] This means that this offence can no longer be charged, as the prosecution will be out of time. Until *R. v J*[171] it was the practice, after the expiry of the 12-month time limit, to charge indecent assault contrary to s.14 of the 1956 Act instead. However, in *R. v J* the House of Lords held that this had the impermissible effect of dispensing with or suspending an unequivocal statutory provision. The decision reversed the law relating to sexual activity with under-age girls as it had operated for many years, although from May 1, 2004, the statutory time-limit was in any event abolished. However, the change in the law effected by this decision will not necessarily give rise to a meritorious ground of appeal in respect of pre-*R. v J* convictions, as it is unlikely that a substantial injustice will have occurred.[172] Moreover, the prohibition in *R. v J* relates to the institution of proceedings rather than to the alternative verdict to rape under s.6(3) of the Criminal Law Act 1967.[173] It follows that if rape is properly charged in respect of a complainant under

---

[169] [2015] EWCA Crim 724.
[170] Sexual Offences Act 1956 s.37 and Sch.2.
[171] [2004] UKHL 42, discussed in para.4.03, above.
[172] See *Cottrell; Fletcher* [2007] EWCA Crim 2016. The Court did, however, feel obliged to allow an appeal where a count of indecent assault was added, rather left as an alternative to rape. *R. v WR* [2005] EWCA Crim 1907 followed.
[173] *Timmins* [2005] EWCA Crim 2909; *Phillips* [2007] EWCA Crim 485.

the age of 16, a jury could, in appropriate circumstances, still reach an alternative verdict of indecent assault.

Gross indecency with a child

30.158 Gross indecency with a child, contrary to s.1 of the Indecency with Children Act 1960.

Until September 30, 1997, the offence could be committed only in relation to a child under 14 and the maximum sentence was two years' imprisonment. From October 1, 1997, the maximum was 10 years. From January 12, 2001, the protection of the offence was extended to children aged 14 and 15.

Failure to obtain permission to institute proceedings

30.159 Section 8 of the Sexual Offences Act 1967 provides:

"No proceedings shall be instituted except by or with the consent of the Director of Public Prosecutions against any man for the offence of buggery with, or gross indecency with, another man or for aiding, abetting, counselling, procuring or commanding its commission where either of those men was at the time of its commission under the age of twenty-one."

It is not necessary for the DPP personally to consent to the institution of proceedings, as any consent given by a Crown Prosecutor is to be treated as having been given by the DPP.[174]

30.160 It was long thought settled by the decision in *Angel*[175] that if consent was not obtained, proceedings would be a nullity. At one stage there appeared to have been a sea-change in the approach to non-compliance with procedural requirements.[176] However, in *Clarke and McDaid*[177] Lord Brown of Eaton-under-Heywood referred to *Angel* in apparently approving terms, when the House of Lords decided that there could be no valid trial on indictment unless the indictment was duly signed by a proper officer. In *Gowans and Hillman*[178] the Court of Appeal also referred to *Angel* when declaring a conviction for murder should be set aside and annulled as the failure to obtain the Attorney General's consent as required by s.2 of the Law Reform (Year and a Day Rule) Act 1996 vitiated the whole trial. However, *Gowans and Hillman* was a reference to the Court of Appeal by the CCRC. There will be substantial obstacles in the way of any application for leave out of time unless substantial injustice can be demonstrated.[179]

---

[174] Prosecution of Offences Act 1985 s.1(7).
[175] [1968] 1 W.L.R. 669.
[176] See the discussion in paras 8.09 and following, above.
[177] [2006] Crim. L.R 1011.
[178] [2015] EWCA Crim 952.
[179] *Welsh* [2015] EWCA Crim 1516. See also *Ramzan* [2006] EWCA Crim 1974; [2007] 1 Cr. App. R. 150. Hughes LJ, as he then was, explained that an offender seeking to appeal out of time is generally expected to point to something more than the mere fact the law has changed, been corrected, or developed.

SENTENCING DANGEROUS OFFENDERS FOR OFFENCES COMMITTED BEFORE APRIL 4, 2005

When dealing with a dangerous offender for an offence committed before the **30.161** commencement of the sentencing provisions of the Criminal Justice Act 2003 ("CJA 2003") on April 4, 2005, the choice now lies between:
  (i) the "old-style" discretionary life sentence,[180] applying the criteria in *Hodgson* and *Whittaker* (for which see below),
 (ii) the new-style extended sentence under s.226A of the CJA 2003 (inserted by the Legal Aid, Sentencing and Punishment of Offenders Act 2012), which is available for convictions on or after December 3, 2012, irrespective of the date of commission of the offence, or
(iii) the longer than commensurate sentence under s.80(2)(b) of the Powers of Criminal Courts (Sentencing) Act 2000 ("PCC(S)A 2000").

(i) Life sentence

Notwithstanding the multiple statutory amendments governing the sentenc- **30.162** ing of dangerous offenders during the last 10 years, the law remains unchanged as regards "old style" discretionary life sentences in respect of offences committed before April 4, 2005.[181] The criteria for the imposition of such a sentence are set out in *Hodgson*[182] and *Attorney General's Reference (No.32 of 1996) (R. v Whittaker)*.[183] First, the offender must have been convicted of a "very serious offence". The meaning of "very serious offence" was considered in *R. v D*[184] where the Court of Appeal took the view that the *Hodgson/Whittaker* criteria were satisfied where the offender as a youth had broken into his grandmother's home and raped her. Secondly, there should be good grounds for believing that the offender might remain a serious danger to the public for a period which could not be reliably estimated at the date of sentence. It was explained in *Whittaker* that by "serious danger" the Court had in mind particularly serious offences of violence and serious sexual offences.

---

[180] So described by the late Professor David Thomas QC in his commentary on *Saunders* [2013] Crim. L.R. 935.
[181] *Red Saunders* [2013] EWCA Crim 1027. For a fuller discussion of this important case, see paras 1.96 and following, above.
[182] (1968) 52 Cr. App. R. 113; [1968] Crim. L.R. 46.
[183] [1997] 1 Cr. App. R.(S.) 261; [1996] Crim. L.R. 917. For a more recent example of a life sentence approved by the Court of Appeal in an historic case of rape by an intruder, see *Wendell Baker* [2014] EWCA Crim 242.
[184] [2012] EWCA Crim 2370; [2013] 1 Cr. App. R.(S.) 127 (p.674). For fuller discussion of *R. v D*, see paras 1.134 and following, above.

30.163   A good recent illustration of such a sentence is *R. v DP*,[185] in which the appellant pleaded guilty to a number of sexual offences. One was an offence sexual assault on a child under 13 by penetration, contrary to s.6(1) of the Sexual Offences Act 2003, committed between December 2004 and March 2005. It was accepted by the judge and the Court of Appeal that the appellant should be sentenced by reference to the law which existed before April 4, 2005, the relevant legislation being the PCC(S)A 2000 and the early release provisions of the Criminal Justice Act 1991. The complainants were two children of a woman with whom the appellant had formed a relationship. The appellant had a long record of sexual offences against children. He was sentenced to life imprisonment in respect of the s.6 offence with various concurrent determinate sentences for other offences. The Court of Appeal concluded that (i) the offending was of sufficient gravity to warrant a sentence of imprisonment for life, and (ii) the appellant was a serial predatory paedophile, had been so for many years, and at the time of sentence it could not be estimated how long he would remain a danger to younger children.

(ii) Extended sentence

30.164   The new-style extended sentence introduced by the Legal Aid, Sentencing and Punishment of Offenders Act 2012 is available for offenders convicted on or after December 3, 2012. It should be borne in mind that this sentence has replaced the old-style extended sentence under s.85 of the PCC(S)A 2000 with retrospective effect.[186] It is available in respect of sentencing a specified offence whenever committed.

30.165   The extended sentence is a two-part sentence comprising a custodial element and an extended licence period; an extension cannot be added on to two separate custodial terms.[187] If that has occurred, the Court of Appeal is likely to restructure the sentence[188] as the sentence would be unlawful. This is likely to involve aggregating the sentences into the lead offence (which must be a specified offence) when imposing an extended sentence, and thereafter imposing concurrent terms.[189] For offenders sentenced on or after April 13, 2015, the position has been changed again by s.4 of the Criminal Justice and Courts Act 2015. That has the effect that all offenders receiving an extended sentence will now be released at some point between the two-thirds point and the end of the custodial term. For further discussion of the new-style extended sentence, see paras 34.10 and following, below.

---

[185] [2013] EWCA Crim 1143.

[186] See commentary by the late Professor David Thomas QC on *R. v DP* [2013] Crim. L.R. 862. For special custodial sentences under s.236A CJA 2003 for certain offenders of particular concern which apply to certain offences involving penetration of children committed by those aged 18 or over irrespective of when the offences were committed, see para.34.55, below, and *R. v LF and DS* [2016] EWCA Crim 561.

[187] *Brown* [2006] EWCA Crim 1996.

[188] *Smith (Paul)* [2015] EWCA Crim 1627.

[189] This practice was approved by the Court of Appeal in *Pinnell* [2010] EWCA Crim 2848.

(iii) Longer than commensurate sentence

The operation of the provisions relating to longer than commensurate **30.166** sentences under s.80(2)(b) of the PCC(S)A 2000 was examined in *R. v S.*[190] Where the threshold for a life sentence has not been crossed, but the court needs to consider whether it is necessary to protect the public from serious harm in the future, then a longer than commensurate sentence can be passed together with an extended licence period. The anticipated harm likely to be produced by the expected future offences may be either physical or psychological, but must be "serious". The offence which is expected to produce the harm must itself be a violent or sexual offence.

SENTENCING FOR AN OFFENCE WHEN IT IS UNCLEAR WHETHER IT WAS COMMITTED AFTER OR BEFORE APRIL 4, 2005

Indictments should be drafted so as to reflect the significance of April 4, **30.167** 2005. Sentences under the Criminal Justice Act 2003 should only be imposed if the court is satisfied that at least one relevant offence was committed after that date.[191] Otherwise, sentences must be passed under the previous sentencing regime.

[190] [2010] EWCA Crim 1462.
[191] *Harries* [2007] EWCA Crim 1622.

CHAPTER 31

SEXUAL OFFENCES IN THE YOUTH COURT

By Gillian Jones and Naomi Parsons

Introduction...................................... 31.01   Annex 1: Sentencing Options
Preliminary Matters......................... 31.03   Available to the Youth Court.......31.139
Trial in the Youth Court.................. 31.31   Annex 2: Classification of Sexual
Mode of Trial .... 31.64   Offences Involving Youths 31.140
Sentencing Youths for Sexual
    Offences.......................................31.100

INTRODUCTION

Prosecutions of young defendants for sexual offences often raise different **31.01**
issues to those arising in cases brought against adults. This may be the result
of differences in the law applicable to young people or to differences in the
procedure and practice of the youth court, the venue in which the majority
of youth cases are heard. This chapter covers the procedure and practice of
the youth court, highlighting, in particular, those aspects that are relevant to
the hearing of sexual offences. Of course, many of the issues that arise in sex
cases heard in the youth court are not specific to young people and reference
should accordingly be made to other chapters of this book as necessary.

The youth court is part of the magistrates' court system. It has summary **31.02**
jurisdiction to hear charges against defendants aged from 10 to 17 inclusive.[1]
There is a strong presumption that cases involving youths will be heard in the
youth court, and the majority of cases involving sexual offences allegedly
committed by youths will be dealt with there. However, sexual offences form
a very small proportion of youth court cases: in 2013–14, the youth courts
disposed of 1,653 sexual offence cases, around 2 per cent of total disposals.
It follows that not all youth benches necessarily have experience in dealing
with such offences.[2] Also, cases involving sexual offences that are particularly

---

[1] Children and Young Persons Act 1933 s.45.
[2] Youth Justice Board Statistics 2013/14, p.30. See *https://www.gov.uk/government/uploads/system/uploads/attachment_data/file/399379/youth-justice-annual-stats-13-14.pdf* [Accessed April 30, 2016].

serious may be sent to the Crown Court either for trial or for sentence. This occurs only in tightly defined circumstances: see paras 31.72 and following, below.

Preliminary Matters

31.03 This section deals with preliminary matters relating to the youth court. It covers the following:

- Terminology.
- Aims of the youth justice system.
- The decision to prosecute youths.
- Youth cautions and youth conditional cautions.
- First appearance.
- Mode of trial.
- Bail.

Terminology

31.04 This chapter refers to those within the jurisdiction of the youth court (ages 10 to 17 inclusive) as "youths", as a convenient shorthand. As a general rule, youths divide into "children" (under 14) and "young people" (14 to 17 inclusive).[3] In the Sexual Offences Act 2003, children and young people refer to those under 18. The meaning of "child" is offence-specific and refers variously to a person under 13 (ss.5–8), a person under 16 (ss.9–12), or a person under 18 (ss.25–26).

Aim of the Youth Justice System

31.05 The principal aim of the youth justice system is to prevent re-offending. This is set out in s.37 of the Crime and Disorder Act 1998, which provides:

> "(1) The principal aim of the youth justice system shall be to prevent offending by children and young persons
>
>   (2) In addition to any other duty to which they are subject, it shall be the duty of all persons and bodies carrying out functions in relation to the youth justice system to have regard to that aim".

31.06   In every case, the court must consider the welfare of the child or young offender. This is set out in s.44 of the Children and Young Persons Act 1933:

> "Every court in dealing with a child or young person who is brought before it, either as an offender or otherwise, shall have regard to the welfare of the child or young person, and shall in proper cases take steps for removing him from

---

[3] Statutes dealing with children and young people adopt slightly different definitions, and therefore care should be taken to ensure that the definition is correctly understood. In the Powers of Criminal Court (Sentencing) Act 2000, a "child" is anyone under 14, and a "young person" is anyone aged 14–17 inclusive. The various Children and Young Persons Acts (1933, 1963 and 1969) adopt the same definition, except that the age range for a "young person" is 14–16 inclusive for the purposes of bail under the 1969 Act.

undesirable surroundings, and for securing that proper provision is made for his education and training".

Due regard must be paid to these provisions when dealing with youths. They **31.07** are particularly important considerations in determining sentence (see paras 31.120 and following, below). The operation of the youth justice system is monitored at the national level by the Youth Justice Board.[4] At a local level, each local authority (or a combination of local authorities) has a Youth Offending Team (a "YOT"), which is a multi-agency team required to deliver services to the court and young offenders. A YOT is required, for example, to investigate the background and personal circumstances of the young offender, provide bail support, prepare reports and administer many non-custodial sentences.[5]

THE DECISION TO PROSECUTE YOUTHS

Crown prosecutors must be careful to follow relevant guidance in respect of **31.08** the decision to prosecute. This is because the discretion of the CPS to commence, continue or to discontinue proceedings against a youth is subject to judicial review. This was established in *R. v Chief Constable of Kent, Ex p. L*,[6] which held that such decisions are reviewable, but "only where it can be demonstrated that the decision was made regardless of or clearly contrary to a settled policy of the DPP evolved in the public interest, for example, the policy of [reprimands or warnings]".[7] Relevant guidance can be found in three sources:

- Code for Crown Prosecutors.
- Legal Guidance: Youth Offenders.
- Legal Guidance: Rape and Sexual Offences.

The CPS's decision to prosecute youths for sexual offences has been **31.09** challenged by judicial review: see e.g. *S v DPP*,[8] in which the Divisional Court, in upholding the decision to prosecute, considered whether the CPS had followed its own legal guidance both on Youth Offenders and Sexual Offences.

Code for Crown Prosecutors

The decision whether or not to prosecute a child or young person is taken, **31.10** like all other prosecutorial decisions, in accordance with the *Code for Crown Prosecutors* (January 2013 revision).[9]

[4] Crime and Disorder Act 1998 s.41.
[5] Crime and Disorder Act 1998 s.39.
[6] (1991) 93 Cr. App. R. 416.
[7] At 428. The case was decided prior to the abolition of youth cautions under the Crime and Disorder Act 1998 s.67(8), and their replacement with a system of reprimands and warnings: see the Crime and Disorder Act 1998 ss.65 and 66.
[8] [2006] EWHC 2231 (Admin), discussed in para.3.22, above.
[9] The *Code* is available at *http://www.cps.gov.uk/publications/docs/code_2013_accessible_english.pdf* [Accessed April 30, 2016].

31.11   Paragraph 4.12(d) of the *Code for Crown Prosecutors* identifies the age of the suspect as a factor to be considered when assessing if the case passes the public interest stage. It states that:

> "The criminal justice system treats children and young people differently from adults and significant weight must be attached to the age of the suspect if they are a child or young person under 18. The best interests and welfare of the child or young person must be considered including whether a prosecution is likely to have an adverse impact on his or her future prospects that is disproportionate to the seriousness of the offending. Prosecutors must have regard to the principal aim of the youth justice system which is to prevent offending by children and young people Prosecutors must also have regard to the obligations arising under the United Nations 1989 Convention on the Rights of the Child."

The *Code* goes on to say that as a starting point, the younger the suspect, the less likely it is that a prosecution is required. In deciding whether prosecution is in the public interest it appears that particular consideration should be given to the suitability of an out-of-court disposal, as the *Code* continues:

> "However, there may be circumstances which mean that notwithstanding the fact that the suspect is under 18, a prosecution is in the public interest. These include where the offence committed is serious, where the suspect's past record suggests that there are no suitable alternatives to prosecution, or where the absence of an admission means that out-of-court disposals which might have addressed the offending behaviour are not available."

Legal Guidance: Youth Offenders and Legal Guidance: Rape and Sexual Offences

31.12   Detailed guidance on prosecuting youths is found in *Legal Guidance: Youth Offenders*.[10] This includes guidance on the approach to the prosecution of sexual offences. It should be read in conjunction with *Legal Guidance: Rape and Sexual Offences*, Chapter 11, which contains guidance on the approach to the prosecution of sexual offences under the 2003 Act, highlighting where necessary any distinctive approach to be taken with youths.[11]

General factors

31.13   The overarching approach towards the prosecution of sexual offences committed by youths set out in *Legal Guidance: Youth Offenders* is as follows:

> "If an allegation of any sexual abuse committed by a youth offender has been fully investigated and there is sufficient evidence to justify instituting proceedings, the balance of the public interest must always be carefully considered before any prosecution is commenced. Positive action may need to be taken at an early stage of offending of this type. Although a youth caution or youth conditional

---

[10] Available at *http://www.cps.gov.uk/legal/v_to_z/youth_offenders/* [Accessed April 30, 2016].
[11] Available at *http://www.cps.gov.uk/legal/p_to_r/rape_and_sexual_offences/* [Accessed April 30, 2016].

caution may provide an acceptable alternative in some cases, in reaching any decision, the police and the CPS will have to take into account fully the view of other agencies involved in the case, in particular the Social Services. The consequences for the victim of the decision whether or not to prosecute, and any views expressed by the victim or the victim's family, should also be taken into account."[12]

In dealing with the decision to prosecute, the *Guidance* provides: 31.14

"Prosecutors are reminded of the need to consider all the circumstances surrounding the offence and the circumstances of the youth before reaching a decision to prosecute and to apply all relevant CPS policies and documents. Failure to do so may result in proceedings for judicial review: *R v Chief Constable of Kent ex parte L, R v DPP ex parte B* [1991] 93 Cr App R 416."

The *Guidance* then sets out additional factors to consider, including a set of aggravating and mitigating factors. One aggravating feature is that the offence is a sexual offence.

Offences against children under 13 (ss.5–8 of the Sexual Offences Act 2003)

The CPS's *Legal Guidance: Youth Offenders* and *Legal Guidance: Rape and*   31.15
Sexual Offences provide that when reviewing a case in which a youth under 18 is alleged to have committed an offence contrary to ss.5–8 of the 2003 Act, prosecutors should obtain and consider:

- the views of local authority Children's and Young Peoples Service;
- any risk assessment or report conducted by the local authority or youth offending service in respect of sexually harmful behaviour (such as AIM (Assessment, Intervention and Moving On));
- background information and history of the parties; and
- the views of the families of all parties.

Careful regard should be paid to the following factors:

- the relative ages of the parties;
- the existence of and nature of any relationship;
- the sexual and emotional maturity of the parties and any emotional or physical effects as a result of the conduct;
- whether the child under 13 in fact freely consented (even though in law this is not a defence) or a genuine mistake as to age was in fact made;
- whether any element of seduction, breach of any duty of responsibility to the child or other exploitation is disclosed by the evidence; and
- the impact of a prosecution on each child involved.

Legal Guidance: Rape and Sexual Offences provides examples of the   31.16
application of these factors to a decision as follows:

---

[12] *Legal Guidance: Youth Offenders* (under *Sexual Offences and Child Abuse by Young Offenders*).

"If the sexual act or activity was in fact genuinely consensual and the youth and the child under 13 concerned are fairly close in age and development, a prosecution is unlikely to be appropriate. Action falling short of prosecution may be appropriate. In such cases, the parents and/or welfare agencies may be able to deal with the situation informally. There is a fine line between sexual experimentation and offending and in general, children under the age of 13 should not be criminalised for sexual behaviour in the absence of coercion, exploitation or abuse of trust.

However, if a very young child has been seduced by a youth, or a baby-sitter in a position of responsibility has taken advantage of a child under 13 in his/her care, prosecution is likely to be in the public interest. Where a child under 13 has not given ostensible consent to the activity, then a prosecution contrary to sections 5 to 8 is likely to be the appropriate course of action."

31.17   As to whether it is a breach of art.8 of the ECHR to prosecute a youth under s.5 of the 2003 Act when the basis of plea establishes that the offence fell within ss.9–12 and s.13, see *R. v G*,[13] discussed in paras 3.14 and following, above.

Child sex offences (ss.9–12 and s.13 of the Sexual Offences Act 2003)

31.18   The decision whether to prosecute a child for child sex offences under ss.9–12 and s.13 of the 2003 Act is informed by the considerations applicable to offences under ss.5–8 set out above. And, as with ss.5–8, the prosecutor has more discretion when considering whether to prosecute a youth under s.13 than an adult.[14] The approach to child sex offences under ss.9–12 and s.13 is summarised in *Legal Guidance: Rape and Sexual Offences* as follows[15]:

"In summary, where a defendant, for example, is exploitative, or coercive, or much older than the victim, the balance may be in favour of prosecution, whereas if the sexual activity is truly of the victim's own free will the balance may not be in the public interest to prosecute.

In addition, it is not in the public interest to prosecute children who are of the same or similar age and understanding that engage in sexual activity, where the activity is truly consensual for both parties and there are no aggravating features, such as coercion or corruption. In such cases, protection will normally be best achieved by providing education for the children and young people and providing them and their families with access to advisory and counselling services. This is the intention of Parliament."

Familial sex offences (ss.25–26 and ss.64–65 of the Sexual Offences Act 2003)

31.19   The decision whether to prosecute a child for familial sex offences under ss.25–26 or ss.64–65 is informed by similar considerations to decisions

---

[13] [2008] UKHL 37.
[14] *Legal Guidance: Rape and Sexual Offences*, Chapter 2, under *Code for Crown Prosecutors—Adult/child defendants*.
[15] Chapter 2, under *Code for Crown Prosecutors—Adult/child defendants*.

whether to prosecute under ss.5–8 and s.13. *Legal Guidance: Youth Offenders* provides the following by way of guidance[16]:

> "In cases of sexual activity between siblings, care should be taken to balance the public interest in prosecuting such conduct with the interests and welfare of the victim and the family unit. As a general rule, alternatives to prosecution should be sought where the sexual activity was wholly consensual. The welfare agencies will normally intervene."

However, the *Guidance* states that prosecution should be considered where there is evidence of seduction, coercion, exploitation or violence, or a significant disparity in age. In all cases, the effect of a prosecution on the victim and family should be taken into account and the views of the welfare agency sought, if they are not included in the prosecution file. *Legal Guidance: Rape and Sexual Offences* provides guidance only in respect of the child familial sex offences (i.e. ss.25 and 26), noting that in such cases, "prosecutors should bear in mind the specific breach of trust in these offences".

Sexual exploitation of children (ss.47–50 of the Sexual Offences Act 2003)

It has long been recognised that children and young people involved in **31.20** prostitution are to be considered primarily as the victims of abuse.[17] This is now reflected in the wording of the offences of sexual exploitation of children in the 2003 Act. Section 58 of the Serious Crime Act 2015 amended ss.47–50 of the 2003, such that the words "sexual exploitation of a child" have replaced the words "child prostitution" in those sections of the 2003 Act.[18] Diversion from the courts is therefore the principle policy aim. Criminal proceedings against children are taken only when it is "necessary to do so, and in the full knowledge of the circumstances of the individual child".[19] Only where there is persistent and voluntary return to prostitution, and where there is a genuine choice, should a prosecution be considered.[20]

YOUTH CAUTIONS AND YOUTH CONDITIONAL CAUTIONS

Reprimands and warnings (known as the "final warning scheme") were **31.21** abolished[21] and a new form of disposal, the youth caution, was introduced

---

[16] Under *Familial Sexual Offences*.
[17] cf. *Safeguarding Children Involved in Prostitution: Supplementary Guidance to Working Together to Safeguard Children*, (Department of Health, Home Office, Department for Education and Employment, National Assembly for Wales, 2000). See also *Safeguarding Children and Young People Involved in Sexual Exploitation (Department for Children, Schools and Families* (2009), at para.2.9, which re-iterated this policy.
[18] Section 58 of the Serious Crime Act 2015. See also paras 10.01 and 13.30, above.
[19] *Safeguarding Children Involved in Prostitution*, para.3.8.
[20] Legal Guidance: Exploitation of Prostitution (Children), found in CPS Legal Guidance: Prostitution and Exploitation of Prostitution.
[21] By the repeal of the Crime and Disorder Act 1998 ss.65 and 66.

with effect from April 8, 2013, by s.135 of the Legal Aid, Sentencing and Punishment of Offenders Act 2012. The new scheme comprises youth cautions (ss.66ZA of the Crime and Disorder Act 1998 ("1998 Act")) and youth conditional cautions (s.66A). Youth cautions and youth conditional cautions are not court orders. However, familiarity with these pre-court disposal schemes are important in the youth court: not only are they relevant to considerations of bail and sentence, but representations can sometimes be made to adjourn proceedings if a case is one which may suitable for an alternative disposal.[22] CPS decisions on case disposal are judicially reviewable.[23]

Youth cautions

31.22   By s.66ZA(1)(a)–(c) of the 1998 Act, a youth caution can be administered if there is sufficient evidence to charge, the offence is admitted, and the constable does not consider that the offender should be prosecuted or given a youth conditional caution. The police are to consider the seriousness of the offence, as determined by reference to the ACPO Gravity Factor Matrix.[24] The Matrix assigns sexual offences (and other offences) a score of 1, 2, 3 or 4. An offence that attracts a gravity score of 2 or 3 will usually result in a youth being given a youth caution. If the offending behaviour cannot be satisfactorily addressed by a youth caution, the police will consider a youth conditional caution.

31.23   Guidance on such disposals can be found in *Youth Cautions—Guidance for Police and Youth Offending Teams*, issued by the Ministry of Justice and the Youth Justice Board in April 2013.[25] By virtue of ss.80(1)(d) and 113(1) of the 1998 Act, youth cautions trigger notification requirements in relation to the same set of offences that trigger notification where a person is convicted at court. The *Guidance* stresses that the police are responsible for explaining to the youth and appropriate adult that a caution will trigger the notification requirements.[26] The notification requirement is two years.

Youth conditional cautions

31.24   By s.66A–E of the 1998 Act a youth conditional caution can be administered if there is sufficient evidence to charge, the offence is admitted, the effect of the caution is explained to the young person (breach may result in

---

[22] *F. v CPS* (2004) 168 J.P. 93.
[23] See, e.g. *S. v DPP* [2006] EWHC 2231 (Admin) where the court scrutinised the CPS's decision to prosecute a 15-year-old for an offence under ss.9 and 13 of the 2003 Act in light of the CPS guidance *Legal Guidance: Youth Offenders* and *Legal Guidance: Sexual Offences*.
[24] Available at *http://cps.gov.uk/legal/assets/uploads/files/Gravity%20Matrix%20May09.pdf* [Accessed April 30, 2016].
[25] Available at *http://www.justice.gov.uk/downloads/oocd/youth-cautions-guidance-police-yots-oocd.pdf* [Accessed April 30, 2016].
[26] Para.11.10.

prosecution) and the young person signs a document admitting the offence and consenting to the conditions attached to the caution.[27] There is a duty to consult the victim or victims before a youth conditional caution is administered.[28] The decision to administer such a caution has the effect of suspending any criminal proceedings while the young person is given an opportunity to comply with the agreed conditions. Under s.66E(2), if the young person fails without reasonable excuse to comply with conditions, they may be prosecuted for the original offence.

Guidance on the use of youth conditional cautions is to be found in *The Director's Guidance on Youth Conditional Cautions*[29] and the *Code of Practice for Youth Conditional Cautions*[30] (both revised April 2013). The *Director's Guidance* states that conditional cautions can be used for all offences classified (in the case of adults) as summary only or triable either way. Cases which are triable only on indictment in the case of adults must be referred to a prosecutor before a youth conditional caution is given. **31.25**

First Appearance

The youth court is normally the court of first appearance for a youth charged with an offence. However, where the youth is charged with an adult, or with aiding and abetting an adult, or with an offence arising out of the same facts as give rise to a charge against an adult, the court of first appearance will be an adult magistrates' court. **31.26**

Mode of Trial

The procedure for determining mode of trial is modified in respect of youths. There is a presumption that youth cases will be heard in the youth court. A youth court can deal with all forms of offences, whether summary, triable either way or indictable only.[31] The youth has no right to elect Crown Court trial. The only circumstances in which a youth will be tried in the Crown Court is if the magistrates send the case there. So far as sexual offences are concerned, they may do so only if: **31.27**

- The offence is a "grave crime", i.e. one to which s.91 of the Powers of Criminal Courts (Sentencing) Act 2000 ("PCCSA") applies;
- The offender would be sentenced under the "dangerousness provisions" of the Criminal Justice Act 2003 ("CJA 2003"); or
- The offender is charged jointly with an adult.

---

[27] s.66B(3).
[28] s.66BA.
[29] *http://www.cps.gov.uk/publications/directors_guidance/youth_conditional_cautions.html* [Accessed April 30, 2016].
[30] *http://www.justice.gov.uk/downloads/oocd/code-practice-youth-conditional-cautions-oocd.pdf* [Accessed April 30, 2016].
[31] Except homicide and certain firearms offences.

If none of these circumstances apply, there will be no mode of trial hearing for a sexual offence in the youth court. For the procedure when sexual offences do fall into the above categories, see below.

31.28   The *Code for Crown Prosecutors* states as follows as regards the mode of trial of youths[32]:

> "Prosecutors must bear in mind that youths should be tried in the youth court wherever possible. It is the court which is best designed to meet their specific needs. A trial of a youth in the Crown Court should be reserved for the most serious cases or where the interests of justice require a youth to be jointly tried with an adult."

BAIL

31.29   In the first instance bail will generally fall to be determined by the youth court. The Bail Act 1976, including the presumption in favour of bail in s.4 of the Act, applies to youths as it does to adults.[33] Equally, the limitations on bail set out in s.25 of the Criminal Justice and Public Order Act 1994 apply to youths as they do to adults. Thus, if a youth has been charged with or convicted of certain offences and has a previous conviction for any such offence, there must be exceptional circumstances before they are granted bail.[34] In the case of an adult this limitation applies where the adult has been sentenced to a period of imprisonment for the previous offence. In the case of youths, it applies where they have been sentenced for that offence to "long-term detention" under s.91 of the PCCSA 2000.[35]

31.30   Under the Legal Aid, Sentencing and Punishment of Offenders Act 2012 ss.91–102, a court that refuses bail for a child under 18 has two options:

- Remand to local authority accommodation, with or without conditions (ss.92–97). The conditions may include electronic monitoring, where certain requirements are met and the child has been charged with a sexual offence (ss.93(2) and 94).
- Remand to youth detention accommodation (s.102). If the child is charged with a sexual offence, the court can only remand to youth detention if the child has reached the age of 12, and such detention is the only adequate way to protect the public from death or serious personal injury or to prevent the commission of imprisonable offences by the child (s.98).

TRIAL IN THE YOUTH COURT

31.31   This section deals with the following matters relating to trial in the youth court:

---

[32] Above, fn.9, at para.8.3.

[33] Except that a youth may be refused bail for his "own welfare" rather than his "own protection", as is the case with adults: Bail Act 1976 Sch.1, Pt 1, para.3.

[34] Criminal Justice and Public Order Act 1994 s.25, as amended by the Sexual Offences Act 2003 s.139 and Sch.6.

[35] Criminal Justice and Public Order Act 1994 s.25(3).

- Constitution and operation of a youth court.
- Attendance of parent/guardians.
- Press and publicity.
- Disclosure.
- The course of a trial.
- Competence and compellability.
- Oaths.
- Special measures.
- Questioning of young people.

CONSTITUTION AND OPERATION OF A YOUTH COURT

Magistrates must be authorised to sit in youth courts. Section 45 of the 31.32
Children and Young Persons Act 1933 governs the authorisation process. It
aims to ensure that only suitably trained magistrates sit in youth court, given
the specific needs and issues of this age group.

The composition of the youth court is governed by the Youth Courts 31.33
(Constitution of Committees and Rights to Preside) Rules 2007.[36] Rule 10(1)
requires a youth court to consist of either a district judge sitting alone, or not
more than three justices, including at least one man and one woman (unless
either is unavailable and the members present decide that the hearing will be
delayed unreasonably if they do not proceed). Under r.11(1), a youth court
(unless it consists of a district judge sitting alone) must be chaired by a
district judge or by a youth justice who is on the list of approved youth court
chairman. In *R. v Birmingham Justices, Ex p. F (A Juvenile)*,[37] it was held
that the court should consider representations before proceeding with a
single-sex Bench.

Where a youth court retains jurisdiction for a rape trial, the trial may well 31.34
be heard by a circuit judge authorised to try serious sexual cases. This is in
accordance with the *Protocol: Sexual Offences in the Youth Court* (set out in
full at para.31.86, below). Section 66 of the Courts Act 2003 enables a circuit
judge to sit as a district judge. In exceptional cases, for example if a circuit
judge is not available, a district judge may hear the case.

The public are excluded from the youth court. Under s.47(2) of the 31.35
Children and Young Persons Act 1933, the only persons entitled to be
present in a youth court are:
- Members and officers of the court.
- Parties to the case before the court and their legal representatives.
- Witnesses and other persons directly concerned in that case.
- Bona fide representatives of news gathering or reporting organisa-
  tions.

---

[36] SI 2007/1611.
[37] [2000] Crim. L.R. 588.

- Such other persons as the court may specially authorise to be present.

These restrictions are set out in similar terms in the Criminal Procedure Rules 2015 r.24.2(c). By contrast, there are no such restrictions if a youth appears in an adult magistrates' court or in the Crown Court.

Attendance of Parents/Guardians

31.36   Under s.34A(1) of the Children and Young Persons Act 1933, where a youth under the age of 16 is brought before a court, whether as a defendant or a witness, the court must require a parent or guardian of the child to attend during all stages of the proceedings, unless and to the extent that the court is satisfied that it would be unreasonable to require this, having regard to the circumstances of the case.[38] If the youth is aged 16 or over, the court *may* require a parent or guardian to attend, subject to the same exception. The court has a discretion, in the exercise of which it needs to balance the swift disposal of the case with the seriousness of the offence.[39]

Press and Publicity

31.37   We deal under this heading with:
- Automatic reporting restrictions which take effect in the youth court.
- Removal of reporting restrictions.
- Anonymity for the complainant in sexual offences cases.

Automatic reporting restrictions

31.38   Accredited media representatives are allowed to observe and report on youth court proceedings. However, the media are restricted in the details they may report. Section 49 of the Children and Young Persons Act 1933 applies to the youth court only and provides as follows:[40]

> "**49.—Restrictions on reports of proceedings in which children or young persons are concerned**
>
> (1) No matter relating to any child or young person concerned in proceedings to which this section applies shall while he is under the age of 18 be included in any publication if it is likely to lead members of the public to identify him as someone concerned in the proceedings.

[38] By virtue of s.34A(2), these provisions apply to local authorities where the child or young person is in their care or in accommodation provided by them.

[39] See the *Youth Court Bench Book* (January 2013), available from the Judicial College website. See also Appendix A—Magistrates Association Protocol, which sets out factors influencing procedures in youth court trials.

[40] The section is printed here as amended, most recently by the Youth Justice and Criminal Evidence Act 1999 s.48 and Sch.2.

(2) The proceedings to which this section applies are—

(a) proceedings in a youth court;

(b) proceedings on appeal from a youth court (including proceedings by way of case stated);

(c) proceedings in a magistrates' court under Schedule 2 to the Criminal Justice and Immigration Act 2008 (proceedings for breach, revocation or amendment of youth rehabilitation orders);

(d) proceedings on appeal from a magistrates' court arising out of any proceedings mentioned in paragraph (c) (including proceedings by way of case stated).

(3) In this section 'publication' includes any speech, writing, relevant programme or other communication in whatever form, which is addressed to the public at large or any section of the public (and for this purpose every relevant programme shall be taken to be so addressed), but does not include an indictment or other document prepared for use in particular legal proceedings.

(3A) The matters relating to a person in relation to which the restrictions imposed by subsection (1) above apply (if their inclusion in any publication is likely to have the result mentioned in that subsection) include in particular—

(a) his name,

(b) his address,

(c) the identity of any school or other educational establishment attended by him,

(d) the identity of any place of work, and

(e) any still or moving picture of him.

(4) For the purposes of this section a child or young person is 'concerned' in any proceedings if he is—

(a) a person against or in respect of whom the proceedings are taken, or

(b) a person called, or proposed to be called, to give evidence in the proceedings."

Section 49(3), which was substituted with effect from April 13, 2015, by the Youth Justice and Criminal Evidence Act 1999, has the effect of extending the definition of "publication" beyond the print media and sound and television broadcasts, and is capable of covering content published online.

The effect of s.49, for sexual offences as for any other offence, is that nothing may be published that is likely to lead to the identification of any child or young person under the age of 18 who is concerned in youth court proceedings, including their name, address or school and any picture of them. These restrictions apply whether the child or young person is a defendant or a witness. If they turn 18 during the course of proceedings, the restrictions cease to have effect.[41] But if the child or young person is a victim or a witness, then s.45A of the Youth Justice and Criminal Evidence Act 1999 gives the court a discretion to impose lifetime reporting restrictions: see further paras 29.108 and following, above.

If a youth appears in an adult magistrates' court or the Crown Court,   **31.39** reporting restrictions are governed by s.45 of the Youth Justice and Criminal Evidence Act 1999, for which see paras 29.58 and following, above.

---

[41] *T v DPP* [2003] EWHC 2408 (Admin), considered more recently in *R. (on the application of JC) v Central Criminal Court* [2014] EWHC 1041 (Admin).

Removal of reporting restrictions

31.40   The s.49 restrictions are not absolute. The circumstances in which the court can remove them are set out in s.49(4A) and (5):

- Where the child or young person has been convicted of an offence and the court is satisfied that it is in the public interest to dispense with the reporting restriction (s.49(4A));
- Where it is appropriate to do so for the purpose of avoiding injustice to the child or young person subject to the application (s.49(5)(a)); or
- Where a defendant has been charged with or convicted of a violent or sexual offence, or an offence punishable in the case of a person aged 21 or over with imprisonment for 14 years or more, if the defendant is unlawfully at large and it is necessary to identify him in the press for the purpose of apprehending him (s.49(5)–(7)).

The sexual offences to which s.49(5)–(7) refers are those listed in Pt 2 of Sch.15 to the Criminal Justice Act 2003. Accordingly, this exception may apply to the majority of sexual offences.

31.41   Little guidance is available as to when it will be "in the public interest" to remove restrictions under s.49(4A), following conviction in the youth court. What is clear is that this power should be exercised rarely and with the greatest caution. In *McKerry v Teesdale and Wear Valley Justices*,[42] the fact that the defendant constituted a "serious danger to the public" was held to justify the decision to dispense with restrictions. Lord Bingham stated[43]:

> "The power to dispense with anonymity, as permitted in certain circumstances by section 49(4A), must be exercised with very great care, caution and circum-spection. It would be wholly wrong for any court to dispense with a juvenile's prima facie right to anonymity as an additional punishment. It is also very difficult to see any place for 'naming and shaming'. The court must be satisfied that the statutory criterion that it is in the public interest to dispense with the reporting restriction is satisfied. This will very rarely be the case, and justices making an order under section 49(4A) must be clear in their minds why it is in the public interest to dispense with the restrictions."

Anonymity of complainants in sexual offence cases

31.42   The anonymity of complainants of sexual offences is governed by s.1 of the Sexual Offences (Amendment) Act 1992 (for rape and other sexual offences), discussed in Ch.29. The list of sexual offences to which the anonymity provisions apply are set out in s.2(1) of the 1992 Act, as amended by the Sexual Offences Act 2003. All offences under Pt 1 of the Sexual Offences Act 2003 are included, with the exception of those in s.64 (sex with an adult relative), s.65 (sex with an adult relative: consent to penetration), s.69

---

[42] [2001] E.M.L.R 5; [2000] Crim. L.R. 594.
[43] At [17].

(intercourse with an animal), and s.71 (sexual activity in a public lavatory).[44] The right to anonymity is not absolute as there are circumstances in which a court can lift the restrictions, for example to induce a witness to come forward. These circumstances are set out in s.3 of the 1992 Act.

DISCLOSURE

Disclosure is governed by Pt 15 of the Criminal Procedure Rules 2015.[45] As far as prosecution evidence for summary trial in the youth court is concerned, the relevant guidance is to be found in the *Attorney General's Guidelines on Disclosure*,[46] published in December 2013. Paragraphs 44 to 47 deal with disclosure where a trial is to take place. In short, initial disclosure obligations arise after a not guilty plea has been entered (para.44), and once set down for trial, prosecutors should ensure the investigator is requested to supply any outstanding disclosure schedules as a matter of urgency. Prosecutors should serve initial disclosure in sufficient time to ensure the trial date is effective (para.46). **31.43**

As in the Crown Court, disclosure of unused material in the youth court is governed by the Criminal Procedure and Investigations Act 1996 ("CPIA"). The prosecution's obligations arise after a not guilty plea has been entered.[47] The material must, of course, satisfy the appropriate statutory test for disclosure. **31.44**

Disclosure of a defence statement under s.6 of the CPIA is voluntary in the youth court.[48] However, in the absence of a defence statement, the defendant cannot make an application for specific disclosure under s.8 of the CPIA, nor can the youth court make any order for disclosure of unused prosecution material. If there is to be a defence statement, it must comply with s.6A of the CPIA, and standard directions require that it be served within 14 days of date upon which the prosecution has complied with (or purported to comply with) initial disclosure. **31.45**

The *Judicial Protocol on the Disclosure of Unused Material in Criminal Cases*[49] was issued in December 2013. Paragraphs 30 to 37 deal with disclosure of unused material in the magistrates' and youth court. It notes that whilst the statutory disclosure test applies, given the nature of summary trials, it is important that summary trials are not delayed or over-complicated **31.46**

---

[44] Sexual Offences Act 2003 s.139 and Sch.6, para.31.
[45] The Rules are available at *http://www.legislation.gov.uk/uksi/2015/1490/pdfs/uksi_20151490_en.pdf* [Accessed April 30, 2016].
[46] Available at *https://www.gov.uk/government/publications/attorney-generals-guidelines-on-disclosure-2013* [Accessed April 30, 2016].
[47] Except when, pursuant to the common law rules of disclosure, the prosecution ought to disclose unused material in advance of CPIA disclosure, e.g. for a bail application.
[48] CPIA s.6(2).
[49] Available at *https://www.judiciary.gov.uk/publications/protocol-unused-material-criminal-cases/* [Accessed April 30, 2016].

by misconceived applications for, or inappropriate disclosure of, prosecution material.[50]

The Course of a Trial[51]

31.47 The youth court procedure is the same as that of the adult magistrates' court. The trial procedure is governed by Pt 24 of the Criminal Procedure Rules 2015. That Part applies to all magistrates' courts. It does, however, contain some modifications in respect of youths. In particular, "finding of guilt" is to be used in place of "conviction", and "an order made on a finding of guilt" is to be used in place of "sentence" (r.24.2), and the general rule that a court may proceed in the absence of a defendant does not apply to those under 18 (r.24.12(3)(b)).

31.48 The youth court is intended to be designed in such a way as to ensure that the court proceedings are accessible to this age group. The court layout and procedure will be less formal: for example, first names will be used, the defendant will not normally be in the dock and witnesses will be seated whilst giving evidence.[52] Further guidance is to be found in *R. (TP) v West London Youth Court*,[53] which involved a 15-year-old defendant with an IQ of an eight-year-old. He applied to stay proceedings as an abuse of process on the basis that his intellectual capacity was such that he could not effectively participate in the proceedings in accordance with art.6 ECHR. This application was dismissed, owing to the fact that the youth court was designed to facilitate participation. Baker LJ noted the following steps that should be taken to that end[54]:

> "i) keeping the claimant's level of cognitive functioning in mind;
> ii) using concise and simple language;
> iii) having regular breaks;
> iv) taking additional time to explain court proceedings;
> v) being proactive in ensuring the claimant has access to support;
> vi) explaining and ensuring the claimant understands the ingredients of the charge;

---

[50] para.30.
[51] See the CPS Guidance *Safeguarding Children as Victims and Witnesses*, Annex 2, for a trial checklist when dealing with children or other vulnerable victims of rape. The checklist can be applied to other sexual offences. See also the Equal Treatment Bench Book 2013, Ch.5, which sets out how to adapt criminal proceedings to accommodate children. The Guidance is available at *https://www.cps.gov.uk/legal/v_to_z/safeguarding_children_as_victims_and_witnesses/* [Accessed April 30, 2016].
[52] See the *Youth Court Bench Book* (January 2013), para.12. The *Bench Book* available on the Judicial College website. See also the Magistrates' Association Protocol, Appendix A, which sets out factors influencing procedures in youth court trials.
[53] [2005] EWHC 2583 (Admin). Note that if a youth appears as a defendant in the Crown Court, the court must be adapted in accordance with the Criminal Practice Direction, General matters 3D: Vulnerable People in the Courts. This follows the decision in *SC v UK* (2005) 40 E.H.R.R. 226, which found a breach of art.6 on the basis that the young defendant could not participate effectively at trial.
[54] At [26].

vii) explaining the possible outcomes and sentences;
viii) ensuring that cross-examination is carefully controlled so that questions are short and clear and frustration is minimised".

The court has a duty to ensure that the defendant receives a fair trial, **31.49** which includes the ability to participate effectively at trial.[55] For the use of special measures, and the inherent power of the court to take such steps as are necessary to ensure that the defendant receives a fair trial and to assist the defendant to give his best evidence, see Ch.27. The steps to be taken include "being pro-active in ensuring that the claimant had access to support".[56] This applies not simply to the trial itself, but also, where appropriate, in case preparation and the run up to the trial.[57]

Under s.33A of the Youth Justice and Criminal Evidence Act 1999 **31.50** ("YJCEA"), the court may, on application and if certain conditions are met, direct that the accused give evidence by live link. In the case of those under 18, those conditions are that the accused's:

"(a) ability to participate effectively in the proceedings as a witness giving oral evidence in court is compromised by his level of intellectual ability or social functioning, and
(b) use of a live link would enable him to participate more effectively in the proceedings as a witness (whether by improving the quality of his evidence or otherwise)."[58]

Section 33BA of the YJCEA, when commenced, will enable the court to **31.51** direct that the examination of the accused be conducted through an intermediary. As with the live link provisions, this power will be available where the accused's ability to participate effectively in the proceedings as a witness giving oral evidence in court is compromised by his level of intellectual ability or social functioning.[59]

COMPETENCE AND COMPELLABILITY

By virtue of s.53 of the YJCEA, all persons (whatever their age) are **31.52** competent to give evidence in criminal proceedings. However, a person is not competent to give evidence if it appears to the court that he is not a person who is able to understand questions put to him as a witness, or give answers to them which can be understood.[60] The question of competence is determined by the court. In doing so, it will take into account any special measures directions. Where the witness is a child or vulnerable adult, the court should watch any video-recorded interview before determining the

---

[55] Criminal Procedure Rules 2015, overriding objective, r.1.1(2)(b) and r.3.10(3)(b).
[56] *R. (on the application of P) v West London Youth Court* [2006] 1 W.L.R. 1219, at [26].
[57] *R. (on the application of C) v Sevenoaks Youth Court* [2009] EWHC 3088 (Admin) at [17] (where the court examined steps to be taken to ensure participation of the defendant, in particular the use of intermediaries).
[58] See further paras 27.26 and following, above.
[59] See further paras 27.36 and following, above.
[60] YJCEA 1999 s.53(3).

issue.[61] Expert evidence may well be necessary to inform the decision, and material from medical or school records may also assist.

31.53 Any issue of competence should be raised before the witness is sworn or begins to give evidence. This will usually be at the start of the trial or on earlier notice, but may be dealt with during the course of the trial if it becomes clear only then that competence is an issue. Cases involving very young witnesses should be fast-tracked to avoid any effect on their competence.[62]

31.54 As a general rule, all competent witnesses are compellable. There are no exceptions on the basis of the age of the witness.

OATHS

31.55 A witness aged 14 or over, who appreciates the solemnity of the occasion and the particular responsibility to tell the truth which is involved in taking an oath, must give sworn evidence. A person under the age of 18 uses the words "I promise" in place of "I swear" when taking the oath or affirming.[63] A witness under the age of 14 (or otherwise incapable of giving sworn evidence) is not permitted to give sworn evidence. The court should be satisfied that such a witness is otherwise competent, and knows the difference between truth and lies.

SPECIAL MEASURES

31.56 Special measures are available for vulnerable and intimidated witnesses (other than defendants) to ensure that they are able to give their best evidence at court. The relevant statutory provisions are to be found in ss.16–32 of the YJCEA. Under ss.16 and 17, the following groups of witness are eligible for special measures:
- those under 18 at the time of the hearing (s.16(1)(a));
- vulnerable witnesses (other than those under 18) (s.16(1)(b));
- intimidated witnesses (s.17(1));
- complainants of sexual offences (s.17(4)).

31.57 For detailed discussion of these provisions, see Ch.27. The provisions, and the types of special measures that are most relevant to the youth court and sexual offences, are summarised below. Some options are available to the court to facilitate best evidence for defendants. These do not technically fall under the "special measures" provisions, but arise from the inherent power of the court to protect the rights of the defendant and ensure effective participation.

---

[61] YJCEA 1999 s.54(3); and *MacPherson* [2005] EWCA Crim 3605.
[62] *Powell (Michael John)* [2006] 1 Cr. App. R. 31.
[63] YJCEA 1999 ss.55(2) and 56(2).

Persons eligible for special measures

The persons eligible for special measures can be divided into four groups: **31.58**
- Those under 18. Under s.16(1)(a), those under 18 at the time of the special measures hearing are automatically eligible for special measures.[64]
- Other vulnerable witnesses. Under s.16(1)(b), vulnerable witnesses (those with a mental disorder or other significant impairment of intelligence and social functioning, or those with a physical disability), whatever their age, are eligible if by virtue of that disorder etc. the quality of their evidence is likely to be diminished.[65]
- Intimidated witnesses. Under s.17(1), a person will be eligible for special measures if the court is satisfied that the quality of evidence given by them is likely to be diminished by reason of fear or distress on their part in connection with testifying in the proceedings. The court must take into account various factors including the views, age, cultural background etc. of the witness.[66]
- Complainants of sexual offences. Under s.17(4), a witness who is a complainant of a sexual offence will automatically be deemed eligible for special measures, unless they do not wish to be so eligible.[67]

Types of special measures

Once the eligibility criteria have been met, the court must consider whether   **31.59**
any special measures will be likely to improve the quality of the evidence, and
if so, which measure(s). The types of special measure available are set out in
ss.23–30 of the Act. Measures relevant to the youth court are:
- screens (s.23);
- evidence via live link (s.24);
- video recorded evidence-in-chief (s.27);
- examination of a witness through an intermediary (s.29); and
- devices to aid communication (s.30).

Section 28 of the YJCEA, which provides for pre-recorded cross-examina-   **31.60**
tion where a special measures direction provides for video-recorded
examination-in-chief under s.27 of the Act, is not in force as of the date of
writing (October 2015).

The "primary rule", namely that the court must give a special measures   **31.61**
direction in relation to an eligible witness, applies to child witnesses involved

---

[64] Eligibility used to apply to those under 17 but was extended to those under 18 by an amendment of s.16(1)(a) made by the Coroners and Justice Act 2009 s.98, with effect from June 27, 2011.
[65] YJCEA s.16(1)(b), (2).
[66] See YJCEA, s.17(2), for a full non-exhaustive list of factors the court must consider.
[67] YJCEA s.17(4).

in sexual offence proceedings.[68] Under s.21(3), they will automatically be entitled to give their evidence-in-chief by pre-recorded video, and all other evidence by live link (including evidence-in-chief if it has not been possible to pre-record it). These witnesses are known as children "in need of special protection". By virtue of s.22, these provisions apply to those aged 18 and over, so long as the witness was under 18 at the time of recording. The sexual offences to which this rule applies are set out in s.35(3)(a) of the YJCEA as:

- offences under ss.33–36 of the Sexual Offences Act 1956;
- offences under Part 1 of 2003 Act;
- offences under the Protection of Children Act 1978.

Procedure

31.62 The use of special measures in the youth court is dealt with in Pt 18 of the Criminal Procedure Rules 2015. Even where a witness is automatically eligible for special measures, an application must still be made. An application should be made within 28 days of a defendant's not guilty plea.[69]

QUESTIONING OF YOUNG PEOPLE

31.63 Prosecutions for sexual offences in the youth court often involve young complainants and/or witnesses. Children often have difficulties in understanding questions at court. They are also unlikely to admit that they do not understand questions.[70] The best way to address this problem may be through an intermediary (see s.29 of the Youth Justice and Criminal Evidence Act 1999). However, where the witness or defendant is not eligible for such assistance, the advocates and the court must ensure that the questions are understood. Ground rules hearings can be conducted in youth courts. In particular, these should address the limits of cross-examination, the length of cross-examination and the terminology of the questions, so as to minimise the risk of unreliable answers.[71] The *Equal Treatment Bench Book* suggests how criminal proceedings can be adapted for the questioning of children, whether witnesses or defendants. It stresses the need for flexibility in approach, for example, ensuring sessions are short and there are regular breaks.[72] As far as questions are concerned, they should be phrased simply, and witnesses asked to express answers shortly so the evidence can be followed. Courts should consider allowing children to write or draw

---

[68] YJCEA s.21. A child witnesses is a witness under the age of 18 at the time of the special measures hearing: YJCEA s.16(1)(a), (3).
[69] Criminal Procedure Rules 2015 rr.18.3 and 18.9.
[70] See generally Ch.27.
[71] Equal Treatment Bench Book (Judicial College, 2013), Ch 5, para.64.
[72] Equal Treatment Bench Book (Judicial College, 2013), Ch.5, para.6.

answers.[73] The "Advocates Gateway" provides "toolkits" for questioning of young people including in relation to sensitive issues, many of which arise in sexual offences.[74] One such issue is questions that deal with intimate touching. CPS policy is that "it is almost always inappropriate and unnecessary to have the child point to parts of their own bodies. Consider using diagrams or body maps".[75] A diagram should be used in conjunction with open questioning, such as "You said he touched you. Can you show me on the drawing where he touched you?" This should be followed up by more detailed questioning, such as "Do you have a name for that place? Tell me about it/Tell me what happened?". For detailed consideration of this subject, see Ch.28.

MODE OF TRIAL

THE STATUTORY PRESUMPTION AND ITS EXCEPTIONS

There is a statutory presumption that those under 18 will be tried in the youth court. Section 24(1) of the Magistrates' Court Act 1980[76] provides: **31.64**

> "Where a person under the age of 18 years appears or is brought before a magistrates' court on an information charging him with an indictable offence he shall, subject to sections 51 and 51A of the Crime and Disorder Act 1998 and subject to sections 24A and 24B below, be tried summarily".

There are, however, circumstances in which the presumption does not apply. **31.65**
Section 51A(3) of the Crime and Disorder Act 1998[77] sets out the conditions on the basis of which the court shall send the child or young person forthwith to the Crown Court for trial. They are as follows:

(a) the offence falls within s.51A(12), i.e. it is an offence of homicide that attracts a minimum sentence under s.51A of the Firearms Act 1968 or s.29(3) of the Violent Crime Reduction Act 2006;

(b) the offence is mentioned in s.91(1) of the PCC(S)A 2000 (other than an offence mentioned in (d), below, in relation to which it appears to the court as mentioned there) and the court considers that if the child or young person is found guilty of the offence it ought to be possible to sentence him in pursuance of s.91(3) of that Act;

---

[73] Equal Treatment Bench Book (Judicial College, 2013), Ch.5, para 8.

[74] The Advocates Gateway is a website which provides access to practical, evidence-based guidance on vulnerable witnesses and defendants. The website is hosted by the Advocacy Training Council. See *http://www.theadvocatesgateway.org.*

[75] *Safeguarding Children as Victims and Witnesses* (CPS, November 2009).

[76] As substituted by the Criminal Justice Act 2003 s.41 and Sch.3, para.9 (brought into force in relation to specified local justice areas by SI 2012/1320 and SI 2012/2574 and, so far as not already in force, by SI 2013/1103).

[77] As substituted by the Criminal Justice Act 2003 s.41 and Sch.3, para.18 (brought into force in relation to specified local justice areas by SI 2012/1320 and SI 2012/2574 and, so far as not already in force, by SI 2013/1103).

(c) notice is given to the court under s.51B or s.51C of the 1998 Act, which concern respectively serious or complex fraud cases and cases involving an alleged offence under inter alia the Sexual Offences Act 1956, the Protection of Children Act 1978 or the Sexual Offences Act 2003, where the welfare of a child witness requires the case to proceed without delay to the Crown Court; or

(d) the offence is a specified offence (within the meaning of s.224 of the Criminal Justice Act 2003) and it appears to the court that if the child or young person is found guilty the criteria for the imposition of a sentence under s.226B of that Act would be met (under which young persons convicted on indictment of certain grave crimes may be sentenced to be detained for long periods).

31.66   In addition, s.51(7)(b) of the 1998 Act[78] provides that where the court sends an adult ("A") for trial and:

> "... a child or young person appears or is brought before the court on the same or a subsequent occasion charged jointly with A with an indictable offence for which A is sent to trial ... or an indictable offence which appears to the court to be related to that offence, the court shall, if it considers it necessary in the interests of justice to do so, send the child or young person forthwith to the Crown Court for trial for the indictable offence."

31.67   In the context of sexual offences, the circumstances in which a young person may be sent to the Crown Court for trial can be grouped as follows:

- Section 91 PCCSA 2000: Grave crimes
- "Specified" offences: dangerous offenders
- Young people charged alongside an adult

We deal with these in turn below, after addressing two procedural points.

Procedure for determining mode of trial

31.68 The procedure for determining the mode of trial of youths was modified on the coming into force of ss.24A–24D of the Magistrates' Courts Act 1980 on June 18, 2012. The effect of those provisions, which were enacted in the Criminal Justice Act 2003 ("CJA 2003"), was to introduce a mode of trial procedure similar to that for adults. Thus, where there is a possibility that the youth may be tried in the Crown Court (in one of the limited circumstances explained above), the youth will be invited to plead guilty or not guilty. If a guilty plea is entered, the youth court can proceed to the sentencing stage. This will take place in the youth court, unless sentencing powers are insufficient (see paras 31.101 and following, below). If a not guilty plea is entered, the youth court will determine mode of trial as set out above.

31.69   Prior to the amendment of the PCCSA 2000 by s.53 of the Criminal Justice and Courts Act 2015, if the youth court accepted jurisdiction, it had no

---

[78] As substituted by the Criminal Justice Act 2003 s.41 and Sch.3, para.18 (see last note).

power to commit the defendant to the Crown Court for sentence. Accordingly, the mode of trial procedure could have a significant impact on sentence. However, its impact is now reduced in light of s.3B(1) of the PCCSA 2000, which has been amended so as to permit committal of a child or young person to the Crown Court for sentence under s.91 after trial in a youth court.

The decision as to jurisdiction is taken by the youth court. A person under **31.70** 18 does not have the right to elect trial by jury. The *Code for Crown Prosecutors*[79] states that youths should be tried in the youth court wherever possible, as that is the court best designed to meet their specific needs. It goes on to state that a trial in the Crown Court should be reserved for the most serious of offences or where the interests of justice require that the youth is tried jointly with an adult.

Mode of trial where accused turns 18 in the course of proceedings

The youth court has jurisdiction to deal with those aged 10 to 17 inclusive.[80] **31.71** If the defendant turns 18 after charge but before first appearance, then the youth court has no jurisdiction to deal with him.[81] If the defendant is charged with an indictable offence and turns 18 after his first court appearance, then, for the purpose of determining mode of trial, the relevant age will be his age on the day mode of trial is determined.[82] In the vast majority of cases this will be the same date as the first appearance. Thus, if a defendant is aged 18 on the day on which mode of trial is determined, he will be able to elect a jury trial. If not, mode of trial will be determined in accordance with s.24 of the Magistrates' Court Act 1980.

SECTION 91 PCCSA 2000: GRAVE CRIMES

The most common exception to the general rule that a person under 18 will **31.72** be dealt with in the youth court is found in s.51A(3) of the 1998 Act: the grave crimes exception. The term "grave crimes" was originally found in s.24(1) of the Magistrates' Courts Act 1980, which referred to s.91(1) of the PCCSA 2000 as a provision "under which young persons convicted on indictment of certain grave crimes may be sentenced to be detained for long periods". However, s.91 of the PCCSA 2000 does not itself use the term "grave crimes", instead referring to "serious offences". To further complicate matters, the term "grave crimes" was removed from s.24(1) of the 1980 Act

---

[79] Para.8.3. The *Code* is available at *http://www.cps.gov.uk/publications/docs/code_2013_accessible_english.pdf* [Accessed April 30, 2016].

[80] The court is under a duty to establish that the defendant is aged between 10 and 17. In the unlikely event that the age of the defendant cannot be ascertained, the issue will be dealt with in accordance with the statutory procedure set out in the Children and Young Persons Act 1933, s.99(1).

[81] *R. v Uxbridge Youth Court, Ex p. H* (1998) 162 J.P. 327.

[82] *R. v Islington North Juvenile Court, Ex p. Daley* [1983] 1 A.C. 347.

when that provision was substituted by the Criminal Justice Act 2003 (see para.31.91, below). The term is, however, still in common use, and accordingly references to "grave crimes" in this and subsequent paragraphs should be read as a reference to offences under s.91(1) of the PCC(S)A 2000.

31.73   There are two categories of grave crimes:
- crimes punishable with a maximum term of imprisonment of 14 years or more for an adult (but not an offence for which the sentence is fixed by law) (s.91(1)(a)), and
- a selection of sexual offences not punishable with imprisonment for 14 years or more (s.91(1)(b)).

31.74   The following offences in the Sexual Offences Act 2003 carry a maximum term of imprisonment of 14 years or more and so fall within s.91(1)(a)[83]:
- rape (s.1),
- assault by penetration (s.2),
- causing a person to engage in penetrative sexual activity (s.4(1) and (4)),
- rape of a child under 13 (s.5),
- assault by penetration of a child under 13 (s.6),
- sexual assault of a child under 13 (s.7),
- causing or inciting a child under 13 to engage in sexual activity (s.8),
- arranging or facilitating a child sex offence (s.14),
- certain sexual offences against mentally disordered people (ss.30–31, ss.34–35, and ss.38–39),
- certain child sexual exploitation offences (ss.47–50),
- committing an offence of kidnapping or false imprisonment with intent to commit a sexual offence (s.62),
- aiding, abetting, etc. or attempting the above offences,
- burglary with intent to commit rape (if a dwelling) (s.9 of the Theft Act 1968).

31.75   Section 91(1)(b)–(e) sets out those offences that are not punishable with a maximum term of imprisonment of 14 years or more but are nevertheless grave crimes. They are all sexual offences under the 2003 Act:
- sexual assault (s.3),
- child sex offences committed by children or young persons (s.13),
- sexual activity with a child family member (s.25), and
- inciting a child family member to engage in sexual activity (s.26).

Powers of punishment

31.76   If a person under 18 is charged with a "grave crime", then s.51A(3) of the 1998 Act requires the youth court to consider whether, if the person is

---

[83] Offences under the Sexual Offence Act 1956 which were repealed and replaced by the Sexual Offences Act 2003 are not set out.

convicted, the court has sufficient powers of sentencing, or whether it ought to be possible for the defendant to be sentenced to a period of detention under s.91(3) of the PCCSA 2000.

As regards the sufficiency of the youth court's own sentencing powers: **31.77**

- the court has no power to impose a custodial sentence on those aged 10 and 11,
- it has no power to impose a custodial sentence on those aged 12 to 14 (inclusive) unless they are "persistent offenders",[84] in which case the maximum sentence is a detention and training order for 24 months (PCCSA 2000 s.100), and
- the maximum sentence it may impose in respect of defendants aged 15, 16 or 17 is a detention and training order for 24 months (PCCSA 2000 s.101(1), (4)).

Section 91(3) of the PCCSA 2000 provides: **31.78**

> "If the court is of the opinion that neither a youth rehabilitation order nor a detention and training order is suitable, the court may sentence the offender to be detained for such period, not exceeding the maximum term of imprisonment with which the offence is punishable in the case of a person aged 21 or over, as may be specified in the sentence."

Thus, s.51A(3) of the 1998 Act and s.91 of the PCSSA 2000 together   **31.79** overcome the limitations on the youth court's sentencing powers, in that they enable a child or young person to be sent for trial to the Crown Court which may (i) impose a sentence of detention for longer than 24 months, and (ii) impose a sentence of detention where it would not otherwise be possible (those under the age of 12, and those aged 12–14 who are not persistent offenders). Note that in *R(P) v Derby Youth Court*,[85] it was found that a youth may not be committed under s.51A(3) of the 1998 Act for offences falling within s.91 of the PCCSA 2000 if there is evidence before the youth court that the defendant is unfit to stand trial. This is because the defendant would not be "convicted" and could not therefore be "sentenced" pursuant to that s.91.

The application of the "grave crimes" exception

Guidance as to the general approach to be taken to the exception by the   **31.80** youth court was set out in *R. (H, A and O) v Southampton Youth Court*[86]:

> "The general policy of the legislature is that those who are under 18 years of age and in particular children of under 15 years of age should, wherever possible, be

---

[84] There is no statutory definition of "persistent offender". A court may take into account offences for which the offender received a caution (or reprimand or warning): *AD (a juvenile)* (2001) 1 Cr. App. R.(S.) 59. A court may treat an offender as persistent if just two offences were committed in a short space of time: *Smith* (2000) 164 J.P. 681. A court should not treat an offender as persistent if the offence before the court for sentence is of a different character to a previous offence: *R. v JD* (2001) 165 J.P. 1.
[85] [2015] EWHC 573 (Admin) at [8].
[86] [2004] EWHC 2912 at [33]–[35].

tried in the youth court. It is the court which is best designed to meet their specific needs. A trial in the Crown Court with the inevitably greater formality and greatly increased number of people involved (including a jury and the public) should be reserved for the most serious cases.

It is a further policy of the legislature that, generally speaking, first time offenders aged 12 to 14 and all offenders under 12 should not be detained in custody and decisions as to jurisdiction should have regard to the fact that the exceptional power to detain for grave offences should not be used to water down the general principle. Those under 15 will rarely attract a period of detention and, even more rarely, those who are under 12.

In each case the court should ask itself whether there is a real prospect, having regard to his or her age, that this defendant whose case they are considering might require a sentence of, or in excess of, two years or, alternatively, whether although the sentence might be less than two years, there is some unusual feature of the case which justifies declining jurisdiction, bearing in mind that the absence of a power to impose a detention and training order because the defendant is under 15 is not an unusual feature."

31.81   It will therefore be seen that (i) there is a strong presumption in favour of trial in the youth court as it is the court best designed to meet the need of this age group; (ii) for the "grave crimes" exception to apply, there must be a "real prospect" of a sentence of more than two years' detention at the Crown Court,[87] and (iii) in considering what sentence might be required, the youth court should bear in mind that those under 15 will rarely attract a period of detention and, even more rarely, those who are under 12. In *R (DPP) v South Tyneside Youth Court*,[88] the Divisional Court commented on the use of the "real prospect" test in the context of amendments to s.3B(1) of the PCCSA 2000 introduced by s.53 of the Criminal Justice and Courts Act 2015. The amendments permit the youth court to commit a youth to the Crown Court for sentence after trial in the youth court. The Court said that whilst there are cases in which the alleged offending is so grave that a sentence in excess of two years would be a "real prospect", such cases will be rare. In most cases, the severity will only become apparent after the court has determined the full facts and circumstances of the offence and has a greater understanding of the offender. Since the youth court now has the option of committing a defendant for sentence after conviction, it would generally be at that point when the assessment could and should be made. The Court confirmed that this approach was entirely consistent with the statement in *R. (H, A and O) v Southampton Youth Court* that trial of a youth in the Crown Court "should be reserved for the most serious cases".

31.82   In practical terms, the youth court will consider the prosecution case and all the information before it in order to anticipate sentence. This includes any relevant sentencing guideline, the age and maturity of the child or young person, their previous good character or previous convictions and, if

---

[87] A vague or theoretical possibility is insufficient: *R. (C and D) v Sheffield Youth Court* [2003] EWHC Admin 35.
[88] *R. (DPP) v South Tyneside Youth Court* [2015] EWHC 1455 (Admin).

applicable, any anticipated guilty plea.[89] If the youth court concludes that it ought to be possible to sentence the child or young person under s.91, then the court "shall" commit the case to the Crown Court for trial. There is no discretion once the test is satisfied.

Where more than one defendant is charged, the decision as regards mode **31.83** of trial falls to be considered separately in relation to each.[90] One possible outcome is that one alleged offender may go for trial in the youth court while another might go for trial at the Crown Court, even though the offences are factually linked.[91]

The decision to retain a case in a youth court is not necessarily inconsistent **31.84** with a finding of seriousness.[92] Thus, a youth court can retain jurisdiction, finding that the "grave crime" test is not satisfied, but then commit to the Crown Court for sentence under the dangerousness provisions (see paras 31.91 and following, below).

Grave crimes: rape and other sexual offences in the youth court

The decision in *Billam*[93] established a rule that rape trials were not to be **31.85** conducted in the youth court. This rule no longer applies in absolute terms. In *R. (W, S and B) v Brent, Enfield and Richmond Youth Courts*,[94] Leveson J (as he then was) stated:

> "I doubt that there should be such a hard and fast rule in the case of a child aged 12. We were reminded that, at the time of *Billam*, the offence of rape could be committed only by a male of 14 years or over. At that time a boy of 12 or 13 could not be charged with rape. It appears to me that now that a boy of 12 or 13 can be charged with rape, there may well be some cases in which it will not be appropriate to commit such a defendant to the Crown Court. I suggest perhaps that the rule set out in *Billam* . . . could now properly be modified so as to indicate that in the case of very young defendants it may be appropriate to accept jurisdiction."

That the youth court should in appropriate cases accept jurisdiction in a **31.86** rape case was confirmed by the *Protocol: Rape Cases in the Youth Court*, issued by the Senior Presiding Judge in November 2007. The Protocol was superseded in March 2010 by the *Protocol: Sexual Offences in the Youth*

[89] *R. (W, S and B) v Brent, Enfield and Richmond Youth Courts* [2006] EWHC 95 (Admin).
[90] [2006] EWHC 95 (Admin).
[91] *R. (on the application of W) v Oldham Youth Court* [2010] EWHC 661 (Admin): two young defendants were charged with rape, in related offences committed on separate occasions. The failure to consider M's mode of trial separately from that of W led to the quashing of the decision to commit M.
[92] *W v Warrington Magistrates' Court* [2009] EWHC 1538 (Admin). The youth court retained jurisdiction, based on the information it had before it. As a result of facts that emerged during the trial, the case was committed for sentence at the Crown Court under the dangerousness provisions. This did not invalidate the original decision to retain jurisdiction: there was no inconsistency between the decision not to commit, applying the correct test, and the judge's subsequent finding that a sentence of IPP was required.
[93] [1986] 1 W.L.R. 349.
[94] [2006] EWHC 95 (Admin) at 44.

Court, which deals with all sexual offences and not only rape. It provides as follows:

"Sexual Offences in the Youth Court

A Protocol issued by the Senior Presiding Judge

Introduction

1. This protocol sets out the procedure to be applied in the Youth Court in all cases involving allegations of sexual offences which are capable of being committed for trial at the Crown Court under the grave crime provisions.
2. This protocol applies to all cases involving such charges, irrespective of the gravity of the allegation, the age of the defendant and/or the antecedent history of the defendant.1
3. This protocol does not alter the test that the Youth Court must apply when determining whether a case is a 'grave crime'.
4. This Protocol has been written in consultation with the Senior District Judge, the Magistrates' Association, the National Bench Chairmen's Forum, the Justices' Clerks' Society, HMCS and the CPS.

Commencement and amendment

5. The protocol will take effect forthwith and may be amended as appropriate by the Senior Presiding Judge.
6. This Protocol supersedes the Protocol on Rape Cases, issued in November 2007.

Background

7. Historically, the position was that the Youth Court should never accept jurisdiction in a rape case.3 More recent developments in case law and the wider definition of rape under the Sexual Offences Act 2003 now mean that certain rape cases may not fall within the grave crime exception and can appropriately be tried in the Youth Court.
8. In light of those developments the Rape Protocol was issued in November 2007. That protocol provided that such cases should be heard by a Circuit Judge, authorised to try serious sexual offences, sitting as a District Judge (Magistrates' Court). No explicit provision was made for the trial of alleged sexual offences other than rape.
9. In the Crown Court, cases involving allegations of sexual offences frequently involve complex and sensitive issues and only those Circuit Judges and Recorders who have been specifically authorised and who have attended the appropriate JSB course may try this type of work, although it is open to a Resident Judge to decide that any particular, less serious case, may be tried by any Judge or Recorder.
10. A number of District Judges (Magistrates' Courts) have now undertaken training in dealing with these difficult cases and have been specifically authorised to hear cases involving serious sexual offences which fall short of requiring committal to the Crown Court ("an authorised DJ(MC)"). As such, a procedure similar to that of the Crown Court will now apply to allegations of sexual offences in the Youth Court.

Procedure

11. The determination of venue in the Youth Court is governed by section 24 of the Magistrates' Courts Act 1980, which provides that the youth must be tried summarily unless charged with such a grave crime that long term detention is a

realistic possibility,5 or that one of the other exceptions to this presumption arises.

12. Wherever possible such cases should be listed before an authorised DJ(MC), to decide whether the case falls within the grave crime provisions and should therefore be committed for trial. If jurisdiction is retained and the allegation involves actual, or attempted, penetrative activity, the case must be tried by an authorised DJ(MC). In all other cases, the authorised DJ(MC) must consider whether the case is so serious and/or complex that it must be tried by an authorised DJ(MC), or whether the case can be heard by any DJ(MC) or any Youth Court Bench.

13. If it is not practicable for an authorised DJ(MC) to determine venue, any DJ(MC) or any Youth Court Bench may consider that issue. If jurisdiction is retained, appropriate directions may be given but the case papers, including a detailed case summary and a note of any representations made by the parties, must be sent to an authorised DJ(MC) to consider. As soon as possible the authorised DJ(MC) must decide whether the case must be tried by an authorised DJ(MC) or whether the case is suitable to be heard by any DJ(MC) or any Youth Court Bench; however, if the case involves actual, or alleged, penetrative activity, the trial must be heard by an authorised DJ(MC).

14. Once an authorised DJ(MC) has decided that the case is one which must be tried by an authorised DJ(MC), and in all cases involving actual or alleged penetrative activity, all further procedural hearings should, so far as practicable, be heard by an authorised DJ(MC).

15. Committal proceedings and other hearings in cases in which jurisdiction has been declined may be dealt with by any District Judge or any Youth Court Bench.

Cases remitted for sentence

16. All cases which are remitted for sentence from the Crown Court to the Youth Court should be listed for sentence before an authorised DJ(MC).

Arrangements for an authorised DJ(MC) to be appointed

17. Where a case is to be tried by an authorised DJ(MC) but no such Judge is available, the Bench Legal Adviser should contact the Chief Magistrates Office (*GL-CMO.DDJDeployment@hmcourts-service.gsi.gov.uk* or by telephone on 020 7805 1038) for an authorised DJ(MC) to be assigned.

Footnotes

1. So, for example, every allegation of sexual touching, under s.3 of the Sexual Offences Act 2003, is covered by this protocol.
2. Set out in the Sentencing Guidelines Council's definitive guideline, entitled "Overarching Principles—Sentencing Youths". Published by the Sentencing Guidelines Council in November 2009; available from *http://www.sentencing-guidelines.gov.uk*
3. *R. v Billam* (1986) 1 All ER 985
4. For example, *R. (on the application of B & others) v. The Richmond on Thames Youth Court* (2006) EWHC 95 and Stones' Justices Manual now mean that certain rape cases may not fall within the grave crimes exception and can appropriately be tried in the Youth Court.
5. Section 24(1)(a) of the Magistrates Court Act 1980."

The Protocol does not mean that a very young defendant will never be **31.87** committed to the Crown Court for trial for rape or another serious sexual offence. As Pill LJ observed in *W v Warrington Magistrates Court*, in relation to the 2007 Protocol[95]:

> "Valuable though the procedure encouraged by the Protocol may be, however, the court must apply the statutory test in section [24(1)] of the 1980 Act and not be diverted from it. Parliament has seen fit to grant a right to a Crown Court hearing (including trial by jury) to young offenders in certain circumstances and that cannot be defeated administratively. There will be alleged sexual offences involving very young defendants where committal to the Crown Court is the correct decision."

31.88   Where the youth court retains jurisdiction, it will be limited by its own sentencing powers (subject to a finding of "dangerousness", in which case the matter will be sent up for sentence under s.3C of the PCCSA 2000). In practical terms, this may mean that a first time offender aged under 15 convicted in the youth court of rape automatically receives a referral order.[96]

Examples of youth court decisions on rape

31.89   Decisions to retain jurisdiction or to commit to the Crown Court are frequently the subject of judicial review. There have in recent years been a number of challenges to decisions relating to young defendants charged with rape.[97] As the judgments make clear, each case turns on it own facts: the youth court should consider trying a rape case, but the Crown Court should remain the venue for the most serious offences, notwithstanding the fact that the defendant may be very young. For example, in *R. (on the application of W) v Oldham Youth Court*,[98] W, aged 11, was charged on two counts of rape and one of sexual assault relating to a four-year-old boy. The decision to commit his case to the Crown Court was upheld. The Divisional Court set out the factors which made the case suitable for Crown Court trial:

> "amongst the features which a court is entitled should it wish to do so to regard as aggravating, are the age of the victim, the difference in age between

---

[95] [2009] EWHC 1538 (Admin) at [34].

[96] PCCSA 2000 ss.16–17, as amended by s.35 of the Criminal Justice and Immigration Act 2008.

[97] For examples of decisions to commit being upheld by the Divisional Court, see *R. (W, S and B) v Brent, Enfield and Richmond Youth Courts* [2006] EWHC 95 (Admin); *R. (on the application of W) v Oldham Youth Court* [2010] EWHC 661 (Admin). For examples of decisions to commit being quashed, see *R. (H, A and O) v Southampton Youth Court* [2004] EWHC 2912 (Admin) (a charge of indecent assault); *R. (D) v Manchester City Youth Court* [2003] 1 Cr. App. R.(S.) 323; *R. (H) v South and South East Hants Youth Court Justices & the CPS* [2006] EWHC 1147 (Admin); *R. (on the application of the CPS (Redbridge Section)) v Redbridge Youth Court* [2005] EWHC 1390 (Admin) (where the wrong test was applied, although the Court suggested that on the facts the Crown Court would be the appropriate venue); and *R. (on the application of BH) (A Child v Llandudno Youth Court)* [2014] EWHC 1833 (Admin). For an example of a decision to retain jurisdiction being upheld, see: *W. v Warrington Magistrates' Court* [2009] EWHC 1538 (Admin). For an example of a decision to retain being quashed, see *R. (on the application of W) v Thetford Youth Court* [2002] EWHC 1252 (Admin).

[98] [2010] EWHC 661 (Admin).

perpetrator and victim, the nature and situation of the sexual activity engaged in, the number of occasions when penetration occurred, any remorse shown and the offender's maturity and, it almost goes without saying, a guilty plea."[99]

In *R. v W and M*,[100] two 11-year-old boys were tried at the Central Criminal Court for the rape and attempted rape of an eight-year-old girl. They were convicted of attempted rape and each was sentenced to a three year supervision order; their parents were made subject to a 12-month parenting order. Each was ordered to sign the sex offenders register for two-and-a-half years but, given the boys' young age, the notification requirement was placed on their mothers. The case put under the microscope the issue of jurisdiction and where young defendants charged with rape should be tried. On appeal, Hughes LJ stated:[101]

31.90

"We pass no comment on the decision that this particular charge needed to be brought in a case of this kind, rather than some lesser offence which if proved would more than adequately equip the court with powers to deal with the children accused. We are not privy to that decision and it is not for us. But even if this charge had to be brought, we are unable at present to see why it could not be tried in the Youth Court. We are told that the view was taken by the Crown Prosecution Service that because rape was a 'grave crime', that is to say one within section 91 of the Powers of Criminal Courts (Sentencing) Act 2000, the necessity for committal followed. That proposition having been put to the Justices, as we understand it, they agreed. That however is not the test. All those who are concerned with cases involving children as young as this, if they ever arise, need to have in their briefcases the report of *R (on the application of) H, A and O v Southampton Youth Court* [2004] EWHC 2912 (Admin). The judgment of the court delivered by Leveson J (as he then was) makes clear at paragraph 33 the following three cardinal principles:

1. The general policy of the legislature is that those who are under 18 years of age and particularly children of under 15 should, wherever possible, be tried in the Youth Court. It is that court which is best designed to meet their specific needs. A trial in the Crown Court with the inevitably greater formality and greatly increased number of people involved, including a jury and the public, should be reserved for the most serious cases.

2. It is a further policy of the legislature that, generally speaking, first-time offenders aged 12 to 14, and all offenders under 12, should not be detained in custody and decisions as to jurisdiction should have regard to the fact that the exceptional power to detain for grave offences should not be used to water down that general principle.

3. Those under 15 will rarely attract a period of detention and even more rarely those who are under 12.

The test, in other words, is the real likelihood of a sentence which would be beyond the powers of the Youth Court. If the Justices' minds were not in this case directed to that test, then they should have been. The Youth Court is particularly attuned to enquiries into the alleged activities of children, whether as witnesses, or as defendants, or both. It is staffed by judges who are used to dealing with them. It does not have to sit in a formal courtroom. It can adapt the court premises so as to make the necessary exercise of the trial one more suited

---

[99] *R. (on the application of W) v Oldham Youth Court* [2010] EWHC 661 (Admin) at [22].
[100] *R. v W and M* [2010] EWCA Crim 1926.
[101] At [39]–[40].

to the very young. It has judges who may well have encountered very similar factual disputes also in the family jurisdiction where this kind of thing is not in the least uncommon. We do express the hope that if similar facts should recur again those principles will be kept in mind and every effort be made to keep the proceedings as low key as possibly can be done."

"Specified" Offences: Dangerous Offenders

31.91 The second exception to the general rule that youth cases must be heard in the youth court is when the youth court is of the view that, if convicted, the offender would meet the "dangerousness" criteria in the Criminal Justice Act 2003 ("CJA 2003").[102] This exception is to be found in s.51A(2) and (3)(d) of the Crime and Disorder Act 1998,[103] which provides, so far as material:

"(2) Where a child or young person appears or is brought before a magistrates' court ('the court') charged with an offence and any of the conditions mentioned in subsection (3) below is satisfied, the court shall send him forthwith to the Crown Court for trial for the offence.
(3) Those conditions are— . . .
(d) that the offence is a specified offence (within the meaning of s.224 of the Criminal Justice Act 2003) and it appears to the court that if he is found guilty of the offence the criteria for the imposition of a sentence under s.226B of that Act would be met".

An offence is a "specified" offence if it is listed in Pt 2 of Sch.15 to the CJA 2003. The majority of offences in the Sexual Offences Act 2003 are so listed.

31.92 Section 226B of the CJA 2003[104] provides for the imposition on a person under 18 of an extended sentence for certain violent or sexual offences:

"(1) This section applies where—
(a) a person aged under 18 is convicted of a specified offence (whether the offence was committed before or after this section comes into force),
(b) the court considers that there is a significant risk to members of the public of serious harm occasioned by the commission by the offender of further specified offences,
(c) the court is not required by section 226(2) to impose a sentence of detention for life under section 91 of the Sentencing Act, and
(d) if the court were to impose an extended sentence of detention, the term that it would specify as the appropriate custodial term would be at least 4 years."

31.93 As to whether there is a "significant risk to members of the public of serious harm occasioned by the commission by the offender of further specified offences", as required by s.226B(b), s.229 of the CJA 2003[105] provides the following (known as the "dangerousness test"):

[102] For which see Ch.27.
[103] Inserted by Criminal Justice Act 2003 s.179 and Sch.8, para.15.
[104] Inserted by the Legal Aid, Sentencing and Punishment of Offenders Act 2012 s.124, with effect from December 3, 2012 (SI 2012/2906).
[105] As amended by Criminal Justice and Immigration Act 2008 s.149 and Sch.28(2), para.1, with effect from July 14, 2008 (SI 2008/1586).

"(1) This section applies where—
  (a) a person has been convicted of a specified offence, and
  (b) it falls to a court to assess under any of sections 225 to 228 whether there is a significant risk to members of the public of serious harm occasioned by the commission by him of further such offences.
(2) The court in making the assessment referred to in subsection (1)(b)—
  (a) must take into account all such information as is available to it about the nature and circumstances of the offence,
  (aa)may take into account all such information as is available to it about the nature and circumstances of any other offences of which the offender has been convicted by a court anywhere in the world,
  (b) may take into account any information which is before it about any pattern of behaviour of which any of the offences mentioned in paragraph (a) or (aa) forms part, and
  (c) may take into account any information about the offender which is before it."

Accordingly, in deciding whether the "dangerousness" provisions are engaged, the court must take into account the nature and circumstances of the offence (s.229(2)(a)). It may take into account the offender's previous convictions (s.229(2)(aa))[106] and any information about the offender (s.229(2)(c)). Since children and young people may not have an offending history, the pre-sentence report may well include evidence of violence or sexual aggression at school, at home or among the offender's peers, even if it did not result in a conviction.[107] **31.94**

In so far as the assessment of dangerousness involves considerations particular to children and young people, the Court of Appeal noted in *Lang*[108] that it is necessary, when sentencing young offenders, to bear in mind that, within a shorter time than adults, they might change and develop. This and their level of maturity might be highly pertinent when assessing what their future conduct might be and whether it might give rise to significant risk of serious harm. **31.95**

The application of the "dangerous offenders" exception

Guidance as to whether to commit to the Crown Court under s.51A(2) and (3)(d) was given in *R. (CPS) v South East Surrey Youth Court.*[109] The justices should bear in mind: **31.96**
  • The policy of the legislature that those who are under 18 should, wherever possible, be tried in a youth court, which is best designed for their specific needs;

[106] Any previous conviction may be relevant in the assessment of whether a person is a dangerous offender, whether the offence was specified or not: *Johnson* [2006] EWCA Crim 2486 at 10(iv). An assessment of offender history includes the offence type, facts of the offence and sentence passed: *Lang* [2005] EWCA Crim 2864 at 17(ii).
[107] See *Criminal Justice Act 2003, "Dangerousness" and the New Sentences for Public Protection—Guidance for Youth Offending Teams*, (Youth Justice Board, 2006), p.9.
[108] [2005] EWCA Crim 2864 at [17].
[109] [2005] EWHC 2929 (Admin).

- The guidance given in *Lang*,[110] particularly in relation to non-serious specified offences;[111]
- The need to be particularly rigorous in relation to those under 18 before concluding that there is a significant risk of serious harm by the commission of further offences. Such a conclusion is unlikely to be appropriate in the absence of a pre-sentence report following assessment by a Young Offender Team; and
- In most cases where a non-serious specified offence is charged, an assessment of dangerousness will not be appropriate until after conviction, when, if the dangerousness criteria are met, the defendant can be committed to the Crown Court for sentence—a procedure with which the Crown Court has, for many years, been familiar.[112]

31.97   The only circumstances in which the youth court has power to commit a young defendant to the Crown Court for sentence *after* trial is (i) when the offender is assessed as dangerous (the youth will be sent to the Crown Court under s.3C of the PCCSA 2000), or (ii) with a view to sentence at the Crown Court under s.91 of the PCCSA 2000 (the youth will be sent to the Crown Court under s.3B(1) of the PCCSA 2000).[113]

Grave crimes and specified offences

31.98   There is a large overlap between the sexual offences defined as "grave" and those that are "specified". All grave crimes of a sexual nature are specified offences for the purposes of the dangerousness provisions. However, not all specified offences are grave crimes. Very few sexual offences fall into neither category.[114] Where an offence is both specified and grave, both procedures must be considered.[115] It has been held that the decision to retain a case for trial in the youth court is not necessarily inconsistent with a later finding of seriousness, following which the youth is committed to the Crown Court for sentence.[116]

---

[110] [2005] EWCA Crim 2864.

[111] At 17(iv).

[112] This guidance is reflected in CPS guidance on youth offenders, which repeats the advice in *R. (CPS) v South East Surrey Youth Court* and adds that there will be few cases in which it will be appropriate to commit under s.51A: see *http://www.cps.gov.uk/legal/v_to_z/youth_offenders/£a33* [Accessed April 30, 2016].

[113] Section 3B(1) was introduced by s.53 of the Criminal Justice and Courts Act 2015. Prior to its introduction, the only circumstance in which a youth court could commit a youth to the Crown Court for sentence following trial was pursuant to the dangerousness provisions.

[114] The following offences in the 2003 Act fall into neither category: s.51A (soliciting), s.53A (paying for sexual services of a prostitute subjected to force etc), s.71 (sexual activity in a public lavatory). Sexual offences involving brothels and prostitution are not generally specified offences, although s.33A of the 1956 Act is a specified offence for the purposes of the Criminal Justice Act 2003.

[115] *R. (CPS) v South East Surrey Youth Court* [2005] EWHC 2929 (Admin). The legislation does not state the order in which the procedures must be considered, but in practice the courts have applied the "grave crimes" exception first.

[116] *W v Warrington Magistrates' Court* [2009] EWHC 1538 (Admin).

Young People Charged Alongside an Adult

The third exception to the general rule that youth cases must be tried in the **31.99** youth court is when the youth is charged with an indictable offence alongside an adult and it is necessary in the interests of justice for them to be tried together. Section 51(7)(b) of the Crime and Disorder Act 1998[117] provides that where the court sends an adult ("A") for trial and:

> "... a child or young person appears or is brought before the court on the same or a subsequent occasion charged jointly with A with an indictable offence for which A is sent to trial ... or an indictable offence which appears to the court to be related to that offence, the court shall, if it considers it necessary in the interests of justice to do so, send the child or young person forthwith to the Crown Court for trial for the indictable offence."

In *R. (CPS) v South East Surrey Youth Court*,[118] the Divisional Court noted that when a youth under 18 is jointly charged with an adult, an exercise of judgment will be called for by the youth court when assessing the competing presumptions in favour of (a) joint trial of those jointly charged and (b) the trial of youths in the youth court. Factors relevant to that judgment will include the age and maturity of the youth, the comparative culpability of the two in relation to the offence, their previous convictions and whether the trial can be severed without either injustice or undue inconvenience to witnesses. Once a youth has been committed to the Crown Court for trial with an adult, there is no provision for the Crown Court to remit the youth to the youth court even when the adult pleads guilty.[119]

Sentencing Youths for Sexual Offences

This section explains the differences in the sentencing of youths and adults **31.100** for sexual offences. It covers:
- Youth court sentencing: powers and procedure.
- Approach to sentence.
- Sentencing guidelines.
- Notification.
- Ancillary orders.

Youth Court Sentencing: Powers and Procedure

A youth will normally be sentenced in the youth court. Occasionally the **31.101** youth court passes sentence in cases remitted from the Crown Court,[120] and

---

[117] As substituted by the Criminal Justice Act 2003 s.41 and Sch.3, para.18.
[118] [2005] EWHC 2929 (Admin).
[119] *R. (on the application of W) v Leeds Crown Court* [2011] EWHC 2326 (Admin).
[120] PCCSA 2000 s.8(2). The Crown Court retains a discretion whether to sentence following conviction in the Crown Court.

it does so frequently in cases remitted from the adult magistrates' court.[121] The youth court has no power to commit a youth to the Crown Court for sentence following conviction, unless the offender meets the "dangerousness" criteria, in which case the youth court must commit the offender to the Crown Court for sentence,[122] or unless the court considers it ought to be possible for the Crown Court to sentence pursuant to s.91 of the PCCSA 2000.[123]

31.102   The youth court has at its disposal all the sentences and orders provided by statute for sentencing youths, except (i) detention under s.90 of the PCCSA 2000 (murder and sentences for which life imprisonment can be imposed), (ii) detention under s.91 of the PCCSA 2000 ("long-term detention") and (iii) sentences for dangerous young offenders under ss.226 and 226B of the CJA 2003. These are available only to the Crown Court. The sentencing options available to the youth court will depend on the age of the defendant at the time of conviction. The options are summarised in Annex 1 to this chapter. They are broadly similar to the options available for adults. Those which are specific to youths are dealt with below. They are:

- Detention and Training Orders.
- Youth Rehabilitation Orders.
- Referral Orders.

31.103   Before passing sentence, the court must give youth and their parents, guardian or other supporting adult, if present, an opportunity to make representations and introduce evidence relevant to sentence.[124] The court will usually obtain a pre-sentence report before sentencing a youth. By virtue of s.156(5) of the CJA 2003, it must do so if it is minded to impose a Detention and Training Order or a Youth Rehabilitation Order (unless there exists a previous report and the court has had regard to it and/or the most recent of such reports). The preparation of reports falls to the local authority Youth Offending Team ("YOT").

Detention and Training Orders[125]

31.104   A Detention and Training Orders ("DTO") is the only custodial sentence available to a youth court. It is made up of a period of detention and training followed by a period of supervision once the offender is released from custody back into the community. A DTO can only be for a prescribed

---

[121] Criminal Procedure Rules 2015 r.24.11(2)(b), and PCCSA 2000 s.8(6). The adult magistrates' court must remit the case to the youth court for sentence, except in the limited circumstances set out in PCSSA 2000 s.8(7), (8).
[122] Under PCCSA 2000 s.3C. For a case in which the defendant successfully judicially reviewed the youth court for committing him to sentence at the Crown Court pursuant to s.3C of the PCCSA 2000, see *R. (on the application of W) v Caernarfon Youth Court* [2013] EWHC 1466 (Admin). The case involved an 11-year-old defendant who had pleaded guilty to rape and sexual assault of a six-year-old girl.
[123] Under PCCSA 2000 s.3B(1).
[124] Criminal Procedure Rules 2015 r.24.11(7).
[125] The relevant statutory provisions are found in PCCSA 2000 ss.100–107.

period of 4, 6, 8, 10, 12, 18 or 24 months and cannot be for more than 24 months.[126] The custodial element is normally half of the term imposed.[127] A DTO cannot be imposed on those convicted when aged 10 or 11 (at present),[128] and can only be imposed on those convicted when aged 12–14 if they are "persistent offenders".[129] A written pre-sentence report must be obtained before sentencing to custody.[130] This report will be prepared by the YOT.

DTOs are subject to the statutory restrictions on the imposition of **31.105** custodial sentences. A DTO must be a last resort, and accordingly, a youth can only be sentenced to a DTO if:

- the offence is (or offences are) "so serious that neither a fine alone nor a community sentence can be justified for the offence" (CJA 2003 s.152(2)),
- a Youth Rehabilitation Order with intensive supervision and surveillance or with fostering cannot be justified (CJA 2003 s.174(4B)),[131]
- there has been a "wilful and persistent failure" to comply with a Youth Rehabilitation Order.[132]

Provided the above criteria are met, the most serious sexual offences sentenced in the youth court are likely to be dealt with by way of a DTO.[133]

For the purposes of the notification provisions of the Sexual Offences Act **31.106** 2003, the period of "imprisonment" under a DTO is the period in detention and training, i.e. half the length of the order.[134]

---

[126] PCCSA 2000 s.101(1), (4). Consecutive DTOs may be imposed leading to an aggregate that is not one of the permitted terms, provided the total does not exceed the maximum period.

[127] PCCSA 2000 s.102(2).

[128] When the PCCSA 2000 s.100(2)(b), comes into force, the court will be able to make a DTO in relation to a person under 12 if it is (i) of the opinion that only a custodial sentence would be adequate to protect the public from further offending by him; and (ii) the offence was committed on or after such date as the Secretary of State may by order appoint.

[129] There is no statutory definition of a "persistent offender". The Sentencing Guidelines Council's publication *Overarching Principles— Sentencing Youths* (2009), para.6.5, states that "a court should consider the simple test of whether the young person is one who persists in offending . . . i) in most circumstances, the normal expectation is that the offender will have had some contact with authority in which the offending conduct was challenged before being classed as "persistent"; ii) a young offender is certainly likely to be found to be persistent (and, in relation to a custodial sentence, the test of being a measure of last resort is most likely to be satisfied) where the offender has been convicted of, or made subject to a pre-court disposal that involves an admission or finding of guilt in relation to, imprisonable offences on at least 3 occasions in the past 12 months."

[130] CJA 2003 s.156(3). No report will be required if there exists a previous report and the court has regard to it, and/or the most recent of such reports.

[131] CJA 2003 s.174(4B), inserted by the Criminal Justice and Immigration Act 2008 Sch.4, para.80(3).

[132] Criminal Justice and Immigration Act 2008 Sch.2, paras 6–8.

[133] See *Overarching Principles—Sentencing Youths* (Sentencing Guidelines Council, 2009), Part 11, for full details of the approach to custodial sentences and length of custodial sentences to be imposed on youths.

[134] Sexual Offences Act 2003 s.131.

Youth Rehabilitation Orders

31.107   Youth Rehabilitation Orders ("YROs") were introduced by the Criminal Justice and Immigration Act 2008 ("CJIA 2008"). A YRO is a community sentence for young offenders within which a court may include one or more of the requirements set out in s.1 of the CJIA 2008. A YRO can last for a maximum of three years, but requirements may last for different periods, subject to any statutory limits on their duration (for which see Annex 2 to this chapter). There are two types of YRO that are specifically to be used as an alternative to custody:

- a YRO with intensive supervision and surveillance ("ISS") (s.1(3)(a) of the CJIA 2008). This type of YRO must include supervision, curfew, electronic monitoring and an "extended activity requirement" (90–180 days). The order must be for a minimum of six months' duration.
- a YRO with fostering (s.1(3)(b) of the CJIA 2008). This type of YRO requires the offender to reside with a local authority foster parent for a specified period. The YRO must include a supervision requirement.

31.108   In general, a court must not impose a YRO unless the offence is (or offences are) "serious enough to warrant such a sentence", although it is not obliged to impose a YRO in such circumstances.[135] More specifically, a YRO with ISS or with fostering cannot be imposed unless:

- the offence is imprisonable,
- the offence is (or offences are) "so serious" that but for the availability of such a YRO a custodial sentence would be appropriate, and
- if the offender is aged under 15, they are a "persistent offender".[136]

31.109   Provision for breach, revocation and amendment of YROs is made in Sch.2 to the CJIA 2008. A breach can be dealt with in the youth court (i) by way of a fine, (ii) by amending the YRO or (iii) by dealing with the offender in any way in which the court could originally have dealt with the offender for the offence. Where the court proposes to re-sentence, it has additional powers if the offender has "wilfully and persistently" failed to comply with the YRO. Thus the court may impose a YRO with ISS even though a custodial sentence would not have originally been appropriate, or the original offence was not imprisonable.

Referral Orders

31.110   Referrals orders are provided for by the PCCSA 2000 ss.16–17.[137] A referral order is an order by which the youth is referred to a Youth Offender Panel,

---

[135] CJA 2003 s.148(1), (5).
[136] CJIA 2008 s.1(4).
[137] As amended by the CJIA 2008 s.35. See *Overarching Principles: Sentencing Youths* (Sentencing Guidelines Council, 2009), Part 10, for full factors to be considered before imposing a YRO.

which investigates the causes and consequences of the offending with the youth and their family. A contract is agreed between the Panel and the youth, which includes reparation and a programme of activities aimed at preventing re-offending. Referral orders last for between three and 12 months.

A referral order is mandatory if the "compulsory referral conditions" are **31.111** met:

- the offender pleads guilty to an imprisonable offence (PCCSA s.17(1)), and
- the offender has not previously been convicted (PCCSA s.17(1)(b)),[138] and
- the offence does not have a sentence fixed in law (PCCSA s.16(1)(a)), and
- the court is proposing to impose a custodial sentence, hospital order or absolute discharge (PCCSA s.16(1)(b)–(c)).

A referral order is discretionary in a wider range of circumstances, if the **31.112** discretionary referral conditions are met. These are:

- the offender has a previous conviction, but
- the offender pleaded guilty to the offence, or, if more than one offence, the offender pleaded guilty to at least one offences (PCCSA s.17(2)(b)).[139]

Other sentencing options

Absolute and conditional discharges are at the disposal of the youth court as **31.113** they are in other courts. As far as fines are concerned, a person under 18 can be fined a maximum of £1,000 and a person under 14 can be fined a maximum of £250.[140]

Relevance of age to youth court jurisdiction and sentencing powers

Where a defendant reaches 18 after conviction, but before sentence, the court **31.114** "may deal with the case and make any order which it could have made if he had not attained that age".[141] Thus, if a defendant is 17 at the time of conviction, but 18 at the time of sentence, a court may still impose a DTO.[142] Alternatively, a youth court has the discretion to remit the case to the adult magistrates' court for sentence,[143] in which case the adult magistrates' court

---

[138] Excludes absolute and conditional discharges, youth cautions and youth conditional cautions.
[139] See *Revised Referral Order Guidance* (Ministry of Justice and the Youth Justice Board), effective from April 13, 2015, for guidance on the use of referral orders. The *Guidance* is available at *https://www.gov.uk/government/publications/young-offenders-referral-orders* [Accessed April 30, 2016].
[140] PCCSA 2000 s.135(1).
[141] Children and Young Persons Act 1963 s.29.
[142] *Aldis v DPP* [2002] 2 Cr. App. R.(S.) 400.
[143] PCCSA 2000 s.9.

"may deal with the case in any way in which it would have power to deal with it if all proceedings relating to the offence which took place before the youth court had taken place before [the adult court]". The youth court may not remit for indictable only offences.[144]

31.115 The availability of sentence type, particularly in the case of custodial sentences, depends upon the age of the defendant. The relevant age for sentence is the age on the date of conviction.[145] This is so unless the defendant crosses a significant age threshold (i.e. one which widens the range of sentences available), in which case, the relevant age for sentence will be the age on the date of commission of the offence. The court must have a good reason if it passes a sentence higher than that which would have been passed at the date of the commission of the offence.[146] Seriousness of the offence does not constitute a "good reason".[147]

Approach to Sentence

31.116 The approach to sentencing youths is the same as for adults, in so far as the court is to consider culpability, harm and aggravating and mitigating features. However, in the case of a youth sentence the court is not required to have regard to the purposes of sentencing set out in the CJA 2003 s.142, but must instead have regard to:

- the principal aim of the youth justice system to prevent re-offending by children and young persons (Crime and Disorder Act 1998 s.37(1)), and
- the welfare of the offender (Children and Young Persons Act 1933 s.44(1)).[148]

31.117 In realising its aim to "prevent re-offending", the court will impose a sentence which makes an impact on the offender whilst also identifying and

---

[144] *R. (Denny) v Acton Youth Court* [2004] 1 W.L.R. 3051.

[145] *Danga* (1992) 13 Cr. App. R. 408; and see *Robson* [2006] EWCA Crim 1414 for the application of this principle to the "dangerousness" provisions: a person is under 18 if he or she was aged 17 or under on the date of conviction.

[146] *Ghafoor* [2002] Crim. L.R. 739; see *R. v NH* [2004] EWCA Crim 2674 for the application of this principle to a youth convicted of a sexual offence. *NH* pleaded guilty to indecent assault on an 18-year-old female. He was 14 on the date of commission of the offence but 15 when convicted. He was sentenced to a DTO of 12 months' duration, the court imposing a higher sentence than that which would have been available if he had been convicted when 14. The Court of Appeal found there was no good reason for such a departure, quashed the DTO and imposed a term of 12 months' supervision.

[147] *R. v NH* [2004] EWCA Crim 2674.

[148] When the Criminal Justice and Immigration Act 2008 s.9, is in force, inserting s.142A into the CJA 2003, the court must also have regard to the purposes of sentencing for those under 18, which are: "(3)(a) the punishment of offenders, (b) the reform and rehabilitation of offenders, (c) the protection of the public, and the making of reparation by offenders to persons affected by their offences." These purposes are the same as those that apply to adults (in s.142 of the CJA 2003), with the exception that the reduction of crime (including its reduction by deterrence) is an additional purpose for adults.

seeking to address any factors which make offending more likely.[149] The sentence must be proportionate to the seriousness of the offence. Accordingly, a court should not impose greater restrictions on liberty simply to address the risk of re-offending.[150]

In addressing the "welfare" of the offender, the court will be alert to, amongst other things, the high incidence of mental health problems, learning difficulties or disabilities, speech and language difficulties, and vulnerability to self-harm among young people in the youth justice system.[151]   **31.118**

The sentencing approach must also be determined in light of Sentencing Council Guidelines,[152] for which see below.   **31.119**

SENTENCING GUIDELINES

By virtue of the Coroners and Justice Act 2009 s.125, every court must have regard to sentencing guidelines: see Ch.33. There are three guidelines and one guide for sentencers and practitioners which are relevant to sentencing children and young people for sexual offences. These are summarised, so far as material, below. The guidelines are: **31.120**

- *Overarching Principles—Sentencing Youths*, Definitive Guideline.
- *Sexual Offences,* Definitive Guideline.
- *Magistrates' Court Guidelines*, Definitive Guideline.

Overarching Principles—Sentencing Youths: Definitive Guideline

This Guideline, published by the Sentencing Guidelines Council, applies to the sentencing of young offenders on or after November 30, 2009.[153] The Guideline re-iterates the statutory obligation to bear in mind the principal aim of the youth justice system, defined in the Crime and Disorder Act 1998 s.37, as "to prevent offending by children and young people",[154] and the need to bear in mind the "welfare" of the offender when sentencing. In addition, it emphasises the need for an individualistic approach. Within the "youth" category, the response to an offence is likely to vary depending on the age of the offender. Further, in many instances, the maturity of the offender will be at least as important as their chronological age.[155]   **31.121**

The Guideline also includes specific reference to the effect on sentence of the offender being a young person. There is a general expectation that "a   **31.122**

---

[149] *Overarching Principles—Sentencing Youths* (Sentencing Guidelines Council, 2009), discussed below, para.2.6.

[150] para.2.2.

[151] para.2.9.

[152] Coroners and Justice Act 2009 s.125.

[153] para.2.5(i). The Sentencing Council is in the process of reviewing and updating the guideline, with the revised guideline due to be published in early 2017: for the consultation paper, see the Sentencing Council's website.

[154] para.2.6.

[155] paras 2.1–2.4.

young person will be dealt with less severely than an adult offender, although this distinction diminishes as the offender approaches age 18".[156] More specifically, the Guideline notes the following in respect of sexual offences:

> "When sentencing a young offender whose offence involves sexual activity but there is no evidence of a coercive or abusive relationship or of anything other than consensual activity, a court will need to be aware that a desire to explore gender identity or sexual orientation may result in offending behaviour. Depending on the seriousness of the offending behaviour, offender mitigation may arise where that behaviour stems from sexual immaturity or confusion."[157]

Sexual Offences: Definitive Guideline

31.123   This Guideline, published by the Sentencing Council, applies to all offenders aged 18 or over, who are sentenced on or after April 1, 2014. In its consultation on the draft Guideline,[158] the Council noted that child sexual offences committed by young offenders can be very different in nature to those committed by adults, not least because of the use of social media. It was also concerned that producing guidelines for this narrow range of youth offending, without considering the wider approach that should be adopted to the sentencing of those under 18, could cause problems when it came to review youth sentencing generally, which it is committed to reviewing.[159] Accordingly, the Council decided not to cover youth offending in the Guideline. In order to minimise the risk of sentencers continuing to follow the previous guideline issued by the Sentencing Guidelines Council ("SGC"), or of creating a sentencing "gap", it included in the published Guideline the following narrative guidance:

> "When sentencing offenders under 18, a court must in particular:
> - follow the definitive guideline *Overarching Principles—Sentencing Youths*;
> - and have regard to:
> - the principal aim of the youth justice system (to prevent offending by children and young people); and
> - the welfare of the young offender."

31.124   The Sentencing Council has, however, maintained part of the SGC guideline, namely *Part 7: Sentencing young offenders—offences with a lower statutory maximum* ("Part 7"). Part 7 deals with the offences of:
- Sexual activity with a child (SOA 2003 s.9)
- Causing or inciting a child to engage in sexual activity (SOA 2003 s.10)

---

[156] para.3.1.

[157] para.3.3.

[158] *Sexual Offences Guideline: Consultation* (December 6, 2012).

[159] At the time of writing (May 2016), the Council is in the process of developing a sentencing guideline for sexual offences committed by youths, for publication in early 2017. A consultation document, published in May 2016, is available on the Council's website.

- Engaging in sexual activity in the presence of a child (SOA 2003 s.11)
- Causing a child to watch a sexual act (SOA 2003 s.12)
- Sexual activity with a child family member (SOA 2003 s.25)
- Inciting a child family member to engage in sexual activity (SOA 2003 s.26).

The Council considered these to be difficult and sensitive offences for which a gap would be left if the SGC guidance was removed but not replaced.[160] Accordingly, Part 7 continues to be relevant to sentencing these offences. For each of them, the maximum sentence for an offender under the age of 18 is five years' imprisonment, rather than 14 or 10 years' for adult offenders. This reflects the general principle in sexual offences that the offence will be less serious when the age gap between victim and offender is relatively narrow. Part 7 makes clear that even within this reduced statutory sentencing framework, additional mitigation may arise as a result of:

- the small age gap between the child and the offender, and
- the youth and immaturity of the offender (which includes sexual development and intelligence).[161]

So far as other sexual offences are concerned, "age and/or lack of maturity **31.125** where it affects the responsibility of the offender" is specified routinely as a mitigating factor in the Sentencing Council guideline.

Magistrates' Court Sentencing Guidelines: Definitive Guideline

This Guideline was updated in October 2009. It covers a range of sexual **31.126** offences more commonly dealt with in the magistrates' court. It is based on the SGC's *Sexual Offences Act 2003: Definitive Guideline*, although it goes into greater detail and thereby provide more guidance by way of sentencing. The offences covered are:

- sexual assault (SOA 2003 s.3 and s.7),
- child sexual exploitation (SOA 2003 ss.48–50),
- sexual exploitation by prostitution (SOA 2003 s.52 and s.53),
- keeping a brothel used for prostitution (s.33A SOA 1956),
- exposure (SOA 2003 s.66),
- voyeurism (SOA 2003 s.67),
- sexual activity in a public lavatory (SOA 2003 s.71),
- indecent photographs of children (Protection of Children Act 1978 s.1 and Criminal Justice Act 1988 s.160), and

---

[160] *Sexual Offences Guideline: Consultation* (December 6, 2012), p.9.

[161] paras 7.7–7.10. For an example of mitigating factors in operation, see *R. v D* [2006] EWCA Crim 111 (appellant, aged 13 at the time of the offences, pleaded guilty to five counts of rape of a child under 13 (s.5(1) of the SOA 2003). Intercourse was consensual, the appellant acted out of curiosity and did not know at the time that his conduct was wrong. Having regard to the appellant's age, his circumstances and the basis of his plea, four years' detention was replaced with a sentence of three years' detention).

- failure to comply with notification requirements or supply of false information for the sex offender register (SOA 2003 s.91).

Notification

31.127 The requirement for sex offenders to notify certain details to the police (commonly known as "registration", by which the offender is placed on the "sex offenders' register") is explained in detail in Ch.35. This section deals specifically with the application of the notification requirement to youths.

31.128 A person is subject to the notification requirements if he is convicted of an offence listed in Sch.3 to the SOA 2003, is found guilty of such an offence by reason of insanity, is found to be under a disability and to have done the act charged against him in respect of such an offence, or is cautioned in respect of such an offence. Offences listed in Sch.3 are "relevant offences". The requirement to notify flows from conviction etc. for a relevant offence and it is not at the discretion of the court.

31.129 For some offences, youths are subject to notification requirements in the same circumstances as an adult. However, for others, youths are treated differently. For example, a youth will only be required to register upon conviction for certain offences if sentenced to a period of imprisonment for 12 months or more, whereas there is no such threshold for adults. The term "imprisonment" for this purpose refers to the period of detention and training, not of supervision.[162] The offences to which the "12 month minimum" applies are:

- sexual assault (SOA 2003 s.3),
- sexual assault of a child under 13 (s.7),
- child sex offences committed by children or young persons (ss.8–12, and s.13),
- arranging or facilitating the commission of a child sex offence (s.14),
- familial sex offences (ss.25–26 and ss.64–65),
- offences by care workers on persons with a mental disorder (ss.38–41),
- paying for the sexual services of a child (s.47),
- trespassing or committing an offence with the intent to commit a sexual offence (ss.62–63),
- exposure (s.66),
- voyeurism (s.67),
- intercourse with an animal (s.68),
- sexual penetration of a corpse (s.69),
- indecent images of children (Protection of Children Act 1978 s.1), if children shown are under 16.

---

[162] SOA 2003 s.131(a); *Slocombe* [2006] 1 Cr. App. R. 33.

The notification requirements apply to those who have been cautioned in   **31.130**
respect of such an offence.[163] Thus, a child or young person will be required
to register on the sex offenders' register in the event of a caution. This
requirement should be explained to the youth, or to the appropriate adult,
before a caution is accepted.[164]

Section 89 of the SOA 2003 empowers a court to direct that a person with   **31.131**
parental responsibility for a youth shall fulfil the obligations of the notification requirements, and ensure that the youth attends at the police station
with him, until the youth reaches the age of 18. The police may also apply for
such a direction. Under s.90, a parental direction can be varied, renewed or
discharged at any time on application to the court by the young offender, the
person with parental responsibility or the chief officer of police for either the
young offender's local police area or an area where he is intending to go. The
Explanatory Notes to the Act states that this may be required where, for
example, the parent can no longer control the young offender and is unable
to ensure that he attends with the parent to notify.[165]

The notification period

The length of the notification period depends on the sentence imposed and   **31.132**
is set out in the Table in s.82(1) of the SOA 2003, reproduced below and
adapted to include notification periods applicable to youths.

Description of relevant offence	Notification period (adults)	Notification period (under 18)
A person who, in respect of the offence, is or has been sentenced to imprisonment for life or for a term of 30 months or more.	An indefinite period beginning with the relevant date.	An indefinite period beginning with the relevant date.
A person who, in respect of the offence, has been made the subject of an order under section 210F(1) of the Criminal Procedure (Scotland) Act 1995 (order for lifelong restriction).	An indefinite period beginning with the relevant date.	An indefinite period beginning with the relevant date.

[163] SOA 2003 s.133(1).
[164] *Youth cautions: guidance for police and Youth Offending Teams* (Youth Justice Board for England & Wales, 2013), pp.21–22.
[165] Explanatory Notes to the Sexual Offences Act 2003 para.180.

Description of relevant offence	Notification period (adults)	Notification period (under 18)
A person who, in respect of the offence or finding, is or has been admitted to a hospital subject to a restriction order.	An indefinite period beginning with the relevant date.	An indefinite period beginning with the relevant date.
A person who, in respect of the offence, is or has been sentenced to imprisonment for a term of more than 6 months but less than 30 months.	10 years beginning with that date.	5 years.
A person who, in respect of the offence, is or has been sentenced to imprisonment for a term of 6 months or less.	7 years beginning with that date.	$3\frac{1}{2}$ years.
A person who, in respect of the offence or finding, is or has been admitted to a hospital without being subject to a restriction order.	7 years beginning with that date.	$3\frac{1}{2}$ years.
A person within section 80(1)(d).	2 years beginning with that date.	1 year.
A person in whose case an order for conditional discharge or, in Scotland, a probation order, is made in respect of the offence.	The period of conditional discharge or, in Scotland, the probation period.	The period of conditional discharge or, in Scotland, the probation period.
A person of any other description.	5 years beginning with the relevant date.	$2\frac{1}{2}$ years.

31.133   An offender qualifies for the reduced notification period if they are under 18 "on the relevant date". The relevant date is the date of conviction.[166] It is

[166] SOA 2003 s.82(6)

unclear what the position is regarding the imposition of notification requirements where the offender turns 18 between the date of the commission of the
offence and the date of conviction. In relation to sentencing, the position is
that no sentence is to be imposed other than that which was available on the
date of the commission of the offence.[167] It is arguable that since notification
requirements do not strictly form part of the sentence, this principle does not
apply.

Ancillary Orders

There are a number of orders that may be made upon conviction for a sexual
offence. These apply to both adults and youths and are explained in Chs 34
and 36. The section deals only with specific provisions or modifications
applicable to youths. The orders referred to below are accordingly sexual
harm prevention orders ("SHPOs"), disqualification orders, Sexual Risk
Orders ("SROs") and parenting orders.   **31.134**

Sexual harm prevention orders

SHPOs are discussed in Ch.36. They are at the discretion of the court and   **31.135**
may be made at the time of dealing with an offender for an offence or on an
application made subsequently. A court may make a SHPO if it is dealing
with an offender for an offence listed in Sch.3 or Sch.5 to the SOA 2003. A
SHPO may be made against a child, i.e. a person under the age of 18, as they
can against adults. However, courts should be mindful to ensure that a SHPO
imposed on a youth contains proportionate conditions. In *R. v J*,[168] the
appellant pleaded guilty to one offence of attempted rape. He was 14 at the
time of the offence and 15 at the time of sentence. He was sentenced to an
extended sentence of detention pursuant to ss.85 and 91 of the PCCSA 2000,
and made subject to a SOPO which prevented him for a period of six years
from having unsupervised contact with children younger than himself. The
Court of Appeal held that this prohibition was counter-productive, stating:[169]

> "It seems to us that it is unrealistic in the case of a 15-year-old boy to expect that
> he will not be in contact to some degree with children of about his own age and
> sometimes younger. We consider that the extended licence provisions ought to be
> adequate to enable those responsible for the upbringing and supervision of this
> appellant to ensure that inappropriate contact does not occur . . . we consider it
> is unrealistic to expect that a person of the age of this appellant would not have
> contact with other children, albeit some of them may be younger. We think that
> is just counter productive to the rehabilitation of the appellant."

---

[167] *Ghafoor* [2002] Crim. L.R. 739.
[168] [2005] EWCA Crim 362 (a SOPO case).
[169] At 16–17.

Barring from working with children and young adults

31.136 The provisions relating to barring an individual from working with children and young persons are dealt with in paras 34.63 and following, below.

Sexual Risk Orders

31.137 Sexual Risk Orders ("SROs") allow the court to prohibit a person from engaging in particular behaviour even in circumstances where he has never committed a criminal offence. They are explained in Ch.36. Unlike their predecessor, the Risk of Sexual Harm Order, SROs may be made against children, i.e. those under the age of 18.

Parenting orders

31.138 The youth court has the power to bind parents over and to make a parenting order (s.8 of the Crime and Disorder Act 1998). The purpose of a parenting order is to impose requirements on parents to prevent, for example, the repetition of the kind of behaviour which leads to the imposition of an ABSO. Such orders are rarely imposed in the context of sexual offences.

Aɴɴᴇx 1

Sᴇɴᴛᴇɴᴄɪɴɢ Oᴘᴛɪᴏɴs Aᴠᴀɪʟᴀʙʟᴇ ᴛᴏ ᴛʜᴇ Yᴏᴜᴛʜ Cᴏᴜʀᴛ

31.139

Sentencing options	10–11 years	12–13 years	14 years	15 years	16–17 years
Pre-court disposals[170]					
Reprimand					
Warning					
Youth Conditional Discharge					

---

[170] The youth court cannot order a youth caution or youth conditional caution—they are available only as pre-court disposals.

Sentencing options	10–11 years	12–13 years	14 years	15 years	16–17 years
First tier disposals					
Absolute discharge	●	●	●	●	●
Conditional discharge[171]	●	●	●	●	●
Fine[172]	● Maximum £250	● Maximum £250	● Maximum £1000	● Maximum £1000	● Maximum £100
Referral order[173]	● 3–12 months	● 3–12 months	● 3–12 months	● 3–12 months	● 3–12 months
Reparation order	● Maximum 24 hours	● Maximum 24 hours	● Maximum 24 hours	● Maximum 24 hours	● Maximum 24 hours
Youth Rehabilitation Order					
Activity requirement[174]	● Maximum 90 days	● Maximum 90 days	● Maximum 90 days	● Maximum 90 days	● Maximum 90 days
Supervision requirement[175]	● Maximum 3 years	● Maximum 3 years	● Maximum 3 years	● Maximum 3 years	● Maximum 3 years
Unpaid work requirement[176]					● 40–240 hours

[171] Existence of a final warning will preclude the imposition of a conditional discharge for a further offence, if that further offence was committed within two years of the reprimand or warning, "unless there are exceptional circumstances relating to the offence which justify its doing so" (s.66(4) CDA 1998).

[172] There is no maximum fine at the Crown Court. The order must be made against the parent/guardian if the youth is under 16, unless this is unreasonable in the circumstances.

[173] The court must make an order requiring the parent/guardian to attend the relevant meetings of the Youth Offender Panel if the offender is under 16 (PCCSA 2000 s.20(1), (2)). This does not apply if in the circumstances of each case it would be unreasonable to require such attendance (s.20(3)).

[174] CJIA 2008 s.1(1)(a) and Sch.1, paras 6–8. The maximum number of days for an activity requirement is 90 days (CJIA 2008 Sch.1, para.6(3)), except for sentences of a YRO with intensive supervision and surveillance, in which case the court can impose an "extended activity requirement" of up to 180 days (Sch.1, para.3(2)).

[175] CJIA 2008 s.1(1)(b) and Sch.1, para.9.

[176] CJIA 2008 s.1(1)(c) and Sch.1, para.10.

Sentencing options	10–11 years	12–13 years	14 years	15 years	16–17 years
Programme requirement[177]	●	●	●	●	●
Attendance centre requirement[178]	● Maximum 12 hours	● Maximum 12 hours	● 12–24 hours	● 12–24 hours	● 12–36 hours
Prohibited activity requirement[179]	●	●	●	●	●
Curfew requirement[180]	● 2–12 hours	● 2–12 hours	● 2–12 hours	● 2–12 hours	● 2–12 hours
Exclusion requirement[181]	● Maximum 3 months	● Maximum 3 months	● Maximum 3 months	● Maximum 3 months	● Maximum 3 months
Residence requirement[182]	● Individual only	● Individual only	● Individual only	● Individual only	● Individual or place
Local authority residence requirement[183]	● Maximum 6 months	● Maximum 6 months	● Maximum 6 months	● Maximum 6 months	● Maximum 6 months
Mental health treatment requirement[184]	●	●	●	●	●

[177] CJIA 2008 s.1(1)(d) and Sch.1, para.11. This order can only be imposed following a recommendation from YOT or probation services (para.11(3)).

[178] CJIA 2008 s.1(1)(e) and Sch.1, para.12. Electronic monitoring may be attached to this requirement (s.1 and Sch.1, para.26(7)).

[179] CJIA 2008 s.1(1)(f) and Sch.1, para.13. This means a requirement that the offender must refrain from participating in activities specified in the order on a day or days so specified, or during a specified period (para.13(1)). A court must consult with YOT or probation before imposing such a requirement (para.13(2)).

[180] CJIA 2008 s.1(1)(g) and Sch.1, para.14. The court must obtain and consider information about the place proposed to be specified in the order (including information as to the attitude of persons likely to be affected by the enforced presence there of the offender) (para.14(4)). Electronic monitoring required (s.1(2), and Sch.1, paras 2 and 26(1)(a), unless para.2(2) is satisfied, which includes when it is "inappropriate" to impose such a condition).

[181] CJIA 2008 s.1(1)(h) and Sch.1, para.15. Electronic monitoring required (s.1(2), and Sch.1 para.2 and para.26(1)(b), unless para.2(2) is satisfied, which includes when it is "inappropriate" to impose such a condition.

[182] CJIA 2008 s.1(1)(i) and Sch.1, para.16.

[183] CJIA 2008 s.1(1)(j) and Sch.1, para.17. The requirement is subject to a 6 month maximum, and it must not apply to a young person once that person attains 18 (para.17(6)(b)).

[184] CJIA 2008 s.1(1)(k) and Sch.1, para.20.

Sentencing options	10–11 years	12–13 years	14 years	15 years	16–17 years
Drug treatment requirement[185]	●	●	●	●	●
Drug testing requirement[186]	●	●	●	●	●
Intoxicating substance treatment requirement[187]	●	●	●	●	●
Education requirement[188]	●	●	●	●	
Electronic monitoring requirement[189]	●	●	●	●	●
Intensive supervision and surveillance[190]	● If persistent offender 6 months–3 years	● If persistent offender 6 months–3 years	● If persistent offender 6 months–3 years	● 6 months–3 years	● 6 months–3 years
Intensive fostering[191]	● If persistent offender	● If persistent offender	● If persistent offender	●	●

[185] CJIA 2008 s.1(1)(l) and Sch.1, para.22.
[186] CJIA 2008 s.1(1)(m) and Sch.1, para.23.
[187] CJIA 2008 s.1(1)(n) and Sch.1, para.24.
[188] CJIA 2008 s.1(1)(o) and Sch.1, para.25. The offender must comply, during a period or periods specified in the order, with approved education arrangements. It must include any period after which the offender has ceased to be of compulsory school age (para.25(5)). This order will therefore apply to 16-year-olds (until the end of June of the academic year in which they turn 16), and will never apply to 17-year-olds.
[189] CJIA 2008 s.1(2) Sch.1, para.26. This is not a standalone requirement. It is a requirement for securing the electronic monitoring of the offender's compliance with other requirements imposed by the order during a period specified in the order or determined by the responsible officer in accordance with the order. It must be imposed alongside a curfew or exclusion requirement; it may be imposed for an attendance centre order (para.26(7)).
[190] CJIA 2008 s.1(3) and Sch.1, para.3.
[191] CJIA 2008 s.1(4) and Sch.1, para.4.

Sentencing options	10–11 years	12–13 years	14 years	15 years	16–17 years
Custodial sentences					
Detention and training order[192]		● If persistent offender 4, 6, 8, 12, 18, 24 months	● If persistent offender 4, 6, 8, 12, 18, 24 months	● 4, 6, 8, 12, 18, 24 months	● 4, 6, 8, 12, 18, 24 months
s.91 long-term detention[193]					
s.226 CJA 2003 (detention for life/public protection)[194]					
s.228 CJA 2003 (extended sentence)[195]					
s.90 detention[196–197]					
Sexual offences ancillary orders					
Notification order	●	●	●	●	●
Sexual offences prevention order	●	●	●	●	●
Sexual risk order	●	●	●	●	●

[192] PCCSA 2000 ss.100–107. Not currently available for those under the age of 12 at the time of conviction, but will be when s.100(2)(b) comes into force, which provides that such a person can receive a DTO if (i) it is of the opinion that only a custodial sentence would be adequate to protect the public from further offending by him; and (ii) the offence was committed on or after such date as the Secretary of State may by order appoint.

[193] Sentence available only to the Crown Court.

[194] Sentence available only to the Crown Court.

[195] Sentence available only to the Crown Court.

[196–197] Sentence available only to the Crown Court in cases of murder or other offences for which the maximum term is life imprisonment. The main sexual offences to which this therefore applies are s.1 (rape), s.2 (assault by penetration), s.4(4) (causing a person to engage in sexual activity without consent), s.5 (rape of a child under 13), s.6 (assault by penetration of a child under 13), s.8(4) (causing a child under 13 to engage in sexual activity without consent).

Sentencing options	10–11 years	12–13 years	14 years	15 years	16–17 years
Other orders					
Compensation order[198]	•	•	•	•	•
Costs[199]					

CLASSIFICATION OF SEXUAL OFFENCES INVOLVING YOUTHS

31.140

Sexual offence	s.91 Grave Crime	Sch.15 Specified Sexual Offence	Sch.15 Serious Sexual Offence	Sch.3 Notification Offence[200]	Sch.3/ Sch.5 SOPO Offence
Sexual Offences Act 2004[201]					
s.1 (rape)	•	•	•	•	•
s.2 (assault by penetration)	•	•	•	•	•
s.3 (sexual assault)[202]	•	•	•	• If sentenced to 12 months' or more imprison- ment	•
s.4 (causing a person to engage in sexual activity without consent)	• If s.4(4)	•	•	•	•

[198] Compensation takes priority over any order for costs.
[199] Costs must not exceed the amount of the fine.
[200] Notification will obviously not be required in the case of reprimands and warnings for those offences where the qualification threshold is 12 months' imprisonment or more. Otherwise, a reprimand or warning will trigger notification in the same way as any other post-court dis- posal.
[201] This chart excludes equivalent provisions preceding the Sexual Offences Act 2003 on the basis that nobody now between the ages of 10–17 would have been above the age of criminal responsibility prior to the commencement of the SOA 2003 on May 1, 2004.
[202] This offence is a "grave crime", notwithstanding the fact that the maximum sentence is less than 14 years (PCCSA 2000 s.91(1)(b)).

Sexual offence	s.91 Grave Crime	Sch.15 Specified Sexual Offence	Sch.15 Serious Sexual Offence	Sch.3 Notification Offence	Sch.3/ Sch.5 SOPO Offence
s.5 (rape of a child under 13)	•	•	•	•	•
s.6 (assault by penetration of a child under 13)	•	•	•	•	•
s.7 (sexual assault of a child under 13)	•	•	•	• If sentenced to 12 months' or more imprison- ment	•
s.8 (causing or inciting a child under 13 to engage in sexual activity without consent)	•	•	•	• If sentenced to 12 months' or more imprison- ment	•
s.9 (sexual activity with a child)[203]	•	•		• If sentenced to 12 months' or more imprison- ment	•
s.10 (causing or inciting a child to engage in sexual activity)[204]	•	•		• If sentenced to 12 months' or more imprison- ment	•

[203] When this offence is committed by a person over 18, this is a serious specified offence.
[204] When this offence is committed by a person over 18, this is a serious specified offence.

Sexual offence	s.91 Grave Crime	Sch.15 Specified Sexual Offence	Sch.15 Serious Sexual Offence	Sch.3 Notification Offence	Sch.3/ Sch.5 SOPO Offence
s.11 (engaging in sexual activity in the presence of a child)[205]	●	●		● If sentenced to 12 months' or more imprison-ment	●
s.12 (causing a child to watch a sexual act)[206]	●	●		● If sentenced to 12 months' or more imprison-ment	●
s.13 (ss.9–12 when committed by an offender under 18)[207]	●	●		● If sentenced to 12 months' or more imprison-ment	●
s.14 (facilitating a child sex offence)	●	●	●	● If sentenced to 12 months' or more imprison-ment	●
s.15 (meeting a child following sexual grooming)[208]	N/a	N/a	N/a	N/a	N/a
s.15A (sexual communication with a child)[209]	N/a	N/a	N/a	N/a	N/a

[205] When this offence is committed by a person over 18, this is a serious specified offence.

[206] When this offence is committed by a person over 18, this is a serious specified offence.

[207] This offence is a "grave crime", notwithstanding the fact that the maximum sentence is less than 14 years (PCCSA 2000 s.91(1)(c)).

[208] This offence cannot be committed by someone under the age of 18 (SOA 2003 s.15(1)).

[209] This offence cannot be committed by someone under the age of 18 (SOA 2003 s.15A(1)).

Sexual offence	s.91 Grave Crime	Sch.15 Specified Sexual Offence	Sch.15 Serious Sexual Offence	Sch.3 Notification Offence	Sch.3/ Sch.5 SOPO Offence
s.16 (abuse of position of trust: sexual activity with a child)[210]	N/a	N/a	N/a	N/a	N/a
s.17 (abuse of position of trust: causing or inciting a child to engage in sexual activity)[211]	N/a	N/a	N/a	N/a	N/a
s.18 (abuse of position of trust: sexual activity in the presence of a child[212]	N/a	N/a	N/a	N/a	N/a
s.19 (abuse of position of trust: causing a child to watch a sexual act)[213]	N/a	N/a	N/a	N/a	N/a
s.25 (sexual activity with a child family member)[214]	●	●		● If sentenced to 12 months' or more imprisonment	●

[210] This offence cannot be committed by someone under the age of 18 (SOA 2003 s.16(1)).
[211] This offence cannot be committed by someone under the age of 18 (SOA 2003 s.17(1)).
[212] This offence cannot be committed by someone under the age of 18 (SOA 2003 s.18(1)).
[213] This offence cannot be committed by someone under the age of 18 (SOA 2003 s.19(1)).

[214] This offence is a "grave crime", notwithstanding the fact that the maximum sentence is less than 14 years (PCCSA 2000 s.91(1)(d)). In the case of those under the age of 18, the statutory maximum is 5 years. Accordingly, it is not a serious specified offence for the purposes of the dangerousness provisions.

Sexual offence	s.91 Grave Crime	Sch.15 Specified Sexual Offence	Sch.15 Serious Sexual Offence	Sch.3 Notification Offence	Sch.3/ Sch.5 SOPO Offence
s.26 (inciting a family member to engage in sexual activity)[215]	●	●		● If sentenced to 12 months' or more imprison-ment	●
s.30 (Sexual activity with a person with a mental disorder)	●	●	●	●	●
s.31 (causing or inciting a person with a mental disorder impeding choice to engage in sexual activity)	●	●	●	●	●
s.32 (engaging in sexual activity in the presence of a person with a mental disorder impeding choice)		●	●	●	●
s.33 (causing a person with a mental disorder impeding choice to watch a sexual act)		●	●	●	●

[215] This offence is a "grave crime", notwithstanding the fact that the maximum sentence is less than 14 years (PCCSA 2000 s.91(1)(e)). In the case of those under the age of 18, the statutory maximum is 5 years. Accordingly, it is not a serious specified offence for the purposes of the dangerousness provisions.

Sexual offence	s.91 Grave Crime	Sch.15 Specified Sexual Offence	Sch.15 Serious Sexual Offence	Sch.3 Notification Offence	Sch.3/ Sch.5 SOPO Offence
s.34 (inducement, threat or deception to procure sexual activity with a person with a mental disorder)	•	•	•	•	•
s.35 (causing a person with a mental disorder to engage or agree to engage in sexual activity by inducement, threat or deception)	•	•	•	•	•
s.36 (engaging in sexual activity in the presence, procured by inducement, threat or deception of a person with a mental disorder)		•	•	•	•
s.37 (causing a person with a mental disorder to watch a sexual act by inducement, threat or deception)		•	•	•	•
s.38 (care workers: sexual activity with a person with a mental disorder)	• If s.38(3)	•	•	• If sentenced to 12 months' or more imprison- ment	•

Sexual offence	s.91 Grave Crime	Sch.15 Specified Sexual Offence	Sch.15 Serious Sexual Offence	Sch.3 Notification Offence	Sch.3/ Sch.5 SOPO Offence
s.39 (care workers: causing or inciting sexual activity)	● If s.39(3)	●	●	● If sentenced to 12 months' or more imprisonment	●
s.40 (care workers: sexual activity in the presence of a person with a mental disorder)		●		● If sentenced to 12 months' or more imprisonment	●
s.41 (care workers: causing a person with a mental disorder to watch a sexual act)		●		● If sentenced to 12 months' or more imprisonment	●
s.47 (paying for sexual services of a child)	● If s.47(3) or (4)	●	● If C. under 16	● If sentenced to 12 months' or more imprisonment	●
s.48 (causing or inciting sexual exploitation of a child)	●	●	●	● If sentenced to 12 months' or more imprisonment	●
s.49 (controlling a child in relation to sexual exploitation)	●	●	●	● If sentenced to 12 months' or more imprisonment	●

Sexual offence	s.91 Grave Crime	Sch.15 Specified Sexual Offence	Sch.15 Serious Sexual Offence	Sch.3 Notification Offence	Sch.3/ Sch.5 SOPO Offence
s.50 (arranging or facilitating sexual exploitation of a child)	●	●	●	● If sentenced to 12 months' or more imprisonment	●
s.51A (soliciting for the purpose of obtaining the sexual services of a prostitute)					
s.52 (causing or inciting prostitution for gain)		●			●
s.53 (controlling prostitution for gain)		●			●
s.53A (paying for sexual services of a prostitute subjected to force)					
s.61 (administering a substance with intent)		●	●	● If sentenced to 12 months' or more imprisonment	●
s.62 (committing an offence with intent to commit a sexual offence)	● If s.62(3)	●	●	● If sentenced to 12 months' or more imprisonment	●

Sexual offence	s.91 Grave Crime	Sch.15 Specified Sexual Offence	Sch.15 Serious Sexual Offence	Sch.3 Notification Offence	Sch.3/ Sch.5 SOPO Offence
s.63 (trespass with intent to commit a sexual offence)		●	●	● If sentenced to 12 months' or more imprison-ment	●
s.64 (sex with an adult relative: penetration)		●		● If sentenced to 12 months' or more imprison-ment	●
s.65 (sex with an adult relative: consenting to penetration)		●		● If sentenced to 12 months' or more imprison-ment	●
s.66 (exposure)		●		● If sentenced to 12 months' or more imprison-ment	●
s.67 (voyeurism)		●		● If sentenced to 12 months' or more imprison-ment	●
s.69 (intercourse with an animal)		●		● If sentenced to 12 months' or more imprison-ment	●

Sexual offence	s.91 Grave Crime	Sch.15 Specified Sexual Offence	Sch.15 Serious Sexual Offence	Sch.3 Notification Offence	Sch.3/ Sch.5 SOPO Offence
s.70 (sexual penetration of a corpse)		●		● If sentenced to 12 months' or more imprison-ment	●
s.71 (sexual activity in a public lavatory)[216]					
Aiding, abetting, counseling, procuring, inciting, conspiring or attempting to commit any of the above offences	● If penalty for maximum offence 10 years' or more	● If specified for substantive offence	● If penalty for maximum offence 10 years' or more	● If sentenced to 12 months' or more imprison-ment	●
Breaches of ancillary orders[217]					
Sexual Offences Act 1956					
s.33 (keeping a brothel)[218]		●			
s.33A (keeping a brothel used for prostitution)[219]		●			
s.34 (landlord letting premises for use as a brothel)[220]					

---

[216] This is a summary only offence.
[217] SOA 2003 ss.91, 113, and 122.
[218] This is a summary only offence.
[219] This offence is triable either way.
[220] This is a summary only offence.

Sexual offence	s.91 Grave Crime	Sch.15 Specified Sexual Offence	Sch.15 Serious Sexual Offence	Sch.3 Notification Offence	Sch.3/ Sch.5 SOPO Offence
s.35 (tenant permitting premises to be used as a brothel)[221]					
s.36 (tenant permitting premises to be used for prostitution)[222]					
Other offences					
s.1 Protection of Children Act 1978 (indecent photographs of children)		●	●	●	●
s.160 Criminal Justice Act 1988 (possession of indecent photographs of children)		●		● If sentenced to 12 months' or more imprison-ment	●
s.9 Theft Act 1968 (burglary with intent to commit rape)	● If a building a dwelling	●	●	●	●
s.3 Children and Young Persons Act 1933 (allowing a person under 16 to be in a brothel)[223]					

---

[221] This is a summary only offence.
[222] This is a summary only offence.
[223] This is a summary only offence.

Sexual offence	s.91 Grave Crime	Sch.15 Specified Sexual Offence	Sch.15 Serious Sexual Offence	Sch.3 Notification Offence	Sch.3/ Sch.5 SOPO Offence
s.44 Metropolitan Police Act 1839 (knowingly permitting prostitutes to meet and remain in house of refreshment)[224]					
s.1 Modern Slavery Act 2015 (slavery, servitutde andforce or compulsory labour)	●	●	●	●	●
s.2 Modern Slavery Act 2015 (human trafficking)[225]	●	●	●	●	●
Offences contrary to common law					
Outraging public decency[226]					
Keeping a disorderly house (see also s.81 Disorderly Houses Act 1751 (keeping a disorderly house))					

[224] Applies only to the Metropolitan Police District. A precisely similar provision relating to premises situated in the City of London is contained in the City of London Police Act 1839 s.28.

[225] An offence under s.2 of the Modern Slavery Act 2015 committed with a view to exploitation that consists of or includes behaviour within s.3(3) of that Act (sexual exploitation) is a specified sexual offence in Pt 2 of Sch.15 to the CJA 2003. All other offences under s.2 are specified violent offences and fall within Pt.1 of Sch.15 to the CJA 2003.

[226] This offence is not a "sexual offence" for the purposes of the CJA 2003 and the dangerousness provisions.

CHAPTER 32

SEXUAL OFFENCES IN NORTHERN IRELAND

By H.H. Judge David McFarland

Introduction..................................... 32.01
Sexual Offences (Northern Ireland)
  Order 2008 .... 32.07
Application of Sexual Offences Act
  2003 to Northern Ireland............. 32.22
Commencement 32.26
Sentencing Provisions 32.29
Sentencing Generally 32.47

Evidence... 32.57
Delay.. 32.69
Receiving verdicts 32.74
Annex: Equivalent Sections in
  Sexual Offences Act 2003 to
  Articles in Sexual Offences (NI)
  Order 2008 .... 32.75

INTRODUCTION

Prior to the commencement of the Sexual Offences (Northern Ireland) Order 2008[1] on February 2, 2009,[2] Northern Ireland lacked any form of codified sexual offences legislation, and in addition to common law offences, offences were found in various pieces of legislation from the United Kingdom Parliament, the Northern Ireland Parliament and Orders in Council.[3] On February 12, 2010, policing and justice powers were devolved to the Northern Ireland Assembly by the Northern Ireland Act 1998 (Devolution of Policing and Justice Functions) Order 2010.[4]   **32.01**

The principle offences were: **32.02**

- The common law offence of rape (extended by art.18(4) of the Criminal Justice (Northern Ireland) Order 2003[5] to include anal penetration). The maximum sentence was life imprisonment.
- The offence of buggery contrary to s.61 of the Offences Against the Person Act 1861 which carried a maximum sentence of life when the

[1] SI 2008/1769 (NI2).
[2] Sexual Offences (Northern Ireland) Order 2008 (Commencement) Order 2008 (SI 2008/510 (c.30)).
[3] A useful list of the existing sexual offences can be found in para.1(2) of Sch.2 to the 2008 Order, and in Category 79—Sexual Offences in B.J.A.C. Valentine's *Booklet of Criminal Offences in Northern Ireland 1998*, 4th edn (Belfast: The Stationery Office, 1998).
[4] SI 2010/976. See also Department of Justice Act (Northern Ireland) 2010 (c.3(NI)).
[5] SI 2003/1247(NI13).

victim was a female or a child under 16 years, and 10 years if the male was over 16.[6] In 2002, the offence of attempted buggery of a female (contrary to s.62 of the 1861 Act) was declared incompatible with art.8 of the ECHR by Kerr J in *Re McR*[7] and this resulted in a general review of the law. Non-consensual anal penetration was included in the offence of rape (see above), and art.19 of the Criminal Justice (Northern Ireland) Order 2003 redefined the offence of buggery. It was no longer an offence for acts between people aged 17 and over, or if the penetrating male was under 17, and the other was 17 or over. This defence was not available if the act took place in a public lavatory.[8] New maximum penalties were introduced depending on the age of the victim and the offender—life imprisonment if the victim was 16 or under, five years if the victim was 16 or 17 and the offender was 21 and over, and two years in all other cases.

- Unlawful carnal knowledge.[9] As in England and Wales, there were two different offences depending on the age of the victim, although the age limits were different in Northern Ireland, the more serious offence being committed against a girl of 13 or under and the less serious against a girl of 16 or under. The maximum penalties were life imprisonment and two years respectively. The defence available in England and Wales known as the "young man's defence" did not apply to Northern Ireland.[10]

- Indecent Assault. The offence against a female[11] carried a maximum sentence of two years for offences up to October 2, 1989, and 10 years thereafter.[12] The offence against a male[13] carried a maximum of 10 years.

- Acts of gross indecency with or towards a child (aged 16 or under)[14] carried a maximum sentence of two years, increased to 10 years for offence on, or after, July 28, 2003.[15]

---

[6] art.3 of the Homosexual Offences (Northern Ireland) Order 1982 (SI 1982/1536 NI 19) provided a defence to those aged 18 and over acting in private with consent.

[7] [2002] NIQB 58.

[8] art.4(b). The non-availability of the defence for acts committed where more than two persons take part or are present (art.4(a)) was repealed by the Sexual Offences Act 2003 Sch.6, para.52.

[9] ss.4 and 5 of the Criminal Law Amendment Act 1885.

[10] s.2 of the Criminal Law (Amendment) Act (Northern Ireland) 1923.

[11] s.52 of the Offences Against the Person Act 1861. In the Republic of Ireland this was held to be a common law offence with s.52 only prescribing the sentence: *People v Brophy* [1992] ILRM 709.

[12] Increased by art.12 of the Treatment of Offenders (Northern Ireland) Order 1989 (SI 1989/1344 NI 15).

[13] s.62 of the Offences Against the Person Act 1861, replaced by art.21 of the Criminal Justice (Northern Ireland) Order 2003.

[14] s.22 of the Children and Young Persons Act (Northern Ireland) 1968 for children aged 13 or under, and increased to children aged 16 or under from November 11, 2001, by art.22 of the Criminal Justice (Northern Ireland) Order 2003.

[15] art.22(1) of the Criminal Justice (Northern Ireland) Order 2003.

- Offences relating to indecent images of children[16] carried a maximum sentence of three years up to January 11, 2001, and then 10 years thereafter[17].

The Court of Appeal in *Wilkinson*[18] stated that when dealing with the **32.03** common law offence of rape, and recklessness as to the defendant's state of mind as to whether the victim was consenting, the form of words approved by the English Court of Appeal in *Adkins*[19] was acceptable, i.e. "a man is reckless as to whether the woman consented to sexual intercourse if you are sure that he neither knew nor cared whether she was consenting or not. In other words his state of mind was that he could not have cared less."

In relation to the offence of unlawful carnal knowledge (contrary to ss.4 **32.04** and 5 of the Criminal Law Amendment Act 1885) the Court of Appeal in *Hamilton*[20] decided that the removal of the "young man's defence"[21] did not contravene any ECHR rights of the defendant. A further argument as to the requirement on the prosecution to prove knowledge of the girl's age was also rejected in *Brown*.[22] This argument was based on a submission that the removal of the defences in the 1885 Act by the Criminal Law Amendment Act (Northern Ireland) 1923 resulted in the legislation being silent on the question of mens rea and therefore required its importation.[23]

The presumption that a boy under the age of 14 was incapable of sexual **32.05** intercourse was abolished by art.23 of the Criminal Justice (Northern Ireland) Order 2003, which came into operation on July 28, 2003.[24]

Doli incapax (the rebuttable presumption that a child aged 10 or over but **32.06** under 14 is incapable of committing a criminal offence) was abolished on December 1, 1998.[25]

SEXUAL OFFENCES (NORTHERN IRELAND) ORDER 2008

The Sexual Offences (Northern Ireland) Order 2008[26] followed in almost **32.07** identical terms the provisions of the Sexual Offences Act 2003, with the new offences of loitering or soliciting for the purposes of prostitution (art.59), kerb crawling (art.60) and persistent soliciting (art.61), which were sourced,

[16] art.3(1) of the Protection of Children (Northern Ireland) Order 1978.
[17] s.41 of the Criminal Justice and Court Services Act 2000.
[18] [2011] NICA 29.
[19] [2000] 2 All E.R. 185.
[20] [2011] NICA 46.
[21] Established in England and Wales for men aged 23 and under by s.2 of the Criminal Law Amendment Act 1922.
[22] [2011] NICA 47 and [2013] UKSC 43.
[23] See, e.g. *B. v DPP* [2000] 2 A.C. 428 and *R. v K* [2001] UKHL 41. However, this argument was regarded as contrived by the Supreme Court: see [2013] UKSC 43 at [36].
[24] Criminal Justice (2003 Order) (Commencement No.2) Order (Northern Ireland) 2003 (SI 2003/352 (c.27)).
[25] arts 1(2) and 3 of the Criminal Justice (Children) (Northern Ireland) Order 1998 (SI 1998/1504 (NI 9)). For a correct direction in relation to doli incapax, see *R. v ML* [2013] NICA 23.
[26] SI 2008/1769 (NI 2).

respectively, from s.1(1) of the Street Offences Act 1959 and s.1(1) and s.2(1) of the Sexual Offences Act 1985.

32.08   Articles 60 and 61 were subsequently repealed by s.20 of the Policing and Crime Act 2009 and replaced by a new art.60 which contains a soliciting offence identical to the offence in England and Wales created by s.19 of the 2009 Act (which inserts s.51A into the Sexual Offences Act 2003). New identical offences of paying for sexual services of a prostitute subjected to force—new art.64A of the 2008 Order (Northern Ireland) and new s.53A of the 2003 Act (England and Wales)—were created by ss.14 and 15 of the 2009 Act. These offences came into force on April 1, 2010.[27]

32.09   However, an act of the NI Assembly bearing the short title of the Human Trafficking and Exploitation (Criminal Justice and Support of Victims) Act (NI) 2015 has since made further legislative changes. It repealed the art.59 offence (loitering or soliciting for the purposes of prostitution) on January 13, 2015.[28] Further, it replaced the art.64A offence of paying for sexual services of a prostitute subjected to force (introduced in April 2010), as from June 1, 2015, with a new art.64A offence of paying for sexual services of a prostitute.[29]

Offence of paying for sexual services of a person

32.10   The new offence is committed when A obtains sexual services from B in exchange for payment if the payment is made or promised by A or is made or promised by a third party and A knows or believes that the payment is made or promised by a third party. The sexual services must involve A and B being in each other's presence, and sexual touching by either of the other, or by B of himself or herself, for the sexual gratification of A. "Payment" means any financial advantage to B, or another person, including the discharge of an obligation to pay or the provision of goods or services (other than sexual services)[30] gratuitously or at a discount. The offence carries a maximum sentence on summary conviction of six months' imprisonment and/or a fine not exceeding the statutory maximum, and on conviction on indictment of 12 months and/or a fine. B does not commit an offence by doing anything to aid, abet, counsel or procure the commission of the offence by A and cannot conspire with A to commit the offence.

Offences of sexual communication with a child and meeting a child following grooming

32.11   The offence of sexual communication with a child (inserted as art.22A of the 2008 Order) was introduced on July 24, 2015, by s.90 of the Justice Act

---

[27] Policing and Crime Act 2009 (Commencement No. 4) Order 2010 (SI 2010/507).
[28] s.15(4).
[29] s.15(5).
[30] Contrast art.58(3) of the 2008 Order which, for the purpose of the offences of causing or inciting prostitution for gain (art.62) and controlling prostitution for gain (art.63), defines "gain" to include the provision of goods or services "including" sexual services.

(Northern Ireland) 2015. It is identical to the offence introduced in England and Wales by the Serious Crime Act 2015.

Section 89 of the Justice Act (Northern Ireland) 2015 amended the art.22   **32.12** offence of meeting a child following sexual grooming by reducing the number of required previous contacts from two or more to one or more.[31]

Human trafficking offences

The provisions of ss.57–59 of the 2003 Act were applied to Northern Ireland   **32.13** under art.11 of the Sexual Offences (NI Consequential Amendments) Order 2008.[32] Section 109 of the Protection of Freedoms Act 2012 (which repealed ss.57–59 and introduced an extended new s.59A) did not apply to Northern Ireland. Section 6 of the Criminal Justice Act (Northern Ireland) 2013 was to introduce a new offence (s.58A of the 2003 Act) of trafficking outside the UK for sexual exploitation. However it was never brought into force. The intended group of offences outlawing all forms of trafficking for sexual exploitation—into the UK (s.57), within the UK (s.58), outside the UK (s.58A) and out of the UK (s.59)—have now been replaced by a new offence under s.2 of the 2015 Act.

The offence is committed if A arranges or facilitates the travel of B with a   **32.14** view to B being exploited. Whether B consents to any act constituting the offence is irrelevant. If A is a UK national, habitually resident in Northern Ireland at the time of the offence, or a body corporate incorporated in any part of the UK, the offence is committed regardless of where the arranging or facilitating takes place, or where the travel takes place. For anyone not falling into these three categories, the offence can only be committed if any part of the arranging or facilitating takes place in the UK, or the travel consists of arrival into, departure from, or travel within the UK.

A further offence under s.4 is committed by committing any criminal   **32.15** offence with intent to commit an offence under s.2. The s.4 offence carries a maximum sentence on indictment of 10 years' imprisonment, and on summary conviction of six months and/or a fine (unless the offence is kidnapping or false imprisonment, when it carries as a maximum discretionary life sentence).[33]

A must intend to exploit B, or must have known or ought to have known   **32.16** that another person is likely to exploit B, in any part of the world during or after the travel.

For the purpose of the new offences, "arranging or facilitating" can   **32.17** include recruiting B, transporting or transferring B, harbouring or receiving B or transferring or exchanging control over B. Travel means arriving in, or entering, departing from, or travelling within any country.

---

[31] Amended in England and Wales by the Criminal Justice and Courts Act 2015.
[32] SI 2008/1779.
[33] s.4.

32.18   B is "exploited" if any one of six categories of exploitation (slavery and forced labour, sexual exploitation, removal of organs, exploitation by force, threats or deception and exploitation of children and vulnerable persons) applies in relation to B.[34] In the context of sexual offences, sexual exploitation is defined as something being done to or in respect of B which involves the commission of an offence under art.3(1)(a) of the Protection of Children (NI) Order 1978[35] (indecent photographs of children) or under any provision of the Sexual Offences (NI) Order 2008, or which would involve the commission of such an offence if it were done in Northern Ireland.[36]

32.19   The offence carries a maximum discretionary life sentence and a mandatory minimum sentence of two years' imprisonment for offenders aged 18 years or over when the offence is committed, unless the court states in open court its opinion that there are exceptional circumstances relating to the offence or the offender.[37] Section 6 also sets out what are aggravating factors which a court must take into account, although this does not add anything to well established general sentencing practice.

32.20   The offence is both a specified and serious offence under the provisions of the Criminal Justice (NI) Order 2008[38] and may, if the offender is considered dangerous under that legislation, attract indeterminate or extended custodial sentences. If the exploitation includes sexual exploitation, the offence is a specified sexual offence (which can attract an extended period under an extended custodial sentence of up to eight years).

32.21   Conviction will also trigger consideration by the court of whether to make a slavery and trafficking prevention order,[39] the provisions relating to such orders being similar to sexual offences prevention orders, serious crime prevention orders and violent offences prevention orders.[40] The test for consideration is the risk of further offending and the necessity for making the order to protect the public from harm (as opposed to serious harm as required for the making of a sexual offences prevention order and violent offences prevention order).[41] The order can contain both prohibitions and requirements.[42]

---

[34] s.3.

[35] SI 1978/1047 (NI 17).

[36] One perhaps unintended consequence of the extra-jurisdictional reach of the s.2 offence and the new offence of paying for sexual services (as an offence under the 2008 Order as opposed to the 2015 Act), is that a UK national anywhere in the world, or a non-national anywhere in the UK, arranging for a person to travel to provide sexual services (e.g. providing a taxi to travel to a hotel), will be guilty of a s.2 trafficking offence carrying a minimum mandatory sentence of two years, and liable to imprisonment for life.

[37] See *Rehman* [2005] EWCA Crim 2056 for the correct approach to the consideration of exceptional circumstances in the context of firearms offences.

[38] SI 2008/1216 (NI 1).

[39] Sch.3.

[40] s.55 of the Justice Act (Northern Ireland) 2015 (not yet in force at the date of writing).

[41] Sch.3, para.1(2).

[42] Sch.3, para.4(1).

APPLICATION OF SEXUAL OFFENCES ACT 2003 TO NORTHERN IRELAND

Parts of the Sexual Offences Act 2003 did apply directly to Northern Ireland, namely offences against children under 18 by persons in a position of trust (ss.15–24), offences relating to the sexual exploitation of children (ss.47–54), exposure, voyeurism, intercourse with an animal, sexual penetration of a corpse and sexual activity in a public lavatory (ss.66–71), and the provision to allow the prosecution in Northern Ireland of offences committed outside the United Kingdom (s.72). These statutory provisions, in so far as they applied to Northern Ireland, have all been repealed by the Sexual Offences (Northern Ireland) Order 2008,[43] but the offences have been re-created in the 2008 Order. **32.22**

In addition, the notification requirements for sexual offenders, and the provisions relating to sexual offences prevention orders, foreign travel orders and risk of sexual harm orders (contained in Pt 2 of the 2003 Act) applied directly to Northern Ireland, and continue to apply.[44] **32.23**

To address the issues raised in the decision of the Supreme Court in *F, R. (on the application of) v Secretary of State for the Home Department*,[45] s.1 of the Criminal Justice Act (Northern Ireland) 2013 inserted a new s.82(7) and Sch.3A in the 2003 Act[46] from March 1, 2014,[47] which provides for a review of an indefinite notification requirement after 15 years (eight years in the case of an offender who was under 18 at the time of the offence). **32.24**

From June 26, 2014,[48] s.2 of the Criminal Justice Act (Northern Ireland) 2013 requires an offender to notify police of any intended absence of more than three days from his home address. **32.25**

COMMENCEMENT

Northern Ireland has therefore two principal commencement dates: May 1, 2004 (for those Sexual Offences Act 2003 offences applying to Northern Ireland) and February 2, 2009 (for the Sexual Offences (Northern Ireland) Order 2008 offences).[49] **32.26**

The Sexual Offences Act 2003 did not repeal any of the existing sexual offences in Northern Ireland. Accordingly, the provisions of s.55 of the **32.27**

---

[43] art.83 and Sch.3.

[44] s.142(2)(c).

[45] [2010] UKSC 17; [2011] 1 A.C. 331.

[46] Equivalent to the new s.91F(1) of the 2003 Act introduced in England and Wales by the Sexual Offences Act 2003 (Remedial) Order 2012 (SI 2012/1883).

[47] Criminal Justice (2013 Act) (Commencement No.3) Order (Northern Ireland) 2014 (SI 2014/53 (c.2)).

[48] Criminal Justice (2013 Act) (Commencement No.4) Order (Northern Ireland) 2014 (SI 2014/179 (c.11)).

[49] Sexual Offences (Northern Ireland) Order 2008 (Commencement) Order 2008 (SI 2008/510 (c.30)).

Violent Crime Reduction Act 2006 (continuity of sexual offences law) would not appear to be operative. In particular, the condition in s.55(1)(c) ("the only thing preventing the defendant from being found guilty of the pre-commencement offence is the fact that it has not been proved beyond a reasonable doubt that that time was before the coming into force of the repeal of the enactment providing for the offence") could not apply as there has been no repeal of a pre-commencement offence.

32.28   Transitional provisions in relation to the commencement of the Sexual Offences (Northern Ireland) Order 2008 are provided for in art.82 and Sch.2, and mirror the provisions set out in s.55 of the Violent Crime Reduction Act 2006. With the repeal of the common law offence of rape by art.5(6), there was a serious lacuna in that Sch.2 omitted any reference to the common law offence of rape as a relevant pre-commencement offence. This was remedied by the Sexual Offences (Northern Ireland) Order 2008 (Transitional Provisions) Order 2009[50] which came into operation on August 10, 2009.

Sentencing Provisions

32.29   The sentencing structure in Northern Ireland was largely governed by the Criminal Justice (Northern Ireland) Order 1996, but, in respect of custodial sentences, this is now in the process of being replaced by the provisions of the Criminal Justice (Northern Ireland) Order 2008. The 1996 Order is loosely based on the Criminal Justice Act 1991, and the 2008 Order introduces a sentencing regime for dangerous offenders that is similar, but not identical, to the amended Criminal Justice Act 2003 provisions.

Offences committed before May 15, 2008

32.30   For offences committed before May 15, 2008, the full provisions of the 1996 Order are available, although life sentences, if available, will be imposed under the provisions of the Life Sentence (Northern Ireland) Order 2001.[51] In terms of sexual offences, the sentences available will be discharges and community sentences,[52] and custodial sentences. Custodial sentences under the 1996 Order can include the following:

Longer than commensurate sentences

32.31   Article 20 provides—

"**20**—(1) This Article applies where a court passes a custodial sentence other than one fixed by law . . .
      (2) . . . the custodial sentence shall be—

---

[50] SR 2009/265.
[51] SI 2001/2564 (NI 2).
[52] arts 4–7 (discharges) and arts 8–17 (community sentences).

(a) for such term (not exceeding the permitted maximum) as in the opinion of the court is commensurate with the seriousness of the offence, or the combination of the offence and one or more offences associated with it; or

(b) where the offence is a violent or sexual offence, for such longer term (not exceeding that maximum) as in the opinion of the court is necessary to protect the public from serious harm from the offender."

"Sexual offence" is defined in art.2(2) as one listed in Sch.1 to the Criminal Justice (Children) (Northern Ireland) Order 1998.[53] In *McColgan*,[54] the Court of Appeal stated that any longer than commensurate term to protect the public from serious harm should not be expressed in the form of a percentage uplift, but the sentencer should focus on the actual period required for public protection.

Custody probation orders

This widely used sentence involves the imposition of a period of custody followed by a period of probation. Article 24 provides: **32.32**

"(1) Where, in the case of a person convicted of an offence punishable with a custodial sentence, other than an offence for which the sentence is fixed by law . . . , a court has formed the opinion under Articles 19 and 20 that a custodial sentence of 12 months or more would be justified for the offence, the court shall consider whether it would be appropriate to make a custody probation order, that is to say, an order requiring him both–

(a) to serve a custodial sentence; and
(b) on his release from custody, to be under the supervision of a probation officer for a period specified in the order, being not less than 12 months nor more than 3 years.

(2) Under a custody probation order the custodial sentence shall be for such term as the court would under Article 20 pass on the offender less such period as the court thinks appropriate to take account of the effect of the offender's supervision by the probation officer on his release from custody in protecting the public from harm from him or for preventing the commission by him of further offences.

(3) A court shall not make a custody probation order in respect of any offender unless the offender consents and, where an offender does not so consent, the court shall not pass a custodial sentence of a greater length than the term the court would otherwise pass under Article 20.

(4) Where in any case a court does not consider a custody probation order to be appropriate, the court shall state in open court that it is of that opinion and why it is of that opinion.

(5) A court which makes a custody probation order shall state the term of the custodial sentence it would have passed under Article 20 if the offender had not consented to the order."

In summary, should the court be considering a custodial sentence of 12 months or more, it must consider a custody probation order, which will, if **32.33**

---

[53] SI 1998/1504 (NI 9). See the Criminal Justice (Northern Ireland) Order 2003 (SI 2003/1247 (NI 13)), Sch.1, para.19.
[54] [2006] NICA 41.

imposed, lead to a reduction in time spent in prison, with a period of time on probation once the offender is released. The relevant criteria are the protection of the public from harm (not "serious" harm) or preventing the commission of further offences. There is no presumption for or against making such an order.[55] *Lunney* provides a useful checklist: criminal record, previous probation orders and response thereto, remorse shown by the offender, contents of the pre-sentence report, length of sentence and the possibility of a change of attitude by the offender. As it is difficult to make such an assessment in the case of a long term prisoner, custody probation orders should be avoided in these cases.[56] If the Probation Board are of the view that the offender is unlikely to require or to respond to probation supervision, then a custody probation order should not be made.[57] The reduction of sentence need not be identical in length to the period of probation, but should bear some relation to it. The custody period should be substantial, and should not be very much shorter than the probation period.[58]

Article 26 licence

32.34   Article 26 provides:

"(1) Where, in the case of an offender who has been sentenced to imprisonment . . . —
(a) the whole or any part of his sentence or order for detention was imposed for a sexual offence, and
(b) the court by which he was sentenced or ordered to be detained for that offence, having regard to—
(i) the need to protect the public from serious harm from him, and
(ii) the desirability of preventing the commission by him of further offences and of securing his re-habilitation,
ordered that this Article shall apply,
instead of being granted remission of his sentence or order for detention under prison rules, the offender shall, on the day on which he might have been discharged if the remission had been granted, be released on licence under the provisions of this Article.
(2) An offender released on licence under this Article shall be under the supervision of a probation officer appointed for or assigned to the petty sessions district within which the offender resides until the date on which he would (but for his release) have served the whole of his sentence or order for detention."

32.35   There is a presumption in favour of art.26 disposals if the conditions apply.[59] It is suggested that a custody probation order is the preferred option for an offender facing a shorter sentence, if it is felt that a period of between 12 and 36 months rehabilitation work is required. On release the offender

[55] *Attorney General's Reference (No.1 of 1998)* [1998] NI 232; *Lunney* [1999] NI 158.
[56] *Devenney* [2001] 10 BNIL 90.
[57] *O'Keefe*, unreported, March 3, 2000; *Benson*, unreported, February 14, 2003.
[58] *McDonnell* [2001] NI 168.
[59] *McGowan* [2000] NIJB 305; *Larmour*, unreported, June 22, 2001.

shall be under the supervision of a probation officer and be subject to such conditions as the Minister for Justice shall specify.[60] The powers under the 1996 Order were limited to a suspension of the licence up to a maximum period of six months. A new art.27 has been substituted[61] and the Crown Court now has the power to revoke the licence in its entirety.

Offences committed on or after May 15, 2008

For offences committed on or after May 15, 2008, extended custodial sentences and indeterminate custodial sentences are available (see paras 32.40 and following, below).[62] In the event of an offender not being considered dangerous, then the offender will be sentenced under the 1996 Order. In those circumstances, if a court is considering options under the 1996 Order including a longer than commensurate sentence or an art.26 licence, this may create some difficulty, as the statutory tests are similar, and having rejected the proposition that "there is a significant risk to members of the public of serious harm occasioned by the commission by the offender of further such offences",[63] it may be difficult to form the opinion that it is necessary to protect the public from serious harm from the offender[64] or to determine that there is a need to protect the public from serious harm from him, and a desirability of preventing the commission by him of further offences and of securing his rehabilitation.[65] It is suggested that this potential conflict can be dealt with in the same way as a court can deal with a SOPO, after determining that an offender is not dangerous: see *Rampley*[66] and *Richards,*[67] i.e. there are two distinct statutory schemes relating to public protection. The test for the custody probation order is not as strict (the future harm need not be "serious" or the order may be solely for the prevention of further offending), and the imposition of such an order should not create any difficulty for the court.

32.36

Offences committed on or after April 1, 2009

For offences committed on or after April 1, 2009, determinate custodial sentences are to be imposed if the determinate term in custody is 12 months

32.37

---

[60] art.26(3), (4).

[61] By art.34 of the Criminal Justice (Northern Ireland) Order 2008 (No 1216 (NI 1)).

[62] Criminal Justice (Northern Ireland) Order 2008 (Commencement No. 1 and Savings and Transitory Provisions) Order 2008 (SI 2008/217 (c.8)). Article 3(3) to the Criminal Justice (Northern Ireland) Order 2008 provides that where an offence if found to have been committed over a period of two or more days, or at some time during a period of two or more days, it shall be taken to have been committed on the last of those days.

[63] art.15(1)(b) of the Criminal Justice (Northern Ireland) Order 2008.

[64] art.20(2)(b) of the Criminal Justice (Northern Ireland) Order 1996.

[65] art.26(1)(b) of the Criminal Justice (Northern Ireland) Order 1996.

[66] [2006] EWCA Crim 2203.

[67] [2006] EWCA Crim 2519.

or more.[68] This new sentence will replace the commensurate sentence, the longer than commensurate sentence, the custody probation order and the art.26 licence under the 1996 Order. Under art.8 of the 2008 Order a court is required:

- First, to determine the sentence, such term (not exceeding the permitted maximum) as in the opinion of the court is commensurate with the seriousness of the offence, or the combination of the offence and one or more offences associated with it.[69]
- Secondly, to deduct from the sentence such period (the "licence period") as the court thinks appropriate to take account of the effect of the offender's supervision by a probation officer on release from custody in protecting the public from harm from the offender and in preventing the commission by the offender of further offences.[70]

The resulting "custodial period" cannot exceed one half of the sentence,[71] and therefore should the court determine that a licence period is not appropriate (an unlikely outcome in the case of sexual offences) there will be a simple mathematical reduction by one half.

32.38   When considering a determinate custodial sentence under art.8 of the Criminal Justice (Northern Ireland) Order 2008, and in particular the licence period and the resulting custodial period, a judge should give brief reasons for a decision should he or she determine that the licence period is more than half of the determinate term.[72] This may be of particular relevance should a judge be considering the suitability of an offender undergoing the Probation Board's sex offenders' programme, which usually has a duration of three years. What is clear is that the court should not attempt to adjust the custody/licence terms merely to reflect mitigating factors without any evidence to support a licence term in excess of 50 per cent of the sentence.

Offender levy

32.39   A levy is now imposed on offenders convicted of offences occurring on or after June 6, 2012, although the current arrangements (£15 in the event of a fine, £25 in the event of immediate imprisonment/detention of two years or less, and £50 in the event of an indeterminate sentence or immediate imprisonment/detention of more than two years) are transitional.[73]

---

[68] art.2 and para.2 of Sch.2 to the Criminal Justice (Northern Ireland) Order 2008 (Commencement No.5 and Saving Provisions) Order 2009 (SI 2009/120 (c.6)).
[69] art.7(2).
[70] art.8(2), (5).
[71] art.8(3).
[72] *McKeown, DPP's Reference (No.2 of 2013)* [2013] NICA 28 at [31].
[73] Ch.1 of Pt 1 of the Justice Act (Northern Ireland) 2011 and the Justice (2011 Act) (Commencement No.4 and Transitory Provision) Order (Northern Ireland) 2012 (SI 2012/214 (c.18)).

Dangerous offenders

The introduction of the extended custodial sentence and the indeterminate **32.40** custodial sentence by the Criminal Justice (Northern Ireland) Order 2008 for offences committed on or after May 15, 2008, and the amendment of the existing provisions of the Criminal Justice Act 2003 by the Criminal Justice and Immigration Act 2008 from July 14, 2008, has in broad terms brought the sentencing regimes for dangerous offenders in Northern Ireland and in England and Wales into line.

If an offender is convicted on indictment of a "serious" or "specified" **32.41** offence on or after May 15, 2008,[74] then he falls to be considered as "dangerous". The list of "serious" and "specified" offences is set out in Schs 1 and 2 to the 2008 Order, with the sexual offences listed in Pt 2 to each Schedule. The new sexual offences created by the Sexual Offences (Northern Ireland) Order 2008 are now added to each list by virtue of para.35 of Sch.1 to that Order. In broad terms, those offences attracting a maximum of 10 years' imprisonment or more are categorised as "serious". All "serious" offences are "specified" offences.

The extended custodial sentence is a sentence comprising a custodial term **32.42** and an extension period. The custodial term shall be for such term (not exceeding the permitted maximum) as in the opinion of the court is commensurate with the seriousness of the offence, or the combination of the offence and one or more offences associated with it, and in the event of a commensurate term of less than 12 months, shall be 12 months.[75] The extension period shall be of such length as the court considers necessary for the purpose of protecting members of the public from serious harm occasioned by the commission by the offender of further specified offences,[76] but cannot exceed eight years in the case of a sexual offence.[77] The custodial term and the extension period cannot exceed the maximum permitted for the offence.[78] The offender will serve at least one half of the custodial term, and thereafter be subject to early release by the Minister for Justice as directed by the Parole Commissioners.[79] The offender will then be subject to supervision by a probation officer during the extension period, and subject to any conditions of his licence as determined by the Minister for Justice, in consultation with the Parole Commissioners.[80]

The indeterminate custodial sentence is a sentence similar in nature to a **32.43** life sentence. The court will specify a period of at least two years as a minimum period to the served by the offender. This period is to satisfy the

[74] arts 13(1)(a) and 14(1)(a).
[75] art.14(4)(b).
[76] art.14(3)(b).
[77] art.14(8)(b).
[78] art.14(9).
[79] art.18(2)(b), (3).
[80] art.24(3)(b), (5).

requirements of retribution and deterrence.[81] After the offender has served this minimum period, he or she shall be released if and when the Parole Commissioners direct the Minister for Justice to release him or her if they are satisfied that it is no longer necessary for the protection of the public that he or she should be confined.[82] The offender will then be subject to supervision by a probation officer for the remainder of his life, and subject to any terms of his licence as determined by the Minister for Justice, in consultation with the Parole Commissioners.[83] The Parole Commissioners can direct the Minister for Justice to discharge the licence after 10 years.[84]

32.44   The assessment of dangerousness is provided for in arts 13(1)(b), 14(1)(b)(i) and 15(1)(b), the test being "whether there is a significant risk to members of the public of serious harm occasioned by the commission by the offender of further specified offences". The Court of Appeal in *EB*[85] approved the approach to assessing dangerousness as was suggested in the English authorities of *Lang*,[86] *Johnson*[87] and *Attorney General's Reference (No.55 of 2008)*.[88]

32.45   If an offender has committed a specified offence, and is considered to be dangerous, the court must impose an extended custodial sentence. If an offender has committed a serious offence, and is considered to be dangerous, the court must then determine if an extended custodial sentence would not be adequate for the purpose of protecting the public from serious harm occasioned by the commission by the offender of further specified offences. If it is considered adequate, it must impose an extended custodial sentence.[89] If the court does not consider that an extended custodial sentence is adequate, then it must impose an indeterminate custodial sentence.[90]

In *Pollins*,[91] it was indicated that in considering the adequacy of an extended custodial sentence, the imposition of an indeterminate custodial sentence should be considered a sentence of last resort. Morgan, LCJ explained the reasoning for such an approach in the following terms[92]:

> "Apart from a discretionary life sentence an indeterminate custodial sentence is the most draconian sentence the court can impose. A discretionary life sentence is reserved for those cases where the seriousness of the offending is so exceptionally high that just punishment requires that the offender should be kept in prison for the rest of his life. It is not a borderline decision ... An indeterminate custodial sentence is primarily concerned with future risk and

[81] art.13(3)(b). For guidance with regard to setting the minimum term to be served under the Life Sentences (Northern Ireland) Order 2001, see *McCandless* [2004] NICA 1.
[82] art.18(2)(a), (3), (4)(b).
[83] art.24(3)(b), (5).
[84] art.22(4).
[85] [2010] NICA 40
[86] [2005] EWCA Crim 2864.
[87] [2006] EWCA Crim 2486.
[88] [2008] EWCA Crim 2790.
[89] arts 13(3) and 14(1)(b)(ii), (2).
[90] art.13(3)(a).
[91] [2014] NICA 62.
[92] At [26]–[27].

public protection ... However, in a case in which a life sentence is not appropriate an indeterminate custodial sentence should not be imposed without full consideration of whether alternative and cumulative methods might provide the necessary public protection against the risk posed by the individual offender. In that sense it is a sentence of last resort. The issue of whether the necessary public protection can be achieved is clearly fact specific. That requires, therefore, a careful evaluation of the methods by which such protection can be achieved under the extended sentence regime."

Transitional arrangements

The commencement and the transitional arrangements with regard to the   **32.46** introduction of the Criminal Justice (Northern Ireland) Order 2008 can be summarised as follows:

Date of Offence	Legislation	Sentence
Before May 15, 2008.	Criminal Justice (Northern Ireland) Order 1996.	• Discharge. • Community order. • Commensurate sentence. • Longer than commensurate sentence. • Custody probation order. • Article 26 Licence.
On or after May 15, 2008 but before April 1, 2009.	Criminal Justice (Northern Ireland) Order 2008.	If offender "dangerous": • Extended custodial sentence. • Indeterminate custodial sentence.
	Criminal Justice (Northern Ireland) Order 1996.	If offender not "dangerous": • Discharge. • Community order. • Commensurate sentence. • Longer than commensurate sentence. • Custody probation order. • Article 26 licence.

Date of Offence	Legislation	Sentence
On or after April 1, 2009.	Criminal Justice (Northern Ireland) Order 2008.	If offender "dangerous": • Extended custodial sentence. • Indeterminate custodial sentence. If offender not "dangerous" and sentence 12 months or more: • Determinate custodial sentence.
	Criminal Justice (Northern Ireland) Order 1996.	If offender not "dangerous" and sentence (if appropriate) is less than 12 months: • Discharge. • Community order. • Commensurate sentence. • Longer than commensurate sentence. • Article 26 licence.[93]

Sentencing Generally

Historic cases

32.47   In *R. v ML*,[94] the Court of Appeal gave guidance to judges on the approach to sentencing in historic cases.[95] Morgan L.C.J. set out the factors that should be taken into account[96]:

(i) the statutory framework applicable at the time of the commission of the offences;

---

[93] A custody probation order is not available as the prerequisite for this order is a sentence of 12 months or more. The longer than commensurate sentence and the art.26 licence would not normally be appropriate if the offender is not considered dangerous and serious harm is not considered.

[94] [2013] NICA 27.

[95] See also *R. v CK* [2009] NICA 17; *Coyles* [2010] NICA 48; *Finnegan* [2014] NICA 20.

[96] At [20].

(ii) the sentencing guidelines at the time at which the sentence is imposed;

(iii) the primary considerations are the culpability of the offender, the harm to the victim and the risk of harm in the future;

(iv) the youth of the offender will be material to the issue of culpability;

(v) the court should not seek to establish what sentence would have been imposed had the offender been detected shortly after the commission of the offences;

(vi) the passage of time may often assist the understanding of the long term effects of the offences on the victim;

(vii) the passage of time may also be relevant to the assessment of risk; and

(viii) the attitude of the offender (when he is of full age) at the time of disclosure/interview is significant and admission will attract significant discount in the sentence.

In *R. v ML*, a man of 35 at the time of sentencing had abused his younger sister when he was 13 and 14 years of age. The sentence was reduced from a custody probation order of 18 months' custody and a three year probation order (a commensurate sentence of four-and-a-half years) to 12 months' custody, with a suggestion that had he faced up to his responsibilities at an earlier stage a non-custodial outcome may have been possible

Differences in approach to England and Wales

The general approach in both jurisdictions to arriving at the commensurate **32.48** sentence and range for all criminal offences has been broadly similar. Historically however, Northern Ireland courts generally adopted higher starting points for sexual offences than courts in England and Wales. The most obvious difference related to the offence of rape, with a starting point of seven years as opposed to five years.[97] Similarly, in *R. v JD*,[98] Nicholson LJ (sitting in the Crown Court) in sentencing remarks stated:

> "As with rape, so in cases of indecent assault, the courts in Northern Ireland should in my view take a more serious view of such offences than in England."

The advice and guidance from the Sentencing Advisory Panel, Sentencing Guidelines Council and, now, the Sentencing Council do not have direct application to Northern Ireland.

During the 2000s, there was a movement towards a more common **32.49** approach in the cases of *O'Connell (Attorney General's Reference (No.2 of*

---

[97] See *McDonald* [1989] NI 37 and *Molloy* [1997] NIJB 241.
[98] [2002] 6 BNIL 98.

2004))[99] and later in *Gilbert (Attorney General's Reference (No.3 of 2006))*.[100] In *Gilbert*, Kerr LCJ stated:[101]

> "Sentencing for rape in Northern Ireland has broadly followed levels in England and Wales although traditionally a somewhat higher starting point had been adopted. Thus a starting point of seven years rather than five years was considered appropriate in *R v Molloy* [1997] NIJB 241 where this court stated:
>> 'We would return to the point which the court adumbrated in *R v JM* (1997, unreported), that in view of the increasing frequency of cases of rape, the courts will have to give serious consideration to reviewing the starting or baseline figure of 7 years for a contested rape. We consider that sentencers should in any event regard it as no more than a general guide, rather than a fixed tariff for rape cases. Certainly in cases where the offence is aggravated by violence, sexual indignities or perversions, the scale should rise steeply and judges should not hesitate to visit such cases with penalties that they consider appropriate.'
>
> More recently, in *Attorney General's reference (No 2 of 2004) (O'Connell)* [2004] NICA 15, it has been stated that sentencers in this jurisdiction should apply the starting points recommended by the Sentencing Advisory Panel in England and Wales in its 2002 guidelines—these are 5 years with no aggravating or mitigating factors and 8 years where a number of enumerated features are present. New draft guidelines have been prepared for sentences for offences (including rape) provided for in the Sexual Offences Act 2003. It may be necessary to review sentencing levels after the new guidelines for England and Wales have been finalised, although, of course, these will not apply directly to Northern Ireland."

32.50   The Northern Ireland Court of Appeal in *Sloan*[102] referred to *Gilbert* as a guideline case, and applied the eight-year tariff for an aggravated attempted rape. In *R. v SG*,[103] the Court of Appeal stated that there is assistance to be derived from the final report of the Sentencing Guidelines Council for similar offences under the 2003 Act. Although quoted with approval in *R. v DM*[104] the Court of Appeal did emphasise that greater assistance could be derived from the case-law. This seemed to herald a change in direction with a series of cases indicating a general falling out of favour of the approach being suggested by the English Sentencing Council in relation to sentencing across a range of offences.[105] In *McCaughey and Smyth*, Morgan LCJ clearly stated that notwithstanding the earlier comments in *R. v SG*, sentencers should adopt a similar approach for sexual offences. This approach was confirmed in *McCormick*[106] and *R. v TH*.[107] The current guidance from the Court of Appeal is therefore approval of only that part of the Sentencing Council's

---

[99] [2004] NICA 15.
[100] [2006] NICA 36.
[101] At [18]–[19].
[102] [2008] NICA 46.
[103] [2010] NICA 32.
[104] [2012] NICA 36 at [11].
[105] *McKeown and Lin* [2013] NICA 28 (drugs); *McCaughey and Smyth* [2014] NICA 61 (burglary); *McGrade* [2014] NICA 8 (death by driving).
[106] [2015] NICA 14.
[107] [2015] NICA 48.

definitive guideline that sets out what are aggravating and mitigating factors. Courts should not follow the tabular approach to sentencing set out in the reports, but rather should follow the case-law and guideline cases emanating from the Court of Appeal. The feeling expressed was that sentencers should not be constrained by the tabular approach to sentencing suggested by the Sentencing Council but should rely on their own experience and the training available to the small full-time Crown Court judiciary in Northern Ireland.

Basis of sentencing

The Court of Appeal indicated its disapproval of the seeking of a special **32.51** verdict from a jury to ascertain the factual basis upon which the jury made its decision, indicating that the judge is entitled to make up his or her own mind on any disputed question of fact for the purpose of sentencing.[108]

Mitigation

In cases involving a campaign of serious sexual violence against, and **32.52** corruption of multiple children, personal circumstances are unlikely to weigh heavily as a mitigating factor.[109]

Suspended sentences

Article 23 of the Criminal Justice (Northern Ireland) Order 1996, which **32.53** makes provision for restricting the use of suspended sentences unless there are exceptional circumstances, has never been brought into operation. Notwithstanding this, sentencers have established categories of offences, particularly in cases of higher culpability or if there is a strong deterrent element, which would normally require exceptional circumstances for a judge to impose a suspended sentence. The Court of Appeal in *R. v DM*[110] observed that the offence of sexual activity with a child between 13 and 16 fell into that category given the need for deterrent sentences to protect young children.

Sexual offences prevention orders

The Northern Ireland Court of Appeal in *R. v CK (a minor)*[111] dealt with **32.54** several aspects arising from the imposition of SOPOs after the defendant's conviction for attempted rape, gross indecency and indecent assault.

---

[108] *McKinnell* [2013] NICA 52. See also *Finnegan* [2014] NICA 20 at [23].
[109] *Finnegan* [2014] NICA 20.
[110] [2012] NICA 36 (in this case a 23-year-old male and a 15-year-old girl). See also *DPP's Reference (No.4 of 2012)* [2013] NICA 10.
[111] [2009] NICA 17.

- *Duration*—Section 107(1)(b) of the Sexual Offences Act 2003 should be interpreted to require the court to specify the period during which the order is to have effect, or, alternatively, state that it is to be until further order.
- *Contact with victims*—The order prohibited the defendant from "having contact whatsoever with the victims 'A' and 'B'". The victims were the defendant's cousins. Whilst sympathising with the desire to keep the defendant away from his victims, the court felt that it is difficult to prescribe for the future in terms of intra-familial relationships. The court amended the order to permit such contact, but only after approval in advance by Social Services or the designated risk manager.
- *Contact with children generally*—The order prohibited the defendant from "having or seeking to have any unsupervised contact with any child under the age of 18 years[112] unless approved by Social Services". The court considered that this would be extremely difficult to enforce and might well prove to be an inhibition to progress while not affording a great deal in the way of practical or effective elimination of risk. This condition was removed.
- *Exclusion from a geographic area*—The order prohibited the defendant from entering a geographic area, delineated on a map, unless for any circumstances approved in advance by Social Services. This condition was removed for the same reasons as the order prohibiting contact with children.

32.55   In *R. v EB*,[113] *Jones*[114] and *Simpson*,[115] it was again emphasised by the Court of Appeal that when SOPOs are being considered there is a need, first, to establish whether or not the necessity for an order is established through risk of recurrence, and, if so, whether it is necessary and proportionate to make an order beyond the statutory minimum period of five years. In *McConnell*[116] the Court of Appeal approved the approach taken by the English Court of Appeal in *Smith*[117] emphasising necessity, proportionality and consideration of protective measures in place resulting from other ancillary orders.

32.56   Section 5 of the Criminal Justice Act (Northern Ireland) 2013 permits a court to include a requirement, in addition to a prohibition, in a SOPO.[118]

---

[112] Despite the reduction of the age of consent to 16, there still remains a tendency to seek prohibitions relating to older children.
[113] [2010] NICA 40.
[114] [2011] NICA 62.
[115] [2014] NICA 83.
[116] [2014] NICA 14.
[117] [2012] EWCA Crim 1772.
[118] Commenced June 24, 2014 by the Criminal Justice (2013 Act) (Commencement No 4) Order (NI) 2014 (SI 2014/179 (c.11)).

EVIDENCE

The reforms in relation to evidence (bad character and hearsay) enacted in **32.57**
the Criminal Justice Act 2003 came into force, in identical terms, in Northern
Ireland with the Criminal Justice (Evidence) (Northern Ireland) Order
2004.[119]

In relation to the evidence of children, art.20 of the Criminal Justice **32.58**
(Children) (Northern Ireland) Order 1998 provides that a child under the age
of 14 shall give evidence unsworn in court. Children aged between 14 and 16
shall have an amended oath using the words "I promise before Almighty
God" in substitution for the oath commencing "I swear by Almighty God"
provided for in s.1 of the Oaths Act 1978.[120] Article 21(1) also permits the
court to be cleared if the evidence of a child is likely to involve any matter of
an indecent or immoral nature.

In relation to committal proceedings (involving sexual or violent offences) **32.59**
in the magistrates' court, a child shall not be called as a witness during a
preliminary investigation.[121] A separate provision also allows for the fast
track committal with an immediate transfer to the Crown Court without the
need for a committal from the magistrates' court. This is available should the
Director of Public Prosecutions certify that the evidence is sufficient, that a
child is the alleged victim or has witnessed the commission of the offence,
and to avoid any prejudice to the welfare of the child the case should be
transferred without delay.[122]

As for recent complaint, it was held in *Greene*[123] that the evidence of **32.60**
disclosure by a complainant (born in 1983) to her mother in 2000, her
boyfriend in 2002 and her doctor in 2004 of alleged events from 1991–1993,
was rightly admitted as evidence, and that the trial judge's directions covering
whether the disclosures had been made, the lapse of time from the alleged
incidents, the circumstances of the disclosures, and the fact that they were not
independent evidence were correct.[124] The Court of Appeal suggested that
the trial judge could have gone beyond the agreed position of both
prosecution and defence that the jury should only consider the evidence on
the issue of the complainant's credibility, as the evidence was also admissible
for the purpose of proving the truth of what had been said. The Court of
Appeal approved such a dual-purpose direction given in *R. v JSK*.[125]

---

[119] SI 2004/1501 (NI 10).
[120] art.19(1).
[121] art.23 of the Criminal Justice (Children) (Northern Ireland) Order 1998.
[122] art.4 of the Children's Evidence (Northern Ireland) Order 1995 (SI 1995/757 (NI 3)).
[123] [2010] NICA 47. For further examples of an approved direction to a jury and relevance of
demeanour during a disclosure, see *R. v WM* [2012] NICA 33 at [19]–[20] and [22], and of a
criticism due to a lack of directions on both issues, see *Chakwane* [2013] NICA 24. For
demeanour of complainant when in the company of the defendant, see *Warnock* [2013] NICA
34.
[124] As to the importance of a specific direction as to a disclosure not providing independent
corroboration, see *R. v AG* [2010] NICA 20 and *R. v JSK* [2011] NICA 44.
[125] [2011] NICA 44.

Special measures

32.61   Articles 4 to 21 of the Criminal Evidence (Northern Ireland) Order 1999[126] enacted the special measures provisions relating to vulnerable witnesses.[127]

32.62   Section 9 of the Justice Act (Northern Ireland) 2011 inserted a new art.10A in the 1999 Order, providing that adult complainants alleging sexual offences are entitled to give video-recorded evidence in chief.

32.63   Section 12 of the Justice Act (Northern Ireland) 2011 introduced a new special measure extending the use of intermediaries to defendants. The new art.21BA, combined with art.17 of the Criminal Evidence (Northern Ireland) Order 1999, now enables intermediaries to assist all witnesses, including defendants when giving evidence, if their use is likely to improve the quality of the witness's evidence, in terms of its completeness, coherence and accuracy.[128]

32.64   Articles 22 to 27 of the 1999 Order enacted the provisions prohibiting the cross-examination of a complainant of a sexual offence by the accused,[129] and arts 28–30 replicate the provisions relating to general cross-examination of the complainant concerning previous sexual history.[130] In *R. v DS*[131] the Northern Ireland Court of Appeal emphasised that applications for leave to cross-examine should be made well in advance and in writing in accordance with the Crown Court Rules.[132] In that case the trial judge refused to allow cross-examination arising out of a statement made by the complainant. In that statement, the fourth made to the police, the complainant had stated that she had had sexual intercourse with other members of her family, which contradicted earlier statements that confined the intercourse to three named relatives (including her father, the defendant). The Court of Appeal held that the omission to mention this in the earlier statements did not relate to sexual behaviour as defined, but to her inconsistent statements about who had sexually abused her. Accordingly the cross-examination should have been permitted, and the appeal was allowed.

32.65   Under art.81A of the Police and Criminal Evidence (Northern Ireland) Order 1989[133] the evidence of children, in the case of a sexual offence against

---

[126] SI 1999/2789 (NI 8). Section 7 of the Justice Act (Northern Ireland) 2011 extended eligibility for special measures for child witnesses aged 16 years to those aged 17.

[127] See Ch.27, above.

[128] A pilot scheme that began on May 13, 2013, for cases relating to offences alleged to have been committed within the Belfast City Council boundary was extended to all of Northern Ireland from November 11, 2013: see the Criminal Evidence (Northern Ireland) Order 1999 (Commencement No.8) Order 2013 (SI 2013/126 (c.8)).

[129] art.81B of the Police and Criminal Evidence (Northern Ireland) Order 1989 (SI 1989/1341 (NI 12)) (as inserted by art.5 of the Children's Evidence (Northern Ireland) Order 1995 (1995/757 (NI 3)) also prohibits such cross-examination by video link of any child who is an alleged victim or has witnessed the commission of the offence.

[130] See ss.41–43 of the Youth Justice and Criminal Evidence Act 1999, discussed in Ch.29, above.

[131] [2008] NICA 19.

[132] r.44H.

[133] SI 1989/1314 (NI 12), inserted by art.5 of the Children's Evidence (Northern Ireland) Order 1995.

a child aged under 17, shall be given by playing a video recording or by live link, with cross-examination by live link. Provided the video recording was made when the child was 17, the cross examination by live link will be permitted if the child has turned 18. In *R. v N*,[134] it was held that the failure to swear a 17-year-old witness (who had been 16 at the time of her video-recorded interview) before her cross-examination was fatal and the evidence was not admissible. The evidence in the video recording was admissible; however, for the purposes of cross-examination only a child under 14 can give evidence unsworn (see para.32.58, above).

Inconsistent statements

The Court of Appeal emphasised in *R. v A*[135] the need for a judge, when   **32.66** faced with a complainant who had previously made false accusations of sexual abuse, needed to ensure that the jury received sufficient guidance and warning at the appropriate time. It stated[136]:

> "a warning to exercise caution arising from inconsistencies in a complainant's case or from the making of false allegations, if it is to be fully meaningful, must be properly expressed in terms to make clear to the jury the need to be especially careful in the weighing up of the evidence. It should be given in the context of the review of the evidence rather than as a set piece at a later stage divorced from the evidence."[137]

Cross-admissibility and collusion

Following the decision in *Hutchinson*,[138] the Judicial Studies Board for   **32.67** Northern Ireland issued guidance to judges in relation to what is cross-admissible bad character evidence.[139] Although not interfering with the verdict, Gillen LJ indicated that the matter was fraught with difficulty and does require a degree of clarity, in relation both to the admissibility of the evidence generally—does it show propensity, or does it negative coincidence and rebut a defence (or both)?—and to the warnings and guidance that are needed, particularly that the jury should consider and dismiss contamination, innocent or otherwise, before considering how, if at all, the evidence of one complainant supports the evidence of the other, or others.

Third party material

The need for the defence to take an appropriate and timely approach to the   **32.68** third party disclosure procedure was emphasised by the Court of Appeal in

---

[134] [1998] NI 261 (following *Sharman* [1998] 1 Cr. App. R. 406).
[135] [2014] NICA 2.
[136] At [21].
[137] See also *Joshi* [2012] NICA 56.
[138] [2014] NICA 75.
[139] New para.4.7B (note 128).

R. v FN.[140] In that case, the judge refused a defence application for further consideration of disclosure that was made after the jury had been sworn and on the day the evidence was due to be heard. The Court of Appeal was critical of the casual approach taken to the issue by the defence, particularly as the focus of the late application had not been raised in the Defence Statement. The Court said that there is, however, an obligation on the trial judge to review disclosure as a trial progresses and new issues emerge, although such issues should be raised by way of an amended Defence Statement.

DELAY

32.69 In cases which involve a substantial delay between the date of the alleged offence and the trial, the Northern Ireland Court of Appeal has emphasised the need for judges to give proper directions to juries as to how they should approach the evidence. The Judicial Studies Board for Northern Ireland has given specific guidance on this.[141] However, the guidance is currently under review in light of the judgments of the Court of Appeal in *R. v W*[142] and *R. v McK.*[143] Previously, the more generalised direction was considered acceptable and no adverse comment was expressed about it in *Greene*[144] and *R. v JSK*,[145] and even in *R. v DS*,[146] where no direction on delay was given at all.[147]

32.70   Girvan LJ in *R. v W* emphasised that the counter-balance to the lack of any limitation period in the criminal justice system has to be the requirement for scrupulous care by the court in ensuring the jury appreciates the potential for unfairness to the defendant. He concluded by stating that counsel for the parties should make submissions to the judge as to the content of the judge's direction to the jury and in particular how the defendant may be prejudiced by the delay, and how the defendant may be prejudiced in relation to particular allegations in the specific context of the charges. Morgan LCJ in *R. v McK* reinforced the comments made in *R. v W* by emphasising that the jury needs to be fully aware of any prejudice, both general and specific, that the defendant may have in defending himself. Judges should also desist from suggesting that the delay, and the absence of witnesses or evidence, could have equally impacted on the prosecution case.

---

[140] [2012] NICA 38.
[141] *http://www.jsbni.com/Publications/BenchBook/Pages/default.aspx* [Accessed April 30, 2016], para.4.25.
[142] [2013] NICA 6.
[143] [2013] NICA 11.
[144] [2010] NICA 47.
[145] [2011] NICA 44.
[146] [2010] NICA 18.
[147] For an example of an approved direction, see *Joshi* [2012] NICA 56.

The Court of Appeal in *R. v SR*[148] held that in cases where there has been **32.71** delay in the trial process, as opposed to delay between the alleged incident and the complaint, due regard should be given to the complexity of the case when considering the period of delay; and that complexity is not confined to legal and factual issues but could include the non-availability for genuine reasons of a central witness. In that case, where the reasons for delay were university examinations and then psychiatric factors which impacted on the complainant's availability to give evidence, the Court allowed a prosecution appeal against an order staying proceedings as an abuse of process.

In addition to warnings concerning prejudice to the defendant resulting **32.72** from delay, in cases where the defendant is of good character, the fact that there have been no other similar allegations between the date of the alleged offences and the trial, is a matter that the jury should be told, and the defendant is entitled to ask the jury to give more than usual weight to his good character.[149]

The Court of Appeal in *R. v DPMC and DJW*[150] declined to admit the **32.73** evidence of an expert in autobiographical memory at the appeal, quoting with approval the England and Wales Court of Appeal in *Bowman*[151]:

"In our judgment it is on the very borderline of admissibility. Essentially the professor's evidence of the results of research into memories goes little further than is common sense and well within normal human experience. He accepted that a traumatic event occurring when a person is under the age of seven can be recalled by that person in adulthood."

Receiving Verdicts

The Court of Appeal have suggested on several occasions that judges should **32.74** not receive the verdicts on some counts on an indictment until such time as a jury has concluded its deliberations completely.[152] In *R. v S and C*,[153] Coughlin LJ stated:

"A jury must give separate consideration to and return a separate verdict in respect of individual counts but the overall evidence in a case may be such that views, for example, on credibility on one count may affect the jury's view on credibility on other counts. Before delivering their verdicts on the various counts, the jury should stand back and review preliminary conclusions on some of the counts which they may ultimately consider they must revisit having regard to conclusions reached in later deliberations on other counts. As happened in this case, once it has announced its verdicts on some counts, whether it be by way of acquittal or conviction, it will not be open to a jury to change its mind on their

[148] [2011] NICA 49. See also *Dyer v Watson* [2004] 1 A.C. 379 and *Konig v Germany* (1978) 2 EHRR 170.
[149] See *Hughes* [2008] NICA 17; *R. v AG* [2010] NICA 20; *McCalmont* [2010] NICA 27.
[150] [2010] NICA 22.
[151] [2006] EWCA Crim 417.
[152] See *Harbinson* [2012] NICA 20; *R. v A* [2014] NICA 2; *R. v S and C* [2015] NICA 51.
[153] *R. v S and C* [2015] NICA 51 at [25].

earlier determinations even if they wish to do so. For this reason trial judges should take care as to the risks of returning separate verdicts at different stages and invite the jury not to return their verdicts until they have concluded their deliberations on all counts."

ANNEX

EQUIVALENT SECTIONS IN SEXUAL OFFENCES ACT 2003 TO ARTICLES IN SEXUAL OFFENCES (NI) ORDER 2008

32.75   **SEXUAL OFFENCES (NI) ORDER 2008**

PART 1
INTRODUCTORY

1. TITLE AND COMMENCEMENT
2. INTERPRETATION – *SECTION 79 OF SEXUAL OFFENCES ACT 2003*
3. "CONSENT" – *SECTION 74*
4. "SEXUAL" – *SECTION 78*

PART 2
NON-CONSENSUAL SEXUAL OFFENCES

5. RAPE – *SECTION 1*
6. ASSAULT BY PENETRATION – *SECTION 2*
7. SEXUAL ASSAULT – *SECTION 3*
8. CAUSING A PERSON TO ENGAGE IN SEXUAL ACTIVITY WITHOUT CONSENT – *SECTION 4*
9. EVIDENTIAL PRESUMPTIONS ABOUT CONSENT – *SECTION 75*
10. CONCLUSIVE PRESUMPTIONS ABOUT CONSENT – *SECTION 76*
11. ARTICLES 9 AND 10: RELEVANT ACTS – *SECTION 77*

PART 3
SEXUAL OFFENCES AGAINST CHILDREN

12. RAPE OF A CHILD UNDER 13 – *SECTION 5*
13. ASSAULT OF A CHILD UNDER 13 BY PENETRATION – *SECTION 6*
14. SEXUAL ASSAULT OF A CHILD UNDER 13 – *SECTION 7*
15. CAUSING OR INCITING A CHILD UNDER 13 TO ENGAGE IN SEXUAL ACTIVITY – *SECTION 8*
16. SEXUAL ACTIVITY WITH A CHILD – *SECTION 9*
17. CAUSING OR INCITING A CHILD TO ENGAGE IN SEXUAL ACTIVITY – *SECTION 10*

18. ENGAGING IN SEXUAL ACTIVITY IN THE PRESENCE OF A CHILD – *SECTION 11*

19. CAUSING A CHILD TO WATCH A SEXUAL ACT – *SECTION 12*

20. SEXUAL OFFENCES AGAINST CHILDREN COMMITTED BY CHILDREN OR YOUNG PERSONS – *SECTION 13*

21. ARRANGING OR FACILITATING COMMISSION OF A SEX OFFENCE AGAINST A CHILD – *SECTION 14*

22. MEETING A CHILD FOLLOWING SEXUAL GROOMING ETC. (AMENDED BY S.89 JUSTICE ACT (NI) 2015 FROM JULY 24, 2015) – *SECTION 15*

22A. SEXUAL COMMUNICATION WITH A CHILD (INSERTED BY JUSTICE ACT (NI) 2015) – *SECTION 15A* (INSERTED BY S.67 SERIOUS CRIME ACT 2015)

23. ABUSE OF POSITION OF TRUST: SEXUAL ACTIVITY WITH A CHILD – *SECTION 16*

24. ABUSE OF POSITION OF TRUST: CAUSING A CHILD TO ENGAGE IN SEXUAL ACTIVITY – *SECTION 17*

25. ABUSE OF POSITION OF TRUST: SEXUAL ACTIVITY IN THE PRESENCE OF A CHILD – *SECTION 18*

26. ABUSE OF POSITION OF TRUST: CAUSING A CHILD TO WATCH A SEXUAL ACT – *SECTION 19*

27. ABUSE OF POSITION OF TRUST: ACTS DONE IN ENGLAND AND WALES OR SCOTLAND – *SECTION 20*

28. POSITIONS OF TRUST – *SECTION 21*

29. POSITIONS OF TRUST: INTERPRETATION – *SECTION 22*

30. ARTICLES 23 TO 26: EXCEPTION FOR SPOUSES AND CIVIL PARTNERS – *SECTION 23*

31. ARTICLES 23 TO 26: SEXUAL RELATIONSHIPS WHICH PRE-DATE POSITION OF TRUST – *SECTION 24*

32. SEXUAL ACTIVITY WITH A CHILD FAMILY MEMBER – *SECTION 25*

33. INCITING A CHILD FAMILY MEMBER TO ENGAGE IN SEXUAL ACTIVITY – *SECTION 26*

34. FAMILY RELATIONSHIPS – *SECTION 27*

35. ARTICLES 32 AND 33: EXCEPTION FOR SPOUSES AND CIVIL PARTNERS – *SECTION 28*

36. ARTICLES 32 AND 33: SEXUAL RELATIONSHIPS PRE-DATING FAMILY RELATIONSHIPS – *SECTION 29*

37. PAYING FOR SEXUAL SERVICES OF A CHILD – *SECTION 47*

38. CAUSING OR INCITING CHILD PROSTITUTION OR PORNOGRAPHY – *SECTION 48*

39. CONTROLLING A CHILD PROSTITUTE OR A CHILD INVOLVED IN PORNOGRAPHY – *SECTION 49*

40. ARRANGING OR FACILITATING CHILD PROSTITUTION OR PORNOGRAPHY – *SECTION 50*

41. ARTICLES 38 TO 40: INTERPRETATION – *SECTION 51*

42. INDECENT PHOTOGRAPHS OF PERSONS AGED 16 OR 17 – *SECTION 45*

PART 4
SEXUAL OFFENCES AGAINST A PERSON WITH A MENTAL DISORDER

43. Sexual activity with a person with a mental disorder impeding choice – Section 30
44. Causing or inciting a person, with a mental disorder impeding choice, to engage in sexual activity – Section 31
45. Engaging in sexual activity in the presence of a person with a mental disorder impeding choice – Section 32
46. Causing a person, with a mental disorder impeding choice, to watch a sexual act – Section 33
47. Inducement, threat or deception to procure sexual activity with a person with a mental disorder – Section 34
48. Causing a person with a mental disorder to engage in or agree to engage in sexual activity by inducement, threat or deception – Section 35
49. Engaging in sexual activity in the presence, procured by inducement, threat or deception, of a person with a mental disorder – Section 36
50. Causing a person with a mental disorder to watch a sexual act by inducement, threat or deception – Section 37
51. Care workers: sexual activity with a person with a mental disorder – Section 38
52. Care workers: causing or inciting sexual activity – Section 39
53. Care workers: sexual activity in the presence of a person with a mental disorder – Section 40
54. Care workers: causing a person with a mental disorder to watch a sexual act – Section 41
55. Care workers: interpretation – Section 42
56. Articles 51 to 54: exception for spouses and civil partners – Section 43
57. Articles 51 to 54: sexual relationships which pre-date care relationships – Section 44

PART 5
PROSTITUTION

58. Interpretation of this Part – Section 54
59. Loitering or soliciting for purposes of prostitution (repealed June 1, 2015) – near equivalent is Section 1(1) Street Offences Act 1959
60. Kerb-crawling – Section 1(1) Sexual Offences Act 1985 (repealed April 1, 2010)
60. Soliciting – Section 51A (inserted by Policing and Crime Act 2009)

61. Persistent soliciting – *Section 2(1) Sexual Offences Act 1985* (repealed April 1, 2010)
62. Causing or inciting prostitution for gain – *Section 52*
63. Controlling prostitution for gain – *Section 53*
64. Keeping a brothel used for prostitution – *Section 55*
64A. Paying for sexual services of a prostitute subject to force (inserted by Policing and Crime Act 2009, repealed June 1, 2015) – *Section 53A*
64A. Paying for sexual services (inserted by Human Trafficking and Exploitation (Criminal Justice and Support for Victims) Act (NI) 2015 from June 1, 2015) – *No equivalent*

PART 6
MISCELLANEOUS SEXUAL OFFENCES

65. Administering a substance with intent – *Section 61*
66. Committing an offence with intent to commit a sexual offence – *Section 62*
67. Trespass with intent to commit a sexual offence – *Section 63*
68. Sex with an adult relative: penetration – *Section 64*
69. Sex with an adult relative: consenting to penetration – *Section 65*
70. Exposure – *Section 66*
71. Voyeurism – *Section 67*
72. Voyeurism: interpretation – *Section 68*
73. Intercourse with an animal – *Section 69*
74. Sexual penetration of a corpse – *Section 70*
75. Sexual activity in a public lavatory – *Section 71*

PART 7
SUPPLEMENTARY AND GENERAL

76. Offences outside the United Kingdom – *Section 72*
77. Exceptions to aiding, abetting and counselling – *Section 73*

CHAPTER 33

THE SENTENCING OF SEX OFFENDERS: THE DEFINITIVE GUIDELINE

Introduction...................................... 33.01
Sentencing under the Sexual
   Offences Act 2003 and Historic
   Cases: General............................. 33.06
Approach to Harm and Culpability 33.12
Ostensible or Apparent Consent...... 33.15
Offences Committed Online 33.18

Increase in Sentencing Levels for
   Some Offences of Rape................ 33.19
Approach to Good Character and/
   or Exemplary Conduct................. 33.20
Other Relevant Guidelines............... 33.21
The Principle in *Canavan*................. 33.24

INTRODUCTION

In 2012, the Sentencing Council commenced a timely review of the *Sexual* **33.01** *Offences Act 2003: Definitive Guideline*, which had been in place since issued by the Sentencing Guidelines Council on April 30, 2007. Following a thorough consultation process, the Council issued a new *Definitive Guideline* on February 12, 2014. This guideline applies to all those aged 18 or over convicted of sexual offences, whenever committed, who are sentenced on or after April 1, 2014. Offenders under 18 will in due course be covered by a separate youth guideline on which the Sentencing Council launched a consultation in May 2016 (the consultation document is available on the Council's website). Until the youth guideline is published, an explanatory note issued by the Council in parallel with the adult guideline[1] explains that, when sentencing offenders under 18, sentencers should continue to follow Pt 7 of the Sentencing Guidelines Council's guideline, which relates to sentencing young offenders for offences with a lower statutory maximum under the Sexual Offences Act 2003.[2]

---

[1] *Sexual offences—offenders under 18: Explanatory note.* The note is available on the Sentencing Council's website.

[2] See further paras 4.151 and following, above. In any event, the guidance given in *R. v H* [2011] EWCA Crim 2753 makes plain that the youth and immaturity of an offender at the time of the offence is to be regarded as personal mitigation.

33.02   We have included the relevant parts of the Sentencing Council's Definitive Guideline in the chapters of this work dealing with specific offences. In this chapter we summarise the main changes.[3]

33.03   The Council considered that a new guideline was needed to reflect developments since the implementation of the Sexual Offences Act 2003 on May 1, 2004. A clearer picture had emerged as to the way offences under the Act were being used by the courts. In addition, there were areas where the nature of offending had changed, e.g. the increased use of technology to facilitate the sexual exploitation and grooming of children. There was a better understanding of offenders' behaviour when targeting children. Furthermore, the Council was conscious of the need for judges and magistrates involved in this complex area of sentencing to have relevant and up-to-date guidance against the background of an increased volume of cases coming before the courts.

33.04   The Council sought views on (i) the main factors that reflect the harm caused to the victim by a sexual offence and the culpability of the offender, which lead the court to decide the starting-point for sentencing the offence, and (ii) the approach and structure of the guidance and how this should be tailored to the offences.

33.05   A key issue to emerge from research commissioned by the Council was a strong desire on the part of victims for the criminal justice system, and in particular the sentencing process, to demonstrate an accurate understanding of the overarching and long-term harmful effects of sexual violence and abuse, and how this impacts on the life of the victim and their family.[4]

SENTENCING UNDER THE SEXUAL OFFENCES ACT 2003 AND HISTORIC CASES: GENERAL

33.06   As noted above, the Sentencing Council's guideline applies in respect of those aged 18 or over convicted of sexual offences, whenever committed,[5] who are sentenced on or after April 1, 2014. It follows that the previous guideline issued by the Sentencing Guidelines Council will only now be relevant in

---

[3] We are grateful to Michelle Crotty, Head of the Office of the Sentencing Council during the consultation and implementation of the Council's guideline, for permission to use her summary of the key changes, which we have paraphrased.

[4] See *Sexual Offences Guideline Consultation,* p.10.

[5] For the principles underpinning the correct approach to sentencing in historic cases, see *R. v H* [2011] EWCA Crim 2753, where Lord Judge CJ stated (at [47(2)]): "Sentence will be imposed at the date of the sentencing hearing on the basis of the legislative principles then current, and by measured reference to any definitive guidelines relevant to the situation revealed by established facts." The principles his Lordship enunciated are set out in Annex B to the Sentencing Council guideline (for which, see Appendix B, below). For an explanation of those principles and the meaning of "measured reference", see *Clifford* [2014] EWCA Crim 2245 and *Attorney General's Reference (No.27 of 2015)* [2015] EWCA Crim 1538. The relevant law is set out more fully in paras 30.109 and following, above.

appeals brought out of time against sentences passed before April 1, 2014.[6]

By s.125(1) of the Coroners and Justice Act 2009, every court must, in sentencing an offender follow any sentencing guidelines relevant to the offender's case "unless the court is satisfied that it would be contrary to the interests of justice to do so".[7] This provision does not restrict any power which enables a court to deal with a mentally disordered offender in the manner it considers to be most appropriate in the circumstances.[8] **33.07**

By s.125(3), the court's duty in all cases includes imposing upon the defendant, in accordance with the relevant guideline, a sentence which is within the offence range. Where the guideline describes categories of case, the court must decide which of the categories most closely resembles the defendant's case in order to identify the starting-point within the offence range, unless the court is of the opinion that none of the categories sufficiently resemble the defendant's case.[9] Where a case concerns an offence for which there is no guideline, it is appropriate to consider an analogous guideline.[10] **33.08**

It is inappropriate for a judge to follow a guideline not yet in force.[11] In *Nicholson*[12] the Court of Appeal emphasised that a judge is obliged to apply the guideline at the time of sentencing even if a more lenient outcome might have resulted under a previous or future guideline. **33.09**

The judge must identify any definitive sentencing guideline relevant to the offender's case and explain how the court discharged any duty imposed on it by s.125 of the Coroners and Justice Act 2009.[13] If the court does not follow the guideline because it is of the opinion that it would be contrary to the interests of justice to do so, it must state why it was of that opinion.[14] The flexibility built into a guideline does not entitle a judge to disregard it on inappropriate grounds.[15] Where a judge falls into serious error by departing from a guideline without explanation and fails properly to reflect the gravity or totality of the offending and the aggravating features, the Attorney **33.10**

---

[6] And to the sentencing of offenders under the age of 18: see para.33.01, above.

[7] Section 172(1) of the Criminal Justice Act 2003, which imposed a duty on every court to have regard to any guidelines which were relevant to the offender's case, was repealed on the coming into force of s.125 of the 2009 Act on April 6, 2010. However, it continues to apply to offences committed before that date: see the Coroners and Justice Act 2009 s.177 and Sch.22, para.27.

[8] Criminal Justice Act 2003 s.125(7).

[9] Criminal Justice Act 2003 s.125(4).

[10] *Kavanagh* [2008] EWCA Crim 855; *Lewis* [2012] EWCA Crim 1071.

[11] *Boakye* [2013] 1 Cr. App. R.(S.) 2. See also *R. v Mark L* [2014] EWCA Crim 1669, where the judge did make inappropriate reference to the guideline which was not yet in force, but the Court of Appeal was satisfied that he applied the current guideline.

[12] [2014] EWCA Crim 834.

[13] Criminal Justice Act 2003 s.174(1)(a), (2)(a), (6).

[14] Criminal Justice Act 2003 s.174(1)(a), (2)(aa), (6).

[15] *Healey* [2012] EWCA Crim 1005.

General may refer the sentence to the Court of Appeal as unduly lenient.[16]

33.11   When it comes to the interpretation of terms used in a guideline, the court
should look at the guideline as finally produced as opposed to the discussions
that took place during the consultation period. For instance, in *Attorney
General's Reference (No.51 of 2015) (Whitmore)*,[17] the defence had
researched the production of the Sentencing Council's guideline for rape and
used the consultation documents to argue that the words of the category 2
factor "the victim is particularly vulnerable due to personal circumstances"
required some kind of condition which was "immutable", for example a
permanent physical disability or vulnerability through age. The judge had
agreed with this approach. The Court of Appeal, however, decided that the
words of the guideline were clear and plainly covered the position of a
complainant who was young, female, alone at night and very intoxicated.

Approach to Harm and Culpability

33.12   The guideline uses a number of models for addressing harm and culpability,
each different from the model used in the previous guideline:

(a) *Baseline of inherent harm and culpability*: The model used for the
majority of offences, including rape and sexual assault, has a lowest
level (a baseline) where inherent harm and culpability are assumed.
The Council sought, to some extent, to move away from the notion
that there is a hierarchy of rape (etc.) reflecting different levels of
seriousness. This has led to the removal of the words "greater" and
"lesser" and "higher" and "lower" when identifying harm and
culpability.

In consequence, the guideline recognises that all rape is harmful
to the victim by making the assumption that there is *always* a
baseline of harm. This assumption is reflected in category 3 harm,
which covers offences in which none of harm factors identified in
categories 1 and 2 is present. Category 3 is designed to indicate to
the sentencer that once an offender has been found guilty of rape,
they do not need to identify additional factors for the offence to be
deemed harmful or serious. The Council felt that the violation of the
victim through the act of rape is harm in itself, and it would be
unhelpful to articulate cases where no category 1 or 2 factors are
present as involving "lesser harm" since these offences are all
inherently harmful. The Council did, however, recognise that the
level of harm caused by rape can vary and so categories 1 and 2
build upon the baseline of harm assumed in category 3.

---

[16] See *Attorney General's Reference. (No.80 of 2015) (Lawrence Fernandes)* [2015] EWCA
Crim 2026.
[17] [2015] EWCA Crim 1699.

In respect of this category of offences, the Council adopted the decision-making process for sentencing that it developed for the *Assault: Definitive Guideline*. It is a step-by-step process which determines the method of setting the offence level. There are nine steps to be followed for each offence. The key drivers at the outset of the process for determining the offence category are harm and culpability. The structure for determining these varies according to the offence concerned, so that the guideline is tailored to the particular offending behaviour.

An exhaustive list of factors under both harm and culpability indicates the severity and so the category level of the offence. The lowest level of harm and culpability is the absence of any of these factors. These offences have a numerical harm category and a culpability category indicated by letter. The overall offence category is a combination of both (e.g. "category 2A") which is read from a grid that cross-references harm and culpability.

(b) *Raised harm and raised culpability*: This model is a variation on the one used by the Sentencing Council in the *Assault: Definitive Guideline*. It identifies factors that indicate raised harm and/or culpability. The highest starting points and ranges, in category 1, are reserved for cases where both raised harm and raised culpability are present; category 2 applies where there is either raised harm or raised culpability and category 3 where there is neither. This model is used for the offences of meeting a child following sexual grooming (s.15); administering a substance with intent (s.61); trespass with intent to commit a sexual offence (s.63); sex with an adult relative (ss.64 and 65); exposure (s.66); and voyeurism (s.67).

(c) *Indecent images of children*: Harm is assessed on the basis of the level of the images involved. However, following discussion with experts from the ACPO grading panel, the Sentencing Council reduced the levels from the five set out in the case of *Oliver, Hartrey and Baldwin*[18] to three. The resultant categories of image are:
Category A: This broadly coincides with *Oliver* levels 4 and 5 (images involving penetrative sexual activity, sexual activity with an animal and sadism).
Category B: This broadly coincides with *Oliver* level 3 (images involving non-penetrative activity).
Category C: This covers other indecent images not falling within either A or B.
Culpability is assessed on the basis of what the offender was doing with the images and is split into three categories of role: possession, distribution and production. For a fuller explanation, see paras 8.18 and following, above.

[18] [2003] 1 Cr. App. R. 28.

Greater focus on harm to the victim whether physical and/or psychological

33.13   The Sentencing Council's guideline focuses on the extent of the harm caused by the offence to the victim, rather than the nature of the physical activity involved. For instance, in the guideline for sexual assault (s.3 of the 2003 Act), if the victim suffered severe psychological or physical harm this will take the offence into the highest sentencing category. Similarly, the vulnerability of the victim is treated as a major indicator of the harm.

33.14   The guideline's approach to determining the offence category directs the sentencing court, as a first step, to consider the main factual elements of the offence in terms of harm to the victim. This approach differs from the SGC's guideline in that gravity is not to be evaluated by considering just the physical nature of the offence. The Sentencing Council was concerned that the use of sentence labels based solely on activity does not fully reflect the seriousness or complexity of the offence.

Ostensible or Apparent Consent

33.15   In *Attorney General's References (Nos 11 and 12 of 2012) (Channer and Monteiro)*,[19] Pitchford LJ said:

> "'Ostensible consent' and 'willingness' are terms which, in the context of offences against the young in particular, are susceptible to misunderstanding and, even if accurately used, are liable to obscure the true nature of the encounter between the offender and the victim . . . ".

The new guideline reflects this in that it moves away from the language of "ostensible consent" so that the focus in relation to children aged between 13 and 15 is placed not on the behaviour of the victim but on the behaviour and culpability of the offender. Accordingly, harm is determined without the need to consider the child's behaviour or their understanding of their "relationship" with the offender.

33.16   It follows that the Sentencing Council has moved away from regarding ostensible consent as a mitigating factor when the victim is under 16. This will apply particularly to offences of sexual activity with a child under s.9 of the Sexual Offences Act 2003, but it will also be highly relevant in rape cases where there has been grooming and psychological coercion and the circumstances have limited or distorted the victim's appreciation or understanding of their role in the sexual relationship and the true nature of what occurred.[20] As Lord Thomas CJ explained in *Attorney General's Reference (No.53 of 2013) (Neil Wilson)*[21]:

> "It has been clear since at least the Offences Against the Person Act 1861, and subsequent nineteenth century legislation, that the purpose of Parliament in

---

[19] [2012] EWCA Crim 1119, at [34].
[20] cf. *Ali* and *Ahshraf* [2015] EWCA Crim 1279.
[21] [2013] EWCA Crim 2544 at [19].

passing legislation to make it a crime punishable with imprisonment to have sexual relations with those under 16 was to protect those under 16. Indeed the Criminal Law Amendments *[sic]* Act 1885 makes it expressly clear that that was the purpose of the legislation. That can be seen from the preamble to the Act and was made clear by this court in *R.* v *Tyrrell* [1894] 1 QB 710.

That long-standing principle is well-known. The reduction of punishment on the basis that the person who needed protection encouraged the commission of an offence is therefore simply wrong. We agree with the submission of the Attorney General that an underage person who encourages sexual relations with her needs more protection, not less. Accepting that as the basis for sentencing for the reasons we have explained, the fact that the offender took advantage of what he asserted the victim did aggravated the offence."

In that case, the offender had pleaded guilty to sexual activity with a child contrary to s.9 of the 2003 Act. At the sentencing hearing, prosecuting counsel had made a fundamental error in describing the 13-year old victim as "predatory", thereby suggesting that the initiation of sexual activity by the victim was a mitigating factor.

This principle would apply equally to cases of rape where young girls with **33.17** troubled upbringings have been targeted and groomed by gangs[22] or where an older man, such as a step-father or an uncle, has groomed a teenager.[23] The guideline reflects greater awareness of the phenomenon of grooming and/or the use of the internet to facilitate sex offending. For example, in respect of rape of a child under 13 (s.5 of the 2003 Act), grooming behaviour will place the offender in the higher level of culpability and therefore attract a higher starting point.

OFFENCES COMMITTED ONLINE

Following on from the consideration given to remote offending in *Prince* **33.18** *(Shayne)*,[24] the guideline confirms that the approach to sentencing and the starting points and ranges apply equally where the offender commits the offence remotely over the internet. Thus the guideline for the offences of sexual activity with a child and causing or inciting a child to engage in sexual activity (ss.9 and 10 of the 2003 Act) provides: "This guideline also applies to offences committed remotely/online." It is, however, regrettable that no similar statement appears in the guideline for the offence of causing or inciting a child under 13 to engage in sexual activity (s.8): see para.3.51, above.

INCREASE IN SENTENCING LEVELS FOR SOME OFFENCES OF RAPE

In some cases the application of the Sentencing Council's guideline may lead **33.19** to higher sentences in respect of rape than under the previous SGC guideline.

[22] See e.g. *Karrar* [2015] EWCA Crim 850.
[23] See e.g. *Robinson* [2011] EWCA Crim 916.
[24] [2013] EWCA Crim 1768.

Where an offender is convicted of a campaign of rape, against single or multiple victims, the courts are directed that a sentence of 20 years or more should be passed. Additionally, the extreme nature of one or more category 2 harm factors or the extreme impact of a combination of those factors may elevate the offence to category 1 harm. Where this is combined with an increased level of culpability, the starting point for a single offence will be 15 years. The worst cases of assault by penetration (s.2 of the 2003 Act) may receive the same sentences as rape because of the physical harm that will be caused where large or dangerous objects are used by the offender.

Approach to good Character and/or Exemplary Conduct

33.20 This factor is retained in the guideline but is subject to two forms of explanatory wording in order to provide transparency as to the way in which judges reflect good character in a sentence. Where the offence carries a statutory maximum of under 14 years, the guideline states:

> "Previous good character/exemplary conduct is different from having no previous convictions. The more serious the offence, the less the weight which should normally be attributed to this factor. Where previous good character/exemplary conduct has been used to facilitate the offence, this mitigation should not normally be allowed and such conduct may constitute an aggravating factor."

A classic example of good character being used to facilitate the offence is the misuse of celebrity status.[25] Where the offence carries a statutory maximum of 14 years or more, the guideline additionally states:

> "In the context of this offence previous good character/exemplary conduct should not normally be given any significant weight and will not normally justify a reduction in what would otherwise be the appropriate sentence."

The principle that only limited weight should be attached to previous good character cannot be avoided by enhancing its value by combining it with the courage shown by entering a plea of guilty.[26]

Other Relevant Guidelines

33.21 There are other guidelines which will be relevant in appropriate circumstances:

Domestic violence

33.22 The *Overarching Principles: Domestic Violence Definitive Guideline* applies to offences sentenced on or after December 18, 2006. For the purpose of this guideline, domestic violence means:

[25] See *Attorney General's Reference (No.38 of 2013) (Stuart Hall)* [2013] EWCA Crim 1450.
[26] *Attorney General's Reference (No.115 of 2014) (Long)* [2015] EWCA Crim 200.

"Any incident of threatening behaviour, violence or abuse [psychological, physical, sexual, financial or emotional] between adults who are or have been intimate partners or family members, regardless of gender or sexuality."

This was definition of "domestic violence" adopted by the Government in 2004. However the definition was revised as follows in 2013[27]:

"Any incident or pattern of incidents of controlling coercive or threatening behaviour, violence or abuse between those aged 16 or over who are or have been intimate partners or family members, regardless of gender or sexuality. This can encompass, but is not limited to, the following types of abuse:
1. psychological
2. physical
3. sexual
4. financial
5. emotional
Controlling behaviour is: a range of acts designed to make a person subordinate and/or dependant by isolating them from sources of support, exploiting their resources and capacities for personal gain, depriving them of the means needed for independence, resistance and escape and regulating their everyday behaviour.
Coercive behaviour is: an act or a pattern of acts of assaults, threats, humiliation and intimidation or other abuse that is used to harm, punish, or frighten their victim.
Family members are defined as mother, father, son, daughter, brother, sister and grandparents whether directly related, in-laws or step-family. However, this is not an exhaustive list and may also be extended to uncles, aunts and cousins etc."

The guideline makes clear that offences committed in a domestic context should be regarded as being no less serious than offences committed in a non-domestic context. Indeed, because an offence has been committed in a domestic context, there are likely to be aggravating factors present that make it more serious.

Young offenders

The *Overarching Principles—Sentencing Youths: Definitive Guideline* applies   **33.23** to the sentencing of young offenders on or after November 30, 2009.[28] In addition, as noted in para.33.01, above, Part 7 of the original Sentencing

---

[27] This is the Government definition of domestic violence as revised in 2013. It is taken from the CPS's *Domestic Abuse Guidelines for Prosecutors*, which are available at *http://www.cps. gov.uk/legal/d_to_g/domestic_abuse_guidelines_for_prosecutors/£a02* [Accessed April 30, 2016].

[28] For a recent example of a case where the Court of Appeal had the opportunity to deal with sentencing a youth aged 15 at the time for rape of a child under 13, see *R. v H* [2015] EWCA Crim 1579. The complainant was aged 12. The appellant pleaded guilty at the first opportunity on the basis that the offences were entirely consensual. In his commentary on the case at [2016] Crim. L.R. 139, Professor Andrew Ashworth points out that the judgment makes no reference to two important paragraphs in the guideline. Paragraph 11.11 reminds sentencers of the statutory requirement that custody should not be imposed unless a youth rehabilitation order with intensive supervision and surveillance cannot be justified. Paragraph 11.2 summarises the law by stating that the statutory tests for custody are likely to be satisfied only where a custodial sentence will be more effective in preventing offending by children and young persons.

Guidelines Council guideline continues to apply to the sentencing of young offenders for offences with a lower statutory maximum under the Sexual Offences Act 2003. This has sometimes been overlooked by those who have assumed that the Sentencing Council's *Definitive Guideline* replaced the previous guideline in its entirety.[29] Furthermore, whenever sentencing an offender aged under 18, a court must have regard to the principal aim of the youth justice system to prevent offending by children and young persons[30] and the welfare of the offender.[31]

The Principle in Canavan: Offender may be Sentenced Only for Offences of which he has been Convicted or which he has Admitted

33.24   It can be especially difficult to frame an indictment in cases involving multiple offences committed against a child over a period of perhaps years, where the complainant is unable to recall other than in perhaps vague terms when the various offences took place. How should the prosecution proceed in such cases? As explained in paras 3.24 and following, above, the aim should be to draft an indictment that identifies the alleged offences as specifically as possible but is not so lengthy and complicated as to make the trial, and the jury's task, unmanageable. One way to achieve this is to rely upon specimen charges. However, in *Canavan*[32] the Court of Appeal held that it is a fundamental principle that a person should be sentenced only for the offences of which he has been convicted, or which he has admitted, and not for other offences of which those were specimens. The Court clearly appreciated that its decision would encourage prosecutors to include more counts in their indictments, so that there would be sufficient proof of the offender's criminality to enable the court to pass an appropriate sentence. However, it did not think this "need be unduly burdensome or render the trial unmanageable". But the decision created a dilemma for prosecutors and the courts in cases involving multiple offences, in which an accurate picture of the defendant's criminality could be given only by framing the indictment in a way that would require the defendant to plead to too many offences, or the jury to bring in verdicts in respect of too many counts. It is inevitable that, in at least some cases, the need to ensure a fair trial and the practicalities of trial management will compel the prosecutor to draw up an indictment that gives something less than the full picture.[33]

33.25   This problem has been mitigated, if not wholly resolved, by the amendment of the Criminal Procedure Rules ("CPR") in 2007 to permit more than

[29] cf. *R. v GB* [2015] EWCA Crim 1501.
[30] Crime and Disorder Act 1998 s.37(1).
[31] Children and Young Persons Act 1933 s.41(1).
[32] [1998] 1 Cr. App. R. 79; and see *Clark* [1996] 2 Cr. App. R.(S.) 351; *Tovey and Smith* [2005] EWCA Crim 530; *A v R. (Rev 2)* [2015] EWCA Crim 177.
[33] cf. *Tovey and Smith* [2005] EWCA Crim 530 at [36].

one incident of the same offence to be charged in a single count if the incidents taken together amount to a course of conduct having regard to the time, place or purpose of their commission: see now r.10.2(2) of the CPR 2015, discussed in paras 19.22 and following, above. The Criminal Procedure Rules Committee stated that this facility may be used "when, for example, a defendant is alleged to have repeatedly assaulted the same victim in the same way over a period of time".[34] The Committee's intention in creating the new rule was to take account, amongst other things, of the potential of the old rules to create a perceived unfairness to a victim of multiple offending where, out of many alleged offences, only a few were prosecuted as examples, giving the impression that the victim's distress had been underestimated or that he or she had not been believed.[35] Valuable guidance on the application of r.10.2(2) was given in *A v R. (Rev 2)*,[36] where Fulford LJ, giving the judgment of the Court of Appeal, said:

> "the purpose underpinning multiple counts . . . is to enable the prosecution to reflect the defendant's alleged criminality when the offences are so similar and numerous that it is inappropriate to indict each occasion, or a large number of different occasions, in separate charges. This provision allows the prosecution to reflect the offending in these circumstances in a single count rather than a number of specimen counts. However, when the prosecution fails to specify a sufficient minimum number of occasions within the multiple incident count or counts, they are not making proper use of this procedure. In cases of sustained abuse, it will often be unhelpful to draft the count as representing, potentially, no more than two incidents. Indeed, in this case, if there had been a multiple incident count alleging, for example *'on not less than five occasions'* with an alternative of one or more specimen counts relating to single incidents for the jury to consider if they were unsure the offending had occurred on multiple occasions, the judge would have had a solid basis for understanding the ambit of the jury's verdict and he would been able to pass an appropriate sentence. Therefore, the prosecution needs to ensure that there are one or more sufficiently broad course of conduct counts, or a mix of individual counts and course of conduct counts, such that the judge will be able to sentence the defendant appropriately on the basis of his criminality as revealed by the counts on which he is convicted. In most cases it will be unnecessary for the counts to be numerous, but they should be sufficient in number to enable the judge to reflect the seriousness of the offending by reference to the central factors in the case: *e.g.* the number of victims, the nature of the offending and the length of time over which it extended. Therefore, in drafting the indictment, a balance needs to be struck between including sufficient counts to give the court adequate sentencing powers and unduly burdening the indictment. As the editors of *Archbold Criminal Pleading Evidence and Practice* 2015 at paragraph 1-225 have observed, the indictment must be drafted in such a way as to leave no room for misinterpretation of a guilty verdict and regard must be had to the possible views reached by the jury and to the position of the judge, so as to enable realistic sentencing."

---

[34] See guidance to the Rules, dated March 27, 2007.

[35] Taken from a note prepared by the Secretariat to the Committee dated March 27, 2007 and published with the guidance, above.

[36] [2015] EWCA Crim 177 at [47].

In *A v R. (Rev 2)* the Court held that, where a multiple-counts indictment under r.10.2(2) failed to specify a minimum number of occasions on which the offending was alleged to have happened, so that the sentencing judge could not know how many times the jury believed the offence to have been committed, fairness would require the judge to sentence on the basis that it was more than once, but no more than twice.

33.26   The fundamental principle set out in *Canavan* is, however, still frequently overlooked by the courts. A good example is *Hartley*,[37] in which the appellant was convicted on two counts alleging that he had sexual intercourse with a neighbour's daughter. The complainant's evidence was that the abuse fell into two periods: a few months in the summer of 1980 when she was 11, and a further period of months in 1981 when she was 12. During both periods, sexual intercourse took place two or three times a week. The first count in the indictment related to the period in 1980 and the second to the period in 1981. Neither count related to an identifiable, specific occasion. When sentencing, the judge rejected the appellant's submission that he had been convicted of only two offences, saying that he had to take into account the whole period of time involved and the entirety of the appellant's relationship with the complainant. On appeal, the Crown accepted that *Canavan* was clear authority that an offender can be sentenced only for that of which he has been convicted, but nonetheless sought, unsuccessfully, to uphold the sentence on two alternative bases.

33.27   First, relying on an exception identified in *Canavan* itself, it argued that the appellant had assented to the two counts being treated as representative of a longer course of conduct and to a guilty verdict being taken as a verdict of guilt of that entire course of conduct. The Court of Appeal accepted that this is in principle a permissible approach. Further, the Crown had from the outset presented the case as one of specimen or representative counts and the Court had little doubt that the judge had left it to the jury on the same basis. However, this approach will work only if the defendant explicitly assents to it, and that had not happened here. One might add that it will be rare for such explicit assent to be given, as there will generally be no advantage to the defendant in giving it; it would certainly be unsafe for a prosecutor to rely on assent being forthcoming or, if given at the outset, being maintained as the case unfolds.[38]

---

[37] [2011] EWCA Crim 1299. See also *R. v A.(N.) (Attorney General's Reference. (No.1 of 2011))* [2011] EWCA Crim 930, in which the defendant was convicted of 16 counts of rape of his wife, but the court sentenced on the basis that he had raped her once or twice a week over a period of two years; *Clifford (Frank Maxwell)* [2014] EWCA Crim 2245, where the judge aggravated the sentence for eight indecent assaults in the light of bad character evidence admitted during the trial, involving young women of a similar age to the victims who gave evidence of assaults of a similar type; *Pipe* [2014] EWCA Crim 2570, discussed in paras 4.43 and following, above.

[38] Though see *R. v BDG* [2012] EWCA Crim 1283, in which the four counts were preferred as specimens, on the basis that the assaults had happened so often that the complainant could not remember them all, and defence counsel expressly invited the judge to sentence on the basis that they had occurred on nine or ten occasions. The resulting sentence was upheld on the basis of the exception identified in *Hartley*.

Alternatively, the Crown argued that the two counts in *Hartley* fell within   **33.28**
what is now r.10.2(2) of the CPR, referred to above. The Court rejected this
argument too, on the basis that the two counts did not charge a course of
conduct but rather single offences. It said that to fall within r.10.2(2), a count
must make it clear that what is charged is a course of conduct and indeed the
period over which the conduct persisted. Whilst such a count may be of
assistance in some cases of sexual misbehaviour persisted in over a period,
the Court drew attention to the necessity that the result is not a verdict which
is impossible to interpret. Further, in the often encountered case of allegations of a course of conduct over a long period where it is a possible
conclusion that there was but a single incident, it will normally be appropriate to include not only a course of conduct count but also a single count
in relation to the same period, so that the basis of any verdict can be
clear.

The Court in *Hartley* went on to consider whether any general assistance   **33.29**
might be given as to the framing of indictments in cases of this sort[39]:

> "This is not a new problem. We accept that it is a very common situation and we
> accept that *Canavan* does create significant difficulties for courts and thus also
> for prosecutors. That is particularly so in cases of sexual offending because a
> great many of them are of allegations of a course of conduct involving multiple
> but unidentified instances; probably rather more are of that kind than are of
> single incidents.
>
> We do not think that it is possible to attempt any general statement of how
> indictments ought to be framed in the very wide range of cases that come before
> the courts. Everything in reality depends on the facts of the individual case, on
> what is alleged and on what issue is raised by the defendant. We have been
> reminded that there exist two new potential procedures. One we have already
> referred to, the Criminal Procedure Rules and we add nothing to what we have
> said about those. There is also now in existence the Domestic Violence (Crime
> and Victims) Act 2004 which in sections 17 to 19 does provide in some cases for
> an order to be made for representative counts to remain on the indictment and
> in the event of conviction for guilt of outstanding instances to be determined by
> the judge without the jury . . . [B]ut we draw attention to the fact that [those
> provisions] are limited in application. There are strict conditions for when they
> can be employed and in particular they can be employed only where otherwise
> the indictment would be of such a size as to be impracticable for the jury to cope
> with. It seems to us much more likely that in general terms the problem of which
> this case is an example can normally be dealt with by the framing of an
> indictment which does not contain an enormous number of counts but does
> contain sufficient to enable the judge to pass sentence on a basis which
> sufficiently represents what really happened. More than that we do not attempt
> to say, beyond perhaps this. Where specific incidents are capable of identification,
> however exiguously, for example 'the time the vase broke', or 'the time we went
> by train to Brighton', then ordinarily we would expect the indictment to contain
> a count referable and identifiably referable to that event so that the jury can
> determine it. That of course is subject to not, if there are hundreds of them,
> overloading the indictment with more counts than the jury can be expected to
> determine. Generally it is necessary for those who are framing indictments to pay

---

[39] At [21]–[22] per the Vice President, Hughes LJ.

attention to any issues flagged up by what the defendant has said either in interview with the police or later in a defence statement. Ordinarily we would suggest where there is simply a complaint of a course of conduct over a period of months, often years, more than a single count for each period is usually appropriate, although one per year may well suffice if the alleged period is extended. But the overall principle is simply that regard must be had in an intelligent way to the possible views of the case at which a jury might arrive and to the position of the judge in due course should there be convictions. If thought is given to those questions we have little doubt that it will normally be possible to frame an indictment in a manner which enables the sentencing to be realistic and complies with the strict rules of law as set out in *R v Canavan*."

33.30   Despite these clear words, indictments are still being preferred that fail to particularise the allegations so as properly to reflect what the complainant says happened, with the result that on conviction the principle in *Canavan* prevents the court imposing a sentence that fully reflects the extent of the offending. An example is *Hobson*,[40] where the appellant was alleged to have indecently assaulted the complainants K and N, two sisters, in the same way on a large number of occasions over a period of years, but the "woefully defective"[41] indictment contained just one specimen count in relation to each complainant. In evidence, the complainants differentiated between various particular incidents by giving details such as the location of the offence, the occasion of it, and who else was there. Nobody suggested amending the indictment to reflect this evidence. It was held on appeal that it had been incumbent on the judge, in those circumstances, to direct the jury that they had to be agreed about a particular occasion before they could convict, and it was not sufficient that some jurors were satisfied in relation to one occasion and others in relation to another. The Court of Appeal said that, as the complainants each alleged repeated conduct over many years, specimen counts were in principle appropriate. Moreover, the defence had made no request with respect to any of the specimen counts for the particulars to be identified with greater precision. Nonetheless, when giving evidence, both complainants spoke with some particularity about particular occasions. Yet in directing the jury, the judge did not tell them that they had to be unanimous about the same incident. Without a direction to that effect, it was possible that the jury were not in fact in agreement, in which case the verdict was unsafe. The Court said[42]:

"No doubt in most cases where a specimen count is relied on, it is enough for the judge to tell the jury, as the judge did in this case, that they may convict if they are sure that the offence has been committed at least once. Where the complainant cannot particularise any specific incident and merely alleges a pattern of similar conduct, the question for the jury will be whether they are sure that the account of the complainant is reliable. There will be no room for the jury to focus on one incident rather than another because no single occasion is

[40] [2013] EWCA Crim 819.
[41] James Richardson QC in *Criminal Law Week*, Issue 28, July 22, 2013, p.1.
[42] At [23]–[25].

sufficiently distinct, and it would be meaningless and unhelpful to tell the jury that they had to be sure in relation to the same incident.

However, where the complainant gives evidence identifying specific occasions alleged to be part of a pattern of conduct and there is evidence before the jury which could cause a reasonable jury to acquit on the specimen charge but convict on the particularised occasion or vice versa, then it is possible that the jury is not at one on any specific occasion. Where that is the case, an obvious solution is for the prosecution to apply to amend the indictment and add the particular incident or incidents as separate counts on the indictment. But if these specific occasions are not particularised in the indictment, it will be incumbent on the judge to tell the jury that they can only convict if they are sure that the offence has been committed on the same occasion, either on an occasion in the course of the unspecified pattern of offending, or on one of the particular occasions identified in the evidence.

[C]ounsel for the prosecution, contended that this would be unduly onerous. We do not agree; it simply requires that a specimen offence should be directed to a pattern of conduct which cannot be particularised in any specific way. It is an elementary principle that the jury should be sure about each element of the offence and that is not the case if it is open to a reasonable jury to convict on the basis of different incidents or occasions. Absent such a direction, it will not be possible to say that the jury were unanimous with respect to the same occasion."

The judge in *Hobson* sentenced the appellant on the basis that he had **33.31** repeatedly assaulted the complainants over many years. The Court of Appeal quashed the convictions and so did not need to consider sentence, but it took the opportunity to emphasise that the judge should have passed sentence in accordance with *Canavan*, i.e. on the basis that the appellant had been guilty of a single offence against each complainant. If, in fact, he had been guilty of a prolonged course of abuse of the sisters, as they had stated in evidence, then that outcome would, of course, have been a travesty of justice. It would be hard to find a clearer illustration of the need for prosecutors to draft indictments with great care in cases of prolonged alleged abuse and to consider applying to amend them in the course of the trial so as to particularise the allegations if the evidence justifies that course.

CHAPTER 34

SENTENCING OF SEX OFFENDERS: GENERAL

By Tim Moloney QC

Introduction	34.01	
Offences Committed on or after April 4, 2005	34.06	
The Dangerousness Provisions	34.06	
"Discretionary" Life Sentence under Section 225 of the Criminal Justice Act 2003	34.07	
Impact of Removal of Imprisonment for Public Protection (IPP) as a Sentencing Option	34.08	
Extended Sentences of Imprisonment	34.10	
Automatic Life Sentence—Statutory Life under Section 224A of the CJA 2003 Following Conviction for a Second Listed Offence	34.17	
How to Determine Dangerousness	34.23	
Pre-Sentence Reports	34.37	
The *Goodyear* procedure	34.38	

The Inter-relationship between Indeterminate and Determinate Sentences	34.40
Offences Committed on Dates Straddling either May 1, 2004 or April 4, 2005	34.52
Sentencing Where the Dates of the Offences Span May 1, 2004	34.52
Sentencing Where the Dates of the Offences Span April 5, 2005	34.53
Special Custodial Sentences for Certain Offenders of Particular Concern—S.236A CJA 2003	34.55
Miscellaneous	34.56
Sentencing False Complaints of Rape	34.56
The Use of Bad Character Evidence in the Sentencing Process	34.58
Barring from Working with Children and Vulnerable Adults	34.63

INTRODUCTION

This chapter explains custodial sentencing options that are of special **34.01** relevance to sexual offences. It does not cover general sentencing options such as determinate custodial sentences, suspended sentences and non-custodial sentences.

The Sentencing Council has issued a *Sexual Offences Definitive Guideline* **34.02** that applies to offenders aged 18 and older who are sentenced on or after April 1, 2014, whenever the offence in question was committed.[1] We have

---

[1] For historic cases, see *R. v H(J)* [2011] EWCA Crim 2753, where Lord Judge CJ summarised the principles underpinning the correct approach to sentencing. These are set out in Annex B of the *Sexual Offences: Definitive Guideline*. See also Ch.30, above.

reproduced the relevant parts of this guideline in the chapters dealing with particular substantive offences. Chapter 33 explains the general principles underpinning the guideline.

34.03   The approach taken by the courts when dealing with sex offenders has been transformed over the last 15 years. Sex offenders have received special attention from successive Parliaments and a number of measures have been introduced with the aim of protecting the public from them.

34.04   Following the White Paper *Protecting the Public*,[2] the Criminal Justice Act 2003 ("CJA 2003") was introduced to replace and build upon the scheme in earlier legislation. It provided for a new indeterminate sentence of imprisonment for public protection ("IPP") for dangerous offenders, and also introduced provisions relating to a new type of extended sentence. There have since been significant refinements to the dangerous offender regime, including the abolition of the sentence of IPP and the introduction of a new form of extended sentence. This applies to all cases sentenced after April 1, 2014, whenever the offence was committed, and the dangerousness criteria are satisfied.

34.05   The proliferation of legislation relevant to the sentencing of sex offenders means that certain dates are critical, in that different regimes will apply according to when the offence in question was committed. In this chapter we consider sentencing options where the offence was committed:

    (A) on or after April 4, 2005, when the sentencing provisions of the CJA 2003, and in particular the dangerousness regime, came into force; and

    (B) on dates straddling either May 1, 2004 (when the Sexual Offences Act 2003 ("SOA 2003") came into force) or April 4, 2005.

For sentencing of offences committed before April 4, 2005, see Ch.30 (Historic cases).

OFFENCES COMMITTED ON OR AFTER APRIL 4, 2005

THE DANGEROUSNESS PROVISIONS

34.06   The CJA 2003, whilst importing many of the key concepts of earlier legislation, established a new regime for the sentencing of dangerous sexual (and violent) offenders, including "discretionary" life sentences, sentences of IPP and changes to extended sentences. The provisions of the CJA 2003 which provide the framework for dealing with such offenders have come to be known as the "dangerousness provisions". The determination of dangerousness is dealt with in paras 34.23 and following, below. There have been significant changes to these provisions since they first came into force. Most important were those brought about by the Legal Aid, Sentencing and

---

[2] *Protecting the Public: Strengthening Protection against Sex Offenders and Reforming the Law on Sexual Offences*, Cm 5668 (Home Office: 2002).

Punishment of Offenders Act 2012 ("LASPO") which introduced a new type of automatic life sentence (whilst retaining the discretionary life sentence under s.225 of the CJA 2003); abolished the sentence of IPP; and provided for a new form of extended sentence. We consider these sentences below.

"DISCRETIONARY" LIFE SENTENCE UNDER SECTION 225 OF THE CRIMINAL JUSTICE ACT 2003

A sentence of life imprisonment may be imposed under s.225(1) and (2) of   **34.07** the CJA 2003 if the court is of the opinion that there is "a significant risk to members of the public occasioned by the commission by [the offender] of further specified offences" and concludes that "the seriousness of the offence, or of the offence and one or more offences associated with it, is such as to justify the imposition of a sentence of imprisonment for life". In *Red Saunders v R.*,[3] Lord Judge CJ, giving the judgment of the Court of Appeal, explained that the sentence of life imprisonment under s.225 continues in force after the changes made to the CJA 2003 by LASPO and has been frequently described as the "discretionary" life sentence, although once the statutory conditions in s.225(1) and (2) are established it "must" be imposed. His Lordship said[4]:

> "In that broad sense, therefore, this sentence, is also statutory, but it may only be imposed if justified by reference to the seriousness of the offence and the protection of the public in accordance with s.225(1) and (2)."

Life imprisonment remains the sentence of last resort. In *Wilkinson*,[5] the Court of Appeal had said:

> "In our judgment it is clear that as a matter of principle the discretionary life sentence under section 225 should continue to be reserved for offences of the utmost gravity. Without being prescriptive, we suggest that the sentence should come into contemplation when the judgment of the court is that the seriousness is such that the life sentence would have . . . a 'denunciatory' value, reflective of public abhorrence of the offence, and where, because of its seriousness, the notional determinate sentence would be very long, measured in very many years."

However, following *Red Saunders* it is no longer necessary for the seriousness of the offence to be such that the life sentence would have a denunciatory value reflective of public abhorrence, before such a sentence may be imposed. For a discussion of life sentences in the context of rape offences, see para 1.92 and following, above.

---

[3] [2013] EWCA Crim 1027.
[4] At [9].
[5] [2009] EWCA Crim 1925, at [19] per Lord Judge CJ.

Impact of Removal of Imprisonment for Public Protection (IPP) as a Sentencing Option

34.08 In *Red Saunders*, Lord Judge CJ explained the impact of the removal of IPP as a sentencing option as follows[6]:

> "The new statutory life sentence[7] has not replaced the IPP. Many offenders who represent a danger to the public may not 'qualify' for the statutory life sentence. Yet, for some offenders, the imperative of public protection continues undiminished, and is not wholly met by the 'new' extended sentence. Very long term public protection must therefore be provided by the imposition of a discretionary life sentence. That is consequent on s.225(1) and (2) which, in the context of the discretionary life sentence for serious offences continue, as we have explained, in full force."

Under the old form of extended sentence, release was automatic half way through the custodial term. In *Red Saunders*, Lord Judge noted that under the new extended sentence the offender will not be released until at least the two-thirds point of the custodial term has been reached. Where that term is 10 years or more, or the offences for which the sentence was imposed include one listed in Sch.15B to the CJA 2003 (for which see Appendix A), the offender will not be released until the Parole Board has directed his release on the ground that his continued incarceration is no longer necessary for public protection.[8] In relation to public protection as it arises under the new extended sentence, once the appropriate custodial term has been assessed, the extension period during which the offender will be subject to licence is limited, in the context of a specified sexual offence, to eight years. Further, in relation to some of the specified sexual offences, the maximum available term is 10 or 14 years' imprisonment, and that term may not be exceeded. His Lordship said that it is therefore clear that in relation to the offender who will continue to represent a significant risk to the safety of the public for an indefinite period, the new extended sentence cannot be treated as a direct replacement for the old IPP. He continued[9]:

> "Accordingly, in cases in which, prior to the enactment of LASPO, the court would have been driven to the conclusion that an IPP was required for public protection (on the basis on a judgment made on the particular facts rather than one to which the court was driven by some of the more troublesome assumptions required by the legislation in its original form) the discretionary life sentence will arise for consideration, and where appropriate, if the necessary level of public protection cannot be achieved by the new extended sentence, ordered. The 'denunciatory' ingredient identified to distinguish between the circumstances in which the discretionary life sentence rather than the IPP should be imposed is no longer apposite. By that we mean that although the 'denunciatory' element of the

[6] [2013] EWCA Crim 1027 at [15].
[7] Under s.224A of the CJA 2003, inserted by s.122 of the Legal Aid, Sentencing and Punishment of Offenders Act 2012: see paras 34.17 and following, below.
[8] As a result of changes made by the Criminal Justice and Courts Act 2015 this restriction now applies to all extended sentences imposed after April 13, 2015: see para.34.13, below.
[9] [2013] EWCA Crim 1027 at [18].

sentencing decision may continue to justify the discretionary life sentence, its absence does not preclude such an order. As every judge appreciates, however, the life sentence remains the sentence of last resort."

In *Attorney General's Reference (No.27 of 2013) (Burinskas),*[10] Lord Thomas CJ endorsed the remarks of Lord Judge in *Red Saunders.* He observed that LASPO had fundamentally altered the statutory context and it was inevitable that the s.225 life sentence would be more frequently imposed than before. Authorities decided prior to 2012 are now of limited value. For further discussion on the impact of the demise of IPP in the context of sentencing in rape cases, see paras 1.94 and following, above. **34.09**

EXTENDED SENTENCES OF IMPRISONMENT

Section 226A of the CJA 2003, inserted in place of s.227 by s.124 of LASPO, provides for extended sentences of imprisonment. The power to pass an extended sentence applies where an offender aged 18 or over is convicted of a specified offence, whether the offence was committed before or after the section came into force on December 3, 2012. The pre-condition that the dangerousness criteria must be satisfied is retained, as are the criteria themselves. In this respect the new extended sentence is similar to the old one. However, the reference in s.227 to Sch.15A is replaced by a reference in s.226A to the new Sch.15B (for which see Appendix A). Schedule 15A has been repealed. **34.10**

Criteria

A court may impose an extended sentence where: **34.11**
   (a) the defendant aged 18 or over is convicted of a specified offence (i.e. one listed in Sch.15 to the CJA 2003, for which see Appendix A); or, where the offence was abolished before April 4, 2005, the offence would have constituted a specified offence if committed on the day of conviction;[11]
   (b) the court considers that there is a significant risk of serious harm occasioned by the commission by the defendant of further specified offences[12];
   (c) the court is not required by s.224A or s.225(2) of the CJA 2003 to impose a sentence of imprisonment for life; and
   (d) condition A or B is met:
        Condition A: at the time the offence was committed, the defendant had been convicted of an offence listed in Sch.15B to the CJA 2003, or

---

[10] [2014] EWCA Crim 334.
[11] CJA 2003 s.226A(1) and (4).
[12] CJA 2003 s.226A(1).

Condition B: if the court were to impose an extended sentence, the period it would specify as the custodial portion of the sentence would be at least four years (s.226A(3) of the CJA 2003).

Composition and length of extended sentences

34.12   An extended sentence of imprisonment is a sentence of imprisonment the term of which is equal to the aggregate of (a) the appropriate custodial term and (b) a further period (the "extension period") for which the offender is to be subject to a licence.[13] The appropriate custodial term is the term of imprisonment that would be imposed in compliance with s.153(2).[14] Section 153(2) provides that the length of a sentence of imprisonment must be the shortest term that is commensurate with the seriousness of the offence or the combination of the offence and one or more offences associated with it. The extension period must be for a period of at least one year[15] and be for a period of such length as the court considers necessary for the purpose of protecting members of the public from serious harm occasioned by the offender of further specified offences.[16] The extension period must not exceed (a) five years in the case of a specified violent offence or (b) eight years in the case of a specified sexual offence.[17] The term of an extended sentence must not exceed the term that, at the time the offence was committed, was the maximum term permitted for the offence.[18]

Release on licence

34.13   There have been significant changes in extended sentences, the most significant relating to release on licence. Under the old system, release was ordinarily at the half-way point of the custodial term. LASPO changed this to the two-thirds point of the custodial term, when release would be automatic unless that term was at least 10 years *or* the extended sentence was imposed for an offence or offences listed in Pt 1 of Sch.15B. In the latter circumstances, the case would be referred to the Parole Board at the two-thirds point for it to consider whether or not the offender should be released. The CJA 2003 has been further amended by the Criminal Justice and Courts Act 2015 with effect from April 13, 2015. The effect of s.4 of the 2015 Act is that there is no longer automatic release for extended sentences imposed after that date.[19] *All* offenders now given extended sentences must therefore be referred to the Parole Board. Under s.246A(6)(b) of the CJA 2003, the Parole Board must not direct the release of the offender unless it is satisfied that it

---

[13] CJA 2003 s.226A(5).
[14] CJA 2003 s.226A(6).
[15] CJA 2003 s.226A(7A).
[16] CJA 2003 s.226A(7).
[17] CJA 2003 s.226A(8).
[18] CJA 2003 s.226A(9).
[19] CJA 2003 s.246A(2), as amended.

is no longer necessary for the protection of the public that the offender should be confined. If an offender subject to an extended sentence is not released on the direction of the Parole Board, he must be released when he has served the whole of the custodial term unless he has already been released on licence and recalled. It therefore follows that the precise date of release from a sentence imposed under s.226A cannot be known at the point of sentence. In *Attorney General's Reference (No.27 of 2013) (Burinskas)*,[20] Lord Thomas CJ said that, whilst a finding of dangerousness was a prerequisite to the imposition of an extended sentence, the option of a determinate sentence should not be forgotten. When fixing the custodial term of the extended sentence, the sentencing judge should disregard the early release provisions.

Extended sentences in respect of defendants aged under 18 at conviction

Section 226B of the CJA 2003 provides for the imposition of extended   **34.14** sentences upon those under the age of 18. The statutory scheme is very similar to that under s.226A, but one important difference is that the minimum appropriate custodial portion must be four years' imprisonment. The alternative condition of a previous conviction of a Sch.15B offence does *not* apply to those aged under 18 at conviction. By virtue of s.235 of the CJA 2003, a person liable to detention under s.226B may be detained in a place as determined by the Secretary of State.

In *R. v BD*,[21] the Court of Appeal emphasised that in deciding whether an   **34.15** extended sentence is necessary, a sentencing judge is required to consider whether there is some other part of the sentence which he is imposing which can adequately address the element of risk. In the particular case before the Court, the sentencing judge should have had in mind the terms of the Sexual Offences Prevention Order he imposed. For further discussion see paras 1.115 and following, above.

The statutory provisions

The provisions of the CJA 2003 dealing with extended sentences are as   **34.16** follows:

> "**226A Extended sentence for certain violent or sexual offences: persons 18 or over**[22]
>
> (1) This section applies where—
> (a) a person aged 18 or over is convicted of a specified offence (whether the offence was committed before or after this section comes into force),

---

[20] [2014] EWCA Crim 334.
[21] [2015] EWCA Crim 1415.
[22] As amended by the Legal Aid, Sentencing and Punishment of Offenders Act 2012 s.124 and Sch.21(2), para.36(2), and the Offender Rehabilitation Act 2014 s.8(2).

(b) the court considers that there is a significant risk to members of the public of serious harm occasioned by the commission by the offender of further specified offences,

(c) the court is not required by section 224A or 225(2) to impose a sentence of imprisonment for life, and

(d) condition A or B is met.

(2) Condition A is that, at the time the offence was committed, the offender had been convicted of an offence listed in Schedule 15B.

(3) Condition B is that, if the court were to impose an extended sentence of imprisonment, the term that it would specify as the appropriate custodial term would be at least 4 years.

(4) The court may impose an extended sentence of imprisonment on the offender.

(5) An extended sentence of imprisonment is a sentence of imprisonment the term of which is equal to the aggregate of—

(a) the appropriate custodial term, and

(b) a further period (the 'extension period') for which the offender is to be subject to a licence.

(6) The appropriate custodial term is the term of imprisonment that would (apart from this section) be imposed in compliance with section 153(2).

(7) The extension period must be a period of such length as the court considers necessary for the purpose of protecting members of the public from serious harm occasioned by the commission by the offender of further specified offences, subject to subsections (7A) to (9).

(7A) The extension period must be at least 1 year.

(8) The extension period must not exceed—

(a) 5 years in the case of a specified violent offence, and

(b) 8 years in the case of a specified sexual offence.

(9) The term of an extended sentence of imprisonment imposed under this section in respect of an offence must not exceed the term that, at the time the offence was committed, was the maximum term permitted for the offence.

(10) In subsections (1)(a) and (8), references to a specified offence, a specified violent offence and a specified sexual offence include an offence that—

(a) was abolished before 4 April 2005, and

(b) would have constituted such an offence if committed on the day on which the offender was convicted of the offence.

(11) Where the offence mentioned in subsection (1)(a) was committed before 4 April 2005—

(a) subsection (1)(c) has effect as if the words 'by section 224A or 225(2)' were omitted, and

(b) subsection (6) has effect as if the words 'in compliance with section 153(2)' were omitted.

(12) In the case of a person aged at least 18 but under 21, this section has effect as if—

(a) the reference in subsection (1)(c) to imprisonment for life were to custody for life, and

(b) other references to imprisonment (including in the expression 'extended sentence of imprisonment') were to detention in a young offender institution.

226B Extended sentence for certain violent or sexual offences: persons under 18[23]

---

[23] As amended by the Legal Aid, Sentencing and Punishment of Offenders Act 2012 s.124 and Sch.21(2), para.36(3), and the Offender Rehabilitation Act 2014 s.8(3).

(1) This section applies where—

(a) a person aged under 18 is convicted of a specified offence (whether the offence was committed before or after this section comes into force),

(b) the court considers that there is a significant risk to members of the public of serious harm occasioned by the commission by the offender of further specified offences,

(c) the court is not required by section 226(2) to impose a sentence of detention for life under section 91 of the Sentencing Act, and

(d) if the court were to impose an extended sentence of detention, the term that it would specify as the appropriate custodial term would be at least 4 years.

(2) The court may impose an extended sentence of detention on the offender.

(3) An extended sentence of detention is a sentence of detention the term of which is equal to the aggregate of—

(a) the appropriate custodial term, and

(b) a further period (the 'extension period') for which the offender is to be subject to a licence.

(4) The appropriate custodial term is the term of detention that would (apart from this section) be imposed in compliance with section 153(2).

(5) The extension period must be a period of such length as the court considers necessary for the purpose of protecting members of the public from serious harm occasioned by the commission by the offender of further specified offences, subject to subsections (5A) to (7).

(5A) The extension period must be at least 1 year.

(6) The extension period must not exceed—

(a) 5 years in the case of a specified violent offence, and

(b) 8 years in the case of a specified sexual offence.

(7) The term of an extended sentence of detention imposed under this section in respect of an offence may not exceed the term that, at the time the offence was committed, was the maximum term of imprisonment permitted for the offence in the case of a person aged 21[24] or over.

(8) In subsections (1)(a) and (6), references to a specified offence, a specified violent offence and a specified sexual offence include an offence that—

(a) was abolished before 4 April 2005, and

(b) would have constituted such an offence if committed on the day on which the offender was convicted of the offence.

(9) Where the offence mentioned in subsection (1)(a) was committed before 4 April 2005—

(a) subsection (1) has effect as if paragraph (c) were omitted, and

(b) subsection (4) has effect as if the words 'in compliance with section 153(2)' were omitted.

246A Release on licence of prisoners serving extended sentence under section 226A or 226B[25]

(1) This section applies to a prisoner ('P') who is serving an extended sentence imposed under section 226A or 226B.

(2) It is the duty of the Secretary of State to release P on licence under this section as soon as P has served the requisite custodial period for the purposes of this section IF

---

[24] The age 21 was substituted for 18 by the 2012 Act.

[25] As amended by the Legal Aid, Sentencing and Punishment of Offenders Act 2012 s.125(3), and the Criminal Justice and Courts Act 2015 s.4(2), (3).

(a) the sentence was imposed before the coming into force of section 4 of the Criminal Justice and Courts Act 2015,

(b) the appropriate custodial term is less than 10 years, and

(c) the sentence was not imposed in respect of an offence listed in Parts 1 to 3 of Schedule 15B or in respect of offences that include one or more offences listed in those Parts of that Schedule.

(3) In any other case, it is the duty of the Secretary of State to release P on licence in accordance with subsections (4) to (7).

(4) The Secretary of State must refer P's case to the Board—

(a) as soon as P has served the requisite custodial period, and

(b) where there has been a previous reference of P's case to the Board under this subsection and the Board did not direct P's release, not later than the second anniversary of the disposal of that reference.

(5) It is the duty of the Secretary of State to release P on licence under this section as soon as—

(a) P has served the requisite custodial period, and

(b) the Board has directed P's release under this section.

(6) The Board must not give a direction under subsection (5) unless—

(a) the Secretary of State has referred P's case to the Board, and

(b) the Board is satisfied that it is no longer necessary for the protection of the public that P should be confined.

(7) It is the duty of the Secretary of State to release P on licence under this section as soon as P has served the appropriate custodial term, unless P has previously been released on licence under this section and recalled under section 254 (provision for the release of such persons being made by section 255C).

(8) For the purposes of this section—

'appropriate custodial term' means the term determined as such by the court under section 226A or 226B (as appropriate);

'the requisite custodial period' means—

(a) in relation to a person serving one sentence, two-thirds of the appropriate custodial term, and

(b) in relation to a person serving two or more concurrent or consecutive sentences, the period determined under sections 263(2) and 264(2)."

Automatic Life Sentence—Statutory Life Under Section 224A of the Criminal Justice Act 2003 Following Conviction for a Second Listed Offence

34.17   Section 224A of the CJA 2003, inserted by s.122 of LASPO, provides for a "life sentence for a second listed offence". The sentence is available where:

(i) a person aged 18 or over is convicted of an offence listed in Pt 1 of the new Sch.15B to the CJA 2003 (for which see below and Appendix A);

(ii) the offence is such that the court would have imposed a determinate sentence of 10 years or more (including an extended sentence where the *custodial* term would have been 10 years or more) after taking into account all relevant considerations, including the offender's plea ("the sentence condition"); and

(iii) the offender has a previous conviction for an offence listed in Sch.15B for which he received a "life sentence" with a minimum term of at least five years or a determinate sentence of 10 years or more (including an extended sentence where the *custodial* term was 10 years or more) ("the previous offence" condition).

The restrictions inherent in the "sentence" and "previous offence" conditions mean that this sentence will have limited application. Where the conditions are satisfied, it is likely that the offence will, in any event, attract a life sentence.

Section 224A(10) specifically incorporates the definition of "life sentence" found in s.34 of the Crime (Sentences) Act 1997, which includes a sentence of IPP. Therefore, a previous conviction that was dealt with by way of IPP with a minimum term of five years or more will be sufficient to bring the offender within the "life sentence for a second listed offence" scheme. **34.18**

The new offence must be listed in Pt 1 of Sch.15B, while the previous offence can be listed anywhere in the Schedule. Accordingly, the previous offence can be an offence of murder or one of a number of offences that have now been repealed. Of particular relevance for present purposes are the repealed sexual offences formerly contained in the Sexual Offences Act 1956. **34.19**

Where the specified conditions are met, a court must impose a life sentence under s.224A unless there are "particular circumstances" relating to either the current offence or the past offence, or to the offender, which would make it "unjust to do so in all the circumstances".[26] This formulation has the effect of conferring a wider discretion on the sentencing court than the reference to "exceptional circumstances" in s.109(2) of the PCC(S)A 2000. **34.20**

Giving the judgment of Court of Appeal in *Attorney General's Reference (No.27 of 2013) (Burinskas)*,[27] Lord Thomas CJ provided guidance as to the approach to be taken in a case where s.224A might be relevant. He observed that there might be a temptation in such a case to move directly to consider the sentence under s.224A without first considering whether the offender is dangerous. However, a sentencing judge should first consider whether the offender is dangerous. If the offender is not dangerous and s.224A does not apply, a determinate sentence should be passed. If the offender is not dangerous but the s.224A conditions are satisfied then the court must impose a sentence under s.224A subject to any decision under s.224A(2). If the offender is dangerous, the court should consider whether the seriousness of the offence justifies a discretionary life sentence. If so, then the court must impose that sentence. If, in addition, s.224A applies, then the judge should make that clear in open court. If a discretionary life sentence is not imposed, then the court should consider whether a sentence under s.224A was available. If so, the court must impose it subject to the qualifications contained within s.224A(2). For further discussion, see paras 1.107 and following, above. **34.21**

---

[26] s.224A(2)(a) and (b).
[27] [2014] EWCA Crim 334.

34.22   Section 224A provides as follows:

"**224A Life sentence for second listed offence**[28]

(1) This section applies where—

(a) a person aged 18 or over is convicted of an offence listed in Part 1 of Schedule 15B,

(b) the offence was committed after this section comes into force, and

(c) the sentence condition and the previous offence condition are met.

(2) The court must impose a sentence of imprisonment for life or, in the case of a person aged at least 18 but under 21, custody for life under section 94 of the Sentencing Act unless the court is of the opinion that there are particular circumstances which—

(a) relate to the offence, to the previous offence referred to in subsection (4) or to the offender, and

(b) would make it unjust to do so in all the circumstances.

(3) The sentence condition is that, but for this section, the court would, in compliance with sections 152(2) and 153(2), impose a sentence of imprisonment for 10 years or more, disregarding any extension period imposed under section 226A.

(4) The previous offence condition is that—

(a) at the time the offence was committed, the offender had been convicted of an offence listed in Schedule 15B ('the previous offence'), and

(b) a relevant life sentence or a relevant sentence of imprisonment or detention for a determinate period was imposed on the offender for the previous offence.

(5) A life sentence is relevant for the purposes of subsection (4)(b) if—

(a) the offender was not eligible for release during the first 5 years of the sentence, or

(b) the offender would not have been eligible for release during that period but for the reduction of the period of ineligibility to take account of a relevant pre-sentence period.

(6) An extended sentence imposed under this Act . . . is relevant for the purposes of subsection (4)(b) if the appropriate custodial term imposed was 10 years or more.

(7) Any other extended sentence is relevant for the purposes of subsection (4)(b) if the custodial term imposed was 10 years or more.

(8) Any other sentence of imprisonment or detention for a determinate period is relevant for the purposes of subsection (4)(b) if it was for a period of 10 years or more.

(9) An extended sentence or other sentence of imprisonment or detention is also relevant if it would have been relevant under subsection (7) or (8) but for the reduction of the sentence, or any part of the sentence, to take account of a relevant pre-sentence period.

(10) For the purposes of subsections (4) to (9)—

'extended sentence' means—

(a) a sentence imposed under section 85 of the Sentencing Act or under section 226A, 226B, 227 or 228 of this Act . . . ;

'life sentence' means–

(a) a life sentence as defined in section 34 of the Crime (Sentences) Act 1997 . . . ""

[28] As amended by the Legal Aid, Sentencing and Punishment of Offenders Act 2012 s.122(1) and Sch.19(2), para. 24(2), and the Criminal Justice and Courts Act 2015 s.5(1).

How to Determine Dangerousness

The starting point for the imposition of sentences of life imprisonment under **34.23** s.225 of the CJA 2003 and extended sentences under s.226A of the CJA 2003 is the assessment of dangerousness.

Section 229 sets out the approach the court must undertake when assessing **34.24** dangerousness, i.e. an assessment of whether there is a significant risk of serious harm to the public from the commission of further specified offences by the offender.[29] The provisions incorporate the concepts previously seen in the Powers of Criminal Courts (Sentencing) Act 2000 ("PCCSA") of "significant risk of serious harm"[30] to "members of the public".[31] Section 229[32] provides:

> "**229.**—(1) This section applies where—
> (a) a person has been convicted of a specified offence, and
> (b) it falls to a court to assess under any of sections 225 to 228 whether there is a significant risk to members of the public of serious harm occasioned by the commission by him of further such offences.
> (2) The Court in making the assessment referred to in subsection 1(b)—
> (a) must take into account all such information as is available to it about the nature and circumstances of the offence,
> (aa) may take into account all such information as is available to it about the nature and circumstances of any other offences of which the offender has been convicted by a court anywhere in the world,
> (b) may take into account any information which is before it about any pattern of behaviour of which any of the offences mentioned in paragraph (a) or (aa) forms part, and
> (c) may take into account any information about the offender which is before it."

It follows from the wording of the Act there is no requirement for a nexus between the particular facts of the particular offence and the finding of dangerousness. In principle, once a defendant has been convicted of a serious offence within the meaning of the Act, whatever the facts and nature of the offence, it is perfectly possible for a finding of dangerousness to be made on the basis of material which has no close relationship to the offence for which the sentence is being passed.[33]

The interpretation and practical application of the provisions in ss.224–229 **34.25** of the CJA 2003 have required a good deal of attention from the Court of Appeal. The well-known case of *Lang*[34] provided invaluable initial guidance. Giving the judgment of the Court, the then Vice President, Rose LJ, set out

---

[29] Section 233 allows for offences under service law to be taken into account for the purposes of s.229.
[30] See para.34.26, below.
[31] See para.34.27, below.
[32] As amended by the Criminal Justice and Immigration Act 2008 s.17.
[33] *Green* [2007] EWCA Crim 2172.
[34] [2005] EWCA Crim 2864.

a number of principles that sentencing judges should have regard to in applying the scheme in ss.224–229.

34.26   First, when a sentencer is assessing for the purposes of s.229 whether a "significant risk" exists, he should take into account the following factors[35]:

"(i) The risk identified must be significant. This is a higher threshold than mere possibility of occurrence and in our view can be taken to mean (as in the Oxford Dictionary) 'noteworthy, of considerable amount or importance'.

(ii) In assessing the risk of further offences being committed, the sentencer should take into account the nature and circumstances of the current offence; the offender's history of offending including not just the kind of offence but its circumstances and the sentence passed, details of which the prosecution must have available, and, whether the offending demonstrates any pattern; social and economic factors in relation to the offender including accommodation, employability, education, associates, relationships and drug or alcohol abuse; and the offender's thinking, attitude towards offending and supervision and emotional state. Information in relation to these matters will most readily, though not exclusively, come from antecedents and pre-sentence probation and medical reports. The Guide for sentence for public protection issued in June 2005 for the National Probation Service affords valuable guidance for probation officers. The guidance in relation to assessment of dangerousness in paragraph 5 is compatible with the terms of this judgment. The sentencer will be guided, but not bound by, the assessment of risk in such reports. A sentencer who contemplates differing from the assessment in such a report should give both counsel the opportunity of addressing the point.

(iii) If the foreseen specified offence is serious, there will clearly be some cases, though not by any means all, in which there may be a significant risk of serious harm. For example, robbery is a serious offence. But it can be committed in a wide variety of ways many of which do not give rise to a significant risk of serious harm. Sentencers must therefore guard against assuming there is a significant risk of serious harm merely because the foreseen specified offence is serious. A pre-sentence report should usually be obtained before any sentence is passed which is based on significant risk of serious harm. In a small number of cases, where the circumstances of the current offence or the history of the offender suggest mental abnormality on his part, a medical report may be necessary before risk can properly be assessed.

(iv) If the foreseen specified offence is not serious, there will be comparatively few cases in which a risk of serious harm will properly be regarded as significant. The huge variety of offences in Schedule 15, includes many which, in themselves, are not suggestive of serious harm. Repetitive violent or sexual offending at a relatively low level without serious harm does not of itself give rise to a significant risk of serious harm in the future. There may, in such cases, be some risk of future victims being more adversely affected than past victims but this, of itself, does not give rise to significant risk of serious harm.

(v) In relation to the rebuttable assumption to which section 229(3) gives rise, the court is accorded a discretion if, in the light of information about the current offence, the offender and his previous offences, it would be unreasonable to conclude that there is a significant risk. The exercise of such a discretion is, historically, at the very heart of judicial sentencing and the language of the statute indicates that judges are expected, albeit starting from the assumption, to

---

[35] [2005] EWCA Crim 2864, at [17].

exercise their ability to reach a reasonable conclusion in the light of the information before them. It is to be noted that the assumption will be rebutted, if at all, as an exercise of judgment: the statute includes no reference to the burden or standard of proof. As we have indicated above, it will usually be unreasonable to conclude that the assumption applies unless information about the offences, pattern of behaviour and offender show a significant risk of serious harm from further offences.

(vi) In relation to offenders under 18 and adults with no relevant previous convictions at the time the specified offence was committed, the court's discretion under section 229(2) is not constrained by any initial assumption such as, under section 229(3),[36] applies to adults with previous convictions. It is still necessary, when sentencing young offenders, to bear in mind that, within a shorter time than adults, they may change and develop. This and their level of maturity may be highly pertinent when assessing what their future conduct may be and whether it may give rise to significant risk of serious harm.

(vii) In relation to a particularly young offender, an indeterminate sentence may be inappropriate even where a serious offence has been committed and there is a significant risk of serious harm from further offences (see for example, *R. v D* [2005] EWCA Crim 2282).

(viii) It cannot have been Parliament's intention, in a statute dealing with the liberty of the subject, to require the imposition of indeterminate sentences for the commission of relatively minor offences. On the contrary, Parliament's repeatedly expressed intention is to protect the public from serious harm (compare the reasoning of the Court in relation to automatic life sentences in *R. v. Offen* [2001] 2 Cr. App. R.(S.) 44, paragraphs 96 to 99.

(ix) Sentencers should usually, and in accordance with section 174(1)(a) of the Criminal Justice Act 2003 give reasons for all their conclusions: in particular, that there is or is not a significant risk of further offences or serious harm; where the assumption under section 229(3) arises for making or not making the assumption which the statute requires unless this would be unreasonable; and for not imposing an extended sentence under sections 227 and 228. Sentencers should, in giving reasons, briefly identify the information which they have taken into account."

Secondly, the risk to be assessed is to "members of the public", which **34.27** seemed to the Court to be an all-embracing term. It is wider than "others", which would exclude the offender himself, and the Court saw no need to construe the term so as to exclude any particular group such as prison officers or staff at mental hospitals.

Finally, the Court advised that if, in relation to a dangerous offender, the **34.28** requirements of the Mental Health Act 1983 are satisfied, the court can dispose of the case under those provisions.

Amplification of the guidance in *Lang*, and clarification of some of the **34.29** potential areas of misunderstanding, was provided in a judgment delivered by Sir Igor Judge P (as he then was) in *Johnson*.[37] Sir Igor cautioned against according statutory status to the judgment in *Lang*. He observed:[38]

---

[36] This provision was repealed by the Criminal Justice and Immigration Act 2008 s.17, with effect from July 14, 2008.

[37] [2006] EWCA Crim 2486.

[38] At [2]. The Court of Appeal drew attention to this aspect of the judgment in *Stannard* [2008] EWCA Crim 2789.

"Invaluable understanding of this complicated piece of legislation was provided in *R. v Lang and others* [2006] 1W.L.R. 2509 in the illuminating judgment given by Rose L.J., the Vice President of the Court of Appeal Criminal Division. Perhaps the fact that the judgment was given in his customary clear and trenchant terms by one of the pre-eminent criminal judges of this generation has led practitioners to conclude, and certainly for some of them to advance arguments which proceed, as if every word of the judgment should be treated as statute. Indeed that was precisely how one counsel appearing before us did describe it, treating the judgment as synonymous with the statute with which the judgment was concerned. However, and unsurprisingly, Rose L.J. himself emphasised that the judgment represented 'an attempt to summarise the approach to sentencing which the Act requires and to give guidance as to its meaning'. He warned against treating it as if it were a 'substitute for looking at the Act's provisions'."

34.30   The Court went on to address a number of specific issues relating to the exercise of powers under ss.224–229, and in particular to the assessment of dangerousness, and gave the following guidance[39]:

"(i) Just as the absence of previous convictions does not preclude a finding of dangerousness, the existence of previous convictions for specified offences does not compel such a finding. There is a presumption that it does so, which may be rebutted.

(ii) If a finding of dangerousness can be made against an offender without previous specified convictions, it also follows that previous offences, not in fact specified for the purposes of section 229, are not disqualified from consideration. Thus, for example, as indeed the statute recognises, a pattern of minor previous offences of gradually escalating seriousness may be significant. In other words, it is not right, as many of the submissions made to us suggested, that unless the previous offences were specified offences they were irrelevant.

(iii) Where the facts of the instant offence, or indeed any specified offences for the purposes of section 229(3) are examined, it may emerge that no harm actually occurred. That may be advantageous to the offender, and some of the cases examined in *Lang* exemplify the point. Another such example is *R. v. Isa* [2006] Crim. L.R. 356. On the other hand the absence of harm may be entirely fortuitous. A victim cowering away from an armed assailant may avoid direct physical injury or serious psychological harm. Faced with such a case, the sentencer considering dangerousness may wish to reflect, for example, on the likely response of the offender if his victim, instead of surrendering, resolutely defended himself. It does not automatically follow from the absence of actual harm caused by the offender to date, that the risk that he will cause serious harm in the future is negligible.

Nothing in the decision in *R. v. Shaffi* [2006] EWCA Crim 418, which was relied on before us, suggests the contrary. Giving the judgment of the court, at paragraph 11, Sir Richard Curtis summarised the various submissions made on behalf of the appellant. One of them was that the appellant's previous convictions demonstrated that although the appellant was carrying a knife and a screwdriver in two of the cases, no harm was actually occasioned. The court accepted the force of the overall submission made by counsel that the sentencer was wrong to find that there was a risk of *serious* harm, and the court was unable to find significant evidence of such harm caused during the commission of the appellant's previous offences. However the conclusion represented a finding of

[39] At [10].

fact in the particular case. *Shaffi* is not authority for the proposition that as a matter of law offences which did not result in harm to the victim should be treated as irrelevant. Indeed if that is what *Shaffi* decided, it would, in effect, have rewritten the statute.

(iv) We considered arguments based on the inadequacy, suggestibility, or vulnerability of the offender, and how these and similar characteristics may bear on dangerousness. Such characteristics may serve to mitigate the offender's culpability. In the final analysis however they may also serve to produce or reinforce the conclusion that the offender is dangerous. In one of the instant cases it was suggested that the sentence was wrong because an inadequate offender had suffered what was described as an 'aberrant moment'. But, as experience shows, aberrant moments may be productive of catastrophe. The sentencer is right to be alert to such risks of aberrant moments in the future, and their consequences.

(v) In *Lang*, Rose L.J. suggested that the prosecution should be in a position to describe the facts of previous specified offences. This is plainly desirable, (see also *Isa*) but this is not always practicable. There is no reason why the prosecution's failure to comply with this good practice, even when it can and should, should either make an adjournment obligatory, or indeed preclude the imposition of the sentence, when appropriate. In any such case, counsel for the defendant should be in a position to explain the circumstances, on the basis of his instructions. If the Crown is not in a position to challenge those instructions, then the court may proceed on the information it has. Equally, there are some situations in which the sentence imposed by the court dealing with earlier specified offences may enable the sentencer to draw inferences about its seriousness, or otherwise. In short, failure to comply with best practice on this point should be discouraged, but it does not normally preclude the imposition of the sentence.

(vi) The effect of the 2003 Act, and *Lang*, has been examined in a number of cases. It is not obligatory for the sentencer to spell out all the details of the earlier specified offences. To the extent that a judge is minded to rely upon a disputed fact in reaching a finding of dangerousness, he should not rely on that fact unless the dispute can fairly be resolved adversely to the defendant. In the end, the requirement is that the sentencing remarks should explain the reasoning which has led the sentencer to the conclusion."

The President also emphasised in *Johnson* that the Court of Appeal will **34.31** not normally interfere with conclusions reached by a sentencer who has accurately identified the relevant principles, and applied his mind to the relevant facts. The Court could not too strongly emphasise that the question to be addressed in the Court of Appeal is not whether it is possible to discover some words used by the sentencer which may be inconsistent with the precise language used in *Lang*, or indeed some failure on his part to deploy identical language to that used in *Lang*, but whether the imposition of the sentence was manifestly excessive or wrong in principle. Notwithstanding the labyrinthine provisions of ss.224–229, and the guidance offered by *Lang*, those essential principles are not affected.

In *Attorney General's Reference (No.55 of 2008) (C and others)*,[40] the **34.32** Court of Appeal emphasised that the principles identified in *Johnson*

---

[40] [2009] 2 Cr. App. R.(S.) 22.

continue to govern decisions in respect of dangerousness. In *Pedley*[41]the Court held that the concept of "significant risk" in s.225(1) of the CJA 2003 contains within it a degree of flexibility. Thus when addressing the question whether a risk of serious harm is "significant", a judge is entitled to balance the probability of harm against the nature of the harm if it occurred. The judge is thus able to conclude that a lower probability of particularly grave harm might be significant and, conversely, that a greater probability of less grave harm might not be. In addition, there is no justification for attempting a redefinition of the plain English expression "significant risk . . . of serious harm". In particular, it would be wholly unhelpful to redefine "significant risk" in terms of numerical probability, whether as more probable than not or by any other percentage of likelihood. No attempt should be made by sentencers to attach arithmetical values to the qualitative assessment which the Act requires of them, which would be inconsistent with the degree of flexibility inherent in the word "significant". The Court also held that the threshold imposed by the test in s.225(1) is not so low that the punishment imposed by a sentence of IPP is contrary to art.3 of the ECHR by way of being disproportionate. Moreover, the fact that each case has to be determined upon its own facts does not mean that such sentences are too uncertain to comply with art.5(1).

The meaning of "information" in s.229 of the Criminal Justice Act 2003

34.33   The sentencing judge is not entitled to reach a finding of guilt in relation to a contested but untried allegation so as to justify a finding of dangerousness. In *Farrar*[42] the 22-year-old appellant had abducted a boy of six and taken him back to his home in May 2005. Once there, he put a pillowcase over the boy's head and bounced him up and down on his knee whilst he masturbated. He pleaded guilty to the abduction and sexual assault of the boy. Psychiatric, psychological and pre-sentence reports were prepared for the purposes of sentence. The appellant was found by the psychologist to have an overall IQ rating of 74. He pretended to the psychiatrist that he could not remember the offences and the pre-sentence report concluded that he posed a very high risk of physical and psychological sexual harm to young boys. The author of the report had discovered that there had been a number of reports to the local VISOR (Violent and Sex Offender Register) team of predatory males approaching young boys, including one in August 2004 involving a seven-year-old boy. The appellant had admitted involvement in each of the incidents but had denied any ill intent. From the outset, the sentencing judge had in mind the possibility of a sentence of IPP but the prospect troubled him because the appellant had no previous convictions of any kind. Section 229(2) of the CJA 2003 sets out express statutory guidance by which the

[41] [2009] 1 W.L.R. 2517.
[42] [2006] EWCA Crim 3261; [2007] 2 Cr. App. R.(S.) 35.

process of assessment of dangerousness should be governed when an offender is either under 18 or has no previous convictions. Under s.229(2), when assessing dangerousness the court "must take into account all such information as is available to it about the nature and circumstances of the offence" and "may take into account any information which is before it about any pattern of behaviour of which the offence forms part". The sentencing judge therefore decided to hear evidence about the August 2004 incident and determine where the truth lay to the criminal standard. He found against the appellant and concluded that his conduct was prompted by a sexual motive. The judge then treated the incident as information about a pattern of behaviour of which the offence formed part under s.229(2)(b) and noted the appellant's continuing interest in contact with children as relevant information about him under s.229(2)(c). He concluded that there was a high risk of the repetition of specified sexual offences against children and that the risk was of serious harm, and he therefore sentenced the appellant to IPP.

The Court of Appeal quashed the sentence and considered it afresh as it   **34.34**
was not open to the sentencing judge to find in the way that he did that the appellant had committed the assault in August 2004. The Court observed[43]:

> "A defendant is not to be convicted of any offence with which he is charged unless and until his guilt is proved. Such guilt may be proved by his own admission or (on indictment) by the verdict of a jury. He may be sentenced only for an offence proved against him (by admission or verdict) or which he has admitted and asked the court to take into consideration when passing sentence: see *Anderson* [[1978] A.C. 964]. If, as we think, these are basic principles underlying the administration of the criminal law, it is not easy to see how a defendant can lawfully be punished for offences for which he has not been indicted and which he has denied or declined to admit. Per Lord Bingham CJ in *Canavan* [1998] 1 Cr. App. R.(S.) 243 at 245–246'.
>
> Nothing in the 2003 Act expressly overrides that principle, unlike section 17 (yet to be in force) of the Domestic Violence, Crime and Victims Act 2004. Does section 229(2)(b) do so impliedly? It will only do so if there is a necessary implication to that effect: 'a necessary implication is one which necessarily follows from the express provisions of the statute construed in their context. It distinguishes between what it would have been sensible or reasonable for Parliament to have included or what Parliament would, if it had thought about it, probably have included and what it is clear that the express language of the statute shows that the statute must have included. A necessary implication is a matter of express language and logic not interpretation.' Per Lord Hobhouse of Woodborough *R (on the application of Morgan Grenfell and Co Ltd) v Special Commissioner of Income Tax* [2003] 1 A.C. 563 at paragraph 45.
>
> Or, as Lord Nicholls put it in *B (a minor) v DPP* [2000] 2 A.C. 428 at 464: '"necessary implication" connotes an implication which is compellingly clear.'
>
> It is neither a matter of express language and logic, nor is it compellingly clear, that section 229(2)(b) has the effect of permitting a judge alone to decide that a defendant is guilty of a discrete offence unconnected with that for which he is to

[43] At [14]–[20].

be sentenced. A 'pattern of behaviour' constituted by discrete offences can just as well be established by conviction by a jury or magistrates' court of the offences as by the finding of a judge alone. Hence, 'language and logic' do not require the implication. Further, it is not 'compellingly clear' that Parliament can be taken to have intended to deprive a defendant of the right to a trial by judge and jury or magistrates' court of a discrete offence by implication.

Accordingly, we hold that it was wrong in principle for the judge to undertake the exercise, and make the finding, that he did in relation to the August 2004 incident.

The principle must not be taken too far. As the court in *Canavan* recognised, full account can be taken of 'acts done in the course of committing that offence or offences even when such acts might have been separately charged'. In the specific case of sexual offences against children, evidence about the offences charged may demonstrate a pattern of behaviour before their commission which includes other criminal conduct, for example conduct which is an offence contrary to sections 14 or 15 of the Sexual Offences Act 2003. Such conduct is clearly part of 'a pattern of behaviour of which the offence forms part'. Nor, in our view, would a judge who had presided over a trial of a defendant charged with a sexual offence at which evidence of similar conduct was given, and must have been accepted by a jury, whether in relation to the same or another complainant, be prevented from taking such behaviour into account under section 229(2)(b). The judge who sentenced Z (see [2003] All E.R. 385) could not realistically have been expected to treat his offence of rape as an isolated incident.

In his sentencing remarks, the judge made it clear that it was his finding about the incident in August 2004 which led him to conclude that the statutory criteria for a sentence of imprisonment for public protection were satisfied. Because the means by which he reached that decision was flawed, we must review it afresh."

34.35   On considering the case afresh, the Court was in receipt of new information relating to the appellant secured for the purposes of the appeal hearing and was able legitimately to impose a sentence of IPP. The new information included a psychiatric report prepared for the purposes of the appeal which revealed that the offender admitted having sexual feelings for the boy he assaulted in the August 2004 incident.

Farrar explained

34.36   In *Considine; Davies*,[44] a five-judge Court of Appeal presided over by the President of the Queen's Bench Division stressed that *Farrar* clearly did not decide that, absent a conviction, the court making the decision as to dangerousness is precluded from considering evidence of previous misconduct which would amount to a criminal offence. The "information" which can be taken into account for the purposes of s.229(2) is not restricted to "evidence", nor to the offender's previous convictions or a pattern of behaviour established by them. Instead, as a matter of statutory construction, relevant information bearing on the assessment of dangerousness may

---

[44] [2007] EWCA Crim 1166; [2007] Crim. L.R. 824.

take the form of material adverse to the offender which is not substantiated or proved by criminal convictions. In fact, ultimately in *Farrar* the Court of Appeal had taken into account material directly related to the August 2004 incident which was contained in the fresh psychiatric report. The Court observed that it was therefore difficult to see how evidence admitted under the bad character provisions of the CJA 2003 for consideration by the jury determining the defendant's guilt could be ignored for the purposes of the assessment under s.229. If such evidence is relevant and admissible as to guilt, then it may plainly provide "information" for a dangerousness assessment. If such evidence would have been admissible for bad character purposes, the defendant could not legitimately circumvent its deployment in the course of a dangerousness assessment by pleading guilty. Equally, if a judge excluded bad character evidence on the basis of lack of relevance or the unfairness which would ensue if it were admitted, the same conclusion would follow. The Court accepted the submissions of the Attorney General that there can be no logical reason for distinguishing between formal evidence, adduced before a jury, and evidence or information which comes before the court through some different route.[45] It stated, following *Johnson*, that when a judge is reaching a conclusion as to dangerousness which is adverse to the defendant, he should not rely on a disputed fact unless it can be resolved "fairly" to the offender. The Court cited an example of unfairness as being when a defendant was undercharged (notwithstanding the availability of evidence to prosecute him for a more serious offence) on the basis that, if convicted of the less serious offence, the court could then be supplied by the prosecution with all the "information" relating to the more serious offence. If the defendant was then treated as if he had been convicted of that offence, that would be unfair to him because he might effectively be convicted in the course of the sentencing process without due process. However, the Court deliberately declined to lay down any hard and fast rules as to how a court should approach the resolution of disputed facts when making the necessary dangerousness risk assessment. The Court was of the view that, in reality, there will be very few cases in which a fair analysis of the information in the prosecution papers, the events at any trial, the judicial assessment of the defendant's character and personality,[46] the mitigation material presented to the court on behalf of the defendant, the pre-sentence report and any

---

[45] The Court entertained reservations as to whether the full ambit of the principle in *Canavan* [1998] 1 Cr. App. R.(S.) 243 (for which see paras 34.58 and following, below) applied to the assessment of dangerousness under s.229. What *Farrar*, in keeping with *Canavan*, prohibits is the introduction of a hybrid arrangement of an effective conviction of a serious criminal offence after trial by judge alone in the course of a sentencing decision. The Court explained that a *Newton* hearing is not an acceptable form of trial for a criminal offence. It is a precondition to a *Newton* hearing that the defendant admits guilt and so it is inappropriate to use a *Newton* hearing to decide whether the offender has committed a similar offence to those before the court when assessing dangerousness.

[46] The Court observed that this is always a critical feature in the assessment.

psychiatric or psychological reports should not provide the judge with sufficient information for his task in relation to s.229.

Pre-Sentence Reports

34.37   In most cases where a sentencer is considering a sentence under the dangerousness provisions, he should secure a pre-sentence report. In *Attorney General's Reference (No.145 of 2006)*,[47] Pitchers J, giving the judgment of a Court presided over by Lord Phillips LCJ, said[48]:

> "The sentencing court has an obligation under section 156(3) of the Act to obtain a report before considering this issue unless it is of the opinion that it is unnecessary to do so. At each extreme of the spectrum of sexual offending, it may be that the answer to the question of risk is so clear that no report need be obtained. However, in most cases the court will need help from the Probation Service who use such risk assessment tools as OASYS and Risk Matrix 2000 which can provide valuable help to the sentencer in taking this crucial sentencing decision."

The Goodyear Procedure

34.38   In *Kulah*,[49] the Court of Appeal overturned a sentence of IPP when inappropriate use of the *Goodyear*[50] procedure meant that the appellant had been sentenced without a pre-sentence report and thus without any proper risk assessment as to dangerousness being carried out. The Court said that if a court decides to give a *Goodyear* indication where an assessment of future risk remains to be made, it should make the following clear[51]:

> "(a) The offence (or one or more of them) is a specified offence listed in Schedule 15 to the [Criminal Justice Act 2003], bringing into operation the 'dangerous offender' provisions contained in Part 12, Chapter 5 of that Act.
> (b) The information and materials necessary to undertake the assessment of future risk which is required by those provisions are not available and that that assessment remains to be conducted.
> (c) If the defendant is later assessed as 'dangerous', the sentences mandated by the provisions—an indeterminate or extended sentence—will be imposed.
> (d) If the defendant is not later assessed as 'dangerous', the indication relates in the ordinary way to the maximum determinate sentence which will be imposed.
> (e) If the offender is later assessed as 'dangerous', the indication can only relate to the notional determinate term which will be used in the calculation of the minimum specified period the offender would have to serve before he may apply to the Parole Board to direct his release; or, in a case where an extended sentence is the only lawful option, it will relate to the appropriate custodial term within

[47] [2007] EWCA Crim 692.
[48] At [18]. The importance of securing a pre-sentence report in most cases where dangerousness is being assessed was re-emphasised in *Considine; Davies* [2007] EWCA Crim 1166.
[49] [2007] EWCA Crim 1701.
[50] [2005] EWCA Crim 888.
[51] At [30].

the extended sentence (that is, the indication does not encompass the length of any extension period during which the offender will be on licence following his release). It must be remembered that where an extended sentence is imposed on any offender, the appropriate custodial term cannot be less than 12 months (subsections 227(3)(b); 228(3)(b)).

(f) If an indeterminate sentence is mandated by the provisions, the actual amount of time the offender will spend in custody is not within the control of the sentencing judge, only its minimum."

The Court added that nevertheless judges may, understandably, feel a reluctance to give a *Goodyear* indication in circumstances where they do not yet know how dangerous the defendant really is.

A court should also be slow to give a *Goodyear* indication where a victim   **34.39** personal statement has not been obtained. Paragraph 1.23 of the Sentencing Guidelines Council's Sexual Offences Definitive Guideline (which is no longer in force) stipulated that "If a victim personal statement has not been produced, the court should enquire whether the victim has been given the opportunity to make one. In the absence of a victim personal statement, the court should not assume that the offence had no impact on the victim". In *Black and Gowan*[52] the Court of Appeal was highly critical of the sentencing of two young men for an offence of rape in the absence of a victim personal statement. In dealing with a reference by the Solicitor General concerned with the leniency of the sentences passed, the Court observed[53]:

"In our view, given the circumstances of the offences and the offenders, these two young men should have been sentenced ... only when the victim impact statement was available to the court. Lord Woolf CJ, in *Millberry* said, in terms, that there are three dimensions to an assessment of the gravity of an offence of rape: the impact of the offence on the victim, the level of culpability of the offender and the level of risk that the offender poses to society. We appreciate that [the learned judge] saw the complainant give evidence during the trial of *Gowan*, but the impact of the offence upon her was not relevant to the trial itself and it seems nothing of significance emerged during it.

In our view, therefore, it was incumbent upon the prosecution to ensure that the judge had as much information as possible about the impact upon the victim of the offence, before proceeding to sentence her rapist and his accomplice, unless, of course, there were compelling reasons to the contrary. Similarly, in our view, it was incumbent upon the judge to call for such a statement before proceeding to sentence. Had the judge had the benefit of the victim impact statement in this case he might, with respect, have appreciated the offence was rather more serious than he seems to have thought. As it was, although the judge's sentencing remarks dwelt, at some length, on the effect of the offence on the offenders and on the offenders' families, he made no mention at either hearing of the lasting effect on the offenders' victim, or indeed on the offenders' victim's family. That was, in our judgment, unfortunate, to say the least. Whether or not a victim impact statement was available to him, it should have been glaringly obvious to him that a 16-year-old girl raped in these circumstances was bound to suffer long-term and grave consequences."

[52] [2006] EWCA Crim 2306.
[53] At [28].

The Inter-Relationship between Indeterminate and Determinate Sentences

34.40   The Court of Appeal has issued extensive guidance at different times to sentencing judges as to the practice to be followed when consecutive sentences are passed which include one of the sentences under ss.224–229 of the CJA 2003. In *O'Brien*[54] the Court was faced with two related questions: first, "Can a sentence of IPP be ordered to run consecutively to another sentence of IPP?" and secondly, "If a defendant has offended whilst on licence and the court wishes to order the defendant to serve the remaining period of a previous sentence of imprisonment pursuant to s.116 of the PCCSA 2000[55] and is also sentencing the defendant to a sentence of IPP, how may that be achieved?". Whilst the sentence of IPP is no longer available, the Court's analysis is still relevant to the question whether a court may impose consecutive indeterminate sentences, or order an indeterminate sentence to be served consecutively to another period of imprisonment. Hooper LJ, giving the judgment of the Court, gave the following detailed explanation of the applicable principles:

"58. We were taken through the statutory provisions relevant to indeterminate sentences and it is agreed that there is no provision which forbids the imposition of consecutive indeterminate sentences or the imposition of an indeterminate sentence consecutive to another period of imprisonment. The situation has not changed since the decision in *Jones* (1962) Cr.App.R.129. Ashworth J. giving the judgment of the Court of Criminal Appeal said (pages 148–149):

'There remains the question of sentence. The learned judge in passing sentence said:

"You have been found guilty now of two crimes, evil to a degree beyond all adjectives, and it is proper that you should serve your sentence for the first crime and that neither as a matter of fact nor of appearance should it cease to be operative. In these circumstances, I pass upon you the sentence according to statute that you can be sentenced to imprisonment for life and for the protection of the public. I think firstly that it should be a sentence to commence upon the expiration of your existing sentence and secondly that it would be lamentable indeed if upon the second sentence you did not serve a far longer time than upon the first."

It was contended before us that the form of the sentence was wrong in principle in that it amounted to a 'sentence of life imprisonment less the unremitted portion of the sentence of fourteen years'. Further, it was contended that the learned judge was in error in supposing that if the sentence of life imprisonment were made to take effect at once, the sentence of fourteen years would merge with it and for practical purposes cease to operate.

We were assisted on this point by the Attorney General as amicus curiae, and he assured us that the two sentences would not merge, if the life sentence were made concurrent, and that the sentence of fourteen years would not be affected in any way. According to him, there was no practical difference whatever between a life sentence made concurrent and one made consecutive,

[54] [2006] EWCA Crim 1741.
[55] Since repealed by the CJA 2003.

but he submitted the view that it is undesirable to make the life sentence consecutive since it achieves no practical result.

We have no doubt that the learned judge had power to make the life sentence consecutive to the earlier sentence of fourteen years, but we accept the Attorney General's submission that a consecutive sentence is undesirable. Since the practical result would be the same in any event, we see no reason to allow the appeal against sentence, and it is dismissed.

We would only add that our attention was called to several unreported judgments of this court in regard to life sentences. It is, in our view, difficult to reconcile all the observations contained in those judgments, but on the present occasion there is no need to attempt the task.'

59. We share the view expressed in that case that it is undesirable to impose consecutive indeterminate sentences or order an indeterminate sentence to be served consecutively to another period of imprisonment. Common sense suggests that a sentence of life imprisonment or of IPP starts immediately on its imposition. Given the difficulties that may be encountered already in determining when a prisoner must be released or is eligible for parole, it seems to us to be much easier not to compound those difficulties by making indeterminate sentences consecutive to other sentences or periods in custody.

60. We are supported in our conclusion by a passage in *Lang and others* where the Vice President said (in paragraph 20) that it 'will not usually be appropriate to impose consecutive extended sentences'. (See also *S* [2005] EWCA Crim 3616, paragraph 30.)

61. We shall consider first the following situation: but for the undesirability of making indeterminate sentences consecutive to other terms, the judge would want the period before which the defendant will become eligible for parole to be consecutive to an existing sentence or to follow a period imposed under section 116 of the Powers of Criminal Courts (Sentencing) Act 2000 (return to prison where offence committed during original sentence). How does the judge ensure that the sentence includes the balance of the existing sentence or the section 116 period?

62. The judge should increase the notional determinate term to reflect that balance or that period. The authority for so doing is *Haywood* (2000) 2 Cr. App. R.(S.) 418. The appellant had been sentenced to 8 years' imprisonment for robbery etc and two days after being sentenced he attacked a prison officer. He pleaded guilty to wounding with intent (section 18). The Recorder of Liverpool sentenced him to life imprisonment, as he was obliged to do and specified: 'the part to be served by reference to the period the appellant would have had to serve if the Recorder had imposed seven years' imprisonment consecutive, as he would have done but for section 2 [automatic life sentence].'

63. The Recorder started with a term of 15 years and halved it and then (wrongly as the Court of Appeal said) reduced that period by the time spent in custody on remand (the appellant had never been in custody anyway for the robbery).

64. In the words of Lord Bingham CJ (pages 432–433):

'In our judgment the Recorder took a logical and obviously sensible step . . . This result is in no way unjust to the appellant who on any showing deserves a measure of punishment for this serious offence, and who clearly presents a continuing risk of danger to the public. We consider that the course which the Recorder adopted promotes the public policy underlying the Act and it furthermore avoided the obvious anomaly which would have arisen had the submissions of counsel been accepted.'

65. If the Recorder had set the notional determinate term to reflect only the section 18 offence, then, in Lord Bingham's words, 'virtually nothing' would have been added to the sentence which the appellant was already serving, a result

which Lord Bingham described as 'obviously absurd' (page 422). The principle in *Haywood* was cited with approval by the Vice President in *Szczerba* [2002] EWCA Crim 440, paragraph 33; [2002] 2 Cr. App. R.(S.) 86, at page 387. The statutory provision in *Haywood* equivalent to what is now section 82A of the Powers of Criminal Courts (Sentencing) Act 2000 (paragraph 31 above) was section 28 of the Crime (Sentences) Act 1997. Given that the two provisions are very similar, the principles laid down in *Haywood* would also apply section 82A.

66. In *Szczerba* the Vice President said (paragraph 33):

'There are, however, circumstances in which more than half may well be appropriate. Dr Thomas identified two examples. In *Hayward* (2000) 2 Cr. App. R.(S.) 418 a life sentence was imposed on a serving prisoner for an offence committed in prison. In such a case the term specified can appropriately be fixed to end at a date after that on which the defendant would have been eligible for release on licence from his original sentence. This may involve identifying a proportion of the notional determinate term up to two-thirds. Another example is where a life sentence is imposed on a defendant for an offence committed during licensed release from an earlier sentence, who is therefore susceptible to return to custody under section 116 of the Powers of Criminal Courts (Sentencing) Act 2000. In such a case the specified period could properly be increased above one-half, to reflect the fact that a specified period cannot be ordered to run consecutively to any other sentence.'

67. On our reading of *Haywood* the Recorder achieved the desired objective by increasing the notional determinate term and not by dividing that term by (up to) two thirds rather than by a half to reach the minimum term. We think that increasing the notional determinate sentence is the better way. Indeed, for cases to which section 244 of the Criminal Justice Act 2003 applies . . . the notional determinate sentence should be divided by half to arrive at the specified minimum term.

68. In our view any section 116 period should be treated in the same way, that is by adding it to the notional determinate term which the judge would otherwise have set. As we understand it, a section 116 period attracts the early release provisions. A defendant sentenced to three years imprisonment to be served following a one year section 116 period will be released after two years. By adding the period to the notional determinate term and then halving it, the prisoner is in the same position as he would have been if the judge had passed a determinate term of the same length as the notional determinate term and made it consecutive to the section 116 period.

69. There is one more practical problem which we should address. Assume that a judge is imposing concurrent indeterminate sentences for two or more offences with corresponding concurrent minimum terms. Assume that, if he had not passed indeterminate sentences he would have passed determinate custodial sentences for those offences consecutive to each other. How does he reflect in the notional determinate term the totality of the offending? The answer is, we believe, either to choose the same notional determinate term for all of the offences or take the most serious and make the notional determinate term reflect the totality of the offending. We return to the *O'Brien* case. The notional determinate term for the robbery should reflect the need to punish both the assault with intent to rob and the robbery. That is why we increased the notional determinate sentence for the robbery in his case. This is in accordance with section 82A(3)(a) of the Powers of Criminal Courts (Sentencing) Act 2000.

70. Finally we wish to say something about appeals. Given our view that it is not unlawful but merely undesirable to make consecutive indeterminate sentences or to make them consecutive to some other term or period of imprisonment, permission to appeal should not normally be granted on this ground only.

Our reason for saying this is that if an appeal succeeds on this point only, then it is unlikely that the length of time which the prisoner will have to serve before being eligible for parole will be altered. In such circumstances there would be no practical point in giving permission to appeal."

O'Brien has since been followed in a number of cases dealing with the **34.41** practical problems associated with sentences under ss.224–229. In *Brown*[56] the Court of Appeal considered problems associated with the imposition of consecutive "old style" extended sentences and the imposition of an extended sentence along with a consecutive determinate sentence. Whilst the court has the power to pass either combination of sentences, difficulty might arise in both situations because of the terms of s.247 of the CJA 2003. That section dictates that a prisoner serving an extended sentence must be released as soon as he has served half of the custodial term of the sentence and the Parole Board has directed his release, being satisfied that it is no longer necessary for the protection of the public that he be confined. If consecutive extended sentences are imposed then considerable problems are created in determining the application of the appropriate licence period once the custodial element has been served. If a determinate sentence was made consecutive to an extended sentence it may be difficult to determine when the custodial element of the extended term ends and the determinate sentence began. The Court therefore advised that consecutive extended sentences and the imposition of a determinate sentence consecutive to an extended sentence are, in general terms, not appropriate and should be avoided. The Court could see no reason to suggest that such problems would arise if an extended sentence were made consecutive to a determinate sentence. Similarly, concurrent extended sentences would not cause such problems, nor would an extended sentence concurrent to a determinate sentence cause insuperable difficulties. However, in the latter case a concurrent determinate sentence longer than the custodial element of the extended sentence might well have the effect of subsuming the extended licence period and thus defeating the object of the extended sentence. It is thus sensible to avoid such a combination of sentences.

In *R. v C*,[57] the Court of Appeal was again dealing with old-style extended **34.42** sentences, but its judgment applies equally to sentences of imprisonment for life. In giving the judgment of the Court, the Vice President, Latham LJ stated:

"In summary, our conclusions as to the practice to be adopted in dealing with consecutive and concurrent sentences in this complex area of sentencing are as follows:

a. There is nothing unlawful about the imposition of a concurrent or consecutive sentence within either regime relating to extended sentences, and indeed, as explained by Hooper L.J. in *R. v O'Brien et al* [2006] EWCA Crim

---

[56] [2006] EWCA Crim 1996.
[57] [2007] EWCA Crim 680.

1741, where sentences of life imprisonment or imprisonment for public protection are imposed under chapter 5, this court will not interfere where extended or indeterminate sentences were justified, unless the practical result is manifestly excessive, or for some reason gives rise to real problems of administration.

b. Nonetheless, judges should try to avoid consecutive sentences if that is at all possible and adjust the custodial term or minimum period within concurrent sentences to reflect the overall criminality if that is possible within other sentencing constraints.

c. If consecutive sentences are considered appropriate, as in the example that we have already given, or necessary, if one or more of those sentences are determinate sentences, the determinate sentences should be imposed first, and the extended sentence or sentences expressed to be consecutive.

d. In shaping the overall sentence, judges should remember that there is no obligation for the sentences to be expressed in historical date order. There is nothing wrong with stating that the sentence for the first offence in point of time should be served consecutively to a sentence or sentences imposed for any later offence or offences."

34.43   In *Ashes*[58] the Court of Appeal gave yet more guidance in this difficult field. Although the Court was primarily concerned with the sentence of IPP, the analysis remains useful. It answered three questions concerned with the imposition of sentences of IPP and determinate sentences. The first ("Issue A") was how, under the existing legislation, a court should set a minimum term when imposing a sentence of IPP where it is imposed upon a prisoner who is already subject to and serving an existing custodial term. The second ("Issue B") was how the court should approach as a matter of principle imposing a sentence of imprisonment upon someone who is already serving a sentence of IPP and whether in the circumstances some adjustment, if it is otherwise permissible, may be made to the term which he is destined to serve before release may be considered. The third ("Issue C") was how in such circumstances, if it is permissible to do either the first or second as a matter of principle, the court should approach the time spent in custody.

34.44   So far as Issue A is concerned, the Court said that in the light of *O'Brien* and *R. v C*, the court should try to impose a term for the sentence of IPP which is concurrent with the existing determinate sentence but which also takes account of:

(a) the period still then remaining to be *served* under the existing determinate term and that should be the period of the sentence still to be served but then halved to take account of the automatic release provisions for determinate sentences;

(b) the appropriate *additional* period as the sentence for the offence in respect of which the court was minded to impose a term of IPP, which should then be halved; and

[58] [2007] EWCA Crim 1848.

(c) the need to ensure that the total of the sentences imposed under sub-paragraphs (a) and (b) above does not offend the principle of totality.

The Court also stressed that the sentencing judge should bear in mind that the period imposed in the sentence of IPP is the period which the offender *must* serve before he or she is considered for parole and that means that the constituent period to be taken into account for ascertaining the determinate sentence at stage (a) above is the period remaining to be *served* (which is now one-half of the sentence) rather than the total sentence imposed.

As for Issue B, the Court (echoing the concerns expressed in *Brown* and *R. v C)* observed that, in the ordinary way, in cases in which the appropriate sentence would be a consecutive sentence to the sentence of IPP, there is a serious problem because a sentencing judge considering imposing such a sentence does not know when the existing sentence of IPP will expire as he or she cannot predict when the Parole Board will agree to release the offender. The court also recognised a further difficulty which is that even if the offender might be safe for release at the end of the sentence of IPP, there is no guarantee that he or she will also be safe to be released at the end of any consecutive determinate sentence. Thus problems arise first as to how to shape a sentence which would overcome this difficulty and second in ascertaining the date when the sentence of IPP ends and when the determinate sentence starts. The Court suggested that there are three possible approaches depending on the circumstances: **34.45**

(a) if the subsequent offence is one for which a sentence of IPP is available, then the sentencing judge could pass a new sentence of IPP so as to take account of not only the balance of the existing minimum term yet to be served but also the principle of totality;

(b) if the offence with which the sentence is concerned is "associated" with the offence of which the sentence of IPP was passed, one other option might be to adjust the minimum term of the sentence of IPP to reflect the criminality of that extra offence but to give no separate sentence for the new offence (see s.226(1) of the CJA 2003); or

(c) the judge could order that the determinate sentence be served first and the sentence of IPP be served consecutively but *only* if he was dealing with them on the same occasion.

The Court also expressed a provisional view that when dealing on a subsequent occasion with a further offence, the sentencing court should impose an appropriate concurrent sentence, be it determinate, indeterminate or extended, depending on the circumstances. In any event the Parole Board would be able to take into consideration the subsequent offence in determining whether to release the offender. The case before them did not require a concluded decision on that issue and the Court considered that it would be more appropriate to await a case in which that issue is a live point. **34.46**

Finally, in relation to Issue C, the answer to the question depends on whether the offender was in custody because he was serving an existing **34.47** sentence when he is sentenced for the second offence. If he was, then his time in custody will not be deducted for the purpose of the second sentence while if he was in custody but not because he was serving an existing sentence, then this time will be deducted from his sentence.[59]

34.48   Where an offender is convicted on two counts of an indictment, the first of which requires a sentence of IPP and the second of which requires an extended sentence, the sentencing court must impose the extended sentence and not order "no separate penalty" on the second count, deeming the criminality to have been covered by the sentence of IPP on the first count. There has to be both a sentence of IPP and an extended sentence, no matter how artificial and cumbersome that may be for the prison service.[60]

34.49   An issue not previously dealt with was resolved in *Hills*.[61] The case was concerned with the situation where an offender falls to be sentenced for an offence committed while serving the minimum term of an indeterminate sentence but where a further indeterminate sentence, if imposed concurrently, could not add in any way to the length of the period before which the offender would be considered for release on parole, in circumstances where it is clear that the interests of justice require in effect a consecutive sentence. The appellant had been serving a sentence of Detention for Public Protection ("DePP") with a minimum term of four years when he assaulted a prison officer causing him actual bodily harm. He was sentenced to three years' imprisonment consecutive to the sentence of DePP. The Court of Appeal rejected submissions that it was wrong in principle to impose a sentence that was deferred to commence at the end of a minimum term and there was no basis in the legislation for the passing of such a sentence. As to the matter of principle, it would be extremely unfortunate if the court were not able to impose a sentence which extended the period before which an offender was to be considered for parole. If that were the case, it would effectively mean that, subject always to consideration by the Parole Board, the offender would not have any punishment for what could be a serious offence committed during the course of imprisonment. In respect of the submission that there was no legal basis for the passing of such a sentence, the court referred to s.154 of the Powers of Criminal Courts (Sentencing) Act 2000, which provides that:

> "A sentence imposed, or other order made, by the Crown Court . . . shall take effect at the beginning of the day on which it was imposed, unless the court otherwise directs."

The Court of Appeal held that s.154 gives the sentencing court the power to direct that a sentence should or could commence at a different date. It further observed that the sentencing regime which has been created in particular by

[59] In reaching that conclusion the Court analysed the provisions of s.240 of the CJA 2003 and the Remand in Custody (Effect of Concurrent and Consecutive Sentences of Imprisonment) Rules 2005 (SI 2005/2054).
[60] *Younas* [2007] EWCA Crim 1676.
[61] [2008] EWCA Crim 1871.

the CJA 2003 provides for clear dates upon which minimum terms will come to an end, which enable a court to identify with precision the date upon which otherwise an offender could be considered for release on parole. There was thus no practical reason why an order should not be made which requires the offender to commence to serve an additional period after the minimum period before he can be considered for parole. The Court concluded that the old authorities to the contrary effect are no longer relevant now that minimum terms are clearly identified.

In respect of extended sentences, the Court of Appeal in *Pinnell*[62] departed substantially from the thrust of the line of authority set out above as a result of the changes made to the extended sentence regime by the Criminal Justice and Immigration Act 2008. The Court noted the concern about consecutive extended sentences set out in *Brown*, namely that the prisoner would only be released from such a sentence after serving half of the custodial term if the Parole Board was satisfied that it was no longer necessary for the protection of the public that he be confined. As a result, if a sentence was made consecutive to an extended sentence, it might be difficult to determine when the custodial element of the extended term ended and the consecutive sentence began. The Court in *Pinnell* observed that this practical objection no longer applied since changes made by the 2008 Act, which required that a prisoner be released from the custodial element of an extended sentence at the half-way point, so that the date of release from the custodial term would be known at the time of sentence. However, the picture has moved again as a result of changes to the extended sentence regime made first by LASPO and more recently by the Criminal Justice and Courts Act 2015, under which the prisoner will only be released at the two-thirds point of the custodial element at the direction of the Parole Board. As a result of these changes, once again the release date cannot be known at the time of sentence, and we therefore suggest that in this respect *Pinnell* ought not to be relied upon. Indeed, the Court of Appeal in *Hibbert*,[63] without referring to *Pinnell*, said that where consecutive sentences are considered necessary and imposed at the same time, if one is a determinate sentence and one an extended sentence, the determinate sentence should be imposed first and the extended sentence expressed to be consecutive to it, precisely because of the problems that can otherwise arise, just as was the position under the "old" form of extended sentence which was replaced by the LASPO provisions. **34.50**

There are, however, are circumstances, such as those in *Hibbert* itself, where the defendant is already serving an extended sentence, when he comes to be sentenced for a further matter. In such a situation, there would be nothing unlawful about the imposition of a determinate sentence consecutive to the extended sentence. Where consecutive extended sentences are appropriate, is not possible to pass consecutive custodial terms with the extended **34.51**

---

[62] [2010] EWCA Crim 2848. See also *Watkins* [2014] EWCA Crim 1677.
[63] [2015] EWCA Crim 507.

licence terms to run concurrently.[64] The court should always make it clear to which offences consecutive extended sentences are attributed, as it is the overall extended term sentence that must be consecutive and not just the custodial terms.[65]

OFFENCES COMMITTED ON DATES STRADDLING EITHER MAY 1, 2004 OR APRIL 4, 2005

SENTENCING WHERE THE DATES OF THE OFFENCES SPAN MAY 1, 2004

34.52 When the SOA 2003 came into force on May 1, 2004, it did so without transitional or saving provisions. Consequently, all repeals of existing statutory provisions took place at the same time. That meant that a person could not be convicted of an offence that was either repealed or enacted on that date unless it could be proved that the offence took place either before or after May 1, 2004 (as the case may be).[66] That profoundly unsatisfactory situation was partially resolved by s.55 of the Violent Crime Reduction Act 2006, which provides as follows:

> **"55 Continuity of sexual offences law**
>
> (1) This section applies where, in any proceedings—
> (a) a person ('the defendant') is charged in respect of the same conduct both with an offence under the Sexual Offences Act 2003 ('the 2003 Act offence') and with an offence specified in subsection (2) ('the pre-commencement offence');
> (b) the only thing preventing the defendant from being found guilty of the 2003 Act offence is the fact that it has not been proved beyond a reasonable doubt that the time when the conduct took place was after the coming into force of the enactment providing for the offence; and
> (c) the only thing preventing the defendant from being found guilty of the pre-commencement offence is the fact that it has not been proved beyond a reasonable doubt that that time was before the coming into force of the repeal of the enactment providing for the offence.
> (2) The offences referred to in subsection (1)(a) are—
> (a) any offence under the Sexual Offences Act 1956;
> (b) an offence under section 4 of the Vagrancy Act 1824 (obscene exposure);
> (c) an offence under section 28 of the Town Police Clauses Act 1847 (indecent exposure);
> (d) an offence under section 61 or 62 of the Offences against the Person Act 1861 (buggery etc.);
> (e) an offence under section 128 of the Mental Health Act 1959 (sexual intercourse with patients);
> (f) an offence under section 1 of the Indecency with Children Act 1960 (indecency with children);

---

[64] *Watkins* [2014] EWCA Crim 1677.
[65] *Pinnell* [2010] EWCA Crim 2848; *Francis and Lawrence* [2014] EWCA Crim 631.
[66] See *A (A Prosecutor's Appeal)* [2005] EWCA Crim 3533.

(g) an offence under section 4 or 5 of the Sexual Offences Act 1967 (procuring a man to commit buggery and living on the earnings of male prostitution);

(h) an offence under section 9 of the Theft Act 1968 (burglary, including entering premises with intent to commit rape);

(i) an offence under section 54 of the Criminal Law Act 1977 (incitement of girl under 16 to commit incest);

(j) an offence under section 1 of the Protection of Children Act 1978 (indecent photographs of children);

(k) an offence under section 3 of the Sexual Offences (Amendment) Act 2000 (abuse of position of trust);

(l) an offence under section 145 of the Nationality, Immigration and Asylum Act 2002 (traffic in prostitution).

(3) For the purpose of determining the guilt of the defendant it shall be conclusively presumed that the time when the conduct took place was—

(a) if the maximum penalty for the pre-commencement offence is less than the maximum penalty for the 2003 Act offence, a time before the coming into force of the repeal of the enactment providing for the pre-commencement offence; and

(b) in any other case, a time after the coming into force of the enactment providing for the 2003 Act offence."

Accordingly, where it is not established whether the offending conduct took place before or after May 1, 2004, the conclusive presumption is that the offence of which the offender is guilty is the one which has the lower maximum penalty. If the offence was committed under the Sexual Offences Act 2003, i.e. on or after May 1, 2004, but before April 4, 2005, the sentencing provisions of the CJA 2003 including the dangerous offender regime will not apply.

SENTENCING WHERE THE DATES OF THE OFFENCES SPAN APRIL 4, 2005

The sentencing provisions under the CJA 2003 came into force on April 4, **34.53** 2005. If a count on an indictment straddles April 4, 2005, then, unless the court is satisfied on conviction that the offence occurred after April 4, 2005, the offender should be sentenced on the basis that the offence occurred prior to that date.[67]

In *Stannard*,[68] the Court of Appeal expressed sympathy with judges who **34.54** were required to sentence offenders for offences falling within the dangerous offender provisions of the CJA 2003 committed before and after April 4, 2005. The Court referred to the apparent suggestion in *Lang*[69] that if a defendant was being sentenced for offences committed both before and after that date, it would generally be preferable to pass sentence for the later offences by reference to the new regime, imposing no separate penalty for the

---

[67] *Re Harries* [2008] 1 Cr. App. R.(S.) 47.
[68] [2008] EWCA Crim 2789.
[69] [2005] EWCA Crim 2864.

earlier offences. The Court in *Stannard* observed that the imposition of no separate penalty for a relatively minor offence when the offender was sentenced for more serious offences was sometimes a convenient way of avoiding some of the extraordinary complexity of current sentencing provisions. But in other circumstances such a practice could cause public concern about the administration of the criminal justice system. It could rarely be appropriate for a serious offence to be the subject of no separate penalty. Usually, the victim of a "serious" or "specified" offence should be vindicated, and an order for no separate penalty would tend to convey to the victim that the court had not properly addressed the impact of the crimes. The problem is plainly less acute when the indictment relates to offending against a single victim.

Special Custodial Sentences for Certain Offenders of Particular Concern—S.236A CJA 2003.

34.55   Section 236A of the Criminal Justice Act 2003 (CJA 2003) was introduced into the CJA 2003 by s.6 and Sch.1 of the Criminal Justice and Courts Act 2015. S.236A applies to those who were over 18 when they committed an offence under s.5 or s.6 of the SOA 2003, i.e. rape or assault by penetration of a child under 13, or a repealed historic offence involving rape or penetration of a child under 13.[69a] It applies to all those sentenced on or after April 13, 2015 irrespective of when the offence was committed. If a sentencer does not impose a life or extended sentence for such an offence or an associated offence, then a sentence of imprisonment imposed must be equal to the aggregate of the appropriate custodial term *and a further period of one year* during which the offender is on licence. The amended release provisions[69b] mean that under such a sentence, the offender will be referred to the Parole Board at the midway point, and the Board will only direct release when satisfied that the offender's further confinement is not necessary for the protection of the public. The offender is only entitled to be released after he has served the full custodial term and he will then be subject to 12 months' licence. This arrangement is designed to ensure that such offenders are always on licence upon release for a minimum of 12 months even though, by

---

[69a] It applies to offences listed in Schedule 18A which includes inchoate offences. In respect of historic cases, it is most likely to occur in respect of offences under s.14 (indecent assault on a woman) and s.15 SOA 1956 (indecent assault on a man). There may be cases under other sections of the SOA 1956: s.1 (rape), s.5 (sexual intercourse upon a girl aged under 13) or s.12 (buggery) might be charged under s.5 or s.6 of SOA 2003. Ideally the threshold ages and penetration alleged should be particularised on the indictment. If not, to pass a s.236A sentence, there would have to be an admission or finding of fact as to threshold ages and penetration. Failure to particularise would not be a fatal impediment if the age and penetration criteria are established: *Harries* [2008] 1 Cr App R (S) 47. See *R. v LF and DS* [2016] EWCA Crim 561 at [4], [10] and [28].
[69b] s.244A CJA 2013 (also introduced into the CJA by s.6 of the Criminal Justice and Courts Act 2015) governs the release of a prisoner serving under s.236A.

definition, they have not been found to be 'dangerous.' In the recent conjoined appeals of *R. v LF and DS*,[69c] the Court of Appeal considered various issues that can arise in s.236A cases and has provided useful guidance. Courts should not suspend a sentence under s.236A. In the unusual event of a case where the court might have considered a suspended sentence, a community sentence should be considered. A s.236A sentence is a single indivisible sentence comprising a custodial term and an extension period, and it should be expressed as a such. It is not possible for one element to run consecutively whilst the other element runs concurrently. All of it must be ordered to run consecutively or concurrently. No problems arise in a multiple offending case if s.236A sentences are ordered to run concurrently or a s.236A sentence is ordered to run consecutively to a determinate sentence. Where consecutive s.236A sentences are passed, consecutive periods of licence must follow. In such a case, the total custodial term for those offences as well as the total further period of licence should be stated at the end of sentencing.

MISCELLANEOUS

SENTENCING FALSE COMPLAINTS OF RAPE

There is no formal guideline case on sentencing false complaints of rape, but in *McKenning*[70] Lord Judge CJ provided an authoritative statement of principle as to the seriousness of such offences and the policy considerations underlying any sentencing decision:

34.56

> "Our attention has been drawn to a number of cases. They were not, as far as we are aware, before the judge; but they do not sufficiently focus on the serious policy question which the judge addressed. The judge noted the effect of this offence on the victim, Mr Holling. He pointed out that the full panoply of measures to help women who were genuinely victims of rape had been deployed; all that was wasted; the victim suffered the humiliation to which we have referred in the course of the narrative. There had been ample opportunity for the applicant to tell the truth and bring the ordeal to an end. He referred to the so called 'low conviction rate' for rape, much of which, the judge said, was ill informed, but he pointed out that when the public knew that people like the applicant were wicked enough falsely to cry rape, that would affect the minds of juries assessing the evidence of genuine victims.
>
> Our view can be briefly summarised. We endorse the approach taken by the judge. This was not, as so many cases involving the offence of doing an act tending or intended to pervert the course of public justice, a case of a guilty man or woman seeking to avoid responsibility for a crime often and frequently a relatively minor motoring offence. That is bad enough; but of its kind this was

---

[69c] [2016] EWCA Crim 561: a failure to impose a s.236A sentence when appropriate will mean that the intention of Parliament has been thwarted. Nevertheless, the Court of Appeal will not impose s s.236A sentence in such a case if it would amount to an increase in sentence. See *R. v LF and DS* [2016] EWCA Crim 561 at [29]. To intervene in such circumstances would fall foul of s.11(3) of the Criminal Appeal Act 1968.
[70] [2008] EWCA Crim 2301, at [15]–[18].

a very serious offence. Sexual intercourse with a woman without her consent is a shameful crime. When proved it merits, and it receives, heavy punishment. The reality must, however, be faced that when rape has taken place it is frequently very difficult to prove. It is also the case that when the defendant is truly innocent, a false allegation can be extremely difficult for him to refute. That is why, after sexual intercourse has taken place between adults, the investigation and prosecution of the allegation of rape presents the police and the Crown Prosecution Service, and, if the matter eventually goes to court, the jury with highly sensitive and sometimes desperately difficult decisions. Currently this is a very serious problem. The consequences for an innocent man against whom the allegation is made are very serious. In this case there was enough independent evidence eventually to enable the investigators to discover that the potential defendant was truly an innocent man. In the end he was fortunate. But for the meantime his entire life must have had a nightmarish quality. That lasted for three months. It could have been brought to an end at any time by one word from the applicant.

However, quite apart from the consequences to Mr Holling, this allegation involves more than the individual victim. Every false allegation of rape increases the plight of those women who have been victims of this dreadful crime. It makes the offence harder to prove and, rightly concerned to avoid the conviction of an innocent man, a jury may find itself unable to be sufficiently sure to return a guilty verdict.

This offence caused great problems for the victim; but it also damaged the administration of justice in general in this extremely sensitive area. In our judgment the sentence imposed by the judge fell within the appropriate range. Accordingly the application for leave to appeal against sentence will be refused."

In that case, the Court upheld a sentence of two years' imprisonment following an early guilty plea to attempting to pervert the course of justice. Lord Judge also made clear that authorities which pre-date *McKenning* are of limited value.

34.57   The approach in *McKenning* has been adopted, and extensively cited, in subsequent cases. In *Day (Jennifer Sylvia)*[71] the Court of Appeal emphasised the policy observation made in *McKenning* and said that a custodial sentence is inevitable in such a case. The Court explained the importance of a guilty plea as it demonstrates not only remorse but the acceptance of full responsibility for the false allegation. In that case the appellant had argued with a man at her front door. She subsequently accused him of rape. Witnesses confirmed that he had not entered the house. When officers asked her about previous false claims of rape, she admitted the latest allegation was untrue. A sentence of two years' imprisonment following a trial was upheld. The Court acknowledged that the offender had mental health and other difficulties but observed that the term of imprisonment could have been longer if the sentencing judge had been aware of the principle in *McKenning*. For further, recent examples of the approach to be taken in sentencing such

[71] [2010] 2 Cr. App. R.(S.) 12.

cases see *Jodie Simpson*[72]; *Ngwata*[73]; *Vine*[74]; *Brustenga-Vilaseca*[75]; and *England*.[76]

THE USE OF BAD CHARACTER EVIDENCE IN THE SENTENCING PROCESS

In *Canavan*,[77] which is considered in detail in paras 33.24 and following, **34.58** above, the Court of Appeal held that where a defendant is convicted after trial it is impermissible to sentence him for conduct which has not formed, expressly or by necessary implication, the subject of charges proved against him. The only exception to that rule is where the offender has explicitly assented to counts on the indictment being treated as representative of a longer course of conduct.[78]

The issue arose in the context of an allegation of murder in an sentencing **34.59** appeal by one Restivo, the facts of which are reported as part of *Oakes*.[79] The allegation against Restivo concerned a murder committed in 2002. During the course of his trial, similar fact evidence was admitted of a murder of another woman which took place in Italy in 1993. By the time of Restivo's trial for the 2002 murder, he had not been convicted of the 1993 murder by an Italian court. Ultimately, Restivo was convicted of the 2002 murder, and in passing sentence the judge said that the evidence proved without doubt that Restivo was also guilty of the 1993 murder. Whilst he recognised that Restivo had not been convicted of that crime and would not sentence him in respect of it, he intended to approach sentence for the 2002 murder on the basis that Restivo had killed before. After taking into account the 1993 killing, he imposed a whole life order.

On appeal, Lord Judge CJ remarked that, subject to certain exceptions, a **34.60** defendant cannot be sentenced for offences for which he has not been convicted, on the basis that he had committed them. He observed[80]:

> " . . . the ability of the judge to make findings that other offences have been committed does not extend to reaching a non jury verdict about allegations put before the jury by way of similar fact evidence, at least unless the jury must have been satisfied that they were proved, or unless the defendant has been convicted of them in the past."

His Lordship continued[81]:

---

[72] [2013] EWCA Crim 1250.
[73] [2012] EWCA Crim 2015.
[74] [2011] EWCA Crim 1860.
[75] [2011] EWCA Crim 1099.
[76] [2011] 1 Cr. App. R.(S.) 51.
[77] [1998] 1 Cr. App. R.(S.) 243.
[78] *R. v BDG* [2012] EWCA Crim 1283.
[79] [2012] EWCA Crim 2435.
[80] At [79].
[81] At [84].

"The principle is clear. Even when evidence which served to establish the defendant's guilt of an offence charged on the indictment is deployed as similar fact evidence, the sentencing decision cannot proceed on the basis that he is guilty of a distinct and separate offence of which he has not been convicted and which he denies. Although we sympathise with the judge's approach, it was inconsistent with what is now an axiomatic principle that . . . the ambit of the sentencing decision cannot extend to reflect a specific, distinct offence of which the offender has not been convicted."

34.61   The issue arose for consideration in the case of *Clifford*.[82] The appellant, Max Clifford, was convicted of a number of sexual offences against young women and girls. In addition to the evidence relating to the counts on the indictment, similar fact evidence was admitted which was not the subject of any counts on the indictment. The evidence was of assaults of young women of a similar age to the victims of the offences charged. The Crown had not charged these assaults because it would not be possible to disprove any claim from the appellant that he believed the encounters to be consensual. Instead, the evidence was admitted to rebut the defence advanced that all the allegations were totally untrue. Moreover, it went to the appellant's propensity to commit the type of offences alleged in the indictment. When sentencing, the judge did not specifically say that he was treating the bad character evidence as an aggravating feature. Instead, he said he would take it into account in so far as it informed him as to the offences for which he had to pass sentence. But the Court of Appeal observed that[83]:

" . . . the judge had also said in terms that he rejected [the] submission that this behaviour should be ignored entirely in the sentencing exercise, and he did set out at some length in his sentencing remarks the details of the bad character evidence. He devoted almost as much time to that as he did to the counts on the indictment. We think that the impression given must have been that the judge regarded this evidence as aggravating the case to some extent, albeit he did not say so in terms. What he did not do was explain what place it had had in the case. If he had said that it confirmed that the appellant was a serial predatory offender who abused his position in order to offend, that could not have been criticised. However the judge did not say that or anything similar; nor did he make clear that the bad character evidence would have no effect on the level of sentencing".

34.62   The Court thus concluded that the judge's comments contravened the principle in *Canavan*. However, the Court also concluded that, even with that error (and one other) on the part of the judge, the overall sentence was not manifestly excessive, and accordingly it was left undisturbed. A similar issue arose in *McCaffrey*,[84] where after conviction on a single count of exposure contrary to s.66 of the SOA 2003, the judge fell into error by sentencing the appellant on the basis that the case was not an isolated incident, but the "last straw" in a series of incidents where he had exposed his penis to the complainant. Clearly this was wrong in principle. The Court of Appeal

[82] [2014] EWCA Crim 2245.
[83] At [53].
[84] [2015] EWCA Crim 792.

accepted that the sentence was manifestly excessive as the sentence had been aggravated by five or six previous unindicted incidents of exposure.

BARRING FROM WORKING WITH CHILDREN AND VULNERABLE ADULTS

The Criminal Justice and Court Services Act 2000 first made provision for **34.63** certain persons to be indefinitely prevented from working with children. The relevant provisions have been superseded by the Safeguarding Vulnerable Groups Act 2006. The scheme of the 2006 Act, in amended form, creates lists of people barred from working with children and vulnerable adults. The lists, one relating to children and one to adults, are operated by the Disclosure and Barring Service ("DBS").[85] Under the statutory scheme, a person who accepts a caution or receives a conviction for a "relevant offence" will, subject to the consideration of representations where permitted, be placed on one or both lists and so barred from working in regulated activity,[86] with children and/or adults. Relevant offences include almost all the offences in Pt 1 of the SOA 2003.[87] A relevant offence is either an automatic barring offence (i.e. an offence in relation to which the person will be automatically barred without the opportunity to make representations) or an automatic inclusion offence (i.e. an offence in relation to which the person may make representations to the DBS before a decision is made on barring). In the case of an automatic barring offence, the person will be placed on one or both barred lists by the DBS irrespective of whether they work in regulated activity. In the case of automatic inclusion offences, barring will depend on the consideration of representations by the DBS and may take place only if the DBS believes that the person has worked, is working or may in future work in regulated activity.

Under s.7 of the 2006 Act, a person commits an offence if he seeks to **34.64** engage in, offers to engage in, or does engage in a regulated activity from which he is barred. By virtue of s.7(3), it is a defence for the person to prove that he did not know, and could not reasonably be expected to know, that he was barred from that activity. It is also a defence for him to prove that he reasonably thought it was necessary for him to engage in the activity for the purpose of preventing harm to a child or vulnerable adult, that he reasonably

---

[85] Originally named the Independent Barring Board, renamed the Independent Safeguarding Authority by s.81 of the Policing and Crime Act 2009. The Authority's functions were transferred to the DBS when that body was established under s.87(1) of the Protection of Freedoms Act 2012.

[86] "Regulated activity" in respect of children and vulnerable adults is to be construed in accordance with Pts 1 and 2 of Sch.4 to the Act respectively.

[87] Defined in Sch.3 to the Act and the Safeguarding Vulnerable Groups Act 2006 (Prescribed Criteria and Miscellaneous Provisions) Regulations 2009 (SI 2009/37), as amended. A list of relevant offences is at *https://www.gov.uk/government/uploads/system/uploads/attachment_data/file/384712/DBS_referrals_guide_-_relevant_offences_v2.4.pdf* [Accessed April 30, 2016].

thought there was no other person who could engage in that activity for that purpose and that he engaged in that activity for no longer than was necessary.[88] Section 9 of the Act creates an offence of permitting a barred person to engage in regulated activity, knowing or having reason to believe the person is barred.

[88] s.7(4).

CHAPTER 35

NOTIFICATION AND NOTIFICATION ORDERS

By Tim Moloney QC

Introduction.. 35.01
Notification.. 35.07
Qualifying Offenders........................ 35.07
Transitional Provisions 35.14
The Notification Period.................. 35.16
Review of Indefinite Notification ... 35.26
Notification Requirements............... 35.30
Changes to the Notified Particulars 35.37

Periodic Re-notification 35.41
Checking the Notified Information . 35.43
Advance Notification of Foreign
 Travel... 35.45
Young Offenders............................. 35.46
Notification Offences...................... 35.48
Notification Orders......................... 35.57

INTRODUCTION

The requirement that sex offenders notify the police of their whereabouts has **35.01**
quickly become regarded by many as an essential feature of any strategy to
combat sex crime. The Sex Offenders Act 1997 introduced the requirement
for convicted sex offenders to notify the police of any change of address. The
legislative scheme was extended on the introduction of sex offender orders by
the Crime and Disorder Act 1998. It was then superseded and strengthened
by the notification provisions of the Sexual Offences Act 2003, which have
since been supplemented with the Sexual Offences Act 2003 (Notification
Requirements) (England and Wales) Regulations 2012.[1]

The 1997 Act required all offenders convicted of, or cautioned for, any **35.02**
offence specified in Sch.1 to the Act to notify the police of their address and
any subsequent changes. Relevant offenders were required to notify their
details to their local police station and the information was kept on the Police
National Computer.

In the wake of the murder of eight-year-old Sarah Payne in 2000, there was **35.03**
a concerted campaign to put the whereabouts of convicted sex offenders into
the public domain as occurs in some parts of the USA. The Government

---

[1] SI 2012/1876.

resisted such calls, primarily on the basis that to do so would drive offenders "underground".[2] Nevertheless, it did recognise some deficiencies in the existing notification scheme, particularly with regard to the time period within which offenders were required to notify any change of address, the frequency of re-notification and the ability to keep track of persons who had been convicted of sexual offences abroad.[3]

35.04   The 2003 Act was designed to improve upon the notification requirements under the 1997 Act by:

- reducing the time period within which an offender must notify the police of any change in his notified details (s.84),
- requiring an offender to re-notify the police of his notified details at least once a year (s.85),
- enabling the Secretary of State to make regulations requiring offenders to notify the police of any plans to travel abroad (s.86),
- allowing for a person with parental responsibility for a young offender to be directed to comply with the notification requirements until the offender reaches the age of 18 (ss.89 and 90),
- empowering the police to apply to a magistrates' court for a notification order to require notification by an offender whose offending has taken place abroad (ss.97–103).

35.05   Finally, the Act made provision for ending the notification requirements applicable to individuals convicted of the now abolished offences under ss.12 and 13 of the Sexual Offences Act 1956 (buggery and gross indecency between men).

35.06   More recently, the Sexual Offences Act 2003 (Notification Requirements) (England and Wales) Regulations 2012[4] introduced measures to extend and strengthen the system of notification requirements placed on registered sex offenders (commonly referred to as the sex offenders' register). The new measures came into force on August 13, 2012, and require offenders subject to the notification requirements under the 2003 Act to notify to the police:

- of any intended travel outside the UK (not just travel of three days or more as previously);
- where they have no sole or main residence, the address or location where they can regularly be found, on a weekly basis (rather than yearly as before);
- any residence or stay of at least 12 hours in a household containing a person aged under 18; and
- any bank account, credit or debit card, passport or other identity document (so that sex offenders can no longer seek to avoid being on the register by changing their name: see further para.35.35, below).

---

[2] See e.g. the White Paper *Protecting the Public: Strengthening protection against sex offenders and reforming the law on sexual offences*, (Home Office: 2002) Ch.1, para.19.
[3] *Protecting the Public*, 2002, paras 20–27.
[4] SI 2012/1876.

NOTIFICATION

QUALIFYING OFFENDERS

Section 80 of the 2003 Act provides that the notification requirements apply   35.07
to a person who is convicted of or cautioned for an offence listed in Sch.3 to
the Act, or found not guilty of such an offence by reason of insanity, or found
to be under a disability and to have done the act charged against him in
respect of such an offence. The notification requirements flow from the fact
of conviction (etc.)—they do not depend on an order of the court and form
no part of the sentence for the offence. It follows that the effect of the
requirements is irrelevant to the sentencing exercise.[5] Further, as the notification requirements are not part of the sentence but arise by operation of law,
they do not fall within the rights of appeal against sentence. However, the
House of Lords in *Longworth*[6] made clear that where a judge purports to
order notification as part of the sentencing process, an appellate court may
simply set aside the purported order if the sentence properly imposed did not
trigger the notification requirements. Rule 28.3 of the Criminal Procedure
Rules 2015 requires a sentencing judge to inform the offender of the
notification requirements he or she will be subject to and the legislation that
imposes those requirements.

Section 80[7] provides: 35.08

"**80. Persons becoming subject to notification requirements**

(1) A person is subject to the notification requirements of this Part for the
period set out in section 82 ('the notification period') if—
(a) he is convicted of an offence listed in Schedule 3;
(b) he is found not guilty of such an offence by reason of insanity;
(c) he is found to be under a disability and to have done the act charged
against him in respect of such an offence; or
(d) in England and Wales or Northern Ireland, he is cautioned in respect of
such an offence.
(2) A person for the time being subject to the notification requirements of this
Part is referred to in this Part as a 'relevant offender'."

By s.134 of the Act, a conviction following commencement, i.e. on or after   35.09
May 1, 2004, which results in a conditional (but not an absolute) discharge
qualifies as a "conviction" for the purposes of the notification requirements.
By contrast, a person conditionally discharged for an offence to which the
Sexual Offences Act 1997 applied was not susceptible to the imposition of
notification requirements.[8]

---

[5] *Attorney General's Reference (No.50 of 1997)* [1998] 2 Cr. App. R.(S.) 155 (*held,* judge had
been wrong to reduce the sentence in order that the offender should be subject to the notification
requirements for a shorter period).
[6] [2006] UKHL 1.
[7] As amended by the Armed Forces Act 2006 ss.378, 383(2) and Sch.16, para.206, Sch.17.
[8] *Longworth* [2006] UKHL 1, reversing the controversial decision to the contrary of the Court
of Appeal reported at [2004] EWCA Crim 2145.

35.10   The offences listed in Sch.3 to the Act, to which the notification provisions apply, are exclusively sexual offences. The offences specified in relation to England and Wales are as follows:[9]

"1.   An offence under section 1 of the Sexual Offences Act 1956 (c.69) (rape).

2.   An offence under section 5 of that Act (intercourse with girl under 13).

3.   An offence under section 6 of that Act (intercourse with girl under 16), if the offender was 20 or over.

4.   An offence under section 10 of that Act (incest by a man), if the victim or (as the case may be) other party was under 18.

5.   An offence under section 12 of that Act (buggery) if—
(a)   the offender was 20 or over, and
(b)   the victim or (as the case may be) other party was under 18.

6.   An offence under section 13 of that Act (indecency between men) if—
(a)   the offender was 20 or over, and
(b)   the victim or (as the case may be) other party was under 18.

7.   An offence under section 14 of that Act (indecent assault on a woman) if—
(a)   the victim or (as the case may be) other party was under 18, or
(b)   the offender, in respect of the offence or finding, is or has been—
       (i)   sentenced to imprisonment for a term of at least 30 months; or
       (ii) admitted to a hospital subject to a restriction order.

8.   An offence under section 15 of that Act (indecent assault on a man) if—
(a)   the victim or (as the case may be) other party was under 18, or
(b)   the offender, in respect of the offence or finding, is or has been—
       (i)   sentenced to imprisonment for a term of at least 30 months; or
       (ii) admitted to a hospital subject to a restriction order.

9.   An offence under section 16 of that Act (assault with intent to commit buggery), if the victim or (as the case may be) other party was under 18.

10.   An offence under section 28 of that Act (causing or encouraging the prostitution of, intercourse with or indecent assault on girl under 16).

11.   An offence under section 1 of the Indecency with Children Act 1960 (c.33) (indecent conduct towards young child).

12.   An offence under section 54 of the Criminal Law Act 1977 (c.45) (inciting girl under 16 to have incestuous sexual intercourse).

13.   An offence under section 1 of the Protection of Children Act 1978 (c.37) (indecent photographs of children), if the indecent photographs or pseudo-photographs showed persons under 16 and—
(a)   the conviction, finding or caution was before the commencement of this Part, or
(b)   the offender—
       (i)   was 18 or over, or
       (ii) is sentenced in respect of the offence to imprisonment for a term of at least 12 months.

14.   An offence under section 170 of the Customs and Excise Management Act 1979 (c.2) (penalty for fraudulent evasion of duty etc.) in relation to goods prohibited to be imported under section 42 of the Customs Consolidation

---

[9] Sch.3 is printed as it applies in England and Wales, as amended by the Sexual Offences Act 2003 (Amendment of Schs 3 and 5) Order 2007 (SI 2007/296), arts 1(1), 2(2); the Serious Crime Act 2007 ss.63(2), 94 and Sch.6, para.63(2) (with Sch.13 para.5); by Criminal Justice and Immigration Act 2008 ss.148(1), 153(7) and Sch.26, para.58(2); by the Coroners and Justice Act 2009 ss.177(1), 182(5) and Sch.21, para.62(2); by the Criminal Justice and Licensing (Scotland) Act 2010 ss.41(3)(b), 206(1); and the Serious Crime Act 2015, s.85 and Sch.4, para.66(1), (3).

Act 1876 (c.36) (indecent or obscene articles), if the prohibited goods included indecent photographs of persons under 16 and—
- (a) the conviction, finding or caution was before the commencement of this Part, or
- (b) the offender—
    - (i) was 18 or over, or
    - (ii) is sentenced in respect of the offence to imprisonment for a term of at least 12 months.

15. An offence under section 160 of the Criminal Justice Act 1988 (c.33) (possession of indecent photograph of a child), if the indecent photographs or pseudo-photographs showed persons under 16 and—
    - (a) the conviction, finding or caution was before the commencement of this Part, or
    - (b) the offender—
        - (i) was 18 or over, or
        - (ii) is sentenced in respect of the offence to imprisonment for a term of at least 12 months.

16. An offence under section 3 of the Sexual Offences (Amendment) Act 2000 (c.44) (abuse of position of trust), if the offender was 20 or over.

17. An offence under section 1 or 2 of this Act (rape, assault by penetration).

18. An offence under section 3 of this Act (sexual assault) if—
    - (a) where the offender was under 18, he is or has been sentenced, in respect of the offence, to imprisonment for a term of at least 12 months;
    - (b) in any other case—
        - (i) the victim was under 18, or
        - (ii) the offender, in respect of the offence or finding, is or has been—
    - (a) sentenced to a term of imprisonment,
    - (b) detained in a hospital, or
    - (c) made the subject of a community sentence of at least 12 months.

19. An offence under any of sections 4 to 6 of this Act (causing sexual activity without consent, rape of a child under 13, assault of a child under 13 by penetration).

20. An offence under section 7 of this Act (sexual assault of a child under 13) if the offender—
    - (a) was 18 or over, or
    - (b) is or has been sentenced in respect of the offence to imprisonment for a term of at least 12 months.

21. An offence under any of sections 8 to 12 of this Act (causing or inciting a child under 13 to engage in sexual activity, child sex offences committed by adults).

22. An offence under section 13 of this Act (child sex offences committed by children or young persons), if the offender is or has been sentenced, in respect of the offence, to imprisonment for a term of at least 12 months.

23. An offence under section 14 of this Act (arranging or facilitating the commission of a child sex offence) if the offender—
    - (a) was 18 or over, or
    - (b) is or has been sentenced, in respect of the offence, to imprisonment for a term of at least 12 months.

24. An offence under section 15 of this Act (meeting a child following sexual grooming etc).

25. An offence under any of sections 16 to 19 of this Act (abuse of a position of trust) if the offender, in respect of the offence, is or has been—

(a) sentenced to a term of imprisonment,

(b) detained in a hospital, or

(c) made the subject of a community sentence of at least 12 months.

26. An offence under section 25 or 26 of this Act (familial child sex offences) if the offender—

(a) was 18 or over, or

(b) is or has been sentenced in respect of the offence to imprisonment for a term of at least 12 months.

27. An offence under any of sections 30 to 37 of this Act (offences against persons with a mental disorder impeding choice, inducements etc. to persons with mental disorder).

28. An offence under any of sections 38 to 41 of this Act (care workers for persons with mental disorder) if —

(a) where the offender was under 18, he is or has been sentenced in respect of the offence to imprisonment for a term of at least 12 months;

(b) in any other case, the offender, in respect of the offence or finding, is or has been—

(i) sentenced to a term of imprisonment,

(ii) detained in a hospital, or

(iii) made the subject of a community sentence of at least 12 months.

29. An offence under section 47 of this Act (paying for sexual services of a child) if the victim or (as the case may be) other party was under 16, and the offender—

(a) was 18 or over, or

(b) is or has been sentenced in respect of the offence to imprisonment for a term of at least 12 months.

29A. An offence under section 48 of this Act (causing or inciting child prostitution or pornography) if the offender—

(a) was 18 or over, or

(b) is or has been sentenced in respect of the offence to imprisonment for a term of at least 12 months.

29B. An offence under section 49 of this Act (controlling a child prostitute or a child involved in pornography) if the offender—

(a) was 18 or over, or

(b) is or has been sentenced in respect of the offence to imprisonment for a term of at least 12 months.

29C. An offence under section 50 of this Act (arranging or facilitating child prostitution or pornography) if the offender—

(a) was 18 or over, or

(b) is or has been sentenced in respect of the offence to imprisonment for a term of at least 12 months.

30. An offence under section 61 of this Act (administering a substance with intent).

31. An offence under section 62 or 63 of this Act (committing an offence or trespassing, with intent to commit a sexual offence) if—

(a) where the offender was under 18, he is or has been sentenced in respect of the offence to imprisonment for a term of at least 12 months;

(b) in any other case—

(i) the intended offence was an offence against a person under 18, or

(ii) the offender, in respect of the offence or finding, is or has been—

(a) sentenced to a term of imprisonment,

(b) detained in a hospital, or

(c) made the subject of a community sentence of at least 12 months.

32. An offence under section 64 or 65 of this Act (sex with an adult relative) if—

(a) where the offender was under 18, he is or has been sentenced in respect of the offence to imprisonment for a term of at least 12 months;

(b) in any other case, the offender, in respect of the offence or finding, is or has been—

    (i) sentenced to a term of imprisonment, or

    (ii) detained in a hospital.

33. An offence under section 66 of this Act (exposure) if—

(a) where the offender was under 18, he is or has been sentenced in respect of the offence to imprisonment for a term of at least 12 months;

(b) in any other case—

    (i) the victim was under 18, or

    (ii) the offender, in respect of the offence or finding, is or has been—

(a) sentenced to a term of imprisonment,

(b) detained in a hospital, or

(c) made the subject of a community sentence of at least 12 months.

34. An offence under section 67 of this Act (voyeurism) if—

(a) where the offender was under 18, he is or has been sentenced in respect of the offence to imprisonment for a term of at least 12 months;

(b) in any other case—

    (i) the victim was under 18, or

    (ii) the offender, in respect of the offence or finding, is or has been—

(a) sentenced to a term of imprisonment,

(b) detained in a hospital, or

(c) made the subject of a community sentence of at least 12 months.

35. An offence under section 69 or 70 of this Act (intercourse with an animal, sexual penetration of a corpse) if —

(a) where the offender was under 18, he is or has been sentenced in respect of the offence to imprisonment for a term of at least 12 months;

(b) in any other case, the offender, in respect of the offence or finding, is or has been—

    (i) sentenced to a term of imprisonment, or

    (ii) detained in a hospital.

35A. An offence under section 63 of the Criminal Justice and Immigration Act 2008 (possession of extreme pornographic images) if the offender—

(a) was 18 or over, and

(b) is sentenced in respect of the offence to imprisonment for a term of at least 2 years.

35B. An offence under section 62(1) of the Coroners and Justice Act 2009 (possession of prohibited images of children) if the offender—

(a) was 18 or over, and

(b) is sentenced in respect of the offence to imprisonment for a term of at least 2 years.

35C. An offence under section 69 of the Serious Crime Act 2015 (possession of paedophile manual) if the offender—

(a) was 18 or over, or

(b) is sentenced in respect of the offence to imprisonment for a term of at least 12 months.

. . .

General

94.   A reference in a preceding paragraph to an offence includes—
(a) a reference to an attempt, conspiracy or incitement to commit that offence, and
(b) except in paragraphs 36 to 43, a reference to aiding, abetting, counselling or procuring the commission of that offence.

94A. A reference in a preceding paragraph to an offence ('offence A') includes a reference to an offence under Part 2 of the Serious Crime Act 2007 in relation to which offence A is the offence (or one of the offences) which the person intended or believed would be committed

95.   A reference in a preceding paragraph to a person's age is—
(a) in the case of an indecent photograph, a reference to the person's age when the photograph was taken;
(b) in any other case, a reference to his age at the time of the offence.

96.   In this Schedule 'community sentence' has—
(a) in relation to England and Wales, the same meaning as in the Powers of Criminal Courts (Sentencing) Act 2000 (c.6), and
(b) in relation to Northern Ireland, the same meaning as in the Criminal Justice (Northern Ireland) Order 1996 (S.I. 1996/3160 (N.I. 24)).

97.   For the purposes of paragraphs 14, 44 and 78—
(a) a person is to be taken to have been under 16 at any time if it appears from the evidence as a whole that he was under that age at that time;
(b) section 7 of the Protection of Children Act 1978 (c.37) (interpretation), subsections (2) to (2C) and (8) to (10) of section 52 of the Civic Government (Scotland) Act 1982 (c.45), and Article 2(2) and (3) of the Protection of Children (Northern Ireland) Order 1978 (S.I. 1978/1047 (N.I. 17)) (interpretation) (respectively) apply as each provision applies for the purposes of the Act or Order of which it forms part.

98.   A determination under paragraph 60 constitutes part of a person's sentence, within the meaning of the Criminal Procedure (Scotland) Act 1995 (c.46), for the purposes of any appeal or review."

35.11   Paragraph 94 does not bring an attempt to incite a sexual offence within Sch.3.[10]

35.12   In *Forbes v Secretary of State for the Home Department*,[11] the Court of Appeal (Civil Division) rejected an argument that the imposition of notification requirements upon a person convicted of an offence contrary to s.170(2)(b) of the Customs and Excise Management Act 1979 was incompatible with art.8 ECHR. The Court held that the fact that for the offence to be made out it was only necessary to show that the offender believed that the goods being imported were prohibited, and did not require any knowledge or belief on his part that they contained pornographic images of children, did not mean that the notification requirements were either too broad or disproportionate. The Court emphasised that it is entirely appropriate that people directly involved in the sexual exploitation of children should be subject to notification requirements. That applies to persons who deliberately

[10] *Parnell* [2005] 1 W.L.R. 853 (decided under the Sex Offenders Act 1997).
[11] [2006] EWCA Civ 962.

import child pornography into this jurisdiction, and equally to those who deliberately import prohibited goods either careless or heedless as to the risk that those goods might contain child pornography. In giving the judgment of the Court, Sir Igor Judge P (as he then was) cited with approval the following dictum from *Re Kevin Gallagher*,[12] in which Kerr J rejected an argument that the automatic imposition of the notification requirements of the Sexual Offences Act 1997 infringed the applicant's art.8 rights:

> "It is inevitable that a scheme which applies to sex offenders generally will bear more heavily on some individuals than others. But to be viable the scheme must contain general provisions that will be universally applied to all who come within its purview. The proportionality of the reporting requirements must be examined principally in relation to its general effect. The particular impact that it has on individuals must be of secondary importance... The automatic nature of the notification requirements is in my judgment a necessary and reasonable element of the scheme. Its purpose is to ensure that the police are aware of the whereabouts of all serious sex offenders. This knowledge is of obvious assistance in the detection of offenders and the prevention of crime."

Where a court imposes a community order under s.177(5) of the Criminal **35.13** Justice Act 1988, specifying a date, not more than three years after the date of the order, by which all the requirements of the order must have been complied with, the duration of the order is the period from the date of the order to the specified date, and not the period from the date of the order until the date when the order's requirements have been complied with. Accordingly, where an offender was convicted of two offences of sexual assault and sentenced to a community order with a requirement to complete 220 hours of unpaid work within the period of 12 months and 2 days from the date of sentence, he was held to be "the subject of a community sentence of at least 12 months" for the purposes of Sch.3, para.18(b)(ii)(c).[13] The Court rejected the argument that, as it was open to the offender to complete the work required by the order within 12 months, in which case the order would cease to be in force, the order was not a sentence of "at least 12 months".

TRANSITIONAL PROVISIONS

Section 81 makes transitional provision for an offender who was subject to **35.14** ongoing notification requirements under the 1997 Act at the time of commencement (May 1, 2004) to be subject to the requirements of the 2003 Act. Like the 1997 Act, the 2003 Act also has partially retroactive provisions embodied in ss.81(3)–(6). Thus the offender will not be subject to notification requirements if the offence was committed before September 1, 1997, unless the conditions set out in those subsections are met. Sections 81(7) and 81(8) ensure that offenders who were subject to a sex offender order, interim sex

---

[12] [2003] NIQB 26.
[13] *Davison* [2008] EWCA Crim 2795, not following *Odam* [2008] EWCA Crim 1087 (where the point was not fully argued).

offender order or restraining order and thus required to notify under the 1997 Act, are subject to the requirements of the 2003 Act.[14]

35.15   Section 81 provides:

"81. Persons formerly subject to Part 1 of the Sex Offenders Act 1997

(1) A person is, from the commencement of this Part until the end of the notification period, subject to the notification requirements of this Part if, before the commencement of this Part—

(a) he was convicted of an offence listed in Schedule 3;

(b) he was found not guilty of such an offence by reason of insanity;

(c) he was found to be under a disability and to have done the act charged against him in respect of such an offence; or

(d) in England and Wales or Northern Ireland, he was cautioned in respect of such an offence.

(2) Subsection (1) does not apply if the notification period ended before the commencement of this Part.

(3) Subsection (1)(a) does not apply to a conviction before 1st September 1997 unless, at the beginning of that day, the person—

(a) had not been dealt with in respect of the offence;

(b) was serving a sentence of imprisonment or was subject to a community order, in respect of the offence;

(c) was subject to supervision, having been released from prison after serving the whole or part of a sentence of imprisonment in respect of the offence; or

(d) was detained in a hospital or was subject to a guardianship order, following the conviction.

(4) Paragraphs (b) and (c) of subsection (1) do not apply to a finding made before 1st September 1997 unless, at the beginning of that day, the person—

(a) had not been dealt with in respect of the finding; or

(b) was detained in a hospital, following the finding.

(5) Subsection (1)(d) does not apply to a caution given before 1st September 1997.

(6) A person who would have been within subsection (3)(b) or (d) or (4)(b) but for the fact that at the beginning of 1st September 1997 he was unlawfully at large or absent without leave, on temporary release or leave of absence, or on bail pending an appeal, is to be treated as being within that provision.

(7) Where, immediately before the commencement of this Part, an order under a provision within subsection (8) was in force in respect of a person, the person is subject to the notification requirements of this Part from that commencement until the order is discharged or otherwise ceases to have effect.

(8) The provisions are—

(a) section 5A of the Sex Offenders Act 1997 (c. 51) (restraining orders);

(b) section 2 of the Crime and Disorder Act 1998 (c. 37) (sex offender orders made in England and Wales);

(c) section 2A of the Crime and Disorder Act 1998 (interim orders made in England and Wales);

(d) section 20 of the Crime and Disorder Act 1998 (sex offender orders and interim orders made in Scotland);

(e) Article 6 of the Criminal Justice (Northern Ireland) Order 1998 (S.I. 1998/2839 (N.I. 20)) (sex offender orders made in Northern Ireland);

---

[14] *Ibbotson v UK* [1999] Crim. L.R. 153; 27 EHRR CD332 establishes that a registration requirement does not amount to a penalty within the meaning of art.7 ECHR.

(f) Article 6A of the Criminal Justice (Northern Ireland) Order 1998 (interim orders made in Northern Ireland)."

THE NOTIFICATION PERIOD

The length of the period during which an offender will be subject to the notification requirements is set out in s.82(1):[15]

35.16

"**82. The notification period**

(1) The notification period for a person within section 80(1) or 81(1) is the period in the second column of the following Table opposite the description that applies to him.

TABLE	
Description of relevant offender	*Notification period*
A person who, in respect of the offence, is or has been sentenced to imprisonment for life, to imprisonment for public protection under section 225 of the Criminal Justice Act 2003 or to imprisonment for a term of 30 months or more.	An indefinite period beginning with the relevant date.
A person who, in respect of the offence, has been made the subject of an order under section 210F(1) of the Criminal Procedure (Scotland) Act 1995 (order for lifelong restriction).	An indefinite period beginning with that date.
A person who, in respect of the offence or finding, is or has been admitted to a hospital subject to a restriction order.	An indefinite period beginning with that date.
A person who, in respect of the offence, is or has been sentenced to imprisonment for a term of more than 6 months but less than 30 months.	10 years beginning with that date.
A person who, in respect of the offence, is or has been sentenced to imprisonment for a term of 6 months or less.	7 years beginning with that date.
A person who, in respect of the offence or finding, is or has been admitted to a hospital without being subject to a restriction order.	7 years beginning with that date.
A person within section 80(1)(d).	2 years beginning with that date.

[15] As amended by the Violent Crime Reduction Act 2006 s.57(1).

TABLE	
Description of relevant offender	*Notification period*
A person in whose case an order for conditional discharge or, in Scotland, a probation order, is made in respect of the offence.	The period of conditional discharge or, in Scotland, the probation period.
A person of any other description.	5 years beginning with the relevant date.

(2) Where a person is under 18 on the relevant date, subsection (1) has effect as if for any reference to a period of 10 years, 7 years, 5 years or 2 years there were substituted a reference to one-half of that period.

(3) Subsection (4) applies where a relevant offender within section 80(1)(a) or 81(1)(a) is or has been sentenced, in respect of two or more offences listed in Schedule 3—

(a) to consecutive terms of imprisonment; or

(b) to terms of imprisonment which are partly concurrent.

(4) Where this subsection applies, subsection (1) has effect as if the relevant offender were or had been sentenced, in respect of each of the offences, to a term of imprisonment which—

(a) in the case of consecutive terms, is equal to the aggregate of those terms;

(b) in the case of partly concurrent terms (X and Y, which overlap for a period Z), is equal to X plus Y minus Z.

(5) Where a relevant offender the subject of a finding within section 80(1)(c) or 81(1)(c) is subsequently tried for the offence, the notification period relating to the finding ends at the conclusion of the trial.

(6) In this Part, 'relevant date' means—

(a) in the case of a person within section 80(1)(a) or 81(1)(a), the date of the conviction;

(b) in the case of a person within section 80(1)(b) or (c) or 81(1)(b) or (c), the date of the finding;

(c) in the case of a person within section 80(1)(d) or 81(1)(d), the date of the caution;

(d) in the case of a person within section 81(7), the date which, for the purposes of Part 1 of the Sex Offenders Act 1997 (c. 51), was the relevant date in relation to that person."

35.17   By virtue of s.82(6), the "relevant date" for the purposes of determining the notification period is the date of the conviction, finding or caution.

35.18   The effect of s.82(2) is that when an offender is under the age of 18 on the relevant date, the appropriate notification period is half that to which an adult would have been made subject.

35.19   The calculation of the notification period that should apply to a person who is sentenced to either consecutive or partially concurrent sentences for two or more offences falling within Sch.3 is explained in subss.82(3) and (4). If consecutive sentences are imposed, then the period is simply that which would apply to the sum of the two sentences. Thus, if an offender is sentenced to four months' imprisonment for one offence and three months' consecutive for another, the sum of those sentences is seven months and thus the appropriate notification period is 10 years.

An offender is serving partly concurrent terms when he is sentenced to a **35.20**
term of imprisonment for a relevant offence whilst already a serving prisoner
for another relevant offence. In those circumstances, the calculation of the
sentence to which the notification period should attach is achieved by adding
the two sentences together and then subtracting any overlap. Thus, if an
offender is serving a 12-month sentence and 8 months into that sentence is
sentenced to a further two years, then the period of custody that would apply
for notification period purposes would be three years (the sum of the two
sentences) minus four months (the overlapping period) to give a total of 32
months. The notification period would therefore be indefinite.

In *R (Minter) v Chief Constable of Hampshire Constabulary*,[16] the Court **35.21**
of Appeal held there was nothing arbitrary or disproportionate about the
imposition of an indefinite notification period given the statutory purpose
and the existence of review provisions in ss.91A–F of the 2003 Act.

It was held in *Slocombe*[17] that when a young offender is made subject to **35.22**
a detention and training order ("DTO"), the length of the notification period
is not determined by the whole of the duration of the DTO (including the
supervision element), but instead simply by reference to the detention and
training period of the order.[18] This is because s.131(a) of the 2003 Act
provides that the notification provisions apply to a "period of detention"
which a person is liable to serve under a DTO as it applies to an equivalent
sentence of imprisonment. Under s.102(2) of the Powers of Criminal Courts
(Sentencing) Act 2000, the period of detention and training under a DTO is
one-half of the term of the order. Accordingly in *Slocombe*, where the length
of the DTO was 12 months, the appellant fell to be treated for the purposes
of the notification provisions as if he had been sentenced to a term of six
months. *Slocombe* was followed in *R. v M, B and H*,[19] where the Court of
Appeal held that the notification requirements did not apply to three
appellants variously aged 15 and 16 who were sentenced to DTOs for
offences of sexual activity with a child, contrary to s.13 of the 2003 Act. H
was sentenced to a DTO of 18 months' duration and M and B to DTOs of
12 months' duration. The judge also purported to make orders requiring the
appellants to comply with the notification requirements, for 10 years in the
case of H and seven years in the cases of B and M. The Court of Appeal,
citing *Longworth*,[20] quashed the purported notification orders on the ground
that the notification requirements apply, if at all, by operation of law and not
by order of the court. It went on to consider whether the requirements
applied in this case. It noted the stipulation in the 2003 Act[21] that an offence

---

[16] [2014] 1 W.L.R. 179.
[17] [2006] 1 Cr. App. R. 33.
[18] *Slocombe* [2006] 1 Cr. App. R. 33.
[19] [2010] EWCA Crim 42.
[20] [2006] UKHL 1, for which see para.35.07, above.
[21] Sch.3, para.22.

under s.13 attracts notification only if the offender is sentenced to imprisonment for a term of at least 12 months. The effect of the law as explained in *Slocombe* was that the period of detention the appellants were liable to serve under their DTOs was the period of time that would actually be served in detention, which by virtue of s.102(2) of the Powers of Criminal Courts (Sentencing) Act 2000 was nine months in the case of H and six months in the cases of B and M. Accordingly, none of the appellants was sentenced to a period of detention sufficient to trigger the notification requirements.

35.23   What is the appropriate period of notification when a suspended sentence is passed? Section 82 of the 2003 Act sets the notification period for an offender who is sentenced to a term of imprisonment by reference to the length of the term. A person who receives a suspended sentence is not in fact imprisoned, and it may be arguable whether they are "A person of any other description" within the rubric at the end of s.82. However, s.189(6) of the Criminal Justice Act 2003 provides that a suspended sentence is to be treated as a sentence of imprisonment for all purposes. This has the result that the notification periods set out in s.82 of the 2003 Act apply to all sentences of imprisonment, whether or not they are suspended.

35.24   In *Alary (Bruno)*,[22] it was held that a sexual offences prevention order ("SOPO") might properly be imposed for a greater length of time than the period fixed by the statutory notification requirements, if this is justified by the facts. This no doubt applies equally to the new Sexual Harm Prevention Order ("SHPO"), the successor to the SOPO (for which see Ch.36).

35.25   Section 82(5) deals with the situation where a person is found to have a disability but subsequently recovers sufficiently to be tried for the alleged offence. If he is acquitted, then the indefinite notification requirement imposed when he was found to have the disability is quashed. If he is convicted, then a new notification period appropriate to the sentence he receives is substituted for the indefinite period.

Review of Indefinite Notification

35.26   The "indefinite period" referred to in the Table in s.82 means the rest of the offender's life.[23] In *R. (F) v Secretary of State for the Home Department*,[24] the Supreme Court upheld a decision of the Court of Appeal (Civil Division)[25] that the absence of a right of review of indefinite notification requirements in the 2003 Act as enacted rendered s.82(1) incompatible with art.8 ECHR. The Supreme Court said that it is obvious that there must be some circumstances where a tribunal could reliably find that the risk of a person committing a further sexual offence could be discounted to the extent that the continuation of notification requirements could no longer be

---

[22] [2012] EWCA Crim 1534.
[23] See the Explanatory Notes to the 2003 Act, p.25.
[24] [2010] UKSC 17; [2011] 1 A.C. 331.
[25] [2010] 1 W.L.R. 76.

justified. Consequently, the current notification scheme represented a disproportionate interference with art.8 rights because there was no provision for review.[26] The Supreme Court agreed with the Court of Appeal that any concern as to the opening of the floodgates to a large number of applications for review of notification requirements could be set at rest by Parliament setting the threshold for review at a suitably high level both as regards the time when an application might first be made, the frequency with which applications might be made and what had to be proved if the notification requirements were to be varied or discharged.

Following the Supreme Court's decision, ss.91A–91F were inserted in the **35.27** 2003 Act by the Sexual Offences Act 2003 (Remedial) Order 2012.[27] They provide a mechanism by which indefinite notification requirements may be reviewed. In short, the offender may apply to the chief officer of police for the area in which the offender lives, or has lived for the most days in the previous 12 months, for a determination that the offender is no longer subject to the indefinite notification requirements (s.91A). An application must be in writing (s.91B). For offenders who were made the subject of the indefinite notification requirements when aged 18 or over, the earliest they may apply under s.91B is 15 years after they first made a required notification.[28] For those who were under 18 at the relevant time, the first date on which they may apply is eight years after they first made a required notification. For the purposes of the determination of an application under s.91B, the offender must satisfy the relevant chief officer of police that it is not necessary for the purpose of protecting the public or any particular members of the public from sexual harm for him to remain subject to the indefinite notification requirements (s.91C). If the chief officer of police determines that the offender should remain subject to the indefinite notification requirements, the offender may not re-apply under s.91B for a period of eight years from the date of the determination, or such longer period, up to a maximum of 15 years, as the chief officer considers to be justified by the risk of sexual harm posed by the offender. Section 91D sets out the factors to be taken into account by a chief officer of police in considering an application under s.91B. These include the seriousness of the offence which gave rise to the indefinite notification requirements to which the offender is subject; any assessment of the risk posed by the offender prepared by any responsible authority; and evidence or submission from a victim of the offence which gave rise to the indefinite notification requirements; and any conviction or other finding

---

[26] The Supreme Court observed that France, Ireland, all seven Australian states, Canada and the United States all had registration requirements for sex offenders and nearly all had provision for review. That suggested that it could not be said that such a review process was not practicable.

[27] SI 2012/1883.

[28] In *Main v Scottish Ministers* [2015] CSIH 41; [2015] S.L.T. 349, the Court of Session dismissed an argument that the absence of a right of review until 15 years after the petitioner's release from prison rendered the notification requirements incompatible with his art.8 rights.

made by a court in relation to the subsequent commission of an offence under Sch.3 to the 2003 Act by the offender. There is a right of appeal against a determination by a chief officer of police that an offender must remain subject to the indefinite notification requirements (s.91E). An appeal may be made to a magistrates' court by complaint within 21 days of receipt of the notice of determination. The Secretary of State is under a statutory duty to issue guidance to chief officers of police in relation to the determination of applications under s.91B (s.91F).[29] The duties of a chief officer of police under ss.91A–91C may be delegated to an officer of the rank of superintendent and above.[30]

35.28   Sections 91A–F provide:

"91A. Review of indefinite notification requirements: qualifying relevant offender

(1) A qualifying relevant offender may apply to the relevant chief officer of police for a determination that the qualifying relevant offender is no longer subject to the indefinite notification requirements ("an application for review").

(2) A qualifying relevant offender means a relevant offender who, on the date on which he makes an application for review, is—

(a) subject to the indefinite notification requirements; and

(b) not subject to a sexual offences prevention order under section 104(1) or an interim sexual offences prevention order under section 109(3).

(3) The "indefinite notification requirements" mean the notification requirements of this Part for an indefinite period by virtue of—

(a) section 80(1);

(b) section 81(1); or

(c) a notification order made under section 97(5).

(4) In this Part, the "relevant chief officer of police" means, subject to subsection (5), the chief officer of police for the police area in which a qualifying relevant offender is recorded as residing or staying in the most recent notification given by him under section 84(1) or 85(1).

(5) Subsection (6) applies if a qualifying relevant offender is recorded as residing or staying at more than one address in the most recent notification given by him under section 84(1) or 85(1).

(6) If this subsection applies, the "relevant chief officer of police" means the chief officer of police for the police area in which, during the relevant period, the qualifying relevant offender has resided or stayed on a number of days which equals or exceeds the number of days on which he has resided or stayed in any other police area.

(7) In subsection (6), "the relevant period" means the period of 12 months ending on the day on which the qualifying relevant offender makes an application for review.

---

[29] See the Home Office's *Guidance on Review of Indefinite Notification Requirements issued under section 91F of the Sexual Offences Act 2003*, available at *https://www.gov.uk/government/uploads/system/uploads/attachment_data/file/98378/review-notification-requirements.pdf* [Accessed April 30, 2016].

[30] *R. (Hamill) v Chelmsford Magistrates' Court* [2014] EWHC 2799 (Admin); [2015] 1 W.L.R. 1798, DC (applying the principle in *Carltona Ltd v Commissioners of Works* [1943] All. E.R. 560).

91B. Review of indefinite notification requirements: application for review and qualifying dates

(1) An application for review must be in writing and may be made on or after the qualifying date or, as the case may be, the further qualifying date.

(2) Subject to subsection (7), the qualifying date is—

(a) where the qualifying relevant offender was 18 or over on the relevant date, the day after the end of the 15 year period beginning with the day on which the qualifying relevant offender gives the relevant notification; or

(b) where the qualifying relevant offender was under 18 on the relevant date, the day after the end of the 8 year period beginning with the day on which the qualifying relevant offender gives the relevant notification.

(3) Subject to subsections (4) to (6), the further qualifying date is the day after the end of the 8 year period beginning with the day on which the relevant chief officer of police makes a determination under section 91C to require a qualifying relevant offender to remain subject to the indefinite notification requirements.

(4) Subsection (5) applies if the relevant chief officer of police, when making a determination under section 91C to require a qualifying relevant offender to remain subject to the indefinite notification requirements, considers that the risk of sexual harm posed by a qualifying relevant offender is sufficient to justify a continuation of those requirements after the end of the 8 year period beginning with the day on which the determination is made.

(5) If this subsection applies, the relevant chief officer of police may make a determination to require a qualifying relevant offender to remain subject to the indefinite notification requirements for a period which may be no longer than the 15 year period beginning with the day on which the determination is made.

(6) If subsection (5) applies, the further qualifying date is the day after the end of the period determined under that subsection.

(7) The qualifying date must not be earlier than the expiry of the fixed period specified in a notification continuation order made in relation to a qualifying relevant offender in accordance with sections 88A to 88I.

(8) The relevant chief officer of police within 14 days of receipt of an application for review—

(a) must give an acknowledgment of receipt of the application to the qualifying relevant offender, and

(b) may notify a responsible body that the application has been made.

(9) Where a responsible body is notified of the application for review under subsection (8)(b) and holds information which it considers to be relevant to the application, the responsible body must give such information to the relevant chief officer of police within 28 days of receipt of the notification.

(10) In this section 'the relevant notification' means the first notification which the relevant offender gives under section 83, 84 or 85 when he is first released after—

(a) being remanded in or committed to custody by an order of a court in relation to the conviction for the offence giving rise to the indefinite notification requirements;

(b) serving a sentence of imprisonment or a term of service detention in relation to that conviction;

(c) being detained in hospital in relation to that conviction.

(11) For the purposes of this Part—

(a) 'responsible body' means—

(i) the probation trust for any area that includes any part of the police area concerned,

(ii) in relation to any part of the police area concerned for which there is no probation trust, each provider of probation services which has been identified as a relevant provider of probation services for the purposes of section 325 of the Criminal Justice Act 2003 by arrangements under section 3 of the Offender Management Act 2007,

(iii) the Minister of the Crown exercising functions in relation to prisons (and for this purpose 'prison' has the same meaning as in the Prison Act 1952), and

(iv) each body mentioned in section 325(6) of the Criminal Justice Act 2003, but as if the references in that subsection to the relevant area were references to the police area concerned;

(b) 'risk of sexual harm' means a risk of physical or psychological harm to the public in the United Kingdom or any particular members of the public caused by the qualifying relevant offender committing one or more of the offences listed in Schedule 3.

91C. Review of indefinite notification requirements: determination of application for review

(1) The relevant chief officer of police must, within 6 weeks of the latest date on which any body to which a notification has been given under section 91B(8)(b) may give information under section 91B(9)—

(a) determine the application for review, and

(b) give notice of the determination to the qualifying relevant offender.

(2) For the purposes of the determination of an application for review under this section, a qualifying relevant offender must satisfy the relevant chief officer of police that it is not necessary for the purpose of protecting the public or any particular members of the public from sexual harm for the qualifying relevant offender to remain subject to the indefinite notification requirements.

(3) If the relevant chief officer of police determines under this section that the qualifying relevant offender should remain subject to the indefinite notification requirements, the notice of the determination must—

(a) contain a statement of reasons for the determination, and

(b) inform the qualifying relevant offender that he may appeal the determination in accordance with section 91E.

(4) If the relevant chief officer of police determines under this section that a qualifying relevant offender should not remain subject to the indefinite notification requirements, the qualifying relevant offender ceases to be subject to the indefinite notification requirements on the date of receipt of the notice of determination.

(5) The Secretary of State may by order amend the period in subsection (1).

91D. Review of indefinite notification requirements: factors applying to determination under section 91C

(1) In determining an application for review under section 91C, the relevant chief officer of police must—

(a) have regard to information (if any) received from a responsible body;

(b) consider the risk of sexual harm posed by the qualifying relevant offender and the effect of a continuation of the indefinite notification requirements on the offender; and

(c) take into account the matters listed in subsection (2).

(2) The matters are—

(a) the seriousness of the offence in relation to which the qualifying relevant offender became subject to the indefinite notification requirements;

(b) the period of time which has elapsed since the qualifying relevant offender committed the offence (or other offences);

(c) where the qualifying relevant offender falls within section 81(1), whether the qualifying relevant offender committed any offence under section 3 of the Sex Offenders Act 1997;

(d) whether the qualifying relevant offender has committed any offence under section 91;

(e) the age of the qualifying relevant offender at the qualifying date or further qualifying date;

(f) the age of the qualifying relevant offender at the time the offence referred to in paragraph (a) was committed;

(g) the age of any person who was a victim of any such offence (where applicable) and the difference in age between the victim and the qualifying relevant offender at the time the offence was committed;

(h) any assessment of the risk posed by the qualifying relevant offender which has been made by a responsible body under the arrangements for managing and assessing risk established under section 325 of the Criminal Justice Act 2003;

(i) any submission or evidence from a victim of the offence giving rise to the indefinite notification requirements;

(j) any convictions or findings made by a court (including by a court in Scotland, Northern Ireland or countries outside the United Kingdom) in respect of the qualifying relevant offender for any offence listed in Schedule 3 other than the one referred to in paragraph (a);

(k) any caution which the qualifying relevant offender has received for an offence (including for an offence in Northern Ireland or countries outside the United Kingdom) which is listed in Schedule 3;

(l) any convictions or findings made by a court in Scotland, Northern Ireland or countries outside the United Kingdom in respect of the qualifying relevant offender for any offence listed in Schedule 5 where the behaviour of the qualifying relevant offender since the date of such conviction or finding indicates a risk of sexual harm;

(m) any other submission or evidence of the risk of sexual harm posed by the qualifying relevant offender;

(n) any evidence presented by or on behalf of the qualifying relevant offender which demonstrates that the qualifying relevant offender does not pose a risk of sexual harm; and

(o) any other matter which the relevant chief officer of police considers to be appropriate.

(3) In this section, a reference to a conviction, finding or caution for an offence committed in a country outside the United Kingdom means a conviction, finding or caution for an act which—

(a) constituted an offence under the law in force in the country concerned, and

(b) would have constituted an offence listed in Schedule 3 or Schedule 5 if it had been done in any part of the United Kingdom.

91E. Review of indefinite notification requirements: appeals

(1) A qualifying relevant offender may appeal against a determination of the relevant chief officer of police under section 91C.

(2) An appeal under this section may be made by complaint to a magistrates' court within the period of 21 days beginning with the day of receipt of the notice of determination.

(3) A qualifying relevant offender may appeal under this section to any magistrates' court in a local justice area which includes any part of the police area for which the chief officer is the relevant chief officer of police.

(4) If the court makes an order that a qualifying relevant offender should not remain subject to the indefinite notification requirements, the qualifying relevant offender ceases to be subject to the indefinite notification requirements on the date of the order.

91F. Review of indefinite notification requirements: guidance

(1) The Secretary of State must issue guidance to relevant chief officers of police in relation to the determination by them of applications made under section 91B.

(2) The Secretary of State may, from time to time, revise the guidance issued under subsection (1).

(3) The Secretary of State must arrange for any guidance issued or revised under this section to be published in such manner as the Secretary of State considers appropriate."

35.29   In *R. (on the application of NE) v Birmingham Magistrates' Court*,[31] the Divisional Court held that where an offender subject to indefinite notification requirements seeks a review of those requirements, the burden of proof lies with the offender to demonstrate, on the balance of probabilities, that a continuation of the requirements is not necessary to protect the public from sexual harm. In addition, and in contrast to the approach taken by the Divisional Court in the earlier case of *R. (Hamill) v Chelmsford Magistrates Court*,[32] the Court held that a proportionality test has no part in such considerations (the issue had not been the subject of argument in *Hamill*). Such a test was not suggested by the decision in *R. (F) v Secretary of State for the Home Department*,[33] nor was it identified in the Statutory Instrument used to modify the law to ensure the level of compatibility required by that decision. Finally, the wording of s.91D(1)(b) did not require the Chief Constable to consider the risk of sexual harm posed by the offender together with the effect on the offender of a continuation of the indefinite notification requirements but, rather, the effect of continuation of the requirements for the purposes of s.91C. As Sir Brian Leveson P explained[34]:

"This construction is supported by a consideration of the possible circumstances in which this issue might arise. Take the case of an offender for whom it is legitimately considered that there remains a risk of his causing sexual harm unless appropriately monitored (i.e. by compliance with the notification provisions). It is, in my view, unarguable that a different conclusion would be reached in relation to such an offender for whom the continuation of the requirements of notification posed little additional burden, (perhaps because the offender was unemployed or had no children) to that in relation to an offender for whom the burden was very greatly increased (because of the risk, raised in one of these cases, of information seeping out and affecting employment, family or both). In both cases, if there is a risk of causing sexual harm, the high threshold test is not met and the notification provisions must remain in place. It might be appropriate to take account of the impact on private life when deciding where to fix the point at which a further application can be made (on the spectrum between 8 and 15

[31] [2015] 2 Cr. App. R.(S.) 25.
[32] [2014] EWHC 2799 (Admin); [2015] 1 W.L.R. 1798.
[33] [2010] UKSC 17; [2011] 1 A.C. 331.
[34] At [22].

years) but the line to be drawn between those who must continue to be subject to the notification provisions and those who are relieved of that responsibility cannot depend on the impact of notification on private and family life; the test remains necessity for the purpose of protecting the public or any particular members of the public from sexual harm."

The Court also observed that an appeal by way of case stated was a more appropriate course in such circumstances than the use of judicial review. Judicial review would only be the more appropriate course in wholly exceptional circumstances. So far as the instant case was concerned, the Court observed that, given that judicial review was sought in *Hamill* without adverse comment, it would not have been right to deprive the claimants of a remedy. But the Court went on to say that the same will not necessarily be so in the future.

NOTIFICATION REQUIREMENTS

The 2003 Act altered what is required of an offender in order to comply with the notification requirements. The Act made changes to: **35.30**
- the details that he must provide on notification,
- the time periods allowed for initial notification and notification of any changes to his details, and
- the frequency with which he must report.

The procedure for initial notification is governed by s.83. By s.83(1), any **35.31** person who is convicted (etc.) of a relevant offence must, within three days, notify to the police the information specified in s.83(5), which includes his name, address and date of birth, unless he is detained or outside the United Kingdom as specified in s.83(6). In those circumstances, the three day period begins to run once the offender is no longer detained or returns to this country.

By s.83(2) and (4), the requirement to notify does not apply if the offender **35.32** is already subject to a notification requirement that will continue for three days or more after his new conviction (etc).

Section 83 provides[35]: **35.33**

"83. Notification requirements: initial notification

(1) A relevant offender must, within the period of 3 days beginning with the relevant date (or, if later, the commencement of this Part), notify to the police the information set out in subsection (5).

(2) Subsection (1) does not apply to a relevant offender in respect of a conviction, finding or caution within section 80(1) if—

(a) immediately before the conviction, finding or caution, he was subject to the notification requirements of this Part as a result of another conviction, finding or caution or an order of a court ("the earlier event"),

---

[35] As amended by the Criminal Justice and Immigration Act 2008 ss.73, 142(1), 148(1), 153(7). Section 83 has been amended in Scotland to include in s.83(5) information about passports and such other information as the Scottish Ministers may prescribe in regulations: see the Police, Public Order and Criminal Justice (Scotland) Act 2006 ss.78(2), 104.

(b) at that time, he had made a notification under subsection (1) in respect of the earlier event, and

(c) throughout the period referred to in subsection (1), he remains subject to the notification requirements as a result of the earlier event.

(3) Subsection (1) does not apply to a relevant offender in respect of a conviction, finding or caution within section 81(1) or an order within section 81(7) if the offender complied with section 2(1) of the Sex Offenders Act 1997 in respect of the conviction, finding, caution or order.

(4) Where a notification order is made in respect of a conviction, finding or caution, subsection (1) does not apply to the relevant offender in respect of the conviction, finding or caution if—

(a) immediately before the order was made, he was subject to the notification requirements of this Part as a result of another conviction, finding or caution or an order of a court ('the earlier event'),

(b) at that time, he had made a notification under subsection (1) in respect of the earlier event, and

(c) throughout the period referred to in subsection (1), he remains subject to the notification requirements as a result of the earlier event.

(5) The information is—

(a) the relevant offender's date of birth;

(b) his national insurance number;

(c) his name on the relevant date and, where he used one or more other names on that date, each of those names;

(d) his home address on the relevant date;

(e) his name on the date on which notification is given and, where he uses one or more other names on that date, each of those names;

(f) his home address on the date on which notification is given;

(g) the address of any other premises in the United Kingdom at which, at the time the notification is given, he regularly resides or stays;

(h) any prescribed information.

(5A) In subsection (5)(h) 'prescribed' means prescribed by regulations made by the Secretary of State.

(6) When determining the period for the purpose of subsection (1), there is to be disregarded any time when the relevant offender is—

(a) remanded in or committed to custody by an order of a court or kept in service custody;

(b) serving a sentence of imprisonment or a term of service detention;

(c) detained in a hospital; or

(d) outside the United Kingdom.

(7) In this Part, 'home address' means, in relation to any person—

(a) the address of his sole or main residence in the United Kingdom, or

(b) where he has no such residence, the address or location of a place in the United Kingdom where he can regularly be found and, if there is more than one such place, such one of those places as the person may select."

35.34   The offender must notify his details at any police station in his "local police area" as may be prescribed by the Secretary of State in regulations made under s.87 of the Act.[36] The regulations currently in force are the Sexual Offences Act 2003 (Prescribed Police Stations) Regulations 2015,[37]

---

[36] A separate version of s.87 has been created for Scotland by the Police, Public Order and Criminal Justice (Scotland) Act 2006 (asp 10), ss.78, 104.

[37] SI 2015/82.

the Sexual Offences Act (Prescribed Police Stations) (Scotland) Regulations 2014[38] and the Sexual Offences Act 2003 (Prescribed Police Stations) Regulations (Northern Ireland) 2012.[39] The offender's "local police area" is defined in s.88(3) of the Act as the police area in which his home address is situated; or in the absence of a home address, the police area in which the home address last notified is situated; and in the absence of a home address or such notification, the police area in which the court which last dealt with the offender for a Sch.3 offence or related matters is situated. Section 87(4) of the Act provides that when the offender attends to notify the police, they may take his fingerprints and/or photograph any part of him, or both. The provision allowing the photograph to be of "any part" of the person would enable a photograph to be taken of his iris.

Offenders are now required to disclose banking details, in order to enhance   **35.35** the ability of the police to trace quickly an individual who fails to comply with notification requirements. Regulations 12 and 13 of the Sexual Offences Act 2003 (Notification Requirements) (England and Wales) Regulations 2012[40] require offenders subject to the notification requirements to notify information about their bank accounts and debit and credit cards. Regulation 12(1) requires relevant offenders to notify the police about whether they hold an account with a banking institution (defined as a bank, building society or any other institution providing banking services), a debit card in relation to such an account, a credit card account or a credit card. If relevant offenders hold an account or card, they are required to notify the information specified in reg.12(2)–(7). In respect of bank accounts, the information is the name of the institution, its address, the number of the account and the sort code. In respect of debit and credit cards, it is the card number, the validation date, the expiry date and, if the card is held jointly with another person or in the name of a business, the name of that person or business. Regulation 13 provides for provision of information where circumstances changed. It applies where an account is opened or closed, a debit or credit card is obtained, no longer held or has expired, and information previously notified by the offender has altered or become inaccurate or incomplete.

Regulation 12 was held to be compatible with art.8 ECHR in *R.*   **35.36** *(Prothero) v Secretary of State for the Home Department.*[41] The Court noted that the information is securely recorded and that possession of it does not entitle the police to examine the details of bank account or credit card transactions: to do so they would ordinarily have to obtain an order from a judge. Accordingly, the interference with art.8, although material, is not nearly as significant as the interference already brought about by the other notification requirements. As to the justification for that interference, the Court was in no doubt that it had a legitimate policy objective, namely

[38] SSI 2014/147.
[39] SI 2012/325.
[40] SI 2012/1876.
[41] [2013] EWHC 2830 (Admin).

enabling the police to trace an offender quickly, to guard against the risk of an offender using another identity or to obtain quick access to a credit card account to investigate offences in relation to indecent images. Further, evidence before the Court as to the use of similar powers in Scotland showed that the objective can be achieved. Accordingly, the Court considered the requirements imposed by reg.12 to be a necessary, practical and proportionate means of preventing other persons becoming potential victims of sex offenders[42]:

> "The materials before the court and other matters well within the knowledge of any court provide sufficient evidence that the means are both appropriate and proportionate. Apart from the specific evidence from Scotland it is, in our view, self-evident that if such details are not provided by an offender, then the only course open to the police to identify the bank or institution at which the offender has a bank or credit card account would be to use their statutory powers to make applications in respect of the many banks and other institutions operating in England and Wales to see which bank or institution held an account in the name of the offender as that name was set out on the Sexual Offenders Register or otherwise known. The process of making such applications would be time consuming and expensive. Moreover, if the offender had changed the name under which he operated the account, the difficulties facing the police would be more considerable. By having details of the bank or other institution at which the offender held an account, the police would quickly be able to trace, by seeking appropriate orders. Any subsequent change of identity could be discovered by the well tested route of 'following the money'."

CHANGES TO THE NOTIFIED PARTICULARS

35.37 By s.84, any person subject to the notification requirements must notify to the police any change of name or home address, or the fact of his residing or staying away from home for a period of seven days, or two or more periods in any period of 12 months which together amount to seven days. That notification must be given within three days of the commencement of the change.[43]

35.38 Advance notification of changes is made possible by s.84(2), provided the offender specifies the date when the change is expected to occur. If the change occurs more than two days before the specified date, then s.84(3) provides that the offender must comply with s.84(1), i.e. notify the police within three days of the actual change. By s.84(4), if the change does not occur within the period of three days beginning with the specified date, then the offender must comply with s.84(1) and must also, within six days of specified date, notify the police that the change did not occur within the three day period beginning with that date.

---

[42] At [27].
[43] For criticism of the notification scheme for enabling notified persons to evade its impact by repeatedly moving, see Alisdair Gillespie, *Registering the loopholes*, NLJ 2007 (Jan), 52–53.

Section 84 provides[44]:   35.39

"**84. Notification requirements: changes**

(1) A relevant offender must, within the period of 3 days beginning with—

(a) his using a name which has not been notified to the police under section 83(1), this subsection, or section 2 of the Sex Offenders Act 1997 (c. 51),

(b) any change of his home address,

(c) his having resided or stayed, for a qualifying period, at any premises in the United Kingdom the address of which has not been notified to the police under section 83(1), this subsection, or section 2 of the Sex Offenders Act 1997,

(ca)any prescribed change of circumstances, or

(d) his release from custody pursuant to an order of a court or from imprisonment, service detention or detention in a hospital,

notify to the police that name, the new home address, the address of those premises, the prescribed details or (as the case may be) the fact that he has been released, and (in addition) the information set out in section 83(5).

(2) A notification under subsection (1) may be given before the name is used, the change of home address or the prescribed change of circumstances occurs or the qualifying period ends, but in that case the relevant offender must also specify the date when the event is expected to occur.

(3) If a notification is given in accordance with subsection (2) and the event to which it relates occurs more than 2 days before the date specified, the notification does not affect the duty imposed by subsection (1).

(4) If a notification is given in accordance with subsection (2) and the event to which it relates has not occurred by the end of the period of 3 days beginning with the date specified—

(a) the notification does not affect the duty imposed by subsection (1), and

(b) the relevant offender must, within the period of 6 days beginning with the date specified, notify to the police the fact that the event did not occur within the period of 3 days beginning with the date specified.

(5) Section 83(6) applies to the determination of the period of 3 days mentioned in subsection (1) and the period of 6 days mentioned in subsection (4)(b), as it applies to the determination of the period mentioned in section 83(1).

(5A) In this section—

(a) 'prescribed change of circumstances' means any change—

(i) occurring in relation to any matter in respect of which information is required to be notified by virtue of section 83(5)(h), and

(ii) of a description prescribed by regulations made by the Secretary of State;

(b) 'the prescribed details', in relation to a prescribed change of circumstances, means such details of the change as may be so prescribed.

(6) In this section, 'qualifying period' means—

(a) a period of 7 days, or

(b) two or more periods, in any period of 12 months, which taken together amount to 7 days."

---

[44] As amended by the Criminal Justice and Immigration Act 2008 ss.73, 142(3)–(5), 153(7). A separate version of s.84 has been created for Scotland by the Police, Public Order and Criminal Justice (Scotland) Act 2006 ss.78, 104.

35.40   Regulations 10 and 11 of the Sexual Offences Act 2003 (Notification Requirements) (England and Wales) Regulations 2012[45] require offenders to notify the police when they reside, or stay for at least 12 hours, at a relevant household. A "relevant household" is a household or other place at which a child (defined as a person aged under 18 years) resides or stays (whether with its parent, guardian or carer, with another child or alone) and to which the public do not have access. The information must include the date on which the offender begins to reside or stay at the relevant household, its address and the period for which the offender intends to reside or stay at that place.

Periodic Re-Notification

35.41 Section 85 requires those subject to the notification requirements to re-notify the information set out in s.83(5) to the police at least once a year. If they have no sole or main residence, they are required by reg.9 of the Sexual Offences Act 2003 (Notification Requirements) (England and Wales) Regulations 2012[46] to notify every seven days the address or location of a place in the UK where they can regularly be found. If a person notifies a change under s.84 at any time during the relevant period, he must re-notify within a year (or seven days) of that notification.

35.42   Section 85 of the 2003 Act as amended (in relation to England, Wales and Northern Ireland)[47] reads as follows:

> **"85. Notification requirements: periodic notification**
>
> (1) A relevant offender must, within the applicable period after each event within subsection (2), notify to the police the information set out in section 83(5), unless within that period he has given a notification under section 84(1).
> (2) The events are—
> (a) the commencement of this Part (but only in the case of a person who is a relevant offender from that commencement);
> (b) any notification given by the relevant offender under section 83(1) or 84(1); and
> (c) any notification given by him under subsection (1).
> (3) Where the applicable period would (apart from this subsection) end whilst subsection (4) applies to the relevant offender, that period is to be treated as continuing until the end of the period of 3 days beginning when subsection (4) first ceases to apply to him.
> (4) This subsection applies to the relevant offender if he is—
> (a) remanded in or committed to custody by an order of a court or kept in service custody,
> (b) serving a sentence of imprisonment or a term of service detention,
> (c) detained in a hospital, or
> (d) outside the United Kingdom.
> (5) In this section, 'the applicable period' means—

---

[45] SI 2012/1876.
[46] SI 2012/1876, made under s.85(5)(a) of the 2003 Act.
[47] By the Criminal Justice and Immigration Act 2008 ss.73, 142(7)–(9), 148(1), 153(7) and Sch.26, para.55.

(a) in any case where subsection (6) applies to the relevant offender, such period as may be prescribed by regulations made by the Secretary of State, and

(b) in any other case, the period of one year.

(6) This subsection applies to the relevant offender if the last home address notified by him under section 83(1) or 84(1) or subsection (1) was the address or location of such a place as is mentioned in section 83(7)(b)."

CHECKING THE NOTIFIED INFORMATION

By virtue of s.94, the police have the power to check the veracity of the information provided in accordance with ss.83 to 85. They can do this by supplying the details to the Secretary of State, a Northern Ireland Department or a person providing services to the Secretary of State or a Northern Ireland Department in connection with social security, child support, employment, training, passports or driver licensing, and asking them to check it against the data held by them. The sharing of information is limited to the stated purpose of enabling the police to verify the details provided. Section 95 does, however, provide that the police may use any data received by them for any purpose relating to the prevention, detection, investigation or prosecution of offences. In addition, s.96 allows the Secretary of State to make regulations requiring those responsible for the detention of an offender to notify other organisations if he is to be released or moved to another institution.   **35.43**

Section 96B of the Act[48] makes provision for the police to enter and search the home of a person subject to the notification requirements, pursuant to a warrant issued by a justice of the peace. In *M v Chief Constable of Hampshire*[49] the Court of Appeal held that the power of the police to obtain a search warrant to enter a sex offender's home without notice under s.96B is compatible with the ECHR. The claimant (M) was a repeat child sex offender and subject to the notification requirements. In 2005 and 2006 he received police visits for the purpose of assessing the risk he posed. Section 96B was enacted in 2007. The visits continued. M found them intrusive and, on the last, he refused to answer questions and told the police officers to leave.   **35.44**

M sought declarations that s.96B could be used only if there was a reasonable suspicion of offending; that a warrant could be sought only if he was given notice; and, alternatively, that s.96B was incompatible with art.8 ECHR. On the latter point, M accepted that s.96B was not itself incompatible with art.8, but argued that the police visits constituted an unlawful interference with his art.8 rights because the existence of the power to obtain a warrant if entry was refused vitiated his consent. He also argued that the

[48] Inserted by the Violent Crime Reduction Act 2006 s.58(1), with effect from May 31, 2007.

[49] [2014] EWCA Civ 1461; [2015] 1 W.L.R. 1176.

absence of any procedure for reviewing the application of s.96B separately from the notification requirements involved a disproportionate and unlawful interference with art.8. The Court of Appeal dismissed the appeal. On M's first argument, it held that in the absence of a warrant or statutory authority, the police had no right to enter a person's home against his will, but that a person could consent to acts that would otherwise involve an infringement of his rights, whether at common law or under art.8. Whether a person had waived his right to refuse entry would depend on the facts. One offender might be happy to allow the police entry regardless of s.96B, while another might consent only because he did not wish to give grounds for an application for a warrant. It was therefore not possible to say that, in all cases, s.96B robbed the offender of the ability to make a free and informed decision. While the knowledge that the police could apply for a warrant if refused entry might influence an offender's thinking, it did not necessarily follow that his will had been overborne so as to render his apparent consent illusory. In any event, an offender's failure to allow entry would not inevitably lead to the issue of a warrant. A senior officer had to apply to the court, and it was implicit that the application would have to be supported by evidence. There was no reason to suppose that the magistrates would not scrutinise applications with appropriate care. Therefore, if an offender allowed the police to enter his home without objection he would almost always have waived his right to refuse entry. Moreover, it was not unlawful for the police to visit an offender's home merely because no prior arrangement had been made. Article 8 might be infringed if the police visited with unreasonable frequency and in circumstances liable to result in the offender's convictions being disclosed to friends or neighbours, but that issue did not arise in M's case. Police made visits to sex offenders in order to protect vulnerable members of society from harm. If the visits engaged art.8 at all, they were proportionate to their purpose and satisfied the criteria in art.8(2). Parliament required arrangements to be in place for carrying out that purpose, and by enacting s.96B it recognised that visiting offenders in their homes was an effective way of achieving it. It would seriously undermine the efficacy of the arrangements if the police had to inform an offender or seek a magistrate's approval before making a visit. A balance had to be struck between the rights of vulnerable people and the rights of offenders, and the State enjoyed a considerable margin of appreciation. The practice of making unannounced visits to offenders' homes seeking entry by consent was proportionate and did not involve an unlawful interference with art.8. As for M's argument that the absence of any procedure for reviewing the application of s.96B separately from the notification requirements involved a disproportionate and unlawful interference with art.8, the Court noted that when Parliament enacted s.96B, it must have intended that the notification requirements and the provisions for assessing continuing risk to be viewed as part of a single scheme for the protection of vulnerable persons. That scheme was not disproportionate because it did not provide for exemption from one

constituent part. The monitoring element largely depended on the co-operation of the offender, and while it was reinforced by provision for compulsory
searches, that was subject to judicial oversight and safeguards which ensured
that the power was used proportionately and only when necessary.

ADVANCE NOTIFICATION OF FOREIGN TRAVEL

By virtue of s.86 of the Act and the Sexual Offences Act 2003 (Travel   **35.45**
Notification Requirements) Regulations 2004,[50] notification must be given by
an offender in advance of foreign travel and on return to the United
Kingdom. An offender who intends to leave the United Kingdom must
notify the date on which he will leave, the country to which he will travel and
his point of arrival in that country. This requirement applied originally to
trips of three days of more but now applies regardless of the length of the
trip.[51] If more than one country is to be visited, the offender must notify his
point of arrival in each additional country. He must also notify the identity
of any carrier or carriers he intends to use, the details of his accommodation
arrangements outside the United Kingdom, the date upon which he intends
to return and the point of arrival. Unless the offender has given a date of
return and the point of arrival, and returns on that date and to the notified
point of arrival, he must give notification of his return within three days of
his return. If the offender knows the information he is required to disclose
more than seven days before the date of his intended departure, he must
notify that information not less than seven days before that date. Where the
relevant offender does not know that information more than seven days
before the departure date, he must notify the information not less than 12
hours before that date.[52]

YOUNG OFFENDERS

Section 89 of the Act allows a court to direct that a person with parental   **35.46**
responsibility for a young offender shall comply with the notification
procedure and take the young offender to the police station with him when
he does so, until the offender reaches the age of 18. The police may also apply
for such a direction.

Under s.90, such a direction can be varied, renewed or discharged at any   **35.47**
time on application to the court by, in England, Wales or Northern Ireland,
the young offender, the person with the parental responsibility or the chief
officer of police for either the young offender's local police area or an area
where the young offender is intending to go.

---

[50] SI 2004/1220, as amended by SI 2012/1876. For Scotland, see the Sexual Offences Act 2003
(Travel Notification Requirements) (Scotland) Regulations 2004 (SSI 2004/205).
[51] SI 2004/1220 reg.5(1), as amended by SI 2012/1876, reg.5(a).
[52] SI 2004/1220 reg.5(3), as amended by SI 2012/1876, reg.5(b).

Notification Offences

35.48 Section 91 makes it an offence to fail without reasonable excuse to comply with any notification requirement. It is for the prosecution to prove the absence of reasonable excuse, though the defendant carries an evidential burden to raise the issue.[53] Section 91(3) has the effect that, even though a person may be prosecuted many times during the course of a notification period, he may only be prosecuted once for a single, continuing failure. The maximum penalty for failure to comply with a notification requirement is five years' imprisonment on conviction on indictment, and on summary conviction it is six months' imprisonment or a fine not exceeding the statutory maximum, or both. As from a day to be appointed the maximum sentence on summary conviction will increase to 12 months' imprisonment.[54] The increase will have no application to offences committed before it takes effect.[55]

35.49 Section 91 provides[56]:

"**91. Offences relating to notification**

(1) A person commits an offence if he—
(a) fails, without reasonable excuse, to comply with section 83(1), 84(1), 84(4)(b), 85(1), 87(4) or 89(2)(b) or any requirement imposed by regulations made under section 86(1); or
(b) notifies to the police, in purported compliance with section 83(1), 84(1) or 85(1) or any requirement imposed by regulations made under section 86(1), any information which he knows to be false.

(2) A person guilty of an offence under this section is liable—
(a) on summary conviction, to imprisonment for a term not exceeding 6 months or a fine not exceeding the statutory maximum or both;
(b) on conviction on indictment, to imprisonment for a term not exceeding 5 years.

(3) A person commits an offence under paragraph (a) of subsection (1) on the day on which he first fails, without reasonable excuse, to comply with section 83(1), 84(1) or 85(1) or a requirement imposed by regulations made under section 86(1), and continues to commit it throughout any period during which the failure continues; but a person must not be prosecuted under subsection (1) more than once in respect of the same failure.

(4) Proceedings for an offence under this section may be commenced in any court having jurisdiction in any place where the person charged with the offence resides or is found."

35.50 There is no sentencing guideline for offences under s.91. It is, however, clear from sentencing decisions of the Court of Appeal that an offence of failing to comply with notification requirements will be aggravated if the offender has attempted to evade the requirements and to avoid being checked

---

[53] cf. *Polychronakis v Richards & Jerrom Ltd* [1998] Env. L.R. 347; *O'Boyle* [1973] R.T.R. 445; *Mallows v Harris* [1979] R.T.R. 404; *Charles* [2010] Crim. L.R. 303.
[54] Criminal Justice Act 2003 s.282(2), (3).
[55] Criminal Justice Act 2003 s.282(4).
[56] A separate version of s.91 has been created for Scotland by the Police, Public Order and Criminal Justice (Scotland) Act 2006 ss.78, 104.

by the authorities. A good example is *Adams*,[57] where the appellant had pleaded guilty to failing to notify a change of address, failing to notify a change of name and obtaining a pecuniary advantage by deception by obtaining employment. He was required to comply with notification requirements as a result of convictions for indecent assault on young boys and possession of indecent images of young boys. Following his release from the custodial term he served for those offences, he had registered his address as being in Manchester. On a routine check by police officers, it was discovered that he had left the address without leaving a forwarding address or notifying any change of address to the authorities. The police eventually found him in a flat in Brighton. He had changed his name from "Daniel Paul Gregory" to "Christopher Adams" and was working as a fairground ride attendant. He had obtained that employment by not disclosing his previous convictions. He was sentenced to two years' imprisonment for the offence of failing to notify a change of address, two years' consecutive for failing to notify his change of name and a further six months' consecutive to the first two terms for obtaining a pecuniary advantage by deception. He appealed against that sentence on the grounds, first, that the first two terms should not have been consecutive to each other and secondly, that the totality was manifestly excessive. In the course of argument, the Court was referred to the case of *Wilcox*[58] where the appellant was subject to notification requirements and a further requirement that, although he was running a business providing an inflatable aeroplane for children's parties, he should not remain at the parties whilst they were ongoing. He breached the latter requirement on a number of occasions and was sentenced to two years' imprisonment, which was reduced to 12 months' on appeal. The Court regarded the offending in *Adams* as far more serious than that in *Wilcox*. Wilcox had not changed his name or address and could be checked by the authorities when appropriate. By contrast, Adams had made a determined effort to avoid the registration requirements and avoid being checked by the authorities. The Court held that there was nothing wrong in principle with consecutive sentences for the first two offences as they were different in nature and occurred at different times. However, the sentence of two years' imprisonment for the offence of failing to notify a change of address was reduced to 12 months', as the totality of four-and-a-half years' imprisonment was manifestly excessive. The appeal was therefore allowed to the extent that the total sentence was reduced to one of three-and-a-half years.

Repeated failure to comply with notification requirements will also **35.51** aggravate a s.91 offence. In *Clarke*,[59] the appellant had failed to comply with notification requirements to which he was subject on six previous occasions between 2003 and 2005 and had been variously sentenced to custodial terms ranging between two and six months' imprisonment. When imposing a

[57] [2003] EWCA Crim 3231.
[58] [2003] 1 Cr. App. R.(S.) 43.
[59] [2006] EWCA Crim 491.

sentence of two years' imprisonment for a further breach, the Recorder said that it called for a sharp increase in the custodial term. On appeal against that sentence, the Court of Appeal agreed with the Recorder's conclusion as to the necessity for a sharp increase in the custodial term, but in the light of the appellant's early plea and his voluntary surrender to a police station to admit that he was in breach of the notification requirements, the appropriate custodial term was one of 15 months.

35.52   In *Grosvenor*,[60] the Court of Appeal underlined the aggravating effect of deliberate or repeated breaches of the notification requirements. The appellant had been sentenced to eight months' imprisonment following a plea of guilty to an offence of failing to comply with notification requirements. He was released from prison in August 2009, failed to comply with a condition of his licence that he reside at a probation hostel, failed to notify the police of his whereabouts and was arrested in October 2009 having been "sofa surfing" at the homes of various associates. When arrested, he initially gave a false name but provided his real name minutes later. On his appeal against sentence, the Court of Appeal (Lord Judge CJ presiding) reviewed the previous decisions of the Court in *Clark*,[61] *R. v B*[62] and *Bowman.*[63] Giving the judgment of the Court, Griffiths-Williams J said[64]:

> "These decisions suggest that the sentencing range following conviction for failing to notify a change of address for periods of up to three months or so is in the range of four to six months, but we would emphasise that such a range is only appropriate in the judgment of this court where there are no aggravating factors. Where a sexual predator deliberately flouts the notification requirements, or there are repeated breaches of the notification requirements, a longer sentence would be appropriate. The fact that an offender chooses to live rough is not necessarily a mitigating factor. While this court recognised in *Bowman* (paragraph 7) the difficulties of complying with the notification requirements when an offender is of no fixed abode, or homeless, the Act imposes a mandatory duty on the offender to notify the police of his whereabouts and so an offender's decision to be of no fixed abode when accommodation is or can be made available to him will rarely mitigate the offence."

Dismissing the appeal, the Court observed that there was no evidence that the appellant was a sexual predator, his whereabouts had been unknown for some five weeks and his use of a false name had been an instinctive reaction from which he had quickly resiled. However, this was the third time he had breached notification requirements and he had previously breached a Sexual Offences Prevention Order. Therefore the judgment of the Court was that he had an indifference to court orders. The Court expressed the view that there is not a ceiling of three months for offences of this kind, particularly when the offender has a settled intention to ignore the provisions. It also said that

---

[60] [2010] EWCA Crim 560.
[61] [2003] 1 Cr. App. R.(S.) 2.
[62] [2005] 2 Cr. App. R.(S.) 65.
[63] [2005] EWCA Crim 3612.
[64] At [15].

it may be appropriate for the issue of the level of sentence for a breach of a notification requirement to be reconsidered by another division of the Court for the purposes of a guideline decision.

The decision in *Grosvenor* was considered in *Carnell*,[65] where the appellant **35.53** had originally pleaded guilty to an offence of voyeurism and was sentenced to a community order with supervision and required to comply with the notification requirements. On two occasions he complied with the notification requirements by notifying the police of his intention to travel to Sweden, where his brother lived. However, on another occasion he travelled there without notifying them. He returned voluntarily to the UK when he learned that the police had been enquiring as to his whereabouts. The appellant pleaded guilty at the first opportunity to failing to comply with the notification requirements and was sentenced to 26 weeks' imprisonment. On appeal, his counsel drew attention to his early guilty plea and the absence of any antecedents apart from the voyeurism conviction itself. It was submitted that there were no aggravating features because, whilst the appellant had left the jurisdiction, which would normally be a serious aggravating matter, he had been to Sweden before with permission and he came back voluntarily on learning of the police enquiries. Finally, there was personal mitigation in that as a result of his conviction the appellant had lost his job and experienced emotional turmoil. The Court of Appeal had regard to *Grosvenor*, which suggested that the sentencing range following conviction for failing to notify a change of address for periods up to three months or so is in the range of four to six months where there are no aggravating factors. The present case fell to be dealt with on the basis of plea, not conviction. The Court noted the importance of the notification requirements being complied with, but on the facts, taking particular account of the appellant's voluntary return, and applying the guidance in *Grosvenor*, it considered that on an early plea the appropriate sentence was 3 months' imprisonment, and it therefore allowed the appeal and substituted that sentence.

Grosvenor was again considered in *Petraitis*,[66] where the appellant had **35.54** originally been convicted for sexual assault on a 13-year-old girl. He was later released on licence and required to comply with the notification requirements for 10 years, but did not do so: he gave the police a false address, did not comply with the reporting requirements and was arrested whilst attempting to leave the UK. The appellant pleaded guilty to failing to comply with the notification requirements and was sentenced to 9 months' imprisonment, i.e. a starting point of 12 months and a 25 per cent credit for the guilty plea. His appeal against sentence was allowed, the Court of Appeal holding that the starting point of 12 months was too high. The case was less serious than *Grosvenor*, in which a starting point of 12 months was considered correct. However, the appellant could not expect to be treated favourably when he

[65] [2012] EWCA Crim 248.
[66] [2013] EWCA Crim 997.

had made it clear from the outset that he was not going to comply with the notification requirements, and any sentence imposed for a breach had to reflect that. A starting point of eight months was appropriate. When the 25 per cent discount was applied, that resulted in a sentence of six months' imprisonment.

35.55   In *McC*,[67] the Court of Appeal reviewed a number of relevant authorities including *Grosvenor, Carnell and Petraitis*, but also *Day*[68] and *Robert Piskadlo*[69] Furthermore, the Court considered that there were important principles to be drawn from the case of *Koli*,[70] a case concerned with Serious Crime Prevention Orders, observing that factors to be taken into account in determining the seriousness of the offending in relation to such an order were also relevant to breaches of the notification requirements. They included (a) the time between the imposition of the order and breach; (b) any history of non-compliance; (c) whether non-compliance had been repeated and come in the face of warnings and requests for information; and (d) whether non-compliance was deliberate or inadvertent. It was particularly important whether the breach was related to the commission of further serious offences and might lead to the conclusion that the failure to comply added to the risk that the particular subject of the order was likely to commit further offences. The court would also have to consider the harm caused by non-compliance for breach. The Court concluded[71]:

> "In our judgment, drawing on the authorities referred to above, the following principles can be identified. If notification requirements are to constitute effective and meaningful protection for the innocent and sometimes most vulnerable members of society, including children, they must be enforced rigorously. As this court said in *R. v Bushell*:
>
> 'The provisions of the Sexual Offenders Act 1997, re-enacted in the Sexual Offences Act 2003, that require notification of the whereabouts of sexual offenders are important. Those provisions are there for the safety of the public, and also in some cases for the protection of the offender. It is vital if the purposes of those provisions of the Sexual Offences Act 2003 are to be fulfilled that the requirements of notification are complied with by offenders. That is signalled by the fact that the maximum sentence for failing to comply with those provisions is one of five years' imprisonment.'
>
> Any substantive breach of notification requirements is likely to warrant an immediate custodial sentence. Although not a guideline case, *R. v Grosvenor* . . . suggests that for non-notification during a period of up to 3 months a starting point of 4 to 6 months' custody is appropriate. Any longer period of non-notification is likely to lead to a longer sentence. Equally, the presence of

---

[67] [2014] EWCA Crim 909.

[68] [2013] EWCA Crim 1648 (deliberate repeated breaches by the appellant over a six month period that afforded significant opportunity of increased risk and harm; but significant mitigation available to the appellant including his age (67); *held*, starting point before credit for a guilty plea reduced from 21 to 12 months).

[69] [2014] EWCA Crim 76 (sixth persistent failure to comply with notification requirements; *held*, starting point of 32 months' custody before guilty plea was manifestly excessive, reduced to 18 months').

[70] [2012] EWCA Crim 1869.

[71] At [20]–[21].

aggravating factors, such as the occasioning of harm, repeated non-compliance and deliberate breaches, will increase the sentence. The time between imposition of the order and the date of breach will also be a relevant factor."

McC was subsequently referred to in *Norton*,[72] where a sentence of two   **35.56**
years' imprisonment for a breach of the notification requirements was reduced to 15 months. The appellant had become subject to the notification requirements as a result of his conviction of three offences of rape when aged 16 in 2000. He had been convicted on 11 previous occasions of failing to comply with the requirements, the longest sentence for any of those offences being one of 12 months' imprisonment imposed in 2012. One year later, he had received a suspended sentence of 16 weeks' imprisonment for a further failure. One month later, he joined a team of itinerant road workers, in consequence of which he failed to comply from then until August 2013, when he was arrested for his part in a fraud. It was held that a sentence of two years' imprisonment for the failure (concurrent to four weeks for the fraud but with the 16-week sentence ordered to run consecutively) was too big a leap from the previous longest sentence. The failure to comply with the requirements was not calculated to provide cover under which further sexual crimes could be perpetrated, nor was this the case with respect to the earlier breaches. However, protection of potential victims was a paramount consideration, and the consequential inconvenience to peripatetic sex offenders was a necessary corollary. Whilst the appellant's history of persistent disregard of the notification requirements was a serious aggravating feature, and a deterrent sentence was entirely justified, bearing in mind the absence of any evidence of any relevant or substantive harm or threat, 18 months' imprisonment would satisfy the demands of totality. Accordingly, the Court reduced the sentence for the fresh offence to 15 months, and activated consecutively the suspended sentence to the extent of three months.

NOTIFICATION ORDERS

Section 97 of the 2003 Act makes provision for persons convicted of sexual   **35.57**
offences abroad to be subject to a notification order, the effect of which is to require them to notify their details in the United Kingdom in much the same way as if the offence had been committed here. The provision covers a number of possible situations, including:
- A United Kingdom citizen or foreign national is residing in the local police area and is known to have committed a relevant offence abroad;
- A United Kingdom citizen imprisoned for a sexual offence abroad is about to be deported home on release from custody; or
- A foreign national whom the police know to have committed sexual offences abroad is about to travel to this country.

[72] [2014] 2 Cr. App. R.(S.) 79.

Applications and grounds

35.58 Section 97(1) provides that a chief officer of police may apply to a magistrates' court for a notification order in respect of a person who is residing in the local police area or intending to come to that area. An application may be made only if it appears to the chief officer that the three conditions set out in s.97(2)–(4) are met. If it is proved that they are, then the court must make the requested order. The first condition is that the person has been convicted, cautioned or had a finding made against him in respect of a "relevant offence". The second condition relates to the date of the conviction (etc.) and, as with s.81 of the Act, is made partially retrospective. The third condition is that the appropriate notification period under s.82 has not expired. So, for example, if the offender was sentenced to five months' imprisonment in France, the appropriate notification period would be seven years[73] and an application made eight years after his going to prison would accordingly fail.

35.59 Section 97 provides:

"**97. Notification orders: applications and grounds**

(1) A chief officer of police may, by complaint to any magistrates' court whose commission area includes any part of his police area, apply for an order under this section (a 'notification order') in respect of a person ('the defendant') if—
  (a) it appears to him that the following three conditions are met with respect to the defendant, and
  (b) the defendant resides in his police area or the chief officer believes that the defendant is in, or is intending to come to, his police area.

(2) The first condition is that under the law in force in a country outside the United Kingdom—
  (a) he has been convicted of a relevant offence (whether or not he has been punished for it),
  (b) a court exercising jurisdiction under that law has made in respect of a relevant offence a finding equivalent to a finding that he is not guilty by reason of insanity,
  (c) such a court has made in respect of a relevant offence a finding equivalent to a finding that he is under a disability and did the act charged against him in respect of the offence, or
  (d) he has been cautioned in respect of a relevant offence.

(3) The second condition is that—
  (a) the first condition is met because of a conviction, finding or caution which occurred on or after 1st September 1997,
  (b) the first condition is met because of a conviction or finding which occurred before that date, but the person was dealt with in respect of the offence or finding on or after that date, or has yet to be dealt with in respect of it, or
  (c) the first condition is met because of a conviction or finding which occurred before that date, but on that date the person was, in respect of the offence or finding, subject under the law in force in the country concerned to

---

[73] See para.35.16, above.

detention, supervision or any other disposal equivalent to any of those mentioned in section 81(3) (read with sections 81(6) and 131).

(4) The third condition is that the period set out in section 82 (as modified by subsections (2) and (3) of section 98) in respect of the relevant offence has not expired.

(5) If on the application it is proved that the conditions in subsections (2) to (4) are met, the court must make a notification order.

(6) In this section and section 98, 'relevant offence' has the meaning given by section 99."

In *Masterman v Commissioner of Police of the Metropolis*,[74] the appellant   **35.60**
was convicted of a relevant offence in the United States before September 1, 1997, absconded to the United Kingdom before sentence, and on September 1, 1997, was held in custody pending extradition. In an appeal against a notification order made on his eventual return to the United Kingdom after serving his sentence in the United States, the Divisional Court held that the second condition for making the order was satisfied since on September 1, 1997, he was subject under United States law to detention within the meaning of s.97(3)(c), having been sentenced to a term of imprisonment. Although he was not on that date serving that sentence, he was plainly liable under the relevant State law of the United States to do so and was hence subject to detention.

"Relevant offence"

Section 99 defines a "relevant offence" in s.97 as an act which is a criminal   **35.61**
offence in the country where it occurred and would have constituted one of the offences set out in Sch.3 to the 2003 Act if it had been done in the United Kingdom. By s.99(3), the court must take it that the act would have constituted a Sch.3 offence unless the defendant puts the point in issue.

Section 99 provides: **35.62**

"**99. Sections 97 and 98: relevant offences**

(1) 'Relevant offence' in sections 97 and 98 means an act which—

(a) constituted an offence under the law in force in the country concerned, and

(b) would have constituted an offence listed in Schedule 3 (other than at paragraph 60) if it had been done in any part of the United Kingdom.

(2) An act punishable under the law in force in a country outside the United Kingdom constitutes an offence under that law for the purposes of subsection (1) however it is described in that law.

(3) Subject to subsection (4), on an application for a notification order the condition in subsection (1)(b) is to be taken as met unless, not later than rules of court may provide, the defendant serves on the applicant a notice—

(a) stating that, on the facts as alleged with respect to the act concerned, the condition is not in his opinion met,

(b) showing his grounds for that opinion, and

---

[74] [2010] EWHC 806 (Admin).

(c) requiring the applicant to prove that the condition is met.

(4) The court, if it thinks fit, may permit the defendant to require the applicant to prove that the condition is met without service of a notice under subsection (3)."

Effect of notification orders

35.63 Under s.98 of the Act, when a notification order is made the offender is subject to the notification requirements for a period equivalent to what would remain if he had been required to notify immediately after his conviction. Thus if an offender had been sentenced to nine months' imprisonment in Germany and came to the United Kingdom some eight years later, he would be subject to the notification requirements for a further year. The requirements he would have to comply with are, subject to minor modifications contained in s.98(3), the same as for an offender subject to notification because of his committing an offence in the United Kingdom. As with domestic offenders, a person subject to a notification order must notify his details within three days of the date of service of the order and re-notify each year.

35.64 Section 98 provides:

"**98. Notification orders: effect**

(1) Where a notification order is made—

(a) the application of this Part to the defendant in respect of the conviction, finding or caution to which the order relates is subject to the modifications set out below, and

(b) subject to those modifications, the defendant becomes or (as the case may be) remains subject to the notification requirements of this Part for the notification period set out in section 82.

(2) The 'relevant date' means—

(a) in the case of a person within section 97(2)(a), the date of the conviction;

(b) in the case of a person within section 97(2)(b) or (c), the date of the finding;

(c) in the case of a person within section 97(2)(d), the date of the caution.

(3) In section 82—

(a) references, except in the Table, to a person (or relevant offender) within any provision of section 80 are to be read as references to the defendant;

(b) the reference in the Table to section 80(1)(d) is to be read as a reference to section 97(2)(d);

(c) references to an order of any description are to be read as references to any corresponding disposal made in relation to the defendant in respect of an offence or finding by reference to which the notification order was made;

(d) the reference to offences listed in Schedule 3 is to be read as a reference to relevant offences.

(4) In sections 83 and 85, references to the commencement of this Part are to be read as references to the date of service of the notification order."

Interim notification orders and appeals

Under s.100, a court may on application make an interim notification order **35.65** should it consider it just to do so. Such an application might be appropriate if, for example, the defendant disputes that his act would constitute a Sch.3 offence and papers need to be secured from abroad. Should an interim order be made, the defendant is subject to the notification requirements as if a full order had been made.

Section 101 provides a right of appeal to the Crown Court against the **35.66** making of a notification order or an interim notification order. No procedure is laid down for such appeals. As a notification order must be made where the s.97 conditions are met, an appeal against the making of such an order will succeed only if the appellant can satisfy the Crown Court that one or more of those conditions was not met. By contrast, an appeal against the making of an interim notification order will succeed if the appellant can satisfy the Crown Court that the magistrates' court wrongly exercised its discretion in considering it just to make the order. There is no right of appeal against a refusal to make an interim order.

CHAPTER 36

SEXUAL HARM PREVENTION ORDERS AND SEXUAL RISK
ORDERS

By H.H. Judge Martin Picton

Introduction...................................... 36.01
Sexual Harm Prevention Orders...... 36.13
Criteria for Making a SHPO........... 36.13
Necessity and Proportionality 36.21
SHPOs and Computers 36.29
Non-Contact Prohibitions 36.38

Relationship between SHPOS and
    Other Sentences............................ 36.48
Effect of a SHPO............................ 36.53
Breach of a SHPO........................... 36.60
Sexual Risk Orders......................... 36.66
Conclusion...................................... 36.76

INTRODUCTION

HISTORICAL PERSPECTIVE

Provisions designed to regulate the future behaviour of offenders (or **36.01** potential offenders) are an important aspect of government strategies that have as their aim the prevention of sexual offending. Preventative orders imposed by the courts have proved problematic in a number of fields, but rarely more so than in respect of those designed to guard against the potential for sexual offending.

The first such orders designed to deal exclusively with sexual offences were **36.02** restraining orders under the Sex Offenders Act 1997 and sex offender orders under the Crime and Disorder Act 1998. The 1997 Act[1] provided that where a Crown Court imposed a sentence of imprisonment on a person convicted of an offence to which Pt I of the Act applied,[2] the Court could make a restraining order if satisfied that it was necessary to do so in order to protect the public in general, or particular members of the public, from serious harm

---

[1] s.5A, inserted by the Criminal Justice and Court Services Act 2000 s.66 and Sch.5, para.6(1), with effect from May 2, 2001.
[2] The offences covered by Pt I are set out in Sch.1 to the Act.

from the offender.[3] The order could prohibit the offender from doing anything described in it for a specified period or until further order.[4] There was a right of appeal against the making of such an order and it was possible to apply to vary or discharge an order.[5] To breach an order was an offence punishable with a maximum of five years' imprisonment.[6]

36.03   The Crime and Disorder Act 1998 enabled chief officers of police to apply to a magistrates' court for a sex offender order when a sex offender had acted, since his conviction, in such a way as to give reasonable cause to believe that such an order was necessary to protect the public from serious harm from him.[7] If the specified conditions were met, the court could prohibit the offender from doing anything described in the order.[8] The only limitation on the nature of such a prohibition was that it had to be "necessary for the purpose of protecting the public, or particular members of the public, from serious harm from the defendant".[9] An offender upon whom such an order was imposed became subject to the notification scheme under the Sex Offenders Act 1997 (if he was not already subject to it).[10] An order had a minimum of five years' duration but could be indefinite. There was provision for orders to be appealed, varied or discharged[11] and, as with restraining orders, any breach of an order without reasonable excuse was an offence punishable with a maximum of five years' imprisonment.[12]

36.04   The 2003 Act replaced and built upon restraining orders and sex offender orders with the creation of the Sexual Offences Prevention Order ("SOPO"), which could be made on application or on conviction for the purpose of protecting the public, or particular members of the public, from serious sexual harm from the subject of the order. In addition the Act introduced two new forms of order, the Foreign Travel Order ("FTO") and the Risk of Sexual Harm Order ("RSHO"). The FTO was designed to prevent an offender from travelling abroad when this was necessary in order to protect a child or children from serious sexual harm from him. The RSHO could be made on an application by the police where the subject had engaged in certain specified forms of behaviour towards a child and the order was necessary to protect a child or children from harm (not necessarily serious sexual harm) from him. The legislative schemes applicable to these orders were otherwise very similar to the schemes they replaced.

---

[3] s.5A(2).
[4] s.5A(3).
[5] s.5A(4)–(7).
[6] s.5A(8), (9).
[7] s.2(1).
[8] s.2(3).
[9] s.2(4).
[10] s.2(5). For notification, see Ch.35.
[11] s.2(7).
[12] s.2(8).

SEXUAL HARM PREVENTION ORDERS AND SEXUAL RISK ORDERS

The 2003 Act orders, and in particular SOPOs, generated a significant body   **36.05**
of case law and also a fair degree of criticism due to the limits on their
applicability. In 2013 an ACPO-commissioned review of the statutory scheme
concluded that it was not fit for purpose and proposed legislative changes.[13]
The following year, the Anti-social Behaviour, Crime and Policing Act 2014
swept away the existing orders and introduced in their place two new
orders—Sexual Harm Prevention Orders ("SHPOs") and Sexual Risk
Orders ("SROs").

SHPOs fall to be made under ss.103A–K of the Sexual Offences Act 2003,   **36.06**
and SROs under ss.122A–K. Sections 104–129 of the Act, dealing with
SOPOs, FTOs and RSHOs, are repealed. The commencement date of the
new provisions was March 8, 2015, and any application made after that date
could only legitimately result in the imposition of a SHPO or SRO.[14] Further,
all SOPOs that are subsisting as at March 8, 2020, will on that date be
converted into SHPOs.[15]

The new orders are similar in their effect to the orders they replace, but   **36.07**
there are potentially important differences in the circumstances in which they
apply.[16] The principal differences between a SHPO and a SOPO are:

- the qualifying risk that has to be made out in order for a SHPO to be
  imposed is of "sexual harm" and not, as in the case of a SOPO,
  "serious sexual harm".

- a SHPO can protect potential victims outside the UK by way of a
  prohibition against foreign travel. Previously the power for prevent
  such travel was only available to the magistrates' court and then only
  on an application by the police for a Foreign Travel Order. Such
  applications were in practice rarely made.

- a SHPO can impose prohibitions of varying length and not, as
  previously with SOPOs, by way of a package of prohibitions that all
  applied for the same period.

SROs, like RSHOs, remain the exclusive province of the magistrates' court.   **36.08**
The principal differences between a SRO and a RSHO are:

- A SRO can be made in respect of a defendant who has done a single
  "act of a sexual nature", whereas previously there had be two acts of
  a nature specified in s.123(3) relating to a child.

---

[13] *Review of Civil Prevention Orders under the Sexual Offences Act 2003* by Hugh Davies OBE
QC (May 15, 2013). The review is available at *http://l3rblaw.com/publication/review-of-civil-
prevention-orders-under-the-sexual-offences-act-2003/* [Accessed April 30, 2016].
[14] The Anti-social Behaviour, Crime and Policing Act 2014 (Commencement No.8, Saving and
Transitional Provisions) Order 2015 and s.114 of the Act.
[15] s.114(5) of the anti-Social Behaviour and Policing Act 2014.
[16] See Terry Thomas and David Thompson, *New Civil Orders to Contain Sexual Offending—A
Matter of "Purposive Logic"?* 177 C.L. & J. 703, questioning the application of the civil standard
of proof to consideration of the need for a SHPO or SRO.

- Defendants aged under 18 may be subject to a SRO whereas a RSHO was available only in relation to those aged 18 and over.
- A SRO can be made to protect adults and not just children, as was the case with a RSHO.
- A SRO made to protect children and vulnerable adults outside the UK may contain a prohibition against foreign travel of up to five years.
- Children are defined as those aged under 18 rather than under 16.

The change from RSHO to SRO has the potential to result in many more orders being made than previously, if the police choose to make use of the greater scope that SROs offer. The fact that orders can be made with a view to protecting adults may obviate the need for those with responsibilities in this field to adopt the perhaps more cumbersome (and certainly more expensive) Family Court procedure of seeking injunctive relief, such as was done, for example, in *Birmingham City Council v Riaz*.[17] The reduction in the number of necessary threshold events, i.e. from two "acts of a sexual nature" to one, coupled with the apparent widening of what might be considered to be such an act, should also encourage greater use of the new order.

36.09   In respect of both SHPOs and SROs initiated by an application to the magistrates' court, such applications may now be brought not only by the relevant chief officer of police but also by the Director General of the National Crime Agency.

36.10   In the past, of the three types of preventative order available to the court, the most frequently made, and in proportionate terms the most frequently appealed, were SOPOs. Particular issues that repeatedly arose in the framing of SOPOs, discussed below, related to access to computers, non-contact prohibitions and prohibitions that amount to compulsions. Many of these issues are now reasonably well settled following interventions by the Court of Appeal, and the body of case law relating to the terms of regularly imposed SOPO prohibitions will continue to be relevant to SHPOs. The imposition of a SHPO will, however, call for the application of drafting discipline of a kind more normally exercised in the civil sphere. Regrettably, the case law in relation to SOPOs demonstrates that such discipline has often been conspicuous by its absence. For this reason SHPOs can be expected, like SOPOs, to generate a significant volume of work in the Court of Appeal.

36.11   The fact that the threshold for the imposition of a SHPO is simply "sexual harm", rather than "serious sexual harm" as with SOPOs, is eye-catching. But in practice this is unlikely to have a substantial impact, as it was rarely argued under the previous regime that the nature of the sexual harm that might be anticipated could not properly be assessed as "serious". That was no doubt on the sensible basis that virtually all "sexual harm" is potentially "serious", and to suggest otherwise is to risk generating criticism.

---

[17] [2014] EWHC 4247 (Fam).

The infrequency of applications for FTOs means that there are few **36.12** appellate cases in which they have been considered.[18] As a protective provision they were very little used: only 50 FTOs were made between 2005 and 2012.[19] Should SROs prove to be as popular as the Government hoped, many more prohibitions against foreign travel will be made in the future, with the likely consequence that orders of this nature will come to be considered in the Court of Appeal.[19a]

SEXUAL HARM PREVENTION ORDERS

CRITERIA FOR MAKING A SHPO

Section 103A of the Sexual Offences Act 2003 sets out the criteria for the **36.13** making of a SHPO:

> "**103A Sexual harm prevention orders: applications and grounds**
>
> (1) A court may make an order under this section (a 'sexual harm prevention order') in respect of a person ('the defendant') where subsection (2) or (3) applies to the defendant.
> (2) This subsection applies to the defendant where—
> (a) the court deals with the defendant in respect of—
>   (i) an offence listed in Schedule 3 or 5, or
>   (ii) a finding that the defendant is not guilty of an offence listed in Schedule 3 or 5 by reason of insanity, or
>   (iii) a finding that the defendant is under a disability and has done the act charged against the defendant in respect of an offence listed in Schedule 3 or 5,
> and
> (b) the court is satisfied that it is necessary to make a sexual harm prevention order, for the purpose of—
>   (i) protecting the public or any particular members of the public from sexual harm from the defendant, or
>   (ii) protecting children or vulnerable adults generally, or any particular children or vulnerable adults, from sexual harm from the defendant outside the United Kingdom.
> (3) This subsection applies to the defendant where—
> (a) an application under subsection (4) has been made in respect of the defendant and it is proved on the application that the defendant is a qualifying offender, and
> (b) the court is satisfied that the defendant's behaviour since the appropriate date makes it necessary to make a sexual harm prevention order, for the purpose of—
>   (i) protecting the public or any particular members of the public from sexual harm from the defendant, or

---

[18] See *Grant (R on the Application of) v The Crown Court at Kingston* [2015] EWHC 767 (Admin).
[19] See the *Review of Civil Prevention Orders under the Sexual Offences Act 2003* by Hugh Davies OBE QC (15 May 2013), p.15, Table A.
[19a] See *R. v PG* [2016] EWCA Crim 250 and para.6.47, below.

(ii) protecting children or vulnerable adults generally, or any particular children or vulnerable adults, from sexual harm from the defendant outside the United Kingdom.

(4) A chief officer of police or the Director General of the National Crime Agency ('the Director General') may by complaint to a magistrates' court apply for a sexual harm prevention order in respect of a person if it appears to the chief officer or the Director General that—

(a) the person is a qualifying offender, and

(b) the person has since the appropriate date acted in such a way as to give reasonable cause to believe that it is necessary for such an order to be made.

(5) A chief officer of police may make an application under subsection (4) only in respect of a person—

(a) who resides in the chief officer's police area, or

(b) who the chief officer believes is in that area or is intending to come to it.

(6) An application under subsection (4) may be made to any magistrates' court acting for a local justice area that includes—

(a) any part of a relevant police area, or

(b) any place where it is alleged that the person acted in a way mentioned in subsection (4)(b).

(7) The Director General must as soon as practicable notify the chief officer of police for a relevant police area of any application that the Director has made under subsection (4).

(8) Where the defendant is a child, a reference in this section to a magistrates' court is to be taken as referring to a youth court (subject to any rules of court made under section 103K(1)).

(9) In this section 'relevant police area' means—

(a) where the applicant is a chief officer of police, the officer's police area;

(b) where the applicant is the Director General—

(i) the police area where the person in question resides, or

(ii) a police area which the Director General believes the person is in or is intending to come to."

36.14   For these purposes, "sexual harm" is defined in s.103B(1) as:

"physical or psychological harm caused—

(a) by the person committing one or more offences listed in Schedule 3, or

(b) (in the context of harm outside the United Kingdom) by the person doing, outside the United Kingdom, anything which would constitute an offence listed in Schedule 3 if done in any part of the United Kingdom."

SHPO Made at Time of Dealing With Offender for an Offence

36.15   For an offender to be eligible for a SHPO there has to be both the commission of an offence listed in Sch.3 or Sch.5 to the Act coupled with a necessity to protect the public or particular members of the public within the UK, or children or vulnerable adults abroad, from sexual harm.[20] The offences listed in Sch.3 are sexual offences and those in Sch.5 are a range of

---

[20] s.103A(2).

other offences including murder. Section 103B(1) defines a "child" as someone under 18 and "vulnerable adult" as a person aged 18 or over "whose ability to protect himself or herself from physical or psychological harm is significantly impaired through physical or mental disability or illness, through old age or otherwise".

Applications for a SHPO triggered by a conviction should be notified in advance of the sentence hearing so as to comply with Part 31 of the CPR. This was emphasised in relation to SOPOs by Maddison J in *Lawrence*:[21]   36.16

> "It is necessary that the prosecution should consider in every case whether it is reasonably arguable that it is necessary for such an order to be made. The prosecution should also consider carefully the evidence upon which they seek to rely in support of any such application. Should it then be decided, as it should be decided well in advance of the sentencing hearing, that an application for such an order should be made, then care should be taken to ensure compliance with the procedural and evidential provisions of Part 50 [now Part 31] of the Criminal Procedure Rules, which are in place for the specific purpose of avoiding the difficulties of the kind that arose in this case and avoiding the possibility that a Sexual Offences Prevention Order might be made without proper consideration of the relevant statutory provisions."

The need for the court and the defence to be informed of the fact of a proposed application for a SOPO (now SHPO) and the terms of any order sought was a point also made forcefully in *Smith*[22]:   36.17

> "Arrangements for the provision of a draft order will necessarily vary from court to court. We say no more than that it is essential that there is a written draft, properly considered in advance of the sentencing hearing. The normal requirement should be that it is served on the court and the defendant before the sentencing hearing—we suggest not less than two clear days before but in any event not at the hearing. This will usually be possible because sentencing in such cases only occasionally follows immediately on conviction. Because the draft is likely to require amendment before it is issued by the court staff, it is sensible for it to be available in electronic as well as paper form. If a judge finds that insufficient time for consideration has been given, he has ample power to put the issue back to another hearing, but this is wasteful and the occasion for it ought to be avoided by prior service of the draft."

A SHPO may be made where instead of being convicted of an offence listed in Sch.3 or Sch.5, a person is (a) found not guilty by reason of insanity or (b) found to be under a disability and to have done the act charged.[23]

SHPO MADE BY MAGISTRATES' COURT ON APPLICATION

An application for a SHPO may be made to the magistrates' court in respect of a "qualifying offender". A "qualifying offender" for these purposes includes, in addition to a defendant convicted of a Sch.3 or Sch.5 offence, a person cautioned for such an offence, found not guilty by reason of insanity   36.18

---

[21] [2011] EWCA Crim 3185 at [16].
[22] [2011] EWCA Crim 1772 at [26].
[23] s.103A(2).

or found to be under a disability and to have done the act charged.[24] Foreign convictions, cautions or findings may also result in a defendant being classed as a "qualifying offender".[25] In addition to the offence requirement, the court must be satisfied that the defendant's behaviour makes it necessary that a SHPO be imposed in order to protect members of the public within the UK and/or children and vulnerable adults outside the jurisdiction[26] from sexual harm. Section 103F provides for the making of an interim SHPO in advance of a final hearing in the magistrates' court.

36.19   An application made in respect of a qualifying offender in the magistrates' court is initiated by way of complaint. When SOPOs were introduced, a summons for a SOPO or interim SOPO was required to be in a prescribed form,[27] but this requirement was removed with effect from September 3, 2012,[28] and has not been reinstated in relation to SHPOs. On an application to a magistrates' court both the fact that the subject of the application is a "qualifying offender" and that he has behaved in a relevant manner have to be "proved" to the criminal standard.[29] That is so despite the fact that the proceedings are civil in their nature.[30] Hearsay evidence is admissible, as in any other civil proceedings, but the court must be "sure" on the evidence before it that the qualifying conditions are met. Section 132A of the Act confirms that evidence provided in support of an application does not have to relate to matters occurring during the six month period preceding the making of the application.

Interim SHPO

36.20   A court may make an interim SHPO, if it considers it just to do so, pending the determination of an application for a full order.[31] An interim order is made for a fixed period and will cease to have effect if the main application is determined before the end of that period. If the fixed period expires before the main application is determined, then a court may renew the interim order for a further fixed period.

Necessity and Proportionality

36.21   In *Collard*,[32] the Court of Appeal set out the high test that had to be satisfied before a court could legitimately impose a SOPO. If applied appropriately,

---

[24] s.103B(1).
[25] s.103B(3).
[26] s.103A(3).
[27] Magistrates' Courts (Sexual Offences Prevention Orders) Rules 2004 (SI 2004/1054).
[28] Magistrates' Courts (Sexual Offences Act 2003) (Miscellaneous Amendments) Rules 2012 (SI 2012/2018).
[29] *Cleveland Police v Haggas* [2009] EWHC 3231 (Admin), applying *B v Chief Constable of Avon and Somerset Constabulary* [2001] 1 All E.R. 562.
[30] *Commissioner of Police of the Metropolis v Ebanks* [2012] EWHC 2368 (Admin).
[31] s.103F.
[32] [2004] EWCA Crim 1664.

the test should result in prohibitions (where required at all) that are necessary, reasonable, proportionate and capable of being both understood and sensibly enforced. It would appear incontrovertible by reference to the number of successful appeals against SOPOs, imposed often without opposition at the point of sentence, that the *Collard* test is often not in fact applied with any, or sufficient, rigour.

The *Collard* test can be stated thus: 36.22

1. A prohibition may be imposed only if it is necessary for the purpose of protecting the public or any particular members of the public from serious[33] sexual harm from the defendant. This is a high threshold. It is not sufficient that it may be considered desirable to impose such a prohibition. There must be material before the judge on the basis of which he can reasonably conclude that a prohibition is necessary for that purpose.

2. The court must consider the number of offences, their duration, the nature of the material, the extent of publication and the use to which the material was put.

3. The court must have regard to the offender's antecedents, his personal circumstances and the risk of his re-offending.

4. Where the court makes an order, its terms must be tailored to meet the danger that this offender presents.

5. The order must be proportionate to the danger presented. In this respect the judge must have regard in particular to the provisions of the European Convention on Human Rights and the Human Rights Act and in particular the right to private life under art.8 of the Convention.

The above test is consistent with the statutory requirement that the only 36.23 prohibitions that may be included in a SHPO are those that are "necessary for the purpose of protecting the public or any particular members of the public from sexual harm".[34] In the case of *Smith*,[35] which is essential reading for anyone considering SHPOs, the Vice President (as he then was) attempted to address the issues identified as being responsible for the multiplicity of appeals with which the Court of Appeal had for years been plagued by reason of the imposition of inappropriate SOPOs. The degree to which that has been achieved, in the sense of stemming the flow of appeals, is open to question. The continuing failure of prosecutors to comply with Pt 31 (formerly Pt 50) of the Criminal Procedure Rules, dealing with behaviour orders after verdict or finding, must be a significant factor. The Rules have now been amended so as to make specific reference to SHPOs and to adopt the observations in *Smith* as to the giving of notice of the application.[36]

[33] The word "serious" is no longer relevant in respect of a SHPO.
[34] s.103A(2), (3).
[35] [2011] EWCA Crim 1772.
[36] CPR 2015 r.31.3.

Overly inventive drafting certainly has played a part in the past, but *Smith* should have discouraged that tendency, at least for the moment.

36.24   The fact that a prohibition may be capable of being formulated in such a way that compliance with it might be regarded as being socially beneficial does not mean that it will be either necessary or proportionate. What might be termed "shopping list SHPOs" are unlikely to find favour if subject to review on appeal. The greater the number of SHPO terms, and the more complex the provisions, the more likely it is that they will be the subject of successful challenge.

36.25   The mere fact that a SHPO could be a useful tool in dealing with an offender does not mean that the statutory criteria for its imposition are made out. In this respect there is no reason why the courts should take a different approach to SHPOs than they took in relation to SOPOs. So in *R. v D*[37] the Court of Appeal emphasised that the word "necessary" imported a higher threshold than, for example, that it was desirable to make a SOPO. In *Terrell*[38] the Court of Appeal held that the extent of the harm occasioned to children by the downloading and viewing of child pornography by adults is uncertain, and care should therefore be taken in such cases to ensure that any SOPO was necessary and proportionate to the risk of harm posed by the offender. The Court of Appeal referred on a number of occasions to the undesirability of making SOPOs the terms of which were wider than necessary to protect against ascertained risks. In *Williamson*,[39] Stanley Burnton LJ said that in tailoring a SOPO to the facts of a case, care should be taken, if it was possible, to interfere with the life of the offender no more than was necessary and to enable him to work and to continue his life reasonably normally. The Court of Appeal on numerous occasions deleted SOPO prohibitions that it regarded as unjustified or redrafted them in less restrictive terms.[40]

36.26   In *Jackson*,[41] the Court of Appeal said that it is the responsibility of the prosecution to put before the judge in a proposed SOPO (now SHPO) provisions which are necessary and proportionate. The Court said it is essential that prosecuting counsel appreciates that he is responsible for putting before the judge an appropriate order which meets the individual case and provides the necessary protection for the future. It is a dereliction of counsel's duty if he fails to consider what is proportionate and what the judge should impose. Furthermore, if there is a question as to what provisions it is

[37] [2006] 1 W.L.R. 1088.
[38] [2008] 2 Cr. App. R.(S.) 49.
[39] [2005] EWCA Crim 2151, at 24.
[40] In addition to the cases discussed in paras 36.29–43, below, see *Owen* [2007] EWCA Crim 694; *Frew* [2008] EWCA Crim 1029; *Gersch* [2008] EWCA Crim 1150; *Williams* [2009] EWCA Crim 1034; and *Helmsley* [2010] EWCA Crim 225. See also the decisions of the Court of Appeal of Northern Ireland in *Shannon* [2008] NICA 38 and *R. v CK* [2009] NICA 17. It was established in *R. v D* [2006] 1 W.L.R. 1088 that the Court of Appeal is able, following an erroneous exercise of the power to make a SOPO, to exercise that power afresh and impose a prohibition.
[41] [2012] EWCA Crim 2602.

appropriate to include in a particular order, or argument as to the extent to which the prohibitions should be imposed, it is essential that the judge is referred to the leading authorities, so that he or she is able to decide what is appropriate.

The making of a SHPO in respect of an offender who falls within s.103A   **36.27**
of the 2003 Act by reason of mental disorder would seem to engage similar issues to those that can arise where an Anti-Social Behaviour Order[42] is made against someone suffering from such a condition.[43] Accordingly, it would seem logical that a SHPO should not be made where the offender's mental impairment is such that he is incapable of understanding or complying with its terms. In such circumstances a SHPO would be incapable of protecting the public and for that reason could not be said to be "necessary" within the meaning of s.103A. Moreover, for a court to make a SHPO knowing that the offender is incapable of complying with it would amount to an improper exercise of the court's discretion. However, although an offender who suffers from a personality disorder might be liable to disobey a SHPO, that is not a sufficient reason for holding that an order which is otherwise necessary to protect the public from sexual harm is not necessary for that purpose, or that the court should not exercise its discretion to make such an order. The position will be less problematic if the insanity or other disability to which the offender was subject at the time of the commission of the offence was temporary, is capable of being treated or is otherwise of a nature that does not make it unreasonable to impose prohibitions.

In *Pashley*,[44] the Court of Appeal approved the making of a SOPO in   **36.28**
respect of an offender found to be permanently under a disability such that there was no prospect of him ever being found fit to plead under s.4 of the Criminal Procedure (Insanity) Act 1964. It rejected the argument that the making of a SOPO in such a situation was wrong in principle because the effect of any future breach would, in the circumstances of that case, only lead to the making of another finding of unfitness with the consequence of the imposition of another supervision order. The Court was not, however, referred to the cases dealing with the making of ASBOs in such circumstances, referred to above. It would also seem from the judgment that the Court was of the view that the offender could understand, at least with the assistance of those responsible for his care and by reference to some amendment of the terms of the SOPO, the nature of the prohibitions imposed upon him such that he might comply with them.

---

[42] s.1C of the Crime and Disorder Act 1998. The ABO has been replaced, in relation to orders made on conviction, by the Criminal Behaviour Order provided for by the Anti-Social Behaviour, Crime and Policing Act 2014, discussed in paras 13.73 and following, above.
[43] cf. *R. (Cooke) v DPP* [2008] EWHC 2703 (Admin) and *Fairweather v Commissioner of Police for the Metropolis* [2008] EWHC 3073 (Admin).
[44] [2015] EWCA Crim 1540.

SHPOs AND COMPUTERS

36.29   Offenders who download indecent images of children (often referred to as "browsers"), distribute such images or otherwise make use of computers when committing scheduled offences have frequently been the subject of SOPO applications and will continue to be the subject of SHPOs. Orders made in respect of such offenders have given rise to numerous appeals. The courts quickly recognised the impracticability of imposing a blanket ban on the ownership and/or use of computers. The nature of permissible prohibitions that might be imposed to address the potential for further offending by the medium of the internet have gone through a variety of permutations,[45] but since *Smith*[46] the older decisions should be regarded as being of academic interest only. The wording of a SHPO relevant to a "browser", or other cases in which the internet is a relevant issue, as settled upon in *Smith* is:

> "The defendant is prohibited from:
> 1. Using any device capable of accessing the internet unless:
>   (i) it has the capacity to retain and display the history of internet use, and
>   (ii) he makes the device available on request for inspection by a police officer;
> 2. Deleting such history;
> 3. Possessing any device capable of storing digital images unless he makes it available on request for inspection by a police officer."

36.30   The use of social networking sites is a common feature of the type of offending that might properly attract the imposition of a SHPO. *Filor*[47] is an example of a case with a *Smith*-type prohibition tailored to address that issue. In that case there was, in addition to the *Smith* retention and inspection clause, a separate prohibition against the offender "accessing social networking sites (chatrooms)". Cases not infrequently feature offenders making contact with actual or potential victims via Facebook and other social networking sites. The use of file sharing sites, which provide ready access to indecent images of children, is also commonplace and their use could legitimately be the subject of a prohibition if the evidence demonstrates such a potential.

36.31   In *Hutchison*,[48] the Court of Appeal had to consider prohibitions in these terms:

> "2. Using any social networking site, including Facebook.
> 3. Having or using any device which has webcam facilities."

The Court recognised the impracticability of both prohibitions in the context of the modern world. Access to social networking sites has become part and

---

[45] see e.g. *Hemsley* [2010] EWCA Crim 225; *Mortimer* [2010] EWCA Crim 1303.
[46] [2011] EWCA Crim 1772. See also Ian Walden and Martin Wasik, *The Internet: Access Denied Controlled!* [2011] Crim. L.R. 377.
[47] [2012] EWCA Crim 850.
[48] [2015] EWCA Crim 947.

parcel of internet usage, which is itself an integral part of everyday life for most people. Virtually all devices capable of accessing the internet have cameras that can operate as webcams integral to their design. The Court therefore adjusted the prohibitions so as to focus them on policing by reference to history retention and also prohibited the defendant from "knowingly" communicating with children under 16 and visiting any internet site specifically intended for such an audience.[49]

There are limitations to the *Smith* formulation. In *Warbutton*[50] the Court **36.32** addressed the potential for a computer to be set automatically to delete the history of internet usage at the end of each session. Set up in that way, the computer would still have the "capacity to retain and display the history of internet use", it just would not do so. The Court suggested that this potential difficulty could be met by the addition of the words "and is at all times set to do so". Even worded in this way, however, the prohibition does not cater for the fact that the default setting of most computers is to retain the history of internet usage for a relatively short period (three to four weeks being typical). With "smart" phones, the retention period may be shorter still.[50a] The frequency of visits by monitoring police officers, even in the case of offenders perceived to be "high risk", varies between different forces, but as little as twice a year is not unknown. Even if browsing history is available to be reviewed, there is a question as to how enlightening such a process will be, not least because of the volume of data produced by someone who makes significant use of the internet. Periods in which the offender did not have the device set to retain the history of internet use are unlikely to be detected by a review of usage carried out by a monitoring officer, as opposed to a full forensic examination of the computer. Further, the *Smith* formula, even with the *Warbutton* variation, is potentially and very easily rendered effectively worthless by an offender utilising the "in private" browser setting, with the result, it would appear, that no "history" recoverable by the police is created at all. All web browsers have the capacity to operate in that mode as standard.

There was for a time a fashion for imposing a prohibition against the **36.33** possession of a computer or other device capable of accessing the internet without notifying the police of that fact. The potential advantage of such a prohibition is that if an offender is found in possession of a device without having given notice, then a breach of the prohibition is easily established. Further, an inference could, in appropriate circumstances, be drawn that the reason for the offender's failure to give notice was the use to which the computer was being put. In *Smith*, however, the Court disapproved of

---

[49] At [15].
[50] [2012] EWCA Crim 3146.
[50a] The case of *R. v PG* [2016] EWCA Crim 250 is an example of the Court of Appeal expressing concern as to the applicability of the *Smith* "browsing" formulation to "smart" phones generally, although the judgment should be approached with some caution as there were no representations from the prosecution nor any detailed analysis of the technical issues engaged.

imposing a prohibition of that nature save in occasional situations where it could be regarded as being the only way to prevent offending. The reason given was that the prohibition places too onerous a burden on both the offender and the police. Given the limitations of the *Smith* formula, there may be an argument in favour of revisiting that position at least in relation to what might be termed a committed offender.

36.34   In some cases there may be potential to impose a prohibition that requires the installation of either filtering or monitoring software. This is sometimes described as software that is "designed to prevent access to child pornography"[51] or "monitoring software (e.g. Securus, Net Nanny) that is approved and monitored by [X] Police or any other police force area in which he resides".[52] The Court in *Smith* suggested that such a prohibition might be appropriate but pointed out that there may be uncertainty as to what is required and that the policing of the prohibition might be attended by some difficulty.[53] There is considerable doubt attaching to the effectiveness of software that might be said to be designed to prevent access to indecent images of children. Given the prevalence of tablet devices and "smart" phones capable of accessing the internet, in respect of which there may be no capacity to install such software, it might be thought necessary for there to be very clear evidence that such software exists and can be installed on relevant devices prior to the imposition of such a prohibition. Not all police forces have approved and/or make use of monitoring software such as that developed by Securus.[54] If an offender can only use a computer that has such software installed upon it and that is approved and monitored by the police force in whose area he resides, then that could effectively be converted into a total ban on computer use should he move to an area where such software is not approved and monitored. Any clause of this kind should be the subject of evidence in support and very careful scrutiny and drafting. There is an as yet unresolved issue as to whether the authorisation regime of the Regulation of Investigatory Powers Act 2000 applies to the use of Securas.[55]

SHPO PROHIBITIONS ON DENYING ENTRY TO PREMISES

36.35   In a number of cases the Court of Appeal has disapproved of SOPO terms that create what amounts to an open-ended search warrant executable at the whim of the police. So in *Thompson*[56] the offender was held to be insufficiently "dangerous or recusant" to justify a term prohibiting him from refusing the police access to his home in order to examine computer equipment that might be on the premises. That was despite the fact that over

---

[51] *Morris* [2011] EWCA Crim 2639.
[52] *Turnbull* [2010] EWCA Crim 3149.
[53] [2011] EWCA Crim 1772 at [20(iv)]; and see *Cilla* [2013] EWCA Crim 1810.
[54] At the time of writing, 16 out of 49 do, with five other forces awaiting funding.
[55] *Jeeves* [2014] EWCA Crim 2059.
[56] [2009] EWCA Crim 3258; see also *Smith (Christopher)* [2009] EWCA Crim 785.

2,500 indecent images of children were found on his computer. The Court of Appeal said there was in that case "no good reason to confer on the police any wider powers of search than are vested in them under the generally applicable law". A contrasting decision is *Hicks*,[57] where the Court of Appeal, having considered *Thompson*, imposed a similar prohibition in a case in which an offender, with a history of making and possessing indecent images of children, posed a serious risk to the public and needed to be regularly and effectively monitored.

There is, however, an element of compulsion in the drafting of the **36.36** prohibition settled upon by the then Vice President in *Smith*,[58] in that the subject of the prohibition is required to make the "device available on request for inspection". With a desktop computer, it is perhaps difficult to imagine how in practical terms that is to be achieved without granting a police officer access to the place where the computer is being used. The justification, adverted to in *Thompson* and confirmed by the approach in *Smith*, is that "the power of the court to impose prohibitions . . . must include the power to impose prohibitions subject to exceptions or conditions".[59] The case of *Hutchinson*[60] is an example of the Court of Appeal choosing of its own volition to add just such a prohibition; and see also *Pashley*[61] where the court did not just leave such a prohibition in place but also amended it to make the effect comprehensible to the offender.

As for police powers of search, it was held in *M. v Chief Constable of* **36.37** *Hampshire Police*[62] that s.96B of the Sexual Offences Act 2003, which provides for the police to obtain a warrant to enter and search a notified person's home address, is compatible with art.8 ECHR. The Divisional Court held that the powers conferred by the section are proportionate, sensible and necessary and that the safeguards are sufficient given that there is provision for judicial oversight prior to the issue of a warrant and such issue would be open to judicial review. The Court rejected an argument that art.8 requires the offender to be given notice of an application under the section and the opportunity to make representations, on the ground that this would defeat the purpose of the application. It also rejected an argument that s.96B offends against art.7 ECHR (prohibition on retroactive penalties), holding that it is a preventative measure and not a punitive one.

Non-Contact Prohibitions

Non-contact prohibitions have frequently been included in SOPOs, but there **36.38** have been many cases in which such a prohibition has had to be amended due

[57] [2009] EWCA Crim 733.
[58] [2011] EWCA Crim 1772. See further on this subject Alasdair A Gillespie, *Sexual Offences Prevention Orders and the Right of Entry* [2009] Crim. L.R. 576.
[59] [2009] EWCA Crim 3258 at [16].
[60] [2015] EWCA Crim 947 at [15].
[61] [2015] EWCA Crim 1540.
[62] [2012] EWHC 4034 (Admin).

to the absence of a saving for incidental contact. This was an issue addressed in *Smith*[63] and the suggested formulation settled upon was:

> "The defendant is prohibited from:
> 1. living in the same household as any child/female under the age of 16 unless with the express approval of Social Services for the area;
> 2. having any unsupervised contact or communication of any kind with any child/ female under the age of 16, other than
>   (i) such as is inadvertent and not reasonably avoidable in the course of lawful daily life, or
>   (ii) with the consent of the child's parent or guardian (who has knowledge of his convictions) *and* with the express approval of Social Services for the area."

36.39   The age specified in the prohibition should be 16 unless the trigger offence or the potential offences for which the prohibition is designed to cater are offences under ss.16–19, 25 or 26 of the 2003 Act.[64] Where what might be termed the offender's "target gender" is apparent, there will be no justification for prohibiting contact with persons of a different gender.[65] The Court in *Smith*[66] emphasised the need to take account of the offender's family circumstances and the risk, if any, that the offender might pose to members of the family, balancing against that the entitlement of, for example, the offender's own children to a family life. As the balance may change over time, the inclusion of a reference to the approval of the Social Services is critical in order to cater for the unforeseeable.

36.40   The imposition of a non-contact prohibition is unlikely to be challenged in the context of an offender who engages in contact offending. The justification for such a clause in respect of "browsers" is more problematic, and there are many examples of non-contact prohibitions being overturned in what might be termed pure "browsing" situations.[67] Such a prohibition may, however, be justifiable if there are grounds upon which the court can conclude that there is a significant risk of the offender progressing from non-contact to contact offending. In one of the conjoined appeals in *Smith*, a non-contact prohibition was upheld in relation to an offender who had been convicted of downloading offences.[68] The case of *Turner*[69] may indicate a growing willingness to find that those who "browse" may legitimately be assessed as having the potential to go on to commit contact offences. In that case, a non-contact prohibition was imposed on a man convicted of possession of indecent images of children. His ex-partner had made a statement describing examples of what she considered to be inappropriate behaviour by the appellant with, and demonstrated sexual interest in, female

[63] [2011] EWCA Crim 1772.
[64] [2011] EWCA Crim 1772 at [21].
[65] *Morris* [2013] EWCA Crim 467, at [33]–[36].
[66] [2011] EWCA Crim 1772.
[67] See, e.g. *Turnbull* [2010] EWCA Crim 3149; *Lea* [2011] EWCA Crim 487; *Fung* [2012] EWCA Crim 761; *James* [2012] EWCA Crim 81.
[68] *Hall* [2011] EWCA Crim 1772, at [34]–[43].
[69] [2013] EWCA Crim 1869.

children. The Court of Appeal upheld the prohibition, stating that whilst it is not acceptable to include such a prohibition "just in case", one may be imposed if the court finds there is a risk of contact offences, and there does not have to be a finding of certainty. In this case, the finding of risk was justified by the combined force of the ex-partner's evidence as to her concerns about the appellant's sexual interest in real young girls, the subsequent discovery of the indecent images, and the appellant's continuing denial of any sexual interest in young girls.

It is beholden on a court imposing a non-contact prohibition in such **36.41** circumstances to explain why it considers it necessary so to do. The case of *Juneidi*[70] is an example of the Court of Appeal concluding that a judge had been wrong to impose a non-contact clause in respect of a "browser" and provides a helpful example of the nature of the factors that may come into play in such cases. The judge in that case was persuaded to impose non-contact prohibitions despite the author of the probation report assessing that the appellant had no potential to progress to contact offending. The Court of Appeal considered both *Smith* and *Turner*, above, and concluded that a prohibition against contact with children was not "necessary".

A form of non-contact prohibition that features not infrequently is one **36.42** which bars an offender from going to parks or swimming pools or hanging around outside schools. Such clauses must be expressed with sufficient clarity that the offender knows where he can and cannot go and also to enable the prohibition to be sensibly policed.

In *R. (on the application of Paul Richards) v Teesside Magistrates' Court* **36.43** *and the Chief Constable of Cleveland*,[71] the use of an electronic tagging device as a method of monitoring and thus enforcing a non-contact prohibition was approved. Such a measure is only likely to be justified in an extreme case.

SHPOs and the Family Court's Jurisdiction

In *R. v D*,[72] the Court of Appeal considered the relationship between a SOPO **36.44** under the Sexual Offences Act 2003 and the powers of a court exercising family jurisdiction under the Children Act 1989. The appellant had pleaded guilty to sexual offences committed against his daughter. A SOPO was imposed which, inter alia, prohibited him from approaching or communicating with his daughter and son. The appellant challenged the condition relating to his son on the basis that there had been no suggestion of any offences committed against him. The Court of Appeal observed that the legislation raises problems where there has been abuse within the family and the court has to consider the protection of a family member who was not a

---

[70] [2014] EWCA Crim 966.
[71] [2015] EWCA Civ 7.
[72] [2006] 1 W.L.R. 1088.

direct target of the offender, such as a sibling of the abused child. A SOPO may lack the flexibility to meet the constantly changing needs and circumstances of such a child. What if the son in this case wanted to have some contact with the offender? The son was not a person specified as being able to apply to the court to vary or discharge the order. The Court noted that in the family courts the welfare of the child is the first and paramount consideration, and said that there may be occasions when a SOPO made to protect a child of the offender should reflect the family court's jurisdiction because of the additional flexibility this will provide. In *R. v D*, the Court accordingly varied the SOPO so that it prohibited the appellant from communicating or seeking to communicate with his son without the order of a judge exercising jurisdiction under the Children Act 1989.

PROHIBITIONS AGAINST FOREIGN TRAVEL

36.45   The court now has power to include in a SHPO a prohibition against foreign travel. Such a prohibition must be for a fixed period of five years but may be subject to extensions of no more than five years on each occasion.[73] A prohibition against foreign travel may relate to a country or countries specified in it or to all foreign countries. The prohibition must require the defendant to surrender his passport to the police at the time of the making of the order or within a reasonable period thereafter, and the police must retain the passport for the duration of the order.[74]

36.46   The Act does not require that the protection of children and vulnerable adults abroad relates to something that would be illegal within the relevant foreign jurisdiction. The Guidance issued by the Home Office in March 2015 states that a "SHPO or SRO can prevent an offender from travelling to a foreign country to engage in sexual activity with a child aged 14 even if sexual activity with a child aged 14 is not an offence in the country concerned".[75]

36.47   The Act does not identify any additional criteria that need to be satisfied in order to justify such a prohibition. It is reasonable to presume that a history of travelling to recognised "sex tourism" destinations may trigger consideration of the imposition of such a prohibition, but the power is unlikely to be limited to such cases. An offender who is assessed as meriting a SHPO governing conduct within the jurisdiction should not, it might be thought, be left with the option of giving themselves a "holiday" from those restrictions by travelling to a foreign country. Prohibitions of this nature are

---

[73] s.103D(1), (3).
[74] s.103D(4), (5).
[75] *https://www.gov.uk/government/uploads/system/uploads/attachment_data/file/409872/2015-03-06_FINAL_Guidance_Part_2_SOA_2003.pdf* [Accessed April 30, 2016].

likely to prove contentious given the impact that such a restriction may have on a defendant and potentially their extended family.[75a]

Relationship between SHPOs and Other Sentences

36.48 A prohibition in a SHPO will not be "necessary" if its effect is merely to duplicate another relevant regime. In *Smith*,[76] the Court of Appeal compared and contrasted the variety of other sentences, orders and conditions to which a sex offender may be expected to be subject as a result of a conviction, and identified the type of overlap that should be avoided. It said that prohibitions should not be expressed in the same terms and/or in a way that had the same effect as a disqualification from working with children imposed under s.26 of the Criminal Justice and Court Services Act 2000 (now repealed) or the "barred list" maintained by the Disclosure and Barring Service (which was established in succession to the Independent Safeguarding Authority by the Protection of Freedoms Act 2012). In *Smith*, the Court also held that it would almost never be necessary to impose a SOPO at the same time as a life sentence or sentence of imprisonment for public protection (now abolished), but that the same did not apply to determinate or extended sentences.[77] The reason is that, whilst conditions may be attached to the offender's licence on release from such a sentence, that licence will have a defined and limited life. By contrast, the SOPO (and now the SHPO) can extend beyond the licence term and this may be necessary to protect the public from further offences and serious sexual harm as a result.

36.49 Since the decision in *Smith*, the position with regard to the potential interaction of prohibitions to other sentences has changed somewhat. Disqualification orders under the Criminal Justice and Court Services Act 2000 have been abolished, and inclusion in a barred list is automatic and not potentially subject to the making of representations where the offender has committed one of the more serious sexual offences.[78] These changes mean that a court could be justified in imposing a SHPO prohibition couched in much the same language as disqualification orders under the 2000 Act were previously expressed, in a case where the offender has committed a relatively low level offence (such as making indecent photographs of children) but it would be legitimate to seek to prohibit contact in a work or other situation.

[75a] See *Burrows* [2015] EWCA Crim 2046 where the prohibition against foreign travel element of a SHPO was overturned in respect of an offender who had lived in the Philippines for 30 years and who regarded that country as his home, notwithstanding the fact that evidence in the case demonstrated offences being committed against children in the Philippines some 20 years prior to the date of trial in respect of historic offending committed within the jurisdiction.

[76] [2011] EWCA Crim 1772 at [9]–[17] and in particular at [25(i)].

[77] [2011] EWCA Crim 1772 at [14]–[15].

[78] See the Safeguarding Vulnerable Groups Act 2006 s.2 and Sch.3, and the Safeguarding Vulnerable Groups Act (Prescribed Criteria and Miscellaneous Provisions) Regulations 2009 (SI 2009/37).

In *Hutchinson*,[79] the Court of Appeal decided that a prohibition expressed so as to cover situations outside the range of the regime established by the Safeguarding Vulnerable Groups Act 2006 ("SVGA") was both proportionate and necessary, identifying the potential for engagement in the voluntary sector to fall outside the range of activities that may be covered by a "barring order". This conclusion was also reached in *Warren*,[80] albeit the terms of the prohibition settled upon by the Court in that case are perhaps not as clear as they might have been. The Court in *Warren* did, however, condescend to attempt to identify in some detail that which an offender may and may not be prevented from doing by reason of being subject to a "barring order". The manner in which the SVGA regime works and is administered is far from clear, albeit the general intention, namely to keep sex offenders away from potential victims generally and the young and vulnerable in particular, is apparent. The fact that the Court of Appeal seem to be moving towards a position of approving forms of prohibitions that at one stage it appeared the decision in *Smith* had rendered redundant is perhaps reflective of a lack of confidence in the capacity of a "barring order" to achieve what it is intended it should do. It should be borne in mind, however, that the Vice President (as he then was) made it clear in *Smith* that " . . . judges should ordinarily require the Crown to justify an application for a SOPO term relating to activity with children by demonstrating what the risk is which is not already catered for by the SVGA".[81]

DURATION OF A SHPO

36.50 A SHPO prohibition has effect either for a fixed period, specified in the order, of at least five years or until further order.[82] The amended legislation allows for prohibitions to be of differing duration.[83] Whilst the introduction of a prohibition against foreign travel necessitated an adjustment to the position as it previously stood with regard to SOPOs, the legislation now allows for any or all prohibitions to be of different lengths. This perhaps has the potential to cater for the situation that might arise where the children of a SHPO subject reach maturity and are no longer to be considered at risk.

36.51   In *Hammond*,[84] it was suggested that it would normally be important for the terms of a SOPO to be consistent with the duration of the notification requirements in Pt 2 of the 2003 Act. One of the effects of being made the subject of a SHPO is that the individual is subject to the notification

---

[79] [2015] EWCA Crim 947.
[80] [2015] EWCA Crim 434.
[81] [2011] EWCA Crim 1772 at [25(i)].
[82] s.103C(2).
[83] s.103C(3)(b).
[84] [2008] EWCA Crim 1358; followed in *Helmsley* [2010] EWCA Crim 225.

requirements for the duration of the order.[85] In *Smith*,[86] the Vice President acknowledged what was said in *Hammond* and continued:

> "We entirely agree that a SOPO must operate in tandem with the statutory notification requirements. It must therefore not conflict with any of those requirements. Secondly, we agree that it is not normally a proper use of the power to impose a SOPO to use it to extend notification requirements beyond the period prescribed by law. Absent some unusual feature, it would therefore be wrong to add to a SOPO terms which although couched as prohibitions amounted in effect to no more than notification requirements, but for a period longer than the law provides for. But it does not follow that the duration of a SOPO ought generally to be the same as the duration of notification requirements. Notification requirements and the conditions of a SOPO are generally two different things. The first require positive action by the defendant, who must report his movements to the police. The second prohibit him from doing specified things. Ordinarily there ought to be little or no overlap between them. If the circumstances require it, we can see no objection to the prohibitory provisions of a SOPO extending beyond the notification requirements of the statute. It may also be possible that a SOPO for less than an indefinite period might be found to be the right order in a case where the notification requirements endure for ever; that also is permissible in law."

See *Juneidi*[87] for a recent example of the Court of Appeal disapproving of an indefinite order.

There is one situation in which a SHPO may not operate so as to result in an offender being subject to notification requirements, and that is by reference to s.103G(5) of the Act which addresses the impact of an offender successfully reviewing an indefinite notification requirement. Following the decision in *R. (on the application of F) v Secretary of State for the Home Department*,[88] holding that indefinite notification orders were not compliant with the Human Rights Act 1998, the Sexual Offences Act 2003 (Remedial Order) 2012[89] amended the 2003 Act so as to enable an offender to seek a review of an order's continuance. An offender may successfully pursue such a review by demonstrating to the relevant chief officer of police that it is no longer necessary in order to protect members of the public or any particular members of the public that he remain subject to the notification requirement. If the review is determined in the offender's favour, he ceases to be subject to the notification requirement consequent upon the conviction that triggered its application, and by reason of s.103G(5) any existing SHPO likewise is brought to an end. Whilst the logic of that position is reasonably obvious, it is perhaps curious that a chief officer of police has the power in effect to overturn a sentence imposed by a judge.

36.52

---

[85] s.103G.
[86] [2011] EWCA Crim 1772 at [16]–[17].
[87] [2014] EWCA Crim 966 at [19]–[20].
[88] [2010] UKSC 17.
[89] SI 2012/1883.

Effect of a SHPO

36.53 The effect of a SHPO is dealt with in s.103C of the Act. By s.103C(1), a SHPO prohibits the subject from doing anything described in the order. However, the only prohibitions that may be included in an order are those that are necessary for the purpose of protecting the public or particular members of the public from sexual harm from the subject, or protecting children or vulnerable adults generally, or particular children or vulnerable adults, from sexual harm from him outside the UK.[90] If the court makes a SHPO in respect of an offender who is already subject to such an order, the earlier order "ceases to have effect".[91] Accordingly, when a "new" SHPO is made, any terms from a pre-existing SHPO that are still relevant and appropriate will have to be included in the new order or they will no longer apply. In *Pelletier*[92] the Court of Appeal underlined the need to check that the order as drawn up by the court clerk actually reflects that which the sentencing judge imposed. In that case, there were differences between the order as enunciated by the judge in court and as drawn up. The Court held that the former was determinative and quashed the appellant's conviction for breaching the order as drawn.

Variation, Renewal and Discharge of a SHPO

36.54 By s.103E, the subject of a SHPO or a relevant chief officer of police may apply to the appropriate court to vary, renew or discharge the order. Orders made in the Crown Court or Court of Appeal may be subject to such an application in the Crown Court. Orders made in the magistrates' court should be dealt with there. An application in relation to a youth court order should be made to that court, unless the defendant has attained 18 years of age when it should be made to an adult magistrates' court. Renewal or variation by the imposition of additional prohibitions is subject to the same test of necessity as the making of the initial order.[93] Orders cannot be discharged before the end of five years beginning with the day on which the order was made without the consent of the defendant and the relevant chief officer of police.[94]

Appeals Against SHPOs

36.55 Appeals against SHPOs and interim SHPOs are governed by s.103H. Orders imposed in the Crown Court may be the subject of an appeal to the Court of

---

[90] s.103C(4).
[91] s.103C(6).
[92] [2012] EWCA Crim 1060.
[93] s.103E(5).
[94] s.103E(7).

Appeal. Orders made in the magistrates' court may be appealed to the Crown Court. In *Hoath and Standage*,[95] the Court of Appeal had occasion to examine the relationship between s.108 of the 2003 Act, which provided for applications to vary SOPOs, and s.110, which provided a right of appeal to the Crown Court in respect of SOPOs imposed in the magistrates' court, and to the Court of Appeal in respect of SOPOs imposed in the Crown Court. As the legislation relating to SHPOs deals with variation and appeal in the same terms as for SOPOs, the position remains as identified in *Hoath and Standage*. In that case, the Court expressed the view that the Crown Court was not the venue in which to address the issue of a SOPO being non-compliant with *Smith*.[96] Simon J suggested that applications to the Crown Court should be for more limited purposes:

"10. Although minor but necessary adjustments to the order may be required, in which case application should be made to the Crown Court to vary the order, in circumstances where a defendant has not appealed to the Court of Appeal, we would not expect the Crown Court to make other than minor adjustments to the term of the order, at least in the short term.

11. Usually the defendant will need to rely on a change of circumstances. In such a case, the Crown Court will need to be satisfied that the order in its original form is no longer necessary for the statutory purpose of protecting the public (or particular members of the public) from serious sexual harm from the defendant, or that those objectives can properly and sufficiently be secured by the proposed variation."

Encouraging appeals to the Court of Appeal rather than variation applications to the Crown Court is perhaps not the most expedient and cost effective way of dealing with pre-*Smith* SOPOs. *Hoath and Standage* was, however, confirmed in later cases.[97] Despite this the Crown Court has on occasion taken it upon itself to vary a SOPO in order to remove a non-*Smith* compliant term: an example is *Beeden*.[98] This may be a convenient course, but, in the light of *Hoath and Standage*, it should not be followed. **36.56**

The Court in *Hoath and Standage* held that there is a right of appeal to the Court of Appeal under s.110(3)(a) (now s.103H(3)(a)) against the refusal of the Crown Court to vary a SOPO.[99] Further, the Court said that such a refusal of an application to vary made under s.108 (now s.103E) was, by reference to s.11(3) of the Criminal Appeal Act 1968, a "sentence", thus permitting the Court to quash the order of the Crown Court and to make "another appropriate order". **36.57**

In *Instone*[100] the Court of Appeal was faced with appeals sought to be advanced out of time against SOPOs imposed at the same time as a sentence **36.58**

---

95 [2011] EWCA Crim 274.
96 [2011] EWCA Crim 1772.
97 *Aldridge and Eaton* [2012] EWCA Crim 1456; *Sadler* [2014] EWHC 1715 (Admin).
98 [2013] EWCA Crim 63.
99 The point was considered in *Warbutton* [2012] EWCA Crim 3146.
100 [2012] EWCA Crim 1792.

of imprisonment for public protection ("IPP"), the basis for the appeals being the decision in *Smith*. The Court set out the position thus:

> "19. However, the fresh guidance given by *Smith* does not provide the basis for a successful appeal against a SOPO imposed long before *Smith* was decided and which, but for the licensing conditions which will be imposed on release, was made with every justification. Sentence is imposed on the basis of the relevant legislation, the principles, practice and guidance, whether from this court or the Sentencing Council, which are current at the date when sentence is imposed. An existing sentence should not be varied on appeal because of subsequent changes to them."

36.59   In *James*,[101] the Court dismissed an appeal against the imposition of a sentence of IPP imposed prior to *Smith*, but declined to remove the SOPO notwithstanding the guidance provided therein. *Neish*[102] and *R. v M*,[103] however, are examples of the Court adjusting SOPOs that were not complaint with *Smith* in order to make them so.

Breach of a SHPO

36.60   Under s.103I, any breach of a SHPO without reasonable excuse is punishable with up to five years' imprisonment on indictment and six months' on summary conviction. It is for the prosecution to prove the absence of reasonable excuse, though the defendant carries an evidential burden to raise the issue.[104]There is no current sentencing guideline for breaching a SOPO/SHPO but the passage from the judgment of Leveson J (as he then was) in *Fenton*[105] is frequently cited. In *Fenton* the Court of Appeal upheld a sentence of two-and-a-half years' imprisonment for the repeated breach of a sex offender order by a man who had been found to have a psychopathic, anti-social and borderline personality disorder, with no insight into his offending behaviour. Psychological and psychiatric reports had concluded that he was dangerous, targeted vulnerable sections of the community and demonstrated abnormally high levels of aggression and irresponsible behaviour, and that there was a high risk of his re-offending. Drawing on the sentencing authorities concerned with breach of anti-social behaviour orders, the Court observed that the maximum sentence that would be available for an offence which corresponded to the behaviour comprising the breach would be a factor to which any sentencing court would have regard. But ultimately the court was sentencing for a breach of the order. Giving the judgment of the Court, Leveson J said[106]:

---

[101] [2013] EWCA Crim 847.
[102] [2012] EWCA Crim 62.
[103] [2012] EWCA Crim 852.
[104] cf. *Polychronakis v Richards & Jerrom Ltd* [1998] Env.L.R. 347; *O'Boyle* [1973] R.T.R. 445; *Mallows v Harris* [1979] R.T.R. 404; *Charles* [2010] Crim. L.R. 303.
[105] [2007] 1 Cr. App. R.(S.) 97.
[106] At 25.

"If the breach does not involve any real or obvious risk to that section of the public who it is intended should be protected by the order, a community penalty which further assists the offender to live within the terms of the order may well be appropriate although repeated breaches will necessarily involve a custodial sentence if only to demonstrate that the orders of the court are not to be ignored and cannot be broken with impunity. Any breach which does create a real or obvious risk to those whom the order is intended to protect must inevitably be treated more seriously and multiple or repeated breaches may well justify sentences that might otherwise have been considered far higher than any specific criminal offence or misconduct would have attracted. That, after all, is the statutory purpose behind the legislation in the first place."

The guidance to be derived from *Fenton* has been applied in numerous cases concerned with the breach of SOPOs. In *Carr*,[107] a sentence of four years' imprisonment imposed for a breach of a SOPO was reduced on appeal to one of 12 months. The offender was the subject of a SOPO made by a magistrates' court because of his practice of following teenage girls. He had previously received a custodial sentence for a breach of the order and received the sentence of four years' imprisonment when he committed a further breach by sending a Christmas card to a teenage girl he had previously followed. A sentence of two years' imprisonment for breach of a SOPO was upheld in *Byrne (Frankie)*.[108] The appellant had been released in 2003 from a sentence of 15 years' imprisonment imposed for offences including buggery and other sexual offences committed against young boys. He was subject to a SOPO which effectively prohibited him from contact with any person under the age of 16 unless it was inadvertent or authorised by a police officer. Over a period of about 16 months, the appellant had regular and frequent contact with two boys aged 14 and 15. He took them to the cinema, where he bought them food and drink, and took one of the boys to shops to buy him presents for his birthday. He bought the same boy a mobile telephone. He also tried to become involved in football at the church which the families of the two boys attended. When the appellant learned that the pastor of the church was conducting necessary criminal record checks, he gave up the football so that the checks were not made. He nonetheless continued to attend the church and church outings and to have substantial contact with the two boys. The Court of Appeal approved the dictum of Leveson J in *Fenton* cited above, stressed the importance of an offender deliberately choosing to ignore the requirements of a SOPO on a wholesale basis, and added:

36.61

"The other aspect that informs an assessment of seriousness is that of harm. Here, the question of an assessment of the risks run by the breach of the SOPO comes into play. In our judgment, that assessment includes not only a consideration of the immediate risks which were generated by the breach to the other people concerned; it also imports a consideration of the nature and magnitude of the underlying general risk posed by the offender, reflected in his previous

[107] [2009] 2 Cr. App. R.(S.) 72.
[108] [2010] Cr. App. R.(S.) 65.

offending. Sexual offending covers a very wide spectrum, all of it serious. But some much more serious than others. It is to be noted that the underlying offending of this appellant was very serious indeed".

The Court of Appeal therefore viewed the appellant's culpability as high. His contacts with the boys were too numerous to particularise, he deliberately flouted the terms of the order and the risk with which the SOPO was concerned was at the top end of seriousness of sexual offending.

36.62 In *Brown*,[109] it was suggested that the quality of the acts constituting the breach are not the only consideration; the protection of children is the foremost issue. In *Moore*,[110] it was said that the sentencing judge is entitled to treat an offender as dangerous and as deliberately breaching the order for a sinister purpose, even if no overtly sexual activity has been established. The Court of Appeal in *Morris*[111] reviewed a range of cases dealing with breach of a SOPO and reduced a sentence of 16 months' imprisonment to one of 10 months' in respect of an offender who had created a situation whereby there was an obvious risk that he might offend by committing a contact offence, albeit he had not in fact done so. The Court observed:

> "The breaches here created real and obvious risks which it is unnecessary to spell out. SOPOs are designed to protect children from such risks. Those who breach such orders must expect to be dealt with severely but proportionately. It is clear that the applicant recognised the purpose of the SOPO in his case but that, nevertheless, he took chances and flouted the order on two separate dates. Accordingly, the sentence of imprisonment was, in our judgment, not wrong in principle."

36.63 In *Beeden*,[112] the offender, who had a history of offending against children and in respect of indecent images, was made subject to a SOPO, one term of which prohibited him from "owning or having personal possession of any piece of equipment or device that is capable of connecting to the internet". He breached this prohibition on two occasions, but by the time the case came to be sentenced the prohibition had been removed in the light of the guidance in *Smith*.[113] Despite the fact that, as the SOPO stood by the time sentence was imposed, his conduct would not have constituted any offence at all, the Court of Appeal still upheld the sentence of immediate custody imposed at first instance. In *Simmonds*[114] the Court said that a breach of an order, as well as potentially putting at risk the very people it is designed to protect, is contemptuous of the court, and where the contempt is gross, the culpability will be the higher.[115]

36.64 As a matter of practice, sentences for SOPO breaches tended to range from nine months' to three years' imprisonment, depending on the facts of the

109 [2001] EWCA Crim 724.
110 [2004] EWCA Crim 2574.
111 [2013] EWCA Crim 350.
112 [2013] EWCA 63.
113 [2011] EWCA Crim 1772.
114 [2015] EWCA Crim 1068.
115 At [14].

breach and the nature of the offender's antecedents. There is no reason to anticipate that the change from SOPOs to SHPOs will impact on the length of sentences imposed.

There is no power to impose a SHPO for a breach offence.[116] If a SHPO 36.65
as originally imposed was clearly invalid then it is suggested that in an extreme case it could be regarded as unenforceable.[117]

SEXUAL RISK ORDERS

CRITERIA FOR MAKING A SRO

A person ("the defendant") may be made the subject of a SRO even though 36.66
no offence has been committed. The legislative scheme is in similar terms to that governing the SHPO, save that a SRO can only be made by way of an application to the magistrates' court. Section 122A sets out the qualifying conditions for the making of an order:

"**122A Sexual risk orders: applications, grounds and effect**

(1) A chief officer of police or the Director General of the National Crime Agency ('the Director General') may by complaint to a magistrates' court apply for an order under this section (a 'sexual risk order') in respect of a person ('the defendant') if it appears to the chief officer or the Director General that the following condition is met.

(2) The condition is that the defendant has, whether before or after the commencement of this Part, done an act of a sexual nature as a result of which there is reasonable cause to believe that it is necessary for a sexual risk order to be made.

(3) A chief officer of police may make an application under subsection (1) only in respect of a person—

(a) who resides in the chief officer's police area, or

(b) who the chief officer believes is in that area or is intending to come to it.

(4) An application under subsection (1) may be made to any magistrates' court acting for a local justice area that includes—

(a) any part of a relevant police area, or

(b) any place where it is alleged that the person acted in a way mentioned in subsection (2).

(5) The Director General must as soon as practicable notify the chief officer of police for a relevant police area of any application that the Director has made under subsection (1).

(6) On an application under subsection (1), the court may make a sexual risk order if it is satisfied that the defendant has, whether before or after the commencement of this Part, done an act of a sexual nature as a result of which it is necessary to make such an order for the purpose of—

(a) protecting the public or any particular members of the public from harm from the defendant, or

---

[116] *Hadley* [2012] EWCA Crim 1997.
[117] *R.(W) v DPP* [2005] EWHC 1333; but see *Proctor* [2014] EWCA Crim 162.

(b) protecting children or vulnerable adults generally, or any particular children or vulnerable adults, from harm from the defendant outside the United Kingdom.

(7) Such an order—

(a) prohibits the defendant from doing anything described in the order;

(b) has effect for a fixed period (not less than 2 years) specified in the order or until further order.

(8) A sexual risk order may specify different periods for different prohibitions.

(9) The only prohibitions that may be imposed are those necessary for the purpose of—

(a) protecting the public or any particular members of the public from harm from the defendant, or

(b) protecting children or vulnerable adults generally, or any particular children or vulnerable adults, from harm from the defendant outside the United Kingdom.

(10) Where a court makes a sexual risk order in relation to a person who is already subject to such an order (whether made by that court or another), the earlier order ceases to have effect."

QUALIFYING CONDITIONS

36.67   Unlike SHPOs, it is not a condition precedent for the issue of a SRO that the defendant must have been convicted of a criminal offence—the only requirement is that he should have done an "act of a sexual nature as a result of which there is reasonable cause to believe that it is necessary for a sexual risk order to be made". A single such act is sufficient. The change from the previous requirement in respect of RSHOs for there to be two "acts" is designed to encourage the use of these protective measures. The broadening of the definition of what may amount to an "act of a sexual nature" is also intended to have that effect.[118] The definitions of "sexual harm", "child" and "vulnerable adult" are the same as for SHPOs.

PROCEDURE

36.68   An application for a SRO is made by way of complaint which can be initiated by either a chief officer of police or the Director General of the National Crime Agency.[119] A court may make an interim SRO, if it considers it just to do so, pending the determination of an application for a full order.[120] The interim order is made for a fixed period and will cease to have effect if the main application is determined before the end of that period. If the fixed period expires before the main application is determined, then a court may renew the interim order for a further fixed period.

---

[118] See the Home Office Guidance at *https://www.gov.uk/government/uploads/system/uploads/attachment_data/file/409872/2015-03-06_FINAL_Guidance_Part_2_SOA_2003.pdf*,   pp.42–43 [Accessed April 30, 2016].

[119] s.122A.

[120] s.122E.

As in the case of SHPOs and RSHOs, whilst the nature of the application **36.69** for a SRO is civil, the standard of proof to be applied is criminal.[121]

NATURE OF ORDER

A SRO may "prohibit the defendant from doing anything described in the **36.70** order".[122] It must be for a fixed period of at least two years but may be indefinite. Prohibitions in a SRO may be of varying durations.[123] An order can be made prohibiting foreign travel in the same terms and for the same time limits as with a SHPO, i.e. for up to five years initially.[124] As with a SHPO prohibition against foreign travel, a defendant is required to surrender his passport on or before the date of the order or within a reasonable time of it being made.[125] A person made the subject of a SRO must, within three days of being served with the order, notify the police of his name and address.[126]

VARIATION OF A SRO

Variations, renewals and discharges are in the same terms as for SHPOs, **36.71** discussed in para.36.54, above.[127] Orders cannot be discharged before the end of two years beginning with the day on which the order was made without the consent of the defendant and the relevant chief officer of police.[128]

APPEALS AGAINST SROS AND INTERIM SROS

Appeals against the making of an order are to the Crown Court.[129] Any **36.72** order of the Crown Court on appeal against the making of a SRO or interim SRO is treated as if it were an order of the court from which the appeal was brought and not the Crown Court.

OFFENCE AND SUPPLEMENTARY ISSUES

Section 122H(1) makes it an offence to breach a SRO or interim SRO **36.73** without reasonable excuse. The offence is also committed by breach of a RSHO or interim RSHO, including such orders made in Scotland under s.2 or s.5 of the Protection of Children and Prevention of Sexual Offences

[121] *Commissioner of Police of the Metropolis v Ebanks* [2012] EWHC 2368 (Admin).
[122] s.122A(7).
[123] s.122A(8).
[124] s.122C.
[125] s.122C(4).
[126] s.122F.
[127] s.122D.
[128] s.122D(5).
[129] s.122G.

(Scotland) Act 2005. As with SHPOs it is for the prosecution to prove the absence of a reasonable excuse. A breach is punishable with up five years' imprisonment on indictment and six months' imprisonment on summary conviction.[130] A court may not impose a conditional discharge for such an offence.[131] If a person is convicted of an offence under s.122H,[132] or found not guilty by reason of insanity, found to be under a disability and to have done the act charged, or cautioned, then he becomes subject to the notification requirements of the Act for the duration of the order.[133] If he is already an offender to whom the notification requirements apply, he will be required to notify until the expiry of the order.[134] If the notification period for his previous offence would continue beyond the expiry of the order, then it will so continue.

36.74   Section 122J requires the Secretary of State to issue guidance to chief officers of police and the Director General of the National Crime Agency in relation to the exercise by them of their powers with regard to SROs and interim SROs. The Home Office issued Guidance in March 2015.[135]

36.75   Rules of court may provide for the youth court to determine an application for a SRO against a person aged 18 or over, if an application has been or is to be made to the youth court for a SRO against a person aged under 18, and the youth court thinks it would be in the interests of justice for the applications to be heard together.[136] Rules of court may also prescribe circumstances in which the youth court may or must retain proceedings relating to the making, variation, renewal or discharge of a SRO or interim SRO in relation to a person who reaches the age of 18 after the proceedings have begun.[137] At the time of writing, no such rules have been made.

Conclusion

36.76   The transformation from SOPO to SHPO may not have as great an impact as perhaps may have been hoped by the authors of the ACPO *Review of Civil Prevention Orders*.[138] The introduction of the power to prohibit foreign travel can be expected to result in the most significant change to the package of prohibitions with which practitioners have become familiar. The availability of a prohibition against foreign travel is likely to generate an increase in the number of offenders prevented from leaving the UK by comparison with that

---

[130] s.122H(3).
[131] s.122H(4).
[132] Or an offence of breaching a RSHO or interim RSHO contrary to s.128 of the 2003 Act or s.7 of the Protection of Children and Prevention of Sexual Offences (Scotland) Act 2005.
[133] s.122I(1), (2), (4).
[134] s.122I(1)-(3).
[135] *https://www.gov.uk/government/uploads/system/uploads/attachment_data/file/409872/2015-03-06_FINAL_Guidance_Part_2_SOA_2003.pdf* [accessed April 30, 2016].
[136] s.122K(1)(a).
[137] s.122K(1)(b).
[138] s.122K(1)(b).

produced by the old FTO. The issue that judges at first instance and in the Court of Appeal may have to wrestle with is, why should a SHPO package not contain such a prohibition? If a defendant merits, for example, a non-contact prohibition within the jurisdiction, where the offender's circumstances are subject to policing by those charged with public protection, why should he be able to go abroad where no such regime will apply? We must wait and see whether a prohibition against foreign travels becomes a standard element of the measures designed to protect potential victims, or whether in practice travel prohibitions will be limited to those in respect of whom there is some evidence of engagement or interest in "sex tourism".

It would seem that RSHOs were even more rarely sought or imposed than **36.77** FTOs.[139] The authors of the ACPO *Review of Civil Prevention Orders* considered that the apparent under-use of the RSHO as a weapon of public protection was due to the number and definition of the "acts of a sexual nature" required before an application for such an order could be made. This issue may be addressed by the introduction of the SRO, with the reduction on the number of required "acts" to one and a broader definition of what may amount to such an "act"; that was certainly the avowed intent. The fact that the SRO regime applies to defendants under the age of 18 is less likely to produce any great increase in the number of orders sought by comparison with the RSHO regime. It can be expected that a SRO will be rarely sought in respect of a young person, given the other tools available to control their behaviour and the legislative imperative for the courts to have regard to the welfare of those under the age of 18.[140] A SRO may seem a better option than an injunctive order of the kind that featured in the case of *Birmingham City Council v Riaz*.[141] Certainly, an application for a SRO is likely to be seen as a more economical use of both time and money than bringing a case for injunctive relief in the Family Court.

---

[139] *Review of Civil Prevention Orders under the Sexual Offences Act 2003* by Hugh Davies OBE QC (15 May 2013), para.8.1.1, available at *http://l3rblaw.com/publication/review-of-civil-prevention-orders-under-the-sexual-offences-act-2003/* [Accessed April 30, 2016].
[140] cf. s.44 of the Children and Young People Act 1933 and s.11 of the Children Act 2004.
[141] [2014] EWHC 4247 (Fam), for which see para.36.08, above.

APPENDIX A

CRIMINAL JUSTICE 2003*

SCHEDULE 15[1]
SPECIFIED OFFENCES FOR PURPOSES OF CHAPTER 5 OF PART 12
Section 224

PART 1
SPECIFIED VIOLENT OFFENCES

1. Manslaughter.
2. Kidnapping.
3. False imprisonment.
4. An offence under section 4 of the Offences against the Person Act 1861 (c. 100) (soliciting murder).
5. An offence under section 16 of that Act (threats to kill).
6. An offence under section 18 of that Act (wounding with intent to cause grievous bodily harm).
7. An offence under section 20 of that Act (malicious wounding).
8. An offence under section 21 of that Act (attempting to choke, suffocate or strangle in order to commit or assist in committing an indictable offence).
9. An offence under section 22 of that Act (using chloroform etc. to commit or assist in the committing of any indictable offence).
10. An offence under section 23 of that Act (maliciously administering poison etc. so as to endanger life or inflict grievous bodily harm).
11. An offence under section 27 of that Act (abandoning children).

A.01

---

* The text below is correct as of May 2, 2016.

[1] **Commencement**: April 4, 2005 (SI 2005/950, art.2, Sch.1, para.37); **Extent**: England, Wales (may extend to the Channel Islands or Isle of Man as specified by Orders in Council made under this Act) — except for 22A, 48A, 59A–D, 60A–C,63A–H, 64, 65, 92A, 152A, 153, where the extent is England and Wales; and 143A where the extent is United Kingdom.

12. An offence under section 28 of that Act (causing bodily injury by explosives).
13. An offence under section 29 of that Act (using explosives etc. with intent to do grievous bodily harm).
14. An offence under section 30 of that Act (placing explosives with intent to do bodily injury).
15. An offence under section 31 of that Act (setting spring guns etc. with intent to do grievous bodily harm).
16. An offence under section 32 of that Act (endangering the safety of railway passengers).
17. An offence under section 35 of that Act (injuring persons by furious driving).
18. An offence under section 37 of that Act (assaulting officer preserving wreck).
19. An offence under section 38 of that Act (assault with intent to resist arrest).
20. An offence under section 47 of that Act (assault occasioning actual bodily harm).
21. An offence under section 2 of the Explosive Substances Act 1883 (c. 3) (causing explosion likely to endanger life or property).
22. An offence under section 3 of that Act (attempt to cause explosion, or making or keeping explosive with intent to endanger life or property).
22A. An offence under section 4 of that Act (making or possession of explosive under suspicious circumstances).[2]
23. An offence under section 1 of the Infant Life (Preservation) Act 1929 (c. 34) (child destruction).
24. An offence under section 1 of the Children and Young Persons Act 1933 (c. 12) (cruelty to children).
25. An offence under section 1 of the Infanticide Act 1938 (c. 36) (infanticide).
26. An offence under section 16 of the Firearms Act 1968 (c. 27) (possession of firearm with intent to endanger life).
27. An offence under section 16A of that Act (possession of firearm with intent to cause fear of violence).
28. An offence under section 17(1) of that Act (use of firearm to resist arrest).
29. An offence under section 17(2) of that Act (possession of firearm at time of committing or being arrested for offence specified in Schedule 1 to that Act).
30. An offence under section 18 of that Act (carrying a firearm with criminal intent).

[2] Added by the Criminal Justice and Courts Act 2015, s.2(2) (April 13, 2015: SI 2015/778. The insertion has effect subject to transitional provisions specified in s.2(8)-(11)).

31. An offence under section 8 of the Theft Act 1968 (c. 60) (robbery or assault with intent to rob).

32. An offence under section 9 of that Act of burglary with intent to—
    (a) inflict grievous bodily harm on a person, or
    (b) do unlawful damage to a building or anything in it.

33. An offence under section 10 of that Act (aggravated burglary).

34. An offence under section 12A of that Act (aggravated vehicle-taking) involving an accident which caused the death of any person.

35. An offence of arson under section 1 of the Criminal Damage Act 1971 (c. 48).

36. An offence under section 1(2) of that Act (destroying or damaging property) other than an offence of arson.

37. An offence under section 1 of the Taking of Hostages Act 1982 (c. 28) (hostage-taking).

38. An offence under section 1 of the Aviation Security Act 1982 (c. 36) (hijacking).

39. An offence under section 2 of that Act (destroying, damaging or endangering safety of aircraft).

40. An offence under section 3 of that Act (other acts endangering or likely to endanger safety of aircraft).

41. An offence under section 4 of that Act (offences in relation to certain dangerous articles).

42. An offence under section 127 of the Mental Health Act 1983 (c. 20) (ill-treatment of patients).

43. An offence under section 1 of the Prohibition of Female Circumcision Act 1985 (c. 38) (prohibition of female circumcision).

44. An offence under section 1 of the Public Order Act 1986 (c. 64) (riot).

45. An offence under section 2 of that Act (violent disorder).

46. An offence under section 3 of that Act (affray).

47. An offence under section 134 of the Criminal Justice Act 1988 (c. 33) (torture).

48. An offence under section 1 of the Road Traffic Act 1988 (c. 52) (causing death by dangerous driving).

48A. An offence under section 3ZC of that Act (causing death by driving: disqualified drivers).[3]

49. An offence under section 3A of that Act (causing death by careless driving when under influence of drink or drugs).

50. An offence under section 1 of the Aviation and Maritime Security Act 1990 (c. 31) (endangering safety at aerodromes).

[3] Inserted by the Criminal Justice and Courts Act 2015, s.29 and Sch.6, para.11 (April 13, 2015: SI 2015/778).

51. An offence under section 9 of that Act (hijacking of ships).

52. An offence under section 10 of that Act (seizing or exercising control of fixed platforms).

53. An offence under section 11 of that Act (destroying fixed platforms or endangering their safety).

54. An offence under section 12 of that Act (other acts endangering or likely to endanger safe navigation).

55. An offence under section 13 of that Act (offences involving threats).

56. An offence under Part II of the Channel Tunnel (Security) Order 1994 (S.I. 1994/570) (offences relating to Channel Tunnel trains and the tunnel system).

57. An offence under section 4 or 4A of the Protection from Harassment Act 1997 (c. 40) (putting people in fear of violence and stalking involving fear of violence or serious alarm or distress.[4]

58. An offence under section 29 of the Crime and Disorder Act 1998 (c. 37) (racially or religiously aggravated assaults).

59. An offence falling within section 31(1)(a) or (b) of that Act (racially or religiously aggravated offences under section 4 or 4A of the Public Order Act 1986 (c. 64)).

59A. An offence under section 54 of the Terrorism Act 2000 (weapons training).[5]

59B. An offence under section 56 of that Act (directing terrorist organisation).[6]

59C. An offence under section 57 of that Act (possession of article for terrorist purposes).[7]

59D. An offence under section 59 of that Act (inciting terrorism overseas).[8]

60. An offence under section 51 or 52 of the International Criminal Court Act 2001 (c. 17) (genocide, crimes against humanity, war crimes and related offences), other than one involving murder.

60A. An offence under section 47 of the Anti-terrorism, Crime and Security Act 2001 (use etc of nuclear weapons).[9]

---

[4] Amended by the Protection of Freedoms Act 2012, s.115(1) and Sch.9, para.147 (November 25, 2012).

[5] Inserted by the Coroners and Justice Act 2009, s.138(2) (January 12, 2010. The insertion has effect subject to transitional provisions specified in the 2009 Act, Sch.22, para.37).

[6] Inserted by the Coroners and Justice Act 2009, s.138(2) (January 12, 2010. The insertion has effect subject to transitional provisions specified in the 2009 Act, Sch.22, para.37).

[7] Inserted by the Coroners and Justice Act 2009, s.138(2) (January 12, 2010. The insertion has effect subject to transitional provisions specified in the 2009 Act, Sch.22, para.37).

[8] Inserted by the Coroners and Justice Act 2009, s.138(2) (January 12, 2010. The insertion has effect subject to transitional provisions specified in the 2009 Act, Sch.22, para.37).

[9] Inserted by the Coroners and Justice Act 2009, s.138(3) (January 12, 2010. The insertion has effect subject to transitional provisions specified in the 2009 Act, Sch.22, para.37).

60B. An offence under section 50 of that Act (assisting or inducing certain weapons-related acts overseas).[10]

60C. An offence under section 113 of that Act (use of noxious substance or thing to cause harm or intimidate).[11]

61. An offence under section 1 of the Female Genital Mutilation Act 2003 (c. 31) (female genital mutilation).

62. An offence under section 2 of that Act (assisting a girl to mutilate her own genitalia).

63. An offence under section 3 of that Act (assisting a non-UK person to mutilate overseas a girl's genitalia).

63A. An offence under section 5 of the Domestic Violence, Crime and Victims Act 2004 (causing or allowing a child or vulnerable adult to die or suffer serious physical harm.[12]

63B. An offence under section 5 of the Terrorism Act 2006 (preparation of terrorist acts).[13]

63C. An offence under section 6 of that Act (training for terrorism).[14]

63D. An offence under section 9 of that Act (making or possession of radioactive device or material).[15]

63E. An offence under section 10 of that Act (use of radioactive device or material for terrorist purposes etc).[16]

63F. An offence under section 11 of that Act (terrorist threats relating to radioactive devices etc).[17]

63G. An offence under section 1 of the Modern Slavery Act 2015 (slavery, servitude and forced or compulsory labour).[18]

63H. An offence under section 2 of that Act (human trafficking) which is not within Part 2 of this Schedule.[19]

64. (1) Aiding, abetting, counselling or procuring the commission of an offence specified in the preceding paragraphs of this Part of this Schedule.

---

[10] Inserted by the Coroners and Justice Act 2009, s.138(3) (January 12, 2010. The insertion has effect subject to transitional provisions specified in the 2009 Act, Sch.22, para.37).

[11] Inserted by the Coroners and Justice Act 2009, s.138(3) (January 12, 2010. The insertion has effect subject to transitional provisions specified in the 2009 Act, Sch.22, para.37).

[12] Added by the Domestic Violence, Crime and Victims Act 2004, s.58(1) and Sch.10, para.65 (March 21, 2005) and the Domestic Violence, Crime and Victims (Amendment) Act 2012, s.3 and Sch.1, para.6 (July 2, 2012).

[13] Inserted by the Coroners and Justice Act 2009, s.138(4) (January 12, 2010. The insertion has effect subject to transitional provisions specified in the 2009 Act, Sch.22, para.37).

[14] Inserted by the Coroners and Justice Act 2009, s.138(4) (January 12, 2010. The insertion has effect subject to transitional provisions specified in the 2009 Act, Sch.22, para.37).

[15] Inserted by the Coroners and Justice Act 2009, s.138(4) (January 12, 2010. The insertion has effect subject to transitional provisions specified in the 2009 Act, Sch.22, para.37).

[16] Inserted by the Coroners and Justice Act 2009, s.138(4) (January 12, 2010. The insertion has effect subject to transitional provisions specified in the 2009 Act, Sch.22, para.37).

[17] Inserted by the Coroners and Justice Act 2009, s.138(4) (January 12, 2010. The insertion has effect subject to transitional provisions specified in the 2009 Act, Sch.22, para.37).

[18] Inserted by the Modern Slavery Act 2015, s.6(2) (July 31, 2015).

[19] Inserted by the Modern Slavery Act 2015, s.6(2) (July 31, 2015).

(2) An attempt to commit such an offence.

(3) Conspiracy to commit such an offence.

(4) Incitement to commit such an offence.

(5) An offence under Part 2 of the Serious Crime Act 2007 in relation to which an offence specified in the preceding paragraphs of this Part of this Schedule is the offence (or one of the offences) which the person intended or believed would be committed.[20]

65. (1) An attempt to commit murder.

(2) Conspiracy to commit murder.

(3) Incitement to commit murder.

(4) An offence under Part 2 of the Serious Crime Act 2007 in relation to which murder is the offence (or one of the offences) which the person intended or believed would be committed.[21]

PART 2
SPECIFIED SEXUAL OFFENCES

A.02

66. An offence under section 1 of the Sexual Offences Act 1956 (c. 69) (rape).

67. An offence under section 2 of that Act (procurement of woman by threats).

68. An offence under section 3 of that Act (procurement of woman by false pretences).

69. An offence under section 4 of that Act (administering drugs to obtain or facilitate intercourse).

70. An offence under section 5 of that Act (intercourse with girl under thirteen).

71. An offence under section 6 of that Act (intercourse with girl under 16).

72. An offence under section 7 of that Act (intercourse with a defective).

73. An offence under section 9 of that Act (procurement of a defective).

74. An offence under section 10 of that Act (incest by a man).

75. An offence under section 11 of that Act (incest by a woman).

76. An offence under section 14 of that Act (indecent assault on a woman).

77. An offence under section 15 of that Act (indecent assault on a man).

[20] Substituted by the Criminal Justice and Courts Act 2015, s.2(3) (April 13, 2015: SI 2015/778. The insertion has effect subject to transitional provisions specified in s.2(8)-(9)).

[21] Substituted by the Criminal Justice and Courts Act 2015, s.2(4) (April 13, 2015: SI 2015/778. The insertion has effect subject to transitional provisions specified in s.2(8)-(11)).

78. An offence under section 16 of that Act (assault with intent to commit buggery).
79. An offence under section 17 of that Act (abduction of woman by force or for the sake of her property).
80. An offence under section 19 of that Act (abduction of unmarried girl under eighteen from parent or guardian).
81. An offence under section 20 of that Act (abduction of unmarried girl under sixteen from parent or guardian).
82. An offence under section 21 of that Act (abduction of defective from parent or guardian).
83. An offence under section 22 of that Act (causing prostitution of women).
84. An offence under section 23 of that Act (procuration of girl under twenty-one).
85. An offence under section 24 of that Act (detention of woman in brothel).
86. An offence under section 25 of that Act (permitting girl under thirteen to use premises for intercourse).
87. An offence under section 26 of that Act (permitting girl under sixteen to use premises for intercourse).
88. An offence under section 27 of that Act (permitting defective to use premises for intercourse).
89. An offence under section 28 of that Act (causing or encouraging the prostitution of, intercourse with or indecent assault on girl under sixteen).
90. An offence under section 29 of that Act (causing or encouraging prostitution of defective).
91. An offence under section 32 of that Act (soliciting by men).

Repealed

92. [Repealed by the Criminal Justice and Courts Act 2015, s.2(5) (April 13, 2015: SI 2015/778. The repeal has effect subject to transitional provisions specified in the 2015 Act, s.2(8)-(9))]
92A. An offence under section 33A of that Act (keeping a brothel used for prostitution).[22]
93. An offence under section 128 of the Mental Health Act 1959 (c. 72) (sexual intercourse with patients).
94. An offence under section 1 of the Indecency with Children Act 1960 (c. 33) (indecent conduct towards young child).
95. An offence under section 4 of the Sexual Offences Act 1967 (c. 60) (procuring others to commit homosexual acts).
96. An offence under section 5 of that Act (living on earnings of male prostitution).

---

[22] Inserted by the Criminal Justice and Courts Act 2015, s.2(6) (April 13, 2015: SI 2015/778. The insertion has effect subject to transitional provisions specified in s.2(8)-(9)).

97. An offence under section 9 of the Theft Act 1968 (c. 60) of burglary with intent to commit rape.

98. An offence under section 54 of the Criminal Law Act 1977 (c. 45) (inciting girl under sixteen to have incestuous sexual intercourse).

99. An offence under section 1 of the Protection of Children Act 1978 (c. 37) (indecent photographs of children).

100. An offence under section 170 of the Customs and Excise Management Act 1979 (c. 2) (penalty for fraudulent evasion of duty etc.) in relation to goods prohibited to be imported under section 42 of the Customs Consolidation Act 1876 (c. 36) (indecent or obscene articles).

101. An offence under section 160 of the Criminal Justice Act 1988 (c. 33) (possession of indecent photograph of a child).

102. An offence under section 1 of the Sexual Offences Act 2003 (c. 42) (rape).

103. An offence under section 2 of that Act (assault by penetration).

104. An offence under section 3 of that Act (sexual assault).

105. An offence under section 4 of that Act (causing a person to engage in sexual activity without consent).

106. An offence under section 5 of that Act (rape of a child under 13).

107. An offence under section 6 of that Act (assault of a child under 13 by penetration).

108. An offence under section 7 of that Act (sexual assault of a child under 13).

109. An offence under section 8 of that Act (causing or inciting a child under 13 to engage in sexual activity).

110. An offence under section 9 of that Act (sexual activity with a child).

111. An offence under section 10 of that Act (causing or inciting a child to engage in sexual activity).

112. An offence under section 11 of that Act (engaging in sexual activity in the presence of a child).

113. An offence under section 12 of that Act (causing a child to watch a sexual act).

114. An offence under section 13 of that Act (child sex offences committed by children or young persons).

115. An offence under section 14 of that Act (arranging or facilitating commission of a child sex offence).

116. An offence under section 15 of that Act (meeting a child following sexual grooming etc.).

117. An offence under section 16 of that Act (abuse of position of trust: sexual activity with a child).

118. An offence under section 17 of that Act (abuse of position of trust: causing or inciting a child to engage in sexual activity).
119. An offence under section 18 of that Act (abuse of position of trust: sexual activity in the presence of a child).
120. An offence under section 19 of that Act (abuse of position of trust: causing a child to watch a sexual act).
121. An offence under section 25 of that Act (sexual activity with a child family member).
122. An offence under section 26 of that Act (inciting a child family member to engage in sexual activity).
123. An offence under section 30 of that Act (sexual activity with a person with a mental disorder impeding choice).
124. An offence under section 31 of that Act (causing or inciting a person with a mental disorder impeding choice to engage in sexual activity).
125. An offence under section 32 of that Act (engaging in sexual activity in the presence of a person with a mental disorder impeding choice).
126. An offence under section 33 of that Act (causing a person with a mental disorder impeding choice to watch a sexual act).
127. An offence under section 34 of that Act (inducement, threat or deception to procure sexual activity with a person with a mental disorder).
128. An offence under section 35 of that Act (causing a person with a mental disorder to engage in or agree to engage in sexual activity by inducement, threat or deception).
129. An offence under section 36 of that Act (engaging in sexual activity in the presence, procured by inducement, threat or deception, of a person with a mental disorder).
130. An offence under section 37 of that Act (causing a person with a mental disorder to watch a sexual act by inducement, threat or deception).
131. An offence under section 38 of that Act (care workers: sexual activity with a person with a mental disorder).
132. An offence under section 39 of that Act (care workers: causing or inciting sexual activity).
133. An offence under section 40 of that Act (care workers: sexual activity in the presence of a person with a mental disorder).
134. An offence under section 41 of that Act (care workers: causing a person with a mental disorder to watch a sexual act).
135. An offence under section 47 of that Act (paying for sexual services of a child).
136. An offence under section 48 of that Act (causing or inciting sexual exploitation of a child or pornography).[23]

[23] Amended by the Serious Crime Act 2015, s.85 and Sch.4, para.68(3) (May 3, 2015).

137. An offence under section 49 of that Act (controlling a child in relation to sexual exploitation).[24]

138. An offence under section 50 of that Act (arranging or facilitating sexual exploitation of a child).[25]

139. An offence under section 52 of that Act (causing or inciting prostitution for gain).

140. An offence under section 53 of that Act (controlling prostitution for gain).

141. An offence under section 57 of that Act (trafficking into the UK for sexual exploitation).

142. An offence under section 58 of that Act (trafficking within the UK for sexual exploitation).

143. An offence under section 59 of that Act (trafficking out of the UK for sexual exploitation).

143A. An offence under section 59A of that Act (trafficking for sexual exploitation).[26]

144. An offence under section 61 of that Act (administering a substance with intent).

145. An offence under section 62 of that Act (committing an offence with intent to commit a sexual offence).

146. An offence under section 63 of that Act (trespass with intent to commit a sexual offence).

147. An offence under section 64 of that Act (sex with an adult relative: penetration).

148. An offence under section 65 of that Act (sex with an adult relative: consenting to penetration).

149. An offence under section 66 of that Act (exposure).

150. An offence under section 67 of that Act (voyeurism).

151. An offence under section 69 of that Act (intercourse with an animal).

152. An offence under section 70 of that Act (sexual penetration of a corpse).

152A. An offence under section 2 of the Modern Slavery Act 2015 (human trafficking) committed with a view to exploitation that consists of or includes behaviour within section 3(3) of that Act (sexual exploitation).[27]

153. (1) Aiding, abetting, counselling or procuring the commission of an offence specified in this Part of this Schedule.

(2) An attempt to commit such an offence.

(3) Conspiracy to commit such an offence.

---

[24] Amended by the Serious Crime Act 2015, s.85 and Sch.4, para.68(4) (May 3, 2015).
[25] Amended by the Serious Crime Act 2015, s.85 and Sch.4, para.68(5) (May 3, 2015).
[26] Inserted by the Protection of Freedoms Act 2012, Sch.9(10), para.139 (April 6, 2013).
[27] Inserted by the Modern Slavery Act 2015, s.6(3) (July 31, 2015).

(4)   Incitement to commit such an offence.

(5)   An offence under Part 2 of the Serious Crime Act 2007 in relation to which an offence specified in this Part of this Schedule is the offence (or one of the offences) which the person intended or believed would be committed.[28]

SCHEDULE 15B[29]
OFFENCES LISTED FOR THE PURPOSES OF SECTIONS 224A, 226A AND 246A
Sections 224A, 226A and 246A

PART 1
OFFENCES UNDER THE LAW OF ENGLAND AND WALES LISTED FOR THE
PURPOSES OF SECTIONS 224A(1), 224A(4), 226A AND 246A

The following offences to the extent that they are offences under the law of England and Wales—   **A.03**

1. Manslaughter.

2. An offence under section 4 of the Offences against the Person Act 1861 (soliciting murder).

3. An offence under section 18 of that Act (wounding with intent to cause grievous bodily harm).

3A. An offence under section 28 of that Act (causing bodily injury by explosives).[30]

3B. An offence under section 29 of that Act (using explosives etc with intent to do grievous bodily harm). [31]

3C. An offence under section 2 of the Explosive Substances Act 1883 (causing explosion likely to endanger life or property).[32]

---

[28] Substituted by the Criminal Justice and Courts Act 2015, s.2(7) (April 13, 2015: SI 2015/778. The insertion has effect subject to transitional provisions specified in s.2(8)-(9)).

[29] Inserted by the Legal Aid, Sentencing and Punishment of Offenders Act 2012, s.122 and Sch.18, para.1 (December 3, 2012). **Extent:** England, Wales.

[30] Inserted by the Criminal Justice and Courts Act 2015, s.3(2) (April 13, 2015: SI 2015/778).

[31] Inserted by the Criminal Justice and Courts Act 2015, s.3(2) (April 13, 2015: SI 2015/778).

[32] Inserted by the Criminal Justice and Courts Act 2015, s.3(2) (April 13, 2015: SI 2015/778).

3D. An offence under section 3 of that Act (attempt to cause explosion, or making or keeping explosive with intent to endanger life or property).[33]

3E. An offence under section 4 of that Act (making or possession of explosive under suspicious circumstances).[34]

4. An offence under section 16 of the Firearms Act 1968 (possession of a firearm with intent to endanger life).

5. An offence under section 17(1) of that Act (use of a firearm to resist arrest).

6. An offence under section 18 of that Act (carrying a firearm with criminal intent).

7. An offence of robbery under section 8 of the Theft Act 1968 where, at some time during the commission of the offence, the offender had in his possession a firearm or an imitation firearm within the meaning of the Firearms Act 1968.

8. An offence under section 1 of the Protection of Children Act 1978 (indecent images of children).

8A. An offence under section 54 of the Terrorism Act 2000 (weapons training).[35]

9. An offence under section 56 of that Act (directing terrorist organisation).[35a]

10. An offence under section 57 of that Act (possession of article for terrorist purposes).

11. An offence under section 59 of that Act (inciting terrorism overseas) if the offender is liable on conviction on indictment to imprisonment for life.

12. An offence under section 47 of the Anti-terrorism, Crime and Security Act 2001 (use etc of nuclear weapons).

13. An offence under section 50 of that Act (assisting or inducing certain weapons-related acts overseas).

14. An offence under section 113 of that Act (use of noxious substance or thing to cause harm or intimidate).

15. An offence under section 1 of the Sexual Offences Act 2003 (rape).

16. An offence under section 2 of that Act (assault by penetration).

---

[33] Inserted by the Criminal Justice and Courts Act 2015, s.3(2) (April 13, 2015: SI 2015/778).
[34] Inserted by the Criminal Justice and Courts Act 2015, s.3(2) (April 13, 2015: SI 2015/778).
[35] Inserted by the Criminal Justice and Courts Act 2015, s.3(3) (April 13, 2015: SI 2015/778).
[35a] Amended by the Criminal Justice and Courts Act 2015, s.3(4) (April 13, 2015: SI 2015/778).

17. An offence under section 4 of that Act (causing a person to engage in sexual activity without consent) if the offender is liable on conviction on indictment to imprisonment for life.

18. An offence under section 5 of that Act (rape of a child under 13).

19. An offence under section 6 of that Act (assault of a child under 13 by penetration).

20. An offence under section 7 of that Act (sexual assault of a child under 13).

21. An offence under section 8 of that Act (causing or inciting a child under 13 to engage in sexual activity).

22. An offence under section 9 of that Act (sexual activity with a child).

23. An offence under section 10 of that Act (causing or inciting a child to engage in sexual activity).

24. An offence under section 11 of that Act (engaging in sexual activity in the presence of a child).

25. An offence under section 12 of that Act (causing a child to watch a sexual act).

26. An offence under section 14 of that Act (arranging or facilitating commission of a child sex offence).

27. An offence under section 15 of that Act (meeting a child following sexual grooming etc).

28. An offence under section 25 of that Act (sexual activity with a child family member) if the offender is aged 18 or over at the time of the offence.

29. An offence under section 26 of that Act (inciting a child family member to engage in sexual activity) if the offender is aged 18 or over at the time of the offence.

30. An offence under section 30 of that Act (sexual activity with a person with a mental disorder impeding choice) if the offender is liable on conviction on indictment to imprisonment for life.

31. An offence under section 31 of that Act (causing or inciting a person with a mental disorder to engage in sexual activity) if the offender is liable on conviction on indictment to imprisonment for life.

32. An offence under section 34 of that Act (inducement, threat or deception to procure sexual activity with a person with a mental disorder) if the offender is liable on conviction on indictment to imprisonment for life.

33. An offence under section 35 of that Act (causing a person with a mental disorder to engage in or agree to engage in sexual activity by inducement etc) if the offender is liable on conviction on indictment to imprisonment for life.

34. An offence under section 47 of that Act (paying for sexual services of a child) against a person aged under 16.
35. An offence under section 48 of that Act (causing or inciting sexual exploitation of a child).[36]
36. An offence under section 49 of that Act (controlling a child in relation to sexual exploitation).[37]
37. An offence under section 50 of that Act (arranging or facilitating sexual exploitation of a child).[38]
38. An offence under section 62 of that Act (committing an offence with intent to commit a sexual offence) if the offender is liable on conviction on indictment to imprisonment for life.
39. An offence under section 5 of the Domestic Violence, Crime and Victims Act 2004 (causing or allowing the death of a child or vulnerable adult).
40. An offence under section 5 of the Terrorism Act 2006 (preparation of terrorist acts).
40A. An offence under section 6 of that Act (training for terrorism).[39]
41. An offence under section 9 of that Act (making or possession of radioactive device or materials).
42. An offence under section 10 of that Act (misuse of radioactive devices or material and misuse and damage of facilities).
43. An offence under section 11 of that Act (terrorist threats relating to radioactive devices, materials or facilities).
43A. An offence under section 1 of the Modern Slavery Act 2015 (slavery, servitude and forced or compulsory labour).[40]
43B. An offence under section 2 of that Act (human trafficking).[41]
44. (1) An attempt to commit an offence specified in the preceding paragraphs of this Part of this Schedule ("a listed offence") or murder.
    (2) Conspiracy to commit a listed offence or murder.
    (3) Incitement to commit a listed offence or murder.
    (4) An offence under Part 2 of the Serious Crime Act 2007 in relation to which a listed offence or murder is the offence (or one of the offences) which the person intended or believed would be committed.
    (5) Aiding, abetting, counselling or procuring the commission of a listed offence.

[36] Amended by the Serious Crime Act 2015, s.85 and Sch.4, para.69(2) (May 3, 2015).
[37] Amended by the Serious Crime Act 2015, s.85 and Sch.4, para.69(3) (May 3, 2015).
[38] Amended by the Serious Crime Act 2015, s.85 and Sch.4, para.69(4) (May 3, 2015).
[39] Inserted by the Criminal Justice and Courts Act 2015, s.3(5) (April 13, 2015: SI 2015/778).
[40] Inserted by the Modern Slavery Act 2015, s.6(4) (July 31, 2015).
[41] Inserted by the Modern Slavery Act 2015, s.6(4) (July 31, 2015).

PART 2
FURTHER OFFENCES UNDER THE LAW OF ENGLAND AND
WALES LISTED FOR
THE PURPOSES OF SECTIONS 224A(4), 226A AND 246A

The following offences to the extent that they are offences under the law of **A.04**
England and Wales—
45. Murder.
46. (1) Any offence that—
    (a) was abolished (with or without savings) before the coming into force of this Schedule, and
    (b) would, if committed on the relevant day, have consti-tuted an offence specified in Part 1 of this Schedule.
  (2) "Relevant day", in relation to an offence, means—
    (a) for the purposes of this paragraph as it applies for the purposes of section 246A(2), the day on which the offender was convicted of that offence, and
    (b) for the purposes of this paragraph as it applies for the purposes of sections 224A(4) and 226A(2), the day on which the offender was convicted of the offence referred to in section 224A(1)(a) or 226A(1)(a) (as appropriate).

PART 3
OFFENCES UNDER SERVICE LAW LISTED FOR THE PURPOSES
OF SECTIONS
224A(4),226A AND 246A

47. An offence under section 70 of the Army Act 1955, section 70 of **A.05**
the Air Force Act 1955 or section 42 of the Naval Discipline Act
1957 as respects which the corresponding civil offence (within the
meaning of the Act in question) is an offence specified in Part 1
or 2 of this Schedule.
48. (1) An offence under section 42 of the Armed Forces Act 2006 as respects which the corresponding offence under the law of England and Wales (within the meaning given by that section) is an offence specified in Part 1 or 2 of this Schedule.
  (2) Section 48 of the Armed Forces Act 2006 (attempts, conspiracy etc) applies for the purposes of this paragraph as if the reference in subsection (3)(b) of that section to any of the following provisions of that Act were a reference to this paragraph.

APPROACH TO SENTENCING HISTORIC SEXUAL OFFENCES[1]

NB Details of the principal offences are set out in the table in Appendix C

When sentencing sexual offences under the Sexual Offences Act 1956, or **B.01** other legislation pre-dating the 2003 Act, the court should apply the following principles:[2]

1. The offender must be sentenced in accordance with the sentencing regime applicable at the date of sentence. Under the Criminal Justice Act 2003[3] the court must have regard to the statutory purposes of sentencing and must base the sentencing exercise on its assessment of the seriousness of the offence.

2. The sentence is limited to the maximum sentence available at the date of the commission of the offence. If the maximum sentence has been reduced, the lower maximum will be applicable.

3. The court should have regard to any applicable sentencing guidelines for equivalent offences under the Sexual Offences Act 2003.

4. The seriousness of the offence, assessed by the culpability of the offender and the harm caused or intended, is the main consideration for the court. The court should not seek to establish the likely sentence had the offender been convicted shortly after the date of the offence.

5. When assessing the culpability of the offender, the court should have regard to relevant culpability factors set out in any applicable guideline.

---

[1] Sexual Offences Definitive Guidelines: Annex B, reproduced with permission of the Sentencing Council.
[2] *R v H and others* [2011] EWCA Crim 2753.
[3] s.143.

6. The court must assess carefully the harm done to the victim based on the facts available to it, having regard to relevant harm factors set out in any applicable guideline. Consideration of the circumstances which brought the offence to light will be of importance.

7. The court must consider the relevance of the passage of time carefully as it has the potential to aggravate or mitigate the seriousness of the offence. It will be an aggravating factor where the offender has continued to commit sexual offences against the victim or others or has continued to prevent the victim reporting the offence.

8. Where there is an absence of further offending over a long period of time, especially combined with evidence of good character, this may be treated by the court as a mitigating factor. However, as with offences dealt with under the Sexual Offences Act 2003, previous good character/exemplary conduct is different from having no previous convictions. The more serious the offence, the less the weight which should normally be attributed to this factor. Where previous good character/exemplary conduct has been used to facilitate the offence, this mitigation should not normally be allowed and such conduct may constitute an aggravating factor.

9. If the offender was very young and immature at the time of the offence, depending on the circumstances of the offence, this may be regarded as personal mitigation.

10. If the offender made admissions at the time of the offence that were not investigated this is likely to be regarded as personal mitigation. Even greater mitigation is available to the offender who reported himself to the police and/or made early admissions.

11. A reduction for an early guilty plea should be made in the usual manner.

APPENDIX C

OFFENCES AND PENALTIES: COMPARATIVE TABLE OF
OFFENCES UNDER THE OLD LAW AND CURRENT LAW[1]

OFFENCE (Sexual Offences Act 1956 unless otherwise stated)	EFFECTIVE DATES	MAXIMUM	OFFENCE under Sexual Offences Act 2003 (1 May 2004– present)	MAXIMUM	C.01
Rape and assault offences					
Rape (section 1): penile penetration of another person's vagina or anus without consent and knows or reckless as to consent[2]	1 January 1957–30 April 2004[3]	Life	Rape: Intentional penetration of the vagina/anus/mouth of another without consent and without reasonable belief as to consent	Life (indictable only)	
Attempted rape (Common law)	Became a statutory offence under s.1(1) Criminal Attempts Act 1981	7 years (increases to life 16 September 1985)[4]	Attempted rape (Criminal Attempts Act 1981)	Life	

[1] Showing offences included in Sexual Offences Definitive Guideline: Annex C Historic offences. This table does not include new offences with no non-recent equivalent.

[2] As of November 3, 1994, s.1 of Sexual Offences Act 1956 was amended by Criminal Justice and Public Order Act 1994, s.142 to include non-consensual anal intercourse with a male or female. All anal intercourse prior to this should be charged as "buggery" and not rape.

R v R [1992] A.C. 599: held that "unlawful did not exclude marital rape."

[3] As of September 20, 1993, the Sexual Offences Act 1993, s.1 abolishes the presumption that a boy under 14 was incapable of sexual intercourse.

[4] The Sexual Offences Act 1956, s.37(3) and Sch.2, para.1(b), provided that attempted rape would carry maximum sentence of seven years. This was increased to life imprisonment by s.3(1) and (2) of the Sexual Offences Act 1985.

OFFENCE (Sexual Offences Act 1956 unless otherwise stated)	EFFECTIVE DATES	MAXIMUM	OFFENCE under Sexual Offences Act 2003 (1 May 2004–present)	MAXIMUM
Buggery with a person or animal (section 12)	1 January 1957–30 April 2004 (from 3 November 1994 non-consensual acts of buggery were defined as rape)[5]	Life	Rape	Life
			Bestiality is now covered by s.69 SOA 2003	2 years
			Consensual anal intercourse is no longer an offence	
Indecent assault on a woman (section 14)	1 January 1957–30 April 2004	1 January 1957–31 December 1960: 2 years 1 January 1961–15 September 1985: 2 years or 5 years if victim under 13 and age stated on indictment;[6] 16 September 1985 onwards: 10 years[7]	Assault by penetration s.2 (of vagina or anus with a part of body or anything else)	Life (indictable only)
			Sexual assault s.3	10 years (either way) (6 months on summary conviction)
Indecent assault upon a man (section 15)	1 January 1957–30 April 2004	10 years	Assault by penetration s.2 (of anus with a part of body or anything else)	Life (indictable only)
			Sexual assault s.3	10 years (either way) (6 months on summary conviction)

[5] The age of consent for male anal sex was reduced to 18 by s.143 of the Criminal Justice and Public Order Act 1994 and 16 by the Sexual Offences (Amendment) Act 2000, ss.1 and 2, which came into effect on May 1, 2004.
[6] Indecency with Children Act 1960, s.2(3).
[7] Sexual Offences Act 1985, s.3(3).

OFFENCE (Sexual Offences Act 1956 unless otherwise stated)	EFFECTIVE DATES	MAXIMUM	OFFENCE under Sexual Offences Act 2003 (1 May 2004–present)	MAXIMUM
Offences against children				
Sexual intercourse with a girl under 13 (section 5)[8]	1 January 1957–30 April 2004	Life	Rape of a child under 13 s.5	Life
			Assault of a child under 13 by penetration s.6	Life
Incest by a male person (section 10)	1 January 1957–30 April 2004	Life if victim under 13; otherwise 7 years	Sex with an adult relative: penetration s.64	2 years (either way)
Incest by a female person (section 11)	1 January 1957–30 April 2004	7 years	Sex with an adult relative: consenting to penetration s.65	2 years (either way)
Gross indecency (section 13)	1 January 1957–30 April 2004	Male offender over 21 with male under age of consent: 5 years Otherwise: 2 years	REPEALED	
Indecency with a child (section 1 of the Indecency with Children Act 1960)	1 January 1961–30 April 2004	1 January 1961–30 September 1997: 2 years 1 October 1997 onwards: 10 years[9] Note: on 11 January 2001 the age definition of a child increased from 14 to 16		

[8] No time limit on prosecutions. The irrebuttable presumption that a boy under 14 was incapable of sexual intercourse (abolished September 20, 1993) would apply where relevant, however he could be convicted of indecent assault.

[9] Indecency with Children Act 1960, s.1(1), as amended by the Crime (Sentences) Act 1997, s.52.

OFFENCE (Sexual Offences Act 1956 unless otherwise stated)	EFFECTIVE DATES	MAXIMUM	OFFENCE under Sexual Offences Act 2003 (1 May 2004–present)	MAXIMUM
Incitement of a girl under 16 to commit incest (section 54 of the Criminal Law Act 1977)	8 September 1977–30 April 2004	2 years	Inciting a child family member to engage in sexual activity s.26	14 years where D is over 18; in other cases, 5 years
Abuse of position of trust (section 3 of the Sexual Offences (Amendment) Act 2000	8 January 2001–30 April 2004	5 years	Abuse of position of trust: sexual activity with a child s.16	5 years (either way)
Indecent images				
Taking indecent photographs of a child (section 1 of the Protection of Children Act 1978)	20 August 1978–present	20 August 1978–10 January 2001: 3 years 11 January 2001 onwards: 10 years[10]	Still current	
Possession of indecent photographs of a child (section 160 of the Criminal Justice Act 1988)	11 January 1988–present	11 January 1988–10 January 2001: 6 months 11 January 2001 onwards: 5 years[11]	Still current	
Exploitation offences				
Procurement of woman by threats (section 2)	1 January 1957–30 April 2004	2 years	REPEALED	
Procurement by false pretences (section 3)	1 January 1957–30 April 2004	2 years	REPEALED	
Causing prostitution of women (section 22)	1 January 1957–30 April 2004	2 years	Causing or inciting prostitution for gain s.52	7 years (either way)

[10] Amended by Criminal Justice and Court Services Act 2000, s.41(1).
[11] Amended by Criminal Justice and Court Services Act 2000, s.41(3)(a).

OFFENCE (Sexual Offences Act 1956 unless otherwise stated)	EFFECTIVE DATES	MAXIMUM	OFFENCE under Sexual Offences Act 2003 (1 May 2004–present)	MAXIMUM
Procuration of girl under 21 for unlawful sexual intercourse in any part of the world (section 23)	1 January 1957–30 April 2004	2 years	Arranging or facilitating child sexual exploitation s.50	14 years (either way)
Detention in a brothel (section 24)	1 January 1957–30 April 2004	2 years	REPEALED	
Permitting a defective to use premises for intercourse (section 27)	1 January 1957–30 April 2004	2 years	(Controlling prostitution for gain s.53)	7 years (either way)
Causing or encouraging prostitution (etc) of a girl under 16 (section 28)	1 January 1957–30 April 2004	2 years	Paying for sexual services of a child s.47	Life if penetration with child under 13 (indictable only); 14 years if penetration with child under 16 (indictable only); 14 years with no penetration (either way); otherwise 7 years
			Causing or inciting child sexual exploitation s.48	14 years (either way)
			Controlling child sexual exploitation s.49	14 years either way
Causing or encouraging prostitution of a defective (section 29)	1 January 1957–30 April 2004	2 years	Causing or inciting prostitution for gain s.52	7 years (either way)

OFFENCE (Sexual Offences Act 1956 unless otherwise stated)	EFFECTIVE DATES	MAXIMUM	OFFENCE under Sexual Offences Act 2003 (1 May 2004– present)	MAXIMUM
Living on earnings of prostitution (section 30)	1 January 1957–30 April 2004	2 years	Controlling prostitution for gain s.53	7 years (either way)
and Woman exercising control over prostitute (section 31)	1 January 1957–30 April 2004	2 years	and Keeping a brothel SOA 1956 s.33A (inserted by SOA 2003 s.55)	7 years (either way)
Trafficking into/ within/out of the UK for sexual exploitation	1 January 1957–30 April 2004 (SOA 1956 ss.2, 3, 22, 24, 28, 30 and 31)	2 years	Human trafficking s.2 Modern Slavery Act 2015	Life
	1 May 2005–5 April 2013 (SOA 2003 ss.57–59)[12]	14 years		
Offences against those with a mental disorder				
Intercourse with a defective (section 7)	1 January 1957–30 April 2004	2 years	Sexual activity with a person with a mental disorder impeding choice s.30	Life if penetration (indictable only) Otherwise 14 years (either way)
Procurement of a defective (section 9)	1 January 1957–30 April 2004	2 years	REPEALED	

[12] s.59A was substituted for ss.57-59 by the Protection of Freedoms Act 2012, s.109(2) (April 6, 2013) and was repealed by the Modern Slavery Act 2015, s.57 and Sch.5, para.5(1), (2) (July 31, 2015).

OFFENCE (Sexual Offences Act 1956 unless otherwise stated)	EFFECTIVE DATES	MAXIMUM	OFFENCE under Sexual Offences Act 2003 (1 May 2004–present)	MAXIMUM
Sexual intercourse with patients (section 128 of the Mental Health Act 1959)	1 November 1960–30 April 2004	2 years	Care workers: sexual activity with a person with a mental disorder s.38	14 years if penetration (indictable only) Otherwise 10 years (either way)
Other offences				
Administering drugs to obtain or facilitate intercourse (section 4)	1 January 1957–30 April 2004	2 years	Administering a substance with intent s.61	10 years (either way)
Burglary with intent to commit rape (section 9 of the Theft Act 1968)	1 January 1969–30 April 2004	14 years if dwelling; otherwise 10 years	Trespass with intent to commit a sexual offence s.63	10 years
			Committing an offence with intent to commit a sexual offence s.62	Life if involving kidnapping or false imprisonment (indictable only) Otherwise 10 years (either way)

APPENDIX D

THE CROWN PROSECUTION SERVICE[1]

The Rape and Sexual Offences guidance replaces the Rape Manual and the **D.01**
separate pieces of guidance on other sexual offences. It has 22 chapters and
six appendices. The chapters and appendices are:
- Chapter 1: CPS Policy Statement
- Chapter 2: Sexual Offences Act 2003 Principal Offences, and Sexual
  Offences Act 1956 Most Commonly Charged Offences
- Chapter 3: Consent
- Chapter 4: Section 41 Youth Justice and Criminal Evidence Act
  1999
- Chapter 5: Victims and Witnesses
- Chapter 6: Special Measures and Video Evidence
- Chapter 7: Pre-Trial Witness Interviews
- Chapter 8: Case Building
- Chapter 9: Forensic, Scientific and Medical Evidence
- Chapter 10: Charging Practice
- Chapter 11: Youths
- Chapter 12: Bail
- Chapter 13: Hearsay
- Chapter 14: Bad Character
- Chapter 15: Disclosure and Third Party Material
- Chapter 16: Briefing & Monitoring the Advocate
- Chapter 17: Indictments
- Chapter 18: Newton Hearings
- Chapter 19: Sentencing
- Chapter 20: Media Guidance for Prosecutors
- Chapter 21: Societal Myths
- Chapter 22: Monitoring Rape Prosecutions
- Appendix A: Advocacy Skills Assessment
- Appendix B: Essential Steps Monitoring

[1] Reproduced from the CPS website: *http://www.cps.gov.uk/* [Accessed April 30, 2016].

1953

- Appendix C: VAW Assurance Tool For Six Monthly Use
- Appendix D: Rape Prosecutions Advice/Review Checklist
- Appendix E: Forensic Medical Examination
- Appendix F: Protocol between the Police and the CPS

CPS LEGAL GUIDANCE: RAPE AND SEXUAL OFFENCES
CHAPTER 11: YOUTHS[1]

The Crown Prosecution Service

Rape and Sexual Offences: Chapter 11: Youths[2]

Contents:
- Youths
- Familial sexual offences committed by young people
- Grave Crimes
- Adult co-defendants
- ECHR points
- Sentencing

Youths

This guidance expands on, and should be read in conjunction with other   **E.01** specific sections elsewhere in this Sexual Offences guidance. Also note the Notification requirements. Any decision to prosecute or not to prosecute should be free of discrimination on the grounds of sexual orientation and gender.

If an allegation of any sexual abuse committed by a youth offender has been fully investigated and there is sufficient evidence to justify instituting proceedings, the balance of the public interest must always be carefully considered before any prosecution is commenced. Positive action may need to be taken at an early stage of offending of this type. Although a reprimand or final warning may provide an acceptable alternative in some cases, in reaching any decision, the police and the CPS will have to take into account

---

[1] Reproduced from the CPS website: *http://www.cps.gov.uk/* [Accessed April 30, 2016].
[2] *http://www.cps.gov.uk/legal/p_to_r/rape_and_sexual_offences/youths/* [Accessed April 30, 2016].

fully the view of other agencies involved in the case, in particular the Social Services. The consequences for the victim of the decision whether or not to prosecute, and any views expressed by the victim or the victim's family should also be taken into account.

In child abuse cases, it will be important to have the views of the Social Services on file if at all possible, as well as any background or history of similar conduct, information about the relationship between the two and the effect a prosecution might have on the victim. Any case referred to the CPS for advice, or in which a prosecution does proceed, must be dealt with as quickly as possible to minimise the delay before the case comes to court.

Irrespective of whether the evidence is sufficient to found a criminal prosecution, The Social Services will consider taking civil action, such as care proceedings, to protect the child. The police and the CPS may well be asked to disclose evidence to assist in this process. Great care should be taken to follow the guidance set out in the section on disclosure to third parties

Chief Crown Prosecutors must be notified of any case where at least one of the complainants and at least one of the suspects are under the age of 13. This includes cases which are diverted from prosecution, whether on evidential or public interest grounds.

All such cases must be reviewed by a prosecutor who is both a rape specialist and a youth specialist. All advocates conducting these cases must have a rape specialism and should also have a youth specialism.

When reviewing a case, in which a youth under 18 is alleged to have committed an offence contrary to sections 5 to 8, prosecutors should obtain and consider:

- the views of local authority Childrens and Young Peoples Service;
- any risk assessment or report conducted by the local authority or youth offending service in respect of sexually harmful behaviour (such as AIM (Assessment, Intervention and Moving On);
- background information and history of the parties ;
- the views of the families of all parties.

Careful regard should be paid to the following factors:

- the relative ages of the parties;
- the existence of and nature of any relationship;
- the sexual and emotional maturity of the parties and any emotional or physical effects as a result of the conduct;

- whether the child under 13 in fact freely consented (even though in law this is not a defence) or a genuine mistake as to age was in fact made;
- whether any element of seduction, breach of any duty of responsibility to the child or other exploitation is disclosed by the evidence;
- the impact of a prosecution on each child involved.

If the sexual act or activity was in fact genuinely consensual and the youth and the child under 13 concerned are fairly close in age and development, a prosecution is unlikely to be appropriate. Action falling short of prosecution may be appropriate. In such cases, the parents and/or welfare agencies may be able to deal with the situation informally. There is a fine line between sexual experimentation and offending and in general, children under the age of 13 should not be criminalised for sexual behaviour in the absence of coercion, exploitation or abuse of trust.

However, if a very young child has been seduced by a youth, or a baby-sitter in a position of responsibility has taken advantage of a child under 13 in his/her care, prosecution is likely to be in the public interest. Where a child under 13 has not given ostensible consent to the activity, then a prosecution contrary to sections 5 to 8 is likely to be the appropriate course of action. Where the Full Code Test is satisfied in a case in which a youth is suspected of committing a sexual offence involving a child under the age of 13, the appropriate charge will be an offence contrary to sections 5 to 8 Sexual Offences Act 2003, depending on the act, and not the lesser offence contrary to section 13 Sexual Offences Act 2003.

Rape of a child under 13 (section 5), assault of a child under 13 by penetration (section 6) and causing or inciting a child under 13 to engage in sexual activity that involves penetration (section 8) are indictable only offences with a maximum sentence of life imprisonment. The offences of sexual assault of a child under 13 (section 7), causing or inciting a child under 13 to engage in sexual activity where there has been no penetration (section 8) are punishable on indictment with imprisonment for a term not exceeding 14 years. They are all 'grave crimes' for the purposes of section 24 Magistrates' Courts Act 1980 and s.91 Powers of Criminal Courts (Sentencing) Act 2000.

It is an offence contrary to section 13 Sexual Offences Act 2003 if a person under 18 does anything which would be an offence under sections 9–12 Sexual Offences Act 2003 See Offences Against Children under 16 : sections 9–13 in Sexual Offences Act elsewhere in this guidance. These offences are punishable on indictment with imprisonment for a term not exceeding 5 years. They are 'grave crimes' for the purposes of section 24 Magistrates' Courts Act 1980 and section 91 Powers of Criminal Courts (Sentencing) Act

2000. Section 13(2)(a) purports to restrict the maximum penalty on summary conviction to a maximum of 6 months imprisonment, although this should be read in the light of section 101(2) Powers of Criminal Courts (Sentencing) Act 2000 to allow a Detention and Training Order of up to 24 months. See Code for Crown Prosecutors considerations and Code for Crown prosecutors – child defendant (under 18) in Sexual Offences elsewhere in this guidance. It should be noted that where both parties to sexual activity are under 16, then they may both have committed a criminal offence. However, the overriding purpose of the legislation is to protect children and it was not Parliament's intention to punish children unnecessarily or for the criminal law to intervene where it was wholly inappropriate. Consensual sexual activity between, for example, a 14 or 15-year-old and a teenage partner would not normally require criminal proceedings in the absence of aggravating features. The relevant considerations include:

- the respective ages of the parties;
- the existence and nature of any relationship their level of maturity;
- whether any duty of care existed;
- whether there was a serious element of exploitation.

Familial Sexual Offences Committed by Young People

E.02   Sections 25 and 26 Sexual Offences Act 2003 create the offences of sexual activity with a child family member and inciting a child family member to engage in sexual activity. These offences are punishable on indictment with imprisonment for a term not exceeding 5 years. They are "grave crimes" for the purposes of section 24 Magistrates' Courts Act 1980 and section 91 Powers of Criminal Courts (Sentencing) Act 2000. Section 25 (5) (b) and 26 (5) (b) purport to restrict the maximum penalty on summary conviction to a maximum of 6 months imprisonment, although this should be read in the light of section 101 (2) Powers of Criminal Courts (Sentencing) Act 2000 to allow a Detention and Training Order of up to 24 months.

Sections 64 and 65 Sexual Offences Act 2003 make it an offence for a person aged 16 or over to penetrate or consent to penetration by a family member who is aged 18 or over. The maximum penalty is imprisonment for a term not exceeding 2 years (sections 64 (5) and 65 (5)).

In cases of sexual activity between siblings, care should be taken to balance the public interest in prosecuting such conduct with the interests and welfare of the victim and the family unit. As a general rule, alternatives to prosecution should be sought where the sexual activity was wholly consensual. The welfare agencies will normally intervene.

Prosecution should be considered where there is evidence of:

- seduction;
- coercion;
- exploitation or violence;
- a significant disparity in age;

In all cases the effect of prosecution on a victim and family should be taken into account and if the views of the welfare agencies are not included with the file they should be sought.

Rape of a child under 13 (section 5), assault of a child under 13 by penetration (section 6) and causing or inciting a child under 13 to engage in sexual activity that involves penetration (section 8) are indictable only offences with a maximum sentence of life imprisonment. The offences of sexual assault of a child under 13 (section 7), causing or inciting a child under 13 to engage in sexual activity where there has been no penetration (section 8) are punishable on indictment with imprisonment for a term not exceeding 14 years. They are all 'grave crimes' for the purposes of section 24 Magistrates' Courts Act 1980 and s.91 Powers of Criminal Courts (Sentencing) Act 2000.

Grave Crimes

A 'grave crime' is defined in section 91(1) Powers of Criminal Courts   E.03
(Sentencing) Act 2000 as:
  (a) an offence punishable in the case of a person aged 21 or over with imprisonment of 14 years or more, not being an offence for which the sentence is fixed by law; OR
  (b) an offence of sexual assault contrary to section 3 Sexual Offences Act 2003; OR
  (c) an offence of child sexual offences committed by children or young persons under 18 contrary to section 13 Sexual Offences Act 2003; OR
  (d) an offence of sexual activity with a child family member contrary to section 25 Sexual Offences Act 2003; OR
  (e) an offence of inciting a child family member to engage in sexual activity contrary to section 26 Sexual Offences Act 2003.

If a youth is convicted on indictment of a 'grave crime', the Crown Court may pass a sentence of detention under section 91(3) Powers of Criminal Courts (Sentencing) Act 2000 for a period that does not exceed the maximum period of imprisonment that can be imposed on a person aged 21 or over.

The Crown Court may only impose a sentence of detention under section 91 Powers of Criminal Courts (Sentencing) Act 2000 if none of the other available sentences are suitable (section 91 (3) Powers of Criminal Courts (Sentencing) Act 2000.

In all cases involving a grave crime, the magistrates should be invited to consider the question of venue (Archbold 5-286), before a plea is taken. The 'allocation' provisions in Schedule 13 Criminal Justice and Immigration Act 2008 to introduce to the youth court plea before venue and committal for sentence have not been brought into force.

The reviewing lawyer should bear in mind the principles set out by Leveson J. with the approval of the Vice President of the Court of Appeal in R on the application of *H, A and O v Southampton Youth Court* [2004] EWHC 2912 Admin when the issue of venue is considered;

1. The general policy of the legislature is that those who are under 18 years of age and in particular children of under 15 years of age should, wherever possible, be tried in the youth court. It is the court which is best designed to meet their specific needs. A trial in the Crown Court with the inevitably greater formality and greatly increased number of people involved (including a jury and the public) should be reserved for the most serious cases.
2. It is a further policy of the legislature that, generally speaking, first time offenders aged 12 to 14 and all offenders under 12 should not be detained in custody and decisions as to jurisdiction should have regard to the fact that the exceptional power to detain for grave offences should not be used to water down the general principle. Those under 15 will rarely attract a period of detention and, even more rarely, those who are under 12.
3. In each case the court should ask itself whether there is a real prospect , having regard to his or her age, that this defendant whose case they are considering might require a sentence of, or in excess of, two years or, alternatively, whether although the sentence might be less than two years, there is some unusual feature of the case which justifies declining jurisdiction, bearing in mind that the absence of a power to impose a detention and training order because the defendant is under 15 is not an unusual feature.

The Sentencing Guidelines Council Definitive Guideline: Overarching Principles – Sentencing Youths paragraph 12.11 sets out the following guidance:

i) a young person aged 10 or 11 (or aged 12-14 but not a persistent offender) should be committed to the Crown Court under this provision (grave crimes) only where charged with an offence of such gravity that, despite the normal prohibition on a custodial sentence for a person of that age, a sentence exceeding two years is a realistic possibility;
ii) a young person aged 12–17 (for which a detention and training order could be imposed) should be committed to the Crown Court

under this provision only where charged with an offence of such gravity that a sentence substantially beyond the 2 year maximum for a detention and training order is a realistic possibility.

Prosecutors should assist the court to determine venue in grave crimes by:

- Drawing to the court's attention relevant sentencing authorities e.g. the Sentencing Guidelines Council Definitive Guideline on Robbery and recent and relevant appellate sentencing cases;
- Informing the court of the aggravating and mitigating features of the offence;
- Providing the court with an accurate and agreed list of the youth's previous convictions, warnings and reprimands. This will assist the court to determine both the nature and length of sentence: *R (on the application of T) v Medway Youth Court* [2003] EWHC 2279 Admin.

Adult Co-defendants

Where a youth offender is jointly charged with an adult, the charge shall be **E.04** heard in the adult magistrates' court: Section 46(1) CYPA 1933. In every either-way or indictable only case, the court must only commit or send the youth offender to the Crown Court for trial with an adult where it is necessary in the interests of justice to do so. In considering whether or not a youth offender should be committed for trial to the Crown Court with an adult co-accused, prosecutors should assist the court to exercise its discretion to commit the youth by making representations. The relevant factors include:

the respective ages of the adult and youth; the respective roles of the youth and adult in the commission of the offence; the likely plea; whether there are existing charges against the youth before the Youth Court; the need to deal with the youth as expeditiously as possible consistent with the interests of justice; and the likely sentence upon conviction.

ECHR Points

There is no reason why youths charged with grave crimes should not, where **E.05** appropriate, be tried in the Crown Court. In *R v United Kingdom* and *T v United Kingdom* [1999] the European Court was asked to consider, inter alia, whether the killers of James Bulger had received a fair trial in the Crown Court in contravention of Article 6, and whether the trial itself amounted to inhuman and degrading treatment in contravention of Article 3.

The Court held that the particular features of the Crown Court trial process did not cause suffering going beyond that inevitably engendered by any attempt to deal with the defendants for the offence in question and therefore Article 3 was not contravened.

However, the Court held that the defendants had not received a fair trial in contravention of Article 6 because of the intense media and public interest prior to the trial, the obvious media and public presence in court during the trial and because insufficient adjustments had been made to the Crown Court trial procedure to enable the defendants to participate fully in the trial bearing in mind their ages, level of maturity and intellectual and emotional capacity. The Court did not rule that youth trials in the Crown Court are unfair per se.

As a consequence of the decision of the European Court, Bingham LCJ issued a Practice Direction addressing the arrangements which should be made for the trial of children in the Crown Court (Practice Direction: (Crown Court: Trial of Children and Young Persons) (2000) (Archbold 4-96a). This takes account of the particular concern expressed by the European Court. Prosecutors should be familiar with the provisions of the Practice Direction and should ensure that a copy is annexed to the brief to counsel instructed to conduct a trial of a youth in the Crown Court.

Both the Divisional Court and the Court of Appeal have confirmed that arguments under the ECHR relating to this issue are matters for the Crown Court judge and he or she will have to determine, in his or her discretion, how to conduct the trial, who to allow into the courtroom and to what extent publicity should be allowed, and that a judge who has considered these issues is entitled to rule that a youth could be fairly tried in the Crown Court: (R v Devizes Youth Court ex parte A and others (2000); (R v C (a Minor) TLR 5/7/2000).

Where a youth is to be tried in the Crown Court, whether alone or jointly with other youths or adults, it is essential that a full record is made on the file, and that note copied in the brief to Counsel showing the detailed considera-tion that has been given to the question of venue .The file endorsement and brief should also include the details of the representations made to the youth court and case law relevant to sentencing.

Sentencing

E.06   Courts must have regard to the Sentencing Guidelines Council Definitive Guideline 'Overarching Principles – Sentencing Youths (November 2009).' This Guideline does not supersede the Sentencing Guidelines Council Definitive Guidelines on Sexual Offences Act 2003 and Robbery, which both set out principles to be applied for young offenders.

In determining the sentence, the key elements for consideration are:

The age of the offender (chronological and emotional); The seriousness of the offence; The likelihood of further offences being committed; The extent of harm likely to result from those further offences. The approach to sentence will be individualistic , Proper regard should be had to the mental health and capability of the young person, and to any learning disability, learning difficulty, speech and language difficulty or other disorder, which is likely to affect the likelihood of these purposes being achieved. (SGC Guideline paragraph 4)

YOUTH OFFENDERS[3]

Sexual Offences and Child Abuse by Young Offenders

This guidance expands on, and should be read in conjunction with other specific sections elsewhere in Legal Guidance, such as Rape and Sexual Offences. Also note the Notification requirements. Any decision to prosecute or not to prosecute should be free of discrimination on the grounds of sexual orientation and gender.   E.07

If an allegation of any sexual abuse committed by a youth offender has been fully investigated and there is sufficient evidence to justify instituting proceedings, the balance of the public interest must always be carefully considered before any prosecution is commenced. Positive action may need to be taken at an early stage of offending of this type. Although a youth caution or youth conditional caution may provide an acceptable alternative in some cases, in reaching any decision, the police and the CPS will have to take into account fully the view of other agencies involved in the case, in particular the Social Services. The consequences for the victim of the decision whether or not to prosecute, and any views expressed by the victim or the victim's family, should also be taken into account.

In child abuse cases, it will be important to have the views of the Social Services on file if at all possible, as well as any background or history of similar conduct, information about the relationship between the two and the effect a prosecution might have on the victim.

Any case referred to the CPS for advice, or in which a prosecution does proceed, must be dealt with as quickly as possible to minimise the delay before the case comes to court.

---

[3] *http://www.cps.gov.uk/legal/v_to_z/youth_offenders/* [Accessed April 30, 2016].

Irrespective of whether the evidence is sufficient to found a criminal prosecution, The Social Services will consider taking civil action, such as care proceedings, to protect the child. The police and the CPS may well be asked to disclose evidence to assist in this process. Great care should be taken to follow the guidance set out in the section on disclosure to third parties Refer to Disclosure of Material to Third Parties.

Rape and other offences against children under 13 (sections 5 to 8 Sexual Offences Act 2003)

E.08   CCPs or DCCPs must be notified of any such case where there are both defendants and victims under the age of 13. This includes cases which are diverted from prosecution, whether on evidential or public interest grounds.

All such cases must be reviewed by a prosecutor who is both a rape specialist and a youth specialist. All advocates conducting these cases must have a rape specialism and should also have a youth specialism. Where the Full Code Test is satisfied in a case in which a youth is suspected of committing a sexual offence involving a child under the age of 13, the appropriate charge will be an offence contrary to sections 5 to 8 Sexual Offences Act 2003, depending on the act, and not the lesser offence contrary to section 13 Sexual Offences Act 2003.

Rape of a child under 13 (section 5), assault of a child under 13 by penetration (section 6) and causing or inciting a child under 13 to engage in sexual activity that involves penetration (section 8) are indictable only offences with a maximum sentence of life imprisonment. The offences of sexual assault of a child under 13 (section 7), causing or inciting a child under 13 to engage in sexual activity where there has been no penetration (section 8) are punishable on indictment with imprisonment for a term not exceeding 14 years. They are all grave crimes for the purposes of section 24 Magistrates Courts Act 1980 and section 91 Powers of Criminal Courts (Sentencing) Act 2000.

A mistaken belief that the child under 13 was 16 or over and consented to intercourse is not a defence to an allegation of rape of a child under 13, assault of a child under 13 by penetration, sexual assault of a child under 13 or causing or inciting a child under 13 to engage in sexual activity contrary to sections 5 to 8 Sexual Offences Act 2003 respectively.

When reviewing a case, in which a youth under 18 is alleged to have committed an offence contrary to sections 5 to 8, prosecutors should obtain and consider:

- the views of local authority Children's and Young People's Service;

- any risk assessment or report conducted by the local authority or youth offending service in respect of sexually harmful behaviour (such as AIM (Assessment, Intervention and Moving On);
- background information and history of the parties;
- the views of the families of all parties.

Careful regard should be paid to the following factors:

- the relative ages of both parties;
- the existence of and nature of any relationship;
- the sexual and emotional maturity of both parties and any emotional or physical effects as a result of the conduct;
- whether the child under 13 in fact freely consented (even though in law this is not a defence) or a genuine mistake as to her age was in fact made;
- whether any element of seduction, breach of any duty of responsibility to the girl or other exploitation is disclosed by the evidence;
- the impact of a prosecution on each child involved.

If the sexual act or activity was in fact genuinely consensual and the youth and the child under 13 concerned are fairly close in age and development, a prosecution is unlikely to be appropriate. Action falling short of prosecution may be appropriate. In such cases, the parents and/or welfare agencies may be able to deal with the situation informally.

However, if a very young child has been seduced by a youth, or a baby-sitter in a position of responsibility has taken advantage of a child under 13 in his/her care, prosecution is likely to be in the public interest. Where a child under 13 has not given ostensible consent to the activity, then a prosecution contrary to sections 5 to 8 is likely to be the appropriate course of action.

There is a fine line between sexual experimentation and offending and in general, children under the age of 13 should not be criminalised for sexual behaviour in the absence of coercion, exploitation or abuse of trust. Refer to Sexual Offences guidance.

Child sex offences committed by children or young persons

Section 13 of the 2003 Act makes it an offence for a youth under 18 to have   **E.09**
sexual activity with a child under 16, cause or incite a child under 16 to engage in sexual activity, engage in sexual activity in the presence of a child under or cause a child under 16 to watch a sexual act. These offences are punishable on indictment with imprisonment for a term not exceeding 5 years. They are grave crimes for the purposes of section 24 Magistrates Courts Act 1980 and section 91 Powers of Criminal Courts (Sentencing) Act

2000. Section 13 (2) (a) purports to restrict the maximum penalty on summary conviction to a maximum of 6 months imprisonment, although this should be read in the light of section 101 (2) Powers of Criminal Courts (Sentencing) Act 2000 to allow a Detention and Training Order of up to 24 months.

An offence is not committed if the child is over 13 but is under 16 and the youth has a reasonable belief that the child is 16 or over.

It should be noted that where both parties to sexual activity are under 16, then they may both have committed a criminal offence. However, the overriding purpose of the legislation is to protect children and it was not Parliaments intention to punish children unnecessarily or for the criminal law to intervene where it was wholly in appropriate. Consensual sexual activity between, for example, a 14 or 15 year-old and a teenage partner would not normally require criminal proceedings in the absence of aggravating features. The relevant considerations include:

- the respective ages of the parties;
- the existence and nature of any relationship
- their level of maturity;
- whether any duty of care existed;
- whether there was a serious element of exploitation.

Refer also to Sexual Offences.

Prostitution

E.10 Youth offender prostitution, whether involving young girls or boys, can be one of the most difficult types of cases to deal with. The young people concerned are likely to be extremely vulnerable and present complex emotional problems.

When reviewing a case involving youth offender prostitution it is *essential* that you are aware of and familiar with the inter-agency guidance entitled Safeguarding Children Involved in Prostitution, published in 2000. See also Prostitution, elsewhere in the Legal Guidance.

The aim of this guidance is to both safeguard and promote the welfare of children, and to encourage the investigation and prosecution of criminal activities by those who coerce, exploit and abuse children through prostitution. One of the key purposes of the guidance is to encourage the agencies and professionals involved to treat a child (defined as a boy or girl under the age of 18) involved in prostitution as primarily a victim of abuse.

Paragraph 6.21 of the guidance states that the approach to be adopted in cases of child prostitution is one of diversion of the child from the criminal justice system and a welfare approach is to be adopted. At paragraphs 6.21-6.30, the guidance sets out the approach to be followed when deciding whether it will be appropriate to prosecute or administer a reprimand or final warning to a child involved in prostitution. This section of the Guidance replaces the Home Office Circular 109/50 insofar as the Circular dealt with the cautioning of a child, male or female, under the age of 18 involved in prostitution.

Familial Sexual Offences

Sections 25 and 26 Sexual Offences Act 2003 create the offences of sexual   E.11
activity with a child family member and inciting a child family member to engage in sexual activity. These offences are punishable on indictment with imprisonment for a term not exceeding 5 years. They are grave crimes for the purposes of section 24 Magistrates Courts Act 1980 and section 91 Powers of Criminal Courts (Sentencing) Act 2000. Section 25 (5) (b) and 26 (5) (b) purport to restrict the maximum penalty on summary conviction to a maximum of 6 months imprisonment, although this should be read in the light of section 101 (2) Powers of Criminal Courts (Sentencing) Act 2000 to allow a Detention and Training Order of up to 24 months.

Sections 64 and 65 Sexual Offences Act 2003 make it an offence for a person aged 16 or over to penetrate or consent to penetration by a family member who is aged 18 or over. The maximum penalty is imprisonment for a term not exceeding 2 years (sections 64 (5) and 65 (5)).

In cases of sexual activity between siblings, care should be taken to balance the public interest in prosecuting such conduct with the interests and welfare of the victim and the family unit. As a general rule, alternatives to prosecution should be sought where the sexual activity was wholly consensual. The welfare agencies will normally intervene.

Prosecution should be considered where there is evidence of:

- seduction;
- coercion;
- exploitation or violence;
- a significant disparity in age;

In all cases the effect of prosecution on a victim and family should be taken into account and if the views of the welfare agencies are not included with the file they should be sought.

GUIDELINES ON PROSECUTING CASES OF CHILD SEXUAL ABUSE[4]

E.12
- Introduction
- Early consultation between the police and CPS
- How cases will be managed within the CPS
- Context and circumstances of child sexual abuse
- Supporting victims and witnesses
  - Before the court case
  - Independent Sexual Violence Advisers
  - Attending court
  - Keeping victims and witnesses informed
- Counselling and therapy
- The statement taking stage
- Telling a victim about other allegations
- The credibility or reliability of a child or young person
- Identifying children who may be at risk of sexual exploitation
- Merits-based approach
- Previous convictions of the child/young witness
- Assessing the credibility of child abuse allegations: circumstances of the suspect
- Other case building issues
- Offending patterns/behaviour of the offender
- Case presentation in court
  - Myths and stereotypes raised in court
  - Defence case statement
- Special measures
- Support given to victims and witnesses in court
- Adult victims of childhood sexual abuse
- Witnesses who withdraw support for the prosecution or indicate that they are no longer willing to give evidence
- Criminal and family proceedings
  - Role of the police and CPS in Family Proceedings
- Third party material
- Protocol with the Local Authority
- Obtaining material relating to Family Court proceedings
- Information sharing between agencies
- Annex A
- Annex B

[4] *http://www.cps.gov.uk/legal/a_to_c/child_sexual_abuse/* [Accessed April 30, 2016].

- Annex C
- Annex D
- Annex E

Introduction

1. These guidelines are designed to set out the approach that prose-   E.13
   cutors should take when dealing with child sexual abuse cases.
   Experience has shown that these cases bring with them particular
   issues that differentiate them from other types of case particularly
   in terms of, for example, a victim's response both to the sexual
   abuse and the subsequent intervention by the police. These guidelines are intended to cover the range of child sexual abuse, including
   the abuse referred to as 'child sexual exploitation' and which
   featured for example in the cases of *R v Safi, Aziz, Hassan and
   others* ('Operation Span') and *R v Jamil, Dogar, Dogar, Hussain,
   Karrar, Karrar and Ahmed* ('Operation Bullfinch'). The guidelines
   are intended to be inclusive and should be applied to cases where a
   sexual offence has been committed against a child or young person,
   unless there are good reasons why not in a particular case and these
   reasons are noted clearly by the prosecutor. The guidelines also
   include cases of adult victims of sexual abuse in childhood. These
   guidelines replace the interim guidelines issued on 11 June 2013 and
   come into immediate effect.
2. The guidelines will on occasion refer to victims as 'she' or 'her'.
   However, we fully recognise that boys as well as girls can be victims
   of child sexual abuse and the principles stated below, where
   relevant, will apply equally to boys as well as girls. Similarly
   offenders are known to be female as well as male, although it is
   recognised that the majority of offenders are male.
3. The guidelines should be read in conjunction with other relevant
   guidance, including the CPS Rape and Sexual Offences (RASO)
   Legal Guidance which sets out the approach to be taken in cases
   involving allegations of rape and sexual assault. Of particular
   relevance are:
   - Chapter 2, RASO Legal Guidance, which sets out the principal
     offences of the Sexual Offences Act 2003;
   - Chapter 3, RASO Legal Guidance, which deals with the issue of
     consent;
   - Chapter 21, RASO Legal Guidance, which discusses some of the
     myths and stereotypes around rape and sexual violence;
   - CPS Youth Offenders Legal Guidance, section Sexual Offences
     and Child Abuse by Young Offenders; and
   - Human Trafficking and Smuggling Legal Guidance, which sets
     out detailed advice on trafficking related issues.

Early consultation between the police and CPS

E.14   4. In large or complex child sexual abuse cases there should be early consultation between the police and the CPS. The CPS should be consulted on and informed of the investigation strategy so that early advice can be provided to the police if necessary. The decision to involve the CPS at an early stage is a matter for the police but experience has shown that early CPS involvement can help address some of the evidential or presentational issues that may arise at a later stage of a case.

5. It is important that the police and CPS work closely together and, in more complex cases, joint case review meetings should take place periodically so that progress can be checked and advice on case matters can be given. The frequency and timing of the meetings will be dictated by the size and scale of the investigation and prosecution. However, it is important that these take place so that a strong prosecution case can be built.

How cases will be managed within the CPS

E.15   6. The relevant CPS point of contact for the police is the Rape and Serious Sexual Offences (RASSO) Unit in each CPS Area. The RASSO Unit is a specialist prosecutor unit which provides a central point of expertise in the CPS Area and conducts the prosecution of all rape and serious sexual offences cases locally, including child sexual abuse cases.

7. In particular, the local police should be aware of the identity and contact details of the CPS Area Child Sexual Abuse (CSA) lead. The Area CSA lead is based in the Area RASSO Unit. They have an important role as they are specialist rape prosecutors who provide particular expertise, guidance and good practice in child sexual abuse cases. The police are encouraged to use the Area CSA lead as the single CPS point of contact in these cases, at least initially until case ownership is allocated within the RASSO Unit.

8. The Area CSA leads are also part of a national CPS network established to ensure that best practice is shared and overseen by the National CSA lead. The roles and responsibilities of the National and Area CSA leads can be found at Annex A. The national CPS network will support and play an important role in raising the level of expertise within the CPS to prosecute child sexual abuse cases and support training initiatives in this area. In addition, the DPP has extended the remit of rape advocates on the Advocates Panel to include other sexual offences involving children. This means that

advocates prosecuting in court in all child sexual abuse cases will now be specialists and will have had appropriate training.

Context and circumstances of child sexual abuse

9. Child sexual abuse covers a range of offending behaviour and types of offenders (which is defined in more detail in Annex B). It is therefore important that prosecutors have regard to the context and circumstances in which the offending is alleged to have taken place, as this will determine how the evidential case should be built and what are relevant lines of enquiry.   E.16

10. There is no one model of child sexual abuse. Sexual abuse of children and young people can be perpetrated by family members, family friends, girlfriends and boyfriends, gangs, 'peer on peer', strangers, adults via the internet and people in positions of trust such as teachers or carers. Institutional sexual abuse may occur in any care, health, religious, or academic setting and may be carried out by an individual or group of individuals. Children who are very young or with special needs may be particularly vulnerable to abuse.

11. Online grooming and abuse can take place through chat rooms and social networking sites and gaming devices which have the ability to connect to the internet. Offenders may target hundreds of children at a time and once initial contact with a child is made this can escalate into threats and intimidation. The online abuse can be an end in itself without any contact offences taking place, but in other cases contact offences can occur.

12. Coercion and manipulation often feature in abusive situations so that the perception of what is happening is sometimes difficult for the child or young person to understand. Offenders may groom not only the child or young person but also their family which can mean that the parent or guardian trusts the offender as a friend of the family or potential boyfriend. Conversely, an offender might make threats to the child or young person or members of their family in order to keep them in an abusive situation.

13. Child sexual abuse comes in a number of different forms. Sexual abuse by coordinated networks is a form of child sexual abuse that has become more prominent recently and is referred to as child sexual exploitation (which is defined in more detail in Annex B). These networks may be informal clusters of people linked through a set of victims or 'friendship' groups or they can be more organised criminal groups or gangs. Children and young people may be groomed into 'party' lifestyles where they go to houses, flats, hotels and bed and breakfast accommodation with numerous men and other child victims. Sometimes a single relationship may be formed, but in some cases, there is no single relationship and instead a

general network exists. The 'parties' are usually organised by adults with young people sometimes being coerced into bringing friends along.

14. Offenders may avoid suspicion by taking victims to be abused only for a short time, or during school hours or returning them home before anyone considers them to be missing or absent. The fact that a victim of abuse is maintaining a seemingly normal routine does not mean that they cannot have been the victim of sexual abuse.

15. Prosecutors should also be aware that offenders may use various control elements as a tool to stop a victim reporting the sexual abuse. For example the control might take the form of threatening to publish photographs or recordings of them, including images of them naked or being abused or threatening harm to the victim and/ or their family. The exertion of control could sometimes be through the offender implicating the victim in other criminal activity (e.g. possession of illegal drugs or shoplifting).

16. Another example of the offender exerting control over the victim, which might be particularly relevant to some Black and Minority Ethnic (BME) communities, is that the offender may claim the victim has brought shame on their family and use this as a means of controlling them. In this regard, prosecutors should be aware of the additional cultural barriers that some BME victims might face in coming forward and reporting abuse, as there may be pressure on the victim about what damage such allegations might do to the standing or 'honour' of their family.

Supporting victims and witnesses

E.17   17. Victims and witnesses should be made aware from the outset of the investigation exactly what is expected of them, particularly in terms of attending court and giving evidence, and they should be offered support to help them in the process. Support for victims and witnesses can be provided in a number of ways before, during, and after criminal proceedings. It is important that the need for support is identified early and kept under close review during the progress of the case. Prosecutors should proactively raise this matter in case discussions with the police and other relevant agencies so that victims and witnesses are given the best possible support. Where appropriate, parents and guardians should also be made aware from the outset what is expected and the support that can be offered. (It would be inappropriate if a parent or guardian was at the centre of the allegations).

18. It is also important to recognise that since many of the victims and witnesses will be children or young people, the support available before, during and after trial in court should be explained to them in age appropriate terms (or developmentally appropriate terms) so

that they understand what is being discussed and, where possible and appropriate, the parents or guardians are involved and the support available is also discussed with them. It should be noted that this support is distinct and separate from counselling (which is dealt with in paragraphs 32 to 34 below).

19. Some police forces may appoint Family Liaison Officers or officers with a similar role to support victims of child sexual abuse.

Before the court case

20. Children and young people who have been the subject of sexual abuse are likely to require a very high level of support. The police will be responsible primarily for facilitating this, although they will not be responsible for delivering emotional or psychological support. Achieving Best Evidence in Criminal Proceedings – Guidance on interviewing victims and witnesses, and guidance on using special measures (ABE) provides guidelines for pre-trial preparation of young victims and witnesses and should be followed closely. The guidance (re-published in 2011) provides assistance for those responsible for conducting video-recorded interviews with vulnerable and intimidated witnesses as well as those tasked with preparing and supporting witnesses during the criminal justice process. **E.18**

21. The prosecutor has an important part to play in ensuring that the requisite support is provided and should be asking questions about this from the outset of their involvement in the case. Prosecutors should be aware of the type of support available and, if necessary, should be able to signpost this support to the child or young person (or their parent/carer) via the police officer in the case or the Witness Care Unit, as appropriate.

22. Specialised support is provided by a range of organisations and such support is likely to be essential in ensuring that the child or young person (and where appropriate, their parents or guardian) maintains their engagement with the criminal justice process. Support can be provided by a wide range of agencies both local and national, e.g. Rape Crisis England and Wales, the Survivor's Trust, National Society for the Prevention of Cruelty to Children, and Barnardo's. In some areas, the Witness Service/Victim Support provides a specialist Young Witness Service, and there are also other specialist support services such as Independent Sexual Violence Advisors (ISVAs) that play an important role and should be considered as a vital source of support.

Independent Sexual Violence Advisers

23. ISVAs support victims of rape and sexual violence, including victims of child sexual abuse. They are victim-focused advocates **E.19**

who work with people who have experienced sexual violence, helping them to access the support services that they may need. They are independent from the police and are distinct from therapists, counsellors and Registered Intermediaries.

24. The support provided by an ISVA will vary from case to case, depending on the requirements of the victim and their particular circumstances. However, the main role of an ISVA includes making sure that victims of sexual abuse have the best possible practical advice on: the counselling and other services available to them; the process involved in reporting a crime to the police; and taking their case through the criminal justice process, should they choose to do so.

25. Prosecutors should know whether ISVAs operate in their area and whether they specifically provide support to victims of child sexual abuse.

Attending court

E.20

26. Attendance at court for trial should be discussed in advance with the victim or witnesses (and where appropriate, their parents/ guardian) in order that any fears can be addressed, such as being cross examined or being seen entering the court building by the defendants and their associates. Wherever possible, practical arrangements should be made to address the concern, e.g. visits to court to take place in advance of the trial so that the victim can familiarise themselves with the venue and processes involved; and by using entrances and/or using vehicles at the trial itself that facilitate discreet arrival and departure from court. This discussion should take place more than once as the victim or witness may change their mind, or have new concerns, the nearer it gets to the date of the trial.

27. With the approval of the court, a victim or witness can have a supporter present when being cross examined in a live link room for the purposes of providing emotional support to reduce anxiety and distress and improve the accuracy of their recall. The Youth Justice and Criminal Evidence Act 1999, as amended by the Coroners and Justice Act 2009, provides that, when making a live links direction and after taking into account the views of the witness, the court may also direct that a person specified by the court can accompany the person when giving evidence by live link. This person could be, for example, a volunteer from Victim Support or the Witness Service or from a more specialised support service such as the NSPCC or an ISVA. There are also a number of smaller local support services who can also provide effective support and should be considered. Where the trial is taking place in a court some

distance away from where the victim or witness usually reside, active consideration should be given as to whether the victim or witness in these circumstances can give evidence by live link from a location nearer to their home.

28. The role of the supporter in the live link room is to provide emotional support and they must have received appropriate training. Victim Support and other support organisations locally may provide this service. The supporter should have a relationship of trust with the witness, should not be a party to, or a witness in, the case and must only have basic information about the case.

29. Supporting and engaging with victims (and where appropriate, their parents/guardian) should continue after the court process has concluded, regardless of the outcome, and is often provided by the relevant support organisations. There may also still be risks to the victim that need to be reduced and managed by the police and other agencies including social services; the victim may still be at risk of further exploitation by others.

Keeping victims and witnesses informed

30. The Code of Practice for Victims of Crime (the Victims' Code) sets   **E.21** out the minimum standard of service and aims to ensure that victims of crime are provided with timely, accurate information about their case at all stages of the criminal justice process. Prosecutors should be aware of these minimum obligations.

31. The nature and sensitivity of child sexual abuse cases will inevitably mean that prosecutors (and the police) should go beyond the minimum requirements of the Victims' Code where appropriate to do so, and this should be agreed, recorded and actioned by the prosecutor and the police in the case.

Counselling and therapy

32. The CPS guidance Provision of Therapy for Child Witnesses Prior   **E.22** to a Criminal Trial is clear that the best interests of the victim or witness are the paramount consideration in decisions about therapy. There is no bar to a victim seeking pre-trial therapy or counselling and neither the police nor the CPS should prevent therapy from taking place prior to a trial. Prosecutors should be familiar with the content of the CPS guidance on pre-trial therapy so that they can advise police and witnesses on the correct approach.

33. Providers of counselling or therapy should ensure that records are kept and that the child or young person (and if relevant, parents or guardian) is advised at the start of the process that there may be a requirement to disclose the fact that counselling has taken place,

particularly if detail of the alleged offending is raised. Experience over a number of years has shown that properly conducted and recorded counselling or therapy has not caused problems with the criminal trial process. Where the therapist or counsellor is known to the investigation, they should be briefed at an early stage to inform them about the court process and their disclosure obligations.

34. Prosecutors have a duty to disclose the fact that a victim has undergone therapy or counselling and to disclose any other matter which is determined by the usual tests as to whether it is relevant to an issue in the case. This is part of the continuing duty on the CPS to disclose.

The statement taking stage

35. Particular care should be given when deciding how to take the victim's statement. A video recorded interview (and subsequent use of the live link in court) is often the most appropriate means but may not always be so. For example, if the abuse of the victim has been filmed and the victim does not want to be videoed as a consequence.

36. Practical matters to consider when visually recording a victim's interview include ensuring that there is a close shot of the head and shoulders of the witness, even if slightly side on, rather than from a distance where facial characteristics are too remote. Consideration should also be given, if possible, to a second camera showing the witness's more general body language.

37. The assistance of a Registered Intermediary should be considered at this stage. They can help the victim give their account in the interview and understand what is being asked of them. The earlier the intervention the more likely it is that successful rapport building will take place and the child or young person will be able to give their best evidence. Even if the victim appears to understand, they are unlikely to be familiar with the terms sometimes used in questions posed in interviews, or may not understand a term in the same way as the interviewer, and an Intermediary can ensure that age appropriate language (or developmentally appropriate language) is used and terms are explained.

38. A victim of child sexual abuse may not give their best and fullest account during their first recorded (ABE) interview or statement. This may be for a variety of reasons: they could have been threatened; they might be fearful for themselves or their family; the offending may have been reported by others and they may be reluctant to cooperate at that stage. They might not have identified themselves as a victim or they could be fearful that the police will not believe their allegations. They may initially distrust the police

and could well use the interview to test the credibility of the police.

39. The account given may take a number of interviews, with the child or young person giving their account piecemeal, sometimes saving the 'worst' till last, having satisfied themselves that they can trust the person to whom they are giving their account.

40. Carefully thought out patient intervention by the police and other agencies can ultimately disrupt and break the link to the offender(s). A seemingly contradictory initial account is therefore not a reason in itself to disbelieve subsequent accounts given by the victim and these contradictory accounts should instead be seen as at least potentially symptomatic of the abuse.

41. The police must inform the victim of their right to make a Victim Personal Statement (VPS) and it would be appropriate to do this at the statement taking stage. Whether and when to make a VPS is a decision for the victim, and it is therefore important that police clearly explain the purpose of the VPS and the way in which it will be used (i.e. that it will be disclosed to the defence, may be read out or played in court and could be reported on in the media). It should also be made clear that if the victim does not wish to make a VPS at the time they give their evidential statement, they may make a VPS later. Careful consideration should be given to when and how to take the VPS, taking into account the issues highlighted in paragraphs above, including talking to the parents or guardian if appropriate.

Telling a victim about other allegations

42. There is no rule which prevents victims being told that they are not the only ones to have made a complaint of abuse. If such a rule existed, and it was taken to its logical conclusion, it would mean that any victim who came forward having learned about offences committed against others could never pursue his or her own complaint. **E.24**

43. In terms of enabling a child or young person to give an account of what has occurred to them, they can be told, in very general terms, that the suspect has been the subject of complaints by others. Doing so may strengthen their resolve to continue their engagement with the criminal justice process.

44. In most circumstances this should only be done after the victim's statement has been given or a video interview has taken place. However, in exceptional circumstances, and with the authorisation of a police officer of at least Superintendent rank, this may take place before the statement has been given or a video interview has

taken place if it is considered to be necessary in all the circumstances of the case.

45. However, the details of the other allegations should not be disclosed and a careful record should be kept of what the child or young person has been told.

46. Informing a victim of the existence of other allegations of a similar nature or proactively contacting a potential victim based on a clear intelligence assessment (e.g. they are known to associate with the suspect) is very different to what is sometimes referred to as 'trawling'.

47. The term 'trawling' is used in this context to describe the process whereby the police contact potential victims even though they have not been named in any of the statements given in the course of the investigation and there is little if any intelligence to suggest the individual might be a potential victim. Such a process should be avoided because of the risk that it may give rise to false allegations. For example, in some cases involving allegations of abuse in a care home, it had been police practice years ago to contact all, or a significant proportion of, those who had been resident in the institution at the time that the offences were alleged to have taken place, rather than taking an intelligence-led approach towards identifying potential victims. This practice of "trawling" was criticised heavily in court and led to a number of cases collapsing, but contacting potential victims on a firm intelligence or evidence led basis is not prevented.

The credibility or reliability of a child or young person

E.25

48. When assessing the credibility of a child or young person, police and prosecutors should focus on the credibility of the allegation, rather than focussing solely on the victim.

49. A number of factors have previously militated against some children and young people being regarded as credible victims of sexual abuse. These include:
    ○ the offence was not reported immediately after its commission;
    ○ the account given was inconsistent;
    ○ the victim 'voluntarily' returned to the alleged abuser;
    ○ the victim has a learning disability or mental illness;
    ○ the victim is perceived as consenting to sexual activity;
    ○ the victim has previously told untruths about other matters; and the victim has been, or is, abusing drink or drugs.

50. These factors have tended to be seen as undermining the credibility of the victim's account. However, these factors may, in fact, point the other way and could be seen as supporting the allegations of sexual abuse, not least because the behaviour set out above are often

seen in victims of abuse. Police and prosecutors should therefore look to build a case which looks more widely at the credibility of the overall allegation rather than focusing primarily on the credibility and/or reliability of the child or young person.

51. A victim's circumstances or experiences will often influence their actions and it is important that prosecutors have an understanding of these issues. Victims of sexual abuse may have a chaotic background or lifestyle and they may not display the 'usual' behaviours that one might expect from a victim of a sexual offence. They may crave love and affection and wrongly attribute such feelings to their abuser. They may develop an allegiance to their abuser as a consequence and not consider themselves to be the victim of any type of sexual abuse. They might initially refuse to identify as a 'victim' of abuse, believing that they were in a genuine, loving and non-abusive relationship.

52. The victim may be reluctant to co-operate with those in authority or to participate in the criminal justice process. Inconsistent accounts are not uncommon in victims of child sexual abuse, especially during initial interviews, possibly because of an 'allegiance' to their abuser. The length of time between an alleged incident of sexual abuse and giving the account to the authorities is not a reliable indication of credibility.

53. Children or young people who have been in the care of, or have come to the attention of, social services will inevitably have a great deal of information about them contained within social services records compared to other children or young people. Every episode of 'bad' behaviour, even of the most minor nature, is likely to be a matter of record. Most children misbehave; but not every child has their misbehaviour recorded. Victims who are, or have been, in the care of the social services should not be disadvantaged in the criminal process by this fact, and prosecutors should be prepared to address this issue as part of the presentation of the prosecution case.

54. All of these factors must be taken into account and understood by prosecutors when reviewing allegations of child sexual abuse. Prosecutors must also have an understanding of the consequences faced by a child if they say 'no' to their abuser and this should form part of the prosecution strategy to address perceived weaknesses or anomalies in the victim's account.

55. Prosecutors should also have regard to whether there is any credible third party evidence to suggest that the complainant has malicious intent to make a false allegation. However, prosecutors should guard against looking for 'corroboration' of the victim's account or using the lack of 'corroboration' as a reason not to proceed with a case.

56. Prosecutors must check with the police and the CPS Case Management System (CMS) to see whether there are any pending allegations involving the same victim or suspect(s). A note that this has been done should form part of the formal review. If there are pending allegations then the details should be obtained to see if there are any links or similarities to the on-going case.

Identifying children who may be at risk of sexual exploitation

E.26   57. In 2012, the Office of the Children's Commissioner in England (OCCE) began an enquiry into child sexual exploitation in gangs and groups. The interim report of this enquiry (I thought I was the only one, the only one in the world) outlines a list of vulnerabilities which may be present in children prior to abuse and a further list of signs and behaviours generally seen in children who are already being sexually exploited. Prosecutors should consider whether the victim whose evidence they are considering demonstrates any of these factors. Whilst the absence of any of these characteristics does not mean that an allegation of exploitation is unlikely to be true, their presence may assist the prosecutor in forming an overall view in the case. The OCCE listed the following (pages 51-52 in the interim report, November 2012):

Typical vulnerabilities in children prior to abuse
- living in a chaotic or dysfunctional household (including parental substance use, domestic violence, parental mental health issues, parental criminality);
- history of abuse (including familial child sexual abuse, risk of forced marriage, risk of 'honour' based violence, physical and emotional abuse and neglect);
- recent bereavement or loss;
- gang association either through relatives, peers or intimate relationships (in cases of gang associated child sexual exploitation only);
- attending school with young people who are sexually exploited;
- learning disabilities;
- unsure about their sexual orientation or unable to disclose sexual orientation to their families;
- friends with young people who are sexually exploited;
- homeless;
- lacking friends from the same age group;
- living in a gang neighbourhood;
- living in residential care;
- living in hostel, bed and breakfast accommodation or a foyer;
- low self-esteem or self-confidence;
- young carer.

The following signs and behaviour are generally seen in children who are already being sexually exploited

- missing from home or care;
- physical injuries;
- drug or alcohol misuse;
- involvement in offending;
- repeat sexually-transmitted infections, pregnancy and terminations;
- absent from school;
- change in physical appearance;
- evidence of sexual bullying and/or vulnerability through the internet and/or social networking sites;
- estranged from their family;
- receipt of gifts from unknown sources;
- recruiting others into exploitative situations;
- poor mental health;
- self-harm;
- thoughts of or attempts at suicide.

Merits-based approach

58. As in all cases you must apply the test prescribed by the Code for   E.27
Crown Prosecutors, namely that there is sufficient evidence to provide a realistic prospect of conviction and a prosecution is required in the public interest. The 'merits-based approach' reminds prosecutors of how to approach the evidential stage of the Code test in that even though past experience might tell a prosecutor that juries can be unwilling to convict in cases where, for example, there has been a lengthy delay in reporting the offence, or the complainant had been drinking at the time the rape was committed. These sorts of prejudices against complainants should not be regarded as determinative for the purposes of deciding whether or not there is a realistic prospect of conviction.

59. In other words, the prosecutor should proceed on the basis of a notional jury which is wholly unaffected by any myths such as, for example, were an allegation really true it would have been reported at the time. The prosecutor must further assume that the jury will faithfully apply directions from the judge, such as the fact that they can still convict even where it is one person's word against another's without any supporting evidence.

Previous convictions of the child/young witness

60. Some victims of child sexual abuse may have previous convictions   E.28
which, on the face of it, may cast doubt upon their reliability as a

witness of truth. Robust enquiries should be made of the police about the circumstances of the offending before coming to any conclusion about the truthfulness or otherwise of the witness testimony.

61. Prosecutors are encouraged to look beyond the previous offending by the victim and consider the drivers and circumstances of the offending behaviour. Victims may sometimes commit what is called 'survival crime', i.e. committing crime to find safety or committing crime to ensure justice. An example of this is damaging property belonging to the offender or an associate. Offending might also be a reaction to the abuse which a child or young person is suffering, i.e. externally expressing their internal trauma. The victim may also have committed an offence whilst under the influence of the abuser and this may be used by the abuser as a means of controlling the victim and deterring them from making a complaint about the abuse they are experiencing.

62. Full details of a victim's previous convictions will be required from the police including:
   ○ type of offence;
   ○ location of offence;
   ○ who they were with, e.g. other young people or adults significantly older than them;
   ○ what explanation they gave to the police at the time of arrest or in interview; and
   ○ any other relevant circumstances.

63. A child or young person may even have played a role in procuring others who are then abused. In past cases there is evidence that this may have been as a direct consequence of violence, threats or coercion or because they were in a vulnerable situation and put in considerable fear. In such circumstances, careful thought must be given as to the role, if any, that child or young person plays in any potential prosecution.

64. It will be an essential part of the prosecution case to provide an explanation to the jury about the circumstances of any relevant offending by the witness, rather than it being put to the witness in the course of any cross examination.

Assessing the credibility of child abuse allegations: circumstances of the suspect

E.29   65. In child sexual abuse cases, the circumstances of the suspect need to be considered as intensely as the reliability of the complainant. Prosecutors should have regard to the following non-exhaustive list of evidential considerations:
   ○ are there any relevant antecedents in respect of the suspect

- o is there relevant police intelligence about the suspect in their local area or elsewhere;
- o has the suspect been the recipient of a child abduction warning notice (formerly known as the 'harbourer's warning') in relation to the victim in this case or any other child and young person;
- o is it likely that the suspect will have come into contact with the victim through the position or employment held by the suspect or the victim's lifestyle;
- o has the suspect been the subject of any other allegations of sexual abuse whether these have resulted in a conviction or not. In many abuse cases, there is often more than one victim and inquiries should be made as to whether there are further victims;
- o are there credible third party accounts supporting the allegations against the suspect or any other allegations made against the suspect;
- o is there any credible evidence showing the suspect in contact with the victim (e.g. CCTV, texts, social media);
- o does the suspect associate with others suspected of committing similar offences;
- o does the suspect have indecent images of children (e.g. on personal computer, mobile phone etc).

66. It is important that the prosecutor checks that the suspect's account has been investigated by the police in interview or through gathering further evidence. The questioning should ascertain whether the suspect deliberately targeted a victim's vulnerability and should disclose what their motivation was. If the suspect confirms that they know the victim, the prosecutor should ensure that the nature of the suspect's relationship with the victim is investigated by the police. This should include assessing whether the suspect is able to give a credible account of how and why they know the victim.

67. An early account should be taken from the suspect and the possibility of having to wait a significant period of time for comprehensive expert medical statements should not prevent an arrest taking place and an early explanation from the suspect.

Other case building issues

68. In some cases, the first complaint may not be from the victim but   E.30
from a concerned individual. The case may need to be built against the suspect before an account is obtained from the child or young person.

69. Partner agencies (e.g. social services, voluntary sector and other local support services) and, if appropriate, parents or carers, should be encouraged to involve the police as early as possible to ensure that information critical to a prosecution case is not lost. It is vital

that information is gathered and collated even in cases where the child or young person has not made a formal complaint. In many cases, the process of supporting a child or young person to recognise the exploitative nature of their relationship with the offender will be lengthy. By the time the child's account is given, crucial information could be lost or destroyed unless there is a strategy of evidence gathering from the outset.

70. Other types of evidence that should be gathered to help build a case before the child or young person gives a statement include: obtaining DNA evidence, including from clothing seized; obtaining mobile phone evidence; CCTV footage; car number plate recognition; house searches; and early consideration of directed or intrusive surveillance. The possibility of information coming from house to house enquiries should not be overlooked. Neighbours may well not have seen anything first hand but they could be a useful source of other information about the wider context. Other useful information could be obtained from friends of the victims and their peer group especially about the wider context.

71. In cases where the victim makes an initial allegation and then becomes uncooperative, a conventional investigation may be difficult. However, a review of the intelligence held by the police on any suspect(s) may be sufficient for a proactive operation to be commenced.

72. Child sexual abuse can involve certain patterns of behaviour; a police officer may be presented with an apparently minor issue which in isolation may not cause concern but which is actually a pattern of abuse. It is also possible that concerns about individual children that on the face of it are unconnected are in reality part of a pattern of abuse by either the same offender or different but connected offenders. Concerns about one child or young person may also raise concerns about other children or young people with whom the suspect has contact. Identifying such patterns depends upon careful, accurate and co-ordinated record keeping by the police and other agencies and also upon prosecutors being alert to the issue and asking the right questions.

Offending patterns/behaviour of the offender

E.31

73. People who abuse are not bound by geographic boundaries. Offenders may move victims from one place to another to be sexually exploited. The young victim may not know where they are when the abuse takes place. They may agree to travel between different locations and there may not be any coercion for them to do so.

74. Moving children and young people around may be part of a deliberate strategy by offenders to prevent any single police force

from obtaining a complete picture of the offending behaviour. The fact that a child or a young person is taken to an unfamiliar location can also make it harder for them to identify the time, date and location of the abuse.

75. Young people under 18 cannot consent to being moved for the commission of a relevant offence under the Sexual Offences Act 2003. The fact of the movement and the intent are sufficient for the offence to be proved. In these circumstances, as well as relevant 'contact offences', prosecutors should consider charges under section 58[5] of the Sexual Offences Act 2003. Fuller guidance on human trafficking and the associated set of issues is set out in the Legal Guidance on Human Trafficking and Smuggling.

Case presentation in court

76. For the reasons outlined above, the ABE interview process may be lengthy and the account by the victim may be given over a number of interviews, with the fullest account not being given until the final interview. The ABE interview is primarily an investigative tool but is also required for evidential purposes, but sometimes this dual purpose can cause presentational difficulties at court. Prosecutors should be familiar with police ABE procedures and mindful of the need for a clear and focused ABE interview to be presented at the trial. This will often mean that careful editing is required, and this should be done by the police and prosecutor as soon as is reasonably practical. (An unedited version of the videoed interview is disclosed to the defence unless Public Interest Immunity considerations apply).   **E.32**

Myths and stereotypes raised in court

77. It is very important that prosecutors use their best endeavours to ensure that 'myths and stereotypes' about child sexual abuse are challenged in court. For example, by ensuring that they are addressed in Counsel's opening speech to the jury, by challenging Defence Counsel, by adducing expert evidence where appropriate, or by asking the judge to give specific directions to the jury.   **E.33**

78. The Crown Court Bench Book sets out specimen directions for use by judges in the Crown Court. Chapter 17 The Trial of Sexual Offences addresses myths, stereotypes and generalisations that may influence jury members in their deliberations. Trial advocates

[5] Now replaced by the Modern Slavery Act 2015.

should take the lead in suggesting to the judge appropriate directions from the Bench Book for inclusion in his or her summing
up.

79. At Annex C, a number of common myths and stereotypes surrounding this type of offending have been set out including the basis
for rebutting them.

Defence case statement

E.34

80. Following service of initial disclosure by the prosecution, the time
limit for service of a defence statement and service of the details of
any defence witnesses is 14 days in the magistrates' court and 28
days in the Crown Court, unless that period has been extended by
the court.

81. The defence statement gives a valuable opportunity for the prosecution to confirm or rebut defence allegations and it is likely to point
the prosecution to other lines of inquiry, for example, the investigation of an alibi, or where forensic expert evidence is involved.

82. Where there is no defence statement, or it is considered inadequate,
the prosecutor should contact the defence indicating that further
disclosure will not take place or will be limited (as appropriate) and
inviting them to specify or clarify the defence case. Where the
defence fails to respond, or refuses to clarify the defence case, the
prosecutor should consider raising the issue at a pre-trial hearing to
invite the court to give a statutory warning under section 6E(2) of
the Criminal Procedure and Investigation Act 1996.

Special measures

E.35

83. There is separate CPS Legal Guidance on Special Measures which
sets out the full range of measures that can be applied for to the
court. By virtue of their age, children are automatically eligible for
special measures, although the measures will not automatically be
available at trial. An application for special measures needs to be
made by the party calling the witness. The decision as to whether
the special measure applied for is granted is a matter for the
court.

84. Prosecutors should discuss with the police, and consider carefully,
which, if any, of the special measures should be used. The views of
the victim (and where appropriate, their parents/guardian) should
be taken into account as well as the type of offending alleged.
Prosecutors should actively raise the issue of special measures with
the police if there is not a note of a discussion with the victim (and
where appropriate, their parents/guardian) and also ensure that the

measures requested are kept under close review as the date of the trial approaches.

85. We have referred to Registered Intermediaries in paragraph 37 above in respect of being involved at the interview stage with the victim. Intermediaries should be considered in all cases of child sexual abuse, not just those involving very young witnesses, and if not involved earlier in the case, they should still be actively considered in advance of the trial as a means of supporting the victim giving evidence in court. Children and young people do not approach communication in the same way as adults and ability across all age ranges can vary considerably.

86. Registered Intermediaries can be crucial in enabling witnesses to give their best evidence both at statement taking/interview stage and during the court process. If an Intermediary has not been used at the interview stage but communication needs are identified at the review stage this does not mean that they cannot be instructed for the court process. However, it is preferable for the need for a Registered Intermediary to be identified early in the process so that there is sufficient time for rapport building to take place.

"The use of intermediaries has introduced fresh insights into the criminal justice process. There was some opposition. It was said, for example, that intermediaries would interfere with the process of cross examination. Others suggested that they were expert witnesses or supporters of the witness. They are not. They are independent and neutral. They are properly registered. Their responsibility is to the court . . . their use is a step which improved the administration of justice and it has done so without a diminution in the entitlement of the defendant to a fair trial."

The Rt. Hon. The Lord Judge, Lord Chief Justice of England and Wales, 7 September 2012, speaking at the 17th Australian Institute of Judicial Administration Conference on 'Vulnerable Witnesses in the Administration of Criminal Justice'.

87. Registered Intermediaries fulfil a different role and purpose to that of a witness 'supporter' and the two roles should not be conflated.

88. Further, more detailed, information can be found in the CPS Special Measures: Intermediaries (including their engagement) Legal Guidance.

Support given to victims and witnesses in court

89. Comprehensive advice can be found on all aspects of case management and preparation for vulnerable victims and witnesses in the   E.36

Advocates' Gateway[6] and prosecutors should read and be familiar with its content, along with the Judicial College Bench Checklist for Young Witness Cases.

90. Prosecutors should assist the courts to ensure that effective time-tabling and case progression of child sexual abuse cases takes place. Cases involving children or young people should be heard as soon as possible, with delay for child victims kept to 'an irreducible minimum' (Part 3D General Matters of the Criminal Practice Directions 2013). Young witnesses should not be kept waiting at court and should know that the time given to attend court is when they give evidence so that they are not kept waiting around.

91. Trial dates should not be vacated unless this is absolutely unavoidable. This includes avoiding any last minute changes in Prosecution Counsel because of the disruption it can cause to victims and witnesses. If a change of Counsel does happen, it should only take place where it is unavoidable (for example, illness).

92. Ground rules hearings about cross examination in court are recommended in any young witness trial but required in any intermediary cases. This includes the defence agreeing who will be the lead counsel to put questions to the victim in cases with more than one defendant and the length of time given to the cross examination. The ground rules hearings should take place in advance of the day of the trial so that everyone, particularly the victim, is aware of what to expect and how long the proceedings in court should take. Prosecutors are reminded of rule 3.10 of the Criminal Procedure Rules that states:

Conduct of a trial

3.10[7] – In order to manage a trial or appeal the court –
   a) must establish, with active assistance of the parties, what are the disputed issues
   b) must consider setting a timetable that –
      i) takes account of those issues, and of any timetable proposed by a party, and
      ii) may limit the duration of any stage of the hearing
   c) may require a party to identify –
      i) which witness that party wants to give evidence in person
      ii) the order in which that party wants those witnesses to give their evidence
      iii) whether the party requires an order compelling the attendance of a witness

[6] See Appendix F.
[7] Now Rule 3.11 in the Criminal Procedure Rules 2015.

    iv) what arrangements are desirable to facilitate the giving of evidence by a witness

    v) what arrangements are desirable to facilitate the participation of any other person including the defendant

    vi) what written evidence that parties intend to introduce

    vii) what other material, if any, that person intends to make available to the court in the presentation of the case, and

    viii) whether the party intends to raise any point of law that could effect the conduct of the trial or appeal; and

  d) may limit –

    i) the examination, cross-examination or re-examination of a witness, and

    ii) the duration of any stage of the hearing.

Prosecutors should also assist the court in dealing with questioning of the victim or witness.

93. The Court of Appeal has addressed restrictions on cross examination:

   ○ where there is a risk of a child acquiescing to leading questions (*R v B* [2010] EWCA Crim 4); and

   ○ on 'putting your case' to a child (*R v Wills* [2011] EWCA Crim 1938 and *R v E* [2011] EWCA Crim 2028).

As the Court of Appeal observed in Wills:

"Some of the most effective cross-examination is conducted without long and complicated questions being posed in a leading or 'tagged' manner."

94. Where limits are 'necessary and appropriate', the Court of Appeal in *Wills* stated that:

   ○ limitations on questioning must be clearly defined;

   ○ the judge has a duty to ensure that limitations are complied with;

   ○ the judge should explain limitations to the jury and reasons for them;

   ○ if the advocate fails to comply with limitations, the judge should give relevant directions to the jury when that occurs; and

   ○ instead of commenting on inconsistencies during cross-examination, the advocate/judge may point out important inconsistencies after (instead of during) the witness's evidence, following discussion with the advocates. The judge should be alert to alleged inconsistencies that are not in fact inconsistent, or are trivial.

95. As set out in paragraphs 92 to 94 above, in multiple defendant cases the judge should be asked to consider whether repeat cross examination on similar points should be restricted. Being accused of lying, particularly if repeated, may cause the witness to give inaccurate answers or to agree simply to bring questioning to an end. It may also have a longer term damaging impact on the child or young person. If such a challenge is essential, it should be addressed separately, in simple language, at the end of cross examination.

Adult victims of childhood sexual abuse

E.37   96. Some victims of sexual abuse may not feel confident or strong enough to report until many years after the abuse has taken place, and often not until they are adults. This delay in reporting can be for a wide range of reasons, but many of the same considerations for child victims will also apply to adults who were victims of sexual abuse in their childhood, particularly around assessing the credibility of the overall allegation and the need for effective and proactive case-building.

97. Prosecutors should be mindful of the potential for severe re-traumatisation faced by some victims. The process of giving an account of the abuse may cause flashbacks where an adult finds themself in the same emotional state as when the sexual abuse took place and with the resilience and understanding of a child of that age. Consistent and effective support should be provided including keeping under constant review whether there is a need for counselling and special measures.

98. It is recognised that some adult victims of childhood sexual abuse may suffer severe mental health problems as a result of their experience and may never be able to give evidence in court. However, it should not be overlooked that they may have important information which might be of assistance in supporting the account given by other victim(s) against the same offender(s).

Witnesses who withdraw support for the prosecution or indicate that they are no longer willing to give evidence

E.38   99. Chapter 5 of the CPS Rape and Sexual Offences Legal Guidance deals with this issue in detail. In child sexual abuse cases, prosecutors must ensure that the reason for a victim's ostensible retraction is thoroughly investigated by the police before a decision about how to proceed is made. Prosecutors must be sure that the victim (and where appropriate, their parents/guardian) has had special measures and reporting restrictions (see the CPS Legal Guidance

Contempt of Court and Reporting Restrictions) explained to them thoroughly and in an age-appropriate way (or developmentally appropriate), as this may influence their decision to continue with the process.

100. Particular regard should be had to the highly organised nature of some offenders who will go to great lengths to ensure that if witness intimidation takes place it is several steps removed from them.

Criminal and family proceedings

101. Cases which involve criminal proceedings and family proceedings,   **E.39** together with their respective investigations, taking place either simultaneously or with some degree of overlap, can present challenges for the different agencies concerned. See Annex D for further information.

102. Proceedings in the Family Courts begin when a statutory body, usually the Local Authority, initiate care proceedings in relation to one or more children within a family unit. Such an application is usually based on the belief that the child or children have or are likely to suffer significant harm as a result of child abuse in one or more of the following: physical abuse; sexual abuse; emotional abuse; or neglect.

103. In any of the above circumstances, a child or children can be removed from the family under emergency powers conferred by either section 44 or 46 of the Children Act 1989.

104. In cases relating to the use of section 44 and 46, it is then the responsibility of the Local Authority under section 47 of the Children Act to make, or cause to be made, such enquiries as they consider necessary to enable them to decide what action they should take to safeguard or promote the child's welfare. This action is commonly known as a 'section 47 investigation' and in the majority of cases, will take the form of a joint enquiry conducted by both police and social workers from the Local Authority Children's Services, with police concentrating on the criminal aspect of the enquiry.

105. If a child is removed into police protection under section 46, then a maximum period of 72 hours is permitted before they must be returned to the family or an application is made to the Family Court for an 'emergency protection order' (EPO) under section 44 in order that further enquiries can be carried out as above. The EPO has effect for a period not exceeding 8 days, including any time already spent under police protection; although it can be extended once for a maximum of 7 days.

106. On expiration of this period, an application can be made to the Family Court for a care order under section 31. Once care

proceedings are issued, a first hearing will take place within three days at which the court may make an interim care order. It is then the responsibility of the court to draw up a timetable with a view to disposing of the application for a care order without delay.

Role of the police and CPS in Family Proceedings

E.40   107. When family proceedings are instituted to decide on the most appropriate care plan for any child or children subject to the proceedings, a number of preliminary hearings take place, followed in the latter stages by a fact finding hearing and a final determination hearing. It is likely that each 'party' to the proceedings will be represented.

      108. Parties to family proceedings are those who have an immediate claim to the care of the child, usually each parent and the Local Authority who have placed the child in care. A children's guardian, appointed by the court to represent a child's best interests, is also a party to the proceedings. Others can, on application to the court, become parties to the proceedings, or an 'intervener', such as potential carers or grandparents. However it is important to note that alleged perpetrators of sexual abuse are sometimes joined as parties or interveners and that where findings are sought in family proceedings against an alleged perpetrator that person is invited routinely by the family court to be so joined. They can be non-family members but are commonly also family members or partners of family members.

      109. The focus in the Family Courts is on establishing the facts and achieving the most appropriate outcome for the child, not on the prosecution of the alleged abuser.

      110. Therefore, despite the fact that police might be conducting a parallel criminal investigation into the actions of one or more of the parties against a child (or a sibling) who is the subject of the family proceedings, neither the police nor the CPS are parties to the family proceedings.

      111. It would neither be appropriate nor desirable for the police or CPS to be present throughout family proceedings. Many aspects of the hearings would be irrelevant to the criminal investigation and contempt issues may arise if the police or CPS make use in the criminal proceedings of material arising in the Family Court proceedings without the permission of the Family Court.

      112. If an alleged abuser were to incriminate himself/herself during the course of the family proceedings they would have the benefit of protection from prosecution by virtue of section 98(2) of the Children Act 1989, whereby a statement or admission made in such proceedings is not admissible against the person making it or his

spouse in criminal proceedings (other than for an offence of perjury).

113. Prosecutors should note that the protection in section 98(2) does not extend to the criminal investigation. The police may put relevant statements and admissions to a suspect in interview. If adopted by the suspect, the statements/admissions are admissible in criminal proceedings (subject to the usual provisions of sections 76 and 78 of the Police and Criminal Evidence Act 1984). Similarly, putting inconsistent statements made in Family Court proceedings to a defendant in cross examination in the criminal case should not be contrary to section 98 of the Children Act 1989.

Third party material

114. Chapter 4 of the Disclosure Manual sets out the procedure to be   E.41
adopted with reference to third party material. It is highly likely that many child sexual abuse cases will involve and require access to third party material when building the evidential case.

115. The following are examples of third party material which may be relevant: medical notes; social services/Children's Services material; education notes; counselling/therapy notes; information or evidence arising in parallel family/civil proceedings; or information kept by voluntary sector organisations.

116. Investigators are under a duty to pursue all reasonable lines of enquiry, whether these point towards or away from a suspect. Reasonable lines of enquiry may include enquiries as to the existence of relevant material in the possession of a third party, for example, the Local Authority.

117. If the third party declines or refuses to allow access to it, the matter should not be left. If, despite any reasons put forward by the third party, it is reasonable to seek production of the material or information and the requirements of section 2 of the Criminal Procedure (Attendance of Witnesses) Act 1965 are satisfied, then prosecutors should apply for a witness summons requiring a representative of the third party to produce the material to the court.

118. Third party material should be sought at an early stage, preferably pre charge, and sufficient time should be set aside to receive and process third party material, especially in particularly large or complex cases. The material may contain information that could enhance and strengthen the prosecution case.

Protocol with the Local Authority

119. Prosecutors and investigators should handle requests for Local   E.42
Authority material in accordance with any applicable local or

national protocol. The protocol will ensure that the Local Authority makes disclosure to the police and CPS to the full extent permitted by law (taking into account the common law of confidentiality, the Data Protection Act 1998 and the Family Procedure Rules 2010, see Annex E). The Local Authority will make all relevant material available to the police at the earliest opportunity, or provide reasons why certain material (listed but not described) is not being made available, for example because it is related to Family Court proceedings. The 2013 Protocol and Good Practice Model: Disclosure of information in cases of alleged child abuse and linked criminal and care directions hearings is available here.[8]

120. The police will take copies of all relevant Local Authority material which will then be scheduled for the CPS on the schedule of sensitive unused material. Where any of the material meets the Criminal Procedure and Investigations Act test for disclosure to the defence, the prosecutor should consult with the Local Authority before disclosure is made. There may be public interest reasons which justify withholding disclosure to the defence and which would require the issue of disclosure of the information to be placed before the court. However, following the decision of the House of Lords in *R v H & C* [2004] 2 AC 134, applications for public interest immunity will be rare. Prosecutors should make disclosure in summarised or redacted form where this is possible.

Obtaining material relating to Family Court proceedings

E.43

121. Relevant material might include statements and admissions made in the Family Court proceedings by defendants and witnesses in the criminal case, or might include expert testimony in the Family Court proceedings. There are a number of ways in which prosecutors will become aware of the existence of relevant material relating to Family Court proceedings. For example:

    o The police may have obtained the material from the Local Authority (or elsewhere) in line with their duties of child protection. Note that, in these circumstances, the police cannot share the material with the CPS (nor can they share with the CPS the information on which documentation is based) without the permission of the Family Court. The police have to simply alert the CPS to the fact that relevant Family Court material exists.

    o In accordance with the terms of a local or national protocol, the Local Authority may have alerted the CPS to the existence of relevant material relating to Family Court proceedings.

---

[8] *http://www.cps.gov.uk/publications/docs/third_party_protocol_2013.pdf* [Accessed April 30, 2016].

122. Prosecutors and investigators will determine whether to apply to the Family Court for permission to access such relevant material. Protocols may provide a streamlined process for making the application to the court; and may provide for the Local Authority to make the application on behalf of the police and CPS; or for the Family Court to make an order for disclosure without the need for an application. Any application to the Family Court should make it clear that the material might need to be shared with the defence and (subject to section 98 of the Children Act 1989) used in evidence.

123. The Family Procedure Rules 2010 provide that the text of summary of a judgment in Family Court proceedings can be disclosed to the police and CPS without the permission of the court. The Local Authority (or others) can disclose to the police and CPS documents which are lodged at the Family Court, or used in the proceedings which already existed.

124. A local or national protocol may provide for linked directions hearings at which directions in concurrent criminal and Family Court proceedings can be made jointly by the same judge. Directions will include disclosure of material between the two jurisdictions, timetabling of the respective proceedings and the coordination of the use of expert witnesses.

Information sharing between agencies

125. Working Together to Safeguard Children – A guide to inter-agency **E.44** working to safeguard and promote the welfare of children (2013) provides guidance about sharing information about children in England (and there is separate similar guidance applicable in Wales). In deciding whether there is a need to share information, professionals need to consider their legal obligations, including whether they have a duty of confidentiality. Where there is such a duty, the professional may lawfully share information if consent is obtained or if there is a public interest of sufficient weight. Where there is a clear risk of significant harm to a child, the public interest test will almost certainly be satisfied. Lack of consent to share information is irrelevant where there is a clear concern about a risk of harm to the child or young person.

126. Prosecutors must be proactive in highlighting to police officers information which is of concern to them. If it is not possible to prosecute a case, but information available causes concern to the prosecutor, they should ensure that this is brought to the attention of the relevant investigating police officers, so that they can in turn share this with the relevant agencies including Local Authorities.

127. Prosecutors who receive relevant cases from the police should check with the police that they have complied with their statutory duties

to share information with Local Authorities and any other relevant bodies. CPS case files should not be closed until this confirmation is received.

128. In addition to applying the above information sharing principles, prosecutors and investigators will need to ensure that disclosure does not prejudice the criminal investigation and prosecution. Material disclosed to the Local Authority will be shared with all parties to the Family Court proceedings and the parties are likely to include the defendant(s) and witnesses in the criminal case. The Local Authority may be able to secure a Family Court order prohibiting onward disclosure to named individuals, i.e. defendants and witnesses in the criminal case. Alternatively, it may be possible to delay disclosure of prosecution material to the Local Authority until a later date (although, other than in exceptional circumstances, the existence of criminal proceedings is not reason to adjourn Family Court proceedings). Prosecutors should consult with the police where the request for disclosure of prosecution material is made to the police.

Crown Prosecution Service
17 October 2013

Annex A

National Child Sexual Abuse lead

E.45 The National Child Sexual Abuse (CSA) lead will:

- oversee the national CSA Network drawing on their expertise in high profile CSA casework;
- encourage good practice and offer best practice guidance in CSA cases via the CSA Network;
- develop close relations with partner agencies, in particular with NPCC;
- liaise and work closely with CPS Headquarters to develop and disseminate good practice and identify aspects for improvement and issues for concern; and
- attend and play a leading part in the CSA review panel.

Area Child Sexual Abuse lead

E.46 The Area CSA lead will:

- meet the criteria set out in the standard for rape specialist prosecutors;

- act as an Area source of expertise, guidance and good practice for colleagues both locally and nationally dealing with child sexual abuse cases;
- be an initial single point of contact for police forces and other relevant agencies in their Area providing general advice and guidance in CSA cases;
- establish liaison with police CSA lead officers in order to review and develop local investigative practice;
- attend local partnership CSA strategic meetings to develop criminal justice improvements for victims and witnesses;
- maintain a CSA caseload;
- liaise and work closely with CPS Headquarters to develop and disseminate good practice and identify aspects for improvement and issues for concern;
- produce brief six monthly reports for the Director as part of the bi-annual VAWG Assurance collated through VAWG Coordinators;
- ensure that an Area overview of CSA investigations and prosecutions is maintained to include information about ethnicity, age, gender and offences where practicable;
- work closely with, and assist in training, the police and relevant voluntary sector agencies in relation to general good practice and procedure in relation to CSA cases;
- be a member of the national CPS CSA network, attending training events and seminars as required and maintaining regular dialogue with other CSA leads; and
- attend the CSA review panel when invited.

Annex B

Definitions

Child / Children / Young Person

Anyone who has not yet reached their 18th birthday. The fact that a child has   **E.47**
reached 16 years of age, is living independently or is in further education, is
a member of the armed forces, is in hospital or in custody in the secure estate,
does not change his/her status or entitlement to services or protection.

Abuse

A form of maltreatment of a child. Somebody may abuse or neglect a child   **E.48**
by inflicting harm, or by failing to prevent harm. Children may be abused in
a family or in an institutional or community setting by those known to them
or, more rarely, by others (e.g. via the internet). They may be abused by an
adult or adults, or another child or children.

Child sexual abuse

E.49 Involves forcing or enticing a child or young person to take part in sexual activities, not necessarily involving a high level of violence, whether or not the child is aware of what is happening. The activities may involve physical contact, including assault by penetration (for example, rape or oral sex) or non-penetrative acts such as masturbation, kissing, rubbing and touching outside of clothing. They may also include non-contact activities, such as involving children in looking at, or in the production of, sexual images, watching sexual activities, encouraging children to behave in sexually inappropriate ways, or grooming a child in preparation for abuse (including via the internet). Sexual abuse is not solely perpetrated by adult males. Women can also commit acts of sexual abuse, as can other children.

Child sexual exploitation

E.50 There is no specific offence of child sexual exploitation (CSE); it is defined in government guidance and policy in this way:

> 'The sexual exploitation of children and young people under 18 involves exploitative situations, contexts and friendships where young people (or a third person or persons) receive 'something' (e.g. food, accommodation, drugs, alcohol, cigarettes, affection, gifts, money) as a result of performing, and/or others performing on them, sexual activities.

> 'Child sexual exploitation can occur through the use of technology without the child's immediate recognition, for example the persuasion to post sexual images on the internet/mobile phones with no immediate payment or gain. In all cases those exploiting the child/young person have power over them by virtue of their age, gender, intellect, physical strength and/or economic or other resources.

> 'Violence, coercion and intimidation are common, involvement in exploitative relationships being characterised in the main by the child or young person's limited availability of choice resulting from their social/economic and/or emotional vulnerability.'

CSE can involve a broad range of exploitative activity, from seemingly 'consensual' relationships and informal exchanges of sex for attention, accommodation, gifts or cigarettes, through to very serious organised crime. Young people do not always receive something tangible in return for sexual activities; the promise of something or apparent love and affection may be all that they receive.

The police should know the nature, extent and type of offending they are investigating and will be expected to indicate whether they consider a case involves CSE. However, prosecutors also have a duty to identify potential CSE cases even if the police have omitted to do so. For example, often a case starts with one suspect and one victim in one location but if properly investigated may grow to meet the CSE criteria.

Grooming

'Grooming' is not a specific form of child sexual exploitation but should be seen as a way in which perpetrators target children and manipulate their environments. It is an approach to exploitation and may be the beginning of a complex process adopted by abusers. Grooming can be defined as developing the trust of a young person or his or her family in order to engage in illegal sexual activity or for others to engage in illegal sexual activity with that child or young person. **E.51**

Annex C

Myths and Stereotypes

It is very important that prosecutors use their best endeavours to ensure that 'myths and stereotypes' about child sexual abuse are challenged in court. If they are left unchallenged, it may lead to members of the jury approaching the victim's evidence with unwarranted scepticism. **E.52**

This Annex lists some of the more common myths and stereotypes and the basis for why they should be challenged. It should be stressed that the list below is non-exhaustive.

(a) The victim invited sex by the way they dressed or acted

This is an attempt to excuse the rape or sexual assault and blame the victim. It assumes that a child or young person who attracts attention by their dress or manner is looking for sex and excuses the behaviour of the abuser. A child or young person under 16 can never consent to sex whatever the circumstances. **E.53**

(b) The victim drank alcohol or used drugs and she was therefore available sexually

This is an attempt to excuse the abuser of rape or sexual assault and blame the victim. It assumes that as the child or young person was drunk or under the influence of drugs they were willing sexual partners. An adult is unable to consent to sex if they are drunk, drugged or unconscious, and a child or young person under 16 can never consent to sex whatever the circumstances. **E.54**

(c) The victim didn't scream, fight or protest and so it can't be sexual assault

E.55 It implies the victim is not telling the truth and invalidates the experience of the victim. Also, a child may experience a 'freeze' response to trauma meaning they become incapable of responding in an active way. It does not take account of how the victim's behaviour may have been influenced by threats whether real or perceived, or how manipulative techniques might have been used by the abuser to intimidate or control the victim. A child or young person under 16 can never consent to sex whatever the circumstances.

(d) If the victim didn't complain immediately it wasn't sexual assault

E.56 It implies the victim is not telling the truth and invalidates the experience of the victim. It does not take account of how the victim's behaviour may have been influenced by threats whether real or perceived, or how manipulative techniques might have been used by the abuser to intimidate or control the victim. A child or young person under 16 can never consent to sex whatever the circumstances.

In addition, the trauma can cause feelings of shame and guilt which might inhibit a victim from making a complaint. This was recognised by the Court of Appeal in **R v D (JA)** [2008] EWCA Crim 2557, where it was held that judges are entitled to direct juries that due to shame and shock, victims of rape might not complain for some time, and that "a late complaint does not necessarily mean it is a false complaint".

(e) A victim in a relationship with the alleged offender is a willing sexual partner

E.57 A child or young person under 16 can never consent to sex whatever the circumstances. It invalidates the experience of the victim and it does not take account of how the victim's relationship may have been influenced by threats whether real or perceived, or how manipulative techniques might have been used by the abuser to intimidate or control the victim. The grooming process can actively distort understanding of consent and is often used for that purpose. Feelings of powerlessness and fatalism are common amongst victims.

(f) A victim who has been sexually assaulted will remember events consistently

E.58 It implies the victim is not telling the truth and invalidates the experience of the victim. It also fails to take account of how children and young people do not have the same standards of logic, understanding and consistency as adults do. They will not have the same experience of life as adults and are less sophisticated in their understanding of what has happened. A child may not fully understand the significance of activity which is sexual and this may be reflected in how they remember or describe it. A child is very likely to have a different perception of time to that of an adult. Also the process by which memories are laid down during a traumatic event may impact on issues such as consistency. A child's memory can fade and their recall of when and in what order events took place may not be accurate. A child may not be able to speak of the context in which the events took place, and this may include having particular difficulty with conceptual questions as to how they felt some time ago, or why they did or did not take a particular course of action.

(h) Parents should know what is happening to the victim and be able to stop it

This is an attempt to excuse the abuser of rape or sexual assault and place the   E.59
blame on the victim's parents. Parents may be unable to identify what is happening. Even if they suspect that something is not right, they may not be in a position to stop it due to the control over the victim exercised by the abuser. There can also be risks to parents when seeking to protect their child and they can need support as well as the child.

(h) Children and young people can consent to their own sexual exploitation

This is an attempt to excuse the abuser of rape or sexual assault and blame   E.60
the victim. A child or young person under 16 can never consent to sex whatever the circumstances. A child or young person under 18 cannot consent to being trafficked for purposes of their own exploitation. Regardless of age, a person is unable to consent to sex if they are drunk, drugged or unconscious.

(i) Sexual exploitation only happens in large towns and cities

Sexual exploitation is a form of child sexual abuse and can happen anywhere   E.61
and it is not confined to particular towns or cities. Children and young people can be trafficked between different areas of the country for the purpose of exploitation.

(j) It only happens to teenage girls by adult men

Sexual abuse and exploitation is not limited to teenage girls by adult men.   E.62
The victims may be either boys or girls and victims are not limited to any particular age and can include very young children. The abusers can include peers the same age of the victim, and sometimes peers, even if not directly

perpetrating rape or sexual assault, can be used to 'recruit' other children and young people to take them to locations where they are introduced to adult abusers.

(k) The victim is usually living in a care home away from their family

E.63   There are different types of child sexual abuse and exploitation and victims come from all parts of society. The victim could be living in a care home, but often the victim is living at home with their parents and family. Many children are living at home when their abuse begins. Children who grow up in loving and secure homes may also be vulnerable to child sexual exploitation if they live in a gang-affected neighbourhood, have a friend who is being sexually exploited, or go to a school where other children have been sexually exploited.

(l) Sexual exploitation is only perpetrated by certain ethnic/cultural communities

E.64   Perpetrators of sexual exploitation come from a range of different backgrounds and it is not restricted to one ethnic or cultural community. There is more than one type of perpetrator, model and approach to child sexual exploitation by gangs and groups. It invalidates the experience of victims abused by perpetrators from other backgrounds and risks such abuse being overlooked. What all perpetrators have in common, regardless of the differences in age, ethnicity, or social background, is their abuse of power in relation to their victims.

(m) It only happens to girls and young women

E.65   Boys and young men are also at risk of sexual abuse and exploitation. It implies the boy or young man is not telling the truth and invalidates the experience of the victim. A child or young person under 16 can never consent to sex whatever the circumstances.

(n) Sexual abuse and exploitation does not happen to children and young people from Black and Minority Ethnic (BME) backgrounds

E.66   Victims of child sexual abuse and exploitation come from a range of ethnic backgrounds and are not restricted to just one ethnicity. What is common to all victims is their powerlessness and vulnerability, not their age, ethnicity, disability or sexual orientation. It implies that children and young people from BME backgrounds are not telling the truth and invalidates their experience. It also risks such abuse being overlooked.

(o) Children who are being abused will show physical evidence of abuse

Research shows that genital injuries are the exception even in cases where the   E.67
abuse has been proven. Even where an injury is sustained it may heal very
quickly.

Annex D

Child Protection systems in England and Wales

Child Protection in England is the overall responsibility of the Department   E.68
for Education which issues guidance to local authorities. The most recent
guidance, issued in March 2013, is Working Together to Safeguard Children.
Local Safeguarding Children's Boards (LSCBs) use this guidance to produce
their own procedures that should be followed by practitioners and professionals who come into contact with children and their families in their
local authority area. Wales has the All Wales Child Protection Procedures
which provides Local Safeguarding Children Boards with a single set of
procedures and a range of protocols from which they all work.

In many cases of child sexual abuse, there will be social services involvement,
often prior to any police involvement. In brief this will involve one, or all, of
the following steps:

1. A referral to local authority children's social care, which can come
   from the child themselves, teachers, a GP, the police, health visitors,
   family members and members of the public.
2. An assessment taking place to establish whether the child requires
   immediate protection and urgent action is required; or, the child is
   in need and should be assessed under section 17 of the Children Act
   1989; or, there is reasonable cause to suspect that the child is
   suffering, or likely to suffer, significant harm, and whether enquiries
   must be made and the child assessed under section 47 of the
   Children Act.
3. If there is a risk to the life of a child or a likelihood of serious
   immediate harm, local authority social workers, the police or
   NSPCC must use their statutory child protection powers to act
   immediately to secure the safety of the child. If the child is identified
   as being in need, a social worker should lead a multi-agency
   assessment under section 17. Where information gathered during an
   assessment results in the social worker suspecting that the child is
   suffering or likely to suffer significant harm, the local authority
   should hold a strategy discussion to enable it to decide, with other
   agencies, whether to initiate enquiries under section 47.

For the purposes of the multi-agency assessments, the police should assist other agencies to carry out their responsibilities where there are concerns about the child's welfare, whether or not a crime has been committed. If a crime has been committed, the police should be informed by the local authority children's social care.

For the purposes of the strategy discussion, the police must discuss the basis for any criminal investigation and any relevant processes that other agencies might need to know about, including the timing and methods of evidence gathering; and lead the criminal investigation where joint enquiries take place. The local authority children's social care has the lead for the section 47 enquiries and assessment of the child's welfare.

Social services involvement will potentially generate a great deal of information which police and prosecutors should make enquiries about. The enquiry should not be from the standpoint of looking for material to undermine the child or young person. There may be material which could enhance and strengthen the prosecution case.

All prosecutors who review child sexual abuse cases should have a good working knowledge of the legislative requirements and expectations on individual services to safeguard and promote the welfare of children. Prosecutors should also be aware of the 2013 Protocol and Good Practice Model: Disclosure of information in cases of alleged child abuse and linked criminal and care directions hearings.

Annex E

Family Procedure Rules Part 12

E.69   Practice Direction 12A is a key piece of guidance for prosecutors. It sets out the Public Law Proceedings Guide to Case Management: April 2010, incorporating the Public Law Outline 2010 (PLO). Where there are parallel criminal and care proceedings, it is vital that prosecutors understand the timetables and processes of the Family Court.

The Practice Direction sets out the stages (Issue and First Appointment; Advocates' Meeting and Case Management Conference; Advocates' Meeting and Issues Resolution Meeting; Final Hearing) and the timescales involved. The PLO forms to be used include information of relevance to prosecutors, such as the Local Authority Case Summary, Draft Case Management Order, Timetable for the Child/Children, Standard Directions, disclosure etc.

Practice Direction 12A states at paragraph 3.9: 'Where there are parallel care proceedings and criminal proceedings against a person connected with the child for a serious offence against the child, linked directions hearings should where practicable take place as the case progresses. The timing of the proceedings in a linked care and criminal case should appear in the Timetable for the Child.'

PLO Form 4 makes specific reference to parallel criminal proceedings.

The Timetable for the Child

The Timetable for the Child includes not only legal steps but also social care,   E.70
health and education steps. Due regard is paid to the Timetable to ensure that the court remains child focussed throughout the progress of the proceedings and that any procedural steps proposed under the PLO are considered in the context of significant events in the child's life.

The expectations are that the proceedings should be finally determined within the timetable fixed by the court in accordance with the Timetable for the Child. The timescales in the PLO being adhered to and being taken as the maximum permissible time for the taking of the step referred to in the Outline, unless the Timetable for the Child demands otherwise.

Prosecutors should ensure that they are aware of the Timetable. They will need to provide information regarding criminal proceedings dates/events and, equally, they should take the contents of the Timetable into account when contributing to their own case management procedures in the criminal proceedings. For example, where a trial appears likely it should not simply be a matter of witness availability, but information should be obtained concerning significant steps in the child's life that are likely to take place during the proceedings (such as exams, revision, special events, Family Court proceedings, etc) and efforts should be made to fix the trial date accordingly.

Such an approach should help both the family court and the criminal court to work in synchronisation in the interests of justice and the welfare of the child.

Other matters of relevance to prosecutors

Case Management Orders will include orders relating to the disclosure of   E.71
documents into the proceedings held by third parties, including medical records, police records and the disclosure of documents and information relating to the proceedings to non-parties.

The court may give directions without a hearing.

Where facilities are available to the court and the parties, the court will consider making full use of technology including electronic information exchange and video or telephone conferencing.

Communication of Information Practice Direction 12G

E.72   Practice Direction 12G sets out what information can be communicated to
       third parties – including the police and CPS. The tables from the old rules
       (Part X, Rules 11.2 – 11.9 of the Family Proceedings [Amendment] [No. 2]
       Rules 2009, which include the Family Proceedings Rules 1991) are
       restated.

       In essence, a party in family proceedings or any person lawfully in receipt of
       information can give 'the text or summary of the whole or part of a judgment
       given in the proceedings' to a police officer for the purposes of a criminal
       investigation or to a member of the CPS 'to enable the Crown Prosecution
       Service to discharge its functions under any enactment.'

       Apart from the judgment, there may also be information contained in family
       court case papers that would be relevant to the criminal case, such as:
       previous consistent or inconsistent statements of witnesses or defendants;
       evidence of similar incidents; material for bad character applications; or
       medical reports/medical expert evidence. Disclosure and use of such docu-
       ments is restricted.

       The Rules permit the communication of information relating to the proceed-
       ings (whether or not contained in a document filed with the court) not only
       where the court gives permission, but also where communication is to
       (amongst others) 'a professional acting in furtherance of the protection of
       children', which is defined as including a police officer who is exercising
       powers under section 46 of the Children Act 1989 (removal and accommoda-
       tion of children in an emergency) or is serving in a child protection unit or
       a paedophile unit of a police force, or a professional person attending a child
       protection conference or review in relation to a child who is the subject of
       proceedings to which the information relates.

       Information or documentation communicated as above 'in furtherance of the
       protection of children' cannot be communicated to CPS without the express
       permission of the Family Court.

THE ADVOCATE'S GATEWAY[1]

Advocate's Gateway (TAG) provides free access to practical, evidence-based guidance on vulnerable witnesses and defendants. TAG is hosted by the Advocacy Training Council (ATC).

The Advocate's Gateway toolkits aim to support the early identification of vulnerability in witnesses and defendants and the making of reasonable adjustments so that the justice system is fair. Effective communication is essential in the legal process. The handling and questioning of vulnerable witnesses and defendants is a specialist skill (Raising the Bar: The Handling of Vulnerable Witnesses, Victims and Defendants in Court 2011). Advocates must ensure that they are suitably trained and that they adhere to their professional conduct rules.

Courts are expected to make reasonable adjustments to remove barriers for people with disabilities giving effect to the Equality Act 2010.

These toolkits draw on the expertise of a wide range of professionals and represent best practice guidance; they are not legal advice and should not be construed as such.

Each toolkit contains the following statement: *"Questioning that contravenes principles for obtaining accurate information from a witness by exploiting his or her developmental limitations is not conducive to a fair trial and would contravene the Codes of Conduct".*

TOOLKITS AVAILABLE

1. **Ground rules hearings and the fair treatment of vulnerable people in court**   F.01

---

[1] Toolkits reproduced with the permission of ACT, The Advocate's Gateway, available at *http://www.theadvocatesgateway.org/toolkits*, and Lexicon Limited, available at *http://lexiconlimited.co.uk/toolkits/* [Accessed April 30, 2016].

Ground rules hearing checklist

1a. Case management when a witness or defendant is vulnerable 1b. Case management in young and other vulnerable witness cases – summary

2. General principles from research, policy and guidance: planning to question a vulnerable person or someone with communication needs

3. Planning to question someone with an autism spectrum disorder including Asperger syndrome

4. Planning to question someone with a learning disability

5. Planning to question someone with 'hidden' disabilities: specific language impairment, dyslexia, dyspraxia, dyscalculia and AD(H)D

6. Planning to question a child or young person

7. Additional factors concerning children under 7 (or functioning at a very young age)

8. Effective participation of young defendants

9. Planning to question someone using a remote link

10. Identifying vulnerability in witnesses and defendants

11. Planning to question someone who is deaf

12. General principles when questioning witnesses and defendants with mental disorder

13. Vulnerable witnesses and parties in the family courts

14. Using communication aids in the criminal justice system

15. Witnesses and defendants with autism: memory and sensory issues

16. Intermediaries step by step

17. Vulnerable witnesses and parties in the civil courts

18. Working with traumatised witnesses, defendants and parties

Below is the content from Toolkits 1, 1a, 1b, 2, 6 and 10

TOOLKIT 1: GROUND RULES HEARINGS AND THE FAIR TREATMENT OF VULNERABLE PEOPLE IN COURT[2]

F.02   This toolkit brings together law, policy, research and guidance relating to:

1. general principles, definitions and context;
2. cases involving an intermediary;
3. ground rules requiring advocates to reduce questions to writing;
4. ground rules on special measures and other adjustments;
5. ground rules relieving a party of putting their case;
6. ground rules on the manner of questioning;
7. ground rules on the duration of questioning;
8. ground rules on questions that may or may not be put;
9. ground rules on allocation of topics to advocates for co-defendants;

[2] February 2015. © ATC The Advocate's Gateway 2015.

10. ground rules on communications aids;

11. extending the use of ground rules hearings (GRHs).

The toolkit contains information about GRHs in the criminal courts and is primarily intended for use by advocates as well as solicitors, police officers, social workers and judges. This toolkit supplements the Ground Rules Hearing Checklist.

Key points include:

- GRHs are commonly used by judges to make directions for the fair treatment and participation of vulnerable defendants and vulnerable witnesses.
- Courts must take reasonable steps to ensure the effective participation of vulnerable defendants and witnesses.
- Where directions for the appropriate treatment and questioning are required the court *must* set ground rules (CPR 3.9(7)(b)).
- Courts have a safeguarding responsibility to children and vulnerable adults.
- When there is an intermediary they *must* be invited to make representations (CPR 3.9(7)(a)), in other words they must be included in the discussion at the GRH.
- Advocates and judges should consider 'special measures', 'additional measures' and other reasonable adjustments throughout proceedings. Thus, it may be necessary to revisit the ground rules set at the start of the proceedings by way of a further GRH.
- Guidance for family courts, including on GRHs, is available in Toolkit 13 Vulnerable witnesses and parties in the family courts.

1. GENERAL PRINCIPLES, DEFINITIONS AND CONTEXT

1.1 GRHs are commonly used by judges to make directions for the fair treatment and participation of vulnerable defendants and vulnerable witnesses.

Advocates should therefore be alert to risk factors which may indicate that a   **F.03** witness or party is vulnerable and that a GRH is required. General risk factors which suggest a witness is vulnerable are outlined in Toolkit 10 Identifying vulnerability in witnesses and defendants. When necessary, expert advice (including an intermediary assessment) should be sought.

1.2 Courts must take every reasonable step to ensure the participation of vulnerable witnesses and defendants.

The Criminal Procedure Rules (CPR) 2014 at CPR 1.1 state 'the overriding   **F.04** objective' is that cases are 'dealt with justly'.[2a] In addition:

[2a] CPR 2014, SI 2014/1610 (L26), rule 1.1(1), 'The overriding objective'.

'In order to prepare for the trial, the court must take every reasonable step—
to encourage and to facilitate the attendance of witnesses when they are needed;
and to facilitate the participation of any person, including the defendant.' (CPR 3.9(3))
'Facilitating the participation of any person includes giving directions for the appropriate treatment and questioning of a witness or the defendant, especially where the court directs that such questioning is to be conducted through an intermediary.' (CPR 3.9(6))
The GRH can help to give effect to the courts' safeguarding responsibility: 'Courts have safeguarding responsibilities in respect of children and vulnerable adults.' (Equal Treatment Benchbook 2013, *'Children and vulnerable adults'*)

1.3 Where directions for appropriate treatment and questioning are required, the court must invite representations by the parties and by any intermediary and must set ground rules.

F.05
- *'The ground rules hearing should cover, amongst other matters, the general care of the witness, if, when and where the witness is to be shown their video interview, when, where and how the parties (and the judge if identified) intend to introduce themselves to the witness, the length of questioning and frequency of breaks and the nature of the questions to be asked.'* (*R v Lubemba; R v JP* [2014] EWCA Crim 2064 para 43)
- In addition, ground rules may include directions about relieving a party of putting their case, the manner of questioning, the duration of questioning, the topics that may or may not be covered, allocations of questions amongst co-defendants and the use of communications aids (in force from 6 April 2015, Criminal Procedure (Amendment) Rules 2015):

  '(7)   Where directions for appropriate treatment and questioning are required, the court must—
  (a) invite representations by the parties and by any intermediary; and
  (b) set ground rules for the conduct of the questioning, which rules may include—
  - *(i) a direction relieving a party of any duty to put that party's case to a witness or a defendant in its entirety,*
  - *(ii) directions about the manner of questioning,*
  - *(iii) directions about the duration of questioning,*
  - *(iv) if necessary, directions about the questions that may or may not be asked,*
  - *(v) where there is more than one defendant, the allocation among them of the topics about which a witness may be asked, and*

> *(vi) directions about the use of models, plans, body maps or similar aids to help communicate a question or an answer.'*
> (CPR 3.9(7))

1.4 A GRH is required in all intermediary trials and is good practice in any case where a witness or defendant has communication needs.

GRHs are recognised by the Criminal Practice Directions (CPD) 2014 as a   F.06
key step in planning the proper questioning of a vulnerable witness or
defendant. Many judges and advocates find them 'invaluable' (Henderson
2014).

- *'Discussion of ground rules is required in all intermediary trials where they must be discussed between the judge or magistrates, advocates and intermediary before the witness gives evidence.'* (CPD 3E.2)
- *'Discussion of ground rules is good practice, even if no intermediary is used, in all young witness cases and in other cases where a witness or defendant has communication needs.'* (CPD 3E.3)
- A GRH is expected in every case where there is a vulnerable witness, save in exceptional circumstances: *'judges are taught, in accordance with the Criminal Practice Directions, that it is best practice to hold hearings in advance of the trial to ensure the smooth running of the trial, to give any special measures directions and to set the ground rules for the treatment of a vulnerable witness. We would expect a ground rules hearing in every case involving a vulnerable witness, save in very exceptional circumstances. If there are any doubts on how to proceed, guidance should be sought from those who have the responsibility for looking after the witness and or an expert.'* (R v Lubemba; R v JP [2014] EWCA Crim 2064 para 42)

1.5 The GRH should take place at least the day before the trial to enable advocates to prepare and, if necessary, to adjust their approach; the judge should state what the ground rules are and they should be recorded; advocates must abide by the ground rules.

- *'Discussion before the day of trial is preferable to give advocates time to*   F.07 *adapt their questions to the witness's needs. It may be helpful for a trial practice note of boundaries to be created at the end of the discussion. The judge may use such a document in ensuring that the agreed ground rules are complied with.'* (CPD 3E.3)
- In *R v Wills* [2011] EWCA Crim 1938 para 22, the Court of Appeal endorsed a recommendation of the Advocacy Training Council report, *Raising the Bar* (2011) that there be 'a trial practice note/trial protocol' clearly recording the limitations imposed by the trial judge on cross-examination.

- The advocate has a duty to abide by court rulings: '*In the forensic process the decision and judgment of this court bind the professions . . . in the course of any trial, like everyone else, the advocate is ultimately bound to abide by the rulings of the court.*' (*R v Farooqi and Others* [2013] EWCA Crim 1649 para 109)

GOOD PRACTICE EXAMPLE: At the GRH the judge directed advocates to be mindful of how they questioned prosecution witnesses so that the defendant could understand and follow the trial. The defendant subsequently elected to give evidence, thus a further GRH was required to agree the ground rules for his questioning.

1.6 The GRH should take place in the courtroom (as opposed to chambers) and should be recorded.

F.08 Given that the personal difficulties of a vulnerable person are being discussed, the court should consider clearing the public gallery. The court should also consider whether technology can be utilised to allow GRH participants to take part from a remote location(s).

2. GRHs INVOLVING AN INTERMEDIARY

2.1 An intermediary must be involved in the ground rules discussion (CPR 3.9 (7)).

F.09 '*Ground rules for questioning must be discussed between the court, the advocates and the intermediary before the witness gives evidence, to establish (a) how questions should be put to help the witness understand them, and (b) how the proposed intermediary will alert the court if the witness has not understood, or needs a break.*' (APPLICATION FOR A SPECIAL MEASURES DIRECTION Part F)

' **[Intermediaries] are used . . . to flag up potential difficulties in advance of the trial.**' (Judge 2011)

In advance of the GRH, advocates should put their proposed cross-examination in writing and invite the intermediary to advise them on how best to communicate the proposed questions to the vulnerable witness/defendant. Advocates should rely on the expertise of the intermediary to help them prepare their questions including for witness competency hearings: '*We do not underestimate the difficulties of questioning vulnerable witnesses . . . The shortcomings of this process seem to us to owe much to a lack of preparation and a lack of ability to respond flexibly to the difficulties which arose. There are now substantial materials available to those who have to deal with the questions of competency and the use of intermediaries.*' (*R v F* [2013] EWCA Crim 424 paras 26 and 27)

In the event of disagreement about the proposed questions, the judge must decide what is appropriate: 'a trial judge is not only entitled, he is duty bound to control the questioning of a witness' (*R v Lubemba; R v JP* [2014] EWCA Crim 2064 para 51)

The trial judge has a duty to intervene if he or she thinks the questioning is inappropriate even if the intermediary does not: ' *[T]he trial judge is responsible for controlling questioning and ensuring that vulnerable witnesses and defendants are enabled to give the best evidence they can. The judge has a duty to intervene, therefore, if an advocate's questioning is confusing or inappropriate.'* (*R v Lubemba; R v JP* [2014] EWCA Crim 2064 para 44)

GOOD PRACTICE EXAMPLE: In what may be the first Court of Appeal hearing which required an intermediary to assist a witness, the Court of Appeal, without holding a face-to-face GRH, set ground rules in accordance with the recommendations in the intermediary's written report. The ground rules provided the framework for the appropriate questioning of a vulnerable witness (who had given evidence at the original trial) via live link to the Court of Appeal. The ground rules included that cross-examination questions should be 'provided to all parties' and to the registered intermediary in advance.

2.2 The trial judge and the advocates should agree the wording of the direction that will be given to the jury about the intermediary's role.

For example: F.10

'Members of the Jury you will see that there are two people in the dock. One is the defendant who sits on the left in the dock, the other person Mr/s [X] is there to assist the Court; the technical term for her position is an "intermediary". The Defendant in this case suffers from disabilities, in particular serious learning difficulties. I have ruled, following representations from both the Prosecution and the Defence who agree on this, that by reason of the Defendant's learning difficulties, there should be an intermediary in court during the evidence to assist communication during the evidence in this case. An intermediary is not an expert, she does not give evidence, she is an independent person, a communication specialist who is present to assist with two-way communication in Court. She will only intervene if a communication issue is identified. For the reasons I have outlined I have directed and it is agreed by both sides, that the evidence in this case will be presented in a simple form; questions asked of any witnesses will be short simple and straightforward and it is likely we will take breaks in the evidence. All this is in order that the defendant will be able to understand fully the evidence in this case and the proceedings. I must stress that the giving of evidence with an intermediary present is perfectly normal in a case such as this; the use of an intermediary is to assist communication and to ensure that the Defendant understands fully the evidence and the proceedings during the trial. The fact that an Intermediary is present in these proceedings must not in any way be considered by you as prejudicial to the accused.'

2.3 Warning the jury about special measures for a witness:

F.11 *'Where on a trial on indictment evidence has been given in accordance with a special measures direction, the judge must give the jury such warning (if any) as the judge considers necessary to ensure that the fact that the direction was given in relation to the witness does not prejudice the accused.'* section 32 Youth Justice and Criminal Evidence Act (YJCEA) 1999

3. GROUND RULES REQUIRING AN ADVOCATE TO REDUCE QUESTIONS TO WRITING

3.1 It is reasonable for judges to ask advocates to write out their proposed questions for the vulnerable witness and share them with judge and the intermediary, if there is one:

F.12 *'So as to avoid any unfortunate misunderstanding at trial, it would be an entirely reasonable step for a judge at the ground rules hearing to invite defence advocates to reduce their questions to writing in advance.'* (*R v Lubemba; R v JP* [2014] EWCA Crim 2064 para 42)

- The decision on the appropriateness of the proposed question is a decision for the judge, after consultation with the advocate who has prepared the questions and the intermediary (if there is one) without disclosure to the opposing advocate or the advocate for the co-defendant unless it relates to a question of admissibility of evidence.
- Disclosure of pre-prepared written questions may be agreed between the parties, but, if it is not, the judge will need to consider what is in the interests of justice.
- In section 28 YJCEA 1999 cases (pre-recorded cross-examination), advocates are required to complete the section 28 Defence GRH Form from the HM Courts and Tribunal Service (HMCTS) which includes space at section 8 to set out for the judge 'all proposed questions which should be drafted taking into account the relevant Toolkit'.
- Where witness cross-examination questions are disclosed in advance and/or discussed at the GRH, it is must be on the understanding that proposed cross-examination will not be 'telegraphed' in advance to the witness.

4. GROUND RULES ABOUT SPECIAL MEASURES AND OTHER ADJUSTMENTS

4.1 A party applying for special measures should have done so in accordance with the rules (including time limits) set out in CPR 29.3

F.13 (and see also CPR 29.10 for the content of the application). Directions for appropriate treatment and questioning are not limited to special measures set out in the legislation. See Toolkit 10 Identifying vulnerability in witnesses and defendants.

GOOD PRACTICE EXAMPLE: The defendant had a phobia about entering crowded rooms; the judge directed that the defendant should be the first to enter the courtroom at the start of the trial and after any break.

4.2 At the GRH the trial judge should consider how special measures/ additional measures and other adjustments will combine.

For example, live link and a screen may be combined if the judge directs that   F.14
the defendant is not going to be allowed to see the witness on the live link screen (CPD 29A.2).

GOOD PRACTICE EXAMPLE: At the GRH the trial judge directed that the intermediary should work with interpreters to familiarise them with the deaf witness's idiosyncratic signs so that together they could convey the witness's answers to the court.

4.3 Even if no party has applied for special measures, the court may of its own motion raise the issue of whether such a direction should be given

(section 19(1)(b) YJCEA 1999).   F.15

5. GROUND RULES RELIEVING A PARTY OF PUTTING THEIR CASE (CPR 3.9(7)(b)(i))

5.1 Defence advocates may be restricted from putting their client's case to the vulnerable witness.

'*It is now generally accepted that if justice is to be done to the vulnerable*   F.16
witness and also to the accused, a radical departure from the traditional style of advocacy will be necessary. Advocates must adapt to the witness, not the other way round. They cannot insist upon any supposed right "to put one's case" or previous inconsistent statements to a vulnerable witness. If there is a right to "put one's case" (about which we have our doubts) it must be modified for young or vulnerable witnesses. It is perfectly possible to ensure the jury are made aware of the defence case and of significant inconsistencies without intimidation or distressing a witness (see for example paragraph 3E.4 of the Criminal Practice Directions).' (*R v Lubemba; R v JP* [2014] EWCA Crim 2064 para 45)
'*Aspects of evidence which undermine or are believed to undermine the child's credibility must, of course, be revealed to the jury, but it is not necessarily appropriate for them to form the subject matter of detailed cross-examination of the child and the advocate may have to forego much of the kind of*

contemporary cross-examination which consists of no more than comment on matters which will be before the jury in any event from different sources.' (*R v B* [2010] EWCA Crim 4 para 42)

In section 28 YJCEA 1999 cases (pre-recorded cross-examination), advocates are required to complete the HMCTS's section 28 Defence GRH Form which includes space at sections 7 and 9 to request direction about putting the case to the vulnerable witness and to the jury.

5.2 Where such a restriction is imposed, it must be clearly defined and explained to the jury

F.17   (*R v Wills* [2011] EWCA Crim 1938 paras 36 and 37 and *R v E* [2011] EWCA Crim 3028). For a demonstration of how this might occur see the training film *A Question of Practice* (Criminal Bar Association 2013).

5.3 Not putting the opposing version to the witness potentially deprives the witness of the opportunity to have their evidence fairly tested.

F.18   Careful thought should be given to how questions might be reworded so that the witness's account can be fairly tested. If questions can be adapted so that the defence case can be put to the witness, then the questions should be put. A judge has no power to insist on defence cross-examination of the witness. The judge (or the prosecutor in re-examination) may ask a question to give the witness 'the chance to deal with the implication in the cross examination' (H v R [2014] EWCA Crim 1555 para 63).

GOOD PRACTICE EXAMPLE: Defence counsel wanted to put to the witness the defendant's case that the incident had not happened at all. The intermediary advised on how this could be done in a way that the witness could deal with.

Questions defence counsel originally wanted to put:

Q: *D didn't put his willy in your mouth, did he?*
Q: *D didn't put his willy in your bottom, did he?*

On the advice of the intermediary, defence counsel's questions were reframed. The traditional statement-plus-tag form was avoided. Instead, two simple statements were followed by a simple question for each of the above, e.g:

S: *You said D put his willy in your mouth.*
S: *D says he didn't put his willy in your mouth.*
Q: *Did D really put his willy in your mouth?*

6. GROUND RULES ON THE MANNER OF QUESTIONING (CPR 3.9(7)(b)(ii))

6.1 Timetabling for the witness's evidence should be addressed at the GRH so as to schedule a 'clean start' to the witness's testimony.

Trial management powers should be exercised to the full where a vulnerable   F.19
witness or defendant is involved (see *Equal Treatment Benchbook* 2013, 'Children and vulnerable adults')

GOOD PRACTICE EXAMPLE:
The witness was taking a significant amount of medication to control psychiatric symptoms. Her ability to give evidence was much improved in the afternoon when her medication had the chance to start working and her mental state was most stable. The schedule was arranged so that she gave her testimony only in the afternoons.

6.2 If tag questions are likely to be problematic for the vulnerable witness/ defendant, the court should direct that they be avoided.

Tag questions are linguistically complex and powerfully suggestive. A 'tag'   F.20
question takes the form of a statement with a question added on at the end, for example, *'You don't like your stepdad, do you?'*, *'That's right, isn't it?'*; as opposed to more linguistically straightforward questions or requests, such as *'Do you like your stepdad?'* or *'Tell me about your stepdad.'*

6.3 Advocates should be reminded that cross-examination should consist of short simple questions, not comment on the evidence.

'It is generally recognised that particularly with child witnesses short and   F.21
untagged questions are best at eliciting the evidence.' (*R v W and M* [2010] EWCA Crim 1926 para 30)

6.4 A succession of short questions, particularly if fast-paced, may sound fierce or intimidating to a vulnerable witness.

Use of signposting together with short questioning can put a vulnerable   F.22
witness at ease and enable best evidence.
'. . . it should not be over-problematic for the advocate to formulate short, simple questions which put the essential elements of the defendant's case to the witness . . . it should not take very lengthy cross-examination to demonstrate, when it is the case, that the child may indeed be fabricating, or fantasising, or imagining, or reciting a well rehearsed untruthful script, learned by rote, or simply just suggestible, or contaminated by or in collusion with others to make false allegations, or making assertions in language which is beyond his or her level of comprehension, and therefore likely to be derived from another source. Comment on the evidence, including comment on evidence which may bear

adversely on the credibility of the child, should be addressed after the child has finished giving evidence.' (*R v B* [2010] EWCA Crim 4 para 42)

6.5   Judges may give directions about cross-examination based on third party disclosure.

F.23   A witness taken by surprise by questions may become distressed because, for example, they were unaware that their GP or social care records had been disclosed to the defence: 'prosecutors [should] satisfy themselves that complainants have consented to their medical records and/or counselling notes being disclosed to the defence' (*Disclosure of Medical Records and Counselling Notes*, HM Crown Prosecution Service Inspectorate July 2013) otherwise the witness should be informed if the judge ordered disclosure of such material to the defence in the absence of their consent. Advocates should consider if and how a witness might be informed of the likely areas of cross-examination all the while bearing in mind that witness coaching is prohibited (see *R v Momodou* [2005] EWCA Crim 177 and advocates' codes of conduct).

In *R v Pipe* [2014] EWCA Crim 2570, the Court of Appeal considered a case where a judge cut short cross-examination before the complainant could be asked about potential inconsistencies between what she had said during her evidence and what she had said at the time of her medical appointments, her medical records having been disclosed to the defence: *'In cases of this sort, it is often unnecessary and inappropriate for a complainant to be dragged through their own medical records in huge detail, particularly where any potential inconsistencies can be identified and be the subject of written admissions.'* (para 27)

7.   GROUND RULES ON THE DURATION OF QUESTIONING (CPR 3.9(7)(b)(iii))

7.1   A trial judge is entitled to set time limits on cross-examination.

F.24   A trial judge may be justified in imposing 'a time limit on the cross-examination of the complainant' (*R v Butt* [2005] EWCA Crim 805) and 'is entitled to and should set reasonable time limits and to interrupt where he considers questioning is inappropriate' *(R v Lubemba; R v JP* [2014] EWCA Crim 2064 para 51). By way of example, in *Lubemba*, the cross-examination of a ten-year-old rape complainant was limited 'to 45 minutes and [the judge] interrupted when he felt her questions were unclear or inappropriate' *(R v Lubemba; R v JP* [2014] EWCA Crim 2064 para 32).

GOOD PRACTICE EXAMPLE: The witness was allowed to have short 'time-out' breaks (usually of just 30 seconds) in a small tent in the live link room when her anxiety peaked, but was not at the point where she needed a full break from giving her evidence. While the witness took this short break the live link was temporarily turned off and the court waited until she was ready to continue. (If the live link remains on, the judge should ensure that the microphones in the court are turned off so that the witness does not hear the conversations in the courtroom.)

8. GROUND RULES ABOUT QUESTIONS THAT MAY OR MAY NOT BE ASKED (CPR 3.9(7)(b)(iv))

8.1 Ground rules should prevent cross-examination based on discredited myths.

For example, in sexual assault cases judges are expected to prevent cross-examination based on: F.25

'*what modern research has proved to be myths . . . It is a myth that a man cannot be raped. It is a myth that rape involves a hooded stranger, or is limited to strangers. It is a myth that if there are no marks on the complainant, and no evidence of distress independently offered, that she cannot have been raped. It is a myth that unless the victim complains immediately she must have consented to sexual intercourse . . . It is a myth that if a woman has imbibed a great deal of alcohol with a man, she must have been willing to have sexual intercourse with him.*' (Judge 2011; see also Crown Prosecution Guidance, Rape and Sexual Offences: Chapter 21: Societal myths)

Sections 41–43 YJCEA 1999 restrict cross-examination on the complainant's sexual history without leave of the court. Applications for leave must be made in writing and within 28 days of disclosure (CPR 36.2).

8.2 Judges should make clear in advance where the boundaries of questioning lie.

'*[T]here is a limit to the extent to which a Judge may properly intervene once   F.26 questioning is underway without running the risk of seeming to descend into the arena and thereby potentially creating the perception of unfairness and—in extreme cases—imperilling any resulting conviction. Far better to have made clear from the start where the boundaries of questioning lie.*' (Leveson 2015, at 8.3.1 'Ground rules approach' para 257)

9. GROUND RULES ALLOCATING TOPICS AMONG ADVOCATES FOR CO-DEFENDANTS (CPR 3.9(7)(b)(v))

9.1 Topics should be allocated to defence counsel to avoid repeat and/or unnecessarily prolonged cross-examination.

'*In advance of the trial, the advocates should divide the topics between them,   F.27 with the advocate for the first defendant leading the questioning, and the advocate(s) for the other defendant(s) asking only ancillary questions relevant to their client's case, without repeating the questioning that has already taken place on behalf of the other defendant(s).*' (CPD 3E.5)

'It will never be in the interests of justice that witnesses should be subjected to bullying and intimidatory tactics by counsel or to deliberately and unnecessarily prolonged cross-examination.' (Leveson 2015, at 8.3.1 'Ground rules approach' para 264)

10. GROUND RULES ABOUT COMMUNICATIONS AIDS (CPR 3.9(7)(b)(vi))

10.1 Communication aids (section 30 YJCEA 1999) may be ordered for eligible vulnerable witnesses.

F.28   GOOD PRACTICE EXAMPLE: the judge directed that a witness could pause cross-examination by pointing to a 'pause' card on the table in the live link room and then the intermediary alerting the judge that a pause has been requested.

GOOD PRACTICE and BODY MAPS

'In particular in a trial of a sexual offence, "body maps" should be provided for the witness' use. If the witness needs to indicate a part of the body, the advocate should ask the witness to point to the relevant part on the body map. In sex cases, judges should not permit advocates to ask the witness to point to a part of the witness' own body. Similarly, photographs of the witness' body should not be shown around the court while the witness is giving evidence.' (CPD 3E.6)

10.2 Communications aids for vulnerable defendants have also been ordered by judges using their inherent jurisdiction.

F.29   GOOD PRACTICE EXAMPLE: 'Post-it' notes may be stuck on to the glass screen in the dock showing the order of events during the trial. These can be changed around and also removed, once a particular event has happened, to help a defendant who has difficulty understanding the order of events.
GOOD PRACTICE EXAMPLE: The defendant who struggled with concepts of time was allowed a timeline to assist cross-examination. The advocates had a duplicate copy and indicated certain points on the timeline when putting questions to the witness.

10.3 Ground rules should consider how the witness supporter or intermediary will assist with communication aids.

F.30   GOOD PRACTICE EXAMPLE: It was directed that the intermediary would hold up to the live link camera the answers written by the partially mute witness and she would also number the pages used by the witness to communicate his answers in writing.
See also Toolkit 14 Communication aids.

11. EXTENDING THE USE OF GRHs

'In due course, consideration should be given to whether or not this [ground   **F.31**
rules hearings] approach may sensibly be extended to other areas of cross-
examination in which it may take place (for example, with expert witnesses).'
(Leveson 2015, at 8.3.1 'Ground rules approach' para 267)

This toolkit was developed for The Advocate's Gateway by Professor
Penny Cooper with assistance from Paula Backen (Registered Intermediary) and Ruth Marchant (Director at Triangle and Registered Intermediary). Contributions were made by Registered Intermediaries Kate Man
and Dr Brendan O'Mahony as well as Sarah Clarke, Paul Garlick QC,
Felicity Gerry QC, HHJ Hopmeier, Angela Rafferty QC and David
Wurtzel.

The toolkit summarises key points from law, policy, research and guidance
including:
Advocacy Training Council (2011) *Raising the Bar: The Handling of
vulnerable witnesses, victims and defendants in court*
Criminal Practice Directions (CPD) 2014
Criminal Procedure (Amendment) Rules 2015)
Criminal Procedure Rules 2014
Henderson, E (November 2014) 'Jewel in the Crown?' *Counsel* 10-12
Cooper, P (2014) *Highs and Lows: The 4th intermediary survey* (Kingston
University)
Cooper, P, Backen, P and Marchant, R (2015 forthcoming), 'Getting to
grips with ground rules hearings: a checklist for judges, advocates and
intermediaries to promote the fair treatment of vulnerable people in court'
Criminal Law Review
Judge, The Rt Hon The Lord, Lord Chief Justice of England and Wales
(2011) 'Vulnerable witnesses in the administration of criminal justice',
17th Australian Institute of Judicial Administration Oration in Judicial
Administration
Judicial College (2013) *Equal Treatment Benchbook*
Leveson, The Rt Hon Sir Brian, President of the Queen's Bench Division
(2015) Review of Efficiency in Criminal Proceedings
Wurtzel, D (November 2012) 'Time to change the rules?' *Counsel* 32

GROUND RULES HEARING CHECKLIST[2b]

The checklist should be read in conjunction with **Toolkit 1 Ground rules**   **F.32**
hearings and the fair treatment of vulnerable people in court.

[2b] This checklist is based on the article 'Getting to grips with ground rules hearings' by P
Cooper, P Backen and R Marchant published in [2015] 6 *Criminal Law Review.*

This is not an exhaustive checklist; it contains key matters which the judge and advocates should consider at a ground rules hearing (GRH) in relation to a vulnerable defendant or witness.

The checklist is written in three sections. One or more of the three parts will be relevant dependant on whether or not there is an intermediary and whether or not there is a vulnerable defendant or witness.

SECTION A: Facilitating the role of the **intermediary**
SECTION B: Participation of the **vulnerable defendant**
SECTION C: Fair **questioning of a vulnerable person** (witness or defendant)

SECTION A: Facilitating the role of the intermediary

If there is an intermediary they must be included in the GRH discussion and in particular their report(s)[3] considered and discussed, especially if a report recommendation is disputed. The intermediary is not a witness and is not required to be in the witness box for the GRH. The hearing is a discussion and the hearing is not for cross-examination of the intermediary. The intermediary is not required to take the intermediary oath at this stage.

At the GRH discuss:

1. Whether advocates have shown the intermediary the wording of their proposed questions and taken advice on the suitability of the wording and communication style.
2. Where the intermediary will stand/sit during the trial (for the defendant) or testimony (if for a witness), so that she is able to observe and intervene to assist with communication whilst all the time being visible to the judge, advocates and jury.
3. If for a defendant, where the intermediary will sit in relation to other defendants (if any) and officers in the dock.
4. Where and when the intermediary will take the intermediary oath.[4]
5. If the intermediary and witness will be in a remote location, practical issues such as who will administer the oath and how exhibits would be made available to the witness. See also Toolkit 9 Planning to question someone using a remote link.

---

[3] Some cases will require an addendum to the original intermediary report, particularly if the witness's/defendant's needs have changed since the initial assessment and the report is many months old by the time of the trial. If the first assessing intermediary is no longer available for the trial, a 'new' intermediary will need to conduct her own assessment and write a report, albeit that only a short addendum to the original report may be required.
[4] Section 29(5) Youth Justice and Criminal Evidence Act 1999 requires the intermediary to make the declaration as specified.

6. How the intermediary will be addressed in court in front of the vulnerable person—for example, it might be by her first name if that is how the witness knows her.
7. How the intermediary will intervene/get the judge's attention if there is a communication issue or the intermediary needs to discuss a communication issue with judge and counsel in the absence of the jury.
8. How the role of the intermediary will be explained to the jury in a way that makes clear they are not a witness but that their role is to assist everyone in achieving complete, accurate and coherent communication with the vulnerable person.
9. If communication aids are to be used, how the intermediary will assist with these.
10. Any other recommendations in the intermediary's report.

*'In the absence of an intermediary for the defendant, trials should not be stayed where an asserted unfairness can be met by the trial judge adapting the trial process with appropriate and necessary caution (*R v Cox *[2012] EWCA Crim 549, [2012] 2 Cr. App. R. 6).'* (CPD 3F.6)

SECTION B: Participation of the vulnerable defendant

If the defendant is vulnerable and, in so far as this has not been covered **F.33** above, discuss (including with the intermediary if there is one):

11. Whether an interpreter is required for the trial.
12. Where the defendant will sit during the trial, for example, in the dock or next to the defence lawyers/if anyone will accompany the defendant in the dock—if they need the support of a nurse, for example.
13. Whether the vulnerable defendant will need assistance in the dock to access/follow written evidence and, if so, how this will be achieved.
14. Start and end times of the trial days.
15. Scheduled breaks during the trial day, including, for example, time to take medication, extra time to go through papers with a defendant who cannot read and extra time to allow counsel to take instructions.
16. How a request for an unscheduled break will be notified, if required.
17. ' *[G]round rules for all witness testimony to help the defendant follow proceedings; for example, directing that all witness evidence be adduced by simple questions.*'[5]

[5] CPD 2014, 3F.6

18. How and when the defendant will be familiarised with the courtroom.[6]

19. Use of communication aids, for example, iPad/tablet, hearing loop, stress/concentration aids, break cards, visual timetable and writing/drawing materials.

20. Whether the jury will be assisted by an explanation about the defendant's condition and its effect on his or her behaviour so as to avoid that behaviour being misinterpreted (for example, see *R v Thompson* [2014] EWCA Crim 836 and the defendant with Asperger syndrome).

Ground rules may need to be revisited if during the trial the defendant's effective participation is still not being achieved. Then, if the defendant later elects to give evidence there would normally be a further GRH specifically to discuss how questioning should be conducted (see next section).

SECTION C: Fair questioning of a vulnerable person (witness or defendant)

F.34 Discuss (including with the intermediary if there is one):

21. Whether an interpreter is required for the person's testimony.

22. Whether it is necessary to appoint a lawyer for an unrepresented defendant to conduct any cross-examination on behalf of the defendant.[7]

23. Whether the person will give evidence on oath or not and any assistance they might need to take the oath.

24. Whether the person will give evidence in court or over a live link.[8]

25. How other special measures,[9] which may have previously been ordered, will be implemented—for example, a screen, evidence given in private, evidence pre-recorded, wigs and gowns removed by judge and advocates, a witness supporter, use of communications aids,[10] such as models of maps, timelines, charts, pictures etc. Use of communication aids, such as body maps, for trial of a sexual offence[11] should also be considered.

26. How special measures and other adjustments may be combined: '*[a] combination of special measures may be appropriate. For example, if a witness who is to give evidence by live link wishes, screens can be used to shield the live link screen from the defendant and the public,*

---

[6] CPD 2014, 3G.2

[7] Sections 34–40 YJCEA 1999.

[8] Section 33A YJCEA 1999 for an eligible defendant and section 24 YJCEA 1999 for an eligible witness.

[9] Sections 23–30 YJCEA 1999 are available for eligible witnesses but not the accused, sections 16–17 YJCEA 1999.

[10] See Toolkit 14 Communication aids.

[11] CPD 2014 3E.6

as would occur if screens were being used for a witness giving evidence in the court room.' (CPD 29A.2)

27. Where the advocates will be when they conduct their questioning, for example, in court over live link or in the live link room.[12]

28. How long cross-examination is likely to take and how long it will be permitted to last, taking into account relevant matters such as the witness's concentration abilities, effects of prescribed medication etc.

29. When there will be scheduled breaks during the trial day, including duration and nature of breaks.

30. How a request for an unscheduled break will be notified, for example, arising from an urgent medical need.

31. Whether all breaks should involve adjourning the court or whether brief breaks may speed proceedings for all. Many courts have agreed breaks of up to three minutes for young children; during a short, non-adjourned break (the court stays sitting) and the microphones and cameras to the live link room are temporarily made visible only to the judge, enabling the witness to take a few minutes in the live link room to re-orientate or calm themselves. This avoids the need for the jury to be sent out and brought back which would be unnecessarily time-consuming;

32. Whether the judge has seen the advocates' proposed questions and determined if they are appropriate (if there is an intermediary they should also have been reduced to writing and shown to the intermediary).

33. How repetitious questioning will be avoided when there are separately represented defendants.[13]

34. If limitations are going to be placed on cross-examination, how these will be explained to the jury.[14]

35. How and when the person will be familiarised with the witness box/live link room/remote live link site, if this has not happened already.[15]

36. How and where and when the person will have their memory refreshed by watching the DVD recording of their achieving best evidence (ABE) interview, if any.[16] Note that there is no requirement for the witness to watch their ABE at the same time as the jury.

37. Whether and how the judge and advocates (preferably together) will meet the vulnerable person beforehand. Discussion may include

---

[12] D Wurtzel (2012) 'Time to change the rules?', *Counsel* November 32.
[13] CPD 2014 3E.5
[14] CPD 2014 3E.4
[15] This should include practising communicating over live link, simply being shown it is not enough: CPD 2014 29B.4
[16] CPD 2014 Evidence 29C: VISUALLY RECORDED INTERVIEWS: MEMORY REFRESHING AND WATCHING AT A DIFFERENT TIME FROM THE JURY.

matters such as whether the judge/advocates will be robed. '*In general, experts recommend that the trial judge should introduce him or herself to the witness in person before any questioning, preferably in the presence of the parties. This seems to us to be an entirely reasonable step to take to put the witness at their ease where possible.*' (*R v Lubemba* [2014] EWCA Crim 2064 para 43)

38. The best time of day for the person's testimony to start.
39. Whether the person will need assistance during testimony, for example, referring to/accessing written material, maps, photos, diagrams, transcripts etc.
40. How the court will be enabled to access the person's nonverbal communication, for example, indicating, pointing, drawing, writing.

'*In due course, consideration should be given to whether or not this [ground rules hearings] approach may sensibly be extended to other areas of cross-examination in which it may take place (for example, with expert witnesses).*' Review of Efficiency in Criminal Proceedings by The Rt Hon Sir Brian Leveson, President of the Queen's Bench Division (2015), at 8.3.1 'Ground rules approach' para 267.

TOOLKIT 1A: CASE MANAGEMENT WHEN A WITNESS OR DEFENDANT IS VULNERABLE[17]

F.35
1. **About this toolkit**
2. Pre-trial
   Initial arrangements
   Familiarisation, special measures and considerations
   Listing
3. **Plea and trial preparation hearing**
   Practical arrangements
   Memory refreshing
   Following the hearing
4. **Supporting the witness in advance of their appearance at court/pre-trial witness interview**
5. **Trial**
   Ground rules hearings
   Cross-examination
   Keeping the witness or defendant informed

1 ABOUT THIS TOOLKIT

F.36   **1.1**   This toolkit brings together policy and guidance relating to:
   • instructions, listing and other tasks;

---

[17] December 2015. © ATC The Advocate's Gateway 2015.

- the needs and wishes of young and/or vulnerable children or persons; and
- special measures.

This toolkit has been designed to assist with case management when a witness or defendant is vulnerable. Guidance and GOOD PRACTICE EXAMPLES are divided according to the stage of the case.

1.2 Vulnerable people include those who are young, those who have experienced trauma, those with autism spectrum disorder, attention deficit (hyperactivity) disorder (AD(H)D), mental health needs, specific learning difficulties and deafness, as well as older people and those with physical disabilities or health conditions which may negatively affect their ability to effectively participate in the trial process. See Toolkit 10 Identifying vulnerability in witnesses and defendants and Toolkit 18 Working with traumatised witnesses, defendants and parties.

1.3 This guidance has been written to assist with case management of cases involving vulnerable people. However, individuals will vary hugely in their needs, wishes and preferences and any adjustments made must respond to these individual needs.

1.4 It is assumed that basic arrangements will be made, such as ensuring that:

- the DVD is playable on court equipment;
- a hearing loop is in operation for deaf children and persons;
- visual or written material printed in large format or produced in braille is provided for blind or partially sighted children and persons; and
- first aid staff are on site for individuals with medical conditions.

It is also assumed that advocates will ensure that the DVD has been viewed by all parties prior to the pre-trial preparation hearing in order to aid decisions on admissibility, editing and refreshing the memory of the vulnerable child or person (section 5.3, Achieving Best Evidence 2011).

1.5 Courts are expected to make reasonable adjustments to remove barriers for people with disabilities, including specific learning difficulties (*Equal Treatment Bench Book* 2013, Mental disabilities, specific learning difficulties and mental capacity, giving effect to the Equality Act 2010). The court is required to take 'every reasonable step' to encourage and facilitate the attendance of witnesses and to facilitate the participation of any person, including the defendant (Criminal Procedure Rules 2015, rule 3.9(3)(a) and (b)). This includes enabling a vulnerable person to give their best evidence and enabling a defendant to comprehend the proceedings and engage fully with his or her defence. The pre-trial and trial process should, as far as necessary, be adapted to meet those ends. (Criminal Practice Directions (CPD): CPD General Matters 3D: Vulnerable people in the courts).

1.6 All witnesses, including the defendant and defence witnesses, should be enabled to give the best evidence they can. In relation to vulnerable people, this may mean departing radically from traditional cross-examination. The form and extent of appropriate cross-examination will vary from case to case. For adult non-vulnerable witnesses the advocate will usually put the case so that the witness will have the opportunity of commenting upon it and/or answering it. When the witness is young or otherwise vulnerable, the court may dispense with the normal practice and impose restrictions on the advocate 'putting the case' where there is a risk of a young or otherwise vulnerable witness failing to understand, becoming distressed or acquiescing to leading questions. Where limitations on questioning are necessary and appropriate, they must be clearly defined. The judge has a duty to ensure that these limitations are complied with and should explain them to the jury and the reasons for them. If the advocate fails to comply with the limitations the judge should intervene to prevent further questioning which does not comply with the ground rules settled in advance and give further directions where appropriate. (CPD General Matters 3E.4: Ground rules hearings to plan the questioning of a vulnerable witness or defendant)

1.7 Instead of commenting on inconsistencies during cross-examination, following discussion between the judge and the advocates, the advocate or judge may point out important inconsistencies after (instead of during) the witness's evidence. The judge should also remind the jury of these during summing up. The judge should be alert to alleged inconsistencies that are not in fact inconsistent, or are trivial. (CPD General Matters 3E.4: Ground rules hearings to plan the questioning of a vulnerable witness or defendant).

1.8 Assessment (by an intermediary) should be considered if a child or young person under 18 seems unlikely to be able to recognise a problematic question or, even if able to do so, may be reluctant to say so to a questioner in a position of authority. Many young witnesses, across all age groups, fall into one or other of these categories. For children aged 11 years and under in particular, there should be a presumption that an intermediary assessment is appropriate. Once the child's individual requirements are known and discussed at the ground rules hearing, the intermediary may agree that his or her presence is not needed for the trial.(CPD General Matters 3F.5: Intermediaries).

1.9 The expression 'judge' here applies also to magistrates and district judges.

For case management issues relating to young defendants, see Toolkit 8 Effective participation of young defendants.[18]

---

[18] See also Judicial College, *Equal Treatment Bench Book* (2013): Children and vulnerable adults and Mental disabilities, specific learning difficulties and mental capacity; Advocacy Training Council *Raising the Bar* (2011); and Family Justice Council, *Guidelines in Relation to Children Giving Evidence in Family Proceedings* (2011).

2   PRE-TRIAL

Initial arrangements

2.1 Section 16 of the Youth Justice and Criminal Evidence Act 1999   F.37
recognises children's vulnerability and automatically classifies child witnesses
as being eligible for special measures. However, despite the use of these
measures, the legal process can still be too slow to afford very young
witnesses the opportunity of providing their best evidence. There is long-
standing guidance on reducing delay for young witnesses and a recent
protocol to get child witnesses under 10 to trial within 12 weeks of
complaint. See Crown Prosecution Service (CPS) guidance: A Protocol
between the Association of Chief Police Officers, the Crown Prosecution
Service and Her Majesty's Courts and Tribunals Service to Expedite Cases
Involving Witnesses under 10 Years.
2.2 Disclosure is predominantly covered by the 2013 protocol, the aim of
which is to facilitate timely and consistent disclosure of information and
documents from the police and the CPS into the Family Justice System. See
the CPS publication 2013 Protocol and Good Practice Model: Disclosure of
information in cases of alleged child abuse and linked criminal and care
directions hearings.
2.3 The vulnerable person should be pointed towards the relevant guid-
ance/information on available special measures, ideally in advance of any pre-
trial familiarisation visit. These explain special measure options. It is not
always helpful to expect a vulnerable witness to consider special measures in
advance of a court familiarisation visit when their views very often change.
A provisional assessment can be made and special measures granted pending
the court visit.[19]
2.4 The Victims' Information Service website gives information about what
a witness can expect at different stages of the proceedings. An intermediary
may need to interpret this information to make it accessible and understandable for some witnesses.

Familiarisation, special measures and considerations

Familiarisation

2.5 The familiarisation visit should normally be supervised or conducted   F.38
by appropriately trained and skilled court staff or the witness service, with
the officer in charge and independent sexual violence advisor or intermediary, if appointed, in attendance.[20] Vulnerable witnesses should be given an

---

[19] See standards 15–17, Witness Charter 2013 and sections 1.23 and 4.11, box 4.3 appendix
and K3, *Achieving Best Evidence* (2011).
[20] See Bar Standards Board, *Guidance on Witness Preparation*.

opportunity to practise using the live link and should see screens in place if possible.[21]

2.6   During the visit the police, Witness Care Unit, Witness Service or prosecutor or defence lawyer should explain the available measures, the advantages and disadvantages of these, and ask for the witness's views.[22] The witness may ask to meet the prosecutor to discuss special measures.[23]

2.7   If an intermediary has been appointed they should accompany the vulnerable person for familiarisation with the court in order to facilitate communication between the vulnerable person and others. The intermediary should provide brief guidance on how best to communicate with the person to aid their understanding and should indicate if they believe the vulnerable person has not understood any element of the visit—particularly where a witness has been asked for their views on available special measures.

Special measures

2.8   Special measures applications must be made within 28 days of entry of a not guilty plea in the Magistrates' Court and within 14 days in the Crown Court.[24]

2.9   An intermediary can be appointed as a special measure. The intermediary will undertake an assessment of the vulnerable person's communication needs and abilities and recommend strategies and question types to achieve the best communication with that individual with the aim of improving the coherence, completeness and accuracy of the evidence they provide (and, for defendants, to enable their participation throughout the trial). The intermediary can also provide guidance on settling the individual and keeping their attention; responding to their emotional state; and steps before and during the interview and pre-trial procedures to help the individual make sense of what is happening.[25]

2.10   If opposing the application, an advocate must raise arguable grounds. Advocates should not take it upon themselves to decide the communications needs of potentially vulnerable witnesses, in particular, of children. If no intermediary was used in interview this is not evidence that one is not needed at trial.[26] If an intermediary apparently took no active part at the police interview this is usually because they provided advice to the interviewer beforehand.

2.11   It is generally extremely helpful for vulnerable witnesses to have a pre-trial familiarisation visit to the court because this can reduce anxiety for the individual and, in turn, improve their ability to communicate. Witnesses are

---

[21] Witness Charter 2013, standard 17.

[22] Witness Charter 2013, standard 11

[23] CPS prosecution policy and guidance, Witnesses: Your meeting with the CPS prosecutor

[24] Criminal Procedure Rules 2015, rule 18.9: Special measures direction for a young witness and Application for Special Measures Direction. See generally Criminal Procedure Rules (2015) at Part 18 Measures to assist a witness or defendant to give evidence.

[25] CPS Special Measures: Intermediaries; Judicial College Bench Checklist: Young witness cases (2012); *Achieving Best Evidence* (2011), box 2.1

[26] *R v Boxer* [2015] EWCA Crim 1684

likely to give better quality evidence when they choose how it is given. A pre-trial visit can also enable the individual, with appropriate support, to express an informed opinion about special measures.[27]

Considerations

2.12 *R v B* [2010] EWCA Crim 4 discussed competence as defined in section 53 of the Youth Justice and Criminal Evidence Act 1999:
These statutory provisions are not limited to the evidence of children. They apply to individuals of unsound mind. They apply to the infirm. The question in each case is whether the individual witness, or, as in this case, the individual child, is competent to give evidence in the particular trial. The question is entirely witness or child specific. There are no presumptions or preconceptions. The witness need not understand the special importance that the truth should be told in court, and the witness need not understand every single question or give a readily understood answer to every question . . . The provisions of the statute are clear and unequivocal, and do not require reinterpretation. (para 38)
2.13 The judge has a continuing duty to keep competency under review. If the vulnerable person seems to satisfy the test, 'the court and the parties should carefully consider whether a competency hearing is, in fact, necessary at the initial stage of the case. In some circumstances such a hearing may serve to do no more than cause delay, increase expense and put unnecessary strain on the witness' (*R v F* [2013] EWCA Crim 424, a case in which the competency test was 'seriously flawed').
2.14 Where a witness fears being seen, by the defendant or for another specific reason, the defendant's monitor may be screened/covered/turned off.[28]
2.15 Where facilities make it difficult to prevent the witness from having to see the defendant or their supporters and where there is particular anxiety regarding this, or a concern about intimidation, consideration should be given to the use of a remote live link (away from the trial court) from another court, non-court facility, or using mobile police equipment.[29] This may also be an option for those who are fearful of the court environment or whose anxiety levels are severely affected by travel. Consider what evidence needs to be taken to the remote site.[30]
2.16 Those not wishing to be seen by the defendant may prefer to give evidence behind screens. A vulnerable witness (or one over 18 to whom sections 21 or 22 of the Youth Justice and Criminal Evidence Act 1999 apply)

---

[27] Application for a Special Measures Direction, parts B5 and 6; *Achieving Best Evidence* (2011), section 4.84; Plea and Case Management Hearing Questionnaire, section 18A; Judicial College Bench Checklist: Young witness cases (2012)
[28] Judicial College Bench Checklist: Young witness cases (2012); *Achieving Best Evidence* (2011), sections 5.2 and B.9.10. See also Toolkit 17 Vulnerable witnesses and parties in the civil courts.
[29] Application for a Special Measures Direction, part C2
[30] Judicial College Bench Checklist: Young witness cases (2012)

may also wish to opt out of recorded evidence in chief and choose live link and secondary requirements (screens) instead (Coroners and Justice Act 2009, section 100).

2.17 Consider evidence in private[31] in particular in sexual offence cases, or if there is a reasonable belief that someone is seeking to intimidate a witness (Youth Justice and Criminal Evidence Act 1999, section 5).

2.18 Section 28 of the Youth Justice and Criminal Evidence Act 1999, providing for the pre-trial cross examination of witnesses, is currently being piloted in three Crown Court areas (Leeds, Liverpool and Kingston Upon Thames Crown Courts).

2.19 Third-party material or public interest immunity applications should be made at an early stage.[32]

2.20 Whether the witness seeks pre-trial therapy is not a decision for the police or prosecutor. The best interests of the witness are the paramount consideration. Careful recording of therapy is essential.[33]

Listing

2.21 Priority listing is particularly important in cases involving vulnerable people.

2.22 A 2015 joint protocol gives clear guidance on expediting cases involving witnesses under 10 (A Protocol between the Association of Chief Police Officers, the Crown Prosecution Service and Her Majesty's Courts and Tribunals Service to Expedite Cases Involving Witnesses under 10 Years).

2.23 Advocates should remind decision-makers to prioritise a vulnerable witness case.[34] The prosecution or defence has a responsibility to ask for this but the defence may not do so if this is not in the defendant's best interests.[35]

2.24 The trials of young and/or vulnerable children and/or persons should be fixed, not double-listed behind another trial or as a 'floater'.

2.25 If the live link is not available in all courtrooms, the courtroom should be fixed when setting the trial date.[36]

2.26 Short hearings in other matters that may delay any part of the trial should not be listed or fixed in that courtroom.

2.27 If an intermediary is appointed and the witness is to give evidence over live link, they should be positioned in the live link room so that the plasma screens in court give a clear view of both the witness and the intermediary in

---

[31] Application for a Special Measures Direction, part D
[32] PTPH Questionnaire, sections 21 and 31; *Achieving Best Evidence* (2011)
[33] *Achieving Best Evidence* (2011), sections 4.58–59; CPS, Provision of Therapy for Child Witnesses Prior to a Criminal Trial, sections 4.3–4, 5.4; CPS, Provision of Therapy for Vulnerable or Intimidated Adult Witnesses Prior to a Criminal Trial, sections 4.3, 4.4, 6.5; *Equal Treatment Bench Book*: Children and vulnerable adults, section 15.
[34] *Achieving Best Evidence* (2011), section 4.83
[35] Witness Charter 2013, standard 13
[36] Judicial College Bench Checklist: Young witness cases (2012)

the live link room. The role of the intermediary should have been explained in advance to the jury.

2.28 If the defence seeks an adjournment the prosecutor should draw the court's attention to the adverse effect of delay on young people and other vulnerable children and/or people.[37]

2.29 A judge's duty to manage all cases to achieve targets cannot override the duty to ensure that litigants receive a fair trial and are guaranteed the support necessary to compensate for any disability. The Court of Appeal found a breach of Article 6 rights where, despite a report recommending special measures, a father of 'limited capacity' gave evidence in family proceedings with only 'unsatisfactory makeshift' arrangements (*In the Matter of M (A Child)* [2012] EWCA Civ 1905).

3. PLEA AND TRIAL PREPARATION HEARING

Practical arrangements

3.1 Review any information about the witness. If it has not been provided, F.39 then you need to request it. Witnesses under 18 years of age are automatically eligible for special measures. Those over 18 who made a DVD statement when under 18 remain eligible.[38]

3.2 It is important to address timetabling and other vulnerable witness issues at first appearance in the Magistrates' Court or at the plea and trial preparation hearing in the Crown Court.[39] To help achieve certainty for the witness, complete the preparation for trial form with up-to-date witness information.[40] This should be based on consultation with the witness and, if appropriate, their carer and supporter.[41]

3.3 Available dates and dates to avoid for the witness should be ascertained (e.g. exams or other important events) and the court must take every reasonable step to facilitate the attendance of the witness[42] and the attendance of any intermediary assisting the witness at trial (likely to have limited availability) and any named supporter in the live link room.[43]

3.4 A neutral supporter, who is trusted by the witness may be present in the live link room. The court must take the witness's wishes into account.[44] This neutral supporter can be anyone who is not a party/has no detailed knowledge of evidence and who is trusted by the witness; ideally, the person

[37] *Achieving Best Evidence* (2011), section 5.18
[38] Coroners and Justice Act 2009, section 100(8)
[39] Judicial College Bench Checklist: Young witness cases (2012)
[40] Ministry of Justice Forms page
[41] *Achieving Best Evidence* (2011), sections 4.76, 5.1, 5.2
[42] Criminal Procedure Rules 2015, rule 3.8(4)(a)
[43] Judicial College Bench Checklist: Young witness cases (2012)
[44] Application for a Special Measures Direction, part C3; Coroners and Justice Act 2009, section 102

preparing the witness for court. Others may be appropriate[45] and need not be an usher or court official.[46]

3.5 Agree a timed witness order in advance, ensuring opening/preliminary points will be finished when witness evidence is due to start[47] as delays are likely to cause anxiety and adversely affect the quality of evidence given.

3.6 Schedule testimony at the best time for the young or vulnerable witness. This is likely to be early in the day before the witness becomes fatigued and/ or more anxious, but may be later if the individual needs time to settle in a space or if doses of particular medications which effect the person's concentration, anxiety or mood, for example, are more effective at certain times of the day or have a cumulative effect. It will be important to take into account the likely length of the person's concentration span—this will usually be shorter than in an assessment situation because of the high-pressure environment of the court.

3.7 Schedule evidence in chief (DVD and additional questions) and cross-examination based on advocates' time estimates.[48]

3.8 Prosecutors are expected to meet a child witness and defence advocates may also find it useful. It is up to the judge whether to meet a child with the advocates.[49] It is important to take account of the young or vulnerable person's wishes about introductions. Though the majority of people would be put more at ease by these introductions, for some people they would be likely to increase their anxieties and therefore lessen their abilities in court. Judges and advocates should consider how they will dress (e.g. in formal or casual clothes) when they meet the child witness. In one case, on the advice of the intermediary, the judge directed that they would all wear casual clothes not only when they met the child but also for the duration of the child's evidence.

3.9 The duration of cross-examination should be developmentally appropriate[50] and the judge is 'fully entitled' to impose reasonable time limits.[51]

3.10 Witness access to/exit from the building (not public entrance), standby arrangements and staggered arrival times should be discussed and arranged to best meet the needs of the vulnerable person.[52]

3.11 If a live link room is to be used, consider what exhibits may be needed in the live link room and how these will be managed.

---

[45] *Achieving Best Evidence* (2011), section 5.34, Appendix L.2.1
[46] CPD 2015 Evidence 18B.2
[47] PTPH questionnaire, section 18A; Witness Charter 2013, standard 24
[48] Judicial College Bench Checklist: Young witness cases (2012)
[49] Judicial College Bench Checklist: Young witness cases (2012)
[50] Judicial College, *Equal Treatment Bench Book* (2013): Children and vulnerable adults, section 27c
[51] Criminal Procedure Rules 2015, rule 3(10(d)
[52] PTPH questionnaire, section 18A; Witness Charter 2013, standard 23; Judicial College Bench Checklist: Young witness cases (2012)

Memory refreshing

3.12   Decide how, when and where the witness's memory should be refreshed: this should take place case by case, with the overriding aim of enabling the witness to give best evidence.[53]

3.13   For a vulnerable witness, watching the DVD can be distressing. Viewing the (edited) DVD in an informal setting may help familiarise the witness with his/her own image. First viewing should not be just before testifying.[54]

3.14   Arrangements for memory refreshing are a police responsibility[55] but should be judicially led.

3.15   There is a risk that a viewing combined with the court familiarisation visit will result in 'information overload' so the decision to do so must be made taking their individual needs into account. Memory refreshing should be the subject of a clear local inter-agency agreement.[56]

Currently, little research has been conducted into the effectiveness of refreshing testimony and only limited information has been collected regarding the delivery of this practice. Two reviews have confirmed that not all vulnerable witnesses are even given the opportunity to refresh their memory however, both reports focused on the experiences of young and vulnerable witnesses only and therefore do not offer any insight into the experiences of typical adult witnesses. (HMCPSI & HMIC, 2012; Plotnikoff & Woolfson, 2004). Practitioner guidelines also offer little instruction on refreshed testimony. The Achieving Best Evidence Guidelines *(2011) offer only broad suggestions on the practice, with few directive instructions. So far, the search for practitioner guidance on refreshing adult witnesses has only highlighted the lack of such information.*[57]

3.16   Someone (usually a police officer, not an intermediary) should be designated to take a note and report to the judge if anything is said by the witness.

3.17   If the DVD is ruled inadmissible, request court guidance on an acceptable alternative way of refreshing memory.[58] Inform the intermediary (if any) because they can often assist in memory refreshing.

3.18   There is no legal requirement that the witness should watch their DVD evidence at the same time as the jury. Provided they were able to concentrate on it at memory refreshing, they may not wish to view it again with the jury

---

[53] CPS Policy Bulletin/Legal Information P/LI/11/10
[54] PTPH questionnaire, section 18A
[55] *Achieving Best Evidence* (2011), sections 4.48, 4.51, 4.52,
[56] Criminal Justice Joint Inspection, *Joint Inspection Report on the Experience of Young Victims and Witnesses in the Criminal Justice Service* (2012)
[57] F Ainsworth and A Memon (2013) 'Refreshing Testimony in England and Wales—The Search for Best Practice' (2013) *International Investigative Interviewing: Research and Practice* 5(1): 1–11
[58] *Achieving Best Evidence* (2011), sections 4.49

and it may be detrimental to their anxiety and concentration levels if they do so.

3.19 Some vulnerable witnesses may prefer to read a transcript of their DVD evidence or to listen to, but not watch, the DVD.

3.20 A witness who has reading difficulties can choose to refresh their memory by having their written statement read over to them by a member of Witness Service.

Following the hearing

3.21 Ensure that the witness is updated after the plea and trial preparation hearing.

3.22 Ensure that all explanations are made in simple language with an opportunity for questions; note that new information may become available, witness preferences may change and ways to enable best evidence may have to be reassessed. Advocates must keep the court informed.[59]

3.23 Early identification of needs applies equally to defence witnesses and to vulnerable defendants. Consider whether a relevant expert should be instructed to consider what adaptations may be necessary.

3.24 Communication aids can help improve the quality of evidence. Intermediaries will, with the permission of the court, advise on the selection of appropriate aids, for example: a visual time line for a vulnerable person being asked to give evidence about different events over time/in different locations; or a body map for a witness asked to clarify intimate touching. It is important to plan the use of any communication aids carefully. Failure to ask a non-verbal witness to identify body parts by reference to drawings was criticised in *R v F* [2013] EWCA Crim 424. There is now a communication aids toolkit: Toolkit 14 Using communication aids in the criminal justice system.

3.25 Even when assured about reporting restrictions, some witnesses remain concerned that sufficient detail will be published to make them identifiable. Prosecution and defence counsel should work collaboratively and also consult the intermediary (where there is one) for advice on how best to formulate their questions. See *Re FA* [2015] EWCA Crim 209. Key guidance includes: Reporting Restrictions: Children and young people as victims, witnesses and defendants (CPS online policy); *Press Association, R (on the application of) v Cambridge Crown Court* [2012] EWCA Crim 2434; Reporting on Court Cases involving Sexual Offences (Press Complaints Commission, 2011), which warns editors to take account of information already in the public domain in order to avoid 'jigsaw identification' of the victim; 'The Family Courts: Media Access and Reporting' (President of the Family Division, Judicial College and Society of Editors, 2011); *The Views of*

---

[59] *Achieving Best Evidence* (2011), section 5.4

Children and Young People Regarding Media Access to the Family Courts
(Children's Commissioner for England, 2010).

3.26 Consider a timetable for editing the DVD and whether a transcript is
needed.[60]

3.27 Produce a thorough cross-examination plan and write questions for
cross-examination in advance. This will help to identify any potential
problems with the witness' understanding. There are specific toolkits on The
Advocate's Gateway website for questioning different types of young and
vulnerable people.

4. SUPPORTING THE WITNESS IN ADVANCE OF THEIR APPEARANCE AT COURT/PRE-TRIAL WITNESS INTERVIEW

4.1 Assessment of prosecution witnesses' needs should be recorded on   F.40
police MG forms;[61] a follow-up Witness Care Unit assessment[62] should ask
for information, if not already provided, about concentration span (likely to
be shorter at court), communication, development and health.[63]

4.2 As a result of the CPS consultation 'Speaking to Witnesses at Court' in
2015 the pre-trial guidance for advocates will change in 2016/2017.[64]

4.3 Current arrangements for recording and disclosing the content of such
meetings will remain in place. In the Crown Court, there will be a
reallocation of resources within the CPS that will provide sufficient paralegal
cover to allow for effective recording of conversations where they happen on
the day at court.

5. TRIAL

Ground rules hearings

5.1 The trial should be preceded by a ground rules hearing with the   F.41
intermediary, judge and advocates. (See Toolkit 1 Ground rules hearings and
the fair treatment of vulnerable people in court; and CPD General Matters
3E: Ground rules hearings to plan the questioning of a vulnerable witness or
defendant).

Cross-examination

5.2 The length of cross-examination must be developmentally appropriate
for young and vulnerable children and/or persons and there may be time
limits imposed.[65]

---

[60] Judicial College Bench Checklist: Young witness cases (2012)
[61] *Achieving Best Evidence* (2011), section 4.40
[62] Witness Charter 2013, standard 10
[63] *Achieving Best Evidence* (2011), section 4.76; Witness Charter 2013, para 13
[64] CPS (2015) 'Consultation on Speaking to Witnesses at Court: Summary of responses'
[65] Judicial College, *Equal Treatment Bench Book* (2013): Children and vulnerable adults;
Criminal Procedure Rules 2015, rule 9, rule 3.10(d)

5.3 Facilitating the participation of any person includes giving directions for the appropriate treatment and questioning of a witness or the defendant, especially where the court directs that such questioning is to be conducted through an intermediary.[66]

5.4 In *R v Sandor Jonas* [2015] EWCA Crim 562, the Court of Appeal refused an appeal based on the submission that the judge had over-restricted the cross-examination of a vulnerable witness by defence counsel in a multi-handed trial. It rejected the suggestion that counsel could conduct 'her own independent cross-examination of whatever length she deemed necessary on behalf of the appellant'. Instead, the court ruled that the judge had been correct in limiting the cross-examination which related to credit after the first defence counsel had been allowed to explore those issues thoroughly:

Advocates must accept that the courts will no longer allow them the freedom to conduct their own cross-examination where it involves simply repeating what others have asked before or exploring precisely the same territory. For these purposes, defence advocates will now be treated as a group and, if necessary, issues divided amongst them provided of course that there is no unfairness in so doing. (*R v Sandor Jonas* [2015] EWCA Crim 562, para 34)

5.5 The Court of Appeal pointed out that had there been a ground rules hearing, many of counsel's complaints 'might never have arisen'. 'Modern best practice' is to consider these matters at a ground rules hearing (para 41).

5.6 Advocates must adapt their questioning style, the complexity of the language used and the length of questions and questioning in line with the needs of the vulnerable young child or person. In *R v Cokesix Lubemba; R v JP* [2014] EWCA Crim 2064, the court upheld the conviction of an appellant at whose trial the judge had controlled both the length and content of questioning of a 10-year-old girl. Although counsel's questions were non-confrontational, 'she fell into the trap of asking questions which were more suited to an adult witness than a child' and some questions were too long and too complex. The judge had not gone too far 'in trying to protect the vulnerable witness'. A trial judge 'is not only entitled, he is duty bound to control the questioning of a witness. He is not obliged to allow a defence advocate to put their case. He is entitled to and should set reasonable time limits and to interrupt where he considers questioning is inappropriate.'

5.7 *R v 'RL'* [2015] EWCA Crim 1215 involved use of an intermediary for one of two children in a section 28 pilot case. The challenges addressed what the defence argued were 'draconian' restrictions on the form of questions to be asked and time limits (compared with the length of the ABE interview) imposed on cross-examination at the section 28 hearing. The defence said that the combined effect was to 'emasculate' cross-examination. The Court of Appeal did not agree.

---

[66] Criminal Procedure Rules 2015, rule 3.9(6)

In support of his argument, Mr Dunning relies on two particular points. First, he draws a contrast between the length of the recorded ABE interviews, which stood as the evidence in chief of the two boys, and the much shorter duration of the cross examination by him which was permitted by the judge's rulings. Secondly, he points to the fact that he was able to cross examine the boys' father in a conventional manner and, as will be recalled, the jury acquitted the applicant of the charge relating to that adult complainant (para 13)

> *. . . It is, we think, significant that in his general challenge to the effect of the judge's rulings, Mr Dunning has not sought to identify a specific example of a question which he says he should have been permitted to ask but was not allowed to do. Nor, in our view, is it entirely fair for Mr Dunning to complain that he was effectively bound by the answers given by the young witnesses. He was able to put his case, he was able to challenge the veracity of the witnesses, and he was of course able, when addressing the jury, to make his forensic points in terms other than those appropriate to the cross examination of young children.* (para 17)

Keeping the witness or defendant informed

5.8   All witnesses but particularly those who are vulnerable should be kept informed of any changes to the schedule or the proposed arrangements (including special measures) for the hearing. Each stage of the trial should be explained to them in appropriate language and they should be informed of what will be happening next and their understanding of this checked. If an intermediary has been appointed, they can insist with this. Any steps that can reasonably be taken to reduce the anxiety of a witness or defendant should be taken as this will be likely to increase the quality of the individual's communication throughout the trial.

The development of this toolkit was funded by The Advocacy Training Council and the Legal Education Foundation. It was written by Carly McAuley, Intermediary, Triangle, with assistance from Ruth Marchant, Kimberley Collins, Michelle Mattison, Vanessa Hurst (Intermediaries with Triangle); Jennie Knight, Barrister; Gabby Henty, Barrister; Rowan Jenkins, Barrister; HHJ Heather Norton; HHJ Janet Waddicor; HHJ Christine Laing; Moira Pook (Intermediary); and Professor Penny Cooper. This toolkit summarises key points from:

Achieving Best Evidence (2011)
Advocacy Training Council, *Raising the Bar* (2011) Application for Special Measures Direction
Bar Standards Board, *Guidance on Witness Preparation*
Coroners and Justice Act 2009, section 100(8)

CPS (2015) 'Consultation on Speaking to Witnesses at Court: Summary of responses'
CPS Prosecution Policy and Guidance, 'Witnesses: Your meeting with the CPS prosecutor' CPS Special Measures: Intermediaries
Criminal Justice Joint Inspection, *Joint Inspection Report on the Experience of Young Victims and Witnesses in the Criminal Justice Service* (2012)
Criminal Procedure Rules and Practice Directions 2015
Family Justice Council, *Guidelines in Relation to Children Giving Evidence in Family Proceedings* (2011) Plea and Case Management Hearing Questionnaire
Provision of Therapy for Child Witnesses Prior to a Criminal Trial
Judicial College, *Bench Checklist: Young witness cases* (2012) Judicial College, *Equal Treatment Bench Book* (2013)
Witness Charter 2013

The original versions of this toolkit (dated 21 October 2013) – Toolkit 1a Case management in young and other vulnerable witness cases and Toolkit 1b Case management in young and other vulnerable witness cases: summary – can be found in the archive section of The Advocate's Gateway website.

TOOLKIT 1(B): SUMMARY: CASE MANAGEMENT IN YOUNG AND OTHER VULNERABLE WITNESS CASES[67]

F.42 *This toolkit brings together policy and guidance relating to:*

> 1. *Instructions, listing and other tasks*
> 2. Witness needs, wishes and special measures

The expression 'judge' here applies also to magistrates and district judges.

For a version of this toolkit with references and hyperlinks, see Toolkit 1(a). For case management issues relating to young defendants, see Toolkit 8, Effective participation of young defendants.

1. INSTRUCTIONS, LISTING AND OTHER TASKS

F.43 **1.1** *Address timetabling and other vulnerable witness issues at first appearance* in magistrates' court or preliminary hearing or PCMH in Crown Court. To help achieve certainty for the witness, complete the PCMH questionnaire/ magistrates' court preparation for trial form:

---

[67] August 2014, © Lexicon Limited.

- based on consultation, with witness and, if appropriate, care and supporter, with up-to-date witness information;
- with availability and dates to avoid for the witness (eg exams or other important events); any Registered Intermediary assisting the witness at trial[68] (likely to have limited availability); and any named supporter in the live link room. The court must take every reasonable step to facilitate witness attendance.

1.2 *Priority listing* Delay adds disproportionately to the vulnerable person's stress:

- where the witness is under 18 or otherwise vulnerable (whether or not special measures have been ordered) the trial date should usually be fixed. The prosecution or defence has a responsibility to ask for this but the defence may not if not in the defendant's best interests;
- remind decision-makers to prioritise a vulnerable witness case. The prosecution or defence will ask the court to give the trial date priority and fix it to a specific day;
- give priority to trials involving young defendants or vulnerable or young witnesses. Delay in a case involving a child complainant should be kept 'to an irreducible minimum';
- if the live link is not available in all courtrooms, fix the courtroom when setting the trial date;
- if an early trial date is desirable/ defendant is young, a preliminary hearing should be listed about 14 days after sending the case to Crown Court.

1.3 *If the defence seeks an adjournment* the prosecutor should draw the court's attention to the adverse effect of delay on young witnesses, those with learning disabilities or conditions such as autism spectrum disorder, mental health problems and specific learning difficulties.

1.4 *A court with plasma screens* will give a clear view of intermediary/ witness interaction.

1.5 *Schedule and adhere to prompt start to witness evidence*

- agree a timed witness order in advance, ensuring opening/ preliminary points will be finished when witness evidence is due to start;
- schedule testimony to start early while the witness is fresh, taking account of concentration span, breaks, length of DVD, effect of any medication and whether there is more than one vulnerable witness.

---

[68] For information about Registered Intermediaries for witnesses, contact the National Crime Agency at 0845 0005463, and by e-mail at soc@nca.pnn.police.uk (by pnn users) or soc@nca.x.gsi.gov.uk (by others). The judiciary may use its inherent jurisdiction to appoint non-registered intermediaries for vulnerable defendants.

Schedule evidence in chief (DVD and additional questions) and cross-examination based on advocates' time estimates;

- short hearings in other matters should not be listed before the start or continuation of trial as they may cause delay;
- take account of witness wishes and judicial preferences about introductions. Prosecutors are expected to meet a witness defence advocates may find it useful. It is up to the judge whether to meet a witness with the advocates;
- duration should be developmentally appropriate and limits may be imposed.

1.6 *DVD interview* Have both parties received the DVD?
- watch *before* PCMH to aid decisions on admissibility, editing and refreshing witness memory;
- is it playable and audible on court equipment? Check before day of trial;
- consider timetable for editing and whether a transcript is needed.

1.7 *Pre-trial familiarisation visit to the court* See section 2.8, below.

1.8 *Third party material or PII* Applications should be made at an early stage. Disclosure of medical/ counselling records engage the witness's Article 8 right to privacy. Check that the police have obtained appropriate consent to gain access to the records. Witnesses must be informed about the purpose of the request. They are entitled to give qualified consent to disclosure (i.e. to the prosecution only, not the defence) or to decline consent but must also be told about the possible consequences for the case outcome.

1.9 *Witness access to/ exit from court building (not public entrance); standby arrangements; and staggered arrival times*

1.10 *Arrangements to refresh witness memory* should be addressed at the PCMH or case management hearing. The witness's first viewing of the DVD can be distressing or distracting. It should not be seen for the first time immediately before giving evidence. Assistance of the intermediary may be needed to establish how memory refreshing should be managed. If the interview is ruled inadmissible, the court must decide what constitutes an acceptable alternative method of memory refreshing. Decisions about how, when and where refreshing should take place should be court led in respect of each witness. General principles to be addressed include:
- the venue for viewing. Refreshing at the same time as the court familiarisation visit may lead to 'information overload'. Refreshing need not take place at court but may be done, for example, at the police interview suite;

- requiring that any viewing is monitored, usually by the officer in the case, who will report to the court about anything said by the witness;
- whether it is necessary for the witness to see the DVD more than once for the purpose of refreshing (the court will ask the advice of the intermediary).

1.11 *There is no legal requirement that the witness should watch the DVD at the same time as the jury* Increasingly, this occurs at a different time, so that breaks can be taken without disrupting the trial and cross-examination starts while the witness is fresh. If watched at a different time:

- an intermediary may be present but should not act as the independent person designated to take a note and report to the court if anything is said;
- the witness is sworn just before cross-examination, asked if (s)he has watched the DVD and if its contents are 'true' (in words tailored to witness understanding).

1.12 *Arrangements for memory refreshing are a police responsibility* and should be the subject of a clear local inter-agency agreement. In the case of a very young child it may be appropriate to record the viewing. Any supporter present for refreshing should generally not have been at the investigative interview, have supported the witness pre-trial or be expected to accompany the witness when giving evidence.

1.13 *Update witness and court post-PCMH* Inform witnesses of case progress:

- ensure explanations are made in simple language with an opportunity for questions;
- new information may become available, witness preferences may change and ways to enable best evidence may have to be reassessed. Advocates must keep the court informed.

1.14 *What exhibits may be needed in the live link room?* How will they be managed?

1.15 *Confirm timetable and ensure all relevant decisions have been made* Consider requesting a pre-trial review.

1.16 *If there are parallel care proceedings* refer to CPS Protocol and Good Practice Model for disclosure of information in cases of alleged child abuse and linked criminal and care directions hearings.

1.17 *There is a duty to inform court at once if any order is not complied with* Overriding Objective, Rule 1, Criminal Procedure Rules 2014.

2. WITNESS NEEDS, WISHES AND SPECIAL MEASURES

F.44   **2.1   *Timely special measures applications*** in magistrates' court within 28 days of entry of not guilty plea and in Crown Court within 14 days. The court can vary time limits. Special measures information is needed to complete the PCMH questionnaire.

2.2   *A judge's duty to manage all cases to achieve targets cannot override the duty to ensure that litigants receives a fair trial and are guaranteed the support necessary to compensate for disability*

2.3   *Review witness information: request it if not provided* Gather information at the earliest stage. Young witnesses are automatically eligible for special measures. Those over 18 who made a DVD statement when under 18 remain eligible.

2.4   *Medical conditions* Consider any relevant precautionary arrangements eg ensuring that someone trained in first aid is available in the court building for someone with epilepsy.

2.5   *Assessment of prosecution witness needs* should be recorded on police MG forms and in a follow-up Witness Care Unit assessment. Ask for information if not provided about concentration span (likely to be shorter at court), communication, development and health.

2.6   *Early identification of needs applies equally to defence witnesses and to vulnerable defendants* Consider whether a relevant expert should be instructed to consider what adaptations may be necessary.

2.7   *Competence is assumed if the witness is capable of giving intelligible testimony*
This may require use of an intermediary. The judge has a continuing duty to keep competency under review. If the witness seems to satisfy the test, the court and parties should consider whether a competency hearing is necessary as it may cause delay, increase expense and put unnecessary strain on the witness.

2.8   *Is witness being helped to express <u>informed</u> opinion about special measures?*
   • witnesses are likely to give better evidence when they choose how it is given. They need preparation and support to make an informed choice. This requires a pretrial familiarisation visit to the court with a live link practice session. They should also see screens in place;
   • the prosecution or defence will ask court staff to make provision for witness needs as a result of disability, medical condition or age. An

accredited interpreter, Registered Intermediary, signer or other assistance will be provided in relation to language or communication needs;

- the police, Witness Care Unit or prosecutor or defence lawyer should explain available measures, and ask for witness views. CPS will take the victim's views into account. The witness may ask to meet the prosecutor to discuss special measures;

2.9 *Witness opt out* Those not wishing to be seen by the defendant may prefer screens. A young witness (or one over 18 to whom sections 21 or 22, Youth Justice and Criminal Evidence Act 1999 apply) may wish to opt out of the primary rule (recorded evidence in chief and live link) and secondary requirement (screens).

2.10 *Remote live link (away from trial court) from another court, non-court facility or using mobile police equipment* (Toolkit 9) Consider this where the witness is anxious about seeing the defendant/ supporters; facilities make it difficult to keep the witness separate; or where there is concern about intimidation/ fear of the court environment. What evidence needs to be taken to the remote site?

2.11 *A neutral supporter (trusted by witness) in live link room* may be specified by the court which *must* take witness wishes into account. This can be anyone who is trusted by the witness and is not a party/ has no detailed knowledge of evidence; ideally, the person preparing the witness for court. Others may be appropriate and need not be an usher or court official.

2.12 *Consider evidence in private* in sex offence cases, or if there is a reasonable belief that someone is seeking to intimidate a witness.

2.13 *Where a witness fears being seen by the defendant, or for another specific reason* the defendant's monitor may be screened/ covered/ turned off.

2.14 *Intermediary special measure to help maximise quality of evidence* A Registered Intermediary's assessment report advises how best to question the witness:

- can the witness recognise a problematic question/ tell the questioner that (s)he has not understood? If not, consider intermediary assessment;
- if opposing the application, raise properly arguable grounds. Do not take it upon yourself to decide the communications needs of potentially vulnerable witnesses, in particular, children. If no intermediary was used in interview this is not evidence that one is not needed at trial. If an intermediary apparently took no active part at the police

interview, this is usually because the (s)he provided advice to the interviewer beforehand;

- part F.1 of the Application for a special measures direction and para 5.2 Magistrates' Court Preparation for Effective Trial, requires discussion of ground rules by the intermediary, judge and advocates (see Toolkit 1(c)[68a] Ground Rules). Advocates may request intermediary advice about adapting specific questions.

2.15 *Communication aids can help improve the quality of evidence* Intermediaries will, with the permission of the court, advise on the selection of appropriate aids e.g. a visual time line for a witness being asked to give evidence about different events over time/ in different locations; or a body map for a witness asked to clarify intimate touching.

2.16 *Whether the witness seeks pretrial therapy* is not a decision for the police or prosecutor. The best interests of the witness are the paramount consideration. Careful recording of therapy is essential.

2.17 *Even when assured about reporting restrictions, children and vulnerable adult witnesses remain concerned that enough detail will be published to make them identifiable* Key guidance is listed in Toolkit 1(a).

TOOLKIT 2: GENERAL PRINCIPLES FROM RESEARCH, POLICY AND GUIDANCE: PLANNING TO QUESTION A VULNERABLE PERSON OR SOMEONE WITH COMMUNICATION NEEDS[69]

INDEX
1. General principles from research, policy and guidance
2. Appropriate questioning styles and strategies
3. Framing and structuring questions appropriately and effectively
4. Inappropriate and ineffective questioning: strategies to avoid

F.45   The Advocate's Gateway provides individual toolkits that outline guidance relating to the questioning of children and young people and those who have particular communication needs within the justice process. This toolkit contains general information about questioning a vulnerable person or somebody with communication needs and is primarily intended for use by advocates and judges, as well as police officers, social workers, solicitors and guardians. For more detailed guidance, please refer to the toolkit most appropriate for the person being questioned.

[68a] Available at *http://lexiconlimited.co.uk/wp-content/uploads/2015/02/1cGroundRulesrevision-050215.pdf* [Accessed April 30, 2016].
[69] November 2015. © ATC The Advocate's Gateway 2015.

This toolkit contains general guidance and is not a replacement for an intermediary assessment which will provide advice specific to the individual. Importantly, an intermediary can help highlight an individual's communication needs. For further guidance on the work of intermediaries please refer to Toolkit 16 Intermediaries: step by step.

1.　GENERAL PRINCIPLES FROM RESEARCH, POLICY AND GUIDANCE

1.1　The **most significant factor in effective communication** with a vulnerable F.46 person or somebody with communication needs is the questioner's ability to adopt an appropriate manner and tailor questions to the needs and abilities of the individual (Agnew et al, 2006; Bull, 2010; Powell et al, 2013), enabling the person to understand questions and give answers that he or she believes to be correct.

1.2　**No two people have the same profile of communication strengths and weaknesses.** Obtaining a full picture of the individual's communication capabilities is essential and an intermediary can help with this, by requesting information, for example:

- about the person's education;
- whether (s)he has a carer; and
- whether (s)he uses signing/communication aids in daily life.

1.3　**Always consider assessment of a vulnerable witness by an intermediary** (Youth Justice and Criminal Evidence Act 1999, section 29) if the person is unlikely to be able to recognise when they do not understand something, or tell you that they have not understood, or has some other communication difficulty, even if no intermediary was used at the investigative interview. The judiciary may use its inherent jurisdiction to appoint an intermediary for a vulnerable defendant.

1.4　**Accuracy, coherence and completeness of testimony** from a vulnerable person or somebody with communication needs can be significantly improved if the person's preferred communication strategies are adopted, including the use of communication aids (see Toolkit 14 Using communication aids in the criminal justice system).

1.5　**The 'rules' of communication should also be explained** *prior to questioning,* for example:

- that the person does not need to agree with suggestions put to them when questioned unless they are true;
- that it is okay to say '*I don't know*' or '*I don't understand*'.

Explanations of communication 'rules' like this should be explored with the person beforehand, rather than first being introduced at the start of questioning. The intermediary can help with this. It is essential that the 'rules', including their wording and their presentation, are adapted to the needs of the vulnerable person (Marchant, 2013).

2. APPROPRIATE QUESTIONING STYLES AND STRATEGIES

F.47 **2.1 Introductions:**
- Being introduced to the vulnerable person prior to them giving evidence is an important opportunity to become familiar with their communication abilities.
- This approach can also help to reduce stress and anxiety associated with vulnerability.
- Explanations to the witness or defendant about their role and the questioner's role are crucial.
- Some vulnerable people may be unaware that that the person asking questions does not know the answers.

2.2 Ensure tone and body language are neutral and maintain attention:
- Do not nod, invite an affirmative response, or express disbelief through facial expression or body language.
- Look at the person and ensure that they know you are speaking to them.
- Eye contact is an important part of communication and should be achieved, unless there are cultural or other specific reasons to avoid it.
- On the live link, look straight at the camera, not at papers.

2.3 Use appropriate pace:
- This means appropriate to the individual. For example, some young children will lose attention or not connect the question with their previous answer if there are long pauses between questions.
- Some witnesses need a 'normal' pace of communication, others need you to speak more slowly or to allow extra thinking time where needed in order to process information before answering a question.
- Do not move on to another question too quickly.
- If there is no response, count to six in your head and then try repeating or rephrasing the question.

2.4 Consider non-verbal communication/use of visual communication aids:
- Communication aids can support and augment a person's communication;
- Asking a witness to demonstrate intimate touching on their own body is inappropriate. Use a body map or diagram.
- Using communication aids almost always requires intermediary involvement and should be explored prior to questioning.

2.5 Be alert for possible miscommunication:

- This includes monitoring non-verbal clues such as a puzzled or frustrated look, knitted eyebrows, downcast eyes and long pauses.
- An intermediary in the live link room often identifies signs of confusion before these are picked up by those in court.
- It is good practice to ask the witness to say so, put up a hand or to point to a 'cue' card if he or does not understand.
- Many vulnerable people will not recognise when difficulties occur or will be too embarrassed to admit this.
- Do not just say 'Do you understand?' If necessary, ask the person to explain what is meant in their own words.

2.6　Check that you and the witness mean the same thing.
- Clarify understanding of words crucial to the evidence.
- For example, the word 'touch' may be interpreted as relating solely to touching by hands.
  Q: 'Did he touch you?' (asked of a six-year-old).
  A: 'No. [later] He licked me.'
- The question may not be understood if it implies that the witness was active in the event.
  Q: 'Did you touch John?'
  A: 'No. [later] He put his willy in my hand and in my mouth.'

2.7　Be alert to loss of concentration and take breaks from questioning.
- Breaks should be based on the person's concentration span. This will vary with time of day, stress levels and situation. An intermediary assessment may assist.
- Be mindful that a person's typical level of concentration is likely to be shorter than usual at court.
- Early signs may not be evident over the live link.
- Do not rely on someone to ask for a break, or to say they need one if asked. They may elect to keep going to 'get it over with'. The person may lack the ability to anticipate when they need a break and may quickly reach overload under cross-examination.
- When a break is requested, it may be needed immediately. This should be accommodated.
- **Draw the court's attention to improper or inappropriate cross-examination:** both the prosecutor and defence advocates have this responsibility.

3.　FRAMING AND STRUCTURING QUESTIONS APPROPRIATELY AND EFFECTIVELY

3.1　Writing out questions in advance will help to identify potential problems.　F.48
An intermediary will be able to advise about appropriate question-framing and structure.

3.2　Use clear and simple language.

- Use simple words with which the witness is familiar.
- Avoid redundant words and phrases (e.g. *'To your knowledge . . .'*; *'I put it to you . . .'*), jargon and complex vocabulary.
- Use the same words consistently in questions.
- Ensure there is a shared understanding of key concepts and phrases.
- Avoid metaphors and non-literal language. For example:
  Q: 'Did you go to Jim's house?'
  A: 'No.'
  Q: 'Did you go to Jim's flat?'
  A: 'Yes.'
- Avoid figures of speech, e.g: *'I am going to run through a few things.'*
- Avoid use of present tense, e.g:
  Q: 'Are you in school now?'
  A: 'No, I'm at court.'
- Avoid figures of speech, which even if understood, may be interpreted literally. For example, *'Is that right?'* should be avoided because the word 'right' has two meaning in this context ('accurate' or 'morally right'). Better alternatives are *'Are you sure?'* or *'Is that true?'*

3.3　Use concrete words.

- Abstract, 'concept' words can be problematic, for example: numbers; measurements; before/after; in front of/below/behind; always /never; different/same; and more/less.
- Use of such words by a vulnerable person does not mean they are understood, for example, the ability to count does not mean that somebody can answer accurately 'How many times?' something happened.
- Tie questions about timing of what happened to events: *'What was on TV?'*
- An intermediary can assess the person's understanding of abstract, concept words, prior to questioning.

3.4　Follow a logical and chronological order.

- Avoid questions that jump around in time or appear to be unconnected, as these require constant re-orientation by the witness.
- Refer to one event per question. Referring to more than one event per question is confusing for the listener.

3.5　Signpost places, names and objects:

- **refer to places:** *'Carol, were you in the kitchen?'* not *'Were you there?'*

- **refer to names:** avoid pronouns, e.g. *'What did Max say?'* not *'What did he say?'*
- **refer to objects:** e.g. *'Was the money in the wallet?'* not *'Was it inside?'*. Questions removing personal references to the witness and/or defendant are more difficult to understand and have a distancing effect, e.g. *'Did you tell the police about what is in that statement about the matter, about the touching of the boobs?'* (asked of an 11-year-old). This can cause comprehension problems even for adults. Better options include: *'You said Jim touched your boobs. Did you tell the police?'*

3.6 Refer to the subject in question and explain when it is about to be changed.
- This gives the person transition time to focus on the next subject.
- For example, *'Now we're going to talk about . . . '*. It can be helpful to schedule a break at a change of subject.

3.7 Keep questions short.
- Ask short, simple questions.
- Avoid 'front-loading', e.g. *'I suggest to you that . . . '*; *'I put it to you . . . '*; *'I believe you told us . . . '*
- Avoid phrases such as *'Do you follow?'* at the end of questions.
- Complex questions are likely to result in incorrect or *'I don't know'* responses, even though the person does know the answer and could respond if the question were phrased simply.
- In order to answer accurately, someone with a learning disability needs to be able to remember and process the whole question.
- Present one topic at a time. The person may have a limited working memory and may be unable to remember all of a multi-part question or decipher embedded clauses.
- Who/what/where questions are usually most easily understood.

4. INAPPROPRIATE AND INEFFECTIVE QUESTIONING: STRATEGIES TO AVOID

4.1 Vulnerable people and people with communication needs are more likely F.49 **to misunderstand or comply with** (i.e. reply 'yes' to):
- questions suggesting the answer (such as a tag or other form of leading question);
- questions requiring a yes/no response;
- questions in the form of statements (assertions);
- questions/assertions that are repeated by authority figures;
- forced choice (closed) questions;
- questions containing one or more negatives;
- questions suggesting the witness is lying or confused;
- *'Do you remember . . . ?'* questions.

4.2   Tag questions make a statement then add a short question inviting confirmation, for example, '*John didn't touch you, did he?*' or '*John didn't touch you, right?*'. They are powerfully suggestive and linguistically complex. Judicial guidance recommends that this form of question be avoided with children and that a direct question be put instead, e.g. '*Did John touch you?*'; '*How did John touch you?*'

4.3   Questions requiring a yes/no response: a series of propositions or leading questions inviting repetition of either 'yes' or 'no' answers is likely to affect accuracy. These questions carry a risk that an acquiescent person (i.e. someone with a tendency to answer 'yes', regardless of the question) will adopt a pattern of replies 'cued' by the questioner and will cease to respond to individual questions, leading to inaccurate replies. If only 'yes'/'no' questions are asked, it is difficult to determine if the person is having problems with the questions.

4.4   Questions in the form of statements (assertions), for example, '*You're not telling the truth, you wanted Jim out of your house*', may not be understood as requiring a response. Better alternatives include: '*Did you want Jim out of your house?*'

4.5   Questions/assertions repeated by authority figures: whether asked/stated consecutively or interspersed with others, these risk reducing the overall accuracy of a vulnerable person or someone with communication needs. For questions, this is because the person is likely to conclude that their first answer is wrong or unsatisfactory because somebody in authority is repeating the question. This may make the person 'go along' with the suggested answer, even if the person disagrees with it. If a question must be repeated (even with changed wording) for clarity, explain that you just want to check your understanding of what the person said, without implying the first answer was wrong: for example, '*Thank you, but I want to be sure I understand. Tell me again.*' (followed by the question). For assertions, when someone in a position of authority formally suggests that something is a fact, it becomes extremely difficult for a person to disagree if necessary and to maintain verbally what they believe to be true. The person is likely to have a particular problem with an assertion in the form of a statement, viewing this as a comment and not appreciating that it requires a response.

4.6   Forced choice (closed) questions: these questions (for example, '*When you went to the flat, did John or Bill open the door?*') create opportunities for error if the correct alternative may be missing. If asked open, free recall questions (e.g. '*What happened?*'), vulnerable people or those with communication needs can provide accounts with accuracy rates broadly similar to the general population. In instances where forced choice questions are necessary, offer '*I don't know*' as a last alternative.

4.7 Questions containing one or more negatives: these questions make it harder to decipher the underlying meaning. Negatives increase complexity and the risk of unreliable responses.

4.8 Questions suggesting the witness is lying or confused: these questions are likely to have an adverse impact on concentration and accuracy of responses because of the heightened anxiety often associated with vulnerable people. For an alternative approach in which such points are explained to the jury but not put to the witness, see Toolkit 1 Ground rules hearings and the fair treatment of vulnerable people in court (section 3).

4.9 If such a challenge is developmentally appropriate, it should:
- be addressed separately, at the end of cross-examination;
- be put in simple, clear language;
- not require the person to identify past emotions or intentions—a question about past emotions or intentions may be developmentally inappropriate for a vulnerable person or someone with communication needs.

4.10 *'Do you remember?'* **questions:** these require the ability to follow and recall the whole question and to identify what the questioner wants to know. This type of question requires complex processing, particularly when the person is asked, not about the event, but about what they said about it to someone else.

The development of this toolkit was funded by The Advocacy Training Council and the Legal Education Foundation. It was written by Dr Michelle Mattison, Intermediary, Triangle, with assistance from Ruth Marchant, Kimberley Collins, Carly McAuley, Vanessa Hurst (Intermediaries with Triangle); Jennie Knight, Barrister; Gabby Henty, Barrister; Rowan Jenkins, Barrister; HHJ Heather Norton; HHJ Janet Waddicor; HHJ Christine Laing; Moira Pook (Intermediary). This toolkit summarises key points from:

Advocacy Training Council (2011) Raising the Bar: The handling of vulnerable witnesses, victims and defendants at court, part 5

Agnew, S E, Powell, M B and Snow, P C (2006) 'An examination of the questioning styles of police officers and caregivers when interviewing children with intellectual disabilities' 11(1) *Legal and Criminological Psychology* 35–53

British Dyslexia Association and Developmental Adult Neuro-Diversity Association (2009) *Good Practice Guide for Justice Professionals: Guidelines for supporting clients and users of the justice system who have dyslexia and other specific learning difficulties* (also deals with autism)

British Institute of Learning Disabilities

Bull, R (2010) 'The investigative interviewing of children and other vulnerable witnesses: psychological research and working/professional practice' 15 *Legal and Criminological Psychology* 5–23

Communication Trust (2009) Sentence trouble

Crown Prosecution Service (2012) Safeguarding children as victims and witnesses Department for Education (2013) Working Together to Safeguard Children

Department of Health (2011) Positive practice, positive outcomes: a handbook for professionals working in the criminal justice system with offenders with a learning disability

Ellison, E (2001) *The Adversarial Process and the Vulnerable Witness* (OUP)

Hanna, K et al (2010) *Child Witnesses in the New Zealand Criminal Courts: A review of practice and implications for policy*, Institute of Public Policy, AUT University and New Zealand Law Foundation

Immigration Law Practitioners' Association (2012) *Working with Children and Young People Subject To Immigration control: Guidelines for best practice*

Judicial College (2012) Bench Checklist: Young witness cases

TOOLKIT 6: PLANNING TO QUESTION A CHILD OR YOUNG PERSON[70]

F.50 **INDEX**

1. **Introduction**
   Tailor your approach to the individual child and be flexible because
   Always consider assessment of a child by an intermediary because
2. **General principles about children's communication**
3. **Case management**
4. **Foundations or 'setting conditions'**
   Adjust the environment if needed because
   Think ahead about visually recorded interviews as evidence-in-chief because
   Keep key people in the child's life informed about what is happening because
   Facilitate a pre-trial visit, including a practice with live link and/or screens because
   Plan memory refreshing carefully including when how and where because
   Introduce yourself to establish rapport before questioning starts because

---

[70] December 2015. © ATC The Advocate's Gateway 2015.

Explain the 'rules' of communication prior to questioning because
Be aware of the impact of stress on communication, because
Be aware of the impact of trauma on communication because
Be aware of the impact of live ink on communication because
Adjust your pace to the child's needs because
Be alert to loss of concentration and take breaks from questioning because
Be alert to possible miscommunication because
Draw the court's attention to improper or inappropriate cross-examination because

5. Expressive communication: making sure you are understood
   Plan questions in topics and be clear about changes of topic because
   Write out draft questions in advance because
   Ask each question once unless there is a good reason to repeat it because
   Ensure tone and body language are neutral, and maintain attention because
   Make sure the content of questions is developmentally appropriate
   Use concrete words and say what you mean because
   Check understanding of crucial evidential words because
   Take care with questions suggesting the child is lying or confused because
   Carefully plan questions about intimate touching or sexual acts because
   Be clear about places, names, objects, and subjects because
   Carefully plan questions about abstract concepts because
   Keep questions short because
   Keep questions simple in structure because
   Ask all questions about past events in the past tense because
   Beware of negative and passive language in questions because
   Be careful about questions in form of statements (assertions) because
   Be particularly cautious about the use of tagged questions because
   Be careful with questions requiring a yes/no response because
   Be careful when asking forced choice (closed) questions because
   Be careful with 'Do you remember?' questions, because

6. Receptive communication: making sure you understand
   Make sure you and the jury can see and hear the child clearly because
   Attend to gestures and actions as well as words because
   Ask for clarification if you don't understand or aren't sure because
   Ask the child to repeat if you didn't hear, but say why because

If you need to check back on what was said, use the child's own words because
Gain some familiarity with the child's communication aids because

1. INTRODUCTION

F.51   **1.1   Tailor your approach to the individual child and be flexible because** no two children have the same profile of communication strengths and weaknesses.

Advocates must adapt to the witness, not the other way round. (R v Cokesix Lubemba; R v JP [2014] EWCA Crim 2064)

Obtaining a full picture of the child's communication capabilities is essential and an intermediary can help with this by requesting information, e.g: about the child's education; whether he or she has additional support at home, school, college and so on.

1.2   Always consider assessment of a child by an intermediary because all children under 18 are eligible to be considered for the intermediary special measure (Ministry of Justice, 2011, *Achieving Best Evidence*; section 16, Youth Justice and Criminal Evidence Act 1999). Just because a child appears to be able to communicate well, does not mean that they will be able to understand complex legal questioning during a cross examination, or feel able to say when they do not understand.

2. GENERAL PRINCIPLES ABOUT CHILDREN'S COMMUNICATION

F.52   **2.1   Child development occurs across four main areas**; physical, cognitive, emotional and social, all of which interact. Due to these factors a range of communication skills are acquired over time, for example:

- the ability to understand what others say and do;
- the ability of the child to express themselves;
- knowing how to communicate in a range of social situations;
- the ability to successfully manage stress and anxiety.

2.2   Children do not approach communication in the same way as adults and do not use, process or understand language in the same way as adults.

2.3   Within the 'normal range' of communication for a child's age, ability can vary widely (Doherty-Sneddon, 2003). Effective communication needs to take account of the individual child's chronological age, developmental stage, emotional state, education and culture, as well as any other condition that affects communication (see other toolkits e.g. Toolkit 3 Planning to question someone with an autism spectrum disorder, Toolkit 4 Planning to question someone with a learning disability, Toolkit 5 Planning to question someone with hidden disabilities and Toolkit 15 Witnesses and defendants with autism: memory and sensory issues).

3. CASE MANAGEMENT

3.1 Information about the individual child's communicative needs is essential and, if not supplied, must be requested. All children under 18 are eligible to be considered for the intermediary special measure (Ministry of Justice, 2011; Youth Justice and Criminal Evidence Act 1999). If a child cannot participate in criminal proceedings or provide their best evidence then assessment by an intermediary should be considered, even if not initially used at interview. Intermediaries should be considered in all child sexual abuse cases.   F.53

3.2 Familiarisation: a trained person should help children understand their witness role, using Young Witness Packbook lets or resources at youand-co.org.uk. They should practice on the live link, and see screens in place, to be able to express an informed view about special measures (Application for Special Measures Direction, parts B5, B6) as research demonstrates that children given a choice about whether or not to use the live link were assessed as giving more effective testimony, irrespective of the method of testimony (Cashmore and De Haas, 1992). The special measures requested should be kept under close review (DPP Interim Guidelines 2013, para 81).

GOOD PRACTICE EXAMPLE:
The prosecutor attended the court visit and asked the child non-evidential questions (prepared by the intermediary) over the live link. This helped the child understand the communication rules at court and contributed to the intermediary's assessment. In another case, an intermediary supplemented the live link experience for a child with face-to-face phone calls using a tablet computer and smart phone.

3.3 A ground rules hearing must be carried out between the intermediary, advocates and the judge (Criminal Practice Directions 2015). Guidance on the format of the ground rules hearing can be found in Toolkit 1 Ground rules hearings and the fair treatment of vulnerable people in court. Ground rules hearings are essential because they allow the intermediary the opportunity to provide clear recommendations and guidance for questioning the child based on their communication assessment. This guidance is there to help the court gain best evidence from the child. Ground rules hearings also allow the judge/advocates the opportunity to ask for clarification and guidance on any of the points raised in the intermediary's report about the child's communication (Criminal Procedure Rules 2015).

3.4 Ensure that equipment is working and sound quality is good before the child enters the live link room. Check camera angles (crucial if the child relies on gesture). Change the angle to get the best picture; do not instead seat the child on additional cushions.

3.5   If the child's understanding of truth and lies is questioned, and this has not been appropriately covered in the Achieving Best Evidence interview, then an intermediary's guidance should be sought about how to assess this in a developmentally appropriate way. See Triangle's *Truth and Lies* DVD for an example of a child-appropriate method for assessing children's understanding of truth and lies.

4.   FOUNDATIONS OR 'SETTING CONDITIONS'

F.54   **4.1**   These basic foundations for effective communication will enable the best evidence of a child witness or the best participation of a young defendant.

4.2   Adjust the environment if needed because ensuring the child feels comfortable can reduce anxiety and facilitate recall. Communication live link allows more control of the immediate environment than in the courtroom but there can be complications. Some people struggle with the slight delay between speaking and being heard, or with the drop in volume when two people speak at once. Others find hearing themselves over the link or seeing themselves on screen very difficult. Practice can help with all of these things as can creative adaptations. The intermediary can also offer guidance on how to adapt the environment to make it more suitable for the individual child:

- screening the defendant's view of the live link screen in cases where a child is very fearful of being seen by the defendant.
- consider using a remote link from another court or non-court site in cases where a child is very anxious or fearful of being in the same building as the defendant (Toolkit 9 Planning to question someone using a remote link);
- consider using child-friendly facilities, with doors the child can open;
- consider using child-sized furniture in the live link room so, for example, a three-year-old could be properly seated with their feet on the floor, with a table for communication aids/calming play materials;
- make sure the camera is adjusted to ensure a closer focus to provide a clear view of the child's face and hands so as to capture non-verbal communication;
- locate microphones appropriately for a child who whispers.

GOOD PRACTICE EXAMPLE:
A child whispered answers using 'rude' words to the intermediary. As agreed at the ground rules hearing, the intermediary repeated the responses with

exact intonation and phrasing and sat near a microphone so that the child's
whispers had the best chance of being picked up.

**4.3 Think ahead about visually recorded interviews as evidence-in-chief
because** they may be too long, or contain sections that are not relevant or not
admissible. Transcripts may not be complete. Editing should take place
before memory refreshing and before the planning of cross-examination
questions. This made memory refreshing quicker and also saved court
time.

GOOD PRACTICE EXAMPLE:
A statement was made to condense a lengthy DVD interview. The intermediary and police officer agreed that the intermediary would review the
statement for vocabulary, grammar phrasing and suggest any amendments.
Then the officer, child or young person and intermediary read through the
statement together.

4.4 Ensure interview transcripts include important non-verbal communication, especially where a child indicates yes/no by nodding and shaking their
head without words. Also ensure that relevant communication through
gesture, drawings or communication aids is clearly referred to in the
transcript. An intermediary can help provide a more complete account of
non-verbal communication, e.g. describing gestures without interpretation
('points at genital area of drawing', 'puts finger in own mouth').

GOOD PRACTICE EXAMPLE:
The judge directed an intermediary who was familiar with the child or young
person's communication techniques to revise the transcript to include a
written record of use of signs and communication aids.

4.5 Minimise transcript passages marked 'inaudible', especially where these
are central to the evidence. An intermediary maybe able to transcribe
sections marked 'inaudible' to assist the court.

**4.6 Keep key people in the child's life informed about what is happening
because** parents and caregivers will have to answer the child's questions prior
to court attendance and may have to explain what to expect. Proper
preparation can help alleviate the child's anxiety and help the child understand what is expected of them. Both of these factors will improve the child's
ability to provide a comprehensive account during questioning. The intermediary and the Witness Service can offer guidance on this information, e.g.
who needs to be informed and what types of information the caregiver and
child will need to know.

4.7 Children and young people should be kept informed as far as is possible
as to any changes to the schedule of the hearing. Each stage of the trial

should be explained to them in appropriate language and they should be informed of what will be happening next and their understanding of this checked. If an intermediary has been appointed, they will take responsibility for arranging this. Any steps that can reasonably be taken to reduce the anxiety of a witness or defendant should be taken as this will be likely to increase the quality of the child's communication throughout the trial.

GOOD PRACTICE EXAMPLE:
A five-year-old was sent a series of photo letters to be shared with her by her foster carers, preparing her for each step pre-trial and at trial.

4.8   Facilitate a pre-trial visit, including a practice with live link and/or screens because people need to properly understand the court process and what is expected for their communication. A pre-court familiarisation visit is essential (Wheatcroft, 2013). Here people are shown the court and live link room and the process is explained to them. They are enabled to make an informed choice about using screens or live link. They are made aware of where they, the intermediary/support person, child and their caregiver will be whilst they are providing testimony (Ministry of Justice, 2011, *Achieving Best Evidence*). A trained person can also help children understand their witness role using the Young Witness Pack booklets. The trained person can be an intermediary or an individual from the Witness Service.

4.9   The pre-trial visit will also provide an opportunity to adjust the environment of the live link to suit the individual child. See above in section 4.2 and below for examples.

4.10   If the child's carer/supporter is not going to be with them when they give evidence, helping children to separate from their accompanying adult at the pretrial visit can help to reduce stress and anxiety. The child needs to know ahead of time:
  • where their accompanying adult will wait;
  • that the child can go to the adult if the child needs to and should practise doing so;
  • that the child can stop the questioning as and when needed and come back when ready.

Good practice examples include giving the child the option to practise with the live link and/or screens by questioning the child about something unconnected with the facts of the case using the court facilities.

4.11   Pre-trial visits and practice with the live link are an extremely important part of court communication preparation with children and young people because children are not familiar with the court environment and lack of familiarity can have a detrimental impact on the detail and accuracy of information provided (Nathanson and Saywitz, 2003; Almerigogna et al, 2007).

GOOD PRACTICE EXAMPLE:
At the pre-trial visit the intermediary asked the court usher to play the role of the advocate and gave him a list of neutral questions about the child witness's recent visit to the beach. The usher then questioned the child over the live link and the child was able to practise responding to questions using this method and was then also familiar with the intermediary's support for communication during questioning.

4.12 If an intermediary is not used then a neutral supporter trusted by the child should always be considered as a special measure because of potential benefits to recall and stress reduction. The court must take the child's wishes into account (Application for Special Measures Direction, part C3; Coroners and Justice Act 2009, section 102). This neutral supporter can be anyone who is not a party or witness, has no detailed knowledge of evidence and is trusted by the child; ideally, the person preparing the witness for court. Others may be appropriate (Ministry of Justice, 2011, *Achieving Best Evidence*, section 5.34, appendix L.2.1) and need not be an usher or court official (CPD 2015 Evidence 18B.2: Witnesses giving evidence by live link).

4.13 Plan memory refreshing carefully including when how and where because the child or young person is entitled to refresh their memory in advance of the trial if appropriate. This should take place in a neutral environment (not home or school for children), in the presence of an appropriately trained person able to provide clear guidance and act as witness if the child extends, clarifies or contradicts their account (CPD 2015 Evidence 18C: Visually Recorded Interviews: Memory refreshing and watching at a different time from the jury).

4.14 Memory refreshment should generally not occur at the same time as the jury watches the DVD (Judicial College, 2010, *Bench Checklist: Young witness cases*). Earlier viewing allows children to take breaks as necessary. In certain circumstances, the child need not watch the DVD at all if there is a better way to refresh their testimony. Some children and young people may prefer to read a transcript of their DVD evidence or to listen to, but not watch, the DVD.

GOOD PRACTICE EXAMPLE
A 13-year-old with significant emotional problems refused to watch his DVD and was allowed instead to read the transcript with the intermediary.

4.15 Children and young people generally watch their evidence-in-chief at a different time than the jury, so that they can control the pacing of the viewing and attend fully. Careful note should be taken of anything the child says or does in response.

4.16   Introduce yourself to establish rapport before questioning starts because children will often feel intimidated by the court environment. This may induce further anxiety and have a negative impact on the accuracy of the information provided.

4.17   Many children are taught not to speak to strangers and may not understand why they should answer questions from someone on a TV screen they have not met. It will also help you to build an understanding of the child's communication techniques before you begin questioning. It is a good opportunity to resolve the wigs and gowns question, if this hasn't yet been done, showing how you look with and without. Some children prefer wigs and gowns to be removed, but others prefer that they are worn.

4.18   For some children this can be a very brief introductory session, for others it may take longer.

GOOD PRACTICE EXAMPLE
One at a time, on a pre-trial visit, the defence advocate and judge spent about 10 minutes with a four-year-old with speech impairment, tuning into his communication with the help of the intermediary.
Some children may need to meet the advocates and judge more than once. *Children may need time, and more than one opportunity, to develop sufficient trust to communicate any concerns they may have, especially if they have a communication impairment, learning disabilities, are very young or are experiencing mental health problems.* (Child Focussed Approach to Safeguarding (London child protection procedures)

4.19   Explain the 'rules' of communication prior to questioning because the rules of court communication are very different to the rules of everyday conversation. Children need to understand that the court does not know what happened and it is their role to answer questions and tell the court what they know. An intermediary or a witness service volunteer or an advocate can help the child understand what is expected of their communication in court and often this is covered in pre-trial preparation.

4.20   It can help to explicitly teach the 'rules', for example, that the child does not need to agree with suggestions put to them when questioned unless they are true; that is it OK to say '*I don't know*' or '*I don't understand*'. Explanations of communication 'rules' like this should be explored with the child beforehand, rather than first being introduced at the start of questioning. The intermediary can help with this. It is essential that the 'rules', including their wording and their presentation, are adapted to the needs of each child (Marchant, 2013). Rules may include:

- 'Tell the truth'–explaining in language familiar to the person, e.g. being honest/not telling fibs/porky pies; only talking about things that really happened, things you're sure about; things you saw/ heard/ felt. Don't leave anything out. No lying/pretending/making things up/guessing;
- 'Say if you don't know', 'Say if you don't remember', 'Say if you don't understand';
- 'Say if I get it wrong'–explaining that sometimes you get muddled up, 'You tell me if I get muddled up';
- 'Stop when you need to'. 'Come back when you're ready'.

4.21 Be aware of the impact of stress on communication because some children and young people have low confidence and self-esteem, rendering them prone to stress reactions where their coping strategies break down and their impairments become even more pronounced.

Frustration and stress are heightened by poor communication, not knowing what is going to happen and delays. Responses may include feelings of panic and mental overload, leading to total shutdown or the urge to provide any answer to bring questioning to an end.

4.22 Children who are experiencing stress may function at a lower level: making it harder for them to remember accurately and think clearly (Almerigogna et al, 2007). Causes of anxiety include: delay before/at trial; fear of seeing the defendant/his or her supporters; feelings of shame or guilt; fear of retribution; and anxiety about giving the wrong answer, not being believed or being overwhelmed by emotion in the presence of strangers. Signs of stress are not restricted to crying and include:
- appearing numb, passive or falling silent;
- agreeing, in order to bring questioning to an end;
- answering with a series of '*I don't know*' and '*I don't remember*' responses;
- other seemingly strange behaviours, e.g. tapping arms or legs, pulling at clothes or hair, inappropriate laughter.

4.23 Be aware of the impact of trauma on communication because children and young people may be traumatised by their experiences and the trauma can negatively affect their ability to participate in questioning, specifically their ability to communicate information and recall sufficient detail.

4.24 Questions relating to traumatic events may trigger responses that effectively shut down the ability to process or use language: for example, to freeze, fight, flee or flop (see Van Der Kolk, 2013). Further information about the presentation and impact of trauma can be found in Toolkit 18 Working with traumatised witnesses, defendants and parties.

GOOD PRACTICE EXAMPLE
A seven-year-old with significant emotional difficulties was helped to manage their own anxiety through quiet, calming, play materials, controlled breathing and use of 'stop', 'pause' and 'go' cards to manage pacing.

GOOD PRACTICE EXAMPLE
A four-year-old was allowed to pause cross-examination by going under the table or behind a curtain in the live link room, or by leaving the room. Resuming cross-examination after a break, the advocate wanted to ask the child 'four more questions'. The child agreed but said he wanted to count them. He and the Intermediary quickly made four playdough candles, to help him count. After the fourth question, the child left the live link room saying *'Candles are all gone'*.

4.25   Be aware of the impact of live link on communication because although live link can improve the detail and accuracy of children's testimony and reduce their suggestibility, live link can also disrupt communication in different ways (e.g. Doherty-Sneddon and McAuley, 2000; Marchant, 2010; 2013):

- Some children and young people find it more difficult to understand/ be understood over the live link and need to practise, or may require help from an intermediary.
- The 'picture in picture' on the child's live link screen (where they see themselves) can be distracting. If this is the case it should be disabled or covered.
- The attention of those in court may need to be drawn to the child's gestures or body language over the link by the intermediary –not interpreting, just commenting (e.g. 'you're nodding' 'you're pointing'). This also provides a record for the audio recording of cross-examination.
- If visual aids are to be used they must be visible over the link.
- Some children and young people are much more effective communicating face to face.
- Early signs of the child's confusion, tiredness or stress are often not apparent over the live link. The person who is supporting the child in the live link room should have an agreed way to alert the court about this. If the child or young person has an intermediary, then this eventuality would be covered in the ground rules hearing.

4.26   Some children's communication is significantly impaired across livelink. Sometimes this can be quickly resolved.

GOOD PRACTICE EXAMPLE
A four-year-old practised over the livelink, including responding to questions that prompted him to point and gesture so he realised he could see and be seen.

4.27 Sometimes this cannot be resolved, and in these situations cross-examination with the advocates in the live link room may be helpful.

GOOD PRACTICE EXAMPLE
The Intermediary assessed a five-year-old who used gestures and facial expressions to support her communication, both to help her explain things and to let others know whether she understood. Her receptive and expressive communication was most effective when she was face-to-face. Practising on the live link revealed that she was less likely to use gesture or facial expressions. The intermediary recommended that the prosecution and defence advocates be in the live link room for cross-examination. This was agreed at the ground rules hearing. The advocates and intermediary had a practice session in order to reorganise chairs and camera angles. A table was provided for photos and the child's drawings, which the child, intermediary and defence advocate could look at together. This innovative process worked well at trial (Wurtzel, 2011) and has since been replicated in many trials in which children's communication, attention or behaviour are better in face-to-face contact.

4.28 Adjust your pace to the child's needs because pacing is key to successful communication. This means the pace of questioning itself as well as the speed at which you speak. Some children and young people need a 'normal' pace of communication, some need everything to go more slowly, some need extra thinking time to process information before answering a question, and others need quite a brisk pace between their answer and the next question or their attention wanders or they no longer connect the next question with the previous answer. Adjust your pace in line with the child's responses.

GOOD PRACTICE EXAMPLE
A 4-year-old was cross-examined in 10-minute bursts, with breaks for calm play in the live link room in between.

4.29 Be prepared to pause during questioning if the child moves out of range of the live link camera because young children need to play and to move around and should not be expected to sit still for long periods. An intermediary can assist with pacing questioning and keeping the child focused.
- Be alert to loss of concentration and take breaks from questioning because breaks should be based on the child's concentration span. This will vary with time of day, stress levels and situation. An intermediary assessment may assist.
- A child's typical level of concentration is likely to be shorter than usual at court.
- Early signs of loss of concentration may not be evident over the live link.

- Do not rely on a child to ask for a break, or to say they need one if asked. They may elect to keep going to 'get it over with'. The child may lack the ability to anticipate when they need a break and may quickly reach overload under cross-examination.
- When a break is requested, it may be needed immediately. This should be accommodated. These can be brief, non-adjourned breaks where the court waits for the child to be ready to resume.
- Children's concentration span is generally shorter than that of adults and some have specific difficulties with attention.
- Some children attend best when engaged in calm play. Others need to give their full attention to the questioner for brief periods in between play.
- When tired children become non-responsive or repeat '*I don't know*' even if they know the answer, using the child's preferred name at the start of questions (find out what the child wants to be called) can help them to focus and attend.

4.30 Be alert to possible miscommunication because minor miscommunications can escalate quickly and can create other difficulties with stress and attention if there is persistent miscommunication.

- An intermediary in the live link room often identifies signs of confusion before these are picked up by those in court.
- Many children and young people will not recognise when difficulties occur or will be too embarrassed to admit this.
- The child may try to answer a question even if they do not understand it or when they have no knowledge about the subject matter.
- Do not rely on children (even adolescents) to say they do not understand. It is good practice to ask children to say when they do not understand a question. However, they often try to answer even if they do not understand or have no knowledge. Reasons for failing to say they do not understand include: reluctance; perception of the questioner as an authority figure; the child does not want to look stupid; and because they think that they understand the question when they do not. Be alert to non-verbal clues of misunderstanding, e.g. puzzled looks, knitted eyebrows, downcast eyes and long pauses. The intermediary can help with this by practicing 'ground rules' with the child prior to questioning. The intermediary can provide visual cues to help the child with this. The intermediary will also monitor the child's verbal and non-verbal communication and can highlight when they think the child might not have understood.

GOOD PRACTICE EXAMPLE
Before trial, a four-year-old was introduced to simple communication rules with symbols. At trial she had them in front of her to help her remember the 'rules' (see Figure 1).

4.31 Draw the court's attention to improper or inappropriate cross-examination because such questions should be immediately challenged as they can create significant miscommunication and inaccuracy and also produce high levels of distress. Both the prosecutor and defence advocates have the responsibility to alert the judge.

4.32 See *R v Cokesix Lubemba; R v JP* [[2014] EWCA Crim 2064: a trial judge 'is not only entitled, he is duty bound to control the questioning of a witness. He is not obliged to allow a defence advocate to put their case. He is entitled to and should set reasonable time limits and to interrupt where he considers questioning is inappropriate.'

GOOD PRACTICE EXAMPLE
A defence barrister asked a six-year-old '*Did you do twerking for the men at the party?*' The prosecution barrister intervened before the child was required to answer, on grounds that this question was inappropriate.

5. EXPRESSIVE COMMUNICATION: MAKING SURE YOU ARE UNDERSTOOD

5.1 At least 50% of young witnesses, across age groups, do not understand questions they are asked at court. This rises to almost 90% for those aged 10 and under (Plotnikoff and Woolfson, 2009). F.55

5.2 The most significant factor in effective communication is the questioner's ability to adapt and respond to the child or young person. The aim is to enable the child to understand questions and give answers that he or she believes to be correct. This means adopting an appropriate manner and tailoring questions to the needs and abilities of the individual child (Agnew et al, 2006; Bull, 2010; Powell et al, 2013).

5.3 Adapting questions requires considerable skill, and questioning children in court is very different to questioning children in a family context. Advanced preparation on the part of the questioners is necessary, as is the ability to respond flexibly during cross-examination. This may require further adaptation or even abandoning of pre-planned questions. An intermediary can provide recommendations for how to question the child based on their individual needs and can help advocates prepare questions prior to questioning in court and provide communication support during questioning (see Toolkit 16 Intermediaries step by step).

5.4 Plan questions in topics and be clear about changes of topic because this helps the child make sense of the process and gives them transition time to focus on the next subject.
  • For example: '*Now we're going to talk about . . .*'It can be helpful to schedule a break at a change of subject.

- For example: *'We've finished talking about when you were at the swimming pool. Now I want to talk about what happened the next day. I want to talk about what you said to Mum about Tom.'*
- Follow a logical, chronological order.
- Signpost the subject and explain when the subject is about to be changed.

GOOD PRACTICE EXAMPLE

The defence advocate prepared 24 questions for a seven-year-old, divided into six topics. The intermediary prepared a card for each topic which was turned over as that topic began.

5.5　Write out draft questions in advance because this will help to identify potential problems in advance. In *R v Lubemba, R v JP* [2014] EWCA Crim 2064 the Court of Appeal (para 43) stated that: 'So as to avoid any unfortunate misunderstanding at trial, it would be an entirely reasonable step for a judge at the GRH [ground rules hearing] to invite defence advocates to reduce their questions to writing in advance.'

5.6　Ask each question once unless there is a good reason to repeat it because . . .

- Questions repeated by one or more authority figures risk reducing the child's overall accuracy. This is the case whether asked consecutively or interspersed with others. Children's and young people's experience from school is that, if the teacher repeats the question, their first answer was wrong or unsatisfactory.
- Anxiety, combined with the desire to please someone in a position of authority, can cause even typically developing children to change their first answers, regardless of initial accuracy. If a question needs to be repeated for clarity (even with changed wording), explain that you want to check your understanding of what the child said, e.g: *'Thank you, but I want to be really sure I understand. Tell me again . . .* '(followed by the question).

5.7　Ensure tone and body language are neutral and maintain attention because the child needs to know that you are speaking to them and listening to them.

- Regularly using the child's preferred first name and looking at the camera (if using live link) can help to maintain attention when questioning.
- Explain when you need time to read or think, so that the child understands the delay.
- Eye contact is an important part of communication but can be disrupted by livelink. Generally, direct eye contact is helpful, so when asking questions look directly at the child or, if using live link, look

Toolkit 6

straight at the camera, not at papers. However, there may be cultural
or other specific reasons to avoid direct eye gaze.

5.8 Ensure tone and body language are neutral because . . .
- assertive non-verbal responses (such as nodding or shaking your head
  or expressing disbelief through facial expression or body language)
  can cause compliance or acquiescence;
- some children will be particularly attuned to your facial expression,
  tone of voice and body language e.g. a seven-year-old asking the
  intermediary about counsel during cross examination: *'Is he cross or
  what?'*

**5.9 Make sure the content of questions is developmentally appropriate—use
simple, everyday words, because** these are much more likely to be understood.
- Children and young people will not be familiar with complex
  language that does not form part of their everyday vocabulary –use
  simple words with which the child is familiar.
- Jargon or complex vocabulary may not be understood.
- It is easier for a child to process questions if the words used are
  consistent throughout.
- Always use the simplest word you can find, e.g. instead of *'Who was
  present at the time of the incident?'* ask *'Who was there when that
  happened?'*; instead of *'Have you ever actually observed your father
  physically assaulting your mother?'* try *'Have you seen your Dad hit
  your Mum?'* and then check *'Did you see that with your own eyes?'*

5.10 Use concrete words and say what you mean because some words have
more than one meaning and this can create significant confusion.
- Instead of *'I want to take you back'*, say *'I want to ask you about.'*
- Metaphors, non-literal language and figures of speech may be inter-
  preted literally;
- Avoid figures of speech, e.g *'I am going to run through a few things.'*
- Deciphering underlying meanings can be problematic, *'Are you sure?'*
  or *'Is that true?'* are better alternatives than *'Is that right?'* because the
  word 'right' has two meaning in this context ('accurate' or 'morally
  right').
- Young children often interpret words in a highly literal way, e.g.
  Q: 'Have you ever seen a "blue movie"?'(asked of a four-year-old)
  A: 'Not just blue.'
  Q: 'Are you OK to go on?'(asked of a five-year-old)
  A: 'What on?'
  Q: 'So is it a cul de sac?'(asked of a 12-year-old)
  *Q: 'Were you told you'd get into trouble for retracting your version of
  events?'* (asked of a 15-year-old).

2069

- Use of abstract words by a vulnerable person does not mean the person understands them. For example, the ability to count does not mean that somebody can answer accurately *'How many times?'* something happened. Good practice example A five-year-old witness to murder was asked at the start of cross-examination *'Do you remember the day Mummy went to hospital?'*. She said no. The intermediary clarified, and the child meant she couldn't remember if it was a Monday or another day. When asked *'Do you remember what happened the day Mummy went to hospital?'*, the child said yes.
- Instead of *'Is that right?'* 'try *'Is that true?'*
- Instead of *'I'm going to jog your memory* 'try *'I'm going to ask about when . . . '*
- Instead of *'Let's get down to the facts* 'try *'Now I'm going to ask you about something important.'*
- Instead of *'Did you see eye to eye with Jane?* 'try *'Did you and Jane agree about things?'* Instead of *'Were you and Jane close?* 'try *'Did you like Jane?'*

5.11   Check understanding of crucial evidential words because these provide the foundation for clear communication about essential evidence. For example, children may have learnt new language for private body parts since their interview; learning disabled adults may use the word 'sex' to mean very different things. A young child may interpret 'touch' quite narrowly, as relating only to hands, e.g:

> *Q:* 'Did he touch you?'(asked of a four-year-old)
> *A:* 'No. He washed me on my private, everywhere.'
> *Q:* 'Did he touch you?'(asked of a six-year-old)
> *A:* 'No' (later) 'He licked me.'

5.12   Take care with questions suggesting the child is lying or confused because these question types are likely to have an adverse impact on concentration and accuracy, particularly if repeated. If a challenge is developmentally appropriate, it should be addressed separately, in simple language, at the end of cross-examination. Children should not be asked *'Do you tell lies?'* unless there are grounds to think that the child or young person is a habitual liar. It is not enough that the child's evidence contradicts that of the defendant (Ministry of Justice, 2011, *Achieving Best Evidence*).

5.13   Carefully plan questions about intimate touching or sexual acts, because it is inappropriate to ask someone to demonstrate intimate touching or sexual acts at court using their own bodies. Such questions can be addressed using the child's own drawings made at interview or a diagram or body map identified by the intermediary, e.g. 'How it is: An image vocabulary for children' (Triangle, 2002). The child or young person has to be able to use a body map correctly for demonstrative purposes. Refer to Toolkit 14 Using communication aids in the criminal justice system and CPD 2015 3E.6: Ground rules hearings to plan the questioning of a vulnerable witness or defendant.

GOOD PRACTICE EXAMPLE
An eight-year-old was reluctant to name the place on her body where she alleged she was touched. The intermediary provided a body outline of an undressable young girl and the child was able to point clearly to indicate the place.

5.14   Be clear about places, names, objects and subjects because pronouns are complex to master and can often be mixed up.
* Instead of he, she, it, there; name the person or place.
* Instead of *'When did he do that?'*, try *'When did Robert break the window?'*
* Instead of *'What did he say?'*, try *'What did Tyrese say?'*
* Instead of *'Was it inside?'*, try *'Was the money in the wallet?'*

5.15   People are less likely to become confused if names are used to identify objects, actions and places, e.g. 'there' is open to interpretation.
   Q: *'Was mummy there?'* (asked of a four-year-old)
   A: *'Yes'.*
This could mean 'in the house' or 'in the room with me' (where the alleged offence took place). Better alternatives include, e.g. *'Where was mummy when Jim came into the bedroom?'* or *'Was mummy with you when Jim came into the bedroom?'* or *'When Jim came into the bedroom, was mummy with you in the bedroom?'* This will help the person keep track of the information you are referring to.

5.16   Using the child's preferred name can also help keep them focused. Identify the police officer (and other relevant people) by the name known to the person. Identify names and places.
   Q: *'How often does she let you do that?'* (asked of a nine-year-old)

Better alternatives include e.g *'How often does your mum let you go to the chip shop?'*

5.17   Carefully plan questions about abstract concepts because understanding of time concepts (dates, duration and frequency of events) and weight, height and age estimates is acquired gradually as children develop and may not have been acquired at all by some people.
* Children begin to use words relating to time (eg now/before /after/ then), distance, relationships, size, positioning etc before they fully understand their meaning.

- Abstract, 'concept' words can be problematic. For example: numbers; measurements; before/after; in front of/below/behind; always/never; different/same; and more/less.
- The child or young person may not connect 'category' and 'sub-category' words and may interpret them literally, e.g:

  Q: *'Did you have your clothes on?'* (asked of a six-year old)
  A: *'No.'*
  Q: *'Did you have your pyjamas on?'*
  A: *'Yes.'*
  Or:
  Q: *'Did you go to Jim's home?'*
  A: *'No. But I went to his flat.'*

- A question about 'how many times' something happened may result in a different answer each time the question is posed. People learn that 'how many' questions seek a number response even if they cannot reliably estimate or count. Unbelievable responses (eg *'It happened 1000 times'*) can simply mean 'lots of times'.
- Some people have limited ability to process 'when' questions. A question about when something happened could be answered 'yesterday', meaning any time in the past. Such questions should be linked to familiar knowledge or concrete events such as: *'How old were you when x?'*; *'Was it light or dark or don't you know?'*; or *'You said that you played football that day, was that before or after you saw Robert?'*
- Consider the use of a visual timeline or similar device if the child is likely to have difficulty in responding to questions about times, dates or separate events or locations.
- If the alleged offence involved several incidents in different locations, the intermediary (if appointed) can prepare prompt cards, each with a photo and symbol to represent each location.
- Young children have few ways to estimate the duration of an event. Again they will learn the words for time concepts (days, hours, minutes) well before they fully understand them. Children can be helped to estimate duration with forced alternatives relating to: familiar time periods (eg did it last longer than school playtime?); holidays, birthdays, home routines (eg meal times): or what was on TV. Even very young children can do this.
- Instead of *'How many?'*, try *'One time or more than one time?'*, using hand gestures.
- Instead of 'when', try, *'Was it before or after you . . . '* or *'Was it daytime or night time or don't you know?'* or *'Was it light or dark outside or something else?'* or *'How old were you when . . . ?'*
- Young children cannot process a question about whether *'they ever saw something'* or *'anything like this'* happened before, as 'any' and 'ever' invite the child to search for every possibility.

5.18   Make sure the structure of questions is developmentally appropriate– –keep questions short because in order to answer accurately, the child needs to be able to remember and process the whole question.

- The child may have difficulty remembering all of a multi-part question.
- 'Front-loaded' questions are more difficult to process, e.g. *'I suggest to you that . . . '*; *'I put it to you . . . '*
- Phrases such as *'Do you follow?'* at the end of questions make it harder for the child to retain the key information they need in order to respond to the question.
- Redundant words and phrases can cause confusion (eg 'in fact', 'to your knowledge', *'I put it to you'*, *'I wonder if you can tell me'*, *'Do you follow?'*).
- Instead of *'When was the last time you say he did this to you before the time on that day in the summer that we have been speaking of?'*, try *'You said that Michael touched you one day in the summer. Did he touch you on any other days?'*
- Instead of *'Is it correct that Susan put you up to making these allegations, because Mr and Mrs Hobbs have refused to allow Susan to live with them?'*, try *'Did Susan want to live with your Dad and Step Mum?'* *'Did your Dad and Step Mum say no to Susan living with them?'*

GOOD PRACTICE EXAMPLE
- At the ground rules hearing for a child who had just turned four, the content and length of three questions asked by the prosecutor and two questions asked by the defence was agreed by the judge, intermediary and both advocates.

5.19   Keep questions simple in structure because complex questions are likely to result in incorrect or 'I don't know' responses, even though the child knows the answer and could respond accurately if the question is phrased simply. A question with multiple topics can cause confusion as the person may have a limited working memory and may be unable to remember all of a multi-part question or decipher embedded clauses.

GOOD PRACTICE EXAMPLE
An advocate wanted to ask a five-year-old a series of specific questions about the detail of an alleged sexual assault, but was unsure how to do this with a very young witness. This issue was raised during the ground rules hearing and the intermediary and advocate were able to spend time prior to the court case going over the most age appropriate way in which to do this.

5.20   Ask all questions about past events in the past tense because

the use of the present tense is likely to cause confusion or distress; instead of *'So you are in bed and he's taken your pyjamas off, now what's happening?'* say: *'You were in bed and he took your pyjamas off, then what happened?'*

5.21   Avoid use of present tense, e.g:
> *Q: 'Are you in school at the moment?'* (asked of a five-year-old across the live link)
> *A: 'No, I'm in this room with the cameras so I can talk to you.'*

5.22   Beware of negative and passive language in questions, because this can reduce clarity and increases the likelihood of confusion and inaccurate responses.

- Questions containing a negative are more difficult for people to understand, e.g. *'That is not a lie?'* (asked of a 12-year-old), or *'It was not dark yet?'* (asked of a 4-year-old), *'Did Dad not like you watching TV?'* (asked of a 7-year-old).
- Double negatives are even more problematic, e.g. *'Doesn't Mr Smith not only allow one child in his car at a time?'* (asked of a 10-year-old with autism) or *'Didn't you dislike that?'*
- Questions in the passive form are unnecessarily complex and difficult to understand. For example, e.g. *'Were you to have been taken to school that day?'*
- Questions which remove personal references and objectify the action are also harder to process, e.g. *'Did you tell the police about what is in that statement about the matter, about the touching of the boobs?'* Better options include: *'Did you tell the police that Tony touched your boobs?'*

5.23   The one exception to this is that some children may give an inaccurate reply if the question implies that the child was active in the event, e.g:
> *Q: 'Did you touch John's willy?'*
> *A: 'No'* (later) *'He put his willy in my hand.'*

5.24   Be careful about questions in the form of statements because these may not be understood as requiring a response. For example, *'You wanted Jim out of your house.'* A better alternatives is *'Did you want Jim out of your house?'*

5.25   When an adult in a position of authority formally suggests that something is a fact, it becomes extremely difficult for children, even 11 or 12-year-olds, to disagree and to maintain verbally what they believe to be true. The younger the child, the riskier 'assertion' questions become. The previous Lord Chief Justice described the use of assertions with children and young people as 'particularly damaging' ('Half a century of change: the evidence of child victims' Toulmin lecture, 20 March 2013, King's College

London). Children have difficulty with these for a number of reasons. For example:

- '*I suggest to you that*', '*I believe you told us*', '*In fact*', '*Isn't it a fact that*') lengthen the question as well as suggest the answer, therefore increasing the likelihood of miscommunication and unreliable responses;
- or '*You saw what happened next, didn't you?*' and '*It was late, wasn't it, when you left the pub?*';
- the child may interpret statements as comments, not as questions that require responses, e.g. '*You didn't want your mum to think you had been naughty.*' (asked of an eight-year-old)

5.26 Be particularly cautious about the use of tagged questions because questions that make a statement and then add a short question inviting confirmation are powerfully suggestive and linguistically complex. Judicial guidance recommends that this form of question be avoided altogether with children and that a direct question be put instead:

- instead of '*John didn't touch you, did he?*', it would be safer to ask '*Did John touch you?*' or '*Did John really touch you?*' or '*Are you sure John touched you?*'
- instead of '*You saw her at the cinema, didn't you?*', try '*Did you see her at the cinema?*'
- Instead of '*And he would sometimes come to your house, is that fair?*', try '*Did X sometimes come to your house?*'
- Instead of '*It was sunny that day, wasn't it?*' try '*Was it sunny that day?*' or '*What was the weather like that day?*' or '*Was it sunny or rainy that day, or don't you know?*'
- Instead of '*Now you had a bruise, did you not?*', try '*Did you have a bruise?*'

See Judicial College (2012) *Bench Checklist: Young witness cases.*

5.27 Children are particularly susceptible to answering incorrectly questions that suggest the answer (Bruck and Ceci, 1999). If a question supplies information that did not originate from the child, it becomes more leading. Research suggests children may agree with the information in the question, even if it is not accurate, for a number of reasons. These include the fact that the child may not remember the answer but does not want to seem stupid, or is feeling intimidated by the process that in turn makes them more likely to agree with the questioner. Potentially problematic question types should always be discussed at a ground rules hearing.

5.28 Be careful with questions requiring a yes/no response, because a series of propositions or leading questions inviting repetition of either 'yes' or 'no' answers is very likely to affect accuracy. These questions carry a risk that an acquiescent child will adopt a pattern of replies 'cued' by the questioner and will cease to respond to individual questions, leading to inaccurate replies.

- If only 'yes'/'no' questions are asked, it is difficult to determine if the person is having problems with the questions.
- Similarly, they may also be interpreted literally if the question starts with 'can', 'do' or 'will'(eg *'Can you tell me who was in the room?'* '*Yes'*; *'Do you know the name of the man?'* '*Yes'*).
- Yes/no questions should be interspersed with open and specific questions to allow the child to stay focused on the topic. This will also help the intermediary monitor his or her understanding.

5.29 If yes/no questions are the only option (because a person is unable to respond to more open question types), then ensuring a mix of yes and no responses (by reversing some questions) will increase the chance of accurate responses. This apparently tiny change can make a big difference to accuracy (see Marchant and Page, 1993). For example, instead of *'Did you used to live with Mummy?'*, 'Yes', *'Do your brothers live with Nanny now?'*, *'Yes'*, you could try *'Did you used to live with Mummy?'*, *'Yes'*, *'Do you still live with Mummy?'*, *'No'*, *'Now do you live with Nanny?'* *'Yes'*.

5.30 Be careful when asking forced choice (closed) questions because these create significant opportunities for error as the correct alternative may be missing. The child or young person may assume that one of the alternatives must be correct, e.g. *'When you went to the flat, did John or Bill open the door?'* In instances where forced choice questions are necessary, offer *'I don't know'* or *'something else'* as a third alternative (eg *'Was it red, blue or another colour?'*, *'Were you under the blanket, on top of the blanket, or something else?'*

5.31 If asked open, free recall questions (eg *'What happened?'*), children or young people can provide accounts with accuracy rates broadly similar to the general population.

5.32 Be careful with *'Do you remember?'* **questions because** these require complex processing. Children are particularly likely to be confused when they are not asked about the event but are asked about what they told someone else. . Use of quotes aggravates the problem, e.g. *'Do you remember when you were being asked by the sergeant what was said, you said that your father said, "He loved me" that's all he really said. Do you remember?'* (asked of an 11-year-old).

5.33 Answers may also be ambiguous, especially with *'Do you remember'* questions that are also tagged, e.g. *'Now you had a bruise, did you not, near one of your breasts? Do you remember that?'* (asked of a 12-year-old). If the child answers 'no' this could mean *'No, I don't remember'* or *'No, I didn't have a bruise there'* or *'Yes, I remember but no I didn't have a bruise there.'*

6.   RECEPTIVE COMMUNICATION: MAKING SURE YOU UNDERSTAND

6.1   Even bright, intellectually able children find court communication meth- **F.56** **ods, and language, challenging simply because of their age.** The 'rules' of court communication are very different from those used in everyday conversation. For example, children are not used to having to provide elaborate accounts. In everyday conversation gist information is enough. In addition, children are often told to listen and wait to speak. They are not used to being the main information providers (Lamb and Brown, 2006).

6.2   Make sure you and the jury can see and hear the child or young person clearly because many children and young people use their faces and hands to support their communication. This may require close in focusing, or moving the microphone closer. Check before your first question.

6.3   Attend to gestures and actions as well as words because children may be more competent to **demonstrate** what happened, rather than just explaining in words (Ministry of Justice, 2011, *Achieving Best Evidence*, section 3.107). Showing and telling can be an important part of communication. If the person realises you are not looking or not noticing or not responding, they may stop showing (Marchant, 2010). Commenting can also assist: e.g. '*You're showing me with your hands.*'

6.4   Ask for clarification if you don't understand or aren't sure because pretending to understand will create further confusion. You may need to request clarification and double check, but be clear that this is what you are doing rather than requesting a different answer.

6.5   Some children's speech may not be easily intelligible, especially at first meeting. Sound substitutions and pronunciation errors are common and use of verbs, pronouns and plurals may be at an early stage. Again, an intermediary can be asked to help clarify what has been said; they will have assessed the person and be more familiar with their communication style.

6.6   Listen to what the child says, and try to understand what the child means. A young child often uses words before fully understanding them.

6.7   Ask the child to repeat what they said if you didn't hear properly, but say why because a child may change their answer if asked to repeat something without knowing the reason. Children sometimes speak very quietly, espe- cially when feeling anxious or fearful, or providing information that they are embarrassed about. Microphones can be relocated closer or higher, or the young child seated lower. However, if you do not hear what the child has said, gently tell them that you cannot hear and ask them to say it again, or ask them to speak a bit louder. It is also possible to ask the intermediary to repeat back what the child has said.

6.8   If you need to check back on what was said, use the child or young person's own words because they may not understand if alternative words are used instead. By using alternative words, you are at risk of creating confusion or suggesting an interpretation of events to the child or young person that may not be accurate. This may affect the accuracy of their subsequent account of events.

6.9.   Gain some familiarity with the person's communication aids because this will enable two-way communication during questioning. Communication aids can support and augment a child's communication;

- Asking a witness to demonstrate intimate touching on their own body is never appropriate –use a body map or diagram (see Toolkit 14 Using communication aids in the criminal justice system);
- Using formal communication aids almost always requires intermediary involvement and should be explored prior to questioning.
- Aids may allow children to both show and tell (see Toolkit 14 Using communication aids in the criminal justice system). The intermediary can help with the selection of appropriate communication aids (See 'How It Is: An image vocabulary for children' (2002) Triangle).
- There are risks and pitfalls as well as advantages (Ministry of Justice, 2011, *Achieving Best Evidence*, sections 3.103–3.122). They 'should be used with caution and never combined with leading questions (section 3.108) and should not prevent the child from gesturing (section 3.111).

6.10   The intermediary can assist in identifying appropriate safe aids and help the child create aids to augment their communication. Examples have included:

- **the child's own drawings of people, places and objects** to clarify who/ where/with what (if produced or used at interview these will be exhibits at trial and copies need to be available to the child at cross-examination);
- **a visual pain scale** with numbers and faces balanced along a scale of 0–5 to clarify how much something hurt;
- **precut gender-neutral 'gingerbread people',** or anatomically accurate drawings, with removable clothes to clarify body parts;
- **small dolls or human figures** (e.g. pipe-cleaner figures in different colours and sizes, with polystyrene heads that can be drawn on to represent different individuals) to clarify positions;
- **small furniture** (eg dolls house furniture or Lego models) to clarify locations; and

- **body maps** (eg 'How It Is: An image vocabulary for children' (2002) Triangle; *Living your Life*, Brook; Plotnikoff and Woolfson (2009), Annex B, 'Good practice guidance in managing young witness cases and planning to question children'). The child has to be able to use a body map correctly for demonstrative purposes.

6.11 Full acquisition of language is a gradual process that evolves overtime. This can have implications for court including the following:

- children cannot remember long and complicated sentences and so questions should contain only a certain number of words suitable for their stage of development–an intermediary can offer guidance on how long questions/sentences should be;
- some adolescents may have delayed language capabilities due to trauma, neglect or insufficient communication support at home (McFadyen and Kitson, 1996). Adolescents are at particular risk of miscommunication because of their reluctance to ask for clarification and adults' higher expectations of their ability to understand.

The development of this toolkit was funded by The Advocacy Training Council and the Legal Education Foundation. It was written by Dr Kimberly Collins, Intermediary, Triangle, with assistance from Ruth Marchant, Carly McAuley, Dr Michelle Mattison, Vanessa Hurst (Intermediaries with Triangle); Jennie Knight, Barrister; Gabby Henty, Barrister; Rowan Jenkins, Barrister; HHJ Heather Norton; HHJ Janet Waddicor; HHJ Christine Laing; Moira Pook (Intermediary). This toolkit summarises key points from:

Agnew, S E, Powell, M B and Snow, P C (2006) 'An examination of the questioning styles of police officers and caregivers when interviewing children with intellectual disabilities' 11(1) *Legal and Criminological Psychology* 35–53

Almerigogna, J, Ost, J, Bull, R and Akehurst, L (2007) 'A state of high anxiety: how non-supportive interviewers can increase the suggestibility of child witnesses' 21 *Applied Cognitive Psychology* 963–974

Bercow Report (2008) *A Review of Services for Children and Young People (0–19) with Speech, Language and Communication Needs*, Department for Children, Schools and Families

Block, S D, Oran, H, Oran, D, Baumrind, N and Goodman, G S (2010) 'Abused and neglected children in court: knowledge and attitudes' 34 *Child Abuse and Neglect* 659–670

Bruck, M and Ceci, S J (1999) 'The suggestibility of children's memory' 50 *Annual Review of Psychology* 419–439

Bull, R (2010) 'The investigative interviewing of children and other vulnerable witnesses: psychological research and working/professional practice' 15 *Legal and Criminological Psychology* 5–23

Cashmore, J and DeHaas, N (1992) *The Use of Closed Circuit Television: Child witnesses in the ACT*, Research Paper, Australian Law Reform Commission, Sydney

Ceci, S J and Friedman, R D (2000) 'The suggestibility of children: scientific research and legal Implications' 86 *Cornell Law Review* 34–108

Criminal Procedure Rules and Practice Directions 2015

Dent, H R (1986) 'Experimental study of the effectiveness of different techniques of questioning child witnesses' 18 *British Journal of Social and Clinical Psychology* 41–51

Doherty-Sneddon, G (2003) *Children's Unspoken Language*, Jessica Kingsley

Doherty-Sneddon, G and McAuley, S (2000) 'Influence of video-mediation on adult-child interviews: implications for the use of the live link with child witnesses' 14 *Applied Cognitive Psychology* 379–392

Felts, B B, Powell, M B and Roberts, K P (2011) 'The effect of event repetition on the production of story grammar in children's event narratives' 35 *Child Abuse and Neglect* 180–187

Judicial College (2013) *Equal Treatment Benchbook*

Lamb, M E and Brown, D A (2006) 'Conversational apprentices: helping children become competent informants about their own experiences' 24 *British Journal of Developmental Psychology* 215– 234

Lamb, M E, La Rooy, D J, Malloy, L C and Katz, C (2011) *Children's Testimony: A handbook of psychological research and forensic practice*, Wiley

Lord Chief Justice (March, 2013) 'Half a century of change: the evidence of child victims' Toulmin lecture, King's College London

Marchant, R (2010) 'Show me what happened: children's unspoken communication' paper presented at International Investigate Interviewing Research Group Conference Stavern, Norway

Marchant, R (2013) 'How young is too young? The evidence of children under 5 in the English criminal justice system' 22(6) Child Abuse Review 432–445

Marchant, R and Page, M (1993) *Bridging the Gap: Child protection work with children with multiple disabilities*, NSPCC

McFadyen, R G and Kitson, W J H (1996) 'Language comprehension and expression among adolescents who have experienced childhood physical abuse' 37 *Journal of Child Psychology and Psychiatry* 551–562

Ministry of Justice. (2011). Achieving Best Evidence in Criminal Proceedings: Guidance on interviewing victims and witnesses, and guidance on using special measures

Ministry of Justice (2012) *Registered Intermediary Procedural Guidance Manual,* Ministry of Justice Nathanson, R and Saywitz, K J (2003) 'The effects of the courtroom context on children's memory and anxiety; 31 *Journal of Psychiatry and Law* 67–98

Plotnikoff J and Woolfson R (2009) *Measuring Up? Evaluating implementation of government commitments to young witnesses in criminal proceedings,* NSPCC and Nuffield Foundation

Powell, M B, Mattison, M L and McVilly, K (2013) 'Guidelines for interviewing people with communication impairments' 67(2) *Australian Police Journal* 58-63

Roberts, K P and Powell, M (2001) 'Describing individual incidents of sexual abuse: a review of research on the effects of multiple sources of information on children's reports' 25 *Child Abuse and Neglect* 1643–1659

Talbot J (2010) *Seen and Heard: Supporting vulnerable children in the youth justice system,* Prison Reform Trust

Triangle (2002) *How It Is: An image vocabulary for children*

Triangle (2012) *Communication Systems in Use with Children in England and Wales*

Van Der Kolk, B (2014) *The Body Keeps the Score: Brain, mind and body in the healing of trauma,* Penguin, New York

Wheatcroft, J M (2013) 'Witness evidence in court: the impact of witness preparation and cross examination on witness testimony accuracy and confidence' 32nd Conference of the ASTC, The M Resort

Wurtzel, D (2012) 'Children and cross-examination: time to change the rules?' (November) *Law in Action,* Counsel Magazine

Youth Justice and Criminal Evidence Act 1999

The original version of this toolkit (dated 21 October 2013) can be found in the archive section of The Advocate's Gateway website.

TOOLKIT 10: IDENTIFYING VULNERABILITY IN WITNESSES AND DEFENDANTS[71]

This toolkit brings together policy, research and guidance relating to: F.57

1. general principles;
2. early identification of possible vulnerability of witnesses and defendants;
3. advocates' duties and responsibilities;
4. obtaining expert advice;
5. special measures, other adjustments and ground rules hearings.

[71] 10 July 2014. © ATC The Advocate's Gateway 2015.

The toolkit contains information about vulnerable witnesses and defendants in criminal proceedings and is primarily intended for use by advocates as well as the Crown Prosecution Service (CPS), defence solicitors, witness supporters, judges, magistrates and police.

This toolkit covers the following key points.

- There is no single agreed definition of who is a 'vulnerable' witness or defendant.
- Vulnerability should be identified at the earliest possible stage and information-sharing is key to achieving this.
- Certain behaviour/characteristics/circumstances are 'risk factors' which indicate potential vulnerability.
- Once vulnerability is suspected, action should be taken to obtain relevant expert advice, for example, from an appropriate medical expert or a Registered Intermediary.
- Research has shown that vulnerability is often missed or not properly acted upon.
- Advocates should not assume that the police/CPS/defence solicitors have already identified a witness's or a defendant's vulnerability.
- Advocates should ensure that the interests of their vulnerable clients are taken into account and their needs are met.
- 'Special measures' and other adjustments must be considered.
- A ground rules hearing must take place if a witness or defendant is vulnerable.

1. GENERAL PRINCIPLES

F.58 **1.1 There is no single agreed definition of who is a 'vulnerable' witness or defendant** Any one single definition of vulnerability based on age, incapacity, impairment or medical condition may not reflect the nature of vulnerability that a particular individual may face at different times and in different environments. Advocates should be alert to risk factors which may indicate that the witness or defendant is vulnerable and, if identified, expert advice should be sought. The court must take 'every reasonable step' to facilitate the participation of any person, including the defendant (Rule 3.8(4)(a) and (b) Criminal Procedure Rules 2013).

1.2 A vulnerable witness or defendant may not be able to participate effectively at court if reasonable steps are not taken to adapt the court process Crucially, they may not give complete, coherent or accurate testimony and, in the case of the defendant, they may also be unable to follow or participate effectively in the hearing. Adjustments should be made without prejudicing the parties and the trial must be fair.

1.3 Risk factors which might bring the person within the definition of 'vulnerable' include:

- being a child;
- lack of fluency in the English language;
- illiteracy;
- learning disabilities;
- hearing impairments;
- speech (or language) impairments;
- mental health conditions or impairments (Judicial College (2012) *Fairness in Courts and Tribunals*).

1.4   It is important to take into account the views of the witness or defendant Vulnerable people are not a homogeneous group and not all of those with a disability will be vulnerable or would wish to be regarded as such. Whether or not a person is vulnerable will depend on the nature of their disability and whether it affects their ability to perform the functions of a witness (2.2.2 *Vulnerable and Intimidated Witnesses: A police service guide* 2011).

1.5   'Self-reporting', i.e. obtaining first-hand information from the witness/ defendant him or herself, may be a better predictor of vulnerability An advocate who suspects a witness/defendant may be vulnerable should consider asking questions of that person or asking others to make enquiries in order to consider this further.

1.6   GOOD PRACTICE EXAMPLE The following questions might help identify risk factors:
- Do you/did you get any extra help at school from a person just for you?
- Do you need extra help managing money?
- Do you need any extra help with getting about or going to appointments?
- Do you need any extra help with listening, speaking or reading?
- Do you need any extra help to stay calm?

And, if the advocate knows the person is taking medication:
- Do you need any extra help taking your medicine?
- How does your medicine affect you?

1.7   The above questions are more likely to elicit useful and reliable information compared to questions such as 'Do you have a learning disability?' or 'Are you disabled?' However, advocates should bear in mind that some witnesses/defendants may be reluctant communicators. This may mean that their vulnerability is missed and that their behaviour is mis-construed as being deliberately difficult or unhelpful. Research suggests that 50–60% of young people who are involved in offending have speech, language and communication difficulties. Many people have undiagnosed conditions. Some disadvantaged people have an attachment disorder, due to erratic parenting and emotional and financial poverty, which then presents as a social communication disorder.

1.8   Certain behaviour/characteristics/circumstances will suggest vulnerability
However, it should be noted that current risk assessment/screening tools appear to have had a limited effect on improving the identification of potential vulnerabilities. Characteristics/behaviour /circumstances which might suggest a witness/defendant is vulnerable are listed below (taken from *Vulnerable and Intimidated Witnesses: A police service guide* 2011).

    a. Behavioural characteristics that may warrant further consideration:
- has no speech or limited speech;
- is difficult to understand;
- finds it difficult to communicate without assistance/interpretation;
- uses signs and gestures to communicate;
- appears to have some difficulty in understanding questions;
- responds inappropriately or inconsistently to questions;
- seems to focus on what could be deemed irrelevant small points rather than important issues;
- appears to have a short attention span;
- cannot read or write;
- has difficulty in telling the time;
- has difficulty in remembering their date of birth, age, address, telephone number;
- has difficulty knowing the day of the week, where they are and whom they are talking to;
- appears very eager to please;
- repeats what is said to them;
- appears over-excited/exuberant;
- appears uninterested/lethargic;
- appears confused by what is said or happening;
- is physically withdrawn;
- is violent;
- expresses strange ideas;
- does not understand common everyday expressions.

    b. Behaviour that may also warrant further consideration:
- unusual appearance of the eye;
- angling head/eyes for viewing;
- failing to search visually for people;
- hesitant in movement/reluctant to move in unfamiliar environment;
- uncontrollable muscular movements.

    c. Circumstances that may warrant further consideration:
- in receipt of Disability Living Allowance;

- resident at a group home or institution or employed in a sheltered workplace;
- living in a group home or residential home or attending a specialist day service or sheltered employment;
- in possession of certain prescription medicine;
- receiving support from a carer;
- receiving support from a social worker/community psychiatric nurse etc. (3.2.1–3.2.4 *Vulnerable and Intimidated Witnesses: A police service guide* 2011).

1.9 In addition, the following points may also warrant further consideration. The witness/defendant:
- attends/attended a special school;
- is/has been excluded from school;
- has/had a Statement of Special Educational Needs/extra support at a mainstream school;
- is/was under a care order to the local authority (because the child may have been taken into care after experiencing trauma);
- readily agrees with what you are saying;
- appears restless/hyperactive;
- appears impulsive;
- appears inattentive;
- had an appropriate adult at the police station (if they were a suspect);
- is/was an asylum seeker (an asylum seeker may have fled from oppressive circumstances and have witnessed trauma in their country of origin and/or been a victim of torture. Such witnesses/defendants may present with physical and mental health problems, may have had very limited access to services in the past and often speak little English);
- is the alleged victim of trafficking (this witness/defendant may have experienced trauma including repeated abuse and may speak little English);
- is the alleged victim of a race/religious/ hate crime;
- is the alleged victim of honour-based violence/forced marriage;
- is the alleged victim of child sexual exploitation;
- is the alleged victim of domestic violence and or sexual violence;
- has witnessed a traumatic incident;
- has a history of self-harming;
- is the alleged victim of financial exploitation.

1.10 Vulnerability may not be constant, consistent or continuous within an individual Someone who would be regarded as vulnerable at the investigation stage of a case might not be at the trial and vice versa. Vulnerability may be transient. Advocates and judges should consider the issue of vulnerability at the time of the relevant hearing.

1.11 The issue of vulnerability should be kept under review Individual personal factors (age, incapacity, impairment or medical condition), environmental factors, or a combination of the two can give rise to vulnerability. For example, an environmental factor, such as being in the courtroom or seeing the defendant, might 'trigger' anxiety and fear which brings a particular witness within the definition of 'vulnerable'.

1.12 GOOD PRACTICE EXAMPLE: The Registered Intermediary carried out an assessment of the witness's communication needs several months before the trial. The intermediary then attended the vulnerable witness's pre-trial court visit and identified additional steps that the court would need to take to facilitate the witness giving her best evidence. The intermediary wrote an addendum report for the court so that the additional recommendations could be addressed at a ground rules hearing.

2. EARLY IDENTIFICATION OF POSSIBLE VULNERABILITY OF WITNESSES AND DEFENDANTS

F.59 **2.1 Advocates should not assume that the police/CPS/defence solicitors have already identified a witness's or defendant's vulnerability** Risk factors may not have been apparent before and, even if they were, identification of vulnerability is poor. Even when identified, vulnerability is not always acted upon (Gudjonsson 2010; Young et al. 2013).

2.2 The police should be the first agency to identify the needs and wishes of the witness/defendant and activate the system for support in their area but this may not have happened.

2.3 POOR PRACTICE EXAMPLE: A 48-year-old male witness with learning disabilities, with limited reading ability and taking medication for anxiety had a written statement taken from him as the officer did not think that a video interview was necessary in this case.

2.4 Information-sharing is key to achieving the goal of identifying and safeguarding vulnerable witnesses and defendants Advocates should check that the police, CPS, Witness Care Unit (WCU), any treating physicians, expert witnesses, intermediaries and the Witness Service have shared necessary information about the vulnerability of the witness/defendant. If in doubt about whether or not to share information, practitioners should refer to *Information Sharing: Guidance for Practitioners and Managers* (Department for Children Schools and Families 2008). During the trial the condition of the witness/defendant should be carefully monitored and professionals should share information if there are any concerns about the witness's/defendant's vulnerability or potential vulnerability.

2.5 POOR PRACTICE EXAMPLE: No one shared with the Witness Service the existing concerns about the witness's serious mental health condition. The Witness Service was unable to carry out a detailed needs assessment or to monitor the risk the witness presented to herself, as it would have done had the witness's condition been known.

2.6 GOOD PRACTICE EXAMPLE: The intermediary for a defendant with autism contacted the treating psychiatrists (who were also expert witnesses in the case) to share information about the defendant's physical and mental condition during the trial.

2.7 For witnesses (including victims), the advocate should check that the WCU has offered a full needs assessment if appropriate The WCU must:
- offer a full needs assessment to those victims who are required to attend court to give evidence to assess what support they may require;
- inform victims of the outcome of a Special Measures Application, if made (part B 2.17 *Code of Practice for Victims of Crime* Ministry of Justice 2013)

2.8 Witnesses who are required to give evidence in court:
- Where appropriate, will be offered a full needs assessment by the Witness Care Unit, police or defence lawyer (page 2 *The Witness Charter* Ministry of Justice 2013)

2.9 Vulnerability is not the same as unreliability Undoubtedly, most vulnerable interviewees, if motivated and co-operative, can give reliable evidence if carefully interviewed and provided with the special assistance they require (Gudjonsson 2010)

2.10 Vulnerability is not the same as not being competent to give evidence Witness competence to give evidence is defined in section 53(3) of the Youth Justice and Criminal Evidence Act 1999 (YJCEA 1999):
'A person is not competent to give evidence in criminal proceedings if it appears to the court that he is not a person who is able to—
(a) understand questions put to him as a witness, and
(b) give answers to them which can be understood.'

2.11 The question of competence is entirely witness-specific. ' [T]he witness need not understand every single question or give a readily understood answer to every question. Many competent adult witnesses would fail such a competency test'—the Lord Chief Justice in *R v B* [2010] EWCA Crim 4 at paragraph 38. In determining the question of witness competence, 'the court shall treat the witness as having the benefit of any special measure/s that have been directed for him/her' (section 53(4) YJCEA 1999). Advocates must prepare their questions carefully for a competency hearing involving a vulnerable witness (*R v F* [2013] EWCA Crim 424).

2.12 Being a vulnerable defendant is not the same as being unfit to plead/ stand trial

- A vulnerable defendant may be fit to plead and stand trial if reasonable steps are taken to support his/her effective participation in the trial.
- It is the judge's responsibility to ensure reasonable steps are taken to adjust the trial process and to ensure there is a fair trial. If such adjustments cannot be made to take into account the incapacity of the defendant, then there can be no fair trial and it is incumbent upon the judge to stop the trial and to consider the issue of fitness to plead (*R v SH* [2003] EWCA Crim 1208 at paragraph 21. See also *R v Cox* [2012] EWCA Crim 549 and *R v Dixon* [2013] EWCA Crim 465).
- The Law Commission is undertaking a project to reform the law on the legal test for unfitness to plead which has 'numerous faults' and ' [g]iven the vulnerability of people with learning disabilities and of those with mental illness, modern criminal law should be informed by modern science, and in particular by modern psychology and psychiatric findings'.

3. ADVOCATES' DUTIES AND RESPONSIBILITIES

F.60   **3.1 Advocates have a responsibility to assist the court to identify and appropriately respond to the vulnerability of witnesses and defendants** This is part of the barrister's core 'duty to the court in the administration of justice'. Barristers also have a responsibility to ensure that the interests of their vulnerable clients are taken into account and their needs are met. Barristers should do what they reasonably can to ensure that the client understands the process and what to expect from it and from their barrister and they should also try to avoid any unnecessary distress for their client (Bar Standards Board Handbook 2014). Similarly, solicitors are obliged to 'uphold the rule of law and the proper administration of justice' and 'provide a proper standard of service to clients', including vulnerable clients (Principles 1 and 5 Solicitors Regulation Authority Code of Conduct 2011).

3.2   Advocates should ask for relevant information about the witness/ defendant from the officer in the case/intermediary/health care professional etc. Some people who appear to be robust and resist assistance may be vulnerable.

3.3   The court 'must identify the needs of witnesses at an early stage' and adapt the pre-trial and trial process accordingly

- The sooner the disadvantage is identified, the easier it is to remedy it.

- The court should, where possible, ensure that information is obtained in advance of a hearing about any disability or medical or other circumstance affecting a person so that individual needs can be accommodated.
- For example, access to interpreters, signers, large print, audiotape, oath-taking in accordance with different belief systems (including non-religious ones), more frequent breaks and special measures for vulnerable witnesses can and should be considered (paragraphs 22 and 23 'General judgecraft principles', *Equal Treatment Benchbook* 2013).

3.4   All advocates should be alert to possible behavioural and psychological changes in the witness's/defendant's presentation at court. For example, factors indicating vulnerability may become apparent for the first time when the witness/defendant is giving evidence. In these circumstances the advocate should inform the judge and seek a short adjournment in order to establish what, if any, adjustments are necessary: ' [Disability] places upon the state (and upon others) the duty to make reasonable accommodation to cater for the special needs of those with disabilities.' (Baroness Hale in *P v Cheshire West and others* [2014] UKSC 19 at paragraph 45).

3.5   Contact should be maintained with the witness beyond their testimony and through to the verdict, helping the person to manage their reaction to the court's decision. Advocates should identify who will maintain contact: this could be, for example, the police officer in charge of the case, the CPS representative, the defence solicitor, or the advocate. If an advocate is concerned that the witness or defendant is at risk of significant harm they should make a referral to the relevant child/adult-safeguarding service.

4.   OBTAINING EXPERT ADVICE

4.1   Expert advice is necessary If there is uncertainty about the existence,   F.61 type or impact of the person's vulnerability, expert advice should be taken. This might be from an expert witness such as a psychologist or psychiatrist, for example. A Registered Intermediary is not an expert witness but can assist by carrying out an assessment of the communication needs and abilities of the witness or defendant.

4.2   GOOD PRACTICE EXAMPLE A police officer interviewed a 40-year-old man who lived independently and had a full-time job. The police officer followed his instinct and requested an assessment by a Registered Intermediary; it transpired that the witness had significant undiagnosed special needs.

4.3   GOOD PRACTICE EXAMPLE The CPS requested a Registered Intermediary assessment. The officer who originally felt he could take a statement without support for the witness, watched the Registered Intermediary assessment being carried out and conceded he had underestimated the witness's comprehension difficulties and he had not appreciated how anxious the process was making the witness.

4.4 GOOD PRACTICE EXAMPLE The intermediary for the defendant provided a report which included a summary of the defendant's communication difficulties. Based on this, the prosecution and defence advocates agreed a form of wording describing the defendant's difficulties and this was read to the jury.

5. SPECIAL MEASURES, OTHER ADJUSTMENTS AND GROUND RULES HEARINGS

F.62 **5.1 Some vulnerable witnesses will be eligible for 'special measures'**
- In respect of eligibility for special measures, 'vulnerable' and 'intimidated' witnesses are defined in section 16 and section 17 of the YJCEA 1999 (as amended by the Coroners and Justice Act 2009); 'vulnerable' includes those under 18 years of age and people with a mental disorder or learning disability, a physical disorder or disability, or who are likely to suffer fear or distress in giving evidence because of their own circumstances or those relating to the case. However, many other people giving evidence in a criminal case, whether as a witness or defendant, may require assistance (3D.1 and 3D.2 Criminal Practice Directions [2013])
- The court must take account of the views of the witness in determining whether they are eligible for special measures (section 16(4) YJCEA 1999).
- When determining whether the quality of the witness's evidence is likely to be diminished in these circumstances, the court has to consider the likely completeness, coherence and accuracy of their testimony (section 16(5) YJCEA 1999).
- Special measures should be applied for at the earliest opportunity and considered at the pleas and case management hearing.

5.2 'Special measures' must be applied for and ordered by the court (Application for Special Measures Direction)

5.3 A vulnerable witness may be eligible for one or more of the following special measures (adapted from CPS guidance on Special Measures).
- A screen may be placed around the witness so that the witness is 'prevented by means of a screen or other arrangement from seeing the accused' (section 23(1) YJCEA 1999).
- A live link enables the witness to give evidence during the trial from outside the court through a televised link to the courtroom—the

witness may be accommodated either within the court building or in a suitable location outside the court (section 24 YJCEA 1999).

- Evidence given in private occurs when the judge excludes from the court members of the public and the press (except for one named person to represent the press) in cases involving sexual offences or intimidation by someone other than the accused (section 25 YJCEA 1999).
- Removal of wigs and gowns by judges and barristers (section 26 YJCEA 1999).
- A video-recorded interview with a vulnerable witness before the trial may be admitted by the court as the witness's evidence-in-chief. For adult complainants in sexual offence trials in the Crown Court a video-recorded interview will be automatically admissible upon application unless this would not be in the interests of justice or would not maximise the quality of the complainant's evidence. Section 103 of the Coroners and Justice Act 2009 relaxes the restrictions on a witness giving additional evidence in chief after the witness's video-recorded interview has been admitted (section 27 YJCEA 1999).
- Examination of the witness through an intermediary. The intermediary can provide communication assistance at the police investigation stage (approval for admission of evidence so taken is then sought retrospectively) and at court to assist the witness to give their evidence. The intermediary is allowed to explain questions or answers so far as is necessary to enable them to be understood by the witness or the questioner but without changing the substance of the evidence (section 29 YJCEA 1999).
- Aids to communication may be permitted to enable a witness to give their best evidence whether through a communicator or interpreter, or through a communication aid (such as an electronic device or picture boards) or technique (such as signing), provided that the communication can be independently verified and understood by the court (section 30 YJCEA 1999).

5.4 Video-recorded cross-examination (section 28) is not yet in force, however, this special measure is being piloted in 2014 in three Crown Courts (Kingston-upon-Thames, Leeds and Liverpool).

5.5 In addition to special measures, the YJCEA 1999 also contains the following provisions intended to enable vulnerable or intimidated witnesses to give their best evidence:

- mandatory protection of witness from cross-examination by the accused in person—a prohibition on an unrepresented defendant cross-examining vulnerable child and adult victims in certain classes of cases involving sexual offences;
- discretionary protection of witness from cross-examination by the accused in person—in other types of offence, the court has a

discretion to prohibit an unrepresented defendant from cross-examining the victim in person;

- restrictions on evidence and questions about complainant's sexual behaviour;
- reporting restrictions—restrictions on the reporting by the media of information likely to lead to the identification of certain adult witnesses in criminal proceedings.

5.6 Some vulnerable defendants will be eligible for the equivalent of special measures and other support The Criminal Practice Directions [2013] (3G: Vulnerable defendants) provide examples of adjustments depending on the nature of the defendant's vulnerability: trying the defendant on their own; pre-trial court familiarisation; practising with the live link; frequent and regular breaks etc.

5.7 The special measures provisions of the YJCEA 1999 do not apply to the accused (section 16(1) and section 17(1)). However, using its wide and flexible inherent powers the court may grant the defendant the equivalent of some of the special measures that are available for witnesses (*R v Camberwell Green Youth Court* [2005] UKHL 4) including an intermediary (*C v Sevenoaks Youth Court* [2009] EWHC 3088 (Admin)). A trial judge should take an active role throughout the proceedings to ensure that the vulnerable defendant is effectively participating in the proceedings (*R v Dixon* [2013] EWCA Crim 465).

5.8 In addition, in some cases the judge will not allow the jury to draw inferences (if the defendant chooses not to give evidence) if it would be harmful for the defendant to give evidence (Section 35(1)(b) Criminal Justice and Public Order Act 1994).

5.9 Where a defendant (or indeed a witness) may have difficulty in recalling all that they want to say to the jury because of their limitations, a very detailed defence statement could be read by the judge to the jury to enable them to hear the defendant''s evidence in that way. Another possibility is to allow the witness (or a defendant) to refer to a document if it assists them to give their evidence properly (*R v SH* [2003] EWCA Crim 1208 at paragraphs 27–29).

5.10 GOOD PRACTICE EXAMPLE A judge requested that the intermediary facilitated communication at the defendant's pre-sentence report interview with the probation service and at the sentencing hearing.

5.11 A ground rules hearing must take place if a witness or defendant is vulnerable In preparation for trial, courts must take 'every reasonable step' to facilitate the participation of witnesses and defendants (Rule 3.8(4)(a) and

(b) Criminal Procedure Rules 2013). One such step is the ground rules hearing: a pre-trial meeting of the trial judge, trial advocates and intermediary (if any) with the aim of deciding how someone who has communication needs or is otherwise vulnerable should be enabled to give their best evidence, or how a vulnerable defendant can participate effectively in the trial. For further guidance, see the toolkit on ground rules hearings.

5.12 Adjustments other than special measures may be necessary to ensure the hearing is fair The list below is not exhaustive. Most of the ideas listed are examples of additional adjustments recommended by an intermediary. These creative solutions were suggested to address the communication needs of a particular witness/defendant. Adjustments must be discussed at a ground rules hearing and, if they are ordered by the court, advocates should ensure that the Witness Service/the dock officer (as appropriate) has been given advance notice of this.

5.13 Examples of additional adjustments ordered by the judge include:
- advocates moving to the live link room to conduct their questioning from there;
- allowing a witness/defendant to pause cross-examination by pointing to a 'pause' card on the table in the live link room and then the intermediary alerting the judge that a pause has been requested;
- use of an eggtimer in the live link room to time short three-minute breaks as required by the witness—the court remaining sitting during these breaks;
- allowing a witness to take a comfort toy into the live link room;
- allowing a defendant to have 'Blu-Tack'/a stress toy/a pen and paper in the dock to help maintain their concentration;
- allowing 'Post-it' notes in the dock which are stuck on to the glass screen showing the order of events during the trial which can be changed around and also removed, once a particular event has happened, to help a defendant who has difficulty understanding the order of events;
- ensuring that the flat screen that is ordinarily visible to the defendant be turned off/covered so that the defendant can hear but not see the vulnerable witness giving evidence.

5.14 GOOD PRACTICE EXAMPLE The witness was taking a significant amount of medication to control psychiatric symptoms. Her ability to give evidence was much improved in the afternoon when her medication had had the chance to start working and her mental state was most stable. The schedule was adjusted so that she gave her testimony only in the afternoons.

5.15 GOOD PRACTICE EXAMPLE The defendant had a phobia of the police. The judge instructed the police officer to attend court in non-uniform.

The officer arrived at the trial in uniform and the judge required him to go away and change his clothes.

5.16 GOOD PRACTICE EXAMPLE The judge allowed a young witness to take a very small tent into the live link room which was not visible on the TV link screen in the courtroom. The witness was allowed to have short "time-out" breaks (usually of just 30 seconds) in the tent when her anxiety peaked, but was not at the point where she needed a full break from giving her evidence. While the witness took this short break the live link was temporarily turned off and the court waited until she was ready to continue. (If the live link remains on, the judge should ensure that the microphones in the court are turned off so that the witness does not hear the conversations in the courtroom.)

5.17 GOOD PRACTICE EXAMPLE The vulnerable defendant struggled with concepts of time, so the defendant (who gave evidence from the live link room) was allowed to take a timeline into the live link room to assist cross-examination. The advocates had a duplicate of the timeline and indicated certain points on the timeline when putting questions to the defendant.

5.18 GOOD PRACTICE EXAMPLE The judge held a ground rules hearing in chambers four weeks before the trial. The judge asked what topics counsel would cover in evidence and as a result the intermediary was asked to provide anatomical dolls and dolls' clothing in order to avoid the difficulties that had arisen during the Achieving Best Evidence interview (where there had been no intermediary and the witness had appeared extremely embarrassed whilst explaining what had happened).

5.19 Advocates should ensure that there is consistency between the adjustments made in the hearing and those made at other times. For example, a vulnerable witness might need the intermediary to be present for witness familiarisation to be effective. Advocates should also seek to ensure consistency between 'upstairs' (in court) and 'downstairs' (in the cells); the judge might approve certain measures in the court itself and the advocate should establish whether reasonable accommodation is also being made in the holding cells.

5.20 POOR PRACTICE EXAMPLE In one case the vulnerable defendant missed lunch as he wasn't able to make himself understood when the custody officers asked him if he wanted any.

5.21 GOOD PRACTICE EXAMPLE The vulnerable defendant was brought to court at the usual time but on this particular day of the trial the case was listed as 'not before 12'. The defendant's legal team made sure that custody officers and the defendant in the cells knew what was happening in order to avoid the defendant becoming highly anxious about the delay.

5.22 POOR PRACTICE EXAMPLE A defendant who could not read and was being held in the cells whilst the jury were deliberating was offered a newspaper to pass the time.

5.23 GOOD PRACTICE EXAMPLE After consultation with the guards, the intermediary was permitted to take a travel-sized board game to help the vulnerable defendant pass the time and manage his anxiety.

5.24 **Advocates and judges should be proactive in identifying the need for an assessment of potential vulnerability and responding to it.** If it appears that the adjustments or special measures are necessary to safeguard the witness or defendant or to ensure they give their best evidence and participate effectively, the advocate should consider inviting the judge to impose these, even if the witness/defendant says that they do not wish to have them.

The development of this toolkit was funded by a grant from the Legal Education Foundation. The author is Professor Penny Cooper. Contributions were made by Jay Breslaw, Dr Jenny Cutler, Gill Darvill, Norma Dempster, Professor Gisli Gudjonsson CBE, HHJ Michael Hopmeier, Ruth Marchant, Michelle Mattison, Dr Brendan O'Mahony, Catherine O'Neill, Dr Emily Phibbs, Dr Kevin Smith, Sue Thurman, Charlotte Triggs and David Wurtzel.

The toolkit summarises key points from:
Bar Standards Board Handbook (2014)
Bradley, K (2009) *The Bradley Report: Lord Bradley's Review of People with Mental Health or Learning Disabilities in the Criminal Justice System* (London: Department of Health)
Criminal Procedure Rules 2013
Bull, R (2010) 'The investigative interviewing of children and other vulnerable witnesses: psychological research and working/professional practice' *Legal and Criminological Psychology* 15: 5–23. doi:10.1348/014466509X440160
Criminal Practice Directions [2013] EWCA Crim 1631
Crown Prosecution Service guidance on Special Measures (London: CPS)
Department for Children, Schools and Families (2008) *Information Sharing: Guidance for Practitioners and Managers* (London: DfES)
Gregory, J and Bryan, K (2011) 'Speech and language therapy intervention with a group of persistent and prolific young offenders in a non-custodial setting with previously undiagnosed speech, language and communication difficulties' *International Journal of Language and Communication Disorders* 46(2): 202–15

Gudjonsson, G (2010), 'Psychological vulnerabilities during police interviews. Why are they important?' *Legal and Criminological Psychology* 15:161–75

Home Office (2013) Police and Criminal Evidence Act 1984 Code C: revised code of practice for the detention, treatment and questioning of persons by police officers (London: Home Office)

Judicial College (2012) Fairness in Courts and Tribunals (London: Judicial College) Judicial College (2013) *Equal Treatment Benchbook* (London: Judicial College)

Ministry of Justice (2011) *Achieving Best Evidence in Criminal Proceedings: Guidance on interviewing victims and witnesses, and guidance on using special measures* (London: MoJ)

Ministry of Justice (2011) *Vulnerable Witnesses: A police service guide* (London: MoJ) Ministry of Justice (2013) *Code of Practice for Victims of Crime* (London: MoJ) Ministry of Justice (2013) *The Witness Charter* (London: MoJ)

Solicitors Regulation Authority Code of Conduct 2011

Surrey County Council Safeguarding Adults Board/H Brown (2014) *The Death of Mrs A: A serious case review*

Young, S et al (2013) 'The effectiveness of police custody assessments in identifying suspects with intellectual disabilities and attention deficit hyperactivity disorder' *BMC Medicine* www.biomedcentral.com/ 1741-7015/11/248

THE CROWN COURT COMPENDIUM
PART I

Jury and trial management and summing up
Legal summaries directions and examples
Maddison Ormerod Tonking Wait[1]

10-2 Corroboration and the special need for caution

ARCHBOLD 4-468; BLACKSTONE'S F5.1

Legal Summary

1. Corroborative evidence is relevant, admissible,[277] and credible[278]   **G.01**
   evidence independent of the source requiring corroboration,[279] and
   which has the effect of implicating the accused.

2. Historically there were specific categories of case where, because of
   the nature of the allegation or the type of witness, a direction was
   required that the jury should look for corroboration of the evidence
   in question: evidence of an accomplice, a complainant in the trial of
   a sexual offence and evidence of a child, but corroboration is now
   required by statute only in cases of treason,[280] perjury,[281] speed-
   ing[282] and attempts to commit such offences.[283]

---

[1] Reproduced with permission and thanks to David Maddison, Professor David Ormerod,
Simon Tonking and HHJ John Wait.(*Please note: footnote numbers in this appendix are the exact
numbers from the original*).
[277] *Scarrott* [1978] QB 1016 at p.1021.
[278] *DPP v Kilbourne* [1973] AC 729 at p.746; *DPP v Hester* [1973] AC 296 at p.315.
[279] *Whitehead* [1929] 1 KB 99.
[280] Treason Act 1795, s.1.
[281] Perjury Act 1911, s.13.
[282] Road Traffic Regulation Act 1984, s.89(2).
[283] Criminal Attempts Act 1981, s.2(2)(g).

3. Although corroboration in the strict sense is now no longer required in support of the categories outlined above, circumstances may nevertheless require the judge, as a matter of discretion in summing up, to give a warning to the jury about the need for caution in the absence of supporting evidence.

4. In *Makanjuola*,[284] Lord Taylor CJ gave the following guidance:

   "To summarise:

   (1) Section 32(1) abrogates the requirement to give a corroboration direction in respect of an alleged accomplice or a complainant of a sexual offence, simply because a witness falls into one of those categories.

   (2) It is a matter for the judge's discretion what, if any warning, he considers appropriate in respect of such a witness as indeed in respect of any other witness in whatever type of case. Whether he chooses to give a warning and in what terms will depend on the circumstances of the case, the issues raised and the content and quality of the witness's evidence.

   (3) In some cases, it may be appropriate for the judge to warn the jury to exercise caution before acting upon the unsupported evidence of a witness. **This will not be so simply because the witness is a complainant of a sexual offence nor will it necessarily be so because a witness is alleged to be an accomplice. There will need to be an evidential basis for suggesting that the evidence of the witness may be unreliable. An evidential basis does not include mere suggestions by cross-examining counsel.**

   (4) If any question arises as to whether the judge should give a special warning in respect of a witness, it is desirable that the question be resolved by discussion with counsel in the absence of the jury before final speeches.

   (5) **Where the judge does decide to give some warning in respect of a witness, it will be appropriate to do so as part of the judge's review of the evidence and his comments as to how the jury should evaluate it rather than as a set-piece legal direction.**

   (6) Where some warning is required, it will be for the judge to decide the strength and terms of the warning. It does not have to be invested with the whole florid regime of the old corroboration rules.

   (7) . . .

   (8) Finally, this Court will be disinclined to interfere with a trial judge's exercise of his discretion save in a case where that exercise is unreasonable in the Wednesbury sense." [emphasis added]

5. The need to consider giving a discretionary warning of the type described in *Makanjuola* arises whenever the need for special

---

[284] [1995] 1 WLR 1348 at p.1351D.

caution before acting on the evidence of certain types of witness, if unsupported, is apparent. The following types of witnesses/categories of case are worth consideration:

(1) Co-defendants: An accused may have a purpose of his own to serve by giving evidence which implicates a co-defendant.[285] In *Jones*,[286] in which each of the defendants in part placed blame on the other, Auld LJ commended counsel's suggestion that in such cases the jury should be directed:

   (a) to consider the cases of each defendant separately;

   (b) the evidence of each defendant was relevant to the case of the other;

   (c) when considering the co-defendant's evidence, the jury should bear in mind that the interest may have an interest to serve; and

   (d) the evidence of a co-defendant should otherwise be assessed in the same way as the evidence of any other witness.

(2) Witnesses tainted by improper motive.[287]

(3) Witnesses of bad character.[288]

(4) Evidence from a witness received after section 73 SOCPA 2005 agreement[289]

(5) Children: Whether to give a direction will depend on the circumstances of the case, including the intelligence of the child and, in the case of unsworn evidence, the extent to which the child understands the duty of speaking the truth. In *R v MH*,[290] a case involving a three year old complainant, the Court of Appeal rejected the suggestion that the judge should have directed the jury that children may imagine, fantasise or misunderstand a situation, may easily be coached, may say what they think their mother wants to hear, or may merely repeat by rote that which has been said on a previous occasion; and that the judge should have warned the jury not to be beguiled by the attractiveness of the child and to bear in mind his extreme youth. It would have been wrong for the judge to

[285] *Cheema* [1994] 1 WLR 147; *Muncaster* [1998] EWCA Crim 296; *Jones* [2003] EWCA Crim 1966.

[286] *Jones* [2003] EWCA Crim 1966 at para.47.

[287] *Beck* [1982] 1 WLR 461 at p.467E (defence making allegations of impropriety against witnesses for the prosecution); *Chan Wai-Keung* [1995] 1 WLR 251 (prisoner awaiting sentence giving evidence in unrelated case); *Ashgar* [1995] 1 Cr App R 223 (defence allegation that prosecution witnesses were protecting one of their number); *Pringle* [2003] UKPC 9 and *Benedetto* [2003] UKPC 27 (cell confession); *Spencer* [1987] UKHL 2 (patients in a secure hospital).

[288] *Spencer* [1987] UKHL 2; *Cairns, Zaidi and Chaudhary* [2002] EWCA Crim 2838.

[289] *Daniels and Others* [2010] EWCA Crim 2740.

[290] [2012] EWCA Crim 2725 at para.50 to 51 per Pitchford LJ.

engage in such generalisations remote from the facts of the case.

(6) Unexplained infant deaths: Such cases may give rise to serious and respectable disagreement between experts as to the conclusions which can be drawn from post mortem findings. Supporting evidence independent of expert opinion may be required.[291]

(7) Inherently unreliable witnesses: for example if it has become clear that a witness has made a false complaint, otherwise lied or given substantially different accounts in the past.

6. Whether a warning is given and the terms of any warning given are matters of judicial discretion.[292] In *Stone*[293] the Court of Appeal reiterated the need to examine the particular circumstances of the case before reaching a judgment as to the terms in which the requirement for caution should be expressed.[294] A possible starting point, drawing on *Turnbull*[295] [see Chapter 15-1] is to warn the jury of the special need for caution before acting on the disputed evidence, and to explain the reason why such caution is required. Where the jury is advised to look for supporting evidence, the judge should identify the evidence which is capable of supporting that of the witness;[296] if there is none, the jury should be directed to that effect.

Directions

G.02

7. In some cases, for example those listed in paragraph 5 above, it may be appropriate for the judge to direct the jury to approach the evidence of a particular witness with caution. The need for and terms of any such direction should be discussed with the advocates in the absence of the jury before closing speeches.

8. It is usually a matter for the judge's discretion whether to give any direction, and if so in what terms. However, if one defendant or suspect in relation to an offence gives evidence against another a

---

[291] *Cannings* [2004] EWCA Crim 1; *Kai-Whitewind* [2005] EWCA Crim 1092 (evidence supporting the experts' opinion as to cause of death was found in post mortem results) and *Hookway* [2011] EWCA Crim 1989 (dispute between experts not whether there was DNA evidence incriminating the appellants but as to the strength of that evidence).

[292] *Laing v The Queen* [2013] UKPC 14 at para.8 citing Lord Taylor CJ in *Makanjuola* [1995] 1 WLR 1348 at p.1351.

[293] [2005] EWCA Crim 105.

[294] The content of the warning is a matter for the judge's discretion in the light of the evidence, the issues and the nature of the particular taint on the evidence of the impugned witness: *Muncaster* [1998] EWCA Crim 296; *L* [1999] Crim LR 489.

[295] [1977] QB 224.

[296] *B (MT)* [2000] Crim LR 181.

cautionary direction will almost always be necessary, as to which see also the final bullet point below.

9. Any such direction is best given as part of the review of the evidence rather than as a set-piece legal direction during the first part of the summing up.

10. The strength and terms of any such direction will depend on the circumstances of the individual case. No set formula is available. The following is offered only by way of general guidance, and is not intended to cover every situation that might arise:

    (1) The witness concerned ('W') should be identified and the reason(s) for the need for caution should be explained.

    (2) Sometimes it will be sufficient simply to direct the jury to approach the evidence of W with caution. If so, the jury should also be directed that they may nevertheless rely on that evidence if, having taken into account the need for caution, they are sure that W is telling the truth.

    (3) Where there is no independent supportive evidence, it may be appropriate to remind the jury of that fact, and possibly to suggest that the jury may have wished for such evidence. In that event the jury should also be directed that they may nevertheless rely on the evidence of W if, having taken into account the need for caution and the absence of any independent supportive evidence, they are sure that W is telling the truth.

    (4) In cases where there *is* potentially independent supportive evidence, that evidence must be identified, adding that it is for the jury to decide whether they accept that evidence and if so whether they regard it as supportive. If they conclude that there is independent supportive evidence they may take this into account when assessing W's evidence, but it does not mean that W is bound to be telling the truth. On the other hand, even if the jury conclude that there is no independent supportive evidence, they may still rely on the evidence of W if, having taken into account the need for caution and the absence of any independent supportive evidence they are sure that W is telling the truth.

    (5) Where co-defendants give evidence against each other, the need for caution needs to be conveyed without unnecessarily diminishing the evidence of either defendant. This can usually be achieved by incorporating directions that the jury should consider the case of each defendant separately; should examine that part of each defendant's evidence which implicates the other with caution, since each may have his / her own purpose to serve; but otherwise should assess each defendant's evidence in the same way as that of any other witness. This approach can

be adapted to cover a case in which one co-defendant gives
evidence against another, but not *vice versa*.

G.03

Example 1: co-defendant[297]

When considering the evidence of D1 and D2 you should bear these points in mind:

1. *First, as I have already explained to you, you must consider the case against and for each D separately.*
2. Secondly, you should decide the case in relation to each D on *all of the evidence, which includes the evidence given by each of the Ds.*
3. Thirdly, you should assess the evidence given by each of the Ds in the same way as you assess the evidence of any other witness in the case.
4. Finally, when the evidence of one D bears upon the case of the other, you should have in mind that the D whose evidence you are considering may have an interest of his own to serve and may have tailored his evidence accordingly. Whether either D has in fact done this is entirely for you to decide.

Example 2: co-defendant who has pleaded guilty and has, by written agreement, assisted the prosecutor by giving evidence[298]

When considering the evidence of W you should bear in mind that he has already pleaded guilty to the offence with which D is charged and gave evidence which implicated D after formally agreeing to help the prosecution by doing so. He did this hoping to get a lesser sentence.

Because this is the situation you should approach W's evidence with caution, knowing that he has an obvious incentive to give evidence which implicates D. You should ask yourselves whether W has, or may have, tailored his evidence to implicate D falsely or whether you can be sure, despite the potential benefit to W of giving evidence against D, that he has told you the truth. If you are sure that he has told the truth, you may rely on his evidence.

---

13. CROSS ADMISSIBILITY

ARCHBOLD 13-9, 38 and 63a; BLACKSTONE'S F12.58

Legal Summary

G.04

1. If the indictment against D comprises more than one count the issue may arise as to whether the evidence relating to one count is

---

[297] This example is based on *Jones and Jenkins* [2003] EWCA Crim 1966.
[298] Serious Organised Crime and Police Act 2005, s.73.

"cross admissible" in relation to another, and if so to what uses it may legitimately be put by the jury.

2. Cross admissibility is not an appropriate term to describe the admissibility of evidence from a previous incident that does not form part of the indictment.[403]

3. CJA 2003 s.112(2) provides: "Where a defendant is charged with two or more offences in the same criminal proceedings, this Chapter (except s.101(3)) has effect as if each offence were charged in separate proceedings; and references to the offence with which the defendant is charged are to be read accordingly."[404]

4. The leading authority is *Freeman and Crawford*[405] which confirms that evidence may be cross admissible in one or both of the following ways[406]

   (1) "(1) The evidence may be relevant to more than one count because it rebuts coincidence, as for example, where the prosecution asserts the unlikelihood of a coincidence that separate and independent complainants have made similar but untrue allegations against the defendant. The jury may be permitted to consider the improbability that those complaints are the product of mere coincidence or malice (i.e. a complainant's evidence in support of one count is relevant to the credibility of another complainant's evidence on another count-an important matter in issue: s.101(1)(d))"; and/or*

   (2) "The jury may be sure of the accused's guilt upon one count and if, but only if, they are also sure that guilt of that offence establishes the accused's propensity to commit that kind of offence, the jury may proceed to consider whether the accused's propensity makes it more likely that he committed an offence of a similar type alleged in another count in the same indictment (evidence of propensity: s.101(1)(d) and s.103(1)(a))."*

5. In both categories the evidence which is being adduced is evidence of bad character against the defendant under CJA 2003, s.101[407] : see Chapter 13.

6. Whichever approach is employed, the jury must reach separate verdicts on each count and for each defendant.

7. Under the coincidence approach:
   (1) Cross admissibility of evidence does **not** involve "propensity" evidence in the way in which that term is used under CJA 2003. The

---

[403] *Suleman* [2012] EWCA Crim 1569.
[404] *Wallace* [2007] EWCA Crim 1760; *Chopra* [2006] EWCA Crim 2133.
[405] [2008] EWCA Crim 1863. *See also the very helpful analysis in McAllister [2008] EWCA Crim 1544 para.31.*
[406] *N(H)*: [2012] EWCA Crim 1568 para.31.
[407] *McAllister* [2008] EWCA Crim 1544 para.13.

jury is not being invited to reason from propensity; they are merely being asked to recognise that the evidence in relation to a particular offence on an indictment may appear stronger and more compelling when all the evidence, including evidence relating to other offences, is looked at as a whole.[408] In *H*[409] Rix LJ pithily observed: "the reality is that independent people do not make false allegations of a like nature against the same person, in the absence of collusion or contamination of their evidence."

(2) The jury will need to exclude collusion or innocent contamination as an explanation for the similarity of the complainants' evidence before they can assess the force of the argument that they are unlikely to be the product of coincidence.[410] The jury is being invited to consider the improbability that the complaints are the product of mere coincidence or malice.[411] The more independent sources of evidence, the less probable the coincidence. That is so only if, the sources are genuinely independent. The jury are not being invited to reason from propensity. If they conclude that D is guilty on other counts they may also have concluded that he has a relevant propensity, but they are not being invited to reason from a propensity that they have found to his guilt.

8. Under the propensity approach evidence from one count is admissible against another under s.101 as if the counts were being tried as separate trials. The jury is being invited to reason that if D is guilty of one incident that demonstrates he has a propensity for such offending and that propensity may be relevant when they consider a further count. They are reasoning from a propensity they have found to liability for other counts.

9. In some rare cases it may be appropriate to direct the jury that the evidence that is cross admissible is capable of being used to rebut coincidence and for propensity type reasoning. The leading case is *N(H)*.[412] Care needed to be taken by the judge before giving both directions. It is important to avoid double accounting—i.e. the jury cannot use evidence from count 1 to rebut coincidence that D committed count 2 and then, having become sure of guilt on count 2, use that as propensity evidence to convict D on count 1.

10. Latham LJ in *Freeman and Crawford* said[413]:
"*In some of the judgments since Hanson, the impression may have been given that the jury, in its decision making process in cross-*

[408] *McAllister* at [14].
[409] *H* [2011] EWCA Crim 2344 para.24.
[410] [2011] EWCA Crim 730.
[411] *Cross* [2012] EWCA Crim 2277.
[412] [2011] EWCA Crim 730 para.31.
[413] [2008] EWCA Crim 1863 para.20.

admissibility cases should first determine whether it is satisfied on the evidence in relation to one of the counts of the defendant's guilt before it can move on to using the evidence in relation to that count in dealing with any other count in the indictment. A good example is the judgment of this court in S.[414] We consider that this is too restrictive an approach. Whilst the jury must be reminded that it has to reach a verdict on each count separately, it is entitled, in determining guilt in respect of any count, to have regard to the evidence in regard to any other count, or any other bad character evidence if that evidence is admissible and relevant in the way we have described. It may be that in some cases the jury will find it easier to decide the guilt of a defendant on the evidence relating to that count alone. That does not mean that it cannot, in other cases, use the evidence in relation to the other count or counts to help it decide on the defendant's guilt in respect of the count that it is considering. To do otherwise would fail to give proper effect to the decision on admissibility."

Directions

11. The terms 'coincidence approach' and 'propensity approach' are   **G.05**
used here in the sense explained in the Legal Summary above.

12. In any case in which a cross-admissibility direction is contemplated, it is essential to discuss with the advocates in the absence of the jury and before closing speeches the need for and form of any such direction. While the Examples in this chapter are expressed as oral directions, the jury will inevitably be assisted by some form of written direction.

13. In a 'coincidence approach' case, the jury should be directed as follows:
(1) They must consider each count separately.
(2) However, the prosecution rely on similarities between the evidence of the complainants [identify the similarities].
(3) If the complainants have or may have concocted false accusations against D, any such similarities would count for nothing, and the jury should reject each complainant's evidence.*
(4) If there was no concoction but a complainant had or may have learned what the other/s had said or were going to say about D, and had or may have been influenced by this, consciously or unconsciously, when making his/her own accusations, any such similarities would count for nothing, and the jury should take this matter into account when deciding how far they accept the evidence of the complainant concerned.*

---

[414] [2008] EWCA Crim 544.

(5) If the jury are sure that there has been no such concoction/ influence they should consider how likely it is that two (or more) people would, independently of each other, make similar accusations and yet both/all be lying / mistaken. If the jury thought this unlikely they could, if they thought it right, treat the evidence of each of the complainants as supporting that of the other/s.*

(6) When deciding how much support, if any, the evidence of one complainant gives to another the jury should take into account how similar their accusations are, since the jury might take the view that the closer the similarities the more likely it is that the complainants were telling the truth.

*The directions in paragraphs (3) and (4) above should only be given if the issue has arisen in evidence. If the issue has not arisen, the direction in paragraph (5) should be modified accordingly. See *Example 1* below.

14. In a 'propensity approach' case the jury direction should be based on Chapter 12-6: Bad Character s.101(1)(d). See also *Example 1* in that chapter; and *Example 2* below.

15. Depending on the evidence and issues in the case, a direction based on both coincidence and propensity approaches may be appropriate. However, such a direction is likely to be complex and, unless great care is taken, confusing. It is suggested that such a direction be given, if at all, only in cases where the evidence on one or more counts is significantly stronger than that on the other(s), and in which the jury might therefore convict on the stronger count(s) first, and then treat that as establishing a propensity on D's part to commit offences of the kind charged in the other count(s). Examples would be where there is a recording of D's committing one of the offences charged in the indictment; where one or more witnesses say that they saw D committing one of the offences charged; or where D is said to have confessed to committing one of the offences charged.

16. If a direction based on both approaches is given, then to avoid the risk of the impermissible double counting referred to in paragraph 3 above, it is suggested that the jury be directed to consider the propensity approach first: see *Example 3* below.

Example 1: The 'coincidence' approach
Scenario: D is charged in count 1 with a sexual assault on V1 and in count 2 with a similar sexual assault on V2. The only prosecution evidence comes from V1 and V2 themselves. D claims that V1 and V2 have concocted false accounts.

I have already told you that you must consider each count separately.

However, the prosecution rely on the similarities between the allegations made by V1 and V2. [Set out the similarities e.g. in relation to the nature, circumstances, periods of time and locations of the alleged offences.]

D claims that the allegations are similar because V1 and V2 have got together to make up false accusations against him. If you decide that this has or may have happened, the similarities would obviously count for nothing, and you would reject the evidence of both V1 and V2.

Even if you are sure that that V1 and V2 have not made up false allegations together, you should consider whether either V1 or V2 might have learned what the other was saying about D and have been influenced, knowingly or unknowingly, when making his/her own allegations. If you decide that this has or may have happened, the similarities between that complainant's evidence and the evidence of the other complainant would not take the prosecution's case any further, and you would have to take any influence of that kind into account when deciding how far you accepted that complainant's evidence.

However, if you are sure that there has been no such concoction or influence, you should consider how likely it is that two people, independently of each other, would make allegations that were similar but untrue. If you decide that this is unlikely, then you could if you think it right, treat V1's evidence as supporting that of V2, and vice versa.

When deciding how far, if at all, the evidence of each supports the other, you should take into account how similar in your opinion their allegations are. This is because you could take the view that the more similar independent allegations are the more likely they are to be true.

Example 2: The 'propensity' approach

Scenario: D is charged in count 1 with a sexual assault on V1 and in count 2 with a sexual assault on V2. The prosecution evidence on count 1 is (a) the account given by V1 and (b) a video recording which the prosecution say was made by D as he committed the offence. The prosecution evidence on count 2 is only the account given by V2. D claims that V1 and V2 have concocted false accounts and denies that he is the person shown in the recording.

I have already told you that you must consider each count separately.

However if, but only if, you are sure that the person shown in the recording of events in count 1 is D and that he committed that offence, you should next consider whether that shows that he has a tendency to commit offences of the kind charged in count 2.

If you are not sure that D has such a tendency then your conclusion that he committed the offence charged in count 1 does not support the prosecution's case on count 2. But if you are sure that D does have such a tendency then you may take this into account when you are deciding whether D is guilty of count 2.

Bear in mind however that even if a person has a tendency to commit a particular kind of offence, it does not follow that he is bound to do so. So if you are sure that D does have a tendency to commit offences of the kind charged in count 2, this is only part of the evidence against him on that count, and you must not convict him wholly or mainly on the strength of it.

Example 3: Both approaches

Scenario: D is charged in count 1 with a sexual assault on V1 and in count 2 with a similar sexual assault on V2. The prosecution evidence on count 1 is (a) the account given by V1 and (b) evidence given by V1's mother that she saw D sexually assaulting her daughter. The prosecution evidence on count 2 is only the account given by V2. D claims that V1 and V2 have concocted false accounts and that V1's mother is lying.

I have already told you that you must consider each count separately.

However there are two ways in which the evidence on one count might support the prosecution's case on the other. You should consider these two ways in the following order.

First consider count 1, where the prosecution rely not only on the evidence of V1 but also on that of her mother. If, having considered their evidence, you are sure that D is guilty of count 1, you should go on to consider whether that shows that he has a tendency to commit offences of the kind charged in count 2.

If you are not sure that D has such a tendency, then your conclusion that he committed the offence in count 1 does not support the prosecution's case on count 2. But if you are sure that D does have such a tendency then you may take this into account when you are deciding whether D is guilty of count 2.

Bear in mind however that even if a person has a tendency to commit a particular kind of offence, it does not follow that he is bound to do so. So if you are sure that D has a tendency to commit offences of the kind charged in count 2, this is only part of the evidence against him on that count, and you must not convict him wholly or mainly on the strength of it.

The second way in which the evidence on one count might support the prosecution's case on the other is this. The prosecution also rely on similarities between the allegations made by V1 and V2, [Set out the similarities e.g. in relation to the nature, circumstances, periods of time and locations of the alleged offences.]

D claims that the allegations are similar because V1 and V2 have got together to make up false accusations against him. If you decide that this has or may have happened, the similarities would obviously count for nothing, and you would reject the evidence of both V1 and V2.

Even if you are sure that V1 and V2 have not made up false allegations together, you should consider whether either V1 or V2 might have learned what the other was saying about D and have been influenced, knowingly or unknowingly, when making her own allegations. If you decide that this has or may have happened, the similarities between that complainant's evidence and the evidence of the other complainant would not take the prosecution's case any further, and you would have to take any influence of that kind into account when deciding how far you accepted that complainant's evidence.

However, if you are sure that there has been no such concoction or influence, you should consider how likely it is that two people, independently of each other, would make allegations that were similar but untrue. If you decide that this is unlikely, then you could, if you think it right, use V1's evidence as support for the evidence of V2. For the same reason, if you had not already reached a conclusion on count 1 on the basis of the evidence of V1 and her mother, you could use the evidence of V2 as support for their evidence.

When deciding how far, if at all, the evidence of each complainant supports the other, you should take into account how similar in your opinion their allegations are. This is because you could take the view that the more similar independent allegations are, the more likely they are to be true.

20.   SEXUAL OFFENCES

20-1 Sexual offences—The dangers of assumptions

ARCHBOLD 20-27a; BLACKSTONE'S B3.39
Legal Summary

1. In D^{780} the Court of Appeal accepted that a judge may give   **G.07**
   appropriate directions to counter the risk of stereotypes and

[780] [2008] EWCA Crim 2557 .se also *Breeze* [2009] EWCA Crim 255.

assumptions about sexual behaviour and reactions to non-consensual sexual conduct. In short, these were that (i) experience shows that people react differently to the trauma of a serious sexual assault, that there is no one classic response; (ii) some may complain immediately whilst others feel shame and shock and not complain for some time; and (iii) a late complaint does not necessarily mean it is a false complaint. The court also acknowledged that a judge is entitled to refer to the particular feelings of shame and embarrassment which may arise when the allegation is of sexual assault by a partner.

2. This approach has been endorsed on numerous occasions by the Court of Appeal, as explained in *Miller*[781]

   "In recent years, the courts have increasingly been prepared to acknowledge the need for a direction that deals with what might be described as stereotypical assumptions about issues such as delay in reporting allegations of sexual crime and distress (see, for example, R v. MM [2007] EWCA Crim 1558, R v. D [2008] EWCA Crim 2557 and R v. Breeze [2009] EWCA Crim 255)."

3. In *Miller*, the Court of Appeal endorsed the following passage from the 2010 Benchbook "Direction the Jury"

   "The experience of judges who try sexual offences is that an image of stereotypical behaviour and demeanour by a victim or the perpetrator of a non-consensual offence such as rape held by some members of the public can be misleading and capable of leading to injustice. That experience has been gained by judges, expert in the field, presiding over many such trials during which guilt has been established but in which the behaviour and demeanour of complainants and defendants, both during the incident giving rise to the charge and in evidence, has been widely variable. Judges have, as a result of their experience, in recent years adopted the course of cautioning juries against applying stereotypical images how an alleged victim or an alleged perpetrator of a sexual offence ought to have behaved at the time, or ought to appear while giving evidence, and to judge the evidence on its intrinsic merits. This is not to invite juries to suspend their own judgement but to approach the evidence without prejudice."

4. The use of such a direction, properly tailored to the case does not offend the common-law principle that judicial notice can be taken only of facts of particular notoriety or common knowledge.[782] Parties are not permitted to adduce generic expert evidence of the range of known reactions to non-consensual sexual offences.

---

[781] [2010] EWCA Crim 1578.
[782] *Miller*

5. This direction may be given at the outset of the case [see Chapter 1-5] or as part of the summing up. Whenever it is given it is advisable to discuss the proposed direction with counsel.[783] Considerable care is needed to craft the direction to reflect the facts of the case[784] and to retain a balanced approach.[785]

6. In *GJB*[786] the CA approved the direction of the trial judge in *Miller* on the delay issue. "We entirely accept that in a suitable case, and this was one, the judge is entitled to and should comment on the reluctance or difficulty of the victim of sexual abuse to speak about it for long afterwards. In this connection, we refer to the judgments of this Court in *D (JA)*[787] and in *Miller*.[788] However, it is important that the comment should not assume the guilt of the defendant, and that his case should be made clear. The direction in *Miller* was a model in this respect. The summing up in that case included the following passage:

"You are entitled to consider why these matters did not come to light sooner. The defence say that it is because they are not true. They say that the allegations are entirely fabricated, untrue and they say that had the allegations been true you would have expected a complaint to be made earlier and certainly once either defendant . . . was out of the way . . . of the complainant. The defence say that she could have complained to her mother or her grandmother before she left the country or to her mother on the plane, or to the headmaster of the school . . . or to the social worker who came on one occasion to speak to her (although again bear in mind there is no evidence that the complainant was ever given any contact details or instructions as to how to make such a complaint, or that she could have complained sooner to a family or extended family member once she was safe in Jamaica.

On the other hand the prosecution say that it is not as simple as that. When children are abused they are often confused about what is happening to them and why it is happening. They are children and if a family member is abusing them in his own home or their own home, to whom can they complain? A sexual assault, if it occurs, will usually occur secretly. A child may have some idea that what is going on is wrong but very often children feel that they are to blame in some way, notwithstanding circumstances which an outsider would not consider for one moment them to be at blame or at fault. A child can be inhibited for a variety of reasons from speaking out. They may be

---

[783] *Miller*
[784] *Smith* [2012] EWCA Crim 404.
[785] *CE* [2012] EWCA Crim 1324
[786] GJB [2011] EWCA Crim 867; *F* [2011] EWCA Crim 1844
[787] [2008] EWCA Crim 2557
[788] [2010] EWCA Crim 1578

fearful that they may not be believed, a child's word against a mature adult, or they may be scared of the consequences or fearful of the effect upon relationships which they have come to know, or their only relationship."

Directions

G.08   7. There is a real danger that juries will make and/or be invited by advocates to make unwarranted assumptions. It is important that the judge should alert the jury to guard against this. This must be done in a fair and balanced way and put in the context of the evidence and the arguments raised by both for the prosecution and the defence. The judge must not give any impression of supporting a particular conclusion but should warn the jury against approaching the evidence with any preconceived assumptions.

8. Depending on the evidence and arguments advanced in the case, guidance may be necessary on one or more of the following supposed indicators relating to the evidence of the complainant:

    (1) Of untruthfulness:
        (a) Delay in making a complaint.
        (b) Complaint made for the first time when giving evidence.
        (c) Inconsistent accounts given by the complainant.
        (d) Lack of emotion/distress when giving evidence.

    (2) Of truthfulness:
        (a) A consistent account given by the complainant.
        (b) Emotion/distress when giving evidence.

    (3) Of consent and/or belief in consent:
        (a) Clothing worn by the complainant said to be revealing or provocative.
        (b) Intoxication (drink and/or drugs) on the part of the complainant whilst in the company of others.
        (c) Previous knowledge of, or friendship/sexual relationship between, the complainant and the defendant. In this regard it may be necessary to alert the jury to the distinction between submission and consent.
        (d) Some consensual sexual activity on the occasion of the alleged offence.

    (4) Of consent and/or belief in consent and/or lack of involvement:
        (a) Lack of any use or threat of force, physical struggle and/or injury. In this regard it will be necessary to alert the jury to the distinction between submission and consent.
        (b) A defendant who is in an established sexual relationship.

9. Such directions must be crafted with care and should always be discussed with the advocates. Thought should be given as to when

may be the most appropriate time to give such directions: at the outset of the trial or in the course of summing up?

10. It is of particular importance in cases of this nature to listen to the closing speeches of the advocates with care and if necessary review the directions to be given.

Examples

1. Delay (in the context of the complainant's allegations)   **G.09**

When you come to consider why this allegation was not made any earlier, you must avoid making an assumption that because it was delayed it must be untrue.

The defence say that the fact that the complaint was not made at the time shows that V is not telling the truth and that she has made up her story. When this was suggested to her in evidence she said {insert e.g. that she was a child aged 12 and afraid to tell anyone because D had told her that if she did so she would not be believed and this was "our little secret"; and that she only overcame her fear when her own daughter was approaching the age that she was when she said D did this to her }.

To decide this point, you should look at all the circumstances including the reason that V gave for not having complained at the time that she says this incident occurred. Different people react to particular situations in different ways. Some, if they have experienced something of the kind complained of in this case, may tell someone about it straight away, whilst others may not be able do so, whether out of shame, shock, confusion or fear of getting into trouble, not being believed, or breaking up the family. In this case, if V's complaint is true, she was a child of 12 when it happened and was living in the same family as D, and you should consider whether or not those things would have affected her ability to complain at that time.

The fact that a complaint is not made at the time does not necessarily mean that it must be untrue any more than the fact that a complaint is made immediately means that it must be true. I mention these points so that you think about them but I am not expressing any opinion. It is for you to decide whether or not V's evidence is true.

2. Complaint made for the first time when giving evidence

It is not in issue that until V gave evidence she had not mentioned {specify} to anyone before. The defence say that this shows that she has invented this allegation: they say that she was "making it up as she went along" [if applicable: and that all of her story is untrue]. The prosecution say that {e.g. it is not surprising that when she was having to think about things which happened a long time ago and answer detailed questions about them this triggered her memory so that she was then able to remember this for the first time}.

No doubt you will want to consider these arguments but you should bear in mind that the fact that someone does not mention something at the outset and only mentions it at a late stage does not mean that she cannot be telling the truth, any more than the fact that someone who consistently makes the same allegation must be doing so.

The memory of someone who has had an experience of the kind about which V complains may be affected in different ways. Such an experience may have a bearing on that person's ability to take in, register and recall it. Also, after such an event, some people may go over and over it in their minds with the result that their memory may become clearer whilst other people may try to avoid thinking about it and consequently, whilst the incident did occur, they may have difficulty in recalling it accurately or, in some cases, at all.

I mention these points so that you think about them but I am not expressing any opinion. It is for you to decide whether or not V's evidence is true; and when you are considering this you should look at all of the circumstances in which V made her original complaint, the way she gave her account to the police officer in the interview, the way she gave evidence and what she said when it was suggested to her that she had invented this [if applicable: *and all of her account.*]

If you are sure that V's account is true then you may rely on it in reaching your verdict. If you are not sure that it is true, or sure that it is untrue, then you cannot rely on it.

3. *Inconsistent accounts*

When you come to consider whether or not this allegation is true, you must avoid making an assumption that because V has said something different to someone else her evidence to you is untrue.

You have heard that when V gave a statement to/was interviewed by the police s/he said {insert} whereas when s/he gave evidence s/he said {insert}.

[Either] *There is no issue that these two accounts are inconsistent with one another and you will have to consider why this is so.*

[Or] *You will have to compare these two accounts and, if you find that they are inconsistent, you will have to consider why this is so.*

The mere fact that V has not been consistent in the accounts that s/he has given does not necessarily mean that her/his evidence is not true. Experience has shown that inconsistencies in accounts can arise whether a person is telling the truth or not. This is because the memory of someone who has had an experience of the kind complained of in this case may be affected by it in different ways and this may have a bearing on that person's ability to take in, register and recall it. Also, after such an event, some people may go over and over it in their minds with the result that their memory may become clearer whilst other people may try to avoid thinking about it and consequently, whilst the incident did occur, they may have difficulty in recalling it accurately.

I mention these points so that you think about them but I am not expressing any opinion. It is for you to decide whether or not V's evidence is true. To answer this question you must look at all of the evidence including any inconsistencies which you find exist and decide what effect these have on V's truthfulness. If you are sure that V's account is true then you are entitled to rely on it. If you are not sure that it is true, or sure that it is untrue, then you cannot rely upon it.

4.   Consistent account

You have been asked to find that V's account is true because s/he has been consistent in what s/he said to {e.g. her sister/the police} and in her evidence about this [alleged] incident. The mere fact that a person gives a consistent account about an event does not necessarily mean that account must be true, any more than the fact that a person who gives inconsistent accounts must mean that the event did not happen.

In deciding whether or not V's account is true you should look at all of the evidence. If, having done so, you are sure that V's account is true then you are entitled to rely on it. If you are not sure that it is true, or sure that it is untrue, then you cannot rely on it.

5.   Lack of emotion/distress when giving evidence

You have been reminded/you will remember that when V gave evidence s/he appeared completely calm and gave his/her account in a matter-of-fact way without showing any emotion. It is entirely for you to decide what you make of V's evidence but it would be wrong to assume that the manner in which he/she appeared to give evidence is an indication of whether or not it is true.

This is because experience has shown that people react to situations and cope with them in different ways. Some people who have experienced an incident of the kind complained of in this case, when they have to speak about it, show obvious signs of emotion and distress, whereas others show no emotion at all. Consequently the presence or absence of a show of emotion or distress when giving evidence is not a reliable pointer to the truthfulness or untruthfulness of what a person is saying.

6. Show of emotion/distress when making a complaint and/or giving evidence

You have been reminded/you will remember that at a number of points in his/her evidence V became distressed and emotional. It is entirely for you to decide whether or not V's evidence is true but you must not simply assume that because V showed distress and emotion it must be true. It is perfectly possible for a witness to become distressed and emotional when describing an incident such as this, whether or not their account is true. The presence or absence of a show of emotion or distress when giving evidence is not a reliable pointer to the truthfulness or untruthfulness of what a person is saying.

7. Clothing worn by the complainant said to be revealing or provocative

[Questioning on this subject should have been restricted, but there will be occasions where such evidence has emerged.]

You have been reminded of/you will remember the fact that when V went out on the evening of {date} she was dressed in {specify}. The defence suggested to her that this was because she was "out on the pull" and looking for sex and you will remember her response that {insert}. You should consider this evidence and decide what you make of it but you must not assume that because V was dressed in that way that she must have been either looking for or willing, if the opportunity presented itself, to have sex. People may dress in a variety of ways for a variety of reasons and the mere fact that someone dresses in revealing clothing does not necessarily mean that that person is inviting or willing to have sex or that someone else who sees and engages with that person could reasonably believe that that person would consent to it.

8. Intoxication (drink and/or drugs) on the part of the complainant whilst in the company of others

V has accepted that she was very drunk on the night of {insert} but it is important that you do not assume that because she got into that state she was either looking for, or willing to have, sex. When it was suggested to her in cross-examination that she was out that night to get drunk and then to have sex she said {insert}. You should consider this evidence and decide what you make of it but you must not assume that because she was drunk she must have wanted sex. People do go out at night and get drunk, sometimes for no apparent reason at all, and it would be wrong to leap to the conclusion that such a person must be out looking for, or willing to have, sex or that someone else who sees and engages with that person could reasonably believe that that person would consent to it.

9.   Previous sexual activity between the complainant and the defendant

It is common ground that V and D knew one another and that, whilst they have not been in an established sexual relationship, they have had sexual intercourse on a number of previous occasions. It is important to recognise that the mere fact that V has had consensual sexual intercourse with D on other occasions does not mean that she must have consented to have sexual intercourse with him on this occasion or that this would have given D grounds for reasonably believing that she consented to it. A person who has freely chosen to have sexual activity with another person in the past does not, as a result, give general consent to have sexual intercourse with that person on any occasion: each occasion is specific and whilst at one time a person may want to have sex, at another time that person may not want it at all and will not consent to it.

Also, if and when you come to consider whether D may reasonably have believed that V consented, you must not assume that because V had had sexual intercourse with him on a number of previous occasions this, in itself, gave him grounds for believing on this occasion. You must resolve this issue by looking at all of the evidence.

10.   Some consensual sexual activity on the occasion of the alleged offence

It is common ground that on the night in question V took D back to her home, gave him a cup of coffee and that for a while they engaged in kissing one another, something to which V consented. According to V she then said she had to get up early the next morning and asked D to leave but he refused to go and then forcibly had sexual intercourse with her against her will. D gave evidence that kissing led to further sexual touching and then to sexual intercourse to which V fully consented.

It is for the prosecution to prove that V did not consent to D having sexual intercourse with her and you must decide this issue by looking at all the evidence. When you do so it is important to recognise that the mere fact that V let D into her home and willingly engaged in kissing D does not mean that she must have wanted to go on to have sexual intercourse and must have consented to it. A person who engages in sexual activity is entitled to choose how far that activity goes and is also entitled to say "No" if the other person tries to go further; the fact that V willingly engaged in kissing does not mean that she must have wanted to have sexual intercourse.

If you are sure that V did not consent to having sexual intercourse with D the prosecution must also prove that D did not reasonably believe in V's consent. This too is an issue which you must resolve by looking at all of the evidence but you must not assume that because V had been kissing him willingly before sexual intercourse took place this in itself gave him grounds for believing that she consented to him having sexual intercourse with her.

11.   Fear, although no use or threat of force, physical struggle and/or injury

It is not suggested that, before or at the time that D had sexual intercourse with V he either threatened her with force or that he used any force upon her and V has accepted that she did not put up any struggle. It is also common ground that V did not suffer any injury.

The defence say that this is because V fully consented to what took place. V on the other hand gave evidence that when D started to undo his trousers and then undid her jeans she was so frightened that she could not move: she said she was "petrified with fear". You will have to resolve this issue by looking at all of the evidence but it is important to recognise that the mere fact that D neither used nor threatened to use any force on V and that she did nothing to prevent D from having sexual intercourse with her and was uninjured does not mean that V consented to what took place or that what V has said about what happened cannot be true.

Experience has shown that different people may respond to unwanted sexual activity in different ways. Some may protest and physically resist throughout the event whilst others may, whether through fear or personality, whilst they did not consent, be unable to do so.

It is important to draw a distinction between consent and submission. A person consents to something if, being capable of making a choice and being free to do so, s/he agrees to it. Consent in some situations may be given enthusiastically, whereas in others it is given with reluctance, but nevertheless it is still consent. But when a person is so overcome by fear that she lacks any capacity either to give consent or to resist, that person does not consent but submits to what takes place.

It is for you to say, having considered all of the evidence, what the situation was in this case, bearing in mind that it is for the prosecution to prove that V did not consent to D having sexual intercourse with her and that D did not reasonably believe that she consented. What they do not have to prove is (a) that D used or threatened to use any force or that V put up a struggle or was injured or (b) that V communicated her lack of consent to D.

12.   *Defendant is in an established sexual relationship with another person*

It is not disputed that V was raped: what is in dispute is that it was D who raped her; and the evidence of identification of D as the person responsible is challenged. As part of the evidence you heard from D and also from his wife that they have a mutually fulfilling sex life, and it is D's case that he had no need to have sexual intercourse with a stranger and much to lose by doing so.

You will of course consider this evidence when you are deciding where the truth lies but you must not assume that a man who is married and, if you find that it is or may be the case, who has a fulfilling sex life cannot resort to sexual activity with any other person. In pointing this out I am not suggesting what you should make of the evidence of D or of his wife, but simply alerting you to the danger of making an assumption which, depending on your assessment of their evidence, might flow from it.

13.   *Defendant is a homosexual man*

You have heard that D is gay and lives with/goes out with {specify}. You have heard this as part of the background to the case. It is not relevant to the issue of guilt.

It is no more likely that a man who lives with another man has a sexual interest in young boys than it is that a man who lives with a woman will have an interest in young girls. The fact that D is gay is of no significance at all.

20-2 Sexual offences—Historical allegations

ARCHBOLD: 4-465, 20-9b and 20-27a; BLACKSTONE'S: B3.73

Legal Summary

1. It is important in historic cases that the judge gives full and detailed reasons for decisions and provides clear guidance for the jury on the difficulties faced by the defence as a result of the lapse of time.   **G.10**

2. As the Court made clear in *PS*.[789] The essential matters that a direction should address were identified as being:
   "i) delay can place a defendant at a material disadvantage in challenging allegations arising out of events that occurred many years before, and this was particularly so in this case when the defence was essentially a simple denial (the defendant was saying that he had not acted as alleged);

[789] [2013] EWCA Crim 992.

> *ii) the longer the delay, the more difficult meeting the allegation often becomes because of fading memories and evidence is no longer available—indeed, it may be unclear what has been lost;*
> *iii) when considering the central question whether the prosecution has proved the defendant's guilt, it is necessary particularly to bear in mind the prejudice that delay can occasion; and*
> *iv) a summary of the main elements of prejudice that were identified during the trial."* [35] per Fulford LJ

3. Having reviewed a number of authorities[790] Fulford LJ remarked that *"no two cases are the same and whether a direction on delay is to be given and the way in which it is formulated will depend on the facts of the case. We stress, therefore, that the need for a direction, its formulation and the matters to be included will depend on the circumstances of, and the issues arising in, the trial."*

4. The court suggested that the problems of delay are:
> *"often (although not necessarily always) best addressed by a short, self-contained direction that focuses on the defendant rather than amalgamating it with other aspects of the relevance of delay, for instance as regards the victim or victims. The risk of combining and interweaving the potential consequences of delay for the accused with the other delay-related considerations ("putting the other side of the coin") is that the direction, as the principal means of protecting the defendant, is diluted and its force is diminished."*[37]

5. As regards the absence of documents and witnesses, see D[791] D was convicted of sexual offences on his nieces and daughter between 39 and 63 years earlier. The Court was clear—the length of delay is nothing more than a statement of fact. What matters is not how long it is since the alleged offence but whether the delay has an effect on the fairness of the trial and the safety of any resultant convictions.

Directions

6. In some cases of alleged historical sexual abuse, complaints may have been made before, sometimes a long time before, the complaint which has given rise to the investigation and prosecution with which they jury are concerned. In some cases such earlier complaints may have been made to a friend or a family member, in others they may have been made to the police or some other person in authority. There may be one or more records of such complaints.

---

[790] *Henry* (1998) 2 Cr App R 61; *Graham* [1999] 2 Cr App R 201; *M* [2000] 1 Cr App R 49.
[791] *D* [2013] EWCA Crim 1592.

7. In these cases, evidence of such complaints may be adduced as hearsay, to establish consistency or inconsistency, to rebut a suggestion of recent fabrication or, possibly, to refresh memory. If such evidence is adduced in this way, appropriate directions must be given: see Chapter 15-12 above.

8. If the jury are being invited to make the assumption that if the allegation were true, complaint would have been made at the time, the jury should be directed accordingly: see Chapter 20-1 above.

9. Such directions must be crafted with care and discussed with the advocates. It may also be necessary to discuss these directions after speeches, depending on the arguments advanced by the advocates.

Examples

See examples provided in Chapters 15-12 and 20-1.   **G.12**

20-3 Sexual offences—grooming of children

ARCHBOLD: 20-91; BLACKSTONE'S: B3-119

Legal Summary

1. Although an offence of meeting a child following sexual grooming **G.13** is created by section 15 Sexual Offences Act 2003, other behaviour, often innocent itself but intended to gain favour with and/or the trust of a child with a view to sexual activity, is properly described as "grooming".

Directions

2. Where grooming is alleged to have occurred, whether or not this **G.14** gives rise to a separate count on the indictment, the concept of grooming and the potential difficulties of a witness' realisation and/ or recollection of innocent attention becoming sexual should be explained.

G.15

Example 1: young child

    The prosecution case is that before he sexually assaulted V he "groomed" her. That is to say he won her trust by doing things which in normal circumstances would be innocent, such as playing games with her including play-fighting and tickling, before he went on to touch her sexually. In this situation, a child is unlikely to realise that she is at any risk at all and, when the nature of touching changes from something "innocent" to something which is sexual, the child may not realise that there is anything wrong and may accept it without any feeling of discomfort or dislike and will not make any complaint about it or resist or protest when it happens again. In these circumstances a child is unlikely to be able to say when touching which had been "innocent" changed to touching which was sexual.

    In making these observations I am not suggesting what you should find did, or did not, happen in this case: I am simply alerting you to a potential difficulty which a child in such a situation could face. Whether or not you find that this was a situation faced by V is entirely for you to decide.

Example 2: older child

    You have heard evidence in this case that V was 12 years of age and in the care of the Local Authority when she met D.

    The prosecution say V was, because of her situation, especially impressionable and vulnerable. She has said in evidence that when she first met D she was impressed by {specify e.g. rides in his car/gifts of alcohol, flattery etc.} and that she liked him and became prepared to do things for him that she would not otherwise have done.

    In many relationships, sexual or otherwise, one party will seek to please the other with gifts but in this case the prosecution say that the purpose of D's gifts was to make V dependent upon him and so effectively to remove her capacity to say no.

    The defence say there was no sexual relationship and that although V was 12 she obtained alcohol from a variety of sources and was in no way dependant on him.

    You must look at the evidence of the relationship between V and D. If you are sure that the gifts etc. were intended to and did make her so dependent on him that she was prepared to submit to {specify} you are entitled to conclude that was not true consent. If you are not sure that was the case and you consider D's account is or may be true then you could not be sure that she did not consent when {specify}.

NOTE: For a further comprehensive direction on the difference between consent and compliance or submission, approved by the CACD, see *R. v. Ali and Ashraf.*[792]

20-4 Sexual offences—consent and reasonable belief in consent

ARCHBOLD 20-10, 25 and 25a; BLACKSTONE'S B3.19, 26, 30 and 33

Legal Summary

1. When the charges involved are those under ss. 1 - 4 of the Sexual   G.16
Offences Act 2003, the Crown must prove that V was not consenting to the act alleged.

General consent cases

2. Otherwise than in the exceptional cases under ss. 75 and 76 [see
below] the jury is to determine whether V was consenting, applying
the definition of consent provided in s. 74:
   *'For the purposes of this part, a person consents if he or she agrees by
   choice and has the freedom and capacity to make that choice'.*

3. An absence of consent can therefore arise by reason of mere lack of
agreement as well as by force, threat of force, fear of force, a lack of
capacity owing to unconsciousness,[793] sleep,[794] drink or drugs: for
capacity and voluntary intoxication see Chapter 20-5.

4. The jury may need to be alerted to the distinction between consent
and mere submission: see *Doyle*[795] in which the Court of Appeal
described the distinction between (i) reluctant but free exercise of
choice, especially in a long-term loving relationship, and (ii) unwilling submission due to fear of worse consequences. In *Zafar,* Pill J
directed that: 'C may not particularly want sexual intercourse on a
particular occasion, but because it is her husband or her partner
who is asking for it, she will consent to sexual intercourse. The fact
that such consent is given reluctantly or out of a sense of duty to her
partner i[t i]s still consent.'

5. There have been a number of recent cases in which judges have had
to direct juries in cases where apparent consent, particularly of
young victims or those in ongoing relationships, arises out of prior
abuse.[796]

---

[792] [2015] EWCA Crim 1279 para 15
[793] See s.75.
[794] See s.75.
[795] [2010] EWCA Crim 119.
[796] See *Robinson* [2011] EWCA Crim 916

6. In some cases, particularly where there is evidence of exploitation of a young and immature person who may not understand the full significance of what he or she is doing, that is a factor the jury can take into account in deciding whether or not there was genuine consent.[797]

7. There is no requirement that V must communicate her lack of consent to D.[798]

8. Where the suggestion is that V lacks mental capacity to consent the jury should be directed that a person lacks capacity if he lacks the capacity to choose, whether because he lacks sufficient understanding of the nature or reasonably foreseeable consequences of what is being done, or for any other reason.[799]

9. It is not necessary for the judge to direct on all aspects of the law of consent when they do not arise on the facts.[800]

Sections 75 and 76

10. When evidential (s. 75) or conclusive (s. 76) presumptions about consent arise (a) the jury must be carefully directed and (b) any such directions must be discussed with the advocates: see example below.

D's reasonable belief in consent

11. Under ss. 1–4 of the Sexual Offences Act 2003, the mental element comprises two questions:
    (1) May D have genuinely believed that V was consenting?
    (2) Was D's belief reasonable in the circumstances?

12. D's intoxication is irrelevant.[801] The reasonableness of D's belief must be evaluated as if he had been sober. Delusional thinking, psychotic or otherwise, can never be considered to be reasonable.[802] There may be cases where the personality and abilities of the accused (short of delusional or psychotic states) are relevant to whether his positive belief in consent was reasonable.[803]

13. It is for the jury to determine whether the belief D held is a reasonable one. It is not a question of whether D thought it was reasonable. There is no obligation on D to have taken any specific

---

[797] Ali [2015] EWCA Crim 1279.
[798] *Malone* [1998] 2 Cr App R 447.
[799] *A(G)* [2014] 2 Cr.App.R. 73(5).
[800] *H* [2006] EWCA Crim 853; *Taran* [2006] EWCA Crim 1498
[801] Grewal [2010] EWCA Crim 2448.
[802] *Braham* [2013] EWCA Crim 3.
[803] *Braham* [2013] EWCA Crim 3.

steps to ascertain consent, but where steps have been taken they must be taken into account by the jury in deciding whether D's belief was reasonable. Depending on the facts of the case, D's age, general sexual experience, sexual experience with this complainant[804] learning disability and any other factor that could have affected his ability to understand the nature and consequences of his actions (particularly the ability to appreciate the risk of non-consent) may be relevant.

Directions

14. The prosecution must prove that V did not consent to the sexual activity alleged.   G.17

15. The prosecution must also prove that D did not reasonably believe that she consented.

16. The absence of consent may be proved by evidence of one or more of the following:
    (1) submission
    (2) fear, without threat or use of force
    (3) D continuing after V made it clear that s/he did not consent.
    (4) express or implied threats*
    (5) oppression (e.g. previous abuse)
    (6) force*
    (7) deceit as to the nature and/or purpose of the act£
    (8) deceit as to the identity of D£.

17. Directions must be tailored to the factual issues in a particular case and the concept of consent explained by reference to those factual issues.

18. Where there has been an allegation of non-consensual sexual activity within or immediately after a long term relationship, further guidance will be required about the distinction between the "give and take" that occurs within a relationship and the absence of consent.
    *Section 75 Sexual Offences Act 2003 provides for evidential presumptions to be made about lack of consent and lack of belief in consent, where it is proved that (i) D did the relevant act (ii) any of these circumstances existed and (iii) D knew that these circumstances existed, provided that there is insufficient evidence to raise an issue as to whether V consented. In reality these criteria seldom arise.

---

[804] *McAllister [1997] Crim LR 233.*

£S.76 Sexual Offences Act 2003 provides for a conclusive presumption to be made about lack of consent and lack of belief in consent, where D intentionally deceived V in one or more of these ways. In reality these criteria seldom arise.

Examples

G.18 *1. Consent*

The prosecution must prove, so that you are sure of it, that when D {specify act}, V did not consent to it. A person consents to something if, being capable of making a choice and being free to do so, s/he agrees to it.

2. Reasonable belief in consent

If the prosecution have proved that V did not consent, they must also prove that D did not reasonably believe that s/he consented.

This involves two questions:

a. Did D genuinely believe, or may he have genuinely believed, that V consented? and
b. If he did, or may have done so, was his belief reasonable?
c.

If you are sure that D did not genuinely believe that V consented, this element of the offence will have been proved and so the question of whether belief was reasonable will not arise.

If you decide that D did genuinely believe that V consented, or may have done so, you must then decide whether his belief was reasonable. Whether or not his belief was reasonable is for you to say, having considered all the evidence; and you must decide whether an ordinary reasonable man, in the same circumstances as D, would have believed she was consenting. This includes looking at any steps D took to find out whether she was consenting or not. [If appropriate: *The fact that D gave evidence that he thought that it was reasonable is something for you to take into account but the question is whether, in your view, it was reasonable, not whether D thought that it was.*]

Sequence of questions for jury (to be provided in writing)
1. Are you sure that when D {specify act}, V did not consent to it?
(i) If your answer is "Yes"—i.e. you are sure that she did not consent - go to question 2.
(ii) If your answer is "No"—i.e. you decide that she did consent or may have consented —your verdict will be "Not Guilty".

2. Are you sure that D did not genuinely believe that V consented?

(i) If your answer is "Yes"—i.e. you are sure that he did not genuinely believe that V consented—your verdict will be "Guilty".
(ii) If your answer is "No"—i.e. you decide that D did genuinely believe or may genuinely have believed that V consented—go to question 3.

3. Are you sure that D's belief in V's consent was unreasonable?
(i) If your answer is "Yes"—i.e. you are sure that D's belief in V's consent was unreasonable— your verdict will be "Guilty".
(ii) If your answer is "No"—i.e. you decide that D's belief in V's consent was or may have been reasonable—your verdict will be "Not Guilty".

3. Submission, without threats or force

V gave evidence that although D did not threaten her or use any force on her, she did not consent to {specify act} but submitted to it, because {specify}. It is important to draw a distinction between consent and submission. Consent in some situations may be given enthusiastically, whereas in others it is given with reluctance, but it is still consent. Where however a person gives in to something against his/her free will, that is not consent but submission. It is for you to say, having considered all of the evidence, where the line is to be drawn in this case bearing in mind that it is for the prosecution to prove that V did not consent to {specify act}.

It is not necessary for the prosecution to prove, in order to prove that V did not consent, that s/he was subjected to threats or violence, or that s/he was overpowered or put up a struggle or that s/he told D that s/he did not consent. What you have to decide is whether the prosecution have made you sure that at the time that {specify act} took place, V did not consent to it.

4. Fear, without threat or use of force

V gave evidence that although D did not threaten her or use any force on her, she did not consent to {specify act} because she was so frightened by what D was doing that she froze and was unable to speak or to move. It is important to draw a distinction between consent and submission. A person consents to something if, being capable of making a choice and being free to do so, s/he agrees to it. Consent in some situations may be given enthusiastically, whereas in others it is given with reluctance, but nevertheless it is still consent. Where however a person is so overcome by fear that she lacks any capacity either to give consent or to resist, that person does not consent but is submitting to what takes place.

5. Express indication that V did not consent; belief in consent

V gave evidence that when D started to touch her breast she made it clear to him that she did not want him to continue, by repeatedly saying "No.

Stop" but he ignored her and carried on. D gave evidence that V said nothing of the kind.

Your conclusions about this will be important when you are looking at two things:
(a) whether you are sure that V did not consent; and
(b) if you are sure that V did not consent, whether you are sure that D did not reasonably believe that she consented;
but your final decision must be based on all the evidence.

6. *Non-consensual sexual activity within or immediately after a long term relationship*

It is common ground that D and V have had a long term sexual relationship. This is plainly relevant to the question of whether or not, on this occasion, V consented to D {specify act}, because the situation between two people who have/have had such a relationship is quite different from a situation in which two people are strangers or have met one another only a few times.

When two people have/have had such a relationship, there is likely to be some give and take between them in relation to any number of things, including their sexual relationship, and sometimes a partner who is not feeling enthusiastic may nevertheless reluctantly give consent.

This is not to say however that when two people are/have been in such a relationship it must follow that both of them will consent to any sexual activity which takes place. One party is fully entitled to say "no" to the other notwithstanding their relationship. What you must decide in this case is (a) whether V consented freely and by choice, albeit reluctantly, to what took place or whether she did not consent but submitted to it and (b) whether, in the light of all of the evidence including the nature of the [previous] relationship between V and D, D may have reasonably believed that she was consenting.

20-5 Sexual offences - capacity and voluntary intoxication

ARCHBOLD 17-116, 20-10; BLACKSTONE'S: B3.22

Legal Summary

G.19   1. When the charges involved are those under ss. 1 - 4 of the Sexual Offences Act 2003, V's voluntary intoxication may be relevant to (a) V's ability to consent or (b) whether V consented to sexual activity. D's voluntary intoxication may be relevant to his belief in consent, but is not relevant to the reasonableness of such belief: see chapter 20-4.

2. If in proceedings for such an offence it is alleged that D did the relevant act, at a time when V was unconscious and D knew that, under s. 75 of the Act V is to be taken not to have consented to the relevant act unless sufficient evidence is adduced to raise an issue as to whether V consented, and D is to be taken not to have reasonably believed that the complainant consented unless sufficient evidence is adduced to raise an issue as to whether he reasonably believed it.[805]

3. Otherwise than in such cases, the jury is to determine whether V was consenting, applying the definition of consent provided in s. 74:
'For the purposes of this part, a person consents if he or she agrees by choice and has the freedom and capacity to make that choice'. V's voluntary intoxication is a factor which may bear upon consent and the issues of capacity and freedom to agree.[806]

4. Applying section 74, if V has voluntarily consumed alcohol and/or drugs but remains capable of choosing whether or not to have sexual activity and agrees to do so, she has consented to it. Consumption of alcohol or drugs may cause someone to become disinhibited and behave differently, but consent given in such a state is still a valid consent if a person has the capacity to agree by choice. Where V through intoxication no longer has the capacity to agree, there will be no consent. V will not have capacity if her understanding and knowledge are so limited that she was not in a position to decide whether or not to agree to the act.

5. The Court of Appeal has addressed the question of how a judge should direct the jury when V was intoxicated and may have lacked capacity. The leading case is that of *Bree*[807] where Lord Judge stated:
"*We should perhaps underline that, as a matter of practical reality, capacity to consent may evaporate well before a complainant becomes unconscious. Whether this is so or not, however, is fact specific, or more accurately, depends on the actual state of mind of the individuals involved on the particular occasion.*"[808]

6. The question of capacity is not dependent on whether V might afterwards have regretted what happened or had a poor recollection of what happened, or behaved irresponsibly.[809]

---

[805] Section 75.
[806] In the case of spiked drinks etc s 75(2)(f) applies.
[807] [2008] QB 131
[808] See also *Coates* [2008] 1 Cr App R 52 at [44] per Sir Igor Judge P.
[809] See Archbold para 20-10.

7. In some cases, it will be necessary to direct the jury as to the distinction between an allegation that V was unconscious, and an allegation that although she was capable of consenting, despite her state, she was not in fact consenting and was giving clear indications that she was rejecting D.

8. Where a question of capacity arises it should be left to the common sense of the jury, with an appropriate direction.[810]

9. When directing a jury as to capacity, the words 'a drunken consent is still a consent' can cause distress and are best avoided.

10. When lack of capacity has not been a live issue, it should not be left to the jury.

11. The Court of Appeal in *Kamki*[811] provided the following guidance:

"*a. A person consents if he or she agrees by choice and has the freedom and capacity to make that choice,*

b. When a person is unconscious, there is no such freedom or capacity to choose,

c. Where a person has not reached a state of unconsciousness and experiences some degree of consciousness, further considerations must be applied,

d. A person can still have the capacity to make a choice and have sex even when they have had a lot to drink (thereby consenting to the act),

e. Alcohol can make people less inhibited than when they are sober and everybody has the choice whether or not to have sex,

f. If through drink a woman has temporarily lost the capacity to choose to have sexual intercourse, she would not be consenting,

g. Before a complete loss of consciousness arises, a state of incapacity to consent can nevertheless be reached. Consideration has to be given to the degree of consciousness or otherwise in order to determine the issue of capacity,

h. ... the jury would have to consider the evidence of [V] to determine what her state of consciousness or unconsciousness was and to determine what effect this would have on her capacity to consent,

i. If it is determined that the complainant did have the capacity to make a choice, it would then have to be considered whether she did or may have consented to sexual intercourse".

---

[810] *Hysa* [2007] EWCA Crim 2056.
[811] [2013] EWCA Crim 2335.

Directions

12. Depending on the evidence, the prosecution may put its case in the alternative: (a) that V lacked the capacity to give consent and (b) that V did not consent, in which event the jury should be given directions about each. The jury should not be directed about lack of capacity if this has not been a live issue in the case. **G.20**
13. If the jury are sure that V was unconscious, she could not have consented because she would not have had the freedom or capacity to do so.
14. If the jury are sure that, although V was not unconscious, s/he was so intoxicated by reason of drink or drugs that s/he was unable to make a free choice, V was not consenting.
15. If the jury consider that V had, or may have had, the capacity to make a choice they must go on to consider whether V did in fact consent bearing in mind:
    (1) that alcohol (and some drugs) can make a person less inhibited than she might be when sober;
    (2) consent given when a person is under the influence of drink and/or drugs is still consent even if it would not have been given when sober.
16. If the jury are sure that V did not consent, when considering whether D reasonably believed that V was consenting:
    (1) whether or not D held that belief is to be decided having regard to D's state, which includes whether s/he was sober or drunk;
    (2) The reasonableness of D's belief is to be decided on the basis of whether it would have been reasonable had D been sober.

Example: V and D intoxicated by alcohol: V's capacity to consent and lack of consent in issue.

It is not in dispute that on the night in question D had sexual intercourse with V. What is in issue is whether she consented to that and, if she did not consent, whether D reasonably believed that she consented. **G.21**

It is not in dispute that both V and D had had a great deal to drink during the preceding evening. According to V, she can remember nothing from the time that {specify until specify}. She cannot say what, if any, sexual activity took place but she says that, if any activity did take place, she would not have consented to it. D has given evidence that he and V had sexual intercourse and that, whilst V did not say anything at all, she did not resist in any way and he believed that she was consenting.

As to V's state of mind: it is for the prosecution to make you sure that V did not consent to sexual intercourse. V will have consented if, being capable of making a choice and being free to do so, she agreed to have sexual intercourse with D, whether or not she expressed that in words.

You will have to decide whether the amount which V had had to drink affected (a) her ability to make a free choice or, if she was able to make such a choice, (b) the decision which she made about whether or not to have sexual intercourse.

If you find that V was so drunk that she was in fact unconscious, then she would not have been able to make a free choice and could not have consented. Also, if you find that, although she was not unconscious, V was so drunk that she was not capable of making any choice, then in this event also she could not have consented.

If on the other hand you find that despite what she had had to drink V was, or may have been, able to make a choice and chose, or may have chosen, to have sexual intercourse then she will have consented: consent which is given when disinhibited by drink, even if it would not have been given if sober, is nevertheless consent. If having considered these things you find that V consented, or may have consented, you will find D not guilty.

As to D's state of mind:

If you are sure that D did not believe that V consented then you will find D guilty. If on the other hand you find that D believed, or may have believed, that she consented you must go on to consider whether that belief was reasonable.

On this question you should look at all of the circumstances, including whether D took any steps to find out whether or not V was consenting. You must take no account of the fact that D was drunk; you must approach this question by considering what he would have believed if he had been sober.

If you are sure either (a) that D should have realised that, because of the state she was in, V was incapable of making any choice about whether or not to have sexual intercourse with him or (b) that if sober he should have realised that she was not agreeing to do so by choice, then his belief will not have been reasonable, and you will find him guilty. If on the other hand you find that his belief was, or may have been, reasonable, you will find him not guilty.

DRAFT DIRECTIONS IN MULTIPLE DEFENDANT GROOMING CASES

The following directions are taken from draft directions given by His Honour **H.01** Judge Rook QC in the Oxford Grooming Case heard at the Old Bailey in early 2013. The case involved multiple sexual allegations by six complainants against nine defendants. An appeal against sentence was considered by the Court of Appeal in *Bassam Karrar* [2015] EWCA Crim 850.

The directions given by HHJ Rook QC in the Oxford case were adopted by HH Judge Lucraft QC in *Ali and Ashraf* and tailored to the circumstances of that case. Appeals against conviction were dismissed by the Court of Appeal at [2015] EWCA Crim 1279. The directions given by HH Judge Lucraft QC (and in particular those on consent) are cited extensively in that judgment.

Directions on the law

RAPE

1. In order to prove rape, the prosecution must make you sure that: **H.02**
    (i) the defendant (whose case you are considering) deliberately penetrated the particular complainant's vagina, anus or mouth with his penis;
    (ii) at the time he did so, the complainant was not consenting; and
    (iii) at the time he did so, he did not reasonably believe that the complainant was consenting.

Joint venture: General

2. An offence may be committed by one person acting alone or more **H.03** than one person acting together with the same criminal purpose. An agreement to act together need not have been expressed in words. It may be the result of planning or a tacit understanding reached on

2133

the spur of the moment. Agreement can be inferred from the circumstances. Those who commit crime together may play different parts to achieve their purpose. The prosecution must prove that each defendant took some part with the appropriate intention.

Joint venture where rape alleged

H.04
3. The prosecution puts its case in 2 ways:
   (i) the defendants were acting together in pursuance of a common design to rape the complainant. Here it does not matter who achieved penetration provided there was a penetration without consent by one and the defendant (whose case you are considering) assisted or encouraged the one who actually committed the act of rape; and/or
   (ii) the defendant (whose case you are considering) penetrated the complainant with his penis (here each is individually guilty of rape independently of whether or not they were acting in pursuit of a common purpose where they penetrated the complainant without her consent).

CONSENT

H.05
4. If the complainant was aged under 13 at the time, the prosecution does not have to prove that the complainant did not consent in order to establish the offence of rape. Where the complainant was over 13, even if the complainant was still a child, the prosecution must prove that the complainant did not consent at the time although the child's age may be highly relevant to whether she was genuinely consenting.

5. Consent has a particular legal meaning. A person (in this case a girl or young woman) consents if she agrees by choice, and she, at the relevant time, has the freedom and capacity to make that choice. It follows that a consent must be a genuine consent. This means that in the case of an allegation of rape where the complainant is over 13, the prosecution must make you sure the particular complainant did not give her agreement by an exercise of free choice.

6. The prosecution do not have to show that the defendant was violent or threatened violence at the time. Use of force and/or the threat of force are not essential ingredients of rape. Nor do the prosecution have to prove that the particular complainant resisted or protested. It follows that the prosecution do not have to prove that a complainant communicated or demonstrated her lack of consent by resisting a defendant physically or by shouting at him. The fact that a complainant did not say "no" does not necessarily mean she was consenting.

7. Since consent involves a free agreement, simply to comply or to submit is not necessarily to consent. Compliance and/or submission should not be confused with consent. For example, submission of free choice to repeated demands is not the same thing as consent. Submission achieved by high level psychological coercion in the context of the encounter and/or any pre-existing relationship between the defendant and the complainant may not amount to free agreement. Here the age gap and differences in levels of maturity between the parties may be relevant.

8. Similarly, the threat of force so that free choice has been overborne will not amount to consent freely given. This might apply where a complainant feels intimidated.

9. It is necessary to focus on the complainant's state of mind in the circumstances and the overall context of the particular sexual activity in question as you find them to have been. In particular, you will need to consider the history of the relationship between the parties and the nature of the sexual encounter. Against that background, you must consider the critical question: did the particular complainant agree to sexual intercourse by choice, and did she have the freedom and capacity to make that choice?

10. It does not follow from the fact that a person may be behaving irresponsibly and exposing themselves to high risk situations, that there is necessarily a genuine consent to sexual activity. Similarly, to state the obvious, if a girl or young woman chooses to wear sexually provocative clothing, it does not mean that they are consenting to sexual activity.

11. It is not the experience of the courts that victims of sexual offences including vaginal rape always have injuries to show for it. In this case the medical evidence is neutral.

12. Experience shows that there is no classic reaction to a demand for unwanted sexual activity. Some people with physical self-confidence and maturity will protest loud and long, some will resist, and others will freeze and/or just comply as the realisation dawns upon them they are in a situation they cannot control. Freezing and/or mere compliance is not the same thing as consent freely given.

13. As a general rule, consent can cover a wide spectrum of mind from actual desire on the one hand to reluctant acquiescence on the other. Reluctant but genuine free agreement is not the same thing as submission, and is still consent, even if reluctantly given.

14. However, you will need to consider how mature a particular complainant was at the time. Where you are considering the position of young immature complainants and where there is

evidence of exploitation, you will need to consider evidence of acquiescence in the context of the circumstances as you find them to be. Context is all-important.

15. You will need to take into account the following factors if you find that they apply in respect of a particular allegation as they may have a bearing on whether there was, in reality, a genuine consent.

16. It is a matter for you whether these factors arise and what weight you give to them. Inevitably these factors overlap:

(a) Age and maturity of the complainant at the time. This will be relevant to a young person's understanding and knowledge of the position she was in, and the significance of what she was being asked to do and/or was doing. This, in turn, is relevant to whether in the circumstances she was able to exercise freedom of choice.

(b) The history of the relationship between the parties at the time and the nature of the sexual encounter. This includes the age of the defendant. You will have to consider the extent to which there was grooming as the prosecution allege. A person may achieve their objective of sex with the employments of gifts, alcohol and/or drugs, insincere compliments, apparent security, a more exciting way of life and/or false promises. Such methods will not necessarily mean that there is a lack of consent where a seduction is successful. However, where there is evidence of exploitation of a young and immature girl who may not understand the full significance of what she is doing, this is conduct you can take into account in deciding whether in reality there was no genuine consent.

(c) If a young complainant received or expected to receive payment for sexual favours, it does not necessarily mean that there was a genuine consent. It is evidence to be considered against the background of the context of the circumstances as you find them to have been at the time.

(d) The consumption of significant amounts of alcohol and/or drugs may also mean that a complainant does not have the capacity to consent. Whilst a drunken consent is still a consent, if a complainant is so drunk and/or affected by drugs that they are not in a position to know what is going on (ie they are "out of it"), they will not have the capacity to make that choice and so will not be consenting. That may occur whilst a person is still conscious. If a person is not conscious they are not in a position to consent.

17. It is, of course, always the right of a person to decide whether to consent to a particular sexual activity at a particular time. Consent to one type of sexual activity does not necessarily mean consent to another. It is always necessary to focus upon a complainant's state of mind at the time of the particular sexual activity alleged.

18. Consent to sexual activity on a previous occasion does not necessarily mean there is consent to sexual activity on a later occasion.

19. It is also the right of a person to decide for themselves whether to consent to a particular sexual activity. Consent cannot be given by a 3rd party.

REASONABLE BELIEF

20. If you are sure that the complainant was not consenting, you next have to consider the defendant's state of mind. The prosecution also have to prove that the defendant did not reasonably believe the complainant was consenting at the time. Whether a belief is reasonable is to be determined by having regard to all the circumstances, including any steps the defendant took to ascertain whether the complainant was in fact consenting. Please note that belief in consent is not the same thing as a hope or expectation that the complainant was consenting or indifference as to whether the complainant was consenting or not.   H.06

21. You need to consider 2 questions:
    (i) May the defendant have genuinely believed that the complainant was consenting? If you are sure the defendant did not have such a belief, the prosecution have proved the mental element of the offence. If on the other hand, the defendant may have had such a belief, you need to go on and consider the next question.
    (ii) May the defendant's belief have been reasonable in all the circumstances? Here it is irrelevant if a defendant was affected by alcohol and/or drugs. You must consider the defendant as if he had been sober.

CONSPIRACY TO RAPE

22. A conspiracy is an agreement between at least 2 or more people to commit a particular criminal offence. Conspirators can join a conspiracy at different times. Their roles may be different. They do not need to know all the details. It is not necessary for each conspirator to have met or communicated with the others or even to know their identities, but it is necessary that each of the conspirators is a party to a common design and is aware that the design involves a larger scheme involving others.   H.07

23. A conspiracy may be proved by inference from conduct, including words spoken in furtherance of common design, circumstantial evidence or by direct evidence of the agreement.

24. For conspiracy to rape to be established there must be an agreement with at least one other (whether a defendant or not) for the complainant's vagina, anus or mouth to be penetrated with at least one man's penis without her consent knowing that the complainant was not consenting. The prosecution must prove that the conspirators actually intended to carry out the agreement to rape.

RAPE OF A CHILD UNDER 13

H.08   25. To prove rape of a child under 13, the prosecution must make you sure that:
    (i) the defendant penetrated the complainant's vagina, anus or mouth with his penis;
    (ii) the complainant was aged under 13 at the time.

The prosecution do *NOT* have to prove:
(iii) that the complainant did not consent; or
(iv) the defendant did not reasonably believe the complainant was over 13 or over 16.

GENERAL APPROACH

H.09   When judging allegations of sexual abuse, experience has shown that it is necessary to keep a cool head. It is easy to feel indignant when such allegations are made, and easy to be sympathetic to a witness who seems to be showing difficulty or distress at having to recall and recount incidents which she says were distressing and unpleasant for her.

   These are wholly understandable emotions, but they do not assist you in deciding whether the prosecution have made you sure of the various allegations.

   As I said to you at the outset of this case you must judge this case on the evidence you have heard in this case. You must put aside any feelings and/or assumptions you have about cases such as these and review the evidence you have heard dispassionately. Your task is to consider the evidence clinically. Emotion and/or prejudice have no part to play in your deliberations.

   Let me give you some examples. It would be understandable if some of you came to this trial with assumptions as to what constitutes rape, what kind of person might be a rapist, or what a person who is being, or has been raped will do or say. I stress that you should leave behind all such assumptions because experience tells the courts that there is no stereotype for a rape, rapist, and victim of rape or how people behave after rape.

   You may have read or heard opinions expressed in the media about whether people who allege they have been abused in their early teenage years, tell the truth or lies. You may have formed a view in advance as to how you would expect a person making such allegations would appear or behave when giving evidence. Any person who has been raped or subject to other types of sexual abuse will have undergone trauma. It is impossible to predict how an individual will react, either in the following days, or when speaking about it publicly. The experience of the courts is that assumptions of any kind are unlikely to assist.

There is NO classic reaction. People react in different ways. Some resist, some may freeze, others do not resist because of the circumstances. Furthermore, experience shows that those who have been the victims of rape react differently to the task of speaking about it in evidence. Some people will show obvious signs of distress, others will not. The reason is that every person has his or her way of coping. Conversely, it does not follow that signs of distress of the witness confirm the truth and accuracy of the evidence given. In other words, demeanour in court is not necessarily a clue to the truth of a witness' account. It all depends upon the character and personality of the individual concerned. You are only concerned with a fair and calm evaluation of the evidence in this case. Your verdict must turn on what you make of the evidence and nothing else.

DELAY

Some of the complainants have given evidence about events said to have   **H.10** occurred some years ago. How should you approach the delay? 3 questions are raised. You will need to consider the position in relation to each complainant.

    (i) Why did the particular complainant wait so long before making a complaint?

   (ii) What effect delay has had on the quality of the evidence?

  (iii) Has any defendant been put at a disadvantage in meeting factual assertions against him, and, if so, how should you make an allowance for that?

Issue (i) You are entitled to consider why many of these matters did not come to light sooner. I will deal with this issue after I have covered the other 2 issues.

Issue (ii) The impact of delay upon the quality of the evidence
We are not dealing with events in the distant past. However sometimes we have been hearing evidence about what is said to have occurred as long as 8 years ago. You will need to consider the effect of delay upon the quality of the evidence. Witnesses, whoever they may be, cannot be expected to remember with great clarity events that occurred some years ago. This has a particular relevance to identification evidence but it may be relevant in other areas where after a passage of time a witness cannot provide details that you might have expected if the incident had taken place more recently.

Issue (iii) You should make allowances for the fact that from a defendant's point of view, the longer the time since the alleged incident or incidents, the more difficult it may be for him to answer it even if you decide that the delay in this case is understandable. If an allegation is made only in very general terms without any detail, it may be difficult for a defendant to meet that allegation. IF you decide that because of this a defendant has been placed at a real disadvantage in putting forward his case, take that into account in his favour when deciding whether the prosecution has made you sure of his guilt.

THE EVIDENCE OF THE COMPLAINANTS

H.11   The allegations in this case substantially depend upon the reliability and credibility of the particular complainant who makes the particular allegation.

The prosecution say that you can be sure of the evidence of each complainant in respect of the allegations they now make. The defence say that they are wholly unreliable and you cannot rely upon the evidence of any of the complainants without independent support, and there is no independent support.

How should you approach a particular complainant's evidence?

(i) look at each one individually and assess their reliability. During the course of my summing up I will be reminding you of the significant points in respect of each complainant and their evidence. It is of critical importance that you look at them as individuals. .

(ii) When you do so, take into account and evaluate the points made as to their lack of credibility/ unreliability

(a) inconsistent complaints made at the time/ inconsistencies between accounts given at the time and their evidence.

(b) lies told at the time (including an admitted false complaint)

(c) the failure to make some allegations until the witness gave evidence

(d) failure to name particular defendants when making allegations against others at the time

(e) their life style at the time including their rejection of parental authority and absconding which occurred before any encounter with the defendants

(f) the effect of drugs and/or alcohol.

(g) in some cases, the failure to give detail.

You need to look at the evidence of each complainant with care. There is a fundamental dispute between the prosecution and the defence as to whether these factors I have mentioned undermine the reliability of the witnesses.

You need to consider how each complainant would have been at the time of the allegations.

The prosecution say they were vulnerable and out of control. That is why they were being targeted. They were serial absconders. On return, sometimes they would lie about what they had been doing or give inconsistent accounts. Lies told in those circumstances at that time of their lives do not mean that they are not now reliable witnesses when they give evidence about what happened to them during those turbulent periods of their young lives. The defence say that the lies were of such nature and scale that their accounts now must be considered to be wholly or partly unreliable.

Inconsistencies

You need to assess their evidence as given at this court bearing these factors in mind. The experience of the courts is that it is unwise to approach the issue of inconsistency with the assumption that a true account is always consistent or an inconsistent account is always untrue.   **H.12**

Please remember that, in any event, it is not uncommon for witnesses to give inconsistent accounts when they have undergone a particularly traumatic episode or episodes. Every person who is a victim of rape suffers trauma to a greater or lesser degree. The quality of our memory is affected by the ability of the mind to take in the details of the experience, register them and recall them afterwards. Trauma can interfere with these processes. Experience tells us that the way in which trauma affects memory varies considerably. It may affect a person's ability accurately to lay down in the memory, in the correct sequence, each of the constituent parts of the ordeal. If the trauma did have such an effect, the ability of the witness to recall events consistently is also likely to be affected. I am sure you will appreciate that someone who is involved in a shocking incident may be affected in this way. After the event, some people ruminate constantly on what happened and by that process reconstruct, accurately or perhaps inaccurately, the events which occurred; others hate to confront their memories and do their best to avoid thinking about them. The result is not always consistent.

If you accept that trauma can affect people, and if a particular complainant did indeed suffer trauma, you might consider her failure of consistent recall understandable.

On the other hand, a person who has made a false complaint may also have difficulty being consistent. The inconsistencies may expose the possibility that the details do not represent a true recall of events but are part of a manufactured account which is difficult to remember consistently. Inconsistent accounts may, therefore, be an indicator that the account as a whole is untrue.

How then should you approach the evidence of a complainant? It depends upon the circumstances and the individual. You need to consider (i) the materiality and extent of any significant inconsistency and (ii) whether it undermines the evidence of the particular complainant in such a way that you cannot rely upon their evidence. I will remind you of the evidence with that task in mind. If, having given due consideration to the defence argument, you are sure that the essential parts of a complainant's account are true, you will no doubt act upon that conclusion. But, if you are left in doubt about the truthfulness of a complainant's account, because the inconsistencies cannot be satisfactorily explained to you, you must not rely on that account.

The defence say that those lies and/or inconsistencies in their accounts mean that it would be unsafe to rely on their evidence now. Witnesses may be looking back at their earlier conduct, feeling shame and regret. This may have led them to give less than reliable accounts when looking back at events with the benefit of hindsight. The defence ask this: If different accounts have been given how can you be sure which is accurate? The prosecution, however, say lies and inconsistent accounts at the time are hardly surprising. Make an allowance for the effect of trauma and the way these witnesses would have been at the time. The witnesses are now looking back and trying to give as accurate accounts as possible about what happened to them.

Allegations made for the first time in evidence

H.13 Even when they made their statements in respect of this case, sometimes a witness will have failed to refer to an episode which they have gone on to describe to you in evidence. You will remember that on occasions defence counsel pointed out to a witness that in this court was the first time the witness had told anybody about this. On the one hand, the defence say that makes that evidence wholly unreliable. If it was a true account you would have expected important allegations such as this particular episode to have been remembered and made earlier. Once an allegation is being made against a particular individual, you would expect all significant points to be covered. On the other hand, the prosecution say that you have to bear in mind that some of the complainants are giving evidence about a whole series of events that took place over a number of years. It may be difficult to cover everything in one or more interviews. The interview may not have been designed for the naming of names such as interviews to give background information.

The prosecution say that it is hardly surprising if memories return in a piecemeal fashion. Talking about an episode may trigger further memories. Witnesses have talked of the blanking out of traumatic events, and the difficulty in then accessing memories, describing them and so reliving the trauma. In respect of repeated behaviour, it may be difficult to identify the detail in respect of one particular allegation.

You will need to look with care at an allegation made for the very first time. As we go through the evidence together I will be reminding you of significant examples. You will wish to bear in mind these factors. Ask yourselves, does this undermine the witness' evidence as the defence suggest, or do you accept the explanation put forward by the witness?

Late allegations

Issue (i) You are entitled to consider why many of these matters did not come   **H.14**
to light sooner. It has been said on behalf of certain defendants that the fact
that a particular complainant did not report what had happened to her as
soon as possible makes it less likely that the complaints she eventually made
were true. It is argued that late reporting in these particular cases suggests
fabrication. In certain cases it is suggested that particular complainants had
ample opportunity to make complaints nearer the time. In certain cases it is
suggested that the witness may have made a complaint about another to the
police or the social services, and yet not complained about a defendant when
she is now alleging a defendant was actually sexually abusing her at the time.
Whether late reporting makes an allegation less likely is entirely a matter for
you.

However, it would be wrong to assume every person who has been the
victim of sexual assaults will report it as soon as possible. As I have said the
experience of the courts is that victims of sexual offences can react in
different ways.

Make an allowance for teenagers. Consider them as individuals. Consider
how a particular individual will have been at the time. Be careful not to make
general assumptions about the behaviour of teenagers, whether complainants
or defendants. A victim, particularly a young victim, may not report for a
variety of different reasons. You have heard various explanations put
forward. It is for you to consider them and to decide whether they provide an
understandable reason or reasons for late disclosure in respect of the
particular witness' evidence you are considering. (i) confusion or lack of
confidence or experience when subjected to offences at a very young age (ii)
a sense of loyalty, however misguided, to the very person or persons who
have committed the offence or offences against them particularly where that
person has appeared to show her affection and support and provided her
with alcohol and/or drugs (iii) inability to resist the compulsion to continue
that way of life and what it appears to offer (iv) concern about the effects of
a fall out with that person which may include fear for herself and/ or her
family (v) the difficulty speaking about such matters and feelings of acute
embarrassment and/ or self-blame about revealing what has happened and
may be still happening (vi)and/or distrust of authority, whether it be the
social services, the police or even their own family.

*Failure to complain about defendants when making an allegation against
others*

You have heard on occasions at the time a particular witness has made   **H.15**
allegations about others. That is not because it is suggested those other
allegations are untrue. The only relevance is that it shows that the particular
complainant was prepared to make an allegation at the time to police, social

worker or person in authority. If so, you need to consider why, if at the same time they were being abused by any of these defendants, did they not mention that.

The defence say that the failure to make allegations against the defendants at the time means they are now false. They say that that it is highly significant that they were prepared at the time to make allegations against others to persons in authority, and yet did not make allegations against those they now say were abusing them at the time. You need to consider this with care. You need to decide what the circumstances were. The context as you judge it to have been will be important. The prosecution say that a complete explanation can be found in the nature of the sexual abuse to which they were being subjected by some of the defendants—the nature of the relationships. You need to look at the dynamics of what may have been complex relationships In part it is said they were seduced by the way of life that was being offered—apparent affection, drink and drugs—they felt in their own words "they owed them." Complainants have spoken of a weird loyalty towards those who had abused them. In some cases, witnesses have said that there was an element of fear and/or actual violence. You need to consider that evidence and whether you accept it.

It follows that your approach is to consider these points and ask yourselves does the failure to complain at the time, and/or the failure to complain when making allegations against others undermine the witness' evidence, or do you accept the explanation given by the particular witness for the delay in making the complaint.

In short, a late complaint does not necessarily signify a false complaint, any more than an immediate complaint necessarily demonstrates a true complaint. It is a matter for you to determine whether, in the case of a particular complainant, the lateness of the complaint assists you at all and, if so, what weight you attach to it.

The complainants' lifestyle at the time

H.16   How do you approach the complainants' lifestyle at the time? The prosecution reminds of you of their evidence that they were in their words "out of control"—at times out of control of their parents, at times out of control of the children's homes, at times out of control of themselves. They may have felt they were taking control of their young lives, but you will remember the description of how soon they discovered they were not actually in control.

The prosecution say that it was their lifestyle combined with their vulnerability that made them such easy prey. Their craving for attention made them easy targets. Their lifestyle and behaviour would mean that those who abused them might think that if any particular girl did make any allegations they would not be taken seriously. On occasions they could not help themselves from going back, even though in part they hated themselves for it. The defence say these were young girls deliberately wanting to do adult things, this would lead them into getting into trouble (absconding/ out after curfew/ drink/ drugs) and their reaction would be falsely to blame others either at the time or even now when looking back at their past with regret and seeking to rationalise it.

The defence remind you that they had started absconding and had met others whilst absconding even before any encounter with any of the defendants. Some were involved with others during the periods when the prosecution say they were being abused by a defendant or defendants. The intake of drugs and/or alcohol may have impacted on their ability accurately to recall.

As always look at the circumstances with care. Always look at the particular witness. Ask yourselves: may they have made false allegations to cover up for their own behaviour and consequences they feared at the time or do you accept that their lifestyle was entirely consistent with the allegations they now make?

Contemporaneous Records

In this case you have heard contemporaneous reports or notes made by social   **H.17**
services, staff at children's homes, police officers who investigated particular incidents at the time, and the police officer who was then gathering intelligence in respect of missing persons. Invariably these will report what a particular complainant has said at that time. They are contemporaneous in the sense that they were made nearer to the time, but they may not necessarily have been written as the witness was giving their particular account.

You will need to consider whether such evidence gives you insight into the reliability of the particular witness. I will be reminding you of some of this material which was put to various witnesses. The defence rely upon some of the contemporaneous records as evidence of significant inconsistency (see directions above.)

Occasionally, the prosecution contend that they shed light onto what had happened to a particular complainant at the time. Whilst the witness was not prepared to make a formal complaint, she was prepared to reveal rather more of what was really happening to the missing persons' officer for example. However, please remember that they are not evidence independent of the complainant. The reports are evidence in the case upon which you can act, but they do not come from an independent source.

You have other examples of when witnesses have spoken of what was said at the time. As I have said, the prosecution accept that on occasions witnesses have told lies. They say it was part of the witness' behaviour at the time lying about what had occurred when they were absconding, not wanting to reveal the true position to people in authority. The prosecution say they were deliberately lying about what was really happening. The defence say that this material wholly undermines the reliability of the particular witness. Lies about what had happened at the time mean that the witness' present account cannot be considered reliable. In particular, it is suggested the witnesses made allegations to avoid getting into trouble.

You will need to consider with care whether if lies were told at the time, the witness' evidence should now be considered unreliable or whether the witness is a reliable witness who told lies at the time against the background of and/or because of what was in reality happening at the time.

"REVENGE PORNOGRAPHY"*

The concept of "revenge pornography" has been informally recognised for a **I.01** number of years, anecdotally increasing with the rise of social media. In October 2014, the CPS issued legal guidance regarding the prosecution of communications sent via social media.[1] They gave additional advice for the application of the guidance in the context of offending that could be termed revenge pornography.[2] This advocated a victim-focussed application of existing statute, including s.1 of the Malicious Communications Act 1988; s.127 of the Communications Act 2003; the Protection from Harassment Act 1997; the Protection of Children Act 1978; and the Sexual Offences Act 2003.

This type of criminality has now been specifically prohibited, as the offence of "disclosing private sexual photographs and films with intent to cause distress", by s.33 of the Criminal Justice and Courts Act 2015,[3] which came into force on April 13, 2015. The offence is defined by s.33(1) as follows:

It is an offence for a person to disclose a private sexual photograph or film if the disclosure is made—

(a) without the consent of an individual who appears in the photograph or film; and

(b) with the intention of causing that individual distress.

The offence carries a maximum sentence of two years' custody on conviction on indictment and of six months' custody on summary conviction (to be increased to 12 months once s.154 of the Criminal Justice Act comes into force). It is committed only if the disclosure is to someone other than the person in the image (s.33(2)). It is not sufficient to prove the intention

* Summary written by Samantha Wright.
[1] *http://www.cps.gov.uk/legal/a_to_c/communications_sent_via_social_media/* [Accessed April 30, 2016].
[2] *http://www.cps.gov.uk/news/latest_news/crown_prosecution_service_offers_clear_guidance_for_prosecutors_on_revenge_pornography/* [Accessed April 30, 2016].
[3] *http://www.legislation.gov.uk/ukpga/2015/2/section/33/enacted* [Accessed April 30, 2016].

required by s.33(1)(b) that distress was a natural and probable consequence of the disclosure (s.33(8)).

There are a number of statutory defences. One is that the person charged had a reasonable belief that disclosure was necessary to prevent, detect or investigate crime (s.33(3)). Another is if the disclosure was made in the course of, or with a view to, the publication of journalistic material and the person charged reasonably believed that that publication was or would be in the public interest (s.33(4)). A further defence is if the person charged reasonably believed that the photograph or film had been previously disclosed for reward, whether by the person in the image or anyone else, and they had no reason to believe that that previous disclosure had been made without consent (s.33(5)).

The burden is on the defendant to prove the defence in s.33(3). For the defences in s.33(4) and (5), the defence must adduce sufficient evidence to raise the issue and will be successful if the contrary is not proved beyond reasonable doubt (s.33(6)).

INDEX

Abduction
see also **Child abduction**
assault by penetration, 2.16
rape, 1.40
Abuse of position of trust
assault by penetration, 2.16
causing children to engage in
    sexual activity
    "causes or incites another
        person . . . ", 5.63
    civil partners, 5.68
    consent, 5.70
    jurisdiction, 5.62
    maximum sentences, 5.54–5.57
    meaning, 5.52–5.53
    mens rea, 5.71–5.774
    mode of trial, 5.54–5.57
    offence, 5.51
    parties to offence, 5.59–5.61
    "position of trust", 5.66
    pre-existing sexual
        relationships, 5.69
    sentencing, 5.58
    spouses, 5.68
    "the activity is sexual", 5.65
    "to engage in an activity", 5.64
    "where subsection (2) applies",
        5.67
causing children to watch sexual
    acts
    "causes", 5.114
    civil partners, 5.119
    consent, 5.121
    jurisdiction, 5.113
    maximum sentences,
        5.105–5.108
    meaning, 5.104

Abuse of position of trust—*cont.*
causing children to watch sexual
    acts—*cont.*
    mens rea, 5.122–5.125
    mode of trial, 5.105–5.108
    offence, 5.103
    parties to offence, 5.110–5.112
    "position of trust", 5.117
    pre-existing sexual
        relationships, 5.120
    sentencing, 5.109
    spouses, 5.119
    "the activity is sexual", 5.116
    "to watch . . .", 5.115
    "where subsection (2) applies",
        5.118
engaging in sexual activity in
    presence of children
    civil partners, 5.95
    consent, 5.97
    "engages in an activity", 5.90
    jurisdiction, 5.89
    maximum sentences, 5.77–5.80
    meaning, 5.76
    mens rea, 5.98–5.102
    mode of trial, 5.77–5.80
    offence, 5.75
    parties to offence, 5.86–5.88
    "position of trust", 5.93
    pre-existing sexual
        relationships, 5.96
    "present or in a place from
        which A can be
        observed", 5.92
    sentencing, 5.81–5.85
    spouses, 5.95
    "the activity is sexual", 5.91

Abuse of position of trust—*cont.*
engaging in sexual activity in
    presence of children—*cont.*
"where subsection (2) applies",
    5.94
introduction, 5.01–5.06
Northern Ireland
    generally, 5.127–5.128
    offence, 5.126
rape, 1.47–1.48
Scotland
    generally, 5.127–5.128
    offence, 5.126
sexual activity with child family
    members, 6.25
sexual activity with children
    civil partners, 5.40–5.41
    consent, 5.46
    jurisdiction, 5.28
    maximum sentences, 5.09–5.13
    meaning, 5.08
    mens rea, 5.47–5.50
    mode of trial, 5.09–5.13
    offence, 5.07
    parties to offence, 5.24–5.27
    "position of trust", 5.31–5.38
    pre-existing sexual
        relationships, 5.42–5.45
    sentencing, 5.14–5.23
    spouses, 5.40–5.41
    "the touching is sexual", 5.30
    "touches another person", 5.29
    "where subsection (2) applies",
        5.39
Abuse of process
decisions to prosecute,
    17.28–17.29
historic offences
    civil court decisions,
        30.50–30.51
    correct approach, 30.28–30.36
    dip sampling, 30.82
    earlier complaints, 30.77–30.78
    examples of application of
        principles, 30.39–30.48

Abuse of process—*cont.*
historic offences—*cont.*
    financial compensation,
        30.79–30.81
    guidance derived from
        authorities, 30.37–30.38
    length of delay, 30.48
    missing documents,
        30.52–30.65
    previous police investigations,
        30.66–30.76
    procedure, 30.26–30.27
    promises not to prosecute,
        30.66–30.76
    significant inconsistencies,
        30.49
    trawling, 30.82
    withdrawn complaints,
        30.77–30.78
prosecution of victims of human
    trafficking, 11.29–11.35
Abusive behaviour
see **Anti-social behaviour**
Accomplices
sexual intercourse with animals,
    15.141–15.142
Actual bodily harm
consent to sexual activity,
    2.109–2.113
Administering substances with intent
consent, 14.31–14.32
introduction, 14.03
jurisdiction, 14.26
maximum sentence, 14.09–14.12
meaning, 14.08, 14.27–14.29
mens rea, 14.33–14.36
mode of trial, 14.09–14.12
sentencing
    aggravating features, 14.19
    ancillary orders, 14.20
    category range, 14.18
    credit for time served, 14.20
    culpability, 14.14–14.17
    dangerousness, 14.20
    examples, 14.21–14.25

Administering substances with intent—*cont.*
sentencing—*cont.*
guilty pleas, 14.20
harm, 14.14–14.17
introduction, 14.13
mitigation, 14.19
proportionality, 14.20
reasons, 14.20
reduction in sentence, 14.20
starting point, 14.18
sexual activity, 14.30

Admissibility
bad character
admissibility agreed, 20.24
cross-admissibility, 20.111–20.138
DNA evidence
blood samples given in confidence, 25.38
Criminal Procedure Rules 2015, 25.29–25.34
generally, 25.24–25.28
hearsay evidence, 25.35–25.36
partial profile, 25.37

Adults
after-care
bacterial STI prophylaxis, 21.48
domestic violence, 21.53–21.54
emergency contraception, 21.42
generally, 21.41
hepatitis B prophylaxis, 21.47
post-exposure prophylaxis, 21.46
pregnancy, 21.43–21.44
psychological issues, 21.50–21.51
safeguarding, 21.52
screening for infection post assault, 21.49
sexually transmitted infections, 21.45
suicide risk, 21.50–21.52

Adults—*cont.*
medical examinations
anatomical terms, 21.30
ano-genital injuries, 21.35–21.36
capacity, 21.20
confidentiality, 21.19
consent, 21.21
disclosure, 21.22
documenting injuries, 21.32–21.34
forensic examination, 21.26–21.29
generally, 21.18
history taking, 21.23–21.25
reporting restrictions
challenges to, 29.136
contravention of, 29.130–29.133
framing direction, 29.135
generally, 29.11, 29.123–29.129
prohibiting identification of adult to protect child, 29.89–29.93
representations by media, 29.134

Advertising
prostitution, 13.54–13.59

Advocacy
vulnerable witnesses
adaptation, 28.10–28.17
case management, 28.31–28.40
confrontation, 28.22–28.30
ground rules hearings, 28.31–28.40
introduction, 28.01–28.09
practical suggestions for questioning, 28.41–28.42
practicalities, 28.43–28.45
suggestive questioning, 28.18–28.21

Affirmations
youth courts, 31.55

After-care
adults
bacterial STI prophylaxis, 21.48
domestic violence, 21.53–21.54
emergency contraception, 21.42
generally, 21.41
hepatitis B prophylaxis, 21.47
post-exposure prophylaxis, 21.46
pregnancy, 21.43–21.44
psychological issues, 21.50–21.51
safeguarding, 21.52
screening for infection post assault, 21.49
sexually transmitted infections, 21.45
suicide risk, 21.50–21.52
children, 22.41

Age
historic offences, 30.115–30.118E
rape
capacity and consent, 1.224
mitigation, 1.72–1.73

Aggravating features
administering substances with intent, 14.19
assault by penetration, 1.59, 2.20
assault by penetration of child under 13, 3.93–3.94
care workers engaging in sexual activity in the presence of mentally disordered persons, 7.260
care workers having sexual activity with mentally disordered persons, 7.217
causing children to engage in sexual activity, 3.147–3.148
causing prostitution for gain, 10.128–10.131
causing sexual activity without consent, 2.94

Aggravating features—*cont.*
causing sexual exploitation of children, 10.51
child sex offenses
committed by children, 4.155
engaging in sexual activity in presence of children, 4.107
meeting children following sexual grooming, 4.201
sexual activity with children, 4.40–4.41
engaging in sexual activity in presence of children, 5.84
engaging in sexual activity in presence of mentally disordered persons, 7.114
engaging in sexual activity in presence procured by inducement, threat or deception of mentally disordered persons, 7.181
exposure, 15.80
human trafficking, 11.86–11.88
keeping brothels, 12.50
paying for sexual services of children, 10.23
procuring sexual activity with mentally disordered persons by inducement, threat or deception, 7.150
rape
alcohol, 1.68
blackmail, 1.62
compulsion to leave home, 1.65
concealment, 1.67
domestic violence, 1.65–1.66
drugs, 1.68
ejaculation, 1.61
intimidation of witnesses, 1.67
location, 1.63
offending on bail, 1.60
previous convictions, 1.60
threats, 1.62
timing, 1.63
weapons, 1.64

Aggravating features—*cont.*
rape of child under 13, 3.47–3.48
sex with adult relatives, 6.80
sexual activity with child family
members, 6.21
sexual activity with children, 5.17
sexual activity with mentally
disordered persons, 7.56
sexual assault, 2.54
sexual assault of child under 13,
3.119–3.120
trespass with intent, 14.63
voyeurism, 15.108
Aircraft
slavery and human trafficking
forfeiture and detention of
land vehicles, ships and
aircraft, 11.118–11.119
Alcohol
familial sex offences
inciting child family member
to engage in sexual
activity, 6.69
sex with adult relatives, 6.93,
6.106
sexual activity with child
family members, 6.50
rape
aggravating features, 1.68
intoxication as defence, 1.402
self-induced intoxication,
1.398–1.401
use on victim to facilitate
offence, 1.46
sexual assault, 2.81–2.82
**All-Party Parliamentary Group on
Prostitution**
see **Prostitution**
**Allowing a person under 16 to be in
a brothel**
see **Brothels**
Alternative verdicts
assault by penetration, 2.14
assault by penetration of child
under 13, 3.87

Alternative verdicts—*cont.*
child abduction, 9.18
committing an offence with
intent to commit a sexual
offence, 14.43
rape, 1.137–1.141
rape of child under 13, 3.38
sexual assault, 2.44
sexual assault of child under 13,
3.112
Ancillary orders
administering substances with
intent, 14.20
assault by penetration, 2.21
assault by penetration of child
under 13, 3.95
care workers engaging in sexual
activity in the presence of
mentally disordered persons,
7.261
care workers having sexual
activity with mentally
disordered persons, 7.218
causing children to engage in
sexual activity, 3.149
causing prostitution for gain,
10.132
causing sexual activity without
consent, 2.95
causing sexual exploitation of
children, 10.52
engaging in sexual activity in
presence of children, 4.108,
5.85
engaging in sexual activity in
presence of mentally
disordered persons, 7.115
engaging in sexual activity in
presence procured by
inducement, threat or
deception of mentally
disordered persons, 7.182
exposure, 15.81
human trafficking, 11.89
keeping brothels, 12.51

2153

Ancillary orders—*cont.*
meeting children following sexual
grooming, 4.202
paying for sexual services of
children, 10.24
procuring sexual activity with
mentally disordered persons
by inducement, threat or
deception, 7.151
rape of child under 13, 3.49
sex with adult relatives, 6.81
sexual activity with child family
members, 6.22
sexual activity with children,
4.42, 5.18
sexual activity with mentally
disordered persons, 7.57
sexual assault, 2.55
sexual assault of child under 13,
3.121
trespass with intent, 14.64
voyeurism, 15.109
youth courts
barring from working with
children and young adults,
31.136
generally, 31.134
parenting orders, 31.138
sexual harm prevention orders,
31.135
sexual risk orders, 31.137
Animals
see **Sexual intercourse with**
animals
Ano-genital
see **Anus; Genitalia**
Anonymity
see also **Reporting restrictions**
between arrest and charge,
29.53–29.57
complainants
Contempt of Court Act 1981,
29.29–29.32
generally, 29.12–29.14
introduction, 29.02–29.03

Anonymity—*cont.*
complainants—*cont.*
Sexual Offences (Amendment)
Act 1992, 29.15–29.28
defendants
children and young persons,
29.47–29.52
generally, 29.33–29.43
introduction, 29.04–29.05
legislative interventions, 29.44
teachers, 29.45–29.46
introduction, 29.01
police guidance, 29.53–29.57
youth courts, 31.42
Anti-social behaviour
abusive or disorderly behaviour
"abusive or disorderly
behaviour", 15.185–15.192
defences, 15.197
going naked in public,
15.186–15.192
"harassment, alarm or
distress", 15.196
human rights, 15.183
maximum sentences, 15.184
meaning, 15.180–15.182
mens rea, 15.197
mode of trial, 15.184
offence, 15.179
"within the sight of a person
likely to be caused",
15.193–15.195
Anti-social behaviour injunctions
prostitution, 13.73–13.82
Anus
adults
ano-genital injuries,
21.35–21.36
anatomy, 22.38
interpretation of ano-genital
findings, 22.42–22.46
signs of sexual abuse in children
bruising, 22.61
dilatation, 22.65–22.66

Anus—*cont.*
signs of sexual abuse in
children—*cont.*
erythema, 22.59
lacerations, 22.62–22.63
perianal venous congestion,
22.60
scars and tags, 22.64
Apparent consent
see **Consent**
Appeals
notification orders, 35.66
sexual harm prevention orders,
36.55–36.59
sexual risk orders, 36.72
Applications
notification orders, 35.58–35.60
reporting restrictions (children)
burden of proof, 29.74
Crown Court, 29.107
High Court, 29.105
sexual harm prevention orders
at time of dealing with
offender for offence,
36.15–36.17
by magistrates' courts on
application, 36.18–36.19
criteria for, 36.13–36.14
Arranging child sex offences
acts done to protect child,
4.180–4.184
"arranges or facilitates",
4.172–4.176
"in any part of the world", 4.177
jurisdiction, 4.171
maximum sentences, 4.163–4.167
meaning, 4.161–4.162
mens rea, 4.185
mode of trial, 4.163–4.167
offence, 4.160
parties to offence, 4.170
"sections 9 to 13", 4.178–4.179
sentencing, 4.168–4.169

**Arranging sexual exploitation of
children**
see also **Sexual exploitation of
children**
"arranges or facilitates", 10.99
"in any part of the world",
10.101
jurisdiction, 10.89
maximum sentences, 10.91–10.95
meaning, 10.89–10.90
mens rea, 10.102–10.104
mode of trial, 10.91–10.95
offence, 10.88
parties to offence, 10.97
sentencing, 10.96
"sexual exploitation", 10.100
Assault by penetration
see also **Assault of child under 13
by penetration**
abduction, 2.16
abuse of position of trust, 2.16
alternative verdicts, 2.14
bail, 2.13
classification, 2.10
consent, 2.31
detention, 2.16
introduction, 2.01–2.03
jurisdiction, 2.25
meaning, 2.07–2.08
mens rea, 2.32–2.37
mode of trial, 2.09
more than one offender acting
together, 2.16
notification requirements, 2.12
parties, 2.24
penalties, 2.11
penetration
"part of his body or anything
else", 2.27–2.28
"penetrates the vagina or anus
of another person", 2.26
"penetration is sexual",
2.29–2.30
sentencing
aggravating features, 1.59, 2.20

Assault by penetration—*cont.*
sentencing—*cont.*
ancillary orders, 2.21
category range, 2.18–2.19
credit for time served, 2.21
culpability, 2.17
dangerousness, 2.21
examples, 2.22–2.23
generally, 2.15–2.16
guilty pleas, 2.21
harm, 2.17
mitigation, 1.59, 2.20
proportionality, 2.21
reduction of sentence, 2.21
starting point, 2.18–2.19
Sexual Offences Review, 2.03
specified offences, 2.11
Assault of child under 13 by penetration
see also **Assault by penetration**
alternative verdicts, 3.87
bail, 3.86
"child under 13", 3.101
classification, 3.83
complex cases, 3.83
consent, 3.102
jurisdiction, 3.98
meaning, 3.79–3.81
mens rea, 3.103
mode of trial, 3.82
notification requirements, 3.85
parties, 3.97
"penetrates the vagina or anus of another person", 3.99
"penetration is sexual", 3.100
sentencing
aggravating features, 3.93–3.94
ancillary orders, 3.95
category range, 3.92
credit for time served, 3.95
culpability, 3.90–3.91
dangerousness, 3.84, 3.95
generally, 3.88–3.89
guilty pleas, 3.95
harm, 3.90–3.91

Assault of child under 13 by penetration —*cont.*
sentencing—*cont.*
life imprisonment, 3.84, 3.95
maximum sentence, 3.82
mitigation, 3.93–3.94
proportionality, 3.95
reasonable belief, 3.96
reasons, 3.95
reduction in sentence, 3.95
starting point, 3.92
systematic abuse, 3.83
Assisting rape
see **Rape**
Attempts
child sex offences
causing children to watch sexual acts, 4.131–4.132
meeting children following sexual grooming, 4.190
sexual communication with children, 4.231
rape
generally, 1.128, 1.404–1.406
historic offences, 30.148–30.151
Autistic spectrum disorder
sexual behaviour of complainant, 26.69
Automatic life imprisonment
rape, 1.107–1.109
sex offenders, 34.17–34.22
Bad character
complainants, 20.144–20.147
Criminal Justice Act 2003, 20.01–20.02
cross-admissibility
case law, 20.113–20.120
collusion, 20–123–20.130
consideration before summing up, 20.131–20.134
generally, 20.111–20.112
propensity, 20.121–20.122
statistical assessment of unlikelihood of coincidence, 20.135–20.138

Bad character—*cont.*
exclusionary discretion
generally, 20.92–20.102
PACE s.78, 20.108
satellite litigation,
20.103–20.107
gateways
adduced by defendant
intentionally, 20.25
admissibility agreed, 20.24
age of previous convictions or
allegations, 20.49–20.53
false impression given by
defendant, 20.82–20.86
generalised history, 20.39–20.40
homosexual disposition,
20.58–20.78
important explanatory
evidence, 20.26–20.30
incidents following date of
allegation being tried,
20.54–20.56
indecent photographs,
20.33–20.38
prior heterosexual offences
where homosexual offence
alleged, 20.57
propensity, 20.41–20.48
relevant to important matter in
issue, 20.31–20.79
substantive probative value of
evidence, 20.80–20.81
third party's character,
20.87–20.91
untruthfulness, 20.79
jury directions, 20.109–20.110
meaning, 20.13–20.23
non-defendants
allegations, 20.148–20.150
complainants, 20.144–20.147
generally, 20.139–20.143
notice requirements, 20.03–20.06
proving details of previous sexual
offence, 20.07–20.12
sex offenders, 34.58–34.62

Bad character—*cont.*
sexual behaviour of complainant
and, 20.151–20.153
Bail
assault by penetration, 2.13
assault by penetration of child
under 13, 3.86
causing children to engage in
sexual activity, 3.141
causing sexual activity without
consent, 2.90
mentally disordered persons
causing mentally disordered
persons to engage in
sexual activity, 7.96
sexual activity with mentally
disordered persons, 7.52
rape
obtaining bail, 1.24–1.25
offending on bail, 1.60
rape of child under 13, 3.36
youth courts, 31.29–31.30
Barred persons
sex offenders, 34.63–34.64
youth courts, 31.136
Bawdy house
see **Keeping disorderly houses**
Binding over
prostitution, 13.83–13.87
Blackmail
aggravating features
rape, 1.62
Breach
sexual harm prevention orders,
36.60–36.65
sexual risk orders, 36.73–36.75
Brothels
see also **Keeping brothels; Keeping**
disorderly houses;
Prostitution; Soliciting
allowing a person under 16 to be
in a brothel
"allows", 12.102
"brothel", 12.103

Brothels—*cont.*
allowing a person under 16 to be
in a brothel—*cont.*
"has attained the age of 4
years and is under the age
of 16 years", 12.101
maximum sentences, 12.98
meaning, 12.97
mode of trial, 12.98
parties to offence, 12.99
"responsibility for", 12.100
landlord letting premises for use
as brothel
"brothel", 12.62
"lessor or landlord . . . or
agent", 12.60–12.61
maximum sentence, 12.58
meaning, 12.57
mode of trial, 12.58
parties to offence, 12.59
"to be willfully a party to that
use continuing", 12.64
"with the knowledge that it is
to be used", 12.63
meaning, 12.27
tenant permitting premises to be
used as brothel
"brothel", 12.73
"knowingly", 12.71
maximum sentences, 12.66
meaning, 12.65
mode of trial, 12.66
parties to offence, 12.67
"permit", 12.72
position of lessor or landlord
where tenant convicted,
12.74–12.75
"tenant or occupier or person
in charge", 12.68–12.70
Byelaws
offences against public morals,
15.199–15.200
Canada
keeping brothels, 12.15–12.20
prostitution, 13.20–13.24

Canada—*cont.*
sexual behaviour of complainant,
26.168–26.176
Capacity
medical examinations
adults, 21.20
mentally disordered persons
burden and standard of proof,
7.23–7.24
sexual intercourse with mental
patients, 7.10–7.11
rape
age, 1.224
common law, 1.226–1.229
generally, 1.222–1.223
issues specific to person or
situation, 1.230–1.237
Mental Capacity Act 1005,
1.233–1.234
mental disorder, 1.225,
1.238–1.242
use of and weight to be given
to information,
1.235–1.237
voluntary intoxication,
1.243–1.254
withdrawal of case from jury,
1.255–1.262
Care workers
see **Social care workers**
Case management
vulnerable witnesses, 28.31–28.40
Category range
see **Sentencing**
**Causing children to engage in sexual
activity**
abuse of position of trust
"causes or incites another
person . . . ", 5.63
civil partners, 5.68
consent, 5.70
jurisdiction, 5.62
maximum sentences, 5.54–5.57
meaning, 5.52–5.53
mens rea, 5.71–5.774

Causing children to engage in sexual activity—*cont.*

abuse of position of trust—*cont.*
mode of trial, 5.54–5.57
offence, 5.51
parties to offence, 5.59–5.61
"position of trust", 5.66
pre-existing sexual
relationships, 5.69
sentencing, 5.58
spouses, 5.68
"the activity is sexual", 5.65
"to engage in an activity", 5.64
"where subsection (2) applies",
5.67
bail, 3.141
"causes or incites another
person", 3.158–3.163, 4.86
"child under 13", 3.166
classification, 3.138
complex cases, 3.138
consent, 3.167, 4.91
jurisdiction, 3.157, 4.85
maximum sentences, 4.71–4.75
meaning, 3.131–3.135, 4.68–4.70
mens rea, 3.168–3.170, 4.92–4.93
mode of trial, 3.136–3.137,
4.71–4.75
notification requirements, 3.140
offence, 4.67
parties, 3.155–3.156, 4.84
"penetration", 4.89
sentencing
aggravating features,
3.147–3.148
ancillary orders, 3.149
category range, 3.146
credit for time served, 3.149
culpability, 3.144–3.145
cybercrime, 3.150–3.151,
4.77–4.80
dangerousness, 3.139, 3.149
generally, 3.142–3.143, 4.76
guilty pleas, 3.149
harm, 3.144–3.145

Causing children to engage in sexual activity—*cont.*

sentencing—*cont.*
incitement, 3.152–3.154
life imprisonment, 3.139, 3.149
lower sentences for incitement,
4.81–4.83
maximum sentence,
3.136–3.137
mitigation, 3.147–3.148
online offending, 3.150–3.151
proportionality, 3.149
reasons, 3.149
reduction in sentence, 3.149
starting point, 3.146
specified offences, 3.139
systematic abuse, 3.138
"the activity is sexual", 3.165,
4.88
"to engage in an activity", 3.164,
4.87
"vagina", 4.90

Causing children to watch sexual acts

abuse of position of trust
"causes", 5.114
civil partners, 5.119
consent, 5.121
jurisdiction, 5.113
maximum sentences,
5.105–5.108
meaning, 5.104
mens rea, 5.122–5.125
mode of trial, 5.105–5.108
offence, 5.103
parties to offence, 5.110–5.112
"position of trust", 5.117
pre-existing sexual
relationships, 5.120
sentencing, 5.109
spouses, 5.119
"the activity is sexual", 5.116
"to watch . . . ", 5.115
"where subsection (2) applies",
5.118

Causing children to watch sexual acts—*cont.*
attempts, 4.131–4.132
"causes", 4.133
consent, 4.138
jurisdiction, 4.130
maximum sentences, 4.123–4.127
meaning, 4.122
mens rea, 4.139–4.143
mode of trial, 4.123–4.127
offences, 4.121
parties to offence, 4.129
sentencing, 4.128
"the activity is sexual", 4.137
"to watch a third person engaging in an activity... ", 4.134–4.136
Causing mentally disordered persons to engage in sexual activity
see **Sexual offences against mentally disordered persons; Social care workers**
Causing mentally disordered persons to watch sexual acts
see **Sexual offences against mentally disordered persons; Social care workers**
Causing prostitution for gain
"causes or incites", 10.134–10.135
"for or in the expectation of gain", 10.140–10.141
"in any part of the world", 10.139
maximum sentences, 10.113–10.117
meaning, 10.112
mens rea, 10.142
mode of trial, 10.113–10.117
offence, 10.111
parties to offence, 10.133
"prostitute", 10.137–10.138
sentencing
    aggravating features, 10.128–10.131

Causing prostitution for gain—*cont.*
sentencing—*cont.*
    ancillary orders, 10.132
    category range, 10.126–10.127
    credit for time served, 10.132
    culpability, 10.122–10.125
    dangerousness, 10.132
    generally, 10.118–10.119
    guilty pleas, 10.132
    harm, 10.120–10.121
    mitigation, 10.128–10.131
    proportionality, 10.132
    reasons, 10.132
    reduction of sentence, 10.132
    starting point, 10.126–10.127
"to become", 10.136
Causing sexual activity without consent
bail, 2.90
"causes another person", 2.98
consent, 2.104
jurisdiction, 2.97
maximum sentence, 2.86
meaning, 2.84
mens rea, 2.105–2.108
mode of trial, 2.85–2.87
notification requirements, 2.89
parties, 2.96
sentencing
    aggravating features, 2.94
    ancillary orders, 2.95
    category range, 2.93
    credit for time served, 2.95
    culpability, 2.92
    dangerousness, 2.95
    generally, 2.91
    guilty pleas, 2.95
    harm, 2.92
    mitigation, 2.94
    proportionality, 2.95
    reduction of sentence, 2.95
    sentencing guideline, 2.91
    starting point, 2.93
Sexual Offences Review, 2.05
specified offences, 2.88

Causing sexual activity without consent—*cont.*
"the activity is sexual", 2.103
"to engage in an activity",
2.99–2.102
Causing sexual exploitation of children
see also **Sexual exploitation of children**
"causes or incites", 10.57–10.58
"in any part of the world", 10.65
jurisdiction, 10.56
maximum sentences, 10.38–10.42
meaning, 10.36–10.37
mens rea, 10.66–10.68
mode of trial, 10.38–10.42
offence, 10.35
parties to offence, 10.55
sentencing
  aggravating features, 10.51
  ancillary orders, 10.52
  category range, 10.49–10.50
  credit for time served, 10.52
  culpability, 10.45–10.48
  dangerousness, 10.52
  examples, 10.53–54
  generally, 10.43–10.44
  guilty pleas, 10.52
  harm, 10.45–10.48
  mitigation, 10.51
  proportionality, 10.52
  reasons, 10.52
  reduction of sentence, 10.52
  starting point, 10.49–10.50
"to be sexually exploited",
10.59–10.64
Cautions
soliciting, 13.51–13.52
Celebrities
historic offences, 30.127–30.132
Child abduction
alternative verdicts, 9.18
child abduction warning notices,
9.12–9.17
"detains", 9.37–9.40

Child abduction—*cont.*
introduction, 9.01–9.06
looked-after children
  child abduction warning
    notices, 9.54
  "keeps away", 9.58
  maximum sentences, 9.53
  mens rea, 9.61
  mode of trial, 9.53
  offence, 9.52
  parties to offence, 9.55
  "responsible person", 9.60
  "run away or stay away", 9.59
  "without lawful authority or
    reasonable excuse",
    9.56–9.57
maximum sentences, 9.10–9.11
meaning, 9.07–9.09
mens rea, 9.45–9.52
mode of trial, 9.10–9.11
parties to offence, 9.24–9.26
"remove from . . . lawful
  control", 9.42–9.44
sentencing, 9.19–9.23
"takes", 9.33–9.36
"under the age of 16", 9.41
"without lawful authority or
  reasonable excuse",
  9.27–9.32
Child sex offences
see also **Abuse of position of trust;
Child sexual abuse; Children;
Familial child sex offences;
Indecent photographs of
children; Sexual exploitation
of children**
arranging child sex offences
  acts done to protect child,
    4.180–4.184
  "arranges or facilitates",
    4.172–4.176
  "in any part of the world",
    4.177
  jurisdiction, 4.171

Child sex offences—*cont.*
arranging child sex
offences—*cont.*
maximum sentences,
4.163–4.167
meaning, 4.161–4.162
mens rea, 4.185
mode of trial, 4.163–4.167
offence, 4.160
parties to offence, 4.170
"sections 9 to 13", 4.178–4.179
sentencing, 4.168–4.169
causing children to engage in
sexual activity
"causes or incites another
person", 4.86
consent, 4.91
cybercrime, 4.77–4.80
incitement, 4.81–4.83
jurisdiction, 4.85
maximum sentences, 4.71–4.75
meaning, 4.68–4.70
mens rea, 4.92–4.93
mode of trial, 4.71–4.75
offence, 4.67
parties to offence, 4.84
"penetration", 4.89
sentencing, 4.76–4.83
"the activity is sexual", 4.88
"to engage in an activity", 4.87
"vagina", 4.90
causing children to watch sexual
acts
attempts, 4.131–4.132
"causes", 4.133
consent, 4.138
jurisdiction, 4.130
maximum sentences,
4.123–4.127
meaning, 4.122
mens rea, 4.139–4.143
mode of trial, 4.123–4.127
offences, 4.121
parties to offence, 4.129
sentencing, 4.128

Child sex offences—*cont.*
causing children to watch sexual
acts—*cont.*
"the activity is sexual", 4.137
"to watch a third person
engaging in an activity . . .
", 4.134–4.136
civil orders to protect children
from sexual exploitation,
4.18
committed by children or young
persons
introduction, 4.10–4.16
jurisdiction, 4.158
maximum sentences,
4.147–4.150
meaning, 4.145–4.146
mens rea, 4.159
mode of trial, 4.147–4.150
offence, 4.144
over 18 at time of sentencing,
4.156
parties to offence, 4.157
sentencing, 4.151–4.156
development of
developments subsequent to
2003 Act, 4.08
overlap with under-13 offences,
4.07
Sexual Offences Review,
4.02–4.06
engaging in sexual activity in
presence of children
consent, 4.116
"engages in sexual activity",
4.112
jurisdiction, 4.111
maximum sentences, 4.95–4.99
mens rea, 4.117–4.120
mode of trial, 4.95–4.99
offences, 4.94
parties to offence, 4.110
"present or . . . in a place from
which A can be
observed", 4.114–4.115

Child sex offences—*cont.*
  engaging in sexual activity in
    presence of children—*cont.*
    sentencing, 4.100–4.109
    "the activity is sexual", 4.113
  introduction, 4.01
  meeting children following sexual
    grooming
    "arranges to meet", 4.217
    attempts, 4.190
    consent, 4.220
    "during or after the meeting",
      4.218
    "has met or communicated",
      4.209–4.212
    jurisdiction, 4.208
    maximum sentences,
      4.191–4.195
    meaning, 4.187–4.189
    mens rea, 4.221–4.224
    mode of trial, 4.191–4.195
    offence, 4.186
    "on one or more occasions",
      4.213–4.215
    parties to offence, 4.207
    "relevant offence", 4.219
    sentencing, 4.196–4.206
    "travels with the intention of
      meeting . . . , 4.216
  multiple offending, 4.19
  possession of paedophile manuals
    "abusing children sexually",
      4.261
    "advice or guidance", 4.260
    defences, 4.262–4.263
    "item", 4.259
    jurisdiction, 4.257
    maximum sentences,
      4.250–4.253
    meaning, 4.249
    mens rea, 4.264
    mode of trial, 4.250–4.253
    offence, 4.248
    parties to offence, 4.256
    "possession", 4.258

Child sex offences—*cont.*
  possession of paedophile
    manuals—*cont.*
    restriction on prosecution,
      4.254
    sentencing, 4.255
  sexual activity with children
    consent, 4.64
    jurisdiction, 4.59
    maximum sentences, 4.26–4.30
    meaning, 4.21–4.25
    mens rea, 4.65–4.66
    mode of trial, 4.26–4.30
    offence, 4.20
    parties to offence, 4.56–4.58
    "penetration", 4.62
    sentencing, 4.31–4.55
    "the touching is sexual", 4.61
    "touches another person", 4.60
    "vagina", 4.63
  sexual communication with
    children
    attempts, 4.231
    "communicates", 4.240–4.242
    consent, 4.245
    "for the purpose of sexual
      gratification", 4.239
    jurisdiction, 4.238
    maximum sentences,
      4.232–4.235
    meaning, 4.226–4.230
    mens rea, 4.246–4.247
    mode of trial, 4.232–4.235
    offence, 4.225
    parties to offence, 4.237
    sentencing, 4.236
    "sexual", 4.243–4.244
  spouses, 4.17
  youth courts, 31.18
Child sexual abuse
  accommodation syndrome, 22.24
  genital signs of sexual abuse in
    boys, 22.58

Child sexual abuse—*cont.*
genital signs of sexual abuse in girls
abrasions, 22.50
bruising, 22.49
clefts and notches of the hymen, 22.53
erythema, 22.47
hymenal bumps or mounds, 22.54
hymenal transections, 22.52
hymenal width, 22.56
labial fusion, 22.57
lacerations, 22.51
oedema, 22.48
size of hymenal orifice, 22.55
Child sexual exploitation
see **Sexual exploitation of children**
Childhood memories
see **Memory**
Children
see also **Abuse of position of trust; Child abduction; Child sex offences; Disqualification from working with children; Familial child sex offences; Indecent photographs of children; Sexual exploitation of children**
after-care, 22.41
anonymity
defendants, 29.47–29.52
prohibiting identification of adult to protect child, 29.89–29.93
child sex offences committed by children
introduction, 4.10–4.16
jurisdiction, 4.158
maximum sentences, 4.147–4.150
meaning, 4.145–4.146
mens rea, 4.159
mode of trial, 4.147–4.150

Children—*cont.*
child sex offences committed by children—*cont.*
offence, 4.144
over 18 at time of sentencing, 4.156
parties to offence, 4.157
sentencing, 4.151–4.156
decisions to prosecute
cases involving, 17.21–17.27
public interest, 17.38–17.40
medical examinations
forensic physician qualifications, 22.08––22.10
location, 22.16
peer reviews, 22.12–22.15
process, 22.25–22.26
genital examination, 22.27–22.31
purposes, 22.05–22.07
single or two-doctor examinations, 22.11
timing, 22.17–22.19
rape, 1.88
reporting restrictions
applications for High Court order, 29.105
burden of proof on application, 29.74
challenging making variation or revocation, 29.86–29.88
concerned in criminal proceedings, 29.64–29.69
contravention, 29.70–29.73
framing directions, 29.83–29.85
inherent jurisdiction of Crown Court, 29.107
introduction, 29.06–29.10
legislative history, 29.58–29.59
lifetime reporting restrictions, 29.108–29.122
media interests, 29.106

Children—*cont.*
  reporting restrictions—*cont.*
    media representations,
      29.80–29.82
    not directly involved in
      proceedings, 29.94–29.107
    offences committed by,
      29.47–29.52
    principles governing decision
      to make, 29.75–29.79
    prohibiting identification of
      adult to protect child,
      29.89–29.93
    section 45 directions,
      29.64–29.93
    transitional provisions,
      29.61–29.63
  special measures, 27.15–26.16
Civil partnerships
  abuse of position of trust
    causing children to engage in
      sexual activity, 5.68
    causing children to watch
      sexual acts, 5.119
    engaging in sexual activity in
      presence of children, 5.95
    sexual activity with children,
      5.40–5.41
  evidence of, 19.123–19.129
  familial sex offences
    inciting child family member
      to engage in sexual
      activity, 6.70
    sexual activity with child
      family members, 6.51
  indecent photographs of children
    possession, 8.143
    taking, 8.75–8.81
  sexual intercourse with mental
    patients, 7.17
  social care workers
    causing mentally disordered
      persons to watch sexual
      acts, 7.287

Civil partnerships—*cont.*
  social care workers—*cont.*
    causing or inciting sexual
      activity, 7.251
    sexual activity in the presence
      of mentally disordered
      persons, 7.271
    sexual activity with mentally
      disordered persons, 7.235
Close relatives
  see **Relatives**
Co-accused
  assault by penetration, 2.16
Code for Crown Prosecutors
  youth courts, 31.10–31.11
Coercion
  sexual intercourse with animals,
    15.138–15.140
Collateral evidence
  generally, 19.91
  identifying, 19.92–19.96
  illustrative cases, 19.97–19.105
Collusion
  bad character
    cross-admissibility,
      20–123–20.130
  criminal evidence
    Northern Ireland, 32.67
  historic offences, 30.107–30.108
**Committing an offence with intent to
  commit a human trafficking
  offence**
  see **Human trafficking**
**Committing an offence with intent to
  commit a sexual offence**
  alternative verdicts, 14.43
  "any offence", 14.47
  introduction, 14.04–14.05
  jurisdiction, 14.46
  maximum sentence, 14.39–14.42
  meaning, 14.37–14.38
  mens rea, 14.48–14.50
  mode of trial, 14.39–14.42
  sentencing, 14.44–14.45

Common law
rape
capacity and consent,
1.226–1.229
Company officers
indecent photographs of children
possession, 8.129
taking, 8.42–8.43
Compellability
youth courts, 31.54
Compensation
historic offences, 30.79–30.81
Competence
vulnerable and intimidated
witnesses
delay in case coming to trial,
27.152–27.154
generally, 27.143–27.151
youth courts, 31.52–31.53
Complainants
see **Victims**
Complex or lengthy cases
assault by penetration of child
under 13, 3.83
causing children to engage in
sexual activity, 3.138
rape of child under 13, 3.33
sexual assault of child under 13,
3.108
Compulsory labour
see **Forced labour; Slavery**
Computers
sexual harm prevention orders,
36.29–36.34
Concealment
aggravating features
rape, 1.67
Conditions
sexual risk orders, 36.67
Confidentiality
disclosure, 18.92–18.98
DNA evidence
blood samples given in
confidence, 25.38

Confidentiality—*cont.*
medical evidence
adults, 21.19
children, 22.20–22.21
Confrontation
vulnerable adults, 28.22–28.30
Consent
abuse of position of trust
causing children to engage in
sexual activity, 5.70
causing children to watch
sexual acts, 5.121
engaging in sexual activity in
presence of children, 5.97
sexual activity with children,
5.46
administering substances with
intent, 14.31–14.32
apparent consent
sentencing sex offenders,
33.15–33.17
assault by penetration, 2.31
assault by penetration of child
under 13, 3.102
causing children to engage in
sexual activity, 3.167
causing sexual activity without
consent, 2.104
child sex offenses
causing children to engage in
sexual activity, 4.91
causing children to watch
sexual acts, 4.138
engaging in sexual activity in
presence of children, 4.116
meeting children following
sexual grooming, 4.220
sexual activity with children,
4.64
sexual communication with
children, 4.245
familial sex offences
inciting child family member
to engage in sexual
activity, 6.67

Consent—*cont.*
  familial sex offences—*cont.*
    sex with adult relatives, 6.91,
      6.104
    sexual activity with child
      family members, 6.46
  human trafficking, 11.108
  indecent photographs of children
    possession, 8.143
    taking, 8.75–8.81
  medical examinations
    adults, 21.21
  ostensible consent
    sentencing sex offenders,
      33.15–33.17
  outraging public decency,
    15.62–15.65
  police inquiries, 16.25–16.30
  rape
    absence of reasonable belief of
      consent, 1.374–1.397,
      1.403
    capacity, 1.222–1.262
    conclusive presumptions,
      1.310–1.370
    evidential presumptions,
      1.263–1.309
    introduction, 1.05–1.09
    meaning, 1.169–1.221
    mental disorder, 1.225,
      1.238–1.242
  rape of child under 13, 3.50–3.54,
    3.76
  sex offenders
    apparent consent, 33.15–33.17
    ostensible consent, 33.15–33.17
  sexual assault
    infliction of actual bodily
      harm, 2.109–2.113
    introduction, 2.06
    mens rea, 2.125–2.132
    reasonable belief, 2.83
    rough sex, 2.121–2.123
    sado-masochism, 2.114–2.120

Consent—*cont.*
  sexual assault—*cont.*
    sexual activity carrying risk to
      health, 2.124
    sexual assault of child under 13,
      3.129
    sexual behaviour of complainant
      contemporaneity, 26.80–26.82
      honest belief, 25.56–26.69
      similarity, 26.83–26.116
    sexual intercourse with animals,
      15.138–15.140
    slavery servitude and forced
      compulsory labour, 11.67
Conspiracy
  rape, 1.407–410
  rape of child under 13, 3.37
Contraception
  after-care for adults, 21.42
**Controlling children in relation to
    sexual exploitation**
  see also **Sexual exploitation of
      children**
  charge or indictment, 10.77
  "controls any of the activities of
    another person . . . ",
    10.81–10.82
  "in any part of the world", 10.84
  jurisdiction, 10.80
  maximum sentences, 10.72–10.76
  meaning, 10.70–10.71
  mens rea, 10.85–10.87
  mode of trial, 10.72–10.76
  offence, 10.69
  parties to offence, 10.79
  sentencing, 10.78
  "sexual exploitation", 10.83
Controlling prostitution for gain
  charge or indictment, 10.149
  "controls any of the activities of
    another person . . . ",
    10.153–10.158
  "for or in the expectation of
    gain", 10.161

Controlling prostitution for gain—*cont.*
"in any part of the world",
10.160
maximum sentences,
10.144–10.148
mens rea, 10.162
mode of trial, 10.144–10.148
offence, 10.143
parties to offence, 10.151–10.152
"prostitution", 10.159
sentencing, 10.150
Coordinated Prostitution Strategy (2006)
see **Keeping brothels; Prostitution**
Corpses
see **Sexual penetration of corpses**
Corroboration
case law, 19.108–19.116
complainant's apparent distress,
19.119–19.122
generally, 19.106–19.107
historic offences, 30.106
Makanjoula warning,
19.117–19.118
Course of conduct
historic offences, 30.18–30.23
rape, 1.30–1.31
Credibility
sexual behaviour of complainant,
26.139–26.149
Credit for time served
administering substances with
intent, 14.20
assault by penetration, 2.21
assault by penetration of child
under 13, 3.95
care workers engaging in sexual
activity in the presence of
mentally disordered persons,
7.261
care workers having sexual
activity with mentally
disordered persons, 7.218

Credit for time served—*cont.*
causing children to engage in
sexual activity, 3.149
causing prostitution for gain,
10.132
causing sexual activity without
consent, 2.95
causing sexual exploitation of
children, 10.52
engaging in sexual activity in
presence of children, 4.108,
5.85
engaging in sexual activity in
presence of mentally
disordered persons, 7.115
engaging in sexual activity in
presence procured by
inducement, threat or
deception of mentally
disordered persons, 7.182
exposure, 15.81
human trafficking, 11.89
keeping brothels, 12.51
meeting children following sexual
grooming, 4.202
paying for sexual services of
children, 10.24
procuring sexual activity with
mentally disordered persons
by inducement, threat or
deception, 7.151
rape of child under 13, 3.49
sex with adult relatives, 6.81
sexual activity with child family
members, 6.22
sexual activity with children,
4.42, 5.18
sexual activity with mentally
disordered persons, 7.57
sexual assault, 2.55
sexual assault of child under 13,
3.121
trespass with intent, 14.64
voyeurism, 15.109

Criminal evidence
civil partners, 19.123–19.129
collateral evidence
generally, 19.91
identifying, 19.92–19.96
illustrative cases, 19.97–19.105
corroboration
case law, 19.108–19.116
complainant's apparent
distress, 19.119–19.122
generally, 19.106–19.107
Makanjoula warning,
19.117–19.118
duplicity, 19.22–19.27
finality
generally, 19.91
identifying, 19.92–19.96
illustrative cases, 19.97–19.105
hearsay evidence
complainant who subsequently
died, 19.41
critical evidence, 19.39–19.40
dead witnesses, 19.51–19.52
earlier disclosure by very
young children,
19.55–19.61
frightened witnesses,
19.49–19.50
generally, 19.28
identifying, 19.29–19.34
interest of justice, 19.53–19.54
mental disorder, 19.47–19.48
res gestae, 19.62–19.63
statements by young child,
19.42–19.46
statutory scheme, 19.35–19.38
inconsistent statements
complainants, 19.67–19.71
earlier complaints by
complainant, 19.72–19.90
evidence of truth, 19.64
hostile witnesses, 19.65–19.66
introduction, 19.01–19.03
joinder, 19.04–19.09
multiple offending, 19.22–19.27

Criminal evidence—*cont.*
Northern Ireland
collusion, 32.67
cross-admissibility, 32.67
generally, 32.57–32.60
previous inconsistent
statements, 32.66
special measures for witnesses,
32.61–32.65
third party material, 32.68
severance
cross-admissibility as pre-
condition to, 19.14–19.17
generally, 19.10–19.13
indictments straddling
implementation of 2003
Act, 19.18–19.21
spouses, 19.123–19.129
warnings about reliance on
complainant's evidence
case law, 19.108–19.116
complainant's apparent
distress, 19.119–19.122
generally, 19.106–19.107
Makanjoula warning,
19.117–19.118
Criminal investigations
taking indecent photographs of
children, 8.82–8.85
Criminal proceedings
taking indecent photographs of
children, 8.82–8.85
"Cross-admissibility"
see also **Admissibility**
bad character
case law, 20.113–20.120
collusion, 20–123–20.130
consideration before summing
up, 20.131–20.134
generally, 20.111–20.112
propensity directions,
20.121–20.122
statistical assessment of
unlikelihood of
coincidence, 20.135–20.138

"Cross-admissibility"—*cont.*
pre-condition to severance,
19.14–19.17
Cross-examination
Northern Ireland, 32.64
special measures
pre-recorded, 27.43–27.48
supplementary questions, 27.54
video-recordings,
27.103–27.104
Crown Prosecution Service
see **Code for Crown Prosecutors;**
Decisions to prosecute
Culpability
administering substances with
intent, 14.14–14.17
assault by penetration, 2.17
assault by penetration of child
under 13, 3.90–3.91
care workers engaging in sexual
activity in the presence of
mentally disordered persons,
7.258
care workers having sexual
activity with mentally
disordered persons, 7.215
causing children to engage in
sexual activity, 3.144–3.145
causing prostitution for gain,
10.122–10.125
causing sexual activity without
consent, 2.92
causing sexual exploitation of
children, 10.45–10.48
engaging in sexual activity in
presence of children, 4.101,
4.105, 5.82
engaging in sexual activity in
presence of mentally
disordered persons, 7.112
engaging in sexual activity in
presence procured by
inducement, threat or
deception of mentally
disordered persons, 7.179

Culpability—*cont.*
exposure, 15.76–15.78
human trafficking, 11.82–11.83
keeping brothels, 12.47–12.48
meeting children following sexual
grooming, 4.197, 4.199
paying for sexual services of
children, 10.19–10.21
procuring sexual activity with
mentally disordered persons
by inducement, threat or
deception, 7.148
rape, 1.36–1.37, 1.44–1.52
rape of child under 13, 3.41–3.43
sex offenders, 33.12
sex with adult relatives, 6.78
sexual activity with child family
members, 6.19
sexual activity with children,
4.33, 4.35–4.38, 5.15
sexual activity with mentally
disordered persons, 7.54
sexual assault, 2.46–2.50
sexual assault of child under 13,
3.115–3.116
trespass with intent, 14.58–14.61
voyeurism, 15.104–15.106
"Custody probation orders"
Northern Ireland, 32.32–32.33
Cybercrime
causing children to engage in
sexual activity, 3.150–3.151,
4.77–4.80
sex offenders, 33.18
Dangerousness
administering substances with
intent, 14.20
assault by penetration, 2.21
assault by penetration of child
under 13, 3.84, 3.95
care workers engaging in sexual
activity in the presence of
mentally disordered persons,
7.261

Dangerousness—*cont.*

care workers having sexual activity with mentally disordered persons, 7.218

causing children to engage in sexual activity, 3.139, 3.149

causing prostitution for gain, 10.132

causing sexual activity without consent, 2.95

causing sexual exploitation of children, 10.52

engaging in sexual activity in presence of children, 4.108, 5.85

engaging in sexual activity in presence of mentally disordered persons, 7.115

engaging in sexual activity in presence procured by inducement, threat or deception of mentally disordered persons, 7.182

exposure, 15.81

historic offences, 30.161–30.166

human trafficking, 11.89

meeting children following sexual grooming, 4.202

Northern Ireland, 32.40–32.45

paying for sexual services of children, 10.24

procuring sexual activity with mentally disordered persons by inducement, threat or deception, 7.151

rape of child under 13, 3.34, 3.49

rape, 1.22, 1.78

sex offenders
determining dangerousness, 34.23–34.36
generally, 34.06

sex with adult relatives, 6.81

sexual activity with child family members, 6.22

Dangerousness—*cont.*

sexual activity with children, 4.42, 5.18

sexual activity with mentally disordered persons, 7.57

sexual assault, 2.55

sexual assault of child under 13, 3.109, 3.121

trespass with intent, 14.64

voyeurism, 15.109

youth courts
application of exception, 31.96–31.97
generally, 31.91–31.95
specified offences, 31.98

Death
hearsay evidence, 19.51–19.52

Deception
causing mentally disordered persons to engage in sexual activity by deception
"causes another person (B) to engage in . . . ", 7.169
"inducement, threat or deception", 7.168
jurisdiction, 7.167
maximum sentences, 7.161–7.164
mens rea, 7.172
"mental disorder", 7.171
mode of trial, 7.161–7.164
offence, 7.160
parties to offence, 7.166
sentencing, 7.165
"the activity is sexual", 7.170
causing mentally disordered persons to watch sexual acts by deception
"causes", 7.201
"inducement, threat or deception", 7.203
jurisdiction, 7.200
maximum sentences, 7.194–7.197
mens rea, 7.206–7.208

Deception—*cont.*
causing mentally disordered
persons to watch sexual acts
by deception—*cont.*
mode of trial, 7.194–7.197
offences, 7.193
parties to offence, 7.199
sentencing, 7.198
"the activity is sexual", 7.204
"to watch a third person
engaging in an activity . . .
", 7.202
engaging in sexual activity in
presence procured by
deception of mentally
disordered persons
"engages in an activity", 7.185
"inducement, threat or
deception", 7.188
jurisdiction, 7.184
maximum sentences,
7.174–7.177
mens rea, 7.190–7.192
"mental disorder", 7.189
mode of trial, 7.174–7.177
offence, 7.173
parties to offence, 7.183
"present or . . . in a place from
which A can be
observed", 7.187
sentencing, 7.178–7.182
"the activity is sexual", 7.186

Decisions to prosecute
abuse of process, 17.28–17.29
children
cases involving, 17.21–17.27
public interest, 17.38–17.40
evidential stage, 17.06–17.16
false allegations
CPS charging standards,
17.58–17.59
difficult issues, 17.60–17.65
generally, 17.48–17.57
full code test, 17.03–17.05

Decisions to prosecute—*cont.*
introduction, 17.01–17.02
public interest stage
child suspects, 17.38–17.40
generally, 17.35–17.37
non-recent cases where
nominal penalty likely,
17.41–17.47
reconsideration of decision not to
prosecute, 17.30–17.32
reporting restriction breaches,
17.66–17.69
victim's right of review scheme,
17.33–17.34
withdrawal of allegations,
17.17–17.20

Defences
indecent photographs of children
possession, 8.144
taking, 8.86–8.90
offensive behaviour
abusive or disorderly
behaviour, 15.197
insulting behaviour with intent
to harass, alarm or
distress, 15.177
possession of paedophile
manuals, 4.262–4.263
rape
voluntary intoxication,
1.398–1.401

Defendants
anonymity
children and young persons,
29.47–29.52
generally, 29.33–29.43
introduction, 29.04–29.05
legislative interventions, 29.44
teachers, 29.45–29.46
special measures
generally, 27.20–27.24
intermediaries, 27.31–27.40
live link, 27.25–27.30

Defendants in person
vulnerable and intimidated
witnesses
cross-examination of,
27.157–27.163
Delay
historic offences
abuse of process, 30.48
directions, 30.84–30.95
Northern Ireland, 32.69–32.73
Detention
assault by penetration, 2.16
Detention and training orders
youth courts, 31.104–31.106
"Determinate sentences"
inter-relationship with
indeterminate sentences,
34.40–34.51
Dip sampling
see **Historic offences**
Directions
historic offences
collusion, 30.107–30.108
corroboration, 30.106
delay, 30.84–30.95
inconsistencies, 30.83
irremediable prejudice, 30.96
late complaints, 30.102–30.105
lines of inquiry closed to
defence, 30.99–30.101
memory, 30.97–30.98
multiple counts, 30.83
Disabilities
rape, 1.52
Discharge
sexual harm prevention orders,
36.54
Disclosure
conclusions, 18.99–18.103
confidentiality, 18.92–18.98
Family Court, documents held by
2013 Protocol, 18.57,
18.67–18.68
circumstances justifying
disclosure, 18.49–18.52

Disclosure—*cont.*
Family Court, documents held
by—*cont.*
Family Procedure Rules,
18.39–18.46
legal professional privilege,
18.54–18.56
linked directions hearings,
18.58–18.66
Practice Direction 12G,
18.47–18.48
privilege against self-
incrimination, 18.53
Family Court, documents not
held by
2013 Protocol, 18.67–18.68
Criminal Procedure
(Attendance of Witnesses)
Act 1965, 18.76–18.81
Criminal Procedure Rules,
18.74–18.75
summons served, 18.82–18.88
test to be applied, 18.89–18.91
third party material in criminal
trial, 18.69–18.73
historic offences, 30.24–30.25
introduction, 18.01–18.09
medical examinations
adults, 21.22
prosecution duty to disclose
Criminal Procedure and
Investigations Act 1996,
18.10–18.21
limiting distribution,
18.26–18.31
public interest immunity,
18.22–18.25
right to respect for private and
family life, 18.92–18.98
third party material
generally, 18.32–18.33
procedure, 18.34–18.38
youth courts, 31.43–31.46
Discretion
see also **Exclusionary discretion**

Discretion—*cont.*
  prosecution of victims of human
      trafficking, 11.25–11.28
Discretionary life imprisonment
  rape, 1.92
  sex offenders, 34.07
Disorderly behaviour
  see **Anti-social behaviour**
Disorderly houses
  see **Keeping disorderly houses**
Disqualification from working with
    children
  sex offenders, 34.63–34.64
  youth courts, 31.136
DNA evidence
  see also **Expert evidence**
  admissibility
    blood samples given in
        confidence, 25.38
    Criminal Procedure Rules
        2015, 25.29–25.34
    generally, 25.24–25.28
    hearsay evidence, 25.35–25.36
    partial profile, 25.37
  assessing weight of
    cases based wholly or partly
        on DNA evidence,
        25.44–25.45
    generally, 25.39–25.43
  close relatives, 25.14
  conventional crime sample
      profile, 25.10
  DNA profiling
    generally, 25.04–25.08
    mixed profiles, 25.16–25.19
    partial profiles, 25.15
  DNA samples
    generally, 25.09
    mixed samples, 25.56–25.59
  Forensic Science Regulator,
      25.60–25.62
  introduction, 25.01
  linked topics, 25.20–25.23
  low template DNA
    contamination, 25.54–25.55

DNA evidence—*cont.*
  low template DNA—*cont.*
    generally, 25.46–25.53
  match probability, 25.13
  mixed profiles, 25.16–25.19
  mixed samples
    computer software, 25.57
    generally, 25.56
    non-statistical evaluation
        opinion, 25.58–25.59
  National DNA Database,
      25.63–25.66
  nature of, 25.02–25.03
  partial profiles, 25.15
  preparing a case involving, 25.67
  statistical evaluation, 25.11–25.12
  touch DNA, 25.21
  wearer's DNA, 25.22
Documents
  historic offences, 30.52–30.65
Doli incapax
  historic offences, 30.12–30.13
  Northern Ireland, 32.06
Domestic violence
  after-care for adults, 21.53–21.54
  aggravating features
    rape, 1.65–1.66
  sentencing sex offenders, 33.22
Double jeopardy
  rape, 1.142–1.143
Drugs
  drug-facilitated sexual assault
    medical evidence, 21.40
  rape
    aggravating features, 1.68
    incapacity, 1.402
    use on victim to facilitate
        offence, 1.46
Duplicity
  evidence, 19.22–19.27
Duration
  sexual harm prevention orders,
      36.50–36.52

Ecclesiastical courts
offences against public morals,
15.202

Elderly persons
historic offences, 30.119–30.126

Encouragement
rape
acting reasonably, 1.417
generally, 1.411–1.416
potential victims, 1.418

**Engaging in sexual activity in
presence of children**
abuse of position of trust
civil partners, 5.95
consent, 5.97
"engages in an activity", 5.90
jurisdiction, 5.89
maximum sentences, 5.77–5.80
meaning, 5.76
mens rea, 5.98–5.102
mode of trial, 5.77–5.80
offence, 5.75
parties to offence, 5.86–5.88
"position of trust", 5.93
pre-existing sexual
relationships, 5.96
"present or in a place from
which A can be
observed", 5.92
sentencing, 5.81–5.85
spouses, 5.95
"the activity is sexual", 5.91
"where subsection (2) applies",
5.94
consent, 4.116
"engages in sexual activity",
4.112
jurisdiction, 4.111
maximum sentences, 4.95–4.99
mens rea, 4.117–4.120
mode of trial, 4.95–4.99
offences, 4.94
parties to offence, 4.110

**Engaging in sexual activity in
presence of children**—*cont.*
"present or . . . in a place from
which A can be observed",
4.114–4.115
sentencing
aggravating features, 4.107
ancillary orders, 4.108
category range, 4.106
credit for time served, 4.108
culpability, 4.101, 4.105
dangerousness, 4.108
examples, 4.109
extended sentences, 4.108
generally, 4.100
guilty pleas, 4.108
harm, 4.101–4.104
mitigation, 4.107
proportionality, 4.108
reasons, 4.108
reduction of sentence, 4.108
starting point, 4.106
"the activity is sexual", 4.113

**Engaging in sexual activity in
presence of mentally disordered
persons**
see **Sexual offences against
mentally disordered persons;
Social care workers**

Evidence
see **Criminal evidence**

Evidence in chief
video recordings
exclusion of in interests of
justice, 27.82–27.85
generally, 27.68–27.81
jury access to video transcripts,
27.96–27.102
primary rule for child
witnesses, 27.50–27.53
replaying the video,
27.89–27.95
witness retraction, 27.86–27.88

Examination-in-chief
video recordings, 27.54

Exclusionary discretion
bad character
generally, 20.92–20.102
PACE s.78, 20.108
satellite litigation,
20.103–20.107
Expert evidence
see also **DNA evidence**
duties of expert, 24.16–24.19
general considerations in sex
cases, 24.20–24.22
introduction, 24.01
meaning, 24.02–24.06
memory
childhood memories,
24.34–24.42
false memory syndrome,
24.43–24.48
generally, 24.31–24.33
memory formation,
24.34–24.42
recovered memories,
24.43–24.48
mental condition
of defendant, 24.50–24.51
of victim, 24.49
psychological effects of sexual
assault, 24.23–24.30
reliability, 24.08–24.15
scope of, 24.07
sexual activity with mentally
disordered persons,
7.84–7.86
Exploitative conduct
causing prostitution for gain
"causes or incites",
10.134–10.135
"for or in the expectation of
gain", 10.140–10.141
"in any part of the world",
10.139
maximum sentences,
10.113–10.117
meaning, 10.112
mens rea, 10.142

Exploitative conduct—*cont.*
causing prostitution for
gain—*cont.*
mode of trial, 10.113–10.117
offence, 10.111
parties to offence, 10.133
"prostitute", 10.137–10.138
sentencing, 10.118–10.132
"to become", 10.136
controlling prostitution for gain
charge or indictment, 10.149
"controls any of the activities
of another person . . . ",
10.153–10.158
"for or in the expectation of
gain", 10.161
"in any part of the world",
10.160
maximum sentences,
10.144–10.148
mens rea, 10.162
mode of trial, 10.144–10.148
offence, 10.143
parties to offence,
10.151–10.152
"prostitution", 10.159
sentencing, 10.150
meaning, 10.169
overview, 10.105–10.110
paying for sexual services of
prostitutes subjected to force
"exploitative conduct", 10.169
"for or in the expectation of
gain", 10.170
maximum sentences, 10.165
mens rea, 10.171
mode of trial, 10.164
offence, 10.163
parties to offence, 10.166
"payment", 10.167
"sexual services of a
prostitute", 10.168
Exposure
"alarm or distress", 15.87
"exposes", 15.83–15.85

Exposure—*cont.*
"genitals", 15.86
introduction, 15.12–15.15
maximum sentences, 15.70–15.73
mens rea, 15.88–15.89
mode of trial, 15.70–15.73
offence, 15.69
parties to offence, 15.74
sentencing
   aggravating features, 15.80
   ancillary orders, 15.81
   category range, 15.79
   credit for time served, 15.81
   culpability, 15.76–15.78
   dangerousness, 15.81
   examples, 15.82
   extended sentences, 15.81
   generally, 15.75
   guilty pleas, 15.81
   harm, 15.76–15.78
   mitigation, 15.80
   proportionality, 15.81
   reasons, 15.81
   reduction of sentence, 15.81
   starting point, 15.79

Extended sentences
see also **Life imprisonment;**
   Maximum sentences;
   Sentencing
administering substances with
   intent, 14.11, 14.20
arranging child sex offences,
   4.165
arranging sexual exploitation of
   children, 10.93
assault by penetration, 2.11, 2.21
assault by penetration of child
   under 13, 3.84, 3.95
care workers causing or inciting
   sexual activity, 7.240
care workers engaging in sexual
   activity in the presence of
   mentally disordered persons,
   7.261

Extended sentences—*cont.*
care workers having sexual
   activity with mentally
   disordered persons, 7.218
causing children to engage in
   sexual activity, 4.73
causing children to watch sexual
   acts, 4.125, 5.107
causing mental disordered
   persons to engage in sexual
   activity, 7.94
causing mental disordered
   persons to engage in sexual
   activity by inducement,
   threat or deception, 7.163
causing mentally disordered
   persons to watch sexual acts,
   7.129, 7.275
causing mentally disordered
   persons to watch sexual acts
   by inducement, threat or
   deception, 7.196
causing prostitution for gain,
   10.115, 10.132
causing sexual activity without
   consent, 2.88, 2.95
causing sexual exploitation of
   children, 10.40, 10.52
committing an offence with
   intent to commit a sexual
   offence, 14.41
controlling children in relation to
   sexual exploitation, 10.74
controlling prostitution for gain,
   10.146
dangerous offenders committing
   offences before 4 April 2005,
   30.161
engaging in sexual activity in
   presence of children, 4.97,
   4.108, 5.79, 5.85
engaging in sexual activity in
   presence of mentally
   disordered persons , 7.109,
   7.115, 7.261

Extended sentences—*cont.*
engaging in sexual activity in
presence procured by
inducement, threat or
deception of mentally
disordered persons, 7.176,
7.182
exposure, 15.71, 15.81
historic offences, 30.164–30.165
human trafficking, 11.75, 11.89
inciting child family member to
engage in sexual activity,
6.59
inciting child under 13 to engage
in sexual activity, 3.139,
3.149
inciting children to engage in
sexual activity, 5.56
meeting children following sexual
grooming, 4.193, 4.202
Northern Ireland, 32.45
paying for sexual services of
children, 10.15, 10.24
procuring sexual activity with
mentally disordered persons
by inducement, threat or
deception, 7.145, 7.151
rape,1.78, 1.115
rape of child under 13, 3.34, 3.49
sex offenders
composition, 34.12
criteria, 34.11
defendants under 18,
34.14–34.15
generally, 34.10
introduction, 34.04
length, 34.12
release on licence, 34.13
statutory provisions, 34.16
sex with adult relatives, 6.75,
6.81, 6.97
sexual activity in the presence of
mentally disordered persons,
7.255, 7.261

Extended sentences—*cont.*
sexual activity with child family
members, 6.16, 6.22
sexual activity with children,
4.28, 4.42, 5.11, 5.18
sexual activity with mentally
disordered persons, 7.50,
7.57, 7.212, 7.218
sexual assault, 2.41, 2.55
sexual assault of child under 13,
3.109, 3.121
slavery, servitude and forced
compulsory labour, 11.61
taking indecent photographs of
children, 8.07, 8.30
trespass with intent, 14.55, 14.64
voyeurism, 15.93, 15.109
youth court, 31.92
Fabrication of evidence
sexual behaviour of complainant,
26.70–26.76
False memory syndrome
see **Memory**
False statements
decisions to prosecute
CPS charging standards,
17.58–17.59
difficult issues, 17.60–17.65
generally, 17.48–17.57
Familial child sex offences
see also **Sex with adult relatives**
eugenic debate, 6.07
"family" unit, 6.04
human rights, 6.08–6.11
introduction, 6.01
inciting child family member to
engage in sexual activity
civil partners, 6.70
consent, 6.67
"incites", 6.64
intoxication, 6.69
maximum sentences, 6.56–6.60
meaning, 6.55
mens rea, 6.68–6.69
mode of trial, 6.56–6.60

Familial child sex offences—*cont.*
inciting child family member to
engage in sexual
activity—*cont.*
offence, 6.54
parties to offence, 6.62–6.63
pre-existing sexual
relationships, 6.71
sentencing, 6.61
"sexual", 6.66
spouses, 6.70
"touch", 6.65
nature of modern family, 6.07
proscribed sexual activity,
6.08–6.11
related offences, 6.03
sexual activity with child family
members
civil partners, 6.51
consent, 6.46
introduction, 6.02
jurisdiction, 6.43
maximum sentences, 6.14–6.17
mens rea, 6.47–6.50
mode of trial, 6.13–6.14
offence, 6.12
parties to offence, 6.28–6.42
pre-existing sexual
relationships, 6.52–6.53
sentencing, 6.18–6.27
"sexual", 6.45
spouses, 6.51
"touches", 6.44
youth courts, 31.19
Family Court
disclosure of documents held by
2013 Protocol, 18.57,
18.67–18.68
circumstances justifying
disclosure, 18.49–18.52
Family Procedure Rules,
18.39–18.46
legal professional privilege,
18.54–18.56

Family Court—*cont.*
disclosure of documents held
by—*cont.*
linked directions hearings,
18.58–18.66
Practice Direction 12G,
18.47–18.48
privilege against self-
incrimination, 18.53
disclosure of documents not held
by
2013 Protocol, 18.67–18.68
Criminal Procedure
(Attendance of Witnesses)
Act 1965, 18.76–18.81
Criminal Procedure Rules,
18.74–18.75
summons served, 18.82–18.88
test to be applied, 18.89–18.91
third party material in criminal
trial, 18.69–18.73
Finality
evidence
generally, 19.91
identifying, 19.92–19.96
illustrative cases, 19.97–19.105
Fitness to plead
sexual assault, 2.43
voyeurism, 15.96–15.101
Forced labour
see also **Human trafficking;**
Slavery
"all the circumstances, 11.66
consent, 11.67
maximum sentences, 11.60–11.64
mens rea, 11.71
mode of trial, 11.60–11.64
offence, 11.59
sentencing, 11.65
victim support, 11.68–11.70
Foreign travel
advance notification, 35.45
Foreign travel orders
history, 36.04

Foreign travel orders—*cont.*
replacement of, 36.05–36.06, 36.12
Foreign travel prohibition requirements
sexual harm prevention orders, 36.45–36.47
Forensic evidence
taking indecent photographs of children, 8.105–8.111
Forensic samples
children, 22.39–22.40
Forensic Science Regulator
role of, 25.60–25.62
Forfeiture
slavery and human trafficking forfeiture and detention of land vehicles, ships and aircraft, 11.118–11.119
Frightened witnesses
see **Hearsay evidence**
Genitalia
anal anatomy, 22.38
ano-genital injuries
adults, 21.35–21.36
interpretation of findings, 22.42–22.46
female genital mutilation, 22.68–22.74
genital examinations of children, 22.27–22.31
females, 22.32–22.35
hymen, 22.52–22.56
interpretation of ano-genital findings, 22.42–22.46
males, 22.36
signs of sexual abuse in boys, 22.58
signs of sexual abuse in girls
abrasions, 22.50
bruising, 22.49
erythema, 22.47
hymen, 22.52–22.56
labial fusion, 22.57
lacerations, 22.51

Genitalia—*cont.*
signs of sexual abuse in girls—*cont.*
oedema, 22.48
Tanner stages, 22.37
Gillick competence
medical evidence of children, 22.22
Good character
see also **Bad character**
sentencing
historic offences, 30.141
sex offenders, 33.20
Goodyear indications
sex offenders, 34.38–34.39
Grave crimes
see **Serious offences**
Grooming
see **Sexual grooming**
Gross indecency
historic offences, 30.158
Ground rules hearings
vulnerable witnesses, 28.31–28.40
Guardians
attendance in youth court, 31.36
Guilty pleas
administering substances with intent, 14.20
assault by penetration, 2.21
assault by penetration of child under 13, 3.95
care workers engaging in sexual activity in the presence of mentally disordered persons, 7.261
care workers having sexual activity with mentally disordered persons, 7.218
causing children to engage in sexual activity, 3.149
causing prostitution for gain, 10.132
causing sexual activity without consent, 2.95

Guilty pleas—*cont.*
causing sexual exploitation of
children, 10.52
engaging in sexual activity in
presence of children, 4.108,
5.85
engaging in sexual activity in
presence of mentally
disordered persons, 7.115
engaging in sexual activity in
presence procured by
inducement, threat or
deception of mentally
disordered persons, 7.182
exposure, 15.81
human trafficking, 11.89
keeping brothels, 12.51
meeting children following sexual
grooming, 4.202
paying for sexual services of
children, 10.24
procuring sexual activity with
mentally disordered persons
by inducement, threat or
deception, 7.151
rape of child under 13, 3.49
sex with adult relatives, 6.81
sexual activity with child family
members, 6.22
sexual activity with children,
4.42, 5.18
sexual activity with mentally
disordered persons, 7.57
sexual assault, 2.55
sexual assault of child under 13,
3.121
trespass with intent, 14.64
voyeurism, 15.109
Harm
see **Psychiatric harm; Sentencing**
Health
historic offences, 30.119–30.126
Hearsay evidence
admissibility, 25.35–25.36

Hearsay evidence—*cont.*
complainant who subsequently
died, 19.41
critical evidence, 19.39–19.40
dead witnesses, 19.51–19.52
earlier disclosure by very young
children, 19.55–19.61
frightened witnesses, 19.49–19.50
generally, 19.28
identifying, 19.29–19.34
interest of justice, 19.53–19.54
mental disorders, 19.47–19.48
res gestae, 19.62–19.63
statements by young child,
19.42–19.46
statutory scheme, 19.35–19.38
Hepatitis
after-care for adults, 21.47
Historic offences
abuse of process
civil court decisions,
30.50–30.51
correct approach, 30.28–30.36
dip sampling, 30.82
earlier complaints, 30.77–30.78
examples of application of
principles, 30.39–30.48
financial compensation,
30.79–30.81
guidance derived from
authorities, 30.37–30.38
length of delay, 30.48
missing documents,
30.52–30.65
previous police investigations,
30.66–30.76
procedure, 30.26–30.27
promises not to prosecute,
30.66–30.76
significant inconsistencies,
30.49
trawling, 30.82
withdrawn complaints,
30.77–30.78
collusion, 30.107–30.108

Historic offences—*cont.*
corroboration, 30.106
continuing course of conduct,
    30.18–30.23
delay
    abuse of process, 30.48
    directions, 30.84–30.95
dip sampling, 30.82
directions
    collusion, 30.107–30.108
    corroboration, 30.106
    delay, 30.84–30.95
    inconsistencies, 30.83
    irremediable prejudice, 30.96
    late complaints, 30.102–30.105
    lines of inquiry closed to
        defence, 30.99–30.101
    memory, 30.97–30.98
    multiple counts, 30.83
disclosure, 30.24–30.25
doli incapax, 30.12–30.13
financial compensation,
    30.79–30.81
inconsistencies
    abuse of process, 30.49
    directions, 30.83
indictments
    continuing course of conduct,
        30.18–30.23
    generally, 30.15–30.17
introduction, 30.01
irremediable prejudice, 30.96
late complaints, 30.102–30.105
limitation periods, 30.08–30.11
memory, 30.97–30.98
missing documents, 30.52–30.65
multiple counts, 30.83
Northern Ireland, 32.47
presumption of incapability of
    intercourse in boys under 14,
    30.14
previous police investigations,
    30.66–30.76
promises not to prosecute,
    30.66–30.76

Historic offences—*cont.*
response of courts, 30.02–30.07
sentencing
    approach to, 30.110–30.114
    attempted rape, 30.148–30.151
    celebrity status, 30.127–30.132
    dangerous offenders,
        30.161–30.166
    declining health, 30.119–30.126
    elderly offenders,
        30.119–30.126
    exceptional circumstances,
        30.133–30.138
    extended sentences,
        30.164–30.165
    failure to obtain permission to
        institute proceedings,
        30.159–30.160
    generally, 30.109
    good character since offending,
        30.141
    gross indecency with a child,
        30.158
    immaturity at time of offence,
        30.115–30.118E
    indecent assault, 30.152–30.155
    lack of clarity on commission
        before or after 4 April
        2005, 30.167
    licensing regime changes,
        30.142
    life sentences, 30.162–30.163
    longer than commensurate
        sentences, 30.166
    maximum sentences,
        30.143–30.160
    medical needs in custody,
        30.139–30.140
    rape, 30.146–30.147
    sex offenders, 33.06–33.11
    sexual intercourse with girls
        under 13 or 16,
        30.156–30.157

Historic offences—*cont.*
sentencing—*cont.*
young offenders,
30.115–30.118E
trawling, 30.82
withdrawn complaints,
30.77–30.78
Honest belief
sexual behaviour of complainant,
25.56–26.69
Honeyball Report
see **Keeping Brothels; Prostitution**
Hostile witnesses
inconsistent statements,
19.65–19.66
Human rights
abusive or disorderly behaviour,
15.183
sexual behaviour of complainant,
26.99–26.101
sexual intercourse with mental
patients, 7.42–7.46
Human trafficking
see also **Slavery**
"arranges of facilitates",
11.96–11.99
committing and offence with
intent to commit a human
trafficking offence
maximum sentence, 11.115
mens rea, 11.116
mode of trial, 11.115
offence, 11.114
consent, 11.108
Council of Europe Trafficking
Convention, 11.09–11.12
EU Directive on Trafficking in
Human Beings
2003 Act offences, 11.16–11.18
generally, 11.13–11.15
secondary legislation,
11.19–11.21
"exploitation", 11.101–11.106
"in any part of the world",
11.107

Human trafficking—*cont.*
jurisdiction, 11.95
maximum sentences, 11.74–11.78
mens rea, 11.110–11.113
mode of trial, 11.74–11.78
offence, 11.72
prosecution of victims of
trafficking
abuse of process, 11.29–11.35
CPS guidance, 11.36
generally, 11.22
prosecutorial discretion,
11.25–11.28
statutory defence under 2015
Act, 11.37–11.43
Trafficking Convention,
11.23–11.24
sentencing
aggravating features,
11.86–11.88
ancillary orders, 11.89
category range, 11.84–11.85
credit for time served, 11.89
culpability, 11.82–11.83
dangerousness, 11.89
examples, 11.90–11.94
generally, 11.79
guilty pleas, 11.89
harm, 11.80–11.81
mitigation, 11.86–11.88
proportionality, 11.89
reasons, 11.89
reduction of sentence, 11.89
starting point, 11.84–11.85
Sexual Offences Act 2003,
11.05–11.08
"travel", 11.100
victim support, 11.109
Hymen
see **Genitalia**
Imprisonment for public protection
rape, 1.93–1.105
sex offenders, 34.08–34.09

Incitement

care workers inciting sexual
   activity

   "causes or incites another
      person . . . to engage in an
      activity", 7.245

   civil partners, 7.251

   jurisdiction, 7.244

   maximum sentences,
      7.238–7.241

   mens rea, 7.248–7.250

   "mental disorder", 7.247

   mode of trial, 7.238–7.241

   offence, 7.237

   parties to offence, 7.243

   pre-existing sexual
      relationships, 7.251

   sentencing, 7.242

   spouses, 7.251

   "the activity is sexual", 7.246

inciting child family member to
   engage in sexual activity

   civil partners, 6.70

   consent, 6.67

   "incites", 6.64

   intoxication, 6.69

   maximum sentences, 6.56–6.60

   meaning, 6.55

   mens rea, 6.68–6.69

   mode of trial, 6.56–6.60

   offence, 6.54

   parties to offence, 6.62–6.63

   pre-existing sexual
      relationships, 6.71

   sentencing, 6.61

   "sexual", 6.66

   spouses, 6.70

   "touch", 6.65

inciting children to engage in
   sexual activity

   bail, 3.141

   "causes or incites another
      person", 3.158–3.163,
      4.86, 5.63

   "child under 13", 3.166

Incitement—*cont.*

inciting children to engage in
   sexual activity—*cont.*

   "where subsection (2) applies",
      5.67

   civil partners, 5.68

   classification, 3.138

   complex cases, 3.138

   consent, 3.167, 4.91, 5.70

   jurisdiction, 3.157, 4.85, 5.62

   maximum sentences, 4.71–4.75,
      5.54–5.57

   meaning, 3.131–3.135,
      4.68–4.70, 5.52–5.53

   mens rea, 3.168–3.170,
      4.92–4.93, 5.71–5.774

   mode of trial, 3.136–3.137,
      4.71–4.75, 5.54–5.57

   notification requirements, 3.140

   offence, 4.67, 5.51

   parties, 3.155–3.156, 4.84,
      5.59–5.61

   "penetration", 4.89

   "position of trust", 5.66

   pre-existing sexual
      relationships, 5.69

   sentencing, 3.139, 3.142–3.154,
      4.76–4.83, 5.58

   specified offences, 3.139

   spouses, 5.68

   systematic abuse, 3.138

   "the activity is sexual", 3.165,
      4.88, 5.65

   "to engage in an activity",
      3.164, 4.87, 5.64

   "vagina", 4.90

inciting mentally disordered
   persons to engage in sexual
   activity

   bail, 7.96

   "because of or for a reason
      related to a mental
      disorder", 7.103

Incitement—*cont.*
  inciting mentally disordered
    persons to engage in sexual
    activity—*cont.*
    "causes or incites another
      person . . . to engage in an
      activity", 7.100
    jurisdiction, 7.99
    maximum sentences, 7.92–7.95
    mens rea, 7.104–7.105
    mode of trial, 7.92–7.95
    offence, 7.91
    parties to offence, 7.98
    sentencing, 7.97
    "the activity is sexual", 7.101
    "unable to refuse, 7.102
  inciting prostitution for gain
    "causes or incites",
      10.134–10.135
    "for or in the expectation of
      gain", 10.140–10.141
    "in any part of the world",
      10.139
    maximum sentences,
      10.113–10.117
    meaning, 10.112
    mens rea, 10.142
    mode of trial, 10.113–10.117
    offence, 10.111
    parties to offence, 10.133
    "prostitute", 10.137–10.138
    sentencing, 10.118–10.132
    "to become", 10.136
  inciting sexual exploitation of
    children
    "causes or incites",
      10.57–10.58
    "in any part of the world",
      10.65
    jurisdiction, 10.56
    maximum sentences,
      10.38–10.42
    meaning, 10.36–10.37
    mens rea, 10.66–10.68
    mode of trial, 10.38–10.42

Incitement—*cont.*
  inciting sexual exploitation of
    children—*cont.*
    offence, 10.35
    parties to offence, 10.55
    sentencing, 10.43–10.54
    "to be sexually exploited",
      10.59–10.64
Inconsistencies
  see **Previous inconsistent
    statements**
Indecent assault
  historic offences, 30.152–30.155
Indecent photographs of children
  introduction, 8.01–8.02
  possession of indecent
    photographs of children
    "child", 8.131–8.133
    company officers, 8.129
    consent within marriage or
      other relationship, 8.143
    defences, 8.144
    form of charge or indictment,
      8.124–8.125
    "indecent photographs or
      pseudo-photographs",
      8.130
    jurisdiction, 8.128–8.129
    maximum sentences,
      8.120–8.122
    mens rea, 8.145
    mode of trial, 8.120–8.122
    offence, 8.119
    parties to offence, 8.127
    "possession", 8.134–8.142
    restriction on prosecution,
      8.123
    sentencing, 8.126
  sex offenders, 33.12
  taking indecent photographs of
    children
    "child", 8.57–8.60
    company officers, 8.42–8.43

Indecent photographs of children—*cont.*
taking indecent photographs of children—*cont.*
consent within marriage or other relationship, 8.75–8.81
criminal proceedings or investigations, 8.82–8.85
defences, 8.86–8.90
"distribute or show", 8.64–8.70
forensic evidence, 8.105–8.111
form of charge or indictment, 8.14
"have in his possession . . . with a view to their being distributed or shown", 8.71–8.73
"indecent", 8.44–8.51
jurisdiction, 8.41–8.43
maximum sentence, 8.04–8.08
mens rea, 8.91–8.104
mode of trial, 8.04–8.08
offence, 8.03
parties to offence, 8.39–8.40
"permit to be taken", 8.63
perverting the course of justice by deleting images, 8.118
"photograph", 8.52–8.53
"pseudo-photograph", 8.54–8.56
"publish or cause to be published", 8.74
recovery of encrypted images, 8.112–8.117
restriction on prosecution, 8.09–8.13
sentencing, 8.15–8.38
"to take . . . or to make", 8.61–8.62
Independent sexual violence advisers
see **Victim support**
Indeterminate sentences
sex offenders, 34.40–34.51

Indictments
causing children to engage in sexual activity
multiple offences, 3.24–3.28
controlling children in relation to sexual exploitation, 10.77
controlling prostitution for gain, 10.149
course of conduct
historic offences, 30.18–30.23
rape, 1.30–1.31
historic offences
course of conduct, 30.18–30.23
generally, 30.15–30.17
indecent photographs of children
possession, 8.124–8.125
taking, 8.14
joinder of counts
rape, 1.146–1.147
multiple counts
historic offences, 30.83
rape, 1.30–1.31
outraging public decency, 15.31
rape
course of conduct, 1.30–1.31
mode of trial, 1.20
multiple incident counts, 1.30–1.31
specimen counts, 1.26–1.29
severance
indictments straddling implementation of 2003 Act, 19.18–19.21
specimen counts
rape, 1.26–1.29
Inducements
causing mentally disordered persons to engage in sexual activity by inducement
"causes another person (B) to engage in . . . ", 7.169
"inducement, threat or deception", 7.168
jurisdiction, 7.167

Inducements—*cont.*
causing mentally disordered
  persons to engage in sexual
  activity by
  inducement—*cont.*
maximum sentences,
  7.161–7.164
mens rea, 7.172
"mental disorder", 7.171
mode of trial, 7.161–7.164
offence, 7.160
parties to offence, 7.166
sentencing, 7.165
"the activity is sexual", 7.170
causing mentally disordered
  persons to watch sexual acts
  by inducement
"causes", 7.201
"inducement, threat or
  deception", 7.203
jurisdiction, 7.200
maximum sentences,
  7.194–7.197
mens rea, 7.206–7.208
mode of trial, 7.194–7.197
offences, 7.193
parties to offence, 7.199
sentencing, 7.198
"the activity is sexual", 7.204
"to watch a third person
  engaging in an activity . . .
  ", 7.202
engaging in sexual activity in
  presence procured by
  inducement of mentally
  disordered persons
"engages in an activity", 7.185
"inducement, threat or
  deception", 7.188
jurisdiction, 7.184
maximum sentences,
  7.174–7.177
mens rea, 7.190–7.192
"mental disorder", 7.189
mode of trial, 7.174–7.177

Inducements—*cont.*
engaging in sexual activity in
  presence procured by
  inducement of mentally
  disordered persons—*cont.*
offence, 7.173
parties to offence, 7.183
"present or . . . in a place from
  which A can be
  observed", 7.187
sentencing, 7.178–7.182
"the activity is sexual", 7.186
Insulting behaviour
see **Offensive behaviour**
Intention
see also **Mens rea; Preparatory
  offences**
sexual assault, 2.78–2.80
Interim orders
notification orders, 35.65–35.66
sexual harm prevention orders,
  36.20
sexual risk orders, 36.72
Intermediaries
Northern Ireland, 32.63
special measures
  defendants, 27.31–27.40
  generally, 27.105–27.114
Internet
sexual harm prevention orders,
  36.29–36.34
Intimidation of witnesses
aggravating features
  rape, 1.67
Intoxication
familial sex offences
  inciting child family member
    to engage in sexual
    activity, 6.69
  sex with adult relatives, 6.93,
    6.106
  sexual activity with child
    family members, 6.50
rape
  alcohol, 1.402

Intoxication—*cont.*
rape—*cont.*
drugs, 1.402
self-induced intoxication,
1.398–1.401
sexual assault, 2.81–2.82
special measures for witnesses,
27.19
Joinder of counts
evidence, 19.04–19.09
rape, 1.146–1.147
Judicial ticketing
see **Vulnerable and intimidated
witnesses**
Jurisdiction
abuse of position of trust
causing children to engage in
sexual activity, 5.62
causing children to watch
sexual acts, 5.113
engaging in sexual activity in
presence of children, 5.89
sexual activity with children,
5.28
administering substances with
intent, 14.26
assault by penetration, 2.25
assault by penetration of child
under 13, 3.98
causing children to engage in
sexual activity, 3.157
causing sexual activity without
consent, 2.97
child sex offences
arranging child sex offences,
4.171
causing children to engage in
sexual activity, 4.85
causing children to watch
sexual acts, 4.130
committed by children, 4.158
engaging in sexual activity in
presence of children, 4.111
meeting children following
sexual grooming, 4.208

Jurisdiction—*cont.*
child sex offences—*cont.*
possession of paedophile
manuals, 4.257
sexual activity with children,
4.59
sexual communication with
children, 4.238
committing an offence with
intent to commit a sexual
offence, 14.46
human trafficking, 11.95
mentally disordered persons
causing mentally disordered
persons to engage in
sexual activity, 7.99
causing mentally disordered
persons to engage in
sexual activity by
inducement, threat or
deception, 7.167
causing mentally disordered
persons to watch sexual
acts, 7.133
causing mentally disordered
persons to watch sexual
acts by inducement, threat
or deception, 7.200
engaging in sexual activity in
presence of mentally
disordered persons, 7.117
engaging in sexual activity in
presence procured by
inducement, threat or
deception of mentally
disordered persons, 7.184
procuring sexual activity with
mentally disordered
persons by inducement,
threat or deception, 7.153
sexual activity with mentally
disordered persons, 7.62
paying for sexual services of
children, 10.26
rape, 1.154

Jurisdiction—*cont.*
rape of child under 13, 3.72
sexual activity with child family
members, 6.43
sexual assault, 2.62
sexual assault of child under 13,
3.126
sexual exploitation of children
arranging or facilitating, 10.89
causing, 10.56
controlling children in relation
to sexual exploitation,
10.80
social care workers
causing mentally disordered
persons to watch sexual
acts, 7.279
causing or inciting sexual
activity, 7.244
sexual activity in the presence
of mentally disordered
persons, 7.263
sexual activity with mentally
disordered persons, 7.223
trespass with intent, 14.67
Jury directions
bad character, 20.109–20.110
Keeping a common bawdy house
see **Keeping disorderly houses**
Keeping brothels
see also **Brothels; Keeping
disorderly houses;
Prostitution; Soliciting**
Canada, 12.15–12.20
charges, 12.24, 12.45
development of law
All-Party Parliamentary Group
on Prostitution,
12.12–12.14
Coordinated Prostitution
Strategy, 12.06–12.08
Honeyball Report, 12.12–12.14
other offences, 12.04–12.05

Keeping brothels—*cont.*
development of law—*cont.*
Sexual Offences Act 1956,
12.02–12.03
Tackling the Demand for
Prostitution: A Review
(2008), 12.09–12.11
introduction, 12.01
maximum sentences
s.33 offence, 12.22–12.23
s.33A offence, 12.43–12.44
meaning
"a house" 12.28–12.30
"brothel", 12.27, 12.54
"for the purposes of
prostitution", 12.33–12.35
generally, 12.21, 12.42
"prostitution", 12.55
"resorted to or used by more
than one woman",
12.31–12.32
"to act or assist in the
management",
12.37–12.39, 12.53
"to keep", 12.26, 12.53
"to manage", 12.36, 12.53
mode of trial, 12.22–12.23,
12.43–12.44
necessity, 12.56
parties to offence, 12.25, 12.52
proof, 12.40–12.41
sentencing
aggravating features, 12.50
ancillary orders, 12.51
category range, 12.49
credit for time served, 12.51
culpability, 12.47–12.48
guideline, 12.46
guilty pleas, 12.51
harm, 12.47–12.48
mitigation, 12.50
proportionality, 12.51
reasons, 12.51
reduction of sentence, 12.51

Keeping brothels—*cont.*
sentencing—*cont.*
starting point, 12.49
Keeping disorderly houses
see also **Brothels; Keeping
brothels; Prostitution;
Soliciting**
"disorderly house", 12.92
introduction, 12.85
"keep", 12.88–12.91
keeping a common bawdy house,
12.96
maximum sentences, 12.86
mens rea, 12.95
mode of trial, 12.86
provision of sexual services,
12.93–12.94
sentencing, 12.87
**Knowingly permitting prostitutes to
meet and remain in house of
refreshment**
see **Prostitution**
Landlords
letting premises for use as brothel
"brothel", 12.62
"lessor or landlord . . . or
agent", 12.60–12.61
maximum sentence, 12.58
meaning, 12.57
mode of trial, 12.58
parties to offence, 12.59
"to be willfully a party to that
use continuing", 12.64
"with the knowledge that it is
to be used", 12.63
Late complaints
historic offences, 30.102–30.105
Learning difficulties
sexual behaviour of complainant,
26.69
Learning disabilities
medical evidence , 21.11
rape
mitigation, 1.74

Legal professional privilege
disclosure, 18.54–18.56
Life imprisonment
see also **Extended sentences;
Maximum sentences;
Sentencing**
arranging child sex offences,
4.165
arranging sexual exploitation of
children, 10.93
assault by penetration, 2.11, 2.21
assault by penetration of child
under 13, 3.84, 3.95
automatic life imprisonment for
sex offenders, 34.17–34.22
causing children to engage in
sexual activity, 3.139, 3.149,
4.73
causing children to watch sexual
acts, 4.125
causing mentally disordered
persons to engage in sexual
activity, 7.94
causing mentally disordered
persons to engage in sexual
activity by inducement,
threat or deception, 7.163
causing sexual exploitation of
children, 10.40, 10.52
committing an offence with
intent to commit a sexual
offence, 14.41
discretionary life imprisonment
for sex offenders, 34.07
controlling children in relation to
sexual exploitation, 10.74
engaging in sexual activity in
presence of children, 4.97,
4.108
historic offences, 30.162–30.163
human trafficking, 11.75, 32.15,
32.19
inciting child family member to
engage in sexual activity,
6.59

Life imprisonment—*cont.*
inciting child under 13 to engage in sexual activity, 3.139, 3.149
meeting children following sexual grooming, 4.193, 4.202
Northern Ireland, 32.15, 32.19, 32.30, 32.43
paying for sexual services of children, 10.15
procuring sexual activity with mentally disordered persons by inducement, threat or deception, 7.145, 7.151
rape
automatic life imprisonment, 1.107–1.109
dangerousness, 1.78
discretionary life imprisonment, 1.92
extended sentences, 1.115
imprisonment for public protection, 1.93–1.105
introduction, 1.91
secondary form of discretionary life sentences, 1.106
whole life orders, 1.110–1.114
rape of child under 13, 3.34, 3.49
sexual activity with child family members, 6.16, 6.22
sexual activity with children, 4.28, 4.42
sexual activity with mentally disordered persons , 7.50, 7.57
sexual assault, 2.41, 2.55
sexual assault of child under 13, 3.109, 3.121
slavery, servitude and forced compulsory labour, 11.61
taking indecent photographs of children, 8.07
Limitation periods
historic offences, 30.08–30.11

Listing
vulnerable and intimidated witnesses, 27.135
Live link evidence
defendants, 27.25–27.30
generally, 27.62–27.65
live link room, 27.141–27.142
Northern Ireland, 32.65
primary rule for child witnesses, 27.50–27.53
vulnerable witnesses, 28.43
Loitering for purposes of prostitution
see **Soliciting**
Looked-after children
child abduction
child abduction warning notices, 9.54
"keeps away", 9.58
maximum sentences, 9.53
mens rea, 9.61
mode of trial, 9.53
offence, 9.52
parties to offence, 9.55
"responsible person", 9.60
"run away or stay away", 9.59
"without lawful authority or reasonable excuse", 9.56–9.57
indecent photographs of children
possession, 8.128–8.129
taking, 8.41–8.43
Low template DNA
see **DNA evidence**
Marital rape
see **Rape; Spouses**
Maximum sentences
see also **Extended sentences; Life imprisonment; Sentencing**
abuse of position of trust
causing children to engage in sexual activity, 5.54–5.57
causing children to watch sexual acts, 5.105–5.108

Maximum sentences—*cont.*
abuse of position of trust—*cont.*
engaging in sexual activity in
presence of children,
5.77–5.80
sexual activity with children,
5.09–5.13
abusive or disorderly behaviour,
15.184
administering substances with
intent, 14.09–14.12
assault by penetration of child
under 13, 3.82
brothels
allowing a person under 16 to
be in a brothel, 12.98
landlord letting premises for
use as brothel, 12.58
tenant permitting premises to
be used as brothel, 12.66
causing children to engage in
sexual activity, 3.136–3.137
child abduction
generally, 9.10–9.11
looked-after children, 9.53
child sex offences
arranging child sex offences,
4.163–4.167
causing children to engage in
sexual activity, 4.71–4.75
causing children to watch
sexual acts, 4.123–4.127
committed by children,
4.147–4.150
engaging in sexual activity in
presence of children,
4.95–4.99
meeting children following
sexual grooming,
4.191–4.195
possession of paedophile
manuals, 4.250–4.253
sexual activity with children,
4.26–4.30

Maximum sentences—*cont.*
child sex offences—*cont.*
sexual communication with
children, 4.232–4.235
committing and offence with
intent to commit a human
trafficking offence, 11.115
committing an offence with
intent to commit a sexual
offence, 14.39–14.42
exposure, 15.70–15.73
familial sex offences
inciting child family member
to engage in sexual
activity, 6.56–6.60
sex with adult relatives,
6.73–6.76, 6.95–6.98
sexual activity with child
family members, 6.14–6.17
historic offences, 30.143–30.160
human trafficking, 11.74–11.78
indecent photographs of children
possession, 8.120–8.122
taking, 8.04–8.08
insulting behaviour, 15.164
insulting behaviour with intent to
harass, alarm or distress,
15.173
keeping brothels
s.33 offence, 12.22–12.23
s.33A offence, 12.43–12.44
keeping disorderly houses, 12.86
mentally disordered persons
causing mentally disordered
persons to engage in
sexual activity, 7.92–7.95
causing mentally disordered
persons to engage in
sexual activity by
inducement, threat or
deception, 7.161–7.164
causing mentally disordered
persons to watch sexual
acts, 7.127–7.130

Maximum sentences—*cont.*
mentally disordered
persons—*cont.*
causing mentally disordered
persons to watch sexual
acts by inducement, threat
or deception, 7.194–7.197
engaging in sexual activity in
presence of mentally
disordered persons,
7.107–7.110
engaging in sexual activity in
presence procured by
inducement, threat or
deception of mentally
disordered persons,
7.174–7.177
procuring sexual activity with
mentally disordered
persons by inducement,
threat or deception,
7.143–7.146
sexual activity with mentally
disordered persons,
7.48–7.51
outraging public decency,
15.28–15.30
paying for sexual services of
children, 10.11–10.16
prostitution
causing prostitution for gain,
10.113–10.117
controlling prostitution for
gain, 10.144–10.148
knowingly permitting
prostitutes to meet and
remain in house of
refreshment, 12.105
paying for sexual services of
prostitutes subjected to
force, 10.165
tenant permitting premises to
be used for prostitution,
12.77
rape, 1.20

Maximum sentences—*cont.*
rape of child under 13, 3.32
sexual activity in public
lavatories, 15.157
sexual exploitation of children
arranging or facilitating,
10.91–10.95
causing, 10.38–10.42
controlling children in relation
to sexual exploitation,
10.72–10.76
sexual intercourse with animals,
15.128–15.130
sexual penetration of corpses,
15.147–15.149
slavery servitude and forced
compulsory labour,
11.60–11.64
social care workers
causing mentally disordered
persons to watch sexual
acts, 7.273–7.276
causing or inciting sexual
activity, 7.238–7.241
sexual activity in the presence
of mentally disordered
persons, 7.253–7.256
sexual activity with mentally
disordered persons,
7.210–7.213
soliciting, 13.26–13.28, 13.63
tenants
tenant permitting premises to
be used as brothel, 12.66
tenant permitting premises to
be used for prostitution,
12.77
trespass with intent, 14.53–14.56
voyeurism, 15.92–15.95
Medical evidence (adults)
after-care
bacterial STI prophylaxis,
21.48
domestic violence, 21.53–21.54
emergency contraception, 21.42

Medical evidence (adults)—*cont.*
after-care—*cont.*
generally, 21.41
hepatitis B prophylaxis, 21.47
post-exposure prophylaxis, 21.46
pregnancy, 21.43–21.44
psychological issues, 21.50–21.51
safeguarding, 21.52
screening for infection post assault, 21.49
sexually transmitted infections, 21.45
suicide risk, 21.50–21.52
drug-facilitated sexual assault, 21.40
forensic samples, 21.37–21.39
introduction, 21.01–21.02
medical examination
anatomical terms, 21.30
ano-genital injuries, 21.35–21.36
capacity, 21.20
confidentiality, 21.19
consent, 21.21
disclosure, 21.22
documenting injuries, 21.32–21.34
forensic examination, 21.26–21.29
generally, 21.18
history taking, 21.23–21.25
presentation, 21.12–21.15
prevalence
generally, 21.04–21.08
learning difficulties, 21.11
men, 21.09–21.10
psychological effects
generally, 21.55
independent sexual violence advisers, 21.56
vicarious trauma, 21.57
sexual assault referral centres
aims, 21.16

Medical evidence (adults)—*cont.*
sexual assault referral centres—*cont.*
self-referrals, 21.17
terminology, 21.03
Medical evidence (children)
after-care, 22.41
anal signs of sexual abuse
bruising, 22.61
dilatation, 22.65–22.66
erythema, 22.59
lacerations, 22.62–22.63
perianal venous congestion, 22.60
scars and tags, 22.64
child sexual abuse accommodation syndrome, 22.24
child sexual exploitation
generally, 22.75–22.77
learning disabilities, 22.78
conclusions, 22.79
consent, 22.20–22.21
female genital mutilation, 22.68–22.74
forensic samples, 22.39–22.40
genital signs of sexual abuse in boys, 22.58
genital signs of sexual abuse in girls
abrasions, 22.50
bruising, 22.49
clefts and notches of the hymen, 22.53
erythema, 22.47
hymenal bumps or mounds, 22.54
hymenal transections, 22.52
hymenal width, 22.56
labial fusion, 22.57
lacerations, 22.51
oedema, 22.48
size of hymenal orifice, 22.55
genitalia
anal anatomy, 22.38

Medical evidence (children)—*cont.*
  genitalia—*cont.*
    females, 22.32–22.35
    males, 22.36
    Tanner stages, 22.37
  Gillick competence, 22.22
  history taking, 22.23
  interpretation of ano-genital
    findings, 22.42–22.46
  introduction, 22.01–22.03
  medical examinations
    forensic physician
      qualifications,
      22.08——22.10
    location, 22.16
    peer reviews, 22.12–22.15
    process, 22.25–22.26
    genital examination,
      22.27–22.31
    purposes, 22.05–22.07
    single or two-doctor
      examinations, 22.11
    timing, 22.17–22.19
  medical response to allegations
    or suspicions, 22.04
  parental responsibility,
    22.20–22.21
  sexually transmitted diseases,
    22.67
Medical examinations
  adults
    anatomical terms, 21.30
    ano-genital injuries,
      21.35–21.36
    capacity, 21.20
    confidentiality, 21.19
    consent, 21.21
    disclosure, 21.22
    documenting injuries,
      21.32–21.34
    forensic examination,
      21.26–21.29
    generally, 21.18
    history taking, 21.23–21.25

Medical examinations—*cont.*
  children
    forensic physician
      qualifications,
      22.08——22.10
    location, 22.16
    peer reviews, 22.12–22.15
    process, 22.25–22.26
    genital examination,
      22.27–22.31
    purposes, 22.05–22.07
    single or two-doctor
      examinations, 22.11
    timing, 22.17–22.19
**Meeting children following sexual
  grooming**
  "arranges to meet", 4.217
  attempts, 4.190
  consent, 4.220
  "during or after the meeting",
    4.218
  "has met or communicated",
    4.209–4.212
  jurisdiction, 4.208
  maximum sentences, 4.191–4.195
  meaning, 4.187–4.189
  mens rea, 4.221–4.224
  mode of trial, 4.191–4.195
  offence, 4.186
  "on one or more occasions",
    4.213–4.215
  parties to offence, 4.207
  "relevant offence", 4.219
  sentencing
    aggravating features, 4.201
    ancillary orders, 4.202
    category range, 4.200
    credit for time served, 4.202
    culpability, 4.197, 4.199
    dangerousness, 4.202
    double counting, 4.203
    extended sentences, 4.202
    generally, 4.196
    guilty pleas, 4.202
    harm, 4.197–4.198

Meeting children following sexual grooming—*cont.*
sentencing—*cont.*
mitigation, 4.201
police or media stings, 4.204–4.206
proportionality, 4.202
reasons, 4.202
reduction of sentence, 4.202
starting point, 4.200
"travels with the intention of meeting . . . , 4.216
"Memory"
expert evidence
childhood memories, 24.34–24.42
false memory syndrome, 24.43–24.48
generally, 24.31–24.33
memory formation, 24.34–24.42
recovered memories, 24.43–24.48
historic offences, 30.97–30.98
Mens rea
abuse of position of trust
causing children to engage in sexual activity, 5.71–5.774
causing children to watch sexual acts, 5.122–5.125
engaging in sexual activity in presence of children, 5.98–5.102
sexual activity with children, 5.47–5.50
abusive or disorderly behaviour, 15.197
administering substances with intent, 14.33–14.36
assault by penetration, 2.32–2.37
assault by penetration of child under 13, 3.103
causing children to engage in sexual activity, 3.168–3.170

Mens rea—*cont.*
causing sexual activity without consent, 2.105–2.108
child abduction
generally, 9.45–9.52
looked-after children, 9.61
child sex offences
arranging child sex offences, 4.185
causing children to engage in sexual activity, 4.92–4.93
causing children to watch sexual acts, 4.139–4.143
committed by children, 4.159
engaging in sexual activity in presence of children, 4.117–4.120
meeting children following sexual grooming, 4.221–4.224
possession of paedophile manuals, 4.264
sexual activity with children, 4.65–4.66
sexual communication with children, 4.246–4.247
committing an offence with intent to commit a human trafficking offence, 11.116
committing an offence with intent to commit a sexual offence, 14.48–14.50
consent to sexual activity, 2.125–2.132
exposure, 15.88–15.89
familial sex offences
inciting child family member to engage in sexual activity, 6.68–6.69
sex with adult relatives, 6.92–6.93, 6.105
sexual activity with child family members, 6.47–6.50
human trafficking, 11.110–11.113

Mens rea—*cont.*
indecent photographs of children
  possession, 8.145
  taking, 8.91–8.104
insulting behaviour, 15.170
insulting behaviour with intent to
  harass, alarm or distress,
  15.178
keeping disorderly houses, 12.95
mentally disordered persons
  causing mentally disordered
    persons to engage in
    sexual activity,
    7.104–7.105
  causing mentally disordered
    persons to engage in
    sexual activity by
    inducement, threat or
    deception, 7.172
  causing mentally disordered
    persons to watch sexual
    acts, 7.139–7.141
  causing mentally disordered
    persons to watch sexual
    acts by inducement, threat
    or deception, 7.206–7.208
  engaging in sexual activity in
    presence of mentally
    disordered persons,
    7.123–7.125
  engaging in sexual activity in
    presence procured by
    inducement, threat or
    deception of mentally
    disordered persons,
    7.190–7.192
  generally, 7.15–7.16
  procuring sexual activity with
    mentally disordered
    persons by inducement,
    threat or deception,
    7.158–7.159
  sexual activity with mentally
    disordered persons,
    7.87–7.90

Mens rea—*cont.*
outraging public decency,
  15.66–15.68
paying for sexual services of
  children, 10.33–10.34
prostitution
  causing prostitution for gain,
    10.142
  controlling prostitution for
    gain, 10.162
  paying for sexual services of
    prostitutes subjected to
    force, 10.171
rape
  absence of reasonable belief,
    1.374–1.397, 1.403
  attempted rape, 1.404–1.406
  conspiracy to rape, 1.407–410
  incapacity through drink or
    drugs, 1.402
  intentional penetration,
    1.371–1.373
  self-induced intoxication,
    1.398–1.401
rape of child under 13, 3.77–3.78
sexual activity in public
  lavatories, 15.162
sexual assault
  consent, 2.83
  intention, 2.78–2.80
  intoxication, 2.81–2.82
sexual assault of child under 13,
  3.130
sexual exploitation of children
  arranging or facilitating,
    10.102–10.104
  causing, 10.66–10.68
  controlling children in relation
    to sexual exploitation,
    10.85–10.87
sexual intercourse with animals,
  15.143–15.144
sexual penetration of corpses,
  15.154–15.155

Mens rea—*cont.*
slavery servitude and forced
compulsory labour, 11.71
social care workers
causing mentally disordered
persons to watch sexual
acts, 7.284–7.286
causing or inciting sexual
activity, 7.248–7.250
sexual activity in the presence
of mentally disordered
persons, 7.268–7.270
sexual activity with mentally
disordered persons,
7.231–7.234
trespass with intent, 14.72–14.74
voyeurism, 15.122–15.125
Mental Capacity Act 1005
rape, 1.233–1.234
Mental disorder
see also **Sexual offences against
mentally disordered persons**
hearsay evidence, 19.47–19.48
rape
consent, 1.225, 1.238–1.242
mitigation, 1.74
special measures for witnesses,
27.17–27.18
Mental distress
psychological effects of sexual
assault
during rape or sexual assault,
23.32–23.35
false statements, 23.78–23.79
following sexual assault,
23.36–23.58
inconsistencies, 23.78–23.79
introduction, 23.01–23.17
late reporting, 23.73–23.75
legal implications, 23.59–23.72
myths, 23.18–23.31
re-traumatisation, 23.76–23.77
stereotypes, 23.18–23.31
trials, 23.80–23.82
victim's needs, 23.83–23.88

Mental distress—*cont.*
special measures for witnesses,
27.19
Mentally disordered persons
see **Sexual offences against
mentally disordered persons;
Social care workers**
Mitigation
administering substances with
intent, 14.19
assault by penetration, 1.59, 2.20
assault by penetration of child
under 13, 3.93–3.94
care workers engaging in sexual
activity in the presence of
mentally disordered persons,
7.260
care workers engaging in sexual
activity with mentally
disordered persons, 7.217
causing children to engage in
sexual activity, 3.147–3.148
causing prostitution for gain,
10.128–10.131
causing sexual activity without
consent, 2.94
causing sexual exploitation of
children, 10.51
committed by children, 4.155
engaging in sexual activity in
presence of children, 4.107,
5.84
engaging in sexual activity in
presence of mentally
disordered persons, 7.114
engaging in sexual activity in
presence procured by
inducement, threat or
deception of mentally
disordered persons, 7.181
exposure, 15.80
human trafficking, 11.86–11.88
keeping brothels, 12.50
meeting children following sexual
grooming, 4.201

Mitigation—*cont.*

Northern Ireland, 32.52

paying for sexual services of
children, 10.23

procuring sexual activity with
mentally disordered persons
by inducement, threat or
deception, 7.150

rape
age, 1.72–1.73

impact on offender's
dependents, 1.76

learning disability, 1.74

maturity, 1.72–1.73

mental disorder, 1.74

prior convictions, 1.69–1.70

remorse, 1.71

request for leniency by victim,
1.75

rape of child under 13, 3.47–3.48

sex with adult relatives, 6.80

sexual activity with child family
members, 6.21

sexual activity with children,
4.40–4.41, 5.17

sexual activity with mentally
disordered persons, 7.56

sexual assault, 2.54

sexual assault of child under 13,
3.119–3.120

trespass with intent, 14.63

voyeurism, 15.108

Mode of trial
abuse of position of trust
causing children to engage in
sexual activity, 5.54–5.57

causing children to watch
sexual acts, 5.105–5.108

engaging in sexual activity in
presence of children,
5.77–5.80

sexual activity with children,
5.09–5.13

Mode of trial—*cont.*

abusive or disorderly behaviour,
15.184

administering substances with
intent, 14.09–14.12

assault by penetration, 2.09

assault by penetration of child
under 13, 3.82

brothels
allowing a person under 16 to
be in a brothel, 12.98

keeping brothels, 12.22–12.23,
12.43–12.44

landlord letting premises for
use as brothel, 12.58

tenant permitting premises to
be used as brothel, 12.66

causing children to engage in
sexual activity, 3.136–3.137

causing sexual activity without
consent, 2.85–2.87

child abduction
generally, 9.10–9.11

looked-after children, 9.53

child sex offences
arranging child sex offences,
4.163–4.167

causing children to engage in
sexual activity, 4.71–4.75

causing children to watch
sexual acts, 4.123–4.127

committed by children,
4.147–4.150

engaging in sexual activity in
presence of children,
4.95–4.99

meeting children following
sexual grooming,
4.191–4.195

possession of paedophile
manuals, 4.250–4.253

sexual activity with children,
4.26–4.30

sexual communication with
children, 4.232–4.235

Mode of trial—*cont.*
committing an offence with
intent to commit a human
trafficking offence, 11.115
committing an offence with
intent to commit a sexual
offence, 14.39–14.42
exposure, 15.70–15.73
familial sex offences
inciting child family member
to engage in sexual
activity, 6.56–6.60
sex with adult relatives,
6.73–6.76, 6.95–6.98
sexual activity with child
family members, 6.13–6.14
human trafficking, 11.74–11.78
indecent photographs of children
possession, 8.120–8.122
taking, 8.04–8.08
insulting behaviour, 15.164
insulting behaviour with intent to
harass, alarm or distress,
15.173
keeping disorderly houses, 12.86
mentally disordered persons
causing mentally disordered
persons to engage in
sexual activity, 7.92–7.95
causing mentally disordered
persons to engage in
sexual activity by
inducement, threat or
deception, 7.161–7.164
causing mentally disordered
persons to watch sexual
acts, 7.127–7.130
causing mentally disordered
persons to watch sexual
acts by inducement, threat
or deception, 7.194–7.197
engaging in sexual activity in
presence of mentally
disordered persons,
7.107–7.110

Mode of trial—*cont.*
mentally disordered
persons—*cont.*
engaging in sexual activity in
presence procured by
inducement, threat or
deception of mentally
disordered persons,
7.174–7.177
procuring sexual activity with
mentally disordered
persons by inducement,
threat or deception,
7.143–7.146
sexual activity with mentally
disordered persons,
7.48–7.51
outraging public decency,
15.28–15.30
paying for sexual services of
children, 10.11–10.16
prostitution
causing prostitution for gain,
10.113–10.117
controlling prostitution for
gain, 10.144–10.148
knowingly permitting
prostitutes to meet and
remain in house of
refreshment, 12.105
paying for sexual services of
prostitutes subjected to
force, 10.164
tenant permitting premises to
be used for prostitution,
12.77
rape
classification for listing, 1.21
dangerousness, 1.22
indictments, 1.20
notification requirements, 1.23
rape of child under 13, 3.32
sexual activity in public
lavatories, 15.157
sexual assault, 2.39

Mode of trial—*cont.*
  sexual assault of child under 13,
    3.107, 3.111
  sexual exploitation of children
    arranging or facilitating,
      10.91–10.95
    causing, 10.38–10.42
    controlling children in relation
      to sexual exploitation,
      10.72–10.76
  sexual intercourse with animals,
    15.128–15.130
  sexual penetration of corpses,
    15.147–15.149
  slavery servitude and forced
    compulsory labour,
    11.60–11.64
  social care workers
    causing mentally disordered
      persons to watch sexual
      acts, 7.273–7.276
    causing or inciting sexual
      activity, 7.238–7.241
    sexual activity in the presence
      of mentally disordered
      persons, 7.253–7.256
    sexual activity with mentally
      disordered persons,
      7.210–7.213
  soliciting, 13.26–13.28, 13.63
  tenants
    permitting premises to be used
      as brothel, 12.66
    permitting premises to be used
      for prostitution, 12.77
  trespass with intent, 14.53–14.56
  voyeurism, 15.92–15.95
  youth courts
    accused turning 18 during
      proceedings, 31.71
    dangerousness, 31.91–31.98
    generally, 31.27–31.28
    grave crimes, 31.72–31.90
    procedure for determining,
      31.68–31.70

Mode of trial—*cont.*
  youth courts—*cont.*
    statutory presumption,
      31.64–31.67
    youths charged alongside
      adults, 31.99
Modern slavery
  see **Slavery**
Multiple offending
  child sex offences, 4.19
National DNA Database
  generally, 25.63–25.66
Necessity
  keeping brothels, 12.56
  sexual harm prevention orders,
    36.21–36.28
"Non-contact"
  sexual harm prevention orders,
    36.38–36.44
Northern Ireland
  abuse of position of trust
    generally, 5.127–5.128
    offence, 5.126
  boys under 14, 32.05
  delay, 32.69–32.73
  doli incapax, 32.06
  evidence
    collusion, 32.67
    cross-admissibility, 32.67
    generally, 32.57–32.60
    inconsistent statements, 32.66
    special measures, 32.61–32.65
    third party material, 32.68
  introduction, 32.01
  principle offences, 32.02
  rape, 32.04
  receiving verdicts, 32.74
  sentencing
    basis of, 32.51
    custody prohibition orders,
      32.32–32.33
    dangerous offenders,
      32.40–32.45
    differences from England and
      Wales, 32.48–32.50

Northern Ireland—*cont.*
  sentencing—*cont.*
    generally, 32.29
    historic offences, 32.47
    mitigation, 32.52
    offences committed before 14
      May 2008, 32.30–32.35
    offences committed on or after
      1 April 2009, 32.37–32.38
    offences committed on or after
      15 May 2008, 32.36
    offender levies, 32.39
    sexual offences prevention
      orders, 32.54–32.56
    suspended sentences, 32.53
    transitional arrangements,
      32.46
  Sexual Offences Act 2003
    application of, 32.22–32.25
    commencement, 32.26–32.28
    equivalent provisions in 2008
      Order, 32.75
  Sexual Offences (Northern
    Ireland) Order 2008
    equivalent provisions in 2003
      Act, 32.75
    generally, 32.07–32.09
    human trafficking, 32.13–32.21
    paying for sexual services,
      32.10
    sexual communication with
      children, 32.11–32.12
    unlawful carnal knowledge, 32.04
Notification
  advance notification of foreign
    travel, 35.45
  bad character, 20.03–20.06
  changes to notified particulars,
    35.37–35.40
  checking the notified
    information, 35.43–35.44
  introduction, 35.01–35.06
  notification offences, 35.48–35.56
  notification orders
    appeals, 35.66

Notification—*cont.*
  notification orders—*cont.*
    applications, 35.58–35.60
    effect of, 35.63–35.64
    generally, 35.57
    grounds, 35.58–35.60
    interim orders, 35.65–35.66
    relevant offences, 35.61–35.62
  notification period, 35.16–35.25
  notification requirements
    assault by penetration, 2.12
    assault by penetration of child
      under 13, 3.85
    causing children to engage in
      sexual activity, 3.140
    causing sexual activity without
      consent, 2.89
    generally, 35.30–35.36
    rape of child under 13, 3.35
    sexual assault of child under
      13, 3.110
    sexual assault, 2.42
  periodic re-notification,
    35.41–35.42
  qualifying offenders, 35.07–35.13
  review of indefinite notification,
    35.26–35.29
  transitional provisions,
    35.14–35.15
  young offenders, 35.46–35.47
Oaths
  youth courts, 31.55
Offences against children
  assault by penetration of child
    under 13
    alternative verdicts, 3.87
    bail, 3.86
    "child under 13", 3.101
    classification, 3.83
    complex cases, 3.83
    consent, 3.102
    dangerousness, 3.84
    jurisdiction, 3.98
    life imprisonment, 3.84
    maximum sentence, 3.82

Offences against children—*cont.*

assault by penetration of child
  under 13—*cont.*
  meaning, 3.79–3.81
  mens rea, 3.103
  mode of trial, 3.82
  notification requirements, 3.85
  parties, 3.97
  "penetrates the vagina or anus
    of another person", 3.99
  "penetration is sexual", 3.100
  sentencing, 3.88–3.96
  systematic abuse, 3.83
background, 3.02–3.03
causing children to engage in
  sexual activity
  bail, 3.141
  "causes or incites another
    person", 3.158–3.163
  "child under 13", 3.166
  classification, 3.138
  complex cases, 3.138
  consent, 3.167
  dangerousness, 3.139
  jurisdiction, 3.157
  life imprisonment, 3.139
  maximum sentence,
    3.136–3.137
  meaning, 3.131–3.135
  mens rea, 3.168–3.170
  mode of trial, 3.136–3.137
  notification requirements, 3.140
  parties, 3.155–3.156
  sentencing, 3.142–3.154
  specified offences, 3.139
  systematic abuse, 3.138
  "the activity is sexual", 3.165
  "to engage in an activity",
    3.164
child sex offences, overlap with,
  3.04–3.05
indictments
  multiple offences, 3.24–3.28
introduction, 3.01
multiple offences, 3.24–3.28

Offences against children—*cont.*

offences committed by children
  CPS charging guidance,
    3.10–3.13
  generally, 3.06–3.09
  right to respect for private and
    family life, 3.14–3.23
rape of child under 13
  alternative verdicts, 3.38
  bail, 3.36
  "child under 13", 3.73–3.75
  classification, 3.33
  complex cases, 3.33
  consent, 3.76
  conspiracy, 3.37
  dangerousness, 3.34
  jurisdiction, 3.72
  life imprisonment, 3.34
  maximum sentences, 3.32
  meaning, 3.29–3.31
  mens rea, 3.77–3.78
  mode of trial, 3.32
  notification requirements, 3.35
  parties, 3.71
  sentencing, 3.39–3.70
  specified offences, 3.34
sexual assault of child under 13
  alternative verdicts, 3.112
  child sexual exploitation, 3.111
  "child under 13", 3.128
  classification, 3.108
  complex cases, 3.108
  consent, 3.129
  dangerousness, 3.109
  jurisdiction, 3.126
  life imprisonment, 3.109
  meaning, 3.104–3.106
  mens rea, 3.130
  mode of trial, 3.107, 3.111
  notification requirements, 3.110
  parties, 3.125
  sentencing, 3.113–3.124
  systematic abuse, 3.108
  "touching is sexual", 3.127
youth courts, 31.15–31.17

Offences against public morals

abusive or disorderly behaviour
  "abusive or disorderly
    behaviour", 15.185–15.192
  defences, 15.197
  going naked in public,
    15.186–15.192
  "harassment, alarm or
    distress", 15.196
  human rights, 15.183
  maximum sentences, 15.184
  meaning, 15.180–15.182
  mens rea, 15.197
  mode of trial, 15.184
  offence, 15.179
  "within the sight of a person
    likely to be caused",
    15.193–15.195
byelaws, 15.199–15.200
ecclesiastical courts, 15.202
exposure
  "alarm or distress", 15.87
  "exposes", 15.83–15.85
  "genitals", 15.86
  introduction, 15.12–15.15
  maximum sentences,
    15.70–15.73
  mens rea, 15.88–15.89
  mode of trial, 15.70–15.73
  offence, 15.69
  parties to offence, 15.74
  sentencing, 15.75–15.82
insulting behaviour
  "immediate unlawful violence",
    15.168
  "insulting behaviour",
    15.166–15.167
  maximum sentences, 15.164
  mens rea, 15.170
  mode of trial, 15.164
  offence, 15.163
  "uses towards another person",
    15.165

**Offences against public
  morals**—*cont.*

insulting behaviour—*cont.*
  "whereby it is likely that such
    violence will be
    provoked", 15.169
insulting behaviour with intent to
  harass, alarm or distress
  "abusive or disorderly", 15.175
  defences, 15.177
  "harassment, alarm or
    distress", 15.176
  "insulting behaviour", 15.174
  maximum sentences, 15.173
  mens rea, 15.178
  mode of trial, 15.173
  offence, 15.171–15.172
introduction, 15.01–15.05
other relevant offences,
  15.199–15.202
outraging public decency
  "a lewd, obscene or disgusting
    act", 1.538–15.41
  charge or indictment, 15.31
  consent, 15.62–15.65
  introduction, 15.06–15.11
  maximum sentences,
    15.28–15.30
  meaning, 15.26–15.27
  mens rea, 15.66–15.68
  mode of trial, 15.28–15.30
  "outrage to public decency",
    15.42–15.50
  parties to offence, 15.37
  publicity requirement,
    15.58–15.61
  sentencing, 15.32–15.36
  "to the great disgust and
    annoyance . . . ", 15.51
  "two person" rule, 15.52–15.57
sexual activity in public lavatories
  "lavatory to which the
    public . . . "15.160
  maximum sentences, 15.157
  mens rea, 15.162

Offences against public morals—*cont.*
sexual activity in public lavatories—*cont.*
mode of trial, 15.157
offence, 15.136
parties to offence, 15.158
sentencing, 15.159
"sexual", 15.161
sexual intercourse with animals
accomplices, 15.141–15.142
coercion, 15.138–15.140
consent, 15.138–15.140
introduction, 15.19–15.22
"living animals", 15.137
maximum sentences,
15.128–15.130
meaning, 15.127
mens rea, 15.143–15.144
mode of trial, 15.128–15.130
offence, 15.126
parties to offence, 15.131
"penetration", 15.135
sentencing,15.132–15.134
"vagina or anus", 15.136
sexual penetration of corpses
introduction, 15.23–15.25
maximum sentences,
15.147–15.149
meaning, 15.146
mens rea, 15.154–15.155
mode of trial, 15.147–15.149
offence, 15.145
parties to offence, 15.150
"penetration", 15.152
sentencing, 15.151
"sexual", 15.153
voyeurism
"consent", 15.119
"doing a private act",
15.113–15.118
fitness to plead, 15.96–15.101
"image", 15.120
introduction, 15.16–15.18

Offences against public morals—*cont.*
voyeurism—*cont.*
maximum sentences,
15.92–15.95
meaning, 15.91
mens rea, 15.122–15.125
mode of trial, 15.92–15.95
"observes", 15.111–15.112
offence, 15.90
parties to offence, 15.102
sentencing, 15.103–15.110
"structure", 15.121
Offender levy
Northern Ireland, 32.39
Offensive behaviour
abusive or disorderly behaviour
"abusive or disorderly
behaviour", 15.185–15.192
defences, 15.197
going naked in public,
15.186–15.192
"harassment, alarm or
distress", 15.196
human rights, 15.183
maximum sentences, 15.184
meaning, 15.180–15.182
mens rea, 15.197
mode of trial, 15.184
offence, 15.179
"within the sight of a person
likely to be caused",
15.193–15.195
insulting behaviour
"immediate unlawful violence",
15.168
"insulting behaviour",
15.166–15.167
maximum sentences, 15.164
mens rea, 15.170
mode of trial, 15.164
offence, 15.163
"uses towards another person",
15.165

Offensive behaviour—*cont.*
  insulting behaviour—*cont.*
    "whereby it is likely that such
      violence will be
      provoked", 15.169
  insulting behaviour with intent to
    harass, alarm or distress
    "abusive or disorderly", 15.175
    defences, 15.177
    "harassment, alarm or
      distress", 15.176
    "insulting behaviour", 15.174
    maximum sentences, 15.173
    mens rea, 15.178
    mode of trial, 15.173
    offence, 15.171–15.172
Ostensible consent
  see **Consent**
Outraging public decency
  "a lewd, obscene or disgusting
    act", 1.538–15.41
  charge or indictment, 15.31
  consent, 15.62–15.65
  introduction, 15.06–15.11
  maximum sentences, 15.28–15.30
  meaning, 15.26–15.27
  mens rea, 15.66–15.68
  mode of trial, 15.28–15.30
  "outrage to public decency",
    15.42–15.50
  parties to offence, 15.37
  publicity requirement,
    15.58–15.61
  sentencing, 15.32–15.36
  "to the great disgust and
    annoyance . . . ", 15.51
  "two person" rule, 15.52–15.57
Parental responsibilities
  medical evidence, 22.20–22.21
Parenting orders
  youth courts, 31.138
Parents
  attendance in youth court, 31.36

Parties
  abuse of position of trust
    causing children to engage in
      sexual activity, 5.59–5.61
    causing children to watch
      sexual acts, 5.110–5.112
    engaging in sexual activity in
      presence of children,
      5.86–5.88
    sexual activity with children,
      5.24–5.27
  assault by penetration, 2.24
  assault by penetration of child
    under 13, 3.97
  brothels
    allowing a person under 16 to
      be in a brothel, 12.99
    keeping brothels, 12.25, 12.52
    landlord letting premises for
      use as brothel, 12.59
    tenant permitting premises to
      be used as brothel, 12.67
  causing sexual activity without
    consent, 2.96
  child sex offences
    arranging child sex offences,
      4.170
    causing children to engage in
      sexual activity,
      3.155–3.156, 4.84
    causing children to watch
      sexual acts, 4.129
    committed by children, 4.157
    engaging in sexual activity in
      presence of children, 4.110
    meeting children following
      sexual grooming, 4.207
    possession of paedophile
      manuals, 4.256
    sexual activity with children,
      4.56–4.58
    sexual communication with
      children, 4.237
  exposure, 15.74

Parties—*cont.*
familial sex offences
inciting child family member
to engage in sexual
activity, 6.62–6.63
sex with adult relatives,
6.83–6.88, 6.100–6.101
sexual activity with child
family members, 6.28–6.42
indecent photographs of children
possession, 8.127
taking, 8.39–8.40
mentally disordered persons
causing mentally disordered
persons to engage in
sexual activity, 7.98
causing mentally disordered
persons to engage in
sexual activity by
inducement, threat or
deception, 7.166
causing mentally disordered
persons to watch sexual
acts, 7.132
causing mentally disordered
persons to watch sexual
acts by inducement, threat
or deception, 7.199
engaging in sexual activity in
presence of mentally
disordered persons, 7.116
engaging in sexual activity in
presence procured by
inducement, threat or
deception of mentally
disordered persons, 7.183
procuring sexual activity with
mentally disordered
persons by inducement,
threat or deception, 7.152
sexual activity with mentally
disordered persons, 7.61
outraging public decency, 15.37
paying for sexual services of
children, 10.25

Parties—*cont.*
prostitution
causing prostitution for gain,
10.133
controlling prostitution for
gain, 10.151–10.152
paying for sexual services of
prostitutes subjected to
force, 10.166
rape, 1.148–1.153
rape of child under 13, 3.71
sexual activity in public
lavatories, 15.158
sexual assault, 2.61
sexual assault of child under 13,
3.125
sexual exploitation of children
arranging or facilitating, 10.97
causing, 10.55
controlling children in relation
to sexual exploitation,
10.79
sexual intercourse with animals,
15.131
sexual penetration of corpses,
15.150
social care workers
causing mentally disordered
persons to watch sexual
acts, 7.278
causing or inciting sexual
activity, 7.243
sexual activity in the presence
of mentally disordered
persons, 7.262
sexual activity with mentally
disordered persons, 7.222
soliciting, 13.29–13.30, 13.64
tenants
permitting premises to be used
as brothel, 12.67
permitting premises to be used
for prostitution, 12.78
voyeurism, 15.102

Paying for sexual services of children
see also **Sexual exploitation of children**
jurisdiction, 10.26
maximum sentences, 10.11–10.16
mens rea, 10.33–10.34
mode of trial, 10.11–10.16
"obtains for himself",
  10.27–10.28
offence, 10.10
parties to offence, 10.25
"payment", 10.32
sentencing
  aggravating features, 10.23
  ancillary orders, 10.24
  category range, 10.22
  credit for time served, 10.24
  culpability, 10.19–10.21
  dangerousness, 10.24
  generally, 10.17–10.18
  guilty pleas, 10.24
  harm, 10.19–10.21
  mitigation, 10.23
  proportionality, 10.24
  reasons, 10.24
  reduction of sentence, 10.24
  starting point, 10.22
"the sexual services of another
  person", 10.29–10.31
**Paying for sexual services of
  prostitutes subjected to force**
see also **Prostitution**
"exploitative conduct", 10.169
"for or in the expectation of
  gain", 10.170
maximum sentences, 10.165
mens rea, 10.171
mode of trial, 10.164
offence, 10.163
parties to offence, 10.166
"payment", 10.167
"sexual services of a prostitute",
  10.168

Penetration
see **Assault by penetration;
  Assault of child under 13 by
  penetration; Sex with adult
  relatives; Sexual penetration
  of corpses**
*see also definitions under
  individual offences*
Perverting the course of justice
deleting indecent images, 8.118
Physical disabilities
special measures for witnesses,
  27.17–27.18
Plea and directions hearings
disclosure
  linked hearings, 18.58–18.66
Police inquiries
conclusions, 16.35–16.36
introduction, 16.01–16.06
investigative process
  consent, 16.25–16.30
  early investigative advice, 16.34
  general evidential
    considerations,
    16.23–16.24
  generally, 16.12–16.15
  identifying risk factors,
    16.16–16.20
  police disposal decision-
    making, 16.31–16.33
  prioritised forensic
    opportunities, 16.21
  specific evidential
    opportunities, 16.22
primary guidance documents,
  16.11
structure of rape investigations,
  16.07–16.10
taking indecent photographs of
  children, 8.82–8.85
Possession
indecent photographs of children
  "child", 8.131–8.133
  company officers, 8.129

Possession—*cont.*
indecent photographs of
children—*cont.*
consent within marriage or
other relationship, 8.143
defences, 8.144
form of charge or indictment,
8.124–8.125
"indecent photographs or
pseudo-photographs",
8.130
jurisdiction, 8.128–8.129
maximum sentences,
8.120–8.122
mens rea, 8.145
mode of trial, 8.120–8.122
offence, 8.119
parties to offence, 8.127
"possession", 8.134–8.142
restriction on prosecution,
8.123
sentencing, 8.126
paedophile manuals
"abusing children sexually",
4.261
"advice or guidance", 4.260
defences, 4.262–4.263
"item", 4.259
jurisdiction, 4.257
maximum sentences,
4.250–4.253
meaning, 4.249
mens rea, 4.264
mode of trial, 4.250–4.253
offence, 4.248
parties to offence, 4.256
"possession", 4.258
restriction on prosecution,
4.254
sentencing, 4.255
Powers of arrest
soliciting, 13.53
Pregnancy
after-care for adults, 21.43–21.44
rape, 1.40

Prejudice
historic offences, 30.96
Preliminary issues
youth courts, 31.03
"Preparatory offences"
administering substances with
intent
consent, 14.31–14.32
introduction, 14.03
jurisdiction, 14.26
maximum sentence,
14.09–14.12
meaning, 14.08, 14.27–14.29
mens rea, 14.33–14.36
mode of trial, 14.09–14.12
sentencing, 14.13–14.25
sexual activity, 14.30
assault with intent to rape, 14.06
committing an offence with
intent to commit a sexual
offence
alternative verdicts, 14.43
"any offence", 14.47
introduction, 14.04–14.05
jurisdiction, 14.46
maximum sentence,
14.39–14.42
meaning, 14.37–14.38
mens rea, 14.48–14.50
mode of trial, 14.39–14.42
sentencing, 14.44–14.45
introduction, 14.01–14.02
trespass with intent
introduction, 14.07
jurisdiction, 14.67
maximum sentence,
14.53–14.56
meaning, 14.51–14.52A
mens rea, 14.72–14.74
mode of trial, 14.53–14.56
"premises", 14.71
sentencing, 14.57–14.66
"trespasser", 14.68–14.70
Pre-sentence reports
sex offenders, 34.37

Press
youth courts, 31.37
Presumptions
consent to rape
conclusive presumptions,
1.310–1.370
evidential presumptions,
1.263–1.309
Previous convictions
rape
aggravating features, 1.60
mitigation, 1.69–1.70
Previous inconsistent statements
evidence
complainants, 19.67–19.71
earlier complaints by
complainant, 19.72–19.90
evidence of truth, 19.64
hostile witnesses, 19.65–19.66
historic offences
abuse of process, 30.49
directions, 30.83
Northern Ireland, 32.66
Privilege against self-incrimination
disclosure, 18.53
Procedure
sexual harm prevention orders
at time of dealing with
offender for offence,
36.15–36.17
by magistrates' courts on
application, 36.18–36.19
sexual risk orders, 36.68–36.69
**Procuring sexual activity with
mentally disordered persons by
inducement, threat or deception**
see **Sexual offences against
mentally disordered persons**
Propensity
bad character
cross-admissibility,
20.121–20.122
gateways, 20.41–20.48

Proportionality
sentencing
administering substances with
intent, 14.20
assault by penetration, 2.21
assault by penetration of child
under 13, 3.95
care workers engaging in
sexual activity in the
presence of mentally
disordered persons, 7.261
care workers having sexual
activity with mentally
disordered persons, 7.218
causing children to engage in
sexual activity, 3.149
causing prostitution for gain,
10.132
causing sexual activity without
consent, 2.95
causing sexual exploitation of
children, 10.52
engaging in sexual activity in
presence of children,
4.108, 5.85
engaging in sexual activity in
presence of mentally
disordered persons, 7.115
engaging in sexual activity in
presence procured by
inducement, threat or
deception of mentally
disordered persons, 7.182
exposure, 15.81
human trafficking, 11.89
keeping brothels, 12.51
meeting children following
sexual grooming, 4.202
paying for sexual services of
children, 10.24
procuring sexual activity with
mentally disordered
persons by inducement,
threat or deception, 7.151
rape, 1.80

Proportionality—*cont.*
  sentencing—*cont.*
    rape of child under 13, 3.49
    sex with adult relatives, 6.81
    sexual activity with child
      family members, 6.22
    sexual activity with children,
      4.42, 5.18
    sexual activity with mentally
      disordered persons, 7.57
    sexual assault, 2.55
    sexual assault of child under
      13, 3.121
    trespass with intent, 14.64
    voyeurism, 15.109
  sexual harm prevention orders,
    36.21–36.28
Prosecution decisions
  see **Decisions to prosecute**
Prosecution disclosure
  see also **Disclosure**
  Criminal Procedure and
    Investigations Act 1996,
    18.10–18.21
  limiting distribution, 18.26–18.31
  public interest immunity,
    18.22–18.25
Prosecution
  see also **Brothels; Keeping
    brothels; Keeping disorderly
    houses; Soliciting**
  advertising, 13.54–13.59
  anti-social behaviour injunctions,
    13.73–13.82
  binding over, 13.83–13.87
  Canada, 13.20–13.24
  causing prostitution for gain
    "causes or incites",
      10.134–10.135
    "for or in the expectation of
      gain", 10.140–10.141
    "in any part of the world",
      10.139
    maximum sentences,
      10.113–10.117

Prostitution—*cont.*
  causing prostitution for
    gain—*cont.*
    meaning, 10.112
    mens rea, 10.142
    mode of trial, 10.113–10.117
    offence, 10.111
    parties to offence, 10.133
    "prostitute", 10.137–10.138
    sentencing, 10.118–10.132
    "to become", 10.136
  controlling prostitution for gain
    charge or indictment, 10.149
    "controls any of the activities
      of another person . . . ",
      10.153–10.158
    "for or in the expectation of
      gain", 10.161
    "in any part of the world",
      10.160
    maximum sentences,
      10.144–10.148
    mens rea, 10.162
    mode of trial, 10.144–10.148
    offence, 10.143
    parties to offence,
      10.151–10.152
    "prostitution", 10.159
    sentencing, 10.150
  development of law
    All-Party Parliamentary Group
      on Prostitution,
      13.17–13.19
    Coordinated Prostitution
      Strategy (2006),
      13.10–13.14
    Honeyball Report, 13.17–13.19
    Policing and Crime Act 2009,
      13.15–13.17
    Sexual Offences Act 1985,
      13.06–13.08
    Sexual Offences Review, 13.09
    Street Offences Act 1959,
      13.04–13.05

Prostitution—*cont.*
development of law—*cont.*
Wolfenden Committee,
13.02–13.03
introduction, 13.01
knowingly permitting prostitutes
to meet and remain in house
of refreshment
"knowingly", 12.107
maximum sentences, 12.105
meaning, 12.104
mode of trial, 12.105
"permit or suffer", 12.108
"place of public resort",
12.106
"prostitute", 12.109
paying for sexual services of
prostitutes subjected to force
"exploitative conduct", 10.169
"for or in the expectation of
gain", 10.170
maximum sentences, 10.165
mens rea, 10.171
mode of trial, 10.164
offence, 10.163
parties to offence, 10.166
"payment", 10.167
"sexual services of a
prostitute", 10.168
rape, 1.87
sexual behaviour of complainant,
26.97–26.98
tenant permitting premises to be
used for prostitution
"for the purposes of habitual
prostitution", 12.84
"knowingly, 12.81
maximum sentences, 12.77
meaning, 12.76
mode of trial, 12.77
parties to offence, 12.78
"permit", 12.82–12.83
"tenant or occupier",
12.79–12.80

Psychiatric harm
administering substances with
intent, 14.14–14.17
assault by penetration, 2.17
assault by penetration of child
under 13, 3.90–3.91
care workers engaging in sexual
activity in the presence of
mentally disordered persons,
7.258
care workers having sexual
activity with mentally
disordered persons, 7.215
causing children to engage in
sexual activity, 3.144–3.145
causing prostitution for gain,
10.120–10.121
causing sexual activity without
consent, 2.92
causing sexual exploitation of
children, 10.45–10.48
engaging in sexual activity in
presence of children,
4.101–4.104, 5.82
engaging in sexual activity in
presence of mentally
disordered persons, 7.112
engaging in sexual activity in
presence of mentally
disordered persons procured
by inducement, threat or
deception, 7.179
exposure, 15.76–15.78
human trafficking, 11.80–11.81
keeping brothels, 12.47–12.48
meeting children following sexual
grooming, 4.197–4.198
paying for sexual services of
children, 10.19–10.21
procuring sexual activity with
mentally disordered persons
by inducement, threat or
deception, 7.148
rape, 1.40
rape of child under 13, 3.41–3.43

Psychiatric harm—*cont.*
sex offenders, 33.12–33.14
sex with adult relatives, 6.78
sexual abuse of adults
    after-care, 21.50–21.51
    generally, 21.55
    independent sexual violence
        advisers, 21.56
    vicarious trauma, 21.57
sexual activity with child family
    members, 6.19
sexual activity with children,
    4.33–4.34, 5.15
sexual activity with mentally
    disordered persons, 7.54
sexual assault, 2.46–2.50
sexual assault of child under 13,
    3.115–3.116
trespass with intent, 14.58–14.61
voyeurism, 15.104–15.106
Psychological effects
see **Mental distress; Psychiatric
    harm**
Public interest
decisions to prosecute
    child suspects, 17.38–17.40
    generally, 17.35–17.37
    non-recent cases where
        nominal penalty likely,
        17.41–17.47
Public interest immunity
prosecution disclosure,
    18.22–18.25
Public policy
consent to sexual activity
    infliction of actual bodily
        harm, 2.109–2.113
    introduction, 2.06
    mens rea, 2.125–2.132
    rough sex, 2.121–2.123
    sadomasochism, 2.114–2.120
    sexual activity carrying risk to
        health, 2.124
Publicity
youth courts, 31.37

Qualifying offences
notification, 35.07–35.13
Questioning
vulnerable witnesses
    generally, 28.41–28.45
    suggestive questioning,
        28.18–28.21
Racially aggravated offences
rape, 1.52
Rape
see also **Rape of child under 13**
abduction, 1.40
abuse of position of trust,
    1.47–1.48
acting with others, 1.45
alcohol, 1.46
alternative verdicts, 1.137–1.141
attempted rape
    generally, 1.128, 1.404–1.406
    historic offences, 30.148–30.151
bail, 1.24–1.25
capacity to consent, 1.222–1.262
children, 1.88
commercial exploitation, 1.51
consent
    absence of reasonable belief of,
        1.374–1.397, 1.403
    capacity, 1.222–1.262
    conclusive presumptions,
        1.310–1.370
    evidential presumptions,
        1.263–1.309
    introduction, 1.05–1.09
    meaning, 1.169–1.221
conviction under wrong statute,
    1.34
culpability, 1.36–1.37, 1.44–1.52
dangerousness, 1.78
disability, 1.52
double jeopardy, 1.142–1.143
drugs, 1.46
encouraging or assisting rape
    acting reasonably, 1.417
    generally, 1.411–1.416

Rape—*cont.*

encouraging or assisting
rape—*cont.*
potential victims, 1.418
exceptional gravity, 1.116–1.127
form of penetration, 1.89
historic offences, 1.129–1.136,
30.146–30.147
home invasion, 1.41–1.42
implementation date for new law,
1.32–1.33
indictments
course of conduct, 1.30–1.31
mode of trial, 1.20
multiple incident counts,
1.30–1.31
specimen counts, 1.26–1.29
introduction, 1.01–1.13
joinder of other offences,
1.146–1.147
joint offence allegations,
1.144–1.145
jurisdiction, 1.154
life imprisonment
automatic life imprisonment,
1.107–1.109
discretionary life
imprisonment, 1.92
extended sentences, 1.115
imprisonment for public
protection, 1.93–1.105
introduction, 1.91
secondary form of
discretionary life
sentences, 1.106
whole life orders, 1.110–1.114
young offenders, 1.90
male/female distinction, 1.82
Northern Ireland, 32.04
marital exception, 1.160–1.168
maximum sentences, 1.20
meaning
evolution of definition,
1.14–1.18
statutory definition, 1.19

Rape—*cont.*

mens rea
absence of reasonable belief of
consent, 1.374–1.397,
1.403
attempted rape, 1.404–1.406
conspiracy to rape, 1.407–410
incapacity through drink or
drugs, 1.402
intentional penetration,
1.371–1.373
self-induced intoxication,
1.398–1.401
mode of trial
classification for listing, 1.21
dangerousness, 1.22
indictments, 1.20
notification requirements, 1.23
parties, 1.148–1.153
penetration, 1.155–1.159
pregnancy, 1.40
presumption of consent
conclusive presumptions,
1.310–1.370
evidential presumptions,
1.263–1.309
previous consensual sexual
activity, 1.86
previous violence against victim,
1.49
proportionality, 1.80
prostitution, 1.87
psychiatric harm, 1.40
racially aggravated offences, 1.52
reasonable belief
Asperger's syndrome,
1.389–1.397
autism, 1.389–1.397
avoidance of reasonable man
test, 1.375–1.378
defendant's characteristics,
1.382–1.397
drink, 1.402
drugs, 1.402
generally, 1.374

Rape—*cont.*
reasonable belief—*cont.*
jury directions, 1.403
New Zealand test compared,
1.379–1.381
psychological conditions
affecting ability to
determine consent,
1.385–1.388
recording offence, 1.50
reduction of sentence, 1.77
relationship between defendant
and victim, 1.83
release on licence, 1.79
sentencing
aggravating features, 1.58,
1.60–1.68
attempted rape, 1.128
children, 1.88
commercial exploitation, 1.51
culpability, 1.36–1.37,
1.44–1.52
dangerousness, 1.78
exceptional gravity,
1.116–1.127
harm, 1.36–1.43
historic cases, 1.129–1.136
life imprisonment, 1.91–1.115
mitigation, 1.69–1.76
proportionality, 1.80
prostitution, 1.87
reduction of sentence, 1.77
release on licence, 1.79
sentences passed under SGC
Definitive Guideline,
1.81–1.90
sex offenders, 33.19,
34.56–34.57
Sexual Offences Review,
1.03–1.04
sexual orientation, 1.52
sexually transmitted diseases,
1.40
significant degree of planning,
1.44

Rape—*cont.*
spouses, 1.84–1.85
statistics, 1.02
threats, 1.40
transgender identity, 1.52
violence, 1.40
vulnerable adults, 1.43
youth courts, 31.85–31.88
Rape of child under 13
see also **Rape**
alternative verdicts, 3.38
bail, 3.36
"child under 13", 3.73–3.75
classification, 3.33
complex cases, 3.33
consent, 3.76
conspiracy, 3.37
jurisdiction, 3.72
meaning, 3.29–3.31
mens rea, 3.77–3.78
mode of trial, 3.32
notification requirements, 3.35
parties, 3.71
sentencing
aggravating features, 3.47–3.48
ancillary orders, 3.49
belief that victim aged 13 to
15, 3.57
belief that victim over 16, 3.56
category range, 3.44–3.46
consent, 3.50–3.54
credit for time served, 3.49
culpability, 3.41–3.43
dangerousness, 3.34, 3.49
examples, 3.58
guilty pleas, 3.49
harm, 3.41–3.43
life imprisonment, 3.34, 3.49
maximum sentences, 3.32
mitigation, 3.47–3.48
ostensible consent, 3.55
proportionality, 3.49
reasonable belief, 3.50–3.54

Rape of child under 13—*cont.*
  sentencing—*cont.*
    reasons, 3.49
    reduction in sentence, 3.49
    sentencing guideline, 3.39–3.40
    very young victims, 3.69–3.70
    victim almost 13, 3.59–3.64
    young offenders, 3.65–3.68
  specified offences, 3.34
  starting point, 3.44–3.46
Reasonable belief
  assault by penetration of child
    under 13, 3.96
  consent to sexual activity, 2.83
  rape
    Asperger's syndrome,
      1.389–1.397
    autism, 1.389–1.397
    avoidance of reasonable man
      test, 1.375–1.378
    defendant's characteristics,
      1.382–1.397
    drink, 1.402
    drugs, 1.402
    generally, 1.374
    jury directions, 1.403
    New Zealand test compared,
      1.379–1.381
    psychological conditions
      affecting ability to
      determine consent,
      1.385–1.388
  rape of child under 13, 3.50–3.54
Reasons
  sentencing
    administering substances with
      intent, 14.20
    assault by penetration of child
      under 13, 3.95
    care workers engaging in
      sexual activity in the
      presence of mentally
      disordered persons, 7.261

Reasons—*cont.*
  sentencing—*cont.*
    care workers having sexual
      activity with mentally
      disordered persons, 7.218
    causing children to engage in
      sexual activity, 3.149
    causing prostitution for gain,
      10.132
    causing sexual exploitation of
      children, 10.52
    engaging in sexual activity in
      presence of children,
      4.108, 5.85
    engaging in sexual activity in
      presence of mentally
      disordered persons, 7.115
    engaging in sexual activity in
      presence of mentally
      disordered persons
      procured by inducement,
      threat or deception, 7.182
    exposure, 15.81
    human trafficking, 11.89
    keeping brothels, 12.51
    meeting children following
      sexual grooming, 4.202
    paying for sexual services of
      children, 10.24
    procuring sexual activity with
      mentally disordered
      persons by inducement,
      threat or deception, 7.151
    rape of child under 13, 3.49
    sex with adult relatives, 6.81
    sexual activity with child
      family members, 6.22
    sexual activity with children,
      4.42, 5.18
    sexual activity with mentally
      disordered persons, 7.57
    sexual assault of child under
      13, 3.121
    trespass with intent, 14.64
    voyeurism, 15.109

Rebuttal evidence
 sexual behaviour of complainant,
   26.117–26.126
Recovered memories
 see **Memory**
Reduction of sentence
 administering substances with
   intent, 14.20
 assault by penetration, 2.21
 assault by penetration of child
   under 13, 3.95
 care workers engaging in sexual
   activity in the presence of
   mentally disordered persons,
   7.261
 care workers having sexual
   activity with mentally
   disordered persons, 7.218
 causing children to engage in
   sexual activity, 3.149
 causing prostitution for gain,
   10.132
 causing sexual activity without
   consent, 2.95
 causing sexual exploitation of
   children, 10.52
 engaging in sexual activity in
   presence of children, 4.108,
   5.85
 engaging in sexual activity in
   presence of mentally
   disordered persons, 7.115
 engaging in sexual activity in
   presence of mentally
   disordered persons procured
   by inducement, threat or
   deception, 7.182
 exposure, 15.81
 human trafficking, 11.89
 keeping brothels, 12.51
 meeting children following sexual
   grooming, 4.202
 paying for sexual services of
   children, 10.24

Reduction of sentence—*cont.*
 procuring sexual activity with
   mentally disordered persons
   by inducement, threat or
   deception, 7.151
 rape, 1.77
 rape of child under 13, 3.49
 sex with adult relatives, 6.81
 sexual activity with child family
   members, 6.22
 sexual activity with children,
   4.42, 5.18
 sexual activity with mentally
   disordered persons, 7.57
 sexual assault, 2.55
 sexual assault of child under 13,
   3.121
 trespass with intent, 14.64
 voyeurism, 15.109
Re-examination
 video recordings, 27.103–27.104
Referral orders
 youth courts, 31.110–31.112
Relatives
 see also **Familial child sex
   offences; Sex with adult
   relatives**
 DNA evidence, 25.14
Release on licence
 rape, 1.79
 sex offenders, 34.13
Renewal
 sexual harm prevention orders,
   36.54
Reporting restrictions
 see also **Anonymity**
 adults
   challenges to, 29.136
   contravention of,
     29.130–29.133
   framing direction, 29.135
   generally, 29.11, 29.123–29.129
   prohibiting identification of
     adult to protect child,
     29.89–29.93

Reporting restrictions—*cont.*
adults—*cont.*
representations by media,
29.134
children and young persons
applications for High Court
order, 29.105
burden of proof on
application, 29.74
challenging making variation
or revocation, 29.86–29.88
concerned in criminal
proceedings, 29.64–29.69
contravention, 29.70–29.73
framing directions, 29.83–29.85
inherent jurisdiction of Crown
Court, 29.107
introduction, 29.06–29.10
legislative history, 29.58–29.59
lifetime reporting restrictions,
29.108–29.122
media interests, 29.106
media representations,
29.80–29.82
not directly involved in
proceedings, 29.94–29.107
offences committed by,
29.47–29.52
principles governing decision
to make, 29.75–29.79
prohibiting identification of
adult to protect child,
29.89–29.93
section 45 directions,
29.64–29.93
transitional provisions,
29.61–29.63
decisions to prosecute,
17.66–17.69
special measures, 27.124
teachers, 29.45–29.46
youth courts, 31.38–31.41
Res gestae
hearsay evidence, 19.62–19.63

Revocation
special measures, 27.123
Risk of sexual harm orders
history, 36.04
replacement of, 36.05–36.11
"Rough sex"
consent to sexual activity,
2.121–2.123
Sadomasochism
consent to sexual activity,
2.114–2.120
Scotland
abuse of position of trust
generally, 5.127–5.128
offence, 5.126
Screens
special measures, 27.57–27.61
Self-induced intoxication
see **Voluntary intoxication**
Sentencing
see also **Extended sentences; Life
imprisonment; Maximum
sentences**
see also under individual offences
aggravating features
administering substances with
intent, 14.19
assault by penetration, 1.59,
2.20
assault by penetration of child
under 13, 3.93–3.94
care workers engaging in
sexual activity in the
presence of mentally
disordered persons, 7.260
care workers having sexual
activity with mentally
disordered persons, 7.217
causing children to engage in
sexual activity,
3.147–3.148
causing prostitution for gain,
10.128–10.131

Sentencing—*cont.*
aggravating features—*cont.*
causing sexual activity without consent, 2.94
causing sexual exploitation of children, 10.51
child sex offences committed by children, 4.155
engaging in sexual activity in presence of children, 4.107, 5.84
engaging in sexual activity in presence of mentally disordered persons, 7.114
engaging in sexual activity in presence procured by inducement, threat or deception of mentally disordered persons, 7.181
exposure, 15.80
human trafficking, 11.86–11.88
keeping brothels, 12.50
meeting children following sexual grooming, 4.201
paying for sexual services of children, 10.23
procuring sexual activity with mentally disordered persons by inducement, threat or deception, 7.150
rape, 1.58, 1.60–1.68
rape of child under 13, 3.47–3.48
sex with adult relatives, 6.80
sexual activity with child family members, 6.21
sexual activity with children, 4.40–4.41, 5.17
sexual activity with mentally disordered persons, 7.56
sexual assault, 2.54
sexual assault of child under 13, 3.119–3.120
trespass with intent, 14.63
voyeurism, 15.108

Sentencing—*cont.*
ancillary orders
administering substances with intent, 14.20
assault by penetration, 2.21
assault by penetration of child under 13, 3.95
care workers engaging in sexual activity in the presence of mentally disordered persons, 7.261
care workers having sexual activity with mentally disordered persons, 7.218
causing children to engage in sexual activity, 3.149
causing prostitution for gain, 10.132
causing sexual activity without consent, 2.95
causing sexual exploitation of children, 10.52
engaging in sexual activity in presence of children, 4.108, 5.85
engaging in sexual activity in presence of mentally disordered persons, 7.115
engaging in sexual activity in presence procured by inducement, threat or deception of mentally disordered persons, 7.182
exposure, 15.81
human trafficking, 11.89
keeping brothels, 12.51
meeting children following sexual grooming, 4.202
paying for sexual services of children, 10.24
procuring sexual activity with mentally disordered persons by inducement, threat or deception, 7.151
rape of child under 13, 3.49

Sentencing—*cont.*
  ancillary orders—*cont.*
    sex with adult relatives, 6.81
    sexual activity with child
      family members, 6.22
    sexual activity with children,
      4.42, 5.18
    sexual activity with mentally
      disordered persons, 7.57
    sexual assault, 2.55
    sexual assault of child under
      13, 3.121
    trespass with intent, 14.64
    voyeurism, 15.109
    youth courts, 31.134–31.138
  bad character
    sex offenders, 34.58–34.62
  barring from working with
    children or vulnerable adults
    sex offenders, 34.63–34.64
  category range
    administering substances with
      intent, 14.18
    assault by penetration,
      2.18–2.18
    assault by penetration of child
      under 13, 3.92
    care workers engaging in
      sexual activity in the
      presence of mentally
      disordered persons, 7.259
    care workers having sexual
      activity with mentally
      disordered persons, 7.216
    causing children to engage in
      sexual activity, 3.146
    causing prostitution for gain,
      10.126–10.127
    causing sexual activity without
      consent, 2.93
    causing sexual exploitation of
      children, 10.49–10.50
    child sex offences committed
      by children, 4.155

Sentencing—*cont.*
  category range—*cont.*
    engaging in sexual activity in
      presence of children,
      4.106, 5.83
    engaging in sexual activity in
      presence of mentally
      disordered persons, 7.113
    engaging in sexual activity in
      presence procured by
      inducement, threat or
      deception of mentally
      disordered persons, 7.180
    exposure, 15.79
    human trafficking, 11.84–11.85
    keeping brothels, 12.49
    meeting children following
      sexual grooming, 4.200
    paying for sexual services of
      children, 10.22
    procuring sexual activity with
      mentally disordered
      persons by inducement,
      threat or deception, 7.149
    rape, 1.53–1.57
    rape of child under 13,
      3.44–3.46
    sex with adult relatives, 6.79
    sexual activity with child
      family members, 6.20
    sexual activity with children,
      4.39, 5.16
    sexual activity with mentally
      disordered persons, 7.55
    sexual assault, 2.51–2.53
    sexual assault of child under
      13, 3.117–3.118
    trespass with intent, 14.62
    voyeurism, 15.107
  credit for time served
    administering substances with
      intent, 14.20
    assault by penetration, 2.21
    assault by penetration of child
      under 13, 3.95

Sentencing—*cont.*
credit for time served—*cont.*
care workers engaging in
sexual activity in the
presence of mentally
disordered persons, 7.261
care workers having sexual
activity with mentally
disordered persons, 7.218
causing children to engage in
sexual activity, 3.149
causing prostitution for gain,
10.132
causing sexual activity without
consent, 2.95
causing sexual exploitation of
children, 10.52
engaging in sexual activity in
presence of children,
4.108, 5.85
engaging in sexual activity in
presence of mentally
disordered persons, 7.115
engaging in sexual activity in
presence procured by
inducement, threat or
deception of mentally
disordered persons, 7.182
exposure, 15.81
human trafficking, 11.89
keeping brothels, 12.51
meeting children following
sexual grooming, 4.202
paying for sexual services of
children, 10.24
procuring sexual activity with
mentally disordered
persons by inducement,
threat or deception, 7.151
rape of child under 13, 3.49
sex with adult relatives, 6.81
sexual activity with child
family members, 6.22
sexual activity with children,
4.42, 5.18

Sentencing—*cont.*
credit for time served—*cont.*
sexual activity with mentally
disordered persons, 7.57
sexual assault, 2.55
sexual assault of child under
13, 3.121
trespass with intent, 14.64
voyeurism, 15.109
culpability
administering substances with
intent, 14.14–14.17
assault by penetration, 2.17
assault by penetration of child
under 13, 3.90–3.91
care workers engaging in
sexual activity in the
presence of mentally
disordered persons, 7.258
care workers having sexual
activity with mentally
disordered persons, 7.215
causing children to engage in
sexual activity,
3.144–3.145
causing prostitution for gain,
10.122–10.125
causing sexual activity without
consent, 2.92
causing sexual exploitation of
children, 10.45–10.48
engaging in sexual activity in
presence of children,
4.101, 4.105, 5.82
engaging in sexual activity in
presence of mentally
disordered persons, 7.112
engaging in sexual activity in
presence procured by
inducement, threat or
deception of mentally
disordered persons, 7.179
exposure, 15.76–15.78
human trafficking, 11.82–11.83
keeping brothels, 12.47–12.48

Sentencing—*cont.*
culpability—*cont.*
meeting children following
sexual grooming, 4.197,
4.199
paying for sexual services of
children, 10.19–10.21
procuring sexual activity with
mentally disordered
persons by inducement,
threat or deception, 7.148
rape, 1.36–1.37, 1.44–1.52
rape of child under 13,
3.41–3.43
sex with adult relatives, 6.78
sexual activity with child
family members, 6.19
sexual activity with children,
4.33, 4.35–4.38, 5.15
sexual activity with mentally
disordered persons, 7.54
sexual assault, 2.46–2.50
sexual assault of child under
13, 3.115–3.116
trespass with intent,
14.58–14.61
voyeurism, 15.104–15.106
custody prohibition orders
Northern Ireland, 32.32–32.33
dangerousness
administering substances with
intent, 14.20
assault by penetration, 2.21
assault by penetration of child
under 13, 3.84, 3.95
care workers engaging in
sexual activity in the
presence of mentally
disordered persons, 7.261
care workers having sexual
activity with mentally
disordered persons, 7.218
causing children to engage in
sexual activity, 3.139,
3.149

Sentencing—*cont.*
dangerousness—*cont.*
causing prostitution for gain,
10.132
causing sexual activity without
consent, 2.95
causing sexual exploitation of
children, 10.52
engaging in sexual activity in
presence of children,
4.108, 5.85
engaging in sexual activity in
presence of mentally
disordered persons, 7.115
engaging in sexual activity in
presence procured by
inducement, threat or
deception of mentally
disordered persons, 7.182
exposure, 15.81
historic offences, 30.161–30.166
human trafficking, 11.89
meeting children following
sexual grooming, 4.202
Northern Ireland, 32.40–32.45
paying for sexual services of
children, 10.24
procuring sexual activity with
mentally disordered
persons by inducement,
threat or deception, 7.151
rape, 1.78
rape of child under 13, 3.34,
3.49
sex offenders, 34.06,
34.23–34.36
sex with adult relatives, 6.81
sexual activity with child
family members, 6.22
sexual activity with children,
4.42, 5.18
sexual activity with mentally
disordered persons, 7.57
sexual assault, 2.55

Sentencing—*cont.*
  dangerousness—*cont.*
    sexual assault of child under
      13, 3.109, 3.121
    trespass with intent, 14.64
    voyeurism, 15.109
  detention and training orders
    youth courts, 31.104–31.106
  determinate sentences
    sex offenders, 34.40–34.51
  double counting
    meeting children following
      sexual grooming, 4.203
  examples
    administering substances with
      intent, 14.21–14.25
    assault by penetration,
      2.22–2.23
    care workers having sexual
      activity with mentally
      disordered persons,
      7.219–7.221
    causing sexual exploitation of
      children, 10.53–54
    engaging in sexual activity in
      presence of children, 4.109
    exposure, 15.82
    human trafficking, 11.90–11.94
    sex with adult relatives, 6.82
    sexual activity with child
      family members, 6.26–6.27
    sexual activity with children,
      4.53–4.55, 5.19–5.23
    sexual activity with mentally
      disordered persons,
      7.58–7.60
    sexual assault, 2.56–2.60
    trespass with intent, 14.66
    voyeurism, 15.110
  exceptional gravity
    rape, 1.116–1.127
  Goodyear indications
    sex offenders, 34.38–34.39

Sentencing—*cont.*
  guilty pleas
    administering substances with
      intent, 14.20
    assault by penetration, 2.21
    assault by penetration of child
      under 13, 3.95
    care workers engaging in
      sexual activity in the
      presence of mentally
      disordered persons, 7.261
    care workers having sexual
      activity with mentally
      disordered persons, 7.218
    causing children to engage in
      sexual activity, 3.149
    causing prostitution for gain,
      10.132
    causing sexual activity without
      consent, 2.95
    causing sexual exploitation of
      children, 10.52
    engaging in sexual activity in
      presence of children,
      4.108, 5.85
    engaging in sexual activity in
      presence of mentally
      disordered persons, 7.115
    engaging in sexual activity in
      presence procured by
      inducement, threat or
      deception of mentally
      disordered persons, 7.182
    exposure, 15.81
    human trafficking, 11.89
    keeping brothels, 12.51
    meeting children following
      sexual grooming, 4.202
    paying for sexual services of
      children, 10.24
    procuring sexual activity with
      mentally disordered
      persons by inducement,
      threat or deception, 7.151
    rape of child under 13, 3.49

Sentencing—*cont.*
  guilty pleas—*cont.*
    sex with adult relatives, 6.81
    sexual activity with child
      family members, 6.22
    sexual activity with children,
      4.42, 5.18
    sexual activity with mentally
      disordered persons, 7.57
    sexual assault, 2.55
    sexual assault of child under
      13, 3.121
    trespass with intent, 14.64
    voyeurism, 15.109
  harm
    administering substances with
      intent, 14.14–14.17
    assault by penetration, 2.17
    assault by penetration of child
      under 13, 3.90–3.91
    care workers engaging in
      sexual activity in the
      presence of mentally
      disordered persons, 7.258
    care workers having sexual
      activity with mentally
      disordered persons, 7.215
    causing children to engage in
      sexual activity,
      3.144–3.145
    causing prostitution for gain,
      10.120–10.121
    causing sexual activity without
      consent, 2.92
    causing sexual exploitation of
      children, 10.45–10.48
    engaging in sexual activity in
      presence of children,
      4.101–4.104, 5.82
    engaging in sexual activity in
      presence of mentally
      disordered persons, 7.112
    engaging in sexual activity in
      presence procured by
      inducement, threat or

      deception of mentally
      disordered persons, 7.179
    exposure, 15.76–15.78
    human trafficking, 11.80–11.81
    keeping brothels, 12.47–12.48
    meeting children following
      sexual grooming,
      4.197–4.198
    paying for sexual services of
      children, 10.19–10.21
    procuring sexual activity with
      mentally disordered
      persons by inducement,
      threat or deception, 7.148
    rape, 1.36–1.43
    rape of child under 13,
      3.41–3.43
    sex with adult relatives, 6.78
    sexual activity with child
      family members, 6.19
    sexual activity with children,
      4.33–4.34, 5.15
    sexual activity with mentally
      disordered persons, 7.54
    sexual assault, 2.46–2.50
    sexual assault of child under
      13, 3.115–3.116
    trespass with intent,
      14.58–14.61
    voyeurism, 15.104–15.106
  historic offences
    approach to, 30.110–30.114
    attempted rape, 30.148–30.151
    celebrity status, 30.127–30.132
    dangerous offenders,
      30.161–30.166
    declining health, 30.119–30.126
    elderly offenders,
      30.119–30.126
    exceptional circumstances,
      30.133–30.138
    extended sentences,
      30.164–30.165

Sentencing—*cont.*
  historic offences—*cont.*
    failure to obtain permission to
      institute proceedings,
      30.159–30.160
    generally, 30.109
    good character since offending,
      30.141
    gross indecency with a child,
      30.158
    immaturity at time of offence,
      30.115–30.118E
    indecent assault, 30.152–30.155
    lack of clarity on commission
      before or after 4 April
      2005, 30.167
    licensing regime changes,
      30.142
    life sentences, 30.162–30.163
    longer than commensurate
      sentences, 30.166
    maximum sentences,
      30.143–30.160
    medical needs in custody,
      30.139–30.140
    Northern Ireland, 32.47
    rape, 1.129–1.136,
      30.146–30.147
    sexual intercourse with girls
      under 13 or 16,
      30.156–30.157
    young offenders,
      30.115–30.118E
  imprisonment for public
    protection
    sex offenders, 34.08–34.09
  indeterminate sentences
    sex offenders, 34.40–34.51
  mitigation
    administering substances with
      intent, 14.19
    assault by penetration, 1.59,
      2.20
    assault by penetration of child
      under 13, 3.93–3.94

Sentencing—*cont.*
  mitigation—*cont.*
    care workers engaging in
      sexual activity in the
      presence of mentally
      disordered persons, 7.260
    care workers having sexual
      activity with mentally
      disordered persons, 7.217
    causing children to engage in
      sexual activity,
      3.147–3.148
    causing prostitution for gain,
      10.128–10.131
    causing sexual activity without
      consent, 2.94
    causing sexual exploitation of
      children, 10.51
    child sex offences committed
      by children, 4.155
    engaging in sexual activity in
      presence of children,
      4.107, 5.84
    engaging in sexual activity in
      presence of mentally
      disordered persons, 7.114
    engaging in sexual activity in
      presence procured by
      inducement, threat or
      deception of mentally
      disordered persons, 7.181
    exposure, 15.80
    human trafficking, 11.86–11.88
    keeping brothels, 12.50
    meeting children following
      sexual grooming, 4.201
    Northern Ireland, 32.52
    paying for sexual services of
      children, 10.23
    procuring sexual activity with
      mentally disordered
      persons by inducement,
      threat or deception, 7.150
    rape, 1.69–1.76

Sentencing—*cont.*
  mitigation—*cont.*
    rape of child under 13,
      3.47–3.48
    sex with adult relatives, 6.80
    sexual activity with child
      family members, 6.21
    sexual activity with children,
      4.40–4.41, 5.17
    sexual activity with mentally
      disordered persons, 7.56
    sexual assault, 2.54
    sexual assault of child under
      13, 3.119–3.120
    trespass with intent, 14.63
    voyeurism, 15.108
  Northern Ireland
    basis of, 32.51
    custody prohibition orders,
      32.32–32.33
    dangerousness, 32.40–32.45
    differences from England and
      Wales, 32.48–32.50
    generally, 32.29
    historic offences, 32.47
    mitigation, 32.52
    offences committed before 14
      May 2008, 32.30–32.35
    offences committed on or after
      1 April 2009, 32.37–32.38
    offences committed on or after
      15 May 2008, 32.36
    offender levy, 32.39
    sexual offences prevention
      orders, 32.54–32.56
    suspended sentences, 32.53
    transitional arrangements,
      32.46
  offences of particular concern,
    34.55
  offender levy
    Northern Ireland, 32.39
  pre-sentence reports, 34.37

Sentencing—*cont.*
  proportionality
    administering substances with
      intent, 14.20
    assault by penetration, 2.21
    assault by penetration of child
      under 13, 3.95
    care workers engaging in
      sexual activity in the
      presence of mentally
      disordered persons, 7.261
    care workers having sexual
      activity with mentally
      disordered persons, 7.218
    causing children to engage in
      sexual activity, 3.149
    causing prostitution for gain,
      10.132
    causing sexual activity without
      consent, 2.95
    causing sexual exploitation of
      children, 10.52
    engaging in sexual activity in
      presence of children,
      4.108, 5.85
    engaging in sexual activity in
      presence of mentally
      disordered persons, 7.115
    engaging in sexual activity in
      presence procured by
      inducement, threat or
      deception of mentally
      disordered persons, 7.182
    exposure, 15.81
    human trafficking, 11.89
    keeping brothels, 12.51
    meeting children following
      sexual grooming, 4.202
    paying for sexual services of
      children, 10.24
    procuring sexual activity with
      mentally disordered
      persons by inducement,
      threat or deception, 7.151
    rape, 1.80

Sentencing—*cont.*
  proportionality—*cont.*
    rape of child under 13, 3.49
    sex with adult relatives, 6.81
    sexual activity with child family members, 6.22
    sexual activity with children, 4.42, 5.18
    sexual activity with mentally disordered persons, 7.57
    sexual assault, 2.55
    sexual assault of child under 13, 3.121
    trespass with intent, 14.64
    voyeurism, 15.109
  reasonable belief
    assault by penetration of child under 13, 3.96
    rape of child under 13, 3.50–3.54
  reasons
    administering substances with intent, 14.20
    assault by penetration of child under 13, 3.95
    care workers engaging in sexual activity in the presence of mentally disordered persons, 7.261
    care workers having sexual activity with mentally disordered persons, 7.218
    causing children to engage in sexual activity, 3.149
    causing prostitution for gain, 10.132
    causing sexual exploitation of children, 10.52
    engaging in sexual activity in presence of children, 4.108, 5.85
    engaging in sexual activity in presence of mentally disordered persons, 7.115

Sentencing—*cont.*
  reasons—*cont.*
    engaging in sexual activity in presence procured by inducement, threat or deception of mentally disordered persons, 7.182
    exposure, 15.81
    human trafficking, 11.89
    keeping brothels, 12.51
    meeting children following sexual grooming, 4.202
    paying for sexual services of children, 10.24
    procuring sexual activity with mentally disordered persons by inducement, threat or deception, 7.151
    rape of child under 13, 3.49
    sex with adult relatives, 6.81
    sexual activity with child family members, 6.22
    sexual activity with children, 4.42, 5.18
    sexual activity with mentally disordered persons, 7.57
    sexual assault of child under 13, 3.121
    trespass with intent, 14.64
    voyeurism, 15.109
  reduction of sentence
    administering substances with intent, 14.20
    assault by penetration, 2.21
    assault by penetration of child under 13, 3.95
    care workers engaging in sexual activity in the presence of mentally disordered persons, 7.261
    care workers having sexual activity with mentally disordered persons, 7.218
    causing children to engage in sexual activity, 3.149

Sentencing—*cont.*
reduction of sentence—*cont.*
causing prostitution for gain,
10.132
causing sexual activity without
consent, 2.95
causing sexual exploitation of
children, 10.52
engaging in sexual activity in
presence of children,
4.108, 5.85
engaging in sexual activity in
presence of mentally
disordered persons, 7.115
engaging in sexual activity in
presence procured by
inducement, threat or
deception of mentally
disordered persons, 7.182
exposure, 15.81
human trafficking, 11.89
keeping brothels, 12.51
meeting children following
sexual grooming, 4.202
paying for sexual services of
children, 10.24
procuring sexual activity with
mentally disordered
persons by inducement,
threat or deception, 7.151
rape, 1.77
rape of child under 13, 3.49
sex with adult relatives, 6.81
sexual activity with child
family members, 6.22
sexual activity with children,
4.42, 5.18
sexual activity with mentally
disordered persons, 7.57
sexual assault, 2.55
sexual assault of child under
13, 3.121
trespass with intent, 14.64
voyeurism, 15.109

Sentencing—*cont.*
referral orders
youth courts, 31.110–31.112
release on licence
rape, 1.79
sex offenders
automatic life imprisonment,
34.17–34.22
bad character evidence,
34.58–34.62
barring from working with
children or vulnerable
adults, 34.63–34.64
dangerousness, 34.06,
34.23–34.36
definitive sentencing guideline,
33.01–33.31
determinate sentences,
34.40–34.51
discretionary life
imprisonment, 34.07
extended sentences,
34.10–34.16
false complaints of rape,
34.56–34.57
Goodyear indications,
34.38–34.39
imprisonment for public
protection, 34.08–34.09
indeterminate sentences,
34.40–34.51
introduction, 34.01–34.05
offences of particular concern,
34.55
offences spanning 1 May 2004,
34.52
offences spanning 4 April
2005, 34.53–34.54
pre-sentence reports, 34.37
sexual offences prevention orders
Northern Ireland, 32.54–32.56
suspended sentences
Northern Ireland, 32.53

Sentencing—*cont.*
starting point
administering substances with
intent, 14.18
assault by penetration,
2.18–2.19
assault by penetration of child
under 13, 3.92
care workers engaging in
sexual activity in the
presence of mentally
disordered persons, 7.259
care workers having sexual
activity with mentally
disordered persons, 7.216
causing children to engage in
sexual activity, 3.146
causing prostitution for gain,
10.126–10.127
causing sexual activity without
consent, 2.93
causing sexual exploitation of
children, 10.49–10.50
child sex offences committed
by children, 4.155
engaging in sexual activity in
presence of children,
4.106, 5.83
engaging in sexual activity in
presence of mentally
disordered persons, 7.113
engaging in sexual activity in
presence procured by
inducement, threat or
deception of mentally
disordered persons, 7.180
exposure, 15.79
human trafficking, 11.84–11.85
keeping brothels, 12.49
meeting children following
sexual grooming, 4.200
paying for sexual services of
children, 10.22
procuring sexual activity with
mentally disordered

persons by inducement,
threat or deception, 7.149
rape, 1.53–1.57
rape of child under 13,
3.44–3.46
sex with adult relatives, 6.79
sexual activity with child
family members, 6.20
sexual activity with children,
4.39, 5.16
sexual activity with mentally
disordered persons, 7.55
sexual assault, 2.51–2.53
sexual assault of child under
13, 3.117–3.118
trespass with intent, 14.62
voyeurism, 15.107
young offenders
historic offences,
30.115–30.118E
rape of child under 13,
3.65–3.68
sexual activity with child
family members, 6.23–6.24
youth courts
ancillary orders, 31.134–31.138
approach to, 31.116–31.119
detention and training orders,
31.104–31.106
guidelines, 31.120–31.125
introduction, 31.100
notification, 31.127–31.133
options, 31.139
other sentencing options,
31.113
powers and procedure,
31.101–31.103
referral orders, 31.110–31.112
relevance of age, 31.114–31.115
youth rehabilitation orders,
31.107–31.109
Serious offences
youth courts
application of exception,
31.80–31.84

Serious offences—*cont.*
 youth courts—*cont.*
  examples of decisions,
   31.89–31.90
  generally, 31.72–31.75
  powers of punishment,
   31.76–31.79
  rape, 31.85–31.88
  sexual offences, 31.85–31.88
Servitude
 see **Slavery**
Severance
 evidence
  cross-admissibility as pre-
   condition to, 19.14–19.17
  generally, 19.10–19.13
  indictments straddling
   implementation of 2003
   Act, 19.18–19.21
Sex offenders
 definitive sentencing guideline
  apparent consent, 33.15–33.17
  Canavan principle, 33.24–33.31
  culpability, 33.12
  cybercrime, 33.18
  domestic violence, 33.22
  exemplary conduct, 33.20
  good character, 33.20
  harm, 33.12–33.14
  historic offences, 33.06–33.11
  indecent photographs of
   children, 33.12
  introduction, 33.01–33.05
  ostensible consent, 33.15–33.17
  other relevant guidelines, 33.21
  rape, 33.19
  young offenders, 33.23
 extended sentences
  composition, 34.12
  criteria, 34.11
  defendants under 18,
   34.14–34.15
  generally, 34.10
  length, 34.12
  release on licence, 34.13

Sex offenders—*cont.*
 extended sentences—*cont.*
  statutory provisions, 34.16
 sentencing
  automatic life imprisonment,
   34.17–34.22
  bad character, 34.58–34.62
  barring from working with
   children or vulnerable
   adults, 34.63–34.64
  dangerousness, 34.06
  determinate sentences,
   34.40–34.51
  determining dangerousness,
   34.23–34.36
  discretionary life
   imprisonment, 34.07
  extended sentences,
   34.10–34.16
  false complaints of rape,
   34.56–34.57
  Goodyear procedure,
   34.38–34.39
  imprisonment for public
   protection, 34.08–34.09
  indeterminate sentences,
   34.40–34.51
  introduction, 34.01–34.05
  offences of particular concern,
   34.55
  offences spanning 1 May 2004,
   34.52
  offences spanning 4 April
   2005, 34.53–34.54
  pre-sentence reports, 34.37
Sex with adult relatives
 see also **Familial child sex
   offences**
 consenting to penetration
  consent, 6.104
  intoxication, 6.106
  maximum sentences, 6.95–6.98
  mens rea, 6.105
  mode of trial, 6.95–6.98
  offence, 6.94

Sex with adult relatives—*cont.*
  consenting to penetration—*cont.*
    parties to offence, 6.100–6.101
    "penetrates A's vagina or
      anus . . . or mouth", 6.102
    sentencing, 6.99
    "sexual", 6.103
  eugenic debate, 6.07
  "family" unit, 6.04
  human rights, 6.08–6.11
  introduction, 6.01
  nature of modern family, 6.07
  penetration
    consent, 6.91
    intoxication, 6.93
    introduction, 6.05–6.06
    maximum sentences, 6.73–6.76
    mens rea, 6.92–6.93
    mode of trial, 6.73–6.76
    offence, 6.72
    parties to offence, 6.83–6.88
    "penetrates another person's
      vagina or anus . . . or
      mouth", 6.89
    sentencing, 6.77–6.82
    "sexual", 6.90
  proscribed sexual activity,
    6.08–6.11
  related offences, 6.03
**Sexual activity with child family
  members**
  civil partners, 6.51
  consent, 6.46
  introduction, 6.02
  jurisdiction, 6.43
  maximum sentences, 6.14–6.17
  mens rea
    generally, 6.47–6.49
    intoxication, 6.50
  mode of trial, 6.13–6.14
  offence, 6.12
  parties to offence
    first category, 6.31–6.32
    generally, 6.28–6.30
    principle in *Tyrrell*, 6.41–6.42

**Sexual activity with child family
  members**—*cont.*
  parties to offence—*cont.*
    second category, 6.33–6.36
    third category, 6.37–6.40
  pre-existing sexual relationships,
    6.52–6.53
  sentencing
    abuse of position of trust, 6.25
    aggravating features, 6.21
    ancillary orders, 6.22
    category range, 6.20
    credit for time served, 6.22
    culpability, 6.19
    dangerousness, 6.22
    examples, 6.26–6.27
    guideline, 6.18
    guilty pleas, 6.22
    harm, 6.19
    mitigation, 6.21
    proportionality, 6.22
    reasons, 6.22
    reduction of sentence, 6.22
    starting point, 6.20
    young offenders, 6.23–6.24
  "sexual", 6.45
  spouses, 6.51
  "touches", 6.44
Sexual activity in public lavatories
  "lavatory to which the public . . .
    "15.160
  maximum sentences, 15.157
  mens rea, 15.162
  mode of trial, 15.157
  offence, 15.136
  parties to offence, 15.158
  sentencing, 15.159
  "sexual", 15.161
Sexual activity with children
  abuse of position of trust
    civil partners, 5.40–5.41
    consent, 5.46
    jurisdiction, 5.28
    maximum sentences, 5.09–5.13
    meaning, 5.08

Sexual activity with children—*cont.*
abuse of position of trust—*cont.*
mens rea, 5.47–5.50
mode of trial, 5.09–5.13
offence, 5.07
parties to offence, 5.24–5.27
"position of trust", 5.31–5.38
pre-existing sexual
relationships, 5.42–5.45
sentencing, 5.14–5.23
spouses, 5.40–5.41
"the touching is sexual", 5.30
"touches another person", 5.29
"where subsection (2) applies",
5.39
consent, 4.64
historic offences, 30.156–30.157
jurisdiction, 4.59
maximum sentences, 4.26–4.30
meaning, 4.21–4.25
mens rea, 4.65–4.66
mode of trial, 4.26–4.30
offence, 4.20
parties to offence
child victims, 4.57–4.58
generally, 4.56
"penetration", 4.62
sentencing
aggravating features, 4.40–4.41
ancillary orders, 4.42
category range, 4.39
convictions or admissions only,
4.43–4.44
credit for time served, 4.42
culpability, 4.33, 4.35–4.38
dangerousness, 4.42
examples, 4.53–4.55
extended sentences, 4.42
gender neutral guideline,
4.50–4.51
generally, 4.31–4.32
grooming behaviour, 4.52
guilty pleas, 4.42
harm, 4.33–4.34
mitigation, 4.40–4.41

Sexual activity with children—*cont.*
sentencing—*cont.*
proportionality, 4.42
reasons, 4.42
reduction of sentence, 4.42
significant disparity in age,
4.52
starting point, 4.39
victims almost 16, 4.45–4.49
"the touching is sexual", 4.61
"touches another person", 4.60
"vagina", 4.63
**Sexual activity with mentally
disordered persons**
see **Sexual offences against
mentally disordered persons;
Social care workers**
Sexual assault
see also **Sexual assault of child
under 13**
alternative verdicts, 2.44
classification, 2.40
consent
capacity, 2.77
infliction of actual bodily
harm, 2.109–2.113
introduction, 2.06
mens rea, 2.125–2.132
reasonable belief, 2.83
rough sex, 2.121–2.123
sado-masochism, 2.114–2.120
sexual activity carrying risk to
health, 2.124
fitness to plead, 2.43
intention, 2.78–2.80
intoxication, 2.81–2.82
jurisdiction, 2.62
meaning, 2.38
mens rea
consent, 2.83
intention, 2.78–2.80
intoxication, 2.81–2.82
mode of trial, 2.39
notification requirements, 2.42
parties, 2.61

Sexual assault—*cont.*
  sentencing
    aggravating features, 2.54
    ancillary orders, 2.55
    category range, 2.51–2.53
    credit for time served, 2.55
    culpability, 2.46–2.50
    dangerousness, 2.55
    examples, 2.56–2.60
    generally, 2.45
    guilty pleas, 2.55
    harm, 2.46–2.50
    mitigation, 2.54
    proportionality, 2.55
    reduction of sentence, 2.55
    starting point, 2.51–2.53
  Sexual Offences Review, 2.04
  specified offences, 2.41
  "touches another person",
    2.63–2.65
  "touching is sexual", 2.66–2.76
Sexual assault of child under 13
  see also **Sexual assault**
  alternative verdicts, 3.112
  child sexual exploitation, 3.111
  "child under 13", 3.128
  classification, 3.108
  complex cases, 3.108
  consent, 3.129
  jurisdiction, 3.126
  meaning, 3.104–3.106
  mens rea, 3.130
  mode of trial, 3.107, 3.111
  notification requirements, 3.110
  parties, 3.125
  sentencing
    aggravating features,
      3.119–3.120
    ancillary orders, 3.121
    category range, 3.117–3.118
    credit for time served, 3.121
    culpability, 3.115–3.116
    dangerousness, 3.109, 3.121
    generally, 3.113–3.114
    guilty pleas, 3.121

**Sexual assault of child under
  13**—*cont.*
  sentencing—*cont.*
    harm, 3.115–3.116
    life imprisonment, 3.109, 3.121
    mitigation, 3.119–3.120
    proportionality, 3.121
    reasons, 3.121
    reduction in sentence, 3.121
    stating point, 3.117–3.118
  systematic abuse, 3.108
  "touching is sexual", 3.127
Sexual assault referral centres
  see **Victim support**
Sexual behaviour
  autistic defendants, 26.69
  background, 26.04–26.07
  bad character and, 20.151–20.153
  bias by complainant against
    defendant, 26.70–26.76
  Canadian experience,
    26.168–26.176
  common law, 26.08–26.09
  consent
    contemporaneity, 26.80–26.82
    honest belief, 25.56–26.69
    similarity, 26.83–26.116
  credibility, 26.139–26.149
  defendant, with;
    prior and subsequent sexual
      behaviour, 26.102–26.111
    subsequent decisions in respect
      of, 26.112–26.116
  fabrication of evidence,
    26.70–26.76
  false complaints, 26.151–26.167
  gateways
    consent and contemporaneity,
      26.80–26.82
    consent and similarity,
      26.83–26.116
    issues other than consent,
      26.54–26.79
    rebuttal evidence,
      26.117–26.126

Sexual behaviour—*cont.*
Heilbron Committee, 26.10–26.13
honest belief of consent,
26.56–26.69
human rights, 26.99–26.101
introduction, 26.01–26.03
learning difficulties, 26.69
prohibition on adducing evidence
of
"any sexual behaviour",
26.26–26.33
application for leave, 26.45
background to, 26.19–26.20
complainant's denial of
previous sexual experience,
26.42
consent and contemporaneity,
26.80–26.82
consent and similarity,
26.83–26.116
court's overriding duty,
26.127–26.138
credibility restriction,
26.139–26.143
future of s.41, 26.177–26.184
gateways, 26.50–26.53
general prohibition, 26.21
issues other than consent,
26.54–26.79
procedure, 26.46–26.48
prosecution's position, 26.49
rebuttal, 26.117–26.126
residual discretion, 26.150
scope and application of s 41,
26.22–26.44
sexual behaviour with
defendant, 26.43
sexual orientation,
26.146–26.148
social networking sites,
26.34–26.41
specific instance restriction,
26.144–26.149
prostitution, 26.97–26.98

Sexual behaviour—*cont.*
rebuttal evidence, 26.117–26.126
residual discretion, 26.150
Sexual Offences (Amendment)
Act 1976, 26.14–26.18
sexual orientation, 26.146–26.148
social networking sites,
26.34–26.41
third party conversations,
26.64–26.68
Sexual communication with children
attempts, 4.231
"communicates", 4.240–4.242
consent, 4.245
"for the purpose of sexual
gratification", 4.239
jurisdiction, 4.238
maximum sentences, 4.232–4.235
meaning, 4.226–4.230
mens rea, 4.246–4.247
mode of trial, 4.232–4.235
offence, 4.225
parties to offence, 4.237
sentencing, 4.236
"sexual", 4.243–4.244
Sexual exploitation of adults
see **Exploitative conduct**
Sexual exploitation of children
arranging or facilitating sexual
exploitation of children
"arranges or facilitates", 10.99
"in any part of the world",
10.101
jurisdiction, 10.89
maximum sentences,
10.91–10.95
meaning, 10.89–10.90
mens rea, 10.102–10.104
mode of trial, 10.91–10.95
offence, 10.88
parties to offence, 10.97
sentencing, 10.96
"sexual exploitation", 10.100

Sexual exploitation of children—*cont.*

causing or inciting sexual exploitation of children
"causes or incites", 10.57–10.58
"in any part of the world", 10.65
jurisdiction, 10.56
maximum sentences, 10.38–10.42
meaning, 10.36–10.37
mens rea, 10.66–10.68
mode of trial, 10.38–10.42
offence, 10.35
parties to offence, 10.55
sentencing, 10.43–10.54
"to be sexually exploited", 10.59–10.64
children under 13, 3.111
civil orders to protect children from, 4.18
controlling children in relation to sexual exploitation
charge or indictment, 10.77
"controls any of the activities of another person . . . ", 10.81–10.82
"in any part of the world", 10.84
jurisdiction, 10.80
maximum sentences, 10.72–10.76
meaning, 10.70–10.71
mens rea, 10.85–10.87
mode of trial, 10.72–10.76
offence, 10.69
parties to offence, 10.79
sentencing, 10.78
"sexual exploitation", 10.83
introduction, 10.01–10.02
medical evidence
generally, 22.75–22.77
learning disabilities, 22.78
overview, 10.03–10.09

Sexual exploitation of children—*cont.*

paying for sexual services of children
jurisdiction, 10.26
maximum sentences, 10.11–10.16
mens rea, 10.33–10.34
mode of trial, 10.11–10.16
"obtains for himself", 10.27–10.28
offence, 10.10
parties to offence, 10.25
"payment", 10.32
sentencing, 10.17–10.24
"the sexual services of another person", 10.29–10.31
youth courts, 31.20
Sexual grooming
meeting children following sexual grooming
"arranges to meet", 4.217
attempts, 4.190
consent, 4.220
"during or after the meeting", 4.218
"has met or communicated", 4.209–4.212
jurisdiction, 4.208
maximum sentences, 4.191–4.195
meaning, 4.187–4.189
mens rea, 4.221–4.224
mode of trial, 4.191–4.195
offence, 4.186
"on one or more occasions", 4.213–4.215
parties to offence, 4.207
"relevant offence", 4.219
sentencing, 4.196–4.206
"travels with the intention of meeting . . . ", 4.216
sexual activity with children, 4.52
Sexual harm prevention orders
appeals, 36.55–36.59

Sexual harm prevention orders—*cont.*
breach, 36.60–36.65
computers, 36.29–36.34
conclusions, 36.76–36.77
discharge, 36.54
duration, 36.50–36.52
effect of, 36.53
entry to premises, 36.35–36.37
foreign travel prohibition requirements, 36.45–36.47
historical perspective, 36.01–36.04
interim orders, 36.20
introduction of, 36.05–36.11
making of
at time of dealing with offender for offence, 36.15–36.17
by magistrates' courts on application, 36.18–36.19
criteria for, 36.13–36.14
necessity, 36.21–36.28
non-contact provisions, 36.38–36.44
proportionality, 36.21–36.28
relationship with other sentences, 36.48–36.49
renewal, 36.54
variation, 36.54
youth courts, 31.135
Sexual history
see **Sexual behaviour**
Sexual intercourse with animals
accomplices, 15.141–15.142
coercion, 15.138–15.140
consent, 15.138–15.140
introduction, 15.19–15.22
"living animals", 15.137
maximum sentences, 15.128–15.130
meaning, 15.127
mens rea, 15.143–15.144
mode of trial, 15.128–15.130
offence, 15.126
parties to offence, 15.131

Sexual intercourse with animals—*cont.*
"penetration", 15.135
sentencing,15.132–15.134
"vagina or anus", 15.136
Sexual Offences Act 2003
Northern Ireland
application of, 32.22–32.25
commencement, 32.26–32.28
equivalent provisions in 2008 Order, 32.75
Sexual offences against mentally disordered persons
see also **Social care workers**
capacity
burden and standard of proof, 7.23–7.24
generally, 7.10–7.11
care workers
offence, 7.209
causing mentally disordered persons to engage in sexual activity
bail, 7.96
"because of or for a reason related to a mental disorder", 7.103
"causes or incites another person . . . to engage in an activity", 7.100
jurisdiction, 7.99
maximum sentences, 7.92–7.95
mens rea, 7.104–7.105
mode of trial, 7.92–7.95
offence, 7.91
parties to offence, 7.98
sentencing, 7.97
"the activity is sexual", 7.101
"unable to refuse, 7.102
causing mentally disordered persons to engage in sexual activity by inducement, threat or deception
"causes another person (B) to engage in . . . ", 7.169

Sexual offences against mentally disordered persons—*cont.*
causing mentally disordered
    persons to engage in sexual
    activity by inducement,
    threat or deception—*cont.*
"inducement, threat or
    deception", 7.168
jurisdiction, 7.167
maximum sentences,
    7.161–7.164
mens rea, 7.172
"mental disorder", 7.171
mode of trial, 7.161–7.164
offence, 7.160
parties to offence, 7.166
sentencing, 7.165
"the activity is sexual", 7.170
causing mentally disordered
    persons to watch sexual acts
"because of or for a reason
    related to a mental
    disorder", 7.138
"causes", 7.134
jurisdiction, 7.133
maximum sentences,
    7.127–7.130
mens rea, 7.139–7.141
mode of trial, 7.127–7.130
offence, 7.126
parties to offence, 7.132
sentencing, 7.131
"the activity is sexual", 7.136
"to watch a third person
    engaging in an activity...
    ", 7.135
"unable to refuse", 7.137
causing mentally disordered
    persons to watch sexual acts
    by inducement, threat or
    deception
"causes", 7.201
"inducement, threat or
    deception", 7.203
jurisdiction, 7.200

Sexual offences against mentally disordered persons—*cont.*
causing mentally disordered
    persons to watch sexual acts
    by inducement, threat or
    deception—*cont.*
maximum sentences,
    7.194–7.197
mens rea, 7.206–7.208
mode of trial, 7.194–7.197
offences, 7.193
parties to offence, 7.199
sentencing, 7.198
"the activity is sexual", 7.204
"to watch a third person
    engaging in an activity...
    ", 7.202
civil partners, 7.17
engaging in sexual activity in
    presence of mentally
    disordered persons
"because of or for a person
    related to a mental
    disorder", 7.122
"engages in activity", 7.118
jurisdiction, 7.117
maximum sentences,
    7.107–7.110
mens rea, 7.123–7.125
mode of trial, 7.107–7.110
offence, 7.106
parties to offence, 7.116
"present or... in a place from
    which A can be
    observed", 7.120
sentencing, 7.111–7.115
"the activity is sexual", 7.119
"unable to refuse", 7.121
engaging in sexual activity in
    presence of mentally
    disordered persons procured
    by inducement, threat or
    deception
"engages in an activity", 7.185

Sexual offences against mentally disordered persons—*cont.*

engaging in sexual activity in presence of mentally disordered persons procured by inducement, threat or deception—*cont.*

"inducement, threat or deception", 7.188

jurisdiction, 7.184

maximum sentences, 7.174–7.177

mens rea, 7.190–7.192

"mental disorder", 7.189

mode of trial, 7.174–7.177

offence, 7.173

parties to offence, 7.183

"present or . . . in a place from which A can be observed", 7.187

sentencing, 7.178–7.182

"the activity is sexual", 7.186

evidential considerations, 7.35–7.40

human rights, 7.42–7.46

introduction, 7.01–7.09

"mental disorder", 7.25–7.28

pre-existing sexual relationship, 7.17

procuring sexual activity with mentally disordered persons by inducement, threat or deception

"inducement, threat or deception", 7.156

jurisdiction, 7.153

maximum sentences, 7.143–7.146

mens rea, 7.158–7.159

"mental disorder", 7.157

mode of trial, 7.143–7.146

offence, 7.142

parties to offence, 7.152

sentencing, 7.147–7.151

"the touching is sexual", 7.155

Sexual offences against mentally disordered persons—*cont.*

procuring sexual activity with mentally disordered persons by inducement, threat or deception—*cont.*

"touches another person", 7.154

sentencing, 7.41

sexual activity with mentally disordered persons

bail, 7.52

expert evidence, 7.84–7.86

"because of or for a reason related to a mental disorder", 7.80–7.83

inability to communicate choice, 7.77–7.79

jurisdiction, 7.62

maximum sentences, 7.48–7.51

mens rea, 7.87–7.90

mode of trial, 7.48–7.51

offence, 7.47

parties to offence, 7.61

sentencing, 7.53–7.60

"touches another person, 7.63

"touching is sexual", 7.64

"unable to refuse", 7.65–7.76

spouses, 7.17

three categories

generally, 7.12–7.14

mens rea, 7.15–7.16

"unable to refuse"

generally, 7.18–7.22

overlap with absence of consent, 7.29–7.34

Sexual Offences (Northern Ireland) Order 2008

equivalent provisions in 2003 Act, 32.75

generally, 32.07–32.09

human trafficking, 32.13–32.21

paying for sexual services, 32.10

sexual communication with children, 32.11–32.12

Sexual offences prevention orders
history, 36.04
Northern Ireland, 32.54–32.56
replacement of, 36.05–36.11
Sexual Offences Review
assault by penetration, 2.03
causing sexual activity without
consent, 2.05
child sex offences, 4.02–4.06
prostitution, 13.09
rape, 1.03–1.04
sexual assault, 2.04
Sexual orientation
bad character
homosexual disposition,
20.58–20.78
prior heterosexual offences
where homosexual offence
alleged, 20.57
rape, 1.52
sexual behaviour of complainant,
26.146–26.148
Sexual penetration of corpses
introduction, 15.23–15.25
maximum sentences,
15.147–15.149
meaning, 15.146
mens rea, 15.154–15.155
mode of trial, 15.147–15.149
offence, 15.145
parties to offence, 15.150
"penetration", 15.152
sentencing, 15.151
"sexual", 15.153
Sexual risk orders
appeals, 36.72
breach, 36.73–36.75
conclusions, 36.76–36.77
conditions, 36.67
criteria for making, 36.66
historical perspective, 36.01–36.04
interim orders, 36.72
introduction of, 36.05–36.12
nature of order, 36.70

Sexual risk orders—*cont.*
procedure, 36.68–36.69
supplementary issues,
36.73–36.75
variation, 36.71
youth courts, 31.137
Sexual violence advisers
see **Victim support**
Sexually transmitted diseases
after-care for adults
bacterial STI prophylaxis,
21.48
generally, 21.45
post-exposure prophylaxis,
21.46
screening for infection post
assault, 21.49
children, 22.67
rape, 1.40
Ships
slavery and human trafficking
forfeiture and detention of
land vehicles, ships and
aircraft, 11.118–11.119
Slavery
see also **Human trafficking**
early international measures,
11.02–11.04
forfeiture and detention of land
vehicles, ships and aircraft,
11.118–11.119
future legislative measures,
11.57–11.58
introduction, 11.01
Modern Slavery Act 2015
commencement, 11.56
introduction, 11.21,
11.44–11.50
overlap of offences,
11.51–11.54
powers available under,
11.117—
territorial extent, 11.55

Slavery—*cont.*
Modern Slavery Act 2015—*cont.*
transitional provisions, 11.56
Sexual Offences Act 2003,
11.05–11.08
slavery and trafficking prevention
orders, 11.120–11.127
slavery and trafficking reparation
orders, 11.117
slavery and trafficking risk
orders, 11.128–11.132
slavery servitude and forced
compulsory labour
"all the circumstances, 11.66
consent, 11.67
maximum sentences,
11.60–11.64
mens rea, 11.71
mode of trial, 11.60–11.64
offence, 11.59
sentencing, 11.65
victim support, 11.68–11.70
statutory defence to prosecution
for victims, 11.37–11.43
Social care workers
see also **Sexual offences against
mentally disordered persons**
causing mentally disordered
persons to watch sexual acts
"causes", 7.280
civil partners, 7.287
jurisdiction, 7.279
maximum sentences,
7.273–7.276
mens rea, 7.284–7.286
"mental disorder", 7.283
mode of trial, 7.273–7.276
offence, 7.272
parties to offence, 7.278
pre-existing sexual
relationships, 7.287
sentencing, 7.277
spouses, 7.287
"the activity is sexual", 7.282

Social care workers—*cont.*
causing mentally disordered
persons to watch sexual
acts—*cont.*
"to watch a third person
engaging in an activity . . .
", 7.281
causing or inciting sexual activity
"causes or incites another
person . . . to engage in an
activity", 7.245
civil partners, 7.251
jurisdiction, 7.244
maximum sentences,
7.238–7.241
mens rea, 7.248–7.250
"mental disorder", 7.247
mode of trial, 7.238–7.241
offence, 7.237
parties to offence, 7.243
pre-existing sexual
relationships, 7.251
sentencing, 7.242
spouses, 7.251
"the activity is sexual", 7.246
sexual activity in the presence of
mentally disordered persons
civil partners, 7.271
"engages in an activity", 7.264
jurisdiction, 7.263
maximum sentences,
7.253–7.256
mens rea, 7.268–7.270
"mental disordered", 7.267
mode of trial, 7.253–7.256
offence, 7.252
parties to offence, 7.262
pre-existing sexual
relationships, 7.271
"present or . . . in a place from
which A can be
observed", 7.266
sentencing, 7.257–7.261
spouses, 7.271
"the activity is sexual", 7.265

Social care workers—*cont.*
sexual activity with mentally
disordered persons
civil partners, 7.235
"involved in B's care",
7.224–7.227
jurisdiction, 7.223
maximum sentences,
7.210–7.213
mens rea, 7.231–7.234
"mental disorder", 7.230
mode of trial, 7.210–7.213
offence, 7.209
parties to offence, 7.222
pre-existing sexual
relationships, 7.236
sentencing, 7.214–7.221
spouses, 7.235
"the touching is sexual", 7.229
"touches another person",
7.228
Social media
sexual behaviour of complainant,
26.34–26.41
Software
mixed DNA profiles, 25.57
Soliciting
see also **Brothels; Keeping
brothels; Prostitution**
for purposes of prostitution
cautions, 13.51–13.52
"for the purpose of
prostitution", 13.45–13.50
"loiter", 13.33
maximum sentences,
13.26–13.28
meaning, 13.25
mode of trial, 13.26–13.28
parties to offence, 13.29–13.30
"persistently", 13.31–13.32
powers of arrest, 13.53
"public place", 13.41–13.44
"solicit", 13.34–13.36
"street", 13.37–13.40

Soliciting—*cont.*
to obtain services of prostitute
"for the purpose of obtaining
B's sexual services as a
prostitute", 13.72
maximum sentences, 13.63
meaning, 13.60–13.62
mode of trial, 13.63
parties to offence, 13.64
"public place", 13.66
"solicit", 13.67–13.71
"street", 13.65
Special measures for witnesses
see also **Vulnerable and
intimidated witnesses**
aids to communication, 27.115
availability, 27.41–27.42
cross-examination
pre-recorded, 27.43–27.48
supplementary questions, 27.54
video-recordings,
27.103–27.104
defendants
generally, 27.20–27.24
intermediaries, 27.31–27.40
live link, 27.25–27.30
determination of appropriate
measure, 27.49
eligibility
children, 27.15–26.16
fear, 27.19
generally, 27.13–27.14
intimidation, 27.19
mental disorder, 27.17–27.18
mental distress, 27.19
physical disabilities,
27.17–27.18
evidence in chief
video recordings, 27.50–27.53,
27.68–27.102
giving evidence in private, 27.66
intermediaries
defendants, 27.31–27.40

Special measures for witnesses—*cont.*
intermediaries—*cont.*
generally, 27.105–27.114
legislation, 27.12
live link
defendants, 27.25–27.30
generally, 27.62–27.65
primary rule for child
witnesses, 27.50–27.53
Northern Ireland, 32.61–32.65
primary rule for child witnesses,
27.50–27.53
procedure, 27.116–27.122
re-examination
video recordings,
27.103–27.104
removal of wigs and gowns,
27.67
reporting restrictions, 27.124
revocation, 27.123
screens, 27.57–27.61
types of, 27.55–27.56
under-use of, 27.04–27.06
variation, 27.123
video-recordings
cross-examination,
27.103–27.104
evidence-in-chief, 27.50–27.53,
27.68–27.102
examination-in-chief, 27.54
re-examination, 27.103–27.104
supplementary questions, 27.54
youth courts
eligible persons, 31.58
generally, 31.56–31.57
procedure, 31.62
types, 31.59–31.61

Spouses
abuse of position of trust
causing children to engage in
sexual activity, 5.68
causing children to watch
sexual acts, 5.119

Spouses—*cont.*
abuse of position of trust—*cont.*
engaging in sexual activity in
presence of children, 5.95
sexual activity with children,
5.40–5.41
evidence by, 19.123–19.129
familial sex offences
inciting child family member
to engage in sexual
activity, 6.70
sexual activity with child
family members, 6.51
indecent photographs of children
possession, 8.143
taking, 8.75–8.81
rape, 1.84–1.85, 1.160–1.168
sexual intercourse with mental
patients, 7.17
social care workers
causing mentally disordered
persons to watch sexual
acts, 7.287
causing or inciting sexual
activity, 7.251
sexual activity in the presence
of mentally disordered
persons, 7.271
sexual activity with mentally
disordered persons, 7.235

Starting point
administering substances with
intent, 14.18
assault by penetration, 2.18–2.19
assault by penetration of child
under 13, 3.92
care workers engaging in sexual
activity in the presence of
mentally disordered persons,
7.259
care workers having sexual
activity with mentally
disordered persons, 7.216
causing children to engage in
sexual activity, 3.146

Starting point—*cont.*
causing prostitution for gain,
10.126–10.127
causing sexual activity without
consent, 2.93
causing sexual exploitation of
children, 10.49–10.50
child sex offences committed by
children, 4.155
engaging in sexual activity in
presence of children, 4.106,
5.83
engaging in sexual activity in
presence of mentally
disordered persons, 7.113
engaging in sexual activity in
presence of mentally
disordered persons procured
by inducement, threat or
deception, 7.180
exposure, 15.79
human trafficking, 11.84–11.85
keeping brothels, 12.49
meeting children following sexual
grooming, 4.200
paying for sexual services of
children, 10.22
procuring sexual activity with
mentally disordered persons
by inducement, threat or
deception, 7.149
rape, 1.53–1.57
rape of child under 13, 3.44–3.46
sex with adult relatives, 6.79
sexual activity with child family
members, 6.20
sexual activity with children,
4.39, 5.16
sexual activity with mentally
disordered persons, 7.55
sexual assault, 2.51–2.53
sexual assault of child under 13,
3.117–3.118
trespass with intent, 14.62
voyeurism, 15.107

Suicide
after-care for adults, 21.50–21.52
Suspended sentences
Northern Ireland, 32.53
"Systematic abuse"
assault by penetration of child
under 13, 3.83
causing children to engage in
sexual activity, 3.138
sexual assault of child under 13,
3.108
Teachers
reporting restrictions, 29.45–29.46
Tenants
permitting premises to be used as
brothel
"brothel", 12.73
"knowingly", 12.71
maximum sentences, 12.66
meaning, 12.65
mode of trial, 12.66
parties to offence, 12.67
"permit", 12.72
position of lessor or landlord
where tenant convicted,
12.74–12.75
"tenant or occupier or person
in charge", 12.68–12.70
permitting premises to be used
for prostitution
"for the purposes of habitual
prostitution", 12.84
"knowingly, 12.81
maximum sentences, 12.77
meaning, 12.76
mode of trial, 12.77
parties to offence, 12.78
"permit", 12.82–12.83
"tenant or occupier",
12.79–12.80
Third party disclosure
criminal trials, 18.69–18.73
generally, 18.32–18.33
procedure, 18.34–18.38

Threats
causing mentally disordered
persons to engage in sexual
activity by threat
"causes another person (B) to
engage in . . . ", 7.169
"inducement, threat or
deception", 7.168
jurisdiction, 7.167
maximum sentences,
7.161–7.164
mens rea, 7.172
"mental disorder", 7.171
mode of trial, 7.161–7.164
offence, 7.160
parties to offence, 7.166
sentencing, 7.165
"the activity is sexual", 7.170
causing mentally disordered
persons to watch sexual acts
by threat
"causes", 7.201
"inducement, threat or
deception", 7.203
jurisdiction, 7.200
maximum sentences,
7.194–7.197
mens rea, 7.206–7.208
mode of trial, 7.194–7.197
offences, 7.193
parties to offence, 7.199
sentencing, 7.198
"the activity is sexual", 7.204
"to watch a third person
engaging in an activity...
", 7.202
engaging in sexual activity in
presence procured by threat
of mentally disordered
persons
"engages in an activity", 7.185
"inducement, threat or
deception", 7.188
jurisdiction, 7.184

Threats—*cont.*
engaging in sexual activity in
presence procured by threat
of mentally disordered
persons—*cont.*
maximum sentences,
7.174–7.177
mens rea, 7.190–7.192
"mental disorder", 7.189
mode of trial, 7.174–7.177
offence, 7.173
parties to offence, 7.183
"present or . . . in a place from
which A can be
observed", 7.187
sentencing, 7.178–7.182
"the activity is sexual", 7.186
rape
aggravating features, 1.62
category 2 harm, 1.40
Touch DNA
see **DNA evidence**
Transcripts
evidence-in-chief
jury access to video transcripts,
27.96–27.102
Trawling
see **Historic offences**
Trespass with intent
introduction, 14.07
jurisdiction, 14.67
maximum sentence, 14.53–14.56
meaning, 14.51–14.52A
mens rea, 14.72–14.74
mode of trial, 14.53–14.56
"premises", 14.71
sentencing
aggravating features, 14.63
ancillary orders, 14.64
category range, 14.62
credit for time served, 14.64
culpability, 14.58–14.61
dangerousness, 14.64
examples, 14.66
guilty pleas, 14.64

Trespass with intent—*cont.*
  sentencing—*cont.*
    harm, 14.58–14.61
    introduction, 14.57
    mitigation, 14.63
    offender going on to commit
      intended offence, 14.65
    proportionality, 14.64
    reasons, 14.64
    reduction in sentence, 14.64
    starting point, 14.62
    "trespasser", 14.68–14.70
Unsworn evidence
  vulnerable and intimidated
    witnesses, 27.155–27.156
Variation
  sexual harm prevention orders,
    36.54
  sexual risk orders, 36.71
Vehicles
  slavery and human trafficking
    forfeiture and detention of
      land vehicles, ships and
      aircraft, 11.118–11.119
Verdicts
  Northern Ireland, 32.74
Victim support
  independent sexual violence
    advisers, 21.56
  sexual assault referral centres
    aims, 21.16
    self-referrals, 21.17
Victims
  see also **Sexual behaviour**
  anonymity
    Contempt of Court Act 1981,
      29.29–29.32
    generally, 29.12–29.14
    introduction, 29.02–29.03
    Sexual Offences (Amendment)
      Act 1992, 29.15–29.28
  bad character, 20.144–20.147
  human trafficking, 11.109

Victims—*cont.*
  inconsistent statements,
    19.67–19.71
  prosecution of victims of
    trafficking
    generally, 11.22
    Trafficking Convention,
      11.23–11.24
    prosecutorial discretion,
      11.25–11.28
    abuse of process, 11.29–11.35
    CPS guidance, 11.36
    statutory defence under 2015
      Act, 11.37–11.43
  slavery
    independent child trafficking
      advocates, 11.69
    other measures of support,
      11.70
    special measures, 11.68
Video evidence
  Northern Ireland, 32.62
Video-recordings
  cross-examination, 27.103–27.104
  evidence-in-chief
    exclusion of in interests of
      justice, 27.82–27.85
    generally, 27.68–27.81
    jury access to video transcripts,
      27.96–27.102
    primary rule for child
      witnesses, 27.50–27.53
    replaying the video,
      27.89–27.95
    witness retraction, 27.86–27.88
  examination-in-chief, 27.54
  re-examination, 27.103–27.104
  supplementary questions, 27.54
Violence
  rape, 1.40
Voluntary intoxication
  rape
    capacity and consent,
      1.243–1.254

Voluntary intoxication—*cont.*
rape—*cont.*
defences, 1.398–1.401
Voyeurism
"consent", 15.119
"doing a private act",
15.113–15.118
fitness to plead, 15.96–15.101
"image", 15.120
introduction, 15.16–15.18
maximum sentences, 15.92–15.95
meaning, 15.91
mens rea, 15.122–15.125
mode of trial, 15.92–15.95
"observes", 15.111–15.112
offence, 15.90
parties to offence, 15.102
sentencing
aggravating features, 15.108
ancillary orders, 15.109
category range, 15.107
credit for time served, 15.109
culpability, 15.104–15.106
dangerousness, 15.109
examples, 15.110
extended sentences, 15.109
generally, 15.103
guilty pleas, 15.109
harm, 15.104–15.106
mitigation, 15.108
proportionality, 15.109
reasons, 15.109
reduction of sentence, 15.109
starting point, 15.107
"structure", 15.121
Vulnerable adults
advocacy
adaptation, 28.10–28.17
case management, 28.31–28.40
confrontation, 28.22–28.30
ground rules hearings,
28.31–28.40
introduction, 28.01–28.09

Vulnerable adults—*cont.*
advocacy—*cont.*
live link evidence, 28.43
practical suggestions for
questioning, 28.41–28.42
practicalities, 28.43–28.45
suggestive questioning,
28.18–28.21
barring from working with,
34.63–34.64
rape, 1.43
Vulnerable and intimidated witnesses
see also **Special measures for
witnesses**
at trial, 27.136–27.140
competence
delay in case coming to trial,
27.152–27.154
generally, 27.143–27.151
defendants in person
cross-examination by,
27.157–27.163
developments, 27.07–27.11
introduction, 27.01
judicial ticketing, 27.128
listing, 27.135
live link room, 27.141–27.142
meetings between advocates
judges and witnesses,
27.129–27.130
practicalities, 27.125–27.127
pre-trial familiarisation visits,
27.134
pre-trial therapy, 27.131–27.133
Speaking Up for Justice,
27.02–27.03
sworn and unsworn evidence,
27.155–27.156
Weapons
aggravating features
rape, 1.64
Wearer's DNA
see **DNA evidence**

Whole life orders
rape, 1.110–1.114
Withdrawn complaints
see **Historic offences**
Witnesses
see **Special measures for
witnesses; Vulnerable and
intimidated witnesses**
Wolfenden Committee
see **Prostitution**
Young offenders
historic offences, 30.115–30.118E
notification, 35.46–35.47
rape, 1.90
rape of child under 13, 3.65–3.68
sex offenders, 33.23
sexual activity with child family
members, 6.23–6.24
Young persons
anonymity
defendants, 29.47–29.52
prohibiting identification of
adult to protect child,
29.89–29.93
child sex offences committed by
introduction, 4.10–4.16
jurisdiction, 4.158
maximum sentences,
4.147–4.150
meaning, 4.145–4.146
mens rea, 4.159
mode of trial, 4.147–4.150
offence, 4.144
over 18 at time of sentencing,
4.156
parties to offence, 4.157
sentencing, 4.151–4.156
reporting restrictions
applications for High Court
order, 29.105
burden of proof on
application, 29.74
challenging making variation
or revocation, 29.86–29.88

Young persons—*cont.*
reporting restrictions—*cont.*
concerned in criminal
proceedings, 29.64–29.69
contravention, 29.70–29.73
framing directions, 29.83–29.85
inherent jurisdiction of Crown
Court, 29.107
introduction, 29.06–29.10
legislative history, 29.58–29.59
lifetime reporting restrictions,
29.108–29.122
media interests, 29.106
media representations,
29.80–29.82
not directly involved in
proceedings, 29.94–29.107
offences committed by,
29.47–29.52
principles governing decision
to make, 29.75–29.79
prohibiting identification of
adult to protect child,
29.89–29.93
section 45 directions,
29.64–29.93
transitional provisions,
29.61–29.63
Youth cautions
generally, 31.21–31.23
Youth conditional cautions
generally, 31.21, 31.24–31.25
Youth courts
ancillary orders
barring from working with
children and young adults,
31.136
generally, 31.134
parenting orders, 31.138
sexual harm prevention orders,
31.135
sexual risk orders, 31.137
bail, 31.29–31.30

Youth courts—*cont.*
child sex offences, 31.18
classification of sexual offences,
31.140
dangerousness
application of exception,
31.96–31.97
generally, 31.91–31.95
specified offences, 31.98
decision to prosecute
Code for Crown Prosecutors,
31.10–31.11
generally, 31.08–31.09
legal guidance, 31.13–31.20
familial child sex offences, 31.19
first appearance, 31.26
introduction, 31.01–31.02
mode of trial
accused turning 18 during
proceedings, 31.71
dangerousness, 31.91–31.98
generally, 31.27–31.28
grave crimes, 31.72–31.90
procedure for determining,
31.68–31.70
statutory presumption,
31.64–31.67
youths charged alongside
adults, 31.99
offences against children under
13, 31.15–31.17
preliminary matters, 31.03
sentencing
ancillary orders, 31.134–31.138
approach to, 31.116–31.119
detention and training orders,
31.104–31.106
guidelines, 31.120–31.125
introduction, 31.100
notification, 31.127–31.133
options, 31.139
other sentencing options,
31.113

Youth courts—*cont.*
sentencing—*cont.*
powers and procedure,
31.101–31.103
referral orders, 31.110–31.112
relevance of age, 31.114–31.115
youth rehabilitation orders,
31.107–31.109
serious offences
application of exception,
31.80–31.84
examples of decisions,
31.89–31.90
generally, 31.72–31.75
powers of punishment,
31.76–31.79
rape, 31.85–31.88
sexual offences, 31.85–31.88
sexual exploitation of children,
31.20
special measures for witnesses
eligible persons, 31.58
generally, 31.56–31.57
procedure, 31.62
types, 31.59–31.61
terminology, 31.04
trials
affirmations, 31.55
anonymity of complainants,
31.42
attendance of parents and
guardians, 31.36
compellability, 31.54
competence, 31.52–31.53
constitution and operation,
31.32–31.35
course of trial, 31.47–31.51
disclosure, 31.43–31.46
introduction, 31.31
oaths, 31.55
press, 31.37
publicity, 31.37
questioning young people,
31.63

Youth courts—*cont.*
trials *—cont.*
reporting restrictions,
31.38–31.41
special measures for witnesses,
31.56–31.62
youth cautions, 31.21–31.23

Youth courts—*cont.*
youth conditional cautions,
31.21, 31.24–31.25
youth justice system
aims, 31.05–31.07
Youth rehabilitation orders
youth courts, 31.107–31.109